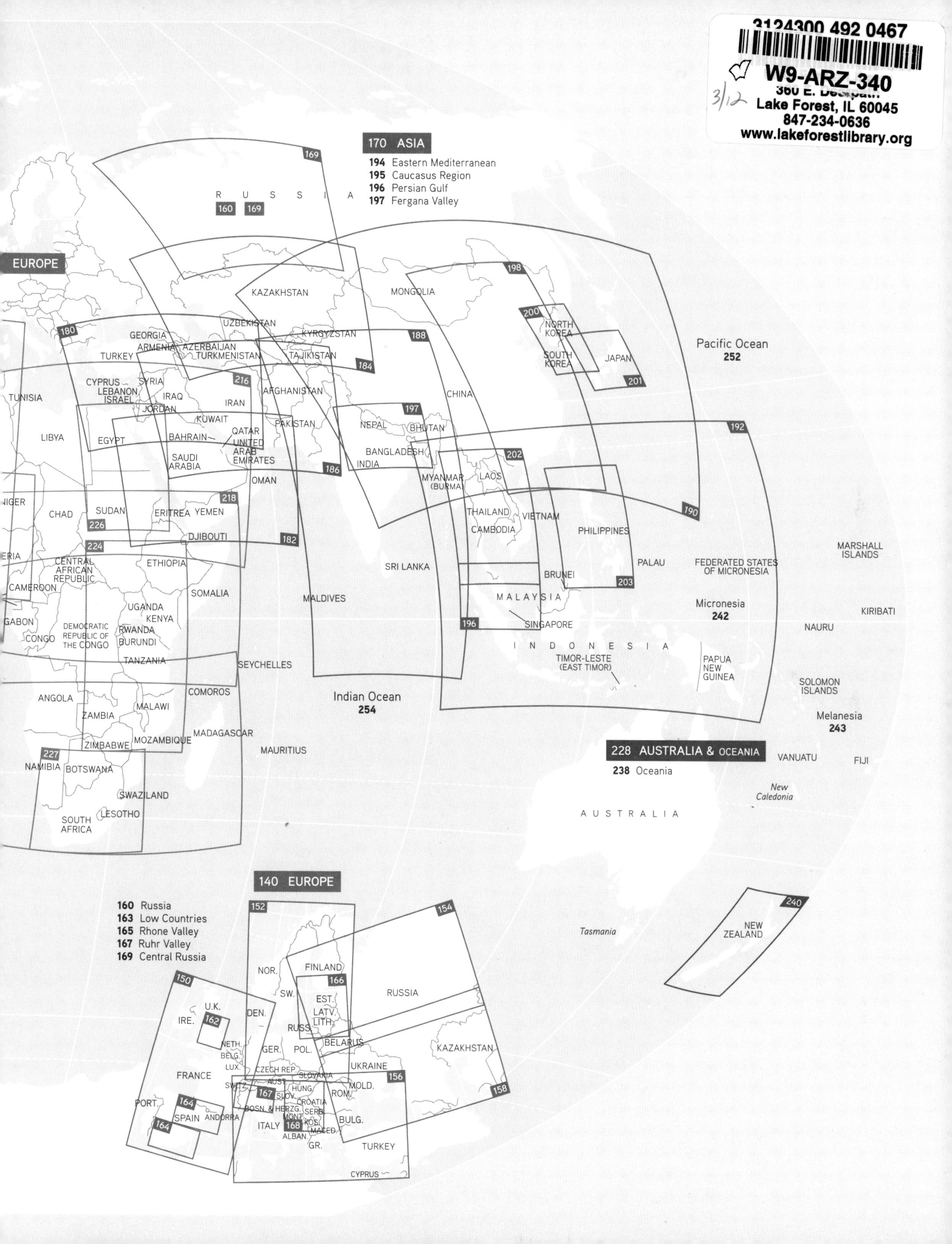
170 ASIA
194 Eastern Mediterranean
195 Caucasus Region
196 Persian Gulf
197 Fergana Valley
R U S S I A
160 169
169
EUROPE
KAZAKHSTAN
MONGOLIA
198
200
NORTH KOREA
SOUTH KOREA
JAPAN
201
Pacific Ocean
252
180
GEORGIA
ARMENIA
AZERBAIJAN
UZBEKISTAN
KYRGYZSTAN
TURKEY
TURKMENISTAN
TAJIKISTAN
184
188
CYPRUS
LEBANON
ISRAEL
SYRIA
IRAQ
JORDAN
216
IRAN
AFGHANISTAN
CHINA
TUNISIA
KUWAIT
PAKISTAN
NEPAL
BHUTAN
197
192
LIBYA
EGYPT
BAHRAIN
QATAR
UNITED ARAB EMIRATES
SAUDI ARABIA
BANGLADESH
INDIA
186
202
OMAN
MYANMAR (BURMA)
LAOS
NIGER
CHAD
SUDAN
226
ERITREA
YEMEN
218
THAILAND
VIETNAM
190
DJIBOUTI
182
CAMBODIA
PHILIPPINES
224
ERIA
CENTRAL AFRICAN REPUBLIC
ETHIOPIA
SRI LANKA
PALAU
FEDERATED STATES OF MICRONESIA
MARSHALL ISLANDS
CAMEROON
SOMALIA
MALDIVES
BRUNEI
203
MALAYSIA
Micronesia
242
UGANDA
KENYA
KIRIBATI
GABON
CONGO
DEMOCRATIC REPUBLIC OF THE CONGO
RWANDA
BURUNDI
196
SINGAPORE
NAURU
TANZANIA
INDONESIA
SEYCHELLES
TIMOR-LESTE (EAST TIMOR)
PAPUA NEW GUINEA
SOLOMON ISLANDS
ANGOLA
COMOROS
Indian Ocean
254
ZAMBIA
MALAWI
Melanesia
243
MOZAMBIQUE
MADAGASCAR
ZIMBABWE
MAURITIUS
228 AUSTRALIA & OCEANIA
238 Oceania
VANUATU
FIJI
227
NAMIBIA
BOTSWANA
New Caledonia
SWAZILAND
LESOTHO
SOUTH AFRICA
AUSTRALIA
140 EUROPE
160 Russia
163 Low Countries
165 Rhone Valley
167 Ruhr Valley
169 Central Russia
152
154
240
NEW ZEALAND
Tasmania
NOR.
FINLAND
166
150
SW.
EST.
LATV.
LITH.
RUSSIA
U.K.
IRE.
162
DEN.
RUSS.
NETH.
BELG.
GER.
POL.
BELARUS
KAZAKHSTAN
LUX.
CZECH REP.
SLOVAKIA
UKRAINE
FRANCE
SWITZ.
AUST.
HUNG.
MOLD.
156
158
PORT.
164
167
SLOV.
CROATIA
ROM.
SPAIN
ANDORRA
BOSN. & HERZG.
SERB.
MONT.
KOS.
164
ITALY
168
BULG.
ALBAN.
MACED.
GR.
TURKEY
CYPRUS

NATIONAL GEOGRAPHIC

Collegiate Atlas OF THE World

SECOND EDITION

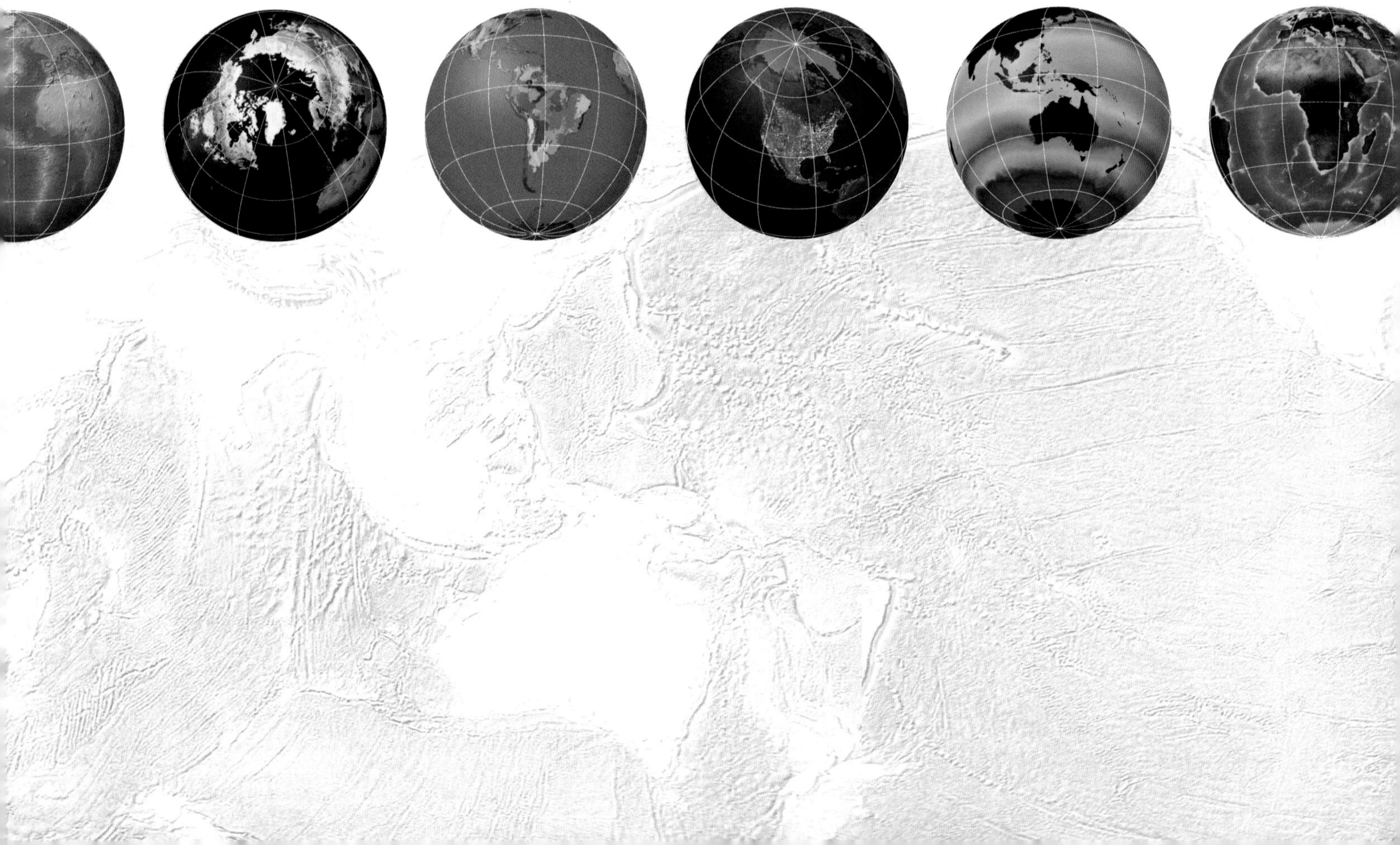

NATIONAL GEOGRAPHIC

Collegiate Atlas OF THE World

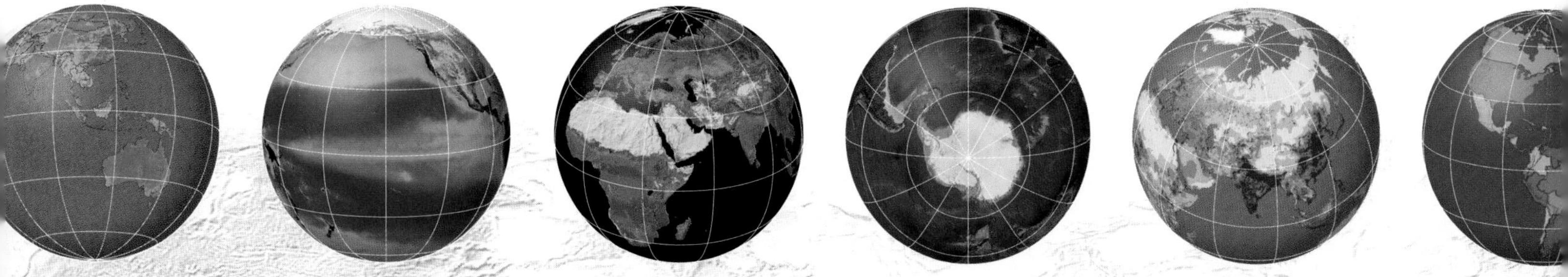

SECOND EDITION

NATIONAL GEOGRAPHIC, WASHINGTON, D.C.

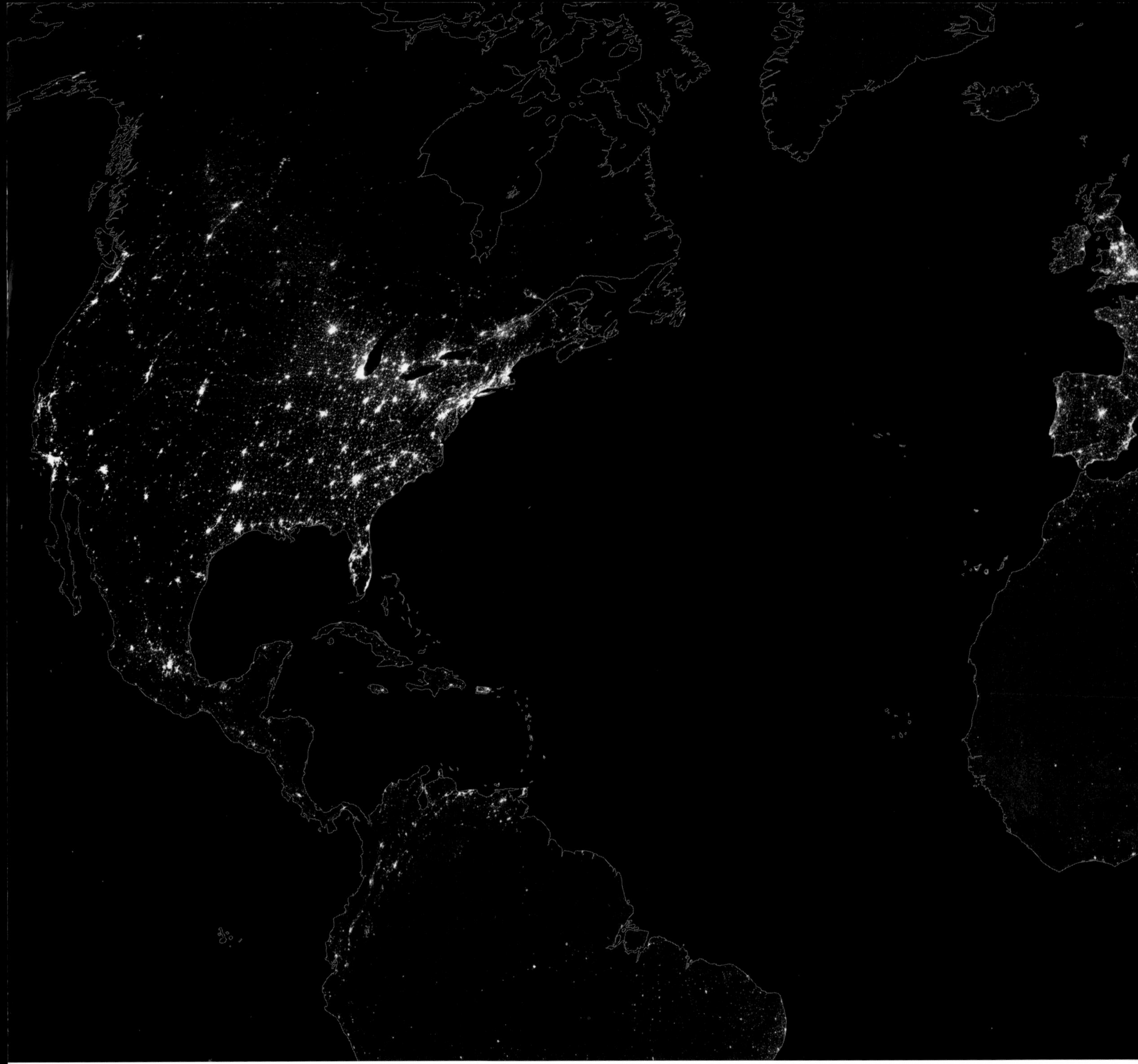

THE URGE TO RECORD our surroundings seems embedded in the human DNA. In the earliest civilizations, the layout of settlements and regions was already being mapped. The world then, and throughout much of human history, was essentially local—the small known universe. Now, the entire planet is so interconnected that national borders and localized concerns have been superseded by far-reaching economic and geopolitical realities. In our century, maps are no longer simple records of a static world—they are fluid, layered representations of forces at work on the ground.

"If geography is prose, maps are iconography," writer and statesman Lennart Meri once said. In this second edition of the *Collegiate Atlas,* we have relied on more than a century of experience in mapmaking to bring you iconic maps that allow you to understand the world as never before, putting at your fingertips a guide to the complicated global realities. Since being founded in 1888, the National Geographic Society's mission has been the increase and diffusion of geographic knowledge, and the current state of technology allows us to do that in ways inconceivable to our predecessors. Satellite data beamed back in an almost constant stream give us the tools to create maps with startling depth and clarity, and each of the map spreads in this 400-page atlas is carefully designed as a portal to some place—and time—on the planet. You'll see in stunning relief everything from the ocean floors to the polar reaches. You'll gain an understanding of how natural forces have shaped and reshaped the Earth over eons and how the human presence is changing life on the planet in our own era. The pressing issues of economics, energy, food security, health and literacy, communications, transportation, and defense and conflict are

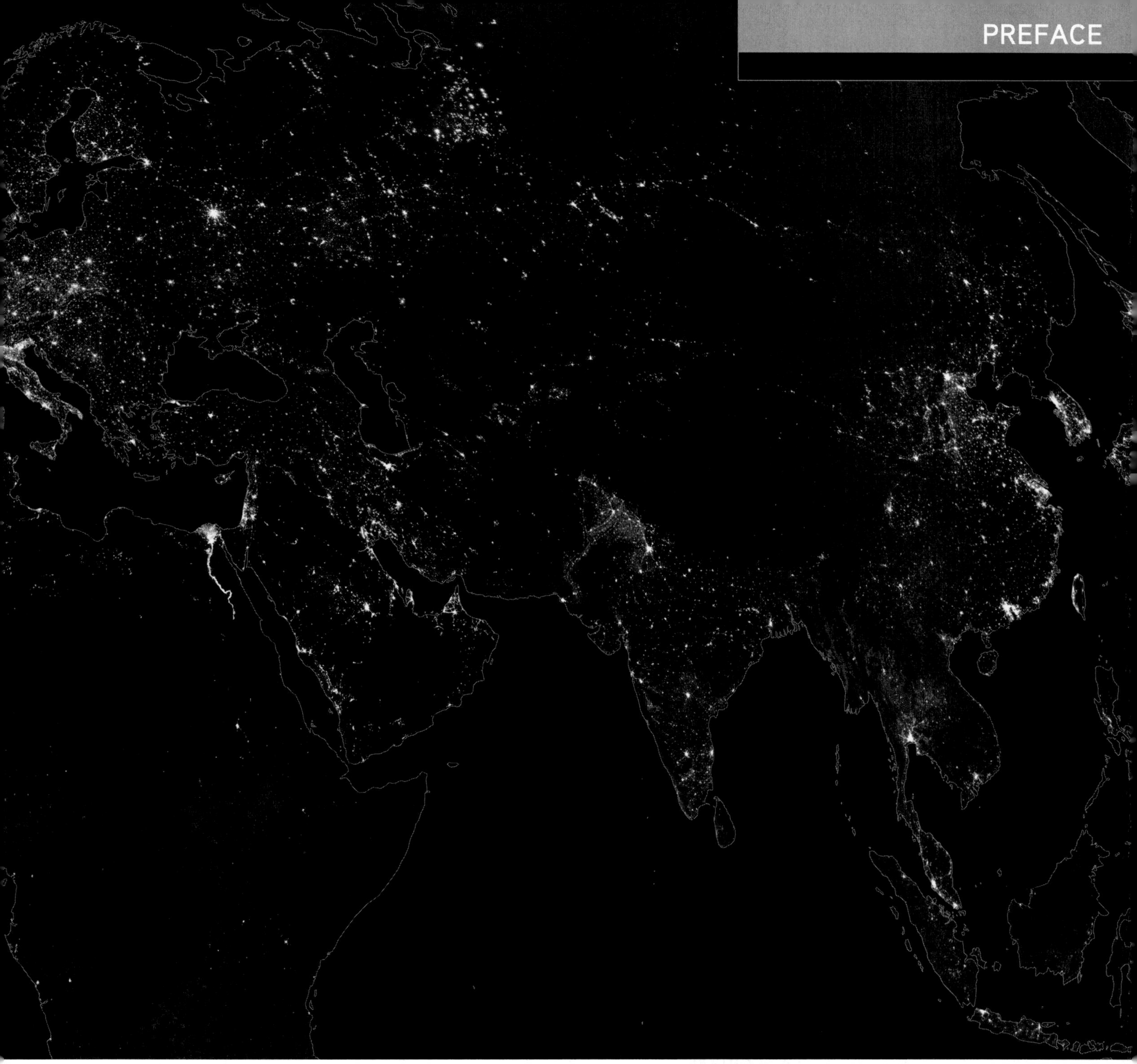

represented in the thematic maps, bringing you a full portrait of each continent and the conditions that both sustain and threaten it. In these 25 world thematic spreads you'll see the planet from all angles—from its physical forms to its cultural and technological features.

Accompanying charts, sidebars, and photographs throughout the atlas add clarity and visual appeal and help you understand where the current global fault lines and hot spots lurk—whether they are tectonic or human. You'll see where volcanoes and earthquakes are likely to strike; where shifting politics and demographics are likely to redefine age-old certainties; how climate change is reshaping coastlines, grasslands, forests, and lifestyles; and how the morphing of cultures, religions, and languages is impacting life in our fast-changing century. In the closing appendix you'll find easy-to-access practical information on foreign terms, geographic comparisons, and the world's most populous urban areas.

A half-century ago, President John Kennedy told the Canadian Parliament, "Geography has made us neighbors. History has made us friends. Economics has made us partners, and necessity has made us allies." Today, as the world grows ever smaller and human abilities and aspirations ever greater, Kennedy's words apply to countries separated by continents and oceans. Understanding that web of interconnection becomes vital. Maps, more than any other single tool, give us the insight we need to appreciate and nurture the complex natural and human wonders of this small but miraculous world.

Declan Moore, Executive Vice President; President, Publishing

Table of Contents

4 Preface
10 Using This Atlas
12 Mapping the Earth
14 World from Above
16 Geospatial Concepts

THEMATIC WORLD 18–69

20 Physical World
22 Political World
24 Plate Tectonics:
Geologic Forces, Global Tectonic Features, Paleogeography
26 Geomorphology:
Eolian Landforms, Ice Ages, Landforms of the World
28 Earth's Surface:
Sea Level Changes, Earth's Highs and Lows, A Slice of Earth
30 Climate:
Hadley Cells, Seasons and Rotation of the Earth, Climatic Zones, Precipitation, Temperatures
32 Weather:
Tracking Weather Patterns, Weather Dynamics
34 Biosphere:
Our Layered Ocean, What Shapes Earth's Climate, Ocean Circulation, Earth's Green Biomass
36 Water:
Water Availability and Primary Watersheds, Access to Fresh Water, Water by Volume
38 Land Cover:
Land Cover Classes
40 Biodiversity:
Major Terrestrial Habitat Types, Major Freshwater and Marine Habitat Types, Threats to Biodiversity, Biodiversity Hotspots
42 Land Use:
Land Use Patterns, Deforestation, Fire, Agricultural Development, Freshwater Loss
44 Human Population:
Population Density, Population Cartogram, Population Pyramids, Regional Population Growth
46 Population Trends:
Fertility, Infant Mortality, Life Expectancy, Population Superlatives, Urban Population, Urban Population Growth
48 Culture:
Major Religions, World Languages, Struggling Cultures
50 Health and Literacy:
Cardiovascular Disease, HIV/AIDS, Doctors Within Borders, Malaria Ravages Tropics, How Do People Die?, Calorie Consumption, Hunger, Literacy
52 Food:
Agriculture, Major Crop Ranges, Genetically Modified Agriculture, World Diet, Fisheries and Aquaculture
54 Economy:
GDP Cartogram, GDP per Capita, GDP Growth, Gross National Income, Labor Migration, World Employment
56 Trade and Globalization:
Trade Flow, Trade Blocs, World Debt, Growth of Trade, Merchandise Imports and Exports
58 Transportation:
Airline Passenger Volume, Measuring Road Networks, Rail Networks, Shipping the World's Goods
60 Communication:
Mapping the Internet, Communications Satellites, Internet Explosion, Rise of the Mobile Phone, Connecting the Planet
62 Energy:
Renewable Energy, Energy Consumption, World Oil Supply, Flow of Oil Worldwide, Alternative Energies
64 Defense and Conflict:
Defense Spending, Biological Weapons, Chemical Weapons, Nuclear Weapons, Measuring Democracy, Flight from Conflict
66 Environment:
Global Warming, Deforestation, Threatened Oceans, Desertification, Ozone Depletion, Carbon Dioxide, Polar Ice Cap, Pollution
68 Protected Areas:
Protected Areas Worldwide, Percentage Protected, Wildest Areas

NORTH AMERICA 70–119

72 Physical and Political Continental Maps

74 Natural Themes
Temperature and Rainfall, Land Cover, Climate Zones, Natural Hazards, Water Availability

76 Human Themes
Population Pyramids, Population Density, Indigenous Languages, Urbanization, Projected Population Change

78 Economic Themes
Imports and Exports, Land Use, Dominant Economy, Economy by Sector, Poverty, Per Capita Energy Consumption

80 Contiguous U.S. Physical Map

82 Contiguous U.S. Political Map

84 United States Natural Themes
Climate Zones, Water Availability, Natural Hazards, National Parks and Reserves

86 United States Human Themes
Religion, Foreign-Born Population, Population Change, Population Density

88 United States Economic Themes
Service Employment, Manufacturing Employment, Farm Area, Median Household Income

90 Northwestern United States
Idaho, Montana, Nebraska, North Dakota, Oregon, South Dakota, Washington, Wyoming

92 Southwestern United States
Arizona, California, Colorado, Kansas, Nevada, New Mexico, Texas, Utah

94 Northeastern United States
Connecticut, Delaware, District of Columbia, Illinois, Indiana, Iowa, Kentucky, Maine, Maryland, Massachusetts, Michigan, Minnesota, Missouri, New Hampshire, New Jersey, New York, Ohio, Pennsylvania, Rhode Island, Vermont, Virginia, West Virginia, Wisconsin

96 Southeastern United States
Alabama, Arkansas, Florida, Georgia, Louisiana, Mississippi, North Carolina, Oklahoma, South Carolina, Tennessee, Texas

98 Alaska, United States

99 Hawai'i, United States and Principal Hawaiian Islands

100 Puget Sound and Central California Coast

101 Southern California

102 Southern Great Lakes

103 Western Gulf Coast

104 Southern New England

105 Peninsular Florida

106 Canada

108 Western Canada
Alberta, British Columbia, Manitoba, Saskatchewan

110 Central Canada
Ontario, Quebec

111 Maritime Canada
New Brunswick, Newfoundland and Labrador, Nova Scotia, Prince Edward Island, Quebec

112 Mexico

114 Central Mexico

115 Central America
Belize, Costa Rica, El Salvador, Guatemala, Honduras, Nicaragua, Panama

116 Caribbean
Antigua and Barbuda, Bahamas, Barbados, Cuba, Dominica, Dominican Republic, Grenada, Haiti, Jamaica, St. Kitts and Nevis, St. Lucia, St. Vincent and the Grenadines, Trinidad and Tobago

118 Bermuda and the West Indies

SOUTH AMERICA 120–139

122 Physical and Political Continental Maps

124 Natural Themes
Temperature and Rainfall, Land Cover, Climate Zones, Natural Hazards, Water Availability

126 Human Themes
Population Pyramids, Population Density, Indigenous Languages, Urbanization, Projected Population Change

128 Economic Themes
Imports and Exports, Land Use, Dominant Economy, Economy by Sector, Poverty, Per Capita Energy Consumption

130 Northern
Brazil, Colombia, Ecuador, French Guiana, Guyana, Peru, Suriname, Venezuela

132 Central
Bolivia, Brazil, Paraguay

134 Southern
Argentina, Chile, Falkland Islands, Uruguay

136 Northern Andes

137 Altiplano

138 Southeastern Brazil

139 River Plate Region

EUROPE 140–169

142 Physical and Political Continental Maps

144 Natural Themes
Temperature and Rainfall, Land Cover, Climate Zones, Natural Hazards, Water Availability

146 Human Themes
Population Pyramids, Population Density, Indigenous Languages, Urbanization, Projected Population Change

148 Economic Themes
Imports and Exports, Land Use, Dominant Economy, Economy by Sector, Poverty, Per Capita Energy Consumption

150 Western
Andorra, Belgium, France, Ireland, Luxembourg, Monaco, Netherlands, Portugal, Spain, United Kingdom

152 Northern
Czech Republic, Denmark, Estonia, Finland, Germany, Latvia, Lithuania, Norway, Poland, Slovakia, Sweden

154 Northeastern
Belarus, Western Russia

156 Southern
Albania, Austria, Bosnia and Herzegovina, Bulgaria, Croatia, Cyprus, Greece, Hungary, Italy, Kosovo, Liechtenstein, Macedonia, Malta, Moldova, Montenegro, Romania, San Marino, Serbia, Slovenia, Switzerland, Turkey, Vatican City

158 Southeastern
Southern Russia, Ukraine

160 Russia

162 Central Britain

163 Low Countries

164 Northeastern and Southern Spain

165 Rhone Valley

166 Baltic States

167 Ruhr and Po Valleys

168 Western Balkans

169 Central Russia

ASIA 170–203

172 Physical and Political Continental Maps

174 Natural Themes
Temperature and Rainfall, Land Cover, Climate Zones, Natural Hazards, Water Availability

176 Human Themes
Population Pyramids, Population Density, Indigenous Languages, Urbanization, Projected Population Change

178 Economic Themes
Imports and Exports, Land Use, Dominant Economy, Economy by Sector, Poverty, Per Capita Energy Consumption

180 Western
Armenia, Azerbaijan, Georgia, Iraq, Israel, Jordan, Kuwait, Lebanon, Syria, Turkey

182 Southwestern
Bahrain, Oman, Qatar, Saudi Arabia, United Arab Emirates, Yemen

184 Central
Kazakhstan, Kyrgyzstan, Tajikistan, Turkmenistan, Uzbekistan

186 South Central
Afghanistan, Iran, Pakistan

188 Southern
Bangladesh, Bhutan, India, Nepal, Sri Lanka

190 Eastern
China, Japan, Mongolia, North Korea, South Korea

192 Southeastern
Brunei, Cambodia, Indonesia, Laos, Malaysia, Myanmar (Burma), Philippines, Singapore, Thailand, Timor-Leste (East Timor), Vietnam

194 Eastern Mediterranean

195 Caucasus Region

196 Persian Gulf and Strait of Malacca

197 Fergana and Ganges Valleys

198 Eastern China

200 Korean Peninsula

201 Central Japan

202 Indochina

203 Philippines

AFRICA 204–227

206 Physical and Political Continental Maps

208 Natural Themes
Temperature and Rainfall, Land Cover, Climate Zones, Natural Hazards, Water Availability

210 Human Themes
Population Pyramids, Population Density, Indigenous Languages, Urbanization, Projected Population Change

212 Economic Themes
Imports and Exports, Land Use, Dominant Economy, Economy by Sector, Poverty, Per Capita Energy Consumption

214 Western
Algeria, Benin, Burkina Faso, Côte d'Ivoire (Ivory Coast), Gambia, Ghana, Guinea, Guinea-Bissau, Liberia, Mali, Mauritania, Morocco, Senegal, Sierra Leone, Togo

216 Northeastern
Chad, Egypt, Libya, Niger, Sudan, Tunisia

218 Central
Burundi, Cameroon, Central African Republic, Chad, Congo, Democratic Republic of the Congo, Djibouti, Equatorial Guinea, Eritrea, Ethiopia, Gabon, Kenya, Nigeria, Rwanda, Sao Tome and Principe, Somalia, Sudan, Tanzania, Uganda

220 Southern
Angola, Botswana, Comoros, Lesotho, Madagascar, Malawi, Mozambique, Namibia, Seychelles, South Africa, Swaziland, Zambia, Zimbabwe

222 Coastal West Africa

224 Central Rift Valley

226 Nile Valley

227 South Africa

AUSTRALIA AND OCEANIA 228–243

230 Australia Physical and Political Continental Maps

232 Natural Themes
Temperature and Rainfall, Land Cover, Climate Zones, Natural Hazards, Water Availability

234 Human Themes
Population Pyramids, Population Density, Indigenous Languages, Urbanization, Projected Population Change

236 Economic Themes
Imports and Exports, Land Use, Dominant Economy, Economy by Sector, Poverty, Per Capita Energy Consumption

238 Oceania
Federated States of Micronesia, Fiji, Kiribati, Marshall Islands, Nauru, Palau, Papua New Guinea, Samoa, Solomon Islands, Tonga, Tuvalu, Vanuatu

240 New Zealand and Polynesia

242 Micronesia and Melanesia

POLAR REGIONS 244–249

246 Arctic

248 Antarctic

OCEANS 250-255

252 Pacific Ocean

253 Atlantic Ocean

254 Indian Ocean

255 Arctic Ocean and Oceans Around Antarctica

PLACE-NAME INDEX 256–388

256 Using This Index

APPENDIX 389–400

389 Map Policies and Notes

390 Abbreviations, Geographic Comparisons, and Metric Conversions

392 Foreign Terms

394 Urban Agglomerations

396 Acknowledgments

Political Map Symbols

BOUNDARIES

Defined

Undefined or disputed

Offshore line of separation

CITIES

Capitals

Towns

TRANSPORTATION

Passenger railroad

UNDER CONSTRUCTION High-speed

UNDER CONSTRUCTION Main line

Tunnel

Railroad ferry

UNDER CONSTRUCTION Superhighway

UNDER CONSTRUCTION Road

Auto ferry

Highway tunnel

Trail

Scheduled air service

Spaceport

WATER FEATURES

Drainage

Intermittent drainage

Intermittent lake

Dry salt lake

Swamp

Channel

Water hole or well

Limit of drift ice

Bank or shoal

Coral reef

302 200 84 Depth curves and soundings in meters

Falls or rapids

PHYSICAL FEATURES

Tundra

Relief

Crater

Lava and volcanic debris

+8850 (29035 ft) Elevation in meters

Pass

Sand

Below sea level

Ice shelf

Glacier

CULTURAL FEATURES

Dam

Wall

Park (water/land extent)

Site

Ruin

Battle

Oil field

UNDER CONSTRUCTION Oil pipeline

Canal

BOUNDARIES AND POLITICAL DIVISIONS

Country type
Lebanon

Double color band
International boundary

Red dots
Claimed boundary line—Syria claims the Golan Heights region, but it is controlled by Israel.

Region type
Disputed or historic region

Broken boundary dots
Disputed boundary—the West Bank border with Israel has been in dispute since 1949.

Single color band
Internal administrative boundary for regions, including provinces and states (see Connecticut-Massachusetts boundary, page 11, under Transportation and Other Features)

Gray color
Disputed region—Israelis and Palestinians dispute the extent and status of the West Bank.

International boundaries and disputed territories, where scale permits, reflect de facto status at time of publication.

CITIES AND TOWNS

The maps in this Atlas depict four categories of cities or towns, based on population.

Small type and town spot
City or town with fewer than 100,000 people

Large type and town spot
City with a population between 100,000 and 1 million

Star with double ring capital spot
National capital—Beijing, China's capital (historic name: Peking); type shown in capital letters because the city population exceeds 5 million

Bull's-eye capital spot
Administrative capital for internal regions in most countries and dependent territories (internal capitals in Australia, Canada, Mexico, U.K., and U.S. show as a ringed star).

Larger type and town spot
City between 1 million and 5 million people

Thematic Maps

WORLD THEMATICS

Thematic maps show the spatial distribution of physical or cultural phenomena in a way that is graphically illuminating and useful. This thematic map on urban growth was created by National Geographic, to show how increasingly urbanized the world is becoming. Some of the world's largest cities are included with population change over time. Thematic maps also can present qualitative or quantitative data for comparison.

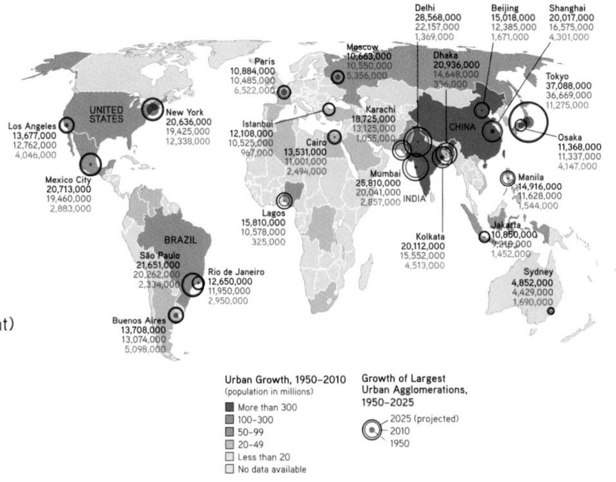

CONTINENTAL THEMATICS

This Atlas contains three spreads of thematic maps for each continent covering human, natural, and economic topics. The map shown here of Africa's vegetation, derived from satellite imagery, on-the-ground analysis, and population data for urban areas, was compiled using data from the University of Maryland Global Land Cover Facility.

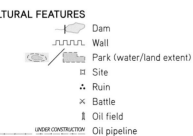

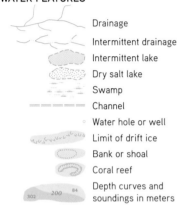

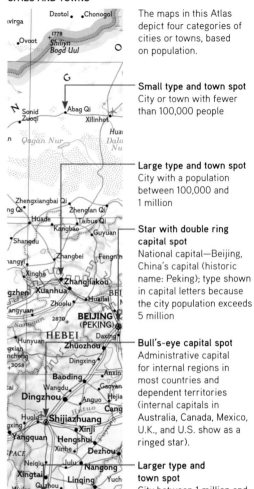

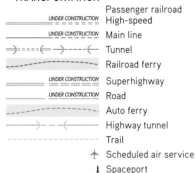

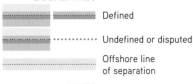

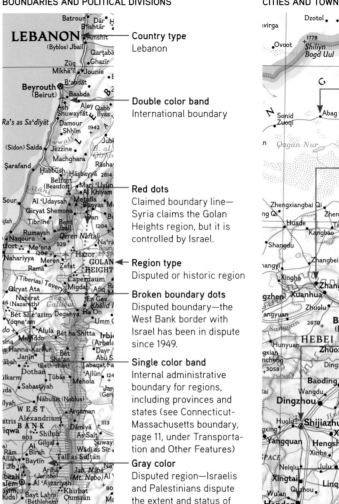

TRANSPORTATION AND OTHER FEATURES

Dashed red line
Trail or track

Red line
Road

Gray line
Passenger railroad

Single color band with black dots
Internal administrative boundary, in this case, the Connecticut-Massachusetts state boundary

Double red line
Superhighway, such as interstates, motorways, and limited-access highways

Double gray line
High-speed passenger railroad

Plane
Airport with scheduled service

Red dots in water
Intracoastal Waterway

Dashed red line in water
Car or passenger ferry

Gray dashes in water
National park extent in water

PHYSICAL FEATURES

Blue dot pattern
Dry salt lake bed

Cross
Mountain summit—elevations in meters (also in feet for highest mountains)

Blue line and dots
Intermittent drainage

Brown random dot pattern
Lava field

Crater symbol
Volcanic or meteor crater

Dashed blue line
Outline for intermittent lakes or dry salt lakes

Brown line pattern
Area below sea level

Blue area with blue outline
Perennial lake

Brown dot pattern
Sand

Blue line
River

Water is key to life on Earth. Lack of water can lead to desertification and human migration.

"When people at a party ask me where I'm from and I say Morocco, the conversation often comes to a complete halt. Even if they know nothing about my country, people could ask where it is. Then they might ask me about its languages or religions or its physical appearance."

Amine Elouazzani, an American college graduate, could have at best been describing how to use the *National Geographic Collegiate Atlas of the World.* A well-educated person should know how to ask good questions and be able to read, understand, and appreciate maps. Use the political and thematic maps in this Atlas to orient yourself to the world at present and to inform your direction for the future.

The maps in the political, or reference, section of this Atlas show international boundaries, cities, national parks, road networks, and other features, organized by continent. In the index, most entries are keyed to place-names on the political maps, citing the page number, followed by their geographic coordinates. The thematic maps at the front of the Atlas explore topics in depth, revealing the rich patchwork and infinite interrelatedness of our changing planet. In selecting from the vast storehouse of knowledge about the Earth, the Atlas editors relied upon proven data sources, detailed in the bibliography.

Other Elements

GRAPHS, CHARTS, AND TABLES

Conveying relationships, facts, and trends quickly and efficiently is the work of these types of displays. They are diagrams that compare information in visual form. Three common types are the bar graph, the line graph, and the circle (or pie) chart. This Atlas uses all three conventions. The bar graph below, from the Health & Literacy thematic spread, compares male and female literacy rates for a range of countries and in relation to world averages. The viewer gains immediate insight not only into the level of literacy in a society but also into the relative value and status accorded to women. These graphic presentations summarize complex data and are most valuable when they generate deep and penetrating inquiry.

Male and Female Literacy Rates
(as a percentage of total population age 15 and over)

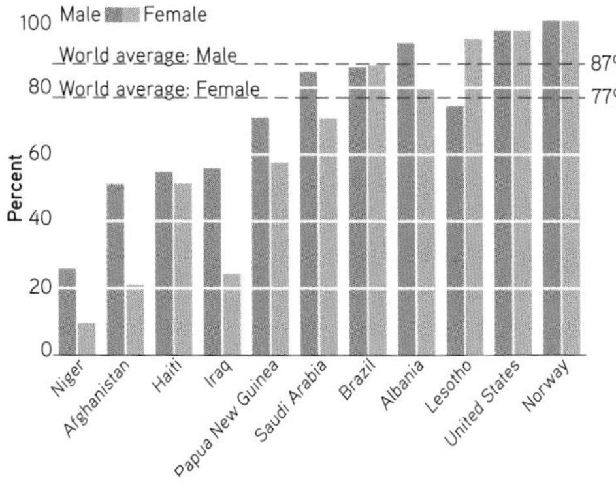

OTHER UNIQUE FEATURES

The Atlas employs a variety of images and mapping techniques to express data. A cartogram, for instance, depicts the size of an object, such as a country, in relation to an attribute, not geographic space. Grounded in research by the Population Reference Bureau, this cartogram represents countries by unit of population, with only a suggestive nod to geographical location. An economic cartogram shows the relative prosperity of the countries of the world. In both cases, editors chose cartograms as the most visually striking way to convey the information. On a map showing the distribution of human population, LandScan global population databases were used, as the most reliable and visually striking tool. While this Atlas is distinguished by its thematic maps, individual thematic maps are, in turn, distinguished by the number of variables analyzed.

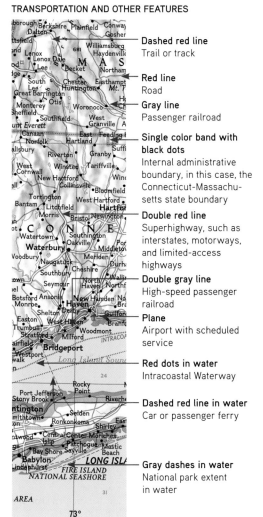

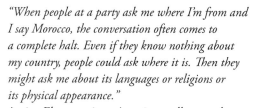

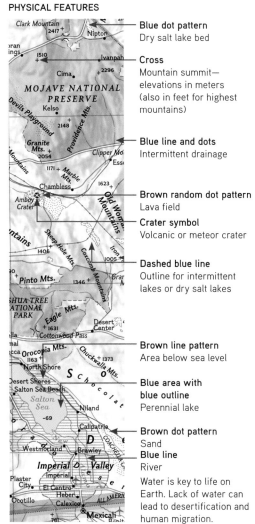

World Population, 2010
1 block = 2 million people

Population Growth Rate (as a percentage of total population)
More than 3%
2.0–2.9%
1.0–1.9%
0–0.9%
Negative growth

TEXT AND GEOBYTES

A blue box on each spread is headed GeoBytes—short, striking facts chosen on a need-to-know or fun-to-know basis. Each thematic spread is introduced with a text block that discusses the theme and alludes to the graphic presentations. Each map or graphic is anchored by explanatory text for a complete and coherent unit.

GeoBytes

UNIQUE SPECIES
Madagascar and the Indian Ocean islands are home to many species found nowhere else. Of the region's 13,000 plant species, more than 89% are endemic, meaning that is the only place on Earth they live.

FRAGILE POPULATIONS
Nearly half of the world's tortoises and freshwater turtles are threatened.

HUMAN HEALTH
Medicines derived from plants and animals are the primary source of health care for 80% of the world's population.

ECONOMIC VALUE
Scientists estimate that ecosystems worldwide provide goods and services, such as nutrient recycling and waste treatment, valued at more than $20 trillion a year.

EXTINCTION RISK
One in every eight birds and one in every four mammals face a high risk of extinction in the near future.

BEETLEMANIA
Beetles are the most diverse life-form on Earth. More than a thousand different kinds can live on a single tree in the forests of South America.

Map Scale Relationships in this Atlas

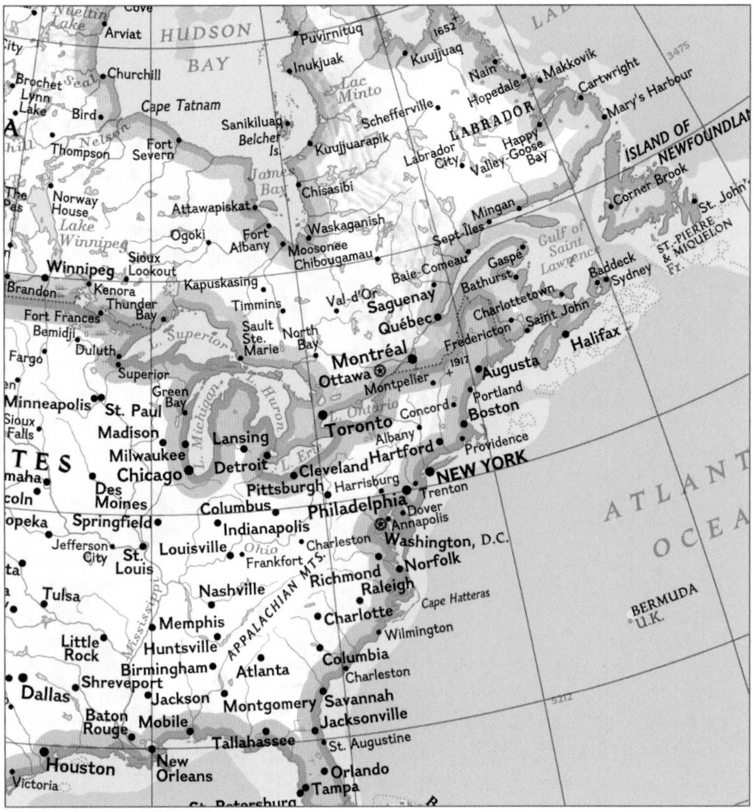

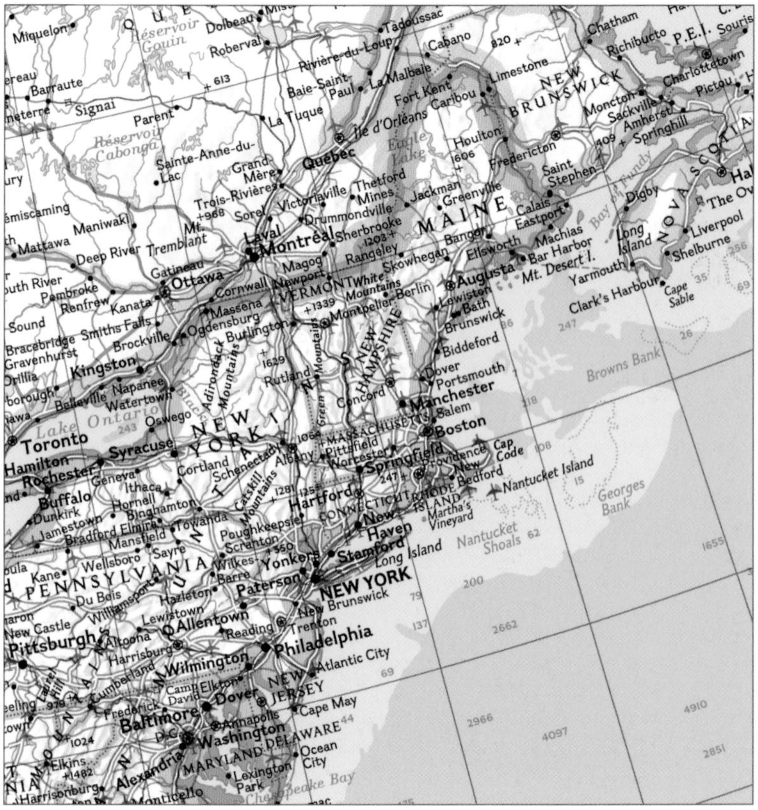

Map Projections

LAMBERT AZIMUTHAL EQUAL-AREA
Distortion away from the center makes this projection a poor choice for world maps but useful for fairly circular regions. It is used on the Trade and Globalization spread, pages 56-57, in the Income Group, 2010, map.

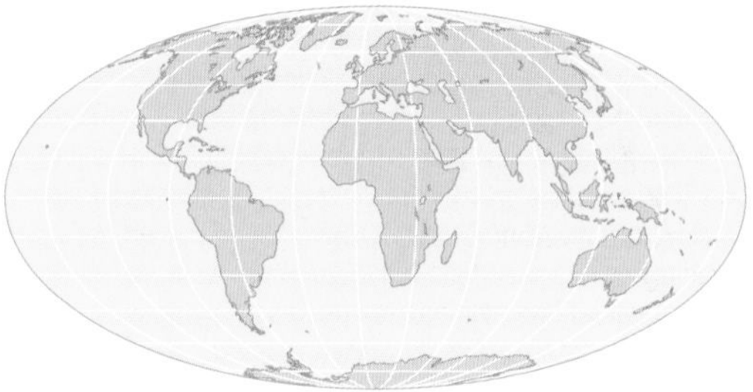

MOLLWEIDE
In 1805, Carl B. Mollweide, a German mathematician, devised this elliptical equal-area projection that represents relative sizes accurately but distorts shapes at the edges. Several thematic maps in the Atlas use the Mollweide.

AZIMUTHAL EQUIDISTANT
Mapmakers can choose any center point, from which directions and distances are true, but in outer areas shapes and sizes are distorted. On this projection, Antarctica, the Arctic Ocean, and several continents appear.

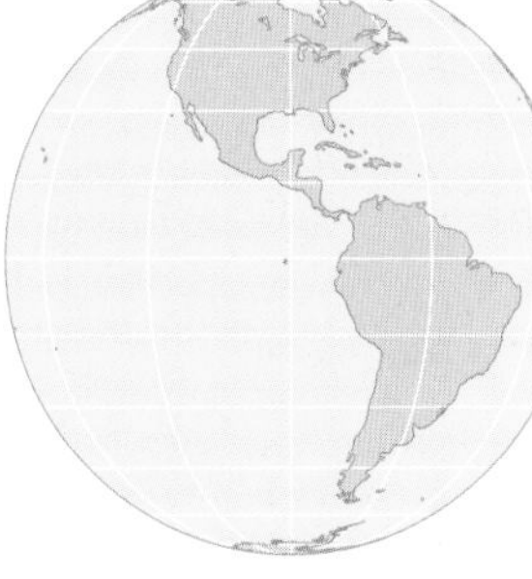

ORTHOGRAPHIC
Designed to show Earth as seen from a distant point in space, the orthographic is usually used to portray hemispheres. Distortion at the edges, however, compresses landmasses.

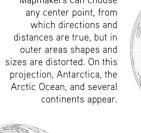

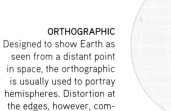

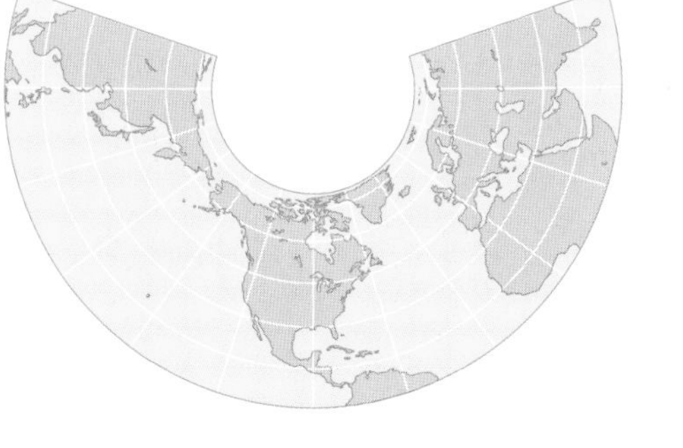

ALBERS CONIC EQUAL-AREA
The Albers is a good format for mapping mid-latitude regions that are larger east to west than north to south. Most maps of the United States in the Atlas appear on this projection.

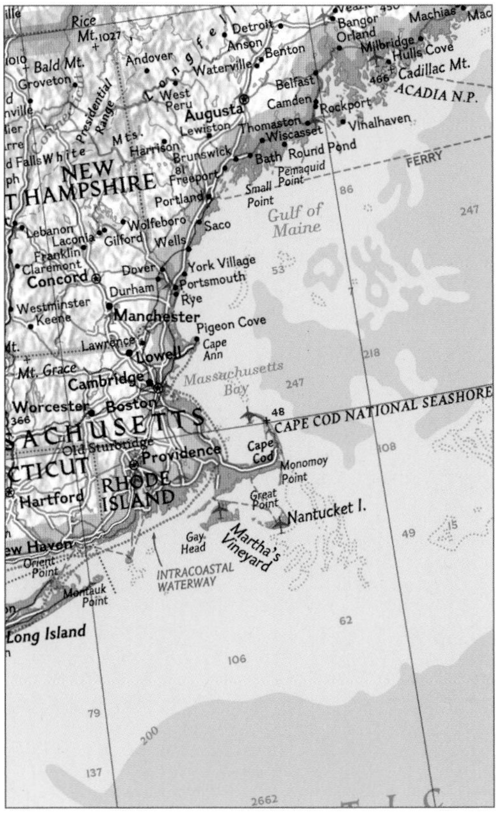

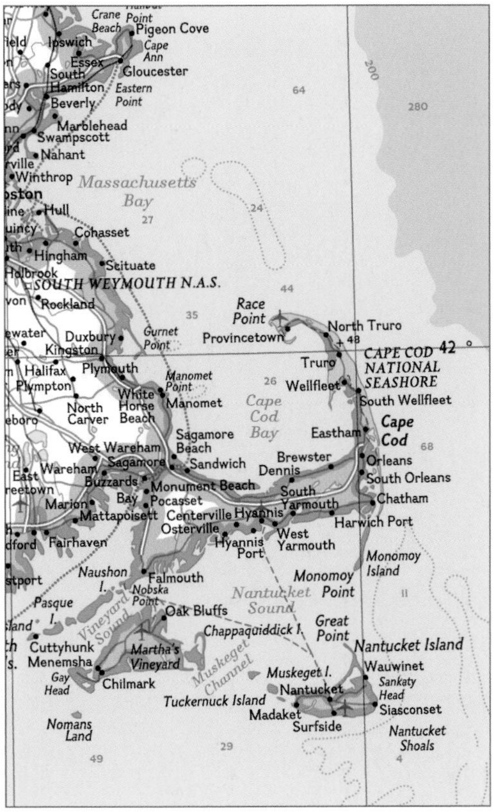

Map scale describes the relationship between distance on a map and distance on the ground. It is usually presented as a ratio or fraction in any of three ways. Verbal scale is a written description of scale, such as "one centimeter equals 100 kilometers," meaning one centimeter on the map is equal to 100 kilometers on the ground. A graphic scale is a bar or line with tick marks showing units such as kilometers or miles that graphically represent scale. A representative fraction (RF) or ratio scale indicates how much the size of a physical area was reduced to fit on the map by showing the relationship between one unit on the map and one unit of the same length on the ground. For example, if the scale is in centimeters and reads 1:10,000,000 (or 1/10,000,000), then each centimeter on the map represents 100 kilometers on the ground.

Political maps in this Atlas were created in a range of scales from global cartographic databases that merged data from maps NGS created in the past. These four maps illustrate the relationship between the scale of a map and the area shown. The area shown decreases as scale increases, while the level of detail shown increases. Smaller scale maps such as the U.S. map on the far left (1:36,000,000) show more area but only the largest features are visible. Large scale maps, such as the map of Cape Cod (1:1,750,000), show a small area but in greater detail.

INTERRUPTED GOODE HOMOLOSINE
To minimize distortion of shape and preserve horizontal scale, this projection interrupts the globe. Its equal-area quality makes it suitable for mapping distributions of various kinds of information.

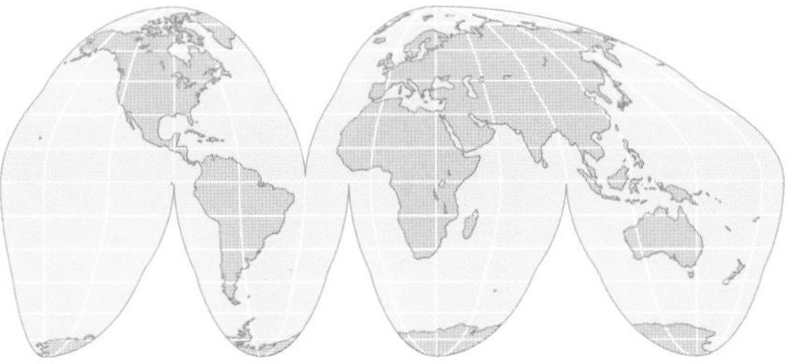

BUCKMINSTER FULLER
Also known as the "Dymaxion map," this projection created by Richard Buckminster Fuller in the mid-20th century mostly retains the relative size of each part of the globe. Because the continents are not split, one can better see continental interconnectedness.

WINKEL TRIPEL
First developed by Oswald Winkel in 1921, this "tripel" projection avoids the congestion and compression of polar areas that are common to many projections. The shapes of countries and islands closely resemble their true shapes as one would see on a globe.

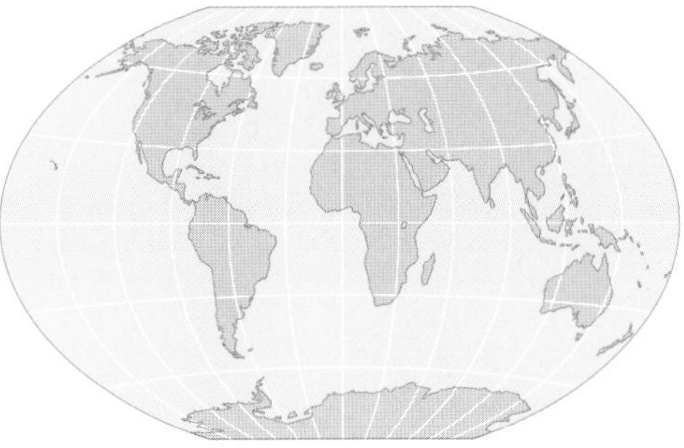

ECKERT EQUAL-AREA
Produced by German educator Max Eckert, this projection represents the Poles by a line one-half the length of the Equator. Polar regions are less compressed than on elliptical projections; low-latitude landmasses are elongated.

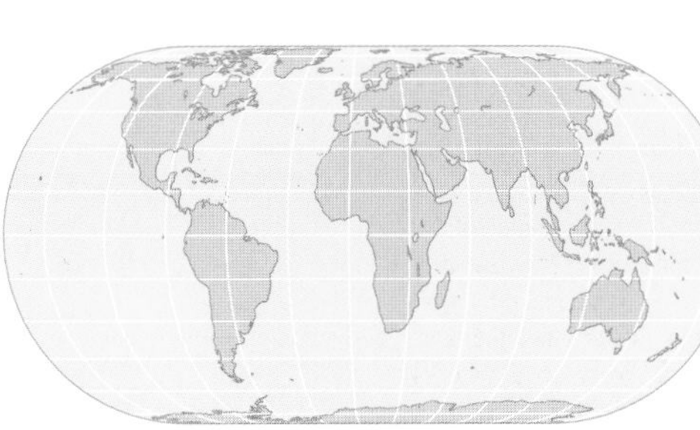

MERCATOR
Named for Gerardus Mercator, the Flemish geographer who invented it in 1569, this most famous of all map projections was intended for navigation. Useful for showing constant bearings as straight lines, the Mercator greatly exaggerates areas at higher latitudes.

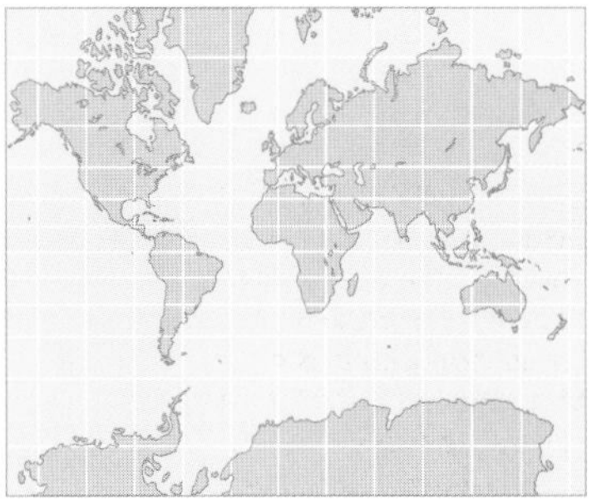

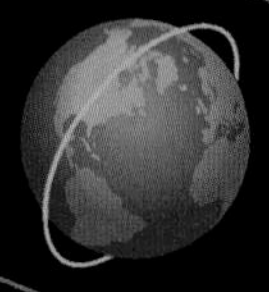

EYES IN THE SKY
Geostationary satellites follow the Earth's path 35,888 kilometers (22,300 miles) above, giving us a wide window to life below. Low-altitude satellites cross the Equator and the Poles many times per day and eventually view most of the planet.

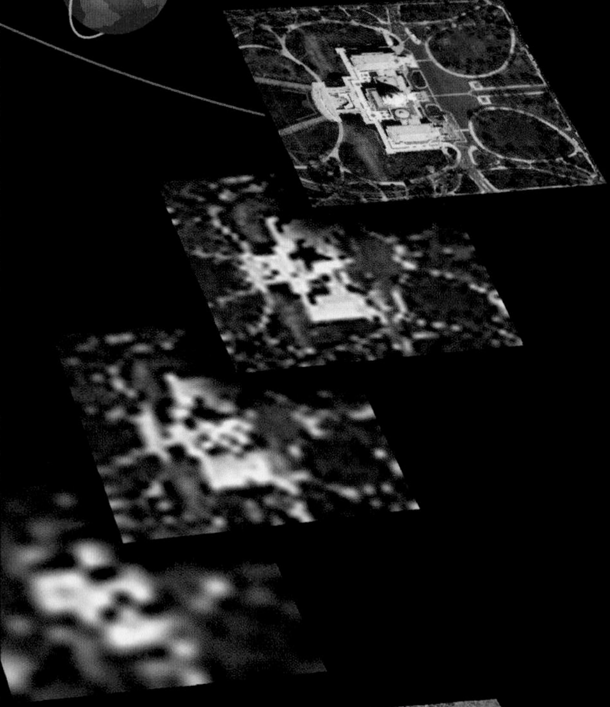

COMING INTO FOCUS
With increased spatial resolution, details emerge in these computer-generated images based on an aerial photograph of the U.S. Capitol in Washington, D.C. From bottom to top, they mimic the 30 (98)-, 15 (49)-, 10 (33)-, and 1-meter (3-feet) resolution of commercial satellites.

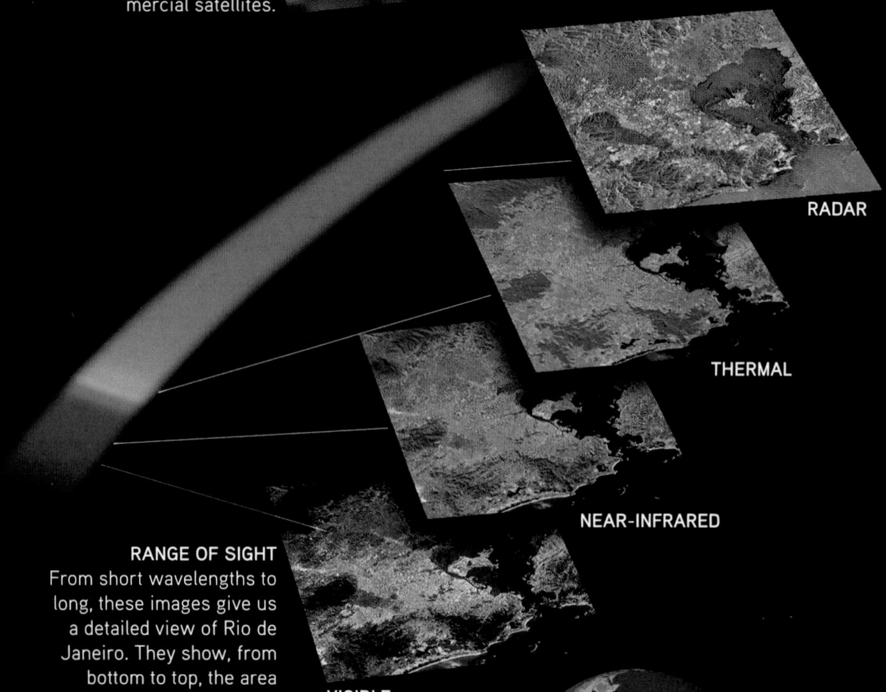

RANGE OF SIGHT
From short wavelengths to long, these images give us a detailed view of Rio de Janeiro. They show, from bottom to top, the area as seen in visible light; vegetation (red) as seen in near-infrared; heat (bright colors) in thermal; and the city's features (black and white) as seen in radar.

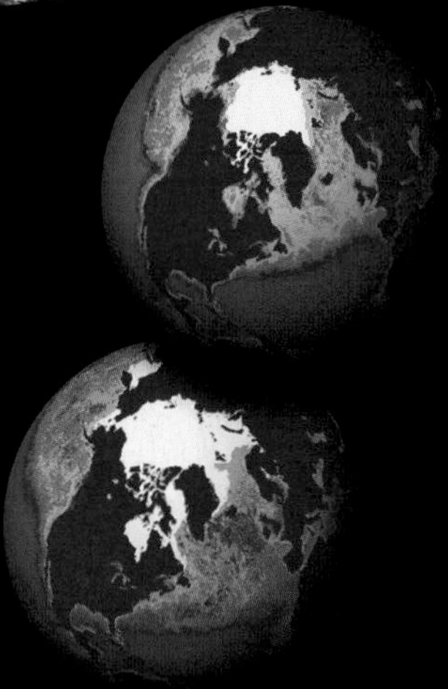

SPOTTING CHANGE
Composite images compiled from low-altitude satellite data illustrate seasonal changes across the globe. Polar ice (white) creeps southward in February (bottom) and by September (top) it has retreated and phytoplankton flourishes (red, orange, and yellow).

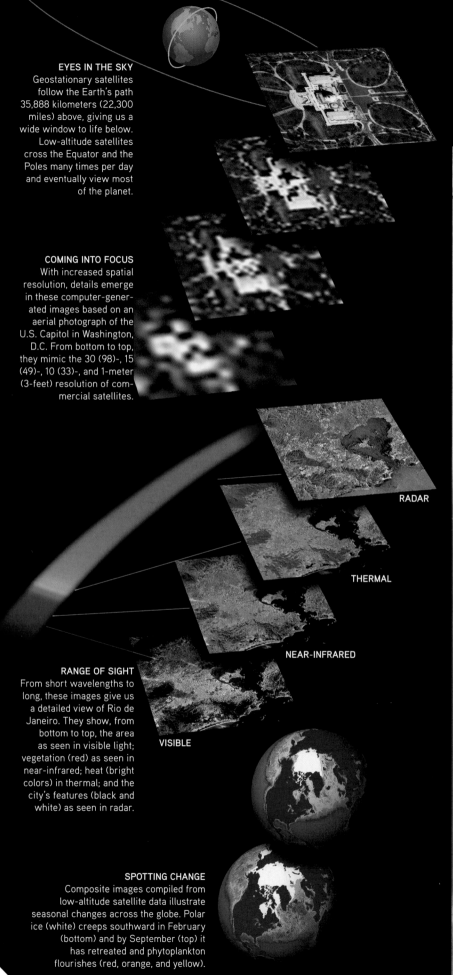

SATELLITE COMPOSITE
The human eye sees only a tiny fraction of the spectrum of electromagnetic radiation that illuminates the world, a narrow band known as "visible" radiation. With the aid of remote sensing, we are able to view a wider range of that spectrum, including infrared, thermal, and microwave bands. From space, we are also able to view large expanses of the Earth, as well as small areas, in great detail. From an altitude of 730 kilometers (454 miles), Landsat 7 can view features as small as 15 meters (49 feet) across. Scientists use remote-sensing satellite data to understand global processes on the Earth's surface, in the oceans, and in the lower atmosphere.

This mosaic image of North America illustrates some of the types of remotely sensed data that scientists have access to today. The eastern third of the continent shows clusters of light on the Earth's surface visible from space at night, helping us better understand urbanization and population density. False-color is used in the middle of the continent to show surface-feature classes. Reds and purples represent different classes or types of vegetation; blues show arid land. Images like this are useful for environmental monitoring. The westernmost part of the continent is in true color. The greener areas are more densely vegetated and less populated. Vibrant colors of the oceans represent sea-surface temperature. Areas in red are the warmest; the blues are the coolest.

To create this image, data were extracted from a number of datasets—the Advanced Very High Resolution Radiometer (AVHRR), the Moderate Resolution Imaging Spectroradiometer (MODIS), and versions 4, 5, and 7 of the Landsat Enhanced Thematic Mapper (ETM). The base of the image was enhanced with shaded relief produced from Shuttle Radar Topography Mission (SRTM) digital elevation model (DEM) data.

A century ago balloonists recorded bird's-eye views of the landscape below on film. Today satellites take increasingly detailed pictures of Earth, penetrating darkness and clouds to create composite images of the land and seafloor and to map once-elusive features such as the ozone hole. Remote sensing—the examination of the Earth from a distance—has widespread applications, from military surveillance to archaeological exposure. And, by layering different sets of remotely sensed data, scientists can study relationships between phenomena such as shrinking polar ice and rising global temperatures.

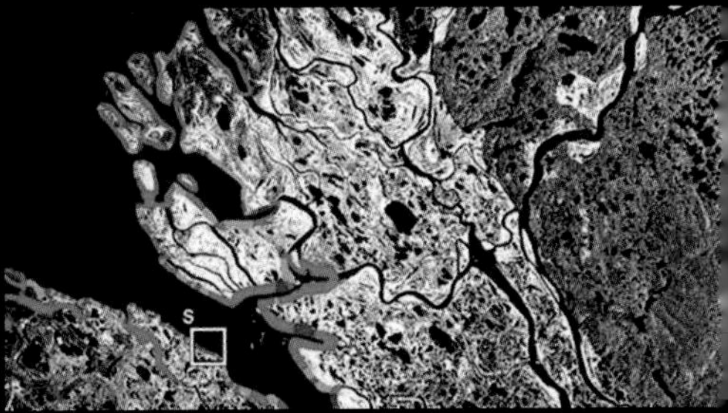

Satellite images from 1973 to 1999 were used to measure change along Canada's Beaufort Sea coastline, an area highly sensitive to erosion. This image illustrates areas o rapid erosion (red), moderate erosion (orange), no detect-able erosion (green), and accretion (blue).

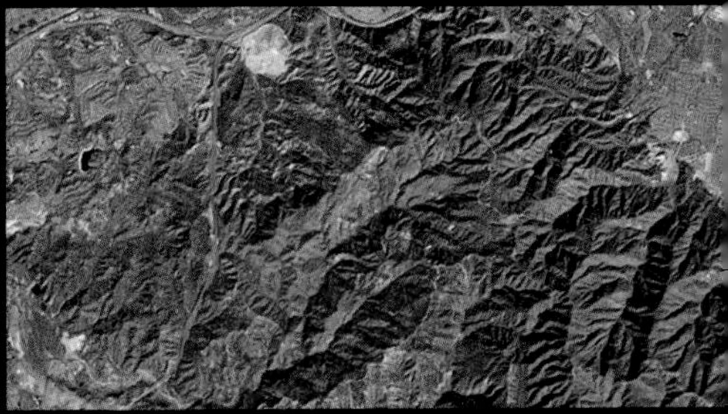

Nearly 4,450 hectares (11,000 acres) burned in the February 2006 Sierra fire in Orange County, California. Deep red tones in the center of this Landsat image show the burned areas on February 12th, the day the fire was contained.

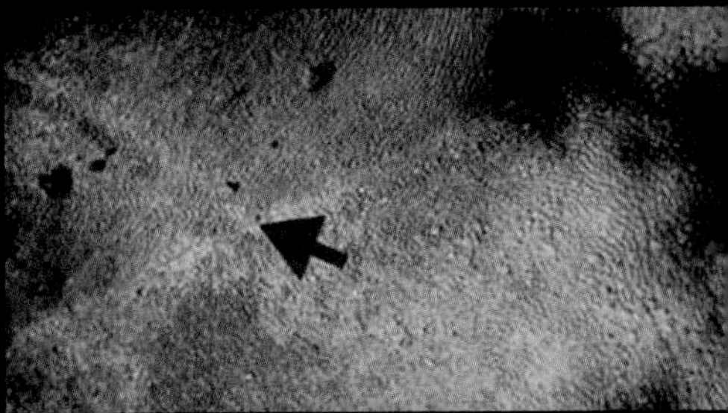

With the help of remote-sensing imagery, archaeologists have identified ancient footpaths in the Arenal Region of Costa Rica. These 2,500-year-old footpaths are being used to study the prehistoric religious, economic, political and social organization of the region.

Geographic Data Layers

GIS enables the layering of data. Vector data represents precise location in terms of a point (a city or airport, for example), a line (roadways, rivers, boundaries), or a polygon (an area such as a body of water or a protected area category). Raster data presents continuous data (such as elevation) or classes of data (for example, population densities) that cover the area in pixels, the discrete elements that make up an image. Vector and raster data are geographically referenced, allowing for overlay.

VECTOR DATA (point)

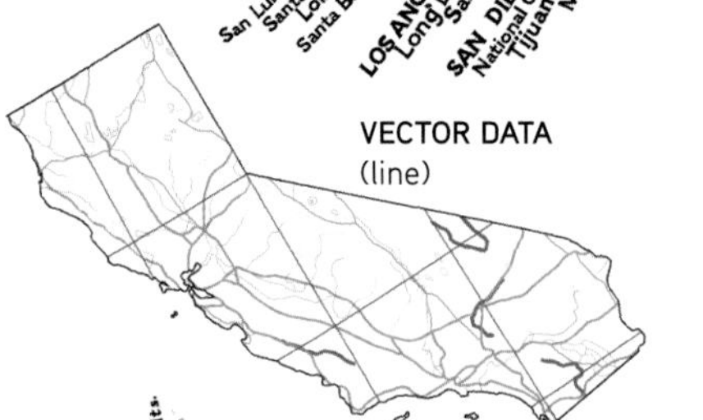
VECTOR DATA (line)

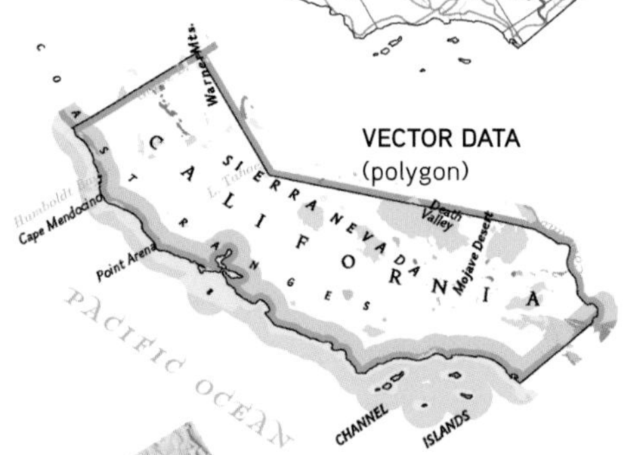

VECTOR DATA (polygon)

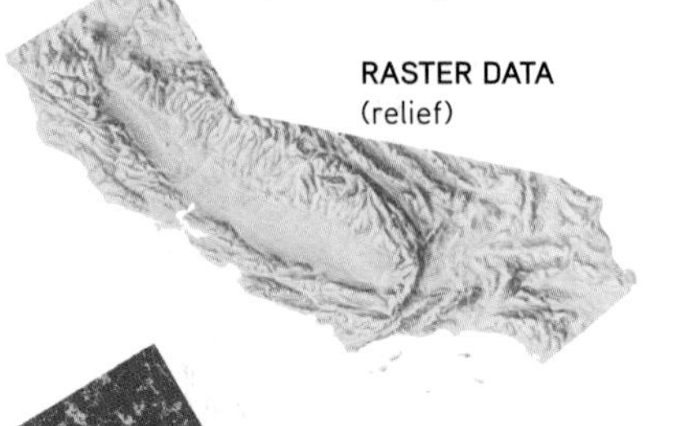
RASTER DATA (relief)

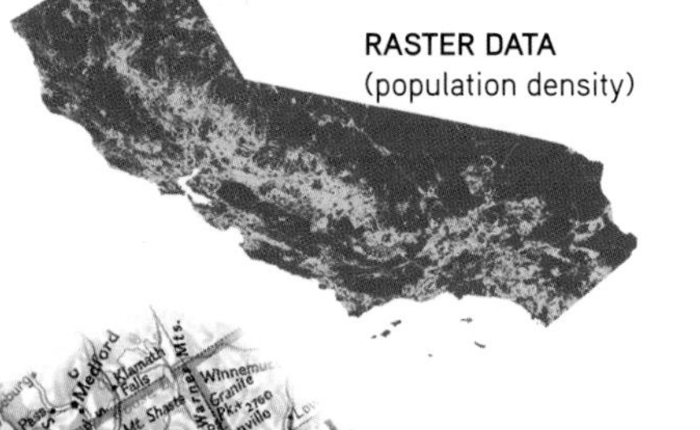
RASTER DATA (population density)

VECTOR AND RASTER DATA COMBINED

Understanding Our World Through GIS

Geographic Information Systems (GIS) is a digitally organized collection of computer hardware, software, methodology, and data assemblage and storage. GIS supports the capture, manipulation, and analysis of place-based information. A highly adaptable tool, GIS provides the means to store and display geographic data and to analyze and describe patterns, distributions, and phenomena. Because so many human and environmental issues can be usefully considered in geographic terms, GIS is becoming increasingly common across a range of enterprises. Foresters use GIS data to inventory trees. Epidemiologists model and predict the spread of disease. Policy makers, environmentalists, and city planners employ GIS technologies to analyze issues and provide dramatic visualizations for matters ranging from wildfire management in the western United States to the rates of suburban sprawl in India's burgeoning cities. The attraction of GIS comes from the magnitude of its analytical capabilities that, in turn, derive from once-unimaginable powers of manipulation of spatial data to suit specific needs. For example, a table with latitude/longitude coordinates of car crashes can be overlaid with a road network to route emergency service vehicles and estimate their arrival time. Combine the crash incident database with other geospatial data, such as terrain, weather, transportation infrastructure, or socioeconomic characteristics, and traffic planners can determine contributing factors to accidents and recommend preventative action. More and more, GIS is the analytical tool for understanding patterns and processes that affect our lives.

GIS Data Structure

GIS data have both spatial and attribute components. Spatial components are mapped features, such as the cities and rivers on this map of South America. Attribute components consist of stored data, as shown in the windows above and below the map. Attribute components might include, for example, socioeconomic characteristics of a city. GIS correlates spatial and attribute data, creating overlays that reveal geospatial relationships. Another use of GIS is digital indexing, which constituted a major advance over laborious and error-prone manual compilation. This Atlas used customized GIS software to coordinate place-names with latitude and longitude (see bubble below).

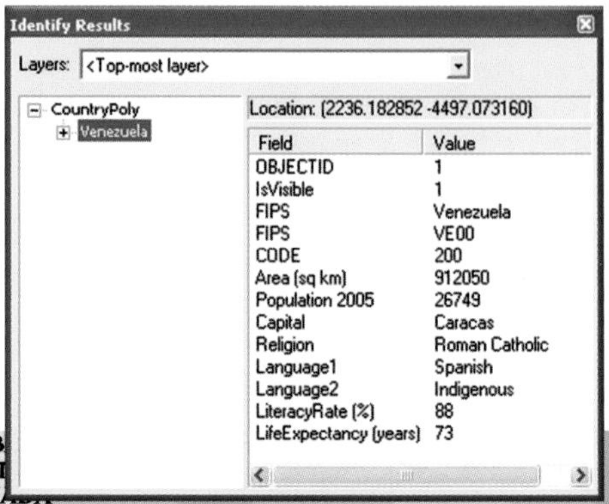

URBAN PLANNING
GIS can be used to inventory and visualize urban land use patterns. The strict code of zoning laws and classifications common to cities and towns requires an accurate database management system. GIS can not only manage the zoning database but can also portray the data in a map. Such visualization can help clarify development issues, plan resource allocations, or identify park and open space needs. Maps with specific GIS overlays can help address questions of, for example, school zones, land ownership, or sprawl.

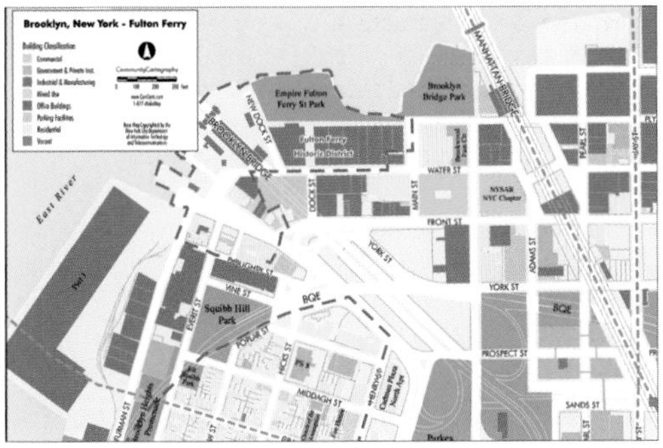

TRANSPORTATION
Many applications of GIS exist within the transportation sector and work particularly well when coupled with the pinpoint accuracy of Global Positioning System (GPS) technology. Freight shipping companies frequently turn to GIS to estimate arrival times of their trucks, using real-time traffic information, digital representations of nationwide transportation infrastructure, and GPS information. Individual drivers have become accustomed to using GIS and GPS for finding directions and avoiding traffic jams.

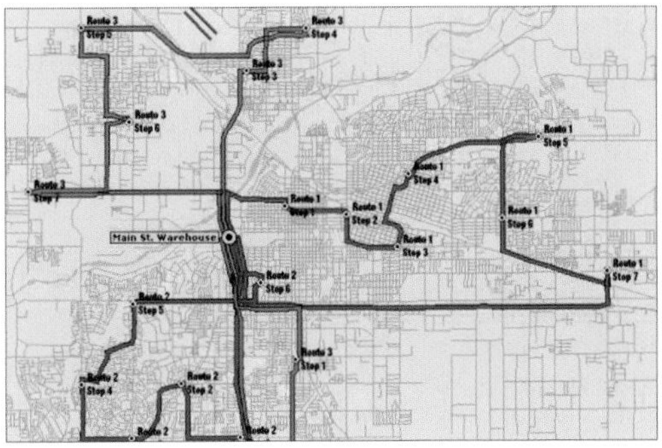

EMERGENCY MANAGEMENT
In emergency management, GIS can be used to model potential disasters, track real-time weather, plan and adjust evacuation routes, define disaster areas, and inventory damage. Predicting and tracking wildfire helps fire management crews plan and allocate resources. GIS can show the before-and-after appearance of the land affected by a disaster, which can help recovery and show how to plan ahead for next time.

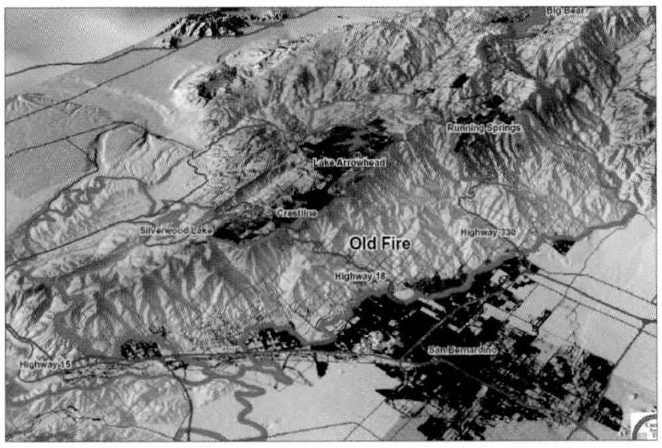

DEMOGRAPHICS AND CENSUS
The U.S. Census Bureau stores demographic and socioeconomic data at numerous levels, even at the county, tract, or city-block level. Applying spatial analysis techniques to such archival data can reveal patterns, trends, and distributions. The findings can be put to various uses, including encouraging economic development or indicating the results of elections.

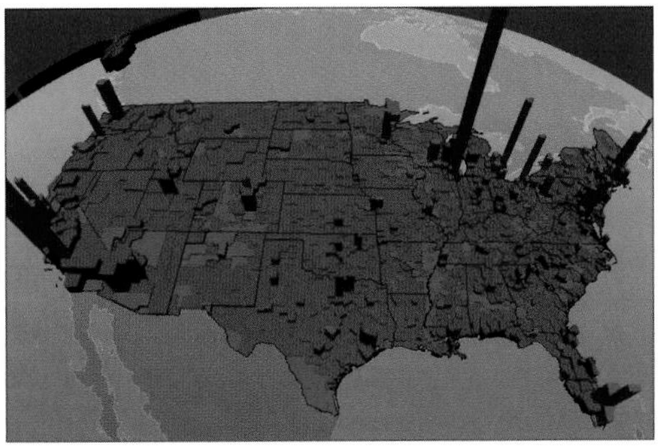

HEALTH
During the 2002-03 SARS outbreak in China, an Internet GIS server allowed for the rapid collection and dissemination of data to health officials and the public. This application tracked the spread of the disease, detected patterns, and distributed accurate information. GIS is currently being used to monitor the H5N1 strain of avian flu around the world, combining outbreaks with pertinent data such as wildfowl migration routes and locations of poultry farms.

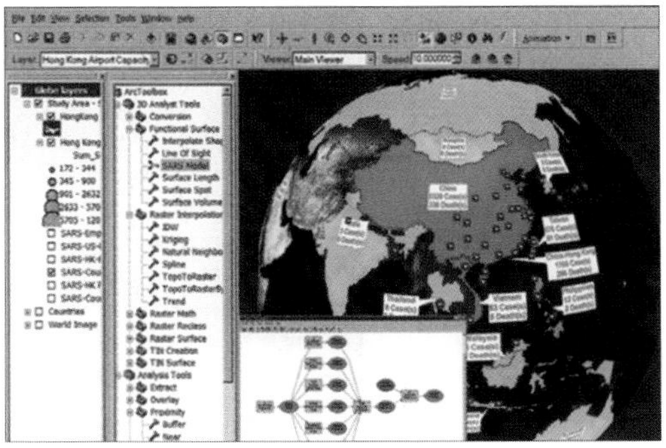

CONSERVATION
Mapping the effects of human population growth and deforestation on Asian elephant habitat highlights the versatility of GIS. Satellite images, demographic data, and elephant locations derived from radio tracking and GPS yielded a comprehensive database and visualization of elephant viability in Myanmar (formerly Burma). The study demonstrated that the rate of deforestation caused by human population growth was lower here than in most countries of Southeast Asia and as a result elephant populations were less affected .

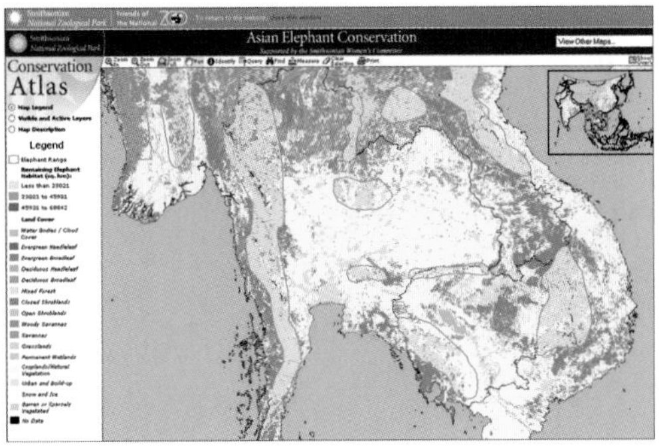

At the dawn of the Age of Exploration, the problem facing mapmakers was a dearth of information. With geospatial data flowing from satellite imagery, aerial photography, on-the-ground surveying, quantitative data, and archival records, the challenge for cartographers became how to manage a wealth of information. Geographic Information Systems (GIS), a sophisticated and versatile digital tool set with a wide range of applications, provides a solution. The data management capabilities of this digital technology make geospatial information readily available for analysis, modeling, and mapping. Scientists use GIS to inventory plant and animal species in their native habitats. Disaster relief managers identify at-risk areas and evacuation routes. The 2004 U.S. presidential election marked the first time that GIS software was used to collate and present near-real-time voting tallies. While GIS allows the layering of information, on-board and handheld Global Positioning System (GPS) devices pinpoint location. Today, geospatial concepts permeate ordinary life to an extraordinary degree.

GeoBytes

BORN IN THE SIXTIES
GIS is a young field, having its beginnings in the 1960s, during the so-called Quantitative Revolution in Geography.

GIS IN COLLEGE
Some 200 universities and colleges offer majors or courses in GIS, with most but not all in Geography departments.

GIS AT WORK
The list of professions that utilize GIS continues to grow and now includes agriculture, archaeology, banking, biology, cartography, civil engineering, ecology, economics, forestry, health care, meteorology, public policy and safety, transportation, urban planning, and utilities.

GIS IN OIL AND GAS
The oil and gas industries use GIS, often combining satellite imagery and radar scans of the Earth's surface to "see through the ground" for new discoveries.

IN SERVICE TO OTHERS
After Hurricanes Katrina and Rita in 2005, nearly a thousand GIS professionals volunteered to gather field data and use GIS to aid recovery on the U.S. Gulf Coast.

MORE THAN MAPS
Anything with a spatial dimension can be recorded, stored, analyzed, and visualized within GIS.

GIS AND GPS TOGETHER
GIS, along with GPS, is used in archaeology to inventory artifacts and digitally recreate ancient sites.

DATA DATA DATA
Local, state, and federal governments are the major producers of GIS data.

HIGH MAINTENANCE
The collection and maintenance of data are the most expensive activities in GIS, sometimes running into the tens of millions of dollars for a field such as transportation asset management.

WHAT ARE MAPS, EXACTLY, and how can we use them to understand our planet? In the pages that proceed we hope to answer that question with pictures that are more than just pictures. The thematic map spreads that follow all show the familiar outlines of coastlines and continents, the traditional arrangements of north to the top of the page and south to the bottom. But each also tells its own unique story based on years of research, oceans of data, and often, the mix of creativity and attention to detail that makes cartography both art and science. Taken together they show, more than anything, the profound and often surprising connections that tie our world and its peoples together.

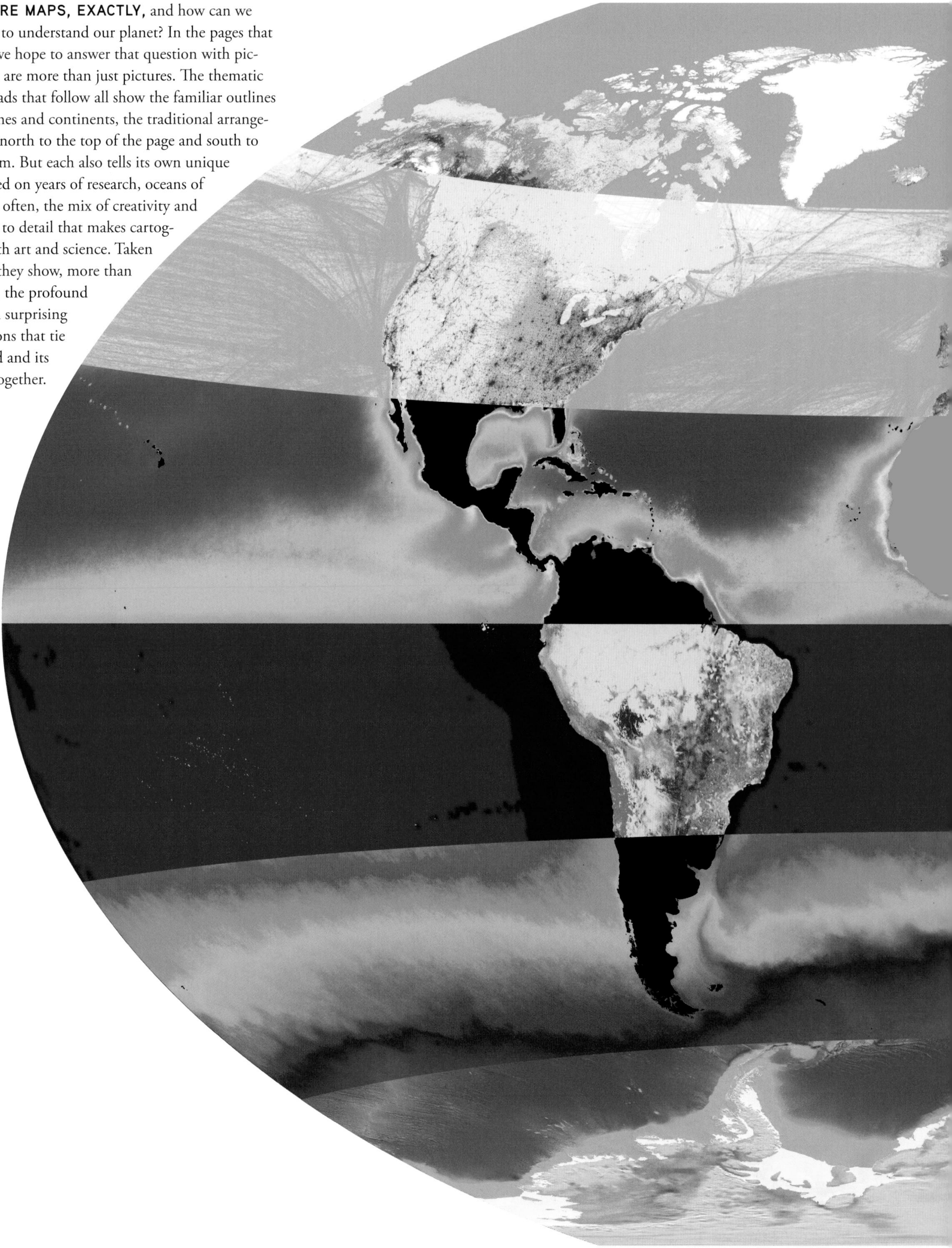

Thematic World

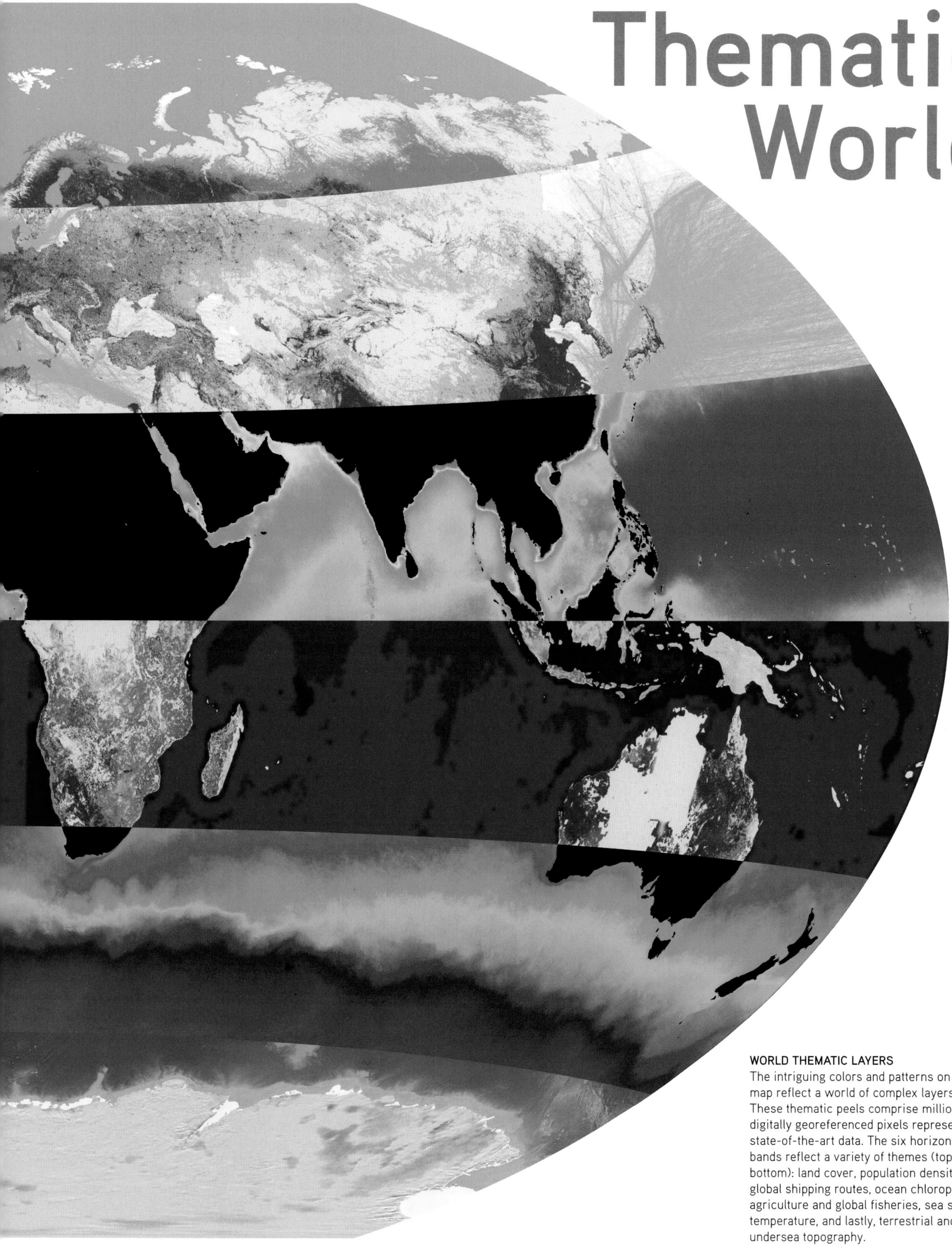

WORLD THEMATIC LAYERS
The intriguing colors and patterns on this map reflect a world of complex layers. These thematic peels comprise millions of digitally georeferenced pixels representing state-of-the-art data. The six horizontal bands reflect a variety of themes (top to bottom): land cover, population density and global shipping routes, ocean chlorophyll, agriculture and global fisheries, sea surface temperature, and lastly, terrestrial and undersea topography.

PHYSICAL REGIONS

This artist-rendered relief map depicts Earth's landforms above and below the surface of the ocean. Major mountain systems are shaded to emphasize their elevation. The Himalaya tower over India's Ganges plain; the Andes and Rocky Mountains reign over the Americas. All are dwarfed by the Mid-Atlantic Ridge, a submarine mountain range that stretches from Iceland to near Antarctica.

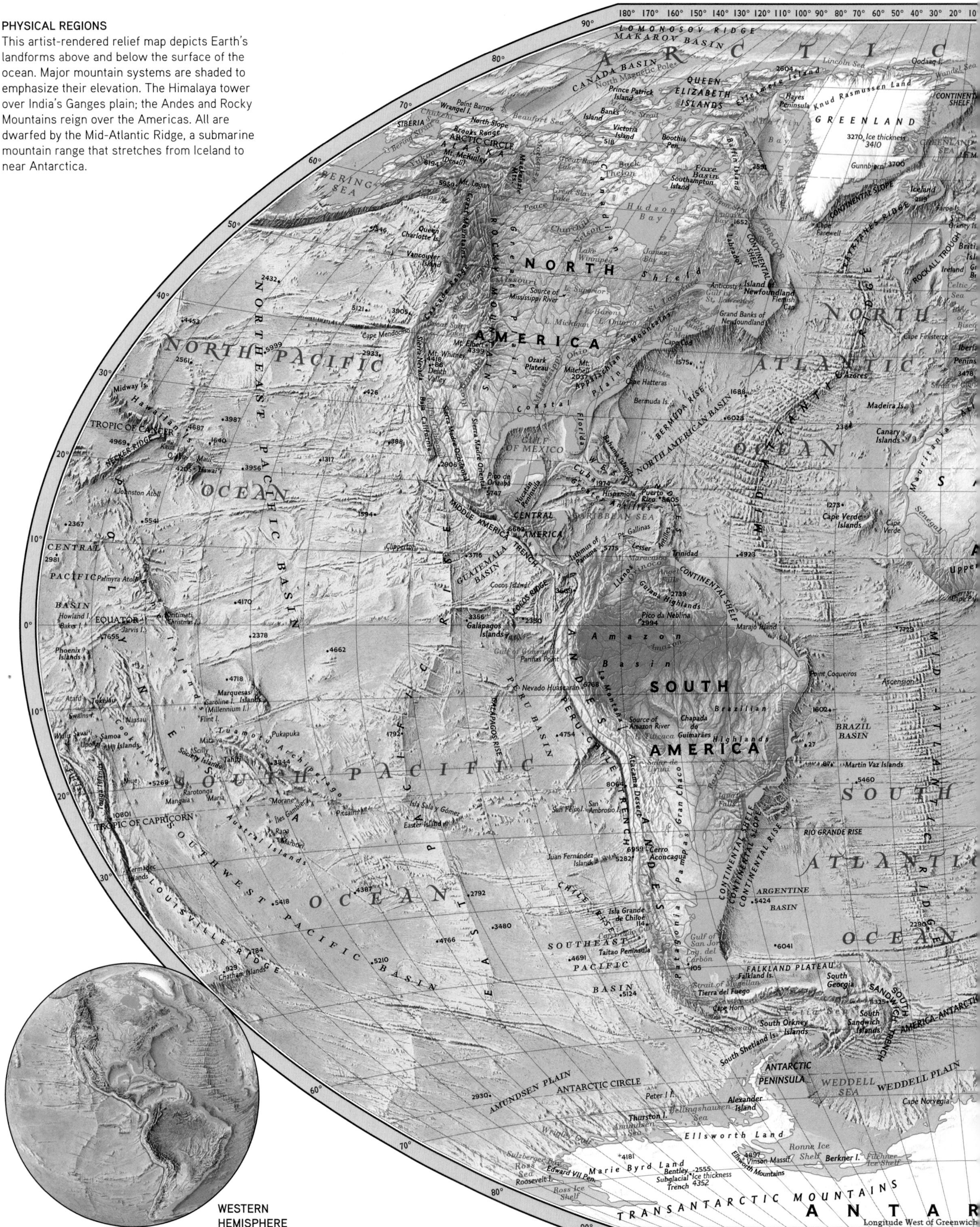

WESTERN HEMISPHERE

WINKEL TRIPEL PROJECTION, CENTRAL MERIDIAN 0°

SCALE 1:96,338,000

1 centimeter = 963 kilometers; 1 inch = 1520 miles at the equator

0 500 1000 1500 2000 2500
KILOMETERS

0 500 1000 1500 2000 2500
STATUTE MILES

EASTERN
HEMISPHERE

POLITICAL BOUNDARIES

The world is divided into 194 independent countries, with colors on the map showing the extents of national sovereignty. International boundaries only occasionally mark true cultural boundaries; they are more often a complex artifact of colonialism, conquest, religious conversion, and conflict. The political map is a useful but all-too-neat construct for a bewilderingly complicated world.

ARCTIC REGION

0 600 km
0 600 mi
Azimuthal Equidistant Projection

WINKEL TRIPEL PROJECTION, CENTRAL MERIDIAN 0°
SCALE 1:96,338,000
1 centimeter = 963 kilometers; 1 inch = 1520 miles at the equator
0 500 1000 1500 2000 2500
KILOMETERS
0 500 1000 1500 2000 2500
STATUTE MILES

ANTARCTIC REGION
0 600 km
0 600 mi
Azimuthal Equidistant Projection
● Research station

GEOLOGIC FORCES

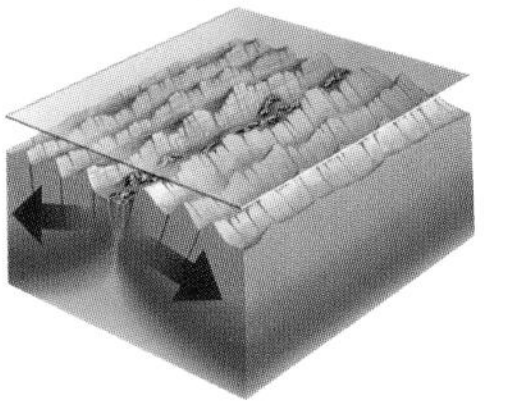

SEAFLOOR SPREADING
Adjacent oceanic plates diverge, at the rate of a few centimeters a year. Along such boundaries—the Mid-Atlantic Ridge and the East Pacific Rise—molten rock (magma) pours forth to form new crust (lithosphere).

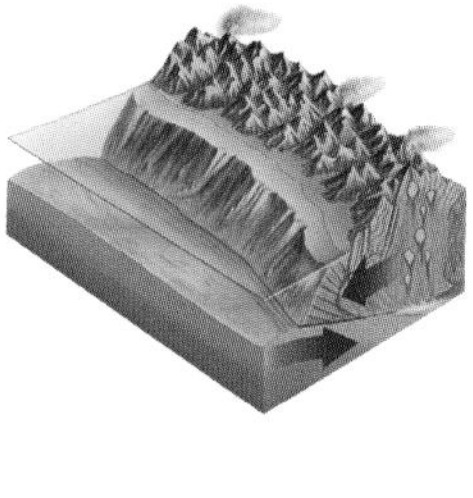

SUBDUCTION
When two massive plates collide, the older, colder, denser one—usually the oceanic plate—takes a dive. Pushed into the Earth, the plate is transformed into molten material that may rise again in volcanic eruption. Subduction also causes earthquakes, raises coastal mountains, and forms island arcs such as the Aleutians and the Lesser Antilles.

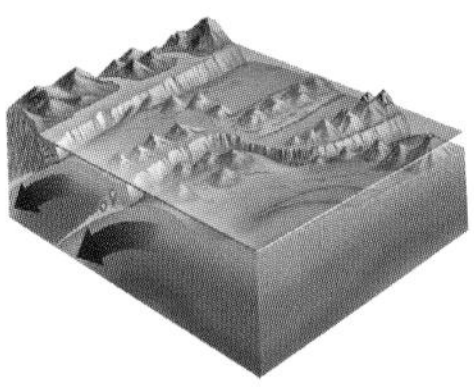

ACCRETION
As ocean plates advance on continental edges or island arcs and slide under them, seamounts on the ocean floor are skimmed off and pile up in submarine trenches. The buildup can fuse with continental plates, as most geologists agree was the case with Alaska and much of western North America.

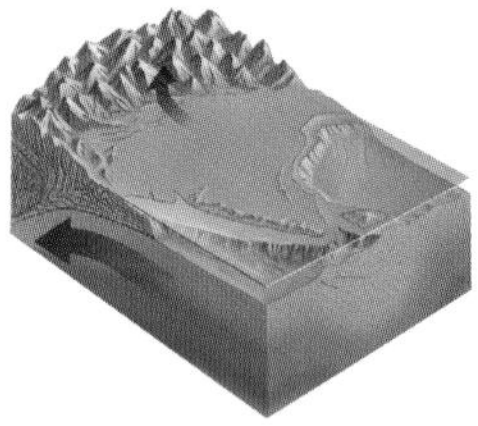

COLLISION
When continental plates meet, the result-ing forces can build impressive mountain ranges. Earth's highest landforms—the Himalaya and adjacent Tibetan Plateau—were born when the Indian plate rammed into the Eurasian plate 50 million years ago.

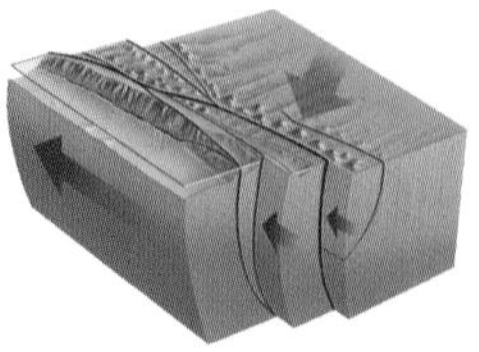

FAULTING
Boundaries where plates slip alongside each other are called transform faults. An example is California's San Andreas fault, which accommodates the stresses between the North American and Pacific plates. Large and sudden displacements can create high-magnitude earthquakes.

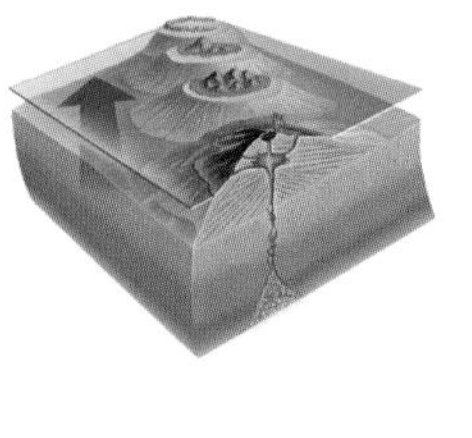

HOT SPOTS
A column of magma rising from deep in the mantle, a hot spot is a thermal plume that literally burns a hole in Earth's rocky crust. The result? Volcanoes, geysers, and new islands. Eruptions occur at plate boundar-ies, such as in Iceland and the Galápagos, as well as within plates, such as the volcanoes of Hawai'i and the geysers of Yellowstone.

GLOBAL TECTONIC FEATURES

Plate Boundary
- ∿ Divergent
- ▲▲ Convergent
- — Transform zone

Plate Motion
- ⬌ Divergent (arrow length proportional to plate motion speed)
- → Convergent
- ○ Hot spot

Major Tectonic Event, Last 100 Years

Earthquake
- ⊙ Ten deadliest
- △ Ten costliest
- ▣ Other

Volcanic Eruption
- ▲ Notable
- ▴ Known during the past 10,000 years

PALEOGEOGRAPHY

With unceasing movement of Earth's tectonic plates, continents "drift" over geologic time—repeatedly breaking apart, reassembling, and fragmenting. Three times during the past billion years, Earth's drifting landmasses have merged to form so-called supercon-tinents. More than 250 million years ago, two land-masses recombined, forming Pangaea. In the Mesozoic era, Pangaea began to split and the Atlantic and Indian Oceans formed. Though the Atlantic is still widening today, scientists predict it will close as the seafloor recycles back into Earth's mantle. A new super-continent, Pangaea Ultima, will eventually form.

600 MILLION YEARS AGO (Late Proterozoic)

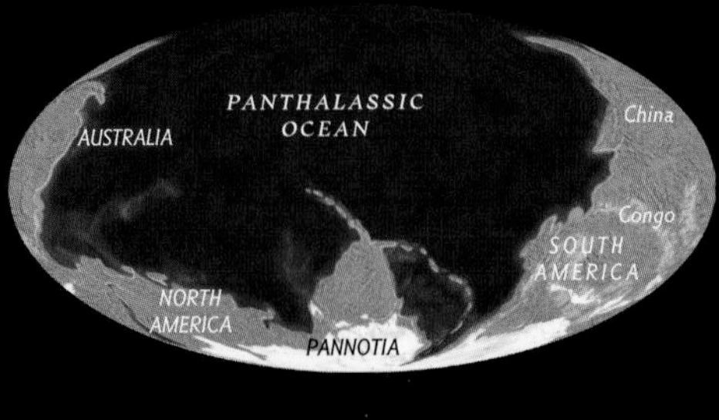

400 MILLION YEARS AGO (Early Devonian)

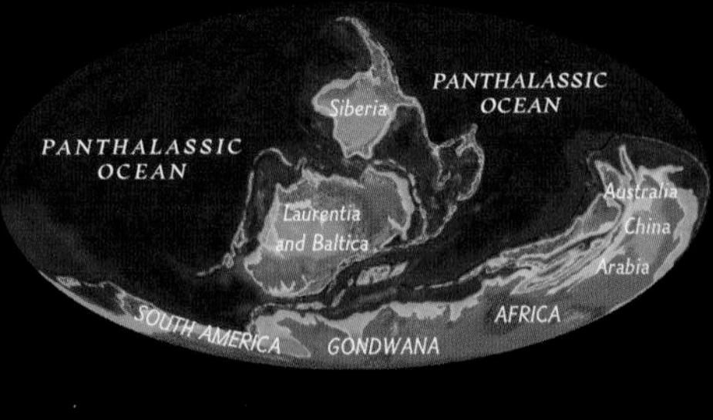

Earth's crust may appear stable and fixed, but, as earthquakes and volcanic activity remind us, Earth's crust is in constant motion, propelled by the heat and pressure of a 2,900-kilometer (1,800-mile)-thick zone of molten rock surrounding a metallic core. Earth's brittle surface—the lithosphere—is cracked into great rafts of rock, called plates, averaging 97 kilometers (60 miles) thick and thousands of kilometers wide. As the plates shift, they change the face of the planet, raising up mountains, generating earthquakes and tsunamis, and firing volcanoes.

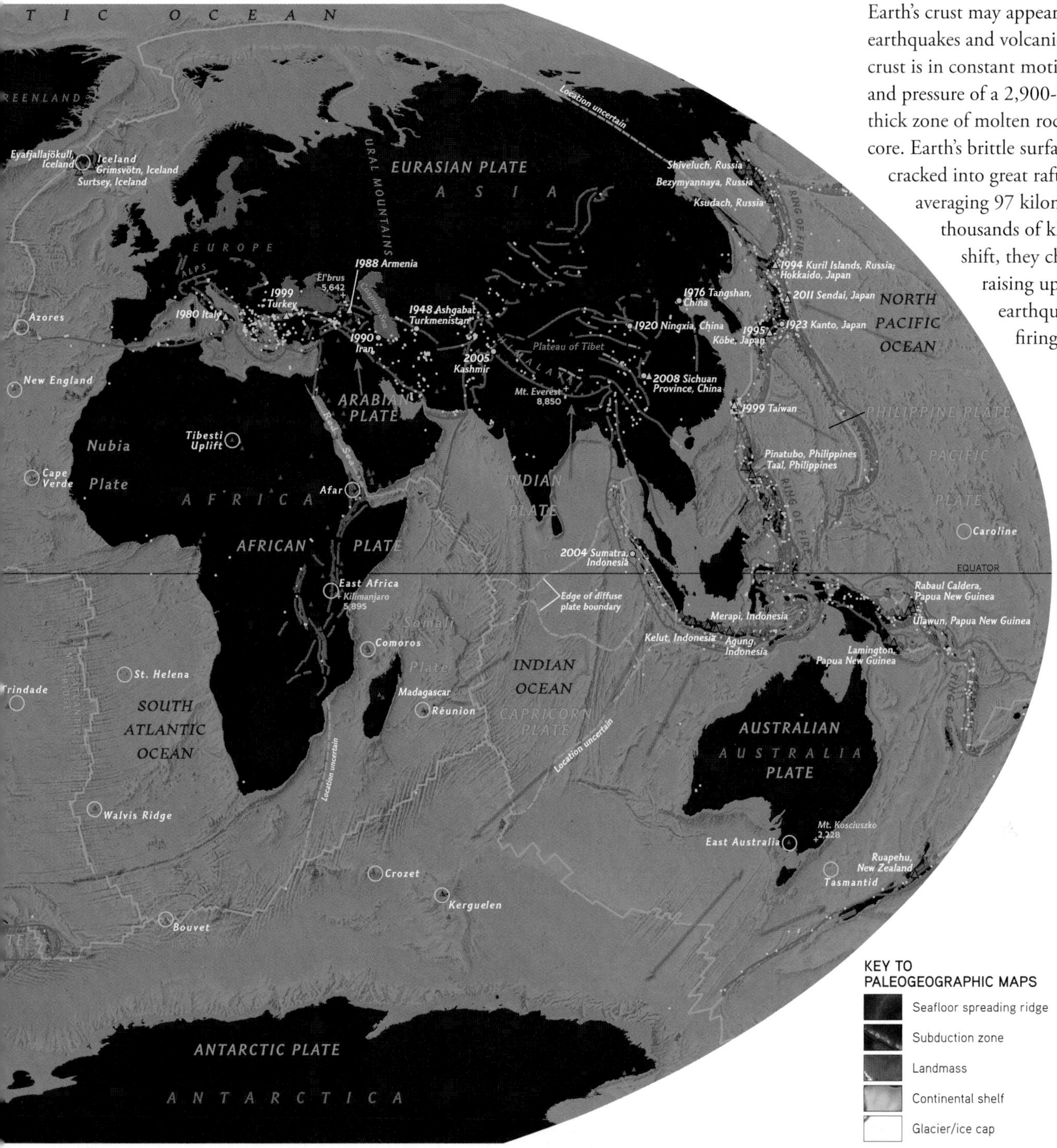

GeoBytes

FIRST SEISMOGRAPH
The Chinese invented the first device to register earthquakes in the first century A.D.

"THE BIG ONE"
The North American West Coast is one of the most earthquake-threatened regions in the world.

TECTONICS THEORY
Plate tectonics has proven as central to Earth sciences as the discovery of the structure of the atom has been to physics and chemistry and the theory of evolution to biology.

NEW NEIGHBORS
Moving slowly to the northwest, the Pacific plate carries a sliver of California, including Los Angeles, which will become a suburb of San Francisco—in a few million years.

RISKY BEHAVIOR
Today, 500 million people live within striking distance of about 550 or so active volcanoes.

KEY TO PALEOGEOGRAPHIC MAPS

- Seafloor spreading ridge
- Subduction zone
- Landmass
- Continental shelf
- Glacier/ice cap

240 MILLION YEARS AGO (Early to Middle Triassic)

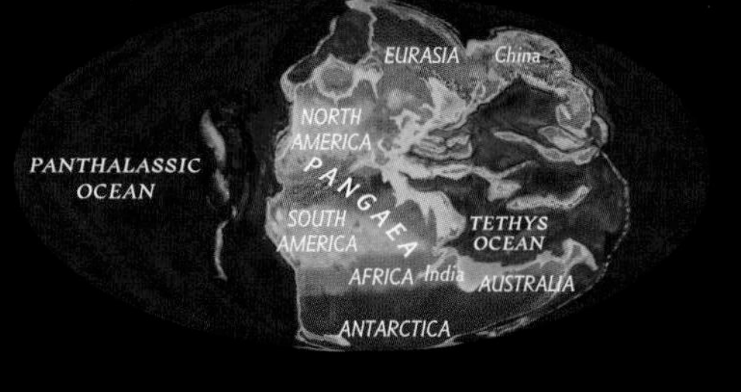

90 MILLION YEARS AGO (Late Cretaceous)

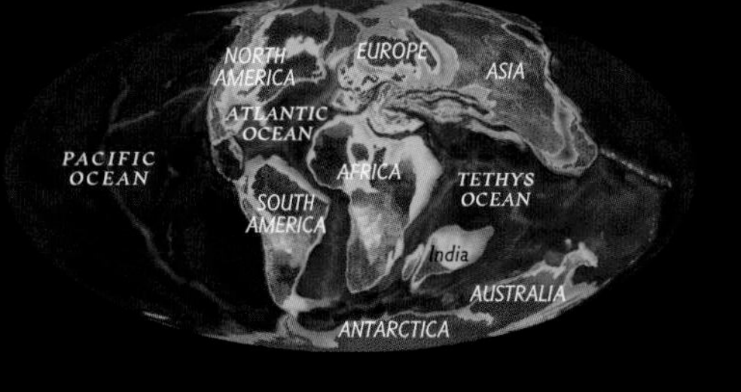

65 MILLION YEARS AGO (Early Paleogene)

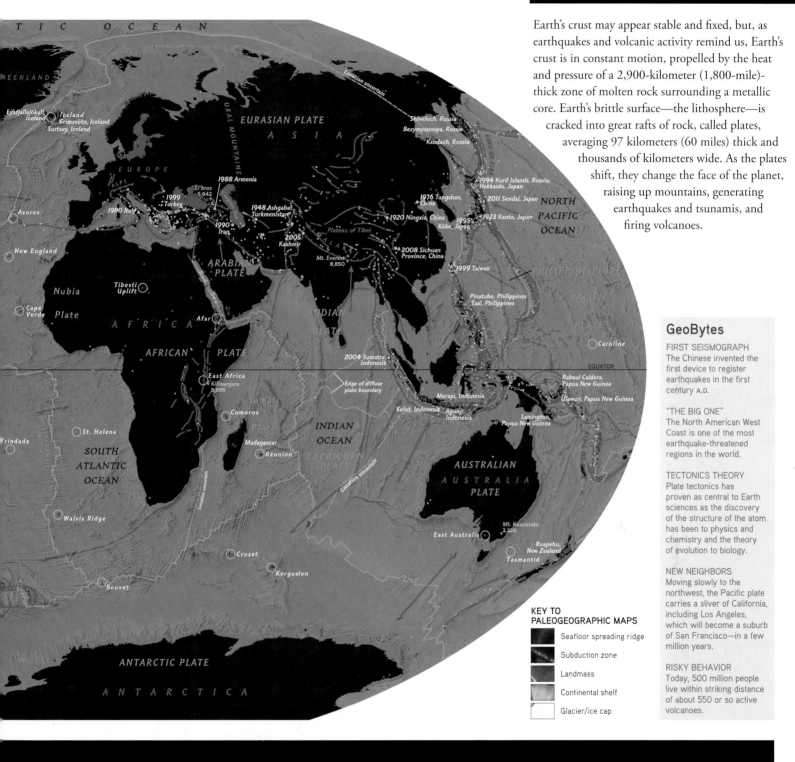

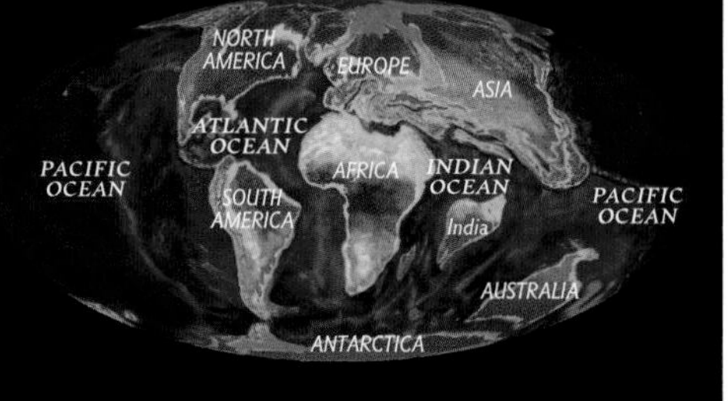

LOESS PLATEAU, CHINA
The thickest known loess (windblown silt) deposits are 335 meters (1,100 feet) deep. The plateau possesses fertile soil and high cliffs.

GANGES RIVER DELTA
The world's largest delta is formed by the Ganges and Brahmaputra Rivers. Its area is about the size of Ireland.

PERU–BOLIVIA ALTIPLANO
Second only to Tibet's plateau in elevation and extent, the Altiplano is a basin 4,000 meters (13,000 feet) high.

LAKE BAIKAL, RUSSIA
This lake lies in the planet's deepest fault-generated trough, a rift about 9 kilometers (5.6 miles) deep.

EOLIAN LANDFORMS
Eolian (from Aeolus, the Greek god of the winds) describes landforms shaped by the wind, and it works best as a geomorphic agent when wind velocity is high—and moisture and vegetation are low. Desert dunes are the most common eolian landform. During the last glaciation, however, strong winds carried vast clouds of silt that were deposited as loess (a fine-grained, fertile soil).

☐ Desert
☐ Loess deposit

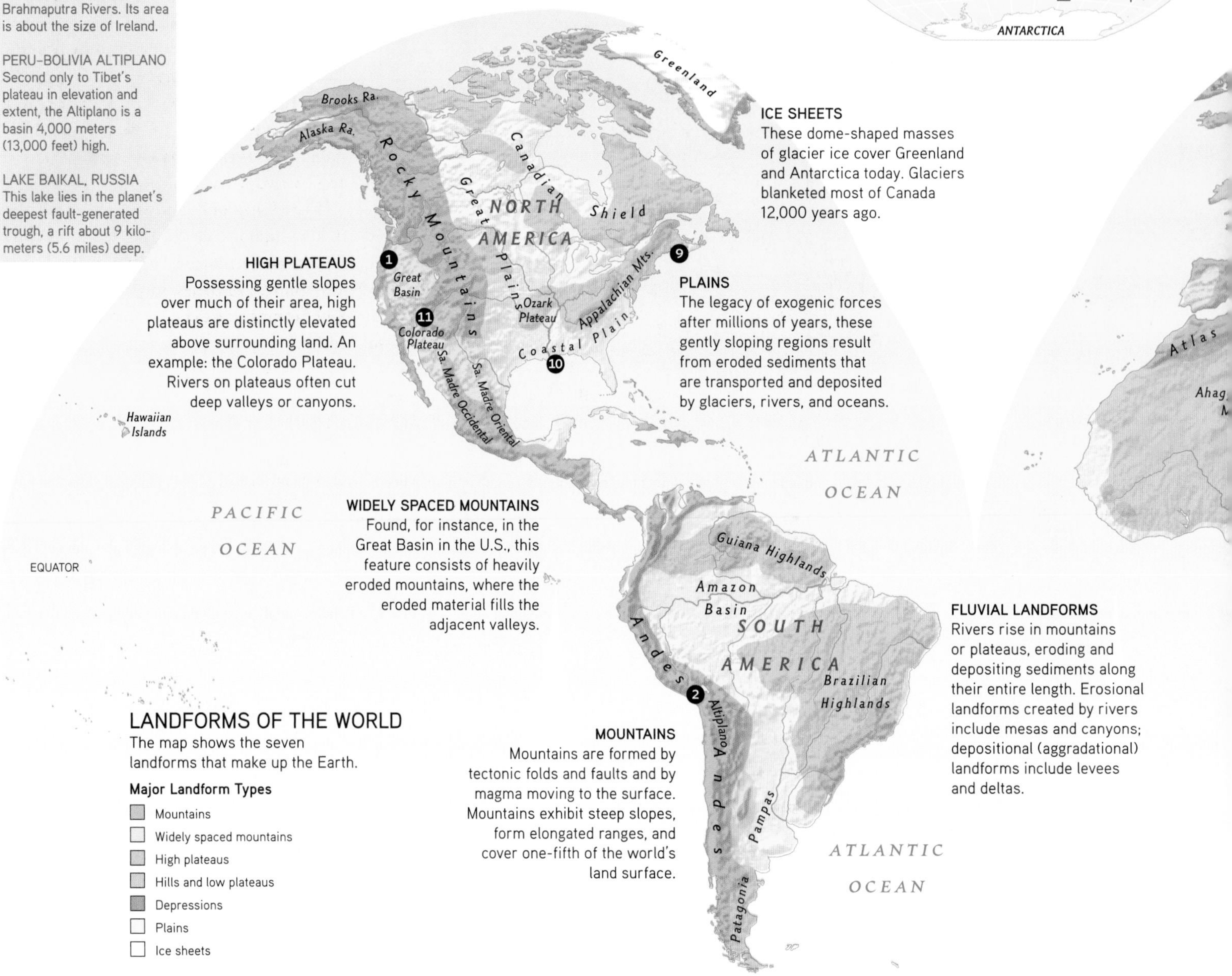

ICE SHEETS
These dome-shaped masses of glacier ice cover Greenland and Antarctica today. Glaciers blanketed most of Canada 12,000 years ago.

HIGH PLATEAUS
Possessing gentle slopes over much of their area, high plateaus are distinctly elevated above surrounding land. An example: the Colorado Plateau. Rivers on plateaus often cut deep valleys or canyons.

PLAINS
The legacy of exogenic forces after millions of years, these gently sloping regions result from eroded sediments that are transported and deposited by glaciers, rivers, and oceans.

WIDELY SPACED MOUNTAINS
Found, for instance, in the Great Basin in the U.S., this feature consists of heavily eroded mountains, where the eroded material fills the adjacent valleys.

FLUVIAL LANDFORMS
Rivers rise in mountains or plateaus, eroding and depositing sediments along their entire length. Erosional landforms created by rivers include mesas and canyons; depositional (aggradational) landforms include levees and deltas.

MOUNTAINS
Mountains are formed by tectonic folds and faults and by magma moving to the surface. Mountains exhibit steep slopes, form elongated ranges, and cover one-fifth of the world's land surface.

LANDFORMS OF THE WORLD
The map shows the seven landforms that make up the Earth.

Major Landform Types
☐ Mountains
☐ Widely spaced mountains
☐ High plateaus
☐ Hills and low plateaus
☐ Depressions
☐ Plains
☐ Ice sheets

Map labels: Greenland, Brooks Ra., Alaska Ra., Rocky Mountains, Canadian Shield, NORTH AMERICA, Great Plains, Great Basin, Ozark Plateau, Colorado Plateau, Appalachian Mts., Coastal Plain, Sa. Madre Occidental, Sa. Madre Oriental, Hawaiian Islands, PACIFIC OCEAN, EQUATOR, ATLANTIC OCEAN, Guiana Highlands, Amazon Basin, SOUTH AMERICA, Andes, Altiplano, Brazilian Highlands, Pampas, Patagonia, ATLANTIC OCEAN, Atlas, Ahag...

VOLCANIC
Crater Lake, Oregon: The caldera, now filled by Crater Lake, was produced by an eruption some 7,000 years ago.

VOLCANIC
Misti Volcano, Peru: A stratovolcano, or composite volcano, it is composed of hardened lava and volcanic ash.

VOLCANIC
Mount Fuji, Japan: Japan's highest peak at 3,776 meters (12,388 feet), it is made up of three superimposed volcanoes.

EXOGENIC
Isle of Skye, Scotland: A pinnacle of basalt lava, known as the Old Man of Storr, resulted from millions of years of erosion.

KARST
Southern China: Steep-sided hills, or tower karst, dominate a karst landscape, where rainfall erodes limestone rock.

ICE AGES

A glacier is a mass of ice moving slowly down a slope or valley. Glacial ice that spreads over vast non-mountainous areas is known as an ice sheet. For millions of years ice sheets have gone through cycles of advancing over continents—and then melting back. The most recent glacial period ended some 10,000 years ago.

NORTH AMERICA
EUROPE
ASIA
AFRICA
SOUTH AMERICA
AUSTRALIA

Glacial maximum 18,000 years ago

ANTARCTICA

What are the many forces that mold the landforms on Earth's surface? Geomorphology is the science that studies the various relief features and the forces that form them. Endogenic forces (internal processes within the planet) produce folding, faulting, and magma movement in the Earth's crust. Subsidence in the crust causes depressions, and uplift builds mountains and plateaus. Exogenic (external) forces hold sway on the surface of the planet. In a process known as weathering, ice, water, and organisms like plant roots break down rock. Weathered rock material is carried great distances by rivers, glaciers, and other erosional agents. These forces of nature are usually gradual, often taking millions of years, but heavy rains and high winds can transform a landscape in a matter of hours. Human activities, such as deforestation and poor farming practices, can rapidly accelerate soil erosion.

Northern European Plain
Ural Mts.
West Siberian Plain
Central Siberian Plateau
Central Range
EUROPE
Alps
Caucasus Mts.
Kazakh Uplands
Lake Baikal
A S I A
Turan Lowland
Tian Shan
Tarim Basin
Kunlun Mts.
Mongolian Plateau
Manchurian Plain
Zagros Mts.
Hindu Kush
Plateau of Tibet
Loess Plateau
Sichuan Basin
Himalaya
Annam Cord.
AFRICA
Ethiopian Highlands
Deccan Plateau
Ganges River Delta
Western Ghats
Congo Basin
Bié Plateau
Anlarana
Drakensberg
INDIAN OCEAN

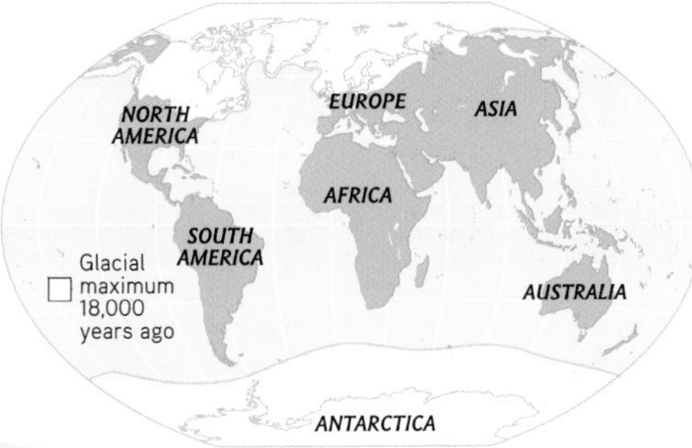

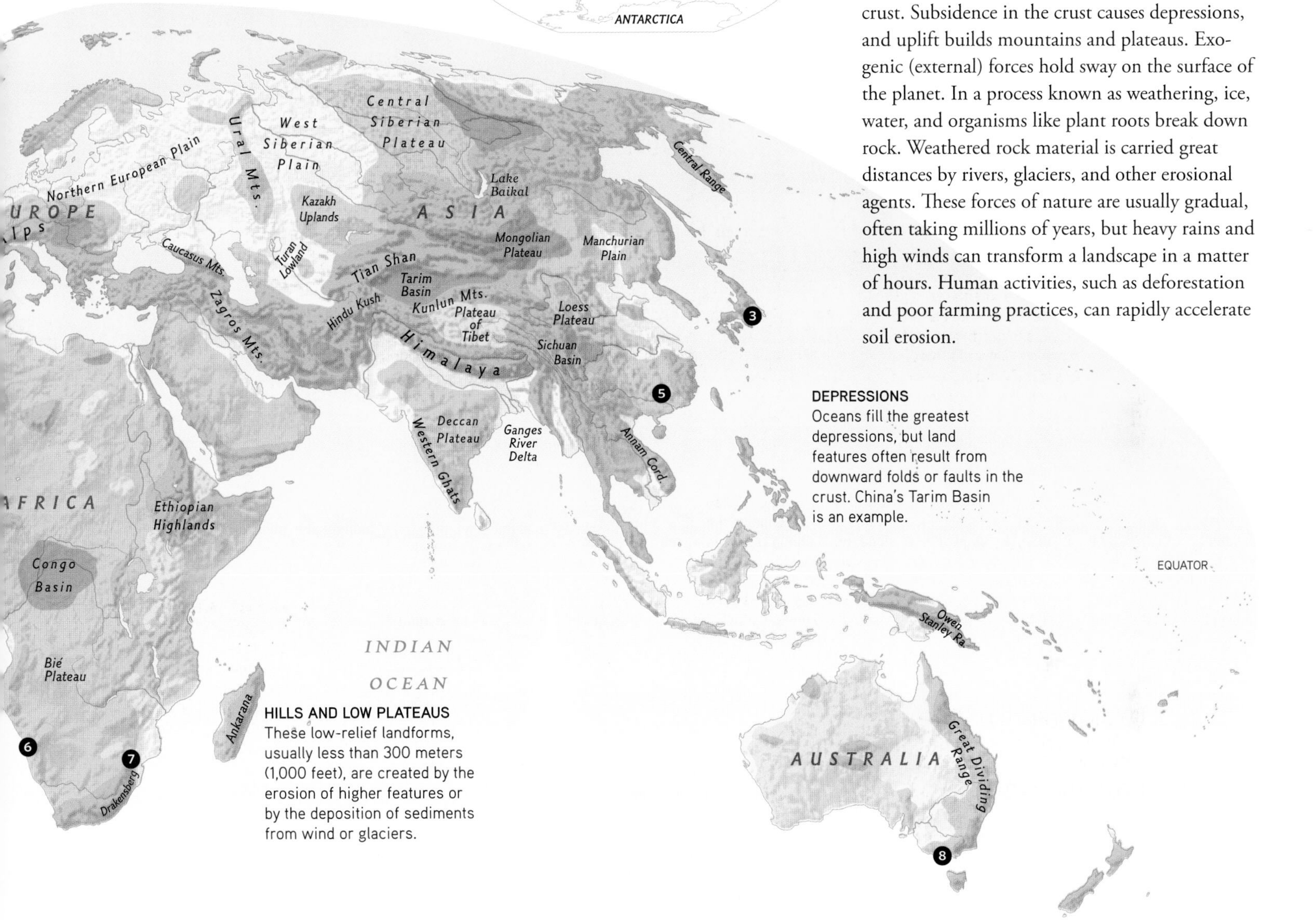

DEPRESSIONS

Oceans fill the greatest depressions, but land features often result from downward folds or faults in the crust. China's Tarim Basin is an example.

EQUATOR

Owen Stanley Ra.

AUSTRALIA
Great Dividing Range

HILLS AND LOW PLATEAUS

These low-relief landforms, usually less than 300 meters (1,000 feet), are created by the erosion of higher features or by the deposition of sediments from wind or glaciers.

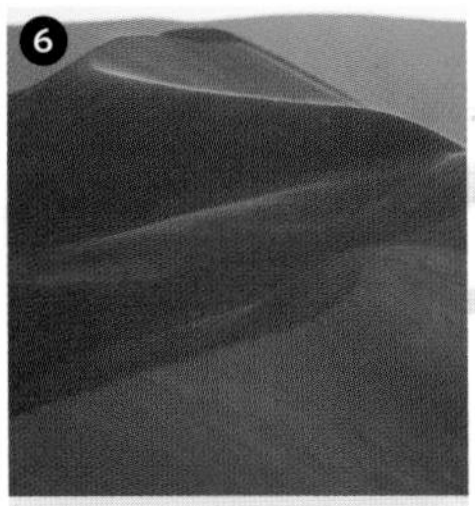

6 EOLIAN
Namibia, Africa: Arid conditions and windstorms combine to build some of the tallest sand dunes in Africa.

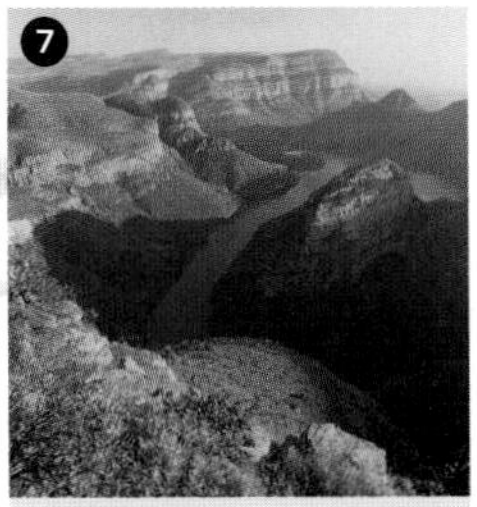

7 FLUVIAL
Blyde River Canyon, Africa: South Africa's Blyde River carved a steep, colorful canyon some 800 meters (2,600 ft) deep.

8 COASTAL
Victoria, Australia: Ocean waves erode coastal cliffs, leaving behind sea stacks made of more resistant rock.

9 POSTGLACIAL
Kejimkujik, Nova Scotia: Drumlins, shaped by overriding glaciers, are elliptical mounds formed by past glacial movement.

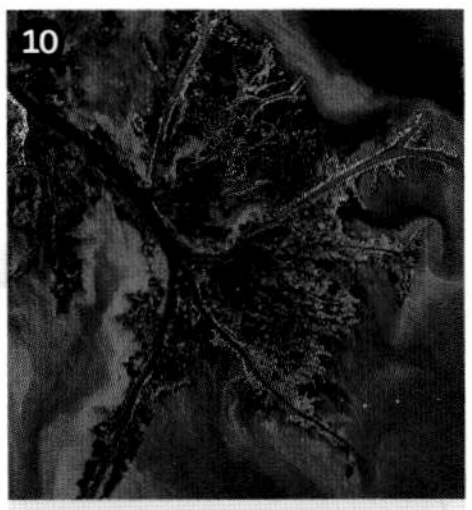

10 FLUVIAL
Mississippi River Delta: Deltas result from deposition of river sediments and vary in shape and size depending on discharge, currents, and waves.

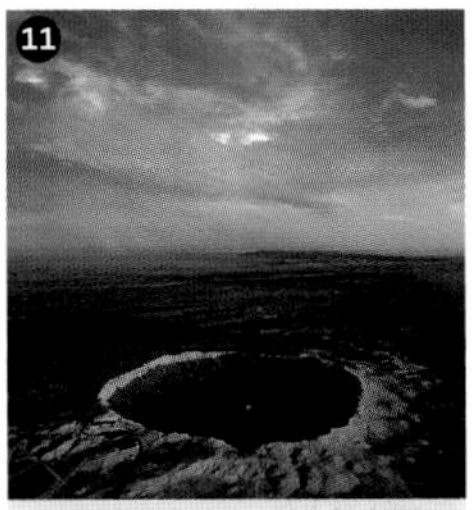

11 OTHER LANDFORMS
Meteor Crater, Arizona: Some 150 visible impact craters exist on Earth; others may have eroded away or been covered.

Sea Level Changes

Earth's hydrologic cycle shows that oceans expand as ice sheets melt and that oceans contract as glaciers grow. Global sea level 20,000 years ago was about 125 meters (410 feet) lower than today—when ice sheets covered much of North America, and the continental shelf was above water. We currently live in an interglacial period (a time of relatively warmer global temperatures). In recent geologic history, global sea level was up to 6 meters (20 feet) higher than today's levels. A future 13-meter (43-foot) rise in sea level, caused primarily by ice sheet melting, would flood areas in the United States affecting about a quarter of the population, mainly in the Gulf and East Coast states.

Sea level 20,000 years ago

Present-day sea level

Projected sea level rise: 13 m (43 ft)

NORTH AMERICA

PACIFIC OCEAN

ATLANTIC OCEAN

SOUTH AMERICA

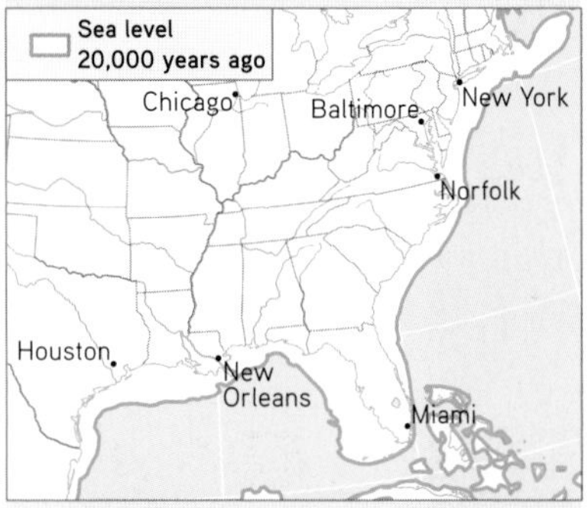

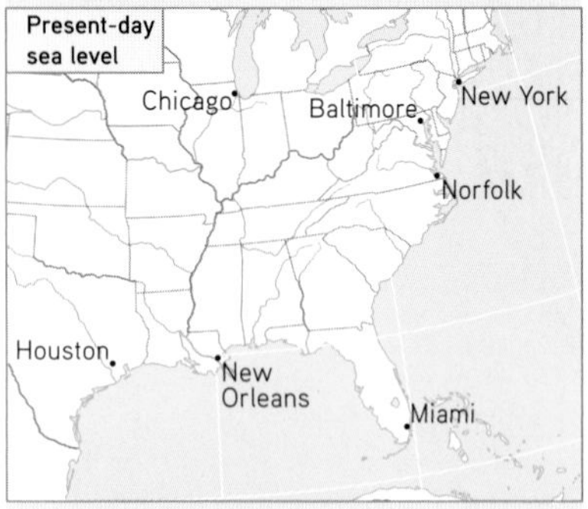

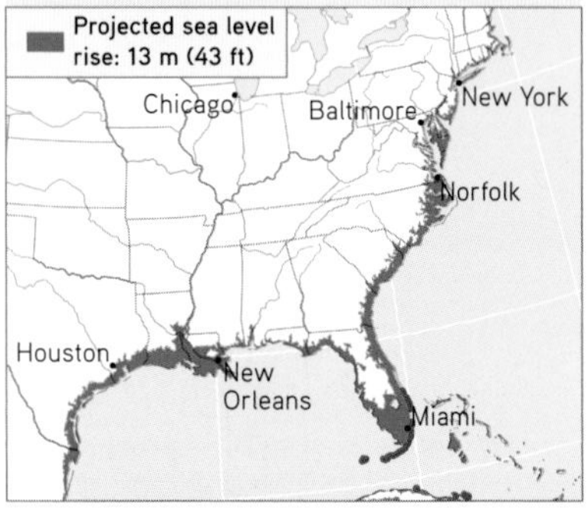

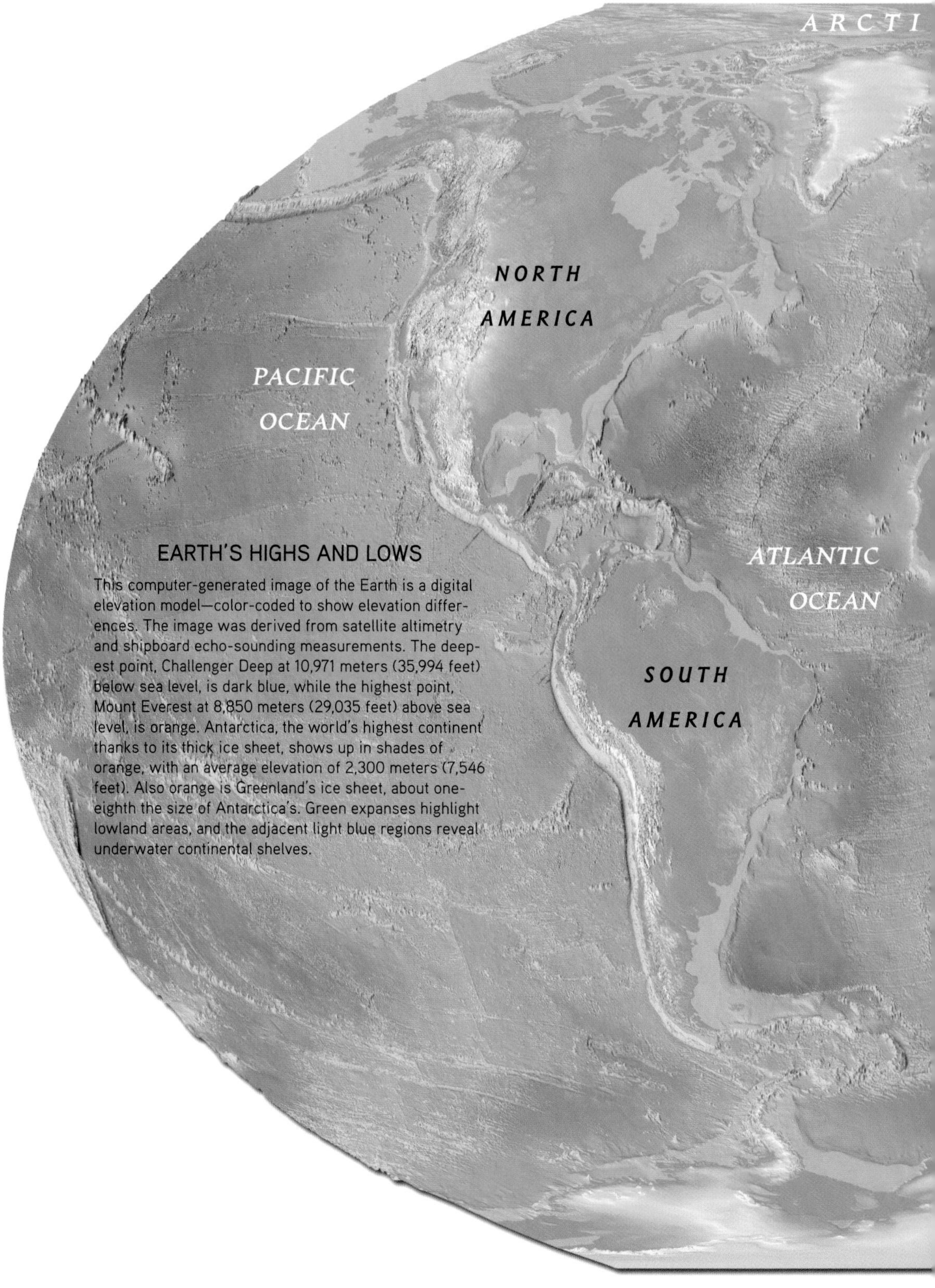

EARTH'S HIGHS AND LOWS

This computer-generated image of the Earth is a digital elevation model—color-coded to show elevation differences. The image was derived from satellite altimetry and shipboard echo-sounding measurements. The deepest point, Challenger Deep at 10,971 meters (35,994 feet) below sea level, is dark blue, while the highest point, Mount Everest at 8,850 meters (29,035 feet) above sea level, is orange. Antarctica, the world's highest continent thanks to its thick ice sheet, shows up in shades of orange, with an average elevation of 2,300 meters (7,546 feet). Also orange is Greenland's ice sheet, about one-eighth the size of Antarctica's. Green expanses highlight lowland areas, and the adjacent light blue regions reveal underwater continental shelves.

A Slice of Earth

A cross section shows that the oceanic crust includes plains, volcanoes, and ridges. The abyssal plains, large, deep areas of the the ocean floor, can reach greater than 3,000 meters (9,840 feet) beneath the surface of the ocean. Underwater volcanoes are called seamounts if they rise more than 1,000 meters (3,300 feet) above the seafloor. The Mid-Atlantic Ridge is a vast submarine mountain range beneath the Atlantic Ocean. Surrounding most continents is an underwater extension of the landmass known as a continental shelf—a shallow, submerged plain. Continental slopes connect the continental shelf with the oceanic crust in the form of giant escarpments that can descend some 2,000 meters (6,600 feet).

Hawaiian Ridge

Rocky Mountains

Middle America Trench

Puerto Rico Trench

Mid-Atlantic Ridge

NORTH AMERICA

PACIFIC OCEAN

ATLANTIC OCEAN

SOUTH AMERICA

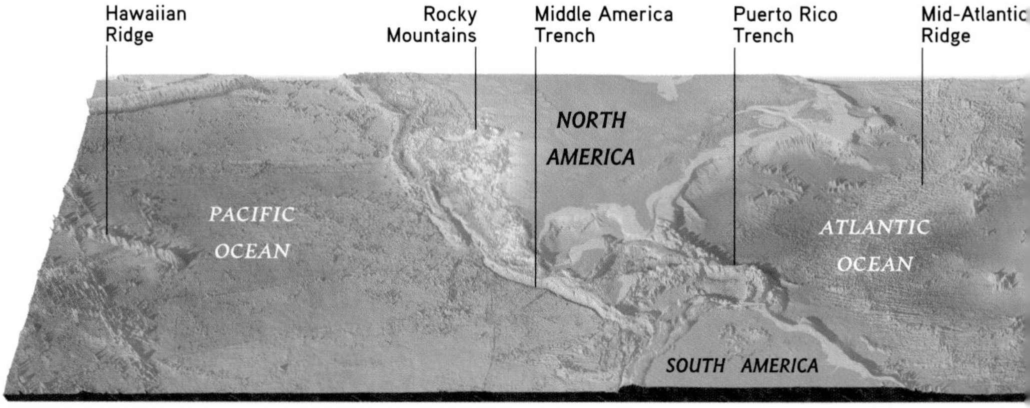

The continental surface and ocean floor have evolved over billions of years, producing enormous variations in relief. From Earth's deepest point, Challenger Deep in the Pacific Ocean's Mariana Trench, to its highest, Mount Everest in the Himalaya, the difference in elevation is 19,821 meters (65,029 feet). About 71% of the planet's surface lies beneath the oceans, and the ocean floor is more varied than the land we can see—with massive volcanoes and near bottomless trenches.

OCEAN

EUROPE

ASIA

AFRICA

PACIFIC
OCEAN

INDIAN
OCEAN

AUSTRALIA

ANTARCTICA

ELEVATION

meters	feet
9,000	30,000
5,000	18,000
3,500	12,000
2,000	6,000
1,000	3,000
0	0
-1,500	-3,000
	-6,000
-3,000	-12,000
-5,000	-18,000
-7,000	-24,000
-9,000	-32,000
-11,000	-36,000

DEPTH

Atlas Mountains

Alps

Mediterranean Ridge

The Steppes

Himalaya

Mount Everest
8,850 m (29,035 ft)

Challenger Deep
-10,971 m
(-35,994 ft)

Kamchatka Peninsula

EUROPE

ASIA

AFRICA

Arabian Sea

Bay of Bengal

PACIFIC OCEAN

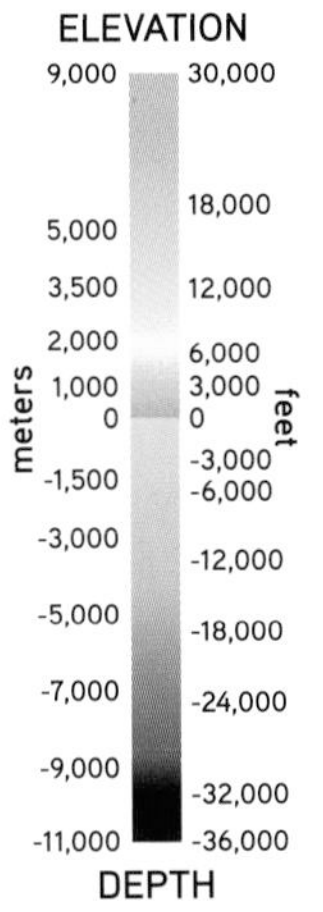

GeoBytes

THE PLATEAU CONTINENT
Africa lacks the long mountain ranges of the other continents. Instead, it is dominated by extensive plateau surfaces. Much of the landmass lies above 1,000 meters (3,300 feet).

THE LOWEST CONTINENT
Australia has an average elevation of only 330 meters (1,080 feet).

ANTARCTIC ICE SHEET
The average elevation is 2,300 meters (7,546 feet), with a maximum ice thickness of more than 4,000 meters (13,120 feet).

LOWEST SURFACE POINT
The Dead Sea lies 422 meters (1,385 feet) below sea level.

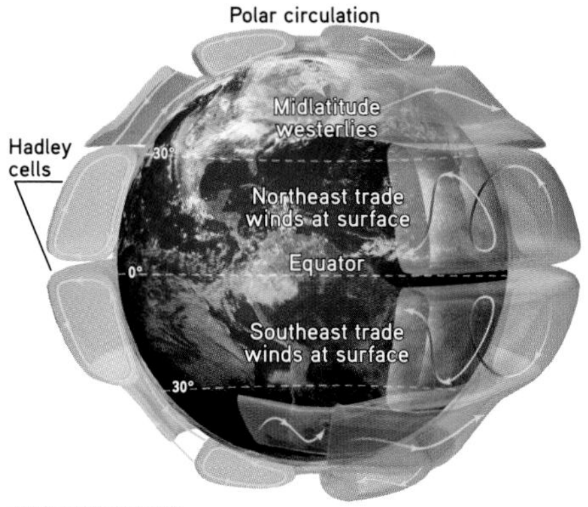

HADLEY CELLS
Air that rises at the Equator and converges in the subtropics forms Hadley cells, while other equatorial trade winds blow east-west. Westerlies dominate higher latitudes.

Polar circulation

Midlatitude westerlies

Hadley cells

Northeast trade winds at surface

Equator

Southeast trade winds at surface

OCEAN CURRENT DYNAMICS
Surface currents along the eastern boundaries of the ocean basins transport colder water equatorward, while western boundary currents carry warmer waters poleward. Warm Gulf Stream water keeps northern Europe warmer than Canada.

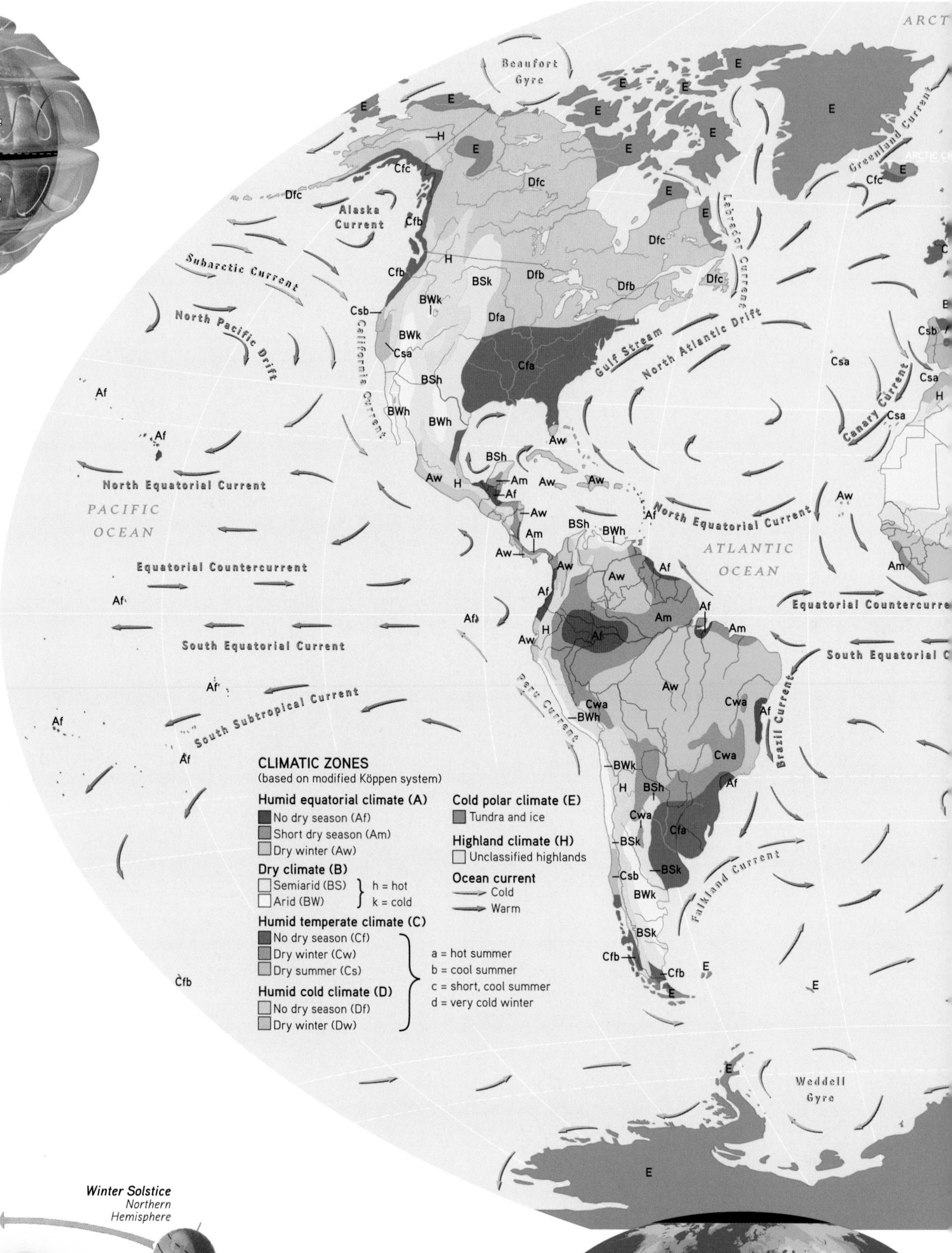

SEASONS AND ROTATION OF THE EARTH
The tilt of the Earth on its axis causes seasonal change. Summer arrives when the rays become more direct and their heat is more concentrated. Winter's cold comes as the sun's rays slant at a steeper angle and cover a larger area.

CLIMATIC ZONES
(based on modified Köppen system)

Humid equatorial climate (A)
- No dry season (Af)
- Short dry season (Am)
- Dry winter (Aw)

Dry climate (B)
- Semiarid (BS)   h = hot
- Arid (BW)   k = cold

Humid temperate climate (C)
- No dry season (Cf)
- Dry winter (Cw)
- Dry summer (Cs)

Humid cold climate (D)
- No dry season (Df)
- Dry winter (Dw)

Cold polar climate (E)
- Tundra and ice

Highland climate (H)
- Unclassified highlands

Ocean current
→ Cold
→ Warm

a = hot summer
b = cool summer
c = short, cool summer
d = very cold winter

Spring Equinox
Northern Hemisphere

Winter Solstice
Northern Hemisphere

Summer Solstice
Northern Hemisphere

Fall Equinox
Northern Hemisphere

North Pole

Tropic of Cancer

Equator

Tropic of Capricorn

South Pole

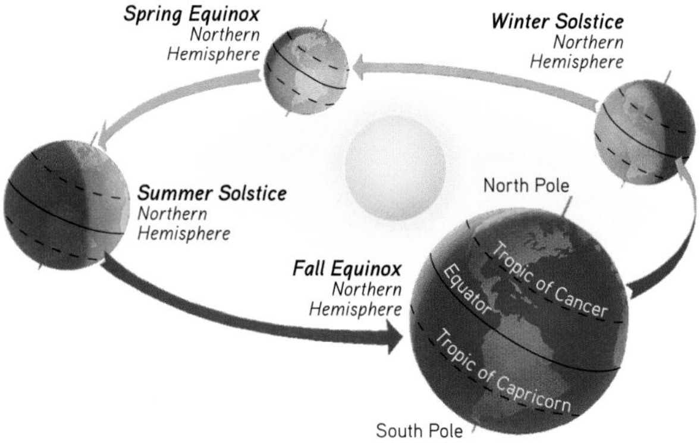

PRECIPITATION
Rainfall hugs the Equator but migrates alternately north-south to the summer hemispheres, when land is warmer than surrounding seas and rising hot air draws in moisture.

Mean annual precipitation
(in thousand millimeters)

More than 3.0 | 2.0 - 3.0 | 1.5 - 2.0 | 1.0 - 1.5 | .60 - 1.0 | .40 - .60 | .20 - .40 | .10 - .20 | Less than .10 | Water area | No data available

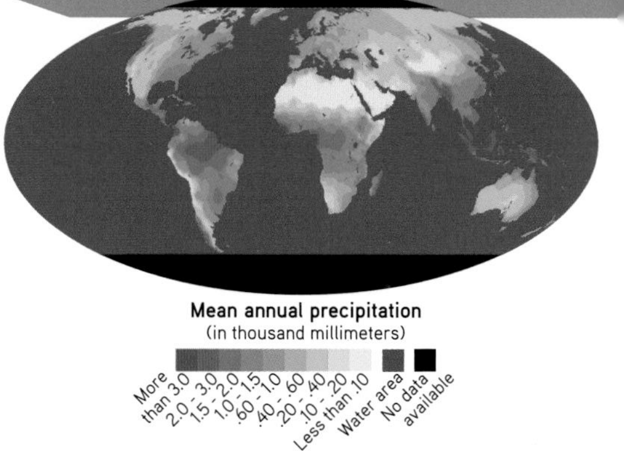

From Arctic desert to equatorial rain forest, climate is the average of the elements of weather over time and dictates conditions for the viability of life. Climatic patterns are established primarily by the energy of the sun and the distribution of solar radiation, which is greatest at the Equator and least at the Poles, and is modified by altitude and distance from the sea. The Köppen system, used here, classifies Earth's climatic zones based on precipitation, temperature, and vegetation. These zones can shift over time. In recent decades, human activities, such as the burning of fossil fuels that increase greenhouse gases in the atmosphere, are contributing to worldwide temperature variations.

GeoBytes

WATTS FROM THE SUN
Each year the sun deposits 324 watts—enough energy for five 60-watt electric bulbs—into every square meter of Earth. Most are absorbed by the tropical zones.

ENERGY BOUNCE
About 30% of the sun's energy is reflected back to space. Only 70% is absorbed by the atmosphere and surface of the planet.

CLOUD BUFFERS
Clouds can cool the planet surface by their shade or warm it by absorbing infrared radiation from the Earth.

INDUSTRY'S ROLE
The world's industrialized areas have produced more than 60% of the carbon dioxide emissions that contribute to global warming.

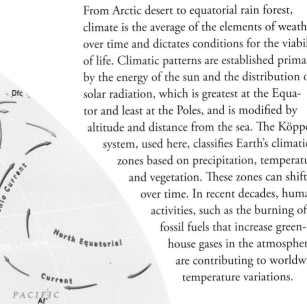

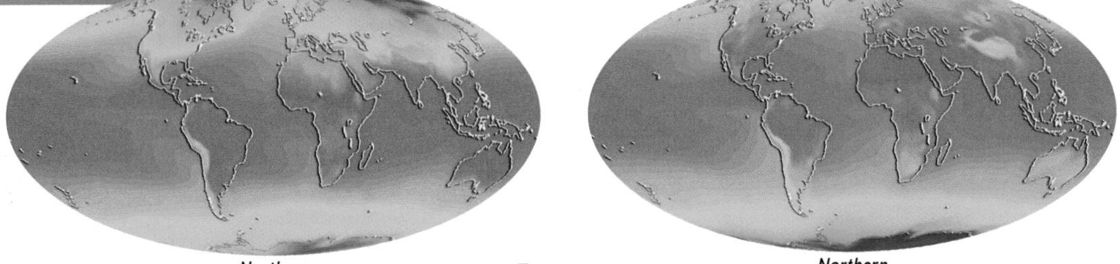

Northern Hemisphere Winter

Northern Hemisphere Summer

Temperature

°C	-63.15	-38.15	-13.5	11.85	36.85
°F	-81.67	-36.67	7.7	53.33	98.33

TEMPERATURES
Temperatures vary seasonally and with latitude as the Earth offers first one, than the other, hemisphere to more direct sunlight. Temperatures are modified by ocean currents and vegetation and are depressed by altitude.

Tracking Weather Patterns

Pressure and Predominant Winds

The sun's direct rays shift from south of the Equator in January to north in July, creating large temperature differences over the globe. These, in turn, lead to air density differences and the creation of high and low pressure areas. Winds result from air attempting to equalize these pressure differences, but the influence of the rotating planet deflects them from a straight line path.

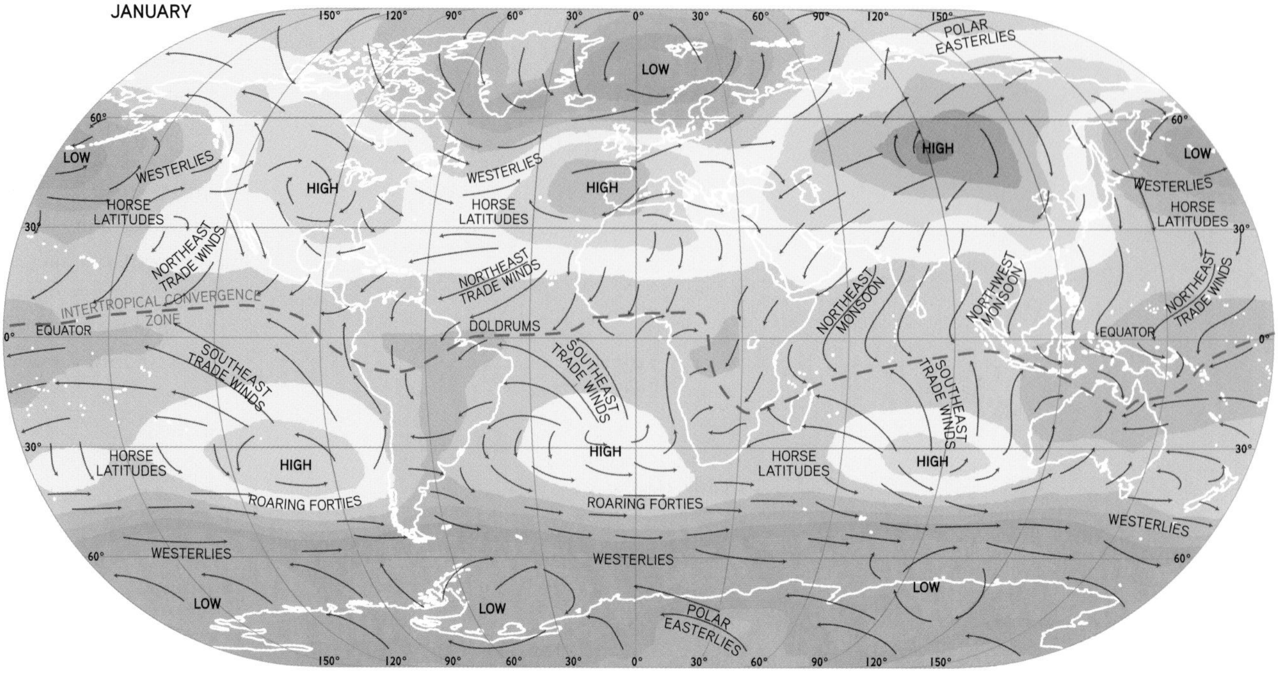

ATMOSPHERIC PRESSURE
(in millibars)

- 1041 - 1045
- 1036 - 1040
- 1031 - 1035
- 1026 - 1030
- 1021 - 1025
- 1016 - 1020
- 1011 - 1015
- 1006 - 1010
- 1001 - 1005
- 996 - 1000
- 991 - 995
- 985 - 990

→ Prevailing wind

JANUARY

JULY

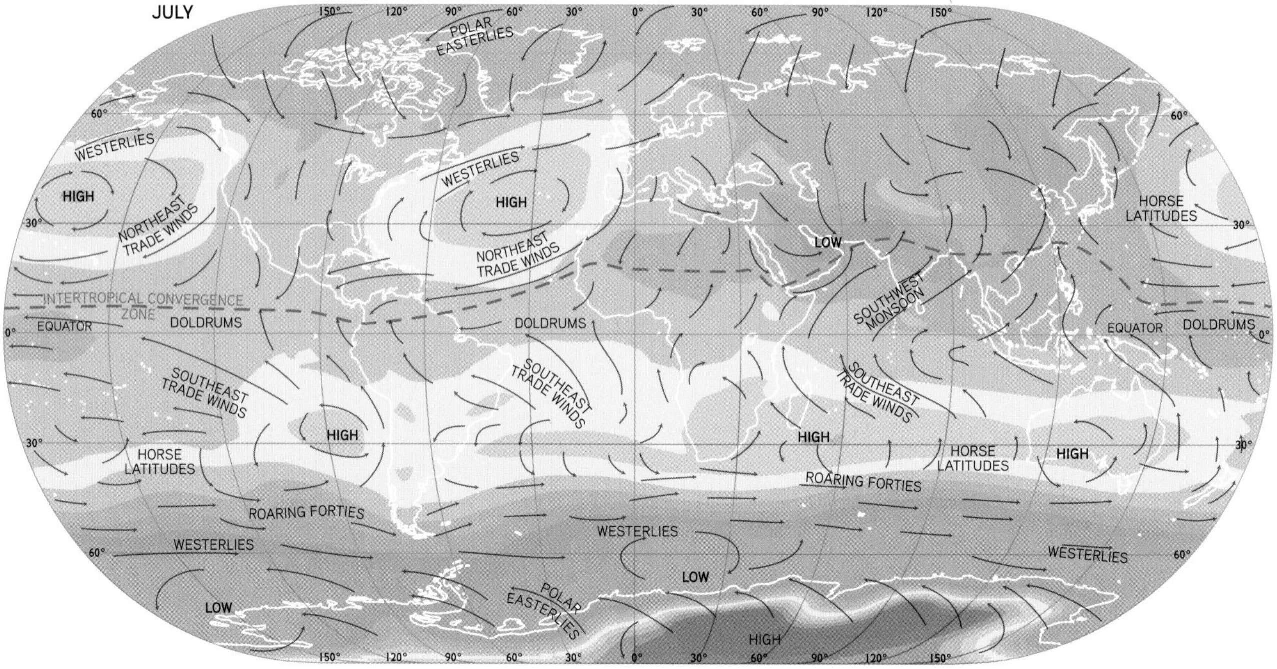

Oceans and Cyclones

Tropical Cyclone Occurance

- High
- Low
- → Cyclone track
- ···· Sea surface temperature can exceed 26.5°C (81°F)

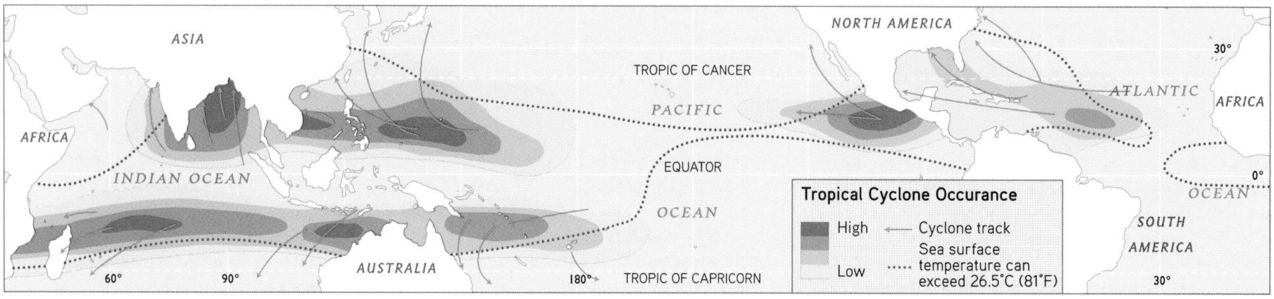

Tropical cyclones—typhoons in the Eastern Hemisphere and hurricanes in the Western—are most likely to occur in areas of greatest heating. Cyclones last until they move over cooler water or hit land. When a cyclone encounters warmer waters it picks up energy and strength.

WEATHER DYNAMICS

EL NIÑO AND LA NIÑA

Sea surface height
anomaly

| cm | -12 | -8 | -4 | 0 | 4 | 8 | 12 |
| in | -5 | -3 | -2 | 0 | 2 | 3 | 5 |

GeoBytes

CHRISTMAS GIFTS
El Niño, The Child, is named for the Christ Child, because the oceanic temperature rise traditionally comes around Christmas.

MONSIEUR CORIOLIS
The Coriolis Effect, the apparent force exerted on winds and ocean currents by the rotation of the earth, was first described by Gastave-Gaspard Coriolis, a French mathematician, in 1835.

SUPER STORMS
One hurricane during its life cycle can expend as much energy as 10,000 nuclear bombs.

BIG STORMS
Frontal systems are the most common weather feature in the mid-latitudes and give precipitation to large, populated areas of the globe. Most occluded fronts have a life of 3 to 6 days.

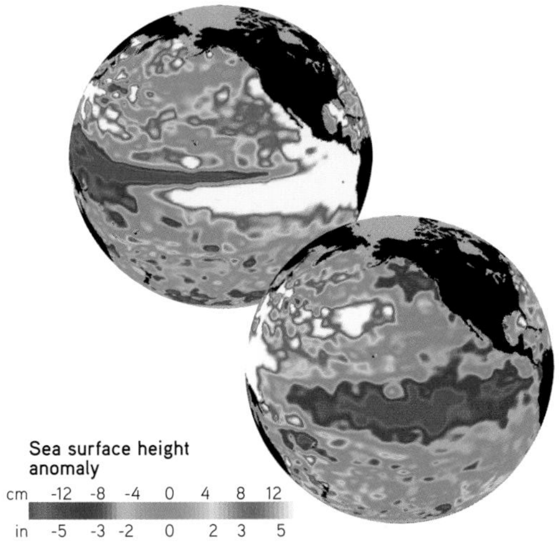

El Niño, an anomaly of sea-surface height or "relief" of the sea, brings warm water to South America's west coast, leading to severe short-term changes in world weather. La Niña, a cooling of those waters, has opposite effects.

Weather is the state of the atmosphere—as indicated by temperature, moisture, wind speed and direction, and barometric pressure—at a specific time and place. Although still frustratingly difficult to predict, weather acts in some known patterns. Variations in ocean temperatures off the South American coast influence storm formation and rainfall around the globe. Jet streams that speed around the planet can usher in winter storms. And the right combination of warm water, wind, and energy from heated water vapor can cook up lethal hurricanes and typhoons that can overwhelm shorelines and cities.

HOW WEATHER HAPPENS

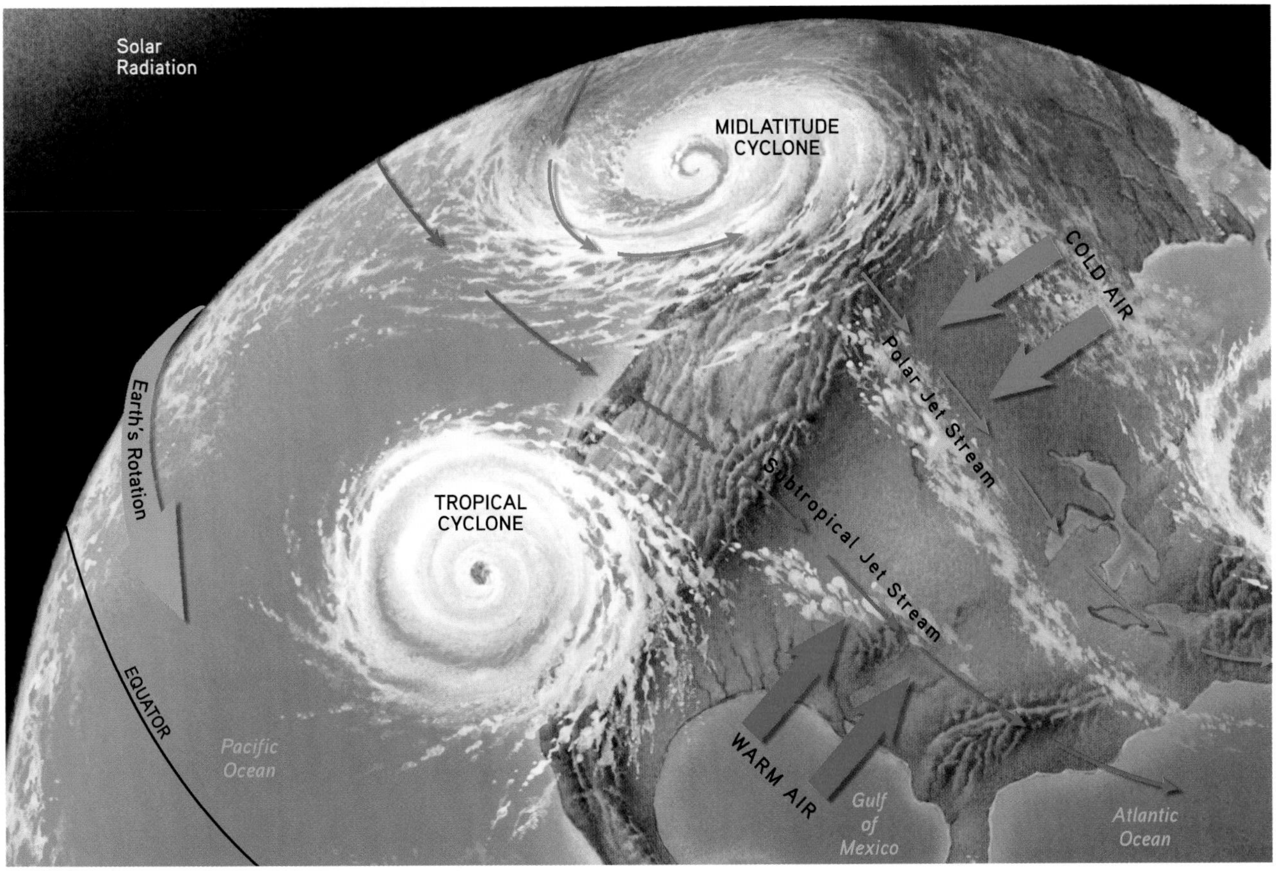

Weather is ultimately the atmospheric response to unequal inputs of solar energy on the globe, as a surplus of heat in low latitudes is transferred to higher latitudes by air motion and by mid-latitude storms. Part of that dynamic are jet streams—rivers of westerly winds speeding as fast as 400 kph (250 mph) in the upper atmosphere, which are also key in the genesis of storms: The Polar Front Jet, which snakes along the front between Arctic and warmer continental air, is instrumental in the formation and direction of cyclonic North Pacific winter storms; the Sub-tropical Jet blows along the boundary of tropical circulation cells and can also abet storm formation, bringing warm, moist air and precipitation into the continent. The different properties of oceans and continents to absorb or reflect heat also influences weather patterns.

FORMATION OF A MID-LATITUDE CYCLONE

1. Stationary polar front

2. Cyclogenesis

3. Low pressure cell—undeveloped

4. Low pressure cell—developed

5. Occlusion

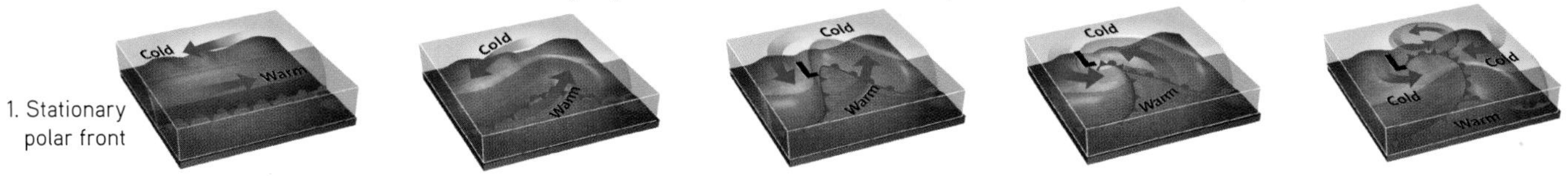

Mid-latitude cyclones are found between 35° and 70° of latitude in the zone of the westerly winds. Most are occluded fronts. (1) Characterized by intense, heavy precipitation, cold polar air—with a boundary known as a front—meets warm tropical air. (2) A wave develops along the frontal boundary as the opposing air masses interact. Cyclogenesis (the birth of a cyclone) begins. (3) The faster-moving cold air forces the warm air to lift above the cold. (4) Full rotation develops, counter-clockwise in the Northern Hemisphere and clockwise in the Southern Hemisphere. (5) Complete occlusion occurs as the warm air, fully caught-up by the cold air, has been lifted away from the surface. Because the warm air is completely separated from the surface, the characteristics of the cold air are felt on the ground in the form of unsteady, windy, and wet weather.

Our Layered Ocean

With depth, the ocean's five layers get colder, darker, saltier, denser, and life becomes scarcer and more adapted to the challenge of survival.

200 METERS (660 FEET)
The epipelagic is the sunlit zone where photosynthesis by plants can take place and where the vast majority of all marine animals live.

1,000 M (3,300 FT)
Only some light penetrates the mesopelagic, or twilight zone. Thus no plants grow, but large fish and whales hunt and bioluminescent fish first appear.

3,960 M (13,000 FT)
No light reaches the midnight zone, or bathypelagic, but sperm whales and rays are known to hunt here for food.

6,100 M (20,000 FT)
Pressure is crushing in the abyssopelagic, or abyss zone, home to bizarre angler fish and invertebrates such as sponges and sea cucumbers.

10,060 M (33,000 FT)
The hadalpelagic zone penetrates into the deepest ocean trenches yet is home to small crustaceans called isopods.

MARINE SEDIMENTS
The vast majority of the Earth's biologically fixed carbon lies in marine sediments trapped at the bottom of the seas. Carbon deposits from past eras are seen in current landforms upthrust from the oceans, such as the white cliffs of Dover.

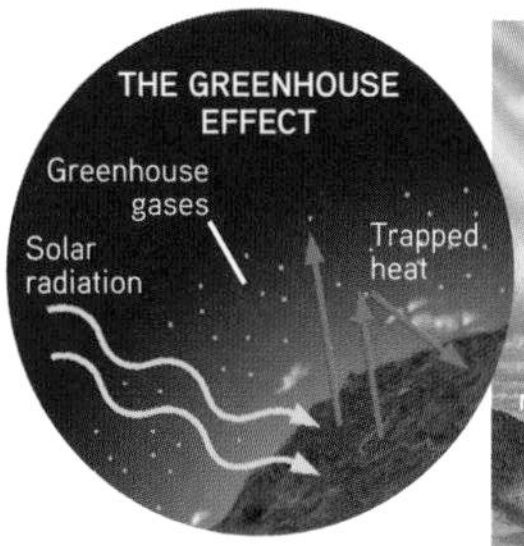

What Shapes Earth's Climate?

THE GREENHOUSE EFFECT
Greenhouse gases
Solar radiation
Trapped heat

1 SOLAR INPUT
Reflected solar radiation
2 THE ATMOSPHERE
5 CLOUDS
Solar radiation
Re-emitted terrestrial radiation
Terrestrial radiation
Phytoplankton (algae)
OCEANS 3
4 THE WATER CYCLE
Precipitation
Ocean evaporation
Sea-ice heat exchange
6 ICE AND SNOW
Runoff and underground water
7 LAND SURFACE
8 HUMAN INFLUENCES

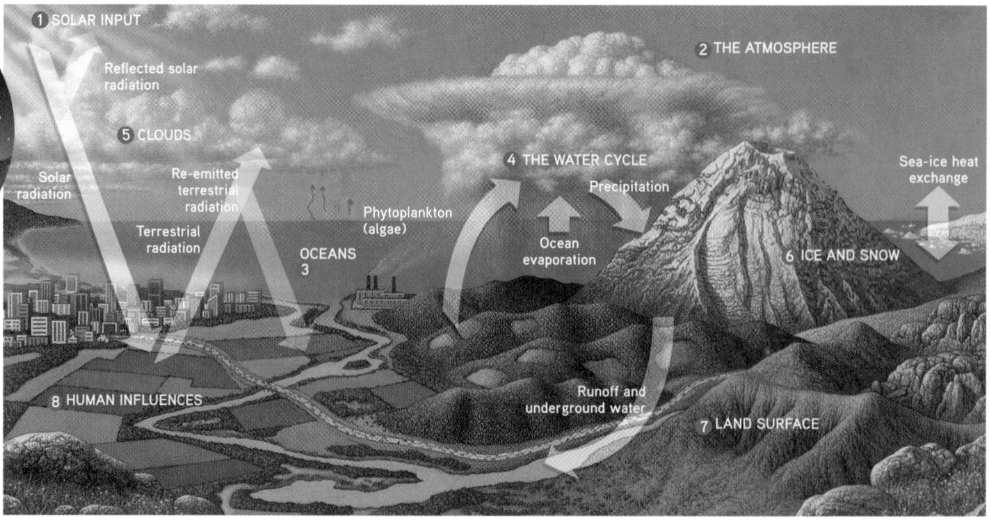

BIOSPHERE AND CLIMATE

Much of the sun's heat (1) is held in the atmosphere (2) by greenhouses gases as well as in the top layer of oceans. Oceans (3) distribute heat; evaporation lifts moisture (4). Clouds (5) reflect heat and cool Earth; they also warm it by trapping heat. Ice and snow (6) reflect sunlight, cooling Earth. Land (7) can influence the formation of clouds, and human use (8) can alter natural processes.

THE GREENHOUSE HEAT TRAP

The atmosphere acts like a greenhouse, allowing sunlight to filter through. Gases such as carbon dioxide, methane, ozone, and nitrous oxide help the atmosphere hold heat. This heating is key in Earth's ability to stay warm and sustain life.

Earth's Green Biomass

Earth's vegetative biomass, the foundation of most life on the planet, is measured by chlorophyll-producing plants. Both land and sea process an equal amount of carbon—50 to 60 billion metric tonnes per year. Photoplankton provides the basis of measurement in the oceans; green-leaf mass on land.

KEY TO IMAGES
Ocean: Chlorophyll concentration

>.01 .05 .2 1 2 5 20 50 (a (mg/m^3))

Land cover: Normalized Difference Vegetation Index (NDVI)

Max.   Min.

Ocean Circulation

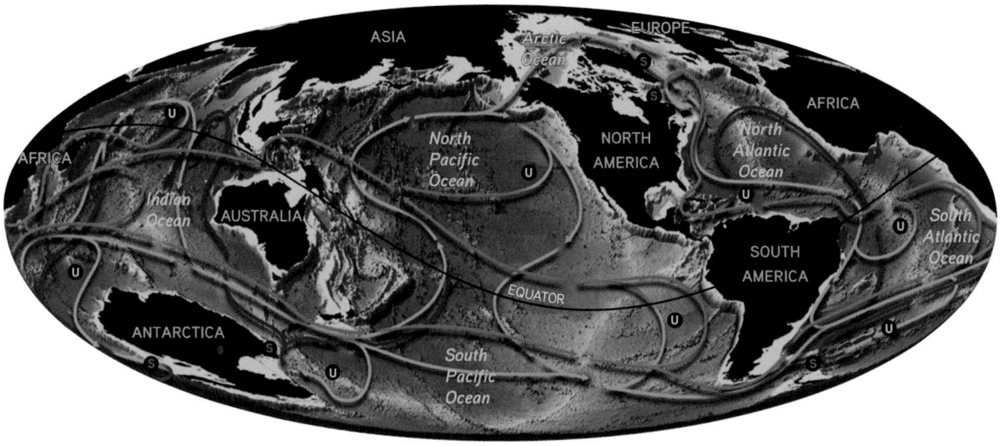

Ocean circulation, driven by wind, density, and Earth's rotation, conveys heat energy around the globe. Tropical surface waters move toward the Poles, cool, sink, and loop around to upwell near the Equator. The Gulf Stream, for example, warms northern Europe. Other, density-driven currents flow vertically to replenish deeper waters.

OCEAN CIRCULATION
- Warmer than 3.5°C (38.3°F)
- 1°C – 3.5°C
- Cooler than 1°C (33.8°F)
- S Sinking
- U Upwelling

BIOSPHERE

The biosphere is Earth's thin layer of life. Containing all known life in the solar system, the biosphere, if viewed from miles above the planet, would be at a scale no thicker than this page. Although the biosphere is 19 kilometers (12 miles) from top to bottom, the bulk of it ocean depths, most living things occupy a three-kilometer-wide (two-mile-wide) band extending from the sunlit ocean layer to the snowline of high mountains. The biosphere—and its communities of plants and animals—interacts with the other key spheres of physical geography: the lithosphere, Earth's solid outer crust; the atmosphere, the layer of air above; and the hydrosphere, the oceans and all water on and within Earth. The ecosystems of the biosphere are in constant flux as the planet turns, as weather and climate shift, and as the human impacts of forestry, agriculture, and urbanization affect the fundamental components of the biosphere—carbon dioxide and other gases, water, and the photosynthesis of plants.

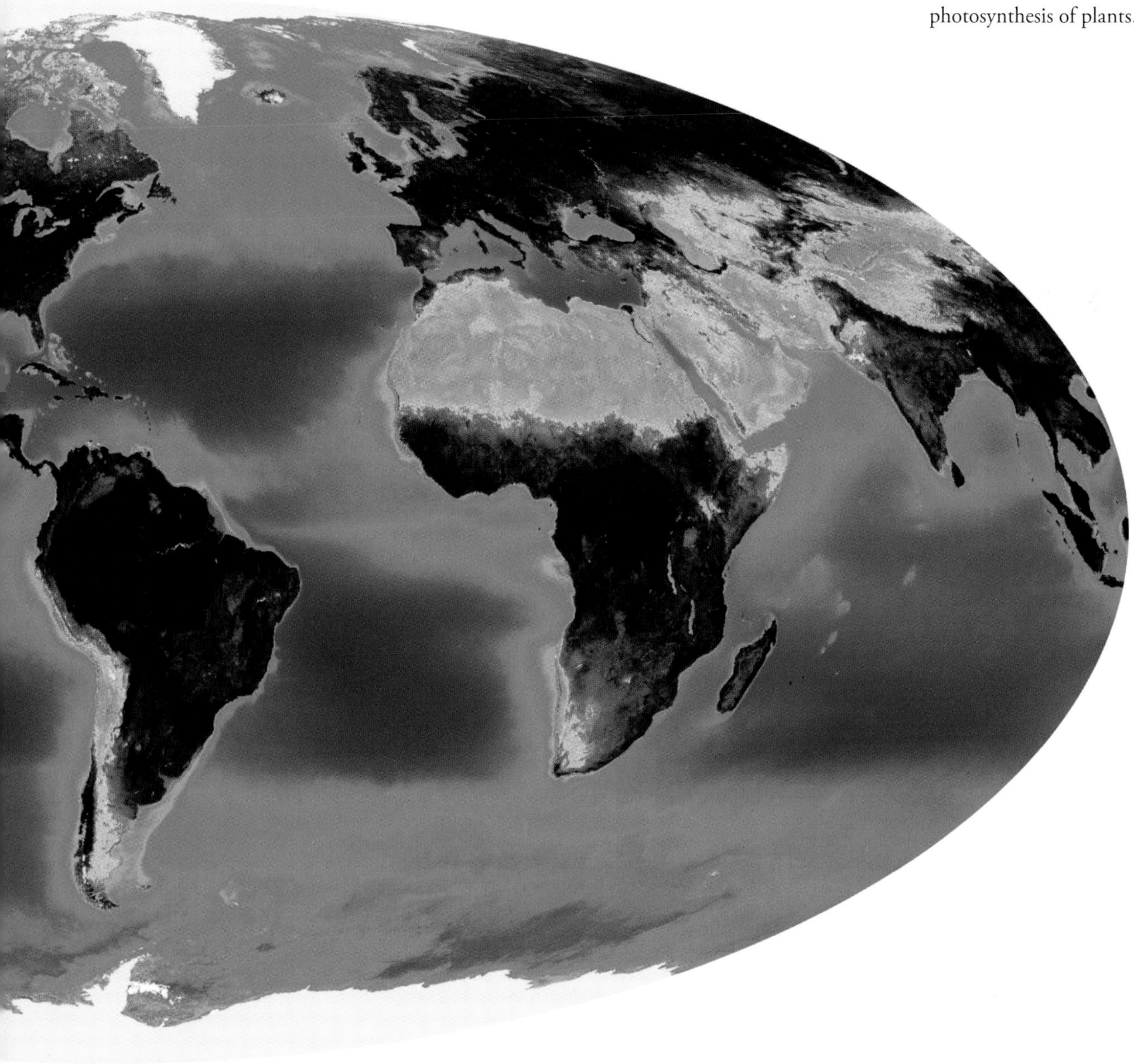

GeoBytes

BIOGENESIS
The evolution of the biosphere is thought to have begun some 3.5 billion years ago.

A NEW SCIENCE
In 1926 a Soviet scientist, Vladimir I. Vernadsky, argued that human reason is capable of ensuring the sustainability of the biosphere.

BOTTOM BIOMASS
The microbes that live deep beneath the Earth's surface could exceed all animal and plant life on the surface by biomass.

WORLD OF BIOMES
Scientists divide the biosphere into a number of biomes that consist of broadly similar flora and fauna. Terrestrial biomes include deserts, forests, and grasslands; oceanic ones are coral reefs, estuaries, oceans, and the deep abyssal zone.

BIRDS SOAR ABOVE
High-flying birds, such as the Ruppell's vulture and the bar-headed geese, are found at altitudes greater than 9,140 meters (30,000 feet).

WATER AVAILABILITY AND PRIMARY WATERSHEDS

One of our most critical resources, fresh water is unequally distributed among the world's population. In wealthy countries, potable water is sprayed on lawns while rainwater gushes down storm drains; in many desert regions and countries, every drop is guarded and carefully used. Water has been and will continue to be a frequent source of conflict around the world—hope rests in better planning and community-scale projects. Watersheds are Earth's rain barrels, collecting precipitation and filtering it as they channel it to streams, rivers, lakes, and aquifers. Many watersheds are stressed by increased industrialization, deforestation, and pollution.

Greenland

NORTH AMERICA

SOUTH AMERICA

ATLANTIC OCEAN

PACIFIC OCEAN

EUROPE
16%
55%
29%

NORTH AMERICA
15%
41%
44%

AFRICA
10% 4%
86%

SOUTH AMERICA
19%
13%
68%

1982
177 killed in protest over dam

2007
Water conflicts between herders and farmers in Burkina Faso

Water Availability
(in millimeters per person per year)
- More than 750
- 251–750
- 26–250
- Less than 26
— Major river
— Primary watershed boundary
• Selected water dispute

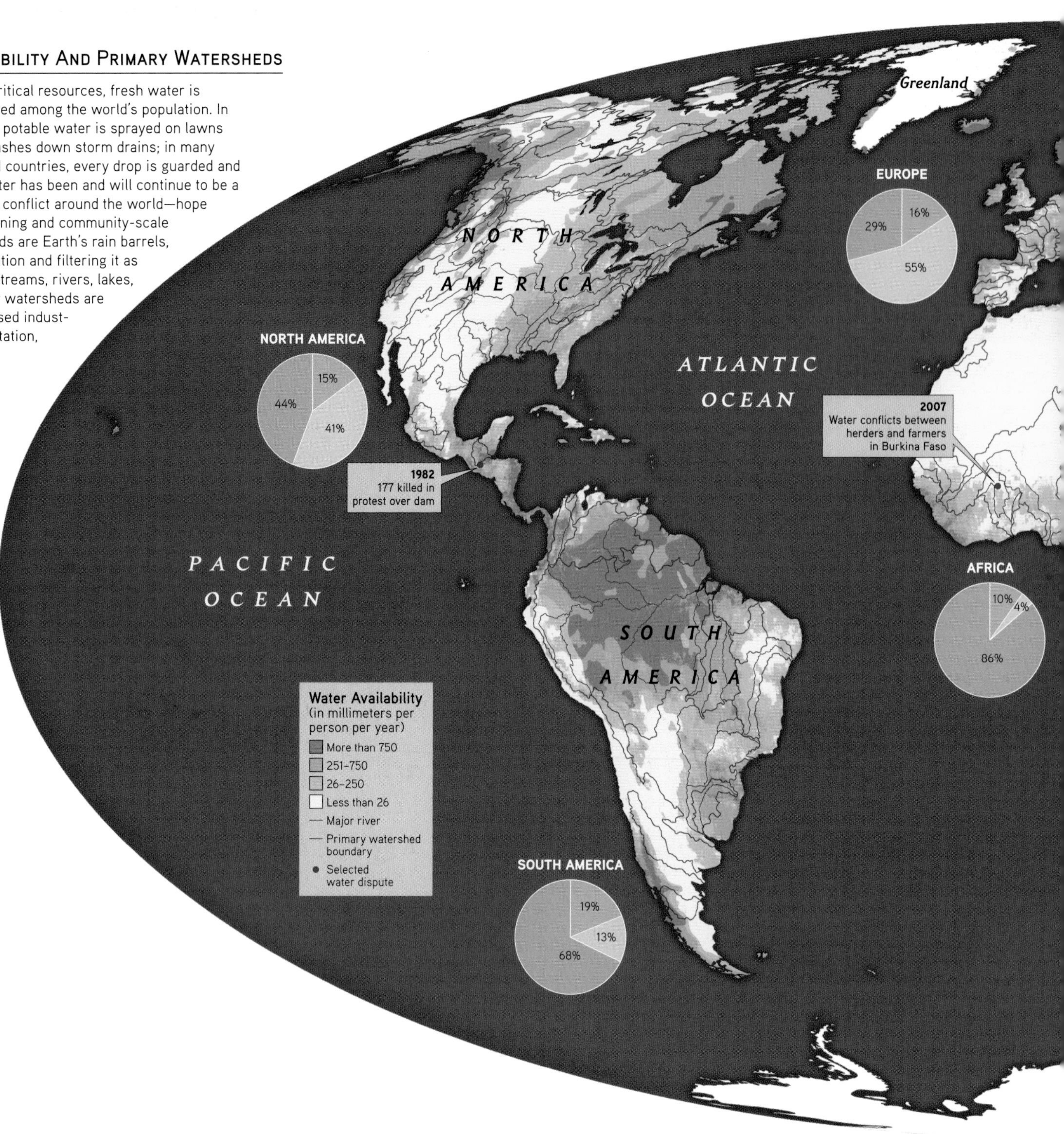

ACCESS TO FRESH WATER

Access to clean fresh water is critical for human health. Yet, in many regions, potable water is becoming scarce because of heavy demands and pollution. Especially worrisome is the poisoning of aquifers—a primary source of water for nearly a third of the world—by sewage, pesticides, and heavy metals.

NORTH AMERICA

EUROPE

ASIA

AFRICA

SOUTH AMERICA

AUSTRALIA

Percent of Total Population Using Improved Drinking Water Sources
- More than 90%
- 76%–90%
- 50%–75%
- Less than 50%
- No data available

It's as vital to life as air. Yet fresh water is one of the rarest resources on Earth. Only 2.5% of Earth's water is fresh, and of that the usable portion for humans is less than 1% of all fresh water, or 0.01% of all water on Earth. Water is constantly recycling through Earth's hydrologic cycle. But population growth and pollution are combining to make less and less available per person per year, while global climate change adds new uncertainty. Efficiency, conservation, and technology can help ensure that the water you absorb today will still be usable and clean hundreds of years from now.

ARCTIC OCEAN

EUROPE

ASIA

ASIA
9%
9%
82%

PACIFIC OCEAN

AFRICA

2010
Pakistan irrigation dispute between tribes kills 116

2007
Injuries at protest over allocation of water to industry in India

1978 onward
Egypt threatens Ethiopia over Nile plans

1999
Villagers killed in Yemen water clash

2006
Sri Lankan rebels cut water supplies to villages

2004–2006
250 killed in violence over water shortage in Ethiopia

2005
90 killed in dispute over water rights in Kenya

INDIAN OCEAN

AUSTRALIA

2007
Australian man murdered in fight over water restrictions

GLOBAL IRRIGATED AREAS AND WATER WITHDRAWALS
Since 1970, global water withdrawals have correlated with the rise in irrigated area. Some 70% of withdrawals are for agriculture, mostly for irrigation that helps produce 40% of the world's food.

OCEANIA
17%
10%
73%

Freshwater Withdrawal
(as a percentage of total water utilization)

Agricultural   Domestic

Industrial

ANTARCTICA

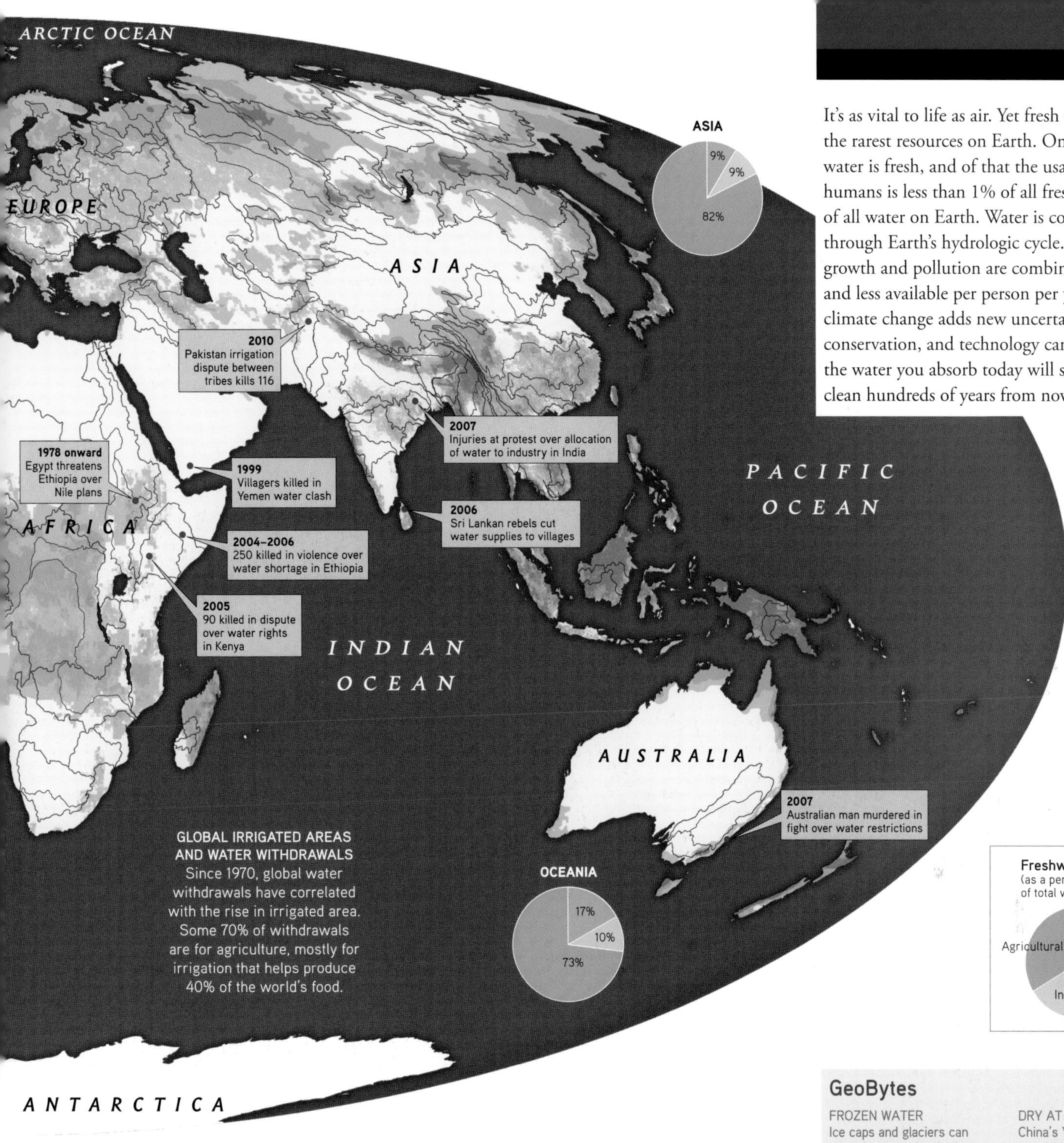

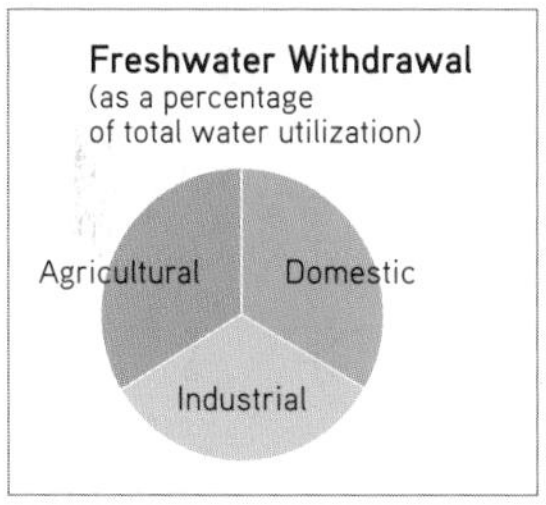

WATER BY VOLUME

Although two-thirds of Earth is covered in water, the fresh water needed for survival, agriculture, and the environment makes up only 2.5% of the Earth's total. Of that paltry amount, much is frozen or deep underground. Overall, less than 1% of the Earth's fresh water is available to humans.

TOTAL WATER
Salt water 97.5%
Fresh water 2.5%

FRESH WATER
Surface and atmospheric water 0.4%
Permafrost 0.8%
Glaciers 68.7%
Groundwater 30.1%

SURFACE AND ATMOSPHERIC WATER
Freshwater lakes 67.4%
Biota 0.8%
Rivers 1.6%
Wetlands 8.5%
Atmosphere 9.5%
Soil moisture 12.2%

WATER WITHDRAWAL
(from groundwater and surface water)
Agriculture 70%
Domestic 11%
Industrial 19%

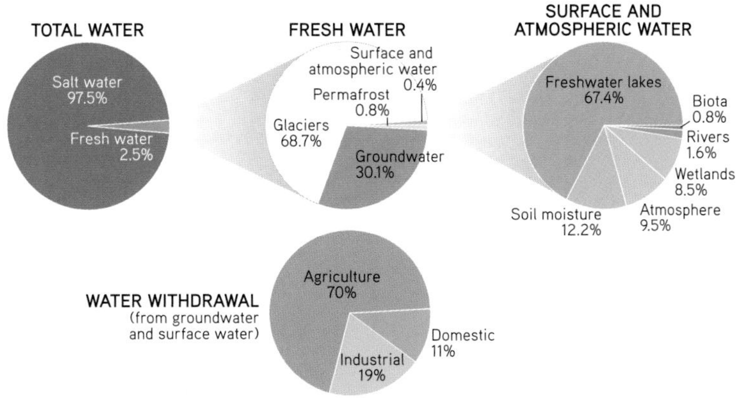

GeoBytes

FROZEN WATER
Ice caps and glaciers can store frozen water for hundreds of thousands of years. In Greenland and Antarctica, glaciers have stored water for millions of years.

LIVING WITH LESS
Australia is the driest inhabited continent.

DYING FOR LACK OF CLEAN WATER
More than 9,000 people–mainly children in Africa and Asia–die every day from water-related illnesses.

OGALLALA AQUIFER
Overpumping has caused the vast aquifer below the Great Plains to drop dramatically in parts of Kansas and Texas.

DRY AT THE MOUTH
China's Yellow River, which is used to irrigate 7.3 million hectares (18 million acres), usually runs dry before reaching the sea.

TIGRIS AND EUPHRATES
More than 4,500 years ago, the Tigris and Euphrates Rivers were the subject of history's only true "water war." Today, dams and irrigation projects cause tension.

DISASTER IN SLOW MOTION
Drought is a slow but inexorable killer that can affect the lives of millions and cost billions of dollars in crop losses.

GeoBytes

PLANT SPECIES
Approximately 250,000 plant species occupy the biomes of the Earth, with an estimated 10 to 15% still to be discovered.

RICH IN BIODIVERSITY
Evergreen broadleaf forests are typical of rain forests, which represent approximately one-half of Earth's remaining forests, occupying 7% of land area worldwide.

THREATS TO FORESTS
Forests everywhere are under pressure from logging, mining, global warming, slash-and-burn agriculture, and desertification.

Land Cover Classes

- Evergreen needleleaf forest
- Evergreen broadleaf forest
- Deciduous needleleaf forest
- Deciduous broadleaf forest
- Mixed forest
- Woody savanna
- Savanna
- Closed shrubland
- Open shrubland
- Grassland
- Cropland
- Barren or sparsely vegetated
- Urban or built-up
- Snow and ice
- Cropland / natural vegetation mosaic
- Wetland

EVERGREEN NEEDLELEAF FOREST
Tree height exceeds 5 m (16 ft); more than 60% is canopied by forest. Example: boreal region. On tree plantations, trees are logged for paper and building products.

EVERGREEN BROADLEAF FOREST
More than 60% of the land is covered by a forest canopy, with tree heights exceeding 5 m (16 ft). Dominant in the tropics; home to great concentrations of biodiversity.

DECIDUOUS NEEDLELEAF FOREST
A forest canopy covers more than 60% of the land; tree height exceeds 5 m (16 ft). This class is dominant only in Siberia, taking the form of larch forests.

DECIDUOUS BROADLEAF FOREST
More than 60% of the land is covered by a forest canopy; tree height exceeds 5 m (16 ft). In temperate regions, much of this forest has been converted to cropland.

MIXED FOREST
Mixed forests can include a mix of leaf types and phenologies (both evergreen and deciduous). Largely found between temperate deciduous and boreal evergreen forests.

WOODY SAVANNA
Land has herbaceous or woody understory; trees exceed 5 m (16 ft) and may be deciduous or evergreen. Highly degraded in long-settled human environments, such as in West Africa.

SAVANNA
Woody or herbaceous understories are punctuated by trees. Examples are African savanna as well as open boreal woodlands marking the border between trees and tundra.

Satellite data provide the most reliable picture of global vegetative cover over time. Few natural communities of plants and animals have remained the same; most have been altered by humans. The "natural" vegetation reflects what would grow there, given ideal conditions. The map at left is based on global satellite imagery from the Moderate Resolution Imaging Spectroradiometer (MODIS), at a spatial resolution of 500 meters. By recording the data at different wavelengths of the electromagnetic spectrum, scientists can derive land cover type through spectral variation. Changes in vegetation are captured in the satellite record, contributing to a rich data bank for Earth studies in areas such as conservation, biodiversity assessments, and land resource management.

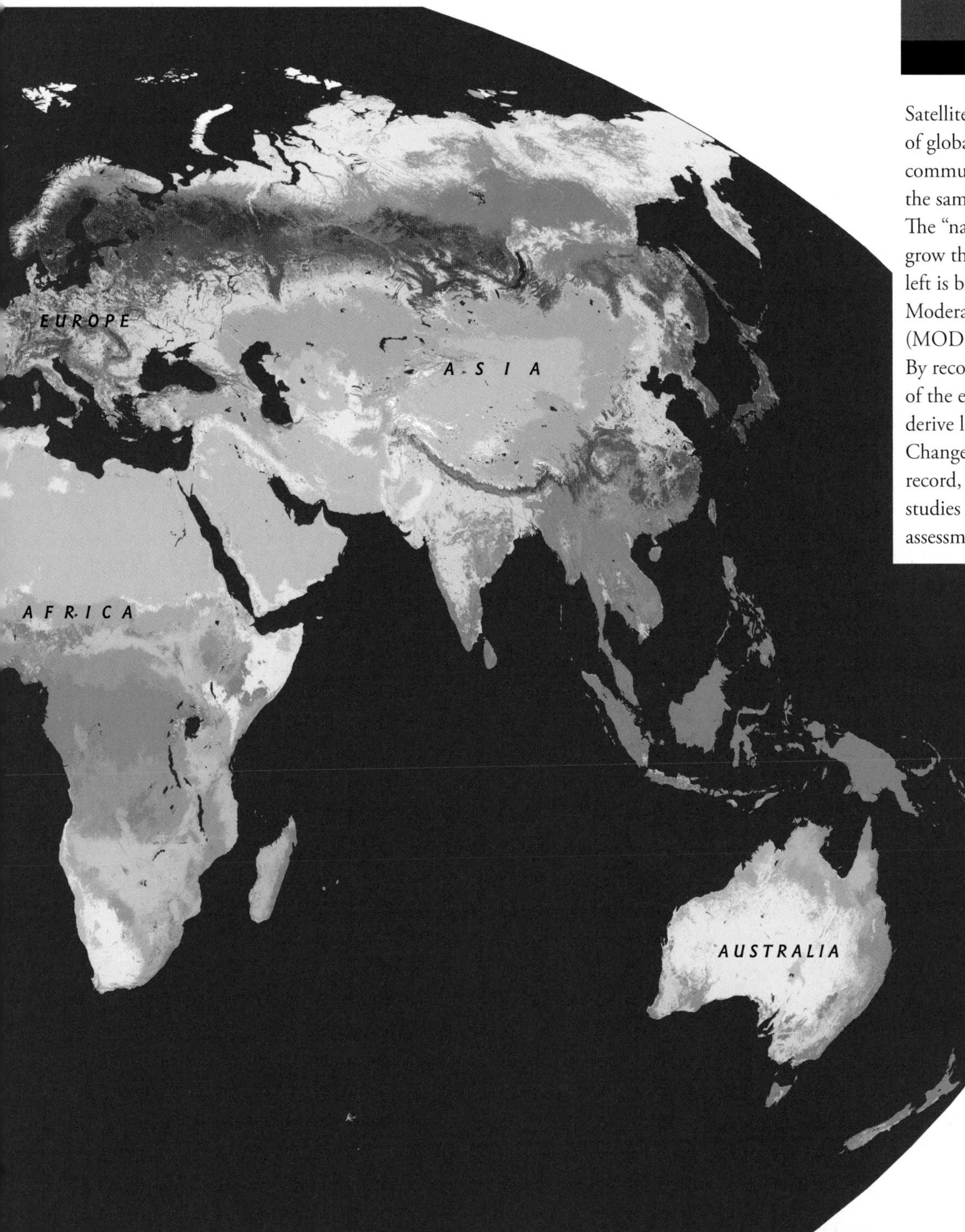

WETLAND
A permanent mixture of water and herbaceous or woody vegetation, in salt, brackish, or fresh water. Examples include the Everglades, Lake Chad, and the Sunderbans.

SNOW AND ICE
Permanent snow cover characterizes this class, the greatest expanses of which are in the polar regions, as well as on high-elevation glaciers in Alaska, the Himalaya, and Iceland.

CLOSED SHRUBLAND
Found where prolonged cold or dry seasons limit plant growth, this cover is dominated by bushes or shrubs not exceeding 5 m (16 ft). Tree canopy is less than 10%.

OPEN SHRUBLAND
Shrubs are dominant, with a canopy cover not exceeding 2 m (6.5 ft) in height. They can be evergreen or deciduous. This land cover type occurs in semiarid or severely cold areas.

GRASSLAND
Occurring in a wide range of habitats, these have continuous herbaceous cover and less than 10% tree or shrub cover. The American Plains and central Russia are the largest examples.

CROPLAND
Crop-producing fields make up more than 80% of the landscape. Temperate regions are home to large areas of mechanized farming; in the developing world, plots are fragmented and smaller.

BARREN/SPARSELY VEGETATED
The land never has more than 10% vegetated cover. True deserts, such as the Sahara, as well as areas succumbing to desertification, are examples.

URBAN AND BUILT-UP
Areas dominated by human occupation for residential, commercial, or transportation purposes. Population densities in these areas are typically much higher than in rural areas.

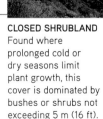

CROPLAND/NATURAL VEGETATION MOSAIC
No one component comprises more than 60% of the landscape. Can be seen in much of the U.S.; examples include southwestern Wisconsin and the Susquehanna Valley.

Major Terrestrial Habitat Types

These 14 major terrestrial habitats—areas with distinct environmental conditions and species communities—represent the broad range of species and ecological processes that make up the diversity of life on Earth's surface. They range from sea-level mangrove forests south of Lagos, Nigeria, to montane grasslands in Tibet.

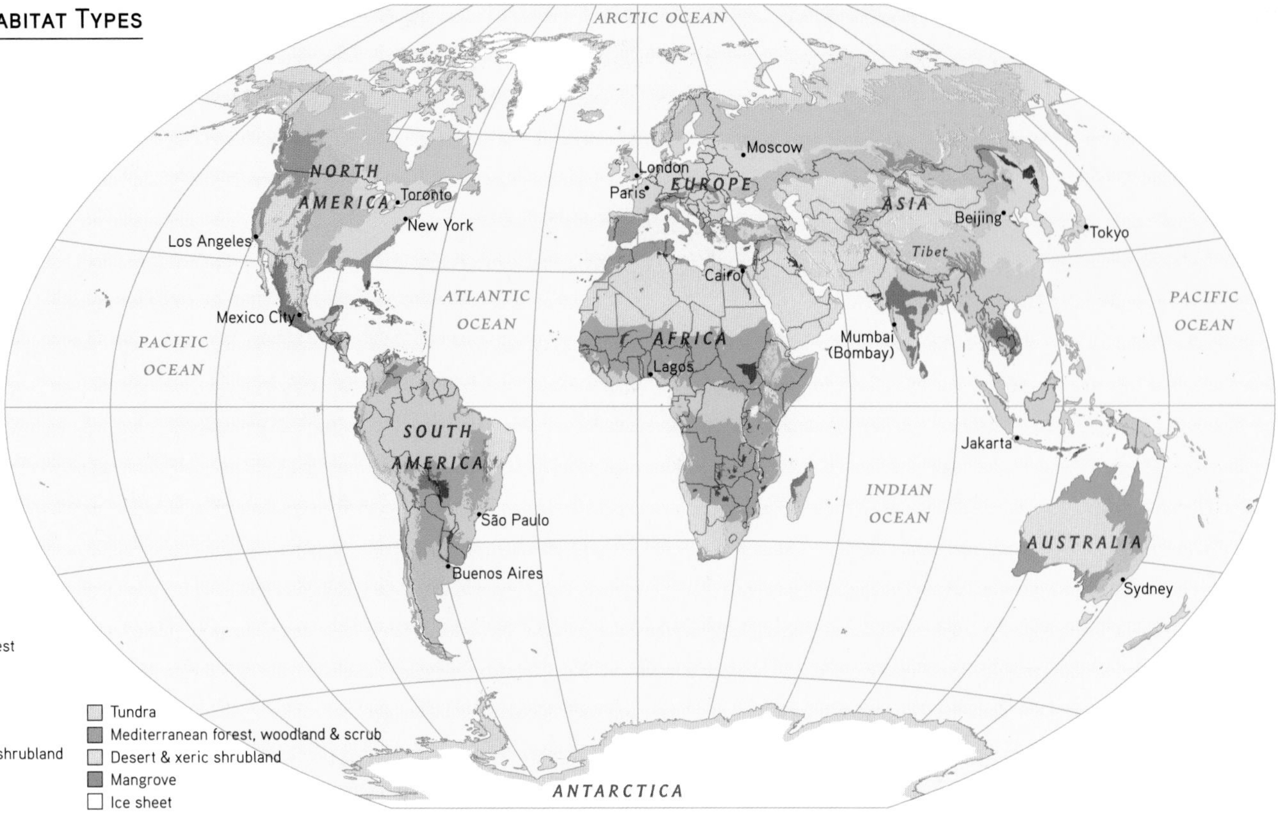

TERRESTRIAL ECOREGION

- Tropical & subtropical moist broadleaf forest
- Tropical & subtropical dry broadleaf forest
- Tropical & subtropical coniferous forest
- Temperate broadleaf & mixed forest
- Temperate conifer forest
- Boreal forest, taiga
- Tropical & subtropical grassland, savanna & shrubland
- Temperate grassland, savanna & shrubland
- Flooded grassland & savanna
- Montane grassland & shrubland
- Tundra
- Mediterranean forest, woodland & scrub
- Desert & xeric shrubland
- Mangrove
- Ice sheet

Major Freshwater and Marine Habitat Types

From coral reefs to river basins, these aqueous habitats illustrate the wide-ranging diversity of the world's freshwater and marine ecoregions, many of which are home to high-priority conservation areas. Examples include Australia's Great Barrier Reef as well as less-well-known habitats, such as small freshwater lakes in the southern Mexican highlands.

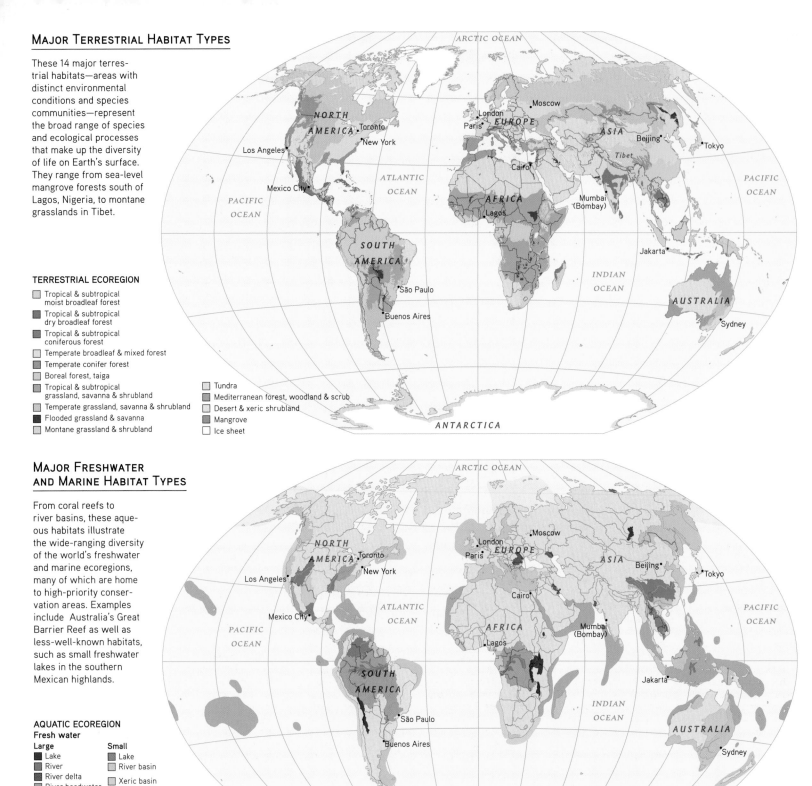

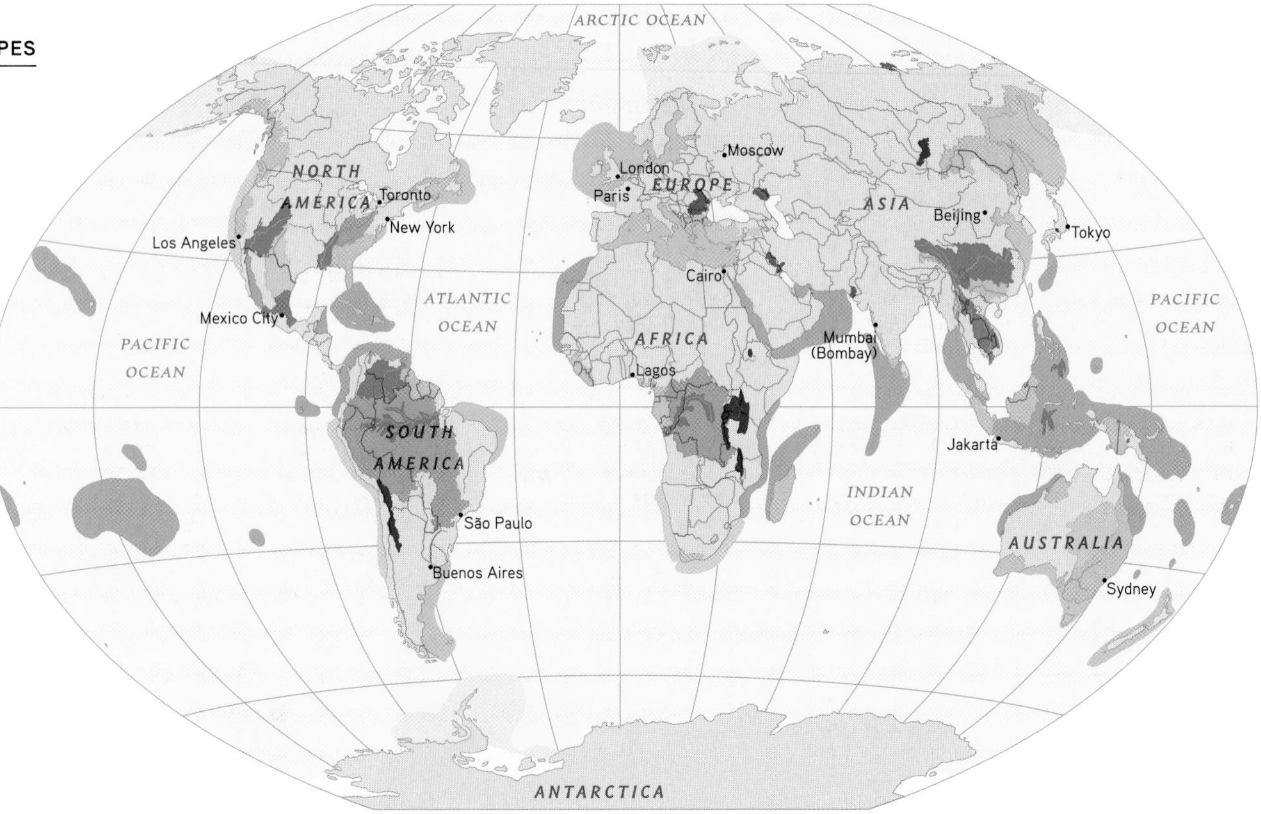

AQUATIC ECOREGION

Fresh water

Large
- Lake
- River
- River delta
- River headwater

Small
- Lake
- River basin
- Xeric basin

Marine-Coastal
- Temperate upwelling
- Tropical upwelling
- Tropical coral
- Temperate shelf & sea
- Polar

GeoBytes

UNIQUE SPECIES
Madagascar and the Indian Ocean islands are home to species found nowhere else. Of the region's 13,000 plant species, more than 89% are endemic, meaning that is the only place on Earth they live.

FRAGILE POPULATIONS
Nearly half of the world's tortoises and freshwater turtles are threatened.

HUMAN HEALTH
Medicines derived from plants and animals are the primary source of health care for 80% of the world's population.

ECONOMIC VALUE
Scientists estimate that ecosystems worldwide provide goods and services, such as nutrient recycling and waste treatment, valued at more than $20 trillion a year.

EXTINCTION RISK
One in every eight birds and one in every four mammals face a high risk of extinction in the near future.

BEETLEMANIA
Beetles are the most diverse life-form on Earth. More than a thousand different kinds can live on a single tree in the forests of South America.

Threats to Biodiversity

The greatest threats to biodiversity—habitat loss and fragmentation, invasion of non-native species, pollution, and unsustainable exploitation—are all caused by human economic activity and population growth.

Projected Status of Biodiversity, 1998–2018
- Critical and endangered
- Threatened
- Relatively stable/intact

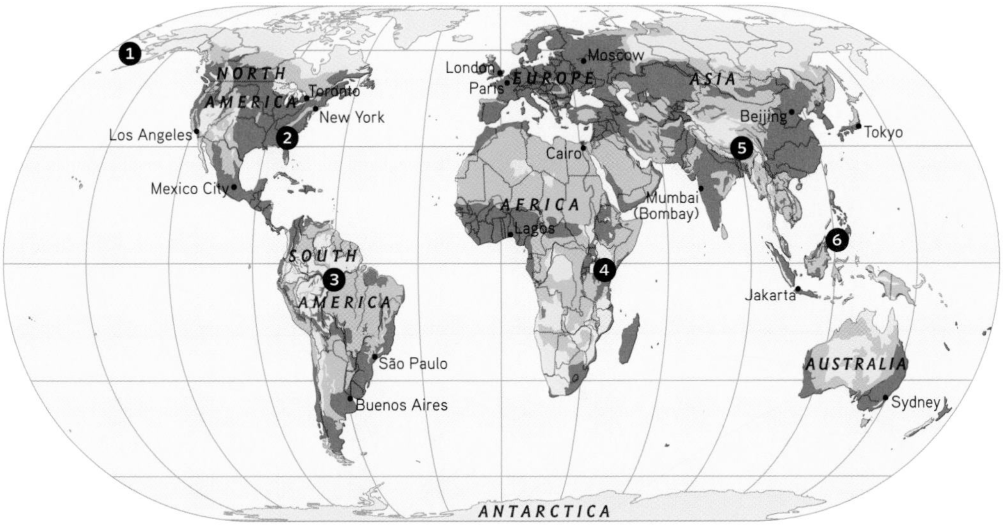

Biodiversity refers to the rich variation among the world's living organisms and the ecological communities they are part of. It includes the number of different species, the genetic diversity within species, and the ecosystems in which species live. Some areas, such as coral reefs, are replete with diversity; others, like the polar regions, lack diversity. The biodiversity of any given place is shaped by biogeographic conditions including local and regional climate, latitude, range of habitats, evolutionary history, and biological productivity—a place's capacity to generate and support life. Experts estimate that species are becoming extinct at a rate of 100 to 1,000 times higher than might be expected from natural extinction. Humans rely on the world's diverse assets for survival—food, medicine, clean air, drinkable water—yet it is our activities that pose the greatest threat to the world's biodiversity.

THE BERING SEA
The Bering Sea, separating Alaska and Russia, is one of the world's most diverse marine environments. Polar bears, seals, sea lions, walruses, whales, enormous populations of seabirds, and more than 400 species of fish, crustaceans, and mollusks live in this ecoregion. It is also home to one of the world's largest salmon runs. Global warming, pollution, overfishing, and mining are major threats to this region's biodiversity.

SOUTHEASTERN U.S. RIVERS AND STREAMS
From Appalachian streams to saltwater marshes along the Atlantic and Gulf coasts, this ecoregion harbors hundreds of species of fish, snails, crayfish, and mussels. A single river in the region, the Cahaba River in Alabama, has more fish species per mile than any other river in North America. Population growth and increasing streamside development, dams, and water diversion for irrigation are threats.

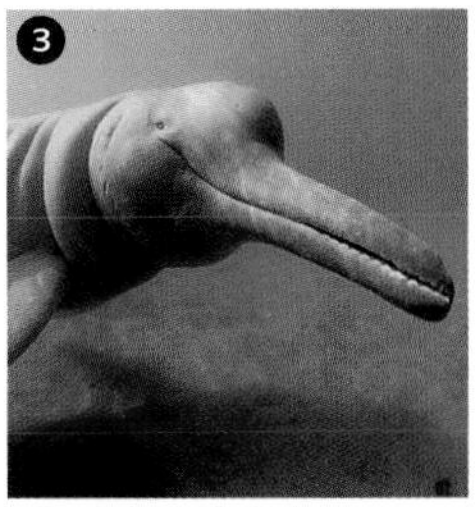

THE AMAZON RIVER AND FLOODED FOREST
More than 3,000 species of freshwater fish and many mammals, including the pink river dolphin, inhabit this ecoregion. The Amazon Basin is Earth's largest watershed and is noted for having the world's largest expanse of seasonally flooded forests, habitat for many of migratory species. Selective logging and the conversion of floodplains for ranching and agricultural use are threats to the region.

RIFT VALLEY LAKES
This cluster of freshwater and alkaline lakes spread across East Africa's Great Lakes region. It is home to nearly 800 species of cichlid fishes, all derived from a common ancestor, a process called species radiation. These radiations are an extraordinary example of evolutionary adaptation. The lakes also provide important bird habitat. Threats include deforestation, pollution, and the spread of non-native species.

EASTERN HIMALAYAN BROADLEAF AND CONIFER FORESTS
Snaking across the lowlands and foothills of the Himalaya, this ecoregion supports a remarkable diversity of plants and animals, including endangered mammals such as the clouded leopard, Himalayan black bear, and the golden langur. These sub-alpine forests are also a significant endemic bird area. Conversion to cropland and timber extraction are serious threats.

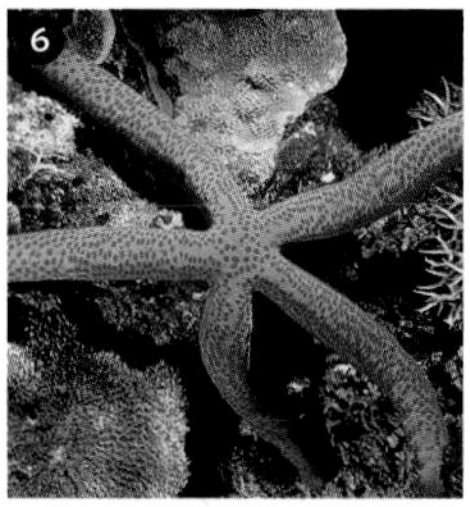

SULU-SULAWESI SEAS
Extensive coral reefs, mangroves, and seagrass beds make this one of the richest habitats for reef animals and plants in the world. More than 450 species of coral, six of the world's eight species of marine turtles, and numerous species of fish, sharks, and whales live in this marine ecoregion between Indonesia, Malaysia, and the Philippines. Reefs continue to be threatened by coastal erosion, pollution, and overfishing.

Biodiversity Hotspots

What areas are vital for conserving biodiversity? Conservation International identified 34 "hotspots," defined as habitat holding at least 1,500 endemic plant species and having lost 70% of its original extent.

Biodiversity Hotspots
- Hotspot region

GeoBytes

SHRINKING FORESTS
Since 1700, about 20% of Earth's forests and woodlands have disappeared.

CARBON DIOXIDE EMISSIONS
Land use has contributed to 35% of human-caused carbon dioxide emissions over the last 150 years.

URBANIZING POPULATION
Urban areas cover roughly 3% of Earth's land but house half of the world's population.

LAND USE PATTERNS

Data from satellite imagery and ground-based records show the impact land use has on the Earth. Food production has had the greatest impact—croplands and pastures now cover nearly 40% of the Earth's surface. Increasing urbanization is poised to alter the landscape further.

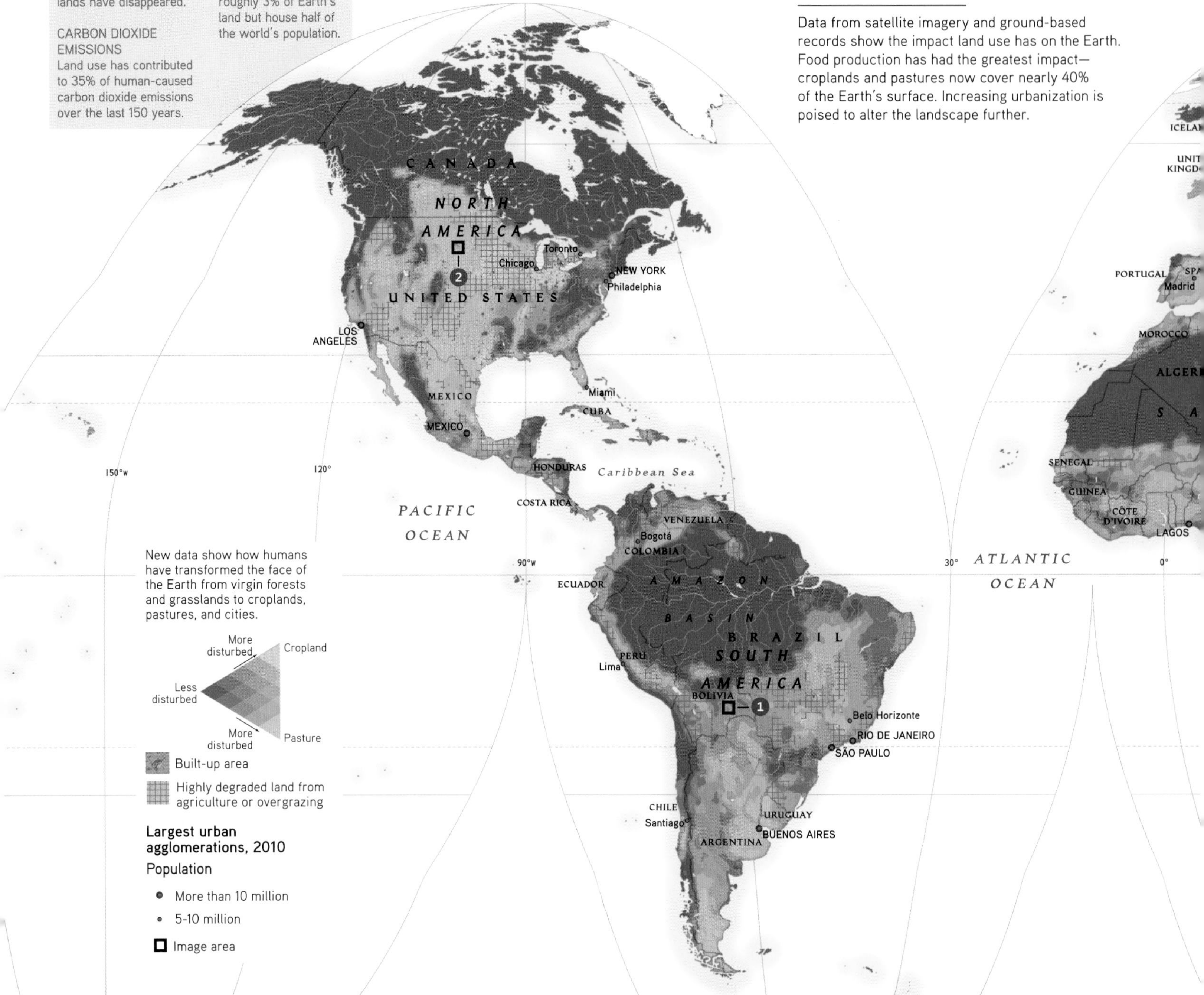

New data show how humans have transformed the face of the Earth from virgin forests and grasslands to croplands, pastures, and cities.

More disturbed — Cropland
Less disturbed
More disturbed — Pasture

Built-up area

Highly degraded land from agriculture or overgrazing

Largest urban agglomerations, 2010
Population

● More than 10 million
· 5-10 million

□ Image area

① DEFORESTATION

These images show the progression of deforestation and increasing agricultural development in Bolivia. The first image (1975) shows a large expanse of solid red, representing tropical dry forest, to the east of Bolivia's second largest city, Santa Cruz. The other two images (1992 and 2000, respectively) show an increasing number of open patches representing small communities and soybean fields, depicted as light-colored rectangles, in areas that were once forested.

② FIRE

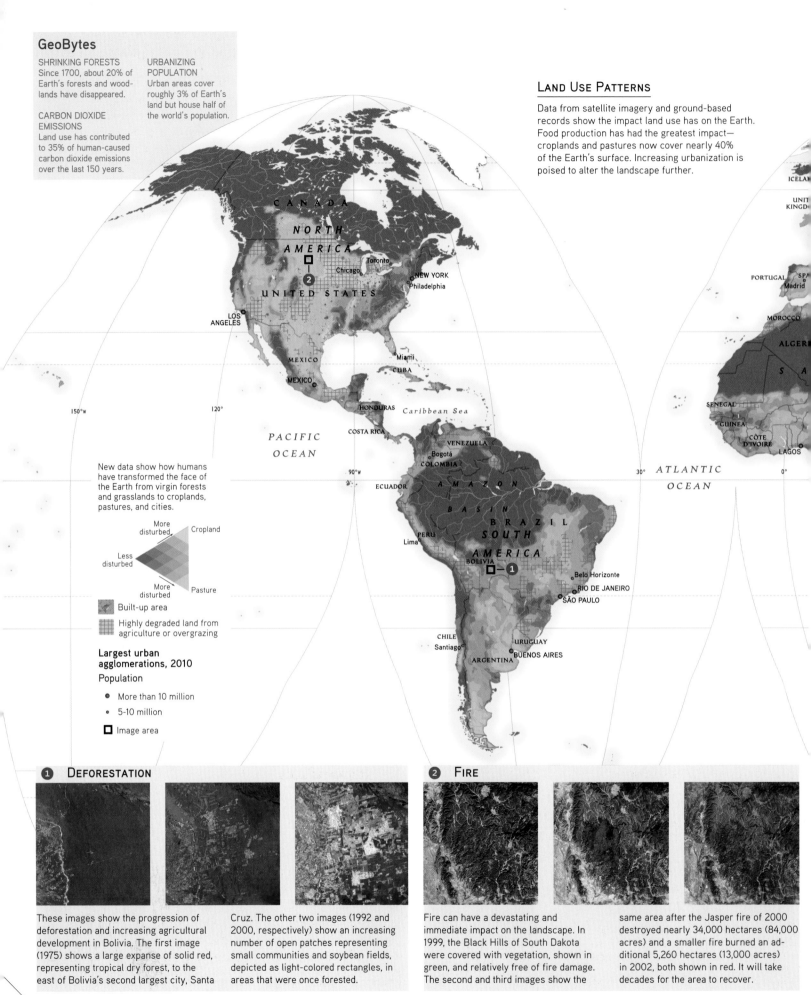

Fire can have a devastating and immediate impact on the landscape. In 1999, the Black Hills of South Dakota were covered with vegetation, shown in green, and relatively free of fire damage. The second and third images show the same area after the Jasper fire of 2000 destroyed nearly 34,000 hectares (84,000 acres) and a smaller fire burned an additional 5,260 hectares (13,000 acres) in 2002, both shown in red. It will take decades for the area to recover.

The intensification of agriculture, increasing consumption of natural resources, and a global trend toward urbanization—partnered with swift population growth—are dramatically transforming Earth's landscape. Practices associated with land use vary widely across the globe, but most fulfill human needs such as food and shelter while having an often negative impact on the natural world, such as climate change, loss of biodiversity, and degradation of soil and water. Lessening these negative impacts is critical to the preservation of the natural world and ultimately to human survival.

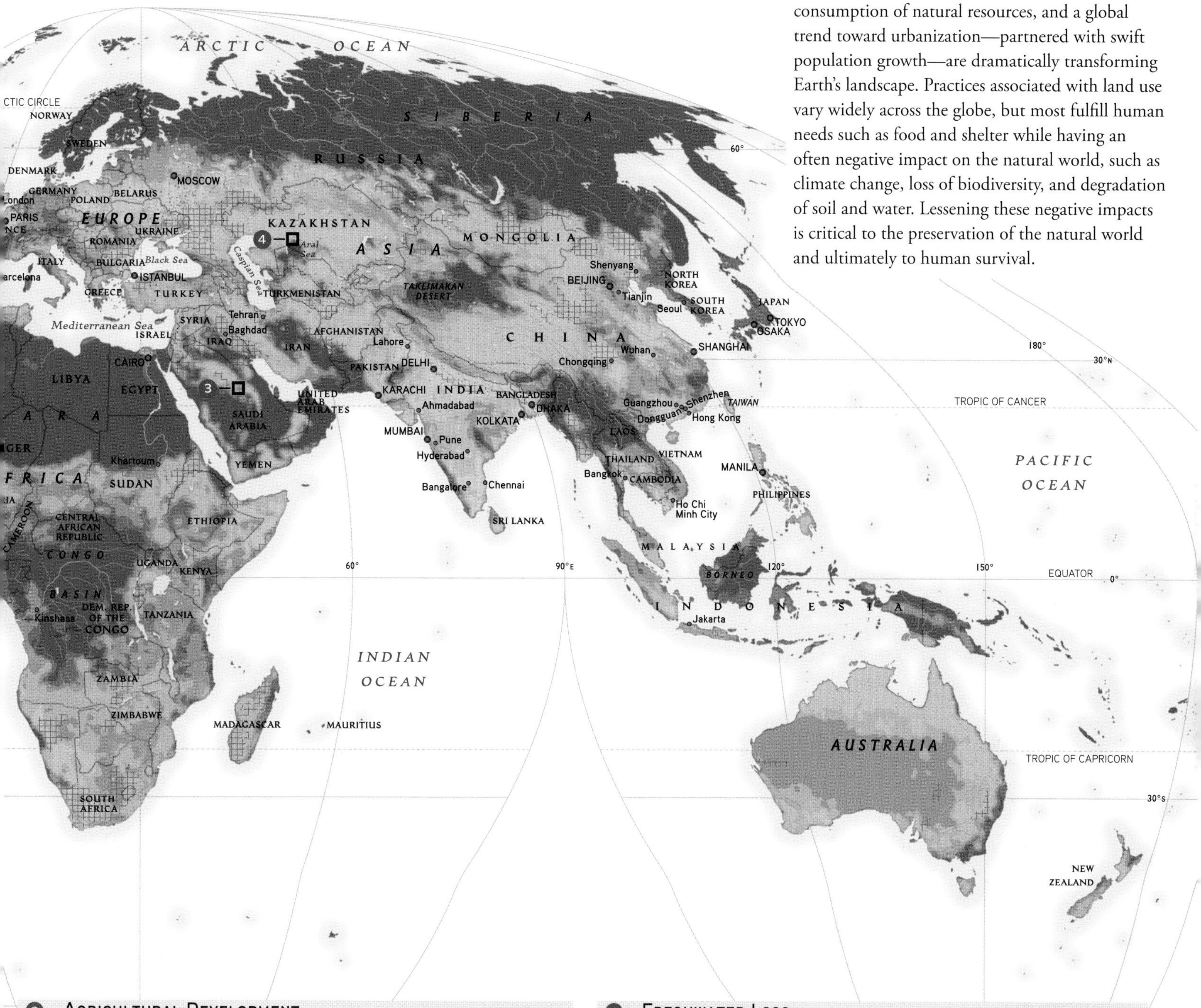

❸ Agricultural Development

Agriculture in Saudi Arabia has undergone dramatic changes in the past few decades. The first image (1972) shows little agricultural development. The oasis cities of Buraydah and 'Unayzah are barely noticeable. By 1986, there is a striking increase in center-pivot irrigation, seen as red circles, for crops such as wheat, and the cities are larger. The 2003 image reveals a vast expansion of irrigated lands surrounding the rapidly growing cities.

❹ Freshwater Loss

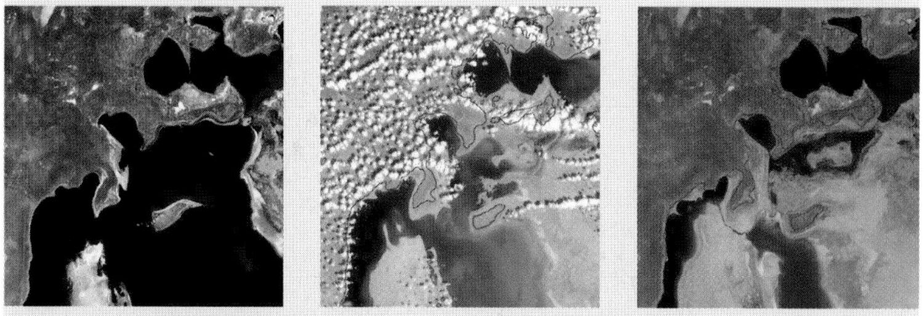

Since 1960, the volume of the Aral Sea has shrunk by 90%. This can be attributed to water being diverted to irrigate cotton and rice fields in Central Asia. These images from 1989, 2000, and 2010, show the drastic changes to the Aral Sea's shoreline. Water level has dropped 26 meters (85 feet), salinity has increased tenfold, and what was once the world's fourth largest lake is now one of its best examples of a human-induced environmental disaster.

GeoBytes

COUNTING HEADS
Most governments conduct a population census every ten years, although the process is expensive and accuracy is difficult to attain for most.

PACKED NEIGHBORHOODS
The most densely populated place in the world is the tiny European principality of Monaco, with 22,083 people per sq km (57,200 people per sq mi). The least dense is Greenland.

IOWA VS. BANGLADESH
Bangladesh's rural population density is 1,459 per sq km (3,779 per sq mi) in an area the size of Iowa. In Iowa, the figure is about 20 per sq km (54 per sq mi).

SHEER NUMBERS
The most populated country is the People's Republic of China, with 1.3 billion. The least populated jurisdiction is Pitcairn Island in the Pacific, with 48 people.

POPULATION CARTOGRAM

The world appears quite different when countries are sized proportional to their populations and mapped. Underpopulated Canada, the world's second largest country, is reduced to a small strip above the United States, while small, crowded Japan looms large. India and China become the global giants.

World Population, 2010
1 block = 2 million people

Population Growth Rate (as a percentage of total population)
- More than 3%
- 2.0–2.9%
- 1.0–1.9%
- 0–0.9%
- Negative growth

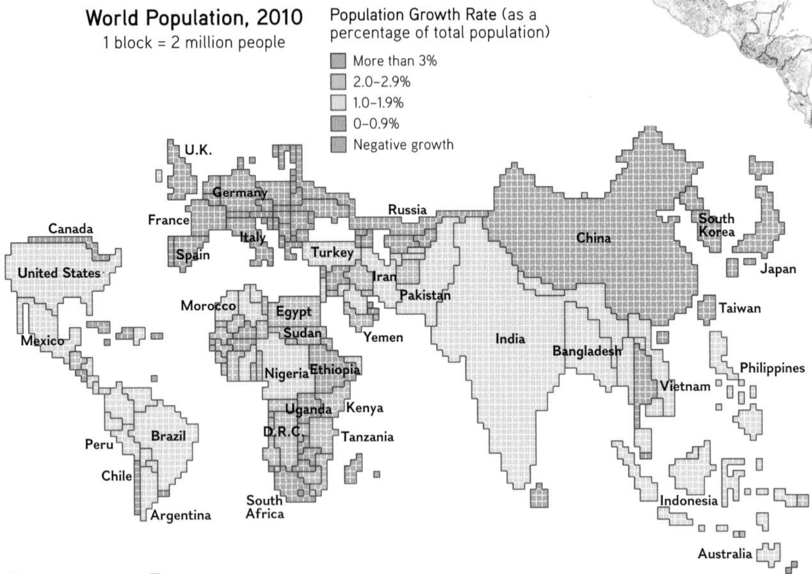

POPULATION PYRAMIDS

When population is expressed in bars representing age and gender and stacked up (males left, females right), country profiles emerge that have ramifications for the future. Countries with high birthrates and high percentages of young, such as Nigeria, look like pyramids. Countries such as Italy, whose birthrate is below the replacement fertility level of 2.1 children per couple, show bulges in the higher age brackets. The United States clearly shows the "baby boom" of children born in the years after World War II.

U.S.   BRAZIL   ITALY   NIGERIA   INDIA   LAOS

Percent of population

Age   80+   60–64   40–44 Male   Female   20–24   0–4

A.D. 1   50   100   150   200   250   300   350   400   450   500   550   600   650   700   750   800   850   900   950

Year

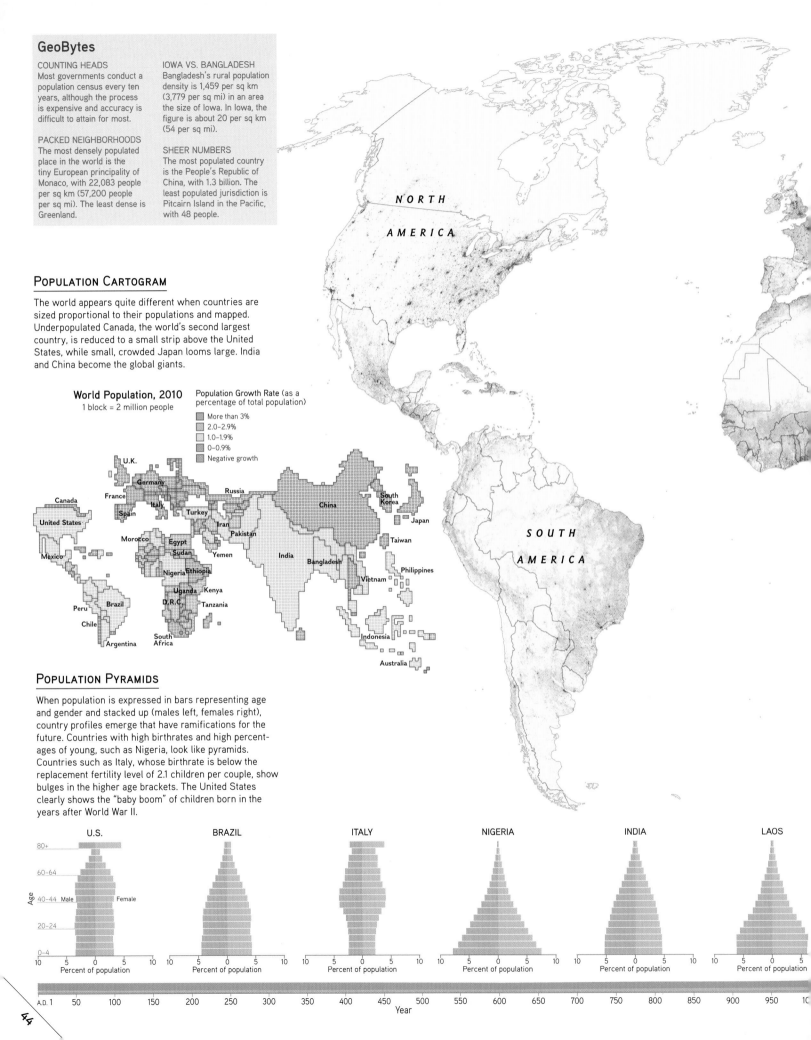

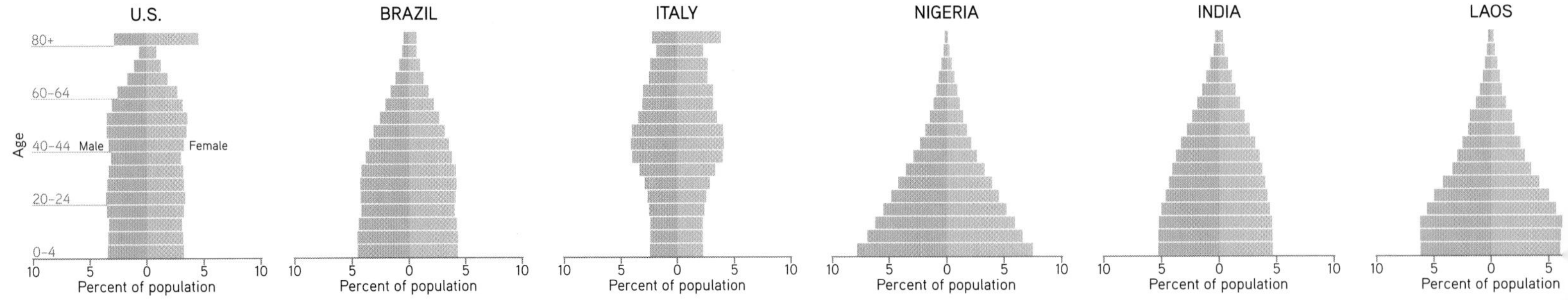

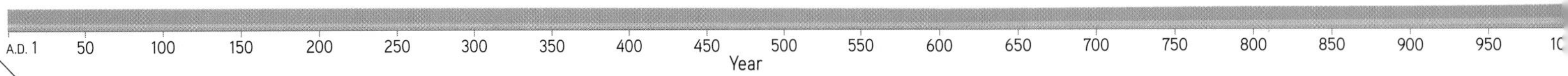

Geographers approach the study of human populations, or demography, from a spatial perspective, asking why density, distribution, resources, births, deaths, and migrations vary from place to place. Earth's population, now at nearly 7 billion, grows by about 80 million a year, or 1.1% annually. The bulk of the increase occurs in developing countries in Asia, Africa, and Latin America. Physiologic density—the number of people per unit of agricultural land—shows concentrations in Asia, in particular in China and India; in Europe, from Britain into Russia; along the eastern seaboard of the United States; in West Africa in Nigeria; and along the Nile Valley.

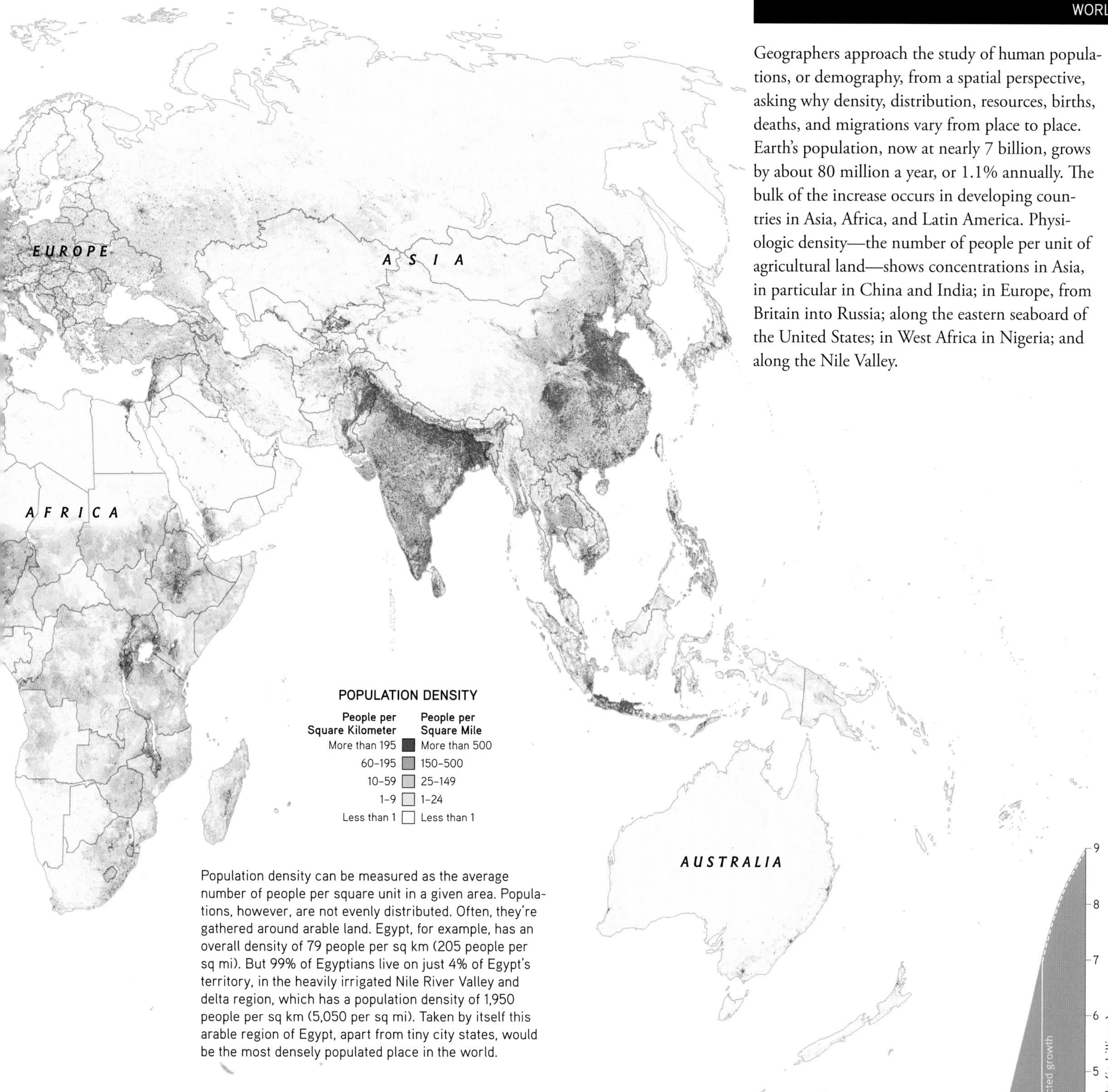

EUROPE

ASIA

AFRICA

POPULATION DENSITY

People per Square Kilometer	People per Square Mile
More than 195	More than 500
60–195	150–500
10–59	25–149
1–9	1–24
Less than 1	Less than 1

Population density can be measured as the average number of people per square unit in a given area. Populations, however, are not evenly distributed. Often, they're gathered around arable land. Egypt, for example, has an overall density of 79 people per sq km (205 people per sq mi). But 99% of Egyptians live on just 4% of Egypt's territory, in the heavily irrigated Nile River Valley and delta region, which has a population density of 1,950 people per sq km (5,050 per sq mi). Taken by itself this arable region of Egypt, apart from tiny city states, would be the most densely populated place in the world.

AUSTRALIA

REGIONAL POPULATION GROWTH
Earth's population has burgeoned since 1800, from approximately one billion to today's seven billion. Africa is sustaining high fertility rates (average number of children per woman) and is projected to contain 21% of the world's population by 2050.

Asia
Africa
Latin America
Europe
North America
Australia & Oceania

Projected growth

Number of people (in billions)

9
8
7
6
5
4
3
2
1
0

Year

1100 1150 1200 1250 1300 1350 1400 1450 1500 1550 1600 1650 1700 1750 1800 1850 1900 1950 2000 2050

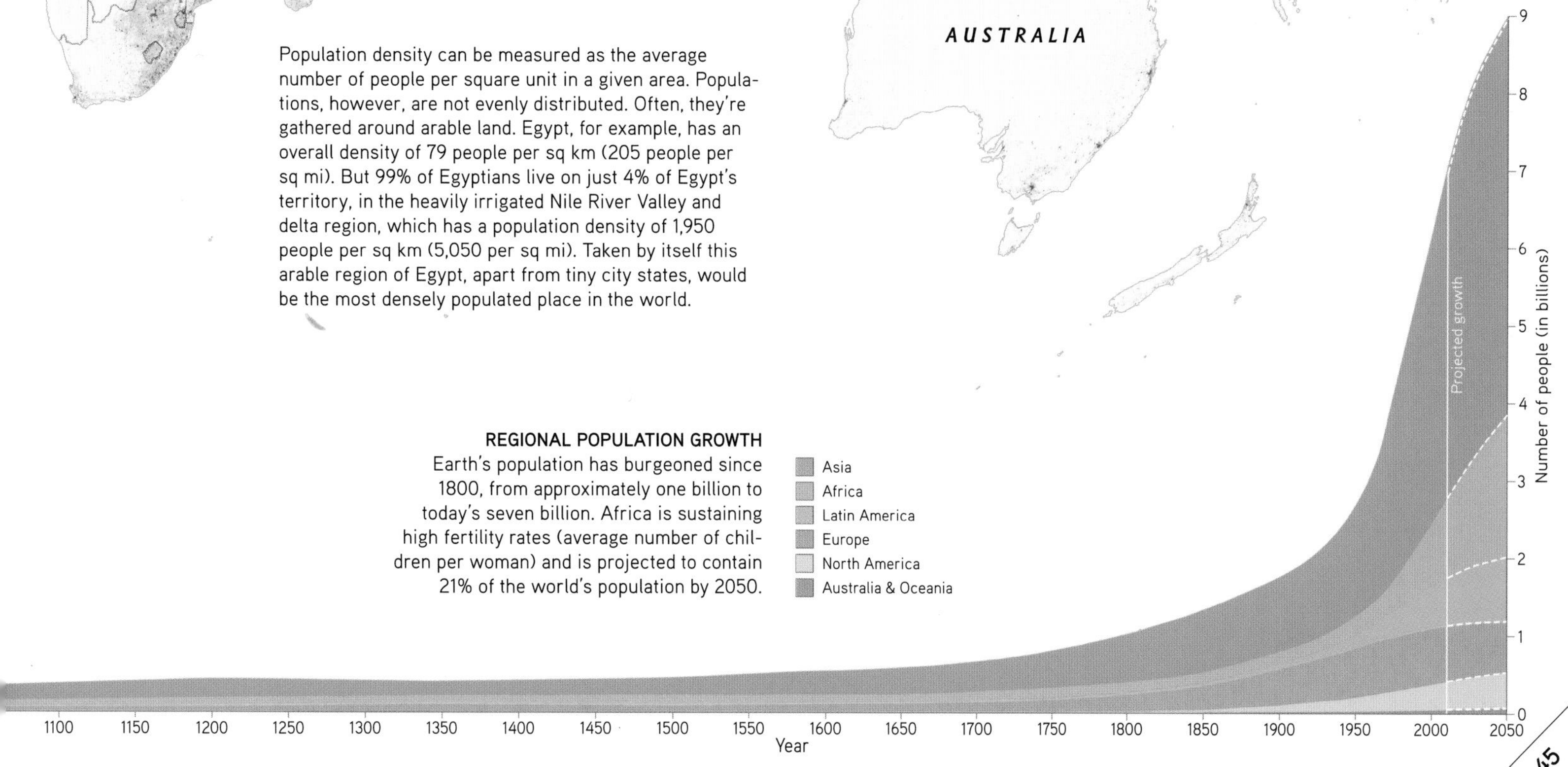

Demographics

Fertility

The nations of central Africa virtually leap off the map as hotbeds of fertility, measured as the average number of children born to women by country. In contrast, northern industrialized nations, such as Japan and the Czech Republic, are not producing enough babies to keep their populations from decreasing.

Total Fertility Rate, 2010

- More than 5.9
- 4.0–5.9
- 2.2–3.9
- 1.6–2.1
- Less than 1.6
- No data

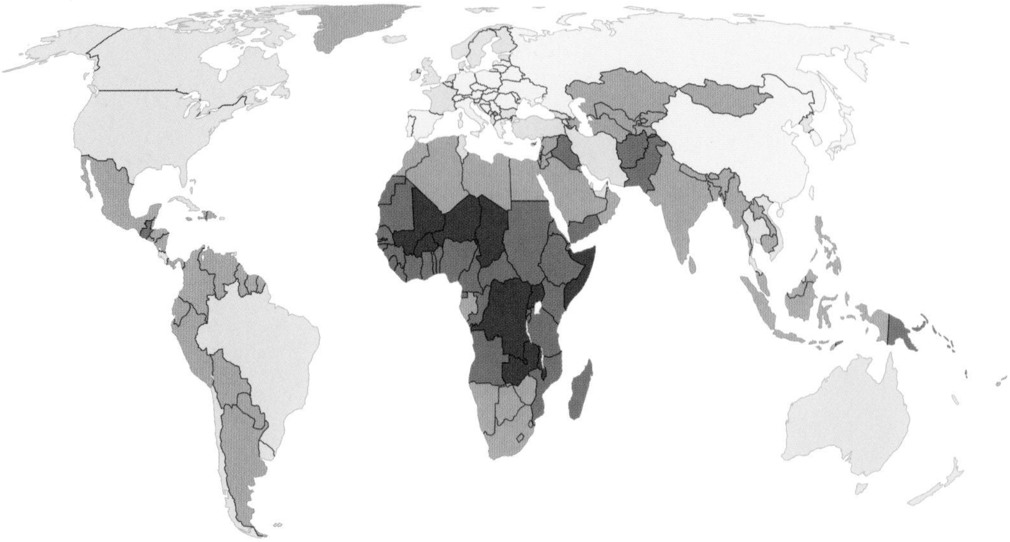

Infant Mortality

Every year, nearly 7 million babies worldwide die before their first birthday. Most are born in poorer countries throughout Africa and parts of Asia. Primary causes of death are respiratory diseases, diarrhea, and infectious diseases. Such illnesses rarely lead to death in more prosperous countries.

Infant Mortality Rate, 2010
(deaths of infants under age 1 per 1,000 live births)

- More than 90
- 45–90
- 30–44
- 15–29
- Less than 15

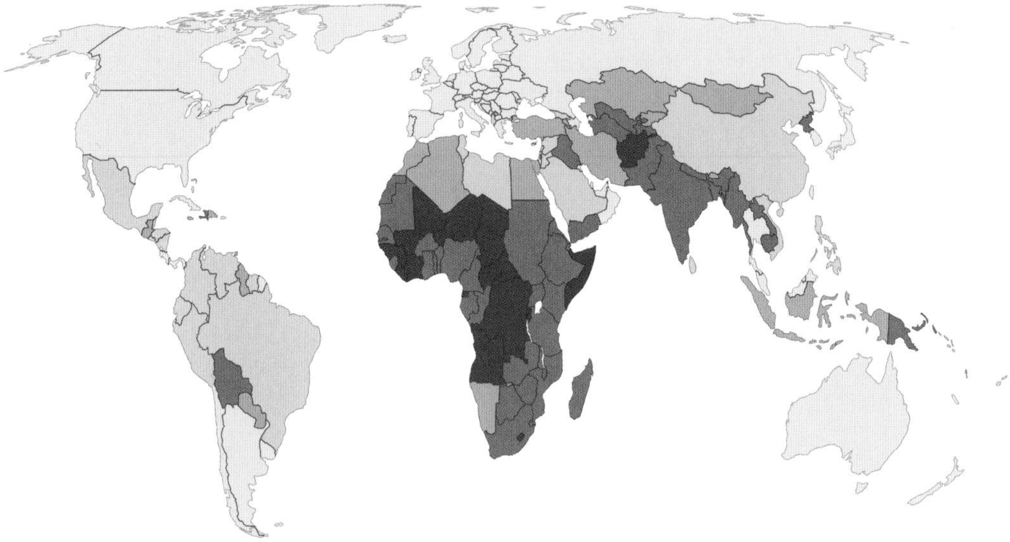

Life Expectancy

The gap in life expectancy between developed and developing nations has narrowed as better medical care and education have lowered the infant mortality rate. Many Africans, however, die early. A Zambian male can expect to live only 42 years, while the average Japanese male ages to 79.

Life Expectancy at Birth, 2010
(in years)

- 76 or older
- 70–75
- 60–69
- 50–59
- 49 or younger

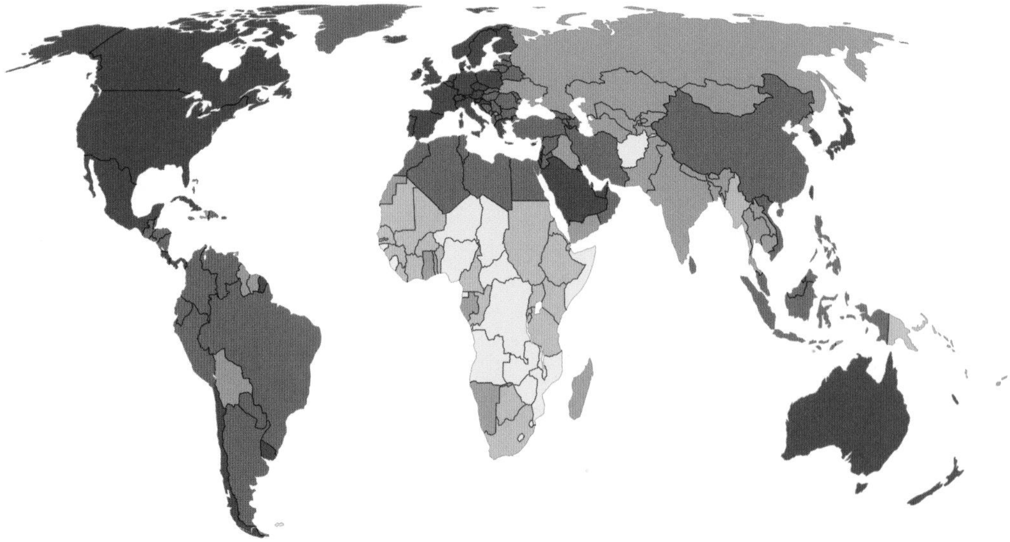

POPULATION SUPERLATIVES

MOST POPULOUS COUNTRIES

1	CHINA*	1,354,146,000
2	INDIA	1,214,464,000
3	UNITED STATES	317,641,000
4	INDONESIA	232,517,000
5	BRAZIL	195,423,000
6	PAKISTAN	184,753,000
7	BANGLADESH	164,425,000
8	NIGERIA	158,259,000
9	RUSSIA	140,367,000
10	JAPAN	126,995,000
11	MEXICO	110,645,000
12	PHILIPPINES	93,617,000
13	VIETNAM	89,029,000
14	ETHIOPIA	84,976,000
15	EGYPT	84,474,000

*not including Hong Kong and Macau

LEAST POPULOUS COUNTRIES

1	VATICAN CITY	1,000
2	TOKELAU	1,000
3	TUVALU	10,000
4	NAURU	10,000
5	PALAU	21,000
6	SAN MARINO	32,000
7	MONACO	33,000
8	LIECHTENSTEIN	36,000
9	ST. KITTS & NEVIS	52,000
10	MARSHALL ISLANDS	63,000
11	DOMINICA	67,000
12	SEYCHELLES	85,000
13	ANDORRA	87,000
14	ANTIGUA & BARBUDA	89,000
15	KIRIBATI	100,000

MOST DENSELY POPULATED PLACES

		Population Density per sq km	(sq mi)
1	MONACO	22,083	(57,200)
2	MACAU (CHINA)	21,061	(54,550)
3	SINGAPORE	7,082	(18,340)
4	HONG KONG (CHINA)	6,433	(16,660)
5	GIBRALTAR (U.K.)	5,179	(13,410)
6	VATICAN CITY	1,784	(4,620)
7	MALTA	1,298	(3,360)
8	BERMUDA (U.K.)	1,226	(3,180)
9	BAHRAIN	1,163	(3,010)
10	BANGLADESH	1,142	(2,960)

LEAST DENSELY POPULATED PLACES

		Population Density per sq km	(sq mi)
1	GREENLAND (DENMARK)	0.1	(0.25)
2	FALKLAND ISLANDS (U.K.)	0.3	(0.78)
3	MONGOLIA	1.7	(4.40)
4	WESTERN SAHARA (MOROCCO)	2.0	(5.20)
5	FRENCH GUIANA (FRANCE)	2.6	(6.70)
6	NAMIBIA	2.7	(7.00)
7	AUSTRALIA	2.8	(7.30)
8	ICELAND	3.2	(8.30)
9	SURINAME	3.2	(8.30)
10	MAURITANIA	3.3	(8.50)

The 21st century will witness substantial world population growth, even as the rate of growth slows, total fertility rates decline, and populations age. Sheer numbers will increase simply because the base population is so great; the milestone figure of 7 billion is expected to be reached in late 2011. By mid-century, up to 10 billion humans may be sharing the planet. Of the 80 million people being added each year, some 90% are born into developing countries. In some African and Muslim countries, one key to limiting growth is improving the status of women and their access to education and contraception. By 2050, the elderly could constitute 22% of the world's population, affecting economies, savings, employment, and health care. The toll of AIDS in sub-Saharan Africa and adult male mortality in some Eastern European countries are disturbing trends.

URBANIZATION

URBAN POPULATION

Cities, notably in developing countries, are growing at nearly twice the rate of the overall world population increase, and almost half the world's people now live in urban areas. Many newcomers hope to escape rural poverty and find work, although lack of skills condemns millions to slums.

Percent Urban Population, 2010
- ■ More than 79%
- ■ 65%–79%
- ▨ 40%–64%
- ▢ 25%–39%
- ▢ Less than 25%

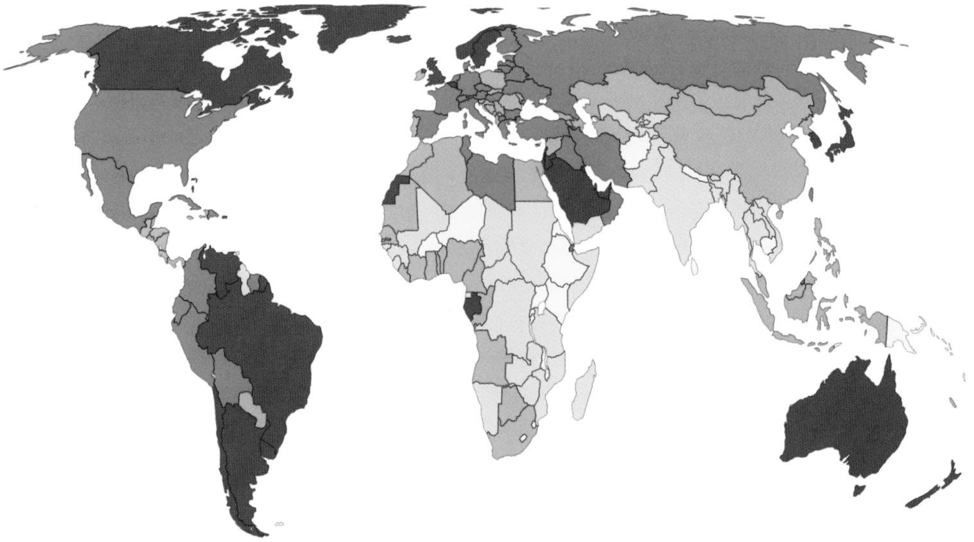

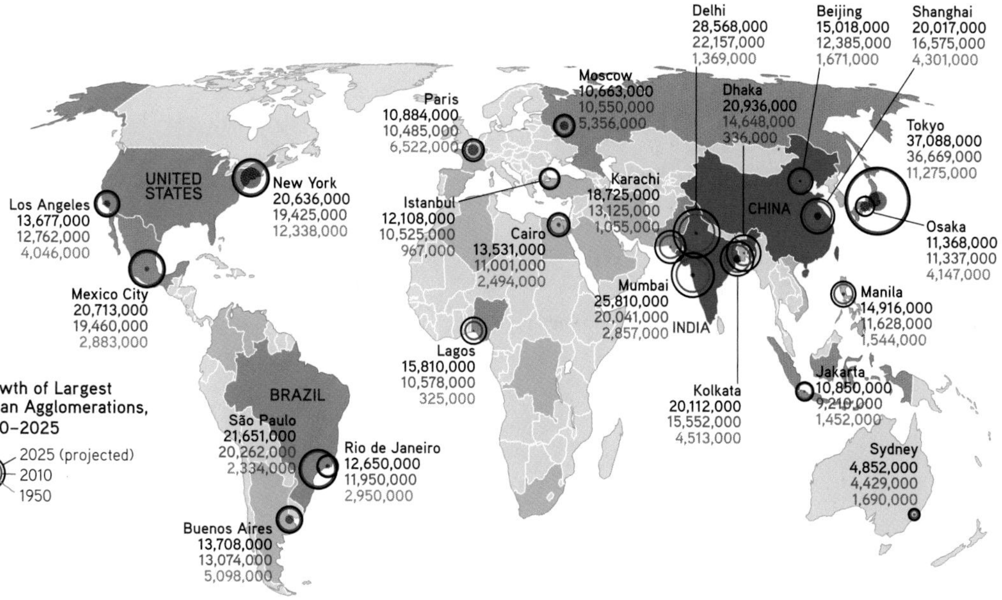

GeoBytes

PEOPLE THROUGH TIME
The total number of humans born since 50,000 B.C. is about 107 billion.

FAST FORWARD
Today the world gains one billion people every 12 years. With current growth rates, world population could reach 10 billion by 2050.

SEVEN BILLION STRONG
In 2011, the world population will reach 7 billion people, or an estimated 6% of the total who have ever lived.

SMALL CITIES
Pre-Industrial Age cities were comparatively small. Rome, the largest city of antiquity, had only 350,000 people.

NATIVITY DISCREPANCY
The death rate of mothers during childbirth in developing countries is 22 times higher than that of women in the developed world.

MOST CHILDREN
In 2010, the the highest fertility rate in the world was in Niger, where women averaged 7.4 children.

URBAN GROWTH

Coal-belt cities in industrialized Europe have stabilized, but Asian and African cities have exploded with growth as millions abandon rural life for the urban promises of prosperity and better health. The population of Lagos, Nigeria, for example, could increase by more than 5 million by 2025.

Delhi
28,568,000
22,157,000
1,369,000

Beijing
15,018,000
12,385,000
1,671,000

Shanghai
20,017,000
16,575,000
4,301,000

Moscow
10,663,000
10,550,000
5,356,000

Paris
10,884,000
10,485,000
6,522,000

Dhaka
20,936,000
14,648,000
336,000

Tokyo
37,088,000
36,669,000
11,275,000

New York
20,636,000
19,425,000
12,338,000

Los Angeles
13,677,000
12,762,000
4,046,000

Istanbul
12,108,000
10,525,000
967,000

Karachi
18,725,000
13,125,000
1,055,000

Osaka
11,368,000
11,337,000
4,147,000

Cairo
13,531,000
11,001,000
2,494,000

Mexico City
20,713,000
19,460,000
2,883,000

Mumbai
25,810,000
20,041,000
2,857,000

Manila
14,916,000
11,628,000
1,544,000

Lagos
15,810,000
10,578,000
325,000

Kolkata
20,112,000
15,552,000
4,513,000

Jakarta
10,850,000
9,210,000
1,452,000

São Paulo
21,651,000
20,262,000
2,334,000

Rio de Janeiro
12,650,000
11,950,000
2,950,000

Sydney
4,852,000
4,429,000
1,690,000

Buenos Aires
13,708,000
13,074,000
5,098,000

Urban Growth, 1950–2010
(population in millions)
- ■ More than 300
- ■ 100–300
- ▨ 50–99
- ▨ 20–49
- ▢ Less than 20
- ▢ No data available

Growth of Largest Urban Agglomerations, 1950–2025
- ◎ 2025 (projected)
- ◉ 2010
- ● 1950

MAJOR RELIGIONS

Christianity has the most adherents of the five major religions; but Islam is growing in Africa and Asia, and migrants increase the number of followers in Europe. Hinduism and Buddhism today maintain wide blocs of the faithful in Asia, while the homeland of Judaism in Israel is a beleaguered bastion.

RELIGIOUS ADHERENCE

The classification of religion and adherents has changed over time. In Western thought and early "world religion" writing, three religions were recognized: Judaism, Christianity, and Paganism. As Eastern history was more understood, other faiths were added to the list of world religions. Around 1800, the "big five" religions were classified as Judaism, Christianity, Islam, Hinduism, and Buddhism. Most recently, nonreligious has been added as an important segment.

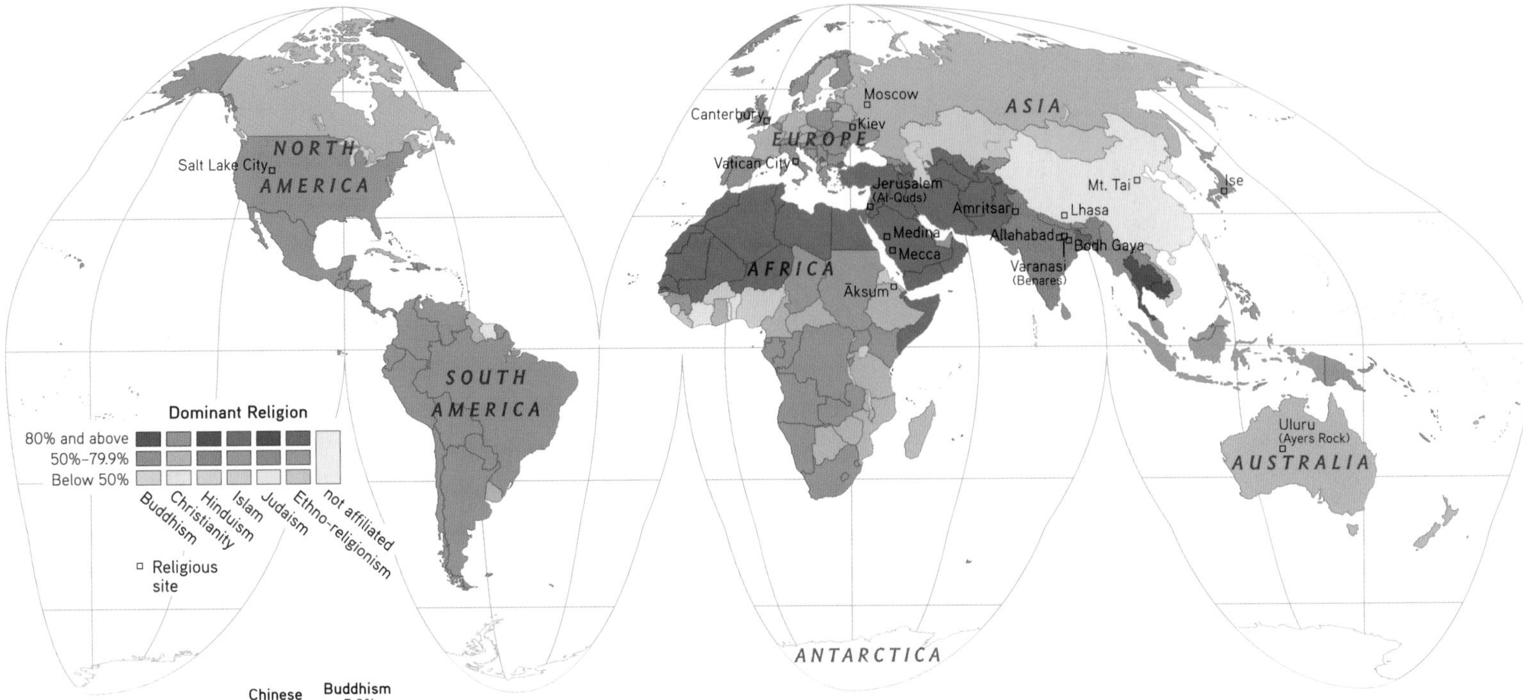

Dominant Religion
80% and above
50%-79.9%
Below 50%
Buddhism · Christianity · Hinduism · Islam · Judaism · Ethno-religionism · not affiliated
□ Religious site

RELIGIOUS ADHERENCE

- Christianity 33.1%
- Islam 20.4%
- Non-religious 14.3%
- Hinduism 13.5%
- Other 6.5%
- Chinese traditional 6.3%
- Buddhism 5.9%

RELIGIOUS ADHERENCE BY REGION

Higher birthrates in Africa and Asia make Islam the world's fastest growing religion; Christianity holds sway on the other continents.

Regions: Africa, Asia, Oceania, Europe, North America, Latin America
Adherents (in millions): 0, 500, 1,000, 1,500, 2,000, 2,500

Legend:
- Buddhists
- Christians
- Hindus
- Muslims
- Jews

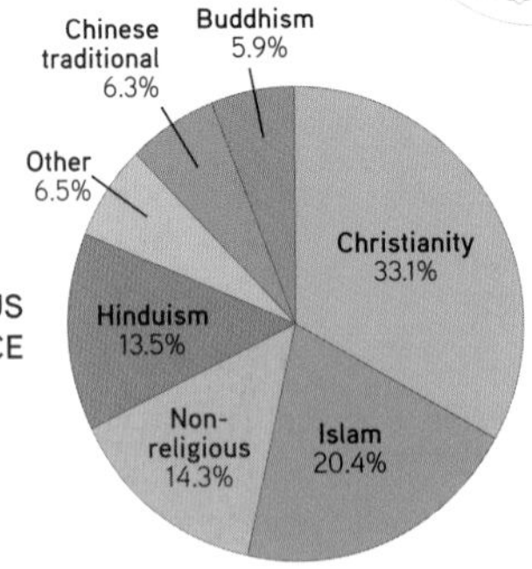

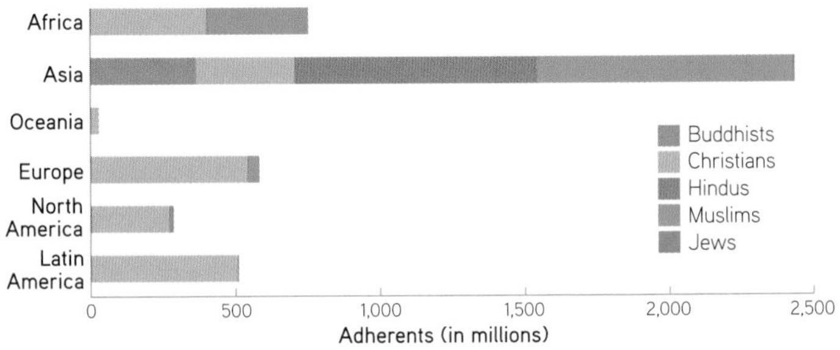

SATELLITE IMAGES OF HOLY SITES

The Old City of Jerusalem surrounds Al' Aqsa Mosque and the Dome of the Rock (lower left). Al' Aqsa is the second oldest mosque in Islam after the Kaaba in Mecca and is third in holiness after the mosques in Mecca and Medina. It holds up to 400,000 worshippers at one time. The shrine of the Dome of the Rock, built in A.D. 692, commemorates the Prophet Muhammad's ascension to heaven. Also visible is the Western (Wailing) Wall of the Jews, the holiest site in the Jewish world. Part of the retaining wall supporting the Temple of Jerusalem built by Herod in 20 B.C., it is visited by Jews from all over the world. Here, too, is the Via Dolorosa, the traditional route of Christ's Crucifixion. Christians pray along the route. The streets of Mecca (lower center) huddle around the Kaaba, Islam's holiest shrine. At Allahabad (lower right), the Ganges and Yamuna Rivers draw more than 30 million Hindus to bathe during the Maha Kumbh Mela, the largest gathering of human beings ever recorded.

OLD CITY OF JERUSALEM, ISRAEL

MECCA, SAUDI ARABIA

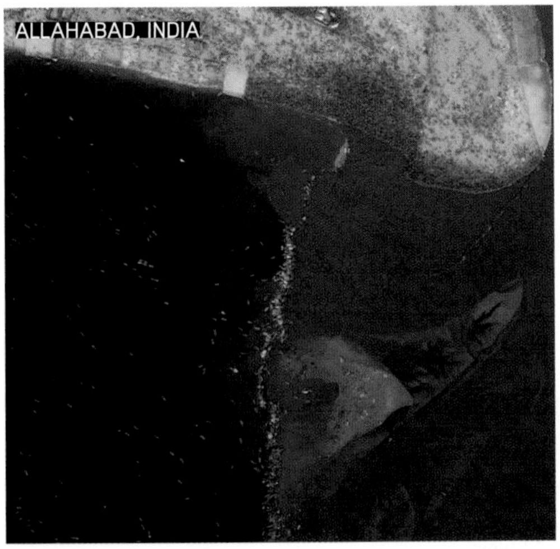

ALLAHABAD, INDIA

WORLD LANGUAGES

Indo-European languages dominate the West, and English has become the language of aviation and technology, but more people speak Mandarin Chinese than speak English, Spanish, German, and French combined. Half of the 6,000 languages in the world today are spoken by fewer than 10,000 people; a quarter by fewer than a thousand. Only a fraction are on the tongues of millions. After Mandarin Chinese, Hindi, Spanish, and English claim the most native speakers.

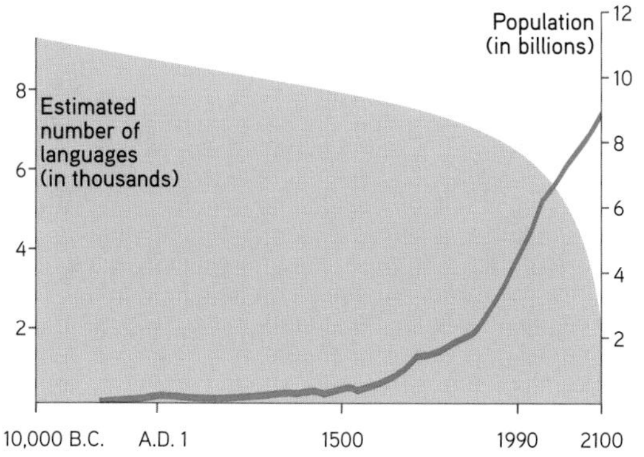

POPULATION VS LANGUAGE
Even as population increases, languages decline. Some 90% of languages today face extinction, potentially leaving only about 600 languages worldwide.

From the food we eat to the values we cherish, culture is at the heart of how we live and understand our human world. Not just a collection of customs, rituals, or artifacts, culture is a complex building up of ideas, innovation, and ideologies. Distinct cultures emerged in river valleys, along coastlines, on islands, and across landmasses, as humans spread to every continent but Antarctica. Conquest and trade helped dominant cultures to expand. Today, electronic communication, transportation networks, and economic globalization bring major cultures closer. Cultural perceptions can play a part in misunderstanding and conflict. Yet cultures arose in the first place in response to a human need for stability and progress.

Major Language Families Today
- Afro-Asiatic
- Altaic
- Austro-Asiatic
- Austronesian
- Dravidian
- Indo-European
- Japanese/Korean
- Kam-Tai
- Niger-Congo
- Nilo-Saharan
- Sino-Tibetan
- Uralic
- Other

STRUGGLING CULTURES

Indigenous Languages
- Extinct
- Endangered
- Vulnerable

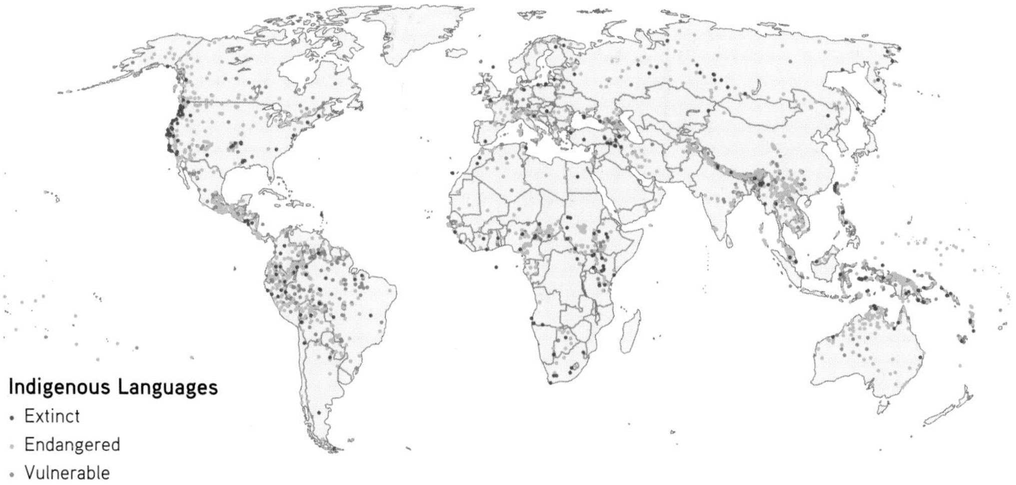

Almost by definition, the world's 5,000 indigenous cultures are struggling. They are the remnants of agricultural and hunter-gatherer societies that existed before modern nation-states. The world has passed them by. Yet, as ethnobiologist Wade Davis has written, "Each language is an old-growth forest of the mind, a watershed of thought, an ecosystem of spiritual possibilities."

GeoBytes

ACROSS THE STRAIT
Walking dry-shod across a land bridge, ancestors of Native Americans crossed into present-day Alaska from Siberia more than 14,000 years ago.

A TROVE OF LANGUAGES
Papua New Guinea is home to more than 800 languages.

CHINA ISOLATED
The rulers of ancient China were so fearful of external influences that they shut off their kingdom for centuries. The quarantine led to technological stagnation.

STONE TOOLS IN AN AGE OF EXPLORATION
In Australia, Africa, South America, and India's Andaman and Nicobar Islands, European explorers found indigenous people with Stone Age technology.

CARDIOVASCULAR DISEASE

Cardiovascular diseases—heart diseases and stroke—seem to be by-products of the more affluent lifestyle that afflicts the developed world, especially in Russia and Eastern Europe. Stress, alcohol abuse, smoking, inactivity, and diets lacking in fruits and vegetables and rich in cholesterol and saturated fats are risk factors that exacerbate the diseases that kill some 13 million people a year, nearly one-fourth of all deaths.

Cardiovascular Deaths (per 100 thousand people)
- More than 500
- 400–500
- 300–399
- 200–299
- Less than 200
- No data available

HIV/AIDS

Acquired immunodeficiency syndrome (AIDS) came to the world's attention in the 1980s. Since then, more than 30 million people have died of the disease, which is carried by the human immunodeficiency virus (HIV). Although HIV/AIDS symptoms can be stabilized by modern drugs, 33 million people remain infected at the end of 2009. Many of these live in countries where poverty, denial, lack of health-delivery systems, and drug production and patent problems limit their access.

Percentage of Adults (ages 15-49) Living with HIV/AIDS
- 20.0%–26.1%
- 10.0%–19.9%
- 5.0%–9.9%
- 1.0%–4.9%
- 0.0%–0.9%
- No data available

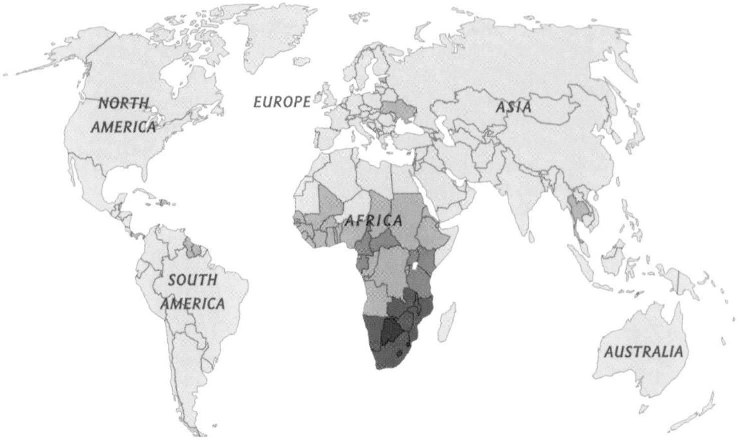

DOCTORS WITHIN BORDERS

The shortage of physicians is critical in sub-Saharan African countries. Thirteen African countries had less than 10 doctors for every 100,000 people in 2009. In contrast, Greece had 540, and Cuba, where health care is centralized, had 640. Now the gap between haves and have-nots is widening as many formerly socialist countries decentralize health care and physicians emigrate from poor societies to wealthier ones.

Physicians (per 100 thousand people)
- More than 400
- 200–400
- 100–199
- 10–99
- Less than 10
- No data available

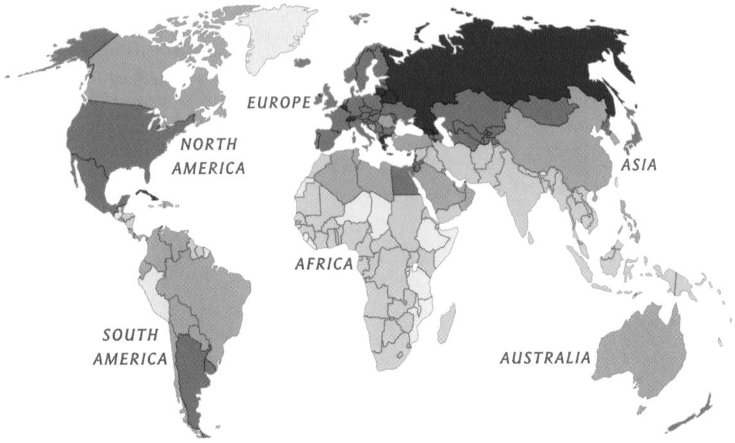

MALARIA RAVAGES TROPICS

Malaria is a mostly tropical, parasitic disease transmitted from human to human by mosquito bites. Worldwide, over 250 million people suffer from illness caused by the malaria parasite. In sub-Saharan Africa exposure to malaria-infected mosquitoes is so intense that nearly one million people die each year. Use of insecticide-treated mosquito nets and new drugs to alleviate the disease will continue to make a difference while scientists work to develop an effective vaccine.

Malaria Endemicity
(range of *Plasmodium falciparum* malaria)
- High
- Low
- No malaria

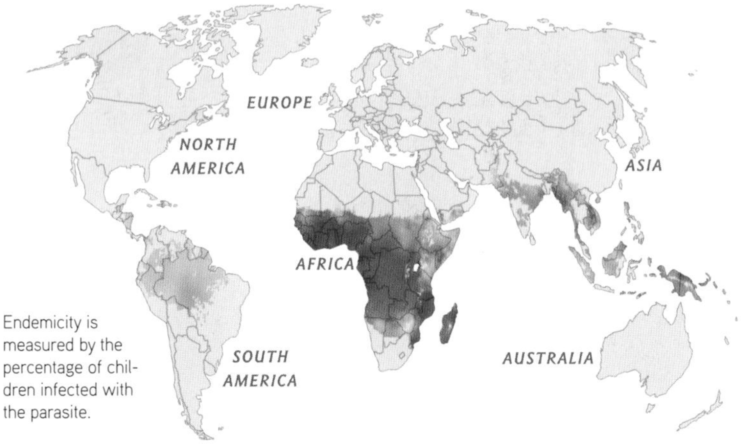

Endemicity is measured by the percentage of children infected with the parasite.

GeoBytes

WHAT IS AN EPIDEMIC?
An epidemic is a sudden outbreak of disease in an area that leads to a high percentage of cases and possibly a large number of deaths.

WHAT IS A PANDEMIC?
A pandemic is an outbreak of disease that spreads over a wide area, possibly even the entire globe.

A WEIGHTY PROBLEM
The percentage of overweight young Americans has more than tripled since 1980. Among Americans aged 6 to 19, 19% (almost 12 million) are considered overweight.

FEAR OF BIRD FLU
A virus strain found in chickens, wild birds, and cats shows that mutation might lead to human-to-human contagion, sparking a pandemic.

KWASHIORKOR
A protein deficiency, this disease kills thousands of children in tropical and subtropical parts of the world.

TRACHOMA
In Africa and parts of Latin America and Asia, this painful and blinding fly-borne disease threatens 70 million, mainly poor women and children living in unsanitary conditions.

HOW DO PEOPLE DIE?

While infectious and parasitic diseases account for about one-quarter of total deaths in developing countries, they result in relatively few deaths in wealthier countries. Over time, as fertility rates fall, social and living conditions improve, the population ages, and further advances are made against infectious diseases in poorer countries, the differences in causes of death between high-income and low-income countries may converge.

Causes of Death
- Infectious & parasitic diseases
- Cardiovascular diseases
- Respiratory infections
- Perinatal conditions
- Unintentional injuries
- Cancers
- Respiratory diseases
- Digestive diseases
- Intentional injuries
- Maternal conditions
- Neuropsychiatric disorders
- Other

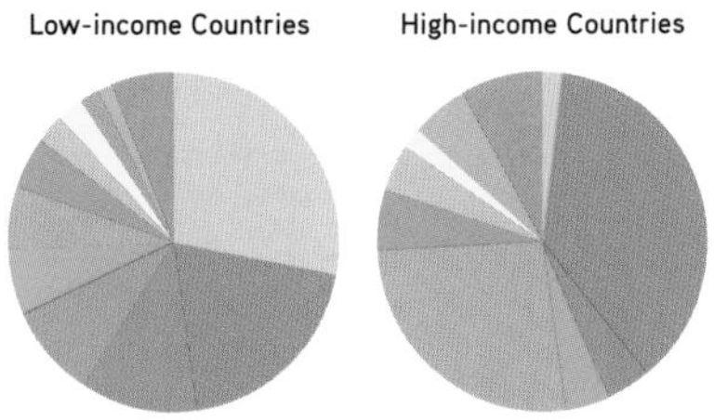

CALORIE CONSUMPTION

How many calories do people need to stay healthy? A minimum of 1,800 per day, according to the Food and Agriculture Organization of the United Nations (FAO). But Eritreans consume a paltry 1,520 a day on average, and one-third of sub-Saharan African children are undernourished. In wealthy countries, such as the United States, high calorie intake means a high rate of obesity—a risk factor for heart disease, diabetes, and cancer. Middle-income countries, such as Mexico and Brazil, are beginning to confront their own epidemics of obesity.

Developed and developing nations show major differences in the rates and causes of death, with AIDS the most significant difference. Cardiovascular disease, the major cause of death in the developed world, is an increasing contributor to mortality in developing nations. Closely tied to health measurements are literacy rates—the percentage of a population who can read—mainly because literacy is an indicator of the reach and effectiveness of a nation's educational system. Educating girls and women improves health indices not only for females but for families. Girls' education makes a difference—in lowered infant mortality and overall mortality rates and in increased rates at which health care is sought.

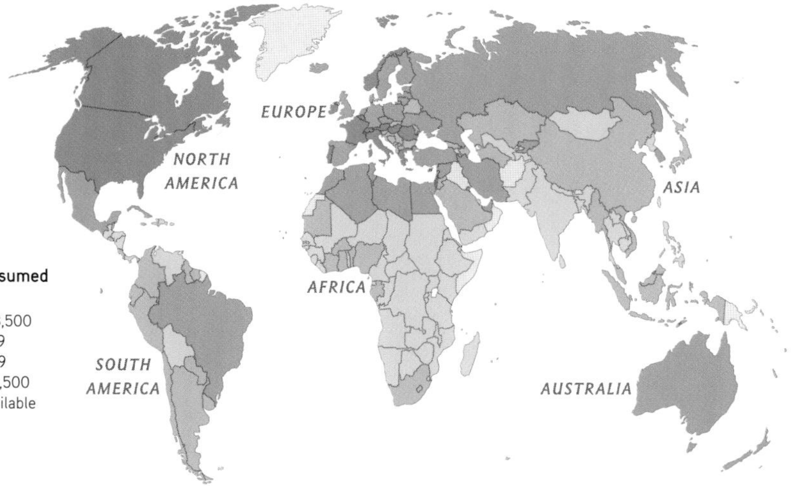

Calories Consumed per Capita
- More than 3,500
- 3,000–3,499
- 2,500–2,999
- Less than 2,500
- No data available

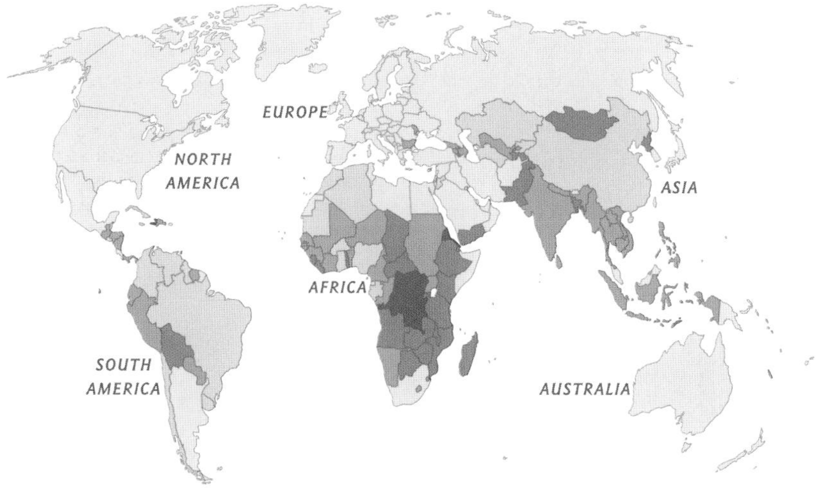

Percentage of Population Undernourished
- 50%–75%
- 25%–49%
- 11%–24%
- 10% or less
- No data available

HUNGER

Although the world produces 20% more food than its population can consume, nearly a billion people suffer from chronic hunger, a condition provoked by drought, war, social conflicts, and inept public policy. Some five million children under age five die each year from lack of food. In sub-Saharan Africa, where desertification has overtaken agricultural lands and there is little irrigation, drought precedes famine.

LITERACY

A nation's success depends on an educated population; thus illiteracy remains strongly tied to poverty. In some regions of Asia, Africa, and the Middle East, women suffer much higher rates of illiteracy than men, a reflection of a systematic social bias against them and a denial or discouragement of women's access to education.

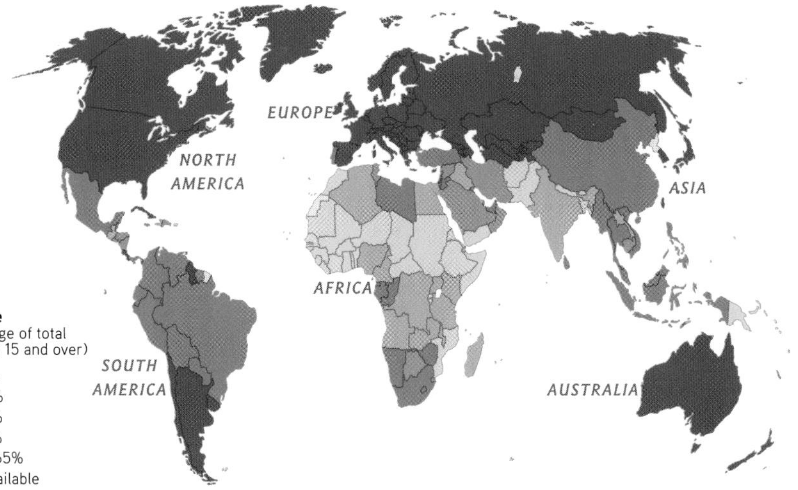

Literacy Rate
(as a percentage of total population age 15 and over)
- 95%–100%
- 85%–94.9%
- 75%–84.9%
- 65%–74.9%
- Less than 65%
- No data available

Male and Female Literacy Rates
(as a percentage of total population age 15 and over)

Male ▮ Female

World average: Male — 87%
World average: Female — 77%

Niger, Afghanistan, Haiti, Iraq, Papua New Guinea, Saudi Arabia, Brazil, Albania, Lesotho, United States, Norway

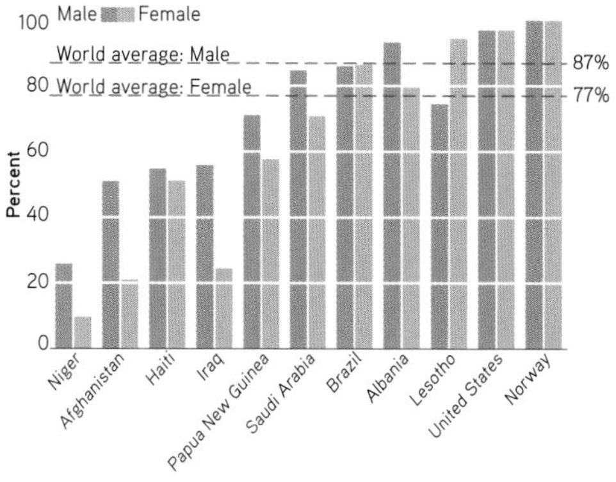

Agriculture

CEREALS

Cereal grains, including barley, maize, millet, rice, rye, sorghum, and wheat, are agricultural staples across the globe. They cover 61% of the world's cultivated land and contribute more calories and protein to the human diet than any other food group.

Percentage of Area Planted in Cereals
- More than 20%
- 2%–20%
- Less than 2%

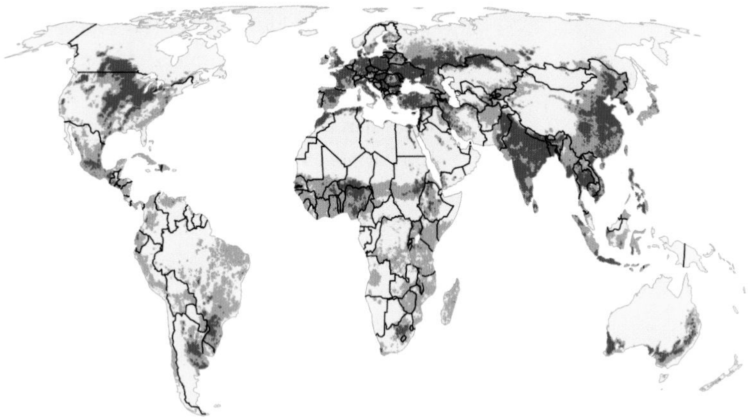

ROOTS AND TUBERS

Although cultivation of tubers such as cassava, potatoes, sweet potatoes, taro, and manioc makes up less than 5% of the world's harvested area, these foods are staples across the globe and are critical to subsistence farming in Africa, Asia, and Latin America.

Percentage of Area Planted in Roots and Tubers
- More than 20%
- 2%–20%
- Less than 2%

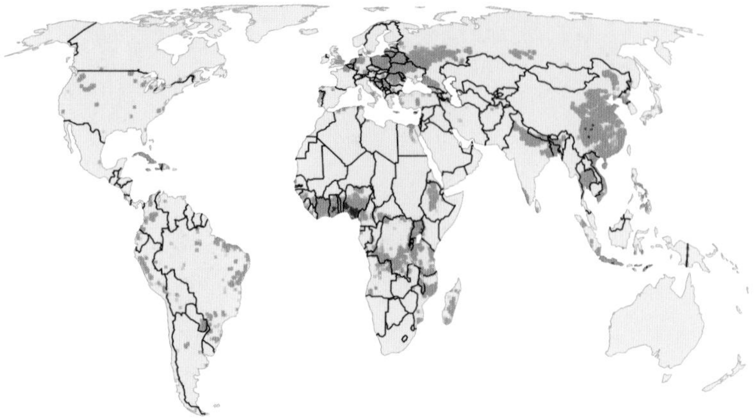

SUGAR-BEARING CROPS

Our taste for sweetness is met by two sugar-bearing crops: sugarcane and sugar beets. Sugarcane is grown in the subtropics, mostly in Brazil and India. Sugar beets thrive in the temperate latitudes of the Northern Hemisphere, primarily in Europe.

Percentage of Area Planted in Sugar-bearing Crops
- More than 20%
- 2%–20%
- Less than 2%

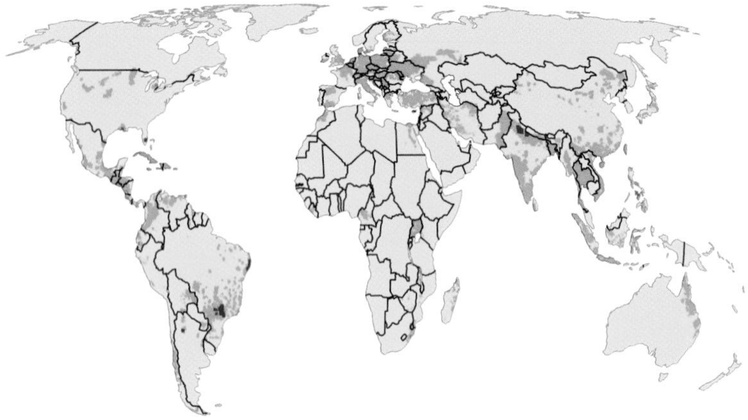

PULSES

Pulses—the edible seeds of legumes such as dry beans, chickpeas, and lentils—have two to three times as much protein as most cereals. They are cultivated broadly, but nearly 90% of the world's crop is consumed in developing countries.

Percentage of Area Planted in Pulses
(edible seeds or beans)
- More than 20%
- 2%–20%
- Less than 2%

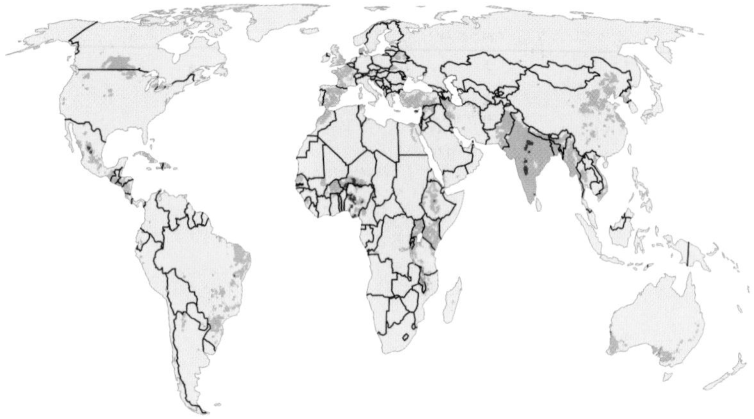

OIL-BEARING CROPS

Major oil-bearing crops—soybeans, groundnuts, rapeseed, sunflower, and oil palm fruit—account for 10% of the total calories available for human consumption. Asia and the Americas are the largest producers of these crops, with soybeans contributing the greatest share.

Percentage of Area Planted in Oil-bearing Crops
- More than 20%
- 2%–20%
- Less than 2%

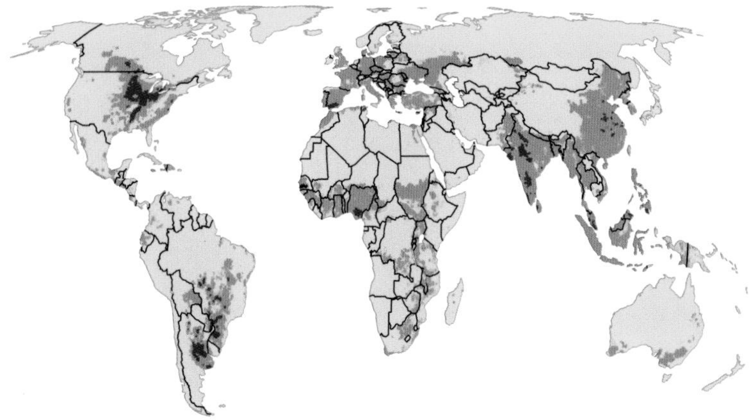

ANIMAL PRODUCTS

Consumption of meat, milk, and eggs, all high-protein foods, is unequal. Wealthier industrialized nations consume 30% more meat than developing nations. With population growth, rising incomes, and urbanization, worldwide demand for animal products is increasing.

Livestock Density
(per sq km)
- More than 100
- 41–100
- 21–40
- 11–20
- 1–10
- Less than 1

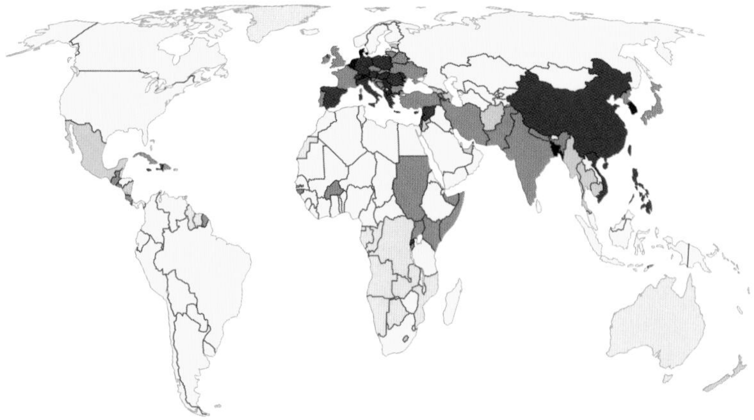

GENETICALLY MODIFIED AGRICULTURE

Genetically modified (GM) or "biotech" crops—mainly soybeans, corn, cotton, and canola—are on the rise, despite continued debate over ecological impacts and human health hazards. GM crops first became an industry in 1996; by 2010, their land area had exceeded one billion hectares (2.5 billion acres), an 87-fold increase.

The U.S., Brazil, and Argentina account for about 78% of total area planted. Some developing nations are beginning to grow GM crops in hopes of increasing output in areas where traditional crops do not meet the needs of the population.

More than 850 million people worldwide do not have access to adequate food. Hunger, found across the globe and even in the richest countries, is chronic in rural areas of the developing world, places not always well suited for agriculture or managed for sustainable yield. Other countries with climates and soils better suited to agriculture, such as the United States, grow and consume far more food than is required to meet the needs of their populations. We are faced with closing this gap between the hungry and the overfed at a time when the world's population, mostly in developing countries, is expected to grow by three billion over the next 50 years. Lack of space for cropland expansion, climate change, and environmental stresses such as deforestation, desertification, and erosion add to the challenge of agricultural management and productivity.

ROMANIA
100,000 ha
(250,000 acres)

U.S.
66.8 million ha
(165.1 million acres)

CHINA
3.5 million ha
(8.6 million acres)

AUSTRALIA
700,000 ha
(1.7 million acres)

Biotech Cropland, 2010
(in million hectares)
- More than 10
- 2.5–10
- 0.5–2.49
- 0.1–0.49
- Less than 0.1
- No data available

SOUTH AFRICA
2.2 million ha
(5.4 million acres)

ARGENTINA
22.9 million ha
(56.6 million acres)

Principal Biotech Crop
- ○ Alfalfa
- ⌒ Canola
- ◇ Cotton
- ▢ Maize
- ▽ Papaya
- ○ Potato
- △ Rice
- ○ Soybean
- ▢ Squash
- ▽ Sugarbeet

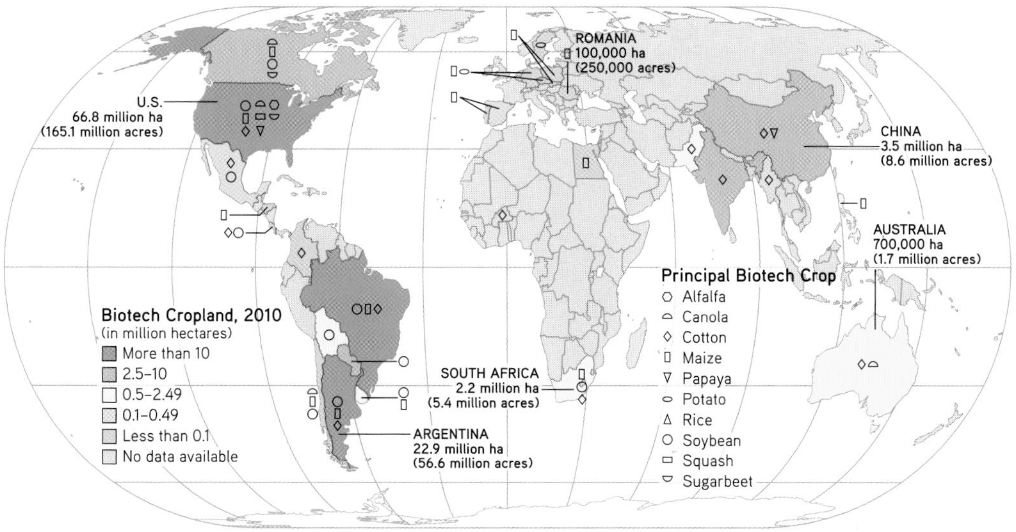

WORLD DIET

The foods people eat vary widely and are chosen on the basis of availability, income, and cultural preference. Cereals, arguably the most significant food source worldwide, make up a large percentage of diets in Africa and Asia. High caloric foods—sugars, meats, and oils—make up a significant portion of diets in Oceania, the Americas, and Europe.

World Diets, 2007
(in kcal/capita/day)

Cereals* - excluding beer
Fruits* - excluding wine
Milk* - excluding butter

Other 338
Milk* 358
Animal fats 120
Cereals* 835
Meat 443
Starchy roots 97
Alcoholic beverages 151
616
Fruits* 118
651
Sweeteners
Vegetable oils

NORTH AMERICA
3,727 kcal/capita/day

293, 311, 174, 352, 190, 108, 1001, 166, 395, 416
EUROPE
3,406 kcal/capita/day

300, 275, 172, 482, 128, 122, 748, 116, 421, 416
AUSTRALIA & OCEANIA
3,180 kcal/capita/day

257, 192, 57, 329, 83, 126, 348, 391, 151, 949
SOUTH AMERICA
2,883 kcal/capita/day

84, 47, 46, 72, 313, 195, 222, 162, 91, 1436
ASIA
2,668 kcal/capita/day

68, 15, 42, 74, 96, 206, 146, 346, 242, 1221
AFRICA
2,456 kcal/capita/day

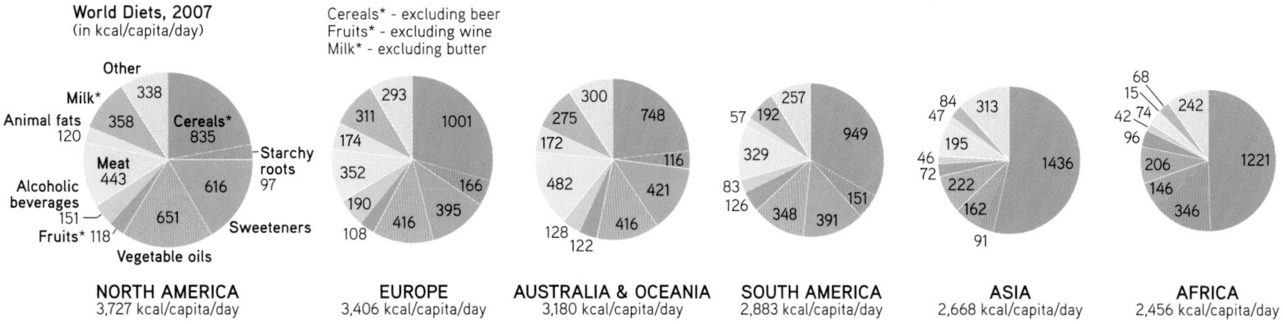

FISHERIES AND AQUACULTURE

Fish is a vital source of protein for much of the world. Yet the world's primary fisheries are under stress from overfishing and environmental degradation. The tonnage of fish caught in the wild has remained relatively stable over the past five years, while tonnage of fish produced by aquaculture has increased markedly. Aquaculture, primarily in freshwater environments, now accounts for more than 30% of total fish production. China leads in aquaculture production, growing more than two-thirds of all farm-raised fish.

Average per Capita Fish Supply, Live Weight Equivalent
(in kilograms per year)

- More than 50
- 25–50
- 15–24
- 5–14
- Less than 5
- No data

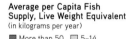

Fish Landings
(in metric tonnes per sq km per year)

- More than 10
- 1–10
- 0.5–0.9

ARCTIC CIRCLE
ARCTIC OCEAN
EUROPE
ASIA
NORTH AMERICA
TROPIC OF CANCER
ATLANTIC OCEAN
AFRICA
PACIFIC OCEAN
EQUATOR
PACIFIC OCEAN
SOUTH AMERICA
INDIAN OCEAN
TROPIC OF CAPRICORN
AUSTRALIA
ANTARCTIC CIRCLE
ANTARCTICA

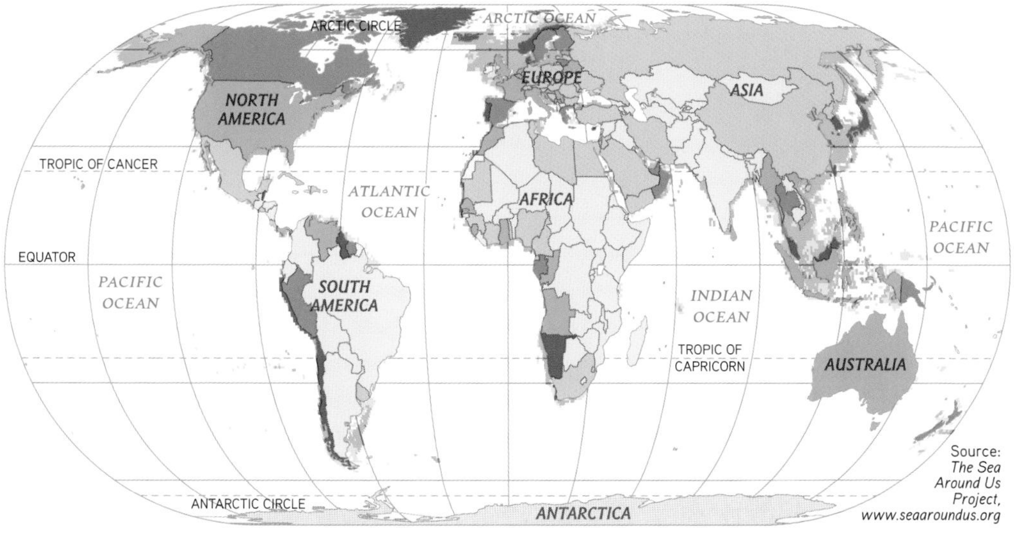

Source:
The Sea Around Us Project,
www.seaaroundus.org

GeoBytes

AGRICULTURAL HEARTLANDS
The world's largest agricultural areas are in China, Australia, the United States, Kazakhstan, the Russian Federation, Brazil, Argentina, India, and Saudi Arabia.

GM CROPS
Genetically modified crops currently account for 10% of the world's cropland, with developing countries leading the GM growth curve.

UNEQUAL CONSUMPTION
On average, people in North America and Europe consume more than 3,000 calories per day, whereas people in some African countries consume barely half that. In countries such as Eritrea, the Democratic Republic of the Congo, and Burundi, up to 70% of the population is undernourished.

CARTOGRAM: GROSS DOMESTIC PRODUCT (GDP) AT PURCHASING POWER PARITY (PPP)

Cartograms are value-by-area maps. As a graphic representation that depicts the size of an object (such as a country) in relation to an attribute (such as gross domestic product at purchasing power parity, or GDP PPP, which compares living standards between countries), cartograms do not delineate geographic space but rather express a thematic relationship. In the cartogram below, each block represents 20 billion U.S. dollars. With some geographical facsimile, countries are associated with neighboring countries and landmasses, but the size of an individual country is related to its GDP PPP, that is, its overall economic buying power. The United States, with the world's largest economy, appears largest, followed by China. Western Europe also stands out, with many countries as large as the entire continent of Africa. Meanwhile Singapore, a tiny island country with a developed economy, stands in contrast to Mongolia, a huge expanse of land that is barely noticeable in terms of its economy. Countries are colored based on income groupings as defined by the World Bank. The World Bank uses these designations for their lending operations and analysis. Other organizations, such as the UN, also employ such groupings as a basis for setting priorities and measures for improved global cooperation and equality.

Gross Domestic Product (GDP) PPP, 2010
■ 1 block = $20 billion U.S.

Income Group, 2010
Gross national income (GNI) per capita in U.S. dollars

High	$12,196 and above
Upper middle	$3,946–$12,195
Lower middle	$996–$3,945
Low	Less than $996
No data available	

Gross Domestic Product (GDP) per Capita, 2010
International ranking
■ Ten highest
■ Ten lowest

U.S. dollars (in thousands)

$145.3

Qatar, Liechtenstein, Luxembourg, Norway, Kuwait, Brunei, United States, Andorra, Switzerland, Zimbabwe, Dem. Rep. Congo, Burundi, Liberia, Somalia, Guinea-Bissau, Niger, Eritrea, Central African Rep., Afghanistan

FASTEST GROWING ECONOMIES

Real Gross Domestic Product (GDP) Growth, 2010

19.4%

Percent

Qatar, Singapore, Turkmenistan, Congo, China, Afghanistan, India, Mozambique, Taiwan, Uzbekistan

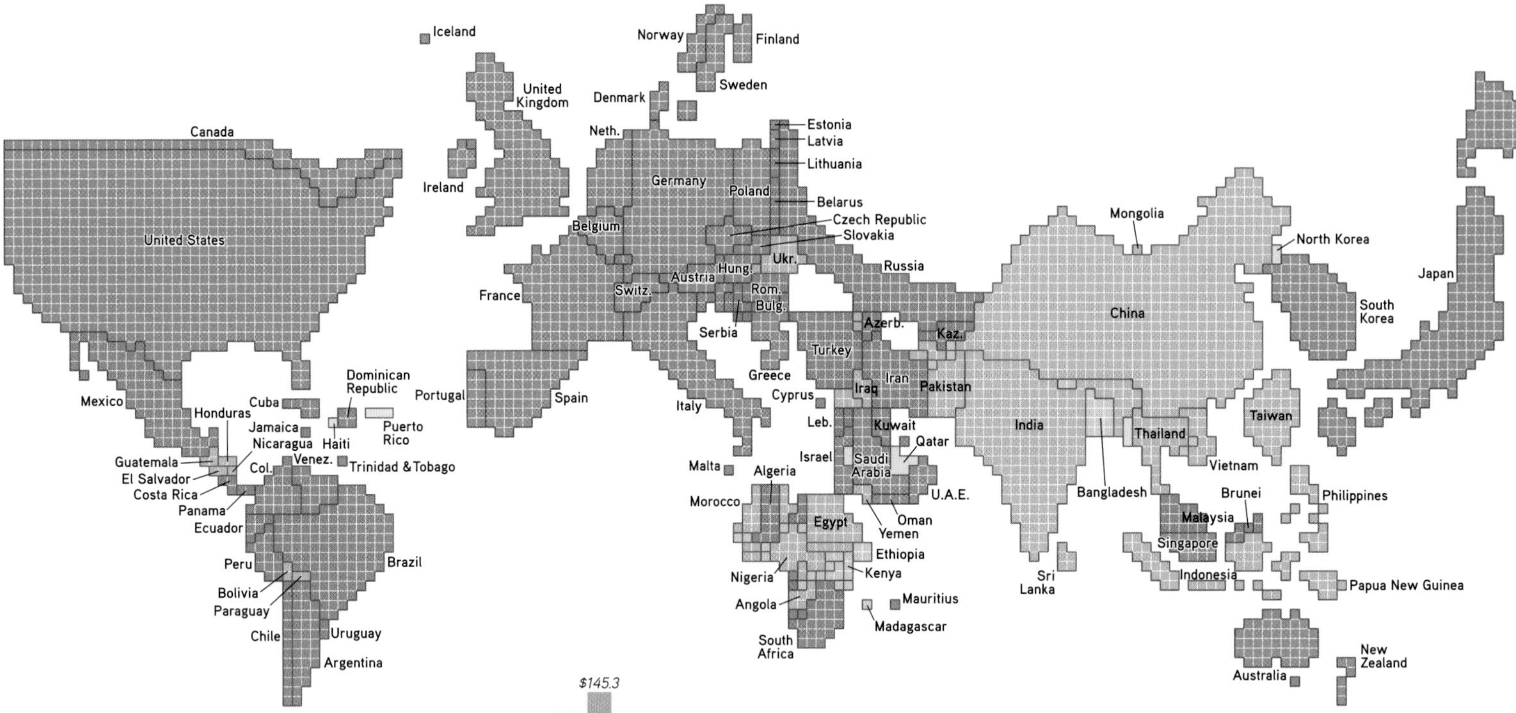

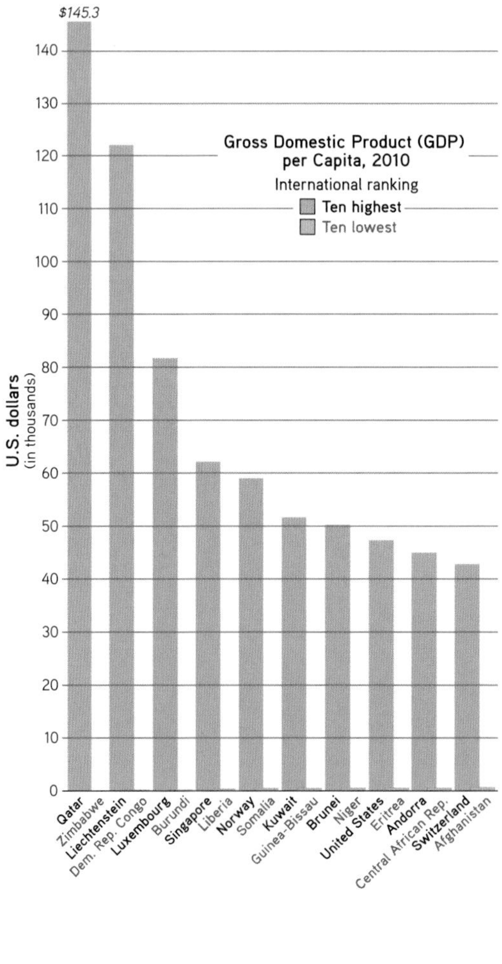

GeoBytes

HUNTING AND GATHERING
This mode of production supported people for more than 95% of the time humans have lived on Earth.

NEOLITHIC REVOLUTION
Around 10,000 B.C., agriculture ushered in settled societies and increasing populations.

FIVE COUNTRIES
The largest deposits of strategic minerals, essential to industry, are concentrated in Canada, the U.S., Russia, South Africa, and Australia.

OIL RESERVES
More than half of all proven oil reserves are in the Middle East region.

OIL CONSUMPTION
The largest consumers of oil are the U.S.—where about 4% of the world's population uses 30% of its energy—Europe, and Japan.

A WIDENING GAP
The gap in income between the world's rich and poor is getting wider, not narrower.

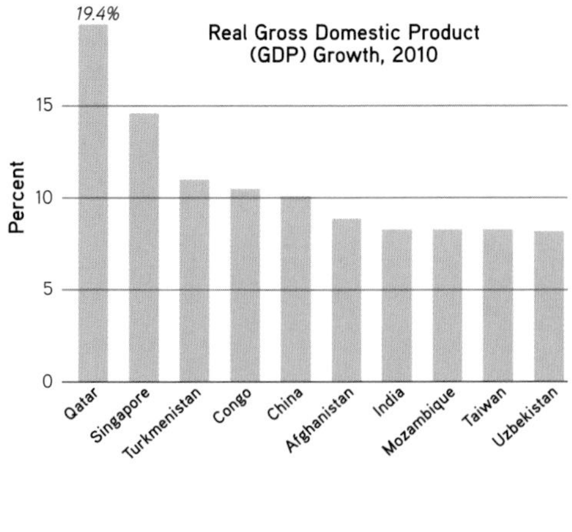

Gross National Income

Broad terms such as First or Third World, or the global North-South divide, conceal as much as they reveal. Yet the division between the haves and the have-nots is real. One measurement is gross national income at purchasing power parity, which measures a currency's buying power based on U.S. dollars. In 2009, per capita values ranged from Luxembourg's high of $59,550 to a low of $290 in Liberia.

Gross National Income (GNI), (PPP) per Capita, 2005–2009
(in U.S. dollars)
- More than $20,000
- $5,000–$20,000
- $2,000–$4,999
- $1,000–$1,999
- Less than $1,000
- No data available

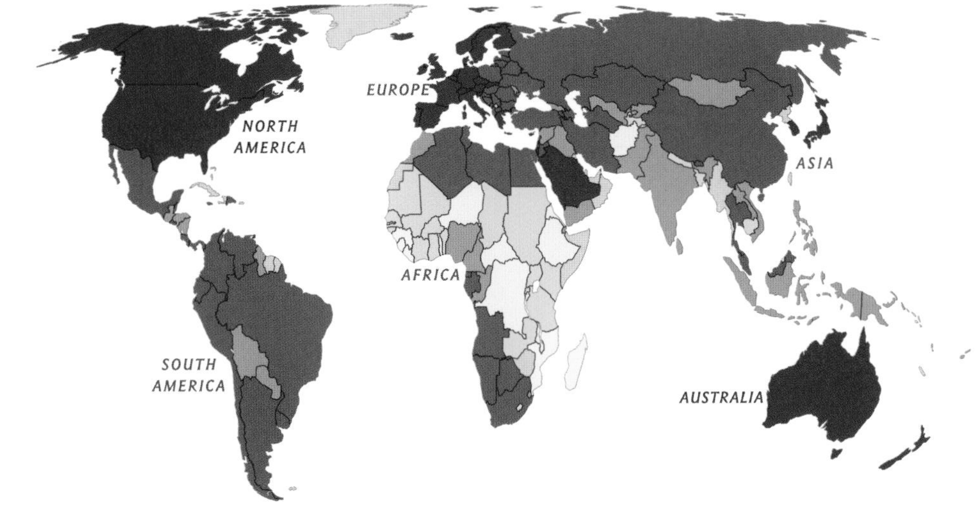

The world's economies are increasingly interrelated. The exchange of farm products, natural resources, manufactured goods, and services benefits trading partners by allowing them to sell what they best produce at home and buy what is economical for them to purchase from overseas. Regional trade is on the rise, as agreements among countries offer each other preferential access to markets, improving the economy of neighboring blocs of countries and the general standard of living. Nevertheless, the stark difference between high- and low-income countries is apparent in a cartogram, which depicts quantitative data not dependent on scale or area. Dominant economies generally occupy the Northern Hemisphere. Oil-rich countries in the Middle East hold their own. The burden of poverty falls mainly on countries in sub-Saharan Africa and in Asia.

Labor Migration

Globalization has made migration from low GDP countries to high GDP countries easier, but integrating this new labor force into the social fabric of destination countries has become a major public policy issue.

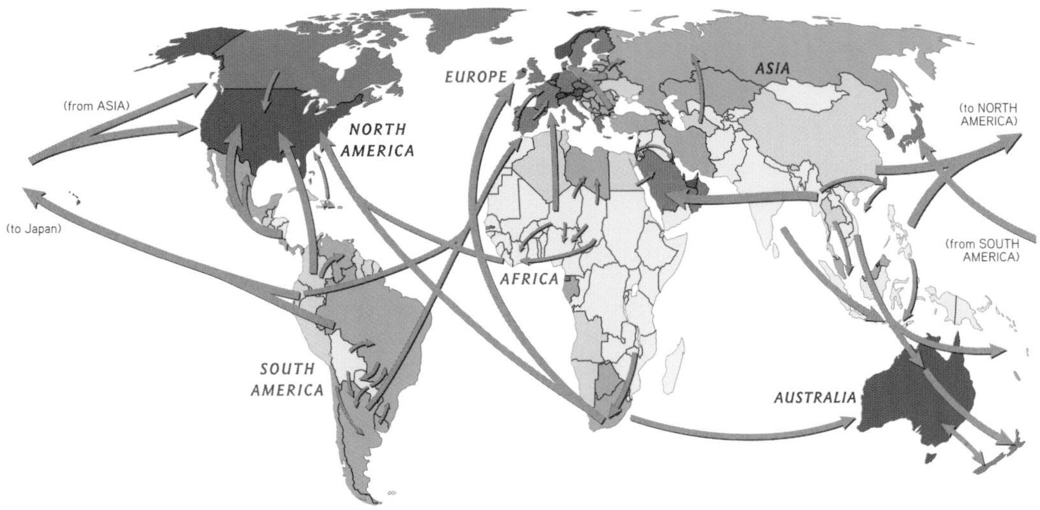

Gross Domestic Product (GDP) per Capita, (PPP)
(in 2010 U.S. dollars)
- More than $40,000
- $20,000–$40,000
- $10,000–$19,999
- $5,000–$9,999
- Less than $5,000
- No data available
- Labor force migration

World Employment

Manufacturing—the production of goods from raw materials—long powered industrialized societies such as the U.S., Europe, and Japan, now more service oriented. Manufacturing is increasingly important in developing economies.

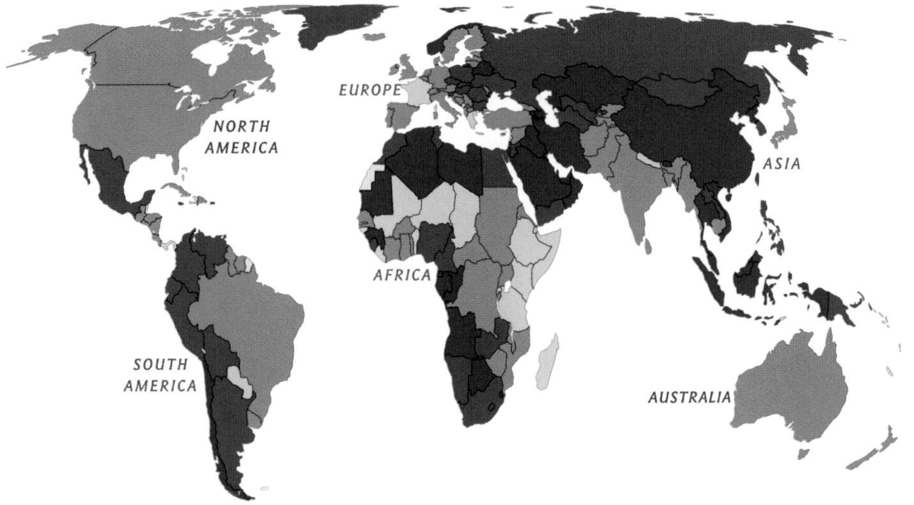

Industry as a Percentage of Gross Domestic Product (GDP), 2011
(includes manufacturing, mining, and construction)
- More than 40%
- 30%–40%
- 20%–29%
- Less than 20%
- No data available

Trade Flow

International trade of goods is a major avenue of globalization. The arrows on the map show the value of trade between major regions of the world. More than half of world trade occurs between high-income areas such as Japan, the United States, and Western Europe. Trade is increasing, however, between these high-income countries and developing countries in Asia, South America, and Africa. Lowered trade barriers offer opportunities for low-income countries, although still limited. Labor-intensive merchandise, such as textiles, can be produced and exported at a low cost from developing nations. Trade in agricultural commodities is a key issue between developing and high-income countries. About one-third of the world's population makes its living from farming. Around 75 countries are dependent on commodities for more than 40% of their export income—in 24 countries the figure is over 80%. Stormy meetings of the World Trade Organization (WTO) focus on making the European Union (EU) and the United States end subsidies to their farmers to increase trade opportunities for developing nations.

Income Group, 2010
Gross national income (GNI) per capita in U.S. dollars

- High — $12,196 and above
- Upper middle — $3,946–$12,195
- Lower middle — $996–$3,945
- Low — Less than $996
- No data available

Interregional Merchandise Trade
(in billions of U.S. dollars)

- $240 and above
- $120–$239
- $60–$119
- $30–$59
- $5–$29

- Stock exchange (World Federation of Exchanges member)

Single-Commodity-Dependent Economies
(commodity comprising more than 40% of total exports)

- Agriculture
- Cotton
- Crude oil and petroleum products
- Fishing
- Gems, metals, and minerals
- Machinery and equipment
- Textiles and apparel

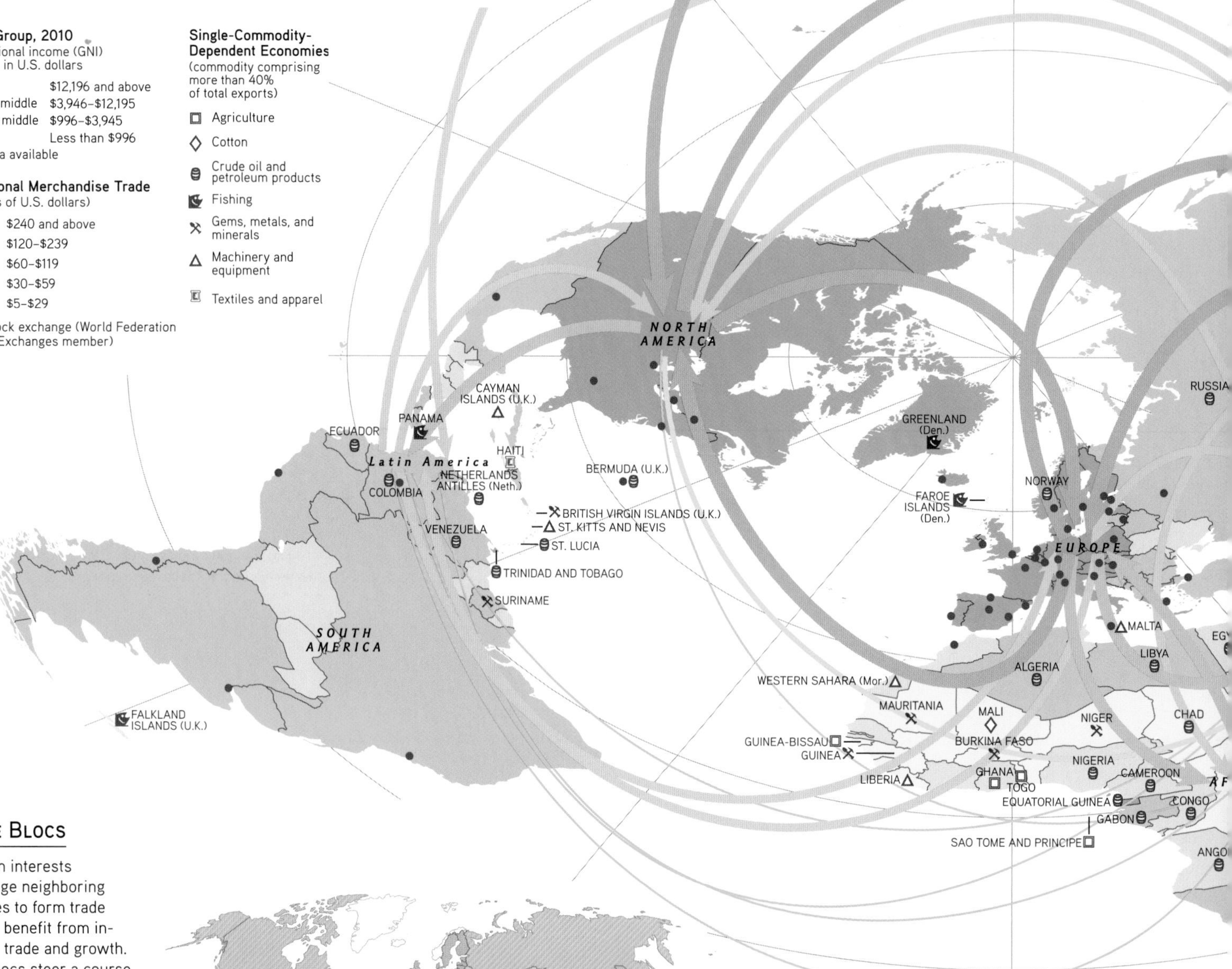

Trade Blocs

Common interests encourage neighboring countries to form trade blocs to benefit from increased trade and growth. Trade blocs steer a course between protectionism and unbridled capitalism. Such agreements fall into two classes: free trade zones, such as NAFTA (North American Free Trade Agreement), which removes internal tariffs but allows participants to set external tariffs; and customs unions, such as the EU (European Union), in which all agree to common outside tariffs.

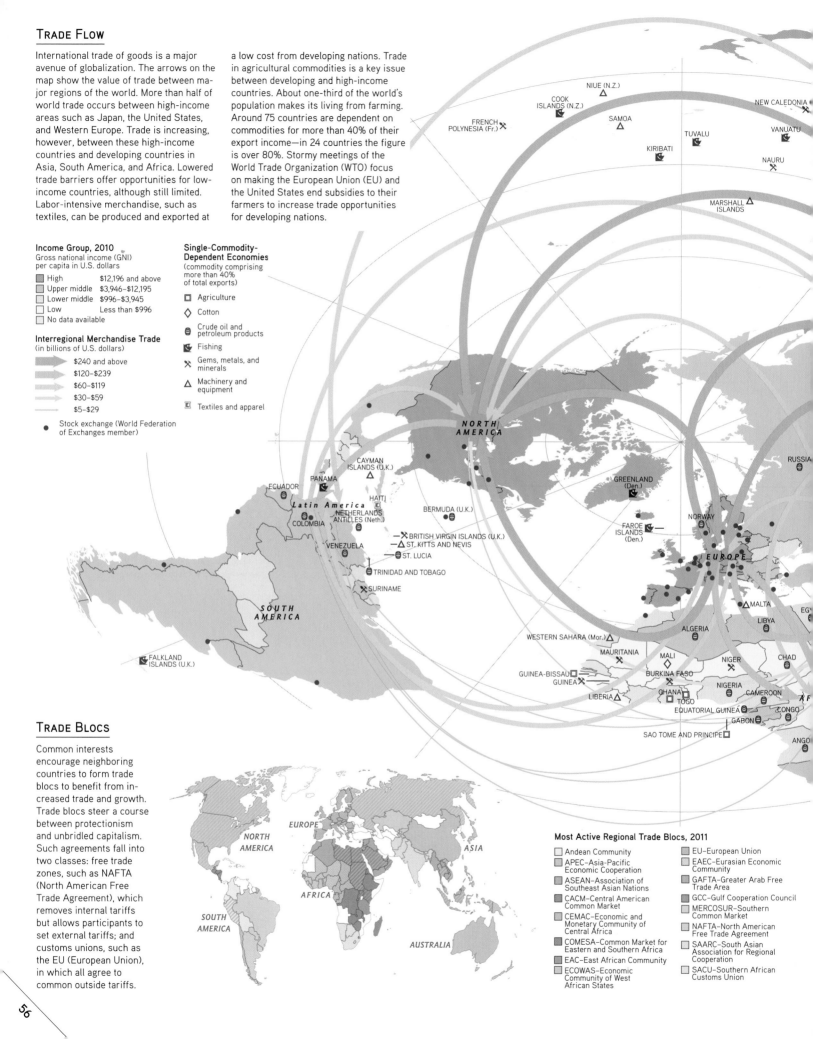

Most Active Regional Trade Blocs, 2011

- Andean Community
- APEC–Asia-Pacific Economic Cooperation
- ASEAN–Association of Southeast Asian Nations
- CACM–Central American Common Market
- CEMAC–Economic and Monetary Community of Central Africa
- COMESA–Common Market for Eastern and Southern Africa
- EAC–East African Community
- ECOWAS–Economic Community of West African States
- EU–European Union
- EAEC–Eurasian Economic Community
- GAFTA–Greater Arab Free Trade Area
- GCC–Gulf Cooperation Council
- MERCOSUR–Southern Common Market
- NAFTA–North American Free Trade Agreement
- SAARC–South Asian Association for Regional Cooperation
- SACU–Southern African Customs Union

GROWTH OF TRADE

Since 1950, manufactured products have grown faster than other exports. Transnational corporations have led the growth and globalization of trade, locating factories and selling products outside their countries of origin. For example, Toyota has 12 plants in Japan, with 51 manufacturing companies in 26 other countries, selling vehicles in more than 170 countries.

Volume of world merchandise exports (logarithmic scale)

Volume indices: 1950 = 100

Manufactured products

Mining products

Agricultural products

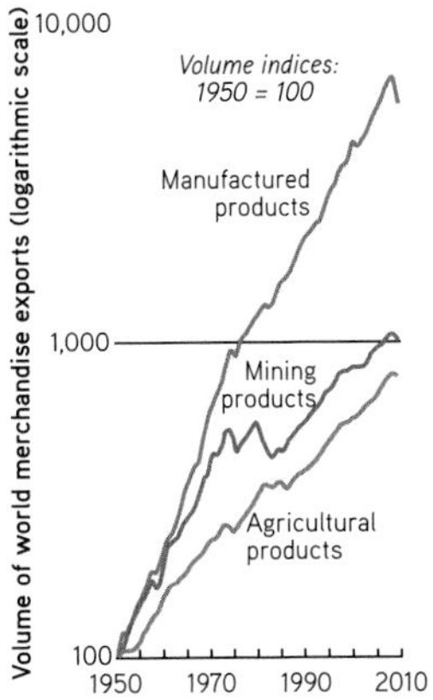

To transnational corporations, globalization means that products can be produced in multiple locations and distributed worldwide. To consumers, globalization means lower prices. To governments, globalization can mean job losses, multinational mergers, and price-fixing cartels. While the benefits of globalization have not been universally shared, it has been a force in bringing economic growth. The World Trade Organization (WTO) works with governments and international organizations to regulate trade and reduce economic inequality among countries. Global integration increases the flow of trade, capital, information, and people across borders by reducing or eliminating trade restrictions and customs barriers. Globalization presents both challenges and opportunities—for new markets, jobs, and export-led growth.

Exports, 2010 estimate (in billions of U.S. dollars)

1,506

China, Germany, United States, Japan, France, South Korea, Italy, Netherlands, Canada, United Kingdom

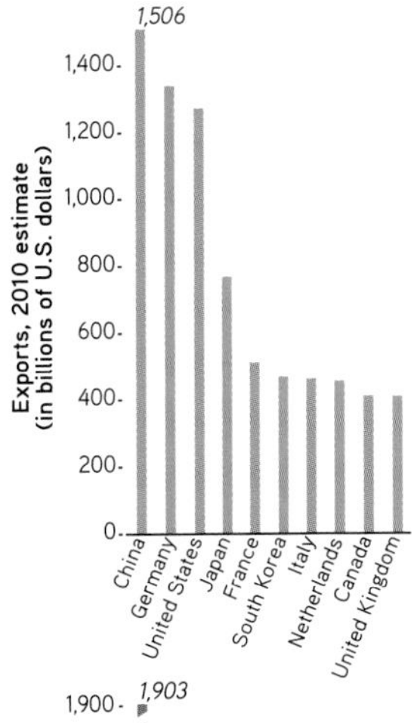

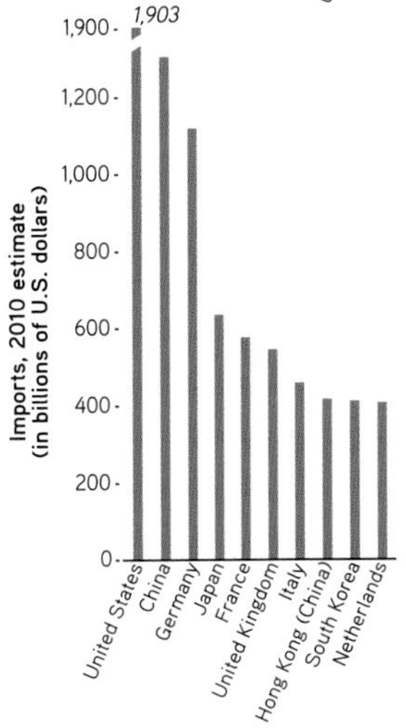

MERCHANDISE IMPORTS AND EXPORTS

China has risen quickly to become the world's largest exporter of merchandise, and its growth rate (at about 10%) exceeds that of any large industrial country. Partly because of government stimulus policies, China rebounded quickly from the world's economic downturn in 2008–2009. The United States is by far the world's largest importer—the U.S. trade deficit (more imports than exports) was $630 billion in 2010. Germany and Japan are also high-ranking importers and exporters, with machinery and transport equipment accounting for a large portion of their trade volumes.

Imports, 2010 estimate (in billions of U.S. dollars)

1,903

United States, China, Germany, Japan, France, United Kingdom, Italy, Hong Kong (China), South Korea, Netherlands

WORLD DEBT

Debt hinders many developing countries. The World Bank classifies countries by debt level. A country with debt at or above 80% of its gross national income (GNI) is classified as severely indebted and in danger of defaulting on loans.

Present Value of External Debt as a Percentage of Gross National Income (GNI), 2006–2010

- More than 80%
- 30%–79%
- 15%–29%
- 5%–14%
- Less than 5%
- No data available
- Countries with no IBRD* or IDA* loans or credits

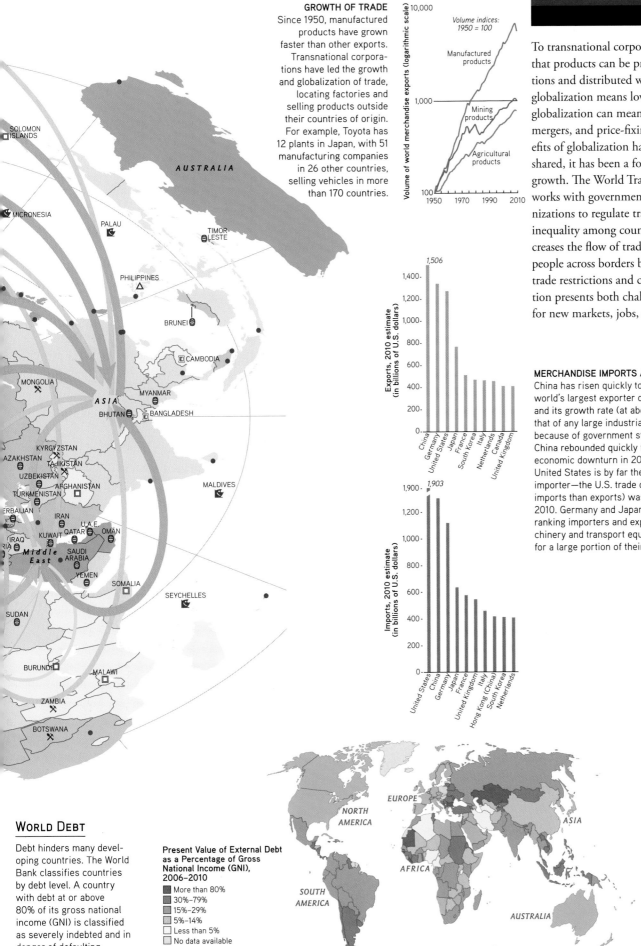

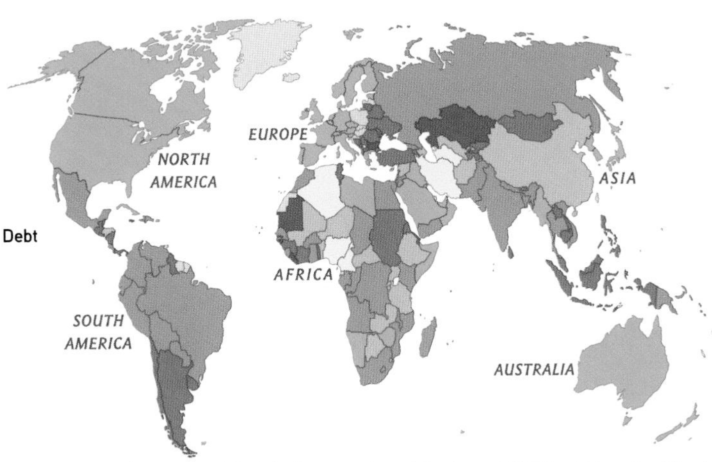

*The World Bank's International Bank for Reconstruction and Development (IBRD) and International Development Association (IDA) provide low-interest loans, interest-free credit, and grants to developing countries.

GeoBytes

LARGEST TRADE BLOC
The European Union (EU) member states account for one-fifth of the global economy, making the EU the largest economic body in the world.

LARGEST ECONOMY
The country with the largest economy is the United States, with an income of more than $14.6 trillion.

LARGEST ASIAN ECONOMY
China has the world's second largest economy at $9.9 trillion—the biggest in Asia.

LARGEST EUROPEAN ECONOMY
Germany maintains the largest economy in Europe, with a national income of more than $3 trillion.

LARGEST SOUTH AMERICAN ECONOMY
The Brazilian economy, at more than $2 trillion, dominates South America.

GeoBytes

SAVING TIME BY CANAL
With the opening of the Suez Canal in 1869, the journey from London to Mumbai (Bombay) shrunk from nearly six months to about two months.

SAVING TIME BY TRAIN
First launched in Japan in 1964, high-speed trains can carry passengers at speeds up to 431 kph (268 mph). Europe, East Asia, and the U.S. have adopted fast trains to provide national, interurban transport.

AIRLINE PASSENGER VOLUME

Air travel, the dominant mode of international passenger transportation, was once limited to the wealthy and those traveling for business. With increased competition, lower fares, and a growing global economy, air travel has boomed over the last 30 years. It is expected to steadily increase over the next five years, particularly in China and other parts of Asia, despite economic instability in the airline industry and concerns over terrorism. Air traffic is concentrated in the Northern Hemisphere between Europe and North America, with increasing volume to East Asia. More than 600 million passengers pass through the doors of the world's ten busiest airports, led by Atlanta, London, Beijing, and Chicago.

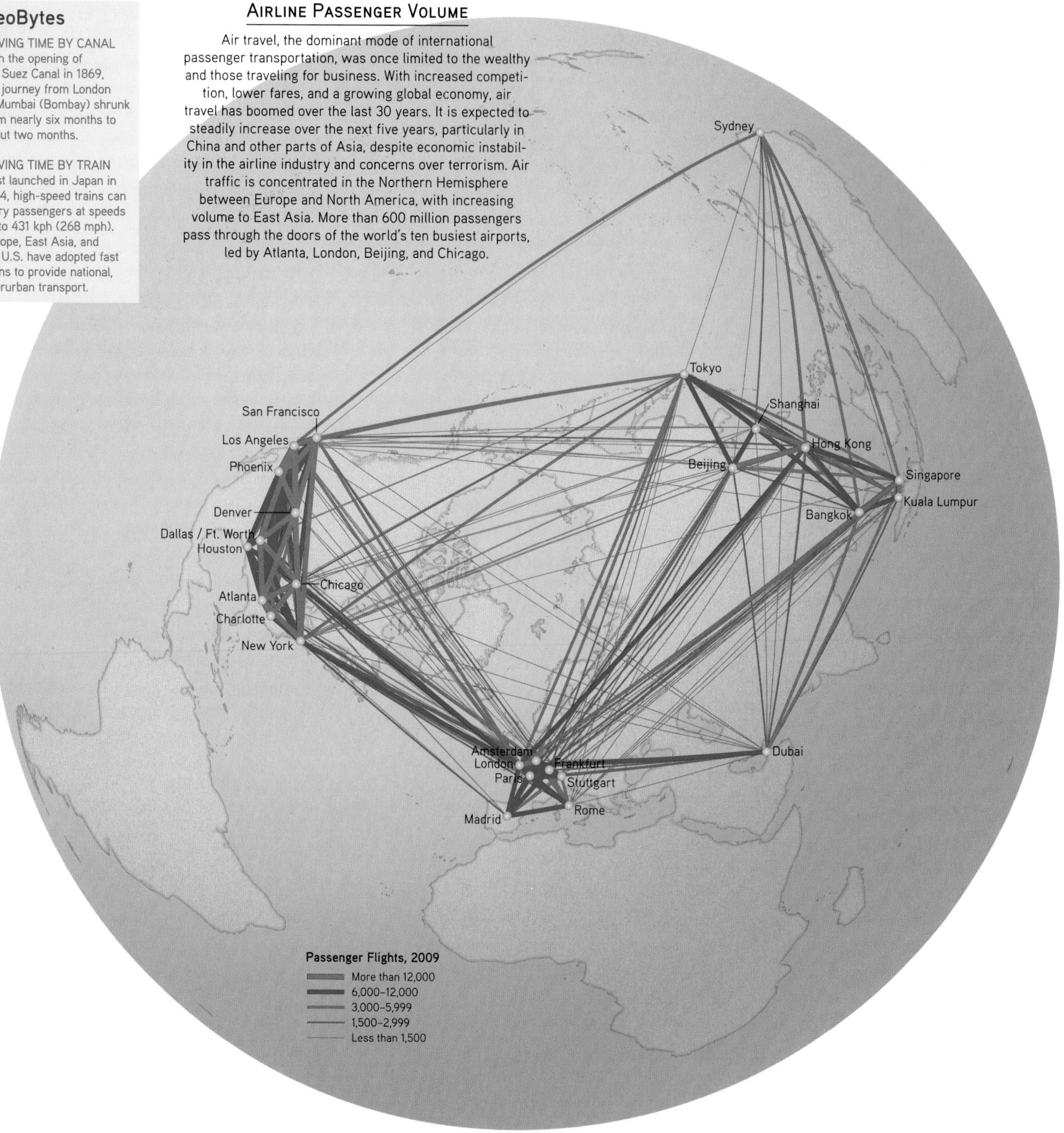

WORLD'S BUSIEST AIRPORTS

Airport	Country	Total annual passengers
1. Atlanta (ATL)	United States	88,032,000
2. London (LHR)	United Kingdom	66,038,000
3. Beijing (PEK)	China	65,372,000
4. Chicago (ORD)	United States	64,158,000
5. Tokyo (HND)	Japan	61,904,000
6. Paris (CDG)	France	57,907,000
7. Los Angeles (LAX)	United States	56,521,000
8. Dallas/Fort Worth (DFW)	United States	56,030,000
9. Frankfurt (FRA)	Germany	50,933,000
10. Denver (DEN)	United States	50,167,000

WORLD'S LARGEST PORTS

Port	Country	Total annual cargo (in tons)
1. Shanghai	China	505,715,000
2. Singapore	Singapore	472,300,000
3. Rotterdam	Netherlands	386,957,000
4. Tianjin	China	381,110,000
5. Ningbo	China	371,540,000
6. Guangzhou	China	364,000,000
7. Qingdao	China	274,304,000
8. Qinhuangdao	China	243,850,000
9. Hong Kong	China	242,967,000
10. Busan	South Korea	226,182,000

Throughout history, the movement of goods and people has linked places and their economies. Early transport was undertaken on foot or by animals such as horses and camels. Long distances were traveled over water by pole and current-propelled boats, then by oar, and later by sail. With the introduction of mechanical means of transport—steamboats, railroad locomotives, and eventually automobiles and airplanes—movement from place to place accelerated rapidly. Speed, efficiency, and safety are some of the important properties of modern transportation systems needed to keep the global economy humming.

MEASURING ROAD NETWORKS

In many countries, such as the United States, the automobile is the most widely used means of transportation for travel and the domestic transport of goods. This is made possible by large networks of roads. Less developed countries often have far fewer kilometers of roads per land area because of the cost of building and maintaining an extensive road network. Some more developed nations such as Russia and Australia have lower densities because of a greater amount of sparsely inhabited land.

Road Network Density
(in km of road per
100 sq km, 2010)

- More than 100
- 50–100
- 25–49
- 10–24
- Less than 10
- No data available

RAIL NETWORKS

Europe leads the world in rail network density overall, with the Czech Republic, Belgium, Luxembourg, and Germany at the top of the list. Japan, India, and China are also known for their railways, and are among the top worldwide in terms of rail passenger transportation. In contrast, the U.S. ranks very low in rail passenger use, but leads the world in freight traffic, just ahead of China and Russia. China claims the longest high-speed rail network, followed by Japan, Spain, and France.

Rail Network Density
(in km of rail per
100 sq km, 2010)

- More than 5
- 2–5
- 1–1.9
- 0.5–0.9
- Less than 0.5
- No data available

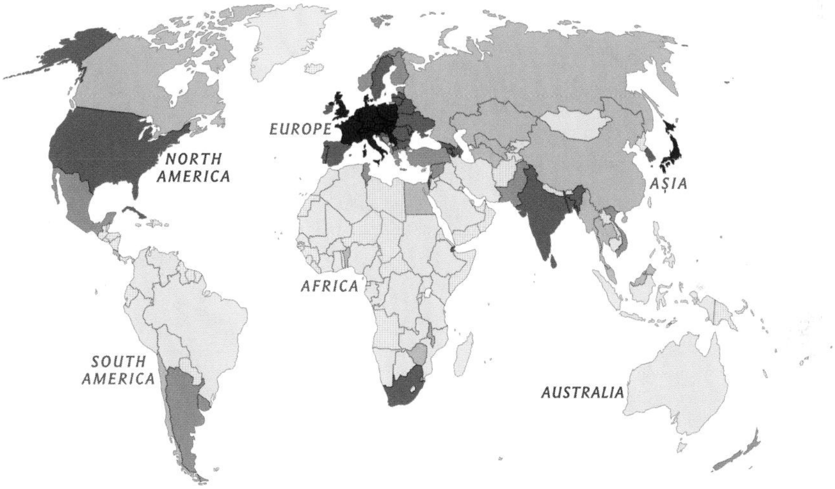

SHIPPING THE WORLD'S GOODS

The world's leading shipping ports are clustered in East Asia. They represent the sending points for the enormous quantities of goods that are produced in the region and then shipped to markets around the world. Shipping continues to be the preferred transportation option for many manufactured goods as it is considerably cheaper than air transport. Key canals such as the Panama and the Suez hold global importance for commerce and trade. Nearly all of the world's freight headed for international destinations is transported via ships in standardized containers. These sealed metal containers have dramatically altered the face of international freight transport. They are designed to be easily transferred from one mode of transport to another—for instance, from a ship to a train, thereby increasing efficiency and reducing cost. As with passenger airline traffic, maritime freight traffic is concentrated. The largest 15 ports, led by Shanghai, Singapore, Rotterdam, Tianjin, and Ningbo, handle more than 50% of global freight traffic.

Top 30 ports, 2009
Total cargo ranked by
volume in tons

- 1–10
- 11–30

8 Qinhuangdao 243,850,000 tons
3 Rotterdam 386,957,000 tons
7 Qingdao 274,304,000 tons
10 Busan 226,182,000 tons
4 Tianjin 381,110,000 tons
1 Shanghai 505,715,000 tons
5 Ningbo 371,540,000 tons
6 Guangzhou 364,000,000 tons
9 Hong Kong 242,967,000 tons
2 Singapore 472,300,000 tons
Suez Canal
Panama Canal

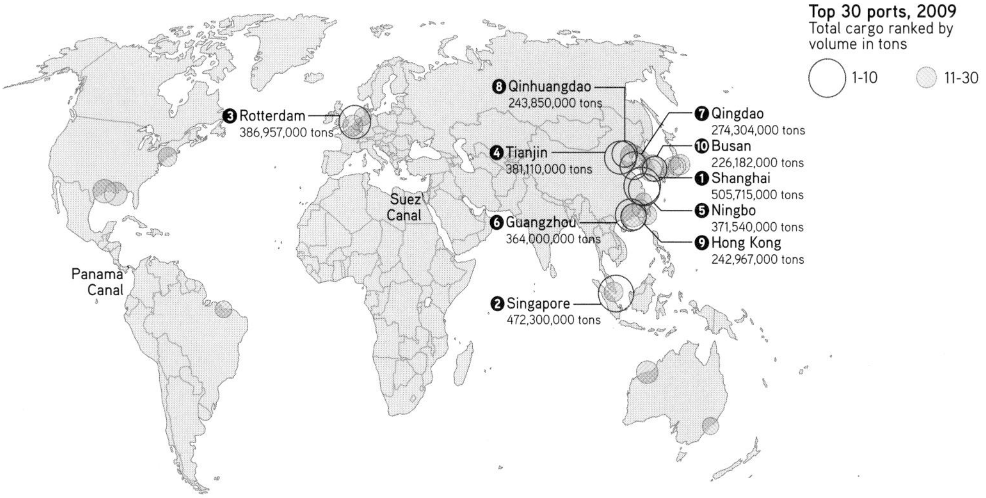

GeoBytes

EXPLOSIVE GROWTH
In 1981, the Internet had barely more than 200 host computers. In 2010, there were more than 760 million, with millions more being added every month.

MOBILE WORLD
More than 90% of the world's population lives within range of a mobile phone network. Mobile subscriptions outnumber fixed telephone lines more than four to one.

TV AND RADIO
In the last 30 years, television viewers in the developing world have multiplied by more than 50. The number of radios per 1,000 habitants has more than doubled.

U.S. OWNS THE SKIES
The United States owns nearly half of the world's satellites, with Russia a distant second. Other satellite holders include Japan and China. Satellites serve a mix of civilian, commercial, and military uses.

MAPPING THE INTERNET
Created by researchers at Lumeta Corporation, this tree-like map shows the paths of most networks on the Internet. It is one of a series of maps in a long-term mapping project documenting how the Internet has grown and changed over time.

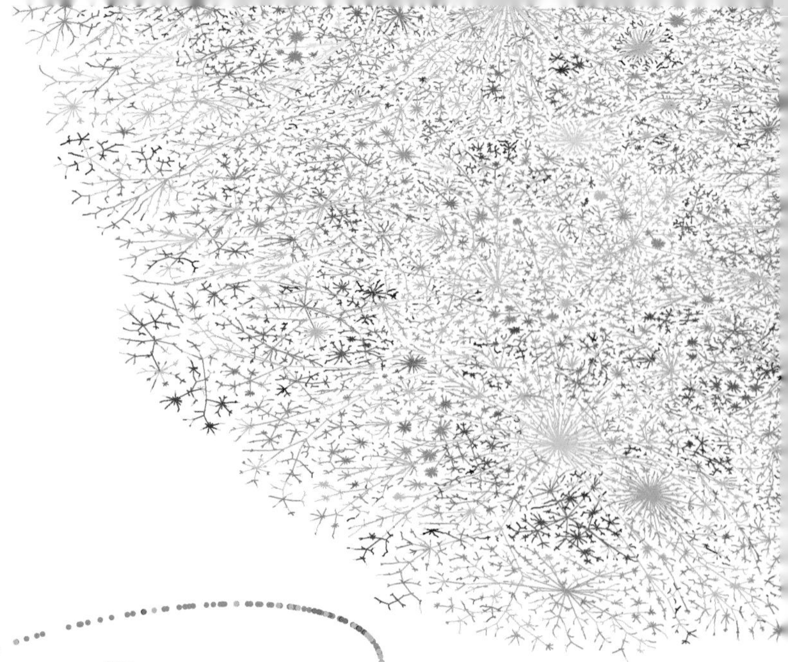

COMMUNICATIONS SATELLITES
Although satellites do not have the voice and data carrying capacity of fiber-optic cables, they remain a vital component of global communication services. They serve large geographic areas, making them well suited to television and radio broadcasting, maritime and aeronautical communications, emergency services, and fleet management. In areas underserved by landlines, including much of Asia and Africa, they provide mobile phone service and Internet connectivity.

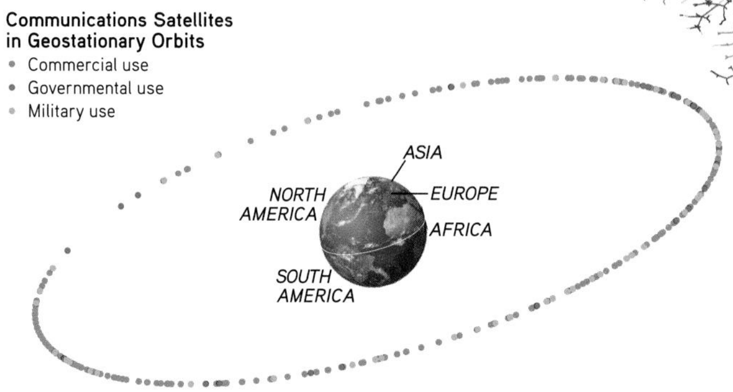

Internet Explosion

With two billion users worldwide, the Internet is a powerful, if unequally distributed, form of global communication. In 2010, China and the U.S. combined to form one-third of all users, with 21% and 12%, respectively. However, only 31% of Chinese citizens were online, while in the U.S. and many other countries the figure was over 75%.

Communications Satellites in Geostationary Orbits
- Commercial use
- Governmental use
- Military use

EUROPE 157.9
ITALY 23.2

NORTH AMERICA 460.6
UNITED STATES 439

ASIA 93.8
JAPAN 54.8

AFRICA 4.6
SOUTH AFRICA 3.8

SOUTH AMERICA 30.6
BRAZIL 19.3

OCEANIA 16.5
AUSTRALIA 13.4

Internet Users, 2009
(per 100 people)
- More than 75
- 50–75
- 25–49
- 10–24
- Less than 10
- No data available

Internet Hosts, 2010
1 block = 1 million hosts

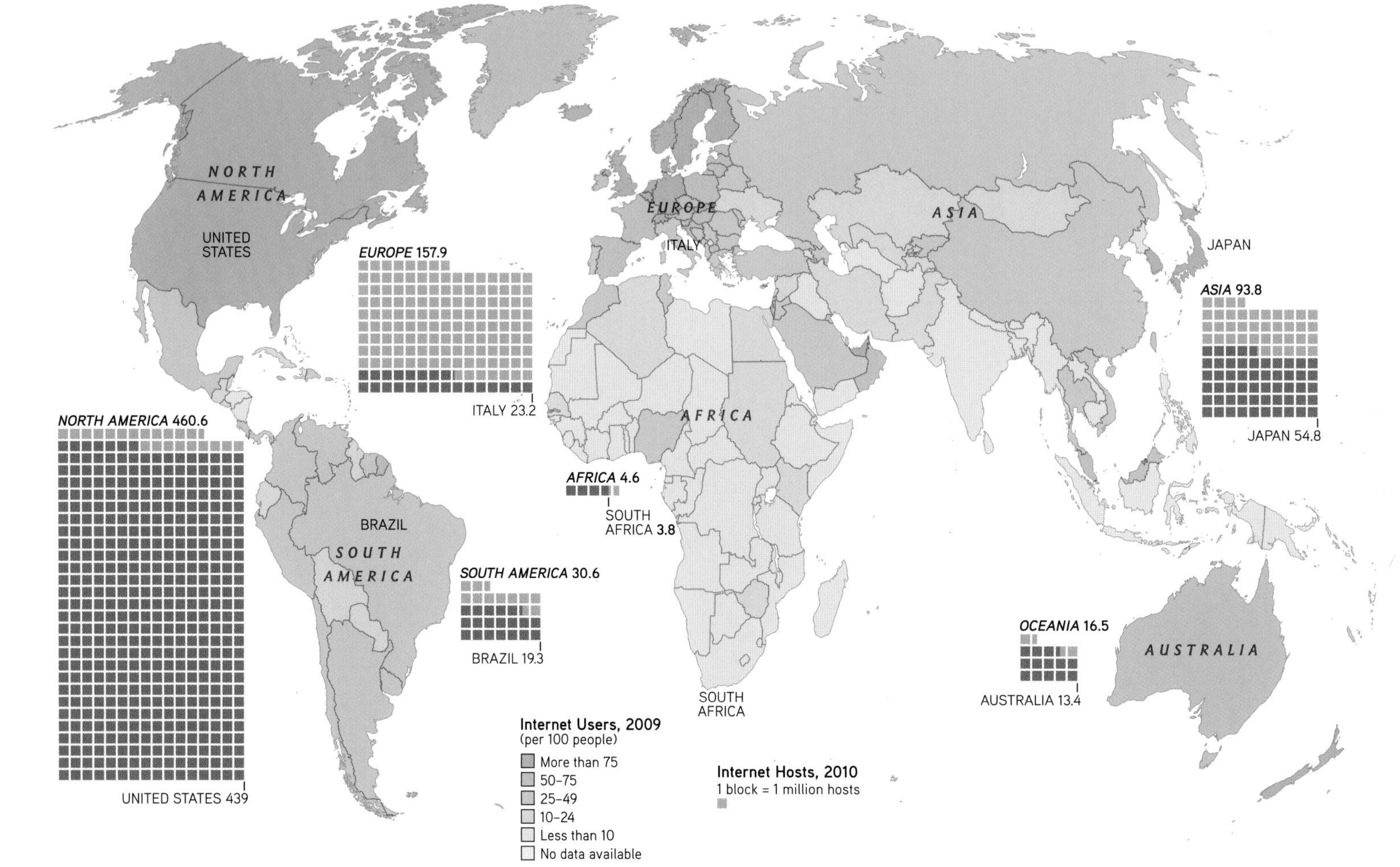

Rise of the Mobile Phone

The number of mobile phone subscriptions surpassed the number of fixed telephone lines by 2002, and the trend continues. Mobile phones are now more numerous in developing countries than are fixed lines in the developed world. In addition to reaching more people in developing countries, where fixed-line infrastructure can be sparse, mobile phones have become almost indispensible to their owners, with advanced devices rivaling personal computers by offering features such as Internet, email, cameras, GPS, text messaging, games, and applications.

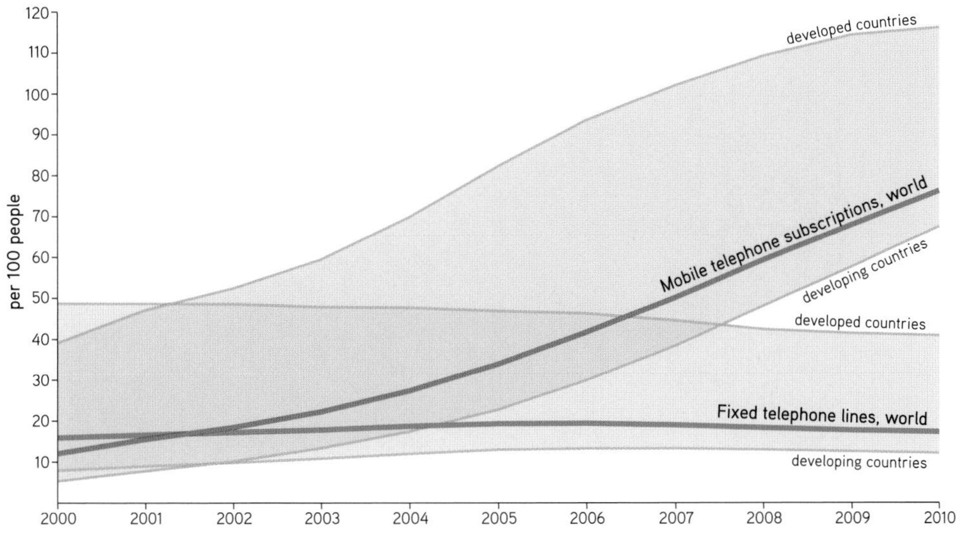

Advances in and widespread use of communication technologies have quickly changed the face of international communication. Enormous amounts of data can be shared nearly instantaneously, and voice communication is now possible across much of the globe. Neither would have been possible a few decades ago when nearly all telecommunication services were carried over copper wire. The Internet has fostered entrepreneurship, helped open new markets, created new industries and jobs, and provided accessibility to and sharing of vast amounts of information. Cellular phones have made voice communication a reality for many who previously had no access to land-line phone service. And without the widespread network of fiber-optic cables, the rapid transmission of volumes of data and crystal-clear voice communication would not be possible. Although these technologies have helped foster communication and economic activity across the globe, they are not truly global. Many areas, both in the developed and developing world, do not have access to these technologies, creating a divide between the digital haves and have-nots.

Connecting the Planet

The world is increasingly connected by underground and undersea fiber-optic cables and cellular networks. Fiber-optic cables allow for lightning-fast transmission of email, data, and voice calls, whereas cellular technology has extended phone service to parts of the world previously lacking any land-line service, including rural regions.

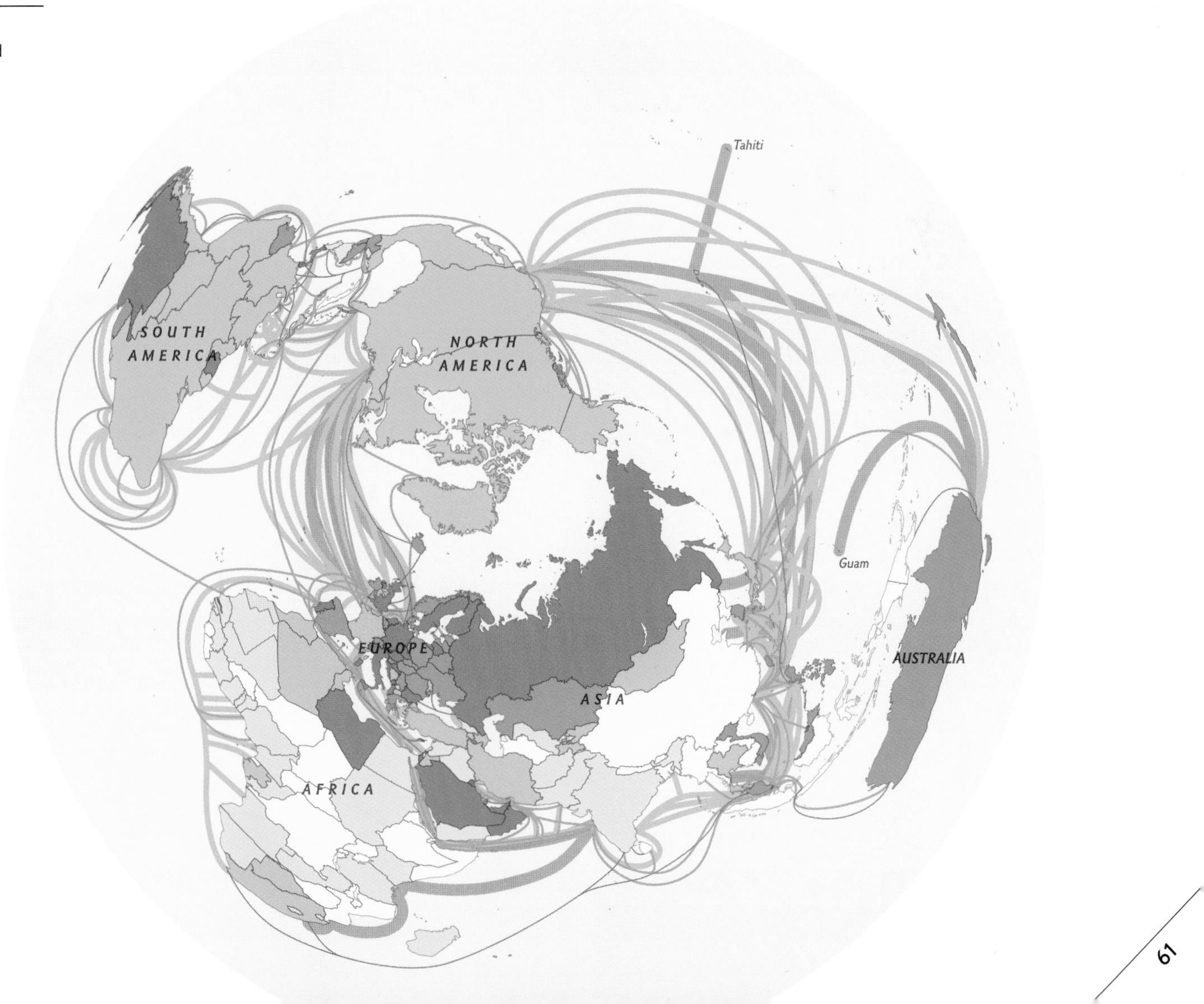

Major Fiber-optic Submarine Cables, 2010
(capacity in gigabits per second)

- More than 500
- 50–500
- 10–49
- Less than 10

Mobile Cellular Subscriptions, 2009
(per 100 people)

- More than 125
- 100–125
- 70–99
- 30–69
- Less than 30
- No data available

Renewable Energy

Renewable sources of energy—geothermal, solar, and wind—make up a small percentage of the world's energy supply. They have a significant impact, however, on local and regional energy supplies, especially for electricity, in places such as the United States, Japan, and Germany. These sources of energy can be regenerated or renewed in a relatively short time, whereas fossil fuels form over geologic time spans.

Annual energy consumption per capita (million Btu)
- More than 300
- 200–299
- 100–199
- 50–99
- 10–49
- Less than 10
- No data available

Major energy deposit
- Coal
- Natural gas
- Oil
- Oil transit chokepoint

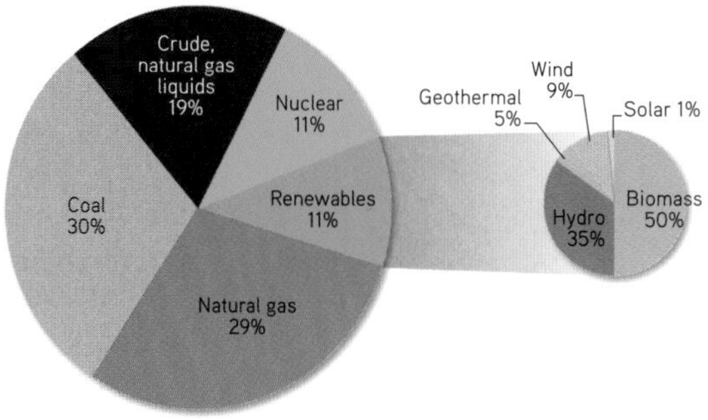

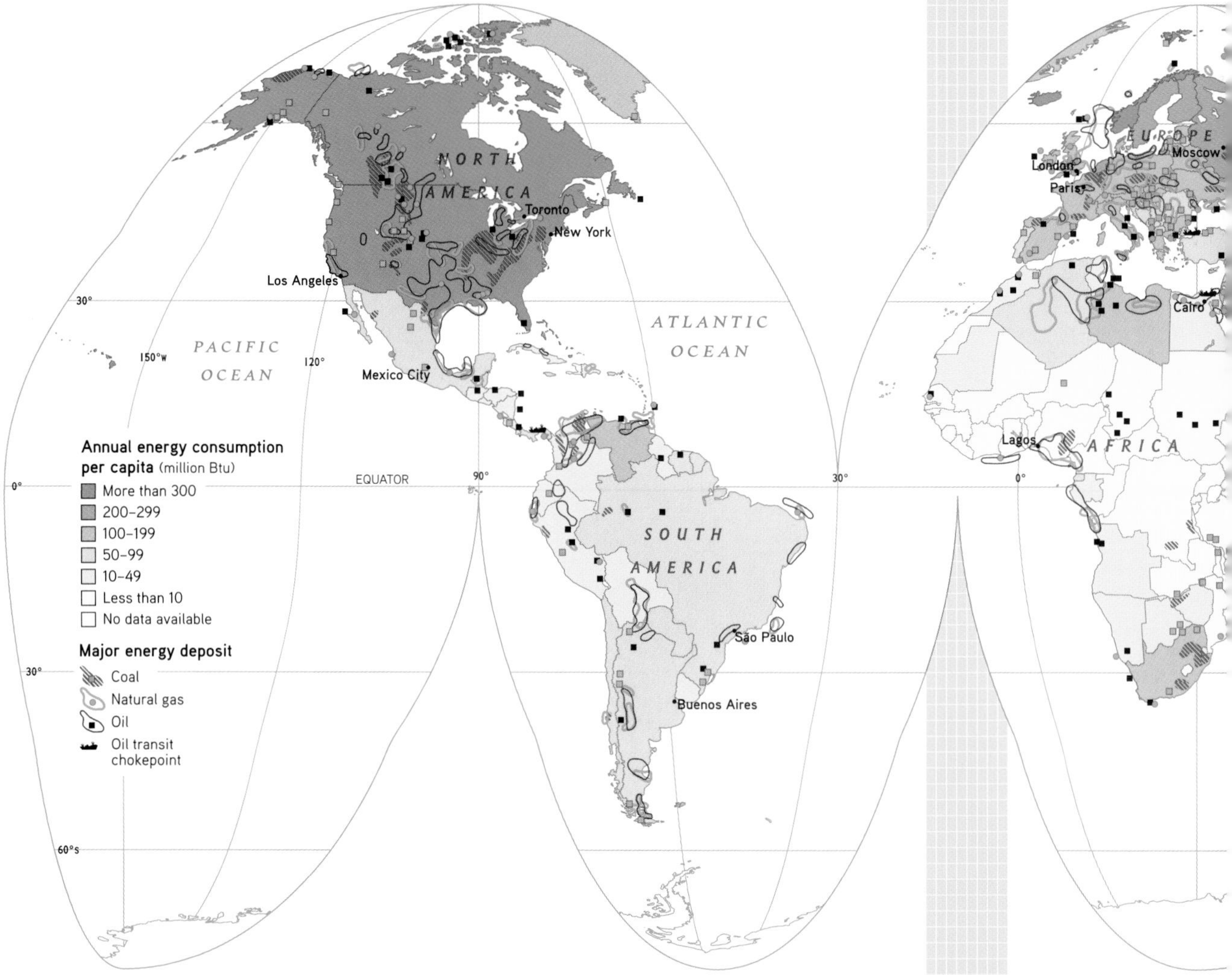

GeoBytes

LACK OF ACCESS
More than one billion people, mostly in the developing world, do not have access to electricity. Increasingly, small-scale wind and solar projects bring power to poor rural areas.

WINDS OF CHANGE
Worldwide, wind supplies less than 1% of electric power, but it is the fastest growing source, especially in Europe. Denmark gets 20% of its electricity from wind.

POWER OF THE SUN
Near Leipzig, Germany, some 550,000 thin-film photovoltaic panels produce up to 40 megawatts of power. It is one of the world's largest solar arrays.

GOING NUCLEAR
France gets 76% of its electricity from nuclear power. Developing nations, such as China and India, are building new reactors to reduce pollution and meet soaring energy demands.

GROWING PAINS
China is fueling its economic growth with huge quantities of coal, and it suffers from energy-related environmental problems. China is the world's largest emitter of greenhouse gases that contribute to global warming.

WORLD OIL SUPPLY
The world's hunger for oil is insatiable, but the supply is finite and unequally distributed, making it one of the world's most valuable commodities. It is the leading source of energy worldwide, and in industrialized countries it accounts for more than one-third of all energy consumed. Pressure on the world's oil supply continues to mount as both industrialized and developing countries grow more dependent on it to meet energy needs.

World Oil

Proven Reserves
1 block = 1 billion barrels

Production
1 block = 2 million barrels per day

Consumption
1 block = 2 million barrels per day

MEXICO | UNITED STATES | CANADA | LATIN AMERICA (excluding MEXICO) | AFRICA | EUROPE | MIDDLE EAST | FORMER SOVIET UNION | ASIA-PACIFIC

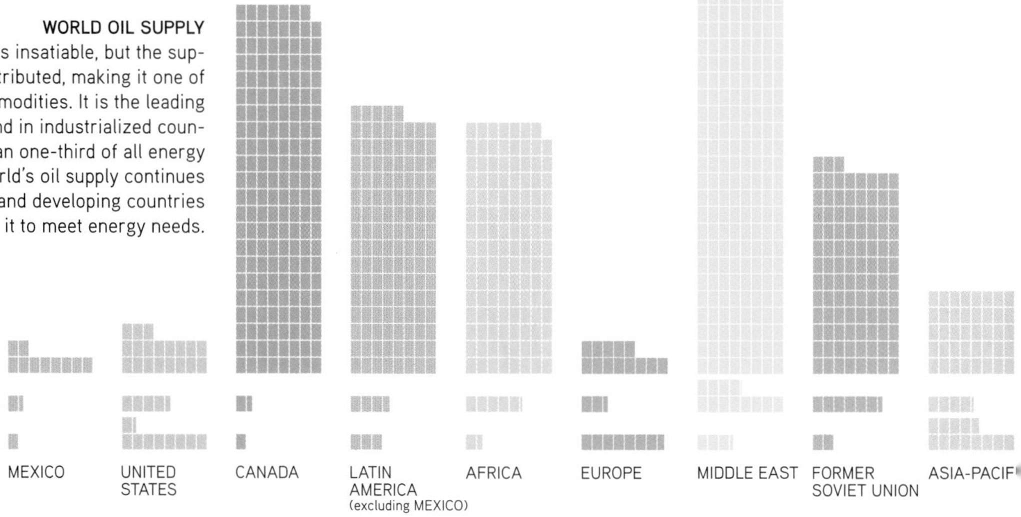

Flow of Oil Worldwide

Major oil reserves are clustered in a handful of countries, more than half of which are in the Middle East, whereas the greatest demand for oil is in the United States, Europe, Japan, and China. Other major oil exporters include Russia, Norway, Nigeria, Canada, Mexico, and Venezuela.

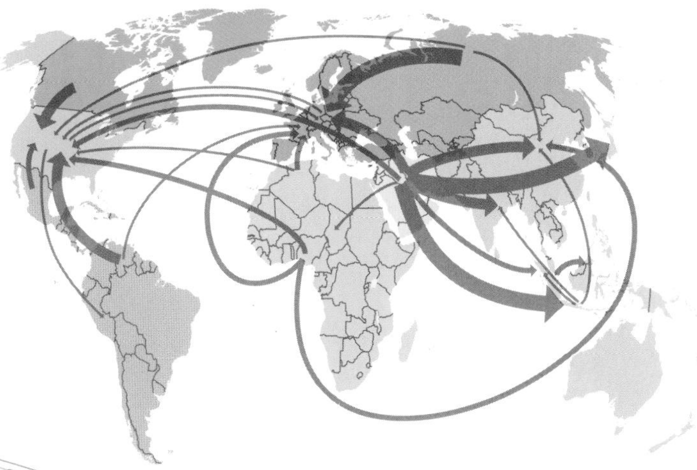

Oil Imports, 2009 (in millions of barrels)

- More than 1,000
- 750–1,000
- 300–749
- Less than 300

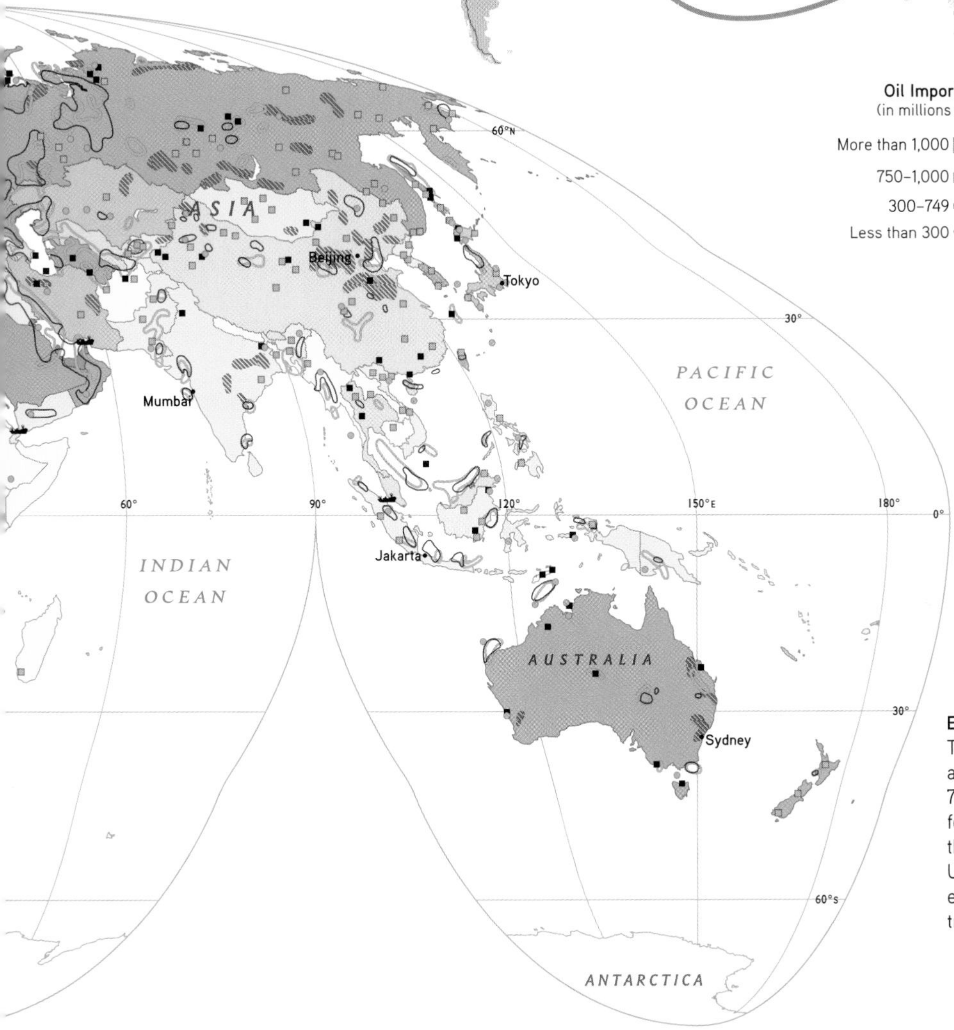

Energy enables us to cook our food, heat our homes, move about our planet, and run industry. Every day the world uses some 54 billion kilowatt-hours of energy—equivalent to each person burning five and a half 60-watt lightbulbs nonstop. Over the next century demand may increase threefold. Consumption is not uniform across the globe. People in industrialized countries consume far greater amounts of energy than those in developing countries. The world's energy supply is still fossil-fuel based, despite advances in alternative energy sources. To meet demand, many countries must import fuels, making the trade of energy a critical, often volatile global political issue. Instability where most oil is found—the Persian Gulf, Nigeria, Venezuela—make this global economic powerline fragile. Insatiable demand where most energy is consumed—the United States, Japan, China, India, Germany—makes national economies increasingly dependent. Furthermore, extraction and use of fossil fuels have serious environmental effects, such as air pollution and global warming. The challenge for the future? Reducing reliance on fossil fuels, developing alternative energies to meet demand, and mediating the trade-offs between the environment and energy.

ENERGY INEQUALITY

The use and availability of primary energy resources are unequally distributed across the globe. More than 78% of energy consumed globally is from nonrenewable fossil fuels—coal, oil, and natural gas. Consumption of these fuels is greatest in industrialized nations, with the U.S. using up nearly one-quarter. Developing countries, especially those in sub-Saharan Africa, rely on more traditional sources of energy, such as firewood and dung.

Alternative Energies

Hydropower provides 16% of the world's electricity, but it is limited to countries with adequate water resources, and it poses threats to local watersheds. Nuclear energy makes up 13% of the world's electricity, but few countries have adopted it because of potential environmental risks and waste disposal issues. Solar and wind energy are inexhaustible and are the focus of new energy technologies and research. Geothermal energy is efficient but limited to countries with ready sources of hot groundwater, such as Iceland.

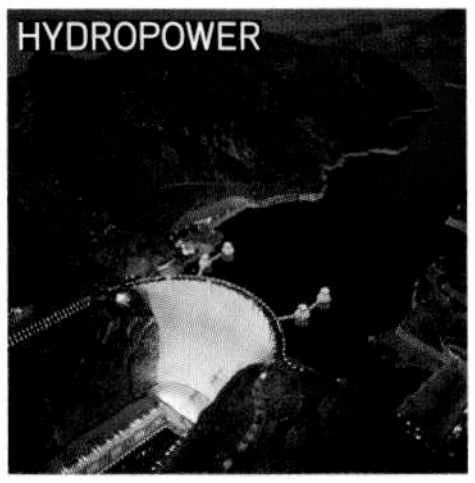

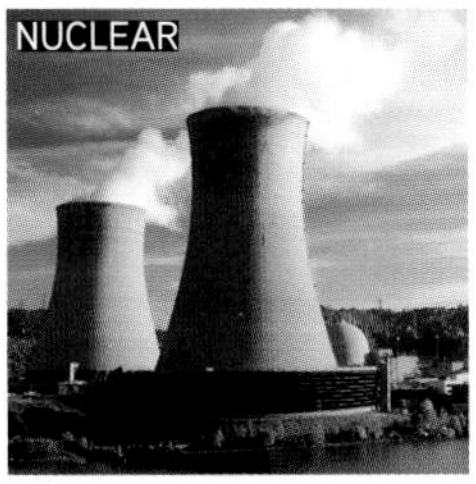

NORTH AMERICA

EUROPE

ASIA

AFRICA

SOUTH AMERICA

AUSTRALIA

3,758

2,540

Uprooted People, 2010

— Country of origin

— Residency

Regime Type, 2011

Autocratic
Governed by an authoritarian leader

Anocratic
Government in transition between autocratic and democratic rule

Democratic
Governed by the people through representatives

Active Military, 2010
(personnel in thousands)

- More than 1,000
- 250–1,000
- 50–249
- 10–49
- Less than 10
- No active military

Number of people (in thousands)

1,000

500

100

0

NORTH AMERICA: Canada, Costa Rica, Cuba, El Salvador, Guatemala, Haiti, Mexico, Panama, United States

S. AMERICA: Colombia, Ecuador, Peru, Venezuela

EUROPE: Albania, Austria, Belarus, Belgium, Bosnia and Herzegovina, Bulgaria, Croatia, Cyprus, Denmark, Finland, France, Germany, Greece, Hungary, Ireland, Italy, Macedonia, Malta, Moldova, Montenegro, Netherlands, Norway, Poland, Russia, Serbia, Spain, Sweden, Switzerland, Ukraine, United Kingdom

AFRICA: Algeria, Angola, Benin, Burundi, Cameroon, Central African Republic, Chad, Congo, Côte d'Ivoire, Democratic Republic of the Congo, Djibouti, Egypt, Eritrea, Ethiopia, Gabon, Gambia, Ghana, Guinea, Guinea-Bissau, Kenya, Liberia, Libya, Malawi, Mali

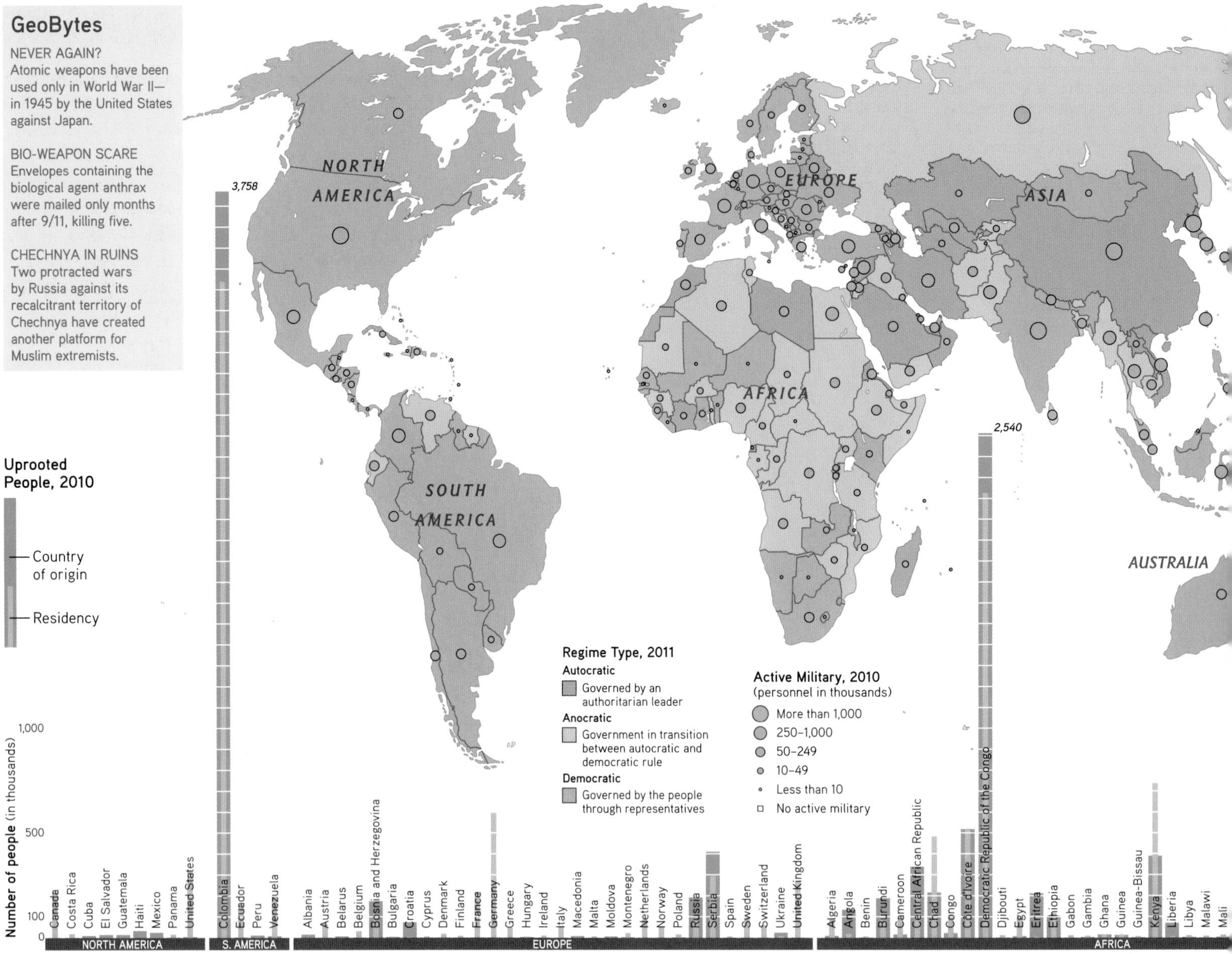

DEFENSE SPENDING

Military spending soaks up a large percentage of GDP (Gross Domestic Product) in many countries that can ill afford it. The states of the Middle East, some with weak economies and beset by popular insurrections, continue to maintain large defense forces. In Sudan, an arms race continues between north and south. A resurgent China flexes new military muscle. The U.S. spends nearly as much on defense as the rest of the world combined. More than 70 countries, headed by both democracies and totalitarian governments, require military service of their young adults.

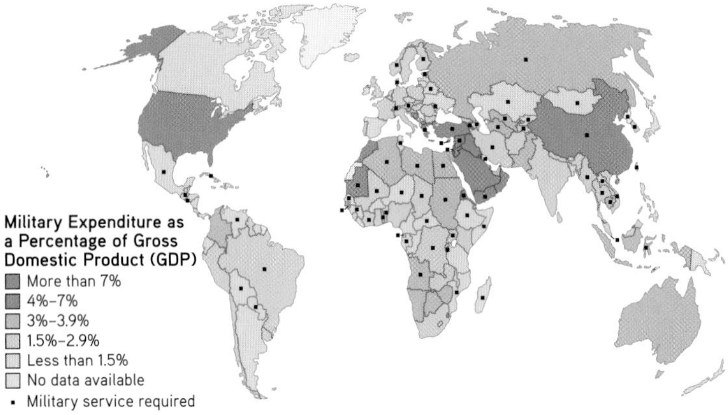

BIOLOGICAL WEAPONS

A very small volume of a toxic biological agent, if properly dispersed, could cause massive casualties in a densely populated area. Moreover, its manufacture could be virtually undetectable, as only a small facility is needed, and much of the material and equipment has legitimate medical and agricultural use. Although only about 8 countries have offensive biological weapons programs, that number is expected to grow with the increased international flow of technology, goods, and information. With this threat, new field tools have been developed to analyze suspect materials.

Military Expenditure as a Percentage of Gross Domestic Product (GDP)
- More than 7%
- 4%–7%
- 3%–3.9%
- 1.5%–2.9%
- Less than 1.5%
- No data available
- • Military service required

Biological Weapons Possession
- Possible
- Possible offensive research program

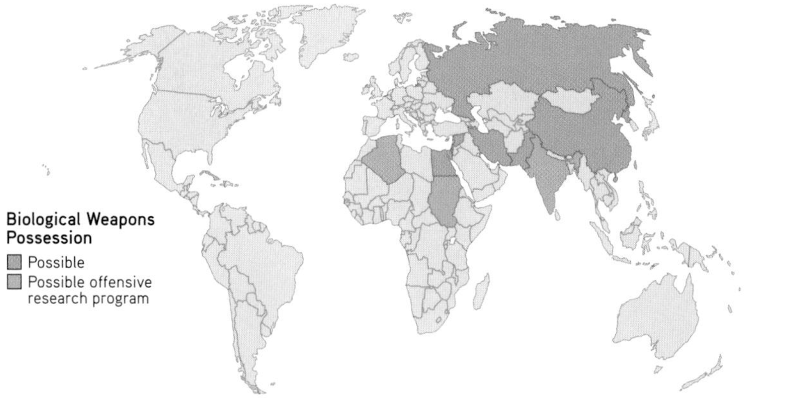

In the late 20th century, the threat of war between sovereign nations had largely given way to war within states—conflicts between rivals to power or involving aggrieved religious, tribal, or ethnic groups. Even more sinister threats involve extremist groups and "terrorists" who seek to disrupt or displace the established order. Not since Iraq rolled into Kuwait in 1991 has one nation tried to forcibly incorporate another, although the Western nations have deployed aerial power to neutralize extremist forces and protect populations in Bosnia, Kosovo, and Libya and, in response to the September 11, 2001, attacks by al Qaeda terrorists, have deployed ground forces in Afghanistan and Iraq. Civil conflicts create humanitarian crises and drive millions to seek shelter abroad. Tensions in the Middle East threaten to disrupt vital oil supplies while nuclear proliferation and accidents pose serious threats to global security.

Measuring Democracy

Democracy surged in the 1990s as Eastern and Central European states emerged from the Soviet Union, while Latin Americans tossed out many of their autocrats and fragile African states embraced the ballot box. Democratic transitions in all regions of the world have transformed the world in the late 20th century; democracy has replaced autocratic rule as the predominant form of governance for the first time in history. Only about two dozen autocracies remain today, and these are mainly communist holdovers, as in Cuba, Vietnam, and China, or oil producing states, such as Saudi Arabia, Iran, and Qatar. The consolidation of recent democratic gains remains vulnerable to periodic instability; however, autocratic rule may finally have become obsolete in the new democratic world order.

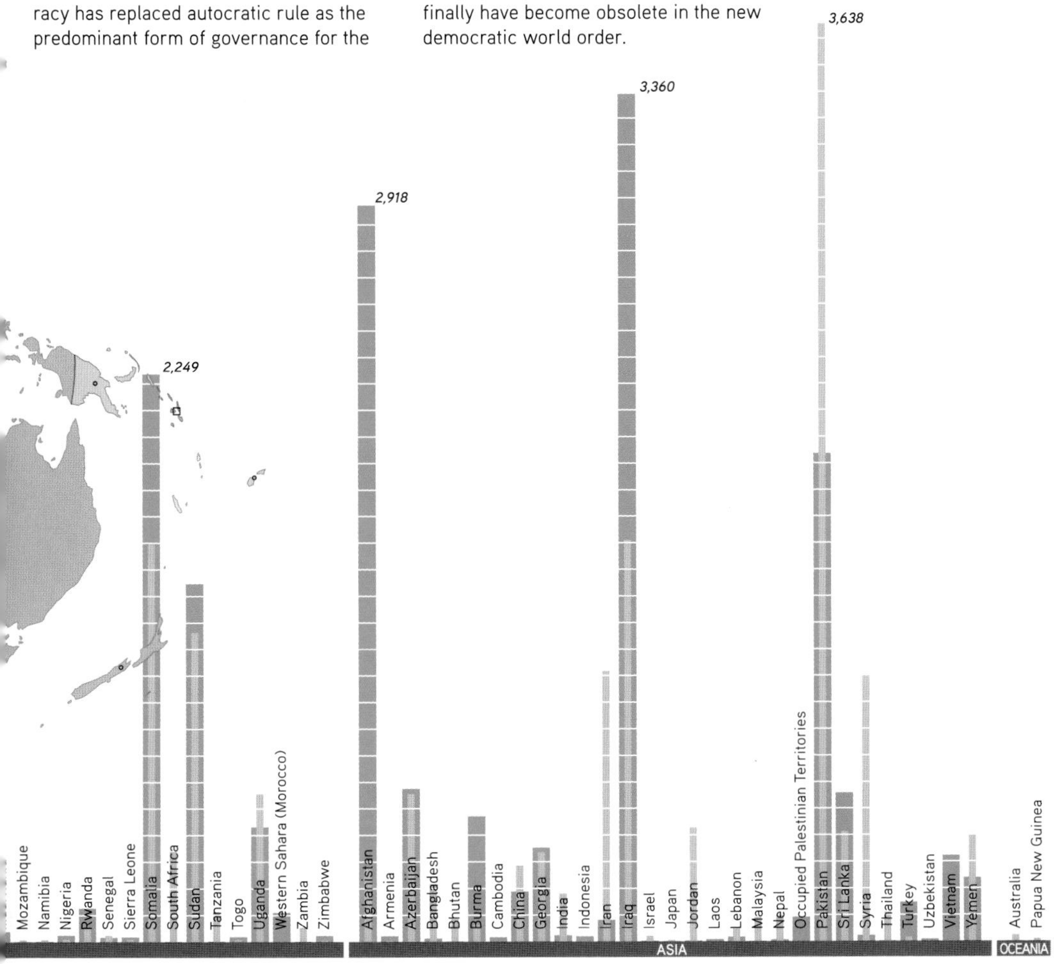

Flight from Conflict

At the end of 2010, the number of uprooted people worldwide numbered nearly 26 million, due to the flows of people who had left their homes because of war, violence, and oppression. The bar graph at left indicates the scale of refugee displacement and sanctuary. In Colombia, decades of conflict have led to a vast number of internally-displaced persons (IDPs), shown by the lighter bar. The darker bar shows the number of Colombians who have fled their homes. Large numbers of Congolese are displaced internally (light bar). Due to conflicts in neighboring countries, Iran has given residence to many (light bar). Germany and the United States shelter refugees from around the world (light bars).

Chemical Weapons

About a dozen countries, including the United States, Russia, South Korea, and India, have acknowledged chemical weapon stockpiles, but most of these weapons have been or are being eliminated. Under the Chemical Weapons Convention (CWC), member countries have been destroying their stockpiles, although several countries have not joined the CWC and likely possess chemical weapons. In addition, terror groups seldom acknowledge international treaties, and materials for chemical weapons are readily available to those who would have them.

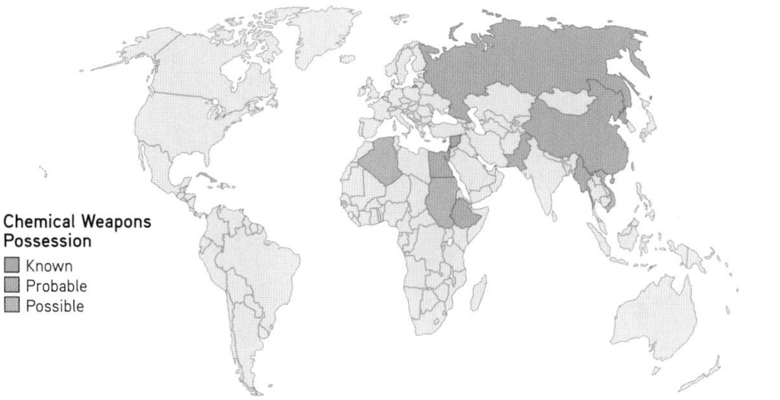

Nuclear Weapons

The United States, United Kingdom, China, France, and Russia remain the world's only declared nuclear weapon states under the Nuclear Non-Proliferation Treaty, but Pakistan and India have conducted nuclear tests, and Israel is also believed to possess them. Libya recently gave up its nuclear program, and Belarus, Kazakhstan, and Ukraine all relinquished Soviet nuclear weapons on their lands. But on October 9, 2006, North Korea tested a nuclear weapon. Iran, another country with nuclear ambitions, is enriching uranium that could be used for weapons.

GLOBAL WARMING

Habitat Loss Due to Global Warming, 21st-century Risk
- Critical
- High
- Low
- City vulnerable to sea level rise
- Melting glacier

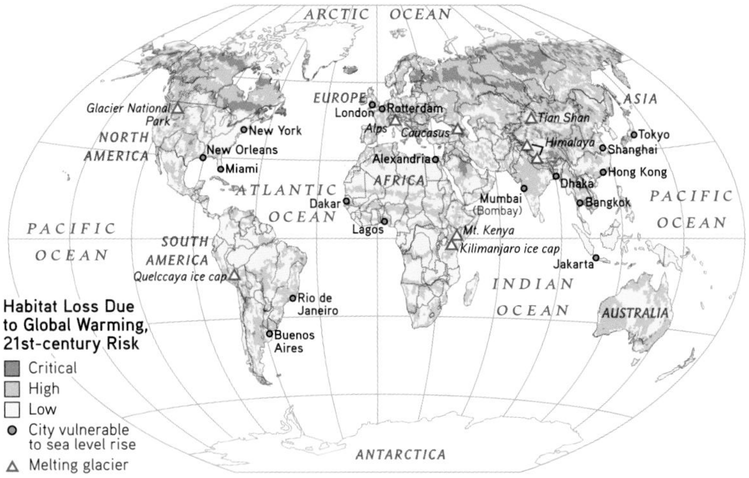

Temperatures across the world are increasing at a rate not seen at any other time in the last 10,000 years. Although climate variation is a natural phenomenon, human activities that release carbon dioxide and other greenhouse gases into the atmosphere—industrial processes, fossil fuel consumption, deforestation, and land use change—are contributing to this warming trend. Scientists predict that if this trend continues, one-third of plant and animal habitats will be dramatically altered and more than one million species will be threatened with extinction in the next 50 years. And even small increases in global temperatures can melt glaciers and polar ice sheets, raising sea levels and flooding coastal cities and towns.

DEFORESTATION

Vanishing Forest
- Frontier forest (large, mostly virgin forest)
- Degraded forest
- Frontier forest 8,000 years ago

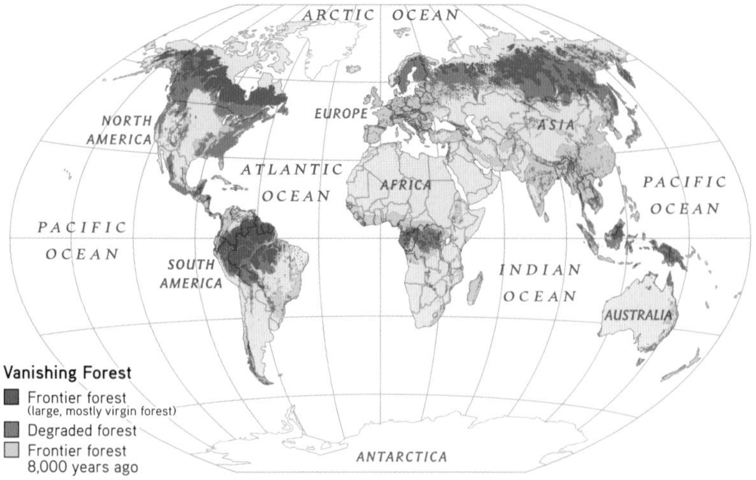

Widespread deforestation in the wet tropics is largely the result of short-term and unsustainable uses. Of the 13 million hectares (32 million acres) of forest lost each year, more than half are in South America and Africa, where many of the world's terrestrial plant and animal species can be found. Loss of habitat in such species-rich areas takes a toll on the world's biodiversity, and forces displaced species into competition with humans for dwelling areas. Deforested areas also release, instead of absorb, carbon dioxide into the atmosphere, contributing to global climate change. On a local or regional scale, deforestation can cause changes in rainfall patterns, and commonly leads to soil erosion and soil nutrient losses.

THREATENED OCEANS

Decline in Fish Catches, Post-1970s
- Cod and cod-like fish (haddock, hake)
- Flatfish (flounder, sole)
- Perch-like fish (grouper, snapper)
- Diseased coral reef

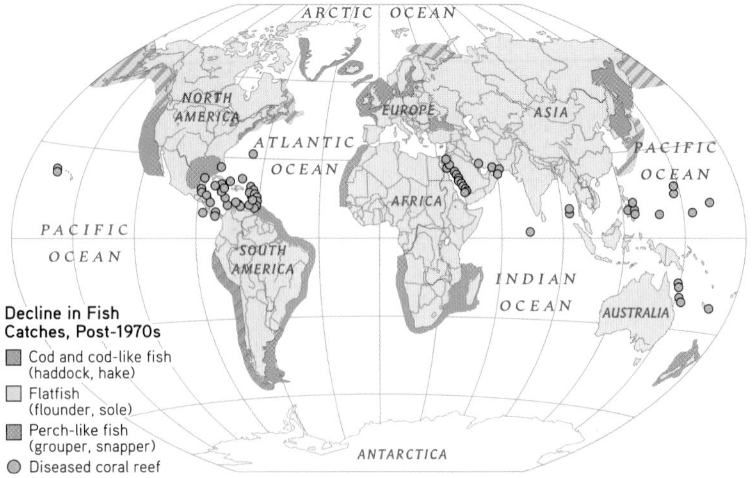

Oceans cover more than two-thirds of the Earth's surface and are home to at least half of the world's biodiversity, yet they are the least understood ecosystems. The combined stresses of overfishing, pollution, increased carbon dioxide emissions, global climate change, and coastal development are having a serious impact on the health of oceans and ocean species. More than 30% of marine fish stocks are now overexploited or depleted (up from 10% in the mid-1970s), while an estimated 25% of coral reefs worldwide are threatened by human activities.

DESERTIFICATION

Risk of Desertification
- Very high
- High
- Moderate
- Low

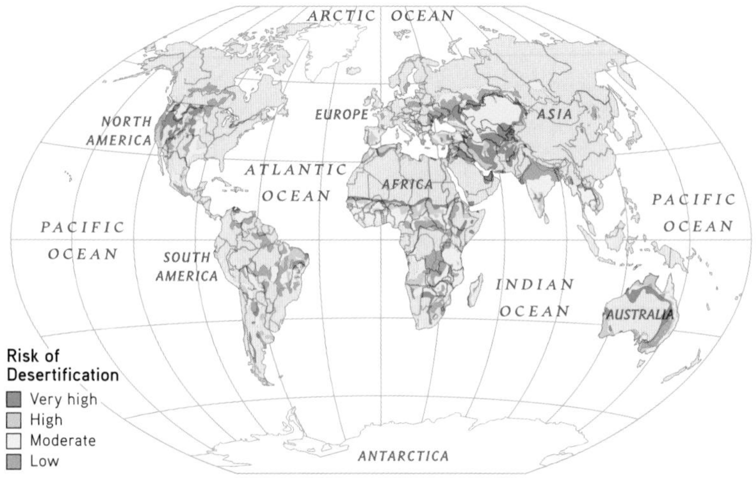

Climate variability and human activities, such as grazing and conversion of natural areas to agricultural use, are leading causes of desertification, the degradation of land in arid, semiarid, and dry subhumid areas. The environmental consequences of desertification are great—loss of topsoil, increased soil salinity, damaged vegetation, regional climate change, and a decline in biodiversity. Equally critical are the social consequences—more than two billion people live in and make a living off these dryland areas, which cover about 41% of the Earth's surface.

OZONE DEPLETION

First noted in the mid-1980s, the springtime "ozone hole" over the Antarctic reached its maximum in 2006. With sustained efforts to restrict chlorofluorocarbons (CFCs) and other ozone-depleting chemicals, scientists have begun to see the beginning of a long-term recovery of the ozone layer. Stratospheric ozone shields the Earth from the sun's ultraviolet radiation. Thinning of this protective layer puts people at risk for skin cancer and cataracts. It also can have devastating effects on the Earth's biological functions.

Atmospheric Ozone (Dobson Unit - DU)
Low — High
100 DU 500

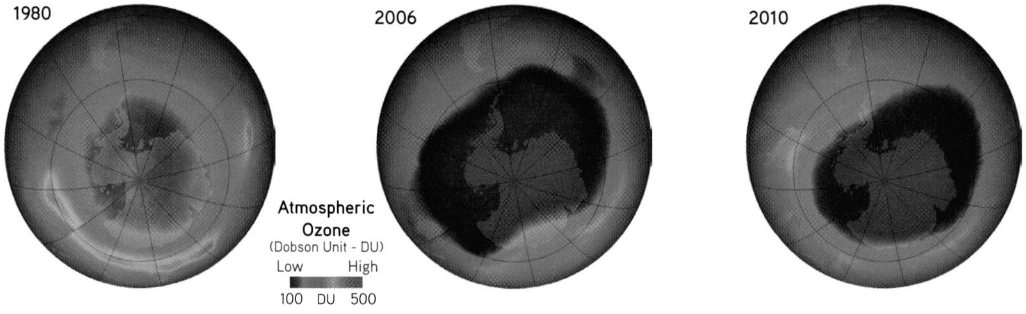

CARBON DIOXIDE

Scientists agree that rising levels of atmospheric carbon dioxide cause higher global temperatures. Solar radiation enters the atmosphere, is absorbed by the surface, then reradiates as heat. That warmth is trapped by the greenhouse gas, contributing to rising temperatures.

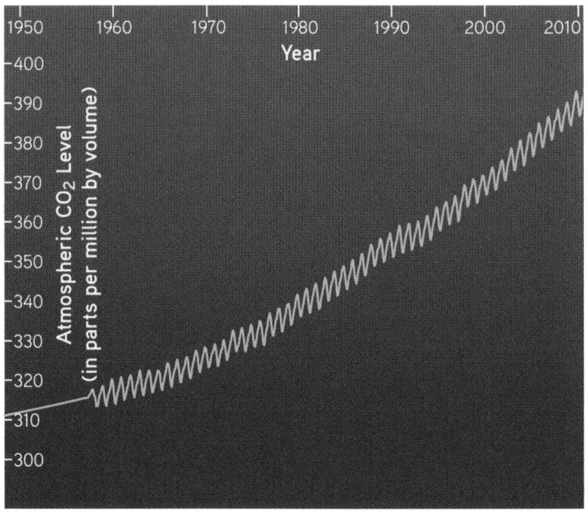

POLAR ICE CAP

Over the last 60 years, the extent of polar sea ice has noticeably decreased. The loss is compounded by a climatic feedback loop, in which less area covered by ice means less solar radiation is bounced back into the atmosphere, and more heat is absorbed by the water.

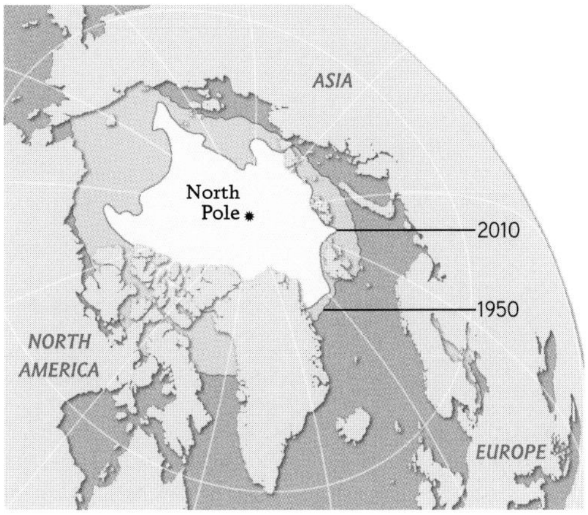

With the growth of scientific recordkeeping, observation, modeling, and analysis, our understanding of Earth's environment is improving. Yet even as we deepen our insight into environmental processes, we are changing what we are studying. At no other time in history have humans altered their environment with such speed and force. Nothing occurs in isolation, and stress in one area has impacts elsewhere. Our agricultural and fishing practices, industrial processes, extraction of resources, and transportation methods are leading to extinctions, destroying habitats, devastating fish stocks, disturbing the soil, and polluting the oceans and the air. As a result, biodiversity is declining, carbon dioxide levels and global temperatures are rising, and polar ice is melting.

POLLUTION

Pollution
- Areas most sensitive to acid rain
- Frequent pollution from shipping
- World's ten most polluted places (based on Blacksmith Institute report)
- World's most polluted cities (by particulate matter)

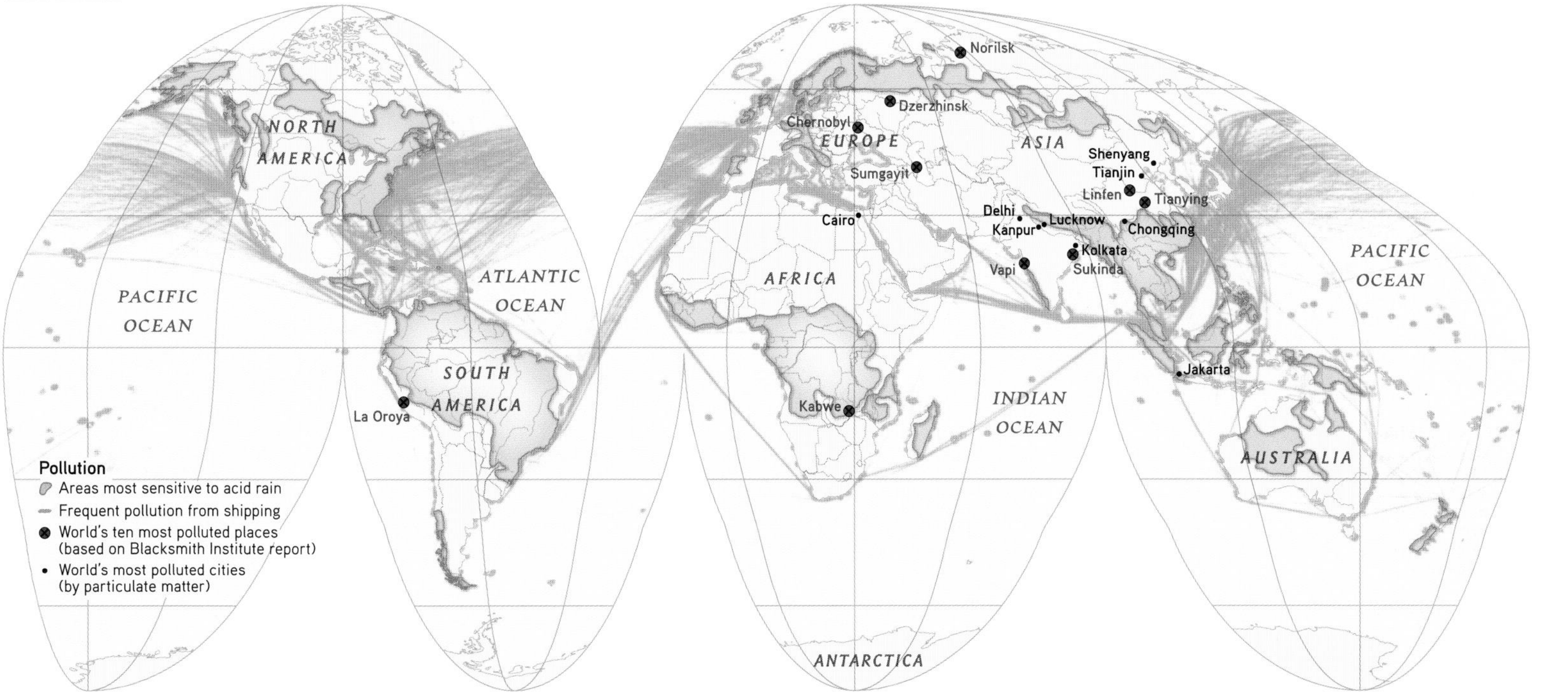

Examples of water and soil pollution include the contamination of groundwater, salinization of irrigated lands in semiarid regions, and the so-called "chemical time bomb" issue, where accumulated toxins are suddenly mobilized following a change in external conditions. Oceans and estuaries are also increasingly polluted. In addition to enormous patches (gyres) of plastic debris in the oceans, a growing problem is the creation of coastal "dead zones," mostly due to agricultural runoff and municipal effluents. Urban air quality likewise remains a serious problem, particularly in developing countries. One of the main reasons is the rapid increase in passenger cars. In some developed countries, successful control measures

have improved air quality over the past 50 years; in others, trends have actually reversed, with brown haze often hanging over metropolitan areas. Solid and hazardous waste disposal is a universal urban strain, and the issue is on many political agendas. In the world's poorest countries, "garbage pickers" (usually women and children) are symbols of abject poverty. In North America, toxic wastes are frequently transported long distances; this introduces the risk of ocean, highway, and rail accidents, causing serious local contamination. Pollution also often occurs as a result of armed conflict. Lebanon, for example, suffered extensive environmental damage after its oil depots were hit by Israeli bombers in 2006.

GeoBytes

ACIDIFYING OCEANS
Oceans are absorbing an unprecedented 30 million metric tons of carbon dioxide each day, increasing the water's acidity at a rate so rapid that marine life will struggle to adapt.

ENDANGERED REEFS
Some 95% of coral reefs in Southeast Asia have been destroyed or are threatened.

RECORD TEMPERATURES
The 10 years since 2000 have all been among the 11 warmest years ever recorded.

WARMING ARCTIC
While the world as a whole has warmed nearly 0.9°C (1.6°F) over the last 100 years, parts of the Arctic have warmed much more in only the last 50 years.

DISAPPEARING RAIN FORESTS
Scientists predict that the world's rain forests will practically disappear within the next hundred years if the current rate of deforestation continues.

OIL POLLUTION
Nearly 1.3 million metric tons of oil seep into the world's oceans each year from the combined sources of natural seepage, extraction, transportation, and consumption, including spills.

ACCIDENTAL DROWNINGS
Entanglement in fishing gear is one of the greatest threats to marine mammals.

A FAREWELL TO FROGS?
Worldwide, the current extinction rate of amphibians is over 200 times the historical rate.

GeoBytes

LARGEST NATIONAL PARK
North East Greenland National Park, 972,000 sq km (375,000 sq mi)

LARGEST MARINE PARK
Northwestern Hawaiian Islands Marine National Monument, U.S., 360,000 sq km (140,000 sq mi)

BIODIVERSITY HOTSPOTS
Conservation International identifies world regions that suffer from a severe loss of biodiversity.

WORLD HERITAGE SITES
The United Nations Educational, Scientific, and Cultural Organization (UNESCO) recognizes natural and cultural sites of "universal value."

Percentage Protected

Protected areas worldwide represent 12% of the Earth's land surface, according to the U.N. Environmental Programme World Conservation Monitoring Centre. Only 6% of territorial waters are within protected areas—an amount considered inadequate by conservationists because of the increasing threats of overfishing and coral reef loss worldwide.

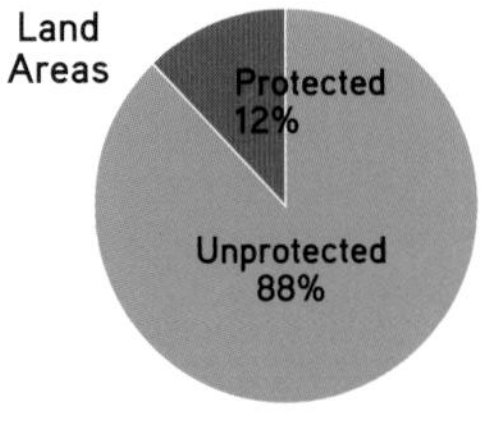

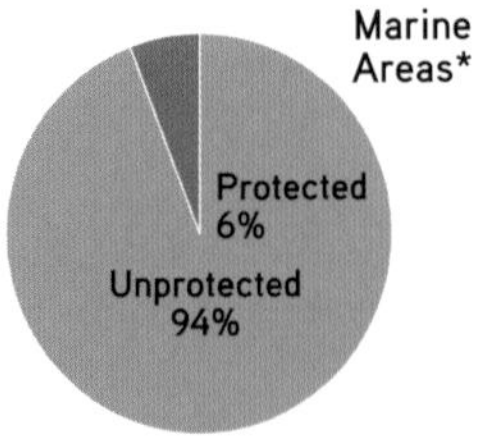

**percentage of territorial waters in a band extending up to 12 nautical miles from shore*

HAWAI'I VOLCANOES NATIONAL PARK, HAWAI'I
The park includes Kilauea, one of the world's most active volcanoes. The landscape shows the results of 70 million years of volcanism, including calderas, lava flows, and black sand beaches. Lava spreads out to build the island, and seawater vaporizes as lava hits the ocean at 1,149°C (2,100° F). The national park, created in 1916, covers about 12.5% of the island of Hawai'i and is a refuge for endangered species, like the hawksbill turtle and Hawaiian goose. It was made a World Heritage site in 1987.

GALÁPAGOS NATIONAL PARK, ECUADOR
Galápago means tortoise in Spanish, and at one time 250,000 giant tortoises roamed the islands. Today about 15,000 remain, and three of the original 14 subspecies are extinct—the Pinta Island tortoise may be extinct soon. In 1959, Ecuador made the volcanic Galápagos Islands a national park, protecting the giant tortoises and other endemic species. The archipelago became a World Heritage site in 1978, and a marine reserve surrounding the islands was added in 2001.

WESTERN UNITED STATES
An intricate public lands pattern—including national forests, wilderness areas, wildlife refuges, and national parks such as Arches (above)—embraces nearly half the surface area of 11 western states. Ten out of 19 World Heritage sites in the United States are found here. It was in the West that the modern national park movement was born in the 19th century with the establishment of Yellowstone and Yosemite National Parks.

MADIDI NATIONAL PARK, BOLIVIA
Macaws may outnumber humans in Madidi, Bolivia's second largest national park, established in 1995. A complex community of plants, animals, and native Indian groups share this 18,900-sq-km (7,300-sq-mi) reserve, part of the Tropical Andes biodiversity hotspot. Indigenous communities benefit from ecotourism.

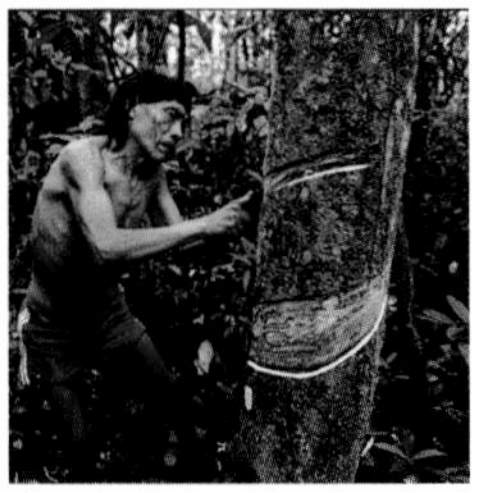

AMAZON BASIN, BRAZIL
Indigenous peoples help manage reserves in Brazil that are linked with Jaú National Park. The park and reserves are part of the Central Amazon Conservation Complex, a World Heritage Site covering more than 60,000 sq km (23,000 sq mi). It is the largest protected area in the Amazon Basin and one of the most biologically rich regions on the planet.

ARCTIC REGIONS
Polar bears find safe havens in Canadian parks, such as on Ellesmere Island, and in Greenland's huge protected area—Earth's largest—that preserves the island's frigid northeast. In 1996 countries with Arctic lands adopted the Circumpolar Protected Areas Network Strategy and Action Plan to help conserve ecosystems.

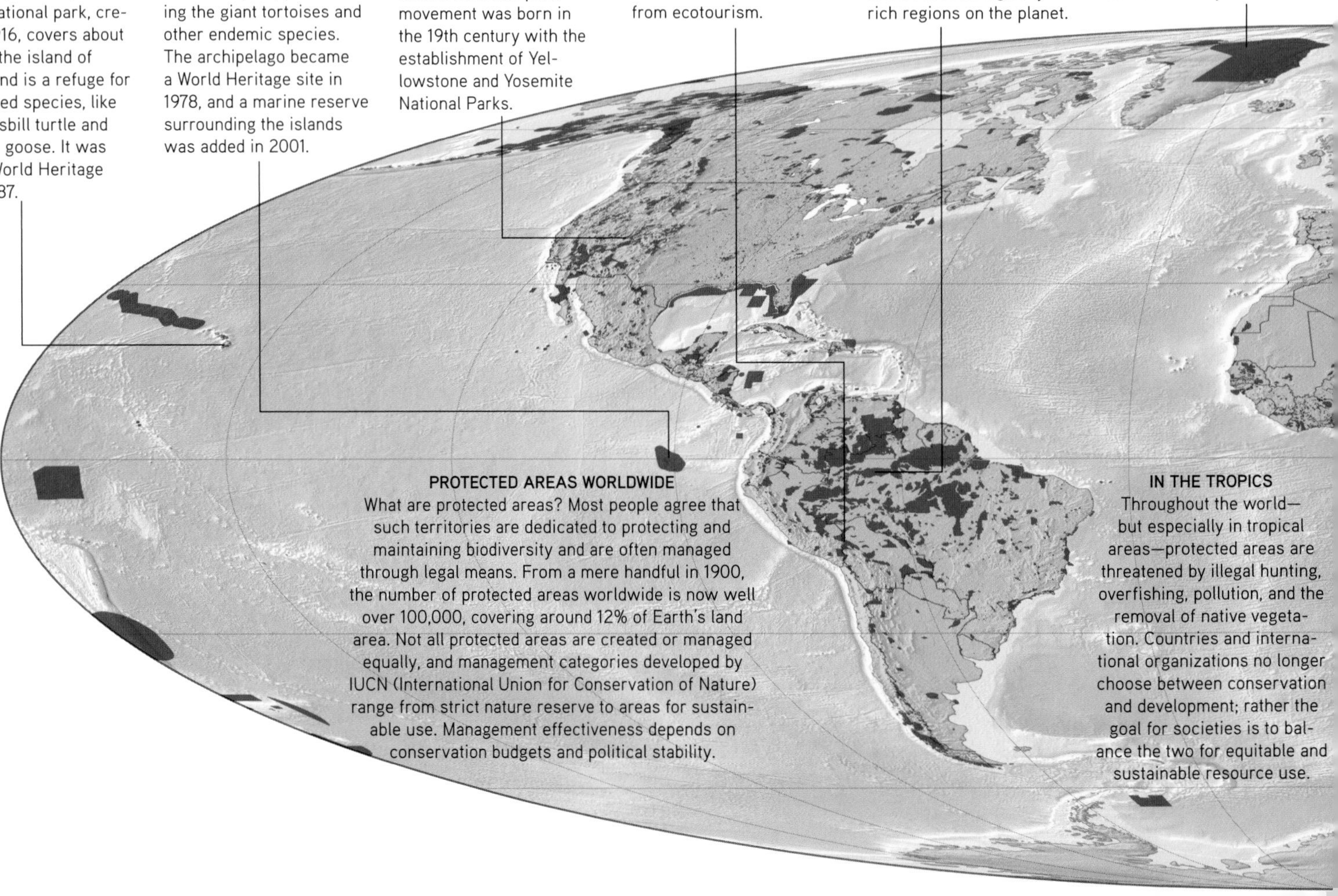

PROTECTED AREAS WORLDWIDE
What are protected areas? Most people agree that such territories are dedicated to protecting and maintaining biodiversity and are often managed through legal means. From a mere handful in 1900, the number of protected areas worldwide is now well over 100,000, covering around 12% of Earth's land area. Not all protected areas are created or managed equally, and management categories developed by IUCN (International Union for Conservation of Nature) range from strict nature reserve to areas for sustainable use. Management effectiveness depends on conservation budgets and political stability.

IN THE TROPICS
Throughout the world—but especially in tropical areas—protected areas are threatened by illegal hunting, overfishing, pollution, and the removal of native vegetation. Countries and international organizations no longer choose between conservation and development; rather the goal for societies is to balance the two for equitable and sustainable resource use.

Wildest Areas

Although generally far from cities, the world's remaining wild places play a vital role in a healthy global ecosystem. The boreal (northern) forests of Canada and Russia, for instance, help cleanse the air we breathe by absorbing carbon dioxide and providing oxygen. With the human population increasing by an estimated one billion over the next 15 years, many wild places could fall within reach of the plow or under a cloud of smog.

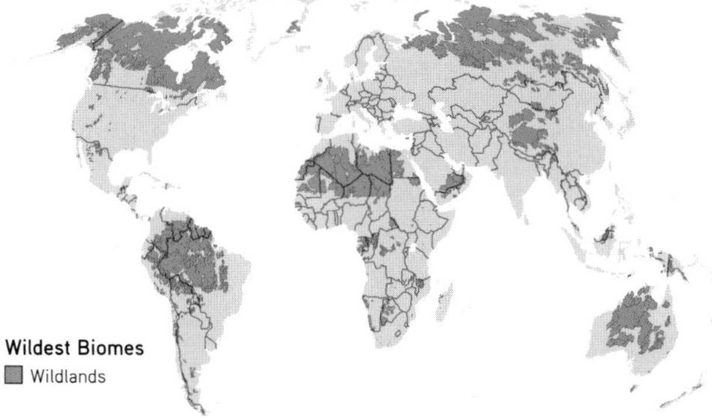

For millennia, lands have been set aside as sacred ground or as hunting reserves for the powerful. Today, great swaths are protected for recreation, habitat conservation, biodiversity preservation, and resource management. Some groups may oppose protected spaces because they want access to resources now. Yet local inhabitants and governments are beginning to see the benefits of conservation efforts and sustainable use for human health and future generations.

SAREKS NATIONAL PARK, SWEDEN
This remote park, established in 1909 to protect the alpine landscape, is a favorite of backcountry hikers. It boasts some 200 mountains over 1,800 m (5,900 ft), and about 100 glaciers. Sareks forms part of the Laponian Area and has been a home to the Saami (or Lapp) people since prehistoric times.

AFRICAN RESERVES
Some 120,000 elephants roam Chobe National Park in northern Botswana. Africa has more than 7,500 national parks, wildlife reserves, and other protected areas, covering about 9% of the continent. Protected areas are under enormous pressure from expanding populations, civil unrest and war, and environmental disasters.

WOLONG NATURE RESERVE, CHINA
Giant pandas freely chomp bamboo in this 2,000-sq-km (772-sq-mi) reserve in Sichuan Province, near the city of Chengdu. Misty bamboo forests host a number of endangered species, but the critically endangered giant panda—among the rarest mammals in the world—is the most famous resident. Only about 1,600 giant pandas exist in the wild.

KAMCHATKA, RUSSIA
Crater lakes, ash-capped cones, and diverse plant and animal species mark this peninsula located between the icy Bering Sea and Sea of Okhotsk. The active volcanoes and glaciers form a dynamic landscape of great beauty, known as "The Land of Fire and Ice." Its remoteness and rugged landscape help fauna to flourish, producing record numbers of salmon species and half of the Steller's sea-eagles on Earth.

GUNUNG PALUNG NATIONAL PARK, INDONESIA
A tree frog's perch could be precarious in this park on the island of Borneo, in the heart of the Sundaland biodiversity hotspot. The biggest threat to trees and animals in the park and region is illegal logging. Gunung Palung contains a wider range of habitats than any other protected area on Borneo, from mangroves to lowland and cloud forests. A number of endangered species, such as orangutans and sun bears, depend on the dense forests.

AUSTRALIA & NEW ZEALAND
Uluru, a red sandstone monolith (formerly known as Ayers Rock), and the vast Great Barrier Reef, one of the largest marine parks in the world, are outstanding examples of Australia's protected areas—which make up more than 10% of the country's area and conserve a diverse range of unique ecosystems. About a third of New Zealand is protected, and it is a biodiversity hotspot because of threats to flightless native birds, such as the kakapo and kiwi. Cats, stoats, and other predators, introduced to New Zealand by settlers, kill thousands of birds each year.

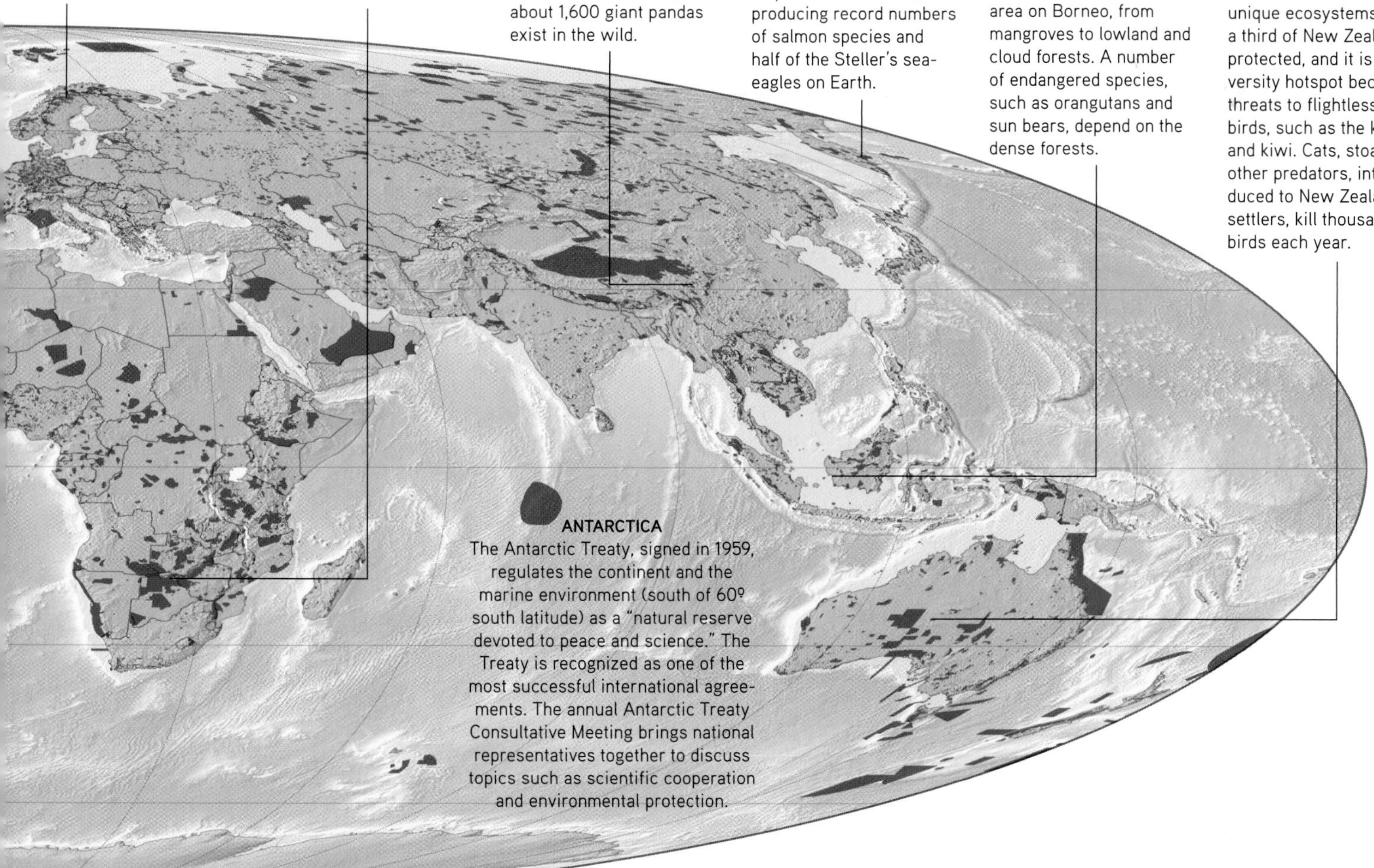

ANTARCTICA
The Antarctic Treaty, signed in 1959, regulates the continent and the marine environment (south of 60º south latitude) as a "natural reserve devoted to peace and science." The Treaty is recognized as one of the most successful international agreements. The annual Antarctic Treaty Consultative Meeting brings national representatives together to discuss topics such as scientific cooperation and environmental protection.

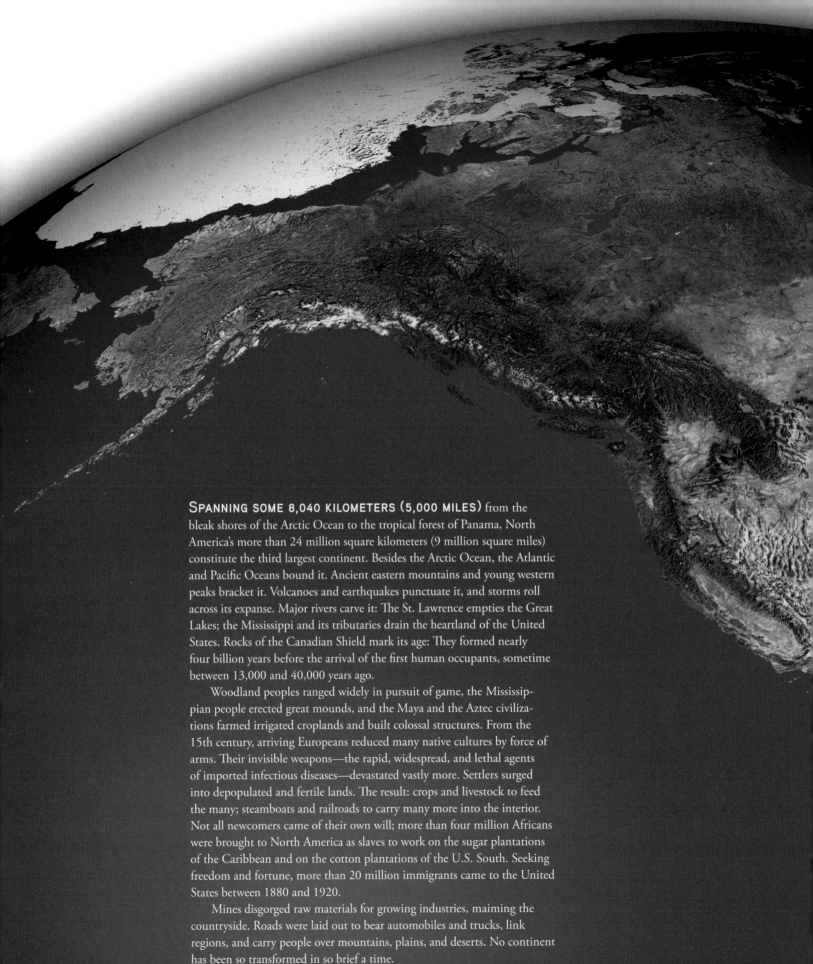

Spanning some 8,040 kilometers (5,000 miles) from the bleak shores of the Arctic Ocean to the tropical forest of Panama, North America's more than 24 million square kilometers (9 million square miles) constitute the third largest continent. Besides the Arctic Ocean, the Atlantic and Pacific Oceans bound it. Ancient eastern mountains and young western peaks bracket it. Volcanoes and earthquakes punctuate it, and storms roll across its expanse. Major rivers carve it: The St. Lawrence empties the Great Lakes; the Mississippi and its tributaries drain the heartland of the United States. Rocks of the Canadian Shield mark its age: They formed nearly four billion years before the arrival of the first human occupants, sometime between 13,000 and 40,000 years ago.

Woodland peoples ranged widely in pursuit of game, the Mississippian people erected great mounds, and the Maya and the Aztec civilizations farmed irrigated croplands and built colossal structures. From the 15th century, arriving Europeans reduced many native cultures by force of arms. Their invisible weapons—the rapid, widespread, and lethal agents of imported infectious diseases—devastated vastly more. Settlers surged into depopulated and fertile lands. The result: crops and livestock to feed the many; steamboats and railroads to carry many more into the interior. Not all newcomers came of their own will; more than four million Africans were brought to North America as slaves to work on the sugar plantations of the Caribbean and on the cotton plantations of the U.S. South. Seeking freedom and fortune, more than 20 million immigrants came to the United States between 1880 and 1920.

Mines disgorged raw materials for growing industries, maiming the countryside. Roads were laid out to bear automobiles and trucks, link regions, and carry people over mountains, plains, and deserts. No continent has been so transformed in so brief a time.

North America

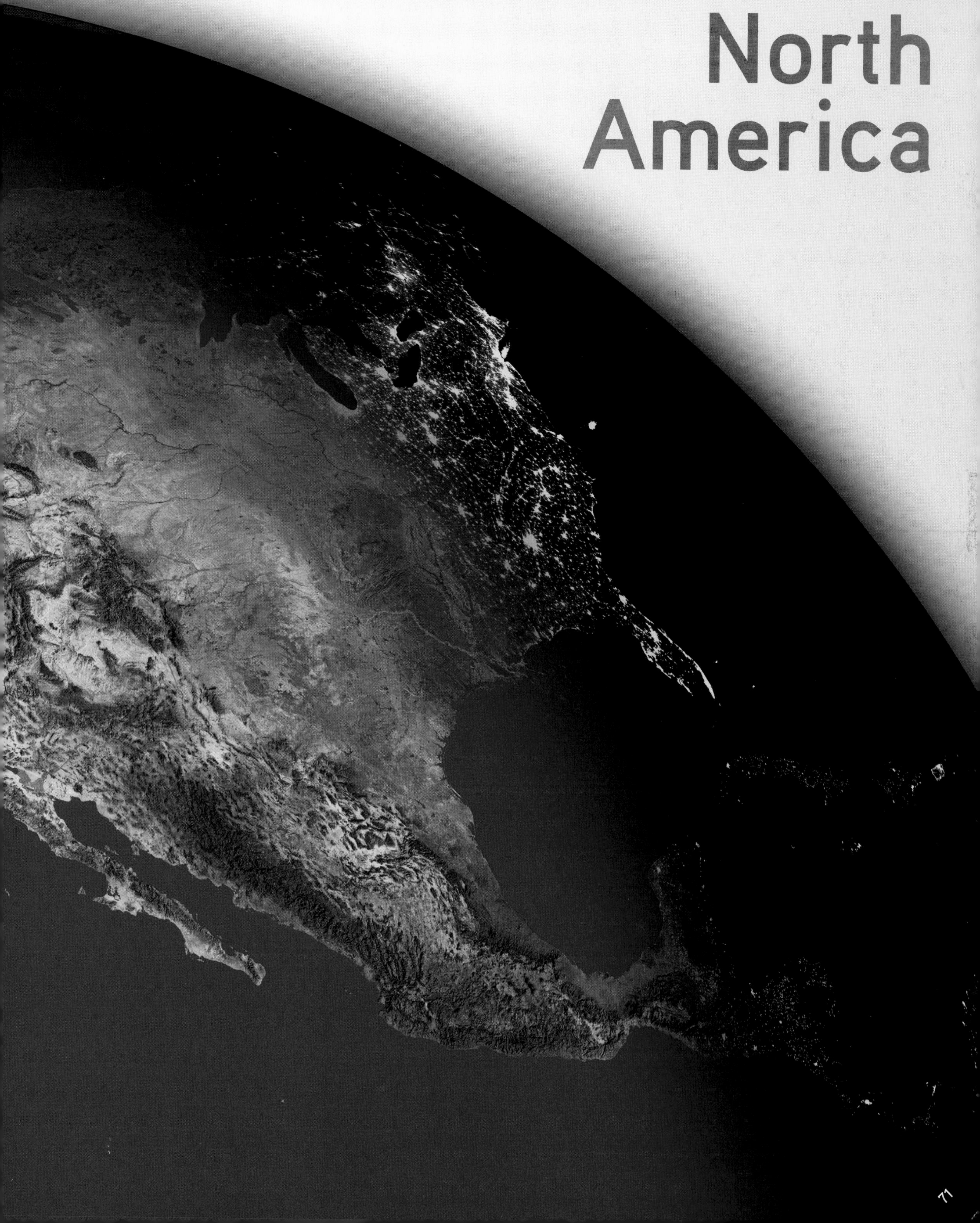

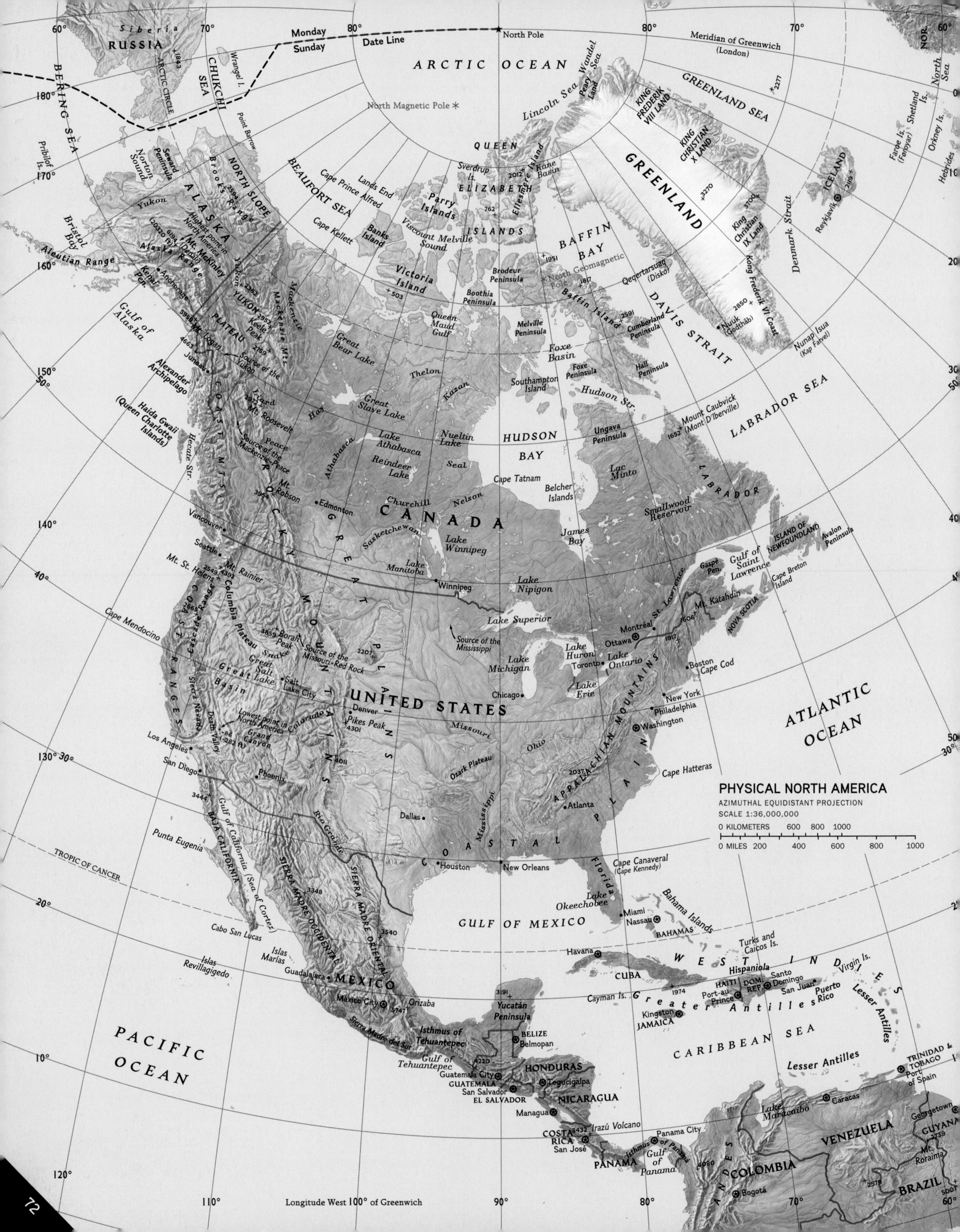

PHYSICAL NORTH AMERICA
AZIMUTHAL EQUIDISTANT PROJECTION
SCALE 1:36,000,000
0 KILOMETERS 600 800 1000
0 MILES 200 400 600 800 1000
ARCTIC OCEAN
North Pole
Monday
Sunday
Date Line
Meridian of Greenwich (London)
North Magnetic Pole
North Geomagnetic Pole
Siberia
RUSSIA
ARCTIC CIRCLE
CHUKCHI SEA
BERING SEA
Wrangel I.
Point Barrow
Pribilof Is.
Norton Sound
Seward Peninsula
Brooks Range
NORTH SLOPE
ALASKA
Yukon
Bristol Bay
Aleutian Range
Alaska Range
Highest point in North America (Mt. McKinley) (Denali) 6194 (20320 ft)
Kenai Pen.
Anchorage
Gulf of Alaska
Mt. Logan
YUKON PLATEAU
Keele Peak
Mackenzie Mts
Mackenzie
Source of the Yukon
Juneau
Alexander Archipelago
Haida Gwaii (Queen Charlotte Islands)
Hecate Str.
COAST MTS
Liard
Mt. Roosevelt
Peace
Source of the Mackenzie-Peace
Mt. Robson
ROCKY MOUNTAINS
BEAUFORT SEA
Cape Prince Alfred
Lands End
Cape Kellett
Banks Island
Parry Islands
Viscount Melville Sound
QUEEN ELIZABETH ISLANDS
Sverdrup Is.
Ellesmere Island
Kane Basin
Lincoln Sea
Peary Land
Wandel Sea
Victoria Island
Great Bear Lake
Queen Maud Gulf
Boothia Peninsula
Brodeur Peninsula
Baffin Island
BAFFIN BAY
Melville Peninsula
Foxe Basin
Foxe Peninsula
Southampton Island
Cumberland Peninsula
Hall Peninsula
Hudson Str.
Thelon
Kazan
Great Slave Lake
Hay
Athabasca
Lake Athabasca
Reindeer Lake
Nueltin Lake
Seal
HUDSON BAY
Cape Tatnam
Belcher Islands
Ungava Peninsula
Lac Minto
LABRADOR
Smallwood Reservoir
Mount Caubvick (Mont D'Iberville)
LABRADOR SEA
DAVIS STRAIT
Qeqertarsuaq (Disko)
Nuuk (Godthåb)
Nunap Isua (Kap Farvel)
GREENLAND
GREENLAND SEA
KING FREDERIK VIII LAND
KING CHRISTIAN X LAND
King Christian IX Land
King Frederik VI Coast
Denmark Strait
ICELAND
Reykjavík
Faroe Is. (Føroyar)
Shetland Is.
Orkney Is.
Hebrides
North Sea
NOR.
CANADA
Edmonton
Churchill
Nelson
Saskatchewan
Lake Winnipeg
Lake Manitoba
Winnipeg
James Bay
Lake Nipigon
Lake Superior
Source of the Mississippi
Vancouver
Seattle
Mt. Rainier
Mt. St. Helens
Columbia Plateau
Columbia
Cascade Range
COAST RANGES
Cape Mendocino
Borah Peak
Snake
Source of the Missouri-Red Rock
Great Salt Lake
Salt Lake City
Great Basin
Sierra Nevada
Death Valley
Lowest point in North America -86 (-282 ft)
Colorado
Grand Canyon
Los Angeles
San Diego
Phoenix
GREAT PLAINS
UNITED STATES
Denver
Pikes Peak 4301
Missouri
Ozark Plateau
Ohio
Mississippi
Dallas
Houston
New Orleans
Rio Grande
COASTAL PLAIN
Lake Michigan
Chicago
Lake Huron
Toronto
Lake Ontario
Lake Erie
Ottawa
Montréal
St. Lawrence
Mt. Katahdin
Boston
Cape Cod
New York
Philadelphia
Washington
APPALACHIAN MOUNTAINS
Atlanta
Cape Hatteras
Florida
Lake Okeechobee
Cape Canaveral (Cape Kennedy)
Miami
Gaspé Pen.
Gulf of Saint Lawrence
ISLAND OF NEWFOUNDLAND
Avalon Peninsula
Cape Breton Island
NOVA SCOTIA
ATLANTIC OCEAN
GULF OF MEXICO
Nassau
BAHAMAS
Bahama Islands
Turks and Caicos Is.
Havana
CUBA
WEST INDIES
Hispaniola
HAITI
Port-au-Prince
DOM. REP.
Santo Domingo
San Juan
Puerto Rico
Virgin Is.
Cayman Is.
Greater Antilles
Kingston
JAMAICA
Lesser Antilles
CARIBBEAN SEA
TRINIDAD & TOBAGO
Port of Spain
Caracas
Lake Maracaibo
VENEZUELA
Georgetown
GUYANA
Mt. Roraima
BRAZIL
COLOMBIA
Bogotá
ANDES
Gulf of Panama
Isthmus of Panama
Panama City
PANAMA
COSTA RICA
San José
Irazú Volcano
NICARAGUA
Managua
HONDURAS
Tegucigalpa
EL SALVADOR
San Salvador
GUATEMALA
Guatemala City
BELIZE
Belmopan
Yucatán Peninsula
Isthmus of Tehuantepec
Gulf of Tehuantepec
Sierra Madre del Sur
Orizaba
Mexico City
MEXICO
Guadalajara
SIERRA MADRE OCCIDENTAL
SIERRA MADRE ORIENTAL
Islas Marías
Islas Revillagigedo
Cabo San Lucas
BAJA CALIFORNIA
Gulf of California (Sea of Cortez)
Punta Eugenia
TROPIC OF CANCER
PACIFIC OCEAN
Longitude West 100° of Greenwich

POLITICAL NORTH AMERICA
AZIMUTHAL EQUIDISTANT PROJECTION
SCALE 1:36,000,000
0 KILOMETERS 600 800 1000
0 MILES 200 400 600 800 1000
ARCTIC OCEAN
North Pole
North Magnetic Pole
Date Line
Monday
Sunday
ARCTIC CIRCLE
TROPIC OF CANCER
Longitude West 100° of Greenwich
RUSSIA
CHUKCHI SEA
BERING SEA
BEAUFORT SEA
Gulf of Alaska
GREENLAND SEA
GREENLAND (KALAALLIT NUNAAT) Denmark
BAFFIN BAY
DAVIS STRAIT
LABRADOR SEA
Hudson Strait
HUDSON BAY
QUEEN ELIZABETH ISLANDS
Parry Islands
Victoria Island
Baffin Island
ICELAND
Reykjavík
UNITED KINGDOM
Faroe Is. (Føroyar) Denmark
ALASKA
NORTH SLOPE
Anchorage
Fairbanks
Mt. McKinley (Denali) 6194
Juneau
Alexander Archipelago
Haida Gwaii (Queen Charlotte Islands)
CANADA
Edmonton
Calgary
Vancouver
Victoria
Regina
Winnipeg
Ottawa
Montréal
Québec
Toronto
Halifax
LABRADOR
ISLAND OF NEWFOUNDLAND
St. John's
ST. PIERRE & MIQUELON Fr.
Gulf of Saint Lawrence
COAST MTS.
ROCKY MTS.
UNITED STATES
Seattle
Portland
Salem
Boise
Salt Lake City
San Francisco
Sacramento
San Jose
Fresno
Bakersfield
Los Angeles
Long Beach
San Diego
Las Vegas
Phoenix
Tucson
Albuquerque
El Paso
Denver
Colorado Springs
Pikes Peak 4301
Cheyenne
Omaha
Lincoln
Topeka
Wichita
Oklahoma City
Tulsa
Dallas
Ft. Worth
Austin
San Antonio
Houston
New Orleans
Baton Rouge
Jackson
Memphis
Little Rock
Shreveport
Minneapolis
St. Paul
Madison
Milwaukee
Chicago
Des Moines
Springfield
St. Louis
Louisville
Indianapolis
Columbus
Detroit
Lansing
Cleveland
Pittsburgh
Nashville
Birmingham
Atlanta
Montgomery
Mobile
Tallahassee
Jacksonville
Orlando
Tampa
St. Petersburg
Miami
Key West
Charlotte
Raleigh
Richmond
Norfolk
Washington, D.C.
Annapolis
Dover
Philadelphia
Harrisburg
Trenton
NEW YORK
Hartford
Providence
Boston
Concord
Albany
Augusta
Cape Hatteras
APPALACHIAN MTS.
SIERRA NEVADA
ATLANTIC OCEAN
BERMUDA U.K.
GULF OF MEXICO
PACIFIC OCEAN
MEXICO
MÉXICO CITY
Guadalajara
Monterrey
Tijuana
Ciudad Juárez
Chihuahua
Torreón
León
Puebla
Veracruz
Acapulco
Mérida
Cancún
BAJA CALIFORNIA
SIERRA MADRE OCCIDENTAL
SIERRA MADRE ORIENTAL
Islas Revillagigedo
BAHAMAS
Nassau
CUBA
La Habana (Havana)
JAMAICA
Kingston
HAITI
Port-au-Prince
DOM. REP.
Santo Domingo
PUERTO RICO U.S.
San Juan
TURKS & CAICOS U.K.
CAYMAN IS. U.K.
Virgin Is. U.S. U.K.
ST. KITTS AND NEVIS
ANTIGUA AND BARBUDA
GUADELOUPE France
DOMINICA
MARTINIQUE Fr.
ST. LUCIA
BARBADOS
ST. VINCENT AND THE GRENADINES
GRENADA
TRINIDAD AND TOBAGO
CARIBBEAN SEA
BELIZE
Belmopan
GUATEMALA
Guatemala City
EL SALVADOR
San Salvador
HONDURAS
Tegucigalpa
NICARAGUA
Managua
COSTA RICA
San José
PANAMA
Panamá City
COLOMBIA
BOGOTÁ
Medellín
Barranquilla
Cartagena
VENEZUELA
Caracas
Maracaibo
GUYANA
Georgetown
BRAZIL
Mount Roraima 2739

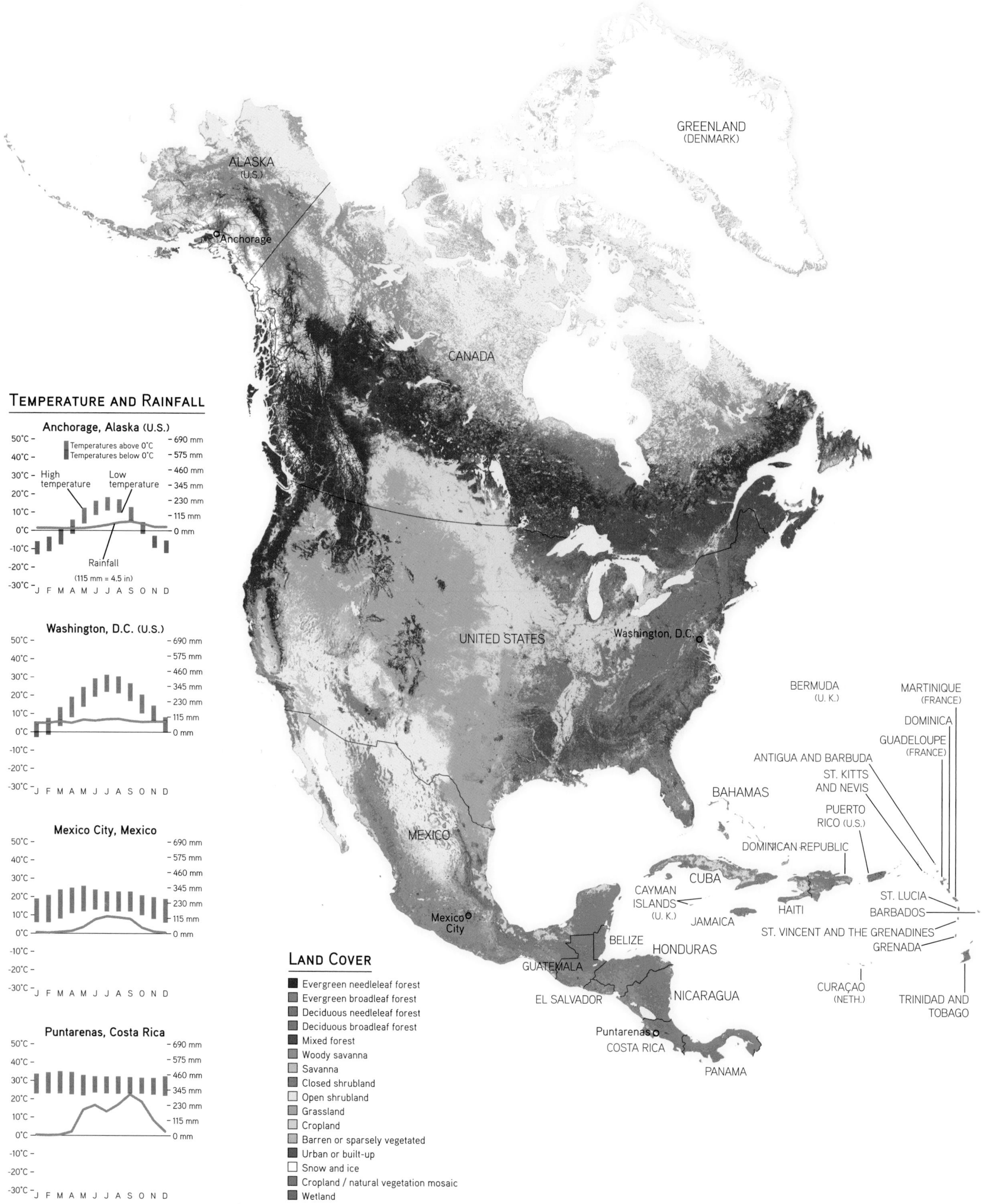
GREENLAND
(DENMARK)
ALASKA
(U.S.)
Anchorage
CANADA
UNITED STATES
Washington, D.C.
MEXICO
Mexico City
BERMUDA
(U. K.)
MARTINIQUE
(FRANCE)
DOMINICA
GUADELOUPE
(FRANCE)
ANTIGUA AND BARBUDA
ST. KITTS AND NEVIS
BAHAMAS
PUERTO RICO (U.S.)
DOMINICAN REPUBLIC
CUBA
CAYMAN ISLANDS
(U. K.)
JAMAICA
HAITI
ST. LUCIA
BARBADOS
ST. VINCENT AND THE GRENADINES
GRENADA
BELIZE
HONDURAS
GUATEMALA
EL SALVADOR
NICARAGUA
CURAÇAO
(NETH.)
TRINIDAD AND TOBAGO
Puntarenas
COSTA RICA
PANAMA
TEMPERATURE AND RAINFALL
Anchorage, Alaska (U.S.)
Temperatures above 0°C
Temperatures below 0°C
High temperature
Low temperature
Rainfall
(115 mm = 4.5 in)
Washington, D.C. (U.S.)
Mexico City, Mexico
Puntarenas, Costa Rica
50°C 40°C 30°C 20°C 10°C 0°C -10°C -20°C -30°C
690 mm 575 mm 460 mm 345 mm 230 mm 115 mm 0 mm
J F M A M J J A S O N D
LAND COVER
Evergreen needleleaf forest
Evergreen broadleaf forest
Deciduous needleleaf forest
Deciduous broadleaf forest
Mixed forest
Woody savanna
Savanna
Closed shrubland
Open shrubland
Grassland
Cropland
Barren or sparsely vegetated
Urban or built-up
Snow and ice
Cropland / natural vegetation mosaic
Wetland

Climate Zones

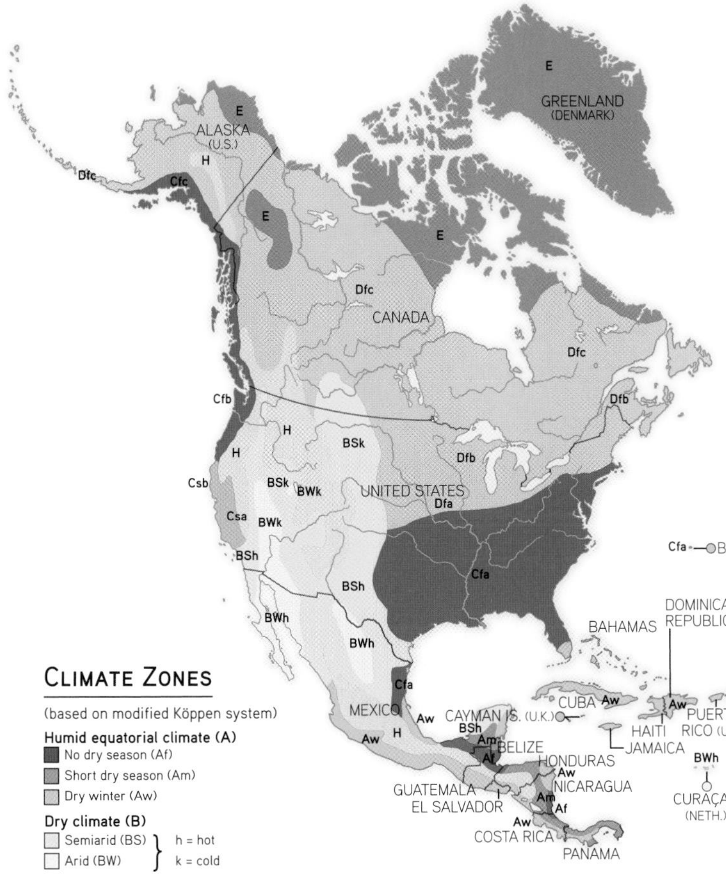

(based on modified Köppen system)

Humid equatorial climate (A)
- No dry season (Af)
- Short dry season (Am)
- Dry winter (Aw)

Dry climate (B)
- Semiarid (BS)
- Arid (BW)

h = hot
k = cold

Humid temperate climate (C)
- No dry season (Cf)
- Dry summer (Cs)

Humid cold climate (D)
- No dry season (Df)

a = hot summer
b = cool summer
c = short, cool summer

Cold climate (E)
- Tundra and ice

Highland climate (H)
- Unclassified highlands

Natural Hazards

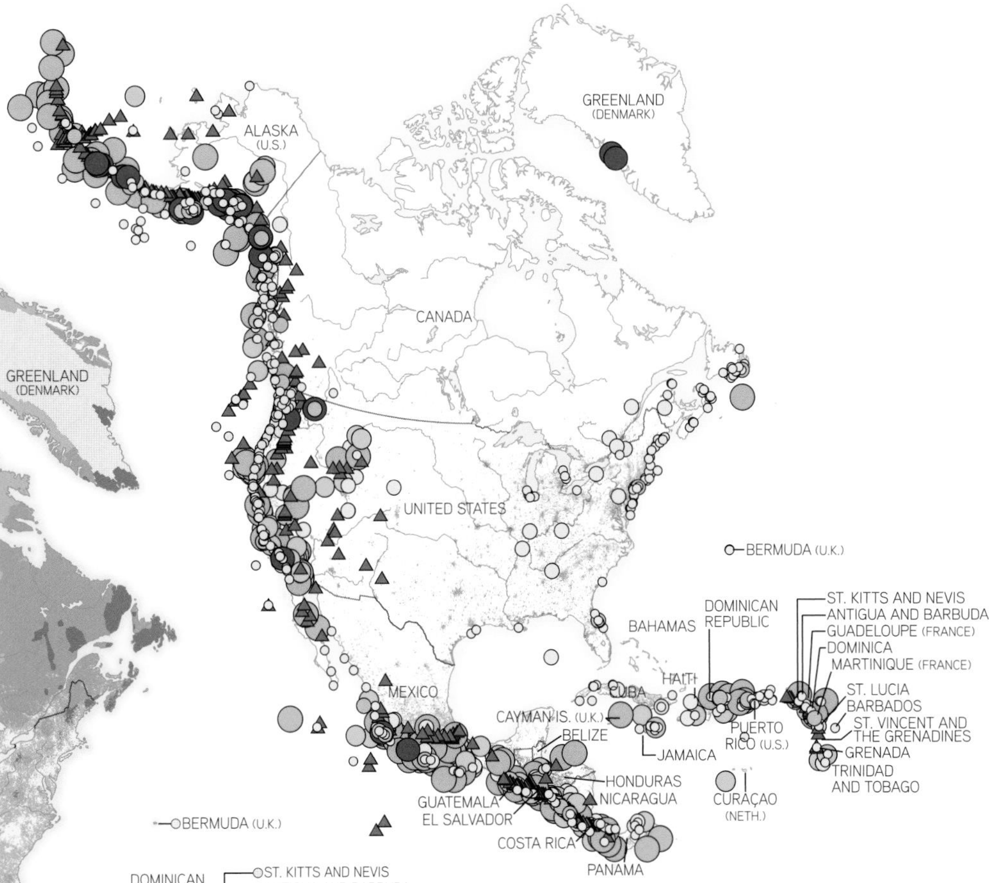

Population Density, 2010

People per square km		People per square mi
More than 1,000		More than 2,500
100–1,000		250–2,500
Less than 100		Less than 250

Fire Intensity
(from gas burn off, slash-and-burn agriculture, or natural causes)
High
Low

Recorded Natural Event

Major Earthquake, 1900-2010
Moment magnitude
- More than 7.0
- 6.0–7.0
- Less than 6.0

Volcano

Tsunami, 1900-2010
Run-up height

Meters	Feet
More than 10	More than 32
5–10	16–32
Less than 5	Less than 16

Water Availability

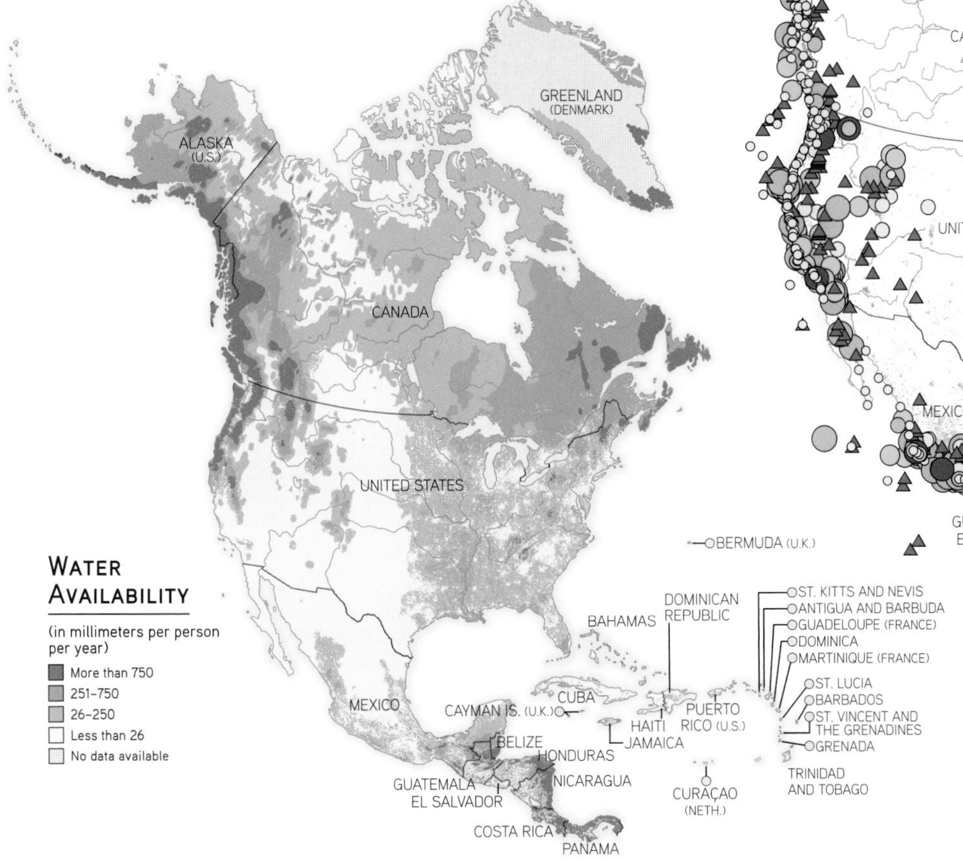

(in millimeters per person per year)
- More than 750
- 251–750
- 26–250
- Less than 26
- No data available

POPULATION PYRAMIDS

CANADA

Age
80+
60–64
40–44 Male   Female
20–24
0–4
10   5   0   5   10
Percent of population

HAITI

Age
80+
60–64
40–44 Male   Female
20–24
0–4
10   5   0   5   10
Percent of population

MEXICO

Age
80+
60–64
40–44 Male   Female
20–24
0–4
10   5   0   5   10
Percent of population

GREENLAND
(DENMARK)

ALASKA
(U.S.)

Nuuk
(Godthåb)

CANADA

Ottawa

UNITED STATES

Washington, D.C.

BERMUDA
(U. K.)

MARTINIQUE
(FRANCE)

DOMINICA

GUADELOUPE
(FRANCE)

ANTIGUA AND BARBUDA

ST. KITTS
AND NEVIS

PUERTO
RICO (U.S.)

BAHAMAS

Nassau

MEXICO

Havana

DOMINICAN REPUBLIC

San
Juan

CUBA

Santo
Domingo

CAYMAN
ISLANDS
(U. K.)

Kingston

Port-au-Prince

HAITI

ST. LUCIA

BARBADOS

Mexico
City

JAMAICA

ST. VINCENT AND THE GRENADINES

GRENADA

Port-of-Spain

Belmopan BELIZE

HONDURAS

Guatemala City

GUATEMALA

Tegucigalpa

CURAÇAO
(NETH.)

TRINIDAD AND
TOBAGO

San Salvador

EL SALVADOR

NICARAGUA

Managua

San José

Panama City

COSTA RICA

PANAMA

POPULATION
DENSITY

People per Square Kilometer	People per Square Mile
More than 195	More than 500
60–195	150–500
10–59	25–149
1–9	1–24
Less than 1	Less than 1

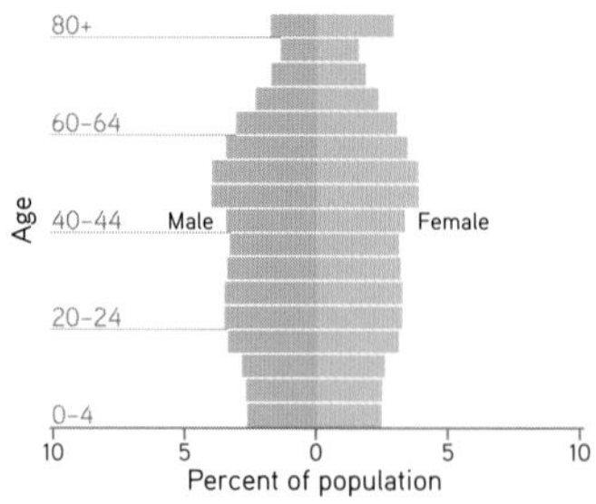

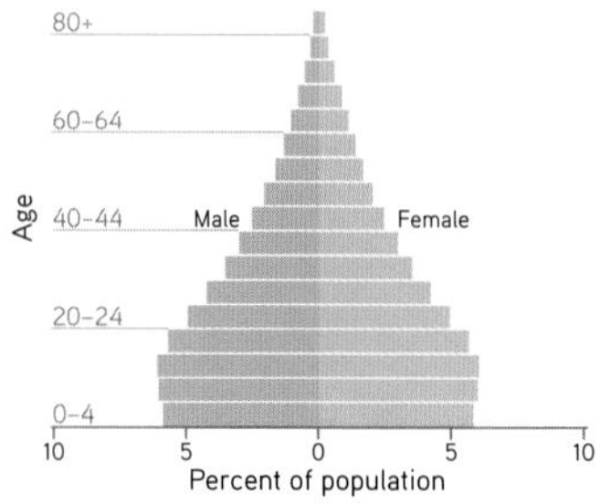

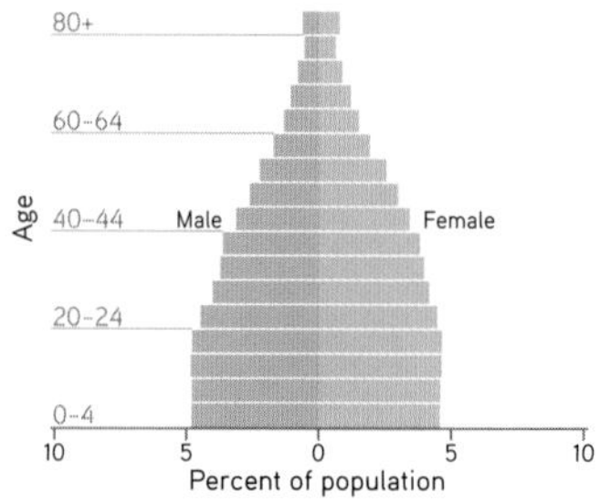

Indigenous Languages

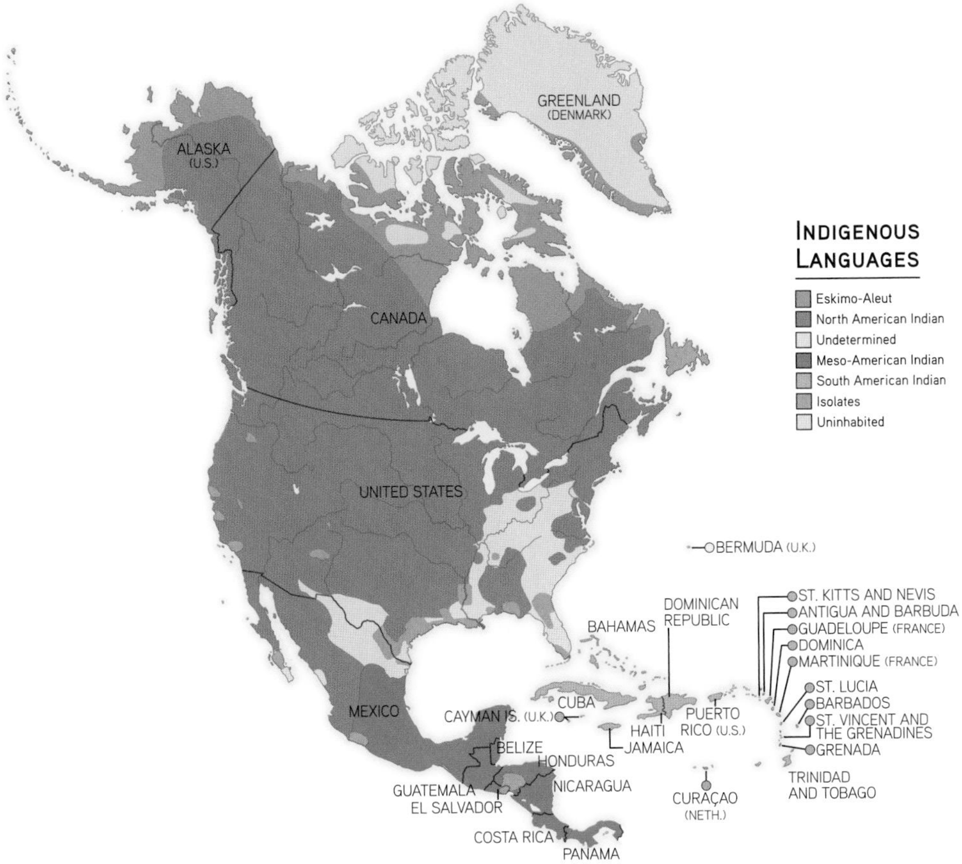

Urbanization

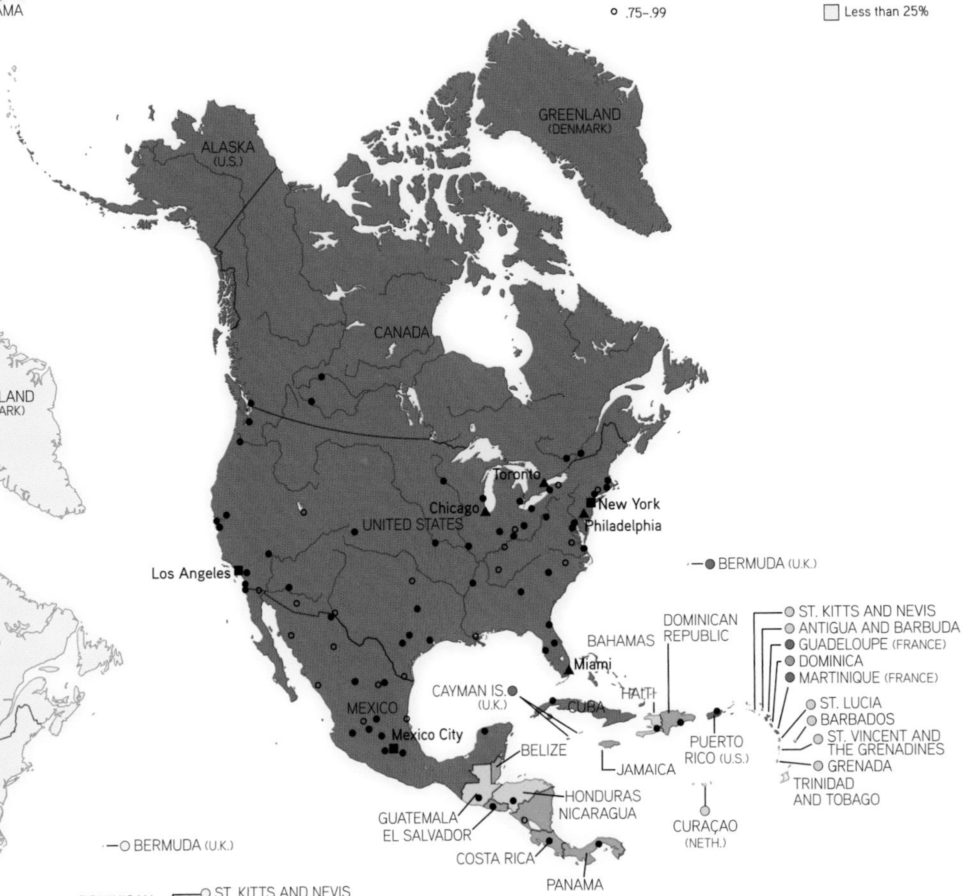

Population Change

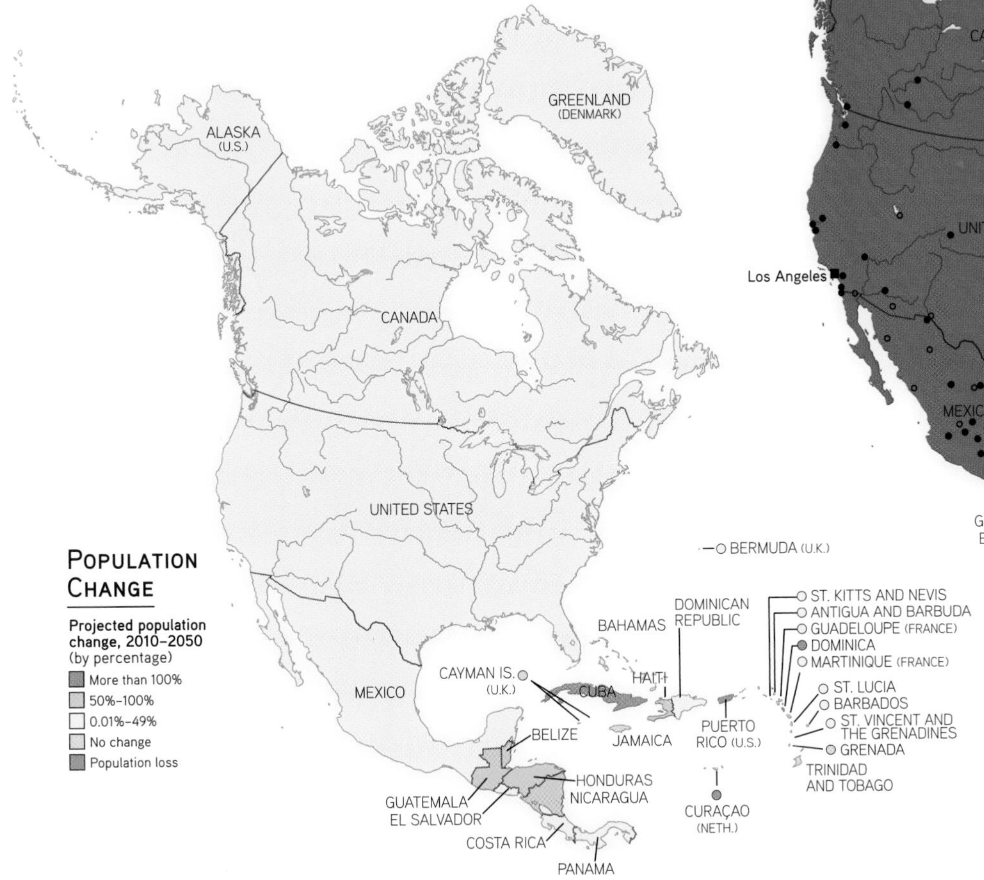

GREENLAND
(DENMARK)

Nuuk
(Godthåb)

ALASKA
(U.S.)

CANADA

IMPORTS AND EXPORTS

VALUE OF IMPORTS

UNITED STATES

Pharmaceutical products 3%
Chemical products 4%
Food 5%
Ores and metals 8%
Other 7%
Machinery and transport equipment 24%
Manufactured goods 18%
Electronic equipment 13%
Petroleum products 18%

CANADA

Pharmaceutical products 3%
Chemical products 4%
Ores and metals 7%
Food 7%
Other 10%
Machinery and transport equipment 31%
Manufactured goods 18%
Electronic equipment 10%
Petroleum products 10%

VALUE OF EXPORTS

UNITED STATES

Pharmaceutical products 3%
Chemical products 6%
Petroleum products 6%
Ores and metals 8%
Food 8%
Other 12%
Machinery and transport equipment 29%
Manufactured goods 16%
Electronic equipment 12%

CANADA

Wood products 4%
Chemical products 4%
Electronic equipment 4%
Manufactured goods 8%
Food 9%
Ores and metals 13%
Other 11%
Petroleum products 24%
Machinery and transport equipment 23%

Ottawa

UNITED STATES

Washington, D.C.

BERMUDA
(U. K.)

MARTINIQUE
(FRANCE)

DOMINICA

GUADELOUPE
(FRANCE)

ANTIGUA AND BARBUDA

ST. KITTS
AND NEVIS

BAHAMAS

PUERTO
RICO (U.S.)

DOMINICAN REPUBLIC

Nassau

Havana

MEXICO

CUBA

Santo
Domingo

San
Juan

CAYMAN
ISLANDS
(U. K.)

Kingston

Port-au-Prince

ST. LUCIA

BARBADOS

JAMAICA

HAITI

ST. VINCENT AND THE GRENADINES

Mexico City

GRENADA

Belmopan

BELIZE

HONDURAS

Port of
Spain

Guatemala City

Tegucigalpa

CURAÇAO
(NETH.)

TRINIDAD AND
TOBAGO

GUATEMALA

San Salvador

NICARAGUA

EL SALVADOR

Managua

LAND USE

More disturbed — Cropland

Less disturbed

More disturbed — Pasture

Built-up area

Irrigated land

San José

Panama City

COSTA RICA

PANAMA

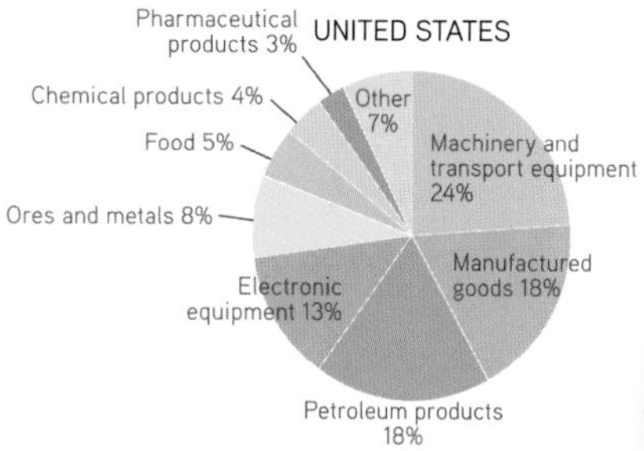

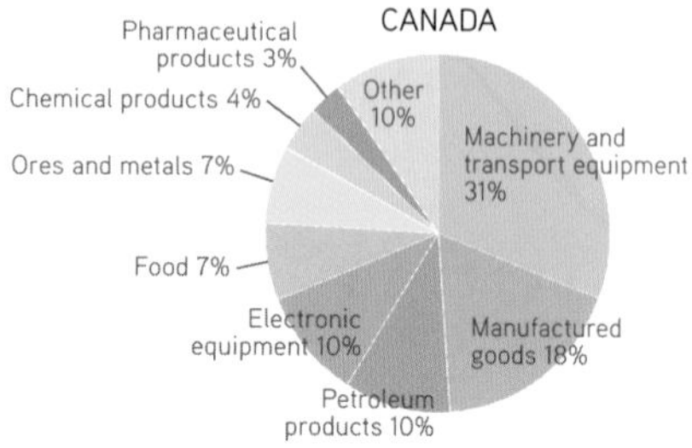

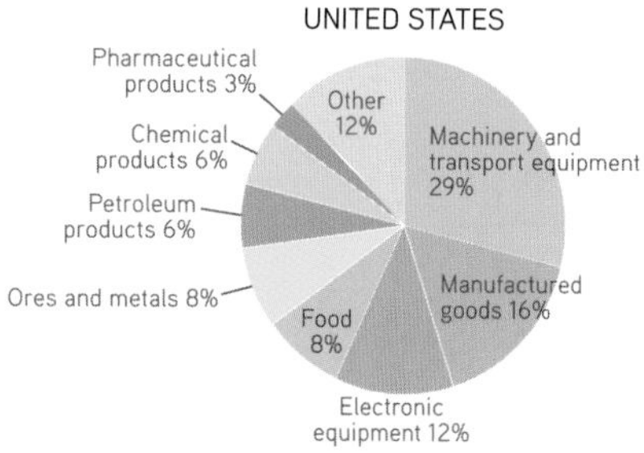

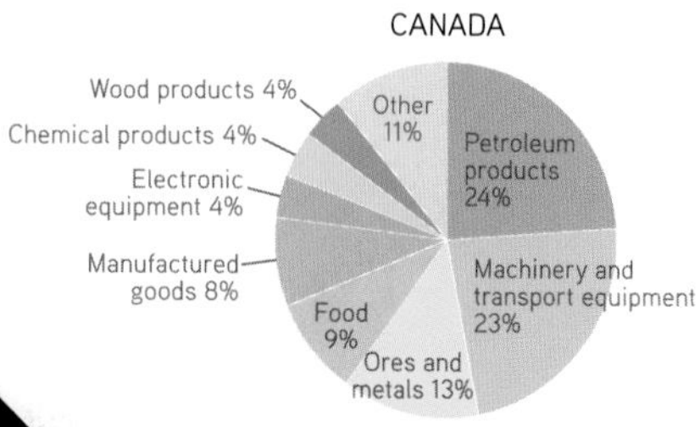

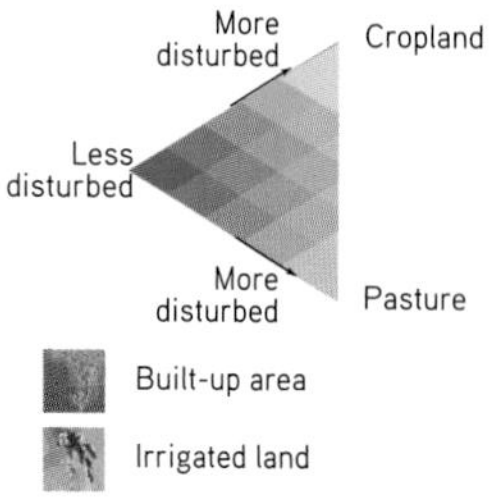

NORTH AMERICA'S ECONOMY

Service
100%

CAYMAN ISLANDS (U.K.)

BELIZE

TRINIDAD
AND TOBAGO

Agricultural
100%

Industrial
100%

per Gross Domestic Product
(GDP) sector

DOMINANT ECONOMY

(per GDP sector)

	Agriculture	Industry*	Services
70%–100%			
50%–69.9%			
0%–49.9%			

*Includes the mining industry

ALASKA (U.S.)

GREENLAND (DENMARK)

CANADA

UNITED STATES

BERMUDA (U.K.)

MEXICO

CAYMAN IS. (U.K.)

CUBA

HAITI

BAHAMAS

DOMINICAN REPUBLIC

BELIZE

JAMAICA

PUERTO RICO (U.S.)

ST. KITTS AND NEVIS
ANTIGUA AND BARBUDA
GUADELOUPE (FRANCE)
DOMINICA
MARTINIQUE (FRANCE)
ST. LUCIA
BARBADOS
ST. VINCENT AND THE GRENADINES
GRENADA

GUATEMALA
EL SALVADOR

HONDURAS
NICARAGUA

COSTA RICA

PANAMA

CURAÇAO (NETH.)

TRINIDAD AND TOBAGO

POVERTY

Percentage of population living
on less than $2 per day

	More than 80%
	60%–80%
	40%–59%
	20%–39%
	Less than 20%
	No data available

GREENLAND (DENMARK)

ALASKA (U.S.)

CANADA

UNITED STATES

BERMUDA (U.K.)

MEXICO

CAYMAN IS. (U.K.)

BAHAMAS

DOMINICAN REPUBLIC

HAITI

CUBA

BELIZE
HONDURAS

JAMAICA

PUERTO RICO (U.S.)

ST. KITTS AND NEVIS
ANTIGUA AND BARBUDA
GUADELOUPE (FRANCE)
DOMINICA
MARTINIQUE (FRANCE)
ST. LUCIA
BARBADOS
ST. VINCENT AND THE GRENADINES
GRENADA

GUATEMALA
EL SALVADOR

NICARAGUA

COSTA RICA

PANAMA

CURAÇAO (NETH.)

TRINIDAD AND TOBAGO

PER CAPITA ENERGY CONSUMPTION

(annual use, in million Btu)

	More than 300
	201–300
	101–200
	30–100
	Less than 30
	No data

Major energy deposit

	Coal
	Natural gas
	Oil
	Oil pipeline
	Oil transit chokepoint

ALASKA (U.S.)

GREENLAND (DENMARK)

CANADA

UNITED STATES

BERMUDA (U.K.)

MEXICO

CAYMAN IS. (U.K.)

CUBA

HAITI

BAHAMAS

DOMINICAN REPUBLIC

BELIZE
HONDURAS

JAMAICA

PUERTO RICO (U.S.)

ST. KITTS AND NEVIS
ANTIGUA AND BARBUDA
GUADELOUPE (FRANCE)
DOMINICA
MARTINIQUE (FRANCE)
ST. LUCIA
BARBADOS
ST. VINCENT AND THE GRENADINES
GRENADA

GUATEMALA
EL SALVADOR

NICARAGUA

COSTA RICA

PANAMA

CURAÇAO (NETH.)

TRINIDAD AND TOBAGO

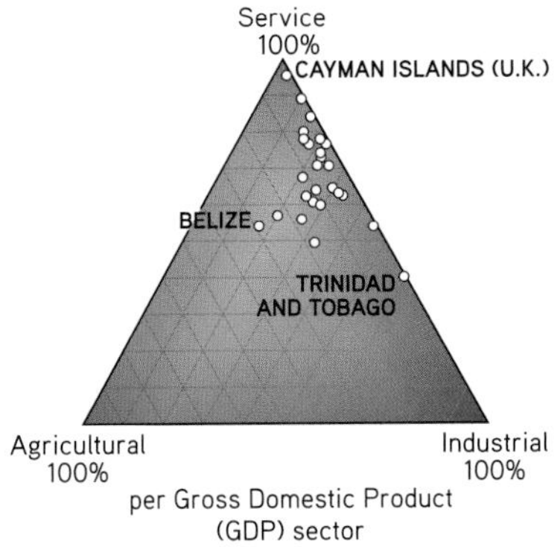

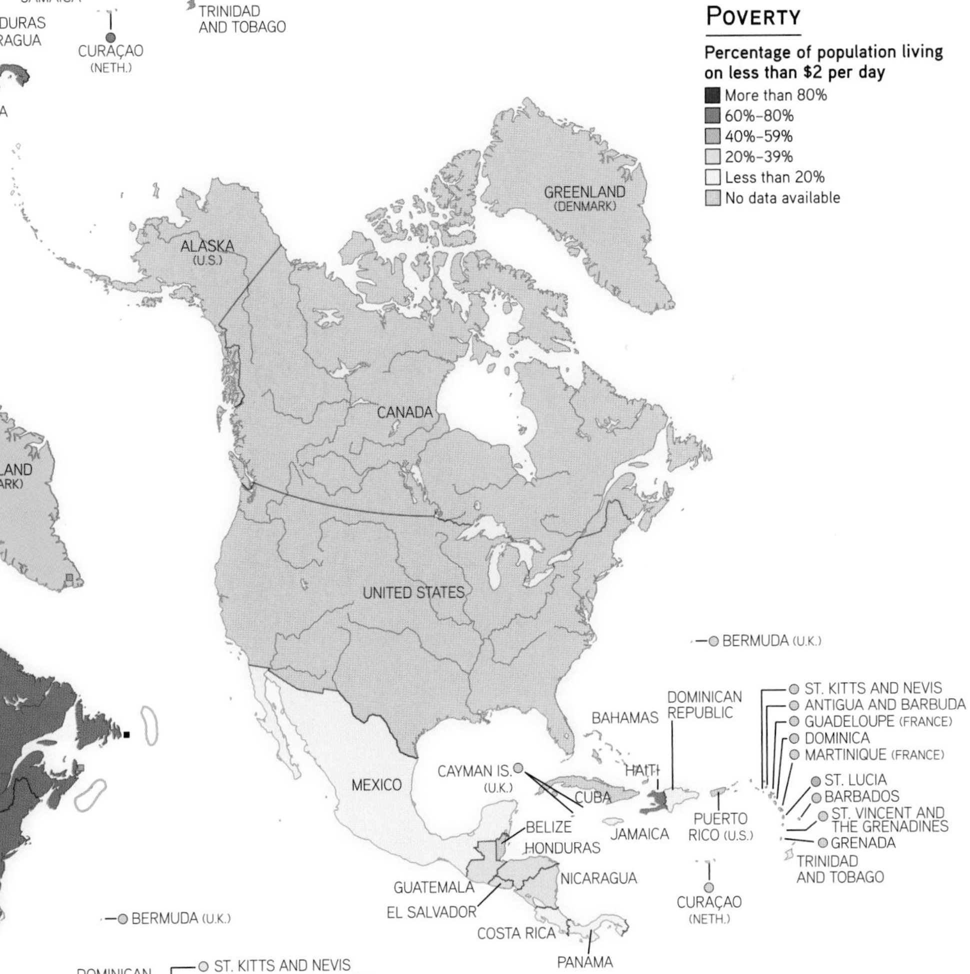

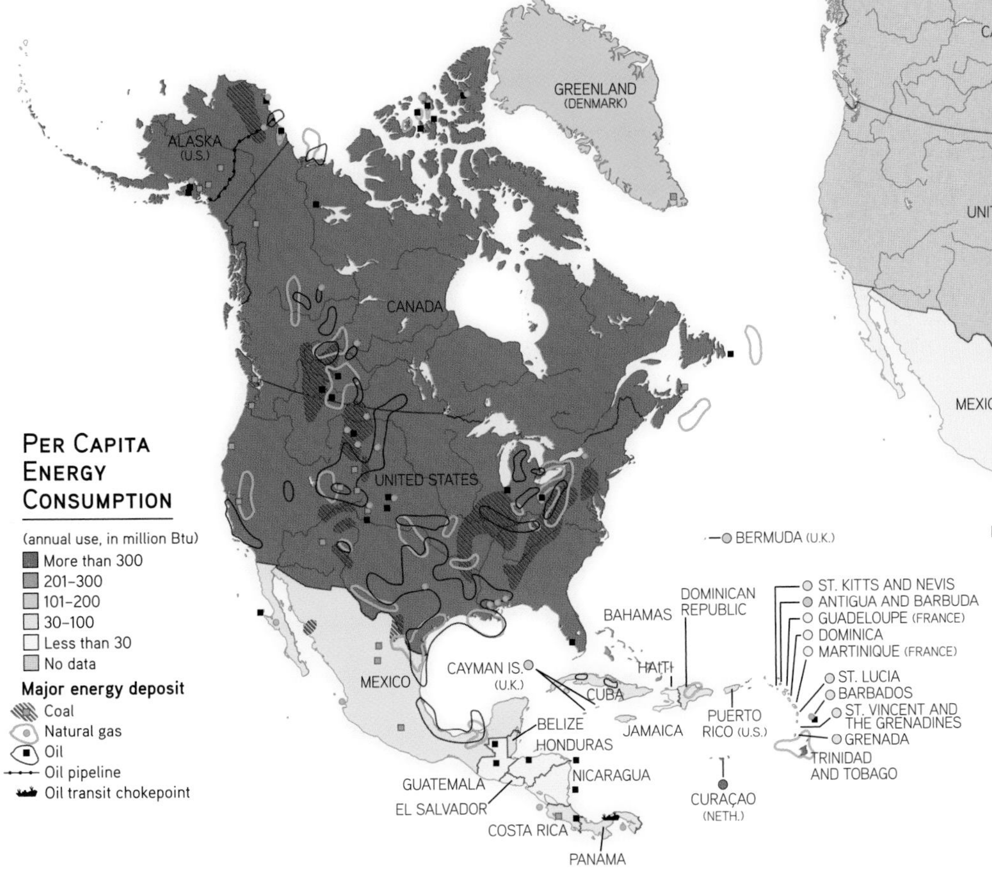

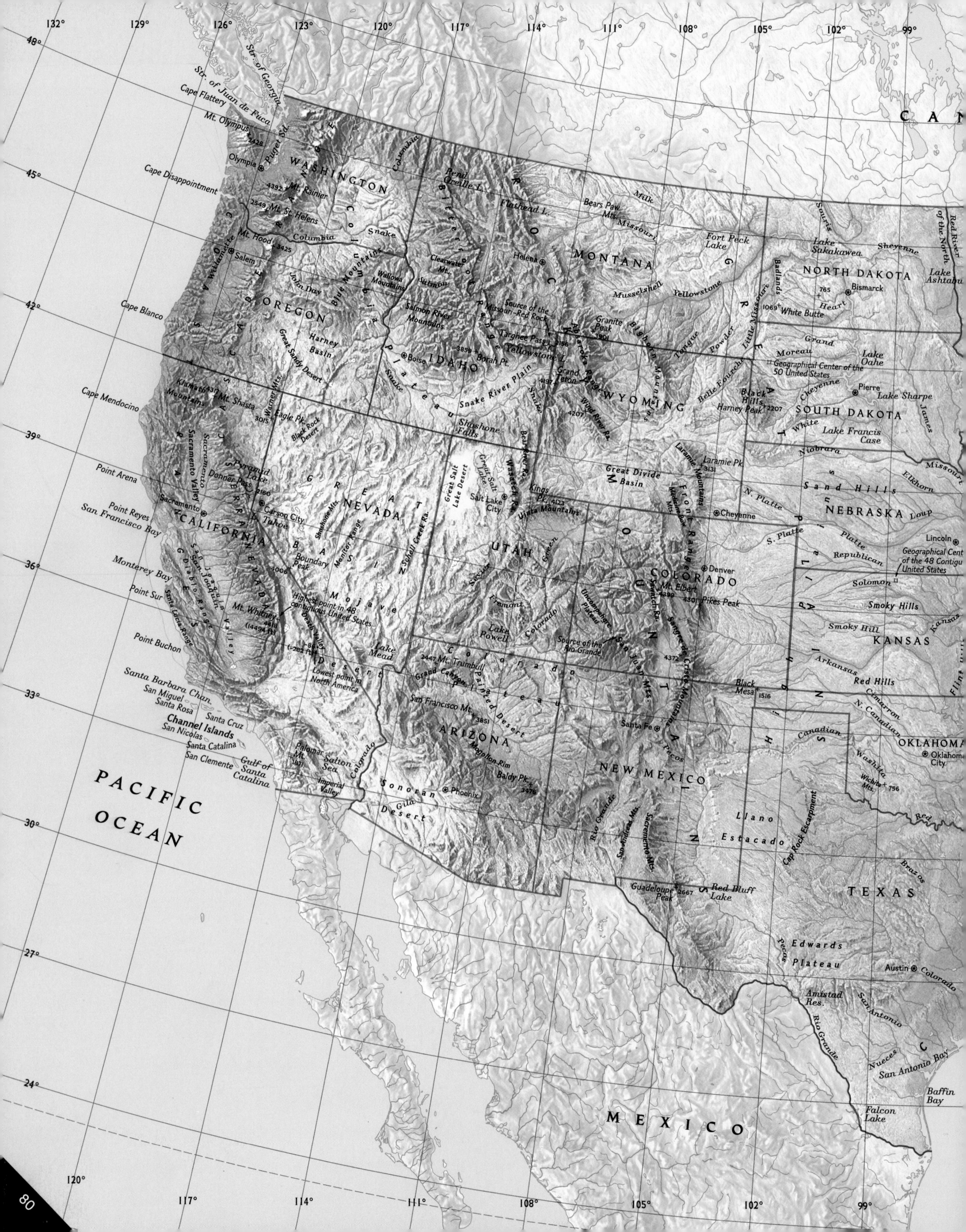
PACIFIC
OCEAN
MEXICO
CAN
WASHINGTON
OREGON
CALIFORNIA
NEVADA
IDAHO
MONTANA
WYOMING
UTAH
COLORADO
ARIZONA
NEW MEXICO
NORTH DAKOTA
SOUTH DAKOTA
NEBRASKA
KANSAS
OKLAHOMA
TEXAS
Str. of Georgia
Str. of Juan de Fuca
Cape Flattery
Mt. Olympus
Puget Sd.
Olympia
Cape Disappointment
Mt. Rainier
Mt. St. Helens
Mt. Hood
Salem
Columbia
Snake
Willamette
John Day
Blue Mountains
Wallowa Mountains
Cape Blanco
Harney Basin
Great Sandy Desert
Cape Mendocino
Klamath Mountains
Mt. Shasta
Warner Mts.
Eagle Pk.
Black Rock Desert
Point Arena
Pyramid Lake
Donner Pass
Sacramento
Sacramento Valley
Carson City
L. Tahoe
Point Reyes
San Francisco Bay
Monterey Bay
Point Sur
Diablo Range
Santa Lucia Range
San Joaquin Valley
Mt. Whitney
Highest point in 48 contiguous United States
Death Valley
Lowest point in North America
Boundary Peak
Point Buchon
Santa Barbara Chan.
San Miguel
Santa Rosa
Santa Cruz
Channel Islands
San Nicolas
Santa Catalina
San Clemente
Gulf of Santa Catalina
Palomar Mt.
Salton Sea
Imperial Valley
Mojave Desert
Lake Mead
Colorado
Shoshone Mts.
Monitor Range
Schell Creek Ra.
Great Salt Lake Desert
Great Salt Lake
Salt Lake City
Wasatch Ra.
Bear River Ra.
Kings Pk.
Uinta Mountains
Sevier
Fremont
Lake Powell
Green
Mt. Trumbull
Grand Canyon
Painted Desert
San Francisco Mt.
Mogollon Rim
Baldy Pk.
Phoenix
Gila
Sonoran Desert
Colorado Plateau
Pend Oreille L.
Bitterroot Range
Clearwater Mts.
Salmon
Salmon River Mountains
Boise
Borah Pt.
Snake River Plain
Shoshone Falls
Targhee Pass
Yellowstone L.
Grand Teton
Source of the Missouri–Red Rock
Flathead L.
Helena
Bears Paw Mts.
Milk
Missouri
Musselshell
Yellowstone
Granite Peak
Absaroka Range
Bighorn Mountains
Wind River Ra.
Tongue
Powder
Belle Fourche
Little Missouri
Fort Peck Lake
Great Divide Basin
Laramie Mountains
Laramie Pk.
Medicine Bow Mts.
Front Range
Cheyenne
Denver
Mt. Elbert
Pikes Peak
Sawatch Ra.
Uncompahgre Plateau
Source of the Rio Grande
San Juan Mts.
Sangre de Cristo Mountains
Santa Fe
Pecos
Rio Grande
San Andres Mts.
Sacramento Mts.
Guadalupe Peak
Red Bluff Lake
Llano Estacado
Cap Rock Escarpment
Black Mesa
ROCKY MOUNTAINS
GREAT PLAINS
GREAT BASIN
CASCADE RANGE
SIERRA NEVADA
Lake Sakakawea
Sheyenne
Souris
Red River of the North
Lake Ashtabula
Bismarck
Badlands
White Butte
Heart
Grand
Moreau
Lake Oahe
Geographical Center of the 50 United States
Cheyenne
Pierre
Lake Sharpe
James
Black Hills
Harney Peak
White
Lake Francis Case
Niobrara
Missouri
Elkhorn
Sand Hills
N. Platte
S. Platte
Platte
Loup
Lincoln
Geographical Center of the 48 Contiguous United States
Republican
Solomon
Smoky Hills
Smoky Hill
Kansas
Arkansas
Red Hills
Cimarron
N. Canadian
Canadian
Washita
Wichita Mts.
Oklahoma City
Red
Flint
Brazos
Edwards Plateau
Austin
Colorado
Amistad Res.
San Antonio
Nueces
San Antonio Bay
Baffin Bay
Falcon Lake
Pecos
Rio Grande

93° 90° 87° 84° 81° 78° 75° 72°

45°

C A N A D A

Lake of the Woods

Upper Red L.

Lower Red L.

Eagle Mt. 701 Isle Royale

Mesabi Ra. Keweenaw Peninsula

Lake Superior

Leech Lake

Source of the Mississippi

MINNESOTA

Mille Lacs L.

Upper Peninsula

Strs. of Mackinac

Georgian Bay

Mt. Katahdin 1606

Moosehead Lake

MAINE

Mt. Desert I.

Augusta

Mt. Washington 1917

Mt. Mansfield 1339 White Mts. N.H.

Lake Champlain Mt. Marcy 1629

Adirondack Mountains Green Mountain

Gulf of Maine

Concord

Boston

Providence R.I. Cape Cod

Nantucket I.

Martha's Vineyard

Menominee

St. Paul

Timms Hill 595

Wolf

MICHIGAN

Lower Peninsula

Muskegon

Saginaw Bay

Lake Huron

Lake Ontario

Niagara Falls

Finger Lakes

NEW YORK

Albany

MASS.

CONN. R.I.

Hartford

Merrimack

Connecticut

Long Island Sd.

WISCONSIN

Lake Winnebago

Madison

Grand Lansing

Lake Michigan

Lake St. Clair

Lake Erie

Catskill Mountains

Hudson

New York

Long Island

Mississippi

Wisconsin

376

Charles Mound

Maumee

Allegheny

PENNSYLVANIA

Harrisburg Susquehanna

Trenton

NEW JERSEY

Pine Barrens

IOWA

Des Moines

Cedar

Iowa

C E N T R A L

Rock

Campbell Hill 472

OHIO

Columbus

Scioto

Mt. Davis 1024

MARYLAND

Washington D.C.

Annapolis Dover

DEL.

Delaware Bay

Chincoteague Bay

Des Moines

ILLINOIS

Springfield

Illinois

L O W L A N D

INDIANA

Indianapolis

Wabash

Gt. Miami

Ohio

WEST VIRGINIA

Charleston

VIRGINIA

Richmond

James

Chesapeake Bay

Potomac

Cape Charles

Topeka

Kaskaskia

Kentucky

Frankfort

Ohio

Great Dismal Swamp

Jefferson City Missouri

Osage

Harry S. Truman Res.

Lake of the Ozarks

MISSOURI 540

Taum Sauk Mt.

KENTUCKY

Lake Cumberland

Black Mt. 1263

Clinch

Roanoke

Raleigh

NORTH CAROLINA

Neuse

Tar

Albemarle Sound

Pamlico Sound

Cape Hatteras

Ozark Plateau

Kentucky Lake

Lake Barkley

Cumberland

Nashville

TENNESSEE

Clingmans Dome 2025

Great Smoky

Mt. Mitchell 2037

ATLANTIC

OCEAN

33°

Boston Mountains

Magazine Mt. 839

Little Rock

White

St. Francis

Woodall Mountain

Tennessee

Coosa

Atlanta

SOUTH CAROLINA

Columbia

Cape Lookout

Cape Fear

Pee Dee

Santee

Ouachita Mountains

Lake Ouachita

ARKANSAS

Black

Cheaha Mt. 734

GEORGIA

Savannah

Pee Dee

30°

Driskill Mt. 163

Yazoo

MISSISSIPPI

Jackson

Tombigbee

ALABAMA

Montgomery

Alabama

Ocmulgee

Oconee

Chattahoochee

Altamaha

Sea Islands

Sulphur

Ouachita

Saline

Red

Pearl

L. Seminole

Okefenokee Swamp

Sabine

Sam Rayburn Res.

LOUISIANA

Baton Rouge

Lake Pontchartrain

Mobile Bay

Pensacola Bay

Cape San Blas

Apalachee Bay

Suwannee

Tallahassee

FLORIDA

Cape Canaveral

27°

Galveston Bay

Marsh I.

Timbalier Bay

Mississippi Sd.

Breton Sound

Mississippi River Delta

Gulf of Mexico

Tampa Bay

Kissimmee

Peace

Lake Okeechobee

Charlotte Harbor

Cape Romano

Biscayne Bay

The Everglades

BAHAMAS

24°

TROPIC OF CANCER

Cape Sable

Dry Tortugas Marquesas Keys Florida Keys

Straits of Florida

72°

LAMBERT CONFORMAL CONIC PROJECTION

SCALE 1:12,000,000

0 KILOMETERS 200 300

0 MILES 100 200 300

PACIFIC
OCEAN
TROPIC OF CANCER
BRITISH COLUMBIA
ALBERTA
SASKATCHEWAN
MANITOBA
WASHINGTON
OREGON
IDAHO
MONTANA
NORTH DAKOTA
SOUTH DAKOTA
WYOMING
NEVADA
UTAH
COLORADO
CALIFORNIA
ARIZONA
NEW MEXICO
NEBRASKA
KANSAS
OKLAHOMA
TEXAS
MEXICO
BAJA CALIFORNIA
BAJA CALIFORNIA SUR
SONORA
CHIHUAHUA
COAHUILA
NUEVO LEÓN
DURANGO
SINALOA
ZACATECAS
TAMAULIPAS
Vancouver
Calgary
Regina
Winnipeg
Seattle
Portland
Boise
Salt Lake City
Denver
Las Vegas
Los Angeles
San Francisco
San Diego
Phoenix
Albuquerque
El Paso
Tucson
Oklahoma City
Fort Worth
San Antonio
Chihuahua
Monterrey
Tijuana
Mexicali
Hermosillo
Pacific Ocean
132°
129°
126°
123°
120°
117°
114°
111°
108°
105°
102°
99°
48°
45°
42°
39°
36°
33°
30°
27°
24°

LAMBERT CONFORMAL CONIC PROJECTION
SCALE 1:12,000,000
0 KILOMETERS 200 300
0 MILES 100 200 300
Longitude West 90° of Greenwich
ATLANTIC OCEAN
Gulf of Mexico
TROPIC OF CANCER
BAHAMAS
ONTARIO
QUEBEC
NEW BRUNSWICK
NOVA SCOTIA
P.E.I.
MAINE
VERMONT
NEW HAMPSHIRE
MASSACHUSETTS
RHODE ISLAND
CONNECTICUT
NEW YORK
PENNSYLVANIA
NEW JERSEY
DELAWARE
MARYLAND
WEST VIRGINIA
VIRGINIA
NORTH CAROLINA
SOUTH CAROLINA
GEORGIA
FLORIDA
ALABAMA
MISSISSIPPI
LOUISIANA
ARKANSAS
TENNESSEE
KENTUCKY
OHIO
INDIANA
ILLINOIS
MICHIGAN
WISCONSIN
IOWA
MISSOURI
Lake Superior
Lake Michigan
Lake Huron
Lake Erie
Lake Ontario
NEW YORK
Washington
Boston
Philadelphia
Baltimore
Chicago
Detroit
Toronto
Montréal
Ottawa
Québec
Atlanta
Miami
New Orleans
Memphis
Nashville
Pittsburgh
Cleveland
Jacksonville
Houston

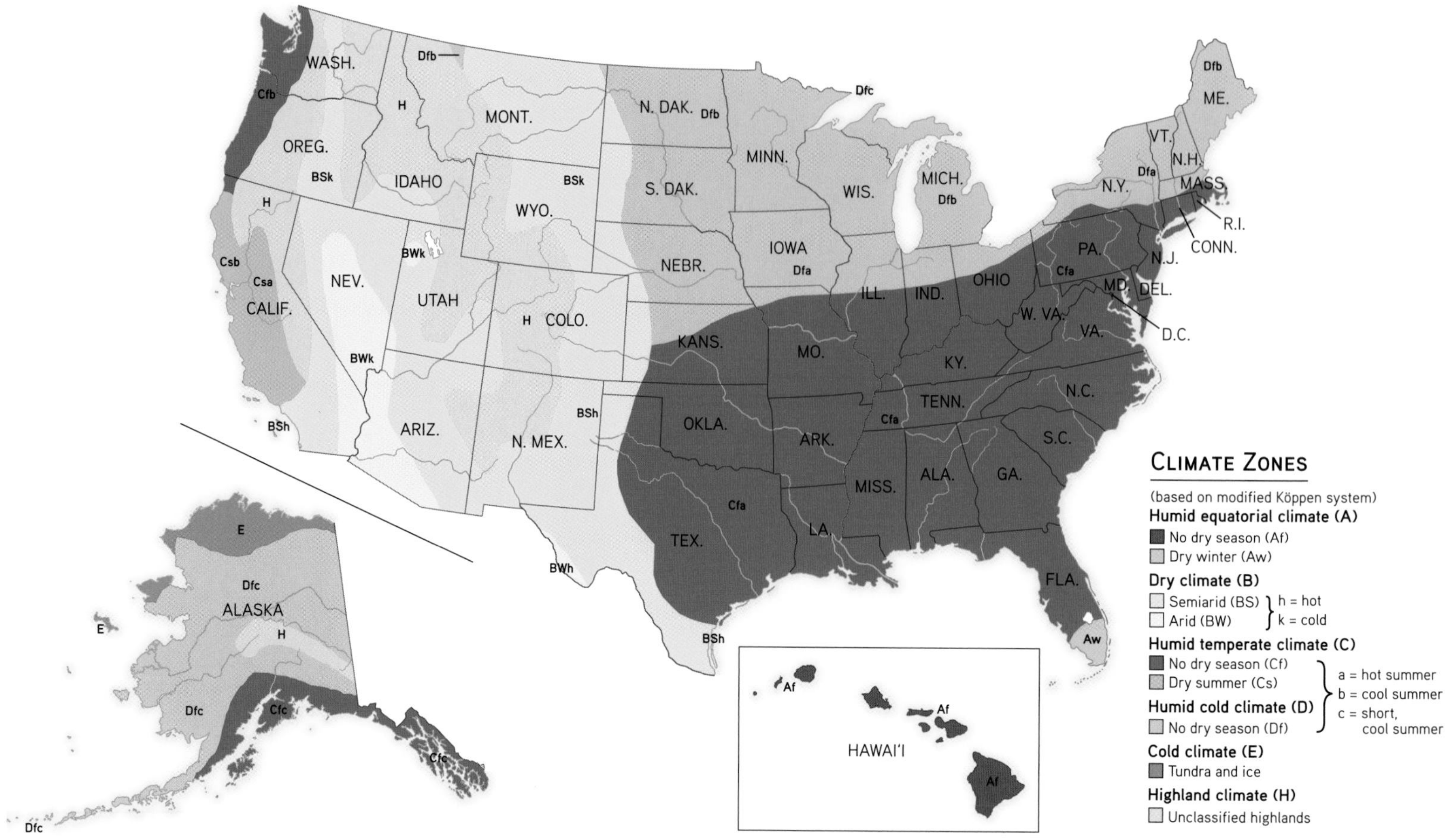

Climate Zones
(based on modified Köppen system)
Humid equatorial climate (A)
No dry season (Af)
Dry winter (Aw)
Dry climate (B)
Semiarid (BS)
Arid (BW)
h = hot
k = cold
Humid temperate climate (C)
No dry season (Cf)
Dry summer (Cs)
a = hot summer
b = cool summer
c = short, cool summer
Humid cold climate (D)
No dry season (Df)
Cold climate (E)
Tundra and ice
Highland climate (H)
Unclassified highlands
WASH.
OREG.
CALIF.
NEV.
IDAHO
MONT.
WYO.
UTAH
COLO.
ARIZ.
N. MEX.
N. DAK.
S. DAK.
NEBR.
KANS.
OKLA.
TEX.
MINN.
IOWA
MO.
ARK.
LA.
WIS.
ILL.
MICH.
IND.
OHIO
KY.
TENN.
MISS.
ALA.
GA.
FLA.
S.C.
N.C.
VA.
W. VA.
MD.
DEL.
D.C.
PA.
N.J.
N.Y.
CONN.
R.I.
MASS.
VT.
N.H.
ME.
ALASKA
HAWAI'I
Cfb
Csb
Csa
BSk
BSh
BWk
BWh
H
Dfb
Dfc
Dfa
Cfa
Aw
Af
E
Cfc

Water Availability
(in millimeters per person per year)
More than 750
251–750
26–250
Less than 26
No data available
WASH.
OREG.
CALIF.
NEV.
IDAHO
MONT.
WYO.
UTAH
COLO.
ARIZ.
N. MEX.
N. DAK.
S. DAK.
NEBR.
KANS.
OKLA.
TEX.
MINN.
IOWA
MO.
ARK.
LA.
WIS.
ILL.
MICH.
IND.
OHIO
KY.
TENN.
MISS.
ALA.
GA.
FLA.
S.C.
N.C.
VA.
W. VA.
MD.
DEL.
D.C.
PA.
N.J.
N.Y.
CONN.
R.I.
MASS.
VT.
N.H.
ME.
ALASKA
HAWAI'I

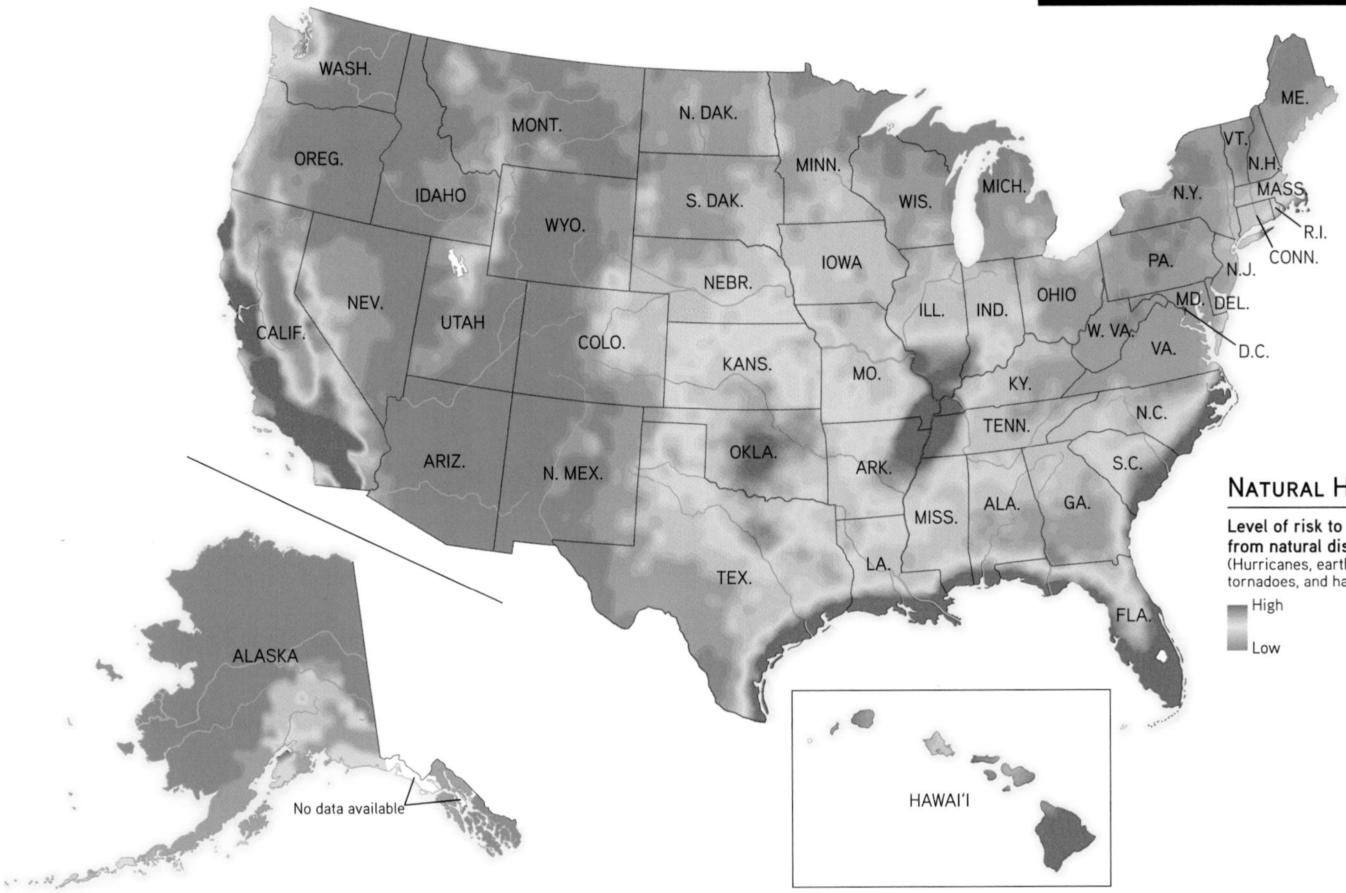

NATURAL HAZARDS

Level of risk to property from natural disasters
(Hurricanes, earthquakes, tornadoes, and hailstorms)

High
Low

NATIONAL PARKS AND RESERVES

- National Park System
- National Forest
- National Wildlife Refuge
- National Grassland
- Bureau of Land Management
- Indian Reservation / Alaskan Native Land
- Military Reservation
- Department of Energy
- National Marine Sanctuary

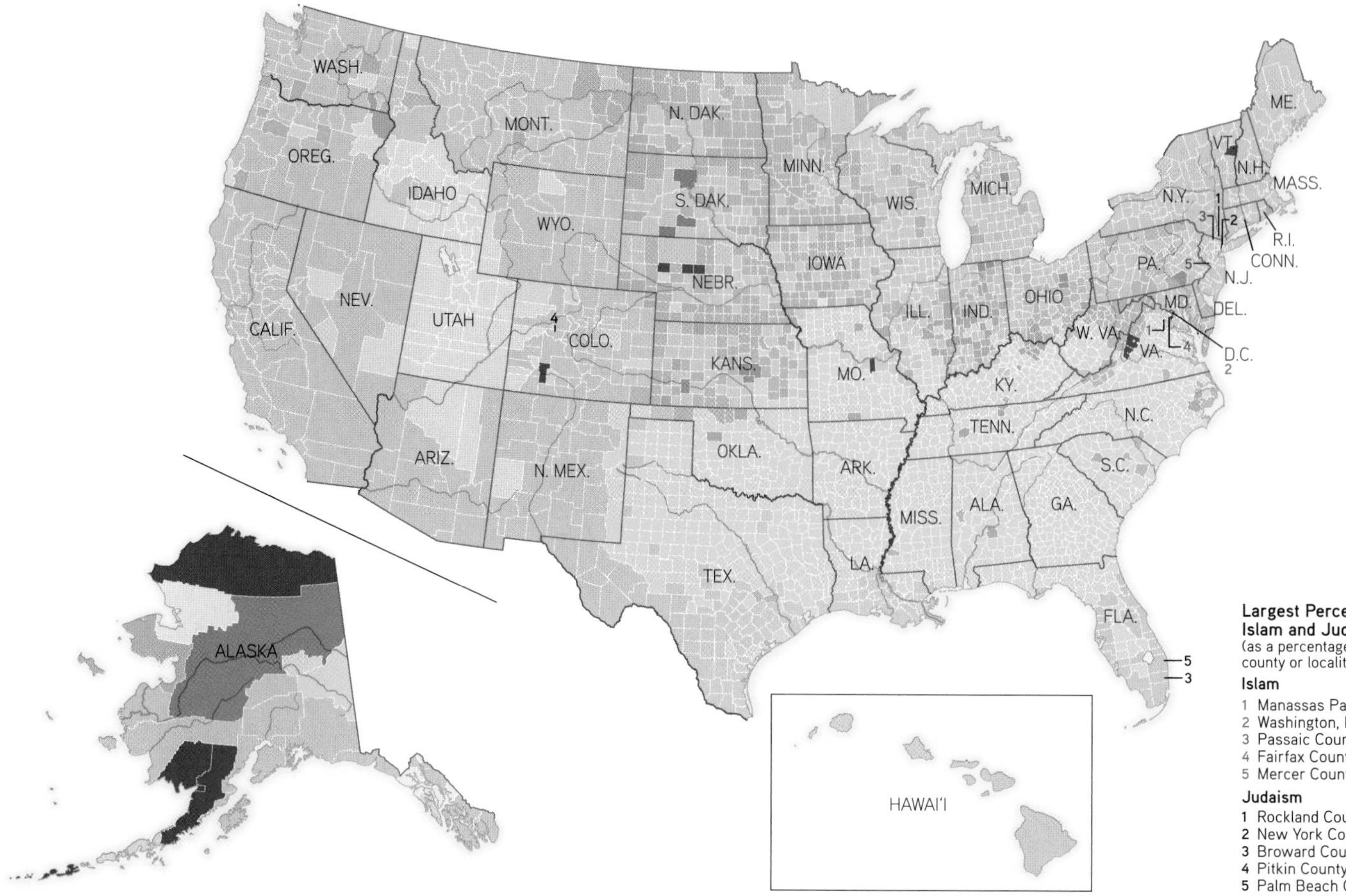

Religion

Most Prevalent Religious Group, 2000
(by county or locality)

- Adventist
- Anglican
- Baptist
- Christian Church and Churches of Christ
- Islam
- Latter-Day Saints
- Lutheran
- Mennonite
- Methodist
- Orthodox
- Pentecostal
- Presbyterian
- Reformed
- Roman Catholic
- United Church of Christ
- Other

Largest Percentage of Adherents to Islam and Judaism, 2000 Estimates
(as a percentage of total adherents by county or locality)

Islam

1	Manassas Park City, VA.	59%
2	Washington, D.C.	14%
3	Passaic County, N.J.	9%
4	Fairfax County, VA.	8%
5	Mercer County, N.J.	7%

Judaism

1	Rockland County, N.Y.	38%
2	New York County, N.Y.	29%
3	Broward County, FLA.	29%
4	Pitkin County, COLO.	27%
5	Palm Beach County, FLA.	26%

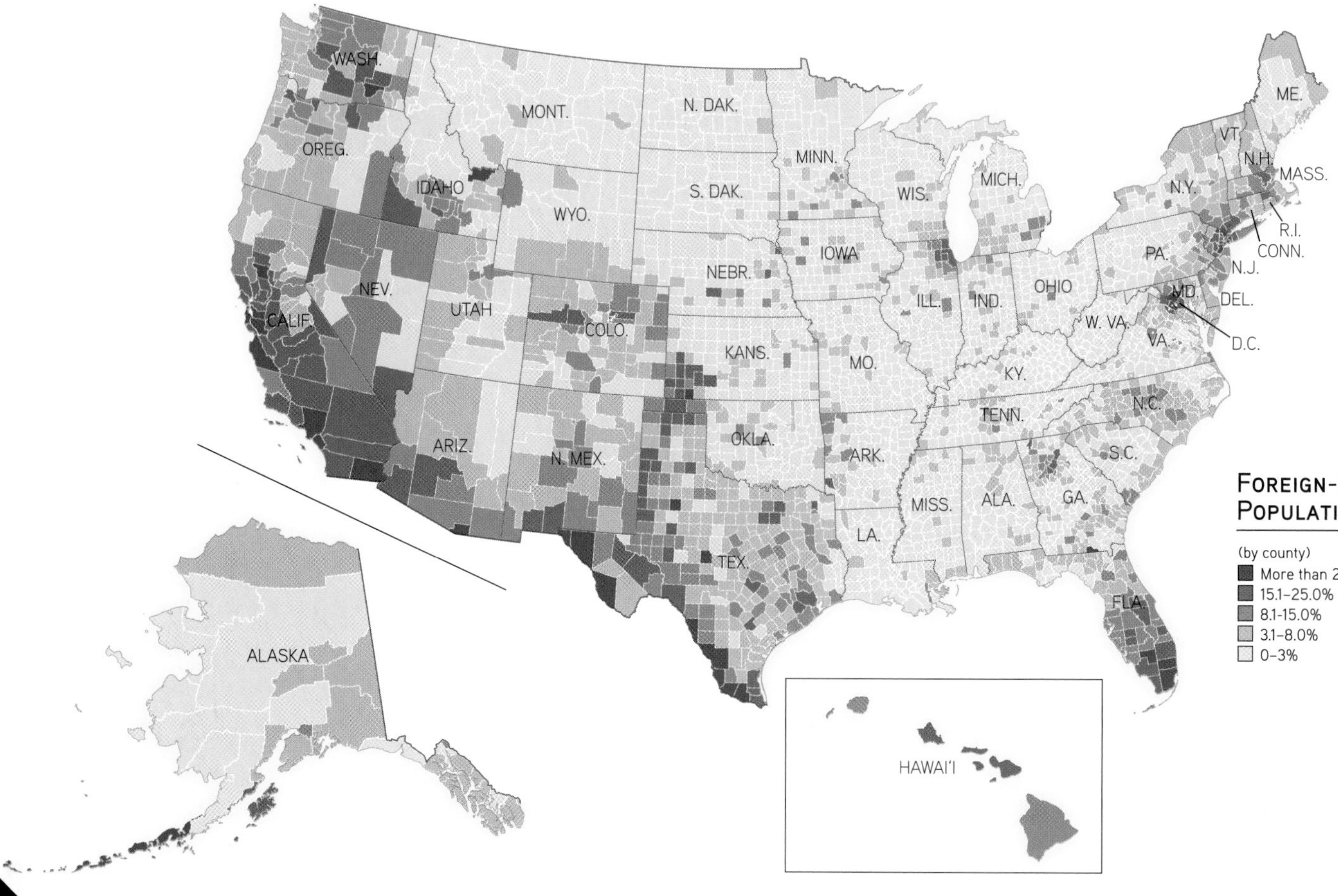

Foreign-Born Population

(by county)

- More than 25.0%
- 15.1–25.0%
- 8.1–15.0%
- 3.1–8.0%
- 0–3%

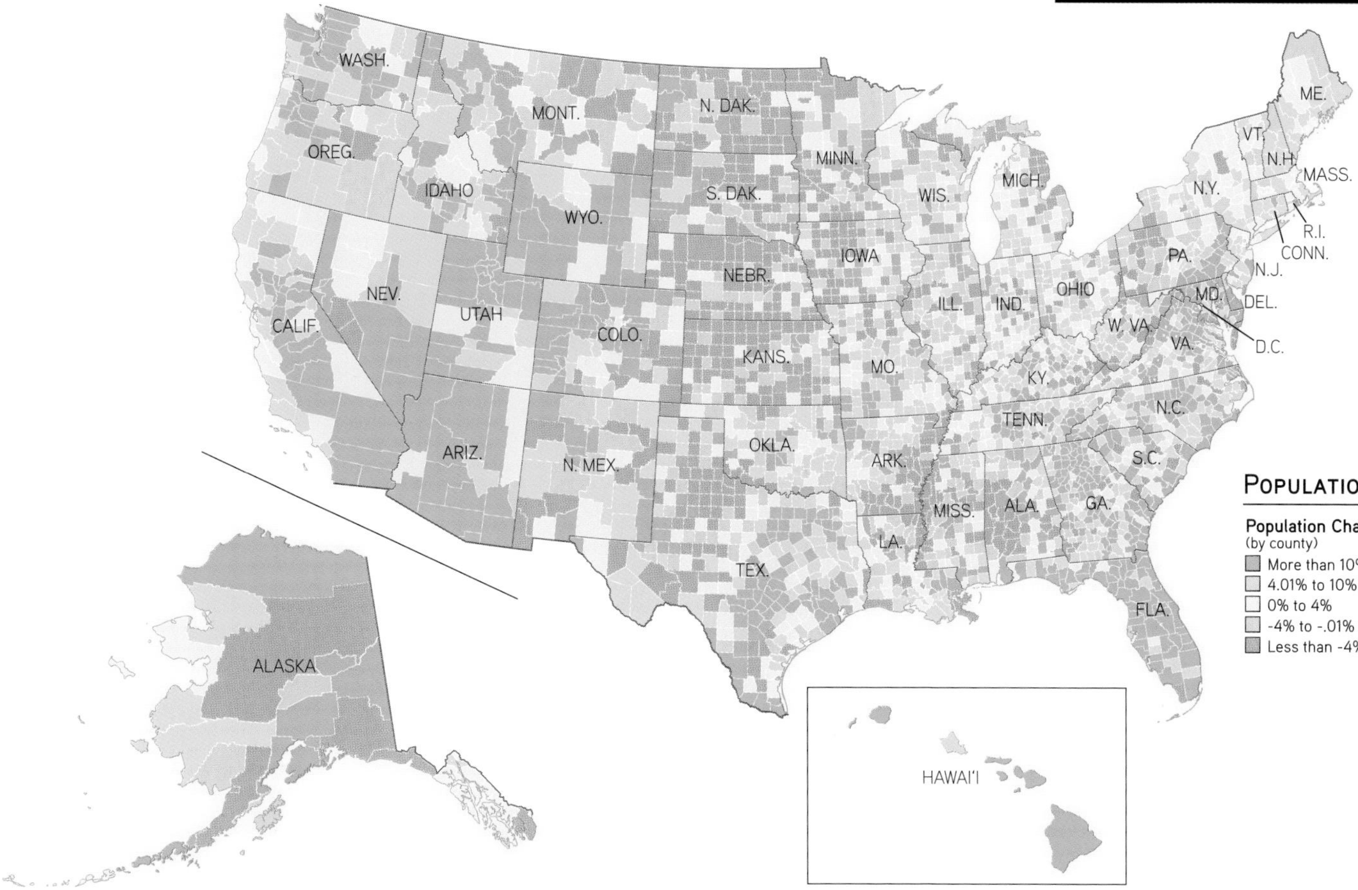

Population Change

Population Change 2000–10
(by county)

- More than 10%
- 4.01% to 10%
- 0% to 4%
- -4% to -.01%
- Less than -4%

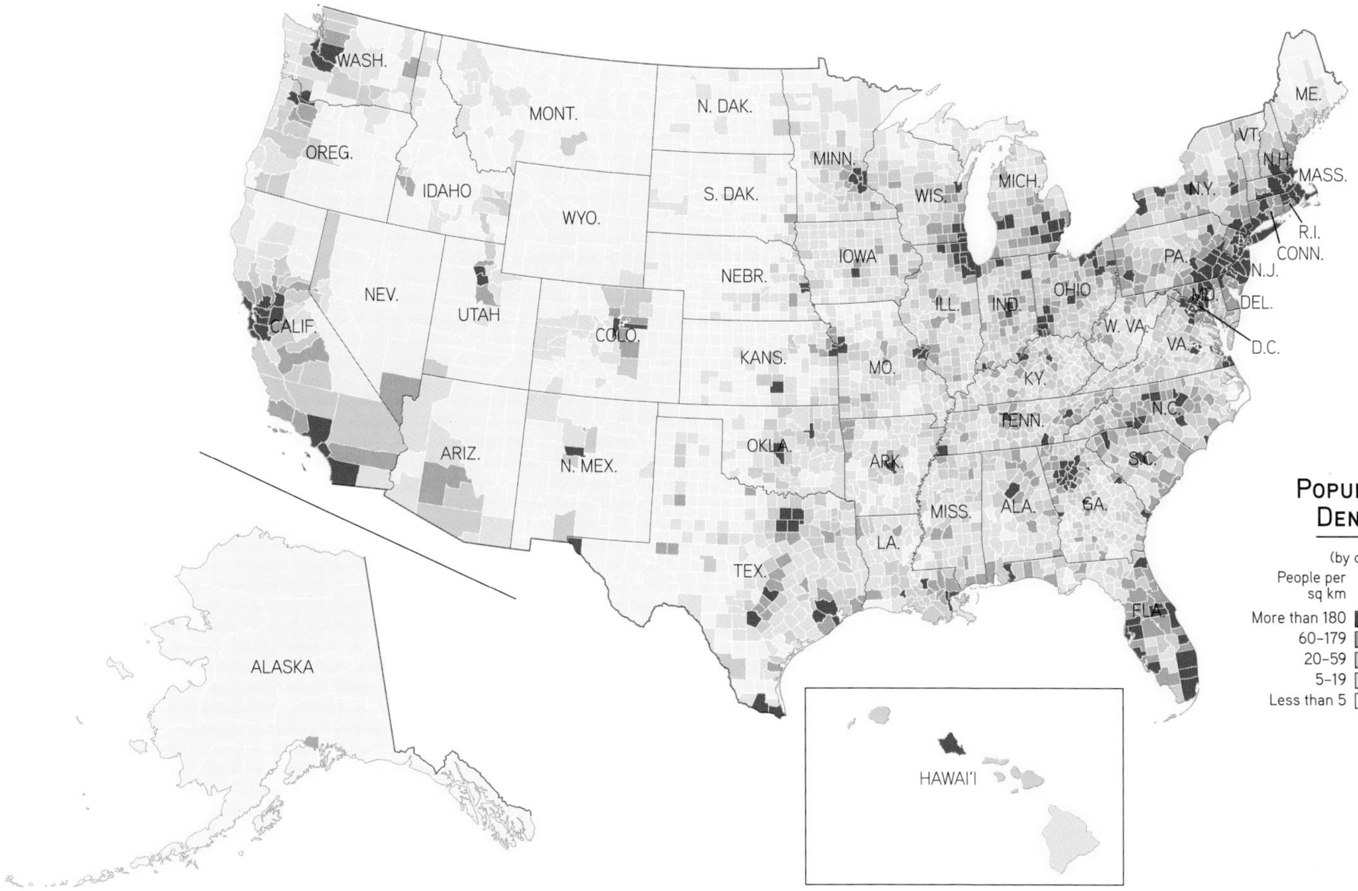

Population Density

(by county)

People per sq km	People per sq mi
More than 180	More than 450
60–179	150–449
20–59	50–149
5–19	15–49
Less than 5	Less than 15

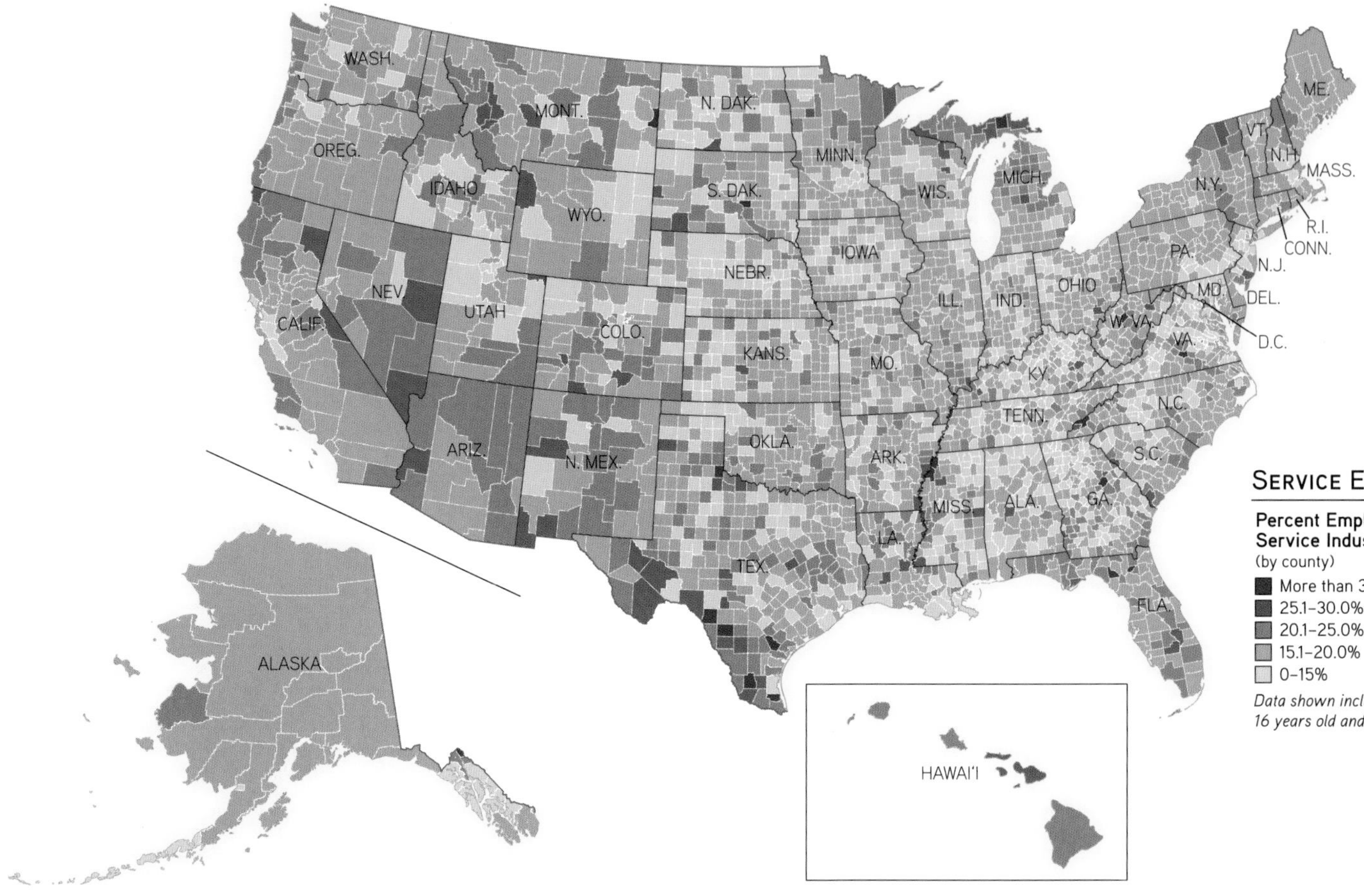

Service Employment

Percent Employed in the Service Industry, 2009
(by county)

- More than 30%
- 25.1–30.0%
- 20.1–25.0%
- 15.1–20.0%
- 0–15%

Data shown includes only civilians 16 years old and older.

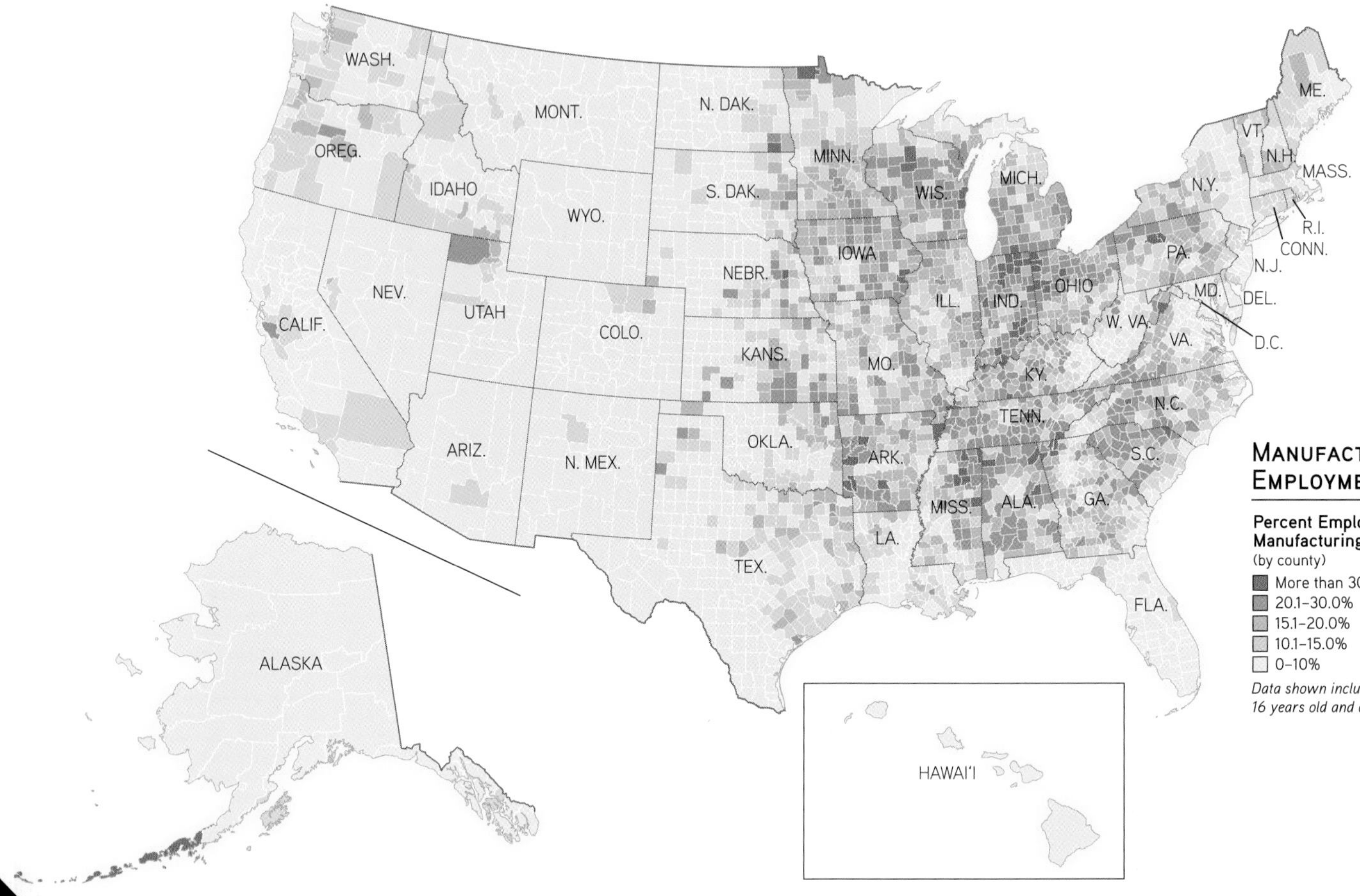

Manufacturing Employment

Percent Employed in the Manufacturing Industry, 2009
(by county)

- More than 30%
- 20.1–30.0%
- 15.1–20.0%
- 10.1–15.0%
- 0–10%

Data shown includes only civilians 16 years old and older.

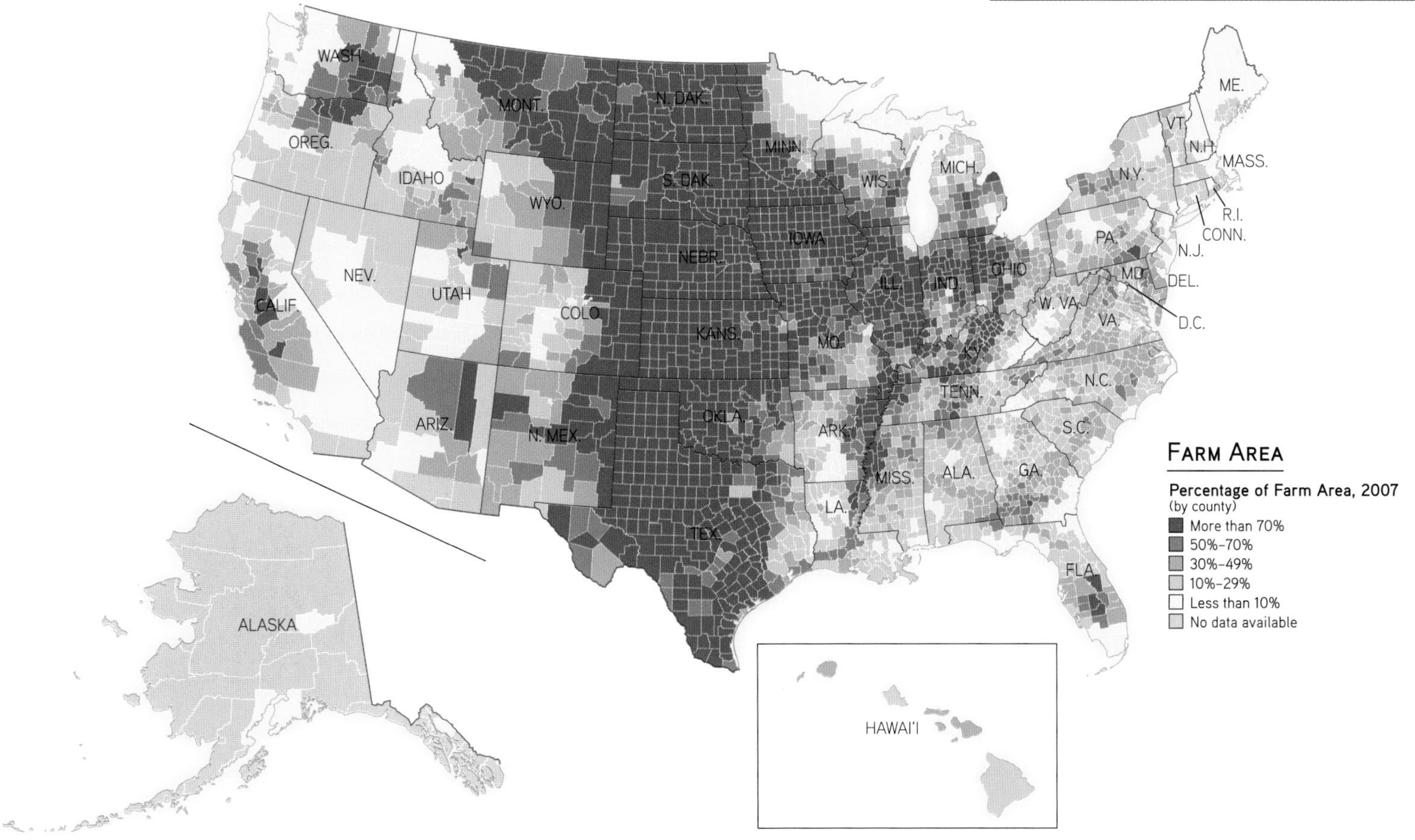
WASH.
OREG.
CALIF.
IDAHO
NEV.
UTAH
ARIZ.
MONT.
WYO.
COLO.
N. MEX.
N. DAK.
S. DAK.
NEBR.
KANS.
OKLA.
TEX.
MINN.
IOWA
MO.
ARK.
LA.
WIS.
ILL.
MICH.
IND.
OHIO
KY.
TENN.
MISS.
ALA.
GA.
FLA.
S.C.
N.C.
VA.
W. VA.
PA.
N.Y.
VT.
N.H.
ME.
MASS.
R.I.
CONN.
N.J.
DEL.
MD.
D.C.
ALASKA
HAWAI'I
Farm Area
Percentage of Farm Area, 2007
(by county)
More than 70%
50%–70%
30%–49%
10%–29%
Less than 10%
No data available

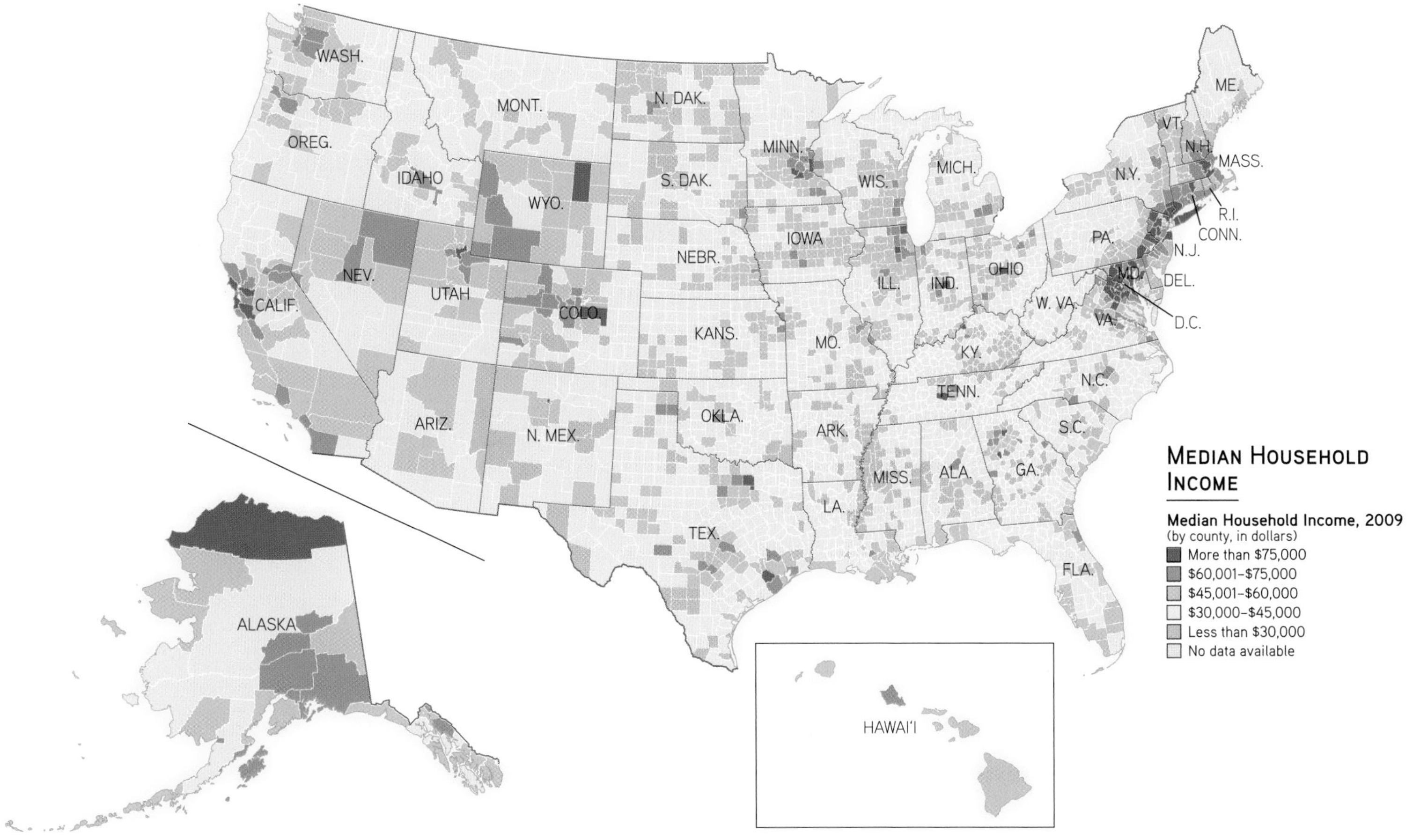
WASH.
OREG.
CALIF.
IDAHO
NEV.
UTAH
ARIZ.
MONT.
WYO.
COLO.
N. MEX.
N. DAK.
S. DAK.
NEBR.
KANS.
OKLA.
TEX.
MINN.
IOWA
MO.
ARK.
LA.
WIS.
ILL.
MICH.
IND.
OHIO
KY.
TENN.
MISS.
ALA.
GA.
FLA.
S.C.
N.C.
VA.
W. VA.
PA.
N.Y.
VT.
N.H.
ME.
MASS.
R.I.
CONN.
N.J.
DEL.
MD.
D.C.
ALASKA
HAWAI'I
Median Household Income
Median Household Income, 2009
(by county, in dollars)
More than $75,000
$60,001–$75,000
$45,001–$60,000
$30,000–$45,000
Less than $30,000
No data available

LAMBERT CONFORMAL CONIC PROJECTION
SCALE 1:6,000,000
0 KILOMETERS 100 150
0 MILES 50 100 150
Longitude West 114° of Greenwich
PACIFIC OCEAN
BRITISH COLUMBIA
ALBERTA
WASHINGTON
OREGON
IDAHO
MONTANA
CALIFORNIA
NEVADA
UTAH
GREAT BASIN
COAST MOUNTAINS
CASCADE RANGE
SIERRA NEVADA
ROCKY MOUNTAINS
BITTERROOT RANGE
KLAMATH MOUNTAINS
VANCOUVER ISLAND
OLYMPIC N.P.
NORTH CASCADES N.P.
MT. RAINIER N.P.
CRATER LAKE N.P.
LASSEN VOLCANIC N.P.
YOSEMITE N.P.
GLACIER N.P.
WATERTON LAKES N.P.
BANFF N.P.
YOHO N.P.
KOOTENAY N.P.
GLACIER N.P.
MT. REVELSTOKE N.P.
PACIFIC RIM N.P. RES.
REDWOOD N.P.
GREAT BASIN N.P.
HELLS CANYON N.R.A.
SAWTOOTH N.R.A.
CRATERS OF THE MOON N.M.
OREGON DUNES N.R.A.
KING RANGE N.C.A.
POINT REYES NAT. SEASHORE
LAVA BEDS N.M.
WW II VALOR IN THE PACIFIC N.M.
OREGON CAVES N.M.
CASCADE SISKIYOU N.M.
WHISKEYTOWN-SHASTA-TRINITY N.R.A.
LAKE ROOSEVELT N.R.A.
Vancouver
Victoria
Seattle
Tacoma
Olympia
Spokane
Portland
Salem
Eugene
Boise
Calgary
Sacramento
San Francisco
Reno
Carson City
Salt Lake City
Provo
Helena
Missoula
Kalispell
Stockton
Berkeley
Hayward
Mt. Rainier 4392
Mt. Shasta 4317
Mt. Hood 3425
Mt. Adams 3751
Mt. Baker 3285
Mt. Jefferson 3199
Three Sisters 3157
Lassen Pk. 3187
Mt. Olympus 2428
Mt. Robson
Mt. Waddington 3994
Great Salt Lake
Columbia
Snake
Salmon River
Harney Basin
Steens Mountain 2967
Lake Tahoe
90

SASKATCHEWAN
MANITOBA
ONTARIO
MONTANA
NORTH DAKOTA
SOUTH DAKOTA
MINNESOTA
WYOMING
NEBRASKA
IOWA
COLORADO
KANSAS
UTAH
MO.
108°
105°
102°
99°
96°
48°
45°
42°
39°
Saskatoon
Regina
Moose Jaw
Swift Current
Medicine Hat
Winnipeg
Brandon
Bismarck
Fargo
Grand Forks
Minot
Williston
Pierre
Sioux Falls
Rapid City
Billings
Cheyenne
Casper
Denver
Lakewood
Arvada
Westminster
Colorado Springs
Pueblo
Fort Collins
Boulder
Lincoln
Omaha
Wichita
Sioux City
Lake Manitoba
Lake Sakakawea
Lake Oahe
Fort Peck Lake
RIDING MOUNTAIN N.P.
GRASSLANDS N.P.
THEODORE ROOSEVELT NAT. PARK
UPPER MISSOURI RIVER BREAKS N.M.
BIGHORN CANYON N.R.A.
YELLOWSTONE N.P.
GRAND TETON N.P.
BADLANDS N.P.
WIND CAVE N.P.
FOSSIL BUTTE N.M.
FLAMING GORGE N.R.A.
DINOSAUR N.M.
ROCKY MT. N.P.
COLORADO N. MEM.
ARCHES N.P.
CANYONLANDS N.P.
GLEN CANYON N.R.A.
BLACK CANYON OF THE GUNNISON N.M.
Black Hills
Bighorn Mountains
Wind River Range
Laramie Mountains
Medicine Bow Mountains
Sawatch Ra.
Sand Hills
Smoky Hills
Flint Hills
Bears Paw Mountains
Killdeer Mountains
Badlands
Missouri
Yellowstone
Platte
Arkansas

OREGON
IDAHO
NEVADA
CALIFORNIA
UTAH
ARIZONA
SONORA
BAJA CALIFORNIA
GREAT BASIN
MOJAVE DESERT
SONORAN DESERT
PACIFIC OCEAN
CHANNEL ISLANDS
GULF OF CALIFORNIA (SEA OF CORTEZ)
SIERRA NEVADA
CASCADE RANGE
COAST RANGES
KLAMATH MOUNTAINS
REDWOOD N.P.
LAVA BEDS N.M.
WW II VALOR IN THE PACIFIC N.M.
WHISKEYTOWN-SHASTA-TRINITY N.R.A.
LASSEN VOLCANIC N.P.
KING RANGE N.C.A.
YOSEMITE N.P.
KINGS CANYON N.P.
SEQUOIA N.P.
DEATH VALLEY N.P.
GREAT BASIN N.P.
MOJAVE NATIONAL PRESERVE
JOSHUA TREE N.P.
LAKE MEAD N.R.A.
PINNACLES NAT. MON.
CARRIZO PLAIN NAT. MON.
CALIFORNIA COASTAL NAT. MON.
MONTEREY BAY NATIONAL MARINE SANCTUARY
CHANNEL ISLANDS N.P.
SANTA MONICA MOUNTAINS N.R.A.
SANTA ROSA AND SAN JACINTO MTS. N.M.
CALIFORNIA SPACEPORT
DRYDEN FLIGHT RESEARCH CENTER
GRAND CANYON-PARASHANT NAT. MON.
GRAND CANYON N.P.
ZION N.P.
BRYCE CANYON N.P.
CAPITOL REEF N.P.
GRAND STAIRCASE ESCALANTE NAT. MON.
VERMILION CLIFFS N.M.
WUPATKI N.M.
AGUA FRIA NAT. MON.
CASA GRANDE RUINS N.M.
IRONWOOD FOREST NAT. MON.
ORGAN PIPE CACTUS NAT. MON.
CONSTITUCIÓN DE 1857 N.P.
SIERRA DE SAN PEDRO MÁRTIR N.P.
San Francisco
Oakland
Sacramento
San Jose
Fresno
Bakersfield
Los Angeles
Long Beach
San Diego
Tijuana
Mexicali
Ensenada
Reno
Carson City
Las Vegas
Salt Lake City
Phoenix
Scottsdale
Mesa
Glendale
Yuma
Flagstaff
Provo
Pacific Crest Trail
LAMBERT CONFORMAL CONIC PROJECTION
SCALE 1:6,000,000
0 KILOMETERS 100 150
0 MILES 50 100 150
Longitude West 117° of Greenwich
126°
123°
120°
117°
114°
39°
36°
33°
30°

WYOMING
COLORADO
ROCKY MOUNTAINS
NEBRASKA
KANSAS
OKLAHOMA
TEXAS
NEW MEXICO
CHIHUAHUA
COAHUILA
MEXICO
Great Divide Basin
Denver
Colorado Springs
Pueblo
Cheyenne
Lincoln
Wichita
Oklahoma City
Albuquerque
Santa Fe
El Paso
Ciudad Juárez
Lubbock
Amarillo
Abilene
Fort Worth
Arlington
Waco
Austin
San Antonio
Laredo
Chihuahua
LLANO ESTACADO
EDWARDS PLATEAU
CAPROCK ESCARPMENT
SIERRA MADRE OCCIDENTAL
SIERRA MADRE ORIENTAL
SANGRE DE CRISTO MOUNTAINS
WHITE SANDS NAT. MON.
CARLSBAD CAVERNS N.P.
GUADALUPE MOUNTAINS N.P.
BIG BEND N.P.
RIO GRANDE WILD & SCENIC RIVER
AMISTAD N.R.A.
ROCKY MOUNTAIN N.P.
MESA VERDE N.P.
CANYONLANDS N.P.
ARCHES N.P.
PETRIFIED FOREST N.P.
CHACO CULTURE N.H.P.
BANDELIER N.M.
LAKE MEREDITH N.R.A.
DINOSAUR NAT. MON.
FLAMING GORGE N.R.A.
108°
105°
102°
99°
39°
36°
33°
30°

99°
96°
93°
90°
87°
84°
48°
45°
42°
39°
36°
MANITOBA
O N T A R I O
NORTH DAKOTA
SOUTH DAKOTA
NEBRASKA
KANSAS
OKLAHOMA
MINNESOTA
IOWA
MISSOURI
ARKANSAS
WISCONSIN
ILLINOIS
INDIANA
MICHIGAN
KENTUCKY
TENN.
Lake Superior
Lake Michigan
Lake Nipigon
Lake of the Woods
Upper Red Lake
Lower Red Lake
Leech Lake
Mille Lacs L.
Thunder Bay
VOYAGEURS N.P.
ISLE ROYALE N.P.
PUKASKWA N.P.
APOSTLE ISLANDS N.L.
PICTURED ROCKS N.L.
SAINT CROIX N.S.R.
Mesabi Range
Vermilion Ra.
Sawtooth Mountains
Gogebic Range
Keweenaw Peninsula
Door Peninsula
Mississippi
Missouri
Wisconsin
Illinois
Ohio
Wabash
Platte
Grand Forks
Fargo
Duluth
Minneapolis
St. Paul
Sioux Falls
Omaha
Lincoln
Des Moines
Cedar Rapids
Madison
Milwaukee
Green Bay
Rockford
Chicago
Joliet
Gary
South Bend
Grand Rapids
Lansing
Detroit
Ann Arbor
Toledo
Fort Wayne
Peoria
Springfield
Indianapolis
Dayton
Columbus
Cincinnati
Louisville
Lexington
Evansville
St. Louis
Kansas City
Independence
Overland Park
Topeka
Wichita
Tulsa
Springfield
Clarksville
OZARK PLATEAU
OZARK N.S.R.
Taum Sauk Mt.
BUFFALO NAT. RIVER
MAMMOTH CAVE N.P.
LAND BETWEEN THE LAKES
CUMBERLAND PLATEAU
BIG S. FORK N.R. & REC. AREA

QUEBEC
CANADA
NEW BRUNSWICK
NOVA SCOTIA
MAINE
NEW HAMPSHIRE
VERMONT
MASSACHUSETTS
CONNECTICUT
RHODE ISLAND
NEW YORK
NEW JERSEY
PENNSYLVANIA
DELAWARE
MARYLAND
WEST VIRGINIA
VIRGINIA
NORTH CAROLINA
ATLANTIC OCEAN
Gulf of Maine
Bay of Fundy
Lake Ontario
Lake Erie
Georgian Bay
Massachusetts Bay
Long Island
Cape Cod
Nantucket I.
Martha's Vineyard
GASPÉ PENINSULA
Adirondack Mountains
Catskill Mountains
Green Mountains
White Mountains
Allegheny Mountains
Blue Ridge
APPALACHIAN MOUNTAINS
Québec
Montréal
Ottawa
Toronto
Boston
Providence
Hartford
New Haven
New York
Philadelphia
Baltimore
Washington
Richmond
Norfolk
Virginia Beach
Pittsburgh
Buffalo
Rochester
Syracuse
Albany
Augusta
Portland
Concord
Cleveland
CAPE COD NATIONAL SEASHORE
ASSATEAGUE ISLAND NATIONAL SEASHORE
ACADIA N.P.
SHENANDOAH N.P.
INTRACOASTAL WATERWAY
Longitude West 81° of Greenwich
78°
75°
72°
69°
48°
45°
42°
39°
36°
LAMBERT CONFORMAL CONIC PROJECTION
SCALE 1:6,000,000
0 KILOMETERS 100 150
0 MILES 50 100 150

COLORADO
KANSAS
MISSOURI
OKLAHOMA
ARKANSAS
TEXAS
LOUISIANA
MISSISSIPPI
MEXICO
COAHUILA
NUEVO LEÓN
TAMAULIPAS
SAN LUIS POTOSÍ
ZACATECAS
GULF OF MEXICO
EDWARDS PLATEAU
LLANO ESTACADO
OZARK PLATEAU
Boston Mountains
Ouachita Mountains
HOT SPRINGS N.P.
BUFFALO NAT. RIVER
OZARK NAT. SCENIC RIVERWAYS
BIG THICKET NAT. PRES.
RIO GRANDE WILD & SCENIC RIVER
AMISTAD N.R.A.
PADRE ISLAND NATIONAL SEASHORE
FLOWER GARDEN BANKS NATIONAL MARINE SANCTUARY
CUMBRES DE MONTERREY N.P.
Amarillo
Lubbock
Abilene
Wichita Falls
Fort Worth
Dallas
Arlington
Plano
Garland
Mesquite
Carrollton
Waco
Austin
San Antonio
Houston
Pasadena
Beaumont
Corpus Christi
Laredo
McAllen
Brownsville
Oklahoma City
Tulsa
Wichita
Springfield
Little Rock
Memphis
Shreveport
Jackson
Baton Rouge
Lafayette
Metairie
New Orleans
Monterrey
Saltillo
Guadalupe
Nuevo Laredo
Reynosa
Matamoros
Monclova
Ciudad Victoria
Longitude West 90° of Greenwich
LAMBERT CONFORMAL CONIC PROJECTION
SCALE 1:6,000,000
0 KILOMETERS 100 150
0 MILES 50 100 150

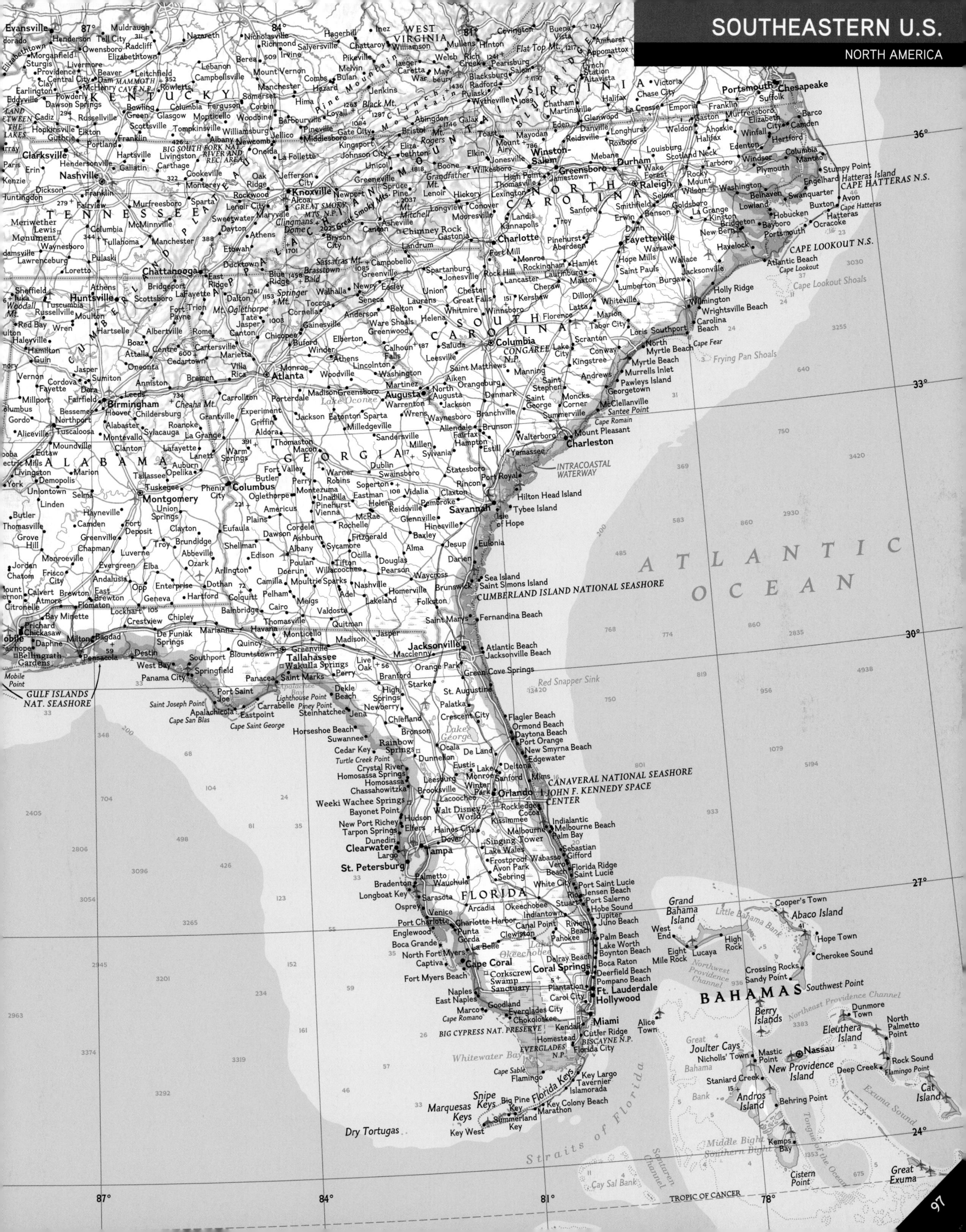

KENTUCKY
TENNESSEE
WEST VIRGINIA
VIRGINIA
NORTH CAROLINA
SOUTH CAROLINA
GEORGIA
ALABAMA
FLORIDA
BAHAMAS
ATLANTIC OCEAN
Straits of Florida
Evansville
Nashville
Knoxville
Chattanooga
Huntsville
Birmingham
Montgomery
Atlanta
Augusta
Columbia
Charlotte
Greensboro
Winston-Salem
Durham
Raleigh
Fayetteville
Wilmington
Charleston
Savannah
Columbus
Macon
Jacksonville
Tallahassee
Pensacola
Orlando
Tampa
St. Petersburg
Clearwater
Cape Coral
Coral Springs
Ft. Lauderdale
Hollywood
Miami
Key West
Nassau
Portsmouth
Chesapeake
CAPE HATTERAS N.S.
CAPE LOOKOUT N.S.
CONGAREE N.P.
INTRACOASTAL WATERWAY
CUMBERLAND ISLAND NATIONAL SEASHORE
CANAVERAL NATIONAL SEASHORE
JOHN F. KENNEDY SPACE CENTER
GULF ISLANDS NAT. SEASHORE
BIG CYPRESS NAT. PRESERVE
EVERGLADES N.P.
BISCAYNE N.P.
GREAT SMOKY MTS. N.P.
BIG SOUTH FORK NAT. RIVER AND REC. AREA
MAMMOTH CAVE N.P.
Lake Okeechobee
Florida Keys
Dry Tortugas
Grand Bahama Island
Abaco Island
Andros Island
Eleuthera Island
New Providence Island
Cat Island
Great Exuma
TROPIC OF CANCER
87°
84°
81°
78°
36°
33°
30°
27°
24°

ALASKA, U.S.
ALBERS CONIC EQUAL-AREA PROJECTION
SCALE 1:10,000,000
0 KILOMETERS 200 300
0 MILES 100 200 300
ARCTIC OCEAN
PACIFIC OCEAN
Beaufort Sea
Chukchi Sea
Bering Sea
Gulf of Alaska
RUSSIA
CANADA
UNITED STATES
ALASKA
YUKON
NORTHWEST TERRITORIES
BRITISH COLUMBIA
NUNAVUT
NORTH SLOPE
BROOKS RANGE
ALASKA RANGE
KUSKOKWIM MOUNTAINS
COAST MOUNTAINS
SEWARD PENINSULA
ALASKA PENINSULA
KENAI PENINSULA
ALEUTIAN RANGE
Aleutian Islands
Fox Islands
ARCTIC CIRCLE
Date Line
Monday
Sunday
Bering Strait
Anchorage
Fairbanks
Juneau
Nome
Barrow
Prudhoe Bay
Kotzebue
Bethel
Kodiak
Valdez
Whitehorse
Dawson (Dawson City)
Mount McKinley (Denali)
DENALI N.P. AND PRESERVE
GATES OF THE ARCTIC N.P. AND PRESERVE
WRANGELL-ST. ELIAS N.P. AND PRESERVE
KATMAI N.P. AND PRESERVE
LAKE CLARK N.P. AND PRESERVE
GLACIER BAY N.P. AND PRESERVE
KENAI FJORDS N.P.
YUKON-CHARLEY RIVERS NATIONAL PRESERVE
Longitude West of Greenwich

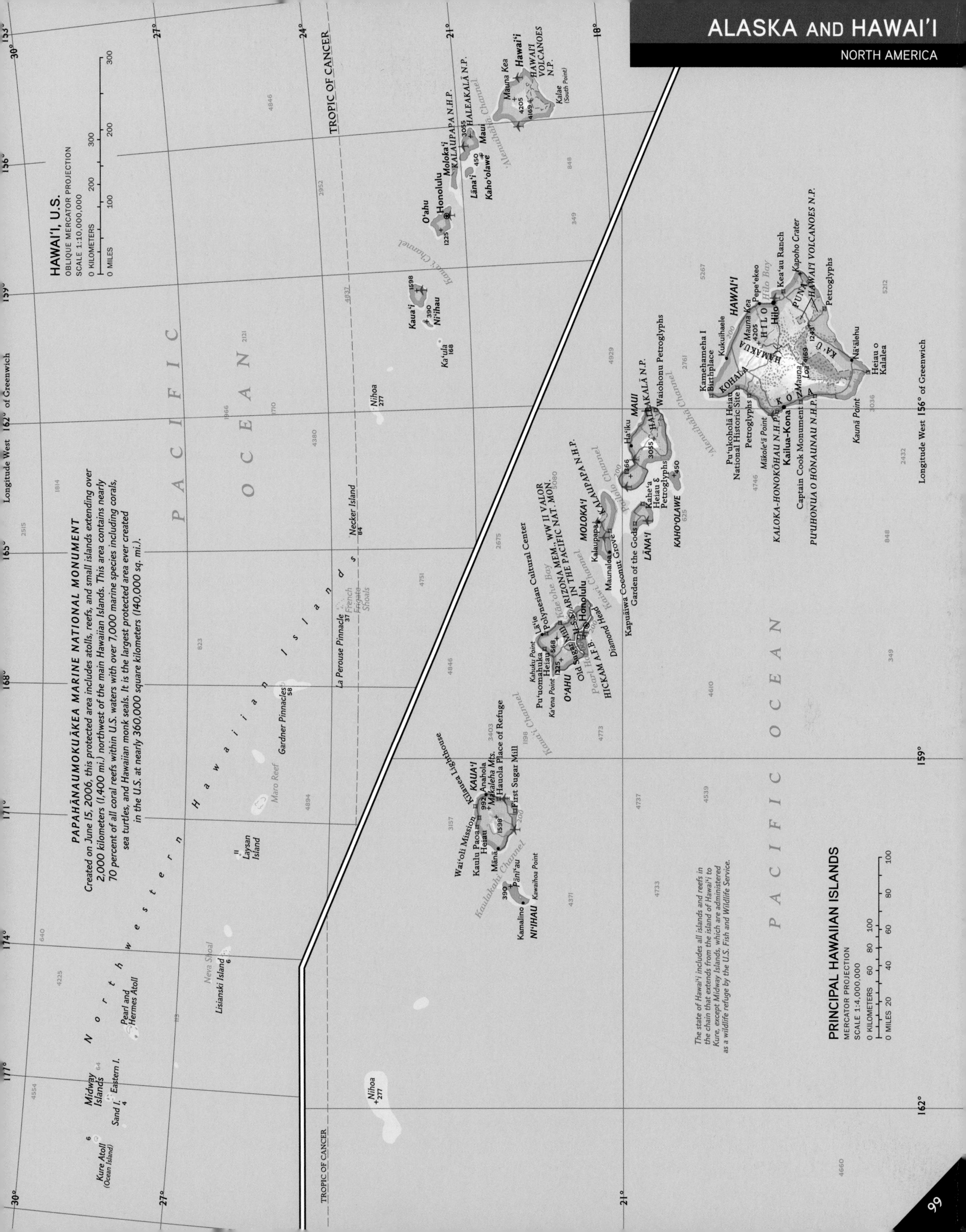
HAWAI'I, U.S.
OBLIQUE MERCATOR PROJECTION
SCALE 1:10,000,000
PAPAHĀNAUMOKUĀKEA MARINE NATIONAL MONUMENT
Created on June 15, 2006, this protected area includes atolls, reefs, and small islands extending over 2,000 kilometers (1,400 mi.) northwest of the main Hawaiian Islands. This area contains nearly 70 percent of all coral reefs within U.S. waters with over 7,000 marine species including corals, sea turtles, and Hawaiian monk seals. It is the largest protected area ever created in the U.S. at nearly 360,000 square kilometers (140,000 sq. mi.).
Northwestern Hawaiian Islands
PACIFIC OCEAN
TROPIC OF CANCER
Kure Atoll (Ocean Island)
Midway Islands
Sand I.
Eastern I.
Pearl and Hermes Atoll
Lisianski Island
Neva Shoal
Laysan Island
Maro Reef
Gardner Pinnacles
French Frigate Shoals
La Perouse Pinnacle
Necker Island
Nihoa
Kaua'i
Ni'ihau
Ka'ula
O'ahu
Honolulu
Moloka'i
Lāna'i
Kaho'olawe
Maui
Hawai'i
Mauna Kea
HAWAI'I VOLCANOES N.P.
KALAUPAPA N.H.P.
HALEAKALĀ N.P.
Kalae (South Point)
Kaua'i Channel
'Alenuihāhā Channel
The state of Hawai'i includes all islands and reefs in the chain that extends from the island of Hawai'i to Kure, except Midway Islands, which are administered as a wildlife refuge by the U.S. Fish and Wildlife Service.
PRINCIPAL HAWAIIAN ISLANDS
MERCATOR PROJECTION
SCALE 1:4,000,000
Longitude West 156° of Greenwich
Longitude West 162° of Greenwich

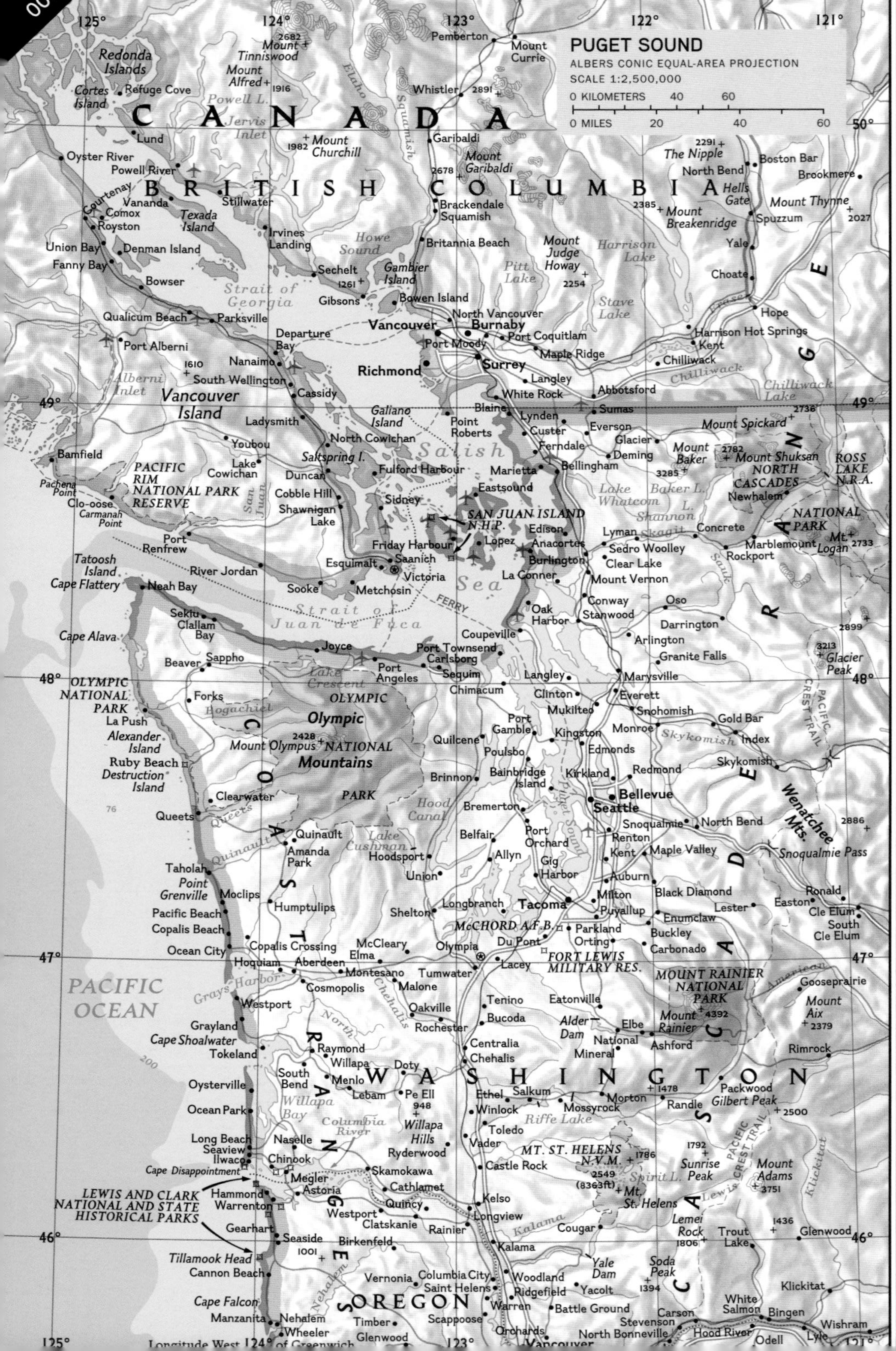
PUGET SOUND
ALBERS CONIC EQUAL-AREA PROJECTION
SCALE 1:2,500,000
0 KILOMETERS 40 60
0 MILES 20 40 60
CANADA
BRITISH COLUMBIA
WASHINGTON
OREGON
COAST RANGES
CASCADE RANGE
PACIFIC OCEAN
Vancouver Island
Strait of Georgia
Strait of Juan de Fuca
Salish Sea
Puget Sound
OLYMPIC NATIONAL PARK
Olympic Mountains
MOUNT RAINIER NATIONAL PARK
NORTH CASCADES NATIONAL PARK
ROSS LAKE N.R.A.
SAN JUAN ISLAND N.H.P.
PACIFIC RIM NATIONAL PARK RESERVE
MT. ST. HELENS N.V.M.
FORT LEWIS MILITARY RES.
McCHORD A.F.B.
LEWIS AND CLARK NATIONAL AND STATE HISTORICAL PARKS
Vancouver
Richmond
Burnaby
Surrey
Victoria
Seattle
Bellevue
Tacoma
Olympia
Bellingham
Everett
Longitude West 124° of Greenwich

CENTRAL CALIFORNIA COAST
ALBERS CONIC EQUAL-AREA PROJECTION
SCALE 1:2,500,000
0 KILOMETERS 40 60
0 MILES 20 40 60
CALIFORNIA
COAST RANGES
SIERRA NEVADA
San Joaquin Valley
PACIFIC OCEAN
MONTEREY BAY NATIONAL MARINE SANCTUARY
Stretching from just north of San Francisco to Cambria, the sanctuary protects California's coastal ecosystem—including the nation's largest kelp forest.
CALIFORNIA COASTAL NATIONAL MONUMENT
The Monument encompasses numerous islands, rocks, exposed reefs, and pinnacles off the California coast.
YOSEMITE NATIONAL PARK
PINNACLES NAT. MON.
CARRIZO PLAIN N.M.
POINT REYES NAT. SEASHORE
VANDENBERG A.F.B.
CALIFORNIA SPACEPORT
Channel Islands
CHANNEL ISLANDS NATIONAL PARK
San Francisco
Oakland
San Jose
Sacramento Valley
Stockton
Modesto
Fresno
Salinas
Monterey
Santa Barbara
Longitude West 120° of Greenwich

SOUTHERN CALIFORNIA
ALBERS CONIC EQUAL-AREA PROJECTION
SCALE 1:2,500,000
0 KILOMETERS 20 40 60
0 MILES 20 40 60
Longitude West 119° of Greenwich
CALIFORNIA
NEVADA
ARIZONA
UTAH
MEXICO
BAJA CALIFORNIA
PACIFIC OCEAN
GREAT BASIN
SIERRA NEVADA
COAST RANGES
MOJAVE DESERT
SONORAN DESERT
MOJAVE NATIONAL PRESERVE
DEATH VALLEY NATIONAL PARK
JOSHUA TREE NATIONAL PARK
CHANNEL ISLANDS NATIONAL PARK
Channel Islands
Santa Barbara Channel
Gulf of Santa Catalina
Salton Sea
Los Angeles
San Diego
Las Vegas
Bakersfield
Fresno
Santa Catalina
San Clemente
San Nicolas
Santa Cruz
Santa Rosa
San Miguel

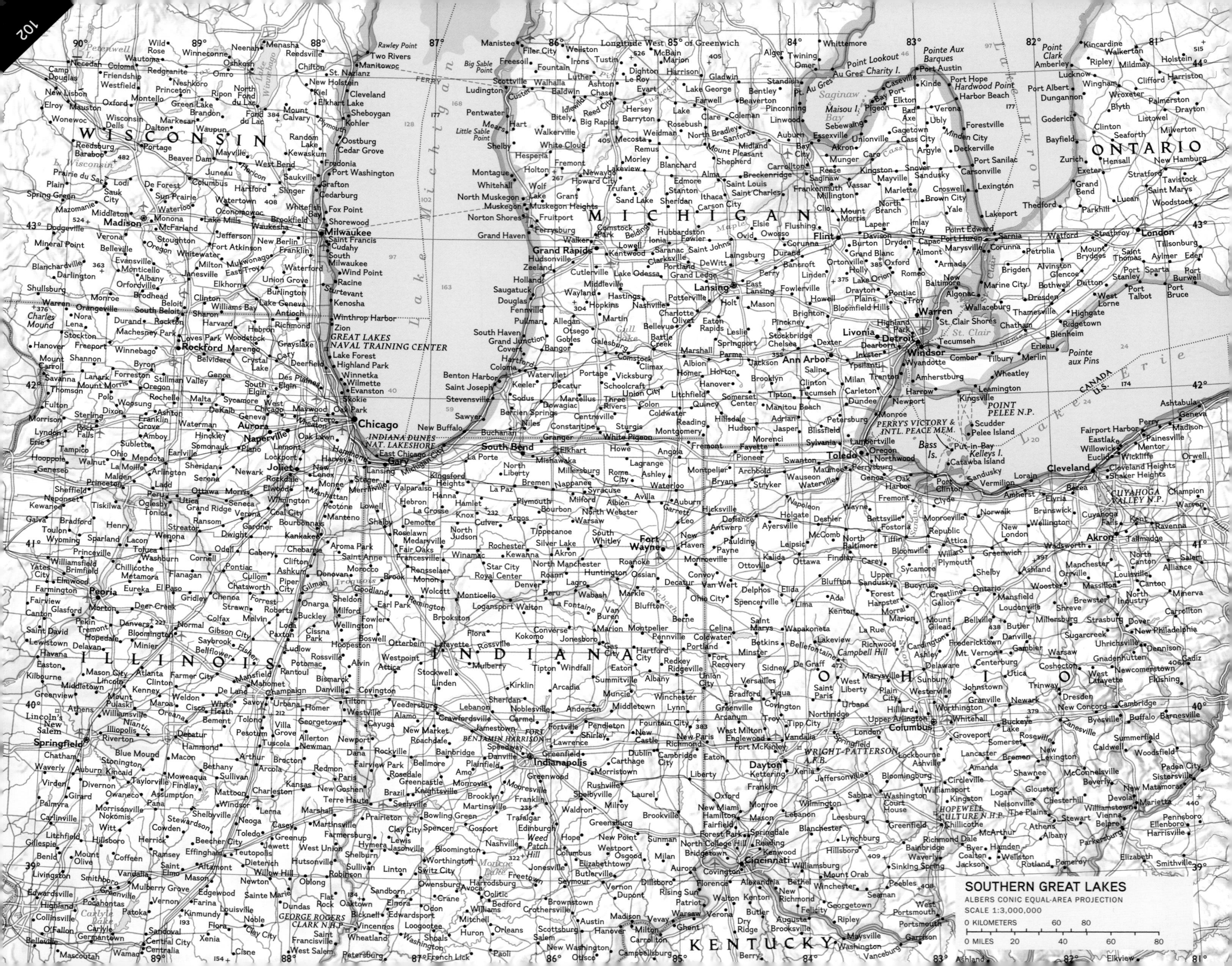
SOUTHERN GREAT LAKES
ALBERS CONIC EQUAL-AREA PROJECTION
SCALE 1:3,000,000
0 KILOMETERS 20 40 60 80
0 MILES 20 40 60 80
Longitude West 85° of Greenwich
WISCONSIN
MICHIGAN
ONTARIO
ILLINOIS
INDIANA
OHIO
KENTUCKY
Lake Michigan
Lake Huron
Lake Erie
Saginaw Bay
L. St. Clair
Lake Winnebago
CANADA
U.S.
Chicago
Milwaukee
Madison
Rockford
Peoria
Springfield
Joliet
Aurora
Naperville
Grand Rapids
Lansing
Flint
Detroit
Warren
Livonia
Ann Arbor
Windsor
London
Toledo
Cleveland
Akron
Columbus
Dayton
Cincinnati
Fort Wayne
South Bend
Gary
Indianapolis
GREAT LAKES NAVAL TRAINING CENTER
INDIANA DUNES NAT. LAKESHORE
POINT PELEE N.P.
PERRY'S VICTORY & INTL. PEACE MEM.
CUYAHOGA VALLEY N.P.
WRIGHT-PATTERSON A.F.B.
HOPEWELL CULTURE N.H.P.
GEORGE ROGERS CLARK N.H.P.
BENJAMIN HARRISON FORT

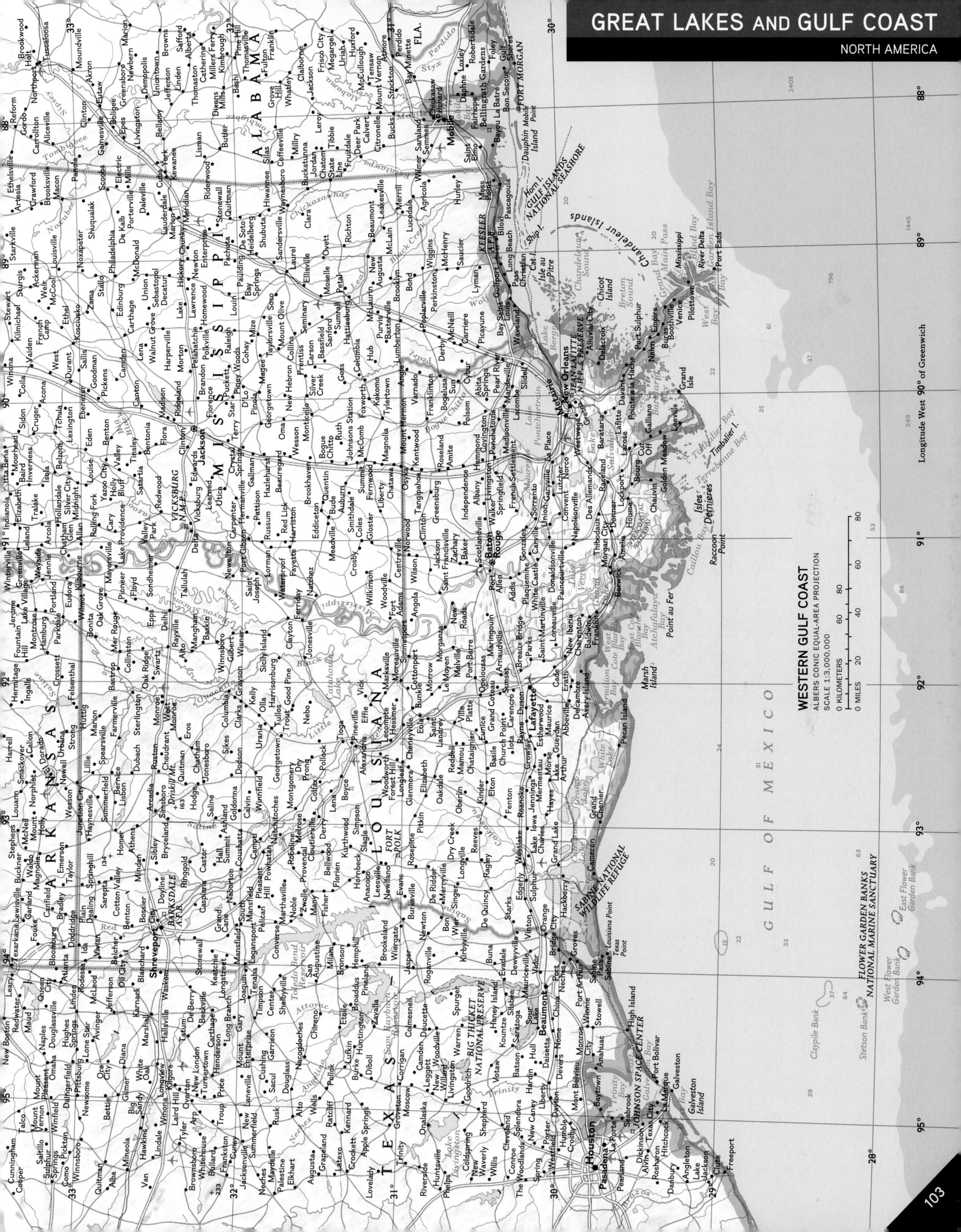
WESTERN GULF COAST
ALBERS CONIC EQUAL-AREA PROJECTION
SCALE 1:3,000,000
0 KILOMETERS 20 40 60 80
0 MILES 20 40 60
GULF OF MEXICO
LOUISIANA
MISSISSIPPI
ALABAMA
ARKANSAS
TEXAS
FLA.
Longitude West 90° of Greenwich

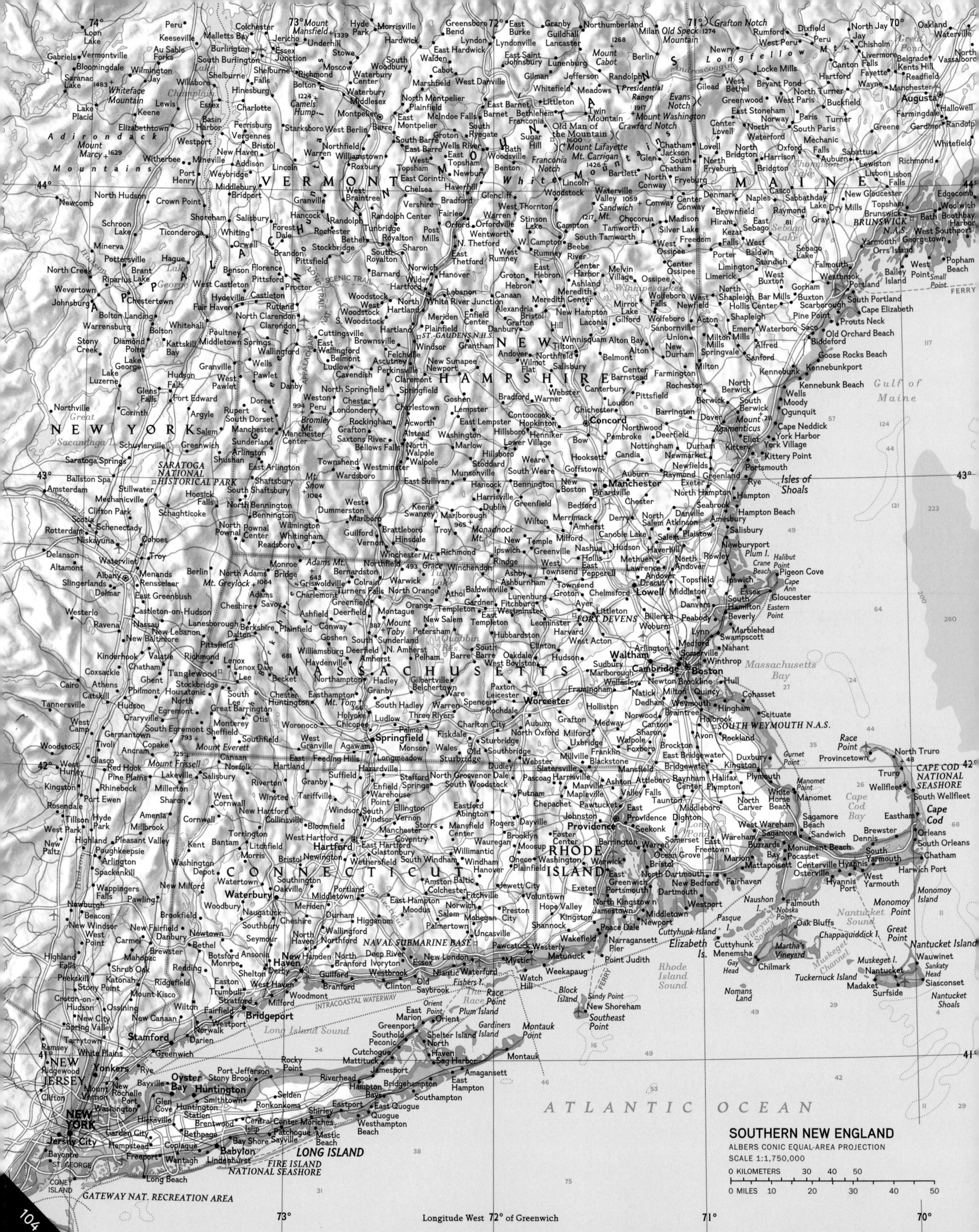
SOUTHERN NEW ENGLAND
ALBERS CONIC EQUAL-AREA PROJECTION
SCALE 1:1,750,000
0 KILOMETERS 30 40 50
0 MILES 10 20 30 40 50
Longitude West 72° of Greenwich
73°
71°
70°
74°
44°
43°
42°
41°
VERMONT
NEW HAMPSHIRE
MAINE
NEW YORK
MASSACHUSETTS
CONNECTICUT
RHODE ISLAND
NEW JERSEY
NEW YORK
ATLANTIC OCEAN
Gulf of Maine
Massachusetts Bay
Long Island Sound
Rhode Island Sound
Nantucket Sound
LONG ISLAND
Adirondack Mountains
White Mountains
Longfellow Mts.
Green Mountains
Boston
Cambridge
Providence
Hartford
Springfield
Worcester
Concord
Manchester
Augusta
Portland
Bridgeport
Albany
Montpelier
New Haven
Stamford
Waterbury
Lowell
Cape Cod
Martha's Vineyard
Nantucket Island
Block Island
CAPE COD NATIONAL SEASHORE
FIRE ISLAND NATIONAL SEASHORE
GATEWAY NAT. RECREATION AREA
SARATOGA NATIONAL HISTORICAL PARK
NAVAL SUBMARINE BASE
SOUTH WEYMOUTH N.A.S.
BRUNSWICK N.A.S.
FORT DEVENS
INTRACOASTAL WATERWAY
Isles of Shoals

PENINSULAR FLORIDA
ALBERS CONIC EQUAL-AREA PROJECTION
SCALE 1:2,500,000
0 KILOMETERS 40 60
0 MILES 20 40 60
Longitude West 81° of Greenwich
83°
82°
81°
80°
29°
28°
27°
26°
25°
FLORIDA
ATLANTIC OCEAN
GULF OF MEXICO
BAHAMAS
Straits of Florida
Florida Keys
CASTILLO DE SAN MARCOS N.M.
FORT MATANZAS N.M.
CANAVERAL N.S.
JOHN F. KENNEDY SPACE CENTER
PATRICK A.F.B.
MACDILL A.F.B.
BIG CYPRESS NATIONAL PRESERVE
EVERGLADES N.P.
BISCAYNE N.P.
DRY TORTUGAS N.P.
FLORIDA'S TURNPIKE
SAINT LUCIE CANAL
INTRACOASTAL WATERWAY
Lake Okeechobee
Lake George
Lake Istokpoga
Lake Placid
Mosquito Lagoon
Tampa Bay
Charlotte Harbor
Biscayne Bay
Florida Bay
Ponce de Leon Bay
Whitewater Bay
Big Cypress Swamp
Okaloacoochee Slough
Suwannee Sound
Waccasassa Bay
Crystal Bay
Horseshoe Cove
Red Snapper Sink
Jacksonville
St. Augustine
Anastasia Island
Gainesville
Ocala
Palatka
Palm Coast
Daytona Beach
Ormond Beach
Port Orange
New Smyrna Beach
Sanford
Orlando
Kissimmee
Walt Disney World
Cape Canaveral (Cape Kennedy)
Cocoa Beach
Melbourne
Palm Bay
Sebastian
Vero Beach
Fort Pierce
Port Saint Lucie
Stuart
Jupiter
West Palm Beach
Palm Beach
Boynton Beach
Delray Beach
Boca Raton
Coral Springs
Pompano Beach
Fort Lauderdale
Hollywood
Hialeah
Miami
Miami Beach
Key Biscayne
Homestead
Florida City
Key Largo
Tavernier
Islamorada
Marathon
Big Pine Key
Key West
Tampa
Clearwater
St. Petersburg
Bradenton
Sarasota
Venice
Punta Gorda
Cape Coral
Fort Myers
Naples
Marco
Everglades City
Flamingo
Cape Sable
Lakeland
Winter Haven
Sebring
Okeechobee
Clewiston
Belle Glade
Immokalee
Lehigh Acres
Arcadia
Wauchula
Cedar Key
Crystal River
Spring Hill
New Port Richey
Dry Tortugas
Marquesas Keys
Grand Bahama Island
Freeport
West End
Bimini Islands
Great Isaac
Mangrove Cay

ARCTIC OCEAN
BERING SEA
BEAUFORT SEA
GULF OF ALASKA
PACIFIC OCEAN
Bristol Bay
Shelikof Str.
Queen Charlotte Sound
Hecate Strait
QUEEN ELIZABETH
PARRY ISLANDS
Banks Island
Victoria Island
Prince of Wales I.
Melville I.
Bathurst I.
Prince Patrick I.
ALASKA
Alaska Peninsula
Alaska Range
Brooks Range
NORTH SLOPE
Mt. McKinley (Denali)
Mt. Michelson
Anchorage
Fairbanks
Nome
Kodiak
Kodiak Island
Juneau
Sitka
Ketchikan
YUKON
Whitehorse
Dawson (Dawson City)
Ogilvie Mountains
Selwyn Mts.
Mackenzie Mountains
NORTHWEST TERRITORIES
Yellowknife
Great Slave Lake
Great Bear Lake
Inuvik
Fort Simpson
Norman Wells
Fort Smith
WOOD BUFFALO NATIONAL PARK
NAHANNI NATIONAL PARK RESERVE
TUKTUT NOGAIT NATIONAL PARK
AULAVIK N.P.
IVVAVIK N.P.
VUNTUT N.P.
YUKON-CHARLEY RIVERS NATIONAL PRESERVE
WRANGELL-ST. ELIAS N.P. AND PRESERVE
KLUANE N.P. AND RESERVE
GLACIER BAY N.P. AND PRESERVE
Mt. St. Elias
Mt. Fairweather
Malaspina Glacier
ARCTIC CIRCLE
Kugluktuk
Cambridge Bay
C A N A D A
BRITISH COLUMBIA
COAST MOUNTAINS
ROCKY MOUNTAINS
Cassiar Mountains
Columbia Mountains
Haida Gwaii (Queen Charlotte Is.)
Vancouver Island
Vancouver
Victoria
Prince Rupert
Prince George
Kamloops
Kelowna
ALBERTA
Edmonton
Calgary
Banff
Jasper
Mt. Robson
JASPER N.P.
BANFF N.P.
YOHO N.P.
KOOTENAY N.P.
GLACIER N.P.
Lake Athabasca
SASKATCHEWAN
Saskatoon
Regina
Prince Albert
PRINCE ALBERT N.P.
MANITOBA
Winnipeg
Lake Winnipeg
Churchill
Baker Lake
UNITED STATES
WASHINGTON
Seattle
Tacoma
Spokane
Olympia
Mt. Rainier
OLYMPIC N.P.
NORTH CASCADES N.P.
MT. RAINIER N.P.
OREGON
Portland
Salem
Eugene
CRATER LAKE N.P.
HELLS CANYON N.R.A.
IDAHO
Boise
SAWTOOTH N.R.A.
CRATERS OF THE MOON N.M.
MONTANA
Helena
Missoula
Billings
WATERTON-GLACIER INTL. PEACE PARK
WYOMING
YELLOWSTONE N.P.
GRAND TETON N.P.
Casper
Cheyenne
NORTH DAKOTA
Bismarck
SOUTH DAKOTA
Pierre
BADLANDS N.P.
NEBRASKA
Lincoln
Omaha
COLORADO
ROCKY MT. N.P.
UTAH
Salt Lake City
GREAT BASIN N.P.
NEVADA
Reno
GREAT BASIN
CALIFORNIA
San Francisco
Sacramento
San Jose
Stockton
Modesto
YOSEMITE N.P.
LASSEN VOLCANIC N.P.
Mt. Shasta
Cape Mendocino
SIERRA NEVADA
Des Moines
Minneapolis

GREENLAND (KALAALLIT NUNAAT)
BAFFIN BAY
DAVIS STRAIT
LABRADOR SEA
ATLANTIC OCEAN
HUDSON BAY
Hudson Strait
NUNAVUT
QUEBEC
ONTARIO
NEWFOUNDLAND AND LABRADOR
NEW BRUNSWICK
NOVA SCOTIA
PRINCE EDWARD I.
MAINE
VT.
N.H.
MASS.
CONN.
RHODE ISLAND
NEW YORK
PENNSYLVANIA
N.J.
OHIO
INDIANA
ILLINOIS
MICHIGAN
WISCONSIN
ST.-PIERRE AND MIQUELON France
ISLAND OF NEWFOUNDLAND
BAFFIN ISLAND
Ellesmere Island
Devon Island
Coburg I.
Bylot I.
Pond Inlet
SIRMILIK NATIONAL PARK
Borden Pen.
Brodeur Peninsula
Clyde River
AUYUITTUQ NATIONAL PARK
Cumberland Peninsula
Cape Dyer
Pangnirtung
Cumberland Sound
Hall Beach
Melville Peninsula
Rowley I.
Spicer Is.
Foley I.
Prince Charles Island
Air Force I.
Rae Isthmus
UKKUSIKSALIK NATIONAL PARK
Foxe Basin
Foxe Peninsula
Cape Dorset
Southampton I.
Coral Harbour
Bell Pen.
Mill Island
Salisbury I.
Nottingham I.
Iqaluit
Meta Incognita Pen.
Kimmirut
Hall Pen.
Frobisher Bay
Resolution Island
Loks Land
Edgell Island
Brevoort Island
Lemieux Islands
Amadjuak Lake
Chesterfield Inlet
Rankin Inlet
Coats I.
Mansel Island
Ivujivik
Salluit
Charles I.
Kangiqsujuaq
Akpatok Island
Cratère du Nouveau-Québec (Chubb Crater)
Ungava Bay
Kangiqsualujjuaq
Kuujjuaq
Button Is.
Port Burwell
North Aulatsivik Island
Mt. D'Iberville (Mt. Caubvick)
Torngat Mts.
Saglek Bay
Cod Island
Okak Islands
S. Aulatsivik I.
Nain
Davis Inlet
Hopedale
Makkovik
Adlavik Islands
Cape Harrison
Indian Harbour
Cartwright
Battle Harbour
Belle Isle
LABRADOR
Churchill Falls
Happy Valley-Goose Bay
North West River
Smallwood Res.
Schefferville
Esker
Labrador City
Lac Payne
Lac Minto
Lac à l'Eau Claire
Lac Guillaume-Delisle
Lac Bienville
Rés. de La Grande 2
Radisson
Sakami
Keyano
Chisasibi
Kuujjuarapik
Inukjuak
Nastapoka Is.
Hopewell Is.
Ottawa Islands
Smith Island
Pointe Cusson
Sleeper Is.
King George Is.
Belcher Is.
N. Belcher Is.
Cape Churchill
WAPUSK NATIONAL PARK
Cape Tatnam
Fort Severn
Shamattawa
Peawanuck
Wabuk Point
Cape Henrietta Maria
Long Island
Big Trout Lake
James Bay
Akimiski I.
Attawapiskat
Charlton Island
Fort Albany
Lansdowne House
Fort Hope
Moosonee
Eastmain
Waskaganish
Nemiscau
Lac Mistassini
Mistassini (Baie-du-Poste)
Chibougamau
Matagami
Lac St.-Jean
Dolbeau-Mistassini
Saguenay
Tadoussac
Baie-Comeau
Sept-Îles
Havre-St.-Pierre
Port-Menier
I. d'Anticosti
Natashquan
St.-Augustin
Blanc-Sablon
Lourdes-de-Blanc-Sablon
St. Anthony
Roddickton
Grey Islands
La Scie
Fogo I.
Port Saunders
GROS MORNE N.P.
Corner Brook
Botwood
Gander
Grand Falls-Windsor
Bonavista
Trinity Bay
Cape Saint Francis
St. John's
Avalon Peninsula
Cape Race
Jerseyside
Stephenville
Channel-Port aux Basques
Cape Ray
Gulf of St. Lawrence
Gaspé
Matane
Gaspé Peninsula
Rimouski
Rivière-du-Loup
Bathurst
Chatham
Îles de la Madeleine Quebec
CAPE BRETON HIGHLANDS N.P.
Cape Breton I.
Sydney
Baddeck
Charlottetown
Moncton
Amherst
Fredericton
Saint John
Halifax
Dartmouth
Windsor
Bridgewater
Liverpool
Yarmouth
Cape Sable
Sable Island Nova Scotia
Gulf of Maine
Bangor
Augusta
Portland
Mount Katahdin
Presque Isle
Québec
Lévis
La Tuque
Shawinigan
Trois-Rivières
LA MAURICIE N.P.
Montréal
Mont-Laurier
GATINEAU PARK
Ottawa
Pembroke
North Bay
Sudbury
Elliot Lake
Sault Ste. Marie
New Liskeard
Kirkland Lake
Rouyn-Noranda
Val-d'Or
Timmins
South Porcupine
Cochrane
Kapuskasing
Hearst
Geraldton
Chapleau
Michipicoten
PUKASKWA NATIONAL PARK
Nipigon
Thunder Bay
ISLE ROYALE N.P.
Lake Superior
Keweenaw Peninsula
Duluth
Superior
Sioux Lookout
Dryden
Lake Nipigon
Marquette
Escanaba
BRUCE PEN. N.P.
Wiarton
Alpena
Lake Huron
Georgian Bay
Peterborough
Kingston
Oshawa
Toronto
Hamilton
Lake Ontario
Rochester
Buffalo
Erie
Lake Erie
Detroit
Lansing
Grand Rapids
Bay City
Muskegon
Lake Michigan
Green Bay
Wausau
Eau Claire
Milwaukee
Madison
Waterloo
Rockford
Chicago
Gary
Cedar Rapids
Rock Island
Davenport
Toledo
Cleveland
Akron
Pittsburgh
Allegheny Mts.
Harrisburg
Philadelphia
Trenton
Baltimore
Elmira
Albany
Hartford
Bridgeport
Long Island
Boston
Providence
Nantucket Island
Concord
Montpelier
Burlington
Adirondack Mts.
Thule Air Base
Qaanaaq
Upernavik
Uummannaq
Ilulissat
Qeqertarsuaq
Aasiaat
Sisimiut
Kangerlussuaq
Maniitsoq
Nuuk (Godthåb)
Paamiut
Qaqortoq
Narsarsuaq
Nanortalik
Tasiilaq
Kap Farvel
ARCTIC CIRCLE
AZIMUTHAL EQUIDISTANT PROJECTION
SCALE 1:16,000,000
0 KILOMETERS 300 400
0 MILES 100 200 300 400
Longitude West 66° of Greenwich

WESTERN CANADA
ALBERS CONIC EQUAL-AREA PROJECTION
SCALE 1:6,000,000
0 KILOMETERS 100 150
0 MILES 50 100 150
YUKON
BRITISH COLUMBIA
ALBERTA
ALASKA
WASHINGTON
IDAHO
PACIFIC OCEAN
VANCOUVER ISLAND
HAIDA GWAII (QUEEN CHARLOTTE ISLANDS)
GWAII HAANAS NAT. PARK RES. AND HAIDA HERITAGE SITE
GLACIER BAY NAT. PARK AND PRESERVE
MISTY FIORDS NAT. MON.
NAHANNI NAT. PARK RESERVE
JASPER NAT. PARK
BANFF NAT. PARK
GLACIER N.P.
MOUNT REVELSTOKE N.P.
KOOTENAY NAT. PARK
WATERTON GLACIER INTERNATIONAL PEACE PARK
PACIFIC RIM N.P. RESERVE
NORTH CASCADES NAT. PARK
OLYMPIC NAT. PARK
COAST MOUNTAINS
ROCKY MOUNTAINS
CASCADE RANGE
Hecate Strait
Queen Charlotte Sound
Prince George
Vancouver
Victoria
Seattle
Juneau
Whitehorse
Fort Nelson
Kamloops
Kelowna
Prince Rupert
Dawson Creek
Fort St. John
Grande Prairie
Revelstoke
Nelson
Banff
Lake Louise
60°
57°
54°
51°
48°
135°
132°
129°
126°
123°
120°
117°

Longitude West 111° of Greenwich
NUNAVUT
NORTHWEST TERRITORIES
HUDSON BAY
MANITOBA
SASKATCHEWAN
CANADA
UNITED STATES
MINNESOTA
NORTH DAKOTA
MONTANA
ONTARIO
WOOD BUFFALO NATIONAL PARK
PRINCE ALBERT NAT. PARK
RIDING MOUNTAIN NATIONAL PARK
GRASSLANDS NATIONAL PARK
WAPUSK NATIONAL PARK
FORT PRINCE OF WALES NATIONAL HISTORICAL PARK
YORK FACTORY NATIONAL HISTORIC SITE
BATOCHE N.H.S.
FORT UNION TRADING POST N.H.S.
KNIFE RIVER INDIAN VILLAGES N.H.S.
UPPER MISSOURI RIVER BREAKS N.M.
WATERTON LAKES
GLACIER N.P.
Lake Athabasca
Lake Winnipeg
Lake Winnipegosis
Lake Manitoba
Reindeer L.
Wollaston L.
Edmonton
Saskatoon
Regina
Winnipeg
Churchill
Brandon
Prince Albert
Lloydminster
Medicine Hat
Moose Jaw
Swift Current
Yorkton
The Pas
Flin Flon
Thompson
Fort McMurray
Uranium City
Minot
Grand Forks
Williston
108°
105°
102°
99°
96°
93°
111°
54°
51°
48°

CENTRAL CANADA
ALBERS CONIC EQUAL-AREA PROJECTION
SCALE 1:6,000,000
0 KILOMETERS 100 150
0 MILES 50 100 150
CANADA
ONTARIO
QUEBEC
NUNAVUT
UNITED STATES
MINNESOTA
WISCONSIN
MICHIGAN
IOWA
ILLINOIS
INDIANA
OHIO
PENNSYLVANIA
NEW YORK
NEW JERSEY
VT.
MASS.
CONN.
JAMES BAY
LAKE SUPERIOR
LAKE MICHIGAN
LAKE HURON
LAKE ERIE
LAKE ONTARIO
GEORGIAN BAY
Saginaw Bay
ISLE ROYALE N.P.
PUKASKWA N.P.
VOYAGEURS N.P.
APOSTLE ISLANDS N.L.
PICTURED ROCKS NATIONAL LAKESHORE
SLEEPING BEAR DUNES N.L.
BRUCE PENINSULA N.P.
GEORGIAN BAY ISLANDS N.P.
POINT PELEE N.P.
CUYAHOGA VALLEY N.P.
SAINT CROIX NATIONAL SCENIC RIVERWAY
LA MAURICIE N.P.
GATINEAU PK.
Thunder Bay
Timmins
Greater Sudbury
Ottawa
Montréal
Toronto
Mississauga
Hamilton
Detroit
Chicago
Milwaukee
Cleveland
Buffalo
New York

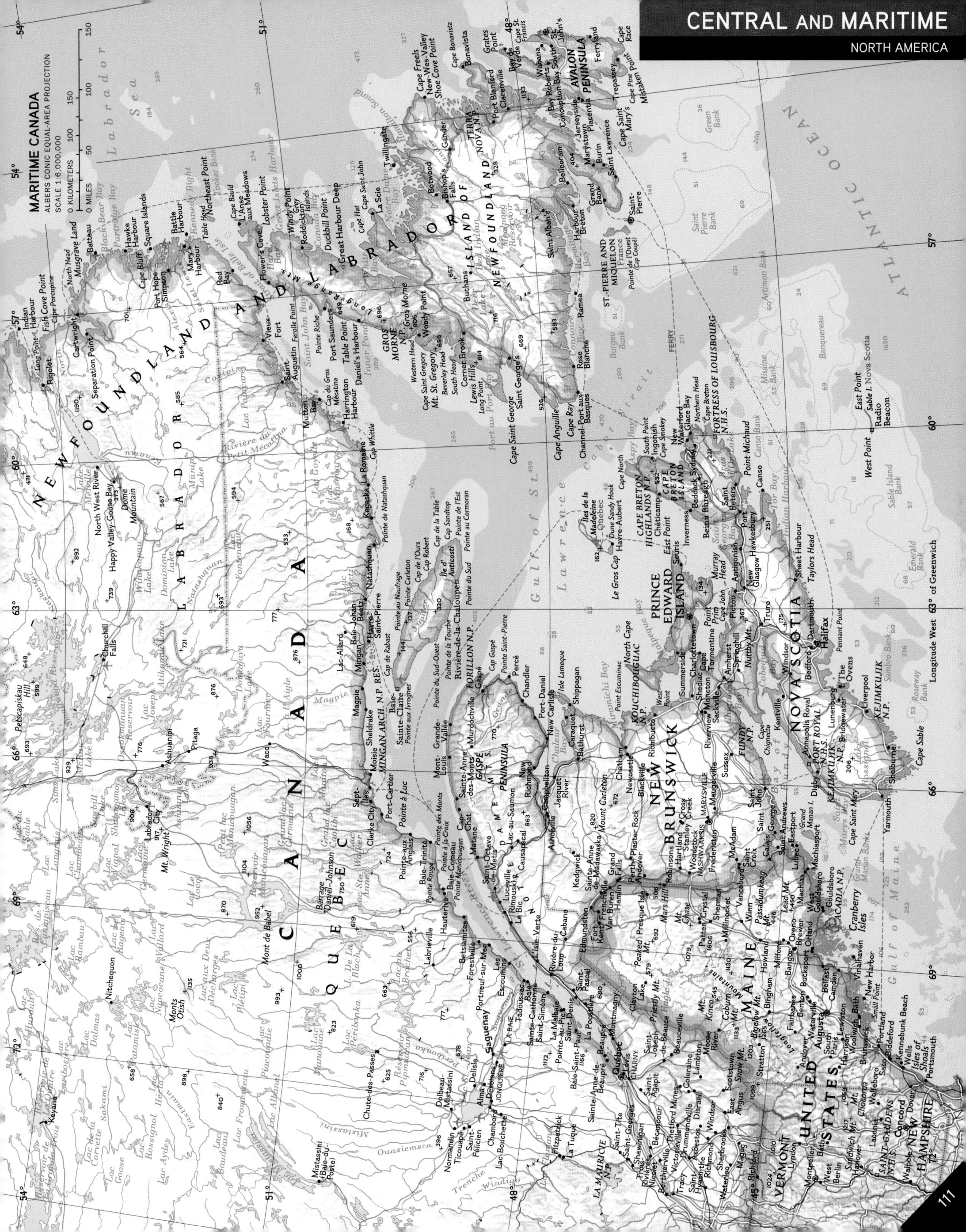
MARITIME CANADA
ALBERS CONIC EQUAL-AREA PROJECTION
SCALE 1:6,000,000
0 KILOMETERS 50 100 150
0 MILES 50 100 150
NEWFOUNDLAND AND LABRADOR
LABRADOR
ISLAND OF NEWFOUNDLAND
QUEBEC
CANADA
NEW BRUNSWICK
NOVA SCOTIA
PRINCE EDWARD ISLAND
MAINE
UNITED STATES
VERMONT
NEW HAMPSHIRE
ST.-PIERRE AND MIQUELON France
ATLANTIC OCEAN
Gulf of St. Lawrence
Labrador Sea
Gulf of Maine
Bay of Fundy
Cabot Strait
ANTICOSTI
GASPÉ PENINSULA
AVALON PENINSULA
CAPE BRETON ISLAND
Longitude West 63° of Greenwich

National Parks of Mexico

(Selected national parks are numbered in blue on the map.)

1 **Cañón de Río Blanco**
2 **Cañón del Sumidero**
3 **Cumbres de Monterrey**
4 **El Gogorrón**
5 **Iztaccíhuatl-Popocatépetl**
6 **Lago de Camécuaro**
7 **Lagunas de Chacahua**
8 **La Malinche**
9 **Los Mármoles**
10 **Nevado de Toluca**
11 **Palenque**
12 **Pico de Orizaba**
13 **Pico de Tancítaro**
14 **Sierra de San Pedro Mártir**
15 **Volcán Nevado de Colima**

UNITED STATES
OKLAHOMA
ARKANSAS
MISSISSIPPI
ALABAMA
GEORGIA
LOUISIANA
TEXAS
FLORIDA
GULF OF MEXICO
ATLANTIC OCEAN
TROPIC OF CANCER
CUBA
La Habana (Havana)
CAMPECHE BANK
YUCATÁN PENINSULA
Caribbean Sea
MEXICO
MEXICO CITY
NUEVO LEÓN
TAMAULIPAS
SAN LUIS POTOSÍ
HIDALGO
PUEBLA
VERACRUZ
OAXACA
GUERRERO
CHIAPAS
TABASCO
CAMPECHE
QUINTANA ROO
YUCATÁN
BELIZE
GUATEMALA
HONDURAS
EL SALVADOR
NICARAGUA
CAYMAN IS. U.K.
Golfo de Tehuantepec
National Parks and Biotopes of Guatemala
(Selected protected areas are numbered in blue on the map.)
16 Sierra del Lacandón
17 Laguna del Tigre–Río Escondido
18 Laguna del Tigre
19 Mirador–Río Azul
20 Naachtún Dos Lagunas
21 Mirador–Río Azul
22 Tikal

CENTRAL MEXICO
ALBERS CONIC EQUAL-AREA PROJECTION
SCALE 1:5,000,000
0 KILOMETERS 80 120
0 MILES 40 80 120
UNITED STATES
TEXAS
PADRE ISLAND NATIONAL SEASHORE
GULF OF MEXICO
PACIFIC OCEAN
TROPIC OF CANCER
MEXICO
CHIHUAHUA
SINALOA
DURANGO
COAHUILA
NUEVO LEÓN
TAMAULIPAS
ZACATECAS
SAN LUIS POTOSÍ
NAYARIT
AGUASCALIENTES
JALISCO
GUANAJUATO
QUERÉTARO
HIDALGO
VERACRUZ
TLAXCALA
PUEBLA
MÉXICO
DISTRITO FED.
MORELOS
MICHOACÁN
COLIMA
GUERRERO
OAXACA
SIERRA MADRE OCCIDENTAL
SIERRA MADRE ORIENTAL
SIERRA MADRE DEL SUR
Istmo de Tehuantepec
Islas Marías
Sierra de los Alamitos
Sierra de Tamaulipas
Laguna Madre
Laguna de Chapala
Bahía de Banderas
Cabo Rojo
Isla de Lobos
Punta de Mita
Punta Roca Partida
Morro de Papanoa
Volcán Ceboruco
Volcán Paricutín
Pico de Orizaba
Popocatépetl
CUMBRES DE MONTERREY N.P.
EL GOGORRÓN N.P.
LOS MÁRMOLES N.P.
VOLCÁN NEVADO DE COLIMA N.P.
PICO DE TANCÍTARO N.P.
NEVADO DE TOLUCA N.P.
IZTACCÍHUATL POPOCATÉPETL N.P.
LA MALINCHE N.P.
PICO DE ORIZABA N.P.
CAÑÓN DEL RÍO BLANCO N.P.
BOSENCHEVE N.P.
LAGO DE CAMÉCUARO N.P.
MEXICO CITY
Monterrey
Guadalupe
Saltillo
Torreón
Gómez Palacio
Durango
Mazatlán
Tepic
Guadalajara
Zacatecas
Aguascalientes
San Luis Potosí
León
Irapuato
Celaya
Querétaro
Morelia
Colima
Puerto Vallarta
Toluca
Cuernavaca
Pachuca
Puebla
Tlalnepantla
Netzahualcóyotl
Xalapa
Veracruz
Orizaba
Tehuacán
Oaxaca
Chilpancingo
Coatzacoalcos
Minatitlán
Poza Rica
Tampico
Ciudad Madero
Ciudad Victoria
Reynosa
Matamoros
Brownsville
McAllen
Nuevo Laredo
Uruapan
Salamanca
Longitude West 102° of Greenwich
105°
102°
99°
96°
24°
21°
18°

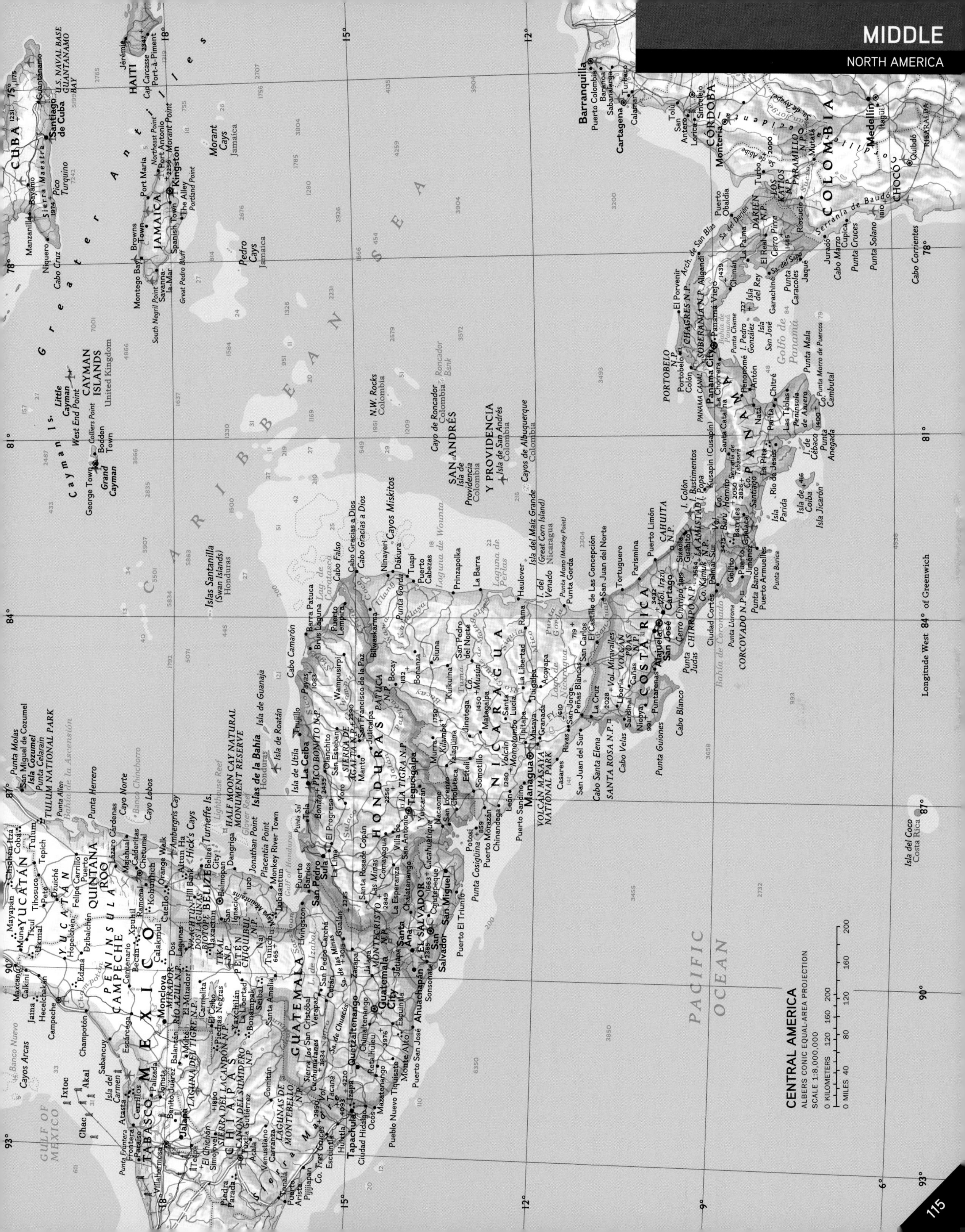
CENTRAL AMERICA
ALBERS CONIC EQUAL-AREA PROJECTION
SCALE 1:8,000,000
0 KILOMETERS 40 80 120 160 200
0 MILES 40 80 120 160 200
Longitude West 84° of Greenwich
CARIBBEAN SEA
PACIFIC OCEAN
GULF OF MEXICO
Greater Antilles
MEXICO
GUATEMALA
BELIZE
HONDURAS
EL SALVADOR
NICARAGUA
COSTA RICA
PANAMA
COLOMBIA
CUBA
JAMAICA
HAITI
CAYMAN ISLANDS
United Kingdom
SAN ANDRÉS Y PROVIDENCIA
Colombia
Islas Santanilla (Swan Islands)
Honduras
Guatemala City
Tegucigalpa
San Salvador
Managua
San José
Panama City
Belmopan
Kingston
Barranquilla
Cartagena
Medellín
Santiago de Cuba
Isla del Coco
Costa Rica

90°
87°
84°
81°
78°
24°
21°
18°
15°
12°
9°
TROPIC OF CAPRICORN
Gulf of Mexico
FLORIDA
UNITED STATES
Port Charlotte
Arcadia
Stuart
West Palm Beach
Fort Myers
Belle Glade
Sanibel Island
Naples
Delray Beach
Pompano Beach
BIG CYPRESS NAT. PRESERVE
Fort Lauderdale
Hollywood
Miami
Cape Romano
Everglades City
Homestead
EVERGLADES N.P.
Ponce de Leon Bay
Cape Sable
Key Largo
Marquesas Keys
Key West
Florida Keys
Marathon
Little Abaco Island
Cooper's Town
Grand Bahama I.
Freeport
High Rock
Tilloo Cay
Moore's I.
Abaco Island
Bimini Islands
Southwest Point
Berry Islands
Nassau
New Providence
Eleuthera Island
Rock Sound
Williams I.
Flamingo Point
Cat Islan
Andros Island
Little San Salvador
Big Wood Cay
Exuma Sound
Deadman's Cays
Dog Rocks
Elbow Cays
Cay Sal Bank
Santaren Channel
Kemps Bay
Gt. Guana Cay
Conception I.
Cistern Point
Great Exuma
Little Exuma
Deadmans Ca
Damas Cays
Anguilla Cays
Archipiélago de Sabana
La Habana (Havana)
GUANABACOA
Matanzas
La Esperanza
Artemisa
LA HABANA
MATANZAS
Corralillo
Quemado de Güines
PINAR DEL RÍO
Pinar del Río
Los Palacios
Península de Zapata
Colón
VILLA CLARA
Cayo Sta. María
Mantua
Ciudad Sandino
Cruces
CIENFUEGOS
Santa Clara
Caibarién
Cayo Coco
CIEGO DE ÁVILA
Arch. de Camagüey
Cabo de San Antonio
Cabo Francés
Cayos de San Felipe
Punta Francés
Nueva Gerona
Cayo Largo
Arch. de los Canarreos
Cienfuegos
Sancti Spíritus
SANCTI SPÍRITUS
Cabaiguán
Bolivia
Ciego de Ávila
Cayo Romano
Cayo Guajaba
Cayo Sabinal
I. DE LA JUVENTUD
Cayo del Rosario
Cayos de Dios
Cayos Ana María
CAMAGÜEY
Camagüey
Minas
CUBA
Cayo Bretón
Cayos Cinco Balas
Cayo Grande
Cayo Anclitas
Contramaestre
Punta Macurijes
Guáimaro
LAS TUNAS
Las Tunas
Gibara
Banes
Antilla
Holguín
HOLGUÍN
Guayabal
Santa Cruz del Sur
Bayamo
GRANMA
Sierra Maestra
SANTIAGO DE CUBA
Santiago de Cuba
Guantánamo
Niquero
Cabo Cruz
G R E A T E R
Little Cayman
West End Point
CAYMAN ISLANDS U.K.
George Town
Grand Cayman
Montego Bay
St. Ann's Bay
Navassa
North Negril Point
South Negril Point
Savanna-la-Mar
Browns Town
Port Maria
Northeast Point
Port Antonio
JAMAICA
Spanish Town
Kingston
Morant Point
Great Pedro Bluff
The Alley
Portland Point
C A R I B B
Islas Santanilla (Swan Islands) Honduras
Half Moon Reefs
North West Rocks Colombia
SAN ANDRÉS
Isla de Providencia Colombia
Roncador Bank
Y PROVIDENCIA
Isla de San Andrés Colombia
Isla Pérez
Arrecife Alacránes
CAMPECHE BANK
Bancos Ingleses
Banco Nuevo
Cayos Arcas
Isla Holbox
Punta Holohit
Punta Yalkubul
Dzilam de Bravo
El Cuyo
Cabo Catoche
Progreso
Chelem
Dzibilchaltún
Dzonot Carretero
Chiquilá
Isla Mujeres
I. Cancún
Sisal
Hunucmá
Mérida
Izamal
Tizimín
Cancún
Umán
Espita
Valladolid
Puerto Morelos
Punta Molas
Isla Cozumel
Maxcanú
Acancéh
Mayapán
Chichén Itzá
Cobá
Calkiní
Muna
Ticul
Tepich
Tulum
Jaina
Uxmal
Peto
Tihosuco
Punta Celarain
Campeche
YUCATÁN
Hopelchén
Dzuiché
Punta Allen
Vigía Chico
Edzná
Champotón
Dzibalchén
Felipe Carrillo Puerto
MEXICO
CAMPECHE
QUINTANA ROO
YUCATÁN PENINSULA
Punta Herrero
Sabancuy
Escárcega
Xpuhil
Majahual
Centenario
Becán
Kohunlich
Chetumal
Calderitas
Cayo Norte
Banco Chinchorro
Cayo Lobos
Monclova
Ramonal
Bahía de Chetumal
Balancán
MIRADOR-RIO AZUL N.P.
Calakmul
Orange Walk
TABASCO
El Mirador
Dos Lagunas
Cuello
Ambergris Cay
San Pedro
LAGUNA DEL TIGRE N.P.
Altun Ha
Tenosique
El Ceibo
Carmelita
Uaxactún
Belize City
Turneffe Is.
Hill Bank
Piedras Negras
TIKAL N.P.
Tikal
Belmopan
Northern Cay
SIERRA DEL LACANDÓN N.P.
San Ignacio
Flores
Lighthouse Reef
Yaxchilán
PETÉN
BELIZE
Dangriga
HALF MOON CAY NATURAL MONUMENT RESERVE
Bonampak
La Libertad
CHIQUIBUL N.P.
Glover Reef
Seibal
Maya Mts.
Jonathan Point
CHIAPAS
Naj Tunich
Placentia Point
Monkey River Town
Santa Amelia
San Luis
Isla de Roatán
Isla de Guanaja
Islas de la Bahía
Gulf of Honduras
GUATEMALA
Livingston
Puerto Barrios
Puerto Cortés
Punta Sal
Isla de Utila
Tela
La Ceiba
Frujillo
Cabo Camarón
Cobán
PICO BONITO N.P.
Payas
Brus Laguna
Barra Patuca
San Pedro Sula
Quimistán
Quiriguá
El Progreso
Olanchito
Sierra de las Minas
Gualán
La Lima
Yoro
San Esteban
SIERRA DE AGALTA N.P.
Laguna de Caratasca
Puerto Lempira
Cabo Falso
Zacapa
Chiquimula
Copán
Wampusirpi
Manto
San Francisco de la Paz
Juticalpa
Cabo Gracias a Dios
Chimaltenango
Guatemala City
Las Minas
HONDURAS
Bilwaskarma
Escuintla
MONTECRISTO N.P.
Comayagua
Villa de San Antonio
PATUCA N.P.
Ninayeri
Cayos Miskitos
Chiquimulilla
Jutiapa
Santa Ana
La Esperanza
LA TIGRA N.P.
Bocay
Punta Gorda
Dákura
San José
Ahuachapán
EL SALVADOR
Tegucigalpa
Tuapí
Puerto Cabezas
Sonsonate
San Salvador
Cojutepeque
Bonanza
Nacaome
San Lorenzo
Murra
Kilambé
Siuna
San Miguel
Puerto El Triunfo
Golfo de Fonseca
Choluteca
Yalagüina
Kuikuina
Punta San Juan
Punta Cosigüina
Potosí
Somotillo
Estelí
Jinotega
Matagalpa
San Pedro del Norte
Prinzapolka
Puerto Morazán
La Trinidad
NICARAGUA
La Barra
Chinandega
Laguna de Perlas
León
Lago de Managua
Islas del Maíz Nicaragua
Managua
Tipitapa
La Libertad
Rama
Haulover
I. del Maíz Grande (Great Corn Island) Nicaragua
Masaya
VOLCÁN MASAYA N.P.
Granada
Acoyapa
Bluefields
I. del Venado
Casares
Rivas
Lago de Nicaragua
Punta Mono (Monkey Point)
Punta Gorda
PACIFIC OCEAN
San Jorge
San Juan del Sur
San Carlos
Peñas Blancas
El Castillo de las Concepción
San Juan del Norte
Cabo Santa Elena
SANTA ROSA N.P.
La Cruz
Golfo de Papagayo
Liberia
Tortuguero
Sardinal
Altamira
TORTUGUERO N.P.
Cabo Velas
Cañas
COSTA RICA
Parismina
Nicoya
Esparza
Puerto Limón
Punta Guiones
Puntarenas
San José
Cartago
CAHUITA N.P.
Cabo Blanco
Golfo de Nicoya
Sixaola
I. Colón
Portobelo
PORTOBELO N.P.
CHIRRIPÓ N.P.
LA AMISTAD N.P.
Isla Bastimentos
I. Cayo Agua
Colón
El Porvenir
Archipiélago de San Blas
Punta Judas
I. Popa
Golfo de los Mosquitos
SOBERANÍA N.P.
CHAGRES N.P.
Ciudad Cortés
Palmar Sur
Kusapin (Cusapín)
Santa Catalina
Bahía de Coronado
PANAMA
Panama City
Lago Bayano
Aligandí
Golfito
Cañas Gordas
Punta Llorona
Puerto Jiménez
CORCOVADO N.P.
Punta Banco
OMAR TORRIJOS N.P.
La Pintada
Golfo de Panamá
Chimán
Puerto Obaldía
Cabo Tiburón
Puerto Armuelles
Antón
I. del Rey
ATLÁNTICO
COLOMBIA
Cartagena
Turbaco
Bahía de Barbacoas
SUCRE
Carmen de Bolívar
Tolú
Sincelejo
Lorica
CÓRDOBA
Montería
Planeta Rica
ANTIOQUIA
ALBERS CONIC EQUAL-AREA PROJECTION
SCALE 1:8,000,000
0 KILOMETERS 120 160 200
0 MILES 40 80 120 160 200
4 Red circled numbers are reference keys to larger scale maps on page 118.

Longitude West 72° of Greenwich
69°
66°
24°
21°
18°
15°
12°
9°
ATLANTIC OCEAN
ANTILLES
CARIBBEAN SEA
San Salvador (Watling)
Rum Cay
Samana Cay
Long Island
Plana Cays (French Cays)
Mayaguana I.
Acklins Island
TURKS AND CAICOS ISLANDS
U.K.
East Caicos
West Caicos
Caicos Is.
Turks Islands
Cockburn Town
Little Inagua Island
Great Inagua Island
Ambergris Cays
Mouchoir Passage
Matthew Town
Punta Guarico
Baracoa
Punta de Maisí
Île de la Tortue
Cabo Isabela
HISPANIOLA
Anse-à-Foleur
Monte Cristi
Jean-Rabel
Cap-à-Foux
Anse-Rouge
Cap-Haïtien
Imbert
Puerto Plata
Cabo Francés Viejo
Abreú
Bahía Escocesa
Mao
Santiago
Cabo Cabrón
Cabo Samaná
Dessalines
HAITI
Cordillera Central
San Francisco de Macorís
Samaná
Cabo San Rafael
Saint-Marc
I. de la Gonâve
Pointe Ouest
Hinche
DOMINICAN REPUBLIC
Sabana de La Mar
El Macao
Anse-à-Galets
Comendador
Cabo Engaño
Grande Cayemite
San Juan
Santo Domingo
Higüey
Massif de la Hotte
Miragoâne
Jacmel
Port-au-Prince
Neiba
Azua
Baní
San Pedro de Macorís
La Romana
Cap Dame-Marie
Port-à-Piment
Les Cayes
Côtes-de-Fer
Duvergé
Cabral
Barahona
Nizao
Isla Saona
Isla Beata
Cabo Beata
Punta Higüero
I. Mona
P.R.
Mayagüez
Cabo Rojo
San Germán
Utuado
Ponce
Cayey
San Juan
PUERTO RICO
United States
Vieques
P.R.
St. Croix
Christiansted
U.S. VIRGIN ISLANDS
U.S.
Charlotte Amalie
St. Thomas
St. John
Tortola
Virgin Gorda
Anegada
Road Town
BRITISH VIRGIN ISLANDS
U.K.
Sombrero
ANGUILLA
U.K.
The Valley
ST. MARTIN France
ST. MAARTEN Neth.
ST. BARTHÉLEMY France
Gustavia
SABA Neth.
ST. EUSTATIUS Neth.
Basseterre
Nevis
ST. KITTS AND NEVIS
Barbuda
ANTIGUA AND BARBUDA
St. John's
Antigua
Montserrat
Plymouth
MONTSERRAT U.K.
Guadeloupe Passage
GUADELOUPE France
Grande-Terre
La Désirade
Basse-Terre
Pointe-à-Pitre
Marie-Galante
Les Saintes
Dominica Passage
LESSER ANTILLES
LEEWARD ISLANDS
DOMINICA
Roseau
Martinique Passage
Mgne. Pelée
Sainte-Marie
Fort-de-France
Martinique
MARTINIQUE France
Pointe d'Enfer
St. Lucia Channel
ST. LUCIA
Castries
WINDWARD ISLANDS
St. Vincent Passage
ST. VINCENT AND THE GRENADINES
Kingstown
Bequia
Canouan
Union
Carriacou
Hillsborough
GRENADA
St. George's
Pt. Salines
Speightstown
Bridgetown
BARBADOS
MONTSERRAT
Eruptions from Soufriere Hills volcano since 1995 have forced the evacuation of southern Montserrat—including its capital, Plymouth.
DUTCH CARIBBEAN ISLANDS
The Netherlands Antilles government was dissolved on October 10, 2010. Today, the islands of Curaçao and St. Maarten, along with Aruba, have local autonomy within the Netherlands realm. The islands of Bonaire, Saba, and St. Eustatius are directly administered by the Netherlands.
ARUBA Neth.
Oranjestad
CURAÇAO Neth.
Willemstad
BONAIRE Neth.
Islas de Aves Venez.
Islas Los Roques Venez.
ARCHIPIÉLAGO LOS ROQUES N.P.
Cayo Grande
La Blanquilla
Los Hermanos
Venezuela
TRINIDAD AND TOBAGO
Tobago
Charlotteville
Canaan
Galera Point
Delaware Bank
Port of Spain
San Fernando
Trinidad
Gulf of Paria
Península de Paria
Macuro
Punta Gallinas
Bahía Honda
Bahía de Portete
Cabo de la Vela
Península de la Guajira
Puerto López
Uribia
Ríohacha
Santa Marta
Cabo de la Aguja
Puerto Colombia
Barranquilla
GUAJIRA
Golfo de Venezuela
Paraguaipoa
San Rafael
Mara
Sierra de Perijá
Valledupar
Maracaibo
Santa Rita
Puerto Mirando
Rosario
Cabimas
Lagunillas
Machiques
Caracolí
CÉSAR
PERIJÁ N.P.
ZULIA
Lago de Maracaibo
Santa Ana
MAGDALENA
Plato
El Banco
Encontrados
BOLÍVAR
NORTE DE SANTANDER
MÉRIDA
Mérida
Cordillera de Mérida
Punto Fijo
Península de Paraguaná
MÉDANOS DE CORO N.P.
Punta Cardón
Coro
La Vela de Coro
Puerto Cumarebo
Mirimire
FALCÓN
Dabajuro
Churuguara
Chichiriviche
MORROCOY N.P.
Tucacas
Puerto Cabello
CARABOBO
VARGAS
La Guaira
Caracas
CAPITAL DIST.
Río Chico
Los Teques
MIRANDA
LARA
San Felipe
Valencia
YARACUY
Maracay
ARAGUA
Barquisimeto
Carora
Mene Grande
TRUJILLO
El Tocuyo
Acarigua
Trujillo
Betijoque
Valera
Bobures
San Carlos
COJEDES
PORTUGUESA
Guanare
Barinas
BARINAS
San Juan de los Morros
Ortiz
Altagracia de Orituco
El Sombrero
VENEZUELA
El Calvario
Calabozo
El Baúl
GUÁRICO
AGUARO-GUARIQUITO N.P.
NUEVA ESPARTA
La Asunción
I. de Margarita
I. Cubagua
I. Coche
Cumaná
Río Caribe
SUCRE
Carúpano
Guanta
Barcelona
Puerto Píritu
Narícual
Maturín
Pedernales
MARIUSA N.P.
Punta Araguapiche
Aragua de Barcelona
San Mateo
Anaco
MONAGAS
Zaraza
Tigre
Nipa
Leona
Tucupita
Coporito
Barrancas
Curiapo
San José de Amacuro
Waini Point
Mabaruma
Morawhanna
DELTA AMACURO
Serranía de Imataca
GUYANA
El Pao
Oficina
ANZOÁTEGUI
Soledad
Ciudad Bolívar
63°
Guarico
Portuguesa

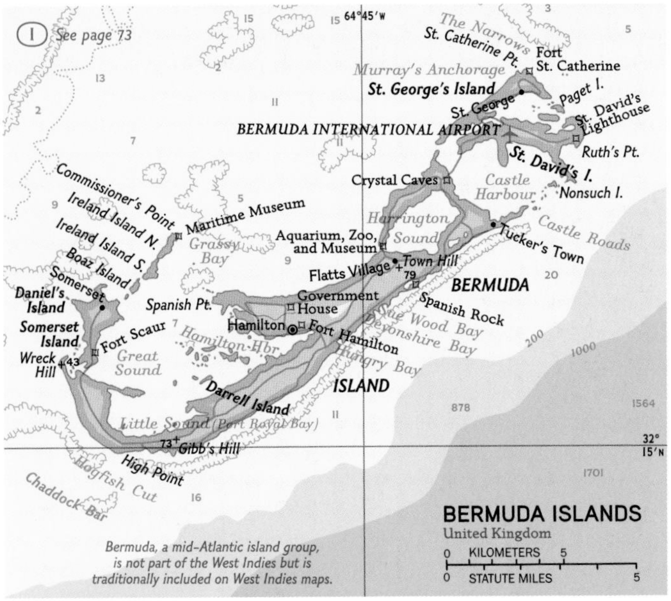

See page 73
BERMUDA ISLANDS
United Kingdom
Bermuda, a mid-Atlantic island group, is not part of the West Indies but is traditionally included on West Indies maps.
KILOMETERS 5
STATUTE MILES 5
St. George's Island
St. Catherine Pt.
Fort St. Catherine
Murray's Anchorage
The Narrows
St. George
Paget I.
St. David's Lighthouse
BERMUDA INTERNATIONAL AIRPORT
St. David's I.
Ruth's Pt.
Nonsuch I.
Crystal Caves
Castle Harbour
Castle Roads
Harrington Sound
Tucker's Town
Commissioner's Point
Maritime Museum
Ireland Island N.
Ireland Island S.
Grassy Bay
Boaz Island
Somerset
Daniel's Island
Somerset Island
Wreck Hill
Fort Scaur
Spanish Pt.
Aquarium, Zoo, and Museum
Flatts Village
Town Hill
Government House
Hamilton
Fort Hamilton
Hamilton Hbr.
Great Sound
BERMUDA
Spanish Rock
Devonshire Bay
Harrington Sound
Darrell Island
ISLAND
Little Sound (Port Royal Bay)
Gibb's Hill
High Point
Hogfish Cut
Chaddock Bar
64°45′W
32° 15′N

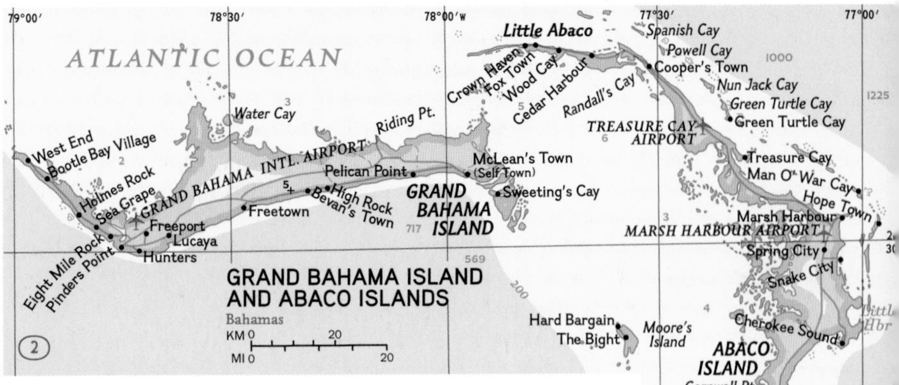

ATLANTIC OCEAN
GRAND BAHAMA ISLAND AND ABACO ISLANDS
Bahamas
KM 0 20
MI 0 20
West End
Bootle Bay Village
Water Cay
GRAND BAHAMA INTL. AIRPORT
Riding Pt.
Holmes Rock
Sea Grape
Freeport
Lucaya
Hunters
Eight Mile Rock
Pinders Point
Freetown
Pelican Point
High Rock
Bevan's Town
GRAND BAHAMA ISLAND
McLean's Town (Self Town)
Sweeting's Cay
Little Abaco
Crown Haven
Fox Town
Wood Cay
Cedar Harbour
Randall's Cay
Spanish Cay
Powell Cay
Cooper's Town
Nun Jack Cay
Green Turtle Cay
TREASURE CAY AIRPORT
Treasure Cay
Man O' War Cay
Hope Town
Marsh Harbour
MARSH HARBOUR AIRPORT
Spring City
Snake City
Hard Bargain
The Bight
Moore's Island
Cherokee Sound
ABACO ISLAND
Cornwall Pt.
Crossing Rocks
Sandy Point
Southwest Point
Conch Sound Point
Hole in the Wall
79°00′
78°30′
78°00′W
77°30′
77°00′

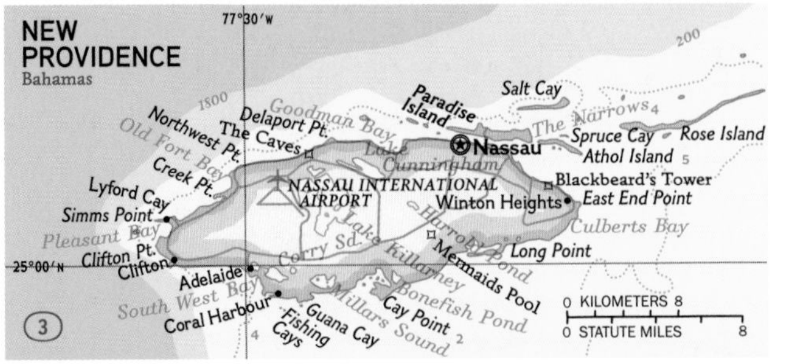

NEW PROVIDENCE
Bahamas
77°30′W
25°00′N
Salt Cay
Paradise Island
Nassau
The Narrows
Spruce Cay
Rose Island
Athol Island
Goodman Bay
Delaport Pt.
Northwest Pt.
The Caves
Old Fort Bay
Creek Pt.
Lake Cunningham
Blackbeard's Tower
East End Point
NASSAU INTERNATIONAL AIRPORT
Winton Heights
Lyford Cay
Simms Point
Pleasant Bay
Clifton Pt.
Clifton
Culberts Bay
Long Point
Adelaide
South West Bay
Corry Sd.
Lake Killarney
Mermaids Pool
Bonefish Pond
Coral Harbour
Fishing Cays
Guana Cay
Cay Point
Millars Sound
KILOMETERS 8
STATUTE MILES 8

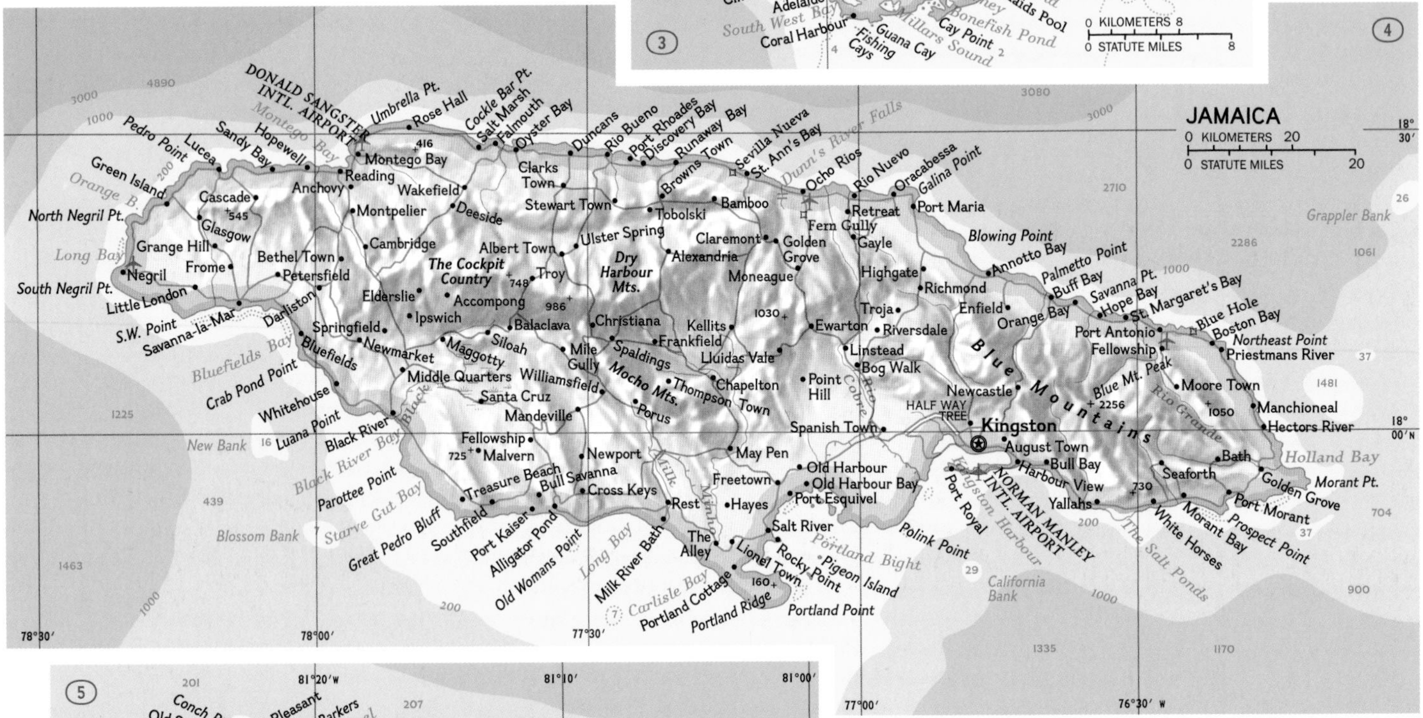

JAMAICA
KILOMETERS 20
STATUTE MILES 20
DONALD SANGSTER INTL. AIRPORT
Montego Bay
Umbrella Pt.
Rose Hall
Cockle Bar Pt.
Salt Marsh
Falmouth
Oyster Bay
Duncans
Rio Bueno
Port Rhoades
Discovery Bay
Runaway Bay
Browns Town
Sevilla Nueva
St. Ann's Bay
Dunn's River Falls
Ocho Rios
Rio Nuevo
Oracabessa
Galina Point
Port Maria
Pedro Point
Lucea
Sandy Bay
Hopewell
Reading
Green Island
Orange B.
Cascade
Anchovy
Wakefield
Clarks Town
Stewart Town
Bamboo
Tobolski
Retreat
North Negril Pt.
Glasgow
Montpelier
Deeside
Fern Gully
Grange Hill
Long Bay
Cambridge
Albert Town
Ulster Spring
Claremont
Golden Grove
Gayle
Blowing Point
Annotto Bay
Frome
Bethel Town
Petersfield
The Cockpit Country
Troy
Dry Harbour Mts.
Alexandria
Moneague
Highgate
Richmond
Palmetto Point
Buff Bay
Negril
South Negril Pt.
Little London
Elderslie
Accompong
Enfield
Orange Bay
Savanna Pt.
Hope Bay
St. Margaret's Bay
Blue Hole
Boston Bay
S.W. Point
Savanna-la-Mar
Darliston
Springfield
Ipswich
Balaclava
Christiana
Kellits
Ewarton
Troja
Riversdale
Port Antonio
Fellowship
Northeast Point
Priestmans River
Bluefields Bay
Bluefields
Newmarket
Maggotty
Siloah
Mile Gully
Spaldings
Frankfield
Lluidas Vale
Linstead
Bog Walk
Blue Mountains
Blue Mt. Peak
Crab Pond Point
Middle Quarters
Williamsfield
Mocho Mts.
Thompson Town
Chapelton
Point Hill
Newcastle
Moore Town
Manchioneal
Whitehouse
Santa Cruz
Mandeville
Porus
HALF WAY TREE
Kingston
Hectors River
Luana Point
Black River
Black River Bay
Spanish Town
August Town
Bull Bay
Holland Bay
New Bank
Fellowship
Malvern
Newport
May Pen
Old Harbour
Harbour View
Bath
Morant Pt.
Parottee Point
Treasure Beach
Bull Savanna
Cross Keys
Freetown
Old Harbour Bay
Yallahs
Seaforth
Golden Grove
Starve Gut Bay
Port Esquivel
NORMAN MANLEY INTL. AIRPORT
Port Royal
Kingston Harbour
Port Morant
Blossom Bank
Great Pedro Bluff
Southfield
Port Kaiser
Alligator Pond
Rest
Hayes
Salt River
Polink Point
White Horses
Morant Bay
Prospect Point
Old Womans Point
Long Bay
Milk River Bath
The Alley
Lionel Town
Rocky Point
Portland Bight
Pigeon Island
The Salt Ponds
California Bank
Carlisle Bay
Portland Cottage
Portland Ridge
Portland Point
Grappler Bank
78°30′
78°00′
77°30′
77°00′
76°30′W
18° 30′
18° 00′N

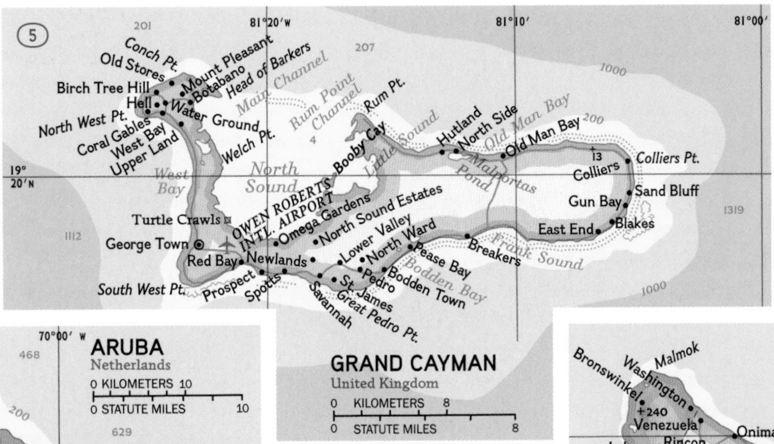

GRAND CAYMAN
United Kingdom
KILOMETERS 8
STATUTE MILES 8
81°20′W
81°10′
81°00′
19° 20′N
Conch Pt.
Old Stores
Mount Pleasant
Botabano
Head of Barkers
Birch Tree Hill
Hell
Water Ground
Main Channel
Rum Point Channel
Rum Pt.
North West Pt.
Coral Gables
West Bay
Upper Land
Welch Pt.
Booby Cay
Little Sound
Hutland
North Side
Old Man Bay
Colliers Pt.
Colliers
Sand Bluff
West Bay
North Sound
Malportas Pond
Gun Bay
Turtle Crawls
OWEN ROBERTS INTL. AIRPORT
Omega Gardens
North Sound Estates
East End
Blakes
George Town
Red Bay
Newlands
Lower Valley
North Ward
Pease Bay
Breakers
Frank Sound
South West Pt.
Prospect
Spotts
Pedro
Bodden Town
Bodden Bay
St. James
Great Pedro Pt.
Savannah

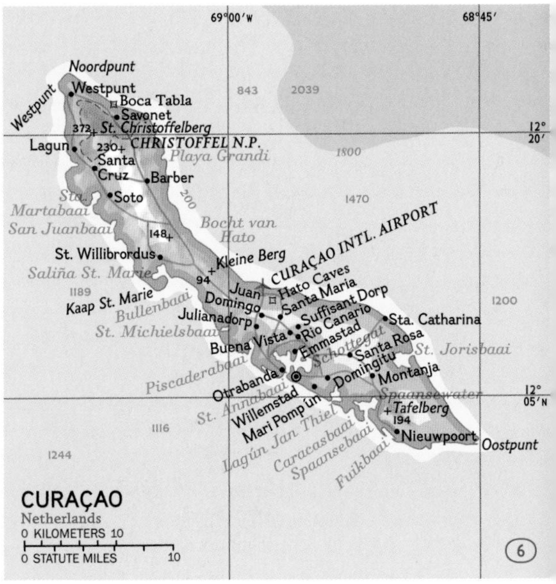

CURAÇAO
Netherlands
KILOMETERS 10
STATUTE MILES 10
69°00′W
68°45′
12° 20′
12° 05′N
Noordpunt
Westpunt
Boca Tabla
Savonet
St. Christoffelberg
CHRISTOFFEL N.P.
Lagun
Santa Cruz
Playa Grandi
Barber
Soto
Sta. Martabaai
San Juanbaai
Bocht van Hato
CURAÇAO INTL. AIRPORT
St. Willibrordus
Kleine Berg
Saliña St. Marie
Kaap St. Marie
Bullenbaai
Juan Domingo
Hato Caves
Santa Maria
Suffisant Dorp
Rio Canario
Sta. Catharina
St. Michielsbaai
Julianadorp
Buena Vista
Emmastad
Santa Rosa
St. Jorisbaai
Piscaderabaai
Otrabanda
Willemstad
Dominguito
Montanja
Spaanse Water
St. Annabaai
Mari Pompún
Tafelberg
Lagún Jan Thiel
Caracasbaai
Spaansebaai
Nieuwpoort
Fuikbaai
Oostpunt

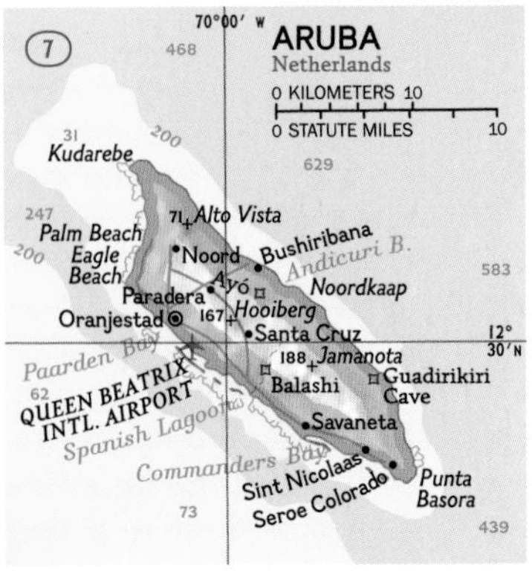

ARUBA
Netherlands
KILOMETERS 10
STATUTE MILES 10
70°00′W
12° 30′N
Kudarebe
Alto Vista
Palm Beach
Eagle Beach
Noord
Bushiribana
Andicuri B.
Noordkaap
Paradera
Ayó
Hooiberg
Oranjestad
Santa Cruz
Jamanota
Paarden Baai
Balashi
Guadirikiri Cave
QUEEN BEATRIX INTL. AIRPORT
Spanish Lagoon
Savaneta
Commanders Baai
Sint Nicolaas
Punta Basora
Seroe Colorado

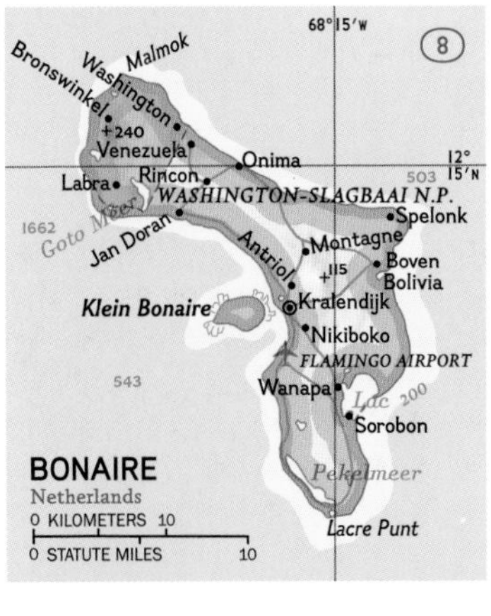

BONAIRE
Netherlands
KILOMETERS 10
STATUTE MILES 10
68°15′W
12° 15′N
Malmok
Washington
Bronswinkel
Venezuela
Labra
Rincon
Onima
WASHINGTON-SLAGBAAI N.P.
Goto Meer
Spelonk
Jan Doran
Antriol
Montagne
Boven Bolivia
Klein Bonaire
Kralendijk
Nikiboko
FLAMINGO AIRPORT
Wanapa
Lac
Sorobon
Pekelmeer
Lacre Punt

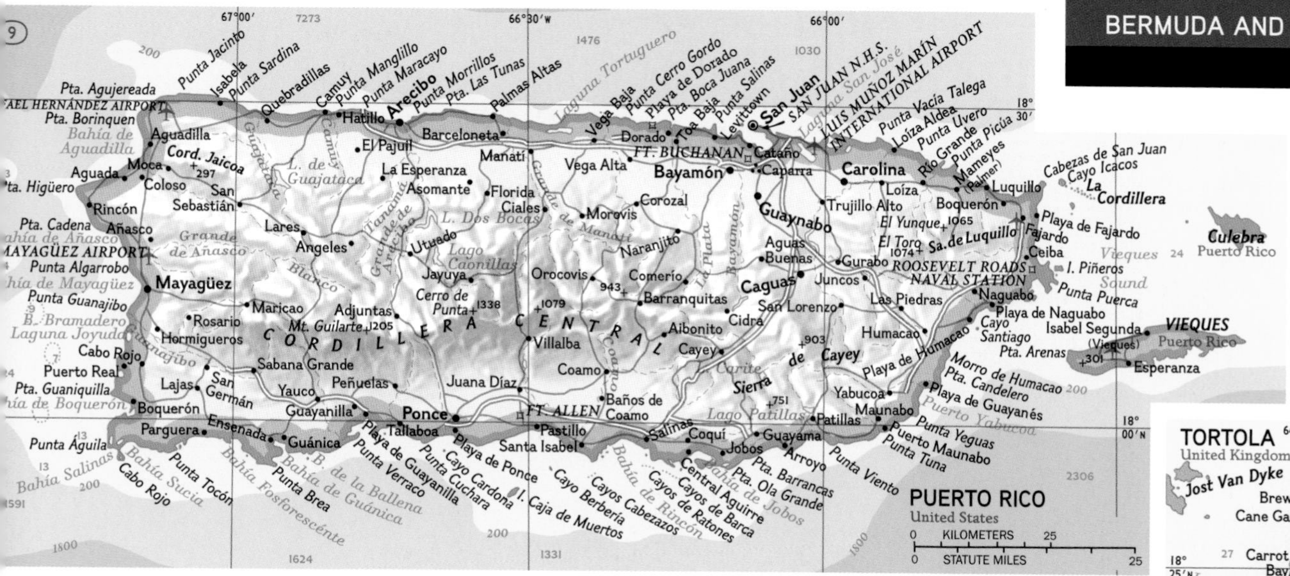
PUERTO RICO
United States
0 KILOMETERS 25
0 STATUTE MILES 25
9
San Juan
Arecibo
Aguadilla
Mayagüez
Ponce
Bayamón
Carolina
Caguas
Guaynabo
Humacao
Fajardo
CORDILLERA CENTRAL
Sierra de Cayey
Sa. de Luquillo
El Yunque
Cerro de Punta 1338
LUIS MUÑOZ MARÍN INTERNATIONAL AIRPORT
RAFAEL HERNÁNDEZ AIRPORT
MAYAGÜEZ AIRPORT
ROOSEVELT ROADS NAVAL STATION
FT. BUCHANAN
FT. ALLEN
SAN JUAN N.H.S.
Culebra
Puerto Rico
VIEQUES
Puerto Rico
Vieques Sound
Esperanza
Isabel Segunda
La Cordillera
Cabezas de San Juan
Cayo Icacos
Laguna Tortuguero
Bahía de Aguadilla
Bahía de Mayagüez
Bahía de Boquerón
Bahía de Jobos
Bahía de Rincón
Bahía Salinas
Bahía Sucia
Bahía Fosforescente
B. de la Ballena
Bahía de Guánica
Caja de Muertos
Cabo Rojo
Punta Tuna
Punta Puerca
Lago Caonillas
L. Dos Bocas
L. de Guajataca
Lago Patillas
18° 30′
18° 00′ N
67° 00′
66° 30′ W
66° 00′

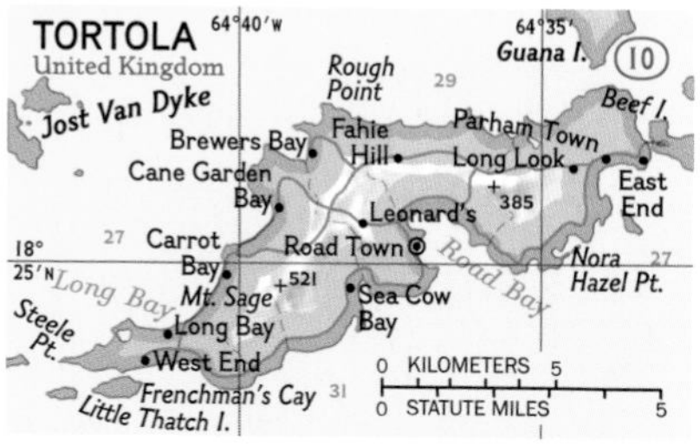
TORTOLA
United Kingdom
10
0 KILOMETERS 5
0 STATUTE MILES 5
Jost Van Dyke
Road Town
Sage Mt. 521
Rough Point
Brewers Bay
Cane Garden Bay
Carrot Bay
Mt. Sage
Long Bay
West End
Frenchman's Cay
Little Thatch I.
Steele Pt.
Fahie Hill
Leonard's
Parham Town
Long Look
East End
Beef I.
Guana I.
Sea Cow Bay
Nora Hazel Pt.
Road Bay
64° 40′ W
64° 35′
18° 25′ N

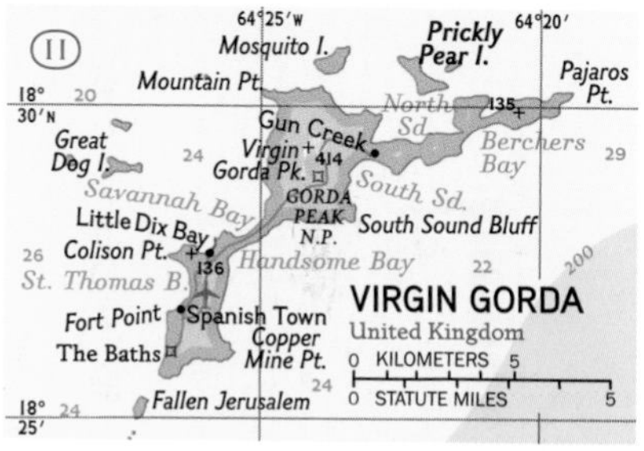
11
VIRGIN GORDA
United Kingdom
0 KILOMETERS 5
0 STATUTE MILES 5
Mosquito I.
Prickly Pear I.
Pajaros Pt.
Mountain Pt.
Gun Creek
Virgin Gorda Pk. 414
GORDA PEAK N.P.
North Sd.
South Sd.
Berchers Bay
Great Dog I.
Savannah Bay
Little Dix Bay
Colison Pt.
St. Thomas B.
Handsome Bay
South Sound Bluff
Fort Point
The Baths
Spanish Town
Copper Mine Pt.
Fallen Jerusalem
64° 25′ W
64° 20′
18° 30′ N
18° 25′

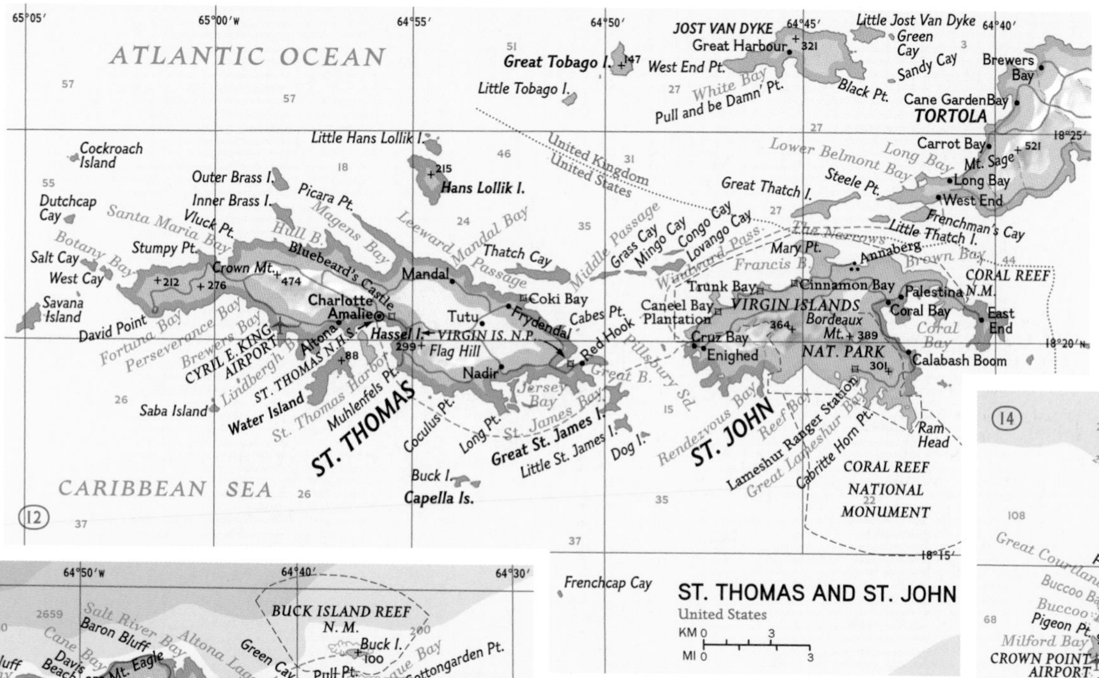
12
ST. THOMAS AND ST. JOHN
United States
KM 0 3
MI 0 3
ATLANTIC OCEAN
CARIBBEAN SEA
ST. THOMAS
ST. JOHN
TORTOLA
JOST VAN DYKE
Charlotte Amalie
CYRIL E. KING AIRPORT
ST. THOMAS N.H.S.
VIRGIN ISLANDS NAT. PARK
VIRGIN IS. N.P.
CORAL REEF NATIONAL MONUMENT
CORAL REEF N.M.
Crown Mt. 474
Bordeaux Mt. 389
Water Island
Hassel I.
Great St. James I.
Little St. James I.
Hans Lollik I.
Little Hans Lollik I.
Great Tobago I.
Little Tobago I.
Great Thatch I.
Cruz Bay
Coral Bay
Red Hook
Frenchcap Cay
Capella Is.
Buck I.
Saba Island
Pillsbury Sd.
Windward Pass.
Middle Passage
Leeward Passage
United Kingdom
United States
65° 05′
65° 00′ W
64° 55′
64° 50′
64° 45′
64° 40′
18° 25′
18° 20′ N
18° 15′

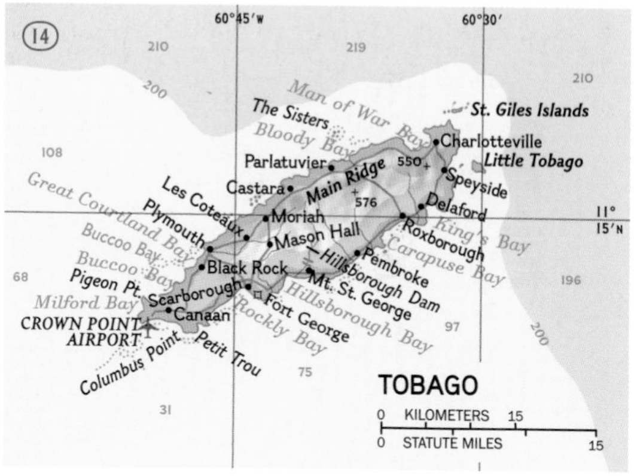
14
TOBAGO
0 KILOMETERS 15
0 STATUTE MILES 15
Scarborough
Main Ridge 576
Charlotteville
Little Tobago
St. Giles Islands
Speyside
Roxborough
Plymouth
CROWN POINT AIRPORT
Canaan
Fort George
Hillsborough Dam
Man of War Bay
Great Courland Bay
King's Bay
Buccoo Bay
Pigeon Pt.
60° 45′ W
60° 30′
11° 15′ N

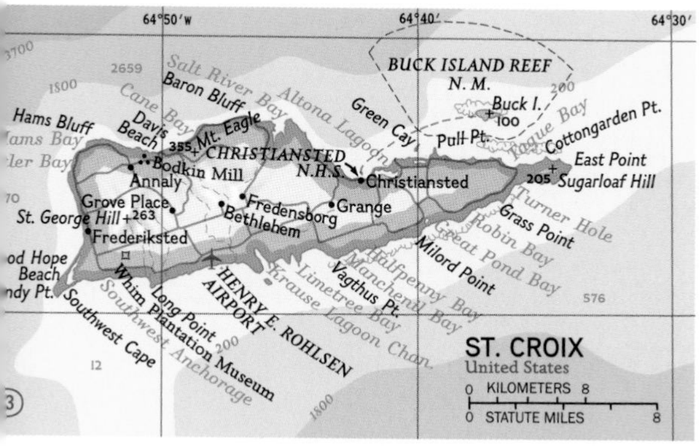
ST. CROIX
United States
0 KILOMETERS 8
0 STATUTE MILES 8
BUCK ISLAND REEF N.M.
Buck I.
Christiansted
CHRISTIANSTED N.H.S.
Frederiksted
HENRY E. ROHLSEN AIRPORT
Mt. Eagle 355
East Point
Sugarloaf Hill
Salt River Bay
Southwest Cape
Whim Plantation Museum
Hams Bluff
Sandy Pt.
64° 50′ W
64° 40′
64° 30′

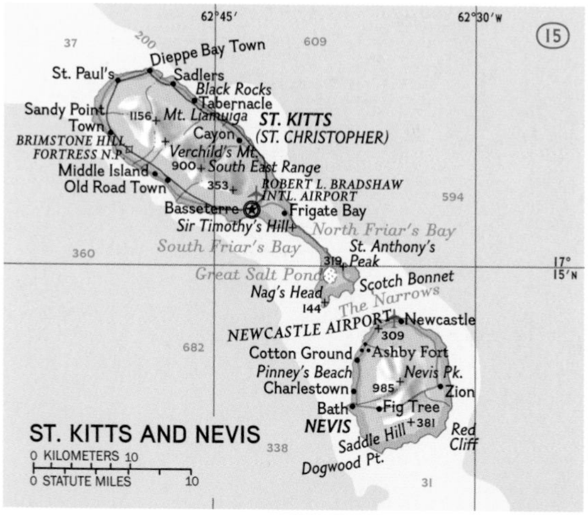
15
ST. KITTS AND NEVIS
0 KILOMETERS 10
0 STATUTE MILES 10
ST. KITTS (ST. CHRISTOPHER)
NEVIS
Basseterre
Charlestown
Mt. Liamuiga 1156
Nevis Pk. 985
BRIMSTONE HILL FORTRESS N.P.
ROBERT L. BRADSHAW INTL. AIRPORT
NEWCASTLE AIRPORT
Dieppe Bay Town
Sandy Point Town
The Narrows
Great Salt Pond
62° 45′
62° 30′ W
17° 15′ N

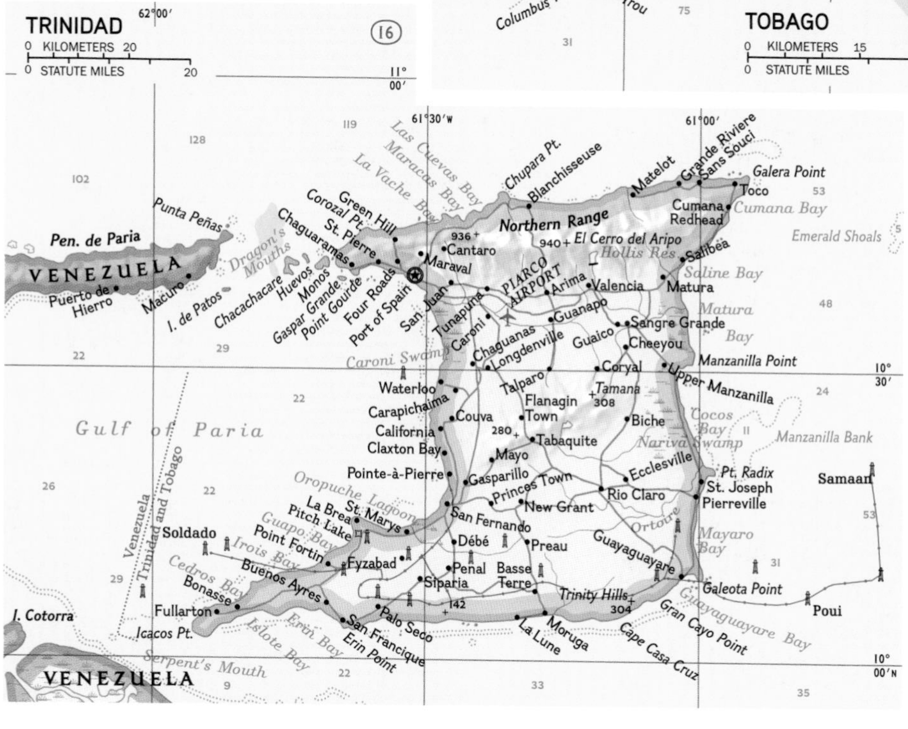
16
TRINIDAD
0 KILOMETERS 20
0 STATUTE MILES 20
Port of Spain
San Fernando
Arima
Chaguanas
Point Fortin
PIARCO AIRPORT
Northern Range
El Cerro del Aripo 940
Pen. de Paria
VENEZUELA
Gulf of Paria
Dragon's Mouths
Serpent's Mouth
Galera Point
Galeota Point
Icacos Pt.
Chacachacare
Monos
Huevos
Gaspar Grande
Caroni Swamp
Nariva Swamp
Pitch Lake
Soldado
Samaan
Poui
Manzanilla Bank
Emerald Shoals
Venezuela
Trinidad and Tobago
61° 30′ W
61° 00′
11° 00′
10° 30′
10° 00′ N

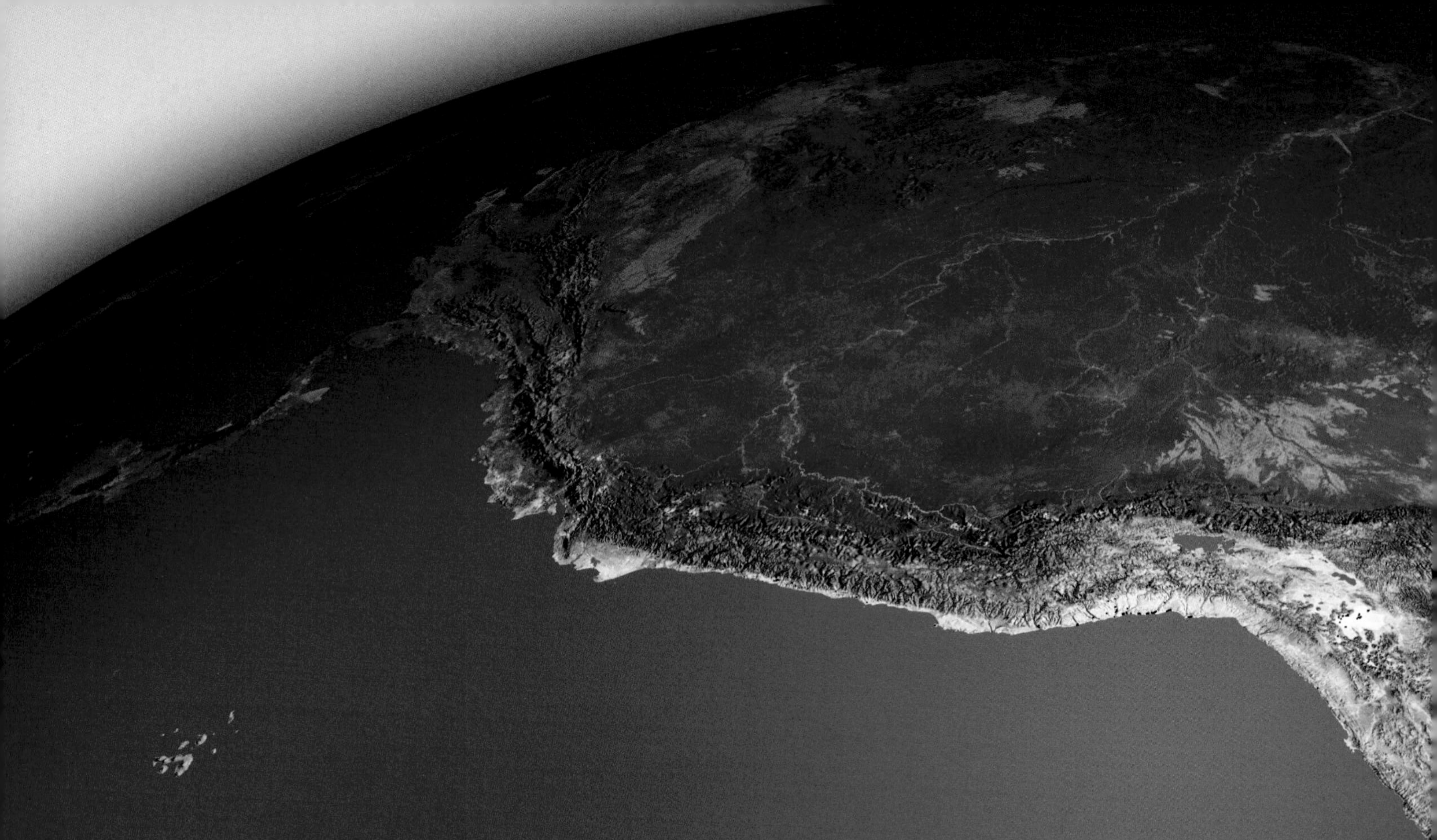

TWO FEATURES DOMINATE SOUTH AMERICA: The Andes, extending 7,242 kilometers (4,500 miles), is the world's longest and second highest mountain range; and the Amazon—the world's largest river by volume and, at 6,679 kilometers (4,150 miles), the second longest—flows through the largest, most biologically rich rain forest on Earth. Some of the people in the Amazon Basin are among the least touched by the modern world, although the press of logging, agriculture, and settlement has devastated much of the forest and its scattered inhabitants. Other South American features also stand out. The Pantanal, spanning parts of Brazil, Paraguay, and Bolivia with flooded grasslands and savannas, is 17 times the size of the Florida Everglades and home to a kaleidoscopic diversity of plant and animal life. The vast grassy plains of the Argentine Pampas nourish livestock, but the Atacama Desert of Chile supports little life. Its dry, clear, thin air, however, makes it ideal for astronomical observatories.

In the Andes, the Inca empire expanded between 1438 and 1527, stretching from modern Colombia to western Argentina. Weakened by internal dissension, the Inca succumbed to Francisco Pizarro's forces in 1533. Spaniards looted its golden treasures and forced native slave labor to work gold and silver mines; Portuguese overlords imported millions of slaves from Africa to work Brazilian plantations. Not until the early 19th century under Simón Bolívar, the Liberator of the Americas, did the desire for independence coalesce and rebellion spread rapidly.

Yet even after the colonial period, strife continued during the 20th century with coups, civil wars, and cross-border disputes. Today mining of industrial mineral ores, fishing, forestry, petroleum extraction, and commercial agriculture support the continent's economies, but prosperity does not reach all its people. Populist leaders in countries such as Venezuela and Bolivia are raising their voices, while indigenous peoples are gaining new influence.

South America

Longitude West 50° of Greenwich
80°
70°
60°
40°
90°
Caribbean Sea
GUATEMALA
HONDURAS
Coco
Tegucigalpa
EL SALVADOR
NICARAGUA
Managua
Irazú Volcano
3412
San José
COSTA RICA
3819
Panama City
PANAMA
Gulf of Panama
Gulf of Venezuela
Lesser Antilles
Barranquilla
5775
Maracaibo
Lake Maracaibo
Caracas
Port of Spain
TRINIDAD AND TOBAGO
Orinoco River Delta
VENEZUELA
LLANOS
Georgetown
Paramaribo
Cayenne
ATLANTIC OCEAN
Angel Falls
2739
Mt. Roraima
GUYANA
SURINAME
FRENCH GUIANA
GUIANA HIGHLANDS
2579
5007
Source of the Orinoco
Serra de Tumucumaque
4080
Medellín
Bogotá
COLOMBIA
Cali
5750
2994
Pico de Neblina
Cape North
Mouths of the Amazon
MARAJÓ ISLAND
Belém
São Marcos Bay
EQUATOR
Quito
Caquetá
AMAZON
Paru
ECUADOR
Putumayo
Napo
Manaus
Amazon
Galápagos Islands
Guayaquil
Gulf of Guayaquil
Amazon (Solimões)
Madeira
Aripuanã
Tapajós
Iriri
Araguaia
Parnaíba
Fortaleza
Point Calcanhar
Pariñas Point
Negra Point
Javari
Juruá
Selvas
Marañón
BASIN
Purus
Ucayali
Juruena
Xingu
BRAZIL
Araguaia
Recife
Teles Pires
Tocantins
Nev. Huascarán
6768
PERU
Lima
BRAZILIAN
Mamoré
1995
Salvador
Source of the Amazon
6425
Nev. Coropuna
Lake Titicaca
La Paz
BOLIVIA
Brasília
Goiânia
HIGHLANDS
1995
Sucre
Pantanal
Belo Horizonte
2890
Bandeira
PACIFIC
Atacama Desert
Campos
Gran Chaco
PARAGUAY
CHILE
Volcán Llullaillaco
6723
Asunción
Cape Frio
Rio de Janeiro
São Paulo
TROPIC OF CAPRICORN
Curitiba
Iguazú Falls
Isla San Félix
Isla San Ambrosio
6880
Cerro Ojos del Salado
OCEAN
6880
Cerro del Toro
Salinas Grandes
Salinas Ambargasta
Paraná
Ríos
Cape Santa Marta Grande
Córdoba
Entre
Porto Alegre
Uruguay
Patos Lagoon
Highest point in South America
Cerro Aconcagua
6959 (22831 ft)
URUGUAY
Islas Juan Fernández
Santiago
Pampas
Buenos Aires
Montevideo
River Plate
ATLANTIC OCEAN
ARGENTINA
4709
Volcán Domuyo
Negro
Blanca Bay
Andes
San Matias Gulf
Patagonia
VALDÉS PENINSULA
Chonos Archipelago
Gulf of San Jorge
AZIMUTHAL EQUIDISTANT PROJECTION
SCALE 1:31,000,000
0 KILOMETERS 600 800
0 MILES 200 400 600 800
C. Tres Puntas
1372
Lowest point in South America
Laguna del Carbón
105 (-344 ft)
Grande Bay
West Falkland
Stanley
East Falkland
Falkland Islands
Strait of Magellan
Tierra del Fuego
Scotia Sea
Cape Disappointment
South Georgia
Cape Horn
10°
0°
20°
30°
40°
50°
100°
90°
80°
70°
60°
50°
40°
30°
20°

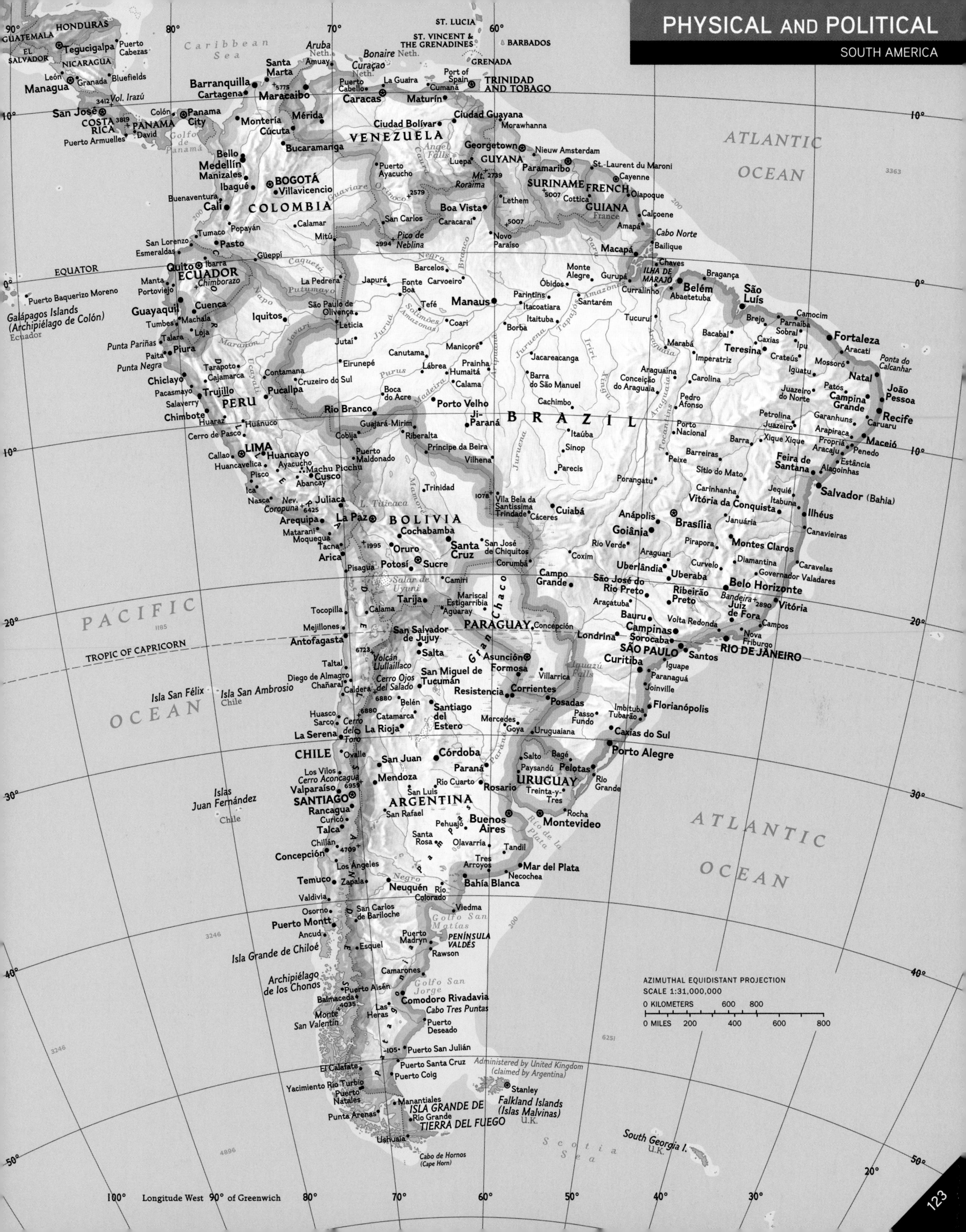
Caribbean Sea
HONDURAS
GUATEMALA
EL SALVADOR
Tegucigalpa
Puerto Cabezas
NICARAGUA
León
Managua
Granada
Bluefields
Vol. Irazú
San José
COSTA RICA
PANAMA
Colón
Panama City
David
Puerto Armuelles
Golfo de Panamá
Aruba Neth.
Amuay
Bonaire Neth.
Curaçao Neth.
ST. LUCIA
ST. VINCENT & THE GRENADINES
BARBADOS
GRENADA
TRINIDAD AND TOBAGO
Port of Spain
Santa Marta
Barranquilla
Cartagena
Maracaibo
Puerto Cabello
La Guaira
Caracas
Cumaná
Maturín
Mérida
Montería
Cúcuta
Ciudad Bolívar
Ciudad Guayana
Morawhanna
VENEZUELA
Bucaramanga
Angel Falls
Georgetown
Nieuw Amsterdam
GUYANA
Paramaribo
St.-Laurent du Maroni
Cayenne
SURINAME
FRENCH GUIANA France
Oiapoque
Bello
Medellín
Manizales
Ibagué
BOGOTÁ
Villavicencio
Puerto Ayacucho
Luepa
Mt. Roraima
Lethem
Cottica
Buenaventura
Cali
COLOMBIA
Guaviare
Orinoco
Boa Vista
Caracaraí
San Carlos
Calamar
Mitú
Pico de Neblina
Novo Paraíso
Calçoene
Amapá
Cabo Norte
Bailique
Macapá
Tumaco
Popayán
Pasto
San Lorenzo
Esmeraldas
Güeppí
Quito
Ibarra
ECUADOR
Chimborazo
EQUATOR
Manta
Portoviejo
Puerto Baquerizo Moreno
Galápagos Islands (Archipiélago de Colón) Ecuador
Guayaquil
Cuenca
Machala
Loja
Tumbes
Talara
Piura
Paita
Punta Pariñas
Punta Negra
Chiclayo
Pacasmayo
Trujillo
Salaverry
Chimbote
Huaraz
Cerro de Pasco
Tarapoto
Cajamarca
PERU
Iquitos
Marañón
Ucayali
Contamana
Pucallpa
Cruzeiro do Sul
Huánuco
LIMA
Callao
Huancayo
Huancavelica
Ayacucho
Machu Picchu
Cusco
Abancay
Pisco
Ica
Nasca
Nev. Coropuna
Juliaca
Arequipa
Matarani
Moquegua
Tacna
Arica
Caquetá
Putumayo
La Pedrera
Japurá
Fonte Boa
Carvoeiro
Barcelos
Negro
Branco
Tefé
Manaus
São Paulo de Olivença
Leticia
Coari
Jutaí
Solimões (Amazonas)
Javari
Juruá
Eirunepé
Canutama
Manicoré
Lábrea
Prainha
Humaitá
Calama
Purus
Boca do Acre
Madeira
Rio Branco
Porto Velho
Ji-Paraná
Guajará-Mirim
Riberalta
Cobija
Puerto Maldonado
Príncipe da Beira
Vilhena
Trinidad
Mamoré
L. Titicaca
La Paz
BOLIVIA
Cochabamba
Oruro
Santa Cruz
San José de Chiquitos
Potosí
Sucre
Corumbá
Pisagua
Salar de Uyuni
Camiri
Tarija
Tocopilla
Calama
Mariscal Estigarribia
Aguaray
Gran Chaco
Vila Bela da Santíssima Trindade
Cáceres
Cuiabá
Óbidos
Monte Alegre
Gurupá
Parintins
Itacoatiara
Santarém
Itaituba
Borba
Amazon
Tapajós
Juruena
Xingu
Iriri
Jacareacanga
Barra do São Manuel
Cachimbo
BRAZIL
Itaúba
Sinop
Parecis
ILHA DE MARAJÓ
Chaves
Curralinho
Belém
Abaetetuba
Bragança
São Luís
Tucuruí
Araguaia
Marabá
Imperatriz
Bacabal
Teresina
Caxias
Araguaína
Conceição do Araguaia
Carolina
Pedro Afonso
Tocantins
Porto Nacional
Barreiras
Peixe
Sítio do Mato
Porangatu
Brejo
Camocim
Parnaíba
Sobral
Ipu
Crateús
Fortaleza
Aracati
Ponta do Calcanhar
Mossoró
Iguatu
Natal
Patos
Campina Grande
João Pessoa
Juazeiro do Norte
Recife
Caruaru
Petrolina
Juazeiro
Garanhuns
Arapiraca
Maceió
Barra
Xique Xique
Propriá
Aracaju
Penedo
Estância
Feira de Santana
Alagoinhas
Jequié
Itabuna
Salvador (Bahia)
Carinhanha
Vitória da Conquista
Januária
Ilhéus
Canavieiras
Anápolis
Brasília
Goiânia
Rio Verde
Araguari
Pirapora
Montes Claros
Diamantina
Caravelas
Coxim
Uberlândia
Curvelo
Governador Valadares
Uberaba
Campo Grande
São José do Rio Preto
Ribeirão Preto
Belo Horizonte
Araçatuba
Bandeira
Juiz de Fora
Vitória
Bauru
Volta Redonda
Campos
Campinas
Sorocaba
Nova Friburgo
RIO DE JANEIRO
SÃO PAULO
Santos
Londrina
PARAGUAY
Concepción
Asunción
Iguazú Falls
Curitiba
Iguape
Paranaguá
Joinville
Villarrica
Formosa
Corrientes
Posadas
Resistencia
Florianópolis
Imbituba
Tubarão
Passo Fundo
Mercedes
Goya
Uruguaiana
Caxias do Sul
Porto Alegre
Salto
Bagé
Paysandú
Pelotas
URUGUAY
Rio Grande
Treinta-y-Tres
Rocha
Montevideo
Río de la Plata
Mejillones
Antofagasta
San Salvador de Jujuy
Salta
Volcán Llullaillaco
Taltal
Cerro Ojos del Salado
Diego de Almagro
Chañaral
Caldera
San Miguel de Tucumán
Belén
Santiago del Estero
Catamarca
Huasco
Sarco
Cerro del Toro
La Rioja
La Serena
CHILE
Ovalle
San Juan
Córdoba
Paraná
Los Vilos
Cerro Aconcagua
Mendoza
Río Cuarto
Rosario
Valparaíso
SANTIAGO
San Luis
ARGENTINA
Rancagua
San Rafael
Curicó
Buenos Aires
Talca
Pehuajó
Santa Rosa
Olavarría
Tandil
Chillán
Concepción
Los Angeles
Tres Arroyos
Mar del Plata
Necochea
Temuco
Zapala
Neuquén
Negro
Bahía Blanca
Valdivia
Río Colorado
Osorno
San Carlos de Bariloche
Viedma
Golfo San Matías
Puerto Montt
Ancud
Puerto Madryn
PENÍNSULA VALDÉS
Rawson
Esquel
Isla Grande de Chiloé
Archipiélago de los Chonos
Camarones
Golfo San Jorge
Puerto Aisén
Comodoro Rivadavia
Balmaceda
Cabo Tres Puntas
Las Heras
Monte San Valentín
Puerto Deseado
Puerto San Julián
Puerto Santa Cruz
Puerto Coig
El Calafate
Yacimiento Río Turbio
Puerto Natales
Administered by United Kingdom (claimed by Argentina)
Stanley
Falkland Islands (Islas Malvinas) U.K.
Manantiales
ISLA GRANDE DE TIERRA DEL FUEGO
Río Grande
Punta Arenas
Ushuaia
Cabo de Hornos (Cape Horn)
Scotia Sea
South Georgia I. U.K.
PACIFIC OCEAN
TROPIC OF CAPRICORN
Isla San Félix
Isla San Ambrosio Chile
Islas Juan Fernández Chile
ATLANTIC OCEAN
AZIMUTHAL EQUIDISTANT PROJECTION
SCALE 1:31,000,000
0 KILOMETERS 200 400 600 800
0 MILES 200 400 600 800
Longitude West 90° of Greenwich

GALÁPAGOS
ISLANDS
(ECUADOR)

VENEZUELA

Caracas

GUYANA

SURINAME

FRENCH
GUIANA
(FRANCE)

COLOMBIA

St. Peter ar
St. Paul Ro
(BRAZIL)

ECUADOR

Atol das
Rocas
(BRAZIL)

Arquipélago
Fernando
de Noronha

PERU

B R A Z I L

Lima

BOLIVIA

P A R A G U A Y

I. de Trindade
(BRAZIL)

Is. Martin Vaz

Rio de Janeiro

I. San
Félix

Isla
San Ambrosio
(CHILE)

URUGUAY

CHILE

Santiago

A R G E N T I N A

ARCHIPIÉLAGO
JUAN FERNÁNDEZ
(CHILE)

FALKLAND
ISLANDS
(U.K.)

Is. Diego
Ramírez
(CHILE)

LAND COVER

- Evergreen needleleaf forest
- Evergreen broadleaf forest
- Deciduous needleleaf forest
- Deciduous broadleaf forest
- Mixed forest
- Woody savanna
- Savanna
- Closed shrubland
- Open shrubland
- Grassland
- Cropland
- Barren or sparsely vegetated
- Urban or built-up
- Snow and ice
- Cropland / natural vegetation mosaic
- Wetland

TEMPERATURE AND RAINFALL

Lima, Peru

50°C –
40°C –
30°C –
20°C –
10°C –
0°C –
-10°C –
-20°C –
-30°C –

– 690 mm
– 575 mm
– 460 mm
– 345 mm
– 230 mm
– 115 mm
– 0 mm

Temperatures above 0°C
Temperatures below 0°C
High
temperature
Low
temperature

Rainfall
(115 mm = 4.5 in)

J F M A M J J A S O N D

Caracas, Venezuela

50°C –
40°C –
30°C –
20°C –
10°C –
0°C –
-10°C –
-20°C –
-30°C –

– 690 m
– 575 m
– 460 m
– 345 m
– 230 m
– 115 mr
– 0 mm

J F M A M J J A S O N D

Santiago, Chile

50°C –
40°C –
30°C –
20°C –
10°C –
0°C –
-10°C –
-20°C –
-30°C –

– 690 mm
– 575 mm
– 460 mm
– 345 mm
– 230 mm
– 115 mm
– 0 mm

J F M A M J J A S O N D

Rio de Janeiro, Brazil

50°C –
40°C –
30°C –
20°C –
10°C –
0°C –
-10°C –
-20°C –
-30°C –

– 690 m
– 575 m
– 460 m
– 345 m
– 230 m
– 115 m
– 0 mm

J F M A M J J A S O N D

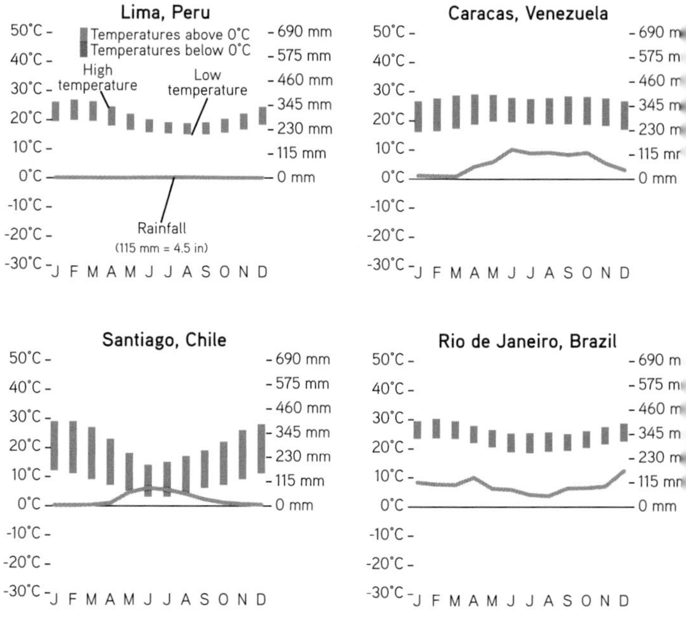

Climate Zones

(based on modified Köppen system)

Humid equatorial climate (A)
- No dry season (Af)
- Short dry season (Am)
- Dry winter (Aw)

Dry climate (B)
- Semiarid (BS) } h = hot
- Arid (BW) } k = cold

Humid temperate climate (C)
- No dry season (Cf) } a = hot summer
- Dry winter (Cw) } b = cool summer
- Dry summer (Cs)

Cold climate (E)
- Tundra and ice

Highland climate (H)
- Unclassified highlands

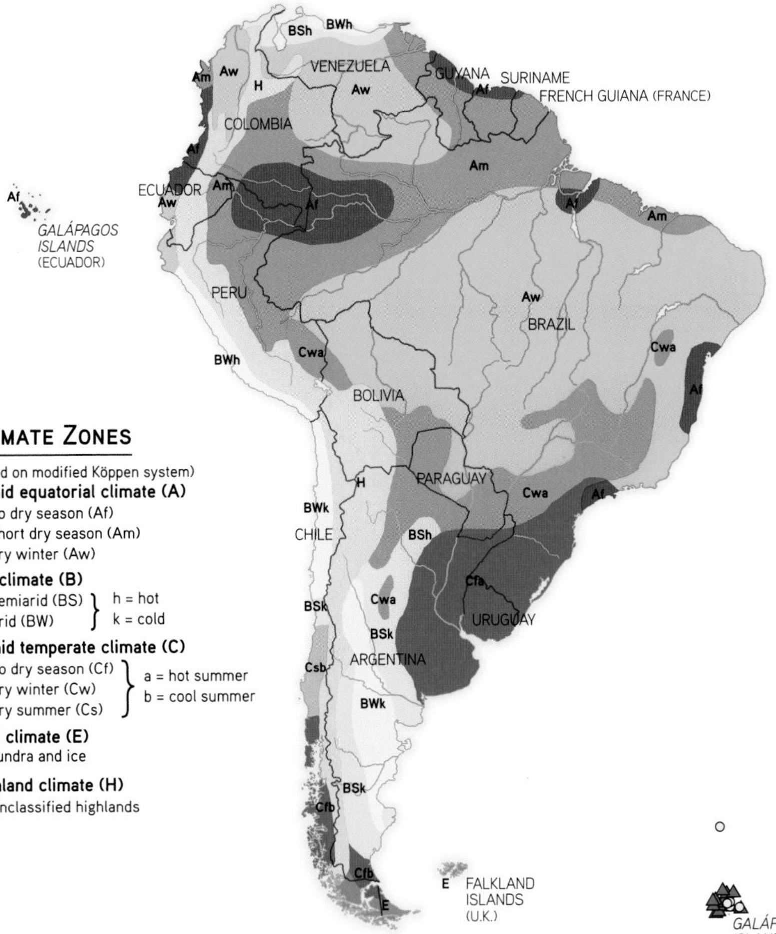

Natural Hazards

Population Density, 2010

People per square km	People per square mi
More than 1,000	More than 2,500
100–1,000	250–2,500
Less than 100	Less than 250

Fire Intensity
(from gas burn off, slash-and-burn agriculture, or natural causes)
High
Low

Recorded Natural Event

Major Earthquake, 1900-2010
Moment magnitude
- More than 7.0
- 6.0–7.0
- Less than 6.0

Volcano

Tsunami, 1900-2010
Run-up height

Meters	Feet
More than 10	More than 32
5–10	16–32
Less than 5	Less than 16

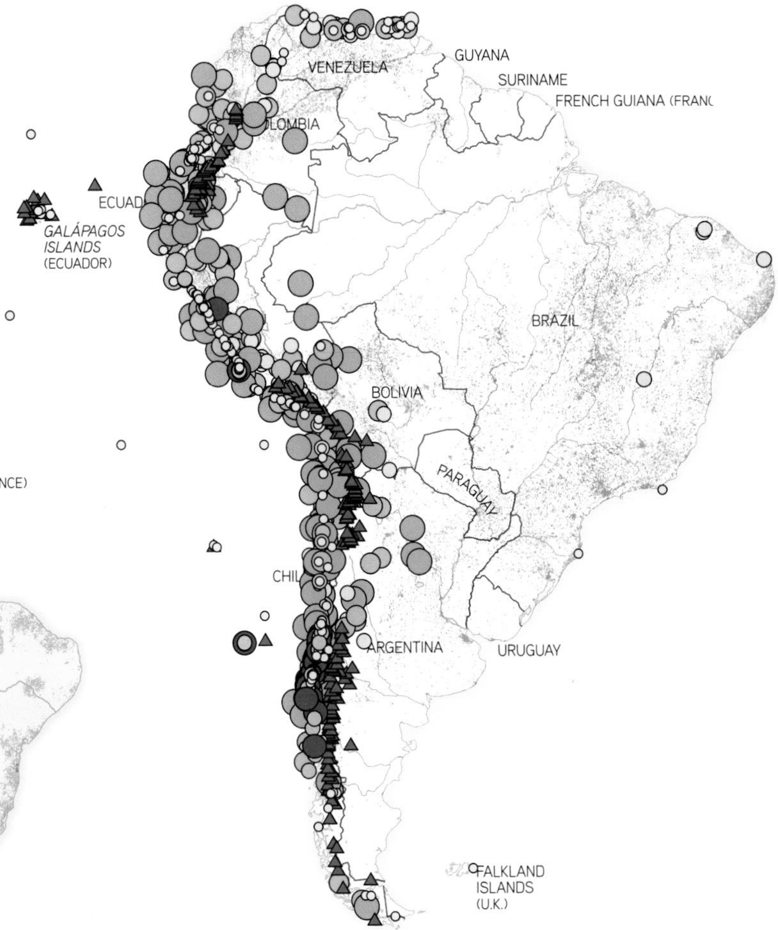

Water Availability

(in millimeters per person per year)
- More than 750
- 251–750
- 26–250
- Less than 26

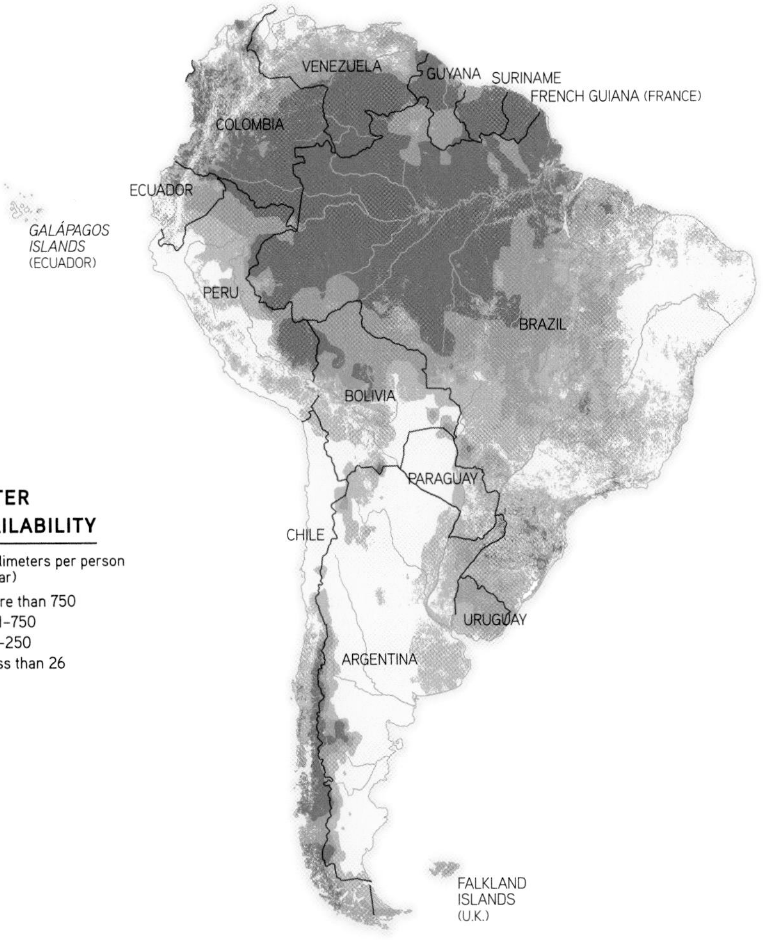

Caracas

VENEZUELA

GUYANA
Georgetown
Paramaribo

FRENCH
GUIANA
(FRANCE)
Cayenne

SURINAME

Bogotá

COLOMBIA

St. Peter ar
St. Paul Roc
(BRAZIL)

GALÁPAGOS
ISLANDS
(ECUADOR)

Quito
ECUADOR

Atol das
Rocas
(BRAZIL)

Arquipélago
Fernando
de Noronha

PERU

B R A Z I L

Lima

La Paz

BOLIVIA

Brasília

Sucre

I. de Trindade   Is. Martin Vaz
(BRAZIL)

P A R A G U A Y

POPULATION PYRAMIDS

COLOMBIA

Asunción

I. San
Félix
(CHILE)

Isla
San Ambrosio

80+

60-64

Age

40-44   Male   Female

20-24

0-4

10   5   0   5   10
Percent of population

BOLIVIA

80+

60-64

Age

40-44   Male   Female

20-24

0-4

10   5   0   5   10
Percent of population

ARGENTINA

80+

60-64

Age

40-44   Male   Female

20-24

0-4

10   5   0   5   10
Percent of population

ARCHIPIÉLAGO
JUAN FERNÁNDEZ
(CHILE)

CHILE
Santiago

URUGUAY

Buenos Aires
Montevideo

A R G E N T I N A

POPULATION
DENSITY

People per Square Kilometer	People per Square Mile	
More than 195		More than 500
60-195		150-500
10-59		25-149
1-9		1-24
Less than 1		Less than 1

Stanley

FALKLAND
ISLANDS
(U.K.)

Is. Diego
Ramírez
(CHILE)

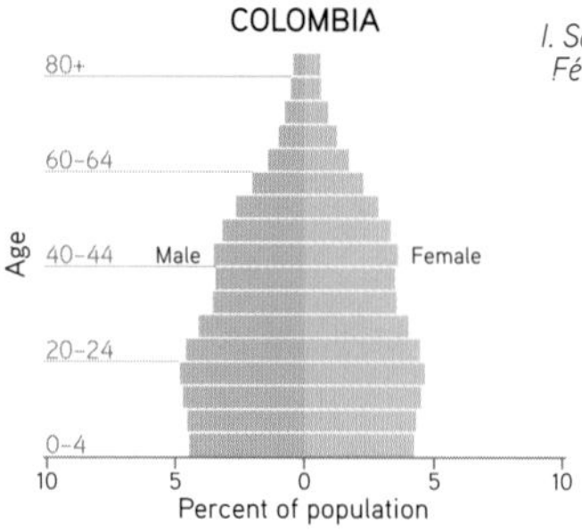

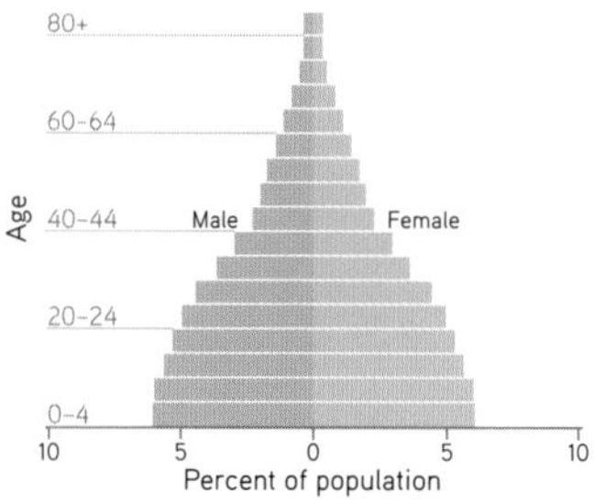

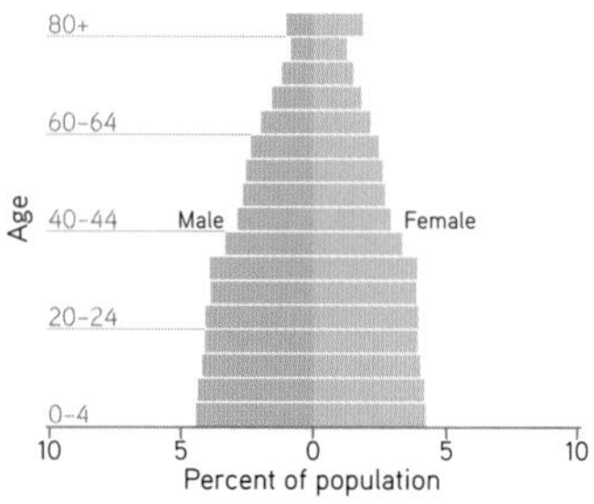

INDIGENOUS LANGUAGES

- ■ Meso-American Indian
- South American Indian
- Isolates
- Other or undetermined

VENEZUELA
GUYANA
SURINAME
FRENCH GUIANA (FRANCE)
COLOMBIA
ECUADOR
GALÁPAGOS ISLANDS (ECUADOR)
PERU
BRAZIL
BOLIVIA
PARAGUAY
CHILE
URUGUAY
ARGENTINA
FALKLAND ISLANDS (U.K.)

URBANIZATION

Urban agglomerations, 2010 (population in millions)
- ■ More than 10.0
- ▲ 5.0–10.0
- ● 1.0–4.9
- ○ .75–.99

Percent urban population, 2010
- ■ More than 75%
- 50%–75%
- 25%–49%
- Less than 25%

VENEZUELA
GUYANA
SURINAME
FRENCH GUIANA (FRANCE)
Bogotá
COLOMBIA
ECUADOR
GALÁPAGOS ISLANDS (ECUADOR)
PERU
Lima
BRAZIL
BOLIVIA
Belo Horizonte
PARAGUAY
São Paolo
Rio de Janeiro
CHILE
Santiago
Buenos Aires
URUGUAY
ARGENTINA
FALKLAND ISLANDS (U.K.)

POPULATION CHANGE

Projected population change, 2010–2050 (by percentage)
- More than 100%
- 50%–100%
- 0.01%–49%
- No change
- Population loss

VENEZUELA
GUYANA
SURINAME
FRENCH GUIANA (FRANCE)
COLOMBIA
ECUADOR
GALÁPAGOS ISLANDS (ECUADOR)
PERU
BRAZIL
BOLIVIA
PARAGUAY
CHILE
ARGENTINA
URUGUAY
FALKLAND ISLANDS (U.K.)

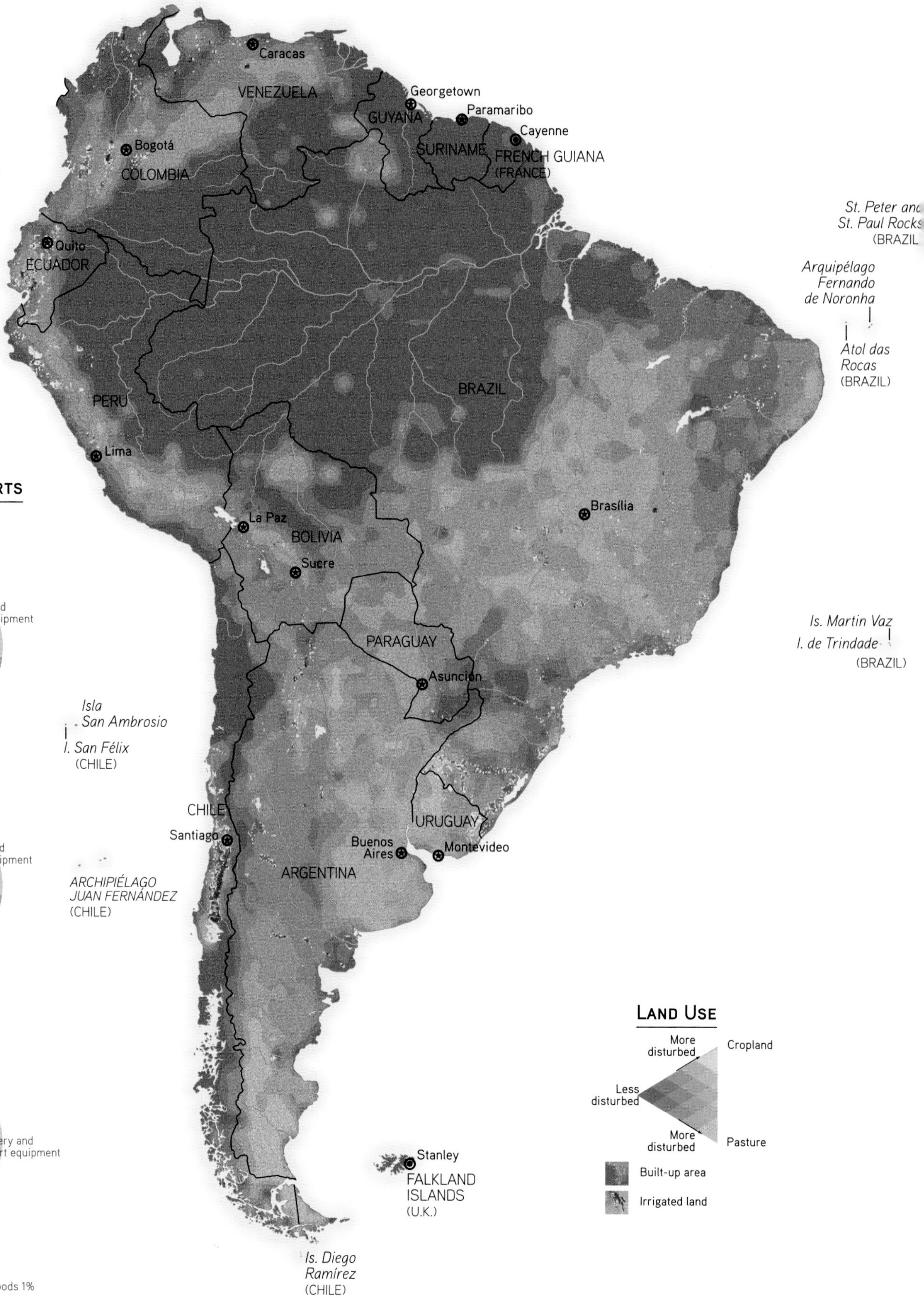

IMPORTS AND EXPORTS

VALUE OF IMPORTS

BRAZIL

- Machinery and transport equipment 27%
- Petroleum products 16%
- Electronic equipment 12%
- Chemical products 10%
- Ores and metals 7%
- Manufactured goods 5%
- Food 4%
- Pharmaceutical products 3%
- Other 16%

CHILE

- Machinery and transport equipment 27%
- Petroleum products 22%
- Manufactured goods 15%
- Electronic equipment 9%
- Food 7%
- Ores and metals 7%
- Chemical products 5%
- Pharmaceutical products 1%
- Other 7%

VALUE OF EXPORTS

BRAZIL

- Ores and metals 22%
- Machinery and transport equipment 14%
- Food 14%
- Petroleum products 10%
- Soybeans and oil seeds 6%
- Sugar 6%
- Chemical products 4%
- Manufactured goods 3%
- Electronic equipment 3%
- Wood products 3%
- Other 15%

VENEZUELA

- Petroleum products 96%
- Ores and metals 3%
- Manufactured goods 1%

LAND USE

More disturbed — Cropland
Less disturbed
More disturbed — Pasture

Built-up area

Irrigated land

Map labels

Caracas
VENEZUELA
Georgetown
GUYANA
Paramaribo
Cayenne
SURINAME
FRENCH GUIANA (FRANCE)
Bogotá
COLOMBIA
Quito
ECUADOR
PERU
Lima
BRAZIL
Brasília
La Paz
BOLIVIA
Sucre
PARAGUAY
Asunción
URUGUAY
Montevideo
Buenos Aires
CHILE
Santiago
ARGENTINA

GALÁPAGOS ISLANDS (ECUADOR)

St. Peter and St. Paul Rocks (BRAZIL)
Arquipélago Fernando de Noronha
Atol das Rocas (BRAZIL)
Is. Martin Vaz
I. de Trindade (BRAZIL)

Isla San Ambrosio
I. San Félix (CHILE)

ARCHIPIÉLAGO JUAN FERNÁNDEZ (CHILE)

Stanley
FALKLAND ISLANDS (U.K.)

Is. Diego Ramírez (CHILE)

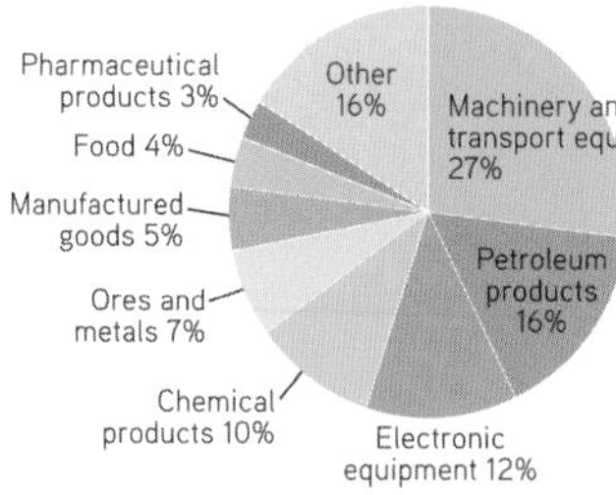

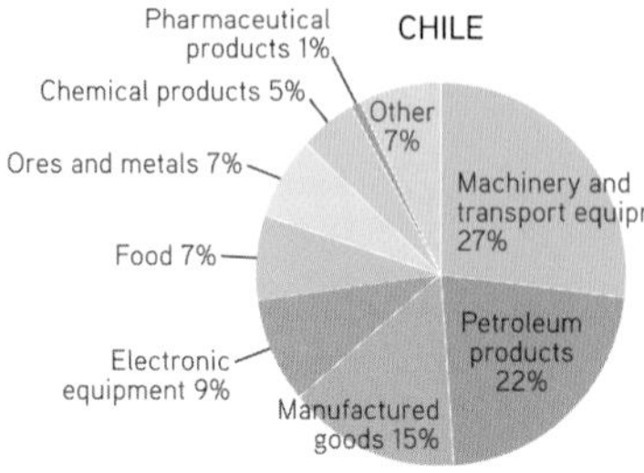

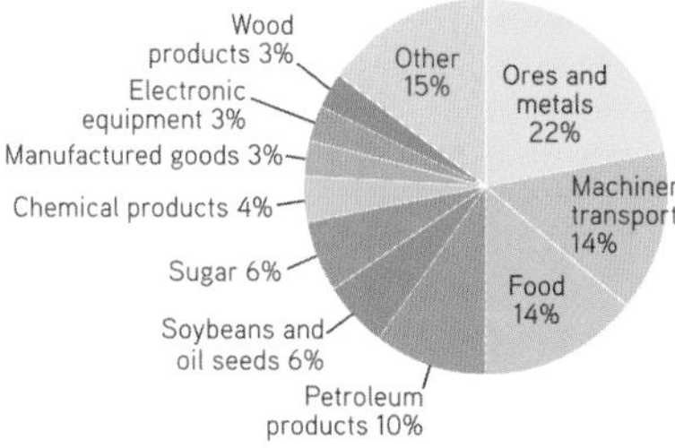

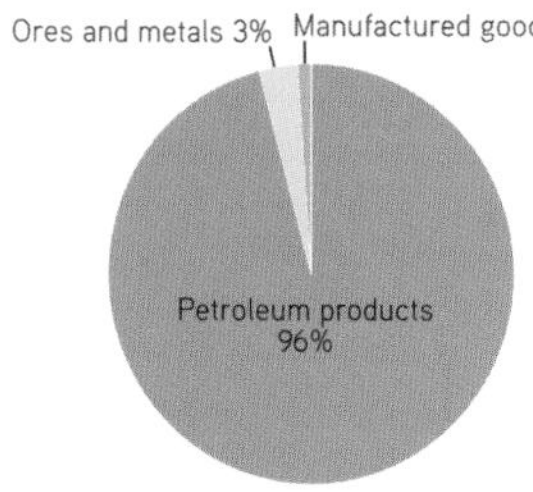

VENEZUELA
GUYANA
SURINAME
FRENCH GUIANA (FRANCE)
COLOMBIA
ECUADOR
GALÁPAGOS ISLANDS (ECUADOR)
PERU
BRAZIL
BOLIVIA
PARAGUAY
CHILE
ARGENTINA
URUGUAY
FALKLAND ISLANDS (U.K.)
DOMINANT ECONOMY
(per GDP sector)
Agriculture Industry* Services
70%–100%
50%–69.9%
0%–49.9%
No data
*Includes the mining industry

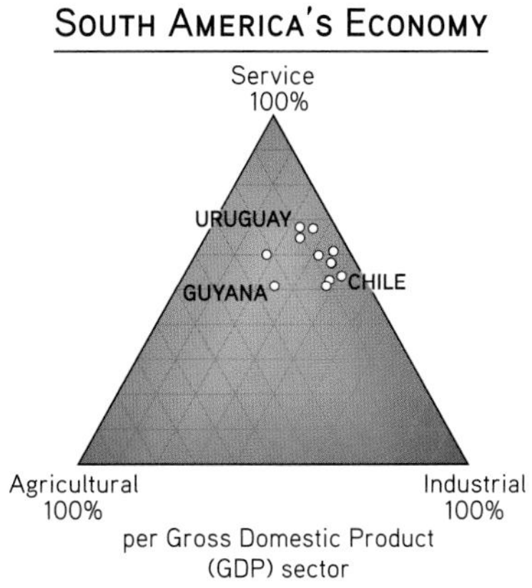
SOUTH AMERICA'S ECONOMY
Service 100%
URUGUAY
CHILE
GUYANA
Agricultural 100%
Industrial 100%
per Gross Domestic Product (GDP) sector

VENEZUELA
GUYANA
SURINAME
FRENCH GUIANA (FRANCE)
COLOMBIA
ECUADOR
GALÁPAGOS ISLANDS (ECUADOR)
PERU
BRAZIL
BOLIVIA
PARAGUAY
CHILE
ARGENTINA
URUGUAY
FALKLAND ISLANDS (U.K.)
POVERTY
Percentage of population living on less than $2 per day
More than 80%
60%–80%
40%–59%
20%–39%
Less than 20%
No data available

VENEZUELA
GUYANA
SURINAME
FRENCH GUIANA (FRANCE)
COLOMBIA
ECUADOR
GALÁPAGOS ISLANDS (ECUADOR)
PERU
BRAZIL
BOLIVIA
PARAGUAY
CHILE
ARGENTINA
URUGUAY
FALKLAND ISLANDS (U.K.)
PER CAPITA ENERGY CONSUMPTION
(annual use, in million Btu)
More than 300
201–300
101–200
30–100
Less than 30
Major energy deposit
Coal
Natural gas
Oil
Oil pipeline

ADMINISTRATIVE AREAS OF VENEZUELA AND THEIR CAPITALS
(Numbered in blue where not labeled on map)
1 Aragua (Maracay)
2 Capital District (Caracas)
3 Miranda (Los Teques)
4 Vargas (La Guaira)
AZIMUTHAL EQUIDISTANT PROJECTION
SCALE 1:12,000,000
0 KILOMETERS 200 300
0 MILES 100 200 300
Longitude West 81° of Greenwich
PACIFIC OCEAN
CARIBBEAN
EQUATOR
GALÁPAGOS ISLANDS
(Archipiélago de Colón)
Ecuador
I. Darwin
I. Wolf
Isla Pinta
Isla Marchena
Isla Genovesa
I. Isabela
I. San Salvador
Fernandina
Isla Santa Cruz
Isla San Cristóbal
Puerto Villamil
Puerto Ayora
Puerto Baquerizo Moreno
Puerto Velasco Ibarra
I. Santa María
Isla Española
Isla del Coco
Costa Rica
I. de Malpelo
Colombia
SAN ANDRÉS Y PROVIDENCIA
I. de Providencia
Roncador Bank
Is. del Maíz
Nicaragua
EL SALVADOR
San Salvador
HONDURAS
NICARAGUA
Managua
León
Masaya
COSTA RICA
San José
PANAMA
Panama City
COLOMBIA
Bogotá
Medellín
Cali
Barranquilla
Cartagena
Santa Marta
Cúcuta
Bucaramanga
Maracaibo
ECUADOR
Quito
Guayaquil
Cuenca
Esmeraldas
Manta
PERU
LIMA
Callao
Trujillo
Chiclayo
Piura
Iquitos
Pucallpa
Huancayo
Ica
Cusco
CORDILLERA OCCIDENTAL
CORDILLERA ORIENTAL
ANDES
AMAZONAS
LORETO
ANTIOQUIA
CHOCÓ
NARIÑO
PUTUMAYO
CAQUETÁ
GUAVIARE
META
CASANARE
ARAUCA
SANTANDER
BOYACÁ
ZULIA
FALCÓN
LA GUAJIRA
MADRE DE DIOS
JUNÍN
HUÁNUCO
ANCASH
LA LIBERTAD
CAJAMARCA
SAN MARTÍN
LAMBAYEQUE
PIURA
TUMBES
AMAZONAS
UCAYALI
PASCO
ICA
HUANCAVELICA
AYACUCHO
APURÍMAC
CUSCO
PUNO
ARUBA
Oranjestad
Neth.
Golfo de Panamá
Golfo de Guayaquil
Golfo de Venezuela
Golfo de los Mosquitos
Golfo de Papagayo
Golfo de Nicoya
Golfo de Chiriquí
Península de Azuero
Isla Puná
Punta Negra
Punta Aguja
93°
90°
87°
84°
81°
78°
75°
72°
12°
9°
6°
3°
0°
3°
6°
9°
12°

ATLANTIC OCEAN
SEA
ANTILLES
WINDWARD ISLANDS
Castries
ST. LUCIA
Kingstown
ST. VINCENT AND THE GRENADINES
Bridgetown
BARBADOS
GRENADA
St. George's
Tobago Basin
Charlotteville
Tobago
TRINIDAD AND TOBAGO
Port of Spain
San Fernando
Trinidad
Gulf of Paria
Punta Araguapiche
BONAIRE Neth.
Is. de Aves Venez.
Is. Los Roques
Isla Blanquilla Venez.
ARCHIPIÉLAGO LOS ROQUES N.P.
NUEVA ESPARTA
I. de Margarita
La Asunción
Isla La Tortuga
MOCHIMA N.P.
Isla Coche
Cumaná
SUCRE
Carúpano
Caripito
Maturín
MONAGAS
Pedernales
MARIUSA N.P.
Tucupita
DELTA AMACURO
Curiapo
San José de Amacuro
Barrancas
Caracas
Petare
La Guaira
Río Chico
Puerto La Cruz
Barcelona
Los Teques
Maracay
MORROCOY N.P.
Chichiriviche
Tucacas
San Felipe
Valencia
CARABOBO
San Juan de los Morros
San Carlos
COJEDES
Ortiz
Valle de la Pascua
Zaraza
San Mateo
Nipa
Leona
El Calvario
Grico
Calabozo
Sabán
El Baúl
GUÁRICO
ANZOÁTEGUI
AGUARO-GUARIQUITO N.P.
San Fernando de Apure
Santa Cruz
Ciudad Bolívar
Ciudad Guayana
Guri Dam
El Pao
Caicara
Cabruta
VENEZUELA
APURE
Guachara
Cunaviche
Ciudad Piar
Aripao
Co. Bolívar
Surama
Cerro Mato
Guasipati
El Callao
El Perú
Tumeremo
Calceta
El Dorado
Serranía de Imataca
Hosororo
Morawhanna
Shell Beach
Mabaruma
Port Kaituma
Matthew's Ridge
Charity
Suddie
Parika
Wakenaam I.
Georgetown
Buxton
Rosignol
New Amsterdam
Bartica
Linden
Mara
Corriverton
Skeldon
Totness
Nieuw Amsterdam
Paramaribo
Meerzorg
Albina
Saint-Laurent du Maroni
Mana
Pointe Isère
GUYANAIS SPACE CENTER
Sinnamary
Kourou
Cayenne
Rémire
Pointe Béhague
Roura
Régina
Cabo Orange
Ponta do Mosquito
Saint-Georges
Oiapoque
Cabo Cassiporé
CABO ORANGE N.P.
Vila Velha
FRENCH GUIANA
France
SURINAME
Brokopondo
Brownsweg
Van Blommestein Meer
Hendrik Top
Wilhelmina Geb.
Granbori
Benzdorp
Camopi
Malavate
Oronoquekamp
Boundary claimed by Suriname
Serra de Tumucumaque
TUMUCUMAQUE N.P.
Tacalé
GUYANA
Pakaraima Mountains
Mahdia
Ituni
Matapi
Kurupukari
Apoteri
Kumaka
Annai
Lethem
Aishalton
Kamoa Mountains
Sa. Acaraí
CINARUCO-CAPANAPARO N.P.
Serranía de La Cerbatana
BOLÍVAR
Puerto Páez
Puerto Carreño
Puerto Ayacucho
CANAIMA N.P.
Auyán Tepui
Co. Venamo
La Gran Sabana
Mt. Roraima
Santa Elena
MONTE ROROIMA N.P.
JAUA SARISARIÑAMA N.P.
Cerro Cutucú
Cacuri
Urimán
Co. Chanaro
Ser. Quinigua
Sierra Pacaraima
Cerro Yumari
YAPACANA N.P.
DUIDA-MARAHUACA N.P.
Co. Marahuaca
San Fernando de Atabapo
Santa Bárbara
Cerro Rana
La Esmeralda
PARIMA
AMAZONAS
Serra Parima
TAPIRAPECÓ NATIONAL PARK
Pico Redondo
Uraricoera
Conceição do Maú
Boa Vista
Sa. Grande (Carauna)
RORAIMA
Caracaraí
Victorino
Maroa
Capibara
Platanal
Cerro Caparro
Solano
San Carlos de Río Negro
San Felipe
SERRANÍA DE LA NEBLINA N.P.
El Carmen
Cucuí
Pico 31 de Março
PICO DA NEBLINA N.P.
Içana
Taraquá
São Gabriel da Cachoeira
Sa. Curicuriari
Tapurucuará
Tomar
Vila Conceição
Barcelos
São José de Anauá
Boiaçu
Moura
Carvoeiro
Represa da Balbina
Santa Maria
JAÚ NATIONAL PARK
Ilhas Macuapanim
Mirapinima
Arquipélago das Anavilhanas
Manaus
Amatari
Itacoatiara
Urucará
Silves
Parintins
Faro
Juruti
Óbidos
Oriximiná
Alenquer
Monte Alegre
Santarém
Alter do Chão
Belterra
Curuá
Prainha
Almeirim
Porto de Moz
Independência
Senador José Porfírio
Vitória
Altamira
Sa. Urubuquara
Tiago
Maloca
Merirumã
Serra do Navio
Teresinha
Porto Grande
Ferreira Gomes
AMAPÁ
Amapá
Calçoene
Cunani
Euca
Ilha de Maracá
Cabo Norte
Ponta Grossa
I. Bailique
Bailique
I. Janaucu
Macapá
Porto Santana
Mazagão
EQUATOR
I. Caviana
Ilha Mexiana
I. Camaleão
Cabo Maguari
Afuá
Santa Cruz do Arai
Ilha de Marajó
Soure
Salvaterra
Anajás
Breves
Boca do Jari
Munguba
San Antonio da Cachoeira
Salinópolis
Maracanã
Primavera
Bragança
Cabo Gurupi
Viseu
Turiaçu
Belém
Castanhal
Abaetetuba
Muaná
Curralinho
Capitão Poço
Cametá
Camiranga
Portel
Mocajuba
Carvalho
Canindé
Ilha Grande de Jutaí
Maloca Timbé
Tucuruí
Serra do Tiracambu
Serra da Desordem
Santa Inês
MARANHÃO
Iguaidade
Japurá
Maraã
Fonte Boa
Tonantins
Santo Antônio do Içá
Alvarães
Tefé
Juruá
São Paulo de Olivença
Renascença
Coari
Codajás
Anori
Anamã
Manacapuru
Careiro da Várzea
Autazes
Beruri
Nova Olinda do Norte
Ilha Tupinambarana
Maués
Urucurituba
Freguesia do Andirá
Boim
Catauara
Aveiro
Brasília Legal
Mucajá
AMAZÔNIA N.P.
Itaituba
Vista Alegre
Canumã
Axinim
Borba
Novo Aripuanã
Tabuleiro
Santa Helena
Laje
Paga Conta
Porto Alegre
Belo Horizonte
PARÁ
AMAZONAS
BRAZIL
Carauari
Aruajá
Imperatriz
Tambaqui
Penha do Tapaua
Arimã
Manicoré
Canumã
Constância dos Baetas
Marari
São Romão
Vista Alegre
Canutama
Tapauá
Paraíso
Natal
Prainha
Lábrea
Crato
Humaitá
Calama
Mamoriá
Pauini
Guajarraã
Boca do Curuquetê
Porto Velho
Foz do Jamari
Samaúma
Boca do Acre
Araras
Rio Branco
Bom Destino
Riozinho
Manoa
Abunã
Fortaleza
Jaci-Paraná
Caritianas
Ariquemes
Jaru
Vila Bella
Vila Murtinho
Yata
Santa Rosa
Brasiléia
Cobija
Bella Flor
Las Piedras
Moreno
Conquista
Ivón
Porvenir
Holanda
Carmen
Sena
San Lorenzo
Apere
Puerto Heath
LA PAZ
BOLIVIA
PANDO
Mayo Mayo
Príncipe da Beira
PACAAS NOVOS NATIONAL PARK
Serra dos Pacaás Novos
RONDÔNIA
Ji-Paraná
Pimenta Bueno
Maloca de Índios
Vilhena
Pedras Negras
Mateguá
Puerto Villazón
NOEL KEMPFF MERCADO N.P.
Yata
Exaltación
Lago Rogagua
BENI
Puerto Saucedo
SANTA CRUZ
MADIDI NATIONAL PARK
Sumaúma
Barracão do Barreto
Canudos
Barra do São Manuel
Santa Júlia
Cachoeira do Rebojo
Cachoeira das Sete Quedas
Aripuanã
Serra do Norte
Serra dos Apiacás
Rancho de Caça dos Tapiúnas
Morro do Sinal
Posto Alto Maniçauá
Porto dos Gaúchos
Sinop
MATO GROSSO
Serra do Tombador
Serra dos Caiabis
Serra Formosa
Utiariti
Lucas do Rio Verde
Porto Artur
Serra do Roncador
Serra do Cachimbo
Cachimbo
Manuelzinho
Cachoeira do Tarerraimbu
Araras
São Félix do Xingu
Serra dos Carajás
Serra da Seringa
Serra dos Gradaús
Gradaús
Marabá
Itupiranga
Jatobal
Remansão
Açailândia
São João do Araguaia
Serra do Gurupi
Imperatriz
São Raimundo do Araguaia
Araguatins
Grajaú
Tocantinópolis
Porto Franco
Serra Negra
São Geraldo do Araguaia
Araguaína
Carolina
Riachão
Filadélfia
Balsas
Palmeirante
Conceição do Araguaia
Couto Magalhães
Itacajá
Araguacema
Santana do Araguaia
Guaraí
Pedro Afonso
Serra do Penitente
Tasso Fragoso
Santa Filomena
Miracema do Norte
Tocantínia
Serra do Estrondo
Chapada das Mangabeiras
Gilbués
Novo Acordo
PIAUÍ
Palmas
ARAGUAIA NATIONAL PARK
Santa Terezinha
Macaúba
Cristalândia
TOCANTINS
Porto Nacional
Pedra de Amolar
Formosa do Rio Prêto
Caripare
Natividade
Almas
Santa Isabel do Morro
Gurupi
Peixe
Alvorada
Paranã
Arraias
Campos Belos
Serra Geral de Goiás
São Miguel do Araguaia
Bandeirante
Estrêla do Norte
Serra Dourada
GOIÁS
BAHIA
Espigão Mestre
66°
63°
60°
57°
54°
51°
48°
12°
9°
6°
3°
0°

COLOMBIA
AMAZONAS
LORETO
PERU
UCAYALI
JUNÍN
HUANCAVELICA
CUSCO
APURÍMAC
AYACUCHO
AREQUIPA
PUNO
MADRE DE DIOS
MOQUEGUA
TACNA
ACRE
PANDO
RONDÔNIA
BRAZIL
PARÁ
MATO GROSSO
MATO GROSSO DO SUL
BOLIVIA
BENI
LA PAZ
COCHABAMBA
SANTA CRUZ
ORURO
POTOSÍ
CHUQUISACA
TARIJA
ARICA Y PARINACOTA
TARAPACÁ
ANTOFAGASTA
ATACAMA
CHILE
PARAGUAY
ARGENTINA
JUJUY
SALTA
FORMOSA
CHACO
TUCUMÁN
CATAMARCA
SANTIAGO DEL ESTERO
LA RIOJA
SANTA FE
CORRIENTES
MISIONES
RIO GRANDE DO SUL
PACIFIC OCEAN
TROPIC OF CAPRICORN
CORDILLERA DE LOS ANDES
Manaus
Porto Velho
Rio Branco
Cuiabá
Campo Grande
Santarém
Itaituba
Iquitos
Pucallpa
Cusco
Arequipa
Juliaca
Tacna
Arica
Iquique
Antofagasta
Calama
La Paz
Cochabamba
Oruro
Sucre
Potosí
Santa Cruz
Tarija
Trinidad
Cobija
Asunción
Salta
San Salvador de Jujuy
San Miguel de Tucumán
Santiago del Estero
Catamarca
Resistencia
Corrientes
Formosa
Posadas
Foz do Iguaçu
Dourados
Corumbá
Ji-Paraná
Rio Verde
Londrina
Presidente Prudente
Cascavel
Guarapuava
Passo Fundo
72°
69°
66°
63°
60°
57°
54°
75°
3°
6°
9°
12°
15°
18°
21°
24°
27°

MARANHÃO
PIAUÍ
CEARÁ
RIO GRANDE DO NORTE
PARAÍBA
PERNAMBUCO
ALAGOAS
SERGIPE
BAHIA
TOCANTINS
MINAS GERAIS
ESPÍRITO SANTO
RIO DE JANEIRO
SÃO PAULO
DISTRITO FED.
ATLANTIC OCEAN
TROPIC OF CAPRICORN
Belém
Castanhal
São Luís
Teresina
Timon
Fortaleza
Caucaia
Natal
Mossoró
João Pessoa
Recife
Olinda
Maceió
Aracaju
Salvador (Bahia)
Feira de Santana
Vitória da Conquista
Brasília
Goiânia
Anápolis
Palmas
Araguaína
Belo Horizonte
Vitória
RIO DE JANEIRO
SÃO PAULO
Campinas
Curitiba
Florianópolis
Uberlândia
Montes Claros
Juiz de Fora
Governador Valadares
Campos
Santos
Sorocaba
Ribeirão Preto
Atol das Rocas Brazil
Arquipélago de Fernando de Noronha Brazil
Trindade
Ilhas Martin Vaz Brazil
Arquipélago dos Abrolhos
LENÇÓIS MARANHENSES N.P.
ALCÂNTARA SPACEPORT
ARAGUAIA N.P.
GRANDE SERTÃO VEREDAS N.P.
MONTE PASCOAL N.P.
SERRA DA BOCAINA N.P.
PLANALTO BRASILEIRO
Chapada Diamantina
Serra do Espinhaço
AZIMUTHAL EQUIDISTANT PROJECTION
SCALE 1:12,000,000
0 KILOMETERS 200 300
0 MILES 100 200 300
Longitude West 45° of Greenwich
48°
45°
42°
39°
36°
33°
30°
27°
3°
6°
9°
12°
15°
18°
21°
24°
27°

PACIFIC OCEAN
TROPIC OF CAPRICORN
Longitude West 60° of Greenwich
BOLIVIA
PARAGUAY
BRAZIL
URUGUAY
ARGENTINA
CHILE
PERU
SÃO PAULO
PARANÁ
SANTA CATARINA
RIO GRANDE DO SUL
MATO GROSSO DO SUL
MINAS GERAIS
BUENOS AIRES
Buenos Aires
Montevideo
Asunción
Santiago
Córdoba
Rosario
Mendoza
Mar del Plata
Porto Alegre
Curitiba
Florianópolis
Campinas
Santos

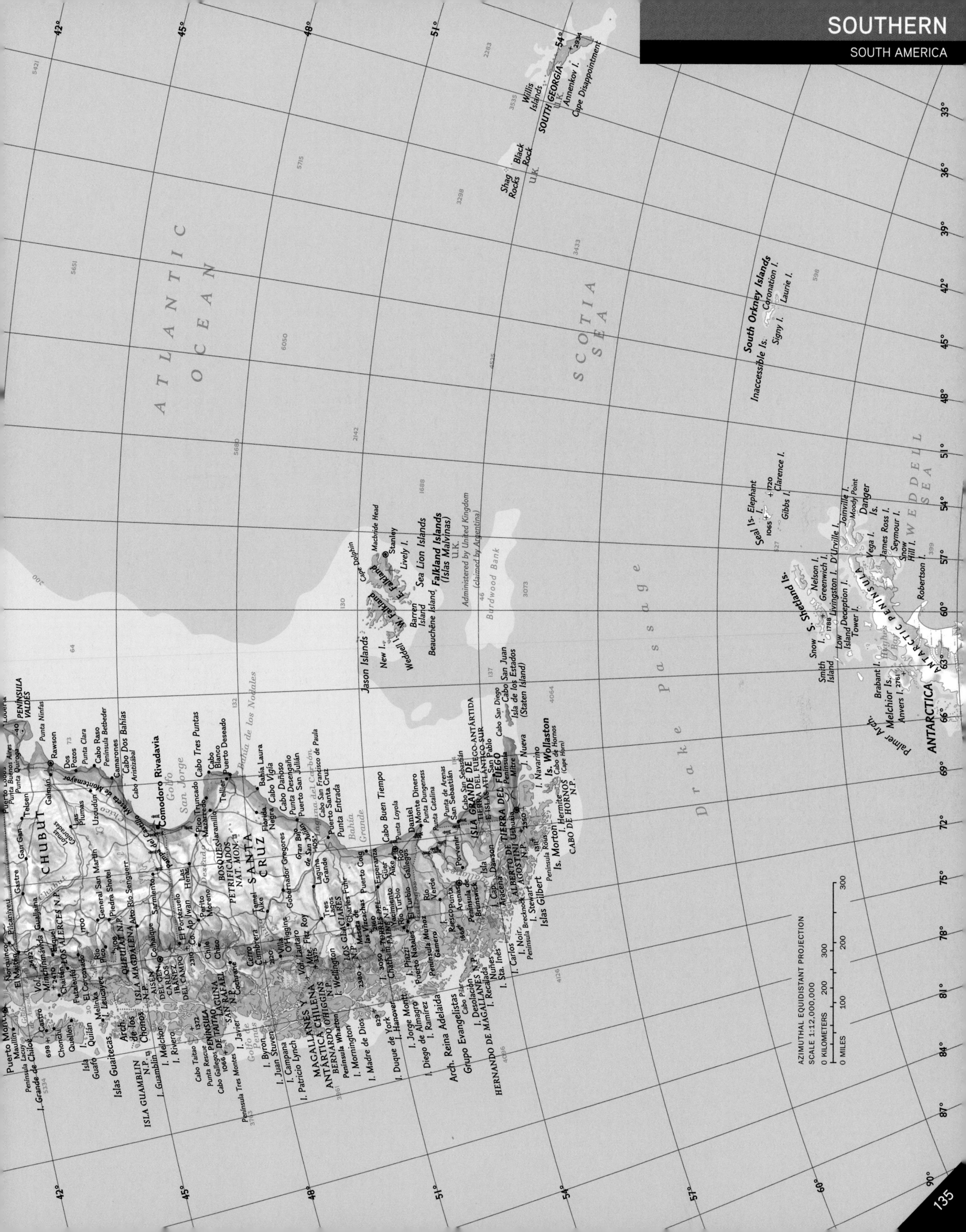
ATLANTIC OCEAN
SCOTIA SEA
Drake Passage
WEDDELL SEA
SOUTH GEORGIA
U.K.
Willis Islands
Annenkov I.
Cape Disappointment
Shag Rocks
Black Rock
U.K.
South Orkney Islands
Inaccessible Is.
Coronation I.
Signy I.
Laurie I.
Falkland Islands
(Islas Malvinas)
U.K.
Administered by United Kingdom
(claimed by Argentina)
Stanley
Cape Dolphin
Macbride Head
Lively I.
Sea Lion Islands
E. Falkland
W. Falkland
Jason Islands
New I.
Weddell I.
Barren Island
Beauchêne Island
Burdwood Bank
Elephant I.
Clarence I.
Gibbs I.
Seal Is.
S. Shetland Is.
Nelson I.
Greenwich I.
Livingston I.
Deception I.
Low Island
Smith Island
Snow I.
Tower I.
D'Urville I.
Joinville I.
Moody Point
Danger Is.
Vega I.
James Ross I.
Seymour I.
Snow Hill I.
Robertson I.
Brabant I.
Melchior Is.
Anvers I.
Palmer Arch.
ANTARCTIC PENINSULA
ANTARCTICA
CHUBUT
SANTA CRUZ
PENÍNSULA VALDÉS
Rawson
Trelew
Gaiman
Comodoro Rivadavia
Golfo San Jorge
Cabo Tres Puntas
Puerto Deseado
Bahía de los Nodales
Puerto San Julián
Puerto Santa Cruz
Bahía Grande
Cabo Buen Tiempo
Río Gallegos
Punta Dungeness
TIERRA DEL FUEGO
ISLA GRANDE DE TIERRA DEL FUEGO
Ushuaia
Isla de los Estados (Staten Island)
Cabo San Juan
Cabo San Diego
I. Navarino
I. Nueva
Is. Wollaston
I. Hermite
Cabo de Hornos (Cape Horn)
CABO DE HORNOS N.P.
Is. Morton
Islas Gilbert
I. Stewart
I. Noir
I. Carlos
I. Sta. Inés
I. Desolación
HERNANDO DE MAGALLANES N.P.
Grupo Evangelistas
Arch. Reina Adelaida
I. Diego de Almagro
I. Duque de York
I. Madre de Dios
I. Mornington
BERNARDO O'HIGGINS N.P.
MAGALLANES Y ANTÁRTICA CHILENA
I. Wellington
LOS GLACIARES N.P.
I. Patricio Lynch
I. Campana
I. Juan Stuven
I. Byron
Golfo de Penas
PENÍNSULA DE TAITAO
LAGUNA SAN RAFAEL N.P.
I. Rivero
I. Melchor
Chonos Arch.
ISLA MAGDALENA N.P.
QUEULAT N.P.
Islas Guaitecas
ISLA GUAMBLIN N.P.
I. Guamblin
I. Grande de Chiloé
Puerto Montt
Castro
Chonchi
Quellón
AISÉN DEL GRAL. CARLOS IBÁÑEZ DEL CAMPO
Coihaique
Cochrane
Puerto Natales
Punta Arenas
Porvenir
Puerto Williams
AZIMUTHAL EQUIDISTANT PROJECTION
SCALE 1:12,000,000
0 KILOMETERS 100 200 300
0 MILES 100 200 300

NORTHERN ANDES
AZIMUTHAL EQUIDISTANT PROJECTION
SCALE 1:7,000,000
0 KILOMETERS 100 150 200
0 MILES 50 100 150 200
Longitude West 75° of Greenwich
78°
72°
69°
66°
12°
9°
6°
3°
0°
CARIBBEAN SEA
PACIFIC OCEAN
COLOMBIA
VENEZUELA
ECUADOR
PERU
BRAZIL
PANAMA
ARUBA Neth.
CURAÇAO Neth.
BONAIRE Neth.
Oranjestad
Willemstad
ARCHIPIÉLAGO LOS ROQUES N.P.
Isla Orchila Venezuela
Islas de Aves Venezuela
Islas Los Roques Venezuela
Isla La Tortuga
Bahía Honda
Bahía de Portete
Punta Gallinas
Puerto Estrella
Punta Espada
Pen. de Paraguaná
Península de la Guajira
Puerto López
Pueblo Nuevo
Punto Fijo
Punta Cardón
Golfo de Venezuela
Golfo de Coro
MÉDANOS DE CORO N.P.
Puerto Cumarebo
Coro
La Vela de Coro
Carrizal
Pájaro
Uribia
Ríohacha
Manaure
Paraguaipoa
Maicao
SIERRA NEVADA DE SANTA MARTA N.P.
GUAJIRA
Santa Marta
Dibulla
Ciénaga
Barranquilla
Soledad
Puerto Colombia
Baranoa
ATLÁNTICO
Fonseca
San Juan del César
Fundación
Valledupar
Cartagena
Turbaco
Arjona
MAGDALENA
Sinamaica
San Rafael
Mara
Maracaibo
Altagracia
Santa Rita
Cabimas
Capatárida
Dabajuro
Quisiro
Mene de Mauroa
FALCÓN
Churuguara
Siquisique
Cerrón
Cabure
Pedregal
Mirimire
San Juan de los Cayos
Tocuyo de la Costa
Chichiriviche
MORROCOY N.P.
Tucacas
Palma Sola
Puerto Cabello
CARABOBO
La Guaira, VARGAS
Caracas
CAPITAL DISTRICT
Higuerote
Río Chico
El Guapo
Los Teques
Maracay
MIRANDA
Ocumare del Tuy
Clarines
ARAGUA
Valencia
San Felipe
YARACUY
Aroa
Barquisimeto
LARA
Carora
Ciudad Ojeda
Lagunillas
Mene Grande
El Tocuyo
La Concepción
Rosario
ZULIA
Machiques
Lago de Maracaibo
Agustín Codazzi
Calamar
Caracolí
San Juan Nepomuceno
Carmen de Bolívar
Plato
CÉSAR
Sierra de Perijá
La Jagua
Chiriguaná
Golfo de Morrosquillo
Tolú
San Antero
Lorica
Corozal
Sincelejo
Magangué
Mompós
Cicuco
El Banco
CATATUMBO-BARÍ N.P.
PERIJÁ N.P.
Tinaco
San Carlos
Acarigua
COJEDES
Libertad
San Juan de los Morros
Ortiz
Altagracia de Orituco
Onoto
Valle de la Pascua
Zaraza
Chaguaramas
El Sombrero
Las Mercedes
Sabán
El Socorro
Grico
El Calvario
Guardatinajas
GUÁRICO
TRUJILLO
La Ceiba
Betijoque
Valera
Boburés
Trujillo
Guanare
Píritu
PORTUGUESA
La Solita
San Carlos del Zulia
SIERRA NEVADA N.P.
Mérida
MÉRIDA
Cordillera de Mérida
Barinas
Obispos
Santa Rosa
Puerto Escondido
Ciénaga de Oro
Montería
San Juan
Mulatos
Necoclí
Sahagún
Caimito
Sucre
SUCRE
San Marcos
Majagual
La Gloria
Tamalameque
Ayacucho
Tibú
Encontrados
Palmira
Casigua
Petrolea
Convención
Aguachica
Ocaña
NORTE DE SANTANDER
CÓRDOBA
Punta Caribana
Acandí
Carreto
Serranía del Darién
La Palma
Turbo
Arquía
Serranía de Abibe
Montelíbano
Ayapel
Nechí
Caucasia
Margento
BOLÍVAR
Simití
PANAMA
Co. Pirre
DARIÉN N.P.
LOS KATÍOS N.P.
PARAMILLO N.P.
Serranía de Ayapel
Jaqué
Serranía del Sapo
Riosucio
Cáceres
Tarazá
Pató
El Bagre
Zaragoza
Cúcuta
San Cristóbal
Rubio
TÁCHIRA
Tovar
San Félix
Pregonero
Ciudad Bolivia
San Silvestre
San Libertad
Puerto de Nutrias
BARINAS
Bruzual
Arismendi
El Samán de Apure
Santa Bárbara
Apurito
San Fernando de Apure
Achaguas
Camaguán
Calabozo
Corozo Pando
Espino
Santa María de Ipire
AGUARO-GUARIQUITO N.P.
La Unión
Cazorla
Guayabal
Santa Rita
Requeña
Cabruta
Caicara
Las Bonitas
Maripa
Cerro Mato
Las Lajitas
Santa Rosalía
San Rafael de Atamaica
Cunaviche
La Urbana
El Yagual
Guachara
El Piñal
Santa Juana
Mantecal
Rincón Hondo
Palmarito
San Antonio de Caparo
La Victoria
EL TAMA N.P.
Guasdualito
Arauquita
Arauca
Elorza
APURE
CINARUCO-CAPANAPARO N.P.
El Porvenir
Capanaparo
Cinaruco
ARAUCA
Jurado
Mutatá
Dabeiba
Valdivia
Yarumal
Amalfi
Puerto Wilches
Barrancabermeja
Pamplona
Bucaramanga
Piedecuesta
Zapatoca
Otú
Cabo Marzo
Punta Cruces
Cupica
ANTIOQUIA
Antioquia
Anzá
Bello
Medellín
Itagüí
Rionegro
Cisneros
Puerto Berrío
La Mugrosa
SANTANDER
Puerto Olaya
Guaca
Málaga
EL COCUY N.P.
El Cocuy
San Lorenzo
El Tigre
Bahía Solano (Puerto Mutis)
Punta Solano
El Valle
CHOCÓ
Venecia
El Carmen
Jericó
Sonsón
Puerto Nare
Vélez
Charalá
Soatá
Chita
Socha
Güepsa
Paz de Río
Barbosa
Duitama
Sogamoso
Cravo Norte
Puerto Rondón
Rondón
Camoruco
Hato Corozal
Paz de Ariporo
Caño Chiquito
Támara
Nunchía
Buena Vista
Culebra
Isidora
Puerto Páez
Puerto Carreño
Parguaza
BOLÍVAR
Meta
San Rafael
Puerto Nuevo
Quibdó
Nuquí
Cabo Corrientes
Cuevita
Bagadó
Aguadas
Río Sucio
La Dorada
Puerto Salgar
Chiquinquirá
Tunja
BOYACÁ
Honda
CALDAS
RISARALDA
Istmina
Bajo Baudó
Baudó
Negría
Ensenada Docampadó
Manizales
Pereira
Armero
Chocontá
Zipaquirá
Sutatenza
Guateque
Tauramena
Yopal
Monterrey
CASANARE
San Luis de Palenque
Maní
Aguaclara
Orocué
Campo Corral
VICHADA
EL TUPARRO NAT. PARK
Puerto Ayacucho
Samariapo
Morganito
Maipures
Cerro Sipapo
Cerro Ovana
Cerro Yumari
Cacuri
Santa Rita
Campo Troco
Sarto
Sucuaro
San José
San Fernando de Atabapo
Serranía Quinigua
Armenia
Ibagué
BOGOTÁ
CUNDINAMARCA
CAPITAL DISTRICT
Medina
Cháviva
Cabuyaro
El Porvenir
Gaviotas
San Pedro de Arimena
Campamento
San José de Ocuné
Zunape
Maleza
Sabana
Punta Charambirá
Zarzal
Sevilla
Tuluá
TOLIMA
Girardot
Restrepo
Villavicencio
Puerto López
Surimena
San Martín
Guamo
Chaparral
SUMAPAZ N.P.
Buenaventura
Buga
VALLE DEL CAUCA
Cali
Palmira
FARALLONES DE CALI N.P.
Puerto Tejada
Caloto
Naya
Alpe
Villavieja
Granada
Uribe
META
Obando
Puerto Inírida
Cerro Rana
La Ceiba
Juan Viego
Santa Bárbara
YAPACANA N.P.
DUIDA-MARAHUACA N.P.
Cerro Marahuaca
San Antonio
AMAZONAS
La Esmeralda
Piedra Lais
Pamoni
Chafurray
Matraca
Bocón
Inírida
GUAINÍA
Yavita
Maroa
San Miguel
Victorino
Cejal
San José
Cabeza de Pava
Cerro Canapiare
Capibara
Boca Mavaca
Curare
Comunidad
Colón
Solano
PARIMA-TAPIRAPECÓ N.P.
El Mango
San Custodio
San Carlos de Río Negro
San Felipe
Altamira
Santa Rosa de Amanadona
Santa Isabel
El Carmen
Cucuí
SERRANÍA DE LA NEBLINA N.P.
Pico 31 de Março
Pico da Neblina
PICO DA NEBLINA N.P.
Micay
Punta Reyes
Punta Guascama
Timbiquí
Guapí
Morales
Piendamó
Santander
Neiva
Campoalegre
CAUCA
Páez
La Plata
Hobo
Popayán
HUILA
Guacamaya
Timbío
Rosas
SANQUIANGA N.P.
CORDILLERA DE LOS PICACHOS N.P.
SERRANÍA DE LA MACARENA N.P.
Puerto Rico
Puerto La Concordia
San José del Guaviare
La Jagua
Mapiripana
Angostura III
Angostura II
Angostura I
Salto Guayabero
Garzón
Altamira
San Agustín
San Vicente de Caguán
Sachene
Las Juntas
Puerto Macaco
Marinuma
Loro
José María
Cerro Caparro
Uarirambá
Vista Alegre
Cuiari
Tapira
Marabitanas
São Marcelino
Calamar
GUAVIARE
Cerro Otare
Palo Negro
Miraflores
Sierra de Chiribiquete
Laguna Chaira
San Antonio
Barbacoas
Bolívar
Mercaderes
La Unión
Florencia
Morelia
Puerto Rico
Sucre
Belén
NARIÑO
Pasto
Junín
Mocoa
Puerto Limón
San Francisco
Valparaíso
Túquerres
Ipiales
Tulcán
El Ángel
San Gabriel
Ibarra
Otavalo
Puerto Umbría
PUTUMAYO
Tres Esquinas
Puerto Príncipe
Puerto Asís
La Bonita
San Miguel
Lago Agrio
LA PAYA N.P.
Concepción
Curiplaya
Puerto Boy
Puerto Huitoto
Macujé
Cunaré
CAQUETÁ
CHIRIBIQUETE NAT. PARK
Macaranay
Raudal Yupurari (Devils Cataract)
Mitú
Jutica
Jibóia
Uacari
Apuí
Acaricuara
VAUPÉS
Lérida
Yavarate
Iauareté
Micuí
Tariana
Iraiti
Samaúma
Taraquá
Cachoeira Ipanoré
Cachoeira Ipadu
Içana
São Gabriel da Cachoeira
São Joaquim
Serra Curicuriari
São Pedro
Putumayo
Hacha
Monclar
Güeppí
La Tagua
Puerto Leguízamo
Aguas Negras
Palermo
Puerto Pizarro
Angostura
Guamareyes
Araracuara
Itiquines
La Chorrera
Mirití
EQUATOR
SUMACO NAPO GALERAS N.P.
Puerto Francisco de Orellana
Loreto
Antisana
YASUNÍ NAT. PARK
Nuevo Rocafuerte
Pantoja
Arcadia
Tena
Puerto Napo
LLANGANATES N.P.
ECUADOR
Puyo
Canelos
Sarayacu
SANGAY N.P.
Sangay
Chiguaza
Macas
Méndez
Yaupi
Capitán Bezada
Andoas
General Leonidas Plaza Gutiérrez
Sinchiyacu
Coronel Portillo
Trozadero
San José
Puerto Salvatierra
Huasaga
Santa Rosa
Soledad
Tempestad
Cononaco
Bellavista
Arica
Río Tigre
Posto Cunambo
Río Corrientes
Posto Bobonaza
Santa María
Todo Santos
El Encanto
Barras
Campuya
Puesto Arturo
Moñoz
Puerto Aurora
Puerto Curaray
Santa Clotilde
Vidal
Flor de Agosto
San Cristóbal
LORETO
Puerto Copal
Puca Barranca
Santa Rosa
Oro Blanco
Francisco de Orellana
Mazán
Intuto
San Antonio
Sargento Lores
Iquitos
PERU
Pebas
Tarma
AMAZONAS
CAHUINARI NAT. PARK
Santa Julia
Indostán
Mediodía
Condar
Puerto Carlos
Puerto Cahuinari
Puerto Miraña
Puerto Córdoba
La Pedrera
Ricaurte
Yauna Moloca
Vila Bittencourt
Arica
Puerto Alfonso
Puca Urco
San Salvador
Tacna
Puerto Carranza
Puerto San Augustín
Puerto Socorro
Santa Clara
Visconde do Rio Branco
Tarapacá
Buenos Aires
AMACAYACU NAT. PARK
Ipiranga
Santa Rita do Weil
São Pedro
Santo Antônio do Içá
Curupaiti
São Paulo de Olivença
Amaturá
Igualdade
Capana
AMAZONAS
BRAZIL
Marcelino
Piquiá
Maraã
Japurá
Lago Paricá
Lago Sapateiro
Foz do Mamoriá
Fonte Boa
Tonantins
Ambrósio
Jutaí
Itaúna
Ipiranga
Juruá
Marauá
Andirá
Amazonas
Japurá
Caquetá
Orinoco
Meta
Vichada
Guaviare
Inírida
Vaupés
Apaporis
Mirití Paraná
Caraparaná
Napo
Curaray
Tigre
Pastaza
Marañón
Yaguas
Atacuari
Içá
Putumayo
Río Negro
Cauca
Magdalena
Atrato
Sinú
Cordillera Occidental
Cordillera Central
Cordillera Oriental
CORDILLERA DE LOS ANDES
SIERRA DE LOS ANDES
5750
5493
4560
5230
5704
3613
3235
2350
1875
1439
1145
1990
2994
2992
2579
2286
2377
2080
1978
2260
1999
1863
1320
1930
3652

Longitude West 69° of Greenwich
72°
75°
69°
66°
9°
12°
15°
18°
21°
BRAZIL
PERU
BOLIVIA
ARGENTINA
CHILE
PACIFIC OCEAN
ACRE
AMAZONAS
RONDÔNIA
UCAYALI
PASCO
HUÁNUCO
JUNÍN
MADRE DE DIOS
CUSCO
APURÍMAC
AYACUCHO
AREQUIPA
MOQUEGUA
TACNA
PUNO
ICA
CORDILLERA OCCIDENTAL
PANDO
BENI
LA PAZ
COCHABAMBA
SANTA CRUZ
ORURO
POTOSÍ
CHUQUISACA
TARIJA
ARICA Y PARINACOTA
TARAPACÁ
ANTOFAGASTA
JUJUY
SERRA DO DIVISOR N.P.
MANU NAT. PARK
BAHUAJA-SONENE N.P.
MADIDI N.P.
PILÓN-LAJA N.P.
ISIBORO SECURE N.P.
BOUNDARY UNDEFINED
CARRASCO ICHILO N.P.
AMBORÓ N.P.
LAUCA N.P.
VOLCAN ISLUGA N.P.
BARITU N.P.
PACAÁS NOVOS N.P.
Source of the Amazon
Lago Titicaca
Lago Poopó
L. de Coipasa
Salar de Coipasa
Salar de Uyuni
Salar de Empexa
Lag. Colorada
Lago Rogaguado
Lago Rogagua
Lag. Huaitunas
Lago de San Luis
Nevado Coropuna
Nevado Ampato
Nevado Chachani
Volcan Misti
Illampu
Illimani
Nevado Sajama
Volcan Ollagüe
Cerro Palpana
Aucanquilcha
Cerro Alcoak
Co. Alcoak
Mount Payne
Cerro de la Mica
Cerro Colupo
Cerro Carrasco
Punta Coles
Cabo Lobos
Punta Madrid
Punta Gruesa
Punta Lobos
Punta Cobija
Punta Gualaguala
Marechal Taumaturgo
Foz do Breu
Foz do Jordão
Puerto Portillo
Progresso
Santa Rosa do Purus
Esperanza
Sena Madureira
Araras
Porto Alegre
Florescência
Horizonte
Porto Acre
Macapá
São José
Riozinho
Bom Comércio
Manoa
Abunã
Mutum-Paraná
Fortaleza
Rio Branco
Bom Destino
Plácido de Castro
Agostinho
Canamari
Amapá
Ulbio
Germânia
São Vicente
Guanabara
Maloca
Assis Brasil
Iñapari
Bolpebra
Xapuri
Brasileia
Cobija
Palmares
Santa Rosa
Vila Murtinho
Villa Bella
Yata
Guajará-Mirim
Cachuela Esperanza
Riberalta
Ivón
Moreno
Nacebe
Bella Flor
Puerto Rico
Porvenir
Costa Rica
Filadelfia
Conquista
Sena
Concepción
Iberia
San Lorenzo
San Miguelito
Holanda
Carmen
Asunción
Bolívar
Apere
Chive
Puerto Pardo
Puerto Heath
Puerto Maldonado
Cavinas
Mayo Mayo
Costa Marques
Príncipe da Beira
Puerto Siles
San Joaquín
Exaltación
San Ramón
Magdalena
Huacaraje
Baures
Rogaguado
El Carmen
Yata
Oriente
Santa Rosa
Ipariá
Ollanta
Cumaría
Sheboya
Bolognesi
Pacaya
Puerto Bermúdez
Termópilas
Atalaya
Colonia Penal del Sepa
Sepahua
Alerta
Satipo
Puerto Prado
Andamarca
Santo Domingo de Acobamba
Camisea
Fitzcarrald
Manú
Itahuanía
Madre de Dios
Sintuya
Inambari
Puerto Carlos
Pampas
Paucarbamba
Teresita
Luisiana
Chancamayo
Huancavelica
Ayna
Quillabamba
Echarate
Acobamba
Huanta
Chaullay
San Miguel
Lircay
Ayacucho
Vilcabamba
Machu Picchu
Cosñipata
Pillcopata
Quince Mil
Astillero
Calca
Pisac
Paucartambo
Marcapata
Anta
Cusco
Abancay
Andahuaylas
Chincheros
Cangallo
Urcos
Ollachea
Lanlacuni Bajo
Madidi
Ixiamas
Cotabambas
Paruro
Acomayo
Querco
Ocoyo
Chapimarca
Chuquibambilla
Macusani
Huari
Limbani
Sandia
Coasa
Crucero
San Ignacio
Tumupasa
Laramate
Aucará
Chalhuanca
Antabamba
Colquemarca
Yanaoca
Sicuani
Santa Rosa
Nuñoa
San José
Asillo
Azángaro
Putina
Sina
Mojos
Pelechuco
Apolo
San Buenaventura
Rurrenabaque
Reyes
Santa Rosa
Nieves
San Miguel
Puerto Leigue
San Pedro
Huachi
San Javier
San Ignacio
San Borja
Trinidad
San Antonio
San Andrés
Loreto
Lucanas
Puquio
Santo Tomás
Corporaque
Yauri
Ayaviri
Nasca
Coracora
Chumpi
Pausa
Alca
Cotahuasi
Caylloma
Ocoruro
Condoroma
Pucará
Lampa
Juliaca
Cojata
Huancané
Villa Juan José Pérez
Chuma
Mapiri
Moho
Guanay
Tipuani
Taraco
Pusi
Puerto Acosta
Santa Ana
San Francisco
San Lorenzo
Limoquije
San Miguel de Huachi
Acarí
Pullo
Jaquí
Puerto de Lomas
Yauca
Atiquipa
Chala
Cabanaconde
Chivay
Capachica
Puerto Carabuco
Sorata
Caranavi
Covendo
Puno
Chuquito
Acora
Ilave
Achacachi
Coroico
Chuquibamba
Aplao
Lluta
Sumbay
Ichuña
Juli
Copacabana
San Pedro
Pucarani
Coripata
Chulumani
Irupana
Atico
Ocoña
Vitor
Arequipa
Quequeña
Puquina
Ubinas
Yunguyo
Tiwanacu
La Paz
Camaná
Pueblo Nuevo
Desaguadero
Guaqui
Mazo Cruz
Viacha
Puerto Patiño
Altamachi
Villa Tunari
Puerto Mamoré
Todos Santos
Puerto Villarroel
Cuatro Ojos
Puerto Velarde
San Pablo
Matarani
Mollendo
Cocachacra
Punta de Bombón
Carumas
Moquegua
Torata
Toquepala
Pizacoma
Calamarca
Sapahaqui
Inquisivi
Independencia
Quime
Luribay
Yaco
Puerto Grether
General Saavedra
Montero
Buena Vista
Santa Cruz
Corocoro
Calacoto
Umala
Sicasica
Colquiri
Quillacollo
Cochabamba
Cliza
Punata
Arani
Tomás Barrón
Pocoma
Tarata
Locumba
Ilo
Las Yaras
Charaña
Pachía
Tacna
Ulloma
San Pedro de Curahuara
Curaguara de Carangas
Paria
Oruro
Arque
Capinota
Totora
Pojo
Comarapa
Mizque
Ayacucho
La Yarada
Chacalluta
Arica
Azapa
Putre
Sajama
Belén
Turco
Machacamarca
Corque
El Choro
Poopó
Llallagua
Uncía
Chayanta
Arampampa
Sacaca
Torotoro
Aiquile
Pasorapa
Pampa Grande
Samaipata
Trigal
Quirusillas
Florida
Vallegrande
Cuya
Codpa
Huachacalla
Negrillos
Sabaya
Orinoca
Pazña
Challapata
Huari
Ocurí
Colquechaca
Ravelo
Poroma
Mojocoya
Presto
Zudañez
Pucará
Curichi
Cabezas
Abapó
Sucre
Yotala
Tarabuco
Villa Serrano
Padilla
Camarones
Miñimiñi
Camiña
Chiapa
Zapiga
Pisagua
Salinas de G. Mendoza
Sevaruyo
Gabriel Vera
Betanzos
Potosí
Chaqui
Masavi
Gutiérrez
Lagunillas
Sopachuy
Monteagudo
Caleta Buena
Negreiros
Tarapacá
Huara
Mamiña
Pozo Almonte
Iquique
Llica
Tagua
Río Mulatos
Porco
Villa Talavera
Caiza
Azurduy
Charagua
Villa Vaca Guzmán
San Lucas
Camiri
Huanchaca
Pulacayo
Uyuni
Vitichi
Toropalca
Tumusla
Boyuibe
Cuevo
Ivo
Anita
Pica
Pintados
Chacarilla
Yonza
Villa Martín
Río Grande
Julaca
Chocaya
Cotagaita
Camargo
Yatina
Ñancorainza
Huacaya
Carandaytí
Machareti
Caleta Pabellón de Pica
Lagunas
Challacollo
Collaguasi
Chiguana
San Cristóbal
Atocha
Villa Abecia
Camatindi
Tarairi
Ollagüe
Oro Ingenio
Opioca
Impora
El Puente
San Lorenzo
Tarija
Entre Ríos
Villamontes
Sanandita
Itaú
Villa Ingavi
Tupiza
Esmoraca
Iscayachi
Uriondo
San Pablo
Moraya
Mojo
Padcaya
Carapari
Quillagua
Oficina Santa Fe
Ascotán
Pan de Azúcar
Santa Catalina
Villazón
La Quiaca
Yavi
Salvador Mazza
Aguarey
Campo Durán
Conchi
Tocopilla
Toco
María Elena
Chuquicamata
Chiuchiu
Rinconada
Santa Victoria
Limal
Tartagal
Calama
Vergara
Gatico
Pedro de Valdivia
Sierra Gorda
Quitor
San Pedro de Atacama
Cochinoca
Iruya
Abra Pampa
Ramos
Tranquitas
Deseada
Coranzuli
Iturbe
ALTIPLANO
AZIMUTHAL EQUIDISTANT PROJECTION
SCALE 1:6,000,000
0 KILOMETERS 100 150
0 MILES 50 100 150

SOUTHEASTERN BRAZIL
AZIMUTHAL EQUIDISTANT PROJECTION
SCALE 1:7,000,000
0 KILOMETERS 100 150 200
0 MILES 50 100 150 200
ATLANTIC OCEAN
TROPIC OF CAPRICORN
Longitude West 45° of Greenwich
BRAZIL
TOCANTINS
BAHIA
MATO GROSSO
GOIÁS
DISTRITO FEDERAL
Brasília
MINAS GERAIS
ESPÍRITO SANTO
RIO DE JANEIRO
SÃO PAULO
MATO GROSSO DO SUL
PARANÁ
SANTA CATARINA
RIO GRANDE DO SUL
PLANALTO BRASILEIRO
Serra do Espinhaço
Serra do Roncador
Espigão Mestre
CHAPADA DOS VEADEIROS N.P.
CHAPADA DIAMANTINA N.P.
GRANDE SERTÃO VEREDAS N.P.
EMAS N.P.
SERRA DA CANASTRA N.P.
MONTE PASCOAL N.P.
SERRA DA BOCAINA NAT. PARK
SÃO JOAQUIM N.P.
IGUAÇU N.P.
Três Marias Dam
Jurumirim Dam
Goiânia
Anápolis
Belo Horizonte
Vitória
Vila Velha (Espírito Santo)
Rio de Janeiro
Niterói
São Paulo
Santo André
Santos
Campinas
Curitiba
Florianópolis
Uberlândia
Uberaba
Ribeirão Preto
São José do Rio Preto
Juiz de Fora
Montes Claros
Vitória da Conquista
Governador Valadares
Londrina
Maringá
Ponta Grossa
Joinville
Blumenau
Campos
Macaé
Cabo Frio
Teófilo Otoni
Patos de Minas
Rio Verde
Presidente Prudente
Bauru
Sorocaba
Jundiaí
Taubaté
São José dos Campos
Volta Redonda
Petrópolis
Nova Iguaçu
Duque de Caxias
Guarapuava
Cascavel
Passo Fundo
Criciúma
Paranaguá
Linhares
Colatina
Cachoeiro do Itapemirim
Jequié
15°
18°
21°
24°
27°
51°
48°
45°
42°
39°

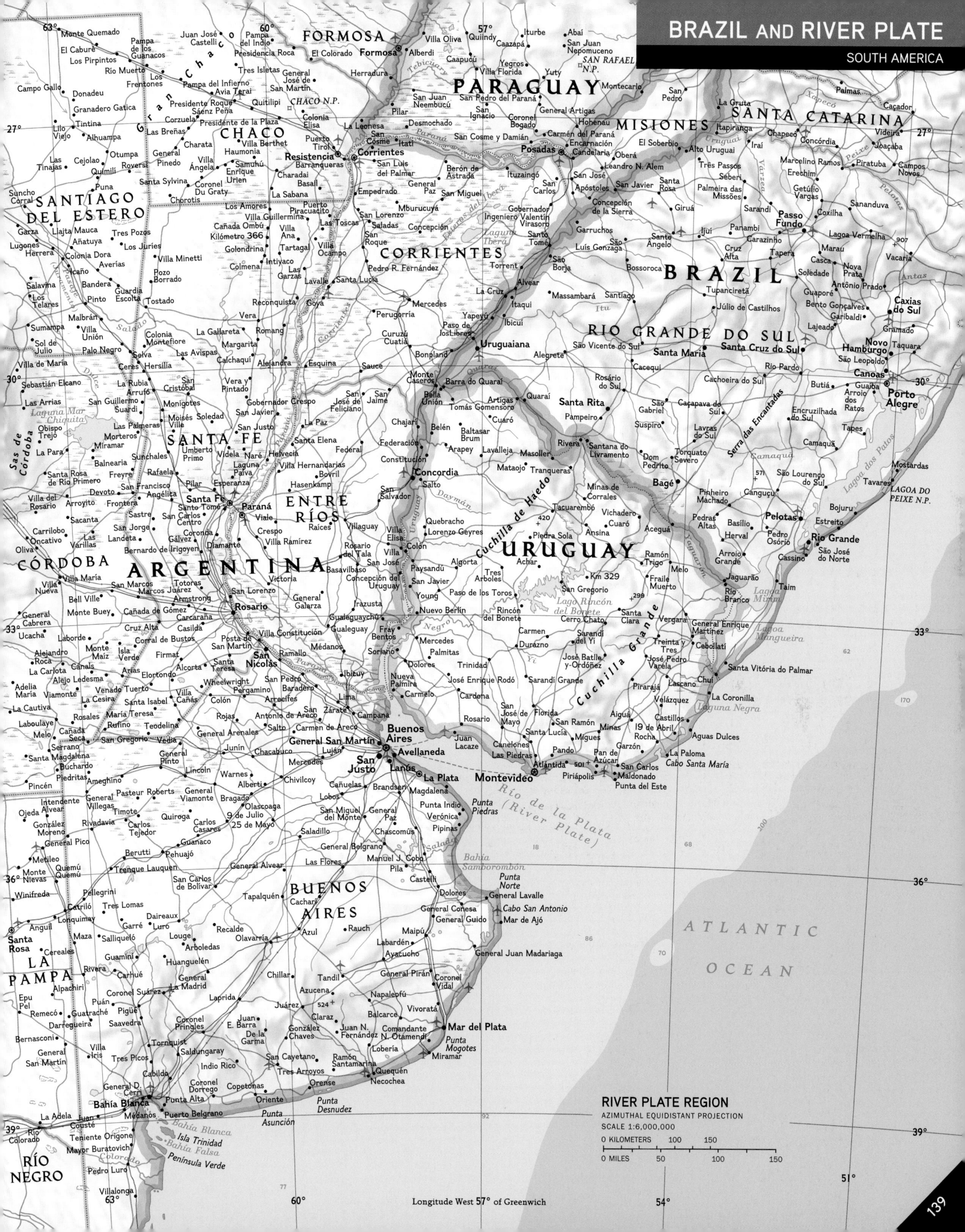
RIVER PLATE REGION
AZIMUTHAL EQUIDISTANT PROJECTION
SCALE 1:6,000,000
0 KILOMETERS 100 150
0 MILES 50 100 150
Longitude West 57° of Greenwich
ATLANTIC OCEAN
BRAZIL
PARAGUAY
URUGUAY
ARGENTINA
FORMOSA
CHACO
SANTIAGO DEL ESTERO
CORRIENTES
MISIONES
SANTA CATARINA
RIO GRANDE DO SUL
SANTA FE
ENTRE RÍOS
CÓRDOBA
BUENOS AIRES
LA PAMPA
RÍO NEGRO
Gran Chaco
Río de la Plata (River Plate)
Cuchilla de Haedo
Cuchilla Grande
Serra das Encantadas
Buenos Aires
Montevideo
Porto Alegre
Rosario
La Plata
Mar del Plata
Bahía Blanca
Corrientes
Resistencia
Posadas
Santa Fe
Paraná
Pelotas
Rio Grande
Santa Maria
Concordia
Uruguaiana
Formosa
Santa Rosa
Laguna Mar Chiquita
Bahía Samborombón
Cabo San Antonio
Punta del Este
Lagoa dos Patos
Lagoa Mirim
Laguna Negra
Lago Rincón del Bonete
Bahía Blanca
Península Verde
CHACO N.P.
SAN RAFAEL N.P.
LAGOA DO PEIXE N.P.

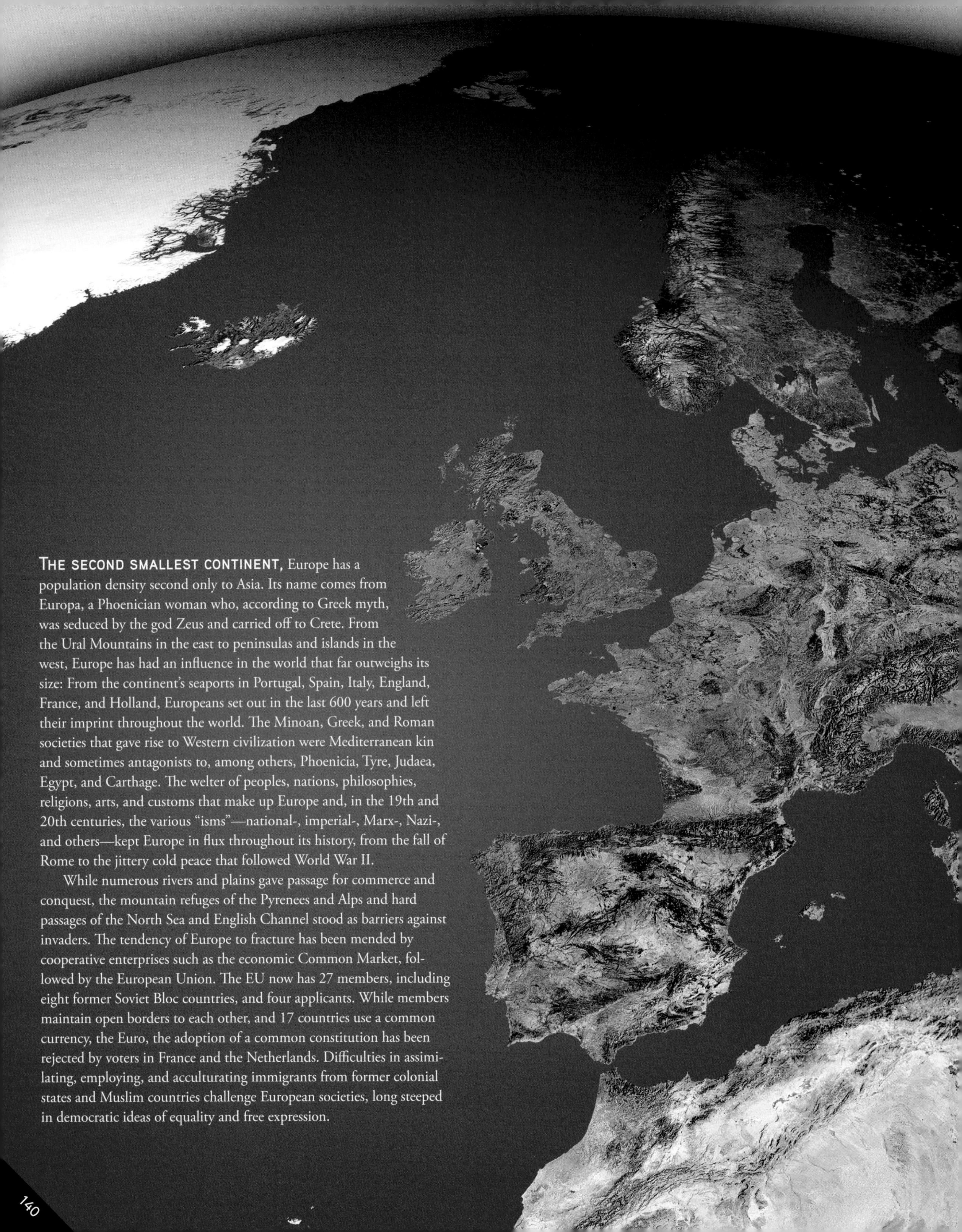

THE SECOND SMALLEST CONTINENT, Europe has a population density second only to Asia. Its name comes from Europa, a Phoenician woman who, according to Greek myth, was seduced by the god Zeus and carried off to Crete. From the Ural Mountains in the east to peninsulas and islands in the west, Europe has had an influence in the world that far outweighs its size: From the continent's seaports in Portugal, Spain, Italy, England, France, and Holland, Europeans set out in the last 600 years and left their imprint throughout the world. The Minoan, Greek, and Roman societies that gave rise to Western civilization were Mediterranean kin and sometimes antagonists to, among others, Phoenicia, Tyre, Judaea, Egypt, and Carthage. The welter of peoples, nations, philosophies, religions, arts, and customs that make up Europe and, in the 19th and 20th centuries, the various "isms"—national-, imperial-, Marx-, Nazi-, and others—kept Europe in flux throughout its history, from the fall of Rome to the jittery cold peace that followed World War II.

While numerous rivers and plains gave passage for commerce and conquest, the mountain refuges of the Pyrenees and Alps and hard passages of the North Sea and English Channel stood as barriers against invaders. The tendency of Europe to fracture has been mended by cooperative enterprises such as the economic Common Market, followed by the European Union. The EU now has 27 members, including eight former Soviet Bloc countries, and four applicants. While members maintain open borders to each other, and 17 countries use a common currency, the Euro, the adoption of a common constitution has been rejected by voters in France and the Netherlands. Difficulties in assimilating, employing, and acculturating immigrants from former colonial states and Muslim countries challenge European societies, long steeped in democratic ideas of equality and free expression.

Europe

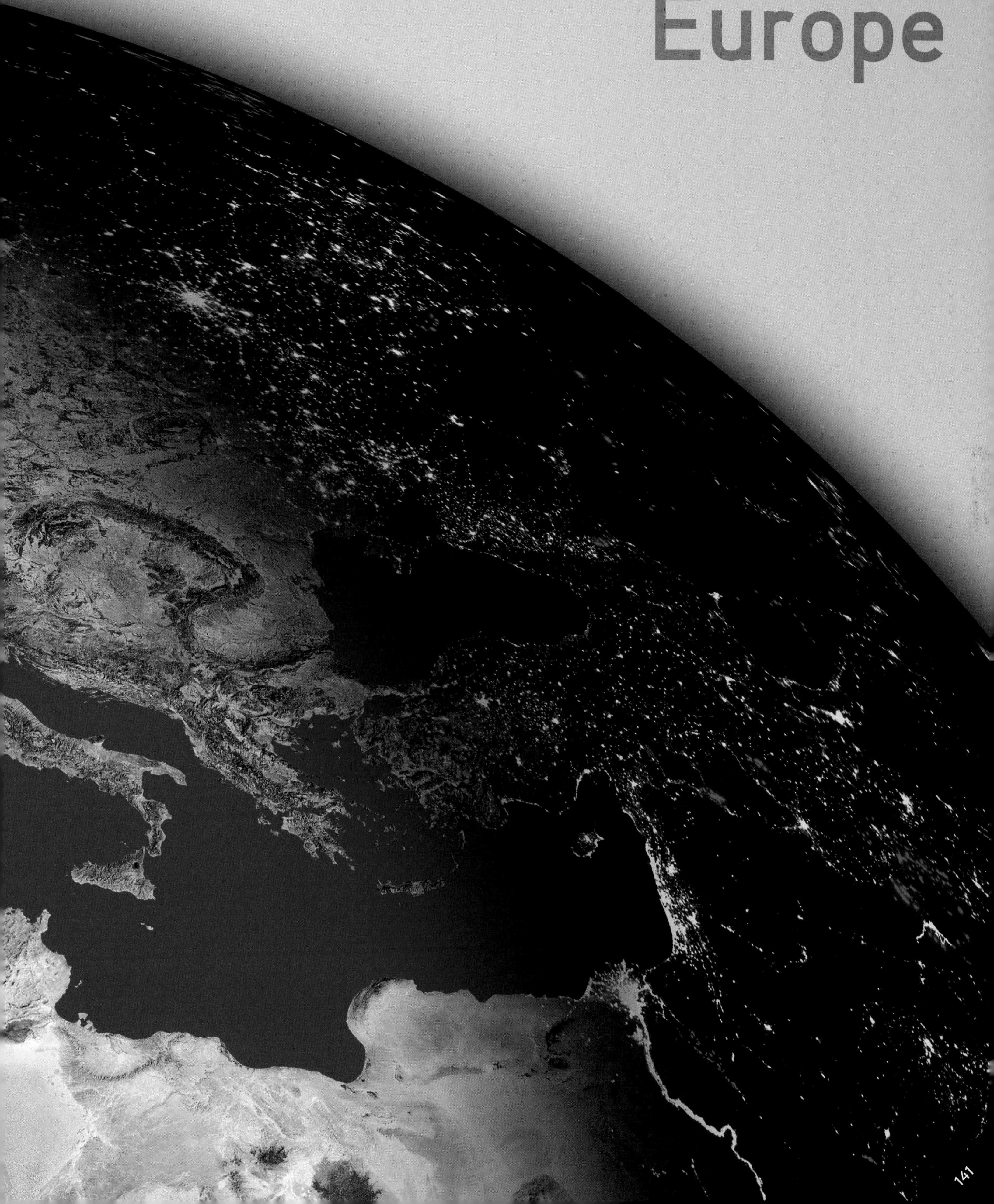

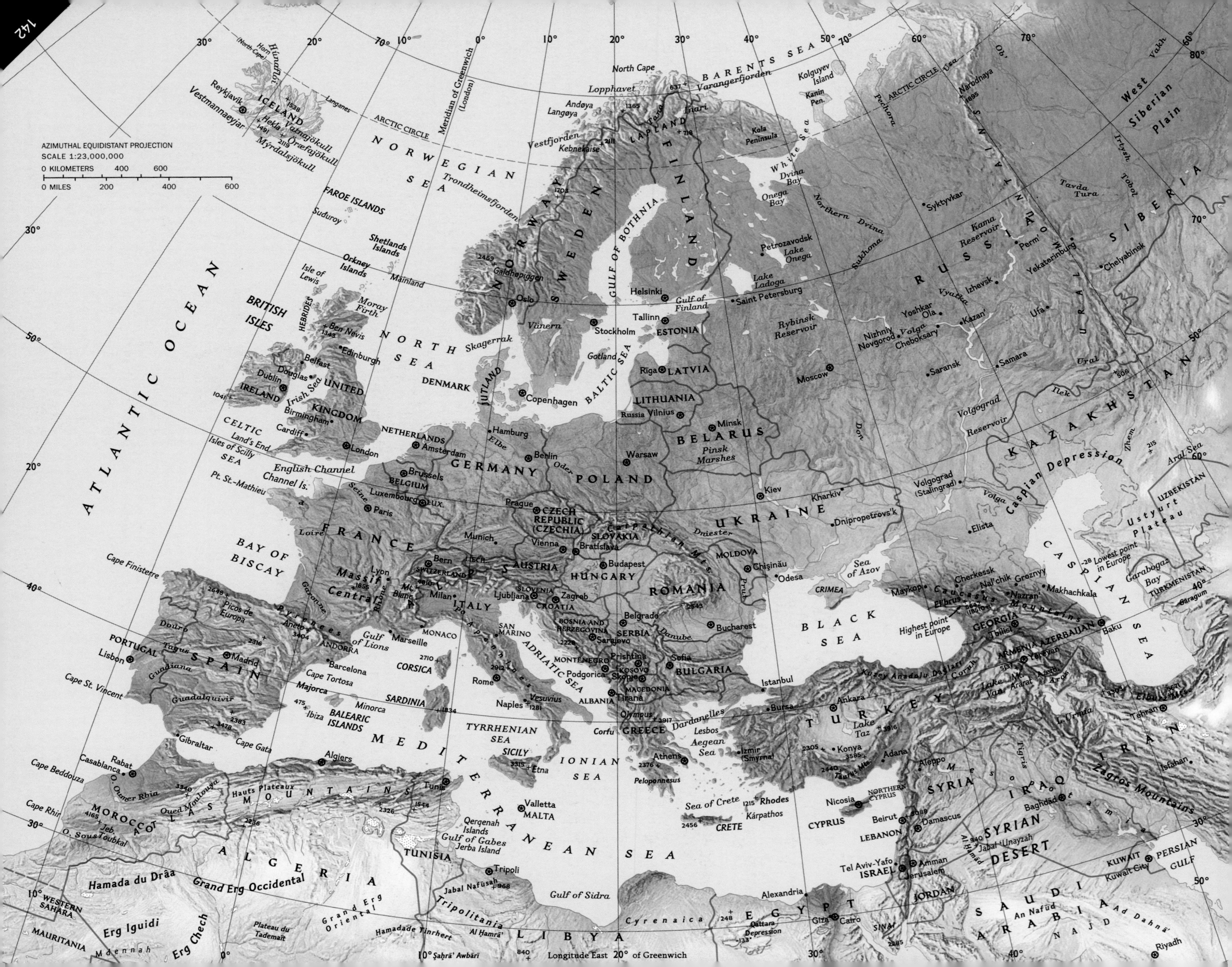
AZIMUTHAL EQUIDISTANT PROJECTION
SCALE 1:23,000,000
0 KILOMETERS 400 600
0 MILES 200 400 600
ATLANTIC OCEAN
NORWEGIAN SEA
NORTH SEA
BARENTS SEA
BALTIC SEA
GULF OF BOTHNIA
BAY OF BISCAY
CELTIC SEA
English Channel
MEDITERRANEAN SEA
TYRRHENIAN SEA
IONIAN SEA
ADRIATIC SEA
Aegean Sea
Sea of Crete
BLACK SEA
Sea of Azov
CASPIAN SEA
Aral Sea
PERSIAN GULF
ARCTIC CIRCLE
Meridian of Greenwich (London)
Longitude East 20° of Greenwich
ICELAND
Reykjavík
FAROE ISLANDS
Shetlands Islands
Orkney Islands
BRITISH ISLES
UNITED KINGDOM
IRELAND
Dublin
Belfast
Edinburgh
London
Birmingham
Cardiff
NORWAY
Oslo
SWEDEN
Stockholm
FINLAND
Helsinki
DENMARK
Copenhagen
ESTONIA
Tallinn
LATVIA
Rīga
LITHUANIA
Vilnius
BELARUS
Minsk
RUSSIA
Moscow
Saint Petersburg
UKRAINE
Kiev
POLAND
Warsaw
GERMANY
Berlin
Hamburg
Munich
NETHERLANDS
Amsterdam
BELGIUM
Brussels
LUX.
Luxembourg
FRANCE
Paris
Lyon
Marseille
SPAIN
Madrid
Barcelona
PORTUGAL
Lisbon
ANDORRA
SWITZERLAND
Bern
ITALY
Rome
Milan
Naples
AUSTRIA
Vienna
CZECH REPUBLIC (CZECHIA)
Prague
SLOVAKIA
Bratislava
HUNGARY
Budapest
SLOVENIA
Ljubljana
CROATIA
Zagreb
BOSNIA AND HERZEGOVINA
Sarajevo
SERBIA
Belgrade
MONTENEGRO
Podgorica
KOSOVO
Prishtina
MACEDONIA
Skopje
ALBANIA
Tirana
GREECE
Athens
BULGARIA
Sofia
ROMANIA
Bucharest
MOLDOVA
Chişinău
TURKEY
Ankara
Istanbul
CYPRUS
Nicosia
GEORGIA
Tbilisi
ARMENIA
Yerevan
AZERBAIJAN
Baku
KAZAKHSTAN
UZBEKISTAN
TURKMENISTAN
IRAN
Tehran
IRAQ
Baghdād
SYRIA
Damascus
LEBANON
Beirut
ISRAEL
JORDAN
Amman
SAUDI ARABIA
Riyadh
KUWAIT
EGYPT
Cairo
LIBYA
Tripoli
TUNISIA
Tunis
ALGERIA
Algiers
MOROCCO
Rabat
WESTERN SAHARA
MAURITANIA
MALTA
Valletta
CORSICA
SARDINIA
SICILY
CRETE
ATLAS MOUNTAINS
URAL MOUNTAINS
Caucasus Mountains
Zagros Mountains
Pyrenees
Apennines
Alps
Carpathian Mts.
Massif Central
West Siberian Plain
Caspian Depression
SYRIAN DESERT
Grand Erg Occidental
Grand Erg Oriental
Highest point in Europe
Lowest point in Europe

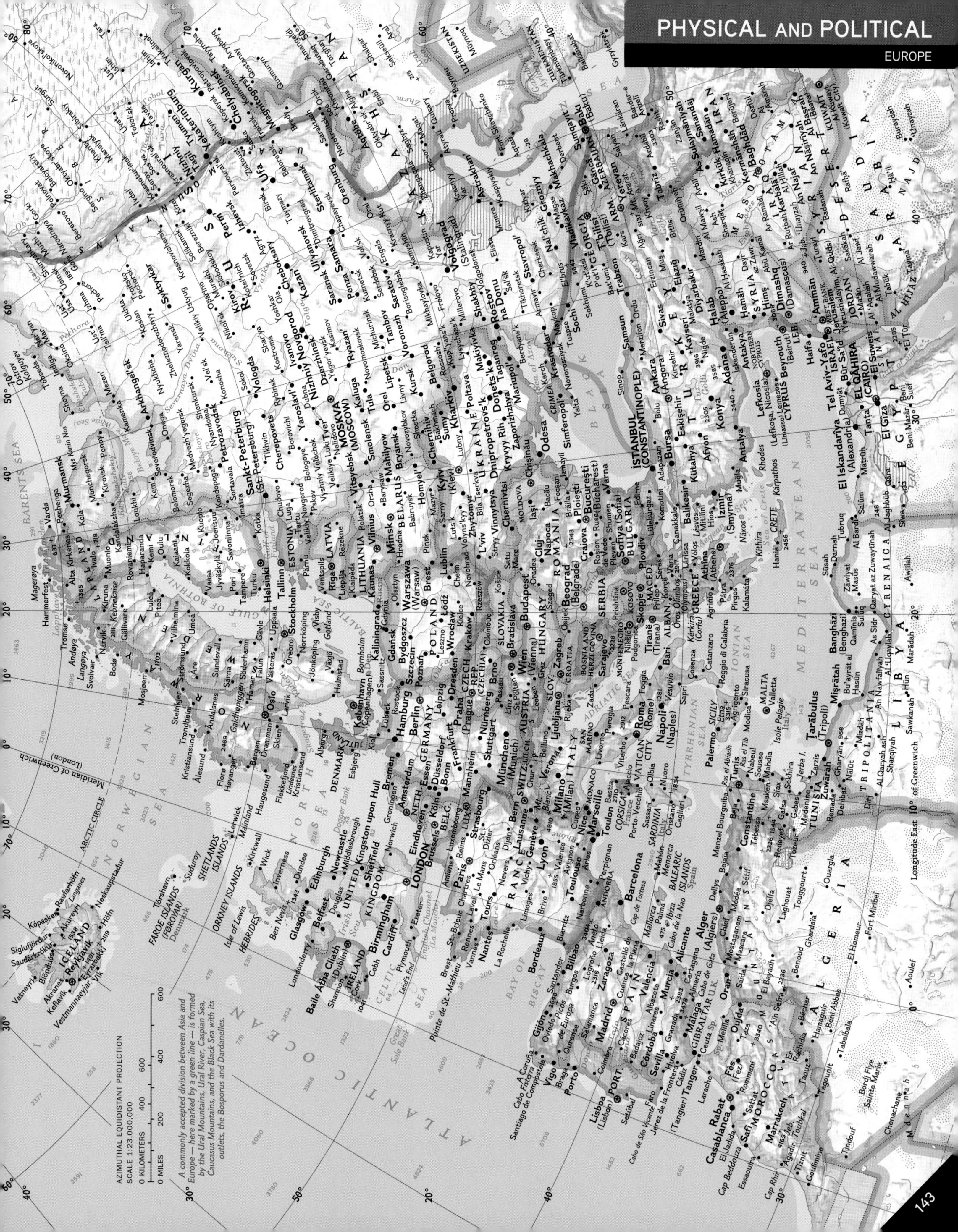
AZIMUTHAL EQUIDISTANT PROJECTION
SCALE 1:23,000,000
0 KILOMETERS 200 400 600
0 MILES 200 400 600
A commonly accepted division between Asia and Europe — here marked by a green line — is formed by the Ural Mountains, Ural River, Caspian Sea, Caucasus Mountains, and the Black Sea with its outlets, the Bosporus and Dardanelles.
ATLANTIC OCEAN
MEDITERRANEAN SEA
BLACK SEA
NORWEGIAN SEA
BARENTS SEA

LAND COVER

- Evergreen needleleaf forest
- Evergreen broadleaf forest
- Deciduous needleleaf forest
- Deciduous broadleaf forest
- Mixed forest
- Woody savanna
- Savanna
- Closed shrubland
- Open shrubland
- Grassland
- Cropland
- Barren or sparsely vegetated
- Urban or built-up
- Snow and ice
- Cropland / natural vegetation mosaic
- Wetland

ICELAND

SVALBARD (NORWAY)

NORWAY

SWEDEN

FINLAND

FAROE ISLANDS (DENMARK)

U.K.

IRELAND

DEN.

NETH.

BELG.

CHANNEL IS. (U.K.)

LUX.

GERMANY

LIECH. Prague○ CZECH REP.

EST.

LAT.

LITH.

RUSS.

BELARUS

○Moscow

R U S S I A

KAZ.

POLAND

SLOVAKIA

FRANCE

SWITZ.

AUSTRIA

HUNGARY

UKRAINE

MOLD.

SLOV.

CROATIA

BOSN. & HERZG.

SERBIA

ROMANIA

AZERB.

GEORGIA

PORTUGAL

○Madrid

ANDORRA

SPAIN

ITALY

MONTENEGRO

KOS.

MACED.

ALBANIA

BULGARIA

Istanbul○

TURKEY

GIBRALTAR (U.K.)

GREECE

MALTA

CYPRUS

TEMPERATURE AND RAINFALL

Madrid, Spain

Temperatures above 0°C
Temperatures below 0°C

High temperature

Low temperature

Rainfall (115 mm = 4.5 in)

50°C – 690 mm
40°C – 575 mm
30°C – 460 mm
20°C – 345 mm
10°C – 230 mm
0°C – 115 mm
-10°C – 0 mm
-20°C
-30°C J F M A M J J A S O N D

Istanbul, Turkey

50°C – 690 mm
40°C – 575 mm
30°C – 460 mm
20°C – 345 mm
10°C – 230 mm
0°C – 115 mm
-10°C – 0 mm
-20°C
-30°C J F M A M J J A S O N D

Prague, Czech Republic

50°C – 690 mm
40°C – 575 mm
30°C – 460 mm
20°C – 345 mm
10°C – 230 mm
0°C – 115 mm
-10°C – 0 mm
-20°C
-30°C J F M A M J J A S O N D

Moscow, Russia

50°C – 690 mm
40°C – 575 mm
30°C – 460 mm
20°C – 345 mm
10°C – 230 mm
0°C – 115 mm
-10°C – 0 mm
-20°C
-30°C J F M A M J J A S O N D

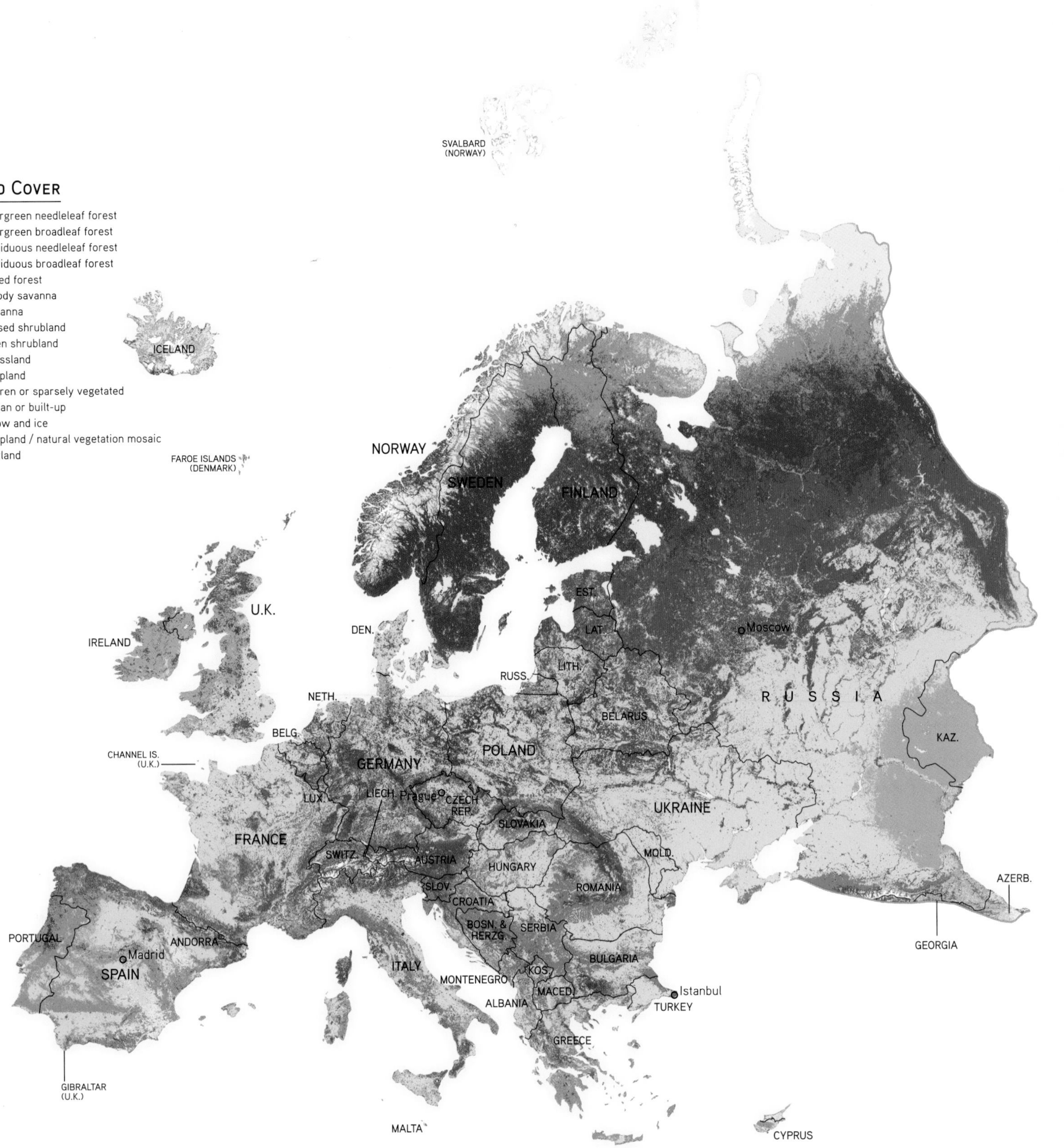

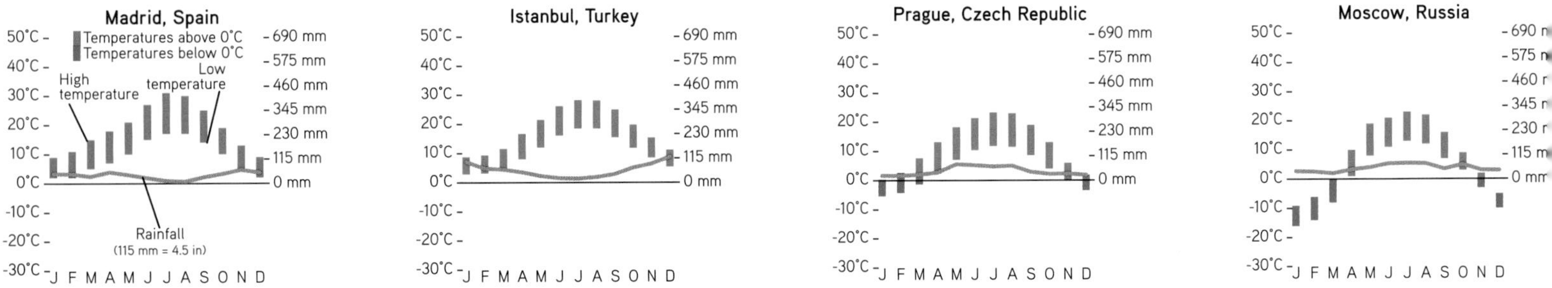

Climate Zones

(based on modified Köppen system)

Dry climate (B)
- Semiarid (BS)
- Arid (BW)

k = cold

Humid temperate climate (C)
- No dry season (Cf)
- Dry summer (Cs)

Humid cold climate (D)
- No dry season (Df)

a = hot summer
b = cool summer
c = short, cool su

Cold climate (E)
- Tundra and ice

Highland climate (H)
- Unclassified highlands

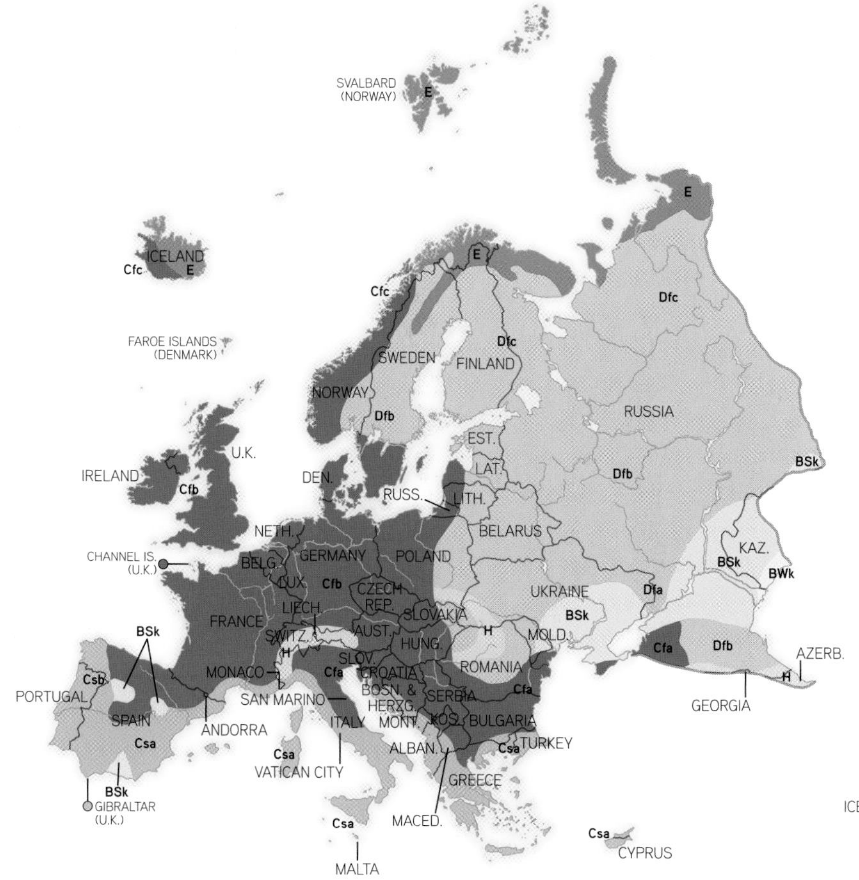

Water Availability

(in millimeters per person per year)
- More than 750
- 251–750
- 26–250
- Less than 26
- No data available

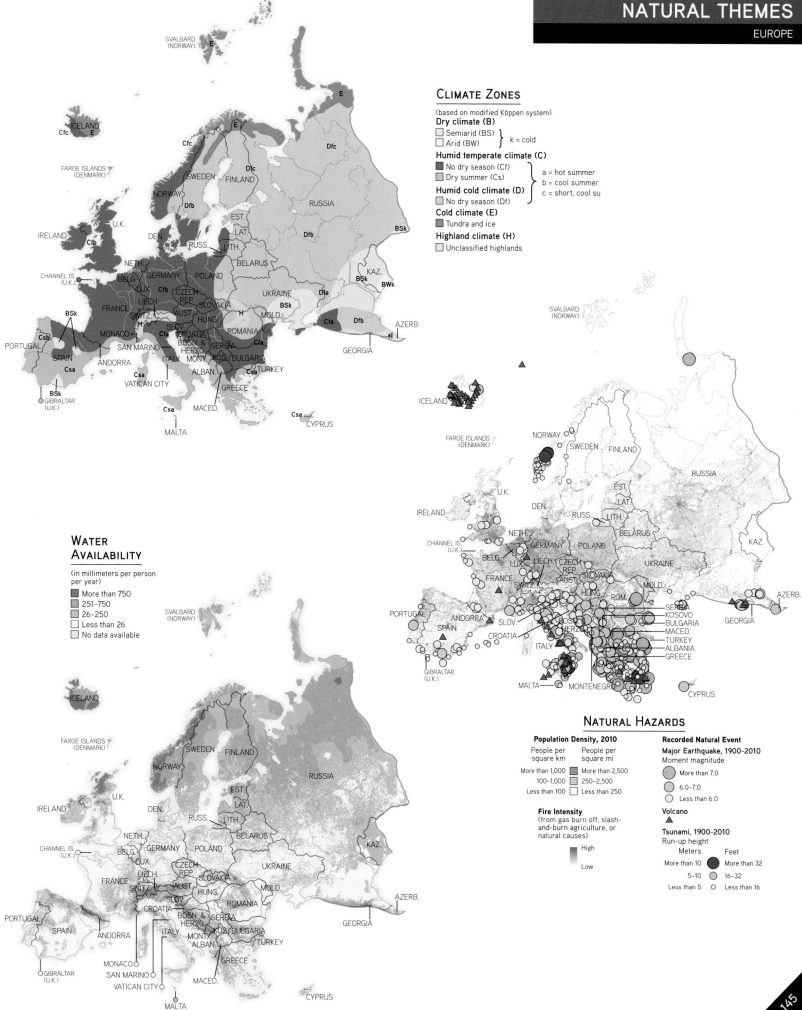

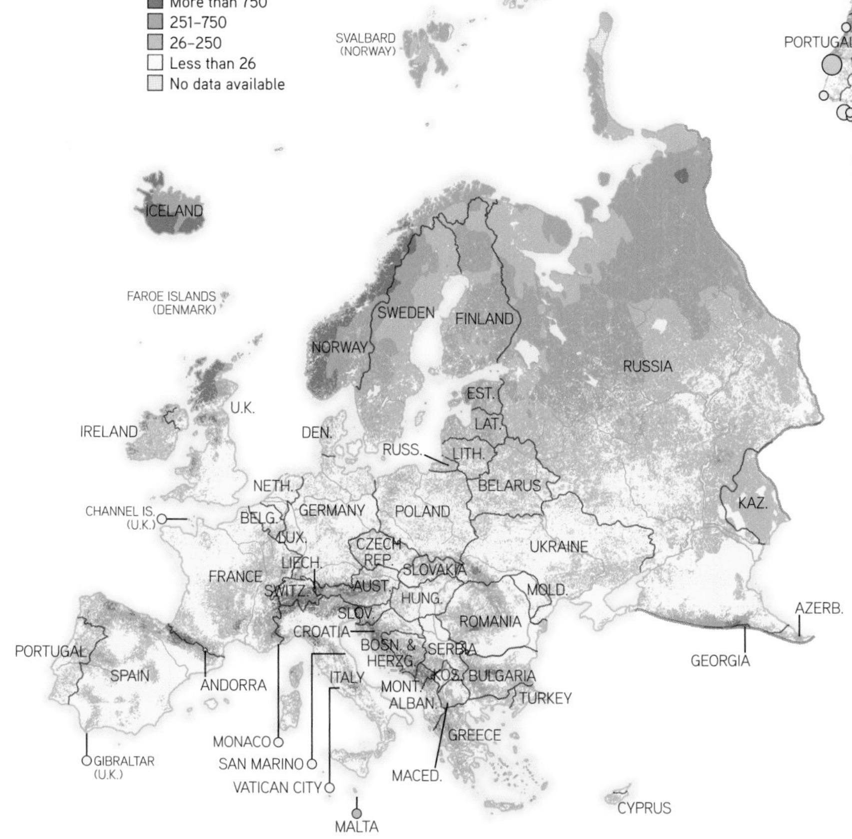

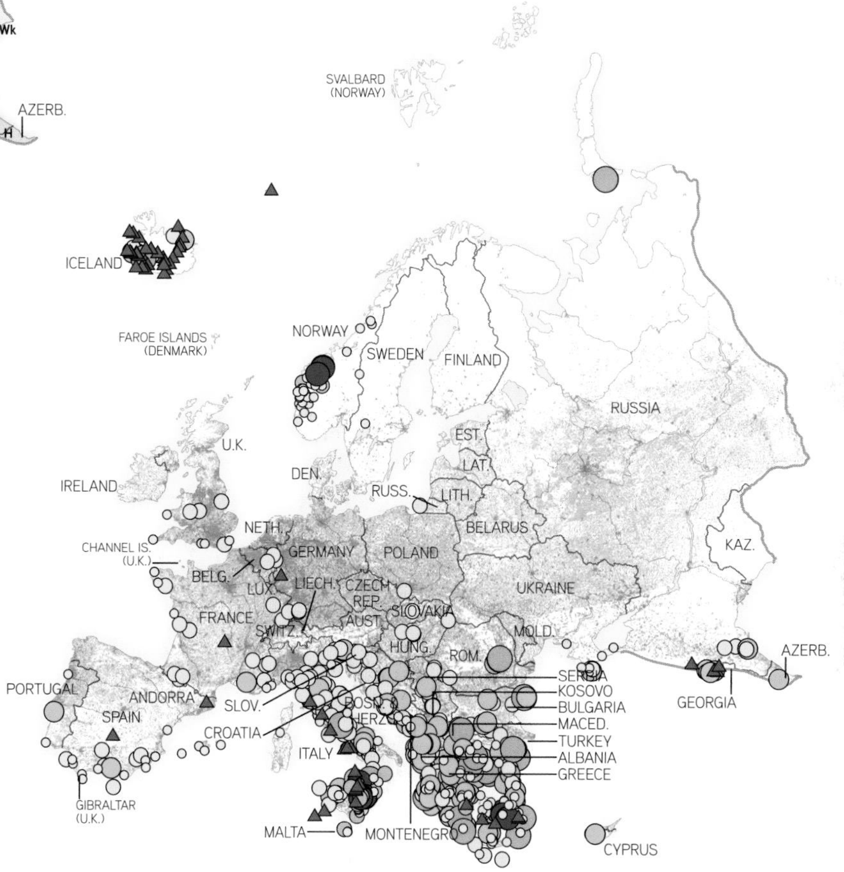

Natural Hazards

Population Density, 2010

People per square km	People per square mi
More than 1,000	More than 2,500
100–1,000	250–2,500
Less than 100	Less than 250

Fire Intensity
(from gas burn off, slash-and-burn agriculture, or natural causes)
High
Low

Recorded Natural Event

Major Earthquake, 1900-2010
Moment magnitude
- More than 7.0
- 6.0–7.0
- Less than 6.0

Volcano

Tsunami, 1900-2010
Run-up height

Meters	Feet
More than 10	More than 32
5–10	16–32
Less than 5	Less than 16

POPULATION DENSITY

People per Square Kilometer / **People per Square Mile**

More than 195	⬛	More than 500
60–195	⬛	150–500
10–59	⬜	25–149
1–9	⬜	1–24
Less than 1	⬜	Less than 1

SVALBARD (NORWAY)

⊛ Reykjavk
ICELAND

NORWAY

FAROE ISLANDS (DENMARK)

SWEDEN

FINLAND

⊛ Helsinki

⊛ Oslo

⊛ Tallinn
EST.

⊛ Stockholm

⊛ Moscow

U.K.

DEN.

RUSS.

Riga
LAT.

R U S S I A

IRELAND

⊛ Dublin

⊛ Copenhagen

LITH.

⊛ Vilnius

⊛ Minsk
BELARUS

KAZ.

London ⊛
NETH.
⊛ Amsterdam

Berlin ⊛

⊛ Warsaw

BELG.

⊛ Brussels

GERMANY

POLAND

⊛ Kiev

CHANNEL IS. (U.K.)

LUX.

LIECH.

Prague ⊛
CZECH REP.

UKRAINE

⊛ Paris

FRANCE

SLOVAKIA

⊛ Bratislava

MOLD.

⊛ Chișinău

⊛ Bern
SWITZ.

Vienna ⊛
AUSTRIA

⊛ Budapest

HUNGARY

Ljubljana ⊛
SLOV.

⊛ Zagreb
CROATIA

ROMANIA

⊛ Bucharest

MONACO

⊛ Belgrade

AZERB.

PORTUGAL

ANDORRA

SAN MARINO

BOSN. & HERZG.
⊛ Sarajevo

SERBIA

GEORGIA

⊛ Madrid

⊛ Podgorica
MONTENEGRO

⊛ Prishtina
KOS.

BULGARIA
⊛ Sofia

⊛ Lisbon

SPAIN

ITALY
⊛ Rome

Skopje
⊛ MACED.

Tirana ⊛
ALBANIA

TURKEY

VATICAN CITY

GREECE

GIBRALTAR (U.K.)

⊛ Athens

MALTA ⊛ Valletta

⊛ Nicosia
CYPRUS

POPULATION PYRAMIDS

BOSNIA AND HERZEGOVINA

Age (80+, 60–64, 40–44, 20–24, 0–4)
Male / Female
10 5 0 5 10
Percent of population

ALBANIA

Age (80+, 60–64, 40–44, 20–24, 0–4)
Male / Female
10 5 0 5 10
Percent of population

MONACO

Age (80+, 60–64, 40–44, 20–24, 0–4)
Male / Female
10 5 0 5 10
Percent of population

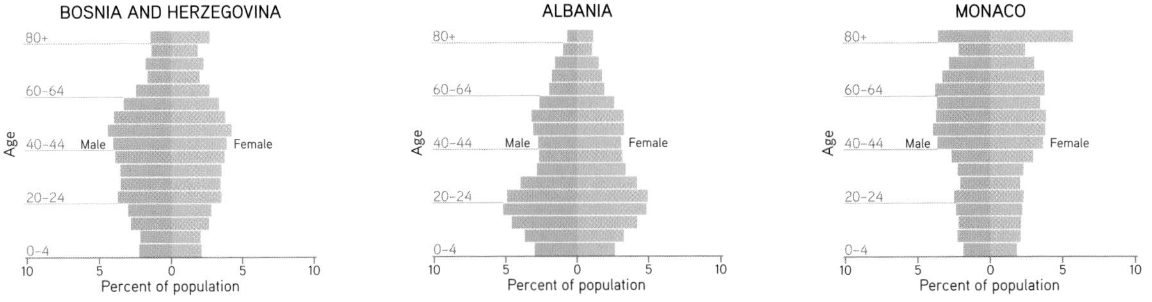

Indigenous Languages

- Altaic
- Caucasian
- Indo-European
- Uralic
- Isolates
- Uninhabited

ICELAND

FAROE ISLANDS (DENMARK)

SWEDEN

FINLAND

NORWAY

RUSSIA

EST.

LAT.

RUSS.

LITH.

U.K.

DEN.

IRELAND

NETH.

BELARUS

CHANNEL IS. (U.K.)

BELG.

GERMANY

POLAND

UKRAINE

KAZ.

LUX.

CZECH REP.

LIECH

SLOVAKIA

FRANCE

AUST.

SWITZ.

HUNG.

MOLD.

SLOV.

ROMANIA

AZERB.

CROATIA

PORTUGAL

BOSN. & HERZG.

SERB.

BULGARIA

GEORGIA

SPAIN

ANDORRA

ITALY

MONT.

KOS.

ALBAN.

TURKEY

MONACO

GREECE

SAN MARINO

VATICAN CITY

MACED.

MALTA

GIBRALTAR (U.K.)

CYPRUS

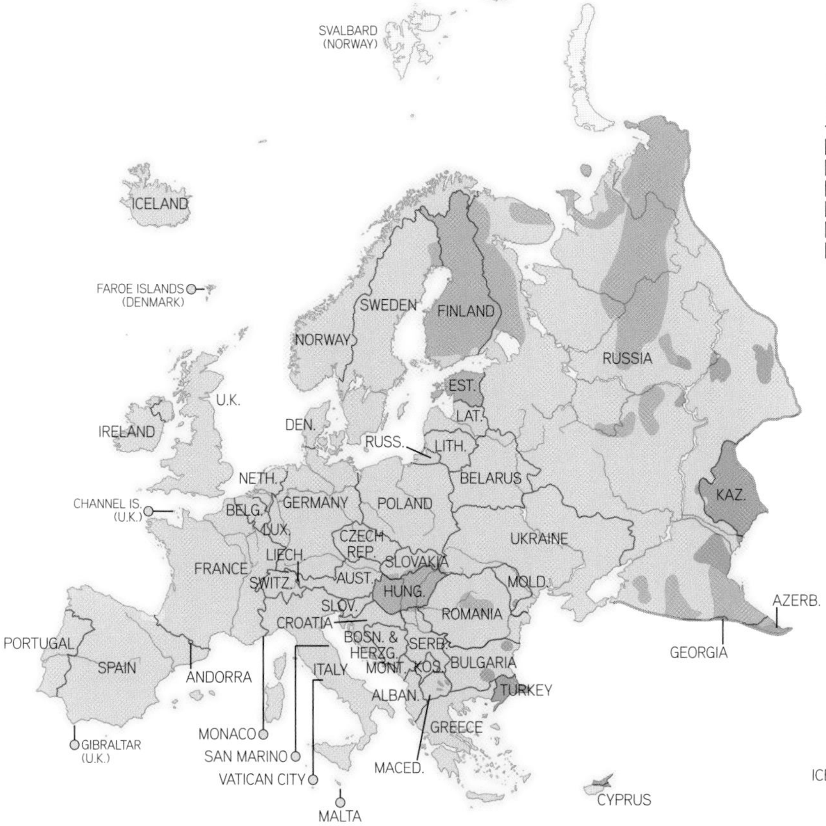

Urbanization

Urban agglomerations, 2010 (population in millions)

- ■ More than 10.0
- ▲ 5.0–10.0
- ● 1.0–4.9
- ○ .75– .99

Percent urban population, 2010

- More than 75%
- 50%–75%
- 25%–49%
- Less than 25%
- No data

SVALBARD (NORWAY)

ICELAND

FAROE ISLANDS (DENMARK)

NORWAY

SWEDEN

FINLAND

RUSSIA

U.K.

EST.

Moscow

IRELAND

DEN.

LAT.

RUSS.

LITH.

NETH.

London

POLAND

BELARUS

CHANNEL IS. (U.K.)

BELG.

GERMANY

CZECH REP.

UKRAINE

KAZ.

Paris

LUX.

FRANCE

SLOVAKIA

MOLD.

SWITZ.

LIECH

AUST.

HUNG.

ROM.

PORTUGAL

SLOV.

AZERB.

ANDORRA

MONACO

CROATIA

SERBIA

Madrid Barcelona

SAN MARINO

KOSOVO

GEORGIA

BULGARIA

VATICAN CITY

ITALY

MACED.

SPAIN

Istanbul

TURKEY

BOSN. & HERZG.

ALBANIA

GREECE

GIBRALTAR (U.K.)

MALTA

MONTENEGRO

CYPRUS

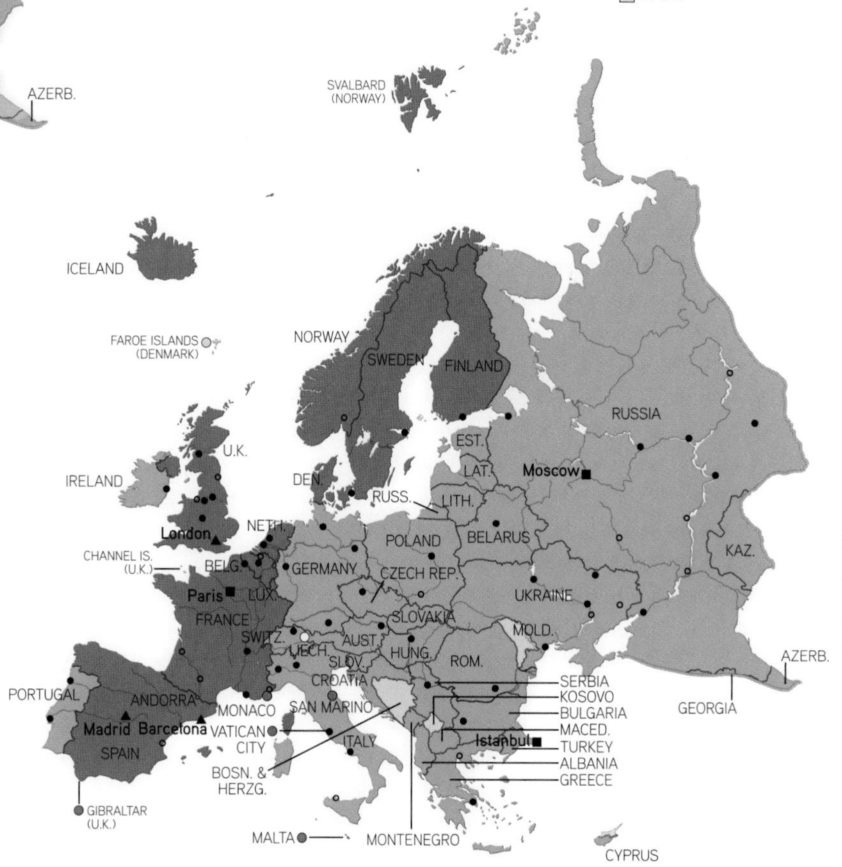

Population Change

Projected population change, 2010–2050 (by percentage)

- More than 100%
- 50%–100%
- 0.01%–49%
- No change
- Population loss

ICELAND

FAROE ISLANDS (DENMARK)

NORWAY

SWEDEN

FINLAND

RUSSIA

U.K.

EST.

IRELAND

DEN.

LAT.

RUSS.

LITH.

NETH.

BELARUS

CHANNEL IS. (U.K.)

BELG.

GERMANY

POLAND

LIECH

LUX.

CZECH REP.

UKRAINE

FRANCE

SLOVAKIA

KAZ.

SWITZ.

AUST.

MOLD.

SLOV.

HUNG.

ROM.

MONACO

CROATIA

SERBIA

AZERB.

SAN MARINO

KOSOVO

PORTUGAL

ANDORRA

BULGARIA

VATICAN CITY

BOSN. & HERZG.

MACED.

GEORGIA

ITALY

TURKEY

SPAIN

ALBANIA

GREECE

GIBRALTAR (U.K.)

MALTA

MONTENEGRO

CYPRUS

Land Use

More disturbed — Cropland
Less disturbed
More disturbed — Pasture

Built-up area

Irrigated land

Franz Josef Land (RUSSIA)

SVALBARD (NORWAY)
Longyearbyen

Novaya Zemlya (RUSSIA)

Reykjavík
ICELAND

FAROE ISLANDS (DENMARK)

SWEDEN
NORWAY
Oslo
Stockholm
FINLAND
Helsinki

RUSSIA

UNITED KINGDOM

IRELAND Dublin

DENMARK
Copenhagen

Tallinn
ESTONIA
Riga LATVIA
LITHUANIA
Vilnius
RUSSIA

Moscow

London

NETHERLANDS
BELGIUM
Amsterdam
Berlin
Brussels
GERMANY

Minsk
BELARUS

KAZAKHSTAN

CHANNEL IS. (U.K.)
Paris
LUXEMBOURG

Prague
CZECH REP.

POLAND
Warsaw

Kiev
UKRAINE

FRANCE
Bern
SWITZERLAND
Ljubljana
SLOVENIA
LIECHTENSTEIN
SAN
MARINO
MONACO

Vienna
AUSTRIA
SLOVAKIA
Bratislava
HUNGARY
Budapest
Zagreb
CROATIA
BOSNIA AND
HERZEGOVINA
Sarajevo

Chișinău
MOLDOVA

GEORGIA
AZERBAIJAN

ROMANIA
Bucharest
Belgrade
SERBIA
Prishtinë

PORTUGAL
Lisbon
Madrid
SPAIN
ANDORRA

VATICAN
CITY
ITALY
Rome
MONTENEGRO
Podgorica
KOSOVO
Tirana
ALBANIA

BULGARIA
Sofia

TURKEY
Istanbul

GIBRALTAR (U.K.)

MACEDONIA
Skopje

GREECE
Athens

Valletta MALTA

Nicosia
CYPRUS

Imports and Exports

VALUE OF IMPORTS

GERMANY

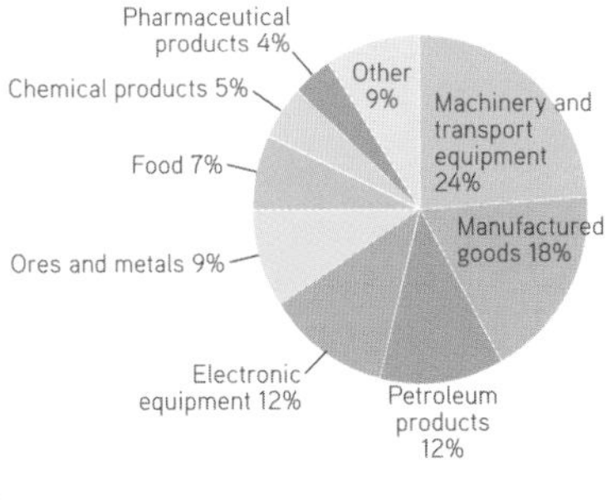

- Pharmaceutical products 4%
- Chemical products 5%
- Food 7%
- Ores and metals 9%
- Electronic equipment 12%
- Petroleum products 12%
- Manufactured goods 18%
- Machinery and transport equipment 24%
- Other 9%

UNITED KINGDOM

- Pharmaceutical products 4%
- Chemical products 5%
- Ores and metals 7%
- Food 9%
- Electronic equipment 10%
- Petroleum products 11%
- Manufactured goods 18%
- Machinery and transport equipment 26%
- Other 10%

VALUE OF EXPORTS

FRANCE

- Petroleum products 4%
- Ores and metals 6%
- Chemical products 6%
- Pharmaceutical products 7%
- Electronic equipment 8%
- Food 11%
- Manufactured goods 16%
- Machinery and transport equipment 30%
- Other 12%

GERMANY

- Petroleum products 2%
- Pharmaceutical products 5%
- Chemical products 5%
- Food 5%
- Ores and metals 6%
- Electronic equipment 11%
- Manufactured goods 18%
- Machinery and transport equipment 38%
- Other 10%

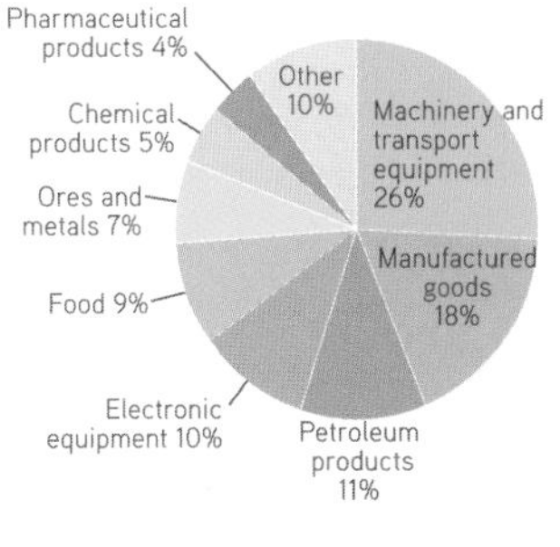

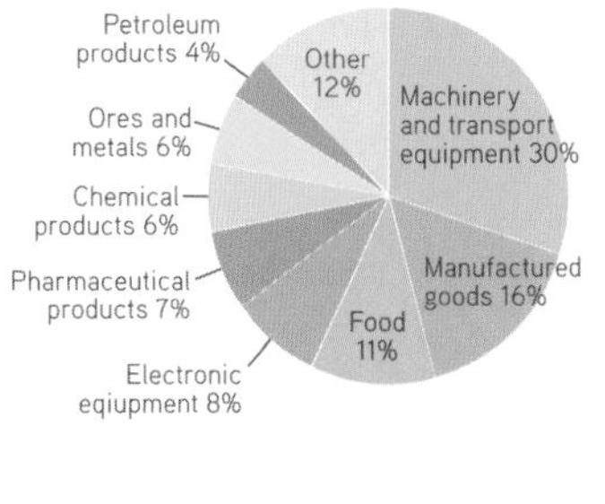

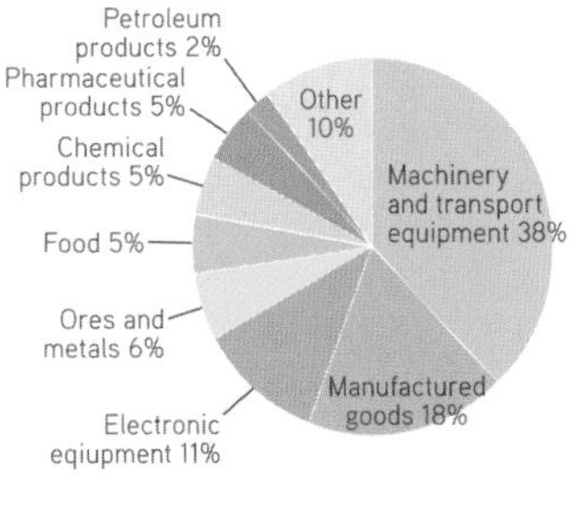

EUROPE'S ECONOMY

Service
100%

MONACO

ALBANIA
BELARUS

Agricultural
100%

Industrial
100%

per Gross Domestic Product
(GDP) sector

SVALBARD
(NORWAY)

ICELAND

FAROE ISLANDS
(DENMARK)

NORWAY

SWEDEN   FINLAND

RUSSIA

U.K.

IRELAND

DEN.

RUSS.

EST.

LAT.

LITH.

NETH.

CHANNEL IS.
(U.K.)

BELG.

LUX.

FRANCE

SWITZ.

GERMANY

LIECH.

CZECH
REP.

AUST.

SLOV.

HUNG.

POLAND

BELARUS

SLOVAKIA

UKRAINE

MOLD.

KAZ.

PORTUGAL

ANDORRA

MONACO

CROATIA

SAN MARINO

VATICAN
CITY   ITALY

BOSN. &
HERZG.

ROM.

SERBIA
KOSOVO
BULGARIA
MACED.
TURKEY
ALBANIA
GREECE

AZERB.

GEORGIA

SPAIN

GIBRALTAR
(U.K.)

MALTA

MONTENEGRO

CYPRUS

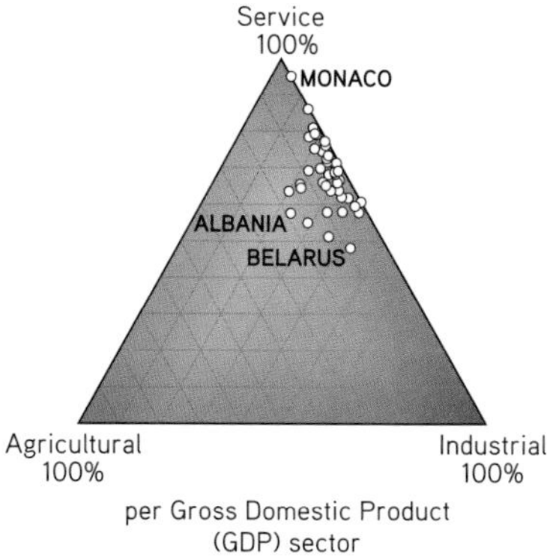

POVERTY

Percentage of population living
on less than $2 per day

- More than 80%
- 60%–80%
- 40%–59%
- 20%–39%
- Less than 20%
- No data available

ICELAND

FAROE ISLANDS
(DENMARK)

NORWAY

SWEDEN   FINLAND

RUSSIA

U.K.

IRELAND

DEN.

RUSS.

EST.
LAT.
LITH.

NETH.

CHANNEL IS.
(U.K.)

BELG.

LUX.

FRANCE

SWITZ.

GERMANY

LIECH.

CZECH
REP.

AUST.

SLOV.

HUNG.

POLAND

BELARUS

SLOVAKIA

UKRAINE

MOLD.

KAZ.

PORTUGAL

ANDORRA

MONACO

CROATIA

SAN MARINO

VATICAN
CITY

ITALY

BOSN. &
HERZG.

ROM.

SERBIA
KOSOVO
BULGARIA
MACED.
TURKEY
ALBANIA
GREECE

AZERB.

GEORGIA

SPAIN

GIBRALTAR
(U.K.)

MALTA

MONTENEGRO

CYPRUS

DOMINANT ECONOMY

(per GDP sector)

	Agriculture	Industry*	Services
70%–100%			
50%–69.9%			
0%–49.9%			
No data			

*Includes the mining industry

SVALBARD
(NORWAY)

ICELAND

FAROE ISLANDS
(DENMARK)

NORWAY

SWEDEN   FINLAND

RUSSIA

U.K.

IRELAND

DEN.

RUSS.

EST.

LAT.

LITH.

NETH.

CHANNEL IS.
(U.K.)

BELG.

LUX.

FRANCE

SWITZ.

GERMANY

LIECH.

CZECH
REP.

AUST.

SLOV.

HUNG.

POLAND

BELARUS

SLOVAKIA

UKRAINE

MOLD.

KAZ.

PORTUGAL

ANDORRA

MONACO

CROATIA

SAN MARINO

VATICAN
CITY   ITALY

BOSN. &
HERZG.

SERBIA

ROM.

KOSOVO
BULGARIA

MACED.

TURKEY

AZERB.

GEORGIA

SPAIN

GREECE

GIBRALTAR
(U.K.)

MALTA

ALBANIA

MONTENEGRO

CYPRUS

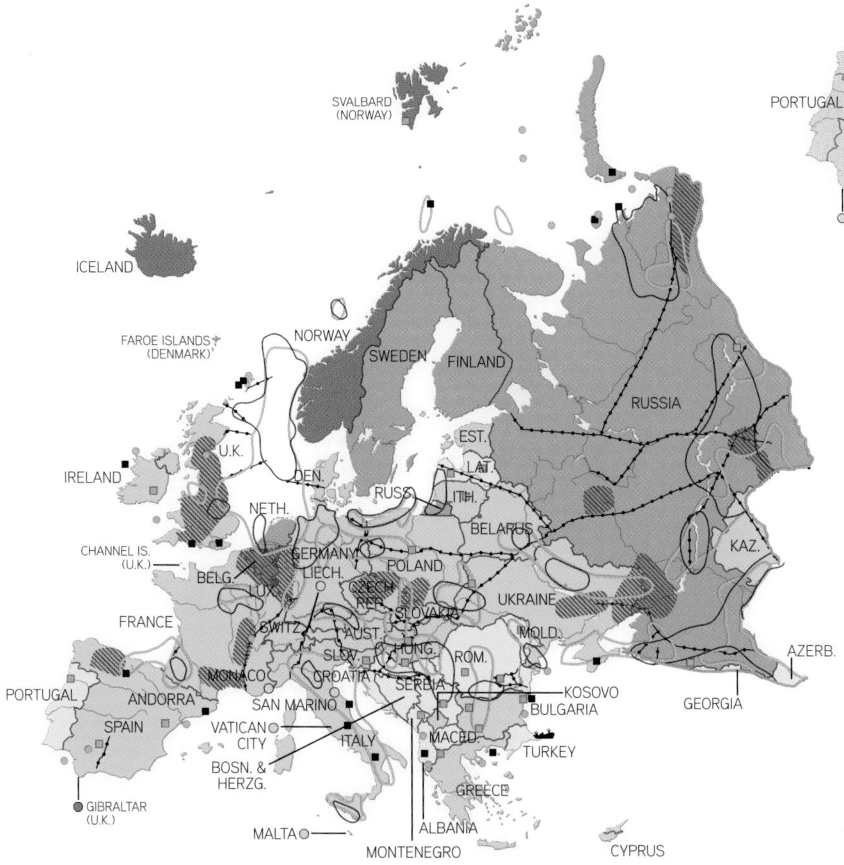

PER CAPITA ENERGY CONSUMPTION

(annual use, in million Btu)

- More than 300
- 201–300
- 101–200
- 30–100
- Less than 30
- No data

Major energy deposit

- Coal
- Natural gas
- Oil
- Oil pipeline
- Oil transit chokepoint

149

UNITED KINGDOM
IRELAND
NORTHERN IRELAND
SCOTLAND
ENGLAND
WALES
GREAT BRITAIN
NORWAY
SWEDEN
DENMARK
NETHERLANDS
BELGIUM
GERMANY
LUX.
NORTH SEA
ATLANTIC OCEAN
Celtic Sea
Irish Sea
ENGLISH CHANNEL (LA MANCHE)
Bristol Channel
North Channel
Sea of the Hebrides
Outer Hebrides
Inner Hebrides
Meridian of Greenwich (London)
Dogger Bank
Channel Islands
LONDON
Dublin
Belfast
Edinburgh
Glasgow
Aberdeen
Cardiff
Birmingham
Manchester
Liverpool
Leeds
Newcastle
Amsterdam
Brussels
Paris
HAUTE NORMANDIE
BASSE-NORMANDIE
BRETAGNE
PAYS DE LA LOIRE
CENTRE
ÎLE-DE-FRANCE
PICARDIE
NORD-PAS-DE-CALAIS
CHAMPAGNE-ARDENNE
LORRAINE
BOURGOGNE
FRANCHE-COMTÉ
NORTH RHINE-WESTPHALIA
RHINELAND-PALATINATE
HESSE
LOWER SAXONY
BADEN-WÜRTTEMBERG
12°
9°
6°
3°
0°
57°
54°
51°
48°

AZIMUTHAL EQUIDISTANT PROJECTION
SCALE 1:6,000,000
0 KILOMETERS 50 100 150
0 MILES 50 100 150
Bay of Biscay
MEDITERRANEAN SEA
Balearic Sea
BALEARIC ISLANDS
Golfe du Lion
Alboran Sea
Golfo de Cádiz
PORTUGAL
SPAIN
ANDORRA
MONACO
MOROCCO
ALGERIA
U.K. GIBRALTAR
Madrid
Lisboa (Lisbon)
Barcelona
Valencia
Sevilla (Seville)
Marseille
Toulouse
Bordeaux
Alger (Algiers)
Longitude West 3° of Greenwich
Longitude East 3° of Greenwich

15° Longitude East 18° of Greenwich
Meridian of Greenwich (London)
AZIMUTHAL EQUIDISTANT PROJECTION
SCALE 1:6,000,000
0 KILOMETERS 100 150
0 MILES 50 100 150
ARCTIC CIRCLE
NORWEGIAN SEA
BARENTS SEA
GULF OF BOTHNIA
NORWAY
SWEDEN
FINLAND
RUSSIA
Lofoten
Vesterålen
Vestfjorden
Trondheim
Bergen
Umeå
Oulu (Uleåborg)
Turku (Åbo)
Espoo (Esbo)
Helsinki
Tampere (Tammerfors)
Sankt-Peterburg (St. Petersburg)
Murmansk
Åland (Ahvenanmaa)
Nordkapp

ESTONIA
LATVIA
LITHUANIA
BELARUS
UKRAINE
ROMANIA
POLAND
SLOVAKIA
HUNGARY
CZECH REPUBLIC
AUSTRIA
GERMANY
DENMARK
NETHERLANDS
BALTIC SEA
NORTH SEA
SKAGERRAK
KATTEGAT
Gulf of Riga
Gotland
Öland
Bornholm
North Frisian Islands
E. Frisian Is.
Stockholm
Riga
Vilnius
Minsk
Warszawa (Warsaw)
Praha (Prague)
Wien (Vienna)
Bratislava
Berlin
København (Copenhagen)
Hamburg
Kaliningrad
KALININGRAD (Russia)

SWEDEN
FINLAND
KARELIYA
ESTONIA
LATVIA
LITHUANIA
BELARUS
POLAND
UKRAINE
KOL'SKIY POLUOSTROV
BELOYE MORE (WHITE SEA)
GULF OF BOTHNIA
BALTIC SEA
GULF OF FINLAND
Gulf of Riga
Ladozhskoye Ozero (L. Ladoga)
Onezhskoye Ozero
Ozero Il'men'
Rybinskoye Vdkhr.
KALININGRAD OBLAST
ÅLAND (AHVENANMAA)
ARKHA
VOLO
NOVGOROD
PSKOV
TVER'
SMOLENSK
MOSKVA
KALUGA
TULA
BRYANSK
OREL
LIPETSK
RYAZAN'
VLADIMIR
YAROSLAVL'
IVANO
MURMANSK
Arkhangel'sk (Archangel)
Severodvinsk
Petrozavodsk
Sankt-Peterburg (St. Petersburg) (Leningrad)
Helsinki
Espoo (Esbo)
Turku (Åbo)
Tampere (Tammerfors)
Oulu (Uleåborg)
Umeå
Tallinn (Reval)
Tartu
Riga
Daugavpils
Vilnius
Kaunas
Klaipėda
Šiauliai
Minsk
Homyel'
Mahilyow
Vitsyebsk
Hrodna
Brest
Białystok
Velikiy Novgorod
Pskov
Velikiye Luki
Tver'
Smolensk
MOSKVA (MOSCOW)
Kaluga
Tula
Bryansk
Orel
Ryazan'
Vologda
Cherepovets
Rybinsk
Yaroslavl'
Ivanovo
Vladimir
Michurinsk
15°
18°
21°
24°
27°
30°
33°
36°
39°
57°
60°
63°

AZIMUTHAL EQUIDISTANT PROJECTION
SCALE 1:6,000,000
0 KILOMETERS 100 150
0 MILES 50 100 150
ARCTIC CIRCLE
Mezenskaya Guba
NENETS
Arkhangel'sk
YAMAL-NENETS
Tyumen'
KHANTY-MANSI
Tyumen'
YUGYD VA NATIONAL PARK
Gora Narodnaya 1895
Gora Neroyka 1646
Pechorskaya Nizmennost'
Timanskiy Kryazh
KOMI
Vychegda
Severnaya Dvina
Sukhona
Pechora
Usa
Sysola
Vyatka
Kama
Belaya
Volga
Ural
Tobol
Severnyye Uvaly
ARKHANGEL'SK
VOLOGDA
KOSTROMA
KIROV
PERM'
SVERDLOVSK
UDMURTIYA
MARIY-EL
CHUVASHIYA
TATARSTAN
BASHKORTOSTAN
CHELYABINSK
KURGAN
ORENBURG
SAMARA
UL'YANOVSK
PENZA
MORDOVIYA
NIZHNIY NOVGOROD
KAZAKHSTAN
QOSTANAY
RUSSIA
URAL MOUNTAINS
Privolzhskaya Vozvyshennost'
Kuybyshevskoye Vdkhr.
Cheboksarskoye Vdkhr.
Gor'kovskoye Vdkhr.
Kamskoye Vdkhr.
Syktyvkar
Ukhta
Sosnogorsk
Pechora
Inta
Vorkuta
Usinsk
Kotlas
Kirov
Perm'
Berezniki
Solikamsk
Nizhniy Tagil
Yekaterinburg
Kamensk Ural'skiy
Pervoural'sk
Chelyabinsk
Kopeysk
Zlatoust
Miass
Magnitogorsk
Izhevsk
Sarapul
Naberezhnyye Chelny
Nizhnekamsk
Kazan'
Al'met'yevsk
Ufa
Sterlitamak
Salavat
Samara
Tol'yatti (Togliatti)
Syzran'
Novokuybyshevsk
Ul'yanovsk
Dimitrovgrad
Cheboksary
Nizhniy Novgorod
Dzerzhinsk
Saransk
Penza
Orenburg
Kineshma
Serov
Krasnotur'insk
Karpinsk
Kachkanar
Murom
Mezen'
Kuloy
Kurgan
Troitsk
Longitude East 45° of Greenwich
45°
48°
51°
54°
57°
60°
63°
60°
57°
54°

GERMANY
BADEN-WÜRTTEMBERG
BAVARIA
FRANCE
FRANCHE-COMTÉ
RHÔNE-ALPES
PROVENCE-ALPES-CÔTE D'AZUR
SWITZERLAND
LIECH.
AUSTRIA
SLOVAKIA
HUNGARY
SLOVENIA
CROATIA
BOSNIA AND HERZEGOVINA
SERBIA
MONTENEGRO
KOSOVO
MACEDONIA
ALBANIA
GREECE
ITALY
TUNISIA
ALGERIA
MALTA
SAN MARINO
VATICAN CITY
MONACO
CORSE
CORSICA France
SARDINIA Italy
SARDEGNA
SICILY
SICILIA
TRENTINO-ALTO ADIGE
LOMBARDY
PIEDMONT
VENETO
FRIULI-VENEZIA GIULIA
EMILIA-ROMAGNA
LIGURIA
TUSCANY
UMBRIA
MARCHES
LAZIO
ABRUZZI
MOLISE
CAMPANIA
APULIA
BASILICATA
CALABRIA
Ligurian Sea
TYRRHENIAN SEA
ADRIATIC SEA
IONIAN SEA
MEDITERRANEAN SEA
Golfo di Genova
GOLFO DI TARANTO
Golfo di Manfredonia
Malta Channel
Milano (Milan)
Torino (Turin)
Genova (Genoa)
Venezia (Venice)
Firenze (Florence)
Roma (Rome)
Napoli (Naples)
Bari
Palermo
Cagliari
Catania
Messina
Siracusa (Syracuse)
Bologna
Trieste
Ljubljana
Zagreb
Sarajevo
Beograd (Belgrade)
Budapest
Bratislava (Pressburg)
(Vienna) Wien
München (Munich)
Tiranë (Tirana)
Skopje
Podgorica
Prishtina (Priština)
Tunis
Valletta
Ajaccio
KOSOVO On February 17, 2008, Kosovo declared its independence. Serbia still claims it as a province.
AZIMUTHAL EQUIDISTANT PROJECTION
SCALE 1:6,000,000
0 KILOMETERS 100 150
0 MILES 50 100 150
Longitude East 21° of Greenwich
12°
15°
18°
42°
39°
36°
45°
48°

UKRAINE
MOLDOVA
ROMANIA
BULGARIA
TURKEY
RUSSIA
SYRIA
LEBANON
CYPRUS
N. CYPRUS
CRIMEA
BLACK SEA
SEA OF AZOV
SEA OF CRETE
TRANSDNIESTRIA
Since the break-up of the Soviet Union, Ukrainian and Russian minorities have been struggling for independence from Moldova.
Odesa
Kherson
Mykolayiv
Sevastopol'
Simferopol'
Kerch
Mariupol'
Berdyans'k
Melitopol'
Krasnodar
Novorossiysk
Chişinău
Bender
Tiraspol
Iaşi
Cluj-Napoca
Braşov
Ploieşti
Bucureşti (Bucharest)
Constanţa
Galaţi
Brăila
Craiova
Varna
Burgas
Sofiya (Sofia)
Plovdiv
Pleven
Edirne (Adrianople)
İSTANBUL (CONSTANTINOPLE)
Bursa
Ankara (Angora)
Eskişehir
İzmir (Smyrna)
Konya (Iconium)
Kayseri
Samsun (Amisus)
Sivas
Adana
Antalya
Aydın
Denizli
Afyon
Kütahya
Zonguldak
Thessaloníki
Athína (Athens)
Pireás (Piraeus)
Iráklio (Candia)
KRÍTI
CRETE
DODEKÁNISSA (DODECANESE)
Kikládes (Cyclades)
Lefkosia (Nicosia, Lefkoşa)
Lemesos (Limassol)
Ḩalab (Aleppo)
Al Lādhiqīyah (Latakia)
Tarābulus (Tripoli)
24°
27°
30°
33°
36°
39°
42°
45°

POLAND
BELARUS
UKRAINE
RUS
MOLDOVA
ROMANIA
BULGARIA
TURKEY
GR.
ABKHAZIA
KARACHA CHERKE
CRIMEA
BLACK SEA
SEA OF AZOV
MOSKVA
SMOLENSK
KALUGA
TULA
RYAZAN'
BRYANSK
OREL
LIPETSK
KURSK
BELGOROD
VORONEZH
ROSTOV
KRASNODAR
ADYGEYA
TRANSNISTRIA
TRANSYLVANIA
BUCOVINA
KUZEY ANADOLU DAĞLARI
Kyiv (Kiev)
Minsk
Chişinău
Bucureşti (Bucharest)
İSTANBUL (CONSTANTINOPLE)
Odesa
Kharkiv
Dnipropetrovs'k
Donets'k
Sevastopol'
Simferopol'
Rostov na Donu
Sochi
Varna
Constanţa
AZIMUTHAL EQUIDISTANT PROJECTION
SCALE 1:6,000,000
0 KILOMETERS 100 150
0 MILES 50 100 150
Longitude East 39° of Greenwich

NIZHNIY NOVGOROD 45°
Ardatov Alatyr' 48°
Kadom Temnikov Pervomaysk Bol'shiye Tarkhany TATARSTAN 51° Bugul'ma 54° Oktyabr'skiy
Kemlya Surskoye Isheyevka Ul'yanovsk Nurlat Klyavlino Bavly Belebey Davlekanovo
Romodanovo Yazykovo Novomalykla Kamyshla Rayevskiy
Shiringushi Insar Ruzayevka 329+ Karsun Dimitrovgrad Surgut Sterlitamak Ishimbay BASHKORTOSTAN CHELYABINSK
MORDOVIYA Saransk UL'YANOVSK Tol'yatti Salavat Bakr Uzyak
Vindrey Ignatovka Sengiley Novyy (Togliatti) 479 Tubinskiy Sibay Kizil'skoye Bredy

Bednodem'yanovsk Inza Barysh Buyan Yelkhovka Pokhvistnevo Fedorovka Voskresenskoye Meleuz Yumaguzino Baymak Prigorodnyy Zhetiqara
+292 Lunino Nikol'sk Zhigulevsk Timashevo Bugurulan Sharlyk Kumertau Mrakovo Krasnoyarskiy Milyutinka
Pachelma Lomov +375 Derzhavino Otradnyy Matveyevka Ponomarevka Tyul'gan 660 Yuldybayevo Energetik QOSTANAY
Kamenka PENZA Gorodishche Chaadayevka Radishchevo Privolzh'ye Grachevka Pavlovka Aleksandrovka Oktyabr'skoye Nikol'skoye Chernyy Otrog Zilair Buribay Novoorsk 51°
Belinskiy Zolotarevka Kuznetsk Khvorostyanka Bol'shaya Sorochinsk Sakmara Perevolotskiy 297+ Novosergiyevka Khalilovo Novotroitsk Orsk Anikhovka
Kirsanov Kondol' Verkhozim Glushitsa ORENBURG Novoorsk Dombarovskiy

Kamenka Serdobsk Petrovsk Bazarnyy Vol'sk Balakovo Pugachev Perelyub Sobolev Krasnoye Ilek Orenburg Dubenskiy Küvandyk Gay Ozernyy Yasnyy
332+ Rtishchevo Karabulak Klintsovka Solyanka Tashla Mustayevo Krasnyy Kholm Belyayevka Mednogorsk Kumak

SARATOV Marx Pervomayskoye Yershov Ozinki Peremetnoye Fedorovka Aqsay Sol'Iletsk Akbulak Khromtaü
Engels Privolzhskiy Pushkino Mokrous Dergachi Kamenka Zashaghan Oral Börili Rodnikovka Aqyrab Qarghaly Badamsha Komsomol'skoye
+316 Pugachev Novorepnoye Oyan Aqzhayyq Burannoye Shkunovka Aqtöbe Alga Starvyy Karabutak Qarabutaq

RUSSIA Krasnyy Kut Zhympity Almaznoe Qobda Il'inka Araltobe
Balashov Kazachka Kalininsk Atkarsk Krasnyy Tekstil'shchik Lübenka Begaly Oktyabr'sk Zhuryn Qumsay Taldyq

KAZAKHSTAN
QAZAQSTAN BATYS Zhalpaqtal Chapaev Mergenevo Kalenyy Miyaly Bayghanin Shubarshi Birshoghyr 657+ 48°
Pallasovka Pyatimarskoe Bazartöbe Antonovo Oyyl Qarabey Mugodzharskaya Kozhasay Shalqar
Saralzhyn Zhanga Taypaq Bazarsholan Qaratöbe Kemer Temir Kengzhaly Embi

VOLGOGRAD
Kamyshin Nikolayevsk Kaztalovka Leninskoe Aqtaysay Aqshataü Shubarquduyq AQTÖBE
+179 Mokraya Ol'khovka Zhänibek Zhangaqala Muqyr Ebeyti Zharkamys Qarazhar Aktogay
Gmelinka Staraya Poltavka Bykovo Aralsor Inderbor Külagino Qazhasay
El'ton Köli

Volgograd Volzhskiy Saygyn KAZAKHSTAN Zelenoe Makhambet Maqat Zhanbike Qaraoba
(Stalingrad) Leninsk Kapustin Yar Verkhniy Baskunchak ATYRAÜ Dossor Komsomol
Krasnoslobodsk Akhtubinsk Nizhniy Baskunchak Novobogatinskoe Eskene Bayshonas Qorsaq Dongyztaü
Krasnoarmeysk Chernyy Yar Aqqystaü Atyraū Qulsary Sorqudyq

ASTRAKHAN' Sasykoli Zhangabek Zhumysker Balyqshy Qosshaghyl Bozoy
Kharabali Khosheutovo Aqköl Zabürün Qaraton Bilkzhal Ülken Borsyq Qumy
Kirovskiy Ganyushkino Tengiz Qaraton Beyneu
KALMYKIYA Astrakhan' Krasnyy Yar Prorva Saryqamys Turysh ARAL SEA
Ikryanoye Oporynyy Matay

CASPIAN SEA Bozashchy Qaraqalpaqstan UZBEKISTAN
Tübegi Qyzan Kamennoe Zhaslyk
Manggystaü Shyghanaghy Sayötesh

STAVROPOL' Neftekumsk Bautino Taushyq Shetpe Zharmysh USTYURT
Fort Shevchenko Tüpqaraghan Tübegi 556 MANGGHYSTAÜ PLATEAU
Budennovsk Staryy Biryuzyak Mys MANGGHYSTAÜ Zhetibay
Arzgir Kochubey Sagyndyk Syghyndy Ozen Zhangaözen
Bryansk Kizlyarskiy Zaliv Manggyystaü Tengge

CHECHNYA Terekli Mektab Lopatin Aqtaü Quryq
INGUSH Kizlyar Agrakhanskiy Poluostrov Mys Karynzharyk (Desert)
Groznyy Babayurt Peschanyy
KABARDINO-BALKARIYA Khasavyurt Sulak Qazaq Shyghanaghy Sarygamysh Köli 42°
Nal'chik Makhachkala Aksu
El'brus Kaspiysk Mys
5642 Buynaksk Achisu Mys Syngyrli 369 Chink Kaplankyr
(18510 ft) Izberbash Sue
NORTH OSSETIA-ALANIA Vladikavkaz DAGESTAN CASPIAN SEA Garabogaz Chagyl
Beslan Magas Shali Khunzakh Kubachi Dagestanskiye Ogni Mys Omchali -19 Gyzylgaya
SOUTH OSSETIA Gunib Kumukh Derbent Garabogaz Aylagy Gyzylsuw
Ts'khinvali Kakhib Berikei Garabogazköl

GEORGIA Kubach 721 Mys Omchali
T'bilisi (Tbilisi) Belidzh Mukhtadir Koshoba
Rust'avi Kasumkent Shollar Xudat TURKMENISTAN
ARMENIA 45° AZERBAIJAN 48° Lahic 51°
Ijevan 500+ Xacmaz Siyäzän 104 54° Koshoba

GREENLAND SEA
NORWEGIAN SEA
NORTH SEA
BALTIC SEA
GULF OF BOTHNIA
BARENTS SEA
KARA SEA
CASPIAN SEA
BLACK SEA
SEA OF AZOV
ARCTIC CIRCLE
North Pole
SVALBARD
Norway
ZEMLYA FRANTSA IOSIFA
(FRANZ JOSEF LAND)
Russia
NOVAYA ZEMLYA
NORWAY
SWEDEN
FINLAND
DENMARK
GERMANY
POLAND
LITHUANIA
LATVIA
ESTONIA
BELARUS
UKRAINE
MOLD.
CRIMEA
GEORGIA
ARMENIA
AZERBAIJAN
KAZAKHSTAN
UZBEKISTAN
TURKMENISTAN
KYRGYZSTAN
TAJIKISTAN
AFGHAN.
IRAN
KARELIYA
KOMI
NENETS
YAMAL-NENETS
KHANTY-MANSI
SVERDLOVSK
TATARSTAN
BASHKORTOSTAN
KALMYKIYA
ALTAY
GORNO-ALTAY
TYVA
KHAKASIYA
XINJIANG UYGUR
R U
Zapadno Sibirskaya Ravnina
Kazakh Uplands
Caspian Depression
Ustyurt Plateau
Garagum
Qizilqum
Moyynqum
Kola Peninsula
Kol'skiy Poluostrov
Poluostrov Yamal
Gydanskiy Poluostrov
Timanskiy Kryazh
Caucasus Mountains
Elburz Mts.
ALTAY
SHAN
KHORASAN
BAYKONUR COSMODROME
Russian-administered
PLESETSK COSMODROME
MOSKVA (MOSCOW)
Sankt-Peterburg (Saint Petersburg)
Helsinki (Helsingfors)
Stockholm
Oslo
København (Copenhagen)
Berlin
Warszawa (Warsaw)
Minsk
Kyiv (Kiev)
Riga
Tallinn
Vilnius
Tbilisi (Tbilisi)
Yerevan
Bakı (Baku)
Astana
Toshkent (Tashkent)
Bishkek
Dushanbe
Aşgabat (Ashgabat)
TEHRĀN
Ürümqi
Almaty
Novosibirsk
Omsk
Yekaterinburg
Chelyabinsk
Perm'
Kazan'
Samara
Ufa
Volgograd (Stalingrad)
Rostov na Donu
Murmansk
Arkhangel'sk (Archangel)
Krasnoyarsk
Tomsk
Kemerovo
Barnaul
Novokuznetsk
Surgut
Tyumen'
Mashhad
Esfahān (Isfahan)
Samarqand
Hami
160

TWO-POINT EQUIDISTANT PROJECTION
SCALE 1:20,000,000
0 KILOMETERS 300 400 500
0 MILES 200 300 400 500
Administrative subdivisions of Russia are outlined on the map; where they are not labeled, they bear the same name as their capitals. Subdivisions in the Caucasus are on plate 195.
KURIL ISLANDS
The southern Kuril Islands of Iturup (Etorofu), Kunashir (Kunashiri), Shikotan, and the Habomai group were lost by Japan to the Soviet Union in 1945. Japan continues to claim these Russian-administered islands.
Date Line
Sunday
Monday
Bering Strait
ARCTIC OCEAN
CHUKCHI SEA
EAST SIBERIAN SEA
LAPTEV SEA
BERING SEA
SEA OF OKHOTSK
PACIFIC OCEAN
SEA OF JAPAN (EAST SEA)
NOVOSIBIRSKIYE OSTROVA (NEW SIBERIAN ISLANDS)
OSTROVA ANZHU
SEVERNAYA ZEMLYA (NORTH LAND)
NORTHERN SEA ROUTE
ARCTIC CIRCLE
Ostrov Vrangelya (Wrangel I.)
CHUKOTSKIY
ANADYRSKIY ZALIV
ALEUTIAN ISLANDS
United States
Near Islands
Rat Islands
Komandorskiye Ostrova (Commander Is.)
KORYAKSKIY
KAMCHATKA
Koryakskoye Nagor'ye
Kolymskoye Nagor'ye
Khrebet Cherskogo
Verkhoyanskiy Khrebet
SAKHA (YAKUTIYA)
SIBERIA
Stanovoy Khrebet
AMUR
SVOBODNYY COSMODROME
OSTROV SAKHALIN
SAKHALIN
KURIL ISLANDS (KURIL'SKIYE OSTROVA)
Khrebet Sikhote Alin'
BURYATIYA
TRANS-BAIKAL
Ozero Baykal
TUNKINSKY N.P.
MONGOLIA
Ulaanbaatar (Ulan Bator)
GOBI
CHINA
HEILONGJIANG
JILIN
LIAONING
NEI MONGOL
HEBEI
NORTH KOREA
SOUTH KOREA
P'yŏngyang
SEOUL
JAPAN
HOKKAIDŌ
HONSHŪ
TOKYO
NAMPŌ SHOTŌ
Yakutsk
Magadan
Petropavlovsk Kamchatskiy
Anadyr'
Khabarovsk
Vladivostok
Blagoveshchensk
Komsomol'sk na Amure
Yuzhno Sakhalinsk
Irkutsk
Chita
Ulan Ude
Harbin
Sapporo
Longitude East 102° of Greenwich

CENTRAL BRITAIN
ALBERS CONIC EQUAL-AREA PROJECTION
SCALE 1:1,750,000
0 KILOMETERS 30 40 50
0 MILES 10 20 30 40 50
NORTH SEA
IRISH SEA
WALES
ENGLAND
Meridian of Greenwich (London)
Longitude West 2° of Greenwich
LAKE DIST. NAT. PARK
YORKSHIRE DALES NAT. PARK
NORTH YORK MOORS NAT. PARK
PEAK DIST. NAT. PARK
SNOWDONIA NATIONAL PARK
BRECON BEACONS NAT. PARK
EXMOOR NAT. PARK
NEW FOREST NAT. PARK
SOUTH DOWNS NAT. PARK
Cambrian Mountains
Lincoln Heights
Chiltern Hills
Cotswold Hills
Mendip Hills
Blackdown Hills
Bristol Channel
Solway Firth
Morecambe Bay
The Wash
River Thames
Flamborough Head
Spurn Head
Outer Dowsing
Dungeness
Carlisle
Sunderland
Newcastle under Lyme
Durham
Middlesbrough
Stockton-on-Tees
Darlington
Redcar
Whitby
Scarborough
York
Leeds
Bradford
Preston
Blackpool
Lancaster
Liverpool
Manchester
Sheffield
Stoke on Trent
Nottingham
Derby
Leicester
Birmingham
Coventry
Wolverhampton
Peterborough
Cambridge
Norwich
Ipswich
Colchester
Chelmsford
Northampton
Milton Keynes
Bedford
Luton
Oxford
Reading
LONDON
Southend-on-Sea
Maidstone
Canterbury
Brighton
Southampton
Portsmouth
Winchester
Salisbury
Bath
Bristol
Gloucester
Cheltenham
Newport
Cardiff (Caerdydd)
Swansea (Abertawe)
Bridgend
Wrexham
Chester
Conwy
Hastings 1066
Bosworth 1485
Naseby 1645
Marston Moor 1644
Sedgemoor 1685

LOW COUNTRIES
ALBERS CONIC EQUAL-AREA PROJECTION
SCALE 1:2,500,000
0 KILOMETERS 40 60 80
0 MILES 20 40 60 80
Longitude East 4° of Greenwich
NORTH SEA
West Frisian Islands
NETHERLANDS
BELGIUM
FRANCE
GERMANY
LUXEMBOURG
ENGLAND
GRONINGEN
FRIESLAND
DRENTHE
NORTH HOLLAND
FLEVOLAND
OVERIJSSEL
GELDERLAND
UTRECHT
SOUTH HOLLAND
ZEELAND
NORTH BRABANT
LIMBURG
FLANDERS
WALLONIA
BRUSSELS CAPITAL
LOWER SAXONY
NORTH RHINE-WESTPHALIA
RHINELAND-PALATINATE
SAARLAND
NORD-PAS-DE-CALAIS
PICARDIE
HAUTE-NORMANDIE
ÎLE-DE-FRANCE
CHAMPAGNE-ARDENNE
LORRAINE
ALSACE
CENTRE
BOURGOGNE
Amsterdam
Den Haag (The Hague)
Rotterdam
Utrecht
Brussels (Bruxelles, Brussel)
Antwerpen (Antwerp)
Gent
Brugge
Lille
Paris
Luxembourg
Köln (Cologne)
Düsseldorf
Strait of Dover
English Channel (La Manche)

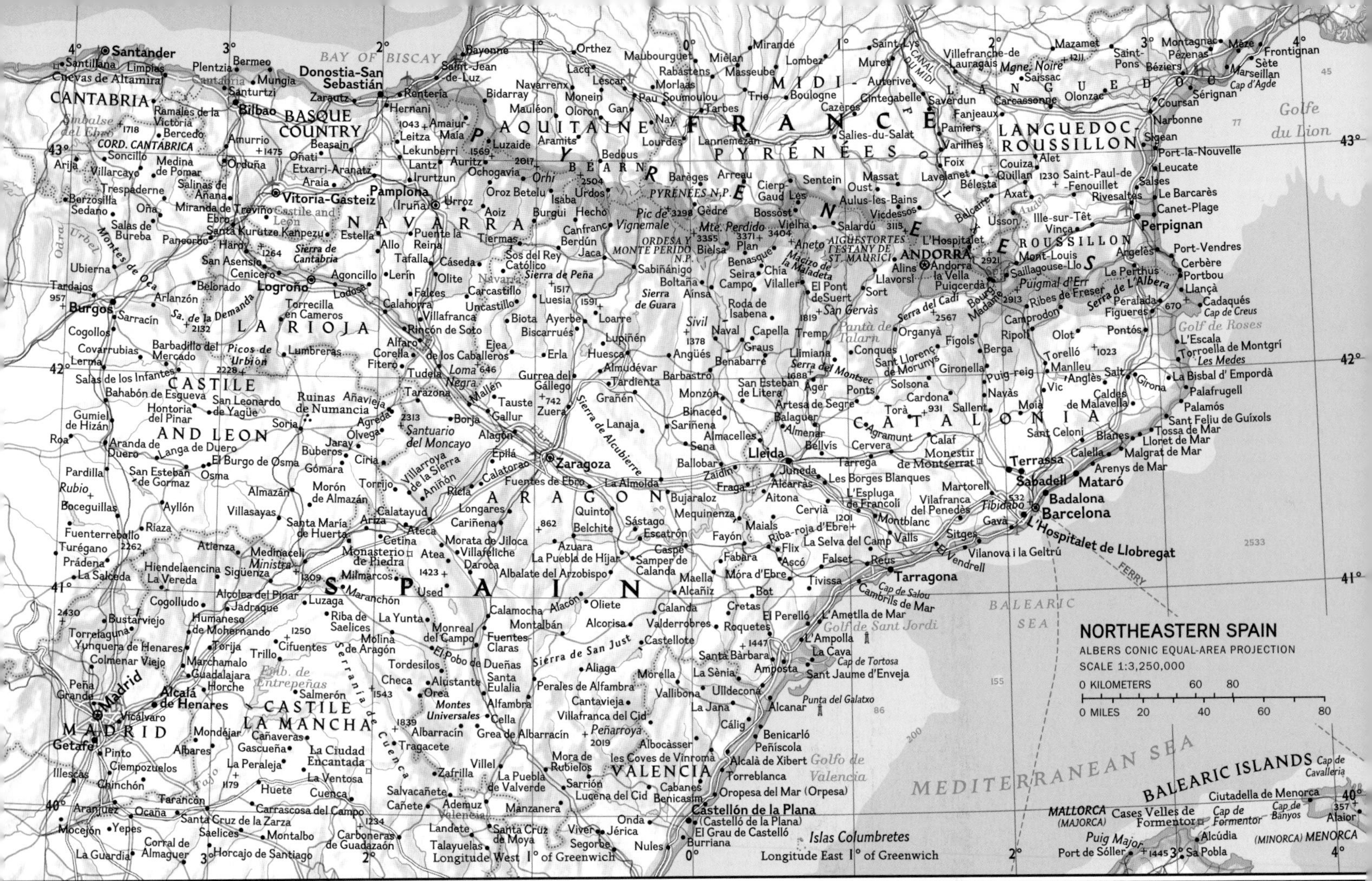
NORTHEASTERN SPAIN
ALBERS CONIC EQUAL-AREA PROJECTION
SCALE 1:3,250,000
0 KILOMETERS 60 80
0 MILES 20 40 60 80
BAY OF BISCAY
CANTABRIA
BASQUE COUNTRY
NAVARRA
LA RIOJA
CASTILE AND LEON
ARAGON
CATALONIA
VALENCIA
CASTILE LA MANCHA
MADRID
SPAIN
FRANCE
AQUITAINE
MIDI-PYRÉNÉES
LANGUEDOC-ROUSSILLON
ANDORRA
MEDITERRANEAN SEA
BALEARIC SEA
BALEARIC ISLANDS
Golfe du Lion
Longitude West 1° of Greenwich
Longitude East 1° of Greenwich

SOUTHERN SPAIN
ALBERS CONIC EQUAL-AREA PROJECTION
SCALE 1:3,250,000
0 KILOMETERS 60 80
0 MILES 20 40 60 80
EXTREMADURA
CASTILE LA MANCHA
VALENCIA
MURCIA
ANDALUSIA
SIERRA MORENA
SPAIN
MEDITERRANEAN SEA
BALEARIC SEA
ALBORAN SEA
ATLANTIC OCEAN
GIBRALTAR U.K.
ALGERIA
Costa del Sol
Longitude West 2° of Greenwich

RHONE VALLEY
ALBERS CONIC EQUAL-AREA PROJECTION
SCALE 1:2,500,000
0 KILOMETERS 40 60
0 MILES 20 40 60
Longitude East 5° of Greenwich
FRANCE
SWITZERLAND
ITALY
GERMANY
MONACO
ÎLE-DE-FRANCE
CHAMPAGNE-ARDENNE
LORRAINE
ALSACE
CENTRE
BOURGOGNE
FRANCHE-COMTÉ
LIMOUSIN
AUVERGNE
RHÔNE-ALPES
MIDI-PYRÉNÉES
LANGUEDOC-ROUSSILLON
PROVENCE-ALPES-CÔTE D'AZUR
PIEDMONT
VALLE D'AOSTA
MASSIF CENTRAL
Golfe du Lion
MEDITERRANEAN SEA
Lyon
Marseille
Toulouse
Genève (Geneva)
Grenoble
Saint-Étienne
Clermont-Ferrand
Montpellier
Nice
Dijon
Besançon
Torino (Turin)

BALTIC STATES
ALBERS CONIC EQUAL-AREA PROJECTION
SCALE 1:3,500,000
0 KILOMETERS 60 80 100
0 MILES 20 40 60 80 100
GULF OF BOTHNIA
Longitude East 24° of Greenwich
FINLAND
KARELIYA
Helsinki
Espoo (Esbo)
Turku (Åbo)
Tampere (Tammerfors)
Åland (Ahvenanmaa)
Mariehamn (Maarianhamina)
SVEALAND
SWEDEN
Uppsala
Stockholm
Gotland
Visby
Gotska Sandön
GOTSKA SANDÖN N.P.
GULF OF FINLAND
Sankt-Peterburg (St. Petersburg, Leningrad)
SANKT-PETERBURG
RUSSIA
PSKOV
NOVGOROD
Pskov
ESTONIA
Tallinn (Reval)
Tartu
Pärnu
LAHEMAA N.P.
MATSALU N.P.
SOOMAA N.P.
VILSANDI N.P.
(Dagö) Hiiumaa
(Ösel) Saaremaa
L. Peipus (Chudskoye Ozero)
Gulf of Riga
Irbe Strait
LATVIA
Riga
GAUJA N.P.
Daugavpils
Liepāja
Ventspils
LITHUANIA
Vilnius
Kaunas
Klaipėda
Šiauliai
Panevėžys
ŽEMAITIJA N.P.
AUKŠTAITIJA N.P.
TRAKAI N.P.
DZŪKIJA N.P.
KURŠIŲ NERIJA N.P.
Curonian Spit
Curonian Lagoon
BALTIC SEA
KALININGRAD OBLAST
Kaliningrad
EAST PRUSSIA
Russia
BELARUS
Minsk
BRASLAV N.P.
POLAND
POMORSKIE
WARMIŃSKO-MAZURSKIE
PODLASKIE
Gdańsk
Gdynia
Gulf of Gdańsk
Vistula Lagoon
Elbląg
FERRY
18° 21° 24° 27° 30°
54° 57° 60°

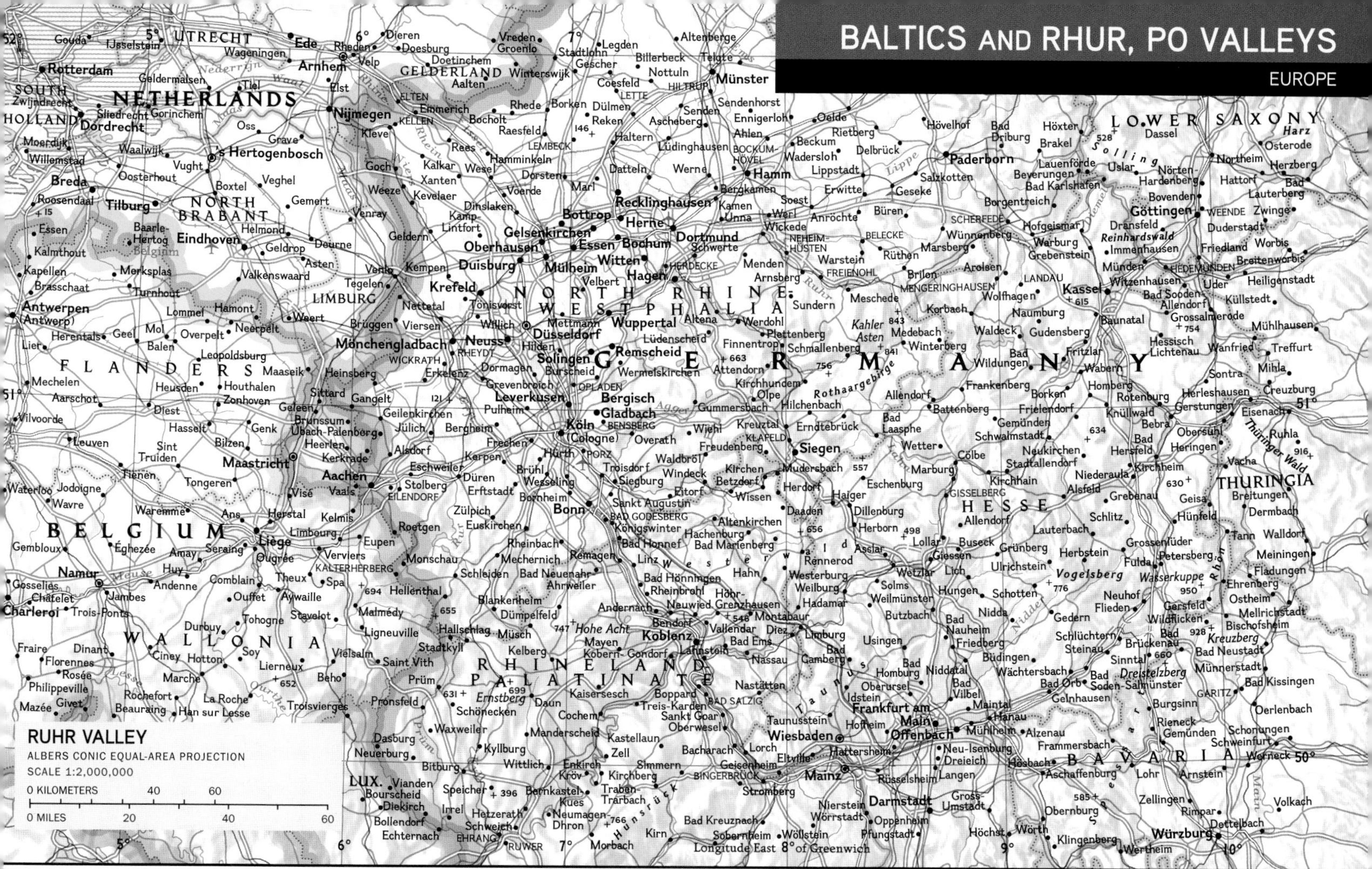
RUHR VALLEY
ALBERS CONIC EQUAL-AREA PROJECTION
SCALE 1:2,000,000
0 KILOMETERS 40 60
0 MILES 20 40 60
NETHERLANDS
NORTH BRABANT
LIMBURG
FLANDERS
BELGIUM
WALLONIA
LUX.
NORTH RHINE-WESTPHALIA
GERMANY
RHINELAND-PALATINATE
HESSE
THURINGIA
LOWER SAXONY
BAVARIA
Rotterdam
Dordrecht
Utrecht
Arnhem
Nijmegen
's Hertogenbosch
Eindhoven
Antwerpen (Antwerp)
Liège
Namur
Charleroi
Maastricht
Aachen
Köln (Cologne)
Bonn
Düsseldorf
Duisburg
Essen
Dortmund
Münster
Paderborn
Kassel
Göttingen
Siegen
Koblenz
Wiesbaden
Mainz
Frankfurt am Main
Darmstadt
Würzburg
Longitude East 8° of Greenwich

PO VALLEY
ALBERS CONIC EQUAL-AREA PROJECTION
SCALE 1:2,800,000
0 KILOMETERS 40
0 MILES 20 40
SWITZERLAND
AUSTRIA
FRANCE
ITALY
CROATIA
TRENTINO-ALTO ADIGE
LOMBARDY
PIEDMONT
VALLE D'AOSTA
VENETO
FRIULI-VENEZIA GIULIA
EMILIA-ROMAGNA
LIGURIA
TUSCANY
MARCHES
RHÔNE-ALPES
PROVENCE-ALPES-CÔTE D'AZUR
LIGURIAN SEA
Gulf of Venice
Golfo di Genova
Bern
Lausanne
Genève (Geneva)
Torino (Turin)
Milano (Milan)
Genova (Genoa)
Venezia (Venice)
Verona
Brescia
Bergamo
Padova (Padua)
Bologna
Parma
Piacenza
Alessandria
Trento
Udine
Ferrara
Ravenna
Rimini
Firenze (Florence)
Pisa
Nice
MONACO
SAN MARINO
Longitude East 9° of Greenwich

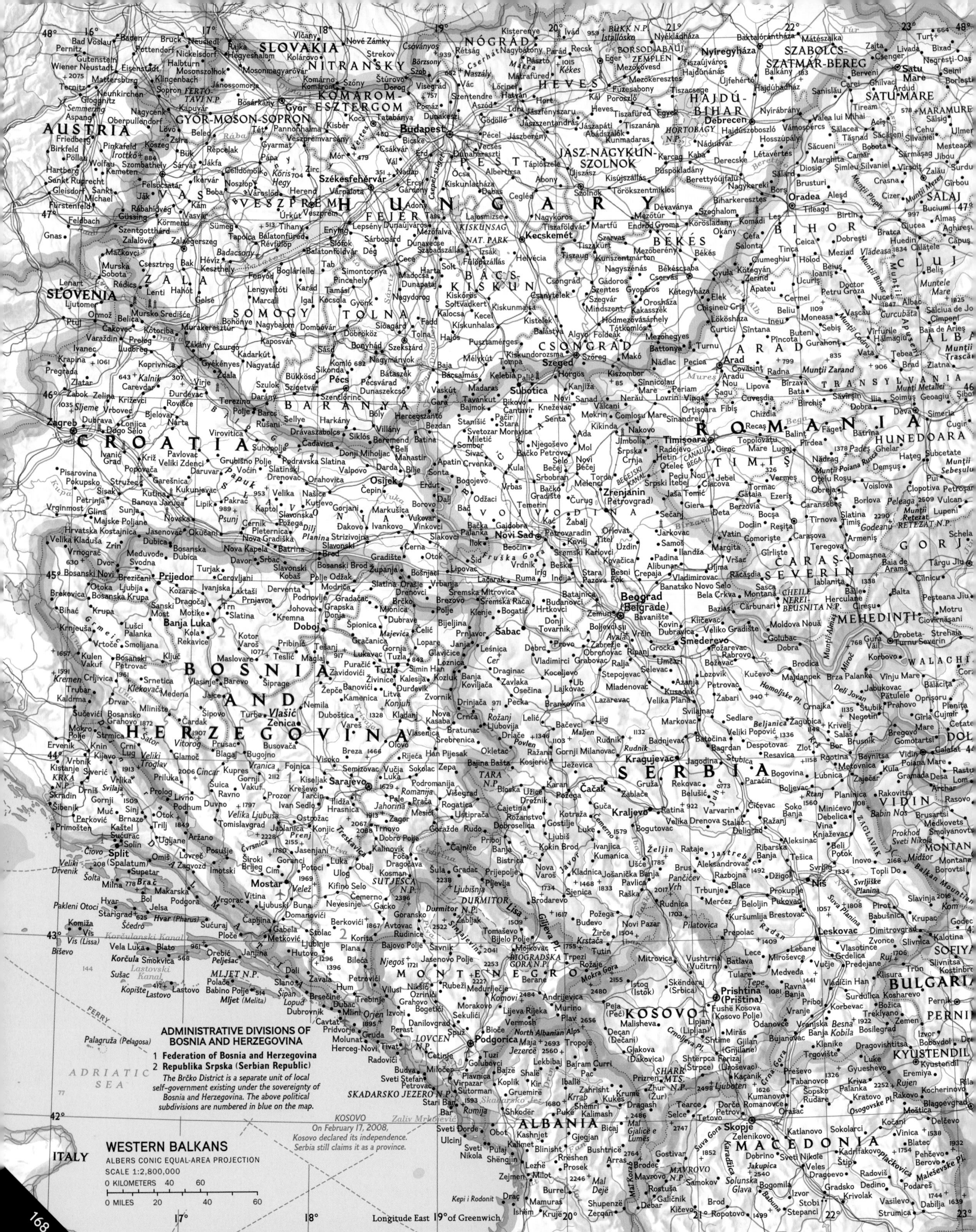
ADMINISTRATIVE DIVISIONS OF BOSNIA AND HERZEGOVINA
1 Federation of Bosnia and Herzegovina
2 Republika Srpska (Serbian Republic)
The Brčko District is a separate unit of local self-government existing under the sovereignty of Bosnia and Herzegovina. The above political subdivisions are numbered in blue on the map.
KOSOVO
On February 17, 2008, Kosovo declared its independence. Serbia still claims it as a province.
WESTERN BALKANS
ALBERS CONIC EQUAL-AREA PROJECTION
SCALE 1:2,800,000
0 KILOMETERS 40 60
0 MILES 20 40 60
Longitude East 19° of Greenwich
AUSTRIA
SLOVAKIA
HUNGARY
SLOVENIA
CROATIA
BOSNIA AND HERZEGOVINA
SERBIA
ROMANIA
MONTENEGRO
KOSOVO
ALBANIA
MACEDONIA
BULGARIA
ITALY
ADRIATIC SEA
Budapest
Zagreb
Sarajevo
Beograd (Belgrade)
Podgorica
Prishtina (Priština)
Skopje

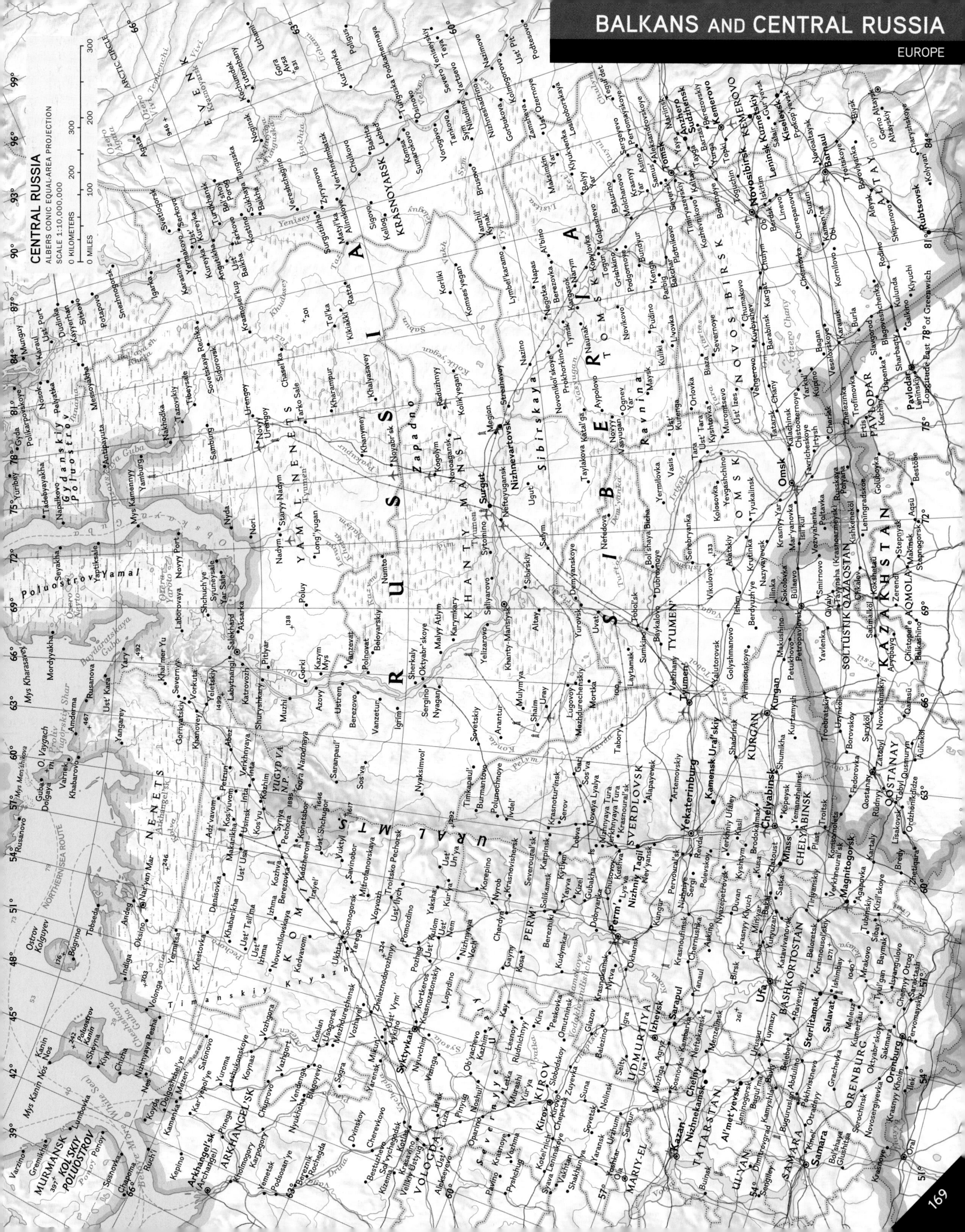
CENTRAL RUSSIA
ALBERS CONIC EQUAL-AREA PROJECTION
SCALE 1:10,000,000
0 KILOMETERS 100 200 300
0 MILES 100 200 300
RUSSIA
KAZAKHSTAN
URAL MTS.
ARCTIC CIRCLE
NORTHERN SEA ROUTE

SO LARGE AND SO DIVERSE—covering almost two-thirds of Earth's land surface and inhabited by 60 percent of humanity—Asia is as much a world as a continent. Earth's most violent tectonic collision continues here, as the Indian subcontinent presses into Asia and thrusts up the Himalaya and the Tibetan Plateau. The resulting land demarcation has effectively isolated large sections of Asia from each other and, in particular, has kept the two most populous countries—China and India, which between them contain half the continent's population—as counterweights to one another, demographically, culturally, economically, and politically.

Asia's vast landmass embraces a wide range of terrain and peoples, from the lightly populated steppes of central Russia to the deserts of the contentious Middle East, from the perilous floodplain of Bangladesh to the teeming western islands of the Indonesian archipelago. Home to the faiths of Judaism, Christianity, Islam, Hinduism, Buddhism, Taoism, Shintoism—and more tongues than religions—the continent supports both megacities and Shangri-La pockets of solitude.

Once primarily a source of raw materials and crops such as rubber, tin, petroleum, timber, and rice, Asia now manufactures goods, from children's toys to high-end electronics, that flood the rest of the world. Japan led the economic boom. China, India, South Korea, Singapore, and others are extending it. Prosperity remains elusive for developing countries, such as Afghanistan and Timor-Leste (East Timor), which have per-capita incomes only one-fourth of that in the region overall. Other regional issues include cross-border migration, trafficking of people and drugs, transboundary spread of diseases, spillover of conflicts, and looming environmental hazards.

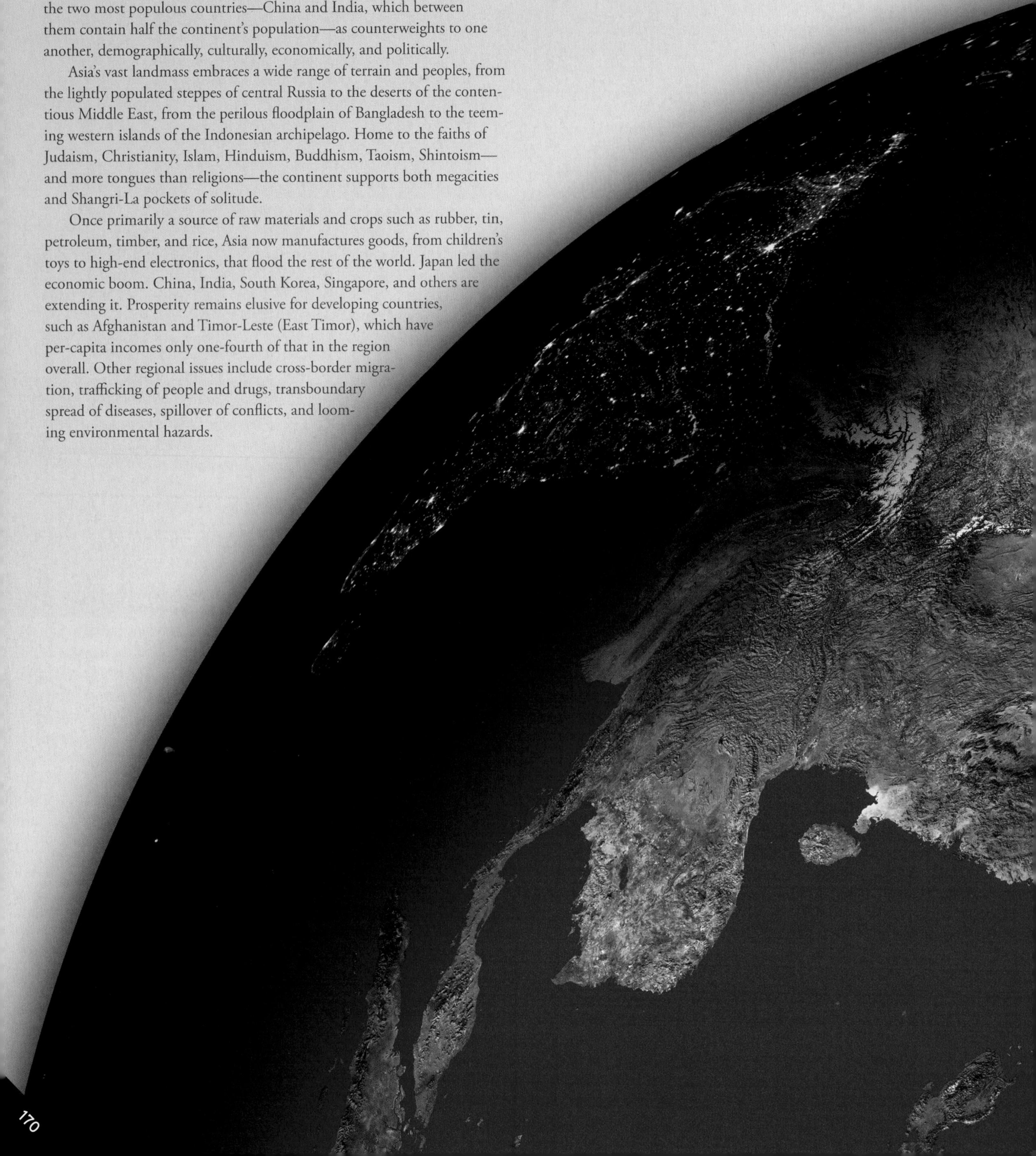

Asia

TWO-POINT EQUIDISTANT PROJECTION
SCALE 1:49,000,000
0 KILOMETERS 1000
0 MILES 400 600 800 1000
Longitude East 110° of Greenwich
North Pole
ARCTIC OCEAN
Date Line
Sunday
Monday
ARCTIC CIRCLE
TROPIC OF CANCER
EQUATOR
Meridian of Greenwich (London)
ATLANTIC OCEAN
PACIFIC OCEAN
INDIAN OCEAN
Norwegian Sea
Barents Sea
Kara Sea
Laptev Sea
East Siberian Sea
Bering Sea
Sea of Okhotsk
Sea of Japan (East Sea)
Yellow Sea
East China Sea
South China Sea
Philippine Sea
Sulu Sea
Celebes Sea
Java Sea
Flores Sea
Banda Sea
Timor Sea
Arafura Sea
Andaman Sea
Bay of Bengal
Arabian Sea
Red Sea
Black Sea
Caspian Sea
Mediterranean Sea
Baltic Sea
North Sea
White Sea
Aral Sea
Persian Gulf
Gulf of Oman
Gulf of Aden
Gulf of Thailand
Gulf of Carpentaria
SVALBARD
Franz Josef Land
NOVAYA ZEMLYA
North Land
New Siberian Islands
Taymyr Peninsula
Yamal Pen.
Gyda Pen.
KAMCHATKA PENINSULA
Kola Pen.
Aleutian Islands
KURIL ISLANDS
Sakhalin
Hokkaido
Honshu
Shikoku
Kyushu
JAPAN
Ryukyu Islands (Nansei Shotō)
Izu Islands
Bonin Islands (Ogasawara Guntō)
Volcano Islands (Kazan Rettō)
Northern Mariana Islands
Guam
Yap Islands
PALAU
Melekeok
PHILIPPINE ISLANDS
PHILIPPINES
Luzon
Mindanao
Manila
TAIWAN
Taipei
Hainan
RUSSIA
SIBERIA
CENTRAL SIBERIAN PLAIN
WEST SIBERIAN PLAIN
NORTHERN EUROPEAN PLAIN
URAL MOUNTAINS
Verkhoyansk Range
Stanovoy Range
Kolyma Range
Koryak Range
Lake Baikal
World's deepest lake −1642 (−5387 ft)
Moscow
KAZAKHSTAN
Astana
Kazakh Uplands
Lake Balkhash
MONGOLIA
Ulaanbaatar
GOBI
ALTAY MOUNTAINS
Dzungarian Basin
TAKLIMAKAN DESERT
KUNLUN MOUNTAINS
PLATEAU OF TIBET
Qaidam Basin
CHINA
Beijing (Peking)
Shanghai
Wuhan
Chongqing
Guangzhou (Canton)
Hong Kong
NORTH KOREA
Pyongyang
SOUTH KOREA
Seoul
Tokyo
HIMALAYA
Mt. Everest 8850 (29035 ft) World's highest point
NEPAL
Kathmandu
BHUTAN
Thimphu
BANGLADESH
Dhaka
INDIA
New Delhi
Mumbai (Bombay)
DECCAN PLATEAU
Western Ghats
Eastern Ghats
SRI LANKA
Colombo
Sri Jayewardenepura Kotte
MALDIVES
Male
PAKISTAN
Islamabad
Karachi
AFGHAN.
Kabul
Hindu Kush
KASHMIR
IRAN
Tehran
Zagros Mountains
TURKMENISTAN
UZBEKISTAN
Tashkent
Dushanbe
Bishkek
MYANMAR (BURMA)
Nay Pyi Taw
Yangon (Rangoon)
THAILAND
Bangkok
LAOS
Vientiane
VIETNAM
Hanoi
CAMBODIA
Phnom Penh
INDOCHINA PENINSULA
MALAY PENINSULA
MALAYSIA
Kuala Lumpur
SINGAPORE
BRUNEI
Bandar Seri Begawan
INDONESIA
Sumatra
Borneo
Celebes
JAVA
Jakarta
GREATER SUNDA ISLANDS
LESSER SUNDA ISLANDS
TIMOR LESTE (EAST TIMOR)
Dili
NEW GUINEA
AUSTRALIA
Darwin
Arnhem Land
SAUDI ARABIA
Riyadh
ARABIAN PENINSULA
Ar Rub' al Khālī (Empty Quarter)
YEMEN
Sanaa
OMAN
Muscat
U.A.E.
Abu Dhabi
QATAR
BAHRAIN
KUWAIT
Kuwait City
IRAQ
Baghdad
SYRIA
Damascus
JORDAN
Amman
ISRAEL
LEBANON
CYPRUS
TURKEY
Ankara
Istanbul
GEORGIA
Caucasus Mts.
UKRAINE
Kyiv
BELARUS
Minsk
POLAND
Warsaw
FINLAND
Helsinki
SWEDEN
Stockholm
NORWAY
Oslo
SCANDINAVIA
EST.
Tallinn
LATV.
Riga
LITH.
Vilnius
GER.
Berlin
FRANCE
Paris
SPAIN
Madrid
PORTUGAL
Lisbon
ITALY
Rome
GREECE
Athens
ROMANIA
Bucharest
BULG.
Sofia
U.K.
London
IRE.
Dublin
EGYPT
Cairo
LIBYA
Tripoli
TUNISIA
Tunis
ALGERIA
Algiers
SUDAN
Khartoum
ERITREA
Asmara
DJIBOUTI
ETHIOPIA
Addis Ababa
SOMALIA
Mogadishu
KENYA
Nairobi
Mt. Kenya
Kilimanjaro
TANZANIA
Dar es Salaam
MADAGASCAR
Antananarivo
COMOROS
Moroni
SEYCHELLES
Victoria
Socotra
Chagos Archipelago (Oil Islands)

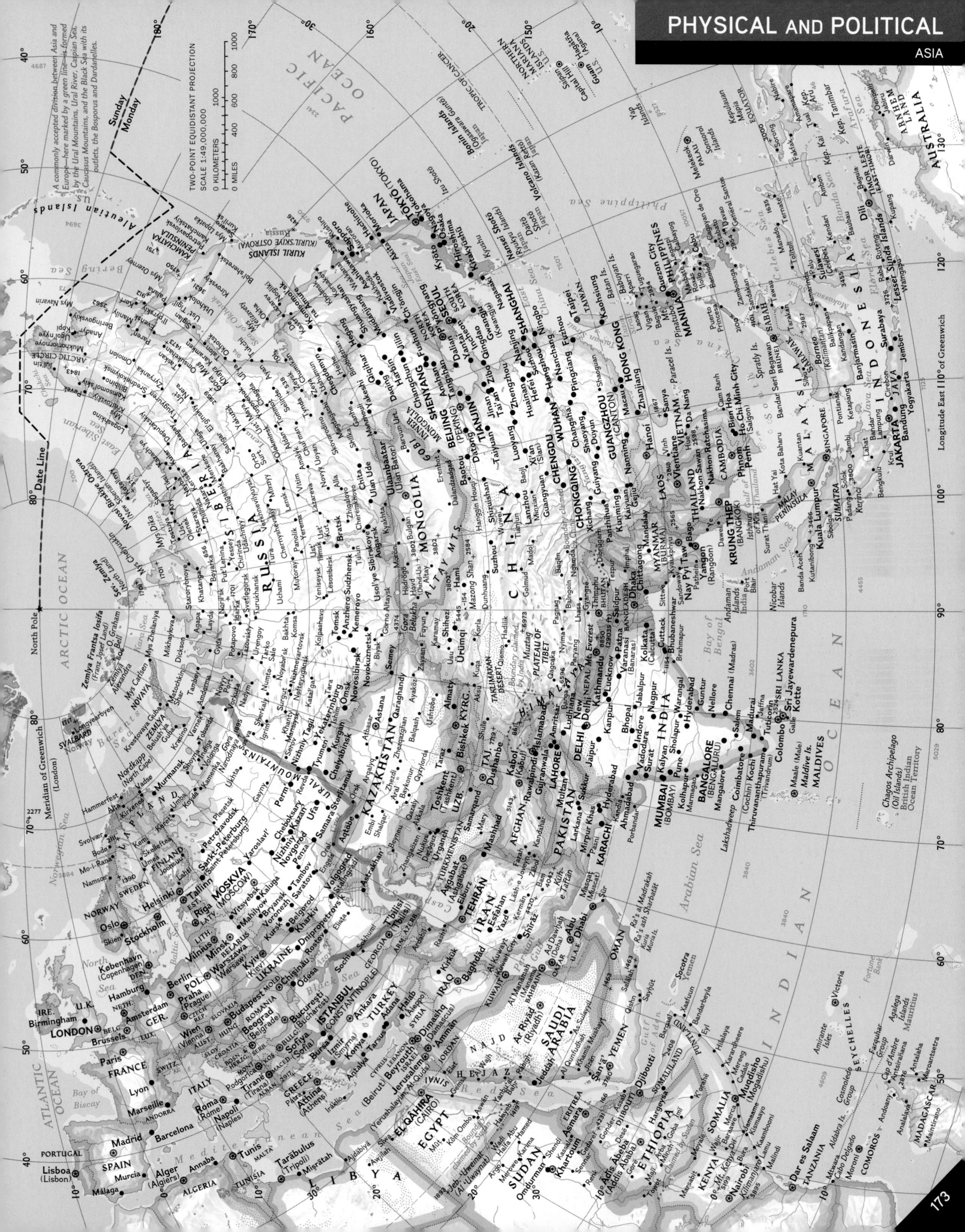
A commonly accepted division between Asia and Europe—here marked by a green line—is formed by the Ural Mountains, Ural River, Caspian Sea, Caucasus Mountains, and the Black Sea with its outlets, the Bosporus and Dardanelles.
TWO-POINT EQUIDISTANT PROJECTION
SCALE 1:49,000,000
0 KILOMETERS 400 600 800 1000
0 MILES 400 600 800 1000
ARCTIC OCEAN
North Pole
Date Line
Sunday
Monday
PACIFIC OCEAN
INDIAN OCEAN
ATLANTIC OCEAN
Meridian of Greenwich (London)
Longitude East 110° of Greenwich
ARCTIC CIRCLE
TROPIC OF CANCER
EQUATOR
RUSSIA
SIBERIA
URAL MOUNTAINS
KAZAKHSTAN
MONGOLIA
CHINA
ALTAY MTS.
GOBI
PLATEAU OF TIBET
HIMALAYA
INDIA
PAKISTAN
AFGHANISTAN
IRAN
IRAQ
SAUDI ARABIA
TURKEY
EGYPT
SUDAN
ETHIOPIA
SOMALIA
KENYA
TANZANIA
YEMEN
OMAN
JAPAN
PHILIPPINES
INDONESIA
MALAYSIA
THAILAND
VIETNAM
MYANMAR (BURMA)
CAMBODIA
LAOS
AUSTRALIA
MADAGASCAR
SPAIN
FRANCE
ITALY
UKRAINE
FINLAND
NORWAY
SWEDEN
LIBYA
ALGERIA
BEIJING (PEKING)
SHANGHAI
TOKYO
SEOUL
HONG KONG
DELHI
MUMBAI (BOMBAY)
KOLKATA (Calcutta)
KARACHI
TEHRĀN
BAGHDĀD
ISTANBUL (CONSTANTINOPLE)
MOSKVA (MOSCOW)
LONDON
EL QÂHIRA (CAIRO)
JAKARTA
MANILA
BANGKOK
Arabian Sea
Bay of Bengal
Bering Sea
Philippine Sea
Black Sea
Caspian Sea
Red Sea
Mediterranean Sea
Aleutian Islands
KURIL ISLANDS
SVALBARD
Maldive Is.
Chagos Archipelago
SEYCHELLES

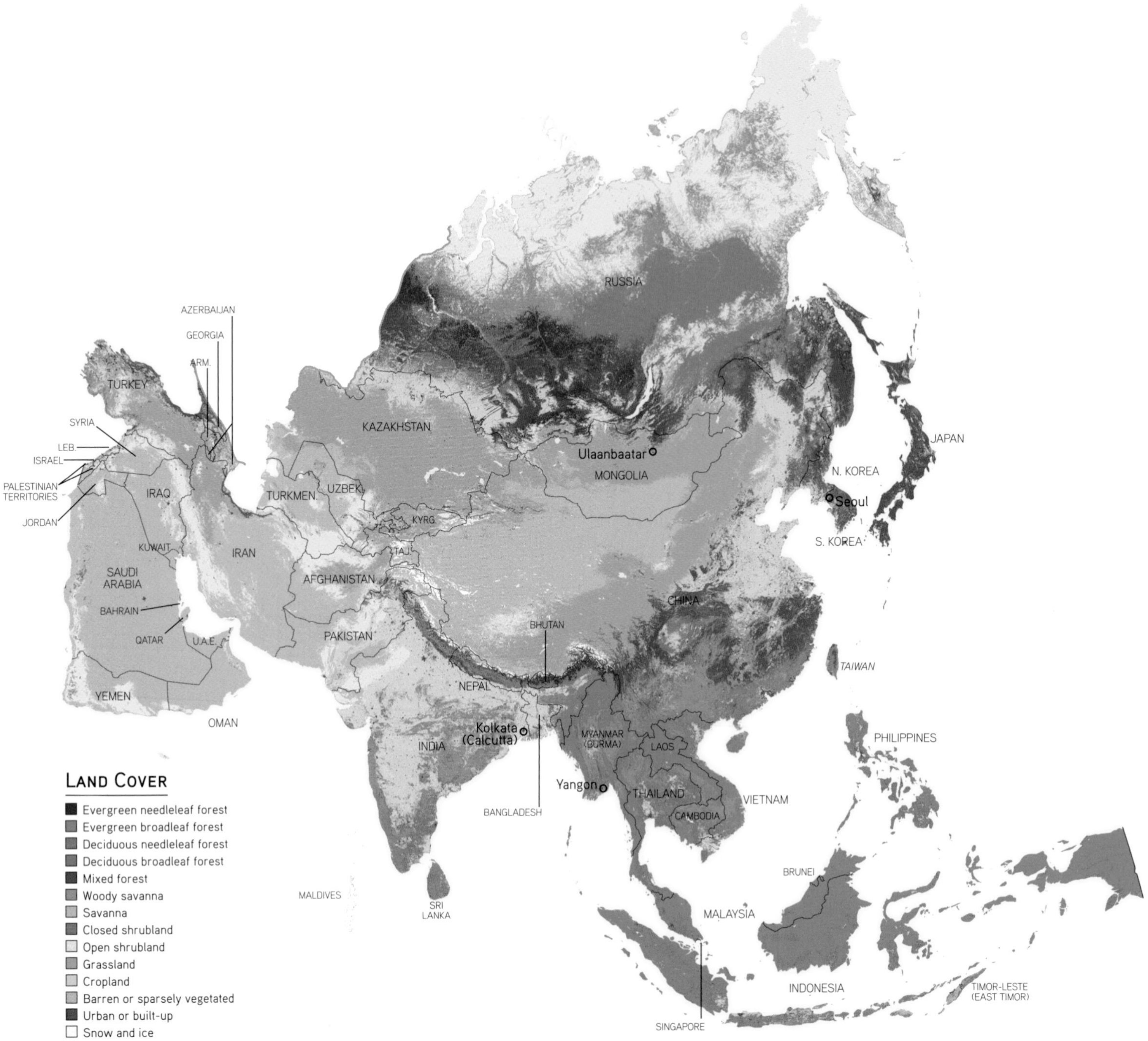

LAND COVER

- Evergreen needleleaf forest
- Evergreen broadleaf forest
- Deciduous needleleaf forest
- Deciduous broadleaf forest
- Mixed forest
- Woody savanna
- Savanna
- Closed shrubland
- Open shrubland
- Grassland
- Cropland
- Barren or sparsely vegetated
- Urban or built-up
- Snow and ice
- Cropland / natural vegetation mosaic
- Wetland

TEMPERATURE AND RAINFALL

Yangon, Myanmar

High temperature
Low temp.
Rainfall
(115 mm = 4.5 in)
Temperatures above 0°C
Temperatures below 0°C

Kolkata (Calcutta), India

Seoul, South Korea

Ulaanbaatar, Mongolia

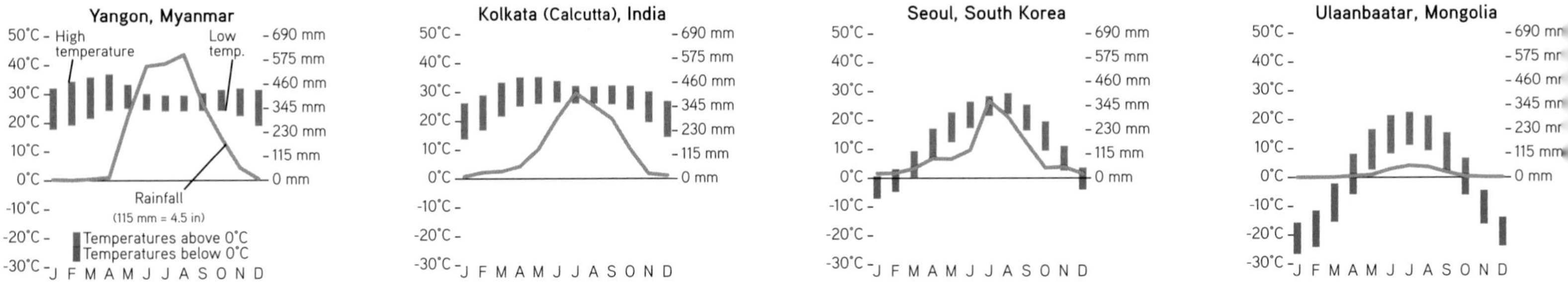

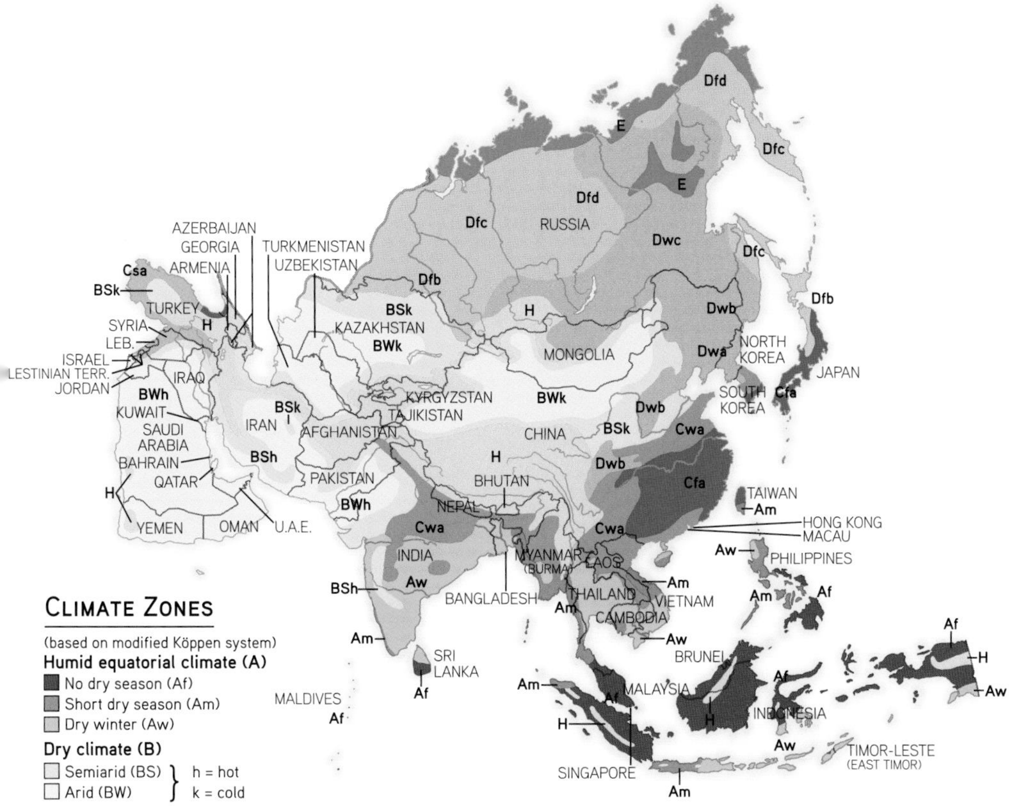

Climate Zones

(based on modified Köppen system)

Humid equatorial climate (A)
- No dry season (Af)
- Short dry season (Am)
- Dry winter (Aw)

Dry climate (B)
- Semiarid (BS)
- Arid (BW)

h = hot
k = cold

Humid temperate climate (C)
- No dry season (Cf)
- Dry winter (Cw)
- Dry summer (Cs)

Humid cold climate (D)
- No dry season (Df)
- Dry winter (Dw)

a = hot summer
b = cool summer
c = short, cool summer
d = very cold winter

Cold climate (E)
- Tundra and ice

Highland climate (H)
- Unclassified highlands

Natural Hazards

Population Density, 2010

People per square km	People per square mi
More than 1,000	More than 2,500
100–1,000	250–2,500
Less than 100	Less than 250

Fire Intensity
(from gas burn off, slash-and-burn agriculture, or natural causes)
High
Low

Recorded Natural Event

Major Earthquake, 1900-2010
Moment magnitude
- More than 7.0
- 6.0–7.0
- Less than 6.0

Volcano

Tsunami, 1900-2010
Run-up height

Meters	Feet
More than 10	More than 32
5–10	16–32
Less than 5	Less than 16

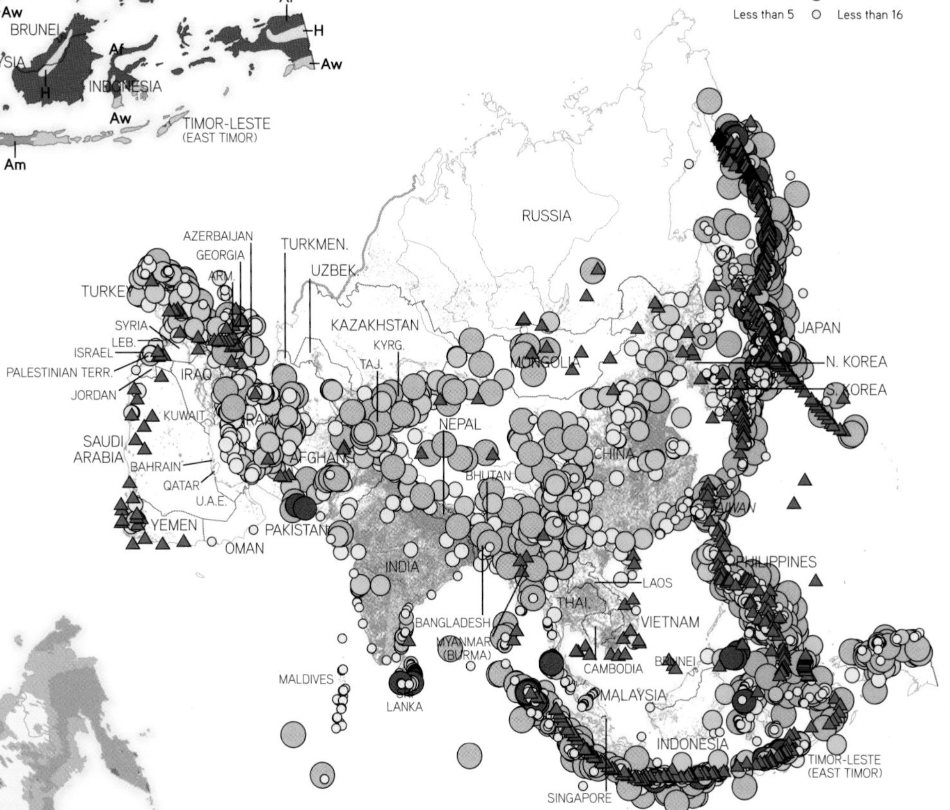

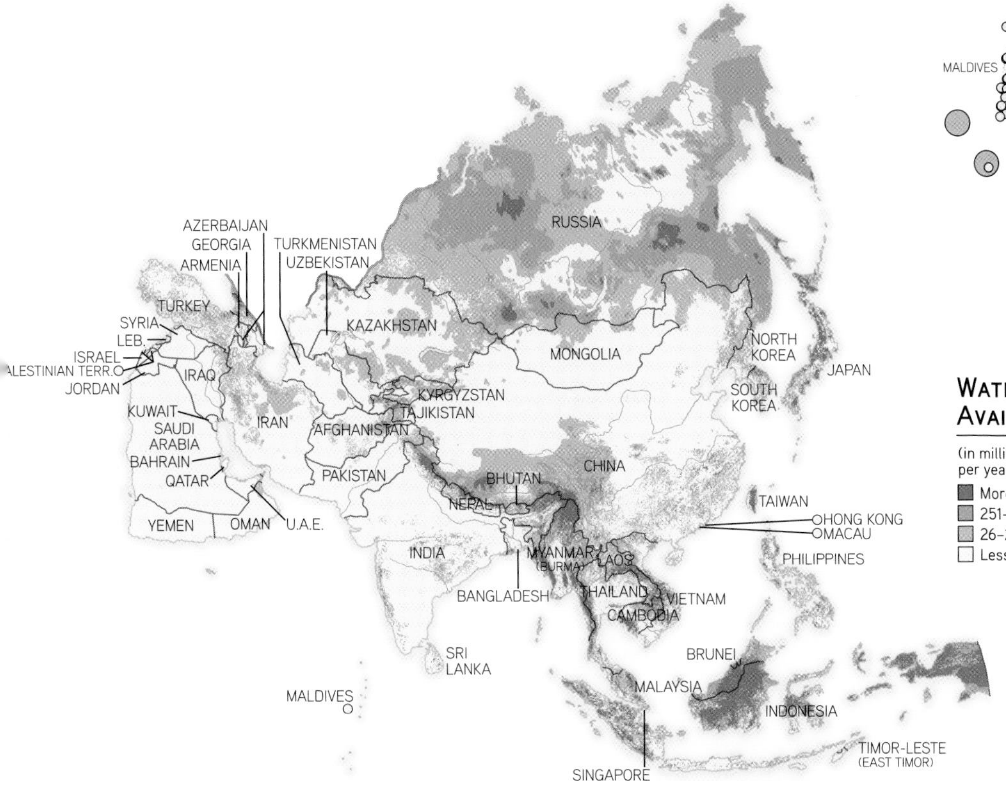

Water Availability

(in millimeters per person per year)
- More than 750
- 251–750
- 26–250
- Less than 26

POPULATION DENSITY

People per Square Kilometer
More than 195
60–195
10–59
1–9
Less than 1

People per Square Mile
More than 500
150–500
25–149
1–24
Less than 1

RUSSIA

AZERBAIJAN
GEORGIA

Ankara ✪
TURKEY
SYRIA
LEB.
Beirut ✪
ISRAEL
Jerusalem ✪
Damascus ✪
Amman ✪
PALESTINIAN
TERRITORIES
JORDAN
IRAQ
Baghdad ✪

Tbilisi ✪
ARM.
Yerevan ✪
Baku ✪

Astana ✪
KAZAKHSTAN

Ulaanbaatar ✪
MONGOLIA

JAPAN
Tokyo ✪

Pyongyang ✪
N. KOREA
Seoul ✪
Beijing ✪
S. KOREA

TURKMEN.
UZBEK.
Bishkek ✪
Ashgabat ✪
Tashkent ✪
KYRG.
Dushanbe ✪
TAJ.

Tehran ✪
IRAN
KUWAIT
Kuwait City ✪
SAUDI ARABIA
Riyadh ✪
BAHRAIN
Manama ✪
Doha ✪
QATAR
Abu Dhabi ✪
U.A.E.
Muscat ✪
OMAN

AFGHANISTAN
Kabul ✪
Islamabad ✪
PAKISTAN

CHINA

Taipei ⊛
TAIWAN

BHUTAN
New Delhi ✪
Kathmandu ✪
Thimphu ✪
NEPAL
Dhaka ✪
INDIA
MYANMAR (BURMA)
Nay Pyi Taw ✪
LAOS
Hanoi ✪
Vientiane ✪
BANGLADESH
Yangon (Rangoon) ✪
THAILAND
Bangkok ✪
CAMBODIA
VIETNAM
Phnom Penh ✪

PHILIPPINES
Manila ✪

Sanaa ✪
YEMEN

Socotra (YEMEN)

SRI LANKA
Colombo ✪
Sri Jayewardenepura Kotte ✪
MALDIVES
Male ✪

Kuala Lumpur ✪
MALAYSIA
Singapore ✪
SINGAPORE
Sumatra
Jakarta ✪
INDONESIA
Java

Bandar Seri Begawan ✪
BRUNEI
Borneo

New Guinea

Dili ✪
TIMOR-LESTE (EAST TIMOR)

POPULATION PYRAMIDS

PALESTINIAN TERRITORIES

Age
80+
60–64
40–44   Male   Female
20–24
0–4
10   5   0   5   10
Percent of population

CHINA

Age
80+
60–64
40–44 Male   Female
20–24
0–4
10   5   0   5   10
Percent of population

JAPAN

Age
80+
60–64
40–44   Male   Female
20–24
0–4
10   5   0   5   10
Percent of population

176

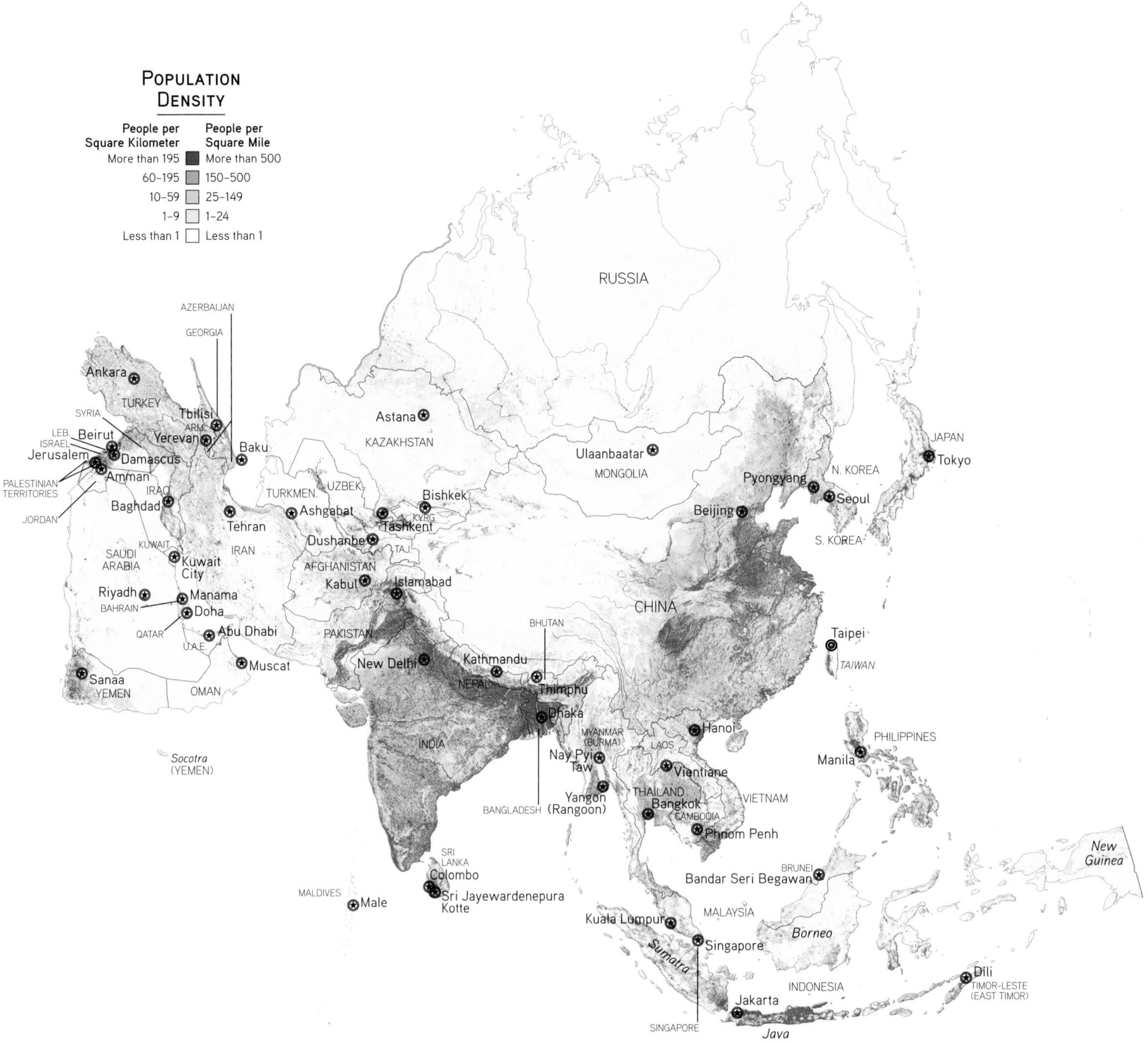

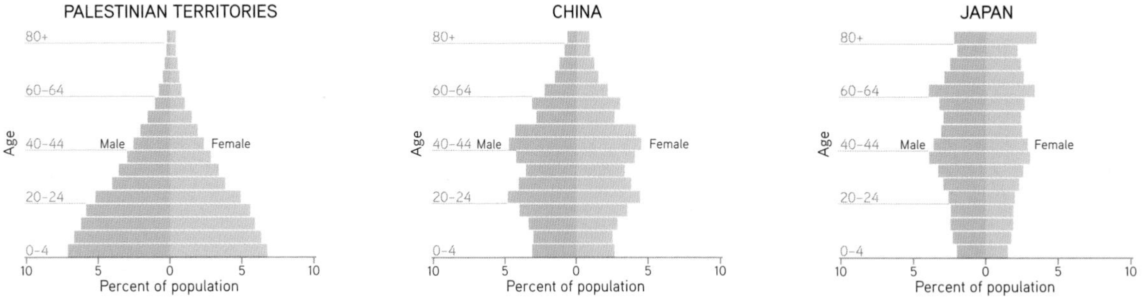

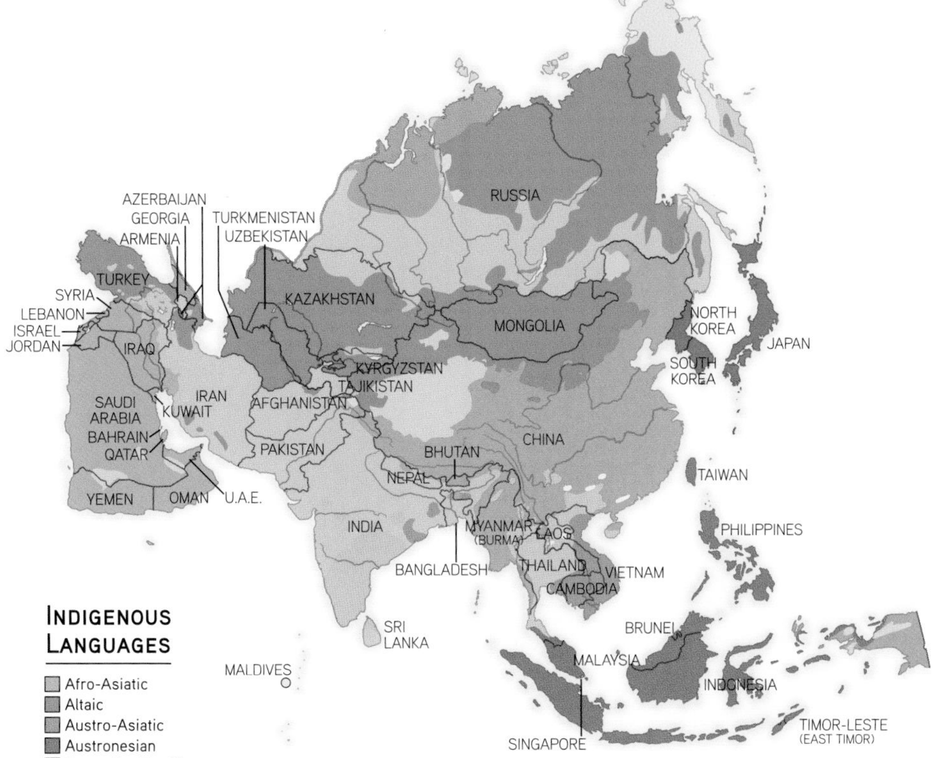

Indigenous Languages

- Afro-Asiatic
- Altaic
- Austro-Asiatic
- Austronesian
- Caucasian Families
- Dravidian
- Eskimo-Aleut
- Hmong-Mien
- Indo-European
- Japanese/Korean
- Kam-Tai
- Papuan Familes
- Sino-Tibetan
- Uralic
- Isolates
- Uninhabited

Urbanization

Urban agglomerations, 2010
(population in millions)
- ■ More than 10.0
- ▲ 5.0–10.0
- ● 1.0–4.9
- ○ .75–.99

Percent urban population, 2010
- More than 75%
- 50%–75%
- 25%–49%
- Less than 25%

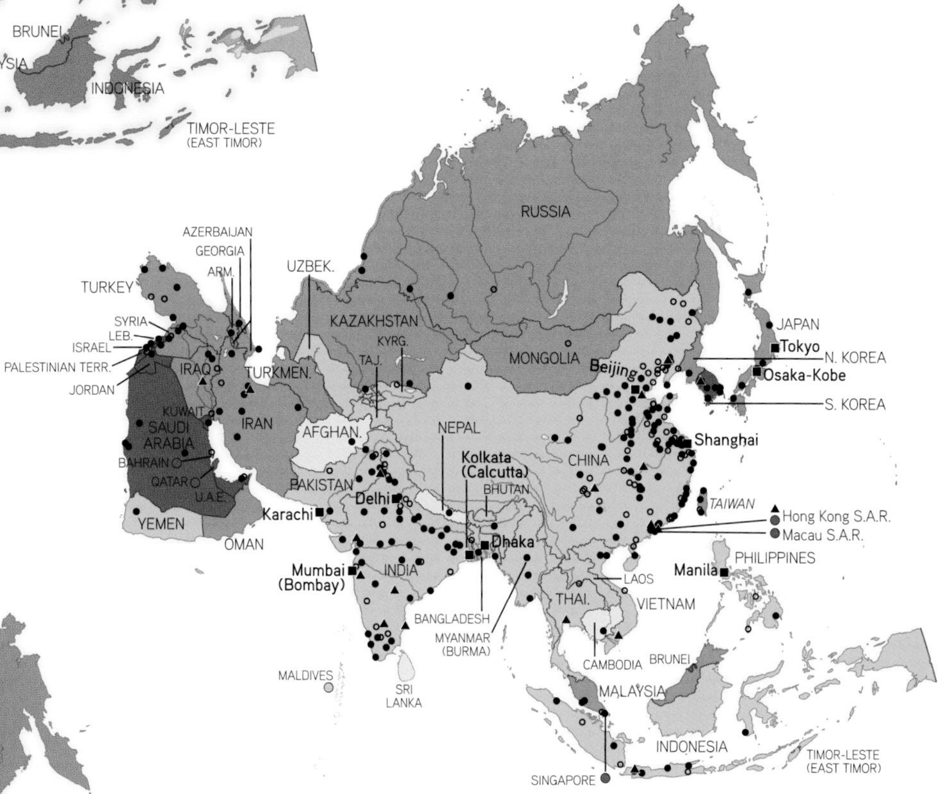

Population Change

Projected population change, 2010–2050
(by percentage)
- More than 100%
- 50%–100%
- 0.01%–49%
- No change
- Population loss

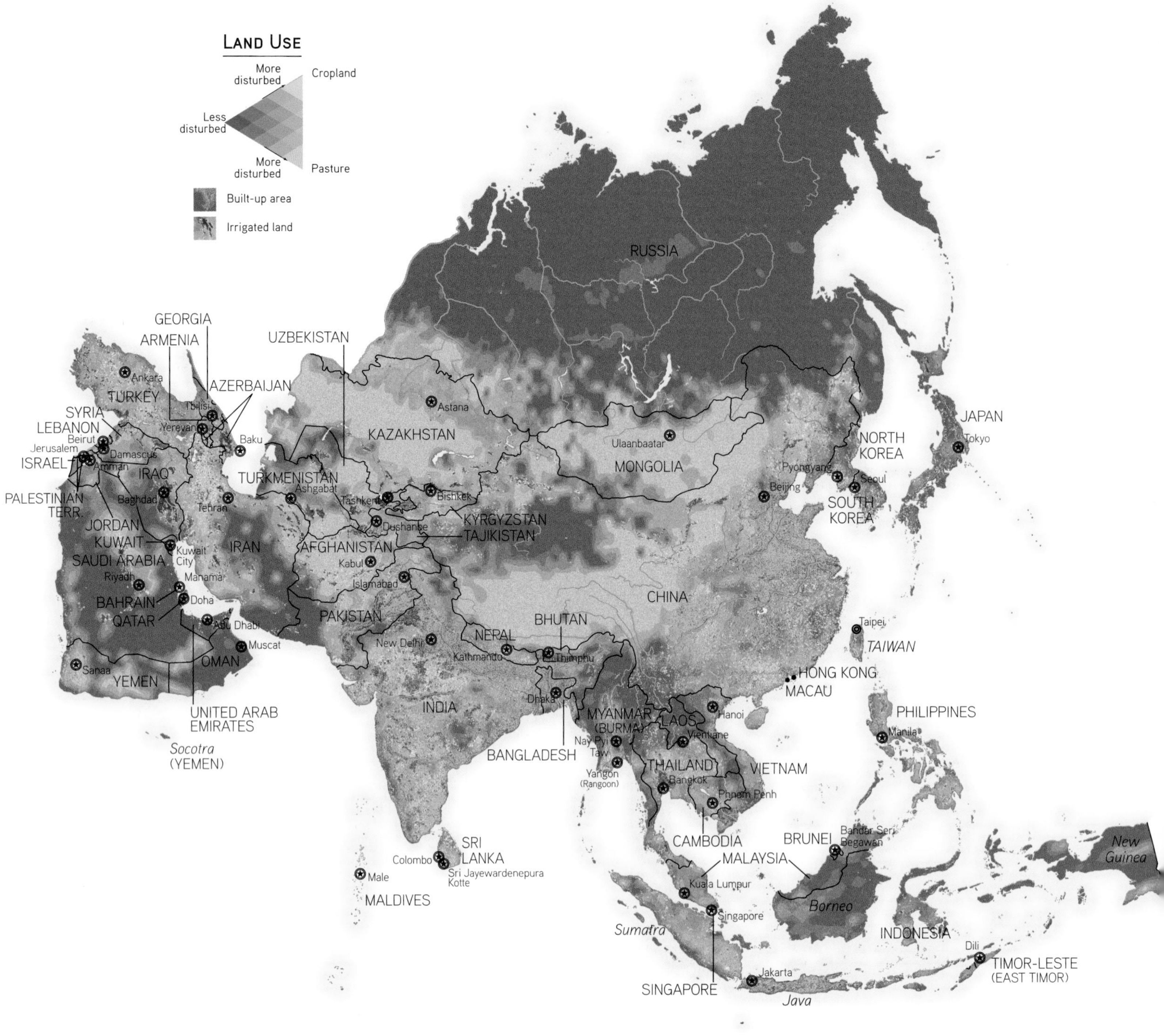

Imports and Exports

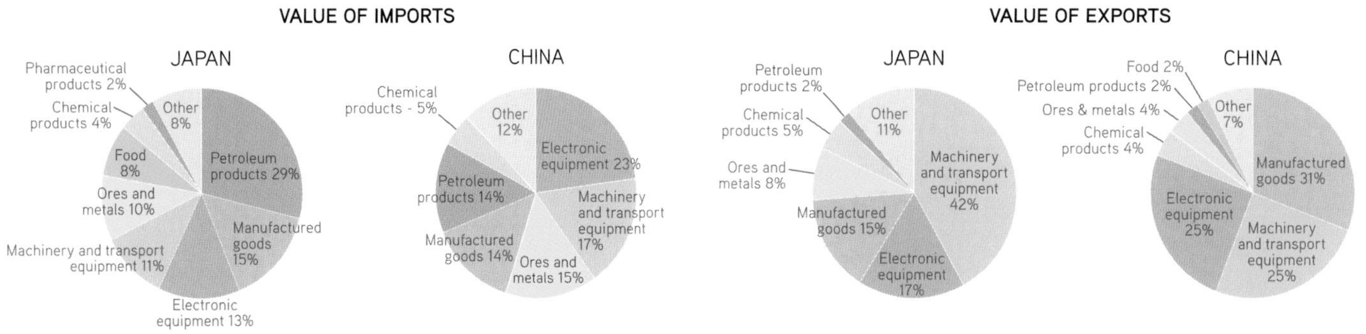

DOMINANT ECONOMY

(per GDP sector)

Agriculture	Industry*	Services
70%–100%		
50%–69.9%		
0%–49.9%		

*Includes the mining industry

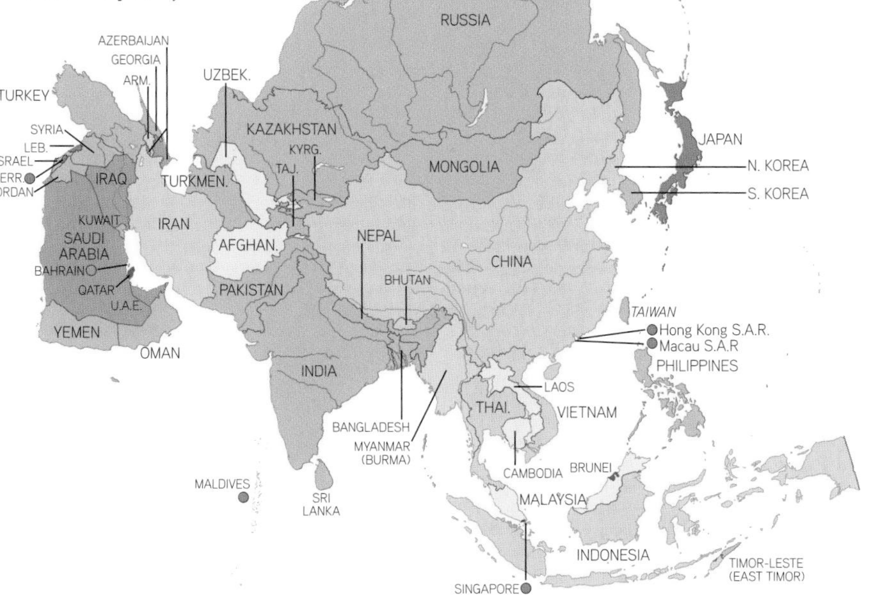

RUSSIA
AZERBAIJAN
GEORGIA
ARM.
TURKEY
UZBEK.
KAZAKHSTAN
KYRG.
SYRIA
LEB.
TAJ.
MONGOLIA
ISRAEL
PALESTINIAN TERR.
JORDAN
IRAQ
TURKMEN.
JAPAN
N. KOREA
S. KOREA
KUWAIT
SAUDI ARABIA
IRAN
AFGHAN.
NEPAL
CHINA
BAHRAIN
QATAR
U.A.E.
PAKISTAN
BHUTAN
YEMEN
OMAN
TAIWAN
Hong Kong S.A.R.
Macau S.A.R.
INDIA
BANGLADESH
MYANMAR (BURMA)
THAI.
LAOS
VIETNAM
PHILIPPINES
MALDIVES
SRI LANKA
CAMBODIA
BRUNEI
MALAYSIA
INDONESIA
TIMOR-LESTE (EAST TIMOR)
SINGAPORE

ASIA'S ECONOMY

Service 100%
MACAU, CHINA
MYANMAR
QATAR
Agricultural 100%
Industrial 100%

per Gross Domestic Product (GDP) sector

PER CAPITA ENERGY CONSUMPTION

(annual use, in million Btu)

- More than 300
- 201–300
- 101–200
- 30–100
- Less than 30

Major energy deposit
- Coal
- Natural gas
- Oil
- Oil pipeline
- Oil transit chokepoint

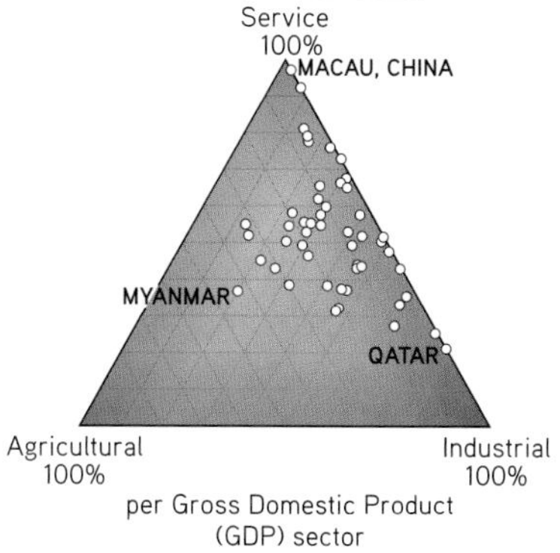

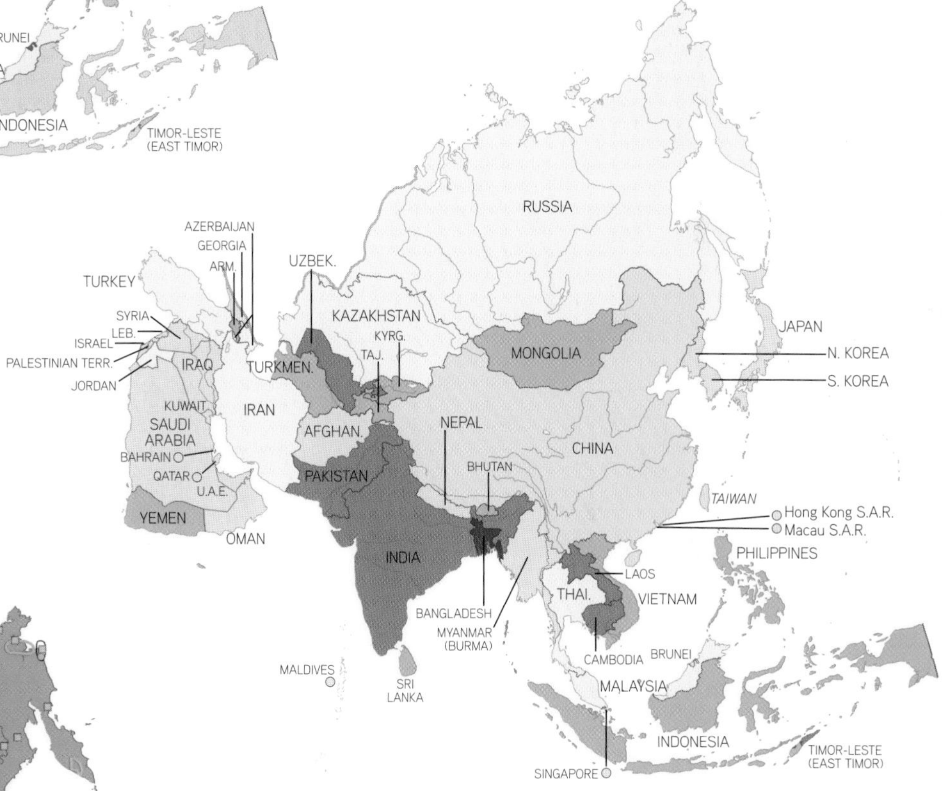

POVERTY

Percentage of population living on less than $2 per day

- More than 80%
- 60%–80%
- 40%–59%
- 20%–39%
- Less than 20%
- No data available

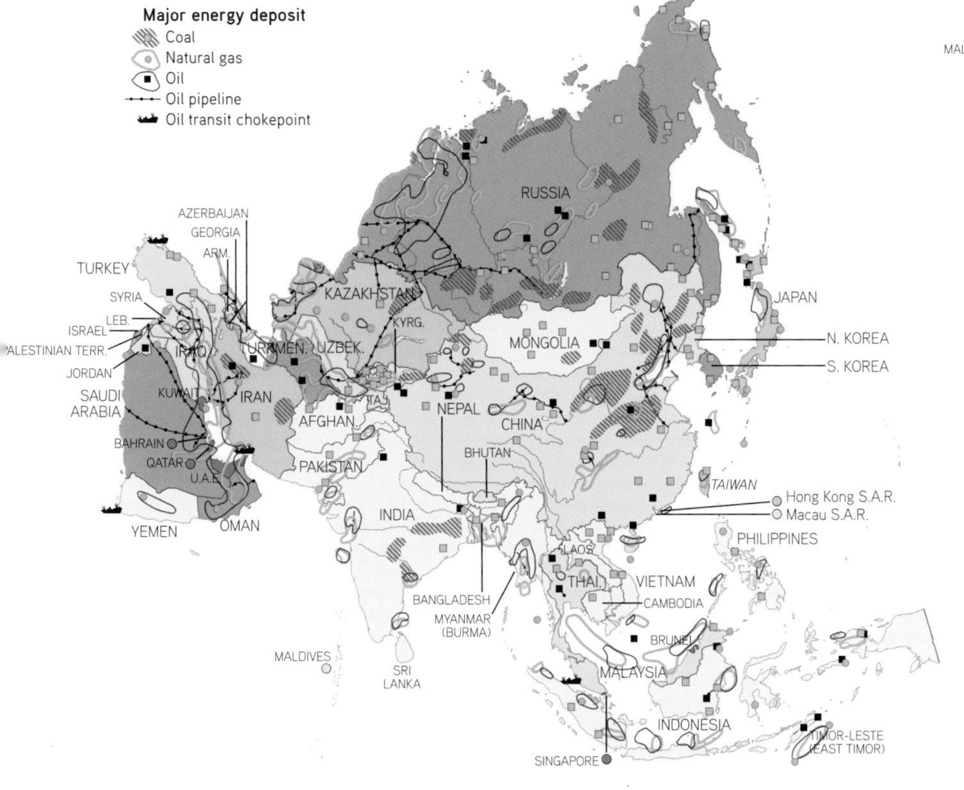

Longitude East 30° of Greenwich
ROMANIA
SERBIA
KOSOVO
Prishtina
BULGARIA
Sofiya (Sofia)
MACEDONIA
Skopje
CRIMEA
UKRAINE
Simferopol'
Sevastopol'
KRASNODAR
Krasnodar
BLACK SEA
ABKHAZIA
Separatists defeated Georgian troops to gain control of this region in 1993—negotiations continue on resolving the conflict.
Constanţa
Varna
Burgas
Plovdiv
Edirne (Adrianople)
Thessaloníki
İSTANBUL (CONSTANTINOPLE)
Marmara Denizi
Kocaeli (İzmit)
Adapazarı
BURSA
Zonguldak
Samsun (Amisus)
Trabzon
Ankara (Angora)
Eskişehir
TURKEY
ANATOLIA
Sivas
Erzurum
Kayseri
Konya (Iconium)
İZMIR (SMYRNA)
Manisa
Denizli
Antalya
Antalya Körfezi
ADANA
Tarsus
İçel (Mersin)
Gaziantep
Şanlıurfa (Edessa)
Diyarbakır
Malatya
Mardin
Kahramanmaraş
İskenderun
(Antioch) Hatay
TOROS DAĞLARI
Balkan Mountains
Rhodope Mountains
Pindus Mountains
GREECE
Athína (Athens)
Peloponnesus
AEGEAN SEA
KIKLÁDES
Dodecanese
Ródos (Rhodes)
Kríti (Crete)
SEA OF CRETE
MEDITERRANEAN SEA
LAMBERT CONFORMAL CONIC PROJECTION
SCALE 1:8,000,000
0 KILOMETERS 120 160 200
0 MILES 40 80 120 160 200
CYPRUS
NORTHERN CYPRUS
Lefkosia (Lefkoşa, Nicosia)
Limassol
Larnaka
SYRIA
Ḩalab (Aleppo)
Ar Raqqah
Al Lādhiqīyah (Latakia)
Ḩamāh (Hamath)
Ḩimş (Homs)
Dimashq (Damascus)
LEBANON
Beyrouth (Beirut)
Trâblous (Tripoli)
ISRAEL
Haifa
Tel Aviv-Yafo
Jerusalem (Yerushalayim, Al-Quds)
WEST BANK
GAZA STRIP
Be'er Sheva
Negev
JORDAN
'Ammān
Az Zarqā'
Irbid
Wādī as Sirḩān
AL ḨAMĀD
SYRIAN DESERT
EGYPT
El Iskandarîya (Alexandria)
Bûr Sa'îd (Port Said)
Dumyât (Damietta)
EL QÂHIRA (CAIRO)
El Giza
El Suweis (Suez)
SUEZ CANAL
Ismâ'ilîya
Țanța
El Manșûra
Zagazig
Munkhafad el Qaţţâra (Qattara Depression)
Libyan Plateau
Libyan Desert
Western Desert
Eastern Desert
Bahr el Nil (Nile)
El Faiyûm
Beni Suef
El Minya
Asyûţ
Sohâg
Qena
SINAI
Gebel el Tîh
Gebel el 'Igma
Gebel Mûsa (Mount Sinai)
Gulf of Suez
Gulf of Aqaba
RAS MUHAMMED N.P.
RED SEA
The Brothers
Hurghada
El Wâḩât el Baḩarîya
El Wâḩât el Farâfra
LIBYA
Al Jaghbūb
SAUDI ARABIA
An Nafūd
AL ḨIJAZ (HEJAZ)
Tabūk
Al 'Aqabah
Elat
Ḩaql
Taymā'
Jabal Shammar
Al Wajh
Şafājah
21° 24° 27° 30° 33° 36° 39°
42° 39° 36° 33° 30° 27°

SOUTH OSSETIA
Georgia lost control of South Ossetia in 1992. Georgia tried to retake South Ossetia in 2008 but was defeated by Russian forces.
NAGORNO-KARABAKH
Since a 1994 cease-fire between Azerbaijani and Armenian forces, ethnic Armenians have controlled Nagorno-Karabakh and surrounding areas (gray). Azerbaijan continues to claim this disputed region.
CASPIAN SEA
-28 (-92 ft)
KAZAKHSTAN
UZBEKISTAN
TURKMENISTAN
AZERBAIJAN
ARMENIA
GEORGIA
RUSSIA
DAGESTAN
CHECHNYA
KALMYKIYA
STAVROPOL'
IRAN
IRAQ
KUWAIT
ARABIA
BAHRAIN
QATAR
U.A.E.
OMAN
AFGHANISTAN
PERSIAN GULF
GULF OF OMAN
Strait of Hormuz
USTYURT PLATEAU
MANGGHYSTAU
Garagum
Turan Lowland
Dasht-e Kavīr (Salt Desert)
Dasht-e Lūt
KHORĀSĀN
Reshteh-ye Alborz (Elburz Mountains)
Kūhhā-ye Zāgros (Zagros Mountains)
Köpetdag Mountains
CAUCASUS MOUNTAINS
TEHRAN
Baku
T'bilisi (Tbilisi)
Yerevan
Baghdād
Ashgabat
Kuwait City
Al Manāmah (Manama)
Esfahan (Isfahan)
Mashhad
Tabrīz
Shīrāz
Bandar 'Abbās
45°
48°
51°
54°
57°
42°
39°
36°
33°
30°
27°

ISRAEL
JORDAN
IRAQ
KUWAIT
EGYPT
SINAI
SAUDI ARABIA
SUDAN
ERITREA
ETHIOPIA
DJIBOUTI
YEMEN
RED SEA
GULF OF ADEN
Helwân
El Faiyûm
Beni Suef
El Minya
Asyût
Sohâg
Qena
Luxor
Aswân
Wadi Halfa
Gebel el Tîh
Gebel el ʽIgma
Gebel Mûsa (Mt. Sinai)
RAS MUHAMMED N.P.
Hurghada
Bûr Safâga
The Brothers
Quseir
Marsa ʽAlam
Eastern Desert
Nubian Desert
Lake Nasser
Lake Nubia
Boundary claimed by Sudan
Halayeb
Oyo
Siyal Islands
Gezâir Marir (Mirear)
Ras Hadarba (Cape Elba)
Mukawwar Island
Port Sudan
Suakin
Suakin Arch.
Tokar
Karora
Massawa
Asmara
Dahlak Arch.
Dahlak Kebir
Massawa Channel
Nile
Bahr el Abyad (White Nile)
Bahr el Azraq
Atbara
Omdurman
Khartoum
Khartoum North
KHARTOUM
KASSALA
Kassala
GEZIRA
Wad Medani
GEDAREF
Gedaref
WHITE NILE
Kosti
SINNAR
Sennar
DINDER NAT. PARK
BLUE NILE
UPPER NILE
RIVER NILE
NORTHERN
Gonder
Bahir Dar
T'ana Hāyk'
Mek'elē
TIGRAY
AMHARA
AFAR
Lalībela
Djibouti
Assab
Bab el Mandab
Golfe de Tadjoura
Al ʽAqabah
Elat
Tabūk
Harrat al ʽUwayrid
HEJAZ
Al Wajh
Umm Lajj
Yanbuʽal Bahr
Al Madīnah (Medina)
Harrat Khaybar
Harrat Rahat
Harrat Kishb
Jeddah
Makkah (Mecca)
At Tāʼif
Tihāmat ash Shām
ʽASĪR
Abhā
Khamīs Mushayt
Jīzān
Farasān
Najrān
Al Hudaydah
Ṣanʽā (Sanaa)
Taʽizz
ʽAdan (Aden)
Al Mukhā
An Nafūd
Jabal Shammar
Hāʼil
Al Qaṣīm
Buraydah
Ar Riyāḍ (Riyadh)
Ad Dahnāʼ
Jabal Ṭuwayq
Nafūd ad Dahy
Wādī ad Dawāsir
ʽUrūq ar Rumaylah
Al Baṣrah
Rumaila
Al Jumaymah
Hafar al Bāṭin
King Khalid Military City
Ar Rawdah
Al Qunfudhah
Al Līth
Kamarān
Jazāʼir az Zubayr
Jazīrat Jabal Zuqar
Hanīsh al Kabīr
Barīm (Perim)
30°
33°
36°
39°
42°
45°
27°
24°
21°
18°
15°
12°

IRAN
PAKISTAN
BALUCHISTAN
PERSIAN GULF
GULF OF OMAN
ARABIAN SEA
GULF OF ADEN
UNITED ARAB EMIRATES
QATAR
BAHRAIN
OMAN
ZUFĀR
ḤAḌRAMAWT
YEMEN
SOMALIA
Rub‘ al Khālī
(Empty Quarter)
Zagros Mountains
Strait of Hormuz
TROPIC OF CANCER
Kermān
Shīrāz
Sīrjān
Bandar ‘Abbās
Būshehr
Ābādān
Persepolis
Jāsk
Chābahār
Gwadar
Pasni
Ormara
Dalbandin
Nok Kundi
Al Manāmah
(Manama)
Ad Dawḥah
(Doha)
Ad Dammām
Al Hufūf
(Hofuf)
Ghawar Oil Field
Abu Dhabi
Dubai
Sharjah
Al ‘Ayn
Masqaṭ (Muscat)
Ṣuḥār
Ra’s al Ḥadd
Jazīrat Maṣīrah
(Masira)
Duqm
Ṣalālah
Mirbāṭ
Kuria Muria Is.
Al Ghayḍah
Ra’s Fartak
Al Mukallā
Sayḥūt
Socotra (Suquṭrá)
Yemen
‘Abd al Kūrī
Yemen
Al Ikhwān
(The Brothers)
Cape
Gwardafuy
Al Ḥadīdah
(meteorite craters)
LAMBERT CONFORMAL CONIC PROJECTION
SCALE 1:8,000,000
0 KILOMETERS 120 160 200
0 MILES 40 80 120 160 200

RYAZAN'
MORDOVIYA
TATARSTAN
LIPETSK
TAMBOV
UL'YANOVSK
PENZA
SAMARA
BASHKORTOSTAN
CHELYABINSK
KURG
RUSSIA
URAL MTS.
VORONEZH
SARATOV
ORENBURG
VOLGOGRAD
Privolzhskaya Vozvyshennost'
ROSTOV
KALMYKIYA
ASTRAKHAN'
BATYS QAZAQSTAN
ATYRAŪ
AQTÖBE
QOSTANAY
KAZAK
Caspian Depression
STAVROPOL'
CHECHNYA
INGUSH.
NORTH OSSETIA-ALANIA
DAGESTAN
GEORGIA
AZERBAIJAN
NAGORNO-KARABAKH
ARM.
IRAN
Caucasus Mts.
CASPIAN SEA
MANGGHYSTAŪ
QORAQALPOG'ISTON (KARAKALPAKSTAN)
QYZYLORDA
UZBEKISTAN
TURKMENISTAN
Garagum
Qizilqum
Turan Lowland
Ustyurt Plateau
Chink Kaplankyr
Karynzharyk Desert
Reshteh-ye Alborz (Elburz Mountains)
Kōpetdag Mts.
Mughalzhar Taūy
Ülken Borsyq Qumy
Aral Mangy Qaraqumy
Dongyztaū Shyngy
Naryn Qum
Bozashchy Tübegi
Tülen Araldary
Tupqaraghan Tübegi
Agrakhanskiy Poluostrov
Apsheron Yarymadasy
Qazaq Shyghanaghy
Garabogaz Aylagy
Türkmenbaşy Aylagy
Ol Qolyq Sory
North Aral Sea
ARAL SEA
Sarygamyş Köli
Aralsor Köli
Shalqar Köli
Saryqopa Köli
Kuybyshevskoye Vodokhranilishche
Volgogradskoye Vodokhranilishche
VOLGA-DON CANAL
GARAGUM CANAL
BAYKONUR COSMODROME Russian-administered
ARAL SEA
Once the world's fourth largest lake, the Aral Sea today is less than half its 1960 extent. Soviet-era irrigation canals divert river water, causing the sea to shrink and changing the former lake bed into a desert. A UN study predicts the Aral Sea could disappear by 2018.
Former shoreline, 2000
Former shoreline, 1960
Railroad Ferry
FERRY
Don
Khoper
Medveditsa
Volga
Samara
Belaya
Ural
Zhayyq
Or
Tobyl
Kuma
Terek
Samur
Qezel Owzan
Atrak
Sumbar
Irghyz
Torghay
Ulyzhylanshyq
Zharman Köli
Lipetsk
Gryazi
Michurinsk
Tambov
Kotovsk
Rasskazovo
Kirsanov
Shatsk
Morshansk
Zemetchino
Kamenka
Nizhniy Lomov
Penza
Kuznetsk
Serdobsk
Ruzayevka
Saransk
Insar
Romodanovo
Ardatov
Alatyr'
Kirya
Buinsk
Tetyushi
Ul'yanovsk
Inza
Nikol'sk
Barysh
Sengiley
Dimitrovgrad
Tol'yatti
Syzran'
Samara
Kinel'
Chapayevsk
Otradnyy
Pokhvistnevo
Kamyshla
Leninogorsk
Al'met'yevsk
Nizhnekamsk
Naberezhnyye Chelny
Zainsk
Urussu
Bavly
Oktyabr'skiy
Tuymazy
Belebey
Abdulino
Rayevskiy
Birsk
Askino
Ufa
Sterlitamak
Salavat
Ishimbay
Meleuz
Kumertau
Krasnousol'skiy
Beloretsk
Asha
Min'yar
Bakal
Satka
Yuryuzan'
Katav-Ivanovsk
Krasnyy Klyuch
Duvan
Nyazepetrovsk
Verkhniy Ufaley
Kasli
Kyshtym
Kusa
Zlatoust
Miass
Chebarkul'
Chelyabinsk
Brodokalmak
Shadrinsk
Kurgan
Shumikha
Kurtamysh
Korkino
Yemanzhelinsk
Plast
Troitsk
Komsomolets
Uzynköl
Borovskoy
Fedorovka
Qostanay
Zatobyl
Rūdnyy
Saryköl
Lisakovsk
Tobyl
Qarasu
Qusmuryn
Äülieköl
Oktyabr'skoe
Ordzhonikidze
Zhetiqara
Muktiköl
Doküchaev
Zhayylma
Ozernyy
Yasnyy
Dombarovskiy
Orsk
Novoorsk
Gay
Iriklinskiy
Kuvandyk
Mednogorsk
Novotroitsk
Magnitogorsk
Agapovka
Verkhneural'sk
Kartaly
Bredy
Tubinskiy
Sibay
Baymak
Kizil'skoye
Mrakovo
Tyul'gan
Isyangulovo
Oktyabr'skoye
Sakmara
Orenburg
Saraktash
Pervomayskiy
Chernyy Otrog
Novosergiyevka
Sorochinsk
Buzuluk
Grachevka
Krasnyy Kholm
Ilek
Sol'-Iletsk
Akbulak
Buzuluk
Bol'shaya Glushitsa
Pugachev
Balakovo
Khvalynsk
Vol'sk
Marx
Engels
Saratov
Krasnoarmeysk
Pushkino
Yershov
Dergachi
Peremetnoe
Oral
Fedorovka
Krasnoye
Aqsay
Kamenka
Krasnyy Kut
Novouzensk
Zhangaghan
Oyan
Aqzhayyq
Alghabas
Shyngghyrlaū
Zhympity
Aleksandrov Gay
Pallasovka
Kaztalovka
Mergenevo
Zhänibek
El'ton
Pyatimarskoe
Saralzhyn
Kalenyy
Zhanga Qazan
Bazartöbe
Taypaq
Kamyshin
Nikolayevsk
Ilovlya
Frolovo
Serafimovich
Dubovka
Volgograd (Stalingrad)
Volzhskiy
Krasnoslobodsk
Sredneakhtubinsk
Saygyn
Akhtubinsk
Chernyy Yar
Nizhniy Baskunchak
Udachnoye
Sasykoli
Tsagan Aman
Sarpa
Seroglazovka
Elista
Priyutnoye
Divnoye
Ulan Erge
Yashkul'
Yuzhnyy
Aqköl
Krasnyy Yar
Zabūrün'e
Astrakhan'
Trudfront
Oranzherei
Mumra
Kirovskiy
Kaspiyskiy
Ulan Khol
Blagodarnyy
Neftekumsk
Budennovsk
Zelenokumsk
Staryy Biryuzyak
Bryansk
Kizlyar
Malgobek
Beslan
Magas
Grozny
Vladikavkaz
Kazbek
Lopatin
Sulak
Buynaksk
Makhachkala
Kaspiysk
Achisu
Izberbash
Gunib
Kumukh
Beriket
Derbent
Tbilisi (Tbilisi)
T'elavi
Tsnori
Tsiteli Tskaro
Agstafa
Tovuz
Qusar
Quba
Xaçmaz
Xudat
Şäki
Gäncä
Yevlax
Mingäçevir
Göyçay
Salyan
Sumqayıt
Sabunçu
Bakı (Baku)
Ağdam
Akna (Ağdam)
Stepanakert (Xankändi)
Karaghbyur (Füzuli)
Goris
Kapan
İmişli
Äli Bayramli
Chalmeh
Salyan
Äläť
Biläsuvar
Banka
Neftçala
Şafarābād
Kaleybar
Ahar
Germi
Port-İliç
Länkäran
Astara
Namin
Şūfiān
Tabrīz
Ardabīl
Sarāb
Nīr
Āzarān
Marāgheh
Bonab
Kargānrūd
Khalkhāl
Mīāneh
Bandar-e Anzalī
Rasht
Lāhījān
Rudsar
Rūdbār
Phraaspa
Shāhīn Dezh
Takāb
Zanjān
Dīvāndarreh
Qazvīn
Tākestān
Tonekābon
Chālūs
Āmol
Bandar-e Torkaman
Gorgān
Gomīshān
Gonbad-e Kāvūs
Āzād Shahr
Nardīn
Chaman Bīd
Bojnūrd
Shīrvān
Bājgīrān
Kaka
Tejen
Mary
Bayramaly
Atamyrat
Kerkiçi
Mukry
Qarshi
Yangi-Nishon
Tollimarjon
Karabekaul
Üçajy
Sayat
Muborak
Türkmenabat (Chärjew)
Seydi
Qorakül
Qorovulbozor
Buxoro (Bukhara)
Navoiy
Qoqtosh
Karmana
Gazli
Gabakly
Zafarobod
Nurota
Darganata
Sarimoy
Gazojak
Mynbulaq
Uchquduq
Zarafshon
Muruntau
Kulkuduk
Türtkül
Beruniy
Khiwa
Daşoguz
Akdepe
Köneürgench
Takhiatosh
Nukus
Khŭjayli
Shumanay
Qunghirot
Chimboy
Uchsay
Zhaslyk
Qaraqalpakstan
Kamennoe
Beyneu
Turysh
Dūghara
Qulandy
Sorqudyq
Akespe
Aral
Sekseūil
Qamystybas
Bögen
Äyteke Bi
Qazaly
Bayqongyr (Baykonur, Leninsk)
Zhosaly
Terengözek
Zhanadarīya
Qyzylorda
Kumkol
Bayqongyr
Togyz
Zhalauly
Shalqar
Sarysay
Yrghyz
Birshoghyr
Kozhasay
Ebeyti
Saghyz
Bayghanīn
Temir
Rodniki
Oktyabr'sk
Shubarquduyq
Oyyl
Miyaly
Qarabey
Kemer
Aqtaysay
Qaratöbe
Qobda
Īl'īnka
Alga
Aqtöbe
Qarghaly
Khromtaū
Badamsha
Almaznoe
Aqyrab
Mortyq
Leninskoe
Komsomol'skoe
Shīlī
Zhaldama
Amangeldi
Qarabutaq
Torghay
Inderbor
Makhambet
Novobogatīnskoe
Atyraū
Zhumysker
Balyqshy
Maqat
Dossor
Qorsaq
Qosshaghyl
Qulsary
Bīikzhal
Zhanbīke
Qaraoba
Qarazhar
Dongyztaū
Qaraton
Tengiz
Prorva
Opornyy
Fort Shevchenko
Qyzan
Taūshyq
Shetpe
Saūtesh
Syghyndy
Aqtaū
Zhetibay
Ozen
Qūryq
Zhangaözen
Aksu
Karabogaz (Bekdash)
Garabogazköl
Dashkuduk
Türkmenbaşy
Gyzylsuw
Koshoba
Gyzylgaya
Oglanly
Uly Balkan Gershi
Çeleken
Balkanabat
Gumdag
Gazanjyk
Gyzylarbat
Darvaza
Yerbent
Bokurdak
Bamy
Archman
Garrygala
Bugdayly
Gamyshlyja
Ekerem
Madaw
Sharlawuk
Maraveh Tappeh
Esenguly
Gyzyletrek
Chaloyuk
Gökdepe
Büzmeyin
Aşgabat (Ashgabat)
Babadaykhan
Tejen
Morozovsk
Oktyabr'skiy
Volgodonsk
Kotel'nikovo
Zavetnoye
Veshenskaya
Mikhaylovka
Novoanninskiy
Uryupinsk
Kalach
Buturlinovka
Borisoglebsk
Povorino
Balashov
Kalininsk
Arkadak
Atkarsk
Muchkapskiy
Zherdevka
Voronezh
54°
42°
45°
48°
51°
54°
57°
60°
63°
51°
48°
45°
42°
39°
36°
329
332
179
250
261
1271
1040
657
-20
-28
556
19
1880
2243
3303
3710
4811
4127
5033
5
11
49
790
1025
781
44
68

TYUMEN
OMSK
Omsk
NOVOSIBIRSK
Novosibirsk
SOLTÜSTIK QAZAQSTAN
Petropavlovsk
Kökshetaū
AQMOLA
Astana
PAVLODAR
Pavlodar
Ekibastuz
ALTAY
Barnaul
Biysk
Prokop'yevsk
KHAKASIYA
TYVA (TUVA)
GORNO-ALTAY
Gorno-Altaysk
UVS
MONGOLIA
BAYAN-ÖLGIY
Rubtsovsk
Semey (Semipalatinsk)
Öskemen (Ust' Kamenogorsk)
SEMIPALATINSK NUCLEAR TEST SITE (closed in 1991)
SHYGHYS QAZAQSTAN
Qaraghandy
Temirtaū
KAZAKH
H S T A N
UPLANDS
QARAGHANDY
Zaysan Köli
Tarbagatay Zhotasy
Tacheng (Qoqek)
Junggar Pendi (Dzungarian Basin)
Karamay
Dzungarian Gate
Balqash Köli
Balqash
Seryesik-Atyraū Qumy
ALMATY
Almaty
Taldyqorghan
BETPAQDALA
Ashchy Köl
Moyynqum
ZHAMBYL
Qaratau Zhotasy
ONGTÜSTIK QAZAQSTAN
Shymkent
Taraz
Bishkek
ALA-ARCHA N.P.
Kyrgyz Range
Ysyk-Köl
KYRGYZSTAN
TIAN SHAN
Khan Tängiri (Khan Tengri)
Jengish Chokusu (Pobedy Peak, Victory Peak)
Boharo Shan
Ürümqi
Shihezi
Changji
Fukang
Yining (Gulja)
Korla
XINJIANG UYGUR (SINKIANG)
CHINA
TARIM PENDI
TAKLIMAKAN SHAMO
Aksu
Kashi (Kashgar)
Shache (Yarkant)
Hotan
Toshkent (Tashkent)
Chirchiq
Angren
Namangan
Andijon
Farg'ona
Qo'qon
Osh
Fergana Valley
Khujand
Jizzax
Samarqand
Zarafshon Range
Turkestan Range
Alay Mts.
TAJIKISTAN
Dushanbe
Qullai Ismoili Somoni (Communism Peak)
Pamirs
Lenin Peak
Kongur Shan
Muztagata
AFGHANISTAN
Khorugh
LAMBERT CONFORMAL CONIC PROJECTION
SCALE 1:8,000,000
0 KILOMETERS 120 160 200
0 MILES 40 80 120 160 200

TURKEY
KURDISTAN
ARMENIA
AZERBAIJAN
NAGORNO-KARABAKH
SYRIA
JORDAN
IRAQ
KUWAIT
SAUDI ARABIA
BAHRAIN
QATAR
UNITED ARAB EMIRATES
IRAN
CASPIAN SEA
PERSIAN GULF
MESOPOTAMIA
ZAGROS MTS.
FARS
Syrian Desert
Reshteh-ye Alborz (Elburz Mountains)
Dasht-e Kavir (Salt Desert)
An Nafūd
Ad Dahnā'
Şahrā' al Ḩijārah
Al Ḩamād
Jabal Shammar
Al Qaşīm
Jabal Ţuwayq
Nafūd ad Dahy
Aş Şummān
As Sanām
Apsheron Yarymadasy
ABU MUSA Island is claimed by Iran and U.A.E. and jointly administered by them.
Erzincan
Erzurum
Sarıkamış
Horasan
Ağrı (Karaköse)
Mt. Ararat
Yerevan
Gäncä
Yevlax
Göyçay
Sumqayıt
Bakı (Baku)
Sabunçu
Elazığ
Malatya
Divriği
Bingöl
Muş
Malazgirt
Patnos
Erciş
Van Gölü
Van
Tatvan
Bitlis
Ahlat
Diyarbakır
Batman
Siirt
Adıyaman
Gaziantep
Şanlıurfa (Edessa)
Viranşehir
Mardin
Midyat
Cizre
Al Qāmishlī
Ceylanpınar
Nizip
Jarābulus
Hakkari
Yüksekova
Şemdinli
Khoy
Marand
Tabrīz
Orūmīyeh (Urmia)
Marāgheh
Ardabīl
Astara
Länkäran
Rasht
Bandar-e Anzalī
Zanjān
Qazvīn
Karaj
Tajrīsh
TEHRAN
Rey
Qolleh-ye Damāvand
Āmol
Bābol
Sārī
Qā'emshahr
Gorgān
Türkmenbaşy
Ar Raqqah
Zenobia
Dayr az Zawr
Al Mayādīn
Tadmur
Abū Kamāl
Al Ḩasakah
Al Mawşil (Mosul)
Arbīl
Karkūk (Kirkūk)
As Sulaymānīyah
Sanandaj
Hamadān (Ecbatana)
Qom (Qum)
Kāshān
Arāk
Borūjerd
Kermānshāh
Īlām
Khorramābād
Sāmarrā'
Baghdād
Al Fallūjah (Fallujah)
Ar Ramādī
Ar Ruţbah
Karbalā'
Babylon
Al Ḩillah
An Najaf (Najaf)
Ad Dīwānīyah
Al Kūt
Al 'Amārah
An Nāşirīyah (Nasiriyah)
Al Başrah (Basra)
Ābādān
Khorramshahr
Dezfūl
Ahvāz (Ahwāz)
Masjed Soleymān
Esfahan (Isfahan)
Khomeynīshahr
Najafābād
Shahrezā
Yazd
Shīrāz
Persepolis
Būshehr
Khārk
Sīrjān
Bandar 'Abbās
Qeshm
Kīsh
Al Kuwayt (Kuwait City)
Al Jumaymah
Ḩafar al Bāţin
King Khalid Military City
Ḩā'il
Buraydah
'Unayzah
Ad Dammām
Al Manāmah (Manama)
Al Hufūf (Hofūf)
Ghawar Oil Field
Ad Dawḩah (Doha)
Ar Riyāḑ (Riyadh)
Al Kharj
Abu Dhabi
Dubai
Sharjah
Al 'Ayn
Liwa
Aţ Ţā'if
39°
42°
45°
48°
51°
54°
36°
33°
30°
27°
24°

TURKMENISTAN

UZBEKISTAN

TAJIKISTAN

KYRGYZ.

CHINA

AFGHANISTAN

PAKISTAN

INDIA

OMAN

KASHMIR

JAMMU AND KASHMIR

AZAD KASHMIR

GILGIT-BALTISTAN

KHYBER-PAKHTUNKHWA

FED. ADMIN. TRIBAL AREAS

PUNJAB

BALOCHISTAN

SINDH

RAJASTHAN

GUJARAT

BALUCHISTAN

SISTAN

HAZARAJAT

FIROZ KOH

ROBAT-E KHOSHK AVEH

PUSHT-I-RUD

Dasht-e Khash

BAND-E-AMIR NAT. PARK

KHUNJERAB NAT. PARK

KIRTHAR NAT. PARK

DESERT N.P.

HINGOL NAT. PARK

GIR N.P.

DACHIGAM N.P.

Thar Desert (Great Indian Desert)

RAJASTHAN CANAL

GARAGUM CANAL

Garagum

Dasht-e Lut

Hamun-e Jaz Murian

GULF OF OMAN

ARABIAN SEA

Sonmiani Bay

Mouths of the Indus

Rann of Kutch

HINDU KUSH

PAMIR

KARAKORAM RANGE

Turkestan Range

Zarafshon Range

Atrak Mts.

Cities and towns:

Ashgabat (Ashgabat), Türkmenabat (Chärjew), Mary, Bayramaly, Tejen, Mashhad, Neyshābūr, Sabzevār, Quchān, Bojnūrd, Birjand, Kermān, Zāhedān, Bam, Herat, Chaghcharan, Kabol (Kabul), Kandahar, Zaranj, Quetta, Multan, Lahore, Faisalabad, Gujranwala, Rawalpindi, Islamabad, Peshawar, Jammu, Srinagar, Amritsar, Jullundur, Bikaner, Ajmer, Udaipur, Ahmadabad, Gandhinagar, Vadodara, Surat, Rajkot, Jamnagar, Bhavnagar, Junagadh, Porbandar, Karachi, Hyderabad, Sukkur, Larkana, Nawabshah, Mirpur Khas, Dushanbe, Samarqand, Buxoro (Bukhara), Navoiy, Qarshi, Termiz, Mazar-e Sharif, Muscat (Masqaṭ)

Navoiy, Jizzax, Nurota, Karmana, Qiziltepa, Gazli, Zafarobod

Physical features & peaks:
Communism Peak (Qullai Ismoili Somoni), 7495, Muztagata, 7649, Rakaposhi 7885, Tirich Mir 7690, Nanga Parbat 8126, Kuh-e Hazārān 4420, Kūh-e Taftān 4042, Kūh-e Bazmān 3489, 3962

Passes:
Khyber Pass, Bolan Pass, Khunjerab Pass, Mingteke Pass, Shandur Pass, Babusar Pass, Kowtal-e Salang, Jaman Pass

LINE OF CONTROL

Boundary claimed by India

Boundary claimed by China

TROPIC OF CANCER

LAMBERT CONFORMAL CONIC PROJECTION

SCALE 1:8,000,000

0 KILOMETERS 120 160 200

0 MILES 40 80 120 160 200

UZBEKISTAN
KAZ.
KYRGYZSTAN
TAJIKISTAN
TURKM.
AFGHANISTAN
PAKISTAN
INDIA
CHINA
NEPAL
BHUTAN
BANGLADESH
MYANMAR (BURMA)
TAKLIMAKAN SHAMO
XINJIANG UYGUR (SINKIANG)
XIZANG (TIBET)
QINGHAI
GANSU
QING ZANG GAOYUAN
ALTUN SHAN
KUNLUN SHAN
HIMALAYA
HINDU KUSH
KASHMIR
AKSAI CHIN
JAMMU AND KASHMIR
GILGIT-BALTISTAN
KHYBER-PAKHTUNKHWA
AZAD KASHMIR
FEDERALLY ADMINISTERED TRIBAL AREAS
ISLAMABAD CAP. TERR.
PUNJAB
HIMACHAL PRADESH
UTTARAKHAND
HARYANA
UTTAR PRADESH
RAJASTHAN
SINDH
BALOCHISTAN
GUJARAT
MADHYA PRADESH
MAHARASHTRA
BIHAR
JHARKHAND
WEST BENGAL
ORISSA
CHHATTISGARH
SIKKIM
ASSAM
MEGHALAYA
ARUNACHAL PRADESH
NAGALAND
MANIPUR
MIZORAM
TRIPURA
DAMAN AND DIU
DADRA AND NAGAR HAVELI
India and Pakistan both claim Kashmir—a disputed region of some 10 million people. India administers only the area south of the line of control; Pakistan controls northwestern Kashmir. China took eastern Kashmir from India in a 1962 war.
LINE OF CONTROL
Boundary claimed by India
Boundary claimed by Pak.
Boundary claimed by China
Mt. Everest (Sagarmatha, Qomolangma) 8850 (29035 ft)
TROPIC OF CANCER
Mouths of the Ganges
Toshkent (Tashkent)
Samarqand
Dushanbe
Kabol (Kabul)
Islamabad
Rawalpindi
Peshawar
LAHORE
KARACHI
Hyderabad
Quetta
Kandahar
Mazar-e Sharif
Srinagar
DELHI
New Delhi
Jaipur
Lucknow
Kanpur
Agra
Ahmadabad
(BOMBAY) MUMBAI
Pune
Nagpur
Bhopal
Indore
Kolkata (Calcutta)
Patna
Varanasi (Banaras)
Kathmandu
Thimphu
Dhaka
Chittagong
Lhasa
Golmud
Dunhuang
Kashi (Kashgar)
Shache (Yarkant)
Hotan
Aksu
Korla
Mandalay
Nay Pyi Taw
Yangon (Rangoon)
63°
66°
69°
72°
75°
78°
81°
84°
87°
90°
93°
96°
99°
39°
36°
33°
30°
27°
24°
21°
18°

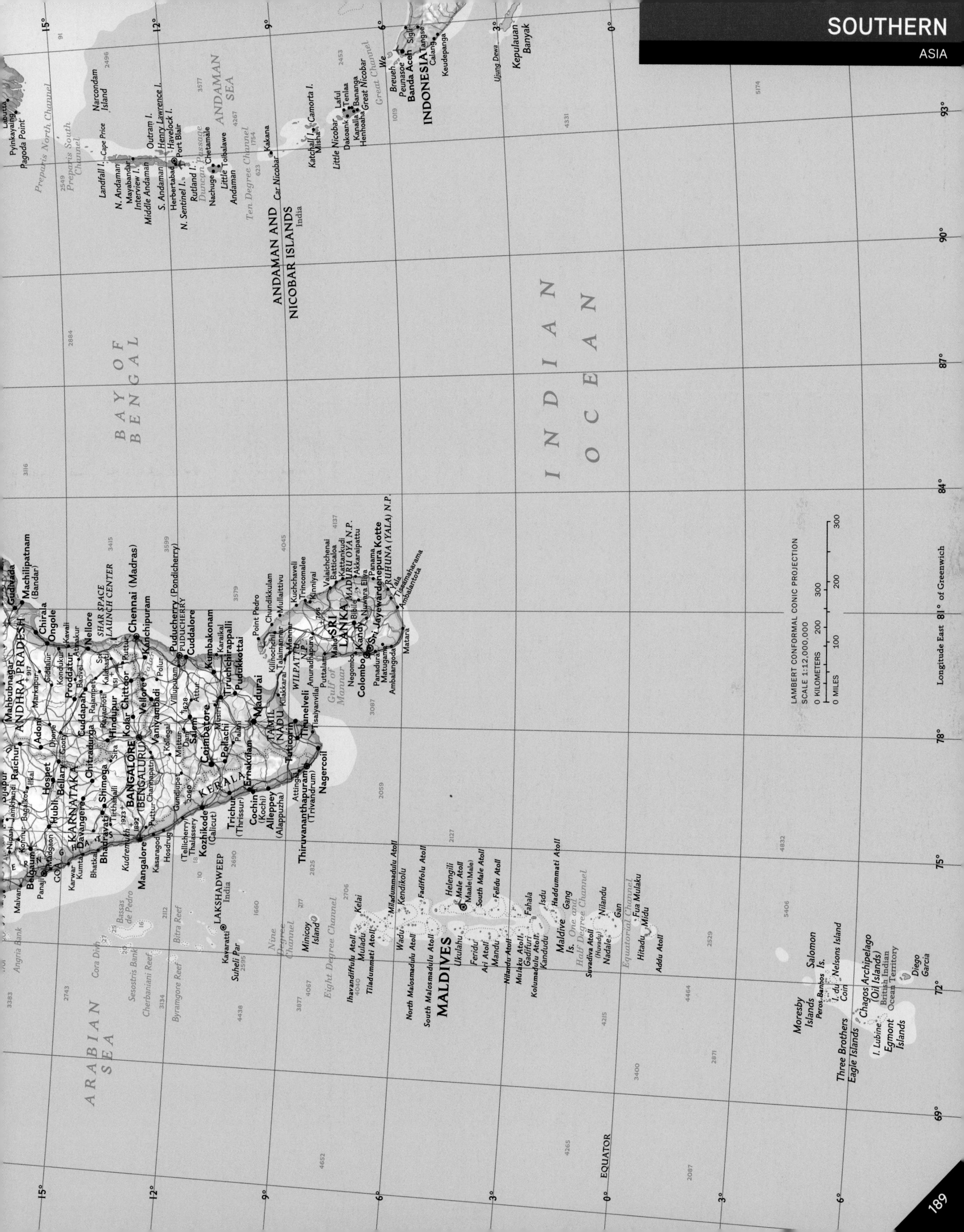

Laburta
Pyinkayaing
Pagoda Point

Preparis North Channel
91
Narcondam Island
2496

Preparis South Channel
2549

Landfall I. Cape Price
N. Andaman
Mayabandar
Interview I.
Middle Andaman
Outram I.
Henry Lawrence I.
Havelock I.
S. Andaman
Herbertabad
Port Blair
Rutland I.
N. Sentinel I.
Duncan Passage
Nachuge
Chetamale
Little
Tottalawe
Andaman
4267

ANDAMAN SEA

3577

Ten Degree Channel
1754
623

Kakana
Katchall I. Camorta I.
Little Nicobar
Misha
Laful
Dakoank
Tenloa
Kanalla
Bananga
Henhoaha
Great Nicobar
Car Nicobar

ANDAMAN AND
NICOBAR ISLANDS
India

Great Channel
1019

Breueh
Peunasoe
We
Sigli
Calang
Banda Aceh
Tangse
Keudepanga

INDONESIA

Ujung Dewa
Kepulauan
Banyak

BAY OF BENGAL

2884

3116

INDIAN OCEAN

5174

Gudivada
Machilipatnam (Bandar)
Mahbubnagar
ANDHRA PRADESH
Raichur
917
Chirala
Ongole
Nellore
SHAR SPACE
LAUNCH CENTER
3415
Chennai (Madras)
Kanchipuram
Puducherry (Pondicherry)
PUDUCHERRY
Cuddalore
3599
Kumbakonam
Karaikal
Tiruchirappalli
Pudukkottai
3579

Point Pedro
Chundikkulam
Kuchchaveli
Trincomalee
Kinniyai
Valaichchenai
Batticaloa
MADURU OYA N.P.
Kattankudi
Akkaraipattu
Bibile
Nuwara Eliya
Panama
RUHUNA (YALA) N.P.
Tissamaharama
Yala
Ambalantota

4137

4045

WILPATTU N.P.
Kilinochchi
Mullaittivu
Talaimannar
Mannar
Anuradhapura
Puttalam
Chilaw
SRI LANKA
Kandy
Negombo
Colombo
Sri Jayewardenepura Kotte
Panadura
Matugama
Ambalangoda
Matara

766

3097

2059

Proddatur
Cuddapah
Rajampet
Kavali
Atmakur
Kondukur
Markapur
Kalahasti
Puttur
Tiruttani
Vellore
Chittoor
Kolar
Polur
Villupuram
Vaniyambadi
Salem
Attur
Mettur
Dam
1628
Coimbatore
Pollachi
Palani
Madurai
TAMIL
NADU
Tuticorin
Tirunelveli
Thoothukudi
Tsalyanvila
Kilakkarai
Gulf of Mannar

Mahbubnagar
Kurnool
Adoni
Dhone
Sira
KARNATAKA
Chitradurga
Hindupur
Tumkur
BANGALORE
BENGALURU
Kolhegal
Mysore
Gundlupet

KERALA
Trichur (Thrissur)
Cochin (Kochi)
Alleppey (Alappuzha)
Thiruvananthapuram (Trivandrum)
Nagercoil
Ernakulam
Kollam
Attingal

1923
1892

Vijayapur
Jamkhandi
Gadag
Ranebennur
Raichur
Hospet
Bellary
Davangere
Shimoga
Bhadravati
Chikmagalur
Tiruthani

Bagalkot
Ilkal
Belgaum
Panaji
GOA
KARNATAKA
Karwar
Kumta
Bhatkal
Kudremukh
Kasaragod
Mangalore
Hosdrug
Kannur
Thalassery (Tellicherry)
Kozhikode (Calicut)

Mahé

Malvan
Ratnagiri
Kolhapur

ARABIAN SEA

3383
2743
Bassas de Pedro
16
Cora Divh
27
3134
Sesostris Bank
Cherbaniani Reef
4438
Byramgore Reef
2112
Bitra Reef
LAKSHADWEEP
India
1660
Kavaratti
Suheli Par
2595
Angria Bank
Agatti

10
2690

Nine Degree Channel

277
Minicoy Island
4067
3877
2825

Eight Degree Channel
Ihavandiffulu Atoll
4040
Muladu
2706
Kelai
Miladummadulu Atoll
Kendikolu
Fadiffolu Atoll
Helengili
Maale (Male)
Male Atoll
South Male Atoll
2127
Felidu Atoll

MALDIVES

Tiladummati Atoll
Wadu
North Malosmadulu Atoll
South Malosmadulu Atoll
Ukulahu
Feridu
Ari Atoll
Nilandu Atoll
Mulaku Atoll
Kolumadulu Atoll
Kandudu
Fahala
Isdu
Haddummati Atoll
Gang
Maldive
Gadifuri
Is. One and
Half Degree Channel
Suvadiva Atoll
(Hundu)
Nadale
Nilandu
Gan
Hitadu
Fua Mulaku
Midu
Addu Atoll

Equatorial Channel

4832

Three Brothers
Eagle Islands
Moresby
Islands
Peros Banhos Is.
Salomon Is.
I. du Coin
Nelsons Island
Chagos Archipelago
I. Lubine
(Oil Islands)
Egmont
Islands
British Indian
Ocean Territory
Diego Garcia

5406

4464
2529
2871
3400

4265

4652

4215

2087

EQUATOR

LAMBERT CONFORMAL CONIC PROJECTION
SCALE 1:12,000,000
0 KILOMETERS 100 200 300
0 MILES 100 200 300

Longitude East 81° of Greenwich

KAZAKHSTAN
Kazakh Uplands
Astana
Pavlodar
Ekibastuz
Qaraghandy
Semey (Semipalatinsk)
Öskemen (Ust' Kamenogorsk)
Ridder (Leninogorsk)
Barnaul
Novokuznetsk
Biysk
Gorno Altaysk
ALTAY
NOVO.
KEMEROVO
KHAKASIYA
Abakan
Minusinsk
KRASNOYARSK
IRKUTSK
Irkutsk
Angarsk
Ulan Ude
Ozero Baykal
RUSSIA
GORNO-ALTAY
TYVA (TUVA)
Kyzyl
BAYKONUR COSMODROME
Russian-administered
Bayqongyr (Baykonur, Leninsk)
Qyzylorda
Moyynqum
Qaratau Zhotasy
Balqash
Balqash Köli
Zaysan Köli
Tarbagatay Zhotasy
Toshkent (Tashkent)
Shymkent
Taraz
UZBEKISTAN
Namangan
Andijon
KYRGYZSTAN
Bishkek
Almaty
Osh
TAJIKISTAN
Dushanbe
Qullai Ismoili Somoni (Communism Peak) 7495
Pamirs
AFGHAN.
HINDU KUSH
Kyber Pass
Peshawar
Islamabad
Rawalpindi
PAKISTAN
Gujranwala
Sialkot
Faisalabad
LAHORE
Ludhiana
Jalandhar
Srinagar
Jammu
Leh
Nanga Parbat 8126
K2 (Godwin Austen, Qogir) 8611
Karakoram Range
AKSAI CHIN
Boundary claimed by India
Boundary claimed by Pakistan
Boundary claimed by China
Kashi (Kashgar)
Shache (Yarkant)
Hotan
Yutian
Minfeng
Aksu
Kuqa
Korla
Ürümqi
Bogda Feng 5445
Turpan (Turfan)
Turpan Depression -154
Hami (Kumul)
Yining
Dzungarian Gate
Junggar Pendi (Dzungarian Basin)
Karamay
XINJIANG UYGUR
TAKLIMAKAN SHAMO
Tarim
Lop Nur
Qiemo
Qarqan
ALTUN SHAN
KUNLUN SHAN
Muztag 6973
Hoh Xil Shan
Dogaicoring Qangco
QING ZANG GAOYUAN
XIZANG (TIBET)
Tanggula Shan
Tanggula Shankou
Gangdisê Shan
Ngangiong Kangri 6720
Gar
Tangra Yumco
Xainza
Lhasa
Xigazê
Gyangzê
Nyainqêntanglha Shan
Yarlung Zangbo (Brahmaputra)
Mt. Everest (Qomolangma, Sagarmatha) 8850 (29035 ft)
Kangto 7089
Dunhuang
Anxi
Yumen (Laojunmiao)
Jiayuguan
JIUQUAN SPACE LAUNCH CENTER
Qilian Shan
Zhangye
GANSU
Wuwei
Golmud
Qaidam Pendi
QINGHAI
Qinghai Hu
Xining
Lanzhou
Kunlun Shankou
Bayan Har Shankou
Bayan Har Shan
Tongtian (Yangtze)
Yushu
Qamdo
Nu (Salween)
Lancang (Mekong)
CHINA
NINGXIA HUIZU
Yinchuan
Baotou
INNER MONGOLIA
SHAANXI
Xi'an
Tianshui
Baoji
Hanzhong
Daba Shan
SICHUAN
CHENGDU
Nanchong
Mianyang
Gongga Shan 7556
XICHANG SPACE LAUNCH CENTER
Xichang
CHONGQING
CHONGQING SHI
Zigong
Yibin
Luzhou
Zunyi
Guiyang
GUIZHOU
Anshun
Panzhihua
YUNNAN
Kunming
Dali
Gejiu
GUANGXI ZHUANG
Nanning
Zhanjiang
Maoming
HAINAN
Gulf of Tonkin
VIETNAM
Hanoi
Haiphong
LAOS
Vientiane
Louangphrabang
THAILAND
Lampang
MYANMAR (BURMA)
Mandalay
Nay Pyi Taw
(Rangoon) Yangon
Myitkyina
Lashio
Arakan Yoma
Sittwe
Chittagong
BAY OF BENGAL
BANGLADESH
Dhaka
Khulna
Kolkata (Calcutta)
Mizo Hills
Naga Hills
Guwahati
Shillong
Imphal
BHUTAN
Thimphu
NEPAL
Kathmandu
Dhaulagiri 8172
HIMALAYA
INDIA
DELHI
New Delhi
Great Indian Desert
Meerut
Moradabad
Bareilly
Dehra Dun
Nanda Devi 7817
Aligarh
Agra
Jaipur
Ajmer
Shahjahanpur
Kanpur
Lucknow
Gwalior
Jhansi
Kota
Gorakhpur
Allahabad
Varanasi (Banaras)
Patna
Gaya
Bhagalpur
Bhopal
Jabalpur
Ranchi
Jamshedpur
Nagpur
Amravati
Akola
Raipur
Cuttack
EASTERN GHATS
Hyderabad
Vishakhapatnam
Kakinada (Cocanada)
Rajahmundry
Vijayawada
Guntur
Nellore
MONGOLIA
ALTAY MTS.
Ulaanbaatar (Ulan Bator)
Hangayn Nuruu
Hovd (Dund-Us)
Ölgiy
Ulaangom
Uliastay
Mörön
Hövsgöl Nuur
Dalandzadgad
Saynshand (Buyant-Uhaa)
Edrengiyn Nuruu
Ejin Qi
GOBI
48°
42°
36°
30°
24°
18°
66°
72°
78°
84°
90°
96°
102°
108°

KURIL ISLANDS
The southern Kuril Islands of Iturup (Etorofu), Kunashir (Kunashiri), Shikotan, and the Habomai group were lost by Japan to the Soviet Union in 1945. Japan continues to claim these Russian-administered islands.
TAIWAN
The People's Republic of China claims Taiwan as its 23rd province. Taiwan's government (Republic of China) maintains that there are two political entities. The islands of Dongsha, Kinmen, Matsu and Penghu are administered by Taiwan.
LAMBERT CONFORMAL CONIC PROJECTION
SCALE 1:16,000,000
0 KILOMETERS 300 400
0 MILES 100 200 300 400
Longitude East 132° of Greenwich
SEA OF OKHOTSK
SEA OF JAPAN (EAST SEA)
YELLOW SEA
EAST CHINA SEA
PHILIPPINE SEA
PACIFIC OCEAN
JAPAN
NORTH KOREA
SOUTH KOREA
TAIWAN
KURIL ISLANDS (KURIL'SKIYE OSTROVA)
OSTROV SAKHALIN
SAKHALIN
AMUR
KHABAROVSK
TRANS-BAIKAL
MARITIME TERRITORY
JEWISH AUTON. REG.
HEILONGJIANG
JILIN
LIAONING
NEI MONGOL
HEBEI
SHANDONG
JIANGSU
ANHUI
ZHEJIANG
JIANGXI
FUJIAN
GUANGDONG
HENAN
HUBEI
Dongbei (Manchuria)
Stanovoy Khrebet
Khrebet Dzhagdy
SVOBODNYY COSMODROME
Da Hinggan Ling
Xiao Hinggan Ling
Khrebet Sikhote Alin'
Tatarskiy Proliv
La Perouse Str.
Tsugaru Kaikyō
Korea Strait
Tsushima Strait
Taiwan Strait
Bashi Channel
Luzon Strait
Demarcation Line, July 27, 1953
BEIJING (PEKING)
TIANJIN (TIENTSIN)
SHANGHAI
SHENYANG
SEOUL
TŌKYŌ
Vladivostok
Khabarovsk
Harbin
Changchun
P'yŏngyang
Busan (Pusan)
Daegu (Taegu)
Daejeon (Taejon)
Incheon (Inch'ŏn)
Dalian (Dairen)
Qingdao
Nanjing
Hangzhou
Fuzhou
Taipei
Kaohsiung
GUANGZHOU (CANTON)
DONGGUAN
SHENZHEN
HONG KONG, S.A.R.
Macau, S.A.R.
WUHAN
Sapporo
Hakodate
Aomori
Sendai
Niigata
Yokohama
Nagoya
Kyōto
Ōsaka
Kōbe
Hiroshima
Kitakyūshū
Fukuoka
Nagasaki
Kagoshima
Naha
Okinawa
HOKKAIDŌ
HONSHŪ
SHIKOKU
KYŪSHŪ
TANEGASHIMA SPACE CENTER
KAGOSHIMA SPACE CENTER
NANSEI SHOTŌ (RYUKYU ISLANDS)
IZU SHOTŌ
Bonin Islands (Ogasawara Guntō)
Volcano Is. (Kazan Rettō) Japan
Iwo Jima (Sulphur Island)
Daitō Islands
Hachijō Jima
Jeju
Jeju-Do S. Korea
Dongsha (Pratas I.)
Batan Is.
Babuyan Is.
LUZON
PHILIPPINES
TROPIC OF CANCER
114°
120°
126°
132°
138°
144°
150°
42°
36°
30°
24°
18°

CHINA
INDIA
BANGLADESH
MYANMAR (BURMA)
LAOS
VIETNAM
THAILAND
CAMBODIA
MALAYSIA
SINGAPORE
BRUNEI
INDONESIA
TAIWAN
YUNNAN
GUIZHOU
GUANGXI ZHUANG
GUANGDONG
HUNAN
JIANGXI
FUJIAN
HAINAN
SABAH
SARAWAK
LUZON
MINDORO
PALAWAN
PANAY
BORNEO (KALIMANTAN)
SUMATRA
JAVA
BALI
LOMBOK
SUMBAWA
FLORES
SUMBA
SULAWESI (CELEBES)
GREATER SUNDA ISLANDS
LESSER SUNDA ISL
BAY OF BENGAL
ANDAMAN SEA
GULF OF THAILAND
SOUTH CHINA SEA
SULU SEA
CELEBES SEA
JAVA SEA
BALI SEA
FLORES SEA
INDIAN OCEAN
Gulf of Martaban
Gulf of Tonkin
Strait of Malacca
Makassar Strait
Taiwan Strait
Bashi Channel
Balabac Strait
Preparis North Channel
Ten Degree Channel
Great Channel
ANDAMAN IS. India
NICOBAR ISLANDS India
North Andaman
Middle Andaman
South Andaman
Little Andaman
Camorta I.
Little Nicobar
Great Nicobar
Mergui Archipelago
Paracel Is.
PARACEL ISLANDS
Occupied by China in 1974, which calls them Xisha Qundao; claimed by Vietnam, which calls them Hoàng Sa.
SPRATLY ISLANDS
The scattered islands and reefs called the Spratly Islands are claimed by Brunei, China, Malaysia, the Philippines, Taiwan, and Vietnam. The Spratlys possess rich fishing grounds and potential oil.
North Luconia Shoals MALAYSIA
Malaysia includes peninsular Malaysia, Sarawak, and Sabah; the capital is Kuala Lumpur.
Kep. Natuna Besar
Kep. Natuna Selatan Indonesia
Kep. Anambas
KEP. RIAU
KEP. LINGGA
Kep. Banyak
Kep. Batu
KEPULAUAN MENTAWAI
Kep. Karimata
Belitung (Billiton)
Bangka
Kep. Masalumbu
Kep. Kangean
Kep. Laut Kecil
Calamian Group
Sulu Archipelago
Christmas Island Australia
Dhaka
Chittagong
Khulna
Mandalay
Yangon (Rangoon)
Nay Pyi Taw
Sittwe
Pathein
Mawlamyine
Hanoi
Haiphong
Vientiane
KRUNG THEP (BANGKOK)
Phnom Penh
Ho Chi Minh City (Saigon)
Da Nang
Kunming
Nanning
GUANGZHOU (CANTON)
DONGGUAN
SHENZHEN
HONG KONG, S.A.R.
Macau S.A.R.
Taipei
Kaohsiung
MANILA
Quezon City
Kuala Lumpur
Putrajaya
George Town
Medan
Padang
Palembang
JAKARTA
Bandung
Surabaya
Semarang
Denpasar
Mataram
Makassar (Ujung Pandang)
Banjarmasin
Pontianak
Kuching
Balikpapan
Samarinda
Kota Kinabalu
Sandakan
Zamboanga
Puerto Princesa
EQUATOR
90°
96°
102°
108°
114°
120°
24°
18°
12°
6°
0°
LAMBERT CONFORMAL CONIC PROJECTION
SCALE 1:16,000,000
0 KILOMETERS 300 400
0 MILES 100 200 300 400

Longitude East 132° of Greenwich
PACIFIC OCEAN
PHILIPPINE SEA
TROPIC OF CANCER
EQUATOR
Naha
Okinawa
NANSEI SHOTŌ (RYUKYU ISLANDS)
Japan
Miyako
Ishigaki
DAITŌ ISLANDS
VOLCANO IS. (KAZAN RETTŌ) Japan
Maug Islands
Agrihan
Pagan
Alamagan
Guguan
Sarigan
Anatahan
NORTHERN MARIANA ISLANDS U.S.
Capital Hill
Saipan
Tinian
Hagåtña (Agana)
Guam U.S.
MICRONESIA
Ulithi Atoll
Yap Islands
Gaferut
Faraulep Atoll
Pigailoe (West Fayu Atoll)
Namonuito Atoll
Nomwin Atoll
Oroluk Atoll
Hall Islands
Ulul
Pikelot
Pulap Atoll
Chuuk (Truk Is.)
Losap Atoll
Ngulu Atoll
Sorol Atoll
PALAU
Babelthuap
Melekeok
Woleai Atoll
Ifalik Atoll
Elato Atoll
Lamotrek Atoll
Puluwat Atoll
Pulusuk
Eauripik Atoll
CAROLINE ISLANDS
FEDERATED STATES OF MICRONESIA
Namoluk Atoll
Etal Atoll
Lukunor Atoll
Mortlock Islands
Sonsorol Islands
Helen Island
PHILIPPINES
Naga
Catanduanes
Legazpi
SAMAR
Calbayog
Tacloban
Cebu
Baybay
Leyte
Siargao
Surigao
Bohol
Dumaguete
Bohol Sea
Dipolog
Iligan
Cagayan de Oro
Ozamis
Marawi
Cotabato
Davao
Mati
Digos
General Santos
MINDANAO
Sarangani Is.
Cape San Agustin
Kep. Nanusa
Beo
Kep. Talaud
Kep. Sangihe
Tahuna
Morotai
Manado
Amurang
Klabat
Kotamobagu
Gorontalo
BOGANI NANI WARTABONE N.P.
Molucca Sea
Tobelo
Jailolo
Ternate
HALMAHERA
Weda
Patani
Kepulauan Asia
Kepulauan Ayu
Kepulauan Mapia
MELANESIA
Waigeo
Gebe
Saonek
Sorong
Wosi
Bacan
Labuha
Salawati
Sailolof
Klamono
Manokwari
Supiori
Biak
Numfoor
Yapen
Serui
Ransiki
Irimi
Obi
Kep. Obi
Misool
Inanwatan
Teluk Berau
Wasior
Waren
Teluk Cenderawasih
Tanjung D'Urville
Sarmi
Demta
Jayapura
Genyem
Peleng
KEP. SULA
Mangole
Taliabu
Kep. Banggai
Sanana
BURU
Namlea
Ceram Sea
CERAM
Piru
Bula
Nif
Fakfak
Kokas
Kaimana
Karufa
Ambon
MANUSELA N.P.
Geser
Leksula
Ambelau
Kep. Banda
Kep. Gorong
Pegunungan Maoke
Puncak Jaya
Puncak Trikora
Puncak Mandala
Kokenau
GUNUNG LORENTZ N.P.
Agats
Taritatu
Kep. Kai
Tual
Dobo
Wokam
Kobroor
KEP. ARU
Trangan
BANDA SEA
Binongko
Molu
Larat
Yamdena
Saumlaki
Selaru
KEP. TANIMBAR
KEP. BARAT DAYA
Damar
Babar
Sermata
Moa
Wetar
Pantar
Alor
Atauro
Dili
Lautem
Tutuala
Lomblen
TIMOR-LESTE (EAST TIMOR)
Makasar
Nikiniki
Kupang
Roti
TIMOR SEA
ARAFURA SEA
Lynedock Bank
DOLAK
Tanjung Vals
Tanahmerah
Kepi
GUINEA
Digul
Muting
Okaba
Merauke
NEW GUINEA
PAPUA NEW GUINEA
Wuvulu Island
Ninigo Group
Sae Is.
Kaniet Islands
ADMIRALTY ISLANDS
Hermit Is.
Manus
Lorengau
Lou
Los Reyes Is.
Rambutyo
Purdy Is.
Ninigo Islands
Mussau Is.
Mussau
Ysabel Channel
New Hanover
Tabar Is.
Tatau
Lihir Group
Djaul
Boang
Schouten Is.
Mushu
Wewak
Manam
Karkar
Bagabag
Central Range
Bismarck Ra.
Ramu
Long I.
Umboi
BISMARCK SEA
BISMARCK ARCHIPELAGO
NEW IRELAND
Rabaul
Gazelle Pen.
Green Islands
Lolobau
Witu Is.
Willaumez Pen.
Cape St. George
Buka
Bougainville
NEW BRITAIN
Awio
Huon Pen.
Lae
SOLOMON SEA
Wau
Morobe
Kikori
Purari
Owen Stanley Ra.
Gulf of Papua
Kiwai
Mt. Victoria
Goodenough I.
TROBRIAND ISLANDS
Kiriwina
Madau
Fergusson I.
Woodlark
Normanby I.
LOUISIADE ARCHIPELAGO
Misima
Calvados Chain
Tagula
Sideia
Goschen Strait
Daru
TORRES STRAIT
Port Moresby
Kwikila
Hood Point
Abau
Boot Reefs
Prince of Wales Island
Cape York
GREAT BARRIER REEF MARINE PARK
Carpentaria Shoal
CORAL SEA
AUSTRALIA
Melville Island
Cobourg Peninsula
Croker Island
Wessel Islands
Marchinbar I.
Goulburn Is.
Elcho I.
Cape Wilberforce
GULF OF CARPENTARIA
Cape York Peninsula

EASTERN MEDITERRANEAN
ALBERS CONIC EQUAL-AREA PROJECTION
SCALE 1:2,250,000
0 KILOMETERS 40 60
0 MILES 20 40 60
Longitude East 33° of Greenwich
DIVIDED CYPRUS
Cyprus was partitioned in 1974 following a coup backed by Greece and an invasion by Turkey. The island is composed of a Greek Cypriot south with an internationally recognized government and a Turkish Cypriot north (gray) with a government recognized only by Turkey. The UN patrols the dividing line and works toward reunification of the island.
PALESTINE
The bounds of the historical region of Palestine have varied through time, but it is generally agreed that the land between the Mediterranean Sea and the Jordan River constitutes its core.
WEST BANK & GAZA STRIP
Captured by Israel in the 1967 Six Day War, a 1993 peace agreement gives areas of the West Bank and Gaza limited Palestinian autonomy. The future for these autonomous areas and 3 million Palestinians is subject to Israeli-Palestinian negotiations.
CYPRUS
NORTHERN CYPRUS
AKROTIRI (WESTERN) SOVEREIGN BASE AREA
U.K. Base
DHEKELIA (EASTERN) SOVEREIGN BASE AREA
MEDITERRANEAN SEA
LEBANON
SYRIA
ISRAEL
JORDAN
EGYPT
SINAI
NEGEV
GOLAN HEIGHTS
WEST BANK
GAZA STRIP
SYRIAN DESERT
Lefkosia (Nicosia, Lefkoşa)
Lemesos (Limassol)
Al Lādhiqīyah (Latakia)
Trâblous (Tripoli)
Beyrouth (Beirut)
Dimashq (Damascus)
Ḩims (Homs)
Ḩamāh (Hamath)
Ḩefa (Haifa)
Tel Aviv-Yafo
Jerusalem (Yerushalayim) (Al-Quds)
'Ammān (Philadelphia)
Ghazzah (Gaza City)
Bûr Sa'îd (Port Said)
Ismâ'ilîya
Be'ér Sheva' (Beersheba)
Dead Sea
Sea of Galilee

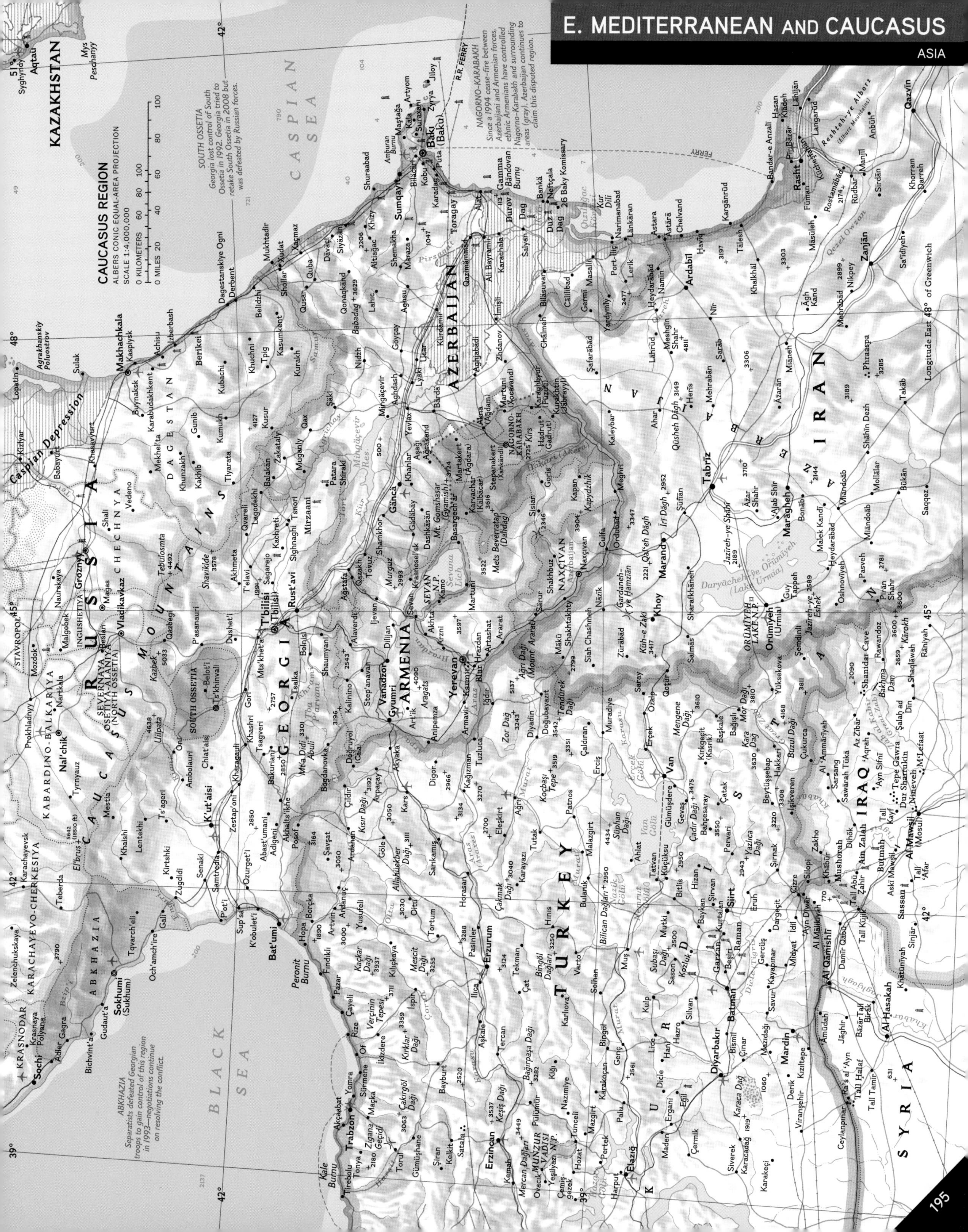
CAUCASUS REGION
ALBERS CONIC EQUAL-AREA PROJECTION
SCALE 1:4,000,000
0 KILOMETERS 20 40 60 80 100
0 MILES 20 40 60 80 100
SOUTH OSSETIA
Georgia lost control of South Ossetia in 1992. Georgia tried to retake South Ossetia in 2008 but was defeated by Russian forces.
NAGORNO-KARABAKH
Since a 1994 cease-fire between Azerbaijani and Armenian forces, ethnic Armenians have controlled Nagorno-Karabakh and surrounding areas (gray). Azerbaijan continues to claim this disputed region.
ABKHAZIA
Separatists defeated Georgian troops to gain control of this region in 1993—negotiations continue on resolving the conflict.
KAZAKHSTAN
CASPIAN SEA
BLACK SEA
RUSSIA
GEORGIA
ARMENIA
AZERBAIJAN
TURKEY
IRAN
IRAQ
SYRIA
CAUCASUS MOUNTAINS
DAGESTAN
CHECHNYA
ABKHAZIA
KURDISTAN
Longitude East 48° of Greenwich

PERSIAN GULF
ALBERS CONIC EQUAL-AREA PROJECTION
SCALE 1:6,000,000
0 KILOMETERS 100 150
0 MILES 50 100 150
Longitude East 54° of Greenwich
IRAQ
KUWAIT
IRAN
SAUDI ARABIA
BAHRAIN
QATAR
UNITED ARAB EMIRATES
OMAN
PERSIAN GULF
Gulf of Bahrain
Strait of Hormuz
GULF OF OMAN
Ad Dahna
Kūhhā-ye Zagros (Zagros Mountains)
FARS
Historically and most commonly known as the Persian Gulf, this body of water is referred to by some as the Arabian Gulf.
ABU MUSA
Island is claimed by Iran and U.A.E. and jointly administered by them.
Tunb Is.
Administered by Iran; claimed by U.A.E.
Abū Mūsá
Iran & U.A.E.
Ābādān
Al Kuwayt (Kuwait City)
Shīrāz
Būshehr
Bandar ʻAbbās
Ad Dammām
Al Manāmah (Manama)
Ad Dawḩah (Doha)
Abu Dhabi
Dubai
Sharjah
Ar Riyāḑ (Riyadh)
Al Hufūf (Hofuf)
Ghawar Oil Field
Masqaţ (Muscat)
Persepolis
Sīrjān
Rafsanjān
Qeshm
Kish
Jazireh-ye Qeshm
Al ʻAyn
Ras al Khaymah
Khaşab
Al Fujayrah
Şuḩār
48°
51°
54°
57°
30°
27°
24°

STRAIT OF MALACCA
ALBERS CONIC EQUAL-AREA PROJECTION
SCALE 1:8,000,000
0 KILOMETERS 120 160 200
0 MILES 40 80 120 160 200
Longitude East 105° of Greenwich
ANDAMAN SEA
Gulf of Thailand
SOUTH CHINA SEA
Strait of Malacca
INDIAN OCEAN
THAILAND
MALAY PENINSULA
MALAYSIA
SINGAPORE
INDONESIA
SUMATRA
Borneo (Kalimantan)
Kuala Lumpur
Medan
George Town (Penang) Pinang
Ipoh
Kota Baharu
Kuala Terengganu
Kuantan
Johor Bahru
Pekanbaru
Padang
Songkhla
Alor Setar
Banda Aceh
Pontianak
TAMAN NEGARA NAT. PARK
GUNUNG LEUSER NAT. PARK
SIBERUT N.P.
KERINCI SEBLAT N.P.
BUKIT TIGAH PULUH NAT. PARK
BERBAK N.P.
Kepulauan Riau
Kepulauan Lingga
Kep. Natuna
Kep. Anambas
Kep. Mentawai
Tioman
EQUATOR
96°
99°
102°
105°
108°
6°
3°
0°

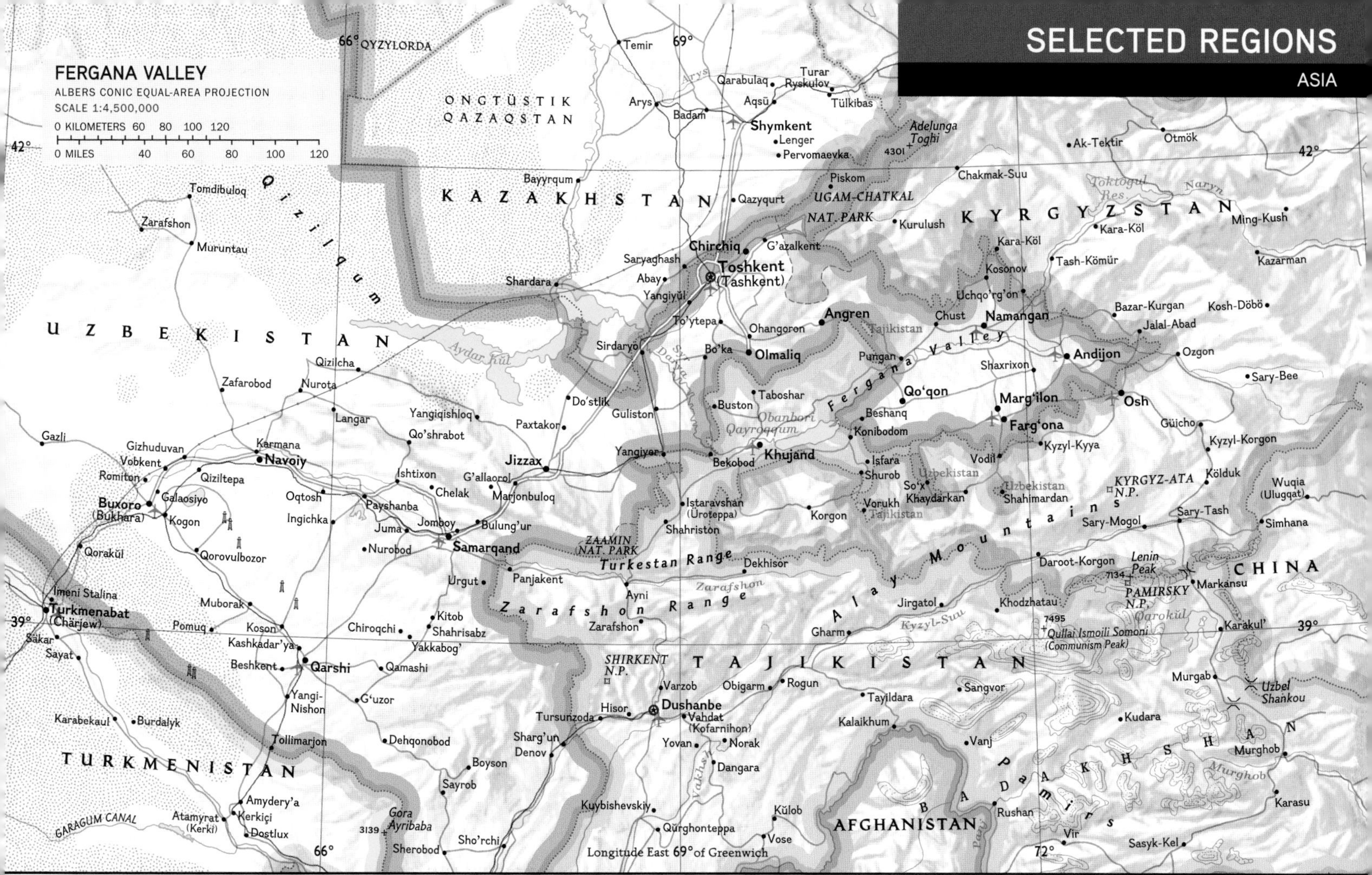
FERGANA VALLEY
ALBERS CONIC EQUAL-AREA PROJECTION
SCALE 1:4,500,000
0 KILOMETERS 60 80 100 120
0 MILES 40 60 80 100 120
KAZAKHSTAN
ONGTÜSTIK QAZAQSTAN
UZBEKISTAN
KYRGYZSTAN
TAJIKISTAN
TURKMENISTAN
AFGHANISTAN
CHINA
Qizilqum
Fergana Valley
Alay Mountains
Turkestan Range
Zarafshon Range
PAMIRS
BADAKHSHAN
Toshkent (Tashkent)
Shymkent
Namangan
Andijon
Osh
Qo'qon
Farg'ona
Marg'ilon
Khujand
Samarqand
Buxoro (Bukhara)
Navoiy
Jizzax
Qarshi
Dushanbe
Turkmenabat (Chärjew)
Angren
Olmaliq
Chirchiq
UGAM-CHATKAL NAT. PARK
ZAAMIN NAT. PARK
SHIRKENT N.P.
KYRGYZ-ATA N.P.
PAMIRSKY N.P.
7495 Qullai Ismoili Somoni (Communism Peak)
7134 Lenin Peak
GARAGUM CANAL
Longitude East 69° of Greenwich

GANGES VALLEY
ALBERS CONIC EQUAL-AREA PROJECTION
SCALE 1:8,000,000
0 KILOMETERS 120 160 200
0 MILES 40 80 120 160 200
MOUNT EVEREST Straddling the Nepal-China border, the mountain is called Sagarmāthā in Nepal and Qomolangma in China.
CHINA
XIZANG
NEPAL
HIMALAYA
INDIA
BHUTAN
BANGLADESH
PUNJAB
HARYANA
UTTARAKHAND
UTTAR PRADESH
RAJASTHAN
MADHYA PRADESH
CHHATTĪSGARH
JHARKHAND
BIHAR
WEST BENGAL
ORISSA
SIKKIM
ASSAM
MEGHALAYA
TRIPURA
ARUNACHAL PRADESH
DELHI
New Delhi
Kathmandu
Dhaka
Kolkata (Calcutta)
Lucknow
Kanpur
Varanasi (Banaras)
Allahabad
Patna
Agra
Jaipur
Bhopal
Indore
Chittagong
Thimphu
Mt. Everest (Sagarmāthā) (Qomolangma) (29035 ft) 8850
Gangdisê Shan
Yarlung Zangbo (Brahmaputra)
BAY OF BENGAL
TROPIC OF CANCER
Longitude East 84° of Greenwich

RUSSIA
MONGOLIA
HEILONGJIANG
DONGBEI (MANCHURIA)
JILIN
LIAONING
NORTH KOREA
SOUTH KOREA
HEBEI
SHANXI
SHAANXI
SHANDONG
NINGXIA HUIZU
BEIJING SHI
TIANJIN SHI
ORHON
DARHAN-UUL
SELENGE
BULGAN
CENTRAL
HENTIY
EASTERN
SÜHBAATAR
GOVĬSÜMBER
MIDDLE GOVĬ
EAST GOVĬ
SOUTH GOVĬ
SOUTH HANGAY
GOBI
MONGOL
Da Hinggan Ling
Ulaanbaatar (Ulan Bator)
BEIJING (PEKING)
TIANJIN (TIENTSIN)
SHENYANG
P'yŏngyang
SEOUL
Harbin
Changchun
Jilin
Qiqihar
Dalian (Dairen)
Qingdao
Jinan
Taiyuan
Shijiazhuang
Hohhot
Baotou
Datong
Zhengzhou (Chengchow)
Luoyang
Xi'an
Lanzhou
Yinchuan
Hailar
Manzhouli
Choybalsan
Erenhot
Zhangjiakou
Chengde
Tangshan
Qinhuangdao
Yantai
Weifang
Zibo
BO HAI
YELLOW SEA
Korea Bay
Liaodong Wan
Mouth of the Yellow River
Demarcation Line, July 27, 1953
TAIYUAN SPACE LAUNCH CENTER
Great Wall
Hulun Nur
Buyr Nuur
Dalai Nur
Qagan Nur
Huang (Yellow)
Kerulen
Taiping Ling
105°
108°
111°
114°
117°
120°
123°
126°
129°
48°
45°
42°
39°
36°

EASTERN CHINA
ALBERS CONIC EQUAL-AREA PROJECTION
SCALE 1:8,000,000
0 KILOMETERS 40 80 120 160 200
0 MILES 40 80 120 160 200
TAIWAN
The People's Republic of China claims Taiwan as its 23rd province. Taiwan's government (Republic of China) maintains that there are two political entities. The islands of Dongsha, Kinmen, Matsu, and Penghu are administered by Taiwan.
EAST CHINA SEA
PHILIPPINE SEA
SOUTH CHINA SEA
TROPIC OF CANCER
Longitude East 114° of Greenwich
Gulf of Tonkin
CHINA
JAPAN
VIETNAM
PHILIPPINES
HONG KONG (XIANGGANG) S.A.R.
MACAU (AOMEN) S.A.R.
SHANGHAI
CHONGQING
WUHAN
GUANGZHOU (CANTON)
SHENZHEN
HONG KONG
Macau
Taipei
Hanoi
Haiphong
Nanjing
Hangzhou
Fuzhou
Nanchang
Changsha
Guiyang
Nanning
Haikou
JIANGSU
ANHUI
ZHEJIANG
FUJIAN
JIANGXI
HUBEI
HUNAN
HENAN
GUANGDONG
GUANGXI ZHUANG
GUIZHOU
SICHUAN
CHONGQING SHI
SHANGHAI SHI
GANSU
HAINAN
TAIWAN

KOREAN PENINSULA
ALBERS CONIC EQUAL-AREA PROJECTION
SCALE 1:4,000,000
0 KILOMETERS 60 80 100
0 MILES 20 40 60 80 100
CHINA
RUSSIA
JAPAN
NORTH KOREA
SOUTH KOREA
JILIN
LIAONING
NEI MONGOL
SEA OF JAPAN
(EAST SEA)
YELLOW SEA
Korea Bay
KOREA STRAIT
TSUSHIMA STRAIT
RAJIN-SEONBONG (RASEON) TRADE ZONE
MUSUDAN MISSILE LAUNCH SITE
MOUNT CHILBO N.P.
MOUNT KUWOL N.P.
MOUNT KUMGANG N.P.
Demarcation Line, July 27, 1953
Northern Limit Line, July 27, 1953
TO CHINA FERRY
TO JEJU ISLAND
SHENYANG
P'yŏngyang
SEOUL
Dokdo
(Takeshima, Liancourt Rocks)
Administered by South Korea;
claimed by Japan
Ulleungdo
(Dagelet)
S. Korea
The Democratic People's Republic of Korea is referred to as North Korea. The Republic of Korea is known as South Korea.
PROVINCES AND PROVINCE-LEVEL CITIES WITH CAPITALS
NORTH KOREA
1 Chagang (Kanggye)
2 Hamgyong, North (Ch'ŏngjin)
3 Hamgyong, South (Hamhŭng)
4 Hwanghae, North (Sariwŏn)
5 Hwanghae, South (Haeju)
6 Kangwon (Wŏnsan)
7 Phyongan, North (Sinŭiju)
8 Phyongan, South (P'yŏng-sŏng)
9 Pyongyang City
10 Raseon City
11 Ryanggang (Hyesan)
SOUTH KOREA
12 Busan City
13 Chungcheong, North (Cheongju)
14 Chungcheong, South (Daejeon)
15 Daegu City
16 Daejeon City
17 Gangwon (Chuncheon)
18 Gwangju City
19 Gyeonggi (Suwon)
20 Gyeongsang, North (Daegu)
21 Gyeongsang, South (Changwon)
22 Incheon City
23 Jeju (Jeju) off map
24 Jeolla, North (Jeonju)
25 Jeolla, South (Namak)
26 Seoul City
27 Ulsan City
The above political subdivisions are numbered in blue on the map.
Longitude East 129° of Greenwich

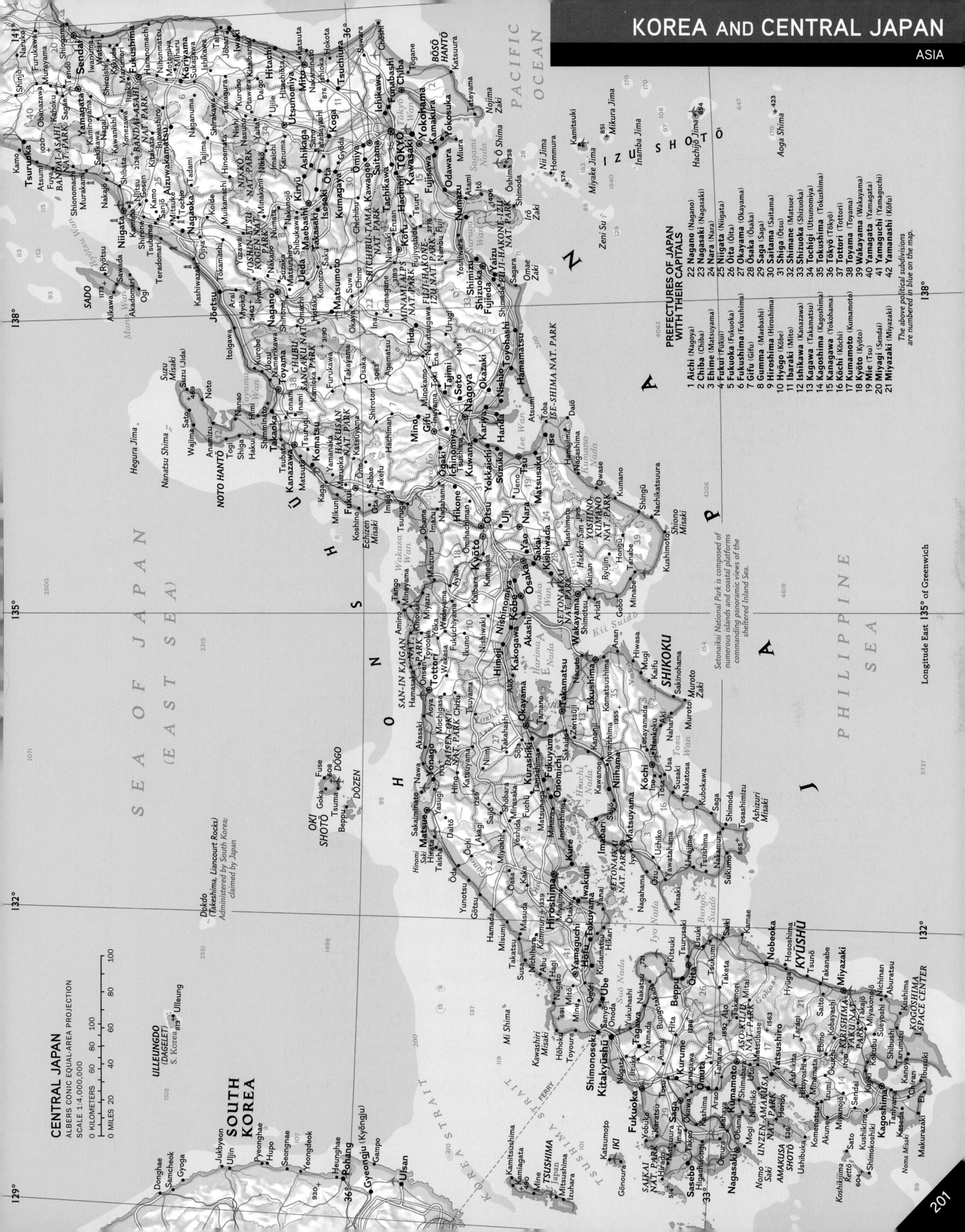
CENTRAL JAPAN
ALBERS CONIC EQUAL-AREA PROJECTION
SCALE 1:4,000,000
0 KILOMETERS 20 40 60 80 100
0 MILES 20 40 60 80 100
PREFECTURES OF JAPAN WITH THEIR CAPITALS
1 Aichi (Nagoya)
2 Chiba (Chiba)
3 Ehime (Matsuyama)
4 Fukui (Fukui)
5 Fukuoka (Fukuoka)
6 Fukushima (Fukushima)
7 Gifu (Gifu)
8 Gumma (Maebashi)
9 Hiroshima (Hiroshima)
10 Hyōgo (Kōbe)
11 Ibaraki (Mito)
12 Ishikawa (Kanazawa)
13 Kagawa (Takamatsu)
14 Kagoshima (Kagoshima)
15 Kanagawa (Yokohama)
16 Kōchi (Kōchi)
17 Kumamoto (Kumamoto)
18 Kyōto (Kyōto)
19 Mie (Tsu)
20 Miyagi (Sendai)
21 Miyazaki (Miyazaki)
22 Nagano (Nagano)
23 Nagasaki (Nagasaki)
24 Nara (Nara)
25 Niigata (Niigata)
26 Ōita (Ōita)
27 Okayama (Okayama)
28 Ōsaka (Ōsaka)
29 Saga (Saga)
30 Saitama (Saitama)
31 Shiga (Ōtsu)
32 Shimane (Matsue)
33 Shizuoka (Shizuoka)
34 Tochigi (Utsunomiya)
35 Tokushima (Tokushima)
36 Tōkyō (Tōkyō)
37 Tottori (Tottori)
38 Toyama (Toyama)
39 Wakayama (Wakayama)
40 Yamagata (Yamagata)
41 Yamaguchi (Yamaguchi)
42 Yamanashi (Kōfu)
The above political subdivisions are numbered in blue on the map.
Setonaikai National Park is composed of numerous islands and coastal platforms commanding panoramic views of the sheltered Inland Sea.
Dokdo (Takeshima, Liancourt Rocks) Administered by South Korea; claimed by Japan
SEA OF JAPAN (EAST SEA)
PACIFIC OCEAN
PHILIPPINE SEA
JAPAN
HONSHU
SHIKOKU
KYŪSHŪ
SOUTH KOREA
KOREA STRAIT
TSUSHIMA STRAIT
IZU SHOTŌ
OKI SHOTŌ
SADO
NOTO HANTŌ
ULLEUNGDO (DAGELET) S. Korea
TSUSHIMA Japan
IKI
Longitude East 135° of Greenwich
Tōkyō
Yokohama
Nagoya
Ōsaka
Kyōto
Kōbe
Hiroshima
Fukuoka
Niigata
Sendai
Busan
Ulsan
Pohang
Gyeongju (Kyŏngju)

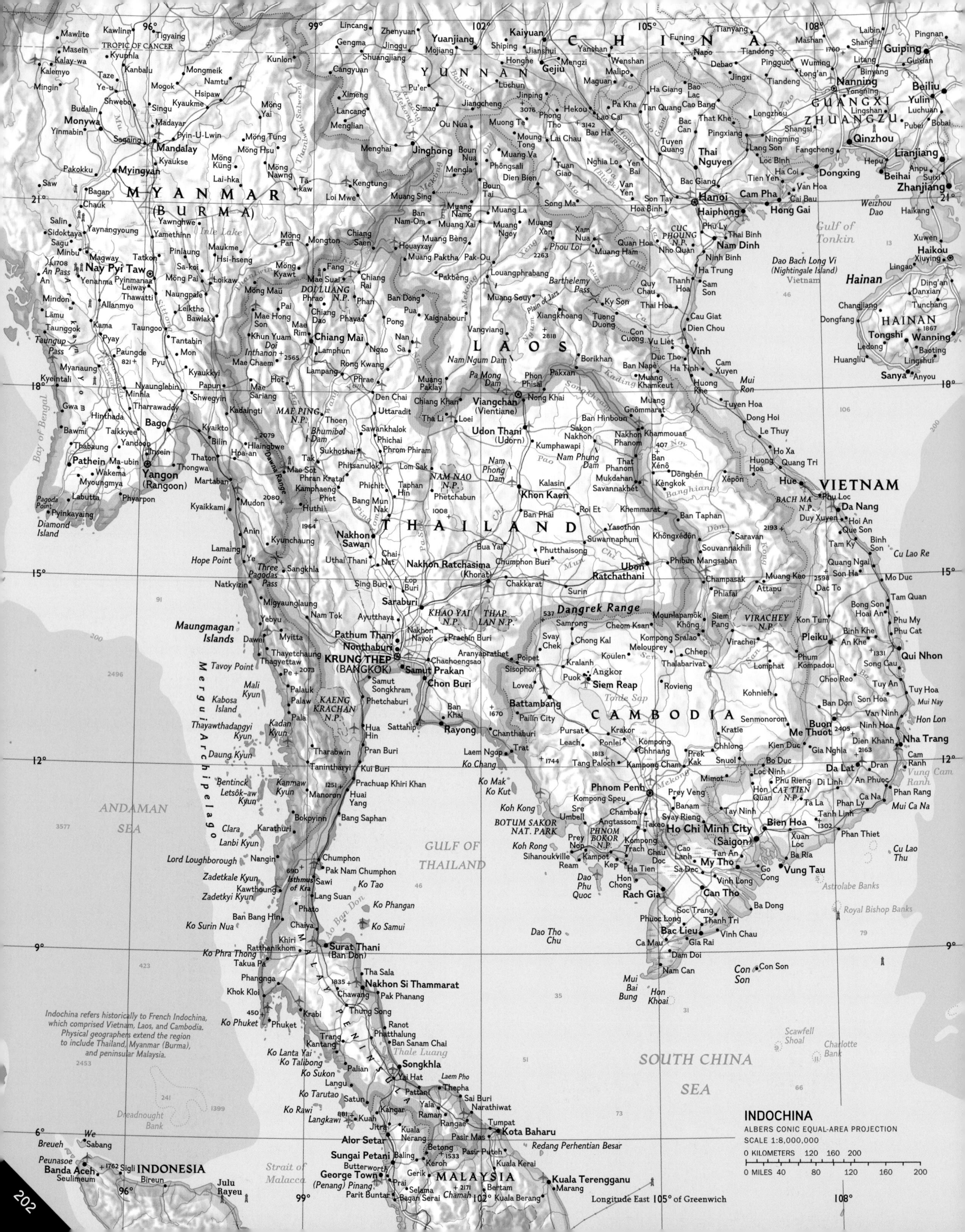
INDOCHINA
ALBERS CONIC EQUAL-AREA PROJECTION
SCALE 1:8,000,000
0 KILOMETERS 120 160 200
0 MILES 40 80 120 160 200
Longitude East 105° of Greenwich
Indochina refers historically to French Indochina, which comprised Vietnam, Laos, and Cambodia. Physical geographers extend the region to include Thailand, Myanmar (Burma), and peninsular Malaysia.
CHINA
YUNNAN
GUANGXI ZHUANGZU
MYANMAR (BURMA)
LAOS
THAILAND
CAMBODIA
VIETNAM
MALAYSIA
INDONESIA
Hainan
HAINAN
ANDAMAN SEA
GULF OF THAILAND
SOUTH CHINA SEA
Gulf of Tonkin
Bay of Bengal
Strait of Malacca
Mergui Archipelago
MALAY PENINSULA
TROPIC OF CANCER
Dangrek Range
Dawna Range
Isthmus of Kra
Tonle Sap
KRUNG THEP (BANGKOK)
Yangon (Rangoon)
Nay Pyi Taw
Mandalay
Viangchan (Vientiane)
Hanoi
Haiphong
Phnom Penh
Ho Chi Minh City (Saigon)
Chiang Mai
Nakhon Ratchasima (Khorat)
Udon Thani (Udorn)
Khon Kaen
Ubon Ratchathani
Surat Thani (Ban Don)
Nakhon Si Thammarat
Songkhla
Hue
Da Nang
Qui Nhon
Nha Trang
Da Lat
Vung Tau
Can Tho
Siem Reap
Battambang
Kunming
Nanning
Zhanjiang
Sanya
George Town
Kota Baharu
Kuala Terengganu
Banda Aceh

PHILIPPINES

ALBERS CONIC EQUAL-AREA PROJECTION

SCALE 1:7,000,000

0 KILOMETERS 100 150 200

0 MILES 50 100 150 200

SPRATLY ISLANDS

The scattered islands and reefs called the Spratly Islands are claimed by Brunei, China, Malaysia, the Philippines, Taiwan, and Vietnam. The Spratlys possess rich fishing grounds and potential oil.

21°

117°

120°

18°

15°

12°

9°

6°

SOUTH CHINA SEA

Vereker Banks

Tungsha Tao (Pratas I.)

Stewart Seamount 430

3557

3932

Macclesfield Banks

4170

Scarborough Shoal

4151

272 Dreyer Banks

4530

5377

4413

SPRATLY ISLANDS

Reed Tablemount

Lys Shoal

Loaita Bank 2238

Tizard Bank

Brown Bank

Seahorse Shoal

Carnatic Reef

Union Reefs

Sabina Shoal

Commodore Reef

Investigator Shoal

PHILIPPINE SEA

Batan Islands

1008 Basco

Luzon Strait

Balintang Channel

1088

543

Babuyan Islands

794

Babuyan Channel

Mayraira Point

Cape Bojeador

Bangui

Claveria

Abulug

Santa Ana

Aparri

Iligan Point

Buguey

Laoag

Bacarra

San Nicolas

Batac

2361 Kabugao

Valley Head

Espiritu

Cabugao

Baguio Point

Bangued

Tuguegarao

Vigan

Narvacan

Mount Sicapoo

Ilagan

Palanan

Aubarede Point

Divilacan Bay

NORTHERN SIERRA MADRE NATIONAL PARK

Lubuagan

Bontoc

Roxas

Candon

Santa Cruz

Bangar

Bachotan

San Fernando

Mount Pulog 2934

Bayombong

LUZON

Sierra Madre

1850 Casiguran

Baguio

Cape Bolinao

Lingayen Gulf

Lingayen

Dagupan

San Jose

Baler

Cape San Ildefonso

Santa Cruz

San Carlos

Cuyapo

Victoria

2037

Masinloc

Tarlac

Gapan

Cape Encanto

Palauig

Angeles

San Fernando

San Narciso

Malolos

Olongapo

MANILA

Quezon City

Cavite

Bataan Peninsula

Corregidor

Manila Bay

Lag. de Bay

Jose Panganiban

Paracale

Santa Cruz

Daet

Pandan

Yog Point

Lucena

Panganiban (Payo)

San Pablo

Lamon Bay

Polillo Islands

Batangas

Lipa

Boac

Calapan

Mulanay

Mt. Isarog

Naga

Mayon Volcano

Virac

Catanduanes

Lubang Island

Paluan

Mount Halcon

Mamburao

2505

Pola

Iriga 2462

Ligao

Legazpi

Sorsogon

Santa Cruz

Sablayan

Marinduque

Burias

Magallanes

Gubat

MINDORO

Mount Baco 2488

Roxas

Romblon

2050 Sibuyan

Masbate

Bulan

Catarman

Palapag

San Jose

Tablas

Santa Fe

Masbate

Ticao Allen

SAMAR

Oras

Sibuyan Sea

Nabas

Cataingan

Calbayog

850

Wright

Sulat

Pandan

Kalibo

Roxas

Visayan Sea

Catbalogan

Calbiga

Busuanga

Bintuan

Culion

Culasi

2117

CCarigara

Basey

General MacArthur

Culion

Calamian Group

Mount Nangtud

PANAY

Ajuy

Cadiz

Bogo

Borbon

Tacloban

1350

Guiuan

El Nido

659

Almodian

Iloilo

908

LEYTE

Cuyo Islands

Cuyo

San Jose

Bacolod

Cebu

CEBU

Baybay

Sogod

Loreto

Taytay

Dao

La Carlota

Isabela

Saint Bernard

Dinagat

703

Roxas

1603

San Carlos

NEGROS

BOHOL

Siargao

Dapa

Cleopatra Needle

Puerto Princesa

PALAWAN

Cauayan

870

Tagbilaran

Guindulman

Surigao

Placer

Aborlan

Inagauan

Sipalay

Tanjay

Oslob

Dumaguete

Lanuza

Birong

1709

Hinoba-an

Siquijor

Mt. Hilonghilong 2012

Quezon

Bayawan

1903

Zamboanguita

1713

Buenavista

Butuan

Malabuñang

Aboabo

Siaton

Salay

Gingoog

Bonobono

2100

Brooke's Point

Dipolog

Baliangao

Cagayan de Oro

Lianga

Hinatuan

Canipaan

Cape Buliluyan

Rio Tuba

Manukan

Oroquieta

Iligan

Malaybalay

Bislig

Balabac

Balabac

Sindangan

Liloy

1224

Ozamis

Tubod

Marawi 2896

Lingig

Cateel

Siocon

Kabasalan

MINDANAO

Baganga

Banggi

Sikuati

Kudat

Senaja

Tandik

1219

Pangutaran

Pangutaran Group

Sibuco

Alicia

Margosatubig

2316 Kibawe

Pagadian

Malabang

Carmen

Tagum

2810 Maco

Caraga

Sibuco

Datu Piang

Cotabato

Mount Apo 2954

Davao

Babak

Manay

Kota Belud

Bandau

Tuaran

4101

Ranau

KINABALU PARK

Kinabalu

Lebak

Isulan

Buluan

Lupon

Mati

Digos

Padada

1633

CROCKER RANGE N.P.

Beaufort

Tambunan

Bingkor

Melalap

Pinangah

Lamag

Lintang

Sukau

Lahad Datu

533

Kota Kinabalu

Kiamba

Palimbang

2083 Tupi

Koronadal

General Santos

Gian

Jose Abad Santos

Weston

Tinaca Point

886

Sarangani Islands

Sandakan

Jolo

Jolo

Luuk

Parang

Tapul

Siasi

Isabela

1011

Lamitan

Basilan

Sulu Archipelago

Tawi Tawi

Bongao

Cagayan Sulu I.

Sulu Sea

Moro Gulf

Basilan Strait

Zamboanga

Illana Bay

Sibuguey Bay

Panguil Bay

Lake Lanao

Tagum

Compostela

Celebes Sea

INDONESIA

Miangas (Palmas)

Kepulauan Nanusa

Kepulauan Karakaralong

Cape San Agustin

Davao Gulf

Sarangani Bay

MALAYSIA

SABAH

BRUNEI

Bandar Seri Begawan

Brunei Bay

Seri Begawan

Longitude East 123° of Greenwich

126°

Benham Seamount

38

5638

5102

7955

10057

5207

4517

9546

5761

2277

Cagayan Islands

Longitude East 123° of Greenwich

Africa

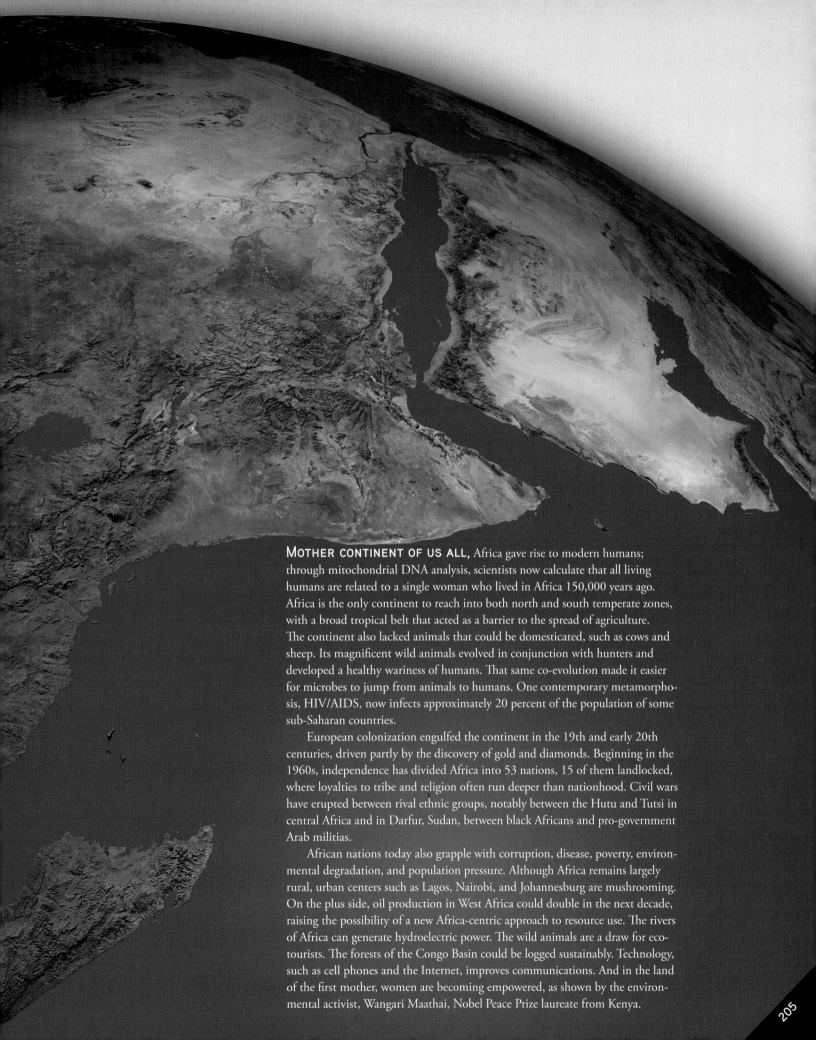

MOTHER CONTINENT OF US ALL, Africa gave rise to modern humans; through mitochondrial DNA analysis, scientists now calculate that all living humans are related to a single woman who lived in Africa 150,000 years ago. Africa is the only continent to reach into both north and south temperate zones, with a broad tropical belt that acted as a barrier to the spread of agriculture. The continent also lacked animals that could be domesticated, such as cows and sheep. Its magnificent wild animals evolved in conjunction with hunters and developed a healthy wariness of humans. That same co-evolution made it easier for microbes to jump from animals to humans. One contemporary metamorphosis, HIV/AIDS, now infects approximately 20 percent of the population of some sub-Saharan countries.

European colonization engulfed the continent in the 19th and early 20th centuries, driven partly by the discovery of gold and diamonds. Beginning in the 1960s, independence has divided Africa into 53 nations, 15 of them landlocked, where loyalties to tribe and religion often run deeper than nationhood. Civil wars have erupted between rival ethnic groups, notably between the Hutu and Tutsi in central Africa and in Darfur, Sudan, between black Africans and pro-government Arab militias.

African nations today also grapple with corruption, disease, poverty, environmental degradation, and population pressure. Although Africa remains largely rural, urban centers such as Lagos, Nairobi, and Johannesburg are mushrooming. On the plus side, oil production in West Africa could double in the next decade, raising the possibility of a new Africa-centric approach to resource use. The rivers of Africa can generate hydroelectric power. The wild animals are a draw for ecotourists. The forests of the Congo Basin could be logged sustainably. Technology, such as cell phones and the Internet, improves communications. And in the land of the first mother, women are becoming empowered, as shown by the environmental activist, Wangari Maathai, Nobel Peace Prize laureate from Kenya.

PHYSICAL AFRICA
AZIMUTHAL EQUIDISTANT PROJECTION
SCALE 1:37,000,000
0 KILOMETERS 600 800 1000
0 MILES 200 400 600 800 1000
ATLANTIC OCEAN
ATLANTIC OCEAN
INDIAN OCEAN
Mediterranean Sea
Black Sea
Caspian Sea
Red Sea
Gulf of Aden
Persian Gulf
Gulf of Guinea
Gulf of Sidra
Bay of Biscay
Sea of Azov
Adriatic Sea
Aegean Sea
Mozambique Channel
TROPIC OF CANCER
TROPIC OF CAPRICORN
EQUATOR
Meridian of Greenwich (London)
Longitude East 30° of Greenwich
FRANCE
SPAIN
PORTUGAL
ITALY
GREECE
TURKEY
UKRAINE
RUSSIA
ROMANIA
BULGARIA
HUNGARY
AUSTRIA
SLOVAKIA
CZECH. REP.
GER.
SWITZ.
SLOVENIA
CROATIA
BOSN. & HERZG.
SERB.
MONT.
KOS.
MACED.
ALBAN.
MOLD.
GEORGIA
ARM.
AZERB.
KAZ.
UZB.
TURK.
SYRIA
IRAQ
IRAN
LEBANON
ISRAEL
JORDAN
KUWAIT
BAHRAIN
QATAR
U.A.E.
SAUDI ARABIA
YEMEN
CYPRUS
N. CYPRUS
MOROCCO
ALGERIA
TUNISIA
LIBYA
EGYPT
WESTERN SAHARA
MAURITANIA
MALI
NIGER
CHAD
SUDAN
ERITREA
DJIBOUTI
ETHIOPIA
SOMALIA
KENYA
UGANDA
RWANDA
BURUNDI
TANZANIA
SENEGAL
GAMBIA
GUINEA-BISSAU
GUINEA
SIERRA LEONE
LIBERIA
CÔTE D'IVOIRE (IVORY COAST)
BURKINA FASO
GHANA
TOGO
BENIN
NIGERIA
CAMEROON
CENTRAL AFRICAN REPUBLIC
EQ. GUINEA
SAO TOME AND PRINCIPE
GABON
CONGO
DEMOCRATIC REPUBLIC OF THE CONGO
CABINDA Angola
ANGOLA
ZAMBIA
MALAWI
MOZAMBIQUE
ZIMBABWE
NAMIBIA
BOTSWANA
SOUTH AFRICA
SWAZILAND
LESOTHO
MADAGASCAR
COMOROS
SEYCHELLES
Paris
Lyon
Marseille
Bern
Vienna
Bratislava
Budapest
Ljubljana
Zagreb
Belgrade
Sarajevo
Podgorica
Skopje
Tirana
Sofia
Bucharest
Chişinău
Athína (Athens)
Istanbul
Ankara
Bursa
İzmir (Smyrna)
Konya
Adana
Tbilisi
Baku
Tehran
Esfahan (Isfahan)
Shīrāz
Baghdad
Aleppo
Beirut
Damascus
Amman
Jerusalem
Nicosia
Kuwait City
Manama
Doha
Riyadh
Jeddah
Sanaa
Madrid
Lisbon
Barcelona
Rome
VATICAN CITY
SAN MARINO
MONACO
ANDORRA
Corsica
Sardinia
Sicily
Balearic Islands
Crete
MALTA
Peloponnesus
CRIMEA
Gibraltar
Strait of Gibraltar
Algiers
Tunis
Tripoli
Rabat
Casablanca
Alexandria
Cairo
Suez Canal
SINAI
Nouakchott
Dakar
Banjul
Bissau
Conakry
Freetown
Monrovia
Yamoussoukro
Abidjan
Accra
Lomé
Porto-Novo
Cotonou
Lagos
Abuja
Bamako
Ouagadougou
Niamey
N'Djamena
Omdurman
Khartoum
Asmara
Djibouti
Addis Ababa
Mogadishu
Nairobi
Kampala
Kigali
Bujumbura
Dodoma
Dar es Salaam
Malabo
Príncipe
São Tomé
Annobón
Libreville
Yaoundé
Bangui
Brazzaville
Kinshasa (Léopoldville)
Luanda
Lusaka
Lilongwe
Harare
Windhoek
Gaborone
Pretoria (Tshwane)
Johannesburg
Maputo
Mbabane
Lobamba
Bloemfontein
Maseru
Cape Town
Antananarivo
Moroni
Azores (Açores)
Madeira Islands
Canary Islands (Islas Canarias)
C. Boujdour
Cape Blanc
Cape Finisterre
Cape St. Vincent
Cape Palmas
Cape Three Points
Cape Fria
Palgrave Point
Cape Columbine
Cape of Good Hope
Cape Agulhas
Cape Saint Lucia
Barra Point
Cape Delgado
C. Ste. Marie
Cap d'Ambre
Tristan da Cunha Group
Aldabra Islands
Farquhar Group
Cosmoledo Group
Glorioso Is.
Mayotte.
Tsaratanana
Pyrenees
Alps
Carpathian Mts.
Caucasus Mts.
Elburz Mts.
Danube
Lake Van
Lake Urmia
Tigris
ATLAS MOUNTAINS
Jebel Toubkal
Great Western Erg
Great Eastern Erg
Hamada de Tinrhert
Erg Iguidi
Erg Chech
El Djouf
SAHARA
TRIPOLITANIA
FEZZAN
CYRENAICA
Libyan Desert
Western Desert
Eastern Desert
Nubian Desert
Lake Nasser
Nile
Jebel 'Uweinat (Al' Uwaynat)
Ahaggar Mts.
Aïr Massif
Ténéré
Tibesti Mts.
Emi Koussi
BORKOU
Ennedi
SAHEL
Sénégal
Niger
Lake Chad
Jebel Marra
Blue Nile
White Nile
Lake Tana
HEJAZ
NAJD
Al Hadīdah (meteorite craters)
Ar Rub' al Khālī (Empty Quarter)
Ogadēn
Jubba
Lowest point in Africa
-156 (-512 ft)
Lotagipi Swamp
Lake Turkana (Lake Rudolf)
Bomu
Ubangi
Congo
CONGO BASIN
Lake Victoria
Sources of the Nile
Mt. Kenya
Kilimanjaro
5895 (19340 ft)
Highest point in Africa
Lake Tanganyika
Mitumba Mountains
KATANGA PLATEAU
Source of the Congo
Lake Malawi (Lake Nyasa)
Zambezi
Lake Kariba
Okavango Delta
Brandberg
NAMIB DESERT
KALAHARI DESERT
Orange
Drakensberg

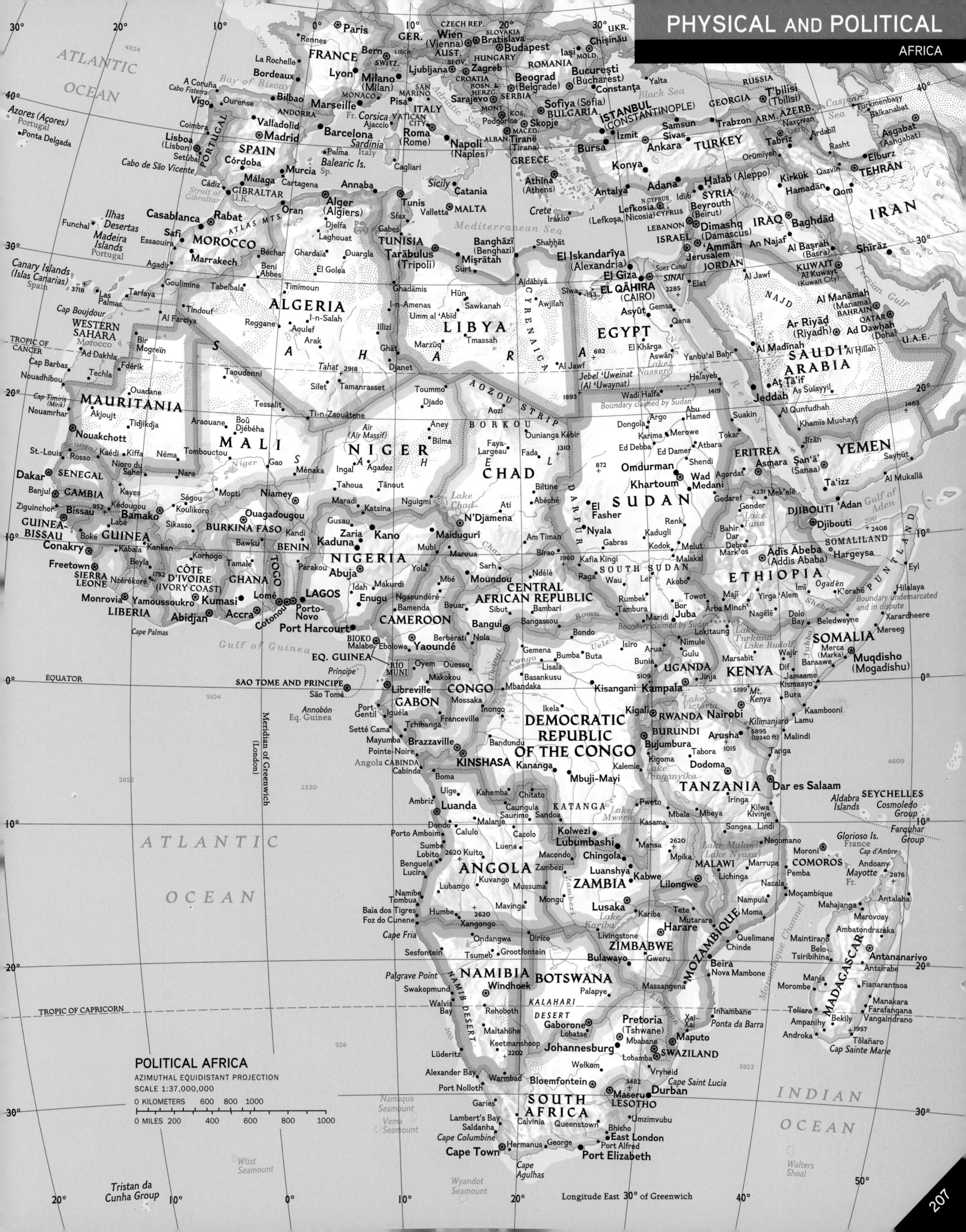
POLITICAL AFRICA
AZIMUTHAL EQUIDISTANT PROJECTION
SCALE 1:37,000,000
0 KILOMETERS 600 800 1000
0 MILES 200 400 600 800 1000
ATLANTIC OCEAN
INDIAN OCEAN
Mediterranean Sea
Gulf of Guinea
TROPIC OF CANCER
EQUATOR
TROPIC OF CAPRICORN
Meridian of Greenwich (London)
Longitude East 30° of Greenwich
MOROCCO
WESTERN SAHARA
ALGERIA
TUNISIA
LIBYA
EGYPT
MAURITANIA
MALI
NIGER
CHAD
SUDAN
SOUTH SUDAN
ERITREA
DJIBOUTI
ETHIOPIA
SOMALIA
SENEGAL
GAMBIA
GUINEA-BISSAU
GUINEA
SIERRA LEONE
LIBERIA
CÔTE D'IVOIRE (IVORY COAST)
BURKINA FASO
GHANA
TOGO
BENIN
NIGERIA
CAMEROON
CENTRAL AFRICAN REPUBLIC
EQ. GUINEA
SAO TOME AND PRINCIPE
GABON
CONGO
DEMOCRATIC REPUBLIC OF THE CONGO
UGANDA
KENYA
RWANDA
BURUNDI
TANZANIA
ANGOLA
ZAMBIA
MALAWI
MOZAMBIQUE
ZIMBABWE
NAMIBIA
BOTSWANA
SOUTH AFRICA
LESOTHO
SWAZILAND
MADAGASCAR
COMOROS
SEYCHELLES
SAUDI ARABIA
YEMEN
IRAN
IRAQ
SYRIA
JORDAN
ISRAEL
LEBANON
TURKEY
SPAIN
PORTUGAL
FRANCE
ITALY
GREECE
SAHARA
KALAHARI DESERT
NAMIB DESERT
Rabat
Alger (Algiers)
Tunis
Tarābulus (Tripoli)
El Qâhira (Cairo)
Nouakchott
Dakar
Banjul
Bissau
Conakry
Freetown
Monrovia
Yamoussoukro
Bamako
Ouagadougou
Niamey
Accra
Lomé
Porto-Novo
Abuja
N'Djamena
Khartoum
Asmara
Djibouti
Ādīs Ābeba (Addis Ababa)
Muqdisho (Mogadishu)
Juba
Bangui
Yaoundé
Malabo
Libreville
Brazzaville
Kinshasa
Kampala
Nairobi
Kigali
Bujumbura
Dodoma
Dar es Salaam
Luanda
Lusaka
Lilongwe
Harare
Windhoek
Gaborone
Pretoria (Tshwane)
Mbabane
Maseru
Cape Town
Antananarivo
Moroni

MOROCCO

TUNISIA

WESTERN
SAHARA
(MOROCCO)

ALGERIA

LIBYA

Cairo

EGYPT

MAURITANIA

MALI

NIGER

CHAD

SUDAN

ERITREA

SENEGAL

GAMBIA

DJIBOUTI

GUINEA-BISSAU

BURKINA
FASO

SOMALIA

GUINEA

BENIN

NIGERIA

ETHIOPIA

SIERRA LEONE

CÔTE
D'IVOIRE
(IVORY COAST)

GHANA

CENTRAL
AFRICAN
REPUBLIC

LIBERIA

Abidjan

TOGO

CAMEROON

UGANDA

KENYA

EQUATORIAL GUINEA

SAO TOME
AND PRINCIPE

GABON

CONGO

SEYCHELLES

RWANDA

DEMOCRATIC
REPUBLIC
OF
THE CONGO

BURUNDI

CABINDA
(ANGOLA)

Kinshasa

TANZANIA

COMOROS

ANGOLA

MALAWI

ZAMBIA

MADAGASCAR

ZIMBABWE

MAURITIUS

NAMIBIA

MOZAMBIQUE

RÉUNION
(FRANCE)

BOTSWANA

SWAZILAND

LESOTHO

SOUTH
AFRICA

Cape Town

LAND COVER

- Evergreen needleleaf forest
- Evergreen broadleaf forest
- Deciduous needleleaf forest
- Deciduous broadleaf forest
- Mixed forest
- Woody savanna
- Savanna
- Closed shrubland
- Open shrubland
- Grassland
- Cropland
- Barren or sparsely vegetated
- Urban or built-up
- Snow and ice
- Cropland / natural vegetation mosaic
- Wetland

TEMPERATURE AND RAINFALL

Abidjan, Côte d'Ivoire (Ivory Coast)

- Temperatures above 0°C
- Temperatures below 0°C

High temperature

Low temperature

Rainfall
(115 mm = 4.5 in)

50°C – 690 mm
40°C – 575 mm
30°C – 460 mm
20°C – 345 mm
10°C – 230 mm
0°C – 115 mm
-10°C – 0 mm
-20°C –
-30°C –

J F M A M J J A S O N D

Kinshasa, Dem. Rep. of Congo

50°C – 690 mm
40°C – 575 mm
30°C – 460 mm
20°C – 345 mm
10°C – 230 mm
0°C – 115 mm
-10°C – 0 mm
-20°C –
-30°C –

J F M A M J J A S O N D

Cape Town, South Africa

50°C – 690 mm
40°C – 575 mm
30°C – 460 mm
20°C – 345 mm
10°C – 230 mm
0°C – 115 mm
-10°C – 0 mm
-20°C –
-30°C –

J F M A M J J A S O N D

Cairo, Egypt

50°C – 690 mm
40°C – 575 mm
30°C – 460 mm
30°C – 345 mm
20°C – 230 mm
10°C – 115 mm
0°C – 0 mm
-10°C –
-20°C –
-30°C –

J F M A M J J A S O N D

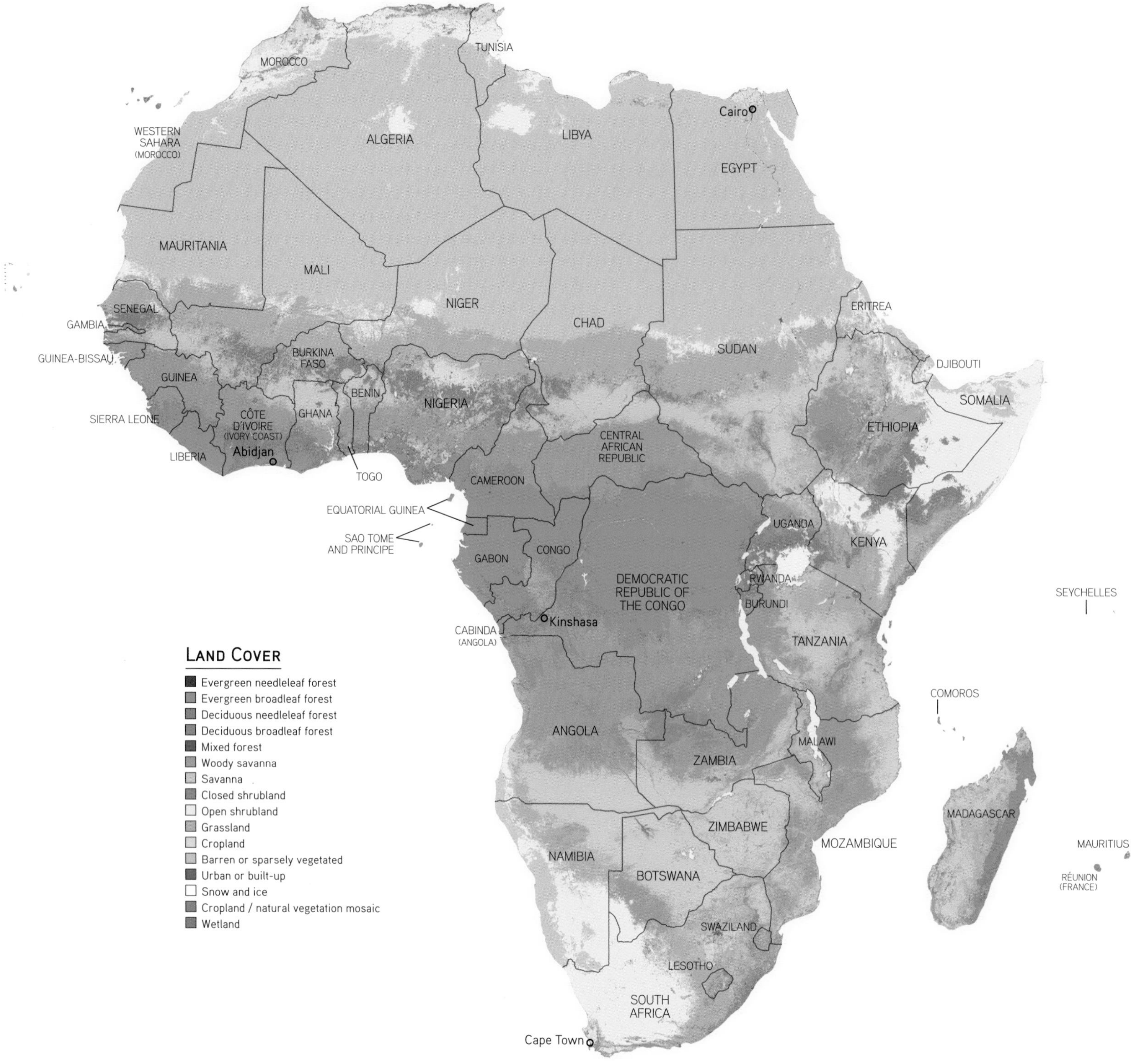

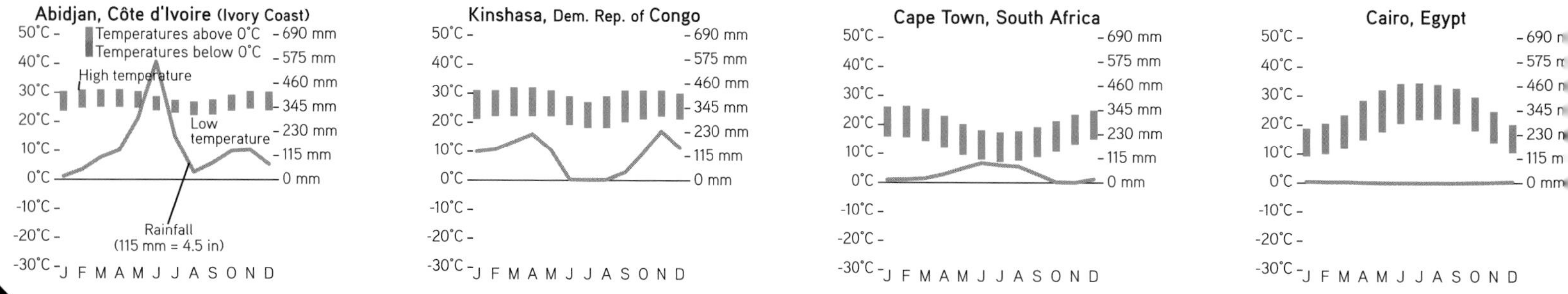

Climate Zones

(based on modified Köppen system)

Humid equatorial climate (A)
- No dry season (Af)
- Short dry season (Am)
- Dry winter (Aw)

Dry climate (B)
- Semiarid (BS)
- Arid (BW)

h = hot
k = cold

Humid temperate climate (C)
- No dry season (Cf)
- Dry winter (Cw)
- Dry summer (Cs)

a = hot summer
b = cool summer

Highland climate (H)
- Unclassified highlands

Natural Hazards

Population Density, 2010

People per square km	People per square mi
More than 1,000	More than 2,500
100–1,000	250–2,500
Less than 100	Less than 250

Fire Intensity
(from gas burn off, slash-and-burn agriculture, or natural causes)
High
Low

Recorded Natural Event

Major Earthquake, 1900-2010
Moment magnitude
- More than 7.0
- 6.0–7.0
- Less than 6.0

Volcano

Tsunami, 1900-2010
Run-up height

Meters	Feet
More than 10	More than 32
5–10	16–32
Less than 5	Less than 16

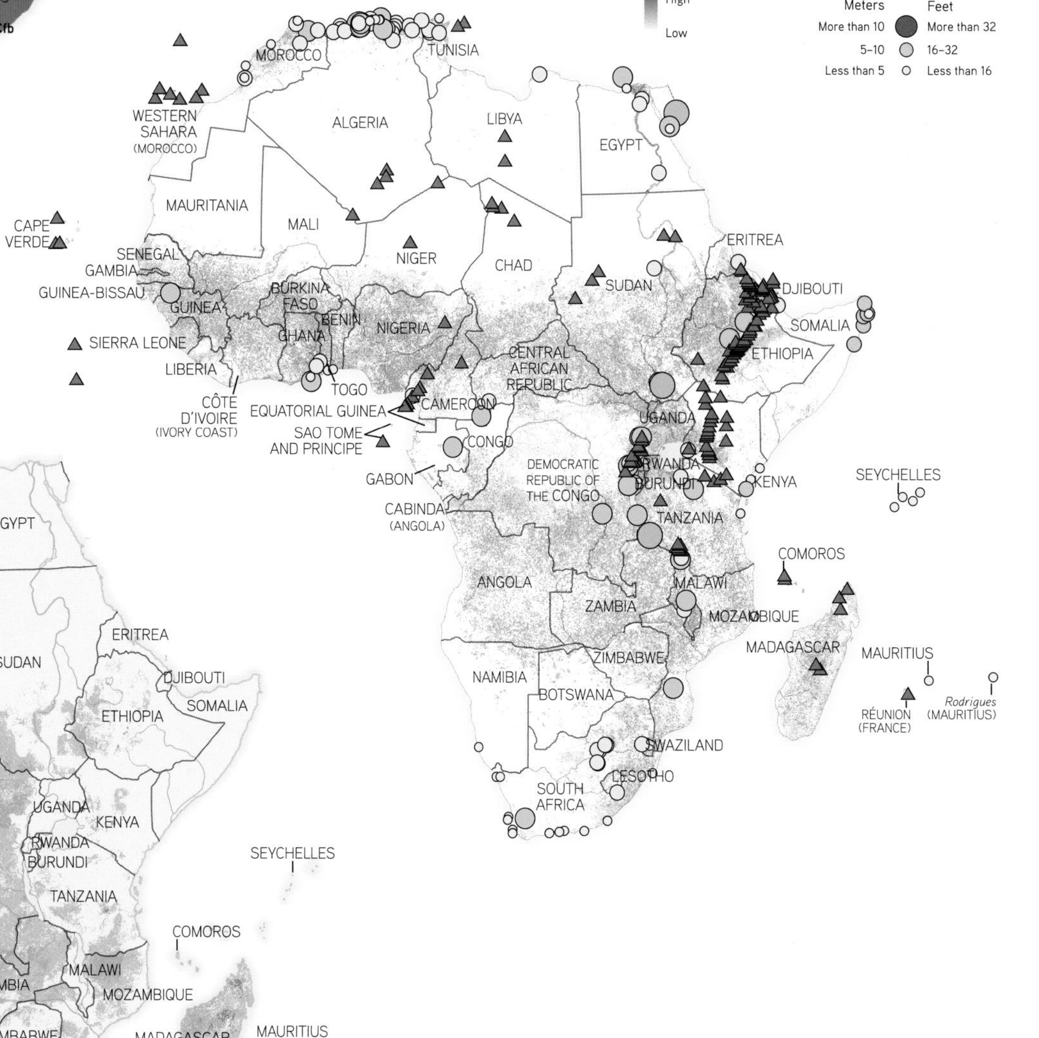

Water Availability

(in millimeters per person per year)
- More than 750
- 251–750
- 26–250
- Less than 26

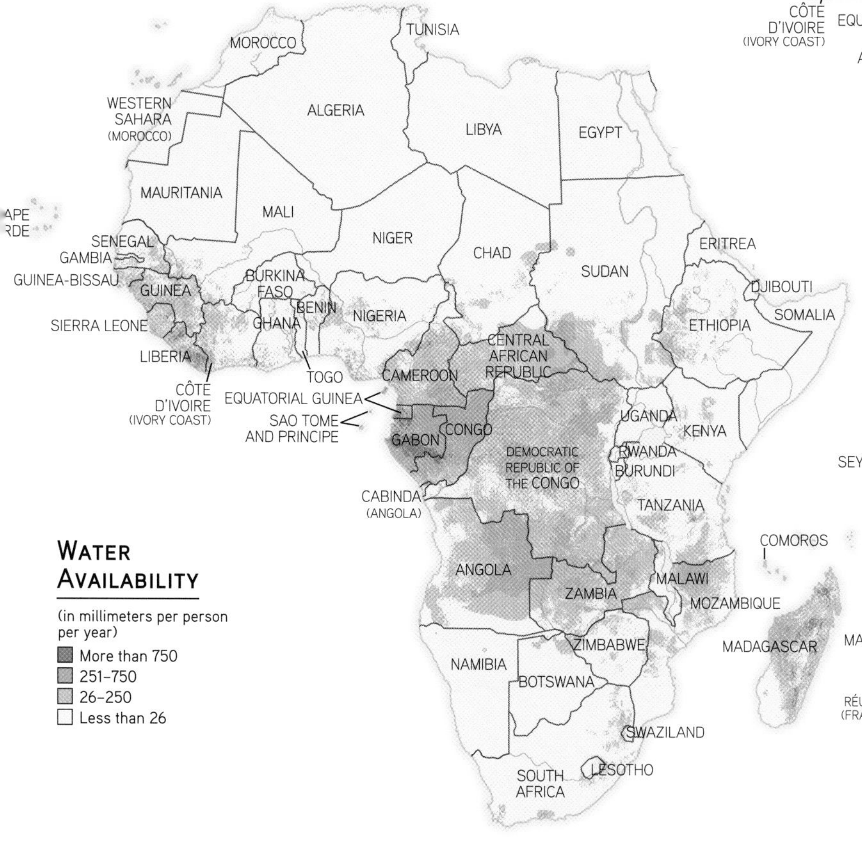

POPULATION DENSITY

People per Square Kilometer / People per Square Mile
- More than 195 / More than 500
- 60–195 / 150–500
- 10–59 / 25–149
- 1–9 / 1–24
- Less than 1 / Less than 1

POPULATION PYRAMIDS

SOMALIA

UGANDA

TUNISIA

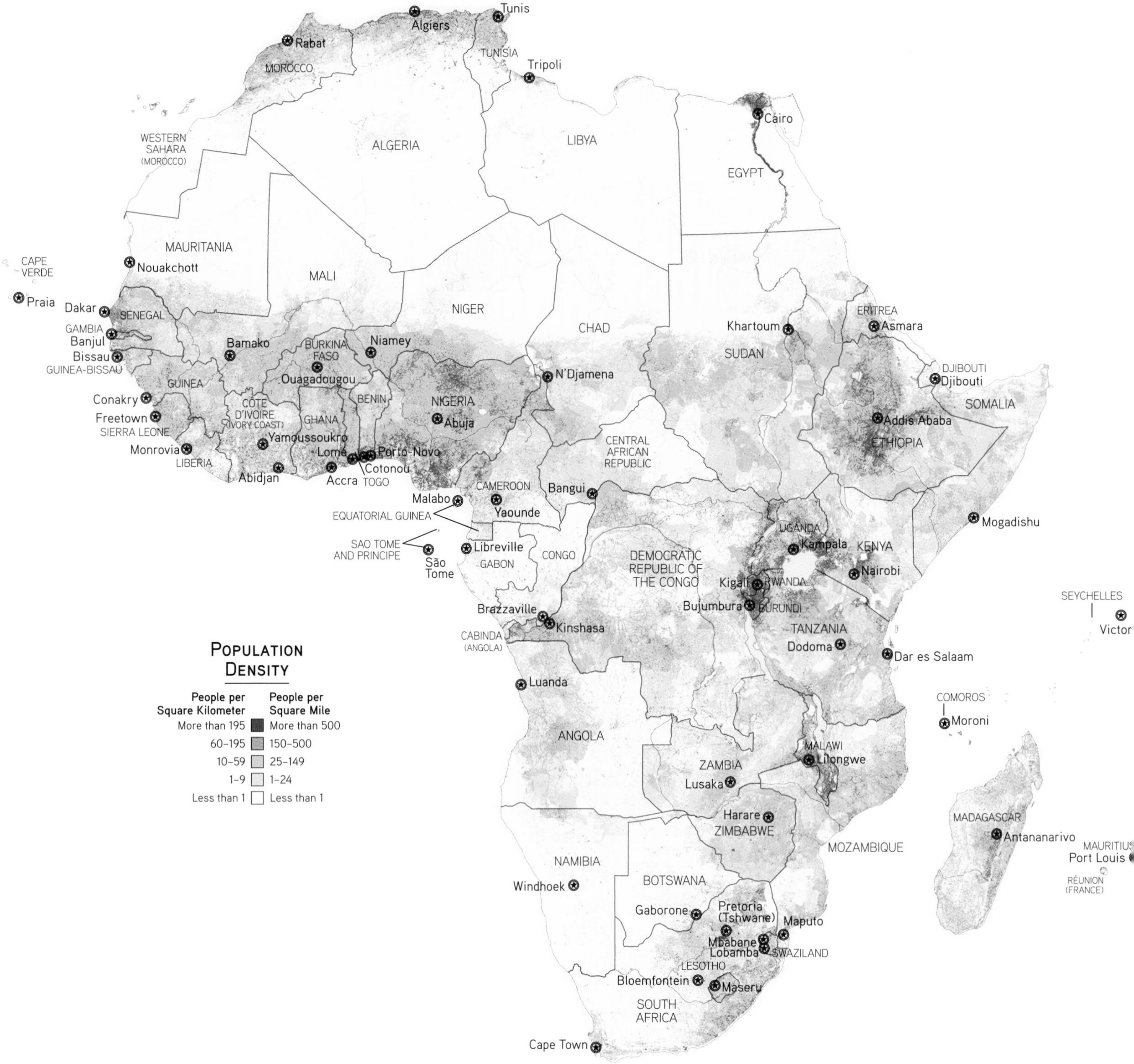

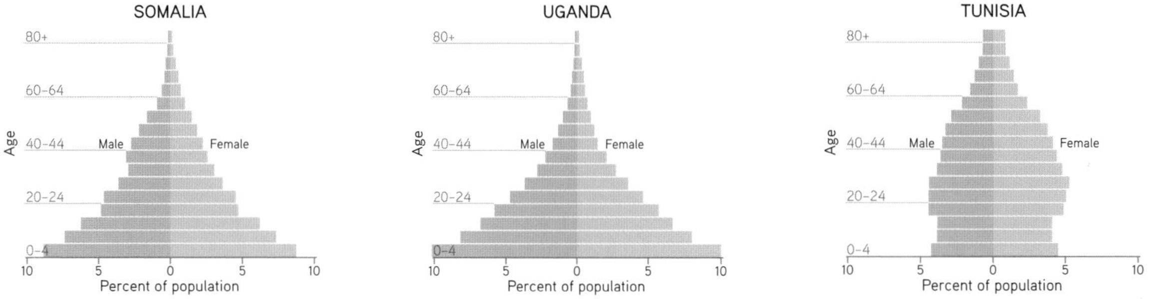

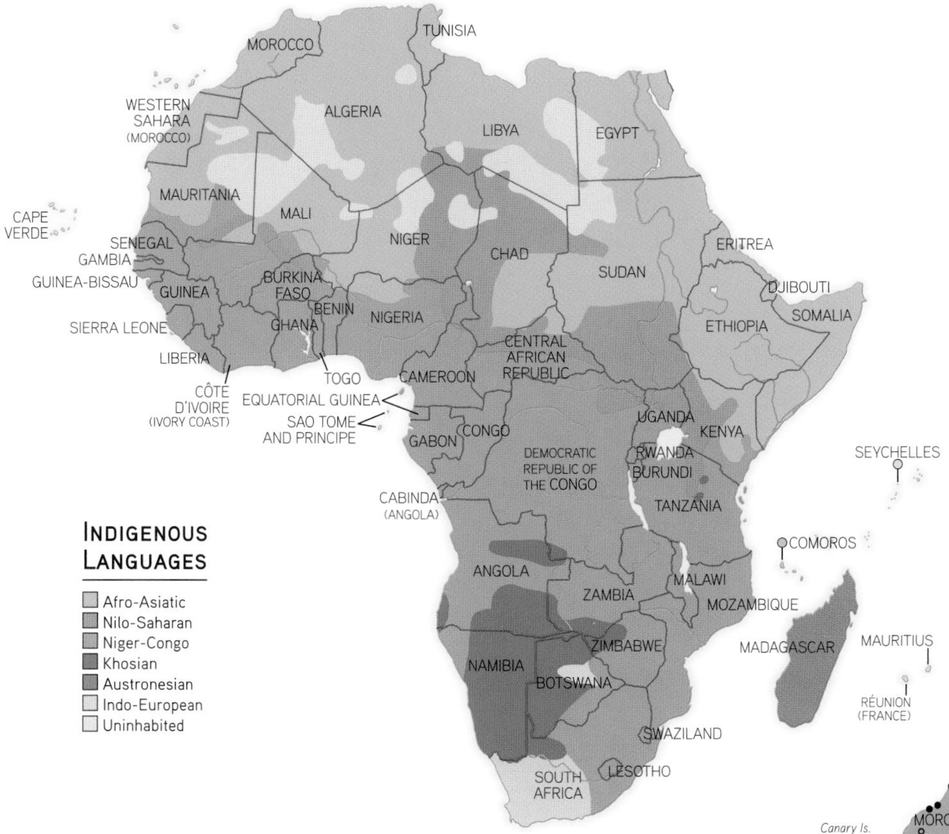

INDIGENOUS LANGUAGES

- Afro-Asiatic
- Nilo-Saharan
- Niger-Congo
- Khosian
- Austronesian
- Indo-European
- Uninhabited

Map labels (Indigenous Languages map)

MOROCCO, TUNISIA, WESTERN SAHARA (MOROCCO), ALGERIA, LIBYA, EGYPT, CAPE VERDE, MAURITANIA, MALI, NIGER, CHAD, SUDAN, ERITREA, DJIBOUTI, SENEGAL, GAMBIA, GUINEA-BISSAU, GUINEA, BURKINA FASO, BENIN, NIGERIA, GHANA, SOMALIA, ETHIOPIA, SIERRA LEONE, LIBERIA, CÔTE D'IVOIRE (IVORY COAST), TOGO, CAMEROON, CENTRAL AFRICAN REPUBLIC, EQUATORIAL GUINEA, SAO TOME AND PRINCIPE, GABON, CONGO, UGANDA, KENYA, DEMOCRATIC REPUBLIC OF THE CONGO, RWANDA, BURUNDI, SEYCHELLES, CABINDA (ANGOLA), TANZANIA, COMOROS, ANGOLA, ZAMBIA, MALAWI, MOZAMBIQUE, MADAGASCAR, MAURITIUS, NAMIBIA, ZIMBABWE, BOTSWANA, RÉUNION (FRANCE), SWAZILAND, SOUTH AFRICA, LESOTHO

URBANIZATION

Urban agglomerations, 2010 (population in millions)
- ■ More than 10.0
- ▲ 5.0–10.0
- ● 1.0–4.9
- ○ .75–.99

Percent urban population, 2010
- More than 75%
- 50%–75%
- 25%–49%
- Less than 25%

Map labels (Urbanization map)

Canary Is. (SPAIN), MOROCCO, TUNISIA, WESTERN SAHARA (MOROCCO), ALGERIA, LIBYA, Cairo, EGYPT, MAURITANIA, MALI, NIGER, CHAD, Khartoum, SUDAN, ERITREA, DJIBOUTI, CAPE VERDE, SENEGAL, GAMBIA, GUINEA-BISSAU, BURKINA FASO, GUINEA, BENIN, GHANA, NIGERIA, SOMALIA, ETHIOPIA, SIERRA LEONE, LIBERIA, CÔTE D'IVOIRE (IVORY COAST), TOGO, EQUATORIAL GUINEA, CAMEROON, CENTRAL AFRICAN REPUBLIC, Lagos, SAO TOME AND PRINCIPE, CONGO, GABON, DEMOCRATIC REPUBLIC OF THE CONGO, UGANDA, KENYA, CABINDA (ANGOLA), Kinshasa, RWANDA, BURUNDI, TANZANIA, SEYCHELLES, COMOROS, ANGOLA, ZAMBIA, MALAWI, MOZAMBIQUE, MADAGASCAR, MAURITIUS, NAMIBIA, ZIMBABWE, BOTSWANA, RÉUNION (FRANCE), SWAZILAND, SOUTH AFRICA, LESOTHO

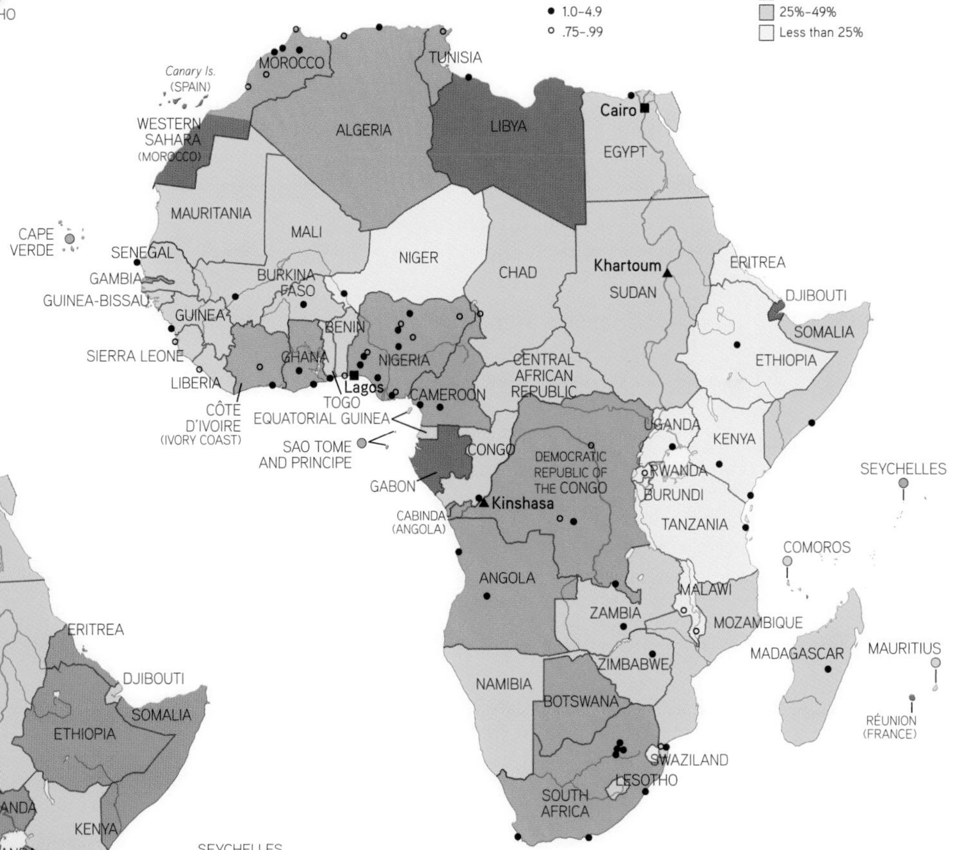

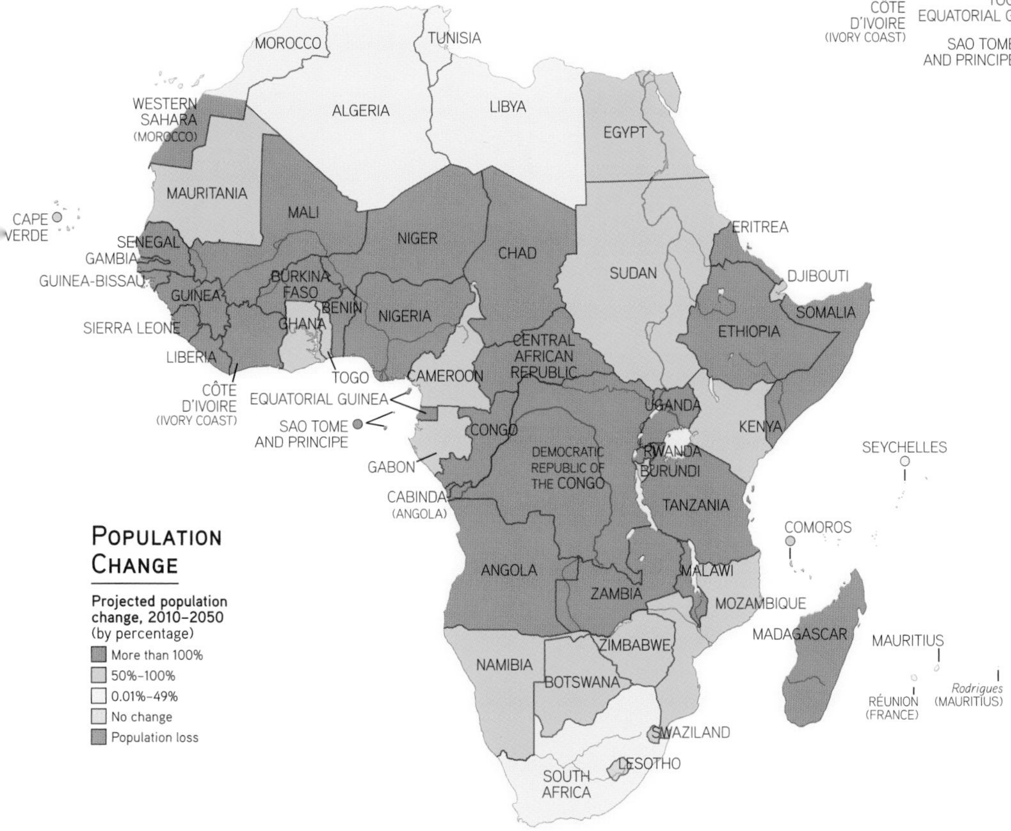

POPULATION CHANGE

Projected population change, 2010–2050 (by percentage)
- More than 100%
- 50%–100%
- 0.01%–49%
- No change
- Population loss

Map labels (Population Change map)

MOROCCO, TUNISIA, WESTERN SAHARA (MOROCCO), ALGERIA, LIBYA, EGYPT, MAURITANIA, MALI, NIGER, CHAD, SUDAN, ERITREA, DJIBOUTI, CAPE VERDE, SENEGAL, GAMBIA, GUINEA-BISSAU, GUINEA, BURKINA FASO, BENIN, GHANA, NIGERIA, CAMEROON, CENTRAL AFRICAN REPUBLIC, ETHIOPIA, SOMALIA, SIERRA LEONE, LIBERIA, CÔTE D'IVOIRE (IVORY COAST), TOGO, EQUATORIAL GUINEA, SAO TOME AND PRINCIPE, GABON, CONGO, DEMOCRATIC REPUBLIC OF THE CONGO, UGANDA, KENYA, CABINDA (ANGOLA), RWANDA, BURUNDI, TANZANIA, SEYCHELLES, COMOROS, ANGOLA, ZAMBIA, MALAWI, MOZAMBIQUE, MADAGASCAR, MAURITIUS, NAMIBIA, ZIMBABWE, BOTSWANA, RÉUNION (FRANCE), Rodrigues (MAURITIUS), SWAZILAND, SOUTH AFRICA, LESOTHO

LAND USE

More disturbed — Cropland

Less disturbed

More disturbed — Pasture

Built-up area

Irrigated land

MADEIRA IS. (PORTUGAL)
CANARY IS. (SPAIN)

Rabat
Algiers
Tunis
Tripoli
Cairo

MOROCCO
TUNISIA
WESTERN SAHARA (MOROCCO)
ALGERIA
LIBYA
EGYPT

Nouakchott
MAURITANIA
MALI
NIGER
CHAD
SUDAN
ERITREA
Asmara
DJIBOUTI
Djibouti

CAPE VERDE
Praia
Dakar
GAMBIA Banjul
SENEGAL
Bamako
BURKINA FASO
Niamey
Khartoum
ETHIOPIA
Addis Ababa
SOMALIA

GUINEA-BISSAU
Bissau
GUINEA
Conakry
Ouagadougou
N'Djamena

Freetown
SIERRA LEONE
CÔTE D'IVOIRE (IVORY COAST)
Yamoussoukro
BENIN
GHANA
TOGO
NIGERIA
Abuja
CENTRAL AFRICAN REPUBLIC
Bangui
UGANDA
KENYA
Mogadishu

Monrovia
LIBERIA
Abidjan
Accra
Lomé
Porto-Novo
Cotonou
CAMEROON
Yaoundé
Kampala
Nairobi

Malabo
EQUATORIAL GUINEA
RIO MUNI
Libreville
CONGO
DEMOCRATIC REPUBLIC OF THE CONGO
Kigali
RWANDA
Bujumbura
BURUNDI
Victoria
SEYCHELL

SAO TOME AND PRINCIPE
São Tomé
GABON
Brazzaville
Kinshasa
Dodoma
TANZANIA
Dar es Salaam

CABINDA (ANGOLA)
Luanda
Moroni
COMOROS

ANGOLA
ZAMBIA
Lilongwe
MALAWI
MOZAMBIQUE
MADAGASCAR
Antananarivo
MAURITIUS

Lusaka
Harare
ZIMBABWE
RÉUNION (FRANCE)
Por Lou

NAMIBIA
Windhoek
BOTSWANA
Gaborone
Pretoria (Tshwane)
Mbabane
Maputo
SWAZILAND
Lobamba

Bloemfontein
Maseru
LESOTHO
SOUTH AFRICA
Cape Town

IMPORTS AND EXPORTS

VALUE OF IMPORTS

NIGERIA

Sugar 1%
Ores & metals 4%
Chemical products 5%
Food 11%
Electronic equipment 12%
Manufactured goods 19%
Machinery & transport equipment 37%
Other 11%

SOUTH AFRICA

Pharmaceutical products 3%
Ores & metals 4%
Chemical products 5%
Food 5%
Electronic equipment 11%
Manufactured goods 14%
Petroleum products 19%
Machinery & transport equipment 25%
Other 14%

VALUE OF EXPORTS

NIGERIA

Other 6%
Food 4%
Petroleum products 90%

SOUTH AFRICA

Other 8%
Chemical products 4%
Manufactured goods 5%
Food 7%
Petroleum products 9%
Machinery and transport equipment 15%
Ores & metals 52%

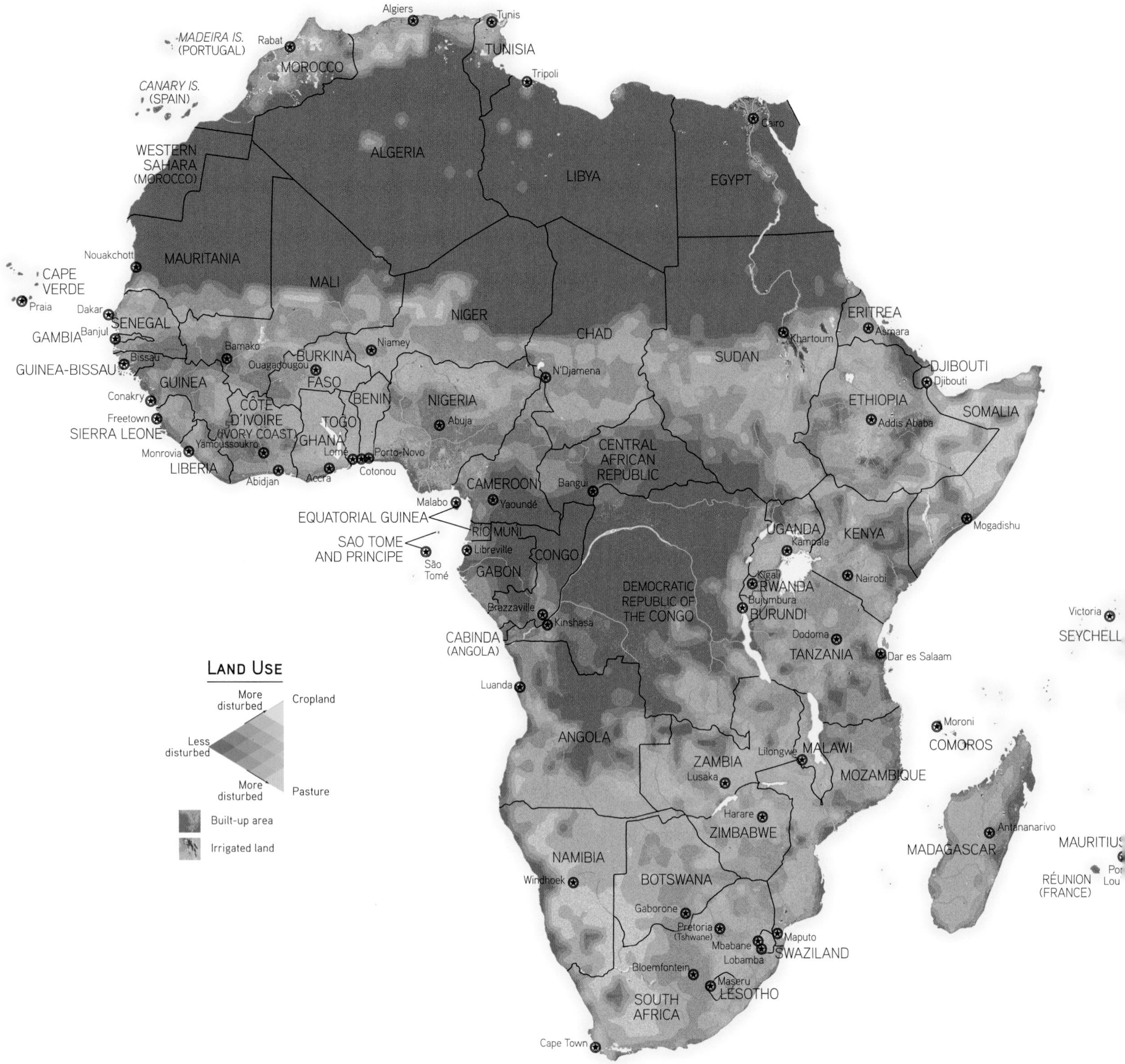

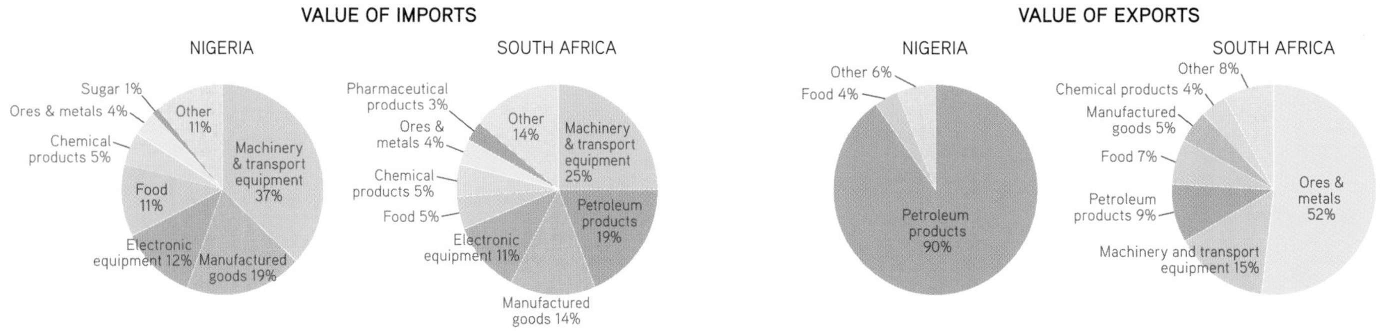

AFRICA'S ECONOMY

Service
100%

DJIBOUTI

LIBERIA

EQUATORIAL GUINEA

Agricultural
100%

Industrial
100%

per Gross Domestic Product
(GDP) sector

DOMINANT ECONOMY

(per GDP sector)

	Agriculture	Industry*	Services
70%–100%			
50%–69.9%			
0%–49.9%			
No data			

*Includes the mining industry

PER CAPITA ENERGY CONSUMPTION

(annual use, in million Btu)

- More than 300
- 201–300
- 101–200
- 30–100
- Less than 30

Major energy deposit

- Coal
- Natural gas
- Oil
- Oil pipeline
- Oil transit chokepoint

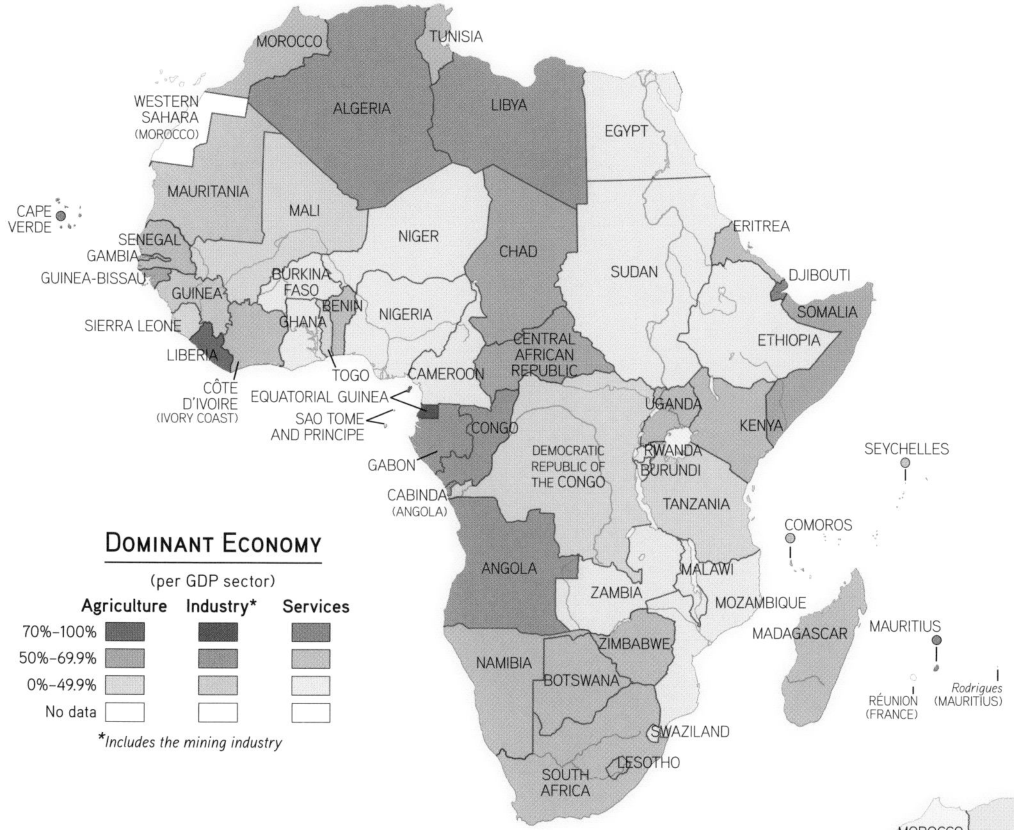

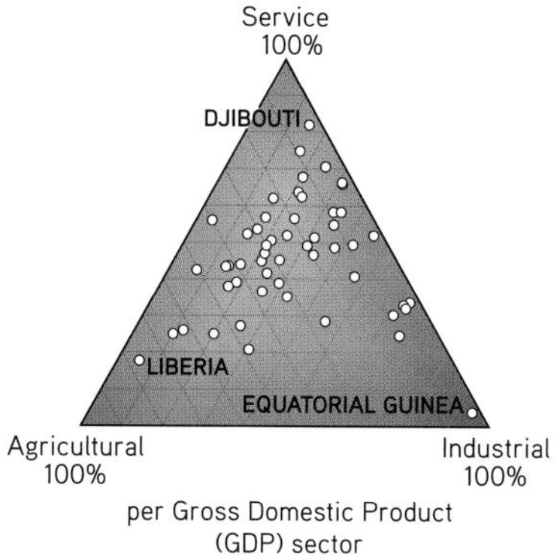

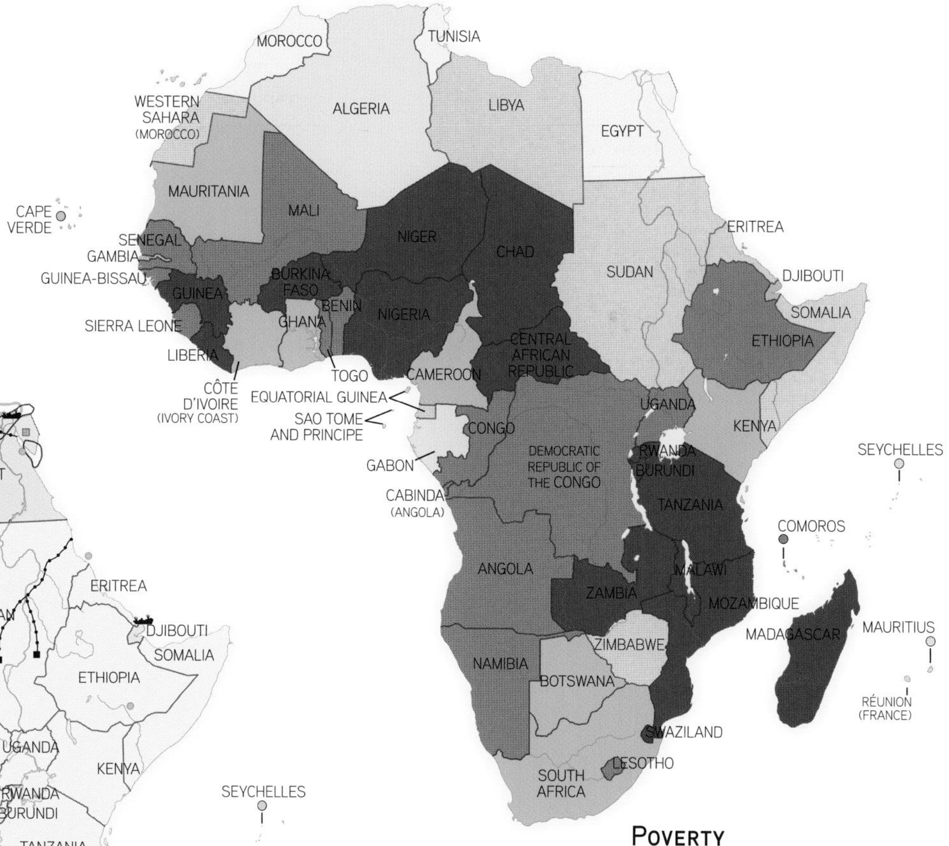

POVERTY

Percentage of population living
on less than $2 per day

- More than 80%
- 60%–80%
- 40%–59%
- 20%–39%
- Less than 20%
- No data available

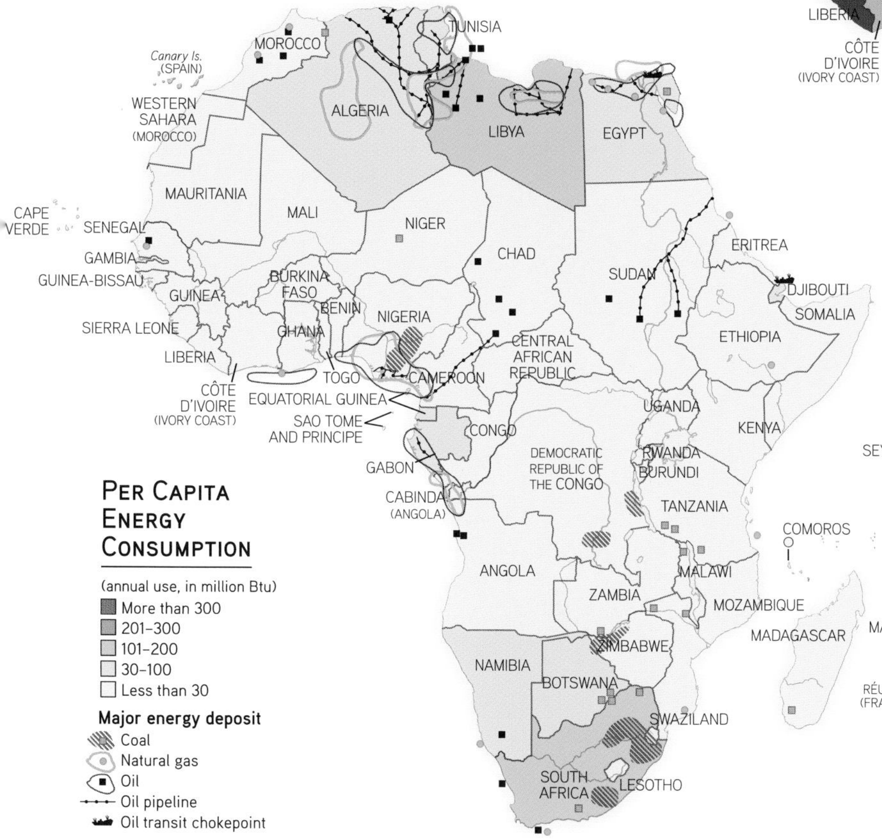

BAY OF BISCAY
FRANCE
SPAIN
PORTUGAL
ITALY
MONACO
ANDORRA
SAN MARINO
VATICAN CITY
GIBRALTAR U.K.
MOROCCO
ALGERIA
TUNISIA
LIBYA
WESTERN SAHARA
MAURITANIA
MEDITERRANEAN SEA
Tyrrhenian Sea
BALEARIC ISLANDS
CORSICA France
SARDINIA Italy
MADEIRA IS. Portugal
Ilhas Selvagens (Salvage Islands) Portugal
CANARY ISLANDS (ISLAS CANARIAS) Spain
ATLANTIC
TROPIC OF CANCER
PYRENEES
Sierra Morena
Er Rif
Moyen Atlas
Haut Atlas
Anti Atlas
Hauts Plateaux
Saharan Atlas
Grand Erg Occidental
Grand Erg Oriental
Plateau du Tademaït
Tanezrouft-n-Ahenet
TASSILI-N-AJJER NATIONAL PARK
AHAGGAR N.P.
Madrid
Lisboa (Lisbon)
Porto (Oporto)
Barcelona
Valencia
Sevilla (Seville)
Marseille
Roma (Rome)
Alger (Algiers)
Tunis
Rabat
Casablanca
Marrakech
Fès (Fez)
Oran
Constantine
Laayoune
Western Sahara, formerly Spanish Sahara, was divided by Morocco and Mauritania in 1976. Morocco has administered the territory since Mauritania's withdrawal in August 1979. The United Nations does not recognize this annexation, and Western Sahara remains in dispute.

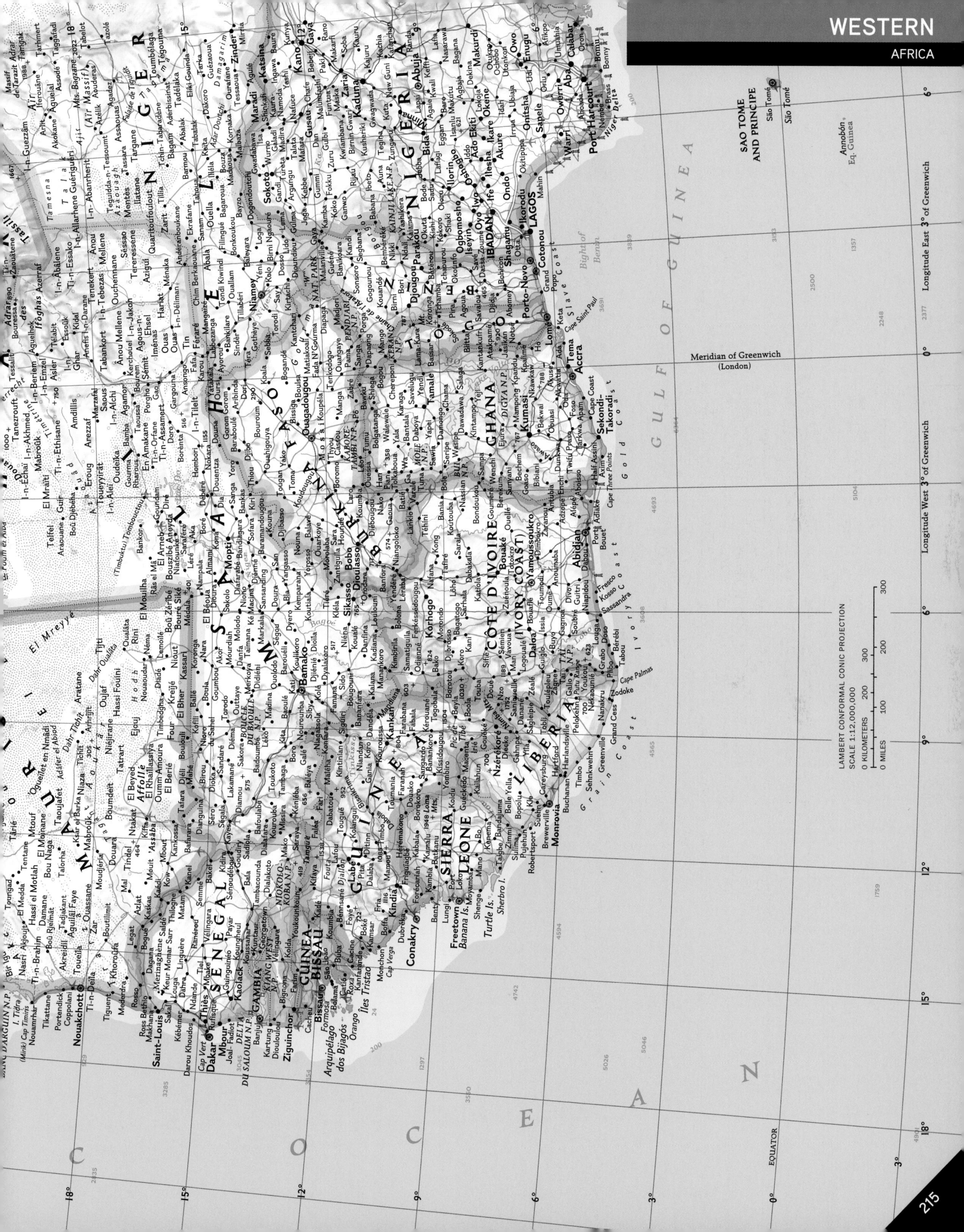

MAURITANIA
MALI
NIGER
SENEGAL
GAMBIA
GUINEA-BISSAU
GUINEA
SIERRA LEONE
LIBERIA
CÔTE D'IVOIRE (IVORY COAST)
BURKINA FASO
GHANA
TOGO
BENIN
NIGERIA
SAO TOME AND PRINCIPE
GULF OF GUINEA
ATLANTIC OCEAN
Bight of Benin
Meridian of Greenwich (London)
EQUATOR
Longitude West 3° of Greenwich
Longitude East 3° of Greenwich
Nouakchott
Dakar
Banjul
Bissau
Conakry
Freetown
Monrovia
Bamako
Ouagadougou
Niamey
Yamoussoukro
Abidjan
Accra
Lomé
Porto-Novo
Cotonou
Abuja
LAGOS
São Tomé
LAMBERT CONFORMAL CONIC PROJECTION
SCALE 1:12,000,000
0 KILOMETERS 100 200 300
0 MILES 100 200 300

LAMBERT CONFORMAL CONIC PROJECTION
SCALE 1:12,000,000
0 KILOMETERS 200 300
0 MILES 100 200 300
MEDITERRANEAN
IONIAN SEA
SICILY
ITALY
MALTA
GREECE
Sea of Crete
ALGERIA
LIBYA
TUNISIA
EGYPT
NIGER
CHAD
NIGERIA
SUDAN
CAMEROON
CENTRAL AFRICAN REPUBLIC
SAHARA
SAHEL
Libyan Desert
Western Desert
Tibesti (Tibesti Mts.)
Aïr (Aïr Massif)
Tassili-n-Ajjer
Tassili Oua-n-Ahaggar
Grand Erg Oriental
Grand Erg Occidental
Grand Erg de Bilma
Erg du Ténéré
Hamada de Tinrhert
Ṣaḥrā' Marzūq
Sarīr Kalanshiyū
Sarir Tibasti
Plateau du Djado
Ennedi
Borkou
AOZOU STRIP
TROPIC OF CANCER
Ṭarābulus (Tripoli)
Banghāzī (Benghazi)
Khalīj Surt (Gulf of Sidra)
Gulf of Gabes
Tunis
Sfax
Sousse
Misrātah
Sabhā
Tubruq (Tobruk)
El Iskandarîya (Alexandria)
Athína (Athens)
Valletta
Constantine
Annaba (Bône)
Ouargla
Touggourt
Ghardaïa
Djelfa
Biskra
Batna
Sétif
Tiaret
N'Djamena
Abéché
Faya
Niamey
Zinder
Maradi
Kano
Kaduna
Abuja
Maiduguri
Sarh
Maroua
Garoua
Geneina
El Fasher
Nyala
WESTERN DARFUR
NORTHERN DARFUR
SOUTHERN DARFUR
WESTERN KORDOFAN
NORTHERN BAHR AL GHAZAL
Al Kufrah (Kufra Oasis)
Jebel 'Uweinat (Al 'Uwaynāt)
Lake Chad
ZAKOUMA N.P.
MANOVO-GOUNDA-SAINT FLORIS N.P.
Qattara Depression
Selima Oasis
3°
6°
9°
12°
15°
18°
21°
24°
27°
33°
30°
27°
24°
21°
18°
15°
12°
9°

TURKEY
SYRIA
CYPRUS
LEBANON
ISRAEL
JORDAN
IRAQ
IRAN
KUWAIT
BAHRAIN
QATAR
UNITED ARAB EMIRATES
SAUDI ARABIA
OMAN
YEMEN
ERITREA
ETHIOPIA
DJIBOUTI
SOMALIA
SOMALILAND
PUNTLAND
RED SEA
PERSIAN GULF
GULF OF ADEN
INDIAN OCEAN
Ar Rub' al Khali (Empty Quarter)
An Nafūd
Syrian Desert
Nubian Desert
TEHRĀN
Baghdād
Dimashq (Damascus)
Beyrouth (Beirut)
'Ammān
Jerusalem
Tel Aviv-Yafo
Ar Riyāḍ (Riyadh)
Jeddah
Makkah (Mecca)
Al Madīnah (Medina)
KUWAIT
Al Manāmah (Manama)
Ad Dawḥah (Doha)
Abu Dhabi
Dubai
Ṣan'ā' (Sanaa)
'Adan (Aden)
Asmara
DJIBOUTI
Khartoum
Omdurman
Port Sudan
Aswân
Halab (Aleppo)
Al Mawṣil (Mosul)
Al Baṣrah (Basra)
Eṣfahan (Isfahan)
Shīrāz
Socotra (Suquṭrā)
33°
36°
39°
42°
45°
48°
51°
9°
12°
15°
18°
21°
24°
30°
33°

NIGER
CHAD
NIGERIA
CAMEROON
CENTRAL AFRICAN REPUBLIC
EQUATORIAL GUINEA
RÍO MUNI
SAO TOME & PRINCIPE
GABON
CONGO
DEMOCRATIC REPUBLIC OF THE CONGO
ANGOLA
MALI
S A H E L
Libyan Desert
Gulf of Guinea
ATLANTIC OCEAN
BIOKO
Annobón Eq. Guinea
Río Muni on the mainland and the islands of Bioko, Annobón, Corisco, and the Elobeies constitute the independent country of Equatorial Guinea.
NORTHERN DARFUR
WESTERN DARFUR
SOUTHERN DARFUR
NORTHERN BAHR AL GHAZAL
WESTERN BAHR AL GHAZAL
ORIENTALE
MANIEMA
KASAÏ ORIENTAL
KASAÏ-OCCIDENTAL
KATANGA
BANDUNDU
BAS-CONGO
KINSHASA
CABINDA
ZAIRE
UÍGE
BENGO
LUANDA
CUANZA NORTE
MALANJE
LUNDA NORTE
LUNDA SUL
N'Djamena
Abuja
Yaoundé
Bangui
Libreville
Brazzaville
KINSHASA (LÉOPOLDVILLE)
Luanda
Malabo
São Tomé
Longitude East 9° of Greenwich

RED SEA
GULF OF ADEN
INDIAN OCEAN
YEMEN
ERITREA
DJIBOUTI
ETHIOPIA
SOMALILAND
SOMALIA
PUNTLAND
SOUTH SUDAN
KENYA
UGANDA
RWANDA
BURUNDI
TANZANIA
SEYCHELLES
Asmara
Djibouti
Ādīs Ābeba (Addis Ababa)
Hargeysa
Muqdisho (Mogadishu)
Nairobi
Kampala
Kigali
Bujumbura
Dodoma
Dar es Salaam
Khartoum
Juba
San'ā' (Sanaa)
Adan (Aden)
EQUATOR
SOUTHERN SUDAN
In January 2011, the people of Southern Sudan voted to form a new independent country to be named South Sudan. It is scheduled to become the newest nation on July 9, 2011.
SOMALILAND
In 1991 the Somali National Movement declared Somaliland an independent republic (in gray) with Hargeysa as the capital. It is not internationally recognized.
Boundary claimed by Sudan
Boundary undemarcated and in dispute
ILEMI TRIANGLE
LAMBERT CONFORMAL CONIC PROJECTION
SCALE 1:12,000,000
0 KILOMETERS 200 300
0 MILES 100 200 300

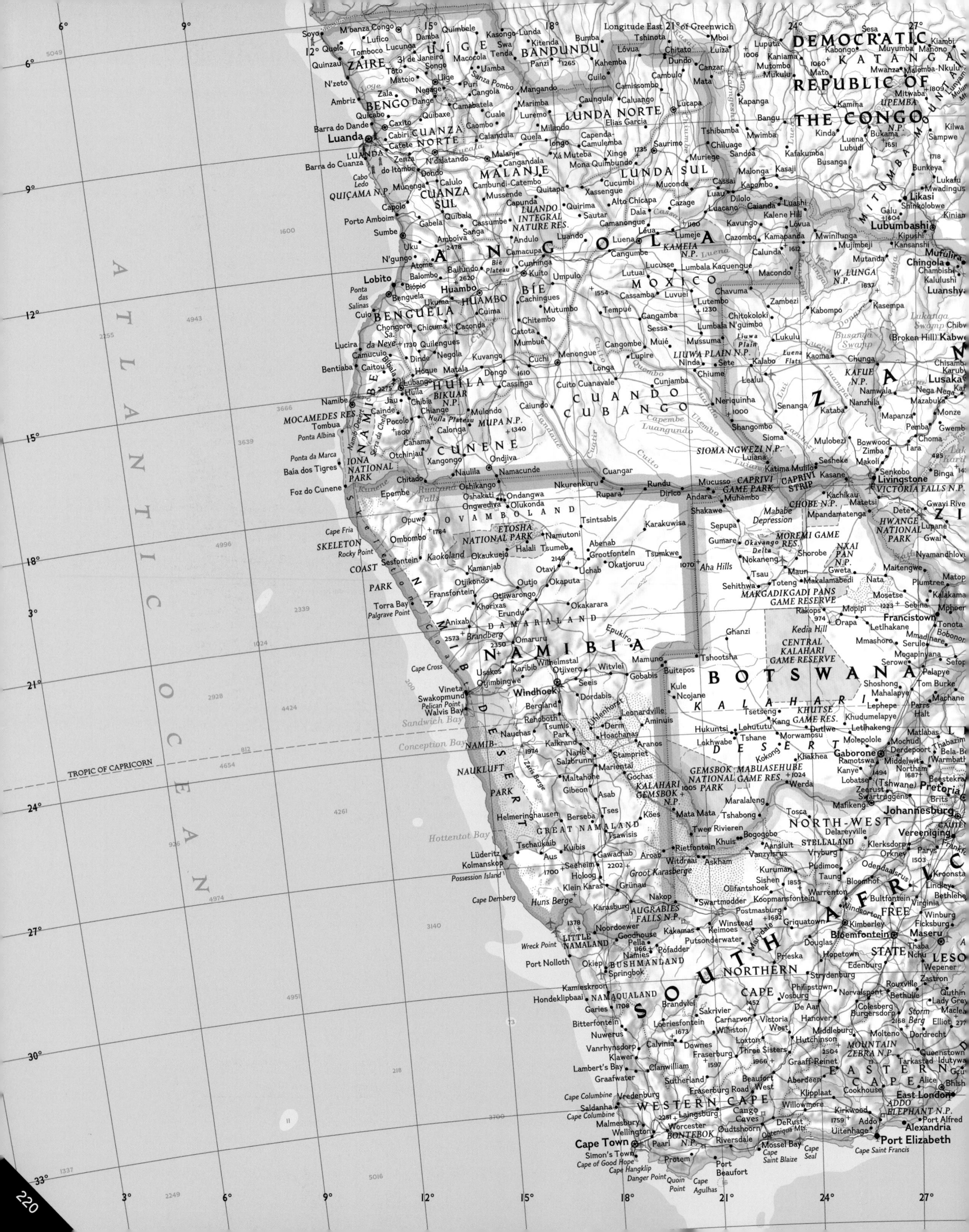
ATLANTIC OCEAN
TROPIC OF CAPRICORN
Longitude East 21° of Greenwich
DEMOCRATIC REPUBLIC OF THE CONGO
ANGOLA
NAMIBIA
BOTSWANA
ZAMBIA
SOUTH AFRICA
KATANGA
UPEMBA N.P.
MITUMBA MOUNTAINS
ZAIRE
UÍGE
BANDUNDU
BENGO
CUANZA NORTE
LUNDA NORTE
LUNDA SUL
MALANJE
CUANZA SUL
LUANDA
QUIÇAMA N.P.
LUANDO INTEGRAL NATURE RES.
BIÉ
Bié Plateau
MOXICO
KAMEIA N.P.
HUAMBO
BENGUELA
HUÍLA
BIKUAR N.P.
Huíla Plateau
MUPA N.P.
NAMIBE
CUNENE
IONA NATIONAL PARK
CUANDO CUBANGO
LIUWA PLAIN N.P.
KAFUE N.P.
W. LUNGA N.P.
SIOMA NGWEZI N.P.
CAPRIVI GAME PARK
CAPRIVI STRIP
CHOBE N.P.
HWANGE NATIONAL PARK
VICTORIA FALLS N.P.
MOREMI GAME RES.
Okavango Delta
NXAI PAN N.P.
MAKGADIKGADI PANS GAME RESERVE
CENTRAL KALAHARI GAME RESERVE
KALAHARI DESERT
KHUTSE GAME RES.
GEMSBOK NATIONAL PARK
MABUASEHUBE GAME RES.
KALAHARI GEMSBOK N.P.
SKELETON COAST PARK
OVAMBOLAND
ETOSHA NATIONAL PARK
Kaokoland
DAMARALAND
NAMIB DESERT
NAMIB-NAUKLUFT PARK
GREAT NAMALAND
AUGRABIES FALLS N.P.
LITTLE NAMALAND
BUSHMANLAND
NAMAQUALAND
NORTHERN CAPE
NORTH-WEST
STELLALAND
FREE STATE
WESTERN CAPE
EASTERN CAPE
MOUNTAIN ZEBRA N.P.
ADDO ELEPHANT N.P.
BONTEBOK N.P.
LESOTHO
Soyo
M'banza Congo
Quelo
Lufico
Tomboco
Quinzau
N'zeto
Ambriz
Luanda
Barra do Dande
Caxito
Barra do Cuanza
Cabo Ledo
Porto Amboim
Sumbe
Lobito
Benguela
Ponta das Salinas
Cuio
Lucira
Bentiaba
Namibe
Tombua
Ponta Albina
Ponta da Marca
Baía dos Tigres
Foz do Cunene
Uíge
Negage
Malanje
Saurimo
Lucapa
Dundo
Chitato
Luena
Kuito
Huambo
Lubango
Menongue
Ondjiva
Cuito Cuanavale
Cazombo
Kahemba
Tshikapa
Kananga
Mbuji-Mayi
Kolwezi
Likasi
Lubumbashi
Chingola
Mufulira
Solwezi
Kabompo
Zambezi
Mongu
Kalabo
Senanga
Sesheke
Livingstone
Katima Mulilo
Kasane
Rundu
Nkurenkuru
Oshakati
Ondangwa
Opuwo
Tsumeb
Grootfontein
Otavi
Outjo
Otjiwarongo
Khorixas
Okahandja
Omaruru
Karibib
Usakos
Swakopmund
Walvis Bay
Windhoek
Gobabis
Rehoboth
Mariental
Maltahöhe
Keetmanshoop
Lüderitz
Kolmanskop
Aus
Bethanie
Karasburg
Noordoewer
Oranjemund
Shakawe
Gumare
Maun
Nata
Francistown
Ghanzi
Kang
Tshabong
Lobatse
Gaborone
Kanye
Mahalapye
Serowe
Palapye
Molepolole
Mafikeng
Zeerust
Pretoria (Tshwane)
Johannesburg
Vereeniging
Kimberley
Bloemfontein
Maseru
Upington
Springbok
Port Nolloth
Kakamas
Prieska
De Aar
Colesberg
Graaff-Reinet
Beaufort West
Calvinia
Vanrhynsdorp
Clanwilliam
Saldanha
Vredenburg
Malmesbury
Wellington
Worcester
Paarl
Stellenbosch
Cape Town
Simon's Town
Cape of Good Hope
Cape Hangklip
Danger Point
Cape Agulhas
Riversdale
Mossel Bay
Oudtshoorn
George
Knysna
Uitenhage
Port Elizabeth
Cape Saint Francis
Alexandria
Port Alfred
East London
Queenstown
Cookhouse
Aberdeen
Middelburg
Cape Columbine
Cape Cross
Cape Fria
Palgrave Point
Torra Bay
Sandwich Bay
Conception Bay
Hottentot Bay
Possession Island
Cape Dernberg
Wreck Point
Brandberg
Huns Berge
Groot Karasberge
Zambezi
Cubango
Kunene
Okavango
Cuando
Ruacana Falls
Epupa
6°
9°
12°
15°
18°
21°
24°
27°
30°
33°
3°

TANZANIA
MOZAMBIQUE
MALAWI
MADAGASCAR
SEYCHELLES
COMOROS
Dar es Salaam
Lilongwe
Harare
Maputo
Antananarivo
Moroni
MOZAMBIQUE CHANNEL
INDIAN OCEAN
LAMBERT CONFORMAL CONIC PROJECTION
SCALE 1:12,000,000
0 KILOMETERS 200 300
0 MILES 100 200 300

MAURITANIA
SENEGAL
GAMBIA
GUINEA-BISSAU
GUINEA
SIERRA LEONE
LIBERIA
CÔTE D'IVOIRE (IVORY COAST)
ATLANTIC OCEAN
WESTERN SAHARA Morocco
Nouadhibou
Nouakchott
Saint-Louis
Dakar
Banjul
Bissau
Conakry
Freetown
Monrovia
Bamako
Yamoussoukro
Abidjan
BANC D'ARGUIN N.P.
DELTA DU SALOUM N.P.
KIANG WEST N.P.
NIOKOLO-KOBA N.P.
BADIAR N.P.
BOUCLE DU BAOULE N.P.
MOUNT SANGBE N.P.
MARAHOUE N.P.
TAÏ N.P.
COMOÉ N.P.
D'ASAGNY N.P.
Arquipélago dos Bijagós
Îles Tristao
Îles de Los
Banana Islands
Turtle Islands
Sherbro Island
Loma Mts.
Nimba Mts.
Fouta Djallon
Grain Coast
Ivory Coast
Cape Palmas
Cap Vert
Cap Blanc
Cap Timiris
Cap Verga
ALBERS CONIC EQUAL-AREA PROJECTION
SCALE 1:8,000,000
0 KILOMETERS 120 160 200
0 MILES 40 80 120 160 200
Longitude West 6° of Greenwich

ALGERIA
SAHARA
NIGER
NIGERIA
BENIN
TOGO
GHANA
BURKINA FASO
CAMEROON
EQUATORIAL GUINEA
BIOKO
GULF OF GUINEA
Bight of Benin
Slave Coast
Gold Coast
Tassili Oua-n-Ahaggar
Adrar des Ifôghas
Aïr (Aïr Massif)
Massif de Tarazit
Erg du Ténéré
Ténéré
Ténéré du Tafassâsset
Tamesna
Talak
Azaouagh
Damergou
Damagarim
Adar Doutchi
Koutous
Manga
Kaouar
Tanezrouft
Timétrine
Erg I-n-Sâkâne
Gourma
Mossi
Lake Chad (Lac Tchad)
Lake Volta
Kainji Lake
"W" NATIONAL PARK
PENDJARI N.P.
KAINJI LAKE N.P.
YANKARI N.P.
CROSS RIVER N.P.
KORUP N.P.
FARO RESERVE
GASHAKA-GUMTI N.P.
MOLE N.P.
DIGYA N.P.
KABORE-TAMBI N.P.
KERAN N.P.
FAZAO-MALFAKASSA N.P.
Niger
Benue
Sirba
Volta
White Volta
Black Volta
Oti
Mono
Ouémé
Okpara
Gongola
Katsina Ala
Niger Delta
Cameroon Mt. 4100
Palm Point
Alantika Mts.
Chaîne de l'Atakora
Mt. Koronga
Niamey
Ouagadougou
Abuja
Accra
Lomé
Porto-Novo
Cotonou
LAGOS
IBADAN
Kano
Kaduna
Zaria
Sokoto
Maiduguri
Jos
Ilorin
Ogbomosho
Oshogbo
Benin City
Onitsha
Enugu
Aba
Port Harcourt
Calabar
Warri
Kumasi
Tamale
Sekondi-Takoradi
Tema
Douala
Yaoundé
Malabo
Bamenda
Garoua
Agadez
Zinder
Maradi
Tahoua
Gao
Arlit
Bilma
Parakou
Djougou
Kara
Meridian of Greenwich (London)
Longitude East 6° of Greenwich
GULF OF GUINEA

SUDAN
SOUTHERN DARFUR
SOUTHERN KORDOFAN
WESTERN KORDOFAN
BLUE NILE
Longitude East 33° of Greenwich
SOUTH SUDAN
UPPER NILE
NORTHERN BAHR AL GHAZAL
UNITY
WARAB
WESTERN BAHR AL GHAZAL
JONGLI
LAKES
WESTERN EQUATORIA
CENTRAL EQUATORIA
EASTERN EQUATORIA
SOUTHERN SUDAN
In January 2011, the people of Southern Sudan voted to form a new independent country to be named South Sudan. It is scheduled to become the newest nation on July 9, 2011.
CEN. AFRICAN REP.
RADOM NATIONAL PARK
SOUTHERN NATIONAL PARK
BOMA NATIONAL PARK
GAMBELA NATIONAL PARK
ILEMI TRIANGLE
ILEMI TRIANGLE Administered by Kenya; conflicting claims by Sudan and Ethiopia
Boundary claimed by Sudan
ETHIOPIA
OROMIA
AMHARA
DJIBOUTI
Ādīs Ābeba (Addis Ababa)
OMO NATIONAL PARK
MAGO N.P.
ABIJATTA-SHALLA LAKES N.P.
AWASH N.P.
YANGUDI RASSA N.P.
MALKA MARI N.P.
SOMALIA
KENYA
EQUATOR
Nairobi
UGANDA
BUGANDA
Kampala
MURCHISON FALLS N.P.
KIDEPO VALLEY N.P.
QUEEN ELIZABETH N.P.
RUWENZORI MTN. N.P.
SIBILOI N.P.
SOUTH ISLAND N.P.
MARSABIT NATURE RESERVE
SAMBURU RES.
MERU N.P.
KORA N.P.
MASAI MARA NATIONAL RESERVE
AMBOSELI NATIONAL PARK
TSAVO NATIONAL PARK
WATAMU MARINE N.P.
LAKE VICTORIA
RWANDA
Kigali
BURUNDI
Bujumbura
MARA
MWANZA
SHINYANGA
KAGERA
ARUSHA
KILIMANJARO N.P.
SERENGETI NATIONAL PARK
AKAGERA N.P.
RUBONDO ISLAND N.P.
DEMOCRATIC REPUBLIC OF THE CONGO
ORIENTALE
NORD-KIVU
SUD-KIVU
MANIEMA
MAIKO N.P.
VIRUNGA NATIONAL PARK
KAHUZI-BIEGA N.P.
GARAMBA NAT. PARK
Kisangani (Stanleyville)
MONTS MITUMBA

INDIAN OCEAN
MOZAMBIQUE CHANNEL
TANZANIA
MALAWI
MOZAMBIQUE
ZAMBIA
ZIMBABWE
BOTSWANA
NAMIBIA
ANGOLA
KATANGA
ALBERS CONIC EQUAL-AREA PROJECTION
SCALE 1:8,000,000
Dar es Salaam
Zanzibar
Dodoma
Lilongwe
Blantyre
Lusaka
Harare
Lubumbashi
Beira
Tete
Quelimane
Nampula
Mbeya
Tabora
Kigoma
Morogoro
LAKE MALAWI (LAKE NYASA)
Ndola
Kitwe
Livingstone

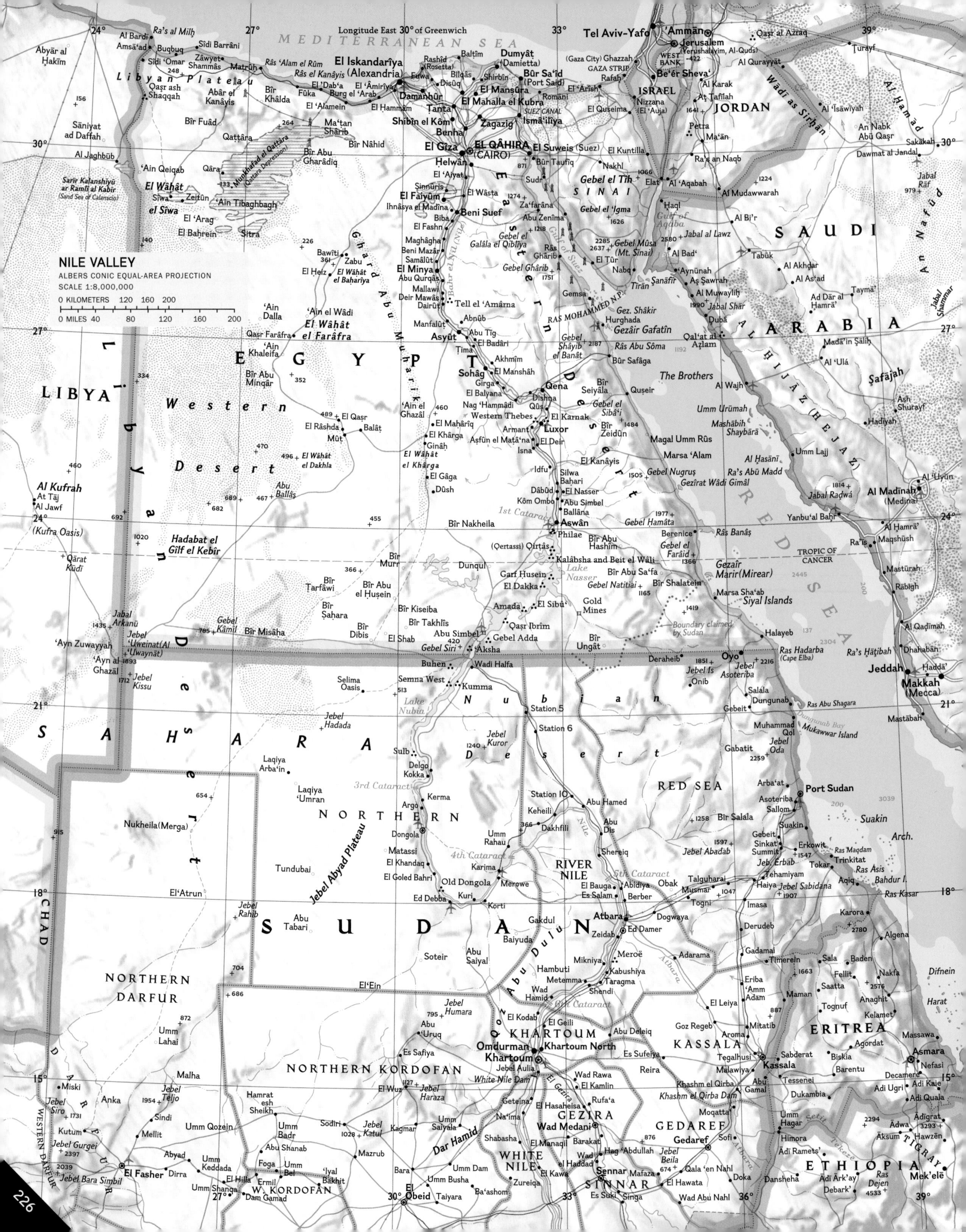

NILE VALLEY
ALBERS CONIC EQUAL-AREA PROJECTION
SCALE 1:8,000,000
0 KILOMETERS 120 160 200
0 MILES 40 80 120 160 200
Longitude East 30° of Greenwich
MEDITERRANEAN SEA
RED SEA
EGYPT
LIBYA
SUDAN
ISRAEL
JORDAN
SAUDI ARABIA
ERITREA
ETHIOPIA
CHAD
Libyan Plateau
Western Desert
Libyan Desert
Eastern Desert
SAHARA Desert
Nubian Desert
SINAI
Al Hijaz (Hejaz)
TROPIC OF CANCER
Wādī as Sirḩān
Al Ḩamād
An Nafūd
El Iskandarîya (Alexandria)
El Qâhira (Cairo)
El Giza
Helwân
Bûr Sa'îd (Port Said)
Dumyât (Damietta)
Rashîd (Rosetta)
El Mansûra
El Mahalla el Kubra
Tanta
Damanhûr
Zagazig
Benha
Shibîn el Kôm
Ismâ'ilîya
El Suweis (Suez)
SUEZ CANAL
Munkhafad el Qaṭṭâra (Qattara Depression)
Qaṭṭâra
Siwa
El Wâhât el Siwa
Al Jaghbūb
Sarīr Kalanshiyū ar Ramlī al Kabīr (Sand Sea of Calanscio)
Salūm
Matrûh
Sîdi Barrâni
Ra's al Milḩ
El Faiyûm
Beni Suef
El Minya
Asyût
Sohâg
Qena
Luxor
Aswân
Idfu
Isna
El Karnak
Western Thebes
Kôm Ombo
Philae
1st Cataract
Lake Nasser
Abu Simbel
El Wâhât el Baḩarîya
El Wâhât el Farâfra
El Wâhât el Dakhla
El Wâhât el Khârga
El Khârga
Ghard Abu Muḩarik
Hadabat el Gilf el Kebîr
Jebel 'Uweinat (Al 'Uwaynāt)
Al Kufrah
(Kufra Oasis)
Gebel el Tîh
Gebel Mûsa (Mt. Sinai)
Sharm el Sheikh
RAS MOHAMMED N.P.
Gulf of Suez
Gulf of Aqaba
El 'Arîsh
Tel Aviv-Yafo
'Ammān
Jerusalem (Yerushalayim, Al-Quds)
WEST BANK
GAZA STRIP
(Gaza City) Ghazzah
Be'ér Sheva'
Elat
Al 'Aqabah
Al Karak
Tabūk
Al Madīnah (Medina)
Yanbu'al Baḩr
Jeddah
Makkah (Mecca)
Rābigh
Al Wajh
Ḑubā
Bûr Safâga
Quṣeir
Marsa 'Alam
Berenice
Râs Banâs
Halayeb
Siyal Islands
Gezâir Marir (Mirear)
The Brothers
Boundary claimed by Sudan
Wadi Halfa
Lake Nubia
Semna West
Kumma
Selima Oasis
Station 5
Station 6
Station 10
Abu Hamed
2nd Cataract
3rd Cataract
4th Cataract
5th Cataract
6th Cataract
Kerma
Dongola
Old Dongola
Karima
Merowe
Ed Debba
Jebel Abyad Plateau
NORTHERN
RIVER NILE
Atbara
Ed Damer
Berber
Shendi
Meroë
Bayuda
Abu Dulu
KHARTOUM
Omdurman
Khartoum
Khartoum North
Jebel Aulia
White Nile Dam
El Gezira
GEZIRA
Wad Medani
Sennar
SINNAR
GEDAREF
Gedaref
KASSALA
Kassala
Khashm el Qirba Dam
Port Sudan
Suakin
Suakin Arch.
Tokar
Trinkitat
Haiya
Muhammad Qol
Dungunab
Dungunab Bay
Mukawwar Island
Jebel Oda
Jebel Elba
Ras Hadarba (Cape Elba)
NORTHERN KORDOFAN
W. KORDOFAN
El Obeid
NORTHERN DARFUR
WESTERN DARFUR
DARFUR
El Fasher
Jebel Marra
WHITE NILE
Dar Hamid
Laqiya Arba'in
Laqiya 'Umran
Nukheila (Merga)
El'Atrun
Asmara
Massawa
Mek'elē
TIGRAY
Dahlak Arch.
Ras Kasar
Bahdur I.
Ras Asis

SOUTH AFRICA
ALBERS CONIC EQUAL-AREA PROJECTION
SCALE 1:8,000,000
0 KILOMETERS 40 80 120 160 200
0 MILES 40 80 120 160 200
SOUTH AFRICA
BOTSWANA
NAMIBIA
ZIMBABWE
MOZAMBIQUE
LESOTHO
SWAZILAND
KALAHARI DESERT
INDIAN OCEAN
ATLANTIC OCEAN
MOZAMBIQUE CHANNEL
NORTHERN CAPE
WESTERN CAPE
EASTERN CAPE
FREE STATE
NORTH-WEST
KWAZULU-NATAL
MPUMALANGA
LIMPOPO
GAUTENG
Pretoria (Tshwane)
Johannesburg
Cape Town
Durban
Port Elizabeth
East London
Bloemfontein
Kimberley
Maseru
Gaborone
Windhoek
Maputo
Bulawayo
CENTRAL KALAHARI GAME RESERVE
KRUGER N.P.
Cape of Good Hope
Cape Agulhas
TROPIC OF CAPRICORN

Australia and Oceania

ISLAND NATION AND SMALLEST, flattest continent, with a territory about the size of the United States, Australia has gone on a planetary walk-about since it broke away from the supercontinent of Gondwana about 65 million years ago. Isolated, dry, and scoured by erosion, Australia developed unique animals, notably marsupials such as kangaroos, and plants, such as more than 600 eucalyptus species. The land surface has been stable enough to preserve some of the world's oldest rocks and mineral deposits, dating to the original formation of Earth's crust. Precambrian fossils include stromatolites—photosynthetic bacteria that generated oxygen in the early atmosphere and whose descendants still grow mounded in shallow lagoons, such as in Shark Bay in western Australia.

In contrast, New Zealand's two principal islands, about the size of Colorado, are younger and tell of a more violent geology that raised high volcanic mountains above deep fjords, leaving landscapes reminiscent of Europe's Alps, Norway's coast, and Scotland's moors. Both nations were first inhabited by seafarers, Australia as long as 50,000 years ago, New Zealand little more than a thousand years ago. From the late 18th to the early 20th century, both were British colonies. Both have transformed themselves from commerce based on exports of beef and hides, lamb and wool, to fully integrated industrialized and service-oriented economies. Both have striven with varying success to accommodate aboriginal peoples, as well as recent immigrants—many from Vietnam and China and many from Muslim countries—as part of a diverse, modern society.

Oceania, roughly those islands of the southwest Pacific that include Polynesia, Micronesia, and Melanesia, was settled by people migrating from east and southeast Asia, sailing in multihulled vessels. These adventurers settled nearly every inhabitable Pacific island and perhaps made landfall as far distant as South America before Europeans appeared over the horizon in the 17th century. Today these islands are in various states of nationhood or dependency, prosperity or poverty, and often ignored if not outright exploited.

PHYSICAL AUSTRALIA
AZIMUTHAL EQUIDISTANT PROJECTION
SCALE 1:19,000,000
0 KILOMETERS 100 200 300 400 500
0 MILES 100 200 300 400 500
Longitude East 130° of Greenwich
TROPIC OF CAPRICORN
INDIAN OCEAN
ARAFURA SEA
TIMOR SEA
CORAL SEA
TASMAN SEA
SOLOMON SEA
GREAT AUSTRALIAN BIGHT
GULF OF CARPENTARIA
BASS STRAIT
TORRES STRAIT
INDONESIA
TIMOR-LESTE (EAST TIMOR)
Dili
PAPUA NEW GUINEA
Port Moresby
NEW GUINEA
Gulf of Papua
Owen Stanley Range
Mt. Victoria
TROBRIAND IS.
D'ENTRECASTEAUX IS.
LOUISIADE ARCHIPELAGO
Surabaya
Bali Sea
Savu Sea
JAVA
BALI
LOMBOK
SUMBAWA
SUMBA
FLORES
TIMOR
WESTERN AUSTRALIA
NORTHERN TERRITORY
SOUTH AUSTRALIA
QUEENSLAND
NEW SOUTH WALES
VICTORIA
TASMANIA
AUSTRALIA
Canberra, A.C.T.
JERVIS BAY TERRITORY
Sydney
Melbourne
Brisbane
Adelaide
Perth
Darwin
Hobart
GREAT DIVIDING RANGE
GREAT ARTESIAN BASIN
CENTRAL LOWLANDS
MURRAY RIVER BASIN
WESTERN PLATEAU
GREAT SANDY DESERT
Gibson Desert
Great Victoria Desert
Simpson Desert
Tanami Desert
Sturt Stony Desert
Barkly Tableland
Nullarbor Plain
Eucla Basin
Kimberley Plateau
ARNHEM LAND
Cape York Peninsula
Eyre Peninsula
LAKE EYRE BASIN
Lake Eyre
Lowest point in Australia
-16 (-52 ft)
Mt. Kosciuszko 2228 (7310 ft)
Highest point in Australia
Australian Alps
Musgrave Ranges
Macdonnell Ranges
Hamersley Range
Flinders Ranges
Gawler Ranges
Uluru (Ayers Rock)
Kata Tjuta (Mt. Olga)
Great Barrier Reef
Groote Eylandt
Kangaroo I.
Melville I.
Bathurst I.
Flinders I.
FURNEAUX GROUP
King Island
Lord Howe I.
Ball's Pyramid
Fraser Island
Moreton I.
N. Stradbroke I.
Shark Bay
Exmouth Gulf
Spencer Gulf
Gulf St. Vincent
Port Phillip Bay
Geographe Bay
Cape Leeuwin
Cape Byron
Cape York
Murray
Darling
Murrumbidgee
Lachlan
Macquarie
Victoria
Mitchell
Houtman Abrolhos
Dampier Archipelago
Nullarbor Plain

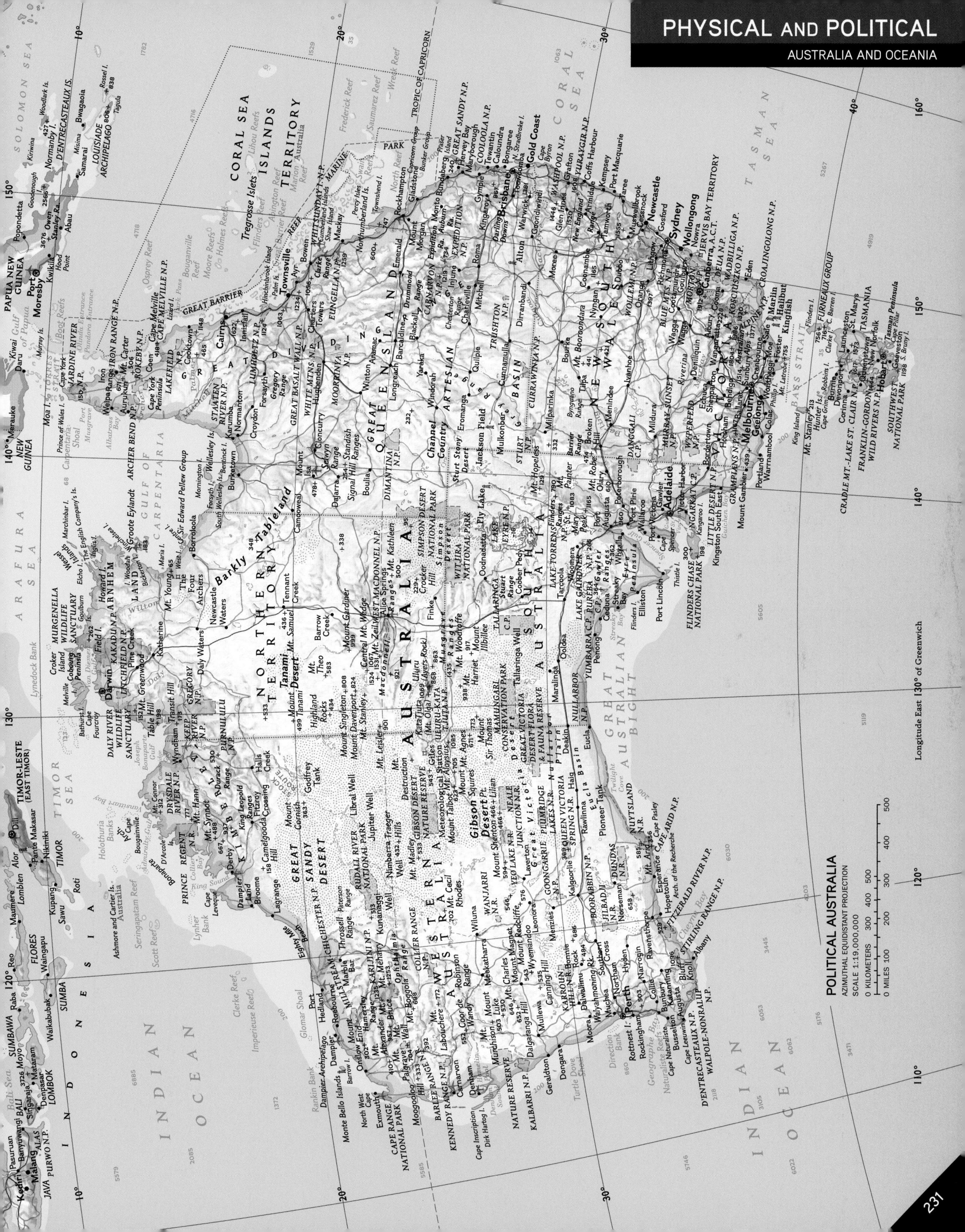
POLITICAL AUSTRALIA
AZIMUTHAL EQUIDISTANT PROJECTION
SCALE 1:19,000,000
0 KILOMETERS 100 200 300 400 500
0 MILES 100 200 300 400 500
Longitude East 130° of Greenwich
INDIAN OCEAN
CORAL SEA
TASMAN SEA
ARAFURA SEA
TIMOR SEA
GULF OF CARPENTARIA
GREAT AUSTRALIAN BIGHT
BASS STRAIT
TROPIC OF CAPRICORN
PAPUA NEW GUINEA
INDONESIA
TIMOR-LESTE (EAST TIMOR)
CORAL SEA ISLANDS TERRITORY
WESTERN AUSTRALIA
NORTHERN TERRITORY
SOUTH AUSTRALIA
QUEENSLAND
NEW SOUTH WALES
VICTORIA
TASMANIA
JERVIS BAY TERRITORY
Canberra, A.C.T.
Perth
Darwin
Adelaide
Melbourne
Sydney
Brisbane
Hobart
Alice Springs
GREAT SANDY DESERT
GIBSON DESERT
GREAT VICTORIA DESERT
SIMPSON DESERT
TANAMI DESERT
NULLARBOR PLAIN
GREAT ARTESIAN BASIN
Barkly Tableland
GREAT BARRIER REEF
KIMBERLEY
ARNHEM LAND
CAPE YORK PENINSULA
GREAT DIVIDING RANGE

FEDERATED STATES OF MICRONESIA

Yap Is.

PALAU

Caroline Islands

Chuuk (Truk Is.)

Enewetak Atoll

MARSHALL ISLANDS

Ralik Chain

Ratak Chain

NAURU

KIRIBATI

Gilbert Islands

HOWLAND I.
BAKER I. (U.S.)

PAPUA NEW GUINEA

Bismarck Archipelago

SOLOMON ISLANDS

Santa Cruz Is.

TUVALU

TOKELAU (N.Z.)

AMERICAN SAMOA (U.S.)

WALLIS & FUTUNA IS. (FR.)

VANUATU

SAMOA

Laucala Bay ○

NEW CALEDONIA (FRANCE)

FIJI

NIUE (N.Z.)

TONGA

NORFOLK I. (AUSTRALIA)

AUSTRALIA

Kermadec Is. (N.Z.)

○ Sydney

Melbourne ○

Auckland ○

TASMANIA

NEW ZEALAND

LAND COVER

- ■ Evergreen needleleaf forest
- ■ Evergreen broadleaf forest
- ■ Deciduous needleleaf forest
- ■ Deciduous broadleaf forest
- ■ Mixed forest
- ■ Woody savanna
- ■ Savanna
- ■ Closed shrubland
- □ Open shrubland
- ■ Grassland
- ■ Cropland
- ■ Barren or sparsely vegetated
- ■ Urban or built-up
- □ Snow and ice
- ■ Cropland / natural vegetation mosaic
- ■ Wetland

Chatham Is. (N.Z.)

TEMPERATURE AND RAINFALL

Laucala Bay, Fiji

■ Temperatures above 0°C
■ Temperatures below 0°C

High temperature — Low temperature
Rainfall
(115 mm = 4.5 in)

Auckland, New Zealand

Rainfall
(115 mm = 4.5 in)

Melbourne, Australia

Sydney, Australia

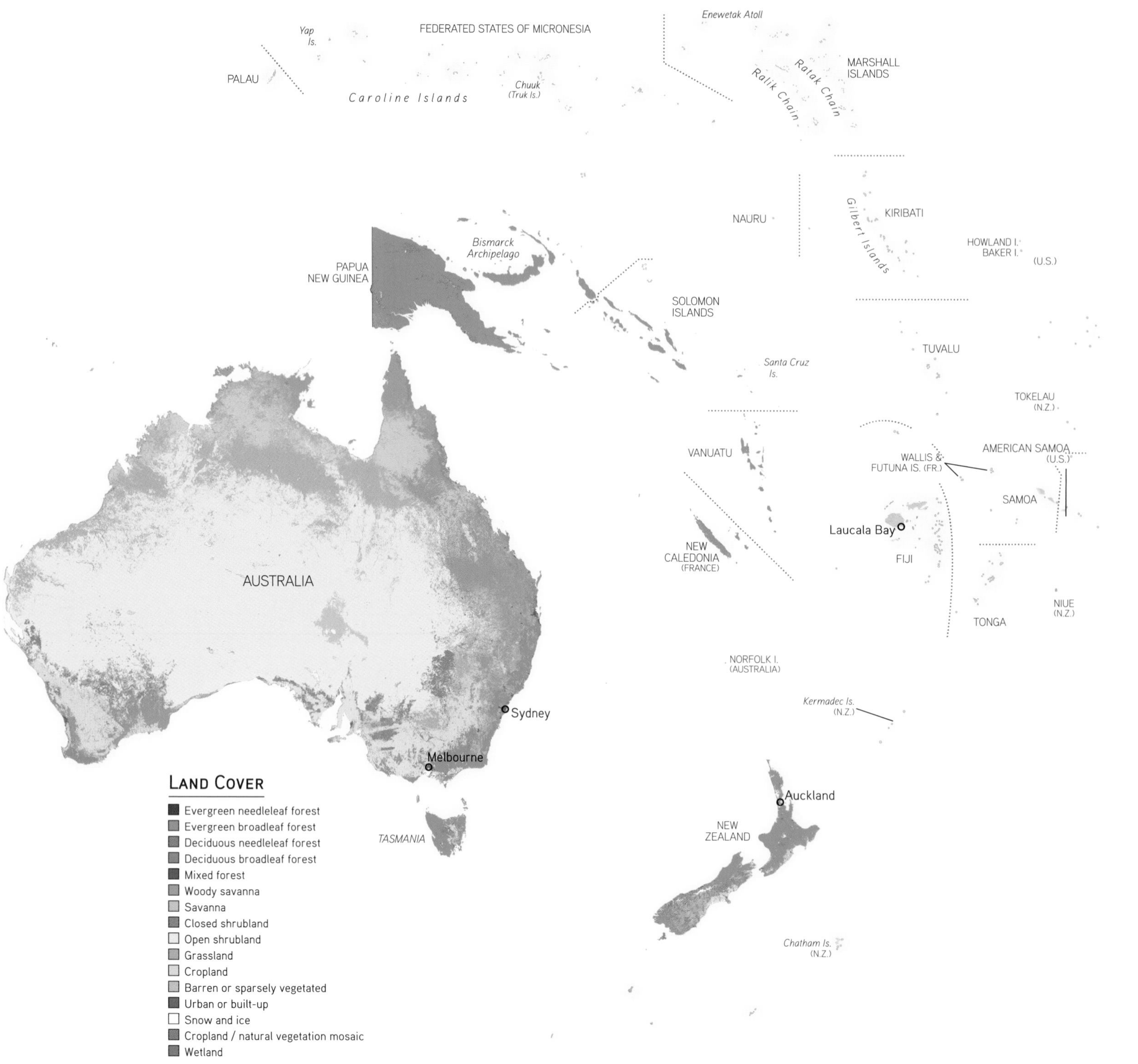

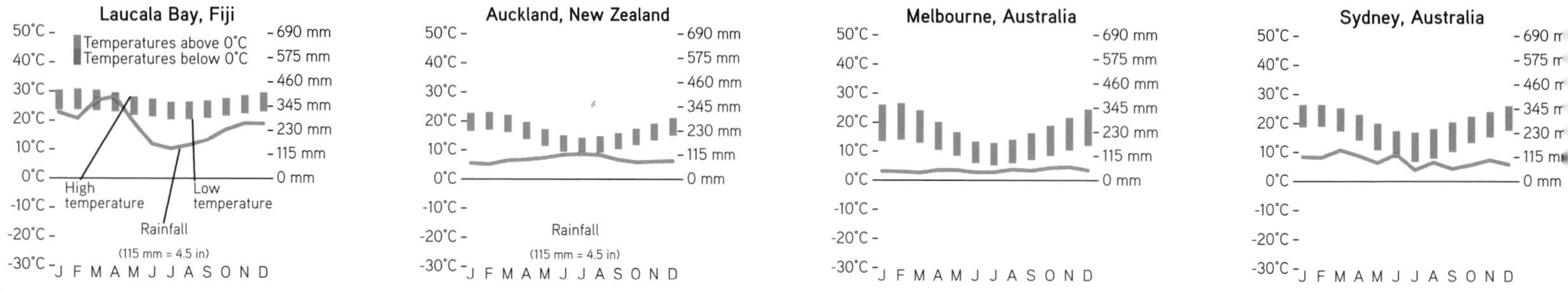

The entire extent of Oceania encompasses the islands of the Central and South Pacific, including Hawai'i, New Zealand, and Australia.

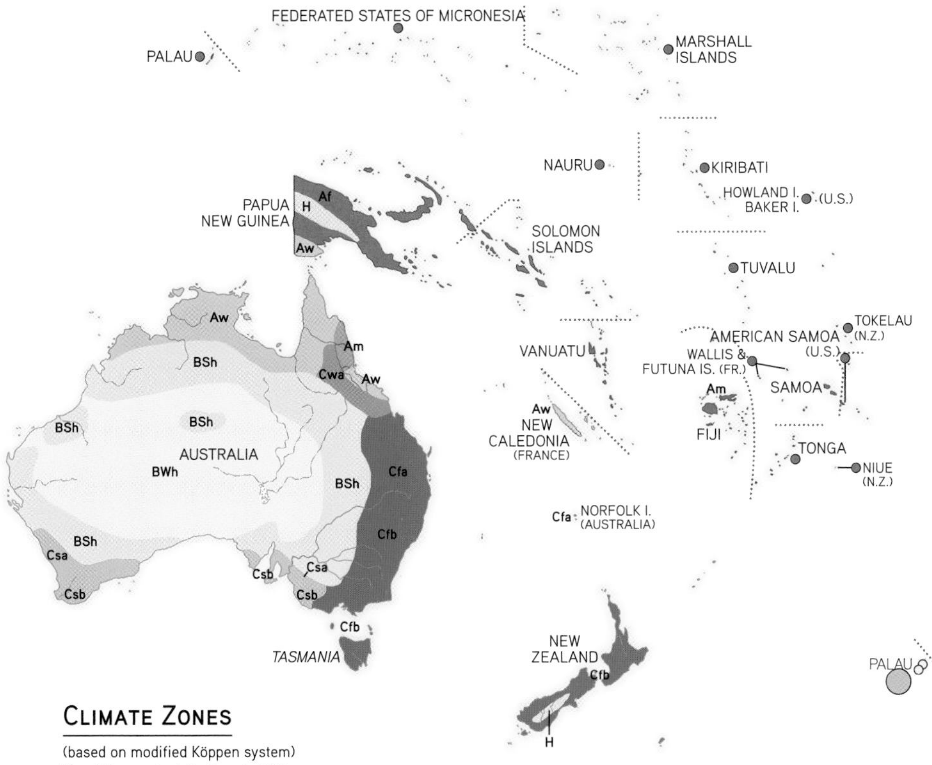

Climate Zones

(based on modified Köppen system)

Humid equatorial climate (A)
- No dry season (Af)
- Short dry season (Am)
- Dry winter (Aw)

Dry climate (B)
- Semiarid (BS)
- Arid (BW)

h = hot
k = cold

Humid temperate climate (C)
- No dry season (Cf)
- Dry summer (Cs)

a = hot summer
b = cool summer

Highland climate (H)
- Unclassified highlands

Natural Hazards

Population Density, 2010

People per square km	People per square mi
More than 1,000	More than 2,500
100–1,000	250–2,500
Less than 100	Less than 250

Fire Intensity
(from gas burn off, slash-and-burn agriculture, or natural causes)
High
Low

Recorded Natural Event

Major Earthquake, 1900-2010
Moment magnitude
- More than 7.0
- 6.0–7.0
- Less than 6.0

Volcano

Tsunami, 1900-2010
Run-up height

Meters	Feet
More than 10	More than 32
5–10	16–32
Less than 5	Less than 16

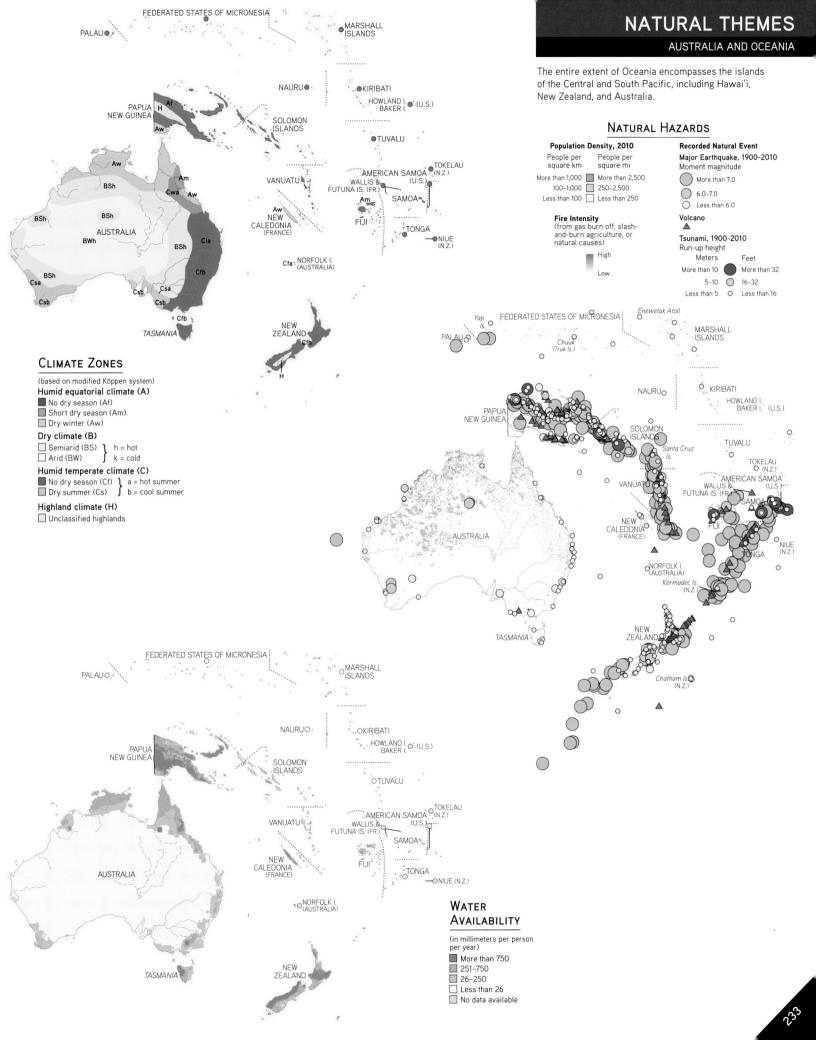

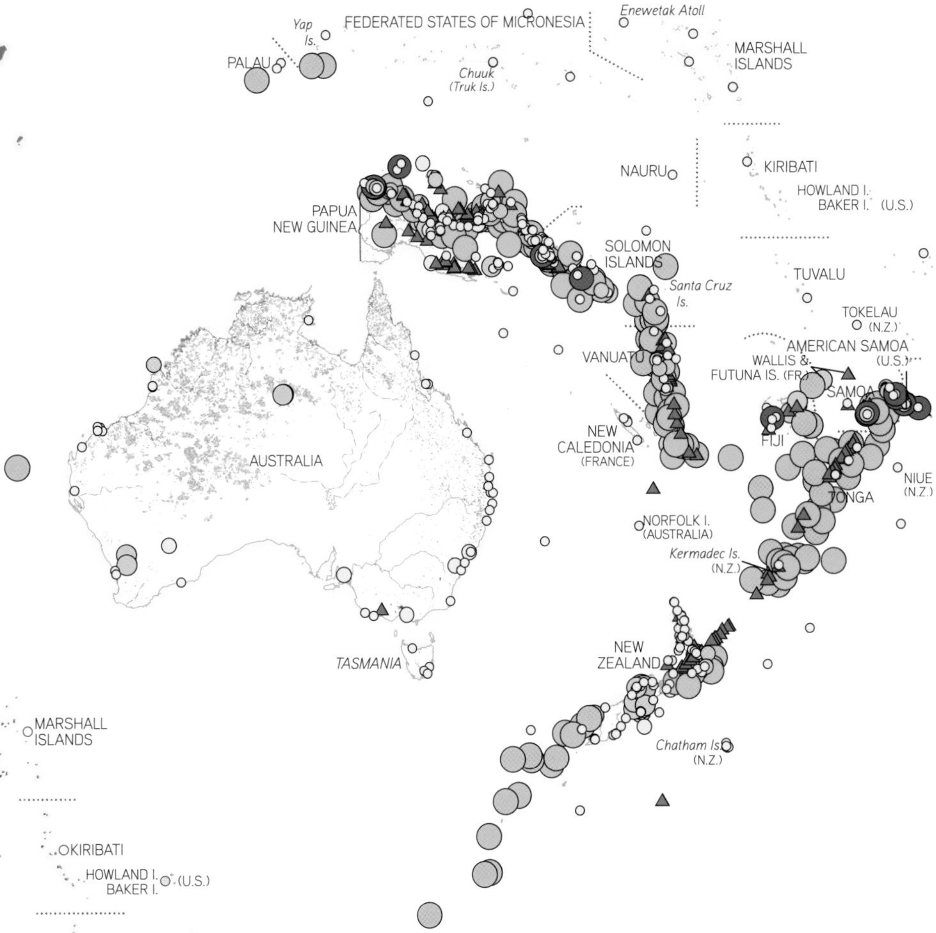

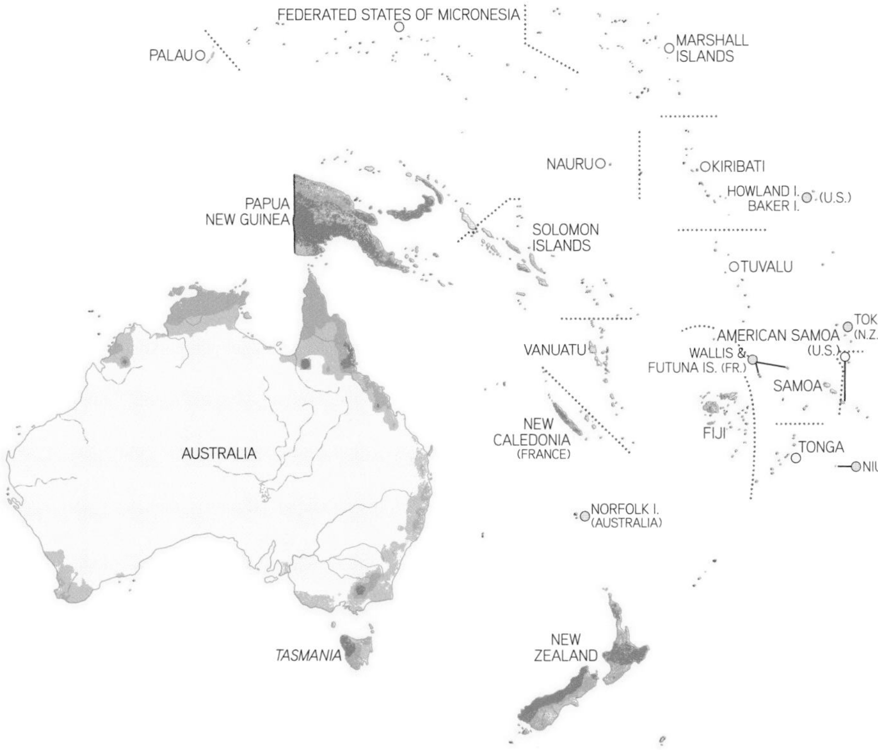

Water Availability

(in millimeters per person per year)
- More than 750
- 251–750
- 26–250
- Less than 26
- No data available

POPULATION DENSITY

People per Square Kilometer	People per Square Mile
More than 195	More than 500
60–195	150–500
10–59	25–149
1–9	1–24
Less than 1	Less than 1

Yap Is.

FEDERATED STATES OF MICRONESIA

Enewetak Atoll

Melekeok
PALAU

Caroline Islands

Chuuk (Truk Is.)

Palikir

MARSHALL ISLANDS

Ralik Chain

Ratak Chain

Majuro

NAURU
Yaren

Tarawa
KIRIBATI

Gilbert Islands

HOWLAND I.
BAKER I. (U.S.)

PAPUA NEW GUINEA

Bismarck Archipelago

Port Moresby

SOLOMON ISLANDS

Honiara

Santa Cruz Is.

TUVALU

Funafuti

TOKELAU (N.Z.)

CORAL SEA ISLANDS TERRITORY (AUSTRALIA)

VANUATU

Port Vila

WALLIS & FUTUNA IS. (FR.)

AMERICAN SAMOA (U.S.)

Apia
SAMOA

Pago Pago

Suva

AUSTRALIA

NEW CALEDONIA (FRANCE)

Nouméa

FIJI

Nukualofa

NIUE (N.Z.)

TONGA

Canberra, A.C.T.

Norfolk I. (AUSTRALIA)

Kermadec Is. (N.Z.)

TASMANIA

NEW ZEALAND

Wellington

Chatham Is. (N.Z.)

POPULATION PYRAMIDS

VANUATU
Age — Male — Female
80+
60–64
40–44
20–24
0–4
10   5   0   5   10
Percent of population

PAPUA NEW GUINEA
Age — Male — Female
80+
60–64
40–44
20–24
0–4
10   5   0   5   10
Percent of population

NEW ZEALAND
Age — Male — Female
80+
60–64
40–44
20–24
0–4
10   5   0   5   10
Percent of population

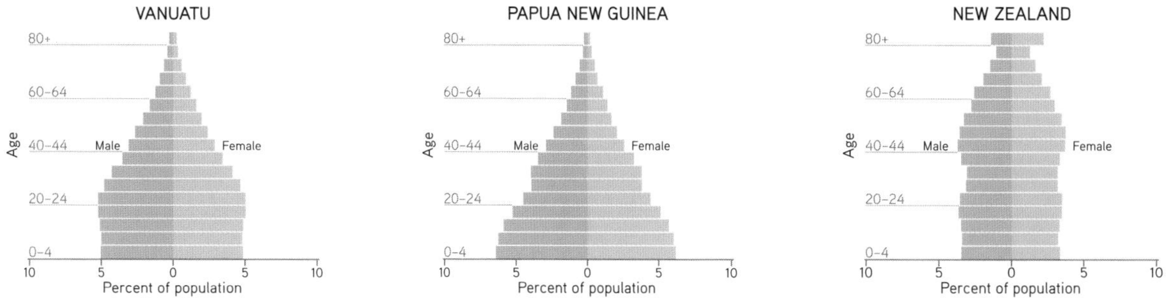

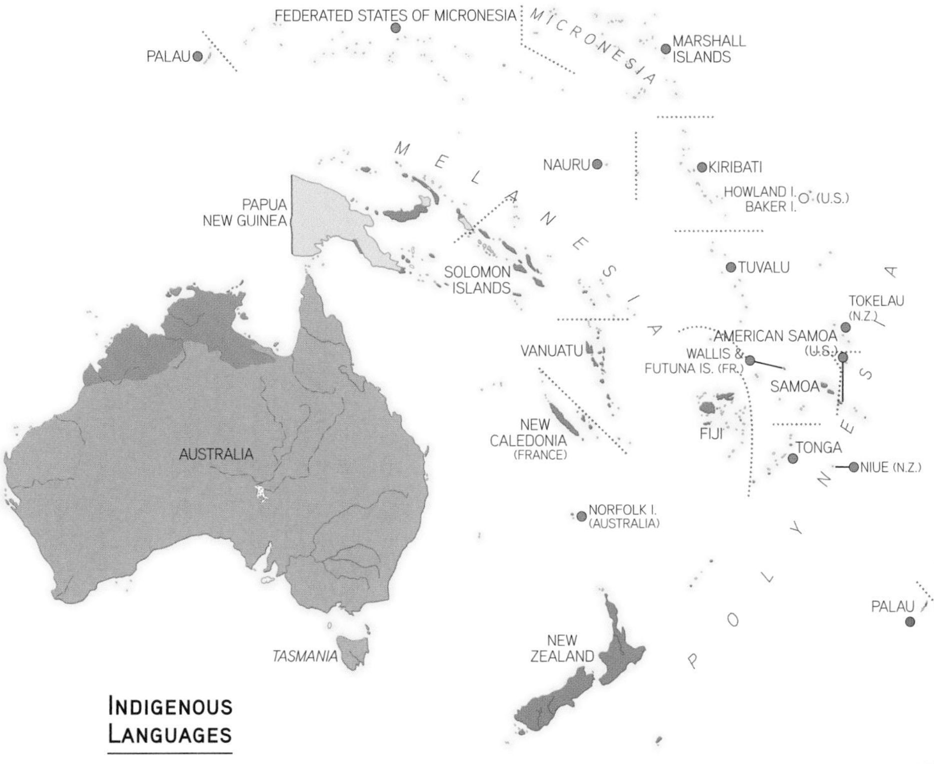

INDIGENOUS LANGUAGES

Australian
- Aboriginal
- Undetermined

- Austronesian
- Papuan
- Uninhabited

URBANIZATION

Urban agglomerations, 2010
(population in millions)
- ■ More than 10.0
- ▲ 5.0–10.0
- ● 1.0–4.9
- ○ .75–.99

Percent urban population, 2010
- More than 75%
- 50%–75%
- 25%–49%
- Less than 25%

POPULATION CHANGE

Projected population change, 2010–2050 (by percentage)
- More than 100%
- 50%–100%
- 0.01%–49%
- No change
- Population loss

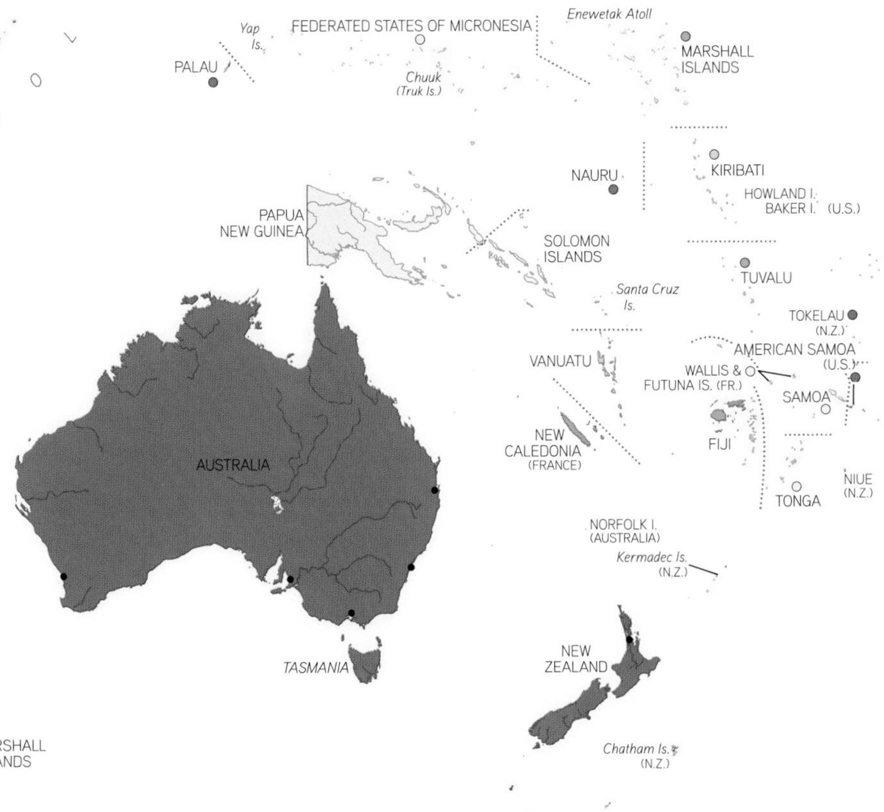

Yap Is.

FEDERATED STATES OF MICRONESIA

Enewetak Atoll

PALAU
Melekeok ✪

Chuuk (Truk Is.)

Caroline Islands

Palikir ✪

Ralik Chain
Ratak Chain

MARSHALL ISLANDS
Majuro ✪

Tarawa ✪
KIRIBATI
Gilbert Islands

Howland I. (U.S.)
Baker I.

BISMARCK ARCHIPELAGO

PAPUA NEW GUINEA

NAURU
Yaren

SOLOMON ISLANDS

Port Moresby ✪

Honiara ✪

Santa Cruz Islands

CORAL SEA ISLANDS TERRITORY (AUSTRALIA)

VANUATU

Port Vila ✪

NEW CALEDONIA (FRANCE)
Nouméa ©

TUVALU
Funafuti ✪

TOKELAU (N.Z.)

WALLIS AND FUTUNA IS. (FR.)

SAMOA
Apia ◎
Pago Pago
AMERICAN SAMOA (U.S.)

FIJI
Suva ●

TONGA
Nuku'alofa ✪

NIUE (N.Z.)

Darwin ●

AUSTRALIA

Brisbane ●

Perth ●

Adelaide ●
Sydney ●
Canberra, A.C.T. ✪
Melbourne ●

Norfolk I. (AUSTRALIA)

Kermadec Is. (N.Z.)

NEW ZEALAND
Wellington ✪

TASMANIA

Hobart ●

Chatham Is. (N.Z.)

Auckland Is. (N.Z.)

LAND USE

More disturbed — Cropland
Less disturbed
More disturbed — Pasture

■ Built-up area
▨ Irrigated land

IMPORTS AND EXPORTS

VALUE OF IMPORTS

AUSTRALIA

- Pharmaceutical products 4%
- Chemical products 4%
- Food 5%
- Ores and metals 7%
- Electronic equipment 11%
- Petroleum products 14%
- Manufactured goods 17%
- Machinery and transport equipment 28%
- Other 10%

NEW ZEALAND

- Pharmaceutical products 3%
- Ores and metals 4%
- Chemical products 4%
- Food 9%
- Electronic equipment 9%
- Petroleum products 15%
- Manufactured goods 19%
- Machinery and transport equipment 25%
- Other 12%

VALUE OF EXPORTS

AUSTRALIA

- Chemical products 3%
- Manufactured goods 4%
- Machinery and transport equipment 4%
- Food 10%
- Petroleum products 29%
- Ores and metals 39%
- Other 11%

NEW ZEALAND

- Electronic equipment 2%
- Petroleum products 5%
- Machinery and transport equipment 6%
- Ores and metals 7%
- Manufactured goods 7%
- Wood products 8%
- Food 52%
- Other 13%

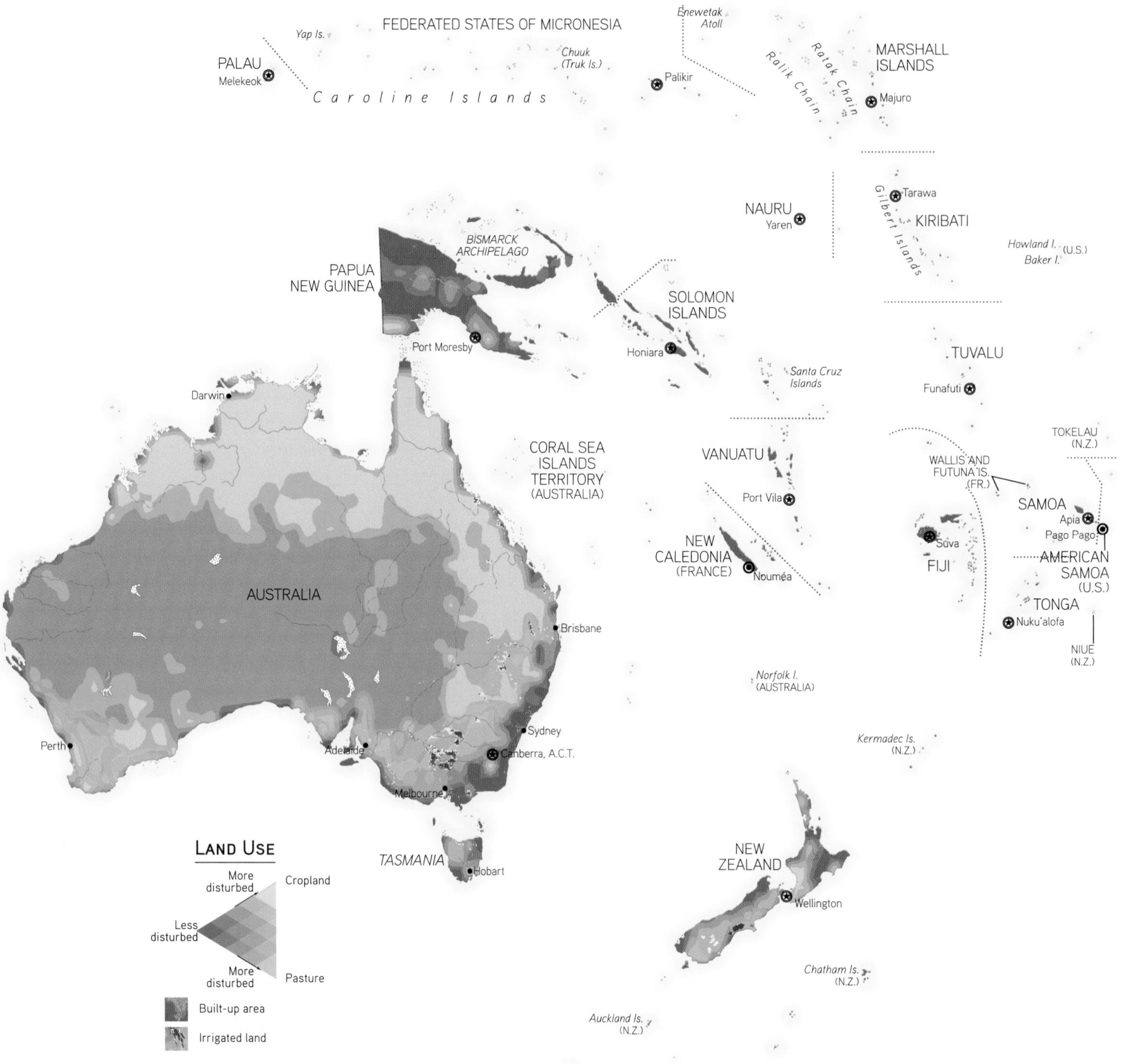

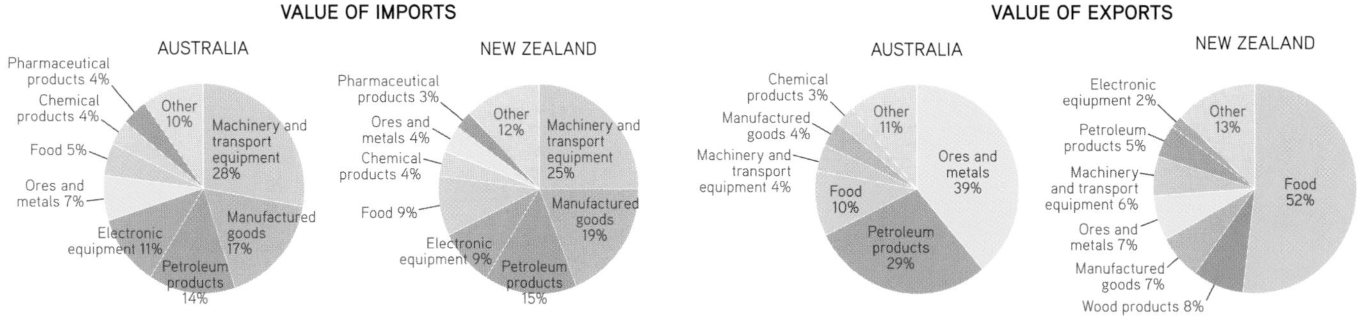

AUSTRALIA AND OCEANIA'S ECONOMY

Service
100%

PALAU

SOLOMON
ISLANDS

PAPUA
NEW GUINEA

Agricultural
100%

Industrial
100%

per Gross Domestic Product
(GDP) sector

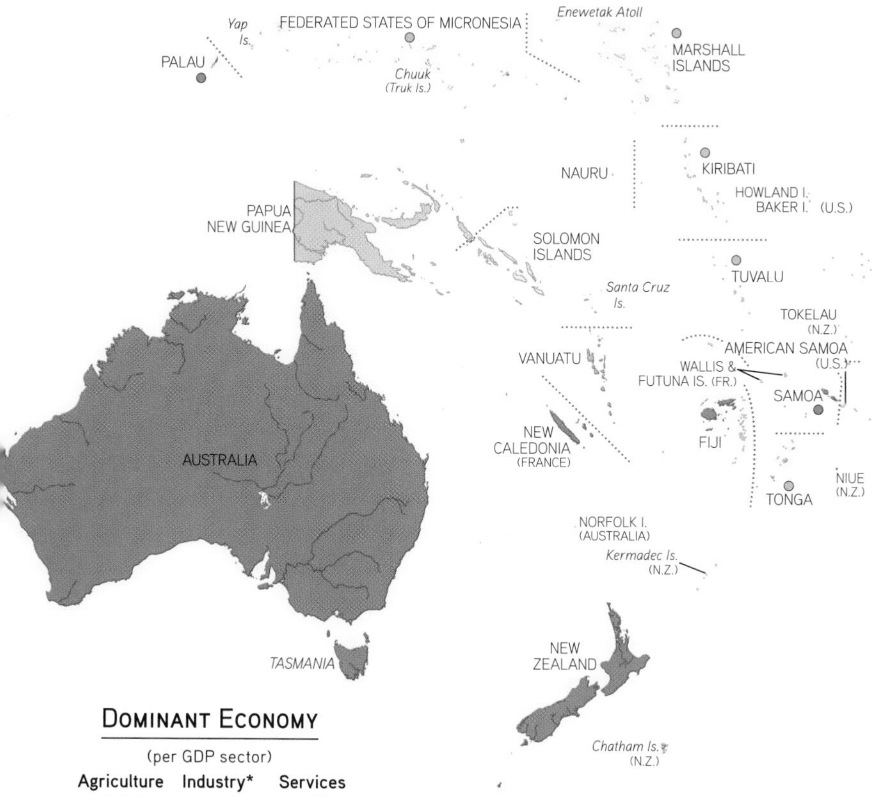

DOMINANT ECONOMY

(per GDP sector)

Agriculture	Industry*	Services
70%–100%		
50%–69.9%		
0%–49.9%		

*Includes the mining industry

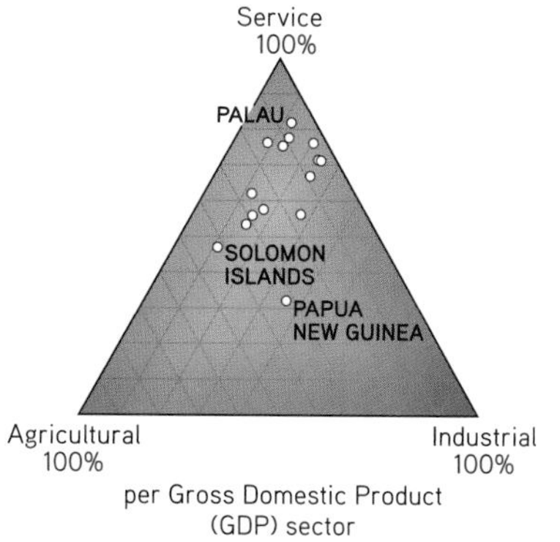

POVERTY

**Percentage of population living
on less than $2 per day**

- More than 80%
- 60%–80%
- 40%–59%
- 20%–39%
- Less than 20%
- No data available

PER CAPITA ENERGY CONSUMPTION

(annual use, in million Btu)

- More than 300
- 201–300
- 101–200
- 30–100
- Less than 30
- No data

Major energy deposit

- Coal
- Natural gas
- Oil
- Oil pipeline
- Oil transit chokepoint

PALAU, Yap Is., FEDERATED STATES OF MICRONESIA, Chuuk (Truk Is.), Enewetak Atoll, MARSHALL ISLANDS, NAURU, KIRIBATI, HOWLAND I., BAKER I. (U.S.), PAPUA NEW GUINEA, SOLOMON ISLANDS, Santa Cruz Is., TUVALU, TOKELAU (N.Z.), VANUATU, WALLIS & FUTUNA IS. (FR.), AMERICAN SAMOA (U.S.), SAMOA, NEW CALEDONIA (FRANCE), FIJI, NIUE (N.Z.), TONGA, AUSTRALIA, NORFOLK I. (AUSTRALIA), Kermadec Is. (N.Z.), TASMANIA, NEW ZEALAND, Chatham Is. (N.Z.)

RUSSIA
MONGOLIA
CHINA
GOBI
NORTH KOREA
SOUTH KOREA
JAPAN
TAIWAN
PHILIPPINES
VIETNAM
MALAYSIA
BRUNEI
INDONESIA
TIMOR-LESTE (EAST TIMOR)
PAPUA NEW GUINEA
AUSTRALIA
SOLOMON ISLANDS
VANUATU
FIJI
NAURU
PALAU
FEDERATED STATES OF MICRONESIA
MARSHALL ISLANDS
GILBERT ISLANDS
TUVALU
NEW CALEDONIA France
NORTHERN MARIANA ISLANDS U.S.
MICRONESIA
MELANESIA
CAROLINE ISLANDS
NORTH
SEA OF OKHOTSK
SEA OF JAPAN (EAST SEA)
YELLOW SEA
EAST CHINA SEA
PHILIPPINE SEA
SOUTH CHINA SEA
Sulu Sea
Celebes Sea
Molucca Sea
Java Sea
Banda Sea
Flores Sea
Bali Sea
Timor Sea
Arafura Sea
Bismarck Sea
Solomon Sea
Coral Sea
INDIAN OCEAN
Gulf of Carpentaria
Gulf of Papua
Joseph Bonaparte Gulf
Huon Gulf
Torres Strait
Luzon Strait
Taiwan Strait
Tartar Strait
La Perouse Strait
Makassar Strait
Great Barrier Reef
GREAT DIVIDING RANGE
Great Sandy Desert
Ulaanbaatar
Ulan Ude
BEIJING (PEKING)
TIANJIN
SHANGHAI
SEOUL
P'yŏngyang
TŌKYŌ
Yokohama
Ōsaka
Kyōto
Kōbe
Nagoya
Sapporo
Vladivostok
Khabarovsk
Harbin
SHENYANG
WUHAN
CHONGQING
GUANGZHOU (CANTON)
HONG KONG
Taipei (Taibei)
MANILA
Quezon City
Ho Chi Minh City (Saigon)
Da Nang
JAKARTA
Bandung
Surabaya
Makassar (Ujung Pandang)
Dili
Port Moresby
Honiara
Port Vila
Nouméa
Darwin
Cairns
Townsville
Majuro
Palikir
Tarawa (Bairiki)
Hagåtña (Agana)
Capital Hill
HOKKAIDŌ
HONSHŪ
KYŪSHŪ
SAKHALIN
KAMCHATKA
KURIL ISLANDS (KURIL'SKIYE OSTROVA)
Nansei Shotō (Ryukyu Islands)
Bonin Islands (Ogasawara Guntō)
Volcano Islands (Kazan Rettō) Japan
Iwo To (Iwo Jima)
Minami Tori Shima (Marcus) Japan
Wake Island U.S.
Guam
Saipan
Tinian
Rota
Yap Islands
Chuuk (Truk Islands)
Pohnpei (Ponape)
Kosrae (Kusaie)
Ralik Chain
Ratak Chain
Enewetak Atoll
Bikini Atoll
Jaluit Atoll
LUZON
MINDANAO
Palawan
BORNEO
SULAWESI
Hainan
JAVA
Timor
Flores
Sumbawa
Lesser Sunda Islands
NEW GUINEA
BISMARCK ARCHIPELAGO
New Britain
New Ireland
Bougainville
Guadalcanal
Louisiade Archipelago
Santa Cruz Islands
Espiritu Santo
Éfaté
Vitu Levu
Loyalty Islands
EQUATOR
Longitude East 160° of Greenwich
110°
120°
130°
140°
150°
160°
170°
50°
40°
20°
10°
0°
10°
20°

170°
160°
150°
140°
130°
120°
110°
Islands of Four Mountains
Unalaska
Fox Islands
Andreanof Is.
ALEUTIAN ISLANDS
United States
Queen Charlotte Islands
Hecate Strait
Mt. Waddington
CANADA
Calgary
Swift Current
Kamloops
Kelowna
Medicine Hat
Lethbridge
Vancouver
Vancouver Island
Victoria
Havre
Missouri
Spokane
Seattle
Tacoma
Olympia
Mt. Rainier
Great Falls
Helena
Missoula
Mt. St. Helens
Walla Walla
Butte
Billings
Portland
Salem
Snake
Borah Peak
Redmond
Boise
Worland
Eugene
Coos Bay
Idaho Falls
COAST MOUNTAINS
ROCKY MOUNTAINS
UNITED STATES
Medford
Klamath Falls
Alturas
Mt. Shasta
Great Salt Lake
Eureka
Lassen Pk.
Salt Lake City
Provo
Cape Mendocino
Reno
SIERRA NEVADA
Carson City
Ely
Sacramento
Oakland
San Francisco
San Jose
Colorado
Fresno
Mt. Whitney
Las Vegas
Bakersfield
Flagstaff
Santa Barbara
Albuquerque
Riverside
Los Angeles
Long Beach
Phoenix
San Diego
Mexicali
Tucson
Tijuana
Douglas
Nogales
BAJA CALIFORNIA
Gulf of California
SIERRA MADRE OCCIDENTAL
I. de Guadeloupe
Mexico
Hermosillo
Guaymas
Punta Eugenia
MEXICO
La Purísima
Los Mochis
TROPIC OF CANCER
La Paz
Cabo San Lucas
Islas Marías
Islas Revillagigedo
Mexico
PACIFIC OCEAN
Midway Islands
Pearl and Hermes Atoll
HAWAI'I
Gardner Pinnacles
United States
Kaua'i
O'ahu
Moloka'i
Honolulu
Maui
Mauna Kea
Hawai'i
Johnston Atoll
U.S.
POLYNESIA
Clipperton
Fr.
Kingman Reef
Palmyra Atoll U.S.
Teraina (Washington I.)
Tabuaeran (Fanning I.)
LINE ISLANDS
Kiritimati (Christmas I.)
Kiribati
Howland Island
U.S.
Baker Island
EQUATOR
Jarvis Island
U.S.
SOUTH PACIFIC OCEAN
PHOENIX ISLANDS
KIRIBATI
TOKELAU N.Z.
MARQUESAS ISLANDS
Ua Huka
Hiva Oa
Pukapuka Atoll (Danger Islands)
AMERICAN SAMOA
U.S.
SAMOA
Savai'i
Apia
Pago Pago
Manu'a Is.
Tutuila
SAMOA ISLANDS
Îles Wallis
Fr.
COOK ISLANDS
TUAMOTU ARCHIPELAGO
Manihi
Rangiroa
Bora Bora
Huahine
Raiatea
Papeete
Tahiti
SOCIETY ISLANDS
FRENCH POLYNESIA
France
Lau Group
TONGA ISLANDS
Niue
New Zealand
Ha'apai Group
Hervey Islands
TONGA
Nuku'alofa
Tongatapu Group
Rarotonga
Îs. du Duc de Glouster
AUSTRAL ISLANDS (TUBUAI IS.)
Groupe Actéon
Îles Gambier
Longitude West 160° of Greenwich
MERCATOR PROJECTION
SCALE 1:35,000,000
0 KILOMETERS 600 800 1000
0 MILES 200 400 600 800 1000
Red circled numbers are reference keys to larger scale maps on pages 241-243.

NEW ZEALAND
ALBERS CONIC EQUAL-AREA PROJECTION
SCALE 1:5,750,000
0 KILOMETERS 100 150
0 MILES 50 100 150
168°
171°
174°
177°
36°
39°
42°
45°
165°
180°
Longitude East 174° of Greenwich
NORTH ISLAND
SOUTH ISLAND
NEW
ZEALAND
TASMAN
SEA
PACIFIC OCEAN
Cape Reinga
North Cape
Te Hapua
Te Kao
Cape Karikari
Ninety Mile Beach
Mangonui
Kaeo
Cape Brett
Ahipara
Mangamuka
Paihia
Pawarenga
Moerewa
Opua
Panguru
Rawene
Kawakawa
Waimamaku
Whakapara
Donnellys Crossing
Pakotai
Hikurangi
Kaihu
Kamo
Whangarei
Waiotira
Marsden Point
Te Kopuru
Waipu
Maungaturoto
Ruawai
Paparoa
Port Fitzroy
Great Barrier I.
Wellsford
Leigh
Cape Colville
Tryphena
North Head
Matakana
East Coast Bays
Helensville
Hauraki Gulf
Colville
Coromandel
Waitakere
Howick
Whitianga
Auckland
COROMANDEL PEN.
Manukau
Papakura
Tairua
Pukekohe
Pokeno
Thames
Tuakau
Waitakaruru
Paeroa
Waihi
Te Kauwhata
Huntly
Te Aroha
Pukemiro
Waitoa
Mount Maunganui
Bay of Plenty
Ngaruawahia
Hamilton
Te Puke
Maketu
Cape Runaway
Hicks Bay
Te Araroa
Te Kaha
East Cape
Raglan
Cambridge
Whakatane
Matata
Hikurangi
Tikitiki
Kawhia
Putaruru
Rotorua
Te Teko
Opotiki
Torere
Ruatoria
Otorohanga
Waitomo Caves
Tokoroa
Mt. Tarawera
Te Puia Springs
Motu
Arowhana
Tokomaru Bay
Te Kuiti
Hangatiki
Atiamuri
TE UREWERA N.P.
Moutohora
Tolaga Bay
Benneydale
Taupo
Te Karaka
Matawai
Ormond
Awakino
Mokau
Ongarue
Ruatahuna
Minginui
Patutahi
Whangara
Taringamotu
Okahukura
Taupo
Ruakituri
Gisborne
Waitara
Uruti
Taumarunui
Kakahi
Turangi
Waitahanui
Tuai
Whakapunake
New Plymouth
Oakura
Urenui
National Park
Tarawera
Raupunga
Frasertown
Mt. Ngauruhoe
EGMONT N.P.
WHANGANUI N.P.
Mt. Ruapehu
Te Pohue
Putorino
Wairoa
Mahia Pen.
Rahotu
(Mt. Egmont) Mt. Taranaki
Toko
TONGARIRO N.P.
Kaweka
Tutira
Opunake
Eltham
Raetihi
Waiouru
Eskdale
Napier
Hawke Bay
Manaia
Hawera
Taihape
Taradale
Cape Kidnappers
Alton
Kakatahi
Utiku
Pakipaki
Kakaramea
Waverley
Mangaweka
Waitotara
Waimarama
Kai Iwi
Wanganui
Waipawa
Pukehou
Castlecliff
Marton
Rata
Takapau
Omakere
Bulls
Feilding
Waipukurau
Palmerston North
Porangahau
Foxton
Pongaroa
Taumatawhakatangihangakoauauotamateapokaiwhenuakitanatahu
Levin
Shannon
Cape Turnagain
Otaki
Ohau
Alfredton
Akitio
Waikanae
Mitre
Mauriceville
Tinui
Carterton
Castlepoint
Porirua
Lower Hutt
Greytown
Wellington
Martinborough
Mount Ross
Cape Palliser
Cape Farewell
Pakawau
Rockville
D'Urville I.
Collingwood
ABEL TASMAN N.P.
French Pass
Takaka
KAHURANGI NATIONAL PARK
Riwaka
Tasman Bay
Mt. Stokes
COOK STRAIT
Karamea
Tasman
Picton
Tapawera
Stoke
Havelock
Blenheim
Ward
Seddonville
Mt. Owen
Tadmor
Granity
Wairau Valley
Cape Campbell
Waimangaroa
Hector
Seddon
Cape Foulwind
Westport
Owen River
Charleston
Murchison
Tapuaenuku
Mt. Uriah
Cronadun
Molesworth
Kekerengu
PAPAROA N.P.
Reefton
NELSON LAKES N.P.
Clarence
Barrytown
Maruia
Rapahoe
Ikamatua
Hanmer Springs
Manakau
Kaikoura
Greymouth
Ngahere
Dobson
Lewis Pass
Waiau
Oaro
Arahura
Moana
Rotherham
Parnassus
Hokitika
Kumara Junction
Culverden
Cheviot
Kowhitirangi
Otira
ARTHUR'S PASS N.P.
Hawarden
Domett
Ross
Arthur's Pass
Omihi
Scargill
Waipara
Amberley
Harihari
Pegasus Bay
Franz Josef Glacier
Springfield
Oxford
Rangiora
WESTLAND (TAI POUTINI) N.P.
Whataroa
Lake Coleridge
Belfast
Christchurch
Fox Glacier
Hororata
Lyttelton
(Mt. Cook) Aoraki
Methven
Rolleston
BANKS PEN.
AORAKI (MT. COOK) N.P.
Lincoln
Rakaia
Mayfield
Akaroa
Haast
Ashburton
Jackson Head
Hinds
Jackson Bay
Lake Tekapo
Geraldine
Canterbury Bight
MT. ASPIRING N.P.
Lake Pukaki
Fairlie
Orari
Pleasant Point
Temuka
Awarua Bay
Twizel
Cave
Lake McKerrow
Mt. Aspiring
Timaru
Mount Tutoko
Omarama
Saint Andrews
Otematata
Waimate
Makikihi
Hakataramea
Studholme Junction
Milford Sound
Coronet Pk.
Kurow
Morven
Glenorchy
Tarras
Glenavy
George Sound
Arrowtown
Duntroon
FIORDLAND
Cromwell
Enfield
Queenstown
Omakau
Totara
Oamaru
The Remarkables
Clyde
Ranfurly
Maheno
Lake Te Anau
Earnscleugh
Herbert
Kakanui
NATIONAL
Kingston
Hampden
Te Anau
Coal Creek Flat
Hyde
Palmerston
L. Manapouri
Athol
Waikouaiti
Manapouri
Roxburgh
Ettrick
Karitane
PARK
Mossburn
Waitati
Edievale
Seacliff
Port Chalmers
Dusky Sound
Mosgiel
Dipton
Kelso
Allanton
Dunedin
Riversdale
Tapanui
Lawrence
Green Island
Waihola
Orawia
Winton
Gore
Waipahi
Milton
Otautau
Balclutha
Thornbury
Browns
Clinton
Kaitangata
Puysegur Point
Wallacetown
Invercargill
Otatara
Tahakopa
Owaka
FOVEAUX STRAIT
Bluff
Tiwai Point
Waikawa
Mt. Anglem
STEWART I. (RAKIURA)
Mason Bay
Half Moon Bay
Mt. Allen
RAKIURA NATIONAL PARK
Mernoo Bank

Polynesia

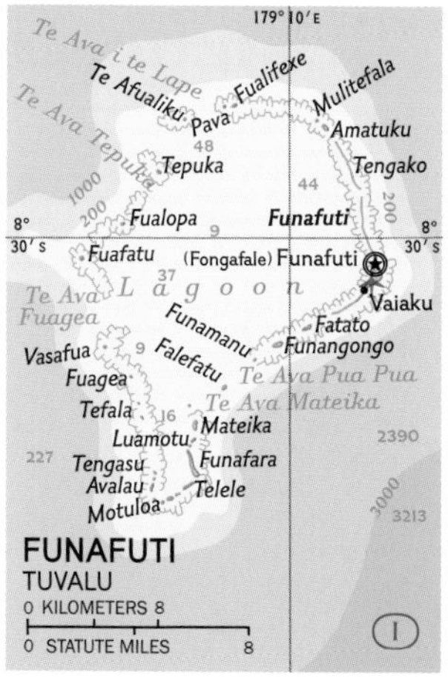
FUNAFUTI
TUVALU
0 KILOMETERS 8
0 STATUTE MILES 8
1
179° 10′ E
8° 30′ S
Te Ava i te Lape
Te Afualiku
Fualifexe
Pava
Mulitefala
Amatuku
Te Ava Tepuka
Tepuka
Tengako
Fualopa
Funafuti
Fuafatu
(Fongafale) Funafuti
Vaiaku
Te Ava Fuagea
Lagoon
Funamanu
Fatato
Funangongo
Vasafua
Falefatu
Te Ava Pua Pua
Fuagea
Te Ava Mateika
Tefala
Mateika
Luamotu
Tengasu
Funafara
Avalau
Telele
Motuloa

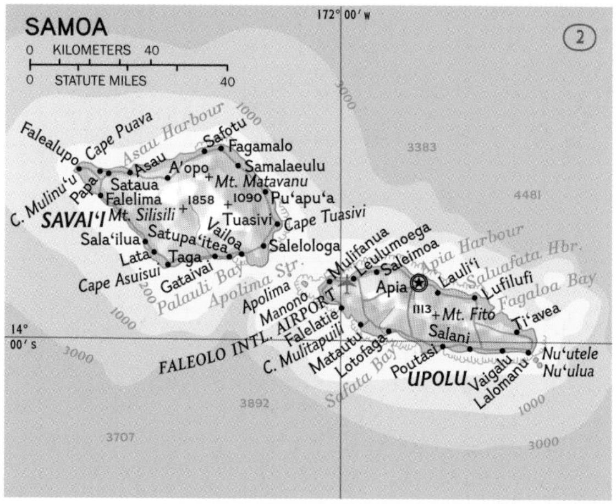
SAMOA
0 KILOMETERS 40
0 STATUTE MILES 40
2
172° 00′ W
14° 00′ S
Falealupo
Cape Puava
Asau Harbour
Safotu
Fagamalo
Samalaeulu
Asau
A'opo
Papa
Sataua
Mt. Matavanu
C. Mulinu'u
Falelima
1858
1090
Pu'apu'a
SAVAI'I
Mt. Silisili
Tuasivi
Cape Tuasivi
Sala'ilua
Satupa'itea
Vailoa
Salelologa
Lata
Taga
Cape Asuisui
Gataivai
Palauli Bay
Apolima Str.
Apolima
Manono
FALEOLO INTL. AIRPORT
Mulifanua
Leulumoega
Saleimoa
Apia Harbour
Apia
Lauli'i
Saluafata Hbr.
Lufilufi
Fagaloa Bay
Mt. Fito
Ti'avea
Falelatai
C. Mulitapuili
Matautu
Lotofaga
Poutasi
Salani
Safata Bay
UPOLU
Vaigalu
Lalomanu
Nu'utele
Nu'ulua

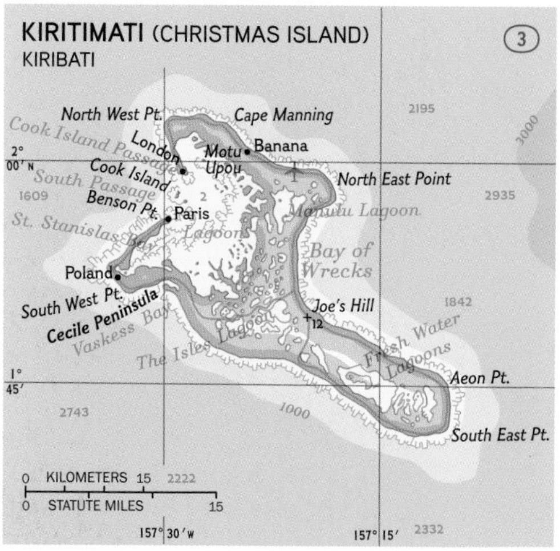
KIRITIMATI (CHRISTMAS ISLAND)
KIRIBATI
3
North West Pt.
Cape Manning
Cook Island Passage
London
Motu Upou
Banana
North East Point
South Passage
Cook Island
Benson Pt.
Paris
St. Stanislas Bay
Lagoon
Manulu Lagoon
Bay of Wrecks
Poland
South West Pt.
Cecile Peninsula
Vaskess Bay
Joe's Hill
The Isles Lagoon
Fresh Water Lagoons
Aeon Pt.
South East Pt.
0 KILOMETERS 15
0 STATUTE MILES 15
157° 30′ W
157° 15′
2° 00′ N
1° 45′

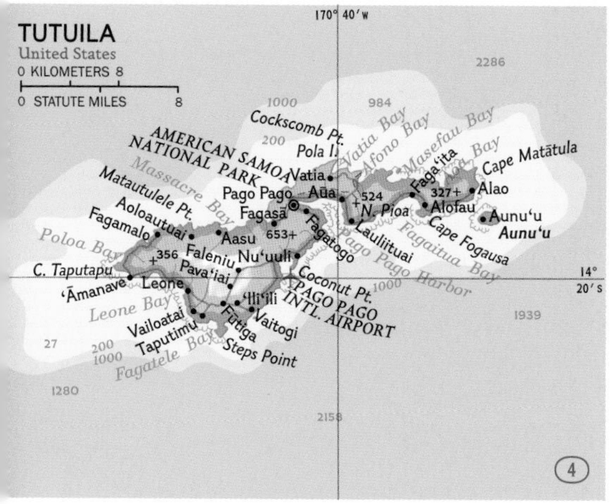
TUTUILA
United States
0 KILOMETERS 8
0 STATUTE MILES 8
170° 40′ W
14° 20′ S
4
Cockscomb Pt.
AMERICAN SAMOA NATIONAL PARK
Pola I.
Vatia Bay
Afono Bay
Masefau Bay
Natia
Faga'itua Bay
Cape Matātula
Massacre Bay
Matautulele Pt.
Pago Pago
Aūa
N. Pioa
Fagasā
Alofau
Alao
Aoloautuai
Aunu'u
Fagamalo
Aasu
Laulituai
Cape Fogausa
Poloa Bay
Faleniu
Nu'uuli
Pago Pago Harbor
C. Taputapu
'Āmanave
Leone
Pava'ia'i
Coconut Pt.
PAGO PAGO INTL. AIRPORT
Leone Bay
'Ili'ili
Vailoatai
Vaitogi
Taputimu
Futiga
Steps Point
Fagatele Bay

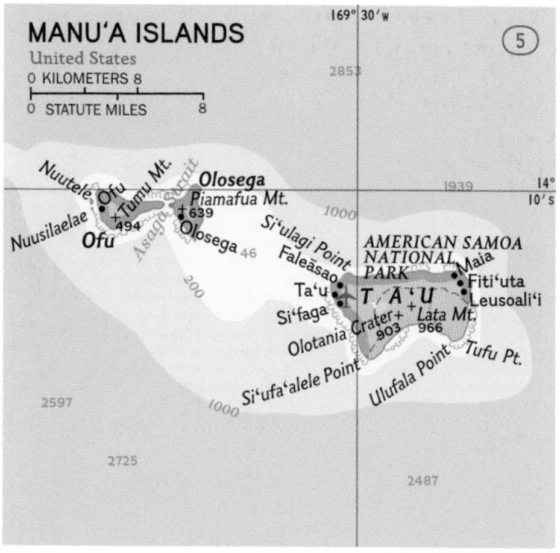
MANU'A ISLANDS
United States
0 KILOMETERS 8
0 STATUTE MILES 8
5
169° 30′ W
14° 10′ S
Nuutele
Ofu
Tumu Mt.
Olosega
Piamafua Mt.
Nuusilaelae
Asaga Strait
Olosega
Si'ulagi Point
AMERICAN SAMOA NATIONAL PARK
Faleāsao
Maia
Fiti'uta
Leusoali'i
Ta'u
TA'U
Si'faga
Lata Mt.
Olotania Crater
Tufu Pt.
Ulufala Point
Si'ufa'alele Point

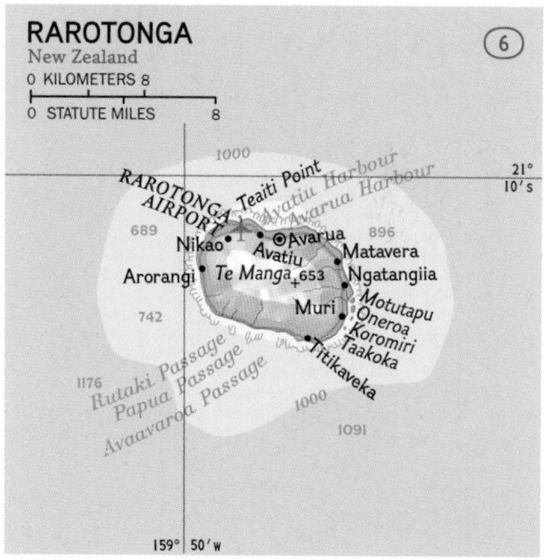
RAROTONGA
New Zealand
0 KILOMETERS 8
0 STATUTE MILES 8
6
21° 10′ S
159° 50′ W
RAROTONGA AIRPORT
Teaiti Point
Avatiu Harbour
Avarua Harbour
Nikao
Avarua
Avatiu
Matavera
Arorangi
Te Manga
Ngatangiia
Muri
Motutapu
Oneroa
Koromiri
Taakoka
Titikaveka
Rutaki Passage
Papua Passage
Avaavaroa Passage

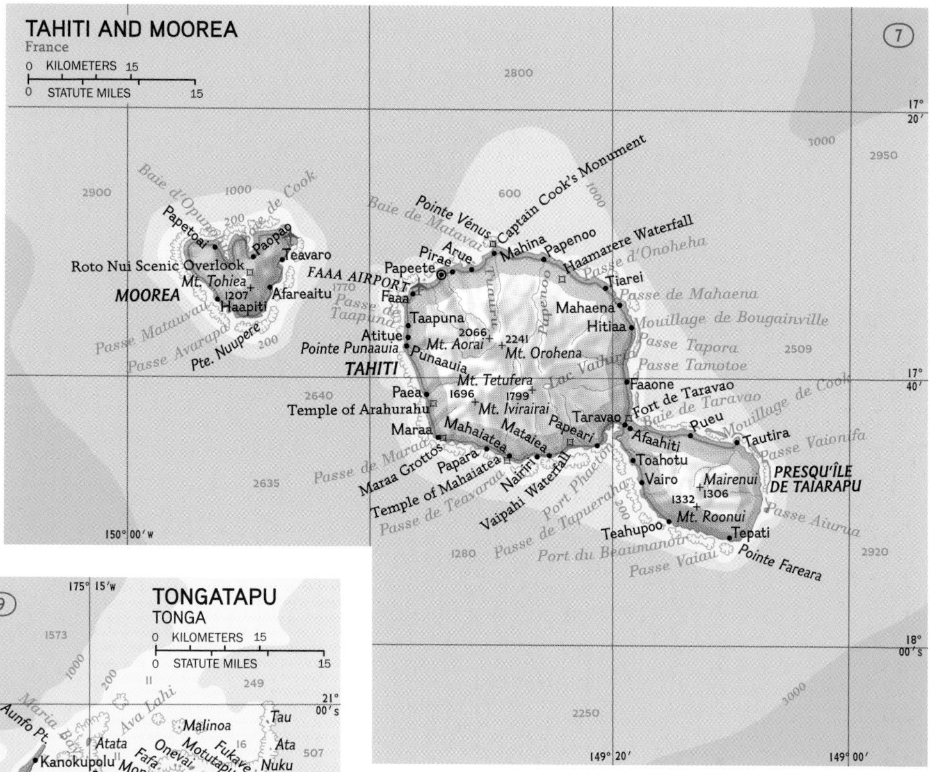
TAHITI AND MOOREA
France
0 KILOMETERS 15
0 STATUTE MILES 15
7
17° 20′
17° 40′
18° 00′ S
150° 00′ W
149° 20′
149° 00′
Baie d'Opunohu
Baie de Cook
Papetoai
Paopao
Teavaro
Roto Nui Scenic Overlook
Mt. Tohiea
MOOREA
Afareaitu
Haapiti
Passe Matauvau
Passe Avarapa
Pte. Nuupere
Pointe Vénus
Captain Cook's Monument
Baie de Matavai
Arue
Mahina
Papenoo
Haamarere Waterfall
Passe d'Onoheha
Pirae
Papeete
FAAA AIRPORT
Tiarei
Passe de Mahaena
Faaa
Passe de Taapuna
Mahaena
Mouillage de Bougainville
Taapuna
Hitiaa
Passe Tapora
Atitue
Mt. Aorai
Mt. Orohena
Passe Tamotoe
Pointe Punaauia
Punaauia
TAHITI
Lac Vaihiria
Faaone
Mt. Tetufera
Paea
Mt. Ivirairai
Fort de Taravao
Temple of Arahurahu
Baie de Taravao
Taravao
Mouillage de Cook
Maraa
Papeari
Pueu
Mahaiatea
Tautira
Passe de Maraa
Matalea
Afaahiti
Passe Vaionifa
Maraa Grottos
Papara
Toahotu
Nairiri
Vairo
Mairenui
PRESQU'ÎLE DE TAIARAPU
Temple of Mahaiatea
Vaipahi Waterfall
Port Phaeton
Passe de Teavaraa
Passe de Tapuerahu
Mt. Roonui
Teahupoo
Passe Aiurua
Tepati
Port du Beaumanoir
Passe Vaiau
Pointe Fareara

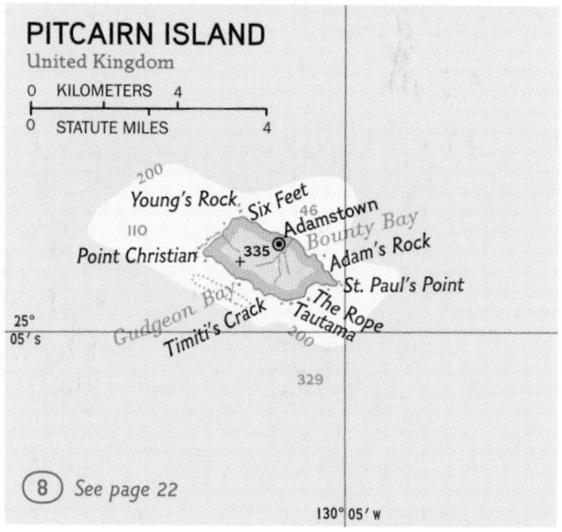
PITCAIRN ISLAND
United Kingdom
0 KILOMETERS 4
0 STATUTE MILES 4
Young's Rock
Six Feet
Adamstown
Bounty Bay
Point Christian
Adam's Rock
St. Paul's Point
Gudgeon Bay
Timiti's Crack
The Rope
Tautama
25° 05′ S
130° 05′ W
8 See page 22

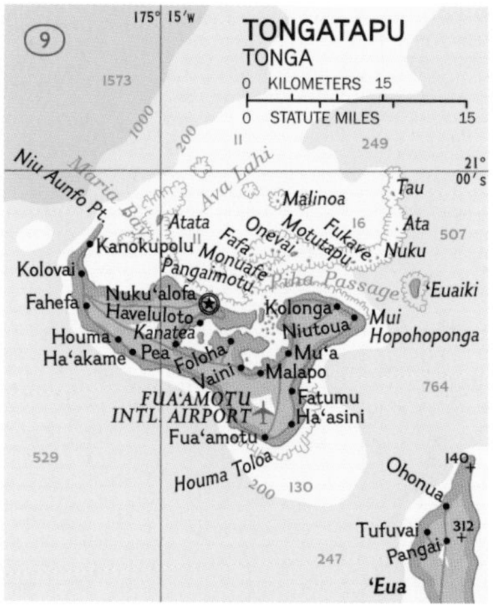
9
175° 15′ W
TONGATAPU
TONGA
0 KILOMETERS 15
0 STATUTE MILES 15
21° 00′ S
Niu Aunfo Pt.
Maria Bay
Ava Lahi
Malinoa
Tau
Atata
Fafa
Onevai
Motutapu
Fukave
Ata
Kanokupolu
Monuafe
Nuku
Kolovai
Pangaimotu
Piha Passage
'Euaiki
Fahefa
Nuku'alofa
Haveluloto
Kolonga
Mui Hopohoponga
Houma
Kanatea
Niutoua
Ha'akame
Pea
Folaha
Mu'a
Vaini
Malapo
FUA'AMOTU INTL. AIRPORT
Fatumu
Ha'asini
Fua'amotu
Houma Toloa
Ohonua
Tufuvai
Pangai
'Eua

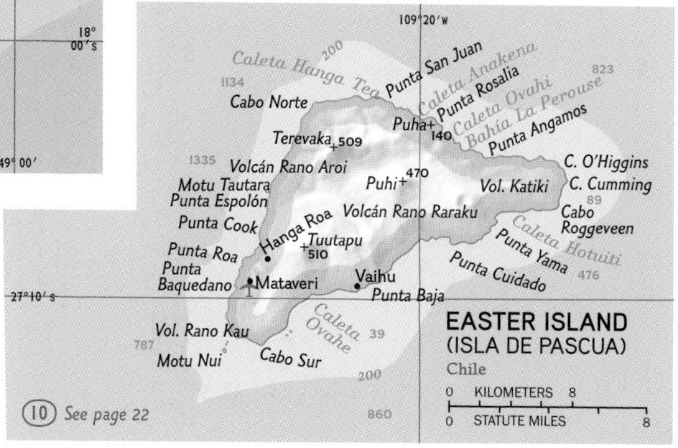
109° 20′ W
Caleta Hanga Tea
Punta San Juan
Caleta Anakena
Cabo Norte
Punta Rosalia
Puha
Caleta Ovahi
Bahía La Perouse
Terevaka
Punta Angamos
Volcán Rano Aroi
C. O'Higgins
Motu Tautara
Puhi
C. Cumming
Punta Espolón
Vol. Katiki
Volcán Rano Raraku
Punta Cook
Hanga Roa
Cabo Roggeveen
Tuutapu
Caleta Hotuiti
Punta Roa
Punta Yama
Punta Baquedano
Vaihu
Punta Cuidado
Mataveri
Punta Baja
27° 10′ S
Caleta Ovahe
Vol. Rano Kau
Motu Nui
Cabo Sur
EASTER ISLAND (ISLA DE PASCUA)
Chile
0 KILOMETERS 8
0 STATUTE MILES 8
10 See page 22

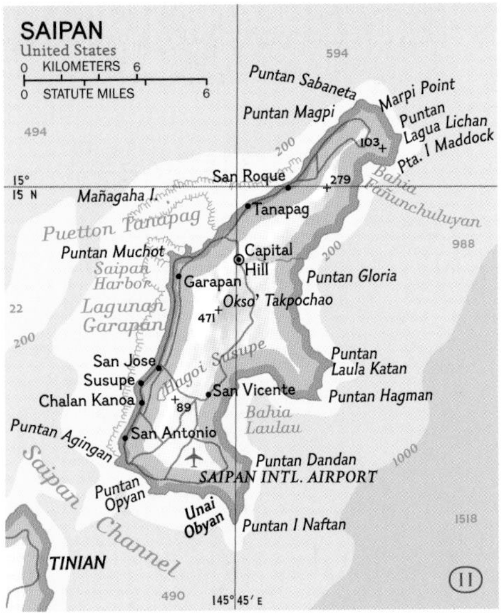
SAIPAN
United States
0 KILOMETERS 6
0 STATUTE MILES 6
Puntan Sabaneta
Marpi Point
Puntan Lagua Lichan
Pta. I Maddock
Puntan Magpi
San Roque
Mañagaha I.
Tanapag
Puetton Tanapag
Bahia Fanunchuluyan
Puntan Muchot
Saipan Harbor
Capital Hill
Garapan
Puntan Gloria
Lagunan Garapan
Okso' Takpochao
San Jose
Susupe
Chalan Kanoa
San Vicente
Puntan Laula Katan
Puntan Hagman
Bahia Laulau
Puntan Agingan
San Antonio
Puntan Dandan
SAIPAN INTL. AIRPORT
Puntan Opyan
Unai Obyan
Puntan I Naftan
Saipan Channel
TINIAN
145° 45′ E
15° 15′ N
11

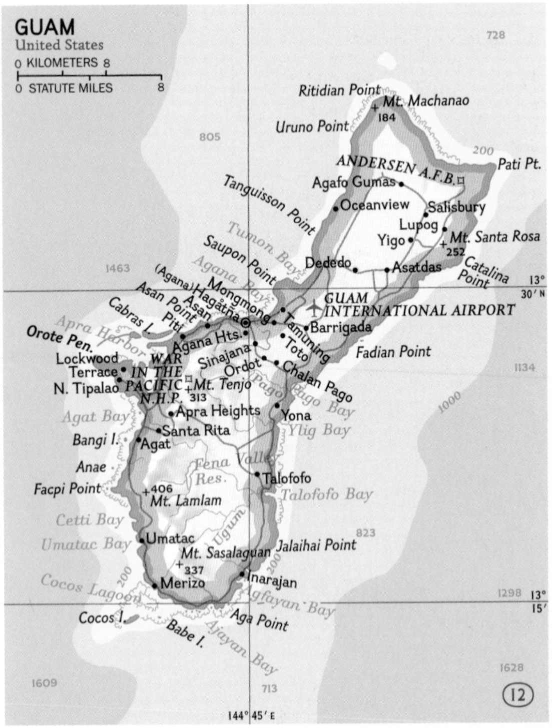
GUAM
United States
0 KILOMETERS 8
0 STATUTE MILES 8
Ritidian Point
Mt. Machanao
Uruno Point
ANDERSEN A.F.B.
Pati Pt.
Tanguisson Point
Agafo Gumas
Oceanview
Salisbury
Lupog
Yigo
Mt. Santa Rosa
Tumon Bay
Saupon Point
Dededo
Asatdas
Catalina Point
Agana Bay
Mongmong
(Agana) Hagåtña
GUAM INTERNATIONAL AIRPORT
Asan Point
Asan
Piti
Cabras I.
Apra Harbor
Orote Pen.
Tamuning
Barrigada
Agana Hts.
Sinajana
Fadian Point
Lockwood Terrace
N. Tipalao
WAR IN THE PACIFIC N.H.P.
Mt. Tenjo
Ordot
Toto
Chalan Pago
Pago Bay
Apra Heights
Agat Bay
Bangi I.
Santa Rita
Agat
Yona
Ylig Bay
Anae
Fena Valley Res.
Facpi Point
Mt. Lamlam
Talofofo
Talofofo Bay
Cetti Bay
Umatac Bay
Umatac
Mt. Sasalaguan
Jalaihai Point
Merizo
Inarajan
Cocos Lagoon
Agfayan Bay
Cocos I.
Babe I.
Aga Point
Ajayan Bay
144° 45′ E
13° 30′ N
13° 15′
12

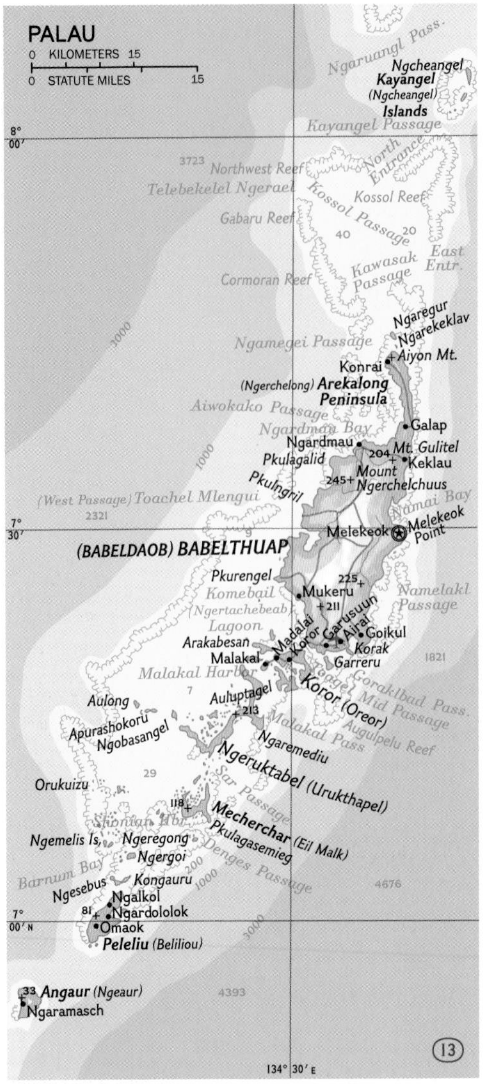
PALAU
0 KILOMETERS 15
0 STATUTE MILES 15
Ngaruangl Pass.
Ngcheangel
Kayangel (Ngcheangel) Islands
Kayangel Passage
North Entrance
Northwest Reef
Telebekelel Ngerael
Kossol Passage
Kossol Reef
Gabaru Reef
Cormoran Reef
Kawasak Passage
East Entr.
Ngaregur
Ngarekeklav
Ngamegei Passage
Konrai
Aiyon Mt.
(Ngerchelong) Arekalong Peninsula
Aiwokako Passage
Ngardmau Bay
Galap
Ngardmau
Mt. Gulitel
Keklau
Pkulagalid
Mount Ngerchelchuus
Pkulngril
(West Passage) Toachel Mlengui
Namai Bay
Melekeok
Melekeok Point
(BABELDAOB) BABELTHUAP
Pkurengel
Komebail (Ngertachebeab) Lagoon
Mukeru
Namelakl Passage
Arakabesan
Malakal
Madalai
Koror
Garusuun
Airai
Goikul
Korak
Garreru
Malakal Harbor
Aulong
Auluptagel
Koror (Oreor)
Goraklbad Pass.
Ngel Mid Passage
Apurashokoru
Ngobasangel
Malakal Pass
Augulpelu Reef
Ngaremediu
Ngeruktabel (Urukthapel)
Orukuizu
Mecherchar (Eil Malk)
Ngemelis Is.
Ngeregong
Ngergoi
Pkulagasemieg
Denges Passage
Barnum Bay
Ngesebus
Kongauru
Ngalkol
Ngardololok
Omaok
Peleliu (Beliliou)
Angaur (Ngeaur)
Ngaramasch
134° 30′ E
8° 00′
7° 30′
7° 00′ N
13

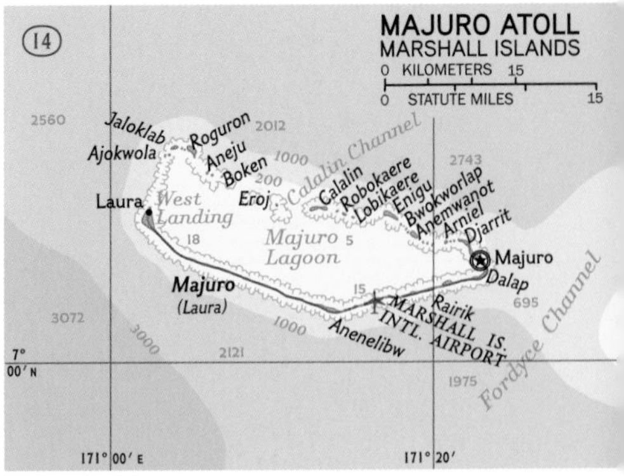
MAJURO ATOLL
MARSHALL ISLANDS
0 KILOMETERS 15
0 STATUTE MILES 15
14
Jaloklab
Ajokwola
Roguron
Aneju
Boken
Laura
West Landing
Eroj
Calalin Channel
Calalin
Robokaere
Lobikaere
Enigu
Bwokworlap
Anemwanot
Arniel
Djarrit
Majuro Lagoon
Majuro
Dalap
Majuro (Laura)
Rairik
MARSHALL IS. INTL. AIRPORT
Anenelibw
Fordyce Channel
171° 00′ E
171° 20′
7° 00′ N

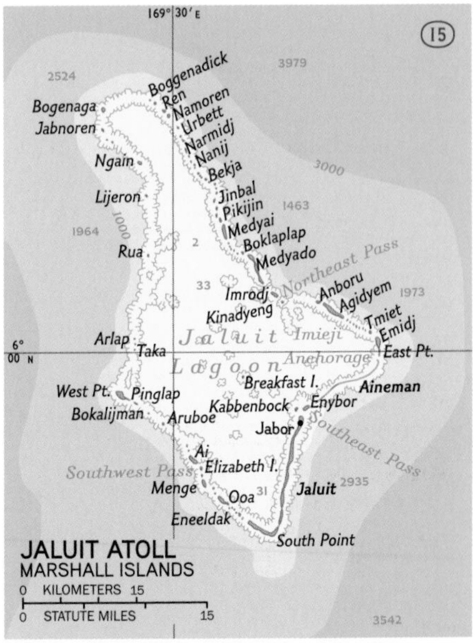
15
Boggenadick
Ren
Namoren
Urbett
Narmidj
Nanij
Bekja
Jinbal
Pikijin
Medyai
Boklaplap
Medyado
Bogenaga
Jabnoren
Ngain
Lijeron
Rua
Northeast Pass
Imrodj
Kinadyeng
Anboru
Agidyem
Tmiet
Emidj
Arlap
Taka
Jaluit Lagoon
Imieji
Anchorage
East Pt.
Breakfast I.
West Pt.
Pinglap
Bokalijman
Aruboe
Kabbenbock
Enybor
Aineman
Jabor
Southeast Pass
Southwest Pass
Ai
Elizabeth I.
Menge
Ooa
Jaluit
Eneeldak
South Point
JALUIT ATOLL
MARSHALL ISLANDS
0 KILOMETERS 15
0 STATUTE MILES 15
169° 30′ E
6° 00′ N

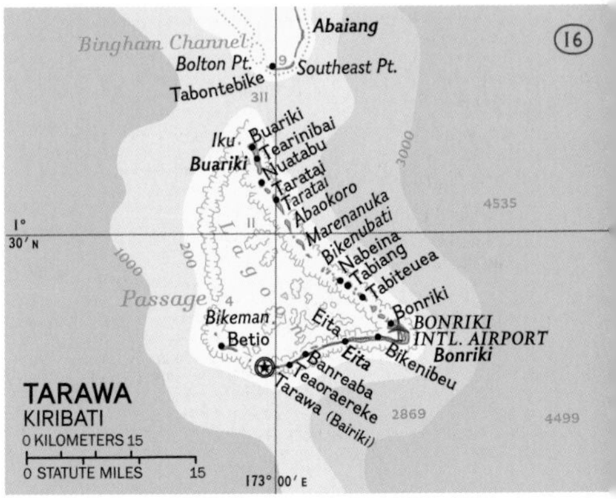
16
Abaiang
Bingham Channel
Bolton Pt.
Southeast Pt.
Tabontebike
Iku
Buariki
Buariki
Tearinibai
Nuatabu
Taratai
Taratai
Abaokoro
Marenanuka
Bikenubati
Nabeina
Tabiang
Tabiteuea
Passage
Bikeman
Betio
Eita
Eita
Bonriki
BONRIKI INTL. AIRPORT
Bonriki
Bikenibeu
Banreaba
Teaoraereke
Tarawa (Bairiki)
TARAWA
KIRIBATI
0 KILOMETERS 15
0 STATUTE MILES 15
173° 00′ E
1° 30′ N

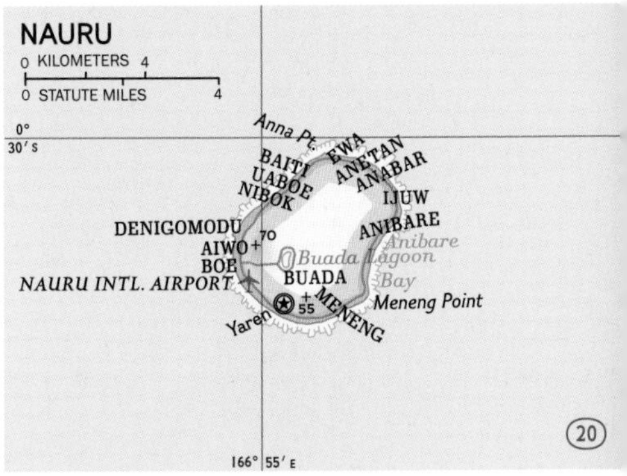
NAURU
0 KILOMETERS 4
0 STATUTE MILES 4
Anna Pt.
EWA
ANETAN
ANABAR
BAITI
UABOE
NIBOK
IJUW
DENIGOMODU
ANIBARE
Anibare Bay
AIWO
BOE
Buada Lagoon
BUADA
NAURU INTL. AIRPORT
Yaren
MENENG
Meneng Point
166° 55′ E
0° 30′ S
20

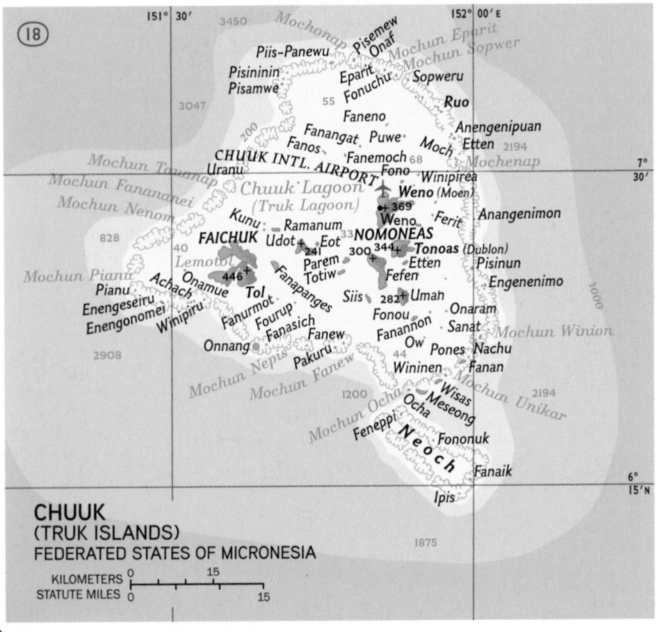
18
151° 30′
152° 00′ E
Mochon Aap
Pisemew
Onaf
Mochun Epwrit
Piis-Panewu
Mochun Sopwer
Pisininin
Pisamwe
Eparit
Fonuchu
Sopweru
Ruo
Faneno
Anengenipuan
Etten
Fanangat
Puwe
Moch
Fanos
Fanemoch
Mochun Tauanap
CHUUK INTL. AIRPORT
Mochenap
Uranu
Fono
Winipirea
Mochun Fananamei
Chuuk Lagoon (Truk Lagoon)
Weno (Moen)
Mochun Nenom
Weno
Ferit
Angenimon
Kunu
Ramanum
FAICHUK
Udot
Eot
NOMONEAS
Tonoas (Dublon)
Pisinun
Parem
Etten
Mochun Piana
Totiw
Fefen
Engenenimo
Achach
Onamue
Tol
Fanapanges
Pianu
Enengeseiru
Enengonomei
Winipiru
Siis
Uman
Onaram
Fanurmot
Fourup
Fonou
Sanat
Mochun Winion
Fanasich
Fananñon
Onnang
Fanew
Ow
Pones
Nachu
Pakuru
Mochun Nepis
Wininen
Fanan
Mochun Fanew
Wisas
Meseong
Mochun Unikar
Mochun Ocha
Ocha
Feneppi
Fononuk
Neoch
Fanaik
Ipis
7° 30′
6° 15′ N
CHUUK
(TRUK ISLANDS)
FEDERATED STATES OF MICRONESIA
KILOMETERS 0 15
STATUTE MILES 0 15

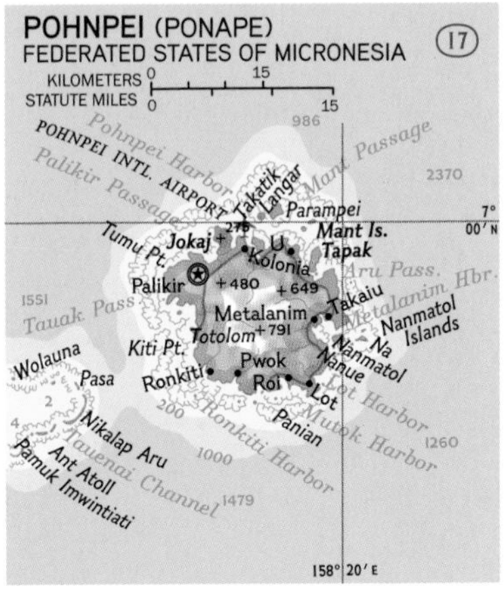
POHNPEI (PONAPE)
FEDERATED STATES OF MICRONESIA
17
KILOMETERS 0 15
STATUTE MILES 0 15
Pohnpei Harbor
POHNPEI INTL. AIRPORT
Takatik
Langar
Mant Passage
Palikir Passage
Parampei
Mant Is.
Tumu Pt.
Jokaj
Tapak
Kolonia
Aru Pass.
Palikir
Metalanim Hbr.
Tauak Pass
Metalanim
Takaiu
Nanmatol Islands
Totolom
Kiti Pt.
Nanmatol
Wolauna
Pwok
Na
Pasa
Ronkiti
Roi
Nanue
Lot Harbor
Panian
Mutok Harbor
Ronkiti Harbor
Nikalap Aru
Ant Atoll
Pamuk Imwintiati
Tauenai Channel
158° 20′ E
7° 00′ N

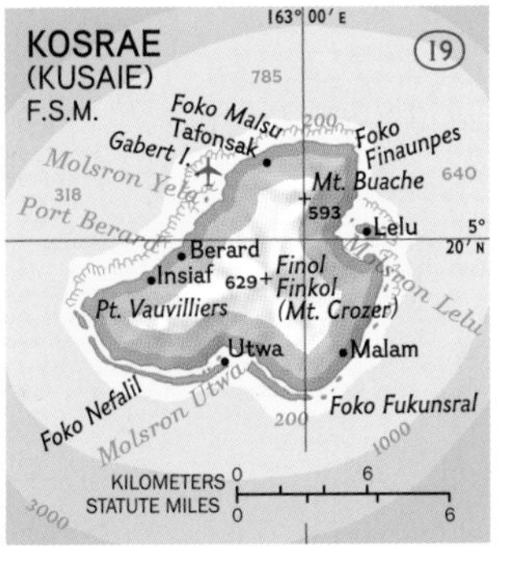
KOSRAE
(KUSAIE)
F.S.M.
19
163° 00′ E
Foko Malsu
Gabert I.
Tafonsak
Foko Finaunpes
Molsron Yela
Mt. Buache
Port Berard
Lelu
Berard
Insiaf
Finol Finkol (Mt. Crozer)
Molsron Lelu
Pt. Vauvilliers
Utwa
Malam
Foko Nefalil
Molsron Utwa
Foko Fukunsral
5° 20′ N
KILOMETERS 0 6
STATUTE MILES 0 6

Melanesia

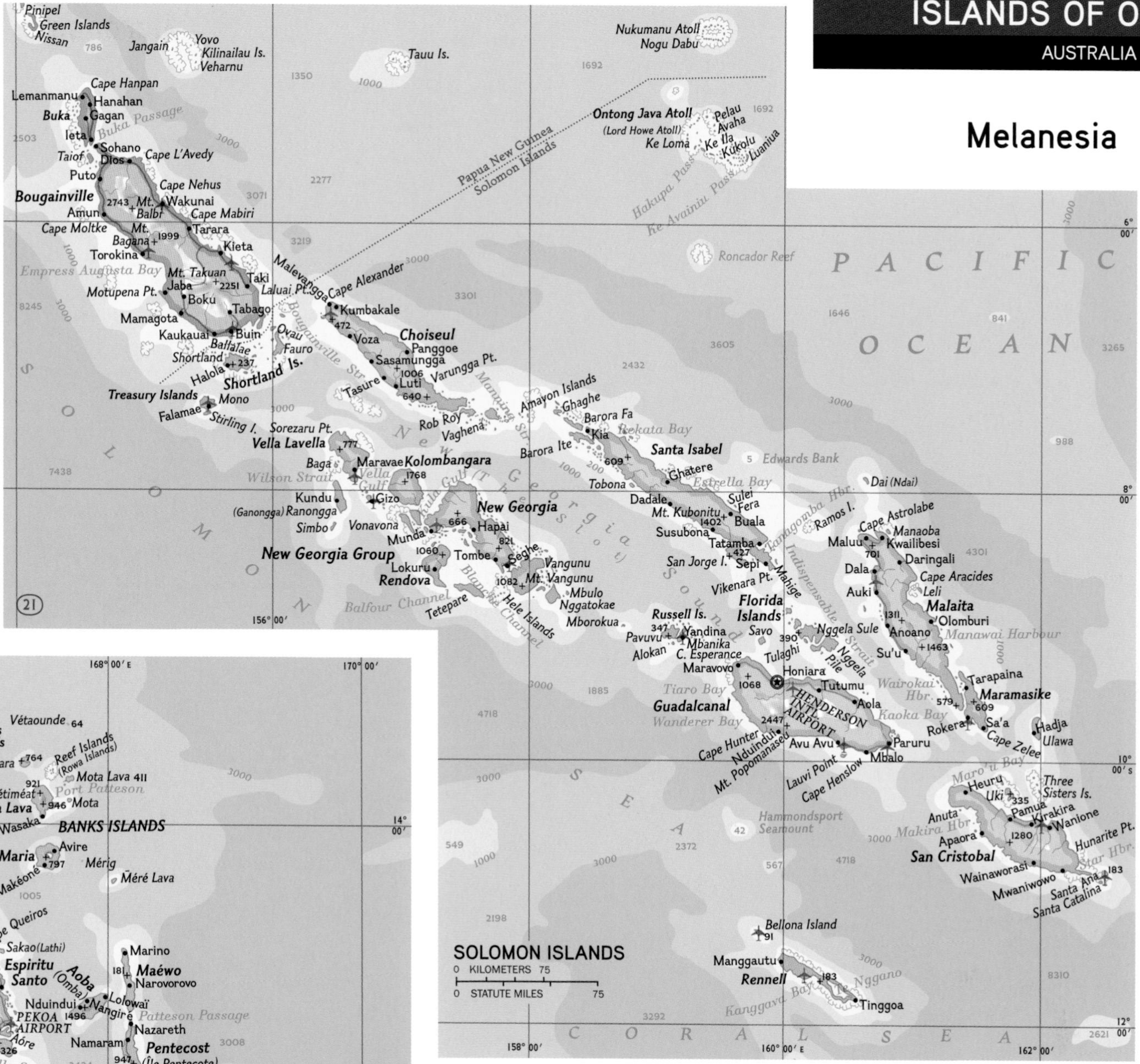
SOLOMON ISLANDS
0 KILOMETERS 75
0 STATUTE MILES 75
PACIFIC OCEAN
SOLOMON SEA
CORAL SEA
Papua New Guinea
Solomon Islands
Pinipel
Green Islands
Nissan
Jangain
Yovo
Kilinailau Is.
Veharnu
Tauu Is.
Nukumanu Atoll
Nogu Dabu
Ontong Java Atoll
(Lord Howe Atoll)
Ke Loma
Pelau
Avaha
Ke Ila
Kukolu
Luaniua
Hakupa Pass
Ke Avainiu Pass
Roncador Reef
Cape Hanpan
Lemanmanu
Hanahan
Buka
Gagan
Buka Passage
Ieta
Taiof
Sohano
Cape L'Avedy
Los
Puto
Cape Nehus
Bougainville
Wakunai
Mt. Balbi
Amun
Cape Mabiri
Cape Moltke
Mt. Bagana
Tarara
Torokina
Kieta
Empress Augusta Bay
Mt. Takuan
Taki
Jaba
Motupena Pt.
Loluai Pt.
Boku
Tabago
Mamagota
Kaukauai
Buin
Ballalae
Ovau
Fauro
Shortland
Halola
Shortland Is.
Treasury Islands
Mono
Falamae
Stirling I.
Bougainville Strait
Malevangga
Cape Alexander
Kumbakale
Voza
Choiseul
Panggoe
Sasamungga
Varungga Pt.
Luti
Tasure
Manning Strait
Rob Roy
Vaghena
Amayon Islands
Ghaghe
Barora Fa
Rekata Bay
Kia
Barora Ite
Santa Isabel
Edwards Bank
Sorezaru Pt.
Vella Lavella
Baga
Maravae
Kolombangara
Vella Gulf
Wilson Strait
Gizo
Kundu
(Ganongga) Ranongga
Simbo
Vonavona
Kula Gulf
New Georgia
Munda
Hapai
New Georgia Group
Lokuru
Tombe
Seghe
Rendova
Tetepare
Vangunu
Mt. Vangunu
Mbulo
Nggatokae
Mborokua
Blanche Channel
Hele Islands
Balfour Channel
The Slot (New Georgia Sound)
Ghatere
Tobona
Estrella Bay
Dadale
Sulei
Fera
Mt. Kubonitu
Buala
Susubona
Tatamba
Tanagomba Hbr.
Ramos I.
San Jorge I.
Sepi
Vikenara Pt.
Mahige
Indispensable Strait
Russell Is.
Pavuvu
Yandina
Mbanika
Alokan
C. Esperance
Florida Islands
Savo
Nggela Sule
Nggela Pile
Tulaghi
Maravovo
Honiara
Tumumu
HENDERSON INTL. AIRPORT
Aola
Tiaro Bay
Guadalcanal
Wanderer Bay
Cape Hunter
Nduindui
Mt. Popomanaseu
Avu Avu
Paruru
Mbalo
Lauvi Point
Cape Henslow
Kaoka Bay
Wairokai Hbr.
Dai (Ndai)
Cape Astrolabe
Manaoba
Maluu
Kwailibesi
Daringali
Dala
Cape Aracides
Leli
Auki
Malaita
Anoano
Olomburi
Manawai Harbour
Su'u
Tarapaina
Maramasike
Rokera
Sa'a
Hadja
Ulawa
Cape Zelee
Maro'u Bay
Heuru
Uki
Three Sisters Is.
Pamua
Kirakira
Wanione
Anuta
Makira Hbr.
Apaora
Hunarite Pt.
San Cristobal
Star Hbr.
Wainaworasi
Mwaniwowo
Santa Ana
Santa Catalina
Hammondsport Seamount
Bellona Island
Manggautu
Rennell
Nggano
Kanggava Bay
Tinggoa
156° 00′
158° 00′
160° 00′ E
162° 00′
6° 00′
8° 00′
10° 00′ S
12° 00′
21

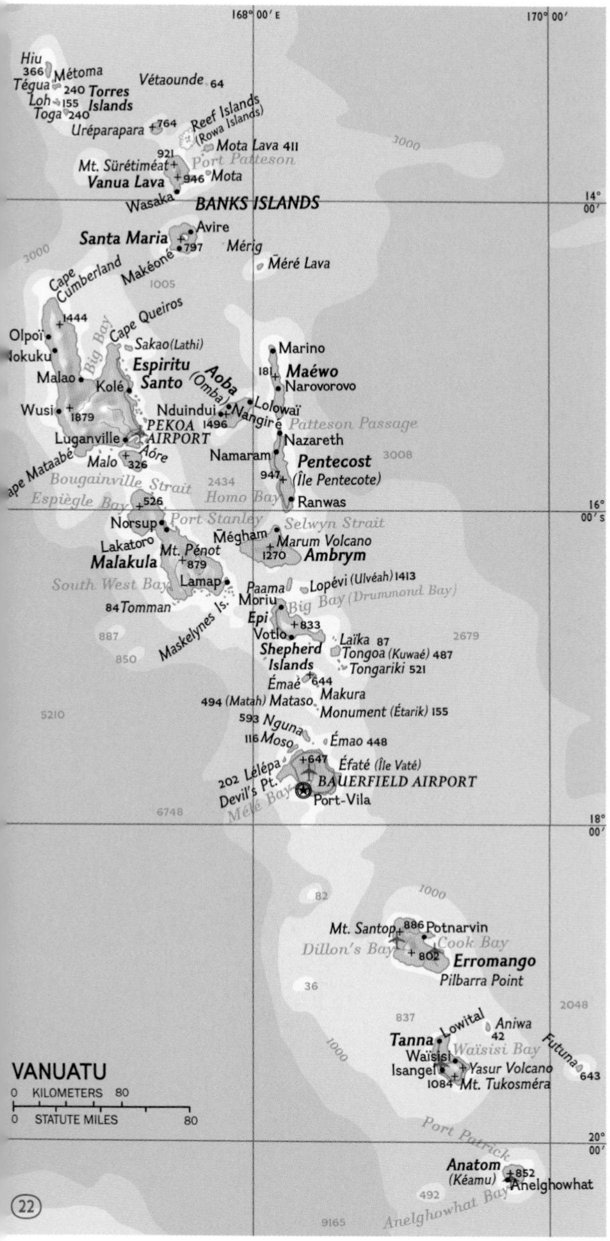
VANUATU
0 KILOMETERS 80
0 STATUTE MILES 80
168° 00′ E
170° 00′
14° 00′
16° 00′ S
18° 00′
20° 00′
Hiu
Tégua
Métoma
Loh
Toga
Torres Islands
Vétaounde
Uréparapara
Reef Islands
(Rowa Islands)
Mota Lava
Port Patteson
Mt. Sürétiméat
Vanua Lava
Mota
Wasaka
BANKS ISLANDS
Santa Maria
Avire
Mérig
Méré Lava
Makéone
Cape Cumberland
Cape Queiros
Big Bay
Olpoï
Nokuku
Sakao (Lathi)
Malao
Espiritu Santo
Kolé
Aoba (Omba)
Marino
Maéwo
Narovorovo
Wusi
Nduindui
Lolowaï
Nangiré
PEKOA AIRPORT
Luganville
Patteson Passage
Nazareth
Namaram
Malo
Aore
Cape Mataabé
Pentecost
(Île Pentecote)
Bougainville Strait
Espiègle Bay
Homo Bay
Ranwas
Port Stanley
Selwyn Strait
Norsup
Lakatoro
Mégham
Marum Volcano
Mt. Pénot
Ambrym
Malakula
South West Bay
Lamap
Paama
Lopévi (Ulvéah)
Moriu
Big Bay (Drummond Bay)
Tomman
Epi
Maskelynes Is.
Votlo
Laïka
Shepherd Islands
Tongoa (Kuwaé)
Tongariki
Émaé
Makura
(Matah) Mataso
Monument (Étarik)
Nguna
Moso
Émao
Éfaté (Île Vaté)
Lélépa
Devil's Pt.
BAUERFIELD AIRPORT
Port-Vila
Mélé Bay
Mt. Santop
Potnarvin
Cook Bay
Dillon's Bay
Erromango
Pilbarra Point
Lowital
Aniwa
Tanna
Waïsisi Bay
Futuna
Waïsisi
Isangel
Yasur Volcano
Mt. Tukosméra
Port Patrick
Anatom
(Kéamu)
Anelghowhat
Anelghowhat Bay
22

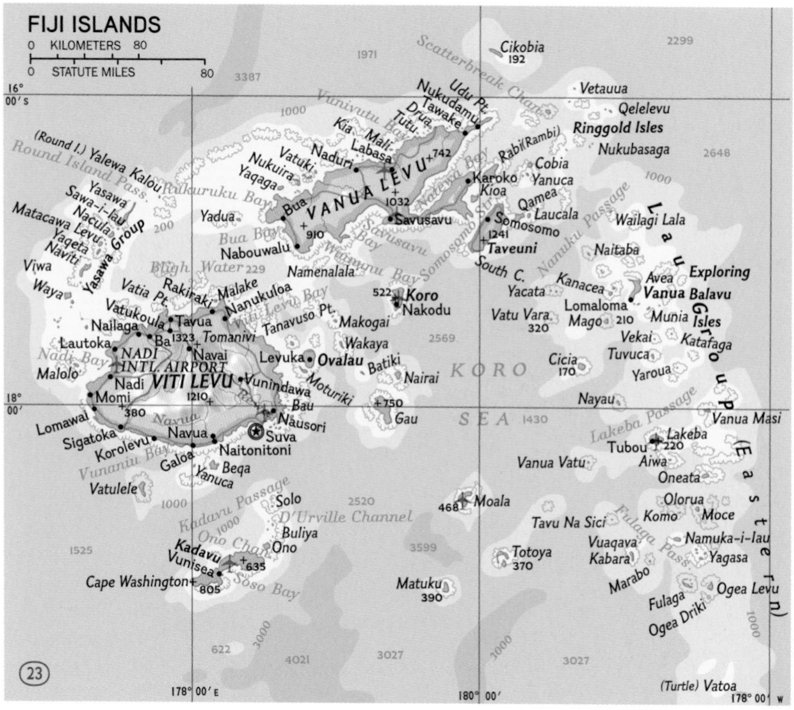
FIJI ISLANDS
0 KILOMETERS 80
0 STATUTE MILES 80
16° 00′ S
18° 00′
178° 00′ E
180° 00′
178° 00′ W
Scatterbreak Channel
Cikobia
Udu Pt.
Nukudamu
Tawake
Drua
Tutu
Kia
Mali
Labasa
Nadurì
Vatuki
Nukuira
Yaqaga
Vanua Levu
Natewa Bay
Rabi (Rambi)
Karoko
Kioa
Vetauua
Qelelevu
Ringgold Isles
Nukubasaga
Cobia
Yanuca
Qamea
Laucala
Somosomo
Taveuni
Somosomo Strait
Savusavu
Savusavu Bay
Bua
Bua Bay
Yadua
Nabouwalu
Wainunu Bay
(Round I.) Yalewa Kalou
Round Island Pass.
Yasawa
Sawa-i-lau
Naviti
Matacawa Levu
Yageta
Naviti
Yasawa Group
Viwa
Waya
Bligh Water
Rakiraki
Malake
Nanukuloa
Namenalala
Koro
Nakodu
Vatia Pt.
Vatukoula
Tavua
Nailaga
Ba
Tomanivi
Tanavuso Pt.
Makogai
Wakaya
Lautoka
Navai
Levuka
Ovalau
Batiki
Nadi Bay
NADI INTL. AIRPORT
Nadi
VITI LEVU
Vunindawa
Moturiki
Nairai
Malolo
Momi
Bau
Gau
Lomawai
Navua
Nausori
Sigatoka
Korolevu
Suva
Naitonitoni
Vunaniu Bay
Galoa
Beqa
Yanuca
Vatulele
Kadavu Passage
Solo
D'Urville Channel
Buliya
Ono
Ono Channel
Kadavu
Vunisea
Soso Bay
Cape Washington
KORO SEA
Moala
Totoya
Matuku
Wailagi Lala
Naitaba
Nanuku Passage
Kanacea
Avea
Exploring Isles
Vanua Balavu
Munia
Katafaga
Lomaloma
Mago
Vatu Vara
Vekai
Tuvuca
Cicia
Yaroua
Nayau
Lau Group (Eastern)
Vanua Masi
Lakeba Passage
Lakeba
Tubou
Aiwa
Vanua Vatu
Oneata
Olorua
Komo
Moce
Tavu Na Sici
Fulaga Passage
Namuka-i-lau
Vuaqava
Kabara
Yagasa
Marabo
Fulaga
Ogea Levu
Ogea Driki
(Turtle) Vatoa
23

Polar Regions

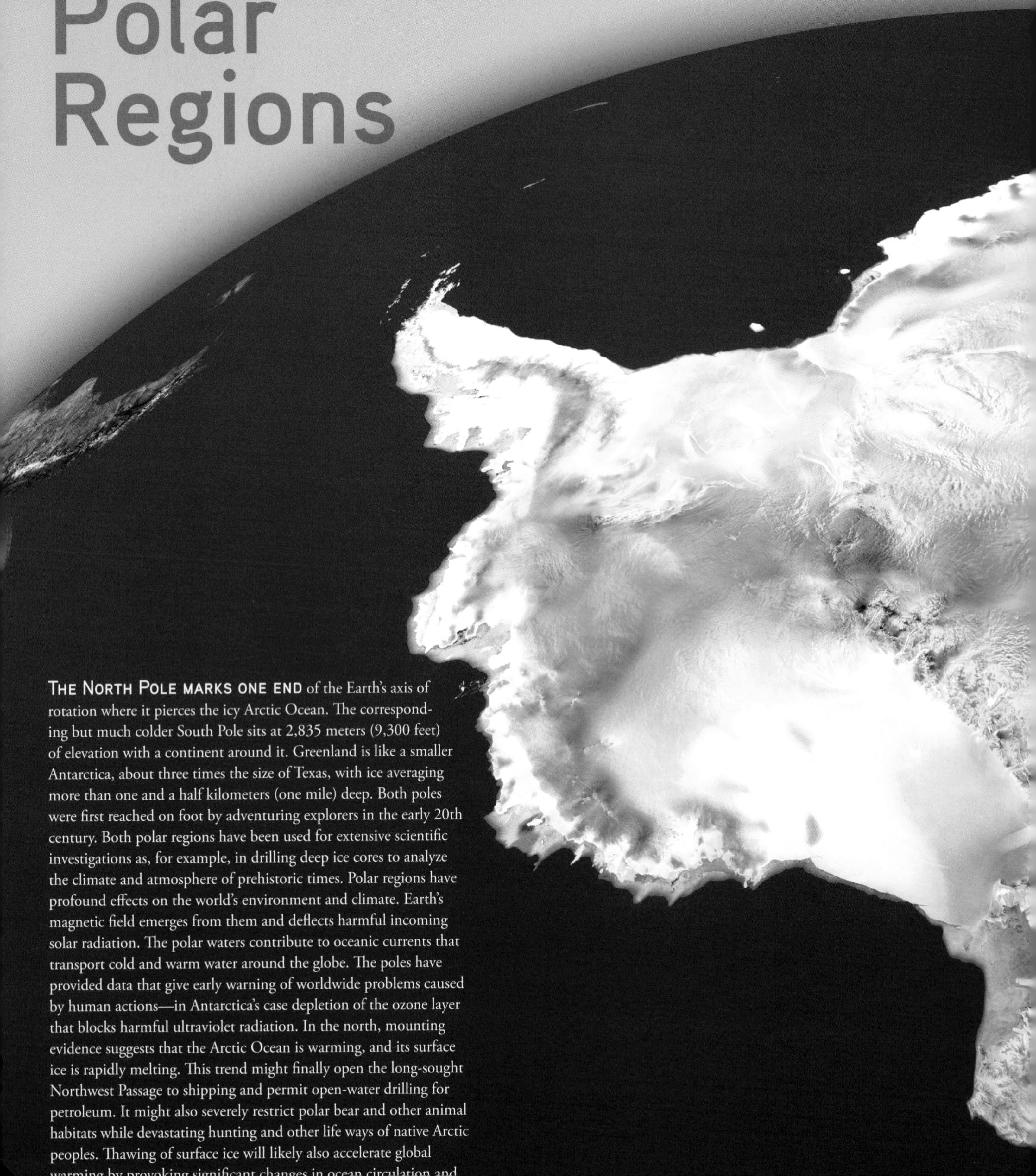

The North Pole marks one end of the Earth's axis of rotation where it pierces the icy Arctic Ocean. The corresponding but much colder South Pole sits at 2,835 meters (9,300 feet) of elevation with a continent around it. Greenland is like a smaller Antarctica, about three times the size of Texas, with ice averaging more than one and a half kilometers (one mile) deep. Both poles were first reached on foot by adventuring explorers in the early 20th century. Both polar regions have been used for extensive scientific investigations as, for example, in drilling deep ice cores to analyze the climate and atmosphere of prehistoric times. Polar regions have profound effects on the world's environment and climate. Earth's magnetic field emerges from them and deflects harmful incoming solar radiation. The polar waters contribute to oceanic currents that transport cold and warm water around the globe. The poles have provided data that give early warning of worldwide problems caused by human actions—in Antarctica's case depletion of the ozone layer that blocks harmful ultraviolet radiation. In the north, mounting evidence suggests that the Arctic Ocean is warming, and its surface ice is rapidly melting. This trend might finally open the long-sought Northwest Passage to shipping and permit open-water drilling for petroleum. It might also severely restrict polar bear and other animal habitats while devastating hunting and other life ways of native Arctic peoples. Thawing of surface ice will likely also accelerate global warming by provoking significant changes in ocean circulation and

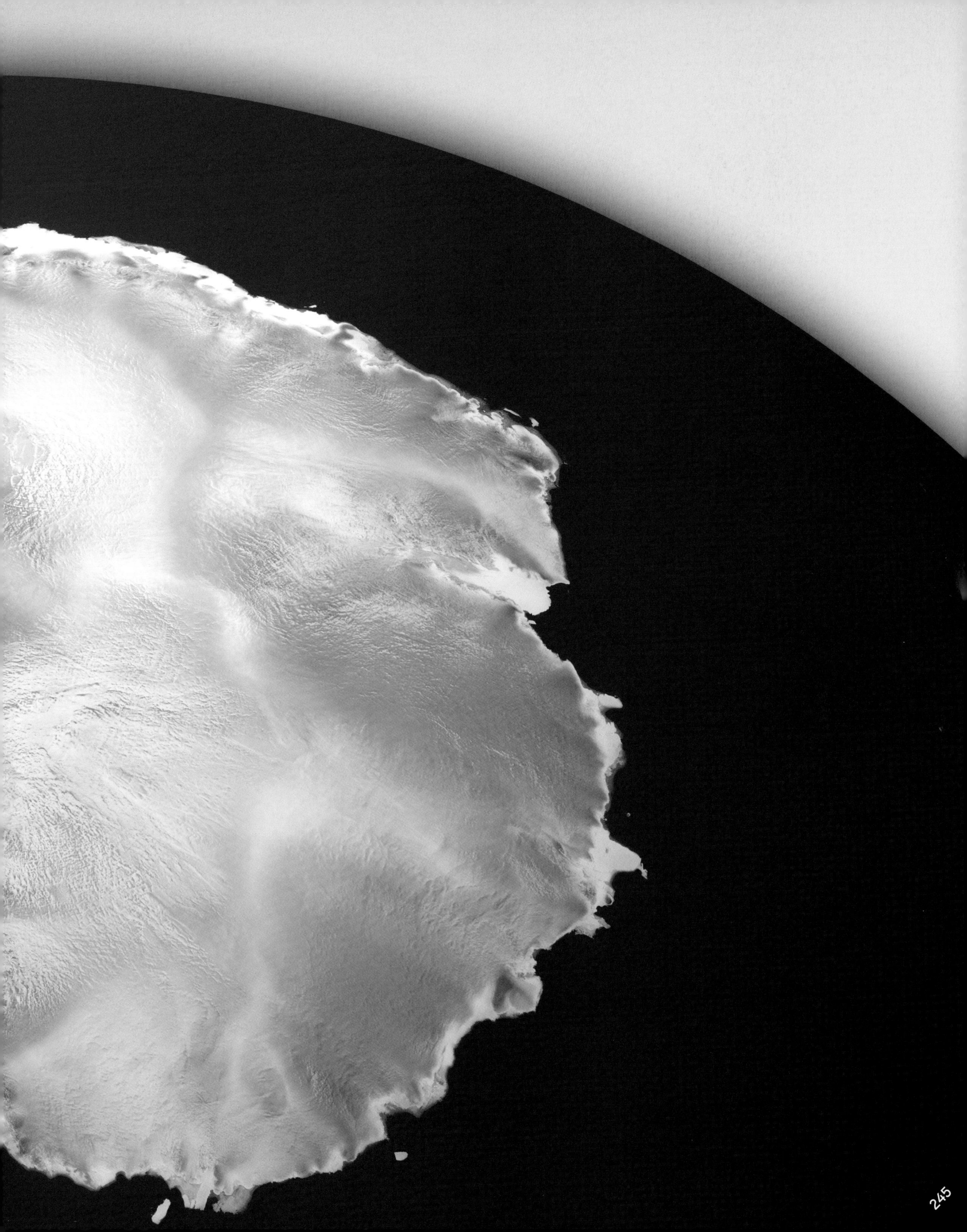

ICE

Pack ice responds to prevailing winds and ocean currents. Tabular icebergs up to 700 sq km (270 sq mi) in area sometimes break away from the northern edge of small ice shelves. These ice islands float slowly in erratic clockwise patterns around the North American side of the Arctic Ocean, completing full circuits in five to ten years, until they disintegrate or move into the Atlantic. Each year hundreds of much smaller bergs break off - calve - from the Greenland ice sheet and Canada's glaciers and move southward into the North Atlantic shipping lanes. After the sinking of the Titanic in 1912, leading maritime nations formed the International Ice Patrol to monitor icebergs and to study polar currents and iceberg dynamics.

AZIMUTHAL EQUIDISTANT PROJECTION
SCALE 1:20,000,000

0 KILOMETERS 300 400 500
0 MILES 200 300 400 500

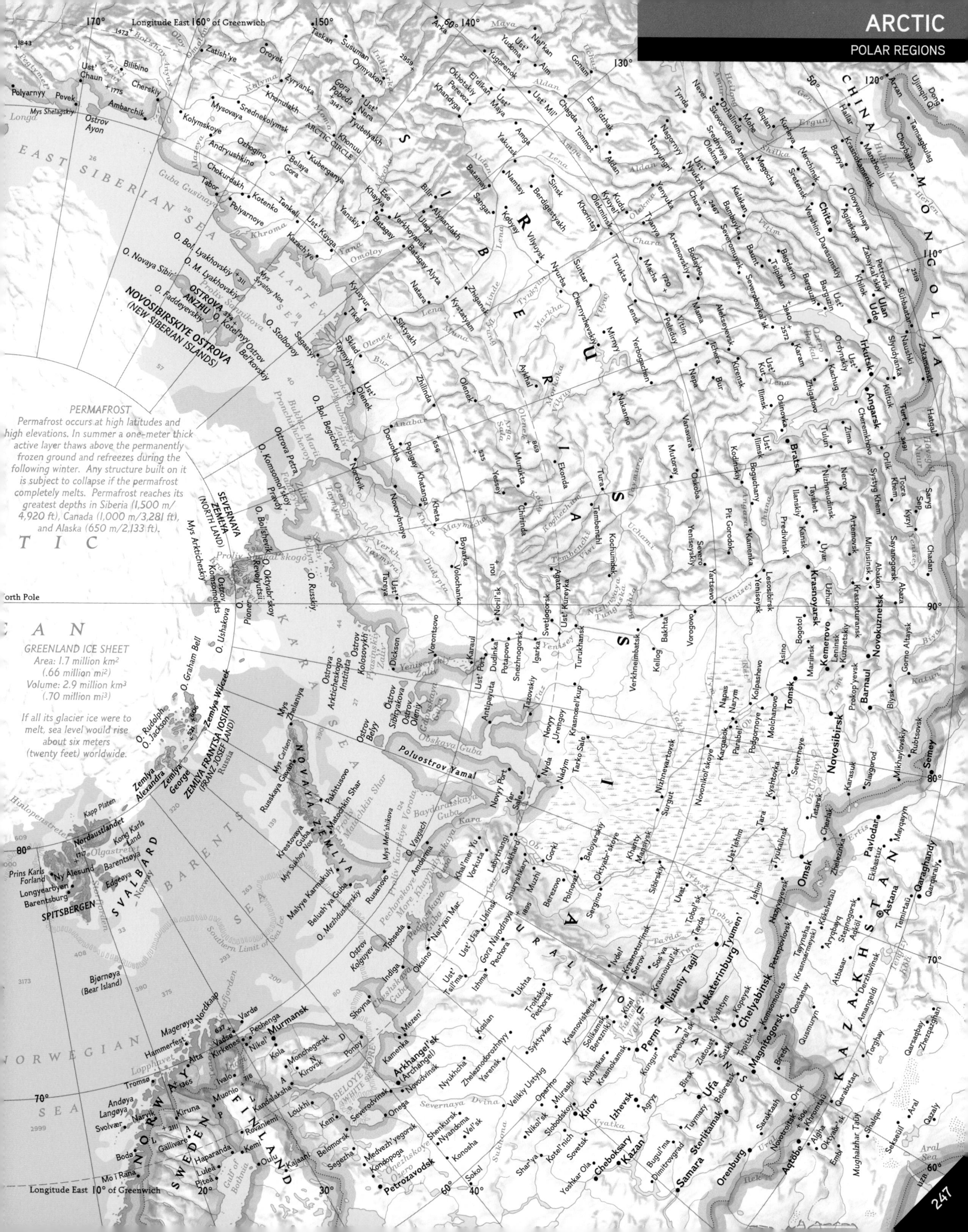

Longitude East 160° of Greenwich
PERMAFROST
Permafrost occurs at high latitudes and high elevations. In summer a one-meter thick active layer thaws above the permanently frozen ground and refreezes during the following winter. Any structure built on it is subject to collapse if the permafrost completely melts. Permafrost reaches its greatest depths in Siberia (1,500 m/ 4,920 ft), Canada (1,000 m/3,281 ft), and Alaska (650 m/2,133 ft).
GREENLAND ICE SHEET
Area: 1.7 million km²
(.66 million mi²)
Volume: 2.9 million km³
(.70 million mi³)
If all its glacier ice were to melt, sea level would rise about six meters (twenty feet) worldwide.
North Pole
EAST SIBERIAN SEA
LAPTEV SEA
KARA SEA
BARENTS SEA
NORWEGIAN SEA
SIBERIA
RUSSIA
URAL MOUNTAINS
CHINA
MONGOLIA
KAZAKHSTAN
NORWAY
SWEDEN
FINLAND
SVALBARD
SPITSBERGEN
NOVOSIBIRSKIYE OSTROVA (NEW SIBERIAN ISLANDS)
SEVERNAYA ZEMLYA (NORTH LAND)
ZEMLYA FRANTSA IOSIFA (FRANZ JOSEF LAND)
NOVAYA ZEMLYA
Poluostrov Yamal
Bjørnøya (Bear Island)
ARCTIC CIRCLE
Murmansk
Arkhangel'sk
Yekaterinburg
Novosibirsk
Krasnoyarsk
Irkutsk
Omsk
Tomsk
Perm'
Chelyabinsk
Astana
Longitude East 10° of Greenwich

ANTARCTIC PENINSULA AREA STATIONS

Argentina
1 Jubany
Brazil
2 Comandante Ferraz
Chile
3 Bernardo O'Higgins
4 Eduardo Frei
5 Estación Marítima Antártica
6 Julio Escudero

China
7 Great Wall
Korea, South
8 King Sejong
Poland
9 Arctowski
Russia
10 Bellingshausen
Uruguay
11 Artigas

Research Stations: ◉ Year-round   ○ Other

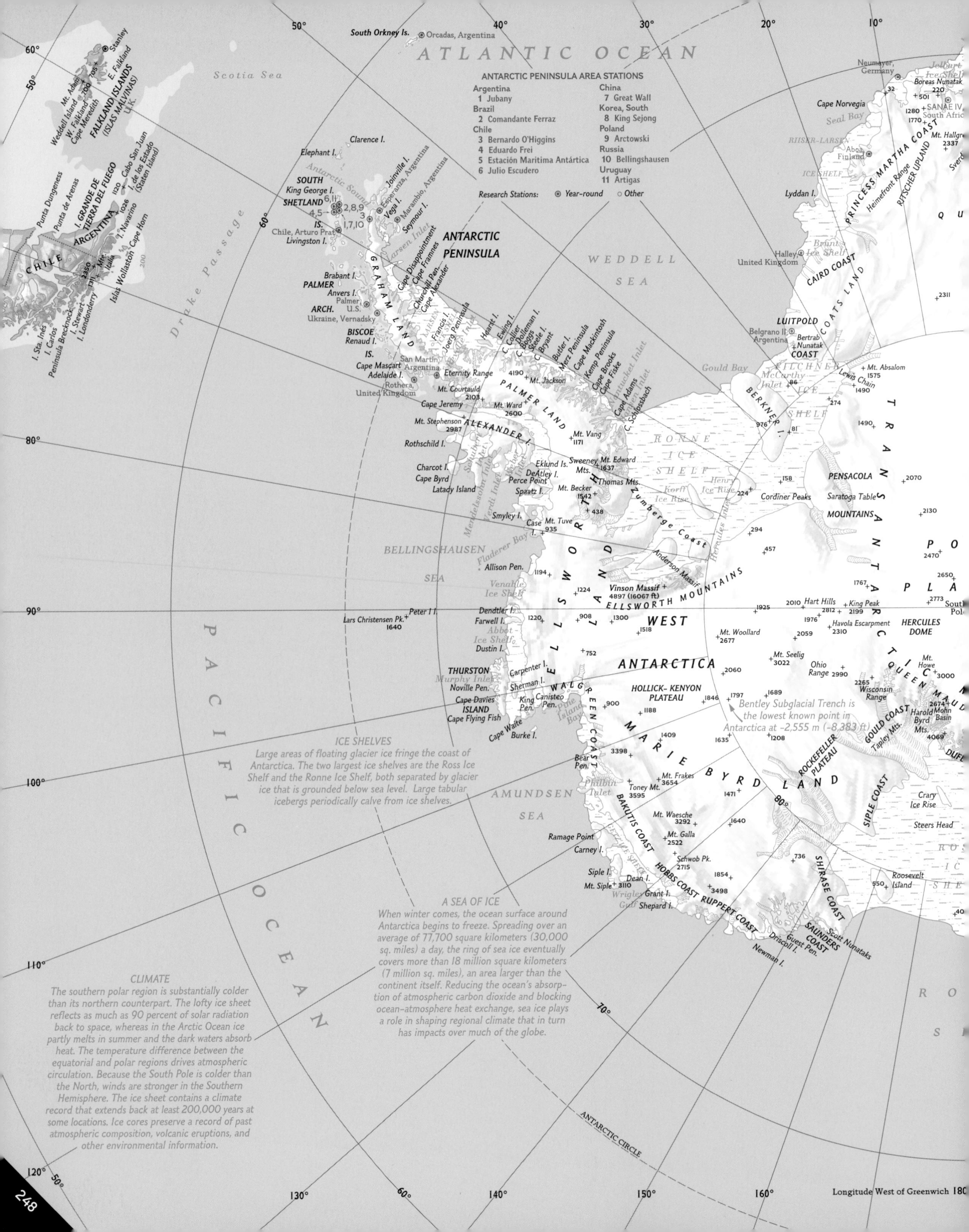

ICE SHELVES
Large areas of floating glacier ice fringe the coast of
Antarctica. The two largest ice shelves are the Ross Ice
Shelf and the Ronne Ice Shelf, both separated by glacier
ice that is grounded below sea level. Large tabular
icebergs periodically calve from ice shelves.

A SEA OF ICE
When winter comes, the ocean surface around
Antarctica begins to freeze. Spreading over an
average of 77,700 square kilometers (30,000
sq. miles) a day, the ring of sea ice eventually
covers more than 18 million square kilometers
(7 million sq. miles), an area larger than the
continent itself. Reducing the ocean's absorp-
tion of atmospheric carbon dioxide and blocking
ocean-atmosphere heat exchange, sea ice plays
a role in shaping regional climate that in turn
has impacts over much of the globe.

CLIMATE
The southern polar region is substantially colder
than its northern counterpart. The lofty ice sheet
reflects as much as 90 percent of solar radiation
back to space, whereas in the Arctic Ocean ice
partly melts in summer and the dark waters absorb
heat. The temperature difference between the
equatorial and polar regions drives atmospheric
circulation. Because the South Pole is colder than
the North, winds are stronger in the Southern
Hemisphere. The ice sheet contains a climate
record that extends back at least 200,000 years at
some locations. Ice cores preserve a record of past
atmospheric composition, volcanic eruptions, and
other environmental information.

Bentley Subglacial Trench is
the lowest known point in
Antarctica at -2,555 m (-8,383 ft)

Longitude West of Greenwich 180

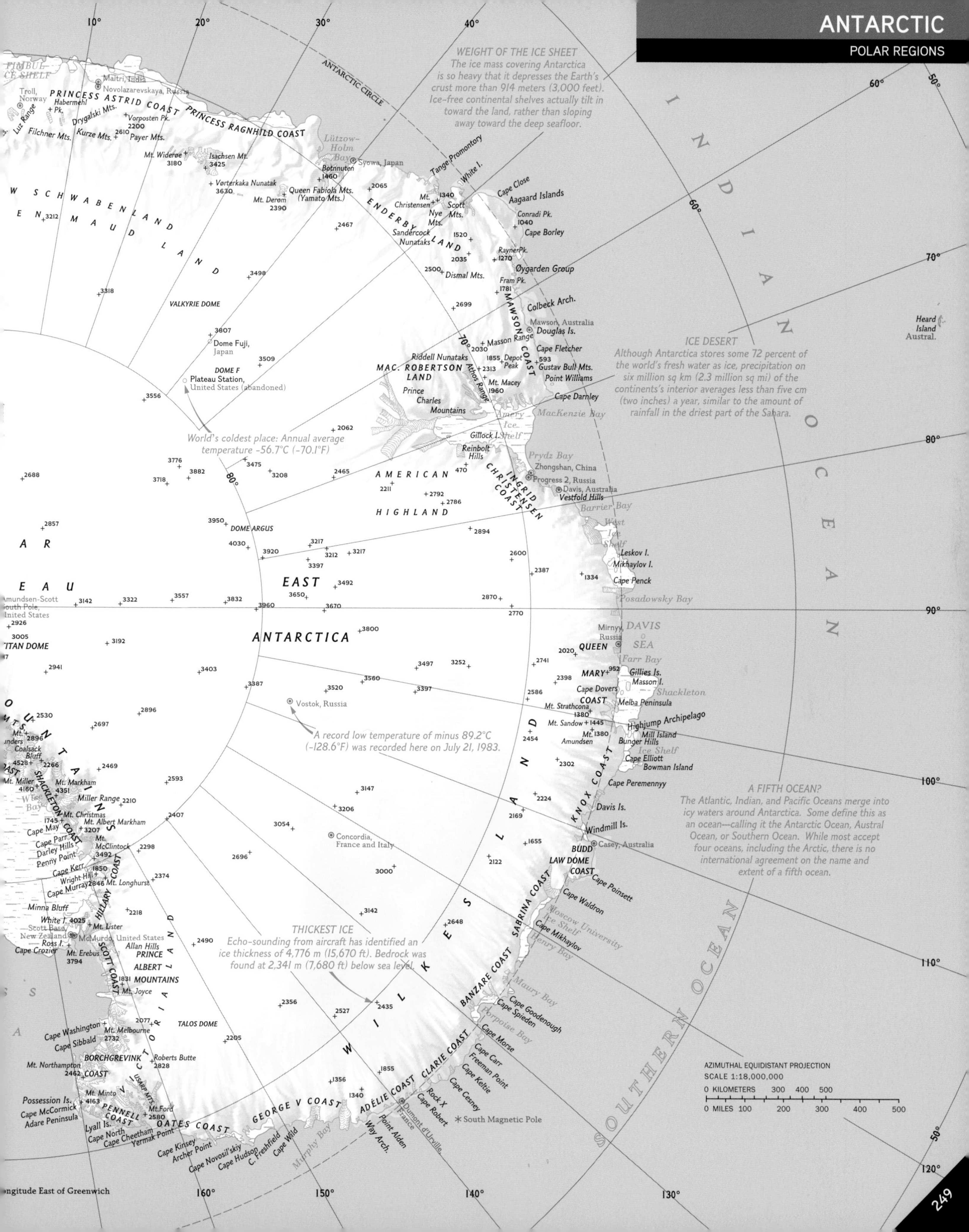
WEIGHT OF THE ICE SHEET
The ice mass covering Antarctica is so heavy that it depresses the Earth's crust more than 914 meters (3,000 feet). Ice-free continental shelves actually tilt in toward the land, rather than sloping away toward the deep seafloor.
ICE DESERT
Although Antarctica stores some 72 percent of the world's fresh water as ice, precipitation on six million sq km (2.3 million sq mi) of the continents's interior averages less than five cm (two inches) a year, similar to the amount of rainfall in the driest part of the Sahara.
World's coldest place: Annual average temperature -56.7°C (-70.1°F)
A record low temperature of minus 89.2°C (-128.6°F) was recorded here on July 21, 1983.
A FIFTH OCEAN?
The Atlantic, Indian, and Pacific Oceans merge into icy waters around Antarctica. Some define this as an ocean—calling it the Antarctic Ocean, Austral Ocean, or Southern Ocean. While most accept four oceans, including the Arctic, there is no international agreement on the name and extent of a fifth ocean.
THICKEST ICE
Echo-sounding from aircraft has identified an ice thickness of 4,776 m (15,670 ft). Bedrock was found at 2,341 m (7,680 ft) below sea level.
AZIMUTHAL EQUIDISTANT PROJECTION
SCALE 1:18,000,000
0 KILOMETERS 300 400 500
0 MILES 100 200 300 400 500
INDIAN OCEAN
SOUTHERN OCEAN
ANTARCTIC CIRCLE
EAST ANTARCTICA
PRINCESS ASTRID COAST
PRINCESS RAGNHILD COAST
ENDERBY LAND
MAC. ROBERTSON LAND
AMERICAN HIGHLAND
INGRID CHRISTENSEN COAST
MAWSON COAST
QUEEN MARY COAST
KNOX COAST
BUDD LAW DOME COAST
SABRINA COAST
BANZARE COAST
CLARIE COAST
ADÉLIE COAST
GEORGE V COAST
OATES COAST
PENNELL COAST
BORCHGREVINK COAST
SCOTT COAST
HILLARY COAST
SHACKLETON COAST
WILKES LAND
VICTORIA LAND
PRINCE ALBERT MOUNTAINS
DOME ARGUS
DOME F
VALKYRIE DOME
TALOS DOME
Dome Fuji, Japan
Plateau Station, United States (abandoned)
Vostok, Russia
Concordia, France and Italy
Maitri, India
Novolazarevskaya, Russia
Troll, Norway
Syowa, Japan
Mawson, Australia
Zhongshan, China
Progress 2, Russia
Davis, Australia
Mirnyy, Russia
Casey, Australia
Dumont d'Urville, France
McMurdo, United States
Scott Base, New Zealand
Amundsen-Scott South Pole, United States
Lützow-Holm Bay
Amery Ice Shelf
MacKenzie Bay
Prydz Bay
Barrier Bay
West Ice Shelf
Posadowsky Bay
DAVIS SEA
Farr Bay
Shackleton Ice Shelf
Moscow University Ice Shelf
Henry Bay
Maury Bay
Porpoise Bay
Murphy Bay
Wise Bay
Prince Charles Mountains
Vestfold Hills
Douglas Is.
Heard Island Austral.
South Magnetic Pole
Mt. Erebus 3794
Longitude East of Greenwich
10° 20° 30° 40° 50° 60° 70° 80° 90° 100° 110° 120° 130° 140° 150° 160°

Oceans

Satellite-derived images (above) depict a ten-year average of the hills and valleys, or shape, of the changing ocean surface. These undulations range over a few meters in height, and flow occurs along the color contours. Such topographic maps are like the weather maps for ocean currents, aiding oceanographers, fishermen, and navigators in studying the ocean and utilizing its resources. The vectors (white arrows) show ocean velocity caused exclusively by the effect of wind on the top layer of the ocean (called the Ekman Drift).

Departure From Mean Sea Level

Meters	-2.6	-2.4	-2.2	-2.0	-1.8	-1.6	-1.4	-1.2	-1.0	-0.8	-0.6	-0.4	-0.2	0.0	0.2	0.4	0.6	0.8	1.0	1.2
Feet	-8.5	-7.9	-7.2	-6.6	-5.9	-5.2	-4.6	-3.9	-3.3	-2.6	-2.0	-1.3	-0.7	0.0	0.7	1.3	2.0	2.6	3.3	3.9

No data available

THE FIRST COLOR IMAGES beamed home from satellites in lunar orbit illustrated with startling visual impact a fact long known: Earth is truly a water planet. The great interconnected oceans cover 70 percent of it. Hidden from plain sight beneath that blue surface lie trenches, ridges, rises, abyssal plains, and immense, snaking mountain ranges. Earth's highest mountain, from base to top, is not Everest, but the almost mile-higher Mauna Kea, a volcano that broke the Pacific Ocean's surface during the creation of Hawai'i. Primitive oceans and atmospheres were born from release and condensation of gases including water vapor spewing from the hot young planet. More water was added by bombardment of water-rich comets. The combination of Earth's size and distance from the Sun allowed water to persist as a liquid and set the stage for the origins of life. Without oceans Earth's climate would be much more extreme, perhaps unlivable, with much hotter hot zones and much colder frigid zones. Ocean currents set in motion by the planet's rotation, shaped by landmasses, and maintained by flow and counterflow between Polar and Equatorial regions keep Earth mostly temperate. Even small variations in these patterns can have large effects. The systematic variation of oceanic patterns in the Pacific called "El Niño" brings stormy weather to the United States and Peru, for instance, while a rise in Atlantic sea surface temperature feeds the formation, frequency, and severity of hurricanes. A matter of present concern is the melting of Arctic sea ice because of global warming accelerated by human activities. Introduction of cold fresh meltwater into the North Atlantic circulation system may suppress or deflect the Gulf Stream. That current warms northwest Europe, and its substantial weakening could lead to widespread economic and political hardships.

PACIFIC OCEAN
MERCATOR PROJECTION
SCALE 1:75,100,000
0 KILOMETERS 1500 2000
0 MILES 500 1000 1500 2000
ASIA
NORTH AMERICA
SOUTH AMERICA
AUSTRALIA
INDIAN OCEAN
SEA OF OKHOTSK
BERING SEA
ALEUTIAN BASIN
ALEUTIAN ISLANDS
ALEUTIAN TRENCH
GULF OF ALASKA
ALASKA PLAIN
TUFTS PLAIN
JUAN DE FUCA RIDGE
HUDSON BAY
NORTH ATLANTIC OCEAN
GULF OF MEXICO
CARIBBEAN SEA
CENTRAL AMERICA
MIDDLE AMERICA TRENCH
PANAMA BASIN
GUATEMALA BASIN
COLÓN RIFT
GALÁPAGOS IS.
GALÁPAGOS RISE
PERU BASIN
PERU-CHILE TRENCH
NASCA RIDGE
SALA Y GÓMEZ RIDGE
EASTER FRACTURE ZONE
CHILE BASIN
CHILE FRACTURE ZONE
CHILE RISE
SOUTHEAST PACIFIC BASIN
EAST PACIFIC RISE
MENARD FRACTURE ZONE
ELTANIN FRACTURE ZONE SYSTEM
UDINTSEV FRACTURE ZONE
SOUTHWEST PACIFIC BASIN
AGASSIZ FRACTURE ZONE
LOUISVILLE RIDGE
NORTHEAST PACIFIC BASIN
MENDOCINO FRACTURE ZONE
PIONEER FRACTURE ZONE
MURRAY FRACTURE ZONE
MOLOKAI FRACTURE ZONE
CLARION FRACTURE ZONE
CLIPPERTON FRACTURE ZONE
GALÁPAGOS FRACTURE ZONE
MARQUESAS FRACTURE ZONE
MARQUESAS IS.
TUAMOTU ARCHIPELAGO
LINE ISLANDS
HAWAIIAN ISLANDS
HAWAIIAN RIDGE
CENTRAL PACIFIC BASIN
MID-PACIFIC MOUNTAINS
EMPEROR SEAMOUNTS
EMPEROR TROUGH
NORTHWEST PACIFIC BASIN
SHATSKY RISE
KURIL-KAMCHATKA TRENCH
JAPAN TRENCH
IZU-OGASAWARA TRENCH
BONIN TRENCH
MARIANA TRENCH
World's greatest ocean depth
Challenger Deep
PHILIPPINE SEA
WEST MARIANA BASIN
EAST MARIANA BASIN
KYUSHU-PALAU RIDGE
RYUKYU TRENCH
PHILIPPINE TRENCH
CAROLINE ISLANDS
MARSHALL ISLANDS
INDONESIA
NEW GUINEA
SOLOMON ISLANDS
CORAL SEA
NEW CALEDONIA BASIN
NORFOLK RIDGE
LORD HOWE RISE
TASMAN SEA
NEW ZEALAND
TONGA TRENCH
KERMADEC TRENCH
CHATHAM RISE
CAMPBELL PLATEAU
SOUTHEAST INDIAN RIDGE
SOUTH AUSTRALIAN BASIN

ATLANTIC OCEAN
MERCATOR PROJECTION
SCALE 1:62,600,000
0 KILOMETERS 1200 1600
0 MILES 400 800 1200 1600
GREENLAND
FOXE BASIN
HUDSON BAY
DAVIS STRAIT
CONTINENTAL SHELF
CONTINENTAL SLOPE
Nuuk (Godthåb)
Tasiilaq (Ammassalik)
DENMARK STRAIT
ICELAND
Reykjavík
Surtsey
ICELAND-FAROE RISE
FAROE ISLANDS
SCANDINAVIA
GULF OF BOTHNIA
Halten Bank
Bergen
Oslo
Stockholm
Helsinki
BALTIC SEA
NORTH SEA
Hamburg
BRITISH ISLES
Dublin
CELTIC SEA
ENGLISH CHANNEL
BAY OF BISCAY
BISCAY PLAIN
PORCUPINE PLAIN
EUROPE
Danube
Marseille
CORSICA
Rome
ADRIATIC SEA
SARDINIA
TYRRHENIAN SEA
BALEARIC IS.
SICILY
MEDITERRANEAN SEA
Athens
CRETE
Algiers
Tripoli
Lisbon
Strait of Gibraltar
Rabat
MADEIRA ISLANDS
CANARY ISLANDS
CAPE VERDE PLAIN
CAPE VERDE ISLANDS
Nouakchott
Dakar
AFRICA
Niger
L. Chad
GAMBIA PLAIN
Freetown
SIERRA LEONE RISE
Abidjan
Accra
Lagos
Bioko
São Tomé
Libreville
Congo
EQUATOR
Congo Canyon
Luanda
ANGOLA PLAIN
St. Helena
Zambezi
WALVIS RIDGE
Orange
CAPE PLAIN
Cape of Good Hope
Cape Town
CONTINENTAL SLOPE
Tristan da Cunha Group
Discovery Tablemount
NORTHWEST ATLANTIC MID-OCEAN CANYON
LABRADOR SEA
Eirik Ridge
IMARSSUAK SEACHANNEL
REYKJANES RIDGE
MAURY SEACHANNEL
WYVILLE THOMSON RIDGE
Rockall
Gloria Ridge
CHARLIE-GIBBS FRACTURE ZONE
MID-ATLANTIC RIDGE
Flemish Cap
St. John's
Grand Banks of Newfoundland
GULF OF ST. LAWRENCE
St. Lawrence
Québec
Montréal
Cape Breton Island
Halifax
Sable Island
Gulf of Maine
Boston
New York
Laurentian Fan
NORTH AMERICA
Chicago
Missouri
Ohio
Mississippi
Hudson Canyon
Cape Hatteras
SOHM PLAIN
New England Seamounts
Corner Seamounts
OCEANOGRAPHER FRACTURE ZONE
AZORES
Pico
Bermuda Islands
BERMUDA RISE
BLAKE PLATEAU
Blake-Bahama Ridge
HATTERAS PLAIN
New Orleans
GULF OF MEXICO
Mexico Basin
Campeche Bank
Miami
BAHAMA ISLANDS
Havana
CUBA
ATLANTIS FRACTURE ZONE
NARES PLAIN
KANE FRACTURE ZONE
Atlantic Ocean's deepest point
PUERTO RICO TRENCH
HISPANIOLA
-8605 (-28232 ft)
Cayman Trench
GREATER ANTILLES
LESSER ANTILLES
AVES RIDGE
CENTRAL AMERICA
MIDDLE AMERICA TRENCH
Panama City
COCOS RIDGE
Trinidad
VEMA FRACTURE ZONE
DEMERARA PLAIN
DOLDRUMS FRACTURE ZONE
Georgetown
Amazon Fan
St. Peter and St. Paul Rocks
CEARA PLAIN
ROMANCHE FRACTURE ZONE
CHAIN FRACTURE ZONE
Fernando de Noronha
Belém
Amazon
GALÁPAGOS ISLANDS
CARNEGIE RIDGE
PERNAMBUCO PLAIN
ASCENSION FRACTURE ZONE
SOUTH AMERICA
Lima
PERU-CHILE TRENCH
NASCA RIDGE
Trindade
Martin Vaz Islands
Vitória Seamount
Paraguay
Rio de Janeiro
São Paulo
Santos Plateau
RIO GRANDE RISE
SOUTH PACIFIC OCEAN
San Félix Island
San Ambrosio Island
Juan Fernández Islands
CHILE RISE
Paraná
Buenos Aires
Montevideo
CONTINENTAL RISE
Zapiola Ridge
ARGENTINE PLAIN
Gulf of San Jorge

INDIAN OCEAN
MERCATOR PROJECTION
SCALE 1:51,400,000
0 KILOMETERS 800 1200
0 MILES 400 800 1200
ASIA
AFRICA
AUSTRALIA
INDIA
ARABIAN PENINSULA
INDONESIA
MEDITERRANEAN SEA
Alexandria
SUEZ CANAL
Dead Sea
-422 (-1385ft)
World's lowest point
Mt. Everest
8850 (29035 ft)
World's highest point
Tigris
Euphrates
Ābādān
PERSIAN GULF
GULF OF OMAN
Muscat
Karachi
Indus
Ganges
Brahmaputra
Kolkata (Calcutta)
Mumbai (Bombay)
Chennai (Madras)
SRI LANKA (CEYLON)
Yangon (Rangoon)
Bangkok
Ho Chi Minh City (Saigon)
Mekong
Yangtze
Shanghai
Hong Kong
Hainan
Taiwan
EAST CHINA SEA
JAPAN
KYUSHU
RYUKYU ISLANDS
RYUKYU TRENCH
PHILIPPINE SEA
PHILIPPINE BASIN
WEST MARIANA BASIN
LUZON
Manila
PHILIPPINE ISLANDS
PHILIPPINE TRENCH
SOUTH CHINA SEA
Paracel Islands
PALAWAN TROUGH
SULU BASIN
MINDANAO
CELEBES BASIN
Palau
PALAU TRENCH
YAP TRENCH
WEST CAROLINE BASIN
EQUATOR
NEW GUINEA
SULAWESI
BANDA SEA
BORNEO
Singapore
SUMATRA
GREATER SUNDA ISLANDS
Jakarta
JAVA
Bali
LESSER SUNDA ISLANDS
TIMOR
Darwin
CONTINENTAL SHELF
JAVA TRENCH (SUNDA TRENCH)
JAVA RIDGE
Christmas I.
-7125 (-23376 ft)
Indian Ocean's deepest point
NORTH AUSTRALIAN BASIN
EXMOUTH PLATEAU
WHARTON BASIN
ZENITH PLATEAU
CUVIER PLATEAU
PERTH BASIN
Perth
NATURALISTE PLATEAU
DIAMANTINA FRACTURE ZONE
CONTINENTAL SLOPE
Adelaide
SOUTH AUSTRALIAN BASIN
EAST INDIAMAN RIDGE
BROKEN RIDGE
INVESTIGATOR RIDGE
NINETYEAST RIDGE
OSBORN PLATEAU
ANDAMAN BASIN
Andaman Islands
Nicobar Islands
BAY OF BENGAL
Ganges Fan
Nikitin Seamount
MID-INDIAN BASIN
CHAGOS TRENCH
Maldive Islands
CHAGOS-LACCADIVE RIDGE
Chagos Archipelago
Diego Garcia
ARABIAN SEA
ARABIAN BASIN
Indus Fan
OWEN FRACTURE ZONE
CARLSBERG RIDGE
Socotra
Error Tablemount
GULF OF ADEN
Aden
Djibouti
RED SEA
Nile
Congo
Lake Victoria
Lake Tanganyika
Lake Malawi
Zambezi
Mogadishu
Mombasa
Zanzibar I.
Dar es Salaam
SOMALI BASIN
COCO-DE-MER SEAMOUNTS
Seychelles
Amirante Isles
AMIRANTE TRENCH
MASCARENE PLATEAU
Agalega Islands
Aldabra Is.
Farquhar Group
Comoro Islands
MASCARENE BASIN
Tromelin
Cargados Carajos Bank
MADAGASCAR
MASCARENE PLAIN
Mauritius
Réunion
MAURITIUS TRENCH
RODRIGUES RIDGE
Rodrigues
EGERIA FRACTURE ZONE
MID-INDIAN RIDGE
MADAGASCAR BASIN
Bassas da India
Europa
Maputo
Durban
MOZAMBIQUE BASIN
MADAGASCAR PLATEAU
MOZAMBIQUE PLATEAU
MOZAMBIQUE ESCARPMENT
Walters Shoal
Agulhas Bank
AGULHAS PLATEAU
AGULHAS BASIN
PRINCE EDWARD FRACTURE ZONE
Prince Edward Islands
INDOMED FRACTURE ZONE
SOUTHWEST INDIAN RIDGE
ATLANTIS II FRACTURE ZONE
CROZET BASIN
CROZET PLATEAU
Crozet Islands
Amsterdam
St. Paul
SOUTHEAST INDIAN RIDGE
Kerguelen Islands
KERGUELEN PLATEAU

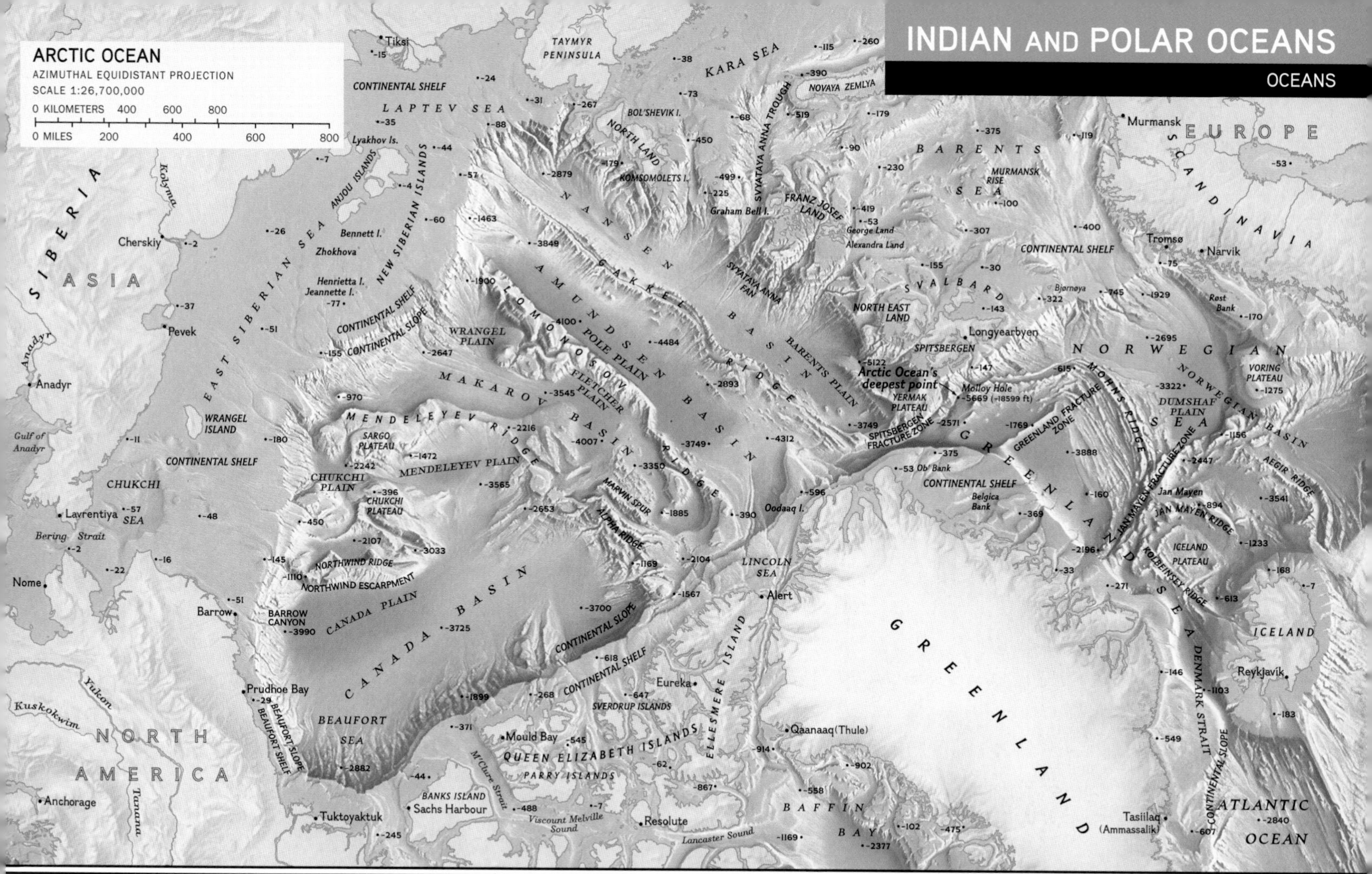
ARCTIC OCEAN
AZIMUTHAL EQUIDISTANT PROJECTION
SCALE 1:26,700,000
0 KILOMETERS 400 600 800
0 MILES 200 400 600 800
SIBERIA
ASIA
EUROPE
SCANDINAVIA
NORTH AMERICA
GREENLAND
LAPTEV SEA
KARA SEA
BARENTS SEA
EAST SIBERIAN SEA
CHUKCHI SEA
BEAUFORT SEA
LINCOLN SEA
BAFFIN BAY
NORWEGIAN SEA
GREENLAND SEA
ATLANTIC OCEAN
NANSEN BASIN
AMUNDSEN BASIN
MAKAROV BASIN
CANADA BASIN
NORWEGIAN BASIN
GAKKEL RIDGE
LOMONOSOV RIDGE
MENDELEYEV RIDGE
ALPHA RIDGE
NORTHWIND RIDGE
MOHNS RIDGE
KOLBEINSEY RIDGE
JAN MAYEN RIDGE
AEGIR RIDGE
CANADA PLAIN
WRANGEL PLAIN
POLE PLAIN
FLETCHER PLAIN
MENDELEYEV PLAIN
CHUKCHI PLAIN
BARENTS PLAIN
CONTINENTAL SHELF
CONTINENTAL SLOPE
NEW SIBERIAN ISLANDS
ANJOU ISLANDS
WRANGEL ISLAND
NOVAYA ZEMLYA
FRANZ JOSEF LAND
SVALBARD
SPITSBERGEN
NORTH LAND
QUEEN ELIZABETH ISLANDS
PARRY ISLANDS
SVERDRUP ISLANDS
ELLESMERE ISLAND
ICELAND
Arctic Ocean's deepest point
Molloy Hole -5669 (-18599 ft)
Murmansk
Tromsø
Narvik
Longyearbyen
Reykjavík
Tiksi
Cherskiy
Pevek
Anadyr
Lavrentiya
Nome
Barrow
Prudhoe Bay
Anchorage
Tuktoyaktuk
Sachs Harbour
Mould Bay
Resolute
Eureka
Alert
Qaanaaq (Thule)
Tasiilaq (Ammassalik)
Bering Strait
Gulf of Anadyr

OCEANS AROUND ANTARCTICA
AZIMUTHAL EQUIDISTANT PROJECTION
SCALE 1:70,000,000
0 KILOMETERS 1200 1600 2000
0 MILES 400 800 1200 1600 2000
SOUTH AMERICA
ANTARCTICA
AUSTRALIA
TASMANIA
WEDDELL SEA
SCOTIA SEA
BELLINGSHAUSEN SEA
AMUNDSEN SEA
ROSS SEA
COSMONAUT SEA
WEDDELL PLAIN
ENDERBY PLAIN
BELLINGSHAUSEN PLAIN
AMUNDSEN PLAIN
SOUTH AUSTRALIAN PLAIN
AUSTRALIAN-ANTARCTIC BASIN
ATLANTIC-INDIAN RIDGE
SOUTHWEST INDIAN RIDGE
MID-INDIAN RIDGE
SOUTHEAST INDIAN RIDGE
NINETYEAST RIDGE
BROKEN RIDGE
PACIFIC-ANTARCTIC RIDGE
EAST PACIFIC RISE
CHILE RISE
PERU-CHILE TRENCH
SALA Y GÓMEZ RIDGE
KERGUELEN PLATEAU
CROZET PLATEAU
FALKLAND PLATEAU
MAUD RISE
ELTANIN FRACTURE ZONE SYSTEM
UDINTSEV FRACTURE ZONE
MENARD FRACTURE ZONE
CHILE FRACTURE ZONE
TASMAN FRACTURE ZONE
DIAMANTINA FRACTURE ZONE
MACQUARIE RIDGE
RONNE ICE SHELF
ROSS ICE SHELF
Punta Arenas
Perth
Hobart
Falkland Islands
South Georgia
South Orkney Is.
Prince Edward Is.
Crozet Is.
Kerguelen Islands
Réunion
Mauritius
Rodrigues
Amsterdam
St. Paul
Macquarie I.
Campbell I.
Auckland Is.
Balleny Is.
Scott I.
Peter I Island
Thurston I.
Alexander I.
Berkner I.
Juan Fernández Islands
Isla Sala y Gómez
Ducie I.
Henderson I.

Place-name Index

Using This Index

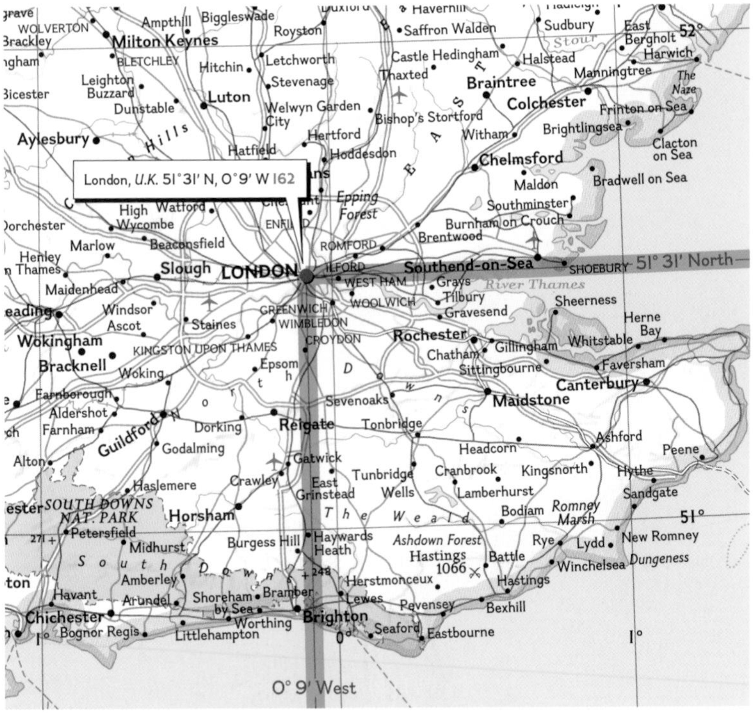

The Following System is used to locate a place on a map in this atlas. The coordinates listed after each name give its geographic location; the boldface, gray type refers to the atlas page on which it can be found. Each map contains a system of gray lines representing specific lines of latitude (north-south position) and longitude (east-west position). These graticule lines, which are often curved, are labeled near the page edges. Each degree of latitude or longitude is divided into 60 equal parts, called minutes, represented by a ' symbol. London's entry, 51° 31' N, 0° 9' W, indicates that it is located about halfway between 51 and 52 degrees north latitude, and just west of 0 degrees longitude. These lines are highlighted in green on the example map at left, with London located at their intersection point.

Useful tips: Page numbers are listed in gray type. When a single map falls across two pages, place-names are indexed to the even-numbered page. A place-name may appear on several maps, but the index generally references the largest-scale applicable map. The name of the country or continent in which a feature lies is shown in italic type, and is often abbreviated; a list of abbreviations appears on page 390.

The index lists more than proper names. Some entries include a feature description after the proper name, as in "**Rendova, island, *Solomon Islands* 8° 35' S, 157° 15' E 242.**" When a place-name can be referred to by more than one name, both may appear in the index with cross-references. For example, the entry for Bombay reads "**Bombay, see Mumbai, *India*, 18° 57' N, 72° 49' E 188.**"

entry name — Bornholm, island, *Den.* 55° 18' N, 14° 51' E 143 — *page number*
feature type — island
country — *Den.*
latitude coordinates — 55° 18' N
longitude coordinates — 14° 51' E

A

150 Mile House, *Can.* 52° 7' N, 121° 57' W 108
19 de Abril, *Uru.* 34° 23' S, 54° 5' W 139
23 August, *Rom.* 43° 55' N, 28° 35' E 156
25 de Mayo, *Arg.* 35° 26' S, 60° 12' W 139
26 Baky Komissary, *Azerb.* 39° 18' N, 49° 10' E 195
2nd Cataract, fall(s), *Sudan* 21° 54' N, 30° 50' E 226
31 de Janeiro, *Angola* 6° 53' S, 15° 18' E 218
31 de Março, Pico, peak, *Braz.* 0° 48' N, 66° 0' W 136
3rd Cataract, fall(s), *Sudan* 19° 55' N, 29° 47' E 226
6th Cataract, fall(s), *Sudan* 16° 29' N, 32° 36' E 182
9 de Julio, *Arg.* 35° 26' S, 60° 54' W 139
A Coruña, *Sp.* 43° 21' N, 8° 27' W 150
Aa, river, *Ger.* 52° 26' N, 7° 28' E 163
Aachen, *Ger.* 50° 46' N, 6° 5' E 167
Aagaard Islands, *Indian Ocean* 65° 36' S, 52° 31' E 248
Aalsmeer, *Neth.* 52° 15' N, 4° 45' E 163
Aalst, *Belg.* 50° 56' N, 4° 2' E 163
Aalten, *Neth.* 51° 55' N, 6° 34' E 167
Äänekoski, *Fin.* 62° 36' N, 25° 41' E 152
Aansluit, *S. Af.* 26° 46' S, 22° 30' E 227
Aapajärvi, *Fin.* 67° 13' N, 27° 16' E 152
Aarau, *Switz.* 47° 22' N, 8° 1' E 156
Aare, river, *Switz.* 47° 6' N, 7° 20' E 165
Aarschot, *Belg.* 50° 58' N, 4° 49' E 167
Aasiaat (Egedesminde), *Den.* 68° 45' N, 52° 53' W 106
Aavasaksa, *Fin.* 66° 23' N, 23° 42' E 152
Aba, *Dem. Rep. of the Congo* 3° 51' N, 30° 17' E 224
Aba, *Nig.* 5° 9' N, 7° 23' E 222
Abā as Sa'ūd, *Saudi Arabia* 17° 27' N, 44° 8' E 182
Abacaxis, river, *Braz.* 5° 29' S, 58° 39' W 130
Abaclia, *Mold.* 46° 22' N, 28° 55' E 156
Abaco Island, *Bahamas* 26° 0' N, 77° 0' W 118
Abaco Islands, *North Atlantic Ocean* 27° 0' N, 77° 0' W 118
Abadab, Jebel, peak, *Sudan* 18° 52' N, 35° 52' E 182
Ābādān, *Iran* 30° 20' N, 48° 21' E 180
Ābādeh, *Iran* 31° 6' N, 52° 39' E 180
Abádszalók, *Hung.* 47° 29' N, 20° 35' E 168
Abaeté, *Braz.* 19° 9' S, 45° 25' W 138
Abaetetuba, *Braz.* 1° 45' S, 48° 54' W 130
Abag Qi (Xin Hot), *China* 44° 1' N, 114° 56' E 198
Abaí, *Parag.* 26° 1' S, 55° 53' W 139
Abaji, *Nig.* 8° 28' N, 6° 55' E 222
Abajo Mountains, *Utah, U.S.* 37° 57' N, 109° 50' W 90
Abajo Peak, *Utah, U.S.* 37° 49' N, 109° 31' W 92
Abak, *Nig.* 4° 57' N, 7° 47' E 222
Abakaliki, *Nig.* 6° 17' N, 8° 5' E 222
Abakan, *Russ.* 53° 42' N, 91° 25' E 184
Abakan, river, *Russ.* 52° 22' N, 89° 24' E 184
Abala, *Congo* 1° 19' S, 15° 34' E 218
Abala, spring, *Niger* 14° 56' N, 3° 27' E 222
Abalak, *Niger* 15° 19' N, 6° 11' E 222
Abalemma, spring, *Alg.* 20° 57' N, 5° 55' E 222
Abalemma, spring, *Niger* 16° 18' N, 7° 49' E 222
Abalessa, *Alg.* 22° 55' N, 4° 49' E 214
Abancay, *Peru* 13° 40' S, 72° 52' W 137
Abapó, *Bol.* 18° 52' S, 63° 30' W 137
Ābār al Hazīm, spring, *Jordan* 31° 35' N, 37° 13' E 194
Abâr el Kanâyis, spring, *Egypt* 31° 0' N, 26° 47' E 180
Abarán, *Sp.* 38° 12' N, 1° 24' W 164
Abarqū, *Iran* 31° 6' N, 53° 19' E 180
Abasān, *Gaza Strip, Israel* 31° 18' N, 34° 21' E 194
Abashiri, *Japan* 43° 53' N, 144° 8' E 190
Abasolo, *Mex.* 27° 10' N, 101° 26' W 96
Abasolo, *Mex.* 25° 18' N, 104° 41' W 114
Abasolo, *Mex.* 24° 2' N, 98° 23' W 114
Abast'umani, *Ga.* 41° 45' N, 42° 48' E 195
Abatskiy, *Russ.* 56° 15' N, 70° 27' E 184
Abau, *P.N.G.* 10° 10' S, 148° 43' E 192
Abava, river, *Latv.* 57° 6' N, 22° 18' E 166
Abay, *Kaz.* 41° 18' N, 68° 51' E 197
Ābay (Blue Nile), river, *Eth.* 11° 15' N, 38° 15' E 224
Ābaya Hāyk', lake, *Eth.* 6° 24' N, 37° 45' E 224
Abaza, *Russ.* 52° 42' N, 90° 7' E 184
Abba, *Cen. Af. Rep.* 5° 18' N, 15° 9' E 218
Abbaye, Point, *Mich., U.S.* 46° 59' N, 88° 13' W 94
Abbeville, *Ala., U.S.* 31° 33' N, 85° 15' W 96
Abbeville, *Fr.* 50° 5' N, 1° 49' E 163
Abbeville, *La., U.S.* 29° 57' N, 92° 8' W 103
Abbey, *Can.* 50° 43' N, 108° 46' W 90
Abbotsford, *Can.* 49° 2' N, 122° 17' W 100
Abbotsford, *Wis., U.S.* 44° 57' N, 90° 19' W 110
Abbotsford, site, *U.K.* 55° 34' N, 2° 51' W 150
Abbottabad, *Pak.* 34° 7' N, 73° 14' E 186
'Abda (Eboda), ruin(s), *Israel* 30° 47' N, 34° 43' E 194
Abdelmalek Ramdan, *Alg.* 36° 6' N, 0° 15' E 150
Abdera, ruin(s), *Gr.* 40° 55' N, 24° 52' E 156
Abdi, *Chad* 12° 40' N, 21° 18' E 216
Abdulino, *Russ.* 53° 38' N, 53° 43' E 154
Ab-e Istadeh-ye Moqor, lake, *Afghan.* 32° 25' N, 66° 51' E 186
Ab-e Vakhan (Oxus), river, *Afghan.* 37° 8' N, 72° 26' E 186
Abéché, *Chad* 13° 48' N, 20° 49' E 216
Ābeltī, *Eth.* 8° 9' N, 37° 32' E 224
Abelvær, *Nor.* 64° 44' N, 11° 14' E 152
Abenab, *Namibia* 19° 19' S, 18° 7' E 220
Abengourou, *Côte d'Ivoire* 6° 41' N, 3° 30' W 222
Abenójar, *Sp.* 38° 52' N, 4° 22' W 164
Abeokuta, *Nig.* 7° 12' N, 3° 22' E 222
Ābera, *Eth.* 7° 12' N, 35° 57' E 224
Aberaeron, *U.K.* 52° 13' N, 4° 15' W 162
Abercorn see Mbala, *Zambia* 8° 53' S, 31° 23' E 224
Aberdare, *U.K.* 51° 42' N, 3° 26' W 162
Aberdeen, *Idaho, U.S.* 42° 57' N, 112° 50' W 90
Aberdeen, *Md., U.S.* 39° 30' N, 76° 11' W 94
Aberdeen, *Miss., U.S.* 33° 49' N, 88° 33' W 96
Aberdeen, *N.C., U.S.* 35° 7' N, 79° 26' W 96
Aberdeen, *Ohio, U.S.* 38° 39' N, 83° 45' W 102
Aberdeen, *S. Af.* 32° 29' S, 24° 4' E 227
Aberdeen, *S. Dak., U.S.* 45° 26' N, 98° 30' W 90
Aberdeen, *U.K.* 57° 8' N, 2° 8' W 150
Aberdeen, *Wash., U.S.* 46° 58' N, 123° 50' W 100
Aberdeen Lake, lake, *Can.* 64° 17' N, 101° 1' W 106
Aberdyfi, *U.K.* 52° 32' N, 4° 2' W 162
Aberedw, *U.K.* 52° 6' N, 3° 20' W 162
Abergavenny, *U.K.* 51° 49' N, 3° 1' W 162
Abergele, *U.K.* 53° 17' N, 3° 35' W 162
Abersychan, *U.K.* 51° 44' N, 3° 3' W 162
Abert, Lake, *Oreg., U.S.* 42° 42' N, 120° 35' W 82
Abertawe see Swansea, *U.K.* 51° 37' N, 3° 57' W 162
Abertillery, *U.K.* 51° 43' N, 3° 8' W 162
Aberystwyth, *U.K.* 52° 25' N, 4° 4' W 162
Abez', *Russ.* 66° 28' N, 61° 49' E 169
Abhā, *Saudi Arabia* 18° 11' N, 42° 30' E 182
Ābhē Bid Hāyk', lake, *Eth.* 11° 2' N, 40° 54' E 216
Abibe, Serranía de, *Col.* 7° 44' N, 76° 42' W 136
'Abidiya, *Sudan* 18° 12' N, 33° 59' E 182
Abidjan, *Côte d'Ivoire* 5° 20' N, 4° 12' W 222
Abijatta-Shalla Lakes National Park, *Eth.* 7° 16' N, 37° 53' E 224
Abilene, *Kans., U.S.* 38° 53' N, 97° 12' W 90
Abilene, *Tex., U.S.* 32° 26' N, 99° 44' W 92
Abingdon, *Mo., U.S.* 40° 47' N, 90° 24' W 94
Abingdon, *U.K.* 51° 40' N, 1° 18' W 162
Abingdon, *Va., U.S.* 36° 42' N, 81° 59' W 96
Abington, *Conn., U.S.* 41° 51' N, 72° 1' W 104
Abiquiu, *N. Mex., U.S.* 36° 11' N, 106° 19' W 92
Abisko, *Nor.* 68° 20' N, 18° 47' E 152
Abita Springs, *La., U.S.* 30° 28' N, 90° 2' W 103
Abitau, river, *Can.* 60° 23' N, 108° 5' W 108
Abitibi, Lake, *Can.* 48° 36' N, 80° 21' W 110
Ābīy Ādī, *Eth.* 13° 34' N, 38° 59' E 182
Abja Paluoja, *Est.* 58° 6' N, 25° 20' E 166
Abkhazia, special sovereignty, *Ga.* 42° 59' N, 41° 14' E 195
Abnûb, *Egypt* 27° 18' N, 31° 8' E 180
Åbo see Turku, *Fin.* 60° 27' N, 22° 15' E 166
Aboa, station, *Antarctica* 73° 4' S, 13° 21' W 248
Aboabo, *Philippines* 9° 9' N, 118° 7' E 203
Abohar, *India* 30° 9' N, 74° 11' E 186
Aboisso, *Côte d'Ivoire* 5° 25' N, 3° 15' W 222
Abomey, *Benin* 7° 13' N, 1° 57' E 222
Abondance, *Fr.* 46° 16' N, 6° 44' E 167
Abong Mbang, *Cameroon* 3° 59' N, 13° 12' E 218
Abongabong, peak, *Indonesia* 4° 14' N, 96° 41' E 196
Abony, *Hung.* 47° 11' N, 20° 1' E 168
Aborlan, *Philippines* 9° 27' N, 118° 33' E 203
Abou Deïa, *Chad* 11° 27' N, 19° 18' E 216
Abou Goulem, *Chad* 13° 35' N, 21° 39' E 216
Abra Pampa, *Arg.* 22° 42' S, 65° 44' W 137
Abrantes, *Port.* 39° 29' N, 8° 16' W 214
Abreojos, Punta, *Mex.* 26° 44' N, 114° 58' W 112
Abreschviller, *Fr.* 48° 38' N, 7° 5' E 163
Abreú, *Dom. Rep.* 19° 41' N, 69° 59' W 116
Abreuvoir Timg'aouine, spring, *Alg.* 21° 40' N, 4° 29' E 222
Abriès, *Fr.* 44° 48' N, 6° 54' E 167
Abrolhos, Arquipélago dos, *South Atlantic Ocean* 18° 35' S, 39° 25' W 132
Abruka Saar, island, *Est.* 58° 0' N, 22° 32' E 166
Abruzzi, adm. division, *It.* 41° 59' N, 13° 13' E 156
Abruzzi, Mount, *Can.* 50° 26' N, 115° 13' W 90
Absalom, Mount, *Antarctica* 80° 26' S, 26° 24' W 248
Absaroka Range, *Wyo., U.S.* 44° 17' N, 110° 13' W 90
Absarokee, *Mont., U.S.* 45° 29' N, 109° 26' W 90
Abu, *Japan* 34° 28' N, 131° 28' E 200
Abū al Abyaḍ, island, *U.A.E.* 24° 17' N, 53° 46' E 182
Abū 'Alī, island, *Saudi Arabia* 27° 21' N, 49° 32' E 180
Abu 'Aweigîla, *Egypt* 30° 50' N, 34° 6' E 194
Abu Ballâṣ, peak, *Egypt* 24° 27' N, 27° 33' E 226
Abū Dālī, *Syr.* 34° 40' N, 36° 53' E 194
Abu Deleiq, *Sudan* 15° 50' N, 33° 45' E 182
Abu Dhabi, *U.A.E.* 24° 25' N, 54° 14' E 196
Abu Dis, *Sudan* 19° 5' N, 33° 38' E 182
Abu Dulu, Qoz, *Sudan* 15° 50' N, 31° 47' E 182
Abu Gabra, *Sudan* 11° 4' N, 26° 43' E 224
Abu Gamal, *Sudan* 15° 6' N, 36° 24' E 182
Abu Gubeiha, *Sudan* 11° 26' N, 31° 17' E 218
Abu Hamed, *Sudan* 19° 31' N, 33° 19' E 182
Abu Hashim, *Sudan* 12° 59' N, 34° 21' E 182
Abū Kamāl, *Syr.* 34° 27' N, 40° 54' E 180
Abu Matariq, *Sudan* 10° 56' N, 26° 14' E 224
Abū Mūsá, island, *Iran* 25° 55' N, 54° 49' E 180
Abū Nā'im, spring, *Lib.* 28° 57' N, 18° 46' E 216
Abu Qurqâṣ, *Egypt* 27° 58' N, 30° 47' E 180
Abu Road, *India* 24° 28' N, 72° 47' E 186
Abu Safah, oil field, *Saudi Arabia* 27° 5' N, 50° 39' E 196
Abu Saiyal, spring, *Sudan* 17° 16' N, 31° 12' E 182
Abu Shagara, Ras, *Sudan* 21° 6' N, 37° 15' E 182
Abu Shanab, *Sudan* 13° 55' N, 27° 43' E 226
Abu Simbel, *Egypt* 24° 25' N, 33° 0' E 182
Abu Simbel, site, *Egypt* 22° 19' N, 31° 29' E 182
Abu Sôma, Râs, *Egypt* 26° 31' N, 34° 1' E 180
Abu Sufyan, *Sudan* 11° 55' N, 26° 21' E 216
Abu Ṣuweir, *Egypt* 30° 32' N, 32° 4' E 194
Abu Tabari, spring, *Sudan* 17° 30' N, 28° 29' E 226
Abu Tîg, *Egypt* 27° 3' N, 31° 14' E 180
Abu 'Uruq, *Sudan* 15° 53' N, 30° 25' E 226

Abu Zabad, *Sudan* 12°20′ N, 29°13′ E 216
Abu Zenīma, *Egypt* 29°2′ N, 33°6′ E 180
Abuja, *Nig.* 9°4′ N, 7°2′ E 222
Abulug, *Philippines* 18°25′ N, 121°26′ E 203
Abumombazi, *Dem. Rep. of the Congo* 3°32′ N, 22°2′ E 218
Abunã, *Braz.* 9°42′ S, 65°22′ W 137
Abunã, river, *South America* 10°24′ S, 67°6′ W 137
Ābūr, *Jordan* 30°48′ N, 35°42′ E 194
Aburatsu, *Japan* 31°34′ N, 131°23′ E 201
Ābuyē Mēda, peak, *Eth.* 10°30′ N, 39°43′ E 224
Abwong, *Sudan* 9°5′ N, 32°9′ E 224
Abyad, *Sudan* 13°44′ N, 26°29′ E 226
Abyad Plateau, Jebel, *Sudan* 19°0′ N, 26°57′ E 226
Abyār al Ḩakīm, spring, *Lib.* 31°35′ N, 23°27′ E 180
Åbybro, *Den.* 57°8′ N, 9°43′ E 150
Abyei, *Sudan* 9°34′ N, 28°26′ E 224
Abyek, *Iran* 36°1′ N, 50°36′ E 180
Açailândia, *Braz.* 4°57′ S, 47°42′ W 130
Acala, *Mex.* 16°34′ N, 92°49′ W 115
Acámbaro, *Mex.* 20°0′ N, 100°43′ W 114
Acancéh, *Mex.* 20°47′ N, 89°27′ W 116
Acandí, *Col.* 8°31′ N, 77°19′ W 136
Acaponeta, *Mex.* 22°29′ N, 105°22′ W 114
Acaponeta, river, *Mex.* 23°39′ N, 105°17′ W 114
Acapulco, *Mex.* 16°51′ N, 99°55′ W 112
Acaraí, Serra, *Guyana* 1°50′ N, 57°38′ W 130
Acaraú, *Braz.* 2°55′ S, 40°7′ W 132
Acarí, *Peru* 15°28′ S, 74°35′ W 137
Acari, river, *Braz.* 5°32′ S, 60°5′ W 130
Acarí, river, *Peru* 15°19′ S, 74°37′ W 137
Acaricuara, *Col.* 0°36′ N, 70°22′ W 136
Acarigua, *Venez.* 9°34′ N, 69°13′ W 136
Acatenango, Volcán de, *Guatemala* 14°28′ N, 90°58′ W 115
Acatlán, *Mex.* 18°11′ N, 98°5′ W 114
Acayucan, *Mex.* 17°56′ N, 94°55′ W 114
Accomac, *Va., U.S.* 37°42′ N, 75°41′ W 94
Accous, *Fr.* 42°58′ N, 0°35′ E 164
Accra, *Ghana* 5°34′ N, 0°22′ E 222
Accrington, *U.K.* 53°45′ N, 2°23′ W 162
Aceguá, *Braz.* 31°52′ S, 54°12′ W 139
Achacachi, *Bol.* 16°8′ S, 68°43′ W 137
Achaguas, *Venez.* 7°47′ N, 68°16′ W 136
Achahoish, *U.K.* 55°56′ N, 5°34′ W 150
Achalpur, *India* 21°17′ N, 77°30′ E 188
Achar, *Uru.* 32°25′ S, 56°10′ W 139
Achegour, spring, *Niger* 19°4′ N, 11°45′ E 222
Acheng, *China* 45°32′ N, 126°55′ E 198
Achénouma, *Niger* 19°14′ N, 12°57′ E 216
Acheux, *Fr.* 50°4′ N, 2°33′ E 163
Achikulak, *Russ.* 44°31′ N, 44°47′ E 158
Achinsk, *Russ.* 56°16′ N, 90°41′ E 169
Achisu, *Russ.* 42°37′ N, 47°45′ E 195
Achit, *Russ.* 56°48′ N, 57°56′ E 154
Achna, *Northern Cyprus, Cyprus* 35°2′ N, 33°46′ E 194
Acht, Hohe, peak, *Ger.* 50°22′ N, 6°58′ E 167
Achuyevo, *Russ.* 45°44′ N, 37°43′ E 156
Achwa (Moroto), river, *Uganda* 2°14′ N, 32°58′ E 224
Achwa, river, *Uganda* 3°31′ N, 32°12′ E 224
Acıgöl, lake, *Turk.* 37°49′ N, 29°43′ E 156
Acıpayam, *Turk.* 37°25′ N, 29°20′ E 156
Acîş, *Rom.* 47°30′ N, 22°48′ E 168
Ackerman, *Miss., U.S.* 33°17′ N, 89°11′ W 103
Ackley, *Iowa, U.S.* 42°32′ N, 93°3′ W 94
Acklins and Crooked Islands, adm. division, *Bahamas* 22°52′ N, 74°50′ W 116
Acklins Island, *Bahamas* 22°22′ N, 75°3′ W 116
Acle, *U.K.* 52°38′ N, 1°32′ E 163
Acobamba, *Peru* 12°53′ S, 74°33′ W 137
Acoma Pueblo, site, *N. Mex., U.S.* 34°54′ N, 107°40′ W 92
Acomayo, *Peru* 13°56′ S, 71°41′ W 137
Acona, *Miss., U.S.* 33°15′ N, 90°2′ W 103
Aconcagua, Cerro, *Arg.* 32°33′ S, 69°57′ W 134
Aconchi, *Mex.* 29°49′ N, 110°14′ W 92
Aconi, Point, *Can.* 46°21′ N, 60°50′ W 111
Acora, *Peru* 16°1′ S, 69°46′ W 137
Açores see Azores, islands, *Port.* 39°29′ N, 27°35′ W 207
Acoyapa, *Nicar.* 11°55′ N, 85°9′ W 115
Acqui Terme, *It.* 44°41′ N, 8°28′ E 167
Acrae, ruin(s), *It.* 37°1′ N, 14°47′ E 156
Acre, adm. division, *Braz.* 9°34′ S, 70°21′ W 137
Acre, river, *Braz.* 10°24′ S, 68°2′ W 137
Acre see ʻAkko, *Israel* 32°55′ N, 35°4′ E 194
Ács, *Hung.* 47°41′ N, 18°2′ E 156
Actéon, Groupe, islands, *South Pacific Ocean* 21°2′ S, 137°14′ W 238
Actium, ruin(s), *Gr.* 38°55′ N, 20°39′ E 156
Acton, *Calif., U.S.* 34°28′ N, 118°13′ W 101
Acton, *Me., U.S.* 43°31′ N, 70°55′ W 104
Actopan, *Mex.* 20°15′ N, 98°56′ W 114
Açuã, river, *Braz.* 7°39′ S, 64°12′ W 130
Acuitzio, *Mex.* 19°29′ N, 101°21′ W 114
Acurauá, river, *Braz.* 8°44′ S, 71°25′ W 130
Açurizal, *Braz.* 15°11′ S, 56°24′ W 132
Acworth, *N.H., U.S.* 43°12′ N, 72°18′ W 104
Ad Dahnā', *Saudi Arabia* 26°39′ N, 46°15′ E 196
Ad Dakhla, *Western Sahara, Mor.* 23°42′ N, 15°58′ W 214
Aḑ Ḑāli', *Yemen* 13°41′ N, 44°44′ E 182
Ad Dammām, *Saudi Arabia* 26°23′ N, 50°5′ E 196
Ad Dār al Ḩamrā', *Saudi Arabia* 27°21′ N, 37°41′ E 180
Ad Dawādimī, *Saudi Arabia* 24°29′ N, 44°23′ E 182
Ad Dawḩah (Doha), *Qatar* 25°13′ N, 51°25′ E 196
Ad Dibdibah, region, *Asia* 28°10′ N, 46°32′ E 180
Ad Dilam, *Saudi Arabia* 23°57′ N, 47°13′ E 196
Ad Dīwānīyah, *Iraq* 31°59′ N, 44°51′ E 180
Ad Durūz, Jabal, peak, *Syr.* 32°39′ N, 36°41′ E 194
Ada, *Ghana* 5°46′ N, 0°34′ E 222
Ada, *Minn., U.S.* 47°16′ N, 96°32′ W 90
Ada, *Ohio, U.S.* 40°45′ N, 83°50′ W 102
Ada, *Okla., U.S.* 34°45′ N, 96°40′ W 92
Ada, *Serb.* 45°48′ N, 20°7′ E 168
Adâfer el Abiod, region, *Africa* 18°47′ N, 10°37′ W 222
Adailo, *Eritrea* 14°26′ N, 40°50′ E 182
Adair, Bahía de, *Mex.* 31°22′ N, 114°33′ W 80
Adair, Cape, *Can.* 71°24′ N, 71°5′ W 106
Adak, *Nor.* 65°20′ N, 18°34′ E 152
Adak, island, *Alas., U.S.* 51°18′ N, 176°44′ W 160
Adaleh, spring, *Eth.* 7°27′ N, 46°22′ E 218
Adam, *Oman* 22°23′ N, 57°30′ E 182
Adam, Mount, *U.K.* 51°37′ S, 60°5′ W 134
Adam Peak, *Nev., U.S.* 41°9′ N, 117°24′ W 90
Adamantina, *Braz.* 21°41′ S, 51°5′ W 138
Adamello, peak, *It.* 46°9′ N, 10°27′ E 167
Adamovka, *Russ.* 51°32′ N, 59°53′ E 154
Adams, *Mass., U.S.* 42°36′ N, 73°8′ W 104
Adams, *Minn., U.S.* 43°33′ N, 92°43′ W 94
Adams, *Wis., U.S.* 43°56′ N, 89°49′ W 94
Adams, Cape, *Antarctica* 75°10′ S, 61°57′ W 248
Adams Lake, *Can.* 51°15′ N, 120°1′ W 90
Adams, Mount, *Wash., U.S.* 46°11′ N, 121°33′ W 100
Adams Mountain, *Mass., U.S.* 42°40′ N, 72°55′ W 104
Adam's Peak, *Sri Lanka* 6°46′ N, 80°24′ E 188
Adams Point, *Mich., U.S.* 45°24′ N, 83°41′ W 94
Adamstown, *Pitcairn Is., U.K.* 25°0′ S, 130°0′ W 241
Adamsville, *Tenn., U.S.* 35°13′ N, 88°23′ W 96
Adamuz, *Sp.* 38°1′ N, 4°32′ W 164
ʻAdan (Aden), *Yemen* 12°46′ N, 44°59′ E 182
ʻAdan aş Şughrá, *Yemen* 12°35′ N, 44°1′ E 182
Adana, *Turk.* 36°59′ N, 35°18′ E 156
Adapazarı, *Turk.* 40°46′ N, 30°25′ E 156
Adar Doutchi, region, *Africa* 14°33′ N, 5°50′ E 222
Adarama, *Sudan* 17°3′ N, 34°54′ E 182
Adare Peninsula, *Antarctica* 71°10′ S, 175°59′ E 248
Addington, *Okla., U.S.* 34°13′ N, 97°58′ W 92
Addis, *La., U.S.* 30°19′ N, 91°17′ W 103
Addis Ababa see Ādīs Ābeba, *Eth.* 8°58′ N, 38°34′ E 224
Addison, *Vt., U.S.* 44°5′ N, 73°19′ W 104
Addo, *S. Af.* 33°34′ S, 25°42′ E 227
Addo Elephant National Park, *S. Af.* 33°31′ S, 25°41′ E 227
Addu Atoll, *Maldives* 0°54′ N, 72°39′ E 188
Addy, *Wash., U.S.* 48°20′ N, 117°50′ W 90
Adel, *Ga., U.S.* 31°7′ N, 83°26′ W 96
Adel, *Oreg., U.S.* 42°11′ N, 119°54′ W 90
Adelaide, *Austral.* 34°59′ S, 138°14′ E 230
Adelaide Island, *Antarctica* 66°56′ S, 72°20′ W 248
Adelaide Peninsula, *Can.* 67°53′ N, 97°8′ W 106
Adelanto, *Calif., U.S.* 34°35′ N, 117°26′ W 101
Adélfi, islands, *Aegean Sea* 36°26′ N, 26°40′ E 156
Adelia María, *Arg.* 33°39′ S, 64°2′ W 139
Adélie Coast, *Antarctica* 66°59′ S, 145°40′ E 248
Adelunga Toghi, peak, *Uzb.* 42°7′ N, 70°59′ E 197
Ademuz, *Sp.* 40°3′ N, 1°18′ W 164
Aden, Gulf of 12°29′ N, 45°45′ E 173
Aden see ʻAdan, *Yemen* 12°46′ N, 44°59′ E 182
Adenau, *Ger.* 50°23′ N, 6°57′ E 163
Aderbissinat, *Niger* 15°39′ N, 7°53′ E 222
Aderg, peak, *Mauritania* 21°24′ N, 11°58′ W 222
Adh Dhayd, *U.A.E.* 25°16′ N, 55°48′ E 196
Adhoi, *India* 23°23′ N, 70°29′ E 186
Ādī Ārk'ay, *Eth.* 13°29′ N, 37°55′ E 182
Adi Kaie, *Eritrea* 14°47′ N, 39°22′ E 182
Adi Quala, *Eritrea* 14°38′ N, 38°49′ E 182
Ādī Ramets', *Eth.* 13°47′ N, 37°22′ E 182
Adi Ugri, *Eritrea* 14°52′ N, 38°50′ E 182
Adiaké, *Côte d'Ivoire* 5°12′ N, 3°20′ W 214
Adie Inlet, *Antarctica* 66°40′ S, 63°15′ W 248
Ādīgala, *Eth.* 10°23′ N, 42°17′ E 224
Adige, river, *It.* 45°11′ N, 11°20′ E 167
Adigeni, *Ga.* 41°41′ N, 42°42′ E 195
Ādīgrat, *Eth.* 14°16′ N, 39°26′ E 182
Adilabad, *India* 19°40′ N, 78°33′ E 188
Adilang, *Uganda* 2°42′ N, 33°28′ E 224
Adin, *Calif., U.S.* 41°11′ N, 120°58′ W 90
Adīrī, *Lib.* 27°32′ N, 13°13′ E 216
Adirondack Mountains, *N.Y., U.S.* 43°57′ N, 76°16′ W 106
Ādīs Ābeba (Addis Ababa), *Eth.* 8°58′ N, 38°34′ E 224
Ādīs ʻAlem, *Eth.* 9°2′ N, 38°21′ E 224
Adıyaman, *Turk.* 37°45′ N, 38°16′ E 180
Adjud, *Rom.* 46°5′ N, 27°10′ E 156
Adlavik Islands, *North Atlantic Ocean* 54°39′ N, 62°27′ W 106
Adler, *Russ.* 43°28′ N, 40°0′ E 195
Admiralty Island, *Alas., U.S.* 57°30′ N, 133°39′ W 106
Admiralty Islands, *Bismarck Sea* 3°32′ S, 145°14′ E 192
Ado, *Nig.* 6°37′ N, 2°55′ E 222
Ado Ekiti, *Nig.* 7°38′ N, 5°13′ E 222
Adobe Flat, *Nev., U.S.* 40°2′ N, 119°8′ W 90
Adok, *Sudan* 8°7′ N, 30°17′ E 224
Adolfo López Mateos, *Mex.* 28°26′ N, 107°23′ W 92
Adolfo López Mateos, Presa, lake, *Mex.* 25°10′ N, 108°53′ W 81
Adoni, *India* 15°38′ N, 77°16′ E 188
Adony, *Hung.* 47°6′ N, 18°51′ E 168
Adorf, *Ger.* 50°19′ N, 12°15′ E 152
Adour, river, *Fr.* 43°24′ N, 1°10′ W 214
Adra, *Sp.* 36°44′ N, 3°1′ W 164
Adranga, *Dem. Rep. of the Congo* 2°53′ N, 30°25′ E 224
Adrar, *Alg.* 27°55′ N, 0°18′ E 214
Adrar, region, *Mauritania* 20°22′ N, 14°7′ W 222
Adraskan, *Afghan.* 33°38′ N, 62°18′ E 186
Adré, *Chad* 13°26′ N, 22°12′ E 216
Adria, *It.* 45°4′ N, 12°1′ E 167
Adrian, *Mich., U.S.* 41°52′ N, 84°2′ W 102
Adrian, *Minn., U.S.* 43°36′ N, 95°56′ W 90
Adrian, *Tex., U.S.* 35°15′ N, 102°40′ W 92
Adrianople see Edirne, *Turk.* 41°39′ N, 26°34′ E 156
Adriatic Sea 41°51′ N, 17°3′ E 156
Adun Gol, *China* 42°4′ N, 107°56′ E 198
Adusa, *Dem. Rep. of the Congo* 1°24′ N, 28°4′ E 224
Ādwa, *Eth.* 14°9′ N, 38°52′ E 182
Adwick le Street, *U.K.* 53°33′ N, 1°12′ W 162
Adycha, river, *Russ.* 66°53′ N, 135°23′ E 160
Adygeya, adm. division, *Russ.* 44°59′ N, 40°1′ E 158
Adzopé, *Côte d'Ivoire* 6°3′ N, 3°52′ W 222
Adz'vavom, *Russ.* 66°36′ N, 59°17′ E 169
Aegae, ruin(s), *Gr.* 38°8′ N, 22°13′ E 156
Aegean Sea 36°34′ N, 23°7′ E 156
Aegir Ridge, *Norwegian Sea* 65°42′ N, 4°7′ W 255
Aegna, island, *Est.* 59°37′ N, 24°35′ E 166
Aegviidu, *Est.* 59°15′ N, 25°35′ E 166
Afadé, *Cameroon* 12°15′ N, 14°39′ E 216
Afam, *Nig.* 4°45′ N, 7°23′ E 222
Afándou, *Gr.* 36°17′ N, 28°10′ E 156
Afar, region, *Africa* 12°59′ N, 40°4′ E 182
Āfdem, *Eth.* 9°27′ N, 41°0′ E 224
Affollé, *Mauritania* 16°21′ N, 11°11′ W 222
Afghanistan 34°0′ N, 66°0′ E 186
Afgooye, *Somalia* 2°5′ N, 45°8′ E 218
Afgooye Caddo, *Somalia* 3°12′ N, 45°33′ E 218
ʻAfif, *Saudi Arabia* 23°53′ N, 42°56′ E 182
Afikpo, *Nig.* 5°55′ N, 7°55′ E 222
Afiq, *Israel* 32°46′ N, 35°42′ E 194
Åfjord, *Nor.* 63°57′ N, 10°14′ E 152
Aflou, *Alg.* 34°6′ N, 2°5′ E 214
Afmadow, *Somalia* 0°28′ N, 42°4′ E 224
Āfodo, *Eth.* 10°13′ N, 34°47′ E 224
Afognak Island, *Alas., U.S.* 57°51′ N, 151°54′ W 98
Afonso Cláudio, *Braz.* 20°6′ S, 41°10′ W 138
Afqā, *Leb.* 34°4′ N, 35°53′ E 194
Africa 1°0′ N, 17°0′ E 207
Afşin, *Turk.* 38°14′ N, 36°53′ E 156
Afton, *Okla., U.S.* 36°41′ N, 94°58′ W 94
Afton, *Wyo., U.S.* 42°42′ N, 110°55′ W 82
Afuá, *Braz.* 0°10′ N, 50°23′ W 130
ʻAfula, *Israel* 32°36′ N, 35°17′ E 194
Afyon, *Turk.* 38°44′ N, 30°31′ E 156
Agadem, *Niger* 16°49′ N, 13°17′ E 216
Agadez, *Niger* 16°59′ N, 7°58′ E 222
Agadir, *Mor.* 30°25′ N, 9°37′ W 214
Agaie, *Nig.* 8°59′ N, 6°18′ E 222
Agalega Islands, *Indian Ocean* 12°45′ S, 55°37′ E 173
Agamenticus, Mount, *Me., U.S.* 43°13′ N, 70°44′ W 104
Agamor, spring, *Mali* 17°16′ N, 3°178′ E 222
Agana see Hagåtña, *Guam, U.S.* 13°0′ N, 145°0′ E 242
Agapa, *Russ.* 71°43′ N, 89°24′ E 173
Agapovka, *Russ.* 53°20′ N, 59°12′ E 154
Agar, *India* 23°43′ N, 76°3′ E 197
Āgaro, *Eth.* 7°49′ N, 36°37′ E 224
Agartala, *India* 23°47′ N, 91°18′ E 197
Agaruut, *Mongolia* 43°18′ N, 109°26′ E 198
Agassiz Fracture Zone, *South Pacific Ocean* 39°32′ S, 131°55′ W 252
Agata, *Russ.* 66°51′ N, 93°40′ E 169
Agata, Ozero, lake, *Russ.* 67°14′ N, 92°22′ E 169
Agate, *Colo., U.S.* 39°27′ N, 103°57′ W 90
Agats, *Indonesia* 5°34′ S, 138°4′ E 192
Agattu, island, *Alas., U.S.* 52°17′ N, 171°43′ E 160
Agawam, *Mass., U.S.* 42°3′ N, 72°37′ W 104
Agbaja, *Nig.* 7°58′ N, 6°38′ E 222
Agboville, *Côte d'Ivoire* 5°51′ N, 4°12′ W 222
Ağdam see Akna, *Azerb.* 39°59′ N, 46°54′ E 195
Ağdara see Martakert, *Asia* 40°12′ N, 46°47′ E 195
Agde, *Fr.* 43°19′ N, 3°27′ E 164
Agde, Cap d', *Fr.* 43°11′ N, 3°30′ E 165
Agdz, *Mor.* 30°41′ N, 6°29′ W 214
Agematsu, *Japan* 35°47′ N, 137°43′ E 201
Agen, *Fr.* 44°14′ N, 0°36′ E 214
Àger, *Sp.* 41°59′ N, 0°46′ E 164
Agere Maryam, *Eth.* 5°37′ N, 38°16′ E 224
Agger, river, *Ger.* 50°55′ N, 7°20′ E 167
Aggi, *Eth.* 7°55′ N, 35°38′ E 224
Āghā Jārī, *Iran* 30°43′ N, 49°53′ E 180
Aghaylas, *Western Sahara, Mor.* 22°28′ N, 14°23′ W 214
Aghdash, *Azerb.* 40°39′ N, 47°28′ E 195
Aghireşu, *Rom.* 46°51′ N, 23°14′ E 168
Aghjabädi, *Azerb.* 40°2′ N, 47°28′ E 195
Aghsu, *Azerb.* 40°34′ N, 48°25′ E 195
Aghwinit, *Western Sahara, Mor.* 22°11′ N, 13°10′ W 214
Agia Napa, *Cyprus* 34°59′ N, 33°59′ E 194
Agiabampo, Estero de 26°15′ N, 110°30′ W 80
Agimont, *Belg.* 50°9′ N, 4°45′ E 163
Agin Buryat, adm. division, *Russ.* 51°4′ N, 114°22′ E 190
Aginskoye, *Russ.* 51°6′ N, 114°30′ E 190
Ágio Óros (Mount Athos), *Gr.* 40°14′ N, 23°2′ E 156
Ágios Nikólaos, *Gr.* 35°12′ N, 25°40′ E 180
Agios Sergios, *Northern Cyprus, Cyprus* 35°11′ N, 33°52′ E 194
Aglat Jrayfiya, spring, *Western Sahara, Mor.* 25°1′ N, 14°18′ W 214
Agliano, *It.* 44°47′ N, 8°13′ E 167
Agmar, *Mauritania* 25°18′ N, 10°48′ W 214
Agnes, Mount, *Austral.* 26°55′ S, 128°44′ E 230
Agnibilékrou, *Côte d'Ivoire* 7°5′ N, 3°12′ W 222
Agnières, *Fr.* 44°41′ N, 5°53′ E 150
Agno, river, *Philippines* 16°6′ N, 120°49′ E 203
Agön, island, *Sw.* 61°29′ N, 17°17′ E 166
Agoncillo, *Sp.* 42°25′ N, 2°18′ W 164
Agordat, *Eritrea* 15°32′ N, 37°53′ E 182
Agordo, *It.* 46°17′ N, 12°2′ E 167
Agostinho, *Braz.* 9°58′ S, 68°33′ W 137
Agoua, *Benin* 8°17′ N, 1°57′ E 222
Agouénit, *Mauritania* 16°41′ N, 7°34′ W 222
Agouma, *Gabon* 1°35′ S, 10°11′ E 218
Agous-n-Ehsel, spring, *Mali* 16°20′ N, 1°44′ E 222
Agout, river, *Fr.* 43°44′ N, 1°47′ E 165
Agra, *India* 27°9′ N, 77°59′ E 197
Agrakhanskiy Poluostrov, *Russ.* 43°41′ N, 47°7′ E 195
Agramunt, *Sp.* 41°46′ N, 1°6′ E 164
Agraouri, spring, *Niger* 18°16′ N, 14°14′ E 222
Agreda, *Sp.* 41°50′ N, 1°55′ W 164
Ağrı Dağı (Ararat, Mount), *Turk.* 39°42′ N, 44°15′ E 195
Ağrı (Karaköse), *Turk.* 39°43′ N, 43°3′ E 195
Agrichay, river, *Azerb.* 41°18′ N, 46°42′ E 195
Agricola, *Miss., U.S.* 30°47′ N, 88°30′ W 103
Agrigento, *It.* 37°18′ N, 13°34′ E 216
Agrihan, island, *U.S.* 18°37′ N, 144°36′ E 192
Agrínio, *Gr.* 38°35′ N, 21°22′ E 143
Agryz, *Russ.* 56°30′ N, 53°2′ E 154
Ağstafa, *Azerb.* 41°6′ N, 45°26′ E 195
Agua Brava, Laguna, lake, *Mex.* 22°8′ N, 105°49′ W 114
Agua Clara, *Braz.* 20°25′ S, 52°56′ W 138
Agua Nueva, *Mex.* 25°5′ N, 101°7′ W 114
Água Preta, river, *Braz.* 1°58′ S, 64°53′ W 130
Agua Prieta, *Mex.* 31°18′ N, 109°34′ W 92
Agua Tibia Mountain, *Calif., U.S.* 33°24′ N, 117°1′ W 101
Agua Verde, *Mex.* 22°55′ N, 105°58′ W 114
Aguachica, *Col.* 8°19′ N, 73°38′ W 136
Aguaclara, *Col.* 4°43′ N, 73°2′ W 136
Aguadas, *Col.* 5°35′ N, 75°26′ W 136
Agualeguas, *Mex.* 26°18′ N, 99°33′ W 114
Aguanga, *Calif., U.S.* 33°26′ N, 116°52′ W 101
Aguapeí, *Braz.* 16°12′ S, 59°41′ W 132
Aguapeí, Serra do, peak, *Braz.* 16°5′ S, 59°29′ W 132
Aguarey, *Arg.* 22°13′ S, 63°51′ W 137
Aguarico, river, *Ecua.* 0°18′ N, 76°27′ W 136
Aguaro-Guariquito National Park, *Venez.* 8°21′ N, 66°34′ W 136
Aguas Blancas, *Chile* 24°11′ S, 69°54′ W 132
Aguas Dulces, *Uru.* 34°20′ S, 53°50′ W 139
Águas Formosas, *Braz.* 17°5′ S, 40°59′ W 138
Aguas Negras, *Peru* 0°27′ N, 75°23′ W 136
Aguascalientes, *Mex.* 21°50′ N, 102°23′ W 114
Aguascalientes, adm. division, *Mex.* 21°45′ N, 102°53′ W 114
Aguelal, spring, *Niger* 18°44′ N, 8°6′ E 222
Aguelhok, *Mali* 19°27′ N, 0°50′ E 222
Agueraktem, spring, *Mauritania* 23°11′ N, 6°24′ W 214
Aguié, *Niger* 13°28′ N, 7°33′ E 222
Aguilâl Faye, spring, *Mauritania* 18°27′ N, 14°47′ W 222
Aguilar, *Colo., U.S.* 37°24′ N, 104°40′ W 92
Aguilar de Campoo, *Sp.* 42°46′ N, 4°16′ W 150
Águilas, *Sp.* 37°24′ N, 1°36′ W 164
Aguililla, *Mex.* 18°44′ N, 102°45′ W 114
Aguja, Cabo de la, *Col.* 11°20′ N, 75°3′ W 116
Aguja, Punta, *Peru* 5°43′ S, 82°17′ W 130
Agujita, *Mex.* 27°52′ N, 101°10′ W 92
Āgula'i, *Eth.* 13°40′ N, 39°36′ E 182
Agulhas Basin, *Indian Ocean* 46°55′ S, 24°17′ E 254
Agulhas, Cape, *S. Af.* 35°7′ S, 20°3′ E 227
Agulhas Plateau, *Indian Ocean* 39°48′ S, 26°43′ E 254
Agustín Codazzi, *Col.* 10°2′ N, 73°16′ W 136
Aha Hills, *Botswana* 19°49′ S, 20°57′ E 220
Ahaggar (Hoggar), *Alg.* 21°56′ N, 4°32′ E 222
Ahaggar National Park, *Alg.* 23°5′ N, 4°38′ E 214
Ahar, *Iran* 38°30′ N, 47°3′ E 195
Ahaus, *Ger.* 52°4′ N, 7°0′ E 163
Ahelleguen, spring, *Alg.* 25°36′ N, 7°2′ E 214
Ahipara, *N.Z.* 35°11′ S, 173°10′ E 240
Ahlainen, *Fin.* 61°40′ N, 21°36′ E 166
Ahlat, *Turk.* 38°43′ N, 42°26′ E 195
Ahlatlıbel, ruin(s), *Turk.* 39°48′ N, 32°38′ E 156
Ahlen, *Ger.* 51°46′ N, 7°54′ E 167
Ahmadabad, *India* 22°59′ N, 72°36′ E 186
Ahmadi, oil field, *Kuwait* 29°2′ N, 48°1′ E 196
Ahmadpur East, *Pak.* 29°9′ N, 71°16′ E 186
Ahmar Mountains, *Eth.* 9°9′ N, 40°49′ E 224
Ahmeyine, spring, *Mauritania* 20°53′ N, 14°28′ W 222
Ahnet, region, *Africa* 25°8′ N, 2°58′ E 214
Ahoada, *Nig.* 5°6′ N, 6°37′ E 222
Ahome, *Mex.* 25°53′ N, 109°10′ W 112
Ahoskie, *N.C., U.S.* 36°17′ N, 77°1′ W 96
Ahram, *Iran* 28°51′ N, 51°20′ E 196
Ahrensburg, *Ger.* 53°40′ N, 10°13′ E 152
Ähtäri, *Fin.* 62°32′ N, 24°4′ E 152
Ahtme, *Est.* 59°17′ N, 27°27′ E 166
Ahua ʻUmi Heiau, site, *Hawaiʻi, U.S.* 19°37′ N, 155°50′ W 99
Ahuacatlán, *Mex.* 21°2′ N, 104°30′ W 114
Ahuachapán, *El Salv.* 13°56′ N, 89°52′ W 115
Ahualulco, *Mex.* 20°41′ N, 103°59′ W 114
Ahvāz (Ahwāz), *Iran* 31°19′ N, 48°41′ E 180
Ahvenanmaa see Åland, island, *Fin.* 60°26′ N, 19°33′ E 166
Ahwahnee, *Calif., U.S.* 37°22′ N, 119°44′ W 100
A'war, *Yemen* 13°32′ N, 46°42′ E 182
Ahwāz see Ahvāz, *Iran* 31°19′ N, 48°41′ E 180
Ai Qurayyāt, *Saudi Arabia* 31°19′ N, 37°20′ E 180
Aiari, river, *Braz.* 1°15′ N, 69°5′ W 136
Aichi, adm. division, *Japan* 35°3′ N, 136°54′ E 201
Aigialousa, *Northern Cyprus, Cyprus* 35°32′ N, 34°11′ E 194
Aigle, *Switz.* 46°20′ N, 6°58′ E 167
Aigle, Lac à l', lake, *Can.* 51°12′ N, 65°54′ W 111
Aigoual, Mont, peak, *Fr.* 44°7′ N, 3°32′ E 165
Aiguá, *Uru.* 34°14′ S, 54°44′ W 139
Aiguebelle, *Fr.* 45°32′ N, 6°18′ E 167
Aigües, *Sp.* 38°29′ N, 0°22′ E 164
Aiguilles, *Fr.* 44°47′ N, 6°51′ E 167
Aijiekebey, *China* 37°11′ N, 75°22′ E 184
Aikawa, *Japan* 38°2′ N, 138°15′ E 201
Aiken, *S.C., U.S.* 33°33′ N, 81°44′ W 96
Aileach, Grianan of, peak, *Ire.* 55°0′ N, 7°33′ W 150
Ailet Jridani, *Tun.* 35°6′ N, 10°1′ E 156
Ailigas, peak, *Fin.* 69°25′ N, 25°49′ E 152
Ailly-sur-Noye, *Fr.* 49°45′ N, 2°20′ E 163
Aim, *Russ.* 58°49′ N, 134°4′ E 160
Aimorés, *Braz.* 19°29′ S, 41°5′ W 138

Aimorés, Serra dos, *Braz.* 18°14′ S, 41°22′ W 132
'Aïn Azaz, spring, *Alg.* 27°5′ N, 3°30′ E 214
Aïn Ben Tili, *Mauritania* 25°57′ N, 9°34′ W 214
Aïn Cheikr, spring, *Alg.* 22°9′ N, 9°535′ E 222
'Ain Dalla, spring, *Egypt* 27°18′ N, 27°19′ E 180
'Aïn Deheb, *Alg.* 34°51′ N, 1°31′ E 214
Aïn Djasser, *Alg.* 35°53′ N, 6°17′ E 150
'Aïn el Berd, *Alg.* 35°20′ N, 0°31′ E 150
'Ain el Ghazâl, spring, *Egypt* 25°47′ N, 30°31′ E 180
'Aïn el Hadjel, *Alg.* 35°36′ N, 3°55′ E 214
'Ain el Qideirât (Kadesh-Barnea), spring, *Egypt* 30°39′ N, 34°25′ E 194
'Ain el Wâdi, spring, *Egypt* 27°22′ N, 28°12′ E 180
'Ain Khaleifa, spring, *Egypt* 26°44′ N, 27°46′ E 180
'Aïn M'lila, *Alg.* 36°0′ N, 6°34′ E 150
'Aïn Oussera, *Alg.* 35°26′ N, 2°55′ E 150
'Ain Qeiqab, spring, *Egypt* 29°35′ N, 24°56′ E 180
Ain, river, *Fr.* 45°52′ N, 5°17′ E 165
'Aïn Sefra, *Alg.* 32°50′ N, 0°39′ E 143
'Aïn Sefra, *Alg.* 32°47′ N, 0°37′ E 214
'Aïn Souf, spring, *Alg.* 28°6′ N, 2°14′ E 214
'Aïn Taïba, spring, *Alg.* 30°18′ N, 5°49′ E 214
'Aïn Temouchent, *Alg.* 35°17′ N, 1°9′ W 150
'Ain Tibaghbagh, spring, *Egypt* 29°6′ N, 26°24′ E 180
'Aïn Tidjoubar, spring, *Alg.* 27°46′ N, 1°22′ E 214
'Aïn Tiguift, spring, *Alg.* 26°12′ N, 3°38′ E 214
Ain Zalah, oil field, *Iraq* 36°44′ N, 42°24′ E 195
Aïna, river, *Congo* 1°30′ N, 13°14′ E 218
Ainaži, *Latv.* 57°51′ N, 24°20′ E 166
Aínos National Park, *Gr.* 38°8′ N, 20°34′ E 156
Aínsa, *Sp.* 42°25′ N, 0°7′ E 164
Ainsworth, *Nebr., U.S.* 42°31′ N, 99°53′ W 90
Aipe, *Col.* 3°13′ N, 75°18′ W 136
Aiquile, *Bol.* 18°12′ S, 65°13′ W 137
Aïr (Aïr Massif), region, *Africa* 17°26′ N, 6°28′ E 222
Air Force Island, *Can.* 67°34′ N, 76°15′ W 106
Aïr Massif see Aïr, region, *Africa* 17°26′ N, 6°28′ E 222
Airaines, *Fr.* 49°57′ N, 1°55′ E 163
Airbangis, *Indonesia* 0°14′ N, 99°22′ E 196
Airdrie, *Can.* 51°18′ N, 114°2′ W 90
Aire, *Fr.* 50°38′ N, 2°24′ E 163
Aire, river, *Fr.* 49°3′ N, 5°9′ E 163
Airiselkä, *Fin.* 66°16′ N, 23°56′ E 152
Airolo, *Switz.* 46°32′ N, 8°36′ E 167
Aisén del General Carlos Ibáñez del Campo, adm. division, *Chile* 48°43′ S, 77°8′ W 134
Aishalton, *Guyana* 2°28′ N, 59°9′ W 130
Aisne, river, *Fr.* 49°22′ N, 2°53′ E 163
Aïssa, Djebel, peak, *Alg.* 32°52′ N, 0°38′ E 214
Aït Baha, *Mor.* 30°3′ N, 9°10′ W 214
Aït Ourir, *Mor.* 31°36′ N, 7°43′ W 214
Aitape, *P.N.G.* 3°14′ S, 142°19′ E 238
Aitkin, *Minn., U.S.* 46°30′ N, 93°43′ W 94
Aitona, *Sp.* 41°29′ N, 0°27′ E 164
Aiviekste, river, *Latv.* 56°47′ N, 26°29′ E 166
Aix, Mount, *Wash., U.S.* 46°46′ N, 121°17′ W 100
Aix-en-Othe, *Fr.* 48°13′ N, 3°45′ E 163
Aix-en-Provence, *Fr.* 43°31′ N, 5°26′ E 150
Aizawl, *India* 23°39′ N, 92°42′ E 197
Aizpute, *Latv.* 56°42′ N, 21°36′ E 166
Aizuwakamatsu, *Japan* 37°29′ N, 139°54′ E 201
'Ajab Shīr, *Iran* 37°28′ N, 45°54′ E 195
Ajaccio, *Fr.* 41°55′ N, 8°41′ E 156
Ajajú, river, *Col.* 0°59′ N, 73°20′ W 136
Ajalpan, *Mex.* 18°21′ N, 97°16′ W 114
Ajax Peak, *Mont., U.S.* 45°18′ N, 113°49′ W 90
Ajdābiyā, *Lib.* 30°44′ N, 20°15′ E 216
Ajir, region, *Africa* 18°0′ N, 6°22′ E 222
Ajka, *Hung.* 47°5′ N, 17°34′ E 168
'Ajlūn, *Jordan* 32°20′ N, 35°44′ E 194
'Ajmān, *U.A.E.* 25°26′ N, 55°28′ E 196
Ajmer, *India* 26°27′ N, 74°38′ E 186
Ajo, *Ariz., U.S.* 32°22′ N, 112°51′ W 92
Ajo, Mount, *Ariz., U.S.* 32°0′ N, 112°45′ W 92
Ajuana, river, *Braz.* 1°1′ S, 65°40′ W 136
Ajuchitlán, *Mex.* 18°7′ N, 100°31′ W 114
Ajuy, *Philippines* 11°11′ N, 122°59′ E 203
Ak Dağlar, peak, *Turk.* 36°30′ N, 29°29′ E 156
Ak Dovurak, *Russ.* 51°7′ N, 90°31′ E 184
Aka, *Mali* 15°25′ N, 4°12′ W 222
Aka, river, *Dem. Rep. of the Congo* 4°3′ N, 29°25′ E 224
Akadomari, *Japan* 37°53′ N, 138°25′ E 201
Akagera National Park, *Rwanda* 1°48′ S, 30°38′ E 224
Akagi, *Japan* 34°59′ N, 132°43′ E 201
Akaki, *Cyprus* 35°7′ N, 33°7′ E 194
Akal, oil field, *Mex.* 19°26′ N, 92°7′ W 115
Akalkot, *India* 17°31′ N, 76°11′ E 188
Akanthou, *Northern Cyprus, Cyprus* 35°21′ N, 33°44′ E 194
Akaroa, *N.Z.* 43°50′ S, 172°58′ E 240
Akasaki, *Japan* 35°28′ N, 133°40′ E 201
Akashi, *Japan* 34°40′ N, 134°59′ E 201
Akaska, *S. Dak., U.S.* 45°19′ N, 100°8′ W 90
Akbulak, *Russ.* 51°1′ N, 55°38′ E 158
Akçaabat, *Turk.* 41°1′ N, 39°31′ E 195
Akçadağ, *Turk.* 38°17′ N, 37°57′ E 180
Akçakışla, *Turk.* 39°31′ N, 36°19′ E 156
Akçakoca, *Turk.* 41°4′ N, 31°8′ E 156
Akçay, *Turk.* 39°35′ N, 26°50′ E 156
Akçay, *Turk.* 36°35′ N, 29°43′ E 156
Akchâr, region, *Africa* 20°12′ N, 15°6′ W 222
Akdağ, peak, *Turk.* 38°29′ N, 26°25′ E 156
Akdağ, peak, *Turk.* 36°47′ N, 32°8′ E 156
Akdağmadeni, *Turk.* 39°39′ N, 35°54′ E 156
Akdepe, *Turkm.* 42°3′ N, 59°23′ E 180
Akelo, *Sudan* 6°55′ N, 33°38′ E 224
Akera see Hakari, river, *Azerb.* 39°28′ N, 46°37′ E 195
Åkernes, *Nor.* 58°44′ N, 7°29′ E 152
Akespe, *Kaz.* 46°48′ N, 60°32′ E 184
Aketi, *Dem. Rep. of the Congo* 2°45′ N, 23°46′ E 224
Akhalts'ikhe, *Ga.* 41°39′ N, 42°57′ E 195
Akhisar, *Turk.* 38°54′ N, 27°50′ E 156
Akhmeta, *Ga.* 42°1′ N, 45°17′ E 195
Akhmîm, *Egypt* 26°38′ N, 31°42′ E 180
Akhta, *Arm.* 40°28′ N, 44°45′ E 195
Akhtopol, *Bulg.* 42°7′ N, 27°54′ E 156
Akhtuba, river, *Russ.* 47°55′ N, 46°29′ E 158
Akhtubinsk, *Russ.* 48°17′ N, 46°10′ E 158
Aki, *Japan* 33°30′ N, 133°54′ E 201
Akie, river, *Can.* 57°15′ N, 124°59′ W 108
Akimiski Island, *Can.* 53°8′ N, 84°10′ W 106
Akita, *Japan* 39°48′ N, 140°10′ E 190
Akitio, *N.Z.* 40°37′ S, 176°23′ E 240
Akjoujt, *Mauritania* 19°43′ N, 14°24′ W 222
Akka, *Mor.* 29°24′ N, 8°15′ W 214
Akkala, *Uzb.* 43°40′ N, 59°32′ E 207
Akkaraipattu, *Sri Lanka* 7°14′ N, 81°52′ E 188
Akkarvik, *Nor.* 70°3′ N, 20°30′ E 152
'Akko (Acre), *Israel* 32°55′ N, 35°4′ E 194
Akkuş, *Turk.* 40°48′ N, 36°59′ E 156
Aklavik, *Can.* 68°13′ N, 135°6′ W 98
Aklera, *India* 24°24′ N, 76°34′ E 197
Akmenė, *Lith.* 56°15′ N, 22°41′ E 166
Akmeqit, *China* 37°7′ N, 77°0′ E 184
Akna (Ağdam), *Azerb.* 39°59′ N, 46°54′ E 195
Aknīste, *Latv.* 56°8′ N, 25°46′ E 166
Akō, *Japan* 34°45′ N, 134°22′ E 201
Akobo, *Sudan* 7°45′ N, 33°0′ E 224
Ākobo, river, *Africa* 7°0′ N, 34°13′ E 224
Akokane, *Niger* 18°43′ N, 7°9′ E 222
Akola, *India* 20°41′ N, 77°1′ E 188
Akom, *Cameroon* 2°50′ N, 10°34′ E 218
Akonolinga, *Cameroon* 3°50′ N, 12°15′ E 218
Akor, *Mali* 14°52′ N, 6°59′ W 222
Akosombo, *Ghana* 6°20′ N, 2°119′ E 222
Akosombo Dam, *Ghana* 6°1′ N, 0°14′ E 222
Akot, *India* 21°6′ N, 77°5′ E 188
Akot, *Sudan* 6°31′ N, 30°4′ E 224
Akpatok Island, *Can.* 60°24′ N, 72°3′ W 106
Akqi, *China* 40°56′ N, 78°33′ E 184
Akrabat, *Turkm.* 35°29′ N, 61°45′ E 186
'Akramah, ruin(s), *Lib.* 31°59′ N, 23°31′ E 180
Akranes, *Ice.* 64°21′ N, 22°0′ W 143
Akreidil, spring, *Mauritania* 18°29′ N, 15°39′ W 222
Akron, *Ala., U.S.* 32°52′ N, 87°44′ W 103
Akron, *Colo., U.S.* 40°9′ N, 103°13′ W 90
Akron, *Ind., U.S.* 41°1′ N, 86°1′ W 102
Akron, *Iowa, U.S.* 42°48′ N, 96°34′ W 90
Akron, *Mich., U.S.* 43°33′ N, 83°31′ W 102
Akron, *Ohio, U.S.* 41°5′ N, 81°31′ W 102
Akrotiri, *Cyprus* 34°35′ N, 32°56′ E 194
Akrotírio Apolitáres, *Gr.* 35°50′ N, 23°21′ E 156
Akrotírio Dafnoúdi, *Gr.* 38°28′ N, 19°38′ E 156
Akrotírio Doukáto, *Gr.* 38°35′ N, 19°40′ E 156
Akrotírio Gérakas, *Gr.* 36°46′ N, 23°7′ E 156
Akrotírio Ginas, *Gr.* 36°4′ N, 28°5′ E 156
Akrotírio Griá, *Gr.* 37°49′ N, 24°58′ E 156
Akrotírio Hélatros, *Gr.* 35°12′ N, 27°2′ E 156
Akrotírio Kafiéas, *Gr.* 38°9′ N, 24°37′ E 156
Akrotírio Kapélo, *Gr.* 36°4′ N, 23°4′ E 156
Akrotírio Katomŕi, *Gr.* 36°50′ N, 24°36′ E 156
Akrotírio Keáli, *Gr.* 35°49′ N, 22°34′ E 156
Akrotírio Kílopas, *Gr.* 37°3′ N, 23°37′ E 156
Akrotírio Korakas, *Gr.* 39°23′ N, 25°29′ E 156
Akrotírio Maléas, *Gr.* 36°22′ N, 23°13′ E 156
Akrotírio Mestá, *Gr.* 38°15′ N, 25°6′ E 156
Akrotírio Moúnda, *Gr.* 37°59′ N, 19°56′ E 156
Akrotírio Pláka, *Gr.* 35°4′ N, 26°19′ E 156
Akrotírio Spánda, *Gr.* 35°41′ N, 23°46′ E 156
Akrotírio Spathí, *Gr.* 36°16′ N, 22°58′ E 156
Akrotírio Stavrí, *Gr.* 37°13′ N, 24°54′ E 156
Akrotírio Stenó, *Gr.* 37°42′ N, 24°58′ E 156
Akrotírio Ténaro (Matapás, Taenarum), *Gr.* 36°13′ N, 21°38′ E 156
Aksaray, *Turk.* 38°21′ N, 34°1′ E 156
Aksarka, *Russ.* 66°29′ N, 67°47′ E 169
Aksay, *China* 39°25′ N, 94°14′ E 188
Aksay, *Russ.* 47°56′ N, 43°59′ E 158
Aksayqin Hu, lake, *China* 35°8′ N, 78°55′ E 188
Akşehir, *Turk.* 38°20′ N, 31°25′ E 156
Akşehir Gölü, lake, *Turk.* 38°32′ N, 31°9′ E 156
Akseki, *Turk.* 37°2′ N, 31°47′ E 156
'Aksha, ruin(s), *Egypt* 22°4′ N, 31°12′ E 182
Ak-Shyyrak, *Kyrg.* 41°54′ N, 78°43′ E 184
Aksu, *China* 41°9′ N, 80°15′ E 184
Aksu, *Kaz.* 42°34′ N, 52°43′ E 158
Aksu, river, *China* 40°58′ N, 80°24′ E 184
Aksū, river, *Kaz.* 45°44′ N, 79°0′ E 184
Āksum, *Eth.* 14°7′ N, 38°41′ E 182
Aktag, peak, *China* 36°43′ N, 84°36′ E 184
Aktash, *Russ.* 50°21′ N, 87°48′ E 184
Ak-Tektir, *Kyrg.* 42°6′ N, 72°26′ E 197
Akto, *China* 39°8′ N, 75°54′ E 184
Aktogay, *Kaz.* 48°51′ N, 60°6′ E 158
Aktsyabrski, *Belarus* 52°36′ N, 28°58′ E 152
Akujärvi, *Fin.* 68°40′ N, 27°42′ E 152
Akula, *Dem. Rep. of the Congo* 2°20′ N, 20°15′ E 218
Akune, *Japan* 32°1′ N, 130°13′ E 201
Akure, *Nig.* 7°18′ N, 5°11′ E 222
Akureyri, *Ice.* 65°41′ N, 18°16′ W 246
Akuse, *Ghana* 6°4′ N, 9°535′ E 222
Akwatia, *Ghana* 6°0′ N, 0°48′ E 214
Akyaka, *Turk.* 40°45′ N, 43°32′ E 195
Āl 'Ābis, *Saudi Arabia* 18°1′ N, 43°9′ E 182
Al 'Adam, *Lib.* 31°53′ N, 23°57′ E 180
Al A'madī, *Kuwait* 29°3′ N, 48°4′ E 180
Al Akhḍar, *Saudi Arabia* 28°3′ N, 37°7′ E 180
Al' Amādīyah, *Iraq* 37°7′ N, 43°29′ E 180
Al' Amārah, *Iraq* 31°53′ N, 47°9′ E 180
Al 'Ammārīyah, *Iraq* 37°6′ N, 43°22′ E 195
Al 'Ānāt, *Syr.* 32°20′ N, 36°48′ E 194
Al 'Aqabah, *Jordan* 29°34′ N, 35°4′ E 180
Al 'Aqīq, *Saudi Arabia* 20°40′ N, 41°22′ E 182
Al 'Arīḍah, *Leb.* 34°38′ N, 35°59′ E 194
Al Arṭāwīyah, *Saudi Arabia* 26°29′ N, 45°23′ E 180
Al As'ad, *Saudi Arabia* 27°50′ N, 37°22′ E 180
Al Ashkharah, *Oman* 21°52′ N, 59°32′ E 182
Al 'Athāmīn, peak, *Iraq* 30°20′ N, 43°33′ E 180
Al 'Ayn, *U.A.E.* 24°10′ N, 55°38′ E 196
Al 'Ayzarīyah, *Israel* 31°45′ N, 35°15′ E 194
Al Bad', *Saudi Arabia* 28°26′ N, 35°4′ E 180
Al Badī', *Saudi Arabia* 22°5′ N, 46°30′ E 207
Al Bā'ah, *Saudi Arabia* 20°3′ N, 41°33′ E 182
Al Ba'rah, spring, *Kuwait* 29°35′ N, 47°59′ E 196
Al Bardī, *Lib.* 31°46′ N, 25°3′ E 180
Al Basīt, Ra's, *Syr.* 35°50′ N, 35°50′ E 156
Al Başrah, *Iraq* 30°29′ N, 47°49′ E 180
Al Bayād, *Saudi Arabia* 23°42′ N, 47°48′ E 196
Al Biqā' (Bekaa Valley), region, *Leb.* 33°43′ N, 35°51′ E 194
Al Bi'r, *Saudi Arabia* 28°51′ N, 36°15′ E 180
Al Bir Lahlou, *Western Sahara, Mor.* 26°23′ N, 9°32′ W 214
Al Bīrah, *West Bank, Israel* 31°53′ N, 35°12′ E 194
Al Birk, *Saudi Arabia* 18°8′ N, 41°36′ E 182
Al Birkah, *Lib.* 24°50′ N, 10°8′ E 216
Al Bunduq, oil field, *U.A.E.* 25°2′ N, 52°25′ E 196
Al Burayj, *Gaza Strip, Israel* 31°25′ N, 34°24′ E 194
Al Buraymī, *Oman* 24°11′ N, 55°49′ E 196
Al Burjayn, *Tun.* 35°40′ N, 10°35′ E 156
Al Dafyānah, *Jordan* 32°18′ N, 36°38′ E 194
Al Fallūjah (Fallujah), *Iraq* 33°19′ N, 43°46′ E 180
Al Farciya, *Western Sahara, Mor.* 27°8′ N, 9°52′ W 214
Al Fāw, *Iraq* 29°59′ N, 48°28′ E 196
Al Fayḍah, *Saudi Arabia* 25°15′ N, 44°25′ E 182
Al Fujayrah, *U.A.E.* 25°10′ N, 56°18′ E 196
Al Fuqahā', *Lib.* 27°50′ N, 16°20′ E 216
Al Furāt (Euphrates), river, *Syr.* 35°43′ N, 39°21′ E 180
Al Furāt, river, *Iraq* 32°17′ N, 44°56′ E 180
Al Ghārīyah, *Syr.* 32°23′ N, 36°39′ E 194
Al Ghayḍah, *Yemen* 16°12′ N, 52°14′ E 182
Al Ghayḍah, *Yemen* 14°55′ N, 49°58′ E 182
Al Ghayl, *Saudi Arabia* 22°33′ N, 46°18′ E 182
Al Ghayl, *Yemen* 16°3′ N, 44°48′ E 182
Al Ghazālah, *Saudi Arabia* 26°42′ N, 41°22′ E 180
Al Ghuwayr, *Jordan* 31°8′ N, 35°45′ E 194
Al Ḥaddār, *Saudi Arabia* 21°56′ N, 45°58′ E 182
Al Ḥadīdah, *Saudi Arabia* 21°32′ N, 50°30′ E 182
Al Ḥadīthah, *Iraq* 34°8′ N, 42°27′ E 180
Al Haggounia, *Western Sahara, Mor.* 27°25′ N, 12°26′ W 214
Al Ḥallānīyah, island, *Oman* 17°35′ N, 55°22′ E 182
Al Ḥamād, *Saudi Arabia* 31°17′ N, 37°38′ E 180
Al Ḥamīdīyah, *Syr.* 34°42′ N, 35°56′ E 194
Al Ḥammār, Hawr, lake, *Iraq* 30°49′ N, 46°38′ E 180
Al Ḥamrā', *Lib.* 29°39′ N, 12°0′ E 216
Al Ḥamrā', *Saudi Arabia* 23°55′ N, 38°51′ E 182
Al Ḥamūd, *Jordan* 31°17′ N, 35°47′ E 194
Al Ḥanākīyah, *Saudi Arabia* 24°50′ N, 40°29′ E 182
Al Ḥaqw, *Saudi Arabia* 17°33′ N, 42°40′ E 182
Al Ḥarīq, *Saudi Arabia* 23°35′ N, 46°33′ E 196
Al Harūj al Aswad, *Lib.* 28°27′ N, 17°15′ E 216
Al Ḥasakah, *Syr.* 36°31′ N, 40°46′ E 195
Al Ḥasānī, island, *Saudi Arabia* 25°1′ N, 36°30′ E 182
Al Ḥawīyah, *Saudi Arabia* 21°26′ N, 40°31′ E 182
Al Ḥawrah, *Yemen* 13°51′ N, 47°33′ E 182
Al Ḥayy, *Iraq* 32°9′ N, 46°5′ E 180
Al Ḥijānah, *Syr.* 33°21′ N, 36°32′ E 194
Al Ḥijāz (Hejaz), region, *Saudi Arabia* 26°54′ N, 36°41′ E 180
Al Ḥillah, *Iraq* 32°27′ N, 44°26′ E 180
Al Ḥillah (Hauta), *Saudi Arabia* 23°28′ N, 46°52′ E 196
Al Ḥimá, spring, *Saudi Arabia* 18°13′ N, 44°30′ E 182
Al Ḥiṣn, *Jordan* 32°28′ N, 35°53′ E 194
Al Hoceima, *Mor.* 35°14′ N, 3°57′ W 150
Al Ḥudaydah, *Yemen* 14°48′ N, 42°56′ E 182
Al Hufūf (Hofuf), *Saudi Arabia* 25°21′ N, 49°34′ E 196
Al Ḥulwah, *Saudi Arabia* 23°23′ N, 46°49′ E 182
Al Ḥunayy, *Saudi Arabia* 24°58′ N, 48°46′ E 196
Al Hūwah, *Saudi Arabia* 23°0′ N, 45°48′ E 182
Al Ikhwān (The Brothers), islands, *Yemen* 11°24′ N, 52°52′ E 182
Al 'Irqah, *Yemen* 13°40′ N, 47°19′ E 182
Al 'Īsāwīyah, *Saudi Arabia* 30°41′ N, 38°1′ E 180
Al Jabalash Sharqī (Anti-Lebanon), *Leb.* 34°5′ N, 36°21′ E 194
Al Jaghbūb, *Lib.* 29°45′ N, 24°30′ E 180
Al Jawf, *Lib.* 24°10′ N, 23°16′ E 216
Al Jawf, *Saudi Arabia* 29°54′ N, 39°51′ E 143
Al Jazīrah, spring, *Lib.* 25°43′ N, 21°7′ E 216
Al Jehrā, *Kuwait* 29°21′ N, 47°40′ E 196
Al Jīb, *West Bank, Israel* 31°50′ N, 35°10′ E 194
Al Jifāra, *Tun.* 32°1′ N, 11°10′ E 214
Al Jīzah, *Jordan* 31°41′ N, 35°57′ E 194
Al Jubayl, *Saudi Arabia* 26°59′ N, 49°39′ E 196
Al Jubaylah, *Saudi Arabia* 24°52′ N, 46°28′ E 196
Al Jumaylīyah, *Qatar* 25°36′ N, 51°7′ E 196
Al Jumaymah, spring, *Saudi Arabia* 29°41′ N, 43°37′ E 180
Al Junaynah, *Saudi Arabia* 20°15′ N, 42°50′ E 182
Al Kahfah, *Saudi Arabia* 27°2′ N, 43°3′ E 180
Al Karak, *Jordan* 31°10′ N, 35°42′ E 194
Al Kawm, *Syr.* 35°12′ N, 38°51′ E 180
Al Khābūrah, *Oman* 23°54′ N, 57°7′ E 196
Al Khalīl (Hebron), *West Bank, Israel* 31°31′ N, 35°6′ E 194
Al Kharfah, *Saudi Arabia* 22°11′ N, 46°41′ E 182
Al Kharj, *Saudi Arabia* 24°10′ N, 47°20′ E 196
Al Khāṣirah, *Saudi Arabia* 23°29′ N, 43°44′ E 182
Al Khawr, *Qatar* 25°41′ N, 51°30′ E 196
Al Khīrān, *Kuwait* 28°36′ N, 48°21′ E 196
Al Khiyam, *Leb.* 33°19′ N, 35°36′ E 194
Al Khubar, *Saudi Arabia* 26°13′ N, 50°8′ E 196
Al Khufayfīyah, *Saudi Arabia* 24°54′ N, 44°44′ E 182
Al Khums, *Lib.* 32°42′ N, 14°16′ E 216
Al Khunn, *Saudi Arabia* 23°16′ N, 49°15′ E 182
Al Khuraybah, *Yemen* 15°7′ N, 48°20′ E 182
Al Khurmah, *Saudi Arabia* 21°51′ N, 42°3′ E 182
Al Kifl, *Iraq* 32°16′ N, 44°24′ E 180
Al Kūfah (Kufah), *Iraq* 32°5′ N, 44°27′ E 186
Al Kufrah (Kufra Oasis), *Lib.* 24°20′ N, 23°44′ E 226
Al Kūt, *Iraq* 32°34′ N, 45°49′ E 180
Al Kuwayt (Kuwait City), *Kuwait* 29°20′ N, 47°52′ E 196
Al La'bān, *Jordan* 30°54′ N, 35°42′ E 194
Al Labwah, *Leb.* 34°11′ N, 36°21′ E 194
Al Lādhiqīyah (Latakia), *Syr.* 35°31′ N, 35°47′ E 194
Al Lajā, *Syr.* 32°53′ N, 36°19′ E 194
Al Lawz, Jabal, peak, *Saudi Arabia* 28°38′ N, 35°13′ E 180
Al Lidām, *Saudi Arabia* 20°27′ N, 44°48′ E 182
Al Līth, *Saudi Arabia* 20°8′ N, 40°18′ E 182
Al Luḥayyah, *Yemen* 15°41′ N, 42°42′ E 182
Al Luwaymī, *Saudi Arabia* 27°54′ N, 42°12′ E 180
Al Ma'ānīyah, spring, *Iraq* 30°42′ N, 42°57′ E 180
Al Madīnah (Medina), *Saudi Arabia* 24°26′ N, 39°34′ E 182
Al Madwar, *Jordan* 32°17′ N, 35°59′ E 194
Al Mafraq, *Jordan* 32°20′ N, 36°12′ E 194
Al Mahbas, *Western Sahara, Mor.* 27°27′ N, 9°2′ W 214
Al Maḥrūqah, *Lib.* 27°29′ N, 14°0′ E 216
Al Majma'ah, *Saudi Arabia* 25°52′ N, 45°23′ E 182
Al Malāqī, spring, *Lib.* 26°53′ N, 16°49′ E 216
Al Mālikīyah, *Syr.* 37°11′ N, 42°4′ E 195
Al Manāmah (Manama), *Bahrain* 26°10′ N, 50°27′ E 196
Al Manzil, *Jordan* 31°3′ N, 36°0′ E 194
Al Marj (Barce), *Lib.* 32°30′ N, 20°53′ E 216
Al Mashrafah, *Syr.* 34°50′ N, 36°52′ E 194
Al Mawşil (Mosul), *Iraq* 36°20′ N, 43°0′ E 195
Al Mayādīn, *Syr.* 35°0′ N, 40°24′ E 180
Al Mayyāh, *Saudi Arabia* 27°50′ N, 42°49′ E 180
Al Mazra'ah, *Jordan* 31°17′ N, 35°32′ E 194
Al Mazzah, *Syr.* 33°30′ N, 36°14′ E 194
Al Mintirib, *Oman* 22°24′ N, 58°49′ E 182
Al Minyah, *Leb.* 34°28′ N, 35°56′ E 194
Al Mismīyah, *Syr.* 33°7′ N, 36°23′ E 194
Al Mubarraz, *Saudi Arabia* 25°27′ N, 49°35′ E 196
Al Mudawwarah, *Jordan* 29°23′ N, 36°2′ E 180
Al Mughayrā', *U.A.E.* 24°3′ N, 53°31′ E 196
Al Mukallā, *Yemen* 14°33′ N, 49°6′ E 182
Al Mukhā, *Yemen* 13°20′ N, 43°14′ E 182
Al Musayyib, *Iraq* 32°47′ N, 44°21′ E 180
Al Mushannaf, *Syr.* 32°44′ N, 36°46′ E 194
Al Muwaqqar, ruin(s), *Jordan* 31°48′ N, 36°2′ E 194
Al Muwayh, *Saudi Arabia* 22°43′ N, 41°37′ E 182
Al Muwayliḥ, *Saudi Arabia* 27°41′ N, 35°28′ E 180
Al Qābil, *Oman* 23°52′ N, 55°51′ E 196
Al Qaḍīmah, *Saudi Arabia* 22°19′ N, 39°8′ E 182
Al Qadmūs, *Syr.* 35°5′ N, 36°9′ E 194
Al Qā'im, *Iraq* 34°17′ N, 41°11′ E 180
Al Qa'īyah, *Saudi Arabia* 24°19′ N, 43°32′ E 182
Al Qā'īyah, spring, *Saudi Arabia* 26°28′ N, 45°33′ E 196
Al Qāmishlī, *Syr.* 37°2′ N, 41°16′ E 195
Al Qārah, *Yemen* 13°41′ N, 45°15′ E 182
Al Qaryah ash Sharqīyah, *Lib.* 30°23′ N, 13°33′ E 216
Al Qaryatayn, *Syr.* 34°10′ N, 37°17′ E 180
Al Qaşr, *Jordan* 31°18′ N, 35°44′ E 194
Al Qaṭīf, *Saudi Arabia* 26°32′ N, 49°59′ E 196
Al Qaṭrānah, *Jordan* 31°14′ N, 36°1′ E 194
Al Qaṭrūn, *Lib.* 24°53′ N, 14°29′ E 216
Al Qawārishah, *Lib.* 32°1′ N, 20°5′ E 216
Al Qaws, site, *Lib.* 30°26′ N, 18°21′ E 216
Al Qayṣūmah, *Saudi Arabia* 28°18′ N, 46°9′ E 196
Al Qunayṭirah (Quneitra), *Syr.* 33°7′ N, 35°49′ E 194
Al Qunfudhah, *Saudi Arabia* 19°6′ N, 41°7′ E 182
Al Qurayni, spring, *Saudi Arabia* 21°51′ N, 53°48′ E 182
Al Qurayyah, *Syr.* 32°32′ N, 36°35′ E 194
Al Qurnah, *Iraq* 30°55′ N, 47°22′ E 180
Al Quşayr, *Syr.* 34°30′ N, 36°34′ E 194
Al Quşūrīyah, *Saudi Arabia* 23°43′ N, 44°37′ E 182
Al Quṭayfah, *Syr.* 33°43′ N, 36°35′ E 194
Al Quway'īyah, *Saudi Arabia* 24°2′ N, 45°15′ E 182
Al 'Ubaylah, *Saudi Arabia* 21°58′ N, 50°56′ E 182
Al 'Udaysah, *Leb.* 33°15′ N, 35°32′ E 194
Al 'Ulá, *Saudi Arabia* 26°36′ N, 37°51′ E 180
Al 'Uqaylah, *Lib.* 30°13′ N, 19°11′ E 216
Al 'Uqayr, *Saudi Arabia* 25°38′ N, 50°8′ E 196
Al 'Uwaynāt see 'Uweinat, Jebel, peak, *Sudan* 21°51′ N, 24°58′ E 226
Al 'Uwaynāt (Serdeles), *Lib.* 25°47′ N, 10°33′ E 216
Al 'Uwaynid, *Saudi Arabia* 24°54′ N, 45°48′ E 182
Al 'Uwayqīlah, *Saudi Arabia* 30°18′ N, 42°12′ E 180
Al 'Uyūn, *Saudi Arabia* 26°30′ N, 43°40′ E 180
Al 'Uyūn, *Saudi Arabia* 24°33′ N, 39°33′ E 182
Al 'Uzayr, *Iraq* 31°19′ N, 47°23′ E 180
Al Wābirīyah, spring, *Lib.* 27°24′ N, 18°5′ E 216
Al Wafra, *Kuwait* 28°35′ N, 47°57′ E 196
Al Wajh, *Saudi Arabia* 26°15′ N, 36°27′ E 180
Al Wakrah, *Qatar* 25°6′ N, 51°35′ E 196
Al Wannān, *Saudi Arabia* 26°53′ N, 48°26′ E 196
Al Waqbah, spring, *Saudi Arabia* 28°52′ N, 45°26′ E 196
Al Warī'ah, *Saudi Arabia* 27°47′ N, 47°32′ E 196
Al Yādūdah, *Jordan* 31°50′ N, 35°54′ E 194
Ala, *It.* 45°45′ N, 11°0′ E 167
Alà, Monti di, *It.* 40°33′ N, 8°47′ E 156
Ala-Archa National Park, site, *Kyrg.* 42°35′ N, 74°19′ E 197
Alabama, adm. division, *Ala., U.S.* 31°51′ N, 88°21′ W 96
Alabama, river, *Ala., U.S.* 31°12′ N, 87°54′ W 103
Alabaster, *Ala., U.S.* 33°14′ N, 86°49′ W 96
Alaca, *Turk.* 40°8′ N, 34°50′ E 156
Alaca Dağ, peak, *Turk.* 37°28′ N, 32°4′ E 156
Alacahöyük, ruin(s), *Turk.* 40°13′ N, 34°37′ E 156
Alaçam, *Turk.* 41°35′ N, 35°36′ E 156

Alacant see Alicante, *Sp.* 38°20′ N, 0°30′ E 164
Alachua, *Fla., U.S.* 29°47′ N, 82°30′ W 105
Alacón, *Sp.* 41°1′ N, 0°43′ E 164
Aladağ, peak, *Turk.* 37°42′ N, 35°5′ E 156
Aladağ, peak, *Turk.* 37°56′ N, 32°0′ E 156
Ālagē, Āmba, peak, *Eth.* 12°57′ N, 39°23′ E 182
Alagir, *Russ.* 43°3′ N, 44°14′ E 180
Alagna Valsesia, *It.* 45°51′ N, 7°56′ E 167
Alagoas, adm. division, *Braz.* 9°35′ S, 37°52′ W 132
Alagoinhas, *Braz.* 12°10′ S, 38°24′ W 132
Alagón, *Sp.* 41°45′ N, 1°8′ W 164
Alai Mountains, *Kyrg.* 39°53′ N, 72°4′ E 184
Alaior, *Sp.* 39°55′ N, 4°8′ E 164
Alajärvi, *Fin.* 62°59′ N, 23°46′ E 152
Alajärvi, *Fin.* 64°58′ N, 28°45′ E 152
Alajuela, *C.R.* 10°0′ N, 84°12′ W 115
Alakanuk, *Alas., U.S.* 62°34′ N, 164°50′ W 98
Alakoko Fishpond, site, *Hawai'i, U.S.* 21°56′ N, 159°25′ W 99
Alaköl, lake, *Kaz.* 46°20′ N, 81°30′ E 184
Alakurtti, *Russ.* 66°58′ N, 30°24′ E 152
Alalakh, ruin(s), *Turk.* 36°11′ N, 36°16′ E 156
Alalaú, river, *Braz.* 0°23′ N, 60°19′ W 130
'Alam el Rûm, Râs, *Egypt* 31°25′ N, 27°18′ E 226
Alama, *Cen. Af. Rep.* 5°29′ N, 21°51′ E 218
Alamagan, island, *U.S.* 17°32′ N, 144°34′ E 192
Alameda, *Calif., U.S.* 37°46′ N, 122°17′ W 100
Alameda, *Can.* 49°15′ N, 102°19′ W 90
Alameda, *N. Mex., U.S.* 35°10′ N, 106°38′ W 92
Alameda, *Sp.* 37°13′ N, 4°40′ W 164
Alamedilla, *Sp.* 37°36′ N, 3°15′ W 164
Alamillo, *Sp.* 38°39′ N, 4°47′ W 164
Alamitos, Sierra de los, peak, *Mex.* 26°19′ N, 102°22′ W 114
Alamo, *Ind., U.S.* 39°58′ N, 87°4′ W 102
Álamo, *Mex.* 20°54′ N, 97°41′ W 114
Alamo, *Tenn., U.S.* 35°48′ N, 89°6′ W 96
Alamo Lake, *Ariz., U.S.* 34°18′ N, 113°36′ W 101
Alamo, river, *Calif., U.S.* 32°55′ N, 115°31′ W 101
Álamo, river, *Mex.* 26°31′ N, 99°57′ W 114
Alamogordo, *N. Mex., U.S.* 32°54′ N, 105°57′ W 92
Álamos, *Mex.* 29°12′ N, 110°8′ W 92
Álamos, river, *Mex.* 26°56′ N, 109°8′ W 80
Alanäs, *Nor.* 64°8′ N, 15°39′ E 152
Åland (Ahvenanmaa), island, *Fin.* 60°26′ N, 19°33′ E 166
Alanís, *Sp.* 38°2′ N, 5°44′ W 164
Alanta, *Lith.* 55°21′ N, 25°17′ E 166
Alantika Mountains, *Cameroon* 8°35′ N, 12°15′ E 216
Alanya (Coracesium), *Turk.* 36°31′ N, 32°1′ E 180
Alapayevsk, *Russ.* 57°50′ N, 61°38′ E 154
Alappuzha see Alleppey, *India* 9°29′ N, 76°20′ E 188
Alaquines, *Mex.* 22°6′ N, 99°36′ W 114
Alarcón, *Sp.* 39°32′ N, 2°5′ W 164
Alas Purwo National Park, *Indonesia* 8°40′ S, 114°4′ E 238
Alas, river, *Indonesia* 3°22′ N, 97°44′ E 196
Alaşehir, *Turk.* 38°21′ N, 28°31′ E 156
Alaska, adm. division, *Alas., U.S.* 64°46′ N, 156°29′ W 98
Alaska, Gulf of 57°56′ N, 149°1′ W 98
Alaska Highway, *Can.* 57°34′ N, 122°49′ W 108
Alaska Peninsula, *North America* 58°0′ N, 157°11′ W 98
Alaska Plain, *North Pacific Ocean* 55°0′ N, 143°0′ W 252
Alaska Range, *North America* 62°13′ N, 153°16′ W 98
Alassio, *It.* 44°0′ N, 8°10′ E 167
Alasuolijärvi, lake, *Fin.* 66°17′ N, 27°9′ E 152
Älät, *Azerb.* 39°56′ N, 49°23′ E 195
Alatoz, *Sp.* 39°5′ N, 1°22′ W 164
Alatyr', *Russ.* 54°47′ N, 46°37′ E 154
Alava, Cape, *Wash., U.S.* 48°4′ N, 124°53′ W 100
Alaverdi, *Arm.* 41°6′ N, 44°38′ E 195
Alāyat Samā'il, *Oman* 23°14′ N, 58°3′ E 182
Alazeya, river, *Russ.* 70°55′ N, 153°45′ E 160
Alba, *It.* 44°41′ N, 8°2′ E 167
Alba, *Tex., U.S.* 32°46′ N, 95°38′ W 103
Alba, adm. division, *Rom.* 46°13′ N, 22°59′ E 156
Alba, Foum el, pass, *Mali* 20°40′ N, 3°37′ W 222
Alba Iulia, *Rom.* 46°3′ N, 23°35′ E 168
Albac, *Rom.* 46°27′ N, 22°58′ E 168
Albacete, *Sp.* 38°58′ N, 1°51′ W 164
Albalá del Caudillo, *Sp.* 39°14′ N, 6°11′ W 164
Albalate del Arzobispo, *Sp.* 41°7′ N, 0°31′ E 164
Albanel, Lac, lake, *Can.* 50°52′ N, 74°31′ W 106
Albania 40°43′ N, 19°44′ E 156
Albano, *Braz.* 2°29′ S, 57°32′ W 130
Albany, *Ga., U.S.* 31°34′ N, 84°10′ W 96
Albany, *Ind., U.S.* 40°18′ N, 85°14′ W 102
Albany, *Ky., U.S.* 36°40′ N, 85°8′ W 96
Albany, *La., U.S.* 30°29′ N, 90°35′ W 103
Albany, *Mo., U.S.* 40°13′ N, 94°19′ W 94
Albany, *N.Y., U.S.* 42°38′ N, 73°50′ W 104
Albany, *Ohio, U.S.* 39°13′ N, 82°13′ W 102
Albany, *Oreg., U.S.* 44°36′ N, 123°6′ W 90
Albany, *Tex., U.S.* 32°43′ N, 99°18′ W 92
Albany, *Wis., U.S.* 42°42′ N, 89°26′ W 102
Albany Island, *Can.* 52°20′ N, 82°53′ W 81
Albany, river, *Can.* 51°8′ N, 89°34′ W 110
Albares, *Sp.* 40°17′ N, 3°0′ W 164
Albarracín, *Sp.* 40°24′ N, 1°28′ W 164
Albemarle Sound 35°57′ N, 77°15′ W 80
Albenga, *It.* 44°3′ N, 8°13′ E 167
Albens, *Fr.* 45°46′ N, 5°56′ E 150
Alberdi, *Parag.* 26°12′ S, 58°4′ W 139
Alberese, *It.* 42°40′ N, 11°5′ E 156
Alberic, *Sp.* 39°6′ N, 0°31′ E 164
Alberni Inlet 48°57′ N, 124°47′ W 100
Albert, *Fr.* 50°0′ N, 2°39′ E 163
Albert Icefield, *Can.* 50°49′ N, 118°18′ W 90
Albert Kanaal, canal, *Belg.* 51°8′ N, 4°47′ E 163
Albert Lea, *Minn., U.S.* 43°37′ N, 93°23′ W 94
Albert Markham, Mount, *Antarctica* 81°20′ S, 159°13′ E 248
Albert, Mount, *Can.* 53°31′ N, 66°47′ W 111
Alberta, *Ala., U.S.* 32°13′ N, 87°25′ W 103
Alberta, adm. division, *Can.* 54°43′ N, 116°17′ W 108
Alberti, *Arg.* 35°1′ S, 60°18′ W 139
Albertirsa, *Hung.* 47°14′ N, 19°37′ E 168
Alberton, *Mont., U.S.* 46°59′ N, 114°29′ W 90
Albertville, *Ala., U.S.* 34°15′ N, 86°12′ W 96
Albi, *Fr.* 43°54′ N, 2°9′ E 150
Albia, *Iowa, U.S.* 41°1′ N, 92°47′ W 94
Albin, *Wyo., U.S.* 41°25′ N, 104°6′ W 90
Albina, *Suriname* 5°31′ N, 54°6′ W 130
Albina, Ponta, *Angola* 15°56′ S, 11°11′ E 220
Albinia, *It.* 42°31′ N, 11°13′ E 156
Albino, *It.* 45°46′ N, 9°47′ E 167
Al'bino, *Russ.* 59°22′ N, 83°4′ E 169
Albion, *Mich., U.S.* 42°14′ N, 84°45′ W 102
Albion, *Nebr., U.S.* 41°39′ N, 98°1′ W 90
Albion, *N.Y., U.S.* 43°14′ N, 78°13′ W 110
Albisola Marina, *It.* 44°19′ N, 8°30′ E 167
Albocàsser, *Sp.* 40°21′ N, 0°2′ E 164
Alborán, Isla de, island, *Sp.* 35°54′ N, 3°2′ W 164
Alboran Sea 35°34′ N, 4°26′ W 150
Alborea, *Sp.* 39°15′ N, 1°23′ W 164
Ålborg, *Den.* 57°1′ N, 9°55′ E 150
Ålborg Bugt 56°51′ N, 9°52′ E 152
Alborz, oil field, *Iran* 34°39′ N, 51°0′ E 180
Alborz, Reshteh-ye (Elburz Mountains), *Iran* 36°43′ N, 49°25′ E 195
Albota de Jos, *Mold.* 45°56′ N, 28°29′ E 158
Albox, *Sp.* 37°23′ N, 2°10′ W 164
Albreda, *Can.* 52°37′ N, 119°10′ W 108
Albuquerque, *N. Mex., U.S.* 35°5′ N, 106°39′ W 92
Albury, *Austral.* 36°4′ S, 146°57′ E 231
Alby, *Nor.* 62°29′ N, 15°27′ E 152
Alca, *Peru* 15°10′ S, 72°46′ W 137
Alcácer do Sal, *Port.* 38°21′ N, 8°31′ W 150
Alcadozo, *Sp.* 38°38′ N, 1°59′ W 164
Alcalà de Xibert, *Sp.* 40°17′ N, 0°12′ E 164
Alcalá de Henares, *Sp.* 40°28′ N, 3°22′ W 164
Alcalá de los Gazules, *Sp.* 36°27′ N, 5°44′ W 150
Alcalá la Real, *Sp.* 37°28′ N, 3°56′ W 164
Alcalde, Punta, *Chile* 28°34′ S, 72°35′ W 134
Alcamo, *It.* 37°59′ N, 12°58′ E 156
Alcanar, *Sp.* 40°32′ N, 0°28′ E 164
Alcañiz, *Sp.* 41°1′ N, 0°7′ E 164
Alcántara, *Sp.* 39°42′ N, 6°53′ W 150
Alcantara Lake, *Can.* 60°55′ N, 109°3′ W 108
Alcântara Spaceport, *Braz.* 2°18′ S, 44°32′ W 132
Alcantarilla, *Sp.* 37°58′ N, 1°14′ W 164
Alcaraz, *Sp.* 38°39′ N, 2°29′ W 164
Alcarràs, *Sp.* 41°33′ N, 0°30′ E 164
Alcaudete, *Sp.* 37°35′ N, 4°5′ W 164
Alcázar de San Juan, *Sp.* 39°23′ N, 3°13′ W 164
Alchevs'k, *Ukr.* 48°27′ N, 38°44′ E 158
Alcoa, *Tenn., U.S.* 35°47′ N, 83°58′ W 96
Alcoak, Cerro, peak, *Bol.* 22°26′ S, 66°54′ W 137
Alcocer, *Sp.* 40°28′ N, 2°36′ W 150
Alcoi see Alcoy, *Sp.* 38°41′ N, 0°29′ E 164
Alcolea, *Sp.* 37°55′ N, 4°41′ W 164
Alcolea del Pinar, *Sp.* 41°1′ N, 2°29′ W 164
Alconbury, *U.K.* 52°21′ N, 0°16′ E 162
Alcorcón, *Sp.* 40°19′ N, 3°51′ W 150
Alcorisa, *Sp.* 40°52′ N, 0°24′ E 164
Alcorta, *Arg.* 33°33′ S, 61°8′ W 139
Alcoutim, *Port.* 37°27′ N, 7°31′ W 150
Alcoy (Alcoi), *Sp.* 38°41′ N, 0°29′ E 164
Alcubierre, Sierra de, *Sp.* 41°44′ N, 0°29′ W 164
Alcúdia, *Sp.* 39°50′ N, 3°7′ E 164
Alcudia, Sierra de, *Sp.* 38°37′ N, 4°35′ W 164
Aldabra Islands, *Indian Ocean* 9°54′ S, 45°17′ E 218
Aldama, *Mex.* 28°49′ N, 105°56′ W 92
Aldama, *Mex.* 22°53′ N, 98°5′ W 114
Aldan, *Russ.* 58°39′ N, 125°29′ E 160
Aldan, river, *Russ.* 58°50′ N, 130°46′ E 160
Aldaz, Mount, *Antarctica* 75°57′ S, 123°51′ W 248
Aldbrough, *U.K.* 53°49′ N, 0°7′ E 162
Aldea Moret, *Sp.* 39°26′ N, 6°24′ W 164
Aldeburgh, *U.K.* 52°9′ N, 1°35′ E 163
Alden, Point, *Antarctica* 66°56′ S, 142°24′ E 248
Alder Dam, *Wash., U.S.* 46°48′ N, 122°26′ W 100
Alder Peak, *Calif., U.S.* 35°52′ N, 121°25′ W 100
Aldershot, *U.K.* 51°14′ N, 0°46′ E 162
Aldora, *Ga., U.S.* 33°2′ N, 84°12′ W 96
Aledo, *Mo., U.S.* 41°12′ N, 90°45′ W 94
Aleg, *Mauritania* 17°3′ N, 13°57′ W 222
Alegranza, island, *Sp.* 29°23′ N, 13°30′ W 214
Alegre, *Braz.* 20°48′ S, 41°35′ W 138
Alegre, *Braz.* 18°18′ S, 47°7′ W 138
Alegre, river, *Braz.* 15°11′ S, 59°48′ W 132
Alegres Mountain, *N. Mex., U.S.* 34°9′ N, 108°16′ W 92
Alegrete, *Braz.* 29°49′ S, 55°50′ W 139
Alejandra, *Arg.* 29°53′ S, 59°50′ W 139
Alejandro Roca, *Arg.* 33°26′ S, 63°43′ W 139
Alejo Ledesma, *Arg.* 33°37′ S, 62°37′ W 139
Alekhovshchina, *Russ.* 60°25′ N, 33°54′ E 154
Aleksandro Nevskiy, *Russ.* 53°26′ N, 40°12′ E 154
Aleksandrov, *Russ.* 56°23′ N, 38°42′ E 154
Aleksandrov Gay, *Russ.* 50°9′ N, 48°35′ E 158
Aleksandrovac, *Serb.* 43°27′ N, 21°2′ E 168
Aleksandrovka, *Russ.* 52°40′ N, 54°25′ E 154
Aleksandrovsk, *Russ.* 59°10′ N, 57°36′ E 154
Aleksandrovsk Sakhalinskiy, *Russ.* 50°47′ N, 142°22′ E 190
Aleksandrovskoye, *Russ.* 56°47′ N, 85°37′ E 169
Alekseyevka, *Russ.* 52°18′ N, 48°3′ E 158
Alekseyevka, *Russ.* 50°40′ N, 38°41′ E 158
Alekseyevka, *Russ.* 52°35′ N, 51°15′ E 154
Alekseyevsk, *Russ.* 57°49′ N, 108°40′ E 160
Aleksin, *Russ.* 54°30′ N, 37°10′ E 154
Aleksinac, *Serb.* 43°32′ N, 21°42′ E 168
Além Paraíba, *Braz.* 21°54′ S, 42°44′ W 138
Alemania, *Arg.* 25°37′ S, 65°38′ W 134
Alenquer, *Braz.* 1°59′ S, 54°49′ W 130
'Alenuihāhā Channel, *Hawai'i, U.S.* 20°17′ N, 156°24′ W 99
Alépé, *Côte d'Ivoire* 5°30′ N, 3°42′ W 222
Aleppo see Ḩalab, *Syr.* 36°11′ N, 37°9′ E 156
Aléria, *Fr.* 42°5′ N, 9°32′ E 156
Alert, *Can.* 82°29′ N, 61°46′ W 246
Alert Bay, *Can.* 50°31′ N, 126°50′ W 90
Alerta, *Peru* 10°46′ S, 71°50′ W 137
Alès, *Fr.* 44°7′ N, 4°4′ E 214
Aleşd, *Rom.* 47°4′ N, 22°23′ E 168
Alessandria, *It.* 44°54′ N, 8°37′ E 167
Ålesund, *Nor.* 62°27′ N, 6°2′ E 160
Alet, *Fr.* 42°59′ N, 2°14′ E 164
Aleutian Basin, *Bering Sea* 56°6′ N, 179°52′ E 252
Aleutian Islands, *Bering Sea* 54°5′ N, 164°2′ W 98
Aleutian Range, *North America* 56°36′ N, 158°49′ W 98
Aleutian Trench, *North Pacific Ocean* 49°58′ N, 174°26′ W 252
Alevina, Mys, *Russ.* 58°36′ N, 148°19′ E 160
Alexander, *N. Dak., U.S.* 47°49′ N, 103°40′ W 90
Alexander Archipelago, *North Pacific Ocean* 56°25′ N, 135°30′ W 98
Alexander Bay, *S. Af.* 28°43′ S, 16°27′ E 207
Alexander, Cape, *Antarctica* 67°21′ S, 61°14′ W 248
Alexander City, *Ala., U.S.* 32°56′ N, 85°57′ W 112
Alexander Island, *Wash., U.S.* 47°44′ N, 124°42′ W 100
Alexander, Mount, *Austral.* 22°39′ S, 115°23′ E 230
Alexandra Falls, *Can.* 60°42′ N, 116°54′ W 108
Alexandra Land, *Russ.* 81°0′ N, 47°0′ E 255
Alexandra, Zemlya, islands, *Zemlya Alexandra* 80°31′ N, 33°19′ E 160
Alexandria, *Can.* 52°38′ N, 122°27′ W 108
Alexandria, *Can.* 45°19′ N, 74°39′ W 94
Alexandria, *Ind., U.S.* 40°16′ N, 85°41′ W 102
Alexandria, *Ky., U.S.* 38°57′ N, 84°24′ W 102
Alexandria, *La., U.S.* 31°17′ N, 92°28′ W 103
Alexandria, *Minn., U.S.* 45°52′ N, 95°23′ W 90
Alexandria, *N.H., U.S.* 43°36′ N, 71°48′ W 104
Alexandria, *Rom.* 43°59′ N, 25°20′ E 156
Alexandria, *S. Af.* 33°39′ S, 26°24′ E 227
Alexandria, *S. Dak., U.S.* 43°37′ N, 97°46′ W 90
Alexandria, *Va., U.S.* 38°48′ N, 77°4′ W 94
Alexandria Bay, *N.Y., U.S.* 44°19′ N, 75°55′ W 94
Alexandria see El Iskandarîya, *Egypt* 31°10′ N, 29°55′ E 180
Alexandrium, ruin(s), *West Bank, Israel* 32°4′ N, 35°26′ E 194
Alexandroúpoli, *Gr.* 40°52′ N, 25°52′ E 180
Alexis Creek, *Can.* 52°5′ N, 123°19′ W 108
Alexis, river, *Can.* 52°28′ N, 57°29′ W 111
Aley, *Leb.* 33°48′ N, 35°36′ E 194
Aleysk, *Russ.* 52°32′ N, 82°53′ E 184
Aleza Lake, *Can.* 54°6′ N, 122°4′ W 108
Alfambra, *Sp.* 40°32′ N, 1°2′ W 164
Alfândega da Fé, *Port.* 41°20′ N, 6°59′ W 150
Alfaro, *Sp.* 42°10′ N, 1°45′ W 164
Alfenas, *Braz.* 21°28′ S, 45°56′ W 138
Alföld, *Hung.* 46°44′ N, 20°4′ E 168
Alfonsine, *It.* 44°29′ N, 12°2′ E 167
Alford, *U.K.* 53°15′ N, 0°11′ E 162
Alfred, *Me., U.S.* 43°28′ N, 70°44′ W 104
Alfred, Mount, *Can.* 50°10′ N, 124°4′ W 100
Alfredo M. Terrazas, *Mex.* 21°26′ N, 98°52′ W 114
Alfredton, *N.Z.* 40°41′ S, 175°53′ E 240
Alfreton, *U.K.* 53°6′ N, 1°24′ W 162
Alfta, *Nor.* 61°19′ N, 16°0′ E 152
Algarrobal, *Arg.* 25°29′ S, 64°1′ W 134
Algeciras, *Sp.* 36°7′ N, 5°28′ W 164
Algemesí, *Sp.* 39°11′ N, 0°26′ E 150
Algena, *Eritrea* 17°15′ N, 38°30′ E 182
Alger, *Mich., U.S.* 44°7′ N, 84°7′ W 102
Alger (Algiers), *Alg.* 36°44′ N, 2°56′ E 150
Alger, Mount, *Can.* 56°55′ N, 130°4′ W 108
Algeria 28°10′ N, 1°37′ W 214
Algha, *Kaz.* 49°57′ N, 57°20′ E 158
Alghabas, *Kaz.* 50°39′ N, 52°4′ E 158
Alghero, *It.* 40°33′ N, 8°19′ E 156
Algiers see Alger, *Alg.* 36°44′ N, 2°56′ E 150
Alginet, *Sp.* 39°16′ N, 0°29′ E 164
Algoa Bay 33°54′ S, 25°43′ E 227
Algodones, *Mex.* 32°42′ N, 114°45′ W 101
Algoma, *Wis., U.S.* 44°35′ N, 87°28′ W 94
Algona, *Iowa, U.S.* 43°3′ N, 94°14′ W 94
Algonac, *Mich., U.S.* 42°36′ N, 82°33′ W 102
Algonquin Park, *Can.* 45°32′ N, 78°35′ W 94
Algorta, *Uru.* 32°26′ S, 57°24′ W 139
Algy o, *Hung.* 46°19′ N, 20°13′ E 168
Alhama de Granada, *Sp.* 37°0′ N, 3°59′ W 164
Alhama de Murcia, *Sp.* 37°50′ N, 1°27′ W 164
Alhambra, *Sp.* 38°53′ N, 3°4′ W 164
Alhaurín el Grande, *Sp.* 36°38′ N, 4°42′ W 164
Alhuampa, *Arg.* 27°7′ S, 62°35′ W 139
Äli Bayramlı, *Azerb.* 39°56′ N, 48°54′ E 195
'Ali Sabîḩ, *Djibouti* 11°7′ N, 42°43′ E 218
Alía, *Sp.* 39°26′ N, 5°13′ W 164
Aliabad, *Iran* 28°33′ N, 55°47′ E 196
Aliaga, *Sp.* 40°40′ N, 0°42′ E 164
Alibunar, *Serb.* 45°5′ N, 20°58′ E 168
Alicante (Alacant), *Sp.* 38°20′ N, 0°30′ E 164
Alice, *S. Af.* 32°47′ S, 26°51′ E 227
Alice, *Tex., U.S.* 27°43′ N, 98°4′ W 92
Alice Arm, *Can.* 55°28′ N, 129°33′ W 108
Alice Creek, river, *Can.* 58°22′ N, 113°21′ W 108
Alice, Punta, *It.* 39°18′ N, 17°11′ E 156
Alice Town, *Bahamas* 25°43′ N, 79°17′ W 105
Alicedale, *S. Af.* 33°18′ S, 26°2′ E 227
Aliceville, *Ala., U.S.* 33°7′ N, 88°9′ W 103
Alicia, *Philippines* 7°33′ N, 122°57′ E 203
Alida, *Can.* 49°22′ N, 101°51′ W 90
Alida, peak, *Gr.* 39°6′ N, 21°11′ E 156
Alif, oil field, *Yemen* 15°45′ N, 46°7′ E 182
Aligandí, *Pan.* 9°13′ N, 78°2′ W 115
Aligarh, *India* 27°52′ N, 78°4′ E 197
Alijos, Rocas, islands, *North Pacific Ocean* 25°9′ N, 116°16′ W 112
'Ālika Cone, peak, *Hawai'i, U.S.* 19°15′ N, 155°47′ W 99
Alima, river, *Congo* 1°21′ S, 15°44′ E 218
Alimodian, *Philippines* 10°50′ N, 122°24′ E 203
Alindao, *Cen. Af. Rep.* 5°3′ N, 21°14′ E 218
Alingsås, *Nor.* 57°55′ N, 12°33′ E 152
Alins, *Sp.* 42°32′ N, 1°18′ E 164
Alinskoye, *Russ.* 63°19′ N, 87°36′ E 169
Alipur, *Pak.* 29°24′ N, 70°54′ E 186
Aliquippa, *Pa., U.S.* 40°37′ N, 80°15′ W 94
Alişar Hüyük (Alishar), ruin(s), *Turk.* 39°34′ N, 35°7′ E 156
Aliseda, *Sp.* 39°25′ N, 6°43′ W 164
Alishar see Alişar Hüyük, ruin(s), *Turk.* 39°34′ N, 35°7′ E 156
Alittjåkko, peak, *Nor.* 67°53′ N, 17°20′ E 152
Alivéri, *Gr.* 38°24′ N, 24°2′ E 156
Aliwal North, *S. Af.* 30°43′ S, 26°42′ E 227
Alix, *Can.* 52°22′ N, 113°11′ W 108
Alkmaar, *Neth.* 52°37′ N, 4°43′ E 163
Alla, *Russ.* 54°43′ N, 110°49′ E 173
Allada, *Benin* 6°45′ N, 2°9′ E 222
Allagash Falls, *Me., U.S.* 46°45′ N, 70°14′ W 94
Allagash Lake, lake, *Me., U.S.* 46°16′ N, 69°59′ W 94
Allahabad, *India* 25°26′ N, 81°49′ E 197
Allahabad, *Pak.* 28°55′ N, 70°53′ E 186
Allahüekber Dağı, peak, *Turk.* 40°33′ N, 42°28′ E 195
Allakaket, *Alas., U.S.* 66°30′ N, 152°26′ W 106
Allan Creek, river, *Can.* 60°20′ N, 130°53′ W 108
Allan Hills, *Antarctica* 76°41′ S, 158°26′ E 248
Allan Mountain, *Idaho, U.S.* 45°34′ N, 114°7′ W 90
Allan Water, *Can.* 50°14′ N, 90°12′ W 94
Allanmyo, *Myanmar* 19°23′ N, 95°12′ E 202
Allanridge, *S. Af.* 27°48′ S, 26°38′ E 227
Allanton, *N.Z.* 45°57′ S, 170°16′ E 240
Allegan, *Mich., U.S.* 42°31′ N, 85°51′ W 102
Alleghe, *It.* 46°25′ N, 12°1′ E 167
Allegheny Mountains, *North America* 37°1′ N, 82°33′ W 96
Allegheny Mountains, *W. Va., U.S.* 39°57′ N, 78°49′ W 106
Allen, *Philippines* 12°31′ N, 124°18′ E 203
Allen, Mount, *N.Z.* 47°8′ S, 167°43′ E 240
Allen, Punta, *Mex.* 19°51′ N, 88°7′ W 115
Allendale, *S.C., U.S.* 33°0′ N, 81°19′ W 96
Allendale Town, *U.K.* 54°53′ N, 2°16′ W 162
Allende, *Mex.* 28°19′ N, 100°51′ W 92
Allende, *Mex.* 25°18′ N, 100°0′ W 114
Allendorf, *Ger.* 50°40′ N, 8°47′ E 167
Allensworth, *Calif., U.S.* 35°51′ N, 119°24′ W 100
Allentown, *Pa., U.S.* 40°35′ N, 75°30′ W 94
Allentsteig, *Aust.* 48°41′ N, 15°20′ E 156
Alleppey (Alappuzha), *India* 9°29′ N, 76°20′ E 188
Allerton, *Ill., U.S.* 39°54′ N, 87°56′ W 102
Allgäuer Alpen, *Ger.* 47°27′ N, 9°48′ E 156
Allia Bay, site, *Kenya* 3°38′ N, 36°16′ E 224
Alliance, *Can.* 52°25′ N, 111°47′ W 108
Alliance, *Nebr., U.S.* 42°5′ N, 102°53′ W 90
Alliance, *Ohio, U.S.* 40°54′ N, 81°7′ W 102
Allier, river, *Fr.* 44°53′ N, 3°36′ E 165
Allison Peninsula, *Antarctica* 73°1′ S, 85°31′ W 248
Alliston, *Can.* 44°8′ N, 79°51′ W 94
Allo, *Sp.* 42°34′ N, 2°2′ W 164
Allos, *Fr.* 44°14′ N, 6°37′ E 167
Alluvial City, *La., U.S.* 29°49′ N, 89°43′ W 103
Allyn, *Wash., U.S.* 47°22′ N, 122°50′ W 100
Alma, *Can.* 48°30′ N, 71°40′ W 94
Alma, *Ga., U.S.* 31°31′ N, 82°28′ W 96
Alma, *Kans., U.S.* 38°59′ N, 96°18′ W 90
Alma, *Mich., U.S.* 43°22′ N, 84°40′ W 102
Alma, *Nebr., U.S.* 40°5′ N, 99°23′ W 90
Alma Peak, *Can.* 56°43′ N, 127°38′ W 108
Almacelles, *Sp.* 41°43′ N, 0°26′ E 164
Almadén, *Sp.* 38°46′ N, 4°51′ W 164
Almagro, *Sp.* 38°52′ N, 3°42′ W 164
Almami, *Mali* 14°55′ N, 5°2′ W 222
Almansa, *Sp.* 38°51′ N, 1°6′ W 164
Almanza, *Sp.* 42°38′ N, 5°4′ W 150
Almanzor, peak, *Sp.* 40°13′ N, 5°23′ W 150
Almas, *Braz.* 11°35′ S, 47°9′ W 130
Almaş, *Rom.* 46°56′ N, 23°8′ E 168
Almaş, Munţii, *Rom.* 44°42′ N, 22°4′ E 168
Almas, river, *Braz.* 15°8′ S, 49°18′ W 138
Almassora see Almazora, *Sp.* 39°57′ N, 0°3′ W 150
Almaty, *Kaz.* 43°15′ N, 76°57′ E 184
Almaty, adm. division, *Kaz.* 44°42′ N, 75°55′ E 184
Almazán, *Sp.* 41°28′ N, 2°32′ W 164
Almaznoe, *Kaz.* 50°13′ N, 54°14′ E 158
Almazora (Almassora), *Sp.* 39°57′ N, 0°3′ W 150
Almeirim, *Braz.* 1°31′ S, 52°36′ W 130
Almelo, *Neth.* 52°20′ N, 6°39′ E 163
Almena, *Kans., U.S.* 39°53′ N, 99°43′ W 90
Almenar, *Sp.* 41°46′ N, 0°34′ E 164
Almenara, *Braz.* 16°11′ S, 40°45′ W 138
Almenara, peak, *Sp.* 38°32′ N, 2°29′ W 164
Almendra, *Sp.* 41°34′ N, 5°54′ W 150
Almendralejo, *Sp.* 38°41′ N, 6°25′ W 164
Almere, *Neth.* 52°20′ N, 5°9′ E 163
Almería, *Sp.* 36°49′ N, 2°28′ W 164
Al'met'yevsk, *Russ.* 54°51′ N, 52°17′ E 154
Almina, Punta, *Sp.* 35°53′ N, 5°17′ W 164
Almo, *Idaho, U.S.* 42°6′ N, 113°38′ W 92
Almonaster la Real, *Sp.* 37°51′ N, 6°48′ W 164

Almond Mountain, *Can.* 49°17' N, 118°42' W 90
Almont, *Mich., U.S.* 42°55' N, 83°4' W 102
Almonte, *Can.* 45°13' N, 76°11' W 94
Almonte, *Sp.* 37°15' N, 6°31' W 164
Almonte, river, *Sp.* 39°32' N, 6°18' W 164
Almoradí, *Sp.* 38°6' N, 0°48' E 164
Almudévar, *Sp.* 42°2' N, 0°36' E 164
Almuñécar, *Sp.* 36°43' N, 3°41' W 164
Almunge, *Sw.* 59°52' N, 18°0' E 166
Almuradiel, *Sp.* 38°30' N, 3°30' W 164
Almus, *Turk.* 40°22' N, 36°53' E 156
Almvik, *Nor.* 57°49' N, 16°27' E 152
Alnif, *Mor.* 31°8' N, 5°12' W 214
Aloja, *Latv.* 57°45' N, 24°52' E 166
Alonsa, *Can.* 50°48' N, 98°59' W 90
Alor, island, *Indonesia* 8°9' S, 124°15' E 192
Alor Setar, *Malaysia* 6°4' N, 100°24' E 196
Álora, *Sp.* 36°49' N, 4°43' W 164
Alot, *India* 23°45' N, 75°31' E 197
Aloysius, Mount, *Austral.* 26°3' S, 128°22' E 230
Alpachiri, *Arg.* 37°25' S, 63°44' W 139
Alpaugh, *Calif., U.S.* 35°53' N, 119°30' W 100
Alpedrinha, *Port.* 40°5' N, 7°29' W 150
Alpena, *Mich., U.S.* 45°3' N, 83°28' W 94
Alpera, *Sp.* 38°56' N, 1°14' W 164
Alpercatas, Serra das, *Braz.* 6°24' S, 46°9' W 130
Alpha Ridge, *Arctic Ocean* 85°33' N, 120°28' W 255
Alpine, *Ariz., U.S.* 33°50' N, 109°7' W 92
Alpine, *Calif., U.S.* 32°50' N, 116°47' W 101
Alpine, *Tex., U.S.* 30°20' N, 103°40' W 92
Alps, mountains, *Europe* 44°14' N, 6°2' E 165
Al-Quds see Jerusalem, *Israel* 31°46' N, 35°9' E 194
Alsace, adm. division, *Fr.* 47°41' N, 7°21' E 150
Alsace, region, *Europe* 48°41' N, 7°17' E 163
Alsask, *Can.* 51°23' N, 109°59' W 90
Alsdorf, *Ger.* 50°52' N, 6°10' E 167
Alsea, river, *Oreg., U.S.* 44°18' N, 124°1' W 90
Alsfeld, *Ger.* 50°45' N, 9°16' E 167
Alstahaug, *Nor.* 65°53' N, 12°23' E 152
Alstead, *N.H., U.S.* 43°8' N, 72°22' W 104
Alston, *U.K.* 54°48' N, 2°26' W 162
Alsunga, *Latv.* 56°58' N, 21°32' E 166
Alta, *Iowa, U.S.* 42°39' N, 95°19' W 90
Alta, *Nor.* 69°56' N, 23°12' E 152
Alta Coloma, peak, *Sp.* 37°34' N, 3°36' W 164
Alta Sierra, *Calif., U.S.* 35°43' N, 118°34' W 101
Altagracia, *Venez.* 10°43' N, 71°32' W 136
Altagracia de Orituco, *Venez.* 9°51' N, 66°25' W 136
Altamachi, *Bol.* 16°54' S, 66°23' W 137
Altamachi, river, *Bol.* 16°4' S, 66°58' W 137
Altamaha, river, *Ga., U.S.* 31°52' N, 82°32' W 80
Altamira, *Braz.* 1°38' N, 67°12' W 136
Altamira, *Braz.* 3°13' S, 52°16' W 130
Altamira, *Chile* 25°48' S, 69°53' W 132
Altamira, *Col.* 2°4' N, 75°50' W 136
Altamira, *C.R.* 10°29' N, 84°22' W 116
Altamira, *Mex.* 22°23' N, 97°56' W 114
Altamont, *Ill., U.S.* 39°3' N, 88°45' W 102
Altamont, *N.Y., U.S.* 42°42' N, 74°3' W 104
Altamura, Isla de, island, *Mex.* 24°52' N, 109°26' W 112
Altan Xiret see Ejin Horo Qi, *China* 39°33' N, 109°44' E 198
Altano, Capo, *It.* 39°15' N, 7°47' E 156
Altar, *Mex.* 30°43' N, 111°51' W 92
Altar, Desierto de, *Mex.* 32°29' N, 114°39' W 101
Altares, *Mex.* 28°50' N, 103°22' W 92
Altata, *Mex.* 24°37' N, 107°56' W 112
Altaville, *Calif., U.S.* 38°5' N, 120°34' W 100
Altavista, *Va., U.S.* 37°6' N, 79°18' W 96
Altay, *China* 47°53' N, 88°12' E 184
Altay, *Mongolia* 46°18' N, 96°16' E 190
Altay, *Russ.* 60°18' N, 68°55' E 169
Altay, adm. division, *Russ.* 52°16' N, 81°43' E 184
Altay Mountains, *Asia* 53°12' N, 81°13' E 184
Altayskiy, *Russ.* 51°57' N, 85°25' E 184
Altdorf, *Ger.* 48°33' N, 12°6' E 152
Altdorf, *Switz.* 46°52' N, 8°38' E 167
Altea, *Sp.* 38°36' N, 0°3' W 164
Altena, *Ger.* 51°16' N, 7°39' E 167
Altenberge, *Ger.* 52°2' N, 7°28' E 167
Altenbruch, *Ger.* 53°48' N, 8°46' E 163
Altenkirchen, *Ger.* 50°41' N, 7°39' E 167
Alter do Chão, *Braz.* 2°30' S, 55°2' W 130
Altıağac, *Azerb.* 40°52' N, 48°57' E 195
Altınekin, *Turk.* 38°17' N, 32°52' E 156
Altıntaş, *Turk.* 39°4' N, 30°7' E 156
Altınyayla, *Turk.* 36°59' N, 29°32' E 156
Altiplano, *Bol.-Peru* 18°49' S, 68°8' W 137
Altkirch, *Fr.* 47°37' N, 7°13' E 150
Alto, *La., U.S.* 32°20' N, 91°52' W 103
Alto, *Tex., U.S.* 31°38' N, 95°5' W 103
Alto Araguaia, *Braz.* 17°22' S, 53°17' W 138
Alto, Cerro, peak, *Tex., U.S.* 31°54' N, 106°1' W 92
Alto Chicapa, *Angola* 10°54' S, 19°12' E 220
Alto Garças, *Braz.* 16°58' S, 53°32' W 138
Alto Ligonha, *Mozambique* 15°32' S, 38°17' E 224
Alto Molócuè, *Mozambique* 15°37' S, 37°42' E 224
Alto Paraguai, *Braz.* 14°36' S, 56°36' W 132
Alto Paraíso de Goias, *Braz.* 14°8' S, 47°31' W 138
Alto Paraná, *Braz.* 23°6' S, 52°30' W 138
Alto Parnaíba, *Braz.* 9°7' S, 45°59' W 132
Alto Purús, river, *Peru* 10°46' S, 71°45' W 137
Alto Río Senguerr, *Arg.* 45°3' S, 70°50' W 134
Alto Sucuriú, *Braz.* 19°17' S, 52°50' W 138
Alto Taquari, *Braz.* 17°52' S, 53°18' W 138
Alto Uruguai, *Braz.* 27°22' S, 54°9' W 139
Alto Yuruá, river, *Braz.* 9°10' S, 72°49' W 137
Alton, *Calif., U.S.* 40°33' N, 124°9' W 90
Alton, *Iowa, U.S.* 42°57' N, 96°2' W 90
Alton, *Mo., U.S.* 38°53' N, 90°11' W 94
Alton, *N.H., U.S.* 43°27' N, 71°14' W 104
Alton, *N.Z.* 39°40' S, 174°25' E 240
Alton, *U.K.* 51°8' N, 0°59' E 162
Alton Bay, *N.H., U.S.* 43°28' N, 71°16' W 104
Alton, oil field, *Austral.* 27°55' S, 149°8' E 230
Altona, *Can.* 49°5' N, 97°34' W 90
Altona, *Ger.* 53°33' N, 9°58' E 150
Altoona, *Wis., U.S.* 44°47' N, 91°26' W 94
Altotonga, *Mex.* 19°45' N, 97°15' W 114
Altrincham, *U.K.* 53°23' N, 2°21' W 162
Altun Ha, ruin(s), *Belize* 17°45' N, 88°29' W 115
Altunhisar, *Turk.* 37°59' N, 34°21' E 156
Alturas, *Calif., U.S.* 41°29' N, 120°34' W 90
Altus, *Okla., U.S.* 34°37' N, 99°20' W 92
Aluk, *Sudan* 8°23' N, 27°29' E 224
Alūksne, *Latv.* 57°25' N, 27°0' E 166
Aluniş, *Rom.* 46°53' N, 24°50' E 156
Alunite, *Nev., U.S.* 35°58' N, 114°55' W 101
Alupka, *Ukr.* 44°25' N, 34°0' E 156
Alushta, *Ukr.* 44°40' N, 34°20' E 156
Alustante, *Sp.* 40°36' N, 1°40' W 164
Alva, *Okla., U.S.* 36°47' N, 98°40' W 92
Alvajärvi, *Fin.* 63°26' N, 25°21' E 152
Alvarado, *Mex.* 18°45' N, 95°45' W 114
Alvarado, *Tex., U.S.* 32°24' N, 97°11' W 96
Alvarães, *Braz.* 3°15' S, 64°56' W 130
Álvaro Obregón, Presa, lake, *Mex.* 28°1' N, 111°16' W 81
Alvdal, *Nor.* 62°5' N, 10°39' E 152
Alvear, *Arg.* 29°4' S, 56°33' W 139
Alvin, *Ill., U.S.* 40°18' N, 87°36' W 102
Alvin, *Tex., U.S.* 29°24' N, 95°14' W 103
Alvinston, *Can.* 42°49' N, 81°51' W 102
Alvito, *Port.* 38°14' N, 8°0' W 150
Alvkarleby, *Sw.* 60°32' N, 17°22' E 166
Alvorada, *Braz.* 12°33' S, 49°9' W 130
Alvord, *Tex., U.S.* 33°21' N, 97°42' W 92
Alvord Desert, *Oreg., U.S.* 42°35' N, 118°19' W 90
Älvros, *Nor.* 62°3' N, 14°37' E 152
Älvsbyn, *Nor.* 65°40' N, 20°58' E 152
Alwar, *India* 27°33' N, 76°36' E 197
Alxa Zuoqi, *China* 38°51' N, 105°44' E 198
Alyangula, *Austral.* 13°52' S, 136°30' E 173
Alysardakh, *Russ.* 65°53' N, 131°29' E 160
Alytus, *Lith.* 54°23' N, 24°1' E 166
Alyzia, ruin(s), *Gr.* 38°40' N, 20°49' E 156
Alzada, *Mont., U.S.* 45°0' N, 104°24' W 90
Alzenau, *Ger.* 50°5' N, 9°3' E 167
Alzira, *Sp.* 39°7' N, 0°29' E 214
Am Dam, *Chad* 12°45' N, 20°28' E 216
Am Djéména, *Chad* 13°6' N, 17°19' E 216
Am Djeress, spring, *Chad* 16°7' N, 22°54' E 226
Am Khoumi, *Chad* 12°48' N, 19°43' E 216
Am Léiouna, *Chad* 12°47' N, 21°49' E 216
Am Timan, *Chad* 11°0' N, 20°18' E 216
Am Zoer, *Chad* 14°11' N, 21°22' E 216
Amacayacu National Park, *Col.* 3°48' S, 70°34' W 136
Amada Gaza, *Cen. Af. Rep.* 4°45' N, 15°10' E 218
Amada, ruin(s), *Egypt* 22°41' N, 32°11' E 182
Amadi, *Dem. Rep. of the Congo* 3°37' N, 26°45' E 224
Amadi, *Sudan* 5°30' N, 30°21' E 218
Amadjuak Lake, *Can.* 64°49' N, 73°51' W 106
Amadora, *Port.* 38°45' N, 9°15' W 150
Amagansett, *N.Y., U.S.* 40°58' N, 72°10' W 104
Amagi, *Japan* 33°24' N, 130°39' E 201
Amaiur-Maia, *Sp.* 43°11' N, 1°28' W 164
Åmål, *Nor.* 59°2' N, 12°38' E 152
Amal, oil field, *Lib.* 29°23' N, 21°3' E 216
Amalfi, *Col.* 6°57' N, 75°5' W 136
Amalyk, *Russ.* 57°31' N, 116°39' E 173
Amamapare, *Indonesia* 4°47' S, 136°38' E 238
Amambaí, *Braz.* 23°6' S, 55°16' W 134
Amambaí, river, *Braz.* 22°48' S, 54°50' W 132
Amambaí, Serra de, *Braz.* 23°18' S, 55°51' W 132
Amami Ō Shima, island, *Japan* 28°23' N, 129°46' E 190
Amamula, *Dem. Rep. of the Congo* 0°19' N, 27°46' E 224
Amanda, *Ohio, U.S.* 39°38' N, 82°45' W 102
Amanda Park, *Wash., U.S.* 47°25' N, 123°53' W 100
Amangeldi, *Kaz.* 50°11' N, 65°13' E 184
Amaniú, river, *Braz.* 1°19' S, 67°42' W 136
Amanos Dağları, *Turk.* 36°14' N, 36°0' E 156
Amantea, *It.* 39°9' N, 16°4' E 156
Amapá, *Braz.* 10°19' S, 69°28' W 137
Amapá, *Braz.* 2°2' N, 50°50' W 130
Amapá, adm. division, *Braz.* 1°12' N, 53°2' W 130
Amarante, *Braz.* 6°17' S, 42°51' W 132
Amardalay, *Mongolia* 46°7' N, 106°22' E 198
Amargosa, *Braz.* 13°1' S, 39°38' W 138
Amargosa Desert, *Nev., U.S.* 36°47' N, 116°46' W 101
Amargosa Range, *Calif., U.S.* 36°17' N, 116°48' W 101
Amargosa Valley, *Nev., U.S.* 36°38' N, 116°25' W 101
Amarillo, *Tex., U.S.* 35°10' N, 101°51' W 92
Amarkantak, *India* 22°40' N, 81°46' E 197
Amaro, Monte, peak, *It.* 42°4' N, 14°1' E 156
Amarpur, *India* 23°30' N, 91°37' E 197
Amarwara, *India* 22°19' N, 79°10' E 197
Amasa, *Mich., U.S.* 46°14' N, 88°27' W 94
Amasia see Amasya, *Turk.* 40°40' N, 35°50' E 156
Amasine, *Western Sahara, Mor.* 25°48' N, 13°20' W 214
Amasra, *Turk.* 41°44' N, 32°24' E 156
Amasya (Amasia), *Turk.* 40°40' N, 35°50' E 156
Amatari, *Braz.* 3°16' S, 58°55' W 130
Amataurá, *Braz.* 3°32' S, 68°4' W 136
Amatepec, *Mex.* 18°38' N, 100°9' W 114
Amathous, ruin(s), *Cyprus* 34°42' N, 33°5' E 194
Amatlán de Cañas, *Mex.* 20°49' N, 104°27' W 114
Amavon Islands, *Solomon Sea* 7°0' S, 158°0' E 242
Amay, *Belg.* 50°33' N, 5°18' E 167
Amazar, *Russ.* 53°50' N, 120°55' E 190
Amazon Fan, *North Atlantic Ocean* 5°17' N, 46°22' W 253
Amazon see Amazonas, river, *Braz.* 3°8' S, 55°59' W 123
Amazonas, adm. division, *Braz.* 5°31' S, 65°36' W 130
Amazonas (Amazon), river, *Braz.* 3°8' S, 55°59' W 123
Amazonas see Solimões, river, *Braz.* 2°50' S, 66°35' W 123
Amazônia National Park, *Braz.* 4°19' S, 57°15' W 130
Amb, *Pak.* 34°14' N, 72°48' E 186
Āmba Gīyorgīs, *Eth.* 12°41' N, 37°37' E 218
Āmba Maryam, *Eth.* 11°23' N, 39°16' E 182
Ambala, *India* 30°21' N, 76°50' E 197
Ambalangoda, *Sri Lanka* 6°16' N, 80°4' E 188
Ambalantota, *Sri Lanka* 6°7' N, 81°4' E 188
Ambarchik, *Russ.* 69°33' N, 162°14' E 160
Ambato, *Ecua.* 1°21' S, 78°48' W 130
Ambato Boeny, *Madagascar* 16°27' S, 46°44' E 220
Ambatolampy, *Madagascar* 19°24' S, 47°27' E 220
Ambatondrazaka, *Madagascar* 18°0' S, 48°24' E 207
Ambazac, *Fr.* 45°57' N, 1°23' E 150
Ambelau, island, *Indonesia* 4°17' S, 127°15' E 192
Ambergris Cay, island, *Belize* 17°58' N, 87°52' W 115
Ambergris Cays, islands, *North Atlantic Ocean* 21°19' N, 72°57' W 116
Amberley, *Can.* 44°1' N, 81°42' W 102
Amberley, *N.Z.* 43°10' S, 172°44' E 240
Amberley, *U.K.* 50°54' N, 0°32' E 162
Ambidédi, *Mali* 14°34' N, 11°50' W 222
Ambikapur, *India* 23°7' N, 83°12' E 197
Ambilobe, *Madagascar* 13°13' S, 49°2' E 220
Ambla, *Est.* 59°10' N, 25°48' E 166
Ambler, *Alas., U.S.* 67°5' N, 157°52' W 98
Ambleside, *U.K.* 54°25' N, 2°58' W 162
Ambleteuse, *Fr.* 50°48' N, 1°36' E 163
Ambo, *Peru* 10°11' S, 76°10' W 130
Amboasary, *Madagascar* 25°4' S, 46°26' E 220
Ambodifotatra, *Madagascar* 16°58' S, 49°51' E 220
Ambohimahasoa, *Madagascar* 21°6' S, 47°13' E 220
Ambohimanga Atsimo, *Madagascar* 20°53' S, 47°36' E 220
Amboise, *Fr.* 47°24' N, 0°58' E 150
Amboiva, *Angola* 11°34' S, 14°44' E 220
Ambolauri, *Ga.* 42°28' N, 43°9' E 195
Ambon, *Indonesia* 3°41' S, 128°3' E 192
Amboró National Park, *Bol.* 17°42' S, 64°48' W 137
Ambarompotsy, *Madagascar* 20°35' S, 46°14' E 220
Amboseli National Park, *Kenya* 2°50' S, 37°15' E 224
Amboy, *Ill., U.S.* 41°42' N, 89°20' W 102
Amboy Crater, *Calif., U.S.* 34°31' N, 115°48' W 101
Ambre, Cap d', *Madagascar* 12°1' S, 49°15' E 220
Ambre, Montagne d', peak, *Madagascar* 12°41' S, 48°58' E 220
Ambriz, *Angola* 7°51' S, 13°6' E 218
Ambrogio, *It.* 44°55' N, 11°55' E 167
Ambrósio, *Braz.* 2°53' S, 68°19' W 136
Amburan Burnu, *Azerb.* 40°36' N, 49°49' E 195
Amchitka, island, *Alas., U.S.* 51°7' N, 177°20' E 160
Amderma, *Russ.* 69°42' N, 61°41' E 169
Amdillis, spring, *Mali* 18°24' N, 0°17' E 222
Amdo, *China* 32°19' N, 91°44' E 188
Ameca, *Mex.* 20°33' N, 104°3' W 114
Ameca, river, *Mex.* 20°55' N, 105°12' W 114
Ameghino, *Arg.* 34°51' S, 62°28' W 139
Ameland, island, *Neth.* 53°28' N, 5°37' E 163
Amelia, *La., U.S.* 29°40' N, 91°7' W 103
Amenia, *N.Y., U.S.* 41°50' N, 73°34' W 104
America-Antarctic Ridge (North Weddell Ridge), *South Atlantic Ocean* 59°0' S, 16°0' W 255
American Highland, *Antarctica* 74°55' S, 76°3' E 248
American, river, *Wash., U.S.* 46°53' N, 121°26' W 100
American Samoa, *United States* 14°0' S, 171°0' W 238
Americus, *Ga., U.S.* 32°3' N, 84°15' W 112
Amersfoort, *S. Af.* 27°2' S, 29°51' E 227
Amery, *Wis., U.S.* 45°18' N, 92°23' W 94
Amery Ice Shelf, *Antarctica* 71°16' S, 69°44' E 248
Ames, *Iowa, U.S.* 42°0' N, 93°37' W 94
Amesbury, *Mass., U.S.* 42°50' N, 70°57' W 104
Amesbury, *U.K.* 51°10' N, 1°47' W 162
Amga, *Russ.* 61°1' N, 131°52' E 160
Amga, river, *Russ.* 59°34' N, 126°34' E 160
Amgu, *Russ.* 45°56' N, 137°30' E 190
Amguema, river, *Russ.* 67°26' N, 178°38' W 98
Amguid, *Alg.* 26°26' N, 5°23' E 214
Amhara, region, *Africa* 12°12' N, 36°11' E 182
Amherst, *Can.* 45°49' N, 64°13' W 111
Amherst, *N.H., U.S.* 42°51' N, 71°38' W 104
Amherst, *N.Y., U.S.* 42°58' N, 78°50' W 94
Amherst, *Ohio, U.S.* 41°23' N, 82°14' W 102
Amherst, *Tex., U.S.* 33°59' N, 102°23' W 92
Amherst, *Va., U.S.* 37°34' N, 79°4' W 96
Amherstburg, *Can.* 42°5' N, 83°6' W 102
Amhovichy, *Belarus* 53°6' N, 27°50' E 158
Amiata, Monte, peak, *It.* 42°53' N, 11°32' E 156
Amidon, *N. Dak., U.S.* 46°27' N, 103°19' W 90
Amiens, *Fr.* 49°52' N, 2°18' E 163
Amili, *India* 28°23' N, 95°50' E 188
Amino, *Japan* 35°39' N, 135°1' E 201
Aminuis, *Namibia* 23°43' S, 19°18' E 227
Amiot Islands, *South Pacific Ocean* 67°26' S, 74°9' W 248
Amioun, *Leb.* 34°17' N, 35°48' E 194
Amirante Isles, *Indian Ocean* 4°41' S, 51°23' E 173
Amirante Trench, *Indian Ocean* 9°12' S, 53°16' E 254
Amisk Lake, lake, *Can.* 54°33' N, 102°35' W 108
Amisk, river, *Can.* 54°40' N, 112°29' W 108
Amistad National Recreation Area, *Tex., U.S.* 29°32' N, 101°42' W 96
Amistad Reservoir, lake, *Tex., U.S.* 29°33' N, 101°44' W 92
Amisus see Samsun, *Turk.* 41°17' N, 36°20' E 158
Amite, *La., U.S.* 30°42' N, 90°31' W 103
Amity, *Ark., U.S.* 34°14' N, 93°28' W 96
Amla, *India* 21°56' N, 78°9' E 197
Åmli, *Nor.* 58°45' N, 8°29' E 152
Amlia, island, *Alas., U.S.* 52°10' N, 173°59' W 160
'Amm Adam, *Sudan* 16°21' N, 36°4' E 182
'Ammān (Philadelphia), *Jordan* 31°56' N, 35°53' E 194
Ammanford, *U.K.* 51°47' N, 4°0' W 162
Ammänsaari, *Fin.* 64°50' N, 28°52' E 152
Ammarfjället, peak, *Nor.* 66°4' N, 15°30' E 152
Ammarnäs, *Nor.* 65°57' N, 16°10' E 152
Ammeloe, *Ger.* 52°4' N, 6°47' E 167
Ammochostos (Famagusta, Gazimagusa), *Northern Cyprus, Cyprus* 35°7' N, 33°56' E 194
Amo, *Ind., U.S.* 39°41' N, 86°37' W 102
Āmol, *Iran* 36°36' N, 52°17' E 180
Amolar, *Braz.* 18°1' S, 57°31' W 132
Amos, *Can.* 48°34' N, 78°8' W 94
Amot, *Mor.* 27°57' N, 10°6' W 214
Åmot, *Nor.* 59°36' N, 7°57' E 152
Åmotfors, *Nor.* 59°47' N, 12°24' E 152
Amoúdia, peak, *Gr.* 37°31' N, 25°56' E 156
Amoy see Xiamen, *China* 24°25' N, 118°6' E 198
Ampani, *India* 19°34' N, 82°36' E 188
Ampanihy, *Madagascar* 24°39' S, 44°42' E 220
Amparafaravola, *Madagascar* 17°36' S, 48°13' E 220
Amparihy Est, *Madagascar* 23°58' S, 47°22' E 220
Amparo, *Braz.* 22°42' S, 46°47' W 138
Ampato, Nevado, peak, *Peru* 15°52' S, 71°55' W 137
Ampere, *Braz.* 25°57' S, 53°30' W 139
Ampezzo, *It.* 46°23' N, 12°47' E 167
Amphiareion, ruin(s), *Gr.* 38°17' N, 23°43' E 156
Amphitrite Point, *Can.* 48°43' N, 125°48' W 90
Amposta, *Sp.* 40°42' N, 0°34' E 164
Ampthill, *U.K.* 52°1' N, 0°30' E 162
Amqui, *Can.* 48°27' N, 67°27' W 94
'Amrān, *Yemen* 15°40' N, 43°57' E 182
Amravati, *India* 20°56' N, 77°46' E 188
Amreli, *India* 21°36' N, 71°12' E 186
'Amrīt (Marathus), ruin(s), *Syr.* 34°50' N, 35°52' E 194
'Amrīt, ruin(s), *Syr.* 34°48' N, 35°49' E 156
Amritsar, *India* 31°39' N, 74°52' E 186
Amroha, *India* 28°54' N, 78°28' E 188
Amsā'ad, *Lib.* 31°37' N, 25°2' E 180
'Amshīt, *Leb.* 34°9' N, 35°38' E 194
Amsterdam, *Neth.* 52°22' N, 4°50' E 163
Amsterdam, *N.Y., U.S.* 42°56' N, 74°12' W 104
Amsterdam, island, *Fr.* 37°45' S, 78°0' E 254
Amstetten, *Aust.* 48°7' N, 14°51' E 152
Amston, *Conn., U.S.* 41°37' N, 72°21' W 104
Amu Darya, river, *Uzb.* 41°1' N, 61°42' E 184
Amuay, *Venez.* 11°51' N, 70°4' W 123
'Āmūdah, *Syr.* 37°6' N, 40°57' E 195
Amukta, island, *Alas., U.S.* 52°4' N, 171°7' W 160
Amuku Mountains, *Guyana* 2°4' N, 58°12' W 130
Amundsen Basin *Arctic Ocean* 88°0' N, 90°0' E 255
Amundsen Gulf 70°20' N, 123°56' W 98
Amundsen, Mount, *Antarctica* 67°13' S, 101°28' E 248
Amundsen Plain *South Pacific Ocean* 65°0' S, 125°0' W 255
Amundsen Sea 73°41' S, 105°21' W 248
Amundsen-Scott South Pole, station, *Antarctica* 89°59' S, 164°21' W 248
Amur, adm. division, *Russ.* 53°36' N, 124°46' E 190
Amur, river, *Russ.* 51°18' N, 138°37' E 190
Amurang, *Indonesia* 1°13' N, 124°28' E 192
Amurrio, *Sp.* 43°2' N, 3°1' W 164
Amusco, *Sp.* 42°10' N, 4°28' W 150
Amvrosiyivka, *Ukr.* 47°44' N, 38°26' E 158
Amydery'a, *Turkm.* 37°56' N, 65°18' E 197
An, *Myanmar* 19°46' N, 94°7' E 202
An Khe, *Vietnam* 13°58' N, 108°40' E 202
An Nabī Shīt, *Leb.* 33°52' N, 36°6' E 194
An Nabk, *Syr.* 34°1' N, 36°44' E 194
An Nabk Abū Qaşr, spring, *Saudi Arabia* 30°18' N, 38°41' E 180
An Nafūd, *Saudi Arabia* 28°35' N, 39°18' E 180
An Najaf (Najaf), *Iraq* 31°58' N, 44°19' E 180
An Namatah, *Jordan* 30°48' N, 35°32' E 194
An Nashshāsh, *U.A.E.* 23°1' N, 54°3' E 182
An Nāşirīyah, *Syr.* 33°52' N, 36°48' E 194
An Nāşirīyah (Nasiriyah), *Iraq* 31°5' N, 46°11' E 180
An Nawfalīyah, *Lib.* 30°41' N, 17°49' E 143
An Nimāş, *Saudi Arabia* 19°2' N, 42°9' E 182
An Nu'ayrīyah, *Saudi Arabia* 27°28' N, 48°27' E 196
An Pass, *Myanmar* 19°59' N, 94°17' E 202
An Phuoc, *Vietnam* 11°36' N, 108°54' E 202
An Uaimh see Navan, *Ire.* 53°38' N, 6°42' W 150
Ana María, Cayos, islands, *Caribbean Sea* 21°11' N, 79°29' W 116
Anabar, river, *Russ.* 70°31' N, 114°9' E 160
Anabarskiy Zaliv 73°25' N, 108°6' E 160
Anacapa Island, *North Pacific Ocean* 34°4' N, 119°29' W 100
Anaco, *Venez.* 9°26' N, 64°30' W 116
Anacoco, *La., U.S.* 31°14' N, 93°21' W 103
Anaconda, *Mont., U.S.* 46°7' N, 112°58' W 90
Anaconda Range, *Mont., U.S.* 45°49' N, 113°46' W 90
Anacortes, *Wash., U.S.* 48°28' N, 122°38' W 100
Anactorium, ruin(s), *Gr.* 38°55' N, 20°45' E 156
Anadyr', *Russ.* 64°38' N, 177°6' E 160
Anadyr, Gulf of see Anadyrskiy Zaliv 66°48' N, 179°18' W 160
Anadyr', river, *Russ.* 66°42' N, 169°30' E 160
Anadyrskiy Zaliv (Anadyr, Gulf of) 66°48' N, 179°18' W 160
Anáfi, *Gr.* 36°20' N, 25°46' E 156
Anáfi, island, *Gr.* 36°24' N, 25°52' E 180
Anagé, *Braz.* 14°45' S, 41°10' W 138
Anaghit, *Eritrea* 16°20' N, 38°35' E 182
'Ānah, *Iraq* 34°25' N, 41°58' E 180
Anaheim, *Calif., U.S.* 33°50' N, 117°56' W 101
Anahim Lake, *Can.* 52°28' N, 125°20' W 108
Anahola, *Hawai'i, U.S.* 22°8' N, 159°19' W 99
Anáhuac, *Mex.* 27°13' N, 100°9' W 96
Anáhuac, *Mex.* 24°27' N, 101°31' W 114

Anahuac, *Tex., U.S.* 29°45′ N, 94°41′ W 103
Anai Mudi, peak, *India* 10°8′ N, 76°55′ E 188
Anaï, spring, *Alg.* 24°9′ N, 11°27′ E 214
Anajás, *Braz.* 1°0′ N, 49°58′ W 130
Anak, *N. Korea* 38°29′ N, 125°29′ E 200
Anaktuvuk Pass, *Alas., U.S.* 68°11′ N, 151°54′ W 98
Analalava, *Madagascar* 14°38′ S, 47°47′ E 220
Analavelona, peak, *Madagascar* 22°36′ S, 44°2′ E 220
Anamã, *Braz.* 3°33′ S, 61°30′ W 130
Anambas, Kepulauan, islands, *South China Sea* 2°41′ N, 105°43′ E 196
Anamizu, *Japan* 37°13′ N, 136°54′ E 201
Anamoose, *N. Dak., U.S.* 47°51′ N, 100°15′ W 90
Anamosa, *Iowa, U.S.* 42°6′ N, 91°17′ W 94
Anamu, river, *Braz.* 0°42′ N, 56°51′ W 130
Anamur, *Turk.* 36°5′ N, 32°51′ E 156
Anamur Burnu, *Azerb.* 36°2′ N, 32°4′ E 156
Anan, *Japan* 33°52′ N, 134°37′ E 201
Ananchichi, *Belarus* 52°31′ N, 27°39′ E 152
Anand, *India* 22°33′ N, 73°0′ E 186
Anan'yiv, *Ukr.* 47°43′ N, 29°58′ E 156
Anapa, *Russ.* 44°54′ N, 37°23′ E 156
Anápolis, *Braz.* 16°21′ S, 48°59′ W 138
Anār, *Iran* 30°51′ N, 55°18′ E 180
Anārak, *Iran* 33°20′ N, 53°43′ E 180
Ånäset, *Nor.* 64°14′ N, 21°2′ E 152
Anastasia Island, *Fla., U.S.* 29°52′ N, 81°16′ W 105
Anatahan, island, *U.S.* 16°12′ N, 144°27′ E 192
Anatolia (Asia Minor), region, *Asia* 38°39′ N, 30°18′ E 180
Anatolikí Makedonía Kai Thráki, adm. division, *Gr.* 41°5′ N, 15°57′ E 156
Anatone, *Wash., U.S.* 46°7′ N, 117°9′ W 90
Añatuya, *Arg.* 28°28′ S, 62°49′ W 139
Anauá, river, *Braz.* 0°57′ N, 60°9′ W 130
Anaurilândia, *Braz.* 22°2′ S, 52°48′ W 138
Añavieja, *Sp.* 41°51′ N, 1°56′ W 164
Anavilhanas, Arquipélago das, *South America* 3°13′ S, 62°22′ W 130
Anbyŏn, *N. Korea* 39°2′ N, 127°31′ E 200
Ancares, Sierra de, *Sp.* 42°54′ N, 7°7′ W 150
Ancash, adm. division, *Peru* 9°4′ S, 78°36′ W 130
Ancasti, Sierra de, *Arg.* 28°4′ S, 65°55′ W 132
Anchieta, *Braz.* 20°51′ S, 40°44′ W 138
Anchorage, *Alas., U.S.* 61°5′ N, 149°53′ W 98
Anchorena, *Arg.* 35°40′ S, 65°23′ W 134
Anclitas, Cayo, island, *Cuba* 20°30′ N, 79°14′ W 116
Ancona, *It.* 43°36′ N, 13°30′ E 167
Ancram, *N.Y., U.S.* 42°2′ N, 73°40′ W 104
Ancuabe, *Mozambique* 13°2′ S, 39°54′ E 224
Ancud, *Chile* 41°59′ S, 73°55′ W 123
Ancud, Golfo de 42°13′ S, 73°45′ W 134
Ancy-le-Franc, *Fr.* 47°46′ N, 4°9′ E 150
Anda, *China* 46°22′ N, 125°24′ E 198
Andacollo, *Arg.* 37°13′ S, 70°40′ W 134
Andahuaylas, *Peru* 13°41′ S, 73°24′ W 137
Andalgalá, *Arg.* 27°36′ S, 66°19′ W 132
Åndalsnes, *Nor.* 62°33′ N, 7°42′ E 152
Andalusia, *Ala., U.S.* 31°18′ N, 86°28′ W 96
Andalusia, adm. division, *Sp.* 37°27′ N, 4°53′ W 164
Andaman and Nicobar Islands, *India* 11°25′ N, 92°50′ E 192
Andaman Basin, *Andaman Sea* 9°56′ N, 95°4′ E 254
Andaman Islands, *Andaman Sea* 12°47′ N, 94°43′ E 202
Andaman Sea 15°15′ N, 94°7′ E 188
Andapa, *Madagascar* 14°39′ S, 49°40′ E 220
Andara, *Namibia* 18°3′ S, 21°32′ E 220
Andaraí, *Braz.* 11°49′ S, 41°21′ W 138
Andavaka, Cap, *Madagascar* 25°40′ S, 46°43′ E 220
Andeg, *Russ.* 67°55′ N, 53°10′ E 169
Andelot-Blancheville, *Fr.* 48°14′ N, 5°17′ E 163
Andenne, *Belg.* 50°29′ N, 5°5′ E 167
Andéranboukane, *Mali* 15°27′ N, 3°2′ E 222
Andermatt, *Switz.* 46°38′ N, 8°36′ E 167
Andernach, *Ger.* 50°26′ N, 7°23′ E 167
Anderson, *Calif., U.S.* 40°26′ N, 122°19′ W 90
Anderson, *Ind., U.S.* 40°5′ N, 85°41′ W 102
Anderson, *Mo., U.S.* 36°38′ N, 94°27′ W 96
Anderson, *S.C., U.S.* 34°29′ N, 82°40′ W 96
Anderson Dome, *Antarctica* 72°28′ S, 87°2′ W 248
Anderson Massif, *Antarctica* 78°56′ S, 82°12′ W 248
Anderson Ranch Dam, *Idaho, U.S.* 43°28′ N, 115°37′ W 90
Anderson, river, *Can.* 68°35′ N, 127°50′ W 98
Andersson Island, *Antarctica* 63°39′ S, 59°14′ W 134
Andes, Cordillera de los, mountains, *South America* 9°47′ S, 74°52′ W 136
Andhra Pradesh, adm. division, *India* 16°19′ N, 79°37′ E 188
Andijon, *Uzb.* 40°46′ N, 72°21′ E 197
Andikíra, *Gr.* 38°22′ N, 22°36′ E 156
Andikíthira, island, *Gr.* 35°48′ N, 22°23′ E 180
Andilálou, ruin(s), *Gr.* 41°29′ N, 24°9′ E 156
Andilamena, *Madagascar* 17°2′ S, 48°33′ E 220
Andir, river, *China* 36°34′ N, 84°8′ E 184
Andirá, *Braz.* 3°45′ S, 66°17′ W 136
Andırın, *Turk.* 37°34′ N, 36°21′ E 156
Andirlangar, *China* 37°37′ N, 83°47′ E 184
Andkhvoy, *Afghan.* 36°55′ N, 65°8′ E 186
Andoany (Hell-Ville), *Madagascar* 13°24′ S, 48°17′ E 207
Andoas, *Peru* 2°57′ S, 76°25′ W 136
Andomskiy Pogost, *Russ.* 61°14′ N, 36°39′ E 154
Andong, *S. Korea* 36°33′ N, 128°43′ E 200
Andorra la Vella, *Andorra* 42°29′ N, 1°26′ E 164
Andorra 42°29′ N, 1°26′ E 164
Andover, *Me., U.S.* 44°37′ N, 70°46′ W 94
Andover, *N.H., U.S.* 43°26′ N, 71°50′ W 104
Andover, *U.K.* 51°12′ N, 1°30′ W 162
Andovoranto, *Madagascar* 18°57′ S, 49°5′ E 220
Andøya, island, *Nor.* 69°24′ N, 14°6′ E 160
Andradina, *Braz.* 20°56′ S, 51°24′ W 138
Andreapol', *Russ.* 56°39′ N, 32°18′ E 154
Andreba, *Madagascar* 17°40′ S, 48°33′ E 220
Andrew, *Can.* 53°52′ N, 112°20′ W 108
Andrews, *Ind., U.S.* 40°50′ N, 85°37′ W 102
Andrews, *S.C., U.S.* 33°26′ N, 79°34′ W 96
Andrews, *Tex., U.S.* 32°18′ N, 102°33′ W 92
Andreyevka, *Russ.* 52°20′ N, 51°50′ E 158
Andrijevica, *Mont.* 42°43′ N, 19°47′ E 168
Androka, *Madagascar* 25°1′ S, 44°7′ E 220
Ándros, island, *Gr.* 37°54′ N, 24°57′ E 180
Androscoggin, river, *Me., U.S.* 44°23′ N, 71°6′ W 104
Andryushino, *Russ.* 59°17′ N, 62°59′ E 154
Andryushkino, *Russ.* 69°9′ N, 154°31′ E 160
Andújar, *Sp.* 38°2′ N, 4°3′ W 164
Andulo, *Angola* 11°31′ S, 16°41′ E 220
Aneby, *Nor.* 57°49′ N, 14°46′ E 152
Anefis I-n-Darane, *Mali* 18°2′ N, 0°37′ E 222
Anegada, island, *U.K.* 18°43′ N, 65°1′ W 116
Anegada, Punta, *Pan.* 7°14′ N, 81°48′ W 115
Añelo, Cuenca del, *Arg.* 37°56′ S, 69°57′ W 134
Anenii Noi, *Mold.* 46°52′ N, 29°13′ E 156
Aneroid, *Can.* 49°42′ N, 107°18′ W 90
Anet, *Fr.* 48°51′ N, 1°26′ E 163
Aneta, *N. Dak., U.S.* 47°39′ N, 98°0′ W 90
Aneto, peak, *Sp.* 42°37′ N, 0°36′ E 164
Aney, *Niger* 19°27′ N, 12°54′ E 216
Anfah, *Leb.* 34°21′ N, 35°44′ E 194
Angamos, Punta, *Chile* 23°1′ S, 71°22′ W 132
Angang, *S. Korea* 35°58′ N, 129°15′ E 200
Angangueo, *Mex.* 19°36′ N, 100°17′ W 114
Ang'angxi, *China* 47°7′ N, 123°48′ E 198
Angara, river, *Russ.* 58°38′ N, 98°21′ E 246
Angarsk, *Russ.* 52°43′ N, 103°32′ E 190
Angaur (Ngeaur), island, *Palau* 7°0′ N, 134°0′ E 242
Ånge, *Nor.* 62°31′ N, 15°37′ E 152
Ángel de la Guarda, Isla, island, *Mex.* 29°35′ N, 113°31′ W 112
Angel Falls, *Venez.* 4°34′ N, 63°39′ W 123
Angeles, *Philippines* 15°8′ N, 120°35′ E 203
Angélica, *Arg.* 31°33′ S, 61°32′ W 139
Angelina, river, *Tex., U.S.* 31°30′ N, 94°50′ W 103
Angels Camp, *Calif., U.S.* 38°4′ N, 120°33′ W 100
Angermünde, *Ger.* 53°1′ N, 14°0′ E 152
Angers, *Fr.* 47°28′ N, 0°33′ E 150
Angerville, *Fr.* 48°18′ N, 1°59′ E 163
Angical, *Braz.* 12°0′ S, 44°40′ W 132
Angie, *La., U.S.* 30°57′ N, 89°49′ W 103
Angkor, ruin(s), *Cambodia* 13°28′ N, 103°45′ E 202
Angle Inlet, *Minn., U.S.* 49°18′ N, 95°7′ W 90
Anglem, Mount, *N.Z.* 46°46′ S, 167°48′ E 240
Anglès, *Sp.* 41°56′ N, 2°38′ E 164
Angleton, *Tex., U.S.* 29°9′ N, 95°26′ W 103
Anglure, *Fr.* 48°35′ N, 3°48′ E 163
Ango, *Dem. Rep. of the Congo* 3°58′ N, 25°52′ E 224
Angoche, *Mozambique* 16°12′ S, 39°57′ E 224
Angohrān, *Iran* 26°33′ N, 57°50′ E 196
Angol, *Chile* 37°49′ S, 72°43′ W 134
Angola 12°18′ S, 17°4′ E 220
Angola, *Ind., U.S.* 41°38′ N, 85°0′ W 102
Angola, *La., U.S.* 30°56′ N, 91°34′ W 103
Angola, *N.Y., U.S.* 42°38′ N, 79°3′ W 94
Angola Plain, *South Atlantic Ocean* 15°4′ S, 3°22′ E 253
Angora see Ankara, *Turk.* 39°55′ N, 32°43′ E 156
Angostura, *Col.* 0°28′ N, 72°30′ W 136
Angostura, *Mex.* 25°21′ N, 108°10′ W 112
Angostura, Presa de la, *Mex.* 30°32′ N, 109°47′ W 92
Angoulême, *Fr.* 45°39′ N, 0°10′ E 150
Angouma, *Gabon* 1°11′ N, 12°19′ E 218
Angoumois, region, *Europe* 45°50′ N, 0°49′ E 165
Angra dos Reis, *Braz.* 23°2′ S, 44°20′ W 138
Angren, *Uzb.* 41°1′ N, 70°14′ E 197
Angtassom, *Cambodia* 11°1′ N, 104°39′ E 202
Angu, *Dem. Rep. of the Congo* 3°27′ N, 24°26′ E 224
Angüés, *Sp.* 42°6′ N, 0°9′ E 164
Anguil, *Arg.* 36°31′ S, 64°2′ W 139
Anguilla, *U.K.* 18°48′ N, 69°45′ W 116
Anguilla Cays, *North Atlantic Ocean* 23°19′ N, 79°28′ W 116
Anguille, Cape, *Can.* 47°49′ N, 60°20′ W 111
Angumu, *Dem. Rep. of the Congo* 0°7′ N, 27°39′ E 224
Anguo, *China* 38°26′ N, 115°21′ E 198
Angutikha, *Russ.* 65°58′ N, 87°24′ E 169
Angvik, *Nor.* 62°53′ N, 8°3′ E 152
Anhua, *China* 28°23′ N, 111°3′ E 198
Anhui, adm. division, *China* 31°34′ N, 117°12′ E 198
Aniak, *Alas., U.S.* 61°24′ N, 159°45′ W 98
Anicuns, *Braz.* 16°32′ S, 49°58′ W 138
Anie, Pic d', peak, *Fr.* 42°55′ N, 0°45′ E 164
Anikhovka, *Russ.* 51°29′ N, 60°15′ E 154
Animas, *N. Mex., U.S.* 31°57′ N, 108°47′ W 92
Animas Peak, *N. Mex., U.S.* 31°33′ N, 108°50′ W 92
Ánimas, Punta de las, *Mex.* 28°44′ N, 114°7′ W 112
Anin, *Myanmar* 15°41′ N, 97°46′ E 202
Aniñón, *Sp.* 41°26′ N, 1°43′ W 164
Anipemza, *Arm.* 40°26′ N, 43°36′ E 195
Anishinabi Lake, lake, *Can.* 50°26′ N, 94°1′ W 90
Anita, *Chile* 20°29′ S, 69°51′ W 137
Anita, *Pa., U.S.* 40°59′ N, 78°59′ W 94
Aniva, Mys, *Russ.* 45°46′ N, 142°25′ E 190
Anivorano, *Madagascar* 18°47′ S, 48°58′ E 220
Anixab, *Namibia* 20°58′ S, 14°46′ E 220
Anjalankoski, *Fin.* 60°41′ N, 26°51′ E 166
Anjiang, *China* 27°16′ N, 110°11′ E 198
Anjosvarden, peak, *Nor.* 61°24′ N, 14°7′ E 152
Anjou Islands, *East Siberian Sea* 74°45′ N, 144°8′ E 255
Anjou, region, *Europe* 47°39′ N, 1°10′ W 150
Anju, *N. Korea* 39°35′ N, 125°44′ E 198
Anka, spring, *Sudan* 14°37′ N, 24°51′ E 226
Ankang, *China* 32°36′ N, 109°3′ E 198
Ankara (Angora), *Turk.* 39°55′ N, 32°43′ E 156
Ankaramena, *Madagascar* 21°58′ S, 46°39′ E 220
Ankarede, *Nor.* 64°49′ N, 14°12′ E 152
Ankasakasa, *Madagascar* 16°22′ S, 44°50′ E 220
Ankazoabo, *Madagascar* 22°15′ S, 44°28′ E 220
Ankazobe, *Madagascar* 18°20′ S, 47°8′ E 220
Anklam, *Ger.* 53°51′ N, 13°41′ E 152
Ānkober, *Eth.* 9°31′ N, 39°42′ E 224
Ankofa, peak, *Madagascar* 16°23′ S, 48°27′ E 220
Ankoro, *Dem. Rep. of the Congo* 6°48′ S, 26°52′ E 224
Ankpa, *Nig.* 7°21′ N, 7°36′ E 222
Anlong, *China* 25°0′ N, 105°26′ E 198
Anlu, *China* 31°14′ N, 113°42′ E 198
Ann Arbor, *Mich., U.S.* 42°15′ N, 83°46′ W 102
Ann, Cape, *Mass., U.S.* 42°36′ N, 70°36′ W 104
Anna, *Mo., U.S.* 37°27′ N, 89°14′ W 96
Anna Paulowna, *Neth.* 52°52′ N, 4°50′ E 163
Annaba (Bône), *Alg.* 36°53′ N, 7°45′ E 156
Annai, *Guyana* 3°55′ N, 59°7′ W 130
Annan, *U.K.* 54°59′ N, 3°16′ W 150
Annapolis, *Md., U.S.* 38°58′ N, 76°37′ W 94
Annapolis Royal, *Can.* 44°43′ N, 65°31′ W 111
Annecy, *Fr.* 45°54′ N, 6°7′ E 167
Annecy, Lac d', lake, *Fr.* 45°52′ N, 6°0′ E 165
Annemasse, *Fr.* 46°11′ N, 6°14′ E 167
Annenkov Island, *U.K.* 54°35′ S, 38°57′ W 134
Annenskiy Most, *Russ.* 60°44′ N, 37°6′ E 154
Annette, *Alas., U.S.* 55°2′ N, 131°38′ W 108
Anniston, *Ala., U.S.* 33°38′ N, 85°50′ W 96
Annobón, island, *Equatorial Guinea* 1°32′ S, 4°43′ E 214
Annweiler, *Ger.* 49°11′ N, 7°56′ E 163
Año Nuevo, Point, *Calif., U.S.* 37°10′ N, 122°33′ W 100
Anoka, *Minn., U.S.* 45°10′ N, 93°22′ W 94
Anole, *Somalia* 0°54′ N, 41°57′ E 224
Anori, *Braz.* 3°49′ S, 61°42′ W 130
Anotaie, river, *Braz.* 3°23′ N, 52°15′ W 130
Ânou Mellene, spring, *Mali* 17°27′ N, 0°32′ E 222
Ânou Mellene, spring, *Mali* 18°0′ N, 3°58′ E 222
Anou Meniet, spring, *Alg.* 24°59′ N, 4°19′ E 214
Anou-I-n-Ouzzal, spring, *Alg.* 20°40′ N, 2°27′ E 222
Anoumaba, *Côte d'Ivoire* 6°14′ N, 4°32′ W 222
Anping, *China* 41°9′ N, 123°28′ E 200
Anpu, *China* 21°25′ N, 110°2′ E 198
Anqing, *China* 30°36′ N, 116°59′ E 198
Anren, *China* 26°42′ N, 113°17′ E 198
Anröchte, *Ger.* 51°33′ N, 8°19′ E 167
Ans, *Belg.* 50°40′ N, 5°29′ E 167
Ansai, *China* 36°53′ N, 109°21′ E 198
Ansan, *S. Korea* 37°18′ N, 126°52′ E 198
Ansbach, *Ger.* 49°18′ N, 10°33′ E 152
Anse-à-Foleur, *Haiti* 19°53′ N, 72°38′ W 116
Anse-à-Galets, *Haiti* 18°50′ N, 72°53′ W 116
Anselmo, *Nebr., U.S.* 41°36′ N, 99°53′ W 90
Anseong, *S. Korea* 37°0′ N, 127°16′ E 200
Anse-Rouge, *Haiti* 19°39′ N, 73°3′ W 116
Anshan, *China* 41°7′ N, 122°59′ E 200
Anshun, *China* 26°16′ N, 105°54′ E 198
Ansina, *Uru.* 31°54′ S, 55°29′ W 139
Ansley, *Nebr., U.S.* 41°16′ N, 99°23′ W 92
Anson, *Me., U.S.* 44°47′ N, 69°55′ W 94
Anson, *Tex., U.S.* 32°44′ N, 99°54′ W 92
Ansongo, *Mali* 15°39′ N, 0°28′ E 222
Ansonia, *Conn., U.S.* 41°20′ N, 73°5′ W 104
Ansonia, *Ohio, U.S.* 40°12′ N, 84°39′ W 102
Ansonville, *Can.* 48°45′ N, 80°42′ W 94
Anta, *Peru* 13°29′ S, 72°9′ W 137
Antabamba, *Peru* 14°24′ S, 72°53′ W 137
Antakya, *Turk.* 36°10′ N, 36°6′ E 143
Antalaha, *Madagascar* 15°1′ S, 50°13′ E 207
Antalya, *Turk.* 36°52′ N, 30°43′ E 156
Antalya Körfezi 36°30′ N, 30°36′ E 180
Antanambe, *Madagascar* 16°27′ S, 49°48′ E 220
Antananarivo, *Madagascar* 18°59′ S, 47°21′ E 220
Antanifotsy, *Madagascar* 19°40′ S, 47°20′ E 220
Antarctic Ridge *South Atlantic Ocean* 62°0′ S, 10°0′ W 255
Antarctic Sound 62°24′ S, 58°49′ W 248
Antarctica 81°0′ S, 0°0′ E 248
Antarctica 71°33′ S, 29°36′ E 248
Antas, river, *Braz.* 28°48′ S, 51°2′ W 139
Antelope, *Oreg., U.S.* 44°53′ N, 120°44′ W 90
Antelope Lake, lake, *Can.* 50°13′ N, 108°54′ W 90
Antelope Peak, *Nev., U.S.* 39°23′ N, 116°33′ W 90
Antelope Point, peak, *Mont., U.S.* 45°45′ N, 109°11′ W 90
Antelope Range, *Nev., U.S.* 39°3′ N, 116°34′ W 90
Antelope Valley, *Calif., U.S.* 34°47′ N, 118°27′ W 101
Antequera, *Parag.* 24°5′ S, 57°12′ W 132
Antequera, *Sp.* 37°1′ N, 4°34′ W 164
Anterselva, *It.* 46°52′ N, 12°5′ E 167
Anthony, *Fla., U.S.* 29°17′ N, 82°7′ W 105
Anthony, *Kans., U.S.* 37°8′ N, 98°2′ W 92
Anthony, *N. Mex., U.S.* 32°1′ N, 106°38′ W 112
Anti Atlas, mountains, *Mor.* 30°17′ N, 8°12′ W 214
Antibes, Cap d', *Fr.* 43°28′ N, 7°8′ E 165
Anticosti, Île d', island, *Can.* 48°50′ N, 63°33′ W 81
Antifer, Cap d', *Fr.* 49°39′ N, 0°14′ E 150
Antigo, *Wis., U.S.* 45°8′ N, 89°9′ W 94
Antigonish, *Can.* 45°36′ N, 62°0′ W 111
Antigua and Barbuda 17°0′ N, 62°0′ W 116
Antigua, island, *Antigua and Barbuda* 17°5′ N, 61°41′ W 116
Antiguo Morelos, *Mex.* 22°32′ N, 99°6′ W 114
Anti-Lebanon see Al Jabalash Sharqī, *Leb.* 34°5′ N, 36°21′ E 194
Antilla, *Cuba* 20°51′ N, 75°44′ W 116
Anti-m-Misaou, spring, *Alg.* 21°57′ N, 3°4′ E 222
Antimony, *Utah, U.S.* 38°6′ N, 111°59′ W 92
Antioch, *Calif., U.S.* 38°0′ N, 121°50′ W 100
Antioch, *Ill., U.S.* 42°28′ N, 88°6′ W 102
Antioch see Hatay, *Turk.* 36°12′ N, 36°8′ E 156
Antioquia, *Col.* 6°34′ N, 75°51′ W 136
Antioquia, adm. division, *Col.* 6°56′ N, 76°39′ W 136
Antipatris, ruin(s), *Israel* 32°5′ N, 34°54′ E 194
Antipayuta, *Russ.* 69°4′ N, 76°54′ E 169
Antisana, peak, *Ecua.* 0°31′ N, 78°23′ W 136
Antler Peak, *Nev., U.S.* 40°35′ N, 117°13′ W 90
Antlers, *Okla., U.S.* 34°12′ N, 95°37′ W 96
Antofagasta, *Chile* 23°40′ S, 70°25′ W 132
Antofagasta, adm. division, *Chile* 22°1′ S, 70°14′ W 137
Antofagasta de la Sierra, *Arg.* 26°5′ S, 67°22′ W 132
Antón, *Pan.* 8°24′ N, 80°16′ W 115
Anton, *Tex., U.S.* 33°48′ N, 102°11′ W 92
Anton Chico, *N. Mex., U.S.* 35°11′ N, 105°10′ W 92
Antón Lizardo, Punta, *Mex.* 18°49′ N, 95°58′ W 114
Antonibe, *Madagascar* 15°8′ S, 47°25′ E 220
Antonina, *Braz.* 25°27′ S, 48°43′ W 138
Antoniny, *Ukr.* 49°48′ N, 26°53′ E 152
Antônio Prado, *Braz.* 28°53′ S, 51°16′ W 139
Antonito, *Colo., U.S.* 37°3′ N, 106°1′ W 92
Antonovo, *Kaz.* 49°21′ N, 51°45′ E 158
Antons, Lac des, lake, *Can.* 52°49′ N, 74°20′ W 111
Antopal', *Belarus* 52°12′ N, 24°45′ E 152
Antrim Mountains, *U.K.* 54°52′ N, 6°38′ W 150
Antropovo, *Russ.* 58°24′ N, 43°6′ E 154
Antsirabe, *Madagascar* 19°53′ S, 47°7′ E 207
Antsirabe, *Madagascar* 14°0′ S, 49°58′ E 220
Antsirañana, *Madagascar* 12°26′ S, 49°16′ E 220
Antsla, *Est.* 57°48′ N, 26°31′ E 166
Antsohihy, *Madagascar* 14°53′ S, 47°59′ E 220
Anttila, *Fin.* 65°7′ N, 29°48′ E 154
Anttila, *Fin.* 61°2′ N, 26°49′ E 166
Anttis, *Nor.* 67°16′ N, 22°48′ E 152
Anttola, *Fin.* 61°34′ N, 27°35′ E 166
Antu, *China* 42°32′ N, 128°18′ E 200
Antubia, *Ghana* 6°18′ N, 2°51′ W 222
Antufash, Jazīrat, island, *Yemen* 15°45′ N, 42°7′ E 182
Antwerp, *Ohio, U.S.* 41°9′ N, 84°44′ W 102
Antwerpen (Antwerp), *Belg.* 51°13′ N, 4°24′ E 167
Anuppur, *India* 23°7′ N, 81°42′ E 197
Anupshahr, *India* 28°20′ N, 78°15′ E 197
Anuradhapura, *Sri Lanka* 8°22′ N, 80°22′ E 188
Anvers Island, *Antarctica* 64°36′ S, 66°3′ W 134
Anvik, *Alas., U.S.* 62°30′ N, 160°23′ W 98
Anxi, *China* 25°5′ N, 118°13′ E 198
Anxi, *China* 40°31′ N, 95°47′ E 188
Anxiang, *China* 29°24′ N, 112°12′ E 198
Anxin, *China* 38°57′ N, 115°54′ E 198
Anyang, *China* 36°5′ N, 114°19′ E 198
Anyang, *S. Korea* 37°22′ N, 126°54′ E 200
Anyi, *China* 28°49′ N, 115°28′ E 198
Anyi, *China* 35°5′ N, 111°4′ E 198
Anykščiai, *Lith.* 55°32′ N, 25°8′ E 166
Anyou, *China* 18°11′ N, 109°34′ E 198
Anyuan, *China* 25°6′ N, 115°24′ E 198
Anyue, *China* 30°5′ N, 105°22′ E 198
Anza, *Calif., U.S.* 33°33′ N, 116°42′ W 101
Anzá, *Col.* 6°18′ N, 75°54′ W 136
Anze, *China* 36°8′ N, 112°10′ E 198
Anzhero Sudzhensk, *Russ.* 56°3′ N, 86°8′ E 169
Anzhu, Ostrova, islands, *Ostrov Kotel'nyy;Ostrov Faddeyevskiy* 75°26′ N, 135°19′ E 160
Anzio, *It.* 41°26′ N, 12°37′ E 156
Anzoátegui, adm. division, *Venez.* 8°48′ N, 64°48′ W 116
Aohan Qi, *China* 42°17′ N, 119°55′ E 198
Aoiz, *Sp.* 42°47′ N, 1°21′ W 164
Aokas, *Alg.* 36°38′ N, 5°14′ E 150
Aomori, *Japan* 40°51′ N, 140°48′ E 190
Aoraki (Cook, Mount), *N.Z.* 43°45′ S, 170°4′ E 240
Aosta, *It.* 45°44′ N, 7°19′ E 167
Aouchich, spring, *Mauritania* 22°4′ N, 12°4′ W 222
Aouderas, *Niger* 17°38′ N, 8°25′ E 222
Aougoundou, Lac, lake, *Mali* 15°47′ N, 5°12′ W 222
'Aouinet Bel Egrâ, spring, *Alg.* 26°52′ N, 6°53′ W 214
Aoukâr, plain, *Mali* 23°48′ N, 5°5′ W 214
Aoukâr, region, *Africa* 17°48′ N, 10°56′ W 222
Aoulef, *Alg.* 26°59′ N, 1°5′ E 214
Aoya, *Japan* 35°29′ N, 133°58′ E 201
Aozi, *Chad* 21°3′ N, 18°40′ E 216
Aozou, *Chad* 21°49′ N, 17°26′ E 216
Ap Iwan, Cerro, peak, *Chile* 46°13′ S, 71°59′ W 134
Apa, river, *South America* 22°10′ S, 57°17′ W 132
Apache, *Okla., U.S.* 34°52′ N, 98°22′ W 96
Apache Mountain, *N. Mex., U.S.* 33°55′ N, 108°41′ W 92
Apache Mountains, *Tex., U.S.* 31°9′ N, 104°30′ W 92
Apahida, *Rom.* 46°48′ N, 23°46′ E 156
Apalachicola, *Fla., U.S.* 29°43′ N, 85°0′ W 96
Apam, *Ghana* 5°19′ N, 0°47′ E 222
Apamea, ruin(s), *Syr.* 35°24′ N, 36°21′ E 194
Apaporis, river, *Col.* 0°17′ N, 71°46′ W 136
Aparecida do Taboado, *Braz.* 20°5′ S, 51°8′ W 138
Aparri, *Philippines* 18°18′ N, 121°40′ E 203
Apateu, *Rom.* 46°37′ N, 21°46′ E 168
Apatin, *Serb.* 45°39′ N, 18°58′ E 168
Apatity, *Russ.* 67°34′ N, 33°28′ E 152
Apatzingán, *Mex.* 19°5′ N, 102°22′ W 114
Apaxtla, *Mex.* 18°8′ N, 99°53′ W 114
Ape, *Latv.* 57°31′ N, 26°43′ E 166
Apeldoorn, *Neth.* 52°13′ N, 5°57′ E 163
Apen, *Ger.* 53°13′ N, 7°50′ E 163
Apere, *Bol.* 12°7′ S, 66°17′ W 137
Apere, river, *Bol.* 15°6′ S, 66°7′ W 137
Aphaea, ruin(s), *Gr.* 37°44′ N, 23°26′ E 156
Api, *Dem. Rep. of the Congo* 3°41′ N, 25°28′ E 224
Apia, *Samoa* 14°0′ S, 172°0′ W 241
Apiacá, river, *Braz.* 9°19′ S, 57°6′ W 130
Apiacás, Serra dos, *Braz.* 9°38′ S, 57°21′ W 130
Apiaí, *Braz.* 24°38′ S, 48°58′ W 138
Apiaú, Serra do, *Braz.* 2°53′ N, 61°48′ W 130
Apidiá, river, *Braz.* 12°33′ S, 61°11′ W 130
Apizaco, *Mex.* 19°23′ N, 98°11′ W 114
Aplao, *Peru* 16°6′ S, 72°31′ W 137
Apo, Mount, *Philippines* 6°59′ N, 125°11′ E 203

Apodaca, *Mex.* 25°46' N, 100°12' W 114
Apodi, Chapada do, *Braz.* 5°8' S, 38°11' W 132
Apollonia, ruin(s), *Alban.* 40°41' N, 19°21' E 156
Apollonia see Sozopol, *Bulg.* 42°25' N, 27°42' E 156
Apollonia see Sūsah, *Lib.* 32°52' N, 21°59' E 143
Apolo, *Bol.* 14°41' S, 68°31' W 137
Apopka, *Fla., U.S.* 28°40' N, 81°31' W 105
Apopka, Lake, *Fla., U.S.* 28°38' N, 81°44' W 105
Aporé, *Braz.* 18°57' S, 52°3' W 138
Aporé, river, *Braz.* 19°9' S, 51°35' W 138
Apostle Islands, *Lake Superior* 47°6' N, 90°53' W 94
Apóstoles, *Arg.* 27°55' S, 55°44' W 139
Apostolos Andreas, Cape, *Northern Cyprus, Cyprus* 35°34' N, 34°34' E 194
Apostolos Andreas Monastery, site, *Northern Cyprus, Cyprus* 35°40' N, 34°32' E 194
Apoteri, *Guyana* 4°0' N, 58°34' W 130
Apozol, *Mex.* 21°28' N, 103°7' W 114
Appalachian Mountains, *North America* 47°54' N, 68°40' W 82
Appennini, mountains, *Europe* 44°37' N, 8°30' E 167
Appiano, *It.* 46°27' N, 11°15' E 167
Apple Springs, *Tex., U.S.* 31°12' N, 94°59' W 103
Apple Valley, *Calif., U.S.* 34°30' N, 117°12' W 101
Appleby, *U.K.* 54°34' N, 2°29' W 162
Appleton, *Wis., U.S.* 44°16' N, 88°25' W 94
Appleton City, *Mo., U.S.* 38°10' N, 94°2' W 94
Apriķi, *Latv.* 56°49' N, 21°31' E 166
Apsheron Yarymadasy, *Azerb.* 40°21' N, 49°19' E 180
Apsheronsk, *Russ.* 44°26' N, 39°48' E 180
Aptera, ruin(s), *Gr.* 35°26' N, 24°1' E 156
Aptos, *Calif., U.S.* 36°59' N, 121°53' W 100
Apuane, Alpi, *It.* 43°57' N, 10°17' E 167
Apucarana, *Braz.* 23°36' S, 51°31' W 138
Apuí, *Braz.* 1°11' N, 69°14' W 136
Apuka, *Russ.* 60°35' N, 169°28' E 160
Apulia, adm. division, *It.* 41°1' N, 15°35' E 156
Apure, adm. division, *Venez.* 7°4' N, 70°6' W 136
Apurímac, adm. division, *Peru* 13°58' S, 73°41' W 137
Apurímac, river, *Peru* 13°27' S, 73°16' W 137
Apurito, *Venez.* 7°55' N, 68°28' W 136
Apuseni, Munţii, *Rom.* 46°38' N, 22°39' E 168
Aq Kopruk, *Afghan.* 36°4' N, 66°54' E 186
Aqaba, Gulf of 28°52' N, 34°11' E 180
Aqadyr, *Kaz.* 48°13' N, 72°52' E 184
Aqchan, *Afghan.* 36°57' N, 66°14' E 186
Aqiq, *Sudan* 18°9' N, 38°7' E 182
Aqköl, *Kaz.* 46°40' N, 49°6' E 158
Aqköl, *Kaz.* 43°24' N, 70°46' E 184
Aqköl, *Kaz.* 45°0' N, 75°39' E 184
Aqköl, *Kaz.* 52°0' N, 70°59' E 184
Aqmola, adm. division, *Kaz.* 51°31' N, 68°23' E 184
Aqqikkol Hu, lake, *China* 37°10' N, 87°39' E 188
Aqqystaū, *Kaz.* 47°14' N, 51°4' E 158
'Aqrah, *Iraq* 36°45' N, 43°47' E 195
Aqsay, *Kaz.* 51°10' N, 52°58' E 158
Aqshataū, *Kaz.* 49°25' N, 54°45' E 158
Aqshataū, *Kaz.* 47°58' N, 73°59' E 184
Aqsū, *Kaz.* 52°27' N, 71°58' E 184
Aqsū, *Kaz.* 42°25' N, 69°50' E 197
Aqsūat, *Kaz.* 47°47' N, 82°49' E 184
Aqsū-Ayuly, *Kaz.* 48°45' N, 73°42' E 184
Aqsūgek, *Kaz.* 44°37' N, 74°28' E 184
Aqtaū, *Kaz.* 43°38' N, 51°14' E 195
Aqtaysay, *Kaz.* 49°40' N, 54°1' E 158
Aqtöbe, *Kaz.* 50°15' N, 57°12' E 158
Aqtöbe, adm. division, *Kaz.* 48°43' N, 56°0' E 158
Aqtoghay, *Kaz.* 48°12' N, 75°2' E 184
Aqtoghay, *Kaz.* 46°55' N, 79°39' E 184
Aquarius Mountains, *Ariz., U.S.* 35°1' N, 113°36' W 101
Aquidauana, *Braz.* 20°29' S, 55°48' W 134
Aquileia, *It.* 45°46' N, 13°21' E 167
Aquiles Serdán, *Mex.* 28°35' N, 105°55' W 92
Aquitaine, adm. division, *Fr.* 44°10' N, 1°18' W 150
Aqyrab, *Kaz.* 50°35' N, 55°8' E 158
Aqzhal, *Kaz.* 49°13' N, 81°23' E 184
Aqzhar, *Kaz.* 47°35' N, 83°45' E 184
Aqzhayyq, *Kaz.* 50°50' N, 51°17' E 158
Ar Horqin Qi (Tianshan), *China* 43°55' N, 120°7' E 198
Ar Rabbah, *Jordan* 31°16' N, 35°44' E 194
Ar Rafīd, *Syr.* 32°57' N, 35°53' E 194
Ar Ramādī, *Iraq* 33°23' N, 43°14' E 180
Ar Ramthā, *Jordan* 32°33' N, 36°0' E 194
Ar Raqqah, *Syr.* 35°54' N, 39°2' E 180
Ar Rashādīyah, *Jordan* 30°42' N, 35°37' E 194
Ar Rass, *Saudi Arabia* 25°50' N, 43°28' E 182
Ar Rastan (Arethusa), *Syr.* 34°55' N, 36°44' E 194
Ar Rawḑah, *Saudi Arabia* 21°12' N, 42°47' E 182
Ar Riyāḑ (Riyadh), *Saudi Arabia* 24°35' N, 46°35' E 186
Ar Riyān, *Yemen* 14°40' N, 49°21' E 182
Ar Rub' al Khālī (Empty Quarter), *Saudi Arabia* 24°33' N, 54°53' E 196
Ar Rummān, *Jordan* 32°9' N, 35°49' E 194
Ar Ruşayfah, *Jordan* 32°1' N, 36°2' E 194
Ar Rustāq, *Oman* 23°23' N, 57°24' E 182
Ar Ruţbah, *Iraq* 33°3' N, 40°14' E 180
Ara, *India* 25°32' N, 84°37' E 197
Ara Bure, *Eth.* 6°31' N, 41°17' E 224
'Arab al Mulk, *Syr.* 35°16' N, 35°55' E 194
'Arabah, Wādī al, *Israel-Jordan* 30°23' N, 35°1' E 194
Arabian Basin, *Arabian Sea* 10°36' N, 65°57' E 254
Arabian Gulf see Persian Gulf 26°40' N, 51°30' E 196
Arabian Sea 13°38' N, 58°38' E 173
Araç, *Turk.* 41°15' N, 33°19' E 156
Araç, river, *Turk.* 41°9' N, 32°58' E 158
Aracaju, *Braz.* 10°54' S, 37°5' W 132
Aracati, *Braz.* 4°35' S, 37°43' W 132
Aracatu, *Braz.* 14°27' S, 41°29' W 138
Araçatuba, *Braz.* 21°11' S, 50°27' W 138
Aracena, *Sp.* 37°53' N, 6°35' W 164
Aracena, Sierra de, *Sp.* 37°58' N, 6°51' W 164
Aracruz, *Braz.* 19°51' S, 40°19' W 132
Araçuaí, *Braz.* 16°52' S, 42°4' W 138
Araçuaí, river, *Braz.* 17°50' S, 43°0' W 138
'Arad, *Israel* 31°14' N, 35°12' E 194
Arad, *Rom.* 46°11' N, 21°19' E 168
Arad, adm. division, *Rom.* 46°9' N, 21°5' E 156
Arada, *Chad* 15°1' N, 20°39' E 216
Araden, ruin(s), *Gr.* 35°12' N, 23°57' E 156
Aradu Nou, *Rom.* 46°9' N, 21°20' E 168
Arafali, *Eritrea* 15°1' N, 39°42' E 182
Arafura Sea 9°12' S, 134°22' E 192
Araga, spring, *Niger* 17°25' N, 11°36' E 222
Aragarças, *Braz.* 15°58' S, 52°14' W 138
Aragats, peak, *Arm.* 40°30' N, 44°8' E 195
Arago, Cape, *Oreg., U.S.* 43°20' N, 124°41' W 90
Aragon, adm. division, *Sp.* 41°26' N, 1°15' W 164
Aragua, adm. division, *Venez.* 10°3' N, 67°40' W 136
Aragua de Barcelona, *Venez.* 9°29' N, 64°52' W 116
Araguacema, *Braz.* 8°50' S, 49°37' W 130
Araguaçu, *Braz.* 12°52' S, 49°56' W 138
Araguaia National Park, *Braz.* 11°14' S, 50°56' W 130
Araguaia, river, *Braz.* 15°22' S, 51°48' W 132
Araguaína, *Braz.* 7°12' S, 48°16' W 130
Araguao, Boca 9°11' N, 61°20' W 116
Araguapiche, Punta, *Venez.* 9°21' N, 60°53' W 116
Araguari, *Braz.* 18°40' S, 48°15' W 138
Araguari, river, *Braz.* 18°56' S, 48°13' W 138
Araguatins, *Braz.* 5°39' S, 48°8' W 130
Arahal, *Sp.* 37°15' N, 5°34' W 164
Arahura, *N.Z.* 42°42' S, 171°4' E 240
Arai, *Japan* 37°0' N, 138°14' E 201
Araia, *Sp.* 42°52' N, 2°19' W 164
Arak, *Alg.* 25°18' N, 3°44' E 214
Arāk, *Iran* 34°6' N, 49°42' E 180
Araka, spring, *Niger* 18°54' N, 15°24' E 216
Arakamchechen, Ostrov, island, *Russ.* 64°44' N, 172°1' W 98
Arakan Yoma, *Myanmar* 19°6' N, 94°18' E 202
Aral, *China* 38°8' N, 90°43' E 188
Aral, *China* 40°40' N, 81°28' E 184
Aral, *Kaz.* 46°54' N, 61°36' E 184
Aral Mangy Qaraqumy, *Kaz.* 47°11' N, 61°51' E 184
Aral Sea, lake 45°32' N, 58°10' E 160
Aralqi, *China* 39°27' N, 87°44' E 188
Aralqum, *Kaz.* 44°8' N, 58°11' E 180
Aralsor Köli, lake, *Kaz.* 49°0' N, 48°1' E 158
Araltobe, *Kaz.* 50°31' N, 60°6' E 158
Aramac, *Austral.* 23°0' S, 145°16' E 231
Aramberri, *Mex.* 24°4' N, 99°50' W 114
Aramits, *Fr.* 43°6' N, 0°44' E 164
Arampampa, *Bol.* 18°0' S, 65°58' W 137
Ārān, *Iran* 34°9' N, 51°30' E 180
Aran Islands, *Celtic Sea* 53°12' N, 10°30' W 150
Aranda de Duero, *Sp.* 41°40' N, 3°44' W 164
Arandas, *Mex.* 20°41' N, 102°22' W 114
Arani, *Bol.* 17°38' S, 65°41' W 137
Aranjuez, *Sp.* 40°1' N, 3°36' W 164
Aranos, *Namibia* 24°5' S, 19°7' E 227
Aransas Pass, *Tex., U.S.* 27°53' N, 97°9' W 96
Arantes, river, *Braz.* 19°25' S, 50°20' W 138
Arantur, *Russ.* 60°59' N, 63°37' E 169
Aranyaprathet, *Thai.* 13°44' N, 102°31' E 202
Arao, *Japan* 32°57' N, 130°26' E 201
Araouane, *Mali* 18°53' N, 3°34' W 222
Arapa, Laguna, lake, *Peru* 15°11' S, 70°11' W 137
Arapaho, *Okla., U.S.* 35°33' N, 98°58' W 96
Arapey, *Uru.* 30°57' S, 57°33' W 139
Arapiraca, *Braz.* 9°45' S, 36°42' W 132
Arapkir, *Turk.* 39°1' N, 38°31' E 180
Arapongas, *Braz.* 23°26' S, 51°28' W 138
Araracuara, *Col.* 0°29' N, 72°17' W 136
Araranguá, *Braz.* 28°58' S, 49°29' W 138
Araraquara, *Braz.* 21°48' S, 48°12' W 138
Araras, *Braz.* 9°5' S, 68°6' W 137
Araras, *Braz.* 6°13' S, 54°34' W 130
Araras, *Braz.* 22°22' S, 47°23' W 138
Ararat, *Arm.* 39°50' N, 44°40' E 195
Ararat, Mount see Ağrı Dağı, *Turk.* 39°39' N, 44°12' E 180
Ararat, Mount see Ağrı Dağı, peak, *Turk.* 39°42' N, 44°15' E 195
Arari, *Braz.* 3°28' S, 44°46' W 132
Araria, *India* 26°5' N, 87°27' E 197
Araripe, Chapada do, *Braz.* 7°34' S, 40°28' W 132
Araruama, *Braz.* 22°52' S, 42°22' W 138
Aras (Araxes), river, *Asia* 40°0' N, 42°18' E 195
Arataca, *Braz.* 15°18' S, 39°24' W 138
Aratane, spring, *Mauritania* 18°24' N, 8°33' W 222
Arataú, river, *Braz.* 3°14' S, 50°37' W 130
Arauã, river, *Braz.* 4°14' S, 64°51' W 130
Arauca, *Col.* 7°0' N, 70°47' W 136
Arauca, adm. division, *Col.* 6°39' N, 71°44' W 136
Arauca, river, *Venez.* 7°27' N, 67°58' W 136
Araucária, *Braz.* 25°36' S, 49°24' W 138
Arauquita, *Col.* 6°58' N, 71°22' W 136
Araxá, *Braz.* 19°36' S, 46°56' W 138
Araxes see Aras, river, *Turk.* 40°0' N, 42°18' E 195
Arayit Dağı, peak, *Turk.* 39°17' N, 31°39' E 156
Ārba Minch', *Eth.* 5°59' N, 37°37' E 224
Arba'at, *Sudan* 19°46' N, 36°57' E 182
Arbazh, *Russ.* 57°41' N, 48°24' E 154
Arbela see Irbid, *Jordan* 32°32' N, 35°51' E 194
Arbīl, *Iraq* 36°10' N, 43°59' E 180
Arboledas, *Arg.* 36°51' S, 61°28' W 139
Arborea, *It.* 39°46' N, 8°34' E 156
Arborfield, *Can.* 53°6' N, 103°40' W 108
Arborg, *Can.* 50°53' N, 97°13' W 90
Arbrå, *Nor.* 61°29' N, 16°19' E 152
Arbre du Ténéré, site, *Niger* 17°44' N, 10°5' E 222
Arbroath, *U.K.* 56°33' N, 2°38' W 150
Arc, *Fr.* 47°27' N, 5°33' E 150
Arc Dome, peak, *Nev., U.S.* 38°49' N, 117°26' W 90
Arc, river, *Fr.* 45°23' N, 6°17' E 165
Arcachon, *Fr.* 44°36' N, 1°15' W 214
Arcadia, *Fla., U.S.* 27°13' N, 81°52' W 105
Arcadia, *Ind., U.S.* 40°10' N, 86°1' W 102
Arcadia, *La., U.S.* 32°31' N, 92°56' W 103
Arcadia, *Mich., U.S.* 44°29' N, 86°14' W 94
Arcadia, *Peru* 1°3' S, 75°18' W 136
Arcadia, *Wis., U.S.* 44°15' N, 91°29' W 94
Arcanum, *Ohio, U.S.* 39°59' N, 84°32' W 102
Arcas, Cayos, islands, *Gulf of Mexico* 20°19' N, 92°6' W 115
Arcata, *Calif., U.S.* 40°52' N, 124°6' W 90
Arcelia, *Mex.* 18°16' N, 100°16' W 114
Archangel see Arkhangel'sk, *Russ.* 64°35' N, 40°37' E 154
Archar, *Bulg.* 43°48' N, 22°54' E 168
Archbold, *Ohio, U.S.* 41°30' N, 84°18' W 102
Archeï, spring, *Chad* 16°53' N, 21°44' E 216
Archena, *Sp.* 38°6' N, 1°19' W 164
Archer, *Fla., U.S.* 29°32' N, 82°32' W 105
Archer Bay 13°40' S, 141°24' E 230
Archer Bend National Park, *Austral.* 13°35' S, 141°56' E 238
Archer City, *Tex., U.S.* 33°34' N, 98°38' W 92
Archer Point, *Antarctica* 68°54' S, 161°17' E 248
Archer, river, *Austral.* 13°39' S, 141°16' E 231
Archer's Post, *Kenya* 0°36' N, 37°40' E 224
Archerwill, *Can.* 52°25' N, 103°52' W 108
Archidona, *Sp.* 37°5' N, 4°24' W 164
Archipiélago de Colón see Galápagos Islands, *Ecuador* 0°13' N, 92°2' W 130
Archipiélago Los Roques National Park, *Caribbean Sea* 11°50' N, 67°27' W 136
Archman, *Turkm.* 38°33' N, 57°9' E 180
Arci, Monte, peak, *It.* 39°46' N, 8°41' E 156
Arcis, *Fr.* 48°32' N, 4°8' E 163
Arco, *Idaho, U.S.* 43°38' N, 113°18' W 90
Arco, *It.* 45°55' N, 10°52' E 167
Arco, Paso del, pass, *Arg.* 38°47' S, 71°6' W 134
Arcola, *Ill., U.S.* 39°41' N, 88°19' W 102
Arcola, *Miss., U.S.* 33°14' N, 90°53' W 103
Arcos, *Braz.* 20°17' S, 45°34' W 138
Arcos de Jalón, *Sp.* 41°12' N, 2°17' W 150
Arcoverde, *Braz.* 8°24' S, 37°1' W 132
Arctic Bay, *Can.* 73°3' N, 85°6' W 73
Arctic Ocean 79°19' N, 170°44' W 246
Arctic Red, river, *Can.* 66°40' N, 132°38' W 98
Arctic Village, *Alas., U.S.* 68°6' N, 145°32' W 98
Arctowski, station, *Antarctica* 62°12' S, 58°12' W 134
Arda, river, *Bulg.* 41°30' N, 25°42' E 156
Ardabīl, *Iran* 38°15' N, 48°18' E 195
Ardahan, *Turk.* 41°5' N, 42°40' E 195
Ardakān, *Iran* 32°14' N, 54°3' E 180
Ardakān, *Iran* 30°14' N, 51°59' E 196
Årdal, *Nor.* 61°14' N, 7°43' E 152
Årdal, *Nor.* 59°8' N, 6°11' E 152
Ardales, *Sp.* 36°51' N, 4°51' W 164
Ardanuç, *Turk.* 41°9' N, 42°2' E 195
Arḑaşşawwān, *Jordan* 30°58' N, 36°46' E 194
Ardatov, *Russ.* 54°47' N, 46°19' E 154
Ardencaple Fjord 74°46' N, 25°23' W 246
Ardestān, *Iran* 33°20' N, 52°25' E 180
Ardmore, *Okla., U.S.* 34°9' N, 97°7' W 92
Ardmore, *S. Dak., U.S.* 43°1' N, 103°40' W 90
Ardres, *Fr.* 50°51' N, 1°58' E 163
Ards Peninsula, *U.K.* 54°21' N, 6°3' W 150
Ardud, *Rom.* 47°38' N, 22°53' E 168
Ardvrach Castle, site, *U.K.* 58°9' N, 5°6' W 150
Ardvule, Rubha, *U.K.* 57°15' N, 8°1' W 150
Åre, *Nor.* 63°24' N, 13°3' E 152
Arena, Point, *U.S.* 38°47' N, 124°3' W 90
Arenápolis, *Braz.* 14°28' S, 56°53' W 132
Arenas, Punta de, *Arg.* 53°3' S, 68°13' W 134
Arendal, *Nor.* 58°27' N, 8°43' E 152
Arendsee, *Ger.* 52°53' N, 11°30' E 152
Arenys de Mar, *Sp.* 41°34' N, 2°33' E 164
Arenzano, *It.* 44°23' N, 8°41' E 167
Arequipa, *Peru* 16°24' S, 71°35' W 137
Arequipa, adm. division, *Peru* 16°8' S, 73°31' W 137
Ārēro, *Eth.* 4°43' N, 38°48' E 224
Arês, *Braz.* 6°14' S, 35°8' W 132
Åreskutan, peak, *Nor.* 63°26' N, 12°55' E 152
Arethusa see Ar Rastan, *Syr.* 34°55' N, 36°44' E 194
Arévalo, *Sp.* 41°3' N, 4°44' W 150
Arezzaf, spring, *Mali* 18°5' N, 1°47' W 222
Arezzo, *It.* 43°27' N, 11°52' E 156
Arga Sala, river, *Russ.* 67°51' N, 107°46' E 160
Argaman, *West Bank, Israel* 32°8' N, 35°30' E 194
Argamasilla de Alba, *Sp.* 39°7' N, 3°7' W 164
Argamasilla de Calatrava, *Sp.* 38°44' N, 4°5' W 164
Argan, *China* 40°6' N, 88°17' E 188
Argatay, *Mongolia* 45°33' N, 108°4' E 198
Argelès, *Fr.* 42°32' N, 3°0' E 164
Argens, river, *Fr.* 43°25' N, 6°3' E 165
Argenta, *It.* 44°36' N, 11°49' E 167
Argentario, Monte, peak, *It.* 42°23' N, 11°5' E 156
Argentera, peak, *It.* 44°10' N, 7°17' E 165
Argenteuil, *Fr.* 48°55' N, 2°13' E 163
Argentina 35°22' S, 67°13' W 134
Argentine Plain, *South Atlantic Ocean* 46°42' S, 48°15' W 253
Argentré, *Fr.* 48°3' N, 0°34' E 150
Argeş, adm. division, *Rom.* 44°57' N, 24°28' E 156
Arghandab Dam, *Afghan.* 32°2' N, 65°50' E 186
Argo, *Sudan* 19°30' N, 30°27' E 226
Argolas, *Braz.* 20°26' S, 40°25' W 138
Argonaut Mountain, *Can.* 51°49' N, 118°25' W 90
Argonne, *Fr.* 49°43' N, 4°51' E 167
Árgos, *Gr.* 37°35' N, 22°41' E 180
Argos, *Ind., U.S.* 41°13' N, 86°14' W 102
Argoub, *Western Sahara, Mor.* 23°35' N, 15°51' W 214
Arguello, Point, *Calif., U.S.* 34°30' N, 120°49' W 100
Arguin, Cap d', *Mauritania* 20°25' N, 16°42' W 214
Argungu, *Nig.* 12°43' N, 4°31' E 222
Argus, *Calif., U.S.* 35°44' N, 117°25' W 101
Argus, Dome, *Antarctica* 79°52' S, 74°47' E 248
Argus Range, *Calif., U.S.* 36°0' N, 117°34' W 101
Arguut, *Mongolia* 45°28' N, 102°18' E 190
Argyle, *Mich., U.S.* 43°33' N, 82°56' W 102
Argyle, *Minn., U.S.* 48°18' N, 96°51' W 90
Argyle, *N.Y., U.S.* 43°14' N, 73°31' W 104
Argyle, Lake, *Austral.* 16°12' S, 128°11' E 230
Arhebeb, spring, *Mali* 21°5' N, 0°8' E 222
Arhrījīt, *Mauritania* 18°21' N, 9°15' W 222
Århus, *Den.* 56°9' N, 10°11' E 150
Ari Atoll, *Maldives* 3°33' N, 72°22' E 188
Ariamsvlei, *Namibia* 28°7' S, 19°50' E 227
Ariana, *Tun.* 36°51' N, 10°11' E 156
Arias, *Arg.* 33°39' S, 62°23' W 139
Aribinda, *Burkina Faso* 14°14' N, 0°52' E 222
Arica, *Chile* 18°34' S, 70°20' W 137
Arica, *Col.* 2°9' S, 71°46' W 136
Arica, *Peru* 1°39' S, 75°12' W 136
Arica y Parinacota, adm. division, *Chile* 18°28' S, 70°18' W 137
Arid, Mount, *Austral.* 34°1' S, 122°58' E 230
Arida, *Japan* 34°4' N, 135°7' E 201
Aridal, *Western Sahara, Mor.* 25°59' N, 13°48' W 214
Arīḩā, *Syr.* 35°48' N, 36°35' E 156
Arīḩā (Jericho), *West Bank, Israel* 31°51' N, 35°27' E 194
Arija, *Sp.* 42°57' N, 3°59' W 164
Arikaree, river, *Colo., U.S.* 39°48' N, 102°40' W 90
Arimã, *Braz.* 5°47' S, 63°42' W 130
Arinos, *Braz.* 15°54' S, 46°4' W 138
Arinos, river, *Braz.* 10°28' S, 58°34' W 132
Ariogala, *Lith.* 55°15' N, 23°29' E 166
Aripao, *Venez.* 7°19' N, 65°4' W 130
Ariporo, river, *Col.* 5°57' N, 71°13' W 136
Aripuanã, *Braz.* 9°59' S, 59°28' W 130
Aripuanã, river, *Braz.* 7°52' S, 60°35' W 130
Aripuanã, river, *Braz.* 11°15' S, 59°41' W 130
Ariquemes, *Braz.* 9°57' S, 63°6' W 130
Arismendi, *Venez.* 8°29' N, 68°22' W 136
Arista, *Mex.* 22°37' N, 100°51' W 114
Aristizábal, Cabo, *Arg.* 45°23' S, 66°29' W 134
Arivechi, *Mex.* 28°54' N, 109°10' W 92
Ariza, *Sp.* 41°18' N, 2°4' W 164
Arizona, adm. division, *Ariz., U.S.* 34°22' N, 112°38' W 92
Arizpe, *Mex.* 30°19' N, 110°12' W 92
Arjona, *Col.* 10°16' N, 75°22' W 136
Ark, The, peak, *Antarctica* 80°43' S, 26°3' W 248
Arka, *Russ.* 60°10' N, 142°13' E 160
Arkadak, *Russ.* 51°53' N, 43°35' E 158
Arkadelphia, *Ark., U.S.* 34°6' N, 93°5' W 96
Arkansas, adm. division, *Ark., U.S.* 35°4' N, 93°21' W 96
Arkansas City, *Kans., U.S.* 37°2' N, 97°3' W 92
Arkansas, river, *Okla., U.S.* 35°13' N, 95°34' W 80
Arkanū, Jabal, peak, *Lib.* 22°16' N, 24°40' E 226
Arkhangel'sk, *Russ.* 64°32' N, 40°34' E 160
Arkhangel'sk, adm. division, *Russ.* 63°2' N, 38°58' E 154
Arkhangel'sk (Archangel), *Russ.* 64°35' N, 40°37' E 154
Arkhangel'skoye, *Russ.* 44°34' N, 44°3' E 158
Arkhangel'skoye, *Russ.* 51°28' N, 40°52' E 158
Arklow, *Ire.* 52°47' N, 6°10' W 150
Arkona, Kap, *Ger.* 54°42' N, 13°34' E 152
Arkösund, *Nor.* 58°28' N, 16°53' E 152
Arkticheskiy, Mys, *Russ.* 81°1' N, 79°59' E 160
Arkticheskogo Instituta, Ostrova, island, *Russ.* 75°29' N, 77°0' E 160
Arkul', *Russ.* 57°19' N, 50°9' E 154
Arlanzón, *Sp.* 42°18' N, 3°27' W 164
Arles, *Fr.* 43°41' N, 4°40' E 214
Arlington, *Ga., U.S.* 31°25' N, 84°43' W 96
Arlington, *Ill., U.S.* 41°28' N, 89°15' W 102
Arlington, *Mass., U.S.* 42°24' N, 71°10' W 104
Arlington, *N.Y., U.S.* 41°41' N, 73°54' W 104
Arlington, *Oreg., U.S.* 45°42' N, 120°12' W 90
Arlington, *S. Dak., U.S.* 44°20' N, 97°9' W 94
Arlington, *Tex., U.S.* 32°43' N, 97°7' W 92
Arlington, *Vt., U.S.* 43°4' N, 73°10' W 104
Arlington, *Wash., U.S.* 48°10' N, 122°7' W 100
Arlit, *Niger* 18°50' N, 7°14' E 222
Arlon, *Belg.* 49°40' N, 5°48' E 163
Arly, river, *Fr.* 45°44' N, 6°31' E 165
Arma, *Kans., U.S.* 37°31' N, 94°42' W 94
Armada, *Mich., U.S.* 42°50' N, 82°53' W 102
Armadale Castle, site, *U.K.* 57°2' N, 6°1' W 150
Armadillo, *Mex.* 22°13' N, 100°40' W 114
Armant, *Egypt* 25°36' N, 32°27' E 182
Armavir, *Arm.* 40°9' N, 44°2' E 195
Armavir, *Russ.* 44°59' N, 41°6' E 158
Armenia 40°14' N, 44°43' E 195
Armenia, *Col.* 4°28' N, 75°45' W 136
Armenia Mountain, *Pa., U.S.* 41°44' N, 77°0' W 94
Armeniş, *Rom.* 45°13' N, 22°18' E 168
Armentières, *Fr.* 50°40' N, 2°53' E 163
Armeria, *Mex.* 18°55' N, 104°0' W 114
Armero, *Col.* 4°57' N, 74°55' W 136
Armijo, *N. Mex., U.S.* 35°2' N, 106°41' W 92
Armilla, *Sp.* 37°8' N, 3°38' W 164
Armit, *Can.* 52°49' N, 101°47' W 108
Armizonskoye, *Russ.* 55°56' N, 67°39' E 184
Armona, *Calif., U.S.* 36°19' N, 119°43' W 100
Armour, *S. Dak., U.S.* 43°18' N, 98°21' W 90
Armstrong, *Arg.* 32°49' S, 61°35' W 139
Armstrong, *Can.* 50°18' N, 89°2' W 110
Armstrong, *Can.* 50°26' N, 119°12' W 90
Armutcuk, *Turk.* 41°20' N, 31°31' E 156
Armyans'k, *Ukr.* 46°5' N, 33°41' E 156

Arnaoutis, Cape, *Cyprus* 35°5′ N, 32°4′ E 194
Arnaud, *Can.* 49°14′ N, 97°6′ W 90
Arnaudville, *La., U.S.* 30°23′ N, 91°57′ W 103
Arnbach, *Aust.* 46°44′ N, 12°23′ E 167
Årnes, *Nor.* 60°7′ N, 11°28′ E 152
Arnett, *Okla., U.S.* 36°7′ N, 99°46′ W 92
Arnhem, *Neth.* 51°59′ N, 5°54′ E 167
Arnhem Land, region, *Australia* 11°54′ S, 131°40′ E 192
Arnold, *Calif., U.S.* 38°15′ N, 120°22′ W 100
Arnold, *Nebr., U.S.* 41°25′ N, 100°12′ W 90
Arnold, river, *Austral.* 14°50′ S, 133°57′ E 230
Arnolds Park, *Iowa, U.S.* 43°21′ N, 95°8′ W 90
Arnoldstein, *Aust.* 46°33′ N, 13°42′ E 167
Arnot, *Can.* 55°45′ N, 96°45′ W 108
Arnsberg, *Ger.* 51°23′ N, 8°4′ E 167
Arnstein, *Ger.* 49°58′ N, 9°58′ E 167
Aroa, *Venez.* 10°25′ N, 68°54′ W 136
Aroab, *Namibia* 26°50′ S, 19°43′ E 227
Aroánia, Óri, peak, *Gr.* 37°57′ N, 22°8′ E 156
Arock, *Oreg., U.S.* 42°55′ N, 117°31′ W 90
Arolsen, *Ger.* 51°23′ N, 9°1′ E 167
Aroma, *Sudan* 15°46′ N, 36°8′ E 182
Aroma Park, *Ill., U.S.* 41°4′ N, 87°48′ W 102
Aron, *India* 25°57′ N, 77°54′ E 197
Arona, *It.* 45°45′ N, 8°32′ E 167
Arosa, *Switz.* 46°46′ N, 9°38′ E 167
Ærøskøbing, *Den.* 54°53′ N, 10°24′ E 150
Arowhana, peak, *N.Z.* 38°8′ S, 177°45′ E 240
Arp, *Tex., U.S.* 32°13′ N, 95°4′ W 103
Arpa, river, *Asia* 40°28′ N, 43°31′ E 195
Arpaçay, *Turk.* 40°52′ N, 43°19′ E 195
Arpajon, *Fr.* 48°35′ N, 2°14′ E 163
Arqalyq, *Kaz.* 50°13′ N, 66°54′ E 184
Arque, *Bol.* 17°51′ S, 66°22′ W 137
Arques, *Fr.* 50°44′ N, 2°18′ E 150
Arquía, *Col.* 7°58′ N, 77°7′ W 136
'Arrābah, *West Bank, Israel* 32°24′ N, 35°11′ E 194
Arraias, *Braz.* 12°56′ S, 46°58′ W 130
Arras, *Alban.* 41°45′ N, 20°18′ E 168
Arras, *Fr.* 50°17′ N, 2°47′ E 163
Arreau, *Fr.* 42°54′ N, 0°20′ E 164
Arrecifes, *Arg.* 34°4′ S, 60°7′ W 139
Arrée, Montagnes d', *Fr.* 48°29′ N, 4°12′ W 150
Arriate, *Sp.* 36°47′ N, 5°9′ W 164
Arris, *Alg.* 35°12′ N, 6°17′ E 150
Arroio dos Ratos, *Braz.* 30°6′ S, 51°44′ W 139
Arroio Grande, *Braz.* 32°12′ S, 53°7′ W 139
Arrojado, river, *Braz.* 13°40′ S, 45°16′ W 138
Arrou, *Fr.* 48°6′ N, 1°7′ E 163
Arroux, river, *Fr.* 46°45′ N, 4°8′ E 165
Arrowhead, river, *Can.* 60°18′ N, 123°11′ W 108
Arrowsmith, *Ill., U.S.* 40°26′ N, 88°38′ W 102
Arrowtown, *N.Z.* 44°57′ S, 168°51′ E 240
Arrowwood, *Can.* 50°44′ N, 113°10′ W 90
Arroyito, *Arg.* 31°27′ S, 63°4′ W 139
Arroyo de la Luz, *Sp.* 39°28′ N, 6°36′ W 164
Arroyo Grande, *Calif., U.S.* 35°8′ N, 120°35′ W 100
Arroyo Hondo, *N. Mex., U.S.* 36°31′ N, 105°40′ W 92
Arroyo Verde see Puerto Lobos, *Arg.* 42°2′ S, 65°5′ W 134
Arroyos y Esteros, *Parag.* 25°5′ S, 57°7′ W 132
Arrufó, *Arg.* 30°13′ S, 61°44′ W 139
Ars-en-Ré, *Fr.* 46°12′ N, 1°33′ W 150
Arshaly, *Kaz.* 50°49′ N, 72°11′ E 184
Arshaty, *Kaz.* 49°17′ N, 86°36′ E 184
Arsiero, *It.* 45°48′ N, 11°20′ E 167
Arsk, *Russ.* 56°7′ N, 49°54′ E 154
Arsuk, *Den.* 61°13′ N, 48°8′ W 106
Artashat, *Arm.* 39°58′ N, 44°32′ E 195
Arteaga, *Mex.* 25°25′ N, 100°52′ W 114
Arteaga, *Mex.* 18°24′ N, 102°16′ W 114
Artem, *Russ.* 43°26′ N, 132°21′ E 190
Artemisa, *Cuba* 22°49′ N, 82°46′ W 116
Artemivs'k, *Ukr.* 48°35′ N, 37°57′ E 158
Artemovsk, *Russ.* 54°24′ N, 93°22′ E 190
Artemovskiy, *Russ.* 58°19′ N, 114°40′ E 160
Artemovskiy, *Russ.* 57°22′ N, 61°47′ E 154
Artenay, *Fr.* 48°4′ N, 1°51′ E 150
Artesa de Segre, *Sp.* 41°53′ N, 1°3′ E 164
Artesia, *Miss., U.S.* 33°23′ N, 88°38′ W 103
Artesia, *N. Mex., U.S.* 32°50′ N, 104°25′ W 92
Artesian, *S. Dak., U.S.* 43°59′ N, 97°57′ W 90
Arthez, *Fr.* 43°28′ N, 0°37′ E 150
Arthog, *U.K.* 52°42′ N, 4°1′ W 162
Arthonnay, *Fr.* 47°55′ N, 4°13′ E 150
Arthur, *Ill., U.S.* 39°42′ N, 88°28′ W 102
Arthur, *Nebr., U.S.* 41°33′ N, 101°42′ W 90
Arthur, Lac, lake, *Can.* 51°6′ N, 62°48′ W 111
Arthur's Pass, *N.Z.* 42°57′ S, 171°33′ E 240
Arti, *Russ.* 56°25′ N, 58°37′ E 154
Artigas, *Uru.* 30°24′ S, 56°31′ W 139
Artigas, station, *Antarctica* 61°59′ S, 58°38′ W 134
Art'ik, *Arm.* 40°37′ N, 43°57′ E 195
Artix, *Fr.* 43°24′ N, 0°33′ E 150
Artois, region, *Europe* 50°17′ N, 1°58′ E 163
Artova, *Turk.* 40°2′ N, 36°16′ E 156
Artrutx, Cabo d', *Sp.* 39°56′ N, 3°27′ E 150
Arturo Prat, Chile, station, *Antarctica* 62°38′ S, 59°39′ W 134
Artux, *China* 39°45′ N, 76°6′ E 184
Artvin, *Turk.* 41°11′ N, 41°49′ E 195
Artyom, *Azerb.* 40°28′ N, 50°19′ E 195
Aru, *Dem. Rep. of the Congo* 2°48′ N, 30°50′ E 224
Aru, Kepulauan, islands, *Arafura Sea* 6°8′ S, 133°44′ E 192
Arua, *Dem. Rep. of the Congo* 3°4′ N, 30°56′ E 207
Aruajá, *Braz.* 5°0′ S, 66°51′ W 130
Aruanã, *Braz.* 14°58′ S, 51°8′ W 138
Aruba, island, *Netherlands* 13°0′ N, 70°0′ W 118
Arun Qi, *China* 48°8′ N, 123°34′ E 198
Arunachal Pradesh, adm. division, *India* 28°39′ N, 94°2′ E 188
Arundel, *U.K.* 50°51′ N, 0°34′ E 162
Arusha, *Tanzania* 3°22′ S, 36°42′ E 224
Arusha, adm. division, *Tanzania* 4°7′ S, 35°4′ E 218
Aruwimi, river, *Dem. Rep. of the Congo* 1°37′ N, 25°21′ E 224
Arvada, *Colo., U.S.* 39°47′ N, 105°6′ W 90
Arvayheer, *Mongolia* 46°12′ N, 102°50′ E 198
Arve, river, *Fr.* 46°3′ N, 6°36′ E 167
Arvi, *India* 20°59′ N, 78°13′ E 188
Arviat, *Can.* 61°5′ N, 94°10′ W 106
Arvika, *Nor.* 59°39′ N, 12°36′ E 152
Arvin, *Calif., U.S.* 35°12′ N, 118°50′ W 101
Arvon, Mount, *Mich., U.S.* 46°44′ N, 88°14′ W 94
Arxan, *China* 47°12′ N, 119°55′ E 198
Ary, *Russ.* 72°50′ N, 122°37′ E 173
Arya Köli, lake, *Kaz.* 45°55′ N, 66°3′ E 184
Aryqbayq, *Kaz.* 52°55′ N, 68°12′ E 184
Arys, *Kaz.* 42°25′ N, 68°47′ E 197
Arys, river, *Kaz.* 42°30′ N, 69°1′ E 197
Arzamas, *Russ.* 55°21′ N, 43°55′ E 154
Aržano, *Croatia* 43°35′ N, 16°58′ E 168
Arzew, *Alg.* 35°50′ N, 0°19′ E 150
Arzgir, *Russ.* 45°21′ N, 44°10′ E 158
Arzni, *Arm.* 40°19′ N, 44°36′ E 195
As Ela, *Djibouti* 10°59′ N, 42°12′ E 224
As Sabkhah, *Syr.* 35°46′ N, 39°19′ E 180
Aş Şāfī, *Jordan* 31°1′ N, 35°27′ E 194
As Salmān, *Iraq* 30°30′ N, 44°32′ E 180
As Salţ, *Jordan* 32°2′ N, 35°43′ E 194
As Salwá, *Saudi Arabia* 24°42′ N, 50°48′ E 196
As Samāwah (Samawah), *Iraq* 31°15′ N, 45°15′ E 180
As Sanām, *Saudi Arabia* 23°34′ N, 51°7′ E 196
Aş Şanamayn, *Syr.* 33°4′ N, 36°11′ E 194
Aş Şaqlabīyah, *Syr.* 35°21′ N, 36°22′ E 194
Aş Şarafand, *Leb.* 33°27′ N, 35°17′ E 194
As Sarfaia, spring, *Lib.* 23°38′ N, 17°11′ E 216
Aş Şawrah, *Saudi Arabia* 27°52′ N, 35°22′ E 180
As Sīb, *Oman* 23°41′ N, 58°11′ E 196
As Sidr, *Lib.* 30°39′ N, 18°18′ E 216
As Sidr, *Saudi Arabia* 23°24′ N, 39°44′ E 182
As Sikr, spring, *Iraq* 30°44′ N, 43°44′ E 180
As Sirḩān, Wādī, *Jordan* 31°9′ N, 36°42′ E 180
Aş Şufuq, spring, *U.A.E.* 23°43′ N, 51°48′ E 196
As Sulaymānīyah, *Iraq* 35°33′ N, 45°25′ E 180
As Sulaymānīyah, *Saudi Arabia* 24°6′ N, 47°16′ E 196
As Sulaymī, *Saudi Arabia* 26°15′ N, 41°23′ E 182
As Sulayyil, *Saudi Arabia* 20°27′ N, 45°34′ E 182
As Sulţān, *Lib.* 31°6′ N, 17°7′ E 216
Aş Şurrah, *Yemen* 13°56′ N, 46°11′ E 182
As Suwāqah, *Jordan* 31°21′ N, 36°6′ E 194
Aş Şuwār, *Syr.* 35°31′ N, 40°38′ E 180
As Suwaydā', *Syr.* 32°42′ N, 36°34′ E 194
As Suwayḩ, *Oman* 22°6′ N, 59°41′ E 182
Asa, river, *Dem. Rep. of the Congo* 4°55′ N, 25°15′ E 224
Asab, *Namibia* 25°27′ S, 17°54′ E 227
Asab, oil field, *U.A.E.* 23°12′ N, 54°8′ E 182
Asadābād, Gardaneh-ye, pass, *Iran* 34°48′ N, 48°10′ E 180
Aşaği Ağcakand, *Azerb.* 40°26′ N, 46°33′ E 195
Asahi, river, *Japan* 35°0′ N, 133°47′ E 201
Asahikawa, *Japan* 43°50′ N, 142°36′ E 190
Āsalē, *Eth.* 14°12′ N, 40°18′ E 182
Asansol, *India* 23°40′ N, 86°59′ E 197
Åsarna, *Nor.* 62°39′ N, 14°20′ E 152
Āsayita, *Eth.* 11°31′ N, 41°25′ E 182
Asbest, *Russ.* 57°2′ N, 61°28′ E 154
Asbestos, *Can.* 45°45′ N, 71°57′ W 94
Ascención, *Bol.* 15°43′ S, 63°8′ W 132
Ascensión, *Mex.* 24°18′ N, 99°55′ W 114
Ascensión, *Mex.* 31°5′ N, 108°0′ W 92
Ascensión, Bahía de la 19°30′ N, 88°2′ W 115
Ascension Fracture Zone, *South Atlantic Ocean* 6°36′ S, 11°59′ W 253
Aschaffenburg, *Ger.* 49°58′ N, 9°9′ E 167
Ascheberg, *Ger.* 51°48′ N, 7°36′ E 167
Aschendorf, *Ger.* 53°3′ N, 7°19′ E 163
Ascira, *Somalia* 10°19′ N, 50°56′ E 216
Ascó, *Sp.* 41°10′ N, 0°33′ E 164
Ascot, *U.K.* 51°24′ N, 0°40′ E 162
Ascotán, *Chile* 21°45′ S, 68°19′ W 137
Ascutney, *Vt., U.S.* 43°24′ N, 72°25′ W 104
Åseda, *Nor.* 57°10′ N, 15°20′ E 152
Asedjrad, *Alg.* 24°55′ N, 1°0′ E 214
Āsela, *Eth.* 7°51′ N, 39°2′ E 224
Åsele, *Nor.* 64°9′ N, 17°19′ E 152
Åseral, *Nor.* 58°36′ N, 7°25′ E 152
Asfeld, *Fr.* 49°27′ N, 4°7′ E 163
Asfûn el Maṭâ'na, *Egypt* 25°25′ N, 32°28′ E 226
Aşgabat (Ashgabat), *Turkm.* 37°54′ N, 58°14′ E 180
Ash Fork, *Ariz., U.S.* 35°11′ N, 112°29′ W 82
Ash Grove, *Mo., U.S.* 37°18′ N, 93°34′ W 94
Ash Mountain, *Can.* 59°16′ N, 130°38′ W 108
Ash, river, *Can.* 50°27′ N, 84°56′ W 94
Ash Shabakah, *Iraq* 30°48′ N, 43°36′ E 180
Ash Sha'rā', *Saudi Arabia* 24°15′ N, 44°11′ E 182
Ash Sharawrah, *Saudi Arabia* 17°54′ N, 47°26′ E 182
Ash Sharqāţ, *Iraq* 35°26′ N, 43°15′ E 180
Ash Shaţrah, *Iraq* 31°25′ N, 46°6′ E 180
Ash Shawbak, *Jordan* 30°31′ N, 35°33′ E 194
Ash Shaykh Badr, *Syr.* 34°59′ N, 36°4′ E 194
Ash Shiḩr, *Yemen* 14°45′ N, 49°33′ E 182
Ash Shināfīyah, *Iraq* 31°37′ N, 44°39′ E 180
Ash Shişar, *Oman* 18°15′ N, 53°39′ E 182
Ash Shumlūl, *Saudi Arabia* 26°29′ N, 47°22′ E 196
Ash Shuqayq, *Saudi Arabia* 17°42′ N, 42°4′ E 182
Ash Shurayf, *Saudi Arabia* 25°42′ N, 39°12′ E 182
Ash Shuwayfāt, *Leb.* 33°48′ N, 35°30′ E 194
Ash Shuwayrif, *Lib.* 29°58′ N, 14°12′ E 216
Asha, *Russ.* 55°3′ N, 57°18′ E 154
Ashbourne, *U.K.* 53°0′ N, 1°45′ W 162
Ashburn, *Ga., U.S.* 31°42′ N, 83°39′ W 96
Ashburnham, *Mass., U.S.* 42°37′ N, 71°55′ W 104
Ashburton, *N.Z.* 43°55′ S, 171°47′ E 240
Ashby, *Mass., U.S.* 42°40′ N, 71°50′ W 104
Ashby de la Zouch, *U.K.* 52°44′ N, 1°29′ W 162
Ashchy Köl, lake, *Kaz.* 45°11′ N, 67°38′ E 184
Ashcroft, *Can.* 50°43′ N, 121°15′ W 90
Ashdod, *Israel* 31°47′ N, 34°39′ E 194
Ashdown, *Ark., U.S.* 33°40′ N, 94°8′ W 96
Ashdown Forest, region, *Europe* 50°57′ N, 0°12′ E 162
Ashern, *Can.* 51°11′ N, 98°21′ W 90
Asherton, *Tex., U.S.* 28°26′ N, 99°45′ W 92
Ashfield, *Mass., U.S.* 42°31′ N, 72°48′ W 104
Ashford, *U.K.* 51°9′ N, 0°52′ E 162
Ashford, *Wash., U.S.* 46°44′ N, 122°2′ W 100
Ashgabat see Aşgabat, *Turkm.* 37°54′ N, 58°14′ E 180
Ashikaga, *Japan* 36°20′ N, 139°27′ E 201
Ashikita, *Japan* 32°18′ N, 130°30′ E 201
Ashizuri Misaki, *Japan* 32°36′ N, 133°0′ E 201
Ashkadar, river, *Russ.* 53°2′ N, 55°16′ E 154
Ashkelon, ruin(s), *Israel* 31°39′ N, 34°30′ E 194
Ashkum, *Ill., U.S.* 40°51′ N, 87°57′ W 102
Ashland, *Kans., U.S.* 37°11′ N, 99°47′ W 92
Ashland, *Ky., U.S.* 38°27′ N, 82°39′ W 102
Ashland, *La., U.S.* 32°7′ N, 93°6′ W 103
Ashland, *Me., U.S.* 46°37′ N, 68°25′ W 94
Ashland, *Mont., U.S.* 45°34′ N, 106°16′ W 90
Ashland, *Nebr., U.S.* 41°1′ N, 96°21′ W 94
Ashland, *N.H., U.S.* 43°41′ N, 71°38′ W 104
Ashland, *Ohio, U.S.* 40°52′ N, 82°18′ W 102
Ashland, *Pa., U.S.* 40°46′ N, 76°22′ W 110
Ashland, *Va., U.S.* 37°45′ N, 77°29′ W 94
Ashland, *Wis., U.S.* 46°35′ N, 90°53′ W 94
Ashland, Mount, *Oreg., U.S.* 42°5′ N, 122°48′ W 90
Ashley, *Ind., U.S.* 41°30′ N, 85°5′ W 102
Ashley, *N. Dak., U.S.* 46°0′ N, 99°24′ W 94
Ashley, *Ohio, U.S.* 40°23′ N, 82°57′ W 102
Ashmont, *Can.* 54°7′ N, 111°35′ W 108
Ashmore Islands, *Indian Ocean* 12°34′ S, 122°16′ E 231
Ashmyany, *Belarus* 54°26′ N, 25°55′ E 166
Ashoknagar, *India* 24°32′ N, 77°44′ E 197
Ashqelon, *Israel* 31°40′ N, 34°34′ E 194
Ashtabula, *Ohio, U.S.* 41°51′ N, 80°48′ W 102
Ashtabula, Lake, *N. Dak., U.S.* 47°10′ N, 98°38′ W 90
Ashton, *Idaho, U.S.* 44°4′ N, 111°27′ W 90
Ashton, *Ill., U.S.* 41°51′ N, 89°14′ W 102
Ashton, *Mich., U.S.* 43°58′ N, 85°30′ W 102
Ashton, *R.I., U.S.* 41°56′ N, 71°26′ W 104
Ashton under Lyne, *U.K.* 53°29′ N, 2°6′ W 162
Ashuanipi, *Can.* 52°45′ N, 66°6′ W 111
Ashuanipi Lake, *Can.* 52°31′ N, 66°34′ W 111
Ashuapmushuan, Lac, lake, *Can.* 49°10′ N, 74°40′ W 94
Ashville, *Can.* 51°10′ N, 100°18′ W 90
Ashville, *Ohio, U.S.* 39°43′ N, 82°57′ W 102
Ashyrymy, Bichänäk, *Arm.* 39°33′ N, 45°7′ E 195
'Āşī (Orontes), river, *Syr.* 35°40′ N, 36°21′ E 194
Asia 3°0′ N, 103°0′ E 173
Asia, Kepulauan, islands, *North Pacific Ocean* 1°12′ N, 129°17′ E 192
Asia Minor see Anatolia, region, *Asia* 38°39′ N, 30°18′ E 180
Asiago, *It.* 45°52′ N, 11°30′ E 167
Asika, *India* 19°38′ N, 84°38′ E 188
Asikkala, *Fin.* 61°11′ N, 25°28′ E 166
Asilah, *Mor.* 35°28′ N, 6°2′ W 150
Asillo, *Peru* 14°50′ S, 70°21′ W 137
Asinara, Isola, island, *It.* 41°4′ N, 7°5′ E 214
Asino, *Russ.* 56°59′ N, 86°9′ E 169
Asipovichy, *Belarus* 53°17′ N, 28°45′ E 152
Asis, Ras, *Sudan* 18°17′ N, 37°36′ E 182
Ask, *Nor.* 60°28′ N, 5°10′ E 152
Aşkale, *Turk.* 39°56′ N, 40°41′ E 195
Askaniya Nova, *Ukr.* 46°27′ N, 33°53′ E 156
Asker, *Nor.* 59°50′ N, 10°26′ E 152
Askham, *S. Af.* 27°2′ S, 20°51′ E 227
Askī Mawşil, *Iraq* 36°31′ N, 42°37′ E 195
Åskilje, *Nor.* 64°53′ N, 17°51′ E 152
Askino, *Russ.* 56°6′ N, 56°35′ E 154
Askiz, *Russ.* 53°10′ N, 90°33′ E 184
Askole, *Pak.* 35°40′ N, 75°50′ E 188
Askrigg, *U.K.* 54°18′ N, 2°5′ W 162
Askvoll, *Nor.* 61°21′ N, 5°4′ E 152
Asler, spring, *Mali* 18°33′ N, 0°9′ E 222
Asmar, *Afghan.* 35°2′ N, 71°27′ E 186
Asmara, *Eritrea* 15°16′ N, 38°48′ E 182
Åsnes, *Nor.* 60°36′ N, 11°57′ E 152
Asni, *Mor.* 31°14′ N, 8°1′ W 214
Aso, peak, *Japan* 32°51′ N, 131°3′ E 201
Asola, *It.* 45°13′ N, 10°25′ E 167
Asopus, ruin(s), *Gr.* 36°41′ N, 22°45′ E 156
Āsosa, *Eth.* 10°2′ N, 34°29′ E 224
Asoteriba, *Sudan* 19°31′ N, 37°5′ E 182
Asoteriba, Jebel, peak, *Sudan* 21°49′ N, 36°24′ E 182
Aspang, *Aust.* 47°33′ N, 16°3′ E 168
Aspatria, *U.K.* 54°46′ N, 3°20′ W 162
Aspeå, *Nor.* 63°22′ N, 17°36′ E 152
Aspen, *Colo., U.S.* 39°11′ N, 106°50′ W 92
Aspen Butte, peak, *Oreg., U.S.* 42°18′ N, 122°11′ W 90
Aspen Range, *Idaho, U.S.* 42°42′ N, 111°34′ W 90
Aspermont, *Tex., U.S.* 33°6′ N, 100°14′ W 92
Aspiring, Mount, *N.Z.* 44°25′ S, 168°39′ E 240
Asprókavos, Ákra, *Gr.* 39°21′ N, 19°35′ E 156
Aspromonte, *It.* 38°1′ N, 15°50′ E 156
Aspy Bay 46°53′ N, 60°50′ W 111
Asquith, *Can.* 52°8′ N, 107°13′ W 90
Assa, *Mor.* 28°37′ N, 9°24′ W 214
Assab, *Eritrea* 12°59′ N, 42°41′ E 182
'Assâba, *Mauritania* 16°36′ N, 12°26′ W 222
Aşşafā, *Syr.* 33°13′ N, 36°48′ E 194
Assaikio, *Nig.* 8°34′ N, 8°53′ E 222
Assala, *Congo* 2°18′ S, 14°28′ E 218
Assam, adm. division, *India* 26°28′ N, 90°56′ E 188
Assaouas, spring, *Niger* 16°53′ N, 7°24′ E 222
Assateague Island National Seashore, *Va., U.S.* 38°4′ N, 75°9′ W 94
Assean Lake, lake, *Can.* 56°7′ N, 97°7′ W 108
Assebroek, *Belg.* 51°10′ N, 3°16′ E 163
Assen, *Neth.* 52°59′ N, 6°33′ E 163
Assiniboia, *Can.* 49°37′ N, 106°0′ W 90
Assiniboine, Mount, *Can.* 50°51′ N, 115°44′ W 90
Assiniboine, river, *Can.* 49°21′ N, 99°32′ W 80
Assinica, Lac, lake, *Can.* 50°30′ N, 75°45′ W 110
Assiou (Azéo), spring, *Alg.* 21°6′ N, 7°35′ E 222
Assis, *Braz.* 22°40′ S, 50°28′ W 138
Assis Brasil, *Peru* 10°56′ S, 69°41′ W 137
Asslar, *Ger.* 50°35′ N, 8°26′ E 167
Assodé, *Niger* 18°29′ N, 8°35′ E 222
Assok-Ngoum, *Gabon* 1°45′ N, 11°35′ E 218
Assos, ruin(s), *Turk.* 39°29′ N, 26°15′ E 156
Assoul, *Mor.* 32°2′ N, 5°17′ W 214
Assumption, *Ill., U.S.* 39°30′ N, 89°2′ W 102
Assumption Island, *Seychelles* 9°51′ S, 46°7′ E 218
Astana, *Kaz.* 51°7′ N, 71°14′ E 184
Astara, *Azerb.* 38°28′ N, 48°50′ E 195
Āstārā, *Iran* 38°25′ N, 48°48′ E 195
Asten, *Neth.* 51°24′ N, 5°44′ E 167
Asti, *It.* 44°54′ N, 8°12′ E 167
Astillero, *Peru* 13°24′ S, 69°38′ W 137
Astillero, Cerro del, peak, *Mex.* 20°16′ N, 99°39′ W 114
Asto, Mont, peak, *Fr.* 42°34′ N, 9°8′ E 156
Astola Island, *Pak.* 24°57′ N, 63°54′ E 182
Astorga, *Sp.* 42°26′ N, 6°4′ W 150
Astoria, *Oreg., U.S.* 46°10′ N, 123°48′ W 100
Astove Island, *Seychelles* 10°29′ S, 47°53′ E 220
Astrakhan', *Russ.* 46°19′ N, 48°4′ E 158
Astrakhan', adm. division, *Russ.* 47°9′ N, 46°39′ E 158
Åsträsk, *Nor.* 64°35′ N, 19°57′ E 152
Astravyets, *Belarus* 54°36′ N, 25°57′ E 166
Astryna, *Belarus* 53°44′ N, 24°34′ E 154
Asturias, adm. division, *Sp.* 43°24′ N, 7°1′ W 150
Asunción, *Bol.* 11°49′ S, 67°52′ W 137
Asunción, *Parag.* 25°19′ S, 57°49′ W 132
Asunción, Punta, *Arg.* 39°7′ S, 60°30′ W 139
Åsunden, lake, *Nor.* 57°53′ N, 15°25′ E 152
Asūne, *Latv.* 56°0′ N, 27°37′ E 166
Åsvær, island, *Nor.* 66°16′ N, 11°14′ E 152
Asvyeya, *Belarus* 56°1′ N, 28°5′ E 166
Asvyeyskaye, Vozyera, lake, *Belarus* 56°1′ N, 27°32′ E 166
Aswân, *Egypt* 24°4′ N, 32°54′ E 182
Asyûţ, *Egypt* 27°8′ N, 31°5′ E 180
Aszód, *Hung.* 47°39′ N, 19°28′ E 168
Aţ Ţafīlah, *Jordan* 30°50′ N, 35°36′ E 194
Aţ Ţā'if, *Saudi Arabia* 21°15′ N, 40°24′ E 182
At Tāj, *Lib.* 24°17′ N, 23°15′ E 216
At Tall, *Syr.* 33°35′ N, 36°18′ E 194
Aţ Ţayyibah, *Jordan* 31°3′ N, 35°36′ E 194
At Turbah, *Yemen* 12°45′ N, 43°29′ E 182
Aţ Ţuwayyah, spring, *Saudi Arabia* 27°41′ N, 40°50′ E 180
Ataa, *Den.* 69°46′ N, 51°1′ W 106
Atacama, adm. division, *Chile* 27°6′ S, 70°45′ W 132
Atacama, Desierto de, *Chile* 25°53′ S, 70°11′ W 132
Atacuari, river, *Peru* 3°25′ S, 71°16′ W 136
Atafu, island, *N.Z.* 8°29′ S, 172°40′ W 252
Atakora, Chaîne de l', *Benin* 10°7′ N, 1°12′ E 222
Atakpamé, *Togo* 7°33′ N, 1°8′ E 222
Atalaia do Norte, *Braz.* 4°19′ S, 70°7′ W 130
Atalaya, *Peru* 10°44′ S, 73°48′ W 137
Ataléia, *Braz.* 18°4′ S, 41°7′ W 138
Atami, *Japan* 35°4′ N, 139°3′ E 201
Atammik, *Den.* 64°51′ N, 52°9′ W 106
Atamyrat, *Turkm.* 37°52′ N, 65°11′ E 160
Atamyrat (Kerki), *Turkm.* 37°49′ N, 65°10′ E 197
Atar, *Mauritania* 20°31′ N, 13°3′ W 222
Atarfe, *Sp.* 37°13′ N, 3°41′ W 164
Atascadero, *Calif., U.S.* 35°29′ N, 120°41′ W 100
Atašiene, *Latv.* 56°32′ N, 26°21′ E 166
Atasta, ruin(s), *Mex.* 18°37′ N, 92°14′ W 115
Atasū, *Kaz.* 48°40′ N, 71°39′ E 184
Atauro, island, *Indonesia* 8°31′ S, 125°42′ E 192
Atáviros, peak, *Gr.* 36°11′ N, 27°47′ E 156
Atbara, *Sudan* 17°42′ N, 34°3′ E 182
Atbara, river, *Sudan* 14°10′ N, 35°57′ E 226
Atbasar, *Kaz.* 51°48′ N, 68°22′ E 184
At-Bashy, *Kyrg.* 41°7′ N, 75°47′ E 184
Atchafalaya Bay 29°27′ N, 91°38′ W 103
Atchison, *Kans., U.S.* 39°32′ N, 95°8′ W 94
Atea, *Sp.* 41°9′ N, 1°33′ W 164
Ateca, *Sp.* 41°19′ N, 1°49′ W 164
Ath, *Belg.* 50°37′ N, 3°47′ E 163
Ath Thumāmah, spring, *Saudi Arabia* 27°41′ N, 45°0′ E 180
Athabasca, *Can.* 54°41′ N, 113°15′ W 108
Athabasca, Lake, *Can.* 59°8′ N, 109°58′ W 108
Athabasca, Mount, *Can.* 52°10′ N, 117°17′ W 108
Athabasca, oil field, *Can.* 56°54′ N, 111°38′ W 108
Athabasca, river, *Can.* 53°26′ N, 117°6′ W 106
Athamánon, peak, *Gr.* 39°31′ N, 21°7′ E 156
Athenry, *Ire.* 53°17′ N, 8°46′ W 150
Athens, *Ala., U.S.* 34°48′ N, 86°58′ W 96
Athens, *Ga., U.S.* 33°57′ N, 83°24′ W 96
Athens, *Ill., U.S.* 39°57′ N, 89°44′ W 102
Athens, *La., U.S.* 32°38′ N, 93°2′ W 103
Athens, *N.Y., U.S.* 42°15′ N, 73°50′ W 104
Athens, *Ohio, U.S.* 39°19′ N, 82°6′ W 102
Athens, *Pa., U.S.* 41°57′ N, 76°32′ W 110
Athens, *Tenn., U.S.* 35°26′ N, 84°36′ W 96
Athens, *Tex., U.S.* 32°11′ N, 95°51′ W 96
Athens see Athína, *Gr.* 37°58′ N, 23°36′ E 156

Atherley, Can. 44°35′ N, 79°21′ W 110
Athi River, Kenya 1°28′ S, 36°59′ E 224
Athi, river, Kenya 2°31′ S, 38°21′ E 224
Athienou, Northern Cyprus, Cyprus 35°4′ N, 33°32′ E 194
Athína (Athens), Gr. 37°58′ N, 23°36′ E 156
Athlone, Ire. 53°25′ N, 7°58′ W 150
Athna, Cyprus 35°2′ N, 33°47′ E 156
Athol, Mass., U.S. 42°35′ N, 72°14′ W 104
Athol, N.Z. 45°30′ S, 168°35′ E 240
Atholl, Kap, Den. 76°6′ N, 73°24′ W 106
Atholville, Can. 47°58′ N, 66°44′ W 94
Áthos, Mount see Ágio Óros, peak, Gr. 40°8′ N, 24°15′ E 156
Athos, Mount see Ágio Óros, region, Gr. 40°14′ N, 23°2′ E 156
Athos Range, Antarctica 70°15′ S, 61°18′ E 248
Ati, Chad 13°15′ N, 18°22′ E 216
Ati Ardébé, Chad 12°45′ N, 17°41′ E 216
Atiak, Uganda 3°14′ N, 32°7′ E 224
Atiamuri, N.Z. 38°26′ S, 176°1′ E 240
Atico, Peru 16°12′ S, 73°38′ W 137
Atienza, Sp. 41°11′ N, 2°52′ W 164
Atik Lake, Can. 55°16′ N, 96°19′ W 108
Atikameg, Can. 55°54′ N, 115°41′ W 108
Atikameg Lake, Can. 53°57′ N, 100°58′ W 108
Atikameg, river, Can. 51°45′ N, 83°34′ W 110
Atikí, adm. division, Gr. 37°26′ N, 23°14′ E 156
Atikokan, Can. 48°44′ N, 91°37′ W 94
Atikonak Lake, Can. 52°30′ N, 65°11′ W 111
Atikwa Lake, lake, Can. 49°27′ N, 93°56′ W 90
Atiquipa, Peru 15°50′ S, 74°22′ W 137
Atka, Alas., U.S. 52°10′ N, 174°12′ W 160
Atka, Russ. 60°51′ N, 151°50′ E 160
Atka, island, Alas., U.S. 51°38′ N, 175°35′ W 160
Atkarsk, Russ. 51°53′ N, 45°2′ E 158
Atkinson, Nebr., U.S. 42°30′ N, 98°59′ W 90
Atkinson, N.H., U.S. 42°50′ N, 71°10′ W 104
Atkinson Lake, Can. 55°57′ N, 95°34′ W 108
Atkinson Point, Can. 69°54′ N, 134°2′ W 98
Atlacomulco, Mex. 19°47′ N, 99°55′ W 114
Atlanta, Ga., U.S. 33°44′ N, 84°29′ W 96
Atlanta, Ill., U.S. 40°15′ N, 89°14′ W 102
Atlanta, Mich., U.S. 45°0′ N, 84°9′ W 94
Atlanta, Tex., U.S. 33°6′ N, 94°10′ W 103
Atlantic, Iowa, U.S. 41°22′ N, 95°1′ W 94
Atlantic Beach, Fla., U.S. 30°19′ N, 81°25′ W 96
Atlantic Beach, N.C., U.S. 34°42′ N, 76°46′ W 96
Atlantic Ocean 38°49′ N, 72°7′ W 253
Atlantic-Indian Ridge, Indian Ocean 53°30′ S, 21°10′ E 255
Atlántico, adm. division, Col. 10°25′ N, 75°5′ W 136
Atlántida, Uru. 34°46′ S, 55°43′ W 139
Atlantis Fracture Zone, North Atlantic Ocean 29°7′ N, 40°8′ W 253
Atlantis II Fracture Zone, Indian Ocean 34°58′ S, 57°3′ E 254
Atlas Mountains, Africa 35°53′ N, 0°28′ E 164
Atlas Saharien, mountains, Alg. 35°5′ N, 3°42′ E 150
Atlin, Can. 59°35′ N, 133°44′ W 108
'Atlit, Israel 32°41′ N, 34°56′ E 194
Atlixco, Mex. 18°51′ N, 98°27′ W 114
Atmakur, India 14°39′ N, 79°38′ E 188
Atmakur, India 18°44′ N, 78°35′ E 188
Atmautluak, Alas., U.S. 60°49′ N, 162°33′ W 98
Atmore, Ala., U.S. 31°0′ N, 87°30′ W 103
Atna Peak, Can. 53°55′ N, 128°10′ W 108
Atocha, Bol. 21°0′ S, 66°20′ W 137
Atoka, N. Mex., U.S. 32°46′ N, 104°24′ W 92
Atoka, Okla., U.S. 34°21′ N, 96°7′ W 96
Atokila, spring, Mali 22°46′ N, 5°56′ W 214
Atome, Angola 11°54′ S, 14°37′ E 220
Atotonilco, Mex. 24°14′ N, 102°50′ W 114
Atotonilco el Alto, Mex. 20°32′ N, 102°32′ W 114
Atoyac, Mex. 20°0′ N, 103°33′ W 114
Atoyac, river, Mex. 17°58′ N, 98°42′ W 114
Atqasuk, Alas., U.S. 70°28′ N, 157°34′ W 98
Atrak, river, Iran 37°20′ N, 57°36′ E 180
Atrato, river, Col. 7°29′ N, 77°11′ W 136
Atsumi, Japan 38°38′ N, 139°37′ E 201
Atsumi, Japan 34°37′ N, 137°7′ E 201
Attachie, Can. 56°12′ N, 121°28′ W 108
Attalla, Ala., U.S. 34°0′ N, 86°6′ W 96
Attapu, Laos 14°55′ N, 106°46′ E 202
Attawapiskat, Can. 52°58′ N, 82°31′ W 106
Attawapiskat, river, Can. 52°3′ N, 87°31′ W 110
Attendorn, Ger. 51°7′ N, 7°54′ E 167
Attica, Ind., U.S. 40°16′ N, 87°15′ W 102
Attica, Kans., U.S. 37°13′ N, 98°14′ W 92
Attica, Ohio, U.S. 41°3′ N, 82°54′ W 102
Attigny, Fr. 49°27′ N, 4°34′ E 163
Attigu, Sudan 4°1′ N, 31°43′ E 224
Attingal, India 8°40′ N, 76°48′ E 188
Attleboro, Mass., U.S. 41°56′ N, 71°17′ W 104
Attleborough, U.K. 52°30′ N, 1°1′ E 162
Attoyac, river, Tex., U.S. 31°37′ N, 94°21′ W 103
Attu, Den. 67°55′ N, 53°39′ W 106
Attu, island, Alas., U.S. 52°47′ N, 171°26′ E 160
Attur, India 11°35′ N, 78°36′ E 188
Attwood Lake, Can. 51°11′ N, 89°9′ W 110
Atuel, river, Arg. 35°38′ S, 67°47′ W 134
Atura, Uganda 2°7′ N, 32°23′ E 224
Atwater, Calif., U.S. 37°21′ N, 120°37′ W 100
Atwood, Kans., U.S. 39°47′ N, 101°4′ W 90
Atwood see Crooked Island, Bahamas 22°39′ N, 76°43′ W 81
Atyashevo, Russ. 54°37′ N, 46°10′ E 154
Atyraū, Kaz. 47°6′ N, 51°53′ E 158
Atyrau, adm. division, Kaz. 47°28′ N, 50°45′ E 158
Atzinging Lake, lake, Can. 60°9′ N, 103°50′ W 108
Au Fer, Point, La., U.S. 29°11′ N, 91°28′ W 103
Au Gres, Mich., U.S. 44°3′ N, 83°42′ W 102
Au Gres, Point, Mich., U.S. 43°51′ N, 83°51′ W 102
Au Sable, Mich., U.S. 44°25′ N, 83°21′ W 94
Au Sable Forks, N.Y., U.S. 44°25′ N, 73°41′ W 104
Au Sable Point, Mich., U.S. 46°21′ N, 86°10′ W 110
Au Sable Point, Mich., U.S. 44°19′ N, 83°40′ W 110
Au Sable, river, Mich., U.S. 44°41′ N, 84°44′ W 80
Auas Mountains, Namibia 22°40′ S, 17°6′ E 227
Aubarede Point, Philippines 17°17′ N, 122°28′ E 203
Aúbe, Mozambique 16°22′ S, 39°46′ E 224
Aube, river, Fr. 48°18′ N, 4°35′ E 163
Aubenton, Fr. 49°49′ N, 4°12′ E 163
Auberry, Calif., U.S. 37°4′ N, 119°30′ W 100
Aubin, Fr. 44°31′ N, 2°13′ E 150
Aubrac, Monts d', Fr. 44°47′ N, 2°47′ E 165
Aubrey Cliffs, Ariz., U.S. 35°51′ N, 113°14′ W 92
Aubrey Falls, Can. 46°44′ N, 83°14′ W 94
Aubry Lake, Can. 67°31′ N, 127°14′ W 98
Auburn, Ala., U.S. 32°36′ N, 85°29′ W 96
Auburn, Calif., U.S. 38°53′ N, 121°6′ W 90
Auburn, Ill., U.S. 39°34′ N, 89°44′ W 102
Auburn, Ind., U.S. 41°21′ N, 85°4′ W 102
Auburn, Me., U.S. 44°5′ N, 70°15′ W 104
Auburn, Mich., U.S. 43°36′ N, 84°5′ W 102
Auburn, Miss., U.S. 31°20′ N, 90°37′ W 103
Auburn, Mo., U.S. 39°34′ N, 89°44′ W 94
Auburn, Nebr., U.S. 40°22′ N, 95°51′ W 90
Auburn, N.H., U.S. 43°0′ N, 71°21′ W 104
Auburn, N.Y., U.S. 42°55′ N, 76°34′ W 94
Auburn, Wash., U.S. 47°17′ N, 122°15′ W 100
Auburn Range, Austral. 25°28′ S, 150°9′ E 230
Auburndale, Fla., U.S. 28°4′ N, 81°48′ W 105
Aucanquilcha, peak, Chile 21°15′ S, 68°34′ W 137
Aucará, Peru 14°18′ S, 74°5′ W 137
Auce, Latv. 56°28′ N, 22°52′ E 166
Auch, Fr. 43°38′ N, 0°34′ E 150
Auchi, Nig. 7°6′ N, 6°13′ E 222
Auckland, N.Z. 36°53′ S, 174°48′ E 240
Aude, river, Fr. 42°54′ N, 2°12′ E 165
Auden, Can. 50°14′ N, 87°52′ W 94
Auderville, Fr. 49°42′ N, 1°57′ W 150
Audoin, Lac, lake, Can. 46°46′ N, 79°8′ W 94
Audubon, Iowa, U.S. 41°41′ N, 94°55′ W 94
Audun-le-Roman, Fr. 49°22′ N, 5°51′ E 163
Aūezov, Kaz. 49°42′ N, 81°30′ E 184
Auffay, Fr. 49°43′ N, 1°6′ E 163
Aughty Mountains, Slieve, Ire. 52°54′ N, 9°21′ W 150
Augrabies Falls National Park, S. Af. 28°38′ S, 20°6′ E 227
Augsburg, Ger. 48°22′ N, 10°53′ E 152
Augusta, Austral. 34°16′ S, 115°10′ E 231
Augusta, Ga., U.S. 33°28′ N, 81°58′ W 96
Augusta, Kans., U.S. 37°39′ N, 96°59′ W 92
Augusta, Ky., U.S. 38°45′ N, 84°1′ W 102
Augusta, Me., U.S. 44°18′ N, 69°49′ W 104
Augusta, Mont., U.S. 47°28′ N, 112°24′ W 90
Augusta, Tex., U.S. 31°30′ N, 95°19′ W 103
Augusta, Wis., U.S. 44°40′ N, 91°7′ W 94
Augusta, Mount, Can. 60°16′ N, 140°39′ W 98
Augusta Victoria, Chile 24°7′ S, 69°25′ W 132
Augusto Lima, Braz. 18°7′ S, 44°18′ W 138
Augustów, Pol. 53°51′ N, 22°58′ E 166
Augustus Island, Austral. 15°21′ S, 122°46′ E 230
Augustus, Mount, Austral. 24°23′ S, 116°37′ E 230
Auk, oil field, North Sea 56°23′ N, 1°57′ E 150
Auke Bay, Alas., U.S. 58°24′ N, 134°41′ W 108
Aukra, Nor. 62°46′ N, 6°54′ E 152
Aukštaitija National Park, Lith. 55°22′ N, 25°37′ E 166
Aul, India 20°40′ N, 86°39′ E 188
Āūlīeköl, Kaz. 52°22′ N, 64°5′ E 184
Aulis, ruin(s), Gr. 38°24′ N, 23°30′ E 156
Aulla, It. 44°12′ N, 9°59′ E 167
Aulneau Peninsula, Can. 49°22′ N, 94°42′ W 90
Ault, Fr. 50°5′ N, 1°27′ E 163
Aultbea, U.K. 57°50′ N, 5°35′ W 150
Aulus-les-Bains, Fr. 42°46′ N, 1°20′ E 164
Aumale, Fr. 49°45′ N, 1°45′ E 163
Auna, Nig. 10°10′ N, 4°42′ E 222
Auneau, Fr. 48°27′ N, 1°45′ E 163
Auneuil, Fr. 49°22′ N, 1°59′ E 163
Auno, Nig. 11°51′ N, 12°55′ E 216
Aups, Fr. 43°37′ N, 6°12′ E 150
Aur, island, Malaysia 2°20′ N, 104°22′ E 196
Aura, Fin. 60°36′ N, 22°32′ E 166
Aura, river, Nor. 62°19′ N, 8°10′ E 152
Auraiya, India 26°26′ N, 79°29′ E 197
Aurdal, Nor. 60°54′ N, 9°25′ E 152
Aure, Nor. 63°15′ N, 8°34′ E 152
Aurich, Ger. 53°28′ N, 7°28′ E 163
Aurillac, Fr. 44°54′ N, 2°27′ E 150
Aurisina, It. 45°45′ N, 13°40′ E 167
Auritz (Burguete), Sp. 42°59′ N, 1°21′ W 164
Auronzo di Cadore, It. 46°32′ N, 12°26′ E 167
Aurora, Can. 43°59′ N, 79°28′ W 110
Aurora, Ill., U.S. 41°45′ N, 88°18′ W 102
Aurora, Ind., U.S. 39°2′ N, 84°56′ W 102
Aurora, Minn., U.S. 47°31′ N, 92°16′ W 94
Aurora, Mo., U.S. 41°45′ N, 88°18′ W 94
Aurora, Mo., U.S. 36°57′ N, 93°43′ W 96
Aurora, Nebr., U.S. 40°51′ N, 98°1′ W 90
Aurora, Ohio, U.S. 41°18′ N, 81°21′ W 102
Aurukun, Austral. 13°9′ S, 141°46′ E 238
Aus, Namibia 26°41′ S, 16°16′ E 227
Austevoll, Nor. 60°5′ N, 5°13′ E 152
Austin, Ind., U.S. 38°45′ N, 85°48′ W 102
Austin, Minn., U.S. 43°39′ N, 93°0′ W 94
Austin, Nev., U.S. 39°30′ N, 117°5′ W 90
Austin, Pa., U.S. 41°37′ N, 78°5′ W 94
Austin, Tex., U.S. 30°14′ N, 97°50′ W 92
Austral Islands (Tubuai Islands), South Pacific Ocean 21°30′ S, 152°33′ W 238
Australia 24°25′ S, 128°31′ E 231
Australia 22°0′ S, 133°0′ E 231
Australian, Can. 52°43′ N, 122°26′ W 108
Australian Alps, Austral. 37°20′ S, 145°56′ E 230
Australian-Antarctic Basin, Indian Ocean 59°4′ S, 115°12′ E 255
Australian Capital Territory, adm. division, Austral. 35°42′ S, 148°21′ E 231
Austråt, Nor. 63°41′ N, 9°45′ E 152
Austria 48°27′ N, 14°52′ E 152
Autazes, Braz. 3°38′ S, 59°8′ W 130
Auterive, Fr. 43°19′ N, 1°27′ E 164
Authon-du-Perche, Fr. 48°11′ N, 0°53′ E 163
Autlán, Mex. 19°46′ N, 104°22′ W 114
Auve, Fr. 49°2′ N, 4°41′ E 163
Auvergne, adm. division, Fr. 45°9′ N, 2°15′ E 150
Auvergne, region, Europe 44°55′ N, 2°13′ E 165
Auvillar, Fr. 44°3′ N, 0°53′ E 150
Aux Sources, Mont, peak, Lesotho 28°56′ S, 28°42′ E 227
Auxerre, Fr. 47°47′ N, 3°33′ E 150
Auxonne, Fr. 47°11′ N, 5°23′ E 156
Auyán Tepuí, peak, Venez. 5°48′ N, 62°42′ W 130
Auyuittuq National Park, Can. 67°30′ N, 66°0′ W 106
Ava, Mo., U.S. 36°57′ N, 92°39′ W 96
Avakubi, Dem. Rep. of the Congo 1°21′ N, 27°39′ E 224
Avala, peak, Serb. 44°42′ N, 20°29′ E 168
Avallon, Fr. 47°28′ N, 3°54′ E 150
Avalon, Calif., U.S. 33°19′ N, 118°20′ W 101
Avalon Peninsula, Can. 47°20′ N, 53°50′ W 111
Avaré, Braz. 23°6′ S, 48°57′ W 138
Avarua, New Zealand 21°0′ S, 160°0′ W 241
Avawatz Mountains, Calif., U.S. 35°36′ N, 116°30′ W 101
Avawatz Pass, Calif., U.S. 35°31′ N, 116°27′ W 101
Avay, Kaz. 49°34′ N, 72°52′ E 184
Avebury, site, U.K. 51°26′ N, 1°53′ W 162
Aveiro, Braz. 3°37′ S, 55°23′ W 130
Aveiro, Port. 40°37′ N, 8°42′ W 214
Aveiro, Port. 40°38′ N, 8°40′ W 150
Aveiro, adm. division, Port. 40°37′ N, 8°58′ W 150
Avellaneda, Arg. 34°42′ S, 58°20′ W 139
Avenal, Calif., U.S. 36°0′ N, 120°9′ W 100
Averías, Arg. 28°45′ S, 62°28′ W 139
Aversa, It. 40°59′ N, 14°12′ E 156
Avery, Calif., U.S. 38°12′ N, 120°23′ W 100
Avery Island, La., U.S. 29°52′ N, 91°56′ W 103
Aves, Islas de, islands, Caribbean Sea 12°7′ N, 67°29′ W 116
Aves Ridge, Caribbean Sea 15°1′ N, 63°37′ W 253
Avesnes, Fr. 50°7′ N, 3°55′ E 163
Avesta, Nor. 60°7′ N, 16°7′ E 152
Aveyron, river, Fr. 44°22′ N, 2°7′ E 165
Avia Terai, Arg. 26°41′ S, 60°46′ W 139
Aviano, It. 46°4′ N, 12°34′ E 167
Avignon, Fr. 43°57′ N, 4°50′ E 214
Ávila, Sp. 40°39′ N, 4°42′ W 150
Avila Beach, Calif., U.S. 35°11′ N, 120°44′ W 100
Ávila, Sierra de, Sp. 40°30′ N, 5°33′ W 150
Avilla, Ind., U.S. 41°21′ N, 85°15′ W 102
Avinger, Tex., U.S. 32°53′ N, 94°35′ W 103
Avinurme, Est. 58°58′ N, 26°53′ E 166
Avize, Fr. 48°57′ N, 4°0′ E 163
Avoca, Ind., U.S. 38°54′ N, 86°34′ W 102
Avoca, Iowa, U.S. 41°26′ N, 95°21′ W 90
Avola, It. 36°54′ N, 15°7′ E 156
Avon, Mass., U.S. 42°7′ N, 71°3′ W 104
Avon, N.C., U.S. 35°21′ N, 75°31′ W 96
Avon Park, Fla., U.S. 27°36′ N, 81°30′ W 105
Avon, river, U.K. 51°27′ N, 2°43′ W 162
Avonlea, Can. 50°0′ N, 105°5′ W 90
Avonmouth, U.K. 51°30′ N, 2°42′ W 162
Avontuur, S. Af. 33°44′ S, 23°11′ E 227
Avraga, Mongolia 47°13′ N, 109°10′ E 198
Avre, river, Fr. 48°41′ N, 0°53′ E 163
Avsa, Gora, peak, Russ. 63°18′ N, 93°27′ E 169
Avtovac, Bosn. and Herzg. 43°8′ N, 18°33′ E 168
Awakino, N.Z. 38°42′ S, 174°39′ E 240
Awali, oil field, Bahrain 25°55′ N, 50°29′ E 196
Āwarē, Eth. 8°13′ N, 44°5′ E 218
Awarua Bay 44°22′ S, 167°39′ E 240
Āwasa, Eth. 6°57′ N, 38°26′ E 224
Āwash, Eth. 8°59′ N, 40°10′ E 224
Āwash National Park, Eth. 8°43′ N, 39°27′ E 224
Awash, river, Eth. 9°38′ N, 40°17′ E 224
Awaso, Ghana 6°13′ N, 2°16′ W 222
Awat, China 40°38′ N, 80°22′ E 184
Awbārī (Ubari), Lib. 26°37′ N, 12°45′ E 216
Awdheegle, Somalia 1°57′ N, 44°50′ E 218
Awe, Nig. 8°9′ N, 9°7′ E 222
Aweil, Sudan 8°46′ N, 27°22′ E 224
Awfist, Western Sahara, Mor. 25°45′ N, 14°38′ W 214
Awgu, Nig. 6°4′ N, 7°26′ E 222
Awio, P.N.G. 6°13′ S, 150°6′ E 192
Awjilah, Lib. 29°9′ N, 21°14′ E 216
Awka, Nig. 6°12′ N, 7°3′ E 222
Awsard, Western Sahara, Mor. 22°39′ N, 14°19′ W 214
Awwalī, river, Leb. 33°35′ N, 35°23′ E 194
Axat, Fr. 42°48′ N, 2°12′ E 164
Axbridge, U.K. 51°16′ N, 2°49′ W 162
Axel Heiberg Island, Can. 80°42′ N, 95°47′ W 246
Axim, Ghana 4°53′ N, 2°14′ W 222
Axinim, Braz. 4°2′ S, 59°25′ W 130
Axmarsbruk, Nor. 61°3′ N, 17°4′ E 152
Axminster, U.K. 50°46′ N, 2°59′ W 162
Axochiapan, Mex. 18°28′ N, 98°45′ W 114
Axos, ruin(s), Gr. 35°17′ N, 24°44′ E 156
Axtell, Nebr., U.S. 40°28′ N, 99°8′ W 90
Ay, Fr. 49°3′ N, 4°0′ E 163
Ay, Kaz. 47°29′ N, 80°35′ E 184
Aya Bentih, Eth. 8°0′ N, 46°36′ E 218
Ayabe, Japan 35°16′ N, 135°15′ E 201
Ayacucho, Arg. 37°9′ S, 58°32′ W 139
Ayacucho, Bol. 17°54′ S, 63°24′ W 137
Ayacucho, Col. 8°35′ N, 73°34′ W 136
Ayacucho, Peru 13°11′ S, 74°15′ W 137
Ayacucho, adm. division, Peru 14°1′ S, 74°38′ W 137
Ayad, oil field, Yemen 15°11′ N, 46°58′ E 182
Ayakkum Hu, lake, China 37°38′ N, 88°29′ E 188
Ayaköz, Kaz. 47°57′ N, 80°22′ E 184
Ayaköz, river, Kaz. 46°55′ N, 79°28′ E 184
Ayamonte, Sp. 37°12′ N, 7°24′ W 150
Ayan, Russ. 56°27′ N, 137°54′ E 160
Ayancık, Turk. 41°56′ N, 34°33′ E 156
Ayanganna Mountain, Guyana 5°16′ N, 60°5′ W 130
Ayangba, Nig. 7°29′ N, 7°8′ E 222
Ayanka, Russ. 63°46′ N, 166°45′ E 160
Ayapel, Col. 8°19′ N, 75°9′ W 136
Ayapel, Serranía de, Col. 7°14′ N, 75°53′ W 136
Ayaş, Turk. 40°1′ N, 32°20′ E 156
Ayaviri, Peru 14°54′ S, 70°34′ W 137
Aybak, Afghan. 36°13′ N, 68°5′ E 186
Aydar Kŭl, lake, Uzb. 40°52′ N, 66°59′ E 197
Ayde, Lac, lake, Can. 52°17′ N, 73°52′ W 111
Aydın, Turk. 37°51′ N, 27°48′ E 156
Aydıncık, Turk. 36°8′ N, 33°19′ E 156
Aydyrlinskiy, Russ. 52°3′ N, 59°50′ E 154
Āyelu Terara, peak, Eth. 10°3′ N, 40°37′ E 224
Ayer, Mass., U.S. 42°33′ N, 71°36′ W 104
Ayerbe, Sp. 42°16′ N, 0°41′ E 164
Ayers Rock see Uluru, peak, Austral. 25°23′ S, 130°52′ E 230
Ayersville, Ohio, U.S. 41°13′ N, 84°17′ W 102
Ayeyarwady (Irrawady), river, Myanmar 21°54′ N, 95°42′ W 202
Āykel, Eth. 12°30′ N, 37°3′ E 182
Aykhal, Russ. 65°55′ N, 111°24′ E 160
Aykino, Russ. 62°12′ N, 49°58′ E 154
Aylesbury, U.K. 51°48′ N, 0°49′ E 162
Ayllón, Sp. 41°24′ N, 3°22′ W 164
Aylmer, Can. 42°46′ N, 80°58′ W 102
Aylmer Lake, lake, Can. 63°39′ N, 108°52′ W 106
Aylmer, Mount, Can. 51°19′ N, 115°31′ W 90
Aylsham, U.K. 52°47′ N, 1°15′ E 162
'Ayn al Ghazāl, spring, Lib. 21°50′ N, 24°52′ E 226
'Ayn Dīwār, Syr. 37°16′ N, 42°9′ E 195
'Ayn Sīdī Muḩammad, spring, Lib. 29°5′ N, 20°12′ E 216
'Ayn Sifnī, Iraq 36°42′ N, 43°14′ E 195
'Ayn Wabrah, spring, Saudi Arabia 27°25′ N, 47°20′ E 196
'Ayn Zuwayyah, spring, Lib. 21°54′ N, 24°48′ E 226
Ayna, Peru 12°43′ S, 73°53′ W 137
Ayna, Sp. 38°32′ N, 2°4′ W 164
Ayni, Taj. 39°22′ N, 68°31′ E 197
'Aynūnah, Saudi Arabia 28°6′ N, 35°10′ E 180
Ayod, Sudan 8°3′ N, 31°22′ E 224
Ayon, Ostrov, island, Russ. 70°5′ N, 164°44′ E 160
Ayora, Sp. 39°3′ N, 1°4′ W 164
Ayorou, Niger 14°40′ N, 0°54′ E 222
Ayos, Cameroon 3°57′ N, 12°31′ E 218
'Ayoûn 'Abd el Mâlek, spring, Mauritania 24°55′ N, 7°28′ W 214
'Ayoûn el 'Atroûs, Mauritania 16°40′ N, 9°35′ W 222
Aypolovo, Russ. 58°46′ N, 76°43′ E 169
Ayr, Austral. 19°33′ S, 147°24′ E 231
Ayr, U.K. 55°27′ N, 4°38′ W 150
'Ayrah, Syr. 32°36′ N, 36°32′ E 194
Ayrancı, Turk. 37°21′ N, 33°39′ E 156
Ayribaba, Gora, peak, Turkm. 37°46′ N, 66°28′ E 197
Āysha, Eth. 10°42′ N, 42°35′ E 224
Āyteke Bī, Kaz. 45°52′ N, 62°8′ E 184
Aytos, Bulg. 42°42′ N, 27°15′ E 156
Ayu, Kepulauan, islands, North Pacific Ocean 0°41′ N, 128°54′ E 192
Ayutla, Mex. 20°7′ N, 104°22′ W 114
Ayutthaya, Thai. 14°21′ N, 100°32′ E 202
Ayvaj, Taj. 36°59′ N, 68°0′ E 186
Ayvalık, Turk. 39°17′ N, 26°43′ E 180
Aywaille, Belg. 50°28′ N, 5°40′ E 167
Az Zabadānī, Syr. 33°43′ N, 36°6′ E 194
Az Ẕāhirīyah, West Bank, Israel 31°24′ N, 34°57′ E 194
Az Ẕahrān (Dhahran), Saudi Arabia 26°15′ N, 50°1′ E 196
Az Zarqā', Jordan 32°3′ N, 36°5′ E 194
Az Zarqā', Jordan 32°3′ N, 36°7′ E 180
Az Zawr, Kuwait 28°43′ N, 48°23′ E 196
Az Zībār, Iraq 36°53′ N, 43°58′ E 195
Az Zilfī, Saudi Arabia 26°17′ N, 44°49′ E 182
Az Zubayr, Iraq 30°20′ N, 47°42′ E 180
Āzād Shahr, Iran 37°11′ N, 55°19′ E 180
Azamgarh, India 26°4′ N, 83°10′ E 197
Azángaro, Peru 14°56′ S, 70°14′ W 137
Azanja, Serb. 44°25′ N, 20°53′ E 168
Azaouâd, region, Africa 17°57′ N, 3°35′ W 222
Azaouagh, region, Africa 16°29′ N, 3°46′ E 222
Azapa, Chile 18°35′ S, 70°14′ W 137
Azapol'ye, Russ. 65°17′ N, 45°11′ E 154
Azara, Nig. 8°20′ N, 9°12′ E 222
Āzarān, Iran 37°30′ N, 47°3′ E 195
Azare, Nig. 11°41′ N, 10°10′ E 222
A'zāz, Syr. 36°35′ N, 37°2′ E 156
Azdavay, Turk. 41°39′ N, 33°16′ E 156
Azefal, Mauritania 20°51′ N, 15°9′ W 222
Azeffoun, Alg. 36°53′ N, 4°25′ E 150
Azélik, Niger 17°34′ N, 6°45′ E 222
Azéo see Assiou, spring, Alg. 21°6′ N, 7°35′ E 222
Azerbaijan 40°19′ N, 46°58′ E 195
Azero, river, Bol. 19°42′ S, 64°7′ W 137
Azerraf, spring, Mali 19°28′ N, 2°29′ E 222
Azigui, spring, Mali 16°38′ N, 2°36′ E 222
Azigzane, spring, Mali 22°20′ N, 3°18′ W 222
Azilal, Mor. 31°58′ N, 6°33′ W 214
Azlat, spring, Mauritania 16°49′ N, 14°5′ W 222
Aznakayevo, Russ. 54°52′ N, 53°8′ E 154

Aznalcóllar, *Sp.* 37°30' N, 6°16' W 164
Azores (Açores), islands, *Port.* 39°29' N, 27°35' W 207
Azov, *Russ.* 47°4' N, 39°25' E 158
Azov, Sea of 45°58' N, 35°0' E 160
Azovy, *Russ.* 64°50' N, 65°11' E 169
Azraq ash Shīshān, *Jordan* 31°49' N, 36°48' E 194
Azrou, *Mor.* 33°30' N, 5°14' W 214
Azua, *Dom. Rep.* 18°28' N, 70°43' W 116
Azuaga, *Sp.* 38°15' N, 5°42' W 164
Azuara, *Sp.* 41°15' N, 0°53' E 164
Azucena, *Arg.* 37°33' S, 59°21' W 139
Azuer, river, *Sp.* 38°55' N, 3°26' W 164
Azuero, Península de, *Pan.* 7°36' N, 80°51' W 115
Azufre Norte, Paso del, pass, *Arg.* 31°16' S, 70°34' W 134
Azul, *Arg.* 36°46' S, 59°50' W 139
Azul, river, *Mex.* 17°9' N, 99°9' W 114
Azurduy, *Bol.* 20°0' S, 64°28' W 137
Azure Lake, lake, *Can.* 52°22' N, 120°23' W 108

B

Ba Dong, *Vietnam* 9°40' N, 106°33' E 202
Ba Ria, *Vietnam* 10°29' N, 107°10' E 202
Ba, river, *Vietnam* 13°25' N, 108°29' E 202
Baabda, *Leb.* 33°50' N, 35°31' E 194
Baalbek, *Leb.* 34°0' N, 36°12' E 194
Baarle-Hertog, *Belg.* 51°26' N, 4°55' E 167
Baarn, *Neth.* 52°12' N, 5°16' E 163
Ba'ashom, *Sudan* 13°25' N, 31°22' E 226
Bab, oil field, *U.A.E.* 23°52' N, 53°43' E 196
Bab Ozero, lake, *Russ.* 68°19' N, 33°38' E 152
Baba Burnu, *Turk.* 39°30' N, 25°37' E 156
Baba Dağ, peak, *Turk.* 36°29' N, 29°6' E 156
Baba, peak, *Bulg.* 42°45' N, 23°54' E 156
Babadag, *Rom.* 44°53' N, 28°43' E 158
Babadag, peak, *Azerb.* 41°0' N, 48°15' E 195
Babadaykhan, *Turkm.* 37°53' N, 60°21' E 180
Babaeski, *Turk.* 41°25' N, 27°4' E 156
Babak, *Philippines* 7°9' N, 125°43' E 203
Babana, *Nig.* 10°27' N, 3°49' E 222
Babanūsa, *Sudan* 11°15' N, 27°46' E 224
Babar, island, *Indonesia* 8°21' S, 129°10' E 192
Babati, *Tanzania* 4°12' S, 35°44' E 224
Babayevo, *Russ.* 59°23' N, 35°59' E 154
Babayurt, *Russ.* 43°34' N, 46°44' E 195
Babb, *Mont., U.S.* 48°51' N, 113°28' W 90
B'abdāt, *Leb.* 33°53' N, 35°40' E 194
Babel, Mont de, peak, *Can.* 51°25' N, 68°49' W 111
Babeldaob see Babelthuap, island, *Palau* 8°0' N, 135°0' E 242
Babelthuap (Babeldaob), island, *Palau* 8°0' N, 135°0' E 242
Baberu, *India* 25°34' N, 80°44' E 197
Babi, island, *Indonesia* 2°3' N, 96°40' E 196
Babia Góra, peak, *Slovakia* 49°33' N, 19°28' E 152
Babian, river, *China* 23°31' N, 101°16' E 202
Babilafuente, *Sp.* 40°58' N, 5°27' W 150
Babin Nos, peak, *Bulg.* 43°41' N, 22°22' E 168
Babine, *Can.* 55°19' N, 126°36' W 108
Babine, river, *Can.* 55°41' N, 127°32' W 108
Babino Polje, *Croatia* 42°43' N, 17°31' E 168
Bābol, *Iran* 36°35' N, 52°43' E 180
Babonã, river, *Braz.* 6°16' S, 67°4' W 130
Baboquivari Peak, *Ariz., U.S.* 31°45' N, 111°39' W 92
Babruysk, *Belarus* 53°5' N, 29°17' E 152
Babson Park, *Fla., U.S.* 27°50' N, 81°31' W 105
Babuna, *Maced.* 41°30' N, 21°24' E 168
Babusar Pass, *Pak.* 35°8' N, 74°2' E 186
Babushkina, *Russ.* 59°44' N, 43°11' E 154
Babušnica, *Serb.* 43°4' N, 22°25' E 168
Babuyan Channel 18°34' N, 121°27' E 203
Babuyan, island, *Philippines* 19°34' N, 122°1' E 198
Babuyan Islands, *South China Sea* 19°8' N, 121°56' E 203
Babylon, *N.Y., U.S.* 40°41' N, 73°19' W 104
Babylon, ruin(s), *Iraq* 32°30' N, 44°16' E 180
Bač, *Serb.* 45°22' N, 19°15' E 168
Bac Can, *Vietnam* 22°9' N, 105°50' E 198
Bac Giang, *Vietnam* 21°16' N, 106°13' E 198
Bac Lieu, *Vietnam* 9°18' N, 105°42' E 202
Bac Ninh, *Vietnam* 21°11' N, 106°2' E 198
Bacaadweyne, *Somalia* 7°10' N, 47°34' E 218
Bacabal, *Braz.* 4°15' S, 44°53' W 132
Bacadéhuachi, *Mex.* 29°41' N, 109°9' W 92
Bacajá, river, *Braz.* 3°51' S, 51°48' W 130
Bacan, island, *Indonesia* 0°38' N, 126°26' E 192
Bacanora, *Mex.* 28°58' N, 109°24' W 92
Bacarra, *Philippines* 18°16' N, 120°37' E 203
Bacău, *Rom.* 46°33' N, 26°55' E 156
Bacău, adm. division, *Rom.* 46°13' N, 26°17' E 156
Baccarat, *Fr.* 48°27' N, 6°45' E 163
Bæccegelhalde, peak, *Nor.* 69°31' N, 21°45' E 152
Baceno, *It.* 46°16' N, 8°18' E 167
Bacerac, *Mex.* 30°20' N, 108°58' W 92
Băceşti, *Rom.* 46°50' N, 27°14' E 156
Bačevci, *Serb.* 44°11' N, 19°55' E 168
Bach, *Mich., U.S.* 43°40' N, 83°21' W 102
Bach Long Vi, Dao (Nightingale Island), *Vietnam* 19°46' N, 107°30' E 198
Bach Ma National Park, *Vietnam* 16°12' N, 108°7' E 202
Bach, Mynydd, peak, *U.K.* 52°17' N, 4°4' W 162
Bacharach, *Ger.* 50°3' N, 7°44' E 167
Bachelor, Mount, *Oreg., U.S.* 43°57' N, 121°47' W 90
Bachíniva, *Mex.* 28°46' N, 107°15' W 92
Bachu, *China* 39°44' N, 78°34' E 184
Baciuty, *Pol.* 53°3' N, 22°58' E 152
Back, river, *Can.* 64°47' N, 105°2' W 106
Bačka Palanka, *Serb.* 45°14' N, 19°23' E 168
Bačka, region, *Serb.* 45°44' N, 18°55' E 168
Backbone Mountain, *Md., U.S.* 39°12' N, 79°34' W 94
Backbone Ranges, *Can.* 61°28' N, 124°16' W 108
Backe, *Nor.* 63°49' N, 16°22' E 152
Bäckefors, *Nor.* 58°49' N, 12°8' E 152
Bačko Gradište, *Serb.* 45°32' N, 20°1' E 168
Bačko Petrovo Selo, *Serb.* 45°42' N, 20°4' E 168
Bacnotan, *Philippines* 16°44' N, 120°20' E 203
Baco, Mount, *Philippines* 12°49' N, 121°6' E 203
Bacoachi, *Mex.* 30°38' N, 109°59' W 92
Bacolod, *Philippines* 10°39' N, 122°57' E 203
Bácsalmás, *Hung.* 46°7' N, 19°20' E 168
Bács-Kiskun, adm. division, *Hung.* 46°31' N, 19°2' E 156
Bad Axe, *Mich., U.S.* 43°47' N, 83°0' W 102
Bad Bentheim, *Ger.* 52°18' N, 7°10' E 163
Bad Bergzabern, *Ger.* 49°6' N, 7°59' E 163
Bad Brückenau, *Ger.* 50°18' N, 9°47' E 167
Bad Camberg, *Ger.* 50°18' N, 8°16' E 167
Bad Driburg, *Ger.* 51°44' N, 9°0' E 167
Bad Ems, *Ger.* 50°20' N, 7°42' E 167
Bad Godesberg, *Ger.* 50°41' N, 7°9' E 167
Bad Hersfeld, *Ger.* 50°51' N, 9°42' E 167
Bad Homburg, *Ger.* 50°14' N, 8°36' E 167
Bad Honnef, *Ger.* 50°38' N, 7°13' E 167
Bad Hönningen, *Ger.* 50°30' N, 7°19' E 167
Bad Iburg, *Ger.* 52°9' N, 8°2' E 163
Bad Ischl, *Aust.* 47°42' N, 13°38' E 156
Bad Karlshafen, *Ger.* 51°38' N, 9°29' E 167
Bad Kissingen, *Ger.* 50°11' N, 10°4' E 167
Bad Kreuznach, *Ger.* 49°50' N, 7°52' E 167
Bad Laasphe, *Ger.* 50°55' N, 8°24' E 167
Bad Lauterberg, *Ger.* 51°37' N, 10°26' E 167
Bad Marienberg, *Ger.* 50°38' N, 7°56' E 167
Bad Nauheim, *Ger.* 50°21' N, 8°43' E 167
Bad Neuenahr-Ahrweiler, *Ger.* 50°33' N, 7°7' E 167
Bad Neustadt, *Ger.* 50°19' N, 10°11' E 167
Bad Orb, *Ger.* 50°13' N, 9°21' E 167
Bad, river, *S. Dak., U.S.* 43°58' N, 101°7' W 90
Bad Salzig, *Ger.* 50°12' N, 7°37' E 167
Bad Soden-Salmünster, *Ger.* 50°16' N, 9°21' E 167
Bad Sooden-Allendorf, *Ger.* 51°16' N, 9°58' E 167
Bad Vilbel, *Ger.* 50°11' N, 8°44' E 167
Bad Vöslau, *Aust.* 47°58' N, 16°12' E 168
Bad Waldsee, *Ger.* 47°55' N, 9°45' E 152
Bad Wildungen, *Ger.* 51°6' N, 9°7' E 167
Badacsony, peak, *Hung.* 46°47' N, 17°26' E 168
Badagri, *Nig.* 6°29' N, 2°55' E 222
Badajoz, *Sp.* 38°51' N, 6°58' W 150
Badalona, *Sp.* 41°26' N, 2°14' E 164
Badalucco, *It.* 43°55' N, 7°51' E 167
Badam, *Kaz.* 42°22' N, 69°13' E 197
Badamsha, *Kaz.* 50°33' N, 58°16' E 158
Badanah, *Saudi Arabia* 30°58' N, 40°57' E 180
Badaohe, *China* 43°11' N, 126°32' E 200
Baddeck, *Can.* 46°6' N, 60°46' W 111
Baddo, river, *Pak.* 28°5' N, 64°35' E 182
Baden, *Aust.* 48°0' N, 16°14' E 168
Baden, *Eritrea* 16°53' N, 37°54' E 182
Baden, *Ger.* 53°0' N, 9°6' E 150
Baden, *Switz.* 47°27' N, 8°18' E 150
Baden-Württemberg, adm. division, *Ger.* 47°47' N, 7°43' E 165
Badger, *Minn., U.S.* 48°45' N, 96°3' W 90
Badger Creek, river, *Mont., U.S.* 48°4' N, 113°13' W 108
Badia Polesine, *It.* 45°5' N, 11°28' E 167
Badiar National Park, *Guinea* 12°23' N, 13°51' W 222
Badin, *Pak.* 24°39' N, 68°48' E 186
Badjoki, *Dem. Rep. of the Congo* 2°53' N, 22°21' E 218
Badjoudé (Dompago), *Benin* 9°42' N, 1°23' E 222
Badlands, *N. Dak., U.S.* 47°2' N, 104°19' W 90
Badlands National Park, *S. Dak., U.S.* 43°15' N, 102°43' W 90
Badnjevac, *Serb.* 44°7' N, 20°58' E 168
Badogo, *Mali* 11°3' N, 8°13' W 222
Badong, *China* 30°58' N, 110°23' E 198
Badoumbé, *Mali* 13°41' N, 10°15' W 222
Badreïna, spring, *Mauritania* 17°47' N, 11°6' W 222
Badueín, *Eth.* 6°30' N, 43°22' E 218
Badupi, *Myanmar* 21°37' N, 93°24' E 188
Badvel, *India* 14°44' N, 79°5' E 188
Bad'ya, *Russ.* 60°29' N, 53°22' E 154
Baena, *Sp.* 37°37' N, 4°21' W 164
Baengnyeongdo, island, *S. Korea* 37°50' N, 123°23' E 198
Baeza, *Sp.* 37°59' N, 3°28' W 164
Bafang, *Cameroon* 5°8' N, 10°10' E 222
Bafarara, *Mali* 15°23' N, 11°29' W 222
Baffin Bay 73°51' N, 73°33' W 106
Bafia, *Cameroon* 4°42' N, 11°14' E 222
Bafing, river, *Guinea* 12°23' N, 10°13' W 222
Bafoulabé, *Mali* 13°49' N, 10°52' W 222
Bafousam, *Cameroon* 5°27' N, 10°23' E 222
Bāfq, *Iran* 31°32' N, 55°22' E 180
Bafra, *Turk.* 41°33' N, 35°54' E 156
Bafra Burnu, *Turk.* 41°45' N, 35°24' E 156
Bāft, *Iran* 29°16' N, 56°39' E 196
Bafuka, *Dem. Rep. of the Congo* 4°9' N, 27°52' E 224
Bafwabalinga, *Dem. Rep. of the Congo* 0°54' N, 27°1' E 224
Bafwaboli, *Dem. Rep. of the Congo* 0°42' N, 26°7' E 224
Bafwasende, *Dem. Rep. of the Congo* 1°8' N, 27°11' E 224
Bagabag, island, *P.N.G.* 4°48' S, 146°17' E 192
Bagadó, *Col.* 5°22' N, 76°28' W 136
Bagalkot, *India* 16°10' N, 75°42' E 188
Bagam, spring, *Niger* 15°40' N, 6°34' E 222
Bagamoyo, *Tanzania* 6°23' S, 38°55' E 224
Bagan, *Russ.* 54°3' N, 77°45' E 184
Bagan Datoh, *Malaysia* 3°58' N, 100°47' E 196
Bagan Serai, *Malaysia* 5°1' N, 100°31' E 196
Bagana, *Nig.* 7°58' N, 7°34' E 222
Baganga, *Philippines* 7°37' N, 126°33' E 203
Bagansiapiapi, *Indonesia* 2°12' N, 100°49' E 196
Bagan'yuvom, *Russ.* 66°5' N, 58°2' E 154
Bagaroua, *Niger* 14°30' N, 4°25' E 222
Bagata, *Dem. Rep. of the Congo* 3°49' S, 17°56' E 218
Bagatogo, *Côte d'Ivoire* 8°42' N, 6°42' W 222
Bagdad, *Ariz., U.S.* 34°34' N, 113°12' W 92
Bagdad, *Fla., U.S.* 30°35' N, 87°2' W 96
Bagdarin, *Russ.* 54°28' N, 113°39' E 190
Bagé, *Braz.* 31°21' S, 54°8' W 139
Bågede, *Nor.* 64°21' N, 14°48' E 152
Baggs, *Wyo., U.S.* 41°2' N, 107°40' W 90
Baghdād, *Iraq* 33°21' N, 44°23' E 180
Bagheria, *It.* 38°4' N, 13°30' E 156
Bāghīn, *Iran* 30°9' N, 56°51' E 196
Baghlan, *Afghan.* 36°11' N, 68°48' E 186
Baghran Khowleh, *Afghan.* 32°57' N, 64°58' E 186
Bağırpaşa Dağı, peak, *Turk.* 39°28' N, 40°2' E 195
Bağışlı, *Turk.* 37°51' N, 44°0' E 195
Bagley, *Minn., U.S.* 47°30' N, 95°25' W 90
Bagni del Masino, *It.* 46°15' N, 9°35' E 167
Bagno di Romagna, *It.* 43°50' N, 11°56' E 167
Bagnols-les-Bains, *Fr.* 44°31' N, 3°40' E 150
Bagnone, *It.* 44°19' N, 9°59' E 167
Bago, *Myanmar* 17°20' N, 96°29' E 202
Bagodar, *India* 24°4' N, 85°49' E 197
Bagoé, river, *Mali* 11°44' N, 6°22' W 222
Bagot, Mount, *Can.* 59°20' N, 135°8' W 108
Bagrationovsk, *Russ.* 54°22' N, 20°31' E 166
Bagrax see Bohu, *China* 41°56' N, 86°40' E 184
Bagrdan, *Serb.* 44°4' N, 21°9' E 168
Baguia, *Timor-Leste* 8°33' S, 126°39' E 238
Baguio, *Philippines* 16°23' N, 120°34' E 203
Baguio Point, *Philippines* 17°31' N, 122°11' E 203
Bagzane, Monts, *Niger* 17°49' N, 8°37' E 222
Bahabón de Esgueva, *Sp.* 41°51' N, 3°44' W 164
Bahama Islands, *North Atlantic Ocean* 23°51' N, 76°7' W 253
Bahamas 26°0' N, 77°0' W 118
Baharak, *Afghan.* 37°0' N, 70°52' E 186
Baharampur, *India* 24°3' N, 88°16' E 188
Baḥarîya, El Wâḥât el, *Egypt* 27°49' N, 28°21' E 180
Bahau, *Malaysia* 2°50' N, 102°24' E 196
Bahawalnagar, *Pak.* 30°2' N, 73°16' E 186
Bahawalpur, *Pak.* 29°24' N, 71°40' E 186
Bahçe, *Turk.* 37°14' N, 36°35' E 156
Bahçesaray, *Turk.* 38°4' N, 42°47' E 195
Bahdanaw, *Belarus* 54°10' N, 26°8' E 166
Bahdur Island, *Sudan* 17°59' N, 37°52' E 182
Bäherden, *Turkm.* 38°22' N, 57°10' E 160
Bahi, *Tanzania* 5°57' S, 35°19' E 224
Bahia, adm. division, *Braz.* 13°49' S, 42°23' W 138
Bahía Blanca, *Arg.* 38°43' S, 62°17' W 139
Bahía de Caráquez, *Ecua.* 0°42' N, 80°19' W 130
Bahía de Loreto National Park, *Mex.* 25°52' N, 111°32' W 238
Bahía de los Ángeles, *Mex.* 28°56' N, 113°37' W 92
Bahía, Islas de la, islands, *Isla de Roatán* 16°27' N, 87°19' W 115
Bahía Kino, *Mex.* 28°49' N, 111°55' W 92
Bahía Laura, *Arg.* 48°22' S, 66°30' W 134
Bahia see Salvador, *Braz.* 12°59' S, 38°28' W 132
Bahía Solano (Puerto Mutis), *Col.* 6°12' N, 77°25' W 136
Bahía Tortugas, *Mex.* 27°41' N, 114°52' W 112
Bahir Dar, *Eth.* 11°31' N, 37°21' E 182
Bahlah, *Oman* 22°57' N, 57°15' E 182
Bahr el 'Arab, river, *Sudan* 10°4' N, 25°6' E 224
Bahr ez Zaraf, river, *Sudan* 7°42' N, 30°43' E 224
Bahr Kéita (Doka), river, *Chad* 9°8' N, 18°38' E 218
Bahr Salamat, river, *Chad* 10°17' N, 19°27' E 216
Bahrah, oil field, *Kuwait* 29°39' N, 47°49' E 196
Bahraich, *India* 27°32' N, 81°36' E 197
Bahrain 26°0' N, 51°0' E 196
Bahrain, Gulf of 25°31' N, 50°13' E 196
Bāhū Kalāt, *Iran* 25°44' N, 61°25' E 182
Bahuaja-Sonene National Park, *Peru* 13°28' S, 69°24' W 137
Bai Bung, Mui, *Vietnam* 8°15' N, 104°19' E 202
Baia, *Rom.* 44°43' N, 28°40' E 156
Baia de Aramă, *Rom.* 44°59' N, 22°49' E 168
Baia de Arieş, *Rom.* 46°21' N, 23°16' E 168
Baía dos Tigres, *Angola* 16°38' S, 11°40' E 220
Baia Mare, *Rom.* 47°39' N, 23°36' E 168
Baibokoum, *Chad* 7°40' N, 15°42' E 218
Baicheng, *China* 45°35' N, 122°50' E 198
Baicheng, *China* 41°46' N, 81°51' E 184
Baidoa see Baydhabo, *Somalia* 3°5' N, 43°41' E 218
Baie-Comeau, *Can.* 49°13' N, 68°10' W 111
Baie-du-Poste see Mistassini, *Can.* 50°24' N, 73°50' W 110
Baie-Johan-Beetz, *Can.* 50°17' N, 62°49' W 111
Baie-Sainte-Catherine, *Can.* 48°6' N, 69°44' W 94
Baie-Sainte-Claire, site, *Can.* 49°52' N, 64°35' W 111
Baie-Saint-Paul, *Can.* 47°26' N, 70°31' W 94
Baihar, *India* 22°7' N, 80°33' E 197
Baihe, *China* 42°22' N, 128°7' E 198
Ba'ījī, *Iraq* 34°54' N, 43°27' E 180
Baijnath, *India* 29°57' N, 79°37' E 188
Baikal, Lake, *Russ.* 52°49' N, 106°59' E 238
Baikha, *Russ.* 64°54' N, 88°0' E 169
Baikonur Cosmodrome, spaceport, *Kaz.* 46°6' N, 63°9' E 184
Baile Átha Cliath see Dublin, *Ire.* 53°18' N, 6°26' W 150
Băile Herculane, *Rom.* 44°54' N, 22°26' E 168
Bailén, *Sp.* 38°5' N, 3°46' W 164
Bailey Island, *Me., U.S.* 43°43' N, 70°0' W 104
Bailingmiao see Darhan Muminggan Lianheqi, *China* 41°41' N, 110°23' E 198
Bailique, *Braz.* 1°0' N, 50°3' W 130
Bailique, Ilha, island, *Braz.* 1°4' N, 49°56' W 130
Bailleul, *Fr.* 50°43' N, 2°44' E 163
Baillie Islands, *Beaufort Sea* 70°39' N, 129°39' W 98
Baillieu Peak, *Antarctica* 67°57' S, 60°27' E 248
Bailong, river, *China* 33°26' N, 104°17' E 198
Bailundo, *Angola* 12°13' S, 15°51' E 220
Bainang, *China* 29°13' N, 89°15' E 197
Bainbridge, *Ga., U.S.* 30°53' N, 84°34' W 96
Bainbridge, *Ind., U.S.* 39°45' N, 86°49' W 102
Bainbridge, *Ohio, U.S.* 39°13' N, 83°16' W 102
Bainbridge Island, *Wash., U.S.* 47°37' N, 122°32' W 100
Baingoin, *China* 31°37' N, 89°51' E 188
Bainville, *Mont., U.S.* 48°7' N, 104°15' W 90
Baiona, *Sp.* 42°6' N, 8°53' W 150
Baiquan, *China* 47°37' N, 126°4' E 198
Bā'ir, *Jordan* 30°45' N, 36°40' E 194
Bairab Co, lake, *China* 34°55' N, 82°29' E 188
Baird, *Miss., U.S.* 33°23' N, 90°36' W 103
Baird, *Tex., U.S.* 32°23' N, 99°24' W 92
Baird Inlet 60°44' N, 164°34' W 98
Baird, Mount, *Idaho, U.S.* 43°21' N, 111°11' W 90
Baird Mountains, *Alas., U.S.* 67°24' N, 161°29' W 98
Bairiki see Tarawa, *Kiribati* 1°15' N, 169°58' E 242
Bairin Youqi, *China* 43°30' N, 118°40' E 198
Bairin Zuoqi, *China* 43°59' N, 119°24' E 198
Bairoil, *Wyo., U.S.* 42°15' N, 107°33' W 90
Baisha, *China* 29°31' N, 119°15' E 198
Baishan, *China* 42°38' N, 127°12' E 200
Baiso, *It.* 44°29' N, 10°37' E 167
Baitadi, *Nepal* 29°34' N, 80°26' E 197
Baixo Guandu, *Braz.* 19°32' S, 40°59' W 138
Baiyin, *China* 36°34' N, 104°15' E 198
Baiyuda, spring, *Sudan* 17°29' N, 32°8' E 182
Baja, *Hung.* 46°10' N, 18°57' E 168
Baja California, region, *North America* 31°27' N, 115°59' W 92
Baja California, adm. division, *Mex.* 30°0' N, 115°0' W 112
Baja California Sur, adm. division, *Mex.* 26°3' N, 112°13' W 112
Baja, Punta, *Mex.* 28°17' N, 111°59' W 92
Baja, Punta, *Mex.* 29°59' N, 115°58' W 92
Bajag, *India* 22°42' N, 81°21' E 197
Baján, *Mex.* 26°32' N, 101°15' W 114
Bājgīrān, *Iran* 37°37' N, 58°24' E 180
Bajiazi, *China* 42°41' N, 129°9' E 200
Bājil, *Yemen* 14°58' N, 43°15' E 182
Bajina Bašta, *Serb.* 43°58' N, 19°35' E 168
Bajitpur, *Bangladesh* 24°9' N, 90°54' E 197
Bajmok, *Serb.* 45°57' N, 19°24' E 168
Bajo Baudó, *Col.* 4°57' N, 77°22' W 136
Bajoga, *Nig.* 10°52' N, 11°17' E 222
Bajovo Polje, *Mont.* 43°0' N, 18°53' E 168
Bajram Curri, *Alban.* 42°21' N, 20°3' E 168
Bajzë, *Alban.* 42°16' N, 19°26' E 168
Bak, *Hung.* 46°43' N, 16°51' E 168
Bakaba, *Chad* 7°43' N, 16°54' E 218
Bakal, *Russ.* 54°59' N, 58°51' E 154
Bakala, *Cen. Af. Rep.* 6°9' N, 20°21' E 218
Bakałarzewo, *Pol.* 54°5' N, 22°38' E 166
Bakaly, *Russ.* 55°11' N, 53°50' E 154
Bakanas, *Kaz.* 44°49' N, 76°17' E 184
Bakaoré, *Chad* 15°17' N, 21°47' E 216
Bakchar, *Russ.* 56°59' N, 82°4' E 169
Bakel, *Senegal* 14°53' N, 12°31' W 222
Baker, *Calif., U.S.* 35°16' N, 116°5' W 101
Baker, *La., U.S.* 30°35' N, 91°10' W 103
Baker, *Mont., U.S.* 46°20' N, 104°18' W 90
Baker, *Nev., U.S.* 39°0' N, 114°8' W 92
Baker, *Oreg., U.S.* 44°46' N, 117°52' W 90
Baker Foreland, *Can.* 62°46' N, 90°36' W 106
Baker Island, *U.S.* 0°18' N, 176°37' W 238
Baker Lake, *Can.* 62°18' N, 99°20' W 106
Baker Lake, *Can.* 64°19' N, 96°7' W 73
Baker Lake, *Wash., U.S.* 48°42' N, 121°52' W 100
Baker, Mount, *Wash., U.S.* 48°46' N, 121°51' W 100
Bakersfield, *Calif., U.S.* 35°22' N, 119°1' W 101
Bakewell, *U.K.* 53°12' N, 1°41' W 162
Bakhanay, *Russ.* 66°16' N, 123°37' E 173
Bakhchysaray, *Ukr.* 44°45' N, 33°51' E 156
Bakhma Dam, *Iraq* 36°31' N, 44°10' E 195
Bakhmach, *Ukr.* 51°11' N, 32°48' E 158
Bakhta, *Russ.* 62°19' N, 89°10' E 160
Bakhta, river, *Russ.* 63°43' N, 90°2' E 169
Bakhtegān, Daryācheh-ye, lake, *Iran* 29°21' N, 53°32' E 196
Bakı (Baku), *Azerb.* 40°23' N, 49°44' E 195
Baki, spring, *Chad* 16°58' N, 21°10' E 216
Bakin Birji, *Niger* 14°10' N, 8°52' E 222
Bakırdağı, *Turk.* 38°12' N, 35°47' E 156
Bako, *Côte d'Ivoire* 9°7' N, 7°36' W 222
Bako, *Eth.* 5°50' N, 36°37' E 224
Bakony, *Hung.* 47°17' N, 17°23' E 168
Bakouma, *Cen. Af. Rep.* 5°42' N, 22°50' E 218
Bakoye, river, *Africa* 12°50' N, 9°26' W 222
Bakr Uzyak, *Russ.* 52°59' N, 58°36' E 154
Baktalórántháza, *Hung.* 48°0' N, 22°3' E 168
Baku see Bakı, *Azerb.* 40°23' N, 49°44' E 195
Bakundi, *Nig.* 8°1' N, 10°45' E 222
Bakungan, *Indonesia* 2°58' N, 97°29' E 196
Bakuriani, *Ga.* 41°44' N, 43°31' E 195
Bakutis Coast, *Antarctica* 75°0' S, 115°49' W 248
Bakwanga see Mbuji-Mayi, *Dem. Rep. of the Congo* 6°10' S, 23°36' E 224
Bala, *Senegal* 14°1' N, 13°11' W 222
Bâlâ, *Turk.* 39°32' N, 33°7' E 156
Bala, *U.K.* 52°54' N, 3°37' W 162
Balabac, *Philippines* 8°1' N, 117°2' E 203
Balabac, island, *Philippines* 7°49' N, 115°56' E 192
Balabac Strait 7°38' N, 116°33' E 203
Bălăciţa, *Rom.* 44°23' N, 23°7' E 168
Balaena Islands, *Indian Ocean* 65°59' S, 112°14' E 248
Balaghat, *India* 21°49' N, 80°13' E 197
Balaguer, *Sp.* 41°47' N, 0°46' E 164
Balaka, *Malawi* 14°54' S, 34°56' E 224

Balakän, Azerb. 41°43′ N, 46°25′ E 195
Balakété, Cen. Af. Rep. 6°54′ N, 19°57′ E 218
Balakhna, Russ. 56°25′ N, 43°37′ E 154
Balaki, Guinea 12°12′ N, 11°52′ W 222
Balaklava, Ukr. 44°30′ N, 33°34′ E 158
Balakliya, Ukr. 49°29′ N, 36°52′ E 158
Balakovo, Russ. 52°0′ N, 47°50′ E 158
Balama, Mozambique 13°15′ S, 38°38′ E 224
Balancán, Mex. 17°47′ N, 91°34′ W 115
Balangir, India 20°42′ N, 83°28′ E 188
Balanikha, Russ. 65°56′ N, 43°19′ E 154
Balao, Ecua. 3°2′ S, 79°48′ W 130
Balashivka, Ukr. 50°59′ N, 26°57′ E 152
Balashov, Russ. 51°29′ N, 43°10′ E 158
Balástya, Hung. 46°25′ N, 20°1′ E 168
Balâṭ, Egypt 25°33′ N, 29°14′ E 226
Balatina, Mold. 47°41′ N, 27°20′ E 158
Balatonföldvár, Hung. 46°50′ N, 17°51′ E 168
Balatonfüred, Hung. 46°57′ N, 17°53′ E 168
Balavé, Burkina Faso 12°23′ N, 4°11′ W 222
Balazote, Sp. 38°53′ N, 2°9′ W 164
Balbina, Represa da, dam, Braz. 1°25′ S, 60°25′ W 130
Balcad, Somalia 2°18′ N, 45°26′ E 218
Balcarce, Arg. 37°51′ S, 58°17′ W 139
Balcarres, Can. 50°47′ N, 103°33′ W 90
Balchik, Bulg. 43°26′ N, 28°11′ E 156
Balclutha, N.Z. 46°15′ S, 169°42′ E 240
Bald Butte, peak, Oreg., U.S. 43°40′ N, 119°27′ W 90
Bald Eagle Mountain, Pa., U.S. 40°59′ N, 77°48′ W 94
Bald Knob, Ark., U.S. 35°17′ N, 91°35′ W 96
Bald Mountain, peak, Calif., U.S. 40°54′ N, 121°11′ W 90
Bald Mountain, peak, Can. 54°5′ N, 61°29′ W 111
Bald Mountain, peak, Idaho, U.S. 44°20′ N, 114°26′ W 90
Bald Mountain, peak, Nev., U.S. 38°34′ N, 117°8′ W 90
Bald Mountain, peak, Oreg., U.S. 44°33′ N, 118°0′ W 90
Bald Mountain, peak, Vt., U.S. 44°45′ N, 72°5′ W 94
Baldhill Dam, N. Dak., U.S. 47°19′ N, 98°45′ W 82
Baldock Lake, Can. 56°32′ N, 98°25′ W 108
Baldone, Latv. 56°44′ N, 24°23′ E 166
Baldwin, La., U.S. 29°49′ N, 91°33′ W 103
Baldwin, Mich., U.S. 43°53′ N, 85°52′ W 102
Baldwinville, Mass., U.S. 42°36′ N, 72°5′ W 104
Baldwyn, Miss., U.S. 34°30′ N, 88°38′ W 96
Baldy Mountain, peak, Can. 51°28′ N, 120°6′ W 90
Baldy Mountain, peak, Can. 51°27′ N, 100°49′ W 90
Baldy Mountain, peak, Can. 49°8′ N, 119°20′ W 90
Baldy Mountain, peak, Mont., U.S. 45°20′ N, 113°7′ W 90
Baldy Peak, Ariz., U.S. 33°53′ N, 109°37′ W 92
Bale Mountains National Park, Eth. 6°33′ N, 38°57′ E 224
Balearic Islands, Sp. 40°4′ N, 3°1′ E 164
Balearic Sea 40°47′ N, 1°23′ E 150
Baleia, Ponta da, Braz. 17°40′ S, 39°9′ W 132
Baleine, Rivière à la, river, Can. 57°24′ N, 67°59′ W 106
Balen, Belg. 51°9′ N, 5°9′ E 167
Baler, Philippines 15°46′ N, 121°32′ E 203
Balerma, Sp. 36°43′ N, 2°54′ W 164
Baleshwar, India 21°29′ N, 86°53′ E 188
Baley, Russ. 51°36′ N, 116°35′ E 238
Baléya, Mali 12°16′ N, 9°58′ W 222
Baleyara, Niger 13°56′ N, 2°50′ E 222
Balezino, Russ. 57°57′ N, 53°5′ E 154
Balguntay, China 42°46′ N, 86°18′ E 184
Bal'āf, Yemen 14°1′ N, 48°10′ E 182
Balho, Djibouti 12°2′ N, 42°12′ E 182
Bali, India 25°13′ N, 73°16′ E 186
Bali, island, Indonesia 9°21′ S, 114°38′ E 192
Bali Sea 7°47′ S, 114°55′ E 192
Baliangao, Philippines 8°40′ N, 123°37′ E 203
Balige, Indonesia 2°21′ N, 99°3′ E 196
Balık Göl, lake, Turk. 41°34′ N, 35°44′ E 156
Balıkesir, Turk. 39°38′ N, 27°51′ E 156
Balikpapan, Indonesia 1°12′ S, 116°46′ E 192
Baling, Malaysia 5°40′ N, 100°54′ E 196
Balinț, Rom. 45°49′ N, 21°51′ E 168
Balintang Channel 19°44′ N, 121°25′ E 203
Balipara, India 26°48′ N, 92°43′ E 188
Baliza, Braz. 16°14′ S, 52°25′ W 138
Balkan Mountians, Bulg. 43°16′ N, 22°39′ E 168
Balkanabat (Nebitdag), Turkm. 39°31′ N, 54°21′ E 180
Balkány, Hung. 47°46′ N, 21°49′ E 168
Balkany, Russ. 53°29′ N, 59°34′ E 154
Balkashīno, Kaz. 52°27′ N, 68°40′ E 184
Balkh, Afghan. 36°46′ N, 66°58′ E 186
Balkhash, Lake, Kaz. 46°0′ N, 69°44′ E 173
Ball Lake, lake, Can. 50°13′ N, 94°17′ W 90
Ballâna, Egypt 24°17′ N, 32°58′ E 182
Ballantine, Mont., U.S. 45°55′ N, 108°9′ W 90
Ballarat, Austral. 37°34′ S, 143°55′ E 231
Ballé, Mali 15°21′ N, 8°36′ W 222
Ballenas, Canal de 29°14′ N, 114°0′ W 92
Balleny Islands, South Pacific Ocean 66°21′ S, 162°20′ E 255
Balleza, Mex. 26°57′ N, 106°22′ W 112
Ballinger, Tex., U.S. 31°43′ N, 99°57′ W 92
Ballobar, Sp. 41°36′ N, 0°11′ E 164
Ball's Pyramid, island, Austral. 32°15′ S, 157°57′ E 230
Ballstad, Nor. 68°4′ N, 13°28′ E 152
Ballston Spa, N.Y., U.S. 43°0′ N, 73°52′ W 104
Balmaceda, Chile 45°59′ S, 71°48′ W 123
Balmertown, Can. 51°3′ N, 93°45′ W 90
Balmoral Castle, site, U.K. 57°0′ N, 3°20′ W 150
Balmorhea, Tex., U.S. 30°57′ N, 103°45′ W 92
Balnearia, Arg. 31°0′ S, 62°40′ W 139
Balneario de los Novillos see I, Mex. 29°22′ N, 101°19′ W 112
Balod, India 20°44′ N, 81°12′ E 188
Balombo, Angola 12°22′ S, 14°47′ E 220
Balonne, river, Austral. 28°41′ S, 147°59′ E 230
Balotra, India 25°51′ N, 72°14′ E 186
Balqash, Kaz. 46°52′ N, 74°58′ E 184
Balqash Köli, lake, Kaz. 45°35′ N, 73°9′ E 190
Balş, Rom. 44°22′ N, 24°4′ E 156
Balsas, Braz. 7°32′ S, 46°3′ W 130
Balsas, Mex. 17°59′ N, 99°46′ W 114
Balsas, river, Braz. 8°24′ S, 46°19′ W 130
Balsas, river, Braz. 10°47′ S, 47°39′ W 130
Balsas, river, Mex. 18°29′ N, 100°56′ W 114
Balta, N. Dak., U.S. 48°9′ N, 100°3′ W 90
Balta, Rom. 44°52′ N, 22°39′ E 168
Balta, Ukr. 47°55′ N, 29°38′ E 156
Balta Albă, Rom. 45°18′ N, 27°16′ E 156
Baltasar Brum, Uru. 30°43′ S, 57°20′ W 139
Bălți, Mold. 47°45′ N, 27°57′ E 152
Baltic Sea 59°13′ N, 17°48′ E 152
Baltîm, Egypt 31°34′ N, 31°4′ E 180
Baltimore, Md., U.S. 39°17′ N, 76°38′ W 94
Baltimore, Ohio, U.S. 39°50′ N, 82°36′ W 102
Baltit, Pak. 36°19′ N, 74°41′ E 186
Baltiysk, Russ. 54°39′ N, 19°54′ E 166
Baltrum, island, Ger. 53°41′ N, 7°26′ E 163
Balumbal, Eth. 8°33′ N, 45°10′ E 218
Balurghat, India 25°12′ N, 88°47′ E 197
Balvi, Latv. 57°6′ N, 27°14′ E 166
Balya, Turk. 39°43′ N, 27°34′ E 156
Balykcha, Russ. 51°18′ N, 87°43′ E 184
Balykchy, Kyrg. 42°26′ N, 76°10′ E 184
Balyksa, Russ. 53°23′ N, 89°8′ E 184
Balyqshy, Kaz. 47°2′ N, 51°52′ E 158
Balzola, It. 45°11′ N, 8°24′ E 167
Bam, Iran 29°2′ N, 58°23′ E 196
Bam Co, lake, China 31°29′ N, 90°37′ E 188
Bama, Nig. 11°32′ N, 13°41′ E 216
Bamako, Mali 12°37′ N, 8°10′ W 222
Bamba, Mali 17°2′ N, 1°26′ W 222
Bambafouga, Guinea 10°11′ N, 11°53′ W 222
Bambamarca, Peru 6°35′ S, 78°34′ W 130
Bambara, Chad 8°54′ N, 18°34′ E 218
Bambara, Mali 13°25′ N, 4°11′ W 222
Bambari, Cen. Af. Rep. 5°45′ N, 20°39′ E 218
Bambesa, Dem. Rep. of the Congo 3°24′ N, 25°43′ E 224
Bambey, Senegal 14°44′ N, 16°19′ W 222
Bambili, Dem. Rep. of the Congo 3°36′ N, 26°7′ E 224
Bambinga, Dem. Rep. of the Congo 3°45′ S, 18°51′ E 218
Bambio, Cen. Af. Rep. 3°59′ N, 16°58′ E 218
Bambouti, Cen. Af. Rep. 5°23′ N, 27°11′ E 224
Bambuí, Braz. 20°2′ S, 45°57′ W 138
Bambuyka, Russ. 55°46′ N, 115°33′ E 190
Bamenda, Cameroon 5°53′ N, 10°9′ E 222
Bamfield, Can. 48°47′ N, 125°8′ W 100
Bamian, Afghan. 34°51′ N, 67°51′ E 186
Bamingui, Cen. Af. Rep. 7°30′ N, 20°12′ E 218
Bampton, U.K. 51°44′ N, 1°33′ W 162
Bampton, U.K. 50°59′ N, 3°29′ W 162
Bamy, Turkm. 38°43′ N, 56°49′ E 180
Ban Bang Hin, Thai. 9°32′ N, 98°35′ E 202
Ban Don, Vietnam 12°54′ N, 107°47′ E 202
Ban Don, Ao 9°17′ N, 99°0′ E 202
Ban Don see Surat Thani, Thai. 9°7′ N, 99°20′ E 202
Ban Dong, Thai. 19°33′ N, 100°57′ E 202
Ban Hinboun, Laos 17°37′ N, 104°37′ E 202
Ban Khai, Thai. 12°47′ N, 101°20′ E 202
Ban Nam-Om, Laos 20°43′ N, 101°4′ E 202
Ban Napè, Laos 18°19′ N, 105°6′ E 202
Ban Phai, Thai. 16°6′ N, 102°41′ E 202
Ban Sanam Chai, Thai. 7°34′ N, 100°25′ E 196
Ban Taphan, Laos 15°56′ N, 105°25′ E 202
Ban Xénô, Laos 16°41′ N, 105°6′ E 202
Bañados de Otuquis, marsh, Braz. 20°54′ S, 60°29′ W 132
Bañados del Izozog, marsh, Bol. 18°55′ S, 62°31′ W 132
Banak, Nor. 70°2′ N, 25°1′ E 152
Banalia, Dem. Rep. of the Congo 1°33′ N, 25°25′ E 224
Banam, Cambodia 11°19′ N, 105°16′ E 202
Banamba, Mali 13°34′ N, 7°26′ W 222
Banana Islands, North Atlantic Ocean 7°56′ N, 13°50′ W 222
Bananfara, Guinea 11°19′ N, 8°56′ W 222
Bananga, India 6°56′ N, 93°58′ E 188
Banankoro, Guinea 9°10′ N, 9°18′ W 222
Banaras see Varanasi, India 25°18′ N, 82°57′ E 197
Banâs, Râs, Egypt 23°52′ N, 35°49′ E 182
Banas, river, India 25°5′ N, 74°2′ E 186
Banatsko Novo Selo, Serb. 44°59′ N, 20°46′ E 168
Banaz, Turk. 38°44′ N, 29°45′ E 156
Banbalah, Tun. 35°42′ N, 10°48′ E 156
Banbān, Saudi Arabia 24°58′ N, 46°36′ E 196
Banbar, China 31°4′ N, 94°46′ E 188
Banbury, U.K. 52°3′ N, 1°21′ W 162
Banco, Punta, C.R. 8°17′ N, 83°54′ W 115
Bancroft, Can. 45°3′ N, 77°52′ W 94
Bancroft, Iowa, U.S. 43°17′ N, 94°14′ W 94
Bancroft, Mich., U.S. 42°51′ N, 84°4′ W 102
Banda, Dem. Rep. of the Congo 4°8′ N, 27°4′ E 224
Banda, India 24°3′ N, 78°57′ E 197
Banda, India 25°27′ N, 80°19′ E 197
Banda Aceh, Indonesia 5°30′ N, 95°20′ E 196
Banda, Kepulauan, islands, Banda Sea 5°8′ S, 129°26′ E 192
Banda Nkwanta, Ghana 8°22′ N, 2°8′ W 222
Banda, Pointe, Gabon 3°46′ S, 10°57′ E 218
Banda Sea 5°42′ S, 127°27′ E 254
Banda Sea 5°13′ S, 123°58′ E 173
Bandai-Asahi National Park, Japan 38°17′ N, 139°38′ E 201
Bandajuma, Sierra Leone 7°35′ N, 11°39′ W 222
Bandān, Iran 31°23′ N, 60°42′ E 186
Bandar 'Abbās, Iran 27°11′ N, 56°13′ E 196
Bandar Murcaayo, Somalia 11°36′ N, 50°26′ E 182
Bandar see Machilipatnam, India 16°11′ N, 81°10′ E 188
Bandar Seri Begawan, Brunei 4°52′ N, 114°50′ E 203
Bandarban, Bangladesh 22°12′ N, 92°11′ E 188
Bandarbeyla, Somalia 9°25′ N, 50°48′ E 216
Bandar-e Anzalī, Iran 37°30′ N, 49°20′ E 195
Bandar-e Chārak, Iran 26°46′ N, 54°17′ E 196
Bandar-e Deylam, Iran 30°2′ N, 50°13′ E 196
Bandar-e Eman Khomeynī, Iran 30°27′ N, 49°3′ E 180
Bandar-e Genāveh, Iran 29°36′ N, 50°29′ E 196
Bandar-e Khoemir, Iran 26°57′ N, 55°34′ E 196
Bandar-e Lengeh, Iran 26°37′ N, 54°54′ E 196
Bandar-e Māh Shahr, Iran 30°38′ N, 49°12′ E 180
Bandar-e Maqām, Iran 26°58′ N, 53°29′ E 196
Bandar-e Rīg, Iran 29°29′ N, 50°39′ E 196
Bandar-e Torkaman, Iran 36°54′ N, 54°3′ E 180
Bandau, Malaysia 6°33′ N, 116°46′ E 203
Band-e-Amir National Park, Afghan. 34°52′ N, 67°30′ E 187
Bandeira, peak, Braz. 20°30′ S, 41°53′ W 138
Bandeirante, Braz. 13°45′ S, 50°51′ W 138
Bandéko, Congo 1°56′ N, 17°27′ E 218
Bandelierkop, S. Af. 23°21′ S, 29°49′ E 227
Bandera, Arg. 28°52′ S, 62°17′ W 139
Bandera, Tex., U.S. 29°43′ N, 99°5′ W 92
Bandiagara, Mali 14°20′ N, 3°38′ W 222
Bandikui, India 27°2′ N, 76°35′ E 197
Bandırma, Turk. 40°19′ N, 27°57′ E 156
Bandon, Oreg., U.S. 43°6′ N, 124°24′ W 90
Bändovan Burnu, Azerb. 39°34′ N, 49°20′ E 195
Bandundu, Dem. Rep. of the Congo 3°24′ S, 17°23′ E 218
Bandundu, adm. division, Dem. Rep. of the Congo 4°38′ S, 16°30′ E 218
Bandung, Indonesia 7°1′ S, 107°32′ E 192
Băneasa, Rom. 45°57′ N, 27°55′ E 156
Bañeres, Sp. 38°43′ N, 0°40′ E 164
Banes, Cuba 20°58′ N, 75°44′ W 116
Banff, Can. 51°11′ N, 115°33′ W 108
Banff National Park, Can. 51°29′ N, 116°37′ W 238
Banfora, Burkina Faso 10°38′ N, 4°47′ W 222
Bang Mun Nak, Thai. 16°1′ N, 100°21′ E 202
Bang Saphan, Thai. 11°14′ N, 99°31′ E 202
Bangalore (Bengaluru), India 12°59′ N, 77°35′ E 188
Bangar, Philippines 16°54′ N, 120°25′ E 203
Bangassou, Cen. Af. Rep. 4°38′ N, 22°48′ E 207
Banggai, Kepulauan, islands, Banda Sea 2°42′ S, 123°39′ E 192
Banggi, island, Malaysia 7°2′ N, 117°21′ E 192
Banghāzī (Benghazi), Lib. 32°6′ N, 20°4′ E 216
Banghiang, river, Laos 16°17′ N, 105°14′ E 202
Bangka, island, Indonesia 2°24′ S, 106°18′ E 192
Bangkaru, island, Indonesia 1°52′ N, 97°4′ E 196
Bangkinang, Indonesia 0°21′ N, 101°1′ E 196
Bangkok see Krung Thep, Thai. 13°44′ N, 100°24′ E 202
Bangladesh 24°0′ N, 90°0′ E 188
Bangor, Me., U.S. 44°48′ N, 68°47′ W 111
Bangor, Mich., U.S. 42°18′ N, 86°7′ W 102
Bangor, U.K. 53°13′ N, 4°7′ W 162
Bangs, Tex., U.S. 31°41′ N, 99°8′ W 92
Bangs, Mount, Ariz., U.S. 36°46′ N, 113°54′ W 101
Bangu, Dem. Rep. of the Congo 9°5′ S, 23°43′ E 224
Bangué, Cameroon 3°12′ N, 15°9′ E 218
Bangued, Philippines 17°37′ N, 120°38′ E 203
Bangui, Cen. Af. Rep. 4°21′ N, 18°22′ E 218
Bangui-Motoba, Congo 2°28′ N, 17°16′ E 218
Bangui, Philippines 18°32′ N, 120°46′ E 203
Banguru, Dem. Rep. of the Congo 0°28′ N, 27°6′ E 224
Bangwade, Dem. Rep. of the Congo 1°0′ N, 25°14′ E 224
Banh, Burkina Faso 14°4′ N, 2°27′ W 222
Banhine National Park, Mozambique 22°54′ S, 32°6′ E 227
Bani, Cen. Af. Rep. 7°7′ N, 22°54′ E 218
Baní, Dom. Rep. 18°16′ N, 70°20′ W 116
Bani, Jebel, Mor. 29°44′ N, 7°57′ W 214
Bani, river, Mali 13°31′ N, 4°52′ W 222
Banī Sharfā, Saudi Arabia 19°38′ N, 41°30′ E 182
Banī Walīd, Lib. 31°46′ N, 14°0′ E 216
Bania, Cen. Af. Rep. 4°6′ N, 16°6′ E 218
Bania, Côte d'Ivoire 9°0′ N, 3°10′ W 222
Banihal Pass, India 33°30′ N, 75°12′ E 186
Banikoara, Benin 11°19′ N, 2°27′ E 222
Baniou, Alg. 35°24′ N, 4°20′ E 150
Banissa, Kenya 3°47′ N, 40°16′ E 224
Bāniyās, Syr. 35°11′ N, 35°57′ E 194
Banja, Serb. 43°33′ N, 19°33′ E 168
Banja Koviljača, Serb. 44°30′ N, 19°9′ E 168
Banja Luka, Bosn. and Herzg. 44°46′ N, 17°10′ E 168
Banjarmasin, Indonesia 3°24′ S, 114°29′ E 192
Banjul, Gambia 13°23′ N, 16°38′ W 222
Bankä, Azerb. 39°25′ N, 49°15′ E 195
Bankas, Mali 14°4′ N, 3°33′ W 222
Banket, Zimb. 17°25′ S, 30°24′ E 224
Bankilare, Niger 14°27′ N, 0°44′ E 222
Bankim, Cameroon 6°4′ N, 11°29′ E 222
Bankor, Mali 16°51′ N, 3°47′ W 222
Banks Island, Can. 53°3′ N, 131°0′ W 98
Banks Island, Can. 73°31′ N, 129°47′ W 106
Banks Islands, Coral Sea 14°34′ S, 168°7′ E 238
Banks Peninsula, N.Z. 43°50′ S, 172°37′ E 240
Bankura, India 23°12′ N, 87°4′ E 197
Bankya, Bulg. 42°42′ N, 23°8′ E 168
Bannalec, Fr. 47°55′ N, 3°42′ W 150
Banner, Wyo., U.S. 44°36′ N, 106°52′ W 90
Banning, Calif., U.S. 33°56′ N, 116°54′ W 101
Bannock Peak, Idaho, U.S. 42°36′ N, 112°46′ W 90
Bannock Range, Idaho, U.S. 42°34′ N, 112°36′ W 90
Bannu, Pak. 32°57′ N, 70°38′ E 186
Banova Jaruga, Croatia 45°26′ N, 16°55′ E 168
Banovići, Bosn. and Herzg. 44°24′ N, 18°28′ E 168
Banow, Afghan. 35°36′ N, 69°20′ E 186
Bánréve, Slovakia 48°18′ N, 20°21′ E 156
Bansang, Gambia 13°25′ N, 14°41′ W 222
Banská Bystrica, Slovakia 48°44′ N, 19°8′ E 152
Banskobystrický, adm. division, Slovakia 48°28′ N, 18°34′ E 152
Bantaeng, Indonesia 5°31′ S, 119°52′ E 192
Bantala, Ghana 9°51′ N, 1°49′ W 222
Bantam, Conn., U.S. 41°43′ N, 73°14′ W 104
Banyak, Kepulauan, islands, Indian Ocean 1°45′ N, 96°30′ E 196
Banyas, Israel 33°14′ N, 35°41′ E 194
Banyo, Cameroon 6°42′ N, 11°48′ E 218
Banyos, Cap de, Sp. 39°51′ N, 3°36′ E 164
Banyuwangi, Indonesia 8°10′ S, 114°21′ E 192
Banzare Coast, Antarctica 68°40′ S, 129°50′ E 248
Bao Bilia, spring, Chad 16°27′ N, 22°56′ E 226
Bao Flala, Mali 12°12′ N, 6°35′ W 222
Bao Ha, Vietnam 22°13′ N, 104°20′ E 202
Bao Lac, Vietnam 22°58′ N, 105°39′ E 198
Baode, China 38°57′ N, 111°2′ E 198
Baoding, China 38°51′ N, 115°28′ E 198
Baofeng, China 33°52′ N, 113°5′ E 198
Baogarada, Chad 12°9′ N, 16°19′ E 216
Baoji, China 34°25′ N, 107°9′ E 198
Baojing, China 28°41′ N, 109°41′ E 198
Baoro, Cen. Af. Rep. 5°39′ N, 15°57′ E 218
Baoshan, China 25°8′ N, 99°8′ E 190
Baoting, China 18°36′ N, 109°39′ E 198
Baotou, China 40°36′ N, 110°0′ E 198
Baoulé, Mali 12°56′ N, 8°36′ W 222
Baoulé, river, Mali 13°57′ N, 9°27′ W 222
Baoying, China 33°16′ N, 119°22′ E 198
Bapaume, Fr. 50°5′ N, 2°50′ E 163
Bapia, Dem. Rep. of the Congo 4°24′ N, 24°57′ E 224
Baqên, China 31°54′ N, 93°59′ E 188
Baqty, Kaz. 46°41′ N, 82°48′ E 184
Ba'qūbah, Iraq 33°43′ N, 44°40′ E 180
Bar, Mont. 42°5′ N, 19°5′ E 168
Bar, Ukr. 49°4′ N, 27°44′ E 152
Bar Harbor, Me., U.S. 44°23′ N, 68°12′ W 82
Bar Mills, Me., U.S. 43°36′ N, 70°33′ W 104
Bara, Sudan 13°41′ N, 30°20′ E 226
Bara Banki, India 26°54′ N, 81°11′ E 197
Bara Simbil, Jebel, peak, Sudan 13°27′ N, 24°10′ E 226
Baraawe, Somalia 1°3′ N, 44°2′ E 218
Barabinsk, Russ. 55°17′ N, 78°23′ E 184
Baraboo, Wis., U.S. 43°28′ N, 89°44′ W 94
Baraboo, river, Wis., U.S. 43°30′ N, 90°5′ W 102
Baraboulé, Burkina Faso 14°13′ N, 1°52′ W 222
Baracoa, Cuba 20°20′ N, 74°30′ W 116
Baradá, river, Syr. 33°36′ N, 36°1′ E 194
Baradero, Arg. 33°51′ S, 59°30′ W 139
Baraga, Mich., U.S. 46°47′ N, 88°31′ W 94
Bărăganul, Rom. 44°15′ N, 26°55′ E 156
Baragoi, Kenya 1°44′ N, 36°47′ E 224
Barahona, Dom. Rep. 18°11′ N, 71°5′ W 116
Barakat, Sudan 14°13′ N, 33°35′ E 182
Baram, river, Malaysia 3°55′ N, 113°58′ E 192
Baramandougou, Mali 13°37′ N, 4°38′ W 222
Baramula, India 34°10′ N, 74°23′ E 186
Baran', Belarus 54°29′ N, 28°40′ E 166
Baran, India 25°5′ N, 76°31′ E 197
Baranama, Guinea 10°11′ N, 8°46′ W 222
Baranavichy, Belarus 53°6′ N, 26°1′ E 152
Baranoa, Col. 10°47′ N, 74°57′ W 136
Baranof Island, Alas., U.S. 56°3′ N, 135°55′ W 98
Baranovka, Russ. 49°55′ N, 46°2′ E 158
Baranya, adm. division, Hung. 45°55′ N, 17°41′ E 156
Barão de Grajaú, Braz. 6°43′ S, 43°3′ W 132
Barão de Melgaço, Braz. 16°15′ S, 55°57′ W 132
Barassoli, spring, Eritrea 13°36′ N, 42°5′ E 182
Barat Daya, Kepulauan, islands, Banda Sea 6°36′ S, 126°45′ E 192
Barataria, La., U.S. 29°43′ N, 90°8′ W 103
Barataria Bay 29°22′ N, 90°11′ W 103
Barbacena, Braz. 21°13′ S, 43°46′ W 138
Barbacoas, Col. 1°38′ N, 78°13′ W 136
Barbadillo, Sp. 40°55′ N, 5°52′ W 150
Barbadillo del Mercado, Sp. 42°2′ N, 3°22′ W 164
Barbados 13°0′ N, 60°0′ W 116
Barbaria, Cap de, Sp. 38°19′ N, 1°24′ E 150
Barbas, Cap, Western Sahara, Mor. 21°56′ N, 16°47′ W 214
Barbastro, Sp. 42°2′ N, 0°7′ E 164
Barbate, Sp. 36°11′ N, 5°57′ W 164
Barbazan, Fr. 43°2′ N, 0°36′ E 164
Bārbele, Latv. 56°26′ N, 24°35′ E 166
Barberton, Ohio, U.S. 41°0′ N, 81°37′ W 110
Barberton, S. Af. 25°50′ S, 31°0′ E 227
Barberville, Fla., U.S. 29°11′ N, 81°26′ W 105
Barbosa, Col. 5°56′ N, 73°39′ W 136
Barbourville, Ky., U.S. 36°52′ N, 83°54′ W 96
Barbuda, island, Antigua and Barbuda 17°45′ N, 61°51′ W 116
Barcarrota, Sp. 38°31′ N, 6°52′ W 164
Barce see Al Marj, Lib. 32°30′ N, 20°53′ E 216
Barcelona, Sp. 41°23′ N, 2°10′ E 164
Barcelona, Venez. 10°5′ N, 64°44′ W 136
Barcelonnette, Fr. 44°23′ N, 6°38′ E 167
Barcelos, Braz. 1°0′ N, 62°58′ W 130
Barco, N.C., U.S. 36°23′ N, 76°0′ W 96
Barcs, Hung. 45°57′ N, 17°28′ E 168
Barczewo, Pol. 53°50′ N, 20°40′ E 166
Bard, Calif., U.S. 32°47′ N, 114°34′ W 101
Bärdä, Azerb. 40°23′ N, 47°6′ E 195
Barda, Russ. 56°56′ N, 55°39′ E 154
Barda Hills, India 21°50′ N, 69°41′ E 186
Bardaale, Somalia 7°0′ N, 47°54′ E 218
Bardaï, Chad 21°20′ N, 17°1′ E 216
Bardas Blancas, Arg. 35°52′ S, 69°50′ W 134
Bardawīl, Sabkhet el 31°7′ N, 33°2′ E 194
Barddhaman, India 23°13′ N, 87°52′ E 197
Bardoli, India 21°8′ N, 73°7′ E 186

Bardon Hill, peak, *U.K.* 52°42′ N, 1°21′ W 162
Bardonecchia, *It.* 45°5′ N, 6°42′ E 167
Bardstown, *Ky., U.S.* 37°47′ N, 85°29′ W 94
Bardwell, *Ky., U.S.* 36°51′ N, 89°1′ W 96
Bare Mountain, *Nev., U.S.* 36°50′ N, 116°43′ W 101
Barèges, *Fr.* 42°53′ N, 6°357′ E 164
Bareilly, *India* 28°20′ N, 79°24′ E 197
Barents Plain, *Arctic Ocean* 83°46′ N, 15°37′ E 255
Barents Sea 71°12′ N, 27°58′ E 152
Barentsburg, *Nor.* 77°58′ N, 14°33′ E 160
Barentsøya, island, *Nor.* 78°41′ N, 22°17′ E 246
Barentu, *Eritrea* 15°6′ N, 37°35′ E 182
Barevo, *Bosn. and Herzg.* 44°25′ N, 17°14′ E 168
Barfleur, Pointe de, *Fr.* 49°39′ N, 1°54′ W 150
Barga, *China* 30°52′ N, 81°19′ E 197
Barga, *It.* 44°5′ N, 10°29′ E 167
Bargaal, *Somalia* 11°13′ N, 51°3′ E 216
Bargarh, *India* 21°19′ N, 83°35′ E 188
Bargē, *Eth.* 6°13′ N, 36°53′ E 224
Bårgo, peak, *Nor.* 66°16′ N, 18°7′ E 152
Barguzin, *Russ.* 53°41′ N, 109°32′ E 190
Barham, Mount, *Can.* 59°44′ N, 133°36′ W 98
Barharwa, *India* 24°51′ N, 87°47′ E 197
Barhi, *India* 24°14′ N, 85°23′ E 197
Barhi, *India* 23°56′ N, 80°51′ E 197
Bari, *Dem. Rep. of the Congo* 3°22′ N, 19°24′ E 218
Bari, *India* 26°37′ N, 77°36′ E 197
Bari, *It.* 41°7′ N, 16°51′ E 156
Barika, *Alg.* 35°21′ N, 5°22′ E 150
Barikowt, *Afghan.* 35°17′ N, 71°32′ E 186
Baril Lake, *Can.* 58°45′ N, 111°57′ W 108
Barīm (Perim), island, *Yemen* 12°36′ N, 42°32′ E 182
Barinas, *Venez.* 8°38′ N, 70°15′ W 136
Barinas, adm. division, *Venez.* 8°23′ N, 70°58′ W 136
Baringa, *Dem. Rep. of the Congo* 0°42′ N, 20°53′ E 218
Baripada, *India* 21°57′ N, 86°43′ E 197
Bariri, *Braz.* 22°5′ S, 48°41′ W 138
Bârîs, *Egypt* 24°40′ N, 30°30′ E 182
Barisal, *Bangladesh* 22°42′ N, 90°17′ E 197
Barisan, Pegunungan, *Indonesia* 1°4′ S, 100°23′ E 196
Barito, river, *Indonesia* 2°13′ S, 114°39′ E 192
Baritú National Park, *Arg.* 22°25′ S, 64°46′ W 137
Bark Lake, *Can.* 46°50′ N, 82°54′ W 94
Bark Point, *Wis., U.S.* 46°40′ N, 91°13′ W 94
Barkā', *Oman* 23°40′ N, 57°54′ E 196
Barkald, *Nor.* 61°59′ N, 10°54′ E 152
Barkley, Lake, *Ky., U.S.* 36°20′ N, 88°40′ W 81
Barkley Sound 48°50′ N, 125°50′ W 108
Barkly East, *S. Af.* 30°58′ S, 27°33′ E 227
Barkly Tableland, *Austral.* 19°43′ S, 136°41′ E 230
Barkly West, *S. Af.* 28°33′ S, 24°31′ E 227
Barkol, *China* 43°31′ N, 92°51′ E 190
Barksdale, *Tex., U.S.* 29°44′ N, 100°2′ W 92
Barksdale Air Force Base, *La., U.S.* 32°27′ N, 93°42′ W 103
Barla Dağı, peak, *Turk.* 38°2′ N, 30°37′ E 156
Bar-le-Duc, *Fr.* 48°46′ N, 5°10′ E 163
Barlee Range Nature Reserve, *Austral.* 23°21′ S, 115°39′ E 238
Barlow Pass, *Oreg., U.S.* 45°16′ N, 121°42′ W 90
Barmer, *India* 25°43′ N, 71°23′ E 186
Barmou, *Niger* 15°8′ N, 5°27′ E 222
Barmouth, *U.K.* 52°43′ N, 4°3′ W 162
Barnard, *Vt., U.S.* 43°43′ N, 72°38′ W 104
Barnaul, *Russ.* 53°23′ N, 83°48′ E 184
Barnegat, *N.J., U.S.* 39°45′ N, 74°14′ W 94
Barnegat Light, *N.J., U.S.* 39°44′ N, 74°7′ W 94
Barnes Ice Cap, *Can.* 68°46′ N, 73°57′ W 106
Barnes Sound 25°13′ N, 80°35′ W 105
Barnesville, *Minn., U.S.* 46°37′ N, 96°26′ W 90
Barnesville, *Ohio, U.S.* 39°58′ N, 81°11′ W 102
Barnet, *Vt., U.S.* 44°17′ N, 72°4′ W 104
Barnhart, *Tex., U.S.* 31°6′ N, 101°10′ W 92
Barnoldswick, *U.K.* 53°55′ N, 2°12′ W 162
Barnsley, *U.K.* 53°32′ N, 1°28′ W 162
Barnstaple, *U.K.* 51°5′ N, 4°3′ W 162
Barnum, *Minn., U.S.* 46°29′ N, 92°44′ W 94
Baro, *Nig.* 8°33′ N, 6°22′ E 222
Barons, *Can.* 49°59′ N, 113°5′ W 90
Barouéli, *Mali* 13°4′ N, 6°50′ W 222
Barpeta, *India* 26°19′ N, 90°57′ E 197
Barques, Pointe aux, *Mich., U.S.* 44°4′ N, 82°55′ W 102
Barquisimeto, *Venez.* 10°0′ N, 69°19′ W 136
Barr, *Fr.* 48°24′ N, 7°26′ E 163
Barra, *Braz.* 10°58′ S, 43°8′ W 123
Barra, *Braz.* 11°6′ S, 43°11′ W 132
Barra da Estiva, *Braz.* 13°39′ S, 41°20′ W 138
Barra de Navidad, *Mex.* 19°12′ N, 104°43′ W 114
Barra de São João, *Braz.* 22°34′ S, 42°0′ W 138
Barra del Tordo, *Mex.* 23°0′ N, 97°47′ W 114
Barra do Bugres, *Braz.* 15°4′ S, 57°13′ W 132
Barra do Corda, *Braz.* 5°33′ S, 45°15′ W 132
Barra do Cuanza, *Angola* 9°18′ S, 13°7′ E 220
Barra do Dande, *Angola* 8°29′ S, 13°21′ E 218
Barra do Garças, *Braz.* 15°53′ S, 52°16′ W 138
Barra do Piraí, *Braz.* 22°30′ S, 43°46′ W 138
Barra do Quaraí, *Uru.* 30°15′ S, 57°34′ W 139
Barra do São Manuel, *Braz.* 7°19′ S, 58°2′ W 130
Barra Head, *U.K.* 56°38′ N, 8°2′ W 150
Barra Mansa, *Braz.* 22°34′ S, 44°9′ W 138
Barra Patuca, *Hond.* 15°48′ N, 84°18′ W 115
Barra, Ponta da, *Mozambique* 23°42′ S, 35°29′ E 227
Barracão do Barreto, *Braz.* 8°50′ S, 58°25′ W 130
Barrage Daniel-Johnson, dam, *Can.* 50°23′ N, 69°12′ W 111
Barrage Gouin, dam, *Can.* 48°7′ N, 74°5′ W 94
Barragem, *Mozambique* 24°24′ S, 32°53′ E 227
Barrancabermeja, *Col.* 7°3′ N, 73°50′ W 136
Barrancas, *Venez.* 8°43′ N, 62°14′ W 116
Barranco Branco, *Braz.* 19°35′ S, 56°8′ W 132
Barranco Branco, *Braz.* 21°7′ S, 57°51′ W 134
Barrancos de Guadalupe, *Mex.* 29°57′ N, 104°45′ W 92
Barranqueras, *Arg.* 27°30′ S, 58°57′ W 139
Barranquilla, *Col.* 10°57′ N, 74°50′ W 136
Barras, *Braz.* 4°17′ S, 42°19′ W 132
Barras, *Col.* 1°46′ S, 73°13′ W 136
Barraute, *Can.* 48°26′ N, 77°40′ W 94
Barrax, *Sp.* 39°2′ N, 2°13′ W 164
Barre, *Mass., U.S.* 42°25′ N, 72°7′ W 104
Barre, *Vt., U.S.* 44°12′ N, 72°31′ W 104
Barreiras, *Braz.* 12°10′ S, 44°58′ W 132
Barreirinha, *Braz.* 2°49′ S, 57°5′ W 130
Barreiro, *Port.* 38°36′ N, 9°8′ W 214
Barrême, *Fr.* 43°57′ N, 6°21′ E 167
Barren Island, *U.S.* 52°44′ S, 60°8′ W 134
Barretos, *Braz.* 20°35′ S, 48°36′ W 138
Barrhead, *Can.* 54°8′ N, 114°25′ W 108
Barrie, *Can.* 44°23′ N, 79°42′ W 94
Barrier Bay 67°42′ S, 78°28′ E 248
Barrier Range, *Austral.* 31°5′ S, 140°54′ E 230
Barriles, ruin(s), *Pan.* 8°42′ N, 82°50′ W 115
Barrington, *Ill., U.S.* 42°9′ N, 88°8′ W 102
Barrington, *N.H., U.S.* 43°13′ N, 71°3′ W 104
Barrington, *R.I., U.S.* 41°44′ N, 71°19′ W 104
Barro Alto, *Braz.* 15°6′ S, 48°58′ W 138
Barrocão, *Braz.* 16°24′ S, 43°16′ W 138
Barron, *Wis., U.S.* 45°23′ N, 91°52′ W 94
Barrow, *Alas., U.S.* 71°8′ N, 156°35′ W 98
Barrow Canyon, *Arctic Ocean* 72°4′ N, 151°21′ W 255
Barrow Creek, *Austral.* 21°33′ S, 133°54′ E 231
Barrow in Furness, *U.K.* 54°7′ N, 3°13′ W 162
Barrow Island, *Austral.* 20°51′ S, 114°19′ E 230
Barrow, Point, *Alas., U.S.* 71°40′ N, 155°42′ W 246
Barrow Strait 74°8′ N, 97°17′ W 106
Barrows, *Can.* 52°49′ N, 101°27′ W 108
Barry, *U.K.* 51°23′ N, 3°17′ W 162
Barry, Lac, lake, *Can.* 48°59′ N, 75°59′ W 94
Barry's Bay, *Can.* 45°28′ N, 77°41′ W 94
Barryton, *Mich., U.S.* 43°44′ N, 85°9′ W 102
Barrytown, *N.Z.* 42°15′ S, 171°20′ E 240
Barshatas, *Kaz.* 48°4′ N, 78°32′ E 184
Barshyn, *Kaz.* 49°37′ N, 69°30′ E 184
Barsi, *India* 18°14′ N, 75°41′ E 188
Barstow, *Calif., U.S.* 34°53′ N, 117°2′ W 101
Bar-sur-Aube, *Fr.* 48°13′ N, 4°43′ E 163
Bārta, *Latv.* 56°21′ N, 21°18′ E 166
Bārta, river, *Latv.* 56°18′ N, 21°2′ E 166
Barter Island, *Alas., U.S.* 70°11′ N, 145°51′ W 106
Barthelemy Pass, *Laos* 19°31′ N, 104°1′ E 202
Bartica, *Guyana* 6°19′ N, 58°41′ W 130
Bartın, *Turk.* 41°38′ N, 32°20′ E 156
Bartlesville, *Okla., U.S.* 36°43′ N, 95°59′ W 96
Bartlett, *Nebr., U.S.* 41°51′ N, 98°33′ W 90
Bartlett, *N.H., U.S.* 44°4′ N, 71°18′ W 104
Bartlett, *Tex., U.S.* 30°46′ N, 97°26′ W 92
Bartolomeu Dias, *Mozambique* 21°12′ S, 35°6′ E 227
Barton, *N. Dak., U.S.* 48°29′ N, 100°12′ W 94
Barton upon Humber, *U.K.* 53°40′ N, 0°27′ E 162
Bartoszyce, *Pol.* 54°14′ N, 20°48′ E 166
Bartow, *Fla., U.S.* 27°50′ N, 81°51′ W 112
Bartow, *Ger.* 53°49′ N, 13°20′ E 152
Barú, Volcán, *Pan.* 8°47′ N, 82°41′ W 115
Barus, *Indonesia* 2°3′ N, 98°22′ E 196
Baruth, *Ger.* 52°4′ N, 13°29′ E 152
Baruun Urt, *Mongolia* 46°40′ N, 113°16′ E 198
Baruunharaa, *Mongolia* 48°58′ N, 106°3′ E 198
Baruunsuu, *Mongolia* 43°45′ N, 105°31′ E 198
Barvinkove, *Ukr.* 48°56′ N, 37°6′ E 158
Barysaw, *Belarus* 54°13′ N, 28°29′ E 166
Barysh, *Russ.* 53°39′ N, 47°13′ E 154
Barzas, *Russ.* 55°45′ N, 86°29′ E 169
Bāsa'īdū, *Iran* 26°37′ N, 55°17′ E 196
Basail, *Arg.* 27°51′ S, 59°18′ W 139
Basal, *Pak.* 33°32′ N, 72°19′ E 186
Basankusu, *Dem. Rep. of the Congo* 1°7′ N, 19°50′ E 207
Basargech'ar, *Arm.* 40°12′ N, 45°42′ E 195
Basaseachic, *Mex.* 28°10′ N, 108°11′ W 92
Basavilbaso, *Arg.* 32°23′ S, 58°51′ W 139
Basco, *Philippines* 20°25′ N, 121°58′ E 203
Bas-Congo, adm. division, *Dem. Rep. of the Congo* 5°10′ S, 13°44′ E 218
Bascuñán, Cabo, *Chile* 28°48′ S, 72°52′ W 134
Basekpio, *Dem. Rep. of the Congo* 4°45′ N, 24°38′ E 224
Basel, *Switz.* 47°33′ N, 7°35′ E 150
Basey, *Philippines* 11°18′ N, 125°3′ E 203
Bashaw, *Can.* 52°35′ N, 112°59′ W 108
Bashi, *Ala., U.S.* 31°57′ N, 87°51′ W 103
Bashi Channel 21°28′ N, 120°30′ E 198
Bashkortostan, adm. division, *Russ.* 54°0′ N, 55°48′ E 154
Basilan, island, *Philippines* 6°14′ N, 122°25′ E 192
Basile, *La., U.S.* 30°28′ N, 92°37′ W 103
Basiliano, *It.* 46°1′ N, 13°5′ E 167
Basilicata, adm. division, *It.* 40°59′ N, 15°38′ E 156
Basílio, *Braz.* 31°53′ S, 53°2′ W 139
Basin, *Wyo., U.S.* 44°21′ N, 108°3′ W 90
Basin Harbor, *Vt., U.S.* 44°11′ N, 73°22′ W 104
Basinger, *Fla., U.S.* 27°23′ N, 81°2′ W 105
Basingstoke, *U.K.* 51°16′ N, 1°6′ W 162
Basirhat, *India* 22°40′ N, 88°48′ E 197
Baška, *Croatia* 44°58′ N, 14°44′ E 156
Başkale, *Turk.* 38°2′ N, 43°56′ E 195
Baskin, *La., U.S.* 32°14′ N, 91°44′ W 103
Baskomutan National Park, *Turk.* 38°51′ N, 30°15′ E 156
Baslow, *U.K.* 53°15′ N, 1°37′ W 162
Basoda, *India* 23°51′ N, 77°56′ E 197
Basoko, *Dem. Rep. of the Congo* 1°17′ N, 23°35′ E 224
Basongo, *Dem. Rep. of the Congo* 4°23′ S, 20°22′ E 218
Basque Country, adm. division, *Sp.* 43°10′ N, 3°2′ W 164
Basra see Al Başrah, *Iraq* 30°30′ N, 47°48′ E 207
Bass Islands, *Lake Erie* 41°36′ N, 83°0′ W 102
Bass Lake, *Calif., U.S.* 37°20′ N, 119°34′ W 100
Bass Strait 39°32′ S, 143°59′ E 231
Bassae, ruin(s), *Gr.* 37°25′ N, 21°42′ E 156
Bassano, *Can.* 50°47′ N, 112°29′ W 90
Bassano del Grappa, *It.* 45°46′ N, 11°44′ E 167
Bassar, *Togo* 9°14′ N, 0°46′ E 222
Bassas da India, adm. division, *Fr.* 21°15′ S, 39°13′ E 220
Basse Santa Su, *Gambia* 13°17′ N, 14°15′ W 222
Basse-Normandie, adm. division, *Fr.* 49°7′ N, 1°9′ W 150
Basse-Terre, *Fr.* 16°0′ N, 61°44′ W 116
Basseterre, *Saint Kitts and Nevis* 17°0′ N, 63°0′ W 118
Basse-Terre, island, *Fr.* 16°10′ N, 62°34′ W 116
Bassett, *Nebr., U.S.* 42°33′ N, 99°33′ W 90
Bassfield, *Miss., U.S.* 31°28′ N, 89°45′ W 103
Bassigibiri, *Cen. Af. Rep.* 5°18′ N, 26°54′ E 224
Bassikounou, *Mauritania* 15°52′ N, 5°58′ W 222
Bastak, *Iran* 27°11′ N, 54°25′ E 196
Bastar, *India* 19°14′ N, 81°58′ E 188
Bastevarre, peak, *Nor.* 68°57′ N, 22°12′ E 152
Basti, *India* 26°46′ N, 82°44′ E 197
Bastia, *Fr.* 42°40′ N, 9°23′ E 214
Bastimentos, Isla, island, *Pan.* 9°23′ N, 82°9′ W 115
Bastrop, *La., U.S.* 32°46′ N, 91°55′ W 103
Bastrop, *Tex., U.S.* 30°6′ N, 97°19′ W 92
Bastuträsk, *Nor.* 64°46′ N, 20°1′ E 152
Bastyn', *Belarus* 52°23′ N, 26°44′ E 152
Basuo see Dongfang, *China* 19°3′ N, 108°38′ E 198
Bat Yam, *Israel* 32°1′ N, 34°44′ E 194
Bata, *Equatorial Guinea* 2°1′ N, 9°47′ E 207
Bata, *Rom.* 46°1′ N, 22°2′ E 168
Batac, *Philippines* 18°4′ N, 120°33′ E 203
Batagay, *Russ.* 67°42′ N, 134°52′ E 160
Batagay Alyta, *Russ.* 67°47′ N, 130°22′ E 160
Batajnica, *Serb.* 44°53′ N, 20°17′ E 168
Batala, *India* 31°47′ N, 75°13′ E 186
Batam, island, *Indonesia* 0°53′ N, 103°40′ E 196
Batama, *Dem. Rep. of the Congo* 0°53′ N, 26°35′ E 224
Batamay, *Russ.* 63°30′ N, 129°24′ E 160
Batamorghab, *Afghan.* 35°37′ N, 63°20′ E 186
Batan, island, *Philippines* 20°30′ N, 122°3′ E 198
Batan Islands, *Philippine Sea* 20°36′ N, 122°2′ E 203
Batang, *China* 30°6′ N, 98°58′ E 190
Batang Ai National Park, *Malaysia* 1°14′ N, 111°42′ E 238
Batang Berjuntai, *Malaysia* 3°22′ N, 101°25′ E 196
Batanga, *Gabon* 0°19′ N, 9°21′ E 218
Batangafo, *Cen. Af. Rep.* 7°15′ N, 18°18′ E 218
Batangas, *Philippines* 13°48′ N, 121°2′ E 203
Batangtoru, *Indonesia* 1°30′ N, 99°4′ E 196
Batara, *Cen. Af. Rep.* 5°50′ N, 16°8′ E 218
Bátaszék, *Hung.* 46°11′ N, 18°42′ E 168
Batatais, *Braz.* 20°55′ S, 47°36′ W 138
Batavia, *N.Y., U.S.* 42°59′ N, 78°11′ W 94
Bataysk, *Russ.* 47°6′ N, 39°46′ E 156
Batchawana Bay, *Can.* 46°56′ N, 84°36′ W 94
Batchawana Mountain, *Can.* 47°5′ N, 84°29′ W 94
Batesville, *Ark., U.S.* 35°45′ N, 91°42′ W 96
Batesville, *Miss., U.S.* 34°17′ N, 89°57′ W 96
Batesville, *Tex., U.S.* 28°56′ N, 99°38′ W 92
Batetskaya, *Russ.* 58°38′ N, 30°22′ E 166
Bath, *Me., U.S.* 43°54′ N, 69°50′ W 104
Bath, *N.H., U.S.* 44°9′ N, 71°58′ W 104
Bath, *N.Y., U.S.* 42°20′ N, 77°20′ W 94
Bath, *U.K.* 51°23′ N, 2°23′ W 162
Bathurst, *Can.* 47°32′ N, 65°44′ W 106
Bathurst, *S. Af.* 33°32′ S, 26°48′ E 227
Bathurst, Cape, *Can.* 70°19′ N, 130°47′ W 98
Bathurst Inlet 67°37′ N, 111°0′ W 106
Bathurst Inlet, *Can.* 66°24′ N, 107°24′ W 73
Bathurst Island, *Austral.* 12°5′ S, 128°51′ E 230
Bathurst Island, *Can.* 74°41′ N, 102°4′ W 106
Batī, *Eth.* 11°12′ N, 40°1′ E 224
Batié, *Burkina Faso* 9°54′ N, 2°58′ W 222
Batina, *Croatia* 45°49′ N, 18°48′ E 168
Batista, Serra da, *Braz.* 6°40′ S, 41°49′ W 132
Batkanu, *Sierra Leone* 9°3′ N, 12°25′ W 222
Batlava, *Serb.* 42°50′ N, 21°14′ E 168
Batley, *U.K.* 53°43′ N, 1°38′ W 162
Batman, *Turk.* 37°53′ N, 41°10′ E 195
Batna, *Alg.* 35°31′ N, 6°8′ E 150
Batoche National Historic Site, *Can.* 52°42′ N, 106°10′ W 108
Batočina, *Serb.* 44°9′ N, 21°3′ E 168
Baton Rouge, *La., U.S.* 30°25′ N, 91°13′ W 103
Batopilas, *Mex.* 27°1′ N, 107°46′ W 112
Batouri, *Cameroon* 4°25′ N, 14°20′ E 218
Batovi see Tamitatoala, river, *Braz.* 14°11′ S, 53°58′ W 132
Batrina, *Croatia* 45°11′ N, 17°39′ E 168
Bătrîna, *Rom.* 45°48′ N, 22°35′ E 168
Batroun, *Leb.* 34°16′ N, 35°40′ E 194
Batsí, *Gr.* 37°51′ N, 24°46′ E 156
Batson, *Tex., U.S.* 30°13′ N, 94°37′ W 103
Battambang, *Cambodia* 13°7′ N, 103°11′ E 202
Battenberg, *Ger.* 51°0′ N, 8°39′ E 167
Batticaloa, *Sri Lanka* 7°44′ N, 81°43′ E 188
Battle, *U.K.* 50°54′ N, 0°29′ E 162
Battle Creek, *Mich., U.S.* 42°18′ N, 85°12′ W 102
Battle Creek, river, *Mont., U.S.* 49°3′ N, 109°29′ W 108
Battle Ground, *Ind., U.S.* 40°30′ N, 86°50′ W 102
Battle Ground, *Wash., U.S.* 45°46′ N, 122°33′ W 100
Battle Harbour, *Can.* 52°15′ N, 55°38′ W 111
Battle Mountain, *Nev., U.S.* 40°43′ N, 117°19′ W 90
Battle, river, *Can.* 52°17′ N, 112°10′ W 80
Battleford, *Can.* 52°43′ N, 108°20′ W 108
Battonya, *Hung.* 46°17′ N, 21°2′ E 168
Batu, Kepulauan, islands, *Tanahmasa* 5°297′ N, 98°10′ E 196
Batu Pahat, *Malaysia* 1°52′ N, 102°56′ E 196
Batu, peak, *Eth.* 6°53′ N, 39°39′ E 224
Bat'umi, *Ga.* 41°38′ N, 41°38′ E 195
Batupanjang, *Indonesia* 1°45′ N, 101°33′ E 196
Baturaja, *Indonesia* 4°10′ S, 104°9′ E 192
Baturino, *Russ.* 57°42′ N, 85°17′ E 169
Baturité, *Braz.* 4°20′ S, 38°54′ W 132
Baturité, Serra de, *Braz.* 4°45′ S, 39°36′ W 132
Batys Qazaqstan, adm. division, *Kaz.* 49°52′ N, 49°51′ E 158
Bau, *Sudan* 11°22′ N, 34°6′ E 216
Baú, river, *Braz.* 6°41′ S, 52°57′ W 130
Baubau, *Indonesia* 5°36′ S, 122°41′ E 192
Bauchi, *Nig.* 10°19′ N, 9°50′ E 222
Baudeau, Lac, lake, *Can.* 51°37′ N, 73°44′ W 110
Baudette, *Minn., U.S.* 48°41′ N, 94°39′ W 90
Baudó, *Col.* 5°1′ N, 77°7′ W 136
Baudó, Serranía de, *Col.* 5°31′ N, 78°6′ W 115
Bauges, *Fr.* 45°34′ N, 5°59′ E 165
Bauld, Cape, *Can.* 51°40′ N, 55°58′ W 111
Baunatal, *Ger.* 51°15′ N, 9°26′ E 167
Baunei, *It.* 40°2′ N, 9°39′ E 156
Baunt, *Russ.* 55°20′ N, 113°12′ E 190
Baure, *Nig.* 12°50′ N, 8°44′ E 222
Baures, *Bol.* 13°39′ S, 63°36′ W 137
Baures, river, *Bol.* 12°43′ S, 64°5′ W 137
Bauru, *Braz.* 22°21′ S, 49°5′ W 138
Baús, *Braz.* 18°27′ S, 53°0′ W 138
Bauska, *Latv.* 56°24′ N, 24°11′ E 166
Bautīno, *Kaz.* 44°33′ N, 50°16′ E 158
Bauya, *Sierra Leone* 8°10′ N, 12°37′ W 222
Baūyrzhan Momyshuly, *Kaz.* 42°37′ N, 70°45′ E 197
Bavanište, *Serb.* 44°48′ N, 20°52′ E 168
Bavaria, adm. division, *Ger.* 49°12′ N, 11°22′ E 167
Bavay, *Fr.* 50°16′ N, 3°48′ E 163
Baviácora, *Mex.* 29°43′ N, 110°11′ W 92
Bavispe, river, *Mex.* 30°27′ N, 109°6′ W 92
Bavly, *Russ.* 54°21′ N, 53°24′ E 154
Bawîti, *Egypt* 28°21′ N, 28°50′ E 180
Bawku, *Ghana* 11°3′ N, 0°16′ E 222
Bawlake, *Myanmar* 19°11′ N, 97°17′ E 202
Bawlf, *Can.* 52°54′ N, 112°28′ W 108
Bawmi, *Myanmar* 17°20′ N, 94°36′ E 202
Bawtry, *U.K.* 53°26′ N, 1°1′ W 162
Baxaya, peak, *Somalia* 11°17′ N, 49°35′ E 218
Baxdo, *Somalia* 5°48′ N, 47°17′ E 218
Baxley, *Ga., U.S.* 31°46′ N, 82°22′ W 96
Baxoi, *China* 30°2′ N, 96°57′ E 188
Baxter, *Minn., U.S.* 46°21′ N, 94°18′ W 94
Baxter Peak, *Colo., U.S.* 39°39′ N, 107°24′ W 90
Baxterville, *Miss., U.S.* 31°4′ N, 89°37′ W 103
Bay City, *Mich., U.S.* 43°35′ N, 83°53′ W 102
Bay City, *Tex., U.S.* 28°58′ N, 95°58′ W 96
Bay City, *Wis., U.S.* 44°35′ N, 92°27′ W 94
Bay de Verde, *Can.* 48°6′ N, 52°54′ W 111
Bay Minette, *Ala., U.S.* 30°51′ N, 87°46′ W 103
Bay Port, *Mich., U.S.* 43°50′ N, 83°23′ W 102
Bay Roberts, *Can.* 47°35′ N, 53°16′ W 111
Bay Saint Louis, *Miss., U.S.* 30°18′ N, 89°20′ W 103
Bay Shore, *N.Y., U.S.* 40°43′ N, 73°16′ W 104
Bay Springs, *Miss., U.S.* 31°58′ N, 89°17′ W 103
Baya, *Dem. Rep. of the Congo* 2°31′ N, 20°17′ E 218
Bay'ah, *Oman* 25°45′ N, 56°18′ E 196
Bayamo, *Cuba* 20°21′ N, 76°38′ W 115
Bayan, *China* 46°3′ N, 127°25′ E 198
Bayan, *Mongolia* 47°11′ N, 107°33′ E 198
Bayan, *Mongolia* 48°27′ N, 111°0′ E 198
Bayan Har Shan, *China* 34°35′ N, 95°13′ E 188
Bayan Har Shankou, pass, *China* 34°10′ N, 97°41′ E 188
Bayan Huxu see Horqin Youyi Zhongqi, *China* 45°5′ N, 121°25′ E 198
Bayan Mod, *China* 40°45′ N, 104°31′ E 198
Bayan Obo, *China* 41°46′ N, 109°58′ E 198
Bayan Ovoo, *Mongolia* 47°49′ N, 112°4′ E 198
Bayan Uul, *Mongolia* 49°5′ N, 112°45′ E 198
Bayana, *India* 26°53′ N, 77°14′ E 197
Bayanaūyl, *Kaz.* 50°45′ N, 75°42′ E 184
Bayanhongor, *Mongolia* 46°37′ N, 100°8′ E 190
Bayano, Lago, lake, *Pan.* 9°0′ N, 79°0′ W 116
Bayan-Ölgiy, adm. division, *Mongolia* 48°37′ N, 89°55′ E 184
Bayan-Ovoo, *Mongolia* 48°57′ N, 111°25′ E 198
Bayard, *Nebr., U.S.* 41°45′ N, 103°21′ W 92
Bayard, *N. Mex., U.S.* 32°44′ N, 108°8′ W 92
Bayasgalant, *Mongolia* 46°57′ N, 112°2′ E 198
Bayat, *Turk.* 38°58′ N, 30°55′ E 156
Bayawan, *Philippines* 9°23′ N, 122°48′ E 203
Baybay, *Philippines* 10°40′ N, 124°50′ E 203
Bayboro, *N.C., U.S.* 35°9′ N, 76°47′ W 96
Bayburt, *Turk.* 40°16′ N, 40°14′ E 195
Baydhabo (Baidoa), *Somalia* 3°5′ N, 43°41′ E 218
Bayerischer Wald, *Ger.* 48°59′ N, 12°19′ E 152
Bayfield, *Can.* 43°32′ N, 81°41′ W 102
Bayfield, *Wis., U.S.* 46°49′ N, 90°50′ W 94
Bayghanīn, *Kaz.* 48°42′ N, 55°53′ E 158
Bayḩan al Qişāb, *Yemen* 14°49′ N, 45°46′ E 182
Baykal, Ozero, lake, *Russ.* 53°48′ N, 103°44′ E 190
Baykalovo, *Russ.* 57°26′ N, 63°42′ E 154
Baykalovo, *Russ.* 57°45′ N, 67°40′ E 169
Baykan, *Turk.* 38°8′ N, 41°47′ E 195
Baykonur see Bayqongyr, *Kaz.* 47°47′ N, 66°0′ E 184
Baykurt, *China* 39°56′ N, 75°32′ E 184
Bayliss, Mount, *Antarctica* 73°30′ S, 62°4′ E 248
Baymak, *Russ.* 52°38′ N, 58°11′ E 154
Baynū, *Leb.* 34°32′ N, 36°10′ E 194
Bayombong, *Philippines* 16°29′ N, 121°8′ E 203
Bayon, *Fr.* 48°28′ N, 6°19′ E 163
Bayonet Point, *Fla., U.S.* 28°19′ N, 82°43′ W 105
Bayonne, *Fr.* 43°29′ N, 1°30′ W 164
Bayonne, *N.J., U.S.* 40°40′ N, 74°8′ W 104
Bayou La Batre, *Ala., U.S.* 30°23′ N, 88°16′ W 103
Bayou Macon, river, *La., U.S.* 32°6′ N, 91°32′ W 103
Bayovar, *Peru* 5°47′ S, 81°4′ W 130
Bayport, *Minn., U.S.* 45°0′ N, 92°48′ W 94

Bayqongyr (Leninsk, Baykonur), Kaz. 47°47′ N, 66°0′ E 184
Bayqongyr, adm. division, Kaz. 46°3′ N, 62°27′ E 184
Bayramaly, Turkm. 37°36′ N, 62°10′ E 184
Bayramiç, Turk. 39°48′ N, 26°35′ E 156
Bayreuth, Ger. 49°56′ N, 11°34′ E 152
Bays, Lake of, Can. 45°15′ N, 79°35′ W 94
Bayshint, Mongolia 49°40′ N, 90°20′ E 184
Bayshonas, Kaz. 47°18′ N, 53°0′ E 158
Bayt al Faqīh, Yemen 14°29′ N, 43°16′ E 182
Bayt Lahiyah, Gaza Strip, Israel 31°33′ N, 34°30′ E 194
Bayt La'm (Bethlehem), West Bank, Israel 31°41′ N, 35°12′ E 194
Baytīn, West Bank, Israel 31°55′ N, 35°14′ E 194
Baytown, Tex., U.S. 29°43′ N, 94°58′ W 103
Bayville, N.Y., U.S. 40°54′ N, 73°34′ W 104
Bayyrqum, Kaz. 41°54′ N, 68°5′ E 184
Bayzo, Niger 13°52′ N, 4°45′ E 222
Baza, Sp. 37°29′ N, 2°48′ W 164
Baza'i Gonbad, Afghan. 37°13′ N, 74°5′ E 186
Bazar-Kurgan, Kyrg. 41°1′ N, 72°46′ E 197
Bazarnyy Karabulak, Russ. 52°15′ N, 46°27′ E 158
Bazarsholan, Kaz. 48°58′ N, 51°55′ E 158
Bazartöbe, Kaz. 49°23′ N, 51°53′ E 158
Bazaruto, Ilha do, island, Mozambique 21°44′ S, 34°29′ E 227
Bazber, Eth. 10°36′ N, 35°7′ E 224
Bazhong, China 31°53′ N, 106°39′ E 198
Baziaş, Rom. 44°48′ N, 21°22′ E 168
Bazin, river, Can. 47°29′ N, 75°0′ W 94
Bazkovskaya, Russ. 49°33′ N, 41°35′ E 158
Bazmān, Kūh-e, peak, Iran 27°51′ N, 60°2′ E 182
Bazzano, It. 44°30′ N, 11°4′ E 167
Bcharre, Leb. 34°14′ N, 36°0′ E 194
Be, Nosy, island, Madagascar 13°24′ S, 47°23′ E 220
Beach, N. Dak., U.S. 46°53′ N, 104°1′ W 90
Beach Haven, N.J., U.S. 39°33′ N, 74°16′ W 94
Beacon, N.Y., U.S. 41°29′ N, 73°59′ W 104
Beaconsfield, U.K. 51°36′ N, 0°39′ E 162
Beade, Sp. 42°19′ N, 8°10′ W 150
Beale Air Force Base, Calif., U.S. 39°8′ N, 121°30′ W 90
Beale, Cape, Can. 48°37′ N, 125°31′ W 90
Beaminster, U.K. 50°48′ N, 2°44′ W 162
Beampingaratra, peak, Madagascar 24°36′ S, 46°39′ E 220
Bear Bay 75°23′ N, 88°10′ W 106
Bear Creek, river, Colo., U.S. 37°26′ N, 102°48′ W 80
Bear Island see Bjørnøya, Nor. 73°46′ N, 15°27′ E 160
Bear Islands see Medvezh'i Ostrova, islands, East Siberian Sea 71°5′ N, 151°1′ E 160
Bear Lake, Can. 55°2′ N, 96°49′ W 108
Bear Lake, Can. 56°6′ N, 127°4′ W 108
Bear Lake, Mich., U.S. 44°24′ N, 86°9′ W 94
Bear Lodge Mountains, Wyo., U.S. 44°39′ N, 104°42′ W 90
Bear Peninsula, Antarctica 74°18′ S, 106°40′ W 248
Bear River, Utah, U.S. 41°37′ N, 112°8′ W 90
Bear, river, Idaho, U.S. 42°27′ N, 111°48′ W 90
Bear River Range, Utah, U.S. 41°18′ N, 111°34′ W 90
Beardmore, Can. 49°37′ N, 87°57′ W 94
Beardstown, Mo., U.S. 40°0′ N, 90°25′ W 94
Béarn, region, Europe 42°57′ N, 0°52′ E 164
Bears Paw Mountains, Mont., U.S. 48°18′ N, 109°52′ W 90
Beas, Sp. 37°25′ N, 6°48′ W 164
Beas de Segura, Sp. 38°14′ N, 2°52′ W 164
Beasain, Sp. 43°2′ N, 2°13′ W 164
Beata, Cabo, Dom. Rep. 17°30′ N, 71°22′ W 116
Beata, Isla, island, Dom. Rep. 17°16′ N, 71°33′ W 116
Beatrice, Nebr., U.S. 40°15′ N, 96°45′ W 90
Beatton River, Can. 57°22′ N, 121°27′ W 108
Beatton, river, Can. 57°18′ N, 121°27′ W 108
Beatty, Nev., U.S. 36°54′ N, 116°47′ W 101
Beattyville, Can. 48°51′ N, 77°10′ W 94
Beatys Butte, peak, Oreg., U.S. 42°23′ N, 119°25′ W 90
Beaucamps, Fr. 49°49′ N, 1°47′ E 163
Beauceville, Can. 46°13′ N, 70°46′ W 111
Beauchêne Island, U.K. 52°56′ S, 61°53′ W 134
Beaufort, Malaysia 5°22′ N, 115°46′ E 203
Beaufort, S.C., U.S. 32°24′ N, 80°53′ W 112
Beaufort Marine Corps Air Station, S.C., U.S. 32°29′ N, 80°48′ W 96
Beaufort Sea 69°54′ N, 141°54′ W 106
Beaufort Sea 72°45′ N, 137°20′ W 255
Beaufort see Belfort, ruin(s), Leb. 33°19′ N, 35°30′ E 194
Beaufort Shelf, Beaufort Sea 70°4′ N, 142°6′ W 255
Beaufort Slope, Beaufort Sea 70°37′ N, 141°34′ W 255
Beaufort West, S. Af. 32°21′ S, 22°35′ E 227
Beaugency, Fr. 47°47′ N, 1°37′ E 150
Beaumaris, U.K. 53°15′ N, 4°5′ W 162
Beaumetz-lès-Loges, Fr. 50°13′ N, 2°38′ E 163
Beaumont, Belg. 50°14′ N, 4°14′ E 163
Beaumont, Calif., U.S. 33°56′ N, 116°59′ W 101
Beaumont, Fr. 49°8′ N, 2°16′ E 163
Beaumont, Miss., U.S. 31°8′ N, 88°54′ W 103
Beaumont, Tex., U.S. 30°4′ N, 94°7′ W 103
Beaumont-le-Roger, Fr. 49°5′ N, 0°47′ E 163
Beaupré, Can. 47°2′ N, 70°54′ W 94
Beauraing, Belg. 50°6′ N, 4°56′ E 167
Beauregard, Miss., U.S. 31°43′ N, 90°24′ W 103
Beausejour, Can. 50°3′ N, 96°31′ W 108
Beauvais, Fr. 49°26′ N, 2°5′ E 163
Beauval, Can. 55°9′ N, 107°39′ W 108
Beauval, Fr. 50°5′ N, 2°20′ E 163
Beauvezer, Fr. 44°8′ N, 6°34′ E 167
Beaver, Alas., U.S. 66°14′ N, 147°28′ W 98
Beaver, Ohio, U.S. 39°1′ N, 82°49′ W 102
Beaver, Okla., U.S. 36°47′ N, 100°32′ W 96
Beaver, Oreg., U.S. 45°16′ N, 123°50′ W 90
Beaver, Pa., U.S. 40°41′ N, 80°19′ W 94
Beaver, Utah, U.S. 38°16′ N, 112°38′ W 90
Beaver, Wash., U.S. 48°2′ N, 124°20′ W 100
Beaver Bay, Minn., U.S. 47°14′ N, 91°20′ W 94
Beaver City, Nebr., U.S. 40°7′ N, 99°50′ W 90
Beaver Creek, Can. 62°24′ N, 140°52′ W 98
Beaver Dam, Ky., U.S. 37°24′ N, 86°53′ W 96
Beaver Dam, Wis., U.S. 43°27′ N, 88°50′ W 102
Beaver Falls, Pa., U.S. 40°44′ N, 80°20′ W 94
Beaver Hill Lake, Can. 54°14′ N, 95°24′ W 108
Beaver Island, Mich., U.S. 45°20′ N, 85°49′ W 81
Beaver Lake, N. Dak., U.S. 46°20′ N, 100°7′ W 90
Beaver, river, Can. 60°29′ N, 126°29′ W 108
Beaver, river, Can. 54°40′ N, 112°3′ W 108
Beaver, river, Can. 53°43′ N, 61°38′ W 111
Beaverdell, Can. 49°25′ N, 119°4′ W 90
Beaverhead Mountains, Mont., U.S. 45°36′ N, 113°50′ W 90
Beaverlodge, Can. 55°12′ N, 119°27′ W 108
Beaverton, Can. 44°25′ N, 79°9′ W 94
Beaverton, Mich., U.S. 43°51′ N, 84°30′ W 102
Beawar, India 26°4′ N, 74°18′ E 186
Bebedouro, Braz. 20°57′ S, 48°30′ W 138
Bebeji, Nig. 11°39′ N, 8°16′ E 222
Bebington, U.K. 53°22′ N, 3°0′ W 162
Béboto, Chad 8°17′ N, 16°55′ E 218
Bebra, Ger. 50°58′ N, 9°46′ E 167
Becán, ruin(s), Mex. 18°33′ N, 89°39′ W 115
Bécancour, Can. 46°21′ N, 72°25′ W 94
Beccles, U.K. 52°26′ N, 1°33′ E 163
Bečej, Serb. 45°37′ N, 20°2′ E 168
Béchar, Alg. 31°39′ N, 2°13′ W 214
Becharof Lake, Alas., U.S. 58°4′ N, 159°33′ W 106
Bechater, Tun. 37°18′ N, 9°45′ E 156
Bechem, Ghana 7°7′ N, 2°3′ W 222
Bechetu, Rom. 43°46′ N, 23°57′ E 156
Becker, Mount, Antarctica 75°9′ S, 72°53′ W 248
Becket, Mass., U.S. 42°19′ N, 73°6′ W 104
Beckley, W. Va., U.S. 37°46′ N, 81°12′ W 94
Beckum, Ger. 51°45′ N, 8°1′ E 167
Beckville, Tex., U.S. 32°14′ N, 94°28′ W 103
Beckwourth Pass, Calif., U.S. 39°47′ N, 120°8′ W 90
Beda, oil field, Lib. 28°14′ N, 18°44′ E 216
Bedale, U.K. 54°17′ N, 1°36′ W 162
Beddgelert, U.K. 53°0′ N, 4°6′ W 162
Beddouza, Cap, Mor. 32°37′ N, 10°38′ W 214
Bedēsa, Eth. 8°51′ N, 40°45′ E 224
Bedford, Can. 44°43′ N, 63°41′ W 111
Bedford, Ind., U.S. 38°52′ N, 86°29′ W 102
Bedford, Iowa, U.S. 40°39′ N, 94°43′ W 94
Bedford, N.H., U.S. 42°56′ N, 71°32′ W 104
Bedford, Pa., U.S. 40°0′ N, 78°31′ W 94
Bedford, S. Af. 32°41′ S, 26°4′ E 227
Bedford, U.K. 52°8′ N, 0°28′ E 162
Bedi, India 22°32′ N, 70°0′ E 186
Bednesti, Can. 53°51′ N, 123°8′ W 108
Bednodem'yanovsk, Russ. 53°53′ N, 43°10′ E 154
Bedonia, It. 44°30′ N, 9°38′ E 167
Bédouaram, Niger 15°44′ N, 13°8′ E 216
Bedous, Fr. 43°0′ N, 0°36′ E 164
Bee Ridge, Fla., U.S. 27°18′ N, 82°27′ W 105
Beebe, Ark., U.S. 35°3′ N, 91°53′ W 96
Beebe River, N.H., U.S. 43°49′ N, 71°40′ W 104
Beech Grove, Ind., U.S. 39°43′ N, 86°5′ W 102
Beecher City, Ill., U.S. 39°10′ N, 88°47′ W 102
Beechy, Can. 50°53′ N, 107°25′ W 90
Beer, Somalia 9°21′ N, 45°48′ E 216
Be'ér 'Ada, spring, Israel 30°19′ N, 34°54′ E 194
Be'ér Ḥafir, spring, Israel 30°43′ N, 34°35′ E 194
Be'ér Sheva, Israel 31°13′ N, 34°50′ E 180
Be'ér Sheva' (Beersheba), Israel 31°14′ N, 34°47′ E 194
Beerberg, Grosser, peak, Ger. 50°38′ N, 10°38′ E 152
Beersheba see Be'ér Sheva', Israel 31°14′ N, 34°47′ E 194
Beestekraal, S. Af. 25°24′ S, 27°35′ E 227
Beeston, U.K. 52°55′ N, 1°14′ W 162
Beetz, Lac, lake, Can. 50°30′ N, 63°11′ W 111
Beeville, Tex., U.S. 28°23′ N, 97°45′ W 92
Befale, Dem. Rep. of the Congo 0°26′ N, 20°58′ E 218
Befandriana, Madagascar 15°15′ S, 48°35′ E 220
Befandriana Atsimo, Madagascar 22°7′ S, 43°51′ E 220
Befori, Dem. Rep. of the Congo 0°9′ N, 22°17′ E 218
Befotaka, Madagascar 23°48′ S, 47°1′ E 220
Bega, river, Rom. 45°51′ N, 21°56′ E 168
Begaly, Kaz. 49°55′ N, 55°17′ E 158
Begejski Kanal, canal, Serb. 45°31′ N, 20°28′ E 168
Bēgī, Eth. 9°20′ N, 34°32′ E 224
Begonte, Sp. 43°8′ N, 7°42′ W 150
Béguégué, Chad 8°53′ N, 18°52′ E 218
Begunitsy, Russ. 59°33′ N, 29°16′ E 152
Behagle see Laï, Chad 9°23′ N, 16°20′ E 216
Béhague, Pointe, Fr. 4°43′ N, 51°56′ W 130
Behan, Can. 55°14′ N, 111°28′ W 108
Behara, Madagascar 24°57′ S, 46°25′ E 220
Behbehān, Iran 30°34′ N, 50°15′ E 180
Behchok, Can. 62°42′ N, 116°26′ W 106
Behm Canal 55°45′ N, 132°3′ W 108
Beho, Belg. 50°14′ N, 5°58′ E 167
Behring Point, Bahamas 24°30′ N, 77°46′ W 96
Behshahr, Iran 36°43′ N, 53°33′ E 180
Bei'an, China 48°16′ N, 126°32′ E 198
Beiarn, Nor. 67°0′ N, 14°35′ E 152
Beida, river, China 39°9′ N, 97°39′ E 188
Beigang, China 42°23′ N, 127°28′ E 200
Beihai, China 21°26′ N, 109°8′ E 198
Beijing, adm. division, China 40°32′ N, 116°8′ E 198
Beijing (Peking), China 39°52′ N, 116°9′ E 198
Beila, Jebel, peak, Sudan 13°41′ N, 34°46′ E 182
Beilen, Neth. 52°51′ N, 6°31′ E 163
Beiliu, China 22°42′ N, 110°19′ E 198
Beilrode, Ger. 51°33′ N, 13°4′ E 152
Beilu, river, China 34°47′ N, 93°23′ E 188
Beilul, Eritrea 13°9′ N, 42°22′ E 182
Beinn Bhreagh, site, Can. 46°4′ N, 60°48′ W 111
Beipiao, China 41°52′ N, 120°47′ E 198
Beira, Mozambique 19°50′ S, 34°53′ E 224
Beirut see Beyrouth, Leb. 33°53′ N, 35°26′ E 194
Beitbridge, Zimb. 22°10′ S, 29°58′ E 227
Beitun, China 47°19′ N, 87°48′ E 184
Beiuş, Rom. 46°40′ N, 22°23′ E 168
Beizhen, China 41°37′ N, 121°50′ E 198
Beja, Port. 38°1′ N, 7°52′ W 150
Beja, Tun. 36°43′ N, 9°11′ E 156
Beja, adm. division, Port. 37°41′ N, 8°36′ W 150
Bejaïa (Bougie), Alg. 36°46′ N, 5°2′ E 150
Béjar, Sp. 40°23′ N, 5°47′ W 150
Bek, river, Cameroon 3°1′ N, 14°23′ E 218
Bekaa Valley see Al Biqā', region, Leb. 33°43′ N, 35°51′ E 194
Bekaie, Dem. Rep. of the Congo 2°29′ S, 18°17′ E 218
Bekdash see Karabogaz, Turkm. 41°32′ N, 52°35′ E 158
Békés, Hung. 46°46′ N, 21°8′ E 168
Békés, adm. division, Hung. 46°50′ N, 20°45′ E 156
Békéscsaba, Hung. 46°40′ N, 21°5′ E 168
Bekily, Madagascar 24°11′ S, 45°17′ E 220
Bekobod, Uzb. 40°12′ N, 69°15′ E 197
Bekodoka, Madagascar 17°1′ S, 45°7′ E 220
Bekoropoka-Antongo, Madagascar 21°27′ S, 43°32′ E 220
Bekwai, Ghana 6°29′ N, 1°34′ W 222
Bela, India 25°53′ N, 81°58′ E 197
Bela, Pak. 26°14′ N, 66°20′ E 186
Bela Crkva, Serb. 44°53′ N, 21°26′ E 168
Bela Vista, Mozambique 26°18′ S, 32°40′ E 227
Bela Vista de Goiás, Braz. 17°1′ S, 48°59′ W 138
Bela-Bela (Warmbaths), S. Af. 24°55′ S, 28°16′ E 227
Bélabo, Cameroon 4°49′ N, 13°16′ E 218
Belalcázar, Sp. 38°34′ N, 5°10′ W 164
Bélanger, river, Can. 53°14′ N, 97°28′ W 108
Belarus 53°57′ N, 27°35′ E 154
Belasica, Gr. 41°23′ N, 23°1′ E 168
Belawan, Indonesia 3°46′ N, 98°42′ E 196
Belaya Glina, Russ. 46°5′ N, 40°52′ E 158
Belaya Gora, Russ. 68°8′ N, 146°6′ E 160
Belaya Kalitva, Russ. 48°10′ N, 40°50′ E 158
Belaya Kholunitsa, Russ. 58°50′ N, 50°52′ E 154
Belaya, peak, Eth. 11°23′ N, 36°4′ E 182
Belaya, river, Russ. 52°52′ N, 56°57′ E 154
Belcaire, Fr. 42°48′ N, 1°56′ E 164
Belcher, La., U.S. 32°44′ N, 93°51′ W 103
Belcher Channel 76°55′ N, 100°16′ W 106
Belcher Islands, Hudson Bay 56°1′ N, 80°5′ W 106
Belcheragh, Afghan. 35°46′ N, 65°13′ E 186
Belchertown, Mass., U.S. 42°16′ N, 72°25′ W 104
Belchite, Sp. 41°17′ N, 0°46′ E 164
Belding, Mich., U.S. 43°6′ N, 85°14′ W 102
Belebey, Russ. 54°6′ N, 54°12′ E 154
Belecke, Ger. 51°28′ N, 8°20′ E 167
Beled, Hung. 47°27′ N, 17°5′ E 168
Beledweyne, Somalia 4°43′ N, 45°10′ E 218
Belej, Croatia 44°47′ N, 14°24′ E 156
Belém, Braz. 1°24′ S, 48°28′ W 130
Belén, Arg. 27°39′ S, 67°3′ W 134
Belén, Chile 18°30′ S, 69°34′ W 137
Belén, Col. 1°25′ N, 75°57′ W 136
Belen, N. Mex., U.S. 34°39′ N, 106°46′ W 92
Belén, Parag. 23°29′ S, 57°18′ W 132
Belén, Uru. 30°49′ S, 57°45′ W 139
Beles, river, Eth. 11°1′ N, 36°15′ E 182
Bélesta, Fr. 42°54′ N, 1°54′ E 164
Belev, Russ. 53°47′ N, 36°5′ E 154
Beleza, river, Braz. 10°11′ S, 51°13′ W 132
Belfair, Wash., U.S. 47°26′ N, 122°49′ W 100
Belfast, Me., U.S. 44°25′ N, 69°2′ W 94
Belfast, N.Z. 43°28′ S, 172°36′ E 240
Belfast, S. Af. 25°42′ S, 30°2′ E 227
Belfast, U.K. 54°34′ N, 6°5′ W 150
Belfield, N. Dak., U.S. 46°52′ N, 103°13′ W 90
Bēlfodiyo, Eth. 10°29′ N, 34°48′ E 224
Belford, U.K. 55°35′ N, 1°50′ W 150
Belfort, Fr. 47°38′ N, 6°50′ E 150
Belfort (Beaufort), ruin(s), Leb. 33°19′ N, 35°30′ E 194
Belgaum, India 15°49′ N, 74°31′ E 188
Belgica Bank, Greenland Sea 78°11′ N, 13°45′ W 255
Belgioioso, It. 45°9′ N, 9°19′ E 167
Belgium 50°41′ N, 4°16′ E 163
Belgorod, Russ. 50°37′ N, 36°32′ E 158
Belgorod, adm. division, Russ. 50°59′ N, 36°52′ E 158
Belgrade, Me., U.S. 44°26′ N, 69°51′ W 104
Belgrade, Mont., U.S. 45°45′ N, 111°11′ W 90
Belgrade see Beograd, Serb. 44°47′ N, 20°24′ E 168
Belgrano II, station, Antarctica 77°55′ S, 34°4′ W 248
Belhaven, N.C., U.S. 35°33′ N, 76°38′ W 96
Belhedan, oil field, Lib. 27°53′ N, 19°10′ E 216
Beli, Nig. 7°49′ N, 10°58′ E 222
Beli Manastir, Croatia 45°44′ N, 18°36′ E 168
Beli Potok, Serb. 43°30′ N, 22°4′ E 168
Belica, Alban. 41°14′ N, 20°23′ E 156
Belica, Croatia 46°25′ N, 16°31′ E 168
Belidzhi, Russ. 41°50′ N, 48°28′ E 195
Beliliou see Paleliu, island, Palau 7°0′ N, 134°15′ E 242
Belinskiy, Russ. 52°57′ N, 43°23′ E 154
Beliş, Rom. 46°39′ N, 23°2′ E 168
Belitung (Billiton), island, Indonesia 3°41′ S, 107°3′ E 192
Beliu, Rom. 46°29′ N, 21°59′ E 168
Belize 16°58′ N, 89°1′ W 115
Belize City, Belize 17°30′ N, 88°13′ W 115
Beljanica, Serb. 44°10′ N, 21°30′ E 168
Bel'kovskiy, Ostrov, island, Russ. 75°28′ N, 126°33′ E 160
Bell Lake, lake, Can. 49°47′ N, 91°13′ W 94
Bell Peninsula, Can. 63°28′ N, 84°36′ W 106
Bell, river, Can. 49°40′ N, 77°37′ W 94
Bell Rock, Can. 60°0′ N, 112°5′ W 108
Bell Ville, Arg. 32°40′ S, 62°38′ W 139
Bella Bella, Can. 52°8′ N, 128°3′ W 108
Bella Flor, Bol. 11°8′ S, 67°49′ W 137
Bella Unión, Uru. 30°17′ S, 57°37′ W 139
Bella Vista, Arg. 28°31′ S, 59°2′ W 132
Bella Vista, Braz. 22°8′ S, 56°24′ W 132
Bellac, Fr. 46°6′ N, 1°3′ E 150
Bellagio, It. 45°58′ N, 9°14′ E 167
Bellaire, Mich., U.S. 44°58′ N, 85°12′ W 94
Bellaire, Tex., U.S. 29°41′ N, 95°29′ W 96
Bellamy, Ala., U.S. 32°26′ N, 88°9′ W 103
Bellary, India 15°8′ N, 76°53′ E 188
Bellavista, Peru 5°33′ S, 78°43′ W 130
Bellavista, Peru 1°35′ S, 75°33′ W 136
Belle Fourche, S. Dak., U.S. 44°38′ N, 103°52′ W 82
Belle Fourche, river, Wyo., U.S. 43°45′ N, 105°45′ W 80
Belle Glade, Fla., U.S. 26°40′ N, 80°41′ W 105
Belle Isle, island, Can. 52°4′ N, 55°26′ W 106
Belle Isle, Strait of 51°28′ N, 56°49′ W 111
Belle Plaine, Iowa, U.S. 41°53′ N, 92°17′ W 94
Belle Plaine, Minn., U.S. 44°36′ N, 93°46′ W 94
Belle Yella, Liberia 7°13′ N, 10°2′ W 222
Belledonne, Chaîne de, Fr. 45°10′ N, 5°50′ E 165
Bellefontaine, Ohio, U.S. 40°21′ N, 83°45′ W 102
Bellefonte, Pa., U.S. 40°53′ N, 77°47′ W 94
Bellenden Ker National Park, Austral. 17°25′ S, 145°31′ E 238
Belleoram, Can. 47°30′ N, 55°25′ W 111
Belleview, Fla., U.S. 29°3′ N, 82°3′ W 105
Belleville, Can. 44°9′ N, 77°22′ W 94
Belleville, Fr. 46°5′ N, 4°43′ E 150
Belleville, Ill., U.S. 38°30′ N, 89°58′ W 102
Belleville, Kans., U.S. 39°48′ N, 97°38′ W 90
Belleville, Mo., U.S. 38°30′ N, 89°58′ W 94
Belleville, Wis., U.S. 42°50′ N, 89°32′ W 102
Bellevue, Congo 2°5′ N, 13°51′ E 218
Bellevue, Idaho, U.S. 43°28′ N, 114°16′ W 90
Bellevue, Iowa, U.S. 42°15′ N, 90°26′ W 94
Bellevue, Mich., U.S. 42°27′ N, 85°1′ W 102
Bellevue, Nebr., U.S. 41°8′ N, 95°54′ W 90
Bellevue, Ohio, U.S. 41°16′ N, 82°50′ W 102
Bellevue, Tex., U.S. 33°36′ N, 98°1′ W 96
Bellevue, Wash., U.S. 47°35′ N, 122°13′ W 100
Bellflower, Ill., U.S. 40°19′ N, 88°32′ W 102
Bellinger, Lac, lake, Can. 51°10′ N, 75°0′ W 110
Bellingham, Wash., U.S. 48°46′ N, 122°29′ W 100
Bellingrath Gardens, site, Ala., U.S. 30°24′ N, 88°11′ W 103
Bellingshausen Plain, South Pacific Ocean 65°21′ S, 112°43′ W 255
Bellingshausen Sea 70°32′ S, 88°38′ W 248
Bellingshausen, station, Antarctica 62°17′ S, 58°44′ W 248
Bellinzona, Switz. 46°11′ N, 9°1′ E 167
Bellmore, Ind., U.S. 39°45′ N, 87°6′ W 102
Bello, Col. 6°20′ N, 75°35′ W 136
Bello Islands, Monte, Indian Ocean 20°10′ S, 113°11′ E 230
Bellona Island, Solomon Islands 11°0′ S, 160°0′ E 242
Bellows Falls, Vt., U.S. 43°7′ N, 72°28′ W 104
Bellpat, Pak. 29°1′ N, 68°5′ E 186
Belluno, It. 46°8′ N, 12°12′ E 167
Bellville, Ohio, U.S. 40°36′ N, 82°31′ W 102
Bellville, Tex., U.S. 29°55′ N, 96°16′ W 96
Bellvís, Sp. 41°39′ N, 0°49′ E 164
Bellwood, La., U.S. 31°29′ N, 93°12′ W 103
Belmar, N.J., U.S. 40°10′ N, 74°2′ W 94
Bélmez, Sp. 38°15′ N, 5°12′ W 164
Belmond, Iowa, U.S. 42°49′ N, 93°36′ W 94
Belmont, N.H., U.S. 43°26′ N, 71°29′ W 104
Belmont, S. Af. 29°27′ S, 24°20′ E 227
Belmont, Vt., U.S. 43°24′ N, 72°50′ W 104
Belmonte, Braz. 15°56′ S, 38°56′ W 132
Belmonte, Sp. 39°33′ N, 2°43′ W 150
Belmopan, Belize 17°10′ N, 88°56′ W 115
Belo, Madagascar 20°48′ S, 44°1′ E 220
Belo Horizonte, Braz. 19°55′ S, 43°55′ W 138
Beloci, Mold. 47°52′ N, 28°56′ E 156
Belogorsk, Russ. 51°2′ N, 128°27′ E 190
Belogorsk, Russ. 54°59′ N, 88°33′ E 169
Belogorskīy, Kaz. 49°26′ N, 83°9′ E 184
Beloha, Madagascar 25°9′ S, 45°2′ E 220
Beloit, Kans., U.S. 39°27′ N, 98°7′ W 90
Beloit, Wis., U.S. 42°31′ N, 89°2′ W 102
Beloljin, Serb. 43°13′ N, 21°23′ E 168
Belomorsk, Russ. 64°28′ N, 34°38′ E 154
Belonia, India 23°12′ N, 91°28′ E 197
Belorado, Sp. 42°24′ N, 3°12′ W 164
Belorechensk, Russ. 44°46′ N, 39°52′ E 158
Beloretsk, Russ. 53°58′ N, 58°23′ E 154
Beloshchel'ye, Russ. 64°56′ N, 46°48′ E 154
Belot'i, Ga. 42°17′ N, 44°7′ E 195
Belo-Tsiribihina, Madagascar 19°41′ S, 44°31′ E 220
Belovo, Russ. 54°22′ N, 86°22′ E 184
Beloyarskiy, Russ. 63°42′ N, 66°58′ E 169
Beloye More (White Sea) 63°17′ N, 35°24′ E 160
Beloye Ozero, lake, Russ. 59°33′ N, 37°43′ E 154
Belozersk, Russ. 59°57′ N, 37°50′ E 154
Belpre, Ohio, U.S. 39°16′ N, 81°35′ W 102
Belt, Mont., U.S. 47°22′ N, 110°56′ W 90
Belterra, Braz. 2°38′ S, 54°59′ W 130
Belton, S.C., U.S. 34°30′ N, 82°31′ W 96
Belton, Tex., U.S. 31°2′ N, 97°27′ W 92
Belukha, Gora, peak, Russ. 49°46′ N, 86°31′ E 184
Belush'ya Guba, Russ. 71°28′ N, 52°29′ E 160
Belush'ye, Russ. 66°52′ N, 47°37′ E 154
Belušić, Serb. 43°47′ N, 21°8′ E 168
Belvidere, Ill., U.S. 42°14′ N, 88°51′ W 102

Belvidere, *S. Dak., U.S.* 43°49′ N, 101°17′ W 90
Belvidere Mountain, *Vt., U.S.* 44°45′ N, 72°39′ W 94
Belvoir, *U.K.* 52°53′ N, 0°48′ E 162
Belyayevka, *Russ.* 51°23′ N, 56°23′ E 158
Belyy, *Russ.* 55°48′ N, 33°1′ E 154
Belyy, Ostrov, island, *Russ.* 73°28′ N, 65°53′ E 160
Belyy, Ostrov, island, *Russ.* 73°26′ N, 70°30′ E 160
Belyy Yar, *Russ.* 58°25′ N, 85°8′ E 169
Belz, *Ukr.* 50°23′ N, 24°1′ E 152
Belzoni, *Miss., U.S.* 33°9′ N, 90°31′ W 103
Bemaraha, *Madagascar* 20°44′ S, 44°42′ E 220
Bembe, *Angola* 7°2′ S, 14°18′ E 218
Bembéréké, *Benin* 10°12′ N, 2°40′ E 222
Bement, *Ill., U.S.* 39°54′ N, 88°34′ W 102
Bemetara, *India* 21°44′ N, 81°31′ E 188
Bemidji, *Minn., U.S.* 47°28′ N, 94°55′ W 90
Bemis, *Tenn., U.S.* 35°33′ N, 88°49′ W 96
Ben Gardane, *Tun.* 33°9′ N, 11°12′ E 214
Ben Lomond, *Calif., U.S.* 37°5′ N, 122°6′ W 100
Ben S'Rour, *Alg.* 35°3′ N, 4°34′ E 150
Ben Zohra, spring, *Alg.* 28°37′ N, 3°50′ W 214
Bena Dibele, *Dem. Rep. of the Congo* 4°8′ S, 22°48′ E 218
Bena Makima, *Dem. Rep. of the Congo* 5°2′ S, 21°7′ E 218
Benabarre, *Sp.* 42°6′ N, 0°28′ E 164
Benalup, *Sp.* 36°21′ N, 5°50′ W 164
Benamaurel, *Sp.* 37°35′ N, 2°41′ W 164
Benamejí, *Sp.* 37°16′ N, 4°33′ W 164
Benasque, *Sp.* 42°35′ N, 0°32′ E 164
Bénat, Cap, *Fr.* 43°1′ N, 6°11′ E 165
Benavente, *Sp.* 42°0′ N, 5°43′ W 150
Benavides, *Tex., U.S.* 27°35′ N, 98°24′ W 92
Benbow, *Calif., U.S.* 40°3′ N, 123°47′ W 90
Benbulbin, peak, *Ire.* 54°20′ N, 8°36′ W 150
Bende, *Nig.* 5°35′ N, 7°38′ E 222
Bender, *Mold.* 46°48′ N, 29°28′ E 156
Bendorf, *Ger.* 50°25′ N, 7°34′ E 167
Bēne, *Latv.* 56°28′ N, 23°1′ E 166
Bené Beraq, *Israel* 32°5′ N, 34°50′ E 194
Benedito Leite, *Braz.* 7°13′ S, 44°36′ W 132
Bénéna, *Mali* 13°7′ N, 4°24′ W 222
Benenitra, *Madagascar* 23°24′ S, 45°3′ E 220
Beneraird, peak, *U.K.* 55°3′ N, 5°2′ W 150
Bénestroff, *Fr.* 48°54′ N, 6°45′ E 163
Benfeld, *Fr.* 48°22′ N, 7°34′ E 163
Bengal, adm. division, *India* 21°51′ N, 88°25′ E 197
Bengal, Bay of 13°12′ N, 85°28′ E 188
Bengaluru see Bangalore, *India* 12°59′ N, 77°35′ E 188
Bengbu, *China* 32°53′ N, 117°21′ E 198
Benghazi see Banghāzī, *Lib.* 32°6′ N, 20°4′ E 216
Bengkalis, *Indonesia* 1°30′ N, 102°7′ E 196
Bengkalis, island, *Indonesia* 1°38′ N, 102°5′ E 196
Bengkayang, *Indonesia* 0°51′ N, 109°27′ E 196
Bengkulu, *Indonesia* 3°49′ S, 102°18′ E 192
Bengo, adm. division, *Angola* 8°8′ S, 13°15′ E 220
Bengough, *Can.* 49°23′ N, 105°8′ W 90
Benguela, *Angola* 12°38′ S, 13°23′ E 220
Benguela, adm. division, *Angola* 13°17′ S, 12°57′ E 220
Benguérua, Ilha, island, *Mozambique* 22°11′ S, 34°56′ E 227
Benha, *Egypt* 30°25′ N, 31°12′ E 180
Beni, *Dem. Rep. of the Congo* 0°24′ N, 29°26′ E 224
Beni Abbes, *Alg.* 30°8′ N, 2°10′ W 214
Beni, adm. division, *Bol.* 13°40′ S, 65°45′ W 137
Beni Mazâr, *Egypt* 28°27′ N, 30°46′ E 180
Beni Mellal, *Mor.* 32°24′ N, 6°22′ W 214
Beni, river, *Bol.* 12°25′ S, 66°55′ W 137
Beni Saf, *Alg.* 35°17′ N, 1°23′ W 150
Beni Suef, *Egypt* 29°4′ N, 31°3′ E 180
Beni Tajit, *Mor.* 32°21′ N, 3°28′ W 214
Benicarló, *Sp.* 40°24′ N, 0°25′ E 164
Benicasim, *Sp.* 40°3′ N, 7°416′ E 164
Benicia, *Calif., U.S.* 38°3′ N, 122°10′ W 100
Benidorm, *Sp.* 38°31′ N, 0°8′ E 164
Benifaió, *Sp.* 39°16′ N, 0°26′ E 164
Benin 10°4′ N, 1°52′ E 214
Benin, Bight of 4°25′ N, 1°49′ E 222
Benin City, *Nig.* 6°23′ N, 5°38′ E 222
Benissa, *Sp.* 38°42′ N, 5°297′ E 164
Benito, *Can.* 51°54′ N, 101°33′ W 108
Benito Juárez, *Mex.* 32°34′ N, 115°0′ W 101
Benito Juárez, *Mex.* 17°49′ N, 92°33′ W 115
Benito Juárez National Park see 2, *Mex.* 17°15′ N, 96°46′ W 112
Benjamin, *Tex., U.S.* 33°34′ N, 99°48′ W 92
Benjamin Constant, *Braz.* 4°25′ S, 70°4′ W 132
Benjamín Hill, *Mex.* 30°11′ N, 111°8′ W 92
Benkelman, *Nebr., U.S.* 40°3′ N, 101°33′ W 90
Benld, *Ill., U.S.* 39°5′ N, 89°49′ W 102
Bennane Head, *U.K.* 55°10′ N, 5°15′ W 150
Bennett, *Can.* 59°51′ N, 134°56′ W 108
Bennett Island, *Russ.* 77°0′ N, 149°0′ E 255
Bennett Lake, lake, *Can.* 53°23′ N, 96°35′ W 108
Benneydale, *N.Z.* 38°31′ S, 175°20′ E 240
Bennington, *N.H., U.S.* 43°0′ N, 71°56′ W 104
Bennington, *Vt., U.S.* 42°52′ N, 73°12′ W 104
Bénnsané, *Guinea* 11°26′ N, 14°1′ W 222
Benom, peak, *Malaysia* 3°50′ N, 102°0′ E 196
Benoud, *Alg.* 32°20′ N, 0°15′ E 214
Benoy, *Chad* 8°57′ N, 16°20′ E 216
Bensberg, *Ger.* 50°58′ N, 7°8′ E 167
Benson, *Ariz., U.S.* 31°57′ N, 110°20′ W 112
Benson, *Minn., U.S.* 45°18′ N, 95°37′ W 90
Benson, *N.C., U.S.* 35°22′ N, 78°34′ W 96
Benson, *Vt., U.S.* 43°42′ N, 73°19′ W 104
Bent Jbail, *Leb.* 33°7′ N, 35°25′ E 194
Benta, *Malaysia* 4°1′ N, 101°58′ E 196
Bentiaba, *Angola* 14°18′ S, 12°22′ E 220
Bentinck Island, *Austral.* 17°25′ S, 137°54′ E 230
Bentinck, island, *Myanmar* 11°30′ N, 97°26′ E 202
Bentinck Point, *Can.* 46°26′ N, 61°17′ W 111
Bentiu, *Sudan* 9°9′ N, 29°47′ E 224
Bentley, *Mich., U.S.* 43°56′ N, 84°9′ W 102
Bento Gonçalves, *Braz.* 29°10′ S, 51°30′ W 139
Benton, *Ark., U.S.* 34°32′ N, 92°36′ W 96
Benton, *Ky., U.S.* 36°51′ N, 88°21′ W 94
Benton, *La., U.S.* 32°40′ N, 93°45′ W 103
Benton, *Me., U.S.* 44°34′ N, 69°34′ W 94
Benton, *Miss., U.S.* 32°48′ N, 90°16′ W 103
Benton, *N.H., U.S.* 44°5′ N, 71°55′ W 104
Benton Harbor, *Mich., U.S.* 42°6′ N, 86°27′ W 102
Bentong, *Malaysia* 3°34′ N, 101°55′ E 196
Bentonia, *Miss., U.S.* 32°37′ N, 90°23′ W 103
Bentonville, *Ark., U.S.* 36°21′ N, 94°13′ W 94
Benty, *Guinea* 9°8′ N, 13°13′ W 222
Benue, river, *Nig.* 8°0′ N, 7°50′ E 222
Benwee Head, *Ire.* 54°21′ N, 10°10′ W 150
Benxi, *China* 41°16′ N, 123°47′ E 200
Benzdorp, *Suriname* 3°42′ N, 54°7′ W 130
Benzú, *Mor.* 35°54′ N, 5°23′ W 150
Beo, *Indonesia* 4°15′ N, 126°52′ E 192
Beograd (Belgrade), *Serb.* 44°47′ N, 20°24′ E 168
Beohari, *India* 24°2′ N, 81°22′ E 197
Beolgyo, *S. Korea* 34°48′ N, 127°21′ E 200
Beowawe, *Nev., U.S.* 40°35′ N, 116°30′ W 90
Beppu, *Japan* 36°7′ N, 133°4′ E 201
Beppu, *Japan* 33°16′ N, 131°29′ E 201
Bequia, island, *Saint Vincent and The Grenadines* 13°0′ N, 61°11′ W 116
Bera Ndjoko, *Congo* 3°15′ N, 16°58′ E 218
Berau, Teluk 2°35′ S, 131°10′ E 192
Berber, *Sudan* 18°0′ N, 34°2′ E 182
Berbera, *Somalia* 10°26′ N, 45°1′ E 219
Berbérati, *Cen. Af. Rep.* 4°18′ N, 15°47′ E 218
Bercedo, *Sp.* 43°4′ N, 3°27′ W 164
Berceto, *It.* 44°30′ N, 9°59′ E 167
Berck, *Fr.* 50°25′ N, 1°35′ E 163
Berdigestyakh, *Russ.* 62°8′ N, 127°5′ E 160
Berdoba, *Chad* 16°0′ N, 22°53′ E 216
Berdsk, *Russ.* 54°46′ N, 83°11′ E 184
Berdún, *Sp.* 42°36′ N, 0°52′ E 164
Berdyans'k, *Ukr.* 46°46′ N, 36°46′ E 156
Berdyaush, *Russ.* 55°11′ N, 59°12′ E 154
Berdychiv, *Ukr.* 49°53′ N, 28°41′ E 152
Berdyuzh'ye, *Russ.* 55°48′ N, 68°20′ E 184
Berea, *Ky., U.S.* 37°33′ N, 84°18′ W 96
Berea, *Ohio, U.S.* 41°21′ N, 81°51′ W 102
Bérébi, *Côte d'Ivoire* 4°40′ N, 7°2′ W 222
Bereeda, *Somalia* 11°44′ N, 51°3′ E 182
Bereku, *Tanzania* 4°27′ S, 35°46′ E 224
Berekum, *Ghana* 7°29′ N, 2°35′ W 222
Beremend, *Hung.* 45°46′ N, 18°25′ E 168
Beren, Liman, lake, *Russ.* 46°52′ N, 44°37′ E 158
Berenda, *Calif., U.S.* 37°2′ N, 120°10′ W 100
Berenice, *Egypt* 23°54′ N, 35°25′ E 182
Berens River, *Can.* 52°21′ N, 96°59′ W 82
Berens, river, *Can.* 51°49′ N, 93°43′ W 110
Berens, river, *Can.* 52°5′ N, 96°53′ W 80
Berestechko, *Ukr.* 50°20′ N, 25°6′ E 158
Bereşti, *Rom.* 46°5′ N, 27°51′ E 156
Berettyó, river, *Rom.* 47°15′ N, 21°39′ E 168
Berettyóújfalu, *Hung.* 47°14′ N, 21°32′ E 168
Berevo, *Madagascar* 19°46′ S, 44°58′ E 220
Berezivka, *Ukr.* 47°16′ N, 30°54′ E 156
Bereznik, *Russ.* 62°49′ N, 42°49′ E 154
Berezniki, *Russ.* 59°24′ N, 56°48′ E 154
Berezovka, *Russ.* 57°38′ N, 57°22′ E 154
Berezovka, *Russ.* 59°20′ N, 82°47′ E 169
Berezovka, *Russ.* 65°0′ N, 56°38′ E 154
Berezovo, *Russ.* 63°58′ N, 65°5′ E 169
Berezovskaya, *Russ.* 50°14′ N, 43°59′ E 158
Berezovskiy, *Russ.* 55°34′ N, 86°18′ E 169
Berga, *Nor.* 57°14′ N, 16°0′ E 152
Berga, *Sp.* 42°6′ N, 1°50′ E 164
Bergama, *Turk.* 39°4′ N, 27°11′ E 180
Bergamo, *It.* 45°42′ N, 9°39′ E 167
Bergedorf, *Ger.* 53°29′ N, 10°12′ E 150
Bergen, *Ger.* 54°25′ N, 13°26′ E 152
Bergen, *Nor.* 60°23′ N, 5°19′ E 152
Bergen aan Zee, *Neth.* 52°40′ N, 4°38′ E 163
Bergen op Zoom, *Neth.* 51°29′ N, 4°17′ E 163
Bergerac, *Fr.* 44°51′ N, 0°28′ E 150
Bergersen, Mount, *Antarctica* 72°6′ S, 25°32′ E 248
Bergheim, *Ger.* 50°57′ N, 6°39′ E 167
Bergisch Gladbach, *Ger.* 50°59′ N, 7°7′ E 167
Bergkamen, *Ger.* 51°37′ N, 7°39′ E 167
Bergland, *Namibia* 23°0′ S, 17°5′ E 227
Bergö, *Fin.* 62°56′ N, 21°9′ E 152
Bergsfjord, *Nor.* 70°15′ N, 21°49′ E 152
Bergshamra, *Sw.* 59°37′ N, 18°35′ E 166
Bergsjö, *Nor.* 61°58′ N, 17°1′ E 152
Berguent, *Mor.* 34°1′ N, 2°0′ W 214
Bergues, *Fr.* 50°57′ N, 2°26′ E 163
Bergum, *Neth.* 53°11′ N, 5°58′ E 163
Bergville, *S. Af.* 28°44′ S, 29°20′ E 227
Berh, *Mongolia* 47°44′ N, 111°8′ E 198
Berhala, Selat 0°50′ N, 103°54′ E 196
Berikei, oil field, *Russ.* 42°20′ N, 47°58′ E 195
Bering Sea 65°53′ N, 166°10′ W 246
Bering Strait 65°53′ N, 168°36′ W 255
Beringil, *Sudan* 12°8′ N, 25°43′ E 216
Beringovskiy, *Russ.* 63°8′ N, 179°6′ E 160
Berja, *Sp.* 36°50′ N, 2°57′ W 164
Berkåk, *Nor.* 62°49′ N, 10°1′ E 152
Berkeley, *Calif., U.S.* 37°52′ N, 122°16′ W 100
Berkner Island, *Antarctica* 78°9′ S, 43°53′ W 248
Berkovići, *Bosn. and Herzg.* 43°4′ N, 18°10′ E 168
Berkshire, *Mass., U.S.* 42°30′ N, 73°12′ W 104
Berkshires, The, *Mass., U.S.* 42°27′ N, 73°8′ W 104
Berland, river, *Can.* 53°40′ N, 118°10′ W 108
Berlikum, *Neth.* 53°14′ N, 5°38′ E 163
Berlin, *Ger.* 52°29′ N, 13°14′ E 152
Berlin, *Md., U.S.* 38°19′ N, 75°14′ W 94
Berlin, *N.H., U.S.* 44°28′ N, 71°12′ W 104
Berlin, *N.Y., U.S.* 42°41′ N, 73°23′ W 104
Berlin, *Wis., U.S.* 43°57′ N, 88°56′ W 94
Berlin, Mount, *Antarctica* 75°56′ S, 135°13′ W 248
Bermeja, Punta, *Arg.* 41°21′ S, 63°11′ W 134
Bermeja, Sierra, *Sp.* 36°33′ N, 5°16′ W 164
Bermejillo, *Mex.* 25°52′ N, 103°39′ W 114
Bermejo, river, *Arg.* 25°37′ S, 60°8′ W 134
Bermeo, *Sp.* 43°23′ N, 2°45′ W 164
Bermuda Islands, *U.K.* 32°0′ N, 65°0′ W 118
Bermuda Rise, *North Atlantic Ocean* 32°2′ N, 64°35′ W 253
Bern, *Switz.* 46°55′ N, 7°21′ E 165
Bernalillo, *N. Mex., U.S.* 35°17′ N, 106°34′ W 82
Bernard Lake, lake, *Can.* 45°41′ N, 79°50′ W 110
Bernardo de Irigoyen, *Arg.* 32°11′ S, 61°8′ W 139
Bernardo de Irigoyen, *Arg.* 26°15′ S, 53°41′ W 139
Bernardston, *Mass., U.S.* 42°40′ N, 72°34′ W 104
Bernasconi, *Arg.* 37°57′ S, 63°42′ W 139
Bernay, *Fr.* 49°5′ N, 0°35′ E 150
Berne, *Ind., U.S.* 40°38′ N, 84°57′ W 102
Berner Alpen, *Switz.* 46°20′ N, 6°59′ E 165
Berneval, *Fr.* 49°57′ N, 1°10′ E 163
Bernice, *La., U.S.* 32°48′ N, 92°40′ W 103
Bernie, *Mo., U.S.* 36°40′ N, 89°58′ W 96
Bernier Bay 70°59′ N, 90°44′ W 106
Bernier Island, *Austral.* 24°41′ S, 111°44′ E 230
Bernina Pass, *Switz.* 46°26′ N, 10°0′ E 167
Bernina, Piz, peak, *Switz.* 46°23′ N, 9°52′ E 167
Bernkastel-Kues, *Ger.* 49°55′ N, 7°5′ E 167
Bernterode, *Ger.* 51°24′ N, 10°29′ E 167
Bero, river, *Angola* 15°3′ S, 12°9′ E 220
Berón de Astrada, *Arg.* 27°33′ S, 57°32′ W 139
Beroroha, *Madagascar* 21°37′ S, 45°9′ E 220
Béroubouay, *Benin* 10°32′ N, 2°41′ E 222
Beroun, *Czech Rep.* 49°58′ N, 14°4′ E 152
Berovo, *Maced.* 41°43′ N, 22°52′ E 168
Berri, oil field, *Saudi Arabia* 27°5′ N, 49°29′ E 196
Berriane, *Alg.* 32°51′ N, 3°45′ E 214
Berrien Springs, *Mich., U.S.* 41°56′ N, 86°21′ W 102
Berrouaghia, *Alg.* 36°7′ N, 2°54′ E 150
Berry, *Ky., U.S.* 38°30′ N, 84°23′ W 102
Berry Creek, river, *Can.* 51°34′ N, 111°39′ W 90
Berry Islands, *Atlantic Ocean* 25°23′ N, 77°42′ W 96
Berry, region, *Europe* 46°51′ N, 1°18′ E 165
Berryville, *Ark., U.S.* 36°21′ N, 93°35′ W 96
Berseba, *Namibia* 26°0′ S, 17°46′ E 227
Bersenbrück, *Ger.* 52°33′ N, 7°57′ E 163
Bershad', *Ukr.* 48°24′ N, 29°38′ E 156
Bertam, *Malaysia* 5°11′ N, 102°1′ E 196
Berthierville, *Can.* 46°5′ N, 73°11′ W 110
Berthold, *N. Dak., U.S.* 48°18′ N, 101°45′ W 90
Berthoud, *Colo., U.S.* 40°18′ N, 105°6′ W 90
Berthoud Pass, *Colo., U.S.* 39°47′ N, 105°47′ W 90
Bertincourt, *Fr.* 50°4′ N, 2°56′ E 163
Bertoua, *Cameroon* 4°32′ N, 13°40′ E 218
Bertrab Nunatak, peak, *Antarctica* 78°26′ S, 36°22′ W 248
Bertrand, *Nebr., U.S.* 40°31′ N, 99°39′ W 92
Bertwell, *Can.* 52°35′ N, 102°36′ W 108
Beru, island, *Kiribati* 1°12′ S, 175°57′ E 252
Beruniy, *Uzb.* 41°43′ N, 60°43′ E 180
Beruri, *Braz.* 3°53′ S, 61°23′ W 130
Berutti, *Arg.* 35°50′ S, 62°29′ W 139
Berveni, *Rom.* 47°45′ N, 22°28′ E 168
Berwick, *La., U.S.* 29°41′ N, 91°15′ W 103
Berwick, *Me., U.S.* 43°16′ N, 70°52′ W 104
Berwick upon Tweed, *U.K.* 55°45′ N, 2°1′ W 150
Berwyn, *Can.* 56°9′ N, 117°44′ W 108
Berwyn, *U.K.* 52°51′ N, 3°26′ W 162
Beryslav, *Ukr.* 46°53′ N, 33°19′ E 156
Bērzaune, *Latv.* 56°48′ N, 26°2′ E 166
Bērze, river, *Latv.* 56°37′ N, 23°18′ E 166
Berzosilla, *Sp.* 42°46′ N, 4°3′ W 164
Berzovia, *Rom.* 45°25′ N, 21°36′ E 168
Besançon, *Fr.* 47°14′ N, 6°1′ E 150
Beserah, *Malaysia* 3°54′ N, 103°20′ E 196
Beshanq, *Uzb.* 40°25′ N, 70°33′ E 197
Beshkent, *Uzb.* 38°47′ N, 65°37′ E 197
Beşiri, *Turk.* 37°54′ N, 41°20′ E 195
Beška, *Serb.* 45°7′ N, 20°4′ E 168
Besko, *Pol.* 49°34′ N, 21°56′ E 152
Besköl, *Kaz.* 54°45′ N, 69°4′ E 184
Beslan, *Russ.* 43°9′ N, 44°32′ E 195
Beslet, peak, *Bulg.* 41°47′ N, 23°48′ E 156
Besna Kobila, peak, *Serb.* 42°31′ N, 22°11′ E 168
Besnard Lake, lake, *Can.* 55°25′ N, 106°33′ W 108
Besni Fok, *Serb.* 44°58′ N, 20°24′ E 168
Beşparmak Dağı, peak, *Turk.* 37°29′ N, 27°30′ E 156
Bessaker, *Nor.* 64°14′ N, 10°20′ E 152
Bessemer, *Ala., U.S.* 33°23′ N, 86°56′ W 96
Bestöbe, *Kaz.* 52°29′ N, 73°8′ E 184
Bestuzhevo, *Russ.* 61°37′ N, 44°1′ E 154
Bet Guvrin, *Israel* 31°36′ N, 34°53′ E 194
Bét ha Shitta, *Israel* 32°33′ N, 35°26′ E 194
Bét She'an (Beth-shan), *Israel* 32°29′ N, 35°30′ E 194
Bét She'arim, ruin(s), *Israel* 32°41′ N, 35°5′ E 194
Bet Shemesh, *Israel* 31°44′ N, 34°59′ E 194
Betafo, *Madagascar* 19°52′ S, 46°51′ E 220
Betamba, *Dem. Rep. of the Congo* 2°16′ S, 21°25′ E 218
Betanty (Faux Cap), *Madagascar* 25°34′ S, 45°31′ E 220
Betanzos, *Bol.* 19°33′ S, 65°23′ W 137
Betanzos, *Sp.* 43°15′ N, 8°14′ W 150
Bétaré Oya, *Cameroon* 5°31′ N, 14°5′ E 218
Betbeder, Península, *Arg.* 44°43′ S, 65°19′ W 134
Bete Hor, *Eth.* 11°33′ N, 38°58′ E 182
Bétera, *Sp.* 39°35′ N, 0°28′ E 164
Bétérou, *Benin* 9°12′ N, 2°13′ E 222
Bethal, *S. Af.* 26°26′ S, 29°25′ E 227
Bethanie, *Namibia* 26°31′ S, 17°9′ E 227
Bethany, *Ill., U.S.* 39°38′ N, 88°45′ W 102
Bethany, *Mo., U.S.* 40°15′ N, 94°1′ W 94
Bethany Beach, *Del., U.S.* 38°31′ N, 75°4′ W 94
Bethel, *Alas., U.S.* 60°45′ N, 161°52′ W 98
Bethel, *Conn., U.S.* 41°22′ N, 73°25′ W 104
Bethel, *Ohio, U.S.* 38°57′ N, 84°5′ W 102
Bethel, *Vt., U.S.* 43°49′ N, 72°38′ W 104
Bethesda, *U.K.* 53°11′ N, 4°3′ W 162
Bethlehem, *N.H., U.S.* 44°16′ N, 71°42′ W 104
Bethlehem, *S. Af.* 28°16′ S, 28°15′ E 227
Bethlehem see Bayt La'm, *West Bank, Israel* 31°41′ N, 35°12′ E 194
Bethpage, *N.Y., U.S.* 40°44′ N, 73°30′ W 104
Beth-shan see Bét She'an, *Israel* 32°29′ N, 35°30′ E 194
Bethulie, *S. Af.* 30°27′ S, 25°59′ E 227
Béthune, *Fr.* 50°31′ N, 2°38′ E 163
Betijoque, *Venez.* 9°22′ N, 70°44′ W 136
Betioky, *Madagascar* 23°43′ S, 44°19′ E 220
Betong, *Thai.* 5°47′ N, 101°4′ E 196
Bétou, *Congo* 3°5′ N, 18°30′ E 218
Betpaqdala, *Asia* 45°34′ N, 64°32′ E 184
Betroka, *Madagascar* 23°13′ S, 46°8′ E 220
Betsiamites, *Can.* 48°56′ N, 68°39′ W 94
Betsiamites, river, *Can.* 49°24′ N, 69°51′ W 94
Bettendorf, *Iowa, U.S.* 41°33′ N, 90°30′ W 94
Bettie, *Tex., U.S.* 32°48′ N, 94°58′ W 103
Bettioua, *Alg.* 35°47′ N, 0°16′ E 150
Bettola, *It.* 44°46′ N, 9°36′ E 167
Bettsville, *Ohio, U.S.* 41°14′ N, 83°13′ W 102
Betul, *India* 21°55′ N, 77°54′ E 197
Betws-y-Coed, *U.K.* 53°5′ N, 3°48′ W 162
Betzdorf, *Ger.* 50°47′ N, 7°52′ E 167
Béu, *Angola* 6°14′ S, 15°27′ E 218
Beuil, *Fr.* 44°5′ N, 6°57′ E 167
Beulah, *Colo., U.S.* 38°5′ N, 105°0′ W 90
Beulah, *N. Dak., U.S.* 47°15′ N, 101°48′ W 90
Beurfou, spring, *Chad* 15°54′ N, 14°58′ E 216
Beverley, *U.K.* 53°50′ N, 0°26′ E 162
Beverley Head, *Can.* 49°11′ N, 59°4′ W 111
Beverly, *Mass., U.S.* 42°32′ N, 70°53′ W 104
Beverly, *Ohio, U.S.* 39°32′ N, 81°38′ W 102
Beverly Hills, *Fla., U.S.* 28°56′ N, 82°27′ W 105
Beverungen, *Ger.* 51°40′ N, 9°22′ E 167
Beverwijk, *Neth.* 52°30′ N, 4°37′ E 163
Bewdley, *U.K.* 52°21′ N, 2°20′ W 162
Bex, *Switz.* 46°15′ N, 7°0′ E 167
Bexhill, *U.K.* 50°50′ N, 0°28′ E 162
Bey Dağları, *Turk.* 36°36′ N, 29°46′ E 156
Bey Dağı, peak, *Turk.* 39°41′ N, 37°47′ E 156
Bey Dağı, peak, *Turk.* 38°16′ N, 35°59′ E 156
Beycesultan, ruin(s), *Turk.* 38°14′ N, 29°33′ E 156
Beyla, *Guinea* 8°39′ N, 8°39′ W 222
Beyneu, *Kaz.* 45°18′ N, 55°13′ E 158
Beypazarı, *Turk.* 40°9′ N, 31°54′ E 156
Beyra, *Somalia* 6°55′ N, 47°25′ E 218
Beyrouth (Beirut), *Leb.* 33°53′ N, 35°26′ E 194
Beyşehir, *Turk.* 37°41′ N, 31°44′ E 156
Beyşehir Gölü, lake, *Turk.* 37°43′ N, 31°9′ E 180
Beysug, river, *Russ.* 45°53′ N, 39°3′ E 156
Beytüşşebap, *Turk.* 37°33′ N, 43°3′ E 195
Bezdan, *Serb.* 45°50′ N, 18°55′ E 168
Bezerra, river, *Braz.* 13°14′ S, 47°29′ W 138
Bezhanitsy, *Russ.* 56°57′ N, 29°52′ E 166
Bezhetsk, *Russ.* 57°44′ N, 36°44′ E 154
Béziers, *Fr.* 43°20′ N, 3°13′ E 164
Bhadarwah, *India* 32°57′ N, 75°45′ E 186
Bhadra, *India* 29°7′ N, 75°10′ E 186
Bhadrakh, *India* 21°5′ N, 86°31′ E 188
Bhadravati, *India* 13°52′ N, 75°44′ E 188
Bhagalpur, *India* 25°13′ N, 87°0′ E 197
Bhairahawa, *Nepal* 27°32′ N, 83°23′ E 197
Bhakkar, *Pak.* 31°37′ N, 71°7′ E 186
Bhaktapur, *Nepal* 27°41′ N, 85°26′ E 197
Bhamo, *Myanmar* 24°17′ N, 97°16′ E 190
Bhandara, *India* 21°2′ N, 79°38′ E 190
Bhanpura, *India* 24°31′ N, 75°46′ E 197
Bharatpur, *India* 27°13′ N, 77°28′ E 197
Bharatpur, *India* 23°46′ N, 81°47′ E 197
Bharthana, *India* 26°43′ N, 79°14′ E 197
Bharuch, *India* 21°42′ N, 72°57′ E 186
Bhatapara, *India* 21°44′ N, 81°56′ E 188
Bhatinda, *India* 30°13′ N, 74°57′ E 186
Bhatkal, *India* 14°0′ N, 74°32′ E 188
Bhatpara, *India* 22°51′ N, 88°25′ E 197
Bhavnagar, *India* 21°46′ N, 72°7′ E 186
Bheigeir, Beinn, peak, *U.K.* 55°43′ N, 6°12′ W 150
Bhera, *Pak.* 32°27′ N, 72°58′ E 186
Bhikangaon, *India* 21°53′ N, 75°58′ E 197
Bhilai, *India* 21°13′ N, 81°21′ E 188
Bhilsa see Vidisha, *India* 23°32′ N, 77°51′ E 197
Bhind, *India* 26°32′ N, 78°46′ E 197
Bhinmal, *India* 24°59′ N, 72°16′ E 186
Bhisho, *S. Af.* 32°49′ S, 27°31′ E 227
Bhiwani, *India* 28°46′ N, 76°9′ E 197
Bhojpur, *Nepal* 27°9′ N, 87°4′ E 197
Bhopal, *India* 23°16′ N, 77°25′ E 197
Bhubaneshwar, *India* 20°17′ N, 85°48′ E 188
Bhumibol Dam, *Thai.* 17°9′ N, 98°57′ E 202
Bhusawal, *India* 21°2′ N, 75°46′ E 188
Bhutan 27°24′ N, 89°54′ E 188
Bia, Monts, *Dem. Rep. of the Congo* 9°32′ S, 26°9′ E 224
Biá, river, *Braz.* 3°24′ S, 67°24′ W 136
Bia, river, *Ghana* 6°27′ N, 2°49′ W 222
Biak, *Indonesia* 1°4′ S, 136°1′ E 192
Biak, island, *Indonesia* 0°45′ N, 135°57′ E 192
Biała Góra, peak, *Pol.* 50°15′ N, 23°16′ E 152
Biała Podlaska, *Pol.* 52°2′ N, 23°6′ E 158
Białogard, *Pol.* 54°0′ N, 15°59′ E 152
Białowieża, *Pol.* 52°2′ N, 23°6′ E 152
Biały Bór, *Pol.* 53°54′ N, 16°49′ E 152

Białystok, *Pol.* 53°8′ N, 23°9′ E 152
Bianco, *It.* 38°6′ N, 16°8′ E 156
Biankouma, *Côte d'Ivoire* 7°38′ N, 7°36′ W 222
Biaora, *India* 23°56′ N, 76°55′ E 197
Biar, *Sp.* 38°37′ N, 0°46′ E 164
Biar Zahr, spring, *Tun.* 31°29′ N, 10°6′ E 214
Bīārjomand, *Iran* 36°2′ N, 55°57′ E 180
Biarritz, *Fr.* 43°25′ N, 1°39′ W 214
Bias, *Fr.* 44°8′ N, 1°15′ W 150
Biasca, *Switz.* 46°21′ N, 8°58′ E 167
Biaza, *Russ.* 56°34′ N, 78°18′ E 169
Biba, *Egypt* 28°55′ N, 30°57′ E 180
Bibai, *Japan* 43°18′ N, 141°52′ E 190
Bibala, *Angola* 14°44′ S, 13°18′ E 220
Bibémi, *Cameroon* 9°18′ N, 13°52′ E 216
Bibiani, *Ghana* 6°28′ N, 2°18′ W 222
Bibile, *Sri Lanka* 7°9′ N, 81°15′ E 188
Bibione, *It.* 45°38′ N, 13°1′ E 167
Bibury, *U.K.* 51°45′ N, 1°50′ W 162
Bicaj, *Alban.* 41°59′ N, 20°25′ E 168
Bicas, *Braz.* 21°43′ S, 43°6′ W 138
Bicaz, *Rom.* 46°54′ N, 26°4′ E 156
Bicester, *U.K.* 51°53′ N, 1°9′ W 162
Biche, Lac la, lake, *Can.* 54°53′ N, 112°30′ W 108
Bichena, *Eth.* 10°23′ N, 38°14′ E 224
Bichi, *Nig.* 12°12′ N, 8°13′ E 222
Bichvint'a, *Ga.* 43°9′ N, 40°20′ E 195
Bickerdike, *Can.* 53°32′ N, 116°39′ W 108
Bickerton Island, *Austral.* 13°39′ S, 134°25′ E 230
Bicknell, *Ind., U.S.* 38°46′ N, 87°18′ W 102
Bicknell, *Utah, U.S.* 38°20′ N, 111°33′ W 90
Bicske, *Hung.* 47°28′ N, 18°39′ E 168
Bida, *Nig.* 9°3′ N, 5°59′ E 222
Bidar, *India* 17°54′ N, 77°32′ E 188
Bidarray, *Fr.* 43°16′ N, 1°21′ W 164
Biddeford, *Me., U.S.* 43°29′ N, 70°28′ W 104
Bidwell, Mount, *Calif., U.S.* 41°57′ N, 120°15′ W 90
Bié, adm. division, *Angola* 12°56′ S, 16°44′ E 220
Bié Plateau, *Angola* 11°41′ S, 15°45′ E 220
Biele Karpaty, *Czech Rep.* 49°5′ N, 17°49′ E 152
Bieler See, lake, *Switz.* 47°5′ N, 7°4′ E 165
Biella, *It.* 45°34′ N, 8°2′ E 167
Bielsa, *Sp.* 42°37′ N, 0°13′ E 164
Bielsk, *Pol.* 52°39′ N, 19°48′ E 152
Bielsk Podlaski, *Pol.* 52°46′ N, 23°10′ E 152
Bielsko-Biała, *Pol.* 49°49′ N, 19°2′ E 152
Bien Hoa, *Vietnam* 10°58′ N, 106°49′ E 202
Bienvenida, *Sp.* 38°18′ N, 6°13′ W 164
Bienville, Lac, lake, *Can.* 54°59′ N, 74°39′ W 106
Biescas, *Sp.* 42°37′ N, 0°19′ E 164
Bieżuń, *Pol.* 52°57′ N, 19°52′ E 152
Bifoum, *Gabon* 0°20′ N, 10°24′ E 218
Big Baldy Mountain, *Mont., U.S.* 46°56′ N, 110°41′ W 90
Big Baldy, peak, *Idaho, U.S.* 44°45′ N, 115°18′ W 90
Big Bay, *Mich., U.S.* 46°48′ N, 87°44′ W 94
Big Bear Lake, *Calif., U.S.* 34°14′ N, 116°57′ W 101
Big Beaver House, *Can.* 52°55′ N, 89°52′ W 82
Big Belt Mountains, *Mont., U.S.* 46°58′ N, 111°39′ W 90
Big Bend National Park, *Tex., U.S.* 29°9′ N, 103°44′ W 72
Big Black, river, *Miss., U.S.* 32°43′ N, 90°14′ W 103
Big Blue, river, *Nebr., U.S.* 41°1′ N, 97°55′ W 80
Big Bog, marsh, *Minn., U.S.* 48°18′ N, 94°29′ W 90
Big Creek, *Calif., U.S.* 37°12′ N, 119°15′ W 100
Big Cypress National Preserve, *Fla., U.S.* 26°5′ N, 81°11′ W 105
Big Cypress Swamp, marsh, *Fla., U.S.* 26°1′ N, 81°12′ W 105
Big Delta, *Alas., U.S.* 64°1′ N, 145°49′ W 98
Big Elk Mountain, *Idaho, U.S.* 43°12′ N, 111°21′ W 90
Big Falls, *Minn., U.S.* 48°9′ N, 93°50′ W 90
Big Fork, river, *Minn., U.S.* 48°4′ N, 94°0′ W 90
Big Horn Peak, *Ariz., U.S.* 33°36′ N, 113°13′ W 92
Big Interior Mountain, *Can.* 49°27′ N, 125°36′ W 90
Big Lake, *Minn., U.S.* 45°18′ N, 93°45′ W 94
Big Lake, *Tex., U.S.* 31°11′ N, 101°28′ W 92
Big Lake Ranch, *Can.* 52°23′ N, 121°52′ W 108
Big Lookout Mountain, *Oreg., U.S.* 44°35′ N, 117°23′ W 90
Big Maria Mountains, *Calif., U.S.* 33°54′ N, 114°56′ W 101
Big Mountain, *Nev., U.S.* 41°16′ N, 119°9′ W 90
Big Pine, *Calif., U.S.* 37°10′ N, 118°19′ W 101
Big Pine Key, *Fla., U.S.* 24°39′ N, 81°22′ W 105
Big Pine Mountain, *Calif., U.S.* 34°41′ N, 119°42′ W 100
Big Piney, *Wyo., U.S.* 42°32′ N, 110°6′ W 90
Big Piskwanish Point, *Can.* 51°44′ N, 80°27′ W 110
Big Port Walter, *Alas., U.S.* 56°23′ N, 134°45′ W 108
Big Rapids, *Mich., U.S.* 43°42′ N, 85°30′ W 102
Big River, *Can.* 53°50′ N, 107°1′ W 108
Big, river, *Mo., U.S.* 38°16′ N, 90°40′ W 80
Big Sable Point, *Mich., U.S.* 44°2′ N, 86°40′ W 102
Big Salmon, river, *Can.* 61°46′ N, 134°30′ W 98
Big Sand Lake, *Can.* 57°33′ N, 100°35′ W 108
Big Sandy, *Mont., U.S.* 48°9′ N, 110°6′ W 90
Big Sandy, *Tex., U.S.* 32°34′ N, 95°7′ W 103
Big Sandy Lake, lake, *Can.* 54°22′ N, 104°45′ W 108
Big Sandy Reservoir, *Wyo., U.S.* 42°17′ N, 109°49′ W 90
Big Sioux, river, *S. Dak., U.S.* 45°17′ N, 97°38′ W 80
Big Smoky Valley, *Nev., U.S.* 38°13′ N, 117°46′ W 90
Big Snowy Mountains, *Mont., U.S.* 46°51′ N, 109°39′ W 90
Big Southern Butte, *Idaho, U.S.* 43°23′ N, 113°6′ W 90
Big Spring, *Tex., U.S.* 32°13′ N, 101°28′ W 92
Big Springs, *Nebr., U.S.* 41°3′ N, 102°6′ W 90
Big Squaw Mountain, *Me., U.S.* 45°28′ N, 69°48′ W 94
Big Stone City, *S. Dak., U.S.* 45°16′ N, 96°30′ W 90
Big Sur, *Calif., U.S.* 36°16′ N, 121°49′ W 100
Big Thicket National Preserve, *Tex., U.S.* 30°26′ N, 94°41′ W 103
Big Timber, *Mont., U.S.* 45°48′ N, 109°58′ W 90
Big Trout Lake, *Can.* 53°51′ N, 92°1′ W 106
Big Trout Lake, *Can.* 53°43′ N, 89°55′ W 106
Big Valley, *Can.* 52°2′ N, 112°46′ W 90
Big Valley Mountains, *Calif., U.S.* 41°10′ N, 121°33′ W 90
Big Wells, *Tex., U.S.* 28°33′ N, 99°35′ W 92
Big White Mountain, *Can.* 49°43′ N, 119°2′ W 90
Big Wood Cay, island, *Bahamas* 24°25′ N, 77°40′ W 116
Biga, *Turk.* 40°13′ N, 27°12′ E 156
Bigadiç, *Turk.* 39°23′ N, 28°7′ E 156
Bigelow Mountain, *Me., U.S.* 45°8′ N, 70°22′ W 94
Bigfork, *Minn., U.S.* 47°42′ N, 93°40′ W 90
Bigfork, *Mont., U.S.* 48°2′ N, 114°7′ W 90
Biggar, *Can.* 52°3′ N, 107°59′ W 90
Bigge Island, *Austral.* 14°23′ S, 124°2′ E 230
Biggeluobbal, *Nor.* 69°22′ N, 23°22′ E 152
Biggleswade, *U.K.* 52°4′ N, 0°16′ E 162
Biggs, *Calif., U.S.* 39°24′ N, 121°43′ W 90
Bighorn Mountains, *Wyo., U.S.* 43°48′ N, 107°26′ W 90
Bignasco, *Switz.* 46°21′ N, 8°36′ E 167
Bigniba, river, *Can.* 49°2′ N, 77°43′ W 94
Bignona, *Senegal* 12°48′ N, 16°10′ W 222
Bigobo, *Dem. Rep. of the Congo* 5°27′ S, 27°34′ E 224
Bigstick Lake, *Can.* 50°16′ N, 109°40′ W 90
Bigstone Lake, lake, *Can.* 53°36′ N, 96°20′ W 108
Bigstone, river, *Can.* 55°28′ N, 95°12′ W 108
Bihać, *Bosn. and Herzg.* 44°49′ N, 15°53′ E 168
Bihar, adm. division, *India* 25°9′ N, 84°25′ E 188
Bihar Sharif, *India* 25°10′ N, 85°30′ E 197
Biharamulo, *Tanzania* 2°40′ S, 31°21′ E 224
Biharkeresztes, *Hung.* 47°7′ N, 21°42′ E 168
Bihor, adm. division, *Rom.* 46°51′ N, 21°40′ E 156
Bihor, Munții, *Rom.* 46°42′ N, 22°25′ E 168
Bihosava, *Belarus* 55°50′ N, 27°42′ E 166
Biĭkzhal, *Kaz.* 46°51′ N, 54°48′ E 158
Bijagós, Arquipélago dos, *North Atlantic Ocean* 10°37′ N, 16°42′ W 222
Bijapur, *India* 18°46′ N, 80°49′ E 188
Bijapur, *India* 16°49′ N, 75°42′ E 188
Bījār, *Iran* 35°50′ N, 47°32′ E 180
Bijauri, *Nepal* 28°5′ N, 82°28′ E 197
Bijawar, *India* 24°37′ N, 79°30′ E 197
Bijeljina, *Bosn. and Herzg.* 44°45′ N, 19°14′ E 168
Bijelo Polje, *Mont.* 43°1′ N, 19°44′ E 168
Bijie, *China* 27°18′ N, 105°19′ E 198
Bikaner, *India* 28°1′ N, 73°20′ E 186
Bikava, *Latv.* 56°44′ N, 27°2′ E 166
Bikin, *Russ.* 46°53′ N, 134°22′ E 190
Bikita, *Zimb.* 20°6′ S, 31°37′ E 227
Bīkkū Bīttī, peak, *Lib.* 22°8′ N, 19°11′ E 216
Bikoro, *Dem. Rep. of the Congo* 0°45′ N, 18°6′ E 218
Bikovo, *Serb.* 46°0′ N, 19°45′ E 168
Bila, river, *China* 49°9′ N, 122°19′ E 198
Bila, Tanjung, *Indonesia* 1°8′ N, 108°39′ E 196
Bila Tserkva, *Ukr.* 49°47′ N, 30°14′ E 158
Biläcäri, *Azerb.* 40°27′ N, 49°47′ E 195
Bilād Banī Bū 'Alī, *Oman* 22°4′ N, 59°18′ E 182
Bilanga, *Burkina Faso* 12°32′ N, 5°296′ W 222
Bilaspur, *India* 22°4′ N, 82°8′ E 197
Biläsuvar, *Azerb.* 39°26′ N, 48°31′ E 195
Bilati, *Dem. Rep. of the Congo* 0°36′ N, 28°47′ E 224
Bilati, river, *Dem. Rep. of the Congo* 0°53′ N, 28°12′ E 224
Bilbao, *Sp.* 43°14′ N, 2°58′ W 150
Bile, *Ukr.* 51°38′ N, 26°4′ E 152
Bileća, *Bosn. and Herzg.* 42°52′ N, 18°24′ E 168
Bilecik, *Turk.* 40°9′ N, 29°58′ E 156
Bilhorod-Dnistrovs'kyy, *Ukr.* 46°11′ N, 30°17′ E 156
Bili, *Dem. Rep. of the Congo* 4°7′ N, 25°3′ E 224
Bili, river, *Dem. Rep. of the Congo* 4°4′ N, 24°28′ E 224
Bilibino, *Russ.* 67°54′ N, 166°13′ E 160
Bilican Dağları, peak, *Turk.* 38°56′ N, 42°6′ E 195
Bilimora, *India* 20°46′ N, 72°56′ E 188
Bilin, *Myanmar* 17°14′ N, 97°12′ E 202
Bilir, *Russ.* 65°29′ N, 131°52′ E 160
Bilis Qooqaani, *Somalia* 0°15′ N, 41°36′ E 224
Bilje, *Croatia* 45°35′ N, 18°45′ E 168
Bill, *Wyo., U.S.* 43°12′ N, 105°16′ W 90
Bill Williams, river, *Ariz., U.S.* 34°18′ N, 113°54′ W 101
Billerbeck, *Ger.* 51°58′ N, 7°17′ E 167
Billerica, *Mass., U.S.* 42°33′ N, 71°17′ W 104
Billingham, *U.K.* 54°35′ N, 1°17′ W 162
Billings, *Mont., U.S.* 45°46′ N, 108°31′ W 90
Billings, *Okla., U.S.* 36°30′ N, 97°25′ W 92
Billiton see Belitung, island, *Indonesia* 3°41′ S, 107°3′ E 192
Bilma, *Niger* 18°42′ N, 12°54′ E 216
Bilma, Grand Erg de, *Niger* 18°42′ N, 13°31′ E 216
Bilo Gora, *Croatia* 45°48′ N, 16°57′ E 168
Bilohirs'k, *Ukr.* 45°5′ N, 34°31′ E 156
Bilohir'ya, *Ukr.* 50°0′ N, 26°24′ E 152
Bilohorodka, *Ukr.* 49°59′ N, 26°38′ E 158
Biloli, *India* 18°45′ N, 77°44′ E 188
Bilopillya, *Ukr.* 51°7′ N, 34°20′ E 158
Biloxi, *Miss., U.S.* 30°23′ N, 88°55′ W 103
Bilqâs, *Egypt* 31°13′ N, 31°21′ E 180
Bil'shivtsi, *Ukr.* 49°9′ N, 24°46′ E 152
Biltine, *Chad* 14°30′ N, 20°55′ E 216
Bilto, *Nor.* 69°28′ N, 21°36′ E 152
Bilüü, *Mongolia* 48°58′ N, 89°21′ E 184
Bilwaskarma, *Nicar.* 14°45′ N, 83°52′ W 115
Bilzen, *Belg.* 50°52′ N, 5°30′ E 167
Bima, river, *Dem. Rep. of the Congo* 3°3′ N, 25°44′ E 224
Bimbila, *Ghana* 8°49′ N, 5°297′ E 222
Bimini, adm. division, *Bahamas* 25°43′ N, 79°27′ W 96
Bimini Islands, *North Atlantic Ocean* 25°45′ N, 79°5′ W 116
Bin Ghunaymah, Jabal, *Lib.* 24°45′ N, 15°21′ E 216
Bina, *India* 24°10′ N, 78°12′ E 197
Binaced, *Sp.* 41°49′ N, 0°12′ E 164
Binasco, *It.* 45°19′ N, 9°5′ E 167
Binche, *Belg.* 50°24′ N, 4°9′ E 163
Bindura, *Zimb.* 17°20′ S, 31°19′ E 224
Binford, *N. Dak., U.S.* 47°32′ N, 98°23′ W 90
Binga, *Zimb.* 17°40′ S, 27°20′ E 224
Bingen, *Wash., U.S.* 45°42′ N, 121°28′ W 100
Binger, *Okla., U.S.* 35°17′ N, 98°22′ W 92
BingerbrÜck, *Ger.* 49°57′ N, 7°52′ E 167
Bingham, *Me., U.S.* 45°2′ N, 69°53′ W 111
Binghamton, *N.Y., U.S.* 42°6′ N, 75°54′ W 110
Bingkor, *Malaysia* 5°25′ N, 116°11′ E 203
Bingley, *U.K.* 53°51′ N, 1°50′ W 162
Bingöl, *Turk.* 38°52′ N, 40°29′ E 195
Bingöl Dağları, peak, *Turk.* 39°19′ N, 41°24′ E 195
Binh Khe, *Vietnam* 13°59′ N, 108°48′ E 202
Binh Son, *Vietnam* 15°19′ N, 108°44′ E 202
Binhai, *China* 34°2′ N, 119°51′ E 198
Binham, *U.K.* 52°55′ N, 0°57′ E 162
Bini Erdi, spring, *Chad* 20°9′ N, 18°1′ E 216
Binjai, *Indonesia* 3°51′ N, 108°13′ E 196
Binjai, *Indonesia* 3°38′ N, 98°29′ E 196
Binna, Raas, *Somalia* 11°10′ N, 51°10′ E 216
Binongko, island, *Indonesia* 6°16′ S, 122°51′ E 192
Bintan, island, *Indonesia* 1°16′ N, 104°33′ E 196
Bintuan, *Philippines* 12°2′ N, 120°2′ E 203
Bintulu, *Malaysia* 3°11′ N, 113°2′ E 192
Binxian, *China* 45°44′ N, 127°29′ E 198
Binxian, *China* 35°2′ N, 108°3′ E 198
Binyamina, *Israel* 32°30′ N, 34°56′ E 194
Binyang, *China* 23°9′ N, 108°46′ E 198
Binza, *Dem. Rep. of the Congo* 4°30′ S, 15°10′ E 218
Binzhou, *China* 37°23′ N, 118°4′ E 198
Bio Addo, *Somalia* 8°10′ N, 49°47′ E 216
BioBío, adm. division, *Chile* 37°12′ S, 73°8′ W 134
Bioče, *Mont.* 42°30′ N, 19°20′ E 168
Bioko, island, *Equatorial Guinea* 3°20′ N, 8°35′ E 253
Bioko, region, *Africa* 3°13′ N, 8°14′ E 218
Biokovo, peak, *Croatia* 43°18′ N, 17°0′ E 168
Biola, *Calif., U.S.* 36°48′ N, 120°2′ W 100
Biópio, *Angola* 12°26′ S, 13°45′ E 220
Bioska, *Serb.* 43°52′ N, 19°39′ E 168
Biota, *Sp.* 42°16′ N, 1°12′ W 164
Bipindi, *Cameroon* 3°14′ N, 10°24′ E 218
Bir, *India* 18°59′ N, 75°46′ E 188
Bîr Abu el Ḥuṣein, spring, *Egypt* 22°52′ N, 29°54′ E 182
Bîr Abu Gharâdiq, spring, *Egypt* 30°5′ N, 28°2′ E 180
Bîr Abu Hashîm, spring, *Egypt* 23°41′ N, 34°3′ E 182
Bîr Abu Minqâr, spring, *Egypt* 26°29′ N, 27°35′ E 180
Bîr Abu Sa'fa, spring, *Egypt* 23°14′ N, 34°48′ E 182
Bi'r adh Dhakar, spring, *Lib.* 25°42′ N, 22°42′ E 226
Bi'r al Ma'rūf, spring, *Lib.* 25°6′ N, 18°31′ E 216
Bi'r al Qāf, spring, *Lib.* 28°16′ N, 15°22′ E 216
Bi'r al Qarḍī, spring, *Yemen* 15°35′ N, 47°18′ E 182
Bi'r 'Allāq, spring, *Lib.* 31°7′ N, 11°54′ E 214
Bir Anzarane, *Western Sahara, Mor.* 23°51′ N, 14°33′ W 214
Bir Bel Guerdâne, spring, *Mauritania* 25°23′ N, 10°31′ W 214
Bir Beressof, spring, *Alg.* 32°33′ N, 7°56′ E 214
Bi'r Bin Ghanīyah, spring, *Lib.* 31°10′ N, 21°52′ E 226
Bi'r Bū Ḥawsh, spring, *Lib.* 25°29′ N, 22°4′ E 216
Bi'r Bū Zurayyiq, spring, *Lib.* 25°34′ N, 22°15′ E 226
Bir Chali, spring, *Mali* 22°58′ N, 5°0′ W 214
Bîr Dibis, spring, *Egypt* 22°11′ N, 29°29′ E 226
Bir ed Deheb, spring, *Alg.* 25°8′ N, 1°58′ W 214
Bîr el 'Abd, *Egypt* 31°0′ N, 32°59′ E 194
Bir el Hadjaj, spring, *Alg.* 26°26′ N, 1°26′ W 214
Bîr el Ḥamma, *Egypt* 30°37′ N, 33°32′ E 194
Bîr el Kaseiba, spring, *Egypt* 30°59′ N, 33°17′ E 194
Bir el Khzaïm, spring, *Mauritania* 24°28′ N, 7°50′ W 214
Bir el Ksaïb, spring, *Mali* 21°16′ N, 5°38′ W 222
Bîr el Maqeibra, spring, *Egypt* 30°52′ N, 32°50′ E 194
Bîr el Qanâdîl, spring, *Egypt* 30°58′ N, 33°7′ E 194
Bîr el Roghwi, spring, *Egypt* 30°46′ N, 33°26′ E 194
Bi'r Fardān, spring, *Saudi Arabia* 22°4′ N, 48°38′ E 182
Bîr Fuâd, spring, *Egypt* 30°25′ N, 26°27′ E 180
Bi'r Ghawdah, spring, *Saudi Arabia* 23°0′ N, 44°17′ E 182
Bîr Gifgâfa, *Egypt* 30°26′ N, 33°11′ E 194
Bîr Ḥasana, *Egypt* 30°27′ N, 33°47′ E 194
Bîr Ḥibeia, spring, *Egypt* 30°27′ N, 32°25′ E 194
Bir Igueni, spring, *Mauritania* 20°27′ N, 14°55′ W 222
Bi'r Juraybī'āt, spring, *Iraq* 29°10′ N, 45°30′ E 196
Bîr Khâlda, spring, *Egypt* 30°48′ N, 27°14′ E 180
Bîr Kiseiba, spring, *Egypt* 22°40′ N, 29°55′ E 182
Bîr Lahfân, *Egypt* 31°0′ N, 33°51′ E 194
Bir Lahmar, *Western Sahara, Mor.* 26°4′ N, 11°4′ W 214
Bir Lahrache, spring, *Alg.* 32°0′ N, 8°13′ E 214
Bir Lemouissat, spring, *Mauritania* 25°3′ N, 10°33′ W 214
Bîr Madkûr, spring, *Egypt* 30°42′ N, 32°31′ E 194
Bîr Misâḥa, spring, *Egypt* 22°11′ N, 27°56′ E 226
Bir Mogreïn (Fort Trinquet), *Mauritania* 25°13′ N, 11°37′ W 214
Bîr Murr, spring, *Egypt* 23°21′ N, 30°4′ E 182
Bîr Nâhid, spring, *Egypt* 30°14′ N, 28°53′ E 180
Bîr Nakheila, spring, *Egypt* 23°59′ N, 30°51′ E 182
Bi'r Nāṣirah, spring, *Lib.* 30°18′ N, 11°23′ E 214
Bir Ould Brini, spring, *Alg.* 25°24′ N, 1°50′ W 214
Bîr Ounâne, spring, *Mali* 21°26′ N, 3°55′ W 222
Bîr Qaṭia, spring, *Egypt* 30°57′ N, 32°44′ E 194
Bir Rhorrafa, spring, *Alg.* 32°20′ N, 8°4′ E 214
Bir Romane, spring, *Tun.* 32°32′ N, 8°21′ E 214
Bîr Ṣahara, spring, *Egypt* 22°50′ N, 28°34′ E 226
Bîr Salala, spring, *Sudan* 19°24′ N, 35°38′ E 182
Bîr Seiyâla, spring, *Egypt* 26°7′ N, 33°54′ E 180
Bîr Shalatein, spring, *Egypt* 23°9′ N, 35°35′ E 182
Bîr Takhlîs, spring, *Egypt* 22°24′ N, 30°7′ E 182
Bîr Ṭarfâwi, spring, *Egypt* 22°56′ N, 28°51′ E 226
Bi'r Tārsīn, spring, *Lib.* 31°41′ N, 13°23′ E 216
Bir Tinkardad, spring, *Western Sahara, Mor.* 23°57′ N, 12°58′ W 214
B'ir Tlakshin, oil field, *Lib.* 30°55′ N, 11°53′ E 143
Bîr Ungât, spring, *Egypt* 22°6′ N, 33°44′ E 182
Bi'r Uoigh, spring, *Lib.* 23°7′ N, 17°20′ E 216
Bi'r Zalṭan, spring, *Lib.* 28°27′ N, 19°44′ E 216
Bîr Zeidûn, spring, *Egypt* 25°42′ N, 33°42′ E 180
Bir Zīrī, spring, *Mauritania* 21°32′ N, 10°47′ W 222
Bir Zreïgat, spring, *Mauritania* 22°28′ N, 8°54′ W 222
Birāk, *Lib.* 27°34′ N, 14°14′ E 216
Birao, *Cen. Af. Rep.* 10°16′ N, 22°47′ E 218
Biratnagar, *Nepal* 26°28′ N, 87°16′ E 197
Birch Creek, *Alas., U.S.* 66°16′ N, 145°51′ W 98
Birch Hills, *Can.* 52°59′ N, 105°27′ W 108
Birch Lake, *Can.* 51°21′ N, 92°57′ W 110
Birch Mountains, *Can.* 57°34′ N, 113°37′ W 108
Birch River, *Can.* 52°23′ N, 101°8′ W 108
Birch, river, *Can.* 58°17′ N, 113°56′ W 108
Birchiș, *Rom.* 45°58′ N, 22°10′ E 168
Birchwood, *Alas., U.S.* 61°25′ N, 149°25′ W 98
Bird, *Can.* 56°29′ N, 94°15′ W 108
Bird City, *Kans., U.S.* 39°45′ N, 101°31′ W 90
Bird Island, *Minn., U.S.* 44°45′ N, 94°55′ W 94
Bird, river, *Can.* 50°34′ N, 95°11′ W 90
Bireun, *Indonesia* 5°11′ N, 96°41′ E 196
Birganj, *Nepal* 27°1′ N, 84°54′ E 197
Biri, river, *Sudan* 7°40′ N, 26°4′ E 224
Biria, river, *Venez.* 1°14′ N, 66°34′ W 136
Birigui, *Braz.* 21°16′ S, 50°20′ W 138
Birilyussy, *Russ.* 57°9′ N, 90°39′ E 169
Birīn, *Syr.* 35°0′ N, 36°39′ E 194
Birine, *Alg.* 35°38′ N, 3°13′ E 150
Birini, *Cen. Af. Rep.* 7°50′ N, 22°26′ E 218
Bīrjand, *Iran* 32°55′ N, 59°17′ E 180
Birkenfeld, *Ger.* 49°38′ N, 7°10′ E 163
Birkenfeld, *Oreg., U.S.* 45°58′ N, 123°19′ W 100
Birkenhead, *U.K.* 53°24′ N, 3°2′ W 162
Birkfeld, *Aust.* 47°20′ N, 15°41′ E 168
Bîrlad, *Rom.* 46°13′ N, 27°40′ E 156
Birlik, *Kaz.* 44°3′ N, 73°33′ E 184
Birmingham, *Ala., U.S.* 33°30′ N, 86°49′ W 96
Birmingham, *U.K.* 52°28′ N, 1°53′ W 162
Birmitrapur, *India* 22°22′ N, 84°43′ E 197
Birni, *Benin* 10°1′ N, 1°30′ E 222
Birni Ngaouré, *Niger* 13°6′ N, 2°55′ E 222
Birni Nkonni, *Niger* 13°47′ N, 5°15′ E 222
Birnie, *Can.* 50°27′ N, 99°27′ W 90
Birnin Gwari, *Nig.* 10°59′ N, 6°47′ E 222
Birnin Kebbi, *Nig.* 12°26′ N, 4°12′ E 222
Birniwa, *Nig.* 12°48′ N, 10°15′ E 222
Birobidzhan, *Russ.* 48°54′ N, 133°0′ E 190
Birong, *Philippines* 9°24′ N, 118°9′ E 203
Birou, *Mali* 15°4′ N, 9°56′ W 222
Birougou, Monts, peak, *Gabon* 1°55′ S, 12°9′ E 218
Birrie, river, *Austral.* 29°22′ S, 146°48′ E 230
Birshoghyr, *Kaz.* 48°24′ N, 58°43′ E 158
Birsk, *Russ.* 55°26′ N, 55°36′ E 154
Birštonas, *Lith.* 54°36′ N, 24°0′ E 166
Birtin, *Rom.* 46°58′ N, 22°32′ E 168
Birtle, *Can.* 50°26′ N, 101°4′ W 90
Biru, *China* 31°32′ N, 93°47′ E 188
Biryakovo, *Russ.* 59°33′ N, 41°29′ E 154
Biržai, *Lith.* 56°11′ N, 24°44′ E 166
Bîrzava, *Rom.* 46°6′ N, 21°59′ E 168
Bîrzava, river, *Rom.* 45°16′ N, 20°56′ E 168
Bisaccia, *It.* 41°1′ N, 15°22′ E 156
Bisbee, *Ariz., U.S.* 31°27′ N, 109°54′ W 92
Bisbee, *N. Dak., U.S.* 48°36′ N, 99°24′ W 90
Biscarrués, *Sp.* 42°13′ N, 0°45′ E 164
Biscay, Bay of 43°48′ N, 7°35′ W 143
Biscay Plain, *North Atlantic Ocean* 45°12′ N, 8°17′ W 253
Biscayne Bay 25°34′ N, 80°28′ W 105
Biscayne, Key, island, *Fla., U.S.* 25°42′ N, 80°10′ W 105
Biscayne National Park, *Atlantic Ocean* 25°34′ N, 80°7′ W 105
Bischleben, *Ger.* 50°56′ N, 10°58′ E 152
Bischofsheim, *Ger.* 50°24′ N, 10°0′ E 167
Bischwiller, *Fr.* 48°46′ N, 7°50′ E 163
Biscotasing, *Can.* 47°18′ N, 82°7′ W 94
Biser, *Bulg.* 41°53′ N, 25°57′ E 156
Biserovo, *Russ.* 59°4′ N, 53°24′ E 154
Bisert', *Russ.* 56°52′ N, 59°4′ E 154
Biševo, island, *Croatia* 42°53′ N, 15°57′ E 168
Bishkek, *Kyrg.* 42°50′ N, 74°26′ E 184
Bishop, *Tex., U.S.* 27°34′ N, 97°48′ W 96
Bishop Auckland, *U.K.* 54°40′ N, 1°42′ W 162
Bishop Creek Reservoir, lake, *Nev., U.S.* 41°13′ N, 115°34′ W 90
Bishops and Clerks, islands, *St George's Channel* 51°42′ N, 6°54′ W 150
Bishop's Castle, *U.K.* 52°28′ N, 2°59′ W 162
Bishop's Falls, *Can.* 49°1′ N, 55°31′ W 111
Bishop's Stortford, *U.K.* 51°51′ N, 0°8′ E 162
Biskia, *Eritrea* 15°28′ N, 37°30′ E 182
Biskintā, *Leb.* 33°56′ N, 35°48′ E 194
Biskra, *Alg.* 34°50′ N, 5°44′ E 214
Bislig, *Philippines* 8°13′ N, 126°16′ E 203
Bismarck, *Ill., U.S.* 40°15′ N, 87°36′ W 102
Bismarck, *N. Dak., U.S.* 46°46′ N, 100°54′ W 90
Bismarck Archipelago, *Bismarck Sea* 1°32′ S, 145°44′ E 192
Bismarck Range, *P.N.G.* 5°1′ S, 144°9′ E 192
Bismarck Sea 4°3′ S, 145°12′ E 192
Bismil, *Turk.* 37°52′ N, 40°42′ E 195
Bison, *S. Dak., U.S.* 45°31′ N, 102°28′ W 90
Bison Lake, *Can.* 57°13′ N, 116°28′ W 108
Bison Peak, *Colo., U.S.* 39°13′ N, 105°34′ W 90
Bissameuttack, *India* 19°30′ N, 83°30′ E 188
Bissau, *Guinea-Bissau* 11°49′ N, 15°45′ W 222
Bissett, *Can.* 51°0′ N, 95°41′ W 90
Bissiga, *Burkina Faso* 12°41′ N, 1°14′ W 222
Bissikrima, *Guinea* 10°53′ N, 10°59′ W 222
Bistcho Lake, *Can.* 59°49′ N, 119°18′ W 108

Bistrica, *Serb.* 43°28′ N, 19°41′ E 168
Bistrița-Năsăud, adm. division, *Rom.* 47°20′ N, 24°9′ E 156
Bistrița, *Rom.* 47°9′ N, 24°29′ E 156
Bistriței, Munții, *Rom.* 47°14′ N, 25°3′ E 156
Biswan, *India* 27°29′ N, 81°0′ E 197
Bita, river, *Col.* 5°39′ N, 69°8′ W 136
Bitburg, *Ger.* 49°58′ N, 6°31′ E 167
Bitche, *Fr.* 49°3′ N, 7°26′ E 163
Bitely, *Mich., U.S.* 43°44′ N, 85°52′ W 102
Bitkin, *Chad* 11°58′ N, 18°18′ E 216
Bitlis, *Turk.* 38°21′ N, 42°3′ E 195
Bitola, *Maced.* 41°1′ N, 21°23′ E 180
Bitter Root Range, *North America* 47°31′ N, 116°18′ W 90
Bitterfeld, *Ger.* 51°37′ N, 12°18′ E 152
Bitterfontein, *S. Af.* 31°3′ S, 18°14′ E 227
Bitterroot Range, *Idaho, U.S.* 47°46′ N, 116°27′ W 80
Bitumount, *Can.* 57°22′ N, 111°36′ W 108
Biu, *Nig.* 10°36′ N, 12°12′ E 216
Bivolu, peak, *Rom.* 47°13′ N, 25°51′ E 156
Bixad, *Rom.* 47°55′ N, 23°22′ E 168
Bixby, *Okla., U.S.* 35°54′ N, 95°54′ W 96
Biya, river, *Russ.* 51°16′ N, 87°47′ E 190
Biyang, *China* 32°44′ N, 113°23′ E 198
Biysk, *Russ.* 52°35′ N, 85°13′ E 184
Bizana, *S. Af.* 30°53′ S, 29°52′ E 227
Bizerte, *Tun.* 37°17′ N, 9°51′ E 156
Bjärnum, *Nor.* 56°18′ N, 13°42′ E 152
Bjelolasica, peak, *Croatia* 45°15′ N, 14°53′ E 156
Bjelovar, *Croatia* 45°53′ N, 16°49′ E 168
Björbo, *Nor.* 60°24′ N, 14°44′ E 152
Björkholmen, *Nor.* 66°47′ N, 19°6′ E 152
Björkö, island, *Sw.* 59°54′ N, 19°3′ E 166
Björköby, *Fin.* 63°19′ N, 21°20′ E 152
Björksele, *Nor.* 64°59′ N, 18°33′ E 152
Björna, *Nor.* 63°32′ N, 18°35′ E 152
Björneborg see Pori, *Fin.* 61°26′ N, 21°44′ E 166
Bjørnøya (Bear Island), *Nor.* 73°46′ N, 15°27′ E 160
Bjørnskinn, *Nor.* 68°59′ N, 15°41′ E 152
Bjuröklubb, *Nor.* 64°28′ N, 21°35′ E 152
Bjuv, *Nor.* 56°6′ N, 12°52′ E 152
Bla, *Mali* 13°0′ N, 5°49′ W 222
Blache, Lac de La, lake, *Can.* 50°5′ N, 69°53′ W 111
Black see Da, river, *Vietnam* 21°11′ N, 104°8′ E 202
Black Bay 48°37′ N, 89°19′ W 80
Black Bay Peninsula, *Can.* 48°34′ N, 88°43′ W 94
Black Bear Bay 53°15′ N, 56°36′ W 111
Black Birch Lake, *Can.* 56°48′ N, 108°45′ W 108
Black Butte, peak, *Calif., U.S.* 39°42′ N, 122°57′ W 90
Black Butte, peak, *Mont., U.S.* 44°52′ N, 111°55′ W 90
Black Creek, *Can.* 52°18′ N, 121°8′ W 108
Black Creek, river, *Miss., U.S.* 31°0′ N, 88°58′ W 103
Black Diamond, *Can.* 50°41′ N, 114°14′ W 90
Black Diamond, *Wash., U.S.* 47°17′ N, 122°0′ W 100
Black Fox Mountain, *Calif., U.S.* 41°20′ N, 121°59′ W 90
Black Hills, *S. Dak., U.S.* 43°30′ N, 103°50′ W 90
Black Island, *Antarctica* 78°21′ S, 166°54′ E 248
Black Lake, *Can.* 59°5′ N, 105°42′ W 108
Black Lake, lake, *Can.* 59°13′ N, 105°39′ W 108
Black Lassic, peak, *Calif., U.S.* 40°19′ N, 123°39′ W 90
Black Mesa, *Ariz., U.S.* 35°57′ N, 111°8′ W 80
Black Mountain, *Colo., U.S.* 40°46′ N, 107°27′ W 90
Black Mountain, *Ky., U.S.* 36°53′ N, 82°58′ W 96
Black Mountain, *Va., U.S.* 36°52′ N, 83°2′ W 80
Black Mountains, *Ariz., U.S.* 34°56′ N, 114°28′ W 101
Black Mountains, *Calif., U.S.* 36°10′ N, 116°46′ W 101
Black Mountains, *U.K.* 52°4′ N, 3°9′ W 162
Black Peak, *Ariz., U.S.* 34°6′ N, 114°15′ W 101
Black Peak, *N. Mex., U.S.* 32°54′ N, 108°14′ W 92
Black Pine Peak, *Idaho, U.S.* 42°8′ N, 113°12′ W 90
Black Range, *N. Mex., U.S.* 33°29′ N, 108°42′ W 112
Black, river, *Ark., U.S.* 35°51′ N, 91°15′ W 80
Black River Falls, *Wis., U.S.* 44°17′ N, 90°52′ W 94
Black, river, *La., U.S.* 31°35′ N, 91°54′ W 103
Black, river, *Minn., U.S.* 48°25′ N, 94°20′ W 90
Black, river, *N.Y., U.S.* 44°3′ N, 75°54′ W 80
Black Rock Desert, *Nev., U.S.* 40°50′ N, 119°26′ W 90
Black Rock Range, *Nev., U.S.* 41°25′ N, 119°9′ W 90
Black Sea 43°19′ N, 33°22′ E 158
Black Volta, river, *Ghana* 8°33′ N, 2°3′ W 222
Black Volta see Mouhoun, river, *Burkina Faso* 11°43′ N, 4°30′ W 222
Black Warrior, river, *Ala., U.S.* 34°6′ N, 88°13′ W 80
Blackall, *Austral.* 24°26′ S, 145°31′ E 231
Blackburn, *U.K.* 53°45′ N, 2°30′ W 162
Blackburn, Mount, *Alas., U.S.* 61°36′ N, 143°37′ W 98
Blackdown Hills, *U.K.* 50°56′ N, 3°7′ W 162
Blackduck, *Minn., U.S.* 47°42′ N, 94°33′ W 90
Blackfoot, *Idaho, U.S.* 43°11′ N, 112°20′ W 90
Blackfoot Mountains, *Idaho, U.S.* 42°58′ N, 111°45′ W 90
Blackie, *Can.* 50°37′ N, 113°37′ W 108
Blackmoor Vale, *U.K.* 50°57′ N, 2°24′ W 162
Blackpool, *U.K.* 53°49′ N, 3°3′ W 162
Blacksburg, *Va., U.S.* 37°13′ N, 80°26′ W 96
Blackstone, *Mass., U.S.* 42°0′ N, 71°33′ W 104
Blackstone, river, *Can.* 61°10′ N, 123°2′ W 108
Blackville, *Can.* 46°44′ N, 65°51′ W 94
Blackwell, *Okla., U.S.* 36°46′ N, 97°17′ W 92
Blackwell, *Tex., U.S.* 32°3′ N, 100°19′ W 92
Blaenau Ffestiniog, *U.K.* 52°59′ N, 3°55′ W 162
Blåfjellhatten, peak, *Nor.* 64°6′ N, 13°15′ E 152
Blagaj, *Bosn. and Herzg.* 44°3′ N, 17°11′ E 168
Blagodarnyy, *Russ.* 45°3′ N, 43°20′ E 158
Blagoevgrad, *Bulg.* 42°1′ N, 23°6′ E 168
Blagoevgrad, adm. division, *Bulg.* 41°27′ N, 23°5′ E 168
Blagopoluchiya, Zaliv 75°8′ N, 58°41′ E 160
Blagoveshchenka, *Russ.* 52°49′ N, 79°55′ E 184
Blagoveshchensk, *Russ.* 50°22′ N, 127°32′ E 198
Blagoveshchenskoye, *Russ.* 61°28′ N, 42°36′ E 154
Blagoyevo, *Russ.* 63°25′ N, 47°57′ E 154
Blaiken, *Nor.* 65°15′ N, 16°49′ E 152
Blaine, *Wash., U.S.* 48°58′ N, 122°44′ W 100
Blainville-sur-l'Eau, *Fr.* 48°32′ N, 6°24′ E 163
Blair, *Nebr., U.S.* 41°31′ N, 96°8′ W 90
Blaj, *Rom.* 46°10′ N, 23°57′ E 156
Blake Plateu, *North Atlantic Ocean* 29°56′ N, 78°19′ W 253
Blake Point, *Mich., U.S.* 47°58′ N, 88°28′ W 110
Blake-Bahama Ridge, *North Atlantic Ocean* 29°6′ N, 73°10′ W 253
Blakeney, *U.K.* 52°57′ N, 1°1′ E 162
Blakeney, *U.K.* 51°45′ N, 2°29′ W 162
Blakiston, Mount, *Can.* 49°4′ N, 114°8′ W 90
Blâmont, *Fr.* 48°34′ N, 6°50′ E 163
Blanc, Cap, *Sp.* 39°9′ N, 2°28′ E 150
Blanc, Cap, *Western Sahara, Mor.* 20°59′ N, 17°36′ W 222
Blanc, Mont, peak, *Fr.-It.* 45°50′ N, 6°49′ E 150
Blanc, Réservoir, lake, *Can.* 47°46′ N, 73°19′ W 94
Blanca, *Bahía* 39°3′ S, 62°43′ W 139
Blanca Peak, Sierra, *N. Mex., U.S.* 33°21′ N, 105°52′ W 92
Blanca, Sierra, peak, *Tex., U.S.* 31°13′ N, 105°30′ W 92
Blanchard, *La., U.S.* 32°34′ N, 93°55′ W 103
Blanchard, *Mich., U.S.* 43°30′ N, 85°5′ W 102
Blanchard, *Okla., U.S.* 35°7′ N, 97°40′ W 92
Blanchardville, *Wis., U.S.* 42°47′ N, 89°52′ W 102
Blanchester, *Ohio, U.S.* 39°17′ N, 83°59′ W 102
Blanchland, *U.K.* 54°51′ N, 2°4′ W 162
Blanco, *Tex., U.S.* 30°5′ N, 98°25′ W 92
Blanco, *Bahía* 29°0′ N, 115°4′ W 92
Blanco, Cabo, *C.R.* 9°31′ N, 85°55′ W 115
Blanco, Cape, *Oreg., U.S.* 42°39′ N, 124°56′ W 90
Blanco, Lago, lake, *Arg.* 45°56′ S, 71°8′ W 134
Blanco, Punta, *Mex.* 29°6′ N, 115°5′ W 92
Blanco, river, *Arg.* 29°28′ S, 69°10′ W 134
Blanco, river, *Bol.* 14°47′ S, 63°37′ W 137
Blandford Forum, *U.K.* 50°51′ N, 2°10′ W 162
Blanding, *Utah, U.S.* 37°37′ N, 109°29′ W 92
Blanes, *Sp.* 41°41′ N, 2°48′ E 164
Blangy, *Fr.* 49°54′ N, 1°37′ E 163
Blankenberge, *Belg.* 51°18′ N, 3°7′ E 163
Blankenheim, *Ger.* 50°26′ N, 6°39′ E 167
Blanquilla, La, island, *Venez.* 11°59′ N, 64°58′ W 116
Blantyre, *Malawi* 15°52′ S, 35°2′ E 224
Blasket Islands, *Atlantic Ocean* 51°59′ N, 11°30′ W 150
Błaszki, *Pol.* 51°39′ N, 18°27′ E 152
Blatec, *Maced.* 41°49′ N, 22°35′ E 168
Blato, *Croatia* 42°55′ N, 16°46′ E 168
Blattnicksele, *Nor.* 65°18′ N, 17°38′ E 152
Bléneau, *Fr.* 47°42′ N, 2°56′ E 150
Blenheim, *Can.* 42°20′ N, 82°0′ W 102
Blenheim, *N.Z.* 41°32′ S, 173°55′ E 240
Blenheim Palace, site, *U.K.* 51°49′ N, 1°23′ W 162
Bletchley, *U.K.* 51°59′ N, 0°45′ E 162
Bleue, *Indonesia* 5°0′ N, 96°13′ E 196
Bleus, Monts, *Dem. Rep. of the Congo* 1°8′ N, 29°35′ E 224
Blexen, *Ger.* 53°31′ N, 8°33′ E 163
Blida, *Alg.* 36°27′ N, 2°49′ E 150
Blind River, *Can.* 46°11′ N, 82°58′ W 94
Blinisht, *Alban.* 41°52′ N, 19°59′ E 168
Blissfield, *Mich., U.S.* 41°49′ N, 83°51′ W 102
Blitta, *Togo* 8°20′ N, 0°58′ E 222
Block Island, *R.I., U.S.* 41°12′ N, 71°43′ W 104
Bloedriver, *S. Af.* 27°56′ S, 30°32′ E 227
Bloemfontein, *S. Af.* 29°9′ S, 26°3′ E 227
Bloemhof, *S. Af.* 27°40′ S, 25°34′ E 227
Blois, *Fr.* 47°35′ N, 1°20′ E 150
Blönduós, *Ice.* 65°39′ N, 20°21′ W 246
Bloodvein, river, *Can.* 51°25′ N, 96°32′ W 108
Bloody Mountain, *Calif., U.S.* 37°32′ N, 119°0′ W 92
Bloody Run Hills, *Nev., U.S.* 41°6′ N, 117°59′ W 90
Bloomburg, *Tex., U.S.* 33°8′ N, 94°4′ W 103
Bloomer, *Wis., U.S.* 45°6′ N, 91°29′ W 94
Bloomfield, *Conn., U.S.* 41°49′ N, 72°44′ W 104
Bloomfield, *Iowa, U.S.* 40°44′ N, 92°25′ W 94
Bloomfield, *Nebr., U.S.* 42°33′ N, 97°39′ W 90
Bloomfield, *N. Mex., U.S.* 36°42′ N, 107°59′ W 92
Bloomfield Hills, *Mich., U.S.* 42°35′ N, 83°16′ W 102
Bloomingburg, *Ohio, U.S.* 39°35′ N, 83°24′ W 102
Bloomingdale, *N.Y., U.S.* 44°24′ N, 74°6′ W 104
Bloomington, *Ill., U.S.* 40°28′ N, 88°59′ W 102
Bloomington, *Ind., U.S.* 39°10′ N, 86°32′ W 102
Bloomington, *Tex., U.S.* 28°38′ N, 96°54′ W 96
Bloomsburg, *Pa., U.S.* 40°59′ N, 76°28′ W 94
Bloomville, *Ohio, U.S.* 41°2′ N, 83°1′ W 102
Blouberg, peak, *S. Af.* 23°5′ S, 28°52′ E 227
Blount Nunatak, peak, *Antarctica* 83°20′ S, 52°56′ W 248
Blue Bell Knoll, peak, *Utah, U.S.* 38°8′ N, 111°34′ W 90
Blue Diamond, *Nev., U.S.* 36°2′ N, 115°25′ W 101
Blue Hill, *Nebr., U.S.* 40°18′ N, 98°27′ W 90
Blue Hill Bay 44°6′ N, 68°45′ W 111
Blue Lagoon National Park, *Zambia* 15°36′ S, 26°55′ E 224
Blue Lake, *Calif., U.S.* 40°53′ N, 124°0′ W 90
Blue Mound, *Ill., U.S.* 39°41′ N, 89°8′ W 102
Blue Mountain, *Pa., U.S.* 40°30′ N, 76°43′ W 94
Blue Mountain Pass, *Oreg., U.S.* 42°18′ N, 117°50′ W 90
Blue Mountain, peak, *Ark., U.S.* 34°38′ N, 94°8′ W 96
Blue Mountain, peak, *Calif., U.S.* 41°49′ N, 120°57′ W 90
Blue Mountain, peak, *Nev., U.S.* 40°58′ N, 118°10′ W 90
Blue Mountain, peak, *Oreg., U.S.* 42°19′ N, 117°58′ W 90
Blue Mountains, *Oreg., U.S.* 45°14′ N, 118°33′ W 90
Blue Nile, adm. division, *Sudan* 11°18′ N, 33°10′ E 182
Blue Nile see Ābay, river, *Eth.* 11°15′ N, 38°15′ E 224
Blue Rapids, *Kans., U.S.* 39°40′ N, 96°40′ W 94
Blue Ridge, *Can.* 54°8′ N, 115°24′ W 108
Blue Ridge, *Ga., U.S.* 34°50′ N, 84°19′ W 96
Blue Ridge, mountains, *North America* 36°39′ N, 80°30′ W 96
Blue River, *Can.* 52°6′ N, 119°19′ W 108
Blue, river, *Can.* 59°23′ N, 129°53′ W 108
Blue Springs, *Nebr., U.S.* 40°7′ N, 96°41′ W 92
Blue Stack Mountains, *Ire.* 54°44′ N, 8°11′ W 150
Bluefields, *Nicar.* 12°1′ N, 83°47′ W 116
Bluenose Lake, *Can.* 68°21′ N, 120°48′ W 98
Bluff, *Alas., U.S.* 64°43′ N, 147°13′ W 98
Bluff, *N.Z.* 46°37′ S, 168°20′ E 240
Bluff, *Utah, U.S.* 37°16′ N, 109°33′ W 92
Bluff, Cape, *Can.* 52°49′ N, 56°38′ W 111
Bluff Knoll, peak, *Austral.* 34°26′ S, 118°1′ E 230
Bluffton, *Ind., U.S.* 40°44′ N, 85°10′ W 102
Bluffton, *Ohio, U.S.* 40°53′ N, 83°53′ W 102
Bluffy Lake, lake, *Can.* 50°46′ N, 93°23′ W 90
Blumenau, *Braz.* 26°57′ S, 49°3′ W 138
Blumenthal, *Ger.* 53°11′ N, 8°34′ E 163
Blunt, *S. Dak., U.S.* 44°30′ N, 99°59′ W 90
Blustry Mountain, *Can.* 50°36′ N, 121°48′ W 90
Bly, *Oreg., U.S.* 42°24′ N, 121°3′ W 90
Blyth, *Can.* 43°44′ N, 81°25′ W 102
Blyth, *U.K.* 53°22′ N, 1°4′ W 162
Blyth Range, *Austral.* 26°54′ S, 129°8′ E 230
Blythe, *Calif., U.S.* 33°36′ N, 114°36′ W 101
Blytheville, *Ark., U.S.* 35°55′ N, 89°56′ W 82
Bø, *Nor.* 59°24′ N, 9°1′ E 152
Bø, *Nor.* 61°8′ N, 5°18′ E 152
Bø, *Nor.* 68°36′ N, 14°34′ E 152
Bo, *Sierra Leone* 7°58′ N, 11°44′ W 222
Bo Duc, *Vietnam* 11°59′ N, 106°48′ E 202
Bo River, *Sudan* 6°50′ N, 27°54′ E 224
Boa Nova, *Braz.* 14°25′ S, 40°11′ W 138
Boa Vista, *Braz.* 2°50′ N, 60°43′ W 130
Boac, *Philippines* 13°28′ N, 121°52′ E 203
Boali, *Cen. Af. Rep.* 4°47′ N, 18°6′ E 218
Boane, *Mozambique* 25°58′ S, 32°19′ E 227
Boang, island, *P.N.G.* 3°20′ S, 153°22′ E 192
Boario Terme, *It.* 45°54′ N, 10°9′ E 167
Boatswain, Baie 51°47′ N, 79°34′ W 110
Boaz, *Ala., U.S.* 34°11′ N, 86°10′ W 96
Boba, *Hung.* 47°10′ N, 17°11′ E 168
Bobai, *China* 22°16′ N, 110°1′ E 198
Bobbio, *It.* 44°45′ N, 9°22′ E 167
Böblingen, *Ger.* 48°40′ N, 9°0′ E 152
Bobo Dioulasso, *Burkina Faso* 11°11′ N, 4°18′ W 222
Bobonaza, river, *Ecua.* 2°7′ S, 76°57′ W 136
Bobonong, *Botswana* 22°0′ S, 28°25′ E 227
Bobota, *Rom.* 47°22′ N, 22°48′ E 168
Bobovdol, *Bulg.* 42°22′ N, 23°0′ E 168
Boboye, *Niger* 13°0′ N, 2°47′ E 222
Bobrov, *Russ.* 51°7′ N, 40°1′ E 158
Bobures, *Venez.* 9°14′ N, 71°11′ W 136
Boby, peak, *Madagascar* 22°13′ S, 46°48′ E 220
Boca del Río, *Mex.* 25°18′ N, 108°32′ W 112
Boca do Acre, *Braz.* 8°48′ S, 67°24′ W 130
Boca do Curuquetê, *Braz.* 8°23′ S, 65°43′ W 130
Boca do Jari, *Braz.* 1°7′ S, 51°58′ W 130
Boca Grande, *Fla., U.S.* 26°45′ N, 82°15′ W 105
Boca Mavaca, *Venez.* 2°30′ N, 65°15′ W 136
Boca Raton, *Fla., U.S.* 26°22′ N, 80°7′ W 105
Bocaiúva, *Braz.* 17°9′ S, 43°47′ W 138
Bocay, *Nicar.* 14°19′ N, 85°8′ W 115
Bocay, river, *Nicar.* 13°34′ N, 85°23′ W 115
Boceguillas, *Sp.* 41°20′ N, 3°38′ W 164
Bocheykovo, *Belarus* 55°1′ N, 29°9′ E 166
Bocholt, *Ger.* 51°50′ N, 6°37′ E 167
Bochum, *Ger.* 51°29′ N, 7°12′ E 167
Bockhorn, *Ger.* 53°23′ N, 8°1′ E 163
Bockum-Hövel, *Ger.* 51°41′ N, 7°44′ E 167
Bocón, river, *Col.* 3°4′ N, 68°58′ W 136
Boçoroca, *Braz.* 28°42′ S, 54°57′ W 139
Bocşa, *Rom.* 45°22′ N, 21°43′ E 168
Boda, *Cen. Af. Rep.* 4°21′ N, 17°26′ E 218
Böda, *Sw.* 57°15′ N, 17°1′ E 152
Bodaybo, *Russ.* 57°59′ N, 114°13′ E 160
Boddam, *U.K.* 57°27′ N, 1°48′ W 150
Bodden Town, *U.K.* 19°18′ N, 81°15′ W 115
Bode, river, *Ger.* 51°55′ N, 11°15′ E 152
Bode Sadu, *Nig.* 8°54′ N, 4°47′ E 222
Bodega Head, *Calif., U.S.* 38°17′ N, 123°21′ W 90
Boden, *Nor.* 65°49′ N, 21°40′ E 152
Bodfish, *Calif., U.S.* 35°35′ N, 118°30′ W 101
Bodhei, *Kenya* 1°51′ S, 40°46′ E 224
Bodiam, *U.K.* 51°0′ N, 0°33′ E 162
Bodle, *Eth.* 5°3′ N, 42°51′ E 218
Bodmin Moor, *U.K.* 50°30′ N, 5°4′ W 150
Bodø, *Nor.* 67°16′ N, 14°41′ E 160
Bodocó, *Braz.* 7°48′ S, 39°56′ W 132
Bodoquena, Serra da, *Braz.* 20°23′ S, 56°53′ W 132
Bodrum, *Turk.* 37°2′ N, 27°24′ E 156
Boeae, ruin(s), *Gr.* 36°30′ N, 22°58′ E 156
Boende, *Dem. Rep. of the Congo* 0°15′ N, 20°50′ E 218
Boerne, *Tex., U.S.* 29°47′ N, 98°45′ W 92
Boeuf, river, *La., U.S.* 32°15′ N, 92°17′ W 80
Boffa, *Guinea* 10°11′ N, 14°6′ W 222
Bofosso, *Guinea* 8°38′ N, 9°43′ W 222
Bogachiel, river, *Wash., U.S.* 47°52′ N, 124°20′ W 100
Bogalusa, *La., U.S.* 30°45′ N, 89°52′ W 103
Bogan, river, *Austral.* 30°31′ S, 147°4′ E 230
Bogandé, *Burkina Faso* 12°56′ N, 0°9′ E 222
Bogangolo, *Cen. Af. Rep.* 5°34′ N, 18°18′ E 218
Bogani Nani Wartabone National Park, *Indonesia* 0°23′ N, 123°11′ E 238
Bogarra, *Sp.* 38°34′ N, 2°13′ W 164
Bogart, Mount, *Can.* 50°55′ N, 115°20′ W 90
Bogatić, *Serb.* 44°50′ N, 19°29′ E 168
Bogatka, *Russ.* 63°16′ N, 44°13′ E 154
Bogazi, *Northern Cyprus, Cyprus* 35°19′ N, 33°57′ E 194
Boğazkale, *Turk.* 40°1′ N, 34°35′ E 156
Boğazlıyan, *Turk.* 39°10′ N, 35°15′ E 156
Bogcang, river, *China* 31°38′ N, 85°48′ E 188
Bogda Feng, peak, *China* 43°51′ N, 88°12′ E 184
Bogdan, peak, *Bulg.* 42°35′ N, 24°23′ E 156
Bogdanovich, *Russ.* 56°47′ N, 62°2′ E 154
Bogdanovka, *Ga.* 41°16′ N, 43°34′ E 195
Bogdanovka, *Russ.* 52°10′ N, 52°33′ E 158
Bögen, *Kaz.* 46°12′ N, 61°16′ E 184
Bogetići, *Mont.* 42°40′ N, 18°58′ E 168
Boggeragh Mountains, *Ire.* 52°0′ N, 9°3′ W 150
Boggola, Mount, *Austral.* 23°49′ S, 117°26′ E 230
Boggs, Cape, *Antarctica* 70°39′ S, 63°52′ W 248
Boghar, *Alg.* 35°54′ N, 2°43′ E 150
Boglárlelle, *Hung.* 46°45′ N, 17°40′ E 168
Bognor Regis, *U.K.* 50°47′ N, 0°40′ E 162
Bogo, *Philippines* 11°3′ N, 124°0′ E 203
Bogogobo, *Botswana* 26°37′ S, 21°54′ E 227
Bogojevo, *Serb.* 45°31′ N, 19°8′ E 168
Bogol Manyo, *Eth.* 4°29′ N, 41°30′ E 224
Bogomila, *Maced.* 41°35′ N, 21°27′ E 168
Bogoroditsk, *Russ.* 53°45′ N, 38°7′ E 154
Bogorodsk, *Russ.* 62°16′ N, 52°36′ E 154
Bogorodskoye, *Russ.* 52°24′ N, 140°35′ E 190
Bogorodskoye, *Russ.* 57°48′ N, 50°50′ E 154
Bogotá, *Col.* 4°36′ N, 74°13′ W 136
Bogotol, *Russ.* 56°13′ N, 89°39′ E 169
Bogou, *Togo* 10°38′ N, 0°9′ E 222
Bogovina, *Serb.* 43°53′ N, 21°55′ E 168
Bogra, *Bangladesh* 24°49′ N, 89°21′ E 197
Boguchany, *Russ.* 58°17′ N, 97°27′ E 160
Boguchar, *Russ.* 49°59′ N, 40°33′ E 158
Bogué, *Mauritania* 16°35′ N, 14°19′ W 222
Bogue Chitto, *Miss., U.S.* 31°26′ N, 90°27′ W 103
Bogue Chitto, river, *La., U.S.* 30°48′ N, 90°14′ W 103
Bogushevsk, *Belarus* 54°51′ N, 30°17′ E 152
Bogutovac, *Serb.* 43°38′ N, 20°32′ E 168
Bohain, *Fr.* 49°59′ N, 3°26′ E 163
Bohe, *China* 21°31′ N, 111°9′ E 198
Bohicon, *Benin* 7°13′ N, 2°3′ E 222
Böhmer Wald, *Ger.* 49°28′ N, 12°14′ E 152
Bohodukhiv, *Ukr.* 50°11′ N, 35°32′ E 158
Bohol, island, *Philippines* 9°7′ N, 123°42′ E 192
Bohol Sea 8°50′ N, 123°36′ E 192
Böhönye, *Hung.* 46°23′ N, 17°23′ E 168
Böhöt, *Mongolia* 45°8′ N, 108°10′ E 198
Bohu (Bagrax), *China* 41°56′ N, 86°40′ E 184
Boi, *Nig.* 9°34′ N, 9°29′ E 222
Boiaçu, *Braz.* 0°28′ N, 61°48′ W 130
Boila, *Mozambique* 16°10′ S, 39°50′ E 224
Boim, *Braz.* 3°4′ S, 55°16′ W 130
Boing, *Sudan* 9°55′ N, 33°45′ E 224
Boinso, *Ghana* 5°31′ N, 2°44′ W 222
Boipeba, Ilha de, island, *Braz.* 14°3′ S, 39°38′ W 132
Bois Blanc Island, *Mich., U.S.* 45°25′ N, 84°20′ W 81
Bois, river, *Braz.* 18°11′ S, 50°8′ W 138
Boise, *Idaho, U.S.* 43°36′ N, 116°20′ W 90
Boise City, *Okla., U.S.* 36°42′ N, 102°31′ W 92
Boissevain, *Can.* 49°14′ N, 100°4′ W 90
Bojeador, Cape, *Philippines* 18°30′ N, 120°11′ E 203
Boji Plain, *Kenya* 1°41′ N, 39°35′ E 224
Bojnūrd, *Iran* 37°28′ N, 57°18′ E 180
Bojo, island, *Indonesia* 0°36′ N, 98°30′ E 196
Bojuru, *Braz.* 31°38′ S, 51°31′ W 139
Boka, *Serb.* 45°21′ N, 20°50′ E 156
Bo'ka, *Uzb.* 40°49′ N, 69°12′ E 197
Bokada, *Dem. Rep. of the Congo* 4°8′ N, 19°21′ E 218
Bokalia, spring, *Chad* 17°24′ N, 19°14′ E 216
Bokani, *Nig.* 9°25′ N, 5°10′ E 222
Bokatola, *Dem. Rep. of the Congo* 0°36′ N, 18°44′ E 218
Boké, *Guinea* 10°55′ N, 14°18′ W 222
Bokito, *Cameroon* 4°29′ N, 10°58′ E 222
Bokol, peak, *Kenya* 1°46′ N, 36°58′ E 224
Bökönbaev, *Kyrg.* 42°7′ N, 77°7′ E 184
Bokongo, *Dem. Rep. of the Congo* 3°21′ N, 20°56′ E 218
Bokoro, *Chad* 12°21′ N, 17°3′ E 216
Bokote, *Dem. Rep. of the Congo* 0°7′ N, 20°5′ E 218
Bokovskaya, *Russ.* 49°14′ N, 41°45′ E 158
Bokpyinn, *Myanmar* 11°15′ N, 98°45′ E 202
Boksitogorsk, *Russ.* 59°28′ N, 33°51′ E 154
Bokungu, *Dem. Rep. of the Congo* 0°45′ N, 22°27′ E 218
Bokurdak, *Turkm.* 38°47′ N, 58°29′ E 180
Bol, *Chad* 13°33′ N, 14°44′ E 216
Bol, *Croatia* 43°15′ N, 16°39′ E 168
Bolaiti, *Dem. Rep. of the Congo* 3°16′ S, 24°51′ E 224
Bolama, *Guinea-Bissau* 11°35′ N, 15°31′ W 222
Bolan Pass, *Pak.* 29°43′ N, 67°33′ E 186
Bolaños, river, *Mex.* 21°18′ N, 103°53′ W 114
Bolderāja, *Latv.* 57°1′ N, 24°1′ E 166
Boldeşti, oil field, *Rom.* 45°2′ N, 25°57′ E 156
Bole, *China* 44°49′ N, 82°9′ E 184
Bole, *Ghana* 9°2′ N, 2°32′ W 222
Boleko, *Dem. Rep. of the Congo* 1°31′ S, 19°50′ E 218
Bolesławiec, *Pol.* 51°15′ N, 15°35′ E 152
Boleszkowice, *Pol.* 52°42′ N, 14°33′ E 152
Bolgatanga, *Ghana* 10°45′ N, 0°53′ E 222
Bolhrad, *Ukr.* 45°41′ N, 28°38′ E 156
Boliden, *Nor.* 64°52′ N, 20°20′ E 152
Boligee, *Ala., U.S.* 32°45′ N, 88°3′ W 103
Bolinao, Cape, *Philippines* 16°20′ N, 119°24′ E 203
Bolívar, *Bol.* 12°9′ S, 67°21′ W 137
Bolívar, *Col.* 1°48′ N, 77°0′ W 136
Bolivar, *Mo., U.S.* 37°36′ N, 93°24′ W 96
Bolívar, *Peru* 7°16′ S, 77°50′ W 130
Bolivar, *Tenn., U.S.* 35°14′ N, 88°59′ W 96
Bolívar, adm. division, *Col.* 9°45′ N, 75°9′ W 115
Bolívar, adm. division, *Venez.* 6°10′ N, 64°34′ W 136
Bolívar, Cerro, peak, *Venez.* 7°20′ N, 63°34′ W 130
Bolivar, Mount, *Oreg., U.S.* 42°46′ N, 123°55′ W 90
Bolívar, Pico, peak, *Venez.* 8°33′ N, 71°7′ W 136
Bolivia 16°4′ S, 66°43′ W 132
Bolivia, *Cuba* 22°4′ N, 78°18′ W 116

Boljevac, *Serb.* 43°50' N, 21°58' E 168
Boljevci, *Serb.* 44°43' N, 20°12' E 168
Bolkhov, *Russ.* 53°26' N, 36°1' E 154
Bollendorf, *Ger.* 49°51' N, 6°21' E 167
Bollnäs, *Nor.* 61°20' N, 16°22' E 152
Bollstabruk, *Nor.* 62°59' N, 17°39' E 152
Bolluk Gölü, lake, *Turk.* 38°27' N, 32°29' E 156
Bollullos Par del Condado, *Sp.* 37°20' N, 6°33' W 164
Bolnisi, *Ga.* 41°25' N, 44°32' E 195
Bolobo, *Dem. Rep. of the Congo* 2°12' S, 16°16' E 218
Bologna, *It.* 44°29' N, 11°20' E 167
Bologne, *Fr.* 48°11' N, 5°8' E 163
Bolognesi, *Peru* 10°3' S, 74°0' W 137
Bologoye, *Russ.* 57°52' N, 34°4' E 154
Bolomba, *Dem. Rep. of the Congo* 0°30' N, 19°9' E 218
Bolona, *Côte d'Ivoire* 10°18' N, 6°26' W 222
Bolong, *Chad* 12°3' N, 17°46' E 216
Bolotnoye, *Russ.* 55°38' N, 84°26' E 169
Bolotovskoye, *Russ.* 58°31' N, 62°26' E 154
Bolpebra, *Bol.* 10°59' S, 69°34' W 137
Bol'shakovo, *Russ.* 54°51' N, 21°38' E 166
Bol'shaya Bicha, *Russ.* 57°56' N, 70°36' E 169
Bol'shaya Chernigovka, *Russ.* 52°7' N, 50°52' E 158
Bol'shaya Glushitsa, *Russ.* 52°24' N, 50°28' E 158
Bol'shaya Kheta, river, *Russ.* 68°22' N, 82°43' E 169
Bol'shaya Pyssa, *Russ.* 64°11' N, 48°44' E 154
Bol'shaya Tovra, *Russ.* 64°5' N, 41°41' E 154
Bol'shaya Ucha, *Russ.* 56°36' N, 52°7' E 154
Bol'shaya Vladimirovka, *Kaz.* 50°53' N, 79°29' E 184
Bol'sheretsk, *Russ.* 52°20' N, 156°22' E 238
Bol'shevik Island, *Russ.* 79°0' N, 102°0' E 255
Bol'shezemel'skaya Tundra, region, *Europe* 66°30' N, 52°39' E 154
Bol'shiye Kozly, *Russ.* 65°18' N, 39°45' E 154
Bol'shiye Sluditsy, *Russ.* 59°16' N, 30°28' E 166
Bol'shiye Tarkhany, *Russ.* 54°42' N, 48°34' E 154
Bol'shoy Anyuy, river, *Russ.* 68°20' N, 161°41' E 160
Bol'shoy Begichev, Ostrov, island, *Russ.* 73°50' N, 113°22' E 160
Bol'shoy Begichev, Ostrov, island, *Russ.* 74°38' N, 106°27' E 160
Bol'shoy Chirk, *Russ.* 63°54' N, 47°7' E 154
Bol'shoy Ental', *Russ.* 60°54' N, 49°40' E 154
Bol'shoy Lyakhovskiy, Ostrov, island, *Russ.* 72°34' N, 143°33' E 160
Bol'shoy Porog, *Russ.* 65°35' N, 90°11' E 169
Bol'shoy Sabsk, *Russ.* 59°8' N, 29°2' E 166
Bol'shoy Shantar, Ostrov, island, *Russ.* 55°15' N, 136°51' E 160
Bol'shoy Tyuters, Ostrov, island, *Russ.* 59°48' N, 27°15' E 166
Bolsover, *U.K.* 53°13' N, 1°18' W 162
Bolsward, *Neth.* 53°4' N, 5°30' E 163
Bolt Head, *U.K.* 50°14' N, 3°49' W 150
Boltaña, *Sp.* 42°26' N, 6°356' E 164
Bolton, *U.K.* 53°34' N, 2°27' W 162
Bolton, *Vt., U.S.* 44°22' N, 72°53' W 104
Bolton Abbey, site, *U.K.* 53°59' N, 1°57' W 162
Bolton Lake, lake, *Can.* 54°10' N, 96°19' W 108
Bolton Landing, *N.Y., U.S.* 43°33' N, 73°41' W 104
Bolu, *Turk.* 40°43' N, 31°36' E 156
Boluo, *China* 23°7' N, 114°16' E 198
Bolvadin, *Turk.* 38°43' N, 31°2' E 156
Bóly, *Hung.* 45°57' N, 18°31' E 168
Bom Comércio, *Braz.* 9°46' S, 65°56' W 137
Bom Despacho, *Braz.* 19°44' S, 45°16' W 138
Bom Destino, *Braz.* 9°46' S, 67°32' W 137
Bom Jesus, *Braz.* 28°39' S, 50°24' W 138
Bom Jesus, *Braz.* 9°4' S, 44°23' W 132
Bom Jesus da Gurguéia, Serra, *Braz.* 8°41' S, 43°40' W 133
Bom Jesus da Lapa, *Braz.* 13°18' S, 43°25' W 138
Bom Jesus do Itabapoana, *Braz.* 21°11' S, 41°41' W 138
Bom Retiro, *Braz.* 27°49' S, 49°30' W 138
Boma, *Angola* 5°58' S, 13°6' E 207
Boma National Park, *Sudan* 6°33' N, 33°45' E 224
Bomana, *Dem. Rep. of the Congo* 1°25' N, 18°25' E 218
Bomassa, *Congo* 2°23' N, 16°10' E 218
Bombay see Mumbai, *India* 18°57' N, 72°49' E 188
Bombo, *Uganda* 0°32' N, 32°30' E 224
Bomdila, *India* 27°18' N, 92°25' E 188
Bomi (Bowo), *China* 29°53' N, 95°40' E 188
Bomili, *Dem. Rep. of the Congo* 1°42' N, 27°5' E 224
Bomokandi, river, *Dem. Rep. of the Congo* 3°15' N, 27°9' E 224
Bomongo, *Dem. Rep. of the Congo* 1°26' N, 18°19' E 218
Bomotu, *Dem. Rep. of the Congo* 3°46' N, 19°1' E 218
Bomu, oil field, *Nig.* 4°37' N, 7°14' E 222
Bomu, river, *Africa* 5°3' N, 23°57' E 206
Bon Secour, *Ala., U.S.* 30°18' N, 87°44' W 103
Bon Wier, *Tex., U.S.* 30°44' N, 93°39' W 103
Bonāb, *Iran* 37°19' N, 46°10' E 195
Bonaire, island, *Netherlands* 12°0' N, 68°0' W 118
Bonampak, ruin(s), *Mex.* 16°39' N, 91°8' W 115
Bonandolok, *Indonesia* 1°51' N, 98°49' E 196
Bonanza, *Nicar.* 14°0' N, 84°35' W 115
Bonanza, *Oreg., U.S.* 42°13' N, 121°26' W 90
Bonanza, *Sp.* 36°48' N, 6°21' W 164
Bonanza, *Utah, U.S.* 40°0' N, 109°10' W 90
Bonaparte Archipelago, *Indian Ocean* 13°15' S, 122°48' E 230
Bonaparte Lake, *Can.* 51°17' N, 121°3' W 90
Bonaparte, Mount, *Wash., U.S.* 48°45' N, 119°13' W 90
Boñar, *Sp.* 42°50' N, 5°20' W 150
Bonaventure, *Can.* 48°9' N, 65°35' W 82
Bonavista, *Can.* 48°38' N, 53°7' W 111
Bonavista, Cape, *Can.* 48°43' N, 53°16' W 111
Bond, *Miss., U.S.* 30°53' N, 89°9' W 103
Bondari, *Russ.* 56°9' N, 28°20' E 166
Bondary, *Russ.* 52°58' N, 41°53' E 154
Bondeno, *It.* 44°54' N, 11°23' E 167
Bondo, *Dem. Rep. of the Congo* 3°49' N, 23°48' E 224
Bondoukou, *Côte d'Ivoire* 8°3' N, 2°49' W 222
Bondyug, *Russ.* 60°30' N, 55°58' E 154
Bone Creek, river, *Can.* 49°50' N, 109°18' W 90
Bône see Annaba, *Alg.* 36°53' N, 7°45' E 156
Bone, Teluk 4°59' S, 120°30' E 192
Bonesteel, *S. Dak., U.S.* 43°4' N, 98°58' W 90
Bonete, *Sp.* 38°52' N, 1°21' W 164
Bonete, Cerro, peak, *Arg.* 27°54' S, 68°55' W 132
Bonfinópolis de Minas, *Braz.* 16°33' S, 46°0' W 138
Bong Son, *Vietnam* 14°27' N, 109°0' E 202
Bonga, *Eth.* 7°12' N, 36°16' E 224
Bongandanga, *Dem. Rep. of the Congo* 1°29' N, 21°1' E 218
Bongao, *Philippines* 5°3' N, 119°44' E 203
Bongo, *Dem. Rep. of the Congo* 2°59' N, 20°1' E 218
Bongo, *Dem. Rep. of the Congo* 1°48' S, 17°39' E 218
Bongo, *Gabon* 2°9' S, 10°15' E 218
Bongolava, *Madagascar* 18°36' S, 45°27' E 220
Bongor, *Chad* 10°18' N, 15°23' E 216
Bongouanou, *Côte d'Ivoire* 6°35' N, 4°14' W 222
Bongoul, river, *Cen. Af. Rep.* 9°2' N, 21°9' E 218
Bonham, *Tex., U.S.* 33°34' N, 96°11' W 96
Bonifacio, *Fr.* 41°23' N, 9°11' E 156
Bonin Islands (Ogasawara Guntō), *North Pacific Ocean* 27°46' N, 140°2' E 190
Bonin Trench, *North Pacific Ocean* 23°46' N, 143°57' E 252
Bonita, *La., U.S.* 32°54' N, 91°41' W 103
Bonita Springs, *Fla., U.S.* 26°20' N, 81°47' W 105
Bonito, *Braz.* 21°9' S, 56°28' W 132
Bonito, peak, *Hond.* 15°35' N, 86°58' W 115
Bonkoukou, *Niger* 14°2' N, 3°10' E 222
Bonn, *Ger.* 50°44' N, 7°5' E 167
Bonne Terre, *Mo., U.S.* 37°55' N, 90°34' W 96
Bonner, *Mont., U.S.* 46°51' N, 113°48' W 90
Bonners Ferry, *Idaho, U.S.* 48°40' N, 116°21' W 90
Bonnet, *Fr.* 46°19' N, 1°54' E 150
Bonnet Plume, river, *Can.* 65°34' N, 134°14' W 98
Bonneval, *Fr.* 48°10' N, 1°24' E 163
Bonneville Salt Flats, *Utah, U.S.* 40°39' N, 114°12' W 90
Bonnie Rock, *Austral.* 30°34' S, 118°22' E 231
Bonny, *Fr.* 47°33' N, 2°50' E 150
Bonny, *Nig.* 4°26' N, 7°9' E 222
Bonny Reservoir, lake, *Colo., U.S.* 39°34' N, 102°37' W 90
Bonnyville, *Can.* 54°15' N, 110°43' W 108
Bonobono, *Philippines* 8°43' N, 117°36' E 203
Bonokoski Lake, lake, *Can.* 59°39' N, 104°7' W 108
Bonpland, *Arg.* 29°49' S, 57°27' W 139
Bonsall, *Calif., U.S.* 33°17' N, 117°15' W 101
Bonsecours, Baie 49°26' N, 64°20' W 111
Bontang, *Indonesia* 0°11' N, 117°21' E 192
Bontebok National Park, *S. Af.* 34°5' S, 20°21' E 227
Bonthe, *Sierra Leone* 7°32' N, 12°33' W 222
Bontoc, *Philippines* 17°6' N, 120°57' E 203
Bonvouloir Islands, *Solomon Sea* 10°6' S, 151°55' E 230
Bonyhád, *Hung.* 46°16' N, 18°31' E 168
Booker, *Tex., U.S.* 36°26' N, 100°33' W 96
Booker T. Washington National Monument, *Va., U.S.* 37°5' N, 79°48' W 96
Boola, *Guinea* 8°18' N, 8°43' W 222
Boomer, *W. Va., U.S.* 38°9' N, 81°18' W 94
Boone, *Colo., U.S.* 38°14' N, 104°16' W 90
Boone, *Iowa, U.S.* 42°3' N, 93°54' W 94
Boone, *N.C., U.S.* 36°13' N, 81°41' W 96
Booneville, *Ark., U.S.* 35°7' N, 93°56' W 96
Boonville, *Ind., U.S.* 38°2' N, 87°16' W 96
Boonville, *N.Y., U.S.* 43°28' N, 75°21' W 94
Boorama, *Somalia* 9°54' N, 43°6' E 216
Booroondara, Mount, *Austral.* 31°6' S, 145°5' E 230
Boothbay Harbor, *Me., U.S.* 43°51' N, 69°38' W 104
Boothia, Gulf of 70°9' N, 92°10' W 106
Boothia Peninsula, *Can.* 70°5' N, 95°32' W 106
Boothville, *La., U.S.* 29°19' N, 89°25' W 103
Booué, *Gabon* 4°237' S, 11°52' E 218
Bopolu, *Liberia* 6°58' N, 10°30' W 222
Boppard, *Ger.* 50°13' N, 7°35' E 167
Boqueirão, Serra do, *Braz.* 11°10' S, 44°0' W 132
Boquerón, *Cuba* 19°58' N, 75°7' W 116
Boquilla, Presa de la, lake, *Mex.* 27°34' N, 106°8' W 81
Boquillas del Carmen, *Mex.* 29°8' N, 103°0' W 92
Bor, *Russ.* 56°21' N, 44°9' E 154
Bor, *Serb.* 44°5' N, 22°6' E 168
Bor, *Sudan* 6°17' N, 31°39' E 207
Bor, *Sudan* 6°11' N, 31°32' E 224
Bor, *Turk.* 37°53' N, 34°31' E 156
Borah Peak, *Idaho, U.S.* 44°7' N, 113°51' W 90
Boralday, *Kaz.* 43°20' N, 76°51' E 184
Boran, *Kaz.* 48°0' N, 85°14' E 184
Boran, region, *Africa* 3°11' N, 38°18' E 224
Borås, *Nor.* 57°43' N, 12°56' E 152
Borau, *Sp.* 42°39' N, 0°36' E 150
Borāzjān, *Iran* 29°14' N, 51°12' E 196
Borba, *Braz.* 4°24' S, 59°36' W 130
Borbon, *Philippines* 10°49' N, 124°1' E 203
Borborema, Planalto da, *Braz.* 7°28' S, 38°3' W 132
Borchgrevink Coast, *Antarctica* 73°11' S, 178°45' W 248
Borçka, *Turk.* 41°22' N, 41°40' E 195
Bordeaux, *Fr.* 44°51' N, 0°36' E 150
Borden Island, *Can.* 79°8' N, 110°41' W 246
Borden Peninsula, *Can.* 72°43' N, 89°38' W 106
Bordertown, *Austral.* 36°18' S, 140°47' E 231
Bordj bou Arreridj, *Alg.* 36°3' N, 4°45' E 150
Bordj Bou Rerhda, *Alg.* 36°8' N, 5°22' E 150
Bordj Flye Sainte Marie, *Alg.* 27°16' N, 2°59' W 214
Bordj le Prieur, *Alg.* 21°20' N, 0°53' E 222
Bordj Messouda, *Alg.* 30°13' N, 9°24' E 216
Bordj Omar Driss, *Alg.* 28°6' N, 6°49' E 214
Bordj Welvert, *Alg.* 35°39' N, 3°52' E 150
Boré, *Mali* 15°7' N, 3°30' W 222
Boreas Nunatak, peak, *Antarctica* 71°27' S, 4°34' W 248
Borènta, *Mali* 15°49' N, 1°19' W 222
Borgå see Porvoo, *Fin.* 60°23' N, 25°40' E 166
Borgafjäll, *Nor.* 64°48' N, 15°1' E 152
Børgefjell, *Nor.* 65°12' N, 13°15' E 152
Børgefjell National Park, *Nor.* 65°12' N, 14°27' E 152
Borgentreich, *Ger.* 51°34' N, 9°15' E 167
Borger, *Neth.* 52°55' N, 6°47' E 163
Borger, *Tex., U.S.* 35°38' N, 101°24' W 92
Borgholm, *Sw.* 56°51' N, 16°37' E 152
Borghorst, *Ger.* 52°7' N, 7°24' E 167
Borgne, Lake 30°1' N, 89°42' W 103
Borgo, *It.* 46°3' N, 11°27' E 167
Borgo San Dalmazzo, *It.* 44°19' N, 7°29' E 167
Borgo San Lorenzo, *It.* 43°57' N, 11°22' E 167
Borgo Val di Taro, *It.* 44°29' N, 9°46' E 167
Borgomanero, *It.* 45°42' N, 8°29' E 167
Borgosesia, *It.* 45°43' N, 8°17' E 167
Borgou, region, *Africa* 10°9' N, 2°49' E 222
Borgsjö, *Nor.* 64°11' N, 17°48' E 152
Borgvattnet, *Nor.* 63°25' N, 15°49' E 154
Borhoyn Tal, *Mongolia* 43°44' N, 111°47' E 198
Bori, *Benin* 9°45' N, 2°25' E 222
Borikhan, *Laos* 18°36' N, 103°42' E 202
Börili, *Kaz.* 51°24' N, 52°44' E 158
Borisoglebsk, *Russ.* 51°21' N, 42°3' E 158
Borisovo Sudskoye, *Russ.* 59°52' N, 36°1' E 154
Boriziny (Port-Bergé), *Madagascar* 15°35' S, 47°43' E 220
Borj el Kessira, *Tun.* 32°14' N, 10°2' E 214
Borja, *Peru* 4°21' S, 77°36' W 130
Borja, *Sp.* 41°48' N, 1°33' W 164
Borjomi, *Ga.* 41°50' N, 43°22' E 180
Borkavichy, *Belarus* 55°39' N, 28°18' E 166
Borken, *Ger.* 51°50' N, 6°52' E 167
Borken, *Ger.* 51°3' N, 9°17' E 167
Borkou, region, *Africa* 19°13' N, 15°50' E 216
Borkovskaya, *Russ.* 65°10' N, 49°27' E 154
Borkum, *Ger.* 53°35' N, 6°40' E 163
Borkum, island, *Ger.* 53°36' N, 6°25' E 163
Borland, Mount, *Antarctica* 74°20' S, 67°18' E 248
Borlänge, *Nor.* 60°28' N, 15°23' E 152
Borleşti, *Rom.* 47°40' N, 23°19' E 168
Borley, Cape, *Antarctica* 65°54' S, 55°17' E 248
Borlova, *Rom.* 45°22' N, 22°23' E 168
Bormio, *It.* 46°28' N, 10°21' E 167
Borneo (Kalimantan), island, *Indonesia* 4°28' S, 111°26' E 192
Bornheim, *Ger.* 50°46' N, 6°59' E 167
Bornholm, island, *Den.* 55°18' N, 14°51' E 143
Borno, *It.* 45°57' N, 10°11' E 167
Bornos, *Sp.* 36°48' N, 5°45' W 164
Boro, *Mali* 12°54' N, 9°24' W 222
Boro, river, *Sudan* 8°28' N, 24°43' E 224
Borodūlikha, *Kaz.* 50°44' N, 80°49' E 184
Borokoro, *Guinea* 9°30' N, 10°23' W 222
Boromo, *Burkina Faso* 11°45' N, 2°57' W 222
Boron, *Calif., U.S.* 35°0' N, 117°40' W 101
Borotou, *Côte d'Ivoire* 8°41' N, 7°29' W 222
Boroughbridge, *U.K.* 54°6' N, 1°24' W 162
Borove, *Ukr.* 51°38' N, 25°51' E 152
Borovichi, *Russ.* 57°57' N, 29°39' E 166
Borovichi, *Russ.* 58°22' N, 33°57' E 154
Borovlyanka, *Russ.* 52°38' N, 84°33' E 184
Borovo, *Croatia* 45°24' N, 18°57' E 168
Borovsk, *Russ.* 55°9' N, 36°31' E 154
Borovskoy, *Kaz.* 53°47' N, 64°10' E 184
Borovtsi, *Bulg.* 43°18' N, 23°9' E 168
Borrego Springs, *Calif., U.S.* 33°15' N, 116°23' W 101
Borroloola, *Austral.* 16°7' S, 136°17' E 238
Borş, *Rom.* 47°6' N, 21°48' E 168
Borsod-Abaúj-Zemplén, adm. division, *Hung.* 48°17' N, 20°26' E 152
Borūjen, *Iran* 31°59' N, 51°20' E 180
Borūjerd, *Iran* 33°54' N, 48°44' E 180
Boryeong, *S. Korea* 36°21' N, 126°36' E 200
Borzna, *Ukr.* 51°13' N, 32°25' E 158
Börzsony, *Hung.* 47°52' N, 18°43' E 168
Borzya, *Russ.* 50°25' N, 116°39' E 190
Bosanska Dubica, *Bosn. and Herzg.* 45°10' N, 16°48' E 168
Bosanska Krupa, *Bosn. and Herzg.* 44°52' N, 16°9' E 168
Bosanski Brod, *Bosn. and Herzg.* 45°7' N, 18°1' E 168
Bosanski Novi, *Bosn. and Herzg.* 45°2' N, 16°22' E 168
Bosanski Petrovac, *Bosn. and Herzg.* 44°32' N, 16°21' E 168
Bosansko Grahovo, *Bosn. and Herzg.* 44°9' N, 16°20' E 168
Bősárkány, *Hung.* 47°41' N, 17°17' E 168
Bosbury, *U.K.* 52°4' N, 2°27' W 162
Bosco Chiesanuova, *It.* 45°36' N, 11°1' E 167
Bose, *China* 23°54' N, 106°32' E 198
Boseong, *S. Korea* 34°43' N, 127°6' E 200
Boshof, *S. Af.* 28°33' S, 25°13' E 227
Boshrūyeh, *Iran* 33°52' N, 57°28' E 180
Bosilegrad, *Serb.* 42°30' N, 22°29' E 168
Bosnia and Herzegovina 44°0' N, 18°0' E 156
Bošnjaci, *Croatia* 45°1' N, 18°45' E 168
Bosobele, *Dem. Rep. of the Congo* 1°11' N, 18°12' E 218
Bosobolo, *Dem. Rep. of the Congo* 4°13' N, 19°54' E 218
Bosques Petrificados Natural Monument, *Arg.* 47°43' S, 68°17' W 134
Bossangoa, *Cen. Af. Rep.* 6°28' N, 17°25' E 218
Bossé Bangou, *Niger* 13°21' N, 1°16' E 222
Bossembélé, *Cen. Af. Rep.* 5°13' N, 17°37' E 218
Bossier City, *La., U.S.* 32°30' N, 93°43' W 103
Bosso, *Niger* 13°44' N, 13°17' E 216
Bossoroca, *Braz.* 28°42' S, 54°57' W 139
Bossòst, *Sp.* 42°46' N, 0°40' E 164
Bost see Lashkar Gah, *Afghan.* 31°35' N, 64°22' E 186
Bosten Hu, lake, *China* 41°57' N, 86°51' E 184
Boston, *Mass., U.S.* 42°20' N, 71°6' W 104
Boston, *U.K.* 52°59' N, 0°1' E 162
Boston Bar, *Can.* 49°51' N, 121°25' W 100
Boston Mountains, *Ark., U.S.* 35°44' N, 94°18' W 96
Bostonnais, Grand lac, lake, *Can.* 47°51' N, 73°8' W 94
Bosut, river, *Croatia* 45°12' N, 18°57' E 168
Boswell, *Ind., U.S.* 40°30' N, 87°23' W 102
Boswell, *Okla., U.S.* 34°0' N, 95°52' W 96
Bosworth, battle, *U.K.* 52°35' N, 1°27' W 162
Bot, *Sp.* 41°0' N, 0°22' E 164
Botesdale, *U.K.* 52°20' N, 1°0' E 162
Botev, peak, *Bulg.* 42°42' N, 24°50' E 156
Botevgrad, *Bulg.* 42°51' N, 23°44' E 180
Bothaville, *S. Af.* 27°22' S, 26°36' E 227
Bothnia, Gulf of 61°26' N, 17°58' E 152
Bothwell, *Can.* 42°37' N, 81°51' W 102
Botkins, *Ohio, U.S.* 40°27' N, 84°11' W 102
Botnnuten, peak, *Antarctica* 70°22' S, 37°37' E 248
Botoşani, adm. division, *Rom.* 47°54' N, 26°10' E 156
Botoşani, *Rom.* 47°43' N, 26°38' E 152
Botsford, *Conn., U.S.* 41°22' N, 73°16' W 104
Botsmark, *Nor.* 64°15' N, 20°14' E 152
Botswana 22°36' S, 24°16' E 220
Bottineau, *N. Dak., U.S.* 48°48' N, 100°29' W 90
Bottrop, *Ger.* 51°31' N, 6°56' E 167
Botucatu, *Braz.* 22°54' S, 48°28' W 138
Botum Sakor National Park, *Cambodia* 10°53' N, 102°34' E 202
Botwood, *Can.* 49°8' N, 55°23' W 111
Bou Akba, spring, *Alg.* 28°48' N, 7°45' W 214
Bou Ali, *Alg.* 27°11' N, 0°12' E 214
Bou Arfa, *Mor.* 32°35' N, 1°56' W 214
Boû Djébéha, *Mali* 18°31' N, 2°46' W 222
Bou Hadjar, *Alg.* 36°30' N, 8°6' E 156
Bou Izakarn, *Mor.* 29°11' N, 9°44' W 214
Bou Naga, spring, *Mauritania* 19°0' N, 13°13' W 222
Boû Rjeïmât, *Mauritania* 19°3' N, 15°8' W 222
Bou Saâda, *Alg.* 35°11' N, 4°10' E 214
Bou Thadi, *Tun.* 35°5' N, 10°14' E 216
Boû Zérîbé, spring, *Mauritania* 16°13' N, 5°25' W 222
Bouaflé, *Côte d'Ivoire* 6°56' N, 5°43' W 222
Bouaké, *Côte d'Ivoire* 7°37' N, 5°3' W 222
Bouala, *Cen. Af. Rep.* 6°18' N, 15°35' E 218
Bouali, *Gabon* 3°7' S, 11°30' E 218
Bouar, *Cen. Af. Rep.* 5°53' N, 15°34' E 218
Boubout, spring, *Alg.* 27°30' N, 4°34' W 214
Bouca, *Cen. Af. Rep.* 6°29' N, 18°18' E 218
Boucau, *Fr.* 43°31' N, 1°30' W 150
Bouchier, Lac, lake, *Can.* 50°2' N, 78°23' W 110
Boucle Du Baoulé National Park, *Mali* 13°39' N, 9°25' W 222
Boudenib, *Mor.* 32°1' N, 3°36' W 214
Boudjellil, *Alg.* 36°19' N, 4°20' E 150
Bouga, *Chad* 8°8' N, 15°34' E 218
Bougainville, Cape, *Austral.* 13°49' S, 126°3' E 231
Bougainville, island, *P.N.G.* 5°54' S, 153°10' E 192
Bougar'oûn, Cap, *Alg.* 37°7' N, 6°26' E 150
Boughzoul, *Alg.* 35°44' N, 2°50' E 150
Bougie see Bejaïa, *Alg.* 36°46' N, 5°2' E 150
Bougouni, *Mali* 11°26' N, 7°30' W 222
Bouilly, *Fr.* 48°10' N, 4°0' E 163
Bouira, *Alg.* 36°21' N, 3°54' E 150
Boujad, *Mor.* 32°50' N, 6°25' W 214
Boujdour, *Western Sahara, Mor.* 26°8' N, 14°29' W 214
Boujdour, Cap, *Western Sahara, Mor.* 26°7' N, 16°1' W 214
Boukombé, *Benin* 10°11' N, 1°6' E 222
Boukoula, *Cameroon* 10°9' N, 13°29' E 216
Boukra, *Western Sahara, Mor.* 26°22' N, 12°53' W 214
Boula, *Mali* 15°4' N, 8°27' W 222
Boulder, *Colo., U.S.* 40°2' N, 105°17' W 90
Boulder, *Mont., U.S.* 46°13' N, 112°7' W 90
Boulder City, *Nev., U.S.* 35°55' N, 114°50' W 82
Boulder Creek, *Calif., U.S.* 37°7' N, 122°9' W 100
Boulder Peak, *Calif., U.S.* 41°34' N, 123°11' W 90
Boulogne, *Fr.* 43°17' N, 0°37' E 164
Boulogne-sur-Mer, *Fr.* 50°44' N, 1°36' E 163
Boulouli, *Mali* 15°36' N, 9°20' W 222
Boulsa, *Burkina Faso* 12°39' N, 0°37' E 222
Boultoum, *Niger* 14°41' N, 10°18' E 222
Boumdeït, spring, *Mauritania* 17°27' N, 11°22' W 222
Boumerdas, *Alg.* 36°45' N, 3°29' E 150
Boun Nua, *Laos* 21°40' N, 101°54' E 202
Boun Tai, *Laos* 21°25' N, 101°58' E 202
Bouna, *Côte d'Ivoire* 9°16' N, 3°0' W 222
Boundary, *Can.* 49°0' N, 109°22' W 90
Boundary Bald Mountain, *Me., U.S.* 45°45' N, 70°18' W 94
Boundary Peak, *Nev., U.S.* 37°50' N, 118°26' W 90
Boundiali, *Côte d'Ivoire* 9°31' N, 6°29' W 222
Boundji, *Congo* 1°2' S, 15°22' E 218
Bountiful Islands, *Gulf of Carpentaria* 17°3' S, 140°1' E 230
Bounty Trough, *South Pacific Ocean* 47°2' S, 178°29' W 252
Bourbon, *Ind., U.S.* 41°17' N, 86°7' W 102
Bourbonnais, *Ill., U.S.* 41°9' N, 87°54' W 102
Bourbonnais, region, *Europe* 46°45' N, 2°23' E 165
Bourbourg, *Fr.* 50°56' N, 2°12' E 163
Bouré Siké, spring, *Mali* 15°50' N, 5°18' W 222
Bourem, *Mali* 16°58' N, 0°20' E 222
Bouressa, *Mali* 19°58' N, 2°13' E 222
Bourg, *La., U.S.* 29°33' N, 90°38' W 103
Bourges, *Fr.* 47°4' N, 2°24' E 150
Bourg-Madame, *Fr.* 42°25' N, 1°56' E 164
Bourgneuf, *Fr.* 47°2' N, 1°57' W 150
Bourgogne, adm. division, *Fr.* 47°19' N, 2°55' E 150
Bourke, *Austral.* 30°8' S, 145°56' E 231
Bourlier, *Alg.* 35°23' N, 1°38' E 150
Bourne, *U.K.* 52°46' N, 0°22' E 162
Bournemouth, *U.K.* 50°43' N, 1°54' W 162
Bouroum, *Burkina Faso* 13°38' N, 0°39' E 222
Bourscheid, *Lux.* 49°53' N, 6°4' E 167

Bourtoutou, *Chad* 11° 14' N, 22° 50' E 218
Bouse, *Ariz., U.S.* 33° 56' N, 114° 1' W 101
Boussens, *Fr.* 43° 10' N, 0° 57' E 164
Bousso, *Chad* 10° 32' N, 16° 43' E 216
Bouszibé Aneyda, spring, *Mali* 16° 14' N, 5° 16' W 222
Boutilimit, *Mauritania* 17° 32' N, 14° 44' W 222
Bouvet Island, *Norway* 54° 28' S, 3° 23' E 255
Bouza, *Niger* 14° 22' N, 5° 55' E 222
Bovec, *Slov.* 46° 20' N, 13° 34' E 167
Bovenden, *Ger.* 51° 35' N, 9° 56' E 167
Boves, *Fr.* 49° 49' N, 2° 22' E 163
Bovill, *Idaho, U.S.* 46° 50' N, 116° 24' W 90
Bovina, *Tex., U.S.* 34° 30' N, 102° 53' W 92
Bovril, *Arg.* 31° 19' S, 59° 25' W 139
Bow, *N.H., U.S.* 43° 9' N, 71° 33' W 104
Bow Island, *Can.* 49° 51' N, 111° 23' W 90
Bow, river, *Can.* 51° 6' N, 114° 34' W 90
Bowbells, *N. Dak., U.S.* 48° 48' N, 102° 15' W 90
Bowdle, *S. Dak., U.S.* 45° 26' N, 99° 41' W 90
Bowdoin Canyon, *Can.* 53° 34' N, 65° 28' W 111
Bowen, *Austral.* 20° 0' S, 148° 15' E 231
Bowen Island, *Can.* 49° 22' N, 123° 21' W 100
Bowes, *U.K.* 54° 31' N, 2° 1' W 162
Bowie, *Ariz., U.S.* 32° 19' N, 109° 28' W 92
Bowie, *Tex., U.S.* 33° 32' N, 97° 51' W 92
Bowling Green, *Fla., U.S.* 27° 38' N, 81° 49' W 105
Bowling Green, *Ind., U.S.* 39° 22' N, 87° 1' W 102
Bowling Green, *Ky., U.S.* 36° 59' N, 86° 27' W 96
Bowling Green, *Ohio, U.S.* 41° 22' N, 83° 39' W 102
Bowling Green, *Va., U.S.* 38° 2' N, 77° 21' W 94
Bowling Green Bay National Park, *Austral.* 19° 34' S, 146° 39' E 238
Bowman, *N. Dak., U.S.* 46° 10' N, 103° 26' W 90
Bowman Bay 65° 33' N, 77° 12' W 106
Bowman Island, *Antarctica* 64° 34' S, 104° 9' E 248
Bowman, Mount, *Can.* 51° 11' N, 121° 52' W 90
Bowness, *U.K.* 54° 21' N, 2° 55' W 162
Bowo see Bomi, *China* 29° 53' N, 95° 40' E 188
Bowser, *Can.* 49° 25' N, 124° 41' W 100
Bowser Lake, *Can.* 56° 24' N, 129° 52' W 108
Bowsman, *Can.* 52° 14' N, 101° 13' W 108
Bowwood, *Zambia* 17° 7' S, 26° 16' E 224
Boxing, *China* 37° 9' N, 118° 7' E 198
Boxtel, *Neth.* 51° 35' N, 5° 19' E 167
Boyabat, *Turk.* 41° 27' N, 34° 45' E 156
Boyacá, adm. division, *Col.* 5° 17' N, 73° 33' W 136
Boyang, *China* 29° 0' N, 116° 38' E 198
Boyarka, *Russ.* 70° 43' N, 97° 24' E 160
Boyce, *La., U.S.* 31° 22' N, 92° 40' W 103
Boyd, *Can.* 55° 53' N, 96° 27' W 108
Boyd Lake, *Can.* 61° 22' N, 104° 4' W 108
Boyer, river, *Can.* 57° 54' N, 117° 43' W 108
Boyes Hot Springs, *Calif., U.S.* 38° 19' N, 122° 29' W 100
Boykétté, *Cen. Af. Rep.* 5° 24' N, 20° 49' E 218
Boyle, *Can.* 54° 35' N, 112° 48' W 108
Boyle, *Ire.* 53° 58' N, 8° 20' W 150
Boyne City, *Mich., U.S.* 45° 12' N, 85° 1' W 94
Boynitsa, *Bulg.* 43° 57' N, 22° 31' E 168
Boynton Beach, *Fla., U.S.* 26° 32' N, 80° 5' W 105
Boyoma Falls, *Dem. Rep. of the Congo* 1° 23' N, 21° 41' E 206
Boyoma Falls (Stanley Falls), *Dem. Rep. of the Congo* 0° 14' N, 25° 9' E 224
Boyson, *Uzb.* 38° 12' N, 67° 12' E 197
Boyuibe, *Bol.* 20° 28' S, 63° 16' W 137
Boz Burun, *Turk.* 40° 32' N, 28° 50' E 156
Boz Dağ, peak, *Turk.* 37° 18' N, 29° 7' E 156
Bozalan Burun, *Turk.* 38° 12' N, 26° 27' E 156
Bozashchy Tübegi, *Kaz.* 45° 9' N, 51° 36' E 158
Bozburun, *Turk.* 36° 41' N, 28° 4' E 156
Bozburun Dağı, peak, *Turk.* 37° 16' N, 31° 0' E 156
Bozdoğan, *Turk.* 37° 39' N, 28° 18' E 156
Bozeman, *Mont., U.S.* 45° 38' N, 111° 3' W 90
Bozene, *Dem. Rep. of the Congo* 2° 58' N, 19° 13' E 218
Boževac, *Serb.* 44° 32' N, 21° 23' E 168
Bozhou, *China* 33° 49' N, 115° 44' E 198
Božica, *Serb.* 42° 36' N, 22° 24' E 168
Bozkır, *Turk.* 37° 11' N, 32° 13' E 156
Bozkurt, *Turk.* 41° 58' N, 34° 1' E 158
Bozoum, *Cen. Af. Rep.* 6° 15' N, 16° 23' E 218
Bozoy, *Kaz.* 46° 10' N, 58° 45' E 158
Bozüyük, *Turk.* 39° 55' N, 30° 1' E 156
Bozzolo, *It.* 45° 5' N, 10° 28' E 167
Bra, *It.* 44° 41' N, 7° 51' E 167
Brabant Island, *Antarctica* 64° 4' S, 64° 38' W 134
Brabant Lake, lake, *Can.* 56° 0' N, 104° 18' W 108
Brač, island, *Croatia* 43° 15' N, 16° 54' E 168
Bracebridge, *Can.* 45° 2' N, 79° 20' W 94
Bräcke, *Nor.* 62° 45' N, 15° 26' E 152
Bracken Lake, lake, *Can.* 53° 35' N, 100° 14' W 108
Brackendale, *Can.* 49° 45' N, 123° 8' W 100
Brackettville, *Tex., U.S.* 29° 18' N, 100° 25' W 92
Brackley, *U.K.* 52° 2' N, 1° 9' W 162
Bracknell, *U.K.* 51° 22' N, 0° 46' E 162
Brackwede, *Ger.* 51° 59' N, 8° 29' E 167
Brad, *Rom.* 46° 7' N, 22° 49' E 168
Bradenton, *Fla., U.S.* 27° 29' N, 82° 35' W 105
Bradenton Beach, *Fla., U.S.* 27° 28' N, 82° 41' W 105
Bradford, *Ill., U.S.* 41° 10' N, 89° 41' W 102
Bradford, *Ohio, U.S.* 40° 7' N, 84° 26' W 102
Bradford, *Pa., U.S.* 41° 57' N, 78° 40' W 94
Bradford, *U.K.* 53° 47' N, 1° 46' W 162
Bradford, *Vt., U.S.* 43° 59' N, 72° 9' W 104
Bradford on Avon, *U.K.* 51° 21' N, 2° 15' W 162
Bradley, *Ark., U.S.* 33° 5' N, 93° 41' W 103
Bradley, *Calif., U.S.* 35° 52' N, 120° 49' W 100
Bradley, *Ill., U.S.* 41° 9' N, 87° 51' W 102
Bradley, *S. Dak., U.S.* 45° 4' N, 97° 40' W 90
Bradley Junction, *Fla., U.S.* 27° 47' N, 81° 59' W 105
Bradninch, *U.K.* 50° 49' N, 3° 26' W 162
Brador, Collines de, peak, *Can.* 51° 33' N, 57° 18' W 111
Bradwell on Sea, *U.K.* 51° 43' N, 0° 54' E 162
Brady, *Nebr., U.S.* 41° 2' N, 100° 21' W 90
Brady, *Tex., U.S.* 31° 7' N, 99° 20' W 92
Brașov, adm. division, *Rom.* 45° 42' N, 24° 42' E 156
Braeside, *Can.* 45° 27' N, 76° 26' W 94
Braga, *Port.* 41° 32' N, 8° 27' W 150
Braga, adm. division, *Port.* 41° 24' N, 8° 40' W 150
Bragado, *Arg.* 35° 7' S, 60° 30' W 139
Bragança, *Braz.* 1° 4' S, 46° 48' W 130
Bragança, *Port.* 41° 46' N, 6° 48' W 214
Bragança, *Port.* 41° 49' N, 6° 47' W 150
Bragança, adm. division, *Port.* 41° 28' N, 7° 16' W 150
Braham, *Minn., U.S.* 45° 42' N, 93° 10' W 94
Brahestad see Raahe, *Fin.* 64° 41' N, 24° 27' E 152
Brahmapur, *India* 19° 19' N, 84° 47' E 188
Brahmaputra, river, *India* 26° 18' N, 92° 11' E 190
Brăila, *Rom.* 45° 16' N, 27° 57' E 156
Brăila, adm. division, *Rom.* 44° 57' N, 27° 19' E 156
Braine, *Fr.* 49° 20' N, 3° 30' E 163
Braine l'Alleud, *Belg.* 50° 41' N, 4° 21' E 163
Brainerd, *Minn., U.S.* 46° 20' N, 94° 11' W 90
Braintree, *Mass., U.S.* 42° 12' N, 71° 1' W 104
Braintree, *U.K.* 51° 53' N, 0° 32' E 162
Brakel, *Ger.* 51° 43' N, 9° 11' E 167
Bräkne-Hoby, *Nor.* 56° 14' N, 15° 8' E 152
Bralorne, *Can.* 50° 47' N, 122° 48' W 90
Bramber, *U.K.* 50° 51' N, 0° 18' E 162
Brampton, *Can.* 43° 41' N, 79° 46' W 94
Bramsche, *Ger.* 52° 24' N, 7° 58' E 163
Branchville, *S.C., U.S.* 33° 14' N, 80° 49' W 96
Branco, river, *Braz.* 13° 41' S, 60° 24' W 130
Brandberg, peak, *Namibia* 21° 10' S, 14° 27' E 220
Brandbu, *Nor.* 60° 24' N, 10° 31' E 152
Brandenburg, adm. division, *Ger.* 52° 36' N, 12° 16' E 152
Brandfort, *S. Af.* 28° 43' S, 26° 25' E 227
Brändö, *Fin.* 60° 24' N, 21° 2' E 166
Brandon, *Can.* 49° 49' N, 99° 57' W 90
Brandon, *Fla., U.S.* 27° 57' N, 82° 16' W 105
Brandon, *Miss., U.S.* 32° 15' N, 90° 0' W 103
Brandon, *U.K.* 52° 26' N, 0° 37' E 162
Brandon, *Vt., U.S.* 43° 47' N, 73° 7' W 104
Brandon, *Wis., U.S.* 43° 43' N, 88° 47' W 102
Brandon Mountain, *Ire.* 52° 13' N, 10° 20' W 150
Brandsen, *Arg.* 35° 9' S, 58° 16' W 139
Brandvlei, *S. Af.* 30° 26' S, 20° 26' E 227
Brandy Peak, *Oreg., U.S.* 42° 35' N, 123° 58' W 90
Branford, *Conn., U.S.* 41° 16' N, 72° 50' W 104
Branford, *Fla., U.S.* 29° 58' N, 82° 56' W 96
Braniewo, *Pol.* 54° 21' N, 19° 48' E 166
Brankovina, *Serb.* 44° 21' N, 19° 52' E 168
Bransfield Island, *Antarctica* 63° 28' S, 58° 57' W 134
Branson, *Mo., U.S.* 36° 38' N, 93° 14' W 96
Brant, *N.Y., U.S.* 42° 34' N, 79° 2' W 110
Brant Lake, *N.Y., U.S.* 43° 40' N, 73° 45' W 104
Brantford, *Can.* 43° 7' N, 80° 16' W 110
Bras Coupé, Lac du, lake, *Can.* 49° 33' N, 75° 43' W 94
Bras d'Or Lake, *Can.* 45° 55' N, 61° 18' W 111
Brasileia, *Braz.* 10° 57' S, 68° 44' W 137
Brasileiro, Planalto, *South America* 17° 41' S, 44° 49' W 138
Brasília, *Braz.* 15° 49' S, 48° 0' W 138
Brasília de Minas, *Braz.* 16° 13' S, 44° 28' W 138
Brasília Legal, *Braz.* 3° 52' S, 55° 39' W 130
Braslav, *Belarus* 55° 38' N, 27° 3' E 166
Braslav National Park, *Belarus* 55° 35' N, 27° 1' E 166
Brașov, *Rom.* 45° 38' N, 25° 35' E 156
Brass, *Nig.* 4° 17' N, 6° 15' E 222
Brasschaat, *Belg.* 51° 17' N, 4° 28' E 167
Brasstown Bald, peak, *Ga., U.S.* 34° 51' N, 83° 53' W 96
Bratan, peak, *Bulg.* 42° 29' N, 25° 4' E 156
Bratca, *Rom.* 46° 54' N, 22° 39' E 168
Bratislava (Pressburg), *Slovakia* 48° 7' N, 16° 57' E 152
Bratislavský, adm. division, *Slovakia* 47° 40' N, 16° 52' E 156
Bratiya, peak, *Bulg.* 42° 34' N, 24° 5' E 156
Bratsk, *Russ.* 56° 24' N, 101° 23' E 160
Brattleboro, *Vt., U.S.* 42° 50' N, 72° 34' W 104
Bratunac, *Bosn. and Herzg.* 44° 12' N, 19° 20' E 168
Brauron, ruin(s), *Gr.* 37° 54' N, 23° 52' E 156
Braux, *Fr.* 49° 50' N, 4° 45' E 163
Brawley, *Calif., U.S.* 32° 59' N, 115° 33' W 101
Bray, *Fr.* 49° 56' N, 2° 42' E 163
Brazeau, Mount, *Can.* 52° 31' N, 117° 27' W 108
Brazeau, river, *Can.* 52° 46' N, 116° 22' W 108
Brazeau see Nordegg, *Can.* 52° 28' N, 116° 7' W 108
Brazil 10° 11' S, 55° 28' W 132
Brazil, *Ind., U.S.* 39° 31' N, 87° 7' W 102
Brazoria, *Tex., U.S.* 29° 2' N, 95° 34' W 96
Brazos Peak, *N. Mex., U.S.* 36° 48' N, 106° 30' W 92
Brazzaville, *Congo* 4° 13' S, 15° 0' E 218
Brčko, *Bosn. and Herzg.* 44° 52' N, 18° 47' E 168
Brea, *Calif., U.S.* 33° 55' N, 117° 55' W 101
Brea, Cerros de la, *Peru* 4° 32' S, 80° 56' W 130
Breakenridge, Mount, *Can.* 49° 42' N, 121° 58' W 100
Breaux Bridge, *La., U.S.* 30° 15' N, 91° 55' W 103
Breaza, *Rom.* 45° 11' N, 25° 38' E 158
Breckenridge, *Mich., U.S.* 43° 23' N, 84° 29' W 102
Breckenridge, *Minn., U.S.* 46° 14' N, 96° 35' W 90
Breckenridge, *Tex., U.S.* 32° 45' N, 98° 55' W 112
Brecknock, Península, *Chile* 54° 36' S, 74° 29' W 134
Břeclav, *Czech Rep.* 48° 45' N, 16° 53' E 152
Brecon, *U.K.* 51° 56' N, 3° 23' W 162
Brecon Beacons, peak, *U.K.* 51° 53' N, 3° 28' W 162
Brecon Beacons National Park, *U.K.* 51° 53' N, 3° 26' W 162
Breda, *Neth.* 51° 34' N, 4° 45' E 167
Bredasdorp, *S. Af.* 34° 32' S, 20° 2' E 227
Bredbyn, *Nor.* 63° 26' N, 18° 6' E 152
Bredene, *Belg.* 51° 13' N, 2° 57' E 150
Bredon Hill, *U.K.* 52° 3' N, 2° 5' W 162
Bredy, *Russ.* 52° 25' N, 60° 17' E 154
Breezewood, *Pa., U.S.* 39° 59' N, 78° 15' W 94
Bregovo, *Bulg.* 44° 9' N, 22° 38' E 168
Breil-sur-Roya, *Fr.* 43° 56' N, 7° 29' E 167
Breitenworbis, *Ger.* 51° 25' N, 10° 25' E 167
Breitungen, *Ger.* 50° 45' N, 10° 18' E 167
Brejo, *Braz.* 3° 41' S, 42° 50' W 132
Brejolândia, *Braz.* 12° 30' S, 43° 58' W 132
Brekovica, *Bosn. and Herzg.* 44° 51' N, 15° 51' E 168
Breloh, *Ger.* 53° 1' N, 10° 5' E 150
Bremangerpollen, *Nor.* 61° 51' N, 4° 58' E 152
Bremen, *Ga., U.S.* 33° 41' N, 85° 8' W 96
Bremen, *Ger.* 53° 5' N, 8° 47' E 163
Bremen, *Ind., U.S.* 41° 26' N, 86° 9' W 102
Bremen, *Ohio, U.S.* 39° 41' N, 82° 26' W 102
Bremen, adm. division, *Ger.* 53° 4' N, 8° 27' E 150
Bremer Bay 34° 47' S, 119° 6' E 230
Bremerhaven, *Ger.* 53° 32' N, 8° 36' E 150
Bremerton, *Wash., U.S.* 47° 32' N, 122° 40' W 100
Bremnes, *Nor.* 59° 46' N, 5° 9' E 152
Bremsnes, *Nor.* 63° 4' N, 7° 39' E 152
Brenes, *Sp.* 37° 32' N, 5° 53' W 164
Brenham, *Tex., U.S.* 30° 9' N, 96° 24' W 96
Brenner Pass, *It.* 47° 0' N, 11° 30' E 167
Breno, *It.* 45° 57' N, 10° 18' E 167
Brenton Bay 11° 34' S, 130° 45' E 230
Brentwood, *Calif., U.S.* 37° 55' N, 121° 43' W 100
Brentwood, *N.Y., U.S.* 40° 47' N, 73° 14' W 104
Brentwood, *U.K.* 51° 37' N, 0° 17' E 162
Brescia, *It.* 45° 32' N, 10° 13' E 167
Breskens, *Neth.* 51° 23' N, 3° 33' E 163
Bresles, *Fr.* 49° 24' N, 2° 15' E 163
Bressanone, *It.* 46° 44' N, 11° 38' E 167
Brest, *Belarus* 52° 5' N, 23° 41' E 152
Brest, *Fr.* 48° 23' N, 4° 30' W 150
Brest, *Pol.* 52° 4' N, 23° 42' E 160
Brestovac, *Serb.* 43° 9' N, 21° 52' E 168
Bretagne, adm. division, *Fr.* 48° 10' N, 4° 8' W 150
Breteuil, *Fr.* 49° 37' N, 2° 17' E 163
Breteuil, *Fr.* 48° 49' N, 0° 54' E 163
Breton, *Can.* 53° 5' N, 114° 29' W 108
Breton, Cape, *Can.* 45° 56' N, 59° 46' W 111
Bretón, Cayo, island, *Cuba* 21° 7' N, 80° 16' W 116
Breton Island, Cape, *Can.* 45° 19' N, 63° 50' W 81
Breton Sound 29° 28' N, 89° 22' W 103
Brett, Cape, *N.Z.* 35° 11' S, 174° 16' E 240
Breu, river, *Braz.* 3° 45' S, 66° 39' W 136
Breu, river, *South America* 9° 25' S, 72° 31' W 137
Breueh, island, *Indonesia* 5° 47' N, 94° 35' E 196
Breuil-Cervinia, *It.* 45° 56' N, 7° 38' E 167
Breves, *Braz.* 1° 39' S, 50° 31' W 130
Brevik, *Nor.* 59° 3' N, 9° 41' E 152
Brevoort Island, *Can.* 63° 4' N, 63° 59' W 106
Brevoort Lake, lake, *Mich., U.S.* 45° 58' N, 85° 25' W 110
Brew, Mount, *Can.* 50° 34' N, 122° 2' W 90
Brewer, *Me., U.S.* 44° 47' N, 68° 46' W 94
Brewerville, *Liberia* 6° 20' N, 10° 47' W 222
Brewster, *Kans., U.S.* 39° 22' N, 101° 24' W 90
Brewster, *Mass., U.S.* 41° 45' N, 70° 5' W 104
Brewster, *Nebr., U.S.* 41° 54' N, 99° 52' W 90
Brewster, *N.Y., U.S.* 41° 23' N, 73° 39' W 104
Brewster, *Ohio, U.S.* 40° 42' N, 81° 36' W 102
Brewster, *Wash., U.S.* 48° 5' N, 119° 49' W 90
Brewster, Mount, *Antarctica* 72° 54' S, 169° 59' E 248
Brewton, *Ala., U.S.* 31° 6' N, 87° 4' W 96
Breza, *Bosn. and Herzg.* 44° 1' N, 18° 15' E 168
Brezičani, *Bosn. and Herzg.* 45° 0' N, 16° 40' E 168
Brezina, *Alg.* 33° 7' N, 1° 14' E 214
Brezno, *Slovakia* 48° 48' N, 19° 39' E 156
Brezolles, *Fr.* 48° 41' N, 1° 4' E 163
Brezovo Polje, *Bosn. and Herzg.* 44° 50' N, 18° 57' E 168
Bria, *Cen. Af. Rep.* 6° 29' N, 22° 2' E 218
Brian Head, peak, *Utah, U.S.* 37° 40' N, 112° 54' W 92
Briançon, *Fr.* 44° 53' N, 6° 38' E 167
Briare, *Fr.* 47° 38' N, 2° 43' E 150
Bribie Island, *Austral.* 27° 17' S, 151° 4' E 230
Bridge City, *Tex., U.S.* 30° 0' N, 93° 52' W 103
Bridgehampton, *N.Y., U.S.* 40° 56' N, 72° 19' W 104
Bridgend, *U.K.* 51° 30' N, 3° 34' W 162
Bridgeport, *Ala., U.S.* 34° 56' N, 85° 43' W 96
Bridgeport, *Calif., U.S.* 38° 15' N, 119° 16' W 100
Bridgeport, *Conn., U.S.* 41° 10' N, 73° 12' W 104
Bridgeport, *Nebr., U.S.* 41° 39' N, 103° 8' W 90
Bridgeport, *Tex., U.S.* 33° 11' N, 97° 45' W 92
Bridgeport, Lake, *Tex., U.S.* 33° 17' N, 98° 40' W 81
Bridger Peak, *Wyo., U.S.* 41° 10' N, 107° 7' W 90
Bridgeton, *N.C., U.S.* 35° 7' N, 77° 2' W 96
Bridgetown, *Barbados* 13° 3' N, 59° 43' W 116
Bridgetown, *Ohio, U.S.* 39° 8' N, 84° 39' W 102
Bridgewater, *Can.* 44° 22' N, 64° 33' W 111
Bridgewater, *Mass., U.S.* 41° 59' N, 70° 59' W 104
Bridgnorth, *U.K.* 52° 31' N, 2° 26' W 162
Bridgton, *Me., U.S.* 44° 3' N, 70° 43' W 104
Bridgwater, *U.K.* 51° 7' N, 3° 1' W 162
Bridlington, *U.K.* 54° 4' N, 0° 14' E 162
Bridport, *Vt., U.S.* 43° 58' N, 73° 20' W 104
Brienne-le-Château, *Fr.* 48° 23' N, 4° 31' E 163
Brienz, *Switz.* 46° 45' N, 8° 0' E 167
Brienzer See, lake, *Switz.* 46° 41' N, 7° 42' E 167
Brig, *Switz.* 46° 20' N, 8° 0' E 167
Brigantine, *N.J., U.S.* 39° 23' N, 74° 24' W 94
Brigden, *Can.* 42° 48' N, 82° 18' W 102
Brigg, *U.K.* 53° 32' N, 0° 29' E 162
Brigham City, *Utah, U.S.* 41° 30' N, 112° 0' W 90
Brighouse, *U.K.* 53° 42' N, 1° 47' W 162
Brightlingsea, *U.K.* 51° 48' N, 1° 1' E 162
Brighton, *Can.* 44° 1' N, 77° 43' W 110
Brighton, *Colo., U.S.* 39° 58' N, 104° 49' W 90
Brighton, *Mich., U.S.* 42° 30' N, 83° 47' W 102
Brighton, *U.K.* 50° 50' N, 0° 9' E 162
Brijuni Otoci (Brioni Islands), *Gulf of Venice* 44° 51' N, 13° 23' E 167
Brikama, *Gambia* 13° 17' N, 16° 33' W 222
Brilon, *Ger.* 51° 24' N, 8° 32' E 167
Brimfield, *Ill., U.S.* 40° 49' N, 89° 54' W 102
Brinkburn Priory, site, *U.K.* 55° 16' N, 1° 55' W 150
Brinkley, *Ark., U.S.* 34° 51' N, 91° 12' W 96
Brinnon, *Wash., U.S.* 47° 39' N, 122° 55' W 100
Brion, Île, island, *Can.* 47° 28' N, 61° 18' W 81
Brioni Islands see Brijuni Otoci, *Gulf of Venice* 44° 51' N, 13° 23' E 167
Brioude, *Fr.* 45° 17' N, 3° 21' E 150
Briouze, *Fr.* 48° 41' N, 0° 23' E 150
Brisbane, *Austral.* 27° 28' S, 152° 53' E 230
Bristol, *Conn., U.S.* 41° 40' N, 72° 56' W 104
Bristol, *Ind., U.S.* 41° 42' N, 85° 50' W 102
Bristol, *N.H., U.S.* 43° 35' N, 71° 45' W 104
Bristol, *R.I., U.S.* 41° 40' N, 71° 17' W 104
Bristol, *S. Dak., U.S.* 45° 19' N, 97° 47' W 90
Bristol, *Tenn., U.S.* 36° 35' N, 82° 12' W 96
Bristol, *U.K.* 51° 26' N, 2° 35' W 162
Bristol, *Vt., U.S.* 44° 8' N, 73° 5' W 104
Bristol Bay 56° 13' N, 160° 33' W 106
Bristol Channel 51° 25' N, 4° 42' W 150
Bristol Mountains, *Calif., U.S.* 34° 58' N, 116° 11' W 101
Bristow, *Okla., U.S.* 35° 47' N, 96° 23' W 94
Britannia Beach, *Can.* 49° 36' N, 123° 12' W 100
British Channel 80° 37' N, 47° 37' E 160
British Columbia, adm. division, *Can.* 54° 39' N, 126° 22' W 106
British Indian Ocean Territory, *United Kingdom* 7° 0' S, 72° 0' E 188
British Mountains, *Can.* 69° 15' N, 141° 7' W 98
British Virgin Islands, *United Kingdom* 18° 31' N, 64° 41' W 116
Brits, *S. Af.* 25° 40' S, 27° 46' E 227
Britstown, *S. Af.* 30° 36' S, 23° 31' E 227
Britt, *Can.* 45° 47' N, 80° 32' W 94
Britt, *Iowa, U.S.* 43° 4' N, 93° 47' W 94
Britton, *S. Dak., U.S.* 45° 46' N, 97° 46' W 94
Brive, *Fr.* 45° 8' N, 1° 31' E 150
Briviesca, *Sp.* 42° 32' N, 3° 21' W 150
Brnaze, *Croatia* 43° 40' N, 16° 39' E 168
Brno, *Czech Rep.* 49° 11' N, 16° 37' E 152
Broadback, river, *Can.* 51° 13' N, 78° 42' W 110
Broaddus, *Tex., U.S.* 31° 17' N, 94° 17' W 103
Broadstairs, *U.K.* 51° 21' N, 1° 25' E 163
Broadus, *Mont., U.S.* 45° 25' N, 105° 26' W 90
Broadview, *Can.* 50° 22' N, 102° 35' W 108
Broadwater, *Nebr., U.S.* 41° 36' N, 102° 52' W 90
Brocēni, *Latv.* 56° 41' N, 22° 33' E 166
Brochet, *Can.* 57° 54' N, 101° 39' W 108
Brochet, Lac au, lake, *Can.* 49° 40' N, 70° 15' W 94
Brochet, Lac, lake, *Can.* 58° 38' N, 101° 52' W 108
Brock Island, *Can.* 78° 23' N, 115° 4' W 246
Brock, river, *Can.* 50° 5' N, 75° 5' W 110
Brocken, peak, *Ger.* 51° 47' N, 10° 30' E 152
Brockport, *N.Y., U.S.* 43° 12' N, 77° 58' W 94
Brockport, *Pa., U.S.* 41° 15' N, 78° 45' W 94
Brockton, *Mass., U.S.* 42° 4' N, 71° 2' W 104
Brockville, *Can.* 44° 36' N, 75° 42' W 110
Brockway, *Mont., U.S.* 47° 16' N, 105° 46' W 90
Brockway, *Pa., U.S.* 41° 14' N, 78° 48' W 94
Brocton, *Ill., U.S.* 39° 43' N, 87° 56' W 102
Brod, *Maced.* 41° 31' N, 21° 12' E 168
Brodarevo, *Serb.* 43° 13' N, 19° 42' E 168
Brodec, *Maced.* 41° 46' N, 20° 41' E 168
Brodeur Peninsula, *Can.* 71° 43' N, 89° 33' W 106
Brodhead, *Wis., U.S.* 42° 37' N, 89° 23' W 102
Brodica, *Serb.* 44° 29' N, 21° 49' E 168
Brodick, *U.K.* 55° 34' N, 5° 9' W 150
Brodilovo, *Bulg.* 42° 5' N, 27° 51' E 156
Brodnytsya, *Ukr.* 51° 45' N, 26° 16' E 152
Brodokalmak, *Russ.* 55° 33' N, 61° 59' E 154
Brody, *Ukr.* 50° 4' N, 25° 8' E 152
Brogan, *Oreg., U.S.* 44° 14' N, 117° 32' W 90
Broken Arrow, *Okla., U.S.* 36° 2' N, 95° 47' W 96
Broken Bow, *Nebr., U.S.* 41° 24' N, 99° 39' W 90
Broken Bow, *Okla., U.S.* 34° 1' N, 94° 45' W 96
Broken Bow Lake, lake, *Okla., U.S.* 34° 10' N, 94° 57' W 96
Broken Hill see Kabwe, *Zambia* 14° 29' S, 28° 25' E 224
Broken Ridge, *Indian Ocean* 31° 50' S, 95° 31' E 254
Brokind, *Nor.* 58° 12' N, 15° 40' E 152
Brokopondo, *Suriname* 5° 4' N, 55° 2' W 130
Bromarv, *Fin.* 59° 58' N, 23° 0' E 166
Bromley Mountain, *Vt., U.S.* 43° 13' N, 72° 58' W 104
Bromyard, *U.K.* 52° 10' N, 2° 31' W 162
Brønderslev, *Den.* 57° 15' N, 9° 56' E 150
Broni, *It.* 45° 4' N, 9° 15' E 167
Brønnøysund, *Nor.* 65° 26' N, 12° 12' E 152
Bronson, *Fla., U.S.* 29° 26' N, 82° 40' W 105
Bronson, *Tex., U.S.* 31° 19' N, 94° 1' W 103
Bronte, *Tex., U.S.* 31° 52' N, 100° 18' W 92
Bronyts'ka Huta, *Ukr.* 50° 54' N, 27° 18' E 152
Brook, *Ind., U.S.* 40° 51' N, 87° 22' W 102
Brookeland, *Tex., U.S.* 31° 7' N, 93° 59' W 103
Brooker, *Fla., U.S.* 29° 53' N, 82° 21' W 105
Brooke's Point, *Philippines* 8° 48' N, 117° 50' E 203
Brookfield, *Conn., U.S.* 41° 28' N, 73° 25' W 104
Brookfield, *Mo., U.S.* 39° 46' N, 93° 3' W 94
Brookfield, *Wis., U.S.* 43° 4' N, 88° 7' W 102
Brookhaven, *Miss., U.S.* 31° 34' N, 90° 26' W 103
Brookhaven National Laboratory, *N.Y., U.S.* 40° 52' N, 72° 54' W 104
Brookings, *Oreg., U.S.* 42° 3' N, 124° 16' W 82
Brookline, *Mass., U.S.* 42° 19' N, 71° 8' W 104
Brooklyn, *Conn., U.S.* 41° 47' N, 71° 58' W 104
Brooklyn, *Ind., U.S.* 39° 32' N, 86° 24' W 102
Brooklyn, *Mich., U.S.* 42° 5' N, 84° 15' W 102
Brooklyn, *Miss., U.S.* 31° 2' N, 89° 10' W 103
Brookmere, *Can.* 49° 48' N, 120° 51' W 100
Brookport, *Mo., U.S.* 37° 7' N, 88° 37' W 96

Brooks, Can. 50°33′ N, 111°55′ W 90
Brooks Bay 50°11′ N, 128°1′ W 108
Brooks Brook, Can. 60°25′ N, 133°10′ W 108
Brooks, Cape, Antarctica 73°53′ S, 60°24′ W 248
Brooks Range, Alas., U.S. 67°30′ N, 153°45′ W 106
Brookston, Ind., U.S. 40°35′ N, 86°52′ W 102
Brooksville, Fla., U.S. 28°34′ N, 82°24′ W 105
Brooksville, Ky., U.S. 38°39′ N, 84°5′ W 102
Brooksville, Miss., U.S. 33°12′ N, 88°35′ W 103
Brookville, Ind., U.S. 39°25′ N, 85°1′ W 102
Brookville, Pa., U.S. 41°9′ N, 79°5′ W 94
Brookville Lake, Ind., U.S. 39°31′ N, 85°1′ W 102
Brookwood, Ala., U.S. 33°16′ N, 87°19′ W 103
Broome, Austral. 17°58′ S, 122°20′ E 238
Broqueles, Punta, Col. 9°13′ N, 76°36′ W 136
Brøstrud, Nor. 60°18′ N, 8°30′ E 152
Brothers, The, islands, North Atlantic Ocean 21°50′ N, 75°43′ W 116
Brothers, The, islands, Red Sea 26°35′ N, 34°31′ E 180
Brou, Fr. 48°12′ N, 1°10′ E 163
Brough, U.K. 54°31′ N, 2°19′ W 162
Broughton in Furness, U.K. 54°17′ N, 3°13′ W 162
Broughton Island see Qikiqtarjuaq, Can. 67°30′ N, 63°52′ W 73
Broulkou, spring, Chad 16°39′ N, 18°11′ E 216
Brouwershaven, Neth. 51°43′ N, 3°53′ E 163
Brovary, Ukr. 50°30′ N, 30°52′ E 158
Browerville, Minn., U.S. 46°4′ N, 94°53′ W 90
Brown City, Mich., U.S. 43°13′ N, 82°59′ W 102
Brown Willy, peak, U.K. 50°34′ N, 4°41′ W 150
Browne Bay 72°57′ N, 100°30′ W 106
Brownfield, Me., U.S. 43°56′ N, 70°56′ W 104
Brownfield, Tex., U.S. 33°9′ N, 102°17′ W 92
Brownhills, U.K. 52°39′ N, 1°56′ W 162
Browning, Mont., U.S. 48°31′ N, 113°2′ W 90
Browns, Ala., U.S. 32°26′ N, 87°22′ W 103
Browns, N.Z. 46°10′ S, 168°25′ E 240
Brown's Cay, island, Bahamas 25°19′ N, 79°26′ W 105
Browns Town, Jam. 18°23′ N, 77°23′ W 115
Browns Valley, Minn., U.S. 45°35′ N, 96°50′ W 90
Brownsboro, Tex., U.S. 32°17′ N, 95°37′ W 103
Brownson Islands, Amundsen Sea 73°56′ S, 104°11′ W 248
Brownstown, Ind., U.S. 38°53′ N, 86°3′ W 102
Brownsville, Tenn., U.S. 35°34′ N, 89°16′ W 96
Brownsville, Tex., U.S. 25°57′ N, 97°28′ W 114
Brownsville, Vt., U.S. 43°28′ N, 72°29′ W 104
Brownsweg, Suriname 4°59′ N, 55°11′ W 130
Brownwood, Tex., U.S. 31°41′ N, 98°58′ W 92
Brownwood, Lake, Tex., U.S. 31°52′ N, 99°50′ W 81
Brsečine, Croatia 42°43′ N, 17°57′ E 168
Bru, Nor. 61°32′ N, 5°12′ E 152
Bruce Mines, Can. 46°18′ N, 83°48′ W 94
Bruce, Mount, Austral. 22°39′ S, 117°57′ E 230
Bruce Peninsula, North America 44°50′ N, 81°23′ W 110
Bruck, Aust. 48°1′ N, 16°47′ E 168
Brugg, Switz. 47°28′ N, 8°13′ E 156
Brugge, Belg. 51°12′ N, 3°13′ E 163
Brüggen, Ger. 51°14′ N, 6°10′ E 167
Brühl, Ger. 50°49′ N, 6°53′ E 167
Bruini, India 29°10′ N, 96°8′ E 188
Brûlé, Lac, lake, Can. 46°54′ N, 77°32′ W 94
Brumado, Braz. 14°15′ S, 41°38′ W 138
Brumath, Fr. 48°44′ N, 7°41′ E 163
Brundidge, Ala., U.S. 31°42′ N, 85°49′ W 96
Bruneau, Idaho, U.S. 42°53′ N, 115°48′ W 90
Bruneau, river, Idaho, U.S. 42°57′ N, 115°48′ W 90
Brunei 5°0′ N, 115°0′ E 192
Brunico, It. 46°47′ N, 11°56′ E 167
Bruno, Can. 52°15′ N, 105°32′ W 108
Bruno, It. 44°46′ N, 8°26′ E 167
Brunson, S.C., U.S. 32°55′ N, 81°12′ W 96
Brunssum, Neth. 50°57′ N, 5°58′ E 167
Brunswick, Ga., U.S. 31°8′ N, 81°30′ W 96
Brunswick, Me., U.S. 43°54′ N, 69°59′ W 104
Brunswick, Ohio, U.S. 41°13′ N, 81°51′ W 102
Brunswick Lake, lake, Can. 48°56′ N, 83°57′ W 94
Brunswick Naval Air Station, Me., U.S. 43°53′ N, 69°58′ W 104
Brunswick, Península de, Chile 53°26′ S, 73°18′ W 134
Brunt Ice Shelf, Antarctica 76°2′ S, 31°32′ W 248
Brus, Serb. 43°22′ N, 21°1′ E 168
Brus Laguna, Hond. 15°44′ N, 84°32′ W 115
Brusartsi, Bulg. 43°39′ N, 23°4′ E 168
Brush, Colo., U.S. 40°15′ N, 103°38′ W 90
Brusnik, Serb. 44°6′ N, 22°27′ E 168
Brusovo, Russ. 60°30′ N, 87°24′ E 169
Brusque, Braz. 27°6′ S, 48°55′ W 138
Brussels (Bruxelles), Belg. 50°50′ N, 4°17′ E 163
Brussels Capital, adm. division, Belg. 50°53′ N, 3°56′ E 150
Brusturi, Rom. 47°9′ N, 22°16′ E 168
Brusy, Pol. 53°53′ N, 17°43′ E 152
Bruxelles see Brussels, Belg. 50°50′ N, 4°17′ E 163
Bruyères, Fr. 48°12′ N, 6°42′ E 163
Bruzgi, Belarus 53°34′ N, 23°42′ E 152
Bruzual, Venez. 8°1′ N, 69°21′ W 136
Bryan, Ohio, U.S. 41°27′ N, 84°33′ W 102
Bryan, Tex., U.S. 30°39′ N, 96°22′ W 96
Bryansk, Russ. 53°12′ N, 34°25′ E 154
Bryansk, Russ. 44°19′ N, 46°58′ E 158
Bryansk, adm. division, Russ. 52°59′ N, 32°4′ E 154
Bryant, Ark., U.S. 34°34′ N, 92°30′ W 96
Bryant, Fla., U.S. 26°49′ N, 80°35′ W 105
Bryant, S. Dak., U.S. 44°33′ N, 97°30′ W 90
Bryant, Cape, Antarctica 71°34′ S, 60°10′ W 248
Bryant Pond, Me., U.S. 44°22′ N, 70°39′ W 104
Bryce Canyon National Park, Utah, U.S. 37°22′ N, 112°11′ W 92
Bryceland, La., U.S. 32°27′ N, 92°59′ W 103
Brykalansk, Russ. 65°28′ N, 54°14′ E 154
Bryne, Nor. 58°44′ N, 5°38′ E 152
Bryson City, N.C., U.S. 35°25′ N, 83°26′ W 96
Bryukhovetskaya, Russ. 45°50′ N, 38°56′ E 156
Brza Palanka, Serb. 44°28′ N, 22°25′ E 168
Brzeg, Pol. 50°50′ N, 17°28′ E 152
Bu Hasa, oil field, U.A.E. 23°27′ N, 53°7′ E 182
Bū Sunbul, Jabal, peak, Lib. 23°8′ N, 22°12′ E 216
Bua, river, Malawi 13°43′ S, 33°25′ E 224
Bua Yai, Thai. 15°35′ N, 102°24′ E 202
Bu'aale, Somalia 1°1′ N, 42°38′ E 224
Buan, S. Korea 35°43′ N, 126°45′ E 200
Buatan, Indonesia 0°44′ N, 101°47′ E 196
Buatyrma, river, Kaz. 49°39′ N, 84°23′ E 184
Bu'ayrāt al Ḩasūn, Lib. 31°23′ N, 15°41′ E 216
Buba, Guinea-Bissau 11°34′ N, 15°2′ W 222
Buberos, Sp. 41°38′ N, 2°12′ W 164
Būbiyān, island, Kuwait 29°40′ N, 48°23′ E 180
Bucak, Turk. 37°26′ N, 30°36′ E 180
Bucakkışla, Turk. 36°56′ N, 33°1′ E 156
Bucaramanga, Col. 7°7′ N, 73°6′ W 136
Buccaneer Archipelago, Indian Ocean 15°46′ S, 122°50′ E 230
Buchach, Ukr. 49°2′ N, 25°24′ E 152
Buchan Gulf 71°43′ N, 76°50′ W 106
Buchanan, Liberia 5°49′ N, 10°3′ W 222
Buchanan, Mich., U.S. 41°48′ N, 86°22′ W 102
Buchanan Bay 78°53′ N, 82°59′ W 246
Buchanan, Lake, Tex., U.S. 30°47′ N, 98°54′ W 92
Buchans, Can. 48°48′ N, 56°52′ W 111
Buchardo, Arg. 34°44′ S, 63°26′ W 139
Bucharest see Bucureşti, Rom. 44°27′ N, 25°57′ E 156
Buchon, Point, U.S. 35°10′ N, 121°14′ W 100
Buchy, Fr. 49°34′ N, 1°21′ E 163
Buciumi, Rom. 47°2′ N, 23°3′ E 168
Buck Point, Can. 52°52′ N, 132°58′ W 108
Buckatunna, Miss., U.S. 31°33′ N, 88°32′ W 103
Buckeye Lake, Ohio, U.S. 39°55′ N, 82°30′ W 102
Buckfield, Me., U.S. 44°16′ N, 70°23′ W 104
Buckingham, U.K. 51°59′ N, 1°0′ E 162
Buckley, Ill., U.S. 40°35′ N, 88°3′ W 102
Buckley, Wash., U.S. 47°8′ N, 122°2′ W 100
Bucklin, Kans., U.S. 37°32′ N, 99°39′ W 90
Buckner, Ark., U.S. 33°21′ N, 93°27′ W 103
Buckner, Mo., U.S. 37°58′ N, 89°1′ W 96
Bucks, Ala., U.S. 31°0′ N, 88°1′ W 103
Buckskin Mountains, Ariz., U.S. 34°7′ N, 114°4′ W 101
Bucksport, Me., U.S. 44°34′ N, 68°48′ W 111
Buco Zau, Angola 4°44′ S, 12°30′ E 218
Bucoda, Wash., U.S. 46°47′ N, 122°53′ W 100
Bucovăţ, Mold. 47°11′ N, 28°28′ E 158
Bucureşti, adm. division, Rom. 44°32′ N, 25°44′ E 156
Bucureşti (Bucharest), Rom. 44°27′ N, 25°57′ E 156
Bucyrus, Ohio, U.S. 40°47′ N, 82°58′ W 102
Bud, Nor. 62°54′ N, 6°55′ E 152
Bud Bud, Somalia 4°12′ N, 46°30′ E 218
Buda, Tex., U.S. 30°3′ N, 97°50′ W 92
Buda, Ukr. 51°14′ N, 27°16′ E 152
Budac, peak, Rom. 47°5′ N, 25°35′ E 156
Budăi, Mold. 45°51′ N, 28°28′ E 156
Budalin, Myanmar 22°24′ N, 95°8′ E 202
Buđanovci, Serb. 44°53′ N, 19°51′ E 168
Budapest, Hung. 47°28′ N, 19°1′ E 168
Budapest, adm. division, Hung. 47°25′ N, 18°44′ E 156
Budaun, India 28°1′ N, 79°8′ E 197
Budd Coast, Antarctica 67°41′ S, 114°55′ E 248
Bude, Miss., U.S. 31°27′ N, 90°51′ W 103
Budennovsk, Russ. 44°44′ N, 44°2′ E 158
Budennovskaya, Russ. 46°51′ N, 41°33′ E 158
Buđevo, Serb. 43°7′ N, 20°3′ E 168
Büdingen, Ger. 50°17′ N, 9°7′ E 167
Budogoshch', Russ. 59°18′ N, 32°30′ E 154
Budrio, It. 44°32′ N, 11°33′ E 167
Budva, Mont. 42°16′ N, 18°50′ E 168
Buech, river, Fr. 44°28′ N, 5°39′ E 165
Bueil, Lac, lake, Can. 50°46′ N, 74°38′ W 110
Buellton, Calif., U.S. 34°37′ N, 120°13′ W 100
Buen Tiempo, Cabo, Arg. 51°29′ S, 68°57′ W 134
Buena Vista, Bol. 17°29′ S, 63°39′ W 137
Buena Vista, Mex. 23°37′ N, 109°39′ W 112
Buena Vista, Venez. 6°11′ N, 68°34′ W 136
Buena Vista, Va., U.S. 37°44′ N, 79°22′ W 96
Buenaventura, Col. 3°49′ N, 77°4′ W 136
Buenaventura, Mex. 29°50′ N, 107°30′ W 92
Buenavista, Philippines 9°0′ N, 125°25′ E 203
Buenópolis, Braz. 17°53′ S, 44°12′ W 138
Buenos Aires, Arg. 34°37′ S, 58°34′ W 139
Buenos Aires, Col. 3°13′ S, 70°2′ W 136
Buenos Aires, adm. division, Arg. 36°12′ S, 61°3′ W 139
Buenos Aires, Punta, Arg. 42°12′ S, 66°20′ W 134
Buey, Cabeza de, peak, Sp. 38°37′ N, 3°15′ W 164
Buffalo, Minn., U.S. 45°9′ N, 93°53′ W 94
Buffalo, Mo., U.S. 37°37′ N, 93°5′ W 96
Buffalo, N.Y., U.S. 42°53′ N, 78°54′ W 94
Buffalo, Ohio, U.S. 39°55′ N, 81°29′ W 102
Buffalo, Okla., U.S. 36°48′ N, 99°38′ W 92
Buffalo, S. Dak., U.S. 45°34′ N, 103°34′ W 90
Buffalo, Tex., U.S. 31°27′ N, 96°4′ W 96
Buffalo, W. Va., U.S. 38°36′ N, 82°0′ W 102
Buffalo, Wyo., U.S. 44°20′ N, 106°42′ W 90
Buffalo Head Prairie, Can. 58°2′ N, 116°21′ W 108
Buffalo Hump, peak, Idaho, U.S. 45°35′ N, 115°46′ W 90
Buffalo Lake, Can. 60°18′ N, 115°54′ W 108
Buffalo Mountain, Nev., U.S. 40°12′ N, 118°13′ W 90
Buffalo Narrows, Can. 55°52′ N, 108°30′ W 108
Buffalo, river, Can. 59°23′ N, 114°33′ W 108
Buford, Ga., U.S. 34°6′ N, 84°1′ W 96
Bug, peninsula, Ger. 54°30′ N, 13°11′ E 152
Buga, Col. 3°54′ N, 76°21′ W 136
Buganda, region, Africa 1°2′ N, 31°15′ E 224
Bugdayly, Turkm. 38°27′ N, 54°23′ E 180
Bugge Islands, Bellingshausen Sea 69°2′ S, 69°44′ W 248
Bugojno, Bosn. and Herzg. 44°2′ N, 17°26′ E 168
Bugrino, Russ. 68°48′ N, 49°11′ E 169
Bugt, China 48°44′ N, 121°57′ E 198
Buguey, Philippines 18°16′ N, 121°49′ E 203
Bugul'ma, Russ. 54°33′ N, 52°52′ E 154
Buguruslan, Russ. 53°38′ N, 52°26′ E 154
Buhăeşti, Rom. 46°46′ N, 27°33′ E 156
Bu'ayrat al'Utaybah, lake, Syr. 33°30′ N, 36°22′ E 194
Buhen, ruin(s), Sudan 21°46′ N, 30°51′ E 182
Buhera, Zimb. 19°21′ S, 31°26′ E 224
Buhl, Idaho, U.S. 42°37′ N, 114°46′ W 90
Buhl, Minn., U.S. 47°29′ N, 92°48′ W 110
Buhuşi, Rom. 46°43′ N, 26°41′ E 158
Bui National Park, Ghana 8°39′ N, 3°8′ W 222
Builth Wells, U.K. 52°8′ N, 3°24′ W 162
Buinsk, Russ. 54°58′ N, 48°17′ E 154
Buitepos, Namibia 22°17′ S, 19°56′ E 227
Bujalance, Sp. 37°53′ N, 4°23′ W 164
Bujanovac, Serb. 42°28′ N, 21°46′ E 168
Bujaraloz, Sp. 41°29′ N, 0°10′ E 164
Bujumbura, Burundi 3°25′ S, 29°11′ E 224
Bük, Hung. 47°22′ N, 16°46′ E 168
Buk, Pol. 52°21′ N, 16°31′ E 152
Buka, island, P.N.G. 5°15′ S, 153°51′ E 192
Bukachivtsi, Ukr. 49°14′ N, 24°30′ E 152
Bukadaban Feng, peak, China 36°12′ N, 90°26′ E 188
Bukama, Dem. Rep. of the Congo 9°15′ S, 25°50′ E 224
Bukanik, Maja, peak, Alban. 41°0′ N, 20°10′ E 156
Bukavu, Dem. Rep. of the Congo 2°32′ S, 28°48′ E 224
Bukcha, Belarus 51°45′ N, 27°38′ E 152
Bukene, Tanzania 4°15′ S, 32°52′ E 224
Bukhara see Buxoro, Uzb. 39°47′ N, 64°25′ E 197
Bukit Baka-Bukit Raya National Park, Indonesia 0°53′ N, 112°3′ E 238
Bukit Tawau National Park, Malaysia 4°28′ N, 117°35′ E 238
Bukit Tigah Puluh National Park, Indonesia 0°58′ N, 102°38′ E 196
Bukittinggi, Indonesia 0°17′ N, 100°22′ E 196
Bükk, Hung. 47°58′ N, 20°23′ E 168
Bükkösd, Hung. 46°6′ N, 17°59′ E 168
Bukmuiža, Latv. 56°10′ N, 27°40′ E 166
Bukoba, Tanzania 1°22′ S, 31°47′ E 224
Bukowiec, Pol. 52°16′ N, 16°14′ E 152
Bukukun, Russ. 49°24′ N, 111°9′ E 198
Bukwiuni, Nig. 12°5′ N, 5°26′ E 222
Bula, Indonesia 3°5′ S, 130°24′ E 192
Bula, Nig. 10°1′ N, 9°36′ E 222
Bülach, Switz. 47°31′ N, 8°32′ E 150
Bulacle, Somalia 5°20′ N, 46°32′ E 218
Bülaevo, Kaz. 54°55′ N, 70°26′ E 184
Bulag, Mongolia 48°12′ N, 108°30′ E 198
Bulan, Ky., U.S. 37°17′ N, 83°10′ W 96
Bulan, Philippines 12°42′ N, 123°53′ E 203
Bulanash, Russ. 57°17′ N, 61°59′ E 154
Bulancak, Turk. 40°57′ N, 38°12′ E 156
Bulandshahr, India 28°24′ N, 77°52′ E 197
Bulanık, Turk. 39°5′ N, 42°14′ E 195
Bulawayo, Zimb. 20°9′ S, 28°36′ E 227
Buldan, Turk. 38°2′ N, 28°49′ E 156
Bulgan, Mongolia 48°49′ N, 103°38′ E 198
Bulgan, Mongolia 44°6′ N, 103°34′ E 198
Bulgan, adm. division, Mongolia 48°20′ N, 102°20′ E 198
Bulgar, Russ. 54°59′ N, 49°17′ E 154
Bulgaria 42°38′ N, 24°1′ E 156
Bulgnéville, Fr. 48°12′ N, 5°49′ E 163
Buliluyan, Cape, Philippines 8°21′ N, 116°45′ E 203
Bull Mountains, Mont., U.S. 46°9′ N, 108°41′ W 90
Bulla Régia, ruin(s), Tun. 36°33′ N, 8°38′ E 156
Bullard, Tex., U.S. 32°7′ N, 95°19′ W 103
Bullas, Sp. 38°2′ N, 1°41′ W 164
Bullaxaar, Somalia 10°20′ N, 44°22′ E 216
Bulle, Switz. 46°37′ N, 7°3′ E 167
Bullhead City, Ariz., U.S. 35°8′ N, 114°34′ W 101
Bullion Mountains, Calif., U.S. 34°28′ N, 116°14′ W 101
Bullmoose Mountain, Can. 55°0′ N, 121°39′ W 108
Bulls, N.Z. 40°11′ S, 175°23′ E 240
Bulls Head, peak, Can. 49°36′ N, 110°55′ W 90
Bully Choop Mountain, Calif., U.S. 40°32′ N, 122°52′ W 90
Bultfontein, S. Af. 28°20′ S, 26°8′ E 227
Buluan, Philippines 6°43′ N, 124°47′ E 203
Bulukumba, Indonesia 5°34′ S, 120°3′ E 192
Bulungkol, China 38°40′ N, 74°55′ E 184
Bulungu, Dem. Rep. of the Congo 4°35′ S, 18°33′ E 218
Bulung'ur, Uzb. 39°45′ N, 67°15′ E 197
Bum La, pass, China 27°49′ N, 91°54′ E 197
Bumba, Dem. Rep. of the Congo 6°56′ S, 19°16′ E 218
Bumba, Dem. Rep. of the Congo 2°11′ N, 22°25′ E 218
Bumbah, Khalīj al 32°18′ N, 22°3′ E 216
Bumbat, Mongolia 46°29′ N, 104°3′ E 198
Bumbuli, Dem. Rep. of the Congo 3°25′ S, 20°29′ E 218
Buna, Bosn. and Herzg. 43°14′ N, 17°49′ E 168
Buna, Dem. Rep. of the Congo 3°18′ S, 18°56′ E 218
Buna, Kenya 2°44′ N, 39°31′ E 224
Buna, Tex., U.S. 30°24′ N, 93°58′ W 103
Bunazi, Tanzania 1°15′ S, 31°25′ E 224
Bunbury, Austral. 33°21′ S, 115°40′ E 231
Bunda, Tanzania 2°0′ S, 33°51′ E 224
Bunde, Ger. 53°10′ N, 7°17′ E 163
Bundi, India 25°25′ N, 75°38′ E 197
Bundoran, Ire. 54°27′ N, 8°18′ W 150
Bundyur, Russ. 57°33′ N, 81°58′ E 169
Bunga, Nig. 11°2′ N, 9°40′ E 222
Bungay, U.K. 52°27′ N, 1°26′ E 163
Bunger Hills, Antarctica 65°28′ S, 101°11′ E 248
Bungle Bungle Range, site, Austral. 17°26′ S, 128°18′ E 230
Bungo, Angola 7°28′ S, 15°22′ E 218
Bungo Suidō 33°1′ N, 132°0′ E 201
Bungoma, Kenya 0°32′ N, 34°34′ E 224
Bungotakada, Japan 33°33′ N, 131°26′ E 201
Bunia, Dem. Rep. of the Congo 1°31′ N, 30°11′ E 224
Bunker, Mo., U.S. 37°27′ N, 91°13′ W 94
Bunker Group, islands, Coral Sea 23°51′ S, 152°40′ E 230
Bunker Hill, Ind., U.S. 40°38′ N, 86°6′ W 102
Bunker Hill, Nev., U.S. 39°15′ N, 117°13′ W 90
Bunkerville, Nev., U.S. 36°46′ N, 114°8′ W 101
Bunkeya, Dem. Rep. of the Congo 10°25′ S, 26°56′ E 224
Bunkie, La., U.S. 30°56′ N, 92°11′ W 103
Bunnell, Fla., U.S. 29°27′ N, 81°17′ W 105
Bunnell Mountain, peak, N.H., U.S. 44°46′ N, 71°34′ W 94
Buñol, Sp. 39°25′ N, 0°48′ E 164
Bünyan, Turk. 38°50′ N, 35°51′ E 156
Bunza, Nig. 12°4′ N, 3°59′ E 222
Bunzoqa, Sudan 12°28′ N, 34°13′ E 182
Buol, Indonesia 1°7′ N, 121°19′ E 192
Buon Me Thuot, Vietnam 12°41′ N, 108°2′ E 202
Buor Khaya, Mys, Russ. 71°47′ N, 131°9′ E 172
Buq'ata, Israel 33°12′ N, 35°46′ E 194
Buqayq, Saudi Arabia 25°56′ N, 49°40′ E 196
Buqbuq, Egypt 31°31′ N, 25°33′ E 226
Bur, Russ. 58°48′ N, 107°4′ E 160
Bûr Fu'ad, Egypt 31°14′ N, 32°19′ E 194
Bur, river, Russ. 70°58′ N, 120°22′ E 160
Bûr Safâga, Egypt 26°44′ N, 33°54′ E 180
Bûr Sa'îd (Port Said), Egypt 31°15′ N, 32°18′ E 194
Bûr Taufîq, Egypt 29°56′ N, 32°30′ E 180
Bura, Kenya 1°6′ S, 39°58′ E 224
Buraan, Somalia 10°10′ N, 48°43′ E 216
Buram, Sudan 10°50′ N, 25°11′ E 224
Buranhém, river, Braz. 16°30′ S, 40°4′ W 138
Burannoye, Russ. 50°59′ N, 54°29′ E 158
Burao (Burco), Somalia 9°34′ N, 45°36′ E 207
Burāq, Syr. 33°10′ N, 36°29′ E 194
Buras, La., U.S. 29°20′ N, 89°32′ W 103
Buratai, Nig. 10°54′ N, 12°4′ E 216
Buraydah, Saudi Arabia 26°21′ N, 44°0′ E 180
Burbach, Ger. 50°44′ N, 8°4′ E 163
Burbank, Calif., U.S. 34°10′ N, 118°18′ W 101
Burco see Burao, Somalia 9°34′ N, 45°36′ E 207
Burdalyk, Turkm. 38°24′ N, 64°22′ E 197
Burden, Mount, Can. 56°9′ N, 123°33′ W 108
Burdesi, Eth. 6°32′ N, 37°13′ E 224
Burditt Lake, lake, Can. 48°53′ N, 94°13′ W 90
Burdur, Turk. 37°42′ N, 30°17′ E 156
Burduy, Russ. 65°39′ N, 48°5′ E 154
Burē, Eth. 8°18′ N, 35°7′ E 224
Burē, Eth. 10°42′ N, 37°3′ E 224
Bure, river, U.K. 52°50′ N, 1°9′ E 162
Büren, Ger. 51°32′ N, 8°33′ E 167
Bürenhayrhan, Mongolia 46°13′ N, 91°34′ E 190
Burford, U.K. 51°48′ N, 1°38′ W 162
Burg, Ger. 54°26′ N, 11°12′ E 152
Burg, Ger. 53°59′ N, 9°16′ E 152
Burg el 'Arab, Egypt 30°54′ N, 29°30′ E 180
Burgan, oil field, Kuwait 28°53′ N, 47°51′ E 196
Burgas, Bulg. 42°30′ N, 27°28′ E 156
Burgas, adm. division, Bulg. 42°44′ N, 26°44′ E 156
Burgaw, N.C., U.S. 34°33′ N, 77°56′ W 96
Burgdorf, Switz. 47°2′ N, 7°37′ E 150
Burgersdorp, S. Af. 31°0′ S, 26°17′ E 227
Burgess Hill, U.K. 50°57′ N, 0°9′ E 162
Burgess, Mount, Can. 66°4′ N, 139°58′ W 98
Burgos, Mex. 24°55′ N, 98°47′ W 114
Burgos, Sp. 42°18′ N, 3°43′ W 164
Burgsinn, Ger. 50°8′ N, 9°38′ E 167
Burgsvik, Sw. 57°2′ N, 18°16′ E 166
Burguete see Auritz, Sp. 42°59′ N, 1°21′ W 164
Burgui, Sp. 42°43′ N, 1°2′ W 164
Burgundy, region, Europe 47°10′ N, 4°11′ E 165
Burhaniye, Turk. 39°30′ N, 26°57′ E 156
Burhanpur, India 21°18′ N, 76°12′ E 188
Burhave, Ger. 53°34′ N, 8°22′ E 163
Buribay, Russ. 51°57′ N, 58°11′ E 154
Burica, Punta, C.R. 7°56′ N, 83°32′ W 115
Burigi, Lake, Tanzania 2°5′ S, 30°45′ E 224
Burin, Can. 47°2′ N, 55°10′ W 111
Buritis, Braz. 15°38′ S, 46°27′ W 138
Burkburnett, Tex., U.S. 34°4′ N, 98°34′ W 92
Burke, S. Dak., U.S. 43°9′ N, 99°18′ W 90
Burke, Tex., U.S. 31°13′ N, 94°47′ W 103
Burke Island, Antarctica 72°57′ S, 105°21′ W 248
Burketown, Austral. 17°46′ S, 139°40′ E 238
Burkett, Mount, Can. 57°9′ N, 132°27′ W 108
Burkeville, Tex., U.S. 30°58′ N, 93°40′ W 103
Burkina Faso 12°40′ N, 1°39′ W 214
Burk's Falls, Can. 45°37′ N, 79°24′ W 94
Burla, Russ. 53°16′ N, 78°23′ E 184
Burleson, Tex., U.S. 32°32′ N, 97°19′ W 96
Burlingame, Kans., U.S. 38°43′ N, 95°50′ W 90
Burlington, Can. 43°19′ N, 79°47′ W 94
Burlington, Colo., U.S. 39°17′ N, 102°16′ W 90
Burlington, N.J., U.S. 40°3′ N, 74°52′ W 94
Burlington, Vt., U.S. 44°28′ N, 73°13′ W 104
Burlington, Wash., U.S. 48°28′ N, 122°20′ W 100
Burlington, Wis., U.S. 42°40′ N, 88°17′ W 102
Burma see Myanmar 21°5′ N, 95°9′ E 192
Burmantovo, Russ. 61°17′ N, 60°29′ E 154
Burnaby, Can. 49°16′ N, 122°57′ W 100
Burnet, Tex., U.S. 30°44′ N, 98°13′ W 96
Burnett Bay 73°53′ N, 127°36′ W 106
Burnett Lake, lake, Can. 59°1′ N, 102°51′ W 108
Burney, Calif., U.S. 40°53′ N, 121°40′ W 90
Burney Mountain, Calif., U.S. 40°47′ N, 121°43′ W 90
Burnham Market, U.K. 52°56′ N, 0°44′ E 162

Burnham on Crouch, *U.K.* 51°37' N, 0°49' E 162
Burnham on Sea, *U.K.* 51°14' N, 2°59' W 162
Burnie, *Austral.* 41°3' S, 145°55' E 231
Burnley, *U.K.* 53°47' N, 2°14' W 162
Burnmouth, *U.K.* 55°50' N, 2°5' W 150
Burns, *Miss., U.S.* 32°6' N, 89°33' W 103
Burns, *Oreg., U.S.* 43°35' N, 119°4' W 90
Burns, *Wyo., U.S.* 41°11' N, 104°22' W 90
Burns Lake, *Can.* 54°13' N, 125°46' W 108
Burnt Peak, *Calif., U.S.* 34°40' N, 118°38' W 101
Burnt, river, *Oreg., U.S.* 44°33' N, 118°8' W 80
Burqin, *China* 47°44' N, 86°53' E 184
Burr, Mount, *Austral.* 37°40' S, 140°15' E 230
Burra, *Nig.* 11°1' N, 8°59' E 222
Burrel, *Alban.* 41°36' N, 20°0' E 168
Burren, region, *Europe* 52°59' N, 9°22' W 150
Burriana, *Sp.* 39°54' N, 0°4' W 164
Burrinjuck Reservoir, lake, *Austral.* 34°54' S, 147°35' E 230
Burro Peak, *N. Mex., U.S.* 32°34' N, 108°30' W 92
Burro, Serranías del, *Mex.* 29°31' N, 102°42' W 112
Burrow Head, *U.K.* 54°42' N, 4°22' W 150
Burrton, *Kans., U.S.* 38°1' N, 97°41' W 90
Bursa, *Turk.* 40°12' N, 29°2' E 156
Burscheid, *Ger.* 51°5' N, 7°6' E 167
Bursey, Mount, *Antarctica* 75°54' S, 131°52' W 248
Burt Lake, lake, *Mich., U.S.* 45°25' N, 84°58' W 94
Burtnieku Ezers, lake, *Latv.* 57°45' N, 24°55' E 166
Burton, *Mich., U.S.* 42°57' N, 83°36' W 102
Burton, *Nebr., U.S.* 42°53' N, 99°36' W 90
Burton Agnes, *U.K.* 54°2' N, 0°20' E 162
Burton upon Trent, *U.K.* 52°48' N, 1°39' W 162
Buru, island, *Indonesia* 3°2' S, 126°2' E 192
Burûn, Râs, *Egypt* 31°13' N, 32°58' E 194
Burun Shibertuy, Gora, peak, *Russ.* 49°36' N, 109°46' E 198
Burundi 3°0' S, 30°0' E 224
Bururi, *Burundi* 3°57' S, 29°38' E 224
Burutu, *Nig.* 5°23' N, 5°31' E 222
Burwash Landing, *Can.* 61°26' N, 139°1' W 98
Burwell, *Nebr., U.S.* 41°45' N, 99°9' W 90
Bury Saint Edmunds, *U.K.* 52°14' N, 0°42' E 162
Buryatiya, adm. division, *Russ.* 53°21' N, 108°28' E 160
Bürylbaytal, *Kaz.* 44°52' N, 74°3' E 184
Burzil Pass, *Pak.* 34°52' N, 75°4' E 186
Busan (Pusan), *S. Korea* 35°6' N, 129°3' E 200
Busan City, adm. division, *S. Korea* 35°8' N, 129°3' E 200
Busanga, *Dem. Rep. of the Congo* 10°13' S, 25°19' E 224
Busanga Swamp, marsh, *Zambia* 14°24' S, 25°16' E 224
Busangu, *Dem. Rep. of the Congo* 8°32' S, 25°27' E 224
Buşayrā, *Jordan* 30°44' N, 35°36' E 194
Busca, *It.* 44°31' N, 7°28' E 167
Buseck, *Ger.* 50°36' N, 8°47' E 167
Būshehr, *Iran* 28°54' N, 50°52' E 196
Bushgan, oil field, *Iran* 28°56' N, 51°53' E 196
Bushmanland, region, *Africa* 29°42' S, 19°4' E 227
Bushnell, *Fla., U.S.* 28°40' N, 82°7' W 105
Bushnell, *Mo., U.S.* 40°32' N, 90°31' W 94
Bushnell, *Nebr., U.S.* 41°13' N, 103°54' W 90
Bushtricë, *Alban.* 41°52' N, 20°25' E 168
Businga, *Dem. Rep. of the Congo* 3°17' N, 20°56' E 218
Busira, river, *Dem. Rep. of the Congo* 0°26' N, 19°3' E 218
Buslē, *Eth.* 5°23' N, 44°20' E 218
Busovača, *Bosn. and Herzg.* 44°6' N, 17°51' E 168
Buşrá al Ḩarīrī, *Syr.* 32°50' N, 36°20' E 194
Buşrá ash Shām, *Syr.* 32°31' N, 36°28' E 194
Busseri, *Sudan* 7°31' N, 27°57' E 224
Busseri, river, *Sudan* 6°38' N, 26°33' E 224
Bussoleno, *It.* 45°8' N, 7°8' E 167
Bussum, *Neth.* 52°16' N, 5°9' E 163
Bustamante, *Mex.* 26°30' N, 100°32' W 114
Bustard Islands, *North America* 45°37' N, 81°16' W 94
Bustarviejo, *Sp.* 40°51' N, 3°42' W 164
Buştenari, oil field, *Rom.* 45°7' N, 25°44' E 156
Bustillos, Laguna, lake, *Mex.* 28°34' N, 107°21' W 92
Busto, Cabo, *Sp.* 43°34' N, 6°28' W 150
Buston, *Taj.* 40°30' N, 69°17' E 197
Busu Mandji, *Dem. Rep. of the Congo* 2°51' N, 21°15' E 218
Busu-Djanoa, *Dem. Rep. of the Congo* 1°39' N, 21°20' E 218
Bususulu, *Dem. Rep. of the Congo* 0°49' N, 20°44' E 218
But e Koritës, peak, *Alban.* 40°45' N, 20°47' E 156
Buta, *Dem. Rep. of the Congo* 2°44' N, 24°44' E 224
Butare, *Rwanda* 2°37' S, 29°42' E 224
Bute Helu, *Kenya* 2°40' N, 39°51' E 224
Bute Inlet 50°34' N, 125°22' W 90
Butembo, *Dem. Rep. of the Congo* 0°6' N, 29°15' E 224
Buteni, *Rom.* 46°20' N, 22°8' E 168
Buthidaung, *Myanmar* 20°54' N, 92°28' E 188
Butiá, *Braz.* 30°8' S, 51°56' W 139
Butiaba, *Uganda* 1°47' N, 31°19' E 224
Butler, *Ala., U.S.* 32°5' N, 88°13' W 103
Butler, *Ga., U.S.* 32°33' N, 84°14' W 96
Butler, *Ky., U.S.* 38°46' N, 84°22' W 102
Butler, *Mo., U.S.* 38°14' N, 94°20' W 94
Butler, *Ohio, U.S.* 40°34' N, 82°26' W 102
Butler, *Pa., U.S.* 40°51' N, 79°54' W 94
Butler Island, *Antarctica* 72°6' S, 60°8' W 248
Butlēŗi, *Latv.* 57°3' N, 25°49' E 166
Butlerville, *Ind., U.S.* 39°1' N, 85°31' W 102
Buţmah, oil field, *Iraq* 36°40' N, 42°36' E 195
Buton, island, *Indonesia* 4°47' S, 123°16' E 192
Butte, *Mont., U.S.* 45°59' N, 112°32' W 82
Butte, *Nebr., U.S.* 42°53' N, 98°52' W 90
Butte Mountains, *Nev., U.S.* 39°43' N, 115°26' W 90
Butterwick, *U.K.* 52°58' N, 7°416' E 162
Butterworth, *Malaysia* 5°24' N, 100°23' E 196
Buttes, Sierra, peak, *Calif., U.S.* 39°34' N, 120°44' W 90
Buttle Lake, lake, *Can.* 49°33' N, 125°56' W 90
Button Islands, *Labrador Sea* 60°23' N, 64°18' W 106
Buttonwillow, *Calif., U.S.* 35°24' N, 119°30' W 100
Butuan, *Philippines* 8°59' N, 125°32' E 203
Buturlinovka, *Russ.* 50°50' N, 40°36' E 158
Butwal, *Nepal* 27°41' N, 83°30' E 197
Butyaalo, *Somalia* 11°26' N, 49°57' E 216
Butzbach, *Ger.* 50°26' N, 8°40' E 167
Buuhoodle, *Somalia* 8°14' N, 46°22' E 218
Buulobarde, *Somalia* 3°48' N, 45°37' E 218
Buur Gaabo, *Somalia* 1°13' S, 41°51' E 224
Buurhakaba, *Somalia* 2°45' N, 44°7' E 218
Buwayḑān, *Syr.* 33°11' N, 36°26' E 194
Buxar, *India* 25°32' N, 83°56' E 197
Buxoro (Bukhara), *Uzb.* 39°47' N, 64°25' E 197
Buxton, *Guyana* 6°39' N, 58°3' W 130
Buxton, *Me., U.S.* 43°38' N, 70°32' W 104
Buxton, *N.C., U.S.* 35°16' N, 75°34' W 96
Buxton, *U.K.* 53°15' N, 1°55' W 162
Buy, *Russ.* 58°29' N, 41°36' E 154
Buyant, *Mongolia* 46°12' N, 110°49' E 198
Buyant Ovoo, *Mongolia* 44°56' N, 107°12' E 198
Buyant-Uhaa see Saynshand, *Mongolia* 44°51' N, 110°9' E 190
Buynaksk, *Russ.* 42°48' N, 47°7' E 195
Buyo, *Côte d'Ivoire* 6°11' N, 7°1' W 222
Buyr Nuur, lake, *Mongolia* 47°49' N, 117°29' E 198
Buyun Shan, peak, *China* 40°4' N, 122°41' E 200
Buzancy, *Fr.* 49°25' N, 4°57' E 163
Buzău, adm. division, *Rom.* 45°26' N, 26°10' E 156
Buzău, Pasul, pass, *Rom.* 45°35' N, 26°9' E 156
Buzaymah, *Lib.* 24°55' N, 22°1' E 216
Buzlove, *Ukr.* 48°19' N, 22°23' E 152
Büzmey'in, *Turkm.* 38°1' N, 58°16' E 180
Buzul Daği, peak, *Turk.* 37°27' N, 43°50' E 195
Buzuluk, *Russ.* 52°46' N, 52°13' E 154
Buzzards Bay, *Mass., U.S.* 41°44' N, 70°38' W 104
Bwendi, *Dem. Rep. of the Congo* 4°1' N, 26°42' E 224
Bwere, river, *Dem. Rep. of the Congo* 3°44' N, 27°19' E 224
Byahoml', *Belarus* 54°43' N, 28°3' E 166
Byala, *Bulg.* 43°28' N, 25°44' E 156
Byala, *Bulg.* 42°52' N, 27°53' E 156
Byalynichy, *Belarus* 54°0' N, 29°43' E 166
Byam Channel 75°15' N, 109°24' W 106
Byam Martin, Cape, *Can.* 73°20' N, 77°1' W 106
Byam Martin Island, *Can.* 74°29' N, 104°57' W 106
Byarezina, river, *Belarus* 53°24' N, 29°5' E 152
Byarezina, river, *Belarus* 54°13' N, 26°34' E 166
Byaroza, *Belarus* 52°31' N, 24°58' E 152
Byblos see Jbail, *Leb.* 34°7' N, 35°39' E 194
Bychikha, *Belarus* 55°40' N, 30°3' E 166
Bydalen, *Nor.* 63°5' N, 13°45' E 152
Bydgoszcz, *Pol.* 53°8' N, 18°1' E 152
Byer, *Ohio, U.S.* 39°9' N, 82°38' W 102
Byerazino, *Belarus* 53°53' N, 29°1' E 166
Byers, *Colo., U.S.* 39°42' N, 104°14' W 90
Byesville, *Ohio, U.S.* 39°57' N, 81°33' W 102
Bygdeå, *Nor.* 64°3' N, 20°51' E 152
Bygstad, *Nor.* 61°22' N, 5°41' E 152
Bykhaw, *Belarus* 53°30' N, 30°18' E 154
Bykovo, *Russ.* 49°37' N, 45°21' E 158
Bykovskiy, *Russ.* 71°43' N, 129°19' E 160
Bylas, *Ariz., U.S.* 33°7' N, 110°7' W 92
Bylot Island, *Can.* 73°51' N, 81°13' W 106
Bylot, island, *Can.* 72°49' N, 75°55' W 106
Byng Inlet, *Can.* 45°44' N, 80°33' W 94
Bynguano Range, *Austral.* 31°8' S, 142°42' E 230
Byram, *Miss., U.S.* 32°10' N, 90°16' W 103
Byrd, Cape, *Antarctica* 69°52' S, 79°21' W 248
Byrd, Lac, lake, *Can.* 47°1' N, 77°12' W 110
Byron, *Calif., U.S.* 37°51' N, 121°39' W 100
Byron, *Ill., U.S.* 42°7' N, 89°16' W 102
Byron, Cape, *Austral.* 28°38' S, 153°45' E 230
Byron, Isla, island, *Chile* 47°44' S, 76°33' W 134
Byrum, *Den.* 57°14' N, 10°59' E 150
Byske, *Nor.* 64°57' N, 21°10' E 152
Bytów, *Pol.* 54°9' N, 17°29' E 152
Byumba, *Rwanda* 1°39' S, 30°2' E 224
Bzip'i, river, *Europe* 43°22' N, 40°37' E 195

C

Ca Mau, *Vietnam* 9°12' N, 105°7' E 202
Ca Na, *Vietnam* 11°22' N, 108°51' E 202
Ca Na, Mui, *Vietnam* 10°56' N, 109°0' E 202
Ca, river, *Vietnam* 19°12' N, 104°44' E 202
C.A. Rosetti, *Rom.* 45°17' N, 29°33' E 156
Caaguazú, *Parag.* 25°27' S, 56°1' W 132
Caamaño Sound 52°48' N, 129°56' W 108
Caapucú, *Parag.* 26°15' S, 57°11' W 139
Caatinga, *Braz.* 17°8' S, 45°58' W 138
Caazapá, *Parag.* 26°9' S, 56°23' W 139
Cabaiguán, *Cuba* 22°5' N, 79°31' W 116
Caballococha, *Peru* 3°58' S, 70°30' W 130
Caballos Mesteños, Llano de los, *Mex.* 28°36' N, 104°37' W 112
Cabana, *Peru* 8°25' S, 78°1' W 130
Cabanaconde, *Peru* 15°40' S, 71°58' W 137
Cabanatuan, *Philippines* 15°28' N, 120°58' E 203
Cabañeros National Park, *Sp.* 39°14' N, 4°33' W 164
Cabanes, *Sp.* 40°9' N, 0°3' E 164
Cabano, *Can.* 47°39' N, 68°55' W 94
Cabedelo, *Braz.* 7°4' S, 34°52' W 132
Cabery, *Ill., U.S.* 40°59' N, 88°13' W 102
Cabeza de Lagarto, Punta, *Peru* 10°15' S, 80°8' W 130
Cabeza de Pava, *Col.* 2°47' N, 69°13' W 136
Cabeza del Buey, *Sp.* 38°43' N, 5°14' W 164
Cabezas, *Bol.* 18°49' S, 63°26' W 137
Cabildo, *Arg.* 38°30' S, 61°57' W 139
Cabimas, *Venez.* 10°24' N, 71°29' W 136
Cabinda, *Angola* 5°35' S, 12°10' E 218
Cabinet Mountains, *Mont., U.S.* 48°20' N, 116°13' W 90
Cabiri, *Angola* 8°53' S, 13°40' E 220
Cable, *Wis., U.S.* 46°12' N, 91°17' W 94
Cabo Blanco, *Arg.* 47°12' S, 65°47' W 134
Cabo Delgado, adm. division, *Mozambique* 12°22' S, 38°34' E 220
Cabo Frio, *Braz.* 22°51' S, 42°1' W 138
Cabo Gracias a Dios, *Nicar.* 14°58' N, 83°14' W 115
Cabo Raso, *Arg.* 44°21' S, 65°17' W 134
Cabo San Lucas, *Mex.* 22°51' N, 109°56' W 112
Cabonga, Réservoir, lake, *Can.* 47°6' N, 78°13' W 81
Cabonga, Réservoir, lake, *Can.* 47°14' N, 78°10' W 106
Cabool, *Mo., U.S.* 37°6' N, 92°6' W 96
Caborca, *Mex.* 30°42' N, 112°11' W 92
Cabot, *Vt., U.S.* 44°23' N, 72°20' W 104
Cabot Head, *Can.* 45°15' N, 81°17' W 94
Cabot, Mount, *N.H., U.S.* 44°29' N, 71°26' W 104
Cabra de Santo Cristo, *Sp.* 37°42' N, 3°16' W 164
Cabral, *Dom. Rep.* 18°14' N, 71°12' W 116
Cabrera Baja, Sierra de la, *Sp.* 42°3' N, 7°8' W 150
Cabrera, island, *Sp.* 38°52' N, 2°54' E 214
Cabri, *Can.* 50°37' N, 108°28' W 90
Cabri Lake, lake, *Can.* 51°4' N, 110°5' W 90
Cabriel, river, *Sp.* 39°23' N, 1°27' W 164
Cabrillo National Monument, *Calif., U.S.* 32°40' N, 117°17' W 101
Cabrobó, *Braz.* 8°31' S, 39°21' W 132
Cabrón, Cabo, *Dom. Rep.* 19°22' N, 69°11' W 116
Cabruta, *Venez.* 7°40' N, 66°16' W 136
Cabugao, *Philippines* 17°49' N, 120°27' E 203
Cabure, *Venez.* 11°9' N, 69°38' W 136
Cabuyaro, *Col.* 4°16' N, 72°48' W 136
Caçador, *Braz.* 26°47' S, 51°0' W 139
Cacahuamilpa, *Mex.* 18°40' N, 99°33' W 114
Cacahuatepec, *Mex.* 16°34' N, 98°11' W 112
Cacahuatique, peak, *El Salv.* 13°45' N, 88°20' W 115
Čačak, *Serb.* 43°52' N, 20°20' E 168
Cacalotán, *Mex.* 23°4' N, 105°50' W 114
Cacaoui, Lac, lake, *Can.* 50°52' N, 67°26' W 111
Caçapava do Sul, *Braz.* 30°30' S, 53°30' W 139
Caccia, Capo, *It.* 40°34' N, 7°24' E 156
Cacequi, *Braz.* 29°55' S, 54°51' W 139
Cáceres, *Braz.* 16°7' S, 57°39' W 132
Cáceres, *Col.* 7°35' N, 75°19' W 136
Cáceres, *Sp.* 39°28' N, 6°23' W 164
Cacharí, *Arg.* 36°23' S, 59°31' W 139
Cache Bay, *Can.* 46°22' N, 79°59' W 94
Cache Peak, *Idaho, U.S.* 42°11' N, 113°43' W 90
Cacheu, *Guinea-Bissau* 12°14' N, 16°7' W 222
Cachimbo, *Braz.* 9°19' S, 54°51' W 130
Cachimbo, Serra do, *Braz.* 7°52' S, 56°39' W 130
Cachingues, *Angola* 13°7' S, 16°43' E 220
Cachisca, Lac, lake, *Can.* 50°24' N, 75°36' W 110
Cachoeira, *Braz.* 14°23' S, 55°34' W 132
Cachoeira Alta, *Braz.* 18°51' S, 50°56' W 138
Cachoeira do Sul, *Braz.* 30°2' S, 52°56' W 139
Cachoeira Ipadu, fall(s), *Braz.* 0°15' N, 67°20' W 136
Cachoeira Ipanoré, fall(s), *Braz.* 0°13' N, 68°29' W 136
Cachoeiro do Itapemirim, *Braz.* 20°54' S, 41°9' W 138
Cachos, Punta, *Chile* 27°41' S, 72°17' W 134
Cachuela Esperanza, *Bol.* 10°36' S, 65°34' W 137
Cacine, *Guinea-Bissau* 11°6' N, 15°2' W 222
Cacolo, *Angola* 10°11' S, 19°13' E 207
Caconda, *Angola* 13°44' S, 15°4' E 220
Cacongo, *Angola* 5°15' S, 12°7' E 218
Cactus, *Tex., U.S.* 36°0' N, 101°59' W 92
Cactus Flat, *Nev., U.S.* 37°52' N, 116°55' W 90
Cactus Range, *Nev., U.S.* 37°54' N, 117°6' W 90
Caçu, *Braz.* 18°35' S, 51°12' W 138
Caculé, *Braz.* 14°34' S, 42°12' W 138
Cacuri, *Venez.* 4°48' N, 65°20' W 136
Cacuso, *Angola* 9°27' S, 15°44' E 218
Cadaadley, *Somalia* 9°44' N, 44°40' E 218
Cadair Idris, peak, *U.K.* 52°41' N, 3°57' W 162
Cadale, *Somalia* 2°44' N, 46°27' E 218
Cadaqués, *Sp.* 42°16' N, 3°16' E 164
Cađavica, *Croatia* 45°45' N, 17°50' E 168
Caddo, *Okla., U.S.* 34°6' N, 96°16' W 96
Caddo Lake, *Tex., U.S.* 32°44' N, 94°30' W 81
Cade, *La., U.S.* 30°2' N, 91°54' W 103
Cadereyta, *Mex.* 25°34' N, 99°59' W 114
Cadí, Serra del, *Sp.* 42°16' N, 1°28' E 164
Cadillac, *Can.* 49°43' N, 107°45' W 90
Cadillac Mountain, *Me., U.S.* 44°20' N, 68°19' W 94
Çadır Dağı, peak, *Turk.* 38°12' N, 43°3' E 195
Cadiz, *Ky., U.S.* 36°52' N, 87°50' W 96
Cadiz, *Ohio, U.S.* 40°15' N, 81°0' W 102
Cadiz, *Philippines* 10°56' N, 123°16' E 203
Cádiz, *Sp.* 36°31' N, 6°18' W 164
Cadomin, *Can.* 53°0' N, 117°20' W 108
Cady Mountains, *Calif., U.S.* 34°57' N, 116°20' W 101
Caen, *Fr.* 49°11' N, 0°22' E 150
Caerdydd see Cardiff, *U.K.* 51°28' N, 3°12' W 162
Caerlaverock Castle, site, *U.K.* 54°58' N, 3°38' W 150
Caerleon, *U.K.* 51°36' N, 2°57' W 162
Caernarfon, *U.K.* 53°9' N, 4°14' W 162
Caerphilly, *U.K.* 51°35' N, 3°13' W 162
Caesarea, ruin(s), *Israel* 32°29' N, 34°51' E 194
Caeté, *Braz.* 19°54' S, 43°35' W 138
Caeté, river, *Braz.* 9°29' S, 69°35' W 130
Caetité, *Braz.* 14°5' S, 42°31' W 138
Cafayate, *Arg.* 26°4' S, 65°58' W 132
Cafuini, river, *Braz.* 1°12' N, 58°27' W 130
Cagayan de Oro, *Philippines* 8°31' N, 124°36' E 203
Cagayan Islands, *Sulu Sea* 9°6' N, 121°20' E 203
Cagayan, river, *Philippines* 18°5' N, 121°37' E 203
Cagayan Sulu Island, *Philippines* 6°52' N, 118°36' E 192
Cagliari, *It.* 39°13' N, 9°6' E 156
Cagnano Varano, *It.* 41°49' N, 15°46' E 156
Caguán, river, *Col.* 1°9' N, 74°44' W 136
Cahama, *Angola* 16°15' S, 14°12' E 220
Cahora Bassa, *Mozambique* 15°38' S, 32°46' E 224
Cahora Bassa Dam, *Mozambique* 15°46' S, 32°3' E 224
Cahore Point, *Ire.* 52°34' N, 6°9' W 150
Cahors, *Fr.* 44°31' N, 1°18' E 214
Cahuinari National Park, *Col.* 1°18' S, 71°54' W 136
Cahuinari, river, *Col.* 1°22' S, 71°29' W 136
Cahuita National Park, *C.R.* 9°42' N, 82°55' W 115
Cahul, *Mold.* 45°54' N, 28°10' E 156
Cai Bau, *Vietnam* 21°8' N, 107°28' E 198
Caia, *Mozambique* 17°49' S, 35°18' E 224
Caiabis, Serra dos, *Braz.* 12°29' S, 56°51' W 130
Caianda, *Angola* 11°4' S, 23°30' E 224
Caiapó, river, *Braz.* 16°33' S, 51°17' W 138
Caiapó, Serra do, *Braz.* 17°38' S, 53°25' W 132
Caiapônia, *Braz.* 16°59' S, 51°49' W 138
Caibarién, *Cuba* 22°29' N, 79°28' W 116
Caicara, *Venez.* 7°36' N, 66°10' W 136
Caicó, *Braz.* 6°30' S, 37°7' W 132
Caicos Islands, *North Atlantic Ocean* 21°25' N, 71°58' W 116
Caijiapo, *China* 34°19' N, 107°33' E 198
Cailloma, *Peru* 15°13' S, 71°45' W 137
Caimito, *Col.* 8°49' N, 75°8' W 136
Cainde, *Angola* 15°34' S, 13°20' E 220
Cains, river, *Can.* 46°20' N, 66°23' W 94
Cainsville, *Mo., U.S.* 40°25' N, 93°46' W 94
Caird Coast, *Antarctica* 76°29' S, 32°29' W 248
Cairngorms Nat. Park, *U.K.* 57°3' N, 4°35' W 150
Cairns, *Austral.* 16°56' S, 145°45' E 231
Cairnwell Pass, *U.K.* 56°52' N, 3°25' W 150
Cairo, *Ga., U.S.* 30°52' N, 84°13' W 96
Cairo, *Mo., U.S.* 37°0' N, 89°10' W 96
Cairo, *N.Y., U.S.* 42°17' N, 74°1' W 104
Cairo see El Qâhira, *Egypt* 30°3' N, 31°8' E 180
Cairo Montenotte, *It.* 44°23' N, 8°16' E 167
Caistor, *U.K.* 53°29' N, 0°19' E 162
Caithness, Ord of, peak, *U.K.* 58°8' N, 3°41' W 150
Caitou, *Angola* 14°31' S, 13°4' E 220
Caiundo, *Angola* 15°44' S, 17°26' E 220
Caiza, *Bol.* 20°4' S, 65°45' W 137
Caiza see Villa Ingavi, *Bol.* 21°47' S, 63°33' W 137
Cajamarca, *Peru* 7°8' S, 78°32' W 130
Cajamarca, adm. division, *Peru* 4°58' S, 79°20' W 130
Cajatambo, *Peru* 10°30' S, 77°1' W 130
Cajàzeiras, *Braz.* 6°54' S, 38°32' W 132
Cajniče, *Bosn. and Herzg.* 43°33' N, 19°4' E 168
Cajon Pass, *Calif., U.S.* 34°20' N, 117°27' W 101
Caju, Ilha do, island, *Braz.* 2°56' S, 42°35' W 132
Çakırgöl Dağı, peak, *Turk.* 40°33' N, 39°38' E 195
Çakmak, *Turk.* 39°10' N, 31°52' E 156
Çakmak Dağı, peak, *Turk.* 39°45' N, 42°9' E 195
Çal, *Turk.* 38°4' N, 29°23' E 156
Cal Madow, Buuraha, peak, *Somalia* 10°56' N, 48°7' E 218
Cala, *Sp.* 37°57' N, 6°19' W 164
Cala Rajada, *Sp.* 39°41' N, 3°27' E 150
Cala see Doğruyol, *Turk.* 41°3' N, 43°20' E 195
Calabar, *Nig.* 4°57' N, 8°20' E 222
Calabozo, *Venez.* 8°55' N, 67°28' W 136
Calabria, adm. division, *It.* 39°5' N, 16°5' E 156
Calaburras, Punta de, *Sp.* 36°20' N, 4°39' W 164
Calacoto, *Bol.* 17°22' S, 68°43' W 137
Calaf, *Sp.* 41°43' N, 1°30' E 164
Calafat, *Rom.* 43°59' N, 22°56' E 168
Calahorra, *Sp.* 42°18' N, 1°58' W 164
Calais, *Fr.* 50°57' N, 1°51' E 163
Calais, *Me., U.S.* 45°10' N, 67°17' W 94
Calakmul, ruin(s), *Mex.* 18°4' N, 89°57' W 115
Calalaste, Sierra de, *Arg.* 25°16' S, 67°50' W 132
Calalzo, *It.* 46°27' N, 12°21' E 167
Calama, *Braz.* 8°3' S, 62°51' W 130
Calama, *Chile* 22°28' S, 68°58' W 137
Calamar, *Col.* 10°13' N, 74°58' W 136
Calamar, *Col.* 1°57' N, 72°34' W 136
Calamarca, *Bol.* 16°59' S, 68°8' W 137
Calamian Group, islands, *Sulu Sea* 11°37' N, 119°18' E 203
Calamocha, *Sp.* 40°54' N, 1°18' W 164
Calamonte, *Sp.* 38°53' N, 6°23' W 164
Calamus, river, *Nebr., U.S.* 42°18' N, 100°3' W 90
Calañas, *Sp.* 37°39' N, 6°54' W 150
Calanda, *Sp.* 40°55' N, 0°15' E 164
Calandula, *Angola* 9°6' S, 15°58' E 218
Calang, *Indonesia* 4°39' N, 95°35' E 196
Calanscio, oil field, *Lib.* 28°1' N, 21°18' E 216
Calapan, *Philippines* 13°24' N, 121°10' E 203
Călăraşi, adm. division, *Rom.* 44°23' N, 26°25' E 156
Călăraşi, *Mold.* 47°16' N, 28°18' E 156
Călăraşi, *Rom.* 44°11' N, 27°19' E 156
Calasparra, *Sp.* 38°13' N, 1°43' W 164
Calatayud, *Sp.* 41°21' N, 1°40' W 164
Călăţele, *Rom.* 46°45' N, 23°1' E 168
Calatorao, *Sp.* 41°31' N, 1°21' W 164
Calavà, Capo, *It.* 38°12' N, 14°19' E 156
Calayan, island, *Philippines* 19°26' N, 120°55' E 198
Calbayog, *Philippines* 12°4' N, 124°35' E 203
Calbiga, *Philippines* 11°37' N, 125°1' E 203
Calca, *Peru* 13°19' S, 71°59' W 137
Calcanhar, Ponta do, *Braz.* 5°8' S, 35°29' W 132
Calcasieu Lake, *La., U.S.* 29°52' N, 93°33' W 103
Calcasieu, river, *La., U.S.* 30°22' N, 93°8' W 103
Calceta, *Venez.* 7°4' N, 62°30' W 130
Calchaquí, *Arg.* 29°50' S, 60°18' W 139
Calcutta see Kolkata, *India* 22°33' N, 88°21' E 197
Caldas, adm. division, *Col.* 5°10' N, 75°51' W 136
Caldas da Rainha, *Port.* 39°23' N, 9°9' W 150
Caldas Novas, *Braz.* 17°48' S, 48°40' W 138
Caldbeck, *U.K.* 54°45' N, 3°3' W 162
Caldera, *Chile* 27°6' S, 70°52' W 132

Calderitas, *Mex.* 18°34′ N, 88°17′ W 115
Caldes de Malavella, *Sp.* 41°50′ N, 2°49′ E 164
Çaldıran, *Turk.* 39°6′ N, 43°50′ E 195
Caldonazzo, *It.* 45°59′ N, 11°14′ E 167
Caldron Snout, lake, *U.K.* 54°40′ N, 2°32′ W 162
Caldwell, *Idaho, U.S.* 43°39′ N, 116°40′ W 82
Caldwell, *Kans., U.S.* 37°0′ N, 97°37′ W 92
Caldwell, *Ohio, U.S.* 39°44′ N, 81°31′ W 102
Caldwell, *Tex., U.S.* 30°31′ N, 96°42′ W 96
Caledon, *S. Af.* 34°13′ S, 19°26′ E 227
Caledonia, *Minn., U.S.* 43°38′ N, 91°29′ W 94
Calella, *Sp.* 41°36′ N, 2°39′ E 164
Caleta Buena, *Chile* 19°53′ S, 70°10′ W 137
Caleta Pabellón de Pica, *Chile* 20°56′ S, 70°10′ W 137
Calexico, *Calif., U.S.* 32°40′ N, 115°30′ W 101
Calf, The, peak, *U.K.* 54°22′ N, 2°33′ W 162
Calgary, *Can.* 51°3′ N, 114°5′ W 90
Calhoun Falls, *S.C., U.S.* 34°5′ N, 82°36′ W 96
Cali, *Col.* 3°24′ N, 76°33′ W 136
Calico Peak, *Nev., U.S.* 41°49′ N, 117°22′ W 90
Calico Rock, *Ark., U.S.* 36°6′ N, 92°10′ W 96
Calicut see Kozhikode, *India* 11°15′ N, 75°46′ E 188
Caliente, *Calif., U.S.* 35°18′ N, 118°38′ W 101
Caliente, *Nev., U.S.* 37°35′ N, 114°30′ W 82
Caliente Range, *Calif., U.S.* 35°0′ N, 119°45′ W 100
California, *Mo., U.S.* 38°37′ N, 92°33′ W 94
California, adm. division, *Calif., U.S.* 36°52′ N, 120°58′ W 92
California City, *Calif., U.S.* 35°7′ N, 117°59′ W 101
California Coastal National Monument, *Pacific Ocean* 37°19′ N, 122°49′ W 100
California, Gulf of (Sea of Cortez),31°12′ N, 114°47′ W 73
California Hot Springs, *Calif., U.S.* 35°53′ N, 118°41′ W 101
California Spaceport, *Calif., U.S.* 34°35′ N, 120°39′ W 100
California Valley, *Calif., U.S.* 35°19′ N, 120°1′ W 100
Cálig, *Sp.* 40°26′ N, 0°20′ E 164
Calilegua, *Arg.* 23°45′ S, 64°46′ W 132
Cälilibad, *Azerb.* 39°12′ N, 48°28′ E 195
Călimani, Munţii, *Rom.* 47°0′ N, 24°32′ E 156
Calion, *Ark., U.S.* 33°18′ N, 92°33′ W 103
Calipatria, *Calif., U.S.* 33°7′ N, 115°31′ W 101
Calispell Peak, *Wash., U.S.* 48°24′ N, 117°36′ W 90
Calkini, *Mex.* 20°23′ N, 90°4′ W 115
Callaghan, Mount, *Nev., U.S.* 39°42′ N, 117°2′ W 90
Callamura, spring, *Austral.* 27°39′ S, 140°53′ E 230
Callander, *Can.* 46°13′ N, 79°22′ W 94
Callao, *Peru* 12°4′ S, 77°9′ W 130
Callaway, *Nebr., U.S.* 41°15′ N, 99°55′ W 90
Calling Lake, *Can.* 55°8′ N, 113°47′ W 108
Calling Lake, *Can.* 55°15′ N, 113°12′ W 108
Callirhoe, ruin(s), *Jordan* 31°35′ N, 35°32′ E 194
Calmar, *Can.* 53°15′ N, 113°49′ W 108
Calnali, *Mex.* 20°52′ N, 98°35′ W 114
Calne, *U.K.* 51°25′ N, 2°1′ W 162
Calonga, *Angola* 16°1′ S, 15°13′ E 220
Caloosahatchee, canal, *Fla., U.S.* 26°45′ N, 81°29′ W 105
Calotmul, *Mex.* 21°0′ N, 88°12′ W 112
Caloto, *Col.* 3°3′ N, 76°24′ W 136
Calpe (Calp), *Sp.* 38°39′ N, 0°3′ E 164
Calpulalpan de Méndez, *Mex.* 17°19′ N, 96°25′ W 114
Çaltı Burnu, *Turk.* 41°17′ N, 37°0′ E 156
Caluango, *Angola* 8°21′ S, 19°36′ E 218
Calulo, *Angola* 10°0′ S, 14°54′ E 220
Calunda, *Angola* 12°8′ S, 23°33′ E 220
Caluso, *It.* 45°18′ N, 7°52′ E 167
Caluula, *Somalia* 11°52′ N, 50°43′ E 182
Calvados Chain, islands, *Solomon Sea* 11°41′ S, 150°22′ E 192
Calvert, *Ala., U.S.* 31°9′ N, 88°0′ W 103
Calvert, *Tex., U.S.* 30°57′ N, 96°40′ W 96
Calvin, *La., U.S.* 31°56′ N, 92°47′ W 103
Calvinia, *S. Af.* 31°28′ S, 19°46′ E 227
Calwa, *Calif., U.S.* 36°42′ N, 119°45′ W 100
Calydon, ruin(s), *Gr.* 38°21′ N, 21°25′ E 156
Çam Burnu, *Turk.* 41°9′ N, 37°45′ E 156
Cam Pha, *Vietnam* 21°2′ N, 107°18′ E 198
Cam Ranh, *Vietnam* 11°53′ N, 109°14′ E 202
Cam Ranh, Vung 11°37′ N, 109°3′ E 202
Cam Xuyen, *Vietnam* 18°15′ N, 106°2′ E 198
Camabatela, *Angola* 8°11′ S, 15°22′ E 218
Camacã, *Braz.* 15°26′ S, 39°29′ W 138
Camachigama, Lac, lake, *Can.* 47°48′ N, 77°5′ W 94
Camacho, *Mex.* 24°25′ N, 102°22′ W 114
Camacupa, *Angola* 12°2′ S, 17°28′ E 220
Camaguán, *Venez.* 8°6′ N, 67°34′ W 136
Camagüey, *Cuba* 21°23′ N, 77°54′ W 116
Camagüey, adm. division, *Cuba* 21°27′ N, 78°32′ W 116
Camagüey, Archipiélago de, *North Atlantic Ocean* 22°40′ N, 78°24′ W 116
Camaleão, Ilha, island, *Braz.* 0°8′ N, 48°50′ W 130
Camaná, *Peru* 16°38′ S, 72°43′ W 137
Camanche Reservoir, lake, *Calif., U.S.* 38°13′ N, 121°8′ W 100
Camanongue, *Angola* 11°26′ S, 20°11′ E 220
Camapuã, *Braz.* 19°32′ S, 54°6′ W 132
Camaquã, *Braz.* 30°52′ S, 51°51′ W 139
Camaquã, river, *Braz.* 31°3′ S, 53°4′ W 139
Camăr, *Rom.* 47°17′ N, 22°38′ E 168
Camarat, Cap, *Fr.* 43°7′ N, 6°40′ E 165
Çamardı, *Turk.* 37°50′ N, 34°58′ E 156
Camargo, *Bol.* 20°40′ S, 65°16′ W 137
Camargo, *Okla., U.S.* 36°0′ N, 99°18′ W 92
Camargue, Île de la, islands, *Golfe Dulion* 43°28′ N, 4°23′ E 165
Camarón, Cabo, *Hond.* 15°59′ N, 85°0′ W 115
Camarones, *Arg.* 44°46′ S, 65°45′ W 134
Camarones, *Chile* 19°3′ S, 69°56′ W 137
Camas, *Sp.* 37°24′ N, 6°3′ W 164
Camas, *Wash., U.S.* 45°34′ N, 122°26′ W 90
Camas Valley, *Oreg., U.S.* 43°1′ N, 123°41′ W 90
Camatindi, *Bol.* 21°0′ S, 63°31′ W 137
Cambeak, point, *U.K.* 50°45′ N, 5°11′ W 150
Camblaya, river, *Bol.* 20°57′ S, 65°16′ W 137
Cambodia 12°37′ N, 103°48′ E 192
Cambona, *Mozambique* 11°47′ S, 36°33′ E 224
Camborne, *U.K.* 50°13′ N, 5°19′ W 150
Cambrai, *Fr.* 50°9′ N, 3°15′ E 163
Cambria, *Calif., U.S.* 35°34′ N, 121°7′ W 100
Cambria Icefield, *Can.* 55°51′ N, 129°25′ W 108
Cambrian Mountains, *U.K.* 52°2′ N, 3°33′ W 162
Cambridge, *Idaho, U.S.* 44°34′ N, 116°41′ W 90
Cambridge, *Nebr., U.S.* 40°16′ N, 100°11′ W 90
Cambridge, *N.Z.* 37°54′ S, 175°29′ E 240
Cambridge, *Ohio, U.S.* 40°1′ N, 81°35′ W 102
Cambridge, *U.K.* 52°11′ N, 0°9′ E 162
Cambridge Bay, *Can.* 69°6′ N, 105°2′ W 106
Cambridge City, *Ind., U.S.* 39°48′ N, 85°11′ W 102
Cambridge Gulf 15°11′ S, 127°52′ E 230
Cambrils de Mar, *Sp.* 41°4′ N, 1°3′ E 164
Cambulo, *Angola* 7°44′ S, 21°14′ E 218
Cambundi-Catembo, *Angola* 10°4′ S, 17°31′ E 220
Cambutal, Cerro, peak, *Pan.* 7°18′ N, 80°38′ W 115
Camden, *Ala., U.S.* 31°59′ N, 87°17′ W 96
Camden, *Ark., U.S.* 33°33′ N, 92°51′ W 96
Camden, *Ind., U.S.* 40°36′ N, 86°32′ W 102
Camden, *Me., U.S.* 44°13′ N, 69°4′ W 94
Camden, *Miss., U.S.* 32°46′ N, 89°51′ W 103
Camden, *N.J., U.S.* 39°56′ N, 75°8′ W 94
Camden, *N.Y., U.S.* 43°20′ N, 75°46′ W 94
Camden, *N.C., U.S.* 36°19′ N, 76°11′ W 96
Camden, *Tex., U.S.* 30°53′ N, 94°45′ W 103
Camden Bay 69°56′ N, 147°43′ W 98
Camdenton, *Mo., U.S.* 37°59′ N, 92°44′ W 94
Camelgooda Hill, *Austral.* 18°31′ S, 123°43′ E 230
Çameli, *Turk.* 37°4′ N, 29°19′ E 156
Camels Hump, peak, *Austral.* 23°51′ S, 131°27′ E 230
Camels Hump, peak, *Vt., U.S.* 44°18′ N, 72°55′ W 104
Camenca, *Transdniestria, Mold.* 48°2′ N, 28°44′ E 156
Cameron, *Ariz., U.S.* 35°51′ N, 111°25′ W 92
Cameron, *La., U.S.* 29°47′ N, 93°20′ W 103
Cameron, *Tex., U.S.* 30°50′ N, 96°58′ W 96
Cameron Falls, *Can.* 49°8′ N, 88°19′ W 94
Cameron Lake, lake, *Can.* 48°59′ N, 84°45′ W 110
Cameroon 4°33′ N, 11°3′ E 218
Cameroon Mountain, *Cameroon* 4°15′ N, 9°4′ E 222
Cametá, *Braz.* 2°14′ S, 49°31′ W 130
Camiguin, island, *Philippines* 18°49′ N, 122°1′ E 198
Camilla, *Ga., U.S.* 31°13′ N, 84°13′ W 96
Camiña, *Chile* 19°18′ S, 69°27′ W 137
Caminha, *Port.* 41°52′ N, 8°51′ W 150
Camiranga, *Braz.* 1°51′ S, 46°18′ W 130
Camiri, *Bol.* 20°7′ S, 63°34′ W 137
Camirus, ruin(s), *Gr.* 36°18′ N, 27°48′ E 156
Camisea, *Peru* 11°43′ S, 73°2′ W 137
Camisea, river, *Peru* 11°57′ S, 72°59′ W 137
Camissombo, *Angola* 8°11′ S, 20°40′ E 218
Camocim, *Braz.* 2°57′ S, 40°52′ W 132
Camooweal, *Austral.* 19°56′ S, 138°8′ E 231
Camopi, *Fr.* 3°11′ N, 52°20′ W 130
Camopi, river, *Braz.* 2°28′ N, 53°20′ W 130
Camorta Island, *India* 7°38′ N, 93°39′ E 188
Camoruco, *Col.* 6°27′ N, 70°31′ W 136
Camousitchouane, Lac, lake, *Can.* 51°2′ N, 76°24′ W 110
Camp Crook, *S. Dak., U.S.* 45°32′ N, 104°0′ W 90
Camp David, site, *Md., U.S.* 39°39′ N, 77°32′ W 94
Camp Douglas, *Wis., U.S.* 43°54′ N, 90°16′ W 102
Camp Nelson, *Calif., U.S.* 36°9′ N, 118°38′ W 101
Camp Pendleton Marine Corps Base, *Calif., U.S.* 33°20′ N, 117°29′ W 101
Camp Point, *Mo., U.S.* 40°1′ N, 91°4′ W 94
Camp Wood, *Tex., U.S.* 29°39′ N, 100°1′ W 92
Campagne-lès-Hesdin, *Fr.* 50°23′ N, 1°52′ E 163
Campamento, *Col.* 4°30′ N, 70°24′ W 136
Campana, *Arg.* 34°11′ S, 58°56′ W 139
Campana, Isla, island, *Chile* 48°13′ S, 77°9′ W 134
Campanario, *Sp.* 38°51′ N, 5°37′ W 164
Campania, adm. division, *It.* 41°12′ N, 13°54′ E 156
Campbell, *Calif., U.S.* 37°17′ N, 121°57′ W 100
Campbell, Cape, *N.Z.* 41°44′ S, 174°12′ E 240
Campbell Hill, *Ohio, U.S.* 40°21′ N, 83°45′ W 102
Campbell Island, *N.Z.* 52°37′ S, 169°0′ E 252
Campbell Plateau, *South Pacific Ocean* 50°28′ S, 171°45′ E 252
Campbell River, *Can.* 50°1′ N, 125°15′ W 90
Campbell's Bay, *Can.* 45°43′ N, 76°36′ W 94
Campbellsburg, *Ind., U.S.* 38°38′ N, 86°16′ W 102
Campbellsburg, *Ky., U.S.* 38°30′ N, 85°13′ W 102
Campbellsville, *Ky., U.S.* 37°19′ N, 85°21′ W 96
Campbellton, *Can.* 47°58′ N, 66°41′ W 94
Campeche, *Mex.* 19°48′ N, 90°40′ W 115
Campeche, adm. division, *Mex.* 18°56′ N, 91°2′ W 112
Campeche Bank, *Gulf of Mexico* 21°58′ N, 90°5′ W 253
Camperville, *Can.* 52°1′ N, 100°12′ W 108
Campidano, *It.* 39°44′ N, 8°33′ E 156
Campina Grande, *Braz.* 7°11′ S, 35°53′ W 123
Campina Verde, *Braz.* 19°33′ S, 49°29′ W 138
Campinas, *Braz.* 22°56′ S, 47°5′ W 138
Campo, *Calif., U.S.* 32°36′ N, 116°29′ W 101
Campo, *Colo., U.S.* 37°6′ N, 102°35′ W 92
Campo, *Mozambique* 17°46′ S, 36°22′ E 224
Campo, *Sp.* 42°24′ N, 0°24′ E 164
Campo Belo, *Braz.* 20°53′ S, 45°15′ W 138
Campo Corral, *Col.* 5°3′ N, 70°43′ W 136
Campo de Criptana, *Sp.* 39°24′ N, 3°7′ W 164
Campo Durán, oil field, *Arg.* 22°15′ S, 63°46′ W 137
Campo Erê, *Braz.* 26°24′ S, 53°1′ W 139
Campo Esperanza, *Parag.* 22°19′ S, 59°38′ W 132
Campo Florido, *Braz.* 19°48′ S, 48°36′ W 138
Campo Gallo, *Arg.* 26°35′ S, 62°50′ W 139
Campo Grande, *Braz.* 20°28′ S, 54°36′ W 132
Campo Largo, *Arg.* 26°47′ S, 60°51′ W 139
Campo Largo, *Braz.* 25°30′ S, 49°34′ W 138
Campo Maior, *Braz.* 4°52′ S, 42°13′ W 132
Campo Mourão, *Braz.* 24°4′ S, 52°24′ W 138
Campo, Punta, *Equatorial Guinea* 2°18′ N, 9°14′ E 218
Campo Troco, *Col.* 4°52′ N, 68°9′ W 136
Campoalegre, *Col.* 2°41′ N, 75°21′ W 136
Campobasso, *It.* 41°34′ N, 14°39′ E 156
Campobello, *S.C., U.S.* 35°6′ N, 82°10′ W 96
Campodolcino, *It.* 46°24′ N, 9°20′ E 167
Campos, *Braz.* 21°48′ S, 41°23′ W 138
Campos Altos, *Braz.* 19°43′ S, 46°12′ W 138
Campos Belos, *Braz.* 13°4′ S, 46°55′ W 138
Campos Novos, *Braz.* 27°25′ S, 51°14′ W 139
Campos, Punta, *Mex.* 18°53′ N, 104°40′ W 114
Camposampiero, *It.* 45°34′ N, 11°55′ E 167
Camprodon, *Sp.* 42°17′ N, 2°22′ E 164
Campti, *La., U.S.* 31°52′ N, 93°7′ W 103
Campton, *N.H., U.S.* 43°51′ N, 71°39′ W 104
Campuya, *Peru* 1°46′ S, 73°31′ W 136
Camrose, *Can.* 53°0′ N, 112°51′ W 108
Camsell Portage, *Can.* 59°37′ N, 109°14′ W 108
Camucuio, *Angola* 14°8′ S, 13°17′ E 220
Çan, *Turk.* 40°1′ N, 27°1′ E 156
Can Tho, *Vietnam* 10°2′ N, 105°44′ E 202
Cana Brava, *Braz.* 17°22′ S, 45°52′ W 138
Canaan, *Conn., U.S.* 42°1′ N, 73°20′ W 104
Canaan, *N.H., U.S.* 43°39′ N, 72°1′ W 104
Canaan, *Trinidad and Tobago* 11°8′ N, 60°49′ W 116
Canada 58°59′ N, 99°52′ W 106
Canada Basin, *Arctic Ocean* 77°38′ N, 139°23′ W 255
Canada Bay 50°40′ N, 56°41′ W 111
Cañada de Gómez, *Arg.* 32°50′ S, 61°21′ W 139
Cañada Honda, *Arg.* 31°59′ S, 68°33′ W 134
Cañada Ombú, *Arg.* 28°19′ S, 60°2′ W 139
Canada Plain, *Arctic Ocean* 76°14′ N, 148°23′ W 255
Cañada Seca, *Arg.* 34°25′ S, 62°57′ W 139
Canadian, *Tex., U.S.* 35°53′ N, 100°24′ W 92
Canadian, river, *Oklahoma-Texas, U.S.* 35°22′ N, 103°1′ W 92
Çanakkale, *Turk.* 40°9′ N, 26°23′ E 156
Çanakkale Boğazı (Dardanelles), *Turk.* 40°9′ N, 24°58′ E 157
Canal du Midi, *Fr.* 43°33′ N, 1°32′ E 165
Canal du Rhône au Rhin, *Fr.* 47°35′ N, 6°53′ E 165
Canal Flats, *Can.* 50°9′ N, 115°48′ W 90
Canal Point, *Fla., U.S.* 26°51′ N, 80°38′ W 105
Canale, *It.* 44°48′ N, 7°59′ E 167
Canals, *Arg.* 33°35′ S, 62°50′ W 139
Canals, *Sp.* 38°57′ N, 0°35′ E 150
Canalul Bega, *Rom.* 45°39′ N, 21°1′ E 168
Canamari, *Braz.* 10°10′ S, 69°16′ W 137
Cañamero, *Sp.* 39°22′ N, 5°23′ W 164
Cananea, *Mex.* 30°57′ N, 110°19′ W 92
Cananéia, *Braz.* 25°1′ S, 47°58′ W 138
Canapiare, Cerro, peak, *Col.* 2°38′ N, 68°32′ W 136
Canárias, Ilha das, island, *Braz.* 2°42′ S, 41°53′ W 132
Canarias, Islas see Canary Islands, *North Atlantic Ocean* 28°47′ N, 16°41′ W 214
Canarreos, Archipiélago de los, *Caribbean Sea* 21°39′ N, 82°40′ W 116
Canary Islands (Canarias, Islas), *North Atlantic Ocean* 28°47′ N, 16°41′ W 214
Cañas, *C.R.* 10°26′ N, 85°7′ W 115
Canastota, *N.Y., U.S.* 43°4′ N, 75°46′ W 94
Canatiba, *Braz.* 13°6′ S, 42°51′ W 138
Canatlán, *Mex.* 24°30′ N, 104°46′ W 114
Cañaveral, *Sp.* 39°47′ N, 6°24′ W 150
Canaveral, Cape (Kennedy, Cape), *Fla., U.S.* 28°24′ N, 80°34′ W 105
Canaveral National Seashore, *Fla., U.S.* 28°37′ N, 80°47′ W 105
Cañaveras, *Sp.* 40°20′ N, 2°25′ W 164
Canavieiras, *Braz.* 15°41′ S, 38°58′ W 132
Canberra, *Austral.* 35°22′ S, 148°43′ E 230
Canby, *Calif., U.S.* 41°26′ N, 120°54′ W 90
Canby, *Minn., U.S.* 44°42′ N, 96°18′ W 90
Cancún, *Mex.* 21°6′ N, 86°52′ W 116
Cancún, Isla, island, *Mex.* 21°12′ N, 86°56′ W 116
Çandarlı, *Turk.* 38°56′ N, 26°56′ E 156
Candeias, *Braz.* 12°41′ S, 38°31′ W 132
Candela, *Mex.* 26°50′ N, 100°41′ W 96
Candelaria, *Arg.* 27°29′ S, 55°45′ W 139
Candelaria, *Tex., U.S.* 30°7′ N, 104°41′ W 92
Candelaria, Punta, *Sp.* 43°43′ N, 8°29′ W 150
Candelaria, river, *Bol.* 16°39′ S, 59°48′ W 132
Candelaria, river, *Mex.* 18°21′ N, 91°35′ W 116
Candia, *N.H., U.S.* 43°4′ N, 71°17′ W 104
Candia see Iráklio, *Gr.* 35°19′ N, 25°7′ E 156
Cándido Aguilar, *Mex.* 25°33′ N, 98°3′ W 114
Cândido Sales, *Braz.* 15°36′ S, 41°14′ W 138
Candle Lake, *Can.* 53°45′ N, 105°46′ W 108
Candle Lake, *Can.* 53°44′ N, 105°17′ W 108
Cando, *Can.* 52°22′ N, 108°13′ W 108
Cando, *N. Dak., U.S.* 48°28′ N, 99°13′ W 90
Candon, *Philippines* 17°12′ N, 120°26′ E 203
Canea see Haniá, *Gr.* 35°25′ N, 23°59′ E 180
Canelas, *Mex.* 25°4′ N, 106°31′ W 114
Canelli, *It.* 44°44′ N, 8°17′ E 167
Canelones, *Uru.* 34°32′ S, 56°16′ W 139
Canelos, *Ecua.* 1°39′ S, 77°47′ W 136
Cañete, *Sp.* 40°2′ N, 1°40′ W 164
Cañete see San Vicente de Cañete, *Peru* 13°5′ S, 76°23′ W 130
Canet-Plage, *Fr.* 42°42′ N, 2°59′ E 164
Caney, *Kans., U.S.* 37°0′ N, 95°56′ W 96
Canfield, *Ark., U.S.* 33°9′ N, 93°39′ W 103
Canfranc, *Sp.* 42°42′ N, 0°32′ E 164
Cangallo, *Peru* 13°39′ S, 74°5′ W 137
Cangamba, *Angola* 13°43′ S, 19°50′ E 220
Cangandala, *Angola* 9°46′ S, 16°32′ E 220
Cangas del Narcea, *Sp.* 43°9′ N, 6°34′ W 150
Cango Caves, site, *S. Af.* 33°22′ S, 22°9′ E 227
Cangola, *Angola* 8°0′ S, 15°53′ E 218
Cangombe, *Angola* 14°25′ S, 19°56′ E 220
Canguaretama, *Braz.* 6°23′ S, 35°9′ W 132
Canguçu, *Braz.* 31°24′ S, 52°40′ W 139
Cangumbe, *Angola* 12°1′ S, 19°9′ E 220
Cangwu, *China* 23°25′ N, 111°13′ E 198
Cangyuan, *China* 23°8′ N, 99°15′ E 202
Cangzhou, *China* 38°15′ N, 116°55′ E 198
Cani Islands, *Mediterranean Sea* 37°26′ N, 9°40′ E 156
Caniapiscau, Réservoir, lake, *Can.* 54°37′ N, 72°3′ W 106
Caniapiscau, river, *Can.* 58°9′ N, 70°2′ W 106
Canicattì, *It.* 37°22′ N, 13°50′ E 156
Caniles, *Sp.* 37°25′ N, 2°43′ W 164
Canim Lake, *Can.* 51°47′ N, 120°55′ W 90
Canindé, *Braz.* 2°35′ S, 46°31′ W 130
Canindé, *Braz.* 4°25′ S, 39°22′ W 132
Canipaan, *Philippines* 8°34′ N, 117°15′ E 203
Canisp, peak, *U.K.* 58°6′ N, 5°10′ W 150
Canisteo, *N.Y., U.S.* 42°15′ N, 77°38′ W 94
Canisteo Peninsula, *Antarctica* 73°45′ S, 96°42′ W 248
Cañitas, *Mex.* 23°35′ N, 102°45′ W 112
Canjáyar, *Sp.* 37°0′ N, 2°46′ W 164
Cankhor, spring, *Somalia* 10°39′ N, 46°11′ E 216
Çankırı, *Turk.* 40°35′ N, 33°35′ E 156
Cankuzo, *Burundi* 3°16′ S, 30°32′ E 224
Canmore, *Can.* 51°6′ N, 115°21′ W 90
Cannae, ruin(s), *It.* 41°16′ N, 16°2′ E 156
Cannes, *Fr.* 43°34′ N, 6°58′ E 214
Canning Hill, *Austral.* 28°52′ S, 117°36′ E 230
Cannobio, *It.* 46°3′ N, 8°40′ E 167
Cannock, *U.K.* 52°41′ N, 2°2′ W 162
Cannon Beach, *Oreg., U.S.* 45°52′ N, 123°57′ W 100
Cannonball, river, *N. Dak., U.S.* 46°7′ N, 102°27′ W 80
Caño Chiquito, *Col.* 5°45′ N, 71°29′ W 136
Canoas, *Braz.* 29°54′ S, 51°11′ W 139
Canoas, Punta, *Mex.* 29°13′ N, 115°27′ W 92
Canoas, river, *Braz.* 27°43′ S, 49°58′ W 138
Canobie Lake, *N.H., U.S.* 42°48′ N, 71°15′ W 104
Canoe Lake, *Can.* 55°4′ N, 108°19′ W 108
Canoe Lake, lake, *Can.* 55°10′ N, 108°39′ W 108
Canoinhas, *Braz.* 26°10′ S, 50°20′ W 138
Cañon City, *Colo., U.S.* 38°27′ N, 105°15′ W 90
Canoochee, river, *Ga., U.S.* 32°45′ N, 82°25′ W 80
Canora, *Can.* 51°38′ N, 102°27′ W 90
Canouan, island, *Saint Vincent and The Grenadines* 12°34′ N, 61°18′ W 116
Canso, *Can.* 45°19′ N, 61°0′ W 111
Canso, Strait of 45°16′ N, 62°42′ W 106
Cantabria, adm. division, *Sp.* 43°13′ N, 4°9′ W 164
Cantabria, Sierra de, *Sp.* 42°34′ N, 2°38′ W 164
Cantábrica, Cordillera, *Sp.* 42°32′ N, 3°58′ W 164
Cantavieja, *Sp.* 40°31′ N, 0°25′ E 164
Cantavir, *Serb.* 45°55′ N, 19°45′ E 168
Canterbury, *N.H., U.S.* 43°20′ N, 71°34′ W 104
Canterbury, *U.K.* 51°16′ N, 1°3′ E 162
Cantil, *Calif., U.S.* 35°18′ N, 117°59′ W 101
Canto do Buriti, *Braz.* 8°7′ S, 42°57′ W 132
Canton, *Ga., U.S.* 34°13′ N, 84°29′ W 96
Canton, *Ill., U.S.* 40°32′ N, 90°2′ W 102
Canton, *Me., U.S.* 44°26′ N, 70°20′ W 104
Canton, *Mass., U.S.* 42°9′ N, 71°10′ W 104
Canton, *Miss., U.S.* 32°36′ N, 90°3′ W 103
Canton, *Mo., U.S.* 40°32′ N, 90°2′ W 94
Canton, *Mo., U.S.* 40°7′ N, 91°32′ W 94
Canton, *N.Y., U.S.* 44°35′ N, 75°11′ W 110
Canton, *N.C., U.S.* 35°32′ N, 82°50′ W 96
Canton, *Ohio, U.S.* 40°47′ N, 81°22′ W 102
Canton, *Okla., U.S.* 36°1′ N, 98°36′ W 92
Canton, *Pa., U.S.* 41°38′ N, 76°52′ W 110
Canton, *S. Dak., U.S.* 43°16′ N, 96°36′ W 90
Canton Lake, *Okla., U.S.* 36°2′ N, 99°34′ W 81
Canton see Guangzhou, *China* 23°6′ N, 113°17′ E 198
Cantù, *It.* 45°43′ N, 9°7′ E 167
Cantua Creek, *Calif., U.S.* 36°30′ N, 120°20′ W 100
Cantwell, *Alas., U.S.* 63°17′ N, 149°2′ W 106
Canudos, *Braz.* 7°18′ S, 58°10′ W 130
Cañuelas, *Arg.* 35°4′ S, 58°47′ W 139
Canumã, *Braz.* 6°11′ S, 60°13′ W 130
Canumã, *Braz.* 4°3′ S, 59°5′ W 130
Canutama, *Braz.* 6°35′ S, 64°25′ W 130
Canutillo, *Mex.* 26°21′ N, 105°23′ W 114
Canyon, *Can.* 60°52′ N, 136°58′ W 98
Canyon, *Tex., U.S.* 34°57′ N, 101°56′ W 92
Canzar, *Angola* 7°36′ S, 21°34′ E 218
Cao Bang, *Vietnam* 22°40′ N, 106°15′ E 198
Cao Lanh, *Vietnam* 10°27′ N, 105°37′ E 202
Caombo, *Angola* 8°44′ S, 16°31′ E 218
Caorle, *It.* 45°35′ N, 12°53′ E 167
Caoshi, *China* 42°17′ N, 125°14′ E 200
Caotibi, Grand lac, lake, *Can.* 50°38′ N, 68°20′ W 111
Caoxian, *China* 34°49′ N, 115°31′ E 198
Cap Barbas, *Western Sahara, Mor.* 22°17′ N, 16°40′ W 214
Capac, *Mich., U.S.* 42°59′ N, 82°55′ W 102
Capachica, *Peru* 15°42′ S, 69°49′ W 137
Cap-à-Foux, *Haiti* 19°44′ N, 74°14′ W 116
Capaia, *Angola* 8°28′ S, 20°12′ E 218
Capana, *Braz.* 1°55′ S, 68°59′ W 136
Capanaparo, river, *Venez.* 6°42′ N, 69°54′ W 136
Capannori, *It.* 43°50′ N, 10°34′ E 167
Capão Alto, *Braz.* 27°57′ S, 50°32′ W 138
Caparro, Cerro, peak, *Braz.* 1°54′ N, 68°11′ W 136
Capatárida, *Venez.* 11°10′ N, 70°39′ W 136
Cap-de-la-Madeleine, *Can.* 46°22′ N, 72°32′ W 94
Capdepera, *Sp.* 39°41′ N, 3°25′ E 150
Cape Barren Island, *Austral.* 40°47′ S, 148°31′ E 230
Cape Canaveral, *Fla., U.S.* 28°24′ N, 80°37′ W 105
Cape Charles, *Va., U.S.* 37°14′ N, 76°1′ W 82
Cape Coast, *Ghana* 5°10′ N, 1°17′ W 222
Cape Cod National Seashore, *Mass., U.S.* 42°5′ N, 70°11′ W 104
Cape Coral, *Fla., U.S.* 26°33′ N, 81°57′ W 105
Cape Dorset, *Can.* 64°11′ N, 76°41′ W 106
Cape Elizabeth, *Me., U.S.* 43°34′ N, 70°13′ W 104
Cape May, *N.J., U.S.* 38°56′ N, 74°56′ W 94
Cape Melville National Park, *Austral.* 14°20′ S, 144°10′ E 238
Cape Neddick, *Me., U.S.* 43°11′ N, 70°38′ W 104
Cape Parry, *Can.* 70°8′ N, 124°37′ W 98
Cape Pole, *Alas., U.S.* 55°57′ N, 133°47′ W 108
Cape Range National Park, *Austral.* 22°22′ S, 113°34′ E 238
Cape Tormentine, *Can.* 46°7′ N, 63°47′ W 111
Cape Town, *S. Af.* 33°57′ S, 18°15′ E 227
Cape Tribulation National Park, *Austral.* 16°10′ S, 145°5′ E 238
Cape Verde 15°0′ N, 24°0′ W
Cape Verde Islands, *North Atlantic Ocean* 16°0′ N, 24°11′ W 253
Cape Verde Plain, *North Atlantic Ocean* 25°19′ N, 23°53′ W 253
Cape Vincent, *N.Y., U.S.* 44°7′ N, 76°21′ W 94
Cape Yakataga, *Alas., U.S.* 60°2′ N, 142°25′ W 98
Capel Curig, *U.K.* 53°6′ N, 3°55′ W 162
Capella, *Sp.* 42°11′ N, 0°23′ E 164
Capembe, river, *Angola* 16°21′ S, 20°13′ E 220
Capenda-Camulemba, *Angola* 9°25′ S, 18°32′ E 218
Capendu, *Fr.* 43°11′ N, 2°32′ E 150
Capernaum, ruin(s), *Israel* 32°53′ N, 35°32′ E 194
Cap-Haïtien, *Haiti* 19°44′ N, 72°16′ W 116
Capibara, *Venez.* 2°33′ N, 66°19′ W 136
Capim, river, *Braz.* 2°56′ S, 47°51′ W 130
Capinópolis, *Braz.* 18°46′ S, 49°39′ W 138
Capinota, *Bol.* 17°48′ S, 66°14′ W 137

Capistrano Beach, *Calif., U.S.* 33°28′ N, 117°41′ W 101
Capital District, adm. division, *Col.* 3°45′ N, 74°24′ W 136
Capital Hill, *Northern Mariana Islands, U.S.* 15°0′ N, 146°0′ E 242
Capitan, *N. Mex., U.S.* 33°32′ N, 105°34′ W 92
Capitán Aracena, Isla, island, *Chile* 54°24′ S, 73°8′ W 134
Capitán Bezada, *Peru* 2°54′ S, 77°7′ W 136
Capitán Pablo Lagerenza, *Parag.* 19°58′ S, 60°48′ W 132
Capitão Poço, *Braz.* 1°42′ S, 46°57′ W 130
Caplani, *Mold.* 46°22′ N, 29°52′ E 156
Capo di Ponte, *It.* 46°2′ N, 10°19′ E 167
Capolo, *Angola* 10°27′ S, 14°5′ E 220
Capraia, island, *It.* 43°6′ N, 9°39′ E 214
Capraia Isola, *It.* 43°3′ N, 9°50′ E 156
Caprara, Punta, *It.* 41°8′ N, 7°41′ E 156
Capreol, *Can.* 46°42′ N, 80°55′ W 94
Capricorn Group, islands, *Coral Sea* 23°7′ S, 150°57′ E 230
Caprivi Game Park, *Namibia* 18°7′ S, 21°48′ E 220
Caprivi Strip, region, *Africa* 18°0′ S, 23°28′ E 224
Caprock Escarpment, *North America* 32°55′ N, 101°38′ W 92
Captain Cook Monument, *Hawai'i, U.S.* 19°28′ N, 155°59′ W 99
Captain Cook's Landing, site, *Hawai'i, U.S.* 21°57′ N, 159°44′ W 99
Captiva, *Fla., U.S.* 26°31′ N, 82°11′ W 105
Captiva Island, *Fla., U.S.* 26°32′ N, 82°30′ W 105
Capulin, *N. Mex., U.S.* 36°43′ N, 104°0′ W 92
Capulin Volcano National Monument, *N. Mex., U.S.* 36°46′ N, 104°3′ W 92
Capunda, *Angola* 10°35′ S, 17°22′ E 220
Căpuş, *Rom.* 46°47′ N, 23°18′ E 168
Caquetá, adm. division, *Col.* 0°33′ N, 74°33′ W 136
Caquetá, river, *Col.* 0°59′ N, 73°44′ W 123
Car Nicobar, island, *India* 9°5′ N, 91°37′ E 188
Carabinani, river, *Braz.* 2°50′ S, 62°44′ W 132
Caracal, *Rom.* 44°7′ N, 24°21′ E 156
Caracaraí, *Braz.* 1°50′ N, 61°10′ W 130
Caracas, *Venez.* 10°25′ N, 67°2′ W 136
Caracol, *Braz.* 9°15′ S, 43°22′ W 132
Caracoles, Punta, *Pan.* 7°37′ N, 79°0′ W 115
Caracolí, *Col.* 10°4′ N, 73°47′ W 136
Caraş-Severin, adm. division, *Rom.* 45°8′ N, 21°34′ E 156
Caraga, *Philippines* 7°23′ N, 126°32′ E 203
Caraglio, *It.* 44°25′ N, 7°26′ E 167
Caraí, *Braz.* 17°12′ S, 41°44′ W 138
Carajari, river, *Braz.* 5°0′ S, 54°20′ W 130
Carajás, Serra dos, *Braz.* 5°42′ S, 52°12′ W 130
Caramulo, Serra do, *Port.* 40°25′ N, 8°47′ W 150
Caranavi, *Bol.* 15°51′ S, 67°37′ W 137
Carandayti, *Bol.* 20°46′ S, 63°6′ W 137
Carangola, *Braz.* 20°45′ S, 42°3′ W 138
Caransebeş, *Rom.* 45°25′ N, 22°14′ E 168
Caraparaná, river, *Col.* 0°35′ N, 74°2′ W 136
Carapari, *Bol.* 21°48′ S, 63°47′ W 137
Caraquet, *Can.* 47°46′ N, 64°57′ W 94
Caraşova, *Rom.* 45°12′ N, 21°51′ E 168
Caratasca, Laguna de 15°14′ N, 84°16′ W 115
Caratinga, *Braz.* 19°49′ S, 42°9′ W 138
Carauari, *Braz.* 4°55′ S, 66°56′ W 130
Caraúbas, *Braz.* 5°49′ S, 37°34′ W 132
Carauna see Grande, Serra, peak, *Braz.* 2°34′ N, 60°46′ W 130
Caravaca de la Cruz, *Sp.* 38°6′ N, 1°52′ W 164
Caravelas, *Braz.* 17°42′ S, 39°15′ W 132
Carazinho, *Braz.* 28°18′ S, 52°48′ W 139
Carberry, *Can.* 49°52′ N, 99°22′ W 90
Carbó, *Mex.* 29°40′ N, 110°58′ W 92
Carbon, *Can.* 51°31′ N, 113°10′ W 90
Carbón, Laguna del, *Arg.* 49°35′ S, 68°21′ W 122
Carbonado, *Wash., U.S.* 47°4′ N, 122°3′ W 100
Carbonara, Capo, *It.* 38°54′ N, 9°33′ E 214
Carbondale, *Mo., U.S.* 37°43′ N, 89°12′ W 96
Carbondale, *Pa., U.S.* 41°33′ N, 75°31′ W 94
Carboneras, *Sp.* 36°59′ N, 1°54′ W 164
Carboneras de Guadazaón, *Sp.* 39°53′ N, 1°50′ W 164
Carbonia, *It.* 39°10′ N, 8°25′ E 214
Carbonville, *Utah, U.S.* 39°37′ N, 110°51′ W 92
Cărbunari, *Rom.* 44°50′ N, 21°44′ E 168
Carcaixent, *Sp.* 39°6′ N, 0°27′ E 164
Carcajou, *Can.* 57°47′ N, 117°5′ W 108
Carcajou, river, *Can.* 64°17′ N, 128°22′ W 98
Carcans, *Fr.* 45°4′ N, 1°4′ W 150
Carcaraña, *Arg.* 32°53′ S, 61°7′ W 139
Carcasse, Cap, *Haiti* 18°16′ N, 75°14′ W 115
Carcassonne, *Fr.* 43°12′ N, 2°20′ E 164
Carcastillo, *Sp.* 42°22′ N, 1°27′ W 164
Carche, peak, *Sp.* 38°24′ N, 1°12′ W 164
Carcross, *Can.* 60°12′ N, 134°42′ W 108
Card Sound 25°18′ N, 80°29′ W 105
Cardeña, *Sp.* 38°16′ N, 4°21′ W 164
Cárdenas, *Cuba* 23°2′ N, 81°14′ W 112
Cárdenas, *Mex.* 21°57′ N, 99°40′ W 114
Cardenete, *Sp.* 39°46′ N, 1°42′ W 150
Cardiff, *U.K.* 51°30′ N, 3°55′ W 143
Cardiff by the Sea, *Calif., U.S.* 33°1′ N, 117°18′ W 101
Cardiff (Caerdydd), *U.K.* 51°28′ N, 3°12′ W 162
Cardigan Bay 52°3′ N, 4°51′ W 150
Cardinal, *Can.* 44°47′ N, 75°25′ W 94
Cardington, *Ohio, U.S.* 40°29′ N, 82°53′ W 102
Cardona, *Sp.* 41°55′ N, 1°39′ E 164
Cardona, *Uru.* 33°54′ S, 57°22′ W 139
Cardston, *Can.* 49°11′ N, 113°18′ W 90
Careen Lake, lake, *Can.* 56°56′ N, 108°43′ W 108
Carei, *Rom.* 47°41′ N, 22°29′ E 168
Careiro da Várzea, *Braz.* 3°13′ S, 59°47′ W 130
Carencro, *La., U.S.* 30°18′ N, 92°4′ W 103
Carentan, *Fr.* 49°19′ N, 1°16′ W 150
Caretta, *W. Va., U.S.* 37°19′ N, 81°41′ W 96
Carevdar, *Croatia* 46°4′ N, 16°40′ E 168
Carey, *Ohio, U.S.* 40°56′ N, 83°22′ W 102
Careysburg, *Liberia* 6°18′ N, 10°33′ W 222
Cargados Carajos Bank, *Indian Ocean* 16°17′ S, 59°38′ E 254
Cargèse, *Fr.* 42°8′ N, 8°37′ E 156
Carhué, *Arg.* 37°10′ S, 62°44′ W 139
Cariacica, *Braz.* 20°15′ S, 40°24′ W 138
Cariati, *It.* 39°29′ N, 16°57′ E 156
Caribana, Punta, *Col.* 8°35′ N, 77°9′ W 136
Caribbean Sea 15°24′ N, 75°30′ W 116
Caribou, *Me., U.S.* 46°51′ N, 68°2′ W 94
Caribou Lake, *Can.* 59°23′ N, 96°38′ W 108
Caribou Lake, lake, *Can.* 50°26′ N, 89°31′ W 110
Caribou Range, *Idaho, U.S.* 43°26′ N, 111°33′ W 90
Carigara, *Philippines* 11°17′ N, 124°40′ E 203
Carignan, *Fr.* 49°38′ N, 5°10′ E 163
Carignano, *It.* 44°54′ N, 7°40′ E 167
Cariñena, *Sp.* 41°20′ N, 1°13′ W 164
Carinhanha, *Braz.* 14°16′ S, 43°53′ W 138
Carinhanha, river, *Braz.* 14°59′ S, 45°40′ W 138
Carinthia, region, *Europe* 46°51′ N, 12°53′ E 167
Cariparé, *Braz.* 11°33′ S, 45°4′ W 130
Caripito, *Venez.* 10°6′ N, 63°6′ W 116
Caritianas, *Braz.* 9°27′ S, 63°6′ W 130
Carlet, *Sp.* 39°12′ N, 0°32′ E 164
Carleton, *Can.* 48°6′ N, 66°8′ W 94
Carleton, *Mich., U.S.* 42°3′ N, 83°23′ W 102
Carleton, Mount, *Can.* 47°21′ N, 66°58′ W 94
Carleton Place, *Can.* 45°7′ N, 76°8′ W 94
Carleton, Pointe, *Can.* 49°45′ N, 62°57′ W 111
Carlin, *Nev., U.S.* 40°42′ N, 116°7′ W 92
Carlinville, *Ill., U.S.* 39°16′ N, 89°53′ W 102
Carlisle, *U.K.* 54°53′ N, 2°56′ W 162
Carlos Casares, *Arg.* 35°36′ S, 61°21′ W 139
Carlos Chagas, *Braz.* 17°42′ S, 40°48′ W 138
Carlos, Isla, island, *Chile* 54°11′ S, 74°54′ W 134
Carlos Tejedor, *Arg.* 35°22′ S, 62°26′ W 139
Carlow, *Ire.* 52°50′ N, 6°56′ W 150
Carlsbad, *Calif., U.S.* 33°9′ N, 117°21′ W 101
Carlsbad, *N. Mex., U.S.* 32°25′ N, 104°14′ W 92
Carlsbad, *Tex., U.S.* 31°34′ N, 100°37′ W 92
Carlsbad Caverns National Park, *N. Mex., U.S.* 31°52′ N, 105°45′ W 112
Carlsberg Ridge, *Arabian Sea* 5°2′ N, 62°6′ E 254
Carlsborg, *Wash., U.S.* 48°4′ N, 123°11′ W 100
Carlsen, Mys, *Russ.* 76°38′ N, 69°32′ E 160
Carlton, *Minn., U.S.* 46°39′ N, 92°27′ W 94
Carlyle, *Can.* 49°37′ N, 102°17′ W 90
Carlyle, *Ill., U.S.* 38°36′ N, 89°22′ W 102
Carlyle Lake, *Ill., U.S.* 38°40′ N, 89°30′ W 102
Carmacks, *Can.* 62°8′ N, 136°13′ W 98
Carmagnola, *It.* 44°50′ N, 7°43′ E 167
Carman, *Can.* 49°28′ N, 98°1′ W 90
Carmanah Point, *Can.* 48°32′ N, 124°54′ W 100
Carmangay, *Can.* 50°7′ N, 113°7′ W 90
Carmanovo, *Mold.* 47°15′ N, 29°30′ E 156
Carmarthen, *U.K.* 51°51′ N, 4°19′ W 162
Carmel, *Ind., U.S.* 39°58′ N, 86°7′ W 102
Carmel, *N.Y., U.S.* 41°24′ N, 73°41′ W 104
Carmel Head, *U.K.* 53°24′ N, 4°56′ W 150
Carmel Highlands, *Calif., U.S.* 36°30′ N, 121°57′ W 100
Carmel, Mount, *Calif., U.S.* 36°22′ N, 121°51′ W 100
Carmel, Mount, *Israel* 32°43′ N, 35°1′ E 194
Carmel, ruin(s), *West Bank, Israel* 31°24′ N, 35°6′ E 194
Carmel-by-the-Sea, *Calif., U.S.* 36°33′ N, 121°56′ W 100
Carmelita, *Guatemala* 17°29′ N, 90°11′ W 115
Carmelo, *Uru.* 33°59′ S, 58°13′ W 139
Carmen, *Bol.* 11°39′ S, 67°51′ W 137
Carmen, *Okla., U.S.* 36°34′ N, 98°28′ W 92
Carmen, *Philippines* 7°24′ N, 125°42′ E 203
Carmen, *Uru.* 33°15′ S, 56°2′ W 139
Carmen de Areco, *Arg.* 34°23′ S, 59°50′ W 139
Carmen de Bolívar, *Col.* 9°41′ N, 75°8′ W 136
Carmén del Paraná, *Parag.* 27°13′ S, 56°9′ W 139
Carmen, Isla del, island, *Mex.* 18°22′ N, 91°42′ W 115
Carmen, Isla, island, *Mex.* 25°50′ N, 111°7′ W 112
Carmen, river, *Mex.* 29°57′ N, 107°3′ W 80
Carmen, Sierra del, *Mex.* 29°11′ N, 102°46′ W 112
Carmi, *Mo., U.S.* 38°4′ N, 88°11′ W 94
Carmo do Paranaíba, *Braz.* 19°4′ S, 46°21′ W 138
Carmona, *Sp.* 37°28′ N, 5°39′ W 164
Carnarvon, *S. Af.* 30°57′ S, 22°6′ E 227
Carnduff, *Can.* 49°9′ N, 101°51′ W 90
Carnegie, *Okla., U.S.* 35°4′ N, 98°37′ W 92
Carnegie Ridge, *South Pacific Ocean* 1°29′ S, 86°58′ W 253
Carney Island, *Antarctica* 73°20′ S, 120°12′ W 248
Carnforth, *U.K.* 54°7′ N, 2°46′ W 162
Carnic Alps, *Aust.* 46°31′ N, 12°32′ E 167
Carno, *U.K.* 52°33′ N, 3°32′ W 162
Carnot, *Cen. Af. Rep.* 4°55′ N, 15°51′ E 218
Caro, *Mich., U.S.* 43°28′ N, 83°23′ W 102
Carol City, *Fla., U.S.* 25°57′ N, 80°16′ W 105
Carolina, *Braz.* 7°19′ S, 47°28′ W 130
Carolina, *P.R., U.S.* 18°0′ N, 66°0′ W 118
Carolina Beach, *N.C., U.S.* 34°2′ N, 77°55′ W 96
Caroline, *Can.* 52°5′ N, 114°46′ W 90
Caroline Island (Millennium I.), *Kiribati* 9°49′ S, 150°9′ W 252
Caroline Islands, *North Pacific Ocean* 4°49′ N, 141°18′ E 192
Carora, *Venez.* 10°11′ N, 70°5′ W 136
Carouge, *Switz.* 46°10′ N, 6°8′ E 167
Carp, *Nev., U.S.* 37°6′ N, 114°31′ W 101
Carp Lake, lake, *Can.* 54°43′ N, 123°45′ W 108
Carpathian Mountains, *Ukr.* 48°52′ N, 24°24′ E 160
Carpatho-Ukraine, region, *Europe* 48°2′ N, 22°41′ E 168
Carpentaria, Gulf of 12°17′ S, 138°12′ E 231
Carpenter, *Miss., U.S.* 32°1′ N, 90°42′ W 103
Carpenter Island, *Antarctica* 72°49′ S, 95°35′ W 248
Carpenter Lake, lake, *Can.* 50°52′ N, 123°11′ W 90
Carpi, *It.* 44°46′ N, 10°51′ E 167
Carpignano Sesia, *It.* 45°32′ N, 8°24′ E 167
Carpinteria, *Calif., U.S.* 34°24′ N, 119°32′ W 101
Carpio, *N. Dak., U.S.* 48°25′ N, 101°45′ W 90
Carr, Cape, *Antarctica* 66°21′ S, 133°24′ E 248
Carr Pond Mountain, *Me., U.S.* 46°44′ N, 68°48′ W 94
Carrabelle, *Fla., U.S.* 29°50′ N, 84°40′ W 96
Carrantuohill, peak, *Ire.* 51°58′ N, 9°51′ W 150
Carrara, *It.* 44°4′ N, 10°5′ E 167
Carrasco, Cerro, peak, *Chile* 20°58′ S, 70°11′ W 137
Carrasco Ichilo National Park, *Bol.* 17°13′ S, 65°59′ W 137
Carrascosa del Campo, *Sp.* 40°2′ N, 2°45′ W 164
Carregal do Sal, *Port.* 40°25′ N, 8°1′ W 150
Carreto, *Pan.* 8°45′ N, 77°36′ W 136
Carriacou, island, *Grenada* 12°20′ N, 62°7′ W 116
Carrick on Shannon, *Ire.* 53°57′ N, 8°6′ W 150
Carriere, *Miss., U.S.* 30°37′ N, 89°39′ W 103
Carrière, Lac, lake, *Can.* 47°12′ N, 77°43′ W 110
Carrigan, Mount, *N.H., U.S.* 44°5′ N, 71°29′ W 104
Carrilobo, *Arg.* 31°55′ S, 63°7′ W 139
Carrington, *N. Dak., U.S.* 47°25′ N, 99°8′ W 90
Carrión de Calatrava, *Sp.* 39°1′ N, 3°49′ W 164
Carrizal, *Col.* 11°59′ N, 72°11′ W 136
Carrizal, *Mex.* 30°34′ N, 106°40′ W 92
Carrizal Bajo, *Chile* 28°6′ S, 71°10′ W 134
Carrizal, river, *Mex.* 23°24′ N, 98°12′ W 114
Carrizo Plain, *Calif., U.S.* 35°17′ N, 120°0′ W 100
Carrizo Plain National Monument, *Calif., U.S.* 35°4′ N, 120°8′ W 100
Carrizozo, *N. Mex., U.S.* 33°38′ N, 105°52′ W 92
Carro, peak, *Sp.* 39°8′ N, 2°27′ W 164
Carroll, *Iowa, U.S.* 42°3′ N, 94°52′ W 94
Carrollton, *Ala., U.S.* 33°16′ N, 88°6′ W 103
Carrollton, *Ga., U.S.* 33°33′ N, 85°5′ W 96
Carrollton, *Ky., U.S.* 38°39′ N, 85°10′ W 102
Carrollton, *Mich., U.S.* 43°27′ N, 83°56′ W 102
Carrollton, *Miss., U.S.* 33°28′ N, 89°56′ W 103
Carrollton, *Mo., U.S.* 39°21′ N, 93°30′ W 94
Carrollton, *Mo., U.S.* 39°17′ N, 90°25′ W 94
Carrollton, *Ohio, U.S.* 40°33′ N, 81°5′ W 102
Carrollton, *Tex., U.S.* 32°57′ N, 96°54′ W 92
Carrot River, *Can.* 53°16′ N, 103°36′ W 108
Carrot, river, *Can.* 53°5′ N, 103°26′ W 108
Carrowmore, ruin(s), *Ire.* 54°13′ N, 8°41′ W 150
Carrù, *It.* 44°28′ N, 7°52′ E 167
Çarşamba, *Turk.* 41°12′ N, 36°44′ E 180
Carson, *Miss., U.S.* 31°31′ N, 89°47′ W 103
Carson, *N. Dak., U.S.* 46°25′ N, 101°34′ W 90
Carson, *Wash., U.S.* 45°42′ N, 121°50′ W 100
Carson City, *Mich., U.S.* 43°10′ N, 84°51′ W 102
Carson City, *Nev., U.S.* 39°9′ N, 119°52′ W 90
Carson Pass, *Calif., U.S.* 38°42′ N, 119°59′ W 90
Carsonville, *Mich., U.S.* 43°25′ N, 82°40′ W 102
Carstairs, *Can.* 51°35′ N, 114°6′ W 90
Carswell Lake, *Can.* 58°40′ N, 109°48′ W 108
Cartagena, *Col.* 10°25′ N, 75°32′ W 136
Cartagena, *Sp.* 37°36′ N, 0°59′ E 164
Cartago, *Calif., U.S.* 36°19′ N, 118°2′ W 101
Cartago, *C.R.* 9°51′ N, 83°54′ W 115
Carter, *Wis., U.S.* 45°22′ N, 88°38′ W 110
Carter, Mount, *Austral.* 13°5′ S, 143°5′ E 230
Cartersville, *Ga., U.S.* 34°9′ N, 84°48′ W 96
Carterton, *N.Z.* 41°3′ S, 175°32′ E 240
Carthage, *Ind., U.S.* 39°43′ N, 85°34′ W 102
Carthage, *Miss., U.S.* 32°42′ N, 89°32′ W 103
Carthage, *Mo., U.S.* 37°9′ N, 94°18′ W 96
Carthage, *Mo., U.S.* 40°24′ N, 91°9′ W 94
Carthage, *N.Y., U.S.* 43°58′ N, 75°37′ W 110
Carthage, *S. Dak., U.S.* 44°9′ N, 97°45′ W 90
Carthage, *Tenn., U.S.* 36°16′ N, 85°57′ W 96
Carthage, *Tex., U.S.* 32°9′ N, 94°21′ W 103
Carthage, ruin(s), *Tun.* 36°50′ N, 10°12′ E 156
Cartmel, *U.K.* 54°12′ N, 2°58′ W 162
Cartwright, *Can.* 53°41′ N, 57°2′ W 106
Caruaru, *Braz.* 8°15′ S, 36°0′ W 132
Carumas, *Peru* 16°51′ S, 70°42′ W 137
Carvalho, *Braz.* 2°19′ S, 51°29′ W 130
Carville, *La., U.S.* 30°12′ N, 91°7′ W 103
Carvoeiro, *Braz.* 1°30′ S, 61°58′ W 130
Carvoeiro, Cabo, *Port.* 39°10′ N, 9°53′ W 150
Cary, *Ill., U.S.* 42°12′ N, 88°16′ W 102
Cary, *Miss., U.S.* 32°47′ N, 90°56′ W 103
Cary, *Mo., U.S.* 42°12′ N, 88°16′ W 110
Casa Grande, *Ariz., U.S.* 32°51′ N, 111°46′ W 112
Casa Grande Ruins National Monument, *Ariz., U.S.* 33°00′ N, 111°32′ W 80
Casablanca, *Mor.* 33°36′ N, 7°37′ W 214
Casale Monferrato, *It.* 45°8′ N, 8°27′ E 167
Casalmaggiore, *It.* 44°59′ N, 10°25′ E 167
Casalpusterlengo, *It.* 45°10′ N, 9°38′ E 167
Casamance, river, *Senegal* 12°37′ N, 15°8′ W 222
Casanare, adm. division, *Col.* 5°33′ N, 72°17′ W 136
Casares, *Nicar.* 11°38′ N, 86°20′ W 115
Casares, *Sp.* 36°26′ N, 5°16′ W 164
Casas, *Mex.* 23°41′ N, 98°44′ W 114
Casas de Juan Núñez, *Sp.* 39°5′ N, 1°34′ W 164
Casas de Ves, *Sp.* 39°14′ N, 1°19′ W 164
Casas Grande Ruins National Monument, *Ariz., U.S.* 32°59′ N, 111°31′ W 92
Casas Grandes, *Mex.* 30°23′ N, 107°59′ W 92
Casas Ibáñez, *Sp.* 39°16′ N, 1°28′ W 164
Casca, *Braz.* 28°39′ S, 52°0′ W 139
Cascada de Basaseachic National Park (6), *Mex.* 28°7′ N, 108°17′ W 112
Cascade, *Idaho, U.S.* 44°30′ N, 116°3′ W 90
Cascade, *Mont., U.S.* 47°14′ N, 111°43′ W 90
Cascade Head, *Oreg., U.S.* 44°52′ N, 123°58′ W 90
Cascade Range, *North America* 49°29′ N, 121°25′ W 100
Cascais, *Port.* 38°42′ N, 9°25′ W 150
Cascalho Rico, *Braz.* 18°33′ S, 47°54′ W 138
Cascavel, *Braz.* 24°56′ S, 53°24′ W 138
Cascavel, *Braz.* 4°10′ S, 38°16′ W 132
Casco, *Me., U.S.* 44°0′ N, 70°32′ W 104
Casco Bay 43°42′ N, 70°51′ W 80
Case Island, *Antarctica* 73°37′ S, 81°22′ W 248
Caseda, *Sp.* 42°31′ N, 1°22′ W 164
Cases Velles de Formentor, site, *Sp.* 39°54′ N, 3°6′ E 164
Caseville, *Mich., U.S.* 43°55′ N, 83°17′ W 102
Casey, *Ill., U.S.* 39°17′ N, 88°0′ W 102
Casey, station, *Antarctica* 66°12′ S, 110°52′ E 248
Casigua, *Venez.* 8°42′ N, 72°35′ W 136
Casiguran, *Philippines* 16°17′ N, 122°9′ E 203
Casilda, *Arg.* 33°3′ S, 61°9′ W 139
Casiquiare, river, *Venez.* 2°27′ N, 66°40′ W 136
Casma, *Peru* 9°28′ S, 78°18′ W 130
Casmalia, *Calif., U.S.* 34°50′ N, 120°33′ W 100
Caspar, *Calif., U.S.* 39°21′ N, 123°49′ W 90
Caspe, *Sp.* 41°14′ N, 0°3′ W 164
Casper, *Wyo., U.S.* 42°50′ N, 106°19′ W 90
Caspian Depression, *Kaz.* 43°48′ N, 46°17′ E 195
Caspian Sea 38°26′ N, 49°1′ E 160
Caspiana, *La., U.S.* 32°16′ N, 93°36′ W 103
Cass, *W. Va., U.S.* 38°24′ N, 79°56′ W 94
Cass City, *Mich., U.S.* 43°35′ N, 83°10′ W 102
Cass Lake, *Minn., U.S.* 47°21′ N, 94°38′ W 90
Cass, river, *Mich., U.S.* 43°28′ N, 83°16′ W 102
Cassai, *Angola* 10°37′ S, 21°59′ E 220
Cassai, river, *Angola* 11°13′ S, 20°20′ E 220
Cassamba, *Angola* 13°7′ S, 20°20′ E 220
Cassel, *Fr.* 50°48′ N, 2°28′ E 163
Casselberry, *Fla., U.S.* 28°40′ N, 81°22′ W 105
Casselton, *N. Dak., U.S.* 46°53′ N, 97°14′ W 90
Cássia, *Braz.* 20°34′ S, 46°58′ W 138
Cassiar, *Can.* 59°17′ N, 129°50′ W 108
Cassiar Mountains, *Can.* 58°18′ N, 129°24′ W 108
Cassidy, *Can.* 49°2′ N, 123°52′ W 100
Cassilândia, *Braz.* 19°7′ S, 51°48′ W 138
Cassinga, *Angola* 15°9′ S, 16°5′ E 220
Cassino, *Braz.* 32°10′ S, 52°13′ W 139
Cassiporé, Cabo, *Braz.* 3°46′ N, 51°3′ W 130
Cassou, *Burkina Faso* 11°34′ N, 2°5′ W 222
Cassumbe, *Angola* 11°6′ S, 16°41′ E 220
Cassville, *Mo., U.S.* 36°40′ N, 93°53′ W 94
Cassville, *Wis., U.S.* 42°42′ N, 90°59′ W 94
Castaic, *Calif., U.S.* 34°30′ N, 118°38′ W 101
Castalla, *Sp.* 38°35′ N, 0°41′ E 164
Castanhal, *Braz.* 1°18′ S, 47°58′ W 130
Castaño Nuevo, *Arg.* 31°2′ S, 69°36′ W 134
Castaños, *Mex.* 26°46′ N, 101°27′ W 96
Casteggio, *It.* 45°0′ N, 9°7′ E 167
Castel Bolognese, *It.* 44°19′ N, 11°46′ E 167
Castel San Giovanni, *It.* 45°3′ N, 9°26′ E 167
Castelfranco Veneto, *It.* 45°40′ N, 11°55′ E 156
Castelli, *Arg.* 36°6′ S, 57°49′ W 139
Castelló de la Plana see Castellón de la Plana, *Sp.* 39°59′ N, 0°2′ W 164
Castellón de la Plana (Castelló de la Plana), *Sp.* 39°59′ N, 0°2′ W 164
Castellote, *Sp.* 40°47′ N, 0°20′ E 164
Castelnovo ne' Monti, *It.* 44°25′ N, 10°23′ E 167
Castelo Branco, *Port.* 39°49′ N, 7°31′ W 150
Castelo Branco, adm. division, *Port.* 39°50′ N, 7°58′ W 150
Casterton, *U.K.* 54°12′ N, 2°34′ W 162
Castets, *Fr.* 43°53′ N, 1°10′ W 150
Castiglione delle Stiviere, *It.* 45°22′ N, 10°29′ E 167
Castile and Leon, adm. division, *Sp.* 41°56′ N, 3°33′ W 164
Castile La Mancha, adm. division, *Sp.* 40°28′ N, 2°58′ W 164
Castilla, Playa de, *Sp.* 37°3′ N, 6°45′ W 164
Castillo de San Marcos National Monument, *Fla., U.S.* 29°53′ N, 81°22′ W 105
Castillo de Teayo, ruin(s), *Mex.* 20°39′ N, 97°45′ W 114
Castillo, Pampa del, *Arg.* 46°18′ S, 68°44′ W 134
Castillos, *Uru.* 34°14′ S, 53°53′ W 139
Castle Acre, *U.K.* 52°42′ N, 0°41′ E 162
Castle Dale, *Utah, U.S.* 39°12′ N, 111°1′ W 90
Castle Hedingham, *U.K.* 51°59′ N, 0°36′ E 162
Castle Mountain, peak, *Alas., U.S.* 56°51′ N, 132°16′ W 108
Castle Mountain, peak, *Calif., U.S.* 35°56′ N, 120°23′ W 100
Castle Mountain, peak, *Can.* 51°19′ N, 116°0′ W 90
Castle Mountain, peak, *Tex., U.S.* 31°15′ N, 102°22′ W 92
Castle Peak, *Colo., U.S.* 38°59′ N, 106°57′ W 90
Castle Peak, *Idaho, U.S.* 44°1′ N, 114°40′ W 90
Castle Rising, *U.K.* 52°47′ N, 0°29′ E 162
Castle Rock, *Colo., U.S.* 39°22′ N, 104°52′ W 90
Castle Rock, *Wash., U.S.* 46°16′ N, 122°54′ W 100
Castle Rock, peak, *Oreg., U.S.* 44°0′ N, 118°16′ W 90
Castle Sinclair, site, *U.K.* 58°26′ N, 3°12′ W 150
Castlebar, *Ire.* 53°51′ N, 9°19′ W 150
Castlebay, *U.K.* 56°57′ N, 7°29′ W 150
Castlecliff, *N.Z.* 39°57′ S, 174°58′ E 240
Castleford, *U.K.* 53°43′ N, 1°21′ W 162
Castlegar, *Can.* 49°18′ N, 117°41′ W 90
Castlepoint, *N.Z.* 40°55′ S, 176°12′ E 240
Castleton, *U.K.* 54°27′ N, 0°57′ E 162
Castleton, *Vt., U.S.* 43°36′ N, 73°11′ W 104
Castleton-on-Hudson, *N.Y., U.S.* 42°31′ N, 73°46′ W 104
Castlewood, *S. Dak., U.S.* 44°42′ N, 97°3′ W 90
Castor, *Can.* 52°12′ N, 111°55′ W 90
Castor, *La., U.S.* 32°14′ N, 93°10′ W 103
Castries, *Saint Lucia* 13°59′ N, 61°8′ W 116
Castril, *Sp.* 37°47′ N, 2°46′ W 164
Castro, *Braz.* 24°46′ S, 50°1′ W 138
Castro, *Chile* 42°27′ S, 73°51′ W 134
Castronuño, *Sp.* 41°22′ N, 5°17′ W 150
Castropol, *Sp.* 43°30′ N, 7°2′ W 150
Castroville, *Calif., U.S.* 36°46′ N, 121°45′ W 100
Castuera, *Sp.* 38°43′ N, 5°34′ W 164
Casula, *Mozambique* 15°23′ S, 33°37′ E 224
Casummit Lake, *Can.* 51°28′ N, 92°22′ W 110
Çat, *Turk.* 39°37′ N, 41°1′ E 195
Cat Island, *Bahamas* 24°30′ N, 75°28′ W 116
Cat Island, *Miss., U.S.* 30°7′ N, 89°7′ W 103
Cat Lake, *Can.* 51°43′ N, 91°48′ W 110
Cat Tien National Park, *Vietnam* 11°20′ N, 106°58′ E 202
Catacaos, *Peru* 5°11′ S, 80°44′ W 130
Cataguases, *Braz.* 21°23′ S, 42°40′ W 138
Catahoula Lake, *La., U.S.* 31°25′ N, 92°27′ W 103
Cataingan, *Philippines* 12°1′ N, 123°58′ E 203
Çatak, *Turk.* 38°0′ N, 43°2′ E 195
Catalão, *Braz.* 18°12′ S, 47°57′ W 138
Catalina, *Chile* 25°14′ S, 69°47′ W 132
Catalina, Punta, *Chile* 52°44′ S, 68°43′ W 134
Catalonia, adm. division, *Sp.* 41°46′ N, 1°7′ E 164
Catamarca, *Arg.* 28°30′ S, 65°47′ W 132
Catamarca, adm. division, *Arg.* 28°47′ S, 68°39′ W 134
Catán Lil, *Arg.* 39°43′ S, 70°37′ W 134
Catandica, *Mozambique* 18°4′ S, 33°10′ E 220
Catanduanes, island, *Philippines* 13°52′ N, 124°26′ E 192
Catanduva, *Braz.* 21°6′ S, 48°58′ W 138
Catania, *It.* 37°30′ N, 15°4′ E 156
Catania, Piana di, *It.* 37°17′ N, 14°26′ E 156
Catanzaro, *It.* 38°53′ N, 16°35′ E 156
Catarina, *Tex., U.S.* 28°20′ N, 99°37′ W 92
Catarman, *Philippines* 12°29′ N, 124°38′ E 203
Catarroja, *Sp.* 39°24′ N, 0°24′ E 164

Catatumbo-Barí National Park, *Col.* 9°0' N, 73°30' W 136
Catauara, *Braz.* 3°19' S, 56°26' W 130
Cataviña, *Mex.* 29°45' N, 114°49' W 92
Catawba Island, *Ohio, U.S.* 41°34' N, 82°50' W 102
Catbalogan, *Philippines* 11°46' N, 124°55' E 203
Cateel, *Philippines* 7°51' N, 126°25' E 203
Catemaco, *Mex.* 18°25' N, 95°7' W 114
Catete, *Angola* 9°8' S, 13°40' E 218
Catete, river, *Braz.* 6°22' S, 54°14' W 130
Cathedral Mountain, *Tex., U.S.* 30°8' N, 103°43' W 92
Catherine, *Ala., U.S.* 32°10' N, 87°29' W 103
Catheys Valley, *Calif., U.S.* 37°25' N, 120°8' W 100
Cathlamet, *Wash., U.S.* 46°11' N, 123°22' W 100
Catinaccio, peak, *It.* 46°28' N, 11°36' E 167
Catió, *Guinea-Bissau* 11°16' N, 15°15' W 222
Catirina, Punta, peak, *It.* 40°28' N, 9°27' E 156
Catlow Valley, *Oreg., U.S.* 42°45' N, 119°7' W 90
Catnip Mountain, *Nev., U.S.* 41°50' N, 119°28' W 90
Catoche, Cabo, *Mex.* 21°28' N, 87°10' W 116
Catoctin Mountain, *Md., U.S.* 39°50' N, 77°35' W 94
Catoctin Mountain Park, *Md., U.S.* 39°37' N, 77°33' W 94
Catorce, *Mex.* 23°39' N, 100°53' W 114
Catota, *Angola* 14°2' S, 17°23' E 220
Catria, Monte, peak, *It.* 43°26' N, 12°37' E 156
Catriló, *Arg.* 36°25' S, 63°27' W 139
Catskill, *N.Y., U.S.* 42°13' N, 73°53' W 104
Catskill Mountains, *N.Y., U.S.* 42°26' N, 74°10' W 104
Catterick, *U.K.* 54°22' N, 1°38' W 162
Cattolica, *It.* 43°58' N, 12°44' E 167
Catuane, *Mozambique* 26°44' S, 32°15' E 227
Catur, *Mozambique* 13°45' S, 35°37' E 224
Cau Giat, *Vietnam* 19°9' N, 105°38' E 202
Cauaburi, river, *Braz.* 4°238' N, 66°19' W 136
Cauayan, *Philippines* 9°58' N, 122°36' E 203
Cauca, adm. division, *Col.* 2°29' N, 77°31' W 136
Cauca, river, *Col.* 6°18' N, 75°46' W 136
Caucaia, *Braz.* 3°44' S, 38°40' W 132
Caucasia, *Col.* 7°57' N, 75°14' W 136
Caucasus Mountains, *Asia-Europe* 42°3' N, 44°7' E 158
Caucete, *Arg.* 31°40' S, 68°18' W 134
Cauchon Lake, *Can.* 55°28' N, 97°4' W 108
Caudéran, *Fr.* 44°51' N, 0°38' E 150
Caudete, *Sp.* 38°42' N, 0°59' E 164
Caudry, *Fr.* 50°7' N, 3°23' E 163
Caungula, *Angola* 8°27' S, 18°38' E 218
Cauquenes, *Chile* 35°59' S, 72°21' W 134
Caura, river, *Venez.* 6°56' N, 64°51' W 130
Caurés, river, *Braz.* 1°16' S, 63°17' W 130
Cauro, *Fr.* 41°54' N, 8°54' E 156
Causapscal, *Can.* 48°20' N, 67°13' W 94
Căuseni, *Mold.* 46°37' N, 29°23' E 156
Cautário, river, *Braz.* 11°47' S, 63°55' W 137
Caution, Cape, *Can.* 50°58' N, 128°14' W 108
Cauto, river, *Cuba* 20°39' N, 76°41' W 116
Cavalaire, *Fr.* 43°10' N, 6°30' E 150
Cavalcante, *Braz.* 13°48' S, 47°31' W 138
Cavalese, *It.* 46°17' N, 11°27' E 167
Cavalier, *N. Dak., U.S.* 48°45' N, 97°39' W 90
Cavalla, river, *Africa* 6°18' N, 7°56' W 222
Cavalleria, Cap de, *Sp.* 40°3' N, 3°48' E 164
Cavallermaggiore, *It.* 44°42' N, 7°41' E 167
Cavallo Pass, *U.S.* 28°17' N, 96°20' W 96
Cavally, river, *Côte d'Ivoire* 6°19' N, 8°14' W 222
Cavan, *Ire.* 53°58' N, 7°22' W 150
Cavarzere, *It.* 45°7' N, 12°4' E 167
Cave, *N.Z.* 44°19' S, 170°59' E 240
Cave Creek, *Ariz., U.S.* 33°49' N, 111°56' W 92
Cave Mountain, *Calif., U.S.* 35°3' N, 116°22' W 101
Cave Point, *U.S.* 44°45' N, 87°9' W 94
Cavendish, *Vt., U.S.* 43°23' N, 72°37' W 104
Caviana, Ilha, island, *Braz.* 0°22' N, 49°54' W 130
Cavignac, *Fr.* 45°5' N, 0°24' E 150
Cavinas, *Bol.* 12°34' S, 66°50' W 137
Cavite, *Philippines* 14°29' N, 120°53' E 203
Cavo, Monte, peak, *It.* 41°44' N, 12°37' E 156
Cavour, *It.* 44°46' N, 7°23' E 167
Cavtat (Epidaurum), *Croatia* 42°34' N, 18°13' E 168
Çavuş Burnu, *Turk.* 36°19' N, 30°32' E 156
Çavuşçu Gölü, lake, *Turk.* 38°25' N, 31°35' E 156
Cawker City, *Kans., U.S.* 39°29' N, 98°27' W 92
Cawood, *U.K.* 53°50' N, 1°8' W 162
Cawston, *U.K.* 52°45' N, 1°9' E 162
Caxambu, *Braz.* 22°0' S, 44°56' W 138
Caxias, *Braz.* 4°29' S, 71°26' W 130
Caxias, *Braz.* 4°47' S, 43°19' W 132
Caxias do Sul, *Braz.* 29°11' S, 51°10' W 139
Caxito, *Angola* 8°35' S, 13°41' E 218
Çay, *Turk.* 38°35' N, 31°1' E 156
Cayacal, Punta, *Mex.* 17°44' N, 102°12' W 114
Çaycuma, *Turk.* 41°25' N, 32°2' E 156
Çayeli, *Turk.* 41°5' N, 40°43' E 195
Cayenne, *Fr. Guiana, Fr.* 4°58' N, 52°19' W 130
Cayeux-sur-Mer, *Fr.* 50°10' N, 1°30' E 163
Cayey, *U.S.* 18°7' N, 66°11' W 116
Çayıralan, *Turk.* 39°18' N, 35°38' E 156
Cayman Trench, *Caribbean Sea* 17°52' N, 80°50' W 253
Caynaba, *Somalia* 8°56' N, 46°25' E 216
Cayo Agua, Isla, island, *Pan.* 9°2' N, 82°0' W 115
Cayucos, *Calif., U.S.* 35°27' N, 120°55' W 100
Cayuga, *Ind., U.S.* 39°56' N, 87°28' W 102
Cayuga Lake, *N.Y., U.S.* 42°41' N, 77°13' W 94
Cazage, *Angola* 11°3' S, 20°44' E 220
Cazalla de la Sierra, *Sp.* 37°55' N, 5°47' W 164
Cazères, *Fr.* 43°12' N, 1°3' E 164
Cazombo, *Angola* 11°55' S, 22°58' E 220
Cazones, river, *Mex.* 20°14' N, 98°10' W 114
Cazorla, *Sp.* 37°54' N, 3°2' W 164
Cazorla, *Venez.* 8°0' N, 67°0' W 136
Ceadîr-Lunga, *Mold.* 46°2' N, 28°50' E 156
Ceará, adm. division, *Braz.* 5°20' S, 40°29' W 132
Ceará Mirim, *Braz.* 5°38' S, 35°26' W 132
Ceara Plain, *South Atlantic Ocean* 0°23' N, 37°43' W 253
Cébaco, Isla de, island, *Pan.* 7°22' N, 81°30' W 115
Ceballos, *Mex.* 26°31' N, 104°9' W 114
Cebollar, *Arg.* 29°6' S, 66°32' W 134
Cebollatí, *Uru.* 33°17' S, 53°51' W 139
Céboruco, Volcán, *Mex.* 21°7' N, 104°32' W 114
Cebu, *Philippines* 10°20' N, 123°54' E 203
Cebu, island, *Philippines* 11°11' N, 123°27' E 192
Cece, *Hung.* 46°45' N, 18°38' E 168
Cecil Lake, *Can.* 56°17' N, 120°35' W 108
Cecil Rhodes, Mount, *Austral.* 25°28' S, 121°15' E 230
Cecina, *It.* 43°18' N, 10°31' E 156
Cedar Creek Peak, *Idaho, U.S.* 42°26' N, 113°8' W 90
Cedar Creek Reservoir, lake, *Tex., U.S.* 32°20' N, 96°47' W 96
Cedar Falls, *Iowa, U.S.* 42°30' N, 92°28' W 94
Cedar Grove, *Calif., U.S.* 36°48' N, 118°41' W 101
Cedar Grove, *Wis., U.S.* 43°34' N, 87°49' W 102
Cedar Key, *Fla., U.S.* 29°8' N, 83°3' W 105
Cedar Lake, *Can.* 53°1' N, 101°7' W 81
Cedar Lake, *Can.* 50°7' N, 93°38' W 90
Cedar Lake, *Ind., U.S.* 41°20' N, 87°28' W 102
Cedar Lake, lake, *Can.* 45°58' N, 78°50' W 94
Cedar Mountains, *Utah, U.S.* 40°35' N, 113°9' W 90
Cedar Pass, *Calif., U.S.* 41°33' N, 120°17' W 90
Cedar Pass, *S. Dak., U.S.* 43°45' N, 101°56' W 90
Cedar Rapids, *Iowa, U.S.* 41°57' N, 91°39' W 94
Cedar Ridge, *Calif., U.S.* 39°11' N, 121°2' W 90
Cedar, river, *Iowa, U.S.* 42°9' N, 92°21' W 80
Cedar Vale, *Kans., U.S.* 37°4' N, 96°30' W 92
Cedarburg, *Wis., U.S.* 43°17' N, 87°59' W 102
Cedars of Lebanon, site, *Leb.* 34°14' N, 36°2' E 194
Cedarvale, *Can.* 55°0' N, 128°19' W 108
Cedarville, *Calif., U.S.* 41°31' N, 120°11' W 90
Cedral, *Mex.* 23°47' N, 100°43' W 114
Cedros, *Mex.* 24°39' N, 101°48' W 114
Cedros, Isla, island, *Mex.* 27°56' N, 115°10' W 112
Cedros Trench, *North Pacific Ocean* 24°2' N, 112°32' W 252
Ceek, *Somalia* 8°55' N, 45°19' E 216
Ceel Afweyn, *Somalia* 9°52' N, 47°15' E 216
Ceel Buur, *Somalia* 4°44' N, 46°35' E 218
Ceel Dhaab, *Somalia* 8°49' N, 46°34' E 216
Ceel Huur, *Somalia* 5°0' N, 48°20' E 218
Ceeldheere, *Somalia* 3°52' N, 47°13' E 218
Ceepeecee, *Can.* 49°53' N, 126°44' W 90
Ceerigaabo (Erigavo), *Somalia* 10°34' N, 47°24' E 218
Cefa, *Rom.* 46°54' N, 21°42' E 168
Cegléd, *Hung.* 47°10' N, 19°49' E 168
Cehegín, *Sp.* 38°5' N, 1°48' W 164
Ceheng, *China* 24°58' N, 105°49' E 198
Cehotina, river, *Europe* 43°30' N, 18°48' E 168
Cehu Silvaniei, *Rom.* 47°24' N, 23°12' E 168
Ceiba Grande, ruin(s), *Mex.* 17°22' N, 93°51' W 115
Ceica, *Rom.* 46°51' N, 22°10' E 168
Cejal, *Col.* 2°42' N, 67°55' W 136
Cejolao, *Arg.* 27°28' S, 62°20' W 139
Çekerek, *Turk.* 40°5' N, 35°29' E 156
Çekerek, river, *Turk.* 40°25' N, 35°18' E 156
Celarain, Punta, *Mex.* 20°10' N, 86°59' W 115
Celaya, *Mex.* 20°30' N, 100°49' W 114
Celebes see Sulawesi, island, *Indonesia* 2°0' S, 121°0' E 192
Celebes Basin, *Celebes Sea* 3°27' N, 121°47' E 254
Celebes Sea 3°49' N, 119°35' E 192
Çeleken, *Turkm.* 39°26' N, 53°8' E 180
Čelić, *Bosn. and Herzg.* 44°43' N, 18°47' E 168
Celina, *Ohio, U.S.* 40°32' N, 84°35' W 102
Celje, *Slov.* 46°14' N, 15°14' E 156
Cella, *Sp.* 40°27' N, 1°18' W 164
Cellar Head, *U.K.* 58°25' N, 6°8' W 150
Celldömölk, *Hung.* 47°15' N, 17°10' E 168
Celle, *Ger.* 52°36' N, 10°5' E 150
Celtic Sea 50°32' N, 8°3' W 150
Cement, *Okla., U.S.* 34°54' N, 98°8' W 92
Cemerno, *Serb.* 43°38' N, 20°13' E 168
Çemişgezek, *Turk.* 39°4' N, 38°54' E 195
Cempoala see Zempoala, ruin(s), *Mex.* 19°23' N, 96°28' W 114
Cenchreae, ruin(s), *Gr.* 37°53' N, 22°55' E 156
Cencia see Ch'ench'a, *Eth.* 6°15' N, 37°38' E 224
Cenderawasih, Teluk 3°0' S, 133°34' E 192
Cenicero, *Sp.* 42°28' N, 2°39' W 164
Centenario, *Mex.* 18°39' N, 90°17' W 115
Centennial Mountains, *Idaho, U.S.* 44°29' N, 112°28' W 90
Center, *Colo., U.S.* 37°44' N, 106°6' W 92
Center, *N. Dak., U.S.* 47°5' N, 101°17' W 90
Center, *Tex., U.S.* 31°46' N, 94°11' W 103
Center Barnstead, *N.H., U.S.* 43°20' N, 71°17' W 104
Center Conway, *N.H., U.S.* 43°59' N, 71°4' W 104
Center Harbor, *N.H., U.S.* 43°42' N, 71°28' W 104
Center Hill, *Fla., U.S.* 28°38' N, 82°0' W 105
Center Lovell, *Me., U.S.* 44°10' N, 70°54' W 104
Center Moriches, *N.Y., U.S.* 40°48' N, 72°48' W 104
Center Ossipee, *N.H., U.S.* 43°45' N, 71°10' W 104
Center Peak, *Calif., U.S.* 36°12' N, 120°40' W 100
Center Point, *Tex., U.S.* 29°54' N, 99°2' W 92
Centerburg, *Ohio, U.S.* 40°17' N, 82°41' W 102
Centerfield, *Utah, U.S.* 39°7' N, 111°48' W 92
Centerville, *Calif., U.S.* 36°43' N, 119°30' W 100
Centerville, *Iowa, U.S.* 40°43' N, 92°53' W 94
Centerville, *Mass., U.S.* 41°38' N, 70°22' W 104
Centerville, *S. Dak., U.S.* 43°5' N, 96°58' W 94
Centerville, *Tex., U.S.* 31°14' N, 95°58' W 96
Centerville, *Utah, U.S.* 40°55' N, 111°52' W 90
Centinela, Picacho del, peak, *Mex.* 29°3' N, 102°42' W 92
Cento, *It.* 44°43' N, 11°17' E 167
Central, *Alas., U.S.* 65°33' N, 144°52' W 98
Central, *Ariz., U.S.* 32°52' N, 109°47' W 92
Central, adm. division, *Mongolia* 46°58' N, 105°11' E 198
Central African Republic 7°1' N, 21°10' E 218
Central Butte, *Can.* 50°48' N, 106°32' W 90
Central City, *Ill., U.S.* 38°32' N, 89°8' W 102
Central City, *Ky., U.S.* 37°17' N, 87°7' W 96
Central City, *Nebr., U.S.* 41°6' N, 98°1' W 92
Central City, *S. Dak., U.S.* 44°22' N, 103°46' W 90
Central, Cordillera, *Dom. Rep.* 19°16' N, 71°38' W 116
Central, Cordillera, *Peru* 6°52' S, 77°30' W 130
Central Equatoria, adm. divison, *Sudan* 5°2' N, 31°32' E 224
Central Islip, *N.Y., U.S.* 40°47' N, 73°12' W 104
Central Kalahari Game Reserve, *Botswana* 22°34' S, 23°16' E 227
Central, Massif, *Europe* 44°5' N, 1°58' E 214
Central Mount Wedge, peak, *Austral.* 22°57' S, 131°37' E 230
Central Pacific Basin, *North Pacific Ocean* 7°5' N, 176°34' W 252
Central Range, *P.N.G.* 5°6' S, 141°26' E 192
Centralia, *Ill., U.S.* 38°31' N, 89°8' W 102
Centralia, *Mo., U.S.* 39°11' N, 92°8' W 94
Centralia, *Wash., U.S.* 46°41' N, 122°58' W 100
Centre, *Ala., U.S.* 34°8' N, 85°41' W 96
Centre, adm. division, *Fr.* 47°39' N, 0°50' E 150
Centre de Marcoule, site, *Fr.* 44°8' N, 4°40' E 165
Centre Island, *Austral.* 16°25' S, 136°48' E 230
Centreville, *Mich., U.S.* 41°54' N, 85°31' W 102
Centreville, *Miss., U.S.* 31°4' N, 91°4' W 103
Cenxi, *China* 22°56' N, 111°1' E 198
Çepan, *Alban.* 40°25' N, 20°15' E 156
Cephalonia see Kefaloniá, adm. division, *Gr.* 38°22' N, 20°3' E 156
Cepin, *Croatia* 45°30' N, 18°32' E 168
Ceprano, *It.* 41°32' N, 13°31' E 156
Cer, peak, *Serb.* 44°35' N, 19°27' E 168
Ceram, island, *Indonesia* 3°48' S, 129°2' E 192
Ceram Sea 2°26' S, 128°3' E 192
Cerbat Mountains, *Ariz., U.S.* 35°29' N, 114°7' W 101
Cerbatana, Serranía de la, *Venez.* 6°31' N, 66°45' W 130
Cerbère, *Fr.* 42°26' N, 3°8' E 164
Cerbicales, Îles, islands, *Tyrrhenian Sea* 41°24' N, 9°24' E 156
Cère, river, *Fr.* 44°50' N, 2°21' E 165
Cerea, *It.* 45°12' N, 11°12' E 167
Cereal, *Can.* 51°26' N, 110°48' W 90
Cereales, *Arg.* 36°52' S, 63°51' W 139
Ceres, *Arg.* 29°53' S, 61°57' W 139
Ceres, *Braz.* 15°21' S, 49°37' W 138
Ceres, *Calif., U.S.* 37°35' N, 120°58' W 100
Ceres, *S. Af.* 33°21' S, 19°18' E 227
Cerf Island, *Seychelles* 9°36' S, 49°54' E 218
Cerigo see Kíthira, island, *Gr.* 36°17' N, 23°3' E 180
Cermei, *Rom.* 46°33' N, 21°50' E 168
Çermik, *Turk.* 38°8' N, 39°27' E 195
Cerna, *Croatia* 45°11' N, 18°41' E 168
Cerne Abbas, *U.K.* 50°48' N, 2°29' W 162
Cernik, *Croatia* 45°17' N, 17°23' E 168
Cerovljani, *Bosn. and Herzg.* 45°3' N, 17°14' E 168
Ceralvo, *Mex.* 26°5' N, 99°37' W 114
Cerralvo, Isla, island, *Mex.* 23°58' N, 109°49' W 112
Cerrillos, ruin(s), *Mex.* 18°33' N, 92°10' W 115
Cerritos, *Mex.* 22°24' N, 100°16' W 114
Cerro Azul, *Mex.* 21°12' N, 97°44' W 114
Cerro Azul, *Peru* 13°2' S, 76°31' W 130
Cerro Chato, *Uru.* 33°5' S, 55°10' W 139
Cerro de Garnica National Park, *Mex.* 19°39' N, 101°5' W 112
Cerro de la Estrella National Park (8), *Mex.* 19°11' N, 99°10' W 112
Cerro de las Mesas, ruin(s), *Mex.* 18°41' N, 96°7' W 114
Cerro de Pasco, *Peru* 10°42' S, 76°16' W 130
Cerro Gordo, *Ill., U.S.* 39°52' N, 88°44' W 102
Cerro Jána, Meseta del, *Venez.* 5°36' N, 65°51' W 136
Cerrón, peak, *Venez.* 10°17' N, 70°44' W 136
Cervales, peak, *Sp.* 39°32' N, 5°21' W 164
Cervera, *Sp.* 41°39' N, 1°16' E 164
Cervia, *It.* 44°15' N, 12°19' E 167
Cervià, *Sp.* 41°26' N, 0°51' E 164
Cervignano, *It.* 45°49' N, 13°19' E 167
Cervo, *Sp.* 43°39' N, 7°26' W 150
Cesana Torinese, *It.* 44°57' N, 6°49' E 167
César, adm. division, *Col.* 9°23' N, 73°54' W 136
Cesena, *It.* 44°8' N, 12°14' E 167
Cesenatico, *It.* 44°11' N, 12°24' E 167
Cesiomaggiore, *It.* 46°5' N, 11°58' E 167
Cēsis, *Latv.* 57°17' N, 25°15' E 166
České Budějovice, *Czech Rep.* 48°59' N, 14°27' E 152
Český Les, *Czech Rep.* 49°28' N, 12°41' E 152
Çeşme, *Turk.* 38°16' N, 26°18' E 156
Cesney, Cape, *Antarctica* 66°10' S, 136°15' E 248
Cess, river, *Liberia* 5°40' N, 8°58' W 222
Cessnock, *Austral.* 32°48' S, 151°22' E 231
Cesvaine, *Latv.* 56°57' N, 26°18' E 166
Cetate, *Rom.* 44°6' N, 23°4' E 168
Cetina, *Sp.* 41°16' N, 1°59' W 164
Cetinje, *Mont.* 42°23' N, 18°54' E 168
Ceuta, *Sp.* 35°53' N, 5°20' W 150
Cévennes, region, *Europe* 45°7' N, 4°13' E 165
Cevio, *Switz.* 46°19' N, 8°35' E 167
Ceyhan, *Turk.* 37°1' N, 35°49' E 156
Ceyhan, river, *Turk.* 37°21' N, 36°16' E 180
Ceylanpınar, *Turk.* 36°50' N, 40°5' E 195
Ceylon, *Can.* 49°27' N, 104°36' W 90
Chaadayevka, *Russ.* 53°8' N, 45°58' E 154
Chābahār, *Iran* 25°18' N, 60°39' E 182
Chaboullié, Lac, lake, *Can.* 50°52' N, 78°32' W 110
Chac, oil field, *Mex.* 19°14' N, 92°33' W 115
Chacabuco, *Arg.* 34°40' S, 60°28' W 139
Chacalluta, *Chile* 18°25' S, 70°20' W 137
Chacarilla, *Chile* 20°39' S, 69°8' W 137
Chachani, Nevado, peak, *Peru* 16°14' S, 71°35' W 137
Chachapoyas, *Peru* 6°9' S, 77°51' W 130
Chachersk, *Belarus* 52°50' N, 30°57' E 154
Chachoengsao, *Thai.* 13°43' N, 101°4' E 202
Chachora, *India* 24°10' N, 77°0' E 197
Chachro, *Pak.* 25°7' N, 70°17' E 186
Chaco, adm. division, *Arg.* 27°11' S, 60°49' W 139
Chaco Culture National Historic Park, *N. Mex., U.S.* 36°6' N, 108°26' W 92
Chaco National Park, *Arg.* 26°54' S, 59°45' W 139
Chacon, Cape, *Alas., U.S.* 54°29' N, 132°5' W 108
Chad 15°25' N, 17°21' E 216
Chad Basain National Park, *Nig.* 12°10' N, 13°45' E 218
Chad, Lake, *Chad* 13°48' N, 13°22' E 216
Chadan, *Russ.* 51°19' N, 91°41' E 184
Chadron, *Nebr., U.S.* 42°49' N, 103°0' W 90
Chadwick, *Mo., U.S.* 36°55' N, 93°3' W 96
Chaedong, *N. Korea* 39°28' N, 126°12' E 200
Chaeronea, ruin(s), *Gr.* 38°28' N, 22°43' E 156
Chaeryŏng, *N. Korea* 38°24' N, 125°38' E 200
Chafarinas, Islas, islands, *Alboran Sea* 35°13' N, 2°52' W 150
Chafe, *Nig.* 11°54' N, 6°55' E 222
Chaffee, *Mo., U.S.* 37°10' N, 89°40' W 96
Chafurray, *Col.* 3°9' N, 73°16' W 136
Chagai, *Pak.* 29°19' N, 64°39' E 182
Chagang, adm. division, *N. Korea* 40°45' N, 126°30' E 200
Chagda, *Russ.* 58°44' N, 130°49' E 160
Chagdo Kangri, peak, *China* 34°10' N, 84°4' E 188
Chaghcharan, *Afghan.* 34°28' N, 65°13' E 186
Chagoda, *Russ.* 59°7' N, 35°18' E 154
Chagos Archipelago (Oil Islands), *Indian Ocean* 6°42' S, 71°25' E 188
Chagos Trench, *Indian Ocean* 10°25' S, 72°50' E 254
Chagos-Laccadive Ridge, *Arabian Sea* 2°17' N, 72°13' E 254
Chaguaramas, *Venez.* 9°20' N, 66°17' W 136
Chagyl, *Turkm.* 40°49' N, 55°17' E 158
Chahar Borj, *Afghan.* 34°20' N, 62°12' E 186
Chahbounia, *Alg.* 35°31' N, 2°36' E 150
Chah-e Ab, *Afghan.* 37°25' N, 69°50' E 186
Ch'aho, *N. Korea* 40°12' N, 128°41' E 200
Chaibasa, *India* 22°32' N, 85°49' E 197
Chaïmane, spring, *Mauritania* 21°4' N, 13°6' W 222
Chain Fracture Zone, *South Atlantic Ocean* 1°56' S, 16°17' W 253
Chaîne de Mitumba, *Dem. Rep. of the Congo 8°5' S, 27°22' E* 224
Chai-Nat, *Thai.* 15°14' N, 100°10' E 202
Chaira, Laguna, lake, *Col.* 1°13' N, 75°21' W 136
Chaitén, *Chile* 42°54' S, 72°45' W 134
Chaiya, *Thai.* 9°23' N, 99°10' E 202
Chajarí, *Arg.* 30°44' S, 57°57' W 139
Chak Chak, *Sudan* 8°36' N, 26°57' E 224
Chakar, river, *Pak.* 29°24' N, 68°7' E 186
Chakaran, *Afghan.* 36°54' N, 71°9' E 186
Chakaria, *Bangladesh* 21°47' N, 92°4' E 188
Chake Chake, *Tanzania* 5°12' S, 39°46' E 218
Chakhansur, *Afghan.* 31°10' N, 62°6' E 186
Chakia, *India* 25°2' N, 83°11' E 188
Chakkarat, *Thai.* 15°2' N, 102°25' E 202
Chakmak-Suu, *Kyrg.* 41°59' N, 71°26' E 197
Chakola, *Russ.* 64°17' N, 44°14' E 154
Chakradharpur, *India* 22°41' N, 85°38' E 197
Chakrata, *India* 30°42' N, 77°53' E 197
Chakwal, *Pak.* 32°55' N, 72°53' E 186
Chala, *Peru* 15°54' S, 74°16' W 137
Chala, *Tanzania* 7°37' S, 31°17' E 224
Chalabesa, *Zambia* 11°23' S, 30°59' E 224
Chalatenango, *El Salv.* 14°1' N, 88°55' W 115
Chalaua, *Mozambique* 16°5' S, 39°13' E 224
Chalbi Desert, *Kenya* 3°33' N, 36°48' E 224
Chalchihuites, *Mex.* 23°27' N, 103°54' W 114
Ch'alchīs Terara, peak, *Eth.* 9°6' N, 36°37' E 224
Chalengkou, *China* 38°1' N, 93°55' E 188
Chaleur Bay 47°51' N, 66°0' W 111
Chalhuanca, *Peru* 14°19' S, 73°15' W 137
Chaling, *China* 26°51' N, 113°31' E 198
Chalkyitsik, *Alas., U.S.* 66°38' N, 143°44' W 98
Challacollo, *Chile* 20°59' S, 69°24' W 137
Challans, *Fr.* 46°51' N, 1°54' W 150
Challapata, *Bol.* 18°55' S, 66°45' W 137
Challenger Deep, *North Pacific Ocean* 10°16' N, 142°13' E 252
Challenger Point, peak, *Colo., U.S.* 37°57' N, 105°40' W 90
Challis, *Idaho, U.S.* 44°30' N, 114°14' W 90
Chālmeh, *Iran* 39°29' N, 48°3' E 195
Chalon, *Fr.* 46°47' N, 4°50' E 150
Châlons-en-Champagne, *Fr.* 48°57' N, 4°22' E 163
Chaloyuk, *Turkm.* 37°26' N, 54°13' E 180
Chālūs, *Iran* 36°41' N, 51°19' E 180
Cham, *Ger.* 49°12' N, 12°40' E 152
Chama, *Ghana* 8°49' N, 0°58' E 222
Chama, *N. Mex., U.S.* 36°53' N, 106°36' W 92
Chamah, peak, *Malaysia* 5°12' N, 101°29' E 196
Chaman, *Pak.* 30°53' N, 66°33' E 186
Chaman Bid, *Iran* 37°28' N, 56°39' E 180
Chamba, *Nepal* 32°34' N, 76°9' E 188
Chamba, *Tanzania* 11°32' S, 37°1' E 224
Chambak, *Cambodia* 11°14' N, 104°47' E 202
Chambeaux, Lac, lake, *Can.* 53°39' N, 69°17' W 111
Chamberlain, *S. Dak., U.S.* 43°47' N, 99°19' W 90
Chamberlain Lake, *Me., U.S.* 46°8' N, 70°3' W 94
Chambers, *Ariz., U.S.* 35°12' N, 109°26' W 92
Chambeshi, river, *Zambia* 11°2' S, 31°11' E 224
Chambira, river, *Peru* 3°58' S, 75°57' W 130
Chambishi, *Zambia* 12°40' S, 28°4' E 224
Chambless, *Calif., U.S.* 34°33' N, 115°33' W 101
Chambley, *Fr.* 49°3' N, 5°53' E 163
Chambord, *Can.* 48°24' N, 72°4' W 94
Chame, Punta, *Pan.* 8°32' N, 79°41' W 115
Chamela, *Mex.* 19°32' N, 105°5' W 114
Chamical, *Arg.* 30°23' S, 66°19' W 134
Chamiss Bay, *Can.* 50°5' N, 127°20' W 90
Chamizal National Memorial, *Tex., U.S.* 31°44' N, 106°30' W 92
Chamonix, *Fr.* 45°55' N, 6°51' E 167
Champa, *India* 22°2' N, 82°40' E 197
Champagne, region, *Europe* 49°46' N, 4°21' E 167
Champagne-Ardenne, adm. division, *Fr.* 48°18' N, 3°36' E 150
Champaign, *Ill., U.S.* 40°6' N, 88°15' W 102
Champasak, *Laos* 14°56' N, 105°50' E 202
Champion, *Can.* 50°14' N, 113°10' W 90
Champion, *Ohio, U.S.* 41°18' N, 80°51' W 102
Champlain, *N.Y., U.S.* 44°59' N, 73°28' W 94
Champotón, *Mex.* 19°21' N, 90°44' W 115
Champotón, river, *Mex.* 19°29' N, 90°38' W 115
Chamzinka, *Russ.* 54°25' N, 45°48' E 154
Chanac, *Fr.* 44°27' N, 3°20' E 150
Chañaral, *Chile* 26°23' S, 70°39' W 132
Chenārān, *Iran* 36°39' N, 59°5' E 180
Chanaro, Cerro, peak, *Venez.* 5°28' N, 64°0' W 130
Chancamayo, *Peru* 12°36' S, 72°26' W 137
Chancay, *Peru* 11°34' S, 77°17' W 130
Chanco, *Chile* 35°44' S, 72°34' W 134
Chandalar, river, *Alas., U.S.* 66°56' N, 149°16' W 98
Chandausi, *India* 28°26' N, 78°46' E 197
Chandeleur Islands, *Gulf of Mexico* 29°39' N, 88°48' W 103
Chandeleur Sound 29°48' N, 89°15' W 103
Chandigarh, *India* 30°43' N, 76°51' E 197

Chandigarh, adm. division, *India* 30°45′ N, 76°18′ E 188
Chandler, *Ariz., U.S.* 33°18′ N, 111°50′ W 92
Chandler, *Can.* 48°20′ N, 64°40′ W 111
Chandler, *Okla., U.S.* 35°40′ N, 96°52′ W 92
Chandler, Mount, *Antarctica* 75°19′ S, 73°25′ W 248
Chandless, river, *Braz.* 10°2′ S, 70°12′ W 137
Chandpur, *Bangladesh* 23°13′ N, 90°41′ E 197
Chandpur, *India* 29°7′ N, 78°15′ E 197
Chandrapur, *India* 20°3′ N, 79°17′ E 190
Chang, Ko, island, *Thai.* 11°52′ N, 101°42′ E 202
Chang La, pass, *India* 34°2′ N, 77°55′ E 188
Changalane, *Mozambique* 26°14′ S, 32°14′ E 227
Changane, river, *Mozambique* 24°3′ S, 34°3′ E 227
Changara, *Mozambique* 16°50′ S, 33°16′ E 224
Changbai, *China* 41°27′ N, 128°12′ E 200
Changchun, *China* 43°52′ N, 125°16′ E 198
Changde, *China* 29°5′ N, 111°43′ E 198
Changhua, *Taiwan, China* 23°59′ N, 120°31′ E 198
Changhŭng, *N. Korea* 40°24′ N, 128°20′ E 200
Changji, *China* 44°3′ N, 87°19′ E 184
Changjiang (Shiliu), *China* 19°13′ N, 109°2′ E 198
Changjin, *N. Korea* 40°21′ N, 127°15′ E 200
Changjin Reservoir, lake, *N. Korea* 40°29′ N, 126°46′ E 200
Changjin, river, *N. Korea* 40°55′ N, 127°15′ E 200
Changle, *China* 25°58′ N, 119°33′ E 198
Changli, *China* 39°43′ N, 119°11′ E 198
Changling, *China* 44°16′ N, 124°1′ E 198
Changma, *China* 39°52′ N, 96°43′ E 188
Changmar, *China* 34°27′ N, 79°57′ E 188
Changni, *S. Korea* 37°19′ N, 128°31′ E 200
Changning, *China* 26°23′ N, 112°24′ E 198
Changping, *China* 40°12′ N, 116°13′ E 198
Changsha, *China* 28°13′ N, 113°1′ E 198
Changshou, *China* 29°51′ N, 107°4′ E 198
Changshu, *China* 31°36′ N, 120°40′ E 198
Changting, *China* 25°50′ N, 116°16′ E 198
Changtu, *China* 42°43′ N, 124°8′ E 200
Changwon, *S. Korea* 35°16′ N, 128°45′ E 200
Changxi, *China* 31°48′ N, 105°59′ E 198
Changxing Dao, island, *China* 39°29′ N, 120°1′ E 198
Changyŏn, *N. Korea* 38°14′ N, 125°5′ E 200
Changzheng, *China* 36°41′ N, 105°2′ E 198
Changzhi, *China* 36°10′ N, 113°6′ E 198
Changzhou, *China* 31°50′ N, 120°0′ E 198
Channapatna, *India* 12°40′ N, 77°11′ E 188
Channel Country, *Austral.* 25°2′ S, 138°35′ E 230
Channel Islands, adm. division, *U.K.* 49°26′ N, 2°48′ W 150
Channel Islands National Park, *Calif., U.S.* 34°5′ N, 120°34′ W 101
Channel-Port aux Basques, *Can.* 47°34′ N, 59°9′ W 111
Chanthaburi, *Thai.* 12°36′ N, 102°9′ E 202
Chantilly, *Fr.* 49°11′ N, 2°28′ E 163
Chantrey Inlet 67°23′ N, 98°31′ W 106
Chanute, *Kans., U.S.* 37°39′ N, 95°28′ W 94
Chany, *Russ.* 55°16′ N, 76°54′ E 184
Chany, Ozero, lake, *Russ.* 54°57′ N, 76°49′ E 184
Chany, Ozero, lake, *Russ.* 54°39′ N, 75°46′ E 160
Chaor, river, *China* 47°14′ N, 121°38′ E 198
Chaoyang, *China* 41°35′ N, 120°24′ E 198
Chaoyang, *China* 23°13′ N, 116°33′ E 198
Chaoyang see Huinan, *China* 42°42′ N, 126°4′ E 200
Chaoyangchuan, *China* 42°51′ N, 129°19′ E 200
Chaozhou, *China* 23°37′ N, 116°33′ E 198
Chapada dos Guimarães, *Braz.* 15°25′ S, 55°47′ W 132
Chapada Dos Veadeiros National Park, *Braz.* 14°10′ S, 47°50′ W 138
Chapadinha, *Braz.* 3°46′ S, 43°20′ W 132
Chapaev, *Kaz.* 50°11′ N, 51°8′ E 158
Chapais, *Can.* 49°48′ N, 74°54′ W 94
Chapala, *Mex.* 20°18′ N, 103°12′ W 112
Chapala, Lago de, lake, *Mex.* 20°2′ N, 103°30′ W 114
Chapare, river, *Bol.* 16°21′ S, 65°2′ W 137
Chaparral, *Col.* 3°41′ N, 75°26′ W 136
Chapayevsk, *Russ.* 52°58′ N, 49°48′ E 154
Chapeau, *Can.* 45°55′ N, 77°4′ W 94
Chapeauroux, *Fr.* 44°49′ N, 3°44′ E 150
Chapecó, *Braz. 27°4′ S, 52°36′ W* 139
Chapimarca, *Peru* 13°59′ S, 73°3′ W 137
Chapleau, *Can.* 47°49′ N, 83°24′ W 94
Chaplin Lake, *Can.* 50°13′ N, 107°8′ W 108
Chapman, *Ala., U.S.* 31°40′ N, 86°43′ W 96
Chapman, *Kans., U.S.* 38°57′ N, 97°2′ W 90
Chapman, Mount, *Antarctica* 82°25′ S, 104°25′ W 248
Chapman, Mount, *Can.* 51°56′ N, 118°24′ W 90
Chapoma, *Russ.* 66°8′ N, 38°44′ E 154
Chappaquiddick Island, *Mass., U.S.* 41°23′ N, 70°27′ W 104
Chappell, *Nebr., U.S.* 41°4′ N, 102°28′ W 90
Chaput Hughes, *Can.* 48°8′ N, 80°4′ W 94
Chaqui, *Bol.* 19°35′ S, 65°28′ W 137
Char, *Mauritania* 21°32′ N, 12°50′ W 222
Chara, *Russ.* 56°48′ N, 118°10′ E 160
Chara, river, *Russ.* 59°0′ N, 118°31′ E 160
Charadai, *Arg.* 27°37′ S, 59°54′ W 139
Charagua, *Bol.* 19°48′ S, 63°18′ W 137
Charalá, *Col.* 6°15′ N, 73°7′ W 136
Charambirá, Punta, *Col.* 4°8′ N, 78°10′ W 136
Charaña, *Bol.* 17°40′ S, 69°27′ W 137
Charanwala, *India* 27°51′ N, 72°11′ E 186
Charata, *Arg.* 27°13′ S, 61°12′ W 139
Charay, *Mex.* 26°0′ N, 108°50′ W 112
Charcoal Lake, *Can.* 58°44′ N, 103°14′ W 108
Charcot Bay 63°49′ S, 61°4′ W 134
Charcot Island, *Antarctica* 70°11′ S, 79°50′ W 248
Chard, *Can.* 55°50′ N, 110°54′ W 108
Chard, *U.K.* 50°52′ N, 2°58′ W 162
Charenton, *La., U.S.* 29°52′ N, 91°32′ W 103
Chari, river, *Africa* 13°9′ N, 14°33′ E 216
Charikar, *Afghan.* 35°1′ N, 69°10′ E 186
Chariton, *Iowa, U.S.* 41°1′ N, 93°19′ W 94
Chariton, river, *Mo., U.S.* 40°44′ N, 93°9′ W 80
Charity, *Guyana* 7°21′ N, 58°37′ W 130
Charity Island, *Mich., U.S.* 43°59′ N, 83°25′ W 102
Chärjew see Türkmenabat, *Turkm.* 39°4′ N, 63°35′ E 184
Charkayuvom, *Russ.* 65°48′ N, 54°51′ E 154
Charlemont, *Mass., U.S.* 42°37′ N, 72°53′ W 104
Charleroi, *Belg.* 50°25′ N, 4°26′ E 167
Charles, Cape, *Va., U.S.* 37°1′ N, 75°57′ W 96
Charles Fuhr, *Arg.* 50°13′ S, 71°53′ W 134
Charles Island, *Can.* 62°36′ N, 77°12′ W 106
Charles Lake, lake, *Can.* 59°45′ N, 111°12′ W 108
Charles Mound, *Ill., U.S.* 42°28′ N, 90°17′ W 102
Charles, Mount, *Austral.* 27°46′ S, 117°13′ E 230
Charlesbourg, *Can.* 46°51′ N, 71°17′ W 94
Charleston, *Ill., U.S.* 39°29′ N, 88°11′ W 102
Charleston, *N.Z.* 41°56′ S, 171°27′ E 240
Charleston, *S.C., U.S.* 32°47′ N, 79°57′ W 96
Charleston, *W. Va., U.S.* 38°19′ N, 81°43′ W 94
Charleston Peak, *Nev., U.S.* 36°15′ N, 115°45′ W 101
Charlestown, *N.H., U.S.* 43°13′ N, 72°26′ W 104
Charleville-Mézières, *Fr.* 49°46′ N, 4°43′ E 163
Charlevoix, *Mich., U.S.* 45°18′ N, 85°16′ W 94
Charlie Lake, *Can.* 56°15′ N, 120°59′ W 108
Charlie-Gibbs Fracture Zone, *North Atlantic Ocean* 51°53′ N, 33°3′ W 253
Charlotte, *Mich., U.S.* 42°33′ N, 84°51′ W 102
Charlotte, *N.C., U.S.* 35°12′ N, 80°51′ W 96
Charlotte, *Tex., U.S.* 28°51′ N, 98°43′ W 96
Charlotte, *Vt., U.S.* 44°18′ N, 73°16′ W 104
Charlotte Amalie, *Virgin Islands, U.S.* 18°0′ N, 65°0′ W 118
Charlotte Harbor 26°42′ N, 83°11′ W 80
Charlotte Harbor, *Fla., U.S.* 26°58′ N, 82°4′ W 105
Charlotte Lake, lake, *Can.* 52°6′ N, 125°48′ W 108
Charlottetown, *Can.* 46°13′ N, 63°16′ W 111
Charlotteville, *Trinidad and Tobago* 11°16′ N, 60°33′ W 116
Charlton City, *Mass., U.S.* 42°8′ N, 72°0′ W 104
Charlton Island, *Can.* 52°5′ N, 80°29′ W 81
Charly, *Fr.* 48°58′ N, 3°16′ E 163
Charmes, *Fr.* 48°21′ N, 6°17′ E 163
Charny, *Can.* 46°43′ N, 71°16′ W 94
Charouine, *Alg.* 29°2′ N, 0°15′ E 214
Charron Lake, lake, *Can.* 52°39′ N, 95°47′ W 108
Charters Towers, *Austral.* 20°7′ S, 146°17′ E 231
Chartres, *Fr.* 48°27′ N, 1°27′ E 163
Charyshskoye, *Russ.* 51°26′ N, 83°43′ E 184
Chascomús, *Arg.* 35°34′ S, 58°1′ W 139
Chase, *Alas., U.S.* 62°27′ N, 150°6′ W 98
Chase, *Can.* 50°49′ N, 119°40′ W 90
Chase, *Mich., U.S.* 43°53′ N, 85°38′ W 102
Chase City, *Va., U.S.* 36°47′ N, 78°28′ W 96
Chase, Mount, *Me., U.S.* 46°5′ N, 68°34′ W 94
Chase Mountain, *Can.* 56°32′ N, 125°22′ W 108
Chasel'ka, *Russ.* 65°7′ N, 81°26′ E 169
Chashniki, *Belarus* 54°51′ N, 29°13′ E 166
Chaska, *Minn., U.S.* 44°46′ N, 93°38′ W 94
Chasŏng, *N. Korea* 41°26′ N, 126°38′ E 200
Chasovo, *Russ.* 62°2′ N, 50°40′ E 154
Chassahowitzka, *Fla., U.S.* 28°41′ N, 82°35′ W 105
Chastyye, *Russ.* 57°16′ N, 55°4′ E 154
Chataignier, *La., U.S.* 30°32′ N, 92°20′ W 103
Chatawa, *Miss., U.S.* 31°2′ N, 90°29′ W 103
Châteaumeillant, *Fr.* 46°34′ N, 2°11′ E 150
Châteauneuf-en-Thymerais, *Fr.* 48°34′ N, 1°14′ E 163
Château-Porcien, *Fr.* 49°32′ N, 4°14′ E 163
Châteauroux, *Fr.* 46°49′ N, 1°41′ E 150
Château-Salins, *Fr.* 48°49′ N, 6°30′ E 163
Châteauvert, Lac, lake, *Can.* 47°34′ N, 74°36′ W 110
Chateh, *Can.* 58°41′ N, 118°48′ W 108
Châtel, *Fr.* 46°16′ N, 6°49′ E 167
Châtelet, *Belg.* 50°24′ N, 4°32′ E 167
Châtellerault, *Fr.* 46°48′ N, 0°31′ E 150
Châtel-Saint-Denis, *Switz.* 46°33′ N, 6°55′ E 167
Châtel-sur-Moselle, *Fr.* 48°18′ N, 6°24′ E 163
Châtenois, *Fr.* 48°17′ N, 5°49′ E 163
Chatfield, *Minn., U.S.* 43°50′ N, 92°12′ W 110
Chatham, *Can.* 47°1′ N, 65°28′ W 94
Chatham, *Can.* 42°23′ N, 82°11′ W 102
Chatham, *Ill., U.S.* 39°39′ N, 89°42′ W 102
Chatham, *La., U.S.* 32°18′ N, 92°29′ W 103
Chatham, *Mass., U.S.* 41°40′ N, 69°58′ W 104
Chatham, *Miss., U.S.* 33°4′ N, 91°7′ W 103
Chatham, *Mo., U.S.* 39°39′ N, 89°42′ W 94
Chatham, *N.H., U.S.* 44°9′ N, 71°1′ W 104
Chatham, *N.Y., U.S.* 42°21′ N, 73°37′ W 104
Chatham, *U.K.* 51°21′ N, 0°30′ E 162
Chatham, *Va., U.S.* 36°48′ N, 79°25′ W 96
Chatham, Isla, island, *Chile* 51°9′ S, 74°8′ W 134
Chatham Rise, *South Pacific Ocean* 43°29′ S, 178°25′ W 252
Châtillon, *Fr.* 49°6′ N, 3°46′ E 163
Chatom, *Ala., U.S.* 31°27′ N, 88°15′ W 103
Chatra, *India* 24°11′ N, 84°51′ E 197
Chatsu, *India* 26°35′ N, 75°57′ E 197
Chatsworth, *Ill., U.S.* 40°45′ N, 88°19′ W 102
Chattahoochee, *Fla., U.S.* 30°40′ N, 84°54′ W 112
Chattahoochee, river, *U.S.* 32°4′ N, 85°8′ W 80
Chattanooga, *Tenn., U.S.* 35°1′ N, 85°19′ W 96
Chattaroy, *W. Va., U.S.* 37°42′ N, 82°18′ W 96
Chatteris, *U.K.* 52°27′ N, 5°297′ E 162
Chatyr-Tash, *Kyrg.* 40°54′ N, 76°26′ E 184
Chau Doc, *Vietnam* 10°41′ N, 105°7′ E 202
Chauk, *Myanmar* 20°53′ N, 94°50′ E 202
Chaullay, *Peru* 13°1′ S, 72°39′ W 137
Chaulnes, *Fr.* 49°48′ N, 2°47′ E 163
Chaumont, *Fr.* 48°6′ N, 5°8′ E 150
Chaumont-en-Vexin, *Fr.* 49°16′ N, 1°53′ E 163
Chaumu, *India* 27°10′ N, 75°42′ E 197
Chauncey, *Ohio, U.S.* 39°24′ N, 82°8′ W 102
Chaunskaya Guba 69°10′ N, 165°0′ E 160
Chauny, *Fr.* 49°37′ N, 3°14′ E 163
Chauvin, *Can.* 52°41′ N, 110°9′ W 108
Chauvin, *La., U.S.* 29°26′ N, 90°36′ W 103
Chavan'ga, *Russ.* 66°8′ N, 37°40′ E 154
Chaves, *Braz.* 0°24′ N, 49°48′ W 123
Chaves, *Port.* 41°44′ N, 7°30′ W 150
Chaveslândia, *Braz.* 18°58′ S, 50°36′ W 138
Cháviva, *Col.* 4°18′ N, 72°18′ W 136
Chavuma, *Zambia* 13°5′ S, 22°43′ E 220
Chavusy, *Belarus* 53°46′ N, 31°0′ E 154
Chawang, *Thai.* 8°26′ N, 99°31′ E 202
Chayanta, *Bol.* 18°28′ S, 66°28′ W 137
Chaykovskiy, *Russ.* 56°48′ N, 54°9′ E 154
Cheadle, *U.K.* 52°59′ N, 2°0′ W 162
Cheaha Mountain, *Ala., U.S.* 33°27′ N, 85°53′ W 96
Cheapside, *Va., U.S.* 37°12′ N, 75°59′ W 96
Cheb, *Czech Rep.* 50°4′ N, 12°22′ E 152
Chebanse, *Ill., U.S.* 41°0′ N, 87°55′ W 102
Chebarkul', *Russ.* 55°0′ N, 60°19′ E 154
Chebeague Island, *Me., U.S.* 43°44′ N, 70°8′ W 104
Cheboksary, *Russ.* 56°5′ N, 47°11′ E 154
Cheboygan, *Mich., U.S.* 45°38′ N, 84°30′ W 94
Chebsara, *Russ.* 59°10′ N, 38°49′ E 154
Checa, *Sp.* 40°34′ N, 1°47′ W 164
Chech, Erg, *Alg.* 23°26′ N, 4°20′ W 206
Chechnya, adm. division, *Russ.* 43°33′ N, 44°59′ E 158
Checotah, *Okla., U.S.* 35°27′ N, 95°32′ W 96
Cheddar, *U.K.* 51°16′ N, 2°47′ W 162
Cheduba Island, *Myanmar* 18°29′ N, 92°36′ E 188
Chedworth, *U.K.* 51°48′ N, 1°55′ W 162
Cheecham, *Can.* 56°16′ N, 110°53′ W 108
Cheepash, river, *Can.* 50°42′ N, 82°33′ W 110
Cheepay, river, *Can.* 51°7′ N, 83°35′ W 110
Cheetham, Cape, *Antarctica* 69°54′ S, 167°30′ E 248
Chefornak, *Alas., U.S.* 60°12′ N, 164°14′ W 98
Chegdomyn, *Russ.* 51°6′ N, 133°12′ E 238
Chegga, spring, *Mauritania* 25°22′ N, 5°47′ W 214
Chegutu, *Zimb.* 18°9′ S, 30°10′ E 224
Chehalis, *Wash., U.S.* 46°39′ N, 122°58′ W 100
Chehalis, river, *Wash., U.S.* 46°59′ N, 123°25′ W 100
Chehar Borjak, *Afghan.* 30°17′ N, 62°7′ E 186
Cheïkria, spring, *Alg.* 25°29′ N, 5°28′ W 214
Cheju see Jeju, *S. Korea* 33°29′ N, 126°32′ E 200
Chela, Serra da, *Angola* 16°7′ S, 12°39′ E 220
Ch'elago, *Eth.* 4°9′ N, 40°3′ E 224
Chelak, *Uzb.* 39°58′ N, 66°51′ E 197
Chelan, *Wash., U.S.* 47°50′ N, 120°1′ W 90
Chelan Falls, *Wash., U.S.* 47°47′ N, 119°59′ W 108
Chelem, *Mex.* 21°15′ N, 89°44′ W 116
Chelforó, *Arg.* 39°6′ S, 66°31′ W 134
Chellal, *Alg.* 35°30′ N, 4°23′ E 150
Chełm, *Pol.* 51°7′ N, 23°27′ E 152
Chełmża, *Pol.* 53°21′ N, 18°26′ E 152
Chelmsford, *Mass., U.S.* 42°35′ N, 71°22′ W 104
Chelmsford, *U.K.* 51°44′ N, 0°29′ E 162
Chelmuzhi, *Russ.* 62°32′ N, 35°43′ E 154
Chelsea, *Mich., U.S.* 42°18′ N, 84°2′ W 102
Chelsea, *Okla., U.S.* 36°31′ N, 95°26′ W 96
Chelsea, *Vt., U.S.* 43°59′ N, 72°27′ W 104
Cheltenham, *U.K.* 51°53′ N, 2°5′ W 162
Chelva, *Sp.* 39°44′ N, 1°0′ E 150
Chelyabinsk, *Russ.* 55°9′ N, 61°25′ E 154
Chelyabinsk, adm. division, *Russ.* 53°58′ N, 59°14′ E 154
Chelyuskin, Mys, *Russ.* 76°44′ N, 103°34′ E 172
Chemaïa, *Mor.* 32°5′ N, 8°40′ W 214
Chemba, *Mozambique* 17°11′ S, 34°50′ E 224
Chemehuevi Peak, *Calif., U.S.* 34°32′ N, 114°36′ W 101
Chémery, *Fr.* 49°35′ N, 4°50′ E 163
Chemnitz, *Ger.* 50°48′ N, 12°55′ E 160
Chemtou, ruin(s), *Tun.* 36°28′ N, 8°29′ E 156
Chemult, *Oreg., U.S.* 43°13′ N, 121°48′ W 90
Chen Barag Qi, *China* 49°17′ N, 119°24′ E 198
Chenab, river, *Pak.* 31°18′ N, 72°22′ E 186
Chenachane, *Alg.* 26°3′ N, 4°14′ W 214
Chenango Bridge, *N.Y., U.S.* 42°10′ N, 75°53′ W 94
Chenārān, *Iran* 36°39′ N, 59°5′ E 180
Ch'ench'a (Cencia), *Eth.* 6°15′ N, 37°38′ E 224
Chénérailles, *Fr.* 46°7′ N, 2°10′ E 150
Cheney, *Wash., U.S.* 47°28′ N, 117°36′ W 90
Cheneyville, *La., U.S.* 30°59′ N, 92°18′ W 103
Chengbu, *China* 26°22′ N, 110°19′ E 198
Chengchow see Zhengzhou, *China* 34°46′ N, 113°36′ E 198
Chengde, *China* 41°0′ N, 117°55′ E 198
Chengdu, *China* 30°43′ N, 104°2′ E 190
Chengele, *India* 28°47′ N, 96°17′ E 188
Chenggu, *China* 33°8′ N, 107°19′ E 198
Chenghai, *China* 23°29′ N, 116°48′ E 198
Chengkou, *China* 31°54′ N, 108°39′ E 198
Ch'engkung, *Taiwan, China* 23°8′ N, 121°24′ E 198
Chengshan Jiao, *China* 37°24′ N, 122°45′ E 198
Chengxian, *China* 33°44′ N, 105°40′ E 198
Chennai (Madras), *India* 13°5′ N, 80°16′ E 188
Chenoa, *Ill., U.S.* 40°44′ N, 88°43′ W 102
Chenxi, *China* 28°2′ N, 110°12′ E 198
Chenxiangtun, *China* 41°33′ N, 123°29′ E 200
Chenzhou, *China* 25°48′ N, 113°2′ E 198
Cheo Reo, *Vietnam* 13°23′ N, 108°25′ E 202
Cheom Ksan, *Cambodia* 14°16′ N, 104°56′ E 202
Cheonan, *S. Korea* 36°47′ N, 127°8′ E 200
Cheongeong, *S. Korea* 36°26′ N, 129°6′ E 200
Cheongju, *S. Korea* 36°37′ N, 127°30′ E 200
Cheongyang, *S. Korea* 36°26′ N, 126°48′ E 200
Cheorwon, *S. Korea* 38°14′ N, 127°13′ E 200
Chepachet, *R.I., U.S.* 41°54′ N, 71°41′ W 104
Chepes, *Arg.* 31°20′ S, 66°35′ W 134
Chepstow, *U.K.* 51°38′ N, 2°41′ W 162
Cheptsa, river, *Russ.* 58°8′ N, 52°54′ E 154
Cher, river, *Fr.* 46°54′ N, 2°17′ E 165
Cherán, *Mex.* 19°40′ N, 101°57′ W 114
Cherangany Hills, *Kenya* 1°32′ N, 35°1′ E 224
Cherari, *Eth.* 9°55′ N, 35°52′ E 224
Cheraw, *S.C., U.S.* 34°40′ N, 79°55′ W 96
Cherbourg-Octeville, *Fr.* 49°37′ N, 1°55′ W 150
Cherchell, *Alg.* 36°35′ N, 2°12′ E 150
Cherdyn', *Russ.* 60°24′ N, 56°25′ E 154
Cheremkhovo, *Russ.* 53°16′ N, 102°55′ E 190
Cheremukhovo, *Russ.* 60°21′ N, 59°59′ E 154
Cherepanovo, *Russ.* 54°14′ N, 83°29′ E 184
Chereponi, *Ghana* 10°7′ N, 0°17′ E 222
Cherepovets, *Russ.* 59°7′ N, 37°55′ E 154
Cherevkovo, *Russ.* 61°46′ N, 45°17′ E 154
Chereya, *Belarus* 54°36′ N, 29°20′ E 166
Chéri, *Niger* 13°25′ N, 11°21′ E 222
Cheriton, *Va., U.S.* 37°17′ N, 75°58′ W 96
Cherkasy, *Ukr.* 49°26′ N, 32°3′ E 158
Cherkessk, *Russ.* 44°14′ N, 42°3′ E 158
Cherla, *India* 18°4′ N, 80°50′ E 188
Cherlak, *Russ.* 54°9′ N, 74°53′ E 184
Chermenino, *Russ.* 59°2′ N, 43°59′ E 154
Chermoz, *Russ.* 58°46′ N, 56°5′ E 154
Chern', *Russ.* 53°25′ N, 36°57′ E 154
Chernaya Kholunitsa, *Russ.* 58°52′ N, 51°46′ E 154
Chernevichi, *Belarus* 54°1′ N, 28°49′ E 166
Chernevo, *Russ.* 58°39′ N, 28°12′ E 166
Cherni Vrŭkh, peak, *Bulg.* 42°32′ N, 23°12′ E 156
Chernihiv, *Ukr.* 51°27′ N, 31°20′ E 158
Chernivtsi, *Ukr.* 48°17′ N, 25°57′ E 152
Chernoborskaya, *Russ.* 65°8′ N, 53°38′ E 154
Chernofski, *Alas., U.S.* 53°22′ N, 167°34′ W 98
Chernogorsk, *Russ.* 53°49′ N, 91°16′ E 184
Chernorechenskiy, *Russ.* 60°42′ N, 52°15′ E 154
Chernovka, *Russ.* 54°12′ N, 80°5′ E 184
Chernushka, *Russ.* 56°30′ N, 56°1′ E 154
Chernyakhovsk, *Russ.* 54°36′ N, 21°49′ E 152
Chernyanka, *Russ.* 50°55′ N, 37°48′ E 158
Chernyshevskiy, *Russ.* 62°52′ N, 112°40′ E 160
Chernyy Otrog, *Russ.* 51°51′ N, 56°0′ E 158
Chernyy Yar, *Russ.* 48°2′ N, 46°4′ E 158
Cherokee, *Okla., U.S.* 36°44′ N, 98°21′ W 92
Cherokee Sound, *Bahamas* 26°16′ N, 77°3′ W 96
Cherokees, Lake O' The, *Okla., U.S.* 36°42′ N, 95°40′ W 80
Cherrapunji, *India* 25°15′ N, 91°42′ E 197
Cherry Creek Range, *Nev., U.S.* 39°59′ N, 115°6′ W 90
Cherry Creek, river, *S. Dak., U.S.* 44°42′ N, 102°31′ W 90
Cherskaya, *Russ.* 57°39′ N, 28°17′ E 166
Cherskiy, *Russ.* 68°39′ N, 161°29′ E 160
Cherskogo, Khrebet, *Russ.* 66°20′ N, 138°20′ E 160
Chersonesus, ruin(s), *Gr.* 35°18′ N, 25°17′ E 156
Chertkovo, *Russ.* 49°27′ N, 40°8′ E 158
Cherva, *Russ.* 62°16′ N, 48°41′ E 154
Chervonohrad, *Ukr.* 50°22′ N, 24°15′ E 152
Chervyanka, *Russ.* 57°39′ N, 99°28′ E 160
Cherykaw, *Belarus* 53°32′ N, 31°23′ E 154
Chesaning, *Mich., U.S.* 43°10′ N, 84°7′ W 102
Chesapeake, *Va., U.S.* 36°49′ N, 76°17′ W 96
Chesapeake, *W. Va., U.S.* 38°12′ N, 81°34′ W 94
Chesham, *U.K.* 51°42′ N, 0°38′ E 162
Cheshire, *Conn., U.S.* 41°29′ N, 72°54′ W 104
Cheshire, *Mass., U.S.* 42°33′ N, 73°10′ W 104
Cheshskaya Guba 67°9′ N, 44°36′ E 169
Cheshunt, *U.K.* 51°41′ N, 0°3′ E 162
Cheslatta Lake, lake, *Can.* 53°38′ N, 125°40′ W 108
Chesley, *Can.* 44°17′ N, 81°6′ W 110
Chesma, *Russ.* 53°51′ N, 60°32′ E 154
Cheste, *Sp.* 39°29′ N, 0°42′ E 164
Chester, *Mo., U.S.* 37°54′ N, 89°49′ W 96
Chester, *Mont., U.S.* 48°28′ N, 110°59′ W 90
Chester, *N.H., U.S.* 42°57′ N, 71°16′ W 104
Chester, *S.C., U.S.* 34°42′ N, 81°13′ W 96
Chester, *U.K.* 53°12′ N, 2°51′ W 162
Chester, *Vt., U.S.* 43°15′ N, 72°36′ W 104
Chester le Street, *U.K.* 54°51′ N, 1°36′ W 162
Chesterfield, *Ind., U.S.* 40°6′ N, 85°36′ W 102
Chesterfield, *U.K.* 53°14′ N, 1°27′ W 162
Chesterfield, Îles, islands, *Coral Sea* 18°54′ S, 154°49′ E 238
Chesterfield Inlet, *Can.* 63°19′ N, 90°50′ W 106
Chesterhill, *Ohio, U.S.* 39°28′ N, 81°51′ W 102
Chesterton Range, *Austral.* 26°17′ S, 147°27′ E 230
Chestertown, *N.Y., U.S.* 43°38′ N, 73°49′ W 104
Chestnut Ridge, *Pa., U.S.* 40°29′ N, 79°22′ W 94
Chetamale, *India* 10°44′ N, 92°41′ E 188
Chete Safari Area, *Zimb.* 17°30′ S, 27°12′ E 224
Chetek, *Wis., U.S.* 45°18′ N, 91°40′ W 94
Chéticamp, *Can.* 46°36′ N, 61°1′ W 111
Chetumal, *Mex.* 18°30′ N, 88°27′ W 115
Chetwynd, *Can.* 55°41′ N, 121°39′ W 108
Chevillon, *Fr.* 48°31′ N, 5°7′ E 163
Cheviot, *N.Z.* 42°50′ S, 173°16′ E 240
Cheviot Hills, *U.K.* 55°10′ N, 2°47′ W 150
Cheviot, The, peak, *U.K.* 55°27′ N, 2°16′ W 150
Ch'ew Bahir, lake, *Eth.* 4°40′ N, 36°40′ E 224
Chewelah, *Wash., U.S.* 48°15′ N, 117°45′ W 90
Chewore Safari Area, *Zimb.* 15°58′ S, 29°52′ E 224
Cheyenne, *Okla., U.S.* 35°35′ N, 99°40′ W 92
Cheyenne, *Wyo., U.S.* 41°6′ N, 104°55′ W 90
Cheyenne, river, *S. Dak., U.S.* 44°24′ N, 102°2′ W 90
Cheyenne, river, *Wyo., U.S.* 42°53′ N, 104°36′ W 80
Cheyenne Wells, *Colo., U.S.* 38°48′ N, 102°21′ W 90
Chezacut, *Can.* 52°25′ N, 124°2′ W 108
Chhad Bet, site, *Pak.* 24°13′ N, 69°54′ E 186
Chhapra, *India* 25°46′ N, 84°43′ E 197
Chhatarpur, *India* 24°54′ N, 79°35′ E 197
Chhattīsgarh, adm. division, *India* 19°11′ N, 81°20′ E 188
Chhep, *Cambodia* 13°46′ N, 105°27′ E 202
Chhindwara, *India* 22°4′ N, 78°56′ E 197
Chhlong, *Cambodia* 12°14′ N, 105°57′ E 202
Chhukha, *Bhutan* 27°10′ N, 89°30′ E 197
Chi, river, *Thai.* 15°56′ N, 102°18′ E 202
Chía, *Sp.* 42°31′ N, 0°27′ E 164
Chiai, *Taiwan, China* 23°28′ N, 120°25′ E 198
Chiang Dao, *Thai.* 19°23′ N, 98°57′ E 202
Chiang Khan, *Thai.* 17°53′ N, 101°37′ E 202
Chiang Mai, *Thai.* 18°48′ N, 98°58′ E 202
Chiang Rai, *Thai.* 19°55′ N, 99°48′ E 202
Chiang Saen, *Laos* 20°18′ N, 100°3′ E 202
Chiange, *Angola* 15°43′ S, 13°54′ E 220
Chiapa, *Chile* 19°33′ S, 69°14′ W 137
Chiapas, adm. division, *Mex.* 16°28′ N, 93°24′ W 112
Chiari, *It.* 45°32′ N, 9°54′ E 167
Chiasso, *Switz.* 45°51′ N, 9°1′ E 167
Chiat'aisi, *Ga.* 42°14′ N, 43°17′ E 195
Chiautla, *Mex.* 18°15′ N, 98°36′ W 114
Chiavari, *It.* 44°19′ N, 9°20′ E 167
Chiavenna, *It.* 46°19′ N, 9°23′ E 167
Chiba, *Japan* 35°34′ N, 140°9′ E 201
Chiba, adm. division, *Japan* 35°44′ N, 139°54′ E 201
Chibabava, *Mozambique* 20°17′ S, 33°41′ E 227
Chibi, *Zimb.* 20°19′ S, 30°29′ E 227
Chibia, *Angola* 15°14′ S, 13°40′ E 220
Chibougamau, *Can.* 49°54′ N, 74°22′ W 94
Chibougamau, Lac, lake, *Can.* 49°49′ N, 75°44′ W 81
Chibuto, *Mozambique* 24°42′ S, 33°34′ E 227
Chibwe, *Zambia* 14°12′ S, 28°29′ E 224
Chic Chocs Mountains, *Can.* 48°42′ N, 67°1′ W 94
Chicago, *Ill., U.S.* 41°51′ N, 87°37′ W 102
Chicamba, *Angola* 4°59′ S, 12°2′ E 218
Chichagof, *Alas., U.S.* 57°41′ N, 136°8′ W 108
Chichagof Island, *Alas., U.S.* 58°3′ N, 138°7′ W 98
Chichaoua, *Mor.* 31°31′ N, 8°47′ W 214
Chichas, Cordillera de, *Bol.* 20°47′ S, 66°25′ W 132
Chiché, river, *Braz.* 8°54′ S, 54°6′ W 130
Chichén Itzá, ruin(s), *Mex.* 20°40′ N, 88°42′ W 115

Chichester, *N.H., U.S.* 43°14' N, 71°25' W 104
Chichester, *U.K.* 50°50' N, 0°47' E 162
Chichi Jima Rettō, islands, *Philippine Sea* 26°41' N, 142°19' E 190
Chichibu, *Japan* 35°58' N, 139°6' E 201
Chichibu-Tama National Park, *Japan* 35°50' N, 138°11' E 201
Chichihualco, *Mex.* 17°40' N, 99°41' W 114
Chichiriviche, *Venez.* 10°56' N, 68°17' W 136
Chickaloon, *Alas., U.S.* 61°48' N, 148°28' W 98
Chickasaw, *Ala., U.S.* 30°45' N, 88°3' W 103
Chickasha, *Okla., U.S.* 35°2' N, 97°57' W 92
Chiclana de la Frontera, *Sp.* 36°25' N, 6°9' W 164
Chiclayo, *Peru* 6°44' S, 79°51' W 130
Chico, *Calif., U.S.* 39°43' N, 121°51' W 90
Chico, river, *Arg.* 48°23' S, 71°58' W 134
Chico, river, *Arg.* 45°2' S, 67°5' W 134
Chicomo, *Mozambique* 24°31' S, 34°9' E 227
Chicontepec, *Mex.* 20°57' N, 98°10' W 114
Chicopee, *Ga., U.S.* 34°14' N, 83°51' W 96
Chicopee, *Mass., U.S.* 42°8' N, 72°37' W 104
Chicot Island, *La., U.S.* 29°39' N, 89°22' W 103
Chicoutai, Point, *Can.* 50°5' N, 61°8' W 111
Chicoutimi-Nord, *Can.* 48°26' N, 71°6' W 94
Chicualacuala, *Mozambique* 22°4' S, 31°43' E 227
Chicuma, *Angola* 13°26' S, 14°46' E 220
Chidenguele, *Mozambique* 24°54' S, 34°10' E 227
Chiefland, *Fla., U.S.* 29°28' N, 82°51' W 105
Chiengi, *Zambia* 8°41' S, 29°10' E 224
Chietla, *Mex.* 18°29' N, 98°34' W 114
Chifeng, *China* 42°15' N, 118°59' E 198
Chifre, Serra do, *Braz.* 17°46' S, 42°41' W 132
Chignahuapan, *Mex.* 19°48' N, 98°2' W 114
Chignecto Bay 45°35' N, 64°44' W 111
Chignecto, Cape, *Can.* 45°15' N, 65°39' W 111
Chignik, *Alas., U.S.* 56°8' N, 158°13' W 106
Chiguana, *Bol.* 21°7' S, 67°58' W 137
Chiguaza, *Ecua.* 2°2' S, 77°52' W 136
Chigubo, *Mozambique* 22°49' S, 33°30' E 227
Chihertey, *Mongolia* 48°15' N, 89°30' E 184
Chihuahua, *Mex.* 28°35' N, 106°9' W 92
Chihuahua, adm. division, *Mex.* 29°0' N, 107°42' W 92
Chikalda, *India* 21°24' N, 77°19' E 188
Chikhachevo, *Russ.* 57°17' N, 29°55' E 166
Chikhli, *India* 20°21' N, 76°16' E 188
Chikwawa, *Malawi* 16°6' S, 34°45' E 224
Chilac, *Mex.* 18°18' N, 97°22' W 114
Chilako, river, *Can.* 53°31' N, 124°10' W 108
Chilanga, *Malawi* 13°14' S, 33°31' E 224
Chilapa, *Mex.* 17°34' N, 99°10' W 114
Chilas, *Pak.* 35°23' N, 74°7' E 186
Chilcotin, river, *Can.* 52°52' N, 124°49' W 108
Childersburg, *Ala., U.S.* 33°16' N, 86°22' W 96
Childress, *Tex., U.S.* 34°24' N, 100°13' W 92
Chile 36°9' S, 71°58' W 134
Chile Chico, *Chile* 46°31' S, 71°48' W 134
Chile Fracture Zone, *South Pacific Ocean* 34°0' S, 110°0' W 252
Chile Rise, *South Pacific Ocean* 40°45' S, 87°42' W 253
Chilecito, *Arg.* 29°11' S, 67°30' W 134
Chililabombwe, *Zambia* 12°23' S, 27°49' E 224
Chilko, river, *Can.* 51°45' N, 124°9' W 108
Chilkoot Pass, *Can.* 59°40' N, 135°15' W 108
Chillán, *Chile* 36°36' S, 72°7' W 123
Chillar, *Arg.* 37°20' S, 59°58' W 139
Chillicothe, *Ill., U.S.* 40°54' N, 89°31' W 102
Chillicothe, *Mo., U.S.* 39°47' N, 93°33' W 94
Chillicothe, *Ohio, U.S.* 39°19' N, 82°59' W 102
Chillicothe, *Tex., U.S.* 34°14' N, 99°30' W 92
Chilliwack, *Can.* 49°9' N, 121°57' W 100
Chilliwack Lake, *Can.* 49°2' N, 121°43' W 100
Chilliwack, river, *Can.* 49°5' N, 121°53' W 100
Chilmark, *Mass., U.S.* 41°20' N, 70°45' W 104
Chilo, *India* 27°26' N, 73°32' E 186
Chiloé, Isla Grande de, island, *Chile* 42°1' S, 76°28' W 134
Chilonga, *Zambia* 12°2' S, 31°20' E 224
Chiloquin, *Oreg., U.S.* 42°35' N, 121°52' W 90
Chilpancingo, *Mex.* 17°31' N, 99°34' W 114
Chil'tal'd, Gora, peak, *Russ.* 68°17' N, 30°50' E 152
Chiltern Hills, *U.K.* 51°46' N, 0°55' E 162
Chilton, *Wis., U.S.* 44°1' N, 88°11' W 102
Chiluage, *Angola* 9°30' S, 21°46' E 218
Chilumba (Deep Bay), *Malawi* 10°24' S, 34°13' E 224
Chilung (Keelung), *Taiwan, China* 25°6' N, 121°45' E 198
Chilwa, Lake, *Malawi* 15°22' S, 35°26' E 224
Chim Berkaouane, *Niger* 15°8' N, 3°37' E 222
Chimacum, *Wash., U.S.* 48°0' N, 122°46' W 100
Chimaltenango, *Guatemala* 14°39' N, 90°49' W 115
Chimaltitan, *Mex.* 21°48' N, 103°46' W 114
Chimán, *Pan.* 8°42' N, 78°37' W 115
Chimanimani, *Zimb.* 19°50' S, 32°51' E 224
Chimanimani National Park, *Zimb.* 19°55' S, 33°12' E 224
Chimay, *Belg.* 50°2' N, 4°19' E 163
Chimbote, *Peru* 9°5' S, 78°35' W 130
Chimboy, *Uzb.* 42°55' N, 59°47' E 180
Chimney Reservoir, *Nev., U.S.* 41°42' N, 116°53' W 90
Chimney Rock, site, *N.C., U.S.* 35°24' N, 82°22' W 96
Chimoio, *Mozambique* 19°8' S, 33°31' E 224
China 33°31' N, 97°47' E 190
China, *Mex.* 25°41' N, 99°13' W 114
China, *Tex., U.S.* 30°2' N, 94°21' W 103
China Lake, *Calif., U.S.* 35°39' N, 117°40' W 101
China Mountain, peak, *Calif., U.S.* 41°21' N, 122°40' W 90
Chinandega, *Nicar.* 12°36' N, 87°7' W 115
Chinati Mountains, *Tex., U.S.* 29°46' N, 104°36' W 92
Chinati Peak, *Tex., U.S.* 29°54' N, 104°32' W 92
Chinchaga, river, *Can.* 57°11' N, 119°35' W 108
Chincheros, *Peru* 13°34' S, 73°44' W 137
Chinchilla de Monte Aragón, *Sp.* 38°54' N, 1°45' W 164
Chinchón, *Sp.* 40°8' N, 3°26' W 164
Chincoteague, *Va., U.S.* 37°55' N, 75°22' W 94
Chincoteague Bay 37°58' N, 76°35' W 80
Chinde, *Mozambique* 18°36' S, 36°26' E 224
Chindu, *China* 33°21' N, 97°4' E 188
Chindwin, river, *Myanmar* 25°18' N, 95°16' E 190
Chinese Camp, *Calif., U.S.* 37°51' N, 120°27' W 100
Chingola, *Zambia* 12°36' S, 27°49' E 224
Chingpu, *Taiwan, China* 23°28' N, 121°28' E 198
Chinguetti, *Mauritania* 20°27' N, 12°23' W 222
Chinhoyi, *Zimb.* 17°23' S, 30°11' E 224
Chiniot, *Pak.* 31°41' N, 72°57' E 186
Chínipas, *Mex.* 27°23' N, 108°32' W 112
Chinko, river, *Cen. Af. Rep.* 5°41' N, 24°12' E 224
Chinle, *Ariz., U.S.* 36°8' N, 109°33' W 92
Chino, *Japan* 35°58' N, 138°11' E 201
Chino Valley, *Ariz., U.S.* 34°44' N, 112°27' W 92
Chinobampo, *Mex.* 26°18' N, 108°29' W 112
Chinon, *Fr.* 47°10' N, 0°14' E 150
Chinook, *Mont., U.S.* 48°34' N, 109°14' W 90
Chinook, *Wash., U.S.* 46°16' N, 123°56' W 100
Chinsali, *Zambia* 10°35' S, 32°2' E 224
Chinsong, *N. Korea* 41°24' N, 126°50' E 200
Chinteche, *Malawi* 11°52' S, 34°8' E 224
Chiôco, *Mozambique* 16°26' S, 32°50' E 224
Chioggia, *It.* 45°12' N, 12°14' E 167
Chipata, *Zambia* 13°39' S, 32°38' E 224
Chipchase Castle, site, *U.K.* 55°4' N, 2°18' W 150
Chiperceni, *Mold.* 47°30' N, 28°50' E 156
Chipewyan Lake, *Can.* 56°54' N, 113°30' W 108
Chipili, *Zambia* 10°46' S, 29°3' E 224
Chipinge, *Zimb.* 20°11' S, 32°36' E 227
Chipiona, *Sp.* 36°43' N, 6°26' W 164
Chipley, *Fla., U.S.* 30°46' N, 85°33' W 96
Chipman Lake, lake, *Can.* 49°58' N, 86°42' W 94
Chipoka, *Malawi* 13°57' S, 34°30' E 224
Chippenham, *U.K.* 51°28' N, 2°8' W 162
Chippewa, river, *Mich., U.S.* 43°37' N, 85°6' W 102
Chipping Campden, *U.K.* 52°2' N, 1°48' W 162
Chipping Norton, *U.K.* 51°56' N, 1°33' W 162
Chipping Sodbury, *U.K.* 51°32' N, 2°24' W 162
Chiquihuitlán, *Mex.* 17°56' N, 96°50' W 114
Chiquilá, *Mex.* 21°26' N, 87°18' W 116
Chiquimula, *Guatemala* 14°49' N, 89°35' W 116
Chiquimulilla, *Guatemala* 14°5' N, 90°25' W 116
Chiquinquirá, *Col.* 5°37' N, 73°50' W 136
Chiradzulu, *Malawi* 15°41' S, 35°13' E 224
Chirala, *India* 15°49' N, 80°21' E 188
Chiramba, *Mozambique* 16°58' S, 34°39' E 224
Chiran, *Japan* 31°20' N, 130°27' E 201
Chirchiq, *Uzb.* 41°29' N, 69°34' E 197
Chirchirri, *Somalia* 4°43' N, 44°43' E 218
Chiredzi, *Zimb.* 21°8' S, 31°48' E 227
Chireno, *Tex., U.S.* 31°29' N, 94°21' W 103
Chirfa, *Niger* 20°55' N, 12°19' E 222
Chiribiquete National Park, *Col.* 0°11' N, 72°51' W 136
Chiribiquete, Sierra de, *Col.* 1°3' N, 73°33' W 136
Chiricahua Peak, *Ariz., U.S.* 31°50' N, 109°20' W 92
Chiriguaná, *Col.* 9°20' N, 73°38' W 136
Chirikof Island, *Alas., U.S.* 55°35' N, 157°15' W 98
Chirinda, *Russ.* 67°23' N, 100°23' E 169
Chirk, *U.K.* 52°56' N, 3°2' W 162
Chirnogeni, *Rom.* 43°54' N, 28°13' E 158
Chiromo, *Malawi* 16°33' S, 35°7' E 224
Chiroqchi, *Uzb.* 39°3' N, 66°36' E 197
Chirpan, *Bulg.* 42°12' N, 25°19' E 156
Chirripó, Cerro, peak, *C.R.* 9°29' N, 83°34' W 115
Chirripó, river, *C.R.* 10°13' N, 83°45' W 116
Chirundu, *Zambia* 16°2' S, 28°48' E 224
Chisamba, *Zambia* 15°0' S, 28°22' E 224
Chisasibi, *Can.* 53°45' N, 79°1' W 106
Chisembe Lagoon, *Zambia 11°49' S, 28°59' E 224*
Chishan, *Taiwan, China* 22°56' N, 120°29' E 198
Chishmy, *Russ.* 54°35' N, 55°21' E 154
Chisholm, *Can.* 54°54' N, 114°8' W 108
Chisholm, *Me., U.S.* 44°29' N, 70°13' W 104
Chishui, *China* 28°34' N, 105°41' E 198
Chisimayu see Kismaayo, *Somalia* 0°27' N, 42°35' E 224
Chişineu Criş, *Rom.* 46°32' N, 21°32' E 168
Chişinău, *Mold.* 47°0' N, 28°41' E 156
Chisos Mountains, *Tex., U.S.* 29°10' N, 103°26' W 92
Chistochina, *Alas., U.S.* 62°35' N, 144°40' W 98
Chistoozernoye, *Russ.* 54°40' N, 76°39' E 184
Chistopel'e, *Kaz.* 52°32' N, 67°15' E 184
Chistopol', *Russ.* 55°19' N, 50°31' E 154
Chita, *Col.* 6°11' N, 72°30' W 136
Chita, *Russ.* 52°8' N, 113°31' E 190
Chitado, *Angola* 17°18' S, 13°55' E 220
Chitambo, *Zambia* 12°57' S, 30°38' E 224
Chitato, *Angola* 7°20' S, 20°47' E 218
Chitek Lake, lake, *Can.* 52°23' N, 99°49' W 108
Chitembo, *Angola* 13°33' S, 16°43' E 220
Chitimba, *Malawi* 10°33' S, 34°10' E 224
Chitipa (Fort Hill), *Malawi* 9°43' S, 33°14' E 224
Chitokoloki, *Zambia* 13°50' S, 23°14' E 220
Chitose, *Japan* 42°47' N, 141°49' E 238
Chitradurga, *India* 14°13' N, 76°24' E 188
Chitral, *Pak.* 35°50' N, 71°47' E 186
Chitré, *Pan.* 7°59' N, 80°26' W 115
Chittagong, *Bangladesh* 22°19' N, 91°50' E 197
Chittoor, *India* 13°13' N, 79°6' E 188
Chitungwiza, *Zimb.* 17°58' S, 31°3' E 224
Chiuchiu, *Chile* 22°21' S, 68°42' W 137
Chiumbe, river, *Angola* 8°47' S, 21°10' E 220
Chiume, *Angola* 15°3' S, 21°12' E 220
Chiúre, *Mozambique* 13°24' S, 39°58' E 224
Chiusa, *It.* 46°38' N, 11°32' E 167
Chiusaforte, *It.* 46°24' N, 13°18' E 167
Chiuta, Lago, lake, *Mozambique* 14°50' S, 35°36' E 224
Chiva, *Sp.* 39°28' N, 0°43' E 150
Chivapuri, river, *Venez.* 6°28' N, 66°48' W 136
Chivasso, *It.* 45°12' N, 7°52' E 167
Chivay, *Peru* 15°40' S, 71°35' W 137
Chive, *Bol.* 12°23' S, 68°37' W 137
Chivhu, *Zimb.* 19°2' S, 30°52' E 224
Chivilcoy, *Arg.* 34°56' S, 60°3' W 139
Chiwanda, *Tanzania* 11°21' S, 34°58' E 224
Chiwefwe, *Zambia* 13°40' S, 29°27' E 224
Chizdia, *Rom.* 45°56' N, 21°45' E 168
Chizha, *Russ.* 67°8' N, 44°18' E 169
Chizu, *Japan* 35°14' N, 134°12' E 201
Chkalov, *Kaz.* 53°37' N, 70°25' E 184
Chlef, *Alg.* 36°9' N, 1°19' E 150
Chloride, *Ariz., U.S.* 35°24' N, 114°12' W 101
Cho La, pass, *China* 31°55' N, 98°43' E 188
Choate, *Can.* 49°27' N, 121°26' W 100
Chocaya, *Bol.* 20°57' S, 66°23' W 137
Chocó, adm. division, *Col.* 5°57' N, 77°21' W 136
Chocontá, *Col.* 5°7' N, 73°39' W 136
Chocorua, *N.H., U.S.* 43°52' N, 71°14' W 104
Chocorua, Mount, *N.H., U.S.* 43°57' N, 71°18' W 104
Choctawhatchee Bay 30°15' N, 86°29' W 80
Chodzież, *Pol.* 52°59' N, 16°55' E 152
Choele Choel, *Arg.* 39°17' S, 65°40' W 134
Choggar, spring, *Mauritania* 17°20' N, 13°47' W 222
Chogyuryong Sanmaek, *N. Korea* 40°18' N, 126°6' E 200
Choique Mahuida, Sierra, *Arg.* 38°24' S, 67°41' W 134
Choirokoitia, *Cyprus* 34°47' N, 33°20' E 194
Choiseul, island, *Solomon Islands* 7°0' S, 157°0' E 242
Choisy, *Fr.* 48°46' N, 2°24' E 163
Choix, *Mex.* 26°42' N, 108°22' W 112
Chojna, *Pol.* 52°57' N, 14°26' E 152
Chojnice, *Pol.* 53°41' N, 17°33' E 152
Ch'ok'ē, *Eth.* 11°7' N, 36°46' E 182
Chokoloskee, *Fla., U.S.* 25°48' N, 81°22' W 105
Chokoyan, *Chad* 13°20' N, 21°13' E 216
Chókwè, *Mozambique* 24°31' S, 32°58' E 227
Chokurdakh, *Russ.* 70°36' N, 148°1' E 160
Cholovo, *Russ.* 58°57' N, 30°26' E 166
Cholpon-Ata, *Kyrg.* 42°37' N, 76°59' E 184
Ch'ŏlsan, *N. Korea* 39°45' N, 124°38' E 200
Choluteca, *Hond.* 13°17' N, 87°11' W 115
Choma, *Zambia* 16°49' S, 26°57' E 224
Chon Buri, *Thai.* 13°25' N, 101°1' E 202
Chonchi, *Chile* 42°38' S, 73°49' W 134
Chŏnch'ŏn, *N. Korea* 40°39' N, 126°28' E 200
Chone, *Ecua.* 0°48' N, 80°4' W 130
Chong Kal, *Cambodia* 13°58' N, 103°34' E 202
Chong'an, *China* 27°43' N, 118°2' E 198
Ch'ongch'ŏn, river, *N. Korea* 39°45' N, 125°51' E 200
Ch'ŏngdan, *N. Korea* 37°57' N, 125°54' E 200
Ch'ŏngjin, *N. Korea* 41°45' N, 129°44' E 200
Ch'ŏngjŏng, *N. Korea* 39°40' N, 125°22' E 200
Chŏngju, *N. Korea* 39°40' N, 125°12' E 200
Chongming, *China* 31°39' N, 121°27' E 198
Chongming Dao, island, *China* 31°22' N, 121°54' E 198
Chongoene, *Mozambique* 25°0' S, 33°48' E 227
Chongoroi, *Angola* 13°36' S, 13°58' E 220
Chŏngp'yŏng, *N. Korea* 39°46' N, 127°23' E 200
Chongqing, *China* 29°32' N, 106°28' E 198
Chongqing Shi, adm. division, *China* 31°28' N, 108°25' E 198
Ch'ŏngsŏng, *N. Korea* 40°21' N, 124°51' E 200
Chongxin, *China* 35°20' N, 107°2' E 198
Chongyi, *China* 25°40' N, 114°17' E 198
Ch'ŏnnae, *N. Korea* 39°22' N, 127°11' E 200
Chonogol, *Mongolia* 45°52' N, 115°23' E 198
Chonos, Archipiélago de los, *South Pacific Ocean* 44°53' S, 74°46' W 134
Chop, *Ukr.* 48°25' N, 22°10' E 152
Chopim, river, *Braz.* 26°16' S, 52°11' W 139
Chorges, *Fr.* 44°32' N, 6°16' E 167
Chorley, *U.K.* 53°39' N, 2°38' W 162
Chornobyl', *Ukr.* 51°16' N, 30°15' E 158
Chornomors'ke, *Ukr.* 45°29' N, 32°43' E 156
Chornyy Ostriv, *Ukr.* 49°28' N, 26°46' E 152
Chorotis, *Arg.* 27°53' S, 61°24' W 139
Ch'osan, *N. Korea* 40°48' N, 125°46' E 200
Chōshi, *Japan* 35°44' N, 140°49' E 201
Chosica, *Peru* 11°54' S, 76°45' W 130
Choszczno, *Pol.* 53°10' N, 15°25' E 152
Choteau, *Mont., U.S.* 47°47' N, 112°10' W 90
Choudrant, *La., U.S.* 32°29' N, 92°32' W 103
Chouikhia, spring, *Alg.* 27°52' N, 4°16' W 214
Chouzé, *Fr.* 47°14' N, 0°7' E 150
Chowchilla, *Calif., U.S.* 37°6' N, 120°17' W 100
Choybalsan, *Mongolia* 48°4' N, 114°31' E 198
Choyr, *Mongolia* 46°14' N, 108°44' E 198
Chrea National Park, *Alg.* 36°39' N, 3°55' E 150
Christchurch, *N.Z.* 43°33' S, 172°37' E 240
Christensen, Mount, *Antarctica* 68°2' S, 47°46' E 248
Christiana, *S. Af.* 27°55' S, 25°9' E 227
Christianshåb see Qasigiannguit, *Den.* 68°47' N, 51°7' W 106
Christiansted, *U.S.* 17°45' N, 64°43' W 116
Christie Lake, lake, *Can.* 56°52' N, 97°30' W 108
Christie, Mount, *Can.* 62°56' N, 129°59' W 98
Christina Falls, *Can.* 56°38' N, 123°27' W 108
Christmas, *Fla., U.S.* 28°32' N, 81°1' W 105
Christmas Island see Kiritimati, *Kiribati* 2°0' N, 157°24' W 241
Christmas Lake Valley, *Oreg., U.S.* 43°19' N, 120°39' W 90
Christmas, Mount, *Antarctica* 81°50' S, 163°14' E 248
Christopher Lake, *Can.* 53°33' N, 105°45' W 108
Christoval, *Tex., U.S.* 31°11' N, 100°29' W 92
Chu, river, *Laos* 20°3' N, 104°38' E 202
Chuacús, Sierra de, *Guatemala* 15°13' N, 91°12' W 115
Chualar, *Calif., U.S.* 36°34' N, 121°32' W 100
Chubb Crater see Cratère du Nouveau-Québec, *Can.* 61°19' N, 73°41' W 106
Chubu Sangaku National Park, *Japan* 36°22' N, 137°26' E 201
Chubut, adm. division, *Arg.* 43°44' S, 70°18' W 134
Chubut, river, *Arg.* 42°36' S, 69°41' W 134
Chuchi Lake, *Can.* 55°5' N, 124°57' W 108
Chuckwalla Mountains, *Calif., U.S.* 33°37' N, 115°29' W 101
Chudovo, *Russ.* 59°6' N, 31°44' E 152
Chudz'yavr, *Russ.* 68°17' N, 34°19' E 152
Chugach Mountains, *Alas., U.S.* 60°40' N, 144°17' W 98
Chuginadak, island, *Alas., U.S.* 52°52' N, 172°34' W 160
Chugwater, *Wyo., U.S.* 41°46' N, 104°49' W 90
Chuhuyiv, *Ukr.* 49°52' N, 36°43' E 158
Chuí, *Uru. 33°40' S, 53°29' W* 139
Chukai, *Malaysia* 4°15' N, 103°25' E 196
Chukchi Plain, *Arctic Ocean* 76°29' N, 169°2' W 255
Chukchi Plateau, *Arctic Ocean* 78°6' N, 163°16' W 255
Chukchi Sea 70°53' N, 178°53' W 173
Chukchi Shelf, *Chukchi Sea* 69°0' N, 174°0' W 255
Chukhloma, *Russ.* 58°45' N, 42°46' E 154
Chukotskiy, adm. division, *Russ.* 66°20' N, 170°50' E 160
Chukotskiy, Mys, *Russ.* 64°15' N, 173°3' W 98
Chukotskiy Poluostrov, *Russ.* 66°33' N, 176°46' W 98
Chukotskoye Nagor'ye, *Russ.* 64°32' N, 176°36' E 73
Chula Vista, *Calif., U.S.* 32°38' N, 117°6' W 101
Chulkovo, *Russ.* 62°44' N, 88°22' E 169
Chul'man, *Russ.* 56°53' N, 124°50' E 173
Chulmleigh, *U.K.* 50°55' N, 3°52' W 162
Chulo, *Chile* 27°19' S, 70°13' W 137
Chulumani, *Bol.* 16°23' S, 67°30' W 137
Chulym, *Russ.* 55°7' N, 80°52' E 184
Chulym, river, *Russ.* 57°26' N, 88°13' E 169
Chuma, *Bol.* 15°23' S, 68°56' W 137
Chumakovo, *Russ.* 55°39' N, 79°10' E 184
Chumerna, peak, *Bulg.* 42°46' N, 25°53' E 156
Chumikan, *Russ.* 54°35' N, 135°12' E 190
Chumphon, *Thai.* 10°29' N, 99°11' E 202
Chumphon Buri, *Thai.* 15°21' N, 103°14' E 202
Chumpi, *Peru* 15°7' S, 73°45' W 137
Chuna, river, *Russ.* 57°48' N, 95°37' E 160
Chun'an, *China* 29°37' N, 119°9' E 198
Chuncheon, *S. Korea* 37°52' N, 127°44' E 200
Chundikkulam, *Sri Lanka* 9°27' N, 80°36' E 188
Chunga, *Zambia* 15°3' S, 25°58' E 224
Chungcheong, North, adm. division, *S. Korea* 36°45' N, 128°0' E 200
Chungcheong, South, adm. division, *S. Korea* 36°30' N, 127°0' E 200
Chunghwa, *N. Korea* 38°52' N, 125°48' E 200
Chungju, *S. Korea* 36°57' N, 127°56' E 200
Chungli, *Taiwan, China* 24°51' N, 121°8' E 198
Chŭngsan, *N. Korea* 39°5' N, 125°22' E 200
Chunhua, *China* 34°48' N, 108°36' E 198
Chunian, *Pak.* 30°57' N, 73°57' E 186
Chunky, *Miss., U.S.* 32°18' N, 88°55' W 103
Chupa, *Russ.* 66°16' N, 33°2' E 152
Chuprovo, *Russ.* 64°14' N, 46°32' E 154
Chuquibamba, *Peru* 15°53' S, 72°41' W 137
Chuquibambilla, *Peru* 14°8' S, 72°43' W 137
Chuquicamata, *Chile* 22°19' S, 68°58' W 137
Chuquisaca, adm. division, *Bol.* 20°0' S, 65°2' W 137
Chuquito, *Peru* 15°56' S, 69°54' W 137
Chur, *Switz.* 46°51' N, 9°31' E 167
Church Point, *La., U.S.* 30°22' N, 92°14' W 103
Church Stretton, *U.K.* 52°32' N, 2°49' W 162
Churchill, *Can.* 58°45' N, 94°9' W 73
Churchill, Cape, *Can.* 58°48' N, 93°13' W 108
Churchill Falls, *Can.* 53°31' N, 64°1' W 111
Churchill, Mount, *Alas., U.S.* 61°24' N, 141°56' W 98
Churchill, Mount, *Can.* 49°58' N, 123°52' W 100
Churchill Peak, *Can.* 58°12' N, 125°20' W 108
Churchill Peninsula, *Antarctica* 66°54' S, 60°58' W 248
Churchill, river, *Can.* 57°44' N, 95°11' W 108
Churchill, river, *Can.* 55°7' N, 105°1' W 72
Churchill Rocket Research Range, *Can.* 58°39' N, 94°6' W 108
Churki, *India* 23°50' N, 83°10' E 197
Churkino, *Russ.* 64°3' N, 44°17' E 154
Churuguara, *Venez.* 10°49' N, 69°33' W 136
Chushul, *India* 33°34' N, 78°38' E 188
Chuska Mountains, *N. Mex., U.S.* 36°20' N, 109°6' W 92
Chusovoy, *Russ.* 58°17' N, 57°51' E 154
Chusovskoy, *Russ.* 61°10' N, 56°31' E 154
Chust, *Uzb.* 41°0' N, 71°13' E 197
Chute Island, fall(s), *Can.* 52°5' N, 78°59' W 110
Chute-des-Passes, *Can.* 49°52' N, 71°17' W 94
Chutine, river, *Can.* 57°57' N, 132°47' W 108
Chuuk (Truk Islands), *F.S.M.* 7°44' N, 152°5' E 242
Chuvashiya, adm. division, *Russ.* 55°39' N, 46°9' E 154
Chyrvonaya Slabada, *Belarus* 52°49' N, 27°10' E 154
Ciacova, *Rom.* 45°30' N, 21°7' E 168
Cianorte, *Braz.* 23°41' S, 52°42' W 138
Ciasna, *Pol.* 50°45' N, 18°36' E 152
Cibecue, *Ariz., U.S.* 34°2' N, 110°28' W 92
Cibinului, Munţii, *Rom.* 45°33' N, 23°16' E 156
Cibola, *Ariz., U.S.* 33°18' N, 114°40' W 101
Cibolo, *Tex., U.S.* 29°32' N, 98°14' W 96
Çiçekdağı, *Turk.* 39°36' N, 34°24' E 156
Cicero, *Ill., U.S.* 41°49' N, 87°46' W 102
Čićevac, *Serb.* 43°42' N, 21°27' E 168
Cicuco, oil field, *Col.* 9°13' N, 74°36' W 136
Cide, *Turk.* 41°53' N, 33°0' E 156
Ciechanów, *Pol.* 52°52' N, 20°37' E 152
Ciego de Ávila, *Cuba* 21°51' N, 78°46' W 116
Ciego de Ávila, adm. division, *Cuba* 21°59' N, 79°0' W 116
Ciempozuelos, *Sp.* 40°9' N, 3°38' W 164
Ciénaga, *Col.* 10°59' N, 74°14' W 136
Ciénaga de Oro, *Col.* 8°52' N, 75°38' W 136
Cienagas de Catatumbo National Park, *Venez.* 9°19' N, 72°17' W 136
Cienfuegos, *Cuba* 22°10' N, 80°27' W 116
Cienfuegos, adm. division, *Cuba* 22°17' N, 80°54' W 116
Cierp-Gaud, *Fr.* 42°54' N, 0°38' E 164
Cies, Illas, islands, *North Atlantic Ocean* 42°5' N, 9°35' W 150
Cieza, *Sp.* 38°14' N, 1°25' W 164
Cifuentes, *Sp.* 40°46' N, 2°37' W 164
Cihanbeyli, *Turk.* 38°39' N, 32°54' E 156
Cihuatlán, *Mex.* 19°13' N, 104°36' W 114
Ciiradhame, *Somalia* 10°25' N, 49°23' E 216
Çikës, Maja e, peak, *Alban.* 40°11' N, 19°33' E 156
Cilacap, *Indonesia* 7°39' S, 108°54' E 192
Çıldır, *Turk.* 41°7' N, 43°7' E 195
Cilibia, *Rom.* 45°3' N, 27°2' E 156
Cilician Gates, pass, *Turk.* 37°16' N, 34°47' E 156
Cîlnicu, *Rom.* 44°57' N, 23°5' E 168
Cim, *Bosn. and Herzg.* 43°22' N, 17°45' E 168
Cima, *Calif., U.S.* 35°14' N, 115°31' W 101
Cimadle, spring, *Somalia* 5°14' N, 47°1' E 218
Cimarron, *Kans., U.S.* 37°48' N, 100°21' W 90
Cimişlia, *Mold.* 46°31' N, 28°48' E 158
Cimolais, *It.* 46°17' N, 12°26' E 167
Cimone, Monte, peak, *It.* 44°11' N, 10°40' E 167
Cîmpeni, *Rom.* 46°22' N, 23°4' E 168
Çınar, *Turk.* 37°43' N, 40°27' E 195
Cinaruco, river, *Venez.* 6°31' N, 68°40' W 136
Cinaruco-Capanaparo National Park, *Venez.* 6°35' N, 67°42' W 136
Cincar, peak, *Bosn. and Herzg.* 43°53' N, 17°0' E 168
Cincinnati, *Ohio, U.S.* 39°6' N, 84°32' W 102
Cinco Balas, Cayos, islands, *Caribbean Sea* 20°49' N, 80°20' W 116
Cîndrelu, peak, *Rom.* 45°34' N, 23°44' E 156

Çine, Turk. 37°36′ N, 28°1′ E 156
Cinema, Can. 53°10′ N, 122°31′ W 108
Ciney, Belg. 50°18′ N, 5°5′ E 167
Cinnabar Mountain, Idaho, U.S. 42°58′ N, 116°45′ W 90
Cintegabelle, Fr. 43°17′ N, 1°31′ E 164
Cinto, Monte, peak, Fr. 42°22′ N, 8°52′ E 156
Cintruénigo, Sp. 42°4′ N, 1°47′ W 164
Ciovîrnăşani, Rom. 44°45′ N, 22°52′ E 168
Cipoal, Braz. 1°40′ S, 55°29′ W 130
Circeo, Monte, peak, It. 41°13′ N, 12°59′ E 156
Çirçır, Turk. 40°1′ N, 36°49′ E 156
Circle, Alas., U.S. 65°43′ N, 144°18′ W 98
Circle, Mont., U.S. 47°23′ N, 105°37′ W 90
Circle Hot Springs, Alas., U.S. 65°29′ N, 144°39′ W 98
Circleville, Ohio, U.S. 39°35′ N, 82°56′ W 102
Cirebon, Indonesia 6°47′ S, 108°25′ E 192
Cirencester, U.K. 51°42′ N, 1°58′ W 162
Cireşu, Rom. 44°49′ N, 22°33′ E 168
Ciria, Sp. 41°36′ N, 1°58′ W 164
Ciriè, It. 45°13′ N, 7°36′ E 167
Ciriquiri, river, Braz. 7°52′ S, 65°33′ W 132
Cisco, Ill., U.S. 40°0′ N, 88°43′ W 102
Cisco, Tex., U.S. 32°22′ N, 98°59′ W 92
Cisco, Utah, U.S. 38°58′ N, 109°19′ W 90
Cislău, Rom. 45°14′ N, 26°22′ E 156
Cisne, Ill., U.S. 38°30′ N, 88°26′ W 102
Cisneros, Col. 6°33′ N, 75°5′ W 136
Cissna Park, Ill., U.S. 40°33′ N, 87°54′ W 102
Cistern Point, Bahamas 23°39′ N, 77°37′ W 96
Citaré, river, Braz. 1°40′ N, 55°32′ W 130
Citra, Fla., U.S. 29°24′ N, 82°8′ W 105
Citronelle, Ala., U.S. 31°4′ N, 88°14′ W 103
Citrusdal, S. Af. 32°32′ S, 19°1′ E 227
Cittadella, It. 45°39′ N, 11°46′ E 167
City of Refuge National Historical Park see Pu'uhonua O Hōnaunau National Historical Park, Hawai'i, U.S. 19°24′ N, 155°57′ W 99
City Trenton, Mo., U.S. 40°3′ N, 93°37′ W 94
Ciuc, Munţii, Rom. 46°20′ N, 25°49′ E 156
Ciucaş, peak, Rom. 45°30′ N, 25°53′ E 156
Ciucea, Rom. 46°57′ N, 22°51′ E 168
Ciudad Acuña, Mex. 29°17′ N, 100°57′ W 92
Ciudad Altamirano, Mex. 18°20′ N, 100°41′ W 114
Ciudad Bolívar, Venez. 8°4′ N, 63°34′ W 116
Ciudad Bolivia, Venez. 8°19′ N, 70°36′ W 136
Ciudad Camargo, Mex. 27°40′ N, 105°11′ W 112
Ciudad Constituci´on, Mex. 25°0′ N, 111°43′ W 112
Ciudad Cortés, C.R. 8°58′ N, 83°33′ W 115
Ciudad de La Habana, adm. division, Cuba 23°6′ N, 82°47′ W 116
Ciudad del Maíz, Mex. 22°22′ N, 99°37′ W 114
Ciudad Guayana, Venez. 8°23′ N, 62°36′ W 130
Ciudad Guerrero, Mex. 28°31′ N, 107°31′ W 92
Ciudad Guzmán, Mex. 19°41′ N, 103°29′ W 114
Ciudad Hidalgo, Mex. 14°41′ N, 92°11′ W 115
Ciudad Hidalgo, Mex. 19°41′ N, 100°33′ W 114
Ciudad Juárez, Mex. 31°41′ N, 106°30′ W 92
Ciudad Lerdo, Mex. 25°31′ N, 103°30′ W 114
Ciudad Madero, Mex. 22°15′ N, 97°49′ W 114
Ciudad Mante, Mex. 22°44′ N, 98°58′ W 114
Ciudad Mendoza, Mex. 18°46′ N, 97°12′ W 114
Ciudad Obregón, Mex. 27°28′ N, 109°57′ W 112
Ciudad Ojeda, Venez. 10°12′ N, 71°21′ W 136
Ciudad Piar, Venez. 7°24′ N, 63°19′ W 130
Ciudad Real, Sp. 38°58′ N, 3°56′ W 164
Ciudad Sandino, Cuba 22°5′ N, 84°10′ W 116
Ciudad Valles, Mex. 21°58′ N, 99°0′ W 114
Ciudad Victoria, Mex. 23°42′ N, 99°12′ W 114
Ciumeghiu, Rom. 46°44′ N, 21°36′ E 168
Ciutadella de Menorca, Sp. 39°59′ N, 3°50′ E 164
Civa Burnu, Turk. 41°23′ N, 36°28′ E 156
Civitanova Marche, It. 43°18′ N, 13°43′ E 156
Civitavecchia, It. 42°5′ N, 11°47′ E 156
Çivril, Turk. 38°18′ N, 29°43′ E 156
Cixian, China 36°22′ N, 114°24′ E 198
Cizer, Rom. 47°4′ N, 22°53′ E 168
Cizre, Turk. 37°19′ N, 42°8′ E 195
Clach Leathad, peak, U.K. 56°35′ N, 4°58′ W 150
Clacton on Sea, U.K. 51°47′ N, 1°8′ E 162
Claiborne, Ala., U.S. 31°32′ N, 87°31′ W 103
Clairmont, Can. 55°15′ N, 118°48′ W 108
Claise, river, Fr. 46°47′ N, 0°46′ E 150
Clallam Bay, Wash., U.S. 48°13′ N, 124°16′ W 100
Clam Lake, Wis., U.S. 46°10′ N, 90°55′ W 94
Clan Alpine Mountains, Nev., U.S. 39°27′ N, 118°20′ W 90
Clanton, Ala., U.S. 32°50′ N, 86°38′ W 96
Clanwilliam, S. Af. 32°10′ S, 18°54′ E 227
Clapham, U.K. 54°7′ N, 2°24′ W 162
Clara, Miss., U.S. 31°35′ N, 88°42′ W 103
Clara, island, Myanmar 10°45′ N, 97°39′ E 202
Clara, Punta, Arg. 44°11′ S, 65°11′ W 134
Claraz, Arg. 37°53′ S, 59°18′ W 139
Clare, Mich., U.S. 43°48′ N, 84°46′ W 102
Claremont, N.H., U.S. 43°22′ N, 72°21′ W 104
Claremore, Okla., U.S. 36°17′ N, 95°37′ W 96
Clarence, N.Z. 42°9′ S, 173°54′ E 240
Clarence Island, Antarctica 61°30′ S, 54°3′ W 134
Clarendon, Ark., U.S. 34°40′ N, 91°19′ W 96
Clarendon, Tex., U.S. 34°56′ N, 100°54′ W 92
Clarendon, Vt., U.S. 43°31′ N, 72°59′ W 104
Clarenville, Can. 48°9′ N, 53°59′ W 111
Claresholm, Can. 50°1′ N, 113°35′ W 90
Clarie Coast, Antarctica 67°48′ S, 136°42′ E 248
Clarinda, Iowa, U.S. 40°43′ N, 95°3′ W 94
Clarines, Venez. 10°0′ N, 65°10′ W 136
Clarion, Iowa, U.S. 42°42′ N, 93°44′ W 94
Clarion, Pa., U.S. 41°12′ N, 79°23′ W 94
Clarion Fracture Zone, North Pacific Ocean 17°0′ N, 130°47′ W 252
Clarión, Isla, island, Mex. 18°27′ N, 115°40′ W 112
Clark, S. Dak., U.S. 44°52′ N, 97°45′ W 90
Clark Fork, Idaho, U.S. 48°8′ N, 116°11′ W 108
Clark, Mount, peak, Can. 64°21′ N, 124°7′ W 98
Clark Mountain, Calif., U.S. 35°31′ N, 115°37′ W 101
Clark Peak, Colo., U.S. 40°35′ N, 106°0′ W 90
Clark, Point, Can. 44°4′ N, 81°54′ W 102
Clarkdale, Ariz., U.S. 34°46′ N, 112°3′ W 92
Clarke City, Can. 50°10′ N, 66°37′ W 111
Clarke Island, Austral. 41°8′ S, 147°50′ E 230
Clarke Range, Austral. 20°29′ S, 147°39′ E 230
Clarks, La., U.S. 32°0′ N, 92°9′ W 103
Clark's Harbour, Can. 43°22′ N, 65°36′ W 82
Clarks Hill Lake, Ga., U.S. 33°51′ N, 82°55′ W 112
Clarksburg, W. Va., U.S. 39°16′ N, 80°22′ W 94
Clarksdale, Miss., U.S. 34°11′ N, 90°34′ W 96
Clarkson, Nebr., U.S. 41°41′ N, 97°8′ W 90
Clarksville, Mich., U.S. 42°49′ N, 85°15′ W 102
Clarksville, Tenn., U.S. 36°31′ N, 87°21′ W 96
Clarksville, Tex., U.S. 33°36′ N, 95°4′ W 96
Claro, river, Braz. 15°56′ S, 51°12′ W 138
Claro, river, Braz. 18°8′ S, 51°41′ W 138
Clary, Fr. 50°4′ N, 3°24′ E 163
Clatskanie, Oreg., U.S. 46°5′ N, 123°13′ W 100
Claude, Tex., U.S. 35°6′ N, 101°22′ W 92
Claveria, Philippines 18°36′ N, 121°5′ E 203
Clavering Ø, island, Den. 73°50′ N, 19°47′ W 246
Clawson, Utah, U.S. 39°8′ N, 111°6′ W 90
Claxton, Ga., U.S. 32°9′ N, 81°55′ W 96
Clay, Ky., U.S. 37°28′ N, 87°50′ W 96
Clay Center, Kans., U.S. 39°21′ N, 97°8′ W 90
Clay City, Ill., U.S. 38°40′ N, 88°22′ W 102
Clay City, Ind., U.S. 39°16′ N, 87°7′ W 102
Claymore, oil field, U.K. 58°26′ N, 0°26′ E 150
Clayoquot Sound 49°13′ N, 126°37′ W 90
Clayton, Ala., U.S. 31°52′ N, 85°27′ W 96
Clayton, Ind., U.S. 39°40′ N, 86°32′ W 102
Clayton, La., U.S. 31°42′ N, 91°34′ W 103
Clayton, N. Mex., U.S. 36°26′ N, 103°11′ W 92
Clayton, N.Y., U.S. 44°13′ N, 76°5′ W 94
Clayton, Okla., U.S. 34°33′ N, 95°21′ W 96
Clayton Lake, Me., U.S. 46°36′ N, 69°34′ W 94
Cle Elum, Wash., U.S. 47°11′ N, 120°58′ W 100
Clear, Alas., U.S. 64°26′ N, 148°30′ W 73
Clear, Cape, Ire. 51°14′ N, 9°28′ W 150
Clear Hills, Can. 56°29′ N, 119°50′ W 108
Clear Lake, S. Dak., U.S. 44°44′ N, 96°42′ W 90
Clear Lake, Wash., U.S. 48°27′ N, 122°14′ W 100
Clear Lake, Wis., U.S. 45°14′ N, 92°17′ W 110
Clear Lake Reservoir, Calif., U.S. 41°45′ N, 122°46′ W 81
Clearfield, Utah, U.S. 41°6′ N, 112°2′ W 90
Clearmont, Wyo., U.S. 44°36′ N, 106°23′ W 90
Clearwater, Fla., U.S. 27°57′ N, 82°47′ W 105
Clearwater, Wash., U.S. 47°34′ N, 124°16′ W 100
Clearwater Lake, lake, Can. 52°15′ N, 120°43′ W 108
Clearwater Lake, lake, Can. 54°4′ N, 101°37′ W 108
Clearwater Mountains, Idaho, U.S. 45°47′ N, 116°18′ W 90
Clearwater, river, Can. 51°58′ N, 115°52′ W 90
Clearwater, river, Can. 56°41′ N, 111°1′ W 108
Cleburne, Tex., U.S. 32°20′ N, 97°23′ W 92
Clee Hills, U.K. 52°27′ N, 2°39′ W 162
Cleethorpes, U.K. 53°32′ N, 4°237′ W 162
Clemence Massif, Antarctica 72°14′ S, 68°11′ E 248
Clendenin, W. Va., U.S. 38°28′ N, 81°21′ W 102
Cleopatra Needle, peak, Philippines 10°8′ N, 118°55′ E 203
Clermont, Fla., U.S. 28°32′ N, 81°46′ W 105
Clermont, Fr. 49°22′ N, 2°24′ E 163
Clermont-en-Argonne, Fr. 49°6′ N, 5°3′ E 163
Clermont-Ferrand, Fr. 45°46′ N, 3°5′ E 150
Cles, It. 46°22′ N, 11°2′ E 167
Clevedon, U.K. 51°26′ N, 2°51′ W 162
Cleveland, Miss., U.S. 33°45′ N, 90°47′ W 112
Cleveland, Ohio, U.S. 41°29′ N, 81°40′ W 102
Cleveland, Okla., U.S. 36°17′ N, 96°28′ W 96
Cleveland, Tex., U.S. 30°20′ N, 95°5′ W 103
Cleveland, Wis., U.S. 43°54′ N, 87°45′ W 102
Cleveland Heights, Ohio, U.S. 41°29′ N, 81°34′ W 102
Cleveland Hills, U.K. 54°24′ N, 1°7′ W 162
Cleveland, Mount, Mont., U.S. 48°53′ N, 113°56′ W 90
Clevelândia, Braz. 26°23′ S, 52°24′ W 139
Cleveleys, U.K. 53°52′ N, 3°2′ W 162
Clewiston, Fla., U.S. 26°45′ N, 80°56′ W 105
Cliff, N. Mex., U.S. 32°57′ N, 108°36′ W 92
Cliff Palace, site, Colo., U.S. 37°8′ N, 108°32′ W 92
Clifford, Can. 43°57′ N, 80°58′ W 102
Clifton, Ariz., U.S. 33°3′ N, 109°18′ W 112
Clifton, Ill., U.S. 40°55′ N, 87°56′ W 102
Clifton, Kans., U.S. 39°33′ N, 97°17′ W 90
Clifton, N.J., U.S. 40°52′ N, 74°10′ W 104
Clifton, Tex., U.S. 31°45′ N, 97°35′ W 92
Clifton Forge, Va., U.S. 37°48′ N, 79°50′ W 94
Clifton Park, N.Y., U.S. 42°51′ N, 73°47′ W 104
Climax, Can. 49°11′ N, 108°23′ W 90
Climax, Mich., U.S. 42°13′ N, 85°20′ W 102
Clinch Mountain, Va., U.S. 36°44′ N, 82°30′ W 96
Clinch, river, Va., U.S. 36°20′ N, 83°2′ W 80
Clingmans Dome, Tenn., U.S. 35°33′ N, 83°36′ W 96
Clint, Tex., U.S. 31°34′ N, 106°13′ W 92
Clinton, Ala., U.S. 32°54′ N, 87°59′ W 103
Clinton, Can. 51°6′ N, 121°35′ W 90
Clinton, Can. 43°36′ N, 81°33′ W 102
Clinton, Conn., U.S. 41°16′ N, 72°32′ W 104
Clinton, Ill., U.S. 40°9′ N, 88°58′ W 102
Clinton, Ind., U.S. 39°38′ N, 87°25′ W 94
Clinton, Iowa, U.S. 41°50′ N, 90°12′ W 102
Clinton, Ky., U.S. 36°40′ N, 88°58′ W 96
Clinton, La., U.S. 30°51′ N, 91°2′ W 103
Clinton, Mass., U.S. 42°24′ N, 71°42′ W 104
Clinton, Mich., U.S. 42°3′ N, 83°57′ W 102
Clinton, Miss., U.S. 32°19′ N, 90°20′ W 103
Clinton, Mo., U.S. 40°9′ N, 88°58′ W 94
Clinton, Mo., U.S. 38°21′ N, 93°46′ W 94
Clinton, N.Z. 46°14′ S, 169°22′ E 240
Clinton, Okla., U.S. 35°29′ N, 98°59′ W 96
Clinton, Wash., U.S. 47°57′ N, 122°23′ W 100
Clinton, Wis., U.S. 42°33′ N, 88°52′ W 102
Clio, Mich., U.S. 43°10′ N, 83°44′ W 102
Clion, Fr. 46°56′ N, 1°13′ E 150
Clipper Mountains, Calif., U.S. 34°44′ N, 115°26′ W 101
Clipperton Fracture Zone, North Pacific Ocean 6°22′ N, 126°9′ W 252
Clisham, peak, U.K. 57°56′ N, 6°56′ W 150
Clisson, Fr. 47°5′ N, 1°17′ W 150
Clitheroe, U.K. 53°52′ N, 2°23′ W 162
Clitor, ruin(s), Gr. 37°51′ N, 21°56′ E 156
Cliza, Bol. 17°38′ S, 65°49′ W 137
Clodomira, Arg. 27°34′ S, 64°10′ W 132
Clonakilty, Ire. 51°36′ N, 8°54′ W 150
Cloncurry, Austral. 20°38′ S, 140°31′ E 238
Clonmel, Ire. 52°22′ N, 7°42′ W 150
Clo-oose, Can. 48°39′ N, 124°49′ W 100
Clopotiva, Rom. 45°29′ N, 22°51′ E 168
Cloppenburg, Ger. 52°49′ N, 8°3′ E 163
Cloquet, Minn., U.S. 46°42′ N, 92°29′ W 94
Close, Cape, Antarctica 65°52′ S, 49°26′ E 248
Close Lake, lake, Can. 57°52′ N, 105°22′ W 108
Cloud Peak, Wyo., U.S. 44°20′ N, 107°15′ W 90
Cloutierville, La., U.S. 31°32′ N, 92°56′ W 103
Clova, Can. 48°7′ N, 75°22′ W 94
Cloverdale, Oreg., U.S. 45°11′ N, 123°57′ W 90
Clovis, Calif., U.S. 36°49′ N, 119°43′ W 100
Cluff Lake Mine, site, Can. 58°16′ N, 109°42′ W 108
Cluj, adm. division, Rom. 47°1′ N, 23°32′ E 156
Cluj-Napoca, Rom. 46°45′ N, 23°38′ E 168
Clun, U.K. 52°25′ N, 3°1′ W 162
Cluny, Fr. 46°26′ N, 4°38′ E 150
Cluny Castle, site, U.K. 57°10′ N, 2°38′ W 150
Cluny Castle, site, U.K. 57°1′ N, 4°20′ W 150
Cluses, Fr. 46°3′ N, 6°34′ E 167
Clusone, It. 45°53′ N, 9°57′ E 167
Clute, Tex., U.S. 29°0′ N, 95°24′ W 103
Clydach Vale, U.K. 51°38′ N, 3°30′ W 162
Clyde, Can. 54°8′ N, 113°38′ W 108
Clyde, Kans., U.S. 39°34′ N, 97°25′ W 90
Clyde, N.Z. 45°11′ S, 169°19′ E 240
Clyde, Ohio, U.S. 41°18′ N, 82°58′ W 102
Clyde, Tex., U.S. 32°24′ N, 99°30′ W 92
Clyde River, Can. 70°28′ N, 68°35′ W 106
Ćmielów, Pol. 50°52′ N, 21°31′ E 152
Cnalwa, Western Sahara, Mor. 24°51′ N, 13°55′ W 214
Cnoc Moy, peak, U.K. 55°21′ N, 5°53′ W 150
Cnossus (Knosós), ruin(s), Gr. 35°16′ N, 25°4′ E 156
Coachella, Calif., U.S. 33°41′ N, 116°11′ W 101
Coacoachou, Lac, lake, Can. 50°20′ N, 60°58′ W 111
Coahoma, Tex., U.S. 32°17′ N, 101°19′ W 92
Coahuayana, Mex. 18°42′ N, 103°42′ W 114
Coahuila, adm. division, Mex. 25°38′ N, 102°51′ W 114
Coal City, Ill., U.S. 41°16′ N, 88°17′ W 102
Coal Creek, Colo., U.S. 38°21′ N, 105°9′ W 92
Coal Creek Flat, N.Z. 45°30′ S, 169°17′ E 240
Coal River, Can. 59°39′ N, 126°54′ W 108
Coal, river, Can. 60°59′ N, 127°40′ W 108
Coalane, Mozambique 17°50′ S, 36°58′ E 224
Coalcomán, Mex. 18°46′ N, 103°9′ W 114
Coaldale, Can. 49°43′ N, 112°37′ W 90
Coaldale, Nev., U.S. 38°2′ N, 117°54′ W 90
Coalgate, Okla., U.S. 34°30′ N, 96°13′ W 96
Coalinga, Calif., U.S. 36°8′ N, 120°23′ W 100
Coalsack Bluff, peak, Antarctica 84°10′ S, 164°12′ E 248
Coalspur, Can. 53°10′ N, 117°3′ W 108
Coalton, Ohio, U.S. 39°6′ N, 82°37′ W 102
Coalville, U.K. 52°43′ N, 1°23′ W 162
Coaraci, Braz. 14°38′ S, 39°34′ W 138
Coarsegold, Calif., U.S. 37°15′ N, 119°43′ W 100
Coasa, Peru 14°9′ S, 70°1′ W 137
Coast Mountains, North America 50°29′ N, 123°30′ W 90
Coast Ranges, North America 35°42′ N, 120°54′ W 100
Coats Island, Can. 62°25′ N, 86°9′ W 106
Coats Land, region, Antarctica 77°21′ S, 31°9′ W 248
Coatzacoalcos, Mex. 18°7′ N, 94°26′ W 114
Cobá, ruin(s), Mex. 20°32′ N, 87°45′ W 115
Cobadin, Rom. 44°3′ N, 28°13′ E 156
Cobalt, Can. 47°23′ N, 79°40′ W 94
Cobán, Guatemala 15°30′ N, 90°21′ W 115
Cobble Hill, Can. 48°40′ N, 123°38′ W 100
Cobden, Mo., U.S. 37°31′ N, 89°15′ W 96
Cobequid Bay 45°15′ N, 63°36′ W 111
Cobh, Ire. 51°58′ N, 8°7′ W 143
Cobham, river, Can. 52°55′ N, 95°12′ W 108
Cobija, Bol. 11°1′ S, 68°46′ W 137
Cobija, Punta, Chile 22°49′ S, 70°20′ W 137
Cobol, Alas., U.S. 57°30′ N, 135°52′ W 108
Cobos, Mex. 20°54′ N, 97°22′ W 114
Cobourg, Can. 43°57′ N, 78°11′ W 94
Cobourg Peninsula, Austral. 11°33′ S, 131°12′ E 192
Cobre, Barranca de, Mex. 27°14′ N, 108°19′ W 112
Cóbuè, Mozambique 12°9′ S, 34°47′ E 224
Coburg Island, Can. 75°37′ N, 78°52′ W 106
Coburn Mountain, Me., U.S. 45°27′ N, 70°13′ W 94
Coca, river, Ecua. 8°474′ S, 77°17′ W 136
Cocachacra, Peru 17°9′ S, 71°45′ W 137
Cocalinho, Braz. 14°21′ S, 51°3′ W 138
Cocanada see Kakinada, India 16°59′ N, 82°15′ E 188
Cocentaina, Sp. 38°44′ N, 0°27′ E 164
Cochabamba, Bol. 17°25′ S, 66°4′ W 137
Cochabamba, adm. division, Bol. 17°21′ S, 66°50′ W 137
Coche, Isla, island, Venez. 10°35′ N, 64°7′ W 116
Cochem, Ger. 50°8′ N, 7°8′ E 167
Cochetopa Hills, Colo., U.S. 38°19′ N, 106°38′ W 90
Cochinoca, Arg. 22°44′ S, 65°55′ W 137
Cochise Head, peak, Ariz., U.S. 32°2′ N, 109°21′ W 92
Cochrane, Can. 51°12′ N, 114°28′ W 90
Cochrane, Can. 49°4′ N, 81°3′ W 94
Cochrane, Chile 47°12′ S, 72°34′ W 134
Cochrane, river, Can. 57°55′ N, 101°12′ W 108
Cockburn Town, Turks & Caicos Is., U.K. 21°26′ N, 71°9′ W 116
Cockermouth, U.K. 54°40′ N, 3°21′ W 162
Coco, Cayo, island, Cuba 22°29′ N, 78°16′ W 116
Coco, Isla del, island, C.R. 5°31′ N, 87°1′ W 115
Coco, river, North America 14°43′ N, 83°44′ W 115
Cocoa, Fla., U.S. 28°22′ N, 80°45′ W 105
Cocoa Beach, Fla., U.S. 28°19′ N, 80°37′ W 105
Cocobeach, Gabon 0°59′ N, 9°36′ E 218
Coco-de-Mer Seamounts, Indian Ocean 0°41′ N, 55°21′ E 254
Coconino Plateau, Ariz., U.S. 35°28′ N, 112°21′ W 92
Cócorit, Mex. 27°33′ N, 109°58′ W 112
Cocos, Braz. 14°9′ S, 44°33′ W 138
Cocos Ridge, North Pacific Ocean 5°28′ N, 84°55′ W 253
Cocula, Mex. 18°13′ N, 99°39′ W 114
Cocula, Mex. 20°21′ N, 103°51′ W 114
Cocxá, river, Braz. 14°48′ S, 45°0′ W 138
Cod Bay, Cape 41°48′ N, 70°19′ W 104
Cod, Cape, U.S. 41°36′ N, 70°38′ W 104
Cod Island, Can. 57°41′ N, 61°35′ W 106
Coda Cavallo, Capo, It. 40°49′ N, 9°44′ E 156
Codajás, Braz. 3°50′ S, 62°4′ W 130
Codigoro, It. 44°50′ N, 12°6′ E 167
Codó, Braz. 4°30′ S, 43°53′ W 132
Codogno, It. 45°9′ N, 9°41′ E 167
Codpa, Chile 18°51′ S, 69°47′ W 137
Codrington, Mount, Antarctica 66°22′ S, 52°35′ E 248
Codroipo, It. 45°57′ N, 12°59′ E 167
Codru, Munţii, Rom. 46°22′ N, 22°20′ E 168
Cody, Nebr., U.S. 42°55′ N, 101°15′ W 90
Cody, Wyo., U.S. 44°30′ N, 109°3′ W 90
Coelho Neto, Braz. 4°18′ S, 43°3′ W 132
Coen, Austral. 13°58′ S, 143°12′ E 238
Coen, river, Austral. 13°29′ S, 142°21′ E 230
Coesfeld, Ger. 51°57′ N, 7°9′ E 167
Coeur d'Alene, Idaho, U.S. 47°39′ N, 116°47′ W 82
Coevorden, Neth. 52°40′ N, 6°43′ E 163
Coffeen, Ill., U.S. 39°6′ N, 89°24′ W 102
Coffeeville, Ala., U.S. 31°44′ N, 88°5′ W 103
Cofre de Perote (Nauhcampatépetl), peak, Mex. 19°27′ N, 97°13′ W 114
Cofrentes, Sp. 39°13′ N, 1°5′ W 164
Cogealac, Rom. 44°33′ N, 28°32′ E 156
Coglar Buttes, peak, Oreg., U.S. 42°40′ N, 120°29′ W 90
Cogoleto, It. 44°23′ N, 8°39′ E 156
Cogollos, Sp. 42°11′ N, 3°42′ W 164
Cogolludo, Sp. 40°56′ N, 3°5′ W 164
Cohagen, Mont., U.S. 47°2′ N, 106°38′ W 90
Cohasset, Mass., U.S. 42°14′ N, 70°49′ W 104
Cohay, Miss., U.S. 31°55′ N, 89°36′ W 103
Cohoes, N.Y., U.S. 42°46′ N, 73°44′ W 104
Coiba, Isla de, island, Pan. 7°41′ N, 81°59′ W 115
Coihaique, Chile 45°30′ S, 72°4′ W 134
Coila, Miss., U.S. 33°22′ N, 89°57′ W 103
Coimbatore, India 11°1′ N, 76°55′ E 188
Coimbra, Port. 40°12′ N, 8°26′ W 150
Coimbra, adm. division, Port. 40°6′ N, 8°53′ W 150
Coín, Sp. 36°38′ N, 4°46′ W 164
Coin, Île du, island, U.K. 5°53′ S, 71°36′ E 188
Coipasa, Lago de, lake, Bol. 19°15′ S, 68°35′ W 137
Cojata, Peru 15°5′ S, 69°23′ W 137
Cojedes, adm. division, Venez. 9°19′ N, 68°47′ W 136
Cojedes, river, Venez. 9°21′ N, 68°59′ W 136
Cojimíes, Boca de 0°10′ N, 80°30′ W 130
Cojocna, Rom. 46°45′ N, 23°50′ E 156
Cojutepeque, El Salv. 13°43′ N, 88°58′ W 115
Cokato, Minn., U.S. 45°3′ N, 94°12′ W 90
Cokeville, Wyo., U.S. 42°5′ N, 110°56′ W 90
Coki, Senegal 15°31′ N, 15°59′ W 222
Colatina, Braz. 19°37′ S, 40°40′ W 138
Cölbe, Ger. 50°51′ N, 8°46′ E 167
Colbeck Archipelago, islands, Indian Ocean 66°50′ S, 61°31′ E 248
Colborne, Can. 44°0′ N, 77°53′ W 94
Colby, Kans., U.S. 39°23′ N, 101°4′ W 90
Colby, Wis., U.S. 44°54′ N, 90°19′ W 94
Colchester, Conn., U.S. 41°34′ N, 72°20′ W 104
Colchester, U.K. 51°53′ N, 0°53′ E 162
Colchester, Vt., U.S. 44°32′ N, 73°9′ W 104
Cold Lake, Can. 55°7′ N, 101°8′ W 108
Cold Lake, Can. 54°26′ N, 110°12′ W 108
Cold Spring, Minn., U.S. 45°26′ N, 94°27′ W 90
Coldspring, Tex., U.S. 30°34′ N, 95°8′ W 103
Coldwater, Kans., U.S. 37°15′ N, 99°20′ W 96
Coldwater, Mich., U.S. 41°56′ N, 85°0′ W 102
Coldwater, Ohio, U.S. 40°28′ N, 84°37′ W 102
Coleman, Fla., U.S. 28°47′ N, 82°5′ W 105
Coleman, Mich., U.S. 43°45′ N, 84°35′ W 102
Coleman, Tex., U.S. 31°48′ N, 99°26′ W 92
Coleraine, Can. 45°57′ N, 71°22′ W 111
Coles, Miss., U.S. 31°15′ N, 91°1′ W 103
Coles, Punta, Peru 17°53′ S, 71°41′ W 137
Colesberg, S. Af. 30°42′ S, 25°4′ E 227
Coleville, Can. 51°44′ N, 109°15′ W 90
Colfax, Calif., U.S. 39°6′ N, 120°58′ W 90
Colfax, Ill., U.S. 40°33′ N, 88°37′ W 102
Colfax, Iowa, U.S. 41°39′ N, 93°14′ W 94
Colfax, La., U.S. 31°30′ N, 92°43′ W 103
Colfax, Wash., U.S. 46°51′ N, 117°23′ W 90
Colico, It. 46°8′ N, 9°22′ E 167
Colima, Mex. 19°12′ N, 103°46′ W 114
Colima, adm. division, Mex. 18°57′ N, 104°8′ W 114
Colima, Nevado de, peak, Mex. 19°32′ N, 103°40′ W 114
Colin Lake, lake, Can. 59°31′ N, 110°38′ W 108
Colinas, Braz. 6°5′ S, 44°15′ W 132
Colinton, Can. 54°37′ N, 113°16′ W 108
Collaguasi, Chile 21°0′ S, 68°45′ W 137
Colleen Bawn, Zimb. 20°57′ S, 29°12′ E 227
Colleymount, Can. 54°2′ N, 126°11′ W 108
Collie, Austral. 33°20′ S, 116°11′ E 231
Collier Bay 16°14′ S, 122°5′ E 238
Collier, Cape, Antarctica 70°14′ S, 60°48′ W 248
Colliers Point, U.K. 19°15′ N, 81°4′ W 115
Collierville, Tenn., U.S. 35°2′ N, 89°40′ W 96
Collingwood, Can. 44°29′ N, 80°12′ W 94
Collingwood, N.Z. 40°44′ S, 172°40′ E 240
Collins, Can. 50°17′ N, 89°27′ W 94
Collins, Miss., U.S. 31°39′ N, 89°33′ W 103
Collinson Peninsula, Can. 69°51′ N, 101°10′ W 106
Collinston, La., U.S. 32°40′ N, 91°52′ W 103
Collinsville, Conn., U.S. 41°48′ N, 72°55′ W 104
Collinsville, Ill., U.S. 38°39′ N, 89°59′ W 102
Collinsville, Va., U.S. 36°43′ N, 79°56′ W 94
Collipulli, Chile 37°58′ S, 72°29′ W 134
Colmar, Fr. 48°4′ N, 7°21′ E 150
Colmena, Arg. 28°43′ S, 60°8′ W 139
Colmenar, Sp. 36°54′ N, 4°21′ W 164
Colmenar Viejo, Sp. 40°38′ N, 3°46′ W 164
Colmesneil, Tex., U.S. 30°53′ N, 94°25′ W 103
Colne, U.K. 53°51′ N, 2°10′ W 162
Cologne see Köln, Ger. 50°56′ N, 6°57′ E 167
Coloma, Mich., U.S. 42°10′ N, 86°17′ W 102
Coloma, Wis., U.S. 44°1′ N, 89°31′ W 102
Colombey-les-Belles, Fr. 48°31′ N, 5°53′ E 163
Colombey-les-Deux-Églises, Fr. 48°13′ N, 4°52′ E 163
Colombia 3°30′ N, 74°40′ W 130
Colombia, Braz. 20°12′ S, 48°41′ W 138
Colombo, Sri Lanka 6°51′ N, 79°38′ E 188
Colón, Arg. 32°14′ S, 58°8′ W 139

Colón, *Arg.* 33°55′ S, 61°4′ W 139
Colón, *Cuba* 22°43′ N, 80°54′ W 116
Colon, *Mich., U.S.* 41°56′ N, 85°19′ W 102
Colón, *Pan.* 9°22′ N, 79°54′ W 115
Colón, *Venez.* 2°7′ N, 67°7′ W 136
Colón, Isla, island, *Pan.* 9°4′ N, 82°35′ W 115
Colón Ridge, *North Pacific Ocean* 1°22′ N, 94°53′ W 252
Colonet, *Mex.* 31°0′ N, 116°14′ W 92
Colonia 25 de Mayo, *Arg.* 37°50′ S, 67°42′ W 134
Colonia Dora, *Arg.* 28°36′ S, 62°58′ W 139
Colonia Elisa, *Arg.* 26°55′ S, 59°31′ W 139
Colonia Montefiore, *Arg.* 29°41′ S, 61°51′ W 139
Colonia Morelos, *Mex.* 30°48′ N, 109°12′ W 92
Colonia Penal del Sepa, *Peru* 10°51′ S, 73°15′ W 137
Colophon, ruin(s), *Turk.* 38°4′ N, 27°2′ E 156
Colorada, Laguna, lake, *Arg.* 44°50′ S, 69°0′ W 134
Colorada, Laguna, lake, *Bol.* 22°12′ S, 68°5′ W 137
Coloradas, Lomas, *Arg.* 43°26′ S, 67°31′ W 134
Colorado, adm. division, *Colo., U.S.* 38°49′ N, 106°40′ W 92
Colorado City, *Tex., U.S.* 32°23′ N, 100°52′ W 96
Colorado Desert, *Calif., U.S.* 33°8′ N, 116°5′ W 101
Colorado Plateau, *North America* 36°28′ N, 113°46′ W 101
Colorado, river, *Arg.* 39°27′ S, 63°4′ W 139
Colorado, river, *Braz.* 13°1′ S, 62°22′ W 132
Colorado, river, *Mex.-U.S.* 36°51′ N, 109°48′ W 238
Colorado Springs, *Colo., U.S.* 38°49′ N, 104°49′ W 90
Colorno, *It.* 44°55′ N, 10°21′ E 167
Colotepec, *Mex.* 15°52′ N, 96°57′ W 112
Colotlán, *Mex.* 22°6′ N, 103°15′ W 114
Colotlán, river, *Mex.* 22°1′ N, 103°44′ W 114
Colquechaca, *Bol.* 18°43′ S, 66°3′ W 137
Colquemarca, *Peru* 14°20′ S, 72°3′ W 137
Colquiri, *Bol.* 17°27′ S, 67°10′ W 137
Colquitt, *Ga., U.S.* 31°9′ N, 84°43′ W 96
Colrain, *Mass., U.S.* 42°40′ N, 72°42′ W 104
Colstrip, *Mont., U.S.* 45°52′ N, 106°39′ W 90
Columbia, *Calif., U.S.* 38°2′ N, 120°25′ W 100
Columbia, *Ky., U.S.* 37°5′ N, 85°18′ W 96
Columbia, *La., U.S.* 32°4′ N, 92°5′ W 103
Columbia, *Miss., U.S.* 31°15′ N, 89°51′ W 103
Columbia, *Mo., U.S.* 38°56′ N, 92°20′ W 94
Columbia, *N.C., U.S.* 35°54′ N, 76°16′ W 96
Columbia, *S.C., U.S.* 33°58′ N, 81°6′ W 96
Columbia, *Tenn., U.S.* 35°36′ N, 87°2′ W 96
Columbia, Cape, *Can.* 82°47′ N, 87°54′ W 246
Columbia City, *Oreg., U.S.* 45°52′ N, 122°50′ W 100
Columbia Lake, *Can.* 50°11′ N, 116°15′ W 108
Columbia, Mount, *Can.* 52°7′ N, 117°34′ W 108
Columbia Mountains, *Can.* 51°18′ N, 119°5′ W 80
Columbine, Cape, *S. Af.* 32°46′ S, 17°14′ E 227
Columbretes, Islas, islands, *Balearic Sea* 39°48′ N, 0°44′ E 164
Columbus, *Ga., U.S.* 32°27′ N, 84°59′ W 96
Columbus, *Ind., U.S.* 39°12′ N, 85°54′ W 102
Columbus, *Miss., U.S.* 33°28′ N, 88°25′ W 96
Columbus, *Mont., U.S.* 45°38′ N, 109°14′ W 90
Columbus, *Nebr., U.S.* 41°25′ N, 97°22′ W 90
Columbus, *N. Mex., U.S.* 31°49′ N, 107°38′ W 92
Columbus, *N. Dak., U.S.* 48°52′ N, 102°47′ W 90
Columbus, *Ohio, U.S.* 39°57′ N, 83°4′ W 102
Columbus, *Tex., U.S.* 29°41′ N, 96°32′ W 96
Columbus, *Wis., U.S.* 43°20′ N, 89°2′ W 102
Columbus Grove, *Ohio, U.S.* 40°54′ N, 84°4′ W 102
Columbus Monument, site, *Bahamas* 24°4′ N, 74°33′ W 116
Colupo, Cerro, peak, *Chile* 22°27′ S, 70°5′ W 137
Colville, *N.Z.* 36°40′ S, 175°29′ E 240
Colville, *Wash., U.S.* 48°32′ N, 117°54′ W 90
Colville, Cape, *N.Z.* 36°28′ S, 175°4′ E 240
Colville Lake, *Can.* 67°11′ N, 127°42′ W 98
Colville Lake, *Can.* 67°8′ N, 126°23′ W 98
Colville, river, *Alas., U.S.* 68°56′ N, 154°2′ W 98
Colwyn Bay, *U.K.* 53°17′ N, 3°43′ W 162
Comacchio, *It.* 44°42′ N, 12°11′ E 167
Comai, *China* 28°26′ N, 91°30′ E 197
Comala, *Mex.* 19°19′ N, 103°46′ W 114
Comallo, *Arg.* 41°0′ S, 70°15′ W 134
Coman, Mount, *Antarctica* 73°52′ S, 64°56′ W 248
Comanche, *Okla., U.S.* 34°21′ N, 97°57′ W 92
Comanche, *Tex., U.S.* 31°53′ N, 98°36′ W 92
Comandante Ferraz, station, *Antarctica* 62°2′ S, 58°22′ W 134
Comandante Fontana, *Arg.* 25°22′ S, 59°39′ W 132
Comandante N. Otamendi, *Arg.* 38°8′ S, 57°51′ W 139
Comarapa, *Bol.* 17°56′ S, 64°34′ W 137
Comaton, *Eth.* 7°39′ N, 34°23′ E 224
Comayagua, *Hond.* 14°27′ N, 87°37′ W 115
Combe Martin, *U.K.* 51°12′ N, 4°1′ W 162
Comber, *Can.* 42°14′ N, 82°33′ W 102
Comblain, *Belg.* 50°29′ N, 5°34′ E 167
Combs, *Ky., U.S.* 37°16′ N, 83°14′ W 96
Comendador, *Dom. Rep.* 18°53′ N, 71°41′ W 116
Comercinho, *Braz.* 16°18′ S, 41°50′ W 138
Comfort, *Tex., U.S.* 29°57′ N, 98°55′ W 92
Comilla, *Bangladesh* 23°24′ N, 91°6′ E 197
Comino, Capo, *It.* 40°27′ N, 9°51′ E 156
Comitán, *Mex.* 16°15′ N, 92°8′ W 115
Comloşu Mare, *Rom.* 45°52′ N, 20°38′ E 168
Commander Islands see Komandorskiye Ostrova, *Bering Sea* 53°42′ N, 162°31′ E 160
Commerce, *Okla., U.S.* 36°55′ N, 94°53′ W 96
Commercy, *Fr.* 48°45′ N, 5°34′ E 163
Commissaires, Lac des, lake, *Can.* 48°6′ N, 73°11′ W 111
Committee Bay 68°41′ N, 89°55′ W 106
Communism Peak see Ismoili Somoni, Qullai, *Taj.* 39°3′ N, 72°1′ E 197
Como, *It.* 45°48′ N, 9°5′ E 167
Como, *Miss., U.S.* 34°30′ N, 89°56′ W 96
Como, *Tex., U.S.* 33°3′ N, 95°28′ W 103
Como Bluff Fossil Beds, site, *Wyo., U.S.* 41°51′ N, 106°8′ W 90
Como, Lago di, lake, *It.* 46°3′ N, 9°1′ E 167
Como, Mount, *Nev., U.S.* 39°0′ N, 119°34′ W 90
Comodoro Rivadavia, *Arg.* 45°49′ S, 67°32′ W 134
Comoé National Park, *Côte d'Ivoire* 9°10′ N, 3°55′ W 222
Comorişte, *Rom.* 45°11′ N, 21°33′ E 168
Comoros 12°0′ S, 43°0′ E 220
Comoros, islands, *Mozambique Channel* 11°7′ S, 41°17′ E 207
Comox, *Can.* 49°40′ N, 124°54′ W 100
Compiègne, *Fr.* 49°24′ N, 2°49′ E 163
Compostela, *Mex.* 21°14′ N, 104°55′ W 114
Compostela, *Philippines* 7°42′ N, 126°3′ E 203
Comrat, *Mold.* 46°17′ N, 28°39′ E 156
Comstock, *Mich., U.S.* 42°17′ N, 85°30′ W 102
Comstock Park, *Mich., U.S.* 43°2′ N, 85°41′ W 102
Comunidad, *Venez.* 2°22′ N, 67°12′ W 136
Con Cuong, *Vietnam* 19°2′ N, 104°53′ E 202
Con Son, *Vietnam* 8°43′ N, 106°38′ E 202
Cona, *China* 27°58′ N, 91°56′ E 197
Cona Niyeu, *Arg.* 41°46′ S, 67°13′ W 134
Conakry, *Guinea* 9°29′ N, 13°52′ W 222
Conambo, river, *Ecua.* 1°50′ S, 76°55′ W 136
Concarneau, *Fr.* 47°52′ N, 3°56′ W 150
Conceição, *Braz.* 7°31′ S, 38°25′ W 132
Conceição da Barra, *Braz.* 18°37′ S, 39°45′ W 138
Conceição das Alagoas, *Braz.* 19°56′ S, 48°24′ W 138
Conceição do Araguaia, *Braz.* 8°16′ S, 49°20′ W 130
Conceição do Maú, *Braz.* 3°35′ N, 59°52′ W 130
Concepción, *Arg.* 28°23′ S, 57°54′ W 139
Concepción, *Arg.* 27°23′ S, 65°36′ W 132
Concepción, *Bol.* 16°17′ S, 62°4′ W 132
Concepción, *Bol.* 11°31′ S, 66°32′ W 137
Concepción, *Chile* 36°49′ S, 73°3′ W 134
Concepción, *Col.* 0°5′ N, 75°38′ W 136
Concepción, *Parag.* 23°21′ S, 57°26′ W 134
Concepción de la Sierra, *Arg.* 27°58′ S, 55°30′ W 139
Concepción del Oro, *Mex.* 24°35′ N, 101°26′ W 114
Concepción del Uruguay, *Arg.* 32°30′ S, 58°13′ W 139
Concepción, Laguna, lake, *Bol.* 14°23′ S, 63°39′ W 132
Concepción, Punta, *Mex.* 26°55′ N, 111°50′ W 112
Conception Bay 24°7′ S, 14°14′ E 220
Conception Bay South, *Can.* 47°31′ N, 52°58′ W 111
Conception Island, *Bahamas* 23°44′ N, 75°16′ W 116
Conception, Point, *Calif., U.S.* 34°23′ N, 120°43′ W 100
Conchas Dam, *N. Mex., U.S.* 35°22′ N, 104°10′ W 92
Conchas Lake, *N. Mex., U.S.* 35°25′ N, 104°49′ W 81
Conches, *Fr.* 48°57′ N, 0°56′ E 163
Conchi, *Chile* 22°1′ S, 68°40′ W 137
Concho, *Ariz., U.S.* 34°29′ N, 109°36′ W 92
Concho, river, *Tex., U.S.* 31°11′ N, 100°33′ W 80
Conchos, *Mex.* 27°56′ N, 105°18′ W 92
Conchos, river, *Mex.* 29°7′ N, 105°10′ W 92
Conchos, river, *Mex.* 24°57′ N, 98°56′ W 114
Conchy-les-Pots, *Fr.* 49°34′ N, 2°41′ E 163
Concord, *Calif., U.S.* 37°58′ N, 122°3′ W 100
Concord, *N.H., U.S.* 43°11′ N, 71°35′ W 104
Concord, *N.C., U.S.* 35°21′ N, 80°36′ W 82
Concordia, *Arg.* 31°21′ S, 58°1′ W 139
Concórdia, *Braz.* 27°14′ S, 52°2′ W 139
Concordia, *Mex.* 25°46′ N, 103°7′ W 114
Concordia, *Mex.* 23°17′ N, 106°4′ W 114
Concordia, *Peru* 4°32′ S, 74°46′ W 130
Concordia, station, *Antarctica* 75°3′ S, 123°12′ E 248
Concrete, *Wash., U.S.* 48°31′ N, 121°46′ W 100
Condar, *Col.* 1°34′ S, 72°2′ W 136
Conde, *Braz.* 11°50′ S, 37°37′ W 132
Conde, *S. Dak., U.S.* 45°8′ N, 98°7′ W 90
Condeúba, *Braz.* 14°56′ S, 41°58′ W 138
Condon, *Oreg., U.S.* 45°13′ N, 120°11′ W 90
Condoroma, *Peru* 15°17′ S, 71°3′ W 137
Cone Peak, *Calif., U.S.* 36°2′ N, 121°33′ W 100
Conecuh, river, *Ala., U.S.* 31°7′ N, 87°4′ W 80
Conegliano, *It.* 45°52′ N, 12°16′ E 167
Conejos, *Colo., U.S.* 37°5′ N, 106°1′ W 92
Conero, Monte, peak, *It.* 43°32′ N, 13°31′ E 156
Coneto de Comonfort, *Mex.* 24°57′ N, 104°46′ W 114
Coney Island, *N.Y., U.S.* 40°34′ N, 73°59′ W 104
Conflict Group, islands, *Solomon Sea* 11°5′ S, 149°10′ E 230
Confusion Range, *Utah, U.S.* 39°21′ N, 113°58′ W 90
Confuso, river, *Parag.* 24°34′ S, 59°10′ W 134
Congaree National Park, *S.C., U.S.* 33°48′ N, 80°47′ W 97
Congaz, *Mold.* 46°7′ N, 28°36′ E 156
Conghua, *China* 23°31′ N, 113°33′ E 198
Congjiang, *China* 25°41′ N, 108°52′ E 198
Congleton, *U.K.* 53°9′ N, 2°13′ W 162
Congo 2°118′ S, 15°13′ E 218
Congo Canyon, *Gulf of Guinea* 6°12′ S, 10°30′ E 253
Congo, Democratic Republic of the 2°26′ S, 5°7′ E 218
Congo see Lualaba, river, *Dem. Rep. of the Congo* 5°35′ S, 27°7′ E 224
Congress, *Ariz., U.S.* 34°9′ N, 112°51′ W 92
Conibear Lake, *Can.* 59°35′ N, 114°3′ W 108
Conie, river, *Fr.* 48°7′ N, 1°25′ E 163
Conil de la Frontera, *Sp.* 36°16′ N, 6°6′ W 164
Coniston, *Can.* 46°29′ N, 80°51′ W 94
Coniston, *U.K.* 54°21′ N, 3°5′ W 162
Conklin, *Can.* 55°36′ N, 111°9′ W 108
Connantre, *Fr.* 48°43′ N, 3°56′ E 163
Connecticut, adm. division, *Conn., U.S.* 41°38′ N, 73°9′ W 104
Connecticut, river, *U.S.* 42°37′ N, 72°43′ W 80
Connell, Mount, *Can.* 49°16′ N, 115°43′ W 90
Connerré, *Fr.* 48°3′ N, 0°29′ E 150
Connersville, *Ind., U.S.* 39°38′ N, 85°9′ W 102
Conness, Mount, *Calif., U.S.* 37°57′ N, 119°22′ W 100
Connoire Bay 47°34′ N, 58°5′ W 111
Connor, Mount, *Austral.* 25°31′ S, 131°43′ E 230
Connor, Mount, *Austral.* 14°36′ S, 125°53′ E 230
Connors Pass, *Nev., U.S.* 39°2′ N, 114°39′ W 90
Cononaco, *Ecua.* 1°35′ S, 75°38′ W 136
Cononaco, river, *Ecua.* 1°17′ S, 76°17′ W 136
Conorochite, river, *Venez.* 2°33′ N, 67°23′ W 136
Conover, *N.C., U.S.* 35°42′ N, 81°13′ W 96
Conques, *Sp.* 42°6′ N, 1°1′ E 164
Conquista, *Bol.* 11°26′ S, 67°11′ W 137
Conquista, *Sp.* 38°24′ N, 4°30′ W 150
Conrad, *Mont., U.S.* 48°9′ N, 111°55′ W 90
Conradi Peak, *Antarctica* 66°12′ S, 54°14′ E 248
Conroe, *Tex., U.S.* 30°17′ N, 95°27′ W 103
Conroe, Lake, *Tex., U.S.* 30°18′ N, 95°53′ W 96
Conselheiro Lafaiete, *Braz.* 20°40′ S, 43°48′ W 138
Conselheiro Pena, *Braz.* 19°13′ S, 41°28′ W 138
Conselice, *It.* 44°31′ N, 11°48′ E 167
Consett, *U.K.* 54°50′ N, 1°51′ W 162
Consort, *Can.* 52°2′ N, 110°47′ W 90
Constância dos Baetas, *Braz.* 6°13′ S, 62°17′ W 130
Constanţa, adm. division, *Rom.* 44°3′ N, 27°29′ E 156
Constanţa, *Rom.* 44°10′ N, 28°38′ E 156
Constantina, *Sp.* 37°52′ N, 5°38′ W 164
Constantine, *Mich., U.S.* 41°48′ N, 85°39′ W 102
Constantinople see İstanbul, *Turk.* 41°1′ N, 28°55′ E 156
Constitución, *Uru.* 31°5′ S, 57°49′ W 139
Constitución de 1857, park, *Mex.* 31°57′ N, 116°16′ W 238
Consuegra, *Sp.* 39°27′ N, 3°37′ W 164
Consul, *Can.* 49°17′ N, 109°31′ W 90
Contact, *Nev., U.S.* 41°46′ N, 114°46′ W 90
Contai, *India* 21°49′ N, 87°45′ E 197
Contamana, *Peru* 7°22′ S, 75°2′ W 130
Contas, river, *Braz.* 13°57′ S, 40°34′ W 138
Continental, *Ohio, U.S.* 41°5′ N, 84°17′ W 102
Contoocook, *N.H., U.S.* 43°12′ N, 71°43′ W 104
Contramaestre, *Cuba* 21°11′ N, 77°56′ W 116
Contrexéville, *Fr.* 48°10′ N, 5°53′ E 163
Contria, *Braz.* 18°10′ S, 44°33′ W 138
Control Dam, *Can.* 50°23′ N, 88°27′ W 110
Control Dam, *Can.* 49°6′ N, 87°29′ W 110
Contwoyto Lake, *Can.* 65°29′ N, 112°11′ W 106
Convención, *Col.* 8°28′ N, 73°23′ W 136
Convent, *La., U.S.* 30°0′ N, 90°50′ W 103
Converse, *Ind., U.S.* 40°34′ N, 85°53′ W 102
Converse, *La., U.S.* 31°46′ N, 93°42′ W 103
Convoy, *Ohio, U.S.* 40°54′ N, 84°42′ W 102
Conway, *Ark., U.S.* 35°4′ N, 92°27′ W 96
Conway, *Mass., U.S.* 42°30′ N, 72°43′ W 104
Conway, *N.H., U.S.* 43°58′ N, 71°8′ W 104
Conway, *S.C., U.S.* 33°49′ N, 79°4′ W 96
Conway, *Wash., U.S.* 48°19′ N, 122°21′ W 100
Conway Range National Park, *Austral.* 20°30′ S, 148°29′ E 238
Conway Springs, *Kans., U.S.* 37°22′ N, 97°39′ W 90
Conwy, *U.K.* 53°17′ N, 3°50′ W 162
Cook, *Minn., U.S.* 47°50′ N, 92°41′ W 94
Cook, Cape, *Can.* 49°54′ N, 128°17′ W 90
Cook Inlet 58°41′ N, 154°24′ W 73
Cook Islands, *N.Z.* 13°19′ S, 163°15′ W 238
Cook, Mount see Aoraki, *N.Z.* 43°45′ S, 170°4′ E 240
Cook Strait 40°32′ S, 173°31′ E 240
Cookes Peak, *N. Mex., U.S.* 32°31′ N, 107°48′ W 92
Cookeville, *Tenn., U.S.* 36°9′ N, 85°31′ W 96
Cookhouse, *S. Af.* 32°46′ S, 25°48′ E 227
Cooktown, *Austral.* 15°34′ S, 145°15′ E 238
Coolidge, *Ariz., U.S.* 32°58′ N, 111°33′ W 82
Coolville, *Ohio, U.S.* 39°11′ N, 81°48′ W 102
Cooma, *Austral.* 36°14′ S, 149°10′ E 231
Cooper, *Tex., U.S.* 33°21′ N, 95°42′ W 103
Cooper, Mount, *Can.* 50°10′ N, 117°18′ W 90
Cooper's Town, *Bahamas* 26°51′ N, 77°31′ W 96
Cooperstown, *N.Y., U.S.* 42°41′ N, 74°57′ W 94
Cooperstown, *N. Dak., U.S.* 47°24′ N, 98°9′ W 90
Coor de Wandy, peak, *Austral.* 25°46′ S, 115°58′ E 230
Coorong, The 36°3′ S, 138°4′ E 230
Coos Bay, *Oreg., U.S.* 43°22′ N, 124°17′ W 82
Coosa, river, *Ala., U.S.* 33°46′ N, 85°51′ W 112
Copacabana, *Bol.* 16°13′ S, 69°3′ W 137
Copake, *N.Y., U.S.* 42°5′ N, 73°34′ W 104
Copalis Beach, *Wash., U.S.* 47°5′ N, 124°10′ W 100
Copalis Crossing, *Wash., U.S.* 47°5′ N, 124°4′ W 100
Copan, *Okla., U.S.* 36°52′ N, 95°56′ W 96
Cope, *Colo., U.S.* 39°39′ N, 102°51′ W 90
Cope, Cabo, *Sp.* 37°18′ N, 1°29′ W 164
Copenhagen see København, *Den.* 55°40′ N, 12°23′ E 152
Copero, *Sp.* 37°18′ N, 6°1′ W 164
Copetonas, *Arg.* 38°42′ S, 60°27′ W 139
Copiague, *N.Y., U.S.* 40°40′ N, 73°24′ W 104
Copiapó, *Chile* 27°21′ S, 70°21′ W 132
Coporito, *Venez.* 8°53′ N, 62°0′ W 116
Copp Lake, *Can.* 60°9′ N, 115°13′ W 108
Copper Butte, peak, *Wash., U.S.* 48°41′ N, 118°34′ W 90
Copper Harbor, *Mich., U.S.* 47°28′ N, 87°55′ W 110
Copper Mountain, *Nev., U.S.* 41°45′ N, 115°36′ W 90
Copper Nunataks, *Antarctica* 73°41′ S, 68°29′ W 248
Copper River, *Can.* 54°30′ N, 128°30′ W 108
Copperas Cove, *Tex., U.S.* 31°6′ N, 97°54′ W 92
Coppolani, *Mauritania* 18°20′ N, 16°4′ W 222
Copulhue, Paso de, pass, *Chile* 37°34′ S, 71°9′ W 134
Coqên, *China* 31°14′ N, 85°12′ E 188
Coquilhatville see Mbandaka, *Dem. Rep. of the Congo* 2°119′ N, 18°17′ E 218
Coquille Point, *Oreg., U.S.* 43°7′ N, 124°44′ W 90
Coquimatlán, *Mex.* 19°12′ N, 103°48′ W 114
Coquimbo, *Chile* 29°59′ S, 71°23′ W 134
Coquimbo, adm. division, *Chile* 32°2′ S, 71°15′ W 134
Corabia, *Rom.* 43°47′ N, 24°30′ E 156
Coração de Jesus, *Braz.* 16°43′ S, 44°23′ W 138
Coracesium see Alanya, *Turk.* 36°31′ N, 32°1′ E 180
Coracora, *Peru* 15°2′ S, 73°48′ W 137
Coral, *Can.* 50°12′ N, 81°43′ W 94
Coral Gables, *Fla., U.S.* 25°44′ N, 80°17′ W 105
Coral Harbour, *Can.* 64°9′ N, 83°16′ W 106
Coral Sea 28°58′ S, 154°59′ E 231
Coral Sea Basin, *Coral Sea* 13°56′ S, 151°11′ E 252
Coral Sea Islands, adm. division, *Austral.* 18°0′ S, 148°0′ E 231
Coral Springs, *Fla., U.S.* 26°17′ N, 80°13′ W 105
Coranzuli, *Arg.* 23°2′ S, 66°27′ W 137
Corbeil Point, *Can.* 46°52′ N, 84°58′ W 94
Corbett National Park, *India* 29°34′ N, 78°41′ E 197
Corbie, *Fr.* 49°54′ N, 2°30′ E 163
Corbières, *Fr.* 43°6′ N, 2°18′ E 165
Corbin, *Ky., U.S.* 36°56′ N, 84°6′ W 96
Corbu, *Mold.* 48°15′ N, 27°35′ E 152
Corby, *U.K.* 52°29′ N, 0°41′ E 162
Corcaigh see Cork, *Ire.* 51°54′ N, 8°28′ W 150
Corcoran, *Calif., U.S.* 36°6′ N, 119°35′ W 100
Corcovado National Park, *C.R.* 8°25′ N, 83°24′ W 115
Cordele, *Ga., U.S.* 31°57′ N, 83°47′ W 96
Cordell, *Okla., U.S.* 35°16′ N, 99°0′ W 92
Cordillera de Los Picachos National Park, *Col.* 2°44′ N, 75°5′ W 136
Cordiner Peaks, *Antarctica* 82°2′ S, 68°40′ W 248
Córdoba, *Arg.* 31°23′ S, 64°10′ W 134
Córdoba, *Mex.* 18°51′ N, 96°56′ W 114
Córdoba, *Mex.* 26°15′ N, 103°26′ W 114
Córdoba, *Sp.* 37°53′ N, 4°47′ W 164
Córdoba, *Sp.* 37°54′ N, 4°48′ W 214
Córdoba, adm. division, *Arg.* 32°19′ S, 63°57′ W 139
Córdoba, adm. division, *Col.* 8°22′ N, 76°13′ W 136
Córdoba, Sierras de, *Arg.* 32°56′ S, 65°9′ W 134
Cordova, *Ala., U.S.* 33°45′ N, 87°11′ W 96
Cordova, *Alas., U.S.* 60°25′ N, 145°42′ W 98
Cordova Bay 54°48′ N, 132°49′ W 108
Corduente, *Sp.* 40°50′ N, 1°59′ W 164
Corella, *Sp.* 42°6′ N, 1°47′ W 164
Coreses, *Sp.* 41°33′ N, 5°38′ W 150
Corey Peak, *Nev., U.S.* 38°26′ N, 118°52′ W 90
Corfu see Kérkira, island, *Gr.* 39°10′ N, 16°33′ E 143
Corguinho, *Braz.* 19°51′ S, 54°54′ W 132
Coria, *Sp.* 39°58′ N, 6°34′ W 150
Coria del Río, *Sp.* 37°16′ N, 6°5′ W 164
Coribe, *Braz.* 13°51′ S, 44°29′ W 138
Coringa Islets, *Coral Sea* 17°26′ S, 148°17′ E 230
Corinth, *Miss., U.S.* 34°54′ N, 88°31′ W 96
Corinth, *N.Y., U.S.* 43°14′ N, 73°51′ W 104
Corinto, *Braz.* 18°22′ S, 44°31′ W 138
Coripata, *Bol.* 16°19′ S, 67°35′ W 137
Corisco, island, *Equatorial Guinea* 0°58′ N, 8°40′ E 218
Cork (Corcaigh), *Ire.* 51°54′ N, 8°28′ W 150
Corkscrew Swamp Sanctuary, site, *Fla., U.S.* 26°22′ N, 81°40′ W 105
Çorlu, *Turk.* 41°9′ N, 27°47′ E 156
Cormack Lake, *Can.* 60°56′ N, 122°28′ W 108
Cormòns, *It.* 45°57′ N, 13°29′ E 167
Cormoran, Pointe au, *Can.* 48°59′ N, 61°56′ W 111
Cormorant, *Can.* 54°13′ N, 100°37′ W 108
Cornelia, *Ga., U.S.* 34°30′ N, 83°32′ W 96
Cornélio Procópio, *Braz.* 23°9′ S, 50°43′ W 138
Cornell, *Ill., U.S.* 40°58′ N, 88°44′ W 102
Cornell, *Wis., U.S.* 45°10′ N, 91°9′ W 94
Corner Brook, *Can.* 48°57′ N, 57°58′ W 111
Corner Seamounts, *North Atlantic Ocean* 35°31′ N, 51°30′ W 253
Corning, *Ark., U.S.* 36°24′ N, 90°36′ W 96
Corning, *Calif., U.S.* 39°55′ N, 122°12′ W 92
Corning, *Iowa, U.S.* 40°58′ N, 94°46′ W 94
Corning, *N.Y., U.S.* 42°8′ N, 77°5′ W 94
Cornish, Mount, *Austral.* 20°16′ S, 126°16′ E 230
Cornwall, *Can.* 45°1′ N, 74°47′ W 110
Cornwall, *Conn., U.S.* 41°50′ N, 73°20′ W 104
Cornwallis Island, *Can.* 74°24′ N, 100°42′ W 106
Coro, *Venez.* 11°23′ N, 69°41′ W 136
Coro, Golfete de 11°28′ N, 70°9′ W 136
Coroaci, *Braz.* 18°37′ S, 42°18′ W 138
Corocoro, *Bol.* 17°16′ S, 68°30′ W 137
Coroico, *Bol.* 16°11′ S, 67°49′ W 137
Coromandel, *Braz.* 18°28′ S, 47°13′ W 138
Coromandel, *N.Z.* 36°47′ S, 175°30′ E 240
Coromandel Peninsula, *N.Z.* 36°59′ S, 175°18′ E 240
Corona, *Calif., U.S.* 33°52′ N, 117°35′ W 101
Corona, *N. Mex., U.S.* 34°15′ N, 105°35′ W 92
Coronado, *Calif., U.S.* 32°41′ N, 117°11′ W 101
Coronado, Bahía de 8°50′ N, 84°21′ W 115
Coronados, Islas, islands, *Pacific Ocean* 32°27′ N, 117°47′ W 101
Coronation, *Can.* 52°5′ N, 111°28′ W 90
Coronation Gulf 67°43′ N, 113°4′ W 106
Coronation Island, *Antarctica* 60°32′ S, 45°25′ W 134
Coronation Islands, *Indian Ocean* 15°22′ S, 125°6′ E 230
Coronda, *Arg.* 31°59′ S, 60°54′ W 139
Coronel Bogado, *Parag.* 27°10′ S, 56°16′ W 139
Coronel Dorrego, *Arg.* 38°44′ S, 61°17′ W 139
Coronel du Graty, *Arg.* 27°41′ S, 60°57′ W 139
Coronel Fabriciano, *Braz.* 19°31′ S, 42°34′ W 138
Coronel Oviedo, *Parag.* 25°25′ S, 56°28′ W 132
Coronel Portillo, *Peru* 3°20′ S, 76°36′ W 136
Coronel Pringles, *Arg.* 37°58′ S, 61°24′ W 139
Coronel Suárez, *Arg.* 37°28′ S, 61°59′ W 139
Coronel Vidal, *Arg.* 37°27′ S, 57°46′ W 139
Coronet Peak, *N.Z.* 44°56′ S, 168°39′ E 240
Coronie see Totness, *Suriname* 5°49′ N, 56°18′ W 130
Coropceni, *Rom.* 46°55′ N, 27°49′ E 156
Coropuna, Nevado, peak, *Peru* 15°32′ S, 72°47′ W 137
Corozal, *Col.* 9°18′ N, 75°18′ W 136
Corozo Pando, *Venez.* 8°29′ N, 67°35′ W 136
Corporaque, *Peru* 14°50′ S, 71°33′ W 137
Corpus Christi, *Tex., U.S.* 27°46′ N, 97°25′ W 96
Corque, *Bol.* 18°21′ S, 67°43′ W 137
Corral, *Chile* 39°54′ S, 73°28′ W 134
Corral de Almaguer, *Sp.* 39°45′ N, 3°10′ W 164
Corral de Bustos, *Arg.* 33°17′ S, 62°10′ W 139
Corrales, *N. Mex., U.S.* 35°14′ N, 106°37′ W 92
Corralillo, *Cuba* 22°59′ N, 80°35′ W 116
Corrane, *Mozambique* 15°29′ S, 39°39′ E 224
Correggio, *It.* 44°46′ N, 10°46′ E 167
Corrente, river, *Braz.* 18°30′ S, 52°3′ W 138
Corrente, river, *Braz.* 13°20′ S, 44°8′ W 138
Corrente, river, *Braz.* 14°24′ S, 46°59′ W 138
Correntes, river, *Braz.* 17°32′ S, 55°5′ W 132
Correntina, *Braz.* 13°23′ S, 44°42′ W 138
Correntina see Éguas, river, *Braz.* 13°42′ S, 45°43′ W 138
Corrientes, *Arg.* 27°29′ S, 58°48′ W 139
Corrientes, adm. division, *Arg.* 28°39′ S, 58°48′ W 139
Corrientes, Cabo, *Col.* 5°19′ N, 78°9′ W 136
Corrientes, Cabo, *Mex.* 20°17′ N, 106°42′ W 112
Corrientes, river, *Arg.* 29°44′ S, 59°19′ W 139
Corrientes, river, *Peru* 3°2′ S, 75°44′ W 136
Corrigan, *Tex., U.S.* 30°59′ N, 94°50′ W 103
Corriverton, *Guyana* 5°49′ N, 57°11′ W 130
Corrubedo, Cabo, *Sp.* 42°25′ N, 9°40′ W 150
Corse, adm. division, *Fr.* 42°20′ N, 8°39′ E 156
Corse, Cap, *Fr.* 43°2′ N, 8°54′ E 156
Corsham, *U.K.* 51°25′ N, 2°11′ W 162
Corsica, *S. Dak., U.S.* 43°24′ N, 98°25′ W 90
Corsica, island, *Fr.* 41°40′ N, 6°21′ E 143
Corsicana, *Tex., U.S.* 32°4′ N, 96°28′ W 96
Cort Adelaer, Kap, *Den.* 61°51′ N, 42°1′ W 106
Cortazar, *Mex.* 20°27′ N, 100°58′ W 114
Corte, *Fr.* 42°18′ N, 9°9′ E 156
Cortemaggiore, *It.* 44°59′ N, 9°55′ E 167
Cortes de la Frontera, *Sp.* 36°36′ N, 5°21′ W 164
Cortes Island, *Can.* 50°4′ N, 124°52′ W 100
Cortez, *Colo., U.S.* 37°20′ N, 108°36′ W 92

Cortez Mountains, *Nev., U.S.* 40°20′ N, 116°34′ W 90
Cortez, Sea of,31°12′ N, 114°47′ W 73
Cortina d'Ampezzo, *It.* 46°32′ N, 12°8′ E 167
Cortland, *N.Y., U.S.* 42°35′ N, 76°12′ W 94
Coruche, *Port.* 38°57′ N, 8°33′ W 150
Çoruh, river, *Turk.* 40°21′ N, 40°41′ E 195
Çorum, *Turk.* 40°33′ N, 34°57′ E 156
Corumbá, *Braz.* 19°1′ S, 57°42′ W 132
Corumbá de Goiás, *Braz.* 15°59′ S, 48°50′ W 138
Corumbá, river, *Braz.* 18°4′ S, 48°36′ W 138
Corumbaíba, *Braz.* 18°12′ S, 48°37′ W 138
Corunna, *Can.* 42°53′ N, 82°27′ W 102
Corunna, *Mich., U.S.* 42°57′ N, 84°8′ W 102
Corvallis, *Mont., U.S.* 46°17′ N, 114°7′ W 90
Corvallis, *Oreg., U.S.* 44°33′ N, 123°16′ W 90
Corvette, Lac de la, lake, *Can.* 53°24′ N, 74°31′ W 111
Corwen, *U.K.* 52°58′ N, 3°22′ W 162
Corydon, *Iowa, U.S.* 40°45′ N, 93°19′ W 94
Corzu, *Rom.* 44°27′ N, 23°10′ E 168
Corzuela, *Arg.* 26°57′ S, 60°59′ W 139
Cosalá, *Mex.* 24°23′ N, 106°42′ W 114
Cosamaloapan, *Mex.* 18°22′ N, 95°48′ W 114
Coşava, *Rom.* 45°51′ N, 22°18′ E 168
Coscomatepec, *Mex.* 19°2′ N, 97°3′ W 114
Cosenza, *It.* 39°17′ N, 16°15′ E 156
Coshocton, *Ohio, U.S.* 40°15′ N, 81°51′ W 102
Cosigüina, Punta, *Nicar.* 12°51′ N, 88°44′ W 115
Cosío, *Mex.* 22°21′ N, 102°18′ W 114
Cosmoledo Group, islands, *Indian Ocean* 9°18′ S, 46°45′ E 218
Cosmonaut Sea 62°48′ S, 40°53′ E 255
Cosmopolis, *Wash., U.S.* 46°56′ N, 123°47′ W 100
Cosñipata, *Peru* 13°2′ S, 71°14′ W 137
Coso Range, *Calif., U.S.* 36°9′ N, 117°44′ W 101
Cosoleacaque, *Mex.* 18°1′ N, 94°38′ W 112
Cossato, *It.* 45°34′ N, 8°11′ E 167
Cosson, river, *Fr.* 47°39′ N, 1°34′ E 165
Cossonay, *Switz.* 46°36′ N, 6°31′ E 167
Costa Marques, *Braz.* 12°30′ S, 64°14′ W 137
Costa Mesa, *Calif., U.S.* 33°39′ N, 117°55′ W 101
Costa Rica 10°0′ N, 84°0′ W 115
Costa Rica, *Bol.* 11°15′ S, 68°16′ W 137
Costa Rica, *Mex.* 31°19′ N, 112°37′ W 92
Costigan Lake, *Can.* 56°54′ N, 106°39′ W 108
Coswig, *Ger.* 51°52′ N, 12°27′ E 152
Cotabambas, *Peru* 13°47′ S, 72°22′ W 137
Cotabato, *Philippines* 7°14′ N, 124°13′ E 203
Cotagaita, *Bol.* 20°50′ S, 65°43′ W 137
Cotahuasi, *Peru* 15°16′ S, 72°55′ W 137
Cotati, *Calif., U.S.* 38°19′ N, 122°43′ W 100
Côte d'Ivoire (Ivory Coast) 7°26′ N, 6°9′ W 214
Côte d'Or, *Fr.* 46°59′ N, 4°33′ E 165
Cotentin, *Fr.* 49°29′ N, 1°52′ W 150
Côtes-de-Fer, *Haiti* 18°12′ N, 73°0′ W 116
Cotija, *Mex.* 19°47′ N, 102°43′ W 114
Cotonou, *Benin* 6°23′ N, 2°15′ E 222
Cotopaxi National Park, *Ecua.* 0°40′ N, 78°44′ W 130
Cotopaxi, peak, *Ecua.* 0°47′ N, 78°43′ W 130
Cotorro, *Cuba* 23°3′ N, 82°16′ W 116
Cotswold Hills, *U.K.* 51°58′ N, 1°59′ W 162
Cottage Grove, *Oreg., U.S.* 43°47′ N, 123°3′ W 90
Cottageville, *W. Va., U.S.* 38°51′ N, 81°50′ W 102
Cottbus, *Ger.* 51°45′ N, 14°19′ E 152
Cotter, *Ark., U.S.* 36°15′ N, 92°33′ W 96
Cottian Alps, *It.* 45°16′ N, 6°59′ E 165
Cottica, *Suriname* 3°40′ N, 54°5′ W 123
Cottingham, *U.K.* 53°46′ N, 0°26′ E 162
Cotton Valley, *La., U.S.* 32°48′ N, 93°25′ W 103
Cottonport, *La., U.S.* 30°57′ N, 92°3′ W 103
Cottonwood, *Calif., U.S.* 40°23′ N, 122°18′ W 90
Cottonwood Mountains, *Calif., U.S.* 36°41′ N, 117°26′ W 101
Cottonwood Pass, *Calif., U.S.* 35°46′ N, 120°14′ W 100
Cottonwood Pass, *Calif., U.S.* 33°43′ N, 115°50′ W 101
Cotulla, *Tex., U.S.* 28°26′ N, 99°14′ W 92
Coucy-Auffrique, *Fr.* 49°31′ N, 3°18′ E 163
Cougar, *Wash., U.S.* 46°3′ N, 122°18′ W 100
Cougar Peak, *Oreg., U.S.* 42°18′ N, 120°44′ W 90
Couiza, *Fr.* 42°56′ N, 2°14′ E 164
Coulee Dam, *Wash., U.S.* 47°57′ N, 118°57′ W 90
Coulman Island, *Antarctica* 73°28′ S, 175°10′ E 248
Coulmiers, *Alg.* 36°8′ N, 6°7′ E 150
Coulommiers, *Fr.* 48°49′ N, 3°4′ E 163
Coulonge, river, *Can.* 46°54′ N, 77°24′ W 94
Coulterville, *Calif., U.S.* 37°42′ N, 120°13′ W 100
Council, *Alas., U.S.* 64°53′ N, 163°41′ W 98
Council, *Idaho, U.S.* 44°43′ N, 116°26′ W 90
Council Grove, *Kans., U.S.* 38°38′ N, 96°30′ W 92
Council Mountain, *Idaho, U.S.* 44°41′ N, 116°22′ W 90
Coupé, Cap see Ouest, Pointe de l', *Fr.* 46°48′ N, 57°0′ W 111
Coupeville, *Wash., U.S.* 48°11′ N, 122°41′ W 100
Courcellete Peak, *Can.* 50°16′ N, 114°54′ W 90
Couronne, Cap, *Fr.* 43°14′ N, 5°0′ E 165
Coursan, *Fr.* 43°13′ N, 3°1′ E 164
Courtauld, Mount, *Antarctica* 70°19′ S, 68°3′ W 248
Courtenay, *Can.* 49°40′ N, 125°0′ W 100
Courtisols, *Fr.* 48°58′ N, 4°29′ E 163
Courtland, *Calif., U.S.* 38°19′ N, 121°34′ W 100
Courtright, *Can.* 42°48′ N, 82°28′ W 94
Coushatta, *La., U.S.* 31°59′ N, 93°20′ W 103
Couterne, *Fr.* 48°31′ N, 0°26′ E 150
Couto Magalhães, *Braz.* 8°20′ S, 49°17′ W 130
Coutts, *Can.* 49°0′ N, 111°59′ W 90
Covadonga, site, *Sp.* 43°18′ N, 5°8′ W 150
Covarrubias, *Sp.* 42°3′ N, 3°32′ W 164
Covăsinţ, *Rom.* 46°11′ N, 21°38′ E 168
Covasna, adm. division, *Rom.* 45°55′ N, 25°36′ E 156
Cove, *Oreg., U.S.* 45°17′ N, 117°49′ W 90
Covendo, *Bol.* 15°53′ S, 67°6′ W 137
Coventry, *Conn., U.S.* 41°46′ N, 72°19′ W 104
Coventry, *U.K.* 52°24′ N, 1°31′ W 162
Coventry Lake, *Can.* 61°7′ N, 107°1′ W 108
Covert, *Mich., U.S.* 42°17′ N, 86°16′ W 102
Coves del Drac, site, *Sp.* 39°31′ N, 3°15′ E 150
Covilhã, *Port.* 40°15′ N, 7°34′ W 214
Covington, *Ga., U.S.* 33°35′ N, 83°54′ W 112
Covington, *Ind., U.S.* 40°7′ N, 87°24′ W 102
Covington, *Ky., U.S.* 39°3′ N, 84°32′ W 102
Covington, *La., U.S.* 30°28′ N, 90°7′ W 103
Covington, *Ohio, U.S.* 40°7′ N, 84°21′ W 102
Covington, *Okla., U.S.* 36°17′ N, 97°35′ W 92
Covington, *Tenn., U.S.* 35°33′ N, 89°40′ W 96
Covington, *Va., U.S.* 37°47′ N, 80°0′ W 96
Cowan, *Can.* 52°1′ N, 100°39′ W 108
Cowan Lake, lake, *Can.* 53°58′ N, 107°43′ W 108
Cowan, Mount, *Mont., U.S.* 45°22′ N, 110°32′ W 90
Cowansville, *Can.* 45°12′ N, 72°45′ W 94
Cowbridge, *U.K.* 51°27′ N, 3°27′ W 162
Cowden, *Ill., U.S.* 39°15′ N, 88°52′ W 102
Cowes, *Austral.* 50°45′ N, 1°18′ W 150
Coweta, *Okla., U.S.* 35°55′ N, 95°39′ W 96
Cowhorn Mountain, *Oreg., U.S.* 43°22′ N, 122°8′ W 90
Cowley, *Can.* 49°34′ N, 114°5′ W 90
Cowley, *Wyo., U.S.* 44°52′ N, 108°29′ W 90
Cox, *S. Af.* 27°56′ S, 22°51′ E 227
Coxcatlán, *Mex.* 18°16′ N, 97°11′ W 114
Coxcomb Mountains, *Calif., U.S.* 34°19′ N, 115°34′ W 101
Coxilha, *Braz.* 28°6′ S, 52°18′ W 139
Coxim, *Braz.* 18°28′ S, 54°46′ W 132
Coxim, river, *Braz.* 18°46′ S, 54°28′ W 132
Coxipi, Lac, lake, *Can.* 51°30′ N, 58°47′ W 111
Coxipi, river, *Can.* 52°9′ N, 58°34′ W 111
Coxsackie, *N.Y., U.S.* 42°20′ N, 73°50′ W 104
Coxwold, *U.K.* 54°11′ N, 1°11′ W 162
Coyah, *Guinea* 9°41′ N, 13°25′ W 222
Coyotitán, *Mex.* 23°45′ N, 106°37′ W 112
Cozad, *Nebr., U.S.* 40°50′ N, 100°0′ W 90
Cozón, Cerro, peak, *Mex.* 31°13′ N, 112°39′ W 92
Cozumel, Isla, island, *Mex.* 20°25′ N, 86°45′ W 115
Cradock, *S. Af.* 32°12′ S, 25°36′ E 227
Craig, *Alas., U.S.* 55°28′ N, 133°9′ W 108
Craig, *Colo., U.S.* 40°31′ N, 107°34′ W 90
Crail, *U.K.* 56°15′ N, 2°38′ W 150
Craiova, *Rom.* 44°19′ N, 23°48′ E 156
Cranberry Isles, *Atlantic Ocean* 43°58′ N, 68°17′ W 94
Cranberry Portage, *Can.* 54°35′ N, 101°24′ W 108
Cranbrook, *Can.* 49°30′ N, 115°45′ W 90
Cranbrook, *U.K.* 51°5′ N, 0°32′ E 162
Crane, *Ind., U.S.* 38°53′ N, 86°54′ W 102
Crane, *Oreg., U.S.* 43°24′ N, 118°35′ W 90
Crane, *Tex., U.S.* 31°22′ N, 102°21′ W 92
Crane Beach, *Mass., U.S.* 42°40′ N, 70°45′ W 104
Crane Lake, *Minn., U.S.* 48°14′ N, 92°31′ W 94
Crane Lake, lake, *Can.* 50°1′ N, 109°28′ W 90
Crane Mountain, *Oreg., U.S.* 42°3′ N, 120°19′ W 90
Cranii, ruin(s), *Gr.* 38°10′ N, 20°24′ E 156
Cranwell, *U.K.* 53°2′ N, 0°28′ E 162
Craon, *Fr.* 47°50′ N, 0°57′ E 150
Craonne, *Fr.* 49°26′ N, 3°46′ E 163
Crary Ice Rise, islands, *South Pacific Ocean* 82°38′ S, 174°28′ W 248
Craryville, *N.Y., U.S.* 42°9′ N, 73°37′ W 104
Crasna, *Rom.* 46°30′ N, 27°50′ E 156
Crasna, *Rom.* 47°9′ N, 22°54′ E 168
Crasna, river, *Rom.* 47°35′ N, 22°44′ E 168
Crasnencoe, *Mold.* 47°50′ N, 29°8′ E 156
Crater Mountain, *Calif., U.S.* 40°37′ N, 121°8′ W 90
Crater Peak, *Calif., U.S.* 40°41′ N, 121°42′ W 90
Cratère du Nouveau-Québec (Chubb Crater), *Can.* 61°19′ N, 73°41′ W 106
Crateús, *Braz.* 5°16′ S, 40°26′ W 123
Crato, *Braz.* 7°15′ S, 39°27′ W 132
Crato, *Braz.* 7°28′ S, 63°6′ W 130
Cravari, river, *Braz.* 12°28′ S, 58°10′ W 132
Cravo Norte, *Col.* 6°19′ N, 70°12′ W 136
Cravo Norte, river, *Col.* 6°32′ N, 71°37′ W 136
Cravo Sur, river, *Col.* 4°59′ N, 72°3′ W 136
Crawford, *Miss., U.S.* 33°16′ N, 88°37′ W 103
Crawford, *Nebr., U.S.* 42°40′ N, 103°25′ W 90
Crawford Notch, pass, *N.H., U.S.* 44°11′ N, 71°25′ W 104
Crawfordsville, *Ind., U.S.* 40°1′ N, 86°54′ W 102
Crawley, *U.K.* 51°7′ N, 0°12′ E 162
Crayke, *U.K.* 54°7′ N, 1°9′ W 162
Crazy Mountains, *Mont., U.S.* 46°17′ N, 110°29′ W 90
Crazy Peak, *Mont., U.S.* 45°58′ N, 110°22′ W 90
Crean Lake, lake, *Can.* 54°6′ N, 106°26′ W 108
Crécy, *Fr.* 49°42′ N, 3°37′ E 163
Crécy-en-Ponthieu, *Fr.* 50°14′ N, 1°52′ E 163
Crécy-la-Chapelle, *Fr.* 48°51′ N, 2°54′ E 163
Crediton, *U.K.* 50°47′ N, 3°39′ W 162
Cree Lake, *Can.* 57°20′ N, 106°52′ W 108
Cree Lake, *Can.* 57°24′ N, 106°51′ W 108
Cree, river, *Can.* 57°38′ N, 105°55′ W 106
Creede, *Colo., U.S.* 37°51′ N, 106°56′ W 92
Creek Butte, Rock, peak, *Oreg., U.S.* 44°47′ N, 118°11′ W 90
Creil, *Fr.* 49°15′ N, 2°28′ E 163
Crema, *It.* 45°21′ N, 9°40′ E 167
Cremona, *It.* 45°7′ N, 10°1′ E 156
Crepaja, *Serb.* 45°0′ N, 20°38′ E 168
Crépeau, Lac, lake, *Can.* 53°53′ N, 71°13′ W 111
Crepori, river, *Braz.* 6°54′ S, 56°32′ W 130
Crépy, *Fr.* 49°35′ N, 3°30′ E 163
Crépy-en-Valois, *Fr.* 49°14′ N, 2°52′ E 163
Cresbard, *S. Dak., U.S.* 45°9′ N, 98°58′ W 90
Crescent, *Okla., U.S.* 35°55′ N, 97°36′ W 92
Crescent City, *Calif., U.S.* 41°44′ N, 124°8′ W 106
Crescent City, *Fla., U.S.* 29°26′ N, 81°32′ W 105
Crescent Junction, *Utah, U.S.* 38°57′ N, 109°49′ W 92
Crescent, Lake, *Wash., U.S.* 48°3′ N, 123°59′ W 100
Crescent Spur, *Can.* 53°33′ N, 120°43′ W 108
Cresco, *Iowa, U.S.* 43°22′ N, 92°7′ W 94
Crespo, *Arg.* 32°2′ S, 60°19′ W 139
Crestline, *Calif., U.S.* 34°15′ N, 117°17′ W 101
Crestline, *Ohio, U.S.* 40°46′ N, 82°45′ W 102
Creston, *Calif., U.S.* 35°32′ N, 120°32′ W 100
Creston, *Can.* 49°5′ N, 116°32′ W 90
Creston, *Iowa, U.S.* 41°2′ N, 94°22′ W 94
Crestview, *Fla., U.S.* 30°45′ N, 86°34′ W 96
Creswell, *Oreg., U.S.* 43°54′ N, 123°2′ W 90
Creswell Bay 72°20′ N, 93°54′ W 106
Cretas, *Sp.* 40°55′ N, 0°13′ E 164
Crete, *Nebr., U.S.* 40°36′ N, 96°57′ W 90
Crete see Kríti, island, *Gr.* 35°36′ N, 24°6′ E 180
Crete, Sea of 35°24′ N, 22°56′ E 156
Creus, Cap de, *Sp.* 42°8′ N, 3°19′ E 164
Creuzburg, *Ger.* 51°3′ N, 10°14′ E 167
Crèvecour, *Fr.* 49°36′ N, 2°4′ E 163
Crevillente, *Sp.* 38°14′ N, 0°49′ E 164
Crewe, *U.K.* 53°5′ N, 2°26′ W 162
Crewe, *Va., U.S.* 37°10′ N, 78°7′ W 96
Crewkerne, *U.K.* 50°53′ N, 2°48′ W 162
Criciúma, *Braz.* 28°42′ S, 49°21′ W 138
Crickhowell, *U.K.* 51°51′ N, 3°7′ W 162
Cridersville, *Ohio, U.S.* 40°39′ N, 84°9′ W 102
Criel-sur-Mer, *Fr.* 50°0′ N, 1°18′ E 163
Criffell, peak, *U.K.* 54°55′ N, 3°43′ W 150
Crillon, Mount, *Alas., U.S.* 58°37′ N, 137°13′ W 108
Crimea, region, *Europe* 45°25′ N, 33°20′ E 156
Crinan, *U.K.* 56°4′ N, 5°34′ W 150
Cripple Creek, *Colo., U.S.* 38°44′ N, 105°11′ W 90
Crishy Swash, *Bahamas* 26°47′ N, 78°51′ W 105
Cristal, Monts de, *Gabon* 0°31′ N, 9°45′ E 218
Cristalândia, *Braz.* 10°36′ S, 49°12′ W 130
Cristalina, *Braz.* 16°48′ S, 47°39′ W 138
Cristalino, river, *Braz.* 13°56′ S, 51°11′ W 138
Cristo Mountains, *N. Mex., U.S.* 38°3′ N, 105°42′ W 90
Crişul Alb, river, *Rom.* 46°38′ N, 21°22′ E 168
Criuleni, *Mold.* 47°12′ N, 29°10′ E 156
Crixás, *Braz.* 14°29′ S, 49°59′ W 138
Crixás Açu, river, *Braz.* 14°45′ S, 49°49′ W 138
Crixás Mirim, river, *Braz.* 13°57′ S, 50°43′ W 138
Crljivica, *Bosn. and Herzg.* 44°25′ N, 16°23′ E 168
Crna Gora, *Serb.* 42°20′ N, 21°23′ E 168
Crnajka, *Serb.* 44°17′ N, 22°9′ E 168
Crnča, *Serb.* 44°17′ N, 19°16′ E 168
Crni Lug, *Bosn. and Herzg.* 44°4′ N, 16°35′ E 168
Crnoljeva Planina, *Serb.* 42°29′ N, 20°43′ E 168
Croatia 45°46′ N, 16°12′ E 156
Crocker Hill, *Austral.* 24°55′ S, 135°24′ E 230
Crocker Range National Park, *Malaysia* 5°32′ N, 115°22′ E 203
Crocker Range National Park, *Malaysia* 5°35′ N, 115°49′ E 238
Crockett, *Tex., U.S.* 31°17′ N, 95°27′ W 103
Crocodile Islands, *Arafura Sea* 12°30′ S, 133°42′ E 230
Crofton, *Nebr., U.S.* 42°42′ N, 97°31′ W 90
Croisette, Cap, *Fr.* 43°8′ N, 5°6′ E 165
Croisic, Pointe du, *Fr.* 47°1′ N, 2°58′ W 150
Croix, Pointe à la, *Can.* 49°11′ N, 67°49′ W 111
Croker Bay 74°14′ N, 84°17′ W 106
Croker Island, *Austral.* 11°6′ S, 132°40′ E 192
Crombie, Mount, *Austral.* 26°43′ S, 130°36′ E 230
Cromer, *U.K.* 52°55′ N, 1°17′ E 162
Cromwell, *N.Z.* 45°4′ S, 169°12′ E 240
Cronadun, *N.Z.* 42°3′ S, 171°52′ E 240
Cronin, Mount, *Can.* 54°55′ N, 126°59′ W 108
Crook, *Colo., U.S.* 40°51′ N, 102°49′ W 90
Crook, *U.K.* 54°43′ N, 1°46′ W 162
Crooked Island (Atwood), *Bahamas* 22°39′ N, 76°43′ W 81
Crooked River, *Can.* 52°50′ N, 103°47′ W 108
Crooked, river, *Can.* 54°46′ N, 122°49′ W 108
Crookston, *Minn., U.S.* 47°46′ N, 96°38′ W 82
Crooksville, *Ohio, U.S.* 39°45′ N, 82°6′ W 102
Crosby, *Miss., U.S.* 31°15′ N, 91°4′ W 103
Crosby, *N. Dak., U.S.* 48°53′ N, 103°18′ W 90
Crosby, *Tex., U.S.* 29°54′ N, 95°4′ W 103
Crosby, *U.K.* 53°29′ N, 3°1′ W 162
Crosbyton, *Tex., U.S.* 33°38′ N, 101°15′ W 92
Cross, Cape, *Namibia* 22°13′ S, 13°26′ E 220
Cross City, *Fla., U.S.* 29°37′ N, 83°9′ W 105
Cross Creek, *Can.* 46°18′ N, 66°43′ W 94
Cross Fell, peak, *U.K.* 54°42′ N, 2°32′ W 162
Cross Hands, *U.K.* 51°47′ N, 4°5′ W 162
Cross Lake, *Can.* 54°37′ N, 97°46′ W 108
Cross Lake, lake, *Can.* 46°52′ N, 80°17′ W 94
Cross Plains, *Tex., U.S.* 32°7′ N, 99°10′ W 96
Cross River National Park, *Nig.* 5°28′ N, 7°48′ E 222
Crossett, *Ark., U.S.* 33°7′ N, 91°59′ W 103
Crossfield, *Can.* 51°26′ N, 114°2′ W 90
Crossing Rocks, *Bahamas* 26°7′ N, 77°14′ W 96
Crossman Peak, *Ariz., U.S.* 34°32′ N, 114°14′ W 101
Croswell, *Mich., U.S.* 43°16′ N, 82°36′ W 102
Crothersville, *Ind., U.S.* 38°47′ N, 85°50′ W 102
Crotone, *It.* 39°4′ N, 17°7′ E 156
Croton-on-Hudson, *N.Y., U.S.* 41°11′ N, 73°54′ W 104
Crouy-sur-Ourcq, *Fr.* 49°4′ N, 3°4′ E 163
Crow Agency, *Mont., U.S.* 45°35′ N, 107°27′ W 90
Crow Peak, *Mont., U.S.* 46°15′ N, 111°59′ W 90
Crow, river, *Can.* 60°16′ N, 125°47′ W 108
Crowell, *Tex., U.S.* 33°57′ N, 99°44′ W 92
Crowland, *U.K.* 52°40′ N, 0°9′ E 162
Crowle, *U.K.* 53°36′ N, 0°51′ E 162
Crowley, *La., U.S.* 30°11′ N, 92°23′ W 103
Crowleys Ridge, *Ark., U.S.* 36°2′ N, 90°38′ W 96
Crown City, *Ohio, U.S.* 38°35′ N, 82°18′ W 102
Crown Point, *Ind., U.S.* 41°24′ N, 87°21′ W 102
Crown Point, *N.Y., U.S.* 43°56′ N, 73°27′ W 104
Crownpoint, *N. Mex., U.S.* 35°40′ N, 108°9′ W 92
Crows Landing, *Calif., U.S.* 37°23′ N, 121°6′ W 100
Crowsnest Mountain, *Can.* 49°41′ N, 114°40′ W 90
Crowsnest Pass, *Can.* 49°36′ N, 114°26′ W 90
Croydon, *Austral.* 18°12′ S, 142°14′ E 231
Croydon, *U.K.* 51°22′ N, 9°534′ W 162
Crozet Basin, *Indian Ocean* 40°18′ S, 59°51′ E 254
Crozet Islands, *Indian Ocean* 46°18′ S, 51°8′ E 254
Crozet Plateau, *Indian Ocean* 45°27′ S, 50°24′ E 254
Crozier, Cape, *Antarctica* 77°1′ S, 179°30′ E 248
Crucero, *Peru* 14°22′ S, 70°1′ W 137
Cruces, *Cuba* 22°20′ N, 80°16′ W 116
Cruces, Punta, *Col.* 6°28′ N, 77°32′ W 136
Cruger, *Miss., U.S.* 33°17′ N, 90°14′ W 103
Cruillas, *Mex.* 24°44′ N, 98°31′ W 114
Cruta, river, *Hond.* 14°52′ N, 83°45′ W 115
Cruz Alta, *Arg.* 33°1′ S, 61°48′ W 139
Cruz Alta, *Braz.* 28°40′ S, 53°36′ W 139
Cruz, Cabo, *Cuba* 19°51′ N, 78°25′ W 115
Cruz del Eje, *Arg.* 30°46′ S, 64°48′ W 134
Cruz Grande, *Chile* 29°27′ S, 71°19′ W 134
Cruzeiro, *Braz.* 22°38′ S, 44°58′ W 138
Cruzeiro do Oeste, *Braz.* 23°45′ S, 53°3′ W 138
Cruzeiro do Sul, *Braz.* 7°40′ S, 72°42′ W 132
Crvenka, *Serb.* 45°37′ N, 19°27′ E 168
Cry Lake, *Can.* 58°47′ N, 129°13′ W 108
Crysdale, Mount, *Can.* 55°53′ N, 123°33′ W 108
Crystal, *Me., U.S.* 46°0′ N, 68°23′ W 111
Crystal Bay 28°51′ N, 82°49′ W 105
Crystal City, *Can.* 49°8′ N, 98°58′ W 90
Crystal City, *Tex., U.S.* 28°41′ N, 99°50′ W 92
Crystal Falls, *Mich., U.S.* 46°5′ N, 88°20′ W 94
Crystal Lake, *Ill., U.S.* 42°14′ N, 88°19′ W 102
Crystal River, *Fla., U.S.* 28°54′ N, 82°36′ W 105
Crystal Springs, *Miss., U.S.* 31°59′ N, 90°21′ W 103
Csákvár, *Hung.* 47°24′ N, 18°28′ E 168
Csanytelek, *Hung.* 46°36′ N, 20°7′ E 168
Csenger, *Hung.* 47°51′ N, 22°41′ E 168
Csepel-sziget, *Hung.* 47°7′ N, 18°57′ E 168
Cserhát, *Hung.* 47°51′ N, 19°8′ E 168
Csesztreg, *Hung.* 46°42′ N, 16°31′ E 168
Csongrád, *Hung.* 46°42′ N, 20°8′ E 168
Csongrád, adm. division, *Hung.* 46°12′ N, 19°42′ E 156
Csorna, *Hung.* 47°35′ N, 17°16′ E 156
Csorvás, *Hung.* 46°38′ N, 20°49′ E 168
Csóványos, peak, *Hung.* 47°55′ N, 18°56′ E 168
Csurgó, *Hung.* 46°15′ N, 17°6′ E 168
Cuale, *Angola* 8°24′ S, 16°10′ E 220
Cuamba, *Mozambique* 14°50′ S, 36°33′ E 224
Cuando Cubango, adm. division, *Angola* 17°53′ S, 19°15′ E 220
Cuando, river, *Angola* 15°31′ S, 21°12′ E 220
Cuangar, *Angola* 17°35′ S, 18°39′ E 220
Cuango, *Angola* 6°17′ S, 16°39′ E 218
Cuango, *Angola* 9°10′ S, 18°2′ E 218
Cuanza Norte, adm. division, *Angola* 8°42′ S, 14°20′ E 218
Cuanza Sul, adm. division, *Angola* 10°29′ S, 13°38′ E 220
Cuaró, *Uru.* 31°55′ S, 55°11′ W 139
Cuaró, *Uru.* 30°37′ S, 56°55′ W 139
Cuatir, river, *Angola* 17°10′ S, 18°18′ E 220
Cuatro Ciénegas, *Mex.* 26°59′ N, 102°6′ W 82
Cuatro Ojos, *Bol.* 16°52′ S, 63°38′ W 137
Cuauhtémoc, *Mex.* 19°19′ N, 103°36′ W 114
Cuauhtémoc, *Mex.* 28°24′ N, 106°52′ W 112
Cuautepec, *Mex.* 20°1′ N, 98°17′ W 114
Cuautitlán, *Mex.* 19°26′ N, 104°24′ W 114
Cuautla, *Mex.* 18°47′ N, 98°56′ W 114
Cub Hills, peak, *Can.* 54°13′ N, 104°49′ W 108
Cuba 21°4′ N, 77°43′ W 116
Cuba, *Ala., U.S.* 32°26′ N, 88°23′ W 103
Cuba, *Port.* 38°9′ N, 7°55′ W 150
Cubabi, Cerro, peak, *Mex.* 31°42′ N, 112°54′ W 92
Cubagua, Isla, island, *Venez.* 10°41′ N, 64°50′ W 116
Çubuk, *Turk.* 40°14′ N, 33°2′ E 156
Cuchi, *Angola* 14°41′ S, 16°54′ E 220
Cuchillo Parado, *Mex.* 29°27′ N, 104°52′ W 92
Cuchivero, river, *Venez.* 6°28′ N, 65°56′ W 136
Cuchumatanes, Sierra los, *Guatemala* 15°39′ N, 91°48′ W 115
Cucuí, *Braz.* 1°7′ N, 66°49′ W 136
Cucumbi, *Angola* 10°17′ S, 19°3′ E 220
Cucurpé, *Mex.* 30°20′ N, 110°43′ W 92
Cúcuta, *Col.* 7°54′ N, 72°30′ W 136
Cudahy, *Wis., U.S.* 42°57′ N, 87°52′ W 102
Cuddalore, *India* 11°44′ N, 79°45′ E 188
Cuddapah, *India* 14°27′ N, 78°51′ E 188
Cuduyari, river, *Col.* 1°24′ N, 70°41′ W 136
Cudworth, *Can.* 52°29′ N, 105°45′ W 108
Cuéllar, *Sp.* 41°23′ N, 4°19′ W 150
Cuello, ruin(s), *Belize* 18°3′ N, 88°45′ W 115
Cuenca, *Ecua.* 2°58′ S, 79°3′ W 130
Cuenca, *Sp.* 40°4′ N, 2°8′ W 164
Cuenca, Serranía de, *Sp.* 39°38′ N, 1°55′ W 164
Cuencamé, *Mex.* 24°51′ N, 103°43′ W 114
Cuernavaca, *Mex.* 18°52′ N, 99°18′ W 114
Cuero, *Tex., U.S.* 29°4′ N, 97°18′ W 96
Cuervo, *N. Mex., U.S.* 35°2′ N, 104°24′ W 92
Cuervos, *Mex.* 32°37′ N, 114°52′ W 101
Cuetzalan, *Mex.* 20°2′ N, 97°31′ W 114
Cuevas, Cerro, peak, *Mex.* 29°10′ N, 111°29′ W 92
Cuevas de Altamira, site, *Sp.* 43°22′ N, 4°10′ W 164
Cuevita, *Col.* 5°28′ N, 77°27′ W 136
Cuevitas, *Chile* 23°26′ S, 70°0′ W 134
Cuevo, *Bol.* 20°27′ S, 63°33′ W 137
Cugir, *Rom.* 45°49′ N, 23°21′ E 168
Cuiabá, *Braz.* 15°33′ S, 56°7′ W 132
Cuiabá, river, *Braz.* 17°6′ S, 56°39′ W 132
Cuiari, *Braz.* 1°28′ N, 68°11′ W 136
Cuicatlán, *Mex.* 17°49′ N, 96°58′ W 114
Cuilcagh, peak, *U.K.* 54°11′ N, 7°55′ W 150
Cuillin Hills, *U.K.* 57°14′ N, 6°18′ W 150
Cuilo, *Angola* 7°42′ S, 19°23′ E 218
Cuiluan, *China* 47°42′ N, 128°42′ E 198
Cuima, *Angola* 13°18′ S, 15°38′ E 220
Cuio, *Angola* 13°0′ S, 12°58′ E 220
Cuito Cuanavale, *Angola* 15°9′ S, 19°8′ E 220
Cuito, river, *Angola* 14°7′ S, 18°39′ E 220
Cuitzeo, *Mex.* 19°57′ N, 101°8′ W 114
Cuiuni, river, *Braz.* 1°19′ S, 64°10′ W 130
Cuizăuca, *Mold.* 47°36′ N, 28°49′ E 156
Cujmir, *Rom.* 44°13′ N, 22°56′ E 168
Çukurca, *Turk.* 37°14′ N, 43°30′ E 195
Cùl Mór, peak, *U.K.* 58°2′ N, 5°13′ W 150
Culasi, *Philippines* 11°25′ N, 122°5′ E 203
Culbertson, *Nebr., U.S.* 40°13′ N, 100°51′ W 90
Culebra, *Col.* 6°6′ N, 69°25′ W 136
Culebra, island, *P.R., U.S.* 18°0′ N, 65°0′ W 118
Culebra, Sierra de la, *Sp.* 41°47′ N, 6°49′ W 150
Culfa, *Azerb.* 38°58′ N, 45°38′ E 195
Culgoa, river, *Austral.* 29°14′ S, 147°34′ E 230
Culiacán, *Mex.* 24°44′ N, 107°34′ W 112
Culiacán, Cerro, peak, *Mex.* 20°18′ N, 101°3′ W 114
Culion, *Philippines* 11°53′ N, 119°59′ E 203
Culiseu, river, *Braz.* 13°23′ S, 53°44′ W 130
Cúllar-Baza, *Sp.* 37°34′ N, 2°34′ W 164
Cullera, *Sp.* 39°9′ N, 0°16′ E 164
Cullman, *Ala., U.S.* 34°12′ N, 86°54′ W 112
Culloden Moor, battle, *U.K.* 57°26′ N, 4°17′ W 150
Cullom, *Ill., U.S.* 40°52′ N, 88°16′ W 102
Cullompton, *U.K.* 50°51′ N, 3°24′ W 162
Culuene, river, *Braz.* 15°7′ S, 54°17′ W 132
Culver, *Ind., U.S.* 41°12′ N, 86°26′ W 102
Culverden, *N.Z.* 42°48′ S, 172°50′ E 240
Cumaná, *Venez.* 10°26′ N, 64°11′ W 116
Cumari, *Braz.* 18°18′ S, 48°11′ W 138
Cumaría, *Peru* 9°54′ S, 73°56′ W 137
Cumberland, *Md., U.S.* 39°39′ N, 78°46′ W 94
Cumberland, *Wis., U.S.* 45°31′ N, 92°1′ W 110

Cumberland House, Can. 53°56′ N, 102°17′ W 108
Cumberland Island, Ga., U.S. 30°47′ N, 81°23′ W 112
Cumberland Island National Seashore, Ga., U.S. 30°38′ N, 81°26′ W 96
Cumberland Islands, Coral Sea 20°47′ S, 149°43′ E 230
Cumberland, Lake, Ky., U.S. 36°52′ N, 85°35′ W 94
Cumberland Peninsula, Can. 66°44′ N, 73°46′ W 106
Cumberland Plateau, North America 34°11′ N, 87°21′ W 96
Cumberland Point, Mich., U.S. 47°38′ N, 89°17′ W 110
Cumberland Sound 64°31′ N, 72°15′ W 73
Cumbrera, Cerro, peak, Chile 48°6′ S, 72°55′ W 134
Cumbres de Majalca National Park see 11, Mex. 28°57′ N, 106°43′ W 112
Cumbres del Ajusco National Park see 10, Mex. 19°12′ N, 99°24′ W 112
Cumbrian Mountains, U.K. 54°43′ N, 3°25′ W 162
Cumming, Mount, Antarctica 76°35′ S, 125°8′ W 248
Cummins Peak, Oreg., U.S. 44°12′ N, 124°4′ W 90
Cúmpas, Mex. 29°58′ N, 109°47′ W 92
Çumra, Turk. 37°33′ N, 32°47′ E 156
Cumshewa Head, Can. 53°4′ N, 131°42′ W 108
Cumuruxatiba, Braz. 17°6′ S, 39°12′ W 132
Cunani, Braz. 2°53′ N, 51°8′ W 130
Cunãré, Col. 0°51′ N, 72°35′ W 136
Cunaviche, Venez. 7°19′ N, 67°27′ W 136
Cunco, Chile 38°55′ S, 72°1′ W 134
Cundinamarca, adm. division, Col. 4°8′ N, 74°27′ W 136
Cunene, adm. division, Angola 17°30′ S, 15°28′ E 220
Cunene, river, Angola 14°3′ S, 15°29′ E 220
Cuneo, It. 44°22′ N, 7°32′ E 167
Cuney, Tex., U.S. 32°1′ N, 95°25′ W 103
Cunhinga, Angola 12°15′ S, 16°46′ E 220
Cunjamba, Angola 15°23′ S, 20°4′ E 220
Cunningham, Tex., U.S. 33°24′ N, 95°22′ W 103
Cunningham Landing, Can. 60°4′ N, 112°8′ W 108
Cunningham Mountain, Ariz., U.S. 33°33′ N, 114°23′ W 101
Cuokkarassa, peak, Nor. 69°57′ N, 24°22′ E 152
Cuorgnè, It. 45°23′ N, 7°38′ E 167
Cupar, U.K. 56°19′ N, 3°1′ W 150
Cupcini, Mold. 48°4′ N, 27°21′ E 152
Cupica, Col. 6°44′ N, 77°32′ W 136
Cúpula, Pico, peak, Mex. 24°45′ N, 110°50′ W 112
Curaçá, Braz. 9°1′ S, 39°52′ W 132
Curaçao, island, Neth. 12°0′ N, 69°0′ W 118
Curaguara de Carangas, Bol. 17°57′ S, 68°23′ W 137
Curale, Eth. 7°38′ N, 44°21′ E 218
Curanilahue, Chile 37°28′ S, 73°25′ W 134
Curanja, river, Peru 10°6′ S, 71°39′ W 137
Curaray, river, Ecua.-Peru 1°24′ S, 77°1′ W 136
Curare, Venez. 2°13′ N, 66°29′ W 136
Curcubăta, peak, Rom. 46°27′ N, 22°37′ E 168
Cure, Eth. 5°47′ N, 36°28′ E 224
Curiapo, Venez. 8°33′ N, 61°2′ W 116
Curichi, Bol. 18°43′ S, 63°17′ W 137
Curicó, Chile 34°57′ S, 71°15′ W 134
Curicuriari, river, Braz. 0°32′ N, 68°34′ W 136
Curicuriari, Serra, peak, Braz. 0°22′ N, 66°57′ W 136
Curiplaya, Col. 0°16′ N, 74°52′ W 136
Curitiba, Braz. 25°25′ S, 49°18′ W 138
Curium, ruin(s), Cyprus 34°40′ N, 32°50′ E 194
Curley Cut Cays, North Atlantic Ocean 23°20′ N, 78°3′ W 116
Curonian Lagoon, Lith.-Russ. 55°9′ N, 20°55′ E 166
Curonian Spit, Lith.-Russ. 55°11′ N, 20°37′ E 166
Currais Novos, Braz. 6°17′ S, 36°32′ W 132
Curralinho, Braz. 1°47′ S, 49°50′ W 130
Currant Mountain, Nev., U.S. 38°53′ N, 115°30′ W 90
Currant, pass, Colo., U.S. 38°51′ N, 105°39′ W 90
Curraun Peninsula, Ire. 53°50′ N, 10°32′ W 150
Currie Lake, lake, Can. 57°45′ N, 98°3′ W 108
Curtici, Rom. 46°21′ N, 21°18′ E 168
Curtis, Nebr., U.S. 40°38′ N, 100°31′ W 90
Curtis Group, islands, Bass Strait 39°55′ S, 144°45′ E 231
Curtis Island, Austral. 24°5′ S, 150°2′ E 230
Curuá, Braz. 2°25′ S, 54°4′ W 130
Curuá, Ilha, island, Braz. 0°52′ N, 50°57′ W 130
Curuá, river, Braz. 0°27′ N, 54°52′ W 130
Curuaés, river, Braz. 7°58′ S, 54°33′ W 130
Curuçá, river, South America 5°12′ S, 71°29′ W 132
Curug, Serb. 45°28′ N, 20°3′ E 168
Curupaiti, Braz. 3°25′ S, 68°53′ W 136
Curupira, Serra, Braz. 1°36′ N, 64°19′ W 130
Cururu, river, Braz. 8°4′ S, 57°21′ W 130
Cururupu, Braz. 1°47′ S, 44°54′ W 132
Curutú, Cerro, peak, Venez. 4°16′ N, 63°45′ W 130
Curuzú Cuatiá, Arg. 29°46′ S, 58°3′ W 139
Curvelo, Braz. 18°45′ S, 44°27′ W 138
Cusárare, Mex. 27°33′ N, 107°33′ W 82
Cusco, Peru 13°33′ S, 71°57′ W 137
Cusco, adm. division, Peru 13°5′ S, 72°47′ W 137
Cushing, Okla., U.S. 35°57′ N, 96°45′ W 96
Cushing, Tex., U.S. 31°48′ N, 94°50′ W 103
Cushing, Mount, Can. 57°36′ N, 126°57′ W 108
Cushman, Lake, Wash., U.S. 47°29′ N, 123°26′ W 100
Cusiana, river, Col. 4°44′ N, 72°25′ W 136
Cusihuiriachic, Mex. 28°14′ N, 106°51′ W 92
Cusset, Fr. 46°8′ N, 3°27′ E 150
Cusson, Pointe, Can. 60°11′ N, 77°35′ W 106
Custer, Mich., U.S. 43°56′ N, 86°13′ W 102
Custer, Mont., U.S. 46°7′ N, 107°33′ W 90
Custer, Wash., U.S. 48°54′ N, 122°39′ W 100
Cut Bank, Mont., U.S. 48°37′ N, 112°20′ W 90
Cut Beaver Lake, Can. 53°47′ N, 103°9′ W 108
Cut Knife, Can. 52°45′ N, 109°1′ W 108
Cut Off, La., U.S. 29°32′ N, 90°20′ W 103
Cutbank, river, Can. 54°21′ N, 119°20′ W 108
Cutchogue, N.Y., U.S. 41°0′ N, 72°30′ W 104
Cutler, Calif., U.S. 36°31′ N, 119°18′ W 100
Cutler Ridge, Fla., U.S. 25°33′ N, 80°22′ W 105
Cutlerville, Mich., U.S. 42°49′ N, 85°40′ W 102
Cuttack, India 20°25′ N, 85°52′ E 188
Cuttingsville, Vt., U.S. 43°29′ N, 72°53′ W 104
Cuttyhunk, Mass., U.S. 41°25′ N, 70°57′ W 104
Cuttyhunk Island, Mass., U.S. 41°25′ N, 71°15′ W 104
Cutzamala, Mex. 18°26′ N, 100°36′ W 114
Cuveşdia, Rom. 45°57′ N, 21°42′ E 168
Cuvier Plateau, Indian Ocean 24°32′ S, 108°34′ E 254
Cuxhaven, Ger. 53°51′ N, 8°42′ E 150
Cuya, Chile 19°12′ S, 70°12′ W 137
Cuyahoga Falls, Ohio, U.S. 41°9′ N, 81°29′ W 102
Cuyama, Calif., U.S. 34°56′ N, 119°38′ W 100
Cuyapo, Philippines 15°47′ N, 120°39′ E 203
Cuyuna Range, Minn., U.S. 46°24′ N, 94°0′ W 90
Cuyuni, river, Guyana 6°50′ N, 60°6′ W 130
Cvrsnica, Bosn. and Herzg. 43°31′ N, 17°25′ E 168
Cwmbran, U.K. 51°38′ N, 3°1′ W 162
Cybur, Miss., U.S. 30°36′ N, 89°46′ W 103
Cyclades see Kikládes, islands, Mediterranean Sea 36°31′ N, 24°28′ E 156
Cygnet Lake, lake, Can. 56°45′ N, 95°21′ W 108
Cynthiana, Ky., U.S. 38°23′ N, 84°17′ W 94
Cypress Hills, Can. 49°34′ N, 110°46′ W 80
Cypress Lake, Can. 49°29′ N, 109°47′ W 90
Cyprus 35°2′ N, 33°17′ E 194
Cyrenaica, region, Africa 26°14′ N, 24°46′ E 180
Cyrene see Shahhât, Lib. 32°50′ N, 21°50′ E 216
Cyrus Field Bay 62°29′ N, 66°6′ W 106
Czech Republic (Czechia) 49°41′ N, 14°5′ E 152
Czechia see Czech Republic 49°41′ N, 14°5′ E 152
Czempiń, Pol. 52°8′ N, 16°46′ E 152
Czeremcha, Pol. 52°31′ N, 23°18′ E 154
Czersk, Pol. 53°47′ N, 17°58′ E 152
Czerwin, Pol. 52°55′ N, 21°44′ E 152
Częstochowa, Pol. 50°48′ N, 19°6′ E 152
Czyżewo, Pol. 52°48′ N, 22°17′ E 152

D

Da (Black), river, Vietnam 21°11′ N, 104°8′ E 202
Da Lat, Vietnam 11°56′ N, 108°26′ E 202
Da Nang, Vietnam 16°2′ N, 108°12′ E 202
Da Qaidam, China 37°52′ N, 95°25′ E 188
Daaden, Ger. 50°43′ N, 7°58′ E 167
Da'an, China 45°28′ N, 124°20′ E 198
Dabaga, Tanzania 8°5′ S, 35°55′ E 224
Ḑab'ah, Jordan 31°35′ N, 36°2′ E 194
Dabajuro, Venez. 11°2′ N, 70°42′ W 136
Dabakala, Côte d'Ivoire 8°21′ N, 4°27′ W 222
Dabas, Hung. 47°10′ N, 19°20′ E 168
Dabat, Eth. 12°58′ N, 37°42′ E 182
Dabatou, Guinea 11°49′ N, 10°41′ W 222
Dabeiba, Col. 7°2′ N, 76°17′ W 136
Dabhoi, India 22°5′ N, 73°27′ E 186
Dabilja, Maced. 41°27′ N, 22°42′ E 168
Daboji, China 42°57′ N, 126°51′ E 200
Dabola, Guinea 10°44′ N, 11°9′ W 222
Daborow, Somalia 6°21′ N, 48°43′ E 218
Dabou, Côte d'Ivoire 5°19′ N, 4°23′ W 222
Daboya, Ghana 9°31′ N, 1°26′ W 222
Dabqig see Uxin Qi, China 38°24′ N, 108°59′ E 198
Dabsan Hu, lake, China 37°1′ N, 94°22′ E 188
Dâbûd, Egypt 24°34′ N, 32°55′ E 182
Dabuli, Eth. 7°48′ N, 41°8′ E 224
Dabus, river, Eth. 9°44′ N, 34°54′ E 224
Dabwali, India 29°57′ N, 74°45′ E 186
Dac To, Vietnam 14°43′ N, 107°47′ E 202
Dachang, China 24°50′ N, 107°31′ E 198
Dachigam National Park, India 34°9′ N, 74°57′ E 186
Daday, Turk. 41°30′ N, 33°26′ E 156
Dadda'to, Djibouti 12°20′ N, 42°46′ E 182
Dade City, Fla., U.S. 28°21′ N, 82°12′ W 105
Dadhar, Pak. 29°30′ N, 67°41′ E 186
Dadianzi, China 42°52′ N, 128°17′ E 200
Dadiya, Nig. 9°36′ N, 11°26′ E 222
Ḑadnah, U.A.E. 25°32′ N, 56°16′ E 196
Dadu, Pak. 26°43′ N, 67°50′ E 186
Daegu (Taegu), S. Korea 35°51′ N, 128°37′ E 200
Daegu City, adm. division, S. Korea 35°48′ N, 128°33′ E 200
Daejeon (Taejŏn), S. Korea 36°18′ N, 127°27′ E 200
Daejeon City, adm. division, S. Korea 36°20′ N, 127°25′ E 200
Dăeni, Rom. 44°50′ N, 28°6′ E 156
Daet, Philippines 14°7′ N, 122°56′ E 203
Dafang, China 27°8′ N, 105°33′ E 198
Dafeng, China 33°15′ N, 120°29′ E 198
Dafoe, Can. 51°44′ N, 104°31′ W 90
Dafoe Lake, lake, Can. 55°38′ N, 96°50′ W 108
Dafoe, river, Can. 55°44′ N, 95°16′ W 108
Daga Medo, Eth. 7°57′ N, 42°59′ E 218
Daga Post, Sudan 9°11′ N, 33°57′ E 224
Dagaio, Eth. 6°10′ N, 40°42′ E 224
Dagana, Senegal 16°30′ N, 15°33′ W 222
Dagda, Latv. 56°5′ N, 27°30′ E 166
Dagestan, adm. division, Russ. 42°34′ N, 46°10′ E 195
Dagestanskiye Ogni, Russ. 42°4′ N, 48°17′ E 195
Daggett, Calif., U.S. 34°51′ N, 116°54′ W 101
Daggett, Mich., U.S. 45°27′ N, 87°36′ W 94
Dagö see Hiiumaa, island, Est. 58°49′ N, 21°20′ E 166
Dagongcha, China 39°44′ N, 96°6′ E 188
Dagujiazi, China 42°18′ N, 123°24′ E 200
Dagupan, Philippines 16°2′ N, 120°19′ E 203
Dagzê, China 29°40′ N, 91°19′ E 197
Dahaneh-ye Ghowri, Afghan. 35°54′ N, 68°33′ E 186
Dahlak Archipelago, Red Sea 16°13′ N, 39°29′ E 182
Dahlak Kebir, island, Eritrea 15°28′ N, 39°33′ E 182
Dahmouni, Alg. 35°24′ N, 1°28′ E 150
Dahn, Ger. 49°8′ N, 7°46′ E 163
Dahod, India 22°48′ N, 74°15′ E 188
Dahongliutan, China 36°0′ N, 79°19′ E 188
Dahra, Senegal 15°22′ N, 15°29′ W 222
Dahra, oil field, Lib. 29°27′ N, 17°37′ E 216
Dahuofang Shuiku, lake, China 41°55′ N, 123°58′ E 200
Dahy, Nafūd ad, Saudi Arabia 21°51′ N, 45°20′ E 182
Daïet Abeidi, spring, Mali 21°42′ N, 5°43′ W 222
Daigo, Japan 36°45′ N, 140°20′ E 201
Dailekh, Nepal 28°50′ N, 81°44′ E 197
Daimiel, Sp. 39°3′ N, 3°38′ W 164
Daingerfield, Tex., U.S. 33°1′ N, 94°44′ W 103
Dainkog, China 32°30′ N, 97°52′ E 188
Daintree River National Park, Austral. 16°21′ S, 144°50′ E 238
Daiō, Japan 34°17′ N, 136°53′ E 201
Dair, Jebel ed, peak, Sudan 12°27′ N, 30°36′ E 218
Daireaux, Arg. 36°37′ S, 61°42′ W 139
Dairen see Dalian, China 38°56′ N, 121°33′ E 198
Dairûţ, Egypt 27°35′ N, 30°47′ E 180
Daisen-Oki National Park, Japan 35°16′ N, 133°3′ E 201
Daisetta, Tex., U.S. 30°6′ N, 94°39′ W 103
Daitō, Japan 35°18′ N, 132°58′ E 201
Daitō Islands, Philippine Sea 24°48′ N, 129°27′ E 190
Daixian, China 39°3′ N, 112°55′ E 198
Dajarra, Austral. 21°41′ S, 139°34′ E 231
Dajt, Mal, peak, Alban. 41°21′ N, 19°50′ E 156
Dajt National Park, Alban. 41°20′ N, 19°52′ E 156
Dakar, Senegal 14°39′ N, 17°13′ W 222
Daketa, river, Eth. 8°52′ N, 42°24′ E 224
Dakhfili, Sudan 19°15′ N, 32°32′ E 182
Dakhla, El Wâhât el, Egypt 25°35′ N, 28°10′ E 180
Dakingari, Nig. 11°38′ N, 4°4′ E 222
Dakoank, India 7°4′ N, 93°45′ E 188
Dakoro, Niger 14°35′ N, 6°48′ E 222
Đakovica see Gjakova, Kosovo 42°23′ N, 20°26′ E 168
Đakovo, Croatia 45°18′ N, 18°24′ E 168
Dákura, Nicar. 14°22′ N, 83°14′ W 115
Dakwa, Dem. Rep. of the Congo 3°59′ N, 26°29′ E 224
Dala, Angola 11°5′ S, 20°14′ E 220
Dalaba, Guinea 10°41′ N, 12°18′ W 222
Dalai Nur, lake, China 43°13′ N, 116°7′ E 198
Dalandzadgad, Mongolia 43°33′ N, 104°23′ E 198
Dalane, region, Europe 58°31′ N, 6°0′ E 150
Dalarö, Sw. 59°8′ N, 18°23′ E 166
Dalbandin, Pak. 28°55′ N, 64°27′ E 182
Dalbosjön, lake, Nor. 58°41′ N, 12°30′ E 152
Dale, Nor. 60°35′ N, 5°47′ E 152
Dale, Nor. 61°27′ N, 7°25′ E 152
Dale Country, region, Europe 53°35′ N, 1°46′ W 162
Dale Hollow Lake, U.S. 36°33′ N, 86°33′ W 82
Dalen, Nor. 59°27′ N, 7°58′ E 152
Dalet, Myanmar 19°59′ N, 93°57′ E 188
Daleville, Miss., U.S. 32°33′ N, 88°41′ W 103
Dalfors, Nor. 61°12′ N, 15°24′ E 152
Dalgaranga Hill, Austral. 27°54′ S, 116°54′ E 230
Dalhart, Tex., U.S. 36°3′ N, 102°32′ W 92
Dalhousie, Cape, Can. 70°7′ N, 132°37′ W 98
Dali, China 34°50′ N, 109°57′ E 198
Dali, China 25°40′ N, 99°58′ E 190
Dali, Cyprus 35°1′ N, 33°25′ E 194
Dalian (Dairen), China 38°56′ N, 121°33′ E 198
Dalias, Sp. 36°49′ N, 2°52′ W 164
Dalidag see Mets Beverratap, peak, Azerb. 39°54′ N, 46°0′ E 195
Dalizi, China 41°44′ N, 126°48′ E 200
Dalj, Croatia 45°29′ N, 18°57′ E 168
Dall Island, Alas., U.S. 54°35′ N, 135°26′ W 106
Dall, river, Can. 58°41′ N, 127°56′ W 108
Dallas, Oreg., U.S. 44°54′ N, 123°21′ W 82
Dallas, Tex., U.S. 32°46′ N, 96°48′ W 96
Dallas Naval Air Station, Tex., U.S. 32°41′ N, 97°0′ W 92
Dalmā, island, U.A.E. 24°34′ N, 51°58′ E 182
Dalmas, Lac, lake, Can. 53°27′ N, 72°16′ W 111
Dalmatia, region, Adriatic Sea 42°51′ N, 17°2′ E 168
Dal'negorsk, Russ. 44°34′ N, 135°35′ E 238
Dal'nerechensk, Russ. 45°53′ N, 133°51′ E 190
Daloa, Côte d'Ivoire 6°48′ N, 6°27′ W 222
Dalol, Eth. 14°8′ N, 40°15′ E 182
Dalqān, spring, Saudi Arabia 24°17′ N, 45°32′ E 182
Dalsbruk (Taalintehdas), Fin. 60°1′ N, 22°31′ E 166
Daltenganj, India 24°1′ N, 84°8′ E 197
Dalton, Ga., U.S. 34°45′ N, 84°57′ W 96
Dalton, Mass., U.S. 42°28′ N, 73°10′ W 104
Dalton, Nebr., U.S. 41°24′ N, 102°59′ W 90
Dalton, Wis., U.S. 43°38′ N, 89°12′ W 102
Dalton in Furness, U.K. 54°9′ N, 3°11′ W 162
Dalton, Kap, Den. 69°11′ N, 24°2′ W 246
Dalum, Ger. 52°35′ N, 7°13′ E 163
Dalupiri, island, Philippines 19°10′ N, 120°43′ E 198
Dalwallinu, Austral. 30°16′ S, 116°41′ E 231
Daly City, Calif., U.S. 37°42′ N, 122°29′ W 100
Daly Lake, lake, Can. 56°26′ N, 106°4′ W 108
Daly, river, Austral. 13°35′ S, 130°35′ E 231
Daly River Wildlife Sanctuary, Austral. 13°42′ S, 129°44′ E 238
Daly Waters, Austral. 16°15′ S, 133°20′ E 231
Dam Doi, Vietnam 9°2′ N, 105°10′ E 202
Dam Gamad, Sudan 13°14′ N, 27°26′ E 226
Damagarim, region, Africa 14°13′ N, 7°35′ E 222
Daman and Diu, adm. division, India 20°18′ N, 71°51′ E 188
Daman (Damão), India 20°25′ N, 72°52′ E 186
Damanava, Belarus 52°49′ N, 25°30′ E 152
Damane, spring, Mauritania 19°20′ N, 14°33′ W 222
Damanhûr, Egypt 31°1′ N, 30°22′ E 180
Damão see Daman, India 20°25′ N, 72°52′ E 186
Damar, island, Indonesia 7°28′ S, 127°44′ E 192
Damara, Cen. Af. Rep. 4°57′ N, 18°43′ E 218
Damaraland, region, Africa 21°4′ S, 15°26′ E 227
Damas Cays, North Atlantic Ocean 23°23′ N, 80°1′ W 116
Damasak, Nig. 13°8′ N, 12°33′ E 216
Damascus see Dimashq, Syr. 33°30′ N, 36°14′ E 194
Damaturu, Nig. 11°44′ N, 11°55′ E 222
Damāvand, Qolleh-ye, peak, Iran 35°58′ N, 52°0′ E 180
Damba, Angola 6°41′ S, 15°7′ E 218
Dambarta, Nig. 12°26′ N, 8°31′ E 222
Damboa, Nig. 11°10′ N, 12°49′ E 216
Damergou, region, Africa 14°49′ N, 9°0′ E 222
Dāmghān, Iran 36°11′ N, 54°19′ E 180
Damietta see Dumyâţ, Egypt 31°25′ N, 31°49′ E 180
Daming, China 36°15′ N, 115°8′ E 198
Damingzhen, China 42°32′ N, 123°40′ E 200
Damīr Qābū, Syr. 36°57′ N, 41°52′ E 195
Dāmiyā, Jordan 32°6′ N, 35°33′ E 194
Dammarie, Fr. 48°20′ N, 1°29′ E 163
Dammartin-en-Goële, Fr. 49°2′ N, 2°40′ E 163
Damme, Ger. 52°31′ N, 8°12′ E 163
Damongo, Ghana 9°4′ N, 1°49′ W 222
Damour, Leb. 33°43′ N, 35°27′ E 194
Damous, Alg. 36°32′ N, 1°43′ E 150
Dampier, Austral. 20°40′ S, 116°43′ E 231
Dampier Archipelago, Indian Ocean 20°18′ S, 117°11′ E 230
Dampier Land, Austral. 17°35′ S, 122°12′ E 230
Dampierre, Fr. 48°32′ N, 4°21′ E 163
Damqawt, Yemen 16°35′ N, 52°49′ E 182
Damsarkhū, Syr. 35°32′ N, 35°46′ E 194
Damvillers, Fr. 49°20′ N, 5°23′ E 163
Damxung, China 30°35′ N, 91°9′ E 197
Damyang, S. Korea 35°18′ N, 126°59′ E 200
Dan, Israel 33°13′ N, 35°38′ E 194
Dan Gulbi, Nig. 11°35′ N, 6°16′ E 222
Dan, river, N.C., U.S. 36°35′ N, 79°20′ W 80
Dana, Ind., U.S. 39°48′ N, 87°30′ W 102
Ḑānā, Jordan 30°40′ N, 35°36′ E 194
Dana, Mount, Calif., U.S. 37°53′ N, 119°16′ W 100
Dana Point, Calif., U.S. 33°28′ N, 117°43′ W 101
Danané, Côte d'Ivoire 7°8′ N, 8°9′ W 222
Danbury, Conn., U.S. 41°23′ N, 73°28′ W 104
Danbury, Iowa, U.S. 42°13′ N, 95°44′ W 90
Danbury, N.H., U.S. 43°31′ N, 71°53′ W 104
Danbury, Tex., U.S. 29°13′ N, 95°21′ W 103
Danby, Vt., U.S. 43°20′ N, 73°0′ W 104
Dancheng, China 33°37′ N, 115°14′ E 198
Danco Coast, Antarctica 64°6′ S, 61°55′ W 134
Dandéla, Guinea 10°55′ N, 8°24′ W 222
Dandeldhura, Nepal 29°16′ N, 80°34′ E 197
Dandong, China 40°10′ N, 124°24′ E 200
Dandurand, Lac, lake, Can. 47°48′ N, 75°9′ W 94
Dane, Can. 48°5′ N, 80°1′ W 94
Danfa, Mali 14°9′ N, 7°30′ W 222
Danfeng, China 33°42′ N, 110°24′ E 198
Danfina, Mali 11°2′ N, 7°9′ W 222
Danfort Hills, Colo., U.S. 40°20′ N, 108°25′ W 90
Danforth, Me., U.S. 45°39′ N, 67°52′ W 94
Dangara, Taj. 38°15′ N, 69°16′ E 197
Dangchang, China 33°55′ N, 104°25′ E 198
Dange, Angola 7°58′ S, 15°1′ E 218
Danger Islands, Weddell Sea 63°57′ S, 54°20′ W 134
Danger Islands see Pukapuka Atoll, South Pacific Ocean 10°35′ S, 167°12′ W 238
Danger Point, S. Af. 34°53′ S, 19°1′ E 227
Dangé-Saint-Romain, Fr. 46°56′ N, 0°37′ E 150
Dangila, Eth. 11°15′ N, 36°52′ E 182
Dangjin Shankou, pass, China 39°17′ N, 94°15′ E 188
Dango, Sudan 9°58′ N, 24°43′ E 224
Dango, Qoz, Sudan 10°29′ N, 24°11′ E 224
Dangrek Range, Thai. 14°34′ N, 103°21′ E 202
Dangriga, Belize 16°57′ N, 88°15′ W 115
Dangshan, China 34°27′ N, 116°21′ E 198
Dangtu, China 31°34′ N, 118°28′ E 198
Danguya, Cen. Af. Rep. 6°27′ N, 22°41′ E 218
Daniel, Wyo., U.S. 42°52′ N, 110°4′ W 90
Daniel, oil field, Arg. 52°17′ S, 68°54′ W 134
Daniel's Harbour, Can. 50°14′ N, 57°35′ W 111
Danilov, Russ. 58°11′ N, 40°8′ E 154
Danilovgrad, Mont. 42°32′ N, 19°7′ E 168
Danilovka, Russ. 64°42′ N, 57°47′ E 154
Danjiangkou, China 32°34′ N, 111°31′ E 198
Ḑank, Oman 23°32′ N, 56°17′ E 196
Dankov, Russ. 53°14′ N, 39°1′ E 154
Danlí, Hond. 14°1′ N, 86°31′ W 112
Danmark Havn, Den. 76°46′ N, 18°35′ W 246
Dannemora, N.Y., U.S. 44°42′ N, 73°44′ W 94
Dañoso, Cabo, Arg. 49°2′ S, 67°13′ W 134
Dansheha, Eth. 13°30′ N, 36°54′ E 182
Dansville, N.Y., U.S. 42°33′ N, 77°43′ W 94
Danu, Mold. 47°51′ N, 27°30′ E 152
Danube, river, Europe 44°29′ N, 21°15′ E 143
Danvers, Ill., U.S. 40°30′ N, 89°11′ W 102
Danvers, Mass., U.S. 42°33′ N, 70°57′ W 104
Danville, Ill., U.S. 40°9′ N, 87°37′ W 102
Danville, Ind., U.S. 39°45′ N, 86°32′ W 102
Danville, Ky., U.S. 37°38′ N, 84°46′ W 94
Danville, N.H., U.S. 42°54′ N, 71°8′ W 104
Danville, Ohio, U.S. 40°26′ N, 82°16′ W 102
Danville, Va., U.S. 36°34′ N, 79°25′ W 96
Danxian (Nada), China 19°28′ N, 109°34′ E 198
Danzhai, China 26°11′ N, 107°47′ E 198
Dao, Philippines 10°30′ N, 121°57′ E 203
Dao Timmi, Niger 20°33′ N, 13°31′ E 216
Daoxian, China 25°32′ N, 111°34′ E 198
Daozhen, China 28°52′ N, 107°40′ E 198
Dapa, Philippines 9°47′ N, 126°3′ E 203
Dapaong, Togo 10°50′ N, 0°11′ E 222
Dapchi, Nig. 12°29′ N, 11°31′ E 222
Daphne, Ala., U.S. 30°35′ N, 87°54′ W 103
Dapp, Can. 54°20′ N, 113°56′ W 108
Dapuchaihe, China 42°50′ N, 128°1′ E 200
Daqing, China 46°33′ N, 125°6′ E 198
Daqqaq, Sudan 12°57′ N, 26°53′ E 216
Dār B'ishtār, Leb. 34°15′ N, 35°47′ E 194
Dar es Salaam, Tanzania 6°49′ S, 39°6′ E 224
Dar et Touibia, Tun. 35°19′ N, 10°12′ E 156
Dar Rounga, region, Africa 10°24′ N, 23°37′ E 224
Dar'ā (Edrei), Syr. 32°37′ N, 36°6′ E 194
Dārāb, Iran 28°45′ N, 54°33′ E 196
Daraban, Pak. 31°42′ N, 70°22′ E 186
Daraina, Madagascar 13°17′ S, 49°38′ E 220
Darakhiv, Ukr. 49°17′ N, 25°33′ E 152
Darakht-e Yahya, Pak. 31°48′ N, 68°10′ E 186

Darány, *Hung.* 45°59′ N, 17°34′ E 168
Darâw, *Egypt* 24°22′ N, 32°54′ E 182
Darazo, *Nig.* 10°58′ N, 10°25′ E 222
Darbandi Khan Dam, *Iraq* 34°44′ N, 45°3′ E 180
Darbėnai, *Lith.* 56°1′ N, 21°12′ E 166
Darbhanga, *India* 26°10′ N, 85°53′ E 197
D'Arcole Islands, *Indian Ocean* 15°0′ S, 122°41′ E 230
Darda, *Croatia* 45°37′ N, 18°40′ E 168
Dardanelle, *Ark., U.S.* 35°12′ N, 93°10′ W 96
Dardanelle, *Calif., U.S.* 38°20′ N, 119°52′ W 100
Dardanelles see Çanakkale Boğazı, *Turk.* 40°9′ N, 24°58′ E 157
Darende, *Turk.* 38°33′ N, 37°28′ E 156
Darero, river, *Somalia* 9°15′ N, 47°47′ E 218
Darfur, region, *Africa* 11°6′ N, 23°28′ E 224
Darganata, *Turkm.* 40°27′ N, 62°9′ E 180
Dargaz, *Iran* 37°27′ N, 59°6′ E 180
Dargeçit, *Turk.* 37°33′ N, 41°46′ E 195
Dargol, *Niger* 13°54′ N, 1°12′ E 222
Darhan, *Mongolia* 46°43′ N, 109°15′ E 198
Darhan, *Mongolia* 49°31′ N, 105°58′ E 198
Darhan Muminggan Lianheqi (Bailingmiao), *China* 41°41′ N, 110°23′ E 198
Darhan-Uul, adm. division, *Mongolia* 49°29′ N, 105°55′ E 198
Darien, *Conn., U.S.* 41°4′ N, 73°28′ W 104
Darien, *Ga., U.S.* 31°21′ N, 81°27′ W 96
Darién National Park, *Pan.* 7°23′ N, 78°0′ W 136
Darién, Serranía del, *Pan.* 8°31′ N, 77°58′ W 136
Darjiling, *India* 26°58′ N, 88°14′ E 197
Dark Canyon, *Utah, U.S.* 37°48′ N, 110°0′ W 92
Darley Hills, *Antarctica* 80°41′ S, 172°40′ E 248
Darling, *S. Af.* 33°22′ S, 18°19′ E 227
Darling Downs, *Austral.* 27°20′ S, 149°55′ E 230
Darling, river, *Austral.* 31°16′ S, 144°40′ E 230
Darlington, *U.K.* 54°31′ N, 1°34′ W 162
Darlington, *Wis., U.S.* 42°40′ N, 90°6′ W 102
Darmstadt, *Ger.* 49°52′ N, 8°38′ E 167
Darnah (Derna), *Lib.* 32°44′ N, 22°38′ E 216
Darney, *Fr.* 48°5′ N, 6°1′ E 150
Darnley Bay 69°23′ N, 124°25′ W 106
Daroca, *Sp.* 41°6′ N, 1°25′ W 164
Daroot-Korgon, *Kyrg.* 39°32′ N, 72°3′ E 197
Daror, *Eth.* 8°12′ N, 44°30′ E 218
Darou Khoudos, *Senegal* 15°7′ N, 16°40′ W 222
Darovskoy, *Russ.* 58°43′ N, 47°56′ E 154
Darregueira, *Arg.* 37°45′ S, 63°9′ W 139
Darreh Gaz, *Iran* 37°26′ N, 59°4′ E 180
Darrington, *Wash., U.S.* 48°13′ N, 121°38′ W 100
Darrouzett, *Tex., U.S.* 36°25′ N, 100°21′ W 92
Darss, *Ger.* 54°18′ N, 12°27′ E 152
Dartmoor, region, *Europe* 50°45′ N, 4°7′ W 162
Dartmouth, *Can.* 44°40′ N, 63°35′ W 111
Dartmouth, *Mass., U.S.* 41°34′ N, 71°1′ W 104
Daru, *P.N.G.* 9°9′ S, 143°11′ E 192
Daruvar, *Croatia* 45°35′ N, 17°12′ E 168
Darvaza, *Turkm.* 40°5′ N, 58°30′ E 180
Darvel Bay 4°50′ N, 117°51′ E 203
Darwen, *U.K.* 53°42′ N, 2°28′ W 162
Darwendale, *Zimb.* 17°45′ S, 30°32′ E 224
Darwin, *Austral.* 12°30′ S, 130°37′ E 230
Darwin, *Calif., U.S.* 36°15′ N, 117°37′ W 101
Darwin, Isla, island, *Ecua.* 1°8′ N, 92°28′ W 130
Darwin, Mount, *Calif., U.S.* 37°10′ N, 118°43′ W 101
Darya Khan, *Pak.* 31°47′ N, 71°11′ E 186
Dārzīn, *Iran* 29°6′ N, 58°8′ E 196
Das, *Pak.* 35°6′ N, 75°5′ E 186
D'Asagny National Park, *Côte d'Ivoire* 5°11′ N, 4°56′ W 222
Dasburg, *Ger.* 50°2′ N, 6°8′ E 167
Dashbalbar, *Mongolia* 49°31′ N, 114°22′ E 198
Dashkäsän, *Azerb.* 40°30′ N, 46°3′ E 195
Dashkuduk, *Turkm.* 40°37′ N, 52°53′ E 158
Dasht, river, *Pak.* 25°37′ N, 61°59′ E 182
Dasht-e Navar, marsh, *Afghan.* 33°40′ N, 67°7′ E 186
Daşköpri, *Turkm.* 36°18′ N, 62°36′ E 186
Daşoguz, *Turkm.* 41°51′ N, 59°58′ E 180
Dassa-Zoume, *Benin* 7°44′ N, 2°12′ E 222
Dassel, *Ger.* 51°47′ N, 9°40′ E 167
Datça, *Turk.* 36°44′ N, 27°39′ E 156
Dateland, *Ariz., U.S.* 32°47′ N, 113°32′ W 101
Datia, *India* 25°38′ N, 78°26′ E 197
Datian, *China* 25°40′ N, 117°51′ E 198
Datong, *China* 40°7′ N, 113°14′ E 198
Datteln, *Ger.* 51°39′ N, 7°20′ E 167
Datu Piang, *Philippines* 7°2′ N, 124°28′ E 203
Datu, Tanjong, *Malaysia* 2°8′ N, 109°23′ E 196
Datuk, island, *Indonesia* 0°12′ N, 108°14′ E 196
Daud Khel, *Pak.* 32°52′ N, 71°40′ E 186
Daudnagar, *India* 25°0′ N, 84°23′ E 197
Daugaard-Jensen Land, *Den.* 80°8′ N, 63°33′ W 246
Daugai, *Lith.* 54°22′ N, 24°20′ E 166
Daugava, river, *Latv.* 56°17′ N, 26°13′ E 166
Daugava, river, *Latv.* 56°46′ N, 24°10′ E 166
Daugavpils, *Latv.* 55°51′ N, 26°30′ E 166
Dauli, *Somalia* 8°48′ N, 50°26′ E 216
Daun, *Ger.* 50°11′ N, 6°49′ E 167
D'Aunay Bugt 68°49′ N, 28°49′ W 246
Daung Kyun, island, *Myanmar* 12°6′ N, 98°7′ E 202
Dauphin, *Can.* 51°8′ N, 100°3′ W 90
Dauphin Island, *Ala., U.S.* 30°6′ N, 88°18′ W 103
Dauphin Lake, *Can.* 51°16′ N, 100°32′ W 81
Dauphin, Péninsule du, *Can.* 51°18′ N, 72°54′ W 110
Dauphiné, region, *Europe* 44°22′ N, 4°50′ E 165
Däväçi, *Azerb.* 41°11′ N, 48°59′ E 195
Davangere, *India* 14°27′ N, 75°55′ E 188
Davant, *La., U.S.* 29°36′ N, 89°53′ W 103
Davao, *Philippines* 7°7′ N, 125°36′ E 203
Dāvar Panāh, *Iran* 27°18′ N, 62°21′ E 182
Davegoriale, *Somalia* 8°43′ N, 44°52′ E 218
Davenport, *Calif., U.S.* 37°0′ N, 122°12′ W 100
Davenport, *Fla., U.S.* 28°9′ N, 81°37′ W 105
Davenport, *Iowa, U.S.* 41°32′ N, 90°37′ W 110
Davenport, Mount, *Austral.* 22°28′ S, 130°38′ E 230
Daventry, *U.K.* 52°15′ N, 1°10′ W 162
David, *Pan.* 8°22′ N, 82°19′ W 123
Davidson, *Can.* 51°16′ N, 106°0′ W 90
Davie, *Fla., U.S.* 26°3′ N, 80°15′ W 105
Davies, Cape, *Antarctica* 71°35′ S, 100°20′ W 248
Davis, *Calif., U.S.* 38°32′ N, 121°46′ W 90
Davis, *Okla., U.S.* 34°29′ N, 97°7′ W 92
Davis Dam, *Ariz., U.S.* 35°10′ N, 114°34′ W 101
Davis Dam, *Nev., U.S.* 35°12′ N, 114°37′ W 101
Davis Inlet, *Can.* 55°53′ N, 60°48′ W 106
Davis Islands, *Indian Ocean* 66°35′ S, 108°0′ E 248
Davis, Mount, *Pa., U.S.* 39°46′ N, 79°16′ W 94
Davis Mountains, *Tex., U.S.* 30°44′ N, 104°13′ W 92
Davis Sea 66°31′ S, 89°40′ E 248
Davis, station, *Antarctica* 68°30′ S, 78°25′ E 248
Davis Strait 70°31′ N, 60°40′ W 73
Davison, *Mich., U.S.* 43°1′ N, 83°30′ W 102
Davlekanovo, *Russ.* 54°14′ N, 54°58′ E 154
Davlos, *Northern Cyprus, Cyprus* 35°24′ N, 33°54′ E 194
Davor, *Croatia* 45°7′ N, 17°29′ E 168
Davos, *Switz.* 46°47′ N, 9°47′ E 167
Davy Lake, *Can.* 58°51′ N, 108°49′ W 108
Dawa, river, *Eth.* 4°42′ N, 39°44′ E 224
Dawadawa, *Ghana* 8°21′ N, 1°35′ W 222
Dawei, *Myanmar* 14°5′ N, 98°13′ E 202
Dawhinava, *Belarus* 54°39′ N, 27°26′ E 166
Dawkah, *Oman* 18°41′ N, 53°58′ E 182
Dawmat al Jandal, *Saudi Arabia* 29°47′ N, 39°53′ E 180
Dawna Range, *Myanmar* 16°49′ N, 98°1′ E 202
Dawqah, *Saudi Arabia* 19°35′ N, 40°55′ E 182
Dawra, *Western Sahara, Mor.* 27°27′ N, 13°0′ W 214
Dawros Head, *Ire.* 54°48′ N, 8°57′ W 150
Dawson, *Can.* 64°5′ N, 139°18′ W 98
Dawson City see Dawson, *Can.* 64°5′ N, 139°18′ W 98
Dawson, *Ga., U.S.* 31°45′ N, 84°27′ W 96
Dawson, *Minn., U.S.* 44°55′ N, 96°4′ W 90
Dawson, *N. Dak., U.S.* 46°51′ N, 99°46′ W 90
Dawson, *Tex., U.S.* 31°52′ N, 96°41′ W 96
Dawson Bay 52°50′ N, 101°22′ W 108
Dawson Creek, *Can.* 55°44′ N, 120°16′ W 108
Dawson, Isla, island, *Chile* 54°10′ S, 70°9′ W 134
Dawson, Mount, *Can.* 51°8′ N, 117°32′ W 90
Dawson Springs, *Ky., U.S.* 37°9′ N, 87°41′ W 96
Dawu, *China* 31°30′ N, 114°4′ E 198
Dawukou see Shizuishan, *China* 39°4′ N, 106°25′ E 198
Dawwah, *Oman* 20°39′ N, 58°53′ E 182
Dax, *Fr.* 43°42′ N, 1°3′ W 150
Daxian, *China* 31°15′ N, 107°24′ E 198
Daxing, *China* 39°44′ N, 116°19′ E 198
Dayang, river, *China* 40°15′ N, 123°18′ E 200
Dayet el Khadra, spring, *Alg.* 27°25′ N, 8°30′ W 214
Daying, *China* 42°8′ N, 127°17′ E 200
Daylight Pass, *Calif., U.S.* 36°46′ N, 116°57′ W 101
Daymán, river, *Uru.* 31°34′ S, 57°40′ W 139
Dayong, *China* 29°8′ N, 110°35′ E 198
Dayr Abū Sa'īd, *Jordan* 32°29′ N, 35°41′ E 194
Dayr al A'mar, *Leb.* 34°7′ N, 36°7′ E 194
Dayr al Balaḩ, *Gaza Strip, Israel* 31°25′ N, 34°21′ E 194
Dayr 'Aţīyah, *Syr.* 34°5′ N, 36°46′ E 194
Dayr az Zawr, *Syr.* 35°19′ N, 40°5′ E 180
Daysland, *Can.* 52°51′ N, 112°17′ W 108
Dayton, *Nev., U.S.* 39°15′ N, 119°37′ W 90
Dayton, *Ohio, U.S.* 39°44′ N, 84°11′ W 102
Dayton, *Tenn., U.S.* 35°29′ N, 85°1′ W 96
Dayton, *Tex., U.S.* 30°1′ N, 94°54′ W 103
Dayton, *Wash., U.S.* 46°18′ N, 117°58′ W 82
Dayton, *Wyo., U.S.* 44°50′ N, 107°16′ W 90
Daytona Beach, *Fla., U.S.* 29°13′ N, 81°3′ W 105
Dayu, *China* 25°24′ N, 114°19′ E 198
Dayville, *Conn., U.S.* 41°50′ N, 71°54′ W 104
Dazhu, *China* 30°46′ N, 107°15′ E 198
Dazkırı, *Turk.* 37°54′ N, 29°51′ E 156
Dazu, *China* 29°46′ N, 105°44′ E 198
Dchira, *Western Sahara, Mor.* 27°1′ N, 13°3′ W 214
De Aar, *S. Af.* 30°39′ S, 23°59′ E 227
De Beque, *Colo., U.S.* 39°20′ N, 108°13′ W 90
De Berry, *Tex., U.S.* 32°17′ N, 94°11′ W 103
De Cocksdorp, *Neth.* 53°9′ N, 4°51′ E 163
De Forest, *Wis., U.S.* 43°15′ N, 89°21′ W 102
De Graff, *Ohio, U.S.* 40°18′ N, 83°55′ W 102
De Kalb, *Miss., U.S.* 32°44′ N, 88°39′ W 103
De Kalb, *Tex., U.S.* 33°30′ N, 94°38′ W 96
De Kastri, *Russ.* 51°38′ N, 140°35′ E 190
De la Garma, *Arg.* 37°58′ S, 60°25′ W 139
De Land, *Fla., U.S.* 29°1′ N, 81°19′ W 105
De Land, *Ill., U.S.* 40°6′ N, 88°39′ W 102
De Leon Springs, *Fla., U.S.* 29°6′ N, 81°22′ W 105
De Long Mountains, *Alas., U.S.* 68°7′ N, 164°15′ W 98
De Long, Ostrova, islands, *East Siberian Sea* 75°48′ N, 158°9′ E 160
De Queen, *Ark., U.S.* 34°0′ N, 94°21′ W 96
De Quincy, *La., U.S.* 30°26′ N, 93°27′ W 103
De Ridder, *La., U.S.* 30°49′ N, 93°18′ W 103
De Smet, *S. Dak., U.S.* 44°22′ N, 97°35′ W 90
De Soto, *Miss., U.S.* 31°58′ N, 88°43′ W 103
De Soto, *Mo., U.S.* 38°7′ N, 90°34′ W 94
De Soto, *Wis., U.S.* 43°25′ N, 91°12′ W 94
De Tour Village, *Mich., U.S.* 45°59′ N, 83°55′ W 94
De Witt, *Ark., U.S.* 34°16′ N, 91°21′ W 96
De Witt, *Iowa, U.S.* 41°49′ N, 90°32′ W 94
Dead Horse Point, site, *Utah, U.S.* 38°30′ N, 109°47′ W 90
Dead Indian Peak, *Wyo., U.S.* 44°35′ N, 109°42′ W 90
Dead Mountains, *Calif., U.S.* 35°6′ N, 114°50′ W 101
Dead Sea, lake, *Jordan* 31°28′ N, 35°24′ E 194
Deadmans Cay, *Bahamas* 23°7′ N, 75°4′ W 116
Deadman's Cays, *North Atlantic Ocean* 24°6′ N, 80°37′ W 116
Deadmen Valley, *Can.* 61°2′ N, 124°23′ W 108
Deadwood, *Can.* 56°44′ N, 117°30′ W 108
Deadwood, *S. Dak., U.S.* 44°22′ N, 103°42′ W 82
Deadwood Lake, *Can.* 59°0′ N, 129°12′ W 108
Deadwood Reservoir, *Idaho, U.S.* 44°19′ N, 116°4′ W 90
Deakin, *Austral.* 30°46′ S, 128°57′ E 231
Deal, *U.K.* 51°13′ N, 1°23′ E 163
De'an, *China* 29°18′ N, 115°45′ E 198
Dean Channel 52°33′ N, 127°44′ W 108
Deán Funes, *Arg.* 30°25′ S, 64°21′ W 134
Dean Island, *Antarctica* 74°22′ S, 126°8′ W 248
Dean, river, *Can.* 52°53′ N, 126°11′ W 108
Dearborn, *Mich., U.S.* 42°18′ N, 83°13′ W 102
Dearg, Beinn, peak, *U.K.* 56°51′ N, 4°0′ W 150
Dearg, Beinn, peak, *U.K.* 57°45′ N, 5°3′ W 150
Dease Arm 66°42′ N, 120°16′ W 98
Dease Inlet 70°56′ N, 156°54′ W 98
Dease Lake, *Can.* 58°27′ N, 130°4′ W 108
Dease, river, *Can.* 58°54′ N, 130°11′ W 108
Dease Strait 69°0′ N, 106°42′ W 246
Death Valley, *Calif., U.S.* 36°27′ N, 116°53′ W 101
Death Valley Junction, *Calif., U.S.* 36°17′ N, 116°26′ W 101
Death Valley National Park (Devils Hole), *Nev., U.S.* 36°25′ N, 116°19′ W 101
Deatley Island, *Antarctica* 73°45′ S, 73°41′ W 248
Debao, *China* 23°16′ N, 106°34′ E 198
Debar, *Maced.* 41°31′ N, 20°32′ E 168
Debark', *Eth.* 13°12′ N, 37°51′ E 182
Debary, *Fla., U.S.* 28°53′ N, 81°19′ W 105
Debden, *Can.* 53°31′ N, 106°52′ W 108
Debdou, *Mor.* 34°0′ N, 3°2′ W 214
Dębek, *Pol.* 54°48′ N, 18°5′ E 152
Debelica, *Serb.* 43°39′ N, 22°15′ E 168
Debenham, *U.K.* 52°13′ N, 1°10′ E 162
Débéré, *Mali* 15°5′ N, 3°1′ W 222
Debikut, *India* 25°21′ N, 88°32′ E 197
Debin, *Russ.* 62°18′ N, 150°29′ E 160
Debir, ruin(s), *Israel* 31°27′ N, 34°51′ E 194
Dęblin, *Pol.* 51°33′ N, 21°50′ E 152
Débo, Lake, *Mali* 15°13′ N, 4°26′ W 222
Debrc, *Serb.* 44°36′ N, 19°53′ E 168
Debre Birhan, *Eth.* 9°39′ N, 39°31′ E 224
Debre Mark'os, *Eth.* 10°19′ N, 37°42′ E 224
Debre Tabor, *Eth.* 11°50′ N, 38°0′ E 182
Debre Zebīt, *Eth.* 11°48′ N, 38°35′ E 182
Debre Zeyit, *Eth.* 10°36′ N, 35°42′ E 224
Debrecen, *Hung.* 47°31′ N, 21°38′ E 168
Debrzno, *Pol.* 53°32′ N, 17°14′ E 152
Decamere, *Eritrea* 15°4′ N, 39°4′ E 182
Deçan (Dečani), *Kosovo* 42°31′ N, 20°18′ E 168
Dečani see Deçan, *Kosovo* 42°31′ N, 20°18′ E 168
Decatur, *Ill., U.S.* 39°50′ N, 88°57′ W 102
Decatur, *Ind., U.S.* 40°49′ N, 84°56′ W 102
Decatur, *Mich., U.S.* 42°6′ N, 85°58′ W 102
Decatur, *Miss., U.S.* 32°25′ N, 89°7′ W 103
Decatur, *Mo., U.S.* 39°50′ N, 88°57′ W 94
Decatur, *Tex., U.S.* 33°13′ N, 97°35′ W 92
Deception Island, *Antarctica* 63°16′ S, 60°43′ W 134
Dechu, *India* 26°47′ N, 72°19′ E 186
Deckerville, *Mich., U.S.* 43°31′ N, 82°44′ W 102
Decorah, *Iowa, U.S.* 43°17′ N, 91°48′ W 94
Deddington, *U.K.* 51°58′ N, 1°20′ W 162
Dededo, *Guam, U.S.* 14°0′ N, 147°0′ E 242
Dedegöl Dağı, peak, *Turk.* 37°37′ N, 31°12′ E 156
Deder, *Eth.* 9°17′ N, 41°26′ E 224
Dedham, *Mass., U.S.* 42°14′ N, 71°11′ W 104
Dedino, *Maced.* 41°34′ N, 22°25′ E 168
Dédougou, *Burkina Faso* 12°27′ N, 3°28′ W 222
Dedovichi, *Russ.* 57°32′ N, 30°0′ E 166
Dedu, *China* 48°30′ N, 126°9′ E 198
Dedza, *Malawi* 14°23′ S, 34°16′ E 224
Dee, river, *Ire.* 53°51′ N, 6°42′ W 150
Dee, river, *U.K.* 53°5′ N, 2°53′ W 162
Deep Bay 61°13′ N, 117°11′ W 108
Deep Bay see Chilumba, *Malawi* 10°24′ S, 34°13′ E 224
Deep Crater, *Calif., U.S.* 41°26′ N, 121°38′ W 90
Deep Creek, *Bahamas* 24°49′ N, 76°17′ W 96
Deep Creek Peak, *Idaho, U.S.* 42°28′ N, 112°43′ W 90
Deep Creek Range, *Utah, U.S.* 39°36′ N, 114°20′ W 90
Deep River, *Can.* 46°6′ N, 77°31′ W 94
Deep River, *Conn., U.S.* 41°23′ N, 72°27′ W 104
Deer Creek, *Ill., U.S.* 40°37′ N, 89°20′ W 102
Deer Lake, *Can.* 52°40′ N, 94°59′ W 81
Deer Lake, *Can.* 49°1′ N, 58°2′ W 111
Deer Lodge, *Mont., U.S.* 46°23′ N, 112°44′ W 90
Deer Park, *Ala., U.S.* 31°12′ N, 88°19′ W 103
Deer River, *Minn., U.S.* 47°19′ N, 93°49′ W 94
Deer, river, *Can.* 57°36′ N, 94°32′ W 108
Deer Trail, *Colo., U.S.* 39°36′ N, 104°3′ W 90
Deerfield, *Ill., U.S.* 42°10′ N, 87°52′ W 102
Deerfield, *Mass., U.S.* 42°31′ N, 72°37′ W 104
Deerfield, *N.H., U.S.* 43°8′ N, 71°14′ W 104
Deerfield Beach, *Fla., U.S.* 26°18′ N, 80°7′ W 105
Deerhurst, *U.K.* 51°57′ N, 2°11′ W 162
Deering, *Alas., U.S.* 65°54′ N, 162°50′ W 98
Deeth, *Nev., U.S.* 41°4′ N, 115°17′ W 90
Defa, oil field, *Lib.* 27°45′ N, 19°46′ E 216
Defensores del Chaco National Park, *Parag.* 20°12′ S, 62°1′ W 132
Defiance, *Ohio, U.S.* 41°15′ N, 84°23′ W 102
Défirou, spring, *Niger* 20°33′ N, 15°3′ E 216
Dég, *Hung.* 46°51′ N, 18°27′ E 168
Degana, *India* 26°53′ N, 74°19′ E 186
Deganya, *Israel* 32°41′ N, 35°34′ E 194
Dêgê, *China* 31°51′ N, 98°37′ E 190
Degeh Bur, *Eth.* 8°10′ N, 43°30′ E 218
Degelen, peak, *Kaz.* 49°52′ N, 77°51′ E 184
Degerby, *Fin.* 60°4′ N, 24°9′ E 166
Degerfors, *Nor.* 59°14′ N, 14°22′ E 152
Degerhamn, *Sw.* 56°21′ N, 16°23′ E 152
Dego, *It.* 44°26′ N, 8°19′ E 167
Deh Bīd, *Iran* 30°36′ N, 53°11′ E 180
Deh Khavak, *Afghan.* 35°39′ N, 69°55′ E 186
Deh Mollā, *Iran* 30°33′ N, 49°38′ E 186
Deh Shu, *Afghan.* 30°23′ N, 63°19′ E 186
Dehgam, *India* 23°9′ N, 72°48′ E 186
Dehibat, *Tun.* 32°2′ N, 10°41′ E 214
Dehqonobod, *Uzb.* 38°21′ N, 66°30′ E 197
Dehra Dun, *India* 30°20′ N, 78°2′ E 197
Dehui, *China* 44°30′ N, 125°40′ E 198
Deim Zubeir, *Sudan* 7°42′ N, 26°13′ E 224
Deinze, *Belg.* 50°58′ N, 3°31′ E 163
Deir Mawâs, *Egypt* 27°40′ N, 30°46′ E 180
Dej, *Rom.* 47°8′ N, 23°55′ E 156
Dejë, Mal, peak, *Alban.* 41°41′ N, 20°7′ E 168
Dejen, Ras, peak, *Eth.* 13°11′ N, 38°19′ E 182
Dejiang, *China* 28°16′ N, 108°6′ E 198
Dekalb, *Ill., U.S.* 41°55′ N, 88°44′ W 102
Dekese, *Dem. Rep. of the Congo* 3°29′ S, 21°24′ E 218
Dekhisor, *Taj.* 39°27′ N, 69°32′ E 197
Dekina, *Nig.* 7°38′ N, 7°0′ E 222
Dekle Beach, *Fla., U.S.* 29°51′ N, 83°37′ W 105
Dekoa, *Cen. Af. Rep.* 6°14′ N, 19°3′ E 218
Del Rio, *Tex., U.S.* 29°21′ N, 100°55′ W 112
Del Verme Falls, *Eth.* 5°9′ N, 40°15′ E 224
Delacroix, *La., U.S.* 29°45′ N, 89°48′ W 103
Delamar Mountains, *Nev., U.S.* 37°8′ N, 114°58′ W 101
Delami, *Sudan* 11°50′ N, 30°28′ E 218
Delano, *Calif., U.S.* 35°46′ N, 119°14′ W 100
Delano Peak, *Utah, U.S.* 38°21′ N, 112°26′ W 90
Delanson, *N.Y., U.S.* 42°44′ N, 74°12′ W 104
Delaram, *Afghan.* 32°14′ N, 63°26′ E 186
Delareyville, *S. Af.* 26°42′ S, 25°25′ E 220
Delavan, *Ill., U.S.* 40°21′ N, 89°33′ W 102
Delaware, *Ohio, U.S.* 40°17′ N, 83°5′ W 102
Delaware, adm. division, *Del., U.S.* 39°36′ N, 75°46′ W 94
Delaware Bay 38°16′ N, 76°18′ W 94
Delaware Mountains, *Tex., U.S.* 31°54′ N, 104°55′ W 92
Delbrück, *Ger.* 51°45′ N, 8°32′ E 167
Delcambre, *La., U.S.* 29°56′ N, 92°0′ W 103
Delčevo, *Maced.* 41°57′ N, 22°46′ E 168
Delémont, *Switz.* 47°22′ N, 7°19′ E 156
Delesseps Lake, lake, *Can.* 50°41′ N, 91°15′ W 110
Delft, *Neth.* 52°1′ N, 4°21′ E 163
Delfzijl, *Neth.* 53°20′ N, 6°55′ E 163
Delgada, Point, *Calif., U.S.* 39°51′ N, 124°30′ W 90
Delgado, Cabo, *Mozambique* 10°43′ S, 40°42′ E 224
Delgerhet, *Mongolia* 45°50′ N, 110°29′ E 198
Delgo, *Sudan* 20°6′ N, 30°36′ E 226
Delhi, *Calif., U.S.* 37°25′ N, 120°47′ W 100
Delhi, *India* 28°41′ N, 77°10′ E 197
Delhi, *La., U.S.* 32°26′ N, 91°30′ W 103
Delhi, *N.Y., U.S.* 42°16′ N, 74°56′ W 94
Delhi, adm. division, *India* 28°37′ N, 76°44′ E 188
Deli Jovan, *Serb.* 44°21′ N, 22°12′ E 168
Delia, *Can.* 51°39′ N, 112°23′ W 90
Délices, *Fr.* 4°43′ N, 53°47′ W 130
Delicias, *Mex.* 28°9′ N, 105°29′ W 92
Deligrad, *Serb.* 43°36′ N, 21°35′ E 168
Delījān, *Iran* 34°0′ N, 50°40′ E 180
Deliktaş, *Turk.* 39°19′ N, 37°12′ E 156
Déline, *Can.* 65°13′ N, 123°26′ W 98
Delingha, *China* 37°22′ N, 97°29′ E 188
Delisle, *Can.* 51°55′ N, 107°8′ W 90
Delisle, *Can.* 48°37′ N, 71°42′ W 94
Delium, battle, *Gr.* 38°19′ N, 23°32′ E 156
Dell, *U.K.* 58°28′ N, 6°20′ W 150
Dell Rapids, *S. Dak., U.S.* 43°48′ N, 96°43′ W 90
Delle, *Fr.* 47°30′ N, 6°59′ E 150
Dellenbaugh, Mount, *Ariz., U.S.* 36°6′ N, 113°34′ W 101
Dellys, *Alg.* 36°54′ N, 3°54′ E 150
Delmar, *Md., U.S.* 38°27′ N, 75°35′ W 94
Delmar, *N.Y., U.S.* 42°37′ N, 73°51′ W 104
Deloraine, *Can.* 49°11′ N, 100°30′ W 90
Delos, ruin(s), *Gr.* 37°22′ N, 25°10′ E 156
Delphi, ruin(s), *Gr.* 38°28′ N, 22°24′ E 156
Delphos, *Ohio, U.S.* 40°50′ N, 84°21′ W 102
Delray Beach, *Fla., U.S.* 26°28′ N, 80°6′ W 105
Delta, *Colo., U.S.* 38°44′ N, 108°4′ W 90
Delta, *La., U.S.* 32°18′ N, 90°56′ W 103
Delta, *Utah, U.S.* 39°20′ N, 112°34′ W 90
Delta Amacuro, adm. division, *Venez.* 8°57′ N, 61°48′ W 130
Delta du Saloum National Park, *Senegal* 13°39′ N, 16°27′ W 222
Deltona, *Fla., U.S.* 28°53′ N, 81°15′ W 105
Dema, river, *Russ.* 54°28′ N, 55°29′ E 154
Demanda, Sierra de la, *Sp.* 42°19′ N, 3°14′ W 164
Demange-aux-Eaux, *Fr.* 48°34′ N, 5°27′ E 163
Demarcation Point, *Can.* 69°34′ N, 143°59′ W 98
Demba, *Dem. Rep. of the Congo* 5°30′ S, 22°13′ E 218
Dembech'a, *Eth.* 10°31′ N, 37°28′ E 224
Dembī Dolo, *Eth.* 8°31′ N, 34°47′ E 224
Dembia, *Dem. Rep. of the Congo* 3°29′ N, 25°51′ E 224
Demerara Plain, *North Atlantic Ocean* 9°25′ N, 48°41′ W 253
Demetrias, ruin(s), *Gr.* 39°20′ N, 22°52′ E 156
Demidov, *Russ.* 55°14′ N, 31°31′ E 154
Demidovo, *Russ.* 56°45′ N, 29°33′ E 166
Deming, *N. Mex., U.S.* 32°15′ N, 107°45′ W 92
Deming, *Wash., U.S.* 48°49′ N, 122°13′ W 100
Demini, river, *Braz.* 1°24′ N, 63°13′ W 130
Demirci, *Turk.* 39°3′ N, 28°38′ E 156
Demirköprü Barajı, dam, *Turk.* 38°48′ N, 28°0′ E 156
Demirtaş, *Turk.* 36°25′ N, 32°10′ E 156
Demiti, river, *Braz.* 0°51′ N, 67°4′ W 136
Demmitt, *Can.* 55°25′ N, 119°55′ W 108
Democratic Republic of the Congo 1°57′ S, 17°24′ E 218
Demon, *Ghana* 9°29′ N, 0°11′ E 222
Demonte, *It.* 44°18′ N, 7°17′ E 167

Demopolis, *Ala., U.S.* 32°32′ N, 87°50′ W 103
Demotte, *Ind., U.S.* 41°11′ N, 87°13′ W 102
Demşuş, *Rom.* 45°34′ N, 22°48′ E 168
Demta, *Indonesia* 2°23′ S, 140°10′ E 192
Dem'yanka, river, *Russ.* 58°52′ N, 71°21′ E 169
Demyansk, *Russ.* 57°37′ N, 32°28′ E 154
Dem'yanskoye, *Russ.* 59°32′ N, 69°25′ E 169
Demydivka, *Ukr.* 50°24′ N, 25°20′ E 152
Den Burg, *Neth.* 53°3′ N, 4°46′ E 163
Den Chai, *Thai.* 17°59′ N, 100°3′ E 202
Den Haag (The Hague), *Neth.* 52°5′ N, 4°18′ E 163
Den Helder, *Neth.* 52°57′ N, 4°45′ E 163
Den Oever, *Neth.* 52°55′ N, 5°1′ E 163
Denain, *Fr.* 50°19′ N, 3°23′ E 163
Denair, *Calif., U.S.* 37°31′ N, 120°49′ W 100
Denakil, region, *Africa* 12°35′ N, 40°8′ E 182
Denali see McKinley, Mount, *Alas., U.S.* 62°54′ N, 151°17′ W 98
Denan, *Eth.* 6°27′ N, 43°29′ E 218
Denare Beach, *Can.* 54°40′ N, 102°4′ W 108
Denbigh, *U.K.* 53°11′ N, 3°24′ W 162
Dendtler Island, *Antarctica* 72°46′ S, 90°30′ W 248
Denekamp, *Neth.* 52°23′ N, 7°0′ E 163
Deng Deng, *Cameroon* 5°8′ N, 13°28′ E 218
Dengkou, *China* 40°18′ N, 106°54′ E 198
Dêngqên, *China* 31°33′ N, 95°35′ E 188
Dengu, river, *Dem. Rep. of the Congo* 4°30′ N, 24°14′ E 224
Dengzhou, *China* 32°39′ N, 112°5′ E 198
Denham Springs, *La., U.S.* 30°28′ N, 90°58′ W 96
Denholm, *Can.* 52°39′ N, 108°2′ W 108
Denia, *Sp.* 38°51′ N, 0°7′ E 164
Deniliquin, *Austral.* 35°31′ S, 144°55′ E 231
Denio, *Nev., U.S.* 41°59′ N, 118°39′ W 90
Denis, *Gabon* 0°17′ N, 9°22′ E 218
Denison, *Iowa, U.S.* 41°59′ N, 95°21′ W 90
Denison, *Tex., U.S.* 33°44′ N, 96°32′ W 96
Denisovka, *Russ.* 66°14′ N, 55°19′ E 154
Denisovskaya, *Russ.* 60°18′ N, 41°34′ E 154
Denizli, *Turk.* 37°45′ N, 29°5′ E 156
Denman Island, *Can.* 49°32′ N, 124°49′ W 100
Denmark 56°12′ N, 8°45′ E 152
Denmark, *Me., U.S.* 43°58′ N, 70°49′ W 104
Denmark, *S.C., U.S.* 33°18′ N, 81°9′ W 96
Denmark Strait 64°13′ N, 38°21′ W 246
Dennis, *Mass., U.S.* 41°44′ N, 70°12′ W 104
Dennison, *Ohio, U.S.* 40°23′ N, 81°20′ W 102
Denov, *Uzb.* 38°17′ N, 67°54′ E 197
Denpasar, *Indonesia* 8°44′ S, 115°1′ E 192
Denso, *Mali* 10°27′ N, 8°5′ W 222
Denton, *Md., U.S.* 38°52′ N, 75°50′ W 94
Denton, *Tex., U.S.* 33°12′ N, 97°8′ W 92
D'Entrecasteaux Islands, *Solomon Sea* 9°50′ S, 151°24′ E 231
Denver, *Colo., U.S.* 39°43′ N, 105°6′ W 90
Denver, *Ind., U.S.* 40°51′ N, 86°5′ W 102
Denver City, *Tex., U.S.* 32°56′ N, 102°50′ W 92
Denzil, *Can.* 52°13′ N, 109°38′ W 108
Deoband, *India* 29°40′ N, 77°41′ E 197
Deobhog, *India* 19°56′ N, 82°39′ E 188
Deoghar, *India* 24°27′ N, 86°42′ E 197
Deoria, *India* 26°29′ N, 83°47′ E 197
Departure Bay, *Can.* 49°11′ N, 123°58′ W 100
Deposit, *N.Y., U.S.* 42°3′ N, 75°26′ W 110
Depot Harbour, *Can.* 45°18′ N, 80°5′ W 94
Depot Peak, *Antarctica* 69°6′ S, 64°14′ E 248
Deputatskiy, *Russ.* 69°16′ N, 139°52′ E 173
Deqing, *China* 30°33′ N, 120°4′ E 198
Deqing, *China* 23°10′ N, 111°46′ E 198
Dera Ghazi Khan, *Pak.* 30°3′ N, 70°41′ E 186
Dera Ismail Khan, *Pak.* 31°47′ N, 70°55′ E 186
Deraheib, *Sudan* 21°55′ N, 35°8′ E 182
Derati, spring, *Kenya* 3°47′ N, 36°23′ E 224
Derbent, *Russ.* 42°0′ N, 48°20′ E 195
Derbisaka, *Cen. Af. Rep.* 5°43′ N, 24°52′ E 224
Derby, *Austral.* 17°23′ S, 123°43′ E 238
Derby, *Conn., U.S.* 41°19′ N, 73°6′ W 104
Derby, *Kans., U.S.* 37°31′ N, 97°16′ W 90
Derby, *Miss., U.S.* 30°45′ N, 89°35′ W 103
Derby, *U.K.* 52°55′ N, 1°29′ W 162
Derby Acres, *Calif., U.S.* 35°15′ N, 119°37′ W 101
Derdara, *Mor.* 35°7′ N, 5°18′ W 150
Derdepoort, *S. Af.* 24°41′ S, 26°21′ E 227
Derecske, *Hung.* 47°21′ N, 21°34′ E 168
Dérégoué, *Burkina Faso* 10°46′ N, 4°9′ W 222
Dereisa, *Sudan* 12°43′ N, 22°47′ E 216
Derevyansk, *Russ.* 61°44′ N, 53°23′ E 154
Dergachi, *Russ.* 51°12′ N, 48°48′ E 158
Derhachi, *Ukr.* 50°7′ N, 36°7′ E 158
Derik, *Turk.* 37°20′ N, 40°19′ E 195
Derm, *Namibia* 23°40′ S, 18°13′ E 227
Dermbach, *Ger.* 50°42′ N, 10°6′ E 167
Dermott, *Ark., U.S.* 33°30′ N, 91°27′ W 96
Derna see Darnah, *Lib.* 32°44′ N, 22°38′ E 216
Dernberg, Cape, *Namibia* 27°44′ S, 15°33′ E 227
Dernieres, Isles, *Gulf of Mexico* 29°3′ N, 90°55′ W 103
Derom, Mount, *Antarctica* 71°36′ S, 35°22′ E 248
Derri, *Somalia* 4°21′ N, 46°38′ E 218
Derry, *La., U.S.* 31°30′ N, 92°58′ W 103
Derry, *N.H., U.S.* 42°52′ N, 71°20′ W 104
Derudeb, *Sudan* 17°29′ N, 36°4′ E 182
Derust, *S. Af.* 33°27′ S, 22°32′ E 227
Derval, *Fr.* 47°39′ N, 1°41′ W 150
Derventa, *Bosn. and Herzg.* 44°58′ N, 17°53′ E 168
Derwent, *Can.* 53°38′ N, 110°58′ W 108
Derwent, river, *U.K.* 54°11′ N, 0°44′ E 162
Derwent Water, lake, *U.K.* 54°33′ N, 3°22′ W 162
Deryneia, *Northern Cyprus, Cyprus* 35°3′ N, 33°57′ E 194
Derzhavino, *Russ.* 53°14′ N, 52°19′ E 154
Derzhavīnsk, *Kaz.* 51°6′ N, 66°18′ E 184
Des Allemands, *La., U.S.* 29°50′ N, 90°29′ W 103
Des Moines, *Iowa, U.S.* 41°33′ N, 93°40′ W 94
Des Moines, *N. Mex., U.S.* 36°44′ N, 103°50′ W 92
Des Moines, river, *Iowa, U.S.* 43°26′ N, 95°10′ W 80
Des Plaines, *Ill., U.S.* 42°2′ N, 87°54′ W 102
Desa, *Rom.* 43°53′ N, 23°1′ E 168
Desaguadero, *Peru* 16°39′ S, 69°5′ W 137
Desatoya Mountains, *Nev., U.S.* 39°31′ N, 117°53′ W 90
Desbiens, *Can.* 48°24′ N, 71°57′ W 94
Descalvado, *Braz.* 21°57′ S, 47°38′ W 138
Descanso, *Calif., U.S.* 32°51′ N, 116°37′ W 101
Deschutes, river, *Oreg., U.S.* 44°13′ N, 121°5′ W 80
Desē, *Eth.* 11°5′ N, 39°36′ E 224
Deseada, *Chile* 22°53′ S, 69°51′ W 137
Deseado, river, *Arg.* 46°54′ S, 69°39′ W 134
Desemboque, *Mex.* 30°34′ N, 113°3′ W 92
Desengaño, Punta, *Arg.* 49°15′ S, 67°33′ W 134
Deseret, *Utah, U.S.* 39°16′ N, 112°39′ W 90
Deseret Peak, *Utah, U.S.* 40°26′ N, 112°41′ W 90
Deseronto, *Can.* 44°12′ N, 77°3′ W 94
Desert Center, *Calif., U.S.* 33°43′ N, 115°25′ W 101
Desert Hot Springs, *Calif., U.S.* 33°57′ N, 116°31′ W 101
Desert Island, Mount, *Me., U.S.* 43°48′ N, 68°16′ W 81
Désert, Lac, lake, *Can.* 46°34′ N, 76°44′ W 94
Desert National Park, *India* 26°16′ N, 70°18′ E 186
Desert Peak, *Utah, U.S.* 41°10′ N, 113°26′ W 90
Desert Range, *Nev., U.S.* 36°51′ N, 115°27′ W 101
Desert Shores, *Calif., U.S.* 33°24′ N, 116°3′ W 101
Desert Valley, *Nev., U.S.* 41°12′ N, 118°30′ W 90
Desertas, Ilhas, islands, *North Atlantic Ocean* 33°17′ N, 17°23′ W 214
Deserters Peak, *Can.* 56°56′ N, 125°0′ W 108
Deshler, *Nebr., U.S.* 40°6′ N, 97°45′ W 90
Deshler, *Ohio, U.S.* 41°12′ N, 83°54′ W 102
Deshnoke, *India* 27°48′ N, 73°21′ E 186
Desierto del Carmen National Park see 13, *Mex.* 18°52′ N, 99°38′ W 112
Désirade, La, island, *Fr.* 16°15′ N, 60°59′ W 116
Deskenatlata Lake, *Can.* 60°55′ N, 113°9′ W 108
Desloge, *Mo., U.S.* 37°51′ N, 90°31′ W 94
Desmarais, Point, *Can.* 60°50′ N, 117°6′ W 108
Desmaraisville, *Can.* 49°30′ N, 76°12′ W 94
Desmochado, *Parag.* 27°7′ S, 58°5′ W 139
Desna, river, *Russ.* 54°20′ N, 32°53′ E 154
Desna, river, *Ukr.* 51°6′ N, 31°7′ E 158
Desnogorsk, *Russ.* 54°8′ N, 33°13′ E 154
Desnudez, Punta, *Arg.* 38°59′ S, 59°37′ W 139
Desolación, Isla, island, *Chile* 53°2′ S, 76°38′ W 134
Desolation Canyon, *Utah, U.S.* 39°42′ N, 110°18′ W 90
Desordem, Serra da, *Braz.* 3°15′ S, 47°0′ W 130
Despotovac, *Serb.* 44°5′ N, 21°25′ E 168
Desroches, islands, *Indian Ocean* 6°36′ S, 51°11′ E 218
Dessalines, *Haiti* 19°17′ N, 72°32′ W 116
Dessau, *Ger.* 51°50′ N, 12°15′ E 152
Destruction Island, *Wash., U.S.* 47°34′ N, 124°36′ W 100
Destruction, Mount, *Austral.* 24°35′ S, 127°45′ E 230
Desvres, *Fr.* 50°39′ N, 1°50′ E 163
Deta, *Rom.* 45°24′ N, 21°13′ E 168
Dete, *Zimb.* 18°38′ S, 26°50′ E 224
Detour, Point, *U.S.* 45°27′ N, 86°34′ W 94
Detroit, *Me., U.S.* 44°47′ N, 69°19′ W 94
Detroit, *Mich., U.S.* 42°20′ N, 83°3′ W 102
Dettelbach, *Ger.* 49°47′ N, 10°8′ E 167
Deurne, *Neth.* 51°28′ N, 5°46′ E 167
Deux Balé National Park, *Burkina Faso* 11°34′ N, 3°2′ W 222
Deux Décharges, Lac aux, lake, *Can.* 51°58′ N, 71°19′ W 111
Deva, *Rom.* 45°53′ N, 22°55′ E 168
Devarkonda, *India* 16°41′ N, 78°57′ E 188
Dévaványa, *Hung.* 47°1′ N, 20°58′ E 168
Deveci Dağı, peak, *Turk.* 40°5′ N, 35°51′ E 156
Devecser, *Hung.* 47°5′ N, 17°26′ E 168
Develi, *Turk.* 38°22′ N, 35°31′ E 156
Deventer, *Neth.* 52°15′ N, 6°8′ E 163
Devenyns, Lac, lake, *Can.* 47°3′ N, 74°25′ W 94
Devers, *Tex., U.S.* 30°0′ N, 94°36′ W 103
Devgarh, *India* 25°30′ N, 73°59′ E 186
Devi, river, *India* 20°33′ N, 85°53′ E 188
Devil's Bridge, *U.K.* 52°21′ N, 3°51′ W 162
Devils Cataract see Raudal Yupurari, fall(s), *Col.* 0°58′ N, 71°28′ W 136
Devils Gate, pass, *Calif., U.S.* 38°21′ N, 119°23′ W 100
Devils Hole see Death Valley National Park, *Nev., U.S.* 36°25′ N, 116°19′ W 101
Devils Lake, *N. Dak., U.S.* 48°5′ N, 98°52′ W 90
Devils Paw, mountain, *Can.-U.S.* 58°42′ N, 134°2′ W 108
Devils Playground, *Calif., U.S.* 35°1′ N, 115°54′ W 101
Devils Postpile National Monument, *Calif., U.S.* 37°36′ N, 119°11′ W 92
Devils, river, *Tex., U.S.* 29°58′ N, 101°18′ W 92
Devilsbit Mountain, *Ire.* 52°48′ N, 8°1′ W 150
Devine, *Tex., U.S.* 29°7′ N, 98°55′ W 96
Devine, Mount, *Ariz., U.S.* 32°7′ N, 111°52′ W 92
Devizes, *U.K.* 51°21′ N, 2°0′ W 162
Devli, *India* 25°45′ N, 75°23′ E 197
Devola, *Ohio, U.S.* 39°27′ N, 81°28′ W 102
Devon Island, *Can.* 75°13′ N, 79°17′ W 106
Devoto, *Arg.* 31°27′ S, 62°19′ W 139
Devrek, *Turk.* 41°13′ N, 31°54′ E 156
Devrekâni, *Turk.* 41°36′ N, 33°49′ E 156
Đevrske, *Croatia* 43°56′ N, 15°50′ E 156
Dewa, Ujung, *Indonesia* 2°58′ N, 95°46′ E 196
Dewar, *Okla., U.S.* 35°26′ N, 95°57′ W 96
Dewas, *India* 22°58′ N, 76°3′ E 197
Dewetsdorp, *S. Af.* 29°37′ S, 26°36′ E 227
Dewey, *Okla., U.S.* 36°46′ N, 95°57′ W 96
Dewey Lake, *Ky., U.S.* 37°27′ N, 83°21′ W 81
Deweyville, *Tex., U.S.* 30°16′ N, 93°45′ W 103
Dewitt, *Mich., U.S.* 42°50′ N, 84°34′ W 102
Dewsbury, *U.K.* 53°41′ N, 1°38′ W 162
Dexter, *Me., U.S.* 45°1′ N, 69°18′ W 94
Dexter, *Mich., U.S.* 42°19′ N, 83°54′ W 102
Dexter, *Mo., U.S.* 36°47′ N, 89°57′ W 96
Deyhūk, *Iran* 33°16′ N, 57°31′ E 180
Deyyer, *Iran* 27°49′ N, 51°56′ E 196
Dez, river, *Iran* 33°0′ N, 48°44′ E 180
Dezfūl, *Iran* 32°23′ N, 48°23′ E 180
Dezhneva, Mys (East Cape), *Russ.* 65°45′ N, 169°46′ W 98
Dezhou, *China* 37°28′ N, 116°18′ E 198
Dgūqara, *Kaz.* 46°1′ N, 55°58′ E 158
Dhahabān, *Saudi Arabia* 21°56′ N, 39°5′ E 182
Dhahran see Az̧ Z̧ahrān, *Saudi Arabia* 26°15′ N, 50°1′ E 196
Dhaka, *Bangladesh* 23°38′ N, 90°17′ E 197
Dhamār, *Yemen* 14°30′ N, 44°27′ E 182
Dhanbad, *India* 23°47′ N, 86°24′ E 197
Dhandhuka, *India* 22°16′ N, 71°58′ E 186
Dhangadhi, *Nepal* 28°40′ N, 80°39′ E 197
D'Hanis, *Tex., U.S.* 29°19′ N, 99°16′ W 92
Dhankuta, *Nepal* 26°57′ N, 87°19′ E 197
Dhanora, *India* 20°15′ N, 80°20′ E 188
Dharan Bazar, *Nepal* 26°45′ N, 87°11′ E 197
Dharmjaygarh, *India* 22°29′ N, 83°13′ E 197
Dhasan, river, *India* 24°11′ N, 78°46′ E 197
Dhāt Ra's, *Jordan* 30°59′ N, 35°44′ E 194
Dhaulagiri, peak, *Nepal* 28°41′ N, 83°29′ E 197
Dhebar Lake, *India* 24°16′ N, 73°41′ E 186
Dhërmi, *Alban.* 40°9′ N, 19°38′ E 156
Dhībān (Dibon), *Jordan* 31°29′ N, 35°46′ E 194
Dhone, *India* 15°24′ N, 77°52′ E 188
Dhorain, Beinn, peak, *U.K.* 58°6′ N, 3°57′ W 150
Dhule, *India* 20°52′ N, 74°45′ E 188
Dhupgarh, peak, *India* 22°25′ N, 78°19′ E 197
Dhuusamarreeb (Dusa Marreb), *Somalia* 5°31′ N, 46°24′ E 218
Di Linh, *Vietnam* 11°35′ N, 108°4′ E 202
Dia, *Mali* 14°53′ N, 3°17′ W 222
Diablo, Cerro, peak, *Tex., U.S.* 31°51′ N, 105°28′ W 92
Diablo, El Picacho del, peak, *Mex.* 30°56′ N, 115°27′ W 92
Diablo, Mount, *Calif., U.S.* 37°52′ N, 121°57′ W 100
Diablo Peak, *Oreg., U.S.* 42°57′ N, 120°40′ W 90
Diablo Range, *Calif., U.S.* 37°13′ N, 121°39′ W 100
Diablo, Sierra, *Tex., U.S.* 31°3′ N, 105°0′ W 92
Diadé, *Mauritania* 16°15′ N, 7°33′ W 222
Diafarabé, *Mali* 14°11′ N, 5°0′ W 222
Diala, *Mali* 14°13′ N, 10°10′ W 222
Dialafara, *Mali* 13°28′ N, 11°25′ W 222
Dialakoto, *Senegal* 13°18′ N, 13°20′ W 222
Diamante, *Arg.* 32°3′ S, 60°34′ W 139
Diamantina, *Braz.* 18°16′ S, 43°35′ W 138
Diamantina, Chapada, *Braz.* 12°50′ S, 42°58′ W 138
Diamantina Fracture Zone, *Indian Ocean* 36°3′ S, 105°25′ E 254
Diamantino, *Braz.* 16°32′ S, 53°14′ W 138
Diamantino, *Braz.* 14°28′ S, 56°29′ W 132
Diamond Craters, *Oreg., U.S.* 43°8′ N, 119°2′ W 90
Diamond Harbour, *India* 22°11′ N, 88°12′ E 197
Diamond Head, peak, *Hawai'i, U.S.* 21°14′ N, 157°51′ W 99
Diamond Island, *Myanmar* 15°35′ N, 94°16′ E 202
Diamond Mountains, *Calif., U.S.* 40°7′ N, 120°34′ W 90
Diamond Mountains, *Nev., U.S.* 39°43′ N, 116°5′ W 90
Diamond Peak, *Colo., U.S.* 40°56′ N, 108°57′ W 90
Diamond Peak, *Oreg., U.S.* 43°30′ N, 122°14′ W 90
Diamond Peak, *Wash., U.S.* 46°5′ N, 117°38′ W 90
Diamond Point, *N.Y., U.S.* 43°28′ N, 73°43′ W 104
Diamond Valley, *Nev., U.S.* 39°56′ N, 116°12′ W 90
Diamondville, *Wyo., U.S.* 41°45′ N, 110°32′ W 90
Diamou, *Mali* 14°6′ N, 11°17′ W 222
Diana, *Tex., U.S.* 32°41′ N, 94°46′ W 103
Dianbai, *China* 21°32′ N, 110°59′ E 198
Diandioumé, *Mali* 15°27′ N, 9°21′ W 222
Dianguina, *Mauritania* 15°19′ N, 10°56′ W 222
Dianjiang, *China* 30°18′ N, 107°23′ E 198
Diano d'Alba, *It.* 44°38′ N, 8°2′ E 167
Diapaga, *Burkina Faso* 12°4′ N, 1°46′ E 222
Diar el Haj Hassan, *Tun.* 35°17′ N, 11°3′ E 156
Diarville, *Fr.* 48°22′ N, 6°7′ E 163
Diavolo, Mount, *India* 12°41′ N, 92°54′ E 188
Dībā al Ḩiṣn, *U.A.E.* 25°38′ N, 56°12′ E 196
Dibaya, *Dem. Rep. of the Congo* 6°34′ S, 22°55′ E 218
Dibaya Lubue, *Dem. Rep. of the Congo* 4°14′ S, 19°50′ E 218
Dibbis, *Sudan* 12°33′ N, 24°12′ E 216
Dibella, spring, *Niger* 17°23′ N, 13°13′ E 222
Dibo, *Eth.* 10°46′ N, 38°19′ E 224
Diboll, *Tex., U.S.* 31°9′ N, 94°48′ W 103
Dibon see Dhībān, *Jordan* 31°29′ N, 35°46′ E 194
Dibrugarh, *India* 27°27′ N, 94°56′ E 188
Dibulla, *Col.* 11°14′ N, 73°20′ W 136
Dickens, *Tex., U.S.* 33°35′ N, 100°51′ W 92
Dickey Peak, *Idaho, U.S.* 44°13′ N, 113°57′ W 90
Dickinson, *Tex., U.S.* 29°26′ N, 95°3′ W 103
Dickson, *Russ.* 73°19′ N, 81°0′ E 160
Dickson, *Tenn., U.S.* 36°4′ N, 87°23′ W 96
Dicle, *Turk.* 38°22′ N, 40°5′ E 195
Dicle see Tigris, river, *Turk.* 37°41′ N, 41°7′ E 195
Dicomano, *It.* 43°54′ N, 11°31′ E 167
Didbiran, *Russ.* 52°4′ N, 139°13′ E 190
Didcot, *U.K.* 51°36′ N, 1°15′ W 162
Dider, *Alg.* 25°12′ N, 8°26′ E 214
Dīdēsa, river, *Eth.* 9°31′ N, 35°52′ E 224
Didhav, *Eth.* 12°35′ N, 40°54′ E 182
Didi Abuli, Mt'a, peak, *Ga.* 41°26′ N, 43°35′ E 195
Didia, *Tanzania* 3°50′ S, 33°3′ E 224
Didiéni, *Mali* 13°54′ N, 8°5′ W 222
Dīdīmtu, *Eth.* 8°45′ N, 42°9′ E 224
Didoko, *Côte d'Ivoire* 5°58′ N, 5°19′ W 222
Didsbury, *Can.* 51°41′ N, 114°8′ W 90
Didwana, *India* 27°23′ N, 74°35′ E 186
Diébougou, *Burkina Faso* 10°57′ N, 3°16′ W 222
Diecke, *Guinea* 7°15′ N, 8°59′ W 222
Diefenbaker, Lake, *Can.* 51°15′ N, 107°39′ W 90
Diego de Almagro, *Chile* 26°23′ S, 70°5′ W 134
Diego de Almagro, Isla, island, *Chile* 51°19′ S, 78°10′ W 134
Diego Garcia, island, *U.K.* 7°53′ S, 72°18′ E 188
Diego Garcia, island, *U.K.* 7°17′ S, 72°25′ E 254
Diekirch, *Lux.* 49°52′ N, 6°9′ E 167
Diélé, *Congo* 1°56′ S, 14°37′ E 218
Diéma, *Mali* 14°35′ N, 9°12′ W 222
Diemel, river, *Ger.* 51°30′ N, 9°24′ E 167
Dien Bien, *Vietnam* 21°21′ N, 103°0′ E 202
Dien Chou, *Vietnam* 18°59′ N, 105°35′ E 202
Dien Khanh, *Vietnam* 12°14′ N, 109°6′ E 202
Diepholz, *Ger.* 52°36′ N, 8°22′ E 150
Dieppe, *Fr.* 49°54′ N, 1°3′ E 163
Dieppe Lake, lake, *Can.* 61°37′ N, 116°55′ W 108
Dierdorf, *Ger.* 50°32′ N, 7°39′ E 163
Dieren, *Neth.* 52°3′ N, 6°5′ E 167
Diest, *Belg.* 50°59′ N, 5°2′ E 167
Dieterich, *Ill., U.S.* 39°3′ N, 88°24′ W 102
Dieulouard, *Fr.* 48°50′ N, 6°4′ E 163
Dieuze, *Fr.* 48°49′ N, 6°43′ E 163
Dieveniškės, *Lith.* 54°12′ N, 25°37′ E 166
Diez, *Ger.* 50°22′ N, 8°0′ E 167
Dif, *Kenya* 0°55′ N, 40°55′ E 224
Diffa, *Niger* 13°21′ N, 12°37′ E 216
Differdange, *Lux.* 49°32′ N, 5°53′ E 163
Difnein, island, *Eritrea* 16°29′ N, 38°48′ E 182
Digba, *Dem. Rep. of the Congo* 4°20′ N, 25°47′ E 224
Digboi, *India* 27°23′ N, 95°38′ E 188
Digby, *Can.* 44°37′ N, 65°46′ W 111
Dighton, *Kans., U.S.* 38°29′ N, 100°28′ W 90
Dighton, *Mass., U.S.* 41°48′ N, 71°8′ W 104
Dighton, *Mich., U.S.* 44°5′ N, 85°21′ W 102
Digne, *Fr.* 44°5′ N, 6°14′ E 167
Digny, *Fr.* 48°32′ N, 1°8′ E 163
Digor, *Turk.* 40°22′ N, 43°24′ E 195
Digos, *Philippines* 6°47′ N, 125°20′ E 203
Digri, *Pak.* 25°10′ N, 69°7′ E 186
Digul, river, *Indonesia* 7°13′ S, 139°20′ E 192
Digya National Park, *Ghana* 7°10′ N, 0°48′ E 222
Dihōk, *Iraq* 36°52′ N, 42°52′ E 195
Diinsoor, *Somalia* 2°25′ N, 42°57′ E 218
Dijlah see Tigris, river, *Iraq* 32°8′ N, 46°36′ E 180
Dijon, *Fr.* 47°19′ N, 5°2′ E 150
Dik, *Chad* 9°57′ N, 17°30′ E 216
Dika, Mys, *Russ.* 75°37′ N, 114°26′ E 172
Dikhil, *Djibouti* 11°12′ N, 42°22′ E 224
Dikili, *Turk.* 39°2′ N, 26°53′ E 156
Diksmuide, *Belg.* 51°2′ N, 2°51′ E 163
Dikwa, *Nig.* 12°3′ N, 13°56′ E 216
Dīla, *Eth.* 6°28′ N, 38°18′ E 224
Dildarde Burnu, *Turk.* 36°26′ N, 31°17′ E 156
Dili, *Dem. Rep. of the Congo* 3°25′ N, 26°44′ E 224
Dili, *Timor-Leste* 8°47′ S, 125°17′ E 230
Dilijan, *Arm.* 40°44′ N, 44°50′ E 195
Dilj Planina, *Croatia* 45°16′ N, 17°52′ E 168
Dillenburg, *Ger.* 50°44′ N, 8°16′ E 167
Dilley, *Tex., U.S.* 28°39′ N, 99°10′ W 92
Dilling, *Sudan* 12°1′ N, 29°40′ E 216
Dillingen, *Ger.* 49°21′ N, 6°44′ E 163
Dillingham, *Alas., U.S.* 58°57′ N, 158°36′ W 73
Dillon, *Can.* 55°54′ N, 108°55′ W 108
Dillon, *Mont., U.S.* 45°11′ N, 112°38′ W 90
Dillon, *S.C., U.S.* 34°25′ N, 79°23′ W 96
Dillon, river, *Can.* 55°31′ N, 110°13′ W 108
Dillsboro, *Ind., U.S.* 39°0′ N, 85°3′ W 102
Dilolo, *Dem. Rep. of the Congo* 10°44′ S, 22°22′ E 220
Dilworth, *Minn., U.S.* 46°51′ N, 96°41′ W 90
Dima, *Dem. Rep. of the Congo* 3°19′ S, 17°24′ E 218
Dimapur, *India* 25°52′ N, 93°47′ E 188
Dimas, *Mex.* 23°40′ N, 106°47′ W 114
Dimashq (Damascus), *Syr.* 33°30′ N, 36°14′ E 194
Dimbelenge, *Dem. Rep. of the Congo* 5°32′ S, 23°3′ E 218
Dimbokro, *Côte d'Ivoire* 6°34′ N, 4°42′ W 222
Dimitrovgrad, *Bulg.* 42°3′ N, 25°35′ E 156
Dimitrovgrad, *Russ.* 54°15′ N, 49°34′ E 154
Dimitrovgrad, *Serb.* 43°0′ N, 22°46′ E 168
Dimmitt, *Tex., U.S.* 34°31′ N, 102°19′ W 92
Dimock, *S. Dak., U.S.* 43°26′ N, 97°59′ W 90
Dimona, *Israel* 31°3′ N, 35°0′ E 194
Dīmtu, *Eth.* 5°8′ N, 41°57′ E 224
Dinajpur, *Bangladesh* 25°36′ N, 88°36′ E 197
Dinan, *Fr.* 48°27′ N, 2°4′ W 150
Dinant, *Belg.* 50°16′ N, 4°55′ E 167
Dinar, *Turk.* 38°3′ N, 30°10′ E 156
Dīnār, Kūh-e, peak, *Iran* 30°45′ N, 51°30′ E 180
Dinara, *Bosn. and Herzg.* 43°50′ N, 16°33′ E 168
Dinas Mawddwy, *U.K.* 52°42′ N, 3°42′ W 162
Dinde, *Angola* 14°14′ S, 13°41′ E 220
Dinder National Park, *Sudan* 12°32′ N, 35°8′ E 182
Dinder, river, *Sudan* 12°26′ N, 35°4′ E 182
Dinga, *Dem. Rep. of the Congo* 5°17′ S, 16°39′ E 218
Ding'an, *China* 19°39′ N, 110°19′ E 198
Dingbian, *China* 37°36′ N, 107°36′ E 198
Dinggyê, *China* 28°26′ N, 87°46′ E 197
Dingnan, *China* 24°44′ N, 115°0′ E 198
Dingtao, *China* 35°3′ N, 115°36′ E 198
Dinguiraye, *Guinea* 11°17′ N, 10°44′ W 222
Dingxi, *China* 35°33′ N, 104°32′ E 198
Dingxiang, *China* 38°28′ N, 112°58′ E 198
Dingxing, *China* 39°17′ N, 115°49′ E 198
Dingzhou, *China* 38°31′ N, 114°59′ E 198
Dingzi Gang 36°21′ N, 120°50′ E 198
Dinkey Creek, *Calif., U.S.* 37°5′ N, 119°11′ W 101
Dinklage, *Ger.* 52°39′ N, 8°8′ E 163
Dinorwic, *Can.* 49°41′ N, 92°30′ W 94

Dinorwic Lake, lake, Can. 49°31′ N, 93°7′ W 94
Dinosaur, Colo., U.S. 40°14′ N, 109°1′ W 90
Dinslaken, Ger. 51°33′ N, 6°44′ E 167
Dinuba, Calif., U.S. 36°32′ N, 119°24′ W 100
Dioïla, Mali 12°29′ N, 6°48′ W 222
Dioka, Mali 14°54′ N, 10°7′ W 222
Diona, spring, Chad 17°52′ N, 22°37′ E 216
Diongoï, Mali 14°53′ N, 9°35′ W 222
Dionisio Cerqueira, Arg. 26°17′ S, 53°37′ W 139
Diorbivol, Senegal 16°5′ N, 13°48′ W 222
Dios, Cayos de, Caribbean Sea 21°16′ N, 81°16′ W 116
Diosig, Rom. 47°17′ N, 22°1′ E 168
Diouloulou, Senegal 13°1′ N, 16°31′ W 222
Dioumdiouréré, Mali 14°51′ N, 2°0′ W 222
Dioundiou, Niger 12°35′ N, 3°30′ E 222
Dioura, Mali 14°52′ N, 5°15′ W 222
Diourbel, Senegal 14°39′ N, 16°7′ W 222
Diphu Pass, India 28°14′ N, 97°21′ E 188
Dipkarpaz see Rizokarpaso, Cyprus 35°36′ N, 34°22′ E 194
Diplo, Pak. 24°28′ N, 69°36′ E 186
Dipolog, Philippines 8°36′ N, 123°21′ E 203
Dipton, N.Z. 45°55′ S, 168°23′ E 240
Dir, Pak. 35°11′ N, 71°53′ E 186
Dira, Djebel, peak, Alg. 36°4′ N, 3°34′ E 150
Dirdal, Nor. 58°49′ N, 6°9′ E 152
Dirē, Eth. 10°9′ N, 38°41′ E 224
Diré, Mali 16°17′ N, 3°24′ W 222
Dirē Dawa, Eth. 9°34′ N, 41°51′ E 224
Dirfis, Óros, Gr. 38°32′ N, 23°38′ E 156
Dirico, Angola 17°56′ S, 20°43′ E 220
Dirj, Lib. 30°9′ N, 10°26′ E 214
Dirk Hartog Island, Austral. 26°19′ S, 110°56′ E 230
Dirkou, Niger 19°4′ N, 12°50′ E 216
Dirra, Sudan 13°35′ N, 26°5′ E 226
Dirranbandi, Austral. 28°36′ S, 148°19′ E 231
Disa, India 24°15′ N, 72°11′ E 186
Disappointment, Cape, Wash., U.S. 46°13′ N, 124°26′ W 100
Disaster Bay 37°41′ S, 149°37′ E 231
Discovery Bay 38°20′ S, 139°30′ E 230
Discovery Tablemount, South Atlantic Ocean 42°9′ S, 0°31′ E 253
Disentis-Mustér, Switz. 46°42′ N, 8°50′ E 167
Dishna, Egypt 26°10′ N, 32°25′ E 180
Disko see Qeqertarsuaq, island, Den. 69°31′ N, 62°11′ W 106
Dismal Mountains, Antarctica 68°45′ S, 53°53′ E 248
Dismal, river, Nebr., U.S. 41°45′ N, 101°4′ W 90
Dispur, India 26°6′ N, 91°44′ E 197
Disraëli, Can. 45°53′ N, 71°21′ W 94
Diss, U.K. 52°22′ N, 1°6′ E 162
Disteghil Sar, peak, Pak. 36°16′ N, 75°4′ E 186
District, Lake, region, Europe 54°15′ N, 3°22′ W 162
District of Columbia, adm. division, D.C., U.S. 38°55′ N, 77°12′ W 94
District, Peak, region, Europe 53°17′ N, 1°57′ W 162
Distrito Federal, adm. division, Braz. 15°42′ S, 48°13′ W 138
Distrito Federal, adm. division, Mex. 19°9′ N, 99°21′ W 114
Disûq, Egypt 31°7′ N, 30°39′ E 180
Ditaranto, Golfo 39°48′ N, 16°53′ E 156
Ditinn, Guinea 10°53′ N, 12°13′ W 222
Diu, India 20°41′ N, 70°56′ E 188
Dium, ruin(s), Gr. 40°9′ N, 22°23′ E 156
Dīvāndarreh, Iran 36°0′ N, 46°58′ E 180
Divénié, Congo 2°39′ S, 12°3′ E 218
Divernon, Ill., U.S. 39°32′ N, 89°41′ W 102
Divinhe, Mozambique 20°42′ S, 34°48′ E 227
Divinópolis, Braz. 20°10′ S, 44°55′ W 138
Divisadero Barrancas, Mex. 27°32′ N, 107°48′ W 112
Diviso, Col. 1°22′ N, 78°27′ W 136
Divisor, Serra do, Braz. 8°10′ S, 73°52′ W 130
Divjakë, Alban. 40°59′ N, 19°31′ E 156
Divnoye, Russ. 45°52′ N, 43°10′ E 158
Divo, Côte d'Ivoire 5°47′ N, 5°21′ W 222
Divonne, Fr. 46°21′ N, 6°8′ E 167
Divriği, Turk. 39°20′ N, 38°7′ E 180
Diwal Qol, Afghan. 34°20′ N, 67°57′ E 186
Diwana, Pak. 26°5′ N, 67°19′ E 186
Dixfield, Me., U.S. 44°31′ N, 70°27′ W 104
Dixie Butte, peak, Oreg., U.S. 44°34′ N, 118°42′ W 90
Dixon, Calif., U.S. 38°26′ N, 121°50′ W 90
Dixon, Ill., U.S. 41°49′ N, 89°29′ W 102
Dixon, Ky., U.S. 37°30′ N, 87°42′ W 94
Dixon, Mo., U.S. 37°58′ N, 92°6′ W 94
Dixon, Mont., U.S. 47°17′ N, 114°20′ W 90
Dixon Entrance 54°17′ N, 133°50′ W 108
Dixons Mills, Ala., U.S. 32°3′ N, 87°48′ W 103
Dixonville, Can. 56°32′ N, 117°41′ W 108
Diyadin, Turk. 39°32′ N, 43°41′ E 195
Diyālá, river, Iraq 34°20′ N, 45°5′ E 186
Diyarbakır, Turk. 37°54′ N, 40°17′ E 195
Diz, Pak. 26°36′ N, 63°27′ E 182
Dizy, Fr. 49°3′ N, 3°57′ E 163
Dja, river, Cameroon 3°14′ N, 12°30′ E 218
Dja, river, Cameroon 3°1′ N, 14°6′ E 218
Djado, Niger 21°1′ N, 12°18′ E 222
Djado, Plateau du, Niger 21°41′ N, 11°25′ E 222
Djako, Cen. Af. Rep. 8°18′ N, 22°29′ E 218
Djamaa, Alg. 33°31′ N, 5°57′ E 214
Djambala, Congo 2°32′ S, 14°45′ E 218
Djanet, Alg. 24°23′ N, 9°22′ E 207
Djaul, island, P.N.G. 3°10′ S, 150°7′ E 192
Djebel Onk, Alg. 34°41′ N, 8°2′ E 214
Djédaa, Chad 13°31′ N, 18°36′ E 216
Djelfa, Alg. 34°41′ N, 3°15′ E 214
Djéli Mahé, Mali 15°25′ N, 10°37′ W 222
Djema, Cen. Af. Rep. 5°58′ N, 25°18′ E 224
Djember, Chad 10°26′ N, 17°50′ E 216
Djeniene bou Rezg, Alg. 32°23′ N, 0°47′ E 214
Djénné, Mali 13°55′ N, 4°35′ W 222
Djenoun, Garet el, peak, Alg. 25°2′ N, 5°17′ E 214
Djérem, river, Cameroon 5°58′ N, 12°41′ E 218
Djéroual, Chad 14°29′ N, 18°32′ E 216
Dji, river, Cen. Af. Rep. 6°48′ N, 22°28′ E 218
Djibasso, Burkina Faso 13°8′ N, 4°10′ W 222
Djibo, Burkina Faso 14°5′ N, 1°39′ W 222
Djibouti 12°0′ N, 43°0′ E 216
Djibouti, Djibouti 11°29′ N, 43°0′ E 182
Djibrosso, Côte d'Ivoire 8°45′ N, 7°2′ W 222
Djidja, Benin 7°25′ N, 1°50′ E 222
Djiénié, Mali 12°12′ N, 7°17′ W 222
Djilbé, Cameroon 11°54′ N, 14°39′ E 216
Djirkjik, spring, Chad 16°53′ N, 20°39′ E 216
Djohong, Cameroon 6°47′ N, 14°42′ E 218
Djokupunda, Dem. Rep. of the Congo 5°28′ S, 20°58′ E 218
Djolu, Dem. Rep. of the Congo 0°35′ N, 22°26′ E 218
Djougou, Benin 9°42′ N, 1°41′ E 222
Djouho Battinga, Cen. Af. Rep. 6°37′ N, 20°30′ E 218
Djoum, Cameroon 2°44′ N, 12°40′ E 218
Djugu, Dem. Rep. of the Congo 1°53′ N, 30°30′ E 224
Djupvik, Nor. 69°44′ N, 20°31′ E 152
D'Lo, Miss., U.S. 31°58′ N, 89°55′ W 103
Dmitriyev L'govskiy, Russ. 52°6′ N, 35°7′ E 158
Dmitrov, Russ. 56°20′ N, 37°33′ E 154
Dmitrovsk Orlovskiy, Russ. 52°26′ N, 35°10′ E 158
Dnipropetrovs'k, Ukr. 48°28′ N, 34°59′ E 158
Dno, Russ. 57°48′ N, 30°0′ E 166
Dnyapro, river, Belarus 53°18′ N, 30°37′ E 154
Do Ab-e Mikh-e Zarrin, Afghan. 35°19′ N, 67°59′ E 186
Do, Lac, lake, Mali 15°52′ N, 3°2′ W 222
Do, river, China 34°15′ N, 97°2′ E 188
Doa, Mozambique 16°42′ S, 34°44′ E 224
Doba, Chad 8°39′ N, 16°51′ E 218
Dobane, Cen. Af. Rep. 6°24′ N, 24°39′ E 218
Dobbiaco, It. 46°44′ N, 12°13′ E 167
Dobele, Latv. 56°37′ N, 23°15′ E 166
Dobie Lake, lake, Can. 51°26′ N, 91°24′ W 110
Dobie, river, Can. 51°29′ N, 90°58′ W 110
Dobiegniew, Pol. 52°57′ N, 15°46′ E 152
Dobo, Indonesia 5°48′ S, 134°9′ E 192
Doboj, Bosn. and Herzg. 44°44′ N, 18°3′ E 168
Dobra, Rom. 45°54′ N, 22°35′ E 168
Dobra, Serb. 44°37′ N, 21°54′ E 168
Dobreşti, Rom. 46°50′ N, 22°18′ E 168
Dobrich, Bulg. 43°34′ N, 27°50′ E 156
Dobrich, adm. division, Bulg. 43°38′ N, 27°14′ E 156
Dobrinka, Russ. 50°48′ N, 41°44′ E 158
Dobrino, Maced. 41°48′ N, 21°36′ E 168
Dobro Polje, Bosn. and Herzg. 43°34′ N, 18°29′ E 168
Döbrököz, Hung. 46°25′ N, 18°13′ E 168
Dobroselica, Serb. 43°37′ N, 19°42′ E 168
Dobruchi, Russ. 58°52′ N, 27°53′ E 166
Dobrush, Belarus 52°26′ N, 31°21′ E 158
Dobryanka, Russ. 58°28′ N, 56°21′ E 154
Dobryszyce, Pol. 51°7′ N, 19°25′ E 152
Dobson, N.Z. 42°29′ S, 171°19′ E 240
Docampadó, Ensenada 4°34′ N, 77°43′ W 136
Doce, river, Braz. 19°3′ S, 41°42′ W 138
Doce, river, Braz. 17°46′ S, 51°40′ W 138
Dock Junction, Ga., U.S. 31°11′ N, 81°31′ W 96
Docksta, Nor. 63°2′ N, 18°20′ E 152
Doclin, Rom. 45°18′ N, 21°39′ E 168
Doctor Arroyo, Mex. 23°39′ N, 100°10′ W 114
Doctor Coss, Mex. 25°53′ N, 99°10′ W 114
Doctor González, Mex. 25°50′ N, 99°56′ W 114
Doctor Pedro P. Peña, Parag. 22°27′ S, 62°20′ W 132
Doctor Petru Groza, Rom. 46°32′ N, 22°29′ E 168
Doda, Lac, lake, Can. 49°20′ N, 75°39′ W 110
Doddridge, Ark., U.S. 33°5′ N, 93°55′ W 103
Dodecanese see Dodekánissa, islands, Aegean Sea 35°59′ N, 26°31′ E 180
Dodekánissa (Dodecanese), islands, Aegean Sea 35°26′ N, 27°28′ E 156
Dodge City, Kans., U.S. 37°45′ N, 100°2′ W 90
Dodge Lake, Can. 59°45′ N, 106°15′ W 108
Dodgeville, Wis., U.S. 42°57′ N, 90°8′ W 102
Dodman Point, U.K. 50°3′ N, 4°45′ W 150
Dodola, Eth. 6°57′ N, 39°9′ E 224
Dodoma, Tanzania 6°10′ S, 35°35′ E 224
Dodoma, adm. division, Tanzania 6°43′ S, 35°14′ E 218
Dodona, ruin(s), Gr. 39°31′ N, 20°39′ E 156
Dodsland, Can. 51°49′ N, 108°50′ W 90
Dodson, La., U.S. 32°3′ N, 92°40′ W 103
Dodson, Mont., U.S. 48°23′ N, 108°15′ W 90
Doe Castle, site, Ire. 55°6′ N, 8°0′ W 150
Doe River, Can. 55°59′ N, 120°7′ W 108
Doerun, Ga., U.S. 31°18′ N, 83°55′ W 96
Doesburg, Neth. 52°0′ N, 6°10′ E 167
Doetinchem, Neth. 51°57′ N, 6°18′ E 167
Dog Creek, Can. 51°37′ N, 122°14′ W 90
Dog Lake, Can. 48°48′ N, 89°57′ W 94
Dog Lake, Can. 48°15′ N, 84°26′ W 94
Dog Lake, lake, Can. 50°58′ N, 98°49′ W 90
Dog Rocks, islands, North Atlantic Ocean 24°5′ N, 79°48′ W 116
Dogaicoring Qangco, lake, China 34°25′ N, 88°11′ E 188
Dogface Lake, Can. 60°17′ N, 119°34′ W 108
Dogondoutchi, Niger 13°38′ N, 4°0′ E 222
Doğruyol (Cala), Turk. 41°3′ N, 43°20′ E 195
Doğubayazıt, Turk. 39°30′ N, 44°8′ E 195
Dogwaya, Sudan 17°48′ N, 34°33′ E 182
Doha see Ad Dawḩah, Qatar 25°13′ N, 51°25′ E 196
Dohoukota, Cen. Af. Rep. 6°1′ N, 17°27′ E 218
Doig, river, Can. 56°50′ N, 120°6′ W 108
Doilungdêqên, China 29°49′ N, 90°44′ E 197
Dois Irmãos, Serra, Braz. 8°27′ S, 41°26′ W 132
Doka, Sudan 13°27′ N, 35°45′ E 182
Doka see Bahr Kéita, river, Chad 9°8′ N, 18°38′ E 218
Dokan Dam, Iraq 36°1′ N, 44°37′ E 180
Dokka, Nor. 60°49′ N, 10°3′ E 152
Dokkara, Alg. 35°49′ N, 4°25′ E 150
Dokkum, Neth. 53°19′ N, 6°0′ E 163
Doko, Dem. Rep. of the Congo 3°6′ N, 29°34′ E 224
Dokshytsy, Belarus 54°53′ N, 27°45′ E 166
Dokūchaev, Kaz. 51°40′ N, 64°13′ E 184
Dokuchayevs'k, Ukr. 47°42′ N, 37°37′ E 156
Dolak, island, Indonesia 8°43′ S, 136°42′ E 192
Dolan Springs, Ariz., U.S. 35°35′ N, 114°16′ W 101
Doland, S. Dak., U.S. 44°52′ N, 98°7′ W 90
Dolbeau, Can. 48°49′ N, 72°18′ W 82
Dolbeau-Mistassini, Can. 48°53′ N, 72°11′ W 94
Doldrums Fracture Zone, North Atlantic Ocean 8°41′ N, 33°42′ W 253
Dole, Fr. 47°5′ N, 5°28′ E 150
Doleib Hill, Sudan 9°20′ N, 31°38′ E 224
Dolgoshchel'ye, Russ. 66°3′ N, 43°29′ E 154
Dolhasca, Rom. 47°24′ N, 26°36′ E 156
Doli, Croatia 42°48′ N, 17°48′ E 168
Dolina, Ukr. 48°56′ N, 24°1′ E 152
Dolinsk, Russ. 47°19′ N, 142°44′ E 190
Dolj, adm. division, Rom. 44°2′ N, 23°6′ E 156
Dollard 53°15′ N, 7°1′ E 163
Dolleman Island, Antarctica 70°41′ S, 60°17′ W 248
Dolly Cays, North Atlantic Ocean 23°28′ N, 77°16′ W 116
Dolní Dvořiště, Czech Rep. 48°39′ N, 14°27′ E 152
Dolnośląskie, adm. division, Pol. 51°10′ N, 15°2′ E 152
Dolo, It. 45°25′ N, 12°3′ E 156
Dolo Bay, Eth. 4°10′ N, 42°6′ E 224
Dolomites, It. 46°44′ N, 11°41′ E 167
Doloon, Mongolia 44°25′ N, 105°18′ E 198
Dolores, Arg. 36°17′ S, 57°41′ W 139
Dolores, Colo., U.S. 37°28′ N, 108°30′ W 92
Dolores, Uru. 33°33′ S, 58°9′ W 139
Dolores Hidalgo, Mex. 21°8′ N, 100°57′ W 114
Dolphin and Union Strait 69°9′ N, 118°43′ W 98
Dolphin, Cape, U.K. 51°11′ S, 60°16′ W 134
Dolsan, S. Korea 34°37′ N, 127°45′ E 200
Dolzhanskaya, Russ. 46°38′ N, 37°45′ E 156
Dolzhitsy, Russ. 58°29′ N, 29°5′ E 166
Dolzhok, Ukr. 48°39′ N, 26°30′ E 156
Dom Joaquim, Braz. 18°58′ S, 43°19′ W 138
Dom, peak, Switz. 46°6′ N, 7°49′ E 165
Dom Pedrito, Braz. 31°0′ S, 54°41′ W 139
Dom Pedro, Braz. 5°0′ S, 44°28′ W 132
Domagaya Lake, Can. 51°53′ N, 65°7′ W 111
Domaniç, Turk. 39°47′ N, 29°35′ E 156
Domanovići, Bosn. and Herzg. 43°7′ N, 17°46′ E 168
Domar, China 33°49′ N, 80°14′ E 188
Domart, Fr. 50°4′ N, 2°7′ E 163
Domaşnea, Rom. 45°5′ N, 22°19′ E 168
Dombarovskiy, Russ. 50°45′ N, 59°31′ E 158
Dombe, Mozambique 20°0′ S, 33°23′ E 224
Dombóvár, Hung. 46°22′ N, 18°7′ E 168
Domburg, Neth. 51°33′ N, 3°29′ E 163
Dome, Ariz., U.S. 32°44′ N, 114°22′ W 101
Dome Circe, region, Antarctica 72°58′ S, 129°17′ E 248
Dome Creek, Can. 53°41′ N, 121°2′ W 108
Dome F, Antarctica 77°19′ S, 39°42′ E 249
Dome Fuji, station, Antarctica 77°27′ S, 39°56′ E 248
Dome Mountain, peak, Can. 53°16′ N, 60°38′ W 111
Dome Peak, Can. 61°28′ N, 127°6′ W 98
Dome Peak, Wyo., U.S. 44°33′ N, 107°29′ W 90
Dome Peak, Castle, Ariz., U.S. 33°4′ N, 114°11′ W 101
Dôme, Puy de, peak, Fr. 45°45′ N, 2°55′ E 165
Dome Rock Mountains, Ariz., U.S. 33°37′ N, 114°31′ W 101
Domett, N.Z. 42°53′ S, 173°14′ E 240
Domingo M. Irala, Parag. 25°56′ S, 54°36′ W 139
Dominica 15°25′ N, 61°20′ W 116
Dominican Republic 18°55′ N, 71°0′ W 116
Dominion, Cape, Can. 66°9′ N, 77°33′ W 106
Dominion Lake, Can. 52°40′ N, 62°28′ W 111
Dömitz, Ger. 53°8′ N, 11°15′ E 152
Dommary-Baroncourt, Fr. 49°17′ N, 5°41′ E 163
Domo, Eth. 7°49′ N, 46°55′ E 218
Domodossola, It. 46°7′ N, 8°16′ E 167
Dompago see Badjoudé, Benin 9°42′ N, 1°23′ E 222
Domrémy, Fr. 48°26′ N, 5°40′ E 163
Dömsöd, Hung. 47°5′ N, 19°1′ E 168
Domuyo, Volcán, Arg. 36°38′ S, 70°34′ W 134
Don Benito, Sp. 38°57′ N, 5°52′ W 164
Don Pedro Reservoir, lake, Calif., U.S. 37°43′ N, 120°34′ W 100
Don Peninsula, Can. 52°27′ N, 128°10′ W 108
Dôn, river, Laos 15°43′ N, 105°56′ E 202
Don, river, Russ. 52°0′ N, 39°2′ E 160
Donadeu, Arg. 26°41′ S, 62°42′ W 139
Donald Landing, Can. 54°29′ N, 125°41′ W 108
Donalda, Can. 52°35′ N, 112°34′ W 108
Donaldson, Minn., U.S. 48°33′ N, 96°55′ W 90
Donaldsonville, La., U.S. 30°4′ N, 91°0′ W 103
Donau see Danube, river, Ger. 47°48′ N, 8°25′ E 150
Donauwörth, Ger. 48°43′ N, 10°46′ E 152
Doncaster, U.K. 53°31′ N, 1°9′ W 162
Dondo, Angola 9°41′ S, 14°26′ E 218
Dondo, Mozambique 19°39′ S, 34°43′ E 224
Donets' Kryazh, Ukr. 47°29′ N, 36°35′ E 156
Donets'k, Ukr. 47°57′ N, 37°47′ E 158
Dong Hoi, Vietnam 17°29′ N, 106°36′ E 202
Dong Taijnar Hu, lake, China 37°27′ N, 92°46′ E 188
Dong Ujimqin Qi, China 45°31′ N, 116°57′ E 198
Donga, Nig. 7°41′ N, 10°6′ E 222
Döng-Alysh, Kyrg. 42°17′ N, 74°46′ E 184
Dong'an, China 26°24′ N, 111°13′ E 198
Dongara, Austral. 29°14′ S, 114°57′ E 231
Dongbei (Manchuria), region, Asia 40°34′ N, 122°39′ E 200
Dongfang (Basuo), China 19°3′ N, 108°38′ E 198
Dongfeng, China 42°41′ N, 125°25′ E 200
Donggala, Indonesia 0°37′ N, 119°45′ E 192
Donggang, China 39°53′ N, 124°8′ E 200
Dongguan, China 23°2′ N, 113°44′ E 190
Dongguang, China 37°53′ N, 116°32′ E 198
Donghae, S. Korea 37°33′ N, 129°7′ E 200
Dônghén, Laos 16°43′ N, 105°16′ E 202
Donglan, China 24°28′ N, 107°20′ E 198
Dongo, Angola 14°38′ S, 15°39′ E 220
Dongo, Dem. Rep. of the Congo 2°40′ N, 18°27′ E 218
Dongola, Sudan 19°9′ N, 30°28′ E 182
Dongou, Congo 2°2′ N, 18°3′ E 218
Dongping, China 35°49′ N, 116°22′ E 198
Dongping, China 21°42′ N, 112°15′ E 198
Dongqiao, China 31°58′ N, 90°38′ E 188
Dongsha (Pratas Islands), Taiwan, China 20°43′ N, 116°42′ E 198
Dongshan, China 23°37′ N, 117°23′ E 198
Dongsheng, China 39°51′ N, 109°59′ E 198
Dongtai, China 32°52′ N, 120°17′ E 198
Dongting Hu, lake, China 28°54′ N, 111°45′ E 198
Dongwe, river, Zambia 13°52′ S, 24°59′ E 224
Dongxiang, China 28°12′ N, 116°33′ E 198
Dongxing, China 21°33′ N, 107°59′ E 198
Dongyztaū, Kaz. 46°38′ N, 57°37′ E 158
Dongzhen, China 38°59′ N, 103°40′ E 198
Donington, U.K. 52°54′ N, 0°12′ E 162
Doniphan, Mo., U.S. 36°36′ N, 90°49′ W 96
Donji Kamengrad, Bosn. and Herzg. 44°47′ N, 16°33′ E 168
Donji Miholjac, Croatia 45°44′ N, 18°9′ E 168
Donji Tovarnik, Serb. 44°48′ N, 19°56′ E 168
Donji Vakuf, Bosn. and Herzg. 44°9′ N, 17°24′ E 168
Donkese, Dem. Rep. of the Congo 1°33′ S, 18°28′ E 218
Donnacona, Can. 46°40′ N, 71°45′ W 94
Donnelly, Can. 55°43′ N, 117°8′ W 108
Donnelly Peak, Nev., U.S. 41°5′ N, 119°21′ W 90
Donnellys Crossing, N.Z. 35°43′ S, 173°36′ E 240
Donner, La., U.S. 29°41′ N, 90°57′ W 103
Donner Pass, Calif., U.S. 39°18′ N, 120°20′ W 90
Donnersberg, peak, Ger. 49°36′ N, 7°52′ E 163
Donostia-San Sebastián, Sp. 43°17′ N, 2°1′ W 164
Donovan, Ill., U.S. 40°52′ N, 87°37′ W 102
Donzère, Fr. 44°26′ N, 4°43′ E 150
Doon, river, U.K. 55°23′ N, 4°51′ W 150
Doone Valley, site, U.K. 51°11′ N, 3°47′ W 162
Doonerak, Mount, Alas., U.S. 67°55′ N, 150°54′ W 98
Door Peninsula, Wis., U.S. 44°29′ N, 87°41′ W 94
Door Point, La., U.S. 30°2′ N, 88°52′ W 103
Dora, Ala., U.S. 33°43′ N, 87°6′ W 96
Dora, N. Mex., U.S. 33°55′ N, 103°20′ W 92
Dora Riparia, river, It. 45°6′ N, 6°50′ E 165
Doran Lake, Can. 61°13′ N, 108°32′ W 108
Dorbod, China 46°54′ N, 124°27′ E 198
Đorče Petrov, Maced. 42°1′ N, 21°21′ E 168
Dorchester, U.K. 50°42′ N, 2°27′ W 162
Dorchester, U.K. 51°38′ N, 1°10′ W 162
Dorchester, Cape, Can. 65°29′ N, 81°58′ W 246
Dordabis, Namibia 22°52′ S, 17°34′ E 227
Dordives, Fr. 48°8′ N, 2°45′ E 163
Dordogne, river, Fr. 44°52′ N, 1°31′ E 165
Dordrecht, Neth. 51°47′ N, 4°40′ E 167
Dordrecht, S. Af. 31°24′ S, 27°0′ E 227
Doré Lake, Can. 54°36′ N, 107°21′ W 108
Dores do Indaiá, Braz. 19°27′ S, 45°37′ W 138
Dorfen, Ger. 48°16′ N, 12°9′ E 152
Dorfmark, Ger. 52°54′ N, 9°47′ E 150
Dori, Burkina Faso 14°1′ N, 0°3′ E 222
Dorintosh, Can. 54°21′ N, 108°38′ W 108
Dorking, U.K. 51°14′ N, 0°20′ E 162
Dormaa Ahenkro, Ghana 7°17′ N, 2°53′ W 222
Dormagen, Ger. 51°5′ N, 6°49′ E 167
Dormans, Fr. 49°4′ N, 3°39′ E 163
Dorneşti, Rom. 47°52′ N, 26°0′ E 152
Dorno Djoutougé, Chad 12°29′ N, 22°15′ E 216
Doro, Mali 16°1′ N, 1°5′ W 222
Dorog, Hung. 47°42′ N, 18°43′ E 168
Dorogobuzh, Russ. 54°52′ N, 33°22′ E 154
Dorogorskoye, Russ. 65°39′ N, 44°27′ E 154
Dorohoi, Rom. 47°56′ N, 26°22′ E 152
Dorora, spring, Chad 17°57′ N, 18°41′ E 216
Dorotea, Nor. 64°16′ N, 16°22′ E 152
Dorris, Calif., U.S. 41°57′ N, 121°56′ W 90
Dorset, Vt., U.S. 43°15′ N, 73°7′ W 104
Dorsten, Ger. 51°39′ N, 6°57′ E 167
Dortmund, Ger. 51°30′ N, 7°27′ E 167
Dörtyol, Turk. 36°50′ N, 36°12′ E 156
Dōrud, Iran 33°29′ N, 49°8′ E 186
Doruma, Dem. Rep. of the Congo 4°42′ N, 27°39′ E 224
Doruokha, Russ. 72°6′ N, 113°30′ E 160
Dörverden, Ger. 52°50′ N, 9°14′ E 152
Dos Bahías, Cabo, Arg. 45°7′ S, 65°30′ W 134
Dos Hermanas, Sp. 37°17′ N, 5°56′ W 164
Dos Lagunas, Guatemala 17°43′ N, 89°38′ W 115
Dos Palos, Calif., U.S. 36°58′ N, 120°38′ W 100
Dos Pozos, Arg. 43°53′ S, 65°25′ W 134
Doso, Côte d'Ivoire 4°45′ N, 6°50′ W 222
Dosso, Niger 13°2′ N, 3°11′ E 222
Dossor, Kaz. 47°31′ N, 52°59′ E 158
Do'stlik, Uzb. 40°33′ N, 68°1′ E 197
Dostlux, Turkm. 37°43′ N, 65°22′ E 197
Dostyq, Kaz. 45°14′ N, 82°29′ E 184
Dot Lake, Alas., U.S. 63°41′ N, 144°9′ W 98
Dothan, Ala., U.S. 31°13′ N, 85°23′ W 96
Dothan, ruin(s), West Bank, Israel 32°23′ N, 35°12′ E 194
Dotnuva, Lith. 55°22′ N, 23°51′ E 166
Doty, Wash., U.S. 46°36′ N, 123°17′ W 100
Douai, Fr. 50°21′ N, 3°4′ E 163
Douako, Guinea 9°43′ N, 10°11′ W 222
Douala, Cameroon 4°5′ N, 9°42′ E 222
Douaouir, Mali 20°8′ N, 2°59′ W 222
Douar Sadok, Tun. 35°56′ N, 9°43′ E 156

Douara, spring, *Mauritania* 17°36′ N, 12°47′ W 222
Douarnenez, *Fr.* 48°4′ N, 4°20′ W 150
Double Mountain, *Calif., U.S.* 35°1′ N, 118°32′ W 101
Doubs, river, *Switz.* 47°19′ N, 6°48′ E 165
Doucette, *Tex., U.S.* 30°48′ N, 94°26′ W 103
Doudeville, *Fr.* 49°42′ N, 0°46′ E 163
Doué, *Côte d'Ivoire* 7°42′ N, 7°39′ W 222
Douentza, *Mali* 14°58′ N, 2°59′ W 222
Douglas, *Ariz., U.S.* 31°21′ N, 109°35′ W 112
Douglas, *Ga., U.S.* 31°29′ N, 82°52′ W 96
Douglas, *Mich., U.S.* 42°37′ N, 86°12′ W 102
Douglas, *S. Af.* 29°5′ S, 23°46′ E 227
Douglas, *U.K.* 54°9′ N, 4°29′ W 162
Douglas, *Wyo., U.S.* 42°45′ N, 105°23′ W 82
Douglas Islands, *Indian Ocean* 67°21′ S, 63°31′ E 248
Douglas Lake, *Tenn., U.S.* 35°59′ N, 84°3′ W 81
Douglas Pass, *Colo., U.S.* 39°36′ N, 108°49′ W 90
Douglass, *Kans., U.S.* 37°29′ N, 97°1′ W 92
Douglass, *Tex., U.S.* 31°39′ N, 94°53′ W 103
Douglassville, *Tex., U.S.* 33°11′ N, 94°21′ W 103
Doukoula, *Cameroon* 10°7′ N, 14°56′ E 218
Doulevant-le-Château, *Fr.* 48°22′ N, 4°55′ E 163
Doullens, *Fr.* 50°9′ N, 2°20′ E 163
Doulus Head, *Ire.* 51°58′ N, 10°38′ W 150
Douma, *Leb.* 34°12′ N, 35°50′ E 194
Doumé, *Cameroon* 4°15′ N, 13°27′ E 218
Douna, *Mali* 14°44′ N, 1°43′ W 222
Doura, *Mali* 13°16′ N, 5°58′ W 222
Dourada, Serra, *Braz.* 12°47′ S, 48°59′ W 130
Dourados, *Braz.* 22°15′ S, 54°50′ W 132
Dourados, river, *Braz.* 22°23′ S, 55°26′ W 132
Dourbali, *Chad* 11°48′ N, 15°52′ E 218
Dourdan, *Fr.* 48°31′ N, 2°1′ E 163
Douro, river, *Port.* 40°43′ N, 8°23′ W 143
Douvaine, *Fr.* 46°18′ N, 6°18′ E 167
Douz, *Tun.* 33°28′ N, 9°0′ E 216
Dove Bugt 76°15′ N, 27°0′ W 73
Dove, river, *U.K.* 53°8′ N, 1°52′ W 162
Dover, *Del., U.S.* 39°7′ N, 75°38′ W 94
Dover, *Fla., U.S.* 27°59′ N, 82°12′ W 105
Dover, *N.H., U.S.* 43°12′ N, 70°53′ W 104
Dover, *Ohio, U.S.* 40°31′ N, 81°28′ W 102
Dover, *U.K.* 51°7′ N, 1°17′ E 163
Dover Air Force Base, *Del., U.S.* 39°7′ N, 75°33′ W 94
Dover, Strait of 50°52′ N, 0°56′ E 162
Dover-Foxcroft, *Me., U.S.* 45°11′ N, 69°14′ W 94
Dovers, Cape, *Antarctica* 67°10′ S, 97°16′ E 248
Dovrefjell, *Nor.* 62°5′ N, 9°20′ E 152
Dow Gonbadān, *Iran* 30°20′ N, 50°46′ E 196
Dow Polān, *Iran* 31°54′ N, 50°43′ E 180
Dowa, *Malawi* 13°38′ S, 33°56′ E 224
Dowagiac, *Mich., U.S.* 41°59′ N, 86°7′ W 102
Dowi, Tanjung, *Indonesia* 1°30′ N, 97°0′ E 196
Dowlat Yar, *Afghan.* 34°31′ N, 65°49′ E 186
Dowlatabad, *Afghan.* 36°25′ N, 64°56′ E 186
Dowlatābād, *Iran* 28°17′ N, 56°41′ E 196
Dowling Lake, *Can.* 51°42′ N, 112°39′ W 108
Downes, *S. Af.* 31°30′ S, 19°56′ E 227
Downey, *Calif., U.S.* 33°56′ N, 118°9′ W 101
Downham Market, *U.K.* 52°36′ N, 0°22′ E 162
Downs, *Kans., U.S.* 39°29′ N, 98°34′ W 90
Downs Mountain, *Wyo., U.S.* 43°17′ N, 109°45′ W 90
Dowshi, *Afghan.* 35°36′ N, 68°44′ E 186
Doyang, *S. Korea* 34°32′ N, 127°10′ E 200
Doyline, *La., U.S.* 32°31′ N, 93°25′ W 103
Dozois, Réservoir, lake, *Can.* 47°19′ N, 77°56′ W 94
Drâa, Cap, *Mor.* 28°47′ N, 11°53′ W 214
Drâa, Hamada du, *Alg.* 28°59′ N, 7°8′ W 214
Draç, *Alban.* 41°33′ N, 19°30′ E 168
Dracena, *Braz.* 21°29′ S, 51°30′ W 138
Drachten, *Neth.* 53°6′ N, 6°6′ E 163
Dracut, *Mass., U.S.* 42°40′ N, 71°19′ W 104
Dragash, *Kosovo* 42°3′ N, 20°38′ E 168
Draginac, *Serb.* 44°31′ N, 19°25′ E 168
Dragočaj, *Bosn. and Herzg.* 44°51′ N, 17°8′ E 168
Dragočava, *Bosn. and Herzg.* 43°28′ N, 18°49′ E 168
Dragoevo, *Maced.* 41°40′ N, 22°7′ E 168
Dragovishtitsa, *Bulg.* 42°21′ N, 22°39′ E 168
Dragsfjärd, *Fin.* 60°4′ N, 22°30′ E 166
Drake, *N. Dak., U.S.* 47°53′ N, 100°24′ W 90
Drake Peak, *Oreg., U.S.* 42°17′ N, 120°14′ W 90
Drakensberg, *Africa* 24°47′ S, 30°24′ E 227
Dráma, *Gr.* 41°10′ N, 24°17′ E 180
Drammen, *Nor.* 59°43′ N, 10°11′ E 152
Dran, *Vietnam* 11°52′ N, 108°37′ E 202
Drangedal, *Nor.* 59°6′ N, 9°1′ E 152
Dranov, Lacul, lake, *Rom.* 44°50′ N, 28°48′ E 156
Dransfeld, *Ger.* 51°29′ N, 9°45′ E 167
Dras, *India* 34°26′ N, 75°46′ E 186
Drava, river, *Croatia* 46°19′ N, 16°42′ E 168
Drávaszabolcs, *Hung.* 45°48′ N, 18°12′ E 168
Drawsko, *Pol.* 52°51′ N, 16°3′ E 152
Drayton, *Can.* 43°44′ N, 80°41′ W 102
Drayton, *N. Dak., U.S.* 48°32′ N, 97°12′ W 94
Drayton Plains, *Mich., U.S.* 42°40′ N, 83°22′ W 102
Drayton Valley, *Can.* 53°12′ N, 115°0′ W 108
Drebkau, *Ger.* 51°39′ N, 14°12′ E 152
Dreieich, *Ger.* 50°1′ N, 8°40′ E 167
Dreistelzberg, peak, *Ger.* 50°16′ N, 9°44′ E 167
Dren, *Bulg.* 42°25′ N, 23°9′ E 168
Drenovci, *Croatia* 44°54′ N, 18°54′ E 168
Dresden, *Can.* 42°34′ N, 82°10′ W 102
Dresden, *Ger.* 51°2′ N, 13°44′ E 152
Dresden, *Ohio, U.S.* 40°6′ N, 82°1′ W 102
Dretun', *Belarus* 55°41′ N, 29°10′ E 166
Dreux, *Fr.* 48°44′ N, 1°21′ E 163
Drevsjø, *Nor.* 61°52′ N, 12°2′ E 152
Drezdenko, *Pol.* 52°50′ N, 15°50′ E 152
Drežnik, *Serb.* 43°46′ N, 19°53′ E 168
Driftwood, river, *Can.* 55°55′ N, 126°59′ W 108
Drin, river, *Alban.* 42°11′ N, 19°51′ E 168
Drinjača, *Bosn. and Herzg.* 44°18′ N, 19°9′ E 168
Drinkwater Pass, *Oreg., U.S.* 43°46′ N, 118°17′ W 90
Driscoll Island, *Antarctica* 75°59′ S, 145°33′ W 248
Driskill Mountain, *La., U.S.* 32°24′ N, 92°56′ W 103
Drlače, *Serb.* 44°8′ N, 19°29′ E 168
Drniš, *Croatia* 43°51′ N, 16°8′ E 168
Drobeta-Turnu Severin, *Rom.* 44°37′ N, 22°38′ E 168
Drochia, *Mold.* 48°2′ N, 27°48′ E 156
Droitwich, *U.K.* 52°15′ N, 2°9′ W 162
Dronero, *It.* 44°28′ N, 7°22′ E 167
Dronten, *Neth.* 52°30′ N, 5°43′ E 163
Droué, *Fr.* 48°2′ N, 1°5′ E 150
Drowning, river, *Can.* 50°31′ N, 86°4′ W 110
Droyssig, *Ger.* 51°2′ N, 12°1′ E 152
Drozdyn', *Ukr.* 51°38′ N, 27°14′ E 152
Drūkšių Ežeras, lake, *Lith.* 55°37′ N, 26°8′ E 166
Drum Castle, site, *U.K.* 57°4′ N, 2°27′ W 150
Drumheller, *Can.* 51°28′ N, 112°43′ W 90
Drumlanrig Castle, site, *U.K.* 55°16′ N, 3°55′ W 150
Drummond, *Mont., U.S.* 46°38′ N, 113°9′ W 90
Drummond Island, *Mich., U.S.* 45°53′ N, 85°45′ W 81
Drummond Range, *Austral.* 23°59′ S, 146°26′ E 230
Drummondville, *Can.* 45°51′ N, 72°31′ W 94
Drumochter Pass, *U.K.* 56°51′ N, 4°14′ W 150
Drumright, *Okla., U.S.* 35°57′ N, 96°36′ W 92
Druya, *Belarus* 55°45′ N, 27°26′ E 166
Druzhba, *Ukr.* 52°2′ N, 34°3′ E 158
Druzhnaya Gorka, *Russ.* 59°16′ N, 30°6′ E 166
Drvar, *Bosn. and Herzg.* 44°21′ N, 16°22′ E 168
Dry Bay 59°1′ N, 140°0′ W 98
Dry Creek, *La., U.S.* 30°39′ N, 93°4′ W 103
Dry Falls, site, *Wash., U.S.* 47°33′ N, 119°27′ W 90
Dry Lake, *Nev., U.S.* 36°27′ N, 114°51′ W 101
Dry Mills, *Me., U.S.* 43°55′ N, 70°22′ W 104
Dry Prong, *La., U.S.* 31°33′ N, 92°32′ W 103
Dry Ridge, *Ky., U.S.* 38°40′ N, 84°36′ W 102
Dry Tortugas, islands, *Gulf of Mexico* 24°40′ N, 83°1′ W 105
Dry Tortugas National Park, *Fla., U.S.* 24°38′ N, 82°54′ W 105
Dryanovo, *Bulg.* 42°58′ N, 25°28′ E 156
Dryberry Lake, *Can.* 49°34′ N, 94°22′ W 90
Drybrough, *Can.* 56°32′ N, 101°15′ W 108
Dryden, *Can.* 49°47′ N, 92°50′ W 94
Dryden, *Mich., U.S.* 42°55′ N, 83°8′ W 102
Dryden, *Tex., U.S.* 30°2′ N, 102°7′ W 92
Dryden Flight Research Center, *Calif., U.S.* 34°59′ N, 117°56′ W 101
Drygalski Island, *Antarctica* 64°59′ S, 92°17′ E 248
Drygalski Mountains, *Antarctica* 71°37′ S, 10°5′ E 248
Drysa, river, *Belarus* 55°44′ N, 28°54′ E 166
Drysdale River National Park, *Austral.* 15°7′ S, 126°34′ E 238
Drysvyaty, Vozyera, lake, *Belarus* 55°34′ N, 26°38′ E 166
Dschang, *Cameroon* 5°24′ N, 10°4′ E 222
Du Bois, *Pa., U.S.* 41°7′ N, 78°46′ W 94
Du Pont, *Wash., U.S.* 47°5′ N, 122°34′ W 100
Du Quoin, *Mo., U.S.* 38°0′ N, 89°14′ W 96
Dua, river, *Dem. Rep. of the Congo* 2°54′ N, 21°59′ E 218
Duart Castle, site, *U.K.* 56°25′ N, 5°45′ W 150
Duarte, Pico, peak, *Dom. Rep.* 19°0′ N, 71°3′ W 116
Dub, *Pol.* 50°39′ N, 23°34′ E 158
Ḍubā, *Saudi Arabia* 27°21′ N, 35°43′ E 180
Dubac, *Croatia* 42°37′ N, 18°9′ E 168
Dubach, *La., U.S.* 32°40′ N, 92°40′ W 103
Dubai, *U.A.E.* 25°13′ N, 55°17′ E 196
Dubăsari, *Mold.* 47°15′ N, 29°10′ E 158
Dubawnt Lake, *Can.* 63°2′ N, 103°52′ W 106
Dubawnt, river, *Can.* 60°44′ N, 106°19′ W 108
Dubele, *Dem. Rep. of the Congo* 2°52′ N, 29°33′ E 224
Dubeninki, *Pol.* 54°17′ N, 22°32′ E 166
Dubenskiy, *Russ.* 51°28′ N, 56°35′ E 158
Dubica, *Croatia* 45°11′ N, 16°48′ E 168
Dubičiai, *Lith.* 54°1′ N, 24°44′ E 166
Dubīnskaya, *Kaz.* 43°43′ N, 80°12′ E 184
Dubivtsi, *Ukr.* 49°4′ N, 24°46′ E 152
Dublán, *Mex.* 30°27′ N, 107°55′ W 92
Dublin, *Ga., U.S.* 32°31′ N, 82°55′ W 96
Dublin, *Ind., U.S.* 39°48′ N, 85°13′ W 102
Dublin, *N.H., U.S.* 42°54′ N, 72°5′ W 104
Dublin, *Tex., U.S.* 32°5′ N, 98°21′ W 92
Dublin (Baile Átha Cliath), *Ire.* 53°18′ N, 6°26′ W 150
Dubna, *Russ.* 56°43′ N, 37°12′ E 154
Dubois, *Idaho, U.S.* 44°9′ N, 112°13′ W 90
Dubois, *Wyo., U.S.* 43°32′ N, 109°37′ W 90
Dubose, *Can.* 54°16′ N, 128°40′ W 108
Duboštica, *Bosn. and Herzg.* 44°14′ N, 18°20′ E 168
Dubove, *Ukr.* 51°14′ N, 24°40′ E 152
Dubovka, *Russ.* 49°2′ N, 44°42′ E 158
Dubrava, *Croatia* 45°49′ N, 16°3′ E 168
Dubrave, *Bosn. and Herzg.* 44°48′ N, 18°33′ E 168
Dubravica, *Serb.* 44°41′ N, 21°5′ E 168
Dubréka, *Guinea* 9°47′ N, 13°34′ W 222
Dubrovka, *Russ.* 56°22′ N, 28°39′ E 166
Dubrovnik (Ragusa), *Croatia* 42°38′ N, 18°5′ E 156
Dubrovnoye, *Russ.* 57°54′ N, 69°29′ E 169
Dubrovytsya, *Ukr.* 51°33′ N, 26°32′ E 152
Dubrowna, *Belarus* 54°36′ N, 30°49′ E 154
Dubuque, *Iowa, U.S.* 42°30′ N, 90°40′ W 94
Duc Tho, *Vietnam* 18°30′ N, 105°35′ E 202
Duchesne, *Utah, U.S.* 40°10′ N, 110°24′ W 90
Ducie Island, *U.K.* 24°38′ S, 124°48′ W 255
Duck Bay, *Can.* 52°8′ N, 100°10′ W 108
Duck Hill, *Miss., U.S.* 33°35′ N, 89°43′ W 96
Duck Lake, *Can.* 52°48′ N, 106°13′ W 108
Duck, river, *Tenn., U.S.* 35°41′ N, 87°0′ W 80
Duckbill Point, *Can.* 50°30′ N, 56°13′ W 111
Ducktown, *Tenn., U.S.* 35°2′ N, 84°23′ W 96
Ducor, *Calif., U.S.* 35°53′ N, 119°3′ W 101
Duda, river, *Col.* 2°58′ N, 74°15′ W 136
Dudelange, *Lux.* 49°28′ N, 6°4′ E 163
Duderstadt, *Ger.* 51°31′ N, 10°14′ E 167
Dudhi, *India* 24°12′ N, 83°13′ E 197
Dudhnai, *India* 25°58′ N, 90°45′ E 197
Dudinka, *Russ.* 69°25′ N, 86°24′ E 169
Dudley, *Mass., U.S.* 42°2′ N, 71°56′ W 104
Dudley, *U.K.* 52°30′ N, 2°6′ W 162
Dudleyville, *Ariz., U.S.* 32°56′ N, 110°44′ W 92
Dudo, *Somalia* 9°16′ N, 50°11′ E 216
Dudub, *Eth.* 6°54′ N, 46°44′ E 218
Dudypta, river, *Russ.* 71°10′ N, 91°51′ E 160
Duékoué, *Côte d'Ivoire* 6°39′ N, 7°20′ W 222
Dueodde, *Den.* 54°53′ N, 14°30′ E 152
Duero, river, *Sp.* 41°17′ N, 2°56′ W 214
Dufek Coast, *Antarctica* 84°41′ S, 154°15′ W 248
Dufek Massif, peak, *Antarctica* 82°41′ S, 54°13′ W 248
Duff Islands, *South Pacific Ocean* 9°30′ S, 167°28′ E 238
Dugo Selo, *Croatia* 45°48′ N, 16°13′ E 168
Dugulle, spring, *Somalia* 2°14′ N, 44°30′ E 218
Dugway, *Utah, U.S.* 40°13′ N, 112°45′ W 90
Duida-Marahuaca National Park, *Venez.* 3°36′ N, 65°58′ W 136
Duisburg, *Ger.* 51°25′ N, 6°45′ E 167
Duitama, *Col.* 5°49′ N, 73°3′ W 136
Duiwelskloof, *S. Af.* 23°42′ S, 30°9′ E 227
Dujuuma, *Somalia* 1°10′ N, 42°34′ E 224
Duk Fadiat, *Sudan* 7°42′ N, 31°25′ E 224
Duk Faiwil, *Sudan* 7°30′ N, 31°26′ E 224
Dukafulu, *Eth.* 5°7′ N, 39°7′ E 224
Dukambia, *Eritrea* 14°44′ N, 37°29′ E 182
Dukhān, *Qatar* 25°20′ N, 50°47′ E 196
Dukku, *Nig.* 10°47′ N, 10°46′ E 222
Dūkštas, *Lith.* 55°31′ N, 26°18′ E 166
Dula, *Dem. Rep. of the Congo* 4°41′ N, 20°17′ E 218
Dulan, *China* 36°19′ N, 98°8′ E 188
Dulce, river, *Arg.* 29°58′ S, 62°44′ W 139
Dulion, Golfe 43°2′ N, 3°49′ E 150
Dülmen, *Ger.* 51°50′ N, 7°16′ E 167
Dulovka, *Russ.* 57°30′ N, 28°20′ E 166
Duluth, *Minn., U.S.* 46°47′ N, 92°8′ W 94
Dulverton, *U.K.* 51°2′ N, 3°33′ W 162
Dūmā, *Syr.* 33°34′ N, 36°24′ E 194
Duma, river, *Dem. Rep. of the Congo* 4°32′ N, 26°35′ E 224
Dumaguete, *Philippines* 9°18′ N, 123°14′ E 203
Dumai, *Indonesia* 1°41′ N, 101°27′ E 196
Dumaran, island, *Philippines* 10°19′ N, 119°57′ E 192
Dumas, *Ark., U.S.* 33°52′ N, 91°30′ W 96
Dumas, *Tex., U.S.* 35°50′ N, 101°59′ W 92
Dumas, Peninsula, *Chile* 55°4′ S, 68°22′ W 134
Ḑumayr, *Syr.* 33°38′ N, 36°41′ E 194
Dume, river, *Dem. Rep. of the Congo* 5°3′ N, 24°48′ E 224
Dumfries, *U.K.* 55°4′ N, 3°36′ W 150
Dumka, *India* 24°14′ N, 87°15′ E 197
Dummett, Mount, *Antarctica* 73°16′ S, 63°25′ E 248
Dumoine, Lac, lake, *Can.* 46°51′ N, 78°28′ W 94
Dumont d'Urville, station, *Antarctica* 66°39′ S, 139°39′ E 248
Dümpelfeld, *Ger.* 50°26′ N, 6°57′ E 167
Dumra, *India* 26°33′ N, 85°30′ E 197
Dumshaf Plain, *Norwegian Sea* 69°58′ N, 1°51′ E 255
Dumyât (Damietta), *Egypt* 31°25′ N, 31°49′ E 180
Dun, *Fr.* 49°23′ N, 5°12′ E 163
Dun Aengus, ruin(s), *Ire.* 53°7′ N, 9°55′ W 150
Dún Dealgan see Dundalk, *Ire.* 53°59′ N, 6°24′ W 150
Duna (Danube), river, *Europe* 47°44′ N, 17°37′ E 168
Dunaff Head, *Ire.* 55°17′ N, 7°53′ W 150
Dunaharaszti, *Hung.* 47°21′ N, 19°6′ E 168
Dunakeszi, *Hung.* 47°37′ N, 19°9′ E 168
Dunapataj, *Hung.* 46°38′ N, 19°0′ E 168
Dunărea, river, *Europe* 43°42′ N, 22°49′ E 180
Dunaszekcső, *Hung.* 46°4′ N, 18°44′ E 168
Dunaújváros, *Hung.* 46°58′ N, 18°55′ E 168
Dunavecse, *Hung.* 46°54′ N, 18°58′ E 168
Dunay, *Russ.* 42°53′ N, 132°20′ E 200
Dunayivtsi, *Ukr.* 48°52′ N, 26°51′ E 152
Dunbar, *W. Va., U.S.* 38°21′ N, 81°45′ W 94
Dunblane, *Can.* 51°12′ N, 106°55′ W 90
Duncan, *Ariz., U.S.* 32°42′ N, 109°6′ W 92
Duncan, *Can.* 48°46′ N, 123°41′ W 100
Duncan, *Okla., U.S.* 34°28′ N, 97°58′ W 96
Duncan Passage 10°58′ N, 91°46′ E 188
Dundaga, *Latv.* 57°30′ N, 22°19′ E 166
Dundalk (Dún Dealgan), *Ire.* 53°59′ N, 6°24′ W 150
Dundas, *Ill., U.S.* 38°50′ N, 88°6′ W 102
Dundas Islands, *North Pacific Ocean* 54°35′ N, 130°38′ W 98
Dundas Peninsula, *Can.* 74°29′ N, 116°39′ W 106
Dundbürd, *Mongolia* 47°57′ N, 111°29′ E 198
Dundee, *Fla., U.S.* 28°1′ N, 81°38′ W 105
Dundee, *Mich., U.S.* 41°57′ N, 83°39′ W 102
Dundee, *S. Af.* 28°10′ S, 30°9′ E 227
Dundee, *U.K.* 56°36′ N, 3°10′ W 143
Dundee Island, *Antarctica* 63°49′ S, 58°1′ W 134
Dundo, *Angola* 7°24′ S, 20°47′ E 218
Dundrennan, *U.K.* 54°49′ N, 3°57′ W 162
Dundret, peak, *Nor.* 67°5′ N, 20°23′ E 152
Dund-Urt, *Mongolia* 47°56′ N, 106°12′ E 198
Dund-Us see Hovd, *Mongolia* 48°2′ N, 91°40′ E 190
Dune Sandy Hook, *Can.* 47°11′ N, 61°45′ W 111
Dunedin, *Fla., U.S.* 28°1′ N, 82°46′ W 105
Dunedin, *N.Z.* 45°52′ S, 170°28′ E 240
Dunedin, river, *Can.* 58°56′ N, 124°29′ W 108
Dunes City, *Oreg., U.S.* 43°52′ N, 124°8′ W 90
Dunfermline, *U.K.* 56°4′ N, 3°28′ W 150
Dungannon, *Can.* 43°50′ N, 81°37′ W 102
Dungarpur, *India* 23°50′ N, 73°43′ E 186
Dungas, *Niger* 13°4′ N, 9°19′ E 222
Dungeness, *U.K.* 50°54′ N, 0°58′ E 162
Dungeness, Punta, *Arg.* 52°31′ S, 68°22′ W 134
Dungu, *Dem. Rep. of the Congo* 3°33′ N, 28°34′ E 224
Dungu, river, *Dem. Rep. of the Congo* 3°40′ N, 28°34′ E 224
Dungunab, *Sudan* 21°5′ N, 37°4′ E 182
Dunhua, *China* 43°23′ N, 128°7′ E 198
Dunhuang, *China* 40°10′ N, 94°42′ E 188
Dunilavichy, *Belarus* 55°4′ N, 27°13′ E 166
Dunk Island, *Austral.* 18°2′ S, 146°15′ E 230
Dunkassa, *Benin* 10°19′ N, 3°7′ E 222
Dunkerque (Dunkirk), *Fr.* 51°1′ N, 2°21′ E 163
Dunkery Beacon, peak, *U.K.* 51°9′ N, 3°37′ W 162
Dunkirk, *Ind., U.S.* 40°22′ N, 85°12′ W 94
Dunkirk, *N.Y., U.S.* 42°28′ N, 79°21′ W 94
Dunkirk, river, *Can.* 57°8′ N, 113°2′ W 108
Dunkirk see Dunkerque, *Fr.* 51°1′ N, 2°21′ E 163
Dunkur, *Eth.* 11°54′ N, 35°56′ E 182
Dunkwa, *Ghana* 5°56′ N, 1°48′ W 222
Dunlap, *Iowa, U.S.* 41°50′ N, 95°35′ W 90
Dunlop, *Can.* 54°44′ N, 98°51′ W 108
Dunluce Castle, site, *U.K.* 55°11′ N, 6°41′ W 150
Dunmore Town, *Bahamas* 25°30′ N, 76°38′ W 96
Dunn, *N.C., U.S.* 35°18′ N, 78°37′ W 96
Dunnellon, *Fla., U.S.* 29°3′ N, 82°28′ W 105
Dunning, *Nebr., U.S.* 41°48′ N, 100°7′ W 90
Dunnottar Castle, site, *U.K.* 56°55′ N, 2°19′ W 150
Dunqul, spring, *Egypt* 23°23′ N, 31°39′ E 182
Dunrobin Castle, site, *U.K.* 57°58′ N, 4°5′ W 150
Dunseith, *N. Dak., U.S.* 48°47′ N, 100°4′ W 90
Dunsmuir, *Calif., U.S.* 41°12′ N, 122°18′ W 92
Dunstable, *U.K.* 51°53′ N, 0°32′ E 162
Dunstanburgh Castle, site, *U.K.* 55°28′ N, 1°42′ W 150
Dunster, *Can.* 53°6′ N, 119°53′ W 108
Dunster, *U.K.* 51°11′ N, 3°26′ W 162
Dunte, *Latv.* 57°25′ N, 24°25′ E 166
Duntroon, *N.Z.* 44°53′ S, 170°38′ E 240
Dunvegan, *Can.* 55°57′ N, 118°37′ W 108
Dunvegan Lake, *Can.* 60°10′ N, 107°45′ W 108
Duolun, *China* 42°10′ N, 116°30′ E 198
Duparquet, Lac, lake, *Can.* 48°27′ N, 79°52′ W 110
Dupont, *Ind., U.S.* 38°53′ N, 85°31′ W 102
Dupree, *S. Dak., U.S.* 45°2′ N, 101°37′ W 90
Dupuyer, *Mont., U.S.* 48°9′ N, 112°31′ W 90
Duqm, *Oman* 19°37′ N, 57°41′ E 182
Duque de Caxias, *Braz.* 22°44′ S, 43°18′ W 138
Duque de York, Isla, island, *Chile* 50°51′ S, 77°57′ W 134
Dur Sharrukin, ruin(s), *Iraq* 36°30′ N, 43°3′ E 195
Durack Range, *Austral.* 16°42′ S, 127°6′ E 230
Durance, river, *Fr.* 43°50′ N, 5°55′ E 165
Durance, river, *Fr.* 44°41′ N, 6°35′ E 165
Durand, *Ill., U.S.* 42°25′ N, 89°21′ W 102
Durand, *Mich., U.S.* 42°53′ N, 83°59′ W 102
Durand, *Wis., U.S.* 44°37′ N, 91°58′ W 94
Duranes, peak, *Sp.* 38°50′ N, 4°42′ W 164
Durango, *Colo., U.S.* 37°15′ N, 107°52′ W 92
Durango, *Mex.* 24°0′ N, 104°43′ W 114
Durango, adm. division, *Mex.* 24°46′ N, 105°26′ W 114
Durant, *Miss., U.S.* 33°3′ N, 89°52′ W 103
Durant, *Okla., U.S.* 33°58′ N, 96°23′ W 96
Duraykīsh, *Syr.* 34°54′ N, 36°7′ E 194
Durazno, *Uru.* 33°22′ S, 56°30′ W 139
Durban, *S. Af.* 29°52′ S, 30°57′ E 227
Durbe, *Latv.* 56°35′ N, 21°22′ E 166
Durbuy, *Belg.* 50°21′ N, 5°25′ E 167
Dúrcal, *Sp.* 36°59′ N, 3°34′ W 164
Đurđevac, *Croatia* 46°2′ N, 17°4′ E 168
Đurdevik, *Bosn. and Herzg.* 44°26′ N, 18°38′ E 168
Durduri, *Somalia* 11°14′ N, 48°35′ E 216
Düren, *Ger.* 50°48′ N, 6°29′ E 167
Durham, *Can.* 44°9′ N, 80°49′ W 102
Durham, *Conn., U.S.* 41°28′ N, 72°41′ W 104
Durham, *N.H., U.S.* 43°8′ N, 70°57′ W 104
Durham, *N.C., U.S.* 35°58′ N, 78°55′ W 96
Durham, *U.K.* 54°47′ N, 1°35′ W 162
Duri, oil field, *Indonesia* 1°22′ N, 101°5′ E 196
Durlston Head, *U.K.* 50°23′ N, 1°57′ W 150
Ḑurmā, *Saudi Arabia* 24°35′ N, 46°7′ E 182
Durmitor, mountains, *Mont.* 43°10′ N, 18°54′ E 168
Durmitor National Park, *Mont.* 43°10′ N, 19°21′ E 168
Durov Dag, oil field, *Azerb.* 39°30′ N, 49°4′ E 195
Dursley, *U.K.* 51°40′ N, 2°21′ W 162
Dursunbey, *Turk.* 39°36′ N, 28°37′ E 156
Duru, *Dem. Rep. of the Congo* 4°15′ N, 28°49′ E 224
Duru, river, *Dem. Rep. of the Congo* 3°39′ N, 28°11′ E 224
Dūrū', *Iran* 32°17′ N, 60°33′ E 180
D'Urville Island, *Antarctica* 63°0′ S, 57°29′ W 134
Durwalē, *Eth.* 8°47′ N, 43°4′ E 218
Dusa Marreb see Dhuusamarreeb, *Somalia* 5°31′ N, 46°24′ E 218
Duşak, *Turkm.* 37°12′ N, 60°2′ E 180
Dusetos, *Lith.* 55°44′ N, 25°52′ E 166
Dusey, river, *Can.* 51°10′ N, 87°15′ W 110
Dûsh, *Egypt* 24°34′ N, 30°37′ E 182
Dushan, *China* 25°48′ N, 107°31′ E 198
Dushanbe, *Taj.* 38°34′ N, 68°40′ E 197
Dushanzi (Maytag), *China* 44°17′ N, 84°53′ E 184
Dushet'i, *Ga.* 42°3′ N, 44°41′ E 195
Dŭskotna, *Bulg.* 42°52′ N, 27°11′ E 156
Dusky Sound 45°49′ S, 165°58′ E 240
Duson, *La., U.S.* 30°13′ N, 92°11′ W 103
Düsseldorf, *Ger.* 51°14′ N, 6°47′ E 167
Dustin Island, *Antarctica* 71°52′ S, 94°44′ W 248
Dutch John, *Utah, U.S.* 40°55′ N, 109°24′ W 90
Dutch Mountain, *Utah, U.S.* 40°12′ N, 113°55′ W 90
Dutlwe, *Botswana* 23°56′ S, 23°50′ E 227
Dutovo, *Russ.* 63°49′ N, 56°42′ E 154
Dutse, *Nig.* 11°43′ N, 9°19′ E 222
Dutsin Ma, *Nig.* 12°27′ N, 7°29′ E 222
Dutton, *Can.* 42°38′ N, 81°30′ W 102
Dutton, Mount, *Utah, U.S.* 38°0′ N, 112°17′ W 90
Duvan, *Russ.* 55°42′ N, 57°51′ E 154

Duvergé, *Dom. Rep.* 18°22′ N, 71°33′ W 116
Duvno, *Bosn. and Herzg.* 43°43′ N, 17°13′ E 168
Duwayhin, Khawr 24°14′ N, 51°0′ E 196
Duxbury, *Mass., U.S.* 42°2′ N, 70°41′ W 104
Duxford, *U.K.* 52°5′ N, 0°9′ E 162
Duy Xuyen, *Vietnam* 15°53′ N, 108°15′ E 202
Duyun, *China* 26°16′ N, 107°34′ E 198
Duz Dag, oil field, *Azerb.* 39°22′ N, 49°6′ E 195
Düzce, *Turk.* 40°50′ N, 31°10′ E 156
Dvarets, *Belarus* 53°24′ N, 25°35′ E 152
Dvina, river, *Russ.* 61°15′ N, 46°22′ E 160
Dvinskaya Guba 64°31′ N, 38°23′ E 143
Dvinskoy, *Russ.* 62°11′ N, 45°8′ E 154
Dvor, *Croatia* 45°3′ N, 16°22′ E 168
Dvukh Pilotov, Kosa, *Russ.* 68°5′ N, 178°33′ E 98
Dwarfie Stane, ruin(s), *U.K.* 58°51′ N, 3°28′ W 150
Dwarka, *India* 22°15′ N, 68°59′ E 186
Dwight, *Ill., U.S.* 41°5′ N, 88°25′ W 102
Dwikozy, *Pol.* 50°43′ N, 21°48′ E 152
Dyalakoro, *Mali* 12°3′ N, 7°51′ W 222
Dyat'kovo, *Russ.* 53°32′ N, 34°21′ E 154
Dyce, *Can.* 54°21′ N, 100°11′ W 108
Dyer, Cape, *Can.* 66°20′ N, 61°26′ W 106
Dyero, *Mali* 12°50′ N, 6°30′ W 222
Dyersburg, *Tenn., U.S.* 36°2′ N, 89°23′ W 96
Dymchurch, *U.K.* 51°1′ N, 1°0′ E 162
Dyment, *Can.* 49°37′ N, 92°20′ W 94
Dyrøy, *Nor.* 69°3′ N, 17°30′ E 152
Dytikí Eláda, adm. division, *Gr.* 38°2′ N, 21°22′ E 156
Dytikí Makedonía, adm. division, *Gr.* 40°26′ N, 21°7′ E 156
Dyupkun, Ozero, lake, *Russ.* 67°58′ N, 96°30′ E 169
Dyurtyuli, *Russ.* 55°28′ N, 54°55′ E 154
Dzanga-Ndoki National Park, *Cen. Af. Rep.* 2°30′ N, 15°16′ E 218
Dzavhan, river, *Mongolia* 47°49′ N, 93°37′ E 190
Dzerzhinsk, *Russ.* 56°14′ N, 43°31′ E 154
Dzerzhīnskoe, *Kaz.* 45°48′ N, 81°4′ E 184
Dzhagdy, Khrebet, *Russ.* 53°42′ N, 130°43′ E 190
Dzhalinda, *Russ.* 53°35′ N, 123°57′ E 190
Dzhankoy, *Ukr.* 45°41′ N, 34°20′ E 156
Dzhugdzhur, Khrebet, *Russ.* 57°47′ N, 136°52′ E 160
Działdowo, *Pol.* 53°13′ N, 20°10′ E 152
Dzibalchén, *Mex.* 19°27′ N, 89°45′ W 115
Dzibilchaltún, ruin(s), *Mex.* 21°5′ N, 89°42′ W 116
Džigolj, *Serb.* 43°20′ N, 21°35′ E 168
Dzilam de Bravo, *Mex.* 21°22′ N, 88°55′ W 116
Dzioua, *Alg.* 33°14′ N, 5°16′ E 214
Dzisna, *Belarus* 55°34′ N, 28°9′ E 166
Dzisna, river, *Belarus* 55°26′ N, 27°41′ E 166
Dzivin, *Belarus* 51°56′ N, 24°35′ E 152
Dzodze, *Ghana* 6°14′ N, 0°57′ E 222
Dzogsool, *Mongolia* 46°47′ N, 107°7′ E 198
Dzonot Carretero, *Mex.* 21°24′ N, 87°53′ W 116
Dzotol, *Mongolia* 45°52′ N, 115°5′ E 198
Dzuiché, *Mex.* 19°53′ N, 88°51′ W 115
Dzūkija National Park, *Lith.* 53°56′ N, 24°10′ E 166
Džūkste, *Latv.* 56°47′ N, 23°13′ E 166
Dzungarian Basin, *China* 45°51′ N, 82°34′ E 172
Dzungarian Gate, *Kaz.* 44°59′ N, 73°45′ E 172
Dzüünbayan, *Mongolia* 44°30′ N, 110°7′ E 198
Dzüünbulag, *Mongolia* 47°8′ N, 115°40′ E 198
Dzüünharaa, *Mongolia* 48°55′ N, 106°28′ E 198
Dzuunmod, *Mongolia* 47°41′ N, 107°0′ E 198
Dzvina Zakh, river, *Belarus* 55°34′ N, 28°34′ E 166
Dzyalyatsichy, *Belarus* 53°46′ N, 25°59′ E 158

E

Eabamet Lake, *Can.* 51°31′ N, 89°14′ W 81
Eads, *Colo., U.S.* 38°28′ N, 102°48′ W 90
Eagle, *Alas., U.S.* 64°43′ N, 141°21′ W 98
Eagle, *Colo., U.S.* 39°38′ N, 106°49′ W 90
Eagle Butte, *S. Dak., U.S.* 44°56′ N, 101°15′ W 90
Eagle Cap, peak, *Oreg., U.S.* 45°8′ N, 117°23′ W 90
Eagle Crags, peak, *Calif., U.S.* 35°23′ N, 117°6′ W 101
Eagle Creek, river, *Can.* 52°12′ N, 109°23′ W 80
Eagle Grove, *Iowa, U.S.* 42°39′ N, 93°53′ W 94
Eagle Islands, *Indian Ocean* 6°13′ S, 69°38′ E 188
Eagle Lake, *Calif., U.S.* 40°34′ N, 121°33′ W 81
Eagle Lake, *Can.* 49°32′ N, 93°29′ W 110
Eagle Lake, *Fla., U.S.* 27°58′ N, 81°47′ W 105
Eagle Mountain, *Minn., U.S.* 47°52′ N, 90°40′ W 94
Eagle Mountains, *Calif., U.S.* 33°52′ N, 115°41′ W 101
Eagle Peak, *Calif., U.S.* 41°16′ N, 120°18′ W 90
Eagle Peak, *Calif., U.S.* 38°10′ N, 119°27′ W 100
Eagle Peak, *Mont., U.S.* 47°14′ N, 115°28′ W 90
Eagle Peak, *N. Mex., U.S.* 33°39′ N, 108°38′ W 92
Eagle Peak, *Tex., U.S.* 30°53′ N, 105°9′ W 92
Eagle River, *Mich., U.S.* 47°24′ N, 88°18′ W 94
Eagle, river, *Can.* 52°46′ N, 58°44′ W 111
Eaglesham, *Can.* 55°46′ N, 117°54′ W 108
Eagletail Mountains, *Ariz., U.S.* 33°40′ N, 113°43′ W 101
Ear Falls, *Can.* 50°38′ N, 93°14′ W 90
Earl Park, *Ind., U.S.* 40°40′ N, 87°24′ W 102
Earlimart, *Calif., U.S.* 35°52′ N, 119°17′ W 100
Earlington, *Ky., U.S.* 37°15′ N, 87°31′ W 96
Earlton, *Can.* 47°42′ N, 79°49′ W 94
Earlville, *Ill., U.S.* 41°34′ N, 88°56′ W 102
Earnscleugh, *N.Z.* 45°14′ S, 169°18′ E 240
Earp, *Calif., U.S.* 34°9′ N, 114°19′ W 101
Earth, *Tex., U.S.* 34°12′ N, 102°25′ W 92
Easingwold, *U.K.* 54°7′ N, 1°11′ W 162
Easley, *S.C., U.S.* 34°49′ N, 82°37′ W 96
East Anglia, region, *Europe* 52°26′ N, 0°22′ E 162
East Anglian Heights, *U.K.* 52°23′ N, 0°27′ E 162
East Angus, *Can.* 45°28′ N, 71°40′ W 94
East Antarctica, region, *Antarctica* 75°20′ S, 113°12′ E 248
East Arlington, *Vt., U.S.* 43°3′ N, 73°9′ W 104
East Aurora, *N.Y., U.S.* 42°45′ N, 78°38′ W 94
East Barnet, *Vt., U.S.* 44°19′ N, 72°3′ W 104
East Barre, *Vt., U.S.* 44°9′ N, 72°28′ W 104
East Base, station, *Antarctica* 68°4′ S, 67°16′ W 248
East Bay 28°57′ N, 89°18′ W 103
East Bay 29°31′ N, 94°43′ W 103
East Bergholt, *U.K.* 51°58′ N, 1°1′ E 162
East Beskids, *Pol.* 49°28′ N, 20°46′ E 152
East Brewton, *Ala., U.S.* 31°4′ N, 87°3′ W 96
East Bridgewater, *Mass., U.S.* 42°1′ N, 70°58′ W 104
East Burke, *Vt., U.S.* 44°35′ N, 71°57′ W 104
East Butte, peak, *Idaho, U.S.* 43°29′ N, 112°44′ W 90
East Butte, peak, *Mont., U.S.* 48°50′ N, 111°14′ W 90
East Caicos, island, *U.K.* 21°45′ N, 71°27′ W 116
East Cape, *N.Z.* 37°42′ S, 178°33′ E 240
East Cape see Dezhneva, Mys, *Russ.* 65°45′ N, 169°46′ W 98
East Caroline Basin, *North Pacific Ocean* 2°2′ N, 146°50′ E 252
East Chicago, *Ind., U.S.* 41°37′ N, 87°26′ W 102
East China Sea 30°53′ N, 125°13′ E 190
East Coast Bays, *N.Z.* 36°45′ S, 174°45′ E 240
East Corinth, *Vt., U.S.* 44°3′ N, 72°14′ W 104
East Cote Blanche Bay 29°31′ N, 91°39′ W 103
East Coulee, *Can.* 51°22′ N, 112°31′ W 90
East Dereham, *U.K.* 52°40′ N, 0°56′ E 162
East Dubuque, *Mo., U.S.* 42°29′ N, 90°37′ W 94
East Fairview, *N. Dak., U.S.* 47°50′ N, 104°2′ W 108
East Falkland, island, *Falk. Is., U.K.* 51°14′ S, 58°25′ W 134
East Freetown, *Mass., U.S.* 41°45′ N, 70°58′ W 104
East Frisan Islands, *North Sea* 53°46′ N, 7°12′ E 163
East Glacier Park, *Mont., U.S.* 48°25′ N, 113°14′ W 90
East Govç, adm. division, *Mongolia* 44°17′ N, 108°52′ E 198
East Grand Forks, *Minn., U.S.* 47°55′ N, 97°2′ W 108
East Greenbush, *N.Y., U.S.* 42°34′ N, 73°43′ W 104
East Greenwich, *R.I., U.S.* 41°39′ N, 71°28′ W 104
East Grinstead, *U.K.* 51°7′ N, 1°58′ W 162
East Hampton, *N.Y., U.S.* 40°57′ N, 72°12′ W 104
East Hardwick, *Vt., U.S.* 44°30′ N, 72°19′ W 104
East Hartford, *Conn., U.S.* 41°45′ N, 72°39′ W 104
East Hartland, *Conn., U.S.* 41°59′ N, 72°55′ W 104
East Hebron, *N.H., U.S.* 43°41′ N, 71°47′ W 104
East Isaac, island, *Bahamas* 25°51′ N, 78°53′ W 105
East Jordan, *Mich., U.S.* 45°9′ N, 85°7′ W 94
East Lake, *Mich., U.S.* 44°14′ N, 86°17′ W 102
East Lansing, *Mich., U.S.* 42°44′ N, 84°28′ W 102
East Las Vegas, *Nev., U.S.* 36°5′ N, 115°3′ W 101
East Lempster, *N.H., U.S.* 43°13′ N, 72°11′ W 104
East London, *S. Af.* 32°59′ S, 27°52′ E 227
East Machias, *Me., U.S.* 44°44′ N, 67°25′ W 94
East Mariana Basin, *North Pacific Ocean* 12°38′ N, 151°56′ E 252
East Marion, *N.Y., U.S.* 41°7′ N, 72°21′ W 104
East Montpelier, *Vt., U.S.* 44°16′ N, 72°30′ W 104
East Mountain, *Oreg., U.S.* 44°59′ N, 122°14′ W 90
East Mountain, *Vt., U.S.* 44°38′ N, 71°51′ W 94
East Naples, *Fla., U.S.* 26°6′ N, 81°46′ W 105
East Pacific Rise, *South Pacific Ocean* 25°9′ S, 113°45′ W 252
East Palatka, *Fla., U.S.* 29°38′ N, 81°36′ W 105
East Pepperell, *Mass., U.S.* 42°39′ N, 71°35′ W 104
East Pine, *Can.* 55°42′ N, 121°12′ W 108
East Point, *Can.* 44°2′ N, 60°9′ W 111
East Point, *Can.* 51°21′ N, 80°2′ W 110
East Point, *Can.* 46°29′ N, 62°3′ W 111
East Prairie, *Mo., U.S.* 36°46′ N, 89°23′ W 94
East Providence, *R.I., U.S.* 41°49′ N, 71°23′ W 104
East Quogue, *N.Y., U.S.* 40°50′ N, 72°36′ W 104
East Range, *Nev., U.S.* 40°40′ N, 118°1′ W 90
East Retford, *U.K.* 53°19′ N, 0°57′ E 162
East Ridge, *Tenn., U.S.* 34°59′ N, 85°14′ W 96
East Saint Johnsbury, *Vt., U.S.* 44°26′ N, 71°58′ W 104
East Saint Louis, *Mo., U.S.* 38°36′ N, 90°8′ W 94
East Sea see Japan, Sea of 39°9′ N, 128°12′ E 200
East Sebago, *Me., U.S.* 43°50′ N, 70°39′ W 104
East Siberian Sea 72°23′ N, 162°36′ E 246
East Springfield, *Pa., U.S.* 41°57′ N, 80°25′ W 94
East Stoneham, *Me., U.S.* 44°15′ N, 70°50′ W 104
East Sullivan, *N.H., U.S.* 42°59′ N, 72°13′ W 104
East Tasman Plateau, *Tasman Sea* 43°59′ S, 150°40′ E 252
East Tavaputs Plateau, *Utah, U.S.* 39°28′ N, 110°1′ W 90
East Templeton, *Mass., U.S.* 42°34′ N, 72°3′ W 104
East Thetford, *Vt., U.S.* 43°48′ N, 72°12′ W 104
East Timor see Timor-Leste 9°0′ S, 125°0′ E 192
East Topsham, *Vt., U.S.* 44°7′ N, 72°15′ W 104
East Troy, *Wis., U.S.* 42°47′ N, 88°24′ W 102
East Wallingford, *Vt., U.S.* 43°26′ N, 72°54′ W 104
Eastbourne, *U.K.* 50°46′ N, 0°16′ E 162
Eastend, *Can.* 49°29′ N, 108°50′ W 90
Easter Fracture Zone, *South Pacific Ocean* 22°42′ S, 111°2′ W 252
Easter Group, islands, *Indian Ocean* 28°53′ S, 111°18′ E 230
Easter Island (Pascua, Isla de), *Chile* 27°0′ S, 109°0′ W 241
Eastern, adm. division, *Mongolia* 47°33′ N, 114°13′ E 198
Eastern Cape, adm. division, *S. Af.* 31°43′ S, 25°38′ E 227
Eastern Desert, *Africa* 30°44′ N, 32°4′ E 194
Eastern Equatoria, adm. division, *Sudan* 5°14′ N, 32°41′ E 218
Eastern Ghats, *Asia* 20°12′ N, 83°44′ E 188
Eastern Group, islands, *Great Australian Bight* 34°17′ S, 124°9′ E 230
Eastern Point, *Mass., U.S.* 42°31′ N, 70°41′ W 104
Easterville, *Can.* 53°3′ N, 99°40′ W 108
Eastford, *Conn., U.S.* 41°53′ N, 72°5′ W 104
Eastham, *Mass., U.S.* 41°50′ N, 69°59′ W 104
Easthampton, *Mass., U.S.* 42°15′ N, 72°41′ W 104
Eastlake, *Ohio, U.S.* 41°38′ N, 81°27′ W 102
Eastleigh, *U.K.* 50°58′ N, 1°22′ W 162
Eastmain, *Can.* 52°10′ N, 78°33′ W 106
Eastmain, river, *Can.* 51°58′ N, 73°51′ W 110
Eastmain Un, Réservoir de, lake, *Can.* 51°56′ N, 77°4′ W 110
Eastman, *Ga., U.S.* 32°11′ N, 83°11′ W 96
Easton, *Calif., U.S.* 36°38′ N, 119°48′ W 100
Easton, *Conn., U.S.* 41°14′ N, 73°19′ W 104
Easton, *Ill., U.S.* 40°13′ N, 89°51′ W 102
Easton, *Md., U.S.* 38°46′ N, 76°4′ W 94
Easton, *Pa., U.S.* 40°41′ N, 75°14′ W 94
Easton, *Wash., U.S.* 47°12′ N, 121°12′ W 100
Eastpoint, *Fla., U.S.* 29°45′ N, 84°52′ W 96
Eastport, *Me., U.S.* 44°54′ N, 67°0′ W 94
Eastport, *N.Y., U.S.* 40°49′ N, 72°44′ W 104
Eastsound, *Wash., U.S.* 48°41′ N, 122°55′ W 100
Eaton, *Colo., U.S.* 40°31′ N, 104°44′ W 90
Eaton, *Ohio, U.S.* 39°44′ N, 84°38′ W 102
Eaton Rapids, *Mich., U.S.* 42°31′ N, 84°40′ W 102
Eatonia, *Can.* 51°13′ N, 109°23′ W 90
Eatonton, *Ga., U.S.* 33°18′ N, 83°24′ W 96
Eatonville, *Wash., U.S.* 46°50′ N, 122°17′ W 100
Eau Claire, *Wis., U.S.* 44°48′ N, 91°29′ W 94
Eau Claire, Lac à l', lake, *Can.* 55°52′ N, 76°46′ W 106
Eau Froide, Lac à l', lake, *Can.* 50°49′ N, 73°17′ W 110
Eau Jaune, Lac à l', lake, *Can.* 49°39′ N, 75°29′ W 94
Eauripik Atoll, *F.S.M.* 6°41′ N, 140°4′ E 192
Eauze, *Fr.* 43°51′ N, 0°5′ E 150
Eaval, peak, *U.K.* 57°30′ N, 7°16′ W 150
Ébano, *Mex.* 22°11′ N, 98°23′ W 114
Ebbetts Pass, *Calif., U.S.* 38°33′ N, 119°49′ W 100
Ebbw Vale, *U.K.* 51°46′ N, 3°13′ W 162
Ebenezer, *Miss., U.S.* 32°57′ N, 90°6′ W 103
Ebeyti, *Kaz.* 48°9′ N, 55°24′ E 158
Ebino, *Japan* 32°3′ N, 130°49′ E 201
Ebinur Hu, lake, *China* 44°41′ N, 82°37′ E 184
Eboda see 'Abda, ruin(s), *Israel* 30°47′ N, 34°43′ E 194
Ebola, river, *Dem. Rep. of the Congo* 3°31′ N, 21°25′ E 218
Ebolowa, *Cameroon* 2°57′ N, 11°7′ E 218
Ebro, Embalse del, lake, *Sp.* 43°2′ N, 4°7′ W 164
Ebro, river, *Sp.* 42°42′ N, 3°23′ W 164
Ebruchorr, Gora, *Russ.* 67°43′ N, 31°55′ E 152
Ecbatana see Hamadān, *Iran* 34°48′ N, 48°27′ E 180
Eccleshall, *U.K.* 52°50′ N, 2°15′ W 162
Eceabat, *Turk.* 40°11′ N, 26°19′ E 156
Echallens, *Switz.* 46°38′ N, 6°38′ E 167
Echarate, *Peru* 12°46′ S, 72°35′ W 137
Echizen Misaki, *Japan* 35°53′ N, 135°42′ E 201
Echkill-Tash, *Kyrg.* 42°20′ N, 79°25′ E 184
Echo Bay, *Can.* 66°5′ N, 117°54′ W 106
Echo Bay, *Can.* 46°29′ N, 84°4′ W 94
Echo Cliffs, *Ariz., U.S.* 36°28′ N, 111°36′ W 92
Echo Summit, pass, *Calif., U.S.* 38°48′ N, 120°3′ W 90
Echternach, *Lux.* 49°48′ N, 6°25′ E 167
Echuca, *Austral.* 36°8′ S, 144°48′ E 231
Écija, *Sp.* 37°32′ N, 5°5′ W 164
Eckerö, *Fin.* 60°12′ N, 19°36′ E 166
Écommoy, *Fr.* 47°49′ N, 0°16′ E 150
Ecoporanga, *Braz.* 18°25′ S, 40°53′ W 138
Écorce, Lac de l', lake, *Can.* 47°0′ N, 77°17′ W 94
Ecrins National Park, *Fr.* 44°44′ N, 6°21′ E 167
Ecuador 1°33′ S, 78°58′ W 130
Ecueillé, *Fr.* 47°4′ N, 1°20′ E 150
Ed, *Nor.* 58°54′ N, 11°54′ E 152
Ed Da'ein, *Sudan* 11°25′ N, 26°7′ E 216
Ed Damazin, *Sudan* 11°49′ N, 34°18′ E 182
Ed Damer, *Sudan* 17°31′ N, 34°0′ E 182
Ed Debba, *Sudan* 18°0′ N, 30°57′ E 226
Ed Dueim, *Sudan* 13°56′ N, 32°18′ E 182
Edam, *Can.* 53°11′ N, 108°45′ W 108
Edberg, *Can.* 52°46′ N, 112°47′ W 108
Edd, *Eritrea* 13°55′ N, 41°36′ E 182
Eddiceton, *Miss., U.S.* 31°30′ N, 90°48′ W 103
Eddontenajon, *Can.* 57°47′ N, 129°56′ W 108
Eddy, Mount, *Calif., U.S.* 41°18′ N, 122°35′ W 90
Eddystone Rocks, islands, *English Channel* 50°15′ N, 5°13′ W 150
Eddyville, *Ky., U.S.* 37°5′ N, 88°6′ W 96
Ede, *Neth.* 52°2′ N, 5°39′ E 167
Edéa, *Cameroon* 3°47′ N, 10°9′ E 222
Edehon Lake, *Can.* 60°25′ N, 97°45′ W 108
Eden, *Can.* 42°46′ N, 80°44′ W 102
Eden, *Miss., U.S.* 32°58′ N, 90°21′ W 103
Eden, *N.C., U.S.* 36°30′ N, 79°47′ W 96
Eden, *Tex., U.S.* 31°11′ N, 99°51′ W 92
Eden, *Wyo., U.S.* 42°3′ N, 109°26′ W 90
Eden, river, *U.K.* 54°47′ N, 2°49′ W 162
Edenburg, *S. Af.* 29°46′ S, 25°55′ E 227
Edenton, *N.C., U.S.* 36°3′ N, 76°38′ W 96
Edessa see Şanlıurfa, *Turk.* 37°6′ N, 38°45′ E 180
Edewecht, *Ger.* 53°7′ N, 7°59′ E 163
Edgar, *Nebr., U.S.* 40°21′ N, 97°59′ W 90
Edgecomb, *Me., U.S.* 43°57′ N, 69°38′ W 104
Edgeley, *N. Dak., U.S.* 46°20′ N, 98°44′ W 90
Edgell Island, *Can.* 61°45′ N, 64°46′ W 106
Edgemont, *S. Dak., U.S.* 43°18′ N, 103°49′ W 90
Edgeøya, island, *Nor.* 77°32′ N, 25°31′ E 160
Edgerly, *La., U.S.* 30°13′ N, 93°31′ W 103
Edgerton, *Can.* 52°43′ N, 110°27′ W 108
Edgerton, *Minn., U.S.* 43°51′ N, 96°8′ W 90
Edgerton, *Wis., U.S.* 42°49′ N, 89°5′ W 110
Edgerton, *Wyo., U.S.* 43°24′ N, 106°13′ W 90
Edgewater, *Fla., U.S.* 28°58′ N, 80°54′ W 105
Edgewood, *Ill., U.S.* 38°55′ N, 88°40′ W 102
Edgeworthstown see Mostrim, *Ire.* 53°41′ N, 7°38′ W 150
Edievale, *N.Z.* 45°48′ S, 169°23′ E 240
Edigueri, spring, *Chad* 19°54′ N, 15°54′ E 216
Edina, *Mo., U.S.* 40°9′ N, 92°10′ W 94
Edinburg, *Miss., U.S.* 32°47′ N, 89°21′ W 103
Edinburgh, *Ind., U.S.* 39°21′ N, 85°58′ W 102
Edinburgh, *U.K.* 55°55′ N, 3°22′ W 150
Edirne (Adrianople), *Turk.* 41°39′ N, 26°34′ E 156
Edison, *Calif., U.S.* 35°21′ N, 118°53′ W 101
Edison, *Ga., U.S.* 31°32′ N, 84°44′ W 96
Edison, *N.J., U.S.* 40°30′ N, 74°26′ W 94
Edison, *Wash., U.S.* 48°32′ N, 122°27′ W 100
Edith Cavell, Mount, *Can.* 52°39′ N, 118°8′ W 108
Edith, Mount, *Mont., U.S.* 46°23′ N, 111°15′ W 90
Edjeleh, oil field, *Alg.* 27°49′ N, 9°44′ E 214
Edmond, *Okla., U.S.* 35°37′ N, 97°29′ W 96
Edmonds, *Wash., U.S.* 47°47′ N, 122°22′ W 100
Edmonton, *Can.* 53°33′ N, 113°39′ W 108
Edmore, *Mich., U.S.* 43°24′ N, 85°3′ W 102
Edmore, *N. Dak., U.S.* 48°23′ N, 98°28′ W 90
Edmundston, *Can.* 47°22′ N, 68°19′ W 94
Edna, *Tex., U.S.* 28°58′ N, 96°38′ W 96
Edna Bay, *Alas., U.S.* 55°57′ N, 133°40′ W 108
Edolo, *It.* 46°11′ N, 10°20′ E 167
Edough, Djebel, *Alg.* 36°57′ N, 6°55′ E 150
Edøy, *Nor.* 63°19′ N, 8°2′ E 152
Edrei see Dar'ā, *Syr.* 32°37′ N, 36°6′ E 194
Edremit, *Turk.* 39°34′ N, 27°0′ E 156
Edrengiyn Nuruu, *Mongolia* 44°49′ N, 97°6′ E 190
Edson, *Can.* 53°35′ N, 116°27′ W 108
Edsvalla, *Nor.* 59°26′ N, 13°8′ E 152
Eduardo Castex, *Arg.* 35°54′ S, 64°18′ W 134
Edward, Mount, *Antarctica* 75°6′ S, 70°29′ W 248
Edwards, *Calif., U.S.* 34°56′ N, 117°56′ W 101
Edwards, *Miss., U.S.* 32°18′ N, 90°36′ W 103
Edwards Air Force Base, *Calif., U.S.* 34°54′ N, 117°56′ W 101
Edwards Plateau, *Tex., U.S.* 30°39′ N, 101°4′ W 92
Edwardsport, *Ind., U.S.* 38°48′ N, 87°16′ W 102
Edwardsville, *Ill., U.S.* 38°48′ N, 89°58′ W 102
Edziza, Mount, *Can.* 57°41′ N, 130°45′ W 108
Edzná, ruin(s), *Mex.* 19°33′ N, 90°23′ W 115
Eede, *Neth.* 51°15′ N, 3°27′ E 163
Eeklo, *Belg.* 51°11′ N, 3°33′ E 163
Eel, river, *Ind., U.S.* 39°21′ N, 87°6′ W 102
Effie, *La., U.S.* 31°11′ N, 92°10′ W 103
Effingham, *Ill., U.S.* 39°6′ N, 88°32′ W 102
Eflâni, *Turk.* 41°25′ N, 32°57′ E 156
Eg, *Mongolia* 48°49′ N, 110°5′ E 198
Egadi, Isole, islands, *Tyrrhenian Sea* 37°48′ N, 11°13′ E 156
Egalah, Adrar, peak, *Niger* 18°9′ N, 8°32′ E 222
Egan Range, *Nev., U.S.* 39°49′ N, 115°8′ W 90
Eganville, *Can.* 45°32′ N, 77°6′ W 94
Egedesminde see Aasiaat, *Den.* 68°45′ N, 52°53′ W 106
Egenolf Lake, *Can.* 59°2′ N, 100°32′ W 108
Eger, *Hung.* 47°53′ N, 20°22′ E 168
Egeria Fracture Zone, *Indian Ocean* 19°30′ S, 68°2′ E 254
Egersund, *Nor.* 58°26′ N, 6°0′ E 150
Egg Lake, *Can.* 54°58′ N, 106°50′ W 108
Egg, river, *Can.* 59°58′ N, 95°33′ W 108
Eggan, *Nig.* 8°39′ N, 6°13′ E 222
Eggebek, *Ger.* 54°38′ N, 9°22′ E 150
Eggenburg, *Aust.* 48°38′ N, 15°49′ E 152
Éghezée, *Belg.* 50°35′ N, 4°53′ E 167
Eğil, *Turk.* 38°15′ N, 40°5′ E 195
Egindibulaq, *Kaz.* 49°49′ N, 76°26′ E 184
Egindiköl, *Kaz.* 51°3′ N, 69°31′ E 184
Égio, *Gr.* 38°12′ N, 22°6′ E 180
Eglinton Island, *Can.* 75°24′ N, 126°46′ W 106
Eglon, ruin(s), *Israel* 31°31′ N, 34°41′ E 194
Egmont Islands, *Indian Ocean* 7°21′ S, 70°31′ E 188
Egmont, Mount see Taranaki, Mount, peak, *N.Z.* 39°20′ S, 173°58′ E 240
Egremont, *U.K.* 54°28′ N, 3°32′ W 162
Eğridir, *Turk.* 37°50′ N, 30°49′ E 156
Eğridir Gölü, lake, *Turk.* 38°5′ N, 30°11′ E 180
Eğrigöz Dağı, peak, *Turk.* 39°23′ N, 29°2′ E 156
Éguas (Correntina), river, *Braz.* 13°42′ S, 45°43′ W 138
Egvekinot, *Russ.* 66°17′ N, 179°1′ W 160
Egyek, *Hung.* 47°38′ N, 20°52′ E 168
Egypt 26°46′ N, 27°58′ E 216
Ehime, adm. division, *Japan* 33°37′ N, 132°38′ E 201
Ehingen, *Ger.* 48°16′ N, 9°44′ E 152
Ehrang, *Ger.* 49°48′ N, 6°41′ E 167
Ehrenberg, *Ger.* 50°30′ N, 9°59′ E 167
Ei, *Japan* 31°12′ N, 130°30′ E 201
Eide, *Nor.* 62°53′ N, 7°26′ E 152
Eiderdamm, *Ger.* 54°14′ N, 7°58′ E 150
Eidsbugarden, *Nor.* 61°22′ N, 8°15′ E 152
Eidskog, *Nor.* 60°1′ N, 12°6′ E 152
Eidsvoll, *Nor.* 60°19′ N, 11°12′ E 152
Eifel, region, *Europe* 50°38′ N, 7°3′ E 167
Eige, Càrn, peak, *U.K.* 57°16′ N, 5°13′ W 150
Eigerøy, region, *North Sea* 58°25′ N, 5°35′ E 150
Eight Degree Channel 7°30′ N, 71°39′ E 188
Eight Mile Rock, *Bahamas* 26°31′ N, 78°47′ W 105
Eighty Mile Beach, *Austral.* 20°6′ S, 119°49′ E 231
Eil Malk see Mecherchar, island, *Palau* 7°7′ N, 134°22′ E 242
Eilendorf, *Ger.* 50°46′ N, 6°10′ E 167
Eiler Rasmussen, Cape, *Den.* 81°2′ N, 11°2′ W 246
Eiler Rasmussen, Kap, *Den.* 82°38′ N, 19°35′ W 246
Eilerts de Haan Gebergte, *Suriname* 2°50′ N, 56°17′ W 130
Eina, *Nor.* 60°38′ N, 10°35′ E 152
Eindhoven, *Neth.* 51°26′ N, 5°28′ E 167
Eion, ruin(s), *Gr.* 40°46′ N, 23°46′ E 156

Eirik Ridge, *North Atlantic Ocean* 57°47' N, 44°35' W 253
Eirunepé, *Braz.* 6°40' S, 69°55' W 130
Eisenach, *Ger.* 50°58' N, 10°19' E 167
Eisenstadt, *Aust.* 47°50' N, 16°31' E 168
Eišiškės, *Lith.* 54°10' N, 24°58' E 166
Eitorf, *Ger.* 50°45' N, 7°27' E 167
Eivissa, *Sp.* 38°53' N, 1°25' E 150
Eixe, Sierra do, *Sp.* 42°16' N, 7°23' W 150
Ejea de los Caballeros, *Sp.* 42°7' N, 1°10' W 164
Ejeda, *Madagascar* 24°20' S, 44°30' E 220
Ejin Horo Qi (Altan Xiret), *China* 39°33' N, 109°44' E 198
Ejin Qi, *China* 42°1' N, 101°30' E 190
Ejouj, spring, *Mauritania* 17°1' N, 9°23' W 222
Ejura, *Ghana* 7°25' N, 1°24' W 222
Ekalaka, *Mont., U.S.* 45°52' N, 104°34' W 90
Ekenäs (Tammisaari), *Fin.* 59°58' N, 23°26' E 166
Ekerem, *Turkm.* 38°5' N, 53°50' E 180
Ekeren, *Belg.* 51°16' N, 4°25' E 163
Eket, *Nig.* 4°39' N, 7°56' E 222
Ekibastuz, *Kaz.* 51°44' N, 75°19' E 184
Ekkerøy, *Nor.* 70°4' N, 30°8' E 152
Eklund Islands, *Bellingshausen Sea* 73°25' S, 70°57' W 248
Ekoli, *Dem. Rep. of the Congo* 0°25' N, 24°16' E 224
Ekombe, *Dem. Rep. of the Congo* 1°8' N, 21°32' E 218
Ekonda, *Russ.* 66°5' N, 103°55' E 160
Ekrafane, *Niger* 15°21' N, 3°43' E 222
Ekukola, *Dem. Rep. of the Congo* 0°30' N, 18°53' E 218
Ekwan, river, *Can.* 53°36' N, 84°16' W 106
Ekwendeni, *Malawi* 11°23' S, 33°48' E 224
El Abiadh, Ras, *Tun.* 37°16' N, 9°8' E 156
Ēl Ābrēd, *Eth.* 5°30' N, 45°14' E 218
El Adeb Larache, oil field, *Alg.* 27°23' N, 8°44' E 214
El Agreb, oil field, *Alg.* 30°37' N, 5°30' E 214
El Aïoun, *Mor.* 34°35' N, 2°29' W 214
El 'Aiyaṭ, *Egypt* 29°37' N, 31°12' E 180
El 'Alamein, *Egypt* 30°49' N, 28°52' E 180
El Álamo, *Mex.* 31°32' N, 116°1' W 92
El 'Âmirîya, *Egypt* 31°1' N, 29°48' E 180
El Angel, *Ecua.* 0°36' N, 78°7' W 136
El 'Arag, spring, *Egypt* 28°53' N, 26°27' E 180
El Aricha, *Alg.* 34°13' N, 1°16' W 214
El 'Arîsh (Rhinocolura), *Egypt* 31°6' N, 33°46' E 194
El Arneb, spring, *Mali* 16°19' N, 4°55' W 222
El Atimine, spring, *Alg.* 28°51' N, 3°9' W 214
El Badâri, *Egypt* 27°1' N, 31°23' E 180
El Bagre, *Col.* 7°36' N, 74°47' W 136
El Bah, *Eth.* 9°44' N, 41°47' E 224
El Baḥrein, spring, *Egypt* 28°41' N, 26°30' E 180
El Ballâh, *Egypt* 30°45' N, 32°17' E 194
El Ballestero, *Sp.* 38°50' N, 2°28' W 164
El Balyana, *Egypt* 26°14' N, 31°55' E 180
El Banco, *Col.* 9°1' N, 73°58' W 136
El Bauga, *Sudan* 18°13' N, 33°52' E 182
El Baúl, *Venez.* 8°56' N, 68°20' W 136
El Bayadh, *Alg.* 33°42' N, 1°0' E 214
El Béoua, spring, *Mali* 15°6' N, 6°25' W 222
El Berié, spring, *Mauritania* 16°11' N, 9°57' W 222
El Beru Hagia, *Somalia* 2°47' N, 41°3' E 224
El Beyed, spring, *Mauritania* 16°55' N, 10°3' W 222
El Bher, spring, *Mauritania* 15°59' N, 8°42' W 222
El Biar, *Alg.* 36°44' N, 3°1' E 150
El Bonillo, *Sp.* 38°57' N, 2°33' W 164
El Borma, oil field, *Tun.* 31°36' N, 9°9' E 214
El Bosque, *Sp.* 36°45' N, 5°31' W 164
El Burgo de Osma, *Sp.* 41°35' N, 3°4' W 164
El Cabo de Gata, *Sp.* 36°46' N, 2°15' W 164
El Caburé, *Arg.* 26°2' S, 62°21' W 139
El Caín, *Arg.* 41°37' S, 68°16' W 134
El Calafate (Lago Argentino), *Arg.* 50°26' S, 72°13' W 123
El Callao, *Venez.* 7°22' N, 61°49' W 130
El Calvario, *Venez.* 9°0' N, 66°59' W 136
El Campello, *Sp.* 38°25' N, 0°24' E 164
El Campillo de la Jara, *Sp.* 39°35' N, 5°3' W 164
El Campo, *Tex., U.S.* 29°11' N, 96°17' W 96
El Cap, *Egypt* 30°56' N, 32°17' E 194
El Capitan, peak, *Mont., U.S.* 45°59' N, 114°29' W 90
El Carmen, *Arg.* 24°24' S, 65°18' W 132
El Carmen, *Bol.* 18°49' S, 58°35' W 132
El Carmen, *Bol.* 14°0' S, 63°41' W 137
El Carmen, *Col.* 5°55' N, 76°14' W 136
El Carmen, *Venez.* 1°15' N, 66°50' W 136
El Carpio, *Sp.* 37°56' N, 4°31' W 164
El Castillo de Las Concepción, *Nicar.* 10°58' N, 84°24' W 115
El Ceibo, *Guatemala* 17°16' N, 90°55' W 115
El Centro, *Calif., U.S.* 32°47' N, 115°34' W 101
El Chichón, peak, *Mex.* 17°21' N, 93°23' W 115
El Chico, *Mex.* 20°8' N, 98°54' W 112
El Choro, *Bol.* 18°24' S, 67°9' W 137
El Cimaterio, *Mex.* 20°29' N, 100°27' W 112
El Claro, *Mex.* 30°28' N, 111°11' W 92
El Cocuy, *Col.* 6°24' N, 72°28' W 136
El Cocuy National Park, *Col.* 6°35' N, 72°43' W 136
El Cogoi, *Arg.* 24°48' S, 59°12' W 132
El Colorado, *Arg.* 26°18' S, 59°23' W 139
El Corcovado, *Arg.* 43°30' S, 71°32' W 134
El Cuyo, *Mex.* 21°32' N, 87°42' W 116
El 'Dab'a, *Egypt* 31°1' N, 28°23' E 180
El Dakka, ruin(s), *Egypt* 23°4' N, 32°32' E 182
El Deir, *Egypt* 25°19' N, 32°33' E 182
El Descanso, *Mex.* 32°12' N, 116°54' W 92
El Desemboque, *Mex.* 29°33' N, 112°26' W 92
El Desmonte, *Arg.* 22°42' S, 62°17' W 132
El Djouf, *Mauritania* 19°53' N, 10°5' W 222
El Dorado, *Ark., U.S.* 33°11' N, 92°41' W 103
El Dorado, *Kans., U.S.* 37°47' N, 96°52' W 92
El Dorado, *Venez.* 6°43' N, 61°36' W 130
El Dorado Springs, *Mo., U.S.* 37°51' N, 94°2' W 94
El Egder, spring, *Eth.* 3°51' N, 38°54' E 224
El Eglab, region, *Africa* 25°45' N, 5°58' W 214
El Encanto, *Col.* 1°38' S, 73°14' W 136
El Esfuerzo, *Mex.* 25°23' N, 103°15' W 114
El Faiyûm, *Egypt* 29°16' N, 30°48' E 180
El Farâid, Gebel, peak, *Egypt* 23°31' N, 35°19' E 182
El Fasher, *Sudan* 13°37' N, 25°19' E 226
El Fashn, *Egypt* 28°48' N, 30°50' E 180
El Fifi, *Sudan* 10°3' N, 25°1' E 224
El Fuerte, *Mex.* 23°49' N, 103°8' W 114
El Fula, *Sudan* 11°46' N, 28°20' E 216
El Gâga, *Egypt* 24°48' N, 30°30' E 226
El Gallego, *Mex.* 29°48' N, 106°23' W 92
El Galpón, *Arg.* 25°24' S, 64°39' W 134
El Gassi, oil field, *Alg.* 30°53' N, 5°37' E 214
El Geili, *Sudan* 16°0' N, 32°37' E 182
El Gezira, region, *Africa* 14°22' N, 32°15' E 182
El Ghobena, *Tun.* 35°29' N, 9°38' E 156
El Gîza, *Egypt* 30°1' N, 31°8' E 180
El Golea, *Alg.* 30°33' N, 2°43' E 207
El Goled Bahri, *Sudan* 18°27' N, 30°40' E 226
El Golfo de Santa Clara, *Mex.* 31°41' N, 114°32' W 92
El Grau, *Sp.* 38°59' N, 0°10' E 164
El Grau de Castelló, *Sp.* 39°58' N, 2°0' E 164
El Grullo, *Mex.* 19°48' N, 104°14' W 114
El Guapo, *Venez.* 10°8' N, 66°2' W 136
El Hadjira, *Alg.* 32°37' N, 5°31' E 214
El Hajeb, *Mor.* 33°41' N, 5°25' W 214
El Hamma, *Tun.* 33°55' N, 9°48' E 216
El Ḥammâm, *Egypt* 30°51' N, 29°19' E 180
El Hank, region, *Africa* 24°58' N, 6°26' W 214
El Haouaria, *Tun.* 37°3' N, 11°0' E 156
El Haraïg, *Tun.* 35°47' N, 9°13' E 156
El Harrach, *Alg.* 36°48' N, 3°9' E 214
El Hasaheisa, *Sudan* 14°41' N, 33°17' E 182
El Hawata, *Sudan* 13°24' N, 34°36' E 182
El Ḥeiz, *Egypt* 28°2' N, 28°37' E 180
El Hiaïda, *Mor.* 35°5' N, 6°11' W 150
El Higo, *Mex.* 21°45' N, 98°27' W 114
El Hilla, *Sudan* 13°24' N, 27°5' E 226
El Hobra, *Alg.* 32°10' N, 4°43' E 214
El Homeur, *Alg.* 29°52' N, 1°36' E 214
El Huariche, *Mex.* 24°49' N, 103°9' W 114
El Iskandarîya (Alexandria), *Egypt* 31°10' N, 29°55' E 180
El Jabha (Puerto Capaz), *Mor.* 35°12' N, 4°40' W 150
El Jadida (Mazagan), *Mor.* 33°15' N, 8°33' W 214
El Jardín, *Sp.* 38°48' N, 2°19' W 164
El Jebelein, *Sudan* 12°34' N, 32°52' E 182
El Jemm, *Tun.* 35°18' N, 10°43' E 156
El Kanâyis, spring, *Egypt* 25°0' N, 33°16' E 182
El Karaba, *Sudan* 18°29' N, 33°44' E 182
El Karnak, ruin(s), *Egypt* 25°44' N, 32°37' E 182
El Katulo, spring, *Kenya* 2°26' N, 40°35' E 224
El Kawa, *Sudan* 13°42' N, 32°31' E 182
El Kef, *Tun.* 36°11' N, 8°42' E 156
El Kelaa des Srarhna, *Mor.* 32°5' N, 7°25' W 214
Ēl Kerē, *Eth.* 5°48' N, 42°9' E 224
El Khandaq, *Sudan* 18°36' N, 30°34' E 226
El Khârga, *Egypt* 25°28' N, 30°29' E 182
El Kharrouba, *Tun.* 35°23' N, 9°59' E 156
El Khnâchîch, *Mali* 21°6' N, 5°26' W 222
El Kodab, *Sudan* 16°12' N, 32°30' E 182
El Koin, *Sudan* 19°18' N, 30°33' E 216
El Kseïbat, *Alg.* 27°58' N, 0°30' E 214
El Kseur, *Alg.* 36°40' N, 4°51' E 150
El Ksiba, *Mor.* 32°38' N, 6°3' W 214
El Kuntilla, *Egypt* 29°58' N, 34°41' E 180
El Lagowa, *Sudan* 11°25' N, 29°8' E 216
El Lein, spring, *Kenya* 0°26' N, 40°30' E 224
El Leiya, *Sudan* 16°15' N, 35°26' E 182
El Limón, *Mex.* 22°48' N, 99°1' W 114
El Lucero, *Mex.* 25°56' N, 103°26' W 114
El Macao, *Dom. Rep.* 18°45' N, 68°31' W 116
El Mahalla el Kubra, *Egypt* 30°59' N, 31°8' E 226
El Maḥârîq, *Egypt* 25°39' N, 30°36' E 226
El Mahfoura, spring, *Alg.* 32°34' N, 2°12' E 214
El Maitén, *Arg.* 42°3' S, 71°11' W 134
El Maïz, *Alg.* 28°25' N, 0°15' E 214
El Malpais National Monument, *N. Mex., U.S.* 34°36' N, 110°21' W 92
El Manaqil, *Sudan* 14°12' N, 33°0' E 182
El Mango, *Venez.* 1°54' N, 66°33' W 136
El Manshâh, *Egypt* 26°29' N, 31°42' E 180
El Mansour, *Alg.* 27°38' N, 0°19' E 214
El Manṣûra, *Egypt* 30°58' N, 31°24' E 180
El Maqdaba, spring, *Egypt* 30°53' N, 34°0' E 194
El Mazâr, *Egypt* 31°1' N, 33°23' E 194
El Medda, *Mauritania* 19°56' N, 13°20' W 222
El Meghaïer, *Alg.* 33°56' N, 5°54' E 214
El Melemm, *Sudan* 9°55' N, 28°43' E 224
El Messir, spring, *Chad* 15°43' N, 16°59' E 216
El Mhabes, spring, *Mauritania* 23°43' N, 8°53' W 214
El Milagro, *Arg.* 31°1' S, 65°59' W 134
El Milhas, spring, *Mauritania* 25°25' N, 6°55' W 214
El Milia, *Alg.* 36°48' N, 6°16' E 150
El Mina, *Leb.* 34°27' N, 35°49' E 194
El Mîna, *Leb.* 34°27' N, 35°49' E 156
El Minya, *Egypt* 28°7' N, 30°41' E 180
El Mirador, ruin(s), *Guatemala* 17°43' N, 90°3' W 115
El Mirage, *Ariz., U.S.* 33°37' N, 112°19' W 92
El Moale, spring, *Sudan* 10°20' N, 23°46' E 224
El Moïnane, spring, *Mauritania* 19°10' N, 11°29' W 222
El Morro National Monument, *N. Mex., U.S.* 35°1' N, 108°26' W 92
El Moueïla, *Mauritania* 21°38' N, 10°36' W 222
El Mouilha, spring, *Mali* 16°40' N, 5°6' W 222
El Mraïti, spring, *Mali* 19°12' N, 2°19' W 222
El Mrâyer, spring, *Mauritania* 21°28' N, 8°12' W 222
El Mreïti, spring, *Mauritania* 23°29' N, 7°56' W 214
El Mreyyé, region, *Africa* 18°48' N, 8°16' W 222
El Mughāzī, *Gaza Strip, Israel* 31°23' N, 34°22' E 194
El Mulato, *Mex.* 29°22' N, 104°11' W 92
El Mzereb, spring, *Mali* 24°46' N, 6°23' W 214
El Nasser, *Egypt* 24°34' N, 33°2' E 182
El Nayar, *Mex.* 23°55' N, 104°41' W 114
El Nido, *Philippines* 11°10' N, 119°24' E 203
El Niybo, *Eth.* 4°31' N, 39°54' E 224
El Obeid, *Sudan* 13°8' N, 30°11' E 226
El Oro, *Mex.* 19°46' N, 100°8' W 114
El Oualadji, *Mali* 16°13' N, 3°28' W 214
El Palmito, *Mex.* 25°35' N, 104°59' W 114
El Pao, *Venez.* 8°1' N, 62°38' W 130
El Pao, *Venez.* 8°46' N, 64°39' W 116
El Paso, *Ill., U.S.* 40°43' N, 89°1' W 102
El Paso, *Tex., U.S.* 31°45' N, 106°29' W 92
El Paso Mountains, *Calif., U.S.* 35°23' N, 117°59' W 101
El Payo, *Sp.* 40°18' N, 6°45' W 150
El Perelló, *Sp.* 40°52' N, 0°43' E 164
El Perú, *Venez.* 7°18' N, 61°50' W 130
El Pescadero, *Mex.* 23°20' N, 110°11' W 112
El Picazo, *Sp.* 39°26' N, 2°7' W 164
El Piñal, *Venez.* 7°26' N, 68°41' W 136
El Plomo, *Mex.* 31°14' N, 112°4' W 92
El Pobo de Dueñas, *Sp.* 40°45' N, 1°39' W 164
El Pont de Suert, *Sp.* 42°23' N, 0°44' E 164
El Portal, *Calif., U.S.* 37°41' N, 119°48' W 100
El Portezuelo, *Arg.* 46°2' S, 71°38' W 134
El Porvenir, *Col.* 4°42' N, 71°23' W 136
El Porvenir, *Pan.* 9°34' N, 78°59' W 115
El Porvenir, *Venez.* 6°56' N, 68°43' W 136
El Potosí, *Mex.* 24°50' N, 100°20' W 114
El Potosí National Park, *Mex.* 21°58' N, 100°4' W 112
El Pozo, *Mex.* 30°55' N, 109°16' W 92
El Pozo, *Mex.* 24°54' N, 107°15' W 112
El Progreso, *Hond.* 15°21' N, 87°48' W 115
El Pueblito, *Mex.* 29°5' N, 105°8' W 92
El Puente, *Bol.* 21°14' S, 65°19' W 137
El Qâhira (Cairo), *Egypt* 30°3' N, 31°8' E 180
El Qanṭara, *Egypt* 30°51' N, 32°19' E 194
El Qaṣr, *Egypt* 25°42' N, 28°50' E 180
El Quṣeima, *Egypt* 30°39' N, 34°22' E 194
El Râshda, *Egypt* 25°33' N, 28°54' E 226
El Real, *Pan.* 8°6' N, 77°45' W 115
El Reno, *Okla., U.S.* 35°30' N, 97°57' W 92
El Rhaïlassiya Oumm Amoura, spring, *Mauritania* 16°26' N, 9°24' W 222
El Rio, *Calif., U.S.* 34°14' N, 119°11' W 101
El Rito, *N. Mex., U.S.* 36°21' N, 106°12' W 92
El Roble, *Mex.* 23°13' N, 106°14' W 114
El Ronquillo, *Sp.* 37°43' N, 6°11' W 164
El Rosario, *Mex.* 30°4' N, 115°46' W 92
El Ruâfa, spring, *Egypt* 30°49' N, 34°7' E 194
El Rubio, *Sp.* 37°21' N, 5°0' W 164
El Rucio, *Mex.* 23°23' N, 102°4' W 114
El Rusbayo, *Mex.* 31°1' N, 109°15' W 92
El Sabinal National Park, *Mex.* 26°3' N, 99°47' W 112
El Salado, *Mex.* 24°15' N, 100°51' W 114
El Salto, *Mex.* 20°31' N, 103°11' W 114
El Salto, *Mex.* 23°44' N, 105°22' W 114
El Salvador 14°0' N, 89°0' W 115
El Salvador, *Mex.* 24°28' N, 100°53' W 114
El Samán de Apure, *Venez.* 7°52' N, 68°43' W 136
El Sasabe, *Mex.* 31°28' N, 111°33' W 92
El Sauz, *Mex.* 29°0' N, 106°15' W 92
El Sauzal, *Mex.* 31°53' N, 116°41' W 92
El Seco, *Mex.* 19°6' N, 97°39' W 114
El Shab, spring, *Egypt* 22°18' N, 29°45' E 226
El Sibû', ruin(s), *Egypt* 22°44' N, 32°22' E 182
El Soberbio, *Arg.* 27°21' S, 54°15' W 139
El Socorro, *Venez.* 8°59' N, 65°45' W 136
El Sombrero, *Venez.* 9°23' N, 67°4' W 136
El Sueco, *Mex.* 29°51' N, 106°23' W 92
El Suweis (Suez), *Egypt* 30°1' N, 32°26' E 180
El Tajín, ruin(s), *Mex.* 20°24' N, 97°28' W 114
El Tama National Park, *Venez.* 7°10' N, 72°14' W 136
El Tecuan, *Mex.* 19°21' N, 104°58' W 114
El Teleno, peak, *Sp.* 42°19' N, 6°28' W 150
El Tell el Ahmar, *Egypt* 30°53' N, 32°24' E 194
El Tigre, *Col.* 6°45' N, 71°46' W 136
El Tîna, *Egypt* 31°2' N, 32°17' E 194
El Toboso, *Sp.* 39°31' N, 3°2' W 164
El Tocuyo, *Venez.* 9°45' N, 69°49' W 136
El Tomatal, *Mex.* 28°26' N, 114°6' W 92
El Toro, peak, *Sp.* 39°58' N, 4°5' E 164
El Trébol, *Arg.* 32°13' S, 61°42' W 139
El Triunfo, Pirámide, peak, *Arg.* 25°45' S, 61°51' W 132
El Tuito, *Mex.* 20°19' N, 105°25' W 114
El Tuparro National Park, *Col.* 5°10' N, 67°0' W 136
El Ṭûr, *Egypt* 28°14' N, 33°37' E 180
El Turbio, *Arg.* 51°42' S, 72°8' W 134
El Valle, *Col.* 6°5' N, 77°26' W 136
El Veladero National Park, *Mex.* 16°53' N, 100°0' W 112
El Vendrell, *Sp.* 41°13' N, 1°32' E 164
El Vergel, *Mex.* 26°26' N, 106°24' W 114
El Wak, *Kenya* 2°44' N, 40°53' E 224
El Walamo, *Mex.* 23°6' N, 106°13' W 114
El Wasifîya, *Egypt* 30°33' N, 32°8' E 194
El Wâsṭa, *Egypt* 29°20' N, 31°10' E 180
El Wuz, *Sudan* 15°1' N, 30°12' E 226
El Yagual, *Venez.* 7°29' N, 68°26' W 136
El Zape, *Mex.* 25°46' N, 105°45' W 114
Elaho, river, *Can.* 50°14' N, 123°38' W 100
Elaia, Cape, *Northern Cyprus, Cyprus* 35°16' N, 34°4' E 194
Elan', *Russ.* 57°38' N, 63°38' E 154
Elat, *Israel* 29°35' N, 34°59' E 180
Elato Atoll, *F.S.M.* 6°59' N, 145°34' E 192
El'Atrun, spring, *Sudan* 18°6' N, 26°36' E 226
El'Auja see Nizzana, *Israel* 30°52' N, 34°25' E 194
Elâzığ, *Turk.* 38°39' N, 39°12' E 195
Elba, *Ala., U.S.* 31°24' N, 86°4' W 96
Elba, Cape see Hadarba, Ras, *Egypt* 21°49' N, 36°55' E 182
Elba, island, *It.* 42°54' N, 9°57' E 214
Elbe, *Wash., U.S.* 46°45' N, 122°12' W 100
Elbe, river, *Ger.* 53°7' N, 10°4' E 143
Elbert, Mount, *Colo., U.S.* 39°6' N, 106°31' W 90
Elberta, *Mich., U.S.* 44°35' N, 86°13' W 94
Elbeuf, *Fr.* 49°17' N, 1°0' E 163
Elbistan, *Turk.* 38°11' N, 37°10' E 156
Elbląg, *Pol.* 54°9' N, 19°25' E 166
Elbow, *Can.* 51°8' N, 106°38' W 90
Elbow Cays, *North Atlantic Ocean* 23°56' N, 81°24' W 116
Elbow Lake, *Minn., U.S.* 45°59' N, 95°59' W 90
El'brus, peak, *Russ.* 43°18' N, 42°24' E 195
Elburg, *Neth.* 52°26' N, 5°49' E 163
Elburz, *Iran* 36°26' N, 52°39' E 207
Elburz Mountains see Alborz, Reshteh-ye, *Iran* 36°43' N, 49°25' E 195
Elche de la Sierra, *Sp.* 38°26' N, 2°3' W 164
Elche (Elx), *Sp.* 38°15' N, 0°42' E 164
Elcho Island, *Austral.* 11°51' S, 135°35' E 192
Elda, *Sp.* 38°28' N, 0°49' E 150
Eldama Ravine, *Kenya* 4°238' N, 35°43' E 224
El'dikan, *Russ.* 60°48' N, 135°14' E 160
Eldon, *Iowa, U.S.* 40°55' N, 92°13' W 94
Eldon, *Mo., U.S.* 38°19' N, 92°35' W 94
Eldorado, *Arg.* 26°29' S, 54°42' W 139
Eldorado, *Mex.* 24°18' N, 107°23' W 112
Eldorado, *Mo., U.S.* 37°47' N, 88°26' W 96
Eldorado, *Okla., U.S.* 34°26' N, 99°39' W 96
Eldorado, *Tex., U.S.* 30°51' N, 100°36' W 92
Eldorado Mountains, *Nev., U.S.* 35°49' N, 114°58' W 101
Eldorado Pass, *Oreg., U.S.* 44°20' N, 118°7' W 90
Eldorado Paulista, *Braz.* 24°35' S, 48°9' W 138
Eldoret, *Kenya* 0°28' N, 35°18' E 224
Electra, *Tex., U.S.* 34°0' N, 98°55' W 92
Electric Mills, *Miss., U.S.* 32°44' N, 88°28' W 103
Electric Peak, *Mont., U.S.* 44°59' N, 110°56' W 90
El'Ein, spring, *Sudan* 16°34' N, 29°17' E 226
Eleja, *Latv.* 56°24' N, 23°41' E 166
Elek, *Hung.* 46°32' N, 21°14' E 168
Elektrostal', *Russ.* 55°45' N, 38°30' E 154
Elephant Island, *Antarctica* 61°4' S, 55°14' W 134
Elephant Mountain, *Tex., U.S.* 29°59' N, 103°36' W 92
Elephant Point, *U.S.* 66°15' N, 161°24' W 98
Eleşkirt, *Turk.* 39°47' N, 42°39' E 195
Eleuthera Island, *Bahamas* 25°12' N, 76°7' W 116
Eleutherae, ruin(s), *Gr.* 38°10' N, 23°17' E 156
Eleutherna, ruin(s), *Gr.* 35°18' N, 24°34' E 156
Elfers, *Fla., U.S.* 28°13' N, 82°42' W 105
Elfin Cove, *U.S.* 58°11' N, 136°20' W 98
Elfrida, *Ariz., U.S.* 31°41' N, 109°40' W 92
Elgå, *Nor.* 62°9' N, 11°56' E 152
Elgin, *Ill., U.S.* 42°2' N, 88°16' W 102
Elgin, *Nebr., U.S.* 41°57' N, 98°6' W 90
Elgin, *N. Dak., U.S.* 46°23' N, 101°52' W 90
Elgin, *Oreg., U.S.* 45°33' N, 117°56' W 90
Elgin, *Tex., U.S.* 30°20' N, 97°22' W 92
El'ginskiy, *Russ.* 64°42' N, 142°12' E 173
Elgon, Mount, *Uganda* 1°4' N, 34°29' E 224
Elgoras, Gora, peak, *Russ.* 68°5' N, 31°24' E 152
Elias Garcia, *Angola* 9°3' S, 20°14' E 218
Elida, *N. Mex., U.S.* 33°56' N, 103°40' W 92
Elida, *Ohio, U.S.* 40°46' N, 84°12' W 102
Eliki Gounda, *Niger* 15°3' N, 8°36' E 222
Elikónas (Helicon), peak, *Gr.* 38°17' N, 22°47' E 156
Elila, river, *Dem. Rep. of the Congo* 3°26' S, 27°52' E 224
Elila, river, *Dem. Rep. of the Congo* 2°55' S, 26°23' E 224
Eliot, *Me., U.S.* 43°9' N, 70°48' W 104
Elipa, *Dem. Rep. of the Congo* 1°4' S, 24°19' E 224
Elis, ruin(s), *Gr.* 37°52' N, 21°18' E 156
Élisabethville see Lubumbashi, *Dem. Rep. of the Congo* 11°43' S, 27°26' E 224
Elisenvaara, *Russ.* 61°23' N, 29°45' E 166
Eliseu Martins, *Braz.* 8°11' S, 43°43' W 132
Elista, *Russ.* 46°16' N, 44°9' E 158
Elizabeth, *La., U.S.* 30°51' N, 92°48' W 103
Elizabeth, *Miss., U.S.* 33°24' N, 90°53' W 103
Elizabeth, *N.J., U.S.* 40°39' N, 74°14' W 94
Elizabeth, *W. Va., U.S.* 39°3' N, 81°25' W 102
Elizabeth City, *N.C., U.S.* 36°18' N, 76°16' W 96
Elizabeth Falls, *Can.* 59°20' N, 105°49' W 108
Elizabeth Islands, *Atlantic Ocean* 41°21' N, 71°2' W 104
Elizabeth Mountain, *Utah, U.S.* 40°57' N, 110°48' W 90
Elizabethton, *Tenn., U.S.* 36°20' N, 82°14' W 96
Elizabethtown, *Ind., U.S.* 39°7' N, 85°49' W 102
Elizabethtown, *Ky., U.S.* 37°40' N, 85°52' W 96
Elizabethtown, *Mo., U.S.* 37°27' N, 88°18' W 96
Elizabethtown, *N.Y., U.S.* 44°13' N, 73°37' W 104
Elizondo, *Sp.* 43°8' N, 1°31' W 150
Ełk, *Pol.* 53°50' N, 22°21' E 152
Elk, *Calif., U.S.* 39°8' N, 123°43' W 90
Elk City, *Okla., U.S.* 35°23' N, 99°26' W 92
Elk Creek, river, *S. Dak., U.S.* 44°13' N, 102°53' W 90
Elk Grove, *Calif., U.S.* 38°24' N, 121°23' W 100
Elk Hills, *Calif., U.S.* 35°20' N, 119°31' W 100
Elk Island National Park, *Can.* 53°32' N, 113°12' W 238
Elk Lake, *Can.* 47°43' N, 80°21' W 94
Elk Lake, *Mich., U.S.* 44°47' N, 85°37' W 94
Elk Mountain, *Wyo., U.S.* 41°37' N, 106°36' W 90
Elk Peak, *Mont., U.S.* 46°25' N, 110°50' W 90
Elk Point, *Can.* 53°53' N, 110°55' W 108
Elk Point, *S. Dak., U.S.* 42°39' N, 96°41' W 90
Elk River, *Idaho, U.S.* 46°45' N, 116°13' W 90
Elk River, *Minn., U.S.* 45°17' N, 93°34' W 94
Elk, river, *Can.* 49°23' N, 114°53' W 108
Elk, river, *Colo., U.S.* 40°34' N, 106°58' W 90

Elk, river, *W. Va., U.S.* 38°22′ N, 80°55′ W 80
Elkhart, *Ind., U.S.* 41°40′ N, 85°59′ W 82
Elkhart, *Kans., U.S.* 37°0′ N, 101°54′ W 92
Elkhart, *Tex., U.S.* 31°36′ N, 95°35′ W 103
Elkhart Lake, *Wis., U.S.* 43°49′ N, 88°1′ W 102
Elkhead Mountains, *Colo., U.S.* 40°40′ N, 107°46′ W 90
Elkhorn, *Can.* 49°59′ N, 101°15′ W 90
Elkhorn, *Wis., U.S.* 42°40′ N, 88°33′ W 102
Elkhorn City, *Ky., U.S.* 37°18′ N, 82°22′ W 94
Elkhorn Mountain, *Can.* 49°47′ N, 125°55′ W 90
Elkhorn, river, *Nebr., U.S.* 42°21′ N, 99°26′ W 80
Elkhovo, *Bulg.* 42°10′ N, 26°34′ E 158
Elkin, *N.C., U.S.* 36°14′ N, 80°53′ W 96
Elkins, *N. Mex., U.S.* 33°41′ N, 104°4′ W 92
Elkins, *W. Va., U.S.* 38°55′ N, 79°51′ W 94
Elkland, *Pa., U.S.* 41°59′ N, 77°20′ W 94
Elko, *Can.* 49°18′ N, 115°7′ W 90
Elko, *Nev., U.S.* 40°53′ N, 115°51′ W 106
Elkton, *Fla., U.S.* 29°46′ N, 81°27′ W 105
Elkton, *Ky., U.S.* 36°48′ N, 87°10′ W 96
Elkton, *Md., U.S.* 39°36′ N, 75°51′ W 94
Elkton, *Mich., U.S.* 43°48′ N, 83°11′ W 102
Elkview, *W. Va., U.S.* 38°26′ N, 81°30′ W 102
Ellef Ringnes Island, *Can.* 77°11′ N, 103°31′ W 106
Elleh Creek, river, *Can.* 58°32′ N, 122°26′ W 108
Ellen, Mount, *Utah, U.S.* 38°5′ N, 110°53′ W 90
Ellenboro, *W. Va., U.S.* 39°16′ N, 81°4′ W 102
Ellendale, *N. Dak., U.S.* 46°0′ N, 98°32′ W 90
Ellensburg, *Wash., U.S.* 46°58′ N, 120°35′ W 90
Ellenton, *Fla., U.S.* 27°32′ N, 82°30′ W 105
Ellesmere Island, *Can.* 76°28′ N, 77°40′ W 106
Ellesmere Port, *U.K.* 53°17′ N, 2°54′ W 162
Ellettsville, *Ind., U.S.* 39°13′ N, 86°38′ W 102
Ellila, spring, *Chad* 16°42′ N, 20°20′ E 216
Ellington, *Conn., U.S.* 41°53′ N, 72°29′ W 104
Ellinwood, *Kans., U.S.* 38°20′ N, 98°35′ W 82
Elliot, *S. Af.* 31°21′ S, 27°49′ E 227
Elliot Lake, *Can.* 46°23′ N, 82°40′ W 110
Elliott, Cape, *Antarctica* 65°39′ S, 106°26′ E 248
Elliott Lake, *Can.* 61°1′ N, 100°2′ W 108
Ellis, *Idaho, U.S.* 44°41′ N, 114°2′ W 90
Ellis, *Kans., U.S.* 38°55′ N, 99°34′ W 90
Ellis, Mount, *Mont., U.S.* 45°32′ N, 111°1′ W 90
Ellisburg, *N.Y., U.S.* 43°43′ N, 76°9′ W 110
Ellisland, site, *U.K.* 55°6′ N, 3°46′ W 150
Ellisras see Lephalale, *S. Af.* 23°40′ S, 27°42′ E 227
Elliston, *Austral.* 33°40′ S, 134°54′ E 231
Ellisville, *Miss., U.S.* 31°35′ N, 89°13′ W 103
Ełk, *Pol.* 53°50′ N, 22°20′ E 152
Ellore see Eluru, *India* 16°46′ N, 81°7′ E 188
Ells, river, *Can.* 56°59′ N, 112°21′ W 108
Ellsworth, *Kans., U.S.* 38°43′ N, 98°14′ W 90
Ellsworth, *Me., U.S.* 44°31′ N, 68°24′ W 82
Ellsworth Land, region, *Antarctica* 73°44′ S, 96°14′ W 248
Ellsworth, Mount, *Utah, U.S.* 37°44′ N, 110°42′ W 92
Ellsworth Mountains, *Antarctica* 76°23′ S, 90°19′ W 248
Elm Creek, *Nebr., U.S.* 40°42′ N, 99°23′ W 90
Elma, *Wash., U.S.* 47°0′ N, 123°24′ W 100
Elmadağı, *Turk.* 39°55′ N, 33°14′ E 156
Elmalı, *Turk.* 36°43′ N, 29°55′ E 156
Elmer City, *Wash., U.S.* 47°59′ N, 118°56′ W 90
Elmira, *N.Y., U.S.* 42°5′ N, 76°50′ W 94
Elmo, *Wyo., U.S.* 41°53′ N, 106°31′ W 90
Elmsta, *Sw.* 59°58′ N, 18°42′ E 166
Elmwood, *Ill., U.S.* 40°45′ N, 89°58′ W 102
Elnora, *Ind., U.S.* 38°52′ N, 87°5′ W 102
Elortondo, *Arg.* 33°43′ S, 61°38′ W 139
Elorza, *Venez.* 7°1′ N, 69°31′ W 136
Elos, ruin(s), *Gr.* 36°47′ N, 22°40′ E 156
Elota, *Mex.* 23°56′ N, 106°42′ W 114
Eloy, *Ariz., U.S.* 32°44′ N, 111°34′ W 112
Eloy Alfaro, *Ecua.* 2°16′ S, 79°51′ W 130
Elrose, *Can.* 51°12′ N, 108°4′ W 90
Elroy, *Wis., U.S.* 43°44′ N, 90°17′ W 102
Elsa, *Tex., U.S.* 26°17′ N, 97°59′ W 114
Elsas, *Can.* 48°32′ N, 82°55′ W 94
Elsberry, *Mo., U.S.* 39°9′ N, 90°47′ W 94
Elsdorf, *Ger.* 53°14′ N, 9°22′ E 152
Elsen Nur, lake, *China* 35°14′ N, 91°46′ E 188
Elsie, *Mich., U.S.* 43°4′ N, 84°24′ W 102
Elst, *Neth.* 51°55′ N, 5°50′ E 167
Elstow, *U.K.* 52°7′ N, 0°28′ E 162
Eltanin Fracture Zone System, *South Pacific Ocean* 52°39′ S, 138°6′ W 252
Elten, *Ger.* 51°51′ N, 6°10′ E 167
Eltham, *N.Z.* 39°27′ S, 174°18′ E 240
Elton, *La., U.S.* 30°28′ N, 92°42′ W 103
El'ton, *Russ.* 49°9′ N, 46°47′ E 158
Eltopia, *Wash., U.S.* 46°26′ N, 119°1′ W 90
Eltville, *Ger.* 50°1′ N, 8°6′ E 167
Eluru (Ellore), *India* 16°46′ N, 81°7′ E 188
Elva, *Est.* 58°10′ N, 26°22′ E 166
Elvas, *Port.* 38°52′ N, 7°10′ W 150
Elvenes, *Nor.* 69°40′ N, 30°8′ E 152
Elvins, *Mo., U.S.* 37°49′ N, 90°33′ W 96
Elwell, Lake, *Mont., U.S.* 48°20′ N, 111°36′ W 90
Elwood, *Ill., U.S.* 41°24′ N, 88°7′ W 102
Elwood, *Ind., U.S.* 40°16′ N, 85°50′ W 102
Elwood, *Kans., U.S.* 39°43′ N, 94°53′ W 94
Elwood, *Nebr., U.S.* 40°34′ N, 99°52′ W 90
Elx see Elche, *Sp.* 38°15′ N, 0°42′ E 164
Ely, *Minn., U.S.* 47°53′ N, 91°53′ W 94
Ely, *Nev., U.S.* 39°17′ N, 114°48′ W 238
Ely, *U.K.* 52°23′ N, 0°15′ E 162
Ely, Isle of, *U.K.* 52°24′ N, 0°11′ E 162
Elyria, *Ohio, U.S.* 41°21′ N, 82°5′ W 102
Elyrus, ruin(s), *Gr.* 35°15′ N, 23°42′ E 156
Emådalen, *Nor.* 61°19′ N, 14°42′ E 152
Emajõgi, river, *Est.* 58°24′ N, 26°7′ E 166
Emām Taqī, *Iran* 35°59′ N, 59°23′ E 180
Emas National Park, *Braz.* 18°19′ S, 53°5′ W 138
Embari, river, *Braz.* 0°48′ N, 67°0′ W 136
Embarras Portage, *Can.* 58°24′ N, 111°26′ W 108
Embi, *Kaz.* 48°50′ N, 58°6′ E 158
Embira, river, *Braz.* 9°17′ S, 70°51′ W 137
Embu, *Kenya* 0°33′ N, 37°27′ E 224
Emden, *Ger.* 53°21′ N, 7°12′ E 163
Emel'dzhak, *Russ.* 58°19′ N, 126°40′ E 160
Emerald Island, *Can.* 76°42′ N, 113°8′ W 106
Emero, river, *Bol.* 13°38′ S, 68°3′ W 137
Emerson, *Ark., U.S.* 33°5′ N, 93°12′ W 103
Emerson, *Can.* 49°0′ N, 97°11′ W 90
Emerson Peak, *Calif., U.S.* 41°13′ N, 120°15′ W 90
Emery, *Utah, U.S.* 38°55′ N, 111°14′ W 90
Emery Mills, *Me., U.S.* 43°30′ N, 70°51′ W 104
Emet, *Turk.* 39°21′ N, 29°14′ E 156
Emgayet, oil field, *Lib.* 28°57′ N, 12°45′ E 143
Emigrant Pass, *Nev., U.S.* 40°40′ N, 116°14′ W 90
Emigrant Peak, *Mont., U.S.* 45°14′ N, 110°47′ W 90
Emilia-Romagna, adm. division, *It.* 44°40′ N, 10°18′ E 167
Emilius, Mount, *It.* 45°39′ N, 7°24′ E 165
Emily, *Minn., U.S.* 46°43′ N, 93°58′ W 94
Emily, Mount, *Oreg., U.S.* 45°24′ N, 118°11′ W 90
Emin, *China* 46°29′ N, 83°38′ E 184
Emin, river, *China* 46°24′ N, 83°0′ E 184
Emin, river, *Kaz.* 46°16′ N, 81°53′ E 184
Emir Dağları, peak, *Turk.* 38°50′ N, 31°9′ E 156
Emirdağ, *Turk.* 39°0′ N, 31°6′ E 156
Emisou, Tarso, peak, *Chad* 21°23′ N, 18°32′ E 216
Emlichheim, *Ger.* 52°36′ N, 6°51′ E 163
Emma, Mount, *Ariz., U.S.* 36°15′ N, 113°14′ W 92
Emmaboda, *Nor.* 56°37′ N, 15°31′ E 152
Emmaste, *Est.* 58°43′ N, 22°33′ E 166
Emmaus, *Pa., U.S.* 40°31′ N, 75°30′ W 94
Emmeloord, *Neth.* 52°42′ N, 5°44′ E 163
Emmen, *Neth.* 52°47′ N, 6°53′ E 163
Emmen, *Switz.* 47°3′ N, 8°18′ E 150
Emmerich, *Ger.* 51°49′ N, 6°15′ E 167
Emmetsburg, *Iowa, U.S.* 43°5′ N, 94°41′ W 90
Emmett, *Idaho, U.S.* 43°51′ N, 116°30′ W 90
Emmonak, *Alas., U.S.* 62°42′ N, 164°42′ W 98
Emmons, Mount, *Utah, U.S.* 40°41′ N, 110°23′ W 90
Emo, *Can.* 48°35′ N, 93°50′ W 90
Emory Peak, *Tex., U.S.* 29°12′ N, 103°21′ W 92
Empangeni, *S. Af.* 28°44′ S, 31°51′ E 227
Empedrado, *Arg.* 27°55′ S, 58°48′ W 139
Emperor Seamounts, *North Pacific Ocean* 43°13′ N, 170°0′ E 252
Emperor Trough, *North Pacific Ocean* 44°20′ N, 174°43′ E 252
Empire, *La., U.S.* 29°22′ N, 89°36′ W 103
Empire, *Mich., U.S.* 44°48′ N, 86°3′ W 94
Empoli, *It.* 43°43′ N, 10°57′ E 156
Emporia, *Kans., U.S.* 38°23′ N, 96°11′ W 90
Emporia, *Va., U.S.* 36°41′ N, 77°32′ W 96
Emporio, ruin(s), *Gr.* 38°11′ N, 25°55′ E 156
Emporium, *Pa., U.S.* 41°30′ N, 78°15′ W 94
Empress, *Can.* 50°57′ N, 110°1′ W 90
Empty Quarter see Ar Rubʿ al Khālī, *Saudi Arabia* 18°28′ N, 46°3′ E 182
Ems, river, *Ger.* 52°1′ N, 7°43′ E 167
Emsdetten, *Ger.* 52°10′ N, 7°32′ E 163
En Amakane, spring, *Mali* 16°35′ N, 0°59′ E 222
ʿEn Boqeq, *Israel* 31°11′ N, 35°21′ E 194
ʿEn Gedi, *Israel* 31°27′ N, 35°22′ E 194
ʿEn Gev, *Israel* 32°46′ N, 35°38′ E 194
En Nahud, *Sudan* 12°40′ N, 28°26′ E 226
ʿEn Yahav, *Israel* 30°37′ N, 35°11′ E 194
Ena, *Japan* 35°25′ N, 137°24′ E 201
Ena Lake, *Can.* 59°57′ N, 108°27′ W 108
Enånger, *Nor.* 61°32′ N, 16°58′ E 152
Encantadas, Serra das, *Braz.* 30°51′ S, 53°28′ W 139
Encantado, Cerro, peak, *Mex.* 27°2′ N, 112°38′ W 112
Encanto, Cape, *Philippines* 15°29′ N, 121°37′ E 203
Encarnación, *Parag.* 27°20′ S, 55°50′ W 139
Encarnación de Díaz, *Mex.* 21°30′ N, 102°15′ W 114
Enchi, *Ghana* 5°49′ N, 2°50′ W 222
Encinal, *Tex., U.S.* 28°2′ N, 99°21′ W 92
Encinillas, *Mex.* 29°13′ N, 106°17′ W 92
Encinillas, Laguna de, lake, *Mex.* 29°24′ N, 107°45′ W 81
Encinitas, *Calif., U.S.* 33°2′ N, 117°18′ W 101
Encino, *Tex., U.S.* 26°56′ N, 98°8′ W 96
Encontrados, *Venez.* 9°2′ N, 72°15′ W 136
Encruzilhada, *Braz.* 15°33′ S, 40°55′ W 138
Encruzilhada do Sul, *Braz.* 30°33′ S, 52°34′ W 139
Endako, *Can.* 54°5′ N, 125°1′ W 108
Endau, *Kenya* 1°19′ S, 38°34′ E 224
Endeavour, *Can.* 52°10′ N, 102°40′ W 108
Enderby, *Can.* 50°33′ N, 119°9′ W 90
Enderby Land, region, *Antarctica* 69°55′ S, 39°37′ E 248
Enderby Plain, *Indian Ocean* 58°55′ S, 44°16′ E 255
Enderlin, *N. Dak., U.S.* 46°36′ N, 97°37′ W 90
Endicott Mountains, *Alas., U.S.* 67°34′ N, 155°1′ W 98
Endrőd, *Hung.* 46°56′ N, 20°46′ E 168
Endwell, *N.Y., U.S.* 42°6′ N, 76°1′ W 94
Energetik, *Russ.* 51°44′ N, 58°56′ E 154
Enez, *Turk.* 40°42′ N, 26°3′ E 156
Enfer, Pointe d', *Fr.* 14°17′ N, 61°38′ W 116
Enfida, *Tun.* 36°7′ N, 10°23′ E 156
Enfield, *Conn., U.S.* 41°57′ N, 72°36′ W 104
Enfield, *N.Z.* 45°3′ S, 170°50′ E 240
Enfield, *U.K.* 51°39′ N, 7°415′ W 162
Enfield Center, *N.H., U.S.* 43°35′ N, 72°7′ W 104
Engaño, Cabo, *Dom. Rep.* 18°35′ N, 68°15′ W 116
ʿEn-Gedi, ruin(s), *Israel* 31°27′ N, 35°21′ E 194
Engelberg, *Switz.* 46°48′ N, 8°24′ E 167
Engelhard, *N.C., U.S.* 35°31′ N, 76°1′ W 96
Engels, *Russ.* 51°25′ N, 46°9′ E 158
Engemann Lake, *Can.* 57°49′ N, 107°49′ W 108
Engen, *Can.* 54°1′ N, 124°17′ W 108
Engerdal, *Nor.* 61°45′ N, 11°56′ E 152
Engershand, *Mongolia* 47°44′ N, 107°21′ E 198
Enggano, island, *Indonesia* 5°46′ S, 101°5′ E 192
Enghien, *Belg.* 50°41′ N, 4°2′ E 163
Engizek Dağı, *Turk.* 37°46′ N, 36°29′ E 156
England, adm. division, *U.K.* 52°25′ N, 2°59′ W 143
Englehart, *Can.* 47°50′ N, 79°52′ W 94
Englewood, *Fla., U.S.* 26°58′ N, 82°21′ W 105
Englewood, *Kans., U.S.* 37°1′ N, 100°0′ W 92
Englewood, *Ohio, U.S.* 39°52′ N, 84°19′ W 102
English Channel (La Manche) 49°57′ N, 3°16′ W 150
English River, *Can.* 49°13′ N, 90°58′ W 94
English, river, *Can.* 50°30′ N, 95°13′ W 80
English, river, *Can.* 49°50′ N, 92°1′ W 94
Engure, *Latv.* 57°8′ N, 23°12′ E 166
Engures Ezers, lake, *Latv.* 57°14′ N, 22°50′ E 166
Enid, *Okla., U.S.* 36°22′ N, 97°52′ W 92
Enid, Mount, *Austral.* 21°46′ S, 116°12′ E 230
Enilda, *Can.* 55°24′ N, 116°18′ W 108
Enken, Mys, *Russ.* 56°57′ N, 139°57′ E 172
Enkirch, *Ger.* 49°58′ N, 7°8′ E 167
Enköping, *Nor.* 59°37′ N, 17°3′ E 152
Enmelen, *Russ.* 65°1′ N, 175°51′ W 98
Enna, *It.* 37°34′ N, 14°16′ E 156
Ennadai, *Can.* 61°7′ N, 100°52′ W 108
Ennadai Lake, *Can.* 60°42′ N, 102°23′ W 108
Ennigerloh, *Ger.* 51°49′ N, 8°0′ E 167
Enning, *S. Dak., U.S.* 44°33′ N, 102°34′ W 90
Ennis, *Ire.* 52°50′ N, 9°0′ W 150
Ennis, *Tex., U.S.* 32°18′ N, 96°38′ W 96
Enniskillen, *U.K.* 54°20′ N, 7°38′ W 150
Enns, *Aust.* 48°13′ N, 14°28′ E 156
Eno, *Fin.* 62°45′ N, 30°8′ E 154
Eno, river, *Japan* 34°33′ N, 132°40′ E 201
Enonkoski, *Fin.* 62°4′ N, 28°55′ E 152
Enontekiö, *Fin.* 68°23′ N, 23°35′ E 152
Énos, Óros, peak, *Gr.* 38°7′ N, 20°35′ E 156
Enrique Urien, *Arg.* 27°33′ S, 60°37′ W 139
Enschede, *Neth.* 52°13′ N, 6°53′ E 163
Ensenada, *Mex.* 31°51′ N, 116°38′ W 92
Enshi, *China* 30°14′ N, 109°24′ E 198
Entebbe, *Uganda* 6°357′ N, 32°27′ E 224
Enterprise, *Ala., U.S.* 31°18′ N, 85°51′ W 96
Enterprise, *Can.* 60°40′ N, 116°4′ W 108
Enterprise, *Miss., U.S.* 32°10′ N, 88°48′ W 103
Enterprise, *Utah, U.S.* 37°34′ N, 113°43′ W 92
Entinas, Punta, *Sp.* 36°31′ N, 2°44′ W 150
Entrada, Punta, *Arg.* 50°22′ S, 68°28′ W 134
Entrance, *Can.* 53°21′ N, 117°42′ W 108
Entraunes, *Fr.* 44°10′ N, 6°45′ E 167
Entre Ríos, *Bol.* 21°33′ S, 64°13′ W 137
Entre Ríos, adm. division, *Arg.* 31°43′ S, 59°58′ W 139
Entre-Rios, *Mozambique* 14°58′ S, 37°24′ E 224
Entwistle, *Can.* 53°33′ N, 114°56′ W 108
Enugu, *Nig.* 6°26′ N, 7°29′ E 222
Enumclaw, *Wash., U.S.* 47°10′ N, 121°59′ W 100
Enurmino, *Russ.* 66°55′ N, 171°46′ W 98
Envigado, *Col.* 6°8′ N, 75°37′ W 130
Envira, *Braz.* 7°23′ S, 70°14′ W 130
Enyellé, *Congo* 2°51′ N, 18°4′ E 218
Enying, *Hung.* 46°56′ N, 18°15′ E 168
Enzan, *Japan* 35°41′ N, 138°44′ E 201
Eola, *La., U.S.* 30°53′ N, 92°14′ W 103
Eolie see Lipari, Isole, islands, *Mediterranean Sea* 38°39′ N, 13°46′ E 156
Eonyang, *S. Korea* 35°33′ N, 129°10′ E 200
Epe, *Neth.* 52°21′ N, 5°58′ E 163
Epembe, spring, *Namibia* 17°35′ S, 13°34′ E 220
Epéna, *Congo* 1°23′ N, 17°27′ E 218
Épernay, *Fr.* 49°2′ N, 3°56′ E 163
Épernon, *Fr.* 48°35′ N, 1°40′ E 163
Epes, *Ala., U.S.* 32°41′ N, 88°8′ W 103
Ephesus, ruin(s), *Turk.* 37°55′ N, 27°12′ E 156
Ephraim, *Utah, U.S.* 39°21′ N, 111°35′ W 90
Ephrata, *Wash., U.S.* 47°18′ N, 119°34′ W 90
Epidaurum see Cavtat, *Croatia* 42°34′ N, 18°13′ E 168
Epidaurus Limerás, ruin(s), *Gr.* 36°43′ N, 22°56′ E 156
Épilá, *Sp.* 41°37′ N, 1°17′ W 164
Épinal, *Fr.* 48°10′ N, 6°26′ E 163
Epini, *Dem. Rep. of the Congo* 1°26′ N, 28°21′ E 224
Epirus, region, *Europe* 40°27′ N, 19°28′ E 156
Episkopi, *Cyprus* 34°40′ N, 32°54′ E 194
Epping Forest, *U.K.* 51°38′ N, 2°119′ E 162
Epps, *La., U.S.* 32°35′ N, 91°29′ W 103
Epsom, *U.K.* 51°20′ N, 0°17′ E 162
Epu Pel, *Arg.* 37°36′ S, 64°16′ W 139
Epukiro, *Namibia* 21°45′ S, 19°8′ E 227
Epulu, river, *Dem. Rep. of the Congo* 1°29′ N, 28°42′ E 224
Equator, adm. division, *Dem. Rep. of the Congo* 9°535′ N, 18°55′ E 218
Equatorial Channel 0°14′ N, 72°8′ E 188
Equatorial Guinea 1°38′ N, 10°28′ E 218
Er Rachidia, *Mor.* 31°58′ N, 4°21′ W 143
Er Rahad, *Sudan* 12°43′ N, 30°36′ E 216
Er Rif, *Mor.* 35°15′ N, 5°28′ W 150
Er Roseires, *Sudan* 11°52′ N, 34°24′ E 182
Er Rout Sanihida, spring, *Niger* 21°53′ N, 11°52′ E 222
Eraclea, *It.* 45°34′ N, 12°40′ E 167
Erath, *La., U.S.* 29°56′ N, 92°2′ W 103
Erbaa, *Turk.* 40°40′ N, 36°34′ E 156
Erbab, Jebel, peak, *Sudan* 18°40′ N, 36°59′ E 182
Erçek, *Turk.* 38°37′ N, 43°34′ E 195
Erçek Gölü, lake, *Turk.* 38°39′ N, 43°23′ E 195
Erciş, *Turk.* 38°59′ N, 43°18′ E 195
Erciyeş Dağı, peak, *Turk.* 38°30′ N, 35°22′ E 156
Ercsi, *Hung.* 47°14′ N, 18°53′ E 168
Érd, *Hung.* 47°22′ N, 18°55′ E 168
Erdao, river, *China* 42°44′ N, 127°38′ E 200
Erdaobaihe, *China* 42°26′ N, 128°7′ E 200
Erdébé, Plateau d', *Chad* 17°17′ N, 21°23′ E 216
Erdek, *Turk.* 40°24′ N, 27°45′ E 156
Erdemli, *Turk.* 36°36′ N, 34°18′ E 156
Erdenet, *Mongolia* 48°57′ N, 104°17′ E 198
Erdut, *Croatia* 45°31′ N, 19°2′ E 168
Erebus, Mount, *Antarctica* 77°26′ S, 167°55′ E 248
Erechim, *Braz.* 27°39′ S, 52°18′ W 139
Ereğli, *Turk.* 41°17′ N, 31°25′ E 156
Ereğli, *Turk.* 37°29′ N, 34°2′ E 156
Erego, *Mozambique* 16°3′ S, 37°11′ E 224
Erei, Monti, *It.* 37°23′ N, 14°3′ E 156
Eremiya, *Bulg.* 42°12′ N, 22°50′ E 168
Erenhot, *China* 43°39′ N, 111°57′ E 198
Eresus, ruin(s), *Gr.* 39°7′ N, 25°50′ E 156
Erétria, ruin(s), *Gr.* 38°23′ N, 23°42′ E 156
Ereymentaū, *Kaz.* 51°41′ N, 73°22′ E 184
Erfoud, *Mor.* 31°29′ N, 4°15′ W 214
Erft, river, *Ger.* 51°2′ N, 6°29′ E 167
Erftstadt, *Ger.* 50°47′ N, 6°44′ E 167
Erfurt, *Ger.* 50°59′ N, 11°2′ E 152
'Erg Chech, *Alg.* 25°13′ N, 3°16′ W 214
'Erg el Ahmar, *Mali* 24°14′ N, 4°55′ W 214
'Erg Iguidi, *Alg.* 24°15′ N, 8°24′ W 214
'Erg I-n-Sâkâne, *Mali* 20°43′ N, 0°54′ E 222
Ergani, *Turk.* 38°17′ N, 39°45′ E 195
Ergel, *Mongolia* 43°13′ N, 109°8′ E 198
Ērgļi, *Latv.* 56°53′ N, 25°39′ E 166
Erg-n-Ataram, *Alg.* 23°45′ N, 1°6′ E 214
Ergun, river, *Asia* 50°18′ N, 119°1′ E 190
Eriba, *Sudan* 16°37′ N, 36°3′ E 182
Éric, Lac, lake, *Can.* 51°50′ N, 65°59′ W 111
Erice, *It.* 38°2′ N, 12°35′ E 156
Erick, *Okla., U.S.* 35°11′ N, 99°53′ W 92
Erickson, *Can.* 50°30′ N, 99°54′ W 90
Erie, *Ill., U.S.* 41°38′ N, 90°5′ W 102
Erie, *Pa., U.S.* 42°6′ N, 80°5′ W 94
Erie, Lake 42°11′ N, 83°6′ W 73
Erieau, *Can.* 42°15′ N, 81°56′ W 102
Erigavo see Ceerigaabo, *Somalia* 10°34′ N, 47°24′ E 218
Eriksdale, *Can.* 50°51′ N, 98°6′ W 90
Erímanthos, Óros, peak, *Gr.* 37°58′ N, 21°45′ E 156
Erimi, *Cyprus* 34°40′ N, 32°55′ E 194
Eritrea 15°32′ N, 37°35′ E 218
Erits, river, *Kaz.* 51°34′ N, 77°33′ E 184
Erkelenz, *Ger.* 51°4′ N, 6°19′ E 167
Erkilet, *Turk.* 38°48′ N, 35°27′ E 156
Erkner, *Ger.* 52°24′ N, 13°45′ E 152
Erkowit, *Sudan* 18°45′ N, 37°3′ E 182
Erla, *Sp.* 42°6′ N, 0°57′ E 164
Erlangen, *Ger.* 49°35′ N, 11°0′ E 152
Ermelo, *S. Af.* 26°32′ S, 29°58′ E 227
Ermenek, *Turk.* 36°36′ N, 32°55′ E 156
Ermidas-Sado, *Port.* 37°59′ N, 8°25′ W 150
Ermil, *Sudan* 13°33′ N, 27°38′ E 226
Ermoúpoli, *Gr.* 37°26′ N, 24°56′ E 156
Ernakulam, *India* 9°59′ N, 76°17′ E 188
Erndtebrück, *Ger.* 50°59′ N, 8°15′ E 167
Ernstberg, peak, *Ger.* 50°13′ N, 6°44′ E 167
Eromanga, *Austral.* 26°39′ S, 143°17′ E 231
Erongo Mountains, *Namibia* 21°44′ S, 15°27′ E 227
Eros, *La., U.S.* 32°22′ N, 92°25′ W 103
Eroug, spring, *Mali* 18°20′ N, 2°4′ W 222
Erpengdianzi, *China* 41°10′ N, 125°33′ E 200
Er-Remla, *Tun.* 34°46′ N, 11°14′ E 156
Errigal Mountain, *Ire.* 55°0′ N, 8°13′ W 150
Error Tablemount, *Arabian Sea* 9°58′ N, 56°3′ E 254
Erskine, *Minn., U.S.* 47°38′ N, 96°2′ W 90
Erstein, *Fr.* 48°25′ N, 7°39′ E 163
Ertai, *China* 46°8′ N, 90°7′ E 190
Ertis, *Kaz.* 53°19′ N, 75°27′ E 184
Ertis, river, *Kaz.* 54°12′ N, 74°56′ E 160
Ertix, river, *China* 48°2′ N, 85°34′ E 184
Eruh, *Turk.* 37°44′ N, 42°9′ E 195
Erundu, *Namibia* 20°41′ S, 16°23′ E 227
Ervenik, *Croatia* 44°5′ N, 15°55′ E 168
Erwin, *N.C., U.S.* 35°19′ N, 78°42′ W 96
Erwitte, *Ger.* 51°36′ N, 8°21′ E 167
Erzgebirge, *Czech Rep.* 50°18′ N, 12°34′ E 152
Erzin, *Russ.* 50°14′ N, 95°18′ E 190
Erzincan, *Turk.* 39°44′ N, 39°28′ E 195
Erzurum, *Turk.* 39°54′ N, 41°17′ E 195
Es Bordes, *Sp.* 42°43′ N, 0°42′ E 164
Es Mercadal, *Sp.* 39°59′ N, 4°4′ E 150
Es Safiya, *Sudan* 15°31′ N, 30°6′ E 226
Es Salam, *Sudan* 18°5′ N, 33°53′ E 182
Es Sufeiya, *Sudan* 15°27′ N, 34°40′ E 182
Esa, river, *Belarus* 54°43′ N, 28°30′ E 166
Esbjerg, *Den.* 55°27′ N, 8°36′ E 160
Esbo see Espoo, *Fin.* 60°11′ N, 24°34′ E 166
Escalante, *Utah, U.S.* 37°46′ N, 111°37′ W 92
Escanaba, *Mich., U.S.* 45°48′ N, 87°7′ W 106
Escárcega, *Mex.* 18°36′ N, 90°46′ W 115
Escatawpa, river, *Ala., U.S.* 30°27′ N, 88°27′ W 103
Escatrón, *Sp.* 41°16′ N, 0°20′ E 164
Eschenburg, *Ger.* 50°48′ N, 8°20′ E 167
Eschweiler, *Ger.* 50°48′ N, 6°15′ E 167
Escobedo, *Mex.* 27°11′ N, 101°22′ W 96
Escondido, *Calif., U.S.* 33°7′ N, 117°6′ W 101
Escudero, station, *Antarctica* 62°5′ S, 58°48′ W 134
Escudilla Mountain, *Ariz., U.S.* 33°56′ N, 109°11′ W 92
Escuela de Caza de Morón, *Sp.* 37°9′ N, 5°37′ W 164
Escuinapa, *Mex.* 22°50′ N, 105°47′ W 114
Escuintla, *Guatemala* 14°16′ N, 90°47′ W 115
Escuintla, *Mex.* 15°18′ N, 92°40′ W 115
Escuminac, Point, *Can.* 47°6′ N, 64°49′ W 111
Ese Khayya, *Russ.* 67°28′ N, 134°38′ E 160
Eséka, *Cameroon* 3°41′ N, 10°47′ E 222
Esenguly, *Turkm.* 37°27′ N, 53°57′ E 180

Esens, *Ger.* 53°39′ N, 7°36′ E 163
Esfahan (Isfahan), *Iran* 32°40′ N, 51°38′ E 180
Esfandak, *Iran* 27°5′ N, 62°51′ E 182
Eshkamesh, *Afghan.* 36°27′ N, 69°16′ E 186
Eshkashem, *Taj.* 36°44′ N, 71°34′ E 186
Eshowe, *S. Af.* 28°54′ S, 31°24′ E 227
Esiama, *Ghana* 4°58′ N, 2°21′ W 222
Esik, *Kaz.* 43°21′ N, 77°25′ E 184
Esil, *Kaz.* 51°57′ N, 66°27′ E 184
Esil, river, *Kaz.* 53°18′ N, 66°55′ E 184
Esimi, *Gr.* 41°1′ N, 25°57′ E 156
Esira, *Madagascar* 24°21′ S, 46°47′ E 220
Esk, river, *U.K.* 55°14′ N, 3°17′ W 150
Esk, river, *U.K.* 54°28′ N, 0°54′ E 162
Eskdale, *N.Z.* 39°25′ S, 176°49′ E 240
Eskene, *Kaz.* 47°20′ N, 52°52′ E 158
Esker, *Can.* 54°0′ N, 66°33′ W 106
Eskimo Point, *Can.* 58°49′ N, 94°20′ W 108
Eskipazar, *Turk.* 40°58′ N, 32°32′ E 156
Eskişehir, *Turk.* 39°46′ N, 30°31′ E 156
Eslāmābād, *Iran* 34°9′ N, 46°32′ E 180
Eşler Dağı, peak, *Turk.* 37°39′ N, 29°12′ E 156
Eşme, *Turk.* 38°24′ N, 28°57′ E 156
Esmeralda, river, *Bol.* 13°28′ S, 67°59′ W 137
Esmeraldas, *Ecua.* 0°55′ N, 79°48′ W 130
Esmoraca, *Bol.* 21°41′ S, 66°19′ W 137
Esnagi Lake, *Can.* 48°40′ N, 84°49′ W 94
Espa, *Nor.* 60°34′ N, 11°16′ E 152
Espada, Punta, *Col.* 12°4′ N, 71°8′ W 136
Espakeh, *Iran* 26°46′ N, 60°12′ E 182
Espanola, *Can.* 46°15′ N, 81°46′ W 94
Espanola, *N. Mex., U.S.* 35°59′ N, 106°6′ W 92
Esparza, *C.R.* 9°58′ N, 84°40′ W 116
Esperanza, *Arg.* 31°27′ S, 60°54′ W 139
Esperanza, *Arg.* 51°5′ S, 70°38′ W 134
Esperanza, *Peru* 9°49′ S, 70°44′ W 137
Esperanza Inlet 49°45′ N, 127°40′ W 90
Esperanza, station, *Antarctica* 63°34′ S, 57°4′ W 248
Espichel, Cabo, *Port.* 38°11′ N, 9°37′ W 150
Espiel, *Sp.* 38°11′ N, 5°1′ W 164
Espigão Mestre, *Braz.* 14°41′ S, 46°14′ W 138
Espinal, *Bol.* 17°13′ S, 58°28′ W 132
Espinar see Yauri, *Peru* 14°51′ S, 71°24′ W 137
Espinazo, *Mex.* 26°16′ N, 101°6′ W 114
Espino, *Venez.* 8°32′ N, 66°1′ W 136
Espinosa, *Braz.* 14°59′ S, 42°50′ W 138
Espírito Santo, adm. division, *Braz.* 19°55′ S, 41°11′ W 138
Espírito Santo see Vila Velha, *Braz.* 20°25′ S, 40°21′ W 138
Espiritu, *Philippines* 17°59′ N, 120°39′ E 203
Espita, *Mex.* 21°0′ N, 88°20′ W 116
Espoo (Esbo), *Fin.* 60°11′ N, 24°34′ E 166
Esposende, *Port.* 41°31′ N, 8°48′ W 150
Espuña, peak, *Sp.* 37°51′ N, 1°37′ W 164
Espungabera, *Mozambique* 20°30′ S, 32°47′ E 227
Espy, *Pa., U.S.* 41°0′ N, 76°25′ W 110
Esqueda, *Mex.* 30°41′ N, 109°35′ W 92
Esquel, *Arg.* 42°58′ S, 71°19′ W 123
Esquimalt, *Can.* 48°25′ N, 123°24′ W 100
Esquina, *Arg.* 30°0′ S, 59°33′ W 139
Essaouira, *Mor.* 31°35′ N, 9°39′ W 143
Essé, *Cameroon* 4°6′ N, 11°50′ E 218
Essen, *Belg.* 51°27′ N, 4°29′ E 167
Essen, *Ger.* 51°27′ N, 7°0′ E 167
Essen, *Ger.* 52°44′ N, 7°56′ E 163
Essendon, Mount, *Austral.* 25°2′ S, 120°18′ E 230
Essex, *Calif., U.S.* 34°44′ N, 115°15′ W 101
Essex, *Conn., U.S.* 41°21′ N, 72°24′ W 104
Essex, *Mass., U.S.* 42°37′ N, 70°48′ W 104
Essex, *N.Y., U.S.* 44°18′ N, 73°23′ W 104
Essex Junction, *Vt., U.S.* 44°29′ N, 73°7′ W 104
Essexville, *Mich., U.S.* 43°36′ N, 83°50′ W 102
Esson, *Gabon* 1°14′ N, 11°34′ E 218
Essoûk, *Mali* 18°46′ N, 1°5′ E 222
Est, Cap, *Madagascar* 15°13′ S, 50°28′ E 220
Est, Pointe de l', *Can.* 49°5′ N, 61°39′ W 111
Estacado, Llano, *North America* 34°53′ N, 103°50′ W 92
Estación Marítima Antártica, station, *Chile, Antarctica* 62°12′ S, 58°57′ E 248
Estados, Isla de los (Staten Island), *Arg.* 55°28′ S, 64°48′ W 134
Estahbān, *Iran* 29°5′ N, 54°3′ E 196
Estância, *Braz.* 11°15′ S, 37°28′ W 132
Estancia Rojas Silva, *Parag.* 22°33′ S, 59°5′ W 132
Estancias, peak, *Sp.* 37°34′ N, 2°6′ W 164
Estavayer-le-Lac, *Switz.* 46°50′ N, 6°51′ E 167
Estcourt, *S. Af.* 29°2′ S, 29°51′ E 220
Este, *It.* 45°14′ N, 11°39′ E 167
Estelí, *Nicar.* 13°5′ N, 86°21′ W 115
Estella (Lizarra), *Sp.* 42°39′ N, 2°2′ W 164
Estelline, *S. Dak., U.S.* 44°33′ N, 96°55′ W 90
Estelline, *Tex., U.S.* 34°31′ N, 100°27′ W 92
Estepa, *Sp.* 37°17′ N, 4°54′ W 164
Estepona, *Sp.* 36°25′ N, 5°9′ W 164
Estérel, *Fr.* 43°28′ N, 6°35′ E 165
Esterfeld, *Ger.* 52°41′ N, 7°15′ E 163
Esterhazy, *Can.* 50°38′ N, 102°8′ W 90
Esternay, *Fr.* 48°43′ N, 3°32′ E 163
Estero, Point, *Calif., U.S.* 35°23′ N, 121°7′ W 100
Esteros del Iberá, marsh, *Arg.* 28°15′ S, 58°7′ W 139
Esterwegen, *Ger.* 52°59′ N, 7°37′ E 163
Estes Park, *Colo., U.S.* 40°22′ N, 105°32′ W 90
Estevan, *Can.* 49°7′ N, 103°2′ W 90
Estherville, *Iowa, U.S.* 43°23′ N, 94°49′ W 94
Estherwood, *La., U.S.* 30°10′ N, 92°28′ W 103
Estill, *S.C., U.S.* 32°45′ N, 81°15′ W 96
Estissac, *Fr.* 48°15′ N, 3°48′ E 163
Eston, *Can.* 51°9′ N, 108°45′ W 90
Estonia 58°38′ N, 25°30′ E 166
Estreito, *Braz.* 31°49′ S, 51°45′ W 139
Estreito, Serra do, *Braz.* 10°32′ S, 43°49′ W 132
Estrela do Norte, *Braz.* 13°50′ S, 49°6′ W 138
Estrela, Serra da, *Port.* 39°59′ N, 8°2′ W 150
Estrella, peak, *Sp.* 38°23′ N, 3°39′ W 164
Estrella, Punta, *Mex.* 30°55′ N, 114°43′ W 92
Estrondo, Serra do, *Braz.* 9°16′ S, 49°36′ W 130
Etah, site, *Den.* 78°18′ N, 73°12′ W 246
Étain, *Fr.* 49°12′ N, 5°38′ E 163
Etal Atoll, *F.S.M.* 5°46′ N, 154°5′ E 192
Étampes, *Fr.* 48°25′ N, 2°9′ E 163
Étaples, *Fr.* 50°31′ N, 1°38′ E 163
Etawah, *India* 26°45′ N, 79°0′ E 197
Etawney Lake, *Can.* 57°50′ N, 97°31′ W 108
Etéké, *Gabon* 1°30′ S, 11°33′ E 218
Eternity Range, *Antarctica* 69°10′ S, 68°24′ W 248
Ethel, *Miss., U.S.* 33°6′ N, 89°28′ W 103
Ethel, *Wash., U.S.* 46°30′ N, 122°45′ W 100
Ethel, *W. Va., U.S.* 37°51′ N, 81°55′ W 94
Ethelbert, *Can.* 51°31′ N, 100°25′ W 90
Ethelsville, *Ala., U.S.* 33°23′ N, 88°12′ W 103
Ethiopia 8°36′ N, 37°8′ E 218
Etna, *Wyo., U.S.* 43°2′ N, 111°0′ W 90
Etna, peak, *It.* 37°44′ N, 14°54′ E 156
Etne, *Nor.* 59°39′ N, 5°55′ E 152
Etoile, *Dem. Rep. of the Congo* 11°38′ S, 27°31′ E 224
Etoile, *Tex., U.S.* 31°21′ N, 94°27′ W 103
Etoka, *Dem. Rep. of the Congo* 0°8′ N, 23°17′ E 218
Etosha National Park, *Namibia* 18°57′ S, 14°47′ E 220
Etoumbi, *Congo* 4°237′ S, 14°54′ E 218
Etowah, *Tenn., U.S.* 35°19′ N, 84°32′ W 96
Étrépagny, *Fr.* 49°18′ N, 1°37′ E 163
Ettenheim, *Ger.* 48°14′ N, 7°47′ E 163
Ettersberg, Grosser, peak, *Ger.* 51°0′ N, 11°10′ E 152
Ettrick, *N.Z.* 45°39′ S, 169°21′ E 240
Etulia, *Mold.* 45°32′ N, 28°27′ E 156
Etxarri-Aranatz, *Sp.* 42°55′ N, 2°3′ W 164
Etzatlán, *Mex.* 20°46′ N, 104°7′ W 114
Eu, *Fr.* 50°2′ N, 1°24′ E 163
Euca, *Braz.* 2°38′ N, 50°54′ W 130
Eucla, *Austral.* 31°39′ S, 128°51′ E 231
Euclid, *Ohio, U.S.* 41°34′ N, 81°31′ W 102
Eudora, *Ark., U.S.* 33°5′ N, 91°16′ W 103
Eufaula, *Ala., U.S.* 31°53′ N, 85°9′ W 96
Eufaula, *Okla., U.S.* 35°15′ N, 95°34′ W 96
Eufaula Lake, *Okla., U.S.* 34°58′ N, 96°6′ W 96
Eugene, *Oreg., U.S.* 44°2′ N, 123°7′ W 90
Eugenia, Punta, *Mex.* 27°43′ N, 116°17′ W 112
Eumseong, *S. Korea* 36°55′ N, 127°42′ E 200
Eungella National Park, *Austral.* 21°4′ S, 148°14′ E 238
Eunice, *La., U.S.* 30°28′ N, 92°25′ W 103
Eunice, *N. Mex., U.S.* 32°26′ N, 103°9′ W 92
Eupen, *Belg.* 50°37′ N, 6°2′ E 167
Euphrates, river, *Syr.* 35°33′ N, 40°3′ E 207
Euphrates see Al Furāt, river, *Syr.* 35°43′ N, 39°21′ E 180
Eura, *Fin.* 61°6′ N, 22°9′ E 166
Eurajoki, *Fin.* 61°12′ N, 21°42′ E 166
Eure, river, *Fr.* 49°1′ N, 1°24′ E 163
Eureka, *Calif., U.S.* 40°46′ N, 124°10′ W 90
Eureka, *Can.* 80°2′ N, 85°43′ W 246
Eureka, *Ill., U.S.* 40°42′ N, 89°17′ W 102
Eureka, *Kans., U.S.* 37°48′ N, 96°18′ W 90
Eureka, *Mont., U.S.* 48°52′ N, 115°3′ W 90
Eureka, *Nev., U.S.* 39°31′ N, 115°59′ W 90
Eureka, *S. Dak., U.S.* 45°46′ N, 99°39′ W 90
Eureka, *Utah, U.S.* 39°56′ N, 112°6′ W 90
Eureka Springs, *Ark., U.S.* 36°23′ N, 93°45′ W 94
Eureka Valley, *Calif., U.S.* 37°12′ N, 117°54′ W 101
Europa, Île, *Fr.* 22°44′ S, 39°43′ E 220
Europa, Picos de, peak, *Sp.* 43°10′ N, 4°55′ W 150
Europa Point, *U.K.* 35°58′ N, 5°14′ W 164
Europe 41°0′ N, 28°0′ E 143
Euskirchen, *Ger.* 50°39′ N, 6°47′ E 167
Eustis, *Fla., U.S.* 28°51′ N, 81°41′ W 105
Eutaw, *Ala., U.S.* 32°49′ N, 87°54′ W 103
Eutin, *Ger.* 54°8′ N, 10°37′ E 152
Eutsuk Lake, *Can.* 53°11′ N, 127°16′ W 108
Evadale, *Tex., U.S.* 30°20′ N, 94°4′ W 103
Evangelistas, Grupo, islands, *South Pacific Ocean* 52°34′ S, 78°23′ W 134
Evans, *Colo., U.S.* 40°23′ N, 104°43′ W 90
Evans, *La., U.S.* 30°58′ N, 93°31′ W 103
Evans, Lac, lake, *Can.* 50°46′ N, 77°28′ W 110
Evans, Mount, *Can.* 49°32′ N, 116°23′ W 90
Evans, Mount, *Colo., U.S.* 39°34′ N, 105°42′ W 90
Evans, Mount, *Mont., U.S.* 46°2′ N, 113°18′ W 90
Evans Notch, pass, *Me., U.S.* 44°18′ N, 71°0′ W 104
Evansburg, *Can.* 53°35′ N, 115°2′ W 108
Evanston, *Ill., U.S.* 42°2′ N, 87°41′ W 102
Evanston, *Wyo., U.S.* 41°17′ N, 111°0′ W 90
Evansville, *Ind., U.S.* 37°58′ N, 87°33′ W 96
Evansville, *Wis., U.S.* 42°47′ N, 89°18′ W 102
Evansville, *Wyo., U.S.* 42°51′ N, 106°15′ W 90
Evart, *Mich., U.S.* 43°54′ N, 85°17′ W 102
Evelyn, *Can.* 54°53′ N, 127°19′ W 108
Even Yehuda, *Israel* 32°15′ N, 34°52′ E 194
Evenk, adm. division, *Russ.* 65°19′ N, 91°42′ E 169
Evensk, *Russ.* 61°57′ N, 159°17′ E 173
Everest, Mount (Qomolangma, Sagarmāthā), *China-Nepal* 28°0′ N, 86°53′ E 197
Everett, *Wash., U.S.* 47°58′ N, 122°11′ W 100
Everglades City, *Fla., U.S.* 25°51′ N, 81°24′ W 105
Everglades National Park, *Fla., U.S.* 25°24′ N, 80°54′ W 105
Evergreen, *Ala., U.S.* 31°26′ N, 86°57′ W 96
Everson, *Wash., U.S.* 48°54′ N, 122°20′ W 100
Evesham, *U.K.* 52°6′ N, 1°57′ W 162
Évia, island, *Gr.* 38°45′ N, 23°36′ E 180
Évian, *Fr.* 46°23′ N, 6°35′ E 167
Evje, *Nor.* 58°34′ N, 7°49′ E 152
Évora, *Port.* 38°33′ N, 7°55′ W 150
Évora, adm. division, *Port.* 38°40′ N, 8°25′ W 150
Évreux, *Fr.* 49°1′ N, 1°9′ E 163
Évron, *Fr.* 48°9′ N, 0°25′ E 150
Evrychou, *Cyprus* 35°2′ N, 32°55′ E 194
Ewaso Ngiro, river, *Kenya* 1°16′ S, 35°51′ E 224
Ewenkizu, *China* 49°4′ N, 119°40′ E 198
Ewing, *Nebr., U.S.* 42°14′ N, 98°21′ W 90
Ewing Island, *Antarctica* 69°46′ S, 61°0′ W 248
Ewo, *Congo* 0°51′ N, 14°48′ E 218
Exaltación, *Bol.* 13°18′ S, 65°18′ W 137
Excelsior Mountains, *Nev., U.S.* 38°17′ N, 118°39′ W 90
Exeter, *Calif., U.S.* 36°18′ N, 119°9′ W 101
Exeter, *Can.* 43°21′ N, 81°29′ W 102
Exeter, *Mo., U.S.* 36°40′ N, 93°56′ W 96
Exeter, *N.H., U.S.* 42°58′ N, 70°58′ W 104
Exeter, *R.I., U.S.* 41°34′ N, 71°33′ W 104
Exeter, *U.K.* 50°43′ N, 3°31′ W 162
Exeter Sound 66°3′ N, 64°29′ W 106
Exford, *U.K.* 51°7′ N, 3°38′ W 162
Exmoor, region, *U.K.* 51°8′ N, 3°55′ W 162
Exmoor National Park, *U.K.* 51°10′ N, 3°45′ W 162
Exmouth, *Austral.* 22°5′ S, 114°3′ E 238
Exmouth Gulf 22°8′ S, 113°3′ E 230
Exmouth, Peninsula, *Chile* 49°22′ S, 75°30′ W 134
Exmouth Plateau, *Indian Ocean* 19°26′ S, 112°55′ E 254
Expedition Range, *Austral.* 24°34′ S, 148°33′ E 230
Experiment, *Ga., U.S.* 33°15′ N, 84°17′ W 96
Extremadura, adm. division, *Sp.* 38°59′ N, 6°46′ W 164
Exuma, adm. division, *Bahamas* 23°39′ N, 76°4′ W 96
Exuma Sound 24°7′ N, 76°20′ W 96
Eyasi, Lake, *Tanzania* 3°38′ S, 34°46′ E 224
Eye, *U.K.* 52°19′ N, 1°8′ E 162
Eye Peninsula, *U.K.* 58°12′ N, 6°42′ W 150
Eyl, *Somalia* 7°56′ N, 49°49′ E 218
Eyrarbakki, *Ice.* 63°54′ N, 21°6′ W 143
Eyre Peninsula, *Austral.* 33°21′ S, 135°33′ E 230
Eyumojok, *Cameroon* 5°46′ N, 8°56′ E 222
Ezeriş, *Rom.* 45°24′ N, 21°52′ E 168
Ezeru, peak, *Rom.* 45°27′ N, 24°51′ E 156
Ezine, *Turk.* 39°46′ N, 26°19′ E 156

F

Fabala, *Guinea* 9°43′ N, 9°6′ W 222
Fabara, *Sp.* 41°9′ N, 0°10′ E 164
Faber Lake, *Can.* 63°42′ N, 116°6′ W 246
Facatativá, *Col.* 4°48′ N, 74°22′ W 130
Facha, oil field, *Lib.* 29°21′ N, 17°3′ E 216
Fachi, *Niger* 18°5′ N, 11°33′ E 222
Facho, Pico do, peak, *Port.* 32°55′ N, 16°30′ W 214
Facinas, *Sp.* 36°8′ N, 5°43′ W 164
Facture, *Fr.* 44°38′ N, 0°59′ E 150
Fada, *Chad* 17°11′ N, 21°34′ E 216
Fada N'Gourma, *Burkina Faso* 12°3′ N, 0°19′ E 222
Fadd, *Hung.* 46°27′ N, 18°49′ E 168
Faddeya, Zaliv 76°57′ N, 110°31′ E 246
Faddeyevskiy, Ostrov, island, *Russ.* 76°12′ N, 127°53′ E 160
Fadhili, oil field, *Saudi Arabia* 26°54′ N, 49°6′ E 196
Fadiffolu Atoll, *Maldives* 5°18′ N, 72°47′ E 188
Faenza, *It.* 44°17′ N, 11°51′ E 167
Fafa, *Mali* 15°17′ N, 0°42′ E 222
Făgăraş, Munţii, *Rom.* 45°29′ N, 24°10′ E 156
Fågelsjö, *Nor.* 61°47′ N, 14°39′ E 152
Fagersta, *Nor.* 59°59′ N, 15°45′ E 152
Făget, *Rom.* 45°50′ N, 22°11′ E 168
Făget, Munţii, *Rom.* 47°36′ N, 23°0′ E 168
Faggo, *Nig.* 11°25′ N, 9°57′ E 222
Fagnières, *Fr.* 48°57′ N, 4°20′ E 163
Fahala, island, *Maldives* 2°24′ N, 73°19′ E 188
Fahraj, *Iran* 28°56′ N, 58°50′ E 196
Fahud, oil field, *Oman* 22°11′ N, 56°26′ E 182
Faichuk, island, *Federated States of Micronesia* 7°0′ N, 152°0′ E 242
Fair Haven, *Vt., U.S.* 43°35′ N, 73°17′ W 104
Fair Oaks, *Ind., U.S.* 41°4′ N, 87°16′ W 102
Fairbanks, *Alas., U.S.* 64°49′ N, 147°39′ W 106
Fairbanks, *Me., U.S.* 44°42′ N, 70°11′ W 111
Fairbury, *Mo., U.S.* 40°44′ N, 88°31′ W 94
Fairbury, *Nebr., U.S.* 40°7′ N, 97°11′ W 92
Fairfax, *Okla., U.S.* 36°33′ N, 96°43′ W 94
Fairfax, *S.C., U.S.* 32°57′ N, 81°15′ W 96
Fairfield, *Ala., U.S.* 33°29′ N, 86°53′ W 96
Fairfield, *Calif., U.S.* 38°14′ N, 122°3′ W 100
Fairfield, *Conn., U.S.* 41°8′ N, 73°16′ W 104
Fairfield, *Fla., U.S.* 29°21′ N, 82°16′ W 105
Fairfield, *Idaho, U.S.* 43°21′ N, 114°48′ W 90
Fairfield, *Mo., U.S.* 38°22′ N, 88°22′ W 94
Fairfield, *Mont., U.S.* 47°36′ N, 111°59′ W 90
Fairfield, *Ohio, U.S.* 39°19′ N, 84°35′ W 102
Fairfield, *Tex., U.S.* 31°42′ N, 96°9′ W 96
Fairhaven, *Mass., U.S.* 41°38′ N, 70°55′ W 104
Fairhope, *Ala., U.S.* 30°30′ N, 87°54′ W 103
Fairlawn, *Va., U.S.* 37°8′ N, 80°36′ W 94
Fairlee, *Vt., U.S.* 43°54′ N, 72°10′ W 104
Fairlie, *N.Z.* 44°7′ S, 170°49′ E 240
Fairlight, *Can.* 49°53′ N, 101°40′ W 90
Fairmead, *Calif., U.S.* 37°4′ N, 120°12′ W 100
Fairmont, *Minn., U.S.* 43°38′ N, 94°27′ W 94
Fairmont, *W. Va., U.S.* 39°29′ N, 80°11′ W 94
Fairmount, *Ind., U.S.* 40°24′ N, 85°39′ W 102
Fairport, *Mich., U.S.* 45°37′ N, 86°39′ W 94
Fairport Harbor, *Ohio, U.S.* 41°43′ N, 81°16′ W 102
Fairview, *Can.* 56°4′ N, 118°25′ W 108
Fairview, *Ill., U.S.* 40°37′ N, 90°10′ W 102
Fairview, *Okla., U.S.* 36°15′ N, 98°29′ W 92
Fairview, *Pa., U.S.* 42°1′ N, 80°16′ W 94
Fairview, *Tenn., U.S.* 35°58′ N, 87°7′ W 96
Fairview Park, *Ind., U.S.* 39°40′ N, 87°25′ W 102
Fairview Peak, *Oreg., U.S.* 43°34′ N, 122°44′ W 90
Fairweather, Cape, *Antarctica* 64°57′ S, 60°47′ W 134
Fairweather, Mount, *Alas., U.S.* 58°54′ N, 137°43′ W 98
Faisalabad, *Pak.* 31°24′ N, 73°0′ E 186
Faith, *S. Dak., U.S.* 45°0′ N, 102°4′ W 90
Faizabad, *India* 26°46′ N, 82°6′ E 197
Fakel, *Russ.* 57°36′ N, 53°6′ E 154
Fakenham, *U.K.* 52°49′ N, 0°51′ E 162
Fakfak, *Indonesia* 2°54′ S, 132°11′ E 192
Fakiya, *Bulg.* 42°11′ N, 27°4′ E 156
Fakse Bugt 55°4′ N, 11°41′ E 152
Faku, *China* 42°31′ N, 123°27′ E 200
Falagh, *Sudan* 8°35′ N, 31°5′ E 224
Falakró, Óros, *Gr.* 41°12′ N, 23°39′ E 156
Falam, *Myanmar* 22°50′ N, 93°39′ E 188
Falces, *Sp.* 42°23′ N, 1°49′ W 164
Fălciu, *Rom.* 46°17′ N, 28°7′ E 156
Falcón, adm. division, *Venez.* 10°54′ N, 70°36′ W 136
Falcon, Cape, *Oreg., U.S.* 45°45′ N, 123°58′ W 100
Falcon Lake, *Mex.* 26°52′ N, 99°39′ W 112
Falcone, Capo del, *It.* 40°57′ N, 7°19′ E 156
Falconer, *N.Y., U.S.* 42°7′ N, 79°14′ W 110
Faléa, *Mali* 12°17′ N, 11°18′ W 222
Falémé, river, *Africa* 13°52′ N, 12°10′ W 222
Falenki, *Russ.* 58°22′ N, 51°45′ E 154
Făleşti, *Mold.* 47°34′ N, 27°42′ E 156
Falfurrias, *Tex., U.S.* 27°11′ N, 98°8′ W 96
Falher, *Can.* 55°44′ N, 117°14′ W 108
Falkenberg, *Nor.* 56°54′ N, 12°29′ E 152
Falkirk, *U.K.* 55°59′ N, 3°48′ W 150
Falkland Islands (Islas Malvinas), *Falk. Is., U.K.* 52°18′ S, 62°14′ W 134
Falkland Plateau, *South Atlantic Ocean* 51°7′ S, 49°25′ W 255
Falköping, *Nor.* 58°9′ N, 13°33′ E 152
Fallbrook, *Calif., U.S.* 33°23′ N, 117°16′ W 101
Fallon, *Nev., U.S.* 39°28′ N, 118°48′ W 90
Falls City, *Nebr., U.S.* 40°2′ N, 95°36′ W 90
Fallujah see Al Fallūjah, *Iraq* 33°19′ N, 43°46′ E 180
Falmey, *Niger* 12°40′ N, 2°47′ E 222
Falmouth, *Ky., U.S.* 38°39′ N, 84°20′ W 102
Falmouth, *Mass., U.S.* 41°33′ N, 70°38′ W 104
Falmouth, *Va., U.S.* 38°19′ N, 77°29′ W 94
Falou, *Mali* 14°36′ N, 7°56′ W 222
Falsa, Bahía 39°20′ S, 62°29′ W 139
False Point, *India* 20°17′ N, 86°50′ E 188
Falset, *Sp.* 41°8′ N, 0°48′ E 164
Falso, Cabo, *Hond.* 15°15′ N, 83°23′ W 115
Falso, Cabo, *Mex.* 22°43′ N, 110°51′ W 112
Falun, *Nor.* 60°34′ N, 15°35′ E 152
Famagusta see Ammochostos, *Northern Cyprus, Cyprus* 35°7′ N, 33°56′ E 194
Famaka, *Sudan* 11°18′ N, 34°43′ E 182
Famana, *Mali* 11°51′ N, 7°51′ W 222
Fan, river, *Alban.* 41°47′ N, 19°44′ E 168
Fana, *Mali* 12°47′ N, 7°0′ W 222
Fana, *Nor.* 60°13′ N, 5°23′ E 152
Fanchang, *China* 31°6′ N, 118°12′ E 198
Fandriana, *Madagascar* 20°14′ S, 47°22′ E 220
Fang, *Thai.* 19°57′ N, 99°11′ E 202
Fangak, *Sudan* 9°2′ N, 30°55′ E 224
Fangcheng, *China* 21°48′ N, 108°21′ E 198
Fangcheng, *China* 33°17′ N, 113°4′ E 198
Fangshan, *China* 37°50′ N, 111°16′ E 198
Fanjeaux, *Fr.* 43°11′ N, 2°1′ E 164
Fanny Bay, *Can.* 49°31′ N, 124°51′ W 100
Fano, *It.* 43°49′ N, 13°1′ E 167
Fanshan, *China* 27°22′ N, 120°27′ E 198
Fanshi, *China* 39°13′ N, 113°18′ E 198
Fanūdah, *Saudi Arabia* 25°25′ N, 40°36′ E 182
Fanxian, *China* 35°53′ N, 115°25′ E 198
Far Mountain, *Can.* 52°45′ N, 125°25′ W 108
Farabana, *Guinea* 9°53′ N, 9°8′ W 222
Faradje, *Dem. Rep. of the Congo* 3°43′ N, 29°42′ E 224
Farafangana, *Madagascar* 22°50′ S, 47°50′ E 220
Farâfra, El Wâhât el, *Egypt* 27°18′ N, 28°17′ E 180
Farah, *Afghan.* 32°25′ N, 62°10′ E 186
Farah, river, *Afghan.* 31°54′ N, 61°33′ E 186
Farallon Islands, *Pacific Ocean* 37°28′ N, 123°10′ W 90
Farallones de Cali National Park, *Col.* 2°54′ N, 77°0′ W 136
Faranah, *Guinea* 10°2′ N, 10°45′ W 222
Faraulep Atoll, *F.S.M.* 8°56′ N, 141°38′ E 192
Fareham, *U.K.* 50°51′ N, 1°11′ W 162
Farewell, *Alas., U.S.* 62°22′ N, 153°57′ W 98
Farewell, Cape, *N.Z.* 40°31′ S, 172°44′ E 240
Fargo, *N. Dak., U.S.* 46°49′ N, 97°1′ W 73
Farg'ona, *Uzb.* 40°23′ N, 71°47′ E 197
Fari, *Mali* 12°10′ N, 10°41′ W 222
Faribault, *Minn., U.S.* 44°16′ N, 93°17′ W 94
Faridpur, *Bangladesh* 23°33′ N, 89°51′ E 197
Farim, *Guinea-Bissau* 12°30′ N, 15°13′ W 222
Farīmān, *Iran* 35°44′ N, 59°53′ E 180
Farina, *Ill., U.S.* 38°49′ N, 88°47′ W 102
Færingehavn see Kangerluarsoruseq, *Den.* 63°43′ N, 51°21′ W 106
Farinha, river, *Braz.* 6°52′ S, 47°29′ W 130
Farkhar, *Afghan.* 36°40′ N, 69°50′ E 186
Farkhor, *Taj.* 37°29′ N, 69°22′ E 184
Farkovo, *Russ.* 65°36′ N, 86°58′ E 169
Farkwa, *Tanzania* 5°23′ S, 35°35′ E 224
Farmer City, *Ill., U.S.* 40°14′ N, 88°39′ W 102
Farmersburg, *Ind., U.S.* 39°15′ N, 87°22′ W 102
Farmersville, *Calif., U.S.* 36°18′ N, 119°13′ W 101
Farmerville, *La., U.S.* 32°45′ N, 92°25′ W 103
Farmingdale, *Me., U.S.* 44°14′ N, 69°47′ W 104
Farmington, *Ill., U.S.* 40°41′ N, 90°1′ W 102
Farmington, *N.H., U.S.* 43°23′ N, 71°4′ W 104
Farmington, *N. Mex., U.S.* 36°44′ N, 108°10′ W 82
Farmington, *Utah, U.S.* 40°58′ N, 111°52′ W 90
Farmville, *Va., U.S.* 37°17′ N, 78°25′ W 94

Farnborough, *U.K.* 51° 16′ N, 0° 45′ E 162
Farne Islands, *North Sea* 55° 40′ N, 1° 35′ W 150
Farnham, *U.K.* 51° 12′ N, 0° 48′ E 162
Farnham, Mount, *Can.* 50° 28′ N, 116° 35′ W 90
Faro, *Braz.* 2° 10′ S, 56° 45′ W 130
Faro, *Can.* 62° 15′ N, 133° 24′ W 98
Faro, *Port.* 37° 2′ N, 8° 0′ W 214
Faro, *Port.* 37° 1′ N, 7° 57′ W 150
Faro, adm. division, *Port.* 37° 6′ N, 8° 50′ W 150
Fårö, island, *Sw.* 57° 59′ N, 19° 16′ E 166
Faro, Punta, *Col.* 11° 7′ N, 75° 4′ W 136
Faro, river, *Cameroon* 8° 17′ N, 12° 55′ E 218
Faro, Sierra do, *Sp.* 42° 18′ N, 8° 5′ W 150
Faroe Islands (Føroyar), *North Atlantic Ocean* 62° 34′ N, 11° 40′ W 143
Fårösund, *Sw.* 57° 50′ N, 19° 2′ E 166
Farquhar Group, islands, *Indian Ocean* 9° 52′ S, 50° 31′ E 218
Farr Bay 66° 23′ S, 96° 0′ E 248
Farrāshband, *Iran* 28° 49′ N, 52° 5′ E 196
Farrel, Isla, island, *Chile* 51° 2′ S, 75° 51′ W 134
Farsi, *Afghan.* 33° 44′ N, 63° 15′ E 186
Farsø, *Den.* 56° 46′ N, 9° 20′ E 152
Farsund, *Nor.* 58° 5′ N, 6° 46′ E 150
Fartura, *Braz.* 23° 23′ S, 49° 32′ W 138
Farwell, *Mich., U.S.* 43° 50′ N, 84° 51′ W 102
Farwell, *Tex., U.S.* 34° 22′ N, 103° 2′ W 92
Farwell Island, *Antarctica* 72° 15′ S, 88° 28′ W 248
Fasā, *Iran* 28° 53′ N, 53° 44′ E 196
Fashven, peak, *U.K.* 58° 32′ N, 5° 1′ W 150
Fastiv, *Ukr.* 50° 3′ N, 29° 59′ E 158
Fatala, river, *Guinea* 10° 42′ N, 13° 45′ W 222
Fatehabad, *India* 29° 30′ N, 75° 28′ E 197
Fatehgarh, *India* 27° 22′ N, 79° 33′ E 197
Fatehpur, *India* 27° 59′ N, 74° 59′ E 186
Fatehpur, *India* 25° 54′ N, 80° 49′ E 197
Fatehpur Sikri, *India* 27° 5′ N, 77° 40′ E 197
Fatezh, *Russ.* 52° 3′ N, 35° 49′ E 158
Fathai, *Sudan* 8° 2′ N, 31° 45′ E 224
Father, Lac, lake, *Can.* 49° 20′ N, 75° 52′ W 94
Fátima, *Port.* 39° 36′ N, 8° 40′ W 150
Fatsa, *Turk.* 41° 0′ N, 37° 29′ E 158
Faucille, Col de la, pass, *Fr.* 46° 21′ N, 6° 0′ E 167
Faucilles, Monts, *Fr.* 48° 17′ N, 5° 51′ E 163
Faulkton, *S. Dak., U.S.* 45° 0′ N, 99° 9′ W 90
Faulquemont, *Fr.* 49° 2′ N, 6° 36′ E 163
Fauresmith, *S. Af.* 29° 44′ S, 25° 17′ E 227
Fauro, island, *Solomon Islands* 7° 0′ S, 156° 0′ E 242
Fauske, *Nor.* 67° 15′ N, 15° 22′ E 152
Faust, *Can.* 55° 18′ N, 115° 40′ W 108
Faux Cap see Betanty, *Madagascar* 25° 34′ S, 45° 31′ E 220
Fåvang, *Nor.* 61° 25′ N, 10° 13′ E 152
Faverges, *Fr.* 45° 44′ N, 6° 17′ E 150
Faversham, *U.K.* 51° 18′ N, 0° 53′ E 162
Fawcett, *Can.* 54° 32′ N, 114° 6′ W 108
Faya, *Chad* 17° 54′ N, 19° 6′ E 216
Fayd, *Saudi Arabia* 27° 8′ N, 42° 38′ E 180
Fayette, *Ala., U.S.* 33° 41′ N, 87° 50′ W 96
Fayette, *Me., U.S.* 44° 24′ N, 70° 3′ W 104
Fayette, *Miss., U.S.* 31° 41′ N, 91° 3′ W 103
Fayette, *Mo., U.S.* 39° 8′ N, 92° 41′ W 94
Fayette, *Ohio, U.S.* 41° 39′ N, 84° 20′ W 102
Fayette, *Utah, U.S.* 39° 13′ N, 111° 50′ W 90
Fayetteville, *Ark., U.S.* 36° 3′ N, 94° 10′ W 94
Faynān, ruin(s), *Jordan* 30° 37′ N, 35° 27′ E 194
Fayón, *Sp.* 41° 14′ N, 0° 19′ E 164
Faysh Khābūr, *Iraq* 37° 4′ N, 42° 17′ E 195
Fazao-Malfakassa National Park, *Togo* 8° 39′ N, 0° 14′ E 222
Fazilka, *India* 30° 24′ N, 74° 3′ E 186
Fazran, oil field, *Saudi Arabia* 26° 2′ N, 49° 0′ E 196
Fdérik (Fort Gouraud), *Mauritania* 22° 41′ N, 12° 43′ W 214
Fear, Cape, *N.C., U.S.* 33° 45′ N, 77° 57′ W 96
Feather River Canyon, *Calif., U.S.* 39° 50′ N, 121° 36′ W 90
Fedala see Mohammedia, *Mor.* 33° 43′ N, 7° 22′ W 214
Federación, *Arg.* 30° 59′ S, 57° 54′ W 139
Federal, *Arg.* 30° 55′ S, 58° 45′ W 139
Federally Administered Tribal Areas, adm. division, *Pak.* 32° 7′ N, 69° 33′ E 186
Fedje, *Nor.* 60° 46′ N, 4° 41′ E 152
Fedorovka, *Kaz.* 53° 38′ N, 62° 42′ E 184
Fedorovka, *Kaz.* 51° 10′ N, 51° 59′ E 158
Fedorovka, *Russ.* 53° 10′ N, 55° 12′ E 154
Feeding Hills, *Mass., U.S.* 42° 3′ N, 72° 41′ W 104
Fegen, lake, *Nor.* 57° 10′ N, 12° 51′ E 152
Feia, Lagoa, lake, *Braz.* 22° 1′ S, 41° 34′ W 138
Feijó, *Braz.* 8° 10′ S, 70° 23′ W 130
Feilding, *N.Z.* 40° 13′ S, 175° 33′ E 240
Feira de Santana, *Braz.* 12° 16′ S, 38° 59′ W 132
Feixi, *China* 31° 42′ N, 117° 8′ E 198
Fejér, adm. division, *Hung.* 46° 57′ N, 18° 15′ E 156
Feke, *Turk.* 37° 51′ N, 35° 56′ E 156
Feklistova, Ostrov, island, *Russ.* 55° 7′ N, 134° 15′ E 160
Felanitx, *Sp.* 39° 27′ N, 3° 9′ E 150
Felchville, *Vt., U.S.* 43° 27′ N, 72° 33′ W 104
Feldbach, *Aust.* 46° 56′ N, 15° 53′ E 168
Feldberg, peak, *Ger.* 47° 51′ N, 7° 57′ E 165
Felicity, *Ohio, U.S.* 38° 50′ N, 84° 6′ W 102
Felidu Atoll, *Maldives* 3° 10′ N, 73° 1′ E 188
Felipe Carrillo Puerto, *Mex.* 24° 17′ N, 104° 1′ W 114
Felipe Carrillo Puerto, *Mex.* 19° 34′ N, 88° 4′ W 115
Felixlândia, *Braz.* 18° 46′ S, 44° 54′ W 138
Felixstowe, *U.K.* 51° 57′ N, 1° 20′ E 163
Felizzano, *It.* 44° 54′ N, 8° 26′ E 167
Fellit, *Eritrea* 16° 39′ N, 38° 0′ E 182
Fellows, *Calif., U.S.* 35° 10′ N, 119° 34′ W 100
Fellsmere, *Fla., U.S.* 27° 46′ N, 80° 36′ W 105
Felsenthal, *Ark., U.S.* 33° 2′ N, 92° 10′ W 103
Felsőcsatár, *Hung.* 47° 12′ N, 16° 27′ E 168
Felton, *Calif., U.S.* 37° 3′ N, 122° 6′ W 100
Feltre, *It.* 46° 0′ N, 11° 53′ E 167
Femund, lake, *Nor.* 62° 4′ N, 11° 19′ E 152
Fen, river, *China* 36° 45′ N, 111° 35′ E 198
Fenelon Falls, *Can.* 44° 31′ N, 78° 43′ W 94
Fengari, peak, *Gr.* 40° 27′ N, 25° 29′ E 156
Fengcheng, *China* 28° 10′ N, 115° 43′ E 198
Fengcheng, *China* 40° 26′ N, 124° 3′ E 200
Fengdu, *China* 29° 47′ N, 107° 44′ E 198
Fenggang, *China* 27° 58′ N, 107° 44′ E 198
Fenghuang, *China* 27° 54′ N, 109° 37′ E 198
Fengjie, *China* 31° 5′ N, 109° 34′ E 198
Fengkai, *China* 23° 27′ N, 111° 33′ E 198
Fenglin, *Taiwan, China* 23° 43′ N, 121° 24′ E 198
Fengning, *China* 41° 9′ N, 116° 35′ E 198
Fengshan, *China* 24° 30′ N, 107° 1′ E 198
Fengxian, *China* 33° 52′ N, 106° 37′ E 198
Fengzhen, *China* 40° 26′ N, 113° 7′ E 198
Fennville, *Mich., U.S.* 42° 34′ N, 86° 6′ W 102
Feno, Cap de, *Fr.* 41° 19′ N, 8° 29′ E 156
Feno, Capo di, *Fr.* 41° 58′ N, 7° 55′ E 156
Fenoarivo, *Madagascar* 18° 27′ S, 46° 32′ E 220
Fenoarivo Atsinanana, *Madagascar* 17° 25′ S, 49° 23′ E 220
Fenton, *La., U.S.* 30° 21′ N, 92° 57′ W 103
Fenxi, *China* 36° 38′ N, 111° 31′ E 198
Fenyang, *China* 37° 15′ N, 111° 46′ E 198
Feodosiya, *Ukr.* 45° 2′ N, 35° 18′ E 156
Ferdows, *Iran* 33° 58′ N, 58° 10′ E 180
Fère-Champenoise, *Fr.* 48° 45′ N, 3° 59′ E 163
Féres, *Gr.* 40° 53′ N, 26° 10′ E 156
Fērfēr, *Eth.* 5° 4′ N, 45° 10′ E 218
Fergana Valley, *Asia* 40° 38′ N, 70° 26′ E 197
Fergus Falls, *Minn., U.S.* 46° 16′ N, 96° 5′ W 90
Ferguson, *Ky., U.S.* 37° 3′ N, 84° 36′ W 96
Ferguson Lake, *Ariz., U.S.* 33° 2′ N, 114° 39′ W 101
Ferguson, Mount, *Nev., U.S.* 38° 38′ N, 118° 15′ W 90
Fergusson Island, *P.N.G.* 9° 19′ S, 150° 40′ E 192
Feria, *Sp.* 38° 30′ N, 6° 34′ W 164
Feriana, *Tun.* 34° 56′ N, 8° 34′ E 156
Feridu, island, *Maldives* 3° 46′ N, 72° 0′ E 188
Ferizaj (Uroševac), *Kosovo* 42° 22′ N, 21° 9′ E 168
Ferkéssédougou, *Côte d'Ivoire* 9° 34′ N, 5° 13′ W 222
Fern Grotto, site, *Hawai'i, U.S.* 22° 1′ N, 159° 24′ W 99
Fernández Leal, *Mex.* 30° 49′ N, 108° 16′ W 92
Fernandina Beach, *Fla., U.S.* 30° 39′ N, 81° 28′ W 96
Fernandina, Isla, island, *Ecua.* 0° 39′ N, 92° 41′ W 130
Fernando de Noronha, Arquipélago de, *South Atlantic Ocean* 3° 19′ S, 33° 15′ W 132
Fernandópolis, *Braz.* 20° 17′ S, 50° 15′ W 138
Fernán-Núñez, *Sp.* 37° 40′ N, 4° 45′ W 164
Fernão Dias, *Braz.* 16° 23′ S, 44° 30′ W 138
Fernão Veloso, Baía de 14° 30′ S, 39° 50′ E 224
Ferndale, *Calif., U.S.* 40° 34′ N, 124° 17′ W 92
Ferndale, *Wash., U.S.* 48° 50′ N, 122° 36′ W 100
Fernie, *Can.* 49° 30′ N, 115° 3′ W 90
Fernley, *Nev., U.S.* 39° 36′ N, 119° 17′ W 90
Ferns, *Ire.* 52° 35′ N, 6° 30′ W 150
Fernwood, *Miss., U.S.* 31° 10′ N, 90° 28′ W 103
Ferolle Point, *Can.* 51° 0′ N, 57° 53′ W 111
Ferrara, *It.* 44° 50′ N, 11° 37′ E 167
Ferrara, Mount, *Antarctica* 82° 18′ S, 42° 54′ W 248
Ferrat, Cap, *Alg.* 35° 54′ N, 0° 22′ E 164
Ferreira Gomes, *Braz.* 0° 49′ N, 51° 7′ W 130
Ferrelo, Cape, *Oreg., U.S.* 41° 56′ N, 124° 44′ W 90
Ferret, Cap, *Fr.* 44° 38′ N, 1° 35′ W 150
Ferriday, *La., U.S.* 31° 37′ N, 91° 34′ W 103
Ferris Mountains, *Wyo., U.S.* 42° 21′ N, 107° 23′ W 90
Ferrisburg, *Vt., U.S.* 44° 12′ N, 73° 15′ W 104
Ferro, river, *Braz.* 13° 0′ S, 55° 5′ W 130
Ferro see Hierro, island, *Sp.* 27° 25′ N, 17° 55′ W 214
Ferrol, *Sp.* 43° 30′ N, 8° 17′ W 214
Ferron, *Utah, U.S.* 39° 5′ N, 111° 7′ W 90
Ferros, *Braz.* 19° 16′ S, 43° 3′ W 138
Ferryland, *Can.* 47° 1′ N, 52° 54′ W 111
Ferrysburg, *Mich., U.S.* 43° 5′ N, 86° 12′ W 102
Ferryville see Menzel Bourguiba, *Tun.* 37° 9′ N, 9° 47′ E 156
Fertile, *Minn., U.S.* 47° 31′ N, 96° 18′ W 90
Fès (Fez), *Mor.* 34° 6′ N, 5° 0′ W 214
Feshi, *Dem. Rep. of the Congo* 6° 8′ S, 18° 6′ E 218
Fessenden, *N. Dak., U.S.* 47° 37′ N, 99° 38′ W 90
Fet, *Nor.* 59° 55′ N, 11° 10′ E 152
Fété Bowé, *Senegal* 14° 55′ N, 13° 33′ W 222
Feteşti, *Rom.* 44° 22′ N, 27° 49′ E 156
Fethiye, *Turk.* 36° 34′ N, 29° 9′ E 180
Feuet, spring, *Lib.* 24° 57′ N, 10° 2′ E 214
Feuilles, Rivière aux, river, *Can.* 58° 19′ N, 73° 4′ W 106
Feurs, *Fr.* 45° 44′ N, 4° 13′ E 150
Fevral'sk, *Russ.* 52° 30′ N, 131° 24′ E 190
Feyzabad, *Afghan.* 37° 8′ N, 70° 35′ E 186
Fez see Fès, *Mor.* 34° 6′ N, 5° 0′ W 214
Fezzan, region, *Africa* 29° 39′ N, 9° 56′ E 214
Fezzane, spring, *Niger* 21° 53′ N, 14° 29′ E 222
Ffestiniog, *U.K.* 52° 57′ N, 3° 55′ W 162
Fhada, Beinn, peak, *U.K.* 57° 12′ N, 5° 23′ W 150
Fian, *Ghana* 10° 22′ N, 2° 30′ W 222
Fianarantsoa, *Madagascar* 21° 34′ S, 47° 3′ E 207
Fianga, *Chad* 9° 54′ N, 15° 6′ E 216
Fibiş, *Rom.* 45° 58′ N, 21° 25′ E 168
Fichē, *Eth.* 9° 48′ N, 38° 42′ E 224
Fichtelgebirge, *Ger.* 50° 3′ N, 11° 20′ E 152
Ficksburg, *S. Af.* 28° 52′ S, 27° 51′ E 227
Fidenza, *It.* 44° 51′ N, 10° 4′ E 167
Fidler Lake, *Can.* 57° 10′ N, 97° 26′ W 108
Field Island, *Austral.* 12° 15′ S, 131° 20′ E 230
Field Naval Air Station, *Fla., U.S.* 30° 43′ N, 87° 5′ W 96
Fields Peak, *Oreg., U.S.* 44° 18′ N, 119° 20′ W 90
Fier, *Alban.* 40° 43′ N, 19° 32′ E 156
Fier, river, *Fr.* 45° 54′ N, 5° 55′ E 165
Fiesole, *It.* 43° 48′ N, 11° 17′ E 156
Fiesso, *It.* 44° 58′ N, 11° 36′ E 167
Fife Lake, *Can.* 49° 11′ N, 106° 19′ W 90
Fife Lake, *Mich., U.S.* 44° 34′ N, 85° 21′ W 94
Fife Ness, *U.K.* 56° 17′ N, 2° 34′ W 150
Fifield, *Wis., U.S.* 45° 52′ N, 90° 26′ W 94
Figari, Capo, *It.* 41° 1′ N, 9° 38′ E 156
Figeac, *Fr.* 44° 36′ N, 2° 2′ E 150
Figols, *Sp.* 42° 10′ N, 1° 49′ E 150
Figueira da Foz, *Port.* 40° 8′ N, 8° 53′ W 150
Figueirão, *Braz.* 18° 44′ S, 53° 41′ W 132
Figueres, *Sp.* 42° 15′ N, 2° 57′ E 164
Figuig, *Mor.* 32° 7′ N, 1° 13′ W 214
Figuil, *Cameroon* 9° 44′ N, 13° 56′ E 216
Fihaonana, *Madagascar* 18° 36′ S, 47° 13′ E 220
Fiji 18° 0′ N, 178° 0′ E 242
Fiji Plateau, *South Pacific Ocean* 17° 4′ S, 179° 39′ E 252
Fika, *Nig.* 11° 17′ N, 11° 17′ E 222
Filabres, Sierra de los, *Sp.* 37° 12′ N, 2° 32′ W 164
Filabusi, *Zimb.* 20° 31′ S, 29° 17′ E 227
Filadelfia, *Bol.* 11° 24′ S, 68° 49′ W 137
Filadélfia, *Braz.* 7° 22′ S, 47° 32′ W 130
Filadelfia, *Parag.* 22° 19′ S, 60° 4′ W 132
Fil'akovo, *Slovakia* 48° 15′ N, 19° 50′ E 152
Filattiera, *It.* 44° 19′ N, 9° 56′ E 167
Filchner Mountains, *Antarctica* 72° 42′ S, 4° 23′ E 248
File Axe, Lac, lake, *Can.* 50° 15′ N, 74° 7′ W 110
File Lake, *Can.* 54° 50′ N, 100° 42′ W 108
Filer, *Idaho, U.S.* 42° 34′ N, 114° 37′ W 90
Filer City, *Mich., U.S.* 44° 12′ N, 86° 18′ W 102
Filey, *U.K.* 54° 12′ N, 0° 18′ E 162
Fília, *Gr.* 39° 15′ N, 26° 8′ E 156
Filiaşi, *Rom.* 44° 33′ N, 23° 31′ E 156
Filimon Sîrbu, *Rom.* 45° 5′ N, 27° 15′ E 156
Filingué, *Niger* 14° 23′ N, 3° 17′ E 222
Filipów, *Pol.* 54° 10′ N, 22° 36′ E 152
Filisur, *Switz.* 46° 40′ N, 9° 40′ E 167
Fillmore, *Calif., U.S.* 34° 24′ N, 118° 55′ W 101
Fillmore, *Utah, U.S.* 38° 57′ N, 112° 19′ W 90
Fils, Lac du, lake, *Can.* 46° 38′ N, 78° 36′ W 94
Filton, *U.K.* 51° 30′ N, 2° 35′ W 162
Fītu, *Eth.* 5° 8′ N, 40° 39′ E 224
Filyos, river, *Turk.* 41° 28′ N, 31° 53′ E 180
Fimbul Ice Shelf, *Antarctica* 70° 45′ S, 0° 21′ E 248
Finale Emilia, *It.* 44° 50′ N, 11° 17′ E 167
Fiñana, *Sp.* 37° 9′ N, 2° 51′ W 164
Finarwa, *Eth.* 13° 4′ N, 38° 59′ E 182
Fındıklı, *Turk.* 41° 16′ N, 41° 7′ E 195
Findlay, *Ill., U.S.* 39° 31′ N, 88° 45′ W 102
Findlay, *Ohio, U.S.* 41° 1′ N, 83° 38′ W 102
Findlay, Mount, *Can.* 50° 4′ N, 116° 35′ W 90
Fingoè, *Mozambique* 15° 12′ S, 31° 51′ E 224
Finike, *Turk.* 36° 17′ N, 30° 7′ E 156
Finiq, *Alban.* 39° 54′ N, 20° 3′ E 156
Finke, *Austral.* 25° 37′ S, 134° 36′ E 231
Finland 63° 28′ N, 25° 46′ E 152
Finland, *Minn., U.S.* 47° 24′ N, 91° 16′ W 94
Finland, Gulf of 60° 11′ N, 25° 58′ E 152
Finlay, river, *Can.* 57° 38′ N, 126° 26′ W 108
Finley, *Calif., U.S.* 39° 0′ N, 122° 53′ W 90
Finley, *N. Dak., U.S.* 47° 29′ N, 97° 51′ W 90
Finmoore, *Can.* 53° 56′ N, 123° 37′ W 108
Finne, region, *Europe* 51° 7′ N, 11° 16′ E 152
Finnentrop, *Ger.* 51° 11′ N, 7° 58′ E 167
Finnmarks-vidda, *Nor.* 69° 2′ N, 22° 6′ E 152
Finnskog, *Nor.* 60° 42′ N, 12° 22′ E 152
Finnsnes, *Nor.* 69° 14′ N, 18° 0′ E 152
Finse, *Nor.* 60° 36′ N, 7° 23′ E 152
Finspång, *Nor.* 58° 41′ N, 15° 44′ E 152
Finsteraarhorn, peak, *Switz.* 46° 32′ N, 8° 5′ E 167
Finström, *Fin.* 60° 15′ N, 19° 54′ E 166
Fiordland National Park, *N.Z.* 45° 0′ S, 165° 54′ E 240
Fîrdea, *Rom.* 45° 45′ N, 22° 10′ E 168
Fire Island National Seashore, *Atlantic Ocean* 40° 35′ N, 73° 26′ W 104
Firebag, river, *Can.* 57° 27′ N, 110° 59′ W 108
Firedrake Lake, *Can.* 61° 15′ N, 105° 31′ W 108
Firenze (Florence), *It.* 43° 47′ N, 11° 14′ E 167
Firenzuola, *It.* 44° 7′ N, 11° 22′ E 167
Firmat, *Arg.* 33° 28′ S, 61° 30′ W 139
Firozabad, *India* 27° 7′ N, 78° 22′ E 197
Firozpur, *India* 30° 57′ N, 74° 38′ E 186
First Sugar Mill, site, *Hawai'i, U.S.* 21° 53′ N, 159° 30′ W 99
Fīrūzābād, *Iran* 28° 48′ N, 52° 38′ E 196
Fīrūzkūh, *Iran* 35° 46′ N, 52° 44′ E 180
Fish Camp, *Calif., U.S.* 37° 28′ N, 119° 39′ W 100
Fish Cove Point, *Can.* 54° 4′ N, 57° 19′ W 111
Fish Haven, *Idaho, U.S.* 42° 3′ N, 111° 24′ W 92
Fish River Canyon Nature Reserve, *Namibia* 28° 4′ S, 17° 32′ E 227
Fisher, *Ill., U.S.* 40° 18′ N, 88° 21′ W 102
Fisher, *La., U.S.* 31° 28′ N, 93° 29′ W 103
Fisher Branch, *Can.* 51° 5′ N, 97° 38′ W 90
Fisher Strait 62° 55′ N, 84° 37′ W 106
Fishers Island, *N.Y., U.S.* 41° 15′ N, 72° 12′ W 104
Fishers Peak, *Colo., U.S.* 37° 4′ N, 104° 33′ W 92
Fishing Lake, *Can.* 52° 8′ N, 95° 50′ W 108
Fiskdale, *Mass., U.S.* 42° 6′ N, 72° 8′ W 104
Fiske, Cape, *Antarctica* 74° 15′ S, 60° 22′ W 248
Fiskenæsset see Qeqertarsuatsiaat, *Den.* 63° 6′ N, 50° 43′ W 106
Fismes, *Fr.* 49° 18′ N, 3° 41′ E 163
Fisterra, Cabo, *Sp.* 42° 51′ N, 9° 43′ W 150
Fitchburg, *Mass., U.S.* 42° 34′ N, 71° 48′ W 104
Fitchville, *Conn., U.S.* 41° 33′ N, 72° 9′ W 104
Fitero, *Sp.* 42° 3′ N, 1° 52′ W 164
Fitri, Lac, lake, *Chad* 12° 53′ N, 16° 54′ E 216
Fitz Roy, Monte, peak, *Arg.* 49° 18′ S, 73° 23′ W 134
Fitzcarrald, *Peru* 11° 48′ S, 72° 22′ W 137
Fitzgerald, *Can.* 59° 51′ N, 111° 41′ W 108
Fitzgerald, *Ga., U.S.* 31° 42′ N, 83° 15′ W 96
Fitzpatrick, *Can.* 47° 28′ N, 72° 46′ W 94
Fitzroy Crossing, *Austral.* 18° 15′ S, 125° 32′ E 238
Fiume see Rijeka, *Croatia* 45° 20′ N, 14° 26′ E 156
Fiumicino, *It.* 41° 46′ N, 12° 13′ E 156
Fivizzano, *It.* 44° 14′ N, 10° 8′ E 167
Fizi, *Dem. Rep. of the Congo* 4° 21′ S, 28° 54′ E 224
Fjällåsen, *Nor.* 67° 30′ N, 20° 4′ E 152
Flå, *Nor.* 63° 11′ N, 10° 19′ E 152
Fladerer Bay 73° 19′ S, 84° 19′ W 248
Fladungen, *Ger.* 50° 31′ N, 10° 7′ E 167
Flagler, *Colo., U.S.* 39° 17′ N, 103° 4′ W 90
Flagler Beach, *Fla., U.S.* 29° 28′ N, 81° 9′ W 105
Flagstaff, *Ariz., U.S.* 35° 19′ N, 111° 35′ W 238
Flåm, *Nor.* 60° 50′ N, 7° 7′ E 152
Flamand, Lac, lake, *Can.* 47° 40′ N, 73° 50′ W 94
Flamborough, *U.K.* 54° 6′ N, 0° 7′ E 162
Flamborough Head, *U.K.* 54° 6′ N, 0° 475′ W 162
Flamenco, Isla, island, *Arg.* 40° 29′ S, 62° 7′ W 134
Flamingo, *Fla., U.S.* 25° 8′ N, 80° 56′ W 105
Flamingo Point, *Bahamas* 24° 43′ N, 76° 15′ W 96
Flanagan, *Ill., U.S.* 40° 52′ N, 88° 52′ W 102
Flandreau, *S. Dak., U.S.* 44° 1′ N, 96° 37′ W 90
Flannan Isles, *Atlantic Ocean* 58° 7′ N, 8° 10′ W 150
Flat, *Alas., U.S.* 62° 20′ N, 158° 7′ W 98
Flat River, *Mo., U.S.* 37° 50′ N, 90° 31′ W 96
Flat, river, *Mich., U.S.* 43° 16′ N, 85° 17′ W 102
Flat Rock, *Ill., U.S.* 38° 54′ N, 87° 40′ W 102
Flat Top Mountain, *Va., U.S.* 37° 25′ N, 79° 39′ W 96
Flatbush, *Can.* 54° 41′ N, 114° 9′ W 108
Flateland, *Nor.* 59° 16′ N, 7° 29′ E 152
Flathead Lake, *Mont., U.S.* 47° 49′ N, 114° 45′ W 90
Flathead Range, *Mont., U.S.* 48° 18′ N, 114° 3′ W 90
Flattery, Cape, *Wash., U.S.* 48° 22′ N, 124° 53′ W 100
Flavigny-sur-Ozerain, *Fr.* 47° 30′ N, 4° 31′ E 150
Flavy-le-Martel, *Fr.* 49° 42′ N, 3° 12′ E 163
Flaxton, *N. Dak., U.S.* 48° 53′ N, 102° 24′ W 90
Fleeton, *Va., U.S.* 37° 48′ N, 76° 17′ W 94
Fleetwood, *U.K.* 53° 55′ N, 3° 1′ W 162
Flekkefjord, *Nor.* 58° 13′ N, 6° 40′ E 160
Flemingsburg, *Ky., U.S.* 38° 24′ N, 83° 45′ W 94
Flemish Cap, *North Atlantic Ocean* 47° 7′ N, 44° 36′ W 253
Flen, *Nor.* 59° 3′ N, 16° 33′ E 152
Flensburg, *Ger.* 54° 47′ N, 9° 25′ E 152
Flers, *Fr.* 48° 44′ N, 0° 35′ E 150
Flesberg, *Nor.* 59° 51′ N, 9° 25′ E 152
Fletcher, Cape, *Antarctica* 67° 38′ S, 61° 20′ E 248
Fletcher Lake, *Can.* 58° 11′ N, 94° 38′ W 108
Fletcher Plain, *Arctic Ocean* 86° 43′ N, 162° 1′ E 255
Flett Lake, *Can.* 60° 27′ N, 104° 25′ W 108
Fleurance, *Fr.* 43° 50′ N, 0° 39′ E 150
Fleurier, *Switz.* 46° 54′ N, 6° 35′ E 167
Flevoland, adm. division, *Neth.* 52° 18′ N, 4° 50′ E 150
Flieden, *Ger.* 50° 25′ N, 9° 35′ E 167
Flims, *Switz.* 46° 50′ N, 9° 18′ E 167
Flin Flon, *Can.* 54° 47′ N, 101° 52′ W 108
Flinders Entrance 9° 52′ S, 143° 32′ E 230
Flinders Group, islands, *Coral Sea* 14° 38′ S, 144° 11′ E 230
Flinders Island, *Austral.* 40° 15′ S, 146° 5′ E 230
Flinders Island, *Austral.* 33° 35′ S, 132° 48′ E 230
Flinders Passage 19° 4′ S, 147° 16′ E 230
Flinders Ranges, *Austral.* 30° 14′ S, 138° 14′ E 230
Flint, *Mich., U.S.* 43° 0′ N, 83° 41′ W 102
Flint, *U.K.* 53° 14′ N, 3° 8′ W 162
Flint Creek Range, *Mont., U.S.* 46° 20′ N, 113° 15′ W 90
Flint Hills, *Kans., U.S.* 38° 28′ N, 96° 36′ W 90
Flint Island, *Kiribati* 11° 27′ S, 151° 51′ W 252
Flint Lake, *Can.* 49° 50′ N, 86° 11′ W 94
Flint, river, *Ala., U.S.* 35° 3′ N, 86° 30′ W 96
Flint, river, *Ga., U.S.* 30° 58′ N, 84° 31′ W 112
Flix, *Sp.* 41° 12′ N, 0° 32′ E 164
Flixecourt, *Fr.* 50° 0′ N, 2° 5′ E 163
Flize, *Fr.* 49° 41′ N, 4° 47′ E 163
Flodden, battle, *U.K.* 55° 37′ N, 2° 21′ W 150
Flomaton, *Ala., U.S.* 30° 59′ N, 87° 17′ W 96
Floodwood, *Minn., U.S.* 46° 55′ N, 92° 57′ W 94
Flor de Agosto, *Peru* 2° 24′ S, 73° 8′ W 136
Flora, *Ill., U.S.* 38° 39′ N, 88° 29′ W 102
Flora, *Ind., U.S.* 40° 32′ N, 86° 31′ W 102
Flora, *Miss., U.S.* 32° 31′ N, 90° 19′ W 103
Flora, *Mo., U.S.* 38° 39′ N, 88° 29′ W 94
Flora, *Oreg., U.S.* 45° 53′ N, 117° 20′ W 90
Floral City, *Fla., U.S.* 28° 45′ N, 82° 18′ W 105
Florange, *Fr.* 49° 20′ N, 6° 8′ E 163
Florence, *Ala., U.S.* 34° 48′ N, 87° 43′ W 112
Florence, *Ariz., U.S.* 33° 1′ N, 111° 23′ W 92
Florence, *Colo., U.S.* 38° 23′ N, 105° 7′ W 90
Florence, *Kans., U.S.* 38° 13′ N, 96° 56′ W 90
Florence, *Ky., U.S.* 38° 59′ N, 84° 37′ W 102
Florence, *Miss., U.S.* 32° 9′ N, 90° 7′ W 103
Florence, *Oreg., U.S.* 43° 58′ N, 124° 6′ W 90
Florence, *S.C., U.S.* 34° 11′ N, 79° 47′ W 96
Florence, *Vt., U.S.* 43° 42′ N, 73° 5′ W 104
Florence, *Wis., U.S.* 45° 55′ N, 88° 15′ W 94
Florence Peak, *Calif., U.S.* 36° 24′ N, 118° 36′ W 101
Florence see Firenze, *It.* 43° 47′ N, 11° 14′ E 167
Florencia, *Col.* 1° 37′ N, 75° 38′ W 136
Florennes, *Belg.* 50° 15′ N, 4° 36′ E 167
Florenville, *Belg.* 49° 41′ N, 5° 19′ E 163
Flores, *Braz.* 7° 53′ S, 37° 59′ W 132
Flores, *Guatemala* 16° 57′ N, 89° 53′ W 116
Flores, island, *Indonesia* 9° 22′ S, 120° 40′ E 192
Flores Sea 7° 54′ S, 118° 8′ E 192
Florescência, *Braz.* 9° 39′ S, 68° 45′ W 137
Floriano, *Braz.* 6° 49′ S, 43° 3′ W 132
Florianópolis, *Braz.* 27° 35′ S, 48° 30′ W 138
Florida, *Bol.* 18° 32′ S, 63° 31′ W 137
Florida, *N. Mex., U.S.* 34° 5′ N, 106° 54′ W 92
Florida, *Uru.* 34° 6′ S, 56° 14′ W 139

Florida, adm. division, *Fla., U.S.* 26°39′ N, 82°22′ W 96
Florida Bay 24°55′ N, 80°49′ W 116
Florida Bay 25°4′ N, 80°55′ W 105
Florida City, *Fla., U.S.* 25°26′ N, 80°30′ W 105
Florida Islands, *Solomon Sea* 9°0′ S, 160°0′ E 242
Florida Keys, *Atlantic Ocean* 24°52′ N, 80°55′ W 105
Florida Negra, *Arg.* 48°18′ S, 67°21′ W 134
Florida Ridge, *Fla., U.S.* 27°34′ N, 80°22′ W 105
Florida, Straits of 25°7′ N, 79°48′ W 105
Florida's Turnpike, *Fla., U.S.* 27°49′ N, 81°4′ W 105
Florido, river, *Mex.* 26°41′ N, 105°4′ W 80
Florien, *La., U.S.* 31°25′ N, 93°29′ W 103
Florissant, *Mo., U.S.* 38°47′ N, 90°20′ W 94
Florø, *Nor.* 61°33′ N, 5°1′ E 160
Flötningen, *Nor.* 61°51′ N, 12°12′ E 152
Flower Garden Banks National Marine Sanctuary, *Gulf of Mexico* 28°1′ N, 94°27′ W 103
Flower's Cove, *Can.* 51°18′ N, 56°43′ W 111
Floyd, *La., U.S.* 32°39′ N, 91°25′ W 103
Floyd, *N. Mex., U.S.* 34°12′ N, 103°35′ W 92
Floyd, Mount, *Ariz., U.S.* 35°22′ N, 112°47′ W 92
Floyd, river, *Iowa, U.S.* 42°21′ N, 96°36′ W 80
Floydada, *Tex., U.S.* 33°58′ N, 101°20′ W 92
Flumet, *Fr.* 45°49′ N, 6°30′ E 167
Flushing, *Mich., U.S.* 43°4′ N, 83°50′ W 102
Flushing, *Ohio, U.S.* 40°8′ N, 81°3′ W 102
Flushing see Vlissingen, *Neth.* 51°27′ N, 3°34′ E 163
Fly Lake, oil field, *Austral.* 27°35′ S, 139°26′ E 230
Flying Fish, Cape, *Antarctica* 71°55′ S, 102°43′ W 248
Foam Lake, *Can.* 51°39′ N, 103°32′ W 90
Foča, *Bosn. and Herzg.* 43°29′ N, 18°46′ E 168
Fochi, spring, *Chad* 18°57′ N, 15°56′ E 216
Focşani, *Rom.* 45°42′ N, 27°10′ E 143
Foga, *Sudan* 13°37′ N, 27°59′ E 226
Fogang, *China* 23°48′ N, 113°32′ E 198
Foggaret el Arab, *Alg.* 27°11′ N, 2°48′ E 214
Foggia, *It.* 41°29′ N, 15°33′ E 143
Föglö, *Fin.* 60°0′ N, 20°25′ E 166
Fogo Island, *Can.* 49°43′ N, 54°0′ W 106
Foinaven, peak, *U.K.* 58°23′ N, 5°0′ W 150
Foix, *Fr.* 42°57′ N, 1°37′ E 164
Foix, region, *Europe* 42°58′ N, 1°22′ E 165
Fojnica, *Bosn. and Herzg.* 43°56′ N, 17°53′ E 168
Fokino, *Russ.* 53°23′ N, 34°26′ E 154
Fokku, *Nig.* 11°41′ N, 4°29′ E 222
Földeák, *Hung.* 46°20′ N, 20°30′ E 168
Folégandros, island, *Gr.* 36°28′ N, 24°13′ E 180
Foley, *Ala., U.S.* 30°24′ N, 87°41′ W 103
Foley, *Minn., U.S.* 45°38′ N, 93°56′ W 94
Foley Island, *Can.* 68°24′ N, 77°53′ W 106
Foleyet, *Can.* 48°14′ N, 82°26′ W 94
Foligno, *It.* 42°56′ N, 12°43′ E 156
Folkestone, *U.K.* 51°5′ N, 1°10′ E 163
Folkingham, *U.K.* 52°53′ N, 0°24′ E 162
Follett, *Tex., U.S.* 36°25′ N, 100°8′ W 92
Föllinge, *Nor.* 63°39′ N, 14°37′ E 152
Follonica, *It.* 42°55′ N, 10°45′ E 156
Folsom, *Calif., U.S.* 38°40′ N, 121°11′ W 90
Folsom, *La., U.S.* 30°38′ N, 90°12′ W 103
Folteşti, *Rom.* 45°44′ N, 28°2′ E 158
Fond du Lac, *Wis., U.S.* 43°47′ N, 88°26′ W 102
Fond-du-Lac, *Can.* 59°19′ N, 107°11′ W 108
Fonelas, *Sp.* 37°24′ N, 3°11′ W 164
Fongafale see Funafuti, *Tuvalu* 9°0′ S, 179°0′ E 241
Fongen, peak, *Nor.* 63°9′ N, 11°30′ E 152
Fonseca, *Col.* 10°52′ N, 72°52′ W 136
Fonseca, Golfo de 13°9′ N, 88°27′ W 112
Fontaine Lake, *Can.* 59°38′ N, 107°7′ W 108
Fontainebleau, *Fr.* 48°23′ N, 2°42′ E 163
Fontana, *Calif., U.S.* 34°5′ N, 117°27′ W 101
Fontas, *Can.* 58°17′ N, 121°44′ W 108
Fontas, river, *Can.* 58°10′ N, 121°53′ W 108
Fonte Boa, *Braz.* 2°33′ S, 66°6′ W 136
Fonteneau, Lac, lake, *Can.* 51°54′ N, 62°11′ W 111
Fonyód, *Hung.* 46°43′ N, 17°32′ E 168
Foothills, *Can.* 53°3′ N, 116°49′ W 108
Foping, *China* 33°32′ N, 108°1′ E 198
Foppolo, *It.* 46°3′ N, 9°44′ E 167
Forbes, Mount, *Austral.* 23°44′ S, 130°22′ E 230
Forbes, Mount, *Can.* 51°51′ N, 117°3′ W 90
Forcados, *Nig.* 5°23′ N, 5°26′ E 222
Ford, *U.K.* 56°10′ N, 5°27′ W 150
Ford City, *Calif., U.S.* 35°9′ N, 119°29′ W 100
Ford City, *Pa., U.S.* 40°45′ N, 79°32′ W 94
Ford, Mount, *Antarctica* 70°50′ S, 163°28′ E 248
Førde, *Nor.* 61°26′ N, 5°51′ E 152
Fordingbridge, *U.K.* 50°55′ N, 1°48′ W 162
Fordyce, *Ark., U.S.* 33°47′ N, 92°24′ W 96
Fore, *Nor.* 66°55′ N, 13°38′ E 152
Forécariah, *Guinea* 9°24′ N, 13°7′ W 222
Forel, Mont, peak, *Den.* 66°56′ N, 37°16′ W 106
Foreman, *Ark., U.S.* 33°42′ N, 94°25′ W 96
Foremost, *Can.* 49°28′ N, 111°27′ W 90
Forest, *Can.* 43°4′ N, 82°0′ W 102
Forest, *Miss., U.S.* 32°21′ N, 89°30′ W 112
Forest, *Ohio, U.S.* 40°47′ N, 83°31′ W 102
Forest City, *Iowa, U.S.* 43°14′ N, 93°39′ W 94
Forest Dale, *Vt., U.S.* 43°49′ N, 73°4′ W 104
Forest Grove, *Oreg., U.S.* 45°30′ N, 123°7′ W 90
Forest Hill, *La., U.S.* 31°1′ N, 92°33′ W 103
Forest Park, *Ohio, U.S.* 39°16′ N, 84°30′ W 102
Forester Pass, *Calif., U.S.* 36°42′ N, 118°23′ W 101
Forestville, *Can.* 48°44′ N, 69°5′ W 94
Forestville, *Mich., U.S.* 43°39′ N, 82°37′ W 102
Forez, Monts du, *Fr.* 45°55′ N, 3°30′ E 165
Forgan, *Okla., U.S.* 36°53′ N, 100°32′ W 92
Forges-les-Eaux, *Fr.* 49°36′ N, 1°32′ E 163
Forillon National Park, *Can.* 48°51′ N, 63°58′ W 111
Forks, *Wash., U.S.* 47°55′ N, 124°24′ W 100
Forlì, *It.* 44°13′ N, 12°1′ E 167
Forlimpopoli, *It.* 44°11′ N, 12°6′ E 167
Forman, *N. Dak., U.S.* 46°5′ N, 97°39′ W 90
Formentera, island, *Sp.* 38°27′ N, 1°37′ E 214
Formentor, Cap de, *Sp.* 40°5′ N, 3°19′ E 164
Formerie, *Fr.* 49°38′ N, 1°44′ E 163
Formiga, *Braz.* 20°30′ S, 45°26′ W 138
Formosa, *Arg.* 26°11′ S, 58°11′ W 139
Formosa, *Braz.* 15°34′ S, 47°20′ W 138
Formosa, adm. division, *Arg.* 26°6′ S, 59°40′ W 139
Formosa do Rio Prêto, *Braz.* 11°3′ S, 45°13′ W 130
Formosa, island, *Guinea-Bissau* 11°37′ N, 16°30′ W 222
Formosa, Serra, *Braz.* 12°8′ S, 55°27′ W 130
Formoso, *Braz.* 15°0′ S, 46°15′ W 138
Formoso, *Braz.* 13°38′ S, 48°55′ W 138
Formoso, river, *Braz.* 12°45′ S, 49°34′ W 138
Formoso, river, *Braz.* 14°27′ S, 45°28′ W 138
Forno di Zoldo, *It.* 46°20′ N, 12°9′ E 167
Fornovo di Taro, *It.* 44°40′ N, 10°5′ E 167
Føroyar see Faroe Islands, *North Atlantic Ocean* 62°34′ N, 11°40′ W 143
Forozan, oil field, *Kuwait* 28°44′ N, 49°43′ E 196
Forrest, *Ill., U.S.* 40°44′ N, 88°25′ W 102
Forrest City, *Ark., U.S.* 34°59′ N, 90°48′ W 96
Forrest Lake, *Can.* 57°31′ N, 109°57′ W 108
Forreston, *Ill., U.S.* 42°7′ N, 89°35′ W 102
Fors, *Nor.* 62°59′ N, 16°41′ E 152
Forsand, *Nor.* 58°53′ N, 6°7′ E 152
Forsayth, *Austral.* 18°35′ S, 143°34′ E 231
Forsby, *Fin.* 60°30′ N, 25°57′ E 166
Forse, *Nor.* 63°8′ N, 17°0′ E 154
Forsmark, *Nor.* 65°29′ N, 15°49′ E 152
Forsnäs, *Nor.* 66°14′ N, 18°37′ E 152
Forssa, *Fin.* 60°49′ N, 23°37′ E 166
Forst, *Ger.* 51°44′ N, 14°38′ E 152
Forsyth, *Mo., U.S.* 36°40′ N, 93°7′ W 96
Forsyth, *Mont., U.S.* 46°14′ N, 106°40′ W 90
Forsyth Island, *Austral.* 16°59′ S, 137°1′ E 230
Forsyth Lake, *Can.* 59°31′ N, 107°59′ W 108
Fort Abbas, *Pak.* 29°13′ N, 72°54′ E 186
Fort Adams, *Miss., U.S.* 31°4′ N, 91°34′ W 103
Fort Albany, *Can.* 52°13′ N, 81°39′ W 110
Fort Assiniboine, *Can.* 54°21′ N, 114°47′ W 108
Fort Atkinson, *Wis., U.S.* 42°55′ N, 88°51′ W 102
Fort Belvoir, *Va., U.S.* 38°40′ N, 77°13′ W 94
Fort Benjamin Harrison, *Ind., U.S.* 39°51′ N, 86°4′ W 102
Fort Benning, *Ga., U.S.* 32°19′ N, 85°2′ W 96
Fort Benton, *Mont., U.S.* 47°48′ N, 110°40′ W 90
Fort Black, *Can.* 55°24′ N, 107°45′ W 108
Fort Bragg, *Calif., U.S.* 39°26′ N, 123°48′ W 90
Fort Caroline National Memorial, *Fla., U.S.* 30°20′ N, 81°34′ W 96
Fort Chipewyan, *Can.* 58°43′ N, 111°7′ W 108
Fort Clatsop National Memorial, *Oreg., U.S.* 46°6′ N, 123°55′ W 100
Fort Collins, *Colo., U.S.* 40°34′ N, 105°6′ W 90
Fort Collinson, site, *Can.* 71°36′ N, 118°5′ W 106
Fort Conger, site, *Can.* 81°49′ N, 65°57′ W 246
Fort Defiance, *Ariz., U.S.* 35°43′ N, 109°6′ W 82
Fort Deposit, *Ala., U.S.* 31°59′ N, 86°34′ W 96
Fort Detrick, *Md., U.S.* 39°25′ N, 77°31′ W 94
Fort Devens, *Mass., U.S.* 42°31′ N, 71°38′ W 104
Fort Dick, *Calif., U.S.* 41°51′ N, 124°10′ W 90
Fort Dodge, *Iowa, U.S.* 42°29′ N, 94°11′ W 94
Fort Dorval, Péninsule du, *Can.* 50°56′ N, 73°21′ W 111
Fort Edward, *N.Y., U.S.* 43°15′ N, 73°36′ W 104
Fort Frances, *Can.* 48°40′ N, 93°33′ W 90
Fort Fraser, *Can.* 54°3′ N, 124°31′ W 108
Fort Gay, *W. Va., U.S.* 38°6′ N, 82°37′ W 94
Fort Gibson, *Okla., U.S.* 35°46′ N, 95°15′ W 96
Fort Good Hope, *Can.* 66°14′ N, 128°29′ W 106
Fort Gordon, *Ga., U.S.* 33°22′ N, 82°16′ W 96
Fort Gouraud see Fdérik, *Mauritania* 22°41′ N, 12°43′ W 214
Fort Hall, *Idaho, U.S.* 43°3′ N, 112°26′ W 90
Fort Hill see Chitipa, *Malawi* 9°43′ S, 33°14′ E 224
Fort Hope, *Can.* 51°33′ N, 88°1′ W 110
Fort Irwin, *Calif., U.S.* 35°15′ N, 116°42′ W 101
Fort Kent, *Me., U.S.* 47°15′ N, 68°35′ W 111
Fort Laramie, *Wyo., U.S.* 42°12′ N, 104°31′ W 90
Fort Laramie National Historic Site, *Wyo., U.S.* 42°10′ N, 104°38′ W 90
Fort Lauderdale, *Fla., U.S.* 26°7′ N, 80°10′ W 105
Fort Lewis, *Wash., U.S.* 47°2′ N, 122°36′ W 100
Fort Liard, *Can.* 60°14′ N, 123°26′ W 108
Fort Lupton, *Colo., U.S.* 40°4′ N, 104°49′ W 90
Fort MacKay, *Can.* 57°12′ N, 111°42′ W 108
Fort Macleod, *Can.* 49°42′ N, 113°24′ W 90
Fort Madison, *Iowa, U.S.* 40°38′ N, 91°20′ W 94
Fort Matanzas National Monument, *Fla., U.S.* 29°43′ N, 81°19′ W 105
Fort McKinley, *Ohio, U.S.* 39°47′ N, 84°16′ W 102
Fort McMurray, *Can.* 56°40′ N, 111°23′ W 108
Fort McPherson, *Can.* 67°27′ N, 134°44′ W 98
Fort Mill, *S.C., U.S.* 35°0′ N, 80°56′ W 96
Fort Miribel, *Alg.* 29°26′ N, 3°1′ E 214
Fort Morgan, *Ala., U.S.* 30°13′ N, 88°3′ W 103
Fort Morgan, *Colo., U.S.* 40°15′ N, 103°49′ W 90
Fort Motylinski see Tarhaouhaout, *Alg.* 22°38′ N, 5°55′ E 214
Fort Myers, *Fla., U.S.* 26°38′ N, 81°52′ W 105
Fort Myers Beach, *Fla., U.S.* 26°27′ N, 81°57′ W 105
Fort Necessity National Battlefield, *Pa., U.S.* 39°47′ N, 79°42′ W 94
Fort Nelson, *Can.* 58°42′ N, 122°42′ W 106
Fort Nelson, river, *Can.* 59°20′ N, 123°45′ W 108
Fort Niagara, site, *N.Y., U.S.* 43°14′ N, 79°8′ W 94
Fort Ogden, *Fla., U.S.* 27°5′ N, 81°57′ W 105
Fort Payne, *Ala., U.S.* 34°25′ N, 85°44′ W 96
Fort Peck, *Mont., U.S.* 47°59′ N, 106°28′ W 90
Fort Peck Dam, *Mont., U.S.* 47°43′ N, 106°34′ W 90
Fort Peck Lake, *Mont., U.S.* 47°40′ N, 107°29′ W 90
Fort Pierce, *Fla., U.S.* 27°26′ N, 80°20′ W 105
Fort Pierre, *S. Dak., U.S.* 44°21′ N, 100°23′ W 90
Fort Pierre Bordes see Ti-n-Zaouâtene, *Alg.* 19°58′ N, 2°57′ E 222
Fort Polk, *La., U.S.* 31°0′ N, 93°15′ W 103
Fort Portal, *Uganda* 0°38′ N, 30°16′ E 224
Fort Prince of Wales National Historical Park, *Can.* 58°44′ N, 94°24′ W 108
Fort Providence, *Can.* 61°24′ N, 117°36′ W 108
Fort Qu' Appelle, *Can.* 50°43′ N, 103°50′ W 90
Fort Quitman, site, *Tex., U.S.* 31°3′ N, 105°40′ W 92
Fort Recovery, *Ohio, U.S.* 40°23′ N, 84°46′ W 102
Fort Resolution, *Can.* 61°10′ N, 113°39′ W 108
Fort Ritchie, *Md., U.S.* 39°41′ N, 77°35′ W 94
Fort Rock, *Oreg., U.S.* 43°20′ N, 121°4′ W 90
Fort Saint, *Tun.* 30°16′ N, 9°36′ E 214
Fort Saint James, *Can.* 54°25′ N, 124°12′ W 108
Fort Saint John, *Can.* 56°13′ N, 120°52′ W 108
Fort Sam Houston, *Tex., U.S.* 29°26′ N, 98°31′ W 92
Fort Saskatchewan, *Can.* 53°41′ N, 113°14′ W 108
Fort Scott, *Kans., U.S.* 37°48′ N, 94°42′ W 96
Fort Severn, *Can.* 56°0′ N, 87°42′ W 106
Fort Shafter, *Hawai'i, U.S.* 21°19′ N, 157°56′ W 99
Fort Shawnee, *Ohio, U.S.* 40°40′ N, 84°8′ W 102
Fort Shevchenko, *Kaz.* 44°30′ N, 50°16′ E 158
Fort Sill, *Okla., U.S.* 34°38′ N, 98°29′ W 92
Fort Simcoe, site, *Wash., U.S.* 46°18′ N, 120°57′ W 90
Fort Simpson, *Can.* 61°49′ N, 121°23′ W 106
Fort Smith, *Ark., U.S.* 35°20′ N, 94°25′ W 96
Fort Smith, *Can.* 60°2′ N, 112°11′ W 106
Fort St. John, *Can.* 56°13′ N, 120°53′ W 246
Fort Stockton, *Tex., U.S.* 30°52′ N, 102°53′ W 92
Fort Sumner, *N. Mex., U.S.* 34°28′ N, 104°14′ W 92
Fort Supply, *Okla., U.S.* 36°33′ N, 99°34′ W 92
Fort Supply Lake, *Okla., U.S.* 36°21′ N, 100°49′ W 81
Fort Ternan, *Kenya* 0°13′ N, 35°22′ E 224
Fort Thompson, *S. Dak., U.S.* 44°4′ N, 99°28′ W 90
Fort Trinquet see Bir Mogreïn, *Mauritania* 25°13′ N, 11°37′ W 214
Fort Union National Monument, *N. Mex., U.S.* 35°53′ N, 105°6′ W 92
Fort Valley, *Ga., U.S.* 32°32′ N, 83°53′ W 96
Fort Vermilion, *Can.* 58°22′ N, 115°58′ W 108
Fort Wayne, *Ind., U.S.* 41°3′ N, 85°8′ W 102
Fort White, *Fla., U.S.* 29°55′ N, 82°43′ W 105
Fort Worth, *Tex., U.S.* 32°43′ N, 97°19′ W 92
Fort Yates, *N. Dak., U.S.* 46°4′ N, 100°40′ W 90
Fort Yukon, *Alas., U.S.* 66°32′ N, 145°5′ W 106
Fortaleza, *Bol.* 12°6′ S, 66°51′ W 137
Fortaleza, *Bol.* 9°49′ S, 65°30′ W 137
Fortaleza, *Braz.* 3°46′ S, 38°32′ W 132
Fort-Coulonge, *Can.* 45°50′ N, 76°44′ W 94
Fort-de-France, *Fr.* 14°36′ N, 61°4′ W 116
Forteau, *Can.* 51°26′ N, 56°59′ W 111
Fortezza, *It.* 46°47′ N, 11°35′ E 167
Fortim, *Braz.* 4°30′ S, 37°49′ W 132
Fortín, *Mex.* 18°54′ N, 97°1′ W 114
Fortín Carlos A. López, *Parag.* 21°19′ S, 59°42′ W 132
Fortín General Díaz, *Parag.* 23°31′ S, 60°35′ W 132
Fortín Infante Rivarola, *Parag.* 21°38′ S, 62°25′ W 132
Fortín Madrejón, *Parag.* 20°37′ S, 59°52′ W 132
Fortín Presidente Ayala, *Parag.* 23°29′ S, 59°43′ W 132
Fortín Suárez Arana, *Bol.* 18°39′ S, 60°9′ W 132
Fortín Teniente Américo Picco, *Parag.* 19°39′ S, 59°47′ W 132
Fortress Mountain, *Wyo., U.S.* 44°18′ N, 109°53′ W 90
Fortress of Louisbourg National Historic Site, *Can.* 45°52′ N, 60°7′ W 111
Fortun, *Nor.* 61°30′ N, 7°39′ E 152
Fortuna, *N. Dak., U.S.* 48°53′ N, 103°47′ W 90
Fortune Island see Long Cay, *Bahamas* 22°35′ N, 76°5′ W 116
Fortville, *Ind., U.S.* 39°55′ N, 85°51′ W 102
Forūr, island, *Iran* 26°8′ N, 54°22′ E 180
Foshan, *China* 23°3′ N, 113°6′ E 198
Fosheim Peninsula, *Can.* 79°5′ N, 90°14′ W 246
Fosna, *Nor.* 63°36′ N, 9°53′ E 152
Fosnes, *Nor.* 64°39′ N, 11°17′ E 152
Foso, *Ghana* 5°42′ N, 1°18′ W 222
Fossacesia, *It.* 42°14′ N, 14°28′ E 156
Fossano, *It.* 44°33′ N, 7°42′ E 167
Fossil, *Oreg., U.S.* 44°59′ N, 120°13′ W 82
Fosston, *Minn., U.S.* 47°33′ N, 95°47′ W 90
Foster, *Austral.* 38°38′ S, 146°11′ E 231
Foster Bugt 72°24′ N, 28°4′ W 73
Foster Center, *R.I., U.S.* 41°47′ N, 71°44′ W 104
Foster, Mount, *Can.* 59°45′ N, 135°37′ W 108
Foster Peak, *Can.* 51°3′ N, 116°15′ W 90
Foster, river, *Can.* 56°21′ N, 105°54′ W 108
Fostoria, *Ohio, U.S.* 41°9′ N, 83°24′ W 102
Fota Terara, peak, *Eth.* 9°8′ N, 38°24′ E 224
Fotokol, *Cameroon* 12°26′ N, 14°16′ E 216
Fouke, *Ark., U.S.* 33°15′ N, 93°54′ W 103
Foulweather, Cape, *Oreg., U.S.* 44°47′ N, 124°44′ W 90
Foulwind, Cape, *N.Z.* 41°48′ S, 171°0′ E 240
Foum Tatatouine, *Tun.* 32°57′ N, 10°26′ E 216
Foum Zguid, *Mor.* 30°6′ N, 6°55′ W 214
Foumban, *Cameroon* 5°42′ N, 10°52′ E 222
Fountain, *Colo., U.S.* 38°41′ N, 104°42′ W 92
Fountain, *Mich., U.S.* 44°3′ N, 86°11′ W 102
Fountain City, *Ind., U.S.* 39°57′ N, 84°55′ W 102
Fountain City, *Wis., U.S.* 44°8′ N, 91°42′ W 110
Fountain Hill, *Ark., U.S.* 33°20′ N, 91°52′ W 103
Four Corners Monument, *U.S.* 36°59′ N, 109°6′ W 92
Four, spring, *Mauritania* 16°3′ N, 8°50′ W 222
Fourcroy, Cape, *Austral.* 11°36′ S, 128°59′ E 230
Fourmies, *Fr.* 50°1′ N, 4°2′ E 163
Foúrni, *Gr.* 37°34′ N, 26°29′ E 156
Fournier, Lac, lake, *Can.* 51°28′ N, 66°0′ W 111
Fouta Djallon, region, *Africa* 12°3′ N, 12°50′ W 222
Fowler, *Calif., U.S.* 36°38′ N, 119°42′ W 100
Fowler, *Colo., U.S.* 38°7′ N, 104°2′ W 90
Fowler, *Ind., U.S.* 40°36′ N, 87°19′ W 102
Fowler, *Kans., U.S.* 37°22′ N, 100°12′ W 92
Fowler, *Mich., U.S.* 42°59′ N, 84°45′ W 102
Fowlers Bay 32°11′ S, 131°19′ E 230
Fowlerville, *Mich., U.S.* 42°39′ N, 84°4′ W 102
Fox Creek, *Can.* 54°23′ N, 116°48′ W 108
Fox Glacier, *N.Z.* 43°30′ S, 170°0′ E 240
Fox Islands, *Anadyrskiy Zaliv* 52°57′ N, 168°37′ W 98
Fox Lake, *Can.* 58°26′ N, 114°31′ W 108
Fox Lake, *Wis., U.S.* 43°32′ N, 88°54′ W 102
Fox Mountain, *Nev., U.S.* 41°0′ N, 119°39′ W 90
Fox Point, *Wis., U.S.* 43°9′ N, 87°54′ W 102
Fox, river, *Can.* 55°57′ N, 93°55′ W 108
Fox, river, *Wis., U.S.* 43°56′ N, 89°2′ W 102
Fox Valley, *Can.* 50°28′ N, 109°29′ W 90
Foxboro, *Mass., U.S.* 42°3′ N, 71°16′ W 104
Foxe Basin 67°2′ N, 80°27′ W 106
Foxe Channel 64°14′ N, 82°12′ W 106
Foxe Peninsula, *Can.* 64°50′ N, 80°3′ W 106
Foxton, *N.Z.* 40°29′ S, 175°19′ E 240
Foxworth, *Miss., U.S.* 31°13′ N, 89°53′ W 103
Foyé, *Guinea* 11°17′ N, 13°31′ W 222
Foyn Coast, *Antarctica* 66°58′ S, 64°23′ W 248
Foz do Breu, *Braz.* 9°22′ S, 72°45′ W 137
Foz do Cunene, *Angola* 17°13′ S, 11°46′ E 220
Foz do Jamari, *Braz.* 8°29′ S, 63°30′ W 130
Foz do Jordão, *Braz.* 9°21′ S, 71°58′ W 137
Foz do Mamoriá, *Braz.* 2°26′ S, 66°38′ W 136
Foz do Tarauacá, *Braz.* 6°46′ S, 69°47′ W 130
Frącki, *Pol.* 53°58′ N, 23°17′ E 166
Fraga, *Sp.* 41°31′ N, 0°21′ E 164
Fraile Muerto, *Uru.* 32°30′ S, 54°34′ W 139
Frailes, Cordillera de los, *Bol.* 19°24′ S, 67°12′ W 132
Frailes, Sierra de los, *Mex.* 24°9′ N, 106°0′ W 112
Fraize, *Fr.* 48°11′ N, 7°0′ E 163
Frakes, Mount, *Antarctica* 76°45′ S, 117°2′ W 248
Fram Basin, *Arctic Ocean* 88°9′ N, 0°36′ E 255
Fram Peak, *Antarctica* 68°4′ S, 58°9′ E 248
Framingham, *Mass., U.S.* 42°16′ N, 71°26′ W 104
Frammersbach, *Ger.* 50°3′ N, 9°28′ E 167
Framnes, Cape, *Antarctica* 65°54′ S, 60°39′ W 134
Franca, *Braz.* 20°35′ S, 47°24′ W 138
France 47°30′ N, 1°48′ E 150
France, Île de, island, *Den.* 77°37′ N, 16°49′ W 246
Francés, Cabo, *Cuba* 21°54′ N, 83°58′ W 116
Frances Lake, *Can.* 61°24′ N, 130°41′ W 98
Francés, Punta, *Cuba* 21°32′ N, 83°58′ W 116
Frances, river, *Can.* 60°17′ N, 129°2′ W 108
Francés Viejo, Cabo, *Dom. Rep.* 19°44′ N, 69°57′ W 116
Francesville, *Ind., U.S.* 40°59′ N, 86°53′ W 102
Franceville, *Gabon* 1°43′ S, 13°32′ E 218
Franche-Comté, adm. division, *Fr.* 47°13′ N, 5°31′ E 150
Francis Case, Lake, *S. Dak., U.S.* 43°7′ N, 100°51′ W 106
Francis E. Warren Air Force Base, *Wyo., U.S.* 41°10′ N, 104°58′ W 90
Francis Island, *Antarctica* 67°45′ S, 64°16′ W 248
Francisco de Orellana, *Peru* 3°23′ S, 72°50′ W 136
Francisco I. Madero, *Mex.* 24°24′ N, 104°20′ W 114
Francistown, *Botswana* 21°14′ S, 27°30′ E 227
François, Lacs à, lake, *Can.* 51°41′ N, 66°11′ W 111
François Lake, *Can.* 54°3′ N, 125°46′ W 108
Franconia, *N.H., U.S.* 44°13′ N, 71°45′ W 104
Franconia Notch, pass, *N.H., U.S.* 44°9′ N, 71°41′ W 104
Franconia, region, *Europe* 49°54′ N, 8°2′ E 167
Francs Peak, *Wyo., U.S.* 43°55′ N, 109°25′ W 90
Franeker, *Neth.* 53°11′ N, 5°31′ E 163
Frankenberg, *Ger.* 51°3′ N, 8°48′ E 167
Frankenhöhe, *Ger.* 49°12′ N, 9°48′ E 152
Frankenmuth, *Mich., U.S.* 43°20′ N, 83°44′ W 102
Frankenwald, *Ger.* 50°16′ N, 11°7′ E 152
Frankfort, *Ind., U.S.* 40°16′ N, 86°32′ W 102
Frankfort, *Kans., U.S.* 39°41′ N, 96°25′ W 90
Frankfort, *Ky., U.S.* 38°10′ N, 84°57′ W 94
Frankfort, *Mich., U.S.* 44°38′ N, 86°14′ W 94
Frankfort, *Ohio, U.S.* 39°24′ N, 83°11′ W 102
Frankfort, *S. Af.* 27°16′ S, 28°28′ E 227
Frankfurt am Main, *Ger.* 50°6′ N, 8°40′ E 167
Fränkische Alb, *Ger.* 49°33′ N, 11°12′ E 152
Franklin, *Ala., U.S.* 31°42′ N, 87°24′ W 103
Franklin, *Ariz., U.S.* 32°39′ N, 109°3′ W 92
Franklin, *Idaho, U.S.* 42°1′ N, 111°47′ W 90
Franklin, *Ind., U.S.* 39°28′ N, 86°3′ W 102
Franklin, *La., U.S.* 29°47′ N, 91°31′ W 103
Franklin, *Mass., U.S.* 42°4′ N, 71°25′ W 104
Franklin, *Nebr., U.S.* 40°4′ N, 98°58′ W 90
Franklin, *N.H., U.S.* 43°26′ N, 71°39′ W 94
Franklin, *Ohio, U.S.* 39°32′ N, 84°18′ W 102
Franklin, *Tenn., U.S.* 35°54′ N, 86°52′ W 96
Franklin, *Va., U.S.* 36°40′ N, 76°56′ W 96
Franklin, *Wis., U.S.* 42°52′ N, 88°1′ W 102
Franklin Bay 69°42′ N, 122°26′ W 246
Franklin Grove, *Ill., U.S.* 41°50′ N, 89°18′ W 102
Franklin Lake, *Can.* 59°17′ N, 104°2′ W 108
Franklin Mountains, *Can.* 65°17′ N, 125°31′ W 98
Franklin Strait 71°15′ N, 100°8′ W 106
Franklinton, *La., U.S.* 30°50′ N, 90°10′ W 103
Franklinville, *N.Y., U.S.* 42°20′ N, 78°28′ W 94
Frankston, *Tex., U.S.* 32°2′ N, 95°31′ W 103
Fransfontein, *Namibia* 20°14′ S, 14°59′ E 220
Franske Øer, islands, *Greenland Sea* 78°16′ N, 17°28′ W 246
Fränsta, *Nor.* 62°29′ N, 16°11′ E 152
Franz, *Can.* 48°28′ N, 84°24′ W 94
Franz Josef Glacier, *N.Z.* 43°24′ S, 170°12′ E 240
Franz Josef Land, *Barents Sea* 80°39′ N, 63°19′ E 255
Frasca, Capo della, *It.* 39°41′ N, 7°36′ E 156
Fraser Island, *Austral.* 25°59′ S, 153°16′ E 230
Fraser, river, *Can.* 53°23′ N, 122°46′ W 108
Fraser, river, *Can.* 51°30′ N, 122°24′ W 90
Fraser, river, *Can.* 49°20′ N, 121°40′ W 100

Fraser, river, Can. 53°51′ N, 121°49′ W 108
Fraserburg, S. Af. 31°55′ S, 21°31′ E 227
Fraserburg Road, S. Af. 32°48′ S, 21°57′ E 227
Fraserdale, Can. 49°51′ N, 81°38′ W 94
Frasertown, N.Z. 38°59′ S, 177°26′ E 240
Fray Bentos, Uru. 33°10′ S, 58°15′ W 139
Fray Jorge National Park, Chile 30°42′ S, 71°48′ W 134
Frazee, Minn., U.S. 46°42′ N, 95°43′ W 90
Frazer Lake, Can. 49°13′ N, 88°56′ W 94
Frazier, Mount, Antarctica 77°45′ S, 154°7′ W 248
Frazier Mountain, Calif., U.S. 34°46′ N, 119°1′ W 101
Frazier Park, Calif., U.S. 34°50′ N, 118°58′ W 101
Frechen, Ger. 50°54′ N, 6°48′ E 167
Fredericia, Den. 55°33′ N, 9°43′ E 150
Frederick, Md., U.S. 39°23′ N, 77°25′ W 82
Frederick, Okla., U.S. 34°21′ N, 99°1′ W 92
Frederick, S. Dak., U.S. 45°49′ N, 98°33′ W 90
Frederick Sound 56°54′ N, 133°26′ W 108
Fredericksburg, Tex., U.S. 30°15′ N, 98°52′ W 92
Fredericksburg and Spotsylvania National Military Park, Va., U.S. 38°14′ N, 77°34′ W 94
Fredericktown, Ohio, U.S. 40°28′ N, 82°32′ W 102
Fredericton, Can. 45°55′ N, 66°48′ W 94
Frederikshåb see Paamiut, Den. 62°4′ N, 49°33′ W 106
Frederikshavn, Den. 57°25′ N, 10°29′ E 150
Fredonia, Ariz., U.S. 36°56′ N, 112°31′ W 92
Fredonia, Kans., U.S. 37°30′ N, 95°50′ W 96
Fredonia, N.Y., U.S. 42°26′ N, 79°21′ W 94
Fredonia, Wis., U.S. 43°27′ N, 87°57′ W 102
Fredonyer Pass, Calif., U.S. 40°22′ N, 120°52′ W 90
Fredonyer Peak, Calif., U.S. 40°40′ N, 120°42′ W 90
Fredrikstad, Nor. 59°13′ N, 10°56′ E 152
Free State, adm. division, S. Af. 29°23′ S, 26°36′ E 220
Freedom, N.H., U.S. 43°48′ N, 71°3′ W 104
Freedom, Okla., U.S. 36°45′ N, 99°7′ W 92
Freels, Cape, Can. 49°9′ N, 53°27′ W 111
Freeman Point, Antarctica 65°49′ S, 132°15′ E 248
Freeport, Bahamas 26°31′ N, 78°41′ W 105
Freeport, Ill., U.S. 42°17′ N, 89°37′ W 102
Freeport, Me., U.S. 43°51′ N, 70°7′ W 94
Freeport, Mo., U.S. 42°17′ N, 89°37′ W 94
Freeport, N.Y., U.S. 40°39′ N, 73°35′ W 104
Freeport, Tex., U.S. 28°55′ N, 95°22′ W 103
Freer, Tex., U.S. 27°51′ N, 98°38′ W 92
Freesoil, Mich., U.S. 44°6′ N, 86°13′ W 102
Freetown, Ind., U.S. 38°58′ N, 86°7′ W 102
Freetown, Sierra Leone 8°24′ N, 13°21′ W 222
Freezeout Mountain, Oreg., U.S. 43°36′ N, 117°40′ W 90
Fregenal de la Sierra, Sp. 38°10′ N, 6°40′ W 164
Freguesia do Andirá, Braz. 2°55′ S, 57°0′ W 130
Fréhel, Cap, Fr. 48°29′ N, 2°40′ W 150
Freiburg, Ger. 48°0′ N, 7°51′ E 152
Freienohl, Ger. 51°22′ N, 8°9′ E 167
Freila, Sp. 37°31′ N, 2°54′ W 164
Freising, Ger. 48°24′ N, 11°44′ E 156
Freistadt, Aust. 48°30′ N, 14°29′ E 152
Fremont, Calif., U.S. 37°33′ N, 121°59′ W 100
Fremont, Ind., U.S. 41°43′ N, 84°56′ W 102
Fremont, Mich., U.S. 43°26′ N, 85°57′ W 102
Fremont, Nebr., U.S. 41°24′ N, 96°30′ W 90
Fremont, Ohio, U.S. 41°20′ N, 83°8′ W 102
Fremont Mountains, Oreg., U.S. 42°49′ N, 121°27′ W 90
Fremont Peak, Calif., U.S. 36°46′ N, 121°35′ W 100
Fremont Peak, Wyo., U.S. 43°6′ N, 109°42′ W 90
Fremont, river, Utah, U.S. 38°17′ N, 111°42′ W 80
French Camp, Miss., U.S. 33°16′ N, 89°24′ W 103
French Cays see Plana Cays, North Atlantic Ocean 22°41′ N, 73°33′ W 116
French Guiana, Fr. 3°47′ N, 53°56′ W 130
French Lick, Ind., U.S. 38°32′ N, 86°37′ W 102
French Pass, N.Z. 40°59′ S, 173°50′ E 240
French Polynesia, Fr. 15°4′ S, 145°29′ W 238
French River, Can. 46°1′ N, 80°35′ W 94
French Settlement, La., U.S. 30°17′ N, 90°49′ W 103
Frenchman Butte, Can. 53°35′ N, 109°38′ W 108
Frenchman Flat, Nev., U.S. 36°47′ N, 115°59′ W 101
Frenchman, river, Can. 49°30′ N, 108°41′ W 90
Frenchville, Me., U.S. 47°16′ N, 68°23′ W 94
Freren, Ger. 52°29′ N, 7°33′ E 163
Fresco, Côte d'Ivoire 5°5′ N, 5°32′ W 222
Freshfield, Cape, Antarctica 68°29′ S, 150°37′ E 248
Freshfield Icefield, Can. 51°43′ N, 117°41′ W 90
Fresnillo, Mex. 23°9′ N, 102°53′ W 114
Fresno, Calif., U.S. 36°44′ N, 119°48′ W 100
Fresno Reservoir, lake, Mont., U.S. 48°43′ N, 110°51′ W 90
Fresno Slough, river, Calif., U.S. 36°28′ N, 120°4′ W 101
Fresnoy-le-Grand, Fr. 49°56′ N, 3°25′ E 163
Freudenberg, Ger. 50°53′ N, 7°53′ E 167
Frévent, Fr. 50°16′ N, 2°17′ E 163
Freyre, Arg. 31°10′ S, 62°6′ W 139
Fria, Guinea 10°22′ N, 13°36′ W 222
Fria, Cape, Namibia 18°27′ S, 12°4′ E 220
Friant, Calif., U.S. 36°59′ N, 119°43′ W 100
Frías, Arg. 28°39′ S, 65°7′ W 132
Fribourg, Switz. 46°48′ N, 7°8′ E 167
Friday Creek, river, Can. 49°44′ N, 82°59′ W 94
Friday Harbour, Wash., U.S. 48°31′ N, 123°2′ W 100
Fridtjof Nansen, Mount, Antarctica 85°17′ S, 165°5′ W 248
Friedberg, Aust. 47°26′ N, 16°3′ E 168
Friedberg, Ger. 50°19′ N, 8°45′ E 167
Friedland, Ger. 51°25′ N, 9°55′ E 167
Frielendorf, Ger. 50°58′ N, 9°20′ E 167
Friend, Nebr., U.S. 40°38′ N, 97°18′ W 90
Friendship, Wis., U.S. 43°58′ N, 89°49′ W 102
Friguiagbé, Guinea 9°57′ N, 12°58′ W 222
Frinton on Sea, U.K. 51°50′ N, 1°15′ E 162
Friona, Tex., U.S. 34°37′ N, 102°43′ W 92
Frisco, Colo., U.S. 39°33′ N, 106°6′ W 90
Frisco City, Ala., U.S. 31°25′ N, 87°24′ W 103
Frisco Peak, Utah, U.S. 38°30′ N, 113°21′ W 90
Frissell, Mount, Conn., U.S. 42°2′ N, 73°30′ W 104
Fritzlar, Ger. 51°8′ N, 9°17′ E 167
Friuli-Venezia Giulia, adm. division, It. 46°11′ N, 12°48′ E 167
Froan, islands, Norwegian Sea 64°11′ N, 8°31′ E 152
Frobisher Bay 62°26′ N, 67°19′ W 246
Frobisher Lake, Can. 56°36′ N, 109°20′ W 108
Frog Lake, Can. 53°50′ N, 110°42′ W 108
Frog, river, Can. 58°16′ N, 127°1′ W 108
Frohavet 63°59′ N, 8°38′ E 152
Frolovo, Russ. 49°45′ N, 43°41′ E 158
Fromberg, Mont., U.S. 45°22′ N, 108°55′ W 90
Frombork, Pol. 54°20′ N, 19°40′ E 166
Frome, U.K. 51°13′ N, 2°20′ W 162
Fromenteau, Lac, lake, Can. 51°24′ N, 74°5′ W 111
Front Range, North America 39°3′ N, 105°43′ W 90
Front Royal, Va., U.S. 38°55′ N, 78°13′ W 94
Fronteiras, Braz. 7°6′ S, 40°37′ W 132
Frontenac, Kans., U.S. 37°26′ N, 94°41′ W 94
Frontera, Arg. 31°31′ S, 62°1′ W 139
Frontera, Mex. 18°31′ N, 92°39′ W 115
Frontera, Mex. 26°56′ N, 101°28′ W 112
Frontera, Punta, Mex. 18°38′ N, 93°30′ W 115
Fronteras, Mex. 30°56′ N, 109°33′ W 92
Frontier, Wyo., U.S. 41°50′ N, 110°33′ W 90
Frontignan, Fr. 43°27′ N, 3°44′ E 164
Frostburg, Md., U.S. 39°39′ N, 78°56′ W 94
Frostproof, Fla., U.S. 27°44′ N, 81°32′ W 105
Frotet, Lac, lake, Can. 50°38′ N, 75°16′ W 110
Frövi, Nor. 59°27′ N, 15°20′ E 152
Fruita, Colo., U.S. 39°9′ N, 108°44′ W 90
Fruitdale, Ala., U.S. 31°19′ N, 88°24′ W 103
Fruitport, Mich., U.S. 43°7′ N, 86°10′ W 102
Fruitville, Fla., U.S. 27°21′ N, 82°27′ W 105
Fruška Gora, Serb. 45°10′ N, 19°19′ E 168
Frutal, Braz. 20°3′ S, 48°55′ W 138
Frutigen, Switz. 46°36′ N, 7°38′ E 167
Fryeburg, Me., U.S. 44°0′ N, 70°59′ W 104
Fua Mulaku, island, Maldives 0°27′ N, 73°24′ E 188
Fu'an, China 27°11′ N, 119°40′ E 198
Fubo, Angola 5°28′ S, 12°23′ E 218
Fucecchio, It. 43°44′ N, 10°48′ E 167
Fuchs Dome, peak, Antarctica 80°38′ S, 29°4′ W 248
Fuchū, Japan 34°35′ N, 133°14′ E 201
Fudong, China 42°34′ N, 129°12′ E 200
Fuego Mountain, Oreg., U.S. 42°37′ N, 121°32′ W 90
Fuente, Mex. 28°38′ N, 100°33′ W 92
Fuente de Cantos, Sp. 38°14′ N, 6°19′ W 164
Fuente el Fresno, Sp. 39°13′ N, 3°47′ W 164
Fuente Obejuna, Sp. 38°15′ N, 5°26′ W 164
Fuente-Álamo, Sp. 38°41′ N, 1°26′ W 164
Fuenterrebollo, Sp. 41°17′ N, 3°56′ W 164
Fuentes de Andalucía, Sp. 37°28′ N, 5°22′ W 164
Fuentes de Ebro, Sp. 41°30′ N, 0°40′ E 164
Fuentes-Claras, Sp. 40°51′ N, 1°19′ W 164
Fuerteventura, island, Sp. 28°46′ N, 15°30′ W 214
Fuga, island, Philippines 18°56′ N, 121°27′ E 198
Fugou, China 34°1′ N, 114°24′ E 198
Fugu, China 39°3′ N, 111°2′ E 198
Fuhai, China 47°8′ N, 87°28′ E 184
Fuji, peak, Japan 35°20′ N, 138°41′ E 201
Fujian, adm. division, China 25°27′ N, 116°57′ E 198
Fujieda, Japan 34°52′ N, 138°15′ E 201
Fuji-Hakone-Izu National Park, Japan 34°42′ N, 138°36′ E 201
Fujisawa, Japan 35°19′ N, 139°30′ E 201
Fujiyoshida, Japan 35°27′ N, 138°48′ E 201
Fūka, Egypt 31°3′ N, 27°55′ E 180
Fukang, China 44°8′ N, 87°55′ E 184
Fukuchiyama, Japan 35°15′ N, 135°6′ E 201
Fukui, Japan 36°3′ N, 136°14′ E 201
Fukui, adm. division, Japan 35°49′ N, 136°3′ E 201
Fukuoka, Japan 33°35′ N, 130°24′ E 201
Fukuoka, adm. division, Japan 33°29′ N, 130°11′ E 201
Fukushima, Japan 37°45′ N, 140°26′ E 201
Fukushima, adm. division, Japan 37°20′ N, 139°16′ E 201
Fukushima, Mount, Antarctica 71°18′ S, 35°0′ E 248
Fukuyama, Japan 34°29′ N, 133°22′ E 201
Fulacunda, Guinea-Bissau 11°46′ N, 15°11′ W 222
Fulbourn, U.K. 52°10′ N, 0°13′ E 162
Fulda, Ger. 50°33′ N, 9°41′ E 167
Fulda, Minn., U.S. 43°51′ N, 95°36′ W 90
Fulda, river, Ger. 51°12′ N, 9°28′ E 167
Fulford Harbour, Can. 48°45′ N, 123°27′ W 100
Fuling, China 29°40′ N, 107°19′ E 198
Fullerton, Calif., U.S. 33°52′ N, 117°56′ W 101
Fullerton, Nebr., U.S. 41°21′ N, 97°59′ W 90
Fülöpszállás, Hung. 46°49′ N, 19°14′ E 168
Fulton, Ala., U.S. 31°47′ N, 87°43′ W 103
Fulton, Ill., U.S. 41°51′ N, 90°9′ W 102
Fulton, Ky., U.S. 36°31′ N, 88°52′ W 96
Fulton, Miss., U.S. 34°15′ N, 88°24′ W 96
Fulton, Mo., U.S. 38°50′ N, 91°58′ W 94
Fulton, N.Y., U.S. 43°19′ N, 76°25′ W 110
Fulufjället, peak, Nor. 61°34′ N, 12°29′ E 152
Fūman, Iran 37°14′ N, 49°18′ E 195
Fumane, Mozambique 24°27′ S, 33°58′ E 227
Fumel, Fr. 44°28′ N, 0°56′ E 150
Funabashi, Japan 35°41′ N, 140°0′ E 201
Funafuti, Tuvalu 8°42′ S, 178°24′ E 238
Funafuti (Fongafale), Tuvalu 9°0′ S, 179°0′ E 241
Funafuti, island, Tuvalu 9°0′ S, 179°0′ E 241
Funan, China 32°38′ N, 115°35′ E 198
Funan Gaba, Eth. 4°22′ N, 37°59′ E 224
Funan see Fushun, China 41°44′ N, 123°53′ E 200
Funan see Fusui, China 22°37′ N, 107°54′ E 198
Funäsdalen, Nor. 62°32′ N, 12°35′ E 152
Funauke, Japan 24°14′ N, 123°43′ E 198
Funchal, Port. 32°34′ N, 17°9′ W 207
Fundación, Col. 10°32′ N, 74°12′ W 136
Fundão, Port. 40°8′ N, 7°31′ W 150
Fundong, Cameroon 6°14′ N, 10°10′ E 222
Fundy, Bay of 45°6′ N, 66°10′ W 111
Fundy National Park, Can. 45°26′ N, 65°42′ W 111
Funeral Mountains, Calif., U.S. 36°44′ N, 116°53′ W 101
Funeral Peak, Calif., U.S. 36°5′ N, 116°40′ W 101
Funhalouro, Mozambique 23°2′ S, 34°24′ E 227
Funing, China 23°35′ N, 105°37′ E 198
Funtua, Nig. 11°29′ N, 7°19′ E 222
Fuping, China 34°47′ N, 109°9′ E 198
Fuqing, China 25°43′ N, 119°23′ E 198
Fuquan, China 26°44′ N, 107°30′ E 198
Furancungo, Mozambique 14°55′ S, 33°37′ E 224
Furawiya, spring, Sudan 15°20′ N, 23°41′ E 226
Furillen, island, Sw. 57°41′ N, 19°2′ E 166
Furmanov, Russ. 57°16′ N, 41°5′ E 154
Furnas Dam, Braz. 20°50′ S, 46°15′ W 132
Furneaux Group, islands, Flinders Island 39°48′ S, 148°30′ E 230
Furnes see Veurne, Belg. 51°4′ N, 2°40′ E 150
Furqlus, Syr. 34°36′ N, 37°4′ E 194
Fürstenau, Ger. 52°31′ N, 7°41′ E 163
Fürstenfeld, Aust. 47°3′ N, 16°5′ E 168
Fürth, Ger. 49°27′ N, 10°59′ E 152
Furudal, Nor. 61°10′ N, 15°8′ E 152
Furukawa, Japan 38°35′ N, 140°57′ E 201
Furukawa, Japan 36°14′ N, 137°11′ E 201
Furusund, Sw. 59°40′ N, 18°52′ E 166
Furuvik, Nor. 60°38′ N, 17°17′ E 152
Fuscaldo, It. 39°25′ N, 16°2′ E 156
Fuse, Japan 36°19′ N, 133°21′ E 201
Fushan, China 37°30′ N, 121°13′ E 198
Fushë Kosova (Kosovo Polje), Kosovo 42°38′ N, 21°6′ E 168
Fushimi Lake, Can. 49°47′ N, 84°21′ W 94
Fushun, China 29°13′ N, 104°56′ E 198
Fushun (Funan), China 41°44′ N, 123°53′ E 200
Fusio, Switz. 46°27′ N, 8°38′ E 167
Fusong, China 42°16′ N, 127°18′ E 200
Fusui (Funan), China 22°37′ N, 107°54′ E 198
Futaleufú, Chile 43°12′ S, 71°55′ W 134
Futeau, Fr. 43°26′ N, 5°33′ E 150
Fuwa, Egypt 31°12′ N, 30°32′ E 180
Fuxian, China 36°0′ N, 109°20′ E 198
Fuxin, China 42°4′ N, 121°39′ E 198
Fuya, Japan 38°30′ N, 139°32′ E 201
Fuyang, China 32°52′ N, 115°46′ E 198
Fuyang, river, China 37°46′ N, 115°57′ E 198
Fuyu, China 45°12′ N, 124°53′ E 198
Fuyu, China 47°46′ N, 124°28′ E 198
Fuyun, China 47°3′ N, 89°25′ E 184
Füzesabony, Hung. 47°45′ N, 20°26′ E 168
Fuzhou, China 26°8′ N, 119°20′ E 198
Füzuli see Karaghbyur, Azerb. 39°34′ N, 47°6′ E 195
Fylingdales Moor, site, U.K. 54°21′ N, 0°38′ E 162

G

Ga, Ghana 9°47′ N, 2°30′ W 222
Gaal Goble, Somalia 9°50′ N, 49°50′ E 216
Gaalkacyo (Galcaio), Somalia 6°44′ N, 47°29′ E 218
Gabakly, Turkm. 39°48′ N, 62°31′ E 180
Gabarus, Cape, Can. 45°41′ N, 60°43′ W 111
Gabasawa, Nig. 12°9′ N, 8°54′ E 222
Gabatit, spring, Sudan 20°28′ N, 35°49′ E 182
Gabbac, Raas, Somalia 7°37′ N, 50°3′ E 218
Gabbs, Nev., U.S. 38°52′ N, 117°57′ W 90
Gabbs Valley, Nev., U.S. 38°54′ N, 118°18′ W 90
Gabbs Valley Range, Nev., U.S. 38°37′ N, 118°15′ W 90
Gabela, Angola 10°50′ S, 14°21′ E 220
Gabela, Bosn. and Herzg. 43°3′ N, 17°39′ E 168
Gabes, Tun. 33°53′ N, 10°4′ E 214
Gabes, Gulf of 34°9′ N, 9°36′ E 156
Gabilan Range, Calif., U.S. 36°41′ N, 121°36′ W 100
Gabon 0°41′ N, 11°20′ E 218
Gaborone, Botswana 24°42′ S, 25°45′ E 227
Gabras, Sudan 10°16′ N, 26°15′ E 224
Gabriel, Lac, lake, Can. 49°15′ N, 74°57′ W 94
Gabriel Vera, Bol. 19°15′ S, 65°54′ W 137
Gabriels, N.Y., U.S. 44°25′ N, 74°12′ W 104
Gabro, Eth. 6°16′ N, 43°14′ E 218
Gabrovo, Bulg. 42°52′ N, 25°17′ E 156
Gabrovo, adm. division, Bulg. 42°54′ N, 24°51′ E 156
Gabu, Dem. Rep. of the Congo 3°22′ N, 27°2′ E 224
Gachsaran, oil field, Iran 30°12′ N, 50°51′ E 196
Gackle, N. Dak., U.S. 46°35′ N, 99°9′ W 90
Gacko, Bosn. and Herzg. 43°10′ N, 18°31′ E 168
Gada, river, Dem. Rep. of the Congo 3°21′ N, 28°30′ E 224
Gädäbäy, Azerb. 40°34′ N, 45°48′ E 195
Gadamai, Sudan 17°5′ N, 36°4′ E 182
Gadarwara, India 22°53′ N, 78°46′ E 197
Gadifuri, island, Maldives 2°25′ N, 72°1′ E 188
Gádor, Sierra de, Sp. 36°55′ N, 3°1′ W 164
Gádoros, Hung. 46°40′ N, 20°36′ E 168
Gadra Road, India 25°44′ N, 70°38′ E 186
Gadrut see Hadrut, Azerb. 39°30′ N, 47°0′ E 195
Gadsden, Ariz., U.S. 32°32′ N, 114°46′ W 101
Gadzi, Cen. Af. Rep. 4°46′ N, 16°41′ E 218
Găeşti, Rom. 44°44′ N, 25°18′ E 156
Gafatîn, Gezâir, islands, Red Sea 26°59′ N, 34°2′ E 180
Gaferut, island, F.S.M. 9°22′ N, 144°22′ E 192
Gafsa, Tun. 34°24′ N, 8°48′ E 156
Gagal, Chad 9°1′ N, 15°9′ E 216
Gagarin, Russ. 55°32′ N, 35°1′ E 154
Gagetown, Mich., U.S. 43°38′ N, 83°15′ W 102
Gagino, Russ. 55°13′ N, 45°6′ E 154
Gagliano del Capo, It. 39°50′ N, 18°21′ E 156
Gagnoa, Côte d'Ivoire 6°2′ N, 5°56′ W 222
Gagra, Ga. 43°21′ N, 40°15′ E 195
Gagshor, Russ. 60°47′ N, 50°11′ E 154
Ganta, Liberia 7°5′ N, 9°0′ W 222
Gaibandha, Bangladesh 25°18′ N, 89°29′ E 197
Gaillefontaine, Fr. 49°39′ N, 1°35′ E 163
Gaillimh see Galway, Ire. 53°16′ N, 9°3′ W 150
Gaillon, Fr. 49°9′ N, 1°18′ E 163
Gaimán, Arg. 43°15′ S, 65°30′ W 134
Gainesville, Ala., U.S. 32°47′ N, 88°10′ W 103
Gainesville, Fla., U.S. 29°38′ N, 82°20′ W 105
Gainesville, Ga., U.S. 34°17′ N, 83°50′ W 96
Gainesville, Mo., U.S. 36°35′ N, 92°26′ W 96
Gainesville, Tex., U.S. 33°35′ N, 97°8′ W 92
Gainsborough, Can. 49°10′ N, 101°27′ W 90
Gainsborough, U.K. 53°24′ N, 0°47′ E 162
Gaissane, region, Europe 69°47′ N, 26°1′ E 152
Gaixian, China 40°24′ N, 122°24′ E 198
Gajdobra, Serb. 45°20′ N, 19°27′ E 168
Gajiram, Nig. 12°32′ N, 13°12′ E 216
Gakdul, spring, Sudan 17°36′ N, 32°51′ E 182
Gakkel Ridge, Arctic Ocean 86°39′ N, 68°19′ E 255
Gakona, Alas., U.S. 62°16′ N, 145°16′ W 98
Gakuch, Pak. 36°9′ N, 73°45′ E 186
Gal Tardo, Somalia 3°34′ N, 46°0′ E 218
Galadi, Eth. 5°57′ N, 41°34′ E 224
Galadi, Nig. 13°0′ N, 6°24′ E 222
Galahad, Can. 52°31′ N, 111°57′ W 108
Galaţi, adm. division, Rom. 45°48′ N, 27°19′ E 156
Galâla el Qiblîya, Gebel el, peak, Egypt 28°46′ N, 32°22′ E 180
Galán, Cerro, peak, Arg. 25°57′ S, 67°0′ W 132
Galana, river, Kenya 3°12′ S, 39°14′ E 224
Galaosiyo, Uzb. 39°52′ N, 64°29′ E 197
Galápagos Fracture Zone, South Pacific Ocean 3°38′ S, 139°34′ W 252
Galápagos Islands (Archipiélago de Colón), Ecuador 0°13′ N, 92°2′ W 130
Galápagos Rise, South Pacific Ocean 15°51′ S, 94°41′ W 252
Galateia, Northern Cyprus, Cyprus 35°25′ N, 34°4′ E 194
Galaţi, Rom. 45°27′ N, 28°3′ E 156
Galatxo, Punta del, Sp. 40°24′ N, 0°32′ E 164
Galax, Va., U.S. 36°40′ N, 80°56′ W 96
Galcaio see Gaalkacyo, Somalia 6°44′ N, 47°29′ E 218
Galdhøpiggen, peak, Nor. 61°37′ N, 8°9′ E 152
Galé, Mali 12°37′ N, 9°30′ W 222
Galeana, Mex. 30°6′ N, 107°38′ W 92
Galeana, Mex. 24°49′ N, 100°4′ W 114
Galegu, Sudan 12°33′ N, 35°1′ E 182
Galena, Alas., U.S. 64°37′ N, 156°56′ W 98
Galena, Kans., U.S. 37°3′ N, 94°39′ W 96
Galena, Mo., U.S. 42°24′ N, 90°26′ W 94
Galena Peak, Idaho, U.S. 43°52′ N, 114°40′ W 90
Galera, Sp. 37°43′ N, 2°33′ W 164
Galera Point, Trinidad and Tobago 10°50′ N, 61°24′ W 116
Galera, Punta, Chile 40°4′ S, 75°3′ W 134
Galera, Punta, Ecua. 0°48′ N, 81°14′ W 130
Galera, river, Braz. 14°22′ S, 60°3′ W 132
Galesburg, Mich., U.S. 42°17′ N, 85°25′ W 102
Galesburg, Mo., U.S. 40°57′ N, 90°22′ W 94
Galeton, Can. 51°8′ N, 80°56′ W 110
Galeton, Pa., U.S. 41°44′ N, 77°39′ W 94
Galgate, U.K. 53°59′ N, 2°48′ W 162
Gali, Ga. 42°36′ N, 41°43′ E 195
Galiano Island, Can. 48°56′ N, 123°26′ W 100
Galich, Russ. 58°20′ N, 42°24′ E 154
Galicia, adm. division, Sp. 42°36′ N, 8°44′ W 150
Galičnik, Maced. 41°35′ N, 20°39′ E 168
Galim, Cameroon 7°3′ N, 12°27′ E 218
Galinoporni, Northern Cyprus, Cyprus 35°31′ N, 34°18′ E 194
Galio, Liberia 5°42′ N, 7°34′ W 222
Galion, Ohio, U.S. 40°42′ N, 82°48′ W 102
Galkino, Kaz. 52°20′ N, 78°13′ E 184
Galla, Mount, Antarctica 75°49′ S, 125°18′ W 248
Gallanito, Nor. 68°53′ N, 22°50′ E 152
Gallarate, It. 45°39′ N, 8°47′ E 167
Gallardon, Fr. 48°31′ N, 1°41′ E 163
Gallatin, Mo., U.S. 39°54′ N, 93°58′ W 94
Gallatin, Tenn., U.S. 36°23′ N, 86°27′ W 96
Gallatin Peak, Mont., U.S. 45°20′ N, 111°26′ W 90
Gallatin Range, Mont., U.S. 45°24′ N, 111°13′ W 90
Galle, Sri Lanka 6°8′ N, 80°11′ E 173
Gallegos, Cabo, Chile 46°30′ S, 77°9′ W 134
Gallegos, river, Arg. 52°0′ S, 72°10′ W 134
Galliano, La., U.S. 29°26′ N, 90°18′ W 103
Galliate, It. 45°28′ N, 8°40′ E 167
Gallinas, Punta, Col. 12°27′ N, 71°42′ W 136
Gallipoli, It. 40°3′ N, 17°59′ E 156
Gallipoli see Gelibolu, Turk. 40°25′ N, 26°38′ E 156
Gällivare, Nor. 67°8′ N, 20°39′ E 152
Gallman, Miss., U.S. 31°55′ N, 90°24′ W 103
Gällö, Nor. 62°55′ N, 15°11′ E 152
Gallo, Capo, It. 38°15′ N, 12°42′ E 156
Gallo Mountains, N. Mex., U.S. 34°1′ N, 108°39′ W 92
Gallo, river, Sp. 40°43′ N, 2°3′ W 150
Gallup, N. Mex., U.S. 35°30′ N, 108°44′ W 92
Gallur, Sp. 41°51′ N, 1°19′ W 164
Galma Galla, spring, Kenya 1°14′ S, 40°49′ E 224
Galt, Calif., U.S. 38°14′ N, 121°19′ W 100
Galtat Zemmour, Western Sahara, Mor. 25°9′ N, 12°24′ W 214
Galten, Nor. 70°42′ N, 22°44′ E 152
Galtymore, peak, Ire. 52°21′ N, 8°19′ W 150
Galu, Dem. Rep. of the Congo 11°22′ S, 26°37′ E 224
Galula, Tanzania 8°38′ S, 33°2′ E 224
Galva, Ill., U.S. 41°9′ N, 90°3′ W 102
Galveston, Tex., U.S. 29°16′ N, 94°49′ W 103

Galveston Bay 29°22′ N, 95°48′ W 80
Galveston Island, Tex., U.S. 29°4′ N, 94°58′ W 103
Gálvez, Arg. 32°3′ S, 61°13′ W 139
Galwa, Nepal 29°39′ N, 81°53′ E 197
Galway (Gaillimh), Ire. 53°16′ N, 9°3′ W 150
Gam, river, Vietnam 22°5′ N, 105°11′ E 202
Gamba, China 28°16′ N, 88°31′ E 197
Gamba, Gabon 2°43′ S, 10°0′ E 218
Gambaga, Ghana 10°32′ N, 0°27′ E 222
Gambēla, Eth. 8°14′ N, 34°35′ E 224
Gambela National Park, Eth. 7°42′ N, 33°59′ E 224
Gambell, Alas., U.S. 63°40′ N, 171°50′ W 98
Gambia 13°23′ N, 16°0′ W 214
Gambia, river, Gambia 13°59′ N, 28°49′ W 222
Gambia Plain, North Atlantic Ocean 12°33′ N, 27°53′ W 253
Gambie, river, Senegal 12°54′ N, 13°7′ W 222
Gambier, Ohio, U.S. 40°22′ N, 82°23′ W 102
Gambier, Îles, islands, South Pacific Ocean 22°42′ S, 138°12′ W 238
Gambier Island, Can. 49°32′ N, 123°36′ W 100
Gambier Islands, Great Australian Bight 35°21′ S, 136°39′ E 230
Gamboma, Congo 1°54′ S, 15°51′ E 218
Gamboula, Cen. Af. Rep. 4°10′ N, 15°12′ E 218
Gamdou, Niger 13°27′ N, 10°3′ E 222
Gamlakarleby see Kokkola, Fin. 63°49′ N, 23°5′ E 152
Gamleby, Nor. 57°54′ N, 16°23′ E 152
Gamma, oil field, Azerb. 39°43′ N, 49°19′ E 195
Gammelstad, Nor. 65°37′ N, 22°1′ E 152
Gamoep, S. Af. 29°55′ S, 18°23′ E 227
Gamova, Mys, Russ. 42°24′ N, 131°12′ E 200
Gamph, Slieve (Ox Mountains, The), Ire. 54°2′ N, 9°28′ W 150
Gampo, S. Korea 35°47′ N, 129°32′ E 200
Gamsby, river, Can. 53°5′ N, 127°21′ W 108
Gamud, peak, Eth. 4°1′ N, 38°3′ E 224
Gamyshlyja, Turkm. 38°21′ N, 54°0′ E 180
Gan, Fr. 43°14′ N, 0°23′ E 164
Gan Gan, Arg. 42°29′ S, 68°11′ W 134
Gan, island, Maldives 0°2′ N, 73°22′ E 188
Gan, river, China 26°29′ N, 114°32′ E 198
Gan, river, China 49°20′ N, 124°41′ E 198
Ganado, Ariz., U.S. 35°42′ N, 109°32′ W 92
Ganado, Tex., U.S. 29°2′ N, 96°31′ W 96
Gäncä, Azerb. 40°41′ N, 46°20′ E 195
Gandajika, Dem. Rep. of the Congo 6°46′ S, 23°58′ E 224
Gander, Can. 48°56′ N, 54°29′ W 106
Gander, river, Can. 48°55′ N, 54°53′ W 111
Gandhidham, India 23°5′ N, 70°8′ E 186
Gandhinagar, India 23°19′ N, 72°38′ E 186
Gandi, Nig. 13°2′ N, 4°51′ E 222
Gandia, Sp. 38°57′ N, 0°11′ E 164
Gandino, It. 45°49′ N, 9°54′ E 167
Gandole, Nig. 8°24′ N, 11°37′ E 222
Gandu, Braz. 13°46′ S, 39°30′ W 138
Gang, island, Maldives 1°34′ N, 73°29′ E 188
Ganga (Ganges), river, India 26°9′ N, 81°17′ E 190
Gangala na Bodio, Dem. Rep. of the Congo 3°38′ N, 29°9′ E 224
Ganganagar, India 29°56′ N, 73°54′ E 186
Gangdaba, Tchabal, Cameroon 7°23′ N, 11°49′ E 218
Gangdisê Shan, China 30°58′ N, 83°13′ E 197
Gangelt, Ger. 50°59′ N, 5°59′ E 167
Ganges Fan, Bay of Bengal 14°34′ N, 84°35′ E 254
Ganges, river, India 25°40′ N, 81°12′ E 197
Ganges see Ganga, river, India 26°9′ N, 81°17′ E 190
Ganggyeong, S. Korea 36°9′ N, 127°3′ E 200
Ganghwa, S. Korea 37°44′ N, 126°29′ E 200
Gangi, It. 37°47′ N, 14°12′ E 156
Gangjin, S. Korea 34°37′ N, 126°47′ E 200
Gangneung, S. Korea 37°45′ N, 128°53′ E 200
Gangtok, India 27°23′ N, 88°35′ E 197
Gangu, China 34°43′ N, 105°18′ E 198
Gangwon, adm. division, S. Korea 37°45′ N, 128°15′ E 200
Ganhe, China 50°43′ N, 123°14′ E 238
Gania, Guinea 11°1′ N, 10°21′ W 222
Ganjam, India 19°25′ N, 85°3′ E 188
Gannan, China 47°53′ N, 123°31′ E 198
Gannat, Fr. 46°5′ N, 3°12′ E 150
Gannett Peak, Wyo., U.S. 43°10′ N, 109°45′ W 90
Ganongga see Ranongga, island, Solomon Islands 8°5′ S, 156°30′ E 242
Ganquan, China 36°19′ N, 109°25′ E 198
Ganseong, S. Korea 38°22′ N, 128°27′ E 200
Gansu, adm. division, China 38°17′ N, 101°53′ E 188
Ganta, Liberia 7°5′ N, 9°0′ W 222
Gantgaw, Myanmar 22°12′ N, 94°9′ E 188
Ganwo, Nig. 11°11′ N, 4°37′ E 222
Ganyushkino, Kaz. 46°36′ N, 49°16′ E 158
Ganzhou, China 25°56′ N, 114°57′ E 198
Gao, Mali 16°16′ N, 1°59′ W 222
Gaolan, China 36°22′ N, 103°56′ E 198
Gaoping, China 35°46′ N, 112°53′ E 198
Gaoua, Burkina Faso 10°19′ N, 3°12′ W 222
Gaoual, Guinea 11°46′ N, 13°16′ W 222
Gaoyang, China 38°42′ N, 115°49′ E 198
Gaoyou Hu, lake, China 32°42′ N, 118°40′ E 198
Gap, Fr. 44°32′ N, 6°4′ E 150
Gapan, Philippines 15°19′ N, 120°56′ E 203
Gapyeong, S. Korea 37°49′ N, 127°31′ E 200
Gar, China 32°11′ N, 79°57′ E 188
Gara, Hung. 46°1′ N, 19°3′ E 168
Garabogaz Aylagy, lake, Turkm. 41°4′ N, 51°40′ E 160
Garabogazköl, Turkm. 41°2′ N, 52°55′ E 158
Garacad, Somalia 6°55′ N, 49°23′ E 218
Garachiné, Pan. 8°3′ N, 78°23′ W 115
Garadag, Somalia 9°26′ N, 46°55′ E 216
Garadase, Eth. 5°4′ N, 38°9′ E 224
Garagum, Turkm. 37°50′ N, 63°24′ E 197
Garamba National Park, Dem. Rep. of the Congo 4°27′ N, 28°50′ E 224
Garamba, river, Dem. Rep. of the Congo 3°44′ N, 29°17′ E 224
Garanhuns, Braz. 8°52′ S, 36°31′ W 132
Garapuava, Braz. 16°6′ S, 46°37′ W 138
Garavuti, Taj. 37°31′ N, 68°25′ E 184
Garawe, Liberia 4°37′ N, 7°53′ W 222
Garba Tula, Kenya 0°29′ N, 38°32′ E 224
Garbahaarrey, Somalia 3°7′ N, 42°11′ E 224
Garberville, Calif., U.S. 40°6′ N, 123°48′ W 82
Garbyang, India 30°9′ N, 80°49′ E 197
Garça, Braz. 22°14′ S, 49°43′ W 138
Garças, river, Braz. 8°40′ S, 40°29′ W 132
García de la Cadena, Mex. 21°9′ N, 103°28′ W 114
Garcias, Braz. 20°36′ S, 52°14′ W 138
Garden City, Kans., U.S. 37°58′ N, 100°53′ W 90
Garden City, N.Y., U.S. 40°43′ N, 73°38′ W 104
Garden Creek, Can. 58°43′ N, 113°56′ W 108
Garden Lake, Can. 49°28′ N, 90°15′ W 94
Garden of the Gods, site, Hawai'i, U.S. 20°52′ N, 157°2′ W 99
Garden Peninsula, Mich., U.S. 45°49′ N, 86°42′ W 94
Garden, river, Can. 46°37′ N, 84°5′ W 94
Gardiner, Me., U.S. 44°12′ N, 69°47′ W 104
Gardiner, Mont., U.S. 45°2′ N, 110°42′ W 90
Gardiner, Oreg., U.S. 43°43′ N, 124°6′ W 90
Gardiner Dam, Can. 51°2′ N, 107°12′ W 90
Gardiner, Mount, Austral. 22°15′ S, 132°27′ E 230
Gardiners Island, N.Y., U.S. 41°4′ N, 72°5′ W 104
Gardiz, Afghan. 33°35′ N, 69°12′ E 186
Gardner, Ill., U.S. 41°11′ N, 88°18′ W 102
Gardner, Mass., U.S. 42°34′ N, 72°0′ W 104
Gardner Canal 53°19′ N, 128°44′ W 108
Gardner Pinnacles, Hawai'i, U.S. 24°57′ N, 169°23′ W 99
Gárdony, Hung. 47°12′ N, 18°38′ E 168
Gares see Puente la Reina, Sp. 42°39′ N, 1°49′ W 164
Garešnica, Croatia 45°33′ N, 16°56′ E 168
Garf Ḥusein, ruin(s), Egypt 23°12′ N, 32°42′ E 182
Garfield Mountain, Mont., U.S. 44°29′ N, 112°40′ W 90
Garfield Peak, Wyo., U.S. 42°42′ N, 107°21′ W 90
Gargan, Mont, peak, Fr. 45°36′ N, 1°37′ E 165
Gargano, Promontorio del, It. 41°45′ N, 15°55′ E 168
Gargano, Testa del, It. 41°48′ N, 16°12′ E 168
Gargantua, Cape, Can. 47°34′ N, 85°38′ W 94
Gargouna, Mali 15°59′ N, 0°14′ E 222
Gargždai, Lith. 55°43′ N, 21°23′ E 166
Garhakota, India 23°45′ N, 79°10′ E 197
Gari, Russ. 59°26′ N, 62°21′ E 154
Garibaldi, Braz. 29°16′ S, 51°32′ W 139
Garibaldi, Can. 49°57′ N, 123°9′ W 100
Garibaldi, Mount, Can. 49°49′ N, 123°2′ W 100
Garibaldi, Paso, pass, Arg. 54°35′ S, 67°38′ W 134
Garies, S. Af. 30°34′ S, 17°58′ E 227
Garissa, Kenya 0°30′ N, 39°39′ E 224
Garitz, Ger. 50°11′ N, 10°2′ E 167
Garko, Nig. 11°37′ N, 8°48′ E 222
Garland, Ark., U.S. 33°20′ N, 93°44′ W 103
Garland, Tex., U.S. 32°52′ N, 96°39′ W 96
Garlasco, It. 45°11′ N, 8°54′ E 167
Garliava, Lith. 54°49′ N, 23°51′ E 166
Garlin, Fr. 43°33′ N, 0°17′ E 150
Garmsār, Iran 35°13′ N, 52°15′ E 180
Garner, Iowa, U.S. 43°5′ N, 93°35′ W 94
Garnet Range, Mont., U.S. 46°51′ N, 113°35′ W 90
Garnett, Kans., U.S. 38°15′ N, 95°14′ W 94
Garonne, river, Fr. 44°36′ N, 1°0′ E 143
Garopaba, Braz. 28°4′ S, 48°40′ W 138
Garou, Lac, lake, Mali 16°2′ N, 3°4′ W 222
Garoua, Cameroon 9°18′ N, 13°22′ E 216
Garoua, Niger 13°53′ N, 13°9′ E 216
Garoua Boulaï, Cameroon 5°48′ N, 14°34′ E 218
Garré, Arg. 36°34′ S, 62°35′ W 139
Garrett, Ind., U.S. 41°20′ N, 85°9′ W 102
Garrettsville, Ohio, U.S. 41°16′ N, 81°6′ W 102
Garrison, Ky., U.S. 38°35′ N, 83°10′ W 102
Garrison, N. Dak., U.S. 47°38′ N, 101°26′ W 90
Garrison, Tex., U.S. 31°49′ N, 94°30′ W 103
Garrison, Utah, U.S. 38°55′ N, 114°2′ W 92
Garrucha, Sp. 37°10′ N, 1°50′ W 164
Garruchos, Braz. 28°16′ S, 55°41′ W 139
Garry Lake, Can. 65°58′ N, 102°24′ W 106
Garrygala, Turkm. 38°27′ N, 56°17′ E 180
Garsen, Kenya 2°18′ S, 40°5′ E 224
Garsila, Sudan 12°21′ N, 23°7′ E 216
Garson Lake, Can. 56°14′ N, 110°41′ W 108
Garssen, Ger. 52°39′ N, 10°7′ E 150
Garstang, U.K. 53°54′ N, 2°47′ W 162
Gartow, Ger. 53°1′ N, 11°27′ E 152
Garub, Namibia 26°38′ S, 16°5′ E 227
Garvão, Port. 37°42′ N, 8°21′ W 150
Garwa, India 24°9′ N, 83°48′ E 197
Gary, Ind., U.S. 41°34′ N, 87°22′ W 102
Gary, Tex., U.S. 32°1′ N, 94°23′ W 103
Garyarsa, China 31°36′ N, 80°31′ E 188
Garyville, La., U.S. 30°3′ N, 90°37′ W 103
Garza, Arg. 28°10′ S, 63°34′ W 139
Garzan, oil field, Turk. 37°53′ N, 41°38′ E 195
Garzê, China 31°42′ N, 99°51′ E 190
Garzón, Col. 2°11′ N, 75°40′ W 136
Garzón, Uru. 34°37′ S, 54°34′ W 139
Gas, Kans., U.S. 37°53′ N, 95°21′ W 94
Gas City, Ind., U.S. 40°28′ N, 85°37′ W 102
Gasa, Bhutan 27°54′ N, 89°35′ E 197
Gascony, region, Europe 42°41′ N, 1°18′ E 165
Gascueña, Sp. 40°17′ N, 2°31′ W 164
Gåsefjord 69°54′ N, 29°46′ W 246
Gåseland, Den. 70°12′ N, 32°55′ W 246
Gashagar, Nig. 13°20′ N, 12°46′ E 216
Gashaka, Nig. 7°19′ N, 11°29′ E 222
Gashua, Nig. 12°52′ N, 11°5′ E 222
Gąski, Pol. 53°56′ N, 22°25′ E 166
Gąsocin, Pol. 52°43′ N, 20°41′ E 152
Gasparilla Island, Fla., U.S. 26°43′ N, 82°25′ W 105
Gaspé, Cap, Can. 48°41′ N, 64°8′ W 111
Gaspé Peninsula, Can. 48°18′ N, 67°57′ W 80
Gass Peak, Nev., U.S. 36°22′ N, 115°14′ W 101
Gassol, Nig. 8°31′ N, 10°29′ E 222
Gassville, Ark., U.S. 36°16′ N, 92°30′ W 96
Gastilovtsy, Belarus 53°44′ N, 24°57′ E 152
Gaston, N.C., U.S. 36°30′ N, 77°39′ W 96
Gaston, Lake, Va., U.S. 36°30′ N, 78°23′ W 96
Gastonia, N.C., U.S. 35°15′ N, 81°12′ W 96
Gastre, Arg. 42°19′ S, 69°18′ W 134
Gåsvær, islands, Norwegian Sea 66°1′ N, 10°55′ E 152
Gata, Cabo de, Sp. 36°32′ N, 2°12′ W 164
Gata, Cape, Cyprus 34°29′ N, 32°59′ E 194
Gata de Gorgos, Sp. 38°46′ N, 0°5′ E 164
Gata, Sierra de, Sp. 40°8′ N, 6°50′ W 150
Gataga, river, Can. 58°25′ N, 126°18′ W 108
Gătaia, Rom. 45°26′ N, 21°26′ E 168
Gatchina, Russ. 59°32′ N, 30°5′ E 152
Gate, Okla., U.S. 36°49′ N, 100°2′ W 92
Gate City, Va., U.S. 36°38′ N, 82°36′ W 96
Gatelo, Eth. 5°59′ N, 38°11′ E 224
Gates of the Rocky Mountains, pass, Mont., U.S. 46°51′ N, 111°56′ W 90
Gateshead, U.K. 54°56′ N, 1°37′ W 150
Gateway, Colo., U.S. 38°42′ N, 108°58′ W 90
Gatico, Chile 22°32′ S, 70°17′ W 137
Gâtine, Hauteurs de, Fr. 47°1′ N, 1°14′ W 150
Gatineau, Can. 45°28′ N, 75°40′ W 82
Gatineau, river, Can. 45°55′ N, 76°8′ W 94
Gaṭrūyeh, Iran 29°13′ N, 54°40′ E 196
Gattinara, It. 45°37′ N, 8°21′ E 167
Gatwick, U.K. 51°8′ N, 0°10′ E 162
Gaucín, Sp. 36°30′ N, 5°20′ W 164
Gauer Lake, Can. 57°1′ N, 98°6′ W 108
Gauja, river, Latv. 57°13′ N, 24°50′ E 166
Gauja National Park, Latv. 57°19′ N, 24°42′ E 166
Gaujiena, Latv. 57°30′ N, 26°23′ E 166
Gauré, Lith. 55°14′ N, 22°28′ E 166
Gausta, peak, Nor. 59°50′ N, 8°31′ E 152
Gauteng, adm. division, S. Af. 26°24′ S, 27°21′ E 227
Gavà, Sp. 41°17′ N, 2°1′ E 164
Gavāter, Iran 25°7′ N, 61°29′ E 182
Gāvbandī, Iran 27°8′ N, 53°5′ E 196
Gávdos, island, Gr. 34°37′ N, 23°48′ E 180
Gavião, Port. 39°26′ N, 7°57′ W 150
Gavião, river, Braz. 14°42′ S, 41°0′ W 138
Gaviota, Calif., U.S. 34°28′ N, 120°14′ W 100
Gaviotas, Col. 4°26′ N, 70°47′ W 136
Gavirate, It. 45°51′ N, 8°42′ E 167
Gävle, Sw. 60°40′ N, 16°57′ E 160
Gavrilov Yam, Russ. 57°16′ N, 39°51′ E 154
Gavrilovo, Russ. 69°12′ N, 35°51′ E 152
Gávrovon, peak, Gr. 39°8′ N, 21°15′ E 156
Gavry, Russ. 56°54′ N, 27°52′ E 166
Gawachab, Namibia 27°4′ S, 17°50′ E 227
Gawler, Austral. 34°35′ S, 138°45′ E 231
Gawler Ranges, Austral. 32°9′ S, 135°22′ E 230
Gay, Russ. 51°25′ N, 58°25′ E 158
Gay Head, Mass., U.S. 41°17′ N, 70°55′ W 104
Gaya, India 24°48′ N, 84°59′ E 197
Gaya, Nig. 11°51′ N, 9°1′ E 222
Gaya, Niger 11°55′ N, 3°26′ E 222
Gayaza, Uganda 0°50′ N, 30°47′ E 224
Gaylor Mountain, Ark., U.S. 35°43′ N, 94°11′ W 96
Gaylord, Mich., U.S. 45°1′ N, 84°41′ W 94
Gaylord, Minn., U.S. 44°32′ N, 94°15′ W 90
Gayny, Russ. 60°19′ N, 54°19′ E 154
Gaza, adm. division, Mozambique 23°14′ S, 31°51′ E 220
Gaza City see Ghazzah, Gaza Strip, Israel 31°29′ N, 34°28′ E 194
Gaza Strip, special sovereignity, Israel 31°21′ N, 33°57′ E 194
Gazak, Iran 27°37′ N, 59°57′ E 182
G'azalkent, Uzb. 41°33′ N, 69°44′ E 197
Gazamni, Niger 14°20′ N, 10°31′ E 222
Gazanjyk, Turkm. 39°10′ N, 55°47′ E 180
Gazaoua, Niger 13°35′ N, 7°55′ E 222
Gazelle Peninsula, P.N.G. 4°33′ S, 151°15′ E 192
Gazi, Dem. Rep. of the Congo 1°3′ N, 24°28′ E 224
Gazi, Kenya 4°27′ S, 39°29′ E 224
Gaziantep, Turk. 37°2′ N, 37°25′ E 180
Gazimagusa see Ammochostos, Northern Cyprus, Cyprus 35°7′ N, 33°56′ E 194
Gazipaşa, Turk. 36°17′ N, 32°18′ E 156
Gazli, Uzb. 40°8′ N, 63°28′ E 197
Gazojak, Turkm. 41°10′ N, 61°22′ E 180
Gazū, Kūh-e, peak, Iran 28°16′ N, 61°30′ E 182
Gbadolite, Dem. Rep. of the Congo 4°18′ N, 21°3′ E 218
Gbarnga, Liberia 6°51′ N, 9°33′ W 222
Gberia Fotombu, Sierra Leone 9°51′ N, 11°12′ W 222
Gboko, Nig. 7°19′ N, 8°57′ E 222
Gcuwa, S. Af. 32°21′ S, 28°7′ E 227
Gdańsk, Pol. 54°21′ N, 18°38′ E 166
Gdanskaya Guba 71°3′ N, 74°49′ E 160
Gdov, Russ. 58°44′ N, 27°48′ E 166
Gdynia, Pol. 54°29′ N, 18°31′ E 166
Gearhart, Oreg., U.S. 46°1′ N, 123°54′ W 100
Gearhart Mountain, Oreg., U.S. 42°30′ N, 120°57′ W 90
Gêba, river, Senegal 12°38′ N, 14°29′ W 222
Gebe, island, Indonesia 0°6′ N, 129°13′ E 192
Gebeit, Sudan 18°57′ N, 36°46′ E 182
Gebeit, Sudan 21°4′ N, 36°19′ E 182
Gebel Adda, ruin(s), Egypt 22°12′ N, 31°32′ E 182
Gebiley, Somalia 9°38′ N, 43°36′ E 216
Gebra, Ger. 51°25′ N, 10°37′ E 152
Gebze, Turk. 40°48′ N, 29°26′ E 156
Gech'a, Eth. 7°26′ N, 35°21′ E 224
Gedaref, Sudan 14°0′ N, 35°24′ E 182
Gedaref, adm. division, Sudan 14°5′ N, 34°13′ E 182
Geddes, S. Dak., U.S. 43°14′ N, 98°42′ W 90
Gedern, Ger. 50°25′ N, 9°12′ E 167
Gedid Ras el Fil, Sudan 12°41′ N, 25°43′ E 216
Gediz, Turk. 39°3′ N, 29°24′ E 156
Gedlegubē, Eth. 6°50′ N, 45°2′ E 218
Gēdo, Eth. 8°58′ N, 37°26′ E 224
Gèdre, Fr. 42°48′ N, 0°1′ E 164
Gedser, Den. 54°35′ N, 11°56′ E 152
Geel, Belg. 51°9′ N, 4°58′ E 167
Geelong, Austral. 38°11′ S, 144°23′ E 231
Geelvink Channel 28°34′ S, 112°19′ E 230
Geeste, Ger. 52°36′ N, 7°16′ E 163
Geeveston, Austral. 43°5′ S, 146°56′ E 231
Gê'gyai, China 32°29′ N, 80°58′ E 188
Geidam, Nig. 12°53′ N, 11°56′ E 222
Geikie, river, Can. 57°28′ N, 104°9′ W 108
Geilenkirchen, Ger. 50°58′ N, 6°7′ E 167
Geilo Hills, Kenya 3°12′ N, 40°49′ E 224
Geisa, Ger. 50°43′ N, 9°56′ E 167
Geisenheim, Ger. 49°58′ N, 7°57′ E 167
Geita, Tanzania 2°56′ S, 32°9′ E 224
Gejiu, China 23°18′ N, 103°6′ E 202
Gel, river, Sudan 6°59′ N, 29°3′ E 224
Gela, It. 37°4′ N, 14°14′ E 156
Geladaintong, peak, China 33°6′ N, 90°38′ E 188
Geladī, Eth. 6°57′ N, 46°28′ E 218
Gelahun, Liberia 7°43′ N, 10°28′ W 222
Gelai, peak, Tanzania 2°37′ S, 36°2′ E 224
Gelasa, Selat 3°8′ S, 106°41′ E 192
Geldermalsen, Neth. 51°53′ N, 5°16′ E 167
Geldern, Ger. 51°29′ N, 6°20′ E 167
Geldrop, Neth. 51°25′ N, 5°33′ E 167
Geleen, Neth. 50°58′ N, 5°49′ E 167
Gelendzhik, Russ. 44°34′ N, 38°6′ E 156
Gélengdeng, Chad 10°54′ N, 15°31′ E 216
Gelgaudiškis, Lith. 55°4′ N, 22°57′ E 166
Gelhak, Sudan 11°3′ N, 32°40′ E 182
Gelibolu (Gallipoli), Turk. 40°25′ N, 26°38′ E 156
Gellinsoor, Somalia 6°20′ N, 46°42′ E 218
Gelnhausen, Ger. 50°12′ N, 9°11′ E 167
Gelse, Hung. 46°35′ N, 16°59′ E 168
Gelsenkirchen, Ger. 51°30′ N, 7°5′ E 167
Gemas, Malaysia 2°37′ N, 102°36′ E 196
Gembloux, Belg. 50°34′ N, 4°41′ E 167
Gemena, Dem. Rep. of the Congo 3°12′ N, 19°54′ E 207
Gemerek, Turk. 39°10′ N, 36°3′ E 156
Gemert, Neth. 51°33′ N, 5°40′ E 167
Gemlik, Turk. 40°25′ N, 29°9′ E 156
Gemona del Friuli, It. 46°16′ N, 13°8′ E 167
Gemsa, Egypt 27°40′ N, 33°33′ E 180
Gemsbok National Park, Botswana 25°25′ S, 20°49′ E 227
Gemünden, Ger. 50°58′ N, 8°57′ E 167
Gen, river, China 50°24′ N, 121°3′ E 190
Genalē, river, Eth. 4°55′ N, 41°17′ E 224
Genalē, river, Eth. 6°8′ N, 39°1′ E 224
Genç, Turk. 38°44′ N, 40°32′ E 195
Geneina, Sudan 13°20′ N, 22°29′ E 216
General Alvear, Arg. 36°3′ S, 60°3′ W 139
General Alvear, Arg. 34°57′ S, 67°41′ W 134
General Arenales, Arg. 34°18′ S, 61°17′ W 139
General Artigas, Parag. 26°51′ S, 56°13′ W 139
General Belgrano, Arg. 35°45′ S, 58°30′ W 139
General Bernardo O'Higgins, station, Antarctica 63°26′ S, 57°47′ W 134
General Bravo, Mex. 25°47′ N, 99°10′ W 114
General Cabrera, Arg. 32°49′ S, 63°52′ W 139
General Cepeda, Mex. 25°21′ N, 101°29′ W 114
General Conesa, Arg. 36°29′ S, 57°19′ W 139
General D. Cerri, Arg. 38°44′ S, 62°24′ W 139
General Enrique Martínez, Uru. 33°13′ S, 53°51′ W 139
General Eugenio A. Garay, Parag. 20°33′ S, 62°10′ W 134
General Galarza, Arg. 32°43′ S, 59°22′ W 139
General Galeana, Mex. 25°27′ N, 105°13′ W 114
General Güemes, Arg. 24°40′ S, 65°4′ W 132
General Guido, Arg. 36°38′ S, 57°46′ W 139
General José de San Martín, Arg. 26°33′ S, 59°21′ W 139
General Juan Madariaga, Arg. 37°0′ S, 57°7′ W 139
General La Madrid, Arg. 37°15′ S, 61°17′ W 139
General Lavalle, Arg. 36°25′ S, 56°56′ W 139
General Leonidas Plaza Gutiérrez, Ecua. 3°4′ S, 78°25′ W 136
General Levalle, Arg. 34°3′ S, 63°53′ W 134
General Lorenzo Vintter, Arg. 40°44′ S, 64°28′ W 134
General MacArthur, Philippines 11°16′ N, 125°33′ E 203
General Paz, Arg. 35°31′ S, 58°20′ W 139
General Paz, Arg. 27°45′ S, 57°38′ W 139
General Pico, Arg. 35°39′ S, 63°44′ W 139
General Pinedo, Arg. 27°19′ S, 61°18′ W 139
General Pinto, Arg. 34°46′ S, 61°52′ W 139
General Pirán, Arg. 37°17′ S, 57°49′ W 139
General Saavedra, Bol. 17°15′ S, 63°14′ W 137
General San Martín, Arg. 38°2′ S, 63°34′ W 139
General San Martín, Arg. 34°33′ S, 58°33′ W 139
General San Martín, Arg. 44°5′ S, 70°28′ W 134
General Santos, Philippines 6°9′ N, 125°13′ E 203
General Terán, Mex. 25°15′ N, 99°42′ W 114
General Treviño, Mex. 26°12′ N, 99°29′ W 114
General Trías, Mex. 28°19′ N, 106°23′ W 92
General Viamonte, Arg. 34°59′ S, 61°4′ W 139
General Villegas, Arg. 35°1′ S, 63°1′ W 139
Genesee, Idaho, U.S. 46°32′ N, 116°57′ W 90
Genesee, river, N.Y., U.S. 42°15′ N, 78°17′ W 80
Geneseo, Ill., U.S. 41°27′ N, 90°10′ W 102
Geneseo, N.Y., U.S. 42°47′ N, 77°50′ W 94

Geneva, Ala., U.S. 31°1' N, 85°53' W 96
Geneva, Ill., U.S. 41°52' N, 88°19' W 102
Geneva, Nebr., U.S. 40°30' N, 97°37' W 94
Geneva, N.Y., U.S. 42°52' N, 76°59' W 94
Geneva, Ohio, U.S. 41°47' N, 80°58' W 102
Geneva, Lake, Fr.-Switz. 46°15' N, 6°11' E 142
Genève, Switz. 46°11' N, 6°9' E 167
Gengma, China 23°33' N, 99°22' E 202
Geni, river, Sudan 7°22' N, 32°53' E 224
Genk, Belg. 50°56' N, 5°30' E 167
Gennargentu, Monti del, It. 39°48' N, 8°39' E 156
Genoa, Ill., U.S. 42°4' N, 88°42' W 102
Genoa, Nebr., U.S. 41°26' N, 97°45' W 90
Genoa, Ohio, U.S. 41°30' N, 83°21' W 102
Genoa see Genova, It. 44°24' N, 8°57' E 167
Génolhac, Fr. 44°21' N, 3°56' E 150
Génoto, Senegal 13°35' N, 13°53' W 222
Genova (Genoa), It. 44°24' N, 8°57' E 167
Genova, Golfo di 44°4' N, 7°33' E 150
Gent, Belg. 51°3' N, 3°44' E 163
Genthin, Ger. 52°24' N, 12°9' E 152
Genyem, Indonesia 2°33' S, 140°9' E 192
Geoagiu, Rom. 45°55' N, 23°12' E 168
Geochang, S. Korea 35°41' N, 127°55' E 200
Geographical Society Ø, island, Den. 72°30' N, 21°29' W 246
Geoje, S. Korea 34°51' N, 128°37' E 200
George, S. Af. 33°58' S, 22°26' E 227
George, Lake, Fla., U.S. 29°15' N, 81°41' W 105
George, Lake, N.Y., U.S. 43°36' N, 74°9' W 81
George, river, Can. 57°32' N, 66°1' W 106
George Sound 44°59' S, 167°7' E 240
George Town, Malaysia 5°25' N, 100°17' E 196
George Town, Cayman Is., U.K. 19°18' N, 81°24' W 115
George V Coast, Antarctica 69°8' S, 153°28' E 248
George Washington Birthplace National Monument, Va., U.S. 38°10' N, 77°0' W 94
George West, Tex., U.S. 28°19' N, 98°7' W 92
George, Zemlya, island, Russ. 79°13' N, 47°22' E 160
Georgetown, Austral. 18°17' S, 143°32' E 238
Georgetown, Fla., U.S. 29°23' N, 81°38' W 105
Georgetown, Gambia 13°29' N, 14°48' W 222
Georgetown, Guyana 6°40' N, 58°21' W 130
Georgetown, Ill., U.S. 39°58' N, 87°38' W 102
Georgetown, La., U.S. 31°45' N, 92°23' W 103
Georgetown, Me., U.S. 43°48' N, 69°46' W 104
Georgetown, Miss., U.S. 31°52' N, 90°11' W 103
Georgetown, Ohio, U.S. 38°51' N, 83°54' W 102
Georgetown, S.C., U.S. 33°22' N, 79°19' W 96
Georgetown, Tex., U.S. 30°37' N, 97°40' W 92
Georgia 42°0' N, 44°0' E 195
Georgia, adm. division, Ga., U.S. 32°40' N, 84°11' W 96
Georgia, Strait of 49°53' N, 124°58' W 90
Georgian Bay 45°4' N, 81°13' W 80
Georgīevka, Kaz. 49°19' N, 81°33' E 184
Georgiyevsk, Russ. 44°9' N, 43°28' E 158
Georgiyevskoye, Russ. 58°41' N, 45°6' E 154
Gera, Ger. 50°53' N, 12°5' E 152
Geraardsbergen, Belg. 50°47' N, 3°54' E 163
Geral de Goiás, Serra, Braz. 12°46' S, 46°59' W 130
Geral, Serra, Braz. 25°36' S, 51°43' W 132
Geraldine, Mont., U.S. 47°34' N, 110°17' W 90
Geraldine, N.Z. 44°6' S, 171°14' E 240
Geraldton, Can. 49°44' N, 86°57' W 94
Gerar, ruin(s), Israel 31°21' N, 34°33' E 194
Gerasa see Jarash, Jordan 32°17' N, 35°53' E 194
Gerbéviller, Fr. 48°30' N, 6°30' E 163
Gercüş, Turk. 37°33' N, 41°25' E 195
Gerdine, Mount, Alas., U.S. 61°25' N, 152°42' W 98
Gerede, Turk. 40°48' N, 32°11' E 156
Gereshk, Afghan. 31°48' N, 64°34' E 186
Gérgal, Sp. 37°6' N, 2°33' W 164
Gerik, Malaysia 5°25' N, 101°6' E 196
Gering, Nebr., U.S. 41°49' N, 103°40' W 90
Gerlachovský Štít, peak, Slovakia 49°8' N, 20°3' E 152
Germain, Grand lac, lake, Can. 51°11' N, 67°11' W 111
Germaine, Lac, lake, Can. 52°59' N, 68°16' W 111
Germânia, Braz. 10°36' S, 70°5' W 137
Germania Land, Den. 76°52' N, 17°54' W 246
Germansen Landing, Can. 55°43' N, 124°43' W 108
Germantown, Ill., U.S. 38°32' N, 89°32' W 102
Germantown, N.Y., U.S. 42°8' N, 73°54' W 104
Germantown, Tenn., U.S. 35°4' N, 89°49' W 96
Germany 51°17' N, 7°48' E 150
Germfask, Mich., U.S. 46°16' N, 85°56' W 110
Germī, Iran 39°3' N, 48°6' E 195
Gernsbach, Ger. 48°45' N, 8°19' E 152
Gerolakkos, Cyprus 35°10' N, 33°15' E 194
Gerolstein, Ger. 50°13' N, 6°40' E 163
Gerrard, Can. 50°30' N, 117°18' W 90
Gersfeld, Ger. 50°27' N, 9°55' E 167
Gerstungen, Ger. 50°58' N, 10°3' E 167
Gêrzê, China 32°29' N, 84°3' E 188
Gerze, Turk. 41°48' N, 35°11' E 156
Gescher, Ger. 51°57' N, 7°0' E 167
Geseke, Ger. 51°38' N, 8°29' E 167
Geser, Indonesia 3°57' S, 130°51' E 192
Geta, Fin. 60°21' N, 19°50' E 166
Getafe, Sp. 40°18' N, 3°44' W 164
Geteina, Sudan 14°49' N, 32°23' E 182
Gettysburg, S. Dak., U.S. 44°59' N, 99°59' W 90
Getúlio Vargas, Braz. 27°54' S, 52°13' W 139
Gety, Dem. Rep. of the Congo 1°11' N, 30°11' E 224
Geumpang, Indonesia 4°56' N, 96°6' E 196
Geumsan, S. Korea 36°5' N, 127°29' E 200
Gevaş, Turk. 38°16' N, 43°4' E 195
Gevelsberg, Ger. 51°18' N, 7°20' E 163
Gewanē, Eth. 10°7' N, 40°36' E 224
Gex, Fr. 46°19' N, 6°3' E 167
Geylegphug, Bhutan 26°49' N, 90°37' E 197
Geyve, Turk. 40°30' N, 30°19' E 156
Gézenti, Chad 21°39' N, 18°19' E 216
Gezer, ruin(s), Israel 31°51' N, 34°52' E 194
Gezira, adm. division, Sudan 14°32' N, 32°33' E 182
Ghaba North, oil field, Oman 21°24' N, 57°15' E 182
Ghabāghib, Syr. 33°11' N, 36°12' E 194
Ghabeish, Sudan 12°9' N, 27°18' E 216
Ghadāmis (Ghadames), Lib. 30°7' N, 9°28' E 214
Ghaddūwah, Lib. 26°27' N, 14°18' E 216
Ghagghar, river, India 29°40' N, 75°1' E 197
Ghana 7°51' N, 1°42' W 214
Ghanzi, Botswana 21°41' S, 21°44' E 227
Gharbi Island, Tun. 34°27' N, 10°39' E 214
Ghardaïa, Alg. 32°17' N, 3°34' E 207
Ghârib, Gebel, peak, Egypt 28°6' N, 32°47' E 180
Gharm, Taj. 39°4' N, 70°25' E 197
Gharo, Pak. 24°44' N, 67°37' E 186
Gharyān, Lib. 32°9' N, 13°0' E 216
Ghāt, Lib. 24°57' N, 10°10' E 214
Ghatampur, India 26°9' N, 80°9' E 188
Ghawar Oil Field, Saudi Arabia 25°5' N, 49°15' E 196
Ghaziabad, India 28°40' N, 77°25' E 197
Ghazipur, India 25°35' N, 83°34' E 197
Ghazīr, Leb. 34°1' N, 35°40' E 194
Ghazni, Afghan. 33°34' N, 68°33' E 186
Ghazzah (Gaza City), Gaza Strip, Israel 31°29' N, 34°28' E 194
Ghelar, Rom. 45°42' N, 22°47' E 168
Ghent, Ky., U.S. 38°43' N, 85°3' W 102
Ghent, N.Y., U.S. 42°19' N, 73°38' W 104
Ghilarza, It. 40°8' N, 8°50' E 156
Ghilvaci, Rom. 47°41' N, 22°41' E 168
Ghisonaccia, Fr. 42°0' N, 9°25' E 156
Ghlo, Beinn a', peak, U.K. 56°49' N, 3°48' W 150
Ghost River, Can. 50°9' N, 91°27' W 94
Ghoumrassen, Tun. 33°1' N, 10°15' E 214
Ghraiba, Tun. 34°31' N, 10°12' E 156
Ghunthur, Syr. 34°23' N, 37°8' E 194
Ghurian, Afghan. 34°27' N, 61°30' E 186
Gia Nghia, Vietnam 12°15' N, 107°37' E 202
Gia Rai, Vietnam 9°13' N, 105°28' E 202
Gialo, oil field, Lib. 28°30' N, 21°2' E 216
Giant Forest, Calif., U.S. 36°34' N, 118°47' W 101
Giant's Ring, ruin(s), U.K. 54°31' N, 6°5' W 150
Giarso, Eth. 5°14' N, 37°33' E 224
Gibara, Cuba 21°7' N, 76°11' W 116
Gibbon, Nebr., U.S. 40°44' N, 98°51' W 90
Gibbs Island, Antarctica 61°44' S, 55°25' W 134
Gibeah, ruin(s), Israel 31°48' N, 35°11' E 194
Gibeon, Namibia 25°8' S, 17°46' E 227
Gibraltar, adm. division, U.K. 36°7' N, 5°35' W 164
Gibraltar, Strait of 36°2' N, 6°40' W 150
Gibsland, La., U.S. 32°31' N, 93°3' W 96
Gibson City, Ill., U.S. 40°27' N, 88°22' W 102
Gibson Desert, Austral. 23°7' S, 121°58' E 230
Gibsonburg, Ohio, U.S. 41°22' N, 83°19' W 102
Gibsons, Can. 49°24' N, 123°31' W 100
Gibsonton, Fla., U.S. 27°50' N, 82°22' W 105
Gīdamī, Eth. 8°56' N, 34°33' E 224
Giddalur, India 15°22' N, 78°56' E 188
Giddings, Tex., U.S. 30°10' N, 96°56' W 96
Gīdolē, Eth. 5°37' N, 37°27' E 224
Giel, Sudan 11°20' N, 32°44' E 182
Gien, Fr. 47°41' N, 2°38' E 150
Giera, Rom. 45°25' N, 20°59' E 168
Giessen, Ger. 50°34' N, 8°39' E 167
Gieten, Neth. 53°0' N, 6°45' E 163
Giffard, Lac, lake, Can. 51°7' N, 77°25' W 110
Gifford, Fla., U.S. 27°40' N, 80°25' W 105
Gifford, river, Can. 70°40' N, 84°39' W 106
Gift Lake, Can. 55°53' N, 115°54' W 108
Gifu, Japan 35°24' N, 136°46' E 201
Gifu, adm. division, Japan 35°48' N, 136°49' E 201
Gig Harbor, Wash., U.S. 47°18' N, 122°36' W 100
Gigant, Russ. 46°30' N, 41°14' E 158
Giganta, Sierra de la, Mex. 25°57' N, 111°37' W 112
Gijón, Sp. 43°30' N, 5°42' W 150
Gikongoro, Rwanda 2°31' S, 29°33' E 224
Gila, N. Mex., U.S. 32°57' N, 108°34' W 92
Gila Bend, Ariz., U.S. 32°56' N, 112°43' W 92
Gila Bend Mountains, Ariz., U.S. 33°24' N, 113°42' W 101
Gila Cliff Dwellings National Monument, N. Mex., U.S. 33°13' N, 108°21' W 92
Gila Mountains, Ariz., U.S. 33°9' N, 109°59' W 92
Gila, river, Ariz., U.S. 33°12' N, 110°9' W 80
Gilbâna, Egypt 30°55' N, 32°28' E 194
Gilbert, La., U.S. 32°3' N, 91°40' W 103
Gilbert, Minn., U.S. 47°29' N, 92°29' W 94
Gilbert Islands, North Pacific Ocean 0°46' N, 173°11' E 238
Gilbert, Islas, Drake Passage 55°7' S, 73°15' W 134
Gilbert, Mount, Can. 50°51' N, 124°21' W 90
Gilbert Peak, Utah, U.S. 40°47' N, 110°25' W 90
Gilbert Peak, Wash., U.S. 46°27' N, 121°26' W 100
Gilbert Plains, Can. 51°7' N, 100°30' W 90
Gilbertville, Mass., U.S. 42°18' N, 72°13' W 104
Gilbués, Braz. 9°51' S, 45°23' W 130
Gildeskål, Nor. 67°3' N, 14°2' E 152
Gildford, Mont., U.S. 48°33' N, 110°17' W 90
Gilead, Me., U.S. 44°23' N, 70°59' W 104
Giles Meteorological Station, site, Austral. 25°7' S, 128°4' E 230
Giles, Mount, Antarctica 75°2' S, 137°1' W 248
Gilford, N.H., U.S. 43°32' N, 71°25' W 104
Gilgal, West Bank, Israel 31°58' N, 35°26' E 194
Gilgil, Kenya 0°30' N, 36°19' E 224
Gilgit, Pak. 35°52' N, 74°19' E 186
Gilgit-Baltistan, adm. division, Pak. 36°0' N, 75°0' E 186
Giljeva Planina, Mont. 43°3' N, 19°50' E 168
Gillam, Can. 56°20' N, 94°44' W 108
Gilleleje, Den. 56°6' N, 12°18' E 152
Gillespie, Ill., U.S. 39°7' N, 89°50' W 102
Gillett, Ark., U.S. 34°5' N, 91°23' W 96
Gillette, Wyo., U.S. 44°16' N, 105°30' W 90
Gilliam, Mo., U.S. 39°14' N, 93°0' W 94
Gillies Islands, Davis Sea 66°37' S, 98°44' E 248
Gillingham, U.K. 51°22' N, 0°32' E 162
Gillis Range, Nev., U.S. 38°43' N, 118°40' W 90
Gillock Island, Antarctica 70°22' S, 72°12' E 248
Gills Rock, Wis., U.S. 45°16' N, 87°1' W 94
Gilman, Ill., U.S. 40°45' N, 88°0' W 102
Gilman, Vt., U.S. 44°24' N, 71°44' W 104
Gilmer, Tex., U.S. 32°43' N, 94°58' W 103
Gilo Wenz, river, Eth. 7°40' N, 33°38' E 224
Gilroy, Calif., U.S. 37°0' N, 121°35' W 100
Gīmbī, Eth. 9°8' N, 35°49' E 224
Gimcheon, S. Korea 36°5' N, 128°8' E 200
Gimhae, S. Korea 35°12' N, 128°54' E 200
Gimhwa, S. Korea 38°17' N, 127°28' E 200
Gimje, S. Korea 35°48' N, 126°54' E 200
Gimli, Can. 50°37' N, 97°2' W 90
Gimo, Sw. 60°10' N, 18°8' E 166
Ginâh, Egypt 25°21' N, 30°28' E 226
Gingindlovu, S. Af. 29°2' S, 31°32' E 227
Gingoog, Philippines 8°48' N, 125°7' E 203
Gīnīr, Eth. 7°12' N, 40°43' E 224
Ginostra, It. 38°47' N, 15°11' E 156
Giohar see Jawhar, Somalia 2°47' N, 45°34' E 218
Gióna, Óros, peak, Gr. 38°38' N, 22°10' E 156
Giovinazzo, It. 41°11' N, 16°40' E 156
Ģipka, Latv. 57°34' N, 22°36' E 166
Gir National Park, India 21°15' N, 70°30' E 186
Girard, Ill., U.S. 39°26' N, 89°47' W 102
Girard, Kans., U.S. 37°28' N, 94°50' W 94
Girard, Ohio, U.S. 41°9' N, 80°42' W 94
Girardot, Col. 4°19' N, 74°48' W 136
Girawa, Eth. 9°7' N, 41°51' E 224
Girbanat, Sudan 12°0' N, 33°9' E 182
Gîrbou, Rom. 47°10' N, 23°24' E 168
Gîrbovi, Rom. 44°48' N, 26°45' E 156
Giresun, Turk. 40°55' N, 38°22' E 158
Girga, Egypt 26°19' N, 31°49' E 180
Giridih, India 24°9' N, 86°19' E 197
Gîrla Mare, Rom. 44°12' N, 22°46' E 168
Gîrlişte, Rom. 45°10' N, 21°48' E 168
Girne see Kyrenia, Northern Cyprus, Cyprus 35°20' N, 33°18' E 194
Giroc, Rom. 45°42' N, 21°15' E 168
Girolata, Fr. 42°21' N, 8°37' E 156
Girona, Sp. 41°58' N, 2°50' E 164
Giruá, Braz. 28°5' S, 54°21' W 139
Giruliai, Lith. 55°46' N, 21°6' E 166
Girvas, Russ. 62°28' N, 33°44' E 154
Gisborne, N.Z. 38°40' S, 178°0' E 240
Giscome, Can. 54°3' N, 122°23' W 108
Gisors, Fr. 49°16' N, 1°45' E 163
Gisselberg, Ger. 50°45' N, 8°44' E 167
Gitega, Burundi 3°27' S, 29°55' E 224
Giuba, Isole, islands, Indian Ocean 0°45' N, 41°29' E 224
Giulianova, It. 42°44' N, 13°56' E 156
Giuncarico, It. 42°55' N, 10°58' E 156
Giurgeni, Rom. 44°44' N, 27°51' E 158
Giurgiu, Rom. 43°53' N, 25°56' E 156
Giurgiu, adm. division, Rom. 44°8' N, 25°43' E 156
Give, Den. 55°49' N, 9°13' E 150
Givet, Fr. 50°7' N, 4°48' E 167
Giyani, S. Af. 23°17' S, 30°44' E 227
Giyon, Eth. 8°34' N, 38°1' E 224
Gizab, Afghan. 33°27' N, 66°0' E 186
Gizhiga, Russ. 62°2' N, 160°11' E 160
Gizhduvan, Uzb. 40°6' N, 64°42' E 197
Giżycko, Pol. 54°1' N, 21°45' E 166
Gjakova (Đakovica), Kosovo 42°23' N, 20°26' E 168
Gjalicë e Lumës, Mal, peak, Alban. 42°0' N, 20°25' E 168
Gjegjan, Alban. 41°56' N, 20°0' E 168
Gjelsvik Mountains, Antarctica 72°8' S, 4°59' W 248
Gjerstad, Nor. 58°52' N, 9°0' E 152
Gjilan (Gnjilane), Kosovo 42°27' N, 21°27' E 168
Gjinar, Alban. 41°2' N, 20°12' E 156
Gjoa Haven, Can. 68°36' N, 96°0' W 106
Gjøvdal, Nor. 58°51' N, 8°17' E 152
Gjuhëzës, Kepi i, Alban. 40°27' N, 18°34' E 156
Gjuvikfjell, peak, Nor. 59°57' N, 7°55' E 152
Gkreko, Cape, Cyprus 34°53' N, 33°55' E 194
Gla, ruin(s), Gr. 38°23' N, 23°10' E 156
Glace Bay, Can. 46°11' N, 59°58' W 111
Glacier, Wash., U.S. 48°52' N, 121°58' W 100
Glacier Bay 58°40' N, 136°50' W 108
Glacier Bay National Park and Preserve, Alas., U.S. 58°40' N, 137°23' W 73
Glacier Peak, Wash., U.S. 48°5' N, 121°10' W 100
Glacier Strait 75°57' N, 80°39' W 106
Gladstone, Can. 50°13' N, 98°58' W 90
Gladstone, Mich., U.S. 45°50' N, 87°2' W 94
Gladstone, Oreg., U.S. 45°23' N, 122°37' W 90
Gladwin, Mich., U.S. 43°58' N, 84°29' W 102
Gladys Lake, Can. 59°52' N, 133°39' W 108
Glamoč, Bosn. and Herzg. 44°2' N, 16°50' E 168
Glan, Philippines 5°50' N, 125°11' E 203
Glandore, Ire. 51°34' N, 9°7' W 150
Glandorf, Ger. 52°4' N, 8°0' E 163
Glarus, Switz. 47°2' N, 9°2' E 156
Glas, Lac du, lake, Can. 51°49' N, 75°47' W 110
Glasco, Kans., U.S. 39°20' N, 97°51' W 90
Glasco, N.Y., U.S. 42°1' N, 73°58' W 104
Glasford, Ill., U.S. 40°33' N, 89°48' W 102
Glasgow, Ky., U.S. 37°0' N, 85°55' W 96
Glasgow, Mont., U.S. 48°11' N, 106°39' W 90
Glasgow, U.K. 55°51' N, 4°27' W 143
Glaslyn, Can. 53°21' N, 108°22' W 108
Glass Buttes, peak, Oreg., U.S. 43°32' N, 120°10' W 90
Glass Mountain, Calif., U.S. 37°45' N, 118°47' W 90
Glass Mountain, Calif., U.S. 41°35' N, 121°35' W 90
Glass Mountains, Tex., U.S. 30°30' N, 103°11' W 92
Glastonbury, Conn., U.S. 41°42' N, 72°37' W 104
Glastonbury, U.K. 51°8' N, 2°43' W 162
Glavičice, Bosn. and Herzg. 44°35' N, 19°12' E 168
Glazachevo, Russ. 57°12' N, 30°13' E 166
Glazov, Russ. 58°6' N, 52°43' E 154
Gleichberg, Grosser, peak, Ger. 50°22' N, 10°29' E 152
Gleichen, Can. 50°52' N, 113°4' W 90
Gleisdorf, Aust. 47°6' N, 15°42' E 168
Glen, N.H., U.S. 44°6' N, 71°11' W 104
Glen Allan, Miss., U.S. 33°0' N, 91°2' W 103
Glen Arbor, Mich., U.S. 44°53' N, 85°59' W 94
Glen Cove, N.Y., U.S. 40°52' N, 73°38' W 104
Glen Park, N.Y., U.S. 44°0' N, 75°58' W 94
Glen, river, U.K. 52°47' N, 0°34' E 162
Glen Rose, Tex., U.S. 32°14' N, 97°45' W 92
Glen Ullin, N. Dak., U.S. 46°47' N, 101°51' W 90
Glenada, Oreg., U.S. 43°56' N, 124°6' W 90
Glenavy, N.Z. 44°54' S, 171°5' E 240
Glenboro, Can. 49°32' N, 99°18' W 90
Glencliff, N.H., U.S. 43°58' N, 71°54' W 104
Glencoe, Can. 42°44' N, 81°42' W 102
Glencoe, Minn., U.S. 44°45' N, 94°10' W 94
Glendale, Ariz., U.S. 33°32' N, 112°10' W 92
Glendale, Calif., U.S. 34°8' N, 118°16' W 101
Glendive, Mont., U.S. 47°4' N, 104°44' W 90
Glendo, Wyo., U.S. 42°29' N, 105°1' W 90
Glendon, Can. 54°14' N, 111°10' W 108
Glenfield, U.K. 52°38' N, 1°14' W 162
Glenmora, La., U.S. 30°57' N, 92°36' W 103
Glenn, Mount, Ariz., U.S. 31°56' N, 110°3' W 92
Glenns Ferry, Idaho, U.S. 42°58' N, 115°19' W 90
Glennville, Calif., U.S. 35°44' N, 118°43' W 101
Glennville, Ga., U.S. 31°55' N, 81°56' W 96
Glenora, Can. 57°52' N, 131°26' W 108
Glenorchy, N.Z. 44°52' S, 168°26' E 240
Glenrock, Wyo., U.S. 42°51' N, 105°53' W 90
Glens Falls, N.Y., U.S. 43°18' N, 73°39' W 104
Glenwood, Minn., U.S. 45°38' N, 95°24' W 94
Glenwood, N. Mex., U.S. 33°18' N, 108°52' W 92
Glenwood, Oreg., U.S. 45°38' N, 123°16' W 100
Glenwood, Va., U.S. 36°35' N, 79°23' W 96
Glenwood, Wash., U.S. 46°0' N, 121°18' W 100
Glenwood, W. Va., U.S. 38°34' N, 82°12' W 102
Glidden, Wis., U.S. 46°8' N, 90°36' W 94
Glina, Croatia 45°20' N, 16°6' E 168
Glíthion, Gr. 36°43' N, 22°32' E 216
Glittertind, peak, Nor. 61°38' N, 8°24' E 152
Gliwice, Pol. 50°17' N, 18°38' E 152
Głogów, Pol. 51°39' N, 16°5' E 152
Głomno, Pol. 54°18' N, 20°44' E 152
Globe, Ariz., U.S. 33°24' N, 110°47' W 92
Gloggnitz, Aust. 47°40' N, 15°56' E 168
Glommersträsk, Nor. 65°14' N, 19°40' E 152
Glorenza, It. 46°40' N, 10°33' E 167
Glória, Braz. 9°13' S, 38°20' W 132
Gloria Ridge, North Atlantic Ocean 54°34' N, 45°3' W 253
Glorieuses, Îles, islands, Indian Ocean 11°10' S, 47°2' E 220
Glorioso Islands, Indian Ocean 11°19' S, 44°49' E 207
Gloster, Miss., U.S. 31°11' N, 91°2' W 103
Gloucester, Can. 45°24' N, 75°35' W 94
Gloucester, Mass., U.S. 42°36' N, 70°40' W 104
Gloucester, U.K. 51°51' N, 2°14' W 162
Glouster, Ohio, U.S. 39°29' N, 82°4' W 102
Glubokiy, Russ. 46°58' N, 42°38' E 158
Glubokiy, Russ. 48°32' N, 40°20' E 158
Glūbokoe, Kaz. 50°8' N, 82°18' E 184
Glubokoye, Russ. 56°38' N, 28°59' E 166
Glusk, Belarus 52°52' N, 28°47' E 152
Glyncorrwg, U.K. 51°41' N, 3°37' W 162
Glyndon, Minn., U.S. 46°52' N, 96°37' W 94
Gmelinka, Russ. 50°21' N, 46°52' E 158
Gmünd, Aust. 48°45' N, 14°58' E 152
Gmunden, Aust. 47°55' N, 13°47' E 156
Gnadenhutten, Ohio, U.S. 40°20' N, 81°25' W 102
Gnarp, Nor. 62°4' N, 17°12' E 152
Gnas, Aust. 46°52' N, 15°51' E 168
Gnesta, Nor. 59°2' N, 17°18' E 152
Gnetalovo, Russ. 56°52' N, 29°37' E 166
Gnjilane see Gjilan, Kosovo 42°27' N, 21°27' E 168
Go Cong, Vietnam 10°22' N, 106°41' E 202
Goa, adm. division, India 14°59' N, 74°13' E 188
Goageb, Namibia 26°45' S, 17°12' E 227
Goalpara, India 26°7' N, 90°34' E 197
Goaso, Ghana 6°49' N, 2°32' W 222
Goat Mountain, Mont., U.S. 47°17' N, 113°26' W 90
Goat, river, Can. 49°10' N, 116°12' W 90
Goathland, U.K. 54°24' N, 0°44' E 162
Goba, Eth. 6°58' N, 39°55' E 224
Gobabis, Namibia 22°27' S, 18°58' E 227
Gobernador Crespo, Arg. 30°21' S, 60°24' W 139
Gobernador Duval, Arg. 38°42' S, 66°26' W 134
Gobernador Gregores, Arg. 48°45' S, 70°16' W 134
Gobernador Ingeniero Valentín Virasoro, Arg. 28°3' S, 56°3' W 139
Gobi, Asia 41°49' N, 103°50' E 198
Gobles, Mich., U.S. 42°20' N, 85°52' W 102
Gobō, Japan 33°53' N, 135°9' E 201
Goch, Ger. 51°40' N, 6°10' E 167
Gochang, S. Korea 35°26' N, 126°42' E 200
Gochas, Namibia 24°51' S, 18°44' E 227
Godalming, U.K. 51°11' N, 0°37' E 162
Godbout, Can. 49°19' N, 67°38' W 82
Godda, India 24°49' N, 87°13' E 197
Goddard, Can. 56°50' N, 135°19' W 108
Godeanu, peak, Rom. 45°16' N, 22°38' E 168

Godech, *Bulg.* 43°0' N, 23°4' E 168
Godere, *Eth.* 5°2' N, 43°59' E 218
Goderich, *Can.* 43°43' N, 81°42' W 102
Godfrey, *Mo., U.S.* 38°57' N, 90°12' W 94
Godfrey Tank, spring, *Austral.* 20°15' S, 126°34' E 230
Godhavn see Qeqertarsuaq, *Den.* 69°15' N, 53°30' W 106
Godhra, *India* 22°46' N, 73°35' E 186
Gödöll o, *Hung.* 47°35' N, 19°21' E 168
Gods Lake, *Can.* 54°38' N, 94°12' W 108
Gods, river, *Can.* 55°18' N, 93°23' W 108
Godthåb see Nuuk, *Greenland, Den.* 64°14' N, 51°38' W 106
Godwin Austen see K2, peak, *Pak.* 35°51' N, 76°25' E 186
Godzikowice, *Pol.* 50°54' N, 17°19' E 152
Goéland, Lac au, lake, *Can.* 49°36' N, 78°10' W 81
Goélands, Lac aux, lake, *Can.* 55°13' N, 66°38' W 106
Goes, *Neth.* 51°30' N, 3°52' E 163
Goffstown, *N.H., U.S.* 43°1' N, 71°37' W 104
Gog Magog Hills, *U.K.* 52°4' N, 0°10' E 162
Gogama, *Can.* 47°40' N, 81°43' W 94
Gogebic Range, *Mich., U.S.* 46°32' N, 90°10' W 94
Göggingen, *Ger.* 48°20' N, 10°52' E 152
Gogland, island, *Russ.* 60°6' N, 26°43' E 166
Gogói, *Mozambique* 20°19' S, 33°8' E 227
Gogounou, *Benin* 10°46' N, 2°47' E 222
Gogrial, *Sudan* 8°29' N, 28°7' E 224
Goha, *Eth.* 10°19' N, 34°33' E 224
Gohad, *India* 26°24' N, 78°26' E 197
Goheung, *S. Korea* 34°35' N, 127°18' E 200
Goiandira, *Braz.* 18°10' S, 48°7' W 138
Goianésia, *Braz.* 15°22' S, 49°9' W 138
Goiânia, *Braz.* 16°43' S, 49°17' W 138
Goianinha, *Braz.* 6°17' S, 35°11' W 132
Goiás, *Braz.* 15°55' S, 50°6' W 138
Goiás, adm. division, *Braz.* 16°18' S, 50°32' W 138
Goiatuba, *Braz.* 18°5' S, 49°24' W 138
Goio Erê, *Braz.* 24°12' S, 53°3' W 138
Goioxim, *Braz.* 25°13' S, 52°2' W 138
Goito, *It.* 45°15' N, 10°40' E 167
Gojeb, river, *Eth.* 7°10' N, 36°58' E 224
Gök, river, *Turk.* 41°38' N, 34°30' E 156
Goka, *Japan* 36°18' N, 133°14' E 201
Gokase, river, *Japan* 32°38' N, 131°16' E 201
Gökçeada, island, *Turk.* 39°55' N, 25°30' E 180
Gökdepe, *Turkm.* 38°9' N, 57°58' E 180
Göksu, river, *Turk.* 37°3' N, 32°40' E 156
Göksu, river, *Turk.* 37°56' N, 36°21' E 156
Göksun, *Turk.* 38°2' N, 36°29' E 156
Gokwe, *Zimb.* 18°13' S, 28°57' E 224
Gol, *Nor.* 60°42' N, 8°53' E 152
Gol Bax, *Somalia* 0°19' N, 41°36' E 224
Golaghat, *India* 26°34' N, 93°55' E 188
Golan Heights, region, *Asia* 32°56' N, 35°38' E 194
Gölbaşı, *Turk.* 39°47' N, 32°48' E 156
Golconda, *Nev., U.S.* 40°57' N, 117°30' W 90
Gölcük, *Turk.* 40°43' N, 29°48' E 158
Gold Bar, *Wash., U.S.* 47°50' N, 121°41' W 100
Gold Beach, *Oreg., U.S.* 42°24' N, 124°26' W 82
Gold Coast, *Austral.* 27°58' S, 153°23' E 231
Gold Coast, region, *Africa* 5°10' N, 2°17' W 222
Gold Hill, *Nev., U.S.* 39°17' N, 119°40' W 92
Gold Mines, site, *Egypt* 22°37' N, 33°13' E 182
Gold Rock, *Can.* 49°27' N, 92°42' W 90
Gołdap, *Pol.* 54°17' N, 22°17' E 154
Golden, *Can.* 51°18' N, 116°58' W 108
Golden Hinde, peak, *Can.* 49°38' N, 125°50' W 90
Golden Meadow, *La., U.S.* 29°22' N, 90°17' W 103
Goldendale, *Wash., U.S.* 45°48' N, 120°49' W 90
Goldfield, *Iowa, U.S.* 42°43' N, 93°55' W 94
Goldfield, *Nev., U.S.* 37°40' N, 117°14' W 82
Goldonna, *La., U.S.* 32°0' N, 92°55' W 103
Goldpines, *Can.* 50°39' N, 93°11' W 90
Goldsboro, *N.C., U.S.* 35°23' N, 78°1' W 96
Goldsmith, *Tex., U.S.* 31°57' N, 102°37' W 92
Goldsmith Channel 73°5' N, 111°1' W 106
Goldthwaite, *Tex., U.S.* 31°26' N, 98°34' W 92
Göle, *Turk.* 40°47' N, 42°35' E 195
Golela, *Swaziland* 27°16' S, 31°55' E 227
Goleta, *Calif., U.S.* 34°26' N, 119°51' W 100
Golfito, *C.R.* 8°39' N, 83°11' W 115
Goliad, *Tex., U.S.* 28°39' N, 97°23' W 96
Gölköy, *Turk.* 40°42' N, 37°37' E 156
Golmud, *China* 36°19' N, 94°52' E 190
Golmud, river, *China* 35°44' N, 95°6' E 188
Golondrina, *Arg.* 28°32' S, 60°4' W 139
Gölören, *Turk.* 37°52' N, 33°51' E 156
Golovin, *Alas., U.S.* 64°27' N, 162°59' W 98
Golpāyegān, *Iran* 33°28' N, 50°14' E 180
Gölpazarı, *Turk.* 40°16' N, 30°18' E 158
Golran, *Afghan.* 35°7' N, 61°41' E 186
Golubac, *Serb.* 44°38' N, 21°37' E 168
Golubovci, *Mont.* 42°21' N, 19°13' E 168
Golūboyka, *Kaz.* 53°7' N, 74°12' E 184
Golyam Perelik, peak, *Bulg.* 41°35' N, 24°29' E 156
Golyshmanovo, *Russ.* 56°22' N, 68°24' E 184
Goma, *Dem. Rep. of the Congo* 1°41' S, 29°11' E 224
Gómara, *Sp.* 41°36' N, 2°14' W 164
Gombari, *Dem. Rep. of the Congo* 2°43' N, 29°5' E 224
Gombe, *Nig.* 10°15' N, 11°7' E 222
Gombe National Park, *Tanzania* 4°47' S, 29°34' E 224
Gomera, island, *Sp.* 28°6' N, 18°13' W 214
Gómez Farías, *Mex.* 24°56' N, 101°2' W 114
Gómez Palacio, *Mex.* 25°34' N, 103°31' W 114
Gomīshān, *Iran* 37°4' N, 53°59' E 180
Gomo, *China* 33°57' N, 85°19' E 188
Gomo Co, lake, *China* 34°1' N, 84°47' E 188
Gomoh, *India* 23°51' N, 86°9' E 197
Gomotartsi, *Bulg.* 44°4' N, 22°58' E 168
Gomphi, ruin(s), *Gr.* 39°24' N, 21°30' E 156
Gomshasar, Mt. (Gyamish), peak, *Azerb.* 40°17' N, 46°19' E 195
Gonam, *Russ.* 57°15' N, 130°53' E 160
Gonarezhou National Park, *Zimb.* 21°50' S, 31°35' E 227
Gonâve, Île de la, island, *Haiti* 19°1' N, 74°5' W 116
Gonbad-e Kāvūs, *Iran* 37°22' N, 55°18' E 180
Gonda, *India* 27°7' N, 81°58' E 197
Gondal, *India* 21°57' N, 70°47' E 186
Gonder, *Eth.* 12°34' N, 37°25' E 182
Gondey, *Chad* 9°4' N, 19°21' E 218
Gondia, *India* 21°27' N, 80°10' E 188
Gondola, *Mozambique* 19°10' S, 33°38' E 224
Gondrecourt, *Fr.* 48°30' N, 5°31' E 163
Gönen, *Turk.* 40°6' N, 27°38' E 156
Gong'an, *China* 30°1' N, 112°11' E 198
Gongbo'gyamda, *China* 29°55' N, 93°0' E 190
Gongcheng, *China* 24°52' N, 110°45' E 198
Gongga Shan, peak, *China* 29°38' N, 101°36' E 190
Gonggar, *China* 29°17' N, 90°48' E 197
Gongju, *S. Korea* 36°25' N, 127°9' E 200
Gonglee, *Liberia* 5°43' N, 9°27' W 222
Gongliu, *China* 43°25' N, 82°18' E 184
Gongola, river, *Nig.* 11°5' N, 11°29' E 222
Gongoúe, *Gabon* 0°33' N, 9°15' E 218
Gongxi, *China* 27°38' N, 115°51' E 198
Gongzhuling, *China* 43°30' N, 124°52' E 198
Goniądz, *Pol.* 53°28' N, 22°43' E 158
Gonja, *Tanzania* 4°21' S, 38°5' E 224
Gonjo, *China* 30°52' N, 98°16' E 188
Gōno, river, *Japan* 34°53' N, 132°27' E 201
Gōnoura, *Japan* 33°44' N, 129°41' E 201
Gonzales, *Calif., U.S.* 36°30' N, 121°28' W 100
Gonzales, *La., U.S.* 30°13' N, 90°56' W 103
Gonzales, *Tex., U.S.* 29°29' N, 97°27' W 96
González, *Mex.* 22°48' N, 98°26' W 114
González Chaves, *Arg.* 38°4' S, 60°6' W 139
González Moreno, *Arg.* 35°32' S, 63°20' W 139
Good Hope, Cape of, *S. Af.* 34°33' S, 12°22' E 206
Good Hope Mountain, *Can.* 51°9' N, 124°15' W 90
Good Pine, *La., U.S.* 31°40' N, 92°11' W 103
Goodenough, Cape, *Antarctica* 65°58' S, 126°13' E 248
Goodenough Island, *P.N.G.* 9°15' S, 149°59' E 192
Goodenough, Mount, *Can.* 67°56' N, 135°41' W 98
Goodhouse, *S. Af.* 28°57' S, 18°14' E 227
Gooding, *Idaho, U.S.* 42°57' N, 114°43' W 90
Goodland, *Fla., U.S.* 25°55' N, 81°41' W 105
Goodland, *Ind., U.S.* 40°45' N, 87°18' W 102
Goodland, *Kans., U.S.* 39°20' N, 101°42' W 82
Goodman, *Miss., U.S.* 32°56' N, 89°56' W 103
Goodman, *Wis., U.S.* 45°37' N, 88°22' W 94
Goodnews Bay, *Alas., U.S.* 59°8' N, 161°31' W 106
Goodrich, *Tex., U.S.* 30°35' N, 94°57' W 103
Goodridge, *Minn., U.S.* 48°8' N, 95°50' W 90
Goodsir, Mount, *Can.* 51°11' N, 116°28' W 90
Goodsoil, *Can.* 54°22' N, 109°15' W 108
Goodsprings, *Nev., U.S.* 35°49' N, 115°27' W 101
Goodwell, *Okla., U.S.* 36°34' N, 101°39' W 92
Goole, *U.K.* 53°42' N, 0°54' E 162
Goondiwindi, *Austral.* 28°30' S, 150°21' E 231
Goonhilly Downs, site, *U.K.* 50°0' N, 5°18' W 150
Goor, *Neth.* 52°14' N, 6°35' E 163
Goose, Lac, lake, *Can.* 53°3' N, 74°38' W 111
Goose Lake, *Calif., U.S.* 41°58' N, 121°18' W 81
Goose Lake, *Can.* 51°43' N, 107°47' W 90
Goose, river, *Can.* 54°54' N, 117°3' W 108
Goose Rocks Beach, *Me., U.S.* 43°24' N, 70°25' W 104
Goosenest, peak, *Calif., U.S.* 41°42' N, 122°19' W 90
Gooseprairie, *Wash., U.S.* 46°53' N, 121°17' W 100
Gooty, *India* 15°6' N, 77°40' E 188
Gop, *India* 22°3' N, 69°54' E 186
Gor, *Sp.* 37°21' N, 2°58' W 164
Gorakhpur, *India* 26°43' N, 83°21' E 197
Goranci, *Bosn. and Herzg.* 43°25' N, 17°43' E 168
Goransko, *Mont.* 43°7' N, 18°50' E 168
Goražde, *Bosn. and Herzg.* 43°40' N, 18°58' E 168
Gorbukova, *Russ.* 59°31' N, 89°33' E 169
Gorda, Punta, *Calif., U.S.* 40°5' N, 124°41' W 90
Gorda, Punta, *Nicar.* 14°13' N, 84°2' W 115
Gördalen, *Nor.* 61°35' N, 12°28' E 152
Gordion, ruin(s), *Turk.* 39°35' N, 31°52' E 156
Gordo, *Ala., U.S.* 33°17' N, 87°54' W 103
Gordon, *Nebr., U.S.* 42°47' N, 102°13' W 90
Gordon, *Wis., U.S.* 46°13' N, 91°49' W 94
Gordon Horne Peak, *Can.* 51°47' N, 118°55' W 90
Gordon Lake, *Can.* 56°23' N, 111°4' W 108
Gordondale, *Can.* 55°50' N, 119°34' W 108
Gordon's, *Bahamas* 22°52' N, 74°52' W 116
Goré, *Chad* 7°54' N, 16°38' E 218
Gorē, *Eth.* 8°10' N, 35°31' E 224
Gore, *N.Z.* 46°7' S, 168°56' E 240
Gore Bay, *Can.* 45°55' N, 82°29' W 94
Gore Mountain, *Vt., U.S.* 44°54' N, 71°53' W 94
Gore Range, *Colo., U.S.* 40°5' N, 106°44' W 90
Gorecki, Mount, *Antarctica* 83°23' S, 59°14' W 248
Goree, *Tex., U.S.* 33°27' N, 99°32' W 92
Görele, *Turk.* 41°2' N, 38°59' E 158
Gorey, *Ire.* 49°11' N, 2°3' W 150
Gorgān, *Iran* 36°50' N, 54°25' E 180
Gorgonta, *Arg.* 33°48' S, 66°45' W 134
Gorgora, *Eth.* 12°13' N, 37°17' E 182
Gorgova, *Rom.* 45°10' N, 29°10' E 156
Gorguz, *Mex.* 28°53' N, 111°10' W 92
Gorham, *Me., U.S.* 43°40' N, 70°27' W 104
Gori, *Ga.* 41°57' N, 44°8' E 195
Gori Rit, *Somalia* 8°0' N, 48°8' E 218
Gorinchem, *Neth.* 51°49' N, 4°59' E 167
Goris, *Arm.* 39°30' N, 46°20' E 195
Gorizia, *It.* 45°56' N, 13°36' E 167
Gorj, adm. division, *Rom.* 44°42' N, 23°8' E 156
Gorjani, *Croatia* 45°23' N, 18°21' E 168
Gorkha, *Nepal* 28°2' N, 84°40' E 197
Gorki, *Russ.* 65°4' N, 65°29' E 169
Gorleston, *U.K.* 52°34' N, 1°42' E 163
Görlitz, *Ger.* 51°8' N, 14°58' E 152
Gorman, *Calif., U.S.* 34°45' N, 118°49' W 101
Gorman, *Tex., U.S.* 32°12' N, 98°41' W 92
Gornja Tuzla, *Bosn. and Herzg.* 44°34' N, 18°44' E 168
Gornji Muć, *Croatia* 43°41' N, 16°25' E 168
Gornji Vakuf (Uskoplje), *Bosn. and Herzg.* 43°55' N, 17°33' E 168
Gorno Altaysk, *Russ.* 51°57' N, 86°2' E 184
Gorno-Altay, adm. division, *Russ.* 50°43' N, 85°39' E 184
Gornozavodsk, *Russ.* 46°32' N, 141°52' E 190
Gornyak, *Russ.* 51°0' N, 81°30' E 184
Gornyatskiy, *Russ.* 67°31' N, 64°13' E 169
Gornyy, *Russ.* 51°43' N, 48°36' E 158
Gornyy Balykley, *Russ.* 49°35' N, 45°0' E 158
Goro, river, *Cen. Af. Rep.* 9°13' N, 21°36' E 218
Gorodets, *Russ.* 58°30' N, 29°47' E 166
Gorodets, *Russ.* 56°37' N, 43°35' E 154
Gorodishche, *Russ.* 53°16' N, 45°45' E 154
Gorodishche, *Russ.* 58°14' N, 29°53' E 166
Gorodovikovsk, *Russ.* 46°4' N, 41°48' E 158
Gorom Gorom, *Burkina Faso* 14°27' N, 0°15' E 222
Gorong, Kepulauan, islands, *Banda Sea* 4°39' S, 130°39' E 192
Gorongosa National Park, *Mozambique* 19°13' S, 34°35' E 224
Gorongosa, Serra da, peak, *Mozambique* 18°27' S, 34°0' E 224
Gorontalo, *Indonesia* 0°38' N, 123°2' E 192
Gortyn, ruin(s), *Gr.* 35°3' N, 24°50' E 156
Gorutuba, river, *Braz.* 15°10' S, 43°32' W 138
Goryachiy Klyuch, *Russ.* 44°37' N, 39°6' E 156
Gorzów Wielkopolski, *Pol.* 52°44' N, 15°15' E 152
Górzyca, *Pol.* 52°29' N, 14°40' E 152
Goschen Strait 10°40' S, 150°46' E 192
Gosen, *Japan* 37°43' N, 139°10' E 201
Goseong, *S. Korea* 34°58' N, 128°19' E 200
Gosford, *Austral.* 33°23' S, 151°20' E 231
Gosforth, *U.K.* 54°25' N, 3°26' W 162
Goshen, *Calif., U.S.* 36°21' N, 119°26' W 100
Goshen, *N.H., U.S.* 43°18' N, 72°9' W 104
Goshen, *Utah, U.S.* 39°56' N, 111°54' W 90
Goshute Mountains, *Nev., U.S.* 40°27' N, 114°29' W 90
Gospić, *Croatia* 44°32' N, 15°21' E 156
Gosport, *Ind., U.S.* 39°20' N, 86°40' W 102
Goss, *Miss., U.S.* 31°20' N, 89°54' W 103
Gosselies, *Belg.* 50°28' N, 4°26' E 167
Gossinga, *Sudan* 8°38' N, 25°57' E 224
Gostilje, *Serb.* 43°39' N, 19°50' E 168
Gostiņi, *Latv.* 56°36' N, 25°46' E 166
Gostivar, *Maced.* 41°47' N, 20°54' E 168
Gota, *Eth.* 9°31' N, 41°21' E 224
Götaland, region, *Europe* 58°8' N, 10°51' E 150
Göteborg, *Nor.* 57°41' N, 11°57' E 152
Gotha, *Ger.* 50°57' N, 10°42' E 152
Gothenburg, *Nebr., U.S.* 40°56' N, 100°11' W 92
Gothèye, *Niger* 13°49' N, 1°31' E 222
Gotland, island, *Sw.* 57°33' N, 18°49' E 166
Gotska Sandön, island, *Sw.* 58°24' N, 19°12' E 166
Gotska Sandön National Park, *Sw.* 58°12' N, 19°28' E 166
Gōtsu, *Japan* 35°0' N, 132°13' E 200
Göttingen, *Ger.* 51°32' N, 9°55' E 167
Goubéré, *Cen. Af. Rep.* 5°50' N, 26°43' E 224
Gouda, *Neth.* 52°0' N, 4°42' E 167
Goudiry, *Senegal* 14°10' N, 12°45' W 222
Goudoumaria, *Niger* 13°43' N, 11°8' E 222
Gouéké, *Guinea* 7°57' N, 8°43' W 222
Gouin, Réservoir, lake, *Can.* 48°18' N, 76°31' W 106
Gouin, Réservoir, lake, *Can.* 48°18' N, 76°42' W 81
Goulais, river, *Can.* 46°44' N, 84°41' W 110
Goulburn, *Austral.* 34°46' S, 149°45' E 231
Goulburn Islands, *Arafura Sea* 11°36' S, 133°38' E 192
Gould, *Ark., U.S.* 33°58' N, 91°35' W 96
Gould Bay 77°46' S, 49°17' W 248
Gould Coast, *Antarctica* 84°15' S, 127°3' W 248
Gouldsboro, *Me., U.S.* 44°28' N, 68°3' W 111
Goulimine, *Mor.* 28°57' N, 10°5' W 143
Goulmima, *Mor.* 31°43' N, 4°57' W 214
Goumbou, *Mali* 14°58' N, 7°27' W 222
Gouméré, *Côte d'Ivoire* 7°55' N, 3°0' W 222
Gounarou, *Benin* 10°51' N, 2°49' E 222
Goundam, *Mali* 16°24' N, 3°41' W 222
Goundi, *Chad* 9°20' N, 17°21' E 216
Gounou Gaya, *Chad* 9°39' N, 15°28' E 216
Gouradi, spring, *Chad* 16°24' N, 17°11' E 216
Gouré, *Niger* 14°0' N, 10°15' E 222
Gouring, spring, *Chad* 18°44' N, 19°8' E 216
Gourlay Lake, *Can.* 48°51' N, 85°29' W 94
Gourma, region, *Africa* 12°15' N, 2°118' W 222
Gourma Rharous, *Mali* 16°52' N, 1°55' W 222
Gournay, *Fr.* 49°28' N, 1°43' E 163
Gournia, ruin(s), *Gr.* 35°5' N, 25°42' E 156
Gouro, *Chad* 19°32' N, 19°33' E 216
Gove, *Kans., U.S.* 38°58' N, 100°29' W 90
Govena, Mys, *Russ.* 59°34' N, 165°28' E 160
Governador Valadares, *Braz.* 18°51' S, 41°55' W 138
Governor's Harbour, adm. division, *Bahamas* 25°18' N, 77°33' W 116
Govĭsümber, adm. division, *Mongolia* 46°22' N, 108°22' E 198
Gowanda, *N.Y., U.S.* 42°27' N, 78°57' W 94
Gowen, *Okla., U.S.* 34°51' N, 95°29' W 96
Gower Peninsula, *U.K.* 51°36' N, 4°6' W 162
Gowganda, *Can.* 47°38' N, 80°45' W 110
Gowmal Kalay, *Afghan.* 32°28' N, 69°0' E 186
Goya, *Arg.* 29°10' S, 59°16' W 139
Göyçay, *Azerb.* 40°38' N, 47°44' E 195
Goyeau, Pointe, *Can.* 51°37' N, 78°58' W 110
Goyelle, Lac, lake, *Can.* 50°43' N, 61°15' W 111
Göynük, *Turk.* 40°24' N, 30°48' E 156
Goz Beïda, *Chad* 12°13' N, 21°25' E 216
Goz Pass, *Can.* 64°31' N, 132°24' W 98
Goz Regeb, *Sudan* 16°1' N, 35°34' E 182
Gozo, island, *Malta* 36°4' N, 13°38' E 216
Graaff-Reinet, *S. Af.* 32°17' S, 24°27' E 227
Graafwater, *S. Af.* 32°9' S, 18°34' E 227
Grabo, *Côte d'Ivoire* 4°55' N, 7°30' W 214
Grabovac, *Serb.* 44°35' N, 20°5' E 168
Gračanica, *Bosn. and Herzg.* 44°42' N, 18°17' E 168
Grace, Mount, *Mass., U.S.* 42°41' N, 72°23' W 104
Gracefield, *Can.* 46°6' N, 76°3' W 94
Graceville, *Minn., U.S.* 45°33' N, 96°28' W 90
Grachevka, *Russ.* 52°54' N, 52°54' E 158
Gracias a Dios, Cabo, *Nicar.* 14°51' N, 83°10' W 115
Gradac, *Mont.* 43°22' N, 19°9' E 168
Gradačac, *Bosn. and Herzg.* 44°53' N, 18°25' E 168
Gradaús, *Braz.* 7°41' S, 51°11' W 130
Gradaús, Serra dos, *Braz.* 8°20' S, 51°0' W 130
Gradisca d'Isonzo, *It.* 45°54' N, 13°30' E 167
Gradište, *Croatia* 45°8' N, 18°42' E 168
Grado, *It.* 45°41' N, 13°23' E 167
Gradsko, *Maced.* 41°34' N, 21°57' E 168
Gräfenhainichen, *Ger.* 51°44' N, 12°27' E 152
Grafing, *Ger.* 48°2' N, 11°58' E 152
Graford, *Tex., U.S.* 32°55' N, 98°15' W 92
Grafton, *N. Dak., U.S.* 48°23' N, 97°27' W 90
Grafton, *Vt., U.S.* 43°10' N, 72°37' W 104
Grafton, *W. Va., U.S.* 39°20' N, 80°2' W 94
Grafton, *Wis., U.S.* 43°18' N, 87°58' W 102
Grafton, Mount, *Nev., U.S.* 38°40' N, 114°50' W 90
Grafton Notch, pass, *Me., U.S.* 44°35' N, 70°56' W 104
Graham, *Can.* 49°15' N, 90°34' W 94
Graham, *Tex., U.S.* 33°5' N, 98°34' W 92
Graham Bell, Ostrov, island, *Russ.* 81°26' N, 63°57' E 160
Graham Island, *Can.* 54°11' N, 133°54' W 98
Graham Lake, *Can.* 56°30' N, 115°16' W 108
Graham, Mount, *Ariz., U.S.* 32°41' N, 109°56' W 92
Graham, river, *Can.* 56°31' N, 123°55' W 108
Grahamstown, *S. Af.* 33°18' S, 26°29' E 227
Grahovo, *Mont.* 42°38' N, 18°40' E 168
Graian Alps, *It.* 45°31' N, 6°43' E 165
Grain Coast, region, *Africa* 5°23' N, 9°22' W 222
Grajal de Campos, *Sp.* 42°18' N, 5°3' W 150
Grajaú, river, *Braz.* 5°19' S, 46°2' W 130
Gramada, *Bulg.* 43°50' N, 22°39' E 168
Gramado, *Braz.* 29°20' S, 50°50' W 139
Gramercy, *La., U.S.* 30°3' N, 90°42' W 103
Grámos, Óros, *Gr.* 40°11' N, 20°38' E 156
Grampian Mountains, *U.K.* 56°38' N, 5°6' W 150
Gran, *Nor.* 60°21' N, 10°34' E 152
Gran Bajo de San Julián, *Arg.* 49°23' S, 70°59' W 134
Gran Canaria, island, *Sp.* 27°21' N, 15°22' W 214
Gran Chaco, region, *Parag.* 21°5' S, 61°33' W 134
Gran Morelos, *Mex.* 28°14' N, 106°33' W 92
Gran Pajonal, region, *South America* 10°40' S, 74°28' W 130
Gran Paradiso, peak, *It.* 45°31' N, 7°13' E 165
Gran Sabana, La, *Venez.* 5°4' N, 62°25' W 130
Gran Sasso d'Italia, *It.* 42°24' N, 13°13' E 156
Gran Tarajal, *Sp.* 28°14' N, 14°3' W 214
Granada, *Col.* 3°31' N, 73°44' W 136
Granada, *Colo., U.S.* 38°3' N, 102°19' W 90
Granada, *Nicar.* 11°55' N, 85°59' W 115
Granada, *Sp.* 37°13' N, 3°39' W 143
Granada, *Sp.* 37°11' N, 3°36' W 164
Granadero Gatica, *Arg.* 26°52' S, 62°42' W 139
Granados, *Mex.* 29°51' N, 109°21' W 92
Granbori, *Suriname* 3°48' N, 54°54' W 130
Granbury, *Tex., U.S.* 32°26' N, 97°46' W 92
Granby, *Colo., U.S.* 40°4' N, 105°56' W 90
Granby, *Mass., U.S.* 42°15' N, 72°31' W 104
Granby, *Vt., U.S.* 44°34' N, 71°46' W 104
Grand Bahama, island, *Bahamas* 27°0' N, 78°0' W 118
Grand Bank, *Can.* 47°4' N, 55°48' W 111
Grand Banks of Newfoundland, *North Atlantic Ocean* 45°14' N, 52°41' W 253
Grand Bend, *Can.* 43°18' N, 81°44' W 102
Grand Blanc, *Mich., U.S.* 42°55' N, 83°37' W 102
Grand Cane, *La., U.S.* 32°4' N, 93°49' W 103
Grand Canyon, *Ariz., U.S.* 35°46' N, 113°37' W 101
Grand Canyon National Park, *Ariz., U.S.* 35°50' N, 114°11' W 101
Grand Cayman, island, *U.K.* 19°0' N, 81°0' W 118
Grand Centre, *Can.* 54°23' N, 110°14' W 108
Grand Cess, *Liberia* 4°40' N, 8°11' W 214
Grand Chenier, *La., U.S.* 29°45' N, 92°58' W 103
Grand Coteau, *La., U.S.* 30°24' N, 92°2' W 103
Grand Coulee, *Wash., U.S.* 47°48' N, 119°24' W 90
Grand Coulee, *Wash., U.S.* 47°55' N, 119°1' W 90
Grand Falls, *Can.* 47°1' N, 67°47' W 94
Grand Falls-Windsor, *Can.* 48°53' N, 55°42' W 106
Grand Forks, *Can.* 49°1' N, 118°28' W 108
Grand Forks, *N. Dak., U.S.* 47°53' N, 97°3' W 90
Grand Forks Air Force Base, *N. Dak., U.S.* 47°56' N, 97°31' W 90
Grand Haven, *Mich., U.S.* 43°2' N, 86°14' W 102
Grand Island, *Nebr., U.S.* 40°54' N, 98°22' W 90
Grand Isle, *La., U.S.* 29°15' N, 90°0' W 103
Grand Junction, *Colo., U.S.* 39°4' N, 108°34' W 90
Grand Junction, *Mich., U.S.* 42°23' N, 86°4' W 102
Grand Lake, *Can.* 46°3' N, 66°25' W 94
Grand Lake, *La., U.S.* 29°46' N, 91°28' W 103
Grand Lake, *La., U.S.* 30°0' N, 93°16' W 103
Grand Ledge, *Mich., U.S.* 42°44' N, 84°46' W 102
Grand Manan Island, island, *Can.* 44°42' N, 66°47' W 111
Grand Marais, *Can.* 50°31' N, 96°34' W 90
Grand Marais, *Mich., U.S.* 46°39' N, 86°0' W 94

Grand Marais, *Minn., U.S.* 47°45′ N, 90°23′ W 94
Grand Mesa, *Colo., U.S.* 38°57′ N, 108°22′ W 90
Grand Popo, *Benin* 6°17′ N, 1°51′ E 222
Grand Portage, *Minn., U.S.* 47°57′ N, 89°45′ W 82
Grand Portal Point, *Mich., U.S.* 46°14′ N, 86°30′ W 94
Grand Prairie, *Tex., U.S.* 32°43′ N, 96°58′ W 92
Grand Rapids, *Can.* 53°10′ N, 99°20′ W 108
Grand Rapids, *Mich., U.S.* 42°56′ N, 85°40′ W 102
Grand Rapids, *Minn., U.S.* 47°13′ N, 93°32′ W 90
Grand Ridge, *Ill., U.S.* 41°14′ N, 88°50′ W 102
Grand, river, *Mich., U.S.* 42°57′ N, 85°46′ W 80
Grand, river, *Mo., U.S.* 40°15′ N, 94°24′ W 80
Grand, river, *S. Dak., U.S.* 45°40′ N, 101°46′ W 90
Grand Saline, *Tex., U.S.* 32°39′ N, 95°43′ W 96
Grand-Santi, *Fr.* 4°20′ N, 54°23′ W 130
Grand Teton, peak, *Wyo., U.S.* 43°42′ N, 110°53′ W 90
Grand Traverse Bay 44°59′ N, 86°0′ W 110
Grandas, *Sp.* 43°12′ N, 6°54′ W 150
Grand-Bassam, *Côte d'Ivoire* 5°13′ N, 3°46′ W 222
Grande, Bahía 51°3′ S, 70°13′ W 134
Grande, Baía, lake, *Bol.* 15°28′ S, 60°41′ W 132
Grande Cache, *Can.* 53°53′ N, 119°10′ W 108
Grande Cayemite, island, *Haiti* 18°33′ N, 73°42′ W 116
Grande, Cayo, island, *Cuba* 20°40′ N, 79°37′ W 116
Grande, Cayo, island, *Venez.* 11°32′ N, 66°37′ W 116
Grande, Corno, peak, *It.* 42°27′ N, 13°29′ E 156
Grande, Cuchilla, *Uru.* 33°58′ S, 56°15′ W 139
Grande de Lípez, river, *Bol.* 22°0′ S, 67°21′ W 137
Grande Prairie, *Can.* 55°10′ N, 118°49′ W 108
Grande, Punta, *Chile* 25°7′ S, 70°31′ W 132
Grande, river, *Braz.* 20°30′ S, 48°51′ W 138
Grande, river, *Braz.* 13°5′ S, 45°35′ W 138
Grande, river, *Can.* 48°40′ N, 65°15′ W 111
Grande, Serra, *Braz.* 10°11′ S, 61°36′ W 130
Grande, Serra (Carauna), peak, *Braz.* 2°34′ N, 60°46′ W 130
Grande Sertão Veredas National Park, *Braz.* 15°32′ S, 46°6′ W 138
Grande, Sierra, *Mex.* 29°42′ N, 105°8′ W 112
Grande-Terre, island, *Fr.* 16°32′ N, 61°28′ W 116
Grandfalls, *Tex., U.S.* 31°19′ N, 102°51′ W 92
Grandfather Mountain, *N.C., U.S.* 36°5′ N, 81°54′ W 96
Grandfield, *Okla., U.S.* 34°12′ N, 98°41′ W 92
Grand-Fort-Philippe, *Fr.* 50°59′ N, 2°5′ E 163
Grand-Lahou, *Côte d'Ivoire* 5°8′ N, 5°2′ W 222
Grandpré, *Fr.* 49°20′ N, 4°51′ E 163
Grandview, *Can.* 51°9′ N, 100°43′ W 90
Grandview, *Wash., U.S.* 46°14′ N, 119°55′ W 90
Grandvilliers, *Fr.* 49°39′ N, 1°56′ E 163
Grañén, *Sp.* 41°56′ N, 0°22′ E 164
Grange, *U.K.* 54°10′ N, 2°56′ W 162
Granger, *Ind., U.S.* 41°44′ N, 86°7′ W 102
Granger, *Tex., U.S.* 30°41′ N, 97°27′ W 92
Granger, *Wyo., U.S.* 41°36′ N, 109°58′ W 90
Granges, *Fr.* 48°8′ N, 6°47′ E 163
Grangeville, *Idaho, U.S.* 45°53′ N, 116°7′ W 82
Granisle, *Can.* 54°54′ N, 126°18′ W 108
Granite, *Okla., U.S.* 34°56′ N, 99°24′ W 92
Granite Falls, *Minn., U.S.* 44°46′ N, 95°34′ W 90
Granite Falls, *Wash., U.S.* 48°4′ N, 121°58′ W 100
Granite Mountain, *Nev., U.S.* 40°16′ N, 117°54′ W 90
Granite Mountains, *Wyo., U.S.* 42°44′ N, 108°1′ W 90
Granite Pass, *Calif., U.S.* 35°25′ N, 116°35′ W 101
Granite Peak, *Mont., U.S.* 45°8′ N, 109°53′ W 90
Granite Peak, *Nev., U.S.* 41°38′ N, 117°41′ W 90
Granite Peak, *Nev., U.S.* 40°46′ N, 119°31′ W 90
Granite Peak, *Utah, U.S.* 40°6′ N, 113°20′ W 90
Granite Peak, *Wyo., U.S.* 42°32′ N, 108°57′ W 90
Granity, *N.Z.* 41°40′ S, 171°51′ E 240
Granja, *Braz.* 3°9′ S, 40°51′ W 132
Granja de Torrehermosa, *Sp.* 38°18′ N, 5°37′ W 164
Grankulla (Kauniainen), *Fin.* 60°11′ N, 24°43′ E 152
Granma, *Cuba* 19°51′ N, 77°33′ W 116
Gränna, *Nor.* 58°1′ N, 14°28′ E 152
Grannd Erg Oriental, *Alg.* 33°50′ N, 7°52′ E 156
Gransee, *Ger.* 53°1′ N, 13°8′ E 152
Grant, *Mich., U.S.* 43°19′ N, 85°49′ W 102
Grant, *Nebr., U.S.* 40°50′ N, 101°44′ W 90
Grant City, *Mo., U.S.* 40°27′ N, 94°25′ W 94
Grant Island, *Antarctica* 73°36′ S, 131°2′ W 248
Grant, Mount, *Nev., U.S.* 38°33′ N, 118°53′ W 90
Grant Range, *Nev., U.S.* 38°35′ N, 115°34′ W 90
Grantham, *N.H., U.S.* 43°29′ N, 72°8′ W 104
Grantham, *U.K.* 52°54′ N, 0°39′ E 162
Grant-Kohrs Ranch National Historic Site, *Mont., U.S.* 46°22′ N, 112°52′ W 90
Grants, *N. Mex., U.S.* 35°8′ N, 107°51′ W 112
Grants Pass, *Oreg., U.S.* 42°26′ N, 123°21′ W 90
Grantsburg, *Wis., U.S.* 45°45′ N, 92°41′ W 110
Grantsville, *W. Va., U.S.* 38°55′ N, 81°6′ W 102
Grantville, *Ga., U.S.* 33°13′ N, 84°51′ W 96
Granum, *Can.* 49°52′ N, 113°31′ W 90
Granville, *Fr.* 48°50′ N, 1°36′ W 150
Granville, *N. Dak., U.S.* 48°14′ N, 100°51′ W 90
Granville, *Vt., U.S.* 43°58′ N, 72°51′ W 104
Granville, *W. Va., U.S.* 39°38′ N, 80°0′ W 94
Granville Lake, *Can.* 56°16′ N, 101°37′ W 108
Granvin, *Nor.* 60°34′ N, 6°41′ E 152
Grão Mogol, *Braz.* 16°35′ S, 42°57′ W 138
Grapeland, *Tex., U.S.* 31°28′ N, 95°29′ W 103
Grapevine Mountains, *Calif., U.S.* 36°56′ N, 117°13′ W 101
Grapevine Peak, *Nev., U.S.* 36°57′ N, 117°11′ W 101
Graphite Peak, *Antarctica* 85°15′ S, 167°50′ E 248
Grapska Donja, *Bosn. and Herzg.* 44°47′ N, 18°4′ E 168
Graskop, *S. Af.* 24°58′ S, 30°50′ E 227
Grasmere, *U.K.* 54°27′ N, 3°1′ W 162
Gräsö, island, *Sw.* 60°26′ N, 18°25′ E 166
Grass, river, *Can.* 55°6′ N, 98°33′ W 108
Grass Valley, *Calif., U.S.* 39°12′ N, 121°5′ W 90
Grasset, Lac, lake, *Can.* 49°55′ N, 78°40′ W 94
Grassington, *U.K.* 54°4′ N, 1°59′ W 162
Grassland, *Can.* 54°48′ N, 112°42′ W 108
Grasslands National Park, *Can.* 48°54′ N, 108°0′ W 90
Grassrange, *Mont., U.S.* 47°0′ N, 108°48′ W 90
Grassy Butte, *N. Dak., U.S.* 47°22′ N, 103°17′ W 90
Grassy Island Lake, *Can.* 51°51′ N, 110°51′ W 90
Grassy Key, island, *Fla., U.S.* 24°43′ N, 80°55′ W 105
Grassy Mountain, *Oreg., U.S.* 42°37′ N, 117°25′ W 90
Grästorp, *Nor.* 58°19′ N, 12°39′ E 152
Grates Point, *Can.* 48°11′ N, 53°9′ W 111
Graton, *Calif., U.S.* 38°26′ N, 122°53′ W 92
Gråträsk, *Nor.* 65°28′ N, 19°45′ E 152
Graus, *Sp.* 42°10′ N, 0°19′ E 164
Grave, *Neth.* 51°45′ N, 5°43′ E 167
Grave Peak, *Idaho, U.S.* 46°22′ N, 114°49′ W 90
Gravedona, *It.* 46°9′ N, 9°17′ E 167
Gravelbourg, *Can.* 49°52′ N, 106°34′ W 90
Gravelines, *Fr.* 50°59′ N, 2°8′ E 163
Gravelotte, *S. Af.* 23°56′ S, 30°36′ E 227
Gravenhurst, *Can.* 44°54′ N, 79°22′ W 94
Gravesend, *U.K.* 51°25′ N, 0°21′ E 162
Gravette, *Ark., U.S.* 36°23′ N, 94°28′ W 96
Gravvik, *Nor.* 64°59′ N, 11°48′ E 152
Gray, *Me., U.S.* 43°53′ N, 70°20′ W 104
Gray, Mount, *Antarctica* 74°53′ S, 136°11′ W 248
Grayland, *Wash., U.S.* 46°47′ N, 124°6′ W 100
Grayling, *Alas., U.S.* 62°57′ N, 160°9′ W 98
Grayling, *Mich., U.S.* 44°40′ N, 84°43′ W 94
Grays, *U.K.* 51°29′ N, 0°20′ E 162
Grays Harbor 46°49′ N, 125°15′ W 80
Grays Peak, *Colo., U.S.* 39°36′ N, 105°54′ W 90
Grayslake, *Ill., U.S.* 42°20′ N, 88°3′ W 102
Grayson, *Ky., U.S.* 38°19′ N, 82°57′ W 94
Grayson, *La., U.S.* 32°2′ N, 92°7′ W 103
Grayville, *Mo., U.S.* 38°14′ N, 88°0′ W 94
Grayvoron, *Russ.* 50°28′ N, 35°39′ E 158
Graz, *Aust.* 47°4′ N, 15°26′ E 156
Grazie, Monte le, peak, *It.* 42°10′ N, 11°50′ E 156
Grdelica, *Serb.* 42°53′ N, 22°4′ E 168
Grea de Albarracín, *Sp.* 40°24′ N, 1°22′ W 164
Great Artesian Basin, *Australia* 22°45′ S, 142°18′ E 230
Great Australian Bight 37°7′ S, 130°17′ E 231
Great Badminton, *U.K.* 51°32′ N, 2°17′ W 162
Great Barrier Reef, *Coral Sea* 16°34′ S, 147°16′ E 252
Great Barrier Reef Marine Park, *Coral Sea* 19°12′ S, 147°53′ E 238
Great Barrington, *Mass., U.S.* 42°11′ N, 73°23′ W 104
Great Basalt Wall National Park, *Austral.* 20°7′ S, 144°57′ E 238
Great Basin, *North America* 36°22′ N, 114°27′ W 101
Great Basin National Park, *Nev., U.S.* 38°36′ N, 114°29′ W 90
Great Bear Lake, *Can.* 65°31′ N, 121°54′ W 106
Great Britain, island, *U.K.* 52°5′ N, 1°42′ W 143
Great Channel 6°12′ N, 93°33′ E 188
Great Corn Island see Maíz Grande, Isla del, *Nicar.* 11°44′ N, 83°2′ W 115
Great Crater, *Israel* 30°55′ N, 34°59′ E 194
Great Divide Basin, *Wyo., U.S.* 41°58′ N, 108°11′ W 90
Great Dividing Range, *Australia* 11°52′ S, 142°8′ E 192
Great Driffield, *U.K.* 54°0′ N, 0°26′ E 162
Great Exuma, island, *Bahamas* 23°23′ N, 76°30′ W 116
Great Eastern Erg, *Alg.* 30°0′ N, 7°0′ E 156
Great Falls, *Can.* 50°23′ N, 96°4′ W 90
Great Falls, *Mont., U.S.* 47°30′ N, 111°18′ W 90
Great Falls, *S.C., U.S.* 34°33′ N, 80°54′ W 96
Great Fish, river, *S. Af.* 33°1′ S, 25°53′ E 227
Great Guana Cay, island, *Bahamas* 23°53′ N, 76°37′ W 116
Great Harbour Cay, island, *Bahamas* 25°39′ N, 77°45′ W 81
Great Harbour Deep, *Can.* 50°22′ N, 56°33′ W 111
Great Inagua Island, *Bahamas* 21°14′ N, 73°53′ W 116
Great Indian Desert (Thar Desert), *India* 26°55′ N, 68°30′ E 187
Great Isaac, island, *Bahamas* 26°0′ N, 79°20′ W 105
Great Island, peak, *Can.* 58°59′ N, 96°42′ W 108
Great Islets Harbour 51°7′ N, 56°40′ W 111
Great Kei, river, *S. Af.* 32°22′ S, 27°54′ E 227
Great Lakes Naval Training Center, *Ill., U.S.* 42°17′ N, 87°54′ W 102
Great Namaland, region, *Africa* 26°5′ S, 14°59′ E 227
Great Nicobar, island, *India* 6°29′ N, 93°53′ E 188
Great Orme's Head, *U.K.* 53°20′ N, 4°0′ W 162
Great Ouse, river, *U.K.* 52°36′ N, 0°17′ E 162
Great Pedro Bluff, *Jam.* 17°45′ N, 78°41′ W 115
Great Point, *Mass., U.S.* 41°23′ N, 70°8′ W 104
Great Pond, lake, *Me., U.S.* 44°29′ N, 70°3′ W 104
Great Ruaha, river, *Tanzania* 7°21′ S, 35°14′ E 224
Great Sacandaga Lake, *N.Y., U.S.* 43°17′ N, 74°11′ W 104
Great Salt Lake, *Utah, U.S.* 41°16′ N, 113°26′ W 106
Great Salt Lake Desert, *Utah, U.S.* 40°26′ N, 113°47′ W 90
Great Salt Plains Lake, *Okla., U.S.* 36°45′ N, 99°5′ W 81
Great Sandy Desert, *Australia* 20°22′ S, 122°54′ E 230
Great Sitkin, island, *Alas., U.S.* 52°12′ N, 177°22′ W 160
Great Slave Lake, *Can.* 61°13′ N, 117°25′ W 73
Great Smoky Mountains, *N.C., U.S.* 35°44′ N, 83°34′ W 96
Great Snow Mountain, *Can.* 57°25′ N, 124°12′ W 108
Great Victoria Desert, *Austral.* 28°18′ S, 126°42′ E 230
Great Wall, *China* 39°15′ N, 110°33′ E 198
Great Wall, station, *Antarctica* 62°21′ S, 58°57′ W 134
Great Western Erg, *Alg.* 30°20′ N, 0°0′ W 156
Great Yarmouth, *U.K.* 52°36′ N, 1°42′ E 163
Great Zab, river, *Turk.* 37°27′ N, 43°41′ E 195
Great Zab see Zāb al Kabīr, river, *Iraq* 36°32′ N, 43°40′ E 195
Great Zimbabwe, ruin(s), *Zimb.* 20°24′ S, 30°58′ E 227
Greater Antilles, *Caribbean Sea* 17°49′ N, 73°28′ W 116
Greater Khingan Range, *China* 52°0′ N, 122°48′ E 172
Greater Sudbury, *Can.* 46°29′ N, 81°0′ W 95
Grebbestad, *Nor.* 58°41′ N, 11°15′ E 152
Grebenau, *Ger.* 50°44′ N, 9°27′ E 167
Grebenstein, *Ger.* 51°27′ N, 9°25′ E 167
Gréboun, peak, *Niger* 19°55′ N, 8°29′ E 222
Greco, Monte, peak, *It.* 41°47′ N, 13°54′ E 156
Gredos, Sierra de, *Sp.* 40°16′ N, 5°43′ W 150
Greece 39°6′ N, 21°44′ E 156
Greeley, *Colo., U.S.* 40°25′ N, 104°43′ W 90
Greeley, *Nebr., U.S.* 41°32′ N, 98°33′ W 90
Green Bay 44°38′ N, 87°59′ W 94
Green Island, *N.Z.* 45°53′ S, 170°24′ E 240
Green Islands, *South Pacific Ocean* 3°45′ S, 153°35′ E 192
Green Islands, *South Pacific Ocean* 4°1′ S, 154°11′ E 238
Green Lake, *Can.* 54°18′ N, 107°47′ W 108
Green Lake, *Wis., U.S.* 43°49′ N, 88°57′ W 102
Green Mountains, *Vt., U.S.* 44°2′ N, 73°0′ W 104
Green Mountains, *Wyo., U.S.* 42°27′ N, 107°57′ W 90
Green River, *Utah, U.S.* 38°59′ N, 110°10′ W 92
Green River, *Wyo., U.S.* 41°32′ N, 109°28′ W 90
Green, river, *Ky., U.S.* 37°37′ N, 87°33′ W 94
Green, river, *U.S.* 39°51′ N, 109°57′ W 90
Greenacres, *Calif., U.S.* 35°23′ N, 119°8′ W 101
Greenbush, *Minn., U.S.* 48°40′ N, 96°13′ W 90
Greenbush Lake, *Can.* 50°55′ N, 90°38′ W 110
Greencastle, *Ind., U.S.* 39°38′ N, 86°52′ W 102
Greene, *Me., U.S.* 44°11′ N, 70°8′ W 104
Greeneville, *Tenn., U.S.* 36°9′ N, 82°51′ W 96
Greenfield, *Calif., U.S.* 36°19′ N, 121°15′ W 100
Greenfield, *Ind., U.S.* 39°47′ N, 85°46′ W 102
Greenfield, *Iowa, U.S.* 41°18′ N, 94°27′ W 94
Greenfield, *Mo., U.S.* 37°24′ N, 93°51′ W 96
Greenfield, *N.H., U.S.* 42°56′ N, 71°53′ W 104
Greenfield, *N. Mex., U.S.* 33°9′ N, 104°21′ W 92
Greenfield, *Ohio, U.S.* 39°21′ N, 83°24′ W 102
Greenhorn Mountain, *Colo., U.S.* 37°52′ N, 105°6′ W 90
Greenhorn Mountains, *Calif., U.S.* 35°41′ N, 118°54′ W 92
Greenland (Kalaallit Nunaat), *Den.* 67°11′ N, 50°25′ W 106
Greenland, *N.H., U.S.* 43°1′ N, 70°51′ W 104
Greenland Fracture Zone, *Greenland Sea* 74°53′ N, 2°12′ E 255
Greenland Sea 68°26′ N, 25°49′ W 246
Greenough, Mount, *Alas., U.S.* 69°6′ N, 141°54′ W 98
Greenport, *N.Y., U.S.* 41°6′ N, 72°23′ W 104
Greensboro, *Ala., U.S.* 32°42′ N, 87°36′ W 103
Greensboro, *Ga., U.S.* 33°33′ N, 83°11′ W 96
Greensboro, *N.C., U.S.* 36°3′ N, 79°49′ W 96
Greensboro Bend, *Vt., U.S.* 44°32′ N, 72°16′ W 104
Greensburg, *Ind., U.S.* 39°19′ N, 85°29′ W 102
Greensburg, *Kans., U.S.* 37°35′ N, 99°18′ W 92
Greensburg, *La., U.S.* 30°49′ N, 90°41′ W 103
Greensburg, *Pa., U.S.* 40°17′ N, 79°34′ W 94
Greentown, *Ind., U.S.* 40°28′ N, 85°58′ W 102
Greenup, *Ill., U.S.* 39°13′ N, 88°10′ W 102
Greenup, *Ky., U.S.* 38°33′ N, 82°50′ W 102
Greenview, *Ill., U.S.* 40°4′ N, 89°45′ W 102
Greenville, *Ala., U.S.* 31°49′ N, 86°37′ W 96
Greenville, *Can.* 55°3′ N, 129°36′ W 108
Greenville, *Fla., U.S.* 30°26′ N, 83°38′ W 96
Greenville, *Ill., U.S.* 38°53′ N, 89°24′ W 102
Greenville, *Ky., U.S.* 37°12′ N, 87°11′ W 94
Greenville, *Liberia* 5°0′ N, 9°3′ W 222
Greenville, *Me., U.S.* 45°27′ N, 69°36′ W 94
Greenville, *Mich., U.S.* 43°10′ N, 85°16′ W 102
Greenville, *Miss., U.S.* 33°23′ N, 91°4′ W 103
Greenville, *N.H., U.S.* 42°46′ N, 71°50′ W 104
Greenville, *Ohio, U.S.* 40°5′ N, 84°38′ W 102
Greenville, *Pa., U.S.* 41°24′ N, 80°23′ W 94
Greenville, *S.C., U.S.* 34°50′ N, 82°25′ W 96
Greenville, *Tex., U.S.* 33°6′ N, 96°6′ W 96
Greenwich, *Conn., U.S.* 41°1′ N, 73°38′ W 104
Greenwich, *N.Y., U.S.* 43°5′ N, 73°31′ W 104
Greenwich, *Ohio, U.S.* 41°1′ N, 82°31′ W 102
Greenwich, *U.K.* 51°29′ N, 0°0′ W 162
Greenwich Island, *Antarctica* 62°45′ S, 59°27′ W 134
Greenwood, *Ark., U.S.* 35°11′ N, 94°16′ W 96
Greenwood, *Can.* 49°5′ N, 118°41′ W 90
Greenwood, *Ind., U.S.* 39°37′ N, 86°6′ W 102
Greenwood, *Me., U.S.* 44°18′ N, 70°39′ W 104
Greenwood, *Miss., U.S.* 33°29′ N, 90°11′ W 96
Greenwood, *S.C., U.S.* 34°11′ N, 82°11′ W 112
Greenwood, Mount, *Austral.* 13°47′ S, 129°52′ E 230
Greer, *Ariz., U.S.* 34°1′ N, 109°27′ W 92
Gretsiel, *Ger.* 53°30′ N, 7°5′ E 163
Gregoire Lake, *Can.* 56°27′ N, 111°36′ W 108
Gregório, river, *Braz.* 7°39′ S, 71°13′ W 130
Gregory, *S. Dak., U.S.* 43°12′ N, 99°27′ W 90
Gregory National Park, *Austral.* 16°23′ S, 129°58′ E 238
Gregory Range, *Austral.* 18°43′ S, 142°20′ E 230
Greiffenberg, *Ger.* 53°5′ N, 13°56′ E 152
Greifswald, *Ger.* 54°6′ N, 13°22′ E 152
Gremikha, *Russ.* 68°0′ N, 39°23′ E 169
Gremyachinsk, *Russ.* 58°35′ N, 57°52′ E 154
Grenå, *Den.* 56°25′ N, 10°51′ E 150
Grenada 12°0′ N, 62°0′ W 116
Grenada, *Calif., U.S.* 41°39′ N, 122°32′ W 92
Grenada, *Miss., U.S.* 33°43′ N, 89°49′ W 96
Grenchen, *Switz.* 47°11′ N, 7°22′ E 150
Grenfell, *Can.* 50°24′ N, 102°56′ W 90
Grenoble, *Fr.* 45°11′ N, 5°43′ E 150
Grenora, *N. Dak., U.S.* 48°36′ N, 103°57′ W 90
Grenville, *Can.* 45°37′ N, 74°37′ W 94
Grenville Channel 53°42′ N, 130°45′ W 108
Grenville, Mount, *Can.* 50°58′ N, 124°36′ W 90
Grenville, Point, *Wash., U.S.* 47°13′ N, 124°31′ W 100
Gresford, *U.K.* 53°5′ N, 2°59′ W 162
Gressåmoen National Park, *Nor.* 64°18′ N, 12°52′ E 152
Gretna, *La., U.S.* 29°54′ N, 90°4′ W 103
Greven, *Ger.* 52°5′ N, 7°37′ E 163
Grevenbroich, *Ger.* 51°5′ N, 6°35′ E 167
Grevenmacher, *Lux.* 49°40′ N, 6°25′ E 163
Grevesmühlen, *Ger.* 53°51′ N, 11°12′ E 152
Grey Islands, *Labrador Sea* 50°26′ N, 55°8′ W 106
Grey Range, *Austral.* 28°39′ S, 142°4′ E 230
Greybull, *Wyo., U.S.* 44°28′ N, 108°4′ W 90
Greylock, Mount, *Mass., U.S.* 42°37′ N, 73°12′ W 104
Greymouth, *N.Z.* 42°30′ S, 171°13′ E 240
Greytown, *N.Z.* 41°6′ S, 175°29′ E 240
Grezzana, *It.* 45°30′ N, 11°0′ E 167
Griam More, Ben, peak, *U.K.* 58°18′ N, 4°9′ W 150
Gribanovskiy, *Russ.* 51°27′ N, 41°53′ E 158
Gribe, Mal, *Alban.* 40°15′ N, 19°29′ E 156
Grico, oil field, *Venez.* 8°55′ N, 66°40′ W 136
Gridino, *Russ.* 65°53′ N, 34°28′ E 152
Gridley, *Ill., U.S.* 40°44′ N, 88°53′ W 102
Grieskirchen, *Aust.* 48°13′ N, 13°50′ E 152
Griffin, *Ga., U.S.* 33°13′ N, 84°16′ W 96
Grigorevka, *Kyrg.* 42°44′ N, 77°48′ E 184
Grigoriopol, *Mold.* 47°9′ N, 29°17′ E 158
Grimari, *Cen. Af. Rep.* 5°43′ N, 20°5′ E 218
Grimsby, *Can.* 43°10′ N, 79°34′ W 94
Grimsby, *U.K.* 53°34′ N, 0°5′ E 162
Grimshaw, *Can.* 56°11′ N, 117°37′ W 108
Grimstad, *Nor.* 58°20′ N, 8°34′ E 150
Grindelwald, *Switz.* 46°37′ N, 8°2′ E 167
Grinnell, *Iowa, U.S.* 41°44′ N, 92°43′ W 94
Grinnell Peninsula, *Can.* 76°38′ N, 95°22′ W 106
Griñón, *Sp.* 40°12′ N, 3°51′ W 164
Grintavec, peak, *Slov.* 46°21′ N, 14°28′ E 156
Gripsholm, site, *Nor.* 59°14′ N, 17°5′ E 152
Griquatown, *S. Af.* 28°51′ S, 23°15′ E 227
Grise Fiord, *Can.* 76°21′ N, 82°51′ W 106
Grishkino, *Russ.* 57°57′ N, 82°44′ E 169
Grisslehamn, *Sw.* 60°4′ N, 18°44′ E 166
Griswoldville, *Mass., U.S.* 42°39′ N, 72°43′ W 104
Griva, *Latv.* 55°49′ N, 26°31′ E 166
Griva, *Russ.* 60°34′ N, 50°55′ E 154
Grizim, spring, *Alg.* 25°25′ N, 3°4′ W 214
Grizzly Bear Hills, *Can.* 55°35′ N, 109°42′ W 108
Grizzly Mountain, *Can.* 51°42′ N, 120°20′ W 90
Grmeic, *Bosn. and Herzg.* 44°21′ N, 16°29′ E 168
Grobiņa, *Latv.* 56°32′ N, 21°9′ E 166
Grocka, *Serb.* 44°39′ N, 20°42′ E 168
Groenlo, *Neth.* 52°2′ N, 6°36′ E 167
Grombalia, *Tun.* 36°35′ N, 10°31′ E 214
Gromovo, *Russ.* 60°41′ N, 30°16′ E 166
Grong, *Nor.* 64°27′ N, 12°20′ E 152
Groningen, *Neth.* 53°12′ N, 6°33′ E 163
Gronlid, *Can.* 53°5′ N, 104°28′ W 108
Grønøy, *Nor.* 66°47′ N, 13°25′ E 152
Groom, *Tex., U.S.* 35°13′ N, 101°5′ W 92
Groot Karasberge, peak, *Namibia* 27°12′ S, 18°37′ E 227
Groote Eylandt, island, *Austral.* 14°27′ S, 137°3′ E 230
Grootfontein, *Namibia* 19°32′ S, 18°7′ E 220
Gros Mécatina, Cap du, *Can.* 50°38′ N, 59°8′ W 111
Gros Morne National Park, *Can.* 49°46′ N, 58°30′ W 111
Gros Morne, peak, *Can.* 49°34′ N, 57°52′ W 111
Gros Ventre, *Wyo., U.S.* 43°24′ N, 111°16′ W 80
Gros Ventre Range, *Wyo., U.S.* 43°28′ N, 110°52′ W 90
Grosio, *It.* 46°17′ N, 10°14′ E 167
Grosne, river, *Fr.* 46°32′ N, 4°38′ E 165
Grossa, Ponta, *Braz.* 1°14′ N, 49°54′ W 130
Grossa, Punta, *Sp.* 39°5′ N, 1°16′ E 150
Grossalmerode, *Ger.* 51°15′ N, 9°46′ E 167
Grossefehn, *Ger.* 53°24′ N, 7°36′ E 163
Grossenkneten, *Ger.* 52°56′ N, 8°16′ E 163
Grossenlüder, *Ger.* 50°36′ N, 9°32′ E 167
Grosseto, *It.* 42°45′ N, 11°5′ E 156
Grossglockner, peak, *Aust.* 47°4′ N, 12°37′ E 156
Gross-Umstadt, *Ger.* 49°52′ N, 8°54′ E 167
Grostenquin, *Fr.* 48°57′ N, 6°43′ E 163
Grosvenor Seamount, *North Pacific Ocean* 28°4′ N, 166°46′ E 252
Groton, *Mass., U.S.* 42°36′ N, 71°35′ W 104
Groton, *S. Dak., U.S.* 45°26′ N, 98°7′ W 90
Groton, *Vt., U.S.* 44°12′ N, 72°12′ W 104
Grøtøy, *Nor.* 67°49′ N, 14°42′ E 152
Grottammare, *It.* 42°59′ N, 13°51′ E 156
Grotte de Lascaux, site, *Fr.* 45°2′ N, 1°9′ E 165
Grouard, *Can.* 55°31′ N, 116°8′ W 108
Groundhog, river, *Can.* 49°22′ N, 82°15′ W 94
Grouse Creek, *Utah, U.S.* 41°42′ N, 113°54′ W 92
Grouse Creek Mountain, *Idaho, U.S.* 44°21′ N, 113°59′ W 90
Grouse Creek Mountains, *Utah, U.S.* 41°29′ N, 114°8′ W 90
Grovane, *Nor.* 58°17′ N, 7°58′ E 152
Grove Hill, *Ala., U.S.* 31°42′ N, 87°46′ W 103
Groveland, *Calif., U.S.* 37°49′ N, 120°15′ W 100
Groveland, *Fla., U.S.* 28°33′ N, 81°51′ W 105
Groveport, *Ohio, U.S.* 39°51′ N, 82°53′ W 102
Grover, *Colo., U.S.* 40°52′ N, 104°15′ W 90
Grover, *Pa., U.S.* 41°36′ N, 76°53′ W 94
Grover Beach, *Calif., U.S.* 35°7′ N, 120°38′ W 92
Groves, *Tex., U.S.* 29°55′ N, 93°56′ W 103
Groveton, *N.H., U.S.* 44°36′ N, 71°32′ W 94
Groveton, *Tex., U.S.* 31°2′ N, 95°7′ W 103
Growler Pass, *Ariz., U.S.* 32°10′ N, 112°55′ W 92
Groznyy, *Russ.* 43°18′ N, 45°39′ E 195
Grubišno Polje, *Croatia* 45°41′ N, 17°10′ E 168
Gruda, *Croatia* 42°30′ N, 18°22′ E 168
Grudopole, *Belarus* 52°53′ N, 25°42′ E 152
Grudovo, *Bulg.* 42°20′ N, 27°10′ E 156
Grue, *Nor.* 60°26′ N, 12°2′ E 152
Gruemirë, *Alban.* 42°9′ N, 19°31′ E 168
Gruesa, Punta, *Chile* 20°23′ S, 70°36′ W 137
Grulla, *Tex., U.S.* 26°17′ N, 98°39′ W 114
Grums, *Nor.* 59°21′ N, 13°4′ E 152
Grünau, *Namibia* 27°44′ S, 18°21′ E 227

Grünberg, Ger. 50°35′ N, 8°57′ E 167
Grundforsen, Nor. 61°17′ N, 12°52′ E 152
Gruver, Tex., U.S. 36°14′ N, 101°25′ W 92
Gruža, Serb. 43°54′ N, 20°46′ E 168
Gryazi, Russ. 52°28′ N, 39°48′ E 158
Gryazovets, Russ. 58°52′ N, 40°14′ E 154
Grygla, Minn., U.S. 48°16′ N, 95°39′ W 90
Gryžliny, Pol. 53°37′ N, 20°20′ E 152
Gstaad, Switz. 46°27′ N, 7°18′ E 167
Gua Musang, Malaysia 4°52′ N, 101°58′ E 196
Guabito, Pan. 9°29′ N, 82°36′ W 115
Guaca, Col. 6°50′ N, 72°50′ W 136
Guacamaya, Col. 2°15′ N, 75°1′ W 136
Guachara, Venez. 7°16′ N, 68°23′ W 136
Guachochi, Mex. 26°50′ N, 107°5′ W 112
Guaçui, Braz. 20°49′ S, 41°44′ W 138
Guadalajara, Mex. 20°39′ N, 103°26′ W 114
Guadalajara, Sp. 40°36′ N, 3°10′ W 164
Guadalajara, Sp. 40°37′ N, 3°10′ W 214
Guadalcanal, Sp. 38°5′ N, 5°50′ W 164
Guadalcanal, island, Solomon Islands 10°0′ S, 160°0′ E 242
Guadalquivir, river, Sp. 37°52′ N, 6°2′ W 143
Guadalupe, Braz. 6°49′ S, 43°35′ W 132
Guadalupe, Calif., U.S. 34°57′ N, 120°35′ W 100
Guadalupe, Mex. 25°40′ N, 100°15′ W 114
Guadalupe, Mex. 32°1′ N, 116°40′ W 112
Guadalupe, Mex. 29°22′ N, 110°27′ W 92
Guadalupe, Mex. 22°44′ N, 102°29′ W 114
Guadalupe, Sp. 39°27′ N, 5°19′ W 164
Guadalupe Bravos, Mex. 31°22′ N, 106°7′ W 92
Guadalupe, Isla de, island, Fr. 28°27′ N, 118°49′ W 112
Guadalupe Mountains, N. Mex., U.S. 32°16′ N, 105°7′ W 92
Guadalupe Peak, Tex., U.S. 31°51′ N, 104°56′ W 92
Guadalupe, Sierra de, Sp. 39°15′ N, 5°52′ W 164
Guadarrama, Sierra de, Sp. 41°18′ N, 3°18′ W 164
Guadeloupe, islands, Fr. 16°23′ N, 61°59′ W 116
Guadiana, river, Sp. 38°15′ N, 7°35′ W 143
Guadix, Sp. 37°18′ N, 3°9′ W 164
Guafo, Isla, island, Chile 43°32′ S, 75°41′ W 134
Guaíba, Braz. 30°10′ S, 51°21′ W 139
Guaicuí, Braz. 17°12′ S, 44°51′ W 138
Guáimaro, Cuba 21°3′ N, 77°24′ W 116
Guainía, adm. division, Col. 2°47′ N, 69°53′ W 136
Guainía, river, Col. 2°8′ N, 69°29′ W 136
Guaíra, Braz. 24°7′ S, 54°15′ W 132
Guaitecas, Islas, islands, South Pacific Ocean 43°59′ S, 76°28′ W 134
Guajaba, Cayo, island, Cuba 21°51′ N, 77°26′ W 116
Guajará-Mirim, Braz. 10°49′ S, 65°20′ W 137
Guajarraã, Braz. 7°46′ S, 66°57′ W 130
Guaje, Llano del, Mex. 27°50′ N, 103°43′ W 112
Guajira, adm. division, Col. 11°6′ N, 73°23′ W 136
Guajira, Península de la, Col. 11°58′ N, 72°6′ W 136
Gualaca, Pan. 8°31′ N, 82°18′ W 115
Gualaguala, Punta, Chile 22°47′ S, 70°56′ W 137
Gualala, Calif., U.S. 38°46′ N, 123°32′ W 90
Gualán, Guatemala 15°7′ N, 89°24′ W 115
Gualeguay, Arg. 33°7′ S, 59°18′ W 139
Gualeguaychú, Arg. 33°3′ S, 58°29′ W 139
Gualicho, Gran Bajo del, Arg. 40°15′ S, 67°12′ W 134
Gualjaina, Arg. 42°42′ S, 70°33′ W 134
Guam, U.S. 13°18′ N, 144°15′ E 242
Guamareyes, Col. 0°30′ N, 73°1′ W 136
Guamblin, Isla, island, Chile 45°1′ S, 76°41′ W 134
Guaminí, Arg. 37°2′ S, 62°23′ W 139
Guamo, Col. 3°59′ N, 75°1′ W 136
Guamúchil, Mex. 25°27′ N, 108°5′ W 112
Guanabacoa, Cuba 23°7′ N, 82°18′ W 96
Guanabara, Braz. 10°41′ S, 70°8′ W 137
Guanaceví, Mex. 25°58′ N, 105°57′ W 114
Guanaco, Arg. 35°42′ S, 61°40′ W 139
Guanaco, Paso del, pass, Chile 36°1′ S, 70°23′ W 134
Guanaja, Isla de, island, Hond. 16°31′ N, 85°49′ W 115
Guanajuato, Mex. 20°58′ N, 101°20′ W 114
Guanajuato, adm. division, Mex. 21°2′ N, 101°49′ W 114
Guanambi, Braz. 14°14′ S, 42°46′ W 138
Guanare, Venez. 9°2′ N, 69°47′ W 136
Guanare, river, Venez. 8°44′ N, 69°30′ W 136
Guanay, Bol. 15°28′ S, 67°53′ W 137
Guandacol, Arg. 29°32′ S, 68°32′ W 134
Guangchang, China 26°50′ N, 116°11′ E 198
Guangdong, adm. division, China 23°48′ N, 112°55′ E 198
Guangfeng, China 28°27′ N, 118°13′ E 198
Guanghai, China 21°55′ N, 112°46′ E 198
Guangrao, China 37°6′ N, 118°25′ E 198
Guangshan, China 32°0′ N, 114°52′ E 198
Guangshui, China 31°37′ N, 114°3′ E 198
Guangxi Zhuang, adm. division, China 23°49′ N, 107°53′ E 198
Guangyuan, China 32°23′ N, 105°52′ E 173
Guangzhou (Canton), China 23°6′ N, 113°17′ E 198
Guanhaes, Braz. 18°48′ S, 43°1′ W 138
Guanshui, China 40°52′ N, 124°33′ E 200
Guanta, Venez. 10°14′ N, 64°35′ W 116
Guantánamo, Cuba 20°8′ N, 75°14′ W 116
Guantánamo, adm. division, Cuba 20°8′ N, 75°31′ W 116
Guanyan, China 34°16′ N, 119°14′ E 198
Guanyang, China 25°29′ N, 111°6′ E 198
Guapé, Braz. 20°47′ S, 45°56′ W 138
Guapí, Col. 2°33′ N, 77°57′ W 136
Guaporé, Braz. 28°58′ S, 51°57′ W 139
Guaporé Iténez, river, South America 11°49′ S, 65°5′ W 137
Guaporé, river, Braz. 15°29′ S, 58°50′ W 132
Guaqui, Bol. 16°40′ S, 68°51′ W 137
Guará, river, Braz. 13°26′ S, 45°34′ W 132
Guara, Sierra de, Sp. 42°23′ N, 0°26′ E 164
Guarabira, Braz. 6°52′ S, 35°32′ W 132
Guaraci, Braz. 20°33′ S, 48°56′ W 138
Guarai, Braz. 8°59′ S, 48°13′ W 130
Guarapari, Braz. 20°41′ S, 40°31′ W 138
Guarapuava, Braz. 25°23′ S, 51°29′ W 138
Guaraqueçaba, Braz. 25°18′ S, 48°20′ W 138
Guaratinguetá, Braz. 22°51′ S, 45°10′ W 138
Guaratuba, Braz. 25°55′ S, 48°35′ W 138
Guarda, Port. 40°32′ N, 7°17′ W 150
Guarda, adm. division, Port. 40°43′ N, 7°34′ W 150
Guarda Mor, Braz. 17°48′ S, 47°7′ W 138
Guardatinajas, Venez. 9°1′ N, 67°38′ W 136
Guardia Escolta, Arg. 28°57′ S, 62°11′ W 139
Guaribe, river, Braz. 8°2′ S, 60°33′ W 130
Guárico, adm. division, Venez. 8°47′ N, 67°29′ W 136
Guarico, Punta, Cuba 20°40′ N, 74°44′ W 116
Guarromán, Sp. 38°10′ N, 3°41′ W 164
Guasave, Mex. 25°33′ N, 108°29′ W 82
Guascama, Punta, Col. 2°21′ N, 78°28′ W 136
Guasipati, Venez. 7°27′ N, 61°56′ W 130
Guastalla, It. 44°55′ N, 10°38′ E 167
Guatemala 15°4′ N, 91°3′ W 115
Guatemala City, Guatemala 14°34′ N, 90°40′ W 115
Guatemala Basin, North Pacific Ocean 6°59′ N, 94°28′ W 252
Guateque, Col. 5°0′ N, 73°28′ W 136
Guatraché, Arg. 37°42′ S, 63°29′ W 139
Guaviare, adm. division, Col. 1°43′ N, 73°27′ W 136
Guaviare, river, Col. 3°12′ N, 70°17′ W 136
Guaxupé, Braz. 21°18′ S, 46°43′ W 138
Guayabal, Cuba 20°42′ N, 77°39′ W 116
Guayabal, Venez. 7°58′ N, 67°23′ W 136
Guayabero, river, Col. 2°13′ N, 73°43′ W 136
Guayalejo, river, Mex. 23°24′ N, 99°4′ W 114
Guayaquil, Ecua. 2°17′ S, 79°57′ W 130
Guaymas, Mex. 28°4′ N, 110°50′ W 238
Guaymas, Cerro, peak, Mex. 28°10′ N, 111°14′ W 92
Guaymas, Valle de, Mex. 28°16′ N, 110°51′ W 112
Guaynabo, P.R., U.S. 18°0′ N, 66°0′ W 118
Guba, Dem. Rep. of the Congo 10°38′ S, 26°24′ E 224
Guba, Eth. 11°14′ N, 35°18′ E 182
Guba Dolgaya, Russ. 70°17′ N, 58°45′ E 169
Gubakha, Russ. 58°50′ N, 57°34′ E 169
Guban, region, Africa 10°31′ N, 42°50′ E 216
Gubat, Philippines 12°55′ N, 124°7′ E 203
Gubdor, Russ. 60°13′ N, 56°34′ E 154
Guben, Pol. 51°57′ N, 14°41′ E 152
Gubio, Nig. 12°27′ N, 12°45′ E 216
Gubkin, Russ. 51°15′ N, 37°32′ E 158
Guča, Serb. 43°46′ N, 20°12′ E 168
Gucheng, China 32°15′ N, 111°33′ E 198
Gudaut'a, Ga. 43°6′ N, 40°40′ E 195
Gudbrandsdalen, Nor. 61°58′ N, 9°10′ E 152
Guddu Barrage, dam, Pak. 28°31′ N, 69°35′ E 186
Gudensberg, Ger. 51°11′ N, 9°23′ E 167
Gudivada, India 16°23′ N, 81°1′ E 188
Gudžiūnai, Lith. 55°31′ N, 23°45′ E 166
Guéckédo, Guinea 8°33′ N, 10°9′ W 222
Guedon Dong, oil field, Indonesia 4°51′ N, 97°45′ E 196
Guelph, Can. 43°33′ N, 80°14′ W 94
Guelta Mouri Idié, spring, Chad 23°3′ N, 15°14′ E 216
Guemar, Alg. 33°29′ N, 6°48′ E 214
Guéné, Benin 11°45′ N, 3°14′ E 222
Güeppí, Peru 0°8′ N, 75°13′ W 136
Güepsa, Col. 6°2′ N, 73°37′ W 136
Guer, Fr. 47°54′ N, 2°9′ W 150
Güer Aike, Arg. 51°36′ S, 69°37′ W 134
Guéra, Massif de, peak, Chad 11°55′ N, 18°5′ E 218
Guerara, Alg. 32°47′ N, 4°29′ E 214
Guercif, Mor. 34°16′ N, 3°19′ W 214
Guéréda, Chad 14°29′ N, 22°2′ E 216
Guernsey, island, U.K. 49°27′ N, 2°36′ W 150
Guernsey, Wyo., U.S. 42°16′ N, 104°43′ W 90
Guerrero, adm. division, Mex. 17°45′ N, 100°51′ W 114
Guerzim, Alg. 29°40′ N, 1°40′ W 214
Guest Peninsula, Antarctica 76°20′ S, 149°54′ W 248
Gueydan, La., U.S. 30°1′ N, 92°31′ W 103
Guézaoua, Niger 14°29′ N, 8°47′ E 222
Gugu, peak, Eth. 8°11′ N, 39°50′ E 224
Guguan, island, U.S. 17°22′ N, 146°1′ E 192
Gui, river, China 24°0′ N, 110°41′ E 198
Guia Lopes da Laguna, Braz. 21°28′ S, 56°2′ W 132
Guichen Bay 37°15′ S, 138°16′ E 230
Guichi, China 30°40′ N, 117°27′ E 198
Güicho, Kyrg. 40°18′ N, 73°29′ E 197
Guidan Roumji, Niger 13°41′ N, 6°33′ E 222
Guide, China 35°52′ N, 101°36′ E 190
Guider, Cameroon 9°55′ N, 13°56′ E 218
Guidiguir, Niger 13°41′ N, 9°49′ E 222
Guidimouni, Niger 13°42′ N, 9°26′ E 222
Guiding, China 26°33′ N, 107°14′ E 198
Guidouma, Gabon 1°38′ S, 10°42′ E 218
Guienne, region, Europe 44°10′ N, 1°7′ E 165
Guiglo, Côte d'Ivoire 6°26′ N, 7°30′ W 222
Guijá, Mozambique 24°27′ S, 33°3′ E 227
Guildford, U.K. 51°14′ N, 0°36′ E 162
Guildhall, Vt., U.S. 44°34′ N, 71°35′ W 104
Guilford, Conn., U.S. 41°16′ N, 72°41′ W 104
Guilford, Me., U.S. 45°10′ N, 69°24′ W 94
Guilford, Vt., U.S. 42°48′ N, 72°35′ W 104
Guilin, China 25°17′ N, 110°13′ E 198
Guillaume-Delisle, Lac, lake, Can. 56°7′ N, 79°17′ W 106
Guillaumes, Fr. 44°5′ N, 6°51′ E 167
Guillestre, Fr. 44°39′ N, 6°38′ E 167
Guilvinec, Fr. 47°47′ N, 4°18′ W 150
Guimarães, Braz. 2°6′ S, 44°36′ W 132
Guimarães, Port. 41°26′ N, 8°20′ W 214
Guimi, spring, Mauritania 17°29′ N, 13°18′ W 222
Guin, Ala., U.S. 33°59′ N, 87°55′ W 96
Guindulman, Philippines 9°47′ N, 124°28′ E 203
Guinea 10°20′ N, 10°36′ W 214
Guinea, Gulf of 4°29′ N, 0°6′ E 222
Guinea-Bissau 12°7′ N, 15°13′ W 214
Güines, Cuba 22°50′ N, 82°3′ W 112
Guînes, Fr. 50°51′ N, 1°52′ E 163
Guinguinéo, Senegal 14°16′ N, 15°54′ W 222
Guiones, Punta, C.R. 9°51′ N, 86°34′ W 115
Guiping, China 23°21′ N, 110°1′ E 198
Guir, Hamada du, Alg. 31°41′ N, 3°42′ W 214
Guir, spring, Mali 18°52′ N, 2°51′ W 222
Guiratinga, Braz. 16°23′ S, 53°47′ W 132
Guisborough, U.K. 54°32′ N, 1°3′ W 162
Guise, Fr. 49°54′ N, 3°39′ E 163
Guita Koulouba, Cen. Af. Rep. 5°55′ N, 23°22′ E 218
Guitiriz, Sp. 43°9′ N, 7°57′ W 150
Guitri, Côte d'Ivoire 5°30′ N, 5°14′ W 222
Guiuan, Philippines 11°4′ N, 125°43′ E 203
Guixi, China 28°18′ N, 116°59′ E 198
Guixian, China 23°10′ N, 109°35′ E 198
Guiyang, China 26°36′ N, 106°41′ E 198
Guiyang, China 25°46′ N, 112°43′ E 198
Guizhou, adm. division, China 27°34′ N, 106°15′ E 198
Gujar Khan, Pak. 33°12′ N, 73°18′ E 186
Gujarat, adm. division, India 22°12′ N, 69°57′ E 188
Gujba, Nig. 11°29′ N, 11°52′ E 222
Gujranwala, Pak. 32°8′ N, 74°9′ E 186
Gujrat, Pak. 32°32′ N, 74°6′ E 186
Gulbarga, India 17°19′ N, 76°50′ E 188
Gulbene, Latv. 57°10′ N, 26°45′ E 166
Gulen, Nor. 60°59′ N, 5°5′ E 152
Gulf Hammock, Fla., U.S. 29°14′ N, 82°44′ W 105
Gulf Shores, Ala., U.S. 30°14′ N, 87°42′ W 103
Gulfport, Fla., U.S. 27°45′ N, 82°42′ W 105
Gulfport, Miss., U.S. 30°21′ N, 89°5′ W 103
Gulfport, Mo., U.S. 40°48′ N, 91°4′ W 94
Gulin, China 28°5′ N, 105°52′ E 198
Guling, China 29°36′ N, 115°52′ E 198
Guliston, Uzb. 40°29′ N, 68°47′ E 197
Guliya Shan, peak, China 49°48′ N, 122°21′ E 198
Gulkana, Alas., U.S. 62°18′ N, 145°20′ W 106
Gull Islands, Lake Superior 48°11′ N, 88°12′ W 94
Gull Lake, Can. 50°4′ N, 108°29′ W 90
Gull Lake, Can. 52°30′ N, 114°20′ W 108
Gull Lake, Can. 51°13′ N, 92°16′ W 110
Gull Lake, Mich., U.S. 42°24′ N, 85°30′ W 102
Gullion, Slieve, peak, U.K. 54°6′ N, 6°32′ W 150
Güllük, Turk. 37°13′ N, 27°35′ E 156
Gulma, Nig. 12°37′ N, 4°20′ E 222
Gülnar, Turk. 36°20′ N, 33°24′ E 156
Gülşehir, Turk. 38°44′ N, 34°37′ E 156
Gülshat, Kaz. 46°39′ N, 74°23′ E 184
Gulsvik, Nor. 60°22′ N, 9°36′ E 152
Gulu, Uganda 2°45′ N, 32°17′ E 224
Gulwe, Tanzania 6°26′ S, 36°23′ E 224
Gulyayevo, Russ. 64°30′ N, 40°33′ E 154
Guma see Pishan, China 37°39′ N, 78°22′ E 184
Gumal, river, Pak. 31°45′ N, 69°17′ E 186
Gumare, Botswana 19°21′ S, 22°11′ E 220
Gumban, Eth. 7°37′ N, 43°15′ E 218
Gumdag, Turkm. 39°16′ N, 54°35′ E 180
Gumel, Nig. 12°36′ N, 9°23′ E 222
Gumiel de Hizán, Sp. 41°46′ N, 3°42′ W 164
Gumla, India 23°2′ N, 84°33′ E 197
Gumma, adm. division, Japan 36°32′ N, 138°28′ E 201
Gummersbach, Ger. 51°1′ N, 7°33′ E 167
Gummi, Nig. 12°2′ N, 5°9′ E 222
Gumuru, Sudan 6°36′ N, 32°54′ E 224
Gümüşdere, Turk. 38°22′ N, 43°12′ E 195
Gümüşhane, Turk. 40°26′ N, 39°26′ E 195
Gümüşören, Turk. 38°14′ N, 35°37′ E 156
Gun Cay, island, Bahamas 25°33′ N, 79°29′ W 105
Guna, Eth. 8°17′ N, 39°51′ E 224
Guna, India 24°37′ N, 77°19′ E 197
Guna Terara, peak, Eth. 11°42′ N, 38°7′ E 182
Gundlupet, India 11°49′ N, 76°40′ E 188
Gungu, Dem. Rep. of the Congo 5°46′ S, 19°14′ E 218
Gunib, Russ. 42°20′ N, 46°52′ E 195
Gunisao Lake, Can. 53°30′ N, 96°43′ W 108
Gunnbjørn Fjeld, peak, Den. 68°41′ N, 30°44′ W 73
Gunnison, Utah, U.S. 39°9′ N, 111°48′ W 90
Gunsan, S. Korea 35°57′ N, 126°44′ E 200
Guntersville, Ala., U.S. 34°19′ N, 86°21′ W 112
Guntur, India 16°17′ N, 80°26′ E 190
Gunung Bentuang National Park, Indonesia 1°14′ N, 112°46′ E 238
Gunung Leuser National Park, Indonesia 3°50′ N, 96°48′ E 196
Gunung Lorentz National Park, Indonesia 4°32′ S, 137°12′ E 238
Gunung Mulu National Park, Malaysia 4°2′ N, 114°34′ E 238
Gunung Palung National Park, Indonesia 1°14′ S, 109°51′ E 238
Gunungsitoli, Indonesia 1°20′ N, 97°31′ E 196
Guoyang, China 33°29′ N, 116°11′ E 198
Gupis, Pak. 36°12′ N, 73°25′ E 186
Gura Văil, Rom. 44°40′ N, 22°33′ E 168
Gurage, peak, Eth. 8°14′ N, 38°17′ E 224
Gurahonţ, Rom. 46°16′ N, 22°21′ E 168
Gurais, India 34°35′ N, 74°52′ E 186
Gurba, river, Dem. Rep. of the Congo 4°0′ N, 27°27′ E 224
Gurbis, peak, Nor. 68°57′ N, 24°55′ E 152
Gurdaspur, India 32°3′ N, 75°25′ E 186
Gurdon, Ark., U.S. 33°54′ N, 93°9′ W 96
Güre, Turk. 38°38′ N, 29°7′ E 156
Gurgaon, India 28°26′ N, 77°2′ E 197
Gurgei, Jebel, peak, Sudan 13°49′ N, 24°13′ E 226
Gurghiu, Munţii, Rom. 46°52′ N, 24°42′ E 156
Gurha, India 25°9′ N, 71°39′ E 186
Gurī, Eth. 7°30′ N, 40°35′ E 224
Guri Dam, Venez. 7°24′ N, 63°16′ W 130
Guri i Topit, peak, Alban. 40°46′ N, 20°23′ E 156
Gurig National Park, Austral. 11°34′ S, 131°52′ E 238
Gurinhatã, Braz. 19°14′ S, 49°49′ W 138
Gurktaler Alpen, Aust. 46°50′ N, 13°31′ E 167
Gurnet Point, Mass., U.S. 42°0′ N, 70°37′ W 104
Gurrea del Gállego, Sp. 42°0′ N, 0°46′ E 164
Gürün, Turk. 38°42′ N, 37°15′ E 156
Gurupá, Braz. 1°27′ S, 51°38′ W 132
Gurupi, Braz. 11°47′ S, 49°6′ W 130
Gurupi, Cabo, Braz. 0°54′ N, 46°18′ W 130
Gurupi, river, Braz. 2°55′ S, 46°25′ W 130
Gurupi, Serra do, Braz. 5°4′ S, 48°1′ W 130
Guruve, Zimb. 16°40′ S, 30°42′ E 224
Gur'yevsk, Russ. 54°47′ N, 20°34′ E 166
Gur'yevsk, Russ. 54°17′ N, 86°4′ E 184
Gus' Khrustal'nyy, Russ. 55°35′ N, 40°39′ E 154
Gusau, Nig. 12°10′ N, 6°42′ E 222
Güsen, Ger. 52°21′ N, 11°59′ E 152
Gusev, Russ. 54°36′ N, 22°13′ E 166
Guşgy, Turkm. 35°18′ N, 62°25′ E 186
Guşgy, river, Turkm. 37°12′ N, 62°30′ E 186
Gushan, China 39°53′ N, 123°33′ E 200
Gushi, China 32°10′ N, 115°38′ E 198
Gusinaya, Guba 71°25′ N, 145°37′ E 160
Güssing, Aust. 47°2′ N, 16°19′ E 168
Gustav Bull Mountains, Antarctica 67°41′ S, 65°17′ E 248
Gustav Holm, Kap, Den. 66°28′ N, 34°2′ W 106
Gustavia, St.-Barthelemy, Fr. 17°53′ N, 62°51′ W 116
Gustavo Díaz Ordaz, Mex. 26°13′ N, 98°36′ W 114
Gustavus, Alas., U.S. 58°25′ N, 135°44′ W 108
Gustine, Calif., U.S. 37°15′ N, 121°2′ W 100
Guta, Tanzania 2°8′ S, 33°41′ E 224
Gutâiu, peak, Rom. 47°41′ N, 23°47′ E 156
Gutenstein, Aust. 47°53′ N, 15°53′ E 168
Gütersloh, Ger. 51°54′ N, 8°22′ E 167
Guthrie, Ky., U.S. 36°38′ N, 87°10′ W 96
Guthrie, Okla., U.S. 35°51′ N, 97°24′ W 96
Guthrie, Tex., U.S. 33°36′ N, 100°20′ W 92
Gutian, China 26°36′ N, 118°42′ E 198
Gutiérrez, Bol. 19°28′ S, 63°36′ W 137
Gutiérrez Zamora, Mex. 20°27′ N, 97°6′ W 114
Guttenberg, Iowa, U.S. 42°46′ N, 91°7′ W 94
Gutu, Zimb. 19°41′ S, 31°9′ E 224
Güvem, Turk. 40°35′ N, 32°40′ E 156
Guwahati, India 26°11′ N, 91°42′ E 197
Guyana 5°35′ N, 59°12′ W 130
Guyanais Space Center, Fr. 5°9′ N, 52°52′ W 130
Guyang, China 41°1′ N, 110°5′ E 198
Guymon, Okla., U.S. 36°40′ N, 101°30′ W 92
Guyuan, China 41°40′ N, 115°38′ E 198
Guyuan, China 35°59′ N, 106°14′ E 198
Güzeloluk, Turk. 36°45′ N, 34°5′ E 156
Güzelyurt see Morphou, Turk. 38°15′ N, 34°22′ E 156
Guzhang, China 28°35′ N, 109°57′ E 198
Guzmán, Mex. 31°11′ N, 107°27′ W 92
G'uzor, Uzb. 38°36′ N, 66°15′ E 197
Gwa, Myanmar 17°36′ N, 94°36′ E 202
Gwadabawa, Nig. 13°21′ N, 5°12′ E 222
Gwadar, Pak. 25°8′ N, 62°23′ E 182
Gwagwada, Nig. 10°14′ N, 7°12′ E 222
Gwai, Zimb. 19°19′ S, 27°42′ E 224
Gwaii Haanas National Park Reserve and Haida Heritage Site, Can. 52°10′ N, 130°59′ W 108
Gwalangu, Dem. Rep. of the Congo 2°17′ N, 18°14′ E 218
Gwalior, India 26°14′ N, 78°8′ E 197
Gwanda, Zimb. 20°56′ S, 28°58′ E 227
Gwandu, Nig. 12°31′ N, 4°38′ E 222
Gwane, Dem. Rep. of the Congo 4°41′ N, 25°54′ E 224
Gwane, river, Dem. Rep. of the Congo 4°53′ N, 25°25′ E 218
Gwangju (Kwangju), S. Korea 35°8′ N, 126°56′ E 200
Gwangju City, adm. division, S. Korea 35°10′ N, 126°55′ E 200
Gwangyang, S. Korea 34°56′ N, 127°36′ E 200
Gwardafuy, Cape, Somalia 11°38′ N, 51°18′ E 182
Gwayi River, Zimb. 18°37′ S, 27°11′ E 224
Gwayi, river, Zimb. 18°50′ S, 27°10′ E 224
Gwembe, Zambia 16°30′ S, 27°36′ E 224
Gweru, Zimb. 19°30′ S, 29°47′ E 224
Gweta, Botswana 20°10′ S, 25°15′ E 227
Gwinn, Mich., U.S. 46°17′ N, 87°27′ W 94
Gwinner, N. Dak., U.S. 46°13′ N, 97°41′ W 90
Gwoza, Nig. 11°7′ N, 13°43′ E 216
Gwydir, river, Austral. 29°22′ S, 148°51′ E 230
Gya La Pass, China 28°46′ N, 84°32′ E 197
Gyaca, China 29°7′ N, 92°30′ E 188
Gyamish see Gomshasar, Mt., peak, Azerb. 40°17′ N, 46°19′ E 195
Gyangzê, China 28°57′ N, 89°39′ E 197
Gyaring Hu, lake, China 34°55′ N, 96°23′ E 188
Gyarmat, Hung. 47°27′ N, 17°29′ E 168
Gyda, Russ. 70°50′ N, 78°36′ E 169
Gydanskiy Poluostrov, Russ. 69°23′ N, 74°30′ E 169
Gyékényes, Hung. 46°13′ N, 17°0′ E 168
Gyeonggi, adm. division, S. Korea 37°15′ N, 127°3′ E 200
Gyeonggi (Kyŏnggu), S. Korea 35°48′ N, 129°15′ E 200
Gyeongsang, S. Korea 35°47′ N, 128°46′ E 200
Gyeongsang, North, adm. division, S. Korea 36°20′ N, 128°45′ E 200
Gyeongsang, South, adm. division, S. Korea 35°15′ N, 128°15′ E 200
Gyirong (Zongga), China 28°59′ N, 85°16′ E 197
Gyldenløve Fjord 64°6′ N, 43°28′ W 106
Gylgen, Nor. 66°21′ N, 22°41′ E 152
Gympie, Austral. 26°9′ S, 152°41′ E 231
Gyōda, Japan 36°7′ N, 139°28′ E 201
Gyoga, S. Korea 37°22′ N, 129°15′ E 200
Gyoga, S. Korea 37°28′ N, 127°59′ E 200
Gyoha, S. Korea 37°45′ N, 126°46′ E 200
Gyoma, Hung. 46°56′ N, 20°50′ E 168
Gyönk, Hung. 46°34′ N, 18°28′ E 168

Gyopáros, *Hung.* 46°34′ N, 20°38′ E 168
Győr, *Hung.* 47°39′ N, 17°39′ E 168
Győr-Moson-Sopron, adm. division, *Hung.* 47°29′ N, 16°47′ E 156
Gypsumville, *Can.* 51°46′ N, 98°39′ W 108
Gyueshevo, *Bulg.* 42°13′ N, 22°29′ E 168
Gyula, *Hung.* 46°39′ N, 21°17′ E 168
Gyumri, *Arm.* 40°46′ N, 43°50′ E 195
Gyzylarbat, *Turkm.* 38°58′ N, 56°14′ E 180
Gyzyletrek, *Turkm.* 37°41′ N, 54°44′ E 180
Gyzylgaya, *Turkm.* 40°36′ N, 55°27′ E 158
Gyzylsuw, *Turkm.* 39°46′ N, 53°1′ E 180

H

Ha Coi, *Vietnam* 21°27′ N, 107°43′ E 202
Ha Giang, *Vietnam* 22°48′ N, 104°59′ E 202
Ha On, *Israel* 32°43′ N, 35°37′ E 194
Ha Tien, *Vietnam* 10°26′ N, 104°27′ E 202
Ha Tinh, *Vietnam* 18°21′ N, 105°53′ E 202
Ha Trung, *Vietnam* 20°0′ N, 105°48′ E 198
Häädemeeste, *Est.* 58°4′ N, 24°28′ E 166
Haag, *Aust.* 48°5′ N, 14°35′ E 156
Haamstede, *Neth.* 51°42′ N, 3°44′ E 163
Ha'apai Group, islands, *South Pacific Ocean* 19°16′ S, 177°22′ W 238
Haapajärvi, *Fin.* 63°44′ N, 25°18′ E 152
Haapamäki, *Fin.* 62°14′ N, 24°24′ E 152
Haapasaari, *Fin.* 60°16′ N, 27°12′ E 166
Haapavesi, *Fin.* 64°7′ N, 25°19′ E 152
Haapsalu, *Est.* 58°55′ N, 23°30′ E 166
Haar, *Ger.* 48°6′ N, 11°44′ E 152
Haarlem, *Neth.* 52°23′ N, 4°37′ E 163
Haast, *N.Z.* 43°54′ S, 169°0′ E 240
Haaway, *Somalia* 1°7′ N, 43°45′ E 218
Hab, river, *Pak.* 25°7′ N, 66°55′ E 186
Habahe (Kaba), *China* 48°4′ N, 86°21′ E 184
Ḩabarūt, *Oman* 17°15′ N, 52°48′ E 182
Habaswein, *Kenya* 0°59′ N, 39°30′ E 224
Habay, *Can.* 58°51′ N, 118°47′ W 108
Ḩabbūsh, *Leb.* 33°25′ N, 35°28′ E 194
Habermehl Peak, *Antarctica* 71°54′ S, 6°7′ E 248
Habibas, Îles, islands, *Mediterranean Sea* 35°46′ N, 1°30′ W 150
Habiganj, *Bangladesh* 24°20′ N, 91°20′ E 197
Habomai Islands, *North Pacific Ocean* 42°31′ N, 145°36′ E 190
Ḩabshān, *U.A.E.* 23°51′ N, 53°37′ E 196
Hacha, *Col.* 7°420′ N, 75°31′ W 136
Hachenburg, *Ger.* 50°39′ N, 7°48′ E 167
Hachi, *India* 27°49′ N, 94°1′ E 188
Hachijō Jima, island, *Japan* 33°6′ N, 137°49′ E 190
Hachiman, *Japan* 35°44′ N, 136°57′ E 201
Hachinohe, *Japan* 40°26′ N, 141°30′ E 190
Hachiōji, *Japan* 35°38′ N, 139°20′ E 201
Hachita, *N. Mex., U.S.* 31°55′ N, 108°19′ W 92
Hacıbektaş, *Turk.* 38°56′ N, 34°34′ E 156
Hackås, *Nor.* 62°55′ N, 14°31′ E 152
Hackberry, *Ariz., U.S.* 35°21′ N, 113°44′ W 101
Hackberry, *La., U.S.* 29°59′ N, 93°21′ W 103
Hackness, *U.K.* 54°17′ N, 0°31′ E 162
Hadabat el Gîlf el Kebîr, *Egypt* 24°6′ N, 25°40′ E 226
Hadada, Jebel, peak, *Sudan* 20°46′ N, 28°33′ E 226
Hadamar, *Ger.* 50°26′ N, 8°2′ E 167
Hadarba, Ras (Elba, Cape), *Egypt* 21°49′ N, 36°55′ E 182
Ḩaddā', *Saudi Arabia* 21°27′ N, 39°32′ E 182
Haddo House, site, *U.K.* 57°22′ N, 2°21′ W 150
Haddummati Atoll, *Maldives* 1°47′ N, 72°32′ E 188
Hadejia, *Nig.* 12°30′ N, 10°5′ E 222
Ḩadera, *Israel* 32°26′ N, 34°55′ E 194
Haderslev, *Den.* 55°15′ N, 9°29′ E 150
Hadībоh, *Yemen* 12°37′ N, 53°57′ E 182
Hadid, Cap, *Mor.* 31°45′ N, 10°42′ W 214
Ḩadīd, Jabal, peak, *Lib.* 20°21′ N, 22°11′ E 216
Hadilik, *China* 37°52′ N, 86°6′ E 184
Hadım, *Turk.* 36°59′ N, 32°26′ E 156
Hadīyah, *Saudi Arabia* 25°32′ N, 38°37′ E 182
Hadjadj, *Alg.* 36°5′ N, 0°19′ E 164
Hadleigh, *U.K.* 52°2′ N, 0°56′ E 162
Hadley, *Mass., U.S.* 42°19′ N, 72°36′ W 104
Hadley Bay 72°0′ N, 110°44′ W 106
Hadong, *S. Korea* 35°4′ N, 127°46′ E 200
Ḩadramawt, region, *Asia* 16°17′ N, 49°26′ E 182
Hadrut (Gadrut), *Azerb.* 39°30′ N, 47°0′ E 195
Hadsten, *Den.* 56°19′ N, 10°2′ E 152
Hadsund, *Den.* 56°43′ N, 10°7′ E 150
Hadyach, *Ukr.* 50°20′ N, 33°54′ E 158
Haedo, Cuchilla de, *Uru.* 31°29′ S, 56°45′ W 139
Haeju, *N. Korea* 38°2′ N, 125°42′ E 200
Haeju-man 37°47′ N, 125°42′ E 200
Haemi, *S. Korea* 36°41′ N, 126°33′ E 200
Haenam, *S. Korea* 34°32′ N, 126°37′ E 200
Ḩafar al Bāţin, *Saudi Arabia* 28°24′ N, 46°0′ E 180
Haffkrug, *Ger.* 54°3′ N, 10°45′ E 150
Hafford, *Can.* 52°44′ N, 107°22′ W 108
Hafik, *Turk.* 39°51′ N, 37°23′ E 156
Ḩafīt, Jabal, peak, *U.A.E.* 24°3′ N, 55°41′ E 196
Hafizabad, *Pak.* 32°3′ N, 73°39′ E 186
Haflong, *India* 25°10′ N, 92°59′ E 188
Haft Gel, *Iran* 31°28′ N, 49°34′ E 180
Hag 'Abdullah, *Sudan* 13°55′ N, 33°34′ E 182
Hagadera, *Kenya* 2°119′ N, 40°23′ E 224
Hagåtña (Agana), *Guam, U.S.* 13°0′ N, 145°0′ E 242
Hagemeister Island, *Alas., U.S.* 58°9′ N, 161°42′ W 98
Hagen, *Ger.* 51°22′ N, 7°28′ E 167
Hagen Fjord 81°30′ N, 28°8′ W 246
Hagenower Heide, *Ger.* 53°24′ N, 11°13′ E 150
Hagensborg, *Can.* 52°22′ N, 126°33′ W 108
Hāgere Hiywet, *Eth.* 8°56′ N, 37°54′ E 224
Hagerhill, *Ky., U.S.* 37°46′ N, 82°48′ W 96
Hagerman, *N. Mex., U.S.* 33°6′ N, 104°20′ W 92
Hagerman Fossil Beds National Monument, *Idaho, U.S.* 42°47′ N, 115°2′ W 90
Hagerstown, *Md., U.S.* 39°38′ N, 77°43′ W 94
Hagfors, *Nor.* 60°2′ N, 13°41′ E 152
Häggenås, *Nor.* 63°23′ N, 14°53′ E 152
Häggsjön, *Nor.* 63°54′ N, 14°11′ E 152
Hagi, *Japan* 34°24′ N, 131°25′ E 200
Hagia Triada, ruin(s), *Gr.* 35°2′ N, 24°41′ E 156
Hags Head, *Ire.* 52°46′ N, 9°50′ W 150
Hague, *N.Y., U.S.* 43°44′ N, 73°31′ W 104
Hague, Cap de la, *Fr.* 49°41′ N, 2°29′ W 150
Haguenau, *Fr.* 48°48′ N, 7°47′ E 163
Haha Jima Rettō, islands, *North Pacific Ocean* 26°35′ N, 139°20′ E 190
Hahn, *Ger.* 50°31′ N, 7°53′ E 167
Hahót, *Hung.* 46°38′ N, 16°54′ E 168
Hai'an, *China* 32°32′ N, 120°25′ E 198
Haicheng, *China* 40°52′ N, 122°44′ E 200
Haida Gwaii (Queen Charlotte Is.), *Can.* 53°6′ N, 132°30′ W 98
Haidargarh, *India* 26°35′ N, 81°20′ E 197
Haifa, *Israel* 32°46′ N, 35°0′ E 180
Haifa see Ḩefa, *Israel* 32°47′ N, 35°0′ E 194
Haifeng, *China* 22°57′ N, 115°20′ E 198
Haig, *Austral.* 31°1′ S, 126°4′ E 231
Haiger, *Ger.* 50°44′ N, 8°12′ E 167
Haikang, *China* 20°50′ N, 110°2′ E 198
Haikou, *China* 20°1′ N, 110°19′ E 198
Ha'iku, *Hawai'i, U.S.* 20°55′ N, 156°20′ W 99
Ḩā'il, *Saudi Arabia* 27°30′ N, 41°43′ E 180
Hailar, *China* 49°9′ N, 119°38′ E 198
Hailar, river, *China* 49°32′ N, 121°17′ E 198
Hailesboro, *N.Y., U.S.* 44°17′ N, 75°28′ W 110
Haileybury, *Can.* 47°27′ N, 79°38′ W 94
Hailong, *China* 42°39′ N, 125°50′ E 200
Hails, *China* 41°25′ N, 106°25′ E 198
Hailun, *China* 47°28′ N, 126°58′ E 198
Hailuoto, *Fin.* 65°0′ N, 24°42′ E 152
Hainan, adm. division, *China* 19°22′ N, 108°59′ E 198
Hainan, island, *China* 19°47′ N, 108°42′ E 198
Haines, *Alas., U.S.* 59°14′ N, 135°31′ W 108
Haines City, *Fla., U.S.* 28°6′ N, 81°38′ W 105
Haines Junction, *Can.* 60°53′ N, 137°27′ W 98
Haiphong, *Vietnam* 20°52′ N, 106°39′ E 198
Haitan Dao, island, *China* 25°30′ N, 119°55′ E 198
Haiti 19°8′ N, 72°17′ W 116
Haiwee Reservoir, lake, *Calif., U.S.* 36°9′ N, 118°6′ W 101
Haiya, *Sudan* 18°17′ N, 36°19′ E 182
Haiyan, *China* 30°31′ N, 120°52′ E 198
Haiyuan, *China* 36°35′ N, 105°36′ E 198
Hajdú-Bihar, adm. division, *Hung.* 47°17′ N, 21°10′ E 156
Hajdúhadház, *Hung.* 47°40′ N, 21°40′ E 168
Hajdúnánás, *Hung.* 47°50′ N, 21°26′ E 168
Hajdúszoboszló, *Hung.* 47°26′ N, 21°26′ E 168
Haji Pir Pass, *Pak.* 33°55′ N, 74°4′ E 186
Hajinbu, *S. Korea* 37°37′ N, 128°32′ E 200
Ḩajjah, *Yemen* 15°40′ N, 43°33′ E 182
Ḩājjīābād, *Iran* 28°18′ N, 55°50′ E 196
Hajnówka, *Pol.* 52°44′ N, 23°35′ E 158
Hajós, *Hung.* 46°23′ N, 19°7′ E 168
Hakai Passage 51°41′ N, 128°43′ W 108
Hakansonmonts, *Dem. Rep. of the Congo* 8°49′ S, 25°38′ E 224
Hakari (Akera), river, *Azerb.* 39°28′ N, 46°37′ E 195
Hakataramea, *N.Z.* 44°44′ S, 170°31′ E 240
Hakkâri, *Turk.* 37°33′ N, 43°38′ E 195
Hakkas, *Nor.* 66°54′ N, 21°34′ E 152
Hakken San, peak, *Japan* 34°10′ N, 135°50′ E 201
Hakodate, *Japan* 41°55′ N, 140°33′ E 190
Hakui, *Japan* 36°53′ N, 136°47′ E 201
Hakusan National Park, *Japan* 36°6′ N, 136°33′ E 201
Ḩalab (Aleppo), *Syr.* 36°11′ N, 37°9′ E 180
Ḩalabjah, *Iraq* 35°10′ N, 45°59′ E 180
Halāl, Gebel el, *Egypt* 30°34′ N, 33°53′ E 194
Halali, *Namibia* 19°1′ S, 16°30′ E 220
Halastó, lake, *Hung.* 47°35′ N, 20°48′ E 156
Halayeb, *Egypt* 22°11′ N, 36°35′ E 182
Halba, *Leb.* 34°32′ N, 36°4′ E 194
Halba Desēt, island, *Eritrea* 12°43′ N, 42°12′ E 182
Halbturn, *Aust.* 47°52′ N, 16°58′ E 168
Ḩalbūn, *Syr.* 33°39′ N, 36°14′ E 194
Halcon, Mount, *Philippines* 13°15′ N, 120°55′ E 203
Halden, *Nor.* 59°6′ N, 11°22′ E 152
Haldia, *India* 22°3′ N, 88°4′ E 197
Haldwani, *India* 29°14′ N, 79°30′ E 197
Hale, *Mich., U.S.* 44°22′ N, 83°49′ W 110
Hale Eddy, *N.Y., U.S.* 42°0′ N, 75°24′ W 94
Haleakalā Observatories, site, *Hawai'i, U.S.* 20°41′ N, 156°19′ W 99
Haleki'i-Pihana Heiaus, site, *Hawai'i, U.S.* 20°54′ N, 156°33′ W 99
Halesowen, *U.K.* 52°27′ N, 2°3′ W 162
Halesworth, *U.K.* 52°20′ N, 1°29′ E 163
Haleyville, *Ala., U.S.* 34°13′ N, 87°38′ W 96
Half Assini, *Ghana* 5°4′ N, 2°53′ W 214
Half Moon Bay, *Calif., U.S.* 37°27′ N, 122°27′ W 100
Half Moon Cay Natural Monument Reserve, *Belize* 17°6′ N, 87°41′ W 115
Halfmoon Bay, *N.Z.* 46°55′ S, 168°7′ E 240
Halfway, *Oreg., U.S.* 44°51′ N, 117°8′ W 90
Halfway Point, *Can.* 51°40′ N, 81°4′ W 110
Halfway, river, *Can.* 56°52′ N, 122°50′ W 108
Haliartus, battle, *Gr.* 38°22′ N, 22°56′ E 156
Halibut, oil field, *Austral.* 38°33′ S, 148°18′ E 230
Halibut Point, *Mass., U.S.* 42°41′ N, 70°39′ W 104
Halicz, peak, *Pol.* 49°4′ N, 22°40′ E 152
Halifax, *Can.* 44°37′ N, 63°43′ W 111
Halifax, *Mass., U.S.* 41°59′ N, 70°53′ W 104
Halifax, *N.C., U.S.* 36°19′ N, 77°37′ W 96
Halifax, *Va., U.S.* 36°45′ N, 78°56′ W 96
Halkett, Cape, *Alas., U.S.* 70°44′ N, 152°18′ W 98
Halkida, *Gr.* 38°30′ N, 23°37′ E 180
Halkidiki, *Gr.* 40°35′ N, 22°57′ E 156
Halkirk, *Can.* 52°16′ N, 112°10′ W 108
Hall Beach, *Can.* 68°46′ N, 81°21′ W 73
Hall Islands, *North Pacific Ocean* 8°9′ N, 152°10′ E 192
Hall Peninsula, *Can.* 63°28′ N, 66°19′ W 106
Hall Summit, *La., U.S.* 32°9′ N, 93°18′ W 103
Hälla, *Nor.* 63°55′ N, 17°16′ E 152
Hallam Peak, *Can.* 52°10′ N, 118°53′ W 108
Hallandale, *Fla., U.S.* 25°59′ N, 80°10′ W 105
Halle, *Belg.* 50°44′ N, 4°13′ E 163
Halle, *Ger.* 52°3′ N, 8°22′ E 167
Halle, *Ger.* 51°27′ N, 11°58′ E 152
Hallenberg, *Ger.* 51°6′ N, 8°36′ E 150
Hallendorf, *Ger.* 52°9′ N, 10°21′ E 167
Hallettsville, *Tex., U.S.* 29°25′ N, 96°56′ W 96
Halley, station, *Antarctica* 75°38′ S, 26°34′ W 248
Hallgren, Mount, *Antarctica* 73°26′ S, 3°58′ W 248
Halliday, *N. Dak., U.S.* 47°19′ N, 102°22′ W 90
Halliday Lake, *Can.* 61°19′ N, 109°42′ W 108
Halligen, islands, *North Sea* 54°44′ N, 7°33′ E 152
Hallim, *S. Korea* 33°23′ N, 126°15′ E 198
Hallingdal, *Nor.* 60°26′ N, 8°49′ E 152
Hallingskarvet, peak, *Nor.* 60°35′ N, 7°40′ E 152
Halliste, river, *Est.* 58°27′ N, 24°58′ E 166
Hällnäs, *Nor.* 64°18′ N, 19°37′ E 152
Hallock, *Minn., U.S.* 48°45′ N, 96°59′ W 90
Halloran Springs, *Calif., U.S.* 35°21′ N, 115°54′ W 101
Hallowell, *Me., U.S.* 44°16′ N, 69°49′ W 104
Halls Creek, *Austral.* 18°17′ S, 127°44′ E 238
Hallschlag, *Ger.* 50°21′ N, 6°27′ E 167
Hallsville, *Tex., U.S.* 32°29′ N, 94°35′ W 103
Hălmagiu, *Rom.* 46°16′ N, 22°38′ E 168
Halmahera, island, *Indonesia* 1°32′ N, 128°44′ E 192
Halmeu, *Rom.* 47°58′ N, 23°1′ E 168
Halmstad, *Sw.* 56°42′ N, 12°52′ E 160
Hal'shany, *Belarus* 54°15′ N, 26°1′ E 166
Halstead, *Kans., U.S.* 37°59′ N, 97°31′ W 90
Halstead, *U.K.* 51°56′ N, 0°39′ E 162
Halten Bank, *Norwegian Sea* 65°1′ N, 6°31′ E 253
Haltern, *Ger.* 51°45′ N, 7°10′ E 167
Halulu Heiau, site, *Hawai'i, U.S.* 20°44′ N, 157°1′ W 99
Halus, ruin(s), *Gr.* 39°7′ N, 22°45′ E 156
Ḩaluza, Ḩolot, *Israel* 31°7′ N, 34°16′ E 194
Ham, *Chad* 10°1′ N, 15°42′ E 216
Ham, *Fr.* 49°44′ N, 3°2′ E 163
Hamada, *Japan* 34°53′ N, 132°5′ E 200
Hamadade Tinrhert, *Alg.-Lib.* 28°40′ N, 6°46′ E 214
Hamadān (Ecbatana), *Iran* 34°48′ N, 48°27′ E 180
Hamaguir, *Alg.* 30°51′ N, 3°4′ W 214
Ḩamāh (Hamath), *Syr.* 35°7′ N, 36°45′ E 194
Hamajima, *Japan* 34°18′ N, 136°46′ E 201
Hāmākua, region, *Oceania* 19°34′ N, 155°33′ W 99
Hamamatsu, *Japan* 34°42′ N, 137°45′ E 201
Haman, *S. Korea* 35°13′ N, 128°25′ E 200
Hamar, *Nor.* 60°47′ N, 11°4′ E 152
Hamarøy, *Nor.* 68°3′ N, 15°38′ E 152
Hamasaka, *Japan* 35°36′ N, 134°27′ E 201
Ḩamâta, Gebel, peak, *Egypt* 24°10′ N, 34°56′ E 182
Hamath see Ḩamāh, *Syr.* 35°7′ N, 36°45′ E 194
Hamburg, *Ark., U.S.* 33°12′ N, 91°48′ W 103
Hamburg, *Ger.* 53°33′ N, 10°1′ E 150
Hamburg, *Iowa, U.S.* 40°36′ N, 95°39′ W 90
Hamburg, *N.Y., U.S.* 42°43′ N, 78°50′ W 94
Hamburg, adm. division, *Ger.* 53°34′ N, 9°31′ E 150
Hambuti, spring, *Sudan* 16°50′ N, 32°26′ E 182
Hamchang, *S. Korea* 36°32′ N, 128°11′ E 200
Ḩamḑah, *Saudi Arabia* 18°57′ N, 43°40′ E 182
Ḩamdānah, *Saudi Arabia* 19°57′ N, 40°35′ E 182
Hamden, *Conn., U.S.* 41°22′ N, 72°55′ W 104
Hamden, *Ohio, U.S.* 39°8′ N, 82°32′ W 102
Hämeenkyrö, *Fin.* 61°37′ N, 23°8′ E 166
Hämeenlinna, *Fin.* 61°0′ N, 24°22′ E 166
Hamelin Pool 26°29′ S, 113°37′ E 230
Hameln, *Ger.* 52°6′ N, 9°22′ E 150
Hamer Koke, *Eth.* 5°11′ N, 36°46′ E 224
Hamersley Range, *Austral.* 21°46′ S, 116°17′ E 230
Hamgyong, North, adm. division, *N. Korea* 41°54′ N, 129°24′ E 200
Hamgyong, South, adm. division, *N. Korea* 40°14′ N, 127°31′ E 200
Hamhŭng, *N. Korea* 39°53′ N, 127°32′ E 200
Hami, *China* 42°48′ N, 93°23′ E 190
Hamid, Dar, *Sudan* 13°44′ N, 31°24′ E 182
Hamilton, *Ala., U.S.* 34°8′ N, 87°59′ W 96
Hamilton, *Bermuda Islands, U.K.* 32°0′ N, 65°0′ W 118
Hamilton, *Can.* 43°14′ N, 79°51′ W 110
Hamilton, *Mo., U.S.* 39°43′ N, 94°0′ W 94
Hamilton, *Mo., U.S.* 40°23′ N, 91°21′ W 94
Hamilton, *N.Y., U.S.* 42°49′ N, 75°33′ W 94
Hamilton, *N.Z.* 37°48′ S, 175°15′ E 240
Hamilton, *Ohio, U.S.* 39°23′ N, 84°33′ W 102
Hamilton, *Tex., U.S.* 31°41′ N, 98°7′ W 92
Hamilton, *U.K.* 55°45′ N, 4°3′ W 150
Hamilton Inlet 54°3′ N, 61°3′ W 73
Hamilton, Mount, *Antarctica* 80°38′ S, 159°7′ E 248
Hamilton, Mount, *Nev., U.S.* 39°13′ N, 115°37′ W 90
Hamilton Sound 49°31′ N, 55°5′ W 111
Hamina, *Fin.* 60°34′ N, 27°11′ E 166
Hamiota, *Can.* 50°11′ N, 100°36′ W 90
Hamirpur, *India* 25°54′ N, 80°9′ E 197
Hamjun, *N. Korea* 39°32′ N, 127°13′ E 200
Hamlet, *Ind., U.S.* 41°22′ N, 86°35′ W 102
Hamlet, *N.C., U.S.* 34°52′ N, 79°43′ W 96
Hamlin, *Me., U.S.* 47°3′ N, 67°49′ W 111
Hamlin, *N.Y., U.S.* 43°18′ N, 77°56′ W 94
Hamlin, *Tex., U.S.* 32°52′ N, 100°8′ W 92
Hamm, *Ger.* 51°40′ N, 7°48′ E 167
Hammam Lif, *Tun.* 36°41′ N, 10°19′ E 214
Hammarland, *Fin.* 60°12′ N, 19°43′ E 154
Hammerdal, *Nor.* 63°35′ N, 15°19′ E 152
Hammeren, *Den.* 55°17′ N, 14°49′ E 152
Hammerfest, *Nor.* 70°37′ N, 24°3′ E 160
Hamminkeln, *Ger.* 51°43′ N, 6°35′ E 167
Hammond, *Ill., U.S.* 39°47′ N, 88°36′ W 102
Hammond, *Ind., U.S.* 41°35′ N, 87°29′ W 102
Hammond, *La., U.S.* 30°29′ N, 90°27′ W 103
Hammond, *Mont., U.S.* 45°11′ N, 104°55′ W 90
Hammond, *Oreg., U.S.* 46°10′ N, 123°57′ W 100
Hammonton, *N.J., U.S.* 39°37′ N, 74°49′ W 94
Hamningberg, *Nor.* 70°30′ N, 30°36′ E 152
Hamont, *Belg.* 51°14′ N, 5°32′ E 167
Hampden, *N.Z.* 45°21′ S, 170°47′ E 240
Hampton, *Ark., U.S.* 33°30′ N, 92°29′ W 96
Hampton, *Fla., U.S.* 29°51′ N, 82°9′ W 105
Hampton, *Iowa, U.S.* 42°44′ N, 93°12′ W 94
Hampton, *N.H., U.S.* 42°56′ N, 70°50′ W 104
Hampton, *S.C., U.S.* 32°51′ N, 81°7′ W 96
Hampton, *Va., U.S.* 37°1′ N, 76°22′ W 96
Hampton Bays, *N.Y., U.S.* 40°52′ N, 72°32′ W 104
Hampton Beach, *N.H., U.S.* 42°54′ N, 70°50′ W 104
Hampton Butte, peak, *Oreg., U.S.* 43°45′ N, 120°22′ W 90
Hampton, Mount, *Antarctica* 76°22′ S, 125°11′ W 248
Hampyeong, *S. Korea* 35°2′ N, 126°30′ E 200
Hamrånge, *Nor.* 60°55′ N, 17°1′ E 152
Hamrat esh Sheikh, *Sudan* 14°32′ N, 27°57′ E 226
Hamyang, *S. Korea* 35°30′ N, 127°44′ E 200
Han, *Ghana* 10°41′ N, 2°28′ W 222
Han Pijesak, *Bosn. and Herzg.* 44°4′ N, 18°58′ E 168
Han, river, *China* 23°54′ N, 116°25′ E 198
Han, river, *China* 32°44′ N, 109°0′ E 198
Han, river, *S. Korea* 37°33′ N, 128°29′ E 200
Han sur Lesse, *Belg.* 50°6′ N, 5°12′ E 167
Han Uul, *Mongolia* 47°58′ N, 114°40′ E 198
Hanamalo Point, *U.S.* 19°6′ N, 156°15′ W 99
Hanang, peak, *Tanzania* 4°28′ S, 35°21′ E 224
Hanau, *Ger.* 50°7′ N, 8°55′ E 167
Hancheng, *China* 35°30′ N, 110°25′ E 198
Hanchuan, *China* 30°36′ N, 113°47′ E 198
Hancock, *Mich., U.S.* 47°8′ N, 88°36′ W 94
Hancock, *Minn., U.S.* 45°28′ N, 95°49′ W 90
Hancock, *Vt., U.S.* 43°55′ N, 72°52′ W 104
Handa, *Japan* 34°52′ N, 136°56′ E 201
Handan, *China* 36°37′ N, 114°27′ E 198
Handen, *Sw.* 59°9′ N, 18°9′ E 166
Handies Peak, *Colo., U.S.* 37°53′ N, 107°35′ W 90
Haneti, *Tanzania* 5°29′ S, 35°54′ E 224
Hanford, *Calif., U.S.* 36°20′ N, 119°40′ W 100
Hangatiki, *N.Z.* 38°17′ S, 175°9′ E 240
Hanggin Houqi, *China* 40°51′ N, 107°5′ E 198
Hanggin Qi, *China* 39°51′ N, 108°43′ E 198
Hangklip, Cape, *S. Af.* 34°38′ S, 18°11′ E 227
Hangö (Hanko), *Fin.* 59°49′ N, 22°57′ E 166
Hangu, *China* 39°13′ N, 117°43′ E 198
Hangzhou, *China* 30°21′ N, 120°13′ E 198
Hanhöhiy, *Mongolia* 47°39′ N, 112°7′ E 198
Hani, *Turk.* 38°24′ N, 40°24′ E 195
Haniá (Canea), *Gr.* 35°25′ N, 23°59′ E 180
Ḩanīsh al Kabīr, island, *Yemen* 13°25′ N, 42°45′ E 182
Hankinson, *N. Dak., U.S.* 46°3′ N, 96°55′ W 90
Hanko see Hangö, *Fin.* 59°49′ N, 22°57′ E 166
Hanksville, *Utah, U.S.* 38°21′ N, 110°42′ W 90
Hanle, *India* 32°45′ N, 78°57′ E 188
Hanley, *U.K.* 53°1′ N, 2°11′ W 162
Hanmer Springs, *N.Z.* 42°32′ S, 172°50′ E 240
Hann, Mount, *Austral.* 15°55′ S, 125°35′ E 230
Hanna, *Can.* 51°39′ N, 111°56′ W 90
Hanna, *Ind., U.S.* 41°24′ N, 86°47′ W 102
Hanna, *Wyo., U.S.* 41°52′ N, 106°33′ W 90
Hannibal, *Mo., U.S.* 39°42′ N, 91°23′ W 94
Hannibal, *Ohio, U.S.* 39°39′ N, 80°53′ W 94
Hannover (Hanover), *Ger.* 52°22′ N, 9°45′ E 150
Hanoi, *Vietnam* 21°0′ N, 105°40′ E 198
Hanover, *Can.* 44°8′ N, 81°0′ W 102
Hanover, *Conn., U.S.* 41°38′ N, 72°5′ W 104
Hanover, *Ill., U.S.* 42°14′ N, 90°16′ W 102
Hanover, *Ind., U.S.* 38°42′ N, 85°28′ W 102
Hanover, *Kans., U.S.* 39°52′ N, 96°53′ W 90
Hanover, *Mich., U.S.* 42°5′ N, 84°34′ W 102
Hanover, *N.H., U.S.* 43°42′ N, 72°18′ W 104
Hanover, *N. Mex., U.S.* 32°48′ N, 108°5′ W 92
Hanover, *Pa., U.S.* 39°48′ N, 76°59′ W 94
Hanover, *S. Af.* 31°4′ S, 24°26′ E 227
Hanover, Isla, island, *Chile* 51°9′ S, 76°32′ W 134
Hanover see Hannover, *Ger.* 52°22′ N, 9°45′ E 150
Hanp'o, *N. Korea* 38°12′ N, 126°29′ E 200
Hansard, *Can.* 54°4′ N, 121°55′ W 108
Hansen, *Idaho, U.S.* 42°32′ N, 114°18′ W 90
Hansen Inlet 75°20′ S, 67°43′ W 248
Hansjö, *Nor.* 61°9′ N, 14°34′ E 152
Hantsavichy, *Belarus* 52°45′ N, 26°26′ E 152
Hanumangarh, *India* 29°36′ N, 74°17′ E 186
Hanuy, river, *Mongolia* 48°41′ N, 102°6′ E 198
Hanyang, *China* 30°32′ N, 114°4′ E 198
Hanyin, *China* 32°53′ N, 108°31′ E 198
Hanzhong, *China* 33°6′ N, 107°3′ E 198
Haparanda, *Nor.* 65°49′ N, 24°5′ E 152
Happisburgh, *U.K.* 52°49′ N, 1°31′ E 163
Happy, *Tex., U.S.* 34°43′ N, 101°52′ W 92
Happy Valley-Goose Bay, *Can.* 53°19′ N, 60°22′ W 106
Hapur, *India* 28°42′ N, 77°47′ E 197
Ḩaql, *Saudi Arabia* 29°13′ N, 34°56′ E 180
Har Ayrag, *Mongolia* 45°41′ N, 109°15′ E 198
Har Horin (Karakorum), ruin(s), *Mongolia* 47°14′ N, 102°43′ E 198
Ḩaraḑ, *Saudi Arabia* 24°7′ N, 49°5′ E 196
Haradnaya, *Belarus* 51°51′ N, 26°30′ E 152
Haradok, *Belarus* 55°28′ N, 30°0′ E 166

Harads, Nor. 66°4' N, 20°57' E 152
Haradzyeya, Belarus 53°18' N, 26°32' E 152
Haranomachi, Japan 37°38' N, 140°57' E 201
Harappa, ruin(s), Pak. 30°40' N, 72°45' E 186
Harare, Zimb. 17°53' S, 30°56' E 224
Harat, island, Eritrea 15°53' N, 39°5' E 182
Haraz, Chad 13°57' N, 19°25' E 216
Haraza, Jebel, peak, Sudan 15°3' N, 30°19' E 226
Harazé Mangueigne, Chad 9°54' N, 20°47' E 216
Harbin, China 45°43' N, 126°42' E 198
Harbor Beach, Mich., U.S. 43°50' N, 82°41' W 102
Harbour Breton, Can. 47°28' N, 55°50' W 111
Harcuvar Mountains, Ariz., U.S. 33°56' N, 113°45' W 101
Harda, India 22°22' N, 77°5' E 197
Hardangervidda, Nor. 60°13' N, 7°19' E 152
Hardenberg, Neth. 52°34' N, 6°38' E 163
Harderwijk, Neth. 52°20' N, 5°36' E 163
Hardin, Mo., U.S. 39°8' N, 90°39' W 94
Hardin, Mont., U.S. 45°43' N, 107°37' W 90
Hardin, Tex., U.S. 30°8' N, 94°44' W 103
Harding Lake, Can. 56°7' N, 98°59' W 108
Hardisty, Can. 52°39' N, 111°18' W 108
Hardman, Oreg., U.S. 45°10' N, 119°44' W 90
Hardwick, Mass., U.S. 42°20' N, 72°13' W 104
Hardwick, Vt., U.S. 44°29' N, 72°23' W 104
Hardwood Point, Mich., U.S. 43°54' N, 82°41' W 102
Hardy, Ark., U.S. 36°18' N, 91°29' W 96
Hardy, Peninsula, Chile 55°49' S, 67°37' W 248
Hardy, river, Mex. 32°26' N, 115°17' W 101
Hareid, Nor. 62°21' N, 6°0' E 152
Haren, Ger. 52°48' N, 7°14' E 163
Härer, Eth. 9°15' N, 42°7' E 224
Harewa, Eth. 9°55' N, 42°1' E 224
Harg, Nor. 58°45' N, 16°56' E 152
Hargeysa, Somalia 9°29' N, 44°2' E 216
Harghita, adm. division, Rom. 46°25' N, 25°1' E 156
Harghita, Munţii, Rom. 46°8' N, 25°13' E 156
Hargla, Est. 57°37' N, 26°22' E 166
Hargshamn, Nor. 60°9' N, 18°23' E 152
Hari, river, Indonesia 1°15' S, 101°51' E 196
Haría, Sp. 29°10' N, 13°29' W 214
Hariat, spring, Mali 16°10' N, 2°24' E 222
Haricha, Hamâda el, Mali 22°44' N, 3°50' W 214
Haridwar, India 29°58' N, 78°8' E 197
Harihari, N.Z. 43°11' S, 170°32' E 240
Harirud, river, Afghan. 34°35' N, 65°7' E 186
Harīrūd, river, Asia 35°46' N, 61°16' E 180
Hariyo, Somalia 5°1' N, 47°26' E 218
Harjavalta, Fin. 61°16' N, 22°6' E 166
Harkány, Hung. 45°51' N, 18°13' E 168
Harlan, Iowa, U.S. 41°38' N, 95°20' W 90
Harlandsville, Liberia 5°49' N, 9°58' W 222
Harlem, Mont., U.S. 48°31' N, 108°47' W 90
Harleston, U.K. 52°24' N, 1°17' E 162
Harlingen, Neth. 53°10' N, 5°25' E 163
Harlowton, Mont., U.S. 46°25' N, 109°49' W 82
Harmaliyah, oil field, Saudi Arabia 24°11' N, 49°37' E 196
Harmancık, Turk. 39°41' N, 29°7' E 156
Harmil, island, Eritrea 16°26' N, 40°13' E 182
Harmony, Minn., U.S. 43°33' N, 92°1' W 94
Harnai, India 17°51' N, 73°8' E 188
Harney Basin, Oreg., U.S. 43°35' N, 119°50' W 90
Harney, Lake, Fla., U.S. 28°44' N, 81°14' W 105
Harney Lake, Oreg., U.S. 43°13' N, 119°42' W 81
Harney Peak, S. Dak., U.S. 43°50' N, 103°37' W 90
Härnösand, Nor. 62°37' N, 17°54' E 152
Haro, Sp. 42°33' N, 2°52' W 164
Haro, Cabo, Mex. 27°44' N, 111°40' W 112
Harold Byrd Mountains, Antarctica 85°15' S, 138°26' W 248
Haro-Shiikh, Somalia 9°17' N, 44°48' E 218
Harpanahalli, India 14°49' N, 75°58' E 188
Harper, Liberia 4°32' N, 7°43' W 222
Harper Creek, river, Can. 58°0' N, 114°56' W 108
Harperville, Miss., U.S. 32°28' N, 89°30' W 103
Harpster, Ohio, U.S. 40°43' N, 83°14' W 102
Harput, Turk. 38°42' N, 39°13' E 195
Harqin, China 41°8' N, 119°45' E 198
Harqin Qi, China 41°56' N, 118°39' E 198
Harquahala Mountains, Ariz., U.S. 33°44' N, 115°23' W 112
Ḩarrah, Yemen 14°59' N, 50°18' E 182
Ḩarrākah, Syr. 34°43' N, 37°2' E 194
Harran, Nor. 64°34' N, 12°27' E 152
Harrell, Ark., U.S. 33°29' N, 92°25' W 103
Harricana, river, Can. 50°50' N, 79°33' W 80
Harriet, Mount, Austral. 26°36' S, 130°52' E 230
Harrington, U.K. 54°36' N, 3°35' W 162
Harrington, Wash., U.S. 47°27' N, 118°16' W 90
Harriott Lake, Can. 56°7' N, 103°22' W 108
Harris, Mount, Can. 59°12' N, 136°39' W 108
Harris Park, region, Europe 58°2' N, 6°56' W 150
Harrisburg, Ark., U.S. 35°33' N, 90°44' W 96
Harrisburg, Mo., U.S. 37°43' N, 88°32' W 94
Harrisburg, Nebr., U.S. 41°33' N, 103°46' W 90
Harrisburg, Oreg., U.S. 44°15' N, 123°9' W 90
Harrisburg, Pa., U.S. 40°14' N, 77°0' W 94
Harrislee, Ger. 54°48' N, 9°23' E 150
Harrismith, S. Af. 28°17' S, 29°7' E 227
Harrison, Ark., U.S. 36°13' N, 93°7' W 96
Harrison, Idaho, U.S. 47°26' N, 116°47' W 90
Harrison, Me., U.S. 44°6' N, 70°41' W 104
Harrison, Mich., U.S. 44°1' N, 84°48' W 102
Harrison, Nebr., U.S. 42°41' N, 103°54' W 90
Harrison Bay 70°18' N, 152°41' W 98
Harrison, Cape, Can. 54°48' N, 58°3' W 106
Harrison Hot Springs, Can. 49°17' N, 121°47' W 100
Harrison Lake, Can. 49°34' N, 122°16' W 100
Harrison Pass, Nev., U.S. 40°19' N, 115°31' W 90
Harrisonburg, La., U.S. 31°46' N, 91°50' W 103
Harrisonburg, Va., U.S. 38°26' N, 78°53' W 94
Harriston, Can. 43°53' N, 80°51' W 102
Harriston, Miss., U.S. 31°43' N, 91°1' W 103
Harrisville, Mich., U.S. 44°39' N, 83°19' W 94
Harrisville, R.I., U.S. 41°57' N, 71°41' W 104
Harrisville, W. Va., U.S. 39°12' N, 81°4' W 102
Harrodsburg, Ind., U.S. 39°0' N, 86°33' W 102
Harrogate, U.K. 53°59' N, 1°33' W 162
Harrow, Can. 42°2' N, 82°55' W 102
Harry S. Truman Reservoir, lake, Mo., U.S. 38°18' N, 94°56' W 81
Harsewinkel, Ger. 51°57' N, 8°13' E 167
Harşit, river, Turk. 40°42' N, 38°53' E 195
Harsud, India 22°5' N, 76°45' E 197
Hart, Mich., U.S. 43°41' N, 86°22' W 102
Hart, Tex., U.S. 34°23' N, 102°8' W 92
Hart Fell, peak, U.K. 55°23' N, 3°31' W 150
Hart Hills, Antarctica 84°21' S, 89°48' W 248
Hart Mountain, Oreg., U.S. 42°27' N, 119°49' W 90
Hart, river, Can. 64°56' N, 137°28' W 98
Harta, Hung. 46°42' N, 19°1' E 168
Hartberg, Aust. 47°16' N, 15°56' E 168
Hårteigen, peak, Nor. 60°10' N, 6°56' E 152
Hartford, Ala., U.S. 31°5' N, 85°42' W 96
Hartford, Conn., U.S. 41°45' N, 72°43' W 104
Hartford, Liberia 5°56' N, 10°2' W 222
Hartford, Me., U.S. 44°21' N, 70°21' W 104
Hartford, Mich., U.S. 42°11' N, 86°10' W 102
Hartford, S. Dak., U.S. 43°36' N, 96°57' W 90
Hartford, Vt., U.S. 43°39' N, 72°21' W 104
Hartford, Wis., U.S. 43°18' N, 88°23' W 102
Hartford City, Ind., U.S. 40°27' N, 85°22' W 102
Hartigan, Mount, Antarctica 76°48' S, 125°29' W 248
Hartland, Can. 46°16' N, 67°32' W 94
Hartland, U.K. 50°59' N, 4°29' W 150
Hartland, Vt., U.S. 43°32' N, 72°25' W 104
Hartlepool, U.K. 54°41' N, 1°13' W 162
Hartley, Iowa, U.S. 43°10' N, 95°29' W 94
Hartley, Tex., U.S. 35°51' N, 102°24' W 92
Hartney, Can. 49°28' N, 100°30' W 90
Hartola, Fin. 61°34' N, 26°0' E 166
Harts, river, S. Af. 27°24' S, 25°14' E 227
Hartselle, Ala., U.S. 34°25' N, 86°55' W 96
Hartshorne, Okla., U.S. 34°49' N, 95°33' W 96
Hartsville, Tenn., U.S. 36°23' N, 86°9' W 96
Hartville, Wyo., U.S. 42°19' N, 104°44' W 90
Harut, river, Afghan. 32°36' N, 61°27' E 186
Harūz-e Bālā, Iran 30°42' N, 57°6' E 180
Harvard, Ill., U.S. 42°24' N, 88°36' W 102
Harvard, Mass., U.S. 42°30' N, 71°35' W 104
Harvard, Nebr., U.S. 40°35' N, 98°6' W 94
Harvard, Mount, Colo., U.S. 38°54' N, 106°23' W 90
Harvey, Ill., U.S. 41°35' N, 87°39' W 102
Harvey, N. Dak., U.S. 47°45' N, 99°57' W 94
Harwell, U.K. 51°35' N, 1°18' W 162
Harwich, U.K. 51°56' N, 1°16' E 162
Harwich Port, Mass., U.S. 41°39' N, 70°5' W 104
Haryana, adm. division, India 29°11' N, 76°18' E 186
Harz, Ger. 51°44' N, 9°56' E 167
Hasan Dağı, peak, Turk. 38°6' N, 34°5' E 156
Ḩasan Langī, Iran 27°20' N, 56°51' E 196
Ḩāşbayyā, Leb. 33°23' N, 35°41' E 194
Hasdo, river, India 23°2' N, 82°23' E 197
Haselünne, Ger. 52°40' N, 7°29' E 163
Hasenkamp, Arg. 31°29' S, 59°49' W 139
Hashaat, Mongolia 45°15' N, 104°48' E 198
Hashimoto, Japan 34°20' N, 135°37' E 201
Ḩāsik, Oman 17°25' N, 55°14' E 182
Haskell, Tex., U.S. 33°8' N, 99°44' W 92
Hasle, Den. 55°11' N, 14°42' E 152
Haslemere, U.K. 51°5' N, 0°43' E 162
Ḩaşrūn, Leb. 34°14' N, 35°58' E 194
Hassberge, Ger. 50°16' N, 10°11' E 167
Hassela, Nor. 62°7' N, 16°39' E 152
Hasselt, Belg. 50°56' N, 5°19' E 167
Hassi Allal, spring, Alg. 31°19' N, 2°38' E 214
Hassi bel Guebbour, spring, Alg. 28°49' N, 6°28' E 214
Hassi Berkane, spring, Alg. 31°7' N, 4°30' E 214
Hassi bou Khechba, spring, Alg. 29°44' N, 5°41' E 214
Hassi bou Zid, Alg. 32°6' N, 1°42' E 214
Hassi Chefaïa, spring, Alg. 29°48' N, 4°21' W 214
Hassi Djafou, spring, Alg. 30°50' N, 3°36' E 214
Hassi el Abiod, spring, Alg. 31°48' N, 3°34' E 214
Hassi el Hadjar, spring, Alg. 31°28' N, 4°44' E 214
Hassi el Mislane, spring, Alg. 27°36' N, 9°50' E 214
Hassi el Motlah, spring, Mauritania 19°23' N, 12°46' W 222
Hassi Erg Sedra, spring, Alg. 30°4' N, 2°6' E 214
Hassi Fokra, spring, Alg. 30°12' N, 1°26' W 214
Hassi Fouini, spring, Mauritania 17°21' N, 7°28' W 222
Hassi Guern el Guessaa, spring, Alg. 31°9' N, 0°47' E 214
Hassi Habadra, spring, Alg. 26°32' N, 4°6' E 214
Hassi Imoulaye, spring, Alg. 29°54' N, 9°10' E 214
Hassi I-n-Belrem, spring, Alg. 26°3' N, 3°10' E 214
Hassi Inifel, Alg. 29°50' N, 3°44' E 214
Hassi I-n-Sokki, spring, Alg. 28°34' N, 3°45' E 214
Hassi Issaouane, spring, Alg. 27°0' N, 8°44' E 214
Hassi Koussane, spring, Alg. 25°31' N, 4°50' E 214
Hassi Larrocque, spring, Alg. 30°50' N, 6°18' E 214
Hassi Mameche, Alg. 35°50' N, 7°416' E 164
Hassi Marroket, spring, Alg. 30°13' N, 2°57' E 214
Hassi Mdakane, spring, Alg. 28°27' N, 2°20' W 214
Hassi Messaoud, oil field, Alg. 31°43' N, 5°56' E 214
Hassi Moungar, spring, Alg. 27°35' N, 3°6' E 214
Hassi Nechou, spring, Alg. 30°35' N, 2°8' E 214
Hassi Ouchene, spring, Alg. 30°17' N, 0°33' E 214
Hassi R'mel, Alg. 32°56' N, 3°8' E 214
Hassi Sedjra Touila, spring, Alg. 30°5' N, 4°6' E 214
Hassi Tabaloulet, spring, Alg. 29°5' N, 3°1' E 214
Hassi Tabelbalet, spring, Alg. 27°20' N, 6°54' E 214
Hassi Taïeb, spring, Alg. 32°5' N, 6°8' E 214
Hassi Tanezrouft, spring, Alg. 28°28' N, 6°37' E 214
Hassi Targant, spring, Alg. 28°20' N, 8°33' W 214
Hassi Tartrat, spring, Alg. 30°6' N, 6°32' E 214
Hassi Tiguentourine, spring, Alg. 26°51' N, 2°43' E 214
Hassi Ti-n-Fouchaye, spring, Alg. 29°30' N, 8°50' E 214
Hassi Touareg, spring, Alg. 30°33' N, 6°26' E 214
Hassi Zegdou, spring, Alg. 29°49' N, 4°44' W 214
Hassi Zirara, spring, Alg. 31°15' N, 3°13' E 214
Hastings, Fla., U.S. 29°42' N, 81°32' W 105
Hastings, Mich., U.S. 42°37' N, 85°17' W 102
Hastings, Minn., U.S. 44°45' N, 92°53' W 82
Hastings, U.K. 50°51' N, 0°34' E 162
Hastings, battle, U.K. 50°53' N, 0°24' E 162
Haswell, Colo., U.S. 38°26' N, 103°10' W 90
Hat, Cape, Can. 50°4' N, 56°4' W 111
Hat Yai, Thai. 6°59' N, 100°29' E 202
Hatay (Antioch), Turk. 36°12' N, 36°8' E 156
Hatch, N. Mex., U.S. 32°39' N, 107°9' W 92
Hatchet Lake, Can. 58°37' N, 104°4' W 108
Haţeg, Rom. 45°36' N, 22°58' E 168
Hatfield, Mass., U.S. 42°21' N, 72°37' W 104
Hatfield, U.K. 51°45' N, 0°14' E 162
Hatgal, Mongolia 50°15' N, 100°0' E 190
Hatherleigh, U.K. 50°49' N, 4°4' W 162
Hathras, India 27°34' N, 78°2' E 197
Hato Corozal, Col. 6°9' N, 71°43' W 136
Hatsuki, Belarus 53°19' N, 27°32' E 152
Hatta, India 24°7' N, 79°37' E 197
Hatteras, N.C., U.S. 35°13' N, 75°42' W 96
Hatteras, Cape, N.C., U.S. 35°10' N, 75°31' W 96
Hatteras Plain, North Atlantic Ocean 29°2' N, 69°36' W 253
Hattersheim, Ger. 50°3' N, 8°28' E 167
Hattie, Lake, Wyo., U.S. 41°16' N, 106°9' W 90
Hattiesburg, Miss., U.S. 31°18' N, 89°18' W 103
Hatton, N. Dak., U.S. 47°37' N, 97°29' W 90
Hattorf, Ger. 51°39' N, 10°14' E 167
Hattstedt, Ger. 54°31' N, 9°1' E 150
Hattula, Fin. 61°4' N, 24°23' E 166
Hatvan, Hung. 47°40' N, 19°42' E 168
Haugesund, Nor. 59°24' N, 5°15' E 152
Hauho, Fin. 61°9' N, 24°32' E 166
Haukivuori, Fin. 62°0' N, 27°11' E 166
Haukiappi, Fin. 61°25' N, 28°28' E 166
Haulover, Nicar. 12°18' N, 83°42' W 115
Haultain Lake, Can. 56°46' N, 106°57' W 108
Haultain, river, Can. 55°45' N, 106°26' W 108
Haumonia, Arg. 27°28' S, 60°12' W 139
Hauola Place of Refuge, site, Hawai'i, U.S. 22°1' N, 159°23' W 99
Haus, Nor. 60°27' N, 5°29' E 152
Hauser, Oreg., U.S. 43°30' N, 124°14' W 90
Hausjärvi, Fin. 60°46' N, 24°54' E 166
Hausruck, Aust. 48°7' N, 13°11' E 152
Haut Atlas, Mor. 32°31' N, 5°4' W 214
Hauta see Al Ḩillah, Saudi Arabia 23°28' N, 46°52' E 196
Haute-Normandie, adm. division, Fr. 49°40' N, 0°27' E 150
Hauterive, Can. 49°12' N, 68°15' W 94
Hautmont, Fr. 50°14' N, 3°54' E 163
Hauts Plateaux, Alg. 34°11' N, 0°38' E 214
Havana, Fla., U.S. 30°36' N, 84°25' W 96
Havana, Ill., U.S. 40°17' N, 90°4' W 102
Havana see La Habana, Cuba 23°6' N, 82°33' W 116
Havant, U.K. 50°51' N, 0°59' E 162
Havasu, Lake, Ariz., U.S. 34°24' N, 114°29' W 101
Havdhem, Sw. 57°9' N, 18°19' E 166
Haveli, Pak. 30°26' N, 73°43' E 186
Havelock, Can. 44°26' N, 77°53' W 94
Havelock, N.C., U.S. 34°52' N, 76°55' W 96
Havelock, N.Z. 41°19' S, 173°45' E 240
Havelock Island, India 11°44' N, 93°11' E 188
Haven, Kans., U.S. 37°53' N, 97°48' W 90
Haverhill, Mass., U.S. 42°46' N, 71°5' W 104
Haverhill, N.H., U.S. 44°1' N, 72°5' W 104
Haverhill, U.K. 52°5' N, 0°26' E 162
Haverö, Nor. 62°22' N, 15°4' E 152
Häverödal, Sw. 60°1' N, 18°34' E 166
Haviland, Kans., U.S. 37°36' N, 99°7' W 90
Havirga, Mongolia 45°43' N, 113°4' E 198
Havola Escarpment, Antarctica 84°34' S, 95°24' W 248
Havøysund, Nor. 70°58' N, 24°38' E 152
Havre, Mont., U.S. 48°31' N, 109°40' W 90
Havre-Aubert, Can. 47°12' N, 61°52' W 111
Havre-Saint-Pierre, Can. 50°14' N, 63°37' W 111
Havza, Turk. 40°58' N, 35°38' E 156
Hawai'i, adm. division, Hawai'i, U.S. 20°0' N, 156°0' W 99
Hawai'i, island, Hawai'i, U.S. 19°33' N, 154°52' W 99
Hawai'i Volcanoes National Park, Hawai'i, U.S. 18°57' N, 156°9' W 99
Hawaiian Ridge, North Pacific Ocean 23°8' N, 164°25' W 252
Ḩawār, island, Qatar 25°40' N, 50°15' E 182
Hawarden, Iowa, U.S. 42°58' N, 96°29' W 90
Hawarden, N.Z. 42°55' S, 172°37' E 240
Hawarden, U.K. 53°11' N, 3°2' W 162
Hawera, N.Z. 39°35' S, 174°16' E 240
Hawes, U.K. 54°18' N, 2°12' W 162
Hawesville, Ky., U.S. 37°53' N, 86°45' W 94
Hawke Harbour, Can. 53°2' N, 55°50' W 111
Hawkes, Mount, Antarctica 83°57' S, 58°11' W 248
Hawkins, Tex., U.S. 32°35' N, 95°12' W 103
Hawksbill, peak, Va., U.S. 38°32' N, 78°29' W 94
Hawley, Minn., U.S. 46°52' N, 96°19' W 90
Hawthorne, Fla., U.S. 29°35' N, 82°6' W 105
Hawza, Western Sahara, Mor. 27°9' N, 11°3' W 214
Hawzēn, Eth. 13°57' N, 39°26' E 182
Haxtun, Colo., U.S. 40°38' N, 102°39' W 90
Hay, Mount, peak, Can. 59°12' N, 137°38' W 108
Hay River, Can. 60°45' N, 115°36' W 106
Hay, river, Can. 58°37' N, 117°59' W 246
Hay, river, Can. 59°53' N, 116°49' W 108
Hay, river, Can. 58°15' N, 120°23' W 108
Hay Springs, Nebr., U.S. 42°40' N, 102°42' W 90
Haya, Sp. 36°43' N, 6°5' W 164
Hayang, S. Korea 35°53' N, 128°49' E 200
Hayange, Fr. 49°20' N, 6°2' E 163
Hayden, Colo., U.S. 40°29' N, 107°14' W 90
Hayden Peak, Utah, U.S. 40°44' N, 110°55' W 90
Haydenville, Mass., U.S. 42°22' N, 72°42' W 104
Hayes, La., U.S. 30°5' N, 92°56' W 103
Hayes, S. Dak., U.S. 44°21' N, 101°3' W 90
Hayes Center, Nebr., U.S. 40°29' N, 101°2' W 90
Hayes, Mount, Alas., U.S. 63°36' N, 146°55' W 98
Hayes, river, Can. 55°8' N, 94°7' W 108
Hayes, river, Can. 54°14' N, 96°24' W 108
Hayes, river, Can. 56°43' N, 92°38' W 108
Haylaastay, Mongolia 46°51' N, 113°26' E 198
Haymā', Oman 19°55' N, 56°23' E 182
Haymana, Turk. 39°26' N, 32°30' E 156
Haynesville, La., U.S. 32°56' N, 93°9' W 103
Hayneville, Ala., U.S. 32°10' N, 86°35' W 96
Hayrabolu, Turk. 41°12' N, 27°5' E 156
Hays, Kans., U.S. 38°51' N, 99°20' W 90
Hays, Mont., U.S. 47°57' N, 108°41' W 90
Haystack Mountain, Can. 50°18' N, 88°41' W 94
Haysville, Kans., U.S. 37°33' N, 97°23' W 92
Haysyn, Ukr. 48°48' N, 29°35' E 158
Hayti, Mo., U.S. 36°14' N, 89°45' W 96
Hayvoron, Ukr. 48°22' N, 30°0' E 156
Hayward, Calif., U.S. 37°40' N, 122°6' W 100
Hayward, Wis., U.S. 46°1' N, 91°29' W 94
Haywards Heath, U.K. 50°59' N, 0°7' E 162
Haywood, Mount, Can. 63°48' N, 125°11' W 98
Hazar Gölü, lake, Turk. 38°53' N, 38°57' E 195
Hazārān, Kūh-e, peak, Iran 29°29' N, 57°13' E 196
Hazard, Ky., U.S. 37°15' N, 83°11' W 96
Hazardville, Conn., U.S. 41°59' N, 72°33' W 104
Hazareh Toghay, Afghan. 37°9' N, 67°16' E 186
Hazaribag, India 23°52' N, 85°18' E 190
Hazebrouck, Fr. 50°43' N, 2°32' E 163
Hazelton, Can. 55°15' N, 127°39' W 108
Hazelton, N. Dak., U.S. 46°28' N, 100°17' W 90
Hazen, Ark., U.S. 34°45' N, 91°35' W 96
Hazen, Nev., U.S. 39°33' N, 119°4' W 90
Hazen, N. Dak., U.S. 47°17' N, 101°39' W 90
Hazen Bay 60°52' N, 167°10' W 98
Hazen Strait 77°9' N, 106°1' W 246
Ḩazerim, Israel 31°14' N, 34°41' E 194
Ḩazeva, Israel 30°48' N, 35°14' E 194
Hazlehurst, Miss., U.S. 31°51' N, 90°24' W 103
Hazleton, Ind., U.S. 38°28' N, 87°33' W 102
Hazleton, Pa., U.S. 40°57' N, 76°0' W 94
Hazor, ruin(s), Israel 33°1' N, 35°31' E 194
Hazro, Turk. 38°14' N, 40°47' E 195
Heacham, U.K. 52°54' N, 0°29' E 162
Head, Mount, Can. 50°26' N, 114°44' W 90
Headcorn, U.K. 51°10' N, 0°37' E 162
Headley, Mount, Mont., U.S. 47°42' N, 115°21' W 90
Healaval Beg, peak, U.K. 57°21' N, 6°44' W 150
Healdsburg, Calif., U.S. 38°37' N, 122°52' W 90
Healdton, Okla., U.S. 34°12' N, 97°29' W 96
Healy, Kans., U.S. 38°35' N, 100°38' W 90
Healy Peak, Nev., U.S. 39°40' N, 117°54' W 90
Heard Island and McDonald Islands, Australia 53°0' S, 74°0' E 248
Hearne, Tex., U.S. 30°52' N, 96°35' W 96
Hearne Bay 60°12' N, 100°0' W 108
Hearst, Can. 49°41' N, 83°41' W 94
Hearst Island, Antarctica 69°27' S, 61°32' W 248
Heart Mountain, Wyo., U.S. 44°37' N, 109°12' W 90
Heart Peaks, Can. 58°35' N, 132°6' W 108
Heart, river, N. Dak., U.S. 46°24' N, 101°50' W 80
Heath, Ohio, U.S. 40°1' N, 82°27' W 94
Heath, Pointe, Can. 49°8' N, 62°26' W 111
Heath, river, South America 13°6' S, 69°1' W 137
Heaval, peak, U.K. 56°57' N, 7°34' W 150
Heavener, Okla., U.S. 34°51' N, 94°37' W 96
Hebbronville, Tex., U.S. 27°17' N, 98°40' W 96
Hebei, adm. division, China 40°36' N, 115°19' E 198
Heber, Ariz., U.S. 34°25' N, 110°35' W 92
Heber, Calif., U.S. 32°43' N, 115°33' W 101
Heber City, Utah, U.S. 40°30' N, 111°25' W 90
Hébert, Lac, lake, Can. 49°8' N, 75°46' W 94
Hebi, China 35°57' N, 114°9' E 198
Hebrides, islands, North Atlantic Ocean 57°39' N, 11°49' W 143
Hebrides, Sea of the 56°42' N, 7°40' W 150
Hebron, Ill., U.S. 42°27' N, 88°27' W 102
Hebron, Ind., U.S. 41°18' N, 87°12' W 102
Hebron, Nebr., U.S. 40°9' N, 97°35' W 90
Hebron, N.H., U.S. 43°41' N, 71°49' W 104
Hebron, N. Dak., U.S. 46°53' N, 102°3' W 90
Hebron see Al Khalīl, West Bank, Israel 31°31' N, 35°6' E 194
Hecate Strait 51°44' N, 128°18' W 106
Hecelchakán, Mex. 20°10' N, 90°9' W 115
Heceta Head, Oreg., U.S. 44°6' N, 124°26' W 90
Hechi, China 24°39' N, 108°1' E 198
Hecho, Sp. 42°43' N, 0°45' E 164
Hechuan, China 30°1' N, 106°12' E 198
Hecla, Can. 51°7' N, 96°42' W 90
Hecla, S. Dak., U.S. 45°51' N, 98°10' W 90
Hecla and Griper Bay 75°33' N, 113°59' W 106
Hecla, Cape, Can. 82°56' N, 67°3' W 246
Hécla, Lac, lake, Can. 52°33' N, 72°28' W 111
Hector, N.Z. 41°38' S, 171°54' E 240
Hector, Mount, Can. 51°34' N, 116°19' W 90
Hédé, Fr. 48°17' N, 1°48' W 150

Hede, *Nor.* 62°25′ N, 13°30′ E 152
Hedemünden, *Ger.* 51°23′ N, 9°46′ E 167
Hedley, *Tex., U.S.* 34°50′ N, 100°40′ W 92
Hedmark, region, *Europe* 60°57′ N, 10°38′ E 152
Hedon, *U.K.* 53°43′ N, 0°12′ E 162
Heemstede, *Neth.* 52°21′ N, 4°36′ E 163
Heerde, *Neth.* 52°23′ N, 6°2′ E 163
Heerlen, *Neth.* 50°52′ N, 5°58′ E 167
Ḥefa (Haifa), *Israel* 32°47′ N, 35°0′ E 194
Hefei, *China* 31°53′ N, 117°20′ E 198
Hefeng, *China* 29°54′ N, 110°0′ E 198
Hegang, *China* 47°29′ N, 130°15′ E 190
Hegyeshalom, *Hung.* 47°55′ N, 17°10′ E 168
Heiau o Kalalea, site, *Hawai'i, U.S.* 18°54′ N, 155°44′ W 99
Heide, *Ger.* 54°12′ N, 9°6′ E 150
Heidelberg, *Ger.* 49°24′ N, 8°40′ E 150
Heidelberg, *Miss., U.S.* 31°52′ N, 88°59′ W 103
Heidelberg, *S. Af.* 34°4′ S, 20°55′ E 227
Heihe, *China* 50°9′ N, 127°24′ E 190
Heilbron, *S. Af.* 27°19′ S, 27°56′ E 227
Heilbronn, *Ger.* 49°8′ N, 9°13′ E 152
Heiligenstadt, *Ger.* 51°22′ N, 10°8′ E 167
Heilinzi, *China* 44°34′ N, 126°40′ E 198
Heilong Jiang, river, *China* 51°18′ N, 138°37′ E 190
Heilongjiang, adm. division, *China* 46°58′ N, 128°21′ E 198
Heimdal, *Nor.* 63°19′ N, 10°20′ E 152
Heimefront Range, *Antarctica* 74°46′ S, 11°55′ W 248
Heinävesi, *Fin.* 62°23′ N, 28°35′ E 152
Heinola, *Fin.* 61°12′ N, 26°2′ E 166
Heinsberg, *Ger.* 51°3′ N, 6°5′ E 167
Heinsburg, *Can.* 53°46′ N, 110°32′ W 108
Heishan, *China* 41°42′ N, 122°9′ E 198
Hejaz see Al Ḥijāz, region, *Saudi Arabia* 26°54′ N, 36°41′ E 180
Hejian, *China* 38°29′ N, 116°4′ E 198
Hejiang, *China* 28°50′ N, 105°42′ E 198
Hejing, *China* 42°18′ N, 86°30′ E 184
Hekla, peak, *Ice.* 64°1′ N, 20°7′ W 143
Hekou, *China* 22°34′ N, 103°57′ E 202
Hel, *Pol.* 54°37′ N, 18°49′ E 166
Helagsfjället, peak, *Nor.* 62°56′ N, 12°20′ E 152
Helan Shan, peak, *China* 38°37′ N, 105°47′ E 198
Hele Islands, *Solomon Sea* 9°0′ S, 158°0′ E 242
Helechosa, *Sp.* 39°18′ N, 4°56′ W 164
Helen Island, *Palau* 2°18′ N, 131°51′ E 192
Helen Lake, *Can.* 49°3′ N, 88°38′ W 110
Helen, Mount, *Nev., U.S.* 37°29′ N, 116°50′ W 92
Helena, *Ark., U.S.* 34°31′ N, 90°39′ W 112
Helena, *Ga., U.S.* 32°4′ N, 82°56′ W 96
Helena, *Mont., U.S.* 46°33′ N, 112°10′ W 90
Helena, *Okla., U.S.* 36°32′ N, 98°17′ W 96
Helena, *S.C., U.S.* 34°16′ N, 81°39′ W 96
Helengili, island, *Maldives* 4°18′ N, 73°41′ E 188
Helensville, *N.Z.* 36°41′ S, 174°27′ E 240
Helgoland, island, *Ger.* 54°12′ N, 7°53′ E 152
Helgøy, *Nor.* 70°6′ N, 19°23′ E 152
Helicon see Elikónas, peak, *Gr.* 38°17′ N, 22°47′ E 156
Hellberge, peak, *Ger.* 52°33′ N, 11°12′ E 152
Hellemobotn, *Nor.* 67°49′ N, 16°31′ E 152
Hellenthal, *Ger.* 50°28′ N, 6°25′ E 167
Hellesylt, *Nor.* 62°4′ N, 6°52′ E 152
Helligvær, islands, *Norwegian Sea* 67°27′ N, 12°27′ E 152
Hellín, *Sp.* 38°30′ N, 1°42′ W 164
Hells Canyon, *Oreg., U.S.* 45°30′ N, 116°43′ W 90
Hells Gate, *Can.* 49°43′ N, 121°35′ W 100
Hells Half Acre, site, *Wyo., U.S.* 43°1′ N, 107°9′ W 90
Hell-Ville see Andoany, *Madagascar* 13°24′ S, 48°17′ E 207
Helmand, river, *Afghan.* 30°13′ N, 62°36′ E 186
Helmand, river, *Afghan.* 33°24′ N, 66°12′ E 186
Helmeringhausen, *Namibia* 25°56′ S, 16°54′ E 227
Helmond, *Neth.* 51°28′ N, 5°40′ E 167
Helong, *China* 42°31′ N, 128°58′ E 200
Helper, *Utah, U.S.* 39°40′ N, 110°51′ W 90
Helsingborg, *Nor.* 56°3′ N, 12°43′ E 152
Helsingfors see Helsinki, *Fin.* 60°9′ N, 24°48′ E 166
Helsingør, *Den.* 56°1′ N, 12°34′ E 152
Helsinki, *Fin.* 60°9′ N, 24°48′ E 166
Helska, Mierzeja, *Pol.* 54°45′ N, 18°32′ E 166
Heltermaa, *Est.* 58°51′ N, 23°0′ E 166
Helvecia, *Arg.* 31°6′ S, 60°8′ W 139
Helvécia, *Hung.* 46°49′ N, 19°38′ E 168
Helvellyn, peak, *U.K.* 54°30′ N, 3°3′ W 162
Helvick Head, *Ire.* 51°53′ N, 7°31′ W 150
Ḥelwân, *Egypt* 29°50′ N, 31°19′ E 182
Hemet, *Calif., U.S.* 33°45′ N, 117°0′ W 101
Heming Lake, *Can.* 54°56′ N, 101°7′ W 108
Hemingford, *Nebr., U.S.* 42°19′ N, 103°8′ W 90
Hemis National Park, *India* 33°48′ N, 77°22′ E 188
Hemne, *Nor.* 63°15′ N, 9°5′ E 152
Hemphill, *Tex., U.S.* 31°19′ N, 93°52′ W 103
Hempstead, *N.Y., U.S.* 40°41′ N, 73°38′ W 104
Hempstead, *Tex., U.S.* 30°4′ N, 96°5′ W 96
Hemse, *Sw.* 57°13′ N, 18°22′ E 166
Hemsedal, *Nor.* 60°52′ N, 8°33′ E 152
Hemsedalsfjelli, *Nor.* 60°56′ N, 7°9′ E 152
Henan, adm. division, *China* 33°22′ N, 112°17′ E 198
Hendek, *Turk.* 40°48′ N, 30°46′ E 158
Henderson, *Ky., U.S.* 37°49′ N, 87°35′ W 96
Henderson, *Nev., U.S.* 36°1′ N, 115°0′ W 101
Henderson, *Tenn., U.S.* 35°25′ N, 88°38′ W 96
Henderson, *Tex., U.S.* 32°8′ N, 94°48′ W 103
Henderson, *W. Va., U.S.* 38°48′ N, 82°10′ W 102
Henderson Island, *U.K.* 24°19′ S, 128°22′ W 255
Hendersonville, *Tenn., U.S.* 36°18′ N, 86°37′ W 96
Hendon, *Can.* 52°4′ N, 103°49′ W 108
Hendrik Top, peak, *Suriname* 4°11′ N, 56°21′ W 130
Hengām, island, *Iran* 26°28′ N, 55°51′ E 180
Hengchun, *Taiwan, China* 22°2′ N, 120°45′ E 198
Hengshan, *China* 37°57′ N, 109°18′ E 198
Hengshui, *China* 37°41′ N, 115°43′ E 198
Hengxian, *China* 22°42′ N, 109°13′ E 198
Hengyang, *China* 27°1′ N, 112°27′ E 190
Henhoaha, *India* 6°48′ N, 93°54′ E 188
Heniches'k, *Ukr.* 46°12′ N, 34°46′ E 156
Hénin-Beaumont, *Fr.* 50°24′ N, 2°57′ E 163
Henley on Thames, *U.K.* 51°32′ N, 0°55′ E 162
Hennan, *Nor.* 62°2′ N, 15°52′ E 152
Hennessey, *Okla., U.S.* 36°4′ N, 97°53′ W 92
Henniker, *N.H., U.S.* 43°10′ N, 71°51′ W 104
Henning, *Minn., U.S.* 46°18′ N, 95°28′ W 90
Henrietta, *Tex., U.S.* 33°47′ N, 98°11′ W 92
Henrietta Island, *Can.* 76°54′ N, 157°30′ E 255
Henrietta Maria, Cape, *Can.* 55°5′ N, 82°20′ W 106
Henrieville, *Utah, U.S.* 37°34′ N, 111°59′ W 92
Henry, *Ill., U.S.* 41°6′ N, 89°23′ W 102
Henry Bay 66°28′ S, 121°28′ E 248
Henry, Cape, *Va., U.S.* 36°34′ N, 75°57′ W 80
Henry Kater Peninsula, *Can.* 69°15′ N, 66°31′ W 106
Henry Lawrence Island, *India* 11°59′ N, 93°14′ E 188
Henry Mountains, *Utah, U.S.* 38°3′ N, 110°56′ W 90
Henryetta, *Okla., U.S.* 35°25′ N, 95°59′ W 96
Henryville, *Ind., U.S.* 38°32′ N, 85°45′ W 102
Hensall, *Can.* 43°26′ N, 81°30′ W 102
Henshaw, Lake, *Calif., U.S.* 33°15′ N, 116°53′ W 101
Hentiy, *Mongolia* 48°5′ N, 109°50′ E 198
Hentiy, adm. division, *Mongolia* 48°14′ N, 109°39′ E 198
Hephaestia, ruin(s), *Gr.* 39°56′ N, 25°13′ E 156
Heping, *China* 24°25′ N, 114°56′ E 198
Heppner, *Oreg., U.S.* 45°20′ N, 119°34′ W 90
Hepu, *China* 21°38′ N, 109°14′ E 198
Heraea, ruin(s), *Gr.* 37°36′ N, 21°47′ E 156
Herald Cays, *Coral Sea* 16°47′ S, 147°46′ E 230
Herat, *Afghan.* 34°27′ N, 62°11′ E 186
Herb Lake, *Can.* 54°46′ N, 99°46′ W 108
Herbert, *Can.* 50°25′ N, 107°15′ W 90
Herbert, *N.Z.* 45°14′ S, 170°48′ E 240
Herbertabad, *India* 11°43′ N, 92°46′ E 188
Herbertingen, *Ger.* 48°3′ N, 9°26′ E 156
Herbolzheim, *Ger.* 48°13′ N, 7°45′ E 163
Herborn, *Ger.* 50°40′ N, 8°18′ E 167
Herbstein, *Ger.* 50°34′ N, 9°21′ E 167
Herceg-Novi, *Serb.* 42°27′ N, 18°31′ E 168
Hercegszántó, *Hung.* 45°57′ N, 18°55′ E 168
Herchmer, *Can.* 57°24′ N, 94°12′ W 108
Hercules Dome, *Antarctica* 87°14′ S, 106°58′ W 248
Hercules Inlet 80°22′ S, 80°16′ W 248
Herdecke, *Ger.* 51°24′ N, 7°25′ E 167
Herdorf, *Ger.* 50°46′ N, 7°57′ E 167
Hereford, *Tex., U.S.* 34°47′ N, 102°24′ W 92
Hereford, *U.K.* 52°3′ N, 2°43′ W 162
Herefoss, *Nor.* 58°32′ N, 8°20′ E 152
Hérémakono, *Guinea* 9°53′ N, 11°5′ W 222
Herencia, *Sp.* 39°22′ N, 3°22′ W 164
Herend, *Hung.* 47°7′ N, 17°46′ E 168
Herentals, *Belg.* 51°10′ N, 4°49′ E 167
Heringen, *Ger.* 50°53′ N, 10°0′ E 167
Herington, *Kans., U.S.* 38°38′ N, 96°57′ W 90
Herkimer, *N.Y., U.S.* 43°1′ N, 75°0′ W 94
Herlen, river, *Mongolia* 46°56′ N, 110°48′ E 190
Herlenbayan, *Mongolia* 48°20′ N, 114°11′ E 198
Herleshausen, *Ger.* 51°0′ N, 10°8′ E 167
Hermagor, *Aust.* 46°38′ N, 13°21′ E 167
Herman, *Minn., U.S.* 45°47′ N, 96°10′ W 90
Hermann, *Mo., U.S.* 38°41′ N, 91°26′ W 94
Hermansville, *Mich., U.S.* 45°42′ N, 87°35′ W 110
Hermanus, *S. Af.* 34°23′ S, 19°14′ E 227
Hermanville, *Miss., U.S.* 31°57′ N, 90°51′ W 103
Hermel, *Leb.* 34°23′ N, 36°23′ E 194
Hermies, *Fr.* 50°5′ N, 3°2′ E 163
Hermit Islands, *South Pacific Ocean* 2°1′ S, 144°22′ E 192
Hermitage, *Ark., U.S.* 33°26′ N, 92°11′ W 103
Hermitage Bay 47°32′ N, 56°47′ W 111
Hermitage Castle, site, *U.K.* 55°14′ N, 2°55′ W 150
Hermite, Isla, island, *Chile* 56°9′ S, 69°7′ W 134
Hermleigh, *Tex., U.S.* 32°38′ N, 100°47′ W 96
Hermon, Mount see Shaykh, Jabal ash, peak, *Leb.* 33°24′ N, 35°49′ E 194
Hermosillo, *Mex.* 29°1′ N, 111°3′ W 92
Hernández, *Mex.* 22°59′ N, 102°2′ W 114
Hernani, *Sp.* 43°14′ N, 1°59′ W 164
Herne, *Ger.* 51°32′ N, 7°13′ E 167
Herne Bay, *U.K.* 51°22′ N, 1°7′ E 162
Herning, *Den.* 56°7′ N, 8°56′ E 150
Heron Bay, *Can.* 48°39′ N, 86°17′ W 94
Herøy, *Nor.* 65°57′ N, 12°14′ E 152
Herradura, *Arg.* 26°32′ S, 58°17′ W 139
Herreid, *S. Dak., U.S.* 45°49′ N, 100°6′ W 90
Herrera, *Arg.* 28°28′ S, 63°5′ W 139
Herrera del Duque, *Sp.* 39°9′ N, 5°4′ W 164
Herrero, Punta, *Mex.* 19°12′ N, 87°27′ W 115
Herrick, *Ill., U.S.* 39°13′ N, 88°59′ W 102
Herriot, *Can.* 56°23′ N, 101°17′ W 108
Herrljunga, *Nor.* 58°3′ N, 12°58′ E 152
Herschel Island, *Can.* 69°38′ N, 139°31′ W 98
Herscher, *Ill., U.S.* 41°1′ N, 88°7′ W 102
Hersey, *Mich., U.S.* 43°51′ N, 85°26′ W 102
Hersilia, *Arg.* 29°59′ S, 61°52′ W 139
Hérso, *Gr.* 41°6′ N, 22°47′ E 156
Hersónissos Akrotírio, *Gr.* 35°31′ N, 23°35′ E 156
Herstal, *Belg.* 50°40′ N, 5°37′ E 167
Herstmonceux, *U.K.* 50°52′ N, 0°19′ E 162
Hersvik, *Nor.* 61°11′ N, 4°54′ E 152
Hertford, *N.C., U.S.* 36°11′ N, 76°30′ W 96
Hertford, *U.K.* 51°47′ N, 8°474′ W 162
Herval, *Braz.* 32°2′ S, 53°27′ W 139
Hervey Island, *South Pacific Ocean* 20°47′ S, 160°24′ W 238
Herzberg, *Ger.* 51°38′ N, 10°20′ E 167
Herzebrock-Clarholz, *Ger.* 51°53′ N, 8°14′ E 167
Herzliyya, *Israel* 32°10′ N, 34°49′ E 194
Hesdin, *Fr.* 50°21′ N, 2°2′ E 163
Hesel, *Ger.* 53°18′ N, 7°35′ E 163
Hesepe, *Ger.* 52°26′ N, 7°58′ E 163
Heshui, *China* 35°49′ N, 108°2′ E 198
Heskestad, *Nor.* 58°29′ N, 6°20′ E 152
Hesperia, *Calif., U.S.* 34°25′ N, 117°19′ W 101
Hesperia, *Mich., U.S.* 43°33′ N, 86°3′ W 102
Hess, river, *Can.* 63°10′ N, 131°36′ W 98
Hesse, adm. division, *Ger.* 50°35′ N, 8°9′ E 150
Hessisch Lichtenau, *Ger.* 51°12′ N, 9°44′ E 167
Hessmer, *La., U.S.* 31°2′ N, 92°8′ W 103
Hetin, *Serb.* 45°39′ N, 20°46′ E 168
Hettinger, *N. Dak., U.S.* 46°0′ N, 102°39′ W 90
Hetzerath, *Ger.* 49°52′ N, 6°49′ E 167
Heunghae, *S. Korea* 36°6′ N, 129°23′ E 200
Heusden, *Belg.* 51°2′ N, 5°17′ E 167
Heves, *Hung.* 47°35′ N, 20°17′ E 168
Heves, adm. division, *Hung.* 47°46′ N, 19°46′ E 156
Hévíz, *Hung.* 46°46′ N, 17°11′ E 168
Hexi, *China* 32°28′ N, 105°46′ E 198
Hexian, *China* 24°23′ N, 111°33′ E 198
Hexian, *China* 31°41′ N, 118°21′ E 198
Hexigten Qi (Jingpeng), *China* 43°16′ N, 117°28′ E 198
Heysham, *U.K.* 54°2′ N, 2°54′ W 162
Heyuan, *China* 23°41′ N, 114°41′ E 198
Heyworth, *Ill., U.S.* 40°18′ N, 88°59′ W 102
Heze, *China* 35°14′ N, 115°24′ E 198
Hi Vista, *Calif., U.S.* 34°44′ N, 117°48′ W 101
Hialeah, *Fla., U.S.* 25°51′ N, 80°18′ W 105
Hiawatha, *Kans., U.S.* 39°49′ N, 95°33′ W 90
Hiawatha, *Utah, U.S.* 39°28′ N, 111°1′ W 90
Hickam Air Force Base, *Hawai'i, U.S.* 21°18′ N, 158°0′ W 99
Hickiwan, *Ariz., U.S.* 32°21′ N, 112°27′ W 92
Hickman, Mount, *Can.* 57°15′ N, 131°14′ W 108
Hickmann, *Arg.* 23°11′ S, 63°35′ W 132
Hickory, *Miss., U.S.* 32°18′ N, 89°0′ W 103
Hickory, *N.C., U.S.* 35°44′ N, 81°21′ W 96
Hicks Bay, *N.Z.* 37°37′ S, 178°15′ E 240
Hick's Cays, *Caribbean Sea* 17°45′ N, 87°57′ W 115
Hickson Lake, *Can.* 56°15′ N, 104°57′ W 108
Hicksville, *N.Y., U.S.* 40°46′ N, 73°32′ W 104
Hicksville, *Ohio, U.S.* 41°16′ N, 84°46′ W 102
Hico, *Tex., U.S.* 31°58′ N, 98°2′ W 92
Hidalgo, *Mex.* 27°46′ N, 99°52′ W 96
Hidalgo, *Mex.* 25°56′ N, 100°27′ W 114
Hidalgo, *Mex.* 24°14′ N, 99°28′ W 114
Hidalgo, adm. division, *Mex.* 20°15′ N, 99°40′ W 114
Hidalgo del Parral, *Mex.* 26°56′ N, 105°41′ W 112
Hiddensee, *Ger.* 54°34′ N, 13°6′ E 152
Hididelli, *Eth.* 6°6′ N, 43°29′ E 218
Hidrolândia, *Braz.* 17°0′ S, 49°15′ W 138
Hiendelaencina, *Sp.* 41°4′ N, 3°0′ W 164
Hierro (Ferro), island, *Sp.* 27°25′ N, 17°55′ W 214
Higashisongi, *Japan* 33°3′ N, 129°55′ E 201
Higganum, *Conn., U.S.* 41°29′ N, 72°34′ W 104
Higgins, *Tex., U.S.* 36°5′ N, 100°2′ W 92
Higginsville, *Mo., U.S.* 39°3′ N, 93°43′ W 94
High Falls Reservoir, lake, *Wis., U.S.* 45°16′ N, 88°49′ W 94
High Force, fall(s), *U.K.* 54°38′ N, 2°32′ W 162
High Island, *Tex., U.S.* 29°33′ N, 94°25′ W 103
High Level, *Can.* 58°31′ N, 117°7′ W 108
High Plains, *North America* 45°37′ N, 105°5′ W 90
High Point, *N.C., U.S.* 35°57′ N, 80°1′ W 96
High Point, peak, *N.J., U.S.* 41°18′ N, 74°45′ W 94
High Prairie, *Can.* 55°24′ N, 116°28′ W 108
High River, *Can.* 50°31′ N, 113°48′ W 82
High Rock, *Bahamas* 26°37′ N, 78°19′ W 96
High Springs, *Fla., U.S.* 29°48′ N, 82°36′ W 105
High Willhays, peak, *U.K.* 50°40′ N, 4°7′ W 150
High Wycombe, *U.K.* 51°37′ N, 0°46′ E 162
Highgate, *Can.* 42°29′ N, 81°49′ W 102
Highjump Archipelago, *Antarctica* 66°18′ S, 104°58′ E 248
Highland, *Ill., U.S.* 38°44′ N, 89°40′ W 102
Highland, *N.Y., U.S.* 41°43′ N, 73°59′ W 104
Highland Falls, *N.Y., U.S.* 41°21′ N, 74°0′ W 104
Highland Park, *Ill., U.S.* 42°11′ N, 87°48′ W 102
Highland Park, *Mich., U.S.* 42°23′ N, 83°6′ W 102
Highland Peak, *Nev., U.S.* 37°52′ N, 114°40′ W 90
Highland Rocks, *Austral.* 21°20′ S, 129°18′ E 230
Highrock, *Can.* 55°51′ N, 100°24′ W 108
Highrock Lake, *Can.* 57°3′ N, 106°22′ W 108
Highrock Lake, *Can.* 55°59′ N, 100°21′ W 108
Highway City, *Calif., U.S.* 36°48′ N, 119°54′ W 100
Highwood Baldy, peak, *Mont., U.S.* 47°23′ N, 110°42′ W 90
Higüero, Punta, *U.S.* 18°16′ N, 68°4′ W 116
Higuerote, *Venez.* 10°29′ N, 66°7′ W 136
Higüey, *Dom. Rep.* 18°36′ N, 68°44′ W 116
Hiirola, *Fin.* 61°47′ N, 27°16′ E 166
Hiittinen see Hitis, *Fin.* 59°51′ N, 22°29′ E 166
Hiiumaa (Dagö), island, *Est.* 58°49′ N, 21°20′ E 166
Ḥijānah, Bu'ayrat al, lake, *Syr.* 33°16′ N, 36°21′ E 194
Hikari, *Japan* 33°57′ N, 131°56′ E 200
Hikiau Heiau State Monument, site, *Hawai'i, U.S.* 19°28′ N, 155°58′ W 99
Hiko, *Nev., U.S.* 37°34′ N, 115°15′ W 92
Hikone, *Japan* 35°13′ N, 136°14′ E 201
Hikurangi, *N.Z.* 35°36′ S, 174°17′ E 240
Hikurangi, peak, *N.Z.* 37°57′ S, 177°59′ E 240
Hilalaya, *Somalia* 6°3′ N, 49°1′ E 218
Hilchenbach, *Ger.* 50°59′ N, 8°5′ E 167
Hilden, *Ger.* 51°10′ N, 6°56′ E 167
Hiliotaluwa, *Indonesia* 0°43′ N, 97°50′ E 196
Hilisimaetano, *Indonesia* 0°40′ N, 97°44′ E 196
Hill, *N.H., U.S.* 43°31′ N, 71°43′ W 104
Hill Air Force Base, *Utah, U.S.* 41°6′ N, 112°4′ W 90
Hill Bank, *Belize* 17°36′ N, 88°45′ W 115
Hill City, *Kans., U.S.* 39°21′ N, 99°51′ W 90
Hill City, *Minn., U.S.* 46°58′ N, 93°36′ W 90
Hill City, *S. Dak., U.S.* 43°55′ N, 103°35′ W 90
Hill Island Lake, *Can.* 60°32′ N, 110°57′ W 108
Hillary Coast, *Antarctica* 79°49′ S, 171°48′ E 248
Hilleknuten, peak, *Nor.* 58°58′ N, 6°51′ E 152
Hillers, Mount, *Utah, U.S.* 37°52′ N, 110°46′ W 92
Hillesøy, *Nor.* 69°35′ N, 18°2′ E 152
Hilliard, *Ohio, U.S.* 40°1′ N, 83°9′ W 102
Hillman, *Mich., U.S.* 45°4′ N, 83°54′ W 94
Hillsboro, *Ill., U.S.* 39°8′ N, 89°29′ W 102
Hillsboro, *Kans., U.S.* 38°20′ N, 97°13′ W 90
Hillsboro, *Mo., U.S.* 39°8′ N, 89°29′ W 94
Hillsboro, *N.H., U.S.* 43°6′ N, 71°54′ W 104
Hillsboro, *N. Dak., U.S.* 47°23′ N, 97°4′ W 90
Hillsboro, *Ohio, U.S.* 39°11′ N, 83°37′ W 102
Hillsboro, *Tex., U.S.* 32°0′ N, 97°7′ W 92
Hillsboro, *Wis., U.S.* 43°38′ N, 90°21′ W 102
Hillsboro Lower Village, *N.H., U.S.* 43°6′ N, 71°57′ W 104
Hillsborough, *Grenada* 12°26′ N, 61°28′ W 116
Hillsdale, *Mich., U.S.* 41°54′ N, 84°40′ W 102
Hillsville, *Va., U.S.* 36°45′ N, 80°45′ W 94
Hilo, *Hawai'i, U.S.* 19°43′ N, 155°6′ W 99
Hilo, region, *Oceania* 19°48′ N, 155°25′ W 99
Hilonghilong, Mount, *Philippines* 9°5′ N, 125°37′ E 203
Hilton Head Island, *S.C., U.S.* 32°12′ N, 80°46′ W 96
Hiltrup, *Ger.* 51°54′ N, 7°38′ E 167
Hilversum, *Neth.* 52°12′ N, 5°10′ E 163
Hima, *Ky., U.S.* 37°6′ N, 83°48′ W 96
Himachal Pradesh, adm. division, *India* 32°20′ N, 75°58′ E 188
Himalaya, *Asia* 32°53′ N, 74°1′ E 186
Himanka, *Fin.* 64°3′ N, 23°38′ E 152
Himatnagar, *India* 23°36′ N, 72°58′ E 186
Himeji, *Japan* 34°50′ N, 134°41′ E 201
Himi, *Japan* 36°51′ N, 136°58′ E 201
Himo, *Tanzania* 3°25′ S, 37°33′ E 224
Himora, *Eth.* 14°12′ N, 36°36′ E 182
Ḥimş, Ba'rat, lake, *Syr.* 34°39′ N, 36°29′ E 194
Ḥimş (Homs), *Syr.* 34°43′ N, 36°42′ E 194
Hinatuan, *Philippines* 8°24′ N, 126°16′ E 203
Hinche, *Haiti* 19°8′ N, 72°2′ W 116
Hinchinbrook Island, *Austral.* 18°47′ S, 143°13′ E 231
Hinchinbrook Island National Park, *Coral Sea* 18°32′ S, 145°55′ E 238
Hinckley, *Ill., U.S.* 41°45′ N, 88°39′ W 102
Hinckley, *Minn., U.S.* 46°0′ N, 92°58′ W 94
Hinckley, *U.K.* 52°32′ N, 1°23′ W 162
Hinckley, *Utah, U.S.* 39°19′ N, 112°40′ W 90
Hindon, *U.K.* 51°5′ N, 2°8′ W 162
Hinds, *N.Z.* 44°1′ S, 171°33′ E 240
Hindupur, *India* 13°50′ N, 77°29′ E 188
Hines, *Oreg., U.S.* 43°33′ N, 119°5′ W 90
Hines Creek, *Can.* 56°14′ N, 118°36′ W 108
Hinesburg, *Vt., U.S.* 44°19′ N, 73°7′ W 104
Hinesville, *Ga., U.S.* 31°50′ N, 81°37′ W 96
Hinganghat, *India* 20°31′ N, 78°51′ E 188
Hinggan Ling, Da, *China* 44°15′ N, 118°1′ E 198
Hingham, *Mass., U.S.* 42°14′ N, 70°54′ W 104
Hingol, river, *Pak.* 25°50′ N, 65°26′ E 182
Hingol National Park, *Pak.* 25°30′ N, 65°30′ E 187
Hınıs, *Turk.* 39°22′ N, 41°43′ E 195
Hinkley, *Calif., U.S.* 34°56′ N, 117°13′ W 101
Hinkley Point, site, *U.K.* 51°11′ N, 3°4′ W 162
Hinks, Mount, *Antarctica* 67°54′ S, 65°45′ E 248
Hinlopenstretet 79°46′ N, 9°22′ E 160
Hinnerjoki, *Fin.* 60°59′ N, 21°57′ E 166
Hinnøya, *Norwegian Sea* 68°37′ N, 15°28′ E 152
Hino, *Japan* 35°12′ N, 133°25′ E 201
Hinoba-an, *Philippines* 9°37′ N, 122°29′ E 203
Hinoemata, *Japan* 37°1′ N, 139°22′ E 201
Hinojosa del Duque, *Sp.* 38°29′ N, 5°9′ W 164
Hinomi Saki, *Japan* 35°25′ N, 132°28′ E 201
Hinsdale, *N.H., U.S.* 42°47′ N, 72°30′ W 104
Hinterweidenthal, *Ger.* 49°11′ N, 7°44′ E 163
Hinthada, *Myanmar* 17°38′ N, 95°26′ E 202
Hinton, *Can.* 53°24′ N, 117°35′ W 108
Hinton, *Okla., U.S.* 35°26′ N, 98°22′ W 96
Hinton, *W. Va., U.S.* 37°39′ N, 80°54′ W 96
Hınzır Burnu, *Turk.* 36°18′ N, 35°2′ E 156
Híos, *Gr.* 38°22′ N, 26°6′ E 180
Híos, island, *Gr.* 38°9′ N, 25°31′ E 180
Hippolytushoef, *Neth.* 52°54′ N, 4°57′ E 163
Hirado, *Japan* 33°22′ N, 129°32′ E 201
Hiram, *Me., U.S.* 43°52′ N, 70°49′ W 104
Hirata, *Japan* 35°23′ N, 132°47′ E 201
Hirfanlı Barajı, dam, *Turk.* 39°4′ N, 33°36′ E 156
Hirky, *Ukr.* 51°53′ N, 25°16′ E 154
Hirnyky, *Ukr.* 51°42′ N, 24°27′ E 152
Hirosaki, *Japan* 40°33′ N, 140°25′ E 190
Hiroshima, *Japan* 34°23′ N, 132°27′ E 201
Hiroshima, adm. division, *Japan* 34°32′ N, 132°9′ E 201
Hirson, *Fr.* 49°54′ N, 4°4′ E 163
Hîrşova, *Rom.* 44°41′ N, 27°57′ E 156
Hirtshals, *Den.* 57°34′ N, 9°57′ E 150
Hirvasvaara, *Fin.* 66°32′ N, 28°34′ E 152
Hirvensalmi, *Fin.* 61°37′ N, 26°46′ E 166
Hisar, *India* 29°7′ N, 75°44′ E 197
Hisarönü, *Turk.* 41°34′ N, 32°2′ E 156
Ḥişn al 'Abr, *Yemen* 16°8′ N, 47°18′ E 182
Ḥişn Tāqrifat, *Lib.* 29°12′ N, 17°20′ E 216
Hisor, *Taj.* 38°33′ N, 68°33′ E 197
Hispaniola, island, *Caribbean Sea* 18°54′ N, 71°8′ W 253
Hispaniola, island, *Dom. Rep.* 19°57′ N, 70°50′ W 116
Ḥisyah, *Syr.* 34°24′ N, 36°45′ E 194
Hīt, *Iraq* 33°37′ N, 42°44′ E 180
Hita, *Japan* 33°19′ N, 130°56′ E 201
Hitachi, *Japan* 36°35′ N, 140°38′ E 201
Hitachiōta, *Japan* 36°31′ N, 140°32′ E 201
Hitadu, island, *Maldives* 0°36′ N, 72°17′ E 188

Hitchcock, Tex., U.S. 29°20′ N, 95°2′ W 103
Hitchin, U.K. 51°57′ N, 0°17′ E 162
Hitis (Hiittinen), Fin. 59°51′ N, 22°29′ E 166
Hitoyoshi, Japan 32°13′ N, 130°45′ E 201
Hitra, Nor. 63°35′ N, 8°42′ E 152
Hitterdal, Minn., U.S. 46°56′ N, 96°17′ W 90
Hiuchi Nada 34°5′ N, 133°12′ E 201
Hiusta Meadow, Can. 58°4′ N, 130°59′ W 98
Hiver, Lac de l', lake, Can. 53°55′ N, 72°38′ W 111
Hiwannee, Miss., U.S. 31°47′ N, 88°40′ W 103
Hiwasa, Japan 33°44′ N, 134°31′ E 201
Hixon, Can. 53°26′ N, 122°37′ W 108
Hizan, Turk. 38°9′ N, 42°24′ E 195
Hjallerup, Den. 57°10′ N, 10°8′ E 152
Hjalmar Lake, Can. 61°30′ N, 110°6′ W 108
Hjartdal, Nor. 59°35′ N, 8°39′ E 152
Hjerkinn, Nor. 62°13′ N, 9°35′ E 152
Hjørring, Den. 57°26′ N, 9°58′ E 150
Hlaingbwe, Myanmar 17°8′ N, 97°50′ E 202
Hlohovec, Slovakia 48°25′ N, 17°47′ E 152
Hluhluwe, S. Af. 28°1′ S, 32°16′ E 227
Hlukhiv, Ukr. 51°38′ N, 33°57′ E 158
Hlyboka, Ukr. 48°4′ N, 25°55′ E 152
Hlybokaye, Belarus 55°9′ N, 27°41′ E 166
Ho, Ghana 6°36′ N, 0°28′ E 222
Ho Chi Minh City (Saigon), Vietnam 10°48′ N, 106°40′ E 202
Ho Xa, Vietnam 17°4′ N, 107°2′ E 202
Hoa Binh, Vietnam 20°52′ N, 105°17′ E 202
Hoachanas, Namibia 23°57′ S, 18°4′ E 220
Hoai An, Vietnam 14°23′ N, 108°58′ E 202
Hoare Bay 65°23′ N, 64°55′ W 106
Hoback Peak, Wyo., U.S. 43°4′ N, 110°39′ W 90
Hobart, Austral. 42°53′ S, 146°56′ E 230
Hobart, Okla., U.S. 35°0′ N, 99°6′ W 92
Hobbs, N. Mex., U.S. 32°41′ N, 103°8′ W 92
Hobbs Coast, Antarctica 75°18′ S, 127°36′ W 248
Hobe Sound, Fla., U.S. 27°3′ N, 80°9′ W 105
Hobo, Col. 2°33′ N, 75°29′ W 136
Hoboksar, China 46°47′ N, 85°47′ E 184
Hobot Xar see Xianghuang Qi, China 42°11′ N, 113°53′ E 198
Hobro, Den. 56°38′ N, 9°46′ E 150
Hobucken, N.C., U.S. 35°15′ N, 76°35′ W 96
Hoburgen, Sw. 56°52′ N, 18°10′ E 166
Hobyo, Somalia 5°22′ N, 48°36′ E 218
Hŏch'ŏn, N. Korea 40°38′ N, 128°35′ E 200
Hochschwab, Aust. 47°35′ N, 14°46′ E 156
Höchst, Ger. 49°48′ N, 8°59′ E 167
Hochstetter Forland, Den. 75°16′ N, 18°24′ W 246
Hodda, peak, Somalia 11°30′ N, 50°32′ E 182
Hoddesdon, U.K. 51°45′ N, 2°118′ W 162
Hodge, Calif., U.S. 34°49′ N, 117°12′ W 101
Hodge, La., U.S. 32°16′ N, 92°44′ W 103
Hodges Hill, peak, Can. 49°3′ N, 55°59′ W 111
Hodgeville, Can. 50°6′ N, 106°58′ W 90
Hodgson, Can. 51°12′ N, 97°35′ W 90
Hodh, region, Africa 16°35′ N, 8°36′ W 222
Hódmezővásárhely, Hung. 46°25′ N, 20°20′ E 168
Hodonín, Czech Rep. 48°51′ N, 17°8′ E 152
Hödrögö, Mongolia 48°54′ N, 96°51′ E 173
Hoek van Holland, Neth. 51°58′ N, 4°7′ E 163
Hoeryŏng, N. Korea 42°28′ N, 129°46′ E 200
Hoeyang, N. Korea 38°41′ N, 127°37′ E 200
Hof, Ger. 50°18′ N, 11°55′ E 152
Hoffman, Minn., U.S. 45°48′ N, 95°50′ W 90
Hofgeismar, Ger. 51°30′ N, 9°22′ E 167
Hofheim, Ger. 50°5′ N, 8°26′ E 167
Höfn, Ice. 64°20′ N, 15°13′ W 143
Hofors, Nor. 60°32′ N, 16°18′ E 152
Hofra, oil field, Lib. 29°18′ N, 17°43′ E 216
Hofrat en Nahas, Sudan 9°41′ N, 24°16′ E 224
Hofstad, Nor. 64°12′ N, 10°24′ E 152
Hōfu, Japan 34°2′ N, 131°34′ E 200
Hofuf see Al Hufūf, Saudi Arabia 25°21′ N, 49°34′ E 196
Hogback Mountain, Mont., U.S. 44°52′ N, 112°12′ W 90
Hogback Mountain, Va., U.S. 38°45′ N, 78°20′ W 94
Högby, Sw. 57°10′ N, 16°59′ E 152
Högen, Nor. 58°54′ N, 11°41′ E 152
Hoggar see Ahaggar, Alg. 21°56′ N, 4°32′ E 222
Hogoro, Tanzania 5°54′ S, 36°28′ E 224
Högsby, Nor. 57°10′ N, 16°1′ E 152
Høgstegia, peak, Nor. 62°22′ N, 10°0′ E 152
Hogtinden, peak, Nor. 66°57′ N, 14°24′ E 152
Hogup Mountains, Utah, U.S. 41°26′ N, 113°22′ W 90
Hoh Xil Hu, lake, China 35°37′ N, 90°47′ E 188
Hohenau, Parag. 27°6′ S, 55°42′ W 139
Hohenlimburg, Ger. 51°20′ N, 7°33′ E 167
Hoher Dachstein, peak, Aust. 47°27′ N, 13°30′ E 156
Hohhot, China 40°51′ N, 111°42′ E 198
Hohoe, Ghana 7°10′ N, 0°26′ E 222
Hōhoku, Japan 34°19′ N, 130°55′ E 200
Höhr-Grenzhausen, Ger. 50°25′ N, 7°40′ E 167
Hoi An, Vietnam 15°54′ N, 108°20′ E 202
Hoima, Uganda 1°23′ N, 31°21′ E 224
Hoisington, Kans., U.S. 38°29′ N, 98°47′ W 92
Hok, Nor. 57°30′ N, 14°15′ E 152
Hokitika, N.Z. 42°44′ S, 171°0′ E 240
Hokkaidō, island, Japan 44°1′ N, 139°29′ E 190
Hokksund, Nor. 59°47′ N, 9°54′ E 152
Hokota, Japan 36°9′ N, 140°30′ E 201
Hōkūkano Heiau, site, Hawai'i, U.S. 21°3′ N, 156°54′ W 99
Hol, Nor. 60°34′ N, 8°21′ E 152
Hola, Kenya 1°27′ S, 40°0′ E 224
Hola Prystan', Ukr. 46°30′ N, 32°30′ E 156
Holanda, Bol. 11°50′ S, 68°38′ W 137
Holandsfjord, Nor. 66°43′ N, 13°39′ E 152
Holbeach, U.K. 52°47′ N, 1°59′ E 162
Holberg, Can. 50°39′ N, 128°0′ W 90
Holbox, Isla, island, Mex. 21°39′ N, 87°14′ W 116
Holbrook, Ariz., U.S. 34°54′ N, 110°10′ W 92
Holbrook, Idaho, U.S. 42°11′ N, 112°39′ W 92
Holbrook, Mass., U.S. 42°9′ N, 71°1′ W 104
Holcombe, Wis., U.S. 45°12′ N, 91°7′ W 94
Hold with Hope, peninsula, Greenland, Den. 73°19′ N, 20°18′ W 246
Holden, Can. 53°13′ N, 112°13′ W 108
Holden, Mass., U.S. 42°20′ N, 71°52′ W 104
Holden, Mo., U.S. 38°41′ N, 93°59′ W 94
Holden, Utah, U.S. 39°5′ N, 112°16′ W 90
Holdenville, Okla., U.S. 35°3′ N, 96°24′ W 96
Holdfast, Can. 50°57′ N, 105°26′ W 90
Holdrege, Nebr., U.S. 40°25′ N, 99°23′ W 90
Hole in the Ground, site, Oreg., U.S. 43°22′ N, 121°16′ W 90
Hole in the Mountain Peak, Nev., U.S. 40°56′ N, 115°12′ W 90
Holgate, Ohio, U.S. 41°13′ N, 84°8′ W 102
Holguín, Cuba 20°53′ N, 76°15′ W 115
Holguín, adm. division, Cuba 20°31′ N, 75°55′ W 116
Holinshead Lake, lake, Can. 49°38′ N, 90°16′ W 94
Holladay, Utah, U.S. 40°40′ N, 111°48′ W 90
Holland, Mich., U.S. 42°46′ N, 86°6′ W 102
Hollandale, Miss., U.S. 33°8′ N, 90°51′ W 103
Hollick-Kenyon Peninsula, Antarctica 69°3′ S, 60°55′ W 248
Hollick-Kenyon Plateau, Antarctica 78°34′ S, 104°13′ W 248
Hollis, Alas., U.S. 55°28′ N, 132°45′ W 108
Hollis, N.H., U.S. 42°44′ N, 71°36′ W 104
Hollis, Okla., U.S. 34°39′ N, 99°55′ W 92
Hollis Center, Me., U.S. 43°36′ N, 70°36′ W 104
Hollister, Calif., U.S. 36°50′ N, 121°25′ W 100
Hollister, Mo., U.S. 36°36′ N, 93°13′ W 96
Holliston, Mass., U.S. 42°12′ N, 71°26′ W 104
Holloman Air Force Base, N. Mex., U.S. 32°51′ N, 106°9′ W 92
Hollum, Neth. 53°26′ N, 5°37′ E 163
Holly, Colo., U.S. 38°2′ N, 102°7′ W 90
Holly, Mich., U.S. 42°46′ N, 83°37′ W 102
Holly Bluff, Miss., U.S. 32°48′ N, 90°43′ W 103
Holly Hill, Fla., U.S. 29°14′ N, 81°3′ W 105
Holly Ridge, N.C., U.S. 34°29′ N, 77°34′ W 96
Holly Springs, Miss., U.S. 34°42′ N, 89°27′ W 112
Hollywood, Calif., U.S. 34°6′ N, 118°22′ W 101
Hollywood, Fla., U.S. 26°1′ N, 80°10′ W 105
Holm Land, Den. 80°13′ N, 19°10′ W 246
Holman, Can. 70°42′ N, 117°39′ W 106
Holman, N. Mex., U.S. 36°2′ N, 105°24′ W 92
Hólmavík, Ice. 65°35′ N, 21°53′ W 73
Holmer, Lac, lake, Can. 54°2′ N, 72°13′ W 111
Holmes Lake, Can. 57°3′ N, 97°17′ W 108
Holmes, Mount, Wyo., U.S. 44°47′ N, 110°55′ W 90
Holmestrand, Nor. 59°29′ N, 10°18′ E 152
Holmfors, Nor. 65°13′ N, 18°9′ E 152
Holmudden, Sw. 57°52′ N, 19°12′ E 166
Holoby, Ukr. 51°5′ N, 25°0′ E 152
Holod, Rom. 46°47′ N, 22°8′ E 168
Holohit, Punta, Mex. 21°42′ N, 89°4′ W 116
Holoog, Namibia 27°23′ S, 17°54′ E 227
Holopaw, Fla., U.S. 28°8′ N, 81°5′ W 105
Holstebro, Den. 56°21′ N, 8°36′ E 150
Holstein, Can. 44°3′ N, 80°46′ W 102
Holstein, Iowa, U.S. 42°28′ N, 95°33′ W 94
Holsteinsborg see Sisimiut, Den. 66°56′ N, 53°43′ W 106
Holt, Ala., U.S. 33°13′ N, 87°29′ W 103
Holt, Mich., U.S. 42°37′ N, 84°31′ W 102
Holt, U.K. 52°54′ N, 1°5′ E 162
Holton, Kans., U.S. 39°26′ N, 95°45′ W 90
Holton, Mich., U.S. 43°24′ N, 86°5′ W 102
Holtorf, Ger. 52°41′ N, 9°15′ E 150
Holtville, Calif., U.S. 32°48′ N, 115°23′ W 101
Holtyre, Can. 48°28′ N, 80°17′ W 110
Holwerd, Neth. 53°21′ N, 5°53′ E 163
Holy Cross, Alas., U.S. 62°3′ N, 160°0′ W 98
Holyoke, Colo., U.S. 40°34′ N, 102°18′ W 90
Holyoke, Mass., U.S. 42°12′ N, 72°37′ W 104
Holywell, U.K. 53°16′ N, 3°13′ W 162
Holzminden, Ger. 51°48′ N, 9°27′ E 167
Homa Bay, Kenya 0°35′ N, 34°29′ E 224
Homberg, Ger. 51°2′ N, 9°24′ E 167
Hombori, Mali 15°16′ N, 1°43′ W 222
Homburg, Ger. 49°18′ N, 7°19′ E 163
Home Bay 68°36′ N, 67°37′ W 106
Homedale, Idaho, U.S. 43°37′ N, 116°57′ W 90
Homeland, Fla., U.S. 27°49′ N, 81°49′ W 105
Homeland, Ga., U.S. 30°50′ N, 82°2′ W 96
Homer, Alas., U.S. 59°37′ N, 151°36′ W 98
Homer, Ill., U.S. 40°2′ N, 87°58′ W 102
Homer, La., U.S. 32°46′ N, 93°4′ W 103
Homer, Mich., U.S. 42°8′ N, 84°49′ W 102
Homer, N.Y., U.S. 42°38′ N, 76°12′ W 94
Homerville, Ga., U.S. 31°1′ N, 82°46′ W 96
Homestead, Fla., U.S. 25°28′ N, 80°30′ W 105
Homewood, Miss., U.S. 32°14′ N, 89°30′ W 103
Hominy, Okla., U.S. 36°23′ N, 96°24′ W 92
Hommalinn, Myanmar 24°51′ N, 94°54′ E 188
Hommura, Japan 34°22′ N, 139°16′ E 201
Homnabad, India 17°45′ N, 77°8′ E 188
Homodji, spring, Niger 16°34′ N, 13°40′ E 222
Homoine, Mozambique 23°50′ S, 35°9′ E 227
Homoljske Planina, Serb. 44°18′ N, 21°36′ E 168
Homosassa, Fla., U.S. 28°46′ N, 82°36′ W 105
Homosassa Springs, Fla., U.S. 28°48′ N, 82°35′ W 105
Homs, Syr. 34°32′ N, 36°57′ E 173
Homs see Ḩimş, Syr. 34°43′ N, 36°42′ E 194
Homyel', Belarus 52°25′ N, 31°4′ E 154
Hon Chong, Vietnam 10°10′ N, 104°37′ E 202
Hon Quan, Vietnam 11°41′ N, 106°37′ E 202
Honaz, Turk. 37°44′ N, 29°15′ E 156
Honda, Col. 5°10′ N, 74°46′ W 136
Honda, Bahía 12°19′ N, 72°15′ W 136
Hondeklipbaai, S. Af. 30°20′ S, 17°16′ E 227
Hondo, Can. 55°3′ N, 114°3′ W 108
Hondo, Japan 32°27′ N, 130°10′ E 201
Hondo, N. Mex., U.S. 33°23′ N, 105°16′ W 92
Hondo, Tex., U.S. 29°20′ N, 99°8′ W 96
Honduras 14°39′ N, 87°51′ W 115
Hønefoss, Nor. 60°9′ N, 10°15′ E 152
Honey Grove, Tex., U.S. 33°34′ N, 95°55′ W 96
Honey Island, Tex., U.S. 30°23′ N, 94°27′ W 103
Hong Gai, Vietnam 20°58′ N, 107°5′ E 198
Hong Kong, China 22°15′ N, 114°10′ E 198
Hong Kong (Xianggang), island, China 21°55′ N, 114°15′ E 198
Hong'an, China 31°17′ N, 114°35′ E 198
Hongcheon, S. Korea 37°42′ N, 127°53′ E 200
Honghe, China 23°18′ N, 102°22′ E 202
Honghu, China 29°51′ N, 113°28′ E 198
Hongjiang, China 27°3′ N, 109°55′ E 198
Hongliuyuan, China 41°3′ N, 95°26′ E 188
Hongnong, S. Korea 35°24′ N, 126°34′ E 200
Hongor, Mongolia 45°47′ N, 112°43′ E 198
Hongqiling, China 42°56′ N, 126°24′ E 200
Hongseong, S. Korea 36°35′ N, 126°40′ E 200
Hongshi, China 42°58′ N, 127°7′ E 200
Hongtong, China 36°16′ N, 111°42′ E 198
Hongū, Japan 33°50′ N, 135°44′ E 201
Hongwŏn, N. Korea 40°1′ N, 127°58′ E 200
Hongze Hu, lake, China 32°58′ N, 117°53′ E 198
Honiara, Solomon Islands 9°0′ S, 160°0′ E 242
Honiton, U.K. 50°47′ N, 3°11′ W 162
Honkajoki, Fin. 61°58′ N, 22°13′ E 166
Honkilahti, Fin. 60°56′ N, 22°5′ E 166
Hönö, Sw. 57°41′ N, 11°39′ E 152
Honokōhau, Hawai'i, U.S. 19°39′ N, 156°2′ W 99
Honolulu, Hawai'i, U.S. 21°17′ N, 157°55′ W 99
Honshū, island, Japan 35°3′ N, 130°44′ E 190
Hontoria del Pinar, Sp. 41°51′ N, 3°10′ W 164
Hood, Calif., U.S. 38°21′ N, 121°32′ W 100
Hood Bay, Alas., U.S. 57°23′ N, 134°26′ W 108
Hood Canal 48°6′ N, 122°38′ W 100
Hood, Mount, Oreg., U.S. 45°20′ N, 121°48′ W 90
Hood Point, P.N.G. 10°21′ S, 146°34′ E 192
Hood River, Oreg., U.S. 45°41′ N, 121°33′ W 100
Hoodsport, Wash., U.S. 47°22′ N, 123°9′ W 100
Hoogeveen, Neth. 52°44′ N, 6°28′ E 163
Hoogezand-Sappemeer, Neth. 53°9′ N, 6°47′ E 163
Hook Head, Ire. 51°55′ N, 6°59′ W 150
Hooker, Okla., U.S. 36°50′ N, 101°14′ W 92
Hooksett, N.H., U.S. 43°5′ N, 71°28′ W 104
Hoonah, Alas., U.S. 58°1′ N, 135°23′ W 98
Hooper Bay, Alas., U.S. 61°39′ N, 166°2′ W 73
Hooper, Cape, Can. 68°22′ N, 66°48′ W 106
Hoopeston, Ill., U.S. 40°28′ N, 87°40′ W 102
Hooppole, Ill., U.S. 41°31′ N, 89°55′ W 102
Hoopstad, S. Af. 27°50′ S, 25°54′ E 227
Höör, Nor. 55°56′ N, 13°32′ E 152
Hoorn, Neth. 52°38′ N, 5°4′ E 163
Hoosick Falls, N.Y., U.S. 42°54′ N, 73°22′ W 104
Hoover, Ala., U.S. 33°24′ N, 86°50′ W 96
Hoover Dam, Nev., U.S. 35°55′ N, 114°54′ W 101
Höövör, Mongolia 48°27′ N, 113°23′ E 198
Hopa, Turk. 41°25′ N, 41°25′ E 195
Hope, Ariz., U.S. 33°42′ N, 113°43′ W 101
Hope, Ark., U.S. 33°38′ N, 93°36′ W 96
Hope, Can. 49°21′ N, 121°26′ W 100
Hope, Ind., U.S. 39°17′ N, 85°46′ W 102
Hope, N. Dak., U.S. 47°18′ N, 97°44′ W 90
Hope, Ben, peak, U.K. 58°23′ N, 4°43′ W 150
Hope, Cape, Can. 68°55′ N, 118°27′ W 98
Hope Mills, N.C., U.S. 34°58′ N, 78°58′ W 96
Hope Point, Myanmar 15°5′ N, 97°20′ E 202
Hope Town, Bahamas 26°31′ N, 76°58′ W 96
Hope Valley, R.I., U.S. 41°30′ N, 71°44′ W 104
Hopedale, Can. 55°24′ N, 60°19′ W 106
Hopedale, Ill., U.S. 40°24′ N, 89°25′ W 102
Hopelchén, Mex. 19°44′ N, 89°51′ W 115
Hopeless, Mount, Austral. 29°41′ S, 139°27′ E 230
Hopen, Nor. 63°26′ N, 8°0′ E 152
Hopetoun, Austral. 33°55′ S, 120°8′ E 231
Hopetown, S. Af. 29°37′ S, 24°4′ E 227
Hopewell, Va., U.S. 37°17′ N, 77°18′ W 96
Hopewell Culture National Historic Park, Ohio, U.S. 39°21′ N, 83°4′ W 102
Hopewell Furnace National Historic Site, Pa., U.S. 40°10′ N, 75°52′ W 94
Hopewell Islands, Hudson Bay 58°28′ N, 82°13′ W 106
Hopi Buttes, Ariz., U.S. 35°29′ N, 110°23′ W 92
Hopkins, Mich., U.S. 42°36′ N, 85°45′ W 102
Hopkins, Mount, Ariz., U.S. 31°39′ N, 110°57′ W 92
Hopkinsville, Ky., U.S. 36°51′ N, 87°29′ W 96
Hopkinton, N.H., U.S. 43°11′ N, 71°41′ W 104
Hopseidet, Nor. 70°46′ N, 27°42′ E 152
Hopsten, Ger. 52°23′ N, 7°36′ E 163
Hoque, Angola 14°41′ S, 13°49′ E 220
Hoquiam, Wash., U.S. 46°58′ N, 123°54′ W 100
Hora, Polonyna Runa, peak, Ukr. 48°46′ N, 22°44′ E 152
Horace, Kans., U.S. 38°29′ N, 101°49′ W 90
Horasan, Turk. 40°5′ N, 42°14′ E 195
Horcajo de Santiago, Sp. 39°50′ N, 3°0′ W 164
Horche, Sp. 40°33′ N, 3°4′ W 164
Horgos, Serb. 46°8′ N, 19°58′ E 168
Hörh Uul, peak, Mongolia 42°38′ N, 105°16′ E 198
Horicon, Wis., U.S. 43°26′ N, 88°37′ W 102
Horinger, China 40°22′ N, 111°48′ E 198
Horizonte, Braz. 9°41′ S, 68°27′ W 137
Horki, Belarus 54°17′ N, 30°59′ E 154
Horlivka, Ukr. 48°18′ N, 38°1′ E 158
Ḩormak, Iran 29°57′ N, 60°55′ E 182
Hormoz, island, Iran 26°53′ N, 56°25′ E 180
Hormuz, Strait of 26°20′ N, 55°54′ E 196
Horn, Ben, peak, U.K. 58°1′ N, 4°9′ W 150
Horn, Cape see Hornos, Cabo de, Chile 55°49′ S, 66°59′ W 134
Horn Island, Austral. 10°30′ S, 141°38′ E 230
Horn Island, Miss., U.S. 30°9′ N, 88°44′ W 103
Horn (North Cape), Ice. 66°30′ N, 26°3′ W 246
Horn, river, Can. 61°33′ N, 117°58′ W 108
Horn, The, peak, Austral. 36°53′ S, 146°34′ E 230
Hornachos, Sp. 38°33′ N, 6°5′ W 164
Hornachuelos, Sp. 37°50′ N, 5°15′ W 164
Hornavan, lake, Nor. 65°37′ N, 17°40′ E 152
Hornbeck, La., U.S. 31°19′ N, 93°24′ W 103
Hornbrook, Calif., U.S. 41°54′ N, 122°34′ W 90
Horncastle, U.K. 53°12′ N, 0°7′ E 162
Hornell, N.Y., U.S. 42°18′ N, 77°41′ W 94
Hornepayne, Can. 49°14′ N, 84°47′ W 94
Hornito, Cerro, peak, Pan. 8°41′ N, 82°10′ W 115
Hornos, Cabo de (Horn, Cape), Chile 55°49′ S, 66°59′ W 134
Hornsea, U.K. 53°54′ N, 0°11′ E 162
Hörnsjö, Nor. 63°48′ N, 19°30′ E 154
Hornslandet, Sw. 61°35′ N, 17°29′ E 166
Hornsund 76°46′ N, 11°11′ E 160
Hornu, Belg. 50°25′ N, 3°48′ E 163
Horodnya, Ukr. 51°51′ N, 31°39′ E 158
Horodnytsya, Ukr. 50°49′ N, 27°18′ E 158
Horodok, Ukr. 50°40′ N, 26°7′ E 152
Horodok, Ukr. 49°8′ N, 26°32′ E 152
Horodyshche, Ukr. 49°21′ N, 31°31′ E 158
Horokhiv, Ukr. 50°29′ N, 24°45′ E 152
Hororata, N.Z. 43°33′ S, 171°58′ E 240
Horqin Youyi Zhongqi (Bayan Huxu), China 45°5′ N, 121°25′ E 198
Horqin Zuoyi Houqi, China 42°58′ N, 122°22′ E 198
Horqin Zuoyi Zhongqi, China 44°7′ N, 123°20′ E 198
Horqueta, Parag. 23°19′ S, 57°4′ W 132
Horse Lake, Can. 51°35′ N, 121°40′ W 90
Horse, river, Can. 56°23′ N, 112°24′ W 108
Horsehead Lake, N. Dak., U.S. 46°58′ N, 100°21′ W 90
Horsens, Den. 55°51′ N, 9°49′ E 150
Horseshoe Beach, Fla., U.S. 29°27′ N, 83°18′ W 105
Horseshoe Bend, Idaho, U.S. 43°55′ N, 116°11′ W 90
Horseshoe Cove 29°23′ N, 83°26′ W 105
Horsham, Austral. 36°40′ S, 142°10′ E 231
Horsham, U.K. 51°3′ N, 0°21′ E 162
Horsvær, islands, Norwegian Sea 65°24′ N, 10°32′ E 152
Hort, Hung. 47°41′ N, 19°48′ E 168
Horten, Nor. 59°25′ N, 10°28′ E 152
Horton, Mich., U.S. 42°8′ N, 84°31′ W 102
Horton Lake, Can. 67°30′ N, 124°4′ W 98
Horton, river, Can. 69°0′ N, 125°15′ W 98
Horwood Lake, Can. 47°58′ N, 82°55′ W 94
Hosa'ina, Eth. 7°29′ N, 37°51′ E 224
Hösbach, Ger. 50°0′ N, 9°12′ E 167
Hosdrug, India 12°15′ N, 75°8′ E 188
Hosenofu, spring, Lib. 23°39′ N, 20°58′ E 216
Hoshab, Pak. 26°0′ N, 63°56′ E 182
Hoshiarpur, India 31°32′ N, 75°58′ E 188
Höshööt, Mongolia 48°5′ N, 102°26′ E 198
Hosmer, S. Dak., U.S. 45°34′ N, 99°29′ W 90
Hosororo, Guyana 8°11′ N, 59°46′ W 130
Hososhima, Japan 32°25′ N, 131°39′ E 201
Hospet, India 15°17′ N, 76°23′ E 188
Hossa, Fin. 65°26′ N, 29°33′ E 152
Hosszúpályi, Hung. 47°23′ N, 21°43′ E 168
Hoste, Isla, island, Chile 55°53′ S, 70°2′ W 248
Hot, Thai. 18°7′ N, 98°33′ E 202
Hot Creek Range, Nev., U.S. 38°10′ N, 116°28′ W 90
Hot Springs, Ark., U.S. 34°29′ N, 93°5′ W 112
Hot Springs, S. Dak., U.S. 43°26′ N, 103°29′ W 90
Hot Springs National Park, Ark., U.S. 34°29′ N, 93°9′ W 96
Hot Springs Peak, Calif., U.S. 40°20′ N, 120°12′ W 90
Hot Springs Peak, Nev., U.S. 41°21′ N, 117°31′ W 90
Hotaka, Japan 36°20′ N, 137°53′ E 201
Hotan, China 37°7′ N, 79°51′ E 184
Hotan, river, China 38°20′ N, 80°51′ E 184
Hotchkiss, Can. 57°4′ N, 117°34′ W 108
Hotchkiss, Colo., U.S. 38°48′ N, 107°44′ W 90
Hotchkiss, river, Can. 57°19′ N, 118°33′ W 108
Hotevilla, Ariz., U.S. 35°54′ N, 110°41′ W 92
Hottah Lake, Can. 65°19′ N, 119°32′ W 106
Hotte, Massif de la, Haiti 18°34′ N, 74°30′ W 115
Hottentot Bay 26°20′ S, 14°43′ E 220
Hotton, Belg. 50°15′ N, 5°26′ E 167
Houayxay, Laos 20°18′ N, 100°27′ E 202
Houdan, Fr. 48°47′ N, 1°35′ E 163
Houghton Lake, Mich., U.S. 44°15′ N, 86°0′ W 81
Houghton, Point, Mich., U.S. 47°41′ N, 89°29′ W 94
Houlton, Me., U.S. 46°7′ N, 67°49′ W 82
Houma, China 35°37′ N, 111°21′ E 198
Houma, La., U.S. 29°34′ N, 90°44′ W 103
Houndé, Burkina Faso 11°30′ N, 3°33′ W 222
Housatonic, Mass., U.S. 42°15′ N, 73°23′ W 104
House Range, Utah, U.S. 39°16′ N, 113°32′ W 90
House, river, Can. 55°51′ N, 112°25′ W 108
Houston, Can. 54°24′ N, 126°40′ W 108
Houston, Minn., U.S. 43°44′ N, 91°35′ W 94
Houston, Mo., U.S. 37°19′ N, 91°56′ W 96
Houston, Tex., U.S. 29°44′ N, 95°22′ W 103
Houthalen, Belg. 51°2′ N, 5°22′ E 167
Houtman Abrolhos, islands, Indian Ocean 28°8′ S, 110°9′ E 230
Houtskär, Fin. 60°12′ N, 21°20′ E 166
Hovd (Dund-Us), Mongolia 48°2′ N, 91°40′ E 190
Hovden, Nor. 59°31′ N, 7°21′ E 152
Hövelhof, Ger. 51°49′ N, 8°38′ E 167
Hoven, S. Dak., U.S. 45°13′ N, 99°48′ W 90

Hovenweep National Monument, *Utah, U.S.* 37°17' N, 109°15' W 92
Hoverla, Hora, peak, *Ukr.* 48°7' N, 24°24' E 152
Hoveyzeh, *Iran* 31°26' N, 48°5' E 180
Hövsgöl, *Mongolia* 43°38' N, 109°37' E 198
Hövsgöl Nuur, lake, *Mongolia* 50°48' N, 98°47' E 190
Howard, *Kans., U.S.* 37°27' N, 96°17' W 90
Howard, *S. Dak., U.S.* 43°59' N, 97°34' W 90
Howard City, *Mich., U.S.* 43°23' N, 85°28' W 102
Howard Island, *Austral.* 12°4' S, 135°3' E 230
Howard Lake, *Can.* 62°45' N, 107°53' W 106
Howe, *Ind., U.S.* 41°43' N, 85°25' W 102
Howe, *Okla., U.S.* 34°55' N, 94°39' W 96
Howe, *Tex., U.S.* 33°29' N, 96°36' W 96
Howe, Cape, *Austral.* 38°13' S, 149°59' E 230
Howe, Mount, *Antarctica* 87°17' S, 145°9' W 248
Howe Sound 49°26' N, 123°24' W 100
Howell, *Mich., U.S.* 42°35' N, 83°56' W 102
Howells, *Nebr., U.S.* 41°42' N, 97°1' W 90
Howick, *N.Z.* 36°55' S, 174°56' E 240
Howland Island, *United States* 1°0' N, 177°0' W 238
Howland, *Me., U.S.* 45°13' N, 68°40' W 94
Howth, *Ire.* 53°22' N, 6°4' W 150
Hoxie, *Ark., U.S.* 36°2' N, 90°59' W 96
Hoxie, *Kans., U.S.* 39°20' N, 100°27' W 90
Höxter, *Ger.* 51°46' N, 9°23' E 167
Hoxud, *China* 42°13' N, 86°58' E 184
Høyanger, *Nor.* 61°13' N, 6°4' E 152
Hoyt Peak, *Utah, U.S.* 40°40' N, 111°16' W 90
Hozat, *Turk.* 39°5' N, 39°11' E 195
Hpa-an, *Myanmar* 16°54' N, 97°39' E 202
Hradec Králové, *Czech Rep.* 50°13' N, 15°51' E 152
Hrasnica, *Bosn. and Herzg.* 43°46' N, 18°18' E 168
Hrastnik, *Slov.* 46°8' N, 15°5' E 156
Hrazdan, *Arm.* 40°4' N, 44°25' E 195
Hrazdan, river, *Arm.* 40°16' N, 44°31' E 195
Hrodna, *Belarus* 53°40' N, 23°50' E 152
Hrtkovci, *Serb.* 44°52' N, 19°46' E 168
Hrubieszów, *Pol.* 50°49' N, 23°52' E 152
Hrvatska Kostajnica, *Croatia* 45°13' N, 16°32' E 168
Hrymayliv, *Ukr.* 49°19' N, 26°0' E 158
Hrynyava, *Ukr.* 47°58' N, 24°52' E 152
Hsi-hseng, *Myanmar* 20°10' N, 97°14' E 202
Hsinchu, *Taiwan, China* 24°47' N, 120°57' E 198
Hsinying, *Taiwan, China* 23°18' N, 120°17' E 198
Hsipaw, *Myanmar* 22°39' N, 97°17' E 202
Hu, Har, lake, *China* 38°18' N, 97°6' E 188
Hua Hin, *Thai.* 12°39' N, 99°56' E 202
Huacaraje, *Bol.* 13°36' S, 63°47' W 137
Huacaya, *Bol.* 20°44' S, 63°42' W 137
Huachacalla, *Bol.* 18°48' S, 68°16' W 137
Huachi, *Bol.* 14°16' S, 63°34' W 137
Huachi, *China* 36°26' N, 107°57' E 198
Huacho, *Peru* 11°9' S, 77°36' W 130
Huade, *China* 41°53' N, 114°1' E 198
Huadian, *China* 42°58' N, 126°41' E 200
Huai Yang, *Thai.* 11°37' N, 99°40' E 202
Huaibei, *China* 33°56' N, 116°48' E 198
Huaibin, *China* 32°30' N, 115°23' E 198
Huaiji, *China* 23°51' N, 112°13' E 198
Huailai, *China* 40°25' N, 115°29' E 198
Huainan, *China* 32°38' N, 117°1' E 198
Huaining, *China* 30°23' N, 116°35' E 198
Huairen, *China* 39°50' N, 113°6' E 198
Huaitunas, Laguna, lake, *Bol.* 13°2' S, 66°17' W 137
Huaiyin, *China* 33°33' N, 119°2' E 198
Huajicori, *Mex.* 22°38' N, 105°20' W 114
Huajimic, *Mex.* 21°40' N, 104°19' W 114
Huajuapan de León, *Mex.* 17°48' N, 97°47' W 114
Hualahuises, *Mex.* 24°53' N, 99°41' W 114
Hualālai, peak, *Hawai'i, U.S.* 19°40' N, 155°55' W 99
Hualapai Mountains, *Ariz., U.S.* 35°0' N, 113°57' W 101
Hualfín, *Arg.* 27°13' S, 66°48' W 132
Hualien, *Taiwan, China* 24°1' N, 121°33' E 198
Huamachuco, *Peru* 7°49' S, 78°3' W 130
Huamantla, *Mex.* 19°17' N, 97°57' W 114
Huambo, *Angola* 12°49' S, 15°45' E 220
Huambo, adm. division, *Angola* 13°1' S, 15°14' E 220
Huancané, *Peru* 15°16' S, 69°45' W 137
Huancavelica, *Peru* 12°48' S, 74°59' W 137
Huancayo, *Peru* 12°5' S, 75°12' W 137
Huanchaca, *Bol.* 20°23' S, 66°42' W 137
Huanchaca, Serranía de, *Bol.* 14°6' S, 61°17' W 130
Huang (Yellow), river, *China* 37°14' N, 104°6' E 198
Huangchuan, *China* 32°8' N, 115°0' E 198
Huanggang, *China* 30°30' N, 114°51' E 198
Huanggangliang, peak, *China* 43°32' N, 117°23' E 198
Huanghua, *China* 38°24' N, 117°23' E 198
Huangling, *China* 35°35' N, 109°15' E 198
Huangliu, *China* 18°28' N, 108°47' E 198
Huangnihe, *China* 43°35' N, 128°2' E 198
Huangquqiao, *China* 39°3' N, 106°38' E 198
Huangshan, *China* 29°42' N, 118°14' E 198
Huangshi, *China* 30°9' N, 115°0' E 198
Huanguelén, *Arg.* 37°2' S, 61°57' W 139
Huangxian, *China* 37°41' N, 120°36' E 198
Huangyan, *China* 28°37' N, 121°21' E 198
Huanjiang, *China* 24°48' N, 108°14' E 198
Huanren, *China* 41°15' N, 125°25' E 200
Huanta, *Peru* 12°57' S, 74°15' W 137
Huantai, *China* 36°58' N, 118°9' E 198
Huánuco, *Peru* 9°53' S, 76°18' W 130
Huánuco, adm. division, *Peru* 9°41' S, 74°46' W 137
Huanxian, *China* 36°34' N, 107°21' E 198
Huara, *Chile* 19°59' S, 69°50' W 137
Huaral, *Peru* 11°29' S, 77°14' W 130
Huaraz, *Peru* 9°34' S, 77°31' W 130
Huari, *Bol.* 19°1' S, 66°47' W 137
Huari, *Peru* 13°56' S, 69°20' W 137
Huarmey, *Peru* 10°4' S, 78°10' W 130
Huarong, *China* 29°31' N, 112°32' E 198
Huásabas, *Mex.* 29°54' N, 109°21' W 92
Huasaga, *Peru* 3°41' S, 76°25' W 136
Huascarán, Nevado, peak, *Peru* 9°10' S, 77°44' W 130
Huasco, *Chile* 28°30' S, 71°15' W 134
Huashulinzi, *China* 43°13' N, 127°1' E 200
Huatabampo, *Mex.* 26°47' N, 109°41' W 112
Huatusco, *Mex.* 19°7' N, 96°57' W 114
Huauchinango, *Mex.* 20°10' N, 98°4' W 114
Huaura, *Peru* 11°5' S, 77°36' W 130
Huautla, *Mex.* 21°0' N, 98°17' W 114
Huautla, *Mex.* 18°7' N, 96°51' W 114
Huaxi, *China* 41°23' N, 123°28' E 200
Huaxian, *China* 35°30' N, 114°31' E 198
Huaynamota, river, *Mex.* 21°53' N, 104°25' W 114
Huayuan, *China* 28°32' N, 109°29' E 198
Huazhou, *China* 21°34' N, 110°33' E 198
Hub, *Miss., U.S.* 31°9' N, 89°45' W 103
Hubbard, *Tex., U.S.* 31°49' N, 96°47' W 96
Hubbard Lake, *Mich., U.S.* 44°45' N, 84°46' W 82
Hubbard, Mount, *Alas., U.S.* 60°15' N, 139°17' W 98
Hubbardston, *Mass., U.S.* 42°28' N, 72°1' W 104
Hubbardston, *Mich., U.S.* 43°5' N, 84°50' W 102
Hubbart Point, *Can.* 59°24' N, 94°46' W 108
Hubbell Trading Post National Historic Site, *Ariz., U.S.* 35°41' N, 109°39' W 92
Hubei, adm. division, *China* 31°27' N, 111°33' E 198
Huben, *Aust.* 46°55' N, 12°35' E 167
Hubli, *India* 15°21' N, 75°8' E 188
Hucknall, *U.K.* 53°2' N, 1°12' W 162
Huddersfield, *U.K.* 53°39' N, 1°47' W 162
Hudiksvall, *Nor.* 61°42' N, 17°4' E 152
Hudson, *Can.* 50°5' N, 92°12' W 110
Hudson, *Fla., U.S.* 28°21' N, 82°42' W 105
Hudson, *Mich., U.S.* 41°50' N, 84°23' W 102
Hudson, *N.H., U.S.* 42°45' N, 71°27' W 104
Hudson, *N.Y., U.S.* 42°14' N, 73°48' W 104
Hudson Bay 59°43' N, 86°21' W 253
Hudson Bay 59°11' N, 93°51' W 108
Hudson Bay, *Can.* 52°52' N, 102°25' W 108
Hudson Canyon, *North Atlantic Ocean* 37°8' N, 70°6' W 253
Hudson, Cape, *Antarctica* 68°0' S, 156°56' E 248
Hudson Falls, *N.Y., U.S.* 43°18' N, 73°36' W 104
Hudson, river, *N.Y., U.S.* 41°34' N, 73°59' W 104
Hudson Strait 62°49' N, 79°14' W 106
Hudson's Hope, *Can.* 56°2' N, 121°57' W 108
Hudsonville, *Mich., U.S.* 42°51' N, 85°52' W 102
Hudwin Lake, *Can.* 53°9' N, 96°12' W 108
Hue, *Vietnam* 16°28' N, 107°34' E 202
Huedin, *Rom.* 46°50' N, 23°1' E 168
Huejúcar, *Mex.* 22°20' N, 103°12' W 114
Huejuquilla, *Mex.* 22°37' N, 103°54' W 114
Huejutla, *Mex.* 21°7' N, 98°25' W 114
Huelma, *Sp.* 37°39' N, 3°27' W 164
Huelva, *Sp.* 37°15' N, 6°57' W 150
Huércal-Overa, *Sp.* 37°23' N, 1°57' W 164
Huerta, Sierra de la, *Arg.* 31°43' S, 68°11' W 134
Huertecillas, *Mex.* 24°3' N, 101°9' W 114
Huesca, *Sp.* 42°7' N, 0°25' E 164
Huéscar, *Sp.* 37°48' N, 2°33' W 164
Hueso, Sierra del, *Mex.* 30°19' N, 105°34' W 112
Huetamo, *Mex.* 18°35' N, 100°53' W 114
Huete, *Sp.* 40°8' N, 2°43' W 164
Huff, *N. Dak., U.S.* 46°36' N, 100°41' W 90
Hughes, *Alas., U.S.* 65°53' N, 154°17' W 98
Hughes, *Ark., U.S.* 34°56' N, 90°29' W 96
Hughes Bay 64°31' S, 62°6' W 134
Hughes Springs, *Tex., U.S.* 32°59' N, 94°39' W 103
Hugo, *Colo., U.S.* 39°8' N, 103°29' W 90
Hugo, *Okla., U.S.* 34°0' N, 95°31' W 96
Hugo Lake, *Okla., U.S.* 34°3' N, 95°44' W 96
Hugoton, *Kans., U.S.* 37°10' N, 101°21' W 92
Hui, river, *China* 48°43' N, 118°52' E 198
Hui'an, *China* 25°1' N, 118°46' E 198
Huichang, *China* 25°30' N, 115°37' E 198
Hŭich'ŏn, *N. Korea* 40°9' N, 126°17' E 200
Huidong, *China* 22°54' N, 114°43' E 198
Huife, river, *China* 42°44' N, 126°20' E 200
Huíla, *Angola* 15°6' S, 13°29' E 220
Huíla, adm. division, *Angola* 15°5' S, 13°52' E 220
Huila, adm. division, *Col.* 2°33' N, 75°50' W 136
Huíla Plateau, *Angola* 16°12' S, 14°36' E 220
Huilai, *China* 23°1' N, 116°15' E 198
Huimin, *China* 37°29' N, 117°28' E 198
Huinan (Chaoyang), *China* 42°42' N, 126°4' E 200
Huinca Renancó, *Arg.* 34°51' S, 64°21' W 134
Huining, *China* 35°43' N, 105°2' E 198
Huisachal, *Mex.* 26°45' N, 101°6' W 96
Huishui, *China* 26°9' N, 106°36' E 198
Huitong, *China* 26°53' N, 109°42' E 198
Huittinen, *Fin.* 61°9' N, 22°41' E 166
Huitzuco, *Mex.* 18°16' N, 99°20' W 114
Huixian, *China* 33°45' N, 106°5' E 198
Huixtla, *Mex.* 15°8' N, 92°30' W 115
Huize, *China* 26°20' N, 103°17' E 190
Huizhou, *China* 22°59' N, 114°21' E 198
Hujirt, *Mongolia* 46°35' N, 104°36' E 198
Hujirt, *Mongolia* 46°58' N, 102°44' E 198
Hukuntsi, *Botswana* 24°1' S, 21°46' E 227
Hulan, *China* 46°2' N, 126°39' E 198
Ḩulayfā', *Saudi Arabia* 25°55' N, 40°46' E 182
Hulbert, *Mich., U.S.* 46°21' N, 85°10' W 94
Hulin, *China* 45°57' N, 133°10' E 190
Hull, *Mass., U.S.* 42°18' N, 70°55' W 104
Hull, *Tex., U.S.* 30°8' N, 94°39' W 103
Hull Mountain, *Calif., U.S.* 39°30' N, 123°1' W 90
Hull, river, *U.K.* 53°51' N, 0°24' E 162
Hullo, *Est.* 58°59' N, 23°13' E 166
Hulls Cove, *Me., U.S.* 44°24' N, 68°16' W 94
Hulne Priory, site, *U.K.* 55°25' N, 1°51' W 150
Hulst, *Neth.* 51°17' N, 4°3' E 163
Hulstay, *Mongolia* 48°29' N, 114°52' E 198
Hultsfred, *Nor.* 57°29' N, 15°48' E 152
Hulu, river, *China* 36°1' N, 108°35' E 198
Huludao, *China* 40°47' N, 120°54' E 198
Hulun Nur, lake, *China* 48°59' N, 116°20' E 190
Hulyaypole, *Ukr.* 47°38' N, 36°15' E 156
Hum, *Bosn. and Herzg.* 42°43' N, 18°10' E 168
Huma, *China* 51°40' N, 126°45' E 190
Humahuaca, *Arg.* 23°11' S, 65°19' W 132
Humaitá, *Braz.* 7°31' S, 63°4' W 130
Humaneso de Mohernando, *Sp.* 40°48' N, 3°10' W 164
Humansdorp, *S. Af.* 34°1' S, 24°45' E 227
Ḩumar, *U.A.E.* 23°2' N, 53°35' E 182
Humara, Jebel, peak, *Sudan* 16°10' N, 30°45' E 226
Humaya, river, *Mex.* 25°9' N, 106°59' W 114
Humbe, *Angola* 16°41' S, 14°48' E 207
Humble, *Tex., U.S.* 29°58' N, 95°15' W 103
Humboldt, *Ariz., U.S.* 34°30' N, 112°13' W 92
Humboldt, *Can.* 52°11' N, 105°8' W 108
Humboldt, *Kans., U.S.* 37°47' N, 95°26' W 96
Humboldt, *Nebr., U.S.* 40°7' N, 95°56' W 90
Humboldt, *Tenn., U.S.* 35°50' N, 88°54' W 96
Humboldt Range, *Nev., U.S.* 40°23' N, 118°25' W 90
Hume, *Calif., U.S.* 36°47' N, 118°55' W 101
Hume, *Ill., U.S.* 39°47' N, 87°52' W 102
Hume, river, *Can.* 66°4' N, 130°13' W 98
Hūmedān, *Iran* 25°25' N, 59°40' E 182
Humphreys, Mount, *Calif., U.S.* 37°15' N, 118°46' W 92
Humphreys Peak, *Ariz., U.S.* 35°20' N, 111°44' W 92
Humppila, *Fin.* 60°54' N, 23°20' E 166
Humptulips, *Wash., U.S.* 47°13' N, 123°58' W 100
Humu'ula Saddle, pass, *Hawai'i, U.S.* 19°41' N, 155°30' W 99
Hūn, *Lib.* 29°10' N, 15°53' E 143
Hun, river, *China* 41°20' N, 125°43' E 200
Hun, river, *China* 41°52' N, 123°44' E 200
Húnaflói 65°36' N, 23°17' W 143
Hunan, adm. division, *China* 27°50' N, 110°37' E 198
Hunchun, *China* 42°53' N, 130°21' E 200
Hunedoara, adm. division, *Rom.* 46°7' N, 22°35' E 156
Hünfeld, *Ger.* 50°40' N, 9°46' E 167
Hungary 46°45' N, 18°2' E 156
Hungen, *Ger.* 50°28' N, 8°53' E 167
Hungerford, *U.K.* 51°24' N, 1°31' W 162
Hŭngnam, *N. Korea* 39°51' N, 127°38' E 200
Hŭngsu-ri, *N. Korea* 38°27' N, 126°1' E 200
Hunjiang, *China* 41°51' N, 126°23' E 200
Hunlen Falls, *Can.* 51°53' N, 126°39' W 108
Hunmanby, *U.K.* 54°11' N, 0°20' E 162
Huns Berge, peak, *Namibia* 27°48' S, 17°3' E 227
Hunsrück, *Ger.* 50°3' N, 7°14' E 167
Hunstanton, *U.K.* 52°56' N, 0°29' E 162
Hunt, *Mongolia* 47°59' N, 99°33' E 190
Hunt Mountain, *Wyo., U.S.* 44°42' N, 107°50' W 90
Hunter, *N. Dak., U.S.* 47°11' N, 97°15' W 90
Hunter Island, *Austral.* 40°16' S, 144°40' E 230
Hunter Island, *Can.* 48°14' N, 91°43' W 94
Hunter Islands, *Hunter Island* 40°42' S, 142°25' E 230
Hunters Bay 19°36' N, 93°5' E 188
Hunters Road, *Zimb.* 19°10' S, 29°47' E 224
Huntingdon, *Can.* 45°5' N, 74°11' W 94
Huntingdon, *Pa., U.S.* 40°29' N, 78°1' W 94
Huntingdon, *Tenn., U.S.* 36°1' N, 88°25' W 96
Huntingdon, *U.K.* 52°20' N, 0°11' E 162
Huntington, *Ark., U.S.* 35°4' N, 94°16' W 96
Huntington, *Ind., U.S.* 40°52' N, 85°30' W 102
Huntington, *Mass., U.S.* 42°14' N, 72°53' W 104
Huntington, *N.Y., U.S.* 40°52' N, 73°26' W 104
Huntington, *Oreg., U.S.* 44°20' N, 117°17' W 90
Huntington, *Tex., U.S.* 31°16' N, 94°34' W 103
Huntington, *Utah, U.S.* 39°19' N, 110°59' W 90
Huntington Beach, *Calif., U.S.* 33°40' N, 118°2' W 101
Huntington Station, *N.Y., U.S.* 40°51' N, 73°25' W 104
Huntly, *N.Z.* 37°34' S, 175°9' E 240
Hunts Inlet, *Can.* 54°3' N, 130°28' W 108
Huntsville, *Ala., U.S.* 34°43' N, 86°36' W 96
Huntsville, *Ark., U.S.* 36°4' N, 93°45' W 96
Huntsville, *Can.* 45°20' N, 79°15' W 94
Huntsville, *Mo., U.S.* 39°26' N, 92°32' W 94
Huntsville, *Tex., U.S.* 30°42' N, 95°33' W 103
Huntsville, *Utah, U.S.* 41°15' N, 111°46' W 90
Hunucmá, *Mex.* 20°59' N, 89°54' W 116
Hunyuan, *China* 39°41' N, 113°42' E 198
Huocheng, *China* 44°3' N, 80°54' E 184
Huolin Gol, *China* 45°29' N, 119°44' E 198
Huolin, river, *China* 44°43' N, 121°47' E 198
Huolu, *China* 38°5' N, 114°18' E 198
Huon Gulf 7°27' S, 146°5' E 238
Huon Peninsula, *P.N.G.* 6°30' S, 146°32' E 192
Huong Hoa, *Vietnam* 16°38' N, 106°44' E 202
Huong Khe, *Vietnam* 18°14' N, 105°41' E 202
Huoqiu, *China* 32°21' N, 116°17' E 198
Huoshan, *China* 31°25' N, 116°21' E 198
Huoxian, *China* 36°33' N, 111°44' E 198
Hupo, *S. Korea* 36°41' N, 129°28' E 200
Hurault, Lac, lake, *Can.* 54°16' N, 71°12' W 111
Hurd, Cape, *Can.* 45°1' N, 81°58' W 110
Hurdiyo, *Somalia* 10°31' N, 51°7' E 216
Hure Qi, *China* 42°44' N, 121°47' E 198
Hüremt, *Mongolia* 48°38' N, 102°31' E 198
Hurghada, *Egypt* 27°14' N, 33°47' E 180
Huri Hills, *Kenya* 3°31' N, 37°24' E 224
Hurley, *Miss., U.S.* 30°38' N, 88°28' W 103
Huron, *Calif., U.S.* 36°12' N, 120°7' W 100
Huron, *Ind., U.S.* 38°42' N, 86°40' W 102
Huron, *S. Dak., U.S.* 44°21' N, 98°13' W 90
Huron Islands, *Lake Superior* 47°0' N, 88°6' W 94
Huron, Lake 44°22' N, 83°8' W 107
Huron Mountain, *Mich., U.S.* 46°52' N, 87°52' W 110
Huron Mountains, *Mich., U.S.* 46°43' N, 87°59' W 94
Hurricane, *Alas., U.S.* 62°58' N, 149°39' W 98
Hurricane, *Utah, U.S.* 37°10' N, 113°17' W 92
Hürth, *Ger.* 50°51' N, 6°51' E 167
Hurup, *Den.* 56°43' N, 8°24' E 150
Husainabad, *India* 24°31' N, 84°0' E 197
Huşi, *Rom.* 46°40' N, 28°4' E 156
Huslia, *Alas., U.S.* 65°40' N, 156°25' W 98
Husøy, *Nor.* 61°1' N, 4°40' E 152
Husum, *Ger.* 54°28' N, 9°3' E 150
Husum, *Nor.* 63°19' N, 19°10' E 152
Hutanopan, *Indonesia* 0°43' N, 99°44' E 196
Hutch Mountain, *Ariz., U.S.* 34°48' N, 111°28' W 92
Hutchinson, *Kans., U.S.* 38°2' N, 97°55' W 90
Hutchinson, *Minn., U.S.* 44°51' N, 94°24' W 90
Hutchinson, *S. Af.* 31°31' S, 23°10' E 227
Hutchinson Island, *Fla., U.S.* 27°18' N, 80°13' W 105
Huthi, *Myanmar* 16°11' N, 98°49' E 202
Hutig, Ben, peak, *U.K.* 58°32' N, 4°39' W 150
Hutovo, *Bosn. and Herzg.* 42°57' N, 17°48' E 168
Hutsonville, *Ill., U.S.* 39°6' N, 87°41' W 102
Huttig, *Ark., U.S.* 33°1' N, 92°12' W 103
Hutton, *Can.* 53°58' N, 121°38' W 108
Hutuo, river, *China* 38°12' N, 115°9' E 198
Huuhkala, *Fin.* 61°28' N, 28°15' E 166
Huvadu see Suvadiva Atoll, *Maldives* 0°39' N, 72°35' E 188
Huwaisah, oil field, *Oman* 21°48' N, 56°3' E 182
Huxford, *Ala., U.S.* 31°12' N, 87°27' W 103
Huxian, *China* 34°5' N, 108°35' E 198
Huy, *Belg.* 50°30' N, 5°15' E 167
Hüyük, *Turk.* 37°57' N, 31°36' E 156
Huzhou, *China* 30°49' N, 120°12' E 198
Hvaler, islands, *Norwegian Sea* 58°57' N, 11°11' E 152
Hvar, *Croatia* 43°10' N, 16°26' E 168
Hvar (Pharus), island, *Croatia* 43°3' N, 16°47' E 168
Hwadae, *N. Korea* 40°48' N, 129°32' E 200
Hwajin, *N. Korea* 39°11' N, 125°25' E 200
Hwange, *Zimb.* 18°24' S, 26°30' E 224
Hwange National Park, *Zimb.* 19°17' S, 26°23' E 224
Hwanghae, North, adm. division, *N. Korea* 38°33' N, 126°18' E 200
Hwanghae, South, adm. division, *N. Korea* 38°09' N, 125°34' E 200
Hwangju, *N. Korea* 38°39' N, 125°48' E 200
Hwap'yŏng, *N. Korea* 41°15' N, 126°53' E 200
Hwayang, *S. Korea* 35°38' N, 128°46' E 200
Hyalite Peak, *Mont., U.S.* 45°21' N, 111°1' W 90
Hyannis, *Mass., U.S.* 41°39' N, 70°18' W 104
Hyannis, *Nebr., U.S.* 41°59' N, 101°46' W 90
Hyannis Port, *Mass., U.S.* 41°37' N, 70°19' W 104
Hyargas Nuur, lake, *Mongolia* 49°4' N, 91°34' E 190
Hydaburg, *Alas., U.S.* 55°13' N, 132°48' W 108
Hyde, *N.Z.* 45°19' S, 170°15' E 240
Hyde Park, *N.Y., U.S.* 41°46' N, 73°57' W 104
Hyde Park, *Vt., U.S.* 44°35' N, 72°38' W 104
Hyden, *Austral.* 32°26' S, 118°53' E 231
Hyder, *Alas., U.S.* 55°55' N, 130°7' W 108
Hyderabad, *India* 17°19' N, 78°28' E 188
Hyderabad, *Pak.* 25°24' N, 68°24' E 186
Hydeville, *Vt., U.S.* 43°36' N, 73°15' W 104
Hyeolli, *S. Korea* 37°57' N, 128°21' E 200
Hyères, Îles d' (Les Îles d'Or), islands, *Mediterranean Sea* 42°57' N, 6°33' E 165
Hyesan, *N. Korea* 41°23' N, 128°12' E 200
Hyland Post, *Can.* 57°39' N, 128°10' W 108
Hyland, river, *Can.* 60°11' N, 128°3' W 108
Hyltebruk, *Nor.* 56°59' N, 13°15' E 152
Hymera, *Ind., U.S.* 39°10' N, 87°18' W 102
Hyndman Peak, *Idaho, U.S.* 43°44' N, 114°13' W 90
Hynish, Ben, peak, *U.K.* 56°26' N, 7°2' W 150
Hyōgo, adm. division, *Japan* 35°3' N, 134°26' E 201
Hyrra Banda, *Cen. Af. Rep.* 5°56' N, 22°4' E 218
Hyrynsalmi, *Fin.* 64°40' N, 28°31' E 154
Hysham, *Mont., U.S.* 46°16' N, 107°14' W 90
Hythe, *Can.* 55°19' N, 119°35' W 108
Hythe, *U.K.* 51°4' N, 1°4' E 162
Hyūga, *Japan* 32°25' N, 131°36' E 201
Hyvinkää, *Fin.* 60°37' N, 24°50' E 166

I

Ía, *Gr.* 36°27' N, 25°23' E 156
Iá, river, *Braz.* 0°19' N, 66°47' W 136
Iablaniţa, *Rom.* 44°56' N, 22°18' E 168
Iaciara, *Braz.* 14°12' S, 46°39' W 138
Iaco, river, *Braz.* 10°10' S, 69°7' W 137
Iaçu, *Braz.* 12°46' S, 40°16' W 138
Iaeger, *W. Va., U.S.* 37°27' N, 81°49' W 96
Iakora, *Madagascar* 23°6' S, 46°40' E 220
Ialomiţae, adm. division, *Rom.* 44°39' N, 26°21' E 156
Ialysus see Triánda, *Gr.* 36°24' N, 28°10' E 156
Ianca, *Rom.* 45°7' N, 27°28' E 158
Iar Connaught, region, *Europe* 53°18' N, 9°27' W 150
Iaşi, adm. division, *Rom.* 47°16' N, 26°47' E 156
Iaşi, *Rom.* 47°9' N, 27°37' E 152
Iauaretê, *Braz.* 0°34' N, 69°14' W 136
Ib, *Russ.* 61°16' N, 50°34' E 154
Ibadan, *Nig.* 7°26' N, 3°54' E 222
Ibagué, *Col.* 4°23' N, 75°15' W 136
Ibaiti, *Braz.* 23°50' S, 50°14' W 138
Iballë, *Alban.* 42°11' N, 19°59' E 168
Ibapah, *Utah, U.S.* 40°1' N, 113°59' W 90
Ibapah Peak, *Utah, U.S.* 39°47' N, 114°0' W 90
Ibar, river, *Serb.* 43°35' N, 20°32' E 168
Ibaraki, adm. division, *Japan* 36°17' N, 140°0' E 201
Ibarra, *Ecua.* 0°19' N, 78°16' W 136
Ibb, *Yemen* 13°59' N, 44°10' E 182
Ibba, *Sudan* 4°49' N, 29°7' E 224
Ibba (Tonj), river, *Sudan* 6°16' N, 28°21' E 224

Ibbenbüren, Ger. 52°16′ N, 7°43′ E 150
Iberá, Laguna, lake, Arg. 28°22′ S, 57°22′ W 139
Iberia, Peru 11°23′ S, 69°36′ W 137
Ibestad, Nor. 68°46′ N, 17°8′ E 152
Ibeto, Nig. 10°28′ N, 5°7′ E 222
Ibex Pass, Calif., U.S. 35°47′ N, 116°21′ W 101
Ibi, Nig. 8°8′ N, 9°45′ E 222
Ibi, Sp. 38°37′ N, 0°36′ E 164
Ibiá, Braz. 19°31′ S, 46°33′ W 138
Ibicaraí, Braz. 14°54′ S, 39°37′ W 138
Ibicuí, Braz. 29°24′ S, 56°42′ W 139
Ibicuy, Arg. 33°43′ S, 59°7′ W 139
Ibina, river, Dem. Rep. of the Congo 0°57′ N, 28°35′ E 224
Ibipetuba, Braz. 11°1′ S, 44°32′ W 132
Ibiraba, Braz. 10°47′ S, 42°50′ W 132
Ibirama, Braz. 27°5′ S, 49°30′ W 138
Ibiranhém, Braz. 17°52′ S, 40°10′ W 138
Ibitiara, Braz. 12°39′ S, 42°15′ W 132
Ibiza (Iviza), island, Sp. 39°0′ N, 1°25′ E 214
Iblei, Monti, It. 37°18′ N, 14°25′ E 156
Ibo, Mozambique 12°21′ S, 40°38′ E 220
Iboperenda, Bol. 19°4′ S, 62°38′ W 132
Ibotirama, Braz. 12°11′ S, 43°13′ W 132
Iboundji, Mont, peak, Gabon 1°11′ S, 11°41′ E 218
Ibresi, Russ. 55°18′ N, 47°4′ E 154
'Ibrī, Oman 23°10′ N, 56°29′ E 182
Ibusuki, Japan 31°14′ N, 130°36′ E 201
Ibwe Munyama, Zambia 16°10′ S, 28°31′ E 224
Ica, Peru 14°6′ S, 75°48′ W 130
Ica, adm. division, Peru 15°7′ S, 75°3′ W 137
Ica, river, Peru 13°55′ S, 75°47′ W 130
Içana, Braz. 0°19′ N, 67°23′ W 136
Içana, river, Braz. 1°10′ N, 67°59′ W 136
Icaño, Arg. 28°41′ S, 62°53′ W 139
Icaria, ruin(s), Gr. 38°4′ N, 23°48′ E 156
Ice Age National Scientific Reserve, Wis., U.S. 43°39′ N, 88°13′ W 102
Ice Mountain, Can. 54°24′ N, 121°15′ W 108
İçel (Mersin), Turk. 36°48′ N, 34°36′ E 156
Iceland 65°21′ N, 25°52′ W 246
Iceland-Faroe Rise, North Atlantic Ocean 63°30′ N, 10°2′ W 253
Iceland Plateau, Greenland Sea 69°18′ N, 13°34′ W 255
Icheon, S. Korea 37°16′ N, 127°26′ E 200
Ichera, Russ. 58°36′ N, 109°37′ E 160
Ichikawa, Japan 35°42′ N, 139°56′ E 201
Ichilo, river, Bol. 16°58′ S, 64°44′ W 137
Ichinomiya, Japan 35°17′ N, 136°48′ E 201
Ichinskiy, Russ. 55°41′ N, 156°10′ E 160
Ichnya, Ukr. 50°49′ N, 32°23′ E 158
Ichoa, river, Bol. 15°55′ S, 65°34′ W 137
Ich'ŏn, N. Korea 38°28′ N, 126°54′ E 200
Ichuña, Peru 16°9′ S, 70°31′ W 137
Icó, Braz. 6°27′ S, 38°51′ W 132
Iconium see Konya, Turk. 37°51′ N, 32°29′ E 156
Iconoclast Mountain, Can. 51°27′ N, 117°51′ W 90
Icy Cape, Alas., U.S. 70°12′ N, 163°39′ W 98
Ida, La., U.S. 32°59′ N, 93°54′ W 103
Ida Grove, Iowa, U.S. 42°20′ N, 95°27′ W 94
Idabel, Okla., U.S. 33°53′ N, 94°50′ W 96
Idah, Nig. 7°7′ N, 6°43′ E 222
Idaho, adm. division, Idaho, U.S. 44°25′ N, 114°53′ W 90
Idaho City, Idaho, U.S. 43°49′ N, 115°49′ W 90
Idaho Falls, Idaho, U.S. 43°29′ N, 112°2′ W 90
Idali, Sudan 4°43′ N, 32°41′ E 224
Idalou, Tex., U.S. 33°38′ N, 101°41′ W 96
Idar-Oberstein, Ger. 49°42′ N, 7°19′ E 163
Idawgaw, Nig. 6°54′ N, 2°56′ E 222
Iday, spring, Niger 14°58′ N, 11°32′ E 222
'Idd el Ghanam, Sudan 11°31′ N, 24°19′ E 216
Iddo, Nig. 7°55′ N, 5°11′ E 214
Idel', Russ. 64°12′ N, 34°5′ E 152
Ideles, Alg. 23°48′ N, 5°55′ E 214
Ider, river, Mongolia 48°32′ N, 98°4′ E 190
Idermeg, Mongolia 47°36′ N, 111°22′ E 198
Idfu, Egypt 24°58′ N, 32°47′ E 182
Idi, Indonesia 4°59′ N, 97°43′ E 196
Ídi, Óros (Psiloreítis), peak, Gr. 35°12′ N, 24°41′ E 156
İdil, Turk. 37°20′ N, 41°54′ E 195
Idiofa, Dem. Rep. of the Congo 5°2′ S, 19°36′ E 218
Idle, river, U.K. 53°14′ N, 0°54′ E 162
Idlewild, Mich., U.S. 43°53′ N, 85°46′ W 102
Idlib, Syr. 35°56′ N, 36°36′ E 156
Idria, Calif., U.S. 36°24′ N, 120°41′ W 100
Idritsa, Russ. 56°18′ N, 28°51′ E 166
Idro, It. 45°44′ N, 10°29′ E 167
Idstein, Ger. 50°13′ N, 8°15′ E 167
Idutywa, S. Af. 32°8′ S, 28°17′ E 227
Idyllwild, Calif., U.S. 33°44′ N, 116°44′ W 101
Iecava, Latv. 56°36′ N, 24°11′ E 166
Iepê, Braz. 22°42′ S, 51°7′ W 138
Ieper (Ypres), Belg. 50°50′ N, 2°53′ E 163
Ierápetra, Gr. 35°3′ N, 25°43′ E 180
Iernut, Rom. 46°28′ N, 24°12′ E 156
Ifakara, Tanzania 8°8′ S, 36°39′ E 218
Ifalik Atoll, F.S.M. 6°18′ N, 143°39′ E 192
Ifanadiana, Madagascar 21°18′ S, 47°37′ E 220
Ife, Nig. 7°30′ N, 4°33′ E 222
Iferouâne, Niger 19°3′ N, 8°23′ E 222
Ifôghas, Adrar des, Mali 18°56′ N, 9°53′ E 222
Igal, Hung. 46°31′ N, 17°56′ E 168
Igalukilo, Tanzania 6°1′ S, 30°41′ E 224
Igalula, Tanzania 5°13′ S, 33°0′ E 224
Igan, Malaysia 2°46′ N, 111°44′ E 192
Iganga, Uganda 0°34′ N, 33°27′ E 224
Igarka, Russ. 67°23′ N, 86°42′ E 169
Iğdır, Turk. 39°55′ N, 44°1′ E 195
Igiugig, Alas., U.S. 59°18′ N, 155°54′ W 98
Igli, Alg. 30°27′ N, 2°19′ W 214
Iglino, Russ. 54°51′ N, 56°23′ E 154
Igloolik, Can. 69°13′ N, 81°50′ W 73
'Igma, Gebel el, Egypt 29°3′ N, 33°9′ E 180
Ignace, Can. 49°26′ N, 91°40′ W 94
Ignacio, Colo., U.S. 37°6′ N, 107°38′ W 92
Ignacio Allende, Mex. 24°27′ N, 104°0′ W 114
Ignalina, Lith. 55°20′ N, 26°7′ E 166
Ignatovka, Russ. 53°54′ N, 47°43′ E 154
İğneada, Turk. 41°52′ N, 27°57′ E 158
İğneada Burnu, Turk. 41°48′ N, 28°3′ E 156
Igoma, Tanzania 7°51′ S, 33°20′ E 224
Igombe, river, Tanzania 4°38′ S, 32°1′ E 224
Igra, Russ. 57°33′ N, 53°11′ E 154
Igrim, Russ. 63°9′ N, 64°30′ E 169
Iguala, Mex. 18°19′ N, 99°32′ W 114
Igualdade, Braz. 1°49′ S, 68°29′ W 136
Iguape, Braz. 24°41′ S, 47°37′ W 138
Iguatu, Braz. 6°23′ S, 39°17′ W 132
Iguazú Falls, South America 26°4′ S, 54°13′ W 123
Iguazú National Park, Braz. 25°46′ S, 53°36′ W 138
Iguéla, Gabon 1°58′ S, 9°21′ E 218
Iguidi, Erg, Alg. 24°5′ N, 7°50′ W 206
Igula, Tanzania 7°12′ S, 34°40′ E 224
Igumira, Tanzania 6°49′ S, 33°17′ E 224
Ihbulag, Mongolia 43°13′ N, 107°12′ E 198
Ihdin, Leb. 34°17′ N, 35°57′ E 194
Ihlow, Ger. 53°23′ N, 7°26′ E 163
Ihnâsya el Madîna, Egypt 29°6′ N, 30°56′ E 180
Ihosy, Madagascar 22°24′ S, 46°9′ E 220
Ihsuuj, Mongolia 48°10′ N, 106°6′ E 198
Ihugh, Nig. 6°58′ N, 8°59′ E 222
Ii, Fin. 65°18′ N, 25°23′ E 152
Iida, Japan 35°31′ N, 137°50′ E 201
Iida see Suzu, Japan 37°26′ N, 137°15′ E 201
Iijärvi, lake, Fin. 69°23′ N, 27°17′ E 152
Iisaku, Est. 59°5′ N, 27°17′ E 166
Iisalmi, Fin. 63°33′ N, 27°8′ E 152
Iisvesi, Fin. 62°38′ N, 26°57′ E 152
Iitto, Fin. 68°44′ N, 21°24′ E 152
Iittuarmiit, Den. 63°29′ N, 41°18′ W 106
Iiyama, Japan 36°51′ N, 138°20′ E 201
Iizaka, Japan 37°50′ N, 140°25′ E 201
Iizuka, Japan 33°37′ N, 130°41′ E 201
Ijara, Kenya 1°38′ S, 40°30′ E 224
Ijebu Ode, Nig. 6°54′ N, 3°55′ E 222
Ijevan, Arm. 40°53′ N, 45°7′ E 195
IJmuiden, Neth. 52°27′ N, 4°35′ E 163
IJsselmeer 52°47′ N, 5°7′ E 163
IJsselstein, Neth. 52°0′ N, 5°2′ E 167
Ijuí, Braz. 28°24′ S, 53°56′ W 139
Ik, river, Russ. 55°11′ N, 53°18′ E 154
Ikaalinen, Fin. 61°45′ N, 23°2′ E 166
Ikamatua, N.Z. 42°17′ S, 171°43′ E 240
Ikare, Nig. 7°32′ N, 5°44′ E 222
Ikaría, island, Gr. 37°41′ N, 26°3′ E 180
Ikast, Den. 56°8′ N, 9°8′ E 150
Ikela, Dem. Rep. of the Congo 1°5′ S, 23°4′ E 218
Ikélemba, Congo 1°15′ N, 16°31′ E 218
Ikeq 64°47′ N, 41°4′ W 106
Ikerasassuaq 59°54′ N, 45°2′ W 106
Ikervár, Hung. 47°12′ N, 16°53′ E 168
Iki, Mauna, peak, Hawai'i, U.S. 19°20′ N, 155°25′ W 99
İkizdere, Turk. 40°47′ N, 40°30′ E 195
Ikla, Est. 57°53′ N, 24°21′ E 166
Ikom, Nig. 5°57′ N, 8°42′ E 222
Ikoma, Tanzania 2°7′ S, 34°37′ E 224
Ikongo, Madagascar 21°51′ S, 47°29′ E 220
Ikorodu, Nig. 6°42′ N, 3°29′ E 222
Ikoto, Sudan 4°3′ N, 33°3′ E 224
Ikoyi, Nig. 8°17′ N, 4°9′ E 222
Ikozi, Dem. Rep. of the Congo 2°38′ S, 27°38′ E 224
Ikryanoye, Russ. 46°5′ N, 47°43′ E 158
Iksan, S. Korea 35°55′ N, 126°58′ E 200
Ikungi, Tanzania 5°6′ S, 34°45′ E 224
Ikuno, Japan 35°9′ N, 134°47′ E 201
Ikutha, Kenya 2°5′ S, 38°11′ E 224
Ila, Dem. Rep. of the Congo 2°56′ S, 21°4′ E 218
Ilaferh, spring, Alg. 21°41′ N, 1°58′ E 222
Ilagan, Philippines 17°7′ N, 121°52′ E 203
Īlām, Iran 33°38′ N, 46°25′ E 180
Ilan, Taiwan, China 24°44′ N, 121°42′ E 198
Ilandža, Serb. 45°9′ N, 20°55′ E 168
Ilanskiy, Russ. 56°15′ N, 96°7′ E 160
Ilaro, Nig. 6°58′ N, 3°1′ E 222
Ilatane, spring, Niger 16°33′ N, 4°36′ E 222
Ilava, Slovakia 48°59′ N, 18°15′ E 152
Ilave, Peru 16°7′ S, 69°40′ W 137
Ilchester, U.K. 50°59′ N, 2°40′ W 162
Île de France, region, Europe 49°1′ N, 1°33′ E 163
Île d'Orléans, island, Can. 47°3′ N, 72°9′ W 81
Ile, river, Kaz. 43°54′ N, 79°15′ E 184
Île-à-la-Crosse, Can. 55°27′ N, 107°55′ W 108
Île-à-la-Crosse, Lac, lake, Can. 55°37′ N, 108°36′ W 108
Ilebo, Dem. Rep. of the Congo 4°20′ S, 20°35′ E 218
Île-de-France, adm. division, Fr. 48°43′ N, 1°37′ E 150
Ilek, Russ. 51°33′ N, 53°27′ E 158
Ilek, river, Russ. 50°58′ N, 55°20′ E 158
Ileksa, river, Russ. 63°6′ N, 36°46′ E 154
Ilemi Triangle, Kenya 4°59′ N, 35°19′ E 224
Iles, Lac des, lake, Can. 49°9′ N, 90°7′ W 94
Ilesha, Nig. 7°37′ N, 4°44′ E 222
Ilford, Can. 56°4′ N, 95°38′ W 108
Ilford, U.K. 51°33′ N, 7°416′ E 162
Ilgaz, Turk. 40°55′ N, 33°37′ E 156
Ilgın, Turk. 38°15′ N, 31°55′ E 156
Ilhéus, Braz. 14°49′ S, 39°10′ W 123
Ili, river, China 43°55′ N, 80°49′ E 184
Ilia, Rom. 45°57′ N, 22°40′ E 168
Iliamna Lake, Alas., U.S. 59°58′ N, 157°10′ W 106
Iliamna Volcano, Alas., U.S. 60°0′ N, 153°15′ W 98
Ilıca, Turk. 39°57′ N, 41°6′ E 195
Ilidža, Bosn. and Herzg. 43°48′ N, 18°18′ E 168
Iligan, Philippines 8°16′ N, 124°15′ E 203
Iligan Bay 8°14′ N, 123°55′ E 203
Iligan Point, Philippines 18°29′ N, 122°15′ E 203
'Ili'ili'ōpae Heiau, site, Hawai'i, U.S. 21°4′ N, 156°52′ W 99
Ilimsk, Russ. 56°46′ N, 104°1′ E 246
Il'inka, Kaz. 49°55′ N, 56°13′ E 158
Ilinka, Russ. 55°23′ N, 69°16′ E 184
Ilinska Planina, Maced. 41°18′ N, 20°31′ E 156
Il'inskaya, Russ. 45°45′ N, 40°40′ E 158
Il'insko Podomskoye, Russ. 61°9′ N, 48°2′ E 154
'Ilio Point, U.S. 21°10′ N, 157°33′ W 99
Ilion, N.Y., U.S. 43°0′ N, 75°3′ W 110
Ilkal, India 15°58′ N, 76°9′ E 188
Ilkeston, U.K. 52°57′ N, 1°19′ W 162
Ill, river, Fr. 48°6′ N, 7°28′ E 163
Illampu, peak, Bol. 15°52′ S, 68°41′ W 137
Illana Bay 7°42′ N, 123°18′ E 203
Illbillee, Mount, Austral. 27°4′ S, 132°15′ E 230
Illéla, Niger 14°28′ N, 5°14′ E 222
Illescas, Mex. 23°12′ N, 102°7′ W 114
Illescas, Sp. 40°6′ N, 3°51′ W 164
Ille-sur-Têt, Fr. 42°40′ N, 2°35′ E 164
Illichivs'k, Ukr. 46°19′ N, 30°35′ E 156
Illiers, Fr. 48°17′ N, 1°15′ E 163
Illimani, peak, Bol. 16°40′ S, 67°58′ W 137
Illinois, adm. division, Ill., U.S. 40°33′ N, 89°18′ W 102
Illinois Peak, Mont., U.S. 46°59′ N, 115°9′ W 90
Illinois, river, Ark., U.S. 36°4′ N, 94°51′ W 96
Illiopolis, Ill., U.S. 39°50′ N, 89°15′ W 102
Illizi, Alg. 26°23′ N, 8°18′ E 207
Iłowo, Pol. 53°9′ N, 20°17′ E 152
Illmo, Mo., U.S. 37°13′ N, 89°30′ W 96
Íllora, Sp. 37°16′ N, 3°53′ W 164
Ilminster, U.K. 50°55′ N, 2°54′ W 162
Ilo, Peru 17°41′ S, 71°21′ W 137
Iloilo, Philippines 10°42′ N, 122°32′ E 203
Ilok, Croatia 45°12′ N, 19°22′ E 168
Ilomantsi, Fin. 62°38′ N, 30°55′ E 152
Ilonga, Tanzania 6°43′ S, 37°3′ E 224
Ilorin, Nig. 8°30′ N, 4°33′ E 222
Ilovlya, Russ. 49°18′ N, 43°59′ E 158
Ilpela, Paso de, pass, Arg. 40°10′ S, 71°50′ W 134
Il'pyrskiy, Russ. 60°1′ N, 164°9′ E 160
Ilu, Dem. Rep. of the Congo 4°1′ N, 23°9′ E 218
Ilūkste, Latv. 55°58′ N, 26°16′ E 166
Ilula, Tanzania 3°16′ S, 33°19′ E 224
Ilulissat (Jakobshavn), Den. 69°11′ N, 51°0′ W 106
Ilwaco, Wash., U.S. 46°17′ N, 124°3′ W 100
Il'ya, Belarus 54°25′ N, 27°15′ E 166
Ilych, river, Russ. 62°57′ N, 58°40′ E 154
Imabari, Japan 34°2′ N, 133°0′ E 201
Imabu, river, Braz. 2°0′ N, 57°46′ W 130
Imaichi, Japan 36°42′ N, 139°41′ E 201
Imajō, Japan 35°45′ N, 136°11′ E 201
Imanombo, Madagascar 24°25′ S, 45°50′ E 220
Imari, Japan 33°17′ N, 129°52′ E 201
Imarssuak Seachannel, North Atlantic Ocean 58°30′ N, 38°40′ W 253
Imasa, Sudan 17°58′ N, 36°8′ E 182
Imataca, Serranía de, Venez. 8°6′ N, 62°19′ W 116
Imatra, Fin. 61°9′ N, 28°46′ E 166
Imazu, Japan 35°22′ N, 136°0′ E 201
Imbert, Dom. Rep. 19°46′ N, 70°50′ W 116
Imbituba, Braz. 28°18′ S, 48°42′ W 138
Iménas, spring, Mali 16°21′ N, 0°36′ E 222
Imeni Stalina, Turkm. 39°9′ N, 63°37′ E 197
Imeri, Serra, Venez. 0°47′ N, 66°22′ W 130
Imese, Dem. Rep. of the Congo 2°2′ N, 18°9′ E 218
Īmī, Eth. 6°29′ N, 42°12′ E 224
Imi n 'Tanout, Mor. 31°10′ N, 8°52′ W 214
İmişli, Azerb. 39°51′ N, 48°2′ E 195
Imjin, river, N. Korea 38°44′ N, 126°59′ E 200
Imlay, Nev., U.S. 40°40′ N, 118°10′ W 92
Imlay City, Mich., U.S. 43°0′ N, 83°4′ W 102
Imlily, Western Sahara, Mor. 23°16′ N, 15°55′ W 214
Immenhausen, Ger. 51°26′ N, 9°29′ E 167
Immenstadt, Ger. 47°33′ N, 10°12′ E 156
Immingham, U.K. 53°36′ N, 0°14′ E 162
Immokalee, Fla., U.S. 26°25′ N, 81°25′ W 105
Imnaha, Oreg., U.S. 45°33′ N, 116°50′ W 90
Imola, It. 44°21′ N, 11°42′ E 156
Imotski, Croatia 43°25′ N, 17°12′ E 168
Imperatriz, Braz. 5°18′ S, 67°12′ W 130
Imperatriz, Braz. 5°29′ S, 47°28′ W 130
Imperia, It. 43°53′ N, 8°1′ E 167
Imperial, Calif., U.S. 32°50′ N, 115°35′ W 101
Imperial, Can. 51°22′ N, 105°28′ W 90
Imperial, Nebr., U.S. 40°30′ N, 101°39′ W 90
Imperial, Peru 13°3′ S, 76°20′ W 130
Imperial Beach, Calif., U.S. 32°34′ N, 117°8′ W 101
Imperial Dam, Calif., U.S. 32°48′ N, 114°37′ W 101
Imperial Valley, Calif., U.S. 32°56′ N, 115°52′ W 101
Imphal, India 24°50′ N, 93°55′ E 188
Impiö, Fin. 65°57′ N, 27°10′ E 152
Impora, Bol. 21°28′ S, 65°20′ W 137
Imst, Aust. 47°14′ N, 10°43′ E 156
Imtān, Syr. 32°25′ N, 36°48′ E 194
Imuris, Mex. 30°48′ N, 110°51′ W 92
Imuruan Bay 10°33′ N, 118°50′ E 203
In Azar, spring, Lib. 28°56′ N, 9°57′ E 214
Ina, Japan 35°51′ N, 137°57′ E 201
Ina, river, Pol. 53°25′ N, 14°44′ E 152
I-n-Âbâlene, spring, Mali 18°53′ N, 2°23′ E 222
I-n-Abanrherit, spring, Niger 17°54′ N, 6°2′ E 222
Inaccessible Islands, Scotia Sea 60°37′ S, 47°27′ W 134
I-n-Afarag, Erg, Alg. 23°58′ N, 2°5′ E 214
Inagauan, Philippines 9°33′ N, 118°37′ E 203
Inagua, adm. division, Bahamas 20°59′ N, 73°41′ W 116
I-n-Ahmar, spring, Mauritania 17°18′ N, 9°11′ W 222
Inajá, Braz. 8°56′ S, 37°47′ W 132
I-n-Akhmed, spring, Mali 19°53′ N, 0°54′ E 222
I-n-Alchi, spring, Mali 17°39′ N, 1°11′ W 222
I-n-Aleï, spring, Mali 17°40′ N, 2°34′ W 222
I-n-Allarhene Guériguéri, spring, Niger 18°12′ N, 6°18′ E 222
Inambari, Peru 12°46′ S, 69°41′ W 137
I-n-Amenas, Alg. 28°3′ N, 9°28′ E 214
I-n-Amguel, Alg. 23°37′ N, 5°9′ E 214
Inami, Japan 36°32′ N, 136°58′ E 201
Inanwatan, Indonesia 2°6′ S, 132°5′ E 192
Iñapari, Peru 10°59′ S, 69°39′ W 137
Inari, Fin. 68°54′ N, 27°0′ E 152
Inari, Fin. 63°16′ N, 30°58′ E 154
Inari, lake, Fin. 68°54′ N, 27°1′ E 246
Inauini, river, Braz. 8°17′ S, 68°19′ W 132
Inawashiro, Japan 37°33′ N, 140°6′ E 201
I-n-Azaoua, spring, Alg. 25°43′ N, 7°0′ E 214
I-n-Azaoua, spring, Niger 20°52′ N, 7°28′ E 222
I-n-Belbel, Alg. 27°54′ N, 1°8′ E 214
I-n-Beriem, spring, Mali 19°24′ N, 0°26′ E 222
Inca de Oro, Chile 26°45′ S, 69°56′ W 132
Inca, Paso del, pass, Chile 28°43′ S, 69°44′ W 132
İnce Burun, Turk. 42°1′ N, 34°14′ E 156
İncekum Burnu, Turk. 36°16′ N, 33°57′ E 156
İncesu, Turk. 38°36′ N, 35°11′ E 156
Incheon (Inch'ŏn), S. Korea 37°27′ N, 126°39′ E 200
Incheon City, adm. division, S. Korea 37°27′ N, 126°39′ E 200
Inch'ŏn see Incheon, S. Korea 37°27′ N, 126°39′ E 200
Inchoun, Russ. 66°16′ N, 170°14′ W 98
Incudine, Monte, peak, Fr. 41°50′ N, 9°8′ E 156
Inčukalns, Latv. 57°5′ N, 24°41′ E 166
I-n-Dagouber, spring, Mali 22°13′ N, 2°39′ W 222
Indaiá, river, Braz. 19°9′ S, 45°48′ W 138
Indaial, Braz. 27°0′ S, 49°16′ W 138
Indaparapeo, Mex. 19°45′ N, 100°58′ W 114
Indaw, Myanmar 24°9′ N, 96°6′ E 188
Indawgyi Lake, Myanmar 25°1′ N, 95°22′ E 188
Indé, Mex. 25°51′ N, 105°10′ W 114
I-n-Déliman, Mali 15°52′ N, 1°24′ E 222
Independence, Calif., U.S. 36°48′ N, 118°13′ W 101
Independence, Iowa, U.S. 42°28′ N, 91°53′ W 94
Independence, Kans., U.S. 37°12′ N, 95°43′ W 94
Independence, La., U.S. 30°36′ N, 90°30′ W 103
Independence, Mo., U.S. 39°4′ N, 94°26′ W 94
Independence Mountains, Nev., U.S. 41°4′ N, 116°25′ W 90
Independence Rock, site, Wyo., U.S. 42°29′ N, 107°11′ W 90
Independencia, Bol. 17°2′ S, 66°47′ W 137
Independência, Braz. 5°26′ S, 40°20′ W 132
Independência, Braz. 2°53′ S, 52°5′ W 130
Independencia, Parag. 21°35′ S, 62°9′ W 132
Inder see Jalaid Qi, China 46°41′ N, 122°53′ E 198
Inderapura, Indonesia 2°4′ S, 100°54′ E 192
Index, Wash., U.S. 47°49′ N, 121°34′ W 100
Indi, India 17°9′ N, 75°58′ E 188
India 22°56′ N, 77°2′ E 188
India, Bassas da, islands, Mozambique Channel 21°15′ S, 39°13′ E 220
Indialantic, Fla., U.S. 28°5′ N, 80°36′ W 105
Indian Cabins, Can. 59°53′ N, 117°3′ W 108
Indian Harbour 45°1′ N, 62°26′ W 111
Indian Harbour, Can. 54°26′ N, 57°13′ W 111
Indian Head, Can. 50°31′ N, 103°42′ W 90
Indian Head, peak, Utah, U.S. 39°51′ N, 110°59′ W 90
Indian Lake, Can. 47°5′ N, 82°30′ W 94
Indian Ocean 26°43′ S, 30°5′ E 254
Indian Peak, Utah, U.S. 38°14′ N, 113°57′ W 90
Indian Peak, Wyo., U.S. 44°45′ N, 109°56′ W 90
Indian Springs, Nev., U.S. 36°34′ N, 115°41′ W 101
Indiana, adm. division, Ind., U.S. 40°10′ N, 86°37′ W 102
Indianapolis, Ind., U.S. 39°45′ N, 86°13′ W 102
Indianola, Iowa, U.S. 41°21′ N, 93°33′ W 94
Indianola, Miss., U.S. 33°26′ N, 90°40′ W 103
Indianola, Nebr., U.S. 40°13′ N, 100°26′ W 90
Indianópolis, Braz. 19°2′ S, 47°58′ W 138
Indiantown, Fla., U.S. 27°1′ N, 80°29′ W 105
Indiga, Russ. 67°40′ N, 49°3′ E 169
Indigirka, river, Russ. 63°22′ N, 141°33′ E 160
Indija, Serb. 45°2′ N, 20°5′ E 168
Indio, Calif., U.S. 33°43′ N, 116°14′ W 101
Indio Rico, Arg. 38°20′ S, 60°53′ W 139
Índios, Braz. 27°46′ S, 50°11′ W 138
Índios, Cachoeira dos, fall(s), Braz. 0°18′ N, 63°47′ W 130
Indomed Fracture Zone, Indian Ocean 40°19′ S, 45°6′ E 254
Indonesia 2°19′ S, 115°43′ E 192
Indore, India 22°43′ N, 75°50′ E 197
Indostán, Col. 1°45′ S, 72°13′ W 136
Indra, Latv. 55°52′ N, 27°34′ E 166
Indravati National Park, India 19°13′ N, 80°24′ E 188
Indre, river, Fr. 46°59′ N, 1°4′ E 165
Indus Fan, Arabian Sea 19°1′ N, 65°10′ E 254
Indus, river, China 34°4′ N, 77°38′ E 190
Indus, river, Pak. 35°18′ N, 74°13′ E 186
Indwe, S. Af. 31°29′ S, 27°19′ E 227
I-n-Ebeggi, spring, Alg. 21°42′ N, 6°36′ E 222
İnebolu, Turk. 41°58′ N, 33°44′ E 156
I-n-Échaï, spring, Mali 20°2′ N, 2°7′ W 222
İnegöl, Turk. 40°4′ N, 29°29′ E 156
I-n-Eker, Alg. 24°1′ N, 5°5′ E 214
I-n-Emzel, spring, Mali 19°25′ N, 0°46′ E 222
Ineu, Rom. 46°25′ N, 21°53′ E 168
Ineu, peak, Rom. 47°30′ N, 24°48′ E 156
Inez, Ky., U.S. 37°51′ N, 82°33′ W 96
Inezgane, Mor. 30°21′ N, 9°33′ W 214
I-n-Ezzane, spring, Alg. 23°30′ N, 11°12′ E 214

Infieles, Punta, Chile 26°22′ S, 71°29′ W 132
Infiernillo, Mex. 18°17′ N, 101°53′ W 114
Infiernillo, Presa del, lake, Mex. 18°38′ N, 102°2′ W 114
Infiesto, Sp. 43°20′ N, 5°24′ W 150
Ingal, Niger 16°48′ N, 6°55′ E 222
Ingalls, Ark., U.S. 33°22′ N, 92°10′ W 103
Ingalls, Mich., U.S. 45°22′ N, 87°36′ W 94
Ingalls Lake, Can. 60°18′ N, 105°31′ W 108
Ingalls, Mount, Calif., U.S. 39°58′ N, 120°43′ W 90
Ingawa, Nig. 12°38′ N, 8°2′ E 222
Ingende, Dem. Rep. of the Congo 0°16′ N, 18°54′ E 218
Ingeniero Guillermo N. Juárez, Arg. 23°54′ S, 61°53′ W 132
Ingeniero Luiggi, Arg. 35°25′ S, 64°27′ W 134
Ingenika, river, Can. 56°43′ N, 125°52′ W 108
Ingersoll, Can. 43°2′ N, 80°53′ W 102
Ingettolgoy, Mongolia 49°24′ N, 104°0′ E 198
I-n-Ghar, spring, Mali 18°17′ N, 0°20′ E 222
Ingichka, Uzb. 39°44′ N, 66°0′ E 197
Ingleborough, peak, U.K. 54°10′ N, 2°25′ W 162
Inglefield Land, Den. 78°46′ N, 68°29′ W 246
Ingleside, Tex., U.S. 27°51′ N, 97°13′ W 96
Inglewood, Calif., U.S. 33°58′ N, 118°22′ W 101
Inglis, Fla., U.S. 29°1′ N, 82°40′ W 105
Inglis Island, Austral. 12°16′ S, 136°22′ E 230
Ingololo, Dem. Rep. of the Congo 5°49′ S, 16°49′ E 218
Ingonish, Can. 46°41′ N, 60°23′ W 111
Ingraj Bazar, India 24°57′ N, 88°8′ E 197
Ingram, Tex., U.S. 30°4′ N, 99°14′ W 92
Ingrid Christensen Coast, Antarctica 73°0′ S, 75°59′ E 248
I-n-Guezzâm, spring, Alg. 19°34′ N, 5°42′ E 222
Ingushetiya, adm. division, Russ. 43°15′ N, 44°35′ E 195
Inhaca, Mozambique 25°58′ S, 32°57′ E 227
Inhambane, Mozambique 23°49′ S, 35°25′ E 227
Inhambane, adm. division, Mozambique 23°10′ S, 34°36′ E 220
Inhambupe, Braz. 11°46′ S, 38°21′ W 132
Inharrime, Mozambique 24°26′ S, 35°0′ E 227
Inhassôro, Mozambique 21°32′ S, 35°7′ E 227
Inhaúmas, Braz. 13°3′ S, 44°39′ W 138
I-n-Hihaou, Adrar, peak, Alg. 23°28′ N, 2°26′ E 214
Inhul, river, Ukr. 48°12′ N, 32°11′ E 156
Inhulets, river, Ukr. 47°53′ N, 33°3′ E 156
Inhumas, Braz. 16°22′ S, 49°31′ W 138
Iniesta, Sp. 39°26′ N, 1°45′ W 164
Inírida, river, Col. 2°13′ N, 70°50′ W 136
Inírida, river, Col. 3°9′ N, 68°6′ W 136
Inishturk, peak, Ire. 53°41′ N, 10°13′ W 150
I-n-Jakoh, spring, Mali 16°49′ N, 2°17′ E 222
Injune, Austral. 25°50′ S, 148°32′ E 231
Inkee, Fin. 65°44′ N, 28°31′ E 152
Inklin, river, Can. 58°46′ N, 133°8′ W 108
Inkster, Mich., U.S. 42°16′ N, 83°20′ W 102
Inle Lake, Myanmar 20°28′ N, 96°31′ E 202
Inn, river, Switz. 46°34′ N, 10°2′ E 167
Inner Mongolia, region, Asia 41°40′ N, 103°25′ E 198
Inner Pond, lake, Can. 50°6′ N, 57°56′ W 111
Innisfail, Austral. 17°33′ S, 146°2′ E 231
Innisfail, Can. 52°2′ N, 113°57′ W 90
Innoshima, Japan 34°18′ N, 133°10′ E 201
Ino, Japan 33°33′ N, 133°25′ E 201
Inocência, Braz. 19°47′ S, 51°50′ W 138
Inongo, Dem. Rep. of the Congo 1°58′ S, 18°20′ E 207
İnönü, Turk. 39°49′ N, 30°7′ E 156
Inostrantseva, Zaliv 76°16′ N, 57°48′ E 160
Inovo, Serb. 43°23′ N, 22°26′ E 168
Inowrocław, Pol. 52°46′ N, 18°15′ E 152
Inquisivi, Bol. 17°1′ S, 67°10′ W 137
I-n-Rahr, Alg. 27°5′ N, 1°54′ E 214
I-n-Ghar, spring, Mali 18°17′ N, 0°20′ E 222
I-n-Salah, Alg. 27°13′ N, 2°28′ E 214
Insar, Russ. 53°50′ N, 44°21′ E 154
Inscription, Cape, Austral. 25°30′ S, 111°26′ E 230
Insein, Myanmar 16°57′ N, 96°6′ E 202
Inselsberg, Grosser, peak, Ger. 50°50′ N, 10°25′ E 167
Insjön, Nor. 60°40′ N, 15°5′ E 152
Insurgente José María Morelos y Pavón National Park see 23, Mex. 19°38′ N, 101°11′ W 112
Insurgente Miguel Hidalgo y Costilla National Park see 24, Mex. 19°14′ N, 99°28′ W 112
Inta, Russ. 66°1′ N, 60°8′ E 154
I-n-Tebezas, spring, Mali 17°49′ N, 1°55′ E 222
Intendente Alvear, Arg. 35°16′ S, 63°38′ W 139
International Falls, Minn., U.S. 48°34′ N, 93°28′ W 106
Interview Island, India 12°43′ N, 91°37′ E 188
Inthanon, Doi, peak, Thai. 18°35′ N, 98°23′ E 202
I-n-Tilelt, spring, Mali 15°26′ N, 0°25′ E 222
Intiyaco, Arg. 28°39′ S, 60°6′ W 139
Intuto, Peru 3°34′ S, 74°46′ W 136
Inukjuak, Can. 58°28′ N, 78°9′ W 106
Inuvik, Can. 68°15′ N, 133°59′ W 106
Inuya, river, Peru 10°34′ S, 72°53′ W 137
Inuyama, Japan 35°21′ N, 136°57′ E 201
Invercargill, N.Z. 46°27′ S, 168°22′ E 240
Invermere, Can. 50°29′ N, 116°2′ W 108
Inverness, Can. 46°13′ N, 61°19′ W 111
Inverness, Fla., U.S. 28°50′ N, 82°21′ W 105
Inverness, Miss., U.S. 33°19′ N, 90°36′ W 103
Inverness, U.K. 57°27′ N, 4°15′ W 143
Investigator Group, islands, Great Australian Bight 34°18′ S, 131°19′ E 230
Investigator Ridge, Indian Ocean 11°21′ S, 98°10′ E 254
Inya, Russ. 50°29′ N, 86°43′ E 184
Inyati, Zimb. 19°42′ S, 28°50′ E 224
Inyo, Mount, Calif., U.S. 36°43′ N, 118°2′ W 101
Inyo Mountains, Calif., U.S. 37°11′ N, 118°9′ W 101
Inyokern, Calif., U.S. 35°39′ N, 117°40′ W 101
Inyonga, Tanzania 6°42′ S, 32°3′ E 224
Inza, Russ. 53°49′ N, 46°26′ E 154
Inzana Lake, Can. 54°57′ N, 124°56′ W 108
Inzhavino, Russ. 52°19′ N, 42°25′ E 158
I-n-Ziza, spring, Alg. 23°32′ N, 2°36′ E 214
Ioánina, Gr. 39°40′ N, 20°50′ E 156
Ioaniş, Rom. 46°40′ N, 22°18′ E 168
Iola, Kans., U.S. 37°53′ N, 95°24′ W 96
Iona, Idaho, U.S. 43°32′ N, 111°56′ W 90
Iona National Park, Angola 17°9′ S, 11°53′ E 220
Ione, Calif., U.S. 38°20′ N, 120°57′ W 100
Ione, Nev., U.S. 38°57′ N, 117°36′ W 90
Ione, Oreg., U.S. 45°29′ N, 119°50′ W 90
Ione, Wash., U.S. 48°43′ N, 117°26′ W 108
Iongo, Angola 9°13′ S, 17°44′ E 218
Ionia, Mich., U.S. 42°58′ N, 85°4′ W 102
Ionian Sea 37°56′ N, 17°35′ E 156
Iónioi Nísoi, adm. division, Gr. 38°37′ N, 20°34′ E 156
Ionn N'yug Oayv, Gora, peak, Russ. 68°18′ N, 28°48′ E 152
Iori, river, Ga. 41°8′ N, 46°0′ E 195
Íos, island, Gr. 36°35′ N, 25°24′ E 180
Iota, La., U.S. 30°18′ N, 92°30′ W 103
Iouik, Mauritania 19°53′ N, 16°18′ W 222
Iowa, La., U.S. 30°12′ N, 93°1′ W 103
Iowa, adm. division, Iowa, U.S. 42°18′ N, 93°59′ W 94
Iowa City, Iowa, U.S. 41°39′ N, 91°31′ W 94
Iowa Falls, Iowa, U.S. 42°30′ N, 93°15′ W 94
Iowa, river, Iowa, U.S. 41°52′ N, 92°57′ W 80
Ipameri, Braz. 17°45′ S, 48°12′ W 138
Ipamu, Dem. Rep. of the Congo 4°10′ S, 19°34′ E 218
Ipanema, Braz. 19°54′ S, 41°44′ W 138
Iparia, Peru 9°19′ S, 74°28′ W 137
Ipatovo, Russ. 45°43′ N, 42°44′ E 158
Ipiales, Col. 0°50′ N, 77°49′ W 136
Ipiaú, Braz. 14°10′ S, 39°42′ W 138
Ipiķi, Latv. 57°59′ N, 25°12′ E 166
Ipiranga, Braz. 3°10′ S, 66°6′ W 136
Ipiranga, Braz. 3°1′ S, 69°36′ W 136
Ipiranga, Braz. 25°3′ S, 50°36′ W 138
Ípiros, adm. division, Gr. 39°40′ N, 20°40′ E 156
Ipitinga, river, Braz. 0°21′ N, 53°53′ W 130
Ipixuna, river, Braz. 7°7′ S, 73°20′ W 130
Ipoh, Malaysia 4°37′ N, 101°3′ E 196
Ipole, Tanzania 5°46′ S, 32°45′ E 224
Iporá, Braz. 16°28′ S, 51°8′ W 138
Ippy, Cen. Af. Rep. 6°15′ N, 21°12′ E 218
İpsala, Turk. 40°55′ N, 26°21′ E 156
Ipsalio, Óros, peak, Gr. 40°42′ N, 24°34′ E 156
Ipswich, Mass., U.S. 42°40′ N, 70°51′ W 104
Ipswich, S. Dak., U.S. 45°25′ N, 99°3′ W 90
Ipswich, U.K. 52°3′ N, 1°9′ E 162
Ipu, Braz. 4°19′ S, 40°44′ W 132
Ipueiras, Braz. 4°33′ S, 40°45′ W 132
Ipun, Isla, island, Chile 44°31′ S, 75°24′ W 134
Ipupiara, Braz. 11°50′ S, 42°38′ W 132
Iput', river, Russ. 52°41′ N, 31°48′ E 154
Iqaluit, Can. 63°42′ N, 69°1′ W 106
Iqe, China 38°4′ N, 95°0′ E 188
Iqe, river, China 38°13′ N, 95°23′ E 188
Iquique, Chile 20°15′ S, 70°10′ W 137
Iquitos, Peru 3°48′ S, 73°14′ W 136
Iraan, Tex., U.S. 30°53′ N, 101°53′ W 92
Īrafshān, Iran 26°44′ N, 61°57′ E 182
Iraí, Braz. 27°13′ S, 53°17′ W 139
Iraiti, Braz. 0°12′ N, 69°26′ W 136
Iráklio (Candia), Gr. 35°19′ N, 25°7′ E 156
Iran 32°49′ N, 52°32′ E 180
Īrānshahr, Iran 27°12′ N, 60°41′ E 182
Irapuato, Mex. 20°39′ N, 101°23′ W 114
Iraq 32°28′ N, 43°26′ E 180
Irati, Braz. 25°28′ S, 50°37′ W 138
Irayel', Russ. 64°22′ N, 55°6′ E 154
Irazú, Volcán, C.R. 9°57′ N, 83°55′ W 115
Irazusta, Arg. 32°56′ S, 58°55′ W 139
Irbe Strait 57°43′ N, 21°29′ E 152
Irbid, Jordan 32°32′ N, 35°51′ E 180
Irbid (Arbela), Jordan 32°32′ N, 35°51′ E 194
Irbit, Russ. 57°40′ N, 62°58′ E 154
Irebu, Dem. Rep. of the Congo 0°39′ N, 17°43′ E 218
Irecê, Braz. 11°21′ S, 41°54′ W 132
Ireland 53°17′ N, 8°19′ W 150
Ireland, Mount, Oreg., U.S. 44°48′ N, 118°25′ W 90
Ireng, river, South America 4°26′ N, 60°6′ W 130
Iriba, Chad 15°6′ N, 22°14′ E 216
Irié, Guinea 8°14′ N, 9°11′ W 222
Irig, Serb. 45°5′ N, 19°51′ E 168
Iriga, Philippines 13°25′ N, 123°25′ E 203
Iriklinskiy, Russ. 51°39′ N, 58°38′ E 154
Irimi, Indonesia 1°58′ S, 133°11′ E 192
Iringa, Tanzania 7°46′ S, 35°42′ E 224
Iringa, adm. division, Tanzania 9°28′ S, 34°6′ E 220
Iriomote, island, Japan 23°59′ N, 122°47′ E 190
Iriomote Jima, island, Japan 24°23′ N, 123°23′ E 198
Iriri Novo, river, Braz. 9°52′ S, 53°23′ W 130
Iriri, river, Braz. 7°21′ S, 53°36′ W 132
Irish Mountain, Oreg., U.S. 43°50′ N, 122°3′ W 90
Irish Sea 52°27′ N, 5°55′ W 150
Irkutsk, Russ. 52°24′ N, 104°22′ E 190
Irkutsk, adm. division, Russ. 57°13′ N, 105°42′ E 160
Irma, Can. 52°54′ N, 111°14′ W 108
Iro, Lac, lake, Chad 10°5′ N, 18°58′ E 216
Irō Zaki, Japan 34°28′ N, 138°49′ E 201
Iron Mountain, Oreg., U.S. 43°15′ N, 119°32′ W 90
Iron Mountain, Oreg., U.S. 42°40′ N, 124°14′ W 90
Iron Mountains, Calif., U.S. 34°13′ N, 115°16′ W 101
Iron Range, Austral. 12°51′ S, 143°20′ E 231
Iron Range National Park, Coral Sea 12°43′ S, 143°0′ E 238
Iron River, Mich., U.S. 46°5′ N, 88°39′ W 94
Iron River, Wis., U.S. 46°33′ N, 91°25′ W 94
Irons, Mich., U.S. 44°8′ N, 85°55′ W 102
Ironside Mountain, Oreg., U.S. 44°13′ N, 118°14′ W 90
Ironton, Minn., U.S. 46°27′ N, 93°59′ W 94
Ironton, Mo., U.S. 37°35′ N, 90°38′ W 96
Ironton, Ohio, U.S. 38°31′ N, 82°40′ W 94
Iroquois Falls, Can. 48°45′ N, 80°41′ W 94
Iroquois, river, Can. 68°9′ N, 130°23′ W 98
Iroquois, river, Ind., U.S. 40°49′ N, 87°44′ W 102
Írottkő, peak, Hung. 47°20′ N, 16°25′ E 168
Irpin', Ukr. 50°33′ N, 30°20′ E 158
Irrawady see Ayeyarwady, river, Myanmar 21°54′ N, 95°42′ W 202
Irrel, Ger. 49°50′ N, 6°28′ E 167
Irrua, Nig. 6°50′ N, 6°13′ E 222
Irshava, Ukr. 48°17′ N, 23°1′ E 152
Irtysh, Russ. 54°27′ N, 74°28′ E 184
Irtysh, river, Russ. 59°32′ N, 69°13′ E 169
Irumu, Dem. Rep. of the Congo 1°28′ N, 29°49′ E 224
Iruña see Pamplona, Sp. 42°47′ N, 1°40′ W 164
Irupana, Bol. 16°27′ S, 67°25′ W 137
Irurtzun, Sp. 42°54′ N, 1°50′ W 164
Iruya, Arg. 22°41′ S, 65°13′ W 137
Iruya, river, Arg. 22°37′ S, 65°13′ W 137
Irvine, Calif., U.S. 33°41′ N, 117°49′ W 101
Irvine, Can. 49°57′ N, 110°15′ W 90
Irvine, Ky., U.S. 37°41′ N, 83°59′ W 96
Irvine, U.K. 55°36′ N, 4°40′ W 150
Irvines Landing, Can. 49°38′ N, 124°2′ W 100
Is, Russ. 58°49′ N, 59°44′ E 154
Is, Jebel, peak, Sudan 21°48′ N, 35°36′ E 182
Isa, Nig. 13°11′ N, 6°21′ E 222
Isa Khel, Pak. 32°41′ N, 71°20′ E 186
Isaba, Sp. 42°51′ N, 0°55′ E 164
Isabel, S. Dak., U.S. 45°22′ N, 101°27′ W 90
Isabela, Philippines 6°41′ N, 121°56′ E 203
Isabela, Philippines 10°11′ N, 122°57′ E 203
Isabela, Cabo, Dom. Rep. 20°0′ N, 71°35′ W 116
Isabela, Isla, island, Ecua. 1°17′ S, 92°8′ W 130
Isabella, Minn., U.S. 47°36′ N, 91°23′ W 94
Isabelle, Point, Mich., U.S. 47°8′ N, 87°56′ W 94
Isaccea, Rom. 45°15′ N, 28°26′ E 156
Isachsen, Can. 78°47′ N, 103°28′ W 246
Isachsen Mount, Antarctica 72°18′ S, 26°0′ E 248
Ísafjörður, Ice. 66°8′ N, 23°9′ W 246
Isagarh, India 24°50′ N, 77°54′ E 197
Isahaya, Japan 32°50′ N, 130°2′ E 201
Isaka, Tanzania 3°54′ S, 32°55′ E 224
Isaki, Russ. 56°39′ N, 28°35′ E 166
Isalo, Massif de l', Madagascar 23°10′ S, 44°24′ E 220
Isana, river, Col. 1°48′ N, 69°4′ W 136
Isangano National Park, Zambia 11°21′ S, 30°2′ E 224
Isangi, Dem. Rep. of the Congo 0°45′ N, 24°7′ E 224
Isangila, Dem. Rep. of the Congo 5°18′ S, 13°33′ E 218
Isanlu Makutu, Nig. 8°15′ N, 5°45′ E 222
Isar, river, Ger. 48°35′ N, 12°46′ E 152
Isarog, Mount, Philippines 13°40′ N, 123°16′ E 203
Isbister, river, Can. 53°41′ N, 94°48′ W 108
Íscar, Sp. 41°20′ N, 4°32′ W 150
Iscayachi, Bol. 21°33′ S, 65°2′ W 137
Ischia, It. 40°44′ N, 13°56′ E 156
Isdu, island, Maldives 1°56′ N, 73°36′ E 188
Ise, Japan 34°28′ N, 136°43′ E 201
Ise Wan 34°39′ N, 136°34′ E 201
Iseo, It. 45°39′ N, 10°2′ E 167
Isère, Pointe, Fr. 5°48′ N, 53°50′ W 130
Isère, river, Fr. 44°59′ N, 5°2′ E 165
Isesaki, Japan 36°18′ N, 139°13′ E 201
Ise-Shima National Park, Japan 34°19′ N, 136°29′ E 201
Iset', river, Russ. 56°7′ N, 64°54′ E 184
Iseyin, Nig. 8°1′ N, 3°37′ E 222
Isfahan see Esfahan, Iran 32°40′ N, 51°38′ E 180
Isfara, Taj. 40°8′ N, 70°36′ E 197
Ishëm, Alban. 41°32′ N, 19°34′ E 168
Isheyevka, Russ. 54°25′ N, 48°23′ E 154
Ishigaki, Japan 24°16′ N, 124°9′ E 198
Ishigaki Jima, island, Japan 24°35′ N, 123°54′ E 198
Ishikawa, Japan 37°8′ N, 140°27′ E 201
Ishikawa, adm. division, Japan 36°16′ N, 136°18′ E 201
Ishim, Russ. 56°8′ N, 69°36′ E 184
Ishim, river, Russ. 56°1′ N, 70°27′ E 184
Ishimbay, Russ. 53°28′ N, 56°4′ E 154
Ishinomaki, Japan 38°33′ N, 141°5′ E 190
Ishioka, Japan 36°10′ N, 140°17′ E 201
Ishkuman, Pak. 36°30′ N, 73°47′ E 186
Ishpatina Ridge, Can. 47°20′ N, 80°48′ W 94
Ishpeming, Mich., U.S. 46°29′ N, 87°40′ W 110
Ishtixon, Uzb. 40°0′ N, 66°33′ E 197
Isiboro, river, Bol. 16°16′ S, 65°15′ W 137
Isiboro Sécure National Park, Bol. 16°2′ S, 66°19′ W 137
Isidora, Col. 6°7′ N, 68°31′ W 136
Işık Dağı, peak, Turk. 40°40′ N, 32°40′ E 156
Isikveren, Turk. 37°23′ N, 42°58′ E 195
Isil'kul', Russ. 54°52′ N, 71°18′ E 184
Isiolo, Kenya 0°18′ N, 37°36′ E 224
Isiro (Paulis), Dem. Rep. of the Congo 2°43′ N, 27°39′ E 224
Iskele see Trikomo, N. Cyprus, Cyprus 35°17′ N, 33°53′ E 194
İskenderun, Turk. 36°33′ N, 36°13′ E 180
İskilip, Turk. 40°44′ N, 34°28′ E 156
Iskitim, Russ. 54°39′ N, 83°17′ E 184
Iskrets, Bulg. 42°59′ N, 23°14′ E 168
Iskŭr, river, Bulg. 43°21′ N, 24°5′ E 156
Iskushuban, Somalia 10°11′ N, 50°15′ E 216
Iskut, river, Can. 57°9′ N, 130°24′ W 108
Isla de Lobos, oil field, Mex. 21°20′ N, 97°12′ W 114
Isla Guamblin National Park, site, Chile 44°51′ S, 75°19′ W 134
Isla Isabel National Park, Mex. 21°51′ N, 106°1′ W 112
Isla Mujeres, Mex. 21°17′ N, 86°50′ W 116
Isla Verde, Arg. 33°15′ S, 62°24′ W 139
Islamabad, Pak. 33°37′ N, 73°2′ E 186
Islamkot, Pak. 24°43′ N, 70°11′ E 186
Islamorada, Fla., U.S. 24°55′ N, 80°38′ W 105
Island Falls, Me., U.S. 46°0′ N, 68°16′ W 94
Island Grove, Fla., U.S. 29°27′ N, 82°8′ W 105
Island Lake, Can. 53°51′ N, 94°42′ W 108
Island Lake, Can. 53°58′ N, 95°7′ W 108
Island Lake, Minn., U.S. 47°48′ N, 94°31′ W 90
Island Park, Idaho, U.S. 44°25′ N, 111°22′ W 90
Isle of Hope, Ga., U.S. 31°58′ N, 81°4′ W 96
Isle Pierre, Can. 53°56′ N, 123°16′ W 108
Isle, river, Fr. 45°30′ N, 1°3′ E 165
Isleton, Calif., U.S. 38°9′ N, 121°37′ W 100
Ismâ'ilîya, Egypt 30°35′ N, 32°15′ E 194
Ismoili Somoni, Qullai (Communism Peak), Taj. 39°3′ N, 72°1′ E 197
Isna, Egypt 25°16′ N, 32°29′ E 182
Isoanala, Madagascar 23°48′ S, 45°46′ E 220
Isojoki, Fin. 62°6′ N, 21°55′ E 152
Isoka, Zambia 10°11′ S, 32°36′ E 224
Isola, Miss., U.S. 33°14′ N, 90°36′ W 103
Isola del Cantone, It. 44°39′ N, 8°57′ E 167
Isola della Scala, It. 45°16′ N, 11°0′ E 167
Isola delle Correnti, Capo, It. 36°32′ N, 15°5′ E 156
Isola Peak, Can. 50°6′ N, 114°37′ W 90
Isparta, Turk. 37°44′ N, 30°32′ E 156
Ispica, It. 36°46′ N, 14°53′ E 156
İspir, Turk. 40°29′ N, 41°0′ E 195
Ispra, It. 45°49′ N, 8°36′ E 167
Israel 31°0′ N, 34°41′ E 194
Israelite Bay 33°48′ S, 122°33′ E 230
Isratu, island, Eritrea 16°21′ N, 39°48′ E 182
Issa, river, Russ. 56°18′ N, 28°20′ E 166
Issano, Guyana 5°46′ N, 59°30′ W 130
Issel, river, Ger. 51°47′ N, 6°29′ E 167
Issia, Côte d'Ivoire 6°23′ N, 6°35′ W 222
Issoudun, Fr. 46°56′ N, 1°59′ E 150
Issus, battle, Turk. 36°53′ N, 36°4′ E 156
Istallósko, peak, Hung. 48°2′ N, 20°22′ E 168
İstanbul (Constantinople), Turk. 41°1′ N, 28°55′ E 156
Istaravshan (Üroteppa), Taj. 39°53′ N, 69°0′ E 197
Istmina, Col. 5°10′ N, 76°42′ W 136
Isto, Mount, Alas., U.S. 69°5′ N, 144°8′ W 98
Istok (Istok), Kosovo 42°46′ N, 20°29′ E 168
Istok see Istog, Kosovo 42°46′ N, 20°29′ E 168
Istokpoga, Lake, Fla., U.S. 27°24′ N, 81°25′ W 105
Istres, Fr. 43°29′ N, 4°58′ E 150
Istria, Croatia 45°16′ N, 13°33′ E 167
Isulan, Philippines 6°37′ N, 124°37′ E 203
Isyangulovo, Russ. 52°12′ N, 56°27′ E 154
Itá, Parag. 25°31′ S, 57°21′ W 132
Itabaiana, Braz. 10°37′ S, 37°22′ W 132
Itabaianinha, Braz. 11°17′ S, 37°47′ W 132
Itabapoana, Braz. 21°20′ S, 41°1′ W 138
Itaberaba, Braz. 12°33′ S, 40°21′ W 132
Itaberaí, Braz. 16°6′ S, 49°49′ W 138
Itabira, Braz. 19°39′ S, 43°13′ W 138
Itabirito, Braz. 20°21′ S, 43°48′ W 138
Itabuna, Braz. 14°27′ S, 39°36′ W 123
Itacaiúnas, river, Braz. 5°58′ S, 50°40′ W 130
Itacajá, Braz. 8°22′ S, 47°46′ W 130
Itacarambi, Braz. 15°8′ S, 44°9′ W 138
Itacoatiara, Braz. 3°9′ S, 58°33′ W 130
Itaeté, Braz. 13°1′ S, 41°1′ W 138
Itaguari, river, Braz. 14°36′ S, 45°16′ W 138
Itagüí, Col. 6°11′ N, 75°41′ W 136
Itahuanía, Peru 12°38′ S, 71°9′ W 137
Itaí, Braz. 23°25′ S, 49°8′ W 138
Itaituba, Braz. 4°15′ S, 56°1′ W 130
Itajaí, Braz. 26°56′ S, 48°40′ W 138
Itajimirim, Braz. 16°5′ S, 39°36′ W 138
Itajubá, Braz. 22°24′ S, 45°30′ W 138
Itaka, Tanzania 8°54′ S, 32°48′ E 224
Italia, Monte, peak, Chile 54°48′ S, 69°21′ W 134
Italy 42°58′ N, 11°46′ E 156
Itamaraju, Braz. 17°11′ S, 39°33′ W 138
Itamarandiba, Braz. 17°53′ S, 42°55′ W 138
Itambacuri, Braz. 18°3′ S, 41°42′ W 138
Itambé, Braz. 15°18′ S, 40°40′ W 138
Itambé, Pico de, peak, Braz. 18°27′ S, 43°24′ W 138
Itanagar, India 27°7′ N, 93°46′ E 188
Itanhaém, Braz. 24°11′ S, 46°47′ W 138
Itanhauã, river, Braz. 5°2′ S, 64°50′ W 130
Itanhém, Braz. 17°9′ S, 40°20′ W 138
Itany, river, Suriname 2°48′ N, 54°14′ W 130
Itapaci, Braz. 15°0′ S, 49°37′ W 138
Itapagipe, Braz. 19°56′ S, 49°22′ W 138
Itaparaná, river, Braz. 7°28′ S, 63°50′ W 130
Itaparica, Ilha de, island, Braz. 13°16′ S, 40°1′ W 132
Itapebi, Braz. 15°58′ S, 39°33′ W 138
Itapecerica, Braz. 20°31′ S, 45°8′ W 138
Itapecuru Mirim, Braz. 3°25′ S, 44°22′ W 132
Itapemirim, Braz. 21°5′ S, 40°52′ W 138
Itaperina, Pointe, Madagascar 25°18′ S, 47°14′ E 220
Itaperuna, Braz. 21°13′ S, 41°53′ W 138
Itapetinga, Braz. 15°18′ S, 40°18′ W 138
Itapetininga, Braz. 23°35′ S, 48°5′ W 138
Itapeva, Braz. 23°58′ S, 48°53′ W 138
Itapiranga, Braz. 27°9′ S, 53°44′ W 139
Itápolis, Braz. 21°34′ S, 48°49′ W 138
Itaporanga, Braz. 23°43′ S, 49°31′ W 138
Itapuranga, Braz. 15°35′ S, 49°58′ W 138
Itaqui, Braz. 29°11′ S, 56°36′ W 139
Itararé, Braz. 24°7′ S, 49°19′ W 138
Itararé, river, Braz. 24°16′ S, 49°13′ W 138
Itarsi, India 22°37′ N, 77°46′ E 197
Itarumã, Braz. 18°44′ S, 51°29′ W 138
Itasca, Tex., U.S. 32°8′ N, 97°9′ W 92
Itasca, Lake, Minn., U.S. 47°9′ N, 96°14′ W 82
Itatá, river, Braz. 4°13′ S, 52°7′ W 132
Itatí, Arg. 27°17′ S, 58°13′ W 139
Itatupã, Braz. 0°36′ N, 51°14′ W 130
Itaú, Bol. 21°41′ S, 63°55′ W 137
Itaúba, Braz. 10°55′ S, 55°8′ W 123

Itaúna, *Braz.* 20°5′ S, 44°34′ W 138
Itaúna, *Braz.* 2°59′ S, 66°5′ W 136
Itaúnas, *Braz.* 18°24′ S, 39°44′ W 138
Itbayat, island, *Philippines* 20°44′ N, 121°21′ E 198
Itende, *Tanzania* 6°44′ S, 34°23′ E 224
Itezhi-Tezhi, Lake, *Zambia* 15°55′ S, 25°14′ E 224
Ithaca, *Mich., U.S.* 43°16′ N, 84°37′ W 102
Ithaca, *N.Y., U.S.* 42°26′ N, 76°31′ W 94
Itigi, *Tanzania* 5°39′ S, 34°29′ E 224
Itimbiri, river, *Dem. Rep. of the Congo* 2°20′ N, 23°1′ E 218
Itinga, *Braz.* 16°36′ S, 41°50′ W 138
Itiquines, *Col.* 0°38′ N, 73°15′ W 136
Itiquira, *Braz.* 17°12′ S, 54°9′ W 132
Itiquira, river, *Braz.* 17°15′ S, 56°29′ W 132
Itiruçu, *Braz.* 13°30′ S, 40°10′ W 138
Itiúba, Serra de, *Braz.* 10°6′ S, 40°31′ W 132
Itō, *Japan* 34°57′ N, 139°5′ E 201
Itobo, *Tanzania* 4°12′ S, 33°1′ E 224
Itoigawa, *Japan* 37°2′ N, 137°51′ E 201
Itoko, *Dem. Rep. of the Congo* 1°0′ N, 21°46′ E 218
Iton, river, *Fr.* 49°7′ N, 1°7′ E 163
Itonamas, river, *Bol.* 12°30′ S, 64°25′ W 137
Itta Bena, *Miss., U.S.* 33°28′ N, 90°20′ W 103
Ittoqqortoormiit (Scoresbysund), *Den.* 70°26′ N, 21°53′ W 246
Itu, *Braz.* 23°17′ S, 47°21′ W 138
Itu, river, *Braz.* 29°20′ S, 55°23′ W 139
Ituaçu, *Braz.* 13°51′ S, 41°19′ W 138
Ituí, river, *Braz.* 4°59′ S, 70°47′ W 130
Ituiutaba, *Braz.* 19°1′ S, 49°31′ W 138
Itula, *Dem. Rep. of the Congo* 3°32′ S, 27°49′ E 224
Itumbiara, *Braz.* 18°28′ S, 49°15′ W 138
Ituna, *Can.* 51°9′ N, 103°31′ W 90
Ituni, *Guyana* 5°24′ N, 58°18′ W 130
Itupiranga, *Braz.* 5°12′ S, 49°19′ W 130
Iturama, *Braz.* 19°43′ S, 50°14′ W 138
Iturbe, *Arg.* 23°0′ S, 65°21′ W 137
Iturbe, *Parag.* 26°2′ S, 56°28′ W 139
Iturbide, *Mex.* 24°42′ N, 99°54′ W 114
Ituri, river, *Dem. Rep. of the Congo* 1°41′ N, 27°21′ E 224
Iturup (Etorofu), island, *Russ.* 44°16′ N, 147°11′ E 190
Ituverava, *Braz.* 20°21′ S, 47°50′ W 138
Ituxi, river, *Braz.* 7°58′ S, 65°3′ W 130
Ituzaingó, *Arg.* 27°37′ S, 56°40′ W 139
Itzehoe, *Ger.* 53°55′ N, 9°31′ E 150
Iuka, *Miss., U.S.* 34°47′ N, 88°12′ W 96
Iul'tin, *Russ.* 67°49′ N, 178°46′ W 98
Iulúti, *Mozambique* 15°53′ S, 39°2′ E 224
Iúna, *Braz.* 20°22′ S, 41°35′ W 138
Ivád, *Hung.* 48°1′ N, 20°4′ E 168
Ivaí, river, *Braz.* 23°19′ S, 53°24′ W 138
Ivaipora, *Braz.* 24°16′ S, 51°43′ W 138
Ivalo, *Fin.* 68°37′ N, 27°33′ E 160
Ivan Gorod, *Russ.* 59°21′ N, 28°12′ E 166
Ivan Sedlo, *Bosn. and Herzg.* 43°46′ N, 18°2′ E 168
Ivanava, *Belarus* 52°8′ N, 25°32′ E 152
Ivanchina, *Russ.* 60°3′ N, 54°17′ E 154
Ivanec, *Croatia* 46°13′ N, 16°8′ E 168
Ivangrad, *Mont.* 42°50′ N, 19°50′ E 168
Ivanhoe, *Austral.* 32°53′ S, 144°17′ E 231
Ivanhoe, *Calif., U.S.* 36°23′ N, 119°14′ W 100
Ivanhoe Lake, *Can.* 60°23′ N, 107°8′ W 108
Ivanhoe, river, *Can.* 48°19′ N, 82°29′ W 110
Ivanić Grad, *Croatia* 45°41′ N, 16°24′ E 168
Ivanjica, *Serb.* 43°34′ N, 20°13′ E 168
Ivanjska, *Bosn. and Herzg.* 44°55′ N, 17°4′ E 168
Ivankovo, *Croatia* 45°16′ N, 18°39′ E 168
Ivano-Frankivs'k, *Ukr.* 48°53′ N, 24°41′ E 152
Ivanovo, *Russ.* 57°0′ N, 40°58′ E 154
Ivanovo, adm. division, *Russ.* 56°55′ N, 41°55′ E 154
Ivanpah, *Calif., U.S.* 35°19′ N, 115°20′ W 101
Ivanteyevka, *Russ.* 52°15′ N, 49°8′ E 158
Ivatsevichy, *Belarus* 52°43′ N, 25°22′ E 152
Ivaylovgrad, *Bulg.* 41°31′ N, 26°6′ E 156
Ivdel', *Russ.* 60°40′ N, 60°23′ E 154
Ivi, Cap, *Alg.* 36°6′ N, 0°8′ E 164
Ivinheima, *Braz.* 22°12′ S, 53°33′ W 138
Iviza see Ibiza, island, *Sp.* 39°1′ N, 6°356′ W 214
Ivo, *Bol.* 20°29′ S, 63°28′ W 137
Ivohibe, *Madagascar* 22°29′ S, 46°53′ E 220
Ivón, *Bol.* 11°10′ S, 66°9′ W 137
Ivory Coast, region, *Africa* 5°58′ N, 5°7′ W 222
Ivory Coast see Côte d'Ivoire 7°16′ N, 7°29′ W 214
Ivoryton, *Conn., U.S.* 41°20′ N, 72°27′ W 104
Ivrea, *It.* 45°29′ N, 7°52′ E 167
Ivrognes, Pointe aux, *Can.* 49°42′ N, 65°31′ W 111
Ivujivik, *Can.* 62°22′ N, 78°2′ W 106
Ivyanyets, *Belarus* 53°52′ N, 26°44′ E 166
Ivydale, *W. Va., U.S.* 38°32′ N, 81°3′ W 102
Iwaki, *Japan* 36°58′ N, 140°52′ E 201
Iwanuma, *Japan* 38°7′ N, 140°51′ E 201
Iwembere Steppe, *Tanzania* 4°26′ S, 33°20′ E 224
Iwo, *Nig.* 7°42′ N, 4°11′ E 222
Iwŏn, *N. Korea* 40°20′ N, 128°39′ E 200
Iwye, *Belarus* 53°55′ N, 25°45′ E 166
Ixhuatán, *Mex.* 16°21′ N, 94°30′ W 112
Ixiamas, *Bol.* 13°47′ S, 68°8′ W 137
Ixopo, *S. Af.* 30°11′ S, 30°3′ E 227
Ixpalino, *Mex.* 23°52′ N, 106°39′ W 114
Ixtapa, *Mex.* 17°39′ N, 101°36′ W 114
Ixtapa, Punta, *Mex.* 17°29′ N, 101°52′ W 114
Ixtapan del Oro, *Mex.* 19°14′ N, 100°16′ W 114
Ixtlán, *Mex.* 21°1′ N, 104°22′ W 114
Ixtoc, oil field, *Mex.* 19°36′ N, 92°21′ W 115
'Iyal Bakhit, *Sudan* 13°25′ N, 28°43′ E 226
Iyo, *Japan* 33°44′ N, 132°42′ E 201
Iyo Nada 33°29′ N, 131°49′ E 201
Iyomishima, *Japan* 33°57′ N, 133°31′ E 201
Izabal, Lago de, lake, *Guatemala* 15°22′ N, 89°53′ W 115
Īzadkhāst, *Iran* 31°31′ N, 52°5′ E 180
Izamal, *Mex.* 20°55′ N, 89°2′ W 116
Izapa, ruin(s), *Mex.* 14°53′ N, 92°17′ W 115
Izberbash, *Russ.* 42°31′ N, 47°52′ E 195
Izbica, *Pol.* 50°53′ N, 23°9′ E 152
Izdeshkovo, *Russ.* 55°7′ N, 33°41′ E 154
Izegem, *Belg.* 50°54′ N, 3°12′ E 163
Izhevsk, *Russ.* 56°48′ N, 53°15′ E 154
Izhma, *Russ.* 64°59′ N, 53°53′ E 154
Izhma, river, *Russ.* 64°25′ N, 53°38′ E 154
Izmayil, *Ukr.* 45°21′ N, 28°51′ E 156
İzmir (Smyrna), *Turk.* 38°24′ N, 27°8′ E 156
İzmit see Kocaeli, *Turk.* 40°47′ N, 29°46′ E 180
Iznalloz, *Sp.* 37°24′ N, 3°32′ W 164
İznik, *Turk.* 40°25′ N, 29°43′ E 156
Izobil'nyy, *Russ.* 45°22′ N, 41°37′ E 158
Izola, *Slov.* 45°32′ N, 13°39′ E 167
Izra', *Syr.* 32°52′ N, 36°15′ E 194
Izsák, *Hung.* 46°48′ N, 19°22′ E 168
Izu-Ogasawara Trench, *North Pacific Ocean* 30°26′ N, 142°40′ E 252
Izuhara, *Japan* 34°12′ N, 129°17′ E 201
Izumi, *Japan* 32°4′ N, 130°22′ E 201
Izvor, *Bulg.* 42°26′ N, 22°53′ E 168
Izvor, *Maced.* 41°33′ N, 21°41′ E 168
Izvori, *Mont.* 42°36′ N, 18°45′ E 168
Izyaslav, *Ukr.* 50°5′ N, 26°49′ E 152
Izyum, *Ukr.* 49°14′ N, 37°20′ E 158

J

Jaab Lake, *Can.* 51°6′ N, 83°27′ W 110
Jaala, *Fin.* 61°3′ N, 26°29′ E 166
Jaalanka, *Fin.* 64°33′ N, 27°7′ E 152
Jabal os Saraj, *Afghan.* 35°7′ N, 69°16′ E 186
Jabal Zuqar, Jazīrat, island, *Yemen* 14°5′ N, 42°31′ E 182
Jabalan Nuşayrīyah, *Syr.* 35°39′ N, 36°8′ E 194
Jabalar Ruwāq, *Syr.* 33°42′ N, 36°57′ E 194
Jabalón, river, *Sp.* 38°46′ N, 3°44′ W 164
Jabalpur, *India* 23°8′ N, 79°57′ E 197
Jābir, *Jordan* 32°30′ N, 36°12′ E 194
Jabiru, *Austral.* 12°38′ S, 132°52′ E 238
Jablah, *Syr.* 35°21′ N, 35°55′ E 194
Jablanica, *Bosn. and Herzg.* 43°39′ N, 17°43′ E 168
Jablanica, *Maced.* 41°26′ N, 20°21′ E 168
Jabłonowo, *Pol.* 53°23′ N, 19°10′ E 152
Jablunkovský Průsmyk, pass, *Slovakia* 49°29′ N, 18°46′ E 152
Jaboticabal, *Braz.* 21°13′ S, 48°21′ W 138
Jäbrayyl see Kurakhtin, *Azerb.* 39°24′ N, 47°1′ E 195
Jabukovac, *Serb.* 44°20′ N, 22°23′ E 168
Jabung, Tanjung, *Indonesia* 1°15′ S, 104°23′ E 196
Jaca, *Sp.* 42°33′ N, 0°34′ E 164
Jacareacanga, *Braz.* 6°13′ S, 57°40′ W 123
Jacareí, *Braz.* 23°17′ S, 45°55′ W 138
Jacarèzinho, *Braz.* 23°10′ S, 49°58′ W 138
Jacinto, *Braz.* 16°10′ S, 40°20′ W 138
Jaci-Paraná, *Braz.* 9°19′ S, 64°25′ W 137
Jackfish, river, *Can.* 59°31′ N, 113°37′ W 108
Jackhead Harbour, *Can.* 51°51′ N, 97°19′ W 108
Jackman, *Me., U.S.* 45°38′ N, 70°14′ W 82
Jackpot, *Nev., U.S.* 41°59′ N, 114°40′ W 90
Jacks Mountain, *Pa., U.S.* 40°46′ N, 77°40′ W 94
Jacks Peak, *Utah, U.S.* 38°58′ N, 112°11′ W 90
Jacksboro, *Tex., U.S.* 33°11′ N, 98°10′ W 92
Jackson, *Ala., U.S.* 31°30′ N, 87°54′ W 103
Jackson, *Calif., U.S.* 38°21′ N, 120°47′ W 100
Jackson, *Ga., U.S.* 33°16′ N, 83°58′ W 96
Jackson, *La., U.S.* 30°49′ N, 91°13′ W 103
Jackson, *Mich., U.S.* 42°14′ N, 84°26′ W 102
Jackson, *Minn., U.S.* 43°35′ N, 95°1′ W 94
Jackson, *Miss., U.S.* 32°16′ N, 90°15′ W 103
Jackson, *Mo., U.S.* 37°23′ N, 89°40′ W 94
Jackson, *N.H., U.S.* 44°8′ N, 71°12′ W 104
Jackson, *Ohio, U.S.* 39°2′ N, 82°38′ W 102
Jackson, *S.C., U.S.* 33°18′ N, 81°48′ W 96
Jackson, *Tenn., U.S.* 35°36′ N, 88°48′ W 96
Jackson Bay, *N.Z.* 44°1′ S, 168°37′ E 240
Jackson Field, oil field, *Austral.* 27°37′ S, 142°0′ E 230
Jackson Head, *N.Z.* 43°58′ S, 168°36′ E 240
Jackson, Mount, peak *Antarctica* 71°23′ S, 63°22′ W 248
Jackson Mountains, *Nev., U.S.* 41°28′ N, 118°41′ W 90
Jackson, Ostrov, island, *Russ.* 81°23′ N, 53°33′ E 160
Jacksonville, *Ark., U.S.* 34°51′ N, 92°8′ W 96
Jacksonville, *Fla., U.S.* 30°20′ N, 81°40′ W 96
Jacksonville, *N.C., U.S.* 34°45′ N, 77°26′ W 96
Jacksonville, *Oreg., U.S.* 42°18′ N, 122°59′ W 90
Jacksonville, *Tex., U.S.* 31°56′ N, 95°16′ W 103
Jacksonville Beach, *Fla., U.S.* 30°16′ N, 81°24′ W 96
Jäckvik, *Nor.* 66°22′ N, 16°56′ E 152
Jacmel, *Haiti* 18°15′ N, 72°31′ W 116
Jacob Lake, *Ariz., U.S.* 36°42′ N, 112°12′ W 92
Jacobabad, *Pak.* 28°17′ N, 68°29′ E 186
Jacobina, *Braz.* 11°11′ S, 40°32′ W 132
Jacona, *Mex.* 19°57′ N, 102°18′ W 114
Jacques-Cartier, Mont, peak, *Can.* 48°57′ N, 66°2′ W 94
Jacquet River, *Can.* 47°54′ N, 66°2′ W 94
Jacuí, *Braz.* 21°2′ S, 46°45′ W 138
Jacumba, *Calif., U.S.* 32°37′ N, 116°11′ W 101
Jacupiranga, *Braz.* 24°42′ S, 48°2′ W 138
J.A.D. Jensen Nunatakker, peak, *Den.* 62°50′ N, 49°7′ W 106
Jada, *Nig.* 8°45′ N, 12°8′ E 218
Jaddi, Ras, *Pak.* 25°2′ N, 63°0′ E 182
Jade, *Ger.* 53°20′ N, 8°15′ E 163
Jadraque, *Sp.* 40°55′ N, 2°56′ W 164
Jādū, *Lib.* 31°59′ N, 12°1′ E 216
Jaén, *Sp.* 37°46′ N, 3°48′ W 164
Jaffna, *Sri Lanka* 9°33′ N, 80°8′ E 173
Jagadhri, *India* 30°12′ N, 77°20′ E 197
Jagdalpur, *India* 19°5′ N, 82°1′ E 188
Jagersfontein, *S. Af.* 29°47′ S, 25°26′ E 227
Jāghir Bāzār, *Syr.* 36°52′ N, 40°56′ E 195
Jaghjagh, river, *Syr.* 36°35′ N, 41°11′ E 195
Jagodina, *Serb.* 43°58′ N, 21°14′ E 168
Jaguaquara, *Braz.* 13°33′ S, 39°59′ W 138
Jaguarão, *Braz.* 32°31′ S, 53°24′ W 139
Jaguari, river, *Braz.* 29°45′ S, 54°40′ W 134
Jaguariaíva, *Braz.* 24°18′ S, 49°43′ W 138
Jahanabad, *India* 25°11′ N, 84°59′ E 197
Jahorina, peak, *Bosn. and Herzg.* 43°42′ N, 18°30′ E 168
Jahrom, *Iran* 28°33′ N, 53°34′ E 196
Jaicós, *Braz.* 7°22′ S, 41°8′ W 132
Jaigarh, *India* 17°17′ N, 73°13′ E 188
Jailolo, *Indonesia* 1°4′ N, 127°25′ E 192
Jaina, ruin(s), *Mex.* 20°11′ N, 90°39′ W 115
Jaipur, *India* 26°54′ N, 75°49′ E 188
Jaisalmer, *India* 26°55′ N, 70°58′ E 186
Jajarkot, *Nepal* 28°41′ N, 82°11′ E 197
Jājarm, *Iran* 36°56′ N, 56°24′ E 180
Jajce, *Bosn. and Herzg.* 44°21′ N, 17°15′ E 168
Jajiri, *Niger* 13°38′ N, 11°26′ E 222
Jajpur Road, *India* 20°56′ N, 86°6′ E 188
Ják, *Hung.* 47°8′ N, 16°34′ E 168
Jakar, *Bhutan* 27°31′ N, 90°42′ E 197
Jakarta, *Indonesia* 6°22′ S, 106°14′ E 238
Jakes Corner, *Can.* 60°21′ N, 134°1′ W 98
Jákfa, *Hung.* 47°18′ N, 16°58′ E 168
Jakhal, *India* 29°47′ N, 75°49′ E 197
Jakhau, *India* 23°13′ N, 68°43′ E 186
Jakobshavn see Ilulissat, *Den.* 69°11′ N, 51°0′ W 106
Jakobstad (Pietarsaari), *Fin.* 63°39′ N, 22°39′ E 152
Jakupica, *Maced.* 41°43′ N, 21°22′ E 168
Jal, *N. Mex., U.S.* 32°6′ N, 103°12′ W 92
Jalaaqsi, *Somalia* 3°23′ N, 45°36′ E 218
Jalaid Qi (Inder), *China* 46°41′ N, 122°53′ E 198
Jalālābād, *Afghan.* 34°26′ N, 70°30′ E 186
Jalal-Abad, *Kyrg.* 40°55′ N, 72°59′ E 197
Jalán, river, *Hond.* 14°17′ N, 86°43′ W 115
Jalapa, *Guatemala* 14°38′ N, 90°0′ W 115
Jalapa, *Mex.* 17°43′ N, 92°49′ W 115
Jalasjärvi, *Fin.* 62°29′ N, 22°45′ E 152
Jalcocotán, *Mex.* 21°29′ N, 105°8′ W 114
Jales, *Braz.* 20°12′ S, 50°36′ W 138
Jalesar, *India* 27°25′ N, 78°19′ E 197
Jaleswar, *India* 21°49′ N, 87°13′ E 197
Jalgaon, *India* 21°1′ N, 75°33′ E 188
Jalingo, *Nig.* 8°51′ N, 11°20′ E 222
Jalisco, *Mex.* 21°26′ N, 104°53′ W 114
Jalisco, adm. division, *Mex.* 20°33′ N, 104°13′ W 114
Jalitah Island, *Tun.* 37°31′ N, 7°53′ E 214
Jalkot, *Pak.* 35°17′ N, 73°23′ E 186
Jalna, *India* 19°50′ N, 75°52′ E 188
Jalor, *India* 25°19′ N, 72°38′ E 186
Jalostotitlán, *Mex.* 21°10′ N, 102°29′ W 114
Jałowka, *Pol.* 53°1′ N, 23°54′ E 154
Jalpa, *Mex.* 18°10′ N, 93°5′ W 112
Jalpa, *Mex.* 21°37′ N, 103°0′ W 114
Jalpaiguri, *India* 26°26′ N, 88°40′ E 197
Jalpan, *Mex.* 21°10′ N, 99°33′ W 114
Jáltipan, *Mex.* 17°57′ N, 94°44′ W 114
Jālū, *Lib.* 29°1′ N, 21°30′ E 216
Jaluit Atoll, *Marshall Islands* 6°0′ N, 170°0′ E 242
Jam, *Iran* 27°55′ N, 52°22′ E 196
Jamaame, *Somalia* 2°119′ N, 42°46′ E 218
Jamaica 18°0′ N, 78°0′ W 118
Jämaja, *Est.* 58°0′ N, 22°3′ E 166
Jamalpur, *Bangladesh* 24°53′ N, 89°54′ E 197
Jaman Pass, *Taj.* 37°25′ N, 74°41′ E 197
Jamanari, river, *Braz.* 2°26′ S, 69°13′ W 136
Jamari, river, *Braz.* 8°52′ S, 63°30′ W 130
Jambes, *Belg.* 50°27′ N, 4°53′ E 167
Jambi, *Indonesia* 1°41′ S, 103°33′ E 192
Jambur, oil field, *Iraq* 35°1′ N, 44°31′ E 180
Jambusar, *India* 22°3′ N, 72°48′ E 186
James Bay 52°12′ N, 81°23′ W 110
James City, *Pa., U.S.* 41°36′ N, 78°50′ W 94
James Lake, *Can.* 57°15′ N, 100°15′ W 108
James, river, *Can.* 51°47′ N, 115°9′ W 90
James, river, *N. Dak., U.S.* 46°39′ N, 98°34′ W 90
James, river, *S. Dak., U.S.* 45°3′ N, 98°16′ W 94
James, river, *Va., U.S.* 37°54′ N, 78°33′ W 94
James Ross Island, *Antarctica* 64°13′ S, 57°4′ W 134
Jameson Land, *Den.* 70°56′ N, 23°8′ W 246
Jamesport, *N.Y., U.S.* 40°56′ N, 72°35′ W 104
Jamestown, *Calif., U.S.* 37°56′ N, 120°26′ W 100
Jamestown, *Ind., U.S.* 39°55′ N, 86°38′ W 102
Jamestown, *N.Y., U.S.* 42°6′ N, 79°15′ W 94
Jamestown, *N.C., U.S.* 35°59′ N, 79°57′ W 96
Jamestown, *R.I., U.S.* 41°29′ N, 71°23′ W 104
Jamestown, *S. Af.* 31°7′ S, 26°47′ E 227
Jämijärvi, *Fin.* 61°48′ N, 22°40′ E 166
Jamkhandi, *India* 16°30′ N, 75°16′ E 188
Jammu, *India* 32°44′ N, 74°51′ E 186
Jammu and Kashmir, adm. division, *India* 33°48′ N, 76°20′ E 188
Jamnagar, *India* 22°26′ N, 70°4′ E 186
Jamno, *Pol.* 54°14′ N, 16°11′ E 152
Jampur, *Pak.* 29°33′ N, 70°35′ E 186
Jämsä, *Fin.* 61°51′ N, 25°10′ E 166
Jämsänkoski, *Fin.* 61°54′ N, 25°8′ E 166
Jamshedpur, *India* 22°46′ N, 86°13′ E 197
Jämtlands Sikås, *Nor.* 63°37′ N, 15°13′ E 152
Jamui, *India* 24°54′ N, 86°12′ E 197
Jan Mayen, island, *Nor.* 71°0′ N, 8°0′ W 246
Jan Mayen Fracture Zone, *Norwegian Sea* 70°55′ N, 6°54′ W 255
Jan Mayen Ridge, *Norwegian Sea* 69°26′ N, 8°15′ W 255
Jana, oil field, *Saudi Arabia* 27°23′ N, 49°48′ E 196
Janakkala, *Fin.* 60°53′ N, 24°33′ E 166
Janakpur, *Nepal* 26°40′ N, 85°55′ E 197
Janaúba, *Braz.* 15°47′ S, 43°20′ W 138
Janaucu, Ilha, island, *Braz.* 0°27′ N, 51°15′ W 130
Jandaq, *Iran* 34°2′ N, 54°28′ E 180
Janesville, *Wis., U.S.* 42°42′ N, 89°0′ W 102
Jangamo, *Mozambique* 24°4′ S, 35°18′ E 227
Janghang, *S. Korea* 36°1′ N, 126°44′ E 200
Jangheung, *S. Korea* 34°38′ N, 126°54′ E 200
Janghowon, *S. Korea* 37°6′ N, 127°37′ E 200
Jangpyeong, *S. Korea* 37°35′ N, 128°24′ E 200
Jangseong, *S. Korea* 35°17′ N, 126°51′ E 200
Janikowo, *Pol.* 52°45′ N, 18°7′ E 152
Janīn, *West Bank, Israel* 32°27′ N, 35°18′ E 194
Janja, *Bosn. and Herzg.* 44°40′ N, 19°16′ E 168
Janjina, *Croatia* 42°54′ N, 17°25′ E 168
Jannaale, *Somalia* 1°45′ N, 44°41′ E 218
Janos, *Mex.* 30°51′ N, 108°10′ W 92
Jánossomorja, *Hung.* 47°46′ N, 17°8′ E 168
Jansen, *Colo., U.S.* 37°10′ N, 104°33′ W 92
Jansenville, *S. Af.* 32°54′ S, 24°44′ E 227
Januária, *Braz.* 15°27′ S, 44°26′ W 138
Janville, *Fr.* 48°11′ N, 1°52′ E 163
Jaora, *India* 23°37′ N, 75°9′ E 188
Japan 36°0′ N, 137°35′ E 190
Japan, Sea of (East Sea) 39°9′ N, 128°12′ E 200
Japan Trench, *North Pacific Ocean* 35°43′ N, 143°30′ E 252
Japurá, *Braz.* 1°52′ S, 66°41′ W 136
Jaqué, *Pan.* 7°30′ N, 78°9′ W 136
Jaquí, *Peru* 15°31′ S, 74°27′ W 137
Jarābulus, *Syr.* 36°47′ N, 37°58′ E 180
Jarafuel, *Sp.* 39°8′ N, 1°5′ W 164
Jaraguá, *Braz.* 15°49′ S, 49°23′ W 138
Jaraguá do Sul, *Braz.* 26°29′ S, 49°3′ W 138
Jaraicejo, *Sp.* 39°39′ N, 5°49′ W 150
Jarales, *N. Mex., U.S.* 34°36′ N, 106°46′ W 92
Jaramillo, *Arg.* 47°9′ S, 67°8′ W 134
Jarash (Gerasa), *Jordan* 32°17′ N, 35°53′ E 194
Jarauçu, river, *Braz.* 2°47′ S, 53°6′ W 130
Jaray, *Sp.* 41°41′ N, 2°8′ W 164
Jarbidge, *Nev., U.S.* 41°53′ N, 115°25′ W 90
Jarbidge, river, *Idaho, U.S.* 42°24′ N, 115°39′ W 90
Järbo, *Nor.* 60°41′ N, 16°35′ E 152
Jardim, *Braz.* 21°30′ S, 56°5′ W 132
Jardim do Seridó, *Braz.* 6°38′ S, 36°47′ W 132
Jardine River National Park, *Austral.* 11°20′ S, 142°18′ E 238
Jardinésia, *Braz.* 19°17′ S, 48°44′ W 138
Jæren, region, *Europe* 58°33′ N, 5°32′ E 150
Jargalant, *Mongolia* 46°57′ N, 115°15′ E 198
Jari, river, *Braz.* 1°49′ N, 54°28′ W 130
Jari, river, *Braz.* 0°15′ N, 53°7′ W 130
Jarkovac, *Serb.* 45°16′ N, 20°46′ E 168
Jarny, *Fr.* 49°10′ N, 5°53′ E 163
Jarocin, *Pol.* 51°57′ N, 17°30′ E 152
Järpen, *Nor.* 63°21′ N, 13°28′ E 152
Jars, Plain of, *Laos* 19°24′ N, 103°2′ E 202
Jartai, *China* 39°45′ N, 105°47′ E 198
Jaru, *Braz.* 10°25′ S, 62°30′ W 130
Jaru, river, *Braz.* 10°38′ S, 62°25′ W 132
Jarud Qi, *China* 44°35′ N, 120°55′ E 198
Järva Jaani, *Est.* 59°0′ N, 25°51′ E 166
Järvakandi, *Est.* 58°46′ N, 24°47′ E 166
Järvenpää, *Fin.* 69°27′ N, 28°47′ E 152
Järvenpää, *Fin.* 60°27′ N, 25°4′ E 166
Jarvie, *Can.* 54°26′ N, 113°59′ W 108
Järvsö, *Nor.* 61°42′ N, 16°6′ E 152
Jarwa, *India* 27°38′ N, 82°30′ E 197
Jaša Tomić, *Serb.* 45°27′ N, 20°50′ E 168
Jasdan, *India* 22°1′ N, 71°12′ E 186
Jasenjani, *Bosn. and Herzg.* 43°29′ N, 17°49′ E 168
Jasenovac, *Croatia* 45°16′ N, 16°54′ E 168
Jasenovo Polje, *Mont.* 42°52′ N, 18°58′ E 168
Jashpurnagar, *India* 22°53′ N, 84°8′ E 197
Jasikan, *Ghana* 7°25′ N, 0°28′ E 222
Jašiūnai, *Lith.* 54°27′ N, 25°18′ E 166
Jāsk, *Iran* 25°40′ N, 57°50′ E 196
Jasło, *Pol.* 49°44′ N, 21°28′ E 152
Jasmund National Park, *Ger.* 54°32′ N, 13°33′ E 152
Jason Islands, *South Atlantic Ocean* 51°19′ S, 63°21′ W 134
Jasonville, *Ind., U.S.* 39°9′ N, 87°12′ W 102
Jasper, *Ala., U.S.* 33°48′ N, 87°16′ W 96
Jasper, *Ark., U.S.* 35°59′ N, 93°13′ W 96
Jasper, *Can.* 52°53′ N, 118°8′ W 106
Jasper, *Fla., U.S.* 30°30′ N, 82°58′ W 96
Jasper, *Ga., U.S.* 34°27′ N, 84°26′ W 96
Jasper, *Mich., U.S.* 41°47′ N, 84°2′ W 102
Jasper, *Tex., U.S.* 30°54′ N, 94°0′ W 103
Jasper National Park, *Can.* 53°16′ N, 119°17′ W 108
Jastarnia, *Pol.* 54°42′ N, 18°38′ E 166
Jastrebac, *Serb.* 43°31′ N, 21°5′ E 168
Jastrebarsko, *Croatia* 45°39′ N, 15°39′ E 156
Jastrowie, *Pol.* 53°25′ N, 16°49′ E 152
Jászapáti, *Hung.* 47°30′ N, 20°9′ E 168
Jászberény, *Hung.* 47°29′ N, 19°55′ E 168
Jászfényszaru, *Hung.* 47°34′ N, 19°44′ E 168
Jász-Nagykún-Szolnok, adm. division, *Hung.* 47°26′ N, 19°47′ E 156
Jászszentandrás, *Hung.* 47°34′ N, 20°10′ E 168
Jataí, *Braz.* 17°54′ S, 51°43′ W 138
Jatapu, river, *Braz.* 0°49′ N, 58°59′ W 130
Jath, *India* 17°2′ N, 75°11′ E 188
Jati, *Pak.* 24°21′ N, 68°16′ E 186
Jatobá, river, *Braz.* 13°59′ S, 54°21′ W 130
Jatobal, *Braz.* 4°36′ S, 49°45′ W 130
Jau, *Angola* 15°16′ S, 13°27′ E 220
Jaú, *Braz.* 22°20′ S, 48°36′ W 138
Jaú National Park, *Braz.* 2°36′ S, 62°56′ W 130

Jaú, river, *Braz.* 2°36′ S, 63°25′ W 130
Jauaperi, river, *Braz.* 0°20′ N, 61°1′ W 130
Jaumave, *Mex.* 23°23′ N, 99°23′ W 114
Jaunciems, *Latv.* 57°2′ N, 24°11′ E 166
Jaungulbene, *Latv.* 57°3′ N, 26°34′ E 166
Jaunjelgava, *Latv.* 56°35′ N, 25°4′ E 166
Jaunpiebalga, *Latv.* 57°9′ N, 26°1′ E 166
Jaunpur, *India* 25°43′ N, 82°40′ E 197
Jauru, river, *Braz.* 15°53′ S, 58°17′ W 132
Jauru, river, *Braz.* 18°42′ S, 54°12′ W 132
Java, island, *Indonesia* 8°16′ S, 109°10′ E 192
Java Ridge, *Indian Ocean* 9°48′ S, 112°28′ E 254
Java Sea 4°53′ S, 109°50′ E 192
Java Trench (Sunda Trench), *Indian Ocean* 10°30′ S, 110°0′ E 254
Javari, river, *South America* 6°25′ S, 73°12′ W 130
Jávea (Xàbia), *Sp.* 38°47′ N, 0°9′ E 164
Javier, Isla, island, *Chile* 47°17′ S, 75°35′ W 134
Javor, *Serb.* 43°27′ N, 19°57′ E 168
Jawan, oil field, *Iraq* 35°54′ N, 42°51′ E 180
Jawhar (Giohar), *Somalia* 2°47′ N, 45°34′ E 218
Jawi, *Indonesia* 0°48′ N, 109°14′ E 196
Jay, *Me., U.S.* 44°30′ N, 70°14′ W 104
Jay, *N.Y., U.S.* 44°22′ N, 73°45′ W 104
Jay, *Okla., U.S.* 36°24′ N, 94°48′ W 94
Jay Em, *Wyo., U.S.* 42°28′ N, 104°22′ W 90
Jay Peak, *Vt., U.S.* 44°54′ N, 72°37′ W 94
Jaya, Puncak, peak, *Indonesia* 4°1′ S, 137°0′ E 192
Jayanti, *India* 26°41′ N, 89°32′ E 197
Jayapura, *Indonesia* 2°39′ S, 140°44′ E 192
Jayrūd, *Syr.* 33°48′ N, 36°44′ E 194
Jayton, *Tex., U.S.* 33°14′ N, 100°35′ W 92
Jaz Mūrīān, Hāmūn-e, lake, *Iran* 27°27′ N, 58°26′ E 180
Jazā'ir az Zubayr, island, *Yemen* 14°58′ N, 41°3′ E 182
Jazā'ir Farasān, islands, *Red Sea* 17°8′ N, 41°25′ E 182
Jbail (Byblos), *Leb.* 34°7′ N, 35°39′ E 194
Jbinate, *Mor.* 35°7′ N, 5°58′ W 150
Jdiriya, *Western Sahara, Mor.* 27°17′ N, 10°27′ W 214
Jean, *Nev., U.S.* 35°46′ N, 115°20′ W 101
Jean Lafitte National Historical Park and Preserve, *La., U.S.* 29°55′ N, 90°2′ W 103
Jean Marie River, *Can.* 61°31′ N, 120°39′ W 108
Jeannette Island, *Russ.* 76°39′ N, 159°13′ E 255
Jean-Rabel, *Haiti* 19°52′ N, 73°12′ W 116
Jebāl Bārez, Kūh-e, peak, *Iran* 28°46′ N, 58°7′ E 196
Jebarna, *Tun.* 34°49′ N, 10°28′ E 156
Jebba, *Nig.* 9°7′ N, 4°48′ E 222
Jebel, *Rom.* 45°34′ N, 21°14′ E 168
Jebel Aulia, *Sudan* 15°15′ N, 32°30′ E 182
Jebel, Bahr al, adm. division, *Sudan* 4°21′ N, 30°14′ E 224
Jebel, oil field, *Lib.* 28°32′ N, 19°47′ E 216
Jebibina, *Tun.* 36°7′ N, 10°5′ E 156
Jecheon, *S. Korea* 37°7′ N, 128°13′ E 200
Jeddah, *Saudi Arabia* 21°31′ N, 39°12′ E 182
Jhdrzejów, *Pol.* 50°38′ N, 20°19′ E 152
Jef Jef el Kebir, peak, *Chad* 20°30′ N, 21°13′ E 216
Jefferson, *Ala., U.S.* 32°23′ N, 87°54′ W 103
Jefferson, *N.H., U.S.* 44°24′ N, 71°29′ W 104
Jefferson, *N.Y., U.S.* 42°28′ N, 74°37′ W 94
Jefferson, *Tex., U.S.* 32°46′ N, 94°23′ W 103
Jefferson, *Wis., U.S.* 43°0′ N, 88°47′ W 102
Jefferson City, *Mo., U.S.* 38°31′ N, 92°17′ W 94
Jefferson City, *Tenn., U.S.* 36°7′ N, 83°30′ W 96
Jefferson, Mount, *Nev., U.S.* 38°44′ N, 117°1′ W 90
Jefferson, Mount, *Oreg., U.S.* 44°39′ N, 121°53′ W 90
Jeffersonville, *Ind., U.S.* 38°17′ N, 85°44′ W 94
Jeffersonville, *Ohio, U.S.* 39°39′ N, 83°33′ W 102
Jega, *Nig.* 12°13′ N, 4°23′ E 222
Jeju (Cheju), *S. Korea* 33°29′ N, 126°32′ E 200
Jeju, adm. division, *S. Korea* 35°25′ N, 126°30′ E 200
Jeju-Do, island, *S. Korea* 33°34′ N, 125°54′ E 198
Jēkabpils, *Latv.* 56°30′ N, 25°53′ E 166
Jelbart Ice Shelf, *Antarctica* 70°24′ S, 6°22′ W 248
Jeldēsa, *Eth.* 9°41′ N, 42°9′ E 224
Jelenia Góra, *Pol.* 50°53′ N, 15°44′ E 152
Jelgava, *Latv.* 56°38′ N, 23°40′ E 160
Jelgava (Mitau), *Latv.* 56°38′ N, 23°40′ E 166
Jellico, *Tenn., U.S.* 36°34′ N, 84°8′ W 96
Jellicoe, *Can.* 49°42′ N, 87°32′ W 94
Jelnica, *Pol.* 51°57′ N, 22°40′ E 154
Jelsa, *Croatia* 43°8′ N, 16°41′ E 168
Jema, river, *Eth.* 10°2′ N, 38°32′ E 224
Jemaja, island, *Indonesia* 3°7′ N, 105°17′ E 196
Jember, *Indonesia* 8°8′ S, 113°41′ E 238
Jemez Pueblo, *N. Mex., U.S.* 35°37′ N, 106°43′ W 92
Jeminay, *China* 47°29′ N, 85°52′ E 184
Jena, *Fla., U.S.* 29°39′ N, 83°23′ W 105
Jena, *La., U.S.* 31°40′ N, 92°9′ W 96
Jenaien, *Tun.* 31°44′ N, 10°8′ E 216
Jengish Chokusu see Pobedy Peak, *China* 42°2′ N, 80°3′ E 184
Jenkins, *Ky., U.S.* 37°10′ N, 82°38′ W 96
Jenner, peak, *Ger.* 47°32′ N, 12°56′ E 156
Jennie, *Ark., U.S.* 33°14′ N, 91°17′ W 103
Jennings, *La., U.S.* 30°12′ N, 92°40′ W 103
Jennings, river, *Can.* 59°29′ N, 132°0′ W 108
Jenpeg, *Can.* 54°30′ N, 98°6′ W 108
Jensen, *Utah, U.S.* 40°22′ N, 109°20′ W 82
Jensen Beach, *Fla., U.S.* 27°14′ N, 80°14′ W 105
Jenu, *Indonesia* 0°36′ N, 109°50′ E 196
Jeogu, *S. Korea* 34°44′ N, 128°38′ E 200
Jeolla, North, adm. division, *S. Korea* 35°45′ N, 127°15′ E 200
Jeolla, South, adm. division, *S. Korea* 34°45′ N, 127°0′ E 200
Jeongeup, *S. Korea* 35°33′ N, 126°52′ E 200
Jeongseon, *S. Korea* 37°23′ N, 128°40′ E 200
Jeonju, *S. Korea* 35°48′ N, 127°9′ E 200
Jequié, *Braz.* 13°50′ S, 40°6′ W 138
Jequitaí, *Braz.* 17°15′ S, 44°30′ W 138
Jequitaí, river, *Braz.* 17°22′ S, 44°7′ W 138
Jequitinhonha, *Braz.* 16°27′ S, 41°3′ W 138
Jerantut, *Malaysia* 3°57′ N, 102°21′ E 196
Jerba Island, *Tun.* 34°0′ N, 10°25′ E 214
Jeremoabo, *Braz.* 10°4′ S, 38°21′ W 132
Jeremy, Cape, *Antarctica* 69°14′ S, 72°52′ W 248
Jerez de García Salinas, *Mex.* 22°38′ N, 103°1′ W 114
Jerez de la Frontera, *Sp.* 36°41′ N, 6°9′ W 164
Jeréz de los Caballeros, *Sp.* 38°18′ N, 6°47′ W 164
Jerez, Punta, *Mex.* 22°53′ N, 97°42′ W 114
Jérica, *Sp.* 39°55′ N, 0°34′ E 164
Jericho, *Vt., U.S.* 44°30′ N, 73°0′ W 104
Jericho see Arīḥā, *West Bank, Israel* 31°51′ N, 35°27′ E 194
Jericó, *Col.* 5°46′ N, 75°48′ W 136
Jermyn, *Pa., U.S.* 41°31′ N, 75°34′ W 110
Jerome, *Ariz., U.S.* 34°45′ N, 112°5′ W 112
Jerome, *Ark., U.S.* 33°23′ N, 91°28′ W 103
Jersey, island, *U.K.* 49°13′ N, 2°7′ W 150
Jersey City, *N.J., U.S.* 40°43′ N, 74°4′ W 104
Jerseyside, *Can.* 47°15′ N, 53°57′ W 111
Jerseyville, *Mo., U.S.* 39°6′ N, 90°20′ W 94
Jerusalem (Yerushalayim, Al-Quds), *Israel* 31°46′ N, 35°9′ E 194
Jervis Bay Territory 35°11′ S, 149°35′ E 230
Jervis Inlet 50°0′ N, 124°8′ W 100
Jeseník, *Czech Rep.* 49°45′ N, 17°9′ E 152
Jessen, *Ger.* 51°47′ N, 12°56′ E 152
Jessnitz, *Ger.* 51°41′ N, 12°17′ E 152
Jessore, *Bangladesh* 23°9′ N, 89°9′ E 197
Jesup, *Ga., U.S.* 31°35′ N, 81°54′ W 96
Jesús Carranza, *Mex.* 17°26′ N, 95°1′ W 114
Jesús María, *Arg.* 31°0′ S, 64°8′ W 134
Jesús María, *Mex.* 21°58′ N, 102°21′ W 114
Jesús María, Boca de 24°30′ N, 98°13′ W 114
Jetait, *Can.* 56°3′ N, 101°20′ W 108
Jetmore, *Kans., U.S.* 38°5′ N, 99°55′ W 90
Jetpur, *India* 21°44′ N, 70°36′ E 186
Jeumont, *Fr.* 50°17′ N, 4°5′ E 163
Jeungpyeong, *S. Korea* 36°46′ N, 127°34′ E 200
Jever, *Ger.* 53°34′ N, 7°54′ E 163
Jewell, *Iowa, U.S.* 42°17′ N, 93°38′ W 94
Jewett, *Ill., U.S.* 39°11′ N, 88°15′ W 102
Jewett, *Tex., U.S.* 31°20′ N, 96°8′ W 96
Jewett City, *Conn., U.S.* 41°36′ N, 72°0′ W 104
Jewish Autonomous Region, *Russ.* 49°5′ N, 131°14′ E 160
Jeypore, *India* 18°55′ N, 82°30′ E 190
Jez. Kopań, lake, *Pol.* 54°37′ N, 16°4′ E 152
Jezercë, Maja, peak, *Alban.* 42°26′ N, 19°46′ E 168
Ježevica, *Serb.* 43°56′ N, 20°5′ E 168
Jeżewo, *Pol.* 53°30′ N, 18°28′ E 152
Jezzine, *Leb.* 33°33′ N, 35°34′ E 194
J.F.K. International Airport, *N.Y., U.S.* 40°36′ N, 73°57′ W 94
Jhalawar, *India* 24°34′ N, 76°10′ E 197
Jhang Sadr, *Pak.* 31°15′ N, 72°20′ E 186
Jhansi, *India* 25°25′ N, 78°32′ E 197
Jharkhand, adm. division, *India* 23°44′ N, 85°22′ E 188
Jharsuguda, *India* 21°52′ N, 84°3′ E 188
Jhatpat, *Pak.* 28°25′ N, 68°20′ E 186
Jhelum, *Pak.* 32°54′ N, 73°45′ E 186
Jhelum, river, *Pak.* 32°16′ N, 72°35′ E 186
Jhunjhunun, *India* 28°6′ N, 75°24′ E 197
Jiahe, *China* 25°34′ N, 112°19′ E 198
Jiamusi, *China* 46°53′ N, 130°18′ E 190
Ji'an, *China* 27°8′ N, 114°56′ E 198
Ji'an, *China* 41°8′ N, 126°10′ E 200
Jianchang, *China* 40°50′ N, 119°45′ E 198
Jiang'an, *China* 28°38′ N, 105°2′ E 198
Jiangcheng, *China* 22°34′ N, 101°50′ E 202
Jianghua, *China* 24°55′ N, 111°44′ E 198
Jiangle, *China* 26°48′ N, 117°25′ E 198
Jiangling, *China* 30°23′ N, 112°9′ E 198
Jiangmen, *China* 22°33′ N, 113°1′ E 198
Jiangshan, *China* 28°45′ N, 118°37′ E 198
Jiangsu, adm. division, *China* 33°41′ N, 118°13′ E 198
Jiangxi, adm. division, *China* 27°28′ N, 115°30′ E 198
Jiangyou, *China* 31°47′ N, 104°34′ E 198
Jianli, *China* 29°50′ N, 112°51′ E 198
Jianning, *China* 26°50′ N, 116°45′ E 198
Jianping, *China* 41°23′ N, 119°40′ E 198
Jianshui, *China* 23°33′ N, 102°46′ E 202
Jianyang, *China* 27°18′ N, 118°5′ E 198
Jiaohe, *China* 43°44′ N, 127°25′ E 198
Jiaokou, *China* 36°58′ N, 111°13′ E 198
Jiaonan, *China* 35°53′ N, 119°59′ E 198
Jiaozhou, *China* 36°20′ N, 120°3′ E 198
Jiaozuo, *China* 35°12′ N, 113°11′ E 198
Jiashi, *China* 39°28′ N, 76°37′ E 184
Jiawang, *China* 34°28′ N, 117°23′ E 198
Jiaxian, *China* 38°3′ N, 110°26′ E 198
Jiaxing, *China* 30°44′ N, 120°42′ E 198
Jiayu, *China* 29°58′ N, 113°57′ E 198
Jiayuguan, *China* 39°50′ N, 98°18′ E 188
Jibal, oil field, *Oman* 22°14′ N, 56°1′ E 182
Jibóia, *Braz.* 1°13′ N, 69°34′ W 136
Jibou, *Rom.* 47°15′ N, 23°17′ E 168
Jicarón, Isla, island, *Pan.* 7°10′ N, 82°31′ W 115
Jicatuyo, river, *Hond.* 14°59′ N, 88°43′ W 116
Jičín, *Czech Rep.* 50°26′ N, 15°21′ E 152
Jidali, *Somalia* 10°40′ N, 47°39′ E 216
Jiddat al Ḩarāsīs, *Oman* 19°19′ N, 55°56′ E 182
Jieshou, *China* 33°21′ N, 115°20′ E 198
Jiexiu, *China* 37°1′ N, 111°54′ E 198
Jieyang, *China* 23°31′ N, 116°17′ E 198
Jieznas, *Lith.* 54°36′ N, 24°10′ E 166
Jigme Dorji National Park, *Bhutan* 27°52′ N, 89°53′ E 197
Jihlava, *Czech Rep.* 49°23′ N, 15°35′ E 152
Jihočeský, adm. division, *Czech Rep.* 49°4′ N, 13°42′ E 152
Jihomoravský, adm. division, *Czech Rep.* 48°53′ N, 15°51′ E 152
Jijel, *Alg.* 36°48′ N, 5°45′ E 150
Jijiga, *Eth.* 9°18′ N, 42°44′ E 218
Jilava, *Rom.* 44°21′ N, 26°5′ E 156
Jilib, *Somalia* 0°26′ N, 42°48′ E 218
Jilin, *China* 43°50′ N, 126°35′ E 198
Jilin, adm. division, *China* 43°43′ N, 126°4′ E 198
Jiloy, *Azerb.* 40°19′ N, 50°34′ E 195
Jīma, *Eth.* 7°37′ N, 36°47′ E 224
Jimbolia, *Rom.* 45°47′ N, 20°43′ E 168
Jimena de la Frontera, *Sp.* 36°26′ N, 5°28′ W 164
Jiménez, *Mex.* 27°6′ N, 104°55′ W 112
Jiménez, *Mex.* 29°2′ N, 100°41′ W 92
Jiménez del Teul, *Mex.* 23°8′ N, 104°5′ W 114
Jimo, *China* 36°26′ N, 120°30′ E 198
Jin, river, *China* 28°9′ N, 114°59′ E 198
Jinan, *China* 36°39′ N, 116°58′ E 198
Jinan, *S. Korea* 36°32′ N, 129°3′ E 200
Jinan, *S. Korea* 35°46′ N, 127°26′ E 200
Jincheng, *China* 35°30′ N, 112°49′ E 198
Jindo, *S. Korea* 34°26′ N, 126°15′ E 200
Jing see Jinghe, *China* 44°35′ N, 82°58′ E 184
Jingbian, *China* 37°35′ N, 108°47′ E 198
Jingde, *China* 30°18′ N, 118°33′ E 198
Jingdezhen, *China* 29°19′ N, 117°16′ E 198
Jinggu, *China* 23°30′ N, 100°41′ E 202
Jinghai, *China* 38°57′ N, 117°3′ E 198
Jinghe (Jing), *China* 44°35′ N, 82°58′ E 184
Jinghong, *China* 22°0′ N, 100°45′ E 202
Jingle, *China* 38°20′ N, 111°57′ E 198
Jingmen, *China* 31°0′ N, 112°10′ E 198
Jingpeng see Hexigten Qi, *China* 43°16′ N, 117°28′ E 198
Jingtai, *China* 37°9′ N, 104°7′ E 198
Jingxi, *China* 23°6′ N, 106°27′ E 198
Jingxing, *China* 38°3′ N, 113°58′ E 198
Jingyu, *China* 42°23′ N, 126°49′ E 200
Jingyuan, *China* 36°32′ N, 104°41′ E 198
Jingyuan, *China* 35°27′ N, 106°21′ E 198
Jingzhou, *China* 26°35′ N, 109°39′ E 198
Jinhae, *S. Korea* 35°8′ N, 128°40′ E 200
Jinhua, *China* 29°11′ N, 119°41′ E 198
Jining, *China* 41°4′ N, 113°5′ E 198
Jining, *China* 35°23′ N, 116°38′ E 198
Jinja, *Uganda* 0°24′ N, 33°12′ E 224
Jinjiang, *China* 24°46′ N, 118°35′ E 198
Jinotega, *Nicar.* 13°5′ N, 85°58′ W 115
Jinping, *China* 26°43′ N, 109°10′ E 198
Jinping, *China* 22°48′ N, 103°11′ E 202
Jinsha, *China* 27°23′ N, 106°13′ E 198
Jinsha (Yangtze), river, *China* 25°47′ N, 103°15′ E 190
Jinshan, *China* 30°52′ N, 121°6′ E 198
Jinshi, *China* 29°39′ N, 111°53′ E 198
Jinta, *China* 39°59′ N, 98°58′ E 188
Jinxiang, *China* 35°5′ N, 116°21′ E 198
Jinzhai, *China* 31°43′ N, 115°47′ E 198
Jinzhou, *China* 39°8′ N, 121°47′ E 198
Jinzhou, *China* 41°10′ N, 121°10′ E 198
Ji-Paraná, *Braz.* 10°53′ S, 61°58′ W 130
Jiquilpan, *Mex.* 19°59′ N, 102°44′ W 114
Jirgatol, *Taj.* 39°13′ N, 71°13′ E 197
Jirisan, peak, *S. Korea* 35°19′ N, 127°42′ E 200
Jīroft, *Iran* 28°41′ N, 57°47′ E 196
Jishou, *China* 28°15′ N, 109°43′ E 198
Jishui, *China* 27°15′ N, 115°7′ E 198
Jisr ash Shughūr, *Syr.* 35°48′ N, 36°17′ E 156
Jitra, *Malaysia* 6°15′ N, 100°25′ E 196
Jiu, river, *Rom.* 45°16′ N, 23°19′ E 168
Jiujiang, *China* 29°40′ N, 115°57′ E 198
Jiuquan Space Launch Center, *China* 40°42′ N, 99°37′ E 188
Jiutai, *China* 44°9′ N, 125°48′ E 198
Jiwani, *Pak.* 25°2′ N, 61°48′ E 182
Jixi, *China* 30°4′ N, 118°38′ E 198
Jixi, *China* 45°7′ N, 130°54′ E 190
Jixian, *China* 36°6′ N, 110°40′ E 198
Jixian, *China* 40°2′ N, 117°21′ E 198
Jiyuan, *China* 35°6′ N, 112°32′ E 198
Jīzān, *Saudi Arabia* 16°52′ N, 42°35′ E 182
Jizzax, *Uzb.* 40°6′ N, 67°50′ E 197
Joaçaba, *Braz.* 27°10′ S, 51°32′ W 139
Joaíma, *Braz.* 16°40′ S, 41°4′ W 138
Joal-Fadiot, *Senegal* 14°12′ N, 16°37′ W 222
João Monlevade, *Braz.* 19°52′ S, 43°8′ W 138
João Pessoa, *Braz.* 7°7′ S, 34°53′ W 132
João Pinheiro, *Braz.* 17°43′ S, 46°12′ W 138
Joaquim Távora, *Braz.* 23°29′ S, 49°59′ W 138
Joaquin, *Tex., U.S.* 31°57′ N, 94°3′ W 103
Joaquín V. González, *Arg.* 25°8′ S, 64°9′ W 132
Job Peak, *Nev., U.S.* 39°34′ N, 118°20′ W 90
Jōban, *Japan* 36°59′ N, 140°49′ E 201
Jochiwon, *S. Korea* 36°34′ N, 127°17′ E 200
Joconoxtle, *Mex.* 23°12′ N, 104°26′ W 114
Jocotepec, *Mex.* 20°17′ N, 103°28′ W 114
Jocotepec, *Mex.* 17°32′ N, 95°57′ W 114
Jodar, *Sp.* 37°50′ N, 3°21′ W 164
Jodhpur, *India* 26°15′ N, 73°1′ E 188
Jodoigne, *Belg.* 50°43′ N, 4°51′ E 167
Joensuu, *Fin.* 62°36′ N, 29°43′ E 152
Joerg Peninsula, *Antarctica* 68°21′ S, 64°22′ W 248
Joesjö, *Nor.* 65°43′ N, 14°36′ E 152
Jōetsu, *Japan* 37°8′ N, 138°13′ E 201
Joeuf, *Fr.* 49°13′ N, 6°0′ E 163
Joffre, Mount, *Can.* 50°31′ N, 115°17′ W 90
Jõgeva, *Est.* 58°44′ N, 26°22′ E 166
Johannesburg, *Calif., U.S.* 35°22′ N, 117°39′ W 101
Johannesburg, *S. Af.* 26°12′ S, 28°2′ E 227
John, Cape, *Can.* 45°49′ N, 63°14′ W 111
John Day, *Oreg., U.S.* 44°24′ N, 118°58′ W 90
John Day, river, *Oreg., U.S.* 45°7′ N, 120°3′ W 106
John D'Or Prairie, *Can.* 58°30′ N, 115°8′ W 108
John F. Kennedy Space Center, *Fla., U.S.* 28°30′ N, 80°44′ W 105
John Jay, Mount, *Alas., U.S.* 56°8′ N, 130°36′ W 108
John Long Mountains, *Mont., U.S.* 46°34′ N, 113°48′ W 90
John Muir National Historic Site, *Calif., U.S.* 37°59′ N, 122°9′ W 100
John o'Groats, site, *U.K.* 58°37′ N, 3°11′ W 150
Johnsburg, *N.Y., U.S.* 43°36′ N, 74°0′ W 104
Johnson, *Kans., U.S.* 37°33′ N, 101°46′ W 92
Johnson City, *Tenn., U.S.* 36°18′ N, 82°22′ W 96
Johnson City, *Tex., U.S.* 30°15′ N, 98°25′ W 92
Johnson, Pico de, peak, *Mex.* 29°7′ N, 112°16′ W 92
Johnson Space Center, *Tex., U.S.* 29°30′ N, 95°8′ W 103
Johnsonburg, *Pa., U.S.* 41°28′ N, 78°40′ W 94
Johnsondale, *Calif., U.S.* 35°58′ N, 118°33′ W 101
Johnsons Crossing, *Can.* 60°30′ N, 133°18′ W 108
Johnsons Pass, *Utah, U.S.* 40°19′ N, 112°35′ W 90
Johnsons Station, *Miss., U.S.* 31°20′ N, 90°28′ W 103
Johnston, *R.I., U.S.* 41°49′ N, 71°30′ W 104
Johnston Atoll, *United States* 17°0′ N, 170°0′ W 99
Johnston Falls, *Zambia* 10°39′ S, 28°9′ E 224
Johnston, Mount, *Antarctica* 71°37′ S, 66°55′ E 248
Johnstone Hill, *Austral.* 23°41′ S, 129°48′ E 230
Johnstown, *N.Y., U.S.* 43°0′ N, 74°24′ W 94
Johnstown, *Ohio, U.S.* 40°8′ N, 82°41′ W 102
Johor Bahru, *Malaysia* 1°30′ N, 103°44′ E 196
Johovac, *Bosn. and Herzg.* 44°50′ N, 18°1′ E 168
Jõhvi, *Est.* 59°21′ N, 27°24′ E 166
Joinville, *Braz.* 26°18′ S, 48°50′ W 138
Joinville, *Fr.* 48°26′ N, 5°6′ E 163
Joinville Island, *Antarctica* 63°11′ S, 55°28′ W 134
Jojutla, *Mex.* 18°35′ N, 99°11′ W 114
Jokau, *Sudan* 8°21′ N, 33°50′ E 224
Jokijärvi, *Fin.* 65°28′ N, 28°35′ E 152
Jokioinen, *Fin.* 60°47′ N, 23°26′ E 166
Jokkmokk, *Nor.* 66°36′ N, 19°50′ E 152
Joliet, *Ill., U.S.* 41°31′ N, 88°4′ W 102
Joliette, *Can.* 46°1′ N, 73°27′ W 94
Jolliet, Lac, lake, *Can.* 51°30′ N, 77°25′ W 110
Jolo, *Philippines* 6°3′ N, 120°59′ E 203
Jomboy, *Uzb.* 39°42′ N, 67°4′ E 197
Jomda, *China* 31°29′ N, 98°11′ E 188
Jomppala, *Fin.* 69°46′ N, 26°58′ E 152
Jomu (Tinde), *Tanzania* 3°53′ S, 33°11′ E 224
Jonathan Point, *Belize* 16°35′ N, 88°18′ W 115
Jonava, *Lith.* 55°5′ N, 24°16′ E 166
Jonesboro, *Ark., U.S.* 35°50′ N, 90°42′ W 96
Jonesboro, *Ind., U.S.* 40°28′ N, 85°38′ W 102
Jonesboro, *La., U.S.* 32°13′ N, 92°43′ W 103
Jonesboro, *Mo., U.S.* 37°26′ N, 89°16′ W 96
Jonesville, *Ind., U.S.* 39°5′ N, 85°54′ W 102
Jonesville, *La., U.S.* 31°36′ N, 91°50′ W 103
Jonesville, *N.C., U.S.* 36°13′ N, 80°51′ W 96
Jonesville, *S.C., U.S.* 34°49′ N, 81°42′ W 96
Jonglei, *Sudan* 6°48′ N, 31°15′ E 224
Jongli, adm. division, *Sudan* 7°18′ N, 31°5′ E 218
Joniškėlis, *Lith.* 56°2′ N, 24°9′ E 166
Joniškis, *Lith.* 56°13′ N, 23°35′ E 166
Jönköping, *Nor.* 57°45′ N, 14°8′ E 152
Jonuta, *Mex.* 18°5′ N, 92°9′ W 115
Joplin, *Mont., U.S.* 48°31′ N, 110°47′ W 90
Jora, *India* 26°19′ N, 77°48′ E 197
Jordan 30°42′ N, 36°5′ E 180
Jordan, *Ala., U.S.* 31°29′ N, 88°15′ W 103
Jordan, *Minn., U.S.* 44°39′ N, 93°38′ W 94
Jordan, *Mont., U.S.* 47°18′ N, 106°55′ W 90
Jordan, river, *Asia* 32°0′ N, 36°0′ E 194
Jordânia, *Braz.* 15°56′ S, 40°12′ W 138
Jordet, *Nor.* 61°25′ N, 12°8′ E 152
Jorge Montt, Isla, island, *Chile* 51°22′ S, 74°31′ W 134
Jörn, *Nor.* 65°3′ N, 20°1′ E 152
Jornada del Muerto, *N. Mex., U.S.* 33°10′ N, 106°46′ W 112
Jørpeland, *Nor.* 59°1′ N, 6°2′ E 152
Jos, *Nig.* 9°53′ N, 8°53′ E 222
Jošanička Banja, *Serb.* 43°23′ N, 20°45′ E 168
Jose Abad Santos, *Philippines* 5°55′ N, 125°36′ E 203
José Batlle y-Ordóñez, *Uru.* 33°28′ S, 55°10′ W 139
José Enrique Rodó, *Uru.* 33°43′ S, 57°31′ W 139
José María, *Col.* 2°11′ N, 68°5′ W 136
Jose Panganiban, *Philippines* 14°17′ N, 122°42′ E 203
José Pedro Varela, *Uru.* 33°28′ S, 54°32′ W 139
Joseph, *Oreg., U.S.* 45°21′ N, 117°14′ W 90
Joseph Bonaparte Gulf 13°4′ S, 127°7′ E 231
Joseph City, *Ariz., U.S.* 34°57′ N, 110°20′ W 92
Joseph, Lac, lake, *Can.* 52°49′ N, 65°47′ W 111
Josephine, Mount, *Antarctica* 77°25′ S, 152°0′ W 248
Joshimath, *India* 30°30′ N, 79°34′ E 197
Joshua Tree, *Calif., U.S.* 34°8′ N, 116°20′ W 101
Joshua Tree National Park, *Calif., U.S.* 33°47′ N, 116°0′ W 101
Josipdol, *Croatia* 45°11′ N, 15°17′ E 156
Jøssund, *Nor.* 63°50′ N, 9°47′ E 152
Jotunheimen, *Nor.* 61°27′ N, 7°38′ E 152
Joulter Cays, *Atlantic Ocean* 25°15′ N, 78°52′ W 96
Jounie, *Leb.* 33°58′ N, 35°37′ E 194
Jourdanton, *Tex., U.S.* 28°53′ N, 98°33′ W 92
Joure, *Neth.* 52°58′ N, 5°48′ E 163
Joussard, *Can.* 55°22′ N, 115°59′ W 108
Joutsa, *Fin.* 61°44′ N, 26°6′ E 166
Joutseno, *Fin.* 61°5′ N, 28°28′ E 166
Jowai, *India* 25°24′ N, 92°11′ E 188
Joya, *Mex.* 26°27′ N, 101°13′ W 114
Joyce, *Wash., U.S.* 48°7′ N, 123°44′ W 100
Joyce, Mount, *Antarctica* 75°32′ S, 161°28′ E 248
Ju, river, *China* 31°26′ N, 111°15′ E 198
Juami, river, *Braz.* 2°13′ S, 68°13′ W 136

Juan Aldama, *Mex.* 24°15′ N, 103°25′ W 114
Juan Cousté, *Arg.* 38°55′ S, 63°8′ W 139
Juan de Fuca Ridge, *North Pacific Ocean* 46°49′ N, 129°21′ W 252
Juan de Fuca, Strait of 48°17′ N, 124°1′ W 90
Juan de Nova, Île, island, *France* 17°7′ S, 41°34′ E 224
Juan E. Barra, *Arg.* 37°50′ S, 60°31′ W 139
Juan Fernández, Archipiélago, *South Pacific Ocean* 33°15′ S, 82°48′ W 123
Juan Fernández Islands, *South Pacific Ocean* 33°38′ S, 80°1′ W 253
Juan José Castelli, *Arg.* 25°58′ S, 60°37′ W 139
Juan Lacaze, *Uru.* 34°25′ S, 57°25′ W 139
Juan N. Fernández, *Arg.* 38°1′ S, 59°17′ W 139
Juan Perez Sound 52°30′ N, 132°27′ W 108
Juan Stuven, Isla, island, *Chile* 47°57′ S, 77°11′ W 134
Juan Viego, *Col.* 3°24′ N, 68°18′ W 136
Juankoski, *Fin.* 63°3′ N, 28°18′ E 152
Juárez, *Arg.* 37°42′ S, 59°49′ W 139
Juárez, *Mex.* 30°19′ N, 108°8′ W 92
Juárez, *Mex.* 27°36′ N, 100°44′ W 96
Juárez, Sierra de, *Mex.* 31°47′ N, 116°1′ W 112
Juazeiro, *Braz.* 9°28′ S, 40°32′ W 132
Juazeiro do Norte, *Braz.* 7°13′ S, 39°21′ W 132
Juba, *Sudan* 4°50′ N, 31°34′ E 224
Jubany, station, *Antarctica* 62°18′ S, 58°29′ W 134
Jubayl, *Leb.* 34°6′ N, 35°40′ E 216
Jubb Jannīn, *Leb.* 33°37′ N, 35°47′ E 194
Jubba, river, *Somalia* 1°26′ N, 42°22′ E 206
Jubbah, *Saudi Arabia* 28°0′ N, 40°55′ E 180
Jubilee Pass, *Calif., U.S.* 35°54′ N, 116°36′ W 101
Juby, Cap, *Mor.* 27°48′ N, 13°57′ W 214
Jucás, *Braz.* 6°31′ S, 39°34′ W 132
Juchitán, *Mex.* 16°26′ N, 95°5′ W 112
Juchitlán, *Mex.* 20°4′ N, 104°7′ W 114
Judas, Punta, *C.R.* 9°23′ N, 85°5′ W 115
Judayyidat ʻArʻar, *Saudi Arabia* 31°14′ N, 41°21′ E 180
Judge Howay, Mount, *Can.* 49°28′ N, 122°22′ W 100
Judith Basin, *Mont., U.S.* 47°2′ N, 110°10′ W 90
Judith Gap, *Mont., U.S.* 46°39′ N, 109°46′ W 90
Judith Mountains, *Mont., U.S.* 47°7′ N, 109°16′ W 90
Judsonia, *Ark., U.S.* 35°16′ N, 91°39′ W 96
Jufari, river, *Braz.* 0°20′ N, 62°36′ W 130
Juhaym, spring, *Iraq* 29°37′ N, 45°23′ E 196
Juhor, *Serb.* 43°53′ N, 20°59′ E 168
Juifang, *Taiwan, China* 25°5′ N, 121°51′ E 198
Juigalpa, *Nicar.* 12°6′ N, 85°23′ W 115
Juist, island, *Ger.* 53°40′ N, 6°44′ E 163
Juiz de Fora, *Braz.* 21°44′ S, 43°21′ W 138
Jujuy, adm. division, *Arg.* 22°42′ S, 66°40′ W 137
Jukbyeon, *S. Korea* 37°3′ N, 129°25′ E 200
Jukkasjärvi, *Nor.* 67°50′ N, 20°36′ E 152
Jukuniemi, *Fin.* 61°46′ N, 29°58′ E 166
Julaca, *Bol.* 20°57′ S, 67°33′ W 137
Juli, *Peru* 16°17′ S, 69°27′ W 137
Juliaca, *Peru* 15°31′ S, 70°8′ W 137
Julian, *Calif., U.S.* 33°4′ N, 116°37′ W 101
Julian Alps, *Slov.* 46°26′ N, 13°33′ E 167
Julian Peak, *Can.* 50°27′ N, 124°23′ W 90
Julianehåb see Qaqortoq, *Den.* 60°47′ N, 46°7′ W 106
Jülich, *Ger.* 50°55′ N, 6°21′ E 167
Julimes, *Mex.* 28°24′ N, 105°27′ W 92
Júlio de Castilhos, *Braz.* 29°15′ S, 53°42′ W 139
Jullundur, *India* 31°19′ N, 75°35′ E 186
Julpo, *S. Korea* 35°35′ N, 126°41′ E 200
Julu, *China* 37°13′ N, 115°0′ E 198
Julu Rayeu, oil field, *Indonesia* 4°58′ N, 97°36′ E 196
Juma, *Uzb.* 39°41′ N, 66°38′ E 197
Juma, river, *Braz.* 5°31′ S, 65°2′ W 132
Jumba, *Somalia* 0°18′ N, 42°38′ E 218
Jumbilla, *Peru* 5°49′ S, 77°47′ W 130
Jumbo Peak, *Nev., U.S.* 36°10′ N, 114°15′ W 101
Jumilla, *Sp.* 38°28′ N, 1°21′ W 164
Jumla, *Nepal* 29°17′ N, 82°12′ E 197
Jumunjin, *S. Korea* 37°53′ N, 128°49′ E 200
Junagadh, *India* 21°32′ N, 70°26′ E 186
Junan, *China* 35°13′ N, 118°52′ E 198
Junction, *Tex., U.S.* 30°28′ N, 99°46′ W 92
Junction, *Utah, U.S.* 38°14′ N, 112°13′ W 90
Junction City, *Ark., U.S.* 33°1′ N, 92°44′ W 103
Junction City, *Kans., U.S.* 39°0′ N, 96°51′ W 90
Jundiaí, *Braz.* 23°10′ S, 46°54′ W 138
Juneau, *Alas., U.S.* 58°19′ N, 134°31′ W 108
Juneau, *Wis., U.S.* 43°24′ N, 88°42′ W 102
Juneda, *Sp.* 41°32′ N, 0°48′ E 164
Jungar Qi, *China* 39°39′ N, 110°54′ E 198
Jungfrau, peak, *Switz.* 46°32′ N, 7°56′ E 167
Junggar Pendi, *China* 45°57′ N, 84°44′ E 184
Junín, *Arg.* 34°37′ S, 60°55′ W 139
Junín, *Col.* 1°19′ N, 78°17′ W 136
Junín, adm. division, *Peru* 11°26′ S, 74°42′ W 137
Junín de los Andes, *Arg.* 39°55′ S, 71°6′ W 134
Juniper Mountain, peak, *Oreg., U.S.* 42°55′ N, 120°1′ W 90
Juniper Peak, *Nev., U.S.* 39°46′ N, 119°17′ W 90
Junipero Serra Peak, *Calif., U.S.* 36°8′ N, 121°28′ W 100
Juniville, *Fr.* 49°23′ N, 4°22′ E 163
Junnar, *India* 19°12′ N, 73°53′ E 188
Juno Beach, *Fla., U.S.* 26°52′ N, 80°4′ W 105
Junosuando, *Nor.* 67°25′ N, 22°28′ E 152
Junsele, *Nor.* 63°41′ N, 16°56′ E 152
Juntura, *Oreg., U.S.* 43°44′ N, 118°5′ W 90
Juntusranta, *Fin.* 65°12′ N, 29°27′ E 152
Juodkrantė, *Russ.* 55°34′ N, 21°6′ E 166
Jupaguá, *Braz.* 11°50′ S, 44°20′ W 132
Jupiter, *Fla., U.S.* 26°56′ N, 80°6′ W 105
Jupiter, river, *Can.* 49°40′ N, 63°36′ W 111
Jupiter Well, spring, *Austral.* 22°59′ S, 126°42′ E 230
Juquiá, *Braz.* 24°19′ S, 47°37′ W 138
Jur, river, *Sudan* 8°34′ N, 28°35′ E 224
Jura Mountains, *Switz.* 46°58′ N, 6°23′ E 165
Jura, Paps of, mountain, *U.K.* 55°53′ N, 6°7′ W 150
Juradó, *Col.* 7°7′ N, 77°47′ W 136
Juramento, *Braz.* 16°50′ S, 43°36′ W 138
Juramento see Pasaje, river, *Arg.* 28°44′ S, 62°58′ W 139
Jurbarkas, *Lith.* 55°4′ N, 22°45′ E 166
Jurf ad Darāwīsh, *Jordan* 30°41′ N, 35°51′ E 194
Jurien Bay 30°46′ S, 114°35′ E 230
Jūrmala, *Latv.* 56°57′ N, 23°48′ E 166
Jūrmalciems, *Latv.* 56°18′ N, 21°0′ E 166
Jurmo, *Fin.* 59°49′ N, 21°34′ E 166
Juruá, *Braz.* 3°28′ S, 66°9′ W 136
Juruá, river, *Braz.* 3°1′ S, 66°9′ W 132
Jurumirim Dam, *Braz.* 23°24′ S, 49°18′ W 138
Juruti, *Braz.* 2°10′ S, 56°8′ W 130
Jussey, *Fr.* 47°49′ N, 5°53′ E 150
Justo Daract, *Arg.* 33°53′ S, 65°10′ W 134
Jutaí, *Braz.* 5°11′ S, 68°52′ W 130
Jutai, Ilha Grande de, islands, *South America* 3°21′ S, 49°31′ W 130
Jutaí, river, *Braz.* 3°21′ S, 67°32′ W 136
Jutiapa, *Guatemala* 14°17′ N, 89°52′ W 115
Jutica, *Braz.* 1°4′ N, 69°31′ W 136
Juticalpa, *Hond.* 14°43′ N, 86°12′ W 115
Jutland, peninsula, *Ger.-Den.* 55°35′ N, 8°29′ E 150
Juuru, *Est.* 59°2′ N, 24°56′ E 166
Juva, *Fin.* 61°53′ N, 27°47′ E 166
Juventino Rosas, *Mex.* 20°37′ N, 101°0′ W 114
Juventud, Isla de la, adm. division, *Cuba* 21°24′ N, 83°32′ W 116
Juxian, *China* 35°36′ N, 118°50′ E 198
Juxtlahuaca, *Mex.* 17°19′ N, 98°2′ W 114
Juye, *China* 35°22′ N, 116°6′ E 198
Jūymand, *Iran* 34°20′ N, 58°41′ E 180
Jūyom, *Iran* 28°5′ N, 53°49′ E 196
Juzennecourt, *Fr.* 48°10′ N, 4°58′ E 163
Jwaneng, *Botswana* 24°34′ S, 24°35′ E 227
Jyderup, *Den.* 55°39′ N, 11°24′ E 152
Jyrgalang, *Kyrg.* 42°38′ N, 78°58′ E 184
Jyväskylä, *Fin.* 62°12′ N, 25°42′ E 152

K

K2 (Qoghir, Godwin Austen), peak, *Pak.* 35°51′ N, 76°25′ E 186
Ka, river, *Nig.* 11°38′ N, 5°19′ E 222
Kaʻ Ū, region, *Oceania* 19°15′ N, 155°39′ W 99
Kaabong, *Uganda* 3°30′ N, 34°6′ E 224
Kaa-Iya National Park, *Bol.* 19°25′ S, 61°49′ W 132
Kaamanen, *Fin.* 69°6′ N, 27°12′ E 152
Kaambooni, *Somalia* 1°38′ S, 41°36′ E 224
Kaambooni, Raas, *Somalia* 1°36′ S, 40°53′ E 224
Kaaresuvanto, *Fin.* 68°27′ N, 22°27′ E 152
Kaba, *Hung.* 47°22′ N, 21°16′ E 168
Kaba see Habahe, *China* 48°4′ N, 86°21′ E 184
Kabaena, island, *Indonesia* 5°48′ S, 121°7′ E 192
Kabala, *Sierra Leone* 9°34′ N, 11°34′ W 222
Kabale, *Uganda* 1°19′ S, 29°59′ E 224
Kabalo, *Dem. Rep. of the Congo* 6°4′ S, 26°55′ E 224
Kabambare, *Dem. Rep. of the Congo* 4°44′ S, 27°38′ E 224
Kabanga, *Zambia* 17°30′ S, 26°47′ E 224
Kabangoué, *Côte d'Ivoire* 10°10′ N, 7°33′ W 222
Kabanjahe, *Indonesia* 3°8′ N, 98°29′ E 196
Kabara, *Mali* 16°40′ N, 3°0′ W 222
Kabardino-Balkariya, adm. division, *Russ.* 43°33′ N, 42°31′ E 195
Kabare, *Dem. Rep. of the Congo* 2°32′ S, 28°42′ E 224
Kabarnet, *Kenya* 0°28′ N, 35°45′ E 224
Kabasalan, *Philippines* 7°50′ N, 122°45′ E 203
Kabasha, *Dem. Rep. of the Congo* 0°43′ N, 29°12′ E 224
Kabba, *Nig.* 7°52′ N, 6°3′ E 222
Kåbdalis, *Nor.* 66°8′ N, 19°56′ E 152
Kabenung Lake, *Can.* 48°15′ N, 85°30′ W 94
Kabinakagami Lake, *Can.* 48°47′ N, 86°7′ W 81
Kabinda, *Dem. Rep. of the Congo* 6°11′ S, 24°27′ E 224
Kabīr, river, *Asia* 34°35′ N, 36°7′ E 194
Kabo, *Cen. Af. Rep.* 7°36′ N, 18°36′ E 218
Kabol (Kabul), *Afghan.* 34°34′ N, 69°2′ E 186
Kabompo, *Zambia* 13°37′ S, 24°10′ E 224
Kabompo, river, *Zambia* 13°34′ S, 24°16′ E 224
Kabongo, *Dem. Rep. of the Congo* 7°21′ S, 25°34′ E 224
Kabore-Tambi National Park, *Burkina Faso* 11°10′ N, 1°50′ W 222
Kabosa Island, *Myanmar* 12°51′ N, 97°24′ E 202
Kaboudia, Ras, *Tun.* 35°10′ N, 11°9′ E 156
Kabūd Gombad, *Iran* 37°1′ N, 59°48′ E 180
Kabugao, *Philippines* 18°3′ N, 121°8′ E 203
Kabul see Kabol, *Afghan.* 34°34′ N, 69°2′ E 186
Kabunda, *Dem. Rep. of the Congo* 12°29′ S, 29°20′ E 224
Kabushiya, *Sudan* 16°51′ N, 33°42′ E 182
Kabwe (Broken Hill), *Zambia* 14°29′ S, 28°25′ E 224
Kabylie, region, *Africa* 36°31′ N, 4°4′ E 150
Kać, *Serb.* 45°18′ N, 19°56′ E 168
Kaçanik, *Kosovo* 42°14′ N, 21°15′ E 168
Kachanovo, *Russ.* 57°27′ N, 27°46′ E 166
Kachia, *Nig.* 9°52′ N, 7°57′ E 222
Kachikau, *Botswana* 18°10′ S, 24°28′ E 224
Kachīry, *Kaz.* 53°4′ N, 76°7′ E 184
Kachkanar, *Russ.* 58°44′ N, 59°30′ E 154
Kachreti, *Ga.* 41°39′ N, 45°40′ E 195
Kachug, *Russ.* 54°3′ N, 105°59′ E 190
Kachung, *Uganda* 1°54′ N, 32°56′ E 224
Kaçkar Dağı, peak, *Turk.* 40°50′ N, 41°6′ E 195
Kada, spring, *Chad* 19°21′ N, 19°36′ E 216
Kadaingti, *Myanmar* 17°37′ N, 97°30′ E 202
Kadam, peak, *Uganda* 1°45′ N, 34°37′ E 224
Kadan Kyun, island, *Myanmar* 12°33′ N, 98°29′ E 202
Kadarkút, *Hung.* 46°14′ N, 17°37′ E 168
Kade, *Ghana* 6°6′ N, 0°52′ E 222
Kadé, *Guinea* 12°10′ N, 13°53′ W 222
Kadéï, river, *Cen. Af. Rep.* 3°48′ N, 15°32′ E 218
Kadesh, battle, *Syr.* 34°34′ N, 36°25′ E 194
Kadesh-Barnea see ʻAin el Qideirât, spring, *Egypt* 30°39′ N, 34°25′ E 194
Kadiana, *Mali* 10°44′ N, 6°31′ W 222
Kadıköy, *Turk.* 40°39′ N, 26°52′ E 158
Kadıköy, *Turk.* 40°58′ N, 29°2′ E 158
Kading, river, *Laos* 18°19′ N, 104°10′ E 202
Kadınhanı, *Turk.* 38°13′ N, 32°13′ E 156
Kadiolo, *Mali* 10°33′ N, 5°46′ W 222
Kadiria, *Alg.* 36°31′ N, 3°41′ E 150
Kadirli, *Turk.* 37°21′ N, 36°5′ E 156
Kadivka, *Ukr.* 48°31′ N, 38°36′ E 158
Kadnikov, *Russ.* 59°30′ N, 40°21′ E 154
Kado, *Nig.* 7°37′ N, 9°40′ E 222
Kadom, *Russ.* 54°32′ N, 42°30′ E 154
Kadoma, *Zimb.* 18°21′ S, 29°56′ E 224
Kadrifakovo, *Maced.* 41°48′ N, 22°3′ E 168
Kadugli, *Sudan* 10°57′ N, 29°40′ E 224
Kaduna, *Nig.* 10°30′ N, 7°24′ E 222
Kaduy, *Russ.* 59°10′ N, 37°12′ E 154
Kadyy, *Russ.* 57°47′ N, 43°10′ E 154
Kadzherom, *Russ.* 64°40′ N, 55°48′ E 154
Kaech'ŏn, *N. Korea* 39°42′ N, 125°52′ E 200
Kaédi, *Mauritania* 16°8′ N, 13°36′ W 222
Kaélé, *Cameroon* 10°6′ N, 14°26′ E 216
Kaʻena Point, *Hawaiʻi, U.S.* 21°34′ N, 158°40′ W 99
Kaeng Krachan National Park, *Thai.* 12°44′ N, 98°58′ E 202
Kaeo, *N.Z.* 35°6′ S, 173°47′ E 240
Kaʻeo, peak, *Hawaiʻi, U.S.* 21°53′ N, 160°12′ W 99
Kaesŏng, *N. Korea* 37°58′ N, 126°32′ E 200
Kafakumba, *Dem. Rep. of the Congo* 9°41′ S, 23°45′ E 224
Kafanchan, *Nig.* 9°36′ N, 8°18′ E 222
Kaffrine, *Senegal* 14°6′ N, 15°32′ W 222
Kafia Kingi, *Sudan* 9°15′ N, 24°24′ E 224
Kafin, *Nig.* 9°29′ N, 7°5′ E 222
Kåfjord, *Nor.* 69°56′ N, 23°0′ E 152
Kåfjord, *Nor.* 69°31′ N, 20°51′ E 152
Kafr Buhum, *Syr.* 35°3′ N, 36°41′ E 194
Kafu, river, *Uganda* 1°8′ N, 31°26′ E 224
Kafue, *Zambia* 15°47′ S, 28°10′ E 224
Kafue National Park, *Zambia* 14°52′ S, 25°40′ E 224
Kafue, river, *Zambia* 14°31′ S, 26°26′ E 224
Kafue, river, *Zambia* 15°41′ S, 26°27′ E 224
Kafufu, river, *Tanzania* 7°5′ S, 31°31′ E 224
Kafulwe, *Zambia* 9°0′ S, 29°1′ E 224
Kaga, *Japan* 36°18′ N, 136°17′ E 201
Kaga Bandoro, *Cen. Af. Rep.* 6°54′ N, 19°11′ E 218
Kagan, *Pak.* 34°45′ N, 73°34′ E 186
Kagawa, adm. division, *Japan* 34°11′ N, 133°41′ E 201
Kåge, *Nor.* 64°49′ N, 20°56′ E 152
Kagera, adm. division, *Tanzania* 2°38′ S, 30°33′ E 218
Kagera, river, *Africa* 1°8′ S, 30°42′ E 224
Kagianagami Lake, *Can.* 50°58′ N, 88°38′ W 110
Kağızman, *Turk.* 40°8′ N, 43°6′ E 195
Kagmar, *Sudan* 14°25′ N, 30°23′ E 226
Kagopal, *Chad* 8°15′ N, 16°26′ E 218
Kagoshima, *Japan* 31°34′ N, 130°32′ E 201
Kagoshima, adm. division, *Japan* 31°15′ N, 130°34′ E 201
Kagoshima Space Center, *Japan* 31°16′ N, 131°0′ E 201
Kaguyak, *Alas., U.S.* 56°51′ N, 153°51′ W 98
Kahama, *Tanzania* 3°49′ S, 32°35′ E 224
Kahan, *Pak.* 29°18′ N, 68°57′ E 186
Kahemba, *Dem. Rep. of the Congo* 7°20′ S, 18°59′ E 218
Kāhili, peak, *Hawaiʻi, U.S.* 21°58′ N, 159°33′ W 99
Kahler Asten, peak, *Ger.* 51°10′ N, 8°26′ E 167
Kahlotus, *Wash., U.S.* 46°37′ N, 118°33′ W 90
Kahntah, *Can.* 58°19′ N, 120°55′ W 108
Kahntah, river, *Can.* 57°50′ N, 120°51′ W 108
Kahnūj, *Iran* 27°54′ N, 57°45′ E 196
Kahoku, *Japan* 38°26′ N, 140°18′ E 201
Kahoʻolawe, island, *Hawaiʻi, U.S.* 20°21′ N, 157°18′ W 99
Kahperusvaara, peak, *Fin.* 69°8′ N, 21°1′ E 152
Kahramanmaraş, *Turk.* 37°35′ N, 36°55′ E 156
Kahtla, *Est.* 58°24′ N, 22°59′ E 166
Kahuku Point, *Hawaiʻi, U.S.* 21°44′ N, 158°21′ W 99
Kahurangi National Park, *N.Z.* 41°11′ S, 171°19′ E 240
Kahuzi-Biega National Park, *Dem. Rep. of the Congo* 2°0′ S, 27°14′ E 224
Kai Iwi, *N.Z.* 39°53′ S, 174°54′ E 240
Kai, Kepulauan, islands, *Banda Sea* 5°58′ S, 130°47′ E 192
Kaiama, *Nig.* 9°35′ N, 4°0′ E 222
Kaibara, *Japan* 35°7′ N, 135°3′ E 201
Kāʻid, spring, *Iraq* 32°2′ N, 40°57′ E 180
Kaifeng, *China* 34°48′ N, 114°19′ E 198
Kaifu, *Japan* 33°36′ N, 134°20′ E 201
Kaiholena, peak, *Hawaiʻi, U.S.* 19°10′ N, 155°38′ W 99
Kaihu, *N.Z.* 35°45′ S, 173°42′ E 240
Kaikoura, *N.Z.* 42°25′ S, 173°39′ E 240
Kailahun, *Sierra Leone* 8°14′ N, 10°35′ W 222
Kaili, *China* 26°34′ N, 107°59′ E 198
Kailu, *China* 43°39′ N, 121°16′ E 198
Kaimana, *Indonesia* 3°39′ S, 133°45′ E 192
Käina, *Est.* 58°49′ N, 22°46′ E 166
Kainan, *Japan* 34°9′ N, 135°13′ E 201
Kainji Dam, *Nig.* 9°40′ N, 4°19′ E 222
Kainji Lake National Park, *Nig.* 9°45′ N, 5°4′ E 222
Kainuunkylä, *Fin.* 66°13′ N, 23°47′ E 152
Kairala, *Fin.* 67°10′ N, 27°23′ E 152
Kaisersesch, *Ger.* 50°13′ N, 7°8′ E 167
Kaiserslautern, *Ger.* 49°26′ N, 7°45′ E 163
Kaishantun, *China* 42°42′ N, 129°44′ E 200
Kaišiadorys, *Lith.* 54°52′ N, 24°26′ E 166
Kaitangata, *N.Z.* 46°17′ S, 169°50′ E 240
Kaithal, *India* 29°47′ N, 76°25′ E 197
Kaʻiwaloa Heiau and Olowalu Petroglyphs, site, *Hawaiʻi, U.S.* 20°49′ N, 156°40′ W 99
Kaixian, *China* 31°11′ N, 108°20′ E 198
Kaiyang, *China* 27°4′ N, 107°0′ E 198
Kaiyuan, *China* 42°32′ N, 124°3′ E 200
Kaiyuan, *China* 23°40′ N, 103°9′ E 202
Kajaani, *Fin.* 64°12′ N, 27°39′ E 152
Kajaki, *Afghan.* 32°12′ N, 65°5′ E 186
Kajaki Dam, *Afghan.* 32°1′ N, 64°29′ E 186
Kajang, *Malaysia* 3°0′ N, 101°45′ E 196
Kajiado, *Kenya* 1°52′ S, 36°48′ E 224
Kajiki, *Japan* 31°43′ N, 130°40′ E 201
Kajo Kaji, *Sudan* 3°48′ N, 31°36′ E 224
Kajok, *Sudan* 8°16′ N, 27°58′ E 224
Kajuru, *Nig.* 10°19′ N, 7°38′ E 222
Kaka, *Sudan* 10°37′ N, 32°7′ E 224
Kaka, *Turkm.* 37°21′ N, 59°36′ E 180
Kakada, spring, *Chad* 16°8′ N, 15°29′ E 216
Kakadu National Park, *Austral.* 13°22′ S, 132°5′ E 238
Kakahi, *N.Z.* 38°59′ S, 175°21′ E 240
Kakamas, *S. Af.* 28°47′ S, 20°35′ E 227
Kakamega, *Kenya* 0°15′ N, 34°46′ E 224
Kakana, *India* 9°9′ N, 92°55′ E 188
Kakanj, *Bosn. and Herzg.* 44°9′ N, 18°5′ E 168
Kakanui, *N.Z.* 45°12′ S, 170°53′ E 240
Kakaramea, *N.Z.* 39°43′ S, 174°25′ E 240
Kakasszék, *Hung.* 46°32′ N, 20°36′ E 168
Kakata, *Liberia* 6°25′ N, 10°21′ W 222
Kakatahi, *N.Z.* 39°41′ S, 175°21′ E 240
Kake, *Alas., U.S.* 56°58′ N, 133°57′ W 108
Kake, *Japan* 34°36′ N, 132°20′ E 201
Kaketsa Mountain, *Can.* 58°10′ N, 131°59′ W 108
Kakhib, *Russ.* 42°23′ N, 46°36′ E 195
Kākhk, *Iran* 34°7′ N, 58°38′ E 180
Kakhovka, *Ukr.* 46°48′ N, 33°29′ E 156
Kakhovs'ke Vodoskhovyshche, lake, *Ukr.* 46°59′ N, 32°23′ E 156
Kakinada (Cocanada), *India* 16°59′ N, 82°15′ E 188
Kakisa, *Can.* 60°54′ N, 117°21′ W 108
Kakisa Lake, *Can.* 60°57′ N, 118°37′ W 108
Kakisa, river, *Can.* 60°44′ N, 119°16′ W 108
Kakogawa, *Japan* 34°46′ N, 134°51′ E 201
Kakshaal Range see Kök Shal Tau, *Kyrg.* 41°22′ N, 77°33′ E 184
Kakskerta, *Fin.* 60°20′ N, 22°13′ E 166
Kaktovik, *Alas., U.S.* 69°59′ N, 143°40′ W 98
Kakuda, *Japan* 37°58′ N, 140°45′ E 201
Kakuma, *Kenya* 3°40′ N, 34°50′ E 224
Kakwa, river, *Can.* 54°13′ N, 118°43′ W 108
Kál, *Hung.* 47°43′ N, 20°17′ E 168
Kala, *Azerb.* 40°27′ N, 50°10′ E 195
Kala, *Tanzania* 8°8′ S, 31°0′ E 224
Kalaallit Nunaat see Greenland, *Den.* 67°11′ N, 50°25′ W 106
Kalabagh, *Pak.* 32°59′ N, 71°35′ E 186
Kalabo, *Zambia* 14°59′ S, 22°40′ E 220
Kalābsha and Beit el Wâli, ruin(s), *Egypt* 23°32′ N, 32°42′ E 182
Kalach, *Russ.* 50°25′ N, 40°58′ E 158
Kalach na Donu, *Russ.* 48°43′ N, 43°32′ E 158
Kalachinsk, *Russ.* 54°59′ N, 74°36′ E 184
Kalae (South Point), *Hawaiʻi, U.S.* 18°40′ N, 155°43′ W 99
Kalahari Desert, *Africa* 19°27′ S, 24°2′ E 224
Kalahari Gemsbok National Park, *S. Af.* 26°6′ S, 19°47′ E 227
Kalaikhum, *Taj.* 38°28′ N, 70°47′ E 197
Kalajoki, *Fin.* 64°12′ N, 23°55′ E 152
Kalakamate, *Botswana* 20°39′ S, 27°18′ E 227
Kalakan, *Russ.* 55°11′ N, 116°45′ E 190
Kalakepen, *Indonesia* 2°47′ N, 97°48′ E 196
Kalalua, peak, *Hawaiʻi, U.S.* 19°23′ N, 155°7′ W 99
Kalam, *Pak.* 35°31′ N, 72°36′ E 186
Kalama, *Wash., U.S.* 46°0′ N, 122°50′ W 100
Kalama, river, *Wash., U.S.* 46°1′ N, 122°45′ W 100
Kalamalka Lake, *Can.* 50°5′ N, 119°57′ W 108
Kalamáta, *Gr.* 37°2′ N, 22°7′ E 216
Kalamazoo, *Mich., U.S.* 42°17′ N, 85°36′ W 102
Kalambo Falls, *Zambia* 8°51′ S, 31°17′ E 224
Kalana, *Mali* 10°47′ N, 8°13′ W 222
Kalangala, *Uganda* 0°23′ N, 32°16′ E 224
Kalangali, *Tanzania* 6°6′ S, 33°55′ E 224
Kalanshiyū ar Ramlī al Kabīr, Sarīr (Sand Sea of Calanscio), *Lib.* 28°52′ N, 23°25′ E 180
Kalanshiyū, Sarīr, *Lib.* 26°35′ N, 20°7′ E 216
Kalao, island, *Indonesia* 7°27′ S, 119°55′ E 192
Kalaotoa, island, *Indonesia* 7°28′ S, 121°50′ E 192
Kälarne, *Nor.* 62°59′ N, 16°4′ E 152
Kalasin, *Thai.* 16°28′ N, 103°31′ E 202
Kalat, *Pak.* 29°2′ N, 66°33′ E 186
Kalaupapa National Historic Park, *Hawaiʻi, U.S.* 20°42′ N, 158°0′ W 99
Kalaus, river, *Russ.* 45°50′ N, 43°15′ E 158
Kalawao, site, *Hawaiʻi, U.S.* 21°10′ N, 157°0′ W 99
Kalay'mor, *Turkm.* 35°41′ N, 62°33′ E 186
Kalay-wa, *Myanmar* 23°10′ N, 94°13′ E 202
Kalbā, *U.A.E.* 25°4′ N, 56°17′ E 196
Kälbäcär see Karvachar, *Azerb.* 40°8′ N, 46°1′ E 195
Kalbān, *Oman* 20°17′ N, 58°41′ E 182
Kaldrma, *Bosn. and Herzg.* 44°18′ N, 16°11′ E 168
Kale Burnu, *Turk.* 41°4′ N, 38°54′ E 195
Kale (Myra), *Turk.* 36°13′ N, 29°57′ E 156
Kalecik, *Turk.* 40°6′ N, 33°25′ E 156
Kalehe, *Dem. Rep. of the Congo* 2°7′ S, 28°50′ E 224
Kalemie, *Dem. Rep. of the Congo* 5°57′ S, 29°11′ E 224
Kalemyo, *Myanmar* 23°10′ N, 94°1′ E 202
Kalene Hill, *Zambia* 11°13′ S, 24°10′ E 224
Kalenyy, *Kaz.* 49°32′ N, 51°35′ E 184
Kalesija, *Bosn. and Herzg.* 44°27′ N, 18°55′ E 168
Kaletnik, *Pol.* 54°10′ N, 23°5′ E 152
Kalevala, *Russ.* 65°12′ N, 31°12′ E 152

Kaleybar, *Iran* 38°56′ N, 47°3′ E 195
Kalgachikha, *Russ.* 63°20′ N, 36°48′ E 154
Kalí Límni, peak, *Gr.* 35°34′ N, 27°4′ E 156
Kali Sindh, river, *India* 24°28′ N, 76°7′ E 197
Kaliakoúda, peak, *Gr.* 38°47′ N, 21°40′ E 156
Kaliakra, Nos, *Bulg.* 43°17′ N, 28°17′ E 156
Kalibo, *Philippines* 11°40′ N, 122°22′ E 203
Kalida, *Ohio, U.S.* 40°58′ N, 84°12′ W 102
Kalima, *Dem. Rep. of the Congo* 2°39′ S, 26°35′ E 218
Kalimantan see Borneo, island, *Indonesia* 4°28′ S, 111°26′ E 192
Kalimash, *Alban.* 42°5′ N, 20°18′ E 168
Kálimnos, *Gr.* 36°57′ N, 26°59′ E 156
Kalimpang, *India* 27°4′ N, 88°26′ E 197
Kaliningrad, *Russ.* 54°42′ N, 20°27′ E 166
Kaliningrad Oblast, adm. division, *Russ.* 54°47′ N, 20°9′ E 166
Kalinino, *Arm.* 41°7′ N, 44°15′ E 195
Kalinino, *Russ.* 45°9′ N, 39°1′ E 156
Kalinino, *Russ.* 57°18′ N, 56°23′ E 154
Kalininsk, *Russ.* 51°29′ N, 44°28′ E 158
Kalinivka, *Ukr.* 49°28′ N, 28°42′ E 152
Kalinkavichy, *Belarus* 52°5′ N, 29°26′ E 152
Kalino, *Russ.* 58°14′ N, 57°38′ E 154
Kalinovik, *Bosn. and Herzg.* 43°30′ N, 18°26′ E 168
Kaliro, *Uganda* 0°52′ N, 33°29′ E 224
Kalis, *Somalia* 8°23′ N, 49°3′ E 216
Kalispell, *Mont., U.S.* 48°12′ N, 114°21′ W 106
Kalisz, *Pol.* 51°45′ N, 18°5′ E 152
Kaliua, *Tanzania* 5°4′ S, 31°46′ E 224
Kalix, *Nor.* 65°51′ N, 23°7′ E 154
Kalixälven, river, *Nor.* 67°41′ N, 19°45′ E 152
Kalkan, *Turk.* 36°15′ N, 29°25′ E 156
Kalkar, *Ger.* 51°42′ N, 6°17′ E 167
Kalkaska, *Mich., U.S.* 44°43′ N, 85°11′ W 94
Kalkfeld, *Namibia* 20°55′ S, 16°12′ E 227
Kalkkinen, *Fin.* 61°17′ N, 25°41′ E 166
Kalkrand, *Namibia* 24°5′ S, 17°35′ E 227
Kallam, *India* 18°32′ N, 76°1′ E 188
Kallaste, *Est.* 58°38′ N, 27°7′ E 166
Kallithéa, *Gr.* 37°57′ N, 23°42′ E 156
Kałuszyn, *Pol.* 52°12′ N, 21°47′ E 152
Kallmet, *Alban.* 41°50′ N, 19°41′ E 168
Kallo, *Fin.* 67°25′ N, 24°27′ E 152
Kallunki, *Fin.* 66°38′ N, 28°54′ E 152
Kalmar, *Nor.* 56°39′ N, 16°20′ E 152
Kalmthout, *Belg.* 51°23′ N, 4°28′ E 167
Kalmykiya, adm. division, *Russ.* 46°7′ N, 43°37′ E 158
Kalnai, *India* 22°47′ N, 83°29′ E 197
Kalnik, peak, *Croatia* 46°7′ N, 16°26′ E 168
Kalo Chorio, *Cyprus* 34°50′ N, 33°2′ E 194
Kalocsa, *Hung.* 46°31′ N, 18°58′ E 168
Kaloko-Honokōhau National Historical Park, *Hawai'i, U.S.* 19°40′ N, 156°5′ W 99
Kaloli Point, *U.S.* 19°34′ N, 154°56′ W 99
Kalomo, *Zambia* 17°3′ S, 26°28′ E 224
Kalotina, *Bulg.* 42°59′ N, 22°51′ E 168
Kalpi, *India* 26°6′ N, 79°43′ E 197
Kalpin, *China* 40°34′ N, 78°54′ E 184
Kalsubai, peak, *India* 19°34′ N, 73°34′ E 188
Kaltag, *Alas., U.S.* 64°11′ N, 158°53′ W 98
Kaltay, *Russ.* 56°14′ N, 84°54′ E 169
Kalterherberg, *Ger.* 50°31′ N, 6°12′ E 167
Kaltungo, *Nig.* 9°48′ N, 11°18′ E 222
Kaluga, *Russ.* 54°34′ N, 36°20′ E 154
Kaluga, adm. division, *Russ.* 54°14′ N, 34°5′ E 154
Kalulushi, *Zambia* 12°52′ S, 28°5′ E 224
Kalundu, *Zambia* 10°17′ S, 29°22′ E 224
Kalungwishi, river, *Zambia* 9°40′ S, 29°0′ E 220
Kalush, *Ukr.* 49°0′ N, 24°21′ E 158
Kalvåg, *Nor.* 61°46′ N, 4°51′ E 152
Kalvarija, *Lith.* 54°26′ N, 23°11′ E 166
Kälviä, *Fin.* 63°51′ N, 23°24′ E 152
Kalvitsa, *Fin.* 61°53′ N, 27°15′ E 166
Kalvola, *Fin.* 61°5′ N, 24°7′ E 166
Kalwang, *Aust.* 47°26′ N, 14°46′ E 156
Kalweyn, Ghubbet, *Somalia* 11°7′ N, 46°28′ E 216
Kal'ya, *Russ.* 60°17′ N, 59°54′ E 154
Kalyan, *India* 19°14′ N, 73°8′ E 188
Kalyazin, *Russ.* 57°12′ N, 37°50′ E 154
Kám, *Hung.* 47°5′ N, 16°53′ E 168
Kam, river, *Nig.* 8°10′ N, 11°4′ E 222
Kama, *Dem. Rep. of the Congo* 3°38′ S, 27°7′ E 224
Kama, *Myanmar* 19°3′ N, 95°4′ E 202
Kama, *Russ.* 60°8′ N, 62°1′ E 154
Kama, river, *Dem. Rep. of the Congo* 3°30′ S, 26°55′ E 218
Kama, river, *Russ.* 60°10′ N, 55°25′ E 154
Kamae, *Japan* 32°47′ N, 131°55′ E 201
Kamaing, *Myanmar* 25°29′ N, 96°40′ E 188
Kamaishi, *Japan* 39°17′ N, 141°42′ E 190
Kamakou, peak, *Hawai'i, U.S.* 21°6′ N, 156°55′ W 99
Kamakura, *Japan* 35°18′ N, 139°34′ E 201
Kamalia, *Pak.* 30°45′ N, 72°38′ E 186
Kamalino, *Hawai'i, U.S.* 21°50′ N, 160°15′ W 99
Kamalu, *Sierra Leone* 9°22′ N, 12°17′ W 222
Kaman, *India* 27°38′ N, 77°14′ E 197
Kaman, *Turk.* 39°21′ N, 33°43′ E 156
Kamanjab, *Namibia* 19°40′ S, 14°49′ E 220
Kamanyola, *Dem. Rep. of the Congo* 2°47′ S, 28°57′ E 224
Kamapanda, *Zambia* 12°1′ S, 24°6′ E 224
Kamarān, island, *Yemen* 15°16′ N, 41°57′ E 182
Kamarod, *Pak.* 27°28′ N, 63°36′ E 186
Kamba, *Nig.* 11°51′ N, 3°40′ E 222
Kambarka, *Russ.* 56°16′ N, 54°17′ E 154
Kambaya, *Guinea* 10°40′ N, 13°1′ W 222
Kambia, *Sierra Leone* 9°5′ N, 12°56′ W 222
Kambja, *Est.* 58°12′ N, 26°41′ E 166
Kambove, *Dem. Rep. of the Congo* 10°51′ S, 26°36′ E 224
Kamchatka, adm. division, *Russ.* 43°39′ N, 145°30′ E 160
Kamchatka, Poluostrov, *Asia* 58°47′ N, 161°17′ E 160
Kamchatskiy Zaliv 55°17′ N, 159°46′ E 160
Kameda, *Japan* 37°52′ N, 139°7′ E 201
Kamehameha I Birthplace, site, *Hawai'i, U.S.* 20°14′ N, 155°56′ W 99
Kamen', *Belarus* 53°51′ N, 26°40′ E 166
Kamen, *Ger.* 51°35′ N, 7°39′ E 167
Kamen, Gora, peak, *Russ.* 69°6′ N, 95°4′ E 169
Kamenica, *Bosn. and Herzg.* 44°20′ N, 18°12′ E 168
Kamenka, *Kaz.* 51°5′ N, 50°16′ E 158
Kamenka, *Russ.* 65°53′ N, 44°0′ E 154
Kamenka, *Russ.* 58°29′ N, 95°34′ E 160
Kamenka, *Russ.* 53°9′ N, 44°5′ E 154
Kamenka, *Russ.* 65°52′ N, 43°51′ E 173
Kamen'na Obi, *Russ.* 53°44′ N, 81°27′ E 184
Kamennoe, *Kaz.* 44°55′ N, 54°47′ E 158
Kamennogorsk, *Russ.* 60°57′ N, 29°6′ E 166
Kamensk Shakhtinskiy, *Russ.* 48°16′ N, 40°16′ E 158
Kamensk Ural'skiy, *Russ.* 56°27′ N, 61°47′ E 154
Kamenskiy, *Russ.* 50°50′ N, 45°29′ E 158
Kamenskoye, *Russ.* 62°31′ N, 165°59′ E 160
Kameoka, *Japan* 35°0′ N, 135°34′ E 201
Kameur, river, *Cen. Af. Rep.* 9°42′ N, 21°14′ E 218
Kamiagata, *Japan* 34°38′ N, 129°24′ E 200
Kamieskroon, *S. Af.* 30°12′ S, 17°54′ E 227
Kamiji, *Dem. Rep. of the Congo* 6°37′ S, 23°16′ E 218
Kâmil, Gebel, peak, *Egypt* 22°15′ N, 26°33′ E 226
Kamina, *Dem. Rep. of the Congo* 8°45′ S, 24°58′ E 224
Kaministiquia, *Can.* 48°32′ N, 89°34′ W 94
Kaminoyama, *Japan* 38°9′ N, 140°15′ E 201
Kaminuriak Lake, *Can.* 63°4′ N, 97°47′ W 106
Kamioka, *Japan* 36°20′ N, 137°19′ E 201
Kamitsuki, *Japan* 34°6′ N, 139°32′ E 201
Kamitsushima, *Japan* 34°39′ N, 129°28′ E 200
Kamkhat Mu'aywir, peak, *Jordan* 31°7′ N, 36°28′ E 194
Kamloops, *Can.* 50°39′ N, 120°20′ W 82
Kammuri, peak, *Japan* 34°28′ N, 132°2′ E 200
Kamo, *Arm.* 40°22′ N, 45°5′ E 195
Kamo, *Japan* 37°39′ N, 139°3′ E 201
Kamo, *Japan* 38°46′ N, 139°44′ E 201
Kamo, *N.Z.* 35°42′ S, 174°18′ E 240
Kamoa Mountains, *Guyana* 1°32′ N, 60°5′ W 130
Kampala, *Uganda* 0°14′ N, 32°22′ E 224
Kampar, *Malaysia* 4°18′ N, 101°9′ E 196
Kampene, *Dem. Rep. of the Congo* 3°37′ S, 26°39′ E 224
Kamphaeng Phet, *Thai.* 16°28′ N, 99°28′ E 202
Kamp-Lintfort, *Ger.* 51°29′ N, 6°33′ E 167
Kampolombo, Lake, *Zambia* 11°37′ S, 29°6′ E 224
Kampong Cham, *Cambodia* 11°59′ N, 105°25′ E 202
Kampong Kuala Besut, *Malaysia* 5°48′ N, 102°35′ E 196
Kampos, *Cyprus* 35°1′ N, 32°43′ E 194
Kampot, *Cambodia* 10°37′ N, 104°12′ E 202
Kampti, *Burkina Faso* 10°8′ N, 3°28′ W 222
Kamsack, *Can.* 51°34′ N, 101°56′ W 90
Kamsar, *Guinea* 10°39′ N, 14°35′ W 222
Kamskoye Vdkhr., lake, *Russ.* 58°48′ N, 56°38′ E 246
Kamskoye Vodokhranilishche, lake, *Russ.* 58°35′ N, 54°17′ E 154
Kamsuuma, *Somalia* 0°14′ N, 42°48′ E 218
Kámuk, Cerro, peak, *C.R.* 9°15′ N, 83°6′ W 115
Kam'yanka-Dniprovs'ka, *Ukr.* 47°28′ N, 34°24′ E 156
Kamyshin, *Russ.* 50°6′ N, 45°22′ E 158
Kamyshla, *Russ.* 54°7′ N, 52°9′ E 154
Kamyzyak, *Russ.* 46°5′ N, 48°6′ E 158
Kan, *Sudan* 8°57′ N, 31°47′ E 224
Kanab, *Utah, U.S.* 37°2′ N, 112°32′ W 82
Kanagawa, adm. division, *Japan* 35°20′ N, 139°2′ E 201
Kanak, river, *Turk.* 39°33′ N, 34°58′ E 156
Kanākir, *Syr.* 33°15′ N, 36°5′ E 194
Kanaktok Mountain, *Alas., U.S.* 67°48′ N, 160°12′ W 98
Kanal, *Slov.* 46°5′ N, 13°38′ E 167
Kanalla, *India* 6°53′ N, 93°52′ E 188
Kananga, *Dem. Rep. of the Congo* 5°54′ S, 22°25′ E 218
Kanash, *Russ.* 55°28′ N, 47°29′ E 154
Kanata, *Can.* 45°16′ N, 75°51′ W 82
Kanava, *Russ.* 61°5′ N, 55°4′ E 154
Kanâyis, Râs el, *Egypt* 31°16′ N, 27°50′ E 180
Kanazawa, *Japan* 36°33′ N, 136°40′ E 201
Kanbalu, *Myanmar* 23°11′ N, 95°31′ E 202
Kanchipuram, *India* 12°51′ N, 79°43′ E 188
Kanda Kanda, *Dem. Rep. of the Congo* 6°55′ S, 23°32′ E 218
Kandahar, *Afghan.* 31°36′ N, 65°43′ E 186
Kandalaksha, *Russ.* 67°9′ N, 32°24′ E 152
Kandalakshskiy Zaliv 66°18′ N, 29°7′ E 160
Kandale, *Dem. Rep. of the Congo* 6°2′ S, 19°23′ E 218
Kandang, *Indonesia* 3°6′ N, 97°18′ E 196
Kandangan, *Indonesia* 2°43′ S, 115°13′ E 192
Kandava, *Latv.* 57°2′ N, 22°44′ E 166
Kandel, *Ger.* 49°5′ N, 8°10′ E 152
Kandersteg, *Switz.* 46°29′ N, 7°40′ E 167
Kandhkot, *Pak.* 28°13′ N, 69°12′ E 186
Kandi, *Benin* 11°7′ N, 2°56′ E 222
Kandiaro, *Pak.* 27°6′ N, 68°15′ E 186
Kandıra, *Turk.* 41°4′ N, 30°8′ E 156
Kandla, *India* 23°12′ N, 70°25′ E 173
Kandrach, *Pak.* 25°29′ N, 65°27′ E 182
Kandreho, *Madagascar* 17°31′ S, 46°6′ E 220
Kandudu, island, *Maldives* 2°2′ N, 72°0′ E 188
Kandy, *Sri Lanka* 7°16′ N, 80°40′ E 188
Kane, *Pa., U.S.* 41°39′ N, 78°49′ W 94
Kāne'ākī Heiau, site, *Hawai'i, U.S.* 21°29′ N, 158°14′ W 99
Kāneiolouma Heiau, site, *Hawai'i, U.S.* 21°52′ N, 159°30′ W 99
Kanel, *Senegal* 15°29′ N, 13°14′ W 222
Kanepi, *Est.* 57°58′ N, 26°45′ E 166
Kanevskaya, *Russ.* 46°6′ N, 38°55′ E 156
Kanfarande, *Guinea* 10°51′ N, 14°34′ W 222
Kang, *Afghan.* 31°7′ N, 61°55′ E 186
Kang, *Botswana* 23°41′ S, 22°48′ E 227
Kangaamiut, *Den.* 65°50′ N, 53°21′ W 106
Kangaatsiaq, *Den.* 68°18′ N, 53°25′ W 106
Kangaba, *Mali* 11°57′ N, 8°26′ W 222
Kangal, *Turk.* 39°13′ N, 37°22′ E 156
Kangān, *Iran* 25°49′ N, 57°28′ E 196
Kangan, *Iran* 27°51′ N, 52°7′ E 196
Kangar, *Malaysia* 6°25′ N, 100°12′ E 202
Kangaroo Island, *Austral.* 36°51′ S, 137°17′ E 230
Kangasala, *Fin.* 61°26′ N, 24°2′ E 166
Kangasniemi, *Fin.* 61°58′ N, 26°34′ E 166
Kangatet, *Kenya* 1°55′ N, 36°6′ E 224
Kangāvar, *Iran* 34°26′ N, 47°48′ E 180
Kangbao, *China* 41°51′ N, 114°36′ E 198
Kangdong, *N. Korea* 39°8′ N, 126°5′ E 200
Kangean, Kepulauan, islands, *Java Sea* 6°17′ S, 113°56′ E 192
Kangeeak Point, *Can.* 67°47′ N, 64°28′ W 106
Kangen, river, *Sudan* 6°35′ N, 33°17′ E 224
Kangerluarsoruseq (Færingehavn), *Den.* 63°43′ N, 51°21′ W 106
Kangerlussuaq 67°49′ N, 35°25′ W 246
Kangerlussuaq, *Den.* 67°4′ N, 50°50′ W 106
Kangersuatsiaq, *Den.* 72°16′ N, 55°39′ W 106
Kanggye, *N. Korea* 40°58′ N, 126°35′ E 200
Kangikajiip Agpalia, *Den.* 69°48′ N, 22°11′ W 246
Kangiqsualujjuaq, *Can.* 58°30′ N, 65°54′ W 106
Kangiqsujuaq, *Can.* 61°35′ N, 72°2′ W 106
Kangmar, *China* 28°36′ N, 89°41′ E 197
Kangmar, *China* 30°48′ N, 85°39′ E 197
Kangnyŏng, *N. Korea* 37°53′ N, 125°31′ E 200
Kango, *Gabon* 0°11′ N, 10°8′ E 218
Kangping, *China* 42°45′ N, 123°24′ E 200
Kangrinboqê Feng, peak, *China* 31°4′ N, 81°18′ E 197
Kangsang, *N. Korea* 40°6′ N, 128°23′ E 200
Kangsŏ, *N. Korea* 38°56′ N, 125°30′ E 200
Kangto, peak, *China* 27°40′ N, 92°10′ E 190
Kangwon, adm. division, *N. Korea* 38°42′ N, 127°26′ E 200
Kaniama, *Dem. Rep. of the Congo* 7°33′ S, 24°10′ E 224
Kaniet Islands, *South Pacific Ocean* 0°47′ N, 145°35′ E 192
Kanin Nos, *Russ.* 68°34′ N, 43°22′ E 169
Kanin Nos, Mys, *Russ.* 68°10′ N, 42°25′ E 169
Kanin, Poluostrov, *Russ.* 68°1′ N, 39°33′ E 169
Kanin, Poluostrov, *Russ.* 67°0′ N, 44°14′ E 160
Kanirom, *Chad* 14°26′ N, 13°45′ E 216
Kanish, ruin(s), *Turk.* 38°51′ N, 35°29′ E 156
Kaniv, *Ukr.* 49°43′ N, 31°30′ E 158
Kanjarkot, site, *Pak.* 24°15′ N, 69°5′ E 186
Kanjiža, *Serb.* 46°4′ N, 20°3′ E 168
Kankaanpää, *Fin.* 61°47′ N, 22°23′ E 166
Kankakee, *Ill., U.S.* 41°7′ N, 87°52′ W 102
Kankan, *Guinea* 10°25′ N, 9°19′ W 222
Kankossa, *Mauritania* 15°54′ N, 11°32′ W 222
Kanmaw Kyun, island, *Myanmar* 11°33′ N, 98°32′ E 202
Kanmen, *China* 28°5′ N, 121°16′ E 198
Kannapolis, *N.C., U.S.* 35°29′ N, 80°38′ W 96
Kannauj, *India* 27°1′ N, 79°54′ E 197
Kannod, *India* 22°40′ N, 76°46′ E 197
Kannusuo, *Russ.* 65°8′ N, 31°54′ E 152
Kano, *Nig.* 11°59′ N, 8°30′ E 222
Kanonji, *Japan* 34°7′ N, 133°38′ E 201
Kanopolis, *Kans., U.S.* 38°41′ N, 98°10′ W 90
Kanorado, *Kans., U.S.* 39°20′ N, 102°2′ W 90
Kanosh, *Utah, U.S.* 38°48′ N, 112°26′ W 90
Kanoya, *Japan* 31°21′ N, 130°51′ E 201
Kanpur, *India* 26°25′ N, 80°19′ E 197
Kansanshi, *Zambia* 12°5′ S, 26°22′ E 224
Kansas, *Ill., U.S.* 39°32′ N, 87°56′ W 102
Kansas, adm. division, *Kans., U.S.* 38°7′ N, 100°3′ W 82
Kansas City, *Mo., U.S.* 39°4′ N, 94°33′ W 82
Kansas, river, *Kans., U.S.* 39°18′ N, 96°32′ W 80
Kansk, *Russ.* 56°6′ N, 95°41′ E 160
Kant, *Kyrg.* 42°52′ N, 74°55′ E 184
Kantang, *Thai.* 7°24′ N, 99°31′ E 196
Kantankufri, *Ghana* 7°49′ N, 2°118′ W 222
Kantara Castle, site, *Northern Cyprus, Cyprus* 35°23′ N, 33°53′ E 194
Kantchari, *Burkina Faso* 12°32′ N, 1°33′ E 222
Kanté, *Togo* 9°56′ N, 1°1′ E 222
Kantemirovka, *Russ.* 49°43′ N, 39°53′ E 158
Kanuma, *Japan* 36°33′ N, 139°45′ E 201
Kanyato, *Tanzania* 4°28′ S, 30°15′ E 224
Kanye, *Botswana* 25°0′ S, 25°19′ E 227
Kaohsiung, *Taiwan, China* 22°41′ N, 120°20′ E 198
Kaokoland, *Namibia* 19°17′ S, 13°48′ E 220
Kaolack, *Senegal* 14°11′ N, 16°3′ W 222
Kaoma, *Zambia* 14°49′ S, 24°47′ E 224
Kaongeshi, river, *Dem. Rep. of the Congo* 7°48′ S, 22°22′ E 218
Kaouar, *Niger* 19°41′ N, 12°17′ E 222
Kap Farvel see Nunap Isua, *Den.* 59°20′ N, 43°43′ W 106
Kapalala, *Zambia* 12°24′ S, 29°22′ E 224
Kapan, *Arm.* 39°11′ N, 46°23′ E 195
Kapanga, *Dem. Rep. of the Congo* 8°23′ S, 22°35′ E 218
Kapatu, *Zambia* 9°45′ S, 30°45′ E 224
Kapedo, *Kenya* 1°9′ N, 36°3′ E 224
Kapela, *Croatia* 44°50′ N, 15°10′ E 156
Kapellen, *Belg.* 51°20′ N, 4°25′ E 167
Kapenguria, *Kenya* 1°15′ N, 35°6′ E 224
Kapıdağı, peak, *Turk.* 40°26′ N, 27°43′ E 156
Kapikik Lake, *Can.* 51°30′ N, 92°24′ W 110
Kapili, river, *Dem. Rep. of the Congo* 3°45′ N, 27°51′ E 224
Kapingamarangi Atoll, *North Pacific Ocean* 0°43′ N, 152°44′ E 238
Kapiri Mposhi, *Zambia* 14°0′ S, 28°40′ E 224
Kapisillit, *Den.* 64°23′ N, 50°19′ W 106
Kapiskau, river, *Can.* 52°0′ N, 84°33′ W 110
Kapit, *Malaysia* 1°55′ N, 112°57′ E 192
Kaplan, *La., U.S.* 29°59′ N, 92°18′ W 96
Kaplice, *Czech Rep.* 48°44′ N, 14°28′ E 152
Kapoeta, *Sudan* 4°45′ N, 33°35′ E 224
Kapoho Crater, *Hawai'i, U.S.* 19°29′ N, 154°53′ W 99
Kapombo, *Dem. Rep. of the Congo* 10°39′ S, 23°27′ E 224
Kaposvár, *Hung.* 46°22′ N, 17°47′ E 168
Kappeln, *Ger.* 54°40′ N, 9°56′ E 150
Kappelshamn, *Sw.* 57°50′ N, 18°45′ E 166
Kapsabet, *Kenya* 0°10′ N, 35°8′ E 224
Kapsan, *N. Korea* 41°4′ N, 128°19′ E 200
Kapsowar, *Kenya* 0°57′ N, 35°35′ E 224
Kapterko, spring, *Chad* 16°50′ N, 23°12′ E 226
Kaptol, *Croatia* 45°25′ N, 17°42′ E 168
Kapuāiwa Coconut Grove, site, *Hawai'i, U.S.* 21°5′ N, 157°6′ W 99
Kapuas, river, *Indonesia* 0°28′ N, 110°18′ E 192
Kapulo, *Dem. Rep. of the Congo* 8°18′ S, 29°11′ E 224
Kapuskasing, *Can.* 49°24′ N, 82°24′ W 82
Kapustin Yar, *Russ.* 48°35′ N, 45°45′ E 158
Kaputirr, *Kenya* 2°3′ N, 35°27′ E 224
Kapuvár, *Hung.* 47°35′ N, 17°2′ E 168
Kapydzhik, peak, *Arm.* 39°9′ N, 45°59′ E 195
Kara Balta, *Kyrg.* 42°48′ N, 73°52′ E 184
Kara Burun, *Turk.* 36°40′ N, 31°40′ E 156
Kara Burun, *Turk.* 38°41′ N, 26°21′ E 156
Kara Dağ, peak, *Turk.* 37°40′ N, 43°33′ E 195
Kara Dağ, peak, *Turk.* 37°22′ N, 33°5′ E 156
Kara, river, *Russ.* 69°10′ N, 65°11′ E 246
Kara Sea 78°26′ N, 78°5′ E 160
Karabash, *Russ.* 55°27′ N, 60°19′ E 154
Karabekaul, *Turkm.* 38°25′ N, 64°13′ E 197
Karabiga, *Turk.* 40°24′ N, 27°16′ E 158
Karabogaz (Bekdash), *Turkm.* 41°32′ N, 52°35′ E 158
Karabudakhkent, *Russ.* 42°42′ N, 47°37′ E 195
Karabük, *Turk.* 41°12′ N, 32°36′ E 156
Karaburun, *Alban.* 40°21′ N, 19°4′ E 156
Karaca Dağ, peak, *Turk.* 37°40′ N, 39°50′ E 195
Karacabey, *Turk.* 40°12′ N, 28°20′ E 156
Karacadağ, *Turk.* 37°43′ N, 39°39′ E 195
Karacaköy, *Turk.* 41°24′ N, 28°21′ E 156
Karacasu, *Turk.* 37°43′ N, 28°35′ E 156
Karachala, *Azerb.* 39°48′ N, 48°56′ E 195
Karachayevo-Cherkesiya, adm. division, *Russ.* 43°42′ N, 40°40′ E 195
Karachayevsk, *Russ.* 43°46′ N, 41°55′ E 195
Karachev, *Russ.* 53°3′ N, 35°0′ E 154
Karachi, *Pak.* 24°49′ N, 67°2′ E 186
Karád, *Hung.* 46°40′ N, 17°50′ E 168
Karadag, *Azerb.* 40°17′ N, 49°34′ E 195
Karadžica, *Maced.* 41°54′ N, 21°14′ E 168
Karaga, *Ghana* 9°54′ N, 0°29′ E 222
Karaghbyur (Füzuli), *Azerb.* 39°34′ N, 47°6′ E 195
Karaginskiy, Ostrov, island, *Russ.* 57°53′ N, 163°44′ E 160
Karagosh, Gora, peak, *Russ.* 51°41′ N, 89°17′ E 184
Karahallı, *Turk.* 38°19′ N, 29°31′ E 156
Karahüyük, *Turk.* 37°47′ N, 32°25′ E 156
Karaidel', *Russ.* 55°50′ N, 56°35′ E 154
Karaidel'skiy, *Russ.* 55°50′ N, 57°2′ E 154
Karaikal, *India* 10°56′ N, 79°48′ E 188
Karaisalı, *Turk.* 37°15′ N, 35°2′ E 156
Karaj, *Iran* 35°51′ N, 50°57′ E 186
Karakaralong, Kepulauan, islands, *Philippine Sea* 4°51′ N, 125°34′ E 203
Karakax, river, *China* 36°39′ N, 78°58′ E 184
Karakeçi, *Turk.* 37°26′ N, 39°27′ E 195
Karakoçan, *Turk.* 38°56′ N, 40°2′ E 195
Kara-Köl, *Kyrg.* 41°35′ N, 72°38′ E 197
Karakol, *Kyrg.* 42°27′ N, 78°17′ E 190
Kara-Koo, *Kyrg.* 42°13′ N, 76°36′ E 184
Karakoram Pass, *China* 35°32′ N, 77°52′ E 188
Karakoro, river, *Mauritania* 15°22′ N, 11°47′ W 222
Karakorum see Har Horin, ruin(s), *Mongolia* 47°14′ N, 102°43′ E 198
Karaköse see Ağrı, *Turk.* 39°43′ N, 43°3′ E 195
Karakul', *Taj.* 39°0′ N, 73°34′ E 197
Karakulino, *Russ.* 56°2′ N, 53°43′ E 154
Karakuwisa, *Namibia* 18°54′ S, 19°40′ E 220
Karam, *Russ.* 55°14′ N, 107°37′ E 190
Karaman, *Turk.* 37°10′ N, 33°12′ E 156
Karamay, *China* 45°30′ N, 84°51′ E 184
Karamea, *N.Z.* 41°16′ S, 172°8′ E 240
Karamiran, river, *China* 37°12′ N, 85°3′ E 188
Karamiran Shankou, pass, *China* 36°18′ N, 87°4′ E 188
Karamken, *Russ.* 60°25′ N, 151°27′ E 173
Karamyshevo, *Russ.* 57°45′ N, 28°41′ E 166
Karan, *Serb.* 43°54′ N, 19°53′ E 168
Karan, oil field, *Saudi Arabia* 27°41′ N, 49°45′ E 196
Karapınar, *Turk.* 37°41′ N, 33°33′ E 156
Kara-Say, *Kyrg.* 41°34′ N, 77°57′ E 184
Karasburg, *Namibia* 28°1′ S, 18°42′ E 227
Karašica, river, *Croatia* 45°44′ N, 17°41′ E 156
Karasino, *Russ.* 66°46′ N, 86°56′ E 169
Karasu, *Taj.* 37°57′ N, 73°57′ E 197
Karasu, *Turk.* 41°6′ N, 30°39′ E 156
Karasu, river, *Turk.* 39°54′ N, 40°4′ E 195
Karasu, river, *Turk.* 38°46′ N, 43°37′ E 195
Karasuk, *Russ.* 53°42′ N, 78°4′ E 184
Karasuk Hills, *Kenya* 2°16′ N, 34°57′ E 224
Kara-Suu, *Kyrg.* 41°5′ N, 75°34′ E 184
Karataş, *Turk.* 36°34′ N, 35°22′ E 156
Karathuri, *Myanmar* 10°56′ N, 98°46′ E 202
Karatsu, *Japan* 33°26′ N, 129°57′ E 201
Karaul, *Russ.* 70°5′ N, 83°22′ E 169
Karauli, *India* 26°31′ N, 76°58′ E 197
Kara-Ünkür, *Kyrg.* 41°43′ N, 75°45′ E 184
Karavás, *Gr.* 36°20′ N, 22°57′ E 156

Karavónissia, islands, *Aegean Sea* 35°54′ N, 25°36′ E 156
Karavostasi, *Northern Cyprus, Cyprus* 35°8′ N, 32°49′ E 194
Karawa, *Dem. Rep. of the Congo* 3°14′ N, 20°17′ E 218
Karawanken, *Aust.* 46°31′ N, 13°54′ E 156
Karayazı, *Turk.* 39°40′ N, 42°8′ E 195
Karayün, *Turk.* 39°38′ N, 37°19′ E 156
Karbalā', *Iraq* 32°36′ N, 44°2′ E 180
Kårböle, *Nor.* 61°58′ N, 15°17′ E 152
Karcag, *Hung.* 47°18′ N, 20°54′ E 168
Kardašova Řečice, *Czech Rep.* 49°10′ N, 14°52′ E 152
Kardítsa, *Gr.* 39°20′ N, 21°56′ E 180
Kardiva Channel 4°49′ N, 72°13′ E 188
Kärdla, *Est.* 58°59′ N, 22°42′ E 166
Kareliya, adm. division, *Russ.* 63°15′ N, 33°53′ E 166
Karel'skaya, *Russ.* 62°11′ N, 39°27′ E 154
Karem Shalom, *Israel* 31°13′ N, 34°16′ E 194
Karema, *Tanzania* 6°48′ S, 30°24′ E 224
Karera, *India* 25°28′ N, 78°10′ E 197
Karesuando, *Nor.* 68°26′ N, 22°26′ E 152
Karêt, region, *Africa* 23°35′ N, 9°38′ W 214
Kargānrūd, *Iran* 37°52′ N, 48°56′ E 195
Kargasok, *Russ.* 58°58′ N, 80°50′ E 169
Kargat, *Russ.* 55°10′ N, 80°21′ E 184
Kargı, *Turk.* 41°8′ N, 34°29′ E 156
Kargil, *India* 34°32′ N, 76°7′ E 186
Kargilik see Yecheng, *China* 37°52′ N, 77°31′ E 184
Kargopol', *Russ.* 61°30′ N, 38°53′ E 154
Karhula, *Fin.* 60°30′ N, 26°55′ E 166
Kari, *Nig.* 11°12′ N, 10°35′ E 222
Kariá, *Gr.* 39°59′ N, 22°23′ E 156
Karia, *Gr.* 38°45′ N, 20°38′ E 156
Kariba, *Zimb.* 16°28′ S, 28°51′ E 224
Kariba, Lake, *Zimb.* 17°27′ S, 25°50′ E 207
Karibib, *Namibia* 21°56′ S, 15°52′ E 227
Karijini National Park, *Austral.* 22°48′ S, 117°59′ E 238
Karikari, Cape, *N.Z.* 34°49′ S, 173°25′ E 240
Karima, *Sudan* 18°30′ N, 31°50′ E 182
Karimata, Kepulauan, islands, *Indian Ocean* 1°31′ S, 106°26′ E 192
Karimganj, *India* 24°44′ N, 92°22′ E 188
Karimnagar, *India* 18°25′ N, 79°7′ E 188
Kariniemi, *Fin.* 65°36′ N, 27°56′ E 152
Karis (Karjaa), *Fin.* 60°4′ N, 23°39′ E 166
Karitane, *N.Z.* 45°39′ S, 170°38′ E 240
Kariya, *Japan* 34°57′ N, 137°0′ E 201
Karizak, *Afghan.* 32°26′ N, 61°28′ E 186
Karjaa see Karis, *Fin.* 60°4′ N, 23°39′ E 166
Karjala, *Fin.* 60°46′ N, 22°4′ E 166
Karkaar, *Somalia* 9°42′ N, 48°36′ E 216
Karkar, island, *P.N.G.* 4°49′ S, 145°4′ E 192
Karkas, Kūh-e, peak, *Iran* 33°26′ N, 51°41′ E 180
Karkkila, *Fin.* 60°31′ N, 24°7′ E 166
Karkku, *Fin.* 61°23′ N, 22°57′ E 166
Karkoj, *Sudan* 12°57′ N, 34°2′ E 182
Kärkölä, *Fin.* 60°54′ N, 25°14′ E 166
Karkūk (Kirkūk), *Iraq* 35°27′ N, 44°23′ E 180
Karlholm, *Sw.* 60°30′ N, 17°34′ E 166
Karlino, *Pol.* 54°2′ N, 15°53′ E 152
Karlıova, *Turk.* 39°16′ N, 41°0′ E 195
Karlovac, *Croatia* 45°28′ N, 15°33′ E 156
Karlovarský, adm. division, *Czech Rep.* 49°55′ N, 12°2′ E 152
Karlovka, *Ukr.* 49°29′ N, 35°9′ E 158
Karlovy Vary, *Czech Rep.* 50°13′ N, 12°52′ E 152
Karlsborg, *Nor.* 65°48′ N, 23°16′ E 152
Karlsborg, *Nor.* 58°31′ N, 14°29′ E 152
Karlskrona, *Nor.* 56°9′ N, 15°33′ E 152
Karlsøy, *Nor.* 70°0′ N, 19°54′ E 152
Karlsøyvær, islands, *Norwegian Sea* 67°35′ N, 12°59′ E 152
Karlsruhe, *Ger.* 49°0′ N, 8°24′ E 150
Karlstad, *Minn., U.S.* 48°33′ N, 96°33′ W 90
Karluk, *Alas., U.S.* 57°25′ N, 154°33′ W 98
Karma, *Belarus* 53°5′ N, 30°51′ E 154
Karmana, *Uzb.* 40°9′ N, 65°20′ E 197
Karmir Blur, ruin(s), *Arm.* 40°7′ N, 44°22′ E 195
Karnack, *Tex., U.S.* 32°39′ N, 94°10′ W 103
Karnal, *India* 29°41′ N, 77°1′ E 197
Karnataka, adm. division, *India* 13°56′ N, 74°36′ E 188
Karnes City, *Tex., U.S.* 28°52′ N, 97°54′ W 96
Karoi, *Zimb.* 16°50′ S, 29°39′ E 224
Karokh, *Afghan.* 34°33′ N, 62°30′ E 186
Kārokh, peak, *Iraq* 36°28′ N, 44°36′ E 195
Karonga, *Malawi* 9°55′ S, 33°54′ E 224
Karoo National Park, *S. Af.* 32°30′ S, 21°51′ E 227
Karor, *Pak.* 31°14′ N, 71°0′ E 186
Karora, *Sudan* 17°41′ N, 38°17′ E 182
Karou, *Mali* 15°6′ N, 0°37′ E 222
Karpasia Peninsula, *Northern Cyprus, Cyprus* 35°21′ N, 33°59′ E 194
Kárpathos, island, *Gr.* 35°15′ N, 27°9′ E 180
Karpinsk, *Russ.* 59°45′ N, 60°0′ E 154
Karpogory, *Russ.* 64°1′ N, 44°33′ E 154
Kärrgruvan, *Nor.* 60°4′ N, 15°56′ E 152
Kars, *Turk.* 40°34′ N, 43°10′ E 180
Kärsämäki, *Fin.* 63°58′ N, 25°44′ E 152
Kārsava, *Latv.* 56°47′ N, 27°40′ E 166
Karsiyang, *India* 26°49′ N, 88°17′ E 197
Karskiye Vorota, Proliv 70°38′ N, 59°23′ E 246
Karsun, *Russ.* 54°10′ N, 47°1′ E 154
Kartal, *Turk.* 40°54′ N, 29°10′ E 156
Kartaly, *Russ.* 53°5′ N, 60°35′ E 154
Kartayel', *Russ.* 64°29′ N, 53°12′ E 154
Karttula, *Fin.* 62°50′ N, 27°7′ E 152
Kartung, *Senegal* 13°6′ N, 16°39′ W 222
Karubwe, *Zambia* 15°8′ S, 28°22′ E 224
Karufa, *Indonesia* 3°47′ S, 133°17′ E 192
Karula National Park, *Est.* 57°40′ N, 26°23′ E 166
Karumwa, *Tanzania* 3°12′ S, 32°37′ E 224
Kārūn, river, *Iran* 30°44′ N, 48°16′ E 180
Karuna, *Fin.* 60°15′ N, 22°31′ E 166
Karungu, *Kenya* 0°51′ N, 34°12′ E 224
Karvachar (Kälbäcär), *Azerb.* 40°8′ N, 46°1′ E 195
Karvio, *Fin.* 62°29′ S, 28°38′ E 152
Karwar, *India* 14°47′ N, 74°8′ E 188
Karwi, *India* 25°12′ N, 80°55′ E 197
Karyaí, *Gr.* 40°15′ N, 24°15′ E 156
Kar'yepol'ye, *Russ.* 65°34′ N, 43°42′ E 154
Karymkary, *Russ.* 62°4′ N, 67°38′ E 169
Kas, *Sudan* 12°30′ N, 24°19′ E 216
Kaş, *Turk.* 36°11′ N, 29°37′ E 156
Kas, river, *Russ.* 59°33′ N, 90°5′ E 169
Kas Saar, *Est.* 58°41′ N, 22°52′ E 166
Kasaan, *Alas., U.S.* 55°33′ N, 132°25′ W 108
Kasaba, *Turk.* 36°17′ N, 29°44′ E 156
Kasaba Bay, *Zambia* 8°35′ S, 30°43′ E 224
Kasai, river, *Dem. Rep. of the Congo* 6°48′ S, 20°59′ E 218
Kasaï-Occidental, adm. division, *Dem. Rep. of the Congo* 5°59′ S, 20°39′ E 218
Kasaï-Oriental, adm. division, *Dem. Rep. of the Congo* 4°17′ S, 23°24′ E 218
Kasaji, *Dem. Rep. of the Congo* 10°22′ S, 23°28′ E 224
Kasala, *Fin.* 61°57′ N, 21°21′ E 166
Kasama, *Zambia* 10°13′ S, 31°10′ E 224
Kasane, *Botswana* 17°51′ S, 25°5′ E 224
Kasanga, *Tanzania* 8°27′ S, 31°10′ E 224
Kasanka National Park, *Zambia* 12°48′ S, 29°40′ E 224
Kasar, Ras, *Eritrea* 17°50′ N, 38°34′ E 182
Kasaragod, *India* 12°31′ N, 75°1′ E 188
Kasari, river, *Est.* 58°44′ N, 23°54′ E 166
Kasba Lake, *Can.* 60°2′ N, 103°43′ W 106
Kaseda, *Japan* 31°23′ N, 130°20′ E 201
Kasempa, *Zambia* 13°29′ S, 25°48′ E 224
Kasenga, *Dem. Rep. of the Congo* 10°18′ S, 28°40′ E 224
Kasenye, *Dem. Rep. of the Congo* 1°23′ N, 30°26′ E 224
Kasese, *Dem. Rep. of the Congo* 1°37′ S, 27°13′ E 224
Kasese, *Uganda* 0°10′ N, 30°7′ E 224
Kasganj, *India* 27°48′ N, 78°39′ E 197
Kāshān, *Iran* 34°1′ N, 51°27′ E 180
Kashegelok, *Alas., U.S.* 60°50′ N, 157°48′ W 98
Kashi, *China* 39°31′ N, 75°59′ E 184
Kashima, *Japan* 33°6′ N, 130°5′ E 201
Kashin, *Russ.* 57°18′ N, 37°31′ E 154
Kashipur, *India* 29°11′ N, 78°57′ E 197
Kashira, *Russ.* 54°48′ N, 38°10′ E 154
Kashishibog Lake, *Can.* 49°47′ N, 90°36′ W 94
Kashitu, *Zambia* 13°44′ S, 28°38′ E 224
Kashiwazaki, *Japan* 37°21′ N, 138°33′ E 201
Kashkadar'ya, *Uzb.* 38°55′ N, 65°45′ E 197
Kashkarantsy, *Russ.* 66°21′ N, 35°55′ E 154
Kāshmar, *Iran* 35°13′ N, 58°28′ E 180
Kashmir, region, *Asia* 34°38′ N, 75°56′ E 188
Kashmor, *Pak.* 28°29′ N, 69°34′ E 186
Kashnjet, *Alban.* 41°54′ N, 19°48′ E 168
Kasimov, *Russ.* 54°55′ N, 41°26′ E 154
Kasindi, *Dem. Rep. of the Congo* 2°119′ N, 29°40′ E 224
Kaskas, *Senegal* 16°22′ N, 14°11′ W 222
Kaskaskia, river, *Ill., U.S.* 38°42′ N, 89°26′ W 80
Kaskö (Kaskinen), *Fin.* 62°22′ N, 21°12′ E 152
Kasli, *Russ.* 55°52′ N, 60°45′ E 154
Kaslo, *Can.* 49°54′ N, 116°56′ W 90
Kasmere Lake, *Can.* 59°35′ N, 101°38′ W 108
Kasongo, *Dem. Rep. of the Congo* 4°29′ S, 26°36′ E 224
Kasongo-Lunda, *Dem. Rep. of the Congo* 6°30′ S, 16°49′ E 220
Kaspiysk, *Russ.* 42°51′ N, 47°41′ E 195
Kaspiyskiy, *Russ.* 45°21′ N, 47°21′ E 158
Kasrik see Kırkgeçit, *Turk.* 38°7′ N, 43°27′ E 195
Kassala, *Sudan* 15°25′ N, 36°22′ E 182
Kassala, adm. division, *Sudan* 15°47′ N, 35°39′ E 182
Kassándra, *Gr.* 40°1′ N, 23°7′ E 156
Kassari, spring, *Mauritania* 15°50′ N, 7°54′ W 222
Kassaro, *Mali* 13°0′ N, 8°54′ W 222
Kassel, *Ger.* 51°19′ N, 9°29′ E 167
Kasserine see Qasserine, *Tun.* 35°9′ N, 8°51′ E 156
Kasson, *Minn., U.S.* 44°0′ N, 92°47′ W 94
Kássos, island, *Gr.* 35°11′ N, 26°48′ E 180
Kassouloua, spring, *Niger* 14°29′ N, 11°23′ E 222
Kastamonu, *Turk.* 41°23′ N, 33°45′ E 156
Kaštel Sućurac, *Croatia* 43°32′ N, 16°25′ E 168
Kastellaun, *Ger.* 50°3′ N, 7°25′ E 167
Kastornoye, *Russ.* 51°48′ N, 38°5′ E 158
Kastrossikiá, *Gr.* 39°6′ N, 20°38′ E 156
Kastsyukovichy, *Belarus* 53°19′ N, 32°5′ E 154
Kasulu, *Tanzania* 4°36′ S, 30°6′ E 224
Kasumkent, *Russ.* 41°40′ N, 48°11′ E 195
Kasungu, *Malawi* 13°4′ S, 33°28′ E 224
Kasungu National Park, *Malawi* 12°58′ S, 32°56′ E 224
Kasupe, *Malawi* 15°12′ S, 35°16′ E 224
Kasur, *Pak.* 31°9′ N, 74°26′ E 186
Kata Tjuta (Mount Olga), *Austral.* 25°21′ S, 130°31′ E 230
Kataba, *Zambia* 16°5′ S, 25°6′ E 224
Kataeregi, *Nig.* 9°20′ N, 6°18′ E 222
Katagum, *Nig.* 12°17′ N, 10°21′ E 222
Katahdin, Mount, *Me., U.S.* 45°53′ N, 69°1′ W 94
Katako Kombe, *Dem. Rep. of the Congo* 3°28′ S, 24°21′ E 224
Katal'ga, *Russ.* 59°8′ N, 76°50′ E 169
Katanda, *Russ.* 50°11′ N, 86°14′ E 184
Katanga, adm. division, *Dem. Rep. of the Congo* 8°40′ S, 23°51′ E 220
Katanning, *Austral.* 33°41′ S, 117°33′ E 231
Katav Ivanovsk, *Russ.* 54°45′ N, 58°10′ E 154
Katavi National Park, *Tanzania* 7°21′ S, 30°38′ E 224
Katavía, *Gr.* 35°57′ N, 27°46′ E 156
Katavivanovsk, *Russ.* 54°44′ N, 58°13′ E 184
Katchall Island, *India* 7°40′ N, 92°29′ E 188
Kate, *Tanzania* 7°50′ S, 31°8′ E 224
Katera, *Uganda* 0°55′ N, 31°37′ E 224
Kateríni, *Gr.* 40°15′ N, 22°33′ E 180
Kates Needle, peak, *Can.* 57°2′ N, 132°14′ W 108
Katha, *Myanmar* 24°8′ N, 96°19′ E 188
Katherine, *Austral.* 14°29′ S, 132°20′ E 231
Kathleen, Mount, *Austral.* 23°56′ S, 135°13′ E 230
Kathmandu, *Nepal* 27°46′ N, 85°11′ E 197
Kati, *Mali* 12°44′ N, 8°4′ W 222
Katihar, *India* 25°30′ N, 87°33′ E 197
Katima Mulilo, *Namibia* 17°33′ S, 24°16′ E 224
Katimik Lake, *Can.* 52°51′ N, 99°52′ W 108
Katiola, *Côte d'Ivoire* 8°6′ N, 5°5′ W 222
Kätkäsuvanto, *Fin.* 68°7′ N, 23°20′ E 152
Katlanovo, *Maced.* 41°53′ N, 21°40′ E 168
Katmai, Mount, *Alas., U.S.* 58°10′ N, 155°14′ W 98
Katonah, *N.Y., U.S.* 41°14′ N, 73°42′ W 104
Katondwe, *Zambia* 15°15′ S, 30°12′ E 224
Katonga, river, *Uganda* 3°179′ N, 30°33′ E 224
Katowice, *Pol.* 50°15′ N, 19°1′ E 152
Katrancık Dağı, peak, *Turk.* 37°26′ N, 30°15′ E 156
Katrineholm, *Nor.* 59°0′ N, 16°8′ E 152
Katrovozh, *Russ.* 66°22′ N, 66°9′ E 169
Katsina, *Nig.* 13°0′ N, 7°38′ E 222
Katsina Ala, river, *Nig.* 7°51′ N, 8°33′ E 222
Katsumoto, *Japan* 33°50′ N, 129°42′ E 200
Katsuta, *Japan* 36°23′ N, 140°32′ E 201
Katsuura, *Japan* 35°9′ N, 140°18′ E 201
Katsuyama, *Japan* 35°5′ N, 133°40′ E 201
Katsuyama, *Japan* 36°4′ N, 136°31′ E 201
Kattankudi, *Sri Lanka* 7°34′ N, 81°48′ E 188
Kattegat 55°53′ N, 10°43′ E 150
Katthammarsvik, *Sw.* 57°25′ N, 18°49′ E 166
Kattisavan, *Nor.* 64°46′ N, 18°8′ E 152
Kattskill Bay, *N.Y., U.S.* 43°28′ N, 73°38′ W 104
Katul, Jebel, peak, *Sudan* 14°13′ N, 29°19′ E 226
Katumbi, *Zambia* 10°49′ S, 33°30′ E 220
Katun', river, *Russ.* 51°28′ N, 86°4′ E 184
Katwa, *India* 23°34′ N, 88°6′ E 197
Katwe, *Uganda* 0°10′ N, 29°51′ E 224
Katwijk aan Zee, *Neth.* 52°12′ N, 4°25′ E 163
Kauaʻi, island, *Hawaiʻi, U.S.* 22°7′ N, 160°15′ W 99
Kauakaiakaola Heiau, site, *Hawaiʻi, U.S.* 19°37′ N, 156°1′ W 99
Kaub, *Ger.* 50°5′ N, 7°46′ E 163
Kaugama, *Nig.* 12°28′ N, 9°46′ E 222
Kauhajoki, *Fin.* 62°24′ N, 22°8′ E 154
Kauhako Crater, peak, *Hawaiʻi, U.S.* 21°11′ N, 157°1′ W 99
Kauhava, *Fin.* 63°5′ N, 23°2′ E 152
Kaukonen, *Fin.* 67°29′ N, 24°52′ E 152
Kaʻula, island, *Hawaiʻi, U.S.* 21°27′ N, 160°43′ W 99
Kauliranta, *Fin.* 66°27′ N, 23°40′ E 152
Kaulu Paoa Heiau, site, *Hawaiʻi, U.S.* 22°12′ N, 159°38′ W 99
Kaunā Point, *Hawaiʻi, U.S.* 18°59′ N, 156°18′ W 99
Kaunas, *Lith.* 54°53′ N, 23°54′ E 166
Kaunata, *Latv.* 56°19′ N, 27°33′ E 166
Kaunatava, *Lith.* 55°58′ N, 22°32′ E 166
Kauniainen see Grankulla, *Fin.* 60°11′ N, 24°43′ E 152
Kaunolū, site, *Hawaiʻi, U.S.* 20°43′ N, 157°0′ W 99
Kaʻūpūlehu, site, *Hawaiʻi, U.S.* 19°49′ N, 156°2′ W 99
Kaura-Namoda, *Nig.* 12°36′ N, 6°35′ E 222
Kauru, *Nig.* 10°33′ N, 8°11′ E 222
Kavacha, *Russ.* 60°22′ N, 169°55′ E 160
Kavak, *Turk.* 41°4′ N, 36°2′ E 156
Kavála, *Gr.* 40°57′ N, 24°24′ E 180
Kavali, *India* 14°55′ N, 79°59′ E 188
Kavaratti, *India* 10°34′ N, 72°38′ E 188
Kavarna, *Bulg.* 43°26′ N, 28°19′ E 158
Kavarskas, *Lith.* 55°26′ N, 24°55′ E 166
Kavieng, *P.N.G.* 2°41′ S, 150°59′ E 238
Kavkaz, *Russ.* 45°22′ N, 36°39′ E 156
Kavungo, *Angola* 11°32′ S, 23°2′ E 220
Kawagoe, *Japan* 35°54′ N, 139°29′ E 201
Kawaihoa Point, *Hawaiʻi, U.S.* 21°42′ N, 160°13′ W 99
Kawakawa, *N.Z.* 35°25′ S, 174°5′ E 240
Kawambwa, *Zambia* 9°49′ S, 29°5′ E 224
Kawanishi, *Japan* 38°0′ N, 140°3′ E 201
Kawanoe, *Japan* 34°0′ N, 133°35′ E 201
Kawardha, *India* 22°1′ N, 81°14′ E 197
Kawasaki, *Japan* 35°30′ N, 139°43′ E 201
Kawashiri Misaki, *Japan* 34°23′ N, 130°41′ E 200
Kawaweogama Lake, *Can.* 50°9′ N, 91°3′ W 110
Kaweah, Mount, *Calif., U.S.* 36°31′ N, 118°32′ W 101
Kaweka, peak, *N.Z.* 39°20′ S, 176°18′ E 240
Kawela Place of Refuge, site, *Hawaiʻi, U.S.* 21°4′ N, 157°1′ W 99
Kawhia, *N.Z.* 38°4′ S, 174°48′ E 240
Kawich Peak, *Nev., U.S.* 37°56′ N, 116°33′ W 90
Kawich Range, *Nev., U.S.* 37°53′ N, 116°38′ W 90
Kawlinn, *Myanmar* 23°46′ N, 95°41′ E 202
Kawnipi Lake, *Can.* 48°27′ N, 91°30′ W 94
Kawthoung, *Myanmar* 9°59′ N, 98°32′ E 202
Kax, river, *China* 43°44′ N, 84°4′ E 184
Kay, *Russ.* 59°57′ N, 53°1′ E 154
Kaya, *Burkina Faso* 13°5′ N, 1°6′ W 222
Kayambi, *Zambia* 9°28′ S, 31°59′ E 224
Kayan-Mentarang National Park, *Indonesia* 2°38′ N, 115°12′ E 238
Kayapınar, *Turk.* 37°32′ N, 41°12′ E 195
Kayar, *Senegal* 14°55′ N, 16°52′ W 222
Kayasula, *Russ.* 44°17′ N, 45°0′ E 158
Kaycee, *Wyo., U.S.* 43°42′ N, 106°39′ W 90
Kayenzi, *Tanzania* 3°16′ S, 32°37′ E 224
Kayes, *Congo* 4°12′ S, 13°10′ E 218
Kayes, *Congo* 4°25′ S, 11°39′ E 218
Kayes, *Mali* 14°26′ N, 11°28′ W 222
Kaymaz, *Turk.* 39°31′ N, 31°10′ E 156
Kaynar, *Turk.* 38°53′ N, 36°25′ E 156
Käyrämo, *Fin.* 66°57′ N, 26°17′ E 152
Kaysatskoye, *Russ.* 49°43′ N, 46°46′ E 158
Kayser Gebergte, *Suriname* 3°5′ N, 57°0′ W 130
Kayseri, *Turk.* 38°41′ N, 35°30′ E 156
Kayyerhan, *Russ.* 69°12′ N, 83°53′ E 169
Kaz Dağı, peak, *Turk.* 39°41′ N, 26°47′ E 156
Kazachka, *Russ.* 51°27′ N, 43°57′ E 158
Kazach'ye, *Russ.* 70°40′ N, 136°18′ E 160
Kazakh Uplands, *Asia* 47°30′ N, 69°46′ E 184
Kazakhstan 48°18′ N, 63°42′ E 184
Kazan', *Russ.* 55°45′ N, 49°9′ E 154
Kazan Rettō see Volcano Islands, *Philippine Sea* 23°11′ N, 139°38′ E 190
Kazan, river, *Can.* 63°10′ N, 98°16′ W 72
Kazanlŭk, *Bulg.* 42°35′ N, 25°24′ E 180
Kazanskaya, *Russ.* 49°50′ N, 41°9′ E 158
Kazanskoye, *Russ.* 57°9′ N, 49°9′ E 154
Kazarman, *Kyrg.* 41°22′ N, 74°3′ E 197
Kazbek, peak, *Ga.* 42°40′ N, 44°29′ E 195
Kāzerūn, *Iran* 29°35′ N, 51°37′ E 196
Kazhim, *Russ.* 60°20′ N, 51°36′ E 154
Kazima, *Cen. Af. Rep.* 5°14′ N, 26°13′ E 224
Kazimoto, *Tanzania* 9°6′ S, 36°50′ E 224
Kazlų Rūda, *Lith.* 54°44′ N, 23°26′ E 166
Kaztalovka, *Kaz.* 49°45′ N, 48°41′ E 158
Kazumba, *Dem. Rep. of the Congo* 6°26′ S, 21°59′ E 218
Kazyany, *Belarus* 55°18′ N, 26°51′ E 166
Kazym Mys, *Russ.* 64°45′ N, 65°52′ E 169
Kazym, river, *Russ.* 63°54′ N, 67°41′ E 169
Ké Macina, *Mali* 14°1′ N, 5°22′ W 222
Kéa, *Gr.* 37°38′ N, 24°20′ E 156
Kéa, island, *Gr.* 37°28′ N, 24°23′ E 180
Kea, Mauna, peak, *Hawaiʻi, U.S.* 19°49′ N, 155°31′ W 99
Keaʻau Ranch, site, *Hawaiʻi, U.S.* 19°37′ N, 155°2′ W 99
Keams Canyon, *Ariz., U.S.* 35°48′ N, 110°12′ W 92
Kearney, *Can.* 45°32′ N, 79°13′ W 94
Kearney, *Nebr., U.S.* 40°41′ N, 99°5′ W 90
Kearny, *Ariz., U.S.* 33°3′ N, 110°54′ W 92
Kearsarge, *Mich., U.S.* 47°16′ N, 88°26′ W 94
Keatchie, *La., U.S.* 32°9′ N, 93°55′ W 103
Keauhou Landing, site, *Hawaiʻi, U.S.* 19°16′ N, 155°17′ W 99
Kebbe, *Nig.* 12°4′ N, 4°46′ E 222
Kébémer, *Senegal* 15°24′ N, 16°27′ W 222
Kebili, *Tun.* 33°42′ N, 8°59′ E 214
Kebkabiya, *Sudan* 13°35′ N, 24°5′ E 216
Keble, peak, *Nor.* 67°21′ N, 20°10′ E 152
Kebnekaise, peak, *Nor.* 67°52′ N, 18°23′ E 152
K'ebrī Dehar, *Eth.* 6°46′ N, 44°10′ E 218
Kecel, *Hung.* 46°30′ N, 19°16′ E 168
Kechika, river, *Can.* 59°5′ N, 127°25′ W 108
Keçiborlu, *Turk.* 37°56′ N, 30°18′ E 156
Kecskemét, *Hung.* 46°54′ N, 19°42′ E 168
Kėdainiai, *Lith.* 55°17′ N, 23°56′ E 166
Kedarnath, *India* 30°44′ N, 79°4′ E 197
Kédédéssé, *Chad* 11°8′ N, 16°44′ E 216
Kedgwick, river, *Can.* 48°2′ N, 68°7′ W 94
Kedia Hill, *Botswana* 21°25′ S, 24°28′ E 227
Kediri, *Indonesia* 7°50′ S, 111°54′ E 192
Kédougou, *Senegal* 12°35′ N, 12°13′ W 222
Kedvavom, *Russ.* 64°13′ N, 53°27′ E 154
Keele Peak, *Can.* 63°23′ N, 130°26′ W 98
Keele, river, *Can.* 64°3′ N, 127°57′ W 98
Keeler, *Calif., U.S.* 36°29′ N, 117°53′ W 101
Keeler, *Mich., U.S.* 42°6′ N, 86°9′ W 102
Keeley Lake, *Can.* 54°51′ N, 108°44′ W 108
Keelung see Chilung, *Taiwan, China* 25°6′ N, 121°45′ E 198
Keen, Mount, *U.K.* 56°56′ N, 3°5′ W 150
Keene, *Calif., U.S.* 35°13′ N, 118°35′ W 101
Keene, *N.H., U.S.* 42°55′ N, 72°17′ W 104
Keene, *N.Y., U.S.* 44°15′ N, 73°48′ W 104
Keep R. National Park, *Austral.* 15°55′ S, 128°49′ E 238
Keeper Hill, *Ire.* 52°44′ N, 8°21′ W 150
Keeseville, *N.Y., U.S.* 44°30′ N, 73°30′ W 104
Keesler Air Force Base, *Miss., U.S.* 30°22′ N, 89°0′ W 103
Keetmanshoop, *Namibia* 26°35′ S, 18°7′ E 227
Keewatin, *Can.* 49°45′ N, 94°32′ W 90
Keezhik Lake, *Can.* 51°40′ N, 89°8′ W 110
Kefaloniá (Cephalonia), adm. division, *Gr.* 38°22′ N, 20°3′ E 156
Kefar 'Ezyon, *West Bank, Israel* 31°37′ N, 35°5′ E 194
Kefar Rosh ha Niqra, *Israel* 33°4′ N, 35°6′ E 194
Kefar Sava, *Israel* 32°10′ N, 34°53′ E 194
Kefar Yona, *Israel* 32°19′ N, 34°56′ E 194
Keffi, *Nig.* 8°51′ N, 7°49′ E 222
Keflavík, *Ice.* 63°58′ N, 22°41′ W 143
Keg River, *Can.* 57°43′ N, 117°35′ W 108
Kegaska, Lac, lake, *Can.* 50°17′ N, 61°56′ W 111
Kegen, *Kaz.* 43°1′ N, 79°13′ E 184
Kegha, *Eth.* 5°5′ N, 36°48′ E 224
Keheili, *Sudan* 19°24′ N, 32°49′ E 182
Kehlstein, peak, *Ger.* 47°35′ N, 12°57′ E 156
Kehra, *Est.* 59°19′ N, 25°18′ E 166
Keighley, *U.K.* 53°51′ N, 1°55′ W 162
Keikyä, *Fin.* 61°15′ N, 22°42′ E 166
Keila, *Est.* 59°17′ N, 24°23′ E 166
Keila, river, *Est.* 59°18′ N, 24°28′ E 166
Keimoes, *S. Af.* 28°40′ S, 20°55′ E 227
Keïta, *Niger* 14°40′ N, 5°44′ E 222
Keitele, lake, *Fin.* 62°56′ N, 25°33′ E 152
Keithley Creek, *Can.* 52°44′ N, 121°26′ W 108
Keithsburg, *Mo., U.S.* 41°5′ N, 90°56′ W 94
Keizer, *Oreg., U.S.* 44°59′ N, 123°2′ W 90
Kejimkujik National Park, *Can.* 43°42′ N, 64°46′ W 111
Kekerengu, *N.Z.* 42°0′ S, 174°0′ E 240
Kékes, peak, *Hung.* 47°51′ N, 19°59′ E 168
Kekurskiy, Mys, *Russ.* 69°55′ N, 32°9′ E 152
K'elafo, *Eth.* 5°35′ N, 44°11′ E 218
Kelai, island, *Maldives* 6°43′ N, 73°12′ E 188
Kélakam, *Niger* 13°32′ N, 11°48′ E 222
Kelamet, *Eritrea* 16°4′ N, 38°41′ E 182
Kelang, *Malaysia* 3°3′ N, 101°26′ E 196

Kelberg, *Ger.* 50°17′ N, 6°55′ E 167
Keld, *U.K.* 54°24′ N, 2°11′ W 162
Kelebia, *Hung.* 46°10′ N, 19°37′ E 168
Keleft, *Afghan.* 37°18′ N, 66°15′ E 186
Kelkit, *Turk.* 40°7′ N, 39°26′ E 195
Kelkit, river, *Turk.* 40°0′ N, 38°38′ E 180
Kellé, *Congo* 0°8′ N, 14°31′ E 218
Kéllé, *Niger* 14°15′ N, 10°9′ E 222
Kellen, *Ger.* 51°47′ N, 6°9′ E 167
Keller Lake, *Can.* 63°22′ N, 120°0′ W 246
Kellet, Cape, *Can.* 71°57′ N, 130°22′ W 106
Kellett Strait 75°40′ N, 120°58′ W 106
Kelleys Island, *Ohio, U.S.* 41°37′ N, 82°40′ W 102
Kelliher, *Can.* 51°15′ N, 103°46′ W 90
Kello, *Fin.* 65°6′ N, 25°23′ E 152
Kellog, *Russ.* 62°27′ N, 86°21′ E 169
Kellogora, *Russ.* 64°19′ N, 32°14′ E 152
Kellojärvi, lake, *Fin.* 64°13′ N, 28°24′ E 152
Kelly, *La., U.S.* 31°58′ N, 92°11′ W 103
Kelly Air Force Base, *Tex., U.S.* 29°19′ N, 98°38′ W 92
Kelmė, *Lith.* 55°38′ N, 22°55′ E 166
Kelmis, *Belg.* 50°42′ N, 6°0′ E 167
Kélo, *Chad* 9°18′ N, 15°47′ E 216
Kelottijärvi, *Fin.* 68°31′ N, 22°1′ E 152
Kelowna, *Can.* 49°51′ N, 119°28′ W 106
Kelsall, Mount, *Can.* 59°48′ N, 136°28′ W 108
Kelsey, *Can.* 56°2′ N, 96°31′ W 108
Kelsey Creek, river, *Can.* 57°47′ N, 94°17′ W 108
Kelso, *Calif., U.S.* 35°1′ N, 115°39′ W 101
Kelso, *N.Z.* 45°56′ S, 169°16′ E 240
Kelso, *Wash., U.S.* 46°8′ N, 122°54′ W 100
Keltie, Cape, *Antarctica* 65°44′ S, 135°58′ E 248
Keluang, *Malaysia* 2°3′ N, 103°20′ E 196
Kelvä, *Fin.* 63°3′ N, 30°6′ E 152
Kelvington, *Can.* 52°10′ N, 103°31′ W 108
Kelyexed, *Somalia* 8°45′ N, 49°11′ E 216
Kem′, *Russ.* 64°59′ N, 34°31′ E 152
Kemah, *Turk.* 39°35′ N, 39°2′ E 195
Kemano, *Can.* 53°33′ N, 127°56′ W 108
Kemasik, *Malaysia* 4°26′ N, 103°26′ E 196
Kembé, *Cen. Af. Rep.* 4°35′ N, 21°52′ E 218
Kembolcha, *Eth.* 11°1′ N, 39°46′ E 224
Kemboma, *Gabon* 0°40′ N, 13°31′ E 218
Kemer, *Kaz.* 49°32′ N, 54°58′ E 158
Kemer, *Turk.* 40°24′ N, 27°2′ E 156
Kemer, *Turk.* 36°37′ N, 29°19′ E 156
Kemer, *Turk.* 36°34′ N, 30°34′ E 156
Ķemeri, *Latv.* 56°56′ N, 23°28′ E 166
Kemerovo, *Russ.* 55°17′ N, 86°11′ E 184
Kemeten, *Aust.* 47°14′ N, 16°9′ E 168
Kemi, *Fin.* 65°43′ N, 24°49′ E 160
Kemijärvi, *Fin.* 66°42′ N, 27°23′ E 152
Kemin, *Kyrg.* 42°47′ N, 75°40′ E 184
Kemlya, *Russ.* 54°39′ N, 45°17′ E 154
Kemmerer, *Wyo., U.S.* 41°48′ N, 110°33′ W 90
Kemp, Lake, *Tex., U.S.* 33°45′ N, 99°23′ W 92
Kemp Peninsula, *Antarctica* 73°32′ S, 59°37′ W 248
Kemparana, *Mali* 12°51′ N, 4°57′ W 222
Kempen, *Ger.* 51°22′ N, 6°25′ E 167
Kemps Bay, *Bahamas* 24°2′ N, 77°34′ W 96
Kemps Bay, adm. division, *Bahamas* 24°34′ N, 78°20′ W 116
Kenadsa, *Alg.* 31°34′ N, 2°25′ W 214
Kenai, *Alas., U.S.* 60°27′ N, 151°19′ W 98
Kenai Peninsula, *North America* 60°23′ N, 150°43′ W 98
Kenamu, river, *Can.* 52°45′ N, 60°4′ W 111
Kenamuke Swamp, marsh, *Sudan* 5°52′ N, 33°30′ E 224
Kenansville, *Fla., U.S.* 27°52′ N, 81°0′ W 105
Kenaston, *Can.* 51°31′ N, 106°18′ W 90
Kendal, *U.K.* 54°20′ N, 2°43′ W 162
Kendall, *Fla., U.S.* 25°41′ N, 80°20′ W 105
Kendall, Cape, *Can.* 63°48′ N, 88°54′ W 106
Kendallville, *Ind., U.S.* 41°26′ N, 85°17′ W 102
Kendari, *Indonesia* 3°55′ S, 122°27′ E 192
Kendikolu, island, *Maldives* 5°45′ N, 73°26′ E 188
Këndrevicës, Maja e, peak, *Alban.* 40°16′ N, 19°45′ E 156
Kendrick, *Idaho, U.S.* 46°36′ N, 116°41′ W 90
Kendu Bay, *Kenya* 0°25′ N, 34°40′ E 224
Kenedy, *Tex., U.S.* 28°48′ N, 97°51′ W 92
Kenema, *Sierra Leone* 7°49′ N, 11°12′ W 222
Kenga, *Russ.* 57°24′ N, 81°5′ E 169
Kenge, *Dem. Rep. of the Congo* 4°59′ S, 17°2′ E 218
Kèngkok, *Laos* 16°26′ N, 105°11′ E 202
Kengtung, *Myanmar* 21°18′ N, 99°38′ E 202
Kengyel, *Hung.* 47°5′ N, 20°20′ E 168
Kengzhaly, *Kaz.* 48°57′ N, 56°13′ E 158
Kenhardt, *S. Af.* 29°20′ S, 21°9′ E 227
Kéniéba, *Mali* 12°50′ N, 11°15′ W 222
Kenilworth, *U.K.* 52°20′ N, 1°35′ W 162
Kenitra (Port Lyautey), *Mor.* 34°17′ N, 6°37′ W 214
Kenli, *China* 37°36′ N, 118°35′ E 198
Kenmare, *N. Dak., U.S.* 48°39′ N, 102°4′ W 90
Kenna, *N. Mex., U.S.* 33°50′ N, 103°47′ W 92
Kennard, *Tex., U.S.* 31°20′ N, 95°11′ W 103
Kennebec, *S. Dak., U.S.* 43°54′ N, 99°53′ W 90
Kennebunk, *Me., U.S.* 43°23′ N, 70°33′ W 104
Kennebunk Beach, *Me., U.S.* 43°20′ N, 70°31′ W 104
Kennebunkport, *Me., U.S.* 43°21′ N, 70°29′ W 104
Kennedy, *Can.* 50°0′ N, 102°22′ W 90
Kennedy Bight 52°5′ N, 56°24′ W 111
Kennedy, Cape see Canaveral, Cape, *Fla., U.S.* 28°24′ N, 80°34′ W 105
Kennedy Channel 78°17′ N, 71°33′ W 246
Kennedy, Mount, *Can.* 60°18′ N, 139°5′ W 98
Kennett, *Mo., U.S.* 36°14′ N, 90°3′ W 96
Kenney, *Ill., U.S.* 40°5′ N, 89°5′ W 102
Kenney Dam, *Can.* 53°27′ N, 125°23′ W 108
Kenny, Mount, *Can.* 56°54′ N, 123°58′ W 108
Keno City, see Keno Hill, *Can.* 63°53′ N, 135°25′ W 106
Keno Hill (Keno City), *Can.* 63°53′ N, 135°25′ W 106
Kenogami, river, *Can.* 50°5′ N, 85°54′ W 94
Kenogamissi Lake, *Can.* 48°13′ N, 82°18′ W 94
Kenora, *Can.* 49°47′ N, 94°28′ W 90
Kenosha, *Wis., U.S.* 42°36′ N, 87°50′ W 102
Kenova, *W. Va., U.S.* 38°23′ N, 82°36′ W 94
Kent, *Can.* 49°13′ N, 121°46′ W 100
Kent, *Conn., U.S.* 41°42′ N, 73°29′ W 104
Kent, *Ohio, U.S.* 41°8′ N, 81°21′ W 102
Kent, *Oreg., U.S.* 45°9′ N, 120°42′ W 90
Kent, *Tex., U.S.* 31°2′ N, 104°13′ W 92
Kent, *Wash., U.S.* 47°22′ N, 122°15′ W 100
Kent Group, islands, *Bass Strait* 39°20′ S, 147°14′ E 230
Kent Peninsula, *Can.* 68°39′ N, 107°16′ W 106
Kentaū, *Kaz.* 43°28′ N, 68°26′ E 184
Kentland, *Ind., U.S.* 40°45′ N, 87°27′ W 102
Kenton, *Ky., U.S.* 38°51′ N, 84°28′ W 102
Kenton, *Ohio, U.S.* 40°38′ N, 83°36′ W 102
Kentozero, *Russ.* 64°51′ N, 31°8′ E 152
Kentrikí Makedonía, adm. division, *Gr.* 40°52′ N, 21°59′ E 156
Kents Hill, *Me., U.S.* 44°23′ N, 70°1′ W 104
Kentuck, *W. Va., U.S.* 38°38′ N, 81°37′ W 102
Kentucky, adm. division, *Ky., U.S.* 37°37′ N, 86°20′ W 94
Kentville, *Can.* 45°4′ N, 64°31′ W 111
Kentwood, *La., U.S.* 30°56′ N, 90°31′ W 103
Kentwood, *Mich., U.S.* 42°54′ N, 85°35′ W 102
Kenville, *Can.* 51°59′ N, 101°20′ W 108
Kenwood, *Ohio, U.S.* 39°11′ N, 84°23′ W 102
Kenya 0°37′ N, 37°25′ E 224
Kenya, Mount, *Kenya* 0°10′ N, 37°14′ E 224
Kenzingen, *Ger.* 48°11′ N, 7°45′ E 163
Keokuk, *Iowa, U.S.* 40°24′ N, 91°28′ W 82
Kep, *Cambodia* 10°30′ N, 104°18′ E 202
Kepa, *Russ.* 65°9′ N, 32°9′ E 152
Kepi, *Indonesia* 6°26′ S, 139°11′ E 192
Kepino, *Russ.* 65°24′ N, 41°41′ E 154
Kępno, *Pol.* 51°16′ N, 17°59′ E 152
Keppel Bay 23°35′ S, 149°50′ E 230
Kepsut, *Turk.* 39°40′ N, 28°8′ E 156
Kerälä, *Fin.* 64°45′ N, 28°46′ E 152
Kerala, adm. division, *India* 10°0′ N, 76°29′ E 188
Keran, *India* 34°39′ N, 73°59′ E 186
Kéran National Park, *Togo* 9°51′ N, 0°8′ E 222
Kerava, *Fin.* 60°23′ N, 25°3′ E 166
Kerby, *Oreg., U.S.* 42°12′ N, 123°38′ W 90
Kerch, *Ukr.* 45°24′ N, 36°29′ E 156
Kerchel′, *Russ.* 59°19′ N, 64°43′ E 154
Kerchem′ya, *Russ.* 61°26′ N, 53°59′ E 154
Kerchenskiy Proliv 45°5′ N, 35°45′ E 156
Kerchevskiy, *Russ.* 59°56′ N, 56°16′ E 154
Kerchouel, *Mali* 17°10′ N, 0°15′ E 222
Kerekere, *Dem. Rep. of the Congo* 2°37′ N, 30°33′ E 224
Kerempe Burnu, *Turk.* 42°2′ N, 33°13′ E 156
Keren, *Eritrea* 15°44′ N, 38°27′ E 182
Kerend-e Gharb, *Iran* 34°15′ N, 46°14′ E 180
Kerens, *Tex., U.S.* 32°6′ N, 96°13′ W 96
Keret′, *Russ.* 66°17′ N, 33°38′ E 152
Kericho, *Kenya* 0°22′ N, 35°16′ E 224
Kerimäki, *Fin.* 61°54′ N, 29°16′ E 166
Kerinci, peak, *Indonesia* 1°45′ S, 100°55′ E 192
Keriske, *Russ.* 69°56′ N, 132°21′ E 173
Keriya, river, *China* 36°46′ N, 81°26′ E 184
Keriya see Yutian, *China* 36°55′ N, 81°36′ E 184
Keriya Shankou, pass, *China* 35°9′ N, 81°33′ E 188
Kerki, *Russ.* 63°43′ N, 54°13′ E 154
Kerki see Atamyrat, *Turkm.* 37°49′ N, 65°10′ E 197
Kerkiçi, *Turkm.* 37°52′ N, 65°15′ E 197
Kérkira, *Gr.* 39°37′ N, 19°54′ E 156
Kérkira (Corfu), island, *Gr.* 39°10′ N, 16°33′ E 143
Kerkour Nourene, Massif du, *Chad* 15°41′ N, 21°0′ E 216
Kerkrade, *Neth.* 50°52′ N, 6°3′ E 167
Kerma, *Sudan* 19°38′ N, 30°28′ E 226
Kerman, *Calif., U.S.* 36°43′ N, 120°5′ W 100
Kermānshāh, *Iran* 34°15′ N, 47°0′ E 180
Kermānshāhān, *Iran* 31°16′ N, 54°56′ E 180
Kermit, *Tex., U.S.* 31°50′ N, 103°5′ W 92
Kermode, Mount, *Can.* 52°56′ N, 131°58′ W 108
Kern Canyon, *Calif., U.S.* 36°20′ N, 118°26′ W 101
Kern, river, *Calif., U.S.* 36°22′ N, 118°28′ W 101
Kernville, *Calif., U.S.* 35°45′ N, 118°27′ W 101
Keroh, *Malaysia* 5°41′ N, 101°1′ E 196
Kérouané, *Guinea* 9°17′ N, 9°0′ W 222
Kerpen, *Ger.* 50°51′ N, 6°41′ E 167
Kerr, Cape, *Antarctica* 80°4′ S, 170°43′ E 248
Kerre, *Cen. Af. Rep.* 5°21′ N, 25°35′ E 224
Kerrobert, *Can.* 51°56′ N, 109°9′ W 90
Kerrville, *Tex., U.S.* 30°1′ N, 99°8′ W 92
Kershaw, *S.C., U.S.* 34°32′ N, 80°35′ W 96
Kersilö, *Fin.* 67°34′ N, 26°41′ E 152
Kersley, *Can.* 52°47′ N, 122°25′ W 108
Kertamulia, *Indonesia* 0°20′ N, 109°7′ E 196
Kerulen, river, *Mongolia* 47°22′ N, 111°2′ E 198
Keryneia (Girne), *Northern Cyprus, Cyprus* 35°20′ N, 33°18′ E 194
Keryneia Range, *Northern Cyprus, Cyprus* 35°16′ N, 33°25′ E 194
Kerzaz, *Alg.* 29°30′ N, 1°24′ W 214
Kesagami Lake, *Can.* 50°23′ N, 80°52′ W 94
Kesagami, river, *Can.* 50°27′ N, 80°10′ W 110
Kesälahti, *Fin.* 61°52′ N, 29°48′ E 166
Keşan, *Turk.* 40°49′ N, 26°40′ E 180
Keşap, *Turk.* 40°55′ N, 38°29′ E 158
Keshan, *China* 48°2′ N, 125°50′ E 198
Keşiş Dağı, peak, *Turk.* 39°47′ N, 39°37′ E 195
Keskal, *India* 20°3′ N, 81°36′ E 188
Kes′ma, *Russ.* 58°22′ N, 37°7′ E 154
Kessingland, *U.K.* 52°25′ N, 1°42′ E 163
Kesten′ga, *Russ.* 65°54′ N, 31°51′ E 152
Kestilä, *Fin.* 64°21′ N, 26°14′ E 152
Keswick, *U.K.* 54°35′ N, 3°8′ W 162
Keszthely, *Hung.* 46°45′ N, 17°14′ E 168
Ket′, river, *Russ.* 58°33′ N, 85°20′ E 169
Keta, *Ghana* 5°54′ N, 0°57′ E 222
Ketapang, *Indonesia* 1°57′ S, 109°59′ E 192
Ketchikan, *Alas., U.S.* 55°22′ N, 131°41′ W 108
Ketchum Mountain, *Tex., U.S.* 31°19′ N, 101°7′ W 92
Kétegyháza, *Hung.* 46°33′ N, 21°11′ E 168
Keti Bandar, *Pak.* 24°4′ N, 67°30′ E 186
Kętrzyn, *Pol.* 54°4′ N, 21°23′ E 166
Kettering, *Ohio, U.S.* 39°40′ N, 84°10′ W 102
Kettering, *U.K.* 52°23′ N, 0°43′ E 162
Kettle Lake, *Can.* 47°0′ N, 82°54′ W 110
Kettle Rapids, fall(s), *Can.* 56°23′ N, 94°37′ W 108
Kettle River Range, *Wash., U.S.* 48°10′ N, 118°29′ W 90
Kettleman City, *Calif., U.S.* 36°0′ N, 119°58′ W 100
Keudepanga, *Indonesia* 4°33′ N, 95°41′ E 196
Keur Momar Sarr, *Senegal* 15°58′ N, 16°1′ W 222
Keuruu, *Fin.* 62°14′ N, 24°38′ E 152
Keuruunselkä, lake, *Fin.* 61°53′ N, 23°10′ E 152
Kevelaer, *Ger.* 51°34′ N, 6°14′ E 167
Kewanee, *Ala., U.S.* 32°25′ N, 88°25′ W 103
Kewanee, *Ill., U.S.* 41°14′ N, 89°56′ W 102
Kewanna, *Ind., U.S.* 41°0′ N, 86°25′ W 102
Kewaskum, *Wis., U.S.* 43°30′ N, 88°15′ W 102
Keweenaw Peninsula, *U.S.* 47°1′ N, 89°0′ W 94
Keweenaw Point, *Mich., U.S.* 47°26′ N, 87°44′ W 94
Key Colony Beach, *Fla., U.S.* 24°45′ N, 80°58′ W 105
Key Harbour, *Can.* 45°53′ N, 80°43′ W 94
Key Largo, *Fla., U.S.* 25°6′ N, 80°27′ W 105
Key West, *Fla., U.S.* 24°33′ N, 81°48′ W 105
Keya Paha, river, *S. Dak., U.S.* 43°11′ N, 100°19′ W 90
Keyano, *Can.* 53°50′ N, 73°26′ W 111
Keyes, *Okla., U.S.* 36°48′ N, 102°15′ W 92
Keyi, *China* 42°8′ N, 82°40′ E 184
Keynsham, *U.K.* 51°24′ N, 2°30′ W 162
Keys View, peak, *Calif., U.S.* 33°55′ N, 116°15′ W 101
Keyser, *W. Va., U.S.* 39°26′ N, 78°59′ W 94
Keystone, *W. Va., U.S.* 37°24′ N, 81°27′ W 94
Keystone Heights, *Fla., U.S.* 29°46′ N, 82°3′ W 105
Keystone Peak, *Ariz., U.S.* 31°52′ N, 111°16′ W 92
Kez, *Russ.* 57°53′ N, 53°46′ E 154
Kezar Falls, *Me., U.S.* 43°48′ N, 70°54′ W 104
Khabab, *Syr.* 33°1′ N, 36°16′ E 194
Khabarikha, *Russ.* 65°49′ N, 52°20′ E 154
Khabarovo, *Russ.* 69°35′ N, 60°21′ E 169
Khabarovsk, *Russ.* 48°30′ N, 135°8′ E 190
Khabarovsk, adm. division, *Russ.* 56°15′ N, 135°49′ E 160
Khabrat Umm al Ḩīrān, spring, *Kuwait* 29°25′ N, 47°14′ E 196
Khābūr, river, *Syr.* 36°11′ N, 40°54′ E 195
Khadyzhensk, *Russ.* 44°24′ N, 39°31′ E 158
Khagaria, *India* 25°30′ N, 86°25′ E 197
Khairpur, *Pak.* 27°30′ N, 68°47′ E 186
Khaishi, *Ga.* 42°58′ N, 42°16′ E 195
Khakasiya, adm. division, *Russ.* 53°22′ N, 90°13′ E 169
Khakhea, *Botswana* 24°44′ S, 23°30′ E 227
Khalasa, ruin(s), *Israel* 31°5′ N, 34°35′ E 194
Khalatse, *India* 34°21′ N, 76°54′ E 188
Khālid Ibn al Walīd, dam, *Asia* 32°36′ N, 35°19′ E 194
Khalilovo, *Russ.* 51°20′ N, 58°4′ E 158
Khalkhāl, *Iran* 37°39′ N, 48°33′ E 195
Khal′mer Yu, *Russ.* 67°56′ N, 64°55′ E 169
Khalturin, *Russ.* 58°32′ N, 48°52′ E 154
Khalūf, *Oman* 20°30′ N, 58°2′ E 182
Khalyasavey, *Russ.* 63°22′ N, 78°26′ E 169
Khambhaliya, *India* 22°12′ N, 69°40′ E 186
Khamīs Mushayţ, *Saudi Arabia* 18°17′ N, 42°44′ E 182
Khammam, *India* 17°14′ N, 80°10′ E 188
Khammouan, *Laos* 17°24′ N, 104°49′ E 202
Khamr, *Yemen* 15°59′ N, 43°56′ E 182
Khamsa, *Egypt* 30°26′ N, 32°22′ E 194
Khān Abū Shāmāt, *Syr.* 33°39′ N, 36°53′ E 194
Khān az Zābīb, *Jordan* 31°28′ N, 36°5′ E 194
Khān Shaykhūn, *Syr.* 35°26′ N, 36°38′ E 194
Khan Tängiri (Khan Tengri), peak, *Kyrg.* 42°11′ N, 80°5′ E 184
Khan Tengri see Khan Tängiri, peak, *Kyrg.* 42°11′ N, 80°5′ E 184
Khān Yūnis, *Gaza Strip, Israel* 31°20′ N, 34°18′ E 194
Khanabad, *Afghan.* 36°39′ N, 69°9′ E 186
Khanai, *Pak.* 30°29′ N, 67°15′ E 186
Khānaqīn, *Iraq* 34°21′ N, 45°22′ E 180
Khandwa, *India* 21°49′ N, 76°21′ E 197
Khandyga, *Russ.* 62°32′ N, 135°34′ E 160
Khanewal, *Pak.* 30°19′ N, 71°57′ E 186
Khangarh, *Pak.* 28°21′ N, 71°43′ E 186
Khanka, Ozero, lake, *Russ.* 45°12′ N, 129°53′ E 173
Khanlar, *Azerb.* 40°35′ N, 46°20′ E 195
Khanovey, *Russ.* 67°15′ N, 63°36′ E 169
Khanpur, *Pak.* 28°38′ N, 70°39′ E 186
Khansiir, Raas, *Somalia* 10°50′ N, 44°43′ E 216
Khantaū, *Kaz.* 44°12′ N, 73°48′ E 184
Khantayskoye, Ozero, lake, *Russ.* 68°13′ N, 88°18′ E 169
Khanty-Mansi, adm. division, *Russ.* 62°2′ N, 69°26′ E 169
Khanty-Mansiysk, *Russ.* 61°2′ N, 69°10′ E 169
Khanymey, *Russ.* 63°47′ N, 75°58′ E 169
Khao Yai National Park, *Thai.* 14°17′ N, 101°43′ E 202
Khapalu, *Pak.* 35°8′ N, 76°21′ E 186
Khapcheranga, *Russ.* 49°41′ N, 112°26′ E 198
Kharabali, *Russ.* 47°23′ N, 47°10′ E 158
Kharagauli, *Ga.* 42°0′ N, 43°7′ E 195
Kharagpur, *India* 22°19′ N, 87°19′ E 197
Kharampur, *Russ.* 64°18′ N, 78°12′ E 169
Kharan, *Pak.* 28°36′ N, 65°25′ E 182
Kharānaq, *Iran* 32°20′ N, 54°41′ E 180
Kharasavey, Mys, *Russ.* 70°41′ N, 64°10′ E 169
Khārga, El Wâḥât el, *Egypt* 25°41′ N, 29°48′ E 180
Khargon, *India* 21°47′ N, 75°38′ E 197
Khārk, island, *Iran* 29°4′ N, 50°10′ E 180
Kharkiv, *Ukr.* 49°59′ N, 36°15′ E 158
Kharlovka, *Russ.* 68°44′ N, 37°15′ E 152
Kharlu, *Russ.* 61°47′ N, 30°53′ E 152
Kharsān, *Syr.* 35°17′ N, 37°2′ E 194
Khartoum, *Sudan* 15°27′ N, 32°23′ E 182
Khartoum, adm. division, *Sudan* 15°48′ N, 31°44′ E 216
Khartoum North, *Sudan* 15°37′ N, 32°34′ E 226
Khaşab, *Oman* 26°10′ N, 56°12′ E 196
Khasan, *Russ.* 42°24′ N, 130°41′ E 200
Khasavyurt, *Russ.* 43°12′ N, 46°34′ E 195
Khash, *Afghan.* 31°31′ N, 62°54′ E 186
Khāsh, *Iran* 28°10′ N, 61°11′ E 182
Khash, river, *Afghan.* 32°42′ N, 64°13′ E 186
Khashm el Qirba, *Sudan* 14°55′ N, 35°55′ E 182
Khashm el Qirba Dam, *Sudan* 14°25′ N, 34°49′ E 182
Khashri, *Ga.* 41°57′ N, 43°33′ E 195
Khaskovo, *Bulg.* 41°56′ N, 25°32′ E 156
Khaskovo, adm. division, *Bulg.* 41°52′ N, 25°17′ E 156
Khatanga, *Russ.* 71°57′ N, 102°45′ E 160
Khātūnīyah, *Syr.* 36°23′ N, 41°14′ E 195
Khatyrka, *Russ.* 62°1′ N, 174°56′ E 160
Khaur, *Pak.* 33°16′ N, 72°33′ E 186
Khavda, *India* 23°51′ N, 69°45′ E 186
Khaydarkan, *Kyrg.* 39°56′ N, 71°26′ E 197
Khaypudyrskaya Guba 68°30′ N, 59°0′ E 160
Khayryuzovo, *Russ.* 56°58′ N, 157°7′ E 160
Khed Brahma, *India* 24°3′ N, 73°2′ E 186
Khemmarat, *Thai.* 16°2′ N, 105°12′ E 202
Kherson, *Ukr.* 46°40′ N, 32°35′ E 156
Kheta, *Russ.* 71°31′ N, 99°56′ E 160
Kheta, river, *Russ.* 71°30′ N, 99°5′ E 160
Khewra, *Pak.* 32°37′ N, 73°4′ E 186
Khibiny, *Russ.* 67°49′ N, 33°16′ E 152
Khiitola, *Russ.* 61°13′ N, 29°40′ E 166
Khilchipur, *India* 24°2′ N, 76°34′ E 197
Khilok, *Russ.* 51°30′ N, 110°29′ E 190
Khimki, *Russ.* 55°53′ N, 37°26′ E 154
Khirbat Ad Dayr, ruin(s), *Jordan* 31°32′ N, 35°35′ E 194
Khirbat al Ghazālah, *Syr.* 32°43′ N, 36°12′ E 194
Khirbat aş Şafrā′, ruin(s), *Jordan* 31°37′ N, 35°36′ E 194
Khirbat as Samrā′, ruin(s), *Jordan* 32°10′ N, 36°8′ E 194
Khirbat Qumrān, ruin(s), *West Bank, Israel* 31°43′ N, 35°25′ E 194
Khirbat Umm al Jimāl, ruin(s), *Jordan* 32°19′ N, 36°20′ E 194
Khiri Ratthanikhom, *Thai.* 9°2′ N, 98°53′ E 202
Khislavichi, *Russ.* 54°12′ N, 32°10′ E 154
Khiwa, *Uzb.* 41°23′ N, 60°22′ E 180
Khizy, *Azerb.* 40°54′ N, 49°4′ E 195
Khlevnoye, *Russ.* 52°12′ N, 39°0′ E 158
Khmel′nyts′kyy, *Ukr.* 49°24′ N, 26°58′ E 158
Khoai, Hon, island, *Vietnam* 8°9′ N, 104°40′ E 202
Khodoriv, *Ukr.* 49°23′ N, 24°19′ E 152
Khodzhatau, *Taj.* 39°11′ N, 71°41′ E 197
Khogali, *Sudan* 6°9′ N, 27°46′ E 224
Khok Kloi, *Thai.* 8°17′ N, 98°17′ E 202
Khokhol′skiy, *Russ.* 51°29′ N, 38°42′ E 158
Khokhropar, *Pak.* 25°42′ N, 70°14′ E 186
Kholm, *Afghan.* 36°42′ N, 67°41′ E 186
Kholm, *Russ.* 57°8′ N, 31°12′ E 154
Kholmogorskaya, *Russ.* 63°49′ N, 40°40′ E 154
Kholmogory, *Russ.* 64°13′ N, 41°37′ E 154
Kholmsk, *Russ.* 47°1′ N, 142°5′ E 190
Kholopenichi, *Belarus* 54°30′ N, 29°1′ E 166
Khomeyn, *Iran* 33°42′ N, 50°6′ E 180
Khomeynīshahr, *Iran* 32°44′ N, 51°32′ E 180
Khon Kaen, *Thai.* 16°29′ N, 102°40′ E 202
Không, *Laos* 14°9′ N, 105°49′ E 202
Khôngxédôn, *Laos* 15°37′ N, 105°47′ E 202
Khonsa, *India* 27°37′ N, 93°50′ E 188
Khonulakh, *Russ.* 66°20′ N, 151°26′ E 160
Khonuu, *Russ.* 66°30′ N, 143°15′ E 160
Khoper, river, *Russ.* 52°5′ N, 43°18′ E 158
Khoper, river, *Russ.* 50°14′ N, 41°53′ E 184
Khor, *Russ.* 48°0′ N, 135°5′ E 190
Khorāsān, region, *Asia* 34°30′ N, 53°1′ E 180
Khorat see Nakhon Ratchasima, *Thai.* 14°58′ N, 102°7′ E 202
Khorb el Ethel, spring, *Alg.* 28°34′ N, 6°19′ W 214
Khorintsy, *Russ.* 60°41′ N, 121°20′ E 160
Khorixas, *Namibia* 20°24′ S, 14°55′ E 220
Khormūj, *Iran* 28°35′ N, 51°24′ E 196
Khorof Harar, *Kenya* 2°7′ N, 40°42′ E 224
Khorol, *Ukr.* 49°48′ N, 33°12′ E 158
Khoroûfa, spring, *Mauritania* 17°21′ N, 15°49′ W 222
Khorramābād, *Iran* 33°29′ N, 48°19′ E 180
Khorramshahr, *Iran* 30°29′ N, 48°9′ E 180
Khorugh, *Taj.* 37°29′ N, 71°35′ E 184
Khosheutovo, *Russ.* 47°0′ N, 47°50′ E 158
Khost, *Afghan.* 33°22′ N, 69°58′ E 186
Khost, *Pak.* 30°14′ N, 67°38′ E 186
Khotyn, *Ukr.* 48°30′ N, 26°30′ E 152
Khouribga, *Mor.* 32°56′ N, 6°57′ W 214
Khoy, *Iran* 38°34′ N, 44°55′ E 195
Khoyniki, *Belarus* 51°51′ N, 30°4′ E 158
Khrami, river, *Ga.* 41°31′ N, 44°3′ E 195
Khrenovoye, *Russ.* 51°8′ N, 40°15′ E 158
Khroma, river, *Russ.* 71°50′ N, 144°2′ E 160
Khromtaū, *Kaz.* 50°16′ N, 58°27′ E 158
Khuchni, *Russ.* 41°53′ N, 47°55′ E 195
Khudabad, *Pak.* 36°42′ N, 74°53′ E 186
Khudosey, river, *Russ.* 65°23′ N, 82°18′ E 169
Khudumelapye, *Botswana* 23°53′ S, 24°53′ E 227
Khuff, oil field, *Lib.* 28°8′ N, 18°17′ E 216
Khuis, *Botswana* 26°37′ S, 21°49′ E 227
Khujand, *Taj.* 40°15′ N, 69°41′ E 197
Khŭjayli, *Uzb.* 42°24′ N, 59°27′ E 180
Khulkhuta, *Russ.* 46°16′ N, 46°21′ E 158
Khulna, *Bangladesh* 22°48′ N, 89°28′ E 197

Khun Yuam, *Thai.* 18°53′ N, 97°52′ E 202
Khunjerab National Park, *Pak.* 36°45′ N, 75°20′ E 187
Khunjerab Pass, *China-Pak.* 36°50′ N, 75°26′ E 184
Khunsar, *Iran* 33°14′ N, 50°17′ E 180
Khunti, *India* 23°6′ N, 85°16′ E 197
Khunzakh, *Russ.* 42°29′ N, 46°42′ E 195
Khur, *Iran* 33°49′ N, 55°5′ E 180
Khvormūj, *Iran* 28°35′ N, 51°22′ E 196
Khurais, oil field, *Saudi Arabia* 25°10′ N, 48°1′ E 196
Khushab, *Pak.* 32°18′ N, 72°24′ E 186
Khutse Game Reserve, *Botswana* 23°43′ S, 23°52′ E 227
Khuwei, *Sudan* 13°3′ N, 29°14′ E 216
Khuzdar, *Pak.* 27°43′ N, 66°34′ E 186
Khvāf, *Iran* 34°36′ N, 60°9′ E 180
Khvalynsk, *Russ.* 52°28′ N, 48°6′ E 158
Khvorostyanka, *Russ.* 52°37′ N, 49°0′ E 158
Khvosh Asia, *Afghan.* 32°53′ N, 62°14′ E 186
Khvoynaya, *Russ.* 58°51′ N, 34°40′ E 154
Khyber-Pakhtunkhwa, adm. division, *Pak.* 34°27′ N, 72°30′ E 186
Khyber Pass, *Pak.* 34°6′ N, 71°9′ E 186
Kiabakari, *Tanzania* 1°48′ S, 33°50′ E 224
Kiamba, *Philippines* 6°2′ N, 124°37′ E 203
Kiambi, *Dem. Rep. of the Congo* 7°20′ S, 28°0′ E 224
Kiamichi Mountains, *Okla., U.S.* 34°30′ N, 95°25′ W 96
Kiang West National Park, *Gambia* 13°22′ N, 15°58′ W 222
Kianta, *Fin.* 65°7′ N, 28°54′ E 154
Kibali, river, *Dem. Rep. of the Congo* 3°29′ N, 28°37′ E 224
Kibangou, *Congo* 3°28′ S, 12°18′ E 218
Kibara, Monts, *Dem. Rep. of the Congo* 8°29′ S, 26°39′ E 224
Kibau, *Tanzania* 8°36′ S, 35°18′ E 224
Kibawe, *Philippines* 7°37′ N, 124°59′ E 203
Kibaya, *Tanzania* 5°19′ S, 36°33′ E 224
Kiberashi, *Tanzania* 5°20′ S, 37°25′ E 224
Kiberege, *Tanzania* 7°57′ S, 36°54′ E 224
Kibiti, *Tanzania* 7°41′ S, 38°54′ E 224
Kiboga, *Uganda* 0°53′ N, 31°45′ E 224
Kibombo, *Dem. Rep. of the Congo* 3°59′ S, 25°53′ E 224
Kibondo, *Tanzania* 3°37′ S, 30°42′ E 224
Kibre Mengist, *Eth.* 5°55′ N, 38°58′ E 224
Kibungo, *Rwanda* 2°12′ S, 30°30′ E 224
Kibuye, *Rwanda* 2°7′ S, 29°20′ E 224
Kibwesa, *Tanzania* 6°29′ S, 29°56′ E 224
Kibwezi, *Kenya* 2°27′ S, 37°57′ E 224
Kičevo, *Maced.* 41°31′ N, 20°58′ E 168
Kichi Kichi, spring, *Chad* 17°36′ N, 17°18′ E 216
Kichmengskiy Gorodok, *Russ.* 60°1′ N, 45°52′ E 154
Kidal, *Mali* 18°27′ N, 1°23′ E 222
Kidatu, *Tanzania* 7°43′ S, 37°0′ E 224
Kidderminster, *U.K.* 52°22′ N, 2°15′ W 162
Kidepo, *Sudan* 4°6′ N, 33°14′ E 224
Kidepo Valley National Park, *Uganda* 3°41′ N, 33°22′ E 224
Kidete, *Tanzania* 6°38′ S, 36°45′ E 224
Kidi Faani, *Somalia* 1°6′ S, 41°46′ E 224
Kidika, *Tanzania* 7°28′ S, 36°30′ E 224
Kidira, *Senegal* 14°26′ N, 12°16′ W 222
Kidnappers, Cape, *N.Z.* 39°41′ S, 177°7′ E 240
Kidodi, *Tanzania* 7°38′ S, 37°3′ E 224
Kidsgrove, *U.K.* 53°4′ N, 2°16′ W 162
Kiel, *Ger.* 54°20′ N, 10°8′ E 150
Kiel, *Wis., U.S.* 43°54′ N, 88°3′ W 102
Kielce, *Pol.* 50°52′ N, 20°36′ E 152
Kiémou, *Côte d'Ivoire* 9°3′ N, 5°33′ W 222
Kien Duc, *Vietnam* 12°19′ N, 107°31′ E 202
Kiéré, *Burkina Faso* 11°38′ N, 3°31′ W 222
Kiev see Kyiv, *Ukr.* 50°25′ N, 30°29′ E 158
Kīevka, *Kaz.* 50°16′ N, 71°32′ E 184
Kifaya, *Guinea* 12°10′ N, 13°6′ W 222
Kiffa, *Mauritania* 16°36′ N, 11°26′ W 222
Kifino Selo, *Bosn. and Herzg.* 43°16′ N, 18°11′ E 168
Kigali, *Rwanda* 2°3′ S, 29°56′ E 224
Kiğı, *Turk.* 39°18′ N, 40°19′ E 195
Kigille, *Sudan* 8°38′ N, 34°1′ E 224
Kigoma, *Tanzania* 4°54′ S, 29°36′ E 224
Kihelkonna, *Est.* 58°21′ N, 22°2′ E 166
Kihniö, *Fin.* 62°10′ N, 23°10′ E 152
Kihnu, island, *Est.* 58°8′ N, 23°47′ E 166
Kii Suidō 33°56′ N, 134°39′ E 201
Kiihtelysvaara, *Fin.* 62°29′ N, 30°14′ E 152
Kiikala, *Fin.* 60°27′ N, 23°33′ E 166
Kiistala, *Fin.* 67°51′ N, 25°21′ E 152
Kijevo, *Croatia* 43°58′ N, 16°22′ E 168
Kikiakki, *Russ.* 63°46′ N, 82°42′ E 169
Kikinda, *Serb.* 45°49′ N, 20°28′ E 168
Kiknur, *Russ.* 57°19′ N, 47°14′ E 154
Kikombo, *Tanzania* 6°12′ S, 35°58′ E 224
Kikondja, *Dem. Rep. of the Congo* 8°12′ S, 26°24′ E 224
Kikori, river, *P.N.G.* 6°53′ S, 143°4′ E 192
Kikwit, *Dem. Rep. of the Congo* 5°6′ S, 18°47′ E 218
Kil, *Nor.* 59°31′ N, 13°17′ E 152
Kilafors, *Nor.* 61°14′ N, 16°30′ E 152
Kilakkarai, *India* 9°16′ N, 78°46′ E 188
Kilambé, peak, *Nicar.* 13°33′ N, 85°47′ W 115
Kilani, *Cyprus* 34°49′ N, 32°51′ E 156
Kilar, *India* 33°6′ N, 76°24′ E 188
Kīlauea Lighthouse, site, *U.S.* 22°13′ N, 159°27′ W 94
Kilbaha, *Ire.* 52°33′ N, 9°52′ W 150
Kilbourne, *Ill., U.S.* 40°8′ N, 90°1′ W 102
Kilbourne, *La., U.S.* 32°59′ N, 91°19′ W 103
Kilbride, *Can.* 57°6′ N, 7°22′ W 150
Kilbuck Mountains, *Alas., U.S.* 60°3′ N, 161°24′ W 98
Kilchoman, *U.K.* 55°46′ N, 6°27′ W 150
Kil'din, *Russ.* 69°20′ N, 34°20′ E 152
Kilembe, *Dem. Rep. of the Congo* 5°48′ S, 19°51′ E 218
Kilgore, *Nebr., U.S.* 42°55′ N, 100°57′ W 90
Kilgore, *Tex., U.S.* 32°22′ N, 94°53′ W 103
Kılıçkaya, *Turk.* 40°42′ N, 41°28′ E 195
Kilifi, *Kenya* 3°37′ S, 39°50′ E 224
Kilimanjaro, peak, *Tanzania* 3°6′ S, 37°17′ E 224
Kılınç Tepesi, peak, *Turk.* 40°31′ N, 38°4′ E 156
Kilindoni, *Tanzania* 7°54′ S, 39°40′ E 224
Kilingi Nõmme, *Est.* 58°8′ N, 24°57′ E 166
Kilíni, Óros, peak, *Gr.* 37°55′ N, 22°19′ E 156
Kilinochchi, *Sri Lanka* 9°22′ N, 80°23′ E 188
Kilis, *Turk.* 36°44′ N, 37°6′ E 156
Kiliya, *Ukr.* 45°29′ N, 29°15′ E 156
Kilju, *N. Korea* 40°57′ N, 129°22′ E 200
Kilkádes (Cyclades), islands, *Mediterranean Sea* 36°31′ N, 24°28′ E 156
Kilkee, *Ire.* 52°40′ N, 9°38′ W 150
Kilkenny, *Ire.* 52°39′ N, 7°16′ W 150
Kilkoris, *Kenya* 1°1′ S, 34°53′ E 224
Killala, *Ire.* 54°12′ N, 9°15′ W 150
Killala Lake, *Can.* 49°2′ N, 86°55′ W 94
Killam, *Can.* 52°46′ N, 111°51′ W 108
Killarney, *Can.* 49°10′ N, 99°40′ W 108
Killarney, *Can.* 45°58′ N, 81°29′ W 94
Killdeer, *N. Dak., U.S.* 47°21′ N, 102°46′ W 90
Killdeer Mountains, *N. Dak., U.S.* 47°44′ N, 102°59′ W 90
Killeen, *Tex., U.S.* 31°6′ N, 97°44′ W 92
Killough, *U.K.* 54°14′ N, 5°40′ W 150
Killybegs, *Ire.* 54°37′ N, 8°28′ W 150
Kil'mez', *Russ.* 56°56′ N, 51°8′ E 154
Kilmichael, *Miss., U.S.* 33°25′ N, 89°34′ W 103
Kilo, *Dem. Rep. of the Congo* 1°48′ N, 30°10′ E 224
Kilómetro, *Arg.* 28°26′ S, 60°3′ W 139
Kilosa, *Tanzania* 6°47′ S, 37°0′ E 224
Kilpua, *Fin.* 64°20′ N, 24°54′ E 154
Kilvaxter, *U.K.* 57°38′ N, 6°23′ W 150
Kilwa, *Dem. Rep. of the Congo* 9°18′ S, 28°19′ E 224
Kilwa Kivinje, *Tanzania* 8°45′ S, 39°23′ E 224
Kilwa Masoko, *Tanzania* 8°56′ S, 39°33′ E 224
Kim, *Chad* 9°42′ N, 15°57′ E 216
Kim, *Colo., U.S.* 37°14′ N, 103°21′ W 92
Kima, *Dem. Rep. of the Congo* 1°27′ S, 26°42′ E 224
Kimali, *Tanzania* 3°28′ S, 34°26′ E 224
Kimasozero, *Russ.* 64°21′ N, 31°11′ E 152
Kimball, *Nebr., U.S.* 41°13′ N, 103°41′ W 90
Kimball, *S. Dak., U.S.* 43°43′ N, 99°0′ W 90
Kimball, Mount, *Alas., U.S.* 63°15′ N, 144°51′ W 98
Kimberley, *Can.* 49°40′ N, 115°59′ W 90
Kimberley, *S. Af.* 28°46′ S, 24°47′ E 227
Kimberley, region, *Australia* 18°35′ S, 125°40′ E 230
Kimbirila, *Côte d'Ivoire* 10°22′ N, 7°32′ W 222
Kimbolton, *U.K.* 52°17′ N, 0°24′ E 162
Kimboto, *Congo* 3°17′ S, 14°1′ E 218
Kimbrough, *Ala., U.S.* 32°1′ N, 87°33′ W 103
Kimch'aek (Sŏngjin), *N. Korea* 40°38′ N, 129°11′ E 200
Kiméria, *Gr.* 41°8′ N, 24°56′ E 156
Kimhwa (Kŭmsŏng), *N. Korea* 38°26′ N, 127°36′ E 200
Kimhyŏnggwŏn, *N. Korea* 40°47′ N, 128°10′ E 200
Kími, *Gr.* 38°38′ N, 24°6′ E 156
Kímina, *Gr.* 40°37′ N, 22°41′ E 156
Kimito, *Fin.* 60°9′ N, 22°42′ E 166
Kimjŏngsuk (Sinp'a), *N. Korea* 41°24′ N, 127°48′ E 200
Kimmirut (Lake Harbor), *Can.* 62°52′ N, 69°53′ W 106
Kimovaara, *Russ.* 63°37′ N, 31°1′ E 152
Kimovsk, *Russ.* 53°56′ N, 38°27′ E 154
Kimpese, *Dem. Rep. of the Congo* 5°33′ S, 14°22′ E 218
Kimry, *Russ.* 56°53′ N, 37°21′ E 154
Kimsquit, *Can.* 52°50′ N, 126°56′ W 108
Kimvula, *Dem. Rep. of the Congo* 5°43′ S, 15°57′ E 218
Kinabalu Park, *Malaysia* 6°14′ N, 116°1′ E 203
Kinabalu, peak, *Malaysia* 6°6′ N, 116°29′ E 203
Kinaskan Lake, *Can.* 57°29′ N, 131°2′ W 108
Kincaid, *Can.* 49°38′ N, 107°1′ W 90
Kincaid, *Ill., U.S.* 39°34′ N, 89°25′ W 102
Kincardine, *Can.* 44°9′ N, 81°37′ W 102
Kincolith, *Can.* 55°2′ N, 129°59′ W 108
Kinda, *Dem. Rep. of the Congo* 9°19′ S, 25°2′ E 224
Kindakun Point, *Can.* 53°7′ N, 133°0′ W 108
Kindanba, *Congo* 3°45′ S, 14°34′ E 218
Kinde, *Mich., U.S.* 43°56′ N, 83°0′ W 102
Kinder, *La., U.S.* 30°28′ N, 92°51′ W 103
Kinder Scout, peak, *U.K.* 53°23′ N, 1°54′ W 162
Kinderhook, *N.Y., U.S.* 42°23′ N, 73°43′ W 104
Kindersley, *Can.* 51°29′ N, 109°9′ W 90
Kindia, *Guinea* 10°3′ N, 12°54′ W 222
Kindu, *Dem. Rep. of the Congo* 3°0′ S, 25°54′ E 224
Kinel', *Russ.* 53°14′ N, 50°33′ E 154
Kineo, Mount, *Me., U.S.* 45°41′ N, 69°49′ W 94
Kineshma, *Russ.* 57°24′ N, 42°12′ E 154
Kinesi, *Tanzania* 1°26′ S, 33°54′ E 224
King Arthur's Castle see Tintagel, site, *U.K.* 50°39′ N, 4°49′ W 150
King Christian Ix Land, *Den.* 71°9′ N, 41°7′ W 73
King City, *Calif., U.S.* 36°13′ N, 121°9′ W 100
King City, *Mo., U.S.* 40°2′ N, 94°32′ W 94
King Frederik Vi Coast, *Den.* 64°54′ N, 50°21′ W 73
King George Island, *Antarctica* 61°46′ S, 61°4′ W 248
King George Islands, *Hudson Bay* 57°39′ N, 80°48′ W 106
King George, Mount, *Can.* 50°35′ N, 115°31′ W 90
King Island, *Alas., U.S.* 65°14′ N, 167°26′ W 160
King Island, *Austral.* 39°58′ S, 142°39′ E 230
King Khalid Military City, site, *Saudi Arabia* 27°52′ N, 45°27′ E 180
King Lear Peak, *Nev., U.S.* 41°11′ N, 118°39′ W 90
King Leopold Ranges, *Austral.* 17°39′ S, 125°3′ E 230
King Mountain, *Can.* 58°17′ N, 128°59′ W 108
King Mountain, *Oreg., U.S.* 43°47′ N, 118°57′ W 90
King Mountain, *Oreg., U.S.* 42°40′ N, 123°19′ W 90
King Peak, *Antarctica* 85°20′ S, 90°39′ W 248
King Peak, *Calif., U.S.* 40°8′ N, 124°12′ W 90
King Peninsula, *Antarctica* 73°6′ S, 98°45′ W 248
King Salmon, *Alas., U.S.* 58°37′ N, 156°48′ W 98
King Sejong, station, *Antarctica* 62°8′ S, 58°27′ W 134
King William Island, *Can.* 69°57′ N, 100°41′ W 106
King William's Town, *S. Af.* 32°54′ S, 27°22′ E 227
Kingaroy, *Austral.* 26°33′ S, 151°49′ E 231
Kingcome Inlet, *Can.* 50°57′ N, 126°14′ W 90
Kingfish, oil field, *Austral.* 38°32′ S, 147°57′ E 230
Kingfisher, *Okla., U.S.* 35°49′ N, 97°56′ W 92
Kingisepp, *Russ.* 59°22′ N, 28°38′ E 166
Kingman, *Ariz., U.S.* 35°11′ N, 114°4′ W 101
Kingman, *Kans., U.S.* 37°38′ N, 98°7′ W 90
Kingri, *Pak.* 30°27′ N, 69°52′ E 186
Kings Canyon, *Calif., U.S.* 36°49′ N, 119°2′ W 101
Kings Canyon National Park, *Calif., U.S.* 36°55′ N, 118°58′ W 101
King's Cliffe, *U.K.* 52°33′ N, 0°31′ E 162
King's Lynn, *U.K.* 52°44′ N, 0°24′ E 162
Kings Mountain National Military Park, *S.C., U.S.* 35°8′ N, 81°27′ W 96
Kings Peak, *Utah, U.S.* 40°44′ N, 110°27′ W 90
Kings, river, *Calif., U.S.* 36°23′ N, 119°40′ W 100
Kingsburg, *Calif., U.S.* 36°31′ N, 119°34′ W 100
Kingsford Heights, *Ind., U.S.* 41°28′ N, 86°42′ W 102
Kingsnorth, *U.K.* 51°7′ N, 0°51′ E 162
Kingsport, *Tenn., U.S.* 36°31′ N, 82°33′ W 82
Kingston, *Can.* 44°14′ N, 76°30′ W 94
Kingston, *Jam.* 17°58′ N, 76°55′ W 115
Kingston, *Mich., U.S.* 43°24′ N, 83°11′ W 102
Kingston, *N.Y., U.S.* 41°55′ N, 74°1′ W 104
Kingston, *N.Z.* 45°21′ S, 168°43′ E 240
Kingston, *Ohio, U.S.* 39°28′ N, 82°56′ W 102
Kingston, *Pa., U.S.* 41°15′ N, 75°55′ W 94
Kingston, *R.I., U.S.* 41°28′ N, 71°32′ W 104
Kingston, *Wash., U.S.* 47°47′ N, 122°31′ W 100
Kingston Lake, *Can.* 58°55′ N, 103°6′ W 108
Kingston Peak, *Calif., U.S.* 35°42′ N, 115°57′ W 101
Kingston Range, *Calif., U.S.* 35°46′ N, 116°0′ W 101
Kingston South East, *Austral.* 36°52′ S, 139°53′ E 231
Kingston upon Hull, *U.K.* 53°44′ N, 0°22′ E 162
Kingston Upon Thames, *U.K.* 51°24′ N, 0°18′ E 162
Kingstown, *Saint Vincent and The Grenadines* 13°8′ N, 61°20′ W 116
Kingstree, *S.C., U.S.* 33°39′ N, 79°50′ W 96
Kingsville, *Can.* 42°1′ N, 82°44′ W 102
Kingsville, *Tex., U.S.* 27°30′ N, 97°52′ W 96
Kingungi, *Dem. Rep. of the Congo* 5°20′ S, 17°57′ E 218
Kiniama, *Dem. Rep. of the Congo* 11°32′ S, 28°22′ E 224
Kinistino, *Can.* 52°57′ N, 105°3′ W 108
Kinkala, *Congo* 4°22′ S, 14°45′ E 218
Kinloch Castle, site, *U.K.* 56°59′ N, 6°23′ W 150
Kinloch Lake, *Can.* 51°53′ N, 91°31′ W 110
Kinmen (Quemoy), island, *Taiwan, China* 24°23′ N, 118°32′ E 198
Kinmundy, *Ill., U.S.* 38°45′ N, 88°51′ W 102
Kinnaird Castle, site, *U.K.* 56°41′ N, 2°43′ W 150
Kinniyai, *Sri Lanka* 8°26′ N, 81°12′ E 188
Kinnula, *Fin.* 63°21′ N, 24°56′ E 152
Kino, river, *Japan* 34°16′ N, 135°20′ E 201
Kinoosao, *Can.* 57°5′ N, 102°3′ W 108
Kinosaki, *Japan* 35°36′ N, 134°47′ E 201
Kinosheo, river, *Can.* 51°22′ N, 82°3′ W 110
Kinsey, Cape, *Antarctica* 69°14′ S, 162°35′ E 248
Kinshasa, adm. division, *Dem. Rep. of the Congo* 4°58′ S, 15°25′ E 218
Kinshasa (Léopoldville), *Dem. Rep. of the Congo* 4°24′ S, 15°6′ E 218
Kinsley, *Kans., U.S.* 37°54′ N, 99°25′ W 90
Kinston, *N.C., U.S.* 35°16′ N, 77°36′ W 96
Kintai, *Lith.* 55°25′ N, 21°17′ E 166
Kintampo, *Ghana* 8°3′ N, 1°43′ W 222
Kintinian, *Guinea* 11°37′ N, 9°22′ W 222
Kintla Peak, *Mont., U.S.* 48°54′ N, 114°15′ W 90
Kintyre, *U.K.* 55°25′ N, 5°34′ W 150
Kinuso, *Can.* 55°20′ N, 115°28′ W 108
Kinyang, *Kenya* 0°56′ N, 36°0′ E 224
Kinyangiri, *Tanzania* 4°26′ S, 34°36′ E 224
Kinyeti, peak, *Sudan* 3°55′ N, 32°52′ E 224
Kiokluk Mountains, *Alas., U.S.* 61°29′ N, 158°44′ W 106
Kiomboi, *Tanzania* 4°17′ S, 34°20′ E 224
Kióni, *Gr.* 38°26′ N, 20°41′ E 156
Kiowa, *Colo., U.S.* 39°20′ N, 104°28′ W 90
Kiowa, *Kans., U.S.* 37°1′ N, 98°30′ W 92
Kiparissi, *Gr.* 36°57′ N, 22°58′ E 156
Kipawa, Lac, lake, *Can.* 46°47′ N, 79°27′ W 110
Kipembawe, *Tanzania* 7°42′ S, 33°25′ E 224
Kipengere Range, *Tanzania* 9°34′ S, 34°15′ E 224
Kipili, *Tanzania* 7°27′ S, 30°36′ E 224
Kipilingu, *Dem. Rep. of the Congo* 13°17′ S, 29°1′ E 224
Kipinä, *Fin.* 65°15′ N, 26°27′ E 152
Kipini, *Kenya* 2°32′ S, 40°29′ E 224
Kipiyevo, *Russ.* 65°40′ N, 54°27′ E 154
Kipling, *Can.* 50°6′ N, 102°39′ W 90
Kipushi, *Dem. Rep. of the Congo* 11°48′ S, 27°14′ E 224
Kipushia, *Dem. Rep. of the Congo* 13°1′ S, 29°30′ E 224
Kir, *Alban.* 42°14′ N, 19°41′ E 168
Kiraz, *Turk.* 38°14′ N, 28°12′ E 156
Kirbla, *Est.* 58°42′ N, 23°55′ E 166
Kirbymoorside, *U.K.* 54°16′ N, 0°55′ E 162
Kirbyville, *Tex., U.S.* 30°38′ N, 93°54′ W 103
Kirchberg, *Ger.* 49°56′ N, 7°23′ E 167
Kirchen, *Ger.* 50°48′ N, 7°53′ E 167
Kirchhain, *Ger.* 50°49′ N, 8°55′ E 167
Kirchheim, *Ger.* 50°50′ N, 9°34′ E 167
Kirchheimbolanden, *Ger.* 49°40′ N, 8°0′ E 163
Kirchhundem, *Ger.* 51°5′ N, 8°4′ E 167
Kirensk, *Russ.* 57°35′ N, 107°50′ E 160
Kiri, *Dem. Rep. of the Congo* 1°28′ S, 18°59′ E 218
Kiri, *Mali* 13°57′ N, 3°0′ W 222
Kiriakí, *Gr.* 41°17′ N, 26°12′ E 156
Kiribati 1°4′ S, 172°37′ E 238
Kiridh, *Somalia* 8°54′ N, 46°11′ E 216
Kırıkkale, *Turk.* 39°50′ N, 33°30′ E 156
Kirillov, *Russ.* 59°53′ N, 38°21′ E 154
Kirillovskoye, *Russ.* 60°27′ N, 29°18′ E 166
Kirin, *Eth.* 9°54′ N, 34°22′ E 224
Kirishi, *Russ.* 59°27′ N, 32°6′ E 154
Kirishima-Yaku National Park, *Japan* 31°45′ N, 130°52′ E 201
Kiritimati (Christmas Island), *Kiribati* 2°0′ N, 157°24′ W 241
Kiriwina, island, *P.N.G.* 8°31′ S, 149°58′ E 192
Kırka, *Turk.* 39°17′ N, 30°30′ E 156
Kırkağaç, *Turk.* 39°5′ N, 27°39′ E 156
Kirkbride, *U.K.* 54°53′ N, 3°12′ W 162
Kirkby Lonsdale, *U.K.* 54°12′ N, 2°36′ W 162
Kirkby Stephen, *U.K.* 54°28′ N, 2°22′ W 162
Kirkcudbright, *U.K.* 54°49′ N, 4°3′ W 162
Kirkenes, *Nor.* 69°42′ N, 30°20′ E 160
Kırkgeçit (Kasrik), *Turk.* 38°7′ N, 43°27′ E 195
Kirkham, *U.K.* 53°47′ N, 2°55′ W 162
Kirkkola, *Fin.* 61°37′ N, 26°0′ E 166
Kirkkonummi see Kyrkslätt, *Fin.* 60°7′ N, 24°26′ E 166
Kirkland, *Tex., U.S.* 34°21′ N, 100°5′ W 92
Kirkland, *Wash., U.S.* 47°39′ N, 122°12′ W 100
Kirkland Lake, *Can.* 48°9′ N, 80°0′ W 82
Kırklar Dağı, peak, *Turk.* 40°33′ N, 40°31′ E 195
Kırklareli, *Turk.* 41°42′ N, 27°13′ E 180
Kirklin, *Ind., U.S.* 40°11′ N, 86°21′ W 102
Kirkoswald, *U.K.* 54°46′ N, 2°41′ W 162
Kirksville, *Mo., U.S.* 40°11′ N, 92°34′ W 94
Kirkūk see Karkūk, *Iraq* 35°27′ N, 44°23′ E 180
Kirkwall, *U.K.* 58°59′ N, 3°3′ W 150
Kirkwood, *Mo., U.S.* 38°34′ N, 90°24′ W 94
Kirkwood, *S. Af.* 33°23′ S, 25°23′ E 227
Kirn, *Ger.* 49°47′ N, 7°27′ E 167
Kirotshe, *Dem. Rep. of the Congo* 1°45′ S, 28°57′ E 224
Kirov, *Russ.* 54°0′ N, 34°17′ E 154
Kirov, *Russ.* 58°34′ N, 49°38′ E 154
Kirov, adm. division, *Russ.* 58°45′ N, 48°49′ E 169
Kirovgrad, *Russ.* 57°27′ N, 60°5′ E 154
Kirovo Chepetsk, *Russ.* 58°31′ N, 50°7′ E 154
Kirovohrad, *Ukr.* 48°30′ N, 32°18′ E 156
Kirovsk, *Russ.* 67°35′ N, 33°43′ E 152
Kirovskiy, *Russ.* 45°49′ N, 48°11′ E 158
Kirovskiy, *Russ.* 54°18′ N, 155°43′ E 173
Kirs, *Russ.* 59°19′ N, 52°17′ E 154
Kirs, peak, *Azerb.* 39°38′ N, 46°41′ E 195
Kirsanov, *Russ.* 52°40′ N, 42°39′ E 158
Kırşehir, *Turk.* 39°8′ N, 34°10′ E 143
Kirtachi, *Niger* 12°47′ N, 2°29′ E 222
Kirthar National Park, *Pak.* 25°37′ N, 66°58′ E 186
Kirton in Lindsey, *U.K.* 53°28′ N, 0°36′ E 162
Kirtshki, *Ga.* 42°32′ N, 42°5′ E 195
Kiruna, *Sw.* 68°0′ N, 19°54′ E 160
Kirundu, *Dem. Rep. of the Congo* 0°46′ N, 25°38′ E 224
Kirungu, *Dem. Rep. of the Congo* 7°6′ S, 29°42′ E 224
Kirya, *Russ.* 55°4′ N, 46°54′ E 154
Kiryū, *Japan* 36°24′ N, 139°21′ E 201
Kisaki, *Tanzania* 7°25′ S, 37°42′ E 224
Kisangani (Stanleyville), *Dem. Rep. of the Congo* 0°33′ N, 25°16′ E 224
Kisangire, *Tanzania* 7°21′ S, 38°43′ E 224
Kisaran, *Indonesia* 3°1′ N, 99°37′ E 196
Kisbér, *Hung.* 47°29′ N, 18°2′ E 168
Kiselevsk, *Russ.* 53°59′ N, 86°44′ E 184
Kiseljak, *Bosn. and Herzg.* 43°56′ N, 18°4′ E 168
Kisengwa, *Dem. Rep. of the Congo* 6°1′ S, 25°50′ E 224
Kishanganj, *India* 26°8′ N, 87°55′ E 197
Kishangarh, *India* 26°35′ N, 74°53′ E 188
Kishi, *Nig.* 9°3′ N, 3°50′ E 222
Kishiwada, *Japan* 34°26′ N, 135°22′ E 201
Kishkenekŏl, *Kaz.* 53°38′ N, 72°21′ E 184
Kishorganj, *Bangladesh* 24°21′ N, 90°43′ E 197
Kisigo, river, *Tanzania* 6°52′ S, 35°8′ E 224
Kisii, *Kenya* 0°43′ N, 34°46′ E 224
Kisiju, *Tanzania* 7°18′ S, 39°19′ E 224
Kısır Dağı, peak, *Turk.* 40°56′ N, 43°1′ E 195
Kiska, island, *Alas., U.S.* 51°31′ N, 176°29′ E 160
Kiskittogisu Lake, *Can.* 54°5′ N, 99°6′ W 108
Kiskőrös, *Hung.* 46°37′ N, 19°18′ E 168
Kiskundorozsma, *Hung.* 46°16′ N, 20°4′ E 168
Kiskunhalas, *Hung.* 46°24′ N, 19°29′ E 168
Kiskunlacháza, *Hung.* 47°10′ N, 19°2′ E 168
Kiskunmajsa, *Hung.* 46°29′ N, 19°45′ E 168
Kislovodsk, *Russ.* 43°56′ N, 42°46′ E 158
Kismaayo (Chisimayu), *Somalia* 0°27′ N, 42°35′ E 224
Kiso, river, *Japan* 35°33′ N, 137°31′ E 201
Kisoro, *Uganda* 1°20′ S, 29°40′ E 224
Kispiox, *Can.* 55°23′ N, 127°43′ W 108
Kispiox, river, *Can.* 55°38′ N, 128°38′ W 108
Kissidougou, *Guinea* 9°10′ N, 10°6′ W 222
Kissimmee, *Fla., U.S.* 28°18′ N, 81°25′ W 105
Kissimmee, Lake, *Fla., U.S.* 27°54′ N, 81°30′ W 105
Kissimmee, river, *Fla., U.S.* 27°23′ N, 81°10′ W 105
Kississing Lake, *Can.* 55°14′ N, 101°51′ W 108
Kissu, Jebel, peak, *Sudan* 21°32′ N, 25°3′ E 226
Kistanje, *Croatia* 43°58′ N, 15°56′ E 168
Kistelek, *Hung.* 46°28′ N, 19°58′ E 168
Kisterenye, *Hung.* 48°1′ N, 19°49′ E 168
Kistrand, *Nor.* 70°26′ N, 25°12′ E 152
Kisújszállás, *Hung.* 47°12′ N, 20°46′ E 168
Kisumu, *Kenya* 0°8′ N, 34°46′ E 224
Kisvárda, *Hung.* 48°13′ N, 22°5′ E 156
Kiswere, *Tanzania* 9°27′ S, 39°33′ E 224
Kiszombor, *Hung.* 46°11′ N, 20°26′ E 168
Kit Carson, *Colo., U.S.* 38°45′ N, 102°48′ W 90
Kita, *Mali* 13°2′ N, 9°30′ W 222
Kitaibaraki, *Japan* 36°46′ N, 140°43′ E 201
Kitakata, *Japan* 37°39′ N, 139°51′ E 201
Kitakyūshū, *Japan* 33°52′ N, 130°53′ E 200
Kitale, *Kenya* 1°0′ N, 34°58′ E 224
Kitchener, *Can.* 43°26′ N, 80°29′ W 94
Kitchener Lake, *Can.* 56°59′ N, 128°11′ W 108
Kitchigama, river, *Can.* 50°58′ N, 79°24′ W 80

Kitee, *Fin.* 62° 4' N, 30° 6' E 152
Kitenda, *Dem. Rep. of the Congo* 6° 49' S, 17° 26' E 218
Kitgum, *Uganda* 3° 14' N, 32° 53' E 224
Kithairṓnas, Óros, peak, *Gr.* 38° 10' N, 23° 10' E 156
Kíthira (Cerigo), island, *Gr.* 36° 17' N, 23° 3' E 180
Kíthira, island, *Gr.* 36° 22' N, 23° 6' E 143
Kiti, Cape, *Cyprus* 34° 44' N, 33° 34' E 194
Kitimat, *Can.* 54° 4' N, 128° 42' W 108
Kitlope, river, *Can.* 53° 14' N, 128° 8' W 108
Kitob, *Uzb.* 39° 8' N, 66° 53' E 197
Kitombe, *Dem. Rep. of the Congo* 5° 23' S, 18° 57' E 218
Kitsa, *Russ.* 68° 30' N, 33° 11' E 152
Kitscoty, *Can.* 53° 19' N, 110° 20' W 108
Kitsuki, *Japan* 33° 25' N, 131° 36' E 201
Kittery, *Me., U.S.* 43° 5' N, 70° 45' W 104
Kittery Point, *Me., U.S.* 43° 5' N, 70° 42' W 104
Kittilä, *Fin.* 67° 39' N, 24° 51' E 152
Kittitas, *Wash., U.S.* 46° 57' N, 120° 26' W 90
Kitty Hawk, *N.C., U.S.* 36° 2' N, 75° 41' W 82
Kitui, *Kenya* 1° 23' S, 38° 1' E 224
Kitwanga, *Can.* 55° 5' N, 128° 4' W 108
Kitwe, *Zambia* 12° 50' S, 28° 11' E 224
Kitzbühel, *Aust.* 47° 26' N, 12° 23' E 156
Kitzbüheler Alpen, *Aust.* 47° 22' N, 11° 45' E 156
Kitzingen, *Ger.* 49° 44' N, 10° 8' E 152
Kiukainen, *Fin.* 61° 12' N, 22° 5' E 166
Kiuruvesi, *Fin.* 63° 38' N, 26° 34' E 154
Kiuyu, Ras, *Tanzania* 4° 55' S, 39° 53' E 224
Kivalina, *Alas., U.S.* 67° 40' N, 164° 30' W 98
Kivalo, *Fin.* 65° 43' N, 25° 0' E 152
Kivertsi, *Ukr.* 50° 49' N, 25° 26' E 152
Kivijärvi, *Fin.* 63° 7' N, 25° 5' E 152
Kivik, *Nor.* 55° 40' N, 14° 14' E 152
Kiviõli, *Est.* 59° 20' N, 26° 55' E 166
Kivivaara, *Fin.* 63° 36' N, 30° 10' E 152
Kivumba, *Tanzania* 4° 38' S, 30° 40' E 224
Kiwai, island, *P.N.G.* 8° 51' S, 143° 38' E 192
Kiwalik, *U.S.* 66° 1' N, 161° 55' W 98
Kiya, *Russ.* 67° 36' N, 44° 11' E 169
Kiyāt, *Saudi Arabia* 18° 41' N, 41° 26' E 182
Kıyıköy, *Turk.* 41° 36' N, 28° 5' E 156
Kiyiu Lake, *Can.* 51° 35' N, 109° 24' W 90
Kiyuk Lake, *Can.* 60° 27' N, 100° 55' W 108
Kizel, *Russ.* 59° 0' N, 57° 42' E 154
Kizema, *Russ.* 61° 7' N, 44° 56' E 154
Kızılcahamam, *Turk.* 40° 27' N, 32° 37' E 156
Kızılırmak, *Turk.* 40° 21' N, 33° 58' E 156
Kızılırmak, river, *Turk.* 40° 33' N, 34° 43' E 180
Kızılliman Burnu, *Turk.* 35° 58' N, 32° 26' E 156
Kizil'skoye, *Russ.* 52° 43' N, 58° 49' E 154
Kızıltepe, *Turk.* 37° 11' N, 40° 36' E 195
Kizimkazi, Ras, *Tanzania* 6° 39' S, 39° 0' E 224
Kizlyar, *Russ.* 43° 49' N, 46° 40' E 195
Kizlyarskiy Zaliv 44° 24' N, 46° 34' E 158
Kizner, *Russ.* 56° 16' N, 51° 34' E 154
Kizreka, *Russ.* 65° 32' N, 31° 54' E 152
Kjelvik, *Nor.* 70° 58' N, 26° 7' E 152
Kjøpsvik, *Nor.* 68° 5' N, 16° 21' E 152
Kjya, islands, *Norwegian Sea* 64° 33' N, 9° 43' E 152
Klabat, peak, *Indonesia* 1° 34' N, 124° 51' E 192
Kladanj, *Bosn. and Herzg.* 44° 13' N, 18° 40' E 168
Kladnica, *Serb.* 43° 22' N, 20° 2' E 168
Klafeld, *Ger.* 50° 55' N, 8° 0' E 167
Klaipėda, *Lith.* 55° 42' N, 21° 10' E 166
Klamath, *Calif., U.S.* 41° 31' N, 124° 2' W 90
Klamath, *Calif., U.S.* 40° 45' N, 123° 5' W 90
Klamath Falls, *Oreg., U.S.* 42° 13' N, 121° 46' W 82
Klamath Mountains Mountains, *Calif., U.S.* 42° 1' N, 125° 19' W 80
Klamono, *Indonesia* 1° 4' S, 131° 25' E 192
Klarabro, *Nor.* 60° 46' N, 12° 46' E 152
Klawer, *S. Af.* 31° 50' S, 18° 36' E 227
Kle, *Liberia* 6° 37' N, 10° 54' W 222
Kleczkowski, Lac, lake, *Can.* 50° 47' N, 64° 6' W 111
Klein Karas, *Namibia* 27° 35' S, 18° 3' E 227
Klekovača, peak, *Bosn. and Herzg.* 44° 25' N, 16° 27' E 168
Kléla, *Mali* 11° 43' N, 5° 40' W 222
Klemtu, *Can.* 52° 34' N, 128° 33' W 108
Klenike, *Serb.* 42° 23' N, 21° 54' E 168
Klenje, *Serb.* 44° 48' N, 19° 26' E 168
Klerksdorp, *S. Af.* 26° 53' S, 26° 39' E 227
Klery Creek, *Alas., U.S.* 67° 10' N, 160° 25' W 98
Kleshchevo, *Russ.* 63° 16' N, 39° 11' E 154
Klesiv, *Ukr.* 51° 18' N, 26° 52' E 152
Kleszczele, *Pol.* 52° 36' N, 23° 19' E 154
Kletnya, *Russ.* 53° 19' N, 33° 12' E 154
Kletskiy, *Russ.* 49° 18' N, 43° 3' E 158
Klevan', *Ukr.* 50° 44' N, 25° 57' E 152
Kleve, *Ger.* 51° 47' N, 6° 8' E 167
Klibreck, Ben, peak, *U.K.* 58° 13' N, 4° 31' W 150
Kličevac, *Serb.* 44° 45' N, 21° 17' E 168
Klichaw, *Belarus* 53° 27' N, 29° 23' E 152
Klickitat, *Wash., U.S.* 45° 48' N, 121° 9' W 100
Klickitat, river, *Wash., U.S.* 46° 9' N, 121° 14' W 100
Klimovsk, *Russ.* 55° 17' N, 37° 28' E 154
Klin, *Russ.* 56° 20' N, 36° 42' E 154
Klinaklini, river, *Can.* 51° 15' N, 125° 47' W 108
Klingenbach, *Aust.* 47° 45' N, 16° 32' E 168
Klingenberg, *Ger.* 49° 45' N, 9° 12' E 167
Klintehamn, *Sw.* 57° 23' N, 18° 11' E 166
Klintsovka, *Russ.* 51° 40' N, 49° 15' E 158
Klintsy, *Russ.* 52° 44' N, 32° 14' E 154
Klipplaat, *S. Af.* 33° 0' S, 24° 19' E 227
Klisura, *Serb.* 42° 45' N, 22° 23' E 168
Ključ, *Bosn. and Herzg.* 44° 32' N, 16° 45' E 168
Kłodzko, *Pol.* 50° 25' N, 16° 40' E 152
Kłomnice, *Pol.* 50° 55' N, 19° 21' E 152
Klos, *Alban.* 41° 29' N, 20° 8' E 168
Kloster, *Ger.* 54° 35' N, 13° 7' E 152
Klosters, *Switz.* 46° 52' N, 9° 52' E 167
Klövsjö, *Nor.* 62° 31' N, 14° 8' E 152
Klukshu, *Can.* 60° 17' N, 137° 2' W 98
Klukwan, *Alas., U.S.* 59° 25' N, 135° 48' W 108
Klyastitsa, *Russ.* 55° 47' N, 29° 36' E 166
Klyastitsy, *Belarus* 55° 52' N, 28° 37' E 166
Klyavlino, *Russ.* 54° 15' N, 52° 2' E 154
Klyetsk, *Belarus* 53° 3' N, 26° 40' E 154
Klyuchevoye, *Russ.* 60° 26' N, 28° 44' E 166
Klyuchi, *Russ.* 52° 6' N, 79° 16' E 184
Klyukvenka, *Russ.* 58° 31' N, 85° 57' E 169
Knaresborough, *U.K.* 54° 1' N, 1° 28' W 162
Knee Lake, *Can.* 55° 9' N, 94° 45' W 108
Knee Lake, *Can.* 55° 50' N, 107° 20' W 108
Kneippbyn, *Sw.* 57° 35' N, 18° 13' E 166
Knesebeck, *Ger.* 52° 41' N, 10° 42' E 150
Knife Delta 58° 50' N, 95° 0' W 108
Knife, river, *N. Dak., U.S.* 47° 3' N, 102° 59' W 80
Knighton, *U.K.* 52° 19' N, 3° 3' W 162
Knightsville, *Ind., U.S.* 39° 31' N, 87° 5' W 102
Knin, *Croatia* 44° 2' N, 16° 11' E 168
Knittelfeld, *Aust.* 47° 14' N, 14° 48' E 156
Knjaževac, *Serb.* 43° 33' N, 22° 15' E 168
Knock Farril, ruin(s), *U.K.* 57° 34' N, 4° 38' W 150
Knockadoon Head, *Ire.* 51° 40' N, 7° 53' W 150
Knockboy, peak, *Ire.* 51° 47' N, 9° 32' W 150
Knockmealdown Mountains, *Ire.* 52° 13' N, 8° 1' W 150
Knokke-Heist, *Belg.* 51° 20' N, 3° 18' E 163
Knosós see Cnossus, ruin(s), *Gr.* 35° 16' N, 25° 4' E 156
Knottingley, *U.K.* 53° 42' N, 1° 14' W 162
Knox, *Ind., U.S.* 41° 16' N, 86° 37' W 102
Knox, Cape, *Can.* 53° 59' N, 133° 31' W 108
Knox City, *Tex., U.S.* 33° 24' N, 99° 49' W 92
Knox Coast, *Antarctica* 68° 16' S, 107° 4' E 248
Knoxville, *Iowa, U.S.* 41° 18' N, 93° 5' W 94
Knoxville, *Tenn., U.S.* 35° 58' N, 83° 56' W 96
Knucklas, *U.K.* 52° 21' N, 3° 6' W 162
Knud Rasmussen Land, region, *Arctic Ocean* 77° 1' N, 66° 28' W 106
Knüllwald, *Ger.* 51° 0' N, 9° 28' E 167
Knysna, *S. Af.* 34° 1' S, 23° 3' E 227
Kō Saki, *Japan* 33° 58' N, 129° 1' E 200
Koal, spring, *Chad* 14° 26' N, 16° 26' E 216
Koala, *Burkina Faso* 13° 24' N, 0° 8' E 222
Koani, *Tanzania* 6° 0' S, 39° 20' E 218
Kobayashi, *Japan* 31° 59' N, 130° 58' E 201
Kōbe, *Japan* 34° 41' N, 135° 9' E 201
Kobelyaky, *Ukr.* 49° 11' N, 34° 8' E 158
København (Copenhagen), *Den.* 55° 40' N, 12° 23' E 152
Kobern-Gondorf, *Ger.* 50° 18' N, 7° 27' E 167
Kobi-ri, *N. Korea* 39° 5' N, 126° 1' E 200
Koblenz, *Ger.* 50° 20' N, 7° 34' E 167
K'obo, *Eth.* 12° 7' N, 39° 37' E 182
Kobowen Swamp, marsh, *Sudan* 5° 23' N, 33° 14' E 224
Kobozha, *Russ.* 58° 48' N, 35° 0' E 154
Kobroor, island, *Indonesia* 6° 31' S, 134° 40' E 192
Kobryn, *Belarus* 52° 14' N, 24° 21' E 152
Kobu, *Azerb.* 40° 24' N, 49° 42' E 195
Kobuk, *Alas., U.S.* 66° 49' N, 156° 58' W 98
Kobuk, river, *Alas., U.S.* 66° 55' N, 159° 28' W 98
K'obulet'i, *Ga.* 41° 49' N, 41° 47' E 195
Kobyay, *Russ.* 63° 29' N, 127° 1' E 160
Kocaeli (İzmit), *Turk.* 40° 47' N, 29° 46' E 180
Kočani, *Maced.* 41° 55' N, 22° 24' E 168
Koçbaşı Tepe, peak, *Turk.* 39° 24' N, 43° 18' E 195
Koceljevo, *Serb.* 44° 28' N, 19° 50' E 168
Koch Bihar, *India* 26° 18' N, 89° 23' E 197
Kochi (Cochin), *India* 9° 50' N, 76° 24' E 188
Koch Peak, *Mont., U.S.* 45° 0' N, 111° 32' W 90
Kochas, *India* 25° 13' N, 83° 53' E 188
Kochechum, river, *Russ.* 67° 10' N, 98° 19' E 160
Kochen'ga, *Russ.* 60° 9' N, 43° 33' E 154
Kocherinovo, *Bulg.* 42° 5' N, 23° 4' E 168
Kochevo, *Russ.* 59° 36' N, 54° 20' E 154
Kōchi, *Japan* 33° 34' N, 133° 31' E 201
Kōchi, adm. division, *Japan* 33° 13' N, 132° 48' E 201
Kochkor, *Kyrg.* 42° 8' N, 75° 41' E 184
Kochubey, *Russ.* 44° 23' N, 46° 31' E 158
Kochumdek, *Russ.* 64° 24' N, 93° 11' E 169
Kocie, Góry, *Pol.* 51° 24' N, 16° 2' E 152
Kock, *Pol.* 51° 38' N, 22° 26' E 152
Kocs, *Hung.* 47° 35' N, 18° 11' E 168
Kocsola, *Hung.* 46° 31' N, 18° 10' E 168
Kodesjärvi, *Fin.* 62° 2' N, 22° 4' E 166
Kodiak, *Alas., U.S.* 57° 43' N, 152° 30' W 98
Kodiak Island, *Alas., U.S.* 56° 52' N, 152° 48' W 98
Kodinar, *India* 20° 46' N, 70° 42' E 188
Kodino, *Russ.* 63° 42' N, 39° 43' E 154
Kodinskiy, *Russ.* 58° 34' N, 99° 5' E 160
Kodok, *Sudan* 9° 55' N, 32° 7' E 224
Kōes, *Namibia* 26° 0' S, 19° 7' E 227
Kofa Mountains, *Ariz., U.S.* 33° 19' N, 113° 59' W 101
Kofarnihon see Vahdat, *Taj.* 38° 32' N, 69° 1' E 197
Koffiefontein, *S. Af.* 29° 25' S, 25° 0' E 227
Kofili, *Mali* 15° 15' N, 8° 46' W 222
Koforidua, *Ghana* 6° 6' N, 0° 16' E 222
Kōfu, *Japan* 35° 39' N, 138° 35' E 201
Koga, *Japan* 36° 11' N, 139° 44' E 201
Køge Bugt 55° 23' N, 12° 3' E 152
Kogolym, *Russ.* 62° 20' N, 74° 49' E 169
Kogon, *Uzb.* 39° 43' N, 64° 34' E 197
Kogon, river, *Guinea* 11° 26' N, 14° 29' W 222
Kohala, region, *Oceania* 20° 10' N, 155° 53' W 99
Kohat, *Pak.* 33° 34' N, 71° 29' E 186
Kohila, *Est.* 59° 9' N, 24° 43' E 166
Kohima, *India* 25° 43' N, 94° 9' E 188
Kohler, *Wis., U.S.* 43° 44' N, 87° 47' W 102
Kohlu, *Pak.* 29° 55' N, 69° 16' E 186
Kohnieh, *Cambodia* 13° 6' N, 107° 3' E 202
Kohtla-Järve, *Est.* 59° 22' N, 27° 14' E 166
Kohunlich, ruin(s), *Mex.* 18° 21' N, 89° 4' W 115
Koide, *Japan* 37° 13' N, 138° 58' E 201
Koidern, *Can.* 61° 57' N, 140° 33' W 98
Koidu, *Sierra Leone* 8° 38' N, 10° 59' W 222
Koilani, *Cyprus* 34° 49' N, 32° 51' E 194
Koin, *N. Korea* 40° 29' N, 126° 23' E 200
Koivu, *Fin.* 66° 9' N, 25° 11' E 152
Kojā, river, *Iran* 25° 30' N, 61° 18' E 182
Kok, river, *Asia* 20° 6' N, 99° 28' E 202
Kök Shal Tau (Kakshaal Range), *Kyrg.* 41° 22' N, 77° 33' E 184
Kokanee Peak, *Can.* 49° 42' N, 117° 14' W 90
Kökar, *Fin.* 59° 56' N, 20° 52' E 166
Kokas, *Indonesia* 2° 47' S, 132° 19' E 192
Kök-Aygyr, *Kyrg.* 40° 43' N, 75° 39' E 184
Kōke'e Lodge, site, *Hawai'i, U.S.* 22° 7' N, 159° 43' W 99
Kokemäki, *Fin.* 61° 13' N, 22° 16' E 166
Kokenau, *Indonesia* 4° 37' S, 136° 13' E 192
Košický, adm. division, *Slovakia* 48° 34' N, 20° 35' E 152
Kokin Brod, *Serb.* 43° 29' N, 19° 49' E 168
Kokka, *Sudan* 20° 1' N, 30° 33' E 226
Kokkina, *Northern Cyprus, Cyprus* 35° 10' N, 32° 36' E 194
Kokkola (Gamlakarleby), *Fin.* 63° 49' N, 23° 5' E 152
Koko, *Eth.* 10° 20' N, 36° 3' E 224
Koko, *Nig.* 11° 26' N, 4° 31' E 222
Koko Head, peak, *Hawai'i, U.S.* 21° 14' N, 157° 44' W 99
Kokomo, *Ind., U.S.* 40° 29' N, 86° 8' W 102
Kokomo, *Miss., U.S.* 31° 11' N, 90° 1' W 103
Kokong, *Botswana* 24° 20' S, 23° 4' E 227
Kokoro, *Nig.* 8° 54' N, 3° 9' E 222
Kökpekti, *Kaz.* 48° 44' N, 82° 23' E 184
Kokrines, *Alas., U.S.* 64° 56' N, 154° 41' W 98
Koksan, *N. Korea* 38° 45' N, 126° 40' E 200
Kökshetaū, *Kaz.* 53° 17' N, 69° 25' E 184
Koksovyy, *Russ.* 48° 9' N, 40° 37' E 158
Kokstad, *S. Af.* 30° 35' S, 29° 25' E 227
Köktal, *Kaz.* 44° 6' N, 79° 47' E 184
Köktöbe, *Kaz.* 51° 37' N, 77° 23' E 184
Kokubu, *Japan* 31° 42' N, 130° 45' E 201
Kola, *Bosn. and Herzg.* 44° 42' N, 17° 4' E 168
Kola, *Russ.* 68° 49' N, 33° 14' E 160
Kola Peninsula, *Russ.* 67° 40' N, 28° 12' E 172
Kolahun, *Liberia* 8° 17' N, 10° 6' W 222
Kolaka, *Indonesia* 4° 2' S, 121° 30' E 192
Kolar, *India* 13° 9' N, 78° 8' E 188
Kolari, *Fin.* 67° 21' N, 23° 46' E 152
Kolarovgrad see Shumen, *Bulg.* 43° 16' N, 26° 55' E 156
Kolárovo, *Slovakia* 47° 54' N, 17° 59' E 168
Kolåsen, *Nor.* 63° 45' N, 12° 58' E 152
Kolayat, *India* 27° 50' N, 72° 57' E 186
Kolbio, *Kenya* 1° 11' S, 41° 7' E 224
Kol'chugino, *Russ.* 56° 18' N, 39° 18' E 154
Kolda, *Senegal* 12° 54' N, 14° 58' W 222
Koldewey, Store, island, *Den.* 75° 50' N, 17° 54' W 246
Kolding, *Den.* 55° 28' N, 9° 27' E 150
Kölduk, *Kyrg.* 39° 56' N, 73° 30' E 197
Kole, *Dem. Rep. of the Congo* 2° 4' N, 25° 26' E 224
Kole, *Dem. Rep. of the Congo* 3° 33' S, 22° 27' E 218
Kolé, *Mali* 12° 6' N, 8° 21' W 222
Koler, *Nor.* 65° 28' N, 20° 27' E 152
Kolezhma, *Russ.* 64° 14' N, 35° 45' E 154
Kolga Laht 59° 28' N, 25° 13' E 166
Kolguyev, Ostrov, island, *Russ.* 69° 29' N, 48° 57' E 169
Kolhapur, *India* 16° 41' N, 74° 14' E 188
Kolī, *Eth.* 10° 19' N, 36° 45' E 224
Koli, *Fin.* 63° 6' N, 29° 45' E 152
Koliganek, *Alas., U.S.* 59° 45' N, 157° 20' W 98
Kolik'yegan, *Russ.* 61° 42' N, 79° 8' E 169
Kolik'yegan, river, *Russ.* 61° 31' N, 79° 14' E 169
Kolimbiné, river, *Mali* 14° 49' N, 12° 8' W 222
Kolka, *Latv.* 57° 43' N, 22° 32' E 166
Kolkas Rags, *Latv.* 57° 44' N, 22° 36' E 166
Kolkata (Calcutta), *India* 22° 33' N, 88° 21' E 197
Kolky, *Ukr.* 51° 5' N, 25° 39' E 152
Kollegal, *India* 12° 9' N, 77° 9' E 188
Kollioura, *Gabon* 0° 11' N, 12° 8' E 218
Kolmanskop, *Namibia* 26° 44' S, 15° 14' E 227
Kolmogorovo, *Russ.* 59° 14' N, 91° 15' E 169
Köln (Cologne), *Ger.* 50° 56' N, 6° 57' E 167
Kolo, *Niger* 13° 19' N, 2° 23' E 222
Kołobrzeg, *Pol.* 54° 9' N, 15° 33' E 152
Kolodishchi, *Belarus* 53° 56' N, 27° 46' E 166
Kolodnya, *Russ.* 54° 47' N, 32° 16' E 154
Kologi, *Sudan* 10° 51' N, 31° 0' E 224
Kologriv, *Russ.* 58° 49' N, 44° 22' E 154
Kolokani, *Mali* 13° 36' N, 8° 2' W 222
Kololo, *Eth.* 7° 27' N, 42° 0' E 224
Kolomna, *Russ.* 55° 4' N, 38° 41' E 154
Kolomyya, *Ukr.* 48° 31' N, 25° 2' E 158
Kolosib, *India* 24° 13' N, 92° 38' E 188
Kolosovka, *Russ.* 56° 31' N, 73° 37' E 169
Kolosovykh, Ostrov, island, *Russ.* 74° 9' N, 87° 14' E 160
Kolozhno, Ozero, lake, *Russ.* 67° 44' N, 30° 18' E 152
Kolpakovskiy, *Russ.* 54° 31' N, 155° 58' E 160
Kolpashevo, *Russ.* 58° 19' N, 82° 57' E 169
Kolpino, *Russ.* 59° 44' N, 30° 36' E 166
Kolpny, *Russ.* 52° 13' N, 37° 3' E 158
Kol'skiy Poluostrov, *Russ.* 67° 17' N, 38° 11' E 169
Koluszki, *Pol.* 51° 44' N, 19° 48' E 152
Kolva, river, *Russ.* 60° 47' N, 56° 50' E 154
Kolva, river, *Russ.* 66° 19' N, 56° 53' E 154
Kolvereid, *Nor.* 64° 52' N, 11° 38' E 152
Kolvitsa, *Russ.* 67° 4' N, 33° 0' E 152
Kolwezi, *Dem. Rep. of the Congo* 10° 46' S, 25° 26' E 224
Kolyma, river, *Russ.* 67° 7' N, 152° 3' E 160
Kolyma, river, *Russ.* 65° 53' N, 152° 45' E 172
Kolymskoye, *Russ.* 68° 47' N, 158° 38' E 160
Kolymskoye Nagor'ye, *Russ.* 61° 35' N, 155° 21' E 160
Kolyuchin, Ostrov, island, *Russ.* 67° 21' N, 174° 33' W 98
Kolyuchinskaya Guba 66° 38' N, 178° 0' W 98
Kolyvan', *Russ.* 51° 19' N, 82° 42' E 184
Kôm Dafana, ruin(s), *Egypt* 30° 50' N, 32° 7' E 194
Kôm Ombo, *Egypt* 24° 27' N, 32° 55' E 182
Kom, peak, *Bulg.* 43° 9' N, 23° 1' E 168
Komádi, *Hung.* 47° 0' N, 21° 30' E 168
Komagane, *Japan* 35° 44' N, 137° 56' E 201
Komagvær, *Nor.* 70° 14' N, 30° 36' E 152
Komandorskiye Ostrova (Commander Islands), *Bering Sea* 53° 42' N, 162° 31' E 160
Komarne, *Ukr.* 49° 37' N, 23° 41' E 152
Komárno, *Slovakia* 47° 46' N, 18° 7' E 168
Komárom, *Hung.* 47° 44' N, 18° 7' E 168
Komárom-Esztergom, adm. division, *Hung.* 47° 45' N, 17° 55' E 156
Komarovo, *Russ.* 59° 33' N, 50° 18' E 154
Komatipoort, *S. Af.* 25° 26' S, 31° 56' E 227
Komatsu, *Japan* 36° 24' N, 136° 28' E 201
Komatsushima, *Japan* 33° 59' N, 134° 34' E 201
Komba, *Dem. Rep. of the Congo* 2° 52' N, 24° 3' E 224
Komenotsu, *Japan* 32° 6' N, 130° 20' E 201
Komi, adm. division, *Russ.* 63° 40' N, 52° 9' E 154
Komi-Permyak, adm. division, *Russ.* 60° 27' N, 52° 55' E 169
Komiža, *Croatia* 43° 2' N, 16° 5' E 168
Komló, *Hung.* 46° 10' N, 18° 16' E 168
Komodo, island, *Indonesia* 9° 13' S, 119° 17' E 230
Komoé, river, *Africa* 9° 15' N, 4° 13' W 222
Komoé, river, *Côte d'Ivoire* 5° 40' N, 3° 23' W 222
Komoro, *Japan* 36° 19' N, 138° 26' E 201
Komotiní, *Gr.* 41° 7' N, 25° 24' E 156
Komovi, peak, *Mont.* 42° 40' N, 19° 37' E 168
Kompong Chhnang, *Cambodia* 12° 15' N, 104° 39' E 202
Kompong Speu, *Cambodia* 11° 24' N, 104° 29' E 202
Kompong Sralao, *Cambodia* 14° 5' N, 105° 45' E 202
Kompong Trach, *Cambodia* 10° 34' N, 104° 27' E 202
Komsa, *Russ.* 61° 45' N, 89° 19' E 169
Komses'yegan, *Russ.* 61° 16' N, 83° 32' E 169
Komsomol, *Kaz.* 47° 26' N, 53° 40' E 158
Komsomolets, *Kaz.* 53° 47' N, 62° 3' E 154
Komsomolets, Ostrov, island, *Russ.* 81° 49' N, 109° 24' E 246
Komsomolets Shyghanaghy 45° 19' N, 52° 3' E 158
Komsomol'sk, *Russ.* 57° 2' N, 40° 16' E 154
Komsomol'sk na Amure, *Russ.* 50° 30' N, 136° 57' E 190
Komsomol'skiy, *Russ.* 69° 5' N, 172° 43' E 173
Komsomol'skoe, *Kaz.* 50° 26' N, 60° 27' E 158
Komsomol'skoy Pravdy, Ostrova, islands, *Laptev Sea* 76° 50' N, 108° 45' E 160
Komsomol'skoye, *Russ.* 50° 45' N, 46° 59' E 158
Komu, *Fin.* 63° 40' N, 26° 8' E 152
Komusan, *N. Korea* 42° 7' N, 129° 41' E 200
Kon Tum, *Vietnam* 14° 21' N, 107° 59' E 202
Kona, *Mali* 14° 56' N, 3° 55' W 222
Kona, region, *Oceania* 19° 25' N, 155° 54' W 99
Konakovo, *Russ.* 56° 40' N, 36° 47' E 154
Konakpınar, *Turk.* 38° 54' N, 37° 17' E 156
Konarak, *India* 19° 53' N, 86° 4' E 188
Konawa, *Okla., U.S.* 34° 56' N, 96° 44' W 96
Konch, *India* 25° 58' N, 79° 8' E 197
Konda, river, *Russ.* 60° 42' N, 63° 22' E 169
Kondiás, *Gr.* 39° 51' N, 25° 9' E 156
Kondoa, *Tanzania* 4° 55' S, 35° 48' E 224
Kondol', *Russ.* 52° 47' N, 45° 5' E 158
Kondolole, *Dem. Rep. of the Congo* 1° 20' N, 26° 0' E 224
Kondopoga, *Russ.* 62° 11' N, 34° 22' E 154
Kondoz, *Afghan.* 36° 47' N, 68° 54' E 186
Kondrovo, *Russ.* 54° 49' N, 35° 57' E 154
Konduga, *Nig.* 11° 38' N, 13° 25' E 216
Kondukur, *India* 15° 11' N, 79° 55' E 188
Konergino, *Russ.* 65° 57' N, 178° 47' W 98
Konetsbor, *Russ.* 64° 51' N, 57° 42' E 154
Köneürgench, *Turkm.* 42° 18' N, 59° 10' E 180
Konevo, *Russ.* 62° 6' N, 39° 19' E 154
Konfara, *Guinea* 11° 55' N, 8° 52' W 222
Kong, *Côte d'Ivoire* 9° 9' N, 4° 38' W 222
Kong Christian IX Land, *Den.* 68° 38' N, 33° 55' W 106
Kong Christian X Land, *Den.* 73° 44' N, 52° 49' W 246
Kong Frederik VI Kyst, *Den.* 61° 32' N, 52° 50' W 106
Kong Frederik VIII Land, *Den.* 79° 7' N, 62° 48' W 246
Kong Karls Land, islands, *Barents Sea* 78° 20' N, 30° 46' E 160
Kong Kemul, peak, *Indonesia* 1° 54' N, 115° 51' E 192
Kong, Koh, island, *Cambodia* 11° 20' N, 102° 19' E 202
Kong, river, *Laos* 15° 33' N, 106° 51' E 202
Köngäs, *Fin.* 67° 52' N, 24° 51' E 152
Kongelai, *Kenya* 1° 22' N, 35° 1' E 224
Konginkangas, *Fin.* 62° 45' N, 25° 44' E 154
Konglu, *Myanmar* 27° 17' N, 97° 56' E 188
Kongolo, *Dem. Rep. of the Congo* 5° 25' S, 26° 56' E 224
Kongor, *Sudan* 7° 8' N, 31° 21' E 224
Kongsfjord, *Nor.* 70° 41' N, 29° 20' E 152
Kongsmoen, *Nor.* 64° 52' N, 12° 25' E 152
Kongur Shan, peak, *China* 38° 36' N, 75° 14' E 184
Kongwa, *Tanzania* 6° 9' S, 36° 26' E 224
Konibodom, *Taj.* 40° 18' N, 70° 27' E 197
Königswinter, *Ger.* 50° 40' N, 7° 11' E 167
Konin, *Pol.* 52° 12' N, 18° 14' E 152
Köniz, *Switz.* 46° 54' N, 7° 25' E 167
Konjic, *Bosn. and Herzg.* 43° 38' N, 17° 58' E 168
Konjuh, peak, *Bosn. and Herzg.* 44° 17' N, 18° 30' E 168
Konkouré, river, *Guinea* 10° 17' N, 13° 31' W 222
Konnur, *India* 16° 10' N, 74° 44' E 188
Konosha, *Russ.* 60° 59' N, 40° 12' E 154
Konotop, *Ukr.* 51° 12' N, 33° 16' E 158
Kon'ovo, *Bulg.* 42° 32' N, 26° 10' E 156
Konta, *India* 17° 48' N, 81° 22' E 188
Kontagora, *Nig.* 10° 21' N, 5° 29' E 222
Kontcha, *Cameroon* 7° 54' N, 12° 13' E 218
Kontiomäki, *Fin.* 64° 20' N, 28° 4' E 152
Konya (Iconium), *Turk.* 37° 51' N, 32° 29' E 156
Konz, *Ger.* 49° 41' N, 6° 36' E 163
Konza, *Kenya* 1° 47' S, 37° 7' E 224

Koocanusa, Lake, *Can.* 49°4′ N, 115°56′ W 108
Ko'oko'olau, peak, *Hawai'i, U.S.* 19°36′ N, 155°37′ W 99
Koopmansfontein, *S. Af.* 28°15′ S, 24°3′ E 227
Koosa, *Est.* 58°30′ N, 27°2′ E 166
Koostatak, *Can.* 51°25′ N, 97°22′ W 90
Kootenai, *Idaho, U.S.* 48°17′ N, 116°33′ W 108
Kootenay Lake, *Can.* 49°44′ N, 116°47′ W 108
Kow, *Mauritania* 15°54′ N, 12°47′ W 222
Kopaonik, mountains, *Kos.* 43°15′ N, 20°50′ E 156
Kópasker, *Ice.* 66°21′ N, 16°31′ W 246
Köpbirlik, *Kaz.* 46°27′ N, 77°12′ E 184
Köpekkayası Burnu, *Turk.* 41°56′ N, 31°52′ E 156
Köpenick, *Ger.* 52°27′ N, 13°33′ E 152
Kopetdag Mountains, *Iran* 38°27′ N, 55°37′ E 180
Kopeysk, *Russ.* 55°5′ N, 61°36′ E 154
Köping, *Nor.* 59°29′ N, 15°58′ E 152
Kopište, island, *Croatia* 42°41′ N, 16°33′ E 168
Koplik, *Alban.* 42°12′ N, 19°26′ E 168
Koporskiy Zaliv 59°47′ N, 28°26′ E 166
Koppang, *Nor.* 61°33′ N, 11°3′ E 152
Kopparberg, *Nor.* 59°52′ N, 15°0′ E 152
Kopperå, *Nor.* 63°23′ N, 11°53′ E 152
Koprivnica, *Croatia* 46°10′ N, 16°50′ E 168
Kõpu, *Est.* 58°54′ N, 22°11′ E 166
Kop'ung, *N. Korea* 40°35′ N, 125°55′ E 200
Kopylovka, *Russ.* 58°39′ N, 82°19′ E 169
Kora National Park, *Kenya* 0°29′ N, 38°18′ E 224
Korab, Mal, *Alban.* 41°43′ N, 20°27′ E 168
K'orahē, *Eth.* 6°35′ N, 44°11′ E 218
Korba, *India* 22°22′ N, 82°44′ E 197
Korba, *Tun.* 36°35′ N, 10°51′ E 156
Korbach, *Ger.* 51°16′ N, 8°51′ E 167
Korbevac, *Serb.* 42°34′ N, 22°2′ E 168
Korbol, *Chad* 10°1′ N, 17°42′ E 216
Korbovo, *Serb.* 44°31′ N, 22°42′ E 168
Korçë, *Alban.* 40°37′ N, 20°47′ E 143
Korčula, *Croatia* 42°56′ N, 17°7′ E 156
Korčula, island, *Croatia* 42°52′ N, 16°25′ E 168
Korčulanski Kanal 42°59′ N, 16°23′ E 168
Korday, *Kaz.* 43°3′ N, 74°42′ E 184
Koré Mayroua, *Niger* 13°23′ N, 3°53′ E 222
Korea, North 40°12′ N, 126°16′ E 200
Korea, South 36°43′ N, 127°7′ E 200
Korea Strait (Tsushima Strait) 34°9′ N, 125°22′ E 190
Korem, *Eth.* 12°28′ N, 39°31′ E 182
Korenevo, *Russ.* 51°23′ N, 34°59′ E 158
Korenovsk, *Russ.* 45°31′ N, 39°27′ E 156
Korepino, *Russ.* 61°4′ N, 57°5′ E 154
Korets', *Ukr.* 50°37′ N, 27°7′ E 152
Korf, *Russ.* 60°20′ N, 165°42′ E 173
Korgon, *Kyrg.* 39°51′ N, 70°5′ E 197
Korhogo, *Côte d'Ivoire* 9°26′ N, 5°39′ W 222
Korinthiakós Kólpos 38°23′ N, 21°36′ E 156
Kórinthos, *Gr.* 37°52′ N, 22°55′ E 180
Kőris Hegy, peak, *Hung.* 47°16′ N, 17°43′ E 168
Korita, *Bosn. and Herzg.* 43°2′ N, 18°29′ E 168
Kōriyama, *Japan* 37°23′ N, 140°22′ E 201
Korkino, *Russ.* 54°53′ N, 61°27′ E 154
Korkuteli, *Turk.* 37°4′ N, 30°12′ E 156
Korla, *China* 41°41′ N, 86°14′ E 184
Korliki, *Russ.* 61°30′ N, 82°27′ E 169
Kormakitis, *Northern Cyprus, Cyprus* 35°20′ N, 33°0′ E 194
Kormakitis, Cape, *Northern Cyprus, Cyprus* 35°22′ N, 32°42′ E 194
Körmend, *Hung.* 47°0′ N, 16°37′ E 168
Kornaka, *Niger* 14°8′ N, 6°55′ E 222
Kornilovo, *Russ.* 53°31′ N, 81°13′ E 184
Koro, *Côte d'Ivoire* 8°29′ N, 7°26′ W 222
Koro Kidinga, spring, *Chad* 16°58′ N, 16°56′ E 216
Korocha, *Russ.* 50°48′ N, 37°12′ E 158
Korogwe, *Tanzania* 5°8′ S, 38°29′ E 224
Koronadal, *Philippines* 6°21′ N, 124°46′ E 203
Koronga, *Mali* 15°21′ N, 7°37′ W 222
Koronga, Mont, peak, *Togo* 9°2′ N, 1°10′ E 222
Kóronos, *Gr.* 37°7′ N, 25°33′ E 156
Koror, *Palau* 7°20′ N, 134°30′ E 242
Körösladany, *Hung.* 46°58′ N, 21°4′ E 168
Korosozero, *Russ.* 63°41′ N, 35°21′ E 154
Korosten', *Ukr.* 50°55′ N, 28°45′ E 152
Korotoyak, *Russ.* 50°59′ N, 39°10′ E 158
Korpela, *Russ.* 66°14′ N, 30°1′ E 152
Korpilahti, *Fin.* 62°0′ N, 25°31′ E 166
Korpilombolo, *Nor.* 66°51′ N, 23°1′ E 152
Korpisalmi, *Fin.* 63°57′ N, 29°37′ E 152
Korpisel'kya, *Russ.* 62°19′ N, 30°58′ E 152
Korpo, *Fin.* 60°9′ N, 21°32′ E 166
Korsakov, *Russ.* 46°44′ N, 142°58′ E 190
Korshiv, *Ukr.* 48°37′ N, 24°59′ E 152
Korsnäs, *Fin.* 62°46′ N, 21°9′ E 152
Korsnes, *Nor.* 70°12′ N, 23°15′ E 152
Korsnes, *Nor.* 68°14′ N, 16°1′ E 152
Korsør, *Den.* 55°18′ N, 11°11′ E 152
Korsze, *Pol.* 54°9′ N, 21°8′ E 166
Korti, *Sudan* 18°1′ N, 31°35′ E 182
Kortkeros, *Russ.* 61°49′ N, 51°38′ E 154
Kortrijk, *Belg.* 50°49′ N, 3°17′ E 163
Korup National Park, *Cameroon* 5°10′ N, 9°15′ E 222
Korvatunturi, peak, *Fin.* 68°3′ N, 29°10′ E 152
Koryakskiy, *Russia* 60°0′ N, 165°0′ E 160
Koryakskoye Nagor'ye, *Russ.* 60°46′ N, 165°33′ E 160
Koryazhma, *Russ.* 61°16′ N, 47°15′ E 154
Korytnitsi, *Belarus* 53°52′ N, 29°26′ E 166
Kos, *Gr.* 36°53′ N, 27°17′ E 156
Kosa, *Eth.* 7°50′ N, 36°49′ E 218
Kosa, *Russ.* 59°57′ N, 55°1′ E 154
Kosan, *N. Korea* 38°50′ N, 127°25′ E 200
Kosaya Gora, *Russ.* 54°5′ N, 37°29′ E 154
Kosciusko, *Miss., U.S.* 33°2′ N, 89°35′ W 103
Kosciuszko, Mount, *Austral.* 36°30′ S, 148°2′ E 230
Kose, *Est.* 59°10′ N, 25°7′ E 166
Koserow, *Ger.* 54°2′ N, 14°0′ E 152
Kosh Agach, *Russ.* 49°58′ N, 88°34′ E 184
Kosha, *Eth.* 6°43′ N, 37°18′ E 224
Kosharevo, *Bulg.* 42°40′ N, 22°46′ E 168
Kosh-Döbö, *Kyrg.* 41°2′ N, 74°6′ E 197
Koshino, *Japan* 36°2′ N, 136°1′ E 201
Koshk-e Kohneh, *Afghan.* 34°53′ N, 62°28′ E 186
Koshki, *Russ.* 54°14′ N, 50°22′ E 154
Koshoba, *Turkm.* 40°13′ N, 54°6′ E 158
Koshuya, *Ukr.* 48°3′ N, 25°24′ E 156
Kosi, Lake, *S. Af.* 26°59′ S, 32°26′ E 227
Košice, *Slovakia* 48°43′ N, 21°15′ E 152
Košický, adm. division, *Slovakia* 48°43′ N, 21°6′ E 156
Kosjerić, *Serb.* 44°0′ N, 19°54′ E 168
Koskenpää, *Fin.* 62°3′ N, 25°6′ E 166
Koski, *Fin.* 61°0′ N, 25°7′ E 166
Koski, *Fin.* 60°38′ N, 23°6′ E 166
Koskolovo, *Russ.* 59°39′ N, 28°27′ E 166
Kos'kovo, *Russ.* 56°30′ N, 29°39′ E 166
Koskullskulle, *Nor.* 67°10′ N, 20°41′ E 152
Koslan, *Russ.* 63°33′ N, 48°45′ E 154
Kosma, river, *Russ.* 66°8′ N, 49°26′ E 154
Kosman, *Bosn. and Herzg.* 43°22′ N, 18°46′ E 168
Koson, *Uzb.* 39°3′ N, 65°36′ E 197
Kosŏng, *N. Korea* 38°45′ N, 128°11′ E 200
Kosonov, *Uzb.* 41°17′ N, 71°40′ E 197
Kosovo Polje see Fushë Kosova, *Kosovo* 42°38′ N, 21°6′ E 168
Kosovo 42°38′ N, 20°10′ E 168
Kosrae (Kusaie), island, *F.S.M.* 5°19′ N, 162°59′ E 242
Kosso, *Côte d'Ivoire* 5°4′ N, 5°46′ W 222
Kossou, Lac de, lake, *Côte d'Ivoire* 8°9′ N, 5°55′ W 222
Kosti, *Sudan* 13°7′ N, 32°37′ E 182
Kostin Shar, Proliv 71°7′ N, 47°6′ E 160
Kostinbrod, *Bulg.* 42°49′ N, 23°13′ E 168
Kostino, *Russ.* 65°16′ N, 88°12′ E 169
Kostomuksha, *Russ.* 64°36′ N, 30°36′ E 152
Kostopil', *Ukr.* 50°53′ N, 26°26′ E 152
Kostroma, *Russ.* 57°47′ N, 41°3′ E 154
Kostroma, adm. division, *Russ.* 57°52′ N, 41°34′ E 160
Kostrzyn, *Pol.* 52°35′ N, 14°39′ E 152
Kostyantynivka, *Ukr.* 48°34′ N, 37°40′ E 158
Kos'ya, *Russ.* 58°49′ N, 59°20′ E 154
Kosyń, *Pol.* 51°22′ N, 23°32′ E 152
Kos'yu, *Russ.* 65°38′ N, 58°57′ E 154
Kos'yu, river, *Russ.* 65°24′ N, 58°57′ E 154
Kos'yuvom, *Russ.* 66°16′ N, 59°47′ E 169
Koszalin, *Pol.* 54°11′ N, 16°10′ E 152
Kot Addu, *Pak.* 30°29′ N, 71°1′ E 186
Kot Kapura, *India* 30°35′ N, 74°52′ E 186
Kota, *India* 25°8′ N, 75°51′ E 197
Kota Baharu, *Malaysia* 6°8′ N, 102°16′ E 196
Kota Belud, *Malaysia* 6°23′ N, 116°23′ E 203
Kota Kinabalu, *Malaysia* 5°59′ N, 116°4′ E 203
Kota Tinggi, *Malaysia* 1°42′ N, 103°52′ E 196
Kotabaru, *Indonesia* 1°6′ S, 101°44′ E 196
Kotabaru, *Indonesia* 3°26′ S, 116°11′ E 192
Kotadabok, *Indonesia* 0°29′ N, 104°32′ E 196
Kotadaik, *Indonesia* 0°11′ N, 104°38′ E 196
Kotakoli, *Dem. Rep. of the Congo* 4°7′ N, 21°42′ E 218
Kotamobagu, *Indonesia* 0°49′ N, 124°13′ E 192
Kotapad, *India* 19°7′ N, 82°17′ E 188
Kotatengah, *Indonesia* 1°8′ N, 100°33′ E 196
Kotcho Lake, *Can.* 59°3′ N, 121°52′ W 108
Kotcho, river, *Can.* 58°45′ N, 121°5′ W 108
Kötegyán, *Hung.* 46°44′ N, 21°28′ E 168
Kotel'nich, *Russ.* 58°18′ N, 48°22′ E 154
Kotel'nikovo, *Russ.* 47°35′ N, 43°2′ E 158
Kotel'nyy, *Russ.* 75°53′ N, 137°53′ E 173
Kotel'nyy, Ostrov, island, *Russ.* 74°17′ N, 131°48′ E 160
Kotenko, *Russ.* 70°33′ N, 147°13′ E 160
Kothi, *India* 24°46′ N, 80°47′ E 197
Kothi, *India* 23°19′ N, 82°4′ E 197
Kotido, *Uganda* 2°57′ N, 34°4′ E 224
Kotka, *Fin.* 60°27′ N, 26°55′ E 166
Kotlas, *Russ.* 61°13′ N, 46°42′ E 154
Kotly, *Russ.* 59°34′ N, 28°46′ E 166
Kotonkoro, *Nig.* 10°59′ N, 5°58′ E 222
Kotor Varoš, *Bosn. and Herzg.* 44°37′ N, 17°22′ E 168
Kotoriba, *Croatia* 46°21′ N, 16°48′ E 168
Kotovsk, *Russ.* 52°33′ N, 41°30′ E 158
Kotovs'k, *Ukr.* 47°40′ N, 29°35′ E 156
Kotraža, *Serb.* 43°41′ N, 20°12′ E 168
Kotri, *Pak.* 25°21′ N, 68°17′ E 186
Kötschach, *Aust.* 46°41′ N, 13°0′ E 167
Kotto, river, *Cen. Af. Rep.* 4°48′ N, 21°58′ E 218
Kotuy, river, *Russ.* 71°33′ N, 99°52′ E 172
Kotuy, river, *Russ.* 67°53′ N, 99°10′ E 169
Kotuykan, river, *Russ.* 70°38′ N, 103°26′ E 160
Kotzebue, *Alas., U.S.* 66°45′ N, 162°31′ W 98
Kotzebue Sound 66°23′ N, 163°57′ W 98
Koualé, *Mali* 11°24′ N, 7°2′ W 222
Kouandé, *Benin* 10°18′ N, 1°40′ E 222
Kouba Modounga, *Chad* 15°39′ N, 18°16′ E 216
Kouchibouguac National Park, *Can.* 46°46′ N, 65°38′ W 111
Koudougou, *Burkina Faso* 12°15′ N, 2°24′ W 222
Koufeï, spring, *Niger* 14°49′ N, 13°34′ E 222
Koukdjuak, Great Plain of the, *Can.* 65°48′ N, 79°52′ W 106
Kouki, *Cen. Af. Rep.* 7°7′ N, 17°18′ E 218
Kouklia, *Cyprus* 34°42′ N, 32°34′ E 194
Koukou Angarana, *Chad* 12°0′ N, 21°46′ E 216
Koúla, peak, *Gr.* 41°20′ N, 24°41′ E 156
Koulé, *Guinea* 7°58′ N, 9°2′ W 222
Koulen, *Cambodia* 13°48′ N, 104°32′ E 202
Koulikoro, *Mali* 12°54′ N, 7°36′ W 222
Koulochéra, peak, *Gr.* 36°48′ N, 22°57′ E 156
Koumameyong, *Gabon* 0°11′ N, 11°47′ E 218
Koumása, ruin(s), *Gr.* 34°57′ N, 24°55′ E 156
Koumbia, *Burkina Faso* 11°14′ N, 3°43′ W 222
Koumbia, *Guinea* 11°47′ N, 13°34′ W 222
Koumogo, *Chad* 8°40′ N, 18°16′ E 218
Koumra, *Chad* 8°53′ N, 17°33′ E 218
Kouna, *Burkina Faso* 13°27′ N, 4°4′ W 222
Koundé, *Cen. Af. Rep.* 6°0′ N, 14°38′ E 218
Koungheul, *Senegal* 13°58′ N, 14°49′ W 222
Koungouri, *Chad* 10°44′ N, 18°56′ E 216
Kounkané, *Senegal* 12°55′ N, 14°8′ W 222
Kountze, *Tex., U.S.* 30°21′ N, 94°19′ W 103
Koupéla, *Burkina Faso* 12°9′ N, 0°22′ E 222
Kourou, *French Guiana, Fr.* 5°11′ N, 52°41′ W 130
Kourouadi, spring, *Chad* 17°33′ N, 18°48′ E 216
Kourouba, *Mali* 13°21′ N, 10°58′ W 222
Kouroussa, *Guinea* 10°39′ N, 9°54′ W 222
Kousha, *Leb.* 34°18′ N, 35°50′ E 194
Koussa Arma, spring, *Niger* 16°8′ N, 13°12′ E 222
Koussanar, *Senegal* 13°52′ N, 14°8′ W 222
Kousséri, *Cameroon* 12°3′ N, 14°59′ E 216
Koussi, Emi, peak, *Chad* 19°45′ N, 18°26′ E 216
Koutiala, *Mali* 12°23′ N, 5°28′ W 222
Kouto, *Côte d'Ivoire* 9°53′ N, 6°26′ W 222
Koutouba, *Côte d'Ivoire* 8°41′ N, 3°13′ W 222
Koutous, region, *Africa* 14°20′ N, 9°41′ E 222
Kouvola, *Fin.* 60°51′ N, 26°41′ E 166
Kovačica, *Serb.* 45°7′ N, 20°37′ E 168
Kovd Ozero, lake, *Russ.* 66°27′ N, 31°8′ E 154
Kovdor, *Russ.* 67°33′ N, 30°24′ E 152
Kovel', *Ukr.* 51°11′ N, 24°42′ E 152
Kovero, *Fin.* 62°31′ N, 30°30′ E 152
Kovesjoki, *Fin.* 61°54′ N, 22°43′ E 166
Kovic, Baie 61°15′ N, 78°53′ W 106
Kovilj, *Serb.* 45°12′ N, 20°1′ E 168
Kovin, *Serb.* 44°44′ N, 20°57′ E 168
Kovrov, *Russ.* 56°21′ N, 41°24′ E 154
Kow, *Mauritania* 15°54′ N, 12°47′ W 222
Kowalów, *Pol.* 52°24′ N, 14°46′ E 152
Kowhitirangi, *N.Z.* 42°53′ S, 171°1′ E 240
Kowkcheh, river, *Afghan.* 37°3′ N, 69°44′ E 186
Kowŏn, *N. Korea* 39°26′ N, 127°14′ E 200
Köyceğiz, *Turk.* 36°57′ N, 28°40′ E 156
Koyda, *Russ.* 66°21′ N, 42°33′ E 154
Koygorodok, *Russ.* 60°28′ N, 51°9′ E 154
Koynas, *Russ.* 64°46′ N, 47°26′ E 154
Koyuk, *Alas., U.S.* 64°48′ N, 161°14′ W 98
Koyukuk, river, *Alas., U.S.* 65°51′ N, 155°8′ W 106
Koyukuk, river, *Alas., U.S.* 65°2′ N, 156°36′ W 98
Koyulhisar, *Turk.* 40°18′ N, 37°49′ E 156
Kozan, *Turk.* 37°26′ N, 35°48′ E 156
Kozáni, *Gr.* 40°18′ N, 21°47′ E 156
Kozarac, *Bosn. and Herzg.* 44°57′ N, 16°51′ E 168
Kozel'shchyna, *Ukr.* 49°16′ N, 33°45′ E 158
Kozel'sk, *Russ.* 54°0′ N, 35°46′ E 154
Kozhasay, *Kaz.* 48°15′ N, 57°11′ E 158
Kozhevnikovo, *Russ.* 56°14′ N, 83°59′ E 169
Kozhikode (Calicut), *India* 11°15′ N, 75°46′ E 188
Kozhim, *Russ.* 65°44′ N, 59°31′ E 154
Kozhva, *Russ.* 65°4′ N, 56°59′ E 154
Kozhva, river, *Russ.* 64°32′ N, 54°57′ E 154
Kozjak, peak, *Maced.* 41°22′ N, 21°37′ E 156
Kozlu, *Turk.* 41°25′ N, 31°44′ E 156
Kozluk, *Bosn. and Herzg.* 44°30′ N, 19°7′ E 168
Kozluk, *Turk.* 38°11′ N, 41°31′ E 195
Koz'modem'yansk, *Russ.* 56°13′ N, 46°43′ E 154
Kozova, *Ukr.* 49°25′ N, 25°9′ E 152
Kožuf, *Maced.* 41°8′ N, 22°4′ E 156
Kozyatyn, *Ukr.* 49°45′ N, 29°0′ E 158
Kpalimé, *Togo* 6°55′ N, 0°36′ E 222
Kpandae, *Ghana* 8°26′ N, 2°118′ W 222
Kpandu, *Ghana* 6°59′ N, 0°17′ E 222
Kra, Isthmus of, *Thai.* 10°18′ N, 98°8′ E 192
Krabi, *Thai.* 8°4′ N, 98°55′ E 202
Kragerø, *Nor.* 58°52′ N, 9°22′ E 152
Kragujevac, *Serb.* 44°0′ N, 20°54′ E 168
Krak des Chevaliers, site, *Syr.* 34°45′ N, 36°17′ E 194
Krakor, *Cambodia* 12°31′ N, 104°10′ E 202
Kraków, *Pol.* 50°3′ N, 19°58′ E 152
Kralanh, *Cambodia* 13°36′ N, 103°24′ E 202
Kraljevo, *Serb.* 43°43′ N, 20°41′ E 168
Královéhradecký, adm. division, *Czech Rep.* 50°28′ N, 16°1′ E 153
Kramators'k, *Ukr.* 48°43′ N, 37°27′ E 158
Kramfors, *Nor.* 62°55′ N, 17°47′ E 152
Kramis, Cap, *Alg.* 36°19′ N, 0°28′ E 164
Kranzberg, *Namibia* 21°56′ S, 15°43′ E 227
Krapina, *Croatia* 46°9′ N, 15°53′ E 168
Krasavino, *Russ.* 60°57′ N, 46°30′ E 154
Krasino, *Russ.* 70°47′ N, 54°21′ E 173
Kraskino, *Russ.* 42°42′ N, 130°46′ E 200
Krāslava, *Latv.* 55°53′ N, 27°10′ E 166
Krasnaya Polyana, *Russ.* 43°41′ N, 40°10′ E 195
Krasnaye, *Belarus* 54°14′ N, 27°3′ E 166
Krasneno, *Russ.* 64°38′ N, 174°49′ E 160
Krasnoarmeysk, *Russ.* 48°30′ N, 44°29′ E 158
Krasnoarmeysk, *Russ.* 50°58′ N, 45°40′ E 158
Krasnoarmeyskaya, *Russ.* 45°22′ N, 38°5′ E 158
Krasnodar, *Russ.* 45°4′ N, 39°0′ E 156
Krasnodar, adm. division, *Russ.* 45°40′ N, 38°18′ E 160
Krasnodon, *Ukr.* 48°16′ N, 39°40′ E 158
Krasnogorodskoye, *Russ.* 56°51′ N, 28°19′ E 166
Krasnogorskoye, *Russ.* 52°17′ N, 86°16′ E 184
Krasnohrad, *Ukr.* 49°24′ N, 35°25′ E 158
Krasnokamensk, *Russ.* 50°8′ N, 118°0′ E 190
Krasnokamsk, *Russ.* 58°5′ N, 55°45′ E 154
Krasnolesnyy, *Russ.* 51°51′ N, 39°30′ E 158
Krasnoostrovskiy, *Russ.* 60°16′ N, 28°39′ E 166
Krasnoperekops'k, *Ukr.* 45°57′ N, 33°47′ E 156
Krasnopillya, *Ukr.* 50°43′ N, 35°16′ E 158
Krasnopol, *Pol.* 54°6′ N, 23°12′ E 166
Krasnosel'kup, *Russ.* 65°41′ N, 82°35′ E 169
Krasnosel'sk, *Arm.* 40°36′ N, 45°19′ E 195
Krasnoslobodsk, *Russ.* 48°40′ N, 44°30′ E 158
Krasnoturansk, *Russ.* 54°19′ N, 91°31′ E 190
Krasnotur'insk, *Russ.* 59°46′ N, 60°15′ E 154
Krasnoufimsk, *Russ.* 56°37′ N, 57°47′ E 154
Krasnoural'sk, *Russ.* 58°21′ N, 60°6′ E 154
Krasnousol'skiy, *Russ.* 53°56′ N, 56°23′ E 154
Krasnovishersk, *Russ.* 60°25′ N, 57°9′ E 154
Krasnoy Armii, Proliv 79°41′ N, 91°44′ E 160
Krasnoyarsk, *Russ.* 56°10′ N, 92°39′ E 160
Krasnoyarsk, adm. division, *Russ.* 62°17′ N, 84°57′ E 169
Krasnoyarskiy, *Russ.* 51°57′ N, 59°52′ E 154
Krasnoye, *Belarus* 52°42′ N, 24°24′ E 154
Krasnoye, *Russ.* 59°12′ N, 47°51′ E 154
Krasnoye, *Russ.* 51°37′ N, 51°30′ E 158
Krasnoye, *Russ.* 56°35′ N, 29°21′ E 166
Krasnozatonskiy, *Russ.* 61°42′ N, 51°9′ E 169
Krasnyy, *Russ.* 54°37′ N, 31°30′ E 154
Krasnyy Kholm, *Russ.* 58°2′ N, 37°5′ E 154
Krasnyy Kholm, *Russ.* 51°35′ N, 54°10′ E 158
Krasnyy Klyuch, *Russ.* 55°24′ N, 56°43′ E 154
Krasnyy Kut, *Russ.* 50°56′ N, 46°54′ E 158
Krasnyy Luch, *Ukr.* 48°8′ N, 39°0′ E 158
Krasnyy Lyman, *Ukr.* 49°1′ N, 37°46′ E 158
Krasnyy Steklovar, *Russ.* 56°15′ N, 48°47′ E 154
Krasnyy Sulin, *Russ.* 47°53′ N, 40°5′ E 158
Krasnyy Tekstil'shchik, *Russ.* 51°18′ N, 45°45′ E 158
Krasnyy Yar, *Russ.* 50°39′ N, 44°43′ E 158
Krasnyy Yar, *Russ.* 46°30′ N, 48°22′ E 158
Krasnyy Yar, *Russ.* 55°14′ N, 72°51′ E 184
Krasnyy Yar, *Russ.* 57°4′ N, 84°38′ E 169
Krasnyye Baki, *Russ.* 57°5′ N, 45°12′ E 154
Kratie, *Cambodia* 12°30′ N, 106°3′ E 202
Kratovo, *Maced.* 42°4′ N, 22°11′ E 168
Kraulshavn see Nuussuaq, *Den.* 74°9′ N, 57°1′ W 106
Krefeld, *Ger.* 51°19′ N, 6°34′ E 167
Kreïjé, spring, *Mauritania* 16°4′ N, 8°32′ W 222
Kremen, peak, *Croatia* 44°26′ N, 15°51′ E 168
Kremenchuk, *Ukr.* 49°7′ N, 33°19′ E 158
Kremenchuts'ke Vdskh., lake, *Ukr.* 49°32′ N, 30°53′ E 158
Kremenets', *Ukr.* 50°5′ N, 25°45′ E 152
Kremna, *Bosn. and Herzg.* 44°48′ N, 17°39′ E 168
Kremnica, *Slovakia* 48°41′ N, 18°55′ E 152
Krems, *Aust.* 48°24′ N, 15°36′ E 156
Kreševo, *Bosn. and Herzg.* 43°51′ N, 18°3′ E 168
Kress, *Tex., U.S.* 34°21′ N, 101°46′ W 92
Kresta, Zaliv 65°38′ N, 178°8′ E 160
Krestovaya Guba, *Russ.* 74°2′ N, 55°18′ E 246
Krestovka, *Russ.* 66°23′ N, 52°29′ E 154
Krestovskiy, Mys, *Russ.* 69°24′ N, 143°33′ E 172
Kresttsy, *Russ.* 58°13′ N, 32°32′ E 154
Kretinga, *Lith.* 55°52′ N, 21°15′ E 166
Kreuzberg, peak, *Ger.* 50°22′ N, 9°57′ E 167
Kreuztal, *Ger.* 50°57′ N, 7°59′ E 167
Krieglach, *Aust.* 47°32′ N, 15°33′ E 156
Krim, peak, *Slov.* 45°55′ N, 14°23′ E 156
Krims'ke Hory, *Ukr.* 44°50′ N, 33°47′ E 156
Kristiansand, *Nor.* 58°10′ N, 7°47′ E 160
Kristiansund, *Nor.* 63°5′ N, 7°45′ E 160
Kristiinankaupunki see Kristinestad, *Fin.* 62°15′ N, 21°20′ E 152
Kristineberg, *Nor.* 65°3′ N, 18°34′ E 152
Kristinehamn, *Nor.* 59°18′ N, 14°4′ E 152
Kristinestad (Kristiinankaupunki), *Fin.* 62°15′ N, 21°20′ E 152
Kríti (Crete), island, *Gr.* 35°36′ N, 24°6′ E 180
Kriva Palanka, *Maced.* 42°11′ N, 22°20′ E 168
Krivaja, river, *Bosn. and Herzg.* 44°15′ N, 18°20′ E 168
Krivelj, *Serb.* 44°8′ N, 22°6′ E 168
Krivolak, *Maced.* 41°31′ N, 22°5′ E 168
Krivoy Porog, *Russ.* 65°2′ N, 33°38′ E 152
Križ, *Croatia* 45°39′ N, 16°31′ E 168
Križevci, *Croatia* 46°1′ N, 16°32′ E 168
Krņalovņehradeckņy, adm. division, *Czech Rep.* 50°32′ N, 14°58′ E 152
Krnjeuša, *Bosn. and Herzg.* 44°41′ N, 16°12′ E 168
Krnov, *Czech Rep.* 50°5′ N, 17°42′ E 152
Krognes, *Nor.* 70°24′ N, 30°46′ E 152
Krokom, *Nor.* 63°19′ N, 14°26′ E 152
Krokstrand, *Nor.* 66°27′ N, 15°5′ E 152
Krolevets', *Ukr.* 51°29′ N, 33°28′ E 158
Kromy, *Russ.* 52°39′ N, 35°45′ E 158
Kronoby (Kruunupyy), *Fin.* 63°43′ N, 23°1′ E 152
Kronprins Christian Land, *Den.* 80°7′ N, 38°45′ W 246
Kronprins Frederik Bjerge, *Den.* 67°31′ N, 34°33′ W 246
Kronshtadt, *Russ.* 59°59′ N, 29°45′ E 152
Kroonstad, *S. Af.* 27°40′ S, 27°15′ E 227
Kropotkin, *Russ.* 45°26′ N, 40°29′ E 158
Kroshin, *Belarus* 53°10′ N, 26°10′ E 152
Krosno, *Pol.* 49°39′ N, 21°46′ E 152
Kröv, *Ger.* 49°58′ N, 7°4′ E 167
Krrab, peak, *Alban.* 42°6′ N, 19°56′ E 168
Krrabë, peak, *Alban.* 41°12′ N, 19°56′ E 156
Krš, *Serb.* 44°5′ N, 21°59′ E 168
Krško, *Slov.* 45°58′ N, 15°27′ E 156
Krstača, peak, *Serb.-Mont.* 42°57′ N, 20°4′ E 168
Kruger National Park, *S. Af.* 23°37′ S, 31°8′ E 227
Kruhlaye, *Belarus* 54°14′ N, 29°51′ E 166
Krui, *Indonesia* 5°11′ S, 103°53′ E 192
Krujë, *Alban.* 41°30′ N, 19°47′ E 168
Krumë, *Alban.* 42°11′ N, 20°25′ E 168
Krung Thep (Bangkok), *Thai.* 13°44′ N, 100°24′ E 202
Krupa, *Bosn. and Herzg.* 44°50′ N, 16°10′ E 168
Krupac, *Serb.* 43°6′ N, 22°41′ E 168
Krupanj, *Serb.* 44°22′ N, 19°23′ E 168
Krupište, *Maced.* 41°51′ N, 22°14′ E 168
Krupki, *Belarus* 54°20′ N, 29°12′ E 166
Krutaya, *Russ.* 63°2′ N, 54°46′ E 154
Krutets, *Russ.* 60°18′ N, 39°24′ E 154
Krutinka, *Russ.* 55°58′ N, 71°35′ E 184
Kruunupyy see Kronoby, *Fin.* 63°43′ N, 23°1′ E 152

Kruzof Island, *Alas., U.S.* 57°3′ N, 137°39′ W 98
Krychaw, *Belarus* 53°38′ N, 31°44′ E 154
Krylovskaya, *Russ.* 46°18′ N, 39°57′ E 158
Krymsk, *Russ.* 44°56′ N, 37°55′ E 156
Krynki, *Pol.* 53°16′ N, 23°45′ E 152
Kryvichy, *Belarus* 54°42′ N, 27°16′ E 166
Kryvyy Rih, *Ukr.* 47°56′ N, 33°22′ E 156
Ksabi, *Alg.* 29°6′ N, 0°56′ E 214
Ksabi, *Mor.* 32°55′ N, 4°24′ W 214
Ksar Chellala (Reïbell), *Alg.* 35°12′ N, 2°19′ E 150
Ksar el Barka, *Mauritania* 18°23′ N, 12°16′ W 222
Ksar el Boukhari, *Alg.* 35°54′ N, 2°46′ E 216
Ksar el Hirane, *Alg.* 33°47′ N, 3°14′ E 214
Ksar el Kebir, *Mor.* 35°1′ N, 5°54′ W 214
Ksar Torchane, *Mauritania* 20°41′ N, 13°0′ W 222
Kshwan Mountain, *Can.* 55°40′ N, 129°51′ W 108
Ktima, *Cyprus* 34°46′ N, 32°24′ E 194
Kuah, *Malaysia* 6°19′ N, 99°51′ E 196
Kuaidamao see Tonghua, *China* 41°41′ N, 125°45′ E 200
Kuala, *Indonesia* 2°58′ N, 105°47′ E 196
Kuala, *Indonesia* 3°35′ N, 98°24′ E 196
Kuala Berang, *Malaysia* 5°5′ N, 103°1′ E 196
Kuala Dungun, *Malaysia* 4°46′ N, 103°24′ E 196
Kuala Kelawang, *Malaysia* 2°58′ N, 102°4′ E 196
Kuala Kerai, *Malaysia* 5°32′ N, 102°12′ E 196
Kuala Kubu Baharu, *Malaysia* 3°34′ N, 101°38′ E 196
Kuala Lipis, *Malaysia* 4°12′ N, 102°1′ E 196
Kuala Lumpur, *Malaysia* 3°8′ N, 101°32′ E 196
Kuala Nerang, *Malaysia* 6°14′ N, 100°36′ E 196
Kuala Rompin, *Malaysia* 2°48′ N, 103°27′ E 196
Kuala Selangor, *Malaysia* 3°20′ N, 101°16′ E 196
Kuala Terengganu, *Malaysia* 5°18′ N, 103°7′ E 196
Kualakapuas, *Indonesia* 2°55′ S, 114°14′ E 192
Kualalangsa, *Indonesia* 4°32′ N, 98°1′ E 196
Kualatungkal, *Indonesia* 0°49′ N, 103°29′ E 196
Kuancheng, *China* 40°35′ N, 118°31′ E 198
Kuandian, *China* 40°43′ N, 124°46′ E 200
Kuanshan, *Taiwan, China* 23°1′ N, 121°7′ E 198
Kuantan, *Malaysia* 3°50′ N, 103°19′ E 196
Kubachi, *Russ.* 42°6′ N, 47°40′ E 195
Kuban', river, *Russ.* 45°4′ N, 38°18′ E 156
Kubaybāt, *Syr.* 35°11′ N, 37°9′ E 194
Kubbum, *Sudan* 11°47′ N, 23°44′ E 216
Kubenskoye, *Russ.* 59°24′ N, 39°38′ E 154
Kubenskoye, Ozero, lake, *Russ.* 59°41′ N, 38°13′ E 154
Kuberganya, *Russ.* 67°41′ N, 144°18′ E 160
Kubokawa, *Japan* 33°11′ N, 133°7′ E 201
Kučevo, *Serb.* 44°29′ N, 21°40′ E 168
Kuchaman, *India* 27°8′ N, 74°52′ E 186
Kuchchaveli, *Sri Lanka* 8°48′ N, 81°6′ E 188
Kuchin Tundra, Gora, peak, *Russ.* 69°3′ N, 30°57′ E 152
Kuching, *Malaysia* 1°27′ N, 110°24′ E 192
Kuchva, river, *Russ.* 57°7′ N, 27°57′ E 166
Küçüksu, *Turk.* 38°25′ N, 42°16′ E 195
Kudamatsu, *Japan* 34°0′ N, 131°53′ E 201
Kudara, *Taj.* 38°28′ N, 72°41′ E 197
Kudat, *Malaysia* 6°56′ N, 116°49′ E 203
Kudever', *Russ.* 56°47′ N, 29°26′ E 166
Kudeyevskiy, *Russ.* 54°54′ N, 56°45′ E 154
Kūdī, Qārat, peak, *Lib.* 23°22′ N, 23°45′ E 226
Kudirkos Naumiestis, *Lith.* 54°47′ N, 22°52′ E 166
Kudremukh, peak, *India* 13°5′ N, 75°8′ E 188
Kudu Kyuyel', *Russ.* 59°23′ N, 121°3′ E 160
Kudus, *Indonesia* 6°51′ S, 110°46′ E 192
Kudymkar, *Russ.* 59°0′ N, 54°43′ E 154
Kufah see Al Kūfah, *Iraq* 32°5′ N, 44°27′ E 186
Kufra Oasis see Al Kufrah, *Lib.* 24°20′ N, 23°44′ E 226
Kugluktuk, *Can.* 67°48′ N, 115°16′ W 106
Kugul'ta, *Russ.* 45°21′ N, 42°18′ E 158
Kūhak, *Iran* 27°6′ N, 63°14′ E 182
Kuh-e Sangan, peak, *Afghan.* 33°30′ N, 64°46′ E 186
Kūhestak, *Iran* 26°49′ N, 57°6′ E 196
Kühlung, peak, *Ger.* 54°5′ N, 11°40′ E 152
Kuhmalahti, *Fin.* 61°29′ N, 24°32′ E 166
Kuhmo, *Fin.* 64°5′ N, 29°28′ E 152
Kuhmoinen, *Fin.* 61°33′ N, 25°9′ E 166
Kuhn Ø, island, *Den.* 74°29′ N, 25°0′ W 246
Kūhpāyeh, *Iran* 32°41′ N, 52°28′ E 180
Kui Buri, *Thai.* 12°4′ N, 99°52′ E 202
Kuibis, *Namibia* 26°42′ S, 16°49′ E 227
Kuikuina, *Nicar.* 13°28′ N, 84°48′ W 115
Kū'īlioloa Heiau, site, *Hawai'i, U.S.* 21°25′ N, 158°14′ W 99
Kuitan, *China* 23°4′ N, 115°57′ E 198
Kuito, *Angola* 12°25′ S, 16°56′ E 220
Kuivaniemi, *Fin.* 65°34′ N, 25°11′ E 152
Kuizhuang, *China* 40°3′ N, 118°46′ E 198
Kujang, *N. Korea* 39°52′ N, 126°2′ E 200
Kujawsko-Pomorskie, adm. division, *Pol.* 52°58′ N, 17°33′ E 152
Kukalaya, river, *Nicar.* 14°14′ N, 84°13′ W 115
Kūkaniloko, site, *Hawai'i, U.S.* 21°30′ N, 158°6′ W 99
Kukas, *Russ.* 66°25′ N, 31°20′ E 152
Kukës, *Alban.* 42°5′ N, 20°24′ E 168
Kukisvunchor, *Russ.* 67°39′ N, 33°43′ E 152
Kukmor, *Russ.* 56°11′ N, 50°58′ E 154
Kukuihaele, *Hawai'i, U.S.* 20°7′ N, 155°35′ W 99
Kukukus Lake, *Can.* 49°47′ N, 92°11′ W 110
Kukunjevac, *Croatia* 45°28′ N, 17°6′ E 168
Kula, *Bulg.* 43°53′ N, 22°31′ E 168
Kula, *Serb.* 45°36′ N, 19°33′ E 168
Kula, *Turk.* 38°32′ N, 28°38′ E 156
Kulagino, *Kaz.* 48°15′ N, 51°31′ E 158
Kulal, Mount, *Kenya* 2°40′ N, 36°51′ E 224
Kūlani, peak, *Hawai'i, U.S.* 19°30′ N, 155°21′ W 99
Kular, *Russ.* 70°37′ N, 134°19′ E 173
Kulata, *Bulg.* 41°23′ N, 23°21′ E 156
Kulautuva, *Lith.* 54°58′ N, 23°38′ E 166
Kuldīga, *Latv.* 56°57′ N, 21°57′ E 166
Kuldo, *Can.* 55°51′ N, 127°54′ W 108
Kule, *Botswana* 22°56′ S, 20°6′ E 227
Kulebaki, *Russ.* 55°24′ N, 42°33′ E 154
Kulen Vakuf, *Bosn. and Herzg.* 44°34′ N, 16°5′ E 168
Kuliki, *Russ.* 57°21′ N, 79°0′ E 169
Kulju, *Fin.* 61°22′ N, 23°44′ E 166
Kulkuduk, *Uzb.* 42°33′ N, 63°17′ E 197
Kullaa, *Fin.* 61°27′ N, 22°8′ E 166
Kullen, *Sw.* 56°21′ N, 11°57′ E 152
Kulli, *Est.* 58°21′ N, 23°46′ E 166
Kullorsuaq, *Den.* 74°37′ N, 56°57′ W 106
Küllstedt, *Ger.* 51°17′ N, 10°16′ E 167
Kulm, *N. Dak., U.S.* 46°17′ N, 98°58′ W 90
Kulma Pass, *China* 38°3′ N, 74°50′ E 197
Kŭlob, *Taj.* 37°53′ N, 69°46′ E 197
Kuloy, *Russ.* 60°59′ N, 42°35′ E 154
Kuloy, *Russ.* 65°1′ N, 43°31′ E 154
Kulp, *Turk.* 38°29′ N, 41°2′ E 195
Kultuk, *Russ.* 51°48′ N, 103°53′ E 190
Kulu, *Turk.* 39°4′ N, 33°5′ E 156
Kululli, *Eritrea* 14°22′ N, 40°21′ E 182
Kulunda, *Russ.* 52°32′ N, 79°0′ E 184
Kum, river, *S. Korea* 35°34′ N, 127°29′ E 200
Kuma, river, *Russ.* 44°53′ N, 45°59′ E 158
Kumagaya, *Japan* 36°9′ N, 139°23′ E 201
Kumak, *Russ.* 51°10′ N, 60°10′ E 158
Kumak, river, *Russ.* 51°16′ N, 59°10′ E 158
Kumaka, *Guyana* 3°53′ N, 58°26′ W 130
Kumamoto, *Japan* 32°48′ N, 130°42′ E 201
Kumamoto, adm. division, *Japan* 32°57′ N, 130°25′ E 201
Kumanica, *Serb.* 43°27′ N, 20°13′ E 168
Kumano, *Japan* 33°53′ N, 136°6′ E 201
Kumano Nada 34°2′ N, 136°23′ E 201
Kumanovo, *Maced.* 42°7′ N, 21°41′ E 168
Kumara Junction, *N.Z.* 42°40′ S, 171°11′ E 240
Kumasi, *Ghana* 6°44′ N, 1°38′ W 222
Kumba, *Cameroon* 4°37′ N, 9°24′ E 222
Kumbakonam, *India* 11°0′ N, 79°21′ E 188
Kumbher, *Nepal* 28°15′ N, 81°25′ E 197
Kumbo, *Cameroon* 6°9′ N, 10°38′ E 222
Kŭmch'ŏn, *N. Korea* 38°9′ N, 126°28′ E 200
Kumeny, *Russ.* 58°6′ N, 49°55′ E 154
Kumertau, *Russ.* 52°46′ N, 55°46′ E 154
Kŭmgang, *N. Korea* 38°36′ N, 127°58′ E 200
Kumi, *Uganda* 1°27′ N, 33°54′ E 224
Kumiva Peak, *Nev., U.S.* 40°23′ N, 119°21′ W 90
Kumkol, oil field, *Kaz.* 46°17′ N, 65°22′ E 184
Kumla, *Nor.* 59°7′ N, 15°7′ E 152
Kumlinge, *Fin.* 60°15′ N, 20°47′ E 166
Kumma, ruin(s), *Sudan* 21°30′ N, 30°58′ E 182
Kumo, *Nig.* 10°2′ N, 11°8′ E 222
Kumphawapi, *Thai.* 17°13′ N, 102°54′ E 202
Kumputunturi, peak, *Fin.* 67°41′ N, 25°23′ E 152
Kŭmsŏng see Kimhwa, *N. Korea* 38°26′ N, 127°36′ E 200
Kumta, *India* 14°24′ N, 74°24′ E 188
Kumu, *Dem. Rep. of the Congo* 3°2′ N, 25°14′ E 224
Kumukh, *Russ.* 42°6′ N, 47°4′ E 195
Kumzār, *Oman* 26°19′ N, 56°23′ E 196
Kunanaggi Well, spring, *Austral.* 23°24′ S, 122°31′ E 230
Künas Linchang, *China* 43°12′ N, 84°40′ E 184
Kunashak, *Russ.* 55°41′ N, 61°27′ E 154
Kunashir (Kunashiri), island, *Russ.* 44°21′ N, 144°17′ E 190
Kunchha, *Nepal* 28°9′ N, 84°21′ E 197
Kunda, *Est.* 59°28′ N, 26°29′ E 166
Kundelungu National Park, *Dem. Rep. of the Congo* 10°41′ S, 27°43′ E 224
Kundi, Lake, *Sudan* 10°24′ N, 24°45′ E 224
Kundian, *Pak.* 32°28′ N, 71°33′ E 186
Kundozero, *Russ.* 66°19′ N, 31°10′ E 152
Kundur, island, *Indonesia* 0°30′ N, 103°27′ E 196
Kunene, river, *Africa* 17°33′ S, 11°31′ E 220
Künes, river, *China* 43°30′ N, 82°59′ E 184
Kungsbacka, *Nor.* 57°29′ N, 12°6′ E 152
Kungu, *Dem. Rep. of the Congo* 2°47′ N, 19°10′ E 218
Kungur, *Russ.* 57°26′ N, 57°3′ E 154
Kungutas, *Tanzania* 8°29′ S, 33°16′ E 224
Kungwe Mountain, *Tanzania* 6°12′ S, 29°44′ E 224
Kunlon, *Myanmar* 23°22′ N, 98°36′ E 202
Kunlun Mountains, *Asia* 33°11′ N, 97°38′ E 172
Kunlun Shankou, pass, *China* 35°37′ N, 94°5′ E 188
Kunlunshan, *Asia* 37°6′ N, 84°45′ E 184
Kunmadaras, *Hung.* 47°25′ N, 20°48′ E 168
Kunming, *China* 25°3′ N, 102°41′ E 190
Kunszentmárton, *Hung.* 46°49′ N, 20°18′ E 168
Kuntaur, *Gambia* 13°40′ N, 14°52′ W 222
Kununurra, *Austral.* 15°45′ S, 128°45′ E 238
Kunya, *Nig.* 12°13′ N, 8°32′ E 222
Kuoliovaara, *Fin.* 65°50′ N, 28°49′ E 152
Kuolismaa, *Russ.* 62°41′ N, 31°36′ E 154
Kuopio, *Fin.* 62°53′ N, 27°38′ E 154
Kuorboaivi, peak, *Fin.* 69°40′ N, 27°34′ E 152
Kuorevesi, *Fin.* 61°55′ N, 24°38′ E 166
Kuormakka, peak, *Nor.* 68°9′ N, 21°42′ E 152
Kuortane, *Fin.* 62°47′ N, 23°30′ E 152
Kuoutatjärro, peak, *Nor.* 68°36′ N, 20°10′ E 152
Kupa, river, *Croatia* 45°30′ N, 15°48′ E 168
Kupang, *Indonesia* 10°21′ S, 123°32′ E 192
Kupino, *Russ.* 54°21′ N, 77°18′ E 184
Kupiškis, *Lith.* 55°48′ N, 24°59′ E 166
Kupopolo Heiau, site, *Hawai'i, U.S.* 21°38′ N, 158°7′ W 99
Kupreanof, *Alas., U.S.* 56°50′ N, 133°3′ W 108
Kupres, *Bosn. and Herzg.* 43°58′ N, 17°16′ E 168
Kup''yans'k, *Ukr.* 49°43′ N, 37°33′ E 158
Kuqa, *China* 41°43′ N, 83°3′ E 184
Kur Dili, *Azerb.* 38°51′ N, 49°9′ E 195
Kür, river, *Azerb.* 40°12′ N, 47°24′ E 195
Kurakh, *Russ.* 41°33′ N, 47°47′ E 195
Kurakhtin (Jäbrayyl), *Azerb.* 39°24′ N, 47°1′ E 195
Kūrān Dap, *Iran* 26°4′ N, 59°40′ E 182
Kuranyets, *Belarus* 54°33′ N, 26°58′ E 166
Kurashiki, *Japan* 34°35′ N, 133°46′ E 201
Kürchatov, *Kaz.* 50°46′ N, 78°28′ E 184
Kürdämir, *Azerb.* 40°20′ N, 48°10′ E 195
Kurdoğlu Burnu, *Turk.* 36°31′ N, 28°11′ E 156
Kŭrdzhali, *Bulg.* 41°38′ N, 25°21′ E 156
Kŭrdzhali, adm. division, *Bulg.* 41°24′ N, 25°11′ E 156
Kure, *Japan* 34°14′ N, 132°33′ E 201
Küre, *Turk.* 41°48′ N, 33°42′ E 156
Kurenala, *Fin.* 65°21′ N, 26°57′ E 152
Kuressaare, *Est.* 58°15′ N, 22°28′ E 166
Kureyka, *Russ.* 66°16′ N, 87°17′ E 169
Kureyka, river, *Russ.* 67°53′ N, 96°35′ E 169
Kurgan, *Russ.* 55°30′ N, 65°19′ E 184
Kurgan, adm. division, *Russ.* 55°27′ N, 63°22′ E 169
Kurganinsk, *Russ.* 44°54′ N, 40°30′ E 158
Kurgolovo, *Russ.* 59°45′ N, 28°5′ E 166
Kuria Muria Islands, *Persian Gulf* 17°13′ N, 55°40′ E 182
Kurikka, *Fin.* 62°36′ N, 22°20′ E 152
Kuril Islands (Kuril'skiye Ostrova), *Sea of Okhotsk* 47°9′ N, 148°32′ E 190
Kurilovka, *Russ.* 50°42′ N, 48°0′ E 158
Kuril'skiye Ostrova see Kuril Islands, *Sea of Okhotsk* 47°9′ N, 148°32′ E 190
Kurkiyoki, *Russ.* 61°18′ N, 29°54′ E 166
Kurleya, *Russ.* 52°6′ N, 119°8′ E 190
Kurmuk, *Sudan* 10°35′ N, 34°15′ E 224
Kurobe, *Japan* 36°52′ N, 137°26′ E 201
Kuroiso, *Japan* 36°56′ N, 140°3′ E 201
Kuropta, *Russ.* 67°29′ N, 30°50′ E 152
Kuror, Jebel, peak, *Sudan* 20°29′ N, 31°30′ E 182
Kurow, *N.Z.* 44°45′ S, 170°25′ E 240
Kurów, *Pol.* 51°23′ N, 22°10′ E 152
Kursavka, *Russ.* 44°28′ N, 42°32′ E 158
Kuršėnai, *Lith.* 56°0′ N, 22°56′ E 166
Kurshim, *Kaz.* 48°46′ N, 83°30′ E 184
Kuršių Nerija National Park, *Lith.* 55°29′ N, 20°37′ E 166
Kursk, *Russ.* 51°43′ N, 36°12′ E 158
Kursk, adm. division, *Russ.* 51°39′ N, 34°47′ E 160
Kursu, *Fin.* 66°45′ N, 28°7′ E 152
Kuršumlija, *Serb.* 43°7′ N, 21°16′ E 168
Kurşunlu, *Turk.* 40°51′ N, 33°15′ E 156
Kurtalan, *Turk.* 37°55′ N, 41°43′ E 195
Kurtamysh, *Russ.* 54°53′ N, 64°31′ E 184
Kürten, *Ger.* 51°3′ N, 7°16′ E 163
Kurthwood, *La., U.S.* 31°18′ N, 93°10′ W 103
Kürti, *Kaz.* 43°56′ N, 76°19′ E 184
Kurtti, *Fin.* 65°28′ N, 28°8′ E 152
Kuru, *Fin.* 61°51′ N, 23°39′ E 166
Kuru, river, *Sudan* 7°58′ N, 26°31′ E 224
Kurulush, *Kyrg.* 41°39′ N, 70°53′ E 197
Kuruman, *S. Af.* 27°29′ S, 23°25′ E 227
Kurume, *Japan* 33°17′ N, 130°31′ E 201
Kurupukari, *Guyana* 4°40′ N, 58°40′ W 130
Kur'ya, *Russ.* 61°38′ N, 57°13′ E 154
Kur'ya, *Russ.* 51°36′ N, 82°17′ E 184
Kurze Mountains, *Antarctica* 72°38′ S, 10°13′ E 248
Kurzheksa, *Russ.* 61°25′ N, 36°45′ E 154
Kus Gölü, lake, *Turk.* 40°9′ N, 27°46′ E 156
Kusa, *Eth.* 4°11′ N, 38°58′ E 224
Kusa, *Russ.* 55°21′ N, 59°30′ E 154
Kusadak, *Serb.* 44°24′ N, 20°47′ E 168
Kuşadası, *Turk.* 37°50′ N, 27°14′ E 156
Kusaie see Kosrae, island, *F.S.M.* 5°19′ N, 162°59′ E 242
Kusapin (Cusapín), *Pan.* 9°10′ N, 81°53′ W 115
Kushereka, *Russ.* 63°49′ N, 37°9′ E 154
Kusheriki, *Nig.* 10°32′ N, 6°26′ E 222
Kushikino, *Japan* 31°41′ N, 130°18′ E 201
Kushima, *Japan* 31°26′ N, 131°14′ E 201
Kushimoto, *Japan* 33°28′ N, 135°46′ E 201
Kushiro, *Japan* 43°6′ N, 144°14′ E 190
Kushkushara, *Russ.* 65°0′ N, 40°19′ E 154
Kushnarenkovo, *Russ.* 55°7′ N, 55°24′ E 154
Kushnīya, *Israel* 33°0′ N, 35°48′ E 194
Kushva, *Russ.* 58°18′ N, 59°47′ E 154
Kuskokwim Bay 59°21′ N, 163°25′ W 98
Kuskokwim Mountains, *North America* 61°20′ N, 157°59′ W 98
Kuskokwim, river, *Alas., U.S.* 60°24′ N, 161°42′ W 98
Kusŏng, *N. Korea* 39°58′ N, 125°14′ E 200
Kustavi, *Fin.* 60°33′ N, 21°20′ E 166
Kusur, *Russ.* 41°44′ N, 46°57′ E 195
Kūt Barrage, dam, *Iraq* 32°23′ N, 44°49′ E 216
Kut, Ko, island, *Thai.* 11°30′ N, 102°5′ E 202
Kuta, *Nig.* 9°50′ N, 6°44′ E 222
Kutabuloh, *Indonesia* 3°28′ N, 97°3′ E 196
Kutacane, *Indonesia* 3°31′ N, 97°47′ E 196
Kütahya, *Turk.* 39°26′ N, 29°58′ E 156
Kutai National Park, *Indonesia* 0°15′ N, 116°57′ E 238
K'ut'aisi, *Ga.* 42°13′ N, 42°40′ E 195
Kutanibong, *Indonesia* 3°56′ N, 96°20′ E 173
Kutcho Creek, river, *Can.* 58°35′ N, 128°59′ W 108
Kutina, *Croatia* 45°27′ N, 16°46′ E 168
Kutjevo, *Croatia* 45°24′ N, 17°52′ E 168
Kutno, *Pol.* 52°14′ N, 19°22′ E 152
Kutu, *Dem. Rep. of the Congo* 2°43′ S, 18°6′ E 218
Kutum, *Sudan* 14°9′ N, 24°40′ E 226
Kutuzovo, *Russ.* 54°46′ N, 22°48′ E 166
Kúty, *Slovakia* 48°37′ N, 17°1′ E 156
Kuujjuaq, *Can.* 58°5′ N, 68°38′ W 106
Kuujjuarapik, *Can.* 55°17′ N, 77°47′ W 106
Kuurne, *Belg.* 50°51′ N, 3°19′ E 163
Kuusamo, *Fin.* 65°58′ N, 29°8′ E 152
Kuusankoski, *Fin.* 60°53′ N, 26°36′ E 166
Kuusivaara, *Fin.* 66°39′ N, 27°0′ E 152
Kuusjärvi, *Fin.* 62°41′ N, 28°54′ E 154
Kuusjoki, *Fin.* 60°30′ N, 23°11′ E 166
Kuvandyk, *Russ.* 51°27′ N, 57°20′ E 158
Kuvango, *Angola* 14°32′ S, 16°15′ E 220
Kuvet, river, *Russ.* 69°3′ N, 176°7′ E 98
Kuvshinovo, *Russ.* 57°0′ N, 34°13′ E 154
Kuwait 29°39′ N, 47°15′ E 196
Kuwait City see Al Kuwayt, *Kuwait* 29°20′ N, 47°52′ E 196
Kuwana, *Japan* 35°3′ N, 136°41′ E 201
Kuybishevskiy, *Taj.* 37°56′ N, 68°46′ E 197
Kuybyshev, *Russ.* 55°30′ N, 78°21′ E 184
Kuyeda, *Russ.* 56°27′ N, 55°31′ E 154
Kuytun, *China* 44°29′ N, 84°56′ E 184
Kuyuwini, river, *Guyana* 1°55′ N, 59°25′ W 130
Kuzey Anadolu Dağlarx, *Turk.* 40°38′ N, 36°33′ E 180
Kuz'movka, *Russ.* 62°21′ N, 92°9′ E 169
Kuznetsk, *Russ.* 53°5′ N, 46°37′ E 154
Kuźnica, *Pol.* 53°30′ N, 23°38′ E 152
Kuzomen', *Russ.* 66°17′ N, 36°44′ E 154
Kuzomen', *Russ.* 64°19′ N, 43°4′ E 154
Kvalsund, *Nor.* 70°29′ N, 23°58′ E 152
Kvænangsbotn, *Nor.* 69°43′ N, 22°4′ E 152
Kvarkeno, *Russ.* 52°5′ N, 59°41′ E 154
K'vemo Azhara, *Turk.* 43°8′ N, 41°49′ E 158
Kvernes, *Nor.* 62°59′ N, 7°42′ E 152
Kvikkjokk, *Nor.* 66°56′ N, 17°44′ E 152
Kvikne, *Nor.* 62°34′ N, 10°19′ E 152
Kvisvik, *Nor.* 63°3′ N, 7°58′ E 152
Kwa Mtoro, *Tanzania* 5°12′ S, 35°26′ E 224
Kwadacha, river, *Can.* 57°28′ N, 125°37′ W 108
Kwail (P'ungch'ŏn), *N. Korea* 38°25′ N, 125°1′ E 200
Kwajaffa Babur, *Nig.* 10°27′ N, 12°24′ E 218
Kwaksan, *N. Korea* 39°40′ N, 125°4′ E 200
Kwale, *Kenya* 4°12′ S, 39°27′ E 224
Kwale Station, *Nig.* 5°48′ N, 6°21′ E 222
Kwali, *Nig.* 8°51′ N, 7°0′ E 222
Kwamouth, *Dem. Rep. of the Congo* 3°16′ S, 16°14′ E 218
Kwangju see Gwangju, *S. Korea* 35°8′ N, 126°56′ E 200
Kwania, Lake, *Uganda* 0°52′ N, 32°45′ E 224
Kwazulu-Natal, adm. division, *S. Af.* 29°6′ S, 29°21′ E 227
Kwekwe, *Zimb.* 18°56′ S, 29°47′ E 224
Kwenge, river, *Dem. Rep. of the Congo* 6°16′ S, 18°20′ E 218
Kwiambana, *Nig.* 11°5′ N, 6°33′ E 222
Kwikila, *P.N.G.* 9°48′ S, 147°39′ E 192
Kwilu, river, *Dem. Rep. of the Congo* 3°35′ S, 17°14′ E 218
Kwokullie Lake, *Can.* 59°14′ N, 121°43′ W 108
Ky Son, *Vietnam* 19°24′ N, 104°8′ E 202
Kyabé, *Chad* 9°28′ N, 18°55′ E 216
Kyaikkami, *Myanmar* 16°5′ N, 97°35′ E 202
Kyaikto, *Myanmar* 17°20′ N, 97°1′ E 202
Kyaka, *Tanzania* 1°20′ S, 31°24′ E 224
Kyakhta, *Russ.* 50°26′ N, 106°25′ E 173
Kyango, *Sudan* 7°54′ N, 27°39′ E 224
Kyaukkyi, *Myanmar* 18°21′ N, 96°46′ E 202
Kyaukme, *Myanmar* 22°32′ N, 97°3′ E 202
Kyaukphyu, *Myanmar* 19°23′ N, 93°29′ E 190
Kyaukse, *Myanmar* 21°36′ N, 96°8′ E 202
Kybartai, *Lith.* 54°39′ N, 22°45′ E 166
Kydz'ras'yu, *Russ.* 65°15′ N, 58°13′ E 154
Kyeintali, *Myanmar* 18°0′ N, 94°30′ E 202
Kyenjojo, *Uganda* 0°33′ N, 30°39′ E 224
Kyffhäuser, peak, *Ger.* 51°23′ N, 11°1′ E 152
Kyiv (Kiev), *Ukr.* 50°25′ N, 30°29′ E 158
Kyle, *Can.* 50°50′ N, 108°2′ W 90
Kyle, *Tex., U.S.* 29°57′ N, 97°53′ W 92
Kyll, river, *Ger.* 50°1′ N, 6°34′ E 167
Kyllburg, *Ger.* 50°2′ N, 6°35′ E 167
Kymijoki, river, *Fin.* 60°51′ N, 26°28′ E 166
Kyŏngju see Gyeongju, *S. Korea* 35°48′ N, 129°15′ E 200
Kyŏngsŏng, *N. Korea* 41°35′ N, 129°36′ E 200
Kyōto, *Japan* 35°0′ N, 135°44′ E 201
Kyōto, adm. division, *Japan* 35°18′ N, 134°59′ E 201
Kyperounta, *Cyprus* 34°56′ N, 32°57′ E 194
Kyrenia see Keryneia, *Northern Cyprus, Cyprus* 35°20′ N, 33°18′ E 194
Kyrgyz-Ata National Park, *Kyrg.* 39°57′ N, 72°50′ E 197
Kyrgyz Range, *Kyrg.* 42°53′ N, 71°46′ E 184
Kyrgyzstan 41°38′ N, 73°40′ E 184
Kyrkslätt (Kirkkonummi), *Fin.* 60°7′ N, 24°26′ E 166
Kyrö, *Fin.* 60°42′ N, 22°45′ E 166
Kyrösjärvi, lake, *Fin.* 61°39′ N, 22°50′ E 166
Kyrta, *Russ.* 64°4′ N, 57°40′ E 154
Kyrtym'ya, *Russ.* 59°1′ N, 63°38′ E 154
Kyshtovka, *Russ.* 56°35′ N, 76°34′ E 169
Kyshtym, *Russ.* 55°41′ N, 60°33′ E 154
Kystatyam, *Russ.* 67°34′ N, 123°24′ E 160
Kythrea, *Northern Cyprus, Cyprus* 35°14′ N, 33°28′ E 194
Kytlym, *Russ.* 59°31′ N, 59°11′ E 154
Kytömaki, *Fin.* 64°46′ N, 28°16′ E 154
Kyunchaung, *Myanmar* 15°32′ N, 98°15′ E 202
Kyunhla, *Myanmar* 23°19′ N, 95°13′ E 202
Kyuquot, *Can.* 50°2′ N, 127°22′ W 108
Kyūshū, island, *Japan* 31°5′ N, 128°47′ E 190
Kyustendil, *Bulg.* 42°16′ N, 22°41′ E 168
Kyustendil, adm. division, *Bulg.* 42°18′ N, 22°28′ E 168
Kyusyur, *Russ.* 70°37′ N, 127°39′ E 160
Kyyjärvi, *Fin.* 63°0′ N, 24°31′ E 154
Kyzkl-Oy, *Kyrg.* 42°15′ N, 73°50′ E 197
Kyzyl, *Russ.* 51°36′ N, 94°38′ E 190
Kyzyl-Adyr, *Kyrg.* 42°35′ N, 71°43′ E 197
Kyzyl-Korgon, *Kyrg.* 40°9′ N, 73°32′ E 197
Kyzyl-Kyya, *Kyrg.* 40°14′ N, 72°6′ E 197
Kyzyl-Suu, river, *Taj.* 39°5′ N, 70°52′ E 197

L

La Adela, *Arg.* 38°57′ S, 64°4′ W 139
La Albuera, *Sp.* 38°42′ N, 6°50′ W 164
La Algaba, *Sp.* 37°27′ N, 6°2′ W 164

La Almolda, Sp. 41°32′ N, 0°12′ E 164
La Antiqua, Mex. 19°20′ N, 96°21′ W 114
La Araucanía, adm. division, Chile 39°21′ S, 73°44′ W 134
La Asunción, Venez. 11°3′ N, 63°52′ W 116
La Baie, Can. 48°18′ N, 70°54′ W 94
La Banda, Arg. 27°44′ S, 64°15′ W 132
La Barca, Mex. 20°17′ N, 102°34′ W 114
La Bardelière, Lac, lake, Can. 51°18′ N, 76°6′ W 110
La Barge, Wyo., U.S. 42°15′ N, 110°12′ W 92
La Barra, Nicar. 12°55′ N, 83°33′ W 115
La Baule-Escoublac, Fr. 47°17′ N, 2°25′ W 150
La Belle, Fla., U.S. 26°45′ N, 81°27′ W 105
La Biche, river, Can. 60°29′ N, 124°30′ W 108
La Bisbal d' Empordà, Sp. 41°57′ N, 3°3′ E 164
La Bonita, Ecua. 0°24′ N, 77°39′ W 136
La Brecha, Mex. 25°21′ N, 108°26′ W 82
La Calera, Chile 32°50′ S, 71°15′ W 134
La Campana, Mex. 26°8′ N, 103°31′ W 114
La Cañada de San Urbano, Sp. 36°49′ N, 2°24′ W 164
La Carlota, Arg. 33°27′ S, 63°16′ W 139
La Carlota, Philippines 10°24′ N, 122°54′ E 203
La Carlota, Sp. 37°40′ N, 4°56′ W 164
La Carolina, Sp. 38°16′ N, 3°37′ W 164
La Cautiva, Arg. 34°0′ S, 64°6′ W 139
La Cava, Sp. 40°42′ N, 0°44′ E 164
La Ceiba, Col. 3°32′ N, 67°51′ W 136
La Ceiba, Hond. 15°45′ N, 86°47′ W 115
La Ceiba, Venez. 9°28′ N, 71°5′ W 136
La Cesira, Arg. 33°59′ S, 62°58′ W 139
La Chambre, Fr. 45°21′ N, 6°17′ E 167
La Charité, Fr. 47°10′ N, 3°0′ E 150
La Chorrera, Col. 0°48′ N, 73°1′ W 136
La Chorrera, Pan. 8°54′ N, 79°46′ W 115
La Ciudad Encantada, site, Sp. 40°11′ N, 2°4′ W 164
La Colorada, Mex. 23°48′ N, 102°28′ W 114
La Colorada, Mex. 28°46′ N, 110°33′ W 92
La Concepción, Venez. 10°27′ N, 71°44′ W 136
La Condamine-Châtelard, Fr. 44°27′ N, 6°43′ E 167
La Conner, Wash., U.S. 48°22′ N, 122°29′ W 100
La Copelina, Arg. 37°18′ S, 67°37′ W 134
La Coronilla, Uru. 33°53′ S, 53°34′ W 139
La Crete, Can. 58°12′ N, 116°21′ W 108
La Crosse, Ind., U.S. 41°18′ N, 86°54′ W 102
La Crosse, Kans., U.S. 38°31′ N, 99°20′ W 92
La Crosse, Va., U.S. 36°41′ N, 78°6′ W 96
La Crosse, Wash., U.S. 46°47′ N, 117°54′ W 90
La Crosse, Wis., U.S. 43°48′ N, 91°15′ W 110
La Cruz, Arg. 29°10′ S, 56°41′ W 139
La Cruz, C.R. 11°4′ N, 85°38′ W 115
La Cruz, Mex. 23°52′ N, 106°54′ W 114
La Cuesta, Mex. 28°43′ N, 102°29′ W 92
La Cygne, Kans., U.S. 38°19′ N, 94°45′ W 94
La Dorada, Col. 5°26′ N, 74°42′ W 136
La Esmeralda, Venez. 3°10′ N, 65°32′ W 136
La Esperanza, Cuba 22°45′ N, 83°45′ W 116
La Esperanza, Hond. 14°19′ N, 88°8′ W 115
La Fère, Fr. 49°39′ N, 3°21′ E 163
La Ferté-Gaucher, Fr. 48°47′ N, 3°17′ E 163
La Ferté-Macé, Fr. 48°35′ N, 0°22′ E 150
La Ferté-sous-Jouarre, Fr. 48°56′ N, 3°7′ E 163
La Feuillie, Fr. 49°27′ N, 1°30′ E 163
La Follette, Tenn., U.S. 36°22′ N, 84°8′ W 96
La Font de la Figuera, Sp. 38°48′ N, 0°53′ E 164
La Fontaine, Ind., U.S. 40°39′ N, 85°43′ W 102
La Fuente de San Esteban, Sp. 40°48′ N, 6°15′ W 150
La Gallareta, Arg. 29°31′ S, 60°25′ W 139
La Gineta, Sp. 39°6′ N, 2°0′ W 164
La Glace, Can. 55°23′ N, 119°8′ W 108
La Gloria, Col. 8°38′ N, 73°47′ W 136
La Gorce Peak, peak, Antarctica 77°31′ S, 152°20′ W 248
La Grande, Oreg., U.S. 45°18′ N, 118°5′ W 90
La Grande Deux, Réservoir de , lake, Can. 54°11′ N, 75°50′ W 106
La Grange, Ga., U.S. 33°1′ N, 85°2′ W 112
La Grange, Ky., U.S. 38°24′ N, 85°23′ W 94
La Grange, Mo., U.S. 40°1′ N, 91°31′ W 94
La Grange, N.C., U.S. 35°18′ N, 77°48′ W 96
La Grange, Tex., U.S. 29°53′ N, 96°52′ W 96
La Grange, Wyo., U.S. 41°38′ N, 104°10′ W 90
La Grave, Fr. 45°2′ N, 6°18′ E 167
La Gruta, Arg. 26°50′ S, 53°43′ W 139
La Guaira, Venez. 10°34′ N, 66°56′ W 136
La Guardia, Arg. 29°33′ S, 65°27′ W 134
La Guardia, Sp. 39°47′ N, 3°29′ W 164
La Habana, adm. division, Cuba 22°44′ N, 82°55′ W 116
La Habana (Havana), Cuba 23°6′ N, 82°33′ W 116
La Honda, Calif., U.S. 37°19′ N, 122°17′ W 100
La Huacana, Mex. 18°56′ N, 101°48′ W 114
La Jagua, Col. 9°33′ N, 73°23′ W 136
La Jagua, Col. 2°25′ N, 72°37′ W 136
La Jana, Sp. 40°31′ N, 0°15′ E 164
La Jara, Colo., U.S. 37°16′ N, 105°58′ W 92
La Javie, Fr. 44°10′ N, 6°20′ E 167
La Jolla, Calif., U.S. 32°50′ N, 117°17′ W 101
La Junta, Colo., U.S. 37°58′ N, 103°33′ W 90
La Leonesa, Arg. 27°3′ S, 58°42′ W 139
La Libertad, Ecua. 2°19′ S, 80°57′ W 130
La Libertad, Guatemala 16°47′ N, 90°8′ W 115
La Libertad, Nicar. 12°12′ N, 85°10′ W 115
La Libertad, adm. division, Peru 8°1′ S, 79°16′ W 130
La Ligua, Chile 32°28′ S, 71°17′ W 134
La Lima, Hond. 15°23′ N, 87°55′ W 115
La Loche, Can. 56°28′ N, 109°25′ W 108
La Loupe, Fr. 48°28′ N, 1°0′ E 163
La Louvière, Belg. 50°28′ N, 4°11′ E 163
La Madrid, Arg. 27°39′ S, 65°16′ W 132
La Malbaie, Can. 47°38′ N, 70°11′ W 94
La Malinche National Park, Mex. 19°6′ N, 98°21′ W 72
La Manche see English Channel 49°57′ N, 3°16′ W 150
La Maroma, Arg. 35°13′ S, 66°18′ W 134
La Marque, Tex., U.S. 29°21′ N, 94°58′ W 103
La Mauricie National Park, Can. 46°56′ N, 75°19′ W 94
La Merced, Peru 11°5′ S, 75°21′ W 130
La Mesa, Calif., U.S. 32°46′ N, 117°2′ W 101
La Mesa, N. Mex., U.S. 32°7′ N, 106°43′ W 92
La Misa, Mex. 28°24′ N, 110°32′ W 92
La Moille, Ill., U.S. 41°31′ N, 89°17′ W 102
La Mothe-Saint-Héraye, Fr. 46°21′ N, 0°8′ E 150
La Mugrosa, Col. 6°44′ N, 73°43′ W 136
La Noria, Mex. 23°27′ N, 106°21′ W 114
La Oroya, Peru 11°32′ S, 75°58′ W 130
La Paca, Sp. 37°52′ N, 1°51′ W 164
La Palma, Pan. 8°22′ N, 78°9′ W 136
La Palma, island, Sp. 28°27′ N, 18°53′ W 214
La Paloma, Uru. 34°39′ S, 54°11′ W 139
La Pampa, adm. division, Arg. 37°3′ S, 67°55′ W 134
La Para, Arg. 30°54′ S, 63°2′ W 139
La Paya National Park, Col. 0°15′ N, 75°53′ W 136
La Paz, Arg. 30°43′ S, 59°36′ W 139
La Paz, Arg. 33°29′ S, 67°32′ W 134
La Paz, Bol. 16°33′ S, 68°16′ W 137
La Paz, Ind., U.S. 41°27′ N, 86°19′ W 102
La Paz, Mex. 24°7′ N, 110°26′ W 112
La Paz, Mex. 23°38′ N, 100°43′ W 114
La Paz, adm. division, Bol. 15°11′ S, 68°59′ W 137
La Pedrera, Col. 1°21′ S, 69°42′ W 136
La Peraleja, Sp. 40°14′ N, 2°33′ W 164
La Perla, Mex. 28°13′ N, 104°36′ W 92
La Pérouse, Can. 55°12′ N, 97°59′ W 108
La Pesca, Mex. 23°47′ N, 97°47′ W 114
La Piedad de Cabadas, Mex. 20°19′ N, 102°2′ W 114
La Pine, Oreg., U.S. 43°39′ N, 121°31′ W 90
La Pintada, Pan. 8°37′ N, 80°25′ W 116
La Pita, ruin(s), Pan. 8°5′ N, 81°15′ W 115
La Place, La., U.S. 30°3′ N, 90°28′ W 103
La Placita, Mex. 18°34′ N, 103°39′ W 114
La Plant, S. Dak., U.S. 45°8′ N, 100°41′ W 90
La Plata, Arg. 34°55′ S, 57°58′ W 139
La Plata, Col. 2°23′ N, 75°57′ W 136
La Plata, Mo., U.S. 40°1′ N, 92°29′ W 94
La Pocatière, Can. 47°20′ N, 70°2′ W 94
La Pointe, Wis., U.S. 46°46′ N, 90°47′ W 94
La Porte, Ind., U.S. 41°36′ N, 86°43′ W 102
La Porte, Tex., U.S. 29°38′ N, 95°1′ W 103
La Porte City, Iowa, U.S. 42°16′ N, 92°11′ W 94
La Presa, Mex. 32°27′ N, 116°56′ W 101
La Pryor, Tex., U.S. 28°55′ N, 99°50′ W 92
La Puebla de Hijar, Sp. 41°12′ N, 0°27′ E 164
La Puebla de Valverde, Sp. 40°12′ N, 0°56′ E 164
La Puerta de Segura, Sp. 38°21′ N, 2°44′ W 164
La Purísima, Mex. 26°9′ N, 112°5′ W 112
La Push, Wash., U.S. 47°53′ N, 124°37′ W 100
La Quemada, ruin(s), Mex. 22°26′ N, 102°55′ W 114
La Quiaca, Arg. 22°11′ S, 65°35′ W 137
La Quinta, Calif., U.S. 33°41′ N, 116°19′ W 101
La Rambla, Sp. 37°37′ N, 4°45′ W 164
La Reale, It. 41°3′ N, 8°18′ E 156
La Réole, Fr. 44°34′ N, 5°296′ W 150
La Rioja, Arg. 29°25′ S, 66°49′ W 132
La Rioja, adm. division, Arg. 28°4′ S, 68°58′ W 132
La Rioja, adm. division, Sp. 42°10′ N, 3°5′ W 150
La Roca de la Sierra, Sp. 39°6′ N, 6°42′ W 164
La Roche, Belg. 50°10′ N, 5°33′ E 167
La Roche, Fr. 46°4′ N, 6°18′ E 167
La Rochelle, Fr. 46°7′ N, 1°11′ W 143
La Roda, Sp. 39°12′ N, 2°10′ W 164
La Romaine, Can. 50°13′ N, 60°40′ W 111
La Ronge, Can. 55°7′ N, 105°18′ W 108
La Rubia, Arg. 30°5′ S, 61°48′ W 139
La Rue, Ohio, U.S. 40°34′ N, 83°23′ W 102
La Rumorosa, Mex. 32°33′ N, 116°3′ W 101
La Sabana, Arg. 27°51′ S, 59°58′ W 139
La Sal, Utah, U.S. 38°18′ N, 109°14′ W 90
La Salceda, Sp. 41°2′ N, 3°54′ W 164
La Salle, Ill., U.S. 41°19′ N, 89°6′ W 102
La Sarre, Can. 48°48′ N, 79°13′ W 94
La Saulce, Fr. 44°25′ N, 5°59′ E 150
La Scie, Can. 49°57′ N, 55°36′ W 111
La Selva Beach, Calif., U.S. 36°56′ N, 121°52′ W 100
La Selva del Camp, Sp. 41°12′ N, 1°7′ E 164
La Sènia, Sp. 40°37′ N, 0°17′ E 164
La Serena, Chile 29°56′ S, 71°17′ W 134
La Solana, Sp. 38°56′ N, 3°15′ W 164
La Soledad, Mex. 24°44′ N, 104°55′ W 114
La Solita, Venez. 9°9′ N, 71°49′ W 136
La Souterraine, Fr. 46°14′ N, 1°28′ E 150
La Spezia, It. 44°6′ N, 9°49′ E 167
La Suze, Fr. 47°53′ N, 1°59′ E 150
La Tagua, Col. 0°5′ N, 74°40′ W 136
La Teste, Fr. 44°38′ N, 1°10′ W 150
La Tigra National Park, Hond. 14°11′ N, 87°13′ W 115
La Trinidad, Nicar. 12°56′ N, 86°13′ W 116
La Tuque, Can. 47°25′ N, 72°47′ W 94
La Unión, Bol. 15°20′ S, 61°7′ W 132
La Unión, Chile 40°16′ S, 73°7′ W 134
La Unión, Col. 1°31′ N, 77°10′ W 136
La Unión, Mex. 17°56′ N, 101°48′ W 114
La Unión, Sp. 37°37′ N, 0°54′ E 164
La Unión, Sp. 37°37′ N, 0°55′ E 214
La Unión, Venez. 8°14′ N, 67°47′ W 136
La Unión Morales, Mex. 24°32′ N, 98°59′ W 114
La Urbana, Venez. 7°7′ N, 66°55′ W 136
La Vanoise National Park, Fr. 45°21′ N, 6°49′ E 167
La Vela de Coro, Venez. 11°24′ N, 69°34′ W 136
La Venta, ruin(s), Mex. 18°2′ N, 94°10′ W 112
La Ventana, Mex. 22°59′ N, 100°14′ W 114
La Ventosa, Sp. 40°11′ N, 2°26′ W 164
La Ventura, Mex. 24°36′ N, 100°54′ W 114
La Vereda, Sp. 41°0′ N, 3°21′ W 164
La Verkin, Utah, U.S. 37°12′ N, 113°16′ W 92
La Veta, Colo., U.S. 37°29′ N, 105°1′ W 92
La Victoria, Venez. 7°17′ N, 70°5′ W 136
La Vila Joiosa see Villajoyosa, Sp. 38°29′ N, 0°14′ E 164
La Yarada, Peru 18°18′ S, 70°30′ W 137
La Yesca, Mex. 21°17′ N, 104°2′ W 114
La Yunta, Sp. 40°53′ N, 1°41′ W 164
Laanila, Fin. 68°24′ N, 27°22′ E 152
Laas Dawaco, Somalia 10°25′ N, 49°3′ E 216
Laayoune, W. Sahara 27°6′ N, 13°12′ W 214
Laayoune, Alg. 35°41′ N, 2°0′ E 150
Labadaad, Somalia 0°30′ N, 42°45′ E 218
Labardén, Arg. 36°57′ S, 58°5′ W 139
Labbezanga, Mali 14°58′ N, 0°42′ E 222
Labé, Guinea 11°19′ N, 12°18′ W 222
Labelle, Can. 46°17′ N, 74°45′ W 94
Labenne, Fr. 43°35′ N, 1°28′ W 150
Laberge, Lake, Can. 61°12′ N, 136°23′ W 98
Labinsk, Russ. 44°40′ N, 40°39′ E 158
Labis, Malaysia 2°24′ N, 103°2′ E 196
Laborde, Arg. 33°10′ S, 62°51′ W 139
Laborovaya, Russ. 67°38′ N, 67°46′ E 169
Labouchere, Mount, Austral. 24°50′ S, 117°30′ E 230
Laboulaye, Arg. 34°7′ S, 63°24′ W 139
Labrador City, Can. 52°57′ N, 67°3′ W 106
Labrador, region, Can. 52°2′ N, 63°21′ W 111
Labrador Sea 55°27′ N, 57°22′ W 106
Lábrea, Braz. 7°17′ S, 64°50′ W 130
Labuha, Indonesia 0°35′ N, 127°27′ E 192
Labuhanbatu, Indonesia 2°14′ N, 100°14′ E 196
Labuhanbilik, Indonesia 2°33′ N, 100°10′ E 196
Labutta, Myanmar 16°10′ N, 94°45′ E 202
Labyrinth Lake, Can. 60°40′ N, 107°11′ W 108
Labytnangi, Russ. 66°38′ N, 66°28′ E 169
Lac du Bonnet, Can. 50°14′ N, 96°5′ W 90
Lac du Flambeau, Wis., U.S. 45°58′ N, 89°53′ W 94
Lac La Biche, Can. 54°46′ N, 112°0′ W 108
Lac Seul, Can. 50°20′ N, 92°17′ W 110
Lac-Allard, Can. 50°32′ N, 63°27′ W 111
Lacanau, Fr. 44°58′ N, 1°6′ W 150
Lacanau-Océan, Fr. 45°0′ N, 1°13′ W 150
Lacantun, river, Mex. 16°10′ N, 91°26′ W 115
Laćarak, Serb. 45°0′ N, 19°34′ E 168
Lacaune, Monts de, peak, Fr. 43°40′ N, 2°41′ E 165
Lac-au-Saumon, Can. 48°24′ N, 67°21′ W 94
Lac-Bouchette, Can. 48°16′ N, 72°10′ W 94
Lacepede Islands, Indian Ocean 17°3′ S, 120°1′ E 230
Lacerdónia, Mozambique 18°6′ S, 35°33′ E 224
Lacey, Wash., U.S. 47°0′ N, 122°48′ W 100
Lache, Lac La, lake, Can. 56°29′ N, 110°17′ W 108
Lachish, ruin(s), Israel 31°33′ N, 34°47′ E 194
Lac-Mégantic, Can. 45°34′ N, 70°54′ W 94
Lacombe, La., U.S. 30°18′ N, 89°57′ W 103
Lacon, Ill., U.S. 41°0′ N, 89°24′ W 102
Laconia, N.H., U.S. 43°31′ N, 71°29′ W 104
Lacoochee, Fla., U.S. 28°27′ N, 82°11′ W 105
Lacq, Fr. 43°25′ N, 0°39′ E 164
Lacuy, Península, Chile 41°46′ S, 75°37′ W 134
Ladainha, Braz. 17°39′ S, 41°45′ W 138
Ladd, Ill., U.S. 41°22′ N, 89°13′ W 102
Lâdik, Turk. 40°54′ N, 35°55′ E 156
Ladismith, S. Af. 33°29′ S, 21°13′ E 227
Ladispoli, It. 41°57′ N, 12°4′ E 156
Ladoga, Lake see Ladozhskoye Ozero, lake, Russ. 61°10′ N, 31°29′ E 154
Ladozhskoye Ozero see Ladozhskoye Ozero, lake, Russ. 61°10′ N, 31°29′ E 154
Ladushkin, Russ. 54°33′ N, 20°10′ E 166
Ladva, Russ. 61°20′ N, 34°43′ E 154
Ladva Vetka, Russ. 61°18′ N, 34°32′ E 154
Lady Evelyn Falls, Can. 60°38′ N, 117°43′ W 108
Lady Grey, S. Af. 30°42′ S, 27°12′ E 227
Ladysmith, Can. 48°58′ N, 123°49′ W 100
Ladysmith, S. Af. 28°32′ S, 29°46′ E 227
Ladysmith, Wis., U.S. 45°28′ N, 91°7′ W 94
Lae, P.N.G. 6°47′ S, 146°52′ E 238
Laem Ngop, Thai. 12°12′ N, 102°25′ E 202
Laer, Ger. 52°3′ N, 7°22′ E 163
Lafayette, Ala., U.S. 32°53′ N, 85°25′ W 96
Lafayette, Ga., U.S. 34°41′ N, 85°16′ W 96
Lafayette, Ind., U.S. 40°25′ N, 86°52′ W 102
Lafayette, La., U.S. 30°12′ N, 92°2′ W 103
Lafayette, Tenn., U.S. 36°31′ N, 86°2′ W 94
Lafayette, Mount, peak, N.H., U.S. 44°9′ N, 71°41′ W 104
Lafia, Nig. 8°28′ N, 8°29′ E 222
Lafiagi, Nig. 8°53′ N, 5°18′ E 222
Lafitte, La., U.S. 29°39′ N, 90°6′ W 103
Lafleche, Can. 49°41′ N, 106°34′ W 90
Lafou, Guinea 11°35′ N, 12°30′ W 222
Laful, India 7°9′ N, 93°55′ E 188
Laganya, Ghana 9°9′ N, 3°179′ E 222
Lagartera, Sp. 39°53′ N, 5°13′ W 150
Lagarto, Braz. 10°54′ S, 37°41′ W 132
Laghouat, Alg. 33°50′ N, 2°52′ E 214
Lagny, Fr. 48°52′ N, 2°42′ E 163
Lago Agrio, Ecua. 5°297′ N, 76°47′ W 136
Lago Argentino see El Calafate, Arg. 50°26′ S, 72°13′ W 123
Lago de Camécuaro National Park, Mex. 19°40′ N, 102°37′ W 112
Lago de Nicaragua, lake, Nicar. 11°30′ N, 85°30′ W 116
Lagoa da Prata, Braz. 20°4′ S, 45°32′ W 138
Lagoa do Peixe National Park, Braz. 31°0′ S, 50°42′ W 139
Lagoa Vermelha, Braz. 28°14′ S, 51°30′ W 139
Lagodekhi, Ga. 41°49′ N, 46°16′ E 195
Lagolândia, Braz. 15°38′ S, 49°4′ W 138
Lagos, Nig. 6°30′ N, 3°22′ E 222
Lagos, Port. 37°5′ N, 8°41′ W 150
Lagos de Moreno, Mex. 21°21′ N, 101°57′ W 114
Lagosa, Tanzania 5°59′ S, 29°50′ E 224
Lagrange, Austral. 18°42′ S, 121°47′ E 231
Lagrange, Ind., U.S. 41°37′ N, 85°25′ W 102
Lagrange Bay 18°46′ S, 120°26′ E 230
Lagro, Ind., U.S. 40°49′ N, 85°44′ W 102
Laguna, Braz. 28°30′ S, 48°47′ W 138
Laguna, N. Mex., U.S. 35°2′ N, 107°24′ W 92
Laguna Beach, Calif., U.S. 33°33′ N, 117°49′ W 101
Laguna Blanca, Arg. 25°8′ S, 58°16′ W 132
Laguna Blanca National Park, Arg. 39°0′ S, 70°46′ W 134
Laguna Dam, Calif., U.S. 32°52′ N, 114°33′ W 101
Laguna de Chautengo, Mex. 16°39′ N, 99°4′ W 112
Laguna de la Restinga National Park, Caribbean Sea 10°59′ N, 64°13′ W 116
Laguna del Laja National Park, Chile 37°32′ S, 71°28′ W 134
Laguna Grande, Arg. 49°30′ S, 70°17′ W 134
Laguna Mountains, Calif., U.S. 32°56′ N, 116°32′ W 101
Laguna Paiva, Arg. 31°18′ S, 60°38′ W 139
Laguna San Rafael National Park, Chile 47°28′ S, 74°37′ W 122
Laguna Yema, Arg. 24°15′ S, 61°15′ W 132
Lagunas, Chile 20°59′ S, 69°41′ W 137
Lagunas, Peru 5°15′ S, 75°41′ W 130
Lagunas de Chacahua National Park, Mex. 15°54′ N, 97°59′ W 72
Lagunas de Montebello National Park see 29, Mex. 16°3′ N, 91°50′ W 115
Lagunas de Zempoala National Park, Mex. 18°59′ N, 99°24′ W 112
Lagunilla, Sp. 40°18′ N, 5°58′ W 150
Lagunillas, Bol. 19°42′ S, 63°46′ W 137
Lagunillas, Venez. 10°7′ N, 71°16′ W 136
Lagunitos, Peru 4°35′ S, 81°17′ W 130
Lagwira, Africa 20°53′ N, 17°5′ W 222
Laha, China 48°14′ N, 124°40′ E 198
Lahad Datu, Malaysia 5°4′ N, 118°19′ E 203
Lahainaluna High School, site, Hawaiʻi, U.S. 20°52′ N, 156°43′ W 99
Lahar, India 26°11′ N, 78°56′ E 197
Lahat, Indonesia 3°50′ S, 103°26′ E 192
Lahemaa National Park, Est. 59°33′ N, 26°3′ E 166
Lahewa, Indonesia 1°24′ N, 97°8′ E 196
Lahıc, Azerb. 40°50′ N, 48°22′ E 195
La'ij, Yemen 13°3′ N, 44°52′ E 182
Lāhījān, Iran 37°14′ N, 50°4′ E 195
Lahn, river, Ger. 50°54′ N, 8°27′ E 167
Lahnstein, Ger. 50°18′ N, 7°36′ E 167
Lahore, Pak. 31°35′ N, 74°18′ E 186
Lahoysk, Belarus 54°12′ N, 27°50′ E 166
Lahr, Ger. 48°20′ N, 7°51′ E 163
Lahti, Fin. 60°58′ N, 25°38′ E 166
Laï (Behagle), Chad 9°23′ N, 16°20′ E 216
Lai Chau, Vietnam 22°3′ N, 103°11′ E 202
Laibin, China 23°45′ N, 109°14′ E 198
Laifeng, China 29°32′ N, 109°22′ E 198
L'Aigle, Fr. 48°45′ N, 0°38′ E 150
Laihia, Fin. 62°57′ N, 22°0′ E 154
Lai-hka, Myanmar 21°17′ N, 97°40′ E 202
Laingsburg, Mich., U.S. 42°52′ N, 84°22′ W 102
Laingsburg, S. Af. 33°10′ S, 20°54′ E 227
Laird Hill, Tex., U.S. 32°20′ N, 94°55′ W 103
Lais, Indonesia 3°31′ S, 102°0′ E 192
Laisamis, Kenya 1°35′ N, 37°49′ E 224
Laisvall, Nor. 66°5′ N, 17°9′ E 152
Laitila, Fin. 60°51′ N, 21°42′ E 166
Laiwu, China 36°12′ N, 117°40′ E 198
Laiyang, China 37°0′ N, 120°39′ E 198
Laizhou, China 37°11′ N, 119°57′ E 198
Laja, river, Mex. 21°17′ N, 100°58′ W 114
Laje, Braz. 5°35′ S, 56°51′ W 130
Lajeado, Braz. 29°23′ S, 51°57′ W 139
Lajes, Braz. 14°2′ S, 48°10′ W 138
Lajes, Braz. 27°51′ S, 50°21′ W 138
Lajitas, Tex., U.S. 29°15′ N, 103°47′ W 92
Lajkovac, Serb. 44°22′ N, 20°9′ E 168
Lajosmizse, Hung. 47°1′ N, 19°34′ E 168
Laka, Dem. Rep. of the Congo 4°11′ N, 23°37′ E 224
Lakamané, Mali 14°31′ N, 9°53′ W 222
Lakaträsk, Nor. 66°17′ N, 21°7′ E 152
Lake, Mich., U.S. 43°51′ N, 85°1′ W 102
Lake, Miss., U.S. 32°19′ N, 89°19′ W 103
Lake Andes, S. Dak., U.S. 43°8′ N, 98°33′ W 90
Lake Arrowhead, Calif., U.S. 34°14′ N, 117°12′ W 101
Lake Arthur, La., U.S. 30°4′ N, 92°41′ W 103
Lake Arthur, N. Mex., U.S. 32°59′ N, 104°23′ W 92
Lake Charles, La., U.S. 30°12′ N, 93°13′ W 103
Lake Chelan National Recreation Area, Wash., U.S. 48°18′ N, 121°30′ W 100
Lake City, Colo., U.S. 38°2′ N, 107°20′ W 92
Lake City, Fla., U.S. 30°9′ N, 82°37′ W 112
Lake City, Iowa, U.S. 42°15′ N, 94°44′ W 94
Lake City, Mich., U.S. 44°20′ N, 85°13′ W 94
Lake City, Minn., U.S. 44°25′ N, 92°18′ W 94
Lake City, S.C., U.S. 33°51′ N, 79°46′ W 96
Lake Coleridge, N.Z. 43°23′ S, 171°32′ E 240
Lake Cowichan, Can. 48°48′ N, 124°3′ W 100
Lake Crystal, Minn., U.S. 44°5′ N, 94°13′ W 94
Lake Delton, Wis., U.S. 43°35′ N, 89°47′ W 102
Lake Elsinore, Calif., U.S. 33°40′ N, 117°21′ W 101
Lake Forest, Ill., U.S. 42°14′ N, 87°50′ W 102
Lake Geneva, Wis., U.S. 42°35′ N, 88°27′ W 102
Lake George, Mich., U.S. 43°58′ N, 84°57′ W 102
Lake George, N.Y., U.S. 43°25′ N, 73°44′ W 104
Lake Harbor, Fla., U.S. 26°40′ N, 80°48′ W 105
Lake Harbor see Kimmirut, Can. 62°52′ N, 69°53′ W 106
Lake Havasu City, Ariz., U.S. 34°29′ N, 114°20′ W 101
Lake Helen, Fla., U.S. 28°58′ N, 81°14′ W 105
Lake Hughes, Calif., U.S. 34°40′ N, 118°28′ W 101
Lake Isabella, Calif., U.S. 35°38′ N, 118°29′ W 101
Lake Jackson, Tex., U.S. 29°1′ N, 95°26′ W 103

Lake Louise, Can. 51°26′ N, 116°8′ W 90
Lake Luzerne, N.Y., U.S. 43°18′ N, 73°51′ W 104
Lake Mburo National Park, Uganda 0°48′ N, 30°36′ E 206
Lake Mead National Recreation Area, Nev., U.S. 36°1′ N, 114°39′ W 101
Lake Mills, Iowa, U.S. 43°23′ N, 93°33′ W 94
Lake Mills, Wis., U.S. 43°5′ N, 88°55′ W 102
Lake Minchumina, Alas., U.S. 63°45′ N, 152°22′ W 98
Lake Monroe, Fla., U.S. 28°49′ N, 81°19′ W 105
Lake Nakuru National Park, Kenya 0°29′ N, 35°43′ E 206
Lake Odessa, Mich., U.S. 42°46′ N, 85°8′ W 102
Lake Orion, Mich., U.S. 42°46′ N, 83°15′ W 102
Lake Park, Fla., U.S. 26°48′ N, 80°5′ W 105
Lake Placid, Fla., U.S. 27°17′ N, 81°22′ W 105
Lake Placid, N.Y., U.S. 44°16′ N, 74°0′ W 104
Lake Preston, S. Dak., U.S. 44°20′ N, 97°24′ W 90
Lake Providence, La., U.S. 32°47′ N, 91°11′ W 103
Lake Pukaki, N.Z. 44°12′ S, 170°7′ E 240
Lake Tekapo, N.Z. 44°2′ S, 170°30′ E 240
Lake Traverse, Can. 45°56′ N, 78°5′ W 94
Lake Village, Ark., U.S. 33°18′ N, 91°18′ W 103
Lake Wales, Fla., U.S. 27°54′ N, 81°35′ W 105
Lake Worth, Fla., U.S. 26°37′ N, 80°5′ W 105
Lakefield, Can. 44°25′ N, 78°15′ W 94
Lakefield National Park, Austral. 15°18′ S, 143°57′ E 238
Lakeland, Fla., U.S. 28°2′ N, 81°58′ W 105
Lakeland, Ga., U.S. 31°2′ N, 83°5′ W 96
Lakelse Lake, Can. 54°22′ N, 128°32′ W 108
Lakeport, Mich., U.S. 43°6′ N, 82°30′ W 102
Lakes, adm. division, Sudan 6°24′ N, 29°29′ E 224
Lakeside, Calif., U.S. 32°51′ N, 116°56′ W 101
Lakeside, Nebr., U.S. 42°3′ N, 102°26′ W 90
Lakeside, Ohio, U.S. 41°31′ N, 82°45′ W 102
Lakeside, Oreg., U.S. 43°34′ N, 124°11′ W 90
Lakeview, Mich., U.S. 43°26′ N, 85°17′ W 102
Lakeview, Ohio, U.S. 40°28′ N, 83°56′ W 102
Lakeville, Conn., U.S. 41°58′ N, 73°27′ W 104
Lakeville, Minn., U.S. 44°38′ N, 93°15′ W 94
Lakewood, Colo., U.S. 39°43′ N, 105°5′ W 90
Lakewood, Ohio, U.S. 41°27′ N, 81°51′ W 82
Lakhdenpokh'ya, Russ. 61°30′ N, 30°10′ E 166
Lakhimpur, India 27°54′ N, 80°46′ E 197
Lakhnadon, India 22°36′ N, 79°37′ E 197
Lakhpat, India 23°48′ N, 68°47′ E 186
Lakhva, Belarus 52°12′ N, 27°7′ E 152
Lakí, Gr. 37°7′ N, 26°52′ E 156
Lakin, Kans., U.S. 37°56′ N, 101°17′ W 90
Lákmos, Óri, peak, Gr. 39°40′ N, 21°2′ E 156
Lakota, Côte d'Ivoire 5°47′ N, 5°40′ W 222
Lakota, N. Dak., U.S. 48°1′ N, 98°22′ W 90
Lakselv, Nor. 70°2′ N, 24°56′ E 152
Lakshadweep, islands, Persian Gulf 10°16′ N, 72°31′ E 188
Laktaši, Bosn. and Herzg. 44°54′ N, 17°18′ E 168
Lalago, Tanzania 3°25′ S, 33°56′ E 224
Lalapansi, Zimb. 19°22′ S, 30°10′ E 224
Lalaua, Mozambique 14°24′ S, 38°16′ E 224
Lāleh Zār, Kūh-e, peak, Iran 29°23′ N, 56°45′ E 196
Lalībela, Eth. 12°1′ N, 39°2′ E 182
Lalinde, Fr. 44°50′ N, 0°44′ E 150
Lalitpur, India 24°42′ N, 78°24′ E 197
Lalitpur (Patan), Nepal 27°36′ N, 85°22′ E 197
Laloche, river, Can. 61°36′ N, 112°26′ W 108
Lal'sk, Russ. 60°45′ N, 47°36′ E 154
Lalsot, India 26°32′ N, 76°21′ E 197
Lama, Ozero, lake, Russ. 69°34′ N, 89°20′ E 169
Lamag, Malaysia 5°30′ N, 117°48′ E 203
Lamaing, Myanmar 15°29′ N, 97°50′ E 202
Lama-Kara, Togo 9°36′ N, 1°11′ E 222
Lamar, Colo., U.S. 38°4′ N, 102°37′ W 90
Lamar, Mo., U.S. 37°28′ N, 94°16′ W 96
Lamas, Peru 6°26′ S, 76°35′ W 130
Lamas, Turk. 36°34′ N, 34°14′ E 156
Lambach, Aust. 48°5′ N, 13°52′ E 156
Lambaréné, Gabon 0°44′ N, 10°11′ E 218
Lambasa, Fiji 16°18′ S, 179°25′ E 238
Lambayeque, Peru 6°39′ S, 79°56′ W 130
Lambayeque, adm. division, Peru 5°30′ S, 80°27′ W 130
Lamberhurst, U.K. 51°5′ N, 0°23′ E 162
Lambert Land, Norske Øer 78°56′ N, 27°17′ W 246
Lambert's Bay, S. Af. 32°5′ S, 18°18′ E 227
Lambertville, Mich., U.S. 41°45′ N, 83°38′ W 102
Lambourn, U.K. 51°30′ N, 1°33′ W 162
Lambrecht, Ger. 49°22′ N, 8°4′ E 163
Lambton, Can. 45°49′ N, 71°6′ W 111
Lambton, Cape, Can. 70°53′ N, 127°37′ W 106
Lamé, Chad 9°15′ N, 14°33′ E 216
Lame Deer, Mont., U.S. 45°35′ N, 106°41′ W 90
Lamesa, Tex., U.S. 32°43′ N, 101°57′ W 92
L'Ametlla de Mar, Sp. 40°53′ N, 0°47′ E 164
Lamía, Gr. 38°54′ N, 22°26′ E 156
Lamitan, Philippines 6°40′ N, 122°7′ E 203
Lamjaybir, Africa 25°21′ N, 14°48′ W 214
Lammeulo, Indonesia 5°15′ N, 95°53′ E 196
Lammhult, Nor. 57°9′ N, 14°34′ E 152
Lammi, Fin. 61°4′ N, 25°0′ E 166
Lamoille, Nev., U.S. 40°44′ N, 115°28′ W 90
Lamoille, river, Vt., U.S. 44°41′ N, 73°18′ W 110
Lamon Bay 14°26′ N, 122°0′ E 203
Lamoni, Iowa, U.S. 40°37′ N, 93°56′ W 94
Lamont, Calif., U.S. 35°16′ N, 118°56′ W 101
Lamont, Can. 53°45′ N, 112°47′ W 108
Lamont, Wyo., U.S. 42°12′ N, 107°29′ W 90
Lamotrek Atoll 6°36′ N, 147°0′ E 192
Lamoure, N. Dak., U.S. 46°20′ N, 98°18′ W 90
Lampa, Peru 15°24′ S, 70°21′ W 137
Lampang, Thai. 18°17′ N, 99°31′ E 202
Lampasas, Tex., U.S. 31°3′ N, 98°11′ W 92
Lampaul, Fr. 48°27′ N, 5°6′ W 150
Lampazos, Mex. 27°1′ N, 100°31′ W 96
Lampedusa, island, It. 35°22′ N, 11°14′ E 216
Lampeter, U.K. 52°6′ N, 4°4′ W 162
Lamphun, Thai. 18°36′ N, 99°3′ E 202
L'Ampolla, Sp. 40°48′ N, 0°41′ E 164
Lampozhnya, Russ. 65°42′ N, 44°20′ E 154
Lamskoye, Russ. 52°55′ N, 38°2′ E 154
Lamu, Kenya 2°16′ S, 40°50′ E 224
Lāmu, Myanmar 19°12′ N, 94°12′ E 202
Lan', river, Belarus 52°45′ N, 27°4′ E 154
Lan Yü, island, Taiwan, China 22°6′ N, 121°35′ E 198
Lana, It. 46°36′ N, 11°8′ E 167
Lana, river, Mex. 17°27′ N, 95°38′ W 114
Lānaʻi, island, Hawaiʻi, U.S. 20°35′ N, 157°29′ W 99
Lanaja, Sp. 41°45′ N, 0°19′ E 164
Lanao, Lake, Philippines 7°53′ N, 123°54′ E 203
Lanark, Ill., U.S. 42°6′ N, 89°50′ W 102
Lanbi Kyun, island, Myanmar 10°38′ N, 98°18′ E 202
Lancang, China 22°33′ N, 99°56′ E 202
Lancang (Mekong), river, China 32°3′ N, 97°14′ E 190
Lancaster, Calif., U.S. 34°41′ N, 118°9′ W 101
Lancaster, Mo., U.S. 40°31′ N, 92°31′ W 94
Lancaster, N.H., U.S. 44°29′ N, 71°35′ W 104
Lancaster, N.Y., U.S. 42°53′ N, 78°40′ W 94
Lancaster, Ohio, U.S. 39°43′ N, 82°36′ W 102
Lancaster, S.C., U.S. 34°42′ N, 80°47′ W 96
Lancaster, U.K. 54°2′ N, 2°48′ W 162
Lancaster, Wis., U.S. 42°50′ N, 90°42′ W 110
Lancaster Sound 73°38′ N, 94°47′ W 72
Lance Creek, Wyo., U.S. 43°1′ N, 104°38′ W 90
Land Between the Lakes, Ky., U.S. 37°1′ N, 88°0′ W 80
Land O'Lakes, Fla., U.S. 28°12′ N, 82°28′ W 105
Landau, Ger. 51°21′ N, 9°5′ E 167
Landay, Afghan. 30°29′ N, 63°47′ E 186
Landeck, Aust. 47°8′ N, 10°34′ E 156
Lander, Wyo., U.S. 42°50′ N, 108°44′ W 90
Landers, Calif., U.S. 34°16′ N, 116°25′ W 101
Landeryd, Nor. 57°5′ N, 13°15′ E 152
Landeta, Arg. 32°1′ S, 62°2′ W 139
Landete, Sp. 39°54′ N, 1°23′ W 164
Landfall Island, India 13°40′ N, 92°0′ E 188
Landis, Can. 52°12′ N, 108°28′ W 108
Landis, N.C., U.S. 35°32′ N, 80°37′ W 96
Landrecies, Fr. 50°7′ N, 3°42′ E 163
Landrum, S.C., U.S. 35°10′ N, 82°12′ W 96
Lands End, Can. 76°47′ N, 123°5′ W 246
Land's End, U.K. 50°0′ N, 6°1′ W 150
Lane Mountain, peak, Calif., U.S. 35°4′ N, 116°59′ W 101
Lanercost Priory, site, U.K. 54°57′ N, 2°49′ W 150
Lanesboro, Pa., U.S. 41°57′ N, 75°35′ W 110
Lanesborough, Mass., U.S. 42°30′ N, 73°14′ W 104
Lanett, Ala., U.S. 32°51′ N, 85°12′ W 96
Laneville, Tex., U.S. 31°57′ N, 94°48′ W 103
Lang Son, Vietnam 21°51′ N, 106°44′ E 198
Lang Suan, Thai. 9°55′ N, 99°5′ E 202
Langå, Den. 56°24′ N, 9°51′ E 150
La'nga Co, lake, China 30°37′ N, 80°48′ E 197
Langa de Duero, Sp. 41°36′ N, 3°24′ W 164
Langanes, Ice. 66°23′ N, 14°29′ W 246
Langao, China 32°16′ N, 108°55′ E 198
Langar, Uzb. 40°26′ N, 65°59′ E 197
Langarūd, Iran 37°10′ N, 50°9′ E 195
Långban, Nor. 59°51′ N, 14°15′ E 152
Langdon, N. Dak., U.S. 48°44′ N, 98°24′ W 90
Längelmäki, Fin. 61°41′ N, 24°41′ E 166
Langen, Ger. 49°59′ N, 8°40′ E 167
Langenau, Ger. 48°29′ N, 10°6′ E 152
Langenburg, Can. 50°50′ N, 101°43′ W 90
Langfang, China 39°33′ N, 116°38′ E 198
Langfjordnes, Nor. 70°42′ N, 28°4′ E 152
Långflon, Nor. 61°2′ N, 12°32′ E 152
Langford, S. Dak., U.S. 45°35′ N, 97°51′ W 90
Langham, Can. 52°21′ N, 106°56′ W 108
Langhirano, It. 44°36′ N, 10°14′ E 167
Langjökull, glacier, Ice. 64°48′ N, 29°24′ W 72
Langkawi, island, Malaysia 6°14′ N, 99°5′ E 196
Langley, Can. 49°5′ N, 122°39′ W 100
Langley, Wash., U.S. 48°1′ N, 122°26′ W 100
Langley Air Force Base, Va., U.S. 37°4′ N, 76°26′ W 94
Langley, Mount, peak, Calif., U.S. 36°31′ N, 118°17′ W 101
Langlois, Oreg., U.S. 42°55′ N, 124°27′ W 90
Langøya, island, Nor. 68°55′ N, 11°48′ E 246
Langport, U.K. 51°2′ N, 2°49′ W 162
Langres, Plateau de, Fr. 47°41′ N, 4°44′ E 165
Langsa, Indonesia 4°29′ N, 97°57′ E 196
Långsele, Nor. 64°33′ N, 15°51′ E 154
Långsele, Nor. 63°9′ N, 17°2′ E 152
Langtou, China 40°1′ N, 124°19′ E 200
Långtrask, Nor. 65°21′ N, 20°17′ E 152
Langtry, Tex., U.S. 29°47′ N, 101°35′ W 92
Langu, Thai. 6°52′ N, 99°46′ E 196
Languedoc-Roussillon, adm. division, Fr. 42°36′ N, 2°13′ E 150
Languedog, region, Fr. 44°39′ N, 3°3′ E 165
Langwarden, Ger. 53°36′ N, 8°19′ E 163
Langzhong, China 31°40′ N, 105°51′ E 190
Laniel, Can. 47°3′ N, 79°15′ W 94
Lanigan, Can. 51°51′ N, 105°3′ W 90
Lanín National Park, Arg. 40°54′ S, 71°5′ W 134
Lanjarón, Sp. 36°55′ N, 3°29′ W 164
Länkäran, Azerb. 38°44′ N, 48°49′ E 195
Lankio, Côte d'Ivoire 9°51′ N, 3°26′ W 222
Lankoveri, Nig. 9°1′ N, 11°22′ E 222
Lanlacuni Bajo, Peru 13°33′ S, 70°25′ W 137
Lannemezan, Fr. 43°7′ N, 0°22′ E 164
Lansdale, Pa., U.S. 40°13′ N, 75°18′ W 94
Lansdowne House, Can. 52°11′ N, 87°55′ W 82
L'Anse, Mich., U.S. 46°45′ N, 88°27′ W 94
L'Anse aux Meadows, Can. 51°36′ N, 55°32′ W 111
Lansing, Ill., U.S. 41°33′ N, 87°32′ W 102
Lansing, Iowa, U.S. 43°21′ N, 91°14′ W 94
Lansing, Mich., U.S. 42°42′ N, 84°36′ W 102
Lanta Yai, Ko, island, Thai. 7°20′ N, 98°23′ E 196
Lantana, Fla., U.S. 26°34′ N, 80°5′ W 105
Lantewa, Nig. 12°15′ N, 11°46′ E 222
Lantz, Sp. 42°59′ N, 1°38′ W 164
Lanús, Arg. 34°46′ S, 58°24′ W 139
Lanuza, Philippines 9°15′ N, 126°3′ E 203
Lanxian, China 38°16′ N, 111°36′ E 198
Lanz Peak, Antarctica 77°18′ S, 87°11′ W 248
Lanzai, Nig. 11°20′ N, 10°49′ E 222
Lanzarote, island, Sp. 29°6′ N, 14°51′ W 214
Lanzhou, China 36°3′ N, 103°44′ E 198
Lao Cai, China 22°29′ N, 104°1′ E 202
Laoag, Philippines 18°12′ N, 120°38′ E 198
Laocheng, China 42°37′ N, 124°5′ E 200
Laohekou, China 32°22′ N, 111°40′ E 198
Laon, Fr. 49°33′ N, 3°37′ E 163
Laona, Wis., U.S. 45°34′ N, 88°40′ W 94
Laos 19°46′ N, 102°26′ E 202
Laoshan, China 36°13′ N, 120°25′ E 198
Laotougou, China 42°55′ N, 129°8′ E 200
Laouni, spring, Alg. 20°30′ N, 5°44′ E 222
Lapa, Braz. 25°46′ S, 49°43′ W 138
Lapai, Nig. 9°0′ N, 6°43′ E 222
Lapeer, Mich., U.S. 43°2′ N, 83°18′ W 102
Lapinlahti, Fin. 63°21′ N, 27°22′ E 152
Lapithos 35°20′ N, 33°9′ E 194
Lapovo, Serb. 44°10′ N, 21°3′ E 156
Lappa, ruin(s), Gr. 35°16′ N, 24°15′ E 156
Lappfjärd (Lapväärtti), Fin. 62°13′ N, 21°29′ E 152
Laprida, Arg. 37°35′ S, 60°48′ W 139
Lâpseki, Turk. 40°20′ N, 26°39′ E 156
Laptev Sea 72°2′ N, 139°4′ E 246
Lapua, Fin. 62°57′ N, 22°59′ E 152
Lăpuş, Munţii, Rom. 47°26′ N, 23°26′ E 168
Lăpuşna, Mold. 46°52′ N, 28°25′ E 156
Lapväärtti see Lappfjärd, Fin. 62°13′ N, 21°29′ E 152
Łapy, Pol. 52°59′ N, 22°51′ E 152
Laqiya Arbaʻin, Sudan 20°2′ N, 28°2′ E 226
Laqiya ʻUmran, spring, Sudan 19°52′ N, 28°10′ E 226
L'Aquila, It. 42°21′ N, 13°23′ E 156
Lār, Iran 27°38′ N, 54°16′ E 196
Lara, Gabon 0°19′ N, 11°22′ E 218
Lara, adm. division, Venez. 9°56′ N, 70°30′ W 136
Larabanga, Ghana 9°13′ N, 1°52′ W 222
Laracha, Sp. 43°15′ N, 8°35′ W 150
Larache, Mor. 35°11′ N, 6°10′ W 150
Lārak, island, Iran 26°43′ N, 56°24′ E 180
Laramate, Peru 14°18′ S, 74°51′ W 137
Laramie, Wyo., U.S. 41°19′ N, 105°34′ W 90
Laramie Mountains, Wyo., U.S. 42°32′ N, 106°11′ W 90
Laramie Peak, Wyo., U.S. 42°15′ N, 105°31′ W 90
Laranjeiras do Sul, Braz. 25°27′ S, 52°27′ W 138
Larat, Indonesia 7°15′ S, 131°43′ E 192
Larb Creek, river, Mont., U.S. 48°15′ N, 107°43′ W 90
Lärbro, Sw. 57°47′ N, 18°47′ E 166
Larche, Fr. 44°27′ N, 6°50′ E 167
Larde, Mozambique 16°27′ S, 39°42′ E 224
Larder Lake, Can. 48°6′ N, 79°43′ W 94
Laredo, Sp. 43°23′ N, 3°27′ W 150
Laredo, Tex., U.S. 27°31′ N, 99°28′ W 73
Laredo Sound 52°24′ N, 129°26′ W 108
Largepike Lake, Can. 60°5′ N, 111°15′ W 108
Largo, Fla., U.S. 27°55′ N, 82°46′ W 105
Largo, Cayo, island, Cuba 21°45′ N, 81°42′ W 116
Laribosière, Lac, lake, Can. 53°38′ N, 72°24′ W 111
Larimore, N. Dak., U.S. 47°52′ N, 97°39′ W 90
Larioja, adm. division, Sp. 42°11′ N, 3°3′ W 164
Lárissa, Gr. 39°38′ N, 22°24′ E 156
Lark Pass 15°11′ S, 144°46′ E 230
Larkana, Pak. 27°32′ N, 68°13′ E 186
Larnaka, Cyprus 34°55′ N, 33°38′ E 194
Larned, Kans., U.S. 38°10′ N, 99°6′ W 92
Laro, Burkina Faso 11°17′ N, 2°51′ W 222
Laro, Cameroon 8°15′ N, 12°16′ E 218
Larose, La., U.S. 29°34′ N, 90°23′ W 103
Lars Christensen Peak, Antarctica 68°47′ S, 90°5′ W 248
Larsen Inlet 64°52′ S, 60°11′ W 248
Larsen, Mount, peak, Antarctica 74°44′ S, 162°27′ E 248
Larsen Sound 70°15′ N, 101°52′ W 106
Larsmont, Minn., U.S. 46°58′ N, 91°46′ W 94
Larvik, Nor. 59°3′ N, 10°2′ E 152
Larzac, Causse du, Fr. 43°53′ N, 3°1′ E 165
Las Alpujarras, Sp. 36°44′ N, 3°26′ W 164
Las Animas, Colo., U.S. 38°3′ N, 103°14′ W 90
Las Arrias, Arg. 30°22′ S, 63°38′ W 139
Las Avispas, Arg. 29°51′ S, 61°18′ W 139
Las Bonitas, Venez. 7°48′ N, 65°42′ W 136
Las Breñas, Arg. 27°5′ S, 61°6′ W 139
Las Cabezas de San Juan, Sp. 36°58′ N, 5°57′ W 164
Las Cruces, Mex. 29°25′ N, 107°23′ W 92
Las Cruces, N. Mex., U.S. 32°17′ N, 106°48′ W 112
Las Esperanzas, Mex. 27°44′ N, 101°21′ W 92
Las Flores, Arg. 36°2′ S, 59°9′ W 139
Las Garzas, Arg. 28°49′ S, 59°32′ W 139
Las Heras, Arg. 46°31′ S, 68°55′ W 134
Las Herreras, Mex. 25°7′ N, 105°30′ W 114
Las Juntas, Col. 2°4′ N, 72°14′ W 136
Las Lajitas, Venez. 6°54′ N, 65°42′ W 136
Las Lomitas, Arg. 24°43′ S, 60°36′ W 132
Las Mercedes, Venez. 9°6′ N, 66°24′ W 136
Las Minas, peak, Hond. 14°32′ N, 88°44′ W 115
Las Palmas, Sp. 28°4′ N, 15°29′ W 214
Las Palmeras, Arg. 30°35′ S, 61°39′ W 139
Las Peñas, Mex. 18°3′ N, 102°30′ W 114
Las Piedras, Bol. 11°2′ S, 66°12′ W 130
Las Piedras, Uru. 34°42′ S, 56°12′ W 139
Las Plumas, Arg. 43°39′ S, 67°16′ W 134
Las Tablas, Pan. 7°47′ N, 80°17′ W 115
Las Tinajas, Arg. 27°30′ S, 62°51′ W 139
Las Toscas, Arg. 28°20′ S, 59°16′ W 139
Las Tres Vírgenes, Volcán, peak, Mex. 27°26′ N, 112°43′ W 112
Las Trincheras, Mex. 30°21′ N, 111°33′ W 92
Las Tunas, Cuba 20°57′ N, 76°59′ W 115
Las Tunas, island, Cuba 20°23′ N, 77°42′ W 116
Las Varas, Mex. 28°7′ N, 105°21′ W 92
Las Varas, Mex. 29°28′ N, 108°2′ W 92
Las Varas, Mex. 21°11′ N, 105°10′ W 114
Las Varillas, Arg. 31°54′ S, 62°43′ W 139
Las Vegas, Nev., U.S. 36°9′ N, 115°10′ W 101
Las Vegas, N. Mex., U.S. 35°35′ N, 105°13′ W 92
Las Vegas Valley, Nev., U.S. 36°21′ N, 115°27′ W 101
Las Vigas, Mex. 19°36′ N, 97°6′ W 114
Las Yaras, Peru 17°54′ S, 70°33′ W 137
Las Zorras, Punta, Peru 10°32′ S, 79°30′ W 130
Lascano, Uru. 33°42′ S, 54°13′ W 139
Lasengmiao, China 39°19′ N, 106°54′ E 198
Lashburn, Can. 53°7′ N, 109°36′ W 108
Lāsh-e Joveyn, Afghan. 31°40′ N, 61°42′ E 186
Lashio, Myanmar 22°51′ N, 97°42′ E 190
Lashkar, India 26°10′ N, 78°7′ E 197
Lashkar Gah (Bost), Afghan. 31°35′ N, 64°22′ E 186
Lasia, island, Indonesia 2°12′ N, 96°36′ E 196
Lāsjerd, Iran 35°22′ N, 53°0′ E 180
Łaskarzew, Pol. 51°46′ N, 21°38′ E 152
Laško, Slov. 46°9′ N, 15°14′ E 156
Laskowice, Pol. 53°29′ N, 18°26′ E 152
Läsna, Est. 59°25′ N, 25°53′ E 166
Lassen Peak, Calif., U.S. 40°28′ N, 121°36′ W 90
L'Assomption, Can. 45°49′ N, 73°27′ W 94
Last Chance Range, Calif., U.S. 37°9′ N, 117°46′ W 101
Last Mountain Lake, Can. 51°17′ N, 107°2′ W 80
Last Mountain, peak, Can. 60°45′ N, 126°47′ W 108
Lastoursville, Gabon 0°52′ N, 12°39′ E 218
Lastovo, Croatia 42°45′ N, 16°53′ E 168
Lastovski Kanal 42°45′ N, 16°39′ E 168
Latady Island, Antarctica 70°55′ S, 81°57′ W 248
Latakia see Al Lādhiqīyah, Syr. 35°31′ N, 35°47′ E 194
Latehar, India 23°45′ N, 84°31′ E 197
Latexo, Tex., U.S. 31°22′ N, 95°29′ W 103
Latham Island, Tanzania 7°9′ S, 40°1′ E 224
Lathrop, Calif., U.S. 37°49′ N, 121°17′ W 100
Latina, It. 41°28′ N, 12°52′ E 156
Latisana, It. 45°46′ N, 12°59′ E 167
Lato, ruin(s), Gr. 35°9′ N, 25°32′ E 156
Laton, Calif., U.S. 36°26′ N, 119°43′ W 100
Latouma, spring, Niger 22°12′ N, 14°47′ E 216
Latrobe, Mount, peak, Austral. 39°2′ S, 146°10′ E 230
Latta, S.C., U.S. 34°19′ N, 79°27′ W 96
Latur, India 18°23′ N, 76°33′ E 188
Latvia 56°59′ N, 25°20′ E 166
Latvozero, Russ. 64°49′ N, 29°54′ E 152
Lau, Nig. 9°10′ N, 11°18′ E 222
Lau, Sudan 6°44′ N, 30°25′ E 224
Lau Group, islands, South Pacific Ocean 17°0′ S, 178°20′ W 238
Lau Ridge, South Pacific Ocean 27°20′ S, 178°35′ W 252
Lauca National Park, Chile 18°11′ S, 69°43′ W 137
Lauca, river, Bol. 18°29′ S, 68°50′ W 137
Laudal, Nor. 58°14′ N, 7°28′ E 152
Lauderdale, Miss., U.S. 32°28′ N, 88°32′ W 103
Lauderdale Lakes, Fla., U.S. 26°10′ N, 80°12′ W 105
Ļaudona, Latv. 56°43′ N, 26°10′ E 166
Lauenburg, Ger. 53°22′ N, 10°34′ E 152
Lauenförde, Ger. 51°39′ N, 9°24′ E 167
Laufen, Switz. 47°25′ N, 7°29′ E 150
Laughlan Islands, Solomon Sea 9°41′ S, 152°47′ E 192
Laughlin, Nev., U.S. 35°11′ N, 114°36′ W 101
Laughlin Peak, N. Mex., U.S. 36°36′ N, 104°17′ W 92
Laujar de Andarax, Sp. 36°59′ N, 2°54′ W 164
Laukuva, Lith. 55°37′ N, 22°15′ E 166
Laurel, Del., U.S. 38°32′ N, 75°35′ W 94
Laurel, Ind., U.S. 39°30′ N, 85°11′ W 102
Laurel, Miss., U.S. 31°41′ N, 89°7′ W 103
Laurel, Mont., U.S. 45°39′ N, 108°46′ W 90
Laurel, Nebr., U.S. 42°24′ N, 97°6′ W 90
Laurel Hill, Pa., U.S. 39°57′ N, 79°23′ W 94
Laurens, Iowa, U.S. 42°50′ N, 94°53′ W 90
Laurens, S.C., U.S. 34°29′ N, 82°2′ W 96
Laurentian Fan, North Atlantic Ocean 41°51′ N, 56°17′ W 253
Laurentian Valley, Can. 46°1′ N, 77°28′ W 110
Lauria, It. 40°2′ N, 15°49′ E 156
Laurie Island, Antarctica 61°15′ S, 44°38′ W 134
Laurie River, Can. 56°14′ N, 101°1′ W 108
Laurinburg, N.C., U.S. 34°45′ N, 79°29′ W 96
Lauritsala, Fin. 61°2′ N, 28°14′ E 166
Lausanne, Switz. 46°32′ N, 6°39′ E 150
Laut, island, Indonesia 4°49′ N, 107°51′ E 196
Laut, island, Indonesia 4°6′ S, 116°19′ E 192
Laut Kecil, Kepulauan, islands, Java Sea 4°59′ S, 116°1′ E 192
Lautaro, Volcán, peak, Chile 49°3′ S, 73°43′ W 134
Lautem, Timor-Leste 8°30′ S, 126°56′ E 192
Lauterbach, Ger. 50°38′ N, 9°24′ E 167
Lava Beds National Monument, Calif., U.S. 41°28′ N, 122°46′ W 80
Lava Cast Forest, site, Oreg., U.S. 43°47′ N, 121°22′ W 90
Lava River Cave, site, Oreg., U.S. 43°52′ N, 121°27′ W 90
Laval, Can. 45°36′ N, 73°46′ W 94
Laval, Fr. 48°2′ N, 0°54′ E 143
Lavalle, Arg. 29°2′ S, 59°12′ W 139
Lavalleja, Uru. 31°5′ S, 57°2′ W 139
Lavangen, Nor. 68°46′ N, 17°48′ E 152
Lavassaare, Est. 58°30′ N, 24°20′ E 166
Laveaga Peak, Calif., U.S. 36°52′ N, 121°14′ W 100
Lavelanet, Fr. 42°55′ N, 1°49′ E 164
Lavenham, U.K. 52°6′ N, 0°47′ E 162
Laverne, Okla., U.S. 36°41′ N, 99°54′ W 92

Lavia, Fin. 61°34′ N, 22°35′ E 166
Lavina, Mont., U.S. 46°17′ N, 108°57′ W 90
Lavis, It. 46°9′ N, 11°6′ E 167
Lavoisier Island, Antarctica 66°11′ S, 67°28′ W 248
Lavos, Port. 40°5′ N, 8°51′ W 150
Lavras, Braz. 21°15′ S, 45°0′ W 138
Lavras da Mangabeira, Braz. 6°44′ S, 38°59′ W 132
Lavras do Sul, Braz. 30°51′ S, 53°55′ W 139
Lavrentiya, Russ. 65°37′ N, 171°9′ W 98
Lavushi Manda National Park, Zambia 12°46′ S, 30°57′ E 224
Law Dome, Antarctica 67°27′ S, 114°17′ E 248
Lawabiskau, river, Can. 51°21′ N, 81°25′ W 110
Lawagamau Lake, Can. 49°47′ N, 80°49′ W 94
Lawers, Ben, peak, U.K. 56°32′ N, 4°19′ W 150
Lawford Lake, Can. 54°25′ N, 97°14′ W 108
Lawnhill, Can. 53°25′ N, 132°0′ W 108
Lawqah, Saudi Arabia 29°46′ N, 42°47′ E 180
Lawra, Ghana 10°38′ N, 2°54′ W 222
Lawrence, Ind., U.S. 39°49′ N, 86°1′ W 102
Lawrence, Kans., U.S. 38°56′ N, 95°14′ W 94
Lawrence, Mass., U.S. 42°42′ N, 71°11′ W 104
Lawrence, Miss., U.S. 32°18′ N, 89°13′ W 103
Lawrence, N.Z. 45°55′ S, 169°39′ E 240
Lawrenceburg, Ind., U.S. 39°5′ N, 84°52′ W 94
Lawrenceburg, Tenn., U.S. 35°14′ N, 87°19′ W 96
Lawrenceville, Ill., U.S. 38°43′ N, 87°41′ W 102
Lawyet el Lagâma, spring, Egypt 30°47′ N, 33°26′ E 194
Laxå, Nor. 58°58′ N, 14°36′ E 152
Laxong Co, lake, China 34°18′ N, 84°18′ E 188
Layda, Russ. 71°30′ N, 83°1′ E 173
Laydasalma, Russ. 65°57′ N, 30°55′ E 152
Laysan Island, Hawai'i, U.S. 25°26′ N, 171°52′ W 99
Layshi, Myanmar 25°27′ N, 94°54′ E 188
Laytamak, Russ. 58°26′ N, 67°26′ E 169
Layton, Utah, U.S. 41°3′ N, 111°57′ W 90
Lazarev, Russ. 52°13′ N, 141°17′ E 238
Lazareva, Russ. 57°36′ N, 107°47′ E 173
Lazarevac, Serb. 44°23′ N, 20°15′ E 168
Lazarevskoye, Russ. 43°56′ N, 39°18′ E 158
Lázaro Cárdenas, Mex. 18°55′ N, 88°16′ W 115
Lázaro Cárdenas, Mex. 17°59′ N, 102°13′ W 114
Lázaro Cardenas, Presa, lake, Mex. 25°31′ N, 106°28′ W 80
Lazdijai, Lith. 54°14′ N, 23°30′ E 166
Lazio, adm. division, It. 41°57′ N, 12°5′ E 156
Lbera, Serra de l', Sp. 42°23′ N, 2°32′ E 164
Le Barcarès, Fr. 42°47′ N, 3°0′ E 164
Le Bic, Can. 48°21′ N, 68°42′ W 94
Le Bugue, Fr. 44°55′ N, 0°55′ E 150
Le Cateau, Fr. 50°5′ N, 3°33′ E 163
Le Catelet, Fr. 49°59′ N, 3°15′ E 163
Le Châtelet-en-Brie, Fr. 48°29′ N, 2°47′ E 163
Le Chesne, Fr. 49°31′ N, 4°46′ E 163
Le Cocq, Lac, lake, Can. 52°16′ N, 68°32′ W 111
Le Conquet, Fr. 48°21′ N, 4°47′ W 150
Le Crotoy, Fr. 50°13′ N, 1°39′ E 163
Le Gros Cap, Can. 47°8′ N, 62°50′ W 111
Le Guelta, Alg. 36°20′ N, 0°50′ E 164
Le Havre, Fr. 49°29′ N, 0°6′ E 150
Le Madonie, It. 37°46′ N, 13°33′ E 156
Le Mans, Fr. 48°0′ N, 0°11′ E 150
Le Mars, Iowa, U.S. 42°46′ N, 96°11′ W 94
Le Mont-Saint-Michel, Fr. 48°37′ N, 1°31′ W 150
Le Moyen, La., U.S. 30°46′ N, 92°3′ W 103
Le Perthus, Fr. 42°28′ N, 2°51′ E 164
Le Petit-Quevilly, Fr. 49°24′ N, 1°2′ E 163
Le Puy, Fr. 45°2′ N, 3°53′ E 150
Le Quesnoy, Fr. 50°14′ N, 3°38′ E 163
Le Rageois, Lac, lake, Can. 53°16′ N, 69°31′ W 111
Le Roy, Ill., U.S. 40°20′ N, 88°46′ W 102
Le Roy, Mich., U.S. 44°2′ N, 85°27′ W 102
Le Roy, N.Y., U.S. 42°58′ N, 78°0′ W 94
Le Thuy, Vietnam 17°14′ N, 106°52′ E 202
Le Touquet-Paris-Plage, Fr. 50°31′ N, 1°35′ E 163
Le Tréport, Fr. 50°3′ N, 1°21′ E 163
Le Veneur, Île, Can. 51°36′ N, 74°11′ W 110
Le Verdon-sur-Mer, Fr. 45°32′ N, 1°6′ W 150
Le Vigan, Fr. 43°59′ N, 3°34′ E 150
Leach, Cambodia 12°20′ N, 103°44′ E 202
Leach Lake Mountain, peak, Calif., U.S. 39°54′ N, 123°10′ W 90
Lead, S. Dak., U.S. 44°20′ N, 103°47′ W 82
Lead Mountain, peak, Me., U.S. 44°51′ N, 68°12′ W 94
Leadenham, U.K. 53°3′ N, 0°36′ E 162
Leader, Can. 50°53′ N, 109°32′ W 90
Leadore, Idaho, U.S. 44°39′ N, 113°22′ W 90
Leadville, Colo., U.S. 39°14′ N, 106°17′ W 90
Leaf Rapids, Can. 56°28′ N, 100°3′ W 108
Leaf, river, Miss., U.S. 31°17′ N, 89°14′ W 103
League, Slieve, peak, Ire. 54°38′ N, 8°49′ W 150
Leakesville, Miss., U.S. 31°7′ N, 88°33′ W 103
Leakey, Tex., U.S. 29°42′ N, 99°46′ W 92
Lealui, Zambia 15°13′ S, 23°2′ E 220
Leamington, Can. 42°3′ N, 82°36′ W 102
Leamington, U.K. 52°17′ N, 1°33′ W 162
Leandro N. Alem, Arg. 27°36′ S, 55°20′ W 139
Leaota, peak, Rom. 45°18′ N, 25°13′ E 156
Learned, Miss., U.S. 32°10′ N, 90°34′ W 103
Leatherman Peak, Idaho, U.S. 44°4′ N, 113°48′ W 90
Leavenworth, Kans., U.S. 39°17′ N, 94°56′ W 94
Leavitt Bay 57°10′ N, 107°38′ W 108
Leavitt Peak, Calif., U.S. 38°16′ N, 119°42′ W 100
Łeba, Pol. 54°45′ N, 17°34′ E 152
Lebach, Ger. 49°25′ N, 6°54′ E 163
Lebak, Philippines 6°33′ N, 124°3′ E 203
Lebam, Wash., U.S. 46°33′ N, 123°33′ W 100
Lebane, Serb. 42°55′ N, 21°44′ E 168
Lebango, Congo 0°15′ N, 14°51′ E 218
Lebanon, Ind., U.S. 40°2′ N, 86°28′ W 102
Lebanon, Kans., U.S. 39°48′ N, 98°33′ W 90
Lebanon, Ky., U.S. 37°34′ N, 85°15′ W 96
Lebanon, Leb. 34°27′ N, 36°5′ E 194
Lebanon 34°0′ N, 35°51′ E 194
Lebanon, Mo., U.S. 37°40′ N, 92°40′ W 96
Lebanon, N.H., U.S. 43°38′ N, 72°15′ W 104
Lebanon, Ohio, U.S. 39°25′ N, 84°12′ W 102
Lebanon, Oreg., U.S. 44°31′ N, 122°55′ W 90
Lebanon, Tenn., U.S. 36°11′ N, 86°18′ W 82
Lebec, Calif., U.S. 34°50′ N, 118°53′ W 101
Lebed', Russ. 62°1′ N, 89°15′ E 169
Lebedyan', Russ. 52°59′ N, 39°2′ E 154
Lebedyn, Ukr. 50°34′ N, 34°26′ E 158
Leben, ruin(s), Gr. 34°55′ N, 24°49′ E 156
Lebo, Dem. Rep. of the Congo 4°28′ N, 23°55′ E 224
Lebombo Mountains, S. Af. 24°10′ S, 31°21′ E 227
Lebon Régis, Braz. 26°56′ S, 50°45′ W 139
Lębork, Pol. 54°31′ N, 17°45′ E 152
Lebowakgomo, S. Af. 24°12′ S, 29°31′ E 227
Lebrija, Sp. 36°55′ N, 6°5′ W 164
Lebu, Chile 37°39′ S, 73°40′ W 134
Lecce, It. 40°20′ N, 18°10′ E 156
Lecco, It. 45°51′ N, 9°23′ E 167
Lece, Serb. 42°53′ N, 21°32′ E 168
Lechang, China 25°8′ N, 113°23′ E 198
Lecompte, La., U.S. 31°4′ N, 92°25′ W 103
Léconi, Gabon 1°37′ S, 14°15′ E 218
Léconi, river, Gabon 1°5′ S, 13°17′ E 218
Ledaña, Sp. 39°21′ N, 1°43′ W 164
Ledbury, U.K. 52°2′ N, 2°26′ W 162
Ledo, India 27°19′ N, 95°48′ E 188
Ledo, Indonesia 1°3′ N, 109°34′ E 196
Ledo, Cabo, Angola 9°46′ S, 12°47′ E 218
Ledong, China 18°41′ N, 109°6′ E 198
Leduc, Can. 53°15′ N, 113°33′ W 108
Lee, Mass., U.S. 42°18′ N, 73°15′ W 104
Lee, Nev., U.S. 40°34′ N, 115°36′ W 90
Leech Lake, Minn., U.S. 47°9′ N, 94°56′ W 90
Leedey, Okla., U.S. 35°50′ N, 99°21′ W 92
Leeds, Ala., U.S. 33°32′ N, 86°33′ W 96
Leeds, N. Dak., U.S. 48°16′ N, 99°28′ W 90
Leeds, U.K. 53°48′ N, 1°33′ W 162
Leeds, Utah, U.S. 37°13′ N, 113°21′ W 92
Leek, Neth. 53°10′ N, 6°23′ E 163
Leek, U.K. 53°6′ N, 2°2′ W 162
Leek Spring Hill, peak, Calif., U.S. 38°36′ N, 120°22′ W 90
Leer, Ger. 53°13′ N, 7°27′ E 163
Leesburg, Fla., U.S. 28°48′ N, 81°54′ W 105
Leesburg, Ohio, U.S. 39°20′ N, 83°33′ W 102
Leesburg, Va., U.S. 39°6′ N, 77°34′ W 94
Leeste, Ger. 52°59′ N, 8°48′ E 163
Leesville, La., U.S. 31°7′ N, 93°17′ W 103
Leesville, S.C., U.S. 33°54′ N, 81°31′ W 96
Leeuwarden, Neth. 53°11′ N, 5°46′ E 163
Leeuwin, Cape, Austral. 34°51′ S, 113°51′ E 230
Leeville, La., U.S. 29°15′ N, 90°13′ W 103
Leeward Islands, Caribbean Sea 15°40′ N, 61°42′ W 116
Léfini Faunal Reserve, Congo 2°51′ S, 15°5′ E 206
Lefka 35°6′ N, 32°51′ E 194
Lefká Óri, Gr. 35°15′ N, 23°47′ E 156
Lefkonoiko 35°15′ N, 33°43′ E 194
Lefkoşa see Lefkosia, Cyprus 35°9′ N, 33°18′ E 194
Lefkosia (Nicosia, Lefkoşa), Cyprus 35°9′ N, 33°18′ E 194
Leftrook Lake, Can. 56°2′ N, 99°9′ W 108
Legal, Can. 53°56′ N, 113°35′ W 108
Légaré, Lac, lake, Can. 46°56′ N, 74°25′ W 110
Legat, Mauritania 16°45′ N, 14°52′ W 222
Legazpi, Philippines 13°8′ N, 123°43′ E 203
Legden, Ger. 52°1′ N, 7°6′ E 167
Legges Tor, peak, Austral. 41°34′ S, 147°31′ E 230
Leggett, Tex., U.S. 30°48′ N, 94°52′ W 103
Leghorn see Livorno, It. 43°33′ N, 10°19′ E 156
Legnano, It. 45°35′ N, 8°53′ E 167
Legnica, Pol. 51°12′ N, 16°9′ E 152
Leh, India 34°9′ N, 77°33′ E 190
Lehi, Utah, U.S. 40°23′ N, 111°51′ W 90
Lehigh Acres, Fla., U.S. 26°36′ N, 81°38′ W 105
Lehliu, Rom. 44°29′ N, 26°48′ E 158
Lehman Caves, site, Nev., U.S. 39°0′ N, 114°18′ W 90
Lehr, N. Dak., U.S. 46°16′ N, 99°23′ W 90
Lehtimäki, Fin. 62°45′ N, 23°51′ E 154
Lehututu, Botswana 23°57′ S, 21°52′ E 227
Leiah, Pak. 30°54′ N, 70°59′ E 186
Leicester, Mass., U.S. 42°14′ N, 71°55′ W 104
Leicester, U.K. 52°37′ N, 1°8′ W 162
Leiden, Neth. 52°9′ N, 4°29′ E 163
Leie, river, Belg. 50°57′ N, 3°24′ E 163
Leigh, N.Z. 36°19′ S, 174°47′ E 240
Leigh, U.K. 53°30′ N, 2°31′ W 162
Leighton Buzzard, U.K. 51°55′ N, 0°39′ E 162
Leikanger, Nor. 61°11′ N, 6°46′ E 152
Leiktho, Myanmar 19°14′ N, 96°33′ E 202
Leippe, Ger. 51°24′ N, 14°4′ E 152
Leipsic, Ohio, U.S. 41°5′ N, 83°59′ W 102
Leipzig, Ger. 51°19′ N, 12°22′ E 152
Leirbotn, Nor. 70°6′ N, 23°23′ E 152
Leiria, Port. 39°44′ N, 8°50′ W 150
Leiria, adm. division, Port. 39°53′ N, 8°54′ W 150
Leirpollen, Nor. 70°25′ N, 28°28′ E 152
Leishan, China 26°24′ N, 108°0′ E 198
Leisler, Mount, peak, Austral. 23°21′ S, 129°4′ E 230
Leismer, Can. 55°44′ N, 111°3′ W 108
Leiston, U.K. 52°12′ N, 1°34′ E 163
Leitchfield, Ky., U.S. 37°28′ N, 86°18′ W 96
Leitza, Sp. 43°4′ N, 1°55′ W 164
Leivonmäki, Fin. 61°54′ N, 26°4′ E 166
Leiway, Myanmar 19°38′ N, 96°4′ E 202
Leiyang, China 26°28′ N, 112°51′ E 198
Leizhou Wan 20°35′ N, 110°18′ E 198
Leka, Nor. 65°4′ N, 11°42′ E 152
Lekatero, Dem. Rep. of the Congo 0°41′ N, 23°57′ E 224
Lekbibaj, Alban. 42°18′ N, 19°55′ E 168
Lekemt see Nek'emtē, Eth. 9°2′ N, 36°33′ E 224
Lekhovskoye, Russ. 62°43′ N, 42°50′ E 154
Lekhwair, oil field, Oman 22°41′ N, 55°26′ E 182
Lekmartovskaya, Russ. 60°49′ N, 56°9′ E 154
Léko, Mali 13°36′ N, 9°3′ W 222
Lekshmozero, Russ. 61°46′ N, 38°5′ E 154
Leksula, Indonesia 3°46′ S, 126°30′ E 192
Lekunberri, Sp. 43°0′ N, 1°54′ W 164
Leland, Miss., U.S. 33°22′ N, 90°55′ W 103
Lel'chytsy, Belarus 51°45′ N, 28°22′ E 152
Lelić, Serb. 44°13′ N, 19°49′ E 168
Lely Gebergte, Suriname 4°17′ N, 55°41′ W 130
Lelystad, Neth. 52°30′ N, 5°24′ E 163
Lema, Nig. 12°56′ N, 4°14′ E 222
Lembach, Fr. 48°59′ N, 7°47′ E 163
Lembé, Cameroon 4°16′ N, 12°19′ E 218
Lembeck, Ger. 51°45′ N, 6°59′ E 167
Lembeni, Tanzania 3°46′ S, 37°37′ E 224
Lemberg, Fr. 49°0′ N, 7°22′ E 163
Leme, Braz. 22°10′ S, 47°25′ W 138
Lemei Rock, peak, Wash., U.S. 46°0′ N, 121°49′ W 100
Lemhi Range, Idaho, U.S. 44°45′ N, 113°59′ W 90
Lemieux Islands, Davis Strait 63°50′ N, 63°57′ W 106
Lemitar, N. Mex., U.S. 34°10′ N, 106°55′ W 92
Lemmer, Neth. 52°51′ N, 5°42′ E 163
Lemmon, S. Dak., U.S. 45°54′ N, 102°9′ W 90
Lemmon, Mount, peak, Ariz., U.S. 32°25′ N, 110°51′ W 92
Lemoïlé, Mauritania 16°10′ N, 7°12′ W 222
Lemon Grove, Calif., U.S. 32°44′ N, 117°3′ W 101
Lemoncove, Calif., U.S. 36°23′ N, 119°2′ W 101
Lemont, Ill., U.S. 41°38′ N, 88°1′ W 102
Lemoore, Calif., U.S. 36°18′ N, 119°48′ W 100
Lempäälä, Fin. 61°18′ N, 23°44′ E 166
Lempster, N.H., U.S. 43°14′ N, 72°13′ W 104
Lemsid, Africa 26°31′ N, 13°49′ W 214
Lemtybozh, Russ. 63°51′ N, 57°2′ E 154
Lemva, river, Russ. 65°28′ N, 61°4′ E 154
Lemvig, Den. 56°32′ N, 8°17′ E 150
Lem'yu, Russ. 64°17′ N, 54°59′ E 154
Lem'yu, river, Russ. 64°15′ N, 55°12′ E 154
Lena, Ill., U.S. 42°22′ N, 89°49′ W 102
Lena, La., U.S. 31°26′ N, 92°47′ W 103
Lena, Miss., U.S. 32°34′ N, 89°37′ W 103
Lena, Mount, peak, Utah, U.S. 40°45′ N, 109°29′ W 90
Lena, river, Russ. 69°16′ N, 124°52′ E 172
Lena Tablemount, Indian Ocean 53°10′ S, 44°34′ E 255
Lenart, Slov. 46°35′ N, 15°50′ E 168
Lençóis, Braz. 12°34′ S, 41°24′ W 132
Lençóis Maranhenses National Park, Braz. 2°37′ S, 43°24′ W 122
Lendery, Russ. 63°24′ N, 31°12′ E 152
Lenger, Kaz. 42°10′ N, 69°50′ E 197
Lengerich, Ger. 52°11′ N, 7°52′ E 163
Lenghu, China 38°48′ N, 93°23′ E 188
Lengua de Vaca, Punta, Chile 30°20′ S, 73°37′ W 134
Lengwe National Park, Malawi 16°30′ S, 33°58′ E 224
Lengyeltóti, Hung. 46°39′ N, 17°38′ E 168
Lenhovda, Nor. 56°59′ N, 15°14′ E 152
Lenin Peak, Kyrg. 39°21′ N, 72°46′ E 197
Leningrad see Sankt-Peterburg, Russ. 59°55′ N, 30°17′ E 166
Leningradskaya, Russ. 46°21′ N, 39°23′ E 156
Leningradskiy, Russ. 69°19′ N, 178°23′ E 98
Lenīngradskoe, Kaz. 53°33′ N, 71°31′ E 184
Lenino, Belarus 53°2′ N, 27°13′ E 152
Leninogorsk, Russ. 54°37′ N, 52°32′ E 154
Lenīnogorsk see Ridder, Kaz. 50°21′ N, 83°32′ E 184
Leninpol', Kyrg. 42°28′ N, 71°58′ E 197
Leninsk, Russ. 48°42′ N, 45°12′ E 158
Leninsk Kuznetskiy, Russ. 54°39′ N, 86°18′ E 184
Leninsk see Baykonur, Kaz. 45°50′ N, 63°18′ E 173
Lenīnskīy, Kaz. 52°14′ N, 76°46′ E 184
Leninskiy, Russ. 56°32′ N, 46°3′ E 154
Lenīnskoe, Kaz. 49°5′ N, 49°59′ E 158
Lenīnskoe, Kaz. 50°45′ N, 57°53′ E 158
Leninskoye, Russ. 58°18′ N, 47°7′ E 154
Lenk, Switz. 46°27′ N, 7°28′ E 167
Lennox, S. Dak., U.S. 43°19′ N, 96°54′ W 94
Lenoir, N.C., U.S. 35°54′ N, 81°33′ W 96
Lenoir City, Tenn., U.S. 35°48′ N, 84°16′ W 96
Lenora, Kans., U.S. 39°37′ N, 100°0′ W 90
Lenox, Mass., U.S. 42°21′ N, 73°18′ W 104
Lenox Dale, Mass., U.S. 42°19′ N, 73°16′ W 104
Lens, Fr. 50°25′ N, 2°49′ E 163
Lensk, Russ. 60°44′ N, 114°42′ E 160
Lenskoye, Russ. 58°10′ N, 63°7′ E 154
Lentekhi, Ga. 42°46′ N, 42°43′ E 195
Lenti, Hung. 46°37′ N, 16°32′ E 168
Lentiira, Fin. 64°22′ N, 29°47′ E 152
Lentini, It. 37°16′ N, 15°3′ E 216
Lentvaris, Lith. 54°38′ N, 25°3′ E 166
Lenwood, Calif., U.S. 34°52′ N, 117°8′ W 101
Léo, Burkina Faso 11°5′ N, 2°7′ W 222
Leo, Ind., U.S. 41°13′ N, 85°1′ W 102
Leoben, Aust. 47°22′ N, 15°6′ E 156
Leocadio Paz, Arg. 26°9′ S, 65°19′ W 132
Leola, S. Dak., U.S. 45°42′ N, 98°58′ W 90
Leominster, Mass., U.S. 42°31′ N, 71°46′ W 104
Leominster, U.K. 52°13′ N, 2°44′ W 162
Leon, Iowa, U.S. 40°43′ N, 93°45′ W 94
León, Mex. 21°5′ N, 101°43′ W 112
León, Nicar. 12°25′ N, 86°53′ W 115
León, Sp. 42°36′ N, 5°35′ W 150
León, Sp. 42°34′ N, 5°37′ W 214
León, Cerro, peak, Parag. 20°21′ S, 60°29′ W 132
León, Montes de, Sp. 42°22′ N, 6°30′ W 150
León, Punta, Arg. 50°36′ S, 68°56′ W 134
Leon, river, Tex., U.S. 31°36′ N, 97°52′ W 112
Leona, oil field, Venez. 8°57′ N, 63°57′ W 116
Leonard, Tex., U.S. 33°22′ N, 96°15′ W 96
Leonardville, Namibia 23°31′ S, 18°43′ E 227
Leonarisso 35°28′ N, 34°8′ E 194
Leonding, Aust. 48°16′ N, 14°14′ E 152
Leones, Isla, island, Pan. 7°38′ N, 81°35′ W 115
Leopoldina, Braz. 21°33′ S, 42°40′ W 138
Leopoldo de Bulhões, Braz. 16°39′ S, 48°47′ W 138
Leopoldsburg, Belg. 51°7′ N, 5°16′ E 167
Léopoldville see Kinshasa, Dem. Rep. of the Congo 4°24′ S, 15°6′ E 218
Leoti, Kans., U.S. 38°29′ N, 101°22′ W 90
Leoville, Can. 53°38′ N, 107°31′ W 108
Lepanto, Ark., U.S. 35°36′ N, 90°21′ W 96
Lephalale (Ellisras), S. Af. 23°40′ S, 27°42′ E 227
Lephepe, Botswana 23°19′ S, 25°47′ E 227
Leping, China 28°58′ N, 117°3′ E 198
L'Épiphanie, Can. 45°51′ N, 73°29′ W 94
Lepontine Alps, Switz. 46°17′ N, 8°24′ E 167
Lepperton, N.Z. 39°6′ S, 174°13′ E 240
Lepsény, Hung. 46°59′ N, 18°14′ E 168
Lepsi, Kaz. 46°14′ N, 78°54′ E 184
Lepsi, river, Kaz. 45°59′ N, 79°47′ E 184
Ler, Sudan 8°18′ N, 30°5′ E 224
Léraba, Côte d'Ivoire 10°7′ N, 5°6′ W 222
Léraba, river, Africa 9°55′ N, 5°6′ W 222
Lerdo de Tejada, Mex. 18°37′ N, 95°30′ W 114
Léré, Chad 9°38′ N, 14°14′ E 216
Léré, Mali 15°42′ N, 4°57′ W 222
Lerici, It. 44°4′ N, 9°55′ E 167
Lérida, Col. 0°8′ N, 70°44′ W 136
Lerik, Azerb. 38°45′ N, 48°23′ E 195
Lerín, Sp. 42°28′ N, 1°58′ W 164
Lérins, Îles de, islands, Mediterranean Sea 43°21′ N, 7°0′ E 165
Lerma, Sp. 42°0′ N, 3°45′ W 164
Lerma, river, Mex. 20°23′ N, 102°10′ W 114
Lerna, Ill., U.S. 39°24′ N, 88°17′ W 102
Lerna, ruin(s), Gr. 37°33′ N, 22°36′ E 156
Lérouville, Fr. 48°47′ N, 5°31′ E 163
Leroy, Ala., U.S. 31°30′ N, 87°59′ W 103
Leroy, Can. 52°1′ N, 104°45′ W 90
Leroy, Kans., U.S. 38°3′ N, 95°38′ W 94
Lerwick, U.K. 60°11′ N, 1°17′ W 143
Leş, Rom. 46°57′ N, 21°51′ E 168
Les, Sp. 42°48′ N, 0°41′ E 164
Les Andelys, Fr. 49°14′ N, 1°25′ E 163
Les Borges Blanques, Sp. 41°31′ N, 0°50′ E 164
Les Cabannes, Fr. 42°47′ N, 1°40′ E 164
Les Cayes, Haiti 18°14′ N, 73°46′ W 116
Les Coves de Vinromà, Sp. 40°18′ N, 0°6′ E 164
Les Escoumins, Can. 48°20′ N, 69°26′ W 94
Les Essarts, Fr. 46°46′ N, 1°15′ W 150
Les Landes, region, Fr. 43°32′ N, 1°26′ W 164
Les Sables-d'Olonne, Fr. 46°29′ N, 1°47′ W 150
Les Salines, Tun. 36°4′ N, 8°57′ E 156
L'Escala, Sp. 42°7′ N, 3°6′ E 164
Lescar, Fr. 43°19′ N, 0°26′ E 164
Leseru, Kenya 0°34′ N, 35°10′ E 224
Leshan, China 29°22′ N, 103°49′ E 190
Leshukonskoye, Russ. 64°53′ N, 45°37′ E 154
Lesja, Nor. 62°7′ N, 8°49′ E 152
Leskov Island, Antarctica 66°30′ S, 82°12′ E 248
Leskovac, Serb. 42°59′ N, 21°58′ E 168
Leslie, Ark., U.S. 35°48′ N, 92°34′ W 96
Leslie, Mich., U.S. 42°26′ N, 84°26′ W 102
Leslie, S. Af. 26°25′ S, 28°54′ E 227
Lesmont, Fr. 48°25′ N, 4°24′ E 163
Leśnica, Serb. 44°39′ N, 19°18′ E 168
Lesnoy, Russ. 59°50′ N, 52°8′ E 154
Lesnoye, Russ. 58°16′ N, 35°32′ E 154
Lesogorskiy, Russ. 61°1′ N, 28°56′ E 166
Lesosibirsk, Russ. 58°2′ N, 92°33′ E 160
Lesotho 29°27′ S, 28°14′ E 227
Lesovo, Bulg. 41°59′ N, 26°35′ E 158
Lesozavodsk, Russ. 45°27′ N, 133°20′ E 190
Lesozavodskiy, Russ. 66°43′ N, 32°52′ E 152
L'Espluga de Francolí, Sp. 41°23′ N, 1°3′ E 164
Lessebo, Nor. 56°45′ N, 15°15′ E 152
Lesser Antilles, North Atlantic Ocean 11°25′ N, 62°26′ W 116
Lesser Caucasus, Arm. 40°7′ N, 45°47′ E 180
Lesser Slave Lake, Can. 55°12′ N, 117°10′ W 106
Lesser Sunda Islands, Indian Ocean 10°13′ S, 121°5′ E 238
Lester, Wash., U.S. 47°12′ N, 121°30′ W 100
Lestijärvi, Fin. 63°30′ N, 24°36′ E 152
Lésvos, island, Gr. 38°50′ N, 26°5′ E 180
Leszno, Pol. 51°49′ N, 16°35′ E 152
Letaba, site, S. Af. 23°52′ S, 31°30′ E 227
Létavértes, Hung. 47°23′ N, 21°53′ E 168
Letchworth, U.K. 51°58′ N, 0°14′ E 162
Letea, Rom. 45°18′ N, 29°30′ E 156
Lethbridge, Can. 49°40′ N, 112°49′ W 82
Lethem, Guyana 3°19′ N, 59°48′ W 130
Leticia, Col. 4°8′ S, 69°59′ W 136
Leting, China 39°24′ N, 118°57′ E 198
Letka, Russ. 59°35′ N, 49°24′ E 154
Letlhakane, Botswana 21°25′ S, 25°34′ E 227
Letlhakeng, Botswana 24°6′ S, 25°2′ E 227
Letnerechenskiy, Russ. 64°19′ N, 34°12′ E 152
Letniy Navolok, Russ. 65°8′ N, 36°57′ E 154
Letnyaya Stavka, Russ. 45°22′ N, 43°16′ E 158
Letnyaya Zolotitsa, Russ. 64°58′ N, 36°42′ E 154
Letsôk-aw Kyun, island, Myanmar 11°20′ N, 98°15′ E 202
Lette, Ger. 51°54′ N, 7°11′ E 167
Letur, Sp. 38°22′ N, 2°5′ W 164
Léua, Angola 11°39′ S, 20°24′ E 220
Leucadia, Calif., U.S. 33°4′ N, 117°19′ W 101
Leucate, Fr. 42°54′ N, 3°0′ E 164
Leucayec, Isla, island, Chile 43°55′ S, 73°41′ W 134

Leuk, *Switz.* 46°20′ N, 7°37′ E 167
Leuna, *Ger.* 51°19′ N, 12°1′ E 152
Leuser, peak, *Indonesia* 3°45′ N, 97°5′ E 196
Leuven, *Belg.* 50°52′ N, 4°41′ E 167
Leuze, *Belg.* 50°35′ N, 3°37′ E 163
Lev Tolstoy, *Russ.* 53°11′ N, 39°23′ E 154
Levajok, *Nor.* 69°54′ N, 26°24′ E 152
Levanger, *Nor.* 63°44′ N, 11°17′ E 152
Levant, *Kans., U.S.* 39°23′ N, 101°13′ W 90
Levant, Île du, island, *Fr.* 43°3′ N, 6°30′ E 165
Levanto, *It.* 44°10′ N, 9°37′ E 167
Levaya Khetta, river, *Russ.* 64°9′ N, 71°21′ E 169
Levelland, *Tex., U.S.* 33°34′ N, 102°23′ W 92
Levens, *Fr.* 43°51′ N, 7°12′ E 167
Leveque, Cape, *Austral.* 16°19′ S, 121°59′ E 230
Lever, river, *Braz.* 11°3′ S, 50°17′ W 130
Leverkusen, *Ger.* 51°0′ N, 6°59′ E 167
Levico, *It.* 46°1′ N, 11°18′ E 167
Levídi, *Gr.* 37°41′ N, 22°17′ E 156
Levikha, *Russ.* 57°36′ N, 59°52′ E 154
Levin, *N.Z.* 40°39′ S, 175°17′ E 240
Lévis, *Can.* 46°47′ N, 71°11′ W 94
Levittown, *Pa., U.S.* 40°8′ N, 74°51′ W 94
Levokumskoye, *Russ.* 44°48′ N, 44°38′ E 158
Lévrier, Baie du 20°6′ N, 16°46′ W 222
Lėvuo, river, *Lith.* 55°49′ N, 24°28′ E 166
Lewellen, *Nebr., U.S.* 41°19′ N, 102°10′ W 90
Lewes, *U.K.* 50°52′ N, 2°120′ E 162
Lewis, *Ind., U.S.* 39°15′ N, 87°16′ W 102
Lewis, *Kans., U.S.* 37°56′ N, 99°16′ W 92
Lewis, *N.Y., U.S.* 44°16′ N, 73°35′ W 104
Lewis and Clark Range, *Mont., U.S.* 48°1′ N, 113°19′ W 90
Lewis Chain 80°2′ S, 29°5′ W 248
Lewis Hills, peak, *Can.* 48°48′ N, 58°35′ W 111
Lewis, Isle of, island, *U.K.* 58°31′ N, 8°23′ W 142
Lewis, Mount, peak, *Nev., U.S.* 40°23′ N, 116°57′ W 90
Lewis Pass, *N.Z.* 42°26′ S, 172°23′ E 240
Lewis, river, *Wash., U.S.* 46°7′ N, 121°50′ W 100
Lewiston, *Me., U.S.* 44°6′ N, 70°13′ W 104
Lewistown, *Ill., U.S.* 40°23′ N, 90°9′ W 102
Lewistown, *Pa., U.S.* 40°35′ N, 77°36′ W 94
Lewisville, *Ark., U.S.* 33°21′ N, 93°35′ W 96
Lexington, *Ky., U.S.* 38°1′ N, 84°30′ W 94
Lexington, *Mich., U.S.* 43°16′ N, 82°32′ W 102
Lexington, *Miss., U.S.* 33°5′ N, 90°3′ W 103
Lexington, *Mo., U.S.* 39°10′ N, 93°52′ W 94
Lexington, *Nebr., U.S.* 40°45′ N, 99°45′ W 92
Lexington, *N.C., U.S.* 35°48′ N, 80°16′ W 96
Lexington, *Ohio, U.S.* 40°40′ N, 82°35′ W 102
Lexington, *Oreg., U.S.* 45°26′ N, 119°41′ W 90
Lexington Park, *Md., U.S.* 38°14′ N, 76°28′ W 82
Leyburn, *U.K.* 54°18′ N, 1°50′ W 162
Leye, *China* 24°47′ N, 106°25′ E 198
Leyte, island, *Philippines* 10°16′ N, 125°21′ E 192
Leżajsk, *Pol.* 50°14′ N, 22°25′ E 152
Lezha, *Russ.* 58°56′ N, 40°49′ E 154
Lezhë, *Alban.* 41°47′ N, 19°39′ E 168
Lezhi, *China* 30°15′ N, 105°5′ E 198
Lezuza, *Sp.* 38°56′ N, 2°21′ W 164
L'gov, *Russ.* 51°41′ N, 35°16′ E 158
Lhari, *China* 30°50′ N, 93°22′ E 188
Lhasa, *China* 29°46′ N, 91°3′ E 197
Lhasa, river, *China* 29°20′ N, 90°55′ E 197
Lhazhong, *China* 32°2′ N, 86°46′ E 188
L'Hillil, *Alg.* 35°43′ N, 0°22′ E 150
Lhokseumawe, *Indonesia* 5°10′ N, 97°5′ E 196
Lhorong, *China* 30°44′ N, 95°51′ E 188
L'Hospitalet, *Fr.* 42°35′ N, 1°47′ E 164
L'Hospitalet de Llobregat, *Sp.* 41°21′ N, 2°6′ E 164
Lhozhag, *China* 28°19′ N, 90°50′ E 197
Lhünzê, *China* 28°26′ N, 92°27′ E 197
Lhünzhub, *China* 30°10′ N, 91°13′ E 197
Li, river, *China* 29°23′ N, 110°55′ E 198
Li Yubu, *Sudan* 5°23′ N, 27°17′ E 224
Lian, river, *China* 24°28′ N, 112°44′ E 198
Liancheng, *China* 25°40′ N, 116°44′ E 198
Liancourt, *Fr.* 49°19′ N, 2°28′ E 163
Lianga, *Philippines* 8°40′ N, 126°5′ E 203
Liangcheng, *China* 40°31′ N, 112°30′ E 198
Liangdang, *China* 33°54′ N, 106°19′ E 198
Liangjiangkou, *China* 42°38′ N, 128°2′ E 200
Liangping, *China* 30°37′ N, 107°47′ E 198
Liangshui, *China* 40°58′ N, 125°51′ E 200
Lianjiang, *China* 26°15′ N, 119°33′ E 198
Lianjiang, *China* 21°36′ N, 110°14′ E 198
Lianping, *China* 24°21′ N, 114°27′ E 198
Lianshan, *China* 24°31′ N, 112°6′ E 198
Lianxian, *China* 24°45′ N, 112°24′ E 198
Lianyungang (Xinpu), *China* 34°38′ N, 119°14′ E 198
Liao, river, *China* 42°7′ N, 123°29′ E 200
Liaocheng, *China* 36°25′ N, 115°53′ E 198
Liaodong Wan 40°21′ N, 120°30′ E 198
Liaoning, adm. division, *China* 41°19′ N, 123°22′ E 200
Liaoyang, *China* 41°17′ N, 123°10′ E 200
Liaoyuan, *China* 42°54′ N, 125°8′ E 200
Liaozhong, *China* 41°31′ N, 122°41′ E 200
Liard Island, *Antarctica* 66°36′ S, 67°58′ W 248
Liard River, *Can.* 59°24′ N, 126°6′ W 108
Liard, river, *Can.* 60°45′ N, 123°3′ W 106
Liathach, peak, *U.K.* 57°32′ N, 5°34′ W 150
Libanga, *Dem. Rep. of the Congo* 0°21′ N, 18°43′ E 218
Libby, *Mont., U.S.* 48°22′ N, 115°34′ W 90
Libby Dam, *Mont., U.S.* 48°8′ N, 115°34′ W 90
Libenge, *Dem. Rep. of the Congo* 3°35′ N, 18°41′ E 218
Liberal, *Kans., U.S.* 37°1′ N, 100°56′ W 92
Liberdade, river, *Braz.* 8°19′ S, 71°53′ W 130
Liberdade, river, *Braz.* 11°14′ S, 52°11′ W 130
Liberec, *Czech Rep.* 50°45′ N, 15°2′ E 152
Liberecký, adm. division, *Czech Rep.* 50°47′ N, 15°7′ E 152
Liberia, *C.R.* 10°38′ N, 85°27′ W 115
Liberia 6°38′ N, 10°19′ W 214
Libertad, *Venez.* 9°18′ N, 68°35′ W 136
Libertad, *Venez.* 8°20′ N, 69°37′ W 136
Libertador General Bernardo O'Higgins, adm. division, *Chile* 34°44′ S, 72°20′ W 134
Liberty, *Ind., U.S.* 39°37′ N, 84°56′ W 102
Liberty, *Miss., U.S.* 31°8′ N, 90°48′ W 103
Liberty, *N.Y., U.S.* 41°47′ N, 74°45′ W 94
Liberty, *Tex., U.S.* 30°2′ N, 94°47′ W 103
Libni, Gebel, peak, *Egypt* 30°43′ N, 33°48′ E 194
Libo, *China* 25°24′ N, 107°50′ E 198
Libode, *S. Af.* 31°34′ S, 29°1′ E 227
Liboi, *Kenya* 0°17′ N, 40°49′ E 224
Libourne, *Fr.* 44°55′ N, 0°14′ E 150
Libral Well, spring, *Austral.* 22°8′ S, 125°29′ E 230
Libreville, *Gabon* 0°20′ N, 9°18′ E 218
Libya 26°52′ N, 11°56′ E 216
Libyan Desert, *Lib.* 26°27′ N, 24°26′ E 180
Libyan Plateau, *Egypt* 30°0′ N, 25°33′ E 180
Licantén, *Chile* 34°58′ S, 72°1′ W 134
Lice, *Turk.* 38°27′ N, 40°39′ E 195
Lich, *Ger.* 50°31′ N, 8°49′ E 167
Lichfield, *U.K.* 52°40′ N, 1°50′ W 162
Lichinga, *Mozambique* 13°20′ S, 35°13′ E 224
Lichtenburg, *S. Af.* 26°11′ S, 26°8′ E 227
Lichuan, *China* 30°18′ N, 108°55′ E 198
Lichuan, *China* 27°22′ N, 116°51′ E 198
Licking, *Mo., U.S.* 37°29′ N, 91°51′ W 96
Licosa, Punta, *It.* 40°8′ N, 14°25′ E 156
Licungo, river, *Mozambique* 17°5′ S, 37°3′ E 224
Lida, *Belarus* 53°52′ N, 25°18′ E 166
Liddon Gulf 74°53′ N, 117°12′ W 106
Liden, *Nor.* 62°41′ N, 16°48′ E 152
Lidgerwood, *N. Dak., U.S.* 46°3′ N, 97°10′ W 90
Lidhult, *Nor.* 56°50′ N, 13°25′ E 152
Lidice, *Czech Rep.* 50°7′ N, 14°10′ E 152
Lidingö, *Sw.* 59°21′ N, 18°9′ E 166
Lidköping, *Nor.* 58°29′ N, 13°7′ E 152
Lido, *It.* 45°25′ N, 12°22′ E 167
Lido, *Niger* 12°51′ N, 3°36′ E 222
Lido di Jesolo, *It.* 45°30′ N, 12°38′ E 167
Liebig, Mount, peak, *Austral.* 23°21′ S, 131°16′ E 230
Liechtenstein 47°6′ N, 9°26′ E 156
Liège, *Belg.* 50°38′ N, 5°33′ E 167
Liège Island, *Antarctica* 64°7′ S, 61°45′ W 134
Liége, river, *Can.* 56°55′ N, 114°1′ W 108
Lieksa, *Fin.* 63°17′ N, 29°59′ E 152
Lielvārde, *Latv.* 56°42′ N, 24°51′ E 166
Liénart, *Dem. Rep. of the Congo* 3°0′ N, 25°36′ E 224
Lienz, *Aust.* 46°49′ N, 12°44′ E 167
Liepāja, *Latv.* 56°31′ N, 21°1′ E 166
Liepājas Ezers, lake, *Latv.* 56°25′ N, 20°37′ E 166
Liepna, *Latv.* 57°19′ N, 27°28′ E 166
Lier, *Belg.* 51°8′ N, 4°33′ E 167
Lierneux, *Belg.* 50°16′ N, 5°47′ E 167
Lieşti, *Rom.* 45°37′ N, 27°32′ E 156
Liétor, *Sp.* 38°32′ N, 1°57′ W 164
Liévin, *Fr.* 50°24′ N, 2°46′ E 163
Lifford, *Ire.* 54°49′ N, 7°31′ W 150
Liftāyā, *Syr.* 34°39′ N, 36°27′ E 194
Ligao, *Philippines* 13°14′ N, 123°31′ E 203
Līgatne, *Latv.* 57°10′ N, 25°1′ E 166
Lighthouse Point, *Fla., U.S.* 29°47′ N, 84°30′ W 96
Lighthouse Point, *Fla., U.S.* 26°16′ N, 80°6′ W 105
Ligneuville, *Belg.* 50°22′ N, 6°3′ E 167
Ligny-en-Barrois, *Fr.* 48°41′ N, 5°19′ E 163
Liguria, adm. division, *It.* 44°26′ N, 8°24′ E 167
Ligurian Sea 43°49′ N, 8°37′ E 167
Lihir Group, islands, *South Pacific Ocean* 2°55′ S, 152°47′ E 192
Lihula, *Est.* 58°41′ N, 23°47′ E 166
Lijeva Rijeka, *Mont.* 42°38′ N, 19°29′ E 168
Likasi, *Dem. Rep. of the Congo* 11°0′ S, 26°44′ E 224
Likati, *Dem. Rep. of the Congo* 3°19′ N, 23°56′ E 224
Likati, river, *Dem. Rep. of the Congo* 3°23′ N, 22°32′ E 218
Likely, *Can.* 52°36′ N, 121°34′ W 108
Likely Mountain, peak, *Calif., U.S.* 41°8′ N, 120°40′ W 90
Likėnai, *Lith.* 56°12′ N, 24°37′ E 166
Líkeo, Óros, peak, *Gr.* 37°26′ N, 21°53′ E 156
Likhoslavl', *Russ.* 57°5′ N, 35°30′ E 154
Likódimo, Óros, peak, *Gr.* 36°55′ N, 21°47′ E 156
Likoma Islands, *Malawi* 11°51′ S, 34°22′ E 224
Likoto, *Dem. Rep. of the Congo* 1°12′ S, 24°50′ E 224
Likwangoli, *Sudan* 6°59′ N, 33°2′ E 224
Lilbourn, *Mo., U.S.* 36°35′ N, 89°36′ W 94
L'Île-Rousse, *Fr.* 42°38′ N, 8°56′ E 156
Lilian, Point, peak, *Austral.* 27°43′ S, 125°51′ E 230
Liling, *China* 27°41′ N, 113°27′ E 198
Liljendal, *Fin.* 60°34′ N, 26°3′ E 166
Lille, *Fr.* 50°37′ N, 3°4′ E 163
Lillers, *Fr.* 50°34′ N, 2°28′ E 163
Lillesand, *Nor.* 58°15′ N, 8°21′ E 150
Lillhamra, *Nor.* 61°39′ N, 14°47′ E 152
Lillhärdal, *Nor.* 61°50′ N, 14°2′ E 152
Lillie, *La., U.S.* 32°55′ N, 92°40′ W 103
Lillooet, *Can.* 50°42′ N, 121°57′ W 108
Lillooet Lake, *Can.* 50°16′ N, 122°51′ W 108
Lilo Viejo, *Arg.* 26°56′ S, 62°58′ W 139
Lilongwe, *Malawi* 13°59′ S, 33°39′ E 224
Liloy, *Philippines* 8°8′ N, 122°40′ E 203
Lima, *Arg.* 34°3′ S, 59°10′ W 139
Lima, *Mont., U.S.* 44°38′ N, 112°36′ W 90
Lima, *Ohio, U.S.* 40°44′ N, 84°7′ W 102
Lima, *Parag.* 23°54′ S, 56°28′ W 132
Lima, *Peru* 12°9′ S, 77°12′ W 130
Lima, adm. division, *Peru* 11°45′ S, 77°10′ W 130
Lima Duarte, *Braz.* 21°52′ S, 43°51′ W 138
Lima, river, *Port.* 41°43′ N, 8°47′ W 150
Limal, *Bol.* 22°28′ S, 64°33′ W 137
Liman, *Russ.* 45°44′ N, 47°10′ E 158
Limas, *Indonesia* 0°13′ N, 104°31′ E 196
Limassol, *Cyprus* 34°40′ N, 33°1′ E 194
Limaumanis, *Indonesia* 1°37′ N, 109°19′ E 196
Limay Mahuida, *Arg.* 37°11′ S, 66°40′ W 134
Limbani, *Peru* 14°11′ S, 69°37′ W 137
Limbara, Monte, peak, *It.* 40°50′ N, 9°4′ E 156
Limbaži, *Latv.* 57°30′ N, 24°41′ E 166
Limbe, *Cameroon* 4°4′ N, 9°10′ E 222
Limbe, *Malawi* 15°59′ S, 35°4′ E 224
Limbourg, *Belg.* 50°37′ N, 5°56′ E 167
Limbung, *Indonesia* 0°13′ N, 109°48′ E 196
Limburg, *Ger.* 50°23′ N, 8°3′ E 167
Lime Village, *Alas., U.S.* 61°21′ N, 155°30′ W 98
Limedsforsen, *Nor.* 60°54′ N, 13°21′ E 152
Limeira, *Braz.* 22°34′ S, 47°26′ W 138
Limena, *It.* 45°29′ N, 11°49′ E 167
Limerick, *Can.* 49°38′ N, 106°16′ W 90
Limerick, *Me., U.S.* 43°41′ N, 70°48′ W 104
Limerick (Luimneach), *Ire.* 52°39′ N, 8°37′ W 150
Limestone, *Me., U.S.* 46°53′ N, 67°50′ W 82
Limestone Point, *Can.* 53°31′ N, 98°23′ W 108
Limestone, river, *Can.* 56°38′ N, 94°48′ W 108
Limington, *Me., U.S.* 43°43′ N, 70°43′ W 104
Liminka, *Fin.* 64°48′ N, 25°21′ E 152
Limmared, *Nor.* 57°32′ N, 13°21′ E 152
Límnos, island, *Gr.* 39°42′ N, 25°22′ E 180
Limoges, *Fr.* 45°50′ N, 1°15′ E 150
Limon, *Colo., U.S.* 39°16′ N, 103°41′ W 90
Limone Piemonte, *It.* 44°12′ N, 7°34′ E 167
Limoquije, *Bol.* 15°28′ S, 64°49′ W 137
Limousin, adm. division, *Fr.* 45°39′ N, 1°16′ E 165
Limousin, region, *Fr.* 45°39′ N, 1°5′ E 165
Limpias, *Sp.* 43°21′ N, 3°26′ W 164
Limpopo, adm. division, *S. Af.* 23°30′ S, 28°24′ E 227
Limpopo, river, *Africa* 22°10′ S, 29°16′ E 227
Līnah, *Saudi Arabia* 28°45′ N, 43°47′ E 180
Linakhamari, *Russ.* 69°38′ N, 31°20′ E 152
Lin'an, *China* 30°15′ N, 119°44′ E 198
Linares, *Mex.* 24°50′ N, 99°35′ W 114
Linares, *Sp.* 38°5′ N, 3°42′ W 214
Linares, *Sp.* 38°5′ N, 3°37′ W 164
Linaro, Capo, *It.* 41°57′ N, 11°18′ E 156
Linas, Monte, peak, *It.* 39°26′ N, 8°32′ E 156
Lincang, *China* 23°51′ N, 99°58′ E 202
Linchuan, *China* 27°58′ N, 116°18′ E 198
Linck Nunataks, *Antarctica* 83°20′ S, 104°39′ W 248
Lincoln, *Arg.* 34°53′ S, 61°30′ W 139
Lincoln, *Calif., U.S.* 38°53′ N, 121°19′ W 90
Lincoln, *Ill., U.S.* 40°8′ N, 89°22′ W 102
Lincoln, *Kans., U.S.* 39°1′ N, 98°10′ W 90
Lincoln, *Mich., U.S.* 44°40′ N, 83°26′ W 94
Lincoln, *Mo., U.S.* 40°8′ N, 89°22′ W 94
Lincoln, *Nebr., U.S.* 40°46′ N, 96°49′ W 90
Lincoln, *N.H., U.S.* 44°2′ N, 71°41′ W 104
Lincoln, *N. Mex., U.S.* 33°28′ N, 105°23′ W 92
Lincoln, *N.Z.* 43°40′ S, 172°28′ E 240
Lincoln, *S. Dak., U.S.* 40°39′ N, 97°21′ W 72
Lincoln, *U.K.* 53°13′ N, 0°33′ E 162
Lincoln, *Vt., U.S.* 44°6′ N, 73°0′ W 104
Lincoln Bay 83°25′ N, 56°35′ W 255
Lincoln Boyhood National Monument, *Ind., U.S.* 38°5′ N, 87°4′ W 96
Lincoln City, *Oreg., U.S.* 44°57′ N, 124°1′ W 90
Lincoln Heights, *U.K.* 53°24′ N, 0°40′ E 162
Lincoln Park, *Colo., U.S.* 38°25′ N, 105°13′ W 92
Lincoln Park, *Mich., U.S.* 42°14′ N, 83°11′ W 102
Lincoln Sea 81°13′ N, 60°27′ W 246
Lincoln's New Salem, site, *Ill., U.S.* 39°57′ N, 89°55′ W 102
Lincolnton, *Ga., U.S.* 33°46′ N, 82°29′ W 96
Lind, *Wash., U.S.* 46°58′ N, 118°37′ W 90
Linda, *Calif., U.S.* 39°7′ N, 121°35′ W 90
Lindale, *Tex., U.S.* 32°30′ N, 95°24′ W 103
Linde, river, *Russ.* 66°15′ N, 120°13′ E 160
Linden, *Ala., U.S.* 32°18′ N, 87°49′ W 103
Linden, *Calif., U.S.* 38°1′ N, 121°6′ W 100
Linden, *Guyana* 6°1′ N, 58°21′ W 130
Linden, *Ind., U.S.* 40°11′ N, 86°54′ W 102
Linden, *Mich., U.S.* 42°47′ N, 83°47′ W 102
Linden, *Tex., U.S.* 33°0′ N, 94°23′ W 103
Lindenhurst, *N.Y., U.S.* 40°40′ N, 73°22′ W 104
Lindenow Fjord 60°10′ N, 43°49′ W 106
Lindesberg, *Nor.* 59°35′ N, 15°14′ E 152
Lindesnes, *Nor.* 57°55′ N, 6°21′ E 150
Lindi, *Tanzania* 9°57′ S, 39°38′ E 224
Lindi, adm. division, *Tanzania* 9°36′ S, 37°48′ E 224
Lindi, river, *Dem. Rep. of the Congo* 0°23′ N, 28°1′ E 224
Lindian, *China* 47°11′ N, 124°54′ E 198
Lindley, *S. Af.* 27°56′ S, 27°52′ E 227
Lindsay, *Calif., U.S.* 36°12′ N, 119°6′ W 101
Lindsay, *Can.* 44°21′ N, 78°43′ W 94
Lindsay, *Mont., U.S.* 47°12′ N, 105°10′ W 90
Lindsay, *Okla., U.S.* 34°48′ N, 97°36′ W 92
Lindsborg, *Kans., U.S.* 38°33′ N, 97°41′ W 90
Lindsey Islands, *Amundsen Sea* 73°24′ S, 103°46′ W 248
Linevo, *Russ.* 54°29′ N, 83°25′ E 184
Linfen, *China* 36°6′ N, 111°35′ E 198
Lingao, *China* 19°56′ N, 109°40′ E 198
Lingayen, *Philippines* 15°59′ N, 120°12′ E 203
Lingbao, *China* 34°32′ N, 110°50′ E 198
Lingbi, *China* 33°33′ N, 117°31′ E 198
Lingbo, *Nor.* 61°2′ N, 16°39′ E 152
Lingchuan, *China* 25°31′ N, 110°21′ E 198
Lingen, *Ger.* 52°31′ N, 7°19′ E 163
Lingga, island, *Indonesia* 0°41′ N, 105°0′ E 192
Lingga, Kepulauan, islands, *South China Sea* 0°19′ N, 105°1′ E 196
Lingig, *Philippines* 8°5′ N, 126°24′ E 203
Lingle, *Wyo., U.S.* 42°8′ N, 104°21′ W 90
Lingomo, *Dem. Rep. of the Congo* 0°37′ N, 22°2′ E 218
Lingshan, *China* 22°25′ N, 109°14′ E 198
Lingshui, *China* 18°27′ N, 109°59′ E 198
Lingtai, *China* 35°4′ N, 107°33′ E 198
Linguère, *Senegal* 15°25′ N, 15°8′ W 222
Lingui, *China* 25°11′ N, 110°11′ E 198
Lingwu, *China* 38°6′ N, 106°18′ E 198
Lingxian, *China* 26°30′ N, 113°45′ E 198
Lingyuan, *China* 41°18′ N, 119°26′ E 198
Lingyun, *China* 24°16′ N, 106°33′ E 198
Linhai, *China* 28°49′ N, 121°11′ E 198
Linhares, *Braz.* 19°24′ S, 40°3′ W 138
Linhe, *China* 40°44′ N, 107°22′ E 198
Linjiang, *China* 41°48′ N, 126°55′ E 200
Linkmenys, *Lith.* 55°19′ N, 25°57′ E 166
Linköping, *Nor.* 58°23′ N, 15°35′ E 152
Linkuva, *Lith.* 56°4′ N, 23°57′ E 166
Linn, *Tex., U.S.* 26°34′ N, 98°7′ W 114
Linova, *Belarus* 52°27′ N, 24°30′ E 152
Linqing, *China* 36°50′ N, 115°43′ E 198
Linquan, *China* 33°4′ N, 115°15′ E 198
Linru, *China* 34°10′ N, 112°53′ E 198
Lins, *Braz.* 21°41′ S, 49°46′ W 138
Linsell, *Nor.* 62°8′ N, 13°53′ E 152
Linshui, *China* 30°20′ N, 106°54′ E 198
Lintang, *Malaysia* 5°20′ N, 118°28′ E 203
Linthal, *Switz.* 46°55′ N, 9°0′ E 167
Linton, *Ind., U.S.* 39°1′ N, 87°10′ W 102
Linton, *N. Dak., U.S.* 46°15′ N, 100°14′ W 90
Lintong, *China* 34°22′ N, 109°16′ E 198
Linwood, *Mich., U.S.* 43°44′ N, 83°58′ W 102
Linxi, *China* 39°44′ N, 118°29′ E 198
Linxi, *China* 43°36′ N, 118°2′ E 198
Linxia, *China* 35°29′ N, 103°1′ E 190
Linxian, *China* 37°57′ N, 110°53′ E 198
Linyi, *China* 35°3′ N, 118°20′ E 198
Linyi, *China* 37°8′ N, 116°52′ E 198
Linz, *Aust.* 48°16′ N, 14°18′ E 152
Linz, *Ger.* 50°33′ N, 7°17′ E 167
Lioma, *Mozambique* 15°12′ S, 36°49′ E 224
Lion, Golfe du 42°17′ N, 3°17′ E 142
Lion's Head, *Can.* 44°58′ N, 81°13′ W 94
Liot Point, *Can.* 73°12′ N, 128°57′ W 106
Liouesso, *Congo* 1°1′ N, 15°42′ E 218
Lipa, *Philippines* 13°57′ N, 121°9′ E 203
Lipari, Isole (Eolie), islands, *It.* 38°39′ N, 13°46′ E 156
Lipcani, *Mold.* 48°16′ N, 26°47′ E 152
Lipce, *Pol.* 51°53′ N, 19°57′ E 152
Lipetsk, *Russ.* 52°37′ N, 39°28′ E 154
Lipetsk, adm. division, *Russ.* 53°14′ N, 38°42′ E 154
Lípez, Cordillera de, *Bol.* 21°42′ S, 66°59′ W 132
Lipiany, *Pol.* 53°0′ N, 14°58′ E 152
Lipik, *Croatia* 45°25′ N, 17°9′ E 168
Liping, *China* 26°13′ N, 109°7′ E 198
Lipjan (Lipljan), *Kosovo* 42°31′ N, 21°8′ E 168
Lipljan see Lipjan, *Kosovo* 42°31′ N, 21°8′ E 168
Lipnica, *Pol.* 53°59′ N, 17°25′ E 152
Lipník, *Czech Rep.* 49°31′ N, 17°35′ E 152
Lipnishki, *Belarus* 54°0′ N, 25°36′ E 166
Lipova, *Rom.* 46°5′ N, 21°43′ E 168
Lipovac, *Croatia* 45°3′ N, 19°4′ E 168
Lippe, river, *Ger.* 51°37′ N, 8°5′ E 167
Lippstadt, *Ger.* 51°39′ N, 8°21′ E 167
Lipscomb, *Tex., U.S.* 36°12′ N, 100°16′ W 92
Lipsí, *Gr.* 37°18′ N, 26°46′ E 156
Lipsko, *Pol.* 51°9′ N, 21°39′ E 152
Lipton, *Can.* 50°54′ N, 103°53′ W 90
Liptovský Mikuláš, *Slovakia* 49°4′ N, 19°39′ E 152
Lipu, *China* 24°30′ N, 110°23′ E 198
Lipu Lekh Pass, *China* 30°14′ N, 81°2′ E 197
Lira, *Uganda* 2°13′ N, 32°54′ E 224
Liranga, *Congo* 0°41′ N, 17°30′ E 218
Lircay, *Peru* 13°1′ S, 74°43′ W 137
Liria, *Sudan* 4°36′ N, 32°4′ E 224
Lirik, oil field, *Indonesia* 0°13′ N, 102°8′ E 196
Lirik Ukul, oil field, *Indonesia* 5°296′ S, 101°48′ E 192
Lisa, *Mont.* 43°9′ N, 19°33′ E 168
Līsakovsk, *Kaz.* 52°32′ N, 62°31′ E 184
Lisala, *Dem. Rep. of the Congo* 2°10′ N, 21°28′ E 218
Lisboa (Lisbon), *Port.* 38°42′ N, 9°17′ W 150
Lisbon, *Ill., U.S.* 41°28′ N, 88°30′ W 102
Lisbon, *La., U.S.* 32°47′ N, 92°53′ W 103
Lisbon, *Me., U.S.* 44°1′ N, 70°7′ W 104
Lisbon, *N. Dak., U.S.* 46°26′ N, 97°41′ W 90
Lisboa, adm. division, *Port.* 38°57′ N, 9°25′ W 150
Lisbon Falls, *Me., U.S.* 44°0′ N, 70°4′ W 104
Lisbon see Lisboa, *Port.* 38°42′ N, 9°17′ W 150
Lisburne, Cape, *Alas., U.S.* 69°21′ N, 163°16′ W 246
Lishu, *China* 43°22′ N, 124°20′ E 198
Lishui, *China* 28°29′ N, 119°54′ E 198
Lisieux, *Fr.* 49°8′ N, 0°14′ E 150
Lisino-Korpus, *Russ.* 59°25′ N, 30°41′ E 166
Lisitsa, river, *Russ.* 58°59′ N, 85°2′ E 169
Liski, *Rom.* 46°14′ N, 26°44′ E 156
Liski, *Russ.* 51°1′ N, 39°30′ E 158
L'Isle-Verte, *Can.* 47°59′ N, 69°21′ W 94
Lisman, *Ala., U.S.* 32°11′ N, 88°17′ W 103
Lisok, pass, *Ukr.* 48°47′ N, 23°8′ E 152
Lissa see Vis, island, *Croatia* 42°57′ N, 16°5′ E 168
Lister, Mount, peak, *Antarctica* 77°58′ S, 163°35′ E 248
Listerlandet, *Nor.* 55°55′ N, 14°45′ E 152
Listowel, *Can.* 43°43′ N, 80°57′ W 102
Lit, *Nor.* 63°19′ N, 14°47′ E 152
Litang, *China* 23°9′ N, 109°7′ E 198
Līṭānī, river, *Leb.* 33°20′ N, 35°14′ E 194
Litani, river, *Suriname* 2°12′ N, 54°24′ W 130
Litberg, peak, *Ger.* 53°23′ N, 9°31′ E 150
Litchfield, *Conn., U.S.* 41°44′ N, 73°12′ W 104
Litchfield, *Ill., U.S.* 39°10′ N, 89°39′ W 102
Litchfield, *Mich., U.S.* 42°2′ N, 84°46′ W 102

Litchfield, *Minn., U.S.* 45°7' N, 94°33' W 90
Litchfield, *Mo., U.S.* 39°10' N, 89°39' W 94
Litchfield National Park, *Austral.* 13°22' S, 130°32' E 238
Liteni, *Rom.* 47°30' N, 26°30' E 156
Lithuania 55°20' N, 23°34' E 166
Litija, *Slov.* 46°3' N, 14°49' E 156
Little Abaco, island, *Bahamas* 26°52' N, 77°44' W 118
Little Abitibi Lake, *Can.* 49°21' N, 81°12' W 94
Little Abitibi, river, *Can.* 50°30' N, 81°35' W 94
Little America (historic), site, *Antarctica* 78°27' S, 163°0' W 248
Little Andaman, island, *India* 10°2' N, 91°45' E 188
Little Beaver, river, *Can.* 57°34' N, 97°4' W 108
Little Belt Mountains, *Mont., U.S.* 46°43' N, 110°43' W 90
Little Bighorn, river, *Mont., U.S.* 46°3' N, 108°23' W 80
Little Blue, river, *Nebr., U.S.* 40°31' N, 98°31' W 80
Little Buffalo, *Can.* 56°27' N, 116°10' W 108
Little Buffalo, river, *Can.* 60°48' N, 113°36' W 108
Little Cadotte, river, *Can.* 56°34' N, 117°5' W 108
Little Cayman, island, *Little Cayman* 19°23' N, 80°33' W 115
Little Creek Peak, *Utah, U.S.* 37°51' N, 112°40' W 92
Little Current, *Can.* 45°57' N, 81°57' W 94
Little Current, river, *Can.* 50°31' N, 86°53' W 110
Little Duck Lake, *Can.* 59°23' N, 98°26' W 108
Little Exuma, island, *Bahamas* 23°9' N, 75°51' W 116
Little Falls, *Minn., U.S.* 45°57' N, 94°22' W 90
Little Falls, *N.Y., U.S.* 43°2' N, 74°53' W 110
Little Gombi, *Nig.* 10°9' N, 12°46' E 216
Little Grand Rapids, *Can.* 52°2' N, 95°27' W 108
Little Inagua Island, *Bahamas* 21°36' N, 73°21' W 116
Little Isaac, island, *Bahamas* 25°56' N, 78°59' W 105
Little Juniper Mountain, peak, *Oreg., U.S.* 43°8' N, 119°55' W 90
Little Lake, *Calif., U.S.* 35°56' N, 117°55' W 101
Little Lake, *Mich., U.S.* 46°18' N, 87°21' W 110
Little Longlac, *Can.* 49°41' N, 86°57' W 94
Little Namaland, region, *S. Af.* 28°17' S, 16°49' E 227
Little Nicobar, island, *India* 7°21' N, 92°20' E 188
Little River, *Calif., U.S.* 39°16' N, 123°47' W 90
Little, river, *La., U.S.* 31°35' N, 92°27' W 103
Little, river, *Okla., U.S.* 34°9' N, 95°7' W 112
Little Rock, *Ark., U.S.* 34°40' N, 92°24' W 96
Little Rocky Mountains, *Mont., U.S.* 47°56' N, 108°26' W 90
Little Sable Point, *Mich., U.S.* 43°37' N, 86°41' W 102
Little Saint Bernard Pass, *It.* 45°41' N, 6°54' E 167
Little San Bernardino Mountains, *Calif., U.S.* 34°0' N, 116°19' W 101
Little San Salvador, island, *Bahamas* 24°26' N, 77°1' W 116
Little Seal, river, *Can.* 59°3' N, 95°41' W 108
Little Sioux, river, *Iowa, U.S.* 41°43' N, 96°20' W 80
Little Sitkin, island, *Alas., U.S.* 52°9' N, 178°28' E 160
Little Smoky, *Can.* 54°43' N, 117°7' W 108
Little Smoky, river, *Can.* 54°4' N, 117°46' W 108
Little Suamico, *Wis., U.S.* 44°42' N, 88°1' W 94
Little White Mountain, peak, *Can.* 49°40' N, 119°26' W 90
Littlefield, *Ariz., U.S.* 36°52' N, 113°56' W 101
Littlefield, *Tex., U.S.* 33°55' N, 102°20' W 92
Littlefork, *Minn., U.S.* 48°21' N, 93°32' W 94
Littlehampton, *U.K.* 50°48' N, 0°32' E 162
Littleton, *Colo., U.S.* 39°35' N, 105°2' W 90
Littleton, *Mass., U.S.* 42°32' N, 71°32' W 104
Littleton, *N.H., U.S.* 44°18' N, 71°47' W 104
Litva, *Bosn. and Herzg.* 44°24' N, 18°31' E 168
Lityn, *Ukr.* 49°18' N, 28°13' E 152
Liu, river, *China* 42°25' N, 125°40' E 200
Liu, river, *China* 42°13' N, 122°39' E 200
Liuba, *China* 33°37' N, 106°53' E 198
Liucheng, *China* 24°39' N, 109°16' E 198
Liudaogou, *China* 41°33' N, 127°12' E 200
Liuhe, *China* 42°16' N, 125°45' E 200
Liuli, *Tanzania* 11°5' S, 34°40' E 224
Liupan Shan, peak, *China* 35°30' N, 106°7' E 198
Liúpo, *Mozambique* 15°36' S, 39°59' E 224
Liuwa Plain, *Zambia* 14°33' S, 22°27' E 220
Liuwa Plain National Park, *Zambia* 14°41' S, 22°14' E 206
Liuzhou, *China* 24°18' N, 109°23' E 198
Livada, *Rom.* 47°52' N, 23°6' E 168
Līvāni, *Latv.* 56°20' N, 26°10' E 166
Live Oak, *Fla., U.S.* 30°16' N, 82°59' W 96
Live Oak Springs, *Calif., U.S.* 32°41' N, 116°22' W 101
Lively Island, *Lively Island* 52°14' S, 58°23' W 134
Livermore, *Calif., U.S.* 37°40' N, 121°47' W 100
Livermore, *Ky., U.S.* 37°29' N, 87°9' W 96
Livermore Falls, *Me., U.S.* 44°28' N, 70°12' W 104
Livermore, Mount, peak, *Tex., U.S.* 30°35' N, 104°14' W 92
Liverpool, *Can.* 44°1' N, 64°44' W 111
Liverpool, *N.Y., U.S.* 43°6' N, 76°14' W 110
Liverpool, *U.K.* 53°24' N, 2°59' W 162
Liverpool Bay 70°0' N, 130°43' W 98
Liverpool Land 70°41' N, 21°27' W 246
Livingston, *Ala., U.S.* 32°35' N, 88°12' W 103
Livingston, *Calif., U.S.* 37°23' N, 120°43' W 100
Lívingston, *Guatemala* 15°49' N, 88°49' W 115
Livingston, *Ill., U.S.* 38°58' N, 89°47' W 102
Livingston, *La., U.S.* 30°29' N, 90°46' W 103
Livingston, *Mont., U.S.* 45°39' N, 110°33' W 90
Livingston, *Tenn., U.S.* 36°22' N, 85°19' W 96
Livingston, *Tex., U.S.* 30°41' N, 94°56' W 103
Livingston Island, *Antarctica* 62°59' S, 60°12' W 134
Livingstone, *Zambia* 17°50' S, 25°50' E 224
Livingstone Lake, *Can.* 58°33' N, 108°4' W 108
Livingstone Memorial, site, *Zambia* 12°21' S, 30°13' E 224
Livingstonia, *Malawi* 10°38' S, 34°8' E 224
Livno, *Bosn. and Herzg.* 43°49' N, 17°1' E 168
Livny, *Russ.* 52°24' N, 37°32' E 158
Livo, *Fin.* 65°32' N, 26°56' E 152
Livonia, *Mich., U.S.* 42°22' N, 83°23' W 102
Livorno (Leghorn), *It.* 43°33' N, 10°19' E 156
Livramento do Brumado, *Braz.* 13°38' S, 41°53' W 138
Livron, *Fr.* 44°46' N, 4°50' E 150
Liwale, *Tanzania* 9°46' S, 38°0' E 224
Liwonde, *Malawi* 15°7' S, 35°13' E 224
Lixian, *China* 29°40' N, 111°44' E 198
Lixian, *China* 34°13' N, 105°6' E 198
Lizard Head Peak, *Wyo., U.S.* 42°47' N, 109°17' W 90
Lizard Islands, *Lake Superior* 47°8' N, 85°17' W 94
Lizard Point, *U.K.* 49°44' N, 5°17' W 150
Lizarra see Estella, *Sp.* 42°39' N, 2°2' W 164
Ljig, *Serb.* 44°13' N, 20°14' E 168
Ljubija, *Bosn. and Herzg.* 44°56' N, 16°36' E 168
Ljubinje, *Bosn. and Herzg.* 42°57' N, 18°5' E 168
Ljubiš, *Serb.* 43°36' N, 19°51' E 168
Ljubišnja, peak, *Mont.* 43°18' N, 19°3' E 168
Ljubljana, *Slov.* 46°2' N, 14°21' E 156
Ljuboten, peak, *Kos.* 42°11' N, 21°4' E 168
Ljubovija, *Serb.* 44°12' N, 19°22' E 168
Ljubuski, *Bosn. and Herzg.* 43°11' N, 17°33' E 168
Ljugarn, *Sw.* 57°20' N, 18°40' E 166
Ljungby, *Nor.* 56°50' N, 13°54' E 152
Ljusdal, *Nor.* 61°49' N, 16°6' E 152
Ljusterö, island, *Sw.* 59°31' N, 18°45' E 166
Ljutomer, *Slov.* 46°31' N, 16°10' E 168
Llaima, Volcán, peak, *Chile* 38°44' S, 71°52' W 134
Llajta Mauca, *Arg.* 28°11' S, 63°6' W 139
Llallagua, *Bol.* 18°25' S, 66°42' W 137
Llanbedr, *U.K.* 52°48' N, 4°5' W 162
Llanbister, *U.K.* 52°20' N, 3°18' W 162
Llançà, *Sp.* 42°21' N, 3°9' E 164
Llancanelo, Laguna, lake, *Arg.* 35°37' S, 70°31' W 134
Llanddewi Brefi, *U.K.* 52°10' N, 3°57' W 162
Llandeilo, *U.K.* 51°53' N, 3°59' W 162
Llandovery, *U.K.* 51°59' N, 3°47' W 162
Llandrindod Wells, *U.K.* 52°14' N, 3°23' W 162
Llanelltyd, *U.K.* 52°45' N, 3°54' W 162
Llanenddwyn, *U.K.* 52°47' N, 4°5' W 162
Llanfair Caereinion, *U.K.* 52°38' N, 3°19' W 162
Llanfyllin, *U.K.* 52°45' N, 3°15' W 162
Llangadog, *U.K.* 51°55' N, 3°52' W 162
Llanganates National Park, *Ecua.* 1°28' S, 78°12' W 136
Llangefni, *U.K.* 53°15' N, 4°18' W 162
Llangeitho, *U.K.* 52°12' N, 4°1' W 162
Llangollen, *U.K.* 52°57' N, 3°10' W 162
Llangorse, *U.K.* 51°56' N, 3°15' W 162
Llanidan, *U.K.* 53°13' N, 4°13' W 162
Llanidloes, *U.K.* 52°25' N, 3°32' W 162
Llanilar, *U.K.* 52°20' N, 4°1' W 162
Llanllugan, *U.K.* 52°36' N, 3°23' W 162
Llano, *Tex., U.S.* 30°44' N, 98°40' W 92
Llanrwst, *U.K.* 53°8' N, 3°46' W 162
Llanuwchllyn, *U.K.* 52°51' N, 3°40' W 162
Llanwrtyd Wells, *U.K.* 52°6' N, 3°38' W 162
Llavorsí, *Sp.* 42°29' N, 1°10' E 164
Lleida, *Sp.* 41°37' N, 0°37' E 164
Llera, *Mex.* 23°18' N, 99°1' W 114
Llerena, *Sp.* 38°14' N, 6°2' W 164
Lleyn Peninsula, *U.K.* 52°55' N, 4°14' W 162
Llica, *Bol.* 19°52' S, 68°16' W 137
Llimiana, *Sp.* 42°5' N, 0°54' E 164
łapy, *Pol.* 53°0' N, 23°0' E 152
łaskarzew, *Pol.* 52°0' N, 22°0' E 152
łeba, *Pol.* 55°0' N, 18°0' E 152
łochów, *Pol.* 52°0' N, 22°0' E 152
łódź, *Pol.* 52°0' N, 20°0' E 152
łodźkie, adm. division, *Pol.* 51°0' N, 19°0' E 152
łomża, *Pol.* 53°0' N, 22°0' E 152
łoniów, *Pol.* 52°0' N, 22°0' E 152
łowicz, *Pol.* 52°0' N, 20°0' E 152
łuków, *Pol.* 52°0' N, 22°0' E 152
Llodio, *Sp.* 43°7' N, 2°59' W 164
Lloret de Mar, *Sp.* 41°42' N, 2°51' E 164
Llorona, Punta, *C.R.* 8°41' N, 84°26' W 115
Lloyd, Cape 60°36' S, 55°0' W 248
Lloyd George, Mount, peak, *Can.* 57°52' N, 125°10' W 108
Lloyd Lake, *Can.* 57°20' N, 109°27' W 108
Lloydminster, *Can.* 53°16' N, 109°59' W 108
Llullaillaco National Park, *Chile* 24°58' S, 69°4' W 122
Llullaillaco, Volcán, peak, *Chile* 24°46' S, 68°42' W 132
Lluta, *Peru* 16°4' S, 72°3' W 137
Llyswen, *U.K.* 52°1' N, 3°16' W 162
Lo, river, *China* 22°54' N, 104°33' E 202
Loa, *Utah, U.S.* 38°23' N, 111°38' W 90
Loa, Mauna, peak, *Hawai'i, U.S.* 19°28' N, 155°40' W 99
Loa, river, *Chile* 22°37' S, 69°18' W 137
Loanda, *Braz.* 22°58' S, 53°14' W 138
Loange, river, *Dem. Rep. of the Congo* 4°20' S, 20°8' E 218
Loango, *Congo* 4°42' S, 11°47' E 218
Loano, *It.* 44°7' N, 8°16' E 167
Loarre, *Sp.* 42°18' N, 0°37' E 164
Lobamba, *Swaziland* 26°28' S, 31°3' E 227
Loban, *Russ.* 65°43' N, 45°28' E 154
Lobatse, *Botswana* 25°15' S, 25°35' E 227
Lobería, *Arg.* 42°7' S, 63°48' W 134
Lobería, *Arg.* 38°11' S, 58°47' W 139
Lobito, *Angola* 12°26' S, 13°32' E 220
Lobitos, *Peru* 4°21' S, 81°17' W 130
Lobo, river, *Côte d'Ivoire* 6°27' N, 6°42' W 222
Lobok, *Belarus* 55°51' N, 30°2' E 166
Lobos, *Arg.* 35°9' S, 59°8' W 139
Lobos, Cabo, *Chile* 19°1' S, 70°43' W 137
Lobos, Cabo, *Mex.* 29°43' N, 113°4' W 92
Lobos, Cayo 18°17' N, 87°26' W 115
Lobos de Afuera, Islas, islands, *South Pacific Ocean* 7°20' S, 81°52' W 130
Lobos de Tierra, Isla, island, *Peru* 6°23' S, 82°43' W 130
Lobos, Estero de 27°17' N, 111°33' W 80
Lobos, Isla, island, *Mex.* 27°26' N, 111°21' W 112
Lobos, Point, *U.S.* 36°22' N, 122°16' W 92
Lobos, Punta, *Chile* 21°13' S, 70°29' W 137
Lobster Point, *Can.* 51°13' N, 55°36' W 111
Lobva, *Russ.* 59°14' N, 60°31' E 154
Loc Binh, *Vietnam* 21°46' N, 106°55' E 198
Loc Ninh, *Vietnam* 11°50' N, 106°36' E 202
Locarno, *Switz.* 46°11' N, 8°46' E 167
Loch Lomond and The Trossachs Nat. Park, *U.K.* 56°10' N, 4°40' W 150
Lochem, *Neth.* 52°8' N, 6°24' E 163
Lochinvar National Park, *Zambia* 16°3' S, 26°49' E 224
Łochów, *Pol.* 52°31' N, 21°42' E 152
Lock Haven, *Pa., U.S.* 41°7' N, 77°27' W 94
Lockbourne, *Ohio, U.S.* 39°47' N, 82°58' W 102
Locke Mills, *Me., U.S.* 44°24' N, 70°43' W 104
Lockeford, *Calif., U.S.* 38°9' N, 121°10' W 100
Lockhart, *Ala., U.S.* 31°1' N, 86°21' W 96
Lockhart, *Tex., U.S.* 29°51' N, 97°40' W 92
Lockney, *Tex., U.S.* 34°5' N, 101°26' W 92
Lockport, *Ill., U.S.* 41°35' N, 88°3' W 102
Lockport, *La., U.S.* 29°37' N, 90°32' W 103
Lockwood, *Calif., U.S.* 35°56' N, 121°6' W 100
Loco Mountain, peak, *Mont., U.S.* 46°11' N, 110°24' W 90
Locri, *It.* 38°15' N, 16°15' E 156
Locumba, *Peru* 17°37' S, 70°47' W 137
Lod (Lydda), *Israel* 31°56' N, 34°53' E 194
Loda, *Ill., U.S.* 40°31' N, 88°4' W 102
Lodalskåpa, peak, *Nor.* 61°46' N, 7°4' E 152
Lodeyka, *Russ.* 60°41' N, 45°45' E 154
Lodeynoye Pole, *Russ.* 60°42' N, 33°34' E 154
Lodge Creek, river, *Can.* 49°32' N, 110°34' W 90
Lodge Grass, *Mont., U.S.* 45°17' N, 107°23' W 90
Lodge, Mount, peak, *Can.* 59°3' N, 137°34' W 108
Lodgepole, *Nebr., U.S.* 41°9' N, 102°40' W 92
Lodhran, *Pak.* 29°35' N, 71°38' E 186
Lodi, *Calif., U.S.* 38°7' N, 121°18' W 100
Lodi, *It.* 45°18' N, 9°29' E 167
Lodi, *Wis., U.S.* 43°19' N, 89°31' W 102
Lodja, *Dem. Rep. of the Congo* 3°31' S, 23°32' E 224
Lodore, Canyon of, *Colo., U.S.* 40°18' N, 109°1' W 90
Lodosa, *Sp.* 42°25' N, 2°5' W 164
Lodwar, *Kenya* 3°4' N, 35°35' E 224
Łódź, *Pol.* 51°44' N, 19°27' E 152
Łodzkie, adm. division, *Pol.* 51°30' N, 18°23' E 152
Loei, *Thai.* 17°32' N, 101°32' E 202
Loelli, spring, *Sudan* 5°6' N, 34°41' E 224
Loen, *Nor.* 61°53' N, 6°51' E 152
Loengo, *Dem. Rep. of the Congo* 4°50' S, 26°30' E 224
Loera, river, *Mex.* 26°39' N, 107°32' W 80
Loeriesfontein, *S. Af.* 30°57' S, 19°27' E 227
Lofgren Peninsula 72°44' S, 91°41' W 248
Lofoten, islands, *Norwegian Sea* 67°57' N, 12°59' E 152
Lofthouse, *U.K.* 54°8' N, 1°49' W 162
Loftus, *U.K.* 54°33' N, 0°53' E 162
Log, *Russ.* 49°27' N, 43°49' E 158
Log Lane Village, *Colo., U.S.* 40°15' N, 103°52' W 90
Loga, *Niger* 13°33' N, 3°21' E 222
Logan, *Iowa, U.S.* 41°38' N, 95°48' W 90
Logan, *Kans., U.S.* 39°39' N, 99°34' W 90
Logan, *N. Mex., U.S.* 35°21' N, 103°25' W 92
Logan, *Ohio, U.S.* 39°32' N, 82°24' W 102
Logan, *Utah, U.S.* 41°44' N, 111°48' W 82
Logan, Mount, peak, *Ariz., U.S.* 36°20' N, 113°16' W 92
Logan, Mount, peak, *Can.* 60°37' N, 140°32' W 98
Logan, Mount, peak, *Can.* 48°52' N, 66°44' W 111
Logan, Mount, peak, *Wash., U.S.* 48°31' N, 120°59' W 100
Logan Pass, *Mont., U.S.* 48°41' N, 113°42' W 90
Logandale, *Nev., U.S.* 36°35' N, 114°30' W 101
Logăneşti, *Mold.* 46°55' N, 28°32' E 158
Logansport, *Ind., U.S.* 40°44' N, 86°21' W 102
Logansport, *La., U.S.* 31°57' N, 94°1' W 103
Logashkino, *Russ.* 70°49' N, 153°44' E 173
Loge, river, *Angola* 7°44' S, 13°12' E 220
Logone Birni, *Cameroon* 11°46' N, 15°2' E 216
Logoniégué, *Burkina Faso* 9°54' N, 4°33' W 222
Logoualé, *Côte d'Ivoire* 7°3' N, 7°33' W 222
Logroño, *Sp.* 42°26' N, 2°27' W 164
Logrosán, *Sp.* 39°20' N, 5°30' W 164
Løgstør, *Den.* 56°56' N, 9°14' E 150
Loharano, *Madagascar* 21°45' S, 48°9' E 220
Lohardaga, *India* 23°24' N, 84°41' E 197
Loharghat, *India* 25°57' N, 91°26' E 197
Loharu, *India* 28°26' N, 75°49' E 197
Lohatlha, *S. Af.* 28°3' S, 23°2' E 227
Lohikoski, *Fin.* 61°36' N, 28°42' E 166
Lohiniva, *Fin.* 67°9' N, 24°58' E 152
Lohja (Lojo), *Fin.* 60°14' N, 24°1' E 166
Lôho, *Côte d'Ivoire* 8°38' N, 5°9' W 222
Lohr, *Ger.* 49°59' N, 9°33' E 167
Lohusuu, *Est.* 58°55' N, 27°0' E 166
Loi Mwe, *Myanmar* 21°9' N, 99°46' E 202
Loi, Phou, peak, *Laos* 20°17' N, 103°5' E 202
Loiano, *It.* 44°16' N, 11°18' E 167
Loikaw, *Myanmar* 19°42' N, 97°10' E 202
Loile, river, *Dem. Rep. of the Congo* 1°11' S, 20°17' E 218
Loimaa, *Fin.* 60°49' N, 23°1' E 166
Loir, river, *Fr.* 48°13' N, 1°17' E 163
Loire, river, *Fr.* 46°26' N, 3°56' E 165
Loire, river, *Fr.* 46°48' N, 1°52' W 142
Loire, river, *Fr.* 45°9' N, 3°58' E 165
Loire, river, *Fr.* 48°16' N, 2°37' E 165
Loja, *Ecua.* 4°1' S, 79°13' W 130
Loja, *Sp.* 37°9' N, 4°9' W 164
Lojo see Lohja, *Fin.* 60°14' N, 24°1' E 166
Loka, *Sudan* 4°15' N, 30°57' E 224
Lokachi, *Ukr.* 50°44' N, 24°38' E 152
Lokalahti, *Fin.* 60°40' N, 21°28' E 166
Lokandu, *Dem. Rep. of the Congo* 2°36' S, 25°45' E 224
Lokchim, river, *Russ.* 61°36' N, 51°43' E 154
Lokeren, *Belg.* 51°5' N, 4°0' E 163
Lokhwabe, *Botswana* 24°9' S, 21°50' E 227
Lokichokio, *Kenya* 4°13' N, 34°20' E 224
Lokila, *Sudan* 4°38' N, 32°26' E 224
Lokitaung, *Kenya* 4°12' N, 35°45' E 224
Lokka, *Fin.* 67°47' N, 27°40' E 152
Løkken, *Nor.* 63°5' N, 9°42' E 152
Loknya, *Russ.* 56°50' N, 30°10' E 166
Lokoja, *Nig.* 7°45' N, 6°41' E 222
Lokolama, *Dem. Rep. of the Congo* 2°36' S, 19°51' E 218
Lokolenge, *Dem. Rep. of the Congo* 1°9' N, 22°36' E 218
Lokomo, *Cameroon* 2°52' N, 15°17' E 218
Lököshäza, *Hung.* 46°25' N, 21°14' E 168
Lokossa, *Benin* 6°39' N, 1°40' E 222
Loks Land, island, *Can.* 62°9' N, 64°30' W 106
Loksa, *Est.* 59°33' N, 25°45' E 166
Lokutu, *Dem. Rep. of the Congo* 1°5' N, 23°36' E 224
Lokwakangole, *Kenya* 3°26' N, 35°50' E 224
Lol, river, *Sudan* 8°56' N, 26°15' E 224
Lol, river, *Sudan* 8°48' N, 28°36' E 224
Loleta, *Calif., U.S.* 40°38' N, 124°14' W 90
Lolgorien, *Kenya* 1°14' S, 34°48' E 224
Lolimi, *Sudan* 4°34' N, 34°2' E 224
Loliondo, *Tanzania* 2°3' S, 35°39' E 224
Lollar, *Ger.* 50°38' N, 8°43' E 167
Lolo, Mount, peak, *Can.* 50°48' N, 120°12' W 90
Lolo Pass, *Idaho, U.S.* 46°37' N, 114°36' W 90
Lolobau, island, *P.N.G.* 4°51' S, 150°14' E 192
Lolowau, *Indonesia* 0°57' N, 97°33' E 196
Lom, *Bulg.* 43°49' N, 23°13' E 168
Lom, *Nor.* 61°50' N, 8°31' E 152
Lom Sak, *Thai.* 16°47' N, 101°7' E 202
Loma Mountains, *Sierra Leone* 9°5' N, 11°27' W 222
Lomami, river, *Dem. Rep. of the Congo* 0°47' N, 24°17' E 224
Lomami, river, *Dem. Rep. of the Congo* 4°35' S, 24°49' E 224
Lomami, river, *Dem. Rep. of the Congo* 7°19' S, 25°26' E 224
Lomas del Real, *Mex.* 22°30' N, 97°55' W 114
Lombarda, Serra, *Braz.* 3°17' N, 51°55' W 130
Lombardy, adm. division, *It.* 45°33' N, 9°3' E 167
Lombez, *Fr.* 43°28' N, 0°52' E 164
Lomblen, island, *Indonesia* 8°58' S, 123°36' E 192
Lombok, island, *Indonesia* 9°26' S, 115°17' E 192
Lomé, *Togo* 6°10' N, 1°7' E 222
Lomela, *Dem. Rep. of the Congo* 2°19' S, 23°17' E 218
Lomela, river, *Dem. Rep. of the Congo* 0°35' N, 21°5' E 218
Lometa, *Tex., U.S.* 31°12' N, 98°24' W 92
Lomié, *Cameroon* 3°21' N, 13°37' E 218
Lomira, *Wis., U.S.* 43°35' N, 88°27' W 102
Lommel, *Belg.* 51°13' N, 5°18' E 167
Lomond, Ben, peak, *U.K.* 56°10' N, 4°44' W 150
Lomonosov, *Russ.* 59°51' N, 29°42' E 166
Lomonosov Ridge, *Arctic Ocean* 88°59' N, 116°17' W 255
Lomovoye, *Russ.* 64°2' N, 40°38' E 154
Lomphat, *Cambodia* 13°39' N, 106°57' E 202
Lompoc, *Calif., U.S.* 34°39' N, 120°28' W 100
Łomża, *Pol.* 53°10' N, 22°5' E 152
Lon, Hon, island, *Vietnam* 12°32' N, 109°26' E 202
Lonauli, *India* 18°43' N, 73°24' E 188
Londinières, *Fr.* 49°50' N, 1°24' E 163
London, *Can.* 42°59' N, 81°13' W 102
London, *Ohio, U.S.* 39°52' N, 83°27' W 102
London, *U.K.* 51°31' N, 0°9' W 162
Londonderry, *U.K.* 54°58' N, 7°16' W 143
Londonderry, *Vt., U.S.* 43°13' N, 72°49' W 104
Londonderry, Isla, island, *Chile* 55°33' S, 72°31' W 248
Londres, *Arg.* 27°43' S, 67°9' W 132
Londrina, *Braz.* 23°18' S, 51°11' W 138
Lone Pine, *Calif., U.S.* 36°36' N, 118°5' W 101
Lone Star, *Tex., U.S.* 32°55' N, 94°44' W 103
Lonely Bay 61°39' N, 115°31' W 108
Lonepine, *Mont., U.S.* 47°40' N, 114°40' W 90
Long Barn, *Calif., U.S.* 38°5' N, 120°9' W 100
Long Bay Cays, islands, *North Atlantic Ocean* 23°49' N, 77°0' W 116
Long Beach, *Calif., U.S.* 33°46' N, 118°12' W 101
Long Beach, *Miss., U.S.* 30°20' N, 89°10' W 103
Long Beach, *N.Y., U.S.* 40°35' N, 73°40' W 104
Long Beach, *Wash., U.S.* 46°20' N, 124°3' W 100
Long Branch, *N.J., U.S.* 40°18' N, 74°1' W 94
Long Branch, *Tex., U.S.* 32°4' N, 94°35' W 103
Long Cay (Fortune Island), *Bahamas* 22°35' N, 76°5' W 116
Long Creek, *Oreg., U.S.* 44°41' N, 119°7' W 90
Long Creek, river, *North America* 49°3' N, 103°40' W 90
Long Eaton, *U.K.* 52°53' N, 1°17' W 162
Long Island, *Austral.* 22°4' S, 148°43' E 230
Long Island, *Bahamas* 23°4' N, 74°52' W 116
Long Island, *Can.* 54°23' N, 81°10' W 106
Long Island, *Can.* 44°20' N, 67°13' W 80
Long Island, *N.Y., U.S.* 40°58' N, 73°14' W 104
Long Island, *P.N.G.* 5°35' S, 146°13' E 192
Long Island Sound 41°5' N, 73°6' W 104
Long Key, island, *Fla., U.S.* 24°47' N, 80°49' W 105
Long Lake, *Can.* 49°20' N, 87°26' W 110
Long Meg, ruin(s), *U.K.* 54°43' N, 2°42' W 162
Long Melford, *U.K.* 52°4' N, 0°43' E 162
Long Point, *Can.* 42°30' N, 80°6' W 94
Long Point, *Can.* 54°13' N, 58°6' W 111
Long Point, *Can.* 48°45' N, 59°26' W 111
Long Point, *Can.* 53°2' N, 98°26' W 108
Long Pond, lake, *Mass., U.S.* 41°47' N, 71°5' W 104

Long Prairie, *Minn., U.S.* 45°57′ N, 94°52′ W 90
Long Sutton, *U.K.* 52°46′ N, 0°7′ E 162
Long Xuyen, *Vietnam* 10°19′ N, 105°18′ E 192
Longa, *Angola* 14°43′ S, 18°30′ E 220
Longa, Proliv 70°18′ N, 174°28′ E 160
Long'an, *China* 23°7′ N, 107°39′ E 198
Longares, *Sp.* 41°23′ N, 1°10′ W 164
Longarone, *It.* 46°16′ N, 12°17′ E 167
Longboat Key, *Fla., U.S.* 27°26′ N, 82°40′ W 105
Longbranch, *Wash., U.S.* 47°11′ N, 122°46′ W 100
Longchuan, *China* 24°4′ N, 115°17′ E 198
Longde, *China* 35°37′ N, 106°6′ E 198
Longfellow Mountains, *Me., U.S.* 44°27′ N, 71°10′ W 104
Longford, *Ire.* 53°43′ N, 7°49′ W 150
Longhai, *China* 24°19′ N, 117°51′ E 198
Longhua, *China* 41°21′ N, 117°47′ E 198
Longhurst, *N.C., U.S.* 36°25′ N, 78°59′ W 96
Longhurst, Mount, peak, *Antarctica* 79°19′ S, 158°10′ E 248
Longjiang, *China* 47°23′ N, 123°13′ E 198
Longjing see Yanji, *China* 42°46′ N, 129°24′ E 200
Longju, *India* 28°38′ N, 93°31′ E 188
Longkou, *China* 37°42′ N, 120°25′ E 198
Longlac, *Can.* 49°47′ N, 86°32′ W 110
Longleaf, *La., U.S.* 30°59′ N, 92°34′ W 103
Longli, *China* 26°30′ N, 106°57′ E 198
Longlin, *China* 24°47′ N, 105°19′ E 198
Longmeadow, *Mass., U.S.* 42°3′ N, 72°35′ W 104
Longmen, *China* 23°43′ N, 114°15′ E 198
Longmont, *Colo., U.S.* 40°10′ N, 105°2′ W 106
Longnan, *China* 24°49′ N, 114°49′ E 198
Longobucco, *It.* 39°27′ N, 16°37′ E 156
Longonot, peak, *Kenya* 0°54′ N, 36°22′ E 224
Longquan, *China* 28°6′ N, 119°7′ E 198
Longrais, Lac, lake, *Can.* 54°10′ N, 68°48′ W 111
Longs Peak, *Colo., U.S.* 40°14′ N, 105°41′ W 90
Longshan, *China* 29°28′ N, 109°28′ E 198
Longstreet, *La., U.S.* 32°4′ N, 93°57′ W 103
Longtam, *Sudan* 8°55′ N, 30°44′ E 224
Longueuil, *Can.* 45°31′ N, 73°30′ W 94
Longuyon, *Fr.* 49°26′ N, 5°35′ E 163
Longview, *N.C., U.S.* 35°44′ N, 81°23′ W 96
Longview, *Tex., U.S.* 32°29′ N, 94°44′ W 103
Longview, *Wash., U.S.* 46°7′ N, 122°57′ W 100
Longville, *La., U.S.* 30°35′ N, 93°15′ W 103
Longwy, *Fr.* 49°31′ N, 5°45′ E 163
Longxi, *China* 35°1′ N, 104°36′ E 198
Longxian, *China* 34°53′ N, 106°48′ E 198
Longyan, *China* 25°4′ N, 117°0′ E 198
Longyearbyen, *Nor.* 78°10′ N, 15°34′ E 160
Long"yugan, *Russ.* 64°54′ N, 71°25′ E 169
Longzhen, *China* 48°41′ N, 126°49′ E 198
Longzhou, *China* 22°23′ N, 106°48′ E 198
Löningen, *Ger.* 52°44′ N, 7°45′ E 163
Łoniów, *Pol.* 50°32′ N, 21°31′ E 152
Lonjica, *Croatia* 45°50′ N, 16°20′ E 168
Lonkala, *Dem. Rep. of the Congo* 4°38′ S, 23°15′ E 218
Lonquimay, *Arg.* 36°30′ S, 63°37′ W 139
Lønsdal, *Nor.* 66°44′ N, 15°25′ E 152
Lons-le-Saunier, *Fr.* 46°40′ N, 5°32′ E 150
Loogootee, *Ind., U.S.* 38°40′ N, 86°54′ W 102
Lookeba, *Okla., U.S.* 35°20′ N, 98°22′ W 92
Lookout, Cape, *Alas., U.S.* 54°54′ N, 133°53′ W 108
Lookout, Cape, *Antarctica* 62°6′ S, 55°18′ W 248
Lookout, Cape, *N.C., U.S.* 34°30′ N, 76°32′ W 96
Lookout, Cape, *U.S.* 45°8′ N, 124°26′ W 90
Lookout Mountain, peak, *Can.* 53°35′ N, 64°13′ W 111
Lookout Mountain, peak, *N. Mex., U.S.* 35°12′ N, 108°21′ W 92
Lookout Mountain, peak, *Oreg., U.S.* 45°19′ N, 121°37′ W 90
Lookout, Point, *Mich., U.S.* 44°3′ N, 83°35′ W 102
Loolmalasin, peak, *Tanzania* 3°3′ S, 35°45′ E 224
Loon Lake, *Can.* 54°2′ N, 109°9′ W 108
Loon Lake, *N.Y., U.S.* 44°32′ N, 74°4′ W 104
Loon, Pointe, *Can.* 51°52′ N, 78°39′ W 110
Loon, river, *Can.* 56°33′ N, 115°24′ W 108
Lop, *China* 37°6′ N, 80°6′ E 184
Lop Buri, *Thai.* 14°49′ N, 100°36′ E 202
Lop Nur, lake, *China* 40°35′ N, 89°42′ E 188
Lopare, *Bosn. and Herzg.* 44°38′ N, 18°48′ E 168
Lopatin, *Russ.* 43°50′ N, 47°40′ E 195
Lopatino, *Russ.* 52°36′ N, 45°49′ E 158
Lopatka, Mys, *Russ.* 51°8′ N, 156°37′ E 160
Lopatyn, *Ukr.* 50°11′ N, 24°48′ E 152
Lope Reserve, *Gabon* 0°38′ N, 11°20′ E 206
Lopera, *Sp.* 37°57′ N, 4°13′ W 164
Loperot, *Kenya* 2°17′ N, 35°51′ E 224
Lopez, *Wash., U.S.* 48°30′ N, 122°54′ W 100
López Collada, *Mex.* 31°40′ N, 113°59′ W 92
Lopez Lake, *Calif., U.S.* 35°12′ N, 120°34′ W 101
Lopez Point, *Calif., U.S.* 35°57′ N, 121°42′ W 100
Lopi, *Congo* 2°55′ N, 16°39′ E 218
Loppa, *Nor.* 70°19′ N, 21°26′ E 152
Lopphavet 70°9′ N, 18°9′ E 160
Loppi, *Fin.* 60°41′ N, 24°24′ E 166
Lopshen'ga, *Russ.* 64°59′ N, 37°25′ E 154
Lopud, island, *Croatia* 42°37′ N, 17°49′ E 168
Lopydino, *Russ.* 61°8′ N, 52°8′ E 154
Lora del Río, *Sp.* 37°39′ N, 5°33′ W 164
Lorain, *Ohio, U.S.* 41°26′ N, 82°11′ W 102
Loralai, *Pak.* 30°21′ N, 68°39′ E 186
Lorca, *Sp.* 37°40′ N, 1°42′ W 164
Lorch, *Ger.* 50°2′ N, 7°48′ E 167
Lord Howe Island, *Austral.* 31°31′ S, 156°53′ E 230
Lord Howe Rise, *Tasman Sea* 33°48′ S, 163°25′ E 252
Lord Loughborough, island, *Myanmar* 10°28′ N, 96°37′ E 202
Lord Mayor Bay 69°41′ N, 94°10′ W 106
Lord, river, *Can.* 50°52′ N, 123°36′ W 90
Lordsburg, *N. Mex., U.S.* 32°21′ N, 108°42′ W 92
Lore Lindu National Park, *Indonesia* 1°40′ S, 119°48′ E 238
Loreauville, *La., U.S.* 30°2′ N, 91°45′ W 103
Lorena, *Braz.* 22°46′ S, 45°6′ W 138
Lorengau, *P.N.G.* 2°6′ S, 147°14′ E 192
Lorenzo, *Idaho, U.S.* 43°43′ N, 111°53′ W 90
Lorenzo, *Tex., U.S.* 33°38′ N, 101°32′ W 92
Lorenzo Geyres, *Uru.* 32°2′ S, 57°51′ W 139
Loreo, *It.* 45°3′ N, 12°10′ E 167
Loreto, *Bol.* 15°16′ S, 64°39′ W 137
Loreto, *Braz.* 7°5′ S, 45°9′ W 132
Loreto, *Ecua.* 0°44′ N, 77°21′ W 136
Loreto, *Mex.* 22°16′ N, 101°58′ W 114
Loreto, *Philippines* 10°22′ N, 125°35′ E 203
Loreto, adm. division, *Peru* 3°3′ S, 74°42′ W 136
Loretto, *Tenn., U.S.* 35°3′ N, 87°26′ W 96
Lorian Swamp, marsh, *Kenya* 0°52′ N, 39°6′ E 224
Lorica, *Col.* 9°14′ N, 75°50′ W 136
Lőrinci, *Hung.* 47°44′ N, 19°41′ E 168
Loriol, *Fr.* 44°45′ N, 4°49′ E 150
Loris, *S.C., U.S.* 34°3′ N, 78°54′ W 96
Loriu Plateau, *Kenya* 1°51′ N, 36°13′ E 224
Lorman, *Miss., U.S.* 31°48′ N, 91°3′ W 103
Lormi, *India* 22°17′ N, 81°40′ E 197
Lornel, Pointe de, *Fr.* 50°34′ N, 1°24′ E 163
Loro, *Col.* 2°11′ N, 69°33′ W 136
Lorraine, adm. division, *Fr.* 48°37′ N, 5°1′ E 150
Lorraine, region, *Fr.* 49°50′ N, 4°47′ E 167
Lorukumu, *Kenya* 2°50′ N, 35°12′ E 224
Lorup, *Ger.* 52°55′ N, 7°38′ E 163
Los, *Nor.* 61°43′ N, 15°8′ E 152
Los Alamos, *Calif., U.S.* 34°44′ N, 120°18′ W 100
Los Alamos, *N. Mex., U.S.* 35°52′ N, 106°19′ W 92
Los Alerces National Park, *Arg.* 42°54′ S, 72°10′ W 122
Los Altos, *Calif., U.S.* 37°21′ N, 122°9′ W 100
Los Amores, *Arg.* 28°6′ S, 60°0′ W 139
Los Angeles, *Calif., U.S.* 34°3′ N, 118°16′ W 101
Los Ángeles, *Chile* 37°28′ S, 72°22′ W 134
Los Banos, *Calif., U.S.* 37°3′ N, 120°52′ W 100
Los Barrios, *Sp.* 36°11′ N, 5°30′ W 164
Los Blancos, *Arg.* 23°34′ S, 62°38′ W 132
Los Dolores, *Sp.* 37°38′ N, 1°1′ W 150
Los Frentones, *Arg.* 26°24′ S, 61°27′ W 139
Los Glaciares National Park, *Arg.* 50°6′ S, 73°33′ W 122
Los Hermanos, islands, *Caribbean Sea* 11°55′ N, 64°25′ W 116
Los, Îles de, islands, *North Atlantic Ocean* 9°5′ N, 13°56′ W 222
Los Juríes, *Arg.* 28°27′ S, 62°7′ W 139
Los Katios National Park, *Col.* 7°35′ N, 77°6′ W 136
Los Lagos, adm. division, *Chile* 41°7′ S, 73°59′ W 134
Los Lavaderos, *Mex.* 23°27′ N, 98°3′ W 114
Los Loros, *Chile* 27°51′ S, 70°10′ W 132
Los Mármoles National Park, *Mex.* 20°47′ N, 99°35′ W 72
Los Mochis, *Mex.* 25°45′ N, 109°0′ W 112
Los Monjes, Islas, islands, *Caribbean Sea* 12°0′ N, 71°6′ W 116
Los Monos, ruin(s), *Mex.* 18°9′ N, 100°30′ W 114
Los Ojos, *N. Mex., U.S.* 36°43′ N, 106°34′ W 92
Los Olivos, *Calif., U.S.* 34°40′ N, 120°8′ W 100
Los Organos, *Mex.* 23°43′ N, 103°51′ W 114
Los Osos, *Calif., U.S.* 35°18′ N, 120°51′ W 100
Los Palacios, *Cuba* 22°35′ N, 83°15′ W 116
Los Pirpintos, *Arg.* 26°10′ S, 62°4′ W 139
Los Remedios, *Mex.* 24°34′ N, 106°25′ W 114
Los Remedios National Park, *Mex.* 19°28′ N, 99°23′ W 112
Los Reyes, *Mex.* 19°34′ N, 102°29′ W 114
Los Reyes Islands, *South Pacific Ocean* 1°51′ S, 147°45′ E 192
Los Ríos, adm. division, *Chile* 40°14′ S, 72°40′ W 134
Los Roques, Islas, islands, *Caribbean Sea* 12°4′ N, 66°32′ W 116
Los Santos de Maimona, *Sp.* 38°27′ N, 6°24′ W 164
Los Telares, *Arg.* 29°1′ S, 63°27′ W 139
Los Teques, *Venez.* 10°21′ N, 67°3′ W 136
Los Vilos, *Chile* 31°55′ S, 71°31′ W 134
Los Yébenes, *Sp.* 39°34′ N, 3°53′ W 164
Losada, river, *Col.* 2°19′ N, 74°30′ W 136
Losap Atoll 6°37′ N, 153°19′ E 192
Losha, *Belarus* 53°26′ N, 27°23′ E 152
Łosice, *Pol.* 52°11′ N, 22°43′ E 158
Losinoborskaya, *Russ.* 58°24′ N, 89°23′ E 169
Łoski, *Pol.* 53°55′ N, 23°24′ E 166
Lost Hills, *Calif., U.S.* 35°36′ N, 119°42′ W 100
Lost River Range, *Idaho, U.S.* 44°20′ N, 113°53′ W 90
Lost Springs, *Wyo., U.S.* 42°45′ N, 104°57′ W 90
Lost Trail Pass, *Mont., U.S.* 45°39′ N, 113°57′ W 90
Lost World Caverns, site, *W. Va., U.S.* 37°49′ N, 80°32′ W 96
Lostmans River, *Fla., U.S.* 25°25′ N, 81°21′ W 105
Lot, river, *Fr.* 44°28′ N, 3°3′ E 165
Lota, *Chile* 37°8′ S, 73°9′ W 134
Lotagipi Swamp, marsh, *Kenya* 4°51′ N, 34°29′ E 224
Lothair, *S. Af.* 26°24′ S, 30°25′ E 227
Lotilla, river, *Sudan* 5°40′ N, 32°46′ E 224
Lotmozero, *Russ.* 68°7′ N, 30°11′ E 152
Loto, *Dem. Rep. of the Congo* 2°50′ S, 22°29′ E 218
Lott, *Tex., U.S.* 31°11′ N, 97°2′ W 96
Lotte, *Ger.* 52°16′ N, 7°56′ E 163
Lou, island, *P.N.G.* 2°42′ S, 146°53′ E 192
Louangphrabang, *Laos* 19°51′ N, 102°6′ E 202
Louann, *Ark., U.S.* 33°22′ N, 92°48′ W 103
Loubet Coast, *Antarctica* 67°22′ S, 66°45′ W 248
Loudon, *Malawi* 12°9′ S, 33°27′ E 224
Loudon, *N.H., U.S.* 43°17′ N, 71°28′ W 104
Loudonville, *Ohio, U.S.* 40°37′ N, 82°14′ W 102
Loue, river, *Fr.* 47°1′ N, 5°29′ E 165
Loufan, *China* 38°3′ N, 111°46′ E 198
Louga, *Côte d'Ivoire* 5°4′ N, 6°14′ W 222
Louga, *Senegal* 15°37′ N, 16°14′ W 222
Louge, *Arg.* 36°54′ S, 61°39′ W 139
Loughborough, *U.K.* 52°46′ N, 1°13′ W 162
Lougheed Island, *Can.* 76°50′ N, 107°36′ W 106
Louin, *Miss., U.S.* 32°3′ N, 89°16′ W 103
Louis Trichardt (Makhado), *S. Af.* 23°3′ S, 29°53′ E 227
Louis Ussing, Kap 67°2′ N, 33°5′ W 246
Louisa, *Ky., U.S.* 38°5′ N, 82°37′ W 94
Louisburg, *N.C., U.S.* 36°6′ N, 78°18′ W 96
Louise, *Miss., U.S.* 32°58′ N, 90°36′ W 103
Louise Falls, *Can.* 60°15′ N, 116°34′ W 108
Louisiade Archipelago, islands, *Solomon Sea* 12°43′ S, 154°40′ E 238
Louisiade Archipelago, islands, *Solomon Sea* 12°7′ S, 149°11′ E 192
Louisiana, *Mo., U.S.* 39°26′ N, 91°4′ W 94
Louisiana, adm. division, *La., U.S.* 31°7′ N, 93°7′ W 103
Louisiana Point, *La., U.S.* 29°43′ N, 93°52′ W 103
Louisville, *Ill., U.S.* 38°45′ N, 88°30′ W 102
Louisville, *Ky., U.S.* 38°14′ N, 85°46′ W 94
Louisville, *Miss., U.S.* 33°6′ N, 89°3′ W 103
Louisville, *Ohio, U.S.* 40°49′ N, 81°16′ W 102
Louisville Ridge, *South Pacific Ocean* 31°0′ S, 172°30′ W 252
Louis-Xiv, Pointe, *Can.* 54°27′ N, 79°40′ W 106
Loukhi, *Russ.* 66°4′ N, 33°0′ E 152
Loukouo, *Congo* 3°37′ S, 14°39′ E 218
Loulan Yiji, ruin(s), *China* 40°25′ N, 89°43′ E 188
Loulay, *Fr.* 46°2′ N, 0°32′ E 150
Loulouni, *Mali* 10°54′ N, 5°38′ W 222
Loum, *Cameroon* 4°41′ N, 9°46′ E 222
Lount Lake, *Can.* 50°9′ N, 94°40′ W 90
Louny, *Czech Rep.* 50°20′ N, 13°47′ E 152
Loup City, *Nebr., U.S.* 41°15′ N, 98°59′ W 90
Loup, river, *Nebr., U.S.* 41°14′ N, 97°58′ W 90
Lourdes, *Fr.* 43°6′ N, 4°237′ W 164
Lourdes-de-Blanc-Sablon, *Can.* 51°26′ N, 57°17′ W 106
Louth, *U.K.* 53°21′ N, 3°179′ W 162
Louviers, *Fr.* 49°12′ N, 1°9′ E 163
Louza, *Tun.* 35°3′ N, 10°58′ E 156
Lov Ozero, lake, *Russ.* 67°55′ N, 35°28′ E 152
Lövånger, *Nor.* 64°21′ N, 21°17′ E 152
Lovat', river, *Russ.* 57°29′ N, 31°34′ E 154
Lövberga, *Nor.* 63°57′ N, 15°49′ E 152
Lovea, *Cambodia* 13°21′ N, 102°55′ E 202
Lovech, *Bulg.* 43°8′ N, 24°42′ E 156
Lovech, adm. division, *Bulg.* 42°53′ N, 24°11′ E 156
Lovelady, *Tex., U.S.* 31°6′ N, 95°27′ W 103
Loveland Pass, *Colo., U.S.* 39°39′ N, 105°52′ W 90
Lovell, *Me., U.S.* 44°7′ N, 70°55′ W 104
Lovell, *Wyo., U.S.* 44°49′ N, 108°24′ W 90
Lovelock, *Nev., U.S.* 40°11′ N, 118°29′ W 90
Lovere, *It.* 45°49′ N, 10°4′ E 167
Loverna, *Can.* 51°40′ N, 109°58′ W 90
Loves Park, *Ill., U.S.* 42°18′ N, 89°4′ W 102
Loviisa see Lovisa, *Fin.* 60°26′ N, 26°12′ E 166
Loving, *N. Mex., U.S.* 32°17′ N, 104°6′ W 92
Lovington, *N. Mex., U.S.* 32°56′ N, 103°21′ W 92
Lovisa (Loviisa), *Fin.* 60°26′ N, 26°12′ E 166
Lovlya, *Russ.* 59°55′ N, 49°22′ E 154
Lövő, *Hung.* 47°29′ N, 16°47′ E 168
Lovozero, *Russ.* 68°0′ N, 35°2′ E 152
Lovran, *Croatia* 45°17′ N, 14°15′ E 156
Lovreč, *Croatia* 43°29′ N, 16°58′ E 168
Lovrin, *Rom.* 45°58′ N, 20°47′ E 168
Lóvua, *Angola* 11°38′ S, 23°41′ E 220
Lóvua, *Angola* 7°19′ S, 20°10′ E 218
Low Bush River, *Can.* 48°56′ N, 80°10′ W 94
Low, Cape, *Can.* 62°51′ N, 87°4′ W 106
Low Island, *Antarctica* 63°21′ S, 61°57′ W 134
Lowa, *Dem. Rep. of the Congo* 1°25′ S, 25°50′ E 224
Lowa, river, *Dem. Rep. of the Congo* 1°23′ S, 26°55′ E 224
Lowell, *Ind., U.S.* 41°16′ N, 87°25′ W 102
Lowell, *Mass., U.S.* 42°38′ N, 71°20′ W 104
Lowell, *Mich., U.S.* 42°56′ N, 85°21′ W 102
Lower Arrow Lake, *Can.* 49°29′ N, 118°56′ W 90
Lower Hutt, *N.Z.* 41°13′ S, 174°57′ E 240
Lower Matecumbe Key, island, *Fla., U.S.* 24°50′ N, 80°42′ W 105
Lower Post, *Can.* 59°57′ N, 128°27′ W 108
Lower Red Lake, *Minn., U.S.* 48°0′ N, 95°35′ W 94
Lower Saxony, adm. division, *Ger.* 51°47′ N, 9°27′ E 167
Lower Zambezi National Park, *Zambia* 15°25′ S, 28°48′ E 224
Lowestoft, *U.K.* 52°28′ N, 1°43′ E 163
Łowicz, *Pol.* 52°5′ N, 19°54′ E 152
Lowland, *N.C., U.S.* 35°18′ N, 76°36′ W 96
Lowry, *Minn., U.S.* 45°41′ N, 95°32′ W 90
Lowry, Îles, islands, *Indian Ocean* 12°35′ S, 49°42′ E 220
Lowville, *N.Y., U.S.* 43°47′ N, 75°30′ W 110
Loxley, *Ala., U.S.* 30°36′ N, 87°45′ W 103
Loxton, *S. Af.* 31°30′ S, 22°19′ E 227
Loya, river, *Dem. Rep. of the Congo* 8°475′ N, 27°45′ E 224
Loyal, Ben, peak, *U.K.* 58°23′ N, 4°33′ W 150
Loyall, *Ky., U.S.* 36°50′ N, 83°21′ W 96
Loyalty Islands 20°7′ S, 166°47′ E 238
Loyew, *Belarus* 51°55′ N, 30°53′ E 158
Loyola, Punta, *Arg.* 51°43′ S, 68°54′ W 134
Loyoro, *Uganda* 3°19′ N, 34°13′ E 224
Lozenets, *Bulg.* 42°12′ N, 27°48′ E 156
Loznica, *Serb.* 44°31′ N, 19°12′ E 168
Lozova, *Ukr.* 48°54′ N, 36°19′ E 158
Lozovik, *Serb.* 44°28′ N, 21°4′ E 168
Loz'va, river, *Russ.* 61°47′ N, 59°54′ E 154
Lü Tao, island, *Taiwan, China* 22°30′ N, 121°31′ E 198
Lua Dekere, river, *Dem. Rep. of the Congo* 3°53′ N, 19°30′ E 218
Lua, river, *Dem. Rep. of the Congo* 2°49′ N, 18°31′ E 218
Luabo, *Mozambique* 18°24′ S, 36°8′ E 224
Luacano, *Angola* 11°11′ S, 21°39′ E 220
Luaha-sibuha, *Indonesia* 0°30′ N, 98°27′ E 196
Luahiwa Petroglyphs, site, *Hawai'i, U.S.* 20°47′ N, 156°57′ W 99
Lualaba (Congo), river, *Dem. Rep. of the Congo* 5°35′ S, 27°7′ E 224
Luama, river, *Dem. Rep. of the Congo* 4°41′ S, 27°17′ E 224
Luambe National Park, *Zambia* 12°37′ S, 31°37′ E 224
Luampa, river, *Zambia* 15°16′ S, 24°38′ E 224
Lu'an, *China* 31°44′ N, 116°31′ E 198
Luan, river, *China* 41°27′ N, 117°5′ E 198
Luanda, *Angola* 8°54′ S, 13°3′ E 218
Luanda, adm. division, *Angola* 9°17′ S, 12°39′ E 218
Luando, *Angola* 11°43′ S, 18°33′ E 220
Luando Integral Nature Reserve, *Angola* 11°24′ S, 16°28′ E 220
Luang, Thale, lake, *Thai.* 7°24′ N, 99°51′ E 196
Luangundo, river, *Angola* 16°17′ S, 19°35′ E 220
Luangwa, *Zambia* 15°37′ S, 30°20′ E 224
Luangwa, river, *Zambia* 12°14′ S, 32°10′ E 224
Luanping, *China* 40°54′ N, 117°18′ E 198
Luanshya, *Zambia* 13°8′ S, 28°22′ E 224
Luanxian, *China* 39°46′ N, 118°41′ E 198
Luanza, *Dem. Rep. of the Congo* 8°42′ S, 28°39′ E 224
Luarca, *Sp.* 43°31′ N, 6°34′ W 150
Luashi, *Dem. Rep. of the Congo* 10°56′ S, 23°34′ E 224
Luau, *Angola* 10°44′ S, 22°14′ E 220
Lubaantun, ruin(s), *Belize* 16°15′ N, 89°7′ W 115
Lubamiti, *Dem. Rep. of the Congo* 2°32′ S, 17°46′ E 218
Lubāna, *Latv.* 56°53′ N, 26°42′ E 166
Lubānas Ezers, lake, *Latv.* 56°45′ N, 26°36′ E 166
Lubanda, *Dem. Rep. of the Congo* 5°13′ S, 26°38′ E 224
Lubango, *Angola* 14°57′ S, 13°28′ E 220
Lubao, *Dem. Rep. of the Congo* 5°20′ S, 25°43′ E 224
Lubba Gerih, spring, *Somalia* 10°21′ N, 44°38′ E 216
Lübben, *Ger.* 51°56′ N, 13°53′ E 152
Lubbock, *Tex., U.S.* 33°32′ N, 101°50′ W 92
Lubec, *Me., U.S.* 44°50′ N, 67°0′ W 94
Lübeck, *Ger.* 53°51′ N, 10°42′ E 152
Lubefu, *Dem. Rep. of the Congo* 4°44′ S, 24°24′ E 224
Lubelskie, adm. division, *Pol.* 51°2′ N, 21°49′ E 152
Lübenka, *Kaz.* 50°27′ N, 54°6′ E 158
Lubero, *Dem. Rep. of the Congo* 0°12′ N, 29°11′ E 224
Lubéron, Montagne du, *Fr.* 43°42′ N, 5°16′ E 165
Lubi, river, *Dem. Rep. of the Congo* 5°49′ S, 23°28′ E 224
Lubicon Lake, *Can.* 56°22′ N, 116°23′ W 108
Lubilash, river, *Dem. Rep. of the Congo* 8°21′ S, 24°7′ E 224
Lubine, Île, island, *U.K.* 6°46′ S, 70°20′ E 188
Lublin, *Pol.* 51°15′ N, 22°33′ E 152
Lubliniec, *Pol.* 50°40′ N, 18°41′ E 152
Lubnica, *Serb.* 43°51′ N, 22°12′ E 168
Lubny, *Ukr.* 50°1′ N, 32°56′ E 158
Lubongola, *Dem. Rep. of the Congo* 2°39′ S, 27°52′ E 218
Lubosalma, *Russ.* 63°4′ N, 31°45′ E 152
Lubuagan, *Philippines* 17°21′ N, 121°10′ E 203
Lubudi, *Dem. Rep. of the Congo* 9°58′ S, 25°58′ E 224
Lubudi, river, *Dem. Rep. of the Congo* 9°52′ S, 24°52′ E 224
Lubukbertubung, *Indonesia* 5°297′ N, 102°6′ E 196
Lubuksikaping, *Indonesia* 0°8′ N, 100°10′ E 196
Lubumbashi (Élisabethville), *Dem. Rep. of the Congo* 11°43′ S, 27°26′ E 224
Lubuskie, adm. division, *Pol.* 51°47′ N, 14°40′ E 152
Lubutu, *Dem. Rep. of the Congo* 0°45′ N, 26°32′ E 224
Lubwe, *Zambia* 11°5′ S, 29°34′ E 224
Luc, Pointe à, *Can.* 49°44′ N, 67°4′ W 111
Lucala, river, *Angola* 9°26′ S, 15°21′ E 220
Lucan, *Can.* 43°10′ N, 81°24′ W 102
Lucanas, *Peru* 14°39′ S, 74°15′ W 137
Lucania, Mount, peak, *Can.* 60°59′ N, 140°39′ W 98
Lucapa, *Angola* 8°40′ S, 20°57′ E 218
Lucas, *Kans., U.S.* 39°1′ N, 98°33′ W 90
Lucas do Rio Verde, *Braz.* 13°7′ S, 55°57′ W 130
Lucaya, *Bahamas* 26°31′ N, 78°39′ W 105
Lucca, *It.* 43°50′ N, 10°30′ E 167
Lucedale, *Miss., U.S.* 30°53′ N, 88°36′ W 103
Lucena, *Philippines* 13°56′ N, 121°36′ E 203
Lucena, *Sp.* 37°24′ N, 4°30′ W 164
Lucena del Cid, *Sp.* 40°8′ N, 0°17′ E 164
Lučenec, *Slovakia* 48°19′ N, 19°41′ E 152
Lucerne, *Can.* 52°51′ N, 118°33′ W 108
Lucerne Valley, *Calif., U.S.* 34°27′ N, 116°58′ W 101
Lucero, *Mex.* 30°48′ N, 106°31′ W 92
Luceville, *Can.* 48°30′ N, 68°21′ W 111
Lüchow, *Ger.* 52°58′ N, 11°9′ E 152
Luchuan, *China* 22°22′ N, 110°15′ E 198
Luchulingo, river, *Mozambique* 12°21′ S, 35°30′ E 224
Lüchun, *China* 23°1′ N, 102°16′ E 202
Lučice, *Croatia* 43°49′ N, 15°17′ E 156
Lucie, Lac, lake, *Can.* 50°22′ N, 78°55′ W 94
Lucie, river, *Suriname* 3°37′ N, 57°29′ W 130
Lucira, *Angola* 13°55′ S, 12°31′ E 220
Lucknow, *Can.* 43°57′ N, 81°31′ W 102
Lucknow, *India* 26°47′ N, 80°53′ E 197
Lucky Boy Pass, *Nev., U.S.* 38°26′ N, 118°47′ W 90
Luçon, *Fr.* 46°27′ N, 1°11′ W 150
Lucunga, *Angola* 6°51′ S, 14°35′ E 218
Lucusse, *Angola* 12°34′ S, 20°48′ E 220
Ludborough, *U.K.* 53°26′ N, 4°237′ W 162
Ludbreg, *Croatia* 46°15′ N, 16°36′ E 168
Lüdenscheid, *Ger.* 51°13′ N, 7°37′ E 167
Lüderitz, *Namibia* 26°41′ S, 15°12′ E 220
Ludgershall, *U.K.* 51°14′ N, 1°39′ W 162
Ludhiana, *India* 30°53′ N, 75°53′ E 188
Lüdinghausen, *Ger.* 51°46′ N, 7°26′ E 167
Ludington, *Mich., U.S.* 43°56′ N, 86°26′ W 102
Ludlow, *Calif., U.S.* 34°43′ N, 116°11′ W 101

Ludlow, *Ill., U.S.* 40°23′ N, 88°7′ W 102
Ludlow, *Mass., U.S.* 42°9′ N, 72°29′ W 104
Ludlow, *U.K.* 52°21′ N, 2°44′ W 162
Ludlow, *Vt., U.S.* 43°23′ N, 72°43′ W 104
Ludogorsko Plato, *Bulg.* 43°26′ N, 26°11′ E 156
Ludwigsfelde, *Ger.* 52°18′ N, 13°15′ E 152
Ludwigshafen, *Ger.* 49°28′ N, 8°26′ E 150
Ludza, *Latv.* 56°32′ N, 27°43′ E 166
Luebo, *Dem. Rep. of the Congo* 5°21′ S, 21°26′ E 218
Lueki, *Dem. Rep. of the Congo* 3°26′ S, 25°49′ E 224
Luembe, river, *Dem. Rep. of the Congo* 6°50′ S, 24°24′ E 224
Luena, *Angola* 11°48′ S, 19°55′ E 220
Luena, *Dem. Rep. of the Congo* 9°27′ S, 25°44′ E 224
Luena, *Zambia* 10°37′ S, 30°11′ E 224
Luena Flats, *Zambia* 14°33′ S, 23°29′ E 224
Luena, river, *Angola-Zambia* 12°19′ S, 21°31′ E 220
Lueo, river, *Dem. Rep. of the Congo* 9°33′ S, 23°43′ E 224
Luepa, *Venez.* 5°52′ N, 61°27′ W 123
Luesia, *Sp.* 42°22′ N, 1°1′ W 164
Lufeng, *China* 22°54′ N, 115°38′ E 198
Lufico, *Angola* 6°24′ S, 13°21′ E 218
Lufira, river, *Dem. Rep. of the Congo* 9°40′ S, 27°14′ E 224
Lufkin, *Tex., U.S.* 31°19′ N, 94°43′ W 103
Lufu, *Dem. Rep. of the Congo* 5°41′ S, 13°52′ E 218
Luga, *Russ.* 58°42′ N, 29°49′ E 166
Lugano, *Switz.* 46°0′ N, 8°57′ E 167
Lugg, river, *U.K.* 52°16′ N, 2°57′ W 162
Lugnaquillia, peak, *Ire.* 52°57′ N, 6°34′ W 150
Lugo, *It.* 44°24′ N, 11°54′ E 167
Lugo, *Sp.* 43°0′ N, 7°34′ W 150
Lugoj, *Rom.* 45°42′ N, 21°54′ E 168
Lugones, *Arg.* 28°21′ S, 63°19′ W 139
Lugovaya Proleyka, *Russ.* 49°19′ N, 45°4′ E 158
Lugovoy, *Russ.* 59°40′ N, 65°56′ E 169
Lūgovoy see Qulan, *Kaz.* 42°54′ N, 72°44′ E 184
Lugulu, river, *Dem. Rep. of the Congo* 2°18′ S, 26°54′ E 224
Luguruka, *Tanzania* 9°59′ S, 36°39′ E 224
Luhanka, *Fin.* 61°47′ N, 25°39′ E 166
Luhans'k, *Ukr.* 48°32′ N, 39°14′ E 158
Lui, Ben, peak, *U.K.* 56°22′ N, 4°55′ W 150
Lui, river, *Zambia* 15°50′ S, 23°27′ E 224
Luiana, *Angola* 17°23′ S, 23°0′ E 220
Luiana, river, *Angola* 17°22′ S, 22°1′ E 220
Luilu, river, *Dem. Rep. of the Congo* 7°2′ S, 23°27′ E 224
Luimneach see Limerick, *Ire.* 52°39′ N, 8°37′ W 150
Luino, *It.* 46°0′ N, 8°45′ E 167
Luis Gonzaga, *Mex.* 29°48′ N, 114°28′ W 92
Luis Moya, *Mex.* 22°25′ N, 102°16′ W 114
Luishia, *Dem. Rep. of the Congo* 11°12′ S, 27°1′ E 224
Luisiana, *Peru* 12°43′ S, 73°44′ W 137
Luitpold Coast, *Antarctica* 77°40′ S, 35°8′ W 248
Luiza, *Dem. Rep. of the Congo* 7°13′ S, 22°25′ E 218
Luizi, river, *Dem. Rep. of the Congo* 6°4′ S, 27°33′ E 224
Luján, *Arg.* 34°36′ S, 59°6′ W 139
Luka, *Bosn. and Herzg.* 43°25′ N, 18°7′ E 168
Lukafu, *Dem. Rep. of the Congo* 10°29′ S, 27°29′ E 224
Lukanga Swamp, marsh, *Zambia* 14°27′ S, 27°19′ E 224
Lukashi, river, *Dem. Rep. of the Congo* 6°7′ S, 24°45′ E 224
Lukavac, *Bosn. and Herzg.* 44°34′ N, 18°31′ E 168
Luke, *Maced.* 42°19′ N, 22°16′ E 168
Luke, *Serb.* 43°36′ N, 20°16′ E 168
Luke Air Force Base, *Ariz., U.S.* 33°32′ N, 112°26′ W 92
Luke, Mount, peak, *Austral.* 27°16′ S, 116°39′ E 230
Lukenie, river, *Dem. Rep. of the Congo* 3°33′ S, 22°5′ E 218
Lukeville, *Ariz., U.S.* 31°53′ N, 112°48′ W 92
Lukolela, *Dem. Rep. of the Congo* 1°10′ S, 17°10′ E 218
Lukovë, *Alban.* 39°59′ N, 19°54′ E 156
Łuków, *Pol.* 51°55′ N, 22°21′ E 152
Lukoyanov, *Russ.* 55°1′ N, 44°33′ E 154
Łukta, *Pol.* 53°47′ N, 20°5′ E 166
Lukuga, river, *Dem. Rep. of the Congo* 5°59′ S, 27°21′ E 224
Lukula, *Dem. Rep. of the Congo* 5°26′ S, 12°53′ E 218
Lukuledi, *Tanzania* 10°35′ S, 38°48′ E 224
Lukulu, *Zambia* 14°23′ S, 23°15′ E 220
Lukunor Atoll 5°17′ N, 153°45′ E 192
Lukup, *Indonesia* 4°25′ N, 97°29′ E 196
Lukusuzi National Park, *Zambia* 13°8′ S, 32°20′ E 224
Luleå, *Nor.* 65°35′ N, 22°9′ E 152
Lüleburgaz, *Turk.* 41°24′ N, 27°21′ E 158
Lules, *Arg.* 27°0′ S, 65°22′ W 132
Luling, *Tex., U.S.* 29°39′ N, 97°39′ W 92
Lulonga, *Dem. Rep. of the Congo* 0°32′ N, 18°24′ E 218
Lulu, river, *Dem. Rep. of the Congo* 1°35′ N, 23°48′ E 224
Lulua, river, *Dem. Rep. of the Congo* 8°22′ S, 22°45′ E 218
Lumajangdong Co, lake, *China* 34°0′ N, 80°21′ E 188
Lümanda, *Est.* 58°17′ N, 22°2′ E 166
Lumbala Kaquengue, *Angola* 12°41′ S, 22°38′ E 220
Lumbala N'guimbo, *Angola* 14°8′ S, 21°24′ E 220
Lumberton, *Miss., U.S.* 30°59′ N, 89°28′ W 103
Lumberton, *N.C., U.S.* 34°37′ N, 79°1′ W 96
Lumbo, *Mozambique* 15°4′ S, 40°38′ E 224
Lumbovka, *Russ.* 67°39′ N, 40°33′ E 169
Lumbreras, *Sp.* 42°5′ N, 2°37′ W 164
Lumbres, *Fr.* 50°42′ N, 2°7′ E 163
Lumbwa, *Kenya* 0°10′ N, 35°30′ E 224
Lumding, *India* 25°44′ N, 93°8′ E 188
Lumeje, *Angola* 11°35′ S, 20°48′ E 220
Lumholtz National Park, *Austral.* 18°27′ S, 145°30′ E 238
Lumivaara, peak, *Nor.* 67°32′ N, 22°51′ E 152
Lumparland, *Fin.* 60°5′ N, 20°15′ E 166
Lumuna, *Dem. Rep. of the Congo* 3°50′ S, 26°29′ E 224
Lumut, *Malaysia* 4°12′ N, 100°36′ E 196
Lun, *Croatia* 44°41′ N, 14°45′ E 156
Lün, *Mongolia* 47°24′ N, 102°54′ E 198
Lün, *Mongolia* 47°49′ N, 105°17′ E 198
Luna, *N. Mex., U.S.* 33°48′ N, 108°57′ W 92
Lunar Crater, *Nev., U.S.* 38°23′ N, 116°0′ W 90
Lunavada, *India* 23°7′ N, 73°36′ E 186
Lund, *Can.* 49°59′ N, 124°45′ W 100
Lund, *Nev., U.S.* 38°51′ N, 115°1′ W 90
Lunda Norte, adm. division, *Angola* 8°37′ S, 18°34′ E 218
Lunda Sul, adm. division, *Angola* 9°13′ S, 20°41′ E 218
Lundar, *Can.* 50°41′ N, 98°3′ W 90
Lundazi, *Zambia* 12°16′ S, 33°13′ E 224
Lunde, *Nor.* 62°51′ N, 17°47′ E 152
Lundu, *Malaysia* 1°42′ N, 109°51′ E 196
Lune, river, *U.K.* 54°13′ N, 2°37′ W 162
Lüneburger Heide, region, *Ger.* 53°2′ N, 9°31′ E 150
Lunel, *Fr.* 43°40′ N, 4°7′ E 150
Lünen, *Ger.* 51°37′ N, 7°32′ E 163
Lunenburg, *Can.* 44°21′ N, 64°20′ W 111
Lunenburg, *Mass., U.S.* 42°35′ N, 71°44′ W 104
Lunenburg, *Vt., U.S.* 44°27′ N, 71°42′ W 104
Lunéville, *Fr.* 48°35′ N, 6°30′ E 163
Lunga, river, *Zambia* 13°1′ S, 26°36′ E 224
Lungdo, *China* 33°54′ N, 82°10′ E 188
Lunggar, *China* 31°8′ N, 84°1′ E 188
Lungi, *Sierra Leone* 8°40′ N, 13°14′ W 222
Lunglei, *India* 22°52′ N, 92°42′ E 188
Luni, *India* 26°1′ N, 73°0′ E 186
Luni, river, *India* 25°3′ N, 71°49′ E 186
Lunino, *Russ.* 53°36′ N, 45°15′ E 154
Luninyets, *Belarus* 52°14′ N, 26°47′ E 152
Lunkaransar, *India* 28°29′ N, 73°45′ E 186
Lunsar, *Sierra Leone* 8°41′ N, 12°34′ W 222
Lunsemfwa, river, *Zambia* 15°3′ S, 29°20′ E 224
Luntai, *China* 41°44′ N, 84°17′ E 184
Lunyama, *Dem. Rep. of the Congo* 7°49′ S, 28°20′ E 224
Lunz, *Aust.* 47°51′ N, 15°1′ E 156
Luo, river, *China* 36°39′ N, 108°16′ E 198
Luo, river, *China* 34°16′ N, 111°45′ E 198
Luocheng, *China* 24°46′ N, 108°53′ E 198
Luodian, *China* 25°24′ N, 106°45′ E 198
Luoding, *China* 22°42′ N, 111°35′ E 198
Luohe, *China* 33°37′ N, 114°4′ E 198
Luonan, *China* 34°5′ N, 110°10′ E 198
Luopioinen, *Fin.* 61°22′ N, 24°37′ E 166
Luoshan, *China* 32°13′ N, 114°34′ E 198
Luoyang, *China* 34°41′ N, 112°25′ E 198
Luoyuan, *China* 26°32′ N, 119°33′ E 198
Luozi, *Dem. Rep. of the Congo* 4°56′ S, 14°4′ E 218
Lupa Market, *Tanzania* 8°42′ S, 33°16′ E 224
Lupane, *Zimb.* 18°56′ S, 27°45′ E 224
Lupeni, *Rom.* 45°20′ N, 23°15′ E 168
Lupilichi, *Mozambique* 11°46′ S, 35°15′ E 224
Lupin, *Can.* 65°41′ N, 111°19′ W 106
Lupiñén, *Sp.* 42°9′ N, 0°34′ E 164
Lupire, *Angola* 14°38′ S, 19°28′ E 220
Lupon, *Philippines* 6°55′ N, 126°1′ E 203
Luputa, *Dem. Rep. of the Congo* 7°6′ S, 23°40′ E 224
Lupweji, river, *Dem. Rep. of the Congo* 10°26′ S, 24°13′ E 224
Luque, *Sp.* 37°33′ N, 4°17′ W 164
Luråsen, peak, *Nor.* 62°1′ N, 16°32′ E 152
Lure, *Fr.* 47°41′ N, 6°29′ E 150
Luremo, *Angola* 8°33′ S, 17°52′ E 218
Luribay, *Bol.* 17°8′ S, 67°43′ W 137
Lúrio, *Mozambique* 13°35′ S, 40°33′ E 224
Lúrio, river, *Mozambique* 14°19′ S, 38°43′ E 224
Luro, *Arg.* 36°38′ S, 62°9′ W 139
Lurøy, *Nor.* 66°25′ N, 12°51′ E 152
Lusahunga, *Tanzania* 2°54′ S, 31°14′ E 224
Lusaka, *Zambia* 15°26′ S, 28°10′ E 224
Lusambo, *Dem. Rep. of the Congo* 4°58′ S, 23°25′ E 224
Lusanga, *Dem. Rep. of the Congo* 4°50′ S, 18°39′ E 218
Lušci Palanka, *Bosn. and Herzg.* 44°44′ N, 16°25′ E 168
Luseland, *Can.* 52°5′ N, 109°23′ W 90
Lusenga Plain National Park, *Zambia* 9°45′ S, 29°1′ E 224
Lushi, *China* 34°4′ N, 111°0′ E 198
Lushiko, river, *Angola* 6°26′ S, 19°26′ E 218
Lushoto, *Tanzania* 4°48′ S, 38°19′ E 224
Lüshun (Port Arthur), *China* 38°52′ N, 121°16′ E 198
Lusigny, *Fr.* 48°15′ N, 4°15′ E 163
Lusikisiki, *S. Af.* 31°22′ S, 29°33′ E 227
Lusk, *Wyo., U.S.* 42°45′ N, 104°27′ W 90
Lussanvira, *Braz.* 20°43′ S, 51°9′ W 138
Lustenau, *Aust.* 47°25′ N, 9°39′ E 156
Lūt, Dasht-e, *Iran* 31°50′ N, 56°19′ E 160
Lūţak, *Iran* 30°41′ N, 61°27′ E 186
Lutcher, *La., U.S.* 30°2′ N, 90°44′ W 103
Lutembo, *Angola* 13°29′ S, 21°17′ E 220
Luther, *Mich., U.S.* 44°2′ N, 85°42′ W 102
Luton, *U.K.* 51°52′ N, 0°26′ E 162
Lutriņi, *Latv.* 56°44′ N, 22°23′ E 166
Lutry, *Pol.* 54°0′ N, 20°53′ E 166
Lutsen, *Minn., U.S.* 47°39′ N, 90°42′ W 94
Lutshima, river, *Dem. Rep. of the Congo* 6°29′ S, 18°21′ E 218
Luts'k, *Ukr.* 50°44′ N, 25°18′ E 152
Lutterworth, *U.K.* 52°26′ N, 1°13′ W 162
Lutuai, *Angola* 12°42′ S, 20°7′ E 220
Lututów, *Pol.* 51°22′ N, 18°27′ E 152
Lützow-Holm Bay 69°52′ S, 35°52′ E 248
Lutzputs, *S. Af.* 28°24′ S, 20°43′ E 227
Luuk, *Philippines* 5°58′ N, 121°19′ E 203
Luuq, *Somalia* 3°48′ N, 42°34′ E 224
Luverne, *Ala., U.S.* 31°42′ N, 86°16′ W 96
Luverne, *Minn., U.S.* 43°37′ N, 96°13′ W 90
Luvia, *Fin.* 61°21′ N, 21°35′ E 166
Luvidjo, river, *Dem. Rep. of the Congo* 7°7′ S, 26°25′ E 224
Luvo, *Angola* 5°52′ S, 14°4′ E 218
Luvos, *Nor.* 66°38′ N, 18°51′ E 152
Luvozero, *Russ.* 64°26′ N, 30°40′ E 152
Luvua, river, *Dem. Rep. of the Congo* 6°44′ S, 26°58′ E 224
Luvuei, *Angola* 13°6′ S, 21°12′ E 220
Luwegu, river, *Tanzania* 9°40′ S, 36°30′ E 224
Luwingu, *Zambia* 10°15′ S, 29°53′ E 224
Luwuk, *Indonesia* 0°58′ N, 122°46′ E 192
Luxembourg, *Lux.* 49°46′ N, 6°1′ E 163
Luxembourg 49°43′ N, 5°50′ E 163
Luxeuil, *Fr.* 47°49′ N, 6°23′ E 150
Luxi, *China* 24°25′ N, 98°38′ E 190
Luxi, *China* 28°18′ N, 110°9′ E 198
Luxor, *Egypt* 25°40′ N, 32°38′ E 182
Luyi, *China* 33°52′ N, 115°26′ E 198
Luz, *Braz.* 19°48′ S, 45°42′ W 138
Luz Range, *Antarctica* 72°22′ S, 4°40′ E 248
Luza, *Russ.* 60°40′ N, 47°18′ E 154
Luza, river, *Russ.* 60°20′ N, 48°39′ E 154
Luzaga, *Sp.* 40°57′ N, 2°27′ W 164
Luzaide (Valcarlos), *Fr.* 43°5′ N, 1°19′ W 164
Luzhai, *China* 24°23′ N, 109°43′ E 198
Luzhi, *China* 26°19′ N, 105°16′ E 198
Luzhma, *Russ.* 63°29′ N, 30°33′ E 152
Luzhou, *China* 28°54′ N, 105°22′ E 198
Luziânia, *Braz.* 16°18′ S, 47°58′ W 138
Luzon, island, *Philippines* 17°39′ N, 122°18′ E 190
Luzon Strait 19°39′ N, 119°44′ E 238
L'viv, *Ukr.* 49°50′ N, 24°2′ E 152
L'vovka, *Russ.* 57°9′ N, 78°48′ E 169
Lwiro, *Dem. Rep. of the Congo* 2°17′ S, 28°43′ E 224
Lyady, *Russ.* 58°36′ N, 28°46′ E 166
Lyakhov Islands, *East Siberian Sea* 73°46′ N, 140°46′ E 255
Lyaki, *Azerb.* 40°33′ N, 47°24′ E 195
Lyall Islands, *South Pacific Ocean* 70°47′ S, 166°57′ E 248
Lyall, Mount, peak, *Can.* 50°4′ N, 114°47′ W 90
Lyamtsa, *Russ.* 64°32′ N, 36°54′ E 154
Lyasnaya, *Belarus* 52°59′ N, 25°50′ E 154
Lychkovo, *Russ.* 57°53′ N, 32°25′ E 154
Lycksele, *Nor.* 64°35′ N, 18°39′ E 152
Lycosura, ruin(s), *Gr.* 37°22′ N, 21°56′ E 156
Lydd, *U.K.* 50°56′ N, 0°55′ E 162
Lydda see Lod, *Israel* 31°56′ N, 34°53′ E 194
Lyddal, *Can.* 55°0′ N, 98°25′ W 108
Lyddan Island, *Antarctica* 73°46′ S, 25°33′ W 248
Lydenburg, *S. Af.* 25°6′ S, 30°25′ E 227
Lydney, *U.K.* 51°43′ N, 2°32′ W 162
Lyduvėnai, *Lith.* 55°30′ N, 23°2′ E 166
Lyell Brown, Mount, peak, *Austral.* 23°24′ S, 130°9′ E 230
Lyell, Mount, peak, *Calif., U.S.* 37°43′ N, 119°20′ W 100
Lyepyel', *Belarus* 54°51′ N, 28°40′ E 166
Lyford, *Tex., U.S.* 26°23′ N, 97°47′ W 96
Lyle, *Oreg., U.S.* 45°40′ N, 121°18′ W 100
Lyman, *Miss., U.S.* 30°29′ N, 89°7′ W 103
Lyman, *Utah, U.S.* 38°23′ N, 111°35′ W 92
Lyman, *Wash., U.S.* 48°31′ N, 122°4′ W 100
Lyman, *Wyo., U.S.* 41°21′ N, 110°18′ W 90
Lymbel'karamo, *Russ.* 60°14′ N, 83°47′ E 169
Lynch, *Nebr., U.S.* 42°49′ N, 98°29′ W 90
Lynch Station, *Va., U.S.* 37°8′ N, 79°19′ W 96
Lynchburg, *Ohio, U.S.* 39°14′ N, 83°47′ W 102
Lynden, *Wash., U.S.* 48°57′ N, 122°27′ W 100
Lyndhurst, *U.K.* 50°52′ N, 1°34′ W 162
Lyndon, *Ill., U.S.* 41°42′ N, 89°57′ W 102
Lyndon, *Vt., U.S.* 44°30′ N, 72°2′ W 104
Lyndonville, *Vt., U.S.* 44°31′ N, 72°1′ W 104
Lynn, *Ind., U.S.* 40°3′ N, 84°57′ W 102
Lynn, *Mass., U.S.* 42°27′ N, 70°58′ W 104
Lynn Canal 58°40′ N, 135°29′ W 108
Lynn Lake, *Can.* 56°48′ N, 101°3′ W 106
Lynton, *U.K.* 51°13′ N, 3°49′ W 162
Lyntupy, *Belarus* 55°4′ N, 26°20′ E 166
Lyon, *Fr.* 45°46′ N, 4°51′ E 165
Lyon, *Miss., U.S.* 34°12′ N, 90°33′ W 96
Lyon, Cape, *Can.* 69°41′ N, 122°54′ W 98
Lyonnais, region, *Fr.* 45°45′ N, 3°45′ E 165
Lyons, *Kans., U.S.* 38°20′ N, 98°13′ W 90
Lyons, *Nebr., U.S.* 41°54′ N, 96°29′ W 90
Lyons, *N.Y., U.S.* 43°3′ N, 77°0′ W 110
Lyons, *Ohio, U.S.* 41°41′ N, 84°4′ W 102
Lyons, *Tex., U.S.* 30°22′ N, 96°34′ W 96
Lyozna, *Belarus* 55°3′ N, 30°53′ E 154
Lys, river, *Fr.* 50°34′ N, 2°9′ E 163
Lysekil, *Nor.* 58°17′ N, 11°26′ E 152
Lysi 35°5′ N, 33°41′ E 194
Łysica, *Pol.* 54°22′ N, 19°24′ E 166
Lys'va, *Russ.* 58°6′ N, 57°49′ E 154
Lysychans'k, *Ukr.* 48°51′ N, 38°27′ E 158
Lytham Saint Anne's, *U.K.* 53°45′ N, 3°0′ W 162
Lytle, *Tex., U.S.* 29°11′ N, 98°49′ W 96
Lyttelton, *N.Z.* 43°36′ S, 172°43′ E 240
Lytton, *Can.* 50°14′ N, 121°33′ W 108
Lyttus, ruin(s), *Gr.* 35°10′ N, 25°16′ E 156
Lyuban', *Russ.* 59°21′ N, 31°17′ E 152
Lyubcha, *Belarus* 53°44′ N, 26°4′ E 154
Lyubeshiv, *Ukr.* 51°46′ N, 25°30′ E 152
Lyubim, *Russ.* 58°21′ N, 40°44′ E 154
Lyubytino, *Russ.* 58°48′ N, 33°28′ E 154
Lyubytiv, *Ukr.* 51°7′ N, 24°50′ E 152
Lyudinovo, *Russ.* 53°48′ N, 34°28′ E 154
Lyushcha, *Belarus* 52°25′ N, 26°41′ E 152
Lyzha, river, *Russ.* 65°44′ N, 55°56′ E 154

M

M' Bomou, river, *Africa* 4°36′ N, 23°30′ E 224
Ma, river, *Asia* 20°38′ N, 104°57′ E 202
Maafer, *Alg.* 35°51′ N, 5°21′ E 150
Maale (Male), *Maldives* 4°9′ N, 73°15′ E 188
Ma'āmīr, *Iraq* 30°2′ N, 48°24′ E 196
Ma'ān, *Jordan* 30°10′ N, 35°44′ E 180
Maaninka, *Fin.* 66°26′ N, 28°26′ E 154
Maanīt, *Mongolia* 48°16′ N, 103°27′ E 198
Maanselkä, *Fin.* 67°46′ N, 27°51′ E 152
Ma'anshan, *China* 31°41′ N, 118°32′ E 198
Maardu, *Est.* 59°27′ N, 25°0′ E 166
Maarestunturit, peak, *Fin.* 68°44′ N, 25°31′ E 152
Maarianhamina see Mariehamn, *Fin.* 60°5′ N, 19°55′ E 166
Ma'arrat an Nu'mān, *Syr.* 35°39′ N, 36°41′ E 194
Maas, river, *Neth.* 51°46′ N, 5°19′ E 167
Maaseik, *Belg.* 51°6′ N, 5°46′ E 167
Maastricht, *Neth.* 50°51′ N, 5°43′ E 167
Mababe Depression, *Botswana* 18°50′ S, 23°43′ E 224
Mabalane, *Mozambique* 23°48′ S, 32°39′ E 227
Ma'bar, *Yemen* 14°47′ N, 44°18′ E 182
Mabaruma, *Guyana* 8°12′ N, 59°43′ W 116
Mabel Lake, *Can.* 50°37′ N, 118°59′ W 90
Mabélé, *Cameroon* 6°0′ N, 13°58′ E 218
Mabenga, *Dem. Rep. of the Congo* 3°40′ S, 18°38′ E 218
Mabirou, *Congo* 1°8′ S, 15°45′ E 218
Mablethorpe, *U.K.* 53°19′ N, 0°15′ E 162
Mabote, *Mozambique* 22°2′ S, 34°8′ E 227
Mabroûk, spring, *Mali* 19°29′ N, 1°15′ W 222
Mabroûk, spring, *Mauritania* 17°58′ N, 12°20′ W 222
Mabrous, spring, *Niger* 21°17′ N, 13°34′ E 222
Mabruk, oil field, *Lib.* 29°45′ N, 17°7′ E 216
Mabuasehube Game Reserve, *Botswana* 25°21′ S, 21°41′ E 227
Mabuki, *Tanzania* 2°59′ S, 33°10′ E 224
Mac. Robertson Land, region, *Antarctica* 72°44′ S, 59°21′ E 248
Macachín, *Arg.* 37°10′ S, 63°41′ W 134
Macaé, *Braz.* 22°23′ S, 41°50′ W 138
Macaíba, *Braz.* 5°50′ S, 35°21′ W 132
Macaloge, *Mozambique* 12°29′ S, 35°26′ E 224
MacAlpine Lake, *Can.* 66°32′ N, 105°59′ W 106
Macapá, *Braz.* 7°416′ N, 51°5′ W 130
Macapá, *Braz.* 9°31′ S, 67°30′ W 137
Macará, *Ecua.* 4°16′ S, 79°59′ W 130
Macaranay, *Col.* 0°55′ N, 72°10′ W 136
Macarani, *Braz.* 15°36′ S, 40°27′ W 138
Macareo, river, *Venez.* 9°9′ N, 61°55′ W 116
Macas, *Ecua.* 2°23′ S, 78°10′ W 136
Macau, *Braz.* 5°9′ S, 36°36′ W 132
Macau, *China* 22°10′ N, 113°31′ E 198
Macauã, river, *Braz.* 10°14′ S, 69°54′ W 137
Macaúba, *Braz.* 10°33′ S, 50°32′ W 130
Macaúbas, *Braz.* 13°1′ S, 42°42′ W 138
Macbride Head, *East Falkland* 51°29′ S, 57°44′ W 134
Macclenny, *Fla., U.S.* 30°16′ N, 82°7′ W 96
Macclesfield, *U.K.* 53°15′ N, 2°8′ W 162
Macdiarmid, *Can.* 49°27′ N, 88°6′ W 94
Macdill Air Force Base, *Fla., U.S.* 27°50′ N, 82°30′ W 105
Macdonnell Ranges, *Austral.* 23°31′ S, 131°40′ E 230
Macdui, Ben, peak, *U.K.* 57°3′ N, 3°46′ W 150
Macedonia 41°38′ N, 21°37′ E 168
Maceió, *Braz.* 9°36′ S, 35°42′ W 132
Macenta, *Guinea* 8°30′ N, 9°28′ W 222
Macerata, *It.* 43°18′ N, 13°26′ E 156
Macey, Mount, peak, *Antarctica* 69°58′ S, 64°49′ E 248
Macgillycuddy's Reeks, *Ire.* 51°43′ N, 10°50′ W 150
MacGregor, *Can.* 49°58′ N, 98°46′ W 90
Macha, *Russ.* 59°47′ N, 117°28′ E 160
Machacalis, *Braz.* 17°3′ S, 40°47′ W 138
Machacamarca, *Bol.* 18°12′ S, 67°5′ W 137
Machado, *Braz.* 21°40′ S, 45°54′ W 138
Machadodorp, *S. Af.* 25°43′ S, 30°11′ E 227
Machaerus, ruin(s), *Jordan* 31°33′ N, 35°36′ E 194
Machaíla, *Mozambique* 22°17′ S, 32°57′ E 227
Machakos, *Kenya* 1°32′ S, 37°15′ E 224
Machala, *Ecua.* 3°23′ S, 79°56′ W 130
Machalilla National Park, *Ecua.* 1°42′ S, 80°55′ W 122
Machaneng, *Botswana* 23°9′ S, 27°26′ E 227
Machanga, *Mozambique* 20°56′ S, 34°55′ E 227
Macharetí, *Bol.* 20°49′ S, 63°31′ W 137
Machault, *Fr.* 49°22′ N, 4°30′ E 163
Machawaian Lake, *Can.* 51°50′ N, 88°56′ W 110
Machaze, *Mozambique* 20°53′ S, 33°22′ E 227
Macheke, *Zimb.* 18°10′ S, 31°45′ E 224
Macheng, *China* 31°12′ N, 114°58′ E 198
Machero, peak, *Sp.* 39°19′ N, 4°22′ W 164
Machesney Park, *Ill., U.S.* 42°20′ N, 89°4′ W 102
Machghara, *Leb.* 33°31′ N, 35°38′ E 194
Machias, *Me., U.S.* 44°43′ N, 67°28′ W 94
Machiasport, *Me., U.S.* 44°41′ N, 67°25′ W 94
Machilipatnam (Bandar), *India* 16°11′ N, 81°10′ E 188
Machipongo, *Va., U.S.* 37°24′ N, 75°54′ W 94
Machiques, *Venez.* 10°1′ N, 72°34′ W 136
Machu Picchu, ruin(s), *Peru* 13°11′ S, 72°40′ W 137
Machupo, river, *Bol.* 13°10′ S, 64°44′ W 137
Machynlleth, *U.K.* 52°34′ N, 3°50′ W 162
Macia, *Mozambique* 25°1′ S, 33°7′ E 227
Macintyre, river, *Austral.* 28°52′ S, 148°46′ E 230
Macizo de la Maladeta, *Sp.* 42°29′ N, 0°38′ E 164
Mack, *Colo., U.S.* 39°13′ N, 108°53′ W 90
Mack Lake, *Can.* 58°1′ N, 95°56′ W 108
Maçka, *Turk.* 40°49′ N, 39°37′ E 195
Mackay, *Austral.* 21°15′ S, 149°7′ E 238
Mackay, *Idaho, U.S.* 43°54′ N, 113°37′ W 90

MacKay, river, *Can.* 56°45′ N, 112°13′ W 108
Mackenzie, *Can.* 55°21′ N, 123°3′ W 108
Mackenzie Bay 68°47′ N, 136°30′ W 98
MacKenzie Bay 68°37′ S, 67°9′ E 248
Mackenzie King Island, *Can.* 77°32′ N, 109°35′ W 106
Mackenzie Mountains, *Can.* 63°16′ N, 128°53′ W 108
Mackenzie, river, *Can.* 62°28′ N, 123°8′ W 106
Mackinaw City, *Mich., U.S.* 45°46′ N, 84°44′ W 94
Mackinnon, Cap, *Can.* 50°25′ N, 59°23′ W 111
Mackinnon Road, *Kenya* 3°44′ S, 39°2′ E 224
Mackintosh, Cape, *Antarctica* 72°59′ S, 59°28′ W 248
Macklin, *Can.* 52°20′ N, 109°58′ W 108
Mačkovci, *Slov.* 46°47′ N, 16°10′ E 168
Macksville, *Kans., U.S.* 37°57′ N, 98°58′ W 90
Maclear, *S. Af.* 31°6′ S, 28°19′ E 227
Maclovio Herrera, *Mex.* 28°58′ N, 105°7′ W 92
Maco, *Philippines* 7°24′ N, 125°49′ E 203
Macocola, *Angola* 7°0′ S, 16°7′ E 218
Macomb, *Mo., U.S.* 40°27′ N, 90°41′ W 94
Macomer, *It.* 40°16′ N, 8°46′ E 156
Macomia, *Mozambique* 12°12′ S, 40°8′ E 224
Macon, *Ga., U.S.* 32°48′ N, 83°38′ W 96
Macon, *Ill., U.S.* 39°42′ N, 89°0′ W 102
Macon, *Miss., U.S.* 33°5′ N, 88°33′ W 103
Macon, *Mo., U.S.* 39°43′ N, 92°28′ W 94
Macondo, *Angola* 12°38′ S, 23°46′ E 224
Macossa, *Mozambique* 17°55′ S, 33°55′ E 224
Macoun Lake, *Can.* 56°29′ N, 104°24′ W 108
Macovane, *Mozambique* 21°28′ S, 35°1′ E 227
Macquarie Island, *Austral.* 54°55′ S, 158°31′ E 255
Macquarie Ridge, *South Pacific Ocean* 52°33′ S, 160°15′ E 252
MaCrae, *Can.* 60°37′ N, 134°56′ W 108
MacSwyne's Gun, site, *Ire.* 55°10′ N, 8°7′ W 150
Macuapanim, Ilhas, islands, *Braz.* 3°8′ S, 66°19′ W 130
Macujer, *Col.* 0°23′ N, 73°7′ W 136
Macurijes, Punta, *Cuba* 20°56′ N, 79°8′ W 116
Macuro, *Venez.* 10°41′ N, 61°54′ W 116
Macururé, *Braz.* 9°13′ S, 39°5′ W 132
Macusani, *Peru* 14°4′ S, 70°27′ W 137
Macuze, *Mozambique* 17°44′ S, 37°13′ E 224
Ma'dabā, *Jordan* 31°42′ N, 35°47′ E 194
Madaba, *Tanzania* 8°38′ S, 37°45′ E 224
Madadi, *Chad* 18°29′ N, 20°43′ E 216
Madagascar 18°5′ S, 45°32′ E 220
Madagascar Basin, *Indian Ocean* 27°1′ S, 55°8′ E 254
Madagascar Plateau, *Indian Ocean* 30°16′ S, 46°6′ E 254
Madā'in Şāli', *Saudi Arabia* 26°47′ N, 37°55′ E 180
Madaket, *Mass., U.S.* 41°15′ N, 70°12′ W 104
Madama, *Niger* 21°56′ N, 13°40′ E 216
Madang, *P.N.G.* 5°15′ S, 145°43′ E 238
Madaoua, *Niger* 14°5′ N, 5°55′ E 222
Madara, *Bulg.* 43°15′ N, 27°5′ E 156
Madaras, *Hung.* 46°2′ N, 19°16′ E 168
Madaripur, *Bangladesh* 23°11′ N, 90°11′ E 197
Madarounfa, *Niger* 13°19′ N, 7°4′ E 222
Madau, island, *P.N.G.* 8°54′ S, 152°10′ E 192
Madaure, ruin(s), *Alg.* 36°3′ N, 7°48′ E 156
Madaw, *Turkm.* 38°11′ N, 54°42′ E 180
Madayar, *Myanmar* 22°13′ N, 96°4′ E 202
Maddock, *N. Dak., U.S.* 47°56′ N, 99°32′ W 90
Madeira Islands, *Portugal* 33°23′ N, 18°12′ W 214
Madeira, river, *Braz.* 5°30′ S, 60°51′ W 122
Madeirinha, river, *Braz.* 9°56′ S, 61°3′ W 130
Madeleine, Îles de la, island, *Can.* 47°31′ N, 63°44′ W 106
Madelia, *Minn., U.S.* 44°2′ N, 94°25′ W 90
Maden, *Turk.* 38°22′ N, 39°40′ E 195
Madera, *Calif., U.S.* 36°57′ N, 120°4′ W 100
Madera, *Mex.* 29°11′ N, 108°10′ W 92
Madgaon, *India* 15°16′ N, 73°59′ E 188
Madhya Pradesh, adm. division, *India* 23°57′ N, 78°8′ E 197
Madi Opei, *Uganda* 3°35′ N, 33°4′ E 224
Madibira, *Tanzania* 8°16′ S, 34°47′ E 224
Madida, *China* 42°57′ N, 130°47′ E 200
Madidi, *Bol.* 13°21′ S, 68°37′ W 137
Madidi National Park, *Bol.* 14°46′ S, 68°6′ W 137
Madidi, river, *Bol.* 12°38′ S, 67°26′ W 137
Madill, *Okla., U.S.* 34°4′ N, 96°45′ W 92
Madimba, *Dem. Rep. of the Congo* 5°1′ S, 15°8′ E 218
Madina, *Mali* 13°24′ N, 8°52′ W 222
Madina do Boé, *Guinea-Bissau* 11°46′ N, 14°14′ W 222
Madīnat ash Sha'b, *Yemen* 12°52′ N, 44°52′ E 182
Madingo, *Congo* 4°6′ S, 11°21′ E 218
Madingou, *Congo* 4°12′ S, 13°31′ E 218
Madira, *Nig.* 12°38′ N, 6°29′ E 222
Madirovalo, *Madagascar* 16°26′ S, 46°31′ E 220
Madison, *Fla., U.S.* 30°26′ N, 83°25′ W 96
Madison, *Ga., U.S.* 33°34′ N, 83°28′ W 96
Madison, *Ind., U.S.* 38°44′ N, 85°23′ W 102
Madison, *Kans., U.S.* 38°6′ N, 96°9′ W 90
Madison, *Me., U.S.* 44°47′ N, 69°53′ W 94
Madison, *Miss., U.S.* 32°27′ N, 90°8′ W 103
Madison, *Nebr., U.S.* 41°48′ N, 97°28′ W 90
Madison, *N.H., U.S.* 43°53′ N, 71°10′ W 104
Madison, *Ohio, U.S.* 41°45′ N, 81°3′ W 102
Madison, *S. Dak., U.S.* 43°59′ N, 97°8′ W 90
Madison, *W. Va., U.S.* 38°3′ N, 81°50′ W 94
Madison, *Wis., U.S.* 43°4′ N, 89°27′ W 102
Madison Heights, *Va., U.S.* 37°25′ N, 79°8′ W 94
Madison Range, *Mont., U.S.* 45°12′ N, 111°48′ W 90
Madisonville, *Ky., U.S.* 37°19′ N, 87°31′ W 94
Madisonville, *La., U.S.* 30°23′ N, 90°10′ W 103
Madisonville, *Tex., U.S.* 30°55′ N, 95°55′ W 96
Madjori, *Burkina Faso* 11°27′ N, 1°12′ E 222
Madley, *U.K.* 52°2′ N, 2°52′ W 162
Madley, Mount, peak, *Austral.* 24°37′ S, 123°41′ E 230
Mado Gashi, *Kenya* 0°41′ N, 39°11′ E 224
Madoc, *Can.* 44°29′ N, 77°29′ W 94
Madocsa, *Hung.* 46°41′ N, 18°56′ E 168
Madoi, *China* 34°54′ N, 98°10′ E 188
Madona, *Latv.* 56°50′ N, 26°12′ E 166
Madras, *Oreg., U.S.* 44°37′ N, 121°8′ W 90
Madras see Chennai, *India* 13°5′ N, 80°16′ E 188
Madrasat Lukk, *Lib.* 32°0′ N, 24°43′ E 180
Madre de Dios, *Peru* 12°39′ S, 70°8′ W 137
Madre de Dios, adm. division, *Peru* 12°9′ S, 71°9′ W 137
Madre de Dios, Isla, island, *Chile* 50°5′ S, 77°46′ W 134
Madre de Dios, river, *Bol.* 11°52′ S, 68°3′ W 137
Madre de Dios, river, *Peru* 12°32′ S, 70°34′ W 137
Madre del Sur, Sierra, *Mex.* 18°15′ N, 101°45′ W 114
Madre, Laguna 25°6′ N, 97°56′ W 114
Madre Mountain, peak, *N. Mex., U.S.* 34°17′ N, 107°58′ W 92
Madre, Sierra, *Guatemala* 15°44′ N, 93°15′ W 115
Madre, Sierra, *Philippines* 16°12′ N, 121°14′ E 203
Madre, Sierra, *Wyo., U.S.* 41°4′ N, 107°0′ W 90
Madrid, *Sp.* 40°24′ N, 3°47′ W 164
Madrid, adm. division, *Sp.* 40°20′ N, 3°58′ W 164
Madrid, Punta, *Chile* 19°2′ S, 70°21′ W 137
Madridejos, *Sp.* 39°28′ N, 3°34′ W 164
Madrigalejo, *Sp.* 39°7′ N, 5°38′ W 164
Madrona, Sierra, *Sp.* 38°28′ N, 4°17′ W 164
Madsen, *Can.* 50°57′ N, 93°55′ W 90
Madura, island, *Indonesia* 6°59′ S, 113°19′ E 192
Madurai, *India* 9°54′ N, 78°4′ E 188
Maduru Oya National Park, *Sri Lanka* 7°25′ N, 80°46′ E 172
Madzha, *Russ.* 61°53′ N, 51°32′ E 154
Mae Chaem, *Thai.* 18°29′ N, 98°22′ E 202
Mae Hong Son, *Thai.* 19°18′ N, 97°56′ E 202
Mae Ping National Park, *Thai.* 17°23′ N, 98°20′ E 202
Mae Rim, *Thai.* 18°55′ N, 98°56′ E 202
Mae Sariang, *Thai.* 18°10′ N, 97°55′ E 202
Mae Sot, *Thai.* 16°42′ N, 98°31′ E 202
Mae Suai, *Thai.* 19°48′ N, 99°32′ E 202
Maebashi, *Japan* 36°23′ N, 139°4′ E 201
Maella, *Sp.* 41°7′ N, 0°7′ E 164
Maentwrog, *U.K.* 52°56′ N, 3°59′ W 162
Maeruş, *Rom.* 45°54′ N, 25°32′ E 156
Maesteg, *U.K.* 51°36′ N, 3°39′ W 162
Maestra, Sierra, *Cuba* 20°12′ N, 76°53′ W 115
Maevatanana, *Madagascar* 17°0′ S, 46°51′ E 220
Mafaza, *Sudan* 13°35′ N, 34°32′ E 182
Mafeking, *Can.* 52°41′ N, 101°9′ W 108
Mafeteng, *Lesotho* 29°50′ S, 27°14′ E 227
Mafia Island, *Tanzania* 8°11′ S, 39°52′ E 224
Mafikeng, *S. Af.* 25°51′ S, 25°36′ E 227
Mafra, *Braz.* 26°9′ S, 49°50′ W 138
Magadan, *Russ.* 59°36′ N, 150°33′ E 160
Magadan, adm. division, *Russ.* 61°8′ N, 149°18′ E 160
Magadi, *Kenya* 1°53′ S, 36°21′ E 224
Magal Umm Rûs, spring, *Egypt* 25°28′ N, 34°35′ E 180
Magallanes, Estecho de (Magellan, Strait of), *Chile* 52°41′ S, 72°22′ W 122
Magallanes, *Philippines* 12°49′ N, 123°51′ E 203
Magallanes Y Antártica Chilena, adm. division, *Chile* 49°4′ S, 76°47′ W 134
Magangué, *Col.* 9°13′ N, 74°47′ W 130
Magaria, *Niger* 12°57′ N, 8°54′ E 222
Magazine Mountain, peak, *Ark., U.S.* 35°7′ N, 93°43′ W 96
Magdagachi, *Russ.* 53°29′ N, 125°48′ E 190
Magdalena, *Arg.* 35°4′ S, 57°33′ W 139
Magdalena, *Bol.* 13°21′ S, 64°11′ W 137
Magdalena, *Mex.* 20°54′ N, 103°58′ W 114
Magdalena, *N. Mex., U.S.* 34°6′ N, 107°15′ W 92
Magdalena, adm. division, *Col.* 10°33′ N, 74°45′ W 136
Magdalena, Bahía 24°32′ N, 112°50′ W 112
Magdalena, Isla, island, *Mex.* 25°20′ N, 113°13′ W 112
Magdalena, Llano de la, *Mex.* 24°13′ N, 111°25′ W 112
Magdalena, river, *Mex.* 30°32′ N, 112°42′ W 92
Magdalena de Kino, *Mex.* 30°37′ N, 110°59′ W 92
Magdeburg, *Ger.* 52°7′ N, 11°37′ E 152
Magdelaine Cays, islands, *Coral Sea* 17°5′ S, 150°25′ E 230
Magee, *Miss., U.S.* 31°52′ N, 89°42′ W 103
Magee Island, *U.K.* 54°45′ N, 6°12′ W 150
Magellan Seamounts, *North Pacific Ocean* 15°24′ N, 154°39′ E 252
Magellan, Strait of 52°41′ S, 72°44′ W 122
Magenta, *It.* 45°27′ N, 8°53′ E 167
Magerøya, island, *Nor.* 71°11′ N, 21°17′ E 160
Maggie Mountain, peak, *Calif., U.S.* 36°16′ N, 118°39′ W 101
Maggiorasca, Monte, peak, *It.* 44°32′ N, 9°27′ E 167
Maghâgha, *Egypt* 28°38′ N, 30°48′ E 182
Maghama, *Mauritania* 15°30′ N, 12°55′ W 222
Magid, oil field, *Lib.* 28°15′ N, 22°8′ E 216
Magilligan Point, *U.K.* 54°58′ N, 6°57′ W 150
Magina, peak, *Sp.* 37°43′ N, 3°29′ W 164
Magione, *It.* 43°8′ N, 12°12′ E 156
Magistral, *Mex.* 25°57′ N, 105°21′ W 114
Maglaj, *Bosn. and Herzg.* 44°33′ N, 18°5′ E 168
Maglie, *It.* 40°7′ N, 18°17′ E 156
Magnetic Island National Park, *Austral.* 19°14′ S, 146°30′ E 238
Magnitka, *Russ.* 55°20′ N, 59°44′ E 154
Magnitogorsk, *Russ.* 53°26′ N, 59°8′ E 154
Magnolia, *Ark., U.S.* 33°15′ N, 93°15′ W 103
Magnolia, *Ill., U.S.* 41°6′ N, 89°12′ W 102
Magnolia, *Miss., U.S.* 31°7′ N, 90°29′ W 103
Magnor, *Nor.* 59°57′ N, 12°11′ E 152
Mago National Park, *Eth.* 5°21′ N, 35°30′ E 224
Magog, *Can.* 45°15′ N, 72°9′ W 111
Magosal, *Mex.* 21°37′ N, 97°59′ W 114
Magpie, *Can.* 50°19′ N, 64°30′ W 111
Magpie, river, *Can.* 50°54′ N, 64°47′ W 111
Magrath, *Can.* 49°25′ N, 112°52′ W 90
Magruder Mountain, peak, *Nev., U.S.* 37°24′ N, 117°38′ W 92
Maguan, *China* 22°59′ N, 104°23′ E 202
Maguari, Cabo, *Braz.* 0°28′ N, 49°15′ W 130
Maguarichic, *Mex.* 27°51′ N, 107°58′ W 112
Magude, *Mozambique* 25°0′ S, 32°37′ E 227
Magué, *Mozambique* 15°50′ S, 31°43′ E 224
Maguire, Mount, peak, *Antarctica* 74°5′ S, 66°32′ E 248
Magumeri, *Nig.* 12°6′ N, 12°50′ E 216
Magwa Falls, *S. Af.* 31°14′ S, 28°52′ E 227
Magwa, oil field, *Kuwait* 29°3′ N, 47°52′ E 196
Magway, *Myanmar* 20°9′ N, 94°57′ E 202
Mahābād, *Iran* 36°45′ N, 45°41′ E 195
Mahabo, *Madagascar* 20°21′ S, 44°38′ E 220
Mahagi, *Dem. Rep. of the Congo* 2°15′ N, 30°59′ E 224
Mahajanga, *Madagascar* 15°42′ S, 46°20′ E 220
Mahalapye, *Botswana* 23°4′ S, 26°46′ E 227
Mahale Mountain National Park, *Tanzania* 6°26′ S, 29°29′ E 224
Ma'allāt, *Iran* 33°56′ N, 50°24′ E 180
Mahanadi, river, *India* 20°55′ N, 84°19′ E 190
Mahanoro, *Madagascar* 19°52′ S, 48°46′ E 220
Mahanoy City, *Pa., U.S.* 40°48′ N, 76°9′ W 94
Mahao, *China* 43°11′ N, 128°2′ E 200
Maharajganj, *India* 27°7′ N, 83°32′ E 197
Maharashtra, adm. division, *India* 19°35′ N, 73°17′ E 188
Mahasthan, ruin(s), *Bangladesh* 24°54′ N, 89°13′ E 197
Mahavelona, *Madagascar* 17°40′ S, 49°28′ E 220
Mahbubnagar, *India* 16°43′ N, 77°57′ E 188
Mahd adh Dhahab, *Saudi Arabia* 23°26′ N, 40°53′ E 182
Mahdere Maryam, *Eth.* 11°41′ N, 37°53′ E 182
Mahdia, *Guyana* 5°14′ N, 59°16′ W 130
Mahdia, *Tun.* 35°31′ N, 11°1′ E 156
Mahendra Giri, peak, *India* 18°58′ N, 84°11′ E 188
Mahenge, *Tanzania* 8°39′ S, 36°42′ E 224
Maheno, *N.Z.* 45°12′ S, 170°49′ E 240
Mahesana, *India* 23°33′ N, 72°24′ E 186
Maheshwar, *India* 22°11′ N, 75°34′ E 197
Mahewa, *India* 24°23′ N, 80°10′ E 197
Mahi, river, *India* 23°6′ N, 73°41′ E 186
Mahia Peninsula, *N.Z.* 39°7′ S, 177°45′ E 240
Mahilyow, *Belarus* 53°57′ N, 30°21′ E 154
Mahim, *India* 19°39′ N, 72°45′ E 188
Mahin, *Nig.* 6°16′ N, 4°45′ E 222
Mahires, *Tun.* 34°34′ N, 10°31′ E 156
Mahlberg, *Ger.* 48°17′ N, 7°48′ E 163
Mahmudiye, *Turk.* 39°30′ N, 30°58′ E 156
Mahnomen, *Minn., U.S.* 47°18′ N, 95°58′ W 90
Maho, *Sri Lanka* 7°50′ N, 80°17′ E 188
Mahoba, *India* 25°17′ N, 79°51′ E 197
Mahogany Hills, *Nev., U.S.* 39°26′ N, 116°21′ W 90
Mahogany Mountain, peak, *Oreg., U.S.* 43°13′ N, 117°21′ W 90
Mahomet, *Ill., U.S.* 40°10′ N, 88°24′ W 102
Mahón, *Sp.* 39°54′ N, 4°14′ E 143
Mahopac, *N.Y., U.S.* 41°22′ N, 73°44′ W 104
Mahora, *Sp.* 39°12′ N, 1°44′ W 164
Mahuta, *Tanzania* 10°52′ S, 39°25′ E 224
Mahuva, *India* 21°4′ N, 71°45′ E 188
Maials, *Sp.* 41°22′ N, 0°30′ E 164
Maicao, *Col.* 11°21′ N, 72°15′ W 136
Maicasagi, Lac, lake, *Can.* 49°53′ N, 77°19′ W 94
Maicasagi, river, *Can.* 49°59′ N, 76°54′ W 110
Maiden Castle, ruin(s), *U.K.* 50°40′ N, 2°37′ W 150
Maidenhead, *U.K.* 51°31′ N, 0°44′ E 162
Maidstone, *Can.* 53°5′ N, 109°17′ W 108
Maidstone, *U.K.* 51°16′ N, 0°31′ E 162
Maiduguri, *Nig.* 11°51′ N, 13°9′ E 216
Maigualida, Sierra, *Venez.* 5°34′ N, 65°28′ W 130
Maihar, *India* 24°15′ N, 80°44′ E 197
Maiko National Park, *Dem. Rep. of the Congo* 0°35′ N, 27°15′ E 224
Maiko, river, *Dem. Rep. of the Congo* 0°20′ N, 26°51′ E 224
Maikona, *Kenya* 2°53′ N, 37°30′ E 224
Mailsi, *Pak.* 29°48′ N, 72°11′ E 186
Main Centre, *Can.* 50°35′ N, 107°22′ W 90
Main Channel 45°19′ N, 82°17′ W 110
Main Pass 29°20′ N, 89°20′ W 103
Main, river, *Ger.* 49°59′ N, 10°12′ E 167
Maine, adm. division, *Me., U.S.* 45°16′ N, 69°59′ W 94
Maine, Gulf of 43°8′ N, 67°56′ W 253
Maine, Gulf of 44°10′ N, 69°15′ W 94
Maine, region, *Fr.* 48°25′ N, 0°48′ E 163
Maïné Soroa, *Niger* 13°14′ N, 12°3′ E 222
Maingkwan, *Myanmar* 26°20′ N, 96°35′ E 188
Mainit, Lake, *Philippines* 9°25′ N, 125°15′ E 203
Mainland, island, *U.K.* 59°44′ N, 0°54′ E 142
Mainling, *China* 29°12′ N, 94°6′ E 188
Mainpuri, *India* 27°12′ N, 79°1′ E 197
Maintal, *Ger.* 50°9′ N, 8°49′ E 167
Maintenon, *Fr.* 48°34′ N, 1°34′ E 163
Maintirano, *Madagascar* 18°4′ S, 44°1′ E 220
Mainz, *Ger.* 49°59′ N, 8°15′ E 167
Maipo, Paso de, pass, *Chile* 34°15′ S, 69°52′ W 134
Maipú, *Arg.* 36°52′ S, 57°53′ W 139
Maipures, *Col.* 5°8′ N, 67°51′ W 136
Maisi, Punta de, *Cuba* 20°14′ N, 74°6′ W 116
Maiskhal, island, *Bangladesh* 21°23′ N, 90°54′ E 188
Maisou Island, *Mich., U.S.* 43°46′ N, 83°45′ W 102
Maisse, *Fr.* 48°23′ N, 2°22′ E 163
Maitengwe, *Botswana* 20°8′ S, 27°10′ E 227
Maitri, India, station, *Antarctica* 70°37′ S, 11°36′ E 248
Maíz Grande, Isla del (Great Corn Island), *Nicar.* 11°44′ N, 83°2′ W 115
Maizhokunggar, *China* 29°52′ N, 91°45′ E 197
Maizières, *Fr.* 49°12′ N, 6°9′ E 163
Maizuru, *Japan* 35°24′ N, 135°19′ E 201
Majagual, *Col.* 8°33′ N, 74°37′ W 136
Majahual, *Mex.* 18°45′ N, 87°45′ W 115
Majdal Shams, *Israel* 33°16′ N, 35°46′ E 194
Majdanpek, *Serb.* 44°24′ N, 21°56′ E 168
Majene, *Indonesia* 3°29′ S, 118°54′ E 192
Majevica, *Bosn. and Herzg.* 44°42′ N, 18°31′ E 168
Majī, *Eth.* 6°12′ N, 35°37′ E 224
Majorca see Mallorca, island, *Sp.* 39°38′ N, 2°37′ E 150
Majske Poljane, *Croatia* 45°19′ N, 16°8′ E 168
Majuro, *Marshall Islands* 7°5′ N, 171°22′ E 242
Majuro Atoll, *Marshall Islands* 7°7′ N, 171°10′ E 242
Mak, Ko, island, *Thai.* 11°40′ N, 101°58′ E 202
Maka, *Senegal* 13°40′ N, 14°20′ W 222
Makabana, *Congo* 3°30′ S, 12°36′ E 218
Makaha, *Zimb.* 17°20′ S, 32°34′ E 224
Makalamabedi, *Botswana* 20°20′ S, 23°48′ E 227
Makaleha Mountains, peak, *Hawai'i, U.S.* 22°6′ N, 159°28′ W 99
Makalu, peak, *Nepal* 27°52′ N, 87°2′ E 197
Makalu-Barun National Park, *Nepal* 27°29′ N, 86°21′ E 197
Makandja, *Dem. Rep. of the Congo* 0°46′ N, 23°14′ E 218
Makanya, *Tanzania* 4°22′ S, 37°49′ E 224
Makanza, *Dem. Rep. of the Congo* 1°35′ N, 19°4′ E 218
Makarfi, *Nig.* 11°19′ N, 7°53′ E 222
Makari, *Cameroon* 12°36′ N, 14°29′ E 216
Makarikha, *Russ.* 66°13′ N, 58°23′ E 169
Makarov, *Russ.* 48°34′ N, 142°40′ E 190
Makarov Basin, *Arctic Ocean* 87°7′ N, 170°10′ W 255
Makarska, *Croatia* 43°17′ N, 17°1′ E 168
Makar'yev, *Russ.* 57°53′ N, 43°46′ E 154
Makassar (Ujung Pandang), *Indonesia* 5°11′ S, 119°25′ E 192
Makassar Strait 1°31′ S, 117°0′ E 192
Makeni, *Sierra Leone* 8°54′ N, 12°4′ W 222
Maketu, *N.Z.* 37°48′ S, 176°26′ E 240
Makgadikgadi Pans Game Reserve, *Botswana* 20°54′ S, 24°49′ E 227
Makhachkala, *Russ.* 42°55′ N, 47°35′ E 195
Makhad, *Pak.* 33°8′ N, 71°46′ E 186
Makhado see Louis Trichardt, *S. Af.* 23°3′ S, 29°53′ E 227
Makhambet, *Kaz.* 47°40′ N, 51°33′ E 158
Makhana, *Senegal* 16°8′ N, 16°26′ W 222
Makhfar al Buşayyah, *Iraq* 30°6′ N, 46°5′ E 196
Makhnovka, *Russ.* 57°25′ N, 29°20′ E 166
Makikihi, *N.Z.* 44°39′ S, 171°8′ E 240
Makindu, *Kenya* 2°19′ S, 37°49′ E 224
Makīnsk, *Kaz.* 52°39′ N, 70°25′ E 184
Makiyivka, *Ukr.* 48°2′ N, 37°59′ E 158
Makkah (Mecca), *Saudi Arabia* 21°24′ N, 39°49′ E 182
Makkovik, *Can.* 54°59′ N, 59°10′ W 106
Makó, *Hung.* 46°13′ N, 20°29′ E 168
Mako, *Senegal* 12°53′ N, 12°24′ W 222
Makoino, *Madagascar* 16°21′ S, 48°11′ E 220
Makok, *Gabon* 1°59′ S, 9°36′ E 218
Makokibatan Lake, *Can.* 51°14′ N, 88°52′ W 80
Makokou, *Gabon* 0°31′ N, 12°48′ E 218
Mākole'ā Point, *Hawai'i, U.S.* 19°47′ N, 156°31′ W 99
Makoli, *Zambia* 17°28′ S, 26°3′ E 224
Makongolosi, *Tanzania* 8°25′ S, 33°10′ E 224
Makrai, *India* 22°6′ N, 77°6′ E 197
Makrana, *India* 27°1′ N, 74°43′ E 186
Maksatikha, *Russ.* 57°44′ N, 35°52′ E 154
Maksimkin Yar, *Russ.* 58°42′ N, 86°50′ E 169
Maktau, *Kenya* 3°27′ S, 38°6′ E 224
Mākū, *Iran* 39°20′ N, 44°31′ E 195
Makumbako, *Tanzania* 8°51′ S, 34°49′ E 224
Makung, *Taiwan, China* 23°31′ N, 119°34′ E 198
Makungo, *Somalia* 0°48′ N, 42°33′ E 224
Makunudu Atoll, *Maldives* 5°26′ N, 67°51′ E 172
Makurazaki, *Japan* 31°15′ N, 130°18′ E 201
Makurdi, *Nig.* 7°41′ N, 8°33′ E 222
Makushin Volcano, peak, *Alas., U.S.* 53°51′ N, 167°3′ W 98
Makushino, *Russ.* 55°12′ N, 67°14′ E 184
Mal, *Mauritania* 16°59′ N, 13°25′ W 222
Malá, *Sp.* 37°6′ N, 3°43′ W 164
Mala, Punta, *Pan.* 7°24′ N, 79°59′ W 115
Mala Vyska, *Ukr.* 48°39′ N, 31°39′ E 158
Malabang, *Philippines* 7°39′ N, 124°6′ E 203
Malabo, *Equatorial Guinea* 3°45′ N, 8°40′ E 222
Malabuñgan, *Philippines* 9°2′ N, 117°40′ E 203
Malacca, *Malaysia* 2°13′ N, 102°16′ E 196
Malacca, Strait of 6°12′ N, 97°6′ E 196
Malad City, *Idaho, U.S.* 42°11′ N, 112°14′ W 82
Maladzyechna, *Belarus* 54°18′ N, 26°50′ E 166
Malaga, *Calif., U.S.* 36°40′ N, 119°45′ W 100
Málaga, *Col.* 6°41′ N, 72°45′ W 136
Malaga, *N. Mex., U.S.* 32°13′ N, 104°4′ W 92
Málaga, *Sp.* 36°42′ N, 4°27′ W 164
Málaga, *Sp.* 36°45′ N, 4°28′ W 214
Malagarasi, *Tanzania* 5°6′ S, 30°51′ E 224
Malagón, *Sp.* 39°10′ N, 3°51′ W 164
Malaita, island, *Solomon Islands* 9°0′ S, 161°0′ E 242
Malakal, *Sudan* 9°32′ N, 31°45′ E 224
Malakoff, *Tex., U.S.* 32°9′ N, 96°1′ W 96
Malalbergo, *It.* 44°44′ N, 11°32′ E 167
Malampaya Sound 10°55′ N, 118°41′ E 203
Malang, *Indonesia* 8°2′ S, 112°27′ E 192
Malangali, *Tanzania* 8°35′ S, 34°52′ E 224
Malangen, *Nor.* 69°23′ N, 18°37′ E 152
Malanje, *Angola* 9°34′ S, 16°13′ E 218
Malanje, adm. division, *Angola* 8°41′ S, 15°42′ E 218
Malanville, *Benin* 11°51′ N, 3°23′ E 222
Malargüe, *Arg.* 35°27′ S, 69°36′ W 134
Malartic, *Can.* 48°8′ N, 78°9′ W 94
Malaryta, *Belarus* 51°46′ N, 24°2′ E 154
Malaspina Glacier, *Alas., U.S.* 59°14′ N, 143°10′ W 106
Malatya, *Turk.* 38°20′ N, 38°17′ E 180
Malavate, *South America* 3°16′ N, 54°6′ W 130
Malawi 13°0′ S, 34°0′ E 224
Malawi, Lake (Nyasa, Lake), *Malawi* 34°30′ S, 12°00′ E 21

Malawiya, *Sudan* 15°13′ N, 36°12′ E 182
Malay Peninsula, *Malaysia* 7°4′ N, 99°57′ E 196
Malaya Vishera, *Russ.* 58°48′ N, 32°20′ E 154
Malayagiri, peak, *India* 21°21′ N, 85°8′ E 188
Malaybalay, *Philippines* 8°12′ N, 125°8′ E 203
Malāyer, *Iran* 34°17′ N, 48°51′ E 180
Malaysia 2°20′ N, 112°47′ E 192
Malazgirt, *Turk.* 39°8′ N, 42°30′ E 195
Malbaza, *Niger* 13°58′ N, 5°39′ E 222
Malbork, *Pol.* 54°1′ N, 19°2′ E 166
Malbrán, *Arg.* 29°21′ S, 62°27′ W 139
Mal'chevskaya, *Russ.* 49°2′ N, 40°21′ E 158
Malden, *Ill., U.S.* 41°25′ N, 89°22′ W 102
Malden, *Mo., U.S.* 36°33′ N, 89°58′ W 94
Maldive Islands, *Arabian Sea* 1°14′ N, 72°26′ E 188
Maldives, *Maldives* 2°12′ N, 74°34′ E 188
Maldon, *U.K.* 51°43′ N, 0°39′ E 162
Maldonado, *Uru.* 34°53′ S, 54°59′ W 139
Maldonado, Punta, *Mex.* 15°32′ N, 103°13′ W 72
Malè, *It.* 46°20′ N, 10°55′ E 167
Male Atoll, *Maldives* 4°29′ N, 73°0′ E 188
Malé Karpaty, *Slovakia* 48°25′ N, 17°3′ E 152
Male see Maale, *Maldives* 4°9′ N, 73°15′ E 188
Malegaon, *India* 20°33′ N, 74°33′ E 188
Maléha, *Guinea* 11°50′ N, 9°44′ W 222
Malek, *Sudan* 6°2′ N, 31°38′ E 224
Malela, *Dem. Rep. of the Congo* 2°26′ S, 26°7′ E 224
Malela, *Dem. Rep. of the Congo* 4°23′ S, 26°8′ E 224
Malemba-Nkulu, *Dem. Rep. of the Congo* 8°1′ S, 26°46′ E 224
Malembé, *Congo* 3°5′ S, 12°2′ E 218
Malengoya, *Dem. Rep. of the Congo* 3°26′ N, 25°24′ E 224
Maler Kotla, *India* 30°31′ N, 75°55′ E 197
Maleševske Planina, *Maced.* 41°38′ N, 22°40′ E 168
Malesherbes, *Fr.* 48°16′ N, 2°23′ E 163
Maleza, *Col.* 4°22′ N, 69°25′ W 136
Malfa, *It.* 38°34′ N, 14°49′ E 156
Malgobek, *Russ.* 43°30′ N, 44°33′ E 195
Malgrat de Mar, *Sp.* 41°38′ N, 2°44′ E 164
Malha, spring, *Sudan* 15°4′ N, 26°9′ E 226
Malhada, *Braz.* 14°20′ S, 43°48′ W 138
Malhão, Serra do, *Port.* 37°24′ N, 8°28′ W 150
Malheur Cave, site, *Oreg., U.S.* 43°13′ N, 118°28′ W 90
Mali, *Guinea* 12°6′ N, 12°20′ W 222
Mali 18°26′ N, 2°0′ W 214
Mali Drvenik, island, *Croatia* 43°20′ N, 15°55′ E 168
Mali Kyun, island, *Myanmar* 13°17′ N, 98°7′ E 202
Mali Lošinj, *Croatia* 44°32′ N, 14°27′ E 156
Mali, river, *Myanmar* 25°18′ N, 97°11′ E 188
Malibu, *Calif., U.S.* 34°2′ N, 118°43′ W 101
Målilla, *Nor.* 57°22′ N, 15°48′ E 152
Malimba, Monts, *Dem. Rep. of the Congo* 7°41′ S, 29°8′ E 224
Malinau, *Indonesia* 3°41′ N, 116°30′ E 192
Malindi, *Kenya* 3°13′ S, 40°6′ E 224
Malinyi, *Tanzania* 8°57′ S, 35°59′ E 224
Malipo, *China* 23°5′ N, 104°42′ E 202
Malishevo, *Kos.* 42°32′ N, 20°43′ E 168
Maljen, *Serb.* 44°9′ N, 19°56′ E 168
Malka Mari National Park, *Kenya* 3°54′ N, 40°5′ E 224
Malkaaray, *Somalia* 3°54′ N, 41°53′ E 224
Malkara, *Turk.* 40°53′ N, 26°53′ E 156
Malki, *Russ.* 53°31′ N, 157°39′ E 160
Małkinia Górna, *Pol.* 53°0′ N, 22°0′ E 152
Malko Tŭrnovo, *Bulg.* 41°59′ N, 27°31′ E 156
Mal'kovichi, *Belarus* 52°31′ N, 26°35′ E 152
Mallā', *Syr.* 32°30′ N, 36°50′ E 194
Mallaoua, *Niger* 13°2′ N, 9°36′ E 222
Mallawi, *Egypt* 27°46′ N, 30°46′ E 180
Mallén, *Sp.* 41°52′ N, 1°26′ W 164
Malles Venosta, *It.* 46°42′ N, 10°33′ E 167
Mallet, *Braz.* 25°55′ S, 50°52′ W 139
Malletts Bay, *Vt., U.S.* 44°32′ N, 73°14′ W 104
Mallorca (Majorca), island, *Sp.* 39°38′ N, 2°37′ E 150
Mallory Swamp, marsh, *Fla., U.S.* 29°42′ N, 83°17′ W 105
Malm, *Nor.* 64°4′ N, 11°12′ E 152
Malmédy, *Belg.* 50°26′ N, 6°1′ E 167
Malmesbury, *S. Af.* 33°28′ S, 18°41′ E 227
Malmesbury, *U.K.* 51°35′ N, 2°6′ W 162
Malmö, *Nor.* 55°35′ N, 12°59′ E 152
Malmstrom Air Force Base, *Mont., U.S.* 47°28′ N, 111°16′ W 90
Maloarkhangel'sk, *Russ.* 52°21′ N, 36°30′ E 158
Maloca, *Braz.* 0°42′ N, 55°58′ W 130
Maloca, *Braz.* 10°49′ S, 70°9′ W 137
Maloca de Índios, *Braz.* 11°42′ S, 58°16′ W 130
Maloca Timbé, *Braz.* 3°3′ S, 47°45′ W 130
Maloja, *Switz.* 46°26′ N, 9°42′ E 167
Malole, *Zambia* 10°8′ S, 31°33′ E 224
Malo-les-Bains, *Fr.* 51°1′ N, 2°25′ E 163
Malolos, *Philippines* 14°49′ N, 120°47′ E 203
Malombe, Lake, *Malawi* 14°40′ S, 34°54′ E 224
Malone, *N.Y., U.S.* 44°50′ N, 74°19′ W 94
Malone, *Wash., U.S.* 46°56′ N, 123°20′ W 100
Malonga, *Dem. Rep. of the Congo* 10°26′ S, 23°9′ E 220
Malongwe, *Tanzania* 5°24′ S, 33°39′ E 224
Małopolskie, adm. division, *Pol.* 52°41′ N, 22°0′ E 152
Malorad, *Bulg.* 43°29′ N, 23°41′ E 156
Maloshuyka, *Russ.* 63°44′ N, 37°28′ E 154
Malouin, river, *Can.* 50°9′ N, 79°11′ W 110
Mal'ovitsa, peak, *Bulg.* 42°9′ N, 23°16′ E 156
Måløy, *Nor.* 61°56′ N, 5°6′ E 152
Maloyaz, *Russ.* 55°13′ N, 58°11′ E 154
Malpas, *U.K.* 53°1′ N, 2°46′ W 162
Malpeque Bay 46°28′ N, 64°26′ W 111
Malpura, *India* 26°16′ N, 75°23′ E 197
Malta 35°56′ N, 14°26′ E 156
Malta, *Idaho, U.S.* 42°19′ N, 113°23′ W 90
Malta, *Ill., U.S.* 41°55′ N, 88°52′ W 102
Malta, *Latv.* 56°19′ N, 27°8′ E 166
Malta, *Malta* 35°56′ N, 14°26′ E 156
Malta, *Mont., U.S.* 48°20′ N, 107°53′ W 90
Malta, *Ohio, U.S.* 39°38′ N, 81°53′ W 102
Malta Channel 36°15′ N, 14°16′ E 156
Malta, river, *Latv.* 56°26′ N, 26°47′ E 166
Maltahöhe, *Namibia* 24°50′ S, 16°56′ E 227
Maltby, *U.K.* 53°25′ N, 1°13′ W 162
Maltese Islands, *Malta* 35°30′ N, 14°3′ E 156
Malton, *U.K.* 54°8′ N, 0°48′ E 162
Ma'lūlā, *Syr.* 33°50′ N, 36°32′ E 194
Malumfashi, *Nig.* 11°46′ N, 7°37′ E 222
Malvan, *India* 16°4′ N, 73°29′ E 188
Malvern, *Ark., U.S.* 34°20′ N, 92°50′ W 96
Malvern, *Iowa, U.S.* 41°0′ N, 95°35′ W 90
Malvern, *U.K.* 52°6′ N, 2°20′ W 162
Malvinas, Islas see Falkland Islands, *Falk. Is., U.K.* 53°40′ S, 58°56′ W 134
Malybay, *Kaz.* 43°30′ N, 78°30′ E 184
Malyn, *Ukr.* 50°47′ N, 29°23′ E 158
Malyns'k, *Ukr.* 51°4′ N, 26°32′ E 152
Malyy Anyuy, river, *Russ.* 67°32′ N, 168°13′ E 246
Malyy Atlym, *Russ.* 62°19′ N, 67°4′ E 169
Malyy Lyakhovskiy, Ostrov, island, *Russ.* 74°11′ N, 150°36′ E 246
Malyy, Ostrov, island, *Russ.* 60°3′ N, 28°0′ E 166
Malyy Tyuters, Ostrov, island, *Russ.* 59°37′ N, 26°44′ E 166
Malyye Derbety, *Russ.* 47°56′ N, 44°34′ E 158
Malyye Karmakuly, *Russ.* 72°15′ N, 52°58′ E 160
Mama, *Russ.* 58°17′ N, 112°55′ E 160
Mamadysh, *Russ.* 55°42′ N, 51°16′ E 154
Maman, *Sudan* 16°20′ N, 36°46′ E 182
Mambajao, *Philippines* 9°15′ N, 124°44′ E 203
Mambali, *Tanzania* 4°33′ S, 32°40′ E 224
Mambasa, *Dem. Rep. of the Congo* 1°19′ N, 29°3′ E 224
Mamboya, *Tanzania* 6°15′ S, 37°9′ E 224
Mambrui, *Kenya* 3°7′ S, 40°8′ E 224
Mamburao, *Philippines* 13°15′ N, 120°36′ E 203
Mamfé, *Cameroon* 5°43′ N, 9°17′ E 222
Mamiña, *Chile* 20°3′ S, 69°15′ W 137
Maminas, *Alban.* 41°23′ N, 19°36′ E 156
Mammamattawa, *Can.* 50°27′ N, 84°23′ W 94
Mammoth Cave National Park, *Ky., U.S.* 37°17′ N, 88°6′ W 80
Mamonovo, *Russ.* 54°27′ N, 19°54′ E 166
Mamoré, river, *Bol.* 13°52′ S, 65°11′ W 137
Mamori, Lago, lake, *Braz.* 3°39′ S, 60°46′ W 130
Mamoriá, river, *Braz.* 7°16′ S, 67°19′ W 130
Mamou, *Guinea* 10°23′ N, 12°7′ W 222
Mamou, *La., U.S.* 30°37′ N, 92°26′ W 103
Mampikony, *Madagascar* 16°5′ S, 47°39′ E 220
Mampong, *Ghana* 7°5′ N, 1°26′ W 222
Mamshit, ruin(s), *Israel* 31°0′ N, 35°1′ E 194
Mamuju, *Indonesia* 2°43′ S, 118°47′ E 192
Mamuno, *Botswana* 22°11′ S, 20°2′ E 227
Mamuras, *Alban.* 41°35′ N, 19°40′ E 168
Man, *Côte d'Ivoire* 7°18′ N, 7°34′ W 222
Man Aung, *Myanmar* 18°51′ N, 93°46′ E 188
Man, Isle of 54°17′ N, 4°55′ W 150
Man of War Point, *Can.* 54°25′ N, 58°25′ W 111
Man, river, *China* 42°10′ N, 127°23′ E 200
Mānā, *Hawai'i, U.S.* 22°2′ N, 159°47′ W 99
Mana, *South America* 5°40′ N, 53°50′ W 130
Mana La, pass, *India* 31°4′ N, 79°25′ E 197
Mana Pools National Park, *Zimb.* 16°11′ S, 28°55′ E 224
Manacacías, river, *Col.* 3°42′ N, 72°26′ W 136
Manacapuru, *Braz.* 3°19′ S, 60°36′ W 130
Manacor, *Sp.* 39°34′ N, 3°11′ E 214
Manado, *Indonesia* 1°30′ N, 124°42′ E 192
Managua, *Nicar.* 12°3′ N, 86°24′ W 115
Managua, Lago de, lake, *Nicar.* 12°14′ N, 87°5′ W 116
Manaia, *N.Z.* 39°34′ S, 174°7′ E 240
Manakara, *Madagascar* 22°15′ S, 48°2′ E 207
Manakau, peak, *N.Z.* 42°15′ S, 173°32′ E 240
Manākhah, *Yemen* 15°2′ N, 43°44′ E 182
Manam, island, *P.N.G.* 4°16′ S, 145°8′ E 192
Manama see Al Manāmah, *Bahrain* 26°10′ N, 50°27′ E 196
Manambolo, river, *Madagascar* 19°6′ S, 43°47′ E 220
Manankoro, *Mali* 10°30′ N, 7°27′ W 222
Manantenina, *Madagascar* 24°20′ S, 47°20′ E 220
Manantiales, *Chile* 52°46′ S, 69°16′ W 123
Manapouri, *N.Z.* 45°36′ S, 167°39′ E 240
Manapouri, Lake, *N.Z.* 45°31′ S, 166°52′ E 240
Manas, *China* 44°16′ N, 86°16′ E 184
Manas Hu, lake, *China* 45°38′ N, 85°18′ E 184
Manassa, *Colo., U.S.* 37°9′ N, 105°57′ W 92
Manassas National Battlefield Park, *Va., U.S.* 38°48′ N, 77°37′ W 94
Manatee, river, *Fla., U.S.* 27°25′ N, 82°11′ W 105
Manaus, *Braz.* 3°5′ S, 60°1′ W 130
Manavgat, *Turk.* 36°45′ N, 31°26′ E 180
Manay, *Philippines* 7°14′ N, 126°32′ E 203
Manbazar, *India* 23°4′ N, 86°39′ E 197
Mancha Real, *Sp.* 37°47′ N, 3°37′ W 164
Manchester, *Conn., U.S.* 41°46′ N, 72°32′ W 104
Manchester, *Iowa, U.S.* 42°29′ N, 91°28′ W 94
Manchester, *Ky., U.S.* 37°9′ N, 83°47′ W 96
Manchester, *Me., U.S.* 44°19′ N, 69°52′ W 104
Manchester, *Mich., U.S.* 42°9′ N, 84°2′ W 102
Manchester, *N.H., U.S.* 42°58′ N, 71°28′ W 104
Manchester, *Ohio, U.S.* 40°55′ N, 81°34′ W 102
Manchester, *Tenn., U.S.* 35°28′ N, 86°5′ W 96
Manchester, *U.K.* 53°28′ N, 2°16′ W 162
Manchester, *Vt., U.S.* 43°9′ N, 73°5′ W 104
Manchester Center, *Vt., U.S.* 43°10′ N, 73°4′ W 104
Manchester Lake, *Can.* 61°24′ N, 108°30′ W 108
Manchuria see Dongbei, region 40°34′ N, 122°39′ E 200
Mancos, *Colo., U.S.* 37°20′ N, 108°18′ W 92
Mand, *Pak.* 26°1′ N, 62°7′ E 182
Mand, river, *Iran* 28°19′ N, 51°45′ E 196
Manda, *Tanzania* 7°58′ S, 32°26′ E 224
Manda, *Tanzania* 10°29′ S, 34°35′ E 224
Manda Island, *Kenya* 2°24′ S, 40°58′ E 224
Manda National Park, *Chad* 9°9′ N, 17°26′ E 216
Mandab, Bāb al 12°28′ N, 42°51′ E 182
Mandabe, *Madagascar* 21°3′ S, 44°54′ E 220
Mandaguari, *Braz.* 23°31′ S, 51°49′ W 138
Mandal, *Mongolia* 48°26′ N, 106°42′ E 198
Mandal, *Nor.* 58°1′ N, 7°30′ E 150
Mandala, Puncak, peak, *Indonesia* 4°42′ S, 140°2′ E 192
Mandalay, *Myanmar* 21°58′ N, 96°7′ E 202
Mandalgovĭ, *Mongolia* 45°47′ N, 106°16′ E 198
Mandalī, *Iraq* 33°45′ N, 45°31′ E 180
Mandan, *N. Dak., U.S.* 46°49′ N, 100°54′ W 90
Mandara Mountains, *Cameroon* 9°18′ N, 12°57′ E 216
Mandau, river, *Indonesia* 1°7′ N, 101°17′ E 196
Mandel, *Afghan.* 33°19′ N, 61°52′ E 186
Mandera, *Tanzania* 6°10′ S, 38°23′ E 224
Manderfield, *Utah, U.S.* 38°21′ N, 112°39′ W 90
Manderscheid, *Ger.* 50°5′ N, 6°48′ E 167
Mandeville, *La., U.S.* 30°21′ N, 90°5′ W 103
Mandi, *Nepal* 31°41′ N, 76°56′ E 188
Mandiana, *Guinea* 10°40′ N, 8°42′ W 222
Mandie, *Mozambique* 16°30′ S, 33°33′ E 224
Mandimba, *Mozambique* 14°22′ S, 35°40′ E 224
Mandjafa, *Chad* 11°13′ N, 15°26′ E 216
Mandla, *India* 22°38′ N, 80°22′ E 197
Mandor, *Indonesia* 0°19′ N, 109°18′ E 196
Mandoto, *Madagascar* 19°38′ S, 46°19′ E 220
Mandráki, *Gr.* 36°36′ N, 27°8′ E 156
Mandu, island, *Maldives* 3°19′ N, 72°0′ E 188
Mandvi, *India* 22°50′ N, 69°21′ E 186
Manevichi, *Ukr.* 51°17′ N, 25°31′ E 152
Manfalût, *Egypt* 27°19′ N, 30°52′ E 180
Manfredonia, Golfo di 41°29′ N, 15°9′ E 156
Manga, *Braz.* 14°49′ S, 43°58′ W 138
Manga, *Burkina Faso* 11°40′ N, 1°6′ W 222
Manga, *Mozambique* 19°46′ S, 34°55′ E 224
Manga, region, *Niger* 14°17′ N, 11°19′ E 222
Mangabeiras, Chapada das, *Braz.* 9°35′ S, 46°50′ W 130
Mangai, *Dem. Rep. of the Congo* 4°3′ S, 19°29′ E 218
Mangaia, island, *N.Z.* 21°52′ S, 157°57′ W 252
Mangaïzé, *Niger* 14°54′ N, 2°6′ E 222
Mangalia, *Rom.* 43°49′ N, 28°32′ E 156
Mangalmé, *Chad* 12°24′ N, 19°37′ E 216
Mangalore, *India* 12°52′ N, 74°52′ E 188
Mangamuka, *N.Z.* 35°13′ S, 173°31′ E 240
Mangando, *Angola* 8°4′ S, 17°6′ E 218
Mangawan, *India* 24°42′ N, 81°31′ E 197
Mangaweka, *N.Z.* 39°50′ S, 175°46′ E 240
Mangeigne, *Chad* 10°31′ N, 21°16′ E 216
Mangghystau, adm. division, *Kaz.* 43°56′ N, 51°44′ E 158
Mangghystaū, *Kaz.* 43°40′ N, 51°17′ E 158
Mangham, *La., U.S.* 32°18′ N, 91°47′ W 103
Mangkalihat, Tanjung, *Indonesia* 0°49′ N, 117°56′ E 192
Manglares, Cabo, *Col.* 1°33′ N, 80°27′ W 130
Mangnai, *China* 37°50′ N, 91°45′ E 188
Mangnai Zhen, *China* 38°25′ N, 90°17′ E 188
Mango, *Togo* 10°22′ N, 0°25′ E 222
Mangoche, *Malawi* 14°29′ S, 35°19′ E 224
Mangoky, river, *Madagascar* 22°3′ S, 44°28′ E 220
Mangole, island, *Indonesia* 1°43′ S, 125°43′ E 192
Mangonui, *N.Z.* 35°2′ S, 173°31′ E 240
Mangqystaū Shyghanaghy 44°28′ N, 50°41′ E 158
Mangrol, *India* 21°7′ N, 70°7′ E 188
Mangrove Cay, island, *Bahamas* 26°55′ N, 78°46′ W 105
Mangueira, Lagoa, lake, *Braz.* 33°0′ S, 53°19′ W 139
Manguéni, Plateau de, *Niger* 23°9′ N, 12°2′ E 216
Manguinho, Ponta do, *Braz.* 11°5′ S, 36°25′ W 132
Mangum, *Okla., U.S.* 34°51′ N, 99°31′ W 92
Mangunça, Ilha, island, *Braz.* 1°36′ S, 44°38′ W 132
Mangut, *Russ.* 49°38′ N, 112°38′ E 198
Mangwe, *Zimb.* 20°41′ S, 28°2′ E 227
Manhattan, *Ill., U.S.* 41°24′ N, 87°59′ W 102
Manhattan, *Kans., U.S.* 39°10′ N, 96°34′ W 90
Manhattan, *Nev., U.S.* 38°32′ N, 117°5′ W 90
Manhiça, *Mozambique* 25°21′ S, 32°49′ E 227
Manhuaçu, *Braz.* 20°19′ S, 42°0′ W 138
Maní, *Col.* 4°50′ N, 72°18′ W 136
Mania, river, *Madagascar* 19°58′ S, 45°19′ E 220
Maniamba, *Mozambique* 12°47′ S, 34°58′ E 224
Manic Trois, Réservoir, lake, *Can.* 50°11′ N, 70°32′ W 80
Manica, *Mozambique* 18°57′ S, 32°54′ E 224
Manica, adm. division, *Mozambique* 18°9′ S, 32°59′ E 224
Maniçauá Miçu, river, *Braz.* 11°35′ S, 55°7′ W 132
Manicoré, river, *Braz.* 6°45′ S, 61°2′ W 130
Manicouagan, Petit lac, lake, *Can.* 51°49′ N, 68°45′ W 111
Manicouagan, Pointe, *Can.* 49°1′ N, 68°18′ W 111
Manicouagan, Réservoir, lake, *Can.* 51°39′ N, 69°10′ W 111
Manicouagan, Réservoir, lake, *Can.* 51°19′ N, 70°56′ W 106
Maniema, adm. division, *Dem. Rep. of the Congo* 3°18′ S, 25°0′ E 218
Manīfah, *Saudi Arabia* 27°28′ N, 48°59′ E 196
Manigotagan, *Can.* 51°6′ N, 96°16′ W 90
Manihiki Plateau, *South Pacific Ocean* 10°15′ S, 159°44′ W 252
Maniitsoq (Sukkertoppen) 65°26′ N, 53°0′ W 106
Manikpur, *India* 25°1′ N, 81°6′ E 197
Manila, *Ark., U.S.* 35°52′ N, 90°11′ W 96
Manila, *Philippines* 14°33′ N, 120°53′ E 203
Manilaid, island, *Est.* 58°10′ N, 24°9′ E 166
Manily, *Russ.* 62°34′ N, 165°18′ E 173
Manipur, adm. division, *India* 24°32′ N, 93°6′ E 188
Manisa, *Turk.* 38°34′ N, 27°24′ E 180
Manistee, *Mich., U.S.* 44°13′ N, 86°20′ W 102
Manistee, river, *Mich., U.S.* 44°1′ N, 86°6′ W 82
Manistique, *Mich., U.S.* 45°58′ N, 86°15′ W 94
Manitoba, adm. division, *Can.* 50°5′ N, 99°36′ W 90
Manitoba, Lake, *Can.* 50°18′ N, 98°55′ W 90
Manitou, *Can.* 49°14′ N, 98°32′ W 90
Manitou Beach, *Mich., U.S.* 41°57′ N, 84°19′ W 102
Manitou Islands, *Lake Michigan* 44°29′ N, 86°12′ W 80
Manitou, Lac, lake, *Can.* 50°47′ N, 65°38′ W 111
Manitou Lake, *Can.* 52°43′ N, 110°13′ W 108
Manitoulin Island, *Can.* 45°15′ N, 83°28′ W 80
Manitouwadge, *Can.* 49°8′ N, 85°47′ W 94
Manitowik Lake, *Can.* 48°8′ N, 85°0′ W 94
Manitowoc, *Wis., U.S.* 44°4′ N, 87°41′ W 102
Maniwaki, *Can.* 46°21′ N, 75°58′ W 94
Manizales, *Col.* 5°1′ N, 75°32′ W 136
Manjā, *Jordan* 31°44′ N, 35°51′ E 194
Manja, *Madagascar* 21°30′ S, 44°22′ E 207
Manjacaze, *Mozambique* 24°41′ S, 33°53′ E 227
Mankato, *Kans., U.S.* 39°46′ N, 98°14′ W 90
Mankato, *Minn., U.S.* 44°8′ N, 94°1′ W 94
Mankera, *Pak.* 31°22′ N, 71°29′ E 186
Mankim, *Cameroon* 5°0′ N, 12°1′ E 218
Mankono, *Côte d'Ivoire* 8°1′ N, 6°12′ W 222
Manley Hot Springs, *Alas., U.S.* 64°59′ N, 150°36′ W 98
Manlleu, *Sp.* 42°0′ N, 2°16′ E 164
Manly, *Iowa, U.S.* 43°15′ N, 93°12′ W 94
Mann Ranges, *Austral.* 25°59′ S, 128°46′ E 230
Manna, *Indonesia* 4°27′ S, 102°51′ E 192
Mannar, *Sri Lanka* 8°58′ N, 79°53′ E 188
Mannar, Gulf of 7°42′ N, 78°20′ E 188
Mannheim, *Ger.* 49°29′ N, 8°27′ E 152
Manning, *Can.* 56°54′ N, 117°37′ W 108
Manning, *Iowa, U.S.* 41°53′ N, 95°5′ W 94
Manning, *N. Dak., U.S.* 47°12′ N, 102°47′ W 90
Manning, *S.C., U.S.* 33°40′ N, 80°13′ W 96
Manningtree, *U.K.* 51°56′ N, 1°3′ E 162
Mannsville, *N.Y., U.S.* 43°42′ N, 76°4′ W 94
Mannu, Capo, *It.* 40°1′ N, 7°43′ E 156
Mannville, *Can.* 53°20′ N, 111°11′ W 108
Mano, *Sierra Leone* 8°2′ N, 12°4′ W 222
Mano, river, *Liberia* 7°14′ N, 10°57′ W 222
Manoa, *Bol.* 9°45′ S, 65°27′ W 137
Manoharpur, *India* 22°21′ N, 85°13′ E 197
Manokotak, *Alas., U.S.* 58°58′ N, 159°3′ W 98
Manokwari, *Indonesia* 0°50′ N, 133°55′ E 192
Manombo, *Madagascar* 22°54′ S, 43°24′ E 220
Manomet, *Mass., U.S.* 41°55′ N, 70°34′ W 104
Manomet Point, *Mass., U.S.* 41°55′ N, 70°33′ W 104
Manono, *Dem. Rep. of the Congo* 7°18′ S, 27°23′ E 224
Manoron, *Myanmar* 11°37′ N, 98°59′ E 202
Manouane, *Can.* 47°14′ N, 74°24′ W 94
Manouane, Lac, lake, *Can.* 47°33′ N, 74°43′ W 94
Manouane, Lac, lake, *Can.* 50°32′ N, 71°22′ W 111
Manouba, *Tun.* 36°47′ N, 10°5′ E 156
Manovo, river, *Cen. Af. Rep.* 9°7′ N, 20°15′ E 218
Manovo-Gounda-Saint Floris National Park, *Cen. Af. Rep.* 9°23′ N, 20°58′ E 206
Manp'o, *N. Korea* 41°10′ N, 126°19′ E 200
Manpur, *India* 23°16′ N, 83°35′ E 197
Manresa, *Sp.* 41°43′ N, 1°46′ E 214
Mansa, *Zambia* 11°12′ S, 28°53′ E 224
Mansa Konko, *Gambia* 13°26′ N, 15°30′ W 222
Mansabá, *Guinea-Bissau* 12°18′ N, 15°11′ W 222
Mansalar see Musala, island, *Indonesia* 1°31′ N, 97°47′ E 196
Mansehra, *Pak.* 34°19′ N, 73°15′ E 186
Mansel Island, *Can.* 61°4′ N, 80°49′ W 106
Manseriche, Pongo de, *Peru* 4°16′ S, 78°36′ W 130
Mansfield, *Ill., U.S.* 40°11′ N, 88°31′ W 102
Mansfield, *La., U.S.* 32°1′ N, 93°44′ W 103
Mansfield, *Mass., U.S.* 42°1′ N, 71°14′ W 104
Mansfield, *Mo., U.S.* 37°5′ N, 92°35′ W 96
Mansfield, *Ohio, U.S.* 40°44′ N, 82°30′ W 102
Mansfield, *Pa., U.S.* 41°46′ N, 77°5′ W 82
Mansfield, *U.K.* 53°8′ N, 1°12′ W 162
Mansfield Center, *Conn., U.S.* 41°45′ N, 72°12′ W 104
Mansfield, Mount, peak, *Vt., U.S.* 44°32′ N, 72°51′ W 104
Manso (Rio das Mortes), river, *Braz.* 15°20′ S, 53°1′ W 138
Manson, *Iowa, U.S.* 42°30′ N, 94°33′ W 94
Manson Creek, *Can.* 55°38′ N, 124°31′ W 108
Mansourah, *Alg.* 36°4′ N, 4°28′ E 150
Manta, *Ecua.* 1°4′ S, 80°31′ W 130
Mantakari, *Niger* 13°52′ N, 3°59′ E 222
Mantaro, river, *Peru* 11°55′ S, 74°47′ W 137
Manteca, *Calif., U.S.* 37°47′ N, 121°13′ W 100
Mantecal, *Venez.* 7°33′ N, 69°8′ W 136
Mantena, *Braz.* 18°51′ S, 40°59′ W 138
Manteno, *Ill., U.S.* 41°14′ N, 87°50′ W 102
Manteo, *N.C., U.S.* 35°54′ N, 75°42′ W 96
Mantes-la-Jolie, *Fr.* 48°59′ N, 1°42′ E 163
Manti, *Utah, U.S.* 39°15′ N, 111°38′ W 90
Mantinea 362 B.C., battle, *Gr.* 37°36′ N, 22°17′ E 156
Manto, *Hond.* 14°55′ N, 86°20′ W 115
Manton, *Mich., U.S.* 44°24′ N, 85°25′ W 94
Mantova, *It.* 45°8′ N, 10°47′ E 167
Mäntsälä, *Fin.* 60°37′ N, 25°18′ E 166
Mänttä, *Fin.* 62°0′ N, 24°36′ E 166
Mantua, *Cuba* 22°17′ N, 84°18′ W 116
Manturovo, *Russ.* 58°20′ N, 44°47′ E 154
Mäntyharju, *Fin.* 61°22′ N, 26°48′ E 166
Mäntyluoto, *Fin.* 61°34′ N, 21°28′ E 166
Manú, *Peru* 12°17′ S, 70°55′ W 137
Manu National Park, *Peru* 12°19′ S, 71°54′ W 137
Manu see Mapiri, river, *Bol.* 10°40′ S, 66°53′ W 137
Manu'a Islands, *American Samoa, U.S.* 14°14′ S, 169°35′ W 241

Manuel Alves, river, *Braz.* 11°53′ S, 48°4′ W 130
Manuel Benavides, *Mex.* 29°5′ N, 103°55′ W 92
Manuel J. Cobo, *Arg.* 35°53′ S, 57°54′ W 139
Manuel Ribas, *Braz.* 24°34′ S, 51°40′ W 138
Manuel Vitorino, *Braz.* 14°12′ S, 40°16′ W 138
Manuelzinho, *Braz.* 7°24′ S, 54°54′ W 130
Manukan, *Philippines* 8°32′ N, 123°5′ E 203
Manukau, *N.Z.* 37°3′ S, 174°54′ E 240
Manupari, river, *Bol.* 12°36′ S, 67°42′ W 137
Manuripi, river, *Bol.* 11°42′ S, 68°35′ W 137
Manus, island, *P.N.G.* 2°27′ S, 145°40′ E 192
Manusela National Park, *Indonesia* 3°14′ S, 129°4′ E 238
Manvers, Port 56°47′ N, 63°21′ W 246
Manville, *R.I., U.S.* 41°58′ N, 71°29′ W 104
Many, *La., U.S.* 31°33′ N, 93°29′ W 103
Many Farms, *Ariz., U.S.* 36°21′ N, 109°37′ W 92
Manyara, Lake, *Tanzania* 3°37′ S, 35°16′ E 224
Manyberries, *Can.* 49°24′ N, 110°42′ W 90
Manyinga, river, *Africa* 12°17′ S, 24°1′ E 220
Manyoni, *Tanzania* 5°42′ S, 34°49′ E 224
Manzala, Buheirat el, lake, *Egypt* 31°12′ N, 32°3′ E 194
Manzanares, *Sp.* 38°59′ N, 3°27′ W 214
Manzanera, *Sp.* 40°3′ N, 0°50′ E 164
Manzanillo, *Mex.* 19°2′ N, 104°18′ W 114
Manzanita, *Oreg., U.S.* 45°42′ N, 123°56′ W 100
Manzano Peak, *N. Mex., U.S.* 34°34′ N, 106°31′ W 92
Manzanola, *Colo., U.S.* 38°6′ N, 103°52′ W 92
Manzhouli, *China* 49°34′ N, 117°26′ E 198
Manzini, *Swaziland* 26°31′ S, 31°20′ E 227
Mao, *Chad* 14°6′ N, 15°17′ E 216
Mao, *Dom. Rep.* 19°34′ N, 71°5′ W 116
Maoke, Pegunungan, *Indonesia* 4°23′ S, 135°14′ E 192
Maoming, *China* 21°40′ N, 110°50′ E 198
Maoudass, *Mauritania* 15°33′ N, 10°55′ W 222
Mapai, *Mozambique* 22°49′ S, 32°1′ E 227
Mapam Yumco, lake, *China* 30°45′ N, 80°50′ E 197
Mapanza, *Zambia* 16°17′ S, 26°55′ E 224
Maper, *Sudan* 7°42′ N, 29°38′ E 224
Mapia, Kepulauan, islands, *North Pacific Ocean* 0°52′ N, 134°31′ E 192
Mapimí, *Mex.* 25°47′ N, 103°52′ W 114
Mapimí, Bolsón de, *Mex.* 26°47′ N, 104°34′ W 112
Mapinhane, *Mozambique* 22°19′ S, 35°2′ E 227
Mapiri, *Bol.* 15°13′ S, 68°11′ W 137
Mapiri (Manu), river, *Bol.* 10°40′ S, 66°53′ W 137
Mapiripán, river, *Col.* 3°10′ N, 71°37′ W 136
Mapiripana, *Col.* 2°39′ N, 70°58′ W 136
Maple Creek, *Can.* 49°53′ N, 109°28′ W 90
Maple Ridge, *Can.* 49°13′ N, 122°36′ W 100
Maple, river, *Mich., U.S.* 43°3′ N, 84°41′ W 102
Maple Valley, *Wash., U.S.* 47°23′ N, 122°3′ W 100
Mapleton, *Iowa, U.S.* 42°8′ N, 95°47′ W 90
Mapleville, *R.I., U.S.* 41°56′ N, 71°40′ W 104
Mapmaker Seamounts, *North Pacific Ocean* 26°45′ N, 166°56′ E 252
Mapuera, river, *Braz.* 1°6′ S, 58°10′ W 130
Mapulanguene, *Mozambique* 24°29′ S, 32°7′ E 227
Maputo, *Mozambique* 25°55′ S, 32°27′ E 227
Maputo, adm. division, *Mozambique* 25°22′ S, 32°6′ E 227
Maqanshy, *Kaz.* 46°45′ N, 82°9′ E 184
Maqat, *Kaz.* 47°38′ N, 53°21′ E 158
Maqdam, Ras, *Sudan* 18°48′ N, 36°58′ E 182
Maqên Gangri, peak, *China* 34°24′ N, 99°22′ E 190
Maqnā, *Saudi Arabia* 28°22′ N, 34°45′ E 180
Maqshūsh, *Saudi Arabia* 23°36′ N, 38°41′ E 182
Maquela do Zombo, *Angola* 6°3′ S, 15°4′ E 218
Maquinchao, *Arg.* 41°14′ S, 68°43′ W 134
Maquoketa, *Iowa, U.S.* 42°3′ N, 90°41′ W 94
Mar Chiquita, Laguna, lake, *Arg.* 30°34′ S, 62°57′ W 139
Mar de Ajó, *Arg.* 36°42′ S, 56°43′ W 139
Mar del Plata, *Arg.* 37°59′ S, 57°36′ W 139
Mar, Serra do, *Braz.* 27°45′ S, 48°59′ W 132
Mara, *Guyana* 5°57′ N, 57°37′ W 130
Mara, *India* 28°10′ N, 94°6′ E 188
Mara, adm. division, *Tanzania* 1°45′ S, 33°47′ E 224
Mara, oil field, *Venez.* 10°49′ N, 71°58′ W 136
Mara Rosa, *Braz.* 13°57′ S, 49°10′ W 138
Maraã, *Braz.* 1°50′ S, 65°26′ W 136
Marabá, *Braz.* 5°24′ S, 49°9′ W 130
Marabitanas, *Braz.* 0°56′ N, 66°54′ W 136
Maracá, Ilha de, island, *Braz.* 2°3′ N, 50°17′ W 130
Maracaibo, *Venez.* 10°41′ N, 71°41′ W 136
Maracaibo, Lago de, *Venez.* 9°20′ N, 74°22′ W 73
Maracaju, *Braz.* 21°39′ S, 55°9′ W 132
Maracaju, Serra de, *Braz.-Parag.* 19°12′ S, 55°27′ W 132
Maracanã, *Braz.* 0°47′ N, 47°27′ W 130
Maracás, *Braz.* 13°26′ S, 40°29′ W 138
Maracay, *Venez.* 10°12′ N, 67°38′ W 136
Marādah, *Lib.* 29°14′ N, 19°12′ E 216
Maradi, *Niger* 13°30′ N, 7°7′ E 222
Marāgheh, *Iran* 37°26′ N, 46°15′ E 195
Maragogipe, *Braz.* 12°48′ S, 38°57′ W 132
Marahoué National Park, *Côte d'Ivoire* 7°5′ N, 6°41′ W 222
Marahuaca, Cerro, peak, *Venez.* 3°32′ N, 65°30′ W 136
Marajó, Ilha de, *South America* 0°41′ N, 50°31′ W 123
Maralal, *Kenya* 1°4′ N, 36°42′ E 224
Maralaleng, *Botswana* 25°49′ S, 22°40′ E 227
Marali, *Cen. Af. Rep.* 6°0′ N, 18°23′ E 218
Maralinga, *Austral.* 30°7′ S, 131°24′ E 231
Maramasike, island, *Solomon Islands* 9°35′ S, 161°30′ E 242
Marambio, station, *Antarctica* 64°17′ S, 56°44′ W 134
Maramureş, adm. division, *Rom.* 47°36′ N, 23°20′ E 156
Maramureşului, Munţii, *Rom.* 47°57′ N, 24°19′ E 152
Maran, *Malaysia* 3°36′ N, 102°45′ E 196
Marana, *Ariz., U.S.* 32°26′ N, 111°13′ W 92
Maranchón, *Sp.* 41°2′ N, 2°13′ W 164
Marand, *Iran* 38°29′ N, 45°43′ E 195
Mărăndeni, *Mold.* 47°39′ N, 27°51′ E 152
Marang, *Malaysia* 5°12′ N, 103°12′ E 196
Maranguape, *Braz.* 3°53′ S, 38°41′ W 132
Maranhão, adm. division, *Braz.* 5°35′ S, 47°22′ W 130
Marañón, river, *Peru* 5°34′ S, 76°27′ W 122
Marão, Serra do, *Port.* 41°6′ N, 8°31′ W 150
Mararaba, *Cameroon* 5°37′ N, 13°47′ E 218
Margiu, Capo, *It.* 40°17′ N, 7°38′ E 156
Marari, *Braz.* 5°45′ S, 67°45′ W 130
Mărăşeşti, *Rom.* 45°52′ N, 27°13′ E 156
Marathon 490 B.C., battle, *Gr.* 38°6′ N, 23°51′ E 156
Marathon, *Can.* 48°43′ N, 86°22′ W 94
Marathon, *Fla., U.S.* 24°42′ N, 81°5′ W 105
Marathon, *Tex., U.S.* 30°11′ N, 103°15′ W 92
Marathus see 'Amrīt, ruin(s), *Syr.* 34°50′ N, 35°52′ E 194
Maratua, island, *Indonesia* 2°16′ N, 118°39′ E 192
Marau, *Braz.* 28°32′ S, 52°13′ W 139
Marauá, *Braz.* 3°26′ S, 66°23′ W 136
Marauiá, river, *Braz.* 0°28′ N, 65°22′ W 136
Maravatío, *Mex.* 19°52′ N, 100°27′ W 114
Marāveh Tappeh, *Iran* 37°54′ N, 55°55′ E 180
Marawi, *Philippines* 8°5′ N, 124°19′ E 203
Maraza, *Azerb.* 40°33′ N, 48°55′ E 195
Marbella, *Sp.* 36°30′ N, 4°53′ W 164
Marble, *Minn., U.S.* 47°18′ N, 93°18′ W 94
Marble Bar, *Austral.* 21°10′ S, 119°45′ E 231
Marble Canyon, *Ariz., U.S.* 36°32′ N, 112°1′ W 92
Marble Falls, *Tex., U.S.* 30°33′ N, 98°16′ W 92
Marble Hall, *S. Af.* 24°59′ S, 29°16′ E 227
Marble Mountains, *Calif., U.S.* 34°42′ N, 115°35′ W 101
Marblehead, *Mass., U.S.* 42°30′ N, 70°52′ W 104
Marblemount, *Wash., U.S.* 48°31′ N, 121°28′ W 100
Marbleton, *Wyo., U.S.* 42°34′ N, 110°5′ W 90
Mårbu, *Nor.* 60°11′ N, 8°10′ E 152
Marburg, *Ger.* 50°48′ N, 8°46′ E 167
Marca, Ponta da, *Angola* 16°36′ S, 11°3′ E 220
Marcali, *Hung.* 46°34′ N, 17°24′ E 168
Marcapata, *Peru* 13°34′ S, 70°54′ W 137
Marcaria, *It.* 45°7′ N, 10°32′ E 167
Marcelin, *Can.* 52°56′ N, 106°47′ W 108
Marceline, *Mo., U.S.* 39°42′ N, 92°56′ W 94
Marcelino, *Braz.* 1°48′ S, 66°25′ W 136
Marcelino Ramos, *Braz.* 27°30′ S, 51°57′ W 139
Marcellus, *Mich., U.S.* 42°1′ N, 85°48′ W 102
March, *U.K.* 52°33′ N, 8°475′ E 162
March Air Force Base, *Calif., U.S.* 33°53′ N, 117°17′ W 101
Marchamalo, *Sp.* 40°39′ N, 3°12′ W 164
Marchand, *Can.* 49°26′ N, 96°22′ W 90
Marche, *Belg.* 50°13′ N, 5°20′ E 167
Marche, region, *Fr.* 46°21′ N, 1°10′ E 165
Marchena, *Sp.* 37°19′ N, 5°26′ W 164
Marches, adm. division, *It.* 43°44′ N, 12°22′ E 156
Marchinbar Island, *Austral.* 11°17′ S, 134°53′ E 192
Marck, *Fr.* 50°56′ N, 1°55′ E 163
Marco, *Fla., U.S.* 25°57′ N, 81°43′ W 105
Marcola, *Oreg., U.S.* 44°9′ N, 122°53′ W 90
Marcos Juárez, *Arg.* 32°42′ S, 62°5′ W 139
Marcus, *Wash., U.S.* 48°39′ N, 118°4′ W 90
Marcy, Mount, peak, *N.Y., U.S.* 44°6′ N, 73°57′ W 104
Mardan, *Pak.* 34°11′ N, 72°6′ E 188
Mardin, *Turk.* 37°19′ N, 40°46′ E 195
Mære, *Nor.* 63°55′ N, 11°23′ E 152
Mare, Muntele, peak, *Rom.* 46°29′ N, 23°11′ E 168
Marechal Taumaturgo, *Braz.* 8°58′ S, 72°48′ W 137
Mareer, *Somalia* 1°35′ N, 44°26′ E 218
Marengo, *Can.* 51°29′ N, 109°47′ W 90
Marengo, *Ill., U.S.* 42°14′ N, 88°37′ W 102
Marennes, *Fr.* 45°50′ N, 1°8′ W 150
Mareshah, ruin(s), *Israel* 31°34′ N, 34°50′ E 194
Marevo, *Russ.* 57°17′ N, 32°6′ E 154
Marfa, *Tex., U.S.* 30°17′ N, 104°2′ W 92
Marfa, Massif de, *Chad* 13°2′ N, 20°4′ E 216
Marfino, *Russ.* 46°23′ N, 48°44′ E 158
Margai Caka, lake, *China* 35°6′ N, 86°25′ E 188
Margaret Lake, *Can.* 58°53′ N, 116°9′ W 108
Margaret, Mount, peak, *Austral.* 22°3′ S, 117°39′ E 230
Margarita, *Arg.* 29°39′ S, 60°13′ W 139
Margarita, Isla de, island, *Venez.* 10°47′ N, 63°53′ W 116
Margat (Marghab), ruin(s), *Syr.* 35°9′ N, 35°55′ E 194
Margat, ruin(s), *Syr.* 35°7′ N, 35°52′ E 156
Margate, *S. Af.* 30°52′ S, 30°20′ E 227
Margento, *Col.* 8°2′ N, 74°56′ W 136
Margeride, Monts de la, *Fr.* 45°6′ N, 3°1′ E 165
Marghab see Margat, ruin(s), *Syr.* 35°9′ N, 35°55′ E 194
Margherita Peak, *Dem. Rep. of the Congo* 0°19′ N, 29°46′ E 224
Marghita, *Rom.* 47°20′ N, 22°21′ E 168
Margie, *Can.* 55°24′ N, 111°23′ W 108
Marg'ilon, *Uzb.* 40°27′ N, 71°44′ E 197
Mărgineni, oil field, *Rom.* 44°56′ N, 25°40′ E 156
Margita, *Serb.* 45°12′ N, 21°12′ E 168
Margog Caka, lake, *China* 33°47′ N, 86°6′ E 188
Margosatubig, *Philippines* 7°36′ N, 123°11′ E 203
Marguerite, *Can.* 52°30′ N, 122°25′ W 108
Marhanets', *Ukr.* 47°37′ N, 34°44′ E 156
María, *Sp.* 37°42′ N, 2°9′ W 164
María Elena, *Chile* 22°20′ S, 69°43′ W 137
Maria Island, *Austral.* 14°45′ S, 135°43′ E 230
María Madre, Isla, island, *Mex.* 21°39′ N, 108°7′ W 112
María, peak, *Sp.* 37°40′ N, 2°15′ W 164
María Teresa, *Arg.* 34°3′ S, 61°55′ W 139
Mariakani, *Kenya* 3°54′ S, 39°28′ E 224
Mariana Lake, *Can.* 55°59′ N, 112°2′ W 108
Mariana Trench, *North Pacific Ocean* 16°4′ N, 148°3′ E 252
Marianao, *Cuba* 23°3′ N, 82°29′ W 116
Marianna, *Ark., U.S.* 34°46′ N, 90°47′ W 96
Marianna, *Fla., U.S.* 30°46′ N, 85°14′ W 96
Mariannelund, *Nor.* 57°37′ N, 15°32′ E 152
Marías, Islas, islands, *Mex.* 21°3′ N, 107°18′ W 112
Marias Pass, *Mont., U.S.* 48°18′ N, 113°20′ W 90
Ma'rib, *Yemen* 15°32′ N, 45°19′ E 182
Maribo, *Den.* 54°47′ N, 11°29′ E 152
Maribor, *Slov.* 46°32′ N, 15°39′ E 156
Maricopa, *Ariz., U.S.* 33°3′ N, 112°3′ W 92
Maricopa, *Calif., U.S.* 35°3′ N, 119°25′ W 100
Maridi, *Sudan* 4°56′ N, 29°30′ E 224
Marie Byrd Land, region, *Antarctica* 76°41′ S, 109°34′ W 248
Marié, river, *Braz.* 0°50′ N, 67°36′ W 136
Marie-Galante, island, *Fr.* 15°48′ N, 61°11′ W 116
Mariehamn (Maarianhamina), *Fin.* 60°5′ N, 19°55′ E 166
Marienbourg, *Belg.* 50°5′ N, 4°30′ E 163
Marienhafe, *Ger.* 53°31′ N, 7°17′ E 163
Mariental, *Namibia* 24°38′ S, 17°57′ E 227
Mariestad, *Nor.* 58°42′ N, 13°49′ E 152
Marietta, *Ga., U.S.* 33°57′ N, 84°34′ W 96
Marietta, *Ohio, U.S.* 39°25′ N, 81°27′ W 102
Marietta, *Okla., U.S.* 33°55′ N, 97°6′ W 92
Marietta, *Wash., U.S.* 48°47′ N, 122°34′ W 100
Marigny, *Fr.* 49°5′ N, 1°15′ W 150
Marii Pronchishchevoy, Bukhta 75°46′ N, 120°4′ E 246
Mariinsk, *Russ.* 56°13′ N, 87°45′ E 169
Marijampolė, *Lith.* 54°33′ N, 23°19′ E 166
Marilândia do Sul, *Braz.* 23°47′ S, 51°18′ W 138
Marília, *Braz.* 22°15′ S, 49°59′ W 138
Marilla, *Can.* 53°42′ N, 125°50′ W 108
Marimba, *Angola* 8°25′ S, 17°1′ E 218
Marina, *Calif., U.S.* 36°41′ N, 121°47′ W 100
Marina di Carrara, *It.* 44°2′ N, 10°1′ E 167
Marina di Ravenna, *It.* 44°28′ N, 12°15′ E 167
Marine City, *Mich., U.S.* 42°41′ N, 82°31′ W 102
Marineland, *Fla., U.S.* 29°39′ N, 81°14′ W 105
Marinette, *Wis., U.S.* 45°4′ N, 87°38′ W 94
Maringá, *Braz.* 23°25′ S, 52°0′ W 138
Maringouin, *La., U.S.* 30°28′ N, 91°32′ W 103
Marínguè, *Mozambique* 18°0′ S, 34°23′ E 224
Mar'ino, *Russ.* 51°12′ N, 36°43′ E 158
Mar'insko, *Russ.* 58°47′ N, 28°32′ E 166
Marinuma, *Col.* 2°15′ N, 69°22′ W 136
Marion, *Ala., U.S.* 32°37′ N, 87°20′ W 103
Marion, *Ark., U.S.* 35°12′ N, 90°13′ W 96
Marion, *Ind., U.S.* 40°33′ N, 85°41′ W 102
Marion, *Iowa, U.S.* 42°1′ N, 91°36′ W 94
Marion, *Kans., U.S.* 38°20′ N, 97°2′ W 90
Marion, *La., U.S.* 32°53′ N, 92°15′ W 103
Marion, *Mass., U.S.* 41°41′ N, 70°47′ W 104
Marion, *Mich., U.S.* 44°6′ N, 85°8′ W 102
Marion, *Miss., U.S.* 32°24′ N, 88°39′ W 103
Marion, *Mo., U.S.* 37°43′ N, 88°55′ W 94
Marion, *Ohio, U.S.* 40°34′ N, 83°8′ W 102
Marion, *S.C., U.S.* 34°10′ N, 79°24′ W 96
Marion, *S. Dak., U.S.* 43°24′ N, 97°16′ W 90
Marion, *Va., U.S.* 36°50′ N, 81°32′ W 94
Marion Nunataks 69°34′ S, 79°8′ W 248
Marionville, *Mo., U.S.* 36°59′ N, 93°38′ W 96
Maripa, *Venez.* 7°21′ N, 65°8′ W 136
Mariposa, *Calif., U.S.* 37°29′ N, 119°59′ W 100
Marir, Gezâir (Mirear), islands, *Egypt* 23°5′ N, 35°51′ E 182
Mariscal Estigarribia, *Parag.* 22°2′ S, 60°37′ W 132
Maristova, *Nor.* 61°6′ N, 8°1′ E 152
Maritime Alps, *Fr.* 44°2′ N, 6°45′ E 165
Maritime Territory, adm. division, *Russ.* 45°20′ N, 135°8′ E 190
Mariupol', *Ukr.* 47°5′ N, 37°28′ E 156
Mariusa National Park, *Venez.* 9°23′ N, 61°33′ W 116
Marīvān, *Iran* 35°31′ N, 46°11′ E 180
Mariy-El, adm. division, *Russ.* 56°19′ N, 46°11′ E 154
Mariyets, *Russ.* 56°30′ N, 49°53′ E 154
Marj 'Uyūn, *Leb.* 33°21′ N, 35°35′ E 194
Märjamaa, *Est.* 58°54′ N, 24°23′ E 166
Marjonbuloq, *Uzb.* 39°59′ N, 67°21′ E 197
Marka see Merca, *Somalia* 1°41′ N, 44°53′ E 207
Markala, *Mali* 13°40′ N, 6°4′ W 222
Markansu, *Taj.* 39°19′ N, 73°21′ E 197
Markapur, *India* 15°42′ N, 79°17′ E 188
Markaryd, *Nor.* 56°28′ N, 13°35′ E 152
Markdale, *Can.* 44°18′ N, 80°39′ W 110
Markelsdorfer Huk, *Kattegat* 54°37′ N, 10°49′ E 152
Markesan, *Wis., U.S.* 43°42′ N, 88°59′ W 102
Market Drayton, *U.K.* 52°53′ N, 2°30′ W 162
Market Harborough, *U.K.* 52°28′ N, 0°55′ E 162
Market Rasen, *U.K.* 53°22′ N, 0°21′ E 162
Market Weighton, *U.K.* 53°51′ N, 0°41′ E 162
Markha, river, *Russ.* 64°57′ N, 116°6′ E 160
Markham, *Can.* 43°51′ N, 79°17′ W 94
Markham Bay 63°24′ N, 74°18′ W 106
Markham, Mount, peak, *Antarctica* 82°47′ S, 162°59′ E 248
Markit, *China* 38°57′ N, 77°37′ E 184
Markkina, *Fin.* 68°29′ N, 22°16′ E 152
Markle, *Ind., U.S.* 40°49′ N, 85°20′ W 102
Markounda, *Cen. Af. Rep.* 7°33′ N, 16°57′ E 218
Markovac, *Serb.* 44°13′ N, 21°5′ E 168
Markovo, *Russ.* 64°41′ N, 170°4′ E 160
Marks Butte, peak, *Colo., U.S.* 40°48′ N, 102°36′ W 90
Marksville, *La., U.S.* 31°6′ N, 92°5′ W 103
Markušica, *Croatia* 45°22′ N, 18°41′ E 168
Marl, *Ger.* 51°39′ N, 7°6′ E 167
Marlboro, *Vt., U.S.* 42°51′ N, 72°44′ W 104
Marlborough, *N.H., U.S.* 42°53′ N, 72°13′ W 104
Marlborough, *U.K.* 51°24′ N, 1°44′ W 162
Marle, *Fr.* 49°44′ N, 3°47′ E 163
Marles, *Fr.* 50°30′ N, 2°30′ E 150
Marlette, *Mich., U.S.* 43°19′ N, 83°5′ W 102
Marlin, *Tex., U.S.* 31°17′ N, 96°53′ W 96
Marlin, oil field, *Bass Strait* 38°17′ S, 148°12′ E 230
Marlow, *N.H., U.S.* 43°6′ N, 72°13′ W 104
Marlow, *Okla., U.S.* 34°38′ N, 97°58′ W 92
Marlow, *U.K.* 51°34′ N, 0°47′ E 162
Marmagao, *India* 15°23′ N, 73°48′ E 173
Marmara Denizi, *Turkey* 40°37′ N, 27°43′ E 156
Marmaris, *Turk.* 36°51′ N, 28°14′ E 156
Marmarth, *N. Dak., U.S.* 46°16′ N, 103°54′ W 90
Marmolada, peak, *It.* 46°26′ N, 11°47′ E 167
Marmolejo, *Sp.* 38°2′ N, 4°11′ W 164
Marmul, oil field, *Oman* 18°10′ N, 55°23′ E 182
Marne, river, *Fr.* 48°49′ N, 2°37′ E 163
Maroa, *Ill., U.S.* 40°1′ N, 88°57′ W 102
Maroa, *Venez.* 2°45′ N, 67°33′ W 136
Maroantsetra, *Madagascar* 15°25′ S, 49°41′ E 220
Marol, *Pak.* 34°45′ N, 76°16′ E 186
Marolambo, *Madagascar* 20°4′ S, 48°8′ E 220
Maromandia, *Madagascar* 14°9′ S, 48°5′ E 220
Maromokotro, peak, *Madagascar* 14°4′ S, 48°50′ E 220
Marondera, *Zimb.* 18°14′ S, 31°30′ E 224
Marone, *It.* 45°44′ N, 10°5′ E 167
Marónia, *Gr.* 40°54′ N, 25°31′ E 156
Maronne, river, *Fr.* 45°1′ N, 1°59′ E 165
Maros, *Indonesia* 4°58′ S, 119°32′ E 192
Marotandrano, *Madagascar* 16°11′ S, 48°48′ E 220
Marotiri, island, *Fr.* 27°49′ S, 143°42′ W 252
Maroua, *Cameroon* 10°36′ N, 14°20′ E 216
Marouini, river, *South America* 2°10′ N, 53°57′ W 130
Marovoay, *Madagascar* 16°8′ S, 46°39′ E 220
Marqaköl, lake, *Kaz.* 48°42′ N, 85°14′ E 184
Marquard, *S. Af.* 28°41′ S, 27°23′ E 227
Marquesas Fracture Zone, *South Pacific Ocean* 10°40′ S, 131°47′ W 252
Marquesas Islands, *South Pacific Ocean* 11°28′ S, 141°48′ W 238
Marquesas Keys, islands, *Gulf of Mexico* 24°26′ N, 82°20′ W 105
Marquette, *Mich., U.S.* 46°32′ N, 87°24′ W 94
Marquette, Lac, lake, *Can.* 48°54′ N, 74°33′ W 94
Marquise, *Fr.* 50°49′ N, 1°42′ E 163
Marra, Jebel, peak, *Sudan* 12°50′ N, 23°50′ E 206
Marrakech, *Mor.* 31°39′ N, 8°1′ W 214
Marrasjärvi, *Fin.* 66°53′ N, 25°6′ E 152
Marrecas, Serra das, *Braz.* 9°33′ S, 41°40′ W 132
Marromeu, *Mozambique* 18°19′ S, 35°55′ E 224
Marrupa, *Mozambique* 13°12′ S, 37°30′ E 224
Mars Hill, peak, *Me., U.S.* 46°30′ N, 67°54′ W 94
Marsá al 'Uwayjā', *Lib.* 30°54′ N, 17°51′ E 216
Marsa 'Alam, spring, *Egypt* 25°4′ N, 34°51′ E 182
Marsa Fatma, *Eritrea* 14°51′ N, 40°20′ E 182
Marsa Sha'ab, *Egypt* 22°49′ N, 35°45′ E 182
Marsabit, *Kenya* 2°18′ N, 38°0′ E 224
Marsabit Nature Reserve, *Kenya* 1°54′ N, 37°47′ E 224
Marsala, *It.* 37°48′ N, 12°26′ E 156
Marsberg, *Ger.* 51°27′ N, 8°52′ E 167
Marsden Point, *N.Z.* 35°53′ S, 174°28′ E 240
Marseillan, *Fr.* 43°21′ N, 3°30′ E 164
Marseille, *Fr.* 43°17′ N, 5°22′ E 150
Marsfjället, peak, *Nor.* 65°5′ N, 15°13′ E 152
Marsh Island, *La., U.S.* 29°24′ N, 92°2′ W 103
Marsh Pass, *Ariz., U.S.* 36°38′ N, 110°25′ W 92
Marsh Peak, *Utah, U.S.* 40°41′ N, 109°54′ W 90
Marsh Point, *Can.* 57°5′ N, 92°20′ W 108
Marshall, *Alas., U.S.* 61°52′ N, 162°4′ W 98
Marshall, *Ark., U.S.* 35°53′ N, 92°39′ W 96
Marshall, *Ill., U.S.* 39°23′ N, 87°41′ W 102
Marshall, *Liberia* 6°4′ N, 10°23′ W 222
Marshall, *Mich., U.S.* 42°16′ N, 84°57′ W 102
Marshall, *Minn., U.S.* 44°26′ N, 95°48′ W 90
Marshall, *Mo., U.S.* 39°6′ N, 93°16′ W 82
Marshall, *Tex., U.S.* 32°32′ N, 94°23′ W 103
Marshall Bennett Islands, *Solomon Sea* 8°46′ S, 152°2′ E 230
Marshall Islands, *Marshall Islands* 9°2′ N, 170°3′ E 238
Marshalltown, *Iowa, U.S.* 42°4′ N, 92°53′ W 82
Marshfield, *Mo., U.S.* 37°19′ N, 92°54′ W 94
Marshfield, *Vt., U.S.* 44°21′ N, 72°22′ W 104
Marshfield, *Wis., U.S.* 44°39′ N, 90°11′ W 94
Marsland, *Nebr., U.S.* 42°26′ N, 103°18′ W 90
Mars-la-Tour, *Fr.* 49°6′ N, 5°53′ E 163
Marston Moor, battle, *U.K.* 53°58′ N, 1°16′ W 162
Marstrand, *Sw.* 57°53′ N, 11°33′ E 150
Marsyaty, *Russ.* 60°4′ N, 60°25′ E 154
Mart, *Tex., U.S.* 31°31′ N, 96°49′ W 96
Martaban, *Myanmar* 16°34′ N, 97°35′ E 202
Martaban, Gulf of 15°50′ N, 96°1′ E 192
Martakert (Ägdara), *Asia* 40°12′ N, 46°47′ E 195
Martap, *Cameroon* 6°50′ N, 13°3′ E 218
Martapura, *Indonesia* 3°30′ S, 114°45′ E 192
Marte R. Gómez, Presa, lake, *Mex.* 26°12′ N, 100°24′ W 80
Martem'yanovskaya, *Russ.* 61°58′ N, 39°11′ E 154
Marten Mountain, peak, *Can.* 55°28′ N, 114°50′ W 108
Martés, peak, *Sp.* 39°18′ N, 1°0′ E 164
Martfű, *Hung.* 47°0′ N, 20°17′ E 168
Martha's Vineyard, island, *Mass., U.S.* 41°14′ N, 70°47′ W 104
Marthaville, *La., U.S.* 31°43′ N, 93°25′ W 103
Martigny, *Switz.* 46°6′ N, 7°3′ E 167
Martigues, *Fr.* 43°23′ N, 5°3′ E 150
Martil, *Mor.* 35°37′ N, 5°17′ W 150
Martin, *Mich., U.S.* 42°32′ N, 85°39′ W 102
Martin, *S. Dak., U.S.* 43°10′ N, 101°44′ W 90
Martin, Lake, *Ala., U.S.* 32°51′ N, 86°22′ W 80
Martin, river, *Can.* 61°31′ N, 122°26′ W 108
Martin Vaz Islands, *South Atlantic Ocean* 20°29′ S, 28°57′ W 253
Martinborough, *N.Z.* 41°15′ S, 175°29′ E 240
Martinez, *Calif., U.S.* 38°1′ N, 122°9′ W 100
Martinez, *Ga., U.S.* 33°30′ N, 82°6′ W 96
Martinez Lake, *Ariz., U.S.* 32°58′ N, 114°28′ W 101
Martinique, *Fr.* 14°26′ N, 61°27′ W 116

Martinique Passage 15° 1′ N, 62° 3′ W 116
Martinsburg, *N.Y., U.S.* 43° 44′ N, 75° 29′ W 94
Martinsville, *Ill., U.S.* 39° 19′ N, 87° 53′ W 102
Martinsville, *Ind., U.S.* 39° 25′ N, 86° 26′ W 102
Martinsville, *Va., U.S.* 36° 40′ N, 79° 53′ W 96
Martna, *Est.* 58° 50′ N, 23° 47′ E 166
Marton, *N.Z.* 40° 6′ S, 175° 24′ E 240
Martorell, *Sp.* 41° 27′ N, 1° 54′ E 164
Martos, *Sp.* 37° 43′ N, 3° 59′ W 164
Martti, *Fin.* 67° 28′ N, 28° 21′ E 152
Martuni, *Arm.* 40° 8′ N, 45° 16′ E 195
Martuni (Xocavand), *Azerb.* 39° 48′ N, 47° 5′ E 195
Martyn, Mount, peak, *Antarctica* 69° 19′ S, 157° 39′ E 248
Ma'ruf, *Afghan.* 31° 29′ N, 67° 3′ E 186
Maruia, *N.Z.* 42° 12′ S, 172° 14′ E 240
Marumori, *Japan* 37° 55′ N, 140° 46′ E 201
Marungu, *Dem. Rep. of the Congo* 8° 10′ S, 29° 36′ E 224
Maruoka, *Japan* 36° 8′ N, 136° 16′ E 201
Marv Dasht, *Iran* 29° 55′ N, 52° 56′ E 196
Marvin Spur, *Arctic Ocean* 86° 15′ N, 118° 55′ W 255
Marvine, Mount, peak, *Utah, U.S.* 38° 39′ N, 111° 42′ W 90
Marwar, *India* 25° 43′ N, 73° 37′ E 186
Marx, *Russ.* 51° 36′ N, 46° 42′ E 158
Mary, *Turkm.* 37° 36′ N, 61° 50′ E 180
Mary, river, *Austral.* 25° 36′ S, 152° 13′ E 230
Mar'yanovka, *Russ.* 54° 55′ N, 72° 44′ E 184
Marydale, *S. Af.* 29° 28′ S, 22° 7′ E 227
Maryland, adm. division, *Md., U.S.* 39° 33′ N, 77° 50′ W 94
Maryport, *U.K.* 54° 42′ N, 3° 30′ W 162
Mary's Harbour, *Can.* 52° 24′ N, 55° 58′ W 73
Marystown, *Can.* 47° 10′ N, 55° 9′ W 111
Marysvale, *Utah, U.S.* 38° 26′ N, 112° 13′ W 90
Marysville, *Calif., U.S.* 39° 9′ N, 121° 37′ W 92
Marysville, *Can.* 45° 58′ N, 66° 37′ W 94
Marysville, *Kans., U.S.* 39° 49′ N, 96° 39′ W 92
Marysville, *Mich., U.S.* 42° 53′ N, 82° 30′ W 102
Marysville, *Ohio, U.S.* 40° 13′ N, 83° 22′ W 102
Marysville, *Wash., U.S.* 48° 2′ N, 122° 11′ W 100
Maryville, *Mo., U.S.* 40° 20′ N, 94° 53′ W 82
Maryville, *Tenn., U.S.* 35° 45′ N, 83° 58′ W 96
Marzafal, *Mali* 17° 56′ N, 0° 59′ E 222
Marzo, Cabo, *Col.* 6° 41′ N, 78° 6′ W 136
Marzūq, *Lib.* 25° 55′ N, 13° 53′ E 216
Mas de las Matas, *Sp.* 40° 51′ N, 0° 15′ E 164
Masada, ruin(s), *Israel* 31° 18′ N, 35° 19′ E 194
Masai Mara National Reserve, *Kenya* 1° 27′ S, 35° 5′ E 224
Masai Steppe, *Tanzania* 5° 43′ S, 37° 1′ E 224
Masaka, *Uganda* 0° 22′ N, 31° 43′ E 224
Masalasef, *Chad* 11° 45′ N, 17° 10′ E 216
Masallı, *Azerb.* 39° 1′ N, 48° 39′ E 195
Masalembu, Kepulauan, islands, *Java Sea* 5° 56′ S, 113° 19′ E 192
Masan, *S. Korea* 35° 11′ N, 128° 33′ E 200
Masasi, *Tanzania* 10° 43′ S, 38° 47′ E 224
Masavi, *Bol.* 19° 24′ S, 63° 18′ W 137
Masaya, *Nicar.* 11° 57′ N, 86° 6′ W 115
Masayama, *Sierra Leone* 8° 14′ N, 10° 49′ W 222
Masbate, *Philippines* 12° 20′ N, 123° 36′ E 203
Masbate, island, *Philippines* 11° 55′ N, 122° 11′ E 192
Mascara, *Alg.* 35° 23′ N, 0° 7′ E 150
Mascarene Basin, *Indian Ocean* 13° 57′ S, 55° 8′ E 254
Mascarene Plain, *Indian Ocean* 21° 15′ S, 51° 32′ E 254
Mascart, Cape, *Antarctica* 66° 35′ S, 71° 50′ W 248
Mascota, *Mex.* 20° 31′ N, 104° 48′ W 114
Mascoutah, *Ill., U.S.* 38° 28′ N, 89° 47′ W 102
Masein, *Myanmar* 23° 22′ N, 94° 21′ E 202
Maseru, *Lesotho* 29° 19′ S, 27° 24′ E 227
Masfjorden, *Nor.* 60° 47′ N, 5° 19′ E 152
Mash'abbé Sade, *Israel* 30° 59′ N, 34° 46′ E 194
Mashābih, island, *Saudi Arabia* 25° 35′ N, 35° 47′ E 182
Masham, *U.K.* 54° 13′ N, 1° 40′ W 162
Mashan, *China* 23° 40′ N, 108° 10′ E 198
Mashhad, *Iran* 36° 19′ N, 59° 35′ E 180
Mashigina, Guba 74° 4′ N, 47° 51′ E 160
Mashkai, river, *Pak.* 26° 44′ N, 65° 14′ E 182
Mashuray, *Afghan.* 32° 8′ N, 68° 20′ E 186
Masi, *Nor.* 69° 26′ N, 23° 38′ E 152
Masindi, *Uganda* 1° 38′ N, 31° 42′ E 224
Masindi Port, *Uganda* 1° 39′ N, 32° 4′ E 224
Masinloc, *Philippines* 15° 34′ N, 119° 58′ E 203
Maşīrah, Jazīrat (Masira), island, *Oman* 20° 43′ N, 58° 55′ E 182
Masisea, *Peru* 8° 40′ S, 74° 21′ W 130
Masisi, *Dem. Rep. of the Congo* 1° 24′ S, 28° 47′ E 224
Māsiyah, Tall al, peak, *Syr.* 32° 47′ N, 36° 39′ E 194
Masjed Soleymān, *Iran* 31° 54′ N, 49° 20′ E 180
Maska, *Nig.* 11° 17′ N, 7° 19′ E 222
Maskan, Raas, *Somalia* 11° 9′ N, 43° 34′ E 216
Maskūtān, *Iran* 26° 51′ N, 59° 53′ E 182
Maslen Nos, *Bulg.* 42° 20′ N, 27° 46′ E 156
Maslovare, *Bosn. and Herzg.* 44° 33′ N, 17° 31′ E 168
Maslovo, *Russ.* 60° 9′ N, 60° 31′ E 154
Masoala, Presqu'île de, *Madagascar* 16° 16′ S, 50° 11′ E 220
Masoller, *Uru.* 31° 7′ S, 55° 59′ W 139
Masomeloka, *Madagascar* 20° 17′ S, 48° 37′ E 220
Mason, *Ill., U.S.* 38° 57′ N, 88° 38′ W 102
Mason, *Mich., U.S.* 42° 34′ N, 84° 26′ W 102
Mason, *Ohio, U.S.* 39° 21′ N, 84° 19′ W 102
Mason, *Tex., U.S.* 30° 43′ N, 99° 13′ W 92
Mason Bay 47° 3′ S, 167° 36′ E 240
Mason City, *Ill., U.S.* 40° 12′ N, 89° 42′ W 102
Mason City, *Iowa, U.S.* 43° 7′ N, 93° 12′ W 94
Masqaţ (Muscat), *Oman* 23° 30′ N, 58° 32′ E 196
Massa, *Congo* 3° 46′ S, 15° 27′ E 218
Massa, *It.* 44° 1′ N, 10° 8′ E 167
Massa Lombarda, *It.* 44° 26′ N, 11° 49′ E 167
Massachusetts, adm. division, *Mass., U.S.* 42° 14′ N, 72° 39′ W 104
Massachusetts Bay 42° 11′ N, 70° 43′ W 104
Massafra, *It.* 40° 35′ N, 17° 7′ E 156
Massaguet, *Chad* 12° 31′ N, 15° 25′ E 216
Massakory, *Chad* 13° 0′ N, 15° 42′ E 216
Massambara, *Braz.* 29° 7′ S, 56° 4′ W 139
Massangena, *Mozambique* 21° 33′ S, 33° 2′ E 227
Massat, *Fr.* 42° 52′ N, 1° 20′ E 164
Massava, *Russ.* 60° 38′ N, 62° 5′ E 154
Massawa, *Eritrea* 15° 37′ N, 39° 23′ E 182
Massenya, *Chad* 11° 27′ N, 16° 9′ E 216
Masset, *Can.* 53° 59′ N, 132° 2′ W 98
Masseube, *Fr.* 43° 25′ N, 0° 33′ E 164
Massillon, *Ohio, U.S.* 40° 47′ N, 81° 31′ W 102
Massinga, *Mozambique* 23° 16′ S, 35° 20′ E 227
Massingir, *Mozambique* 23° 47′ S, 32° 7′ E 227
Masson Island, *Antarctica* 66° 3′ S, 96° 8′ E 248
Masson Range, *Antarctica* 68° 32′ S, 59° 23′ E 248
Mastābah, *Saudi Arabia* 20° 49′ N, 39° 26′ E 182
Maştağa, *Azerb.* 40° 33′ N, 49° 59′ E 195
Mastic Beach, *N.Y., U.S.* 40° 45′ N, 72° 51′ W 104
Mastic Point, *Bahamas* 25° 4′ N, 78° 0′ W 96
Mastuj, *Pak.* 36° 15′ N, 72° 33′ E 186
Mastūrah, *Saudi Arabia* 23° 7′ N, 38° 51′ E 182
Masty, *Belarus* 53° 25′ N, 24° 33′ E 152
Masuda, *Japan* 34° 39′ N, 131° 51′ E 200
Masuria, region, *Pol.* 54° 12′ N, 19° 41′ E 166
Masvingo, *Zimb.* 20° 6′ S, 30° 47′ E 227
Maşyāf, *Syr.* 35° 3′ N, 36° 20′ E 194
Mat, river, *Alban.* 41° 38′ N, 19° 38′ E 168
Mata, *Dem. Rep. of the Congo* 7° 55′ S, 21° 56′ E 218
Mata Mata, *S. Af.* 25° 50′ S, 20° 3′ E 227
Mata Ortiz, *Mex.* 30° 7′ N, 108° 4′ W 92
Matachewan, *Can.* 47° 56′ N, 80° 38′ W 94
Matachic, *Mex.* 28° 50′ N, 107° 44′ W 92
Matadi, *Dem. Rep. of the Congo* 5° 49′ S, 13° 27′ E 218
Matador, *Tex., U.S.* 33° 59′ N, 100° 50′ W 92
Matagalpa, *Nicar.* 12° 54′ N, 85° 54′ W 115
Matagami, *Can.* 49° 47′ N, 77° 39′ W 94
Matagami, Lac, lake, *Can.* 50° 0′ N, 78° 4′ W 94
Matagorda, *Tex., U.S.* 28° 41′ N, 95° 58′ W 96
Matagorda Bay 28° 28′ N, 97° 19′ W 80
Matagorda Peninsula, *Tex., U.S.* 28° 31′ N, 96° 26′ W 96
Matak, island, *Indonesia* 3° 25′ N, 106° 17′ E 196
Matakana, *N.Z.* 36° 23′ S, 174° 42′ E 240
Matala, *Angola* 14° 47′ S, 14° 59′ E 220
Matala, ruin(s), *Gr.* 34° 58′ N, 24° 39′ E 156
Matam, *Senegal* 15° 39′ N, 13° 21′ W 222
Matameye, *Niger* 13° 23′ N, 8° 26′ E 222
Matamoros, *Mex.* 18° 34′ N, 98° 29′ W 114
Matamoros, *Mex.* 25° 31′ N, 103° 15′ W 114
Matamoros, *Mex.* 25° 53′ N, 97° 31′ W 114
Ma'ţan al Ḩusayyāt, spring, *Lib.* 30° 21′ N, 20° 33′ E 216
Ma'ţan as Sarra, spring, *Lib.* 21° 35′ N, 21° 52′ E 216
Ma'ţan Bishrah, spring, *Lib.* 23° 0′ N, 22° 41′ E 226
Ma'ţan Shârib, spring, *Egypt* 30° 16′ N, 28° 26′ E 180
Matandu, river, *Tanzania* 8° 52′ S, 38° 38′ E 224
Matane, *Can.* 48° 49′ N, 67° 33′ W 94
Matanzas, *Cuba* 23° 4′ N, 81° 36′ W 96
Matanzas, adm. division, *Cuba* 22° 59′ N, 81° 44′ W 116
Matanzas, island, *Cuba* 22° 5′ N, 82° 46′ W 116
Matão, Serra do, *Braz.* 9° 38′ S, 51° 31′ W 130
Mataojo, *Uru.* 31° 11′ S, 56° 23′ W 139
Matapás see Akrotírio Ténaro, *Gr.* 36° 13′ N, 21° 38′ E 156
Matapi, *Suriname* 4° 59′ N, 57° 21′ W 130
Mataporquera, *Sp.* 42° 52′ N, 4° 11′ W 150
Matapwa, *Tanzania* 9° 42′ S, 39° 24′ E 224
Matara, *Sri Lanka* 5° 58′ N, 80° 32′ E 188
Mataram, *Indonesia* 8° 36′ S, 116° 6′ E 192
Matarani, *Peru* 17° 0′ S, 72° 7′ W 137
Matarka, *Mor.* 33° 21′ N, 2° 42′ W 214
Mataró, *Sp.* 41° 32′ N, 2° 26′ E 164
Matassi, spring, *Sudan* 18° 49′ N, 29° 47′ E 226
Mätäsvaara, *Fin.* 63° 25′ N, 29° 32′ E 152
Matata, *N.Z.* 37° 55′ S, 176° 46′ E 240
Matatiele, *S. Af.* 30° 22′ S, 28° 46′ E 227
Mataurá, river, *Peru* 6° 15′ S, 60° 59′ W 130
Matawai, *N.Z.* 38° 22′ S, 177° 33′ E 240
Matay, *Kaz.* 45° 31′ N, 57° 6′ E 158
Matay, *Kaz.* 45° 52′ N, 78° 41′ E 184
Mateguá, *Bol.* 13° 3′ S, 62° 49′ W 130
Matehuala, *Mex.* 23° 37′ N, 100° 39′ W 96
Matemo, Ilha, island, *Mozambique* 12° 11′ S, 40° 39′ E 224
Matera, *It.* 40° 39′ N, 16° 36′ E 156
Matese, *It.* 41° 26′ N, 14° 7′ E 156
Mátészalka, *Hung.* 47° 56′ N, 22° 21′ E 168
Matetsi, *Zimb.* 18° 19′ S, 25° 56′ E 224
Matfors, *Nor.* 62° 20′ N, 17° 0′ E 152
Matguia, *Tun.* 34° 40′ N, 10° 20′ E 156
Mather, *Calif., U.S.* 37° 52′ N, 119° 52′ W 100
Mather, Mount, peak, *Antarctica* 73° 32′ S, 60° 30′ E 248
Matheson, *Can.* 48° 32′ N, 80° 29′ W 94
Matheson Island, *Can.* 51° 43′ N, 96° 57′ W 108
Mathews, *Va., U.S.* 37° 25′ N, 76° 20′ W 96
Mathews Peak, *Kenya* 1° 13′ N, 37° 14′ E 224
Mathis, *Tex., U.S.* 28° 5′ N, 97° 49′ W 92
Mathura, *India* 27° 27′ N, 77° 38′ E 197
Mati, *Philippines* 6° 59′ N, 126° 12′ E 203
Matiakoali, *Burkina Faso* 12° 21′ N, 1° 3′ E 222
Matias Cardoso, *Braz.* 14° 56′ S, 43° 55′ W 138
Matin, *India* 22° 46′ N, 82° 25′ E 197
Matkasel'kya, *Russ.* 61° 57′ N, 30° 30′ E 152
Matlabas, *S. Af.* 24° 15′ S, 27° 30′ E 227
Matli, *Pak.* 25° 4′ N, 68° 47′ E 186
Matlock, *U.K.* 53° 8′ N, 1° 33′ W 162
Mato, *Dem. Rep. of the Congo* 8° 1′ S, 24° 54′ E 224
Mato, Cerro, peak, *Venez.* 7° 12′ N, 65° 23′ W 136
Mato Grosso, adm. division, *Braz.* 14° 29′ S, 52° 39′ W 138
Mato Grosso do Sul, adm. division, *Braz.* 20° 12′ S, 53° 26′ W 138
Mato Verde, *Braz.* 15° 25′ S, 42° 55′ W 138
Matobo National Park, *Zimb.* 20° 38′ S, 28° 11′ E 206
Matochkin Shar, *Russ.* 73° 21′ N, 56° 33′ E 160
Matochkin Shar, Proliv 72° 52′ N, 49° 46′ E 160
Matoio, *Angola* 7° 28′ S, 14° 37′ E 220
Matola, *Malawi* 13° 39′ S, 34° 55′ E 224
Matombo, *Tanzania* 7° 2′ S, 37° 47′ E 224
Matope, *Malawi* 15° 21′ S, 34° 58′ E 224
Matopos, *Zimb.* 20° 25′ S, 28° 28′ E 227
Matos, river, *Bol.* 14° 30′ S, 66° 0′ W 137
Matosinhos, *Port.* 41° 10′ N, 8° 43′ W 150
Mátra, *Hung.* 47° 47′ N, 19° 43′ E 168
Matraca, *Col.* 3° 1′ N, 69° 7′ W 136
Mátrafüred, *Hung.* 47° 48′ N, 19° 58′ E 168
Maţra', *Oman* 23° 36′ N, 58° 32′ E 182
Matsalu National Park, *Est.* 58° 44′ N, 23° 50′ E 166
Maţrūḩ, *Egypt* 31° 20′ N, 27° 12′ E 180
Matsena, *Nig.* 13° 8′ N, 10° 3′ E 222
Matsu, island, *Taiwan, China* 26° 16′ N, 120° 3′ E 198
Matsubase, *Japan* 32° 37′ N, 130° 41′ E 201
Matsue, *Japan* 35° 27′ N, 133° 3′ E 201
Matsumoto, *Japan* 36° 13′ N, 137° 59′ E 201
Matsunaga, *Japan* 34° 27′ N, 133° 16′ E 201
Matsusaka, *Japan* 34° 33′ N, 136° 33′ E 201
Matsushiro, *Japan* 36° 34′ N, 138° 13′ E 201
Matsutō, *Japan* 36° 30′ N, 136° 33′ E 201
Matsuura, *Japan* 33° 20′ N, 129° 42′ E 201
Matsuyama, *Japan* 33° 49′ N, 132° 46′ E 201
Mattagami Lake, lake, *Can.* 47° 47′ N, 82° 6′ W 110
Mattagami, river, *Can.* 50° 10′ N, 82° 17′ W 110
Mattapoisett, *Mass., U.S.* 41° 39′ N, 70° 50′ W 104
Mattawa, *Can.* 46° 18′ N, 78° 41′ W 94
Matterhorn Peak, *Calif., U.S.* 38° 5′ N, 119° 25′ W 100
Matterhorn, peak, *Nev., U.S.* 41° 48′ N, 115° 28′ W 90
Matterhorn, peak, *Switz.* 45° 59′ N, 7° 37′ E 165
Mattersburg, *Aust.* 47° 43′ N, 16° 24′ E 168
Matthews Peak, *Ariz., U.S.* 36° 21′ N, 109° 13′ W 92
Matthew's Ridge, *Guyana* 7° 27′ N, 60° 6′ W 130
Mattili, *India* 18° 32′ N, 82° 13′ E 188
Mattinata, *It.* 41° 42′ N, 16° 2′ E 168
Mattituck, *N.Y., U.S.* 40° 59′ N, 72° 32′ W 104
Mattoon, *Ill., U.S.* 39° 29′ N, 88° 22′ W 102
Matugama, *Sri Lanka* 6° 30′ N, 80° 7′ E 188
Matunuck, *R.I., U.S.* 41° 22′ N, 71° 33′ W 104
Maturango Peak, *Calif., U.S.* 36° 6′ N, 117° 35′ W 92
Maturín, *Venez.* 9° 42′ N, 63° 12′ W 116
Matusadona National Park, *Zimb.* 17° 10′ S, 28° 4′ E 224
Matveyevka, *Russ.* 53° 29′ N, 53° 35′ E 154
Matxitxako, Cabo, *Sp.* 43° 19′ N, 2° 48′ W 164
Matyl'ka, *Russ.* 63° 20′ N, 85° 34′ E 169
Matzen, oil field, *Aust.* 48° 21′ N, 16° 35′ E 152
Mau, *India* 25° 54′ N, 83° 31′ E 197
Mau Ranipur, *India* 25° 13′ N, 79° 8′ E 197
Mauá, *Mozambique* 13° 52′ S, 37° 10′ E 224
Maubeuge, *Fr.* 50° 16′ N, 3° 58′ E 163
Ma-ubin, *Myanmar* 16° 43′ N, 95° 36′ E 202
Maubourguet, *Fr.* 43° 27′ N, 3° 178′ E 164
Maud, *Tex., U.S.* 33° 19′ N, 94° 22′ W 103
Maud Rise, *South Atlantic Ocean* 65° 26′ S, 4° 0′ E 255
Maude, Cape, *Antarctica* 82° 34′ S, 179° 24′ E 248
Maués, *Braz.* 3° 23′ S, 57° 43′ W 130
Maués, river, *Braz.* 4° 23′ S, 57° 25′ W 130
Maug Islands, *Maug Islands* 20° 2′ N, 145° 20′ E 192
Mauganj, *India* 24° 42′ N, 81° 52′ E 197
Maugerville, *Can.* 45° 53′ N, 66° 28′ W 94
Maui, island, *Hawai'i, U.S.* 20° 39′ N, 156° 2′ W 99
Maukme, *Myanmar* 20° 13′ N, 97° 42′ E 202
Maule, adm. division, *Chile* 35° 44′ S, 72° 37′ W 134
Mauléon, *Fr.* 43° 12′ N, 0° 53′ E 164
Maullín, *Chile* 41° 38′ S, 73° 37′ W 134
Maumakeogh, peak, *Ire.* 54° 15′ N, 9° 36′ W 150
Maumee, *Ohio, U.S.* 41° 33′ N, 83° 40′ W 102
Maumelle, Lake, *Ark., U.S.* 34° 50′ N, 93° 1′ W 96
Maumere, *Indonesia* 8° 47′ S, 122° 13′ E 192
Maun, *Botswana* 19° 59′ S, 23° 23′ E 227
Mauna Kea Observatories, site, *Hawai'i, U.S.* 19° 49′ N, 155° 32′ W 99
Mauna Loa Observatory, site, *Hawai'i, U.S.* 19° 31′ N, 155° 38′ W 99
Maungaturoto, *N.Z.* 36° 7′ S, 174° 21′ E 240
Maungdaw, *Myanmar* 20° 52′ N, 92° 22′ E 188
Maungmagan Islands, *Andaman Sea* 13° 58′ N, 97° 13′ E 202
Maunoir, Lac, lake, *Can.* 67° 36′ N, 118° 28′ W 246
Maurepas, Lake, *La., U.S.* 30° 11′ N, 90° 56′ W 96
Maurepas, Lake, *La., U.S.* 30° 14′ N, 90° 46′ W 103
Maures, Monts des, *Fr.* 43° 19′ N, 5° 52′ E 165
Maurice, *La., U.S.* 30° 5′ N, 92° 8′ W 103
Mauriceville, *N.Z.* 40° 47′ S, 175° 42′ E 240
Mauriceville, *Tex., U.S.* 30° 10′ N, 93° 53′ W 103
Mauritania 20° 5′ N, 14° 29′ W 214
Mauritius 20° 18′ S, 57° 35′ E 254
Mauritius Trench, *Indian Ocean* 22° 23′ S, 56° 10′ E 254
Maurs, *Fr.* 44° 42′ N, 2° 11′ E 150
Maury Bay 66° 27′ S, 127° 0′ E 248
Maury Mountains, peak, *Oreg., U.S.* 44° 1′ N, 120° 27′ W 90
Maury Seachannel, *North Atlantic Ocean* 56° 23′ N, 24° 27′ W 253
Mauston, *Wis., U.S.* 43° 46′ N, 90° 4′ W 102
Mauthen, *Aust.* 46° 39′ N, 13° 0′ E 167
Mavago, *Mozambique* 12° 27′ S, 36° 13′ E 224
Maverick, *Ariz., U.S.* 33° 44′ N, 109° 33′ W 92
Mavinga, *Angola* 15° 47′ S, 20° 11′ E 207
Mavonde, *Mozambique* 18° 33′ S, 33° 3′ E 224
Mavroli, *Cyprus* 35° 3′ N, 32° 27′ E 194
Mavrovo, *Maced.* 41° 40′ N, 20° 45′ E 168
Mavrovo National Park, *Maced.* 41° 13′ N, 20° 50′ E 180
Mavrovouni Mine, site, *Cyprus* 35° 5′ N, 32° 47′ E 194
Mavrovoúni, peak, *Gr.* 39° 26′ N, 22° 31′ E 156
Mawlá Maţar, *Yemen* 14° 48′ N, 48° 38′ E 182
Mawlamyine, *Myanmar* 16° 24′ N, 97° 41′ E 192
Mawlite, *Myanmar* 23° 36′ N, 94° 19′ E 202
Mawlu, *Myanmar* 24° 26′ N, 96° 13′ E 188
Mawqaq, *Saudi Arabia* 27° 25′ N, 41° 9′ E 180
Mawshij, *Yemen* 13° 43′ N, 43° 19′ E 182
Mawson, Australia, station, *Antarctica* 67° 38′ S, 63° 5′ E 248
Mawson, Cape, *Antarctica* 70° 29′ S, 77° 38′ W 248
Mawson Coast, *Antarctica* 67° 50′ S, 61° 7′ E 248
Max, *N. Dak., U.S.* 47° 48′ N, 101° 19′ W 90
Maxaas, *Somalia* 4° 23′ N, 46° 8′ E 218
Maxcanú, *Mex.* 20° 33′ N, 90° 0′ W 115
Maxhamish Lake, *Can.* 59° 48′ N, 124° 19′ W 108
Maxixe, *Mozambique* 23° 45′ S, 35° 18′ E 227
Maxton, *N.C., U.S.* 34° 43′ N, 79° 22′ W 96
Maxwell, *N. Mex., U.S.* 36° 31′ N, 104° 34′ W 92
Maxwell Bay 74° 19′ N, 89° 56′ W 106
Maxwelton House, site, *U.K.* 55° 11′ N, 3° 57′ W 150
May, Cape 81° 35′ S, 173° 55′ E 248
May Point, Cape, *N.J., U.S.* 38° 38′ N, 75° 1′ W 94
Maya, island, *Indonesia* 1° 39′ S, 109° 16′ E 192
Maya, Mesa de, *Colo., U.S.* 37° 1′ N, 103° 46′ W 92
Maya Mountains, *Belize* 16° 41′ N, 89° 8′ W 115
Maya, river, *Russ.* 55° 23′ N, 132° 42′ E 160
Maya, river, *Russ.* 58° 9′ N, 137° 20′ E 160
Mayabandar, *India* 12° 52′ N, 92° 59′ E 188
Mayaguana, adm. division, *Bahamas* 22° 15′ N, 73° 18′ W 116
Mayaguana Island, *Bahamas* 22° 31′ N, 73° 18′ W 116
Mayagüez, *P.R., U.S.* 18° 11′ N, 67° 10′ W 116
Mayahi, *Niger* 13° 52′ N, 7° 31′ E 222
Mayāmey, *Iran* 36° 30′ N, 55° 46′ E 180
Mayang, *China* 27° 54′ N, 109° 48′ E 198
Mayapán, ruin(s), *Mex.* 20° 35′ N, 89° 35′ W 115
Mayarí, *Cuba* 20° 40′ N, 75° 42′ W 116
Maybeury, *W. Va., U.S.* 37° 21′ N, 81° 23′ W 96
Maych'ew, *Eth.* 12° 47′ N, 39° 32′ E 182
Mayda, *Russ.* 66° 20′ N, 41° 53′ E 154
Maydān Ikbiz, *Syr.* 36° 48′ N, 36° 39′ E 156
Maydelle, *Tex., U.S.* 31° 46′ N, 95° 18′ W 103
Maydh, *Somalia* 10° 53′ N, 47° 4′ E 216
Maydh, island, *Somalia* 11° 21′ N, 46° 49′ E 216
Maydī, *Yemen* 16° 18′ N, 42° 52′ E 182
Mayen, *Ger.* 50° 19′ N, 7° 13′ E 167
Mayersville, *Miss., U.S.* 32° 52′ N, 91° 3′ W 103
Mayerthorpe, *Can.* 53° 56′ N, 115° 11′ W 108
Mayevo, *Russ.* 56° 22′ N, 29° 51′ E 166
Mayfa'ah, *Yemen* 14° 19′ N, 47° 31′ E 182
Mayfield, *Ky., U.S.* 36° 44′ N, 88° 40′ W 82
Mayfield, *N.Z.* 43° 51′ S, 171° 25′ E 240
Mayfield Peak, *Idaho, U.S.* 44° 29′ N, 114° 50′ W 90
Mayhill, *N. Mex., U.S.* 32° 53′ N, 105° 29′ W 92
Maykop, *Russ.* 44° 38′ N, 40° 3′ E 156
Maymecha, river, *Russ.* 71° 36′ N, 97° 42′ E 160
Maymont, *Can.* 52° 32′ N, 107° 42′ W 108
Maynooth, *Can.* 45° 14′ N, 77° 57′ W 94
Mayo, *Can.* 63° 32′ N, 136° 2′ W 246
Mayo, Cerro, peak, *Chile* 50° 22′ S, 73° 40′ W 134
Mayo Darlé, *Cameroon* 6° 25′ N, 11° 32′ E 222
Mayo Faran, *Nig.* 8° 56′ N, 12° 5′ E 216
Mayo Mayo, *Bol.* 12° 19′ S, 65° 12′ W 137
Mayo Ndaga, *Nig.* 6° 52′ N, 11° 25′ E 222
Mayodan, *N.C., U.S.* 36° 24′ N, 79° 59′ W 96
Mayon Volcano, peak, *Philippines* 13° 14′ N, 123° 36′ E 203
Mayor Buratovich, *Arg.* 39° 17′ S, 62° 37′ W 139
Mayotte 12° 58′ S, 44° 34′ E 220
Mayotte, Île de, island, *Fr.* 12° 33′ S, 45° 6′ E 220
Mayqayyn, *Kaz.* 51° 28′ N, 75° 47′ E 184
Mayraira Point, *Philippines* 18° 39′ N, 120° 38′ E 203
Maysk, *Russ.* 57° 47′ N, 77° 10′ E 169
Maysville, *Ky., U.S.* 38° 37′ N, 83° 45′ W 102
Maysville, *Mo., U.S.* 39° 52′ N, 94° 22′ W 94
Maytag see Dushanzi, *China* 44° 17′ N, 84° 53′ E 184
Mayum La, pass, *China* 30° 34′ N, 82° 31′ E 197
Mayumba, *Gabon* 3° 29′ S, 10° 40′ E 218
Mayville, *Mich., U.S.* 43° 19′ N, 83° 20′ W 102
Mayville, *N. Dak., U.S.* 47° 28′ N, 97° 20′ W 90
Mayville, *Wis., U.S.* 43° 28′ N, 88° 34′ W 102
Maywood, *Ill., U.S.* 41° 52′ N, 87° 50′ W 102
Maza, *Arg.* 36° 49′ S, 63° 20′ W 139
Mazabuka, *Zambia* 15° 53′ S, 27° 45′ E 224
Mazagan see El Jadida, *Mor.* 33° 15′ N, 8° 33′ W 214
Mazagão, *Braz.* 0° 8′ N, 51° 18′ W 130
Mazalij, oil field, *Saudi Arabia* 24° 24′ N, 48° 26′ E 196
Mazamet, *Fr.* 43° 28′ N, 2° 22′ E 164
Mazán, *Peru* 3° 29′ S, 73° 9′ W 136
Mazán, river, *Peru* 3° 10′ S, 73° 49′ W 136
Mazapil, *Mex.* 24° 37′ N, 101° 34′ W 114
Mazar-e Sharif, *Afghan.* 36° 42′ N, 67° 9′ E 186
Mazarredo, *Arg.* 47° 5′ S, 66° 41′ W 134
Mazarrón, *Sp.* 37° 35′ N, 1° 19′ W 164
Mazatenango, *Guatemala* 14° 30′ N, 91° 30′ W 115
Mazatlán, *Mex.* 23° 10′ N, 106° 24′ W 114
Mazatlán, *Mex.* 29° 1′ N, 110° 10′ W 92
Mazatzal Mountains, *Ariz., U.S.* 34° 11′ N, 111° 34′ W 92
Mazée, *Belg.* 50° 6′ N, 4° 40′ E 167
Mažeikiai, *Lith.* 56° 19′ N, 22° 20′ E 166
Mazgirt, *Turk.* 39° 1′ N, 39° 36′ E 195
Mazıdağı, *Turk.* 37° 30′ N, 40° 32′ E 195
Mazīnān, *Iran* 36° 22′ N, 56° 43′ E 180
Mazirbe, *Latv.* 57° 38′ N, 22° 10′ E 166
Mazo Cruz, *Peru* 16° 47′ S, 69° 44′ W 137
Mazomanie, *Wis., U.S.* 43° 9′ N, 89° 48′ W 102
Mazong Shan, peak, *China* 41° 27′ N, 96° 25′ E 172
Mazowe, *Zimb.* 17° 31′ S, 30° 59′ E 224
Mazowieckie, adm. division, *Pol.* 52° 21′ N, 19° 23′ E 152

Mazrag, oil field, Oman 18°17′ N, 55°30′ E 182
Mazrub, Sudan 13°52′ N, 29°19′ E 226
Mazsalaca, Latv. 57°51′ N, 25°2′ E 166
Mazunga, Zimb. 21°44′ S, 29°53′ E 227
Mazyr, Belarus 52°0′ N, 29°21′ E 152
Mbabane, Swaziland 26°19′ S, 30°58′ E 227
Mbahiakro, Côte d'Ivoire 7°24′ N, 4°21′ W 222
Mbaïki, Cen. Af. Rep. 3°55′ N, 18°2′ E 218
Mbala, Cen. Af. Rep. 7°47′ N, 20°49′ E 218
Mbala (Abercorn), Zambia 8°53′ S, 31°23′ E 224
Mbalabala, Zimb. 20°28′ S, 29°1′ E 227
Mbalambala, Kenya 4°237′ S, 39°4′ E 224
Mbale, Uganda 1°1′ N, 34°7′ E 224
Mbalmayo, Cameroon 3°40′ N, 11°31′ E 222
Mbamba Bay, Tanzania 11°15′ S, 34°50′ E 224
Mbandaka (Coquilhatville), Dem. Rep. of the Congo 2°119′ N, 18°17′ E 218
Mbandjok, Cameroon 4°21′ N, 11°50′ E 218
Mbang, Monts, Cameroon 7°11′ N, 13°29′ E 218
Mbanga, Cameroon 4°30′ N, 9°33′ E 222
Mbanika, island, Solomon Islands 9°5′ S, 159°11′ E 242
M'banza Congo, Angola 6°17′ S, 14°14′ E 218
Mbanza-Ngungu, Dem. Rep. of the Congo 5°18′ S, 14°49′ E 218
Mbarangandu, river, Tanzania 10°4′ S, 36°47′ E 224
Mbarara, Uganda 0°37′ N, 30°40′ E 224
Mbari, river, Cen. Af. Rep. 4°56′ N, 22°52′ E 218
Mbé, Cameroon 7°43′ N, 13°31′ E 218
Mbé, Congo 3°20′ S, 15°52′ E 218
Mbegera, Tanzania 9°34′ S, 34°58′ E 224
Mbengwi, Cameroon 6°2′ N, 10°2′ E 222
Mbeya, Tanzania 8°54′ S, 33°29′ E 224
Mbeya, adm. division, Tanzania 8°32′ S, 32°46′ E 224
M'Binda, Congo 2°10′ S, 12°52′ E 218
Mbinga, Tanzania 10°51′ S, 35°3′ E 224
Mbitao, Cameroon 7°13′ N, 15°14′ E 218
Mbizi, Zimb. 21°24′ S, 31°1′ E 227
Mbogo, Tanzania 7°25′ S, 33°26′ E 224
Mboi, Dem. Rep. of the Congo 6°57′ S, 21°53′ E 218
Mbomo, Congo 0°22′ N, 14°42′ E 218
Mborokua, island, Solomon Islands 9°2′ S, 158°45′ E 242
Mbour, Senegal 14°25′ N, 16°43′ W 222
Mbout, Mauritania 16°1′ N, 12°38′ W 222
Mbrés, Cen. Af. Rep. 6°36′ N, 19°48′ E 218
Mbuji-Mayi (Bakwanga), Dem. Rep. of the Congo 6°10′ S, 23°36′ E 224
Mbulamuti, Uganda 0°47′ N, 33°2′ E 224
Mbulo, island, Solomon Islands 8°45′ S, 158°19′ E 242
Mbulu, Tanzania 3°49′ S, 35°33′ E 224
Mburucuyá, Arg. 28°2′ S, 58°13′ W 139
McAdam, Can. 45°35′ N, 67°19′ W 94
McAfee Peak, Nev., U.S. 41°30′ N, 116°4′ W 90
McAlester, Okla., U.S. 34°54′ N, 95°46′ W 96
McAllen, Tex., U.S. 26°10′ N, 98°13′ W 96
McArthur, Ohio, U.S. 39°13′ N, 82°29′ W 102
McBain, Mich., U.S. 44°11′ N, 85°13′ W 102
McBride, Can. 53°17′ N, 120°12′ W 108
McCall, Idaho, U.S. 44°53′ N, 116°5′ W 90
McCamey, Tex., U.S. 31°7′ N, 102°12′ W 92
McCann Lake, Can. 61°13′ N, 107°4′ W 108
McCarran International Airport, Nev., U.S. 36°2′ N, 115°14′ W 101
McCarthy, Alas., U.S. 61°25′ N, 142°56′ W 98
McCarthy Inlet 78°49′ S, 51°2′ W 248
McChord Air Force Base, Wash., U.S. 47°7′ N, 122°32′ W 100
McCleary, Wash., U.S. 47°2′ N, 123°16′ W 100
McClellanville, S.C., U.S. 33°5′ N, 79°28′ W 96
McClintock, Mount, peak, Antarctica 80°10′ S, 158°39′ E 248
McClure, Lake, Calif., U.S. 37°35′ N, 120°23′ W 100
McComb, Miss., U.S. 31°13′ N, 90°27′ W 103
McComb, Ohio, U.S. 41°6′ N, 83°46′ W 102
McConaughy, Lake, Nebr., U.S. 41°13′ N, 103°23′ W 80
McConnell Air Force Base, Kans., U.S. 37°35′ N, 97°20′ W 90
McConnelsville, Ohio, U.S. 39°38′ N, 81°51′ W 102
McCook, Nebr., U.S. 40°11′ N, 100°39′ W 90
McCool, Miss., U.S. 33°11′ N, 89°20′ W 103
McCormick, Cape, Antarctica 71°28′ S, 176°52′ E 248
McCoy, Mount, peak, Antarctica 75°46′ S, 140°8′ W 248
McCoy Mountains, Calif., U.S. 33°45′ N, 114°52′ W 101
McCrea Lake, Can. 50°49′ N, 90°44′ W 110
McCreary, Can. 50°47′ N, 99°30′ W 90
McCullough, Ala., U.S. 31°9′ N, 87°31′ W 103
McCullough Range, Nev., U.S. 35°31′ N, 115°17′ W 101
McCusker Lake, Can. 51°42′ N, 95°38′ W 108
McDame, Can. 59°12′ N, 129°14′ W 108
McDills, spring, Austral. 25°50′ S, 135°15′ E 230
McDonald, Kans., U.S. 39°46′ N, 101°22′ W 90
McDonald, Miss., U.S. 32°39′ N, 89°8′ W 103
McDonald Peak, Calif., U.S. 40°55′ N, 120°30′ W 90
McEvoy, Mount, peak, Can. 56°45′ N, 128°25′ W 108
McFarland, Calif., U.S. 35°40′ N, 119°15′ W 100
McFarland, Kans., U.S. 39°2′ N, 96°15′ W 90
McFarland, Wis., U.S. 43°0′ N, 89°18′ W 102
McGehee, Ark., U.S. 33°36′ N, 91°23′ W 96
McGill, Nev., U.S. 39°24′ N, 114°47′ W 90
McGrath, Alas., U.S. 63°4′ N, 155°28′ W 73
McGregor, Tex., U.S. 31°25′ N, 97°24′ W 92
McGregor Lake, Can. 50°26′ N, 113°32′ W 90
McGregor, river, Can. 54°14′ N, 121°26′ W 108
McGuire Air Force Base, N.J., U.S. 39°59′ N, 74°41′ W 94
McGuire, Mount, peak, Idaho, U.S. 45°9′ N, 114°41′ W 90
McHenry, Ky., U.S. 37°22′ N, 86°55′ W 96
McHenry, Miss., U.S. 30°41′ N, 89°7′ W 103
Mcherrah, region, Alg. 26°45′ N, 5°3′ W 214
Mchinga, Tanzania 9°46′ S, 39°41′ E 224
Mchinji, Malawi 13°48′ S, 32°54′ E 224
McIndoe Falls, Vt., U.S. 44°15′ N, 72°5′ W 104
McInnes Lake, Can. 52°8′ N, 95°4′ W 80
McIntosh, Fla., U.S. 29°26′ N, 82°15′ W 105
McIntosh, Minn., U.S. 47°36′ N, 95°55′ W 90
McIntosh, S. Dak., U.S. 45°54′ N, 101°22′ W 90
McIvor, river, Can. 57°53′ N, 112°1′ W 108
McKay Lake, Can. 49°33′ N, 86°52′ W 94
McKay Lake, Can. 53°45′ N, 65°58′ W 111
McKay, Mount, peak, Can. 48°19′ N, 89°22′ W 94
McKeesport, Pa., U.S. 40°20′ N, 79°49′ W 82
McKelvey, Mount, peak, Antarctica 85°26′ S, 87°27′ W 248
McKenzie Island, Can. 51°4′ N, 93°49′ W 82
McKenzie Pass, Oreg., U.S. 44°14′ N, 121°48′ W 90
McKerrow, Can. 46°16′ N, 81°45′ W 94
McKerrow, Lake, N.Z. 44°30′ S, 167°28′ E 240
McKinley, Mount (Denali), peak, Alas., U.S. 62°54′ N, 151°17′ W 98
McKinley Peak, Antarctica 77°46′ S, 147°15′ W 248
McKinney, Tex., U.S. 33°12′ N, 96°39′ W 112
McKinnon, Wyo., U.S. 41°2′ N, 109°56′ W 90
McKittrick, Calif., U.S. 35°18′ N, 119°38′ W 100
McLain, Miss., U.S. 31°4′ N, 88°49′ W 103
McLaughlin, S. Dak., U.S. 45°47′ N, 100°50′ W 90
McLaurin, Miss., U.S. 31°9′ N, 89°12′ W 103
McLean, Ill., U.S. 40°18′ N, 89°11′ W 102
McLean, Tex., U.S. 35°12′ N, 100°36′ W 92
McLean Mountain, peak, Me., U.S. 47°6′ N, 68°57′ W 94
McLeansboro, Mo., U.S. 38°5′ N, 88°32′ W 94
McLennan, Can. 55°41′ N, 116°55′ W 108
McLeod, Tex., U.S. 32°55′ N, 94°6′ W 103
McLeod Bay 62°35′ N, 110°40′ W 106
Mcleod Lake, Can. 54°59′ N, 123°2′ W 108
McLeod Valley, Can. 53°44′ N, 116°1′ W 108
M'Clintock Channel 70°55′ N, 106°28′ W 72
McLoughlin, Mount, peak, Oreg., U.S. 42°27′ N, 122°24′ W 90
M'Clure Strait 74°40′ N, 118°17′ W 255
McMechen, W. Va., U.S. 39°58′ N, 80°45′ W 94
McMinnville, Tenn., U.S. 35°41′ N, 85°46′ W 96
McMurdo, U.S., station, Antarctica 77°48′ S, 166°8′ E 248
McNary, Ariz., U.S. 34°3′ N, 109°51′ W 92
McNeil, Ark., U.S. 33°20′ N, 93°13′ W 103
McNeill, Miss., U.S. 30°39′ N, 89°38′ W 103
McPhadyen, river, Can. 53°57′ N, 67°39′ W 111
McPherson, Kans., U.S. 38°21′ N, 97°41′ W 90
McRae, Ark., U.S. 35°5′ N, 91°49′ W 96
McRae, Ga., U.S. 32°3′ N, 82°54′ W 96
McTaggart Lake, Can. 58°2′ N, 109°0′ W 108
McTavish Lake, Can. 55°54′ N, 105°52′ W 108
McVeigh, Can. 56°42′ N, 101°15′ W 108
McVicar Arm 64°55′ N, 122°55′ W 106
McVille, N. Dak., U.S. 47°44′ N, 98°12′ W 90
Mdandu, Tanzania 9°9′ S, 34°41′ E 224
Mdennah, region, Mali 24°19′ N, 6°3′ W 214
Mdiq, Mor. 35°40′ N, 5°20′ W 150
Mead, Lake, Nev., U.S. 36°26′ N, 114°32′ W 101
Meade, Kans., U.S. 37°17′ N, 100°21′ W 92
Meade Peak, Idaho, U.S. 42°29′ N, 111°19′ W 90
Meade, river, Alas., U.S. 69°34′ N, 156°47′ W 98
Meadow Lake, Can. 54°8′ N, 108°26′ W 108
Meadow Valley Wash, river, Nev., U.S. 36°53′ N, 114°44′ W 101
Meadows, Idaho, U.S. 44°56′ N, 116°15′ W 90
Meadows, N.H., U.S. 44°21′ N, 71°29′ W 104
Meadville, Miss., U.S. 31°27′ N, 90°54′ W 103
Meadville, Pa., U.S. 41°38′ N, 80°9′ W 94
Meander River, Can. 59°2′ N, 117°41′ W 108
Meares, Cape, Oreg., U.S. 45°20′ N, 124°24′ W 90
Mears, Mich., U.S. 43°40′ N, 86°25′ W 102
Meath Park, Can. 53°26′ N, 105°25′ W 108
Meaux, Fr. 48°57′ N, 2°53′ E 163
Mebane, N.C., U.S. 36°5′ N, 79°17′ W 96
Mecanhelas, Mozambique 15°11′ S, 35°53′ E 224
Mecca, Calif., U.S. 33°34′ N, 116°6′ W 101
Mecca see Makkah, Saudi Arabia 21°24′ N, 39°49′ E 182
Mechanic Falls, Me., U.S. 44°6′ N, 70°25′ W 104
Mechanicville, N.Y., U.S. 42°54′ N, 73°43′ W 104
Mechelen, Belg. 51°1′ N, 4°29′ E 167
Mechems, region, Alg. 27°0′ N, 8°15′ W 214
Mecheraa Asfa, Alg. 35°22′ N, 1°4′ E 150
Mecherchar (Eil Malk), island, Palau 7°7′ N, 134°22′ E 242
Mecheria, Alg. 33°33′ N, 0°17′ E 214
Mechernich, Ger. 50°35′ N, 6°39′ E 167
Mechetinskaya, Russ. 46°43′ N, 40°26′ E 158
Mechta Gara, Alg. 36°15′ N, 5°25′ E 150
Mechtat el Hiout, Alg. 36°33′ N, 6°40′ E 150
Mecitözü, Turk. 40°31′ N, 35°17′ E 156
Mecklenburg-Western Pomerania, adm. division, Ger. 53°47′ N, 12°32′ E 152
Meconta, Mozambique 14°58′ S, 39°54′ E 224
Mecosta, Mich., U.S. 43°37′ N, 85°14′ W 102
Mecsek, Hung. 46°15′ N, 17°37′ E 168
Mecubúri, Mozambique 14°41′ S, 38°55′ E 224
Mecúfi, Mozambique 13°22′ S, 40°33′ E 224
Mecula, Mozambique 12°6′ S, 37°42′ E 224
Medak, India 18°4′ N, 78°15′ E 188
Medála, Mauritania 15°31′ N, 5°38′ W 222
Medale, Eth. 6°23′ N, 41°54′ E 224
Medan, Indonesia 3°35′ N, 98°40′ E 196
Médanos, Arg. 33°26′ S, 59°4′ W 139
Médanos, Arg. 38°51′ S, 62°42′ W 139
Médanos de Coro National Park, Venez. 11°34′ N, 70°3′ W 122
Medanosa, Punta, Arg. 48°17′ S, 65°58′ W 134
Medaryville, Ind., U.S. 41°3′ N, 86°54′ W 102
Médéa, Alg. 36°15′ N, 2°45′ E 150
Medebach, Ger. 51°11′ N, 8°42′ E 167
Medeiros Neto, Braz. 17°22′ S, 40°15′ W 138
Medellín, Col. 6°13′ N, 75°34′ W 136
Medemblik, Neth. 52°46′ N, 5°6′ E 163
Medena Selišta, Bosn. and Herzg. 44°7′ N, 16°47′ E 168
Medenine, Tun. 33°21′ N, 10°28′ E 214
Meder, Eritrea 14°41′ N, 40°42′ E 182
Mederdra, Mauritania 16°56′ N, 15°42′ W 222
Medes, Les, islands, Sp. 42°5′ N, 3°8′ E 164
Medford, Mass., U.S. 42°25′ N, 71°7′ W 104
Medford, Okla., U.S. 36°47′ N, 97°43′ W 92
Medford, Oreg., U.S. 42°21′ N, 122°50′ W 106
Medford, Wis., U.S. 45°8′ N, 90°20′ W 94
Medgidia, Rom. 44°14′ N, 28°16′ E 156
Mediaş, Rom. 46°10′ N, 24°20′ E 156
Medical Lake, Wash., U.S. 47°33′ N, 117°42′ W 90
Medicina, It. 44°29′ N, 11°36′ E 167
Medicine Bow, Wyo., U.S. 41°54′ N, 106°13′ W 92
Medicine Bow Mountains, Wyo., U.S. 41°44′ N, 106°32′ W 90
Medicine Bow Peak, Wyo., U.S. 41°21′ N, 106°23′ W 90
Medicine Hat, Can. 50°2′ N, 110°43′ W 82
Medicine Lake, Mont., U.S. 48°23′ N, 105°1′ W 90
Medicine Lodge, Kans., U.S. 37°16′ N, 98°37′ W 90
Medicine Rocks, site, Mont., U.S. 45°56′ N, 104°38′ W 90
Medina, Braz. 16°13′ S, 41°33′ W 138
Medina, Col. 4°30′ N, 73°21′ W 136
Medina, N.Y., U.S. 43°12′ N, 78°25′ W 110
Medina, N. Dak., U.S. 46°53′ N, 99°20′ W 90
Medina, Ohio, U.S. 41°7′ N, 81°52′ W 102
Medina, Tex., U.S. 29°47′ N, 99°15′ W 92
Medina de Pomar, Sp. 42°53′ N, 3°29′ W 164
Medina de Rioseco, Sp. 41°51′ N, 5°7′ W 214
Medina del Campo, Sp. 41°18′ N, 4°55′ W 150
Médina Gadaoundou, Guinea 11°51′ N, 11°36′ W 222
Medina see Al Madīnah, Saudi Arabia 24°26′ N, 39°34′ E 182
Medina Sidonia, Sp. 36°28′ N, 5°58′ W 164
Medinaceli, Sp. 41°9′ N, 2°27′ W 164
Médine, Mali 14°22′ N, 11°24′ W 222
Medinipur, India 22°27′ N, 87°20′ E 197
Mediodía, Col. 1°51′ S, 72°9′ W 136
Mediterranean Sea 34°7′ N, 16°43′ E 143
Medje, Dem. Rep. of the Congo 2°24′ N, 27°16′ E 224
Medjerda, Monts de la, Tun. 36°40′ N, 8°6′ E 156
Medkovets, Bulg. 43°37′ N, 23°10′ E 168
Medley, Can. 54°25′ N, 110°16′ W 108
Mednogorsk, Russ. 51°24′ N, 57°34′ E 158
Médoc, region, Fr. 44°43′ N, 1°16′ W 150
Mêdog, China 29°19′ N, 95°24′ E 188
Medstead, Can. 53°17′ N, 108°5′ W 108
Međurječje, Mont. 42°43′ N, 19°22′ E 168
Međuvođe, Bosn. and Herzg. 45°6′ N, 16°46′ E 168
Medveđa, Serb. 42°50′ N, 21°35′ E 168
Medveditsa, river, Russ. 49°40′ N, 43°1′ E 184
Medvedok, Russ. 57°25′ N, 50°10′ E 154
Medvezh'i Ostrova (Bear Islands), East Siberian Sea 71°5′ N, 151°1′ E 160
Medvezh'yegorsk, Russ. 62°54′ N, 34°28′ E 154
Medway, Mass., U.S. 42°8′ N, 71°25′ W 104
Medzhybizh, Ukr. 49°26′ N, 27°26′ E 152
Meehaus, Mount, peak, Can. 58°0′ N, 130°41′ W 108
Meeker, Colo., U.S. 40°2′ N, 107°56′ W 90
Meelpaeg Reservoir, lake, Can. 48°15′ N, 57°26′ W 111
Meerut, India 28°59′ N, 77°40′ E 197
Meerzorg, Suriname 5°47′ N, 55°9′ W 130
Meeteetse, Wyo., U.S. 44°8′ N, 108°51′ W 90
Mefjell Mount, peak, Antarctica 72°10′ S, 24°38′ E 248
Mēga, Eth. 4°1′ N, 38°17′ E 224
Megalo, Eth. 6°52′ N, 40°47′ E 224
Megargel, Ala., U.S. 31°22′ N, 87°25′ W 103
Meghalaya, adm. division, India 25°20′ N, 89°54′ E 197
Meghri, Arm. 38°53′ N, 46°13′ E 195
Megiddo, Israel 32°34′ N, 35°10′ E 194
Megiddo, Tel, peak, Israel 32°34′ N, 35°8′ E 194
Megion, Russ. 61°1′ N, 76°19′ E 169
Mégiscane, Lac, lake, Can. 48°37′ N, 76°28′ W 94
Megler, Wash., U.S. 46°14′ N, 123°51′ W 100
Mehar, Pak. 27°13′ N, 67°50′ E 186
Meharry, Mount, peak, Austral. 22°59′ S, 118°24′ E 230
Meharry, Mount, peak, Austral. 23°10′ S, 118°10′ E 238
Mehedinţi, adm. division, Rom. 44°49′ N, 22°16′ E 156
Mehedinţi, Munţii, Rom. 44°51′ N, 22°25′ E 168
Mehola, West Bank, Israel 32°20′ N, 35°31′ E 194
Mehrīz, Iran 31°32′ N, 54°35′ E 180
Meia Ponte, river, Braz. 18°4′ S, 49°32′ W 138
Meiganga, Cameroon 6°28′ N, 14°17′ E 218
Meighen Island, Can. 79°58′ N, 102°32′ W 246
Meigs, Ga., U.S. 31°3′ N, 84°6′ W 96
Meihekou, China 42°31′ N, 125°37′ E 200
Meikle Says Law, peak, U.K. 55°49′ N, 2°47′ W 150
Meiners Oaks, Calif., U.S. 34°27′ N, 119°17′ W 100
Meiningen, Ger. 50°34′ N, 10°24′ E 167
Meira, Sp. 43°12′ N, 7°19′ W 150
Meiringen, Switz. 46°43′ N, 8°11′ E 167
Meister, river, Can. 60°20′ N, 131°12′ W 108
Meizhou, China 24°19′ N, 116°4′ E 198
Meja, India 25°9′ N, 82°6′ E 197
Mejillones, Chile 23°8′ S, 70°30′ W 132
Mékambo, Gabon 0°59′ N, 13°53′ E 218
Mek'elē, Eth. 13°29′ N, 39°25′ E 182
Mekhel'ta, Russ. 42°44′ N, 46°30′ E 195
Mekhtar, Pak. 30°29′ N, 69°24′ E 186
Mékinac, Lac, lake, Can. 47°1′ N, 73°13′ W 110
Meknassy, Tun. 34°32′ N, 9°36′ E 156
Meko, Nig. 7°28′ N, 2°50′ E 222
Mekong see Lancang, river, China 32°3′ N, 97°14′ E 190
Mekoryuk, Alas., U.S. 60°17′ N, 166°21′ W 98
Mel, It. 46°3′ N, 12°4′ E 167
Melalap, Malaysia 5°15′ N, 116°0′ E 203
Melanesia, islands, Coral Sea 7°19′ S, 149°12′ E 192
Melaque, Mex. 19°14′ N, 104°43′ W 114
Melba Peninsula 65°39′ S, 98°7′ E 248
Melbourne, Austral. 37°51′ S, 144°38′ E 231
Melbourne, Fla., U.S. 28°6′ N, 80°40′ W 105
Melbourne Beach, Fla., U.S. 28°4′ N, 80°35′ W 105
Melbourne, Mount, peak, Antarctica 74°22′ S, 165°18′ E 248
Melbu, Nor. 68°29′ N, 14°49′ E 152
Melchett Lake, Can. 50°42′ N, 87°36′ W 110
Melchior Islands, Weddell Sea 64°16′ S, 65°56′ W 134
Melchor, Isla, island, Chile 45°15′ S, 75°39′ W 134
Melchor Ocampo, Mex. 24°48′ N, 101°39′ W 114
Meldola, It. 44°6′ N, 12°2′ E 167
Meldorf, Ger. 54°5′ N, 9°4′ E 150
Meldrum Creek, Can. 52°6′ N, 122°22′ W 108
Mele, Capo, It. 43°53′ N, 8°10′ E 167
Melegnano, It. 45°20′ N, 9°18′ E 167
Melekeok, Palau 7°10′ N, 133°47′ E 238
Melekeok Point, Palau 7°10′ N, 133°47′ E 242
Melenci, Serb. 45°30′ N, 20°19′ E 168
Melenki, Russ. 55°19′ N, 41°40′ E 154
Meleski, Est. 58°24′ N, 26°5′ E 166
Meletsk, Russ. 57°28′ N, 90°20′ E 169
Meleuz, Russ. 52°58′ N, 55°53′ E 154
Melfi, Chad 11°3′ N, 17°58′ E 216
Melfi, It. 40°59′ N, 15°39′ E 156
Melfort, Can. 52°51′ N, 104°37′ W 108
Melilla, Sp. 35°15′ N, 2°58′ W 214
Melinka, Chile 43°52′ S, 73°49′ W 134
Melita, Can. 49°17′ N, 100°58′ W 90
Melita see Mljet, island, Croatia 42°37′ N, 17°23′ E 168
Melito di Porto Salvo, It. 37°55′ N, 15°47′ E 156
Melitopol', Ukr. 46°50′ N, 35°19′ E 156
Melksham, U.K. 51°21′ N, 2°9′ W 162
Mellakou, Alg. 35°15′ N, 1°14′ E 150
Mellansel, Nor. 63°25′ N, 18°20′ E 152
Mellen, Wis., U.S. 46°19′ N, 90°41′ W 94
Mellerud, Nor. 58°42′ N, 12°26′ E 152
Mellifont Abbey, site, Ire. 53°43′ N, 6°32′ W 150
Mellit, Sudan 14°6′ N, 25°34′ E 226
Mellrichstadt, Ger. 50°26′ N, 10°17′ E 167
Mellum, island, Ger. 53°39′ N, 8°10′ E 163
Melmerby, U.K. 54°43′ N, 2°37′ W 162
Melo, Arg. 34°20′ S, 63°27′ W 139
Melo, Uru. 32°20′ S, 54°13′ W 139
Meloco, Mozambique 13°31′ S, 39°15′ E 224
Melos, ruin(s), Aegean Sea 36°42′ N, 24°20′ E 156
Melouprey, Cambodia 13°49′ N, 105°16′ E 202
Melrose, Fla., U.S. 29°41′ N, 82°3′ W 105
Melrose, La., U.S. 31°36′ N, 92°59′ W 103
Melrose, Mass., U.S. 42°27′ N, 71°4′ W 104
Melrose, Minn., U.S. 45°38′ N, 94°50′ W 90
Melrose, N. Mex., U.S. 34°26′ N, 103°38′ W 92
Melsungen, Ger. 51°7′ N, 9°32′ E 167
Meltaus, Fin. 66°54′ N, 25°20′ E 152
Melton Constable, U.K. 52°51′ N, 1°2′ E 162
Melton Mowbray, U.K. 52°46′ N, 0°53′ E 162
Melun, Fr. 48°31′ N, 2°39′ E 163
Melut, Sudan 10°27′ N, 32°12′ E 224
Melville, Can. 50°55′ N, 102°51′ W 90
Melville, La., U.S. 30°41′ N, 91°46′ W 103
Melville, Cape, Austral. 14°8′ S, 144°30′ E 230
Melville Hills, Can. 69°17′ N, 122°25′ W 106
Melville Island, Austral. 11°9′ S, 131°5′ E 192
Melville Island, Can. 74°39′ N, 109°22′ W 106
Melville Peninsula, Can. 67°59′ N, 85°41′ W 106
Melville Sound 68°17′ N, 103°42′ W 246
Melvin, Ill., U.S. 40°33′ N, 88°15′ W 102
Melvin, Ky., U.S. 37°21′ N, 82°42′ W 96
Melvin, Tex., U.S. 31°10′ N, 99°35′ W 92
Melvin Lake, Can. 57°7′ N, 100°46′ W 108
Melvin, river, Can. 59°0′ N, 117°27′ W 108
Melvin Village, N.H., U.S. 43°41′ N, 71°19′ W 104
Mélykút, Hung. 46°12′ N, 19°23′ E 168
Mêmar Co, lake, China 34°13′ N, 81°36′ E 188
Memba, Mozambique 14°13′ S, 40°31′ E 224
Mēmele, river, Europe 56°21′ N, 24°9′ E 166
Mempawah, Indonesia 0°24′ N, 108°57′ E 196
Memphis, Mo., U.S. 40°27′ N, 92°11′ W 94
Memphis, Tenn., U.S. 35°8′ N, 90°2′ W 96
Memphis, Tex., U.S. 34°42′ N, 100°33′ W 92
Memphis, site, Egypt 29°51′ N, 31°5′ E 180
Mena, Ark., U.S. 34°33′ N, 94°16′ W 96
Mena, Ukr. 51°29′ N, 32°13′ E 158
Menahga, Minn., U.S. 46°43′ N, 95°7′ W 90
Ménaka, Mali 15°52′ N, 2°25′ E 222
Ménalo, Óros, peak, Gr. 37°38′ N, 22°12′ E 156
Menands, N.Y., U.S. 42°41′ N, 73°45′ W 104
Menard, Tex., U.S. 30°55′ N, 99°47′ W 92
Menard Fracture Zone, South Pacific Ocean 49°46′ S, 113°56′ W 252
Menasha, Wis., U.S. 44°12′ N, 88°27′ W 102
Menawashei, Sudan 12°41′ N, 24°57′ E 216
Mende, Fr. 44°30′ N, 3°29′ E 150
Mende, ruin(s), Gr. 39°58′ N, 23°20′ E 156
Mendebo, Eth. 6°21′ N, 38°52′ E 224
Mendeleyev Plain, Arctic Ocean 81°8′ N, 167°15′ W 255
Mendeleyev Ridge, Arctic Ocean 83°35′ N, 172°10′ W 255
Mendeleyevsk, Russ. 55°54′ N, 52°24′ E 154
Mendelssohn Inlet 71°19′ S, 77°46′ W 248
Menden, Ger. 51°26′ N, 7°47′ E 167
Méndez, Ecua. 2°47′ S, 78°23′ W 136
Méndez, Mex. 25°7′ N, 98°35′ W 114
Mendī, Eth. 9°46′ N, 35°4′ E 224
Mendip Hills, U.K. 51°9′ N, 2°41′ W 162
Mendocino, Cape, Calif., U.S. 40°25′ N, 124°58′ W 90
Mendocino Fracture Zone, North Pacific Ocean 40°1′ N, 144°6′ W 252
Mendol, island, Indonesia 0°23′ N, 103°14′ E 196

Mendon, *Ohio, U.S.* 40°39' N, 84°31' W 102
Mendota, *Calif., U.S.* 36°45' N, 120°24' W 100
Mendota, *Ill., U.S.* 41°32' N, 89°7' W 102
Mendoza, *Arg.* 32°52' S, 68°54' W 134
Mendoza, adm. division, *Arg.* 34°30' S, 70°3' W 134
Mendung, *Indonesia* 0°33' N, 103°11' E 196
Mene de Mauroa, *Venez.* 10°43' N, 70°58' W 136
Mene Grande, *Venez.* 9°50' N, 70°55' W 136
Menemen, *Turk.* 38°32' N, 27°2' E 180
Menemsha, *Mass., U.S.* 41°21' N, 70°46' W 104
Menen, *Belg.* 50°47' N, 3°7' E 163
Mengcheng, *China* 33°15' N, 116°32' E 198
Mengen, *Ger.* 48°3' N, 9°19' E 152
Mengen, *Turk.* 40°56' N, 32°10' E 156
Mengene Dağı, peak, *Turk.* 38°13' N, 43°56' E 195
Mengeringhausen, *Ger.* 51°22' N, 8°58' E 167
Menghai, *China* 21°58' N, 100°26' E 202
Mengibar, *Sp.* 37°58' N, 3°48' W 164
Mengla, *China* 21°29' N, 101°30' E 202
Menglian, *China* 22°21' N, 99°32' E 202
Mengoub, *Mor.* 32°20' N, 2°20' W 214
Mengzi, *China* 23°22' N, 103°23' E 202
Menindee, *Austral.* 32°19' S, 142°28' E 231
Menindee Lake, *Austral.* 32°16' S, 141°18' E 230
Menkere, *Russ.* 67°52' N, 123°17' E 173
Menlo, *Wash., U.S.* 46°35' N, 123°40' W 100
Menno, *S. Dak., U.S.* 43°12' N, 97°35' W 90
Menominee, river, *U.S.* 46°11' N, 88°37' W 80
Menomonie, *Wis., U.S.* 44°51' N, 91°55' W 94
Menongue, *Angola* 14°39' S, 17°39' E 220
Menorca, island, *Sp.* 39°29' N, 4°14' E 142
Menorca (Minorca), island, *Sp.* 39°47' N, 3°33' E 164
Menouarar, *Alg.* 31°12' N, 2°16' W 214
Men'shikova, Mys, *Russ.* 70°24' N, 56°10' E 169
Mentasta Lake, *Alas., U.S.* 62°56' N, 143°52' W 98
Mentawai, Kepulauan, islands, *Indian Ocean* 1°1' S, 97°24' E 196
Mentekab, *Malaysia* 3°29' N, 102°20' E 196
Mentès, spring, *Niger* 16°58' N, 4°17' E 222
Mentmore, *N. Mex., U.S.* 35°30' N, 108°50' W 92
Mentor, *Ohio, U.S.* 41°39' N, 81°20' W 102
Menyapa, peak, *Indonesia* 1°6' N, 115°48' E 192
Menza, *Russ.* 49°21' N, 108°51' E 198
Menzel Bourguiba (Ferryville), *Tun.* 37°9' N, 9°47' E 156
Menzel Chaker, *Tun.* 34°59' N, 10°22' E 156
Menzelinsk, *Russ.* 55°40' N, 53°8' E 154
Menzies, *Austral.* 29°42' S, 121°0' E 231
Menzies, Mount, peak, *Antarctica* 73°29' S, 61°23' E 248
Menzies, Mount, peak, *Can.* 50°12' N, 125°35' W 90
Me'ona, *Israel* 33°0' N, 35°15' E 194
Meota, *Can.* 53°2' N, 108°28' W 108
Meppel, *Neth.* 52°41' N, 6°10' E 163
Meppen, *Ger.* 52°42' N, 7°18' E 163
Mequens, river, *Braz.* 12°56' S, 62°11' W 132
Mequinenza, *Sp.* 41°21' N, 0°17' E 164
Mer Rouge, *La., U.S.* 32°45' N, 91°48' W 103
Meråker, *Nor.* 63°25' N, 11°43' E 152
Merano, *It.* 46°40' N, 11°8' E 167
Merauke, *Indonesia* 8°36' S, 140°31' E 192
Merca (Marka), *Somalia* 1°41' N, 44°53' E 207
Mercaderes, *Col.* 1°47' N, 77°14' W 136
Mercan Dağları, peak, *Turk.* 39°32' N, 39°28' E 195
Mercato Saraceno, *It.* 43°57' N, 12°10' E 167
Merced, *Calif., U.S.* 37°18' N, 120°29' W 100
Merced Peak, *Calif., U.S.* 37°37' N, 119°27' W 100
Mercedes, *Arg.* 34°42' S, 59°25' W 139
Mercedes, *Arg.* 29°12' S, 58°3' W 139
Mercedes, *Tex., U.S.* 26°10' N, 97°55' W 114
Mercedes, *Uru.* 33°17' S, 57°59' W 139
Merćez, *Serb.* 43°13' N, 21°4' E 168
Mercoal, *Can.* 53°8' N, 117°7' W 108
Mercury, *Nev., U.S.* 36°39' N, 116°0' W 101
Mercy Bay 73°58' N, 119°36' W 106
Mercy, Cape, *Can.* 64°47' N, 63°27' W 106
Meredith, *N.H., U.S.* 43°38' N, 71°31' W 104
Meredith, Cape, *West Falkland* 52°28' S, 63°10' W 248
Meredith Center, *N.H., U.S.* 43°36' N, 71°33' W 104
Mereeg, *Somalia* 3°44' N, 47°20' E 218
Mereer-Gur, *Somalia* 5°46' N, 46°31' E 218
Merefa, *Ukr.* 49°47' N, 36°9' E 158
Méréville, *Fr.* 48°19' N, 2°4' E 163
Merga see Nukheila, spring, *Sudan* 19°3' N, 26°20' E 226
Mergenevo, *Kaz.* 49°57' N, 51°15' E 158
Mergui Archipelago, islands, *Andaman Sea* 11°3' N, 97°30' E 202
Méri, *Cameroon* 10°51' N, 14°6' E 218
Meriç, *Turk.* 41°10' N, 26°24' E 158
Meriç, river, *Turk.* 41°3' N, 26°22' E 180
Mérida, *Mex.* 20°56' N, 89°44' W 112
Mérida, *Sp.* 38°54' N, 6°24' W 214
Mérida, *Sp.* 38°54' N, 6°20' W 164
Mérida, *Venez.* 8°36' N, 71°10' W 136
Mérida, adm. division, *Venez.* 8°18' N, 71°50' W 136
Mérida, Cordillera de, *Venez.* 9°41' N, 69°46' W 136
Meriden, *Conn., U.S.* 41°32' N, 72°48' W 104
Meriden, *N.H., U.S.* 43°32' N, 72°16' W 104
Meridian, *Miss., U.S.* 32°21' N, 88°42' W 103
Meridian, *Tex., U.S.* 31°54' N, 97°39' W 92
Merijärvi, *Fin.* 64°17' N, 24°25' E 152
Merikarvia, *Fin.* 61°50' N, 21°29' E 166
Měřín, *Czech Rep.* 49°24' N, 15°52' E 152
Merinaghène, ruin(s), *Senegal* 16°1' N, 16°6' W 222
Merino Jarpa, Isla, island, *Chile* 47°44' S, 74°20' W 134
Merirumã, *Braz.* 1°7' N, 54°37' W 130
Merivälja, *Est.* 59°29' N, 24°48' E 166
Meriwether Lewis Monument, *Tenn., U.S.* 35°31' N, 87°33' W 96
Merka, *Eth.* 5°52' N, 37°6' E 224
Merke, *Kaz.* 42°51' N, 73°9' E 184
Merkinė, *Lith.* 54°10' N, 24°12' E 166
Merkoya, *Mali* 13°56' N, 8°13' W 222
Merksplas, *Belg.* 51°20' N, 4°51' E 167
Merkushino, *Russ.* 58°48' N, 61°32' E 154
Merkys, river, *Lith.* 54°21' N, 24°46' E 166
Merlimont, *Fr.* 50°27' N, 1°36' E 163
Merlin, *Can.* 42°14' N, 82°14' W 102
Mermentau, *La., U.S.* 30°10' N, 92°36' W 103
Meroë, ruin(s), *Sudan* 17°3' N, 33°45' E 182
Meron, *Israel* 32°59' N, 35°26' E 194
Merouana, *Alg.* 35°37' N, 5°54' E 150
Merowe, *Sudan* 18°23' N, 31°49' E 182
Merrill, *Miss., U.S.* 30°57' N, 88°43' W 103
Merrill, *Wis., U.S.* 45°10' N, 89°41' W 94
Merrillville, *Ind., U.S.* 41°28' N, 87°21' W 102
Merrimack, *N.H., U.S.* 42°51' N, 71°31' W 104
Merriman, *Nebr., U.S.* 42°55' N, 101°42' W 90
Merritt, *Can.* 50°5' N, 120°46' W 108
Merritt Island, *Fla., U.S.* 28°21' N, 80°42' W 105
Merritt Pass, *Ariz., U.S.* 34°5' N, 112°59' W 92
Merryville, *La., U.S.* 30°44' N, 93°33' W 103
Mers el Kebir, *Alg.* 35°43' N, 0°43' E 150
Mersey, river, *U.K.* 53°22' N, 2°58' W 162
Mersin see İçel, *Turk.* 36°48' N, 34°36' E 156
Mersing, *Malaysia* 2°25' N, 103°49' E 196
Mērsrags, *Latv.* 57°20' N, 23°6' E 166
Merta Road, *India* 26°43' N, 73°55' E 186
Mertert, *Lux.* 49°42' N, 6°30' E 163
Merthyr Tydfil, *U.K.* 51°45' N, 3°22' W 162
Merti, *Kenya* 1°1' N, 38°40' E 224
Mértola, *Port.* 37°38' N, 7°41' W 150
Mertzon, *Tex., U.S.* 31°15' N, 100°50' W 92
Méru, *Fr.* 49°14' N, 2°8' E 163
Meru, *Kenya* 2°0' N, 37°40' E 224
Meru National Park, *Kenya* 2°119' N, 38°27' E 224
Meru, peak, *Tanzania* 3°15' S, 36°41' E 224
Merville, *Fr.* 50°38' N, 2°38' E 163
Méry, *Fr.* 48°30' N, 3°53' E 163
Merz Peninsula 72°30' S, 59°28' W 248
Merzifon, *Turk.* 40°52' N, 35°28' E 156
Merzig, *Ger.* 49°26' N, 6°38' E 163
Mesa, *Ariz., U.S.* 33°25' N, 111°49' W 92
Mesa Verde National Park, *Colo., U.S.* 37°21' N, 111°23' W 80
Mesaaroole, spring, *Somalia* 3°20' N, 45°2' E 218
Mesabi Range, *Minn., U.S.* 47°26' N, 93°37' W 90
Mesach Mellet, *Lib.* 25°30' N, 11°3' E 216
Mésaconane, Pointe, *Can.* 51°31' N, 79°28' W 110
Mesagne, *It.* 40°33' N, 17°50' E 156
Mesai, river, *Col.* 6°357' N, 72°43' W 136
Mesará, *Gr.* 35°0' N, 24°48' E 156
Mescalero, *N. Mex., U.S.* 33°8' N, 105°46' W 92
Meschede, *Ger.* 51°20' N, 8°16' E 167
Mescit Dağı, peak, *Turk.* 40°22' N, 41°8' E 195
Meselefors, *Nor.* 64°25' N, 16°50' E 152
Mesemvria see Nesebŭr, *Bulg.* 42°39' N, 27°44' E 156
Meshchovsk, *Russ.* 54°18' N, 35°18' E 158
Meshkān, *Iran* 36°37' N, 58°7' E 180
Meshra' er Req, *Sudan* 8°24' N, 29°15' E 224
Mesići, *Bosn. and Herzg.* 43°44' N, 18°59' E 168
Mesier, Canal 48°31' S, 75°10' W 134
Mesilinka, river, *Can.* 56°26' N, 126°8' W 108
Mesilla, *N. Mex., U.S.* 32°16' N, 106°49' W 92
Meškuičiai, *Lith.* 56°4' N, 23°26' E 166
Mesola, *It.* 44°55' N, 12°13' E 167
Mesomikenda Lake, *Can.* 47°34' N, 82°41' W 110
Mesopotamia, region, *Iraq* 35°1' N, 40°11' E 180
Mesplet, Lac, lake, *Can.* 48°45' N, 76°18' W 94
Mesquite, *Nev., U.S.* 36°48' N, 114°4' W 101
Mesquite, *Tex., U.S.* 32°45' N, 96°36' W 96
Mesra, *Alg.* 35°50' N, 0°10' E 164
Messaad, *Alg.* 34°12' N, 3°31' E 214
Messalo, river, *Mozambique* 12°3' S, 39°41' E 224
Messdar, oil field, *Alg.* 31°1' N, 6°35' E 214
Messeïed, *Mor.* 27°57' N, 10°51' W 214
Messene, ruin(s), *Gr.* 37°9' N, 21°49' E 156
Messina, *It.* 38°11' N, 15°31' E 156
Messina see Musina, *S. Af.* 22°21' S, 30°1' E 227
Messoyakha, *Russ.* 69°12' N, 82°44' E 169
Mestanza, *Sp.* 38°34' N, 4°4' W 164
Mesteacăn, *Rom.* 47°22' N, 23°32' E 168
Mestia, *Ga.* 43°2' N, 42°43' E 195
Mestre, *It.* 45°29' N, 12°14' E 167
Meszah Peak, *Can.* 58°29' N, 131°34' W 108
Meta, adm. division, *Col.* 3°26' N, 73°20' W 136
Meta Incognita Peninsula, *Can.* 62°38' N, 68°39' W 106
Meta Lake, *Can.* 50°28' N, 87°42' W 110
Meta, river, *Col.* 5°22' N, 70°30' W 136
Metahāra, *Eth.* 8°51' N, 39°55' E 224
Metairie, *La., U.S.* 29°58' N, 90°9' W 103
Metalici, Munții, *Rom.* 46°2' N, 22°43' E 168
Metaline Falls, *Wash., U.S.* 48°51' N, 117°21' W 90
Metallifere, Colline, *It.* 43°8' N, 10°24' E 156
Metamora, *Ill., U.S.* 40°47' N, 89°22' W 102
Metán, *Arg.* 25°31' S, 64°58' W 134
Metangula, *Mozambique* 12°40' S, 34°50' E 224
Métascouac, Lac, lake, *Can.* 47°43' N, 72°23' W 94
Metchosin, *Can.* 48°22' N, 123°33' W 100
Metema, *Eth.* 12°55' N, 36°11' E 182
Metemma, *Sudan* 16°43' N, 33°20' E 182
Meteor Crater, *Ariz., U.S.* 35°1' N, 111°1' W 92
Meteora, ruin(s), *Gr.* 39°43' N, 21°30' E 156
Methánon, *Gr.* 37°34' N, 23°5' E 156
Methone, ruin(s), *Gr.* 40°25' N, 22°29' E 156
Methuen, *Mass., U.S.* 42°43' N, 71°13' W 104
Methven, *N.Z.* 43°40' S, 171°39' E 240
Metileo, *Arg.* 35°47' S, 63°58' W 139
Metković, *Croatia* 43°1' N, 17°37' E 168
Metlakatla, *Alas., U.S.* 55°6' N, 131°37' W 108
Metlaoui, *Tun.* 34°18' N, 8°26' E 156
Metlili Chaamba, *Alg.* 32°20' N, 3°40' E 214
Metovnica, *Serb.* 43°57' N, 22°9' E 168
Metropolis, *Mo., U.S.* 37°9' N, 88°43' W 96
Mets Beverratap (Dalidag), peak, *Azerb.* 39°54' N, 46°0' E 195
Mettingen, *Ger.* 52°19' N, 7°46' E 163
Mettlach, *Ger.* 49°29' N, 6°36' E 163
Mettler, *Calif., U.S.* 35°3' N, 118°58' W 101
Mettmann, *Ger.* 51°16' N, 6°57' E 167
Mettur Dam, *India* 11°47' N, 77°49' E 188
Metuge, *Mozambique* 13°1' S, 40°24' E 224
Metulla, *Israel* 33°15' N, 35°34' E 194
Metz, *Fr.* 49°6' N, 6°9' E 163
Meuaú, river, *Braz.* 1°23' S, 66°42' W 136
Meulaboh, *Indonesia* 4°12' N, 96°5' E 196
Meung, *Fr.* 47°49' N, 1°41' E 150
Meureudu, *Indonesia* 5°15' N, 96°10' E 196
Meurthe, river, *Fr.* 48°26' N, 6°41' E 163
Meuse, river, *Belg.* 50°28' N, 4°55' E 167
Mexborough, *U.K.* 53°29' N, 1°17' W 162
Mexcaltitán, *Mex.* 21°54' N, 105°30' W 114
Mexia, *Tex., U.S.* 31°39' N, 96°29' W 96
Mexiana, Ilha, island, *Braz.* 0°8' N, 49°32' W 130
Mexicali, *Mex.* 32°38' N, 115°32' W 112
Mexican Hat, *Utah, U.S.* 37°9' N, 109°52' W 92
Mexicanos, Laguna de los, lake, *Mex.* 28°10' N, 107°54' W 81
Mexico City, *Mex.* 19°23' N, 99°13' W 114
Mexico 21°24' N, 102°50' W 112
Mexico, *Mo., U.S.* 39°9' N, 91°54' W 94
México, adm. division, *Mex.* 19°21' N, 100°13' W 114
Mexico Basin, *Gulf of Mexico* 24°13' N, 92°2' W 253
Mexico, Gulf of 24°35' N, 91°4' W 113
Meydan Khvolah, *Afghan.* 33°34' N, 69°54' E 186
Meyers Chuck, *Alas., U.S.* 55°44' N, 132°16' W 108
Meymac, *Fr.* 45°32' N, 2°8' E 150
Meymaneh, *Afghan.* 35°55' N, 64°48' E 186
Mezcala, *Mex.* 17°53' N, 99°39' W 114
Mezdra, *Bulg.* 43°9' N, 23°43' E 156
Mèze, *Fr.* 43°26' N, 3°35' E 164
Mezen', *Russ.* 65°51' N, 44°18' E 154
Mezen', river, *Russ.* 64°14' N, 49°8' E 154
Mézenc, Mont, peak, *Fr.* 44°52' N, 4°7' E 165
Mhżenin, *Pol.* 53°5' N, 22°28' E 152
Mezenskaya Guba 66°33' N, 43°17' E 154
Mezeş, Munții, *Rom.* 47°9' N, 22°55' E 168
Mezhdurechensk, *Russ.* 63°8' N, 48°37' E 154
Mezhdurechenskiy, *Russ.* 59°30' N, 66°2' E 169
Mezhdusharskiy, Ostrov, island, *Russ.* 70°47' N, 53°44' E 246
Mezhdusharskiy, Ostrov, island, *Russ.* 70°34' N, 47°7' E 160
Meziad, *Rom.* 46°45' N, 22°25' E 168
Mezőberény, *Hung.* 46°49' N, 21°1' E 168
Mezőfalva, *Hung.* 46°55' N, 18°47' E 168
Mezőhegyes, *Hung.* 46°19' N, 20°49' E 168
Mezőkeresztes, *Hung.* 47°49' N, 20°42' E 168
Mezőkövesd, *Hung.* 47°47' N, 20°34' E 168
Mezőtúr, *Hung.* 47°0' N, 20°37' E 168
Mezquital, *Mex.* 23°26' N, 104°21' W 114
Mezquitic, *Mex.* 22°22' N, 103°44' W 114
Mezzolombardo, *It.* 46°12' N, 11°5' E 167
Mfouati, *Congo* 4°24' S, 13°47' E 218
Mgera, *Tanzania* 5°25' S, 37°34' E 224
Mgeta, *Tanzania* 8°16' S, 36°2' E 224
Mglin, *Russ.* 53°2' N, 32°52' E 158
M'goun, Irhil, peak, *Mor.* 31°29' N, 6°35' W 214
Mhangura, *Zimb.* 16°52' S, 30°8' E 224
Mholach, Beinn, peak 58°14' N, 6°37' W 150
Mhòr, Beinn, peak 57°14' N, 7°23' W 150
Mhow, *India* 22°32' N, 75°45' E 197
Miahuatlán, *Mex.* 18°31' N, 97°25' W 114
Miajadas, *Sp.* 39°8' N, 5°55' W 164
Miami, *Ariz., U.S.* 33°23' N, 110°53' W 112
Miami, *Fla., U.S.* 25°48' N, 80°13' W 105
Miami, *Okla., U.S.* 36°52' N, 94°53' W 82
Miami, *Tex., U.S.* 35°40' N, 100°38' W 92
Miami Beach, *Fla., U.S.* 25°47' N, 80°10' W 105
Miami, river, *Ohio, U.S.* 39°16' N, 84°50' W 80
Mīānābād, *Iran* 37°2' N, 57°28' E 180
Mianchi, *China* 34°45' N, 111°49' E 198
Mīāndoāb, *Iran* 37°1' N, 46°2' E 195
Mianduhe, *China* 49°7' N, 120°58' E 198
Mīāneh, *Iran* 37°26' N, 47°42' E 195
Mianwali, *Pak.* 32°35' N, 71°36' E 186
Mianxian, *China* 33°9' N, 106°41' E 198
Mianyang, *China* 31°25' N, 104°39' E 198
Miaoli, *Taiwan, China* 24°33' N, 120°47' E 198
Miarinarivo, *Madagascar* 16°37' S, 48°14' E 220
Miarinarivo, *Madagascar* 19°0' S, 46°54' E 220
Miass, *Russ.* 54°59' N, 60°7' E 154
Miass, river, *Russ.* 55°21' N, 61°22' E 154
Miastkowo, *Pol.* 53°9' N, 21°49' E 152
Mica, Cerro de la, peak, *Chile* 21°42' S, 70°2' W 137
Mica Creek, *Can.* 52°2' N, 118°34' W 108
Micanopy, *Fla., U.S.* 29°30' N, 82°17' W 105
Micay, *Col.* 3°0' N, 77°38' W 136
Michaichmon', *Russ.* 64°13' N, 50°4' E 154
Michaud, Point 45°27' N, 60°44' W 111
Michel, *Can.* 55°59' N, 109°8' W 108
Michel Peak, *Can.* 53°32' N, 126°35' W 108
Michelson, Mount, peak, *Alas., U.S.* 69°10' N, 144°39' W 98
Michigamme Reservoir, *Mich., U.S.* 46°7' N, 89°1' W 110
Michigan, adm. division, *Mich., U.S.* 42°56' N, 84°53' W 102
Michigan Center, *Mich., U.S.* 42°13' N, 84°19' W 102
Michigan City, *Ind., U.S.* 41°42' N, 86°54' W 102
Michigan, Lake 42°44' N, 87°43' W 110
Michipicoten, *Can.* 47°57' N, 84°54' W 94
Michipicoten Island, *Can.* 47°31' N, 87°15' W 80
Michipicoten River, *Can.* 47°56' N, 84°50' W 94
Michoacán, adm. division, *Mex.* 19°9' N, 102°33' W 114
Michurinsk, *Russ.* 52°53' N, 40°24' E 154
Michurinskoye, *Russ.* 60°35' N, 29°48' E 166
Mico, river, *Nicar.* 11°55' N, 84°38' W 115
Miconje, *Angola* 4°28' S, 12°50' E 218
Micronesia, Federated States of 8°0' N, 147°0' E 192
Micronesia, islands, *North Pacific Ocean* 15°29' N, 140°15' E 190
Micui, *Braz.* 0°29' N, 69°5' W 136
Midai, island, *Indonesia* 3°4' N, 107°25' E 196
Mid-Atlantic Ridge, *North Atlantic Ocean* 3°49' N, 31°17' W 253
Middelburg, *Neth.* 51°29' N, 3°37' E 163
Middelburg, *S. Af.* 25°48' S, 29°27' E 227
Middelfart, *Den.* 55°29' N, 9°44' E 150
Middelkerke, *Belg.* 51°10' N, 2°48' E 163
Middelwit, *S. Af.* 24°52' S, 27°2' E 227
Middenmeer, *Neth.* 52°48' N, 4°59' E 163
Middle America Trench, *North Pacific Ocean* 11°50' N, 89°38' W 253
Middle Andaman, island, *India* 12°25' N, 91°5' E 188
Middle Bight 24°6' N, 78°41' W 96
Middle Butte, peak, *Idaho, U.S.* 43°28' N, 112°49' W 90
Middle Foster Lake, *Can.* 56°34' N, 106°19' W 108
Middle Govç, adm. division, *Mongolia* 45°3' N, 104°54' E 198
Middle Loup, river, *Nebr., U.S.* 42°8' N, 101°26' W 80
Middle River, *Minn., U.S.* 48°23' N, 96°12' W 90
Middle, river, *Iowa, U.S.* 41°11' N, 94°15' W 94
Middleboro, *Mass., U.S.* 41°53' N, 70°55' W 104
Middlebourne, *W. Va., U.S.* 39°29' N, 80°55' W 102
Middleburg, *S. Af.* 31°31' S, 24°58' E 227
Middlebury, *Ind., U.S.* 41°39' N, 85°43' W 102
Middlebury, *Vt., U.S.* 44°0' N, 73°10' W 104
Middleport, *Ohio, U.S.* 38°59' N, 82°4' W 94
Middlesboro, *Ky., U.S.* 36°36' N, 83°43' W 96
Middlesbrough, *U.K.* 54°33' N, 1°15' W 162
Middlesex, *Vt., U.S.* 44°17' N, 72°41' W 104
Middleton, *Idaho, U.S.* 43°42' N, 116°38' W 90
Middleton, *Mass., U.S.* 42°35' N, 71°1' W 104
Middleton, *U.K.* 53°33' N, 2°12' W 162
Middleton, *Wis., U.S.* 43°6' N, 89°30' W 102
Middleton in Teesdale, *U.K.* 54°38' N, 2°6' W 162
Middletown, *Conn., U.S.* 41°33' N, 72°40' W 104
Middletown, *Ill., U.S.* 40°5' N, 89°35' W 102
Middletown, *Ind., U.S.* 40°3' N, 85°32' W 102
Middletown, *N.Y., U.S.* 41°26' N, 74°26' W 94
Middletown, *Ohio, U.S.* 39°29' N, 84°25' W 82
Middletown, *R.I., U.S.* 41°31' N, 71°18' W 104
Middletown Springs, *Vt., U.S.* 43°29' N, 73°8' W 104
Middleville, *Mich., U.S.* 42°41' N, 85°28' W 102
Midhurst, *U.K.* 50°58' N, 0°44' E 162
Mid-Indian Basin, *Indian Ocean* 8°1' S, 79°3' E 254
Mid-Indian Ridge, *Indian Ocean* 13°41' S, 66°4' E 254
Midi-Pyrénées, adm. division, *Fr.* 43°57' N, 0°59' E 150
Midland, *Can.* 44°44' N, 79°53' W 94
Midland, *Mich., U.S.* 43°36' N, 84°14' W 102
Midland, *Tex., U.S.* 31°58' N, 102°3' W 92
Midlothian, *Tex., U.S.* 32°29' N, 97°0' W 96
Midnight, *Miss., U.S.* 33°1' N, 90°35' W 103
Midongy Atsimo, *Madagascar* 23°35' S, 47°2' E 220
Mid-Pacific Mountains, *North Pacific Ocean* 19°40' N, 164°22' E 252
Midpines, *Calif., U.S.* 37°32' N, 119°56' W 100
Midu, island, *Maldives* 0°41' N, 73°11' E 188
Midway, *Utah, U.S.* 40°30' N, 111°28' W 92
Midway Islands, *North Pacific Ocean* 28°27' N, 177°29' W 99
Midwest, *Wyo., U.S.* 43°24' N, 106°16' W 90
Midwest City, *Okla., U.S.* 35°25' N, 97°22' W 92
Midyat, *Turk.* 37°24' N, 41°26' E 195
Midžor, peak, *Serb.* 43°23' N, 22°38' E 168
Mie, adm. division, *Japan* 34°30' N, 136°11' E 201
Miechów, *Pol.* 50°22' N, 20°1' E 152
Miḩdzyrzec Podlaski, *Pol.* 51°58' N, 22°45' E 152
Miḩdzyzdroje, *Pol.* 53°55' N, 14°27' E 152
Miehikkälä, *Fin.* 60°40' N, 27°40' E 166
Miélan, *Fr.* 43°26' N, 0°18' E 164
Mielec, *Pol.* 50°16' N, 21°26' E 152
Mier, *Mex.* 26°27' N, 99°9' W 114
Mier y Noriega, *Mex.* 23°24' N, 100°6' W 114
Miercurea Ciuc, *Rom.* 46°22' N, 25°48' E 156
Mieres, *Sp.* 43°14' N, 5°46' W 150
Mieslahti, *Fin.* 64°23' N, 27°57' E 152
Mī'ēso, *Eth.* 9°12' N, 40°47' E 224
Mifol, *Alban.* 40°36' N, 19°28' E 156
Migdal, *Israel* 32°50' N, 35°30' E 194
Migole, *Tanzania* 7°5' S, 35°52' E 224
Miguel Alemán, Presa, lake, *Mex.* 18°15' N, 96°49' W 114
Miguel Auza, *Mex.* 24°16' N, 103°28' W 114
Miguel Calmon, *Braz.* 11°27' S, 40°37' W 132
Miguelturra, *Sp.* 38°57' N, 3°53' W 164
Migues, *Uru.* 34°29' S, 55°38' W 139
Migyaunglaung, *Myanmar* 14°41' N, 98°9' E 202
Mihai Viteazu, *Rom.* 44°37' N, 28°39' E 156
Mihailovca, *Mold.* 46°32' N, 28°56' E 156
Mihalţ, *Rom.* 46°9' N, 23°44' E 156
Mihara, *Japan* 34°24' N, 133°5' E 201
Miharu, *Japan* 37°26' N, 140°29' E 201
Mihla, *Ger.* 51°4' N, 10°19' E 167
Mijas, *Sp.* 36°35' N, 4°39' W 150
Mijda'ah, *Yemen* 14°2' N, 48°27' E 182
Mijek, *Africa* 23°34' N, 12°56' W 214
Mikashevichy, *Belarus* 52°12' N, 27°27' E 154
Mikese, *Tanzania* 6°42' S, 37°56' E 224
Mikhanavichy, *Belarus* 53°44' N, 27°43' E 154
Mikhaylov, *Russ.* 54°13' N, 38°59' E 154

Mikhaylov, Cape 67°4′ S, 118°8′ E 248
Mikhaylov Island, *Antarctica* 67°19′ S, 86°6′ E 248
Mikhaylova, *Russ.* 75°2′ N, 87°8′ E 173
Mikhaylovka, *Russ.* 50°3′ N, 43°12′ E 158
Mikhaylovskiy, *Russ.* 51°47′ N, 79°32′ E 190
Mikhaylovskoye, *Russ.* 57°3′ N, 28°53′ E 166
Mikindani, *Tanzania* 10°18′ S, 40°4′ E 224
Mikkeli, *Fin.* 61°40′ N, 27°13′ E 166
Mikkolya, *Russ.* 65°13′ N, 31°40′ E 152
Mikkwa, river, *Can.* 57°56′ N, 115°14′ W 108
Mikniya, *Sudan* 16°59′ N, 33°39′ E 226
Mikumi, *Tanzania* 7°26′ S, 36°58′ E 220
Mikumi National Park, *Tanzania* 7°14′ S, 36°41′ E 224
Mikun′, *Russ.* 62°21′ N, 50°12′ E 154
Mikuni, *Japan* 36°12′ N, 136°10′ E 201
Milaca, *Minn., U.S.* 45°44′ N, 93°38′ W 94
Miladummadulu Atoll, *Maldives* 6°13′ N, 73°12′ E 188
Milam, *Tex., U.S.* 31°24′ N, 93°51′ W 103
Milan, *Ind., U.S.* 39°7′ N, 85°8′ W 102
Milan, *Mich., U.S.* 42°5′ N, 83°41′ W 102
Milan, *Mo., U.S.* 41°26′ N, 90°35′ W 94
Milan, *Mo., U.S.* 40°11′ N, 93°6′ W 94
Milan, *N.H., U.S.* 44°34′ N, 71°12′ W 104
Milan see Milano, *It.* 45°27′ N, 9°10′ E 167
Milando, *Angola* 8°51′ S, 17°32′ E 218
Milange, *Mozambique* 16°7′ S, 35°46′ E 224
Milano (Milan), *It.* 45°27′ N, 9°10′ E 167
Milâs, *Turk.* 37°17′ N, 27°45′ E 156
Milbank, *S. Dak., U.S.* 45°12′ N, 96°40′ W 90
Milbridge, *Me., U.S.* 44°31′ N, 67°54′ W 94
Mildenhall, *U.K.* 52°20′ N, 0°30′ E 162
Mildmay, *Can.* 44°2′ N, 81°7′ W 102
Milejewo, *Pol.* 54°13′ N, 19°33′ E 166
Miles, *Tex., U.S.* 31°34′ N, 100°11′ W 92
Miles City, *Mont., U.S.* 46°23′ N, 105°51′ W 90
Milestone, *Can.* 49°59′ N, 104°31′ W 90
Miletto, Monte, peak, *It.* 41°26′ N, 14°17′ E 156
Miletus, ruin(s), *Turk.* 37°29′ N, 27°10′ E 156
Milford, *Conn., U.S.* 41°13′ N, 73°4′ W 104
Milford, *Ill., U.S.* 40°37′ N, 87°42′ W 102
Milford, *Ind., U.S.* 41°24′ N, 85°51′ W 102
Milford, *Iowa, U.S.* 43°19′ N, 95°9′ W 90
Milford, *Me., U.S.* 44°56′ N, 68°38′ W 94
Milford, *Nebr., U.S.* 40°45′ N, 97°5′ W 90
Milford, *N.H., U.S.* 42°49′ N, 71°40′ W 104
Milford, *Utah, U.S.* 38°23′ N, 113°1′ W 90
Milford Sound, *N.Z.* 44°40′ S, 167°56′ E 240
Miliana, *Alg.* 36°18′ N, 2°13′ E 150
Milk River, *Can.* 49°8′ N, 112°5′ W 90
Milk, river, *Mont., U.S.* 48°55′ N, 110°39′ W 90
Milk River Ridge, *Can.* 48°57′ N, 112°24′ W 90
Mil′kovo, *Russ.* 54°49′ N, 158°55′ E 160
Mill Island, *Antarctica* 65°5′ S, 102°22′ E 248
Mill Island, *Can.* 63°40′ N, 79°52′ W 106
Mill Valley, *Calif., U.S.* 37°54′ N, 122°34′ W 100
Millau, *Fr.* 44°6′ N, 3°3′ E 150
Millbrook, *N.Y., U.S.* 41°46′ N, 73°43′ W 104
Mille Lacs, Lac des, lake, *Can.* 48°44′ N, 91°27′ W 94
Milledgeville, *Ga., U.S.* 33°4′ N, 83°12′ W 112
Millen, *Ga., U.S.* 32°47′ N, 81°56′ W 96
Miller, Mount, peak, *Antarctica* 83°18′ S, 167°27′ E 248
Miller Peak, *Ariz., U.S.* 31°23′ N, 110°21′ W 92
Miller Range, *Antarctica* 82°19′ S, 158°47′ E 248
Millerovo, *Russ.* 48°54′ N, 40°25′ E 158
Millers Ferry, *Ala., U.S.* 32°6′ N, 87°22′ W 103
Millersburg, *Ind., U.S.* 41°31′ N, 85°42′ W 102
Millersburg, *Ohio, U.S.* 40°32′ N, 81°54′ W 102
Millerton, *N.Y., U.S.* 41°57′ N, 73°32′ W 104
Millesimo, *It.* 44°22′ N, 8°14′ E 167
Millevaches, Plateau de, *Fr.* 45°18′ N, 1°29′ E 165
Milligan Creek, river, *Can.* 56°43′ N, 121°25′ W 108
Millington, *Mich., U.S.* 43°16′ N, 83°31′ W 102
Millington, *Tenn., U.S.* 35°19′ N, 89°54′ W 96
Millinocket, *Me., U.S.* 45°39′ N, 68°43′ W 111
Millom, *U.K.* 54°12′ N, 3°16′ W 162
Millry, *Ala., U.S.* 31°38′ N, 88°18′ W 103
Mills, *Wyo., U.S.* 42°50′ N, 106°22′ W 90
Millstream-Chichester National Park, *Austral.* 21°30′ S, 117°1′ E 238
Millville, *Mass., U.S.* 42°1′ N, 71°35′ W 104
Millville, *N.J., U.S.* 39°23′ N, 75°3′ W 94
Millwater, *Can.* 54°35′ N, 101°36′ W 108
Millwood Lake, *Ark., U.S.* 33°43′ N, 94°23′ W 96
Milly, *Fr.* 48°23′ N, 2°28′ E 163
Milmarcos, *Sp.* 41°4′ N, 1°52′ W 164
Milna, *Croatia* 43°19′ N, 16°26′ E 168
Milnor, *N. Dak., U.S.* 46°14′ N, 97°28′ W 94
Mīlo, *Eth.* 10°0′ N, 42°2′ E 224
Milo, *Tanzania* 9°55′ S, 34°38′ E 224
Milo, river, *Guinea* 10°11′ N, 9°32′ W 222
Miločer, *Mont.* 42°16′ N, 18°53′ E 168
Mílos, island, *Gr.* 36°37′ N, 23°49′ E 180
Milot, *Alban.* 41°40′ N, 19°43′ E 168
Milparinka, *Austral.* 29°45′ S, 141°55′ E 231
Milpitas, *Calif., U.S.* 37°26′ N, 121°55′ W 100
Milroy, *Ind., U.S.* 39°29′ N, 85°28′ W 102
Milton, *Fla., U.S.* 30°38′ N, 87°2′ W 96
Milton, *Ky., U.S.* 38°42′ N, 85°23′ W 102
Milton, *Mass., U.S.* 42°15′ N, 71°5′ W 104
Milton, *N.H., U.S.* 43°24′ N, 71°0′ W 104
Milton, *N.Z.* 46°8′ S, 169°56′ E 240
Milton, *Pa., U.S.* 41°1′ N, 76°51′ W 94
Milton, *Wash., U.S.* 47°13′ N, 122°19′ W 100
Milton, *Wis., U.S.* 42°46′ N, 88°57′ W 102
Milton Ernest, *U.K.* 52°11′ N, 0°31′ E 162
Milton Keynes, *U.K.* 52°1′ N, 0°46′ E 162
Milton Lake, *Can.* 59°27′ N, 104°22′ W 108
Milton Mills, *N.H., U.S.* 43°30′ N, 70°59′ W 104
Miltonvale, *Kans., U.S.* 39°19′ N, 97°28′ W 92
Milverton, *Can.* 43°33′ N, 80°55′ W 102
Milverton, *U.K.* 51°1′ N, 3°15′ W 162
Milwaukee, *Wis., U.S.* 43°1′ N, 87°56′ W 102
Mīlyutinka, *Kaz.* 51°58′ N, 61°3′ E 154
Milyutino, *Russ.* 58°21′ N, 29°38′ E 166
Mimizan-Plage, *Fr.* 44°13′ N, 1°19′ W 150
Mimongo, *Gabon* 1°40′ S, 11°39′ E 218
Mimot, *Cambodia* 11°49′ N, 106°11′ E 202
Mims, *Fla., U.S.* 28°40′ N, 80°52′ W 105
Min, river, *China* 26°20′ N, 118°32′ E 198
Min, river, *China* 29°27′ N, 104°1′ E 190
Mina, *Nev., U.S.* 38°23′ N, 118°8′ W 90
Mīnā′ al Fa′l, *Oman* 23°34′ N, 58°24′ E 196
Mina Bazar, *Pak.* 31°3′ N, 69°18′ E 186
Mīnā′ Jabal ′Alī, *U.A.E.* 25°1′ N, 55°6′ E 196
Mīnāb, *Iran* 27°5′ N, 57°4′ E 196
Minabe, *Japan* 33°46′ N, 135°19′ E 201
Minagish, oil field, *Kuwait* 28°59′ N, 47°28′ E 196
Minago, river, *Can.* 54°2′ N, 99°40′ W 108
Minakami, *Japan* 36°45′ N, 138°57′ E 201
Minaki, *Can.* 49°58′ N, 94°41′ W 90
Minamata, *Japan* 32°11′ N, 130°24′ E 201
Minami Alps National Park, *Japan* 35°25′ N, 138°3′ E 201
Minas, *Cuba* 21°28′ N, 77°37′ W 116
Minas, *Uru.* 34°23′ S, 55°14′ W 139
Minas de Corrales, *Uru.* 31°35′ S, 55°31′ W 139
Minas Gerais, adm. division, *Braz.* 18°58′ S, 47°16′ W 138
Minas Novas, *Braz.* 17°13′ S, 42°36′ W 138
Minas, oil field, *Indonesia* 0°49′ N, 101°19′ E 196
Minas, Sierra de las, *Guatemala* 15°10′ N, 90°16′ W 115
Minatitlán, *Mex.* 17°58′ N, 94°33′ W 114
Minbu, *Myanmar* 20°11′ N, 94°50′ E 202
Minch, The, channel 58°2′ N, 6°8′ W 150
Minchinmávida, Volcán, peak, *Chile* 42°48′ S, 72°36′ W 134
Minco, *Okla., U.S.* 35°17′ N, 97°56′ W 92
Mindanao, island, *Philippines* 5°26′ N, 123°17′ E 192
Minden, *La., U.S.* 32°36′ N, 93°17′ W 103
Minden, *Nebr., U.S.* 40°29′ N, 98°58′ W 90
Minden City, *Mich., U.S.* 43°40′ N, 82°47′ W 102
Mindif, *Cameroon* 10°24′ N, 14°27′ E 216
Mindon, *Myanmar* 19°20′ N, 94°44′ E 202
Mindoro, island, *Philippines* 12°31′ N, 119°20′ E 192
Mindszent, *Hung.* 46°32′ N, 20°12′ E 168
Mindyak, *Russ.* 54°3′ N, 58°47′ E 154
Mine, *Japan* 34°27′ N, 129°20′ E 200
Mine, *Japan* 34°8′ N, 131°13′ E 200
Mine Centre, *Can.* 48°46′ N, 92°37′ W 94
Minehead, *U.K.* 51°12′ N, 3°28′ W 162
Mineiros, *Braz.* 17°36′ S, 52°34′ W 138
Mineola, *Tex., U.S.* 32°39′ N, 95°30′ W 103
Mineral, *Wash., U.S.* 46°41′ N, 122°12′ W 100
Mineral King, *Calif., U.S.* 36°27′ N, 118°36′ W 101
Mineral Point, *Wis., U.S.* 42°51′ N, 90°10′ W 102
Mineral Wells, *Tex., U.S.* 32°47′ N, 98°7′ W 92
Mineral′nyye Vody, *Russ.* 44°13′ N, 43°10′ E 158
Minersville, *Utah, U.S.* 38°12′ N, 112°55′ W 92
Minerva, *N.Y., U.S.* 43°46′ N, 74°0′ W 104
Minerva, *Ohio, U.S.* 40°43′ N, 81°7′ W 102
Minetto, *N.Y., U.S.* 43°23′ N, 76°30′ W 94
Mineville, *N.Y., U.S.* 44°5′ N, 73°32′ W 104
Mineyama, *Japan* 35°36′ N, 135°3′ E 201
Minfeng, *China* 37°5′ N, 82°38′ E 184
Mingäçevir, *Azerb.* 40°46′ N, 47°3′ E 195
Mingäçevir Reservoir, *Azerb.* 41°2′ N, 46°18′ E 195
Mingan, *Can.* 50°18′ N, 64°2′ W 111
Mingin, *Myanmar* 22°51′ N, 94°24′ E 202
Minginui, *N.Z.* 38°41′ S, 176°45′ E 240
Ming-Kush, *Kyrg.* 41°38′ N, 74°18′ E 197
Minglanilla, *Sp.* 39°31′ N, 1°37′ W 164
Mingoyo, *Tanzania* 10°6′ S, 39°35′ E 224
Mingteke, *China* 37°6′ N, 74°59′ E 186
Mingteke Pass, *China* 37°2′ N, 74°44′ E 184
Mingyuegou, *China* 43°7′ N, 128°54′ E 200
Minhla, *Myanmar* 17°59′ N, 95°41′ E 202
Minićevo, *Serb.* 43°41′ N, 22°17′ E 168
Minicoy Island, *India* 7°59′ N, 72°19′ E 188
Minidoka, *Idaho, U.S.* 42°45′ N, 113°30′ W 90
Minidoka Internment National Monument, *Idaho, U.S.* 42°40′ N, 114°27′ W 90
Minier, *Ill., U.S.* 40°25′ N, 89°20′ W 102
Minimarg, *Pak.* 34°46′ N, 75°3′ E 186
Miñimiñi, *Chile* 19°14′ S, 69°42′ W 137
Miniogbolo, *Sudan* 6°20′ N, 28°44′ E 224
Minipi Lake, *Can.* 52°21′ N, 60°55′ W 111
Ministra, peak, *Sp.* 41°6′ N, 2°32′ W 164
Ministro João Alberto, *Braz.* 14°39′ S, 52°23′ W 138
Minitonas, *Can.* 52°5′ N, 101°3′ W 108
Min′kovo, *Russ.* 59°30′ N, 44°7′ E 154
Minna, *Nig.* 9°36′ N, 6°33′ E 222
Minna Bluff 78°41′ S, 176°42′ E 248
Minneapolis, *Kans., U.S.* 39°6′ N, 97°43′ W 90
Minneapolis, *Minn., U.S.* 44°56′ N, 93°17′ W 94
Minnedosa, *Can.* 50°15′ N, 99°55′ W 82
Minneola, *Kans., U.S.* 37°26′ N, 100°2′ W 92
Minneota, *Minn., U.S.* 44°32′ N, 96°0′ W 90
Minnesota, adm. division, *Minn., U.S.* 46°13′ N, 95°54′ W 94
Minnesota, river, *Minn., U.S.* 44°56′ N, 95°41′ W 80
Minnewaukan, *N. Dak., U.S.* 48°3′ N, 99°16′ W 90
Minnitaki Lake, *Can.* 49°55′ N, 92°40′ W 110
Mino, *Japan* 35°31′ N, 136°56′ E 201
Minokamo, *Japan* 35°25′ N, 137°0′ E 201
Minonk, *Mo., U.S.* 40°53′ N, 89°3′ W 110
Minorca see Menorca, island, *Sp.* 39°47′ N, 3°33′ E 164
Minot, *N. Dak., U.S.* 48°12′ N, 101°20′ W 90
Minqin, *China* 38°46′ N, 103°4′ E 190
Minsen, *Ger.* 53°42′ N, 7°58′ E 163
Minsk, *Belarus* 53°52′ N, 27°26′ E 166
Minster, *Ohio, U.S.* 40°23′ N, 84°23′ W 102
Minta, *Cameroon* 4°33′ N, 12°48′ E 218
Minto, *Can.* 62°37′ N, 136°47′ W 98
Minto, *N. Dak., U.S.* 48°16′ N, 97°24′ W 90
Minto Inlet 71°5′ N, 120°37′ W 106
Minto, Lac, lake, *Can.* 57°22′ N, 75°53′ W 106
Minto, Mount, peak, *Antarctica* 71°48′ S, 170°19′ E 248
Minton, *Can.* 49°9′ N, 104°35′ W 90
Minusinsk, *Russ.* 53°42′ N, 91°46′ E 190
Minuteman Missle National Historic Site, *S. Dak., U.S.* 43°51′ N, 102°2′ W 90
Minvoul, *Gabon* 2°8′ N, 12°8′ E 218
Minwakh, *Yemen* 16°51′ N, 48°4′ E 182
Minxian, *China* 34°22′ N, 104°0′ E 173
Min′yar, *Russ.* 55°7′ N, 57°31′ E 154
Mio, *Mich., U.S.* 44°38′ N, 84°8′ W 94
Miquelon, *Can.* 49°25′ N, 76°26′ W 94
Miquihuana, *Mex.* 23°33′ N, 99°46′ W 114
Mir, *Niger* 14°3′ N, 11°58′ E 222
Mira, *It.* 45°26′ N, 12°6′ E 167
Mirabela, *Braz.* 16°18′ S, 44°12′ W 138
Miracema, *Braz.* 21°26′ S, 42°13′ W 138
Miracema do Norte, *Braz.* 9°34′ S, 48°28′ W 130
Miracle Hot Springs, *Calif., U.S.* 35°34′ N, 118°33′ W 101
Mirador, *Braz.* 6°23′ S, 44°25′ W 132
Miraflores, *Col.* 1°16′ N, 72°5′ W 136
Miragoâne, *Haiti* 18°26′ N, 73°7′ W 116
Miraj, *India* 16°50′ N, 74°39′ E 188
Miram Shah, *Pak.* 32°57′ N, 70°10′ E 186
Miramar, *Arg.* 30°55′ S, 62°39′ W 139
Miramar, *Arg.* 38°16′ S, 57°51′ W 139
Miramar, *Fla., U.S.* 25°59′ N, 80°13′ W 105
Miramar Naval Air Station, *Calif., U.S.* 32°52′ N, 117°10′ W 101
Miramas, *Fr.* 43°34′ N, 5°0′ E 150
Miramonte, *Calif., U.S.* 36°42′ N, 119°4′ W 101
Miran, *China* 39°16′ N, 88°51′ E 188
Miranda, *Braz.* 20°14′ S, 56°22′ W 132
Miranda, adm. division, *Venez.* 10°18′ N, 66°47′ W 136
Miranda de Ebro, *Sp.* 42°41′ N, 2°58′ W 164
Mirande, *Fr.* 43°30′ N, 0°23′ E 164
Mirandola, *It.* 44°52′ N, 11°3′ E 167
Mirandópolis, *Braz.* 21°7′ S, 51°8′ W 138
Mirapinima, *Braz.* 2°14′ S, 61°10′ W 130
Miras, *Alban.* 40°30′ N, 20°54′ E 156
Mirãs, *Kos.* 42°28′ N, 21°12′ E 168
Mirasaka, *Japan* 34°46′ N, 132°57′ E 201
Mirassol, *Braz.* 20°51′ S, 49°31′ W 138
Miravalles, Volcán, peak, *C.R.* 10°43′ N, 85°15′ W 115
Mirbāţ, *Oman* 16°58′ N, 54°45′ E 182
Mirear see Marir, Gezaîr, islands, *Egypt* 23°5′ N, 35°51′ E 182
Mirik see Timiris, Cap, *Mauritania* 19°28′ N, 16°53′ W 222
Mirim, Lagoa, lake, *Braz.* 32°41′ S, 53°9′ W 139
Mirimire, *Venez.* 11°7′ N, 68°45′ W 136
Mírina, *Gr.* 39°52′ N, 25°4′ E 156
Miringa, *Nig.* 10°45′ N, 12°9′ E 216
Mirití, *Col.* 0°25′ N, 71°9′ W 136
Mirití Paraná, river, *Col.* 0°534′ S, 71°31′ W 136
Miritinitsy, *Russ.* 56°38′ N, 29°50′ E 166
Mīrjāveh, *Iran* 28°57′ N, 61°24′ E 182
Mirnyy, *Russ.* 62°27′ N, 113°27′ E 160
Mirnyy, Russia, station, *Antarctica* 66°41′ S, 93°5′ E 248
Miroč, *Serb.* 44°26′ N, 22°14′ E 168
Mirond Lake, *Can.* 55°4′ N, 103°18′ W 108
Miros, *Pol.* 53°21′ N, 16°6′ E 152
Miroševce, *Serb.* 42°51′ N, 21°50′ E 168
Mirpur, *Pak.* 33°10′ N, 73°48′ E 186
Mirpur Batoro, *Pak.* 24°43′ N, 68°18′ E 186
Mirpur Khas, *Pak.* 25°33′ N, 69°3′ E 186
Mirria, *Niger* 13°42′ N, 9°6′ E 222
Mirror, *Can.* 52°27′ N, 113°7′ W 108
Mirror Lake, *N.H., U.S.* 43°37′ N, 71°17′ W 104
Mirsaale, *Somalia* 5°57′ N, 47°57′ E 218
Mirsíni, *Gr.* 37°55′ N, 21°14′ E 156
Miruro, *Mozambique* 15°19′ S, 30°24′ E 224
Miryang, *S. Korea* 35°29′ N, 128°45′ E 200
Mirzaani, oil field, *Ga.* 41°21′ N, 46°7′ E 195
Mirzapur, *India* 25°6′ N, 82°33′ E 197
Misa, river, *Latv.* 56°38′ N, 23°50′ E 166
Misaki, *Japan* 33°23′ N, 132°7′ E 201
Misantla, *Mex.* 19°55′ N, 96°51′ W 114
Misaw Lake, *Can.* 59°51′ N, 102°59′ W 108
Misekumaw Lake, *Can.* 59°4′ N, 104°30′ W 108
Miseno, Capo, *It.* 40°49′ N, 13°26′ E 156
Mish Mountains, Slieve, peak, *Ire.* 52°11′ N, 9°55′ W 150
Misha, *India* 7°59′ N, 93°28′ E 188
Mishahua, river, *Peru* 11°24′ S, 72°40′ W 137
Mishawaka, *Ind., U.S.* 41°38′ N, 86°11′ W 102
Misheguk Mountain, peak, *Alas., U.S.* 68°13′ N, 161°20′ W 98
Mishkino, *Russ.* 55°35′ N, 55°56′ E 154
Misi, *Fin.* 66°36′ N, 26°40′ E 152
Misima, island, *P.N.G.* 10°40′ S, 152°54′ E 192
Misión San José Estero, *Parag.* 23°44′ S, 61°0′ W 132
Misiones, adm. division, *Arg.* 27°5′ S, 55°22′ W 139
Misiones, Sierra de, *Arg.* 26°48′ S, 54°11′ W 139
Miskah, *Saudi Arabia* 24°48′ N, 42°56′ E 182
Miski, *Sudan* 14°50′ N, 24°11′ E 226
Miskitos, Cayos, islands, *Caribbean Sea* 14°20′ N, 82°37′ W 115
Miskolc, *Hung.* 48°6′ N, 20°48′ E 168
Mislea, oil field, *Rom.* 44°48′ N, 25°15′ E 156
Misool, island, *Indonesia* 1°57′ S, 130°29′ E 192
Misquah Hills, peak, *Minn., U.S.* 47°56′ N, 90°35′ W 94
Mişrātah, *Lib.* 32°22′ N, 15°5′ E 216
Misséni, *Mali* 10°20′ N, 6°5′ W 222
Missinaibi Lake, *Can.* 48°22′ N, 84°24′ W 94
Missinaibi, river, *Can.* 49°18′ N, 83°33′ W 80
Missinaibi, river, *Can.* 50°14′ N, 82°43′ W 110
Missinipe, *Can.* 55°34′ N, 104°45′ W 108
Mission, *S. Dak., U.S.* 43°17′ N, 100°40′ W 90
Mission Range, *Mont., U.S.* 47°32′ N, 114°11′ W 90
Mission Viejo, *Calif., U.S.* 33°35′ N, 117°40′ W 101
Missira, *Senegal* 13°6′ N, 11°43′ W 222
Missisa Lake, *Can.* 52°14′ N, 85°45′ W 110
Missisicabi, river, *Can.* 51°12′ N, 79°38′ W 110
Mississauga, *Can.* 43°35′ N, 79°40′ W 94
Mississippi, adm. division, *Miss., U.S.* 32°33′ N, 90°59′ W 96
Mississippi River Delta, *La., U.S.* 29°43′ N, 90°1′ W 103
Mississippi, river, *U.S.* 42°45′ N, 91°52′ W 80
Mississippi State, *Miss., U.S.* 33°24′ N, 88°47′ W 103
Misso, *Est.* 57°36′ N, 27°12′ E 166
Missoula, *Mont., U.S.* 46°51′ N, 114°0′ W 82
Missour, *Mor.* 33°8′ N, 4°0′ W 214
Missouri, adm. division, *Mo., U.S.* 38°21′ N, 93°28′ W 94
Missouri, river, *U.S.* 40°32′ N, 96°8′ W 80
Mistaken Point, *Can.* 46°30′ N, 54°0′ W 111
Mistaouac, Lac, lake, *Can.* 49°23′ N, 79°19′ W 94
Mistassibi, river, *Can.* 50°31′ N, 72°8′ W 110
Mistassini, *Can.* 48°54′ N, 72°13′ W 82
Mistassini (Baie-du-Poste), *Can.* 50°24′ N, 73°50′ W 110
Mistassini, Lac, lake, *Can.* 50°44′ N, 75°0′ W 80
Mistassini, river, *Can.* 49°53′ N, 72°58′ W 94
Mistastin Lake, lake, *Can.* 55°57′ N, 67°21′ W 246
Mistatim, *Can.* 52°51′ N, 103°24′ W 108
Misti, Volcan, peak, *Peru* 16°21′ S, 71°27′ W 137
Mistinikon Lake, *Can.* 47°51′ N, 81°27′ W 94
Misty Fiords National Monument, *Alas., U.S.* 55°47′ N, 131°10′ W 108
Misty Lake, *Can.* 58°51′ N, 102°11′ W 108
Misumi, *Japan* 34°46′ N, 131°58′ E 200
Mita, Punta de, *Mex.* 20°33′ N, 105°46′ W 114
Mitai, *Japan* 32°42′ N, 131°18′ E 201
Mitatib, *Sudan* 15°55′ N, 36°7′ E 182
Mitau see Jelgava, *Latv.* 56°38′ N, 23°40′ E 166
Mitchell, *Austral.* 26°31′ S, 147°57′ E 231
Mitchell, *Can.* 43°26′ N, 81°11′ W 102
Mitchell, *Ind., U.S.* 38°43′ N, 86°28′ W 102
Mitchell, *Nebr., U.S.* 41°56′ N, 103°49′ W 90
Mitchell, *S. Dak., U.S.* 43°41′ N, 98°2′ W 90
Mitchell and Alice Rivers National Park, *Austral.* 15°34′ S, 141°46′ E 238
Mitchell, Mount, peak, *N.C., U.S.* 35°45′ N, 82°21′ W 96
Mitchell Peak, *Antarctica* 76°16′ S, 146°43′ W 248
Mitchell Peak, *Ariz., U.S.* 33°12′ N, 109°26′ W 92
Mitchell, river, *Austral.* 16°17′ S, 142°32′ E 231
Mitchinamécus, Réservoir, lake, *Can.* 47°8′ N, 75°9′ W 94
Mitilíni (Mytilene), *Gr.* 39°6′ N, 26°33′ E 156
Mito, *Japan* 36°21′ N, 140°27′ E 201
Mitō, *Japan* 34°12′ N, 131°22′ E 200
Mitre, peak, *N.Z.* 40°50′ S, 175°24′ E 240
Mitre, Península, *Arg.* 54°44′ S, 67°9′ W 134
Mitrofanovskaya, *Russ.* 63°14′ N, 56°7′ E 154
Mitrovica, *Kosovo* 42°53′ N, 20°51′ E 168
Mitsero, *Cyprus* 35°2′ N, 33°7′ E 194
Mitsikéli, Óros, *Gr.* 39°50′ N, 20°17′ E 156
Mitsinjo, *Madagascar* 16°1′ S, 45°52′ E 220
Mitsio, Nosy, island, *Madagascar* 13°0′ S, 47°23′ E 220
Mitskevichi, *Belarus* 53°16′ N, 25°45′ E 152
Mitsuke, *Japan* 37°31′ N, 138°55′ E 201
Mitsushima, *Japan* 34°16′ N, 129°18′ E 201
Mitú, *Col.* 1°5′ N, 70°4′ W 136
Mitumba, Chaîne de, *Dem. Rep. of the Congo* 8°5′ S, 27°22′ E 224
Mitumba, Monts, *Dem. Rep. of the Congo* 3°49′ S, 28°12′ E 224
Mitwaba, *Dem. Rep. of the Congo* 8°35′ S, 27°18′ E 224
Mityana, *Uganda* 0°23′ N, 32°4′ E 224
Mityayevo, *Russ.* 60°17′ N, 61°3′ E 154
Miura, *Japan* 35°8′ N, 139°38′ E 201
Mi-Wuk Village, *Calif., U.S.* 38°3′ N, 120°13′ W 100
Mixian, *China* 34°29′ N, 113°26′ E 198
Mixteco, river, *Mex.* 17°57′ N, 98°16′ W 114
Miya, river, *Japan* 34°20′ N, 136°17′ E 201
Miyagi, adm. division, *Japan* 38°3′ N, 140°25′ E 201
Miyajima, *Japan* 34°17′ N, 132°19′ E 201
Miyako, island, *Japan* 24°25′ N, 125°29′ E 190
Miyako Jima, island, *Japan* 24°55′ N, 124°58′ E 198
Miyakonojō, *Japan* 31°43′ N, 131°4′ E 201
Mīyaly, *Kaz.* 48°51′ N, 53°54′ E 158
Miyanojō, *Japan* 31°53′ N, 130°27′ E 201
Miyazaki, *Japan* 31°55′ N, 131°25′ E 201
Miyazaki, adm. division, *Japan* 32°2′ N, 130°52′ E 201
Miyazu, *Japan* 35°30′ N, 135°11′ E 201
Miyory, *Belarus* 55°38′ N, 27°37′ E 166
Miyoshi, *Japan* 34°49′ N, 132°51′ E 201
Miyun, *China* 40°25′ N, 116°51′ E 198
Mizdah, *Lib.* 31°28′ N, 12°55′ E 216
Mize, *Miss., U.S.* 31°52′ N, 89°33′ W 103
Mizen Head, *Ire.* 51°15′ N, 9°51′ W 150
Mizhevichy, *Belarus* 52°58′ N, 25°5′ E 154
Mizhi, *China* 37°47′ N, 110°16′ E 198
Miziya, *Bulg.* 43°40′ N, 23°52′ E 156
Mizo Hills, *India* 23°31′ N, 92°24′ E 188
Mizpé Ramon, *Israel* 30°36′ N, 34°48′ E 194
Mizpe Shalem, *West Bank, Israel* 31°35′ N, 35°23′ E 194
Mizque, *Bol.* 17°55′ S, 65°22′ W 137
Mizzen Topsail, peak, *Can.* 49°3′ N, 56°44′ W 111
Mjällom, *Nor.* 62°58′ N, 18°26′ E 152
Mjanji, *Uganda* 0°14′ N, 33°58′ E 224
Mjölby, *Nor.* 58°18′ N, 15°8′ E 152
Mkalama, *Tanzania* 4°8′ S, 34°35′ E 224
Mkangira, *Tanzania* 8°57′ S, 37°27′ E 224
Mkhi, *Russ.* 58°59′ N, 29°54′ E 166
Mkoani, *Tanzania* 5°22′ S, 39°39′ E 224
Mkokotoni, *Tanzania* 5°52′ S, 39°18′ E 218
Mkomazi, *Tanzania* 4°36′ S, 38°4′ E 224

Mkowela, *Tanzania* 10°56' S, 38°5' E 224
Mkumbi, Ras, *Tanzania* 7°53' S, 39°55' E 224
Mkushi, *Zambia* 13°38' S, 29°23' E 224
Mkuze, *S. Af.* 27°35' S, 32°6' E 227
Mladenovac, *Serb.* 44°26' N, 20°41' E 168
M'Lefaat, ruin(s), *Iraq* 36°17' N, 43°21' E 195
Mléhas, spring, *Mauritania* 22°38' N, 7°0' W 214
Mlini, *Croatia* 42°37' N, 18°12' E 168
Mlinište, *Bosn. and Herzg.* 44°14' N, 16°49' E 168
Mljet (Melita), island, *Croatia* 42°37' N, 17°23' E 168
Mljet National Park, *Croatia* 42°45' N, 17°27' E 168
Mława, *Pol.* 53°6' N, 20°21' E 152
Mloa, *Tanzania* 7°40' S, 35°23' E 224
Mmabatho, *Botswana* 25°42' S, 25°39' E 207
Mmadinare, *Botswana* 21°59' S, 27°43' E 227
Mmashoro, *Botswana* 21°56' S, 26°22' E 227
Mnero, *Tanzania* 10°10' S, 38°40' E 224
Mo, *Nor.* 59°28' N, 7°48' E 152
Mo Duc, *Vietnam* 14°54' N, 108°55' E 202
Mo i Rana, *Nor.* 66°15' N, 14°22' E 160
Moa, *Cuba* 20°41' N, 74°58' W 116
Moa, island, *Indonesia* 8°19' S, 128°7' E 192
Moa, river, *Sierra Leone* 7°53' N, 11°2' W 222
Moab, *Utah, U.S.* 38°34' N, 109°32' W 90
Moabi, *Gabon* 2°25' S, 11°0' E 218
Moaco, river, *Braz.* 8°21' S, 69°28' W 130
Moamba, *Mozambique* 25°35' S, 32°17' E 227
Moana, *N.Z.* 42°35' S, 171°28' E 240
Moanda, *Gabon* 1°35' S, 13°8' E 218
Moapa, *Nev., U.S.* 36°39' N, 114°38' W 101
Moar Lake, *Can.* 52°0' N, 95°21' W 108
Moatize, *Mozambique* 16°10' S, 33°42' E 224
Moba, *Dem. Rep. of the Congo* 7°6' S, 29°46' E 224
Mobaye, *Cen. Af. Rep.* 4°23' N, 21°12' E 218
Mobeetie, *Tex., U.S.* 35°29' N, 100°26' W 92
Mobenzélé, *Congo* 0°54' N, 17°49' E 218
Moberly, *Mo., U.S.* 39°24' N, 92°26' W 94
Mobile, *Ala., U.S.* 30°41' N, 88°4' W 103
Mobile Bay 30°25' N, 88°46' W 80
Mobile Point, *Ala., U.S.* 30°7' N, 88°6' W 103
Mobile, river, *Ala., U.S.* 30°59' N, 88°3' W 103
Mobridge, *S. Dak., U.S.* 45°32' N, 100°27' W 90
Mocajuba, *Braz.* 2°37' S, 49°29' W 130
Moçambique, *Mozambique* 15°6' S, 40°41' E 224
Mocamedes Reserve, *Angola* 15°41' S, 12°2' E 206
Moccasin, *Calif., U.S.* 37°47' N, 120°19' W 100
Mocejón, *Sp.* 39°56' N, 3°55' W 164
Mocha, Isla, island, *Chile* 38°32' S, 74°51' W 134
Mochigase, *Japan* 35°19' N, 134°11' E 201
Mochima National Park, *Caribbean Sea* 10°17' N, 64°47' W 122
Mochudi, *Botswana* 24°24' S, 26°6' E 227
Mocímboa da Praia, *Mozambique* 11°23' S, 40°20' E 224
Mocímboa do Rovuma, *Mozambique* 11°19' S, 39°22' E 220
Möckmühl, *Ger.* 49°19' N, 9°21' E 152
Moclips, *Wash., U.S.* 47°12' N, 124°12' W 100
Mocó, river, *Braz.* 2°9' S, 67°22' W 136
Mocoa, *Col.* 1°8' N, 76°39' W 136
Mococa, *Braz.* 21°27' S, 47°2' W 138
Moctezuma, *Mex.* 30°10' N, 106°28' W 92
Moctezuma, *Mex.* 22°44' N, 101°6' W 114
Moctezuma, *Mex.* 29°48' N, 109°43' W 92
Moctezuma, river, *Mex.* 20°38' N, 99°26' W 114
Mocuba, *Mozambique* 16°52' S, 36°59' E 224
Mocupe, *Peru* 7°0' S, 79°39' W 130
Modane, *Fr.* 45°11' N, 6°39' E 167
Model, *Colo., U.S.* 37°22' N, 104°16' W 92
Modesto, *Calif., U.S.* 37°38' N, 121°0' W 100
Modica, *It.* 36°51' N, 14°45' E 156
Modigliana, *It.* 44°9' N, 11°47' E 167
Modimolle (Nylstroom), *S. Af.* 24°44' S, 28°24' E 227
Modjamboli, *Dem. Rep. of the Congo* 2°25' N, 22°8' E 218
Modjigo, region, *Niger* 17°6' N, 12°37' E 216
Modriča, *Bosn. and Herzg.* 44°57' N, 18°17' E 168
Moebase, *Mozambique* 17°7' S, 38°41' E 224
Moenkopi, *Ariz., U.S.* 36°6' N, 111°13' W 92
Moerbeke, *Dem. Rep. of the Congo* 5°31' S, 14°41' E 218
Moerdijk, *Neth.* 51°41' N, 4°37' E 167
Moerewa, *N.Z.* 35°24' S, 174°0' E 240
Moffet Inlet 71°59' N, 87°20' W 106
Mogadishu see Muqdisho, *Somalia* 1°58' N, 45°10' E 218
Mogadouro, *Port.* 41°20' N, 6°44' W 150
Mogalo, *Dem. Rep. of the Congo* 3°12' N, 19°5' E 218
Mogandia, *Congo* 0°39' N, 17°10' E 218
Mogapinyana, *Botswana* 22°20' S, 27°34' E 227
Mogaung, *Myanmar* 25°17' N, 96°59' E 188
Mogen, *Nor.* 60°1' N, 7°56' E 152
Mogi, *Japan* 32°42' N, 129°54' E 201
Mogi Mirim, *Braz.* 22°26' S, 46°57' W 138
Mogilno, *Pol.* 52°39' N, 17°58' E 152
Mogincual, *Mozambique* 15°32' S, 40°25' E 224
Mogocha, *Russ.* 53°46' N, 119°43' E 190
Mogok, *Myanmar* 22°55' N, 96°30' E 202
Mogollon Mountains, *N. Mex., U.S.* 33°13' N, 108°44' W 92
Mogollon Rim, *Ariz., U.S.* 34°15' N, 110°40' W 92
Mogor, *Eth.* 4°49' N, 40°18' E 224
Mogotes, Punta, *Arg.* 38°15' S, 57°34' W 139
Mohales Hoek, *Lesotho* 30°11' S, 27°29' E 227
Mohall, *N. Dak., U.S.* 48°45' N, 101°32' W 90
Mohammadia, *Alg.* 35°35' N, 7°416' E 150
Mohammedia (Fedala), *Mor.* 33°43' N, 7°22' W 214
Mohave, Lake, *Ariz., U.S.* 35°21' N, 114°49' W 101
Mohave Mountains, *Ariz., U.S.* 34°35' N, 114°20' W 101
Mohawk, *N.Y., U.S.* 43°0' N, 75°1' W 94
Mohawk Mountains, *Ariz., U.S.* 32°39' N, 113°46' W 101
Mohawk, river, *N.Y., U.S.* 42°46' N, 75°21' W 80
Mohe, *Russ.* 53°24' N, 122°17' E 190
Moheda, *Nor.* 57°0' N, 14°34' E 152
Mohegan, *Conn., U.S.* 41°28' N, 72°6' W 104
Mohenjo Daro, ruin(s), *Pak.* 27°17' N, 68°1' E 186
Mohican, Cape, *Alas., U.S.* 60°7' N, 169°41' W 98
Möhkö, *Fin.* 62°35' N, 31°14' E 152
Mohn Basin, *Antarctica* 86°24' S, 162°33' W 248
Mohns Ridge, *Norwegian Sea* 72°37' N, 3°17' E 255
Mohnyin, *Myanmar* 24°45' N, 96°23' E 188
Moho, *Peru* 15°24' S, 69°29' W 137
Mohon Peak, *Ariz., U.S.* 34°55' N, 113°22' W 92
Mohoro, *Tanzania* 8°7' S, 39°8' E 224
Mohyliv-Podil's'kyy, *Ukr.* 48°28' N, 27°52' E 152
Moi, *Nor.* 58°26' N, 6°31' E 150
Moià, *Sp.* 41°49' N, 2°5' E 164
Mo-i-Rana, *Nor.* 66°13' N, 14°11' E 173
Mõisaküla, *Est.* 58°4' N, 25°10' E 166
Moisés Ville, *Arg.* 30°44' S, 61°29' W 139
Moisie, *Can.* 50°11' N, 66°7' W 111
Moissac, *Fr.* 44°6' N, 1°5' E 150
Moïssala, *Chad* 8°18' N, 17°45' E 218
Möja, island, *Sw.* 59°26' N, 18°54' E 166
Mojácar, *Sp.* 37°7' N, 1°51' W 164
Mojave, *Calif., U.S.* 35°3' N, 118°11' W 101
Mojave Desert, *Calif., U.S.* 34°34' N, 116°28' W 101
Mojave Nature Preserve, *Calif., U.S.* 35°4' N, 115°40' W 101
Mojave River Wash, *Calif., U.S.* 35°5' N, 116°15' W 101
Mojiang, *China* 23°33' N, 101°32' E 202
Mojkovac, *Mont.* 42°57' N, 19°35' E 168
Mojo, *Bol.* 21°50' S, 65°37' W 137
Mojo, *Eth.* 8°35' N, 39°6' E 224
Mojocoya, *Bol.* 18°44' S, 64°41' W 137
Mojos, *Bol.* 14°33' S, 68°55' W 137
Moju, river, *Braz.* 2°50' S, 48°56' W 130
Mokambo, *Dem. Rep. of the Congo* 12°28' S, 28°20' E 224
Mokau, *N.Z.* 38°44' S, 174°38' E 240
Mokelumne Hill, *Calif., U.S.* 38°17' N, 120°43' W 100
Mokelumne Peak, *Calif., U.S.* 38°31' N, 120°11' W 90
Mokhcha, *Russ.* 64°59' N, 53°41' E 154
Mokhtar, *Alg.* 36°17' N, 6°18' E 150
Moknine, *Tun.* 35°36' N, 10°52' E 156
Mokolo, *Cameroon* 10°44' N, 13°48' E 216
Mokopane (Potgietersrus), *S. Af.* 24°9' S, 28°59' E 227
Mokpo, *S. Korea* 34°48' N, 126°23' E 200
Mokra Gora, *Serb.-Kos.* 42°45' N, 20°6' E 168
Mokraya Ol'khovka, *Russ.* 50°26' N, 44°56' E 158
Mokrin, *Serb.* 45°54' N, 20°25' E 168
Mokro Polje, *Croatia* 44°5' N, 16°1' E 168
Mokrous, *Russ.* 51°12' N, 47°31' E 158
Mol, *Belg.* 51°10' N, 5°7' E 167
Mol, *Serb.* 45°45' N, 20°7' E 168
Molaly, *Kaz.* 45°26' N, 78°21' E 184
Molango, *Mex.* 20°46' N, 98°44' W 114
Molanosa, *Can.* 54°29' N, 105°33' W 108
Molas, Punta, *Mex.* 20°36' N, 86°43' W 115
Molatón, peak, *Sp.* 38°58' N, 1°26' W 164
Molchanovo, *Russ.* 57°31' N, 83°46' E 169
Mold, *U.K.* 53°9' N, 3°8' W 162
Molde, *Nor.* 62°44' N, 7°8' E 152
Moldova 47°17' N, 28°27' E 156
Moldoveanu, peak, *Rom.* 45°35' N, 24°39' E 156
Mole National Park, *Ghana* 9°20' N, 2°18' W 222
Molepolole, *Botswana* 24°27' S, 25°30' E 227
Molesworth, *N.Z.* 42°5' S, 173°16' E 240
Molėtai, *Lith.* 55°13' N, 25°27' E 166
Molihong Shan, peak, *China* 42°8' N, 124°38' E 200
Molina de Aragón, *Sp.* 40°50' N, 1°54' W 164
Molina de Segura, *Sp.* 38°3' N, 1°14' W 164
Moline, *Kans., U.S.* 37°20' N, 96°19' W 90
Moline, *Mo., U.S.* 41°30' N, 90°28' W 94
Molinella, *It.* 44°36' N, 11°39' E 167
Molino de Flores Netzahualcóyotl National Park, *Mex.* 19°27' N, 98°55' W 112
Moliro, *Dem. Rep. of the Congo* 8°14' S, 30°30' E 224
Molise, adm. division, *It.* 41°39' N, 14°13' E 156
Möllbrücke, *Aust.* 46°50' N, 13°21' E 167
Mollendo, *Peru* 17°2' S, 72°2' W 137
Moller, Port 55°48' N, 161°42' W 98
Mollerussa, *Sp.* 41°37' N, 0°53' E 164
Mölln, *Ger.* 53°37' N, 10°41' E 152
Molló, *Sp.* 42°20' N, 2°23' E 150
Molloy Hole, *Greenland Sea* 78°52' N, 4°58' E 255
Mölndal, *Nor.* 57°40' N, 12°3' E 152
Molochans'k, *Ukr.* 47°10' N, 35°34' E 156
Molodezhnaya, Russia, station, *Antarctica* 67°50' S, 46°8' E 248
Molodezhnyy, *Kaz.* 50°38' N, 73°29' E 184
Molodi, *Russ.* 58°1' N, 28°43' E 166
Molodo, *Mali* 14°15' N, 6°3' W 222
Molokai Fracture Zone, *North Pacific Ocean* 22°54' N, 136°36' W 252
Moloka'i, island, *Hawai'i, U.S.* 21°13' N, 157°0' W 99
Molsheim, *Fr.* 48°32' N, 7°29' E 163
Molson, *Wash., U.S.* 48°58' N, 119°12' W 90
Molson Lake, *Can.* 54°13' N, 97°12' W 108
Molteno, *S. Af.* 31°24' S, 26°21' E 227
Molu, island, *Indonesia* 6°58' S, 131°32' E 192
Molucca Sea 1°32' N, 125°12' E 192
Molula, *Dem. Rep. of the Congo* 5°59' S, 29°4' E 224
Molunat, *Croatia* 42°27' N, 18°25' E 168
Molveno, *It.* 46°9' N, 10°57' E 167
Moma, *Dem. Rep. of the Congo* 1°37' S, 23°55' E 218
Moma, *Mozambique* 16°41' S, 39°14' E 224
Moma, river, *Russ.* 65°47' N, 143°26' E 160
Momax, *Mex.* 21°54' N, 103°19' W 114
Mombasa, *Kenya* 4°3' S, 39°38' E 218
Mombetsu, *Japan* 44°24' N, 142°58' E 190
Mombo, *Tanzania* 4°54' S, 38°18' E 224
Mombongo, *Dem. Rep. of the Congo* 1°37' N, 23°4' E 218
Momence, *Ill., U.S.* 41°9' N, 87°40' W 102
Momi, *Dem. Rep. of the Congo* 1°45' S, 27°0' E 224
Mommark, *Den.* 54°56' N, 10°1' E 150
Momotombo, Volcán, peak, *Nicar.* 12°24' N, 86°35' W 115
Mompono, *Dem. Rep. of the Congo* 0°6' N, 21°49' E 218
Mon, *Myanmar* 18°33' N, 96°35' E 202
Mona, Isla, island, *Isla Mona* 17°55' N, 68°6' W 116
Mona Quimbundo, *Angola* 9°55' S, 19°57' E 220
Monaco 43°44' N, 7°24' E 167
Monadhliath Mountains, *U.K.* 57°9' N, 5°11' W 150
Monadnock Mountain, peak, *N.H., U.S.* 42°51' N, 72°9' W 104
Monagas, adm. division, *Venez.* 9°24' N, 63°48' W 116
Monaghan, *Ire.* 54°13' N, 6°58' W 150
Monahans, *Tex., U.S.* 31°34' N, 102°53' W 92
Monapo, *Mozambique* 14°55' S, 40°20' E 224
Monarch Pass, *Colo., U.S.* 38°29' N, 106°20' W 90
Monasterio de Piedra, site, *Sp.* 41°11' N, 1°50' W 164
Monasterio de Yuste, site, *Sp.* 40°6' N, 5°48' W 150
Moncalieri, *It.* 44°59' N, 7°41' E 167
Monchegorsk, *Russ.* 67°55' N, 32°56' E 152
Mönchengladbach, *Ger.* 51°11' N, 6°26' E 167
Monchique, Serra de, *Port.* 37°19' N, 9°15' W 150
Monchon, *Guinea* 10°26' N, 14°30' W 222
Moncks Corner, *S.C., U.S.* 33°11' N, 80°2' W 96
Monckton, Mount, peak, *Can.* 59°40' N, 128°50' W 108
Monclar, *Col.* 4°237' S, 75°8' W 136
Monclova, *Mex.* 18°3' N, 90°52' W 115
Monclova, *Mex.* 26°54' N, 101°26' W 96
Moncouche, Lac, lake, *Can.* 48°43' N, 71°22' W 94
Moncton, *Can.* 46°5' N, 64°48' W 111
Mondego, Cabo, *Port.* 40°12' N, 9°25' W 150
Mondéjar, *Sp.* 40°19' N, 3°6' W 164
Mondo, *Chad* 13°47' N, 15°33' E 216
Mondo, *Tanzania* 4°57' S, 35°56' E 224
Mondolfo, *It.* 43°45' N, 13°6' E 167
Mondonac, Lac, lake, *Can.* 47°22' N, 74°31' W 94
Mondovì, *It.* 44°23' N, 7°50' E 167
Moneasa, *Rom.* 46°26' N, 22°18' E 168
Monee, *Ill., U.S.* 41°24' N, 87°44' W 102
Monein, *Fr.* 43°19' N, 0°35' E 164
Monesterio, *Sp.* 38°5' N, 6°16' W 164
Monestir de Montserrat, site, *Sp.* 41°35' N, 1°47' E 164
Monett, *Mo., U.S.* 36°53' N, 93°56' W 96
Monforte, *Sp.* 42°30' N, 7°35' W 214
Mong Cai, *Vietnam* 21°31' N, 107°55' E 198
Möng Hsu, *Myanmar* 21°54' N, 98°20' E 202
Möng Küng, *Myanmar* 21°35' N, 97°35' E 202
Möng Kyawt, *Myanmar* 19°58' N, 98°44' E 202
Möng Maü, *Myanmar* 19°44' N, 97°57' E 202
Möng Nawng, *Myanmar* 21°40' N, 98°6' E 202
Möng Pai, *Myanmar* 19°44' N, 97°1' E 202
Möng Pan, *Myanmar* 20°19' N, 98°19' E 202
Möng Tung, *Myanmar* 22°1' N, 97°42' E 202
Möng Yai, *Myanmar* 22°24' N, 98°0' E 202
Monga, *Dem. Rep. of the Congo* 4°6' N, 22°54' E 218
Monga, *Tanzania* 9°9' S, 37°55' E 224
Mongala, river, *Dem. Rep. of the Congo* 1°51' N, 19°46' E 218
Mongalla, *Sudan* 5°13' N, 31°51' E 224
Mongana, *Dem. Rep. of the Congo* 2°1' N, 21°40' E 218
Mongar, *Bhutan* 27°16' N, 91°8' E 197
Mongbwalu, *Dem. Rep. of the Congo* 1°55' N, 30°2' E 224
Monggŭmp'o, *N. Korea* 38°9' N, 124°46' E 200
Mongmeik, *Myanmar* 23°4' N, 96°36' E 202
Mongo, *Chad* 12°11' N, 18°40' E 216
Mongolia 47°41' N, 99°29' E 190
Mongororo, *Chad* 11°59' N, 22°30' E 216
Mongoumba, *Cen. Af. Rep.* 3°40' N, 18°32' E 218
Mongstad, *Nor.* 60°47' N, 5°2' E 152
Mongton, *Myanmar* 20°21' N, 98°52' E 202
Mongu, *Zambia* 15°18' S, 23°14' E 207
Moni, *Cyprus* 34°43' N, 33°11' E 194
Moní Agíou, site, *Gr.* 40°13' N, 24°8' E 156
Moní Megístis Lávras, site, *Gr.* 40°9' N, 24°19' E 156
Moní Vatopedíou, site, *Gr.* 40°18' N, 24°8' E 156
Monigotes, *Arg.* 30°28' S, 61°37' W 139
Mõniste, *Est.* 57°34' N, 26°32' E 166
Monitor Peak, *Nev., U.S.* 38°48' N, 116°40' W 90
Monitor Range, *Nev., U.S.* 38°33' N, 116°46' W 90
Monkey Bay, *Malawi* 14°3' S, 34°51' E 224
Monkey Point see Mono, Punta, *Nicar.* 11°24' N, 83°39' W 115
Monkey River Town, *Belize* 16°20' N, 88°33' W 115
Monkman Pass, *Can.* 54°31' N, 121°15' W 108
Monkoto, *Dem. Rep. of the Congo* 1°36' S, 20°40' E 218
Monmouth, *Mo., U.S.* 40°54' N, 90°39' W 94
Monmouth, *U.K.* 51°49' N, 2°43' W 162
Monmouth Mountain, peak, *Can.* 50°59' N, 123°51' W 90
Mono Craters, *Calif., U.S.* 37°52' N, 119°2' W 100
Mono, Punta (Monkey Point), *Nicar.* 11°24' N, 83°39' W 115
Monolith, *Calif., U.S.* 35°7' N, 118°24' W 101
Monomoy Island, *Mass., U.S.* 41°31' N, 69°59' W 104
Monomoy Point, *Mass., U.S.* 41°29' N, 70°7' W 104
Monon, *Ind., U.S.* 40°51' N, 86°53' W 102
Monona, *Wis., U.S.* 43°3' N, 89°20' W 102
Monopoli, *It.* 40°56' N, 17°17' E 156
Monou, *Chad* 16°23' N, 22°10' E 216
Monóvar, *Sp.* 38°26' N, 0°51' E 164
Moñoz, *Peru* 2°6' S, 73°58' W 136
Monreal del Campo, *Sp.* 40°46' N, 1°22' W 164
Monroe, *Conn., U.S.* 41°19' N, 73°13' W 104
Monroe, *Ga., U.S.* 33°46' N, 83°43' W 96
Monroe, *La., U.S.* 32°29' N, 92°7' W 103
Monroe, *Mich., U.S.* 41°53' N, 83°25' W 102
Monroe, *N.C., U.S.* 34°59' N, 80°33' W 96
Monroe, *Ohio, U.S.* 39°26' N, 84°22' W 102
Monroe, *Utah, U.S.* 38°38' N, 112°7' W 92
Monroe, *Wash., U.S.* 47°51' N, 121°59' W 100
Monroe, *Wis., U.S.* 42°35' N, 89°38' W 102
Monroe Bridge, *Mass., U.S.* 42°43' N, 72°57' W 104
Monroe City, *Mo., U.S.* 39°37' N, 91°45' W 94
Monroe City, *Tex., U.S.* 29°46' N, 94°35' W 103
Monroe Lake, *Ind., U.S.* 39°5' N, 86°33' W 102
Monroeville, *Ala., U.S.* 31°31' N, 87°19' W 96
Monroeville, *Ind., U.S.* 40°57' N, 84°52' W 102
Monroeville, *Ohio, U.S.* 41°14' N, 82°43' W 102
Monrovia, *Ind., U.S.* 39°34' N, 86°29' W 102
Monrovia, *Liberia* 6°12' N, 10°51' W 222
Mons, *Belg.* 50°26' N, 3°56' E 163
Møns Klint, *Den.* 54°45' N, 12°43' E 152
Monschau, *Ger.* 50°33' N, 6°14' E 167
Monselice, *It.* 45°14' N, 11°45' E 167
Monserrato, *It.* 39°15' N, 9°8' E 156
Monson, *Mass., U.S.* 42°5' N, 72°20' W 104
Mönsterås, *Nor.* 57°2' N, 16°24' E 152
Mont Belvieu, *Tex., U.S.* 29°50' N, 94°54' W 103
Mont Cenis, Col du, pass, *Fr.* 45°16' N, 6°53' E 167
Mont D'Iberville see Caubvick, Mount, peak, *Can.* 58°48' N, 64°6' W 72
Mont Fouari Reserve, *Congo* 2°49' S, 11°15' E 206
Montabaur, *Ger.* 50°25' N, 7°49' E 167
Montacute, *U.K.* 50°57' N, 2°43' W 162
Montagnac, *Fr.* 43°29' N, 3°28' E 164
Montagnais Point, *Can.* 53°34' N, 60°3' W 111
Montagnana, *It.* 45°13' N, 11°27' E 167
Montagne D'Ambre National Park, *Madagascar* 12°41' S, 49°4' E 220
Montagnes, Lac des, lake, *Can.* 51°37' N, 76°47' W 110
Montagu, *S. Af.* 33°46' S, 20°9' E 227
Montague, *Mass., U.S.* 42°31' N, 72°33' W 104
Montague, *Mich., U.S.* 43°24' N, 86°22' W 102
Montague Island, *Alas., U.S.* 59°35' N, 147°39' W 98
Montague Lake, *Can.* 49°29' N, 106°16' W 90
Montalbán, *Sp.* 40°50' N, 0°50' E 164
Montalbo, *Sp.* 39°52' N, 2°41' W 164
Montana, *Bulg.* 43°25' N, 23°13' E 168
Montana, adm. division, *Bulg.* 43°26' N, 22°50' E 168
Montana, adm. division, *Mont., U.S.* 47°8' N, 111°6' W 90
Montaña, La, *Peru* 6°34' S, 74°22' W 130
Montanha, *Braz.* 18°9' S, 40°23' W 138
Montargis, *Fr.* 47°59' N, 2°44' E 150
Montataire, *Fr.* 49°15' N, 2°26' E 163
Montauban, *Fr.* 44°0' N, 1°20' E 214
Montauk, *N.Y., U.S.* 41°2' N, 71°57' W 104
Montauk Point, *N.Y., U.S.* 41°4' N, 71°52' W 104
Montblanc, *Sp.* 41°21' N, 1°9' E 164
Montcornet, *Fr.* 49°41' N, 4°1' E 163
Mont-de-Marsan, *Fr.* 43°52' N, 0°33' E 214
Montdidier, *Fr.* 49°38' N, 2°34' E 163
Monte Albán, ruin(s), *Mex.* 17°1' N, 96°51' W 114
Monte Alegre, *Braz.* 2°0' S, 54°7' W 130
Monte Alegre de Goiás, *Braz.* 13°17' S, 47°10' W 138
Monte Alegre de Minas, *Braz.* 18°53' S, 48°54' W 138
Monte Alto, ruin(s), *Guatemala* 14°8' N, 91°3' W 115
Monte Azul, *Braz.* 15°10' S, 42°55' W 138
Monte Buey, *Arg.* 32°54' S, 62°29' W 139
Monte Carlo, *Monaco* 43°43' N, 7°24' E 167
Monte Carmelo, *Braz.* 18°45' S, 47°31' W 138
Monte Caseros, *Uru.* 30°15' S, 57°41' W 139
Monte Cristi, *Dom. Rep.* 19°51' N, 71°39' W 116
Monte Dinero, *Arg.* 52°19' S, 68°29' W 134
Monte Escobedo, *Mex.* 22°17' N, 103°33' W 114
Monte Maíz, *Arg.* 33°14' S, 62°35' W 139
Monte Nievas, *Arg.* 35°52' S, 64°7' W 139
Monte Pascoal National Park, *Braz.* 16°43' S, 39°39' W 138
Monte Quemado, *Arg.* 25°50' S, 62°52' W 139
Monte Roraima National Park, *Braz.* 4°34' N, 60°52' W 130
Monte Santu, Capo di, *It.* 40°7' N, 9°44' E 156
Monte Vista, *Colo., U.S.* 37°34' N, 106°9' W 92
Monteagle, Mount, peak, *Antarctica* 73°38' S, 166°1' E 248
Monteagudo, *Bol.* 19°49' S, 63°59' W 137
Montebello, *Can.* 45°39' N, 74°57' W 94
Montebelluna, *It.* 45°46' N, 12°1' E 167
Montecarlo, *Arg.* 26°41' S, 54°48' W 139
Montecatini Terme, *It.* 43°53' N, 10°47' E 167
Montecchio Maggiore, *It.* 45°31' N, 11°25' E 167
Montecito, *Calif., U.S.* 34°25' N, 119°40' W 100
Montecristi, *Ecua.* 1°10' S, 80°31' W 130
Montecristo, island, *It.* 42°7' N, 9°35' E 214
Montecristo National Park, *El Salv.* 14°20' N, 89°28' W 115
Montegiordano Marina, *It.* 40°3' N, 16°33' E 156
Montego Bay, *Jam.* 18°29' N, 77°56' W 115
Montejicar, *Sp.* 37°35' N, 3°30' W 164
Montelíbano, *Col.* 8°2' N, 75°27' W 136
Montélimar, *Fr.* 44°33' N, 4°45' E 150
Montello, *Nev., U.S.* 41°15' N, 114°12' W 90
Montello, *Wis., U.S.* 43°47' N, 89°20' W 102
Montemayor, Meseta de, *Arg.* 45°0' S, 66°39' W 134
Montemorelos, *Mex.* 25°11' N, 99°48' W 96
Montemuro, peak, *Port.* 40°57' N, 8°4' W 150
Montenegro 42°48' N, 18°40' E 168
Montepuez, *Mozambique* 13°8' S, 39°8' E 224
Monterado, *Indonesia* 0°47' N, 109°7' E 196
Montereau, *Fr.* 48°23' N, 2°56' E 163
Monterey, *Calif., U.S.* 36°35' N, 121°55' W 100
Monterey, *Mass., U.S.* 42°10' N, 73°14' W 104
Monterey, *Tenn., U.S.* 36°8' N, 85°16' W 96
Monterey Bay National Marine Sanctuary, *Pacific Ocean* 36°45' N, 122°6' W 100
Montería, *Col.* 8°44' N, 75°53' W 136
Montero, *Bol.* 17°23' S, 63°17' W 137
Monterrey, *Col.* 4°53' N, 72°56' W 136
Monterrey, *Mex.* 25°39' N, 100°24' W 114
Montes Claros, *Braz.* 16°45' S, 43°52' W 138
Montesano, *Wash., U.S.* 46°58' N, 123°36' W 100

Montese, *It.* 44°15′ N, 10°55′ E 167
Montets, Col des, pass, *Fr.* 45°59′ N, 6°54′ E 167
Montevallo, *Ala., U.S.* 33°5′ N, 86°53′ W 96
Montevideo, *Minn., U.S.* 44°56′ N, 95°43′ W 90
Montevideo, *Uru.* 34°55′ S, 56°19′ W 139
Montezuma, *Ga., U.S.* 32°17′ N, 84°2′ W 96
Montezuma, *Iowa, U.S.* 41°34′ N, 92°31′ W 94
Montezuma, *Kans., U.S.* 37°35′ N, 100°28′ W 90
Montezuma Castle National Monument, *Ariz., U.S.* 34°36′ N, 111°53′ W 92
Montezuma Creek, *Utah, U.S.* 37°16′ N, 109°20′ W 92
Montfaucon, *Fr.* 49°15′ N, 5°7′ E 163
Montfort, *Fr.* 48°8′ N, 1°58′ W 150
Montfort, ruin(s), *Israel* 33°1′ N, 35°10′ E 194
Montgomery, *Ala., U.S.* 32°20′ N, 86°24′ W 96
Montgomery, *La., U.S.* 31°39′ N, 92°53′ W 103
Montgomery, *Mich., U.S.* 41°46′ N, 84°48′ W 102
Montgomery, *U.K.* 52°33′ N, 3°9′ W 162
Montgomery Pass, *Nev., U.S.* 37°59′ N, 118°20′ W 90
Monthermé, *Fr.* 49°52′ N, 4°44′ E 163
Monthey, *Switz.* 46°15′ N, 6°56′ E 167
Monticelli d'Ongina, *It.* 45°5′ N, 9°56′ E 167
Monticello, *Ark., U.S.* 33°36′ N, 91°49′ W 112
Monticello, *Fla., U.S.* 30°32′ N, 83°51′ W 96
Monticello, *Ind., U.S.* 40°44′ N, 86°46′ W 102
Monticello, *Iowa, U.S.* 42°13′ N, 91°12′ W 110
Monticello, *Ky., U.S.* 36°50′ N, 84°52′ W 96
Monticello, *Minn., U.S.* 45°16′ N, 93°49′ W 94
Monticello, *Miss., U.S.* 31°33′ N, 90°7′ W 103
Monticello, *Mo., U.S.* 40°0′ N, 91°43′ W 94
Monticello, *N. Mex., U.S.* 33°24′ N, 107°27′ W 92
Monticello, *N.Y., U.S.* 41°38′ N, 74°42′ W 110
Monticello, *Utah, U.S.* 37°51′ N, 109°20′ W 92
Monticello, *Wis., U.S.* 42°44′ N, 89°35′ W 102
Monticello, site, *Va., U.S.* 37°59′ N, 78°32′ W 94
Montichiari, *It.* 45°24′ N, 10°23′ E 167
Montigny, *Fr.* 49°5′ N, 6°9′ E 163
Montijo, *Port.* 38°42′ N, 8°59′ W 150
Montijo, *Sp.* 38°53′ N, 6°37′ W 164
Montilla, *Sp.* 37°35′ N, 4°39′ W 164
Montividiu, *Braz.* 17°29′ S, 51°14′ W 138
Mont-Joli, *Can.* 48°34′ N, 68°11′ W 94
Mont-Laurier, *Can.* 46°31′ N, 75°34′ W 106
Mont-Laurier, *Can.* 46°33′ N, 75°31′ W 94
Mont-Louis, *Can.* 49°13′ N, 65°45′ W 111
Mont-Louis, *Fr.* 42°30′ N, 2°5′ E 164
Montmagny, *Can.* 46°57′ N, 70°36′ W 94
Montmartre, *Can.* 50°14′ N, 103°27′ W 90
Montmédy, *Fr.* 49°31′ N, 5°20′ E 163
Montmirail, *Fr.* 48°52′ N, 3°32′ E 163
Montmort-Lucy, *Fr.* 48°55′ N, 3°47′ E 163
Monto, *Austral.* 24°51′ S, 151°6′ E 231
Montoro, *Sp.* 38°0′ N, 4°23′ W 164
Montour Falls, *N.Y., U.S.* 42°20′ N, 76°50′ W 94
Montpelier, *Idaho, U.S.* 42°18′ N, 111°19′ W 82
Montpelier, *Ind., U.S.* 40°32′ N, 85°18′ W 102
Montpelier, *Ohio, U.S.* 41°34′ N, 84°36′ W 102
Montpelier, *Vt., U.S.* 44°14′ N, 72°37′ W 104
Montpellier, *Fr.* 43°36′ N, 3°52′ E 164
Montréal, *Can.* 45°30′ N, 73°36′ W 94
Montreal, *Wis., U.S.* 46°25′ N, 90°16′ W 110
Montreal Lake, *Can.* 54°3′ N, 105°51′ W 108
Montreal Lake, *Can.* 54°19′ N, 106°9′ W 108
Montreal Point, *Can.* 53°23′ N, 97°57′ W 108
Montreux, *Switz.* 46°26′ N, 6°56′ E 167
Montrichard, *Fr.* 47°20′ N, 1°11′ E 150
Montrose, *Ark., U.S.* 33°17′ N, 91°30′ W 103
Montrose, *Colo., U.S.* 38°28′ N, 107°53′ W 90
Montrose, *Iowa, U.S.* 40°31′ N, 91°25′ W 94
Montrose, *Mich., U.S.* 43°9′ N, 83°53′ W 102
Montrose, *Miss., U.S.* 32°7′ N, 89°13′ W 103
Montrose, *U.K.* 56°43′ N, 2°28′ W 150
Montrose, oil field, *North Sea* 57°22′ N, 1°19′ E 150
Monts des Nementcha, *Alg.* 35°7′ N, 5°41′ E 150
Monts, Pointe des, *Can.* 49°22′ N, 67°43′ W 94
Montsec, Serra del, *Sp.* 42°2′ N, 0°51′ E 164
Montserrat, *U.K.* 16°40′ N, 62°43′ W 116
Montserrat, island, *Montserrat* 16°49′ N, 62°11′ W 116
Montsûrs, *Fr.* 48°7′ N, 0°34′ E 150
Monturque, *Sp.* 37°28′ N, 4°36′ W 164
Monument Beach, *Mass., U.S.* 41°43′ N, 70°37′ W 104
Monument Butte, peak, *Wyo., U.S.* 42°12′ N, 110°2′ W 90
Monument Valley, *Ariz., U.S.* 37°3′ N, 110°8′ W 92
Monumental Buttes, peak, *Idaho, U.S.* 47°0′ N, 115°53′ W 90
Monveda, *Dem. Rep. of the Congo* 2°55′ N, 21°34′ E 218
Monywa, *Myanmar* 22°9′ N, 95°9′ E 202
Monywar, *Myanmar* 22°9′ N, 95°8′ E 190
Monza, *It.* 45°35′ N, 9°15′ E 167
Monze, *Zambia* 16°16′ S, 27°28′ E 224
Monzón, *Sp.* 41°54′ N, 0°11′ E 164
Moodus, *Conn., U.S.* 41°30′ N, 72°27′ W 104
Moody, *Me., U.S.* 43°16′ N, 70°37′ W 104
Moody, *Tex., U.S.* 31°18′ N, 97°21′ W 92
Moody Point, *Antarctica* 63°23′ S, 55°6′ W 134
Moogooloo Hill, peak, *Austral.* 23°39′ S, 114°31′ E 230
Mooketsi, *S. Af.* 23°34′ S, 30°4′ E 227
Mookgophong (Naboomspruit), *S. Af.* 24°31′ S, 28°44′ E 227
Moonie, oil field, *Austral.* 27°47′ S, 150°7′ E 230
Moorcroft, *Wyo., U.S.* 44°14′ N, 104°57′ W 90
Moore, *Okla., U.S.* 35°18′ N, 97°28′ W 92
Moore, *Tex., U.S.* 29°2′ N, 99°1′ W 96
Moore Haven, *Fla., U.S.* 26°50′ N, 81°6′ W 105
Moore, Mount, peak, *Antarctica* 80°18′ S, 96°46′ W 248
Moorea, island, *France* 17°35′ S, 149°50′ W 241
Mooreland, *Okla., U.S.* 36°25′ N, 99°12′ W 96
Moore's Island, *Bahamas* 26°8′ N, 78°13′ W 116
Mooresville, *Ind., U.S.* 39°36′ N, 86°22′ W 102
Mooresville, *N.C., U.S.* 35°35′ N, 80°49′ W 96
Moorfoot Hills, *U.K.* 55°42′ N, 3°33′ W 150
Moorhead, *Minn., U.S.* 46°52′ N, 96°45′ W 82
Moorpark, *Calif., U.S.* 34°17′ N, 118°54′ W 101
Moorrinya National Park, *Austral.* 21°27′ S, 144°33′ E 238
Moors, The, *U.K.* 54°56′ N, 4°58′ W 150
Moose Factory, *Can.* 51°15′ N, 80°37′ W 110
Moose Jaw, *Can.* 50°24′ N, 105°33′ W 90
Moose Jaw, river, *Can.* 50°10′ N, 105°12′ W 90
Moose Lake, *Can.* 53°39′ N, 100°21′ W 108
Moose Lake, *Minn., U.S.* 46°27′ N, 92°46′ W 94
Moose Mountain, peak, *Can.* 49°47′ N, 102°40′ W 90
Moose River, *Can.* 50°47′ N, 81°18′ W 110
Moose River, *Me., U.S.* 45°39′ N, 70°16′ W 111
Moosehead Lake, *Me., U.S.* 45°29′ N, 70°57′ W 80
Moosehorn, *Can.* 51°17′ N, 98°26′ W 90
Moosomin, *Can.* 50°9′ N, 101°41′ W 90
Moosonee, *Can.* 51°17′ N, 80°41′ W 82
Moosup, *Conn., U.S.* 41°43′ N, 71°53′ W 104
Mopeia Velha, *Mozambique* 17°59′ S, 35°43′ E 224
Mopipi, *Botswana* 21°15′ S, 24°52′ E 227
Mopti, *Mali* 14°30′ N, 4°11′ W 222
Moqatta', *Sudan* 14°38′ N, 35°51′ E 182
Moqor, *Afghan.* 32°51′ N, 67°50′ E 186
Moquegua, *Peru* 17°14′ S, 70°56′ W 137
Moquegua, adm. division, *Peru* 16°48′ S, 71°18′ W 137
Mór, *Hung.* 47°22′ N, 18°13′ E 168
Mor Dağı, peak, *Turk.* 37°45′ N, 44°12′ E 195
Mor, Glen, *U.K.* 56°59′ N, 4°49′ W 150
Mora, *Cameroon* 11°2′ N, 14°10′ E 216
Mora, *Minn., U.S.* 45°52′ N, 93°18′ W 94
Mora, *N. Mex., U.S.* 35°57′ N, 105°19′ W 92
Mora, *Nor.* 60°58′ N, 14°31′ E 152
Mora, *Port.* 38°55′ N, 8°10′ W 150
Móra d'Ebre, *Sp.* 41°5′ N, 0°36′ E 164
Morach, *Belarus* 52°50′ N, 26°50′ E 152
Moradabad, *India* 28°48′ N, 78°45′ E 197
Morąg, *Pol.* 53°54′ N, 19°56′ E 166
Moraine Point, *Can.* 61°20′ N, 115°40′ W 108
Morakovo, *Mont.* 42°41′ N, 19°11′ E 168
Morales, *Col.* 2°44′ N, 76°41′ W 136
Morales, Laguna de 23°38′ N, 97°43′ W 114
Moramoria, *Guinea* 10°12′ N, 9°39′ W 222
Morane, island, *Fr.* 23°6′ S, 137°9′ W 252
Morant Cays, islands, *Caribbean Sea* 17°1′ N, 76°7′ W 115
Morant Point, *Jam.* 17°56′ N, 76°8′ W 115
Morata de Jiloca, *Sp.* 41°14′ N, 1°36′ W 164
Moratalla, *Sp.* 38°11′ N, 1°53′ W 164
Moravskoslezský, adm. division, *Czech Rep.* 49°54′ N, 16°50′ E 152
Morawhanna, *Guyana* 8°16′ N, 59°41′ W 116
Moray Firth 57°28′ N, 4°34′ W 142
Moraya, *Bol.* 21°44′ S, 65°32′ W 137
Morbach, *Ger.* 49°48′ N, 7°6′ E 167
Morbegno, *It.* 46°8′ N, 9°33′ E 167
Morbi, *India* 22°48′ N, 70°49′ E 186
Morcenx, *Fr.* 44°1′ N, 0°56′ E 150
Morden, *Can.* 49°10′ N, 98°7′ W 90
Mordino, *Russ.* 61°21′ N, 51°56′ E 154
Mordoviya, adm. division, *Russ.* 54°19′ N, 42°53′ E 154
Mordovo, *Russ.* 52°2′ N, 40°39′ E 158
Mordyyakha, *Russ.* 70°19′ N, 67°29′ E 169
More Assynt, Ben, peak, *U.K.* 58°7′ N, 4°58′ W 150
More, Ben, peak, *U.K.* 56°22′ N, 4°39′ W 150
More Coigach, Ben, peak, *U.K.* 57°58′ N, 5°20′ W 150
Moreau, river, *S. Dak., U.S.* 45°2′ N, 102°50′ W 90
Moreauville, *La., U.S.* 31°0′ N, 92°0′ W 103
Morebeng (Soekmekaar), *S. Af.* 23°30′ S, 29°56′ E 227
Morecambe, *U.K.* 54°3′ N, 2°52′ W 162
Morecambe Bay 54°4′ N, 3°11′ W 162
Morehead, *Ky., U.S.* 38°10′ N, 83°27′ W 94
Morehead City, *N.C., U.S.* 34°43′ N, 76°43′ W 82
Morehouse, *Mo., U.S.* 36°49′ N, 89°40′ W 94
Morelia, *Col.* 1°30′ N, 75°51′ W 136
Morelia, *Mex.* 19°39′ N, 101°15′ W 114
Morella, *Sp.* 40°37′ N, 0°6′ W 164
Morelos, *Mex.* 22°50′ N, 102°38′ W 114
Morelos, *Mex.* 28°23′ N, 100°53′ W 92
Morelos, adm. division, *Mex.* 18°38′ N, 99°28′ W 114
Moremi Game Reserve, *Botswana* 19°20′ S, 23°29′ E 224
Morena, *India* 26°29′ N, 78°0′ E 197
Morena, Sierra, *Sp.* 38°19′ N, 5°6′ W 164
Morenci, *Ariz., U.S.* 33°5′ N, 109°22′ W 92
Morenci, *Mich., U.S.* 41°42′ N, 84°13′ W 102
Moreni, oil field, *Rom.* 45°0′ N, 25°36′ E 156
Moreno, *Bol.* 11°7′ S, 66°13′ W 137
Moreno, Cerro, peak, *Chile* 23°32′ S, 70°46′ W 132
Moreno Valley, *Calif., U.S.* 33°55′ N, 117°11′ W 101
Moresby Island, *Can.* 52°51′ N, 134°23′ W 98
Moresby Islands, *Indian Ocean* 5°3′ S, 70°55′ E 188
Moret, *Fr.* 48°21′ N, 2°48′ E 163
Moreton Island, *Austral.* 27°10′ S, 153°32′ E 230
Morey Peak, *Nev., U.S.* 38°37′ N, 116°22′ W 90
Morez, *Fr.* 46°31′ N, 6°1′ E 167
Morphou (Güzelyurt) 35°11′ N, 32°58′ E 194
Morgam Viibus, peak, *Fin.* 68°37′ N, 25°47′ E 152
Morgan City, *La., U.S.* 29°41′ N, 91°12′ W 103
Morgan Hill, *Calif., U.S.* 37°7′ N, 121°40′ W 100
Morganfield, *Ky., U.S.* 37°40′ N, 87°55′ W 96
Morganito, *Venez.* 5°2′ N, 67°42′ W 136
Morgantina, ruin(s), *It.* 37°23′ N, 14°18′ E 156
Morganza, *La., U.S.* 30°44′ N, 91°37′ W 103
Morges, *Switz.* 46°30′ N, 6°30′ E 167
Morghab, river, *Afghan.* 35°10′ N, 64°35′ E 186
Morhange, *Fr.* 48°55′ N, 6°38′ E 163
Morhiban, Lac de, lake, *Can.* 51°51′ N, 63°21′ W 111
Mori, *It.* 45°51′ N, 10°58′ E 167
Moriah, Mount, peak, *Nev., U.S.* 39°15′ N, 114°17′ W 90
Moriarty, *N. Mex., U.S.* 34°59′ N, 106°3′ W 92
Morice Lake, *Can.* 53°59′ N, 128°1′ W 108
Moricetown, *Can.* 55°1′ N, 127°24′ W 108
Moriki, *Nig.* 12°52′ N, 6°29′ E 222
Morin Dawa (Nirji), *China* 48°27′ N, 124°30′ E 198
Morino, *Russ.* 57°51′ N, 30°23′ E 166
Morinville, *Can.* 53°47′ N, 113°39′ W 108
Morioka, *Japan* 39°40′ N, 141°0′ E 190
Moriri, Tso, lake, *India* 32°55′ N, 77°53′ E 188
Morkoka, river, *Russ.* 65°55′ N, 109°43′ E 160
Morlaas, *Fr.* 43°20′ N, 0°15′ E 164
Morley, *Mich., U.S.* 43°29′ N, 85°27′ W 102
Morley, *U.K.* 53°44′ N, 1°36′ W 162
Mormon Mountain, peak, *Idaho, U.S.* 44°59′ N, 114°58′ W 90
Mormon Mountains, *Nev., U.S.* 36°54′ N, 114°34′ W 101
Mormon Peak, *Nev., U.S.* 36°58′ N, 114°33′ W 101
Mormon Temple, site, *Hawai'i, U.S.* 21°38′ N, 157°59′ W 99
Morning, Mount, peak, *Antarctica* 78°25′ S, 164°24′ E 248
Mornington, Isla, island, *Chile* 49°52′ S, 77°35′ W 134
Mornington Island, *Austral.* 16°11′ S, 138°32′ E 230
Moro, *Pak.* 26°42′ N, 68°1′ E 186
Moro, *Sudan* 10°48′ N, 30°5′ E 224
Moro Gulf 6°56′ N, 123°4′ E 203
Moro, Punta del, *Sp.* 36°31′ N, 3°0′ W 164
Moro, river, *Africa* 7°22′ N, 10°46′ W 222
Morobe, *P.N.G.* 7°48′ S, 147°41′ E 192
Morocco, *Ind., U.S.* 40°56′ N, 87°28′ W 102
Morocco 32°22′ N, 6°40′ W 214
Morogoro, *Tanzania* 6°47′ S, 37°43′ E 224
Morogoro, adm. division, *Tanzania* 8°10′ S, 36°22′ E 224
Morolaba, *Burkina Faso* 11°54′ N, 5°2′ W 222
Moroleón, *Mex.* 20°6′ N, 101°14′ W 114
Morombe, *Madagascar* 21°53′ S, 43°32′ E 207
Mörön, *Mongolia* 47°22′ N, 110°15′ E 198
Mörön, *Mongolia* 49°39′ N, 100°9′ E 190
Morón de Almazán, *Sp.* 41°24′ N, 2°26′ W 164
Morón de la Frontera, *Sp.* 37°7′ N, 5°28′ W 164
Morona, river, *Peru* 3°0′ S, 77°44′ W 136
Morondo, *Côte d'Ivoire* 8°57′ N, 6°46′ W 222
Morongo Valley, *Calif., U.S.* 34°2′ N, 116°36′ W 101
Moroni, *Comoros* 11°49′ S, 43°11′ E 220
Morotai, island, *Indonesia* 2°6′ N, 128°37′ E 192
Moroto, *Uganda* 2°29′ N, 34°39′ E 224
Moroto, Mount, peak, *Uganda* 2°29′ N, 34°38′ E 224
Moroto see Achwa, river, *Uganda* 2°14′ N, 32°58′ E 224
Morozovsk, *Russ.* 48°18′ N, 41°45′ E 158
Morpará, *Braz.* 11°36′ S, 43°16′ W 132
Morphou (Güzelyurt), *Turk.* 38°15′ N, 34°22′ E 156
Morral, *Ohio, U.S.* 40°40′ N, 83°12′ W 102
Morrill, *Nebr., U.S.* 41°57′ N, 103°57′ W 90
Morrinhos, *Braz.* 17°46′ S, 49°8′ W 138
Morrinhos, *Braz.* 3°16′ S, 40°9′ W 132
Morris, *Can.* 49°19′ N, 97°23′ W 90
Morris, *Conn., U.S.* 41°40′ N, 73°12′ W 104
Morris, *Ill., U.S.* 41°21′ N, 88°26′ W 102
Morris, *Minn., U.S.* 45°34′ N, 95°56′ W 90
Morris, *Mo., U.S.* 41°21′ N, 88°26′ W 94
Morris, *Okla., U.S.* 35°35′ N, 95°51′ W 96
Morris Jesup, Kap 82°56′ N, 53°20′ W 246
Morris, Mount, peak, *Austral.* 26°11′ S, 130°52′ E 230
Morrisburg, *Can.* 44°54′ N, 75°12′ W 94
Morrison, *Ill., U.S.* 41°47′ N, 89°58′ W 102
Morrisonville, *Ill., U.S.* 39°24′ N, 89°28′ W 102
Morristown, *Ind., U.S.* 39°39′ N, 85°41′ W 102
Morristown, *N.Y., U.S.* 44°34′ N, 75°40′ W 94
Morristown, *S. Dak., U.S.* 45°55′ N, 101°44′ W 90
Morristown National Historical Park, *N.J., U.S.* 40°44′ N, 74°38′ W 94
Morrisville, *Pa., U.S.* 39°53′ N, 80°10′ W 94
Morrisville, *Vt., U.S.* 44°33′ N, 72°36′ W 104
Morro, *Braz.* 16°1′ S, 44°44′ W 138
Morro Agudo, *Braz.* 20°44′ S, 48°6′ W 138
Morro Bay, *Calif., U.S.* 35°22′ N, 120°52′ W 100
Morro de Puercos, Punta, *Pan.* 7°12′ N, 80°22′ W 115
Morro, Punta, *Chile* 27°6′ S, 71°35′ W 132
Morrocoy National Park, *Venez.* 10°52′ N, 68°23′ W 136
Morros, *Braz.* 2°54′ S, 44°2′ W 132
Morrow, *La., U.S.* 30°49′ N, 92°6′ W 103
Morrumbala, *Mozambique* 17°19′ S, 35°35′ E 224
Morrumbene, *Mozambique* 23°35′ S, 35°18′ E 227
Morse, *Can.* 50°25′ N, 107°4′ W 90
Morse, *La., U.S.* 30°6′ N, 92°31′ W 103
Morse, Cape, *Antarctica* 66°28′ S, 130°6′ E 248
Morshansk, *Russ.* 53°25′ N, 41°42′ E 154
Morskaya Masel'ga, *Russ.* 63°5′ N, 34°57′ E 154
Morson, *Can.* 49°5′ N, 94°19′ W 90
Morsott, *Alg.* 35°40′ N, 8°0′ E 156
Mortara, *It.* 45°14′ N, 8°43′ E 167
Morteros, *Arg.* 30°43′ S, 61°59′ W 139
Mortka, *Russ.* 59°14′ N, 66°8′ E 169
Mortlach, *Can.* 50°26′ N, 106°5′ W 90
Mortlock Islands, *North Pacific Ocean* 4°53′ N, 151°50′ E 192
Morton, *Ill., U.S.* 40°35′ N, 89°27′ W 102
Morton, *Miss., U.S.* 32°19′ N, 89°39′ W 103
Morton, *Tex., U.S.* 33°42′ N, 102°46′ W 92
Morton, *Wash., U.S.* 46°31′ N, 122°17′ W 100
Morton, Islas, islands, *South Pacific Ocean* 55°53′ S, 69°42′ W 134
Morton Pass, *Wyo., U.S.* 41°40′ N, 105°31′ W 90
Mortyq, *Kaz.* 50°45′ N, 56°28′ E 158
Morvan, Monts du, *Fr.* 46°51′ N, 3°43′ E 165
Morven, *N.Z.* 44°51′ S, 171°6′ E 240
Morven, peak, *U.K.* 58°12′ N, 3°49′ W 150
Morven, peak, *U.K.* 57°6′ N, 3°9′ W 150
Morvern, *U.K.* 56°36′ N, 6°2′ W 150
Morwamosu, *Botswana* 24°4′ S, 23°1′ E 227
Morzine, *Fr.* 46°10′ N, 6°41′ E 167
Mosal'sk, *Russ.* 54°29′ N, 34°59′ E 154
Moscow, *Idaho, U.S.* 46°42′ N, 117°1′ W 90
Moscow, *Tex., U.S.* 30°54′ N, 94°50′ W 103
Moscow, *Vt., U.S.* 44°26′ N, 72°44′ W 104
Moskva, adm. division, *Russ.* 55°26′ N, 36°31′ E 154
Moscow Canal, *Russ.* 56°28′ N, 37°14′ E 154
Moscow see Moskva, *Russ.* 55°44′ N, 37°29′ E 154
Moscow University Ice Shelf, *Antarctica* 67°17′ S, 124°55′ E 248
Mosėdis, *Lith.* 56°9′ N, 21°33′ E 166
Moselle, *Miss., U.S.* 31°29′ N, 89°17′ W 103
Moselle, river, *Fr.* 49°2′ N, 6°4′ E 163
Moses Coulee, *Wash., U.S.* 47°37′ N, 119°54′ W 90
Moses Lake, *Wash., U.S.* 47°6′ N, 119°17′ W 90
Moses, Mount, peak, *Nev., U.S.* 40°8′ N, 117°30′ W 90
Mosetse, *Botswana* 20°39′ S, 26°36′ E 227
Mosgiel, *N.Z.* 45°53′ S, 170°20′ E 240
Mosha, *Russ.* 61°44′ N, 40°51′ E 154
Mosha, river, *Russ.* 61°35′ N, 40°57′ E 154
Moshchnyy, Ostrov, island, *Russ.* 60°3′ N, 27°18′ E 166
Moshi, *Tanzania* 3°23′ S, 37°21′ E 224
Mosinee, *Wis., U.S.* 44°47′ N, 89°43′ W 94
Mosi-Oa-Tunya National Park, *Zambia* 17°59′ S, 25°53′ E 224
Mosjøen, *Nor.* 65°48′ N, 13°12′ E 160
Moskal'vo, *Russ.* 53°23′ N, 142°18′ E 160
Moskosel, *Nor.* 65°51′ N, 19°27′ E 152
Moskva, *Taj.* 37°36′ N, 69°37′ E 184
Moskva (Moscow), *Russ.* 55°44′ N, 37°29′ E 154
Moskva, river, *Russ.* 55°33′ N, 36°39′ E 154
Mosonmagyaróvár, *Hung.* 47°51′ N, 17°17′ E 168
Mosonszolnok, *Hung.* 47°50′ N, 17°11′ E 168
Mosquera, *Col.* 2°29′ N, 78°25′ W 130
Mosquero, *N. Mex., U.S.* 35°45′ N, 103°58′ W 82
Mosquito Lagoon, lake, *Fla., U.S.* 28°46′ N, 81°0′ W 105
Mosquito, Ponta do, *Braz.* 4°14′ N, 51°24′ W 130
Moss, *Nor.* 59°26′ N, 10°42′ E 152
Moss Agate Hill, peak, *Wyo., U.S.* 42°38′ N, 105°46′ W 90
Moss Point, *Miss., U.S.* 30°23′ N, 88°30′ W 103
Mossaka, *Congo* 1°16′ S, 16°46′ E 218
Mossbank, *Can.* 49°56′ N, 105°59′ W 90
Mossburn, *N.Z.* 45°42′ S, 168°14′ E 240
Mossel Bay see Mosselbaai, *S. Af.* 34°11′ S, 22°4′ E 227
Mosselbaai (Mossel Bay), *S. Af.* 34°11′ S, 22°4′ E 227
Mossendjo, *Congo* 2°56′ S, 12°41′ E 218
Mossi, region, *Burkina Faso* 12°5′ N, 2°36′ W 222
Mossoró, *Braz.* 5°12′ S, 37°22′ W 132
Mossuril, *Mozambique* 14°59′ S, 40°42′ E 224
Mossy, river, *Can.* 54°1′ N, 103°28′ W 108
Mossyrock, *Wash., U.S.* 46°30′ N, 122°29′ W 100
Most, *Czech Rep.* 50°31′ N, 13°38′ E 152
Mostaganem, *Alg.* 35°55′ N, 9°535′ E 150
Mostar, *Bosn. and Herzg.* 43°20′ N, 17°47′ E 168
Mostardas, *Braz.* 31°5′ S, 50°57′ W 139
Moster, *Nor.* 59°43′ N, 5°20′ E 152
Moštica, *Maced.* 42°3′ N, 22°35′ E 168
Møsting, Kap 63°52′ N, 40°54′ W 106
Mostoos Hills, *Can.* 54°59′ N, 109°21′ W 108
Mostrim (Edgeworthstown), *Ire.* 53°41′ N, 7°38′ W 150
Mosul see Al Mawşil, *Iraq* 36°20′ N, 43°0′ E 195
Mot'a, *Eth.* 11°3′ N, 37°51′ E 224
Mota del Cuervo, *Sp.* 39°29′ N, 2°52′ W 164
Motacucito, *Bol.* 17°37′ S, 61°27′ W 132
Motal', *Belarus* 52°18′ N, 25°37′ E 152
Mother Lode, region, *Calif., U.S.* 37°38′ N, 120°36′ W 100
Motihari, *India* 26°38′ N, 84°54′ E 197
Motike, *Bosn. and Herzg.* 44°48′ N, 17°7′ E 168
Motilla del Palancar, *Sp.* 39°33′ N, 1°56′ W 164
Motomiya, *Japan* 37°31′ N, 140°23′ E 201
Motril, *Sp.* 36°44′ N, 3°32′ W 164
Motru, *Rom.* 44°45′ N, 23°1′ E 168
Mott, *N. Dak., U.S.* 46°22′ N, 102°19′ W 90
Motu, *N.Z.* 38°17′ S, 177°34′ E 240
Motupe, *Peru* 6°5′ S, 79°45′ W 130
Mouali, *Congo* 0°15′ N, 15°33′ E 218
Mouchoir Passage 21°6′ N, 71°34′ W 116
Moudjéria, *Mauritania* 17°52′ N, 12°24′ W 222
Moudon, *Switz.* 46°41′ N, 6°48′ E 167
Mouhijärvi, *Fin.* 61°30′ N, 22°59′ E 166
Mouhoun (Black Volta), river, *Burkina Faso* 11°43′ N, 4°30′ W 222
Mouiat el Behima, spring, *Alg.* 32°55′ N, 6°48′ E 214
Mouila, *Gabon* 1°52′ S, 11°3′ E 218
Mouilah, spring, *Alg.* 26°6′ N, 0°39′ E 214
Mouit, *Mauritania* 16°34′ N, 13°10′ W 222
Mould Bay, *Can.* 76°21′ N, 119°15′ W 106
Mouling National Park, *India* 28°31′ N, 94°46′ E 188
Moulins, *Fr.* 46°34′ N, 3°19′ E 150
Moulouya, Oued, river, *Mor.* 32°0′ N, 3°54′ W 142
Moulton, *Ala., U.S.* 34°28′ N, 87°17′ W 96
Moulton, Mount, peak, *Antarctica* 75°58′ S, 134°21′ W 248
Moultrie, *Ga., U.S.* 31°10′ N, 83°48′ W 96
Moultrie, Lake, *S.C., U.S.* 33°17′ N, 80°40′ W 80
Mounana, *Gabon* 1°25′ S, 13°6′ E 218
Mound City, *Mo., U.S.* 37°5′ N, 89°10′ W 94
Mound City, *Mo., U.S.* 40°7′ N, 95°14′ W 94
Moundou, *Chad* 8°35′ N, 16°4′ E 218
Mounds, *Mo., U.S.* 37°6′ N, 89°12′ W 96
Moundville, *Ala., U.S.* 32°59′ N, 87°38′ W 103
Moung Tong, *Vietnam* 22°10′ N, 102°35′ E 202
Mounlapamôk, *Laos* 14°20′ N, 105°51′ E 202
Mount Airy, *N.C., U.S.* 36°28′ N, 80°37′ W 96
Mount Ayr, *Iowa, U.S.* 40°42′ N, 94°15′ W 94
Mount Baldy, *Calif., U.S.* 34°14′ N, 117°40′ W 101
Mount Brydges, *Can.* 42°53′ N, 81°29′ W 102
Mount Calvary, *Wis., U.S.* 43°49′ N, 88°15′ W 102
Mount Carroll, *Ill., U.S.* 42°5′ N, 89°59′ W 102
Mount Charleston, *Nev., U.S.* 36°15′ N, 115°40′ W 101
Mount Chilbo National Park, *N. Korea* 41°2′ N, 129°26′ E 200

Mount Clemens, *Mich., U.S.* 42°35′ N, 82°54′ W 94
Mount Cook, *N.Z.* 43°45′ S, 170°4′ E 240
Mount Cook see Aoraki, peak, *N.Z.* 43°37′ S, 170°7′ E 240
Mount Currie, *Can.* 50°20′ N, 122°42′ W 100
Mount Darwin, *Zimb.* 16°48′ S, 31°35′ E 224
Mount Dora, *Fla., U.S.* 28°47′ N, 81°38′ W 105
Mount Edgecumbe, *Hecate Strait* 56°59′ N, 135°21′ W 98
Mount Enterprise, *Tex., U.S.* 31°54′ N, 94°41′ W 103
Mount Erie, *Ill., U.S.* 38°30′ N, 88°14′ W 102
Mount Gilead, *Ohio, U.S.* 40°32′ N, 82°50′ W 102
Mount Grace Priory, site, *U.K.* 54°22′ N, 1°21′ W 162
Mount Hermon, *La., U.S.* 30°57′ N, 90°18′ W 103
Mount Holly, *Ark., U.S.* 33°17′ N, 92°57′ W 103
Mount Hope, *W. Va., U.S.* 37°53′ N, 81°11′ W 94
Mount Isa, *Austral.* 20°45′ S, 139°33′ E 238
Mount Kenya National Park, *Kenya* 0°14′ N, 36°59′ E 206
Mount Kisco, *N.Y., U.S.* 41°11′ N, 73°44′ W 104
Mount Kümgang National Park, *N. Korea* 38°32′ N, 128°4′ E 200
Mount Kuwol National Park, *N. Korea* 38°30′ N, 125°15′ E 200
Mount Laguna, *Calif., U.S.* 32°52′ N, 116°26′ W 101
Mount Maunganui, *N.Z.* 37°41′ S, 176°12′ E 240
Mount Morgan, *Austral.* 23°39′ S, 150°23′ E 231
Mount Morris, *Ill., U.S.* 42°2′ N, 89°26′ W 102
Mount Morris, *Mich., U.S.* 43°6′ N, 83°41′ W 102
Mount Morris, *Mo., U.S.* 42°2′ N, 89°26′ W 110
Mount Olive, *Ill., U.S.* 39°3′ N, 89°43′ W 102
Mount Olive, *Miss., U.S.* 31°45′ N, 89°39′ W 103
Mount Olivet, *Ky., U.S.* 38°31′ N, 84°2′ W 102
Mount Orab, *Ohio, U.S.* 39°0′ N, 83°55′ W 102
Mount Pleasant, *Mich., U.S.* 43°35′ N, 84°46′ W 94
Mount Pleasant, *S.C., U.S.* 32°47′ N, 79°53′ W 96
Mount Pleasant, *Tex., U.S.* 33°8′ N, 95°0′ W 103
Mount Pulaski, *Ill., U.S.* 40°0′ N, 89°17′ W 102
Mount Rainier National Park, *Wash., U.S.* 46°54′ N, 121°49′ W 100
Mount Revelstoke National Park, *Can.* 51°4′ N, 118°24′ W 238
Mount Robson, *Can.* 52°59′ N, 119°16′ W 108
Mount Saint Helens National Volcanic Monument, *Wash., U.S.* 46°17′ N, 122°35′ W 100
Mount Sangbe National Park, *Côte d'Ivoire* 7°45′ N, 8°1′ W 222
Mount Sangbe National Park, *Côte d'Ivoire* 7°49′ N, 7°37′ W 206
Mount Shasta, *Calif., U.S.* 41°18′ N, 122°20′ W 90
Mount Somers, *N.Z.* 43°42′ S, 171°24′ E 240
Mount Sterling, *Ohio, U.S.* 39°42′ N, 83°16′ W 102
Mount Stewart, site, *U.K.* 54°32′ N, 5°41′ W 150
Mount Sunapee, *N.H., U.S.* 43°20′ N, 72°5′ W 104
Mount Vernon, *Ala., U.S.* 31°5′ N, 88°0′ W 103
Mount Vernon, *Ky., U.S.* 37°20′ N, 84°21′ W 96
Mount Vernon, *N.Y., U.S.* 40°54′ N, 73°51′ W 104
Mount Vernon, *Ohio, U.S.* 40°23′ N, 82°28′ W 102
Mount Vernon, *Tex., U.S.* 33°10′ N, 95°14′ W 103
Mount Vernon, *Wash., U.S.* 48°24′ N, 122°20′ W 100
Mount Vernon, site, *Va., U.S.* 38°42′ N, 77°10′ W 94
Mountain Center, *Calif., U.S.* 33°41′ N, 116°44′ W 101
Mountain City, *Nev., U.S.* 41°50′ N, 115°58′ W 90
Mountain City, *Tenn., U.S.* 36°28′ N, 81°49′ W 94
Mountain Grove, *Mo., U.S.* 37°7′ N, 92°16′ W 96
Mountain Home, *Ark., U.S.* 36°19′ N, 92°23′ W 96
Mountain Home, *Idaho, U.S.* 43°9′ N, 115°43′ W 82
Mountain Home Air Force Base, *Idaho, U.S.* 43°2′ N, 115°59′ W 90
Mountain Lake, *Minn., U.S.* 43°55′ N, 94°56′ W 94
Mountain Park, *Okla., U.S.* 34°41′ N, 98°57′ W 92
Mountain Pass, *Calif., U.S.* 35°28′ N, 115°35′ W 101
Mountain Point, *Alas., U.S.* 55°20′ N, 131°35′ W 108
Mountain, river, *Can.* 65°41′ N, 129°37′ W 98
Mountain View, *Mo., U.S.* 36°59′ N, 91°42′ W 96
Mountain View, *Wyo., U.S.* 41°17′ N, 110°20′ W 92
Mountain Zebra National Park, *S. Af.* 32°12′ S, 25°23′ E 227
Mountainair, *N. Mex., U.S.* 34°31′ N, 106°14′ W 92
Mountjoy, *Can.* 48°29′ N, 81°23′ W 94
Moupitou, *Congo* 2°26′ S, 11°57′ E 218
Moura, *Braz.* 1°31′ S, 61°40′ W 130
Moura, *Chad* 13°47′ N, 21°11′ E 216
Mourão, *Port.* 38°22′ N, 7°21′ W 150
Mourdi, Dépression du, *Chad* 18°1′ N, 20°25′ E 216
Mourdiah, *Mali* 14°27′ N, 7°28′ W 222
Mourmelon-le-Grand, *Fr.* 49°8′ N, 4°21′ E 163
Mourne Mountains, *U.K.* 54°4′ N, 6°49′ W 150
Mouscron, *Belg.* 50°44′ N, 3°14′ E 163
Moussoro, *Chad* 13°39′ N, 16°31′ E 216
Mouthe, *Fr.* 46°43′ N, 6°10′ E 167
Moutier, *Switz.* 47°17′ N, 7°21′ E 150
Moutohora, *N.Z.* 38°19′ S, 177°33′ E 240
Mouy, *Fr.* 49°18′ N, 2°19′ E 163
Mouzarak, *Chad* 13°19′ N, 15°58′ E 216
Mouzay, *Fr.* 49°28′ N, 5°12′ E 163
Mouzon, *Fr.* 49°36′ N, 5°3′ E 163
Mowchadz', *Belarus* 53°18′ N, 25°41′ E 152
Moweaqua, *Ill., U.S.* 39°36′ N, 89°1′ W 102
Moxico, adm. division, *Angola* 12°22′ S, 23°22′ E 224
Moÿ, *Fr.* 49°43′ N, 3°21′ E 163
Moyahua, *Mex.* 21°14′ N, 103°9′ W 114
Moyalē, *Kenya* 3°28′ N, 39°3′ E 224
Moyamba, *Sierra Leone* 8°8′ N, 12°27′ W 222
Moyen Atlas, *Mor.* 33°3′ N, 5°20′ W 214
Moyie, river, *Idaho, U.S.* 49°2′ N, 116°14′ W 90
Moyo, *Uganda* 3°39′ N, 31°44′ E 224
Moyo, island, *Indonesia* 8°18′ S, 116°47′ E 192
Moyobamba, *Peru* 6°1′ S, 76°59′ W 130
Moyto, *Chad* 12°35′ N, 16°35′ E 216
Moyu, *China* 37°16′ N, 79°42′ E 184
Moyynqum, *Kaz.* 44°16′ N, 72°55′ E 184
Moyynqum, *Kaz.* 43°38′ N, 71°25′ E 184
Moyynty, *Kaz.* 47°11′ N, 73°22′ E 184
Mozambique 17°30′ S, 33°5′ E 220
Mozambique 23°32′ S, 33°38′ E 206
Mozambique Basin, *Indian Ocean* 29°34′ S, 40°22′ E 254
Mozambique Channel 17°57′ S, 38°34′ E 224
Mozambique Escarpment, *Indian Ocean* 35°57′ S, 35°12′ E 254
Mozambique Plateau, *Indian Ocean* 30°54′ S, 36°3′ E 254
Mozarlândia, *Braz.* 14°47′ S, 50°44′ W 138
Mozdok, *Russ.* 43°43′ N, 44°35′ E 195
Mozdūrān, *Iran* 36°10′ N, 60°30′ E 180
Mozhaysk, *Russ.* 55°29′ N, 36°3′ E 154
Mozhga, *Russ.* 56°25′ N, 52°17′ E 154
Mozuli, *Russ.* 56°34′ N, 28°11′ E 166
Mpala, *Dem. Rep. of the Congo* 6°46′ S, 29°32′ E 224
Mpanda, *Tanzania* 6°21′ S, 31°1′ E 224
Mpandamatenga, *Botswana* 18°39′ S, 25°41′ E 224
Mphoengs, *Zimb.* 21°11′ S, 27°51′ E 227
Mpika, *Zambia* 11°49′ S, 31°24′ E 224
Mpoko, river, *Cen. Af. Rep.* 6°1′ N, 17°30′ E 218
Mporokoso, *Zambia* 9°23′ S, 30°7′ E 224
Mpouya, *Congo* 2°37′ S, 16°8′ E 218
Mpui, *Tanzania* 8°20′ S, 31°50′ E 224
Mpulungu, *Zambia* 8°48′ S, 31°6′ E 224
Mpumalanga, adm. division, *S. Af.* 26°16′ S, 28°35′ E 227
Mpwapwa, *Tanzania* 6°19′ S, 36°28′ E 224
Mqanduli, *S. Af.* 31°50′ S, 28°45′ E 227
Mrągowo, *Pol.* 53°51′ N, 21°16′ E 166
Mrakovo, *Russ.* 52°43′ N, 56°29′ E 154
Mrkojević, Zaliv 42°0′ N, 18°51′ E 168
Msaken, *Tun.* 35°43′ N, 10°34′ E 156
M'sila, *Alg.* 35°41′ N, 4°33′ E 150
Msoro, *Zambia* 13°39′ S, 31°53′ E 224
Msta, river, *Russ.* 58°34′ N, 31°50′ E 154
Mstizh, *Belarus* 54°34′ N, 28°9′ E 166
Mstsislaw, *Belarus* 54°1′ N, 31°43′ E 154
Mtama, *Tanzania* 10°18′ S, 39°20′ E 224
Mtouf, spring, *Mauritania* 19°27′ N, 11°24′ W 222
Mtsensk, *Russ.* 53°15′ N, 36°39′ E 154
Mts'khet'a, *Ga.* 41°51′ N, 44°42′ E 195
Mtwara, *Tanzania* 10°20′ S, 40°11′ E 224
Mtwara, adm. division, *Tanzania* 10°52′ S, 38°25′ E 224
Mu, river, *Myanmar* 22°22′ N, 95°24′ E 202
Muaguide, *Mozambique* 12°31′ S, 40°5′ E 224
Mualama, *Mozambique* 16°54′ S, 38°19′ E 224
Muaná, *Braz.* 1°31′ S, 49°14′ W 130
Muang Bèng, *Laos* 20°24′ N, 101°47′ E 202
Muang Gnômmarat, *Laos* 17°37′ N, 105°10′ E 202
Muang Ham, *Laos* 20°21′ N, 103°59′ E 202
Muang Kao, *Laos* 14°55′ N, 106°53′ E 202
Muang Khamkeut, *Laos* 18°15′ N, 104°43′ E 202
Muang La, *Laos* 20°53′ N, 102°7′ E 202
Muang Namo, *Laos* 21°4′ N, 101°49′ E 202
Muang Ngoy, *Laos* 20°44′ N, 102°41′ E 202
Muang Paklay, *Laos* 18°13′ N, 101°23′ E 202
Muang Paktha, *Laos* 20°8′ N, 100°37′ E 202
Muang Sing, *Laos* 21°12′ N, 101°8′ E 202
Muang Souy, *Laos* 19°33′ N, 102°55′ E 202
Muang Va, *Laos* 21°54′ N, 102°19′ E 202
Muang Xai, *Laos* 20°45′ N, 101°58′ E 202
Muang Xon, *Laos* 20°28′ N, 103°16′ E 202
Muar, *Malaysia* 2°4′ N, 102°34′ E 196
Muara, *Indonesia* 0°39′ N, 100°58′ E 196
Muaraenim, *Indonesia* 3°36′ S, 103°36′ E 192
Muarakumpe, *Indonesia* 1°22′ S, 104°1′ E 196
Muarasabak, *Indonesia* 1°8′ S, 103°49′ E 196
Muarasipongi, *Indonesia* 0°38′ N, 99°53′ E 196
Muaratewe, *Indonesia* 0°54′ N, 114°42′ E 192
Muari, Ras, *Pak.* 24°48′ N, 66°18′ E 186
Muatua, *Mozambique* 15°46′ S, 39°45′ E 224
Mubarras, oil field, *Persian Gulf* 24°23′ N, 53°38′ E 196
Mubende, *Uganda* 0°32′ N, 31°23′ E 224
Mubi, *Nig.* 10°15′ N, 13°17′ E 216
Muborak, *Uzb.* 39°11′ N, 65°19′ E 197
Mubur, island, *Indonesia* 3°27′ N, 105°51′ E 196
Mucacata, *Mozambique* 13°25′ S, 39°46′ E 224
Mucajá, *Braz.* 3°58′ S, 57°32′ W 130
Mucajaí, river, *Braz.* 2°49′ N, 62°49′ W 130
Mucajaí, Serra do, *Braz.* 2°3′ N, 62°21′ W 130
Much Wenlock, *U.K.* 52°36′ N, 2°34′ W 162
Muchea, *Austral.* 31°35′ S, 115°59′ E 231
Muchinga Mountains, *Zambia* 10°53′ S, 31°40′ E 224
Muchkapskiy, *Russ.* 51°51′ N, 42°27′ E 158
Muckish Mountain, peak, *Ire.* 55°5′ N, 8°7′ W 150
Mucojo, *Mozambique* 12°4′ S, 40°29′ E 224
Muconda, *Angola* 10°37′ S, 21°19′ E 220
Mucubela, *Mozambique* 16°54′ S, 37°50′ E 224
Mucucuaú, river, *Braz.* 0°29′ N, 61°23′ W 130
Mucuim, river, *Braz.* 7°13′ S, 64°31′ W 130
Mucur, *Turk.* 39°3′ N, 34°22′ E 156
Mucuri, *Braz.* 18°5′ S, 39°36′ W 138
Mucuri, river, *Braz.* 17°26′ S, 41°23′ W 138
Mucurici, *Braz.* 18°5′ S, 40°37′ W 138
Mucusso, *Angola* 17°58′ S, 21°25′ E 220
Mud Lake, *S. Dak., U.S.* 45°43′ N, 98°32′ W 90
Mudanjiang, *China* 44°41′ N, 129°43′ E 190
Muddy Peak, *Nev., U.S.* 36°17′ N, 114°45′ W 101
Muddy, river, *Nev., U.S.* 36°39′ N, 114°32′ W 101
Mudersbach, *Ger.* 50°49′ N, 7°56′ E 167
Mudjatik, river, *Can.* 56°18′ N, 107°33′ W 108
Mudon, *Myanmar* 16°15′ N, 97°43′ E 202
Mudurnu, *Turk.* 40°28′ N, 31°12′ E 156
Mudvær, islands, *Norwegian Sea* 65°41′ N, 10°17′ E 152
Mud'yuga, *Russ.* 63°47′ N, 39°17′ E 154
Muecate, *Mozambique* 14°52′ S, 39°39′ E 224
Mueda, *Mozambique* 11°39′ S, 39°34′ E 224
Muembe, *Mozambique* 13°6′ S, 35°39′ E 224
Muen, peak, *Nor.* 61°42′ N, 10°3′ E 152
Muertos Cays, islands, *North Atlantic Ocean* 24°10′ N, 80°51′ W 82
Mufulira, *Zambia* 12°35′ S, 28°14′ E 220
Mug, river, *China* 34°8′ N, 93°6′ E 188
Muga, Mte., peak, *Sp.* 41°59′ N, 6°55′ W 150
Muganly, *Azerb.* 41°28′ N, 46°29′ E 195
Mugeba, *Mozambique* 16°35′ S, 37°14′ E 224
Mughalzhar Taūy, *Kaz.* 47°23′ N, 56°0′ E 184
Mugharet el Wad, ruin(s), *Israel* 32°38′ N, 34°56′ E 194
Mughayyir, *Jordan* 31°24′ N, 35°46′ E 194
Mugi, *Japan* 33°40′ N, 134°25′ E 201
Mugila, Monts, *Dem. Rep. of the Congo* 7°35′ S, 28°49′ E 224
Muğla, *Turk.* 37°12′ N, 28°20′ E 156
Muglad, *Sudan* 11°3′ N, 27°43′ E 224
Mugodzharskaya, *Kaz.* 48°37′ N, 58°25′ E 158
Mugu, *Nepal* 29°46′ N, 82°37′ E 197
Muhagiriya, *Sudan* 11°56′ N, 25°34′ E 216
Muhamdi, *India* 27°57′ N, 80°12′ E 197
Muhammad Qol, *Sudan* 20°52′ N, 37°6′ E 182
Muḥammad, Râs, *Egypt* 27°30′ N, 34°16′ E 180
Mu'ayy, *Jordan* 30°59′ N, 35°50′ E 194
Muhembo, *Botswana* 18°18′ S, 21°45′ E 220
Muheza, *Tanzania* 5°10′ S, 38°47′ E 224
Mühlhausen, *Ger.* 51°12′ N, 10°27′ E 167
Mühlheim, *Ger.* 50°7′ N, 8°50′ E 167
Muhos, *Fin.* 64°46′ N, 25°58′ E 152
Mu'radah, *Syr.* 35°15′ N, 36°34′ E 194
Muhu, *Est.* 58°35′ N, 23°13′ E 166
Muhu, island, *Est.* 58°39′ N, 23°20′ E 166
Muhu Väin 58°55′ N, 22°51′ E 166
Muhulu, *Dem. Rep. of the Congo* 1°4′ S, 27°13′ E 224
Muhutwe, *Tanzania* 1°35′ S, 31°43′ E 224
Muié, *Angola* 14°26′ S, 20°35′ E 220
Muikamachi, *Japan* 37°3′ N, 138°52′ E 201
Muir Woods National Monument, *Calif., U.S.* 37°52′ N, 122°37′ W 100
Muiron Islands, *Indian Ocean* 21°36′ S, 111°35′ E 230
Muisne, *Ecua.* 0°35′ N, 80°1′ W 130
Muíte, *Mozambique* 14°3′ S, 39°3′ E 224
Mujejärvi, *Fin.* 63°47′ N, 29°26′ E 152
Muji, *China* 38°56′ N, 74°37′ E 184
Mujimbeji, *Zambia* 12°11′ S, 24°55′ E 224
Muju, *S. Korea* 36°0′ N, 127°40′ E 200
Mukacheve, *Ukr.* 48°25′ N, 22°43′ E 152
Mukawwar Island, *Sudan* 20°42′ N, 37°16′ E 182
Mukdahan, *Thai.* 16°33′ N, 104°41′ E 202
Mukhayzināt, Jibāl al, peak, *Jordan* 31°55′ N, 36°31′ E 194
Mukhomornoye, *Russ.* 66°21′ N, 173°19′ E 173
Mukhtadir, *Azerb.* 41°41′ N, 48°43′ E 195
Mukhtolovo, *Russ.* 55°25′ N, 43°14′ E 154
Mukilteo, *Wash., U.S.* 47°55′ N, 122°17′ W 100
Muko Jima Rettō, islands, *Philippine Sea* 27°36′ N, 142°16′ E 190
Mukry, *Turkm.* 37°36′ N, 65°45′ E 184
Muktiköl, *Kaz.* 51°50′ N, 60°52′ E 154
Muktinath, *Nepal* 28°48′ N, 83°54′ E 197
Mukutawa, river, *Can.* 53°3′ N, 97°29′ W 108
Mukwonago, *Wis., U.S.* 42°52′ N, 88°20′ W 102
Mul, *India* 20°3′ N, 79°40′ E 188
Mula, *Sp.* 38°2′ N, 1°29′ W 164
Muladu, island, *Maldives* 6°38′ N, 72°7′ E 188
Mulaku Atoll, *Persian Gulf* 2°38′ N, 72°47′ E 188
Mulan, *China* 45°59′ N, 128°4′ E 198
Mulanay, *Philippines* 13°32′ N, 122°26′ E 203
Mulanje Mountains, *Malawi* 16°0′ S, 35°30′ E 224
Mulatos, *Col.* 8°38′ N, 76°42′ W 136
Mulatos, *Mex.* 28°37′ N, 108°51′ W 92
Mulberry, *Fla., U.S.* 27°54′ N, 81°58′ W 105
Mulberry, *Ind., U.S.* 40°20′ N, 86°40′ W 102
Mulberry, *Kans., U.S.* 37°32′ N, 94°38′ W 96
Mulberry Grove, *Ill., U.S.* 38°55′ N, 89°16′ W 102
Muldraugh, *Ky., U.S.* 37°56′ N, 85°59′ W 96
Muleba, *Tanzania* 1°53′ S, 31°39′ E 224
Mulegé, *Mex.* 26°52′ N, 112°4′ W 112
Muleshoe, *Tex., U.S.* 34°12′ N, 102°44′ W 92
Mulhacén, peak, *Sp.* 37°2′ N, 3°21′ W 164
Mülheim, *Ger.* 51°25′ N, 6°52′ E 167
Muligudje, *Mozambique* 16°31′ S, 38°54′ E 224
Mulkonbar, spring, *Austral.* 27°45′ S, 140°45′ E 230
Mull, Ross of 56°13′ N, 6°46′ W 150
Mullaittivu, *Sri Lanka* 9°14′ N, 80°51′ E 188
Mullen, *Nebr., U.S.* 42°2′ N, 101°3′ W 90
Mullens, *W. Va., U.S.* 37°34′ N, 81°24′ W 96
Mullet Key, island, *Fla., U.S.* 27°34′ N, 82°51′ W 105
Mullet Peninsula, *Atlantic Ocean* 54°8′ N, 10°41′ W 150
Mullewa, *Austral.* 28°31′ S, 115°33′ E 231
Mullikkulam, *Sri Lanka* 8°36′ N, 79°57′ E 188
Mullingar, *Ire.* 53°31′ N, 7°21′ W 150
Mullsjö, *Nor.* 57°54′ N, 13°53′ E 152
Mulobezi, *Zambia* 16°50′ S, 25°11′ E 224
Mulondo, *Angola* 15°39′ S, 15°13′ E 220
Multan, *Pak.* 30°10′ N, 71°28′ E 186
Multé, *Mex.* 17°40′ N, 91°27′ W 115
Mulumbe Mountains, *Dem. Rep. of the Congo* 8°27′ S, 27°53′ E 224
Mulym'ya, *Russ.* 60°34′ N, 64°53′ E 169
Muma, *Dem. Rep. of the Congo* 3°28′ N, 23°17′ E 218
Mumallah, *Sudan* 10°49′ N, 25°30′ E 224
Mumbai (Bombay), *India* 18°57′ N, 72°49′ E 188
Mumbué, *Angola* 13°55′ S, 17°12′ E 220
Mumbwa, *Zambia* 14°59′ S, 27°2′ E 224
Mumra, *Russ.* 45°44′ N, 47°43′ E 158
Mumu, *Sudan* 12°7′ N, 23°42′ E 216
Mun, river, *Thai.* 15°9′ N, 103°28′ E 202
Muna, *Mex.* 20°28′ N, 89°44′ W 115
Muna, island, *Indonesia* 5°9′ S, 121°36′ E 192
Muna, river, *Russ.* 67°48′ N, 119°54′ E 160
München (Munich), *Ger.* 48°8′ N, 11°34′ E 152
Muncho Lake, *Can.* 58°55′ N, 125°47′ W 108
Munch'ŏn, *N. Korea* 39°17′ N, 127°16′ E 200
Muncie, *Ind., U.S.* 40°10′ N, 85°23′ W 102
Muncy, *Pa., U.S.* 41°12′ N, 76°48′ W 94
Muncy Valley, *Pa., U.S.* 41°20′ N, 76°36′ W 94
Mundare, *Can.* 53°34′ N, 112°20′ W 108
Munday, *Tex., U.S.* 33°25′ N, 99°38′ W 92
Mundemba, *Cameroon* 4°53′ N, 8°50′ E 222
Münden, *Ger.* 51°24′ N, 9°40′ E 167
Mundesley, *U.K.* 52°52′ N, 1°25′ E 163
Mundeung-ni, *S. Korea* 38°19′ N, 127°58′ E 200
Mundra, *India* 22°50′ N, 69°44′ E 186
Mundybash, *Russ.* 53°13′ N, 87°24′ E 184
Munenga, *Angola* 10°2′ S, 14°38′ E 220
Munera, *Sp.* 39°2′ N, 2°29′ W 164
Mungári, *Mozambique* 17°12′ S, 33°32′ E 224
Mungbere, *Dem. Rep. of the Congo* 2°38′ N, 28°25′ E 224
Mungeli, *India* 22°4′ N, 81°39′ E 197
Munger, *India* 25°21′ N, 86°29′ E 197
Munger, *Mich., U.S.* 43°30′ N, 83°46′ W 102
Mungia, *Sp.* 43°20′ N, 2°51′ W 164
Mungret, *Ire.* 52°37′ N, 8°42′ W 150
Munguba, *Braz.* 0°58′ N, 52°25′ W 130
Munguy, *Russ.* 70°22′ N, 83°51′ E 169
Mungyeong, *S. Korea* 36°42′ N, 128°6′ E 200
Munhamade, *Mozambique* 16°37′ S, 36°58′ E 224
Munich see München, *Ger.* 48°8′ N, 11°34′ E 152
Munising, *Mich., U.S.* 46°24′ N, 86°41′ W 94
Muniz Freire, *Braz.* 20°28′ S, 41°26′ W 138
Munk, *Can.* 55°59′ N, 95°59′ W 108
Munkedal, *Nor.* 58°27′ N, 11°38′ E 152
Munkelv, *Nor.* 69°38′ N, 29°27′ E 152
Munkfors, *Nor.* 59°51′ N, 13°32′ E 152
Munksund, *Nor.* 65°17′ N, 21°29′ E 152
Münnerstadt, *Ger.* 50°15′ N, 10°10′ E 167
Muñoz Gamero, Península, *Chile* 52°9′ S, 74°21′ W 134
Munroe Lake, *Can.* 59°6′ N, 99°12′ W 108
Munsan, *S. Korea* 37°51′ N, 126°48′ E 200
Münsingen, *Switz.* 46°52′ N, 7°34′ E 167
Munsonville, *N.H., U.S.* 43°0′ N, 72°9′ W 104
Münster, *Ger.* 51°57′ N, 7°38′ E 167
Munsungan Lake, *Me., U.S.* 46°20′ N, 69°36′ W 94
Muntok, *Indonesia* 2°3′ S, 105°11′ E 192
Munzur Vadisi National Park, *Turk.* 39°15′ N, 39°24′ E 195
Muodoslompolo, *Nor.* 67°56′ N, 23°19′ E 152
Muong Te, *Vietnam* 22°24′ N, 102°48′ E 202
Muonio, *Fin.* 67°54′ N, 24°4′ E 160
Mupa National Park, *Angola* 15°34′ S, 14°45′ E 220
Muping, *China* 37°24′ N, 121°37′ E 198
Muqakoori, *Somalia* 4°2′ N, 46°5′ E 218
Muqdisho (Mogadishu), *Somalia* 1°58′ N, 45°10′ E 218
Muqyr, *Kaz.* 48°3′ N, 54°27′ E 158
Mur, river, *Aust.* 47°2′ N, 13°30′ E 156
Mura, river, *Slov.* 46°39′ N, 16°2′ E 168
Muradiye, *Turk.* 38°59′ N, 43°44′ E 195
Murakami, *Japan* 38°13′ N, 139°30′ E 201
Murakeresztúr, *Hung.* 46°21′ N, 16°53′ E 168
Muramvya, *Burundi* 3°16′ S, 29°35′ E 218
Murang'a, *Kenya* 0°44′ N, 37°10′ E 224
Murashi, *Russ.* 59°22′ N, 48°59′ E 154
Murat Dağı, peak, *Turk.* 38°54′ N, 29°40′ E 156
Murat, river, *Turk.* 39°41′ N, 43°11′ E 195
Muratlı, *Turk.* 41°9′ N, 27°28′ E 158
Muravera, *It.* 39°25′ N, 9°35′ E 156
Murayama, *Japan* 38°29′ N, 140°23′ E 201
Murazzano, *It.* 44°28′ N, 8°1′ E 167
Mürcheh Khvort, *Iran* 33°4′ N, 51°30′ E 180
Murchison, *N.Z.* 41°50′ S, 172°20′ E 240
Murchison Falls, *Uganda* 2°25′ N, 31°41′ E 224
Murchison Falls National Park, *Uganda* 2°0′ N, 31°26′ E 224
Murchison, Mount, peak, *Antarctica* 73°22′ S, 166°55′ E 248
Murchison, Mount, peak, *Austral.* 26°49′ S, 116°14′ E 230
Murcia, *Sp.* 37°58′ N, 1°8′ W 164
Murcia, adm. division, *Sp.* 37°51′ N, 1°52′ W 164
Murdo, *S. Dak., U.S.* 43°53′ N, 100°43′ W 90
Murdochville, *Can.* 48°57′ N, 65°32′ W 111
Mureş, adm. division, *Rom.* 46°20′ N, 24°2′ E 156
Mureş, river, *Rom.* 46°7′ N, 21°3′ E 168
Muret, *Fr.* 43°27′ N, 1°19′ E 164
Murewa, *Zimb.* 17°41′ S, 31°46′ E 224
Murfreesboro, *Ark., U.S.* 34°2′ N, 93°41′ W 96
Murfreesboro, *N.C., U.S.* 36°26′ N, 77°7′ W 96
Murfreesboro, *Tenn., U.S.* 35°50′ N, 86°23′ W 96
Murgab, *Taj.* 38°42′ N, 73°30′ E 197
Murgenella Wildlife Sanctuary, *Austral.* 11°48′ S, 132°31′ E 238
Murghob, *Taj.* 38°12′ N, 74°3′ E 197
Murghob, river, *Taj.* 38°7′ N, 73°26′ E 197
Murguz, peak, *Arm.* 40°43′ N, 45°12′ E 195
Muri, *China* 38°9′ N, 99°6′ E 188
Muri, *India* 23°22′ N, 85°50′ E 197
Muri, *Nig.* 9°12′ N, 10°52′ E 222
Muriaé, *Braz.* 21°8′ S, 42°22′ W 138
Muriege, *Angola* 9°56′ S, 21°13′ E 220
Murilo Atoll 8°38′ N, 153°0′ E 192
Murino, *Mont.* 42°39′ N, 19°53′ E 168
Muritiba, *Braz.* 12°39′ S, 39°2′ W 132
Murjek, *Nor.* 66°28′ N, 20°50′ E 152
Murle, *Eth.* 5°5′ N, 36°12′ E 224
Murmansk, *Russ.* 68°58′ N, 33°3′ E 152
Murmansk, adm. division, *Russ.* 67°31′ N, 36°54′ E 169
Murmansk Rise, *Barents Sea* 74°41′ N, 37°39′ E 255
Murmino, *Russ.* 54°37′ N, 40°0′ E 154
Murnei, *Sudan* 12°55′ N, 22°48′ E 218

Muro, Capo di, *Fr.* 41°39′ N, 7°59′ E 156
Murom, *Russ.* 55°33′ N, 42°3′ E 154
Muromtsevo, *Russ.* 56°20′ N, 75°15′ E 169
Muroran, *Japan* 42°26′ N, 140°52′ E 190
Muroto, *Japan* 33°18′ N, 134°9′ E 201
Muroto Zaki, *Japan* 33°9′ N, 134°11′ E 201
Murphy, *Idaho, U.S.* 43°13′ N, 116°34′ W 90
Murphy Bay 67°28′ S, 149°3′ E 248
Murphy Inlet 71°42′ S, 96°56′ W 248
Murphy, Mount, peak, *Antarctica* 75°17′ S, 110°10′ W 248
Murphys, *Calif., U.S.* 38°7′ N, 120°29′ W 100
Murphysboro, *Mo., U.S.* 37°45′ N, 89°21′ W 96
Murra, *Nicar.* 13°42′ N, 86°0′ W 115
Murray, *Ky., U.S.* 36°37′ N, 88°17′ W 96
Murray, Cape 79°16′ S, 171°16′ E 248
Murray Fracture Zone, *North Pacific Ocean* 30°51′ N, 143°25′ W 252
Murray Head, *Can.* 45°53′ N, 62°30′ W 111
Murray Islands, *Coral Sea* 10°20′ S, 144°2′ E 192
Murray, Mount, peak, *Can.* 60°52′ N, 128°58′ W 108
Murray, river, *Can.* 54°50′ N, 121°21′ W 108
Murraysburg, *S. Af.* 31°58′ S, 23°44′ E 227
Murree, *Pak.* 33°53′ N, 73°28′ E 186
Murrells Inlet, *S.C., U.S.* 33°32′ N, 79°3′ W 96
Murro di Porco, Capo, *It.* 36°54′ N, 15°20′ E 156
Murrumbidgee, river, *Austral.* 34°43′ S, 143°38′ E 230
Murrupula, *Mozambique* 15°28′ S, 38°47′ E 224
Murska Sobota, *Slov.* 46°39′ N, 16°9′ E 168
Mursko Središće, *Croatia* 46°30′ N, 16°25′ E 168
Murtovaara, *Fin.* 65°40′ N, 29°20′ E 152
Muru, river, *Braz.* 9°9′ S, 71°27′ W 137
Muruasigar, peak, *Kenya* 3°6′ N, 34°51′ E 224
Murukta, *Russ.* 67°49′ N, 102°25′ E 160
Muruntau, *Uzb.* 41°27′ N, 64°41′ E 197
Murwara, *India* 23°49′ N, 80°23′ E 197
Murygino, *Russ.* 58°44′ N, 49°31′ E 154
Muş, *Turk.* 38°44′ N, 41°31′ E 195
Mus Khaya, Gora, peak, *Russ.* 62°18′ N, 140°8′ E 172
Musa, *Dem. Rep. of the Congo* 2°36′ N, 19°20′ E 218
Musa Ālī Terara, peak, *Eth.* 12°22′ N, 42°15′ E 182
Musa Dağ, peak, *Turk.* 36°9′ N, 35°50′ E 156
Mûsa, Gebel (Sinai, Mount), peak, *Egypt* 28°30′ N, 33°54′ E 226
Mūša, river, *Lith.* 56°18′ N, 24°7′ E 166
Musala (Mansalar), island, *Indonesia* 1°31′ N, 97°47′ E 196
Musala, peak, *Bulg.* 42°10′ N, 23°31′ E 156
Musan, *N. Korea* 42°15′ N, 129°15′ E 200
Musawa, *Nig.* 12°7′ N, 7°38′ E 222
Musaymīr, *Yemen* 13°25′ N, 44°36′ E 182
Muscat see Masqaţ, *Oman* 23°30′ N, 58°32′ E 196
Muscatine, *Iowa, U.S.* 41°25′ N, 91°4′ W 94
Müsch, *Ger.* 50°23′ N, 6°49′ E 167
Muse, *Okla., U.S.* 34°38′ N, 94°46′ W 96
Musgrave Land, *Can.* 53°36′ N, 56°12′ W 111
Musgrave, Port 12°9′ S, 141°2′ E 230
Musgrave Ranges, *Austral.* 25°59′ S, 131°49′ E 230
Mushandike Sanctuary, *Zimb.* 20°13′ S, 30°18′ E 206
Mushâsh el Sirr, spring, *Egypt* 30°37′ N, 33°46′ E 194
Mushenge, *Dem. Rep. of the Congo* 4°29′ S, 21°18′ E 218
Mushie, *Dem. Rep. of the Congo* 3°2′ S, 16°51′ E 218
Mushorah, oil field, *Iraq* 36°55′ N, 42°14′ E 195
Mushu, island, *P.N.G.* 3°39′ S, 142°39′ E 192
Music Mountains, peak, *Ariz., U.S.* 35°31′ N, 113°43′ W 101
Musina (Messina), *S. Af.* 22°21′ S, 30°1′ E 227
Musiri, *India* 10°58′ N, 78°29′ E 188
Muskeg, river, *Can.* 60°16′ N, 123°9′ W 108
Muskeget Channel 41°19′ N, 70°29′ W 104
Muskeget Island, *Mass., U.S.* 41°19′ N, 70°18′ W 104
Muskegon, *Mich., U.S.* 43°13′ N, 86°16′ W 102
Muskegon Heights, *Mich., U.S.* 43°11′ N, 86°15′ W 102
Muskegon, river, *Mich., U.S.* 43°50′ N, 85°18′ W 102
Muskogee, *Okla., U.S.* 35°44′ N, 95°22′ W 96
Muskwa, *Can.* 58°44′ N, 122°43′ W 108
Muskwa, river, *Can.* 56°8′ N, 114°38′ W 108
Muslimbagh, *Pak.* 30°51′ N, 67°45′ E 187
Musmar, *Sudan* 18°11′ N, 35°35′ E 182
Musoma, *Tanzania* 1°31′ S, 33°49′ E 224
Musquaro, Lac, lake, *Can.* 50°29′ N, 61°41′ W 111
Mussau, island, *P.N.G.* 1°31′ S, 149°47′ E 192
Mussau Islands, *P.N.G.* 1°17′ S, 149°36′ E 192
Musselshell, *Mont., U.S.* 46°28′ N, 108°6′ W 90
Musselshell, river, *Mont., U.S.* 46°28′ N, 109°57′ W 90
Mussende, *Angola* 10°33′ S, 16°2′ E 220
Mussuma, *Angola* 14°17′ S, 21°57′ E 220
Mustafakemalpaşa, *Turk.* 40°4′ N, 28°23′ E 180
Mustahīl, *Eth.* 5°14′ N, 44°42′ E 218
Mustang, *Nepal* 29°12′ N, 83°58′ E 197
Mustayevo, *Russ.* 51°47′ N, 53°27′ E 158
Mustio see Svarta, *Fin.* 60°8′ N, 23°51′ E 166
Mustjala, *Est.* 58°27′ N, 22°14′ E 166
Mustla, *Est.* 58°13′ N, 25°50′ E 166
Mustvee, *Est.* 58°50′ N, 26°53′ E 166
Musudan Missile Launch Site, *N. Korea* 40°46′ N, 129°44′ E 200
Musún, Cerro, peak, *Nicar.* 12°58′ N, 85°18′ W 115
Musungu, *Dem. Rep. of the Congo* 2°45′ N, 28°22′ E 224
Muswabik, river, *Can.* 51°56′ N, 85°31′ W 110
Mûţ, *Egypt* 25°28′ N, 28°57′ E 226
Mut, *Turk.* 36°38′ N, 33°26′ E 156
Mutá, Ponta do, *Braz.* 14°23′ S, 38°50′ W 132
Mu'tah, *Jordan* 31°5′ N, 35°41′ E 194
Mutalahti, *Fin.* 62°25′ N, 31°4′ E 152
Mutanda, *Zambia* 12°23′ S, 26°14′ E 224
Mutarara, *Mozambique* 17°27′ S, 35°8′ E 224
Mutare, *Zimb.* 18°58′ S, 32°39′ E 224
Mutatá, *Col.* 7°16′ N, 76°32′ W 136
Mutha, *Kenya* 1°49′ S, 38°24′ E 224
Muting, *Indonesia* 7°21′ S, 140°14′ E 192
Mutki, *Turk.* 38°24′ N, 41°54′ E 195
Mutnyy Materik, *Russ.* 65°55′ N, 55°0′ E 154
Mutoko, *Zimb.* 17°26′ S, 32°13′ E 224
Mutombo Mukulu, *Dem. Rep. of the Congo* 7°58′ S, 23°59′ E 224
Mutoray, *Russ.* 61°27′ N, 100°26′ E 160
Mutriba, oil field, *Kuwait* 29°46′ N, 47°14′ E 196
Mutshatsha, *Dem. Rep. of the Congo* 10°40′ S, 24°26′ E 224
Mutumbo, *Angola* 13°15′ S, 17°18′ E 220
Mutum-Paraná, *Braz.* 9°40′ S, 65°0′ W 137
Mutunópolis, *Braz.* 13°41′ S, 49°17′ W 138
Muurla, *Fin.* 60°20′ N, 23°14′ E 166
Muuruvesi, *Fin.* 63°0′ N, 28°10′ E 152
Muxía, *Sp.* 43°5′ N, 9°14′ W 150
Muyinga, *Burundi* 2°52′ S, 30°19′ E 224
Mŭynoq, *Uzb.* 43°49′ N, 58°56′ E 160
Muyumba, *Dem. Rep. of the Congo* 7°15′ S, 27°1′ E 224
Muzaffarabad, *Pak.* 34°23′ N, 73°33′ E 186
Muzaffargarh, *Pak.* 30°4′ N, 71°12′ E 186
Muzaffarnagar, *India* 29°29′ N, 77°40′ E 197
Muzaffarpur, *India* 26°5′ N, 85°23′ E 197
Muzhi, *Russ.* 65°21′ N, 64°36′ E 169
Muzon, Cape, *Alas., U.S.* 54°29′ N, 132°42′ W 108
Múzquiz, *Mex.* 27°52′ N, 101°31′ W 92
Muztag, peak, *China* 36°24′ N, 87°20′ E 188
Muztag, peak, *China* 35°59′ N, 80°10′ E 188
Muztagata, peak, *China* 38°17′ N, 75°2′ E 184
Muztagh Pass, *China* 35°53′ N, 76°12′ E 186
Mvadhi-Ousyé, *Gabon* 1°12′ N, 13°11′ E 218
Mvolo, *Sudan* 6°3′ N, 29°55′ E 224
Mvomero, *Tanzania* 6°17′ S, 37°26′ E 224
Mvouti, *Congo* 4°16′ S, 12°26′ E 218
Mvuma, *Zimb.* 19°19′ S, 30°29′ E 224
Mwadingusha, *Dem. Rep. of the Congo* 10°45′ S, 27°10′ E 224
Mwadui, *Tanzania* 3°35′ S, 33°39′ E 224
Mwakete, *Tanzania* 9°20′ S, 34°14′ E 224
Mwali (Mohéli), island, *Comoros* 12°34′ S, 43°15′ E 220
Mwami, *Zimb.* 16°41′ S, 29°46′ E 224
Mwanza, *Dem. Rep. of the Congo* 7°51′ S, 26°39′ E 224
Mwanza, *Tanzania* 2°32′ S, 32°55′ E 224
Mwanza, adm. division, *Tanzania* 2°57′ S, 31°56′ E 224
Mwatate, *Kenya* 3°32′ S, 38°21′ E 218
Mwaya, *Tanzania* 9°32′ S, 33°55′ E 224
Mweelrea, peak, *Ire.* 53°36′ N, 9°56′ W 150
Mweka, *Dem. Rep. of the Congo* 4°52′ S, 21°31′ E 218
Mwene-Ditu, *Dem. Rep. of the Congo* 7°1′ S, 23°24′ E 224
Mwenezi, *Zimb.* 21°25′ S, 30°45′ E 227
Mwenezi, river, *Zimb.* 21°45′ S, 31°8′ E 227
Mwenga, *Dem. Rep. of the Congo* 3°4′ S, 28°26′ E 224
Mwenzo, *Zambia* 9°21′ S, 32°41′ E 224
Mweru, Lake, *Dem. Rep. of the Congo* 9°16′ S, 26°39′ E 207
Mweru Wantipa National Park, *Zambia* 9°9′ S, 29°20′ E 224
Mwimba, *Dem. Rep. of the Congo* 9°12′ S, 22°46′ E 218
Mwingi, *Kenya* 0°57′ N, 38°4′ E 224
Mwinilunga, *Zambia* 11°44′ S, 24°25′ E 224
Mwitikira, *Tanzania* 6°30′ S, 35°39′ E 224
Mwombezhi, river, *Zambia* 12°41′ S, 25°43′ E 224
My Tho, *Vietnam* 10°21′ N, 106°21′ E 202
Myadzyel, *Belarus* 54°51′ N, 26°56′ E 166
Myakit, *Russ.* 61°29′ N, 151°59′ E 160
Myakka City, *Fla., U.S.* 27°21′ N, 82°9′ W 105
Myakka, river, *Fla., U.S.* 27°13′ N, 82°22′ W 105
Myaksa, *Russ.* 58°52′ N, 38°15′ E 154
Myanaung, *Myanmar* 18°20′ N, 95°13′ E 202
Myanmar (Burma) 21°5′ N, 95°9′ E 192
Myeik, *Myanmar* 12°35′ N, 98°38′ E 192
Myingyan, *Myanmar* 21°28′ N, 95°25′ E 202
Myitkyinā, *Myanmar* 25°29′ N, 97°20′ E 190
Myitta, *Myanmar* 14°10′ N, 98°30′ E 202
Myken, islands, *Norwegian Sea* 66°43′ N, 11°26′ E 152
Mykhaylivka, *Ukr.* 47°14′ N, 35°15′ E 156
Mykolayiv, *Ukr.* 49°31′ N, 23°57′ E 158
Mykolayiv, *Ukr.* 46°59′ N, 32°2′ E 156
Myla, *Russ.* 65°25′ N, 50°42′ E 154
Mylius Erichsen Land 80°43′ N, 42°2′ W 246
Myllykoski, *Fin.* 60°46′ N, 26°46′ E 166
Mymensingh, *Bangladesh* 24°53′ N, 90°40′ E 197
Mynämäki, *Fin.* 60°40′ N, 21°56′ E 166
Mynbulaq, *Uzb.* 42°12′ N, 62°55′ E 180
Myohaung, *Myanmar* 20°38′ N, 93°10′ E 188
Myohyang Sanmaek, *N. Korea* 39°58′ N, 126°24′ E 200
Myōkō, *Japan* 36°55′ N, 138°12′ E 201
Myoungmya, *Myanmar* 16°34′ N, 94°55′ E 202
Myra see Kale, *Turk.* 36°13′ N, 29°57′ E 156
Mýrdalsjökull, glacier, *Ice.* 63°11′ N, 18°33′ W 142
Myrhorod, *Ukr.* 49°57′ N, 33°31′ E 158
Myrskylä, *Fin.* 60°39′ N, 25°48′ E 166
Myrtle Beach, *S.C., U.S.* 33°39′ N, 78°54′ W 82
Myrtle Creek, *Oreg., U.S.* 43°1′ N, 123°17′ W 90
Myrtle Point, *Oreg., U.S.* 43°3′ N, 124°8′ W 90
Mys Kamennyy, *Russ.* 68°29′ N, 73°26′ E 169
Mys Shmidta, *Russ.* 68°54′ N, 179°31′ W 98
Mys Zhelaniya, *Russ.* 76°50′ N, 68°29′ E 160
Mysen, *Nor.* 59°34′ N, 11°19′ E 152
Myshkino, *Russ.* 57°46′ N, 38°26′ E 154
Myślice, *Pol.* 53°54′ N, 19°30′ E 166
Mysovaya, *Russ.* 67°44′ N, 155°59′ E 160
Mystic, *Conn., U.S.* 41°21′ N, 71°58′ W 104
Mystic, *Iowa, U.S.* 40°46′ N, 92°57′ W 94
Mysy, *Russ.* 60°36′ N, 54°4′ E 154
Mytilene see Mitilíni, *Gr.* 39°6′ N, 26°33′ E 156
Myton, *Utah, U.S.* 40°11′ N, 110°3′ W 90
Myyeldino, *Russ.* 61°48′ N, 54°46′ E 154
Mzima Springs, *Kenya* 2°59′ S, 38°4′ E 224
Mzimba, *Malawi* 11°52′ S, 33°32′ E 224
Mzuzu, *Malawi* 11°27′ S, 33°54′ E 224

N

Nā'ālehu, *Hawai'i, U.S.* 19°3′ N, 155°36′ W 99
Naachtún Dos Lagunas Biotope, *Guatemala* 17°35′ N, 90°14′ W 115
Naama, *Alg.* 33°16′ N, 0°21′ E 214
Naandi, *Sudan* 4°58′ N, 27°49′ E 224
Naantali, *Fin.* 60°28′ N, 22°2′ E 166
Naas, *Ire.* 53°12′ N, 6°40′ W 150
Nabā, Jabal (Nebo, Mount), peak, *Jordan* 31°45′ N, 35°43′ E 194
Nababiep, *S. Af.* 29°36′ S, 17°47′ E 227
Nabas, *Philippines* 11°49′ N, 122°6′ E 203
Naberera, *Tanzania* 4°12′ S, 36°56′ E 224
Naberezhnyye Chelny, *Russ.* 55°40′ N, 52°22′ E 154
Nabeul, *Tun.* 36°27′ N, 10°44′ E 156
Nabilatuk, *Uganda* 2°3′ N, 34°35′ E 224
Nabire, *Indonesia* 3°21′ S, 135°28′ E 238
Nablus see Nābulus, *West Bank, Israel* 32°12′ N, 35°17′ E 194
Naboomspruit see Mookgophong, *S. Af.* 24°31′ S, 28°44′ E 227
Nabordo, *Nig.* 10°11′ N, 9°25′ E 222
Naborton, *La., U.S.* 32°1′ N, 93°35′ W 103
Nabq, *Egypt* 28°7′ N, 34°23′ E 180
Nābulus (Nablus), *West Bank, Israel* 32°12′ N, 35°17′ E 194
Nabúri, *Mozambique* 16°57′ S, 39°0′ E 224
Nacala, *Mozambique* 14°33′ S, 40°43′ E 224
Nacaome, *Hond.* 13°31′ N, 87°29′ W 115
Nacaroa, *Mozambique* 14°18′ S, 39°49′ E 224
Nacebe, *Bol.* 10°58′ S, 67°27′ W 137
Naches, *Wash., U.S.* 46°42′ N, 120°42′ W 90
Nachikatsuura, *Japan* 33°35′ N, 135°54′ E 201
Nachingwea, *Tanzania* 10°25′ S, 38°46′ E 224
Nachna, *India* 27°31′ N, 71°44′ E 186
Náchod, *Czech Rep.* 50°24′ N, 16°10′ E 152
Nachuge, *India* 10°44′ N, 92°31′ E 188
Nacimiento, *Mex.* 28°3′ N, 101°45′ W 92
Nacimiento, Lake, *Calif., U.S.* 35°44′ N, 121°17′ W 100
Naciria, *Alg.* 36°44′ N, 3°50′ E 150
Nacka, *Sw.* 59°17′ N, 18°7′ E 166
Nackhörn, *Ger.* 54°18′ N, 7°50′ E 152
Naco, *Mex.* 31°17′ N, 109°58′ W 92
Nacogdoches, *Tex., U.S.* 31°34′ N, 94°39′ W 103
Nácori Chico, *Mex.* 29°39′ N, 109°5′ W 92
Nacozari, river, *Mex.* 29°23′ N, 109°44′ W 80
Nacozari Viejo, *Mex.* 30°21′ N, 109°39′ W 92
Ñacunday, *Parag.* 26°4′ S, 54°35′ W 139
Nada see Danxian, *China* 19°28′ N, 109°34′ E 198
Nadale, island, *Maldives* 0°16′ N, 72°12′ E 188
Nadanbo, *China* 43°9′ N, 125°27′ E 200
Nadap, *Hung.* 47°15′ N, 18°36′ E 168
Nadiad, *India* 22°41′ N, 72°51′ E 186
Nădlac, *Rom.* 46°10′ N, 20°47′ E 168
Nădrag, *Rom.* 45°40′ N, 22°13′ E 168
Nadu, adm. division, *India* 11°19′ N, 79°30′ E 188
Nádudvar, *Hung.* 47°25′ N, 21°9′ E 168
Nadvoitsy, *Russ.* 63°53′ N, 34°13′ E 152
Nadym, *Russ.* 65°35′ N, 72°33′ E 169
Nadym, river, *Russ.* 63°43′ N, 72°30′ E 169
Nafūsah, Jabal, *Lib.* 31°17′ N, 10°13′ E 214
Nafada, *Nig.* 11°2′ N, 11°19′ E 222
Nafana, *Côte d'Ivoire* 9°11′ N, 4°48′ W 222
Naft Khaneh Naft-e-Shāh, oil field, *Iraq* 34°6′ N, 45°18′ E 180
Naft-e Safid, oil field, *Iran* 31°41′ N, 49°12′ E 180
Nafuce, *Nig.* 12°19′ N, 6°30′ E 222
Nag, *Pak.* 27°21′ N, 65°4′ E 186
Nag 'Hammâdi, *Egypt* 26°3′ N, 32°9′ E 180
Naga, *Philippines* 13°38′ N, 123°10′ E 203
Naga Hills, *Myanmar* 25°34′ N, 94°35′ E 188
Nagagami Lake, *Can.* 49°21′ N, 85°32′ W 94
Nagagami, river, *Can.* 49°45′ N, 84°34′ W 94
Nagagamisis Lake, *Can.* 49°27′ N, 85°16′ W 94
Nagahama, *Japan* 35°22′ N, 136°16′ E 201
Nagahama, *Japan* 33°36′ N, 132°29′ E 201
Nagai, *Japan* 38°6′ N, 140°1′ E 201
Nagano, *Japan* 36°40′ N, 138°12′ E 201
Nagano, adm. division, *Japan* 35°59′ N, 137°38′ E 201
Naganuma, *Japan* 37°17′ N, 140°12′ E 201
Nagaoka, *Japan* 37°26′ N, 138°51′ E 201
Nagar, *India* 32°5′ N, 77°13′ E 188
Nagar Parkar, *Pak.* 24°23′ N, 70°47′ E 186
Nagarzê, *China* 28°58′ N, 90°21′ E 197
Nagas Point, *Can.* 52°1′ N, 131°45′ W 108
Nagasaki, *Japan* 32°45′ N, 129°52′ E 201
Nagasaki, adm. division, *Japan* 32°47′ N, 129°50′ E 201
Nagashima, *Japan* 34°12′ N, 136°20′ E 201
Nagato, *Japan* 34°21′ N, 131°11′ E 200
Nagaur, *India* 27°10′ N, 73°45′ E 186
Nagda, *India* 23°26′ N, 75°27′ E 197
Nagēlē, *Eth.* 5°20′ N, 39°36′ E 224
Nagercoil, *India* 8°10′ N, 77°25′ E 188
Nagina, *India* 29°26′ N, 78°24′ E 197
Nagishot, *Sudan* 4°15′ N, 33°33′ E 224
Nagorno-Karabakh, special sovereignty, *Azerb.* 39°45′ N, 46°34′ E 195
Nagornyy, *Russ.* 55°58′ N, 124°54′ E 160
Nagorsk, *Russ.* 59°19′ N, 50°49′ E 154
Nagoya, *Japan* 35°8′ N, 136°55′ E 201
Nagpur, *India* 21°8′ N, 79°5′ E 188
Nagqu, *China* 31°27′ N, 92°0′ E 188
Nagyatád, *Hung.* 46°13′ N, 17°22′ E 168
Nagybajom, *Hung.* 46°23′ N, 17°30′ E 168
Nagybátony, *Hung.* 47°58′ N, 19°49′ E 168
Nagycenk, *Hung.* 47°36′ N, 16°41′ E 168
Nagydorog, *Hung.* 46°37′ N, 18°39′ E 168
Nagykereki, *Hung.* 47°11′ N, 21°47′ E 168
Nagykőros, *Hung.* 47°1′ N, 19°46′ E 168
Nagymányok, *Hung.* 46°16′ N, 18°28′ E 168
Nagyszénás, *Hung.* 46°41′ N, 20°40′ E 168
Naha, *Japan* 26°13′ N, 127°38′ E 190
Nahal Hever, ruin(s), *Israel* 31°25′ N, 35°17′ E 194
Naḥal 'Oz, *Israel* 31°27′ N, 34°29′ E 194
Nahanni Butte, *Can.* 61°2′ N, 123°23′ W 108
Nahanni National Park Reserve, *Can.* 61°8′ N, 125°57′ W 108
Nahant, *Mass., U.S.* 42°25′ N, 70°55′ W 104
Nahari, *Japan* 33°25′ N, 134°1′ E 201
Nahariyya, *Israel* 33°0′ N, 35°5′ E 194
Nahāvand, *Iran* 34°12′ N, 48°21′ E 180
Nahlin, river, *Can.* 58°48′ N, 131°26′ W 108
Nahrin, *Afghan.* 36°2′ N, 69°8′ E 186
Nahuel Huapí National Park, *Arg.* 41°4′ S, 71°53′ W 122
Naicam, *Can.* 52°25′ N, 104°29′ W 108
Naij Gol, river, *China* 35°52′ N, 92°56′ E 188
Nailsworth, *U.K.* 51°41′ N, 2°13′ W 162
Na'ima, *Sudan* 14°36′ N, 32°15′ E 182
Naiman Qi, *China* 42°48′ N, 120°38′ E 198
Nain, *Can.* 56°29′ N, 61°49′ W 106
Nā'īn, *Iran* 32°50′ N, 53°7′ E 180
Nainpur, *India* 22°25′ N, 80°7′ E 197
Nainwa, *India* 25°47′ N, 75°53′ E 197
Nairn, *La., U.S.* 29°25′ N, 89°37′ W 103
Nairn, *U.K.* 57°35′ N, 3°53′ W 150
Nairobi, *Kenya* 1°20′ S, 36°39′ E 224
Nairobi National Park, *Kenya* 1°28′ S, 36°31′ E 206
Nairôto, *Mozambique* 12°24′ S, 39°6′ E 224
Nais Saar, island, *Est.* 59°32′ N, 23°57′ E 166
Naivasha, *Kenya* 0°45′ N, 36°27′ E 224
Naj Tunich, site, *Guatemala* 16°18′ N, 89°22′ W 115
Najaf see An Najaf, *Iraq* 31°58′ N, 44°19′ E 180
Najafābād, *Iran* 32°38′ N, 51°25′ E 180
Najd, region, *Saudi Arabia* 26°8′ N, 42°8′ E 182
Najrān, *Saudi Arabia* 17°44′ N, 44°27′ E 182
Naju, *S. Korea* 35°0′ N, 126°44′ E 200
Naka, river, *Japan* 33°44′ N, 134°17′ E 201
Nakajō, *Japan* 38°3′ N, 139°24′ E 201
Nakaminato, *Japan* 36°20′ N, 140°36′ E 201
Nakamura, *Japan* 32°58′ N, 132°55′ E 201
Nakanno, *Russ.* 62°57′ N, 108°15′ E 160
Nakano, *Japan* 36°44′ N, 138°22′ E 201
Nakanojō, *Japan* 36°35′ N, 138°50′ E 201
Nakatosa, *Japan* 33°18′ N, 133°12′ E 201
Nakatsu, *Japan* 33°35′ N, 131°12′ E 201
Nakatsugawa, *Japan* 35°28′ N, 137°31′ E 201
Nakfa, *Eritrea* 16°38′ N, 38°25′ E 182
Nakhl, *Egypt* 29°52′ N, 33°47′ E 180
Nakhodka, *Russ.* 67°40′ N, 77°44′ E 169
Nakhodka, *Russ.* 42°51′ N, 132°48′ E 190
Nakhon Nayok, *Thai.* 14°13′ N, 101°12′ E 202
Nakhon Phanom, *Thai.* 17°23′ N, 104°44′ E 202
Nakhon Ratchasima (Khorat), *Thai.* 14°58′ N, 102°7′ E 202
Nakhon Sawan, *Thai.* 15°41′ N, 100°5′ E 202
Nakhon Si Thammarat, *Thai.* 8°26′ N, 99°57′ E 202
Nakina, *Can.* 50°11′ N, 86°38′ W 82
Nakina, river, *Can.* 58°51′ N, 133°3′ W 108
Näkkälä, *Fin.* 68°36′ N, 23°31′ E 152
Naknek, *Alas., U.S.* 58°41′ N, 157°5′ W 98
Nako, *Burkina Faso* 10°39′ N, 3°3′ W 222
Nakonde, *Zambia* 9°23′ S, 32°45′ E 224
Nakop, *Namibia* 28°6′ S, 19°59′ E 227
Nakovo, *Serb.* 45°52′ N, 20°32′ E 168
Nakuru, *Kenya* 0°18′ N, 36°5′ E 224
Nakusp, *Can.* 50°14′ N, 117°49′ W 90
Nal'chik, *Russ.* 43°30′ N, 43°38′ E 195
Nallıhan, *Turk.* 40°11′ N, 31°21′ E 156
Nālūt, *Lib.* 31°54′ N, 10°58′ E 214
Nam Can, *Vietnam* 8°48′ N, 105°1′ E 202
Nam Co, lake, *China* 30°45′ N, 89°50′ E 188
Nam Dinh, *Vietnam* 20°26′ N, 106°8′ E 198
Nam Nao National Park, *Thai.* 16°25′ N, 101°24′ E 202
Nam Ngum Dam, *Laos* 18°42′ N, 102°29′ E 202
Nam Phong Dam, *Thai.* 16°34′ N, 102°8′ E 202
Nam Phung Dam, *Thai.* 16°49′ N, 102°59′ E 202
Nam, river, *S. Korea* 35°17′ N, 128°16′ E 200
Nam Tok, *Thai.* 14°23′ N, 98°57′ E 202
Namaacha, *Mozambique* 25°57′ S, 32°1′ E 227
Namacunde, *Angola* 17°19′ S, 15°49′ E 220
Namacurra, *Mozambique* 17°29′ S, 37°2′ E 224
Namak, *S. Korea* 36°34′ N, 127°46′ E 200
Namanga, *Kenya* 2°33′ S, 36°49′ E 224
Namangan, *Uzb.* 40°59′ N, 71°38′ E 197
Namanyere, *Tanzania* 7°31′ S, 31°2′ E 224
Namapa, *Mozambique* 13°44′ S, 39°51′ E 224
Namaponda, *Mozambique* 15°51′ S, 39°53′ E 224
Namaqualand, region, *S. Af.* 30°11′ S, 17°12′ E 227
Namarrói, *Mozambique* 15°58′ S, 36°49′ E 224
Namasagali, *Uganda* 0°59′ N, 32°58′ E 224
Namatanai, *P.N.G.* 3°41′ S, 152°25′ E 238
Nambinda, *Tanzania* 9°37′ S, 37°37′ E 224
Nambu, *Japan* 35°16′ N, 138°26′ E 201
Namdae, river, *N. Korea* 41°8′ N, 129°4′ E 200
Namdapha National Park, *India* 27°30′ N, 96°34′ E 188
Nameigos Lake, *Can.* 48°45′ N, 85°12′ W 94
Namerikawa, *Japan* 36°45′ N, 137°19′ E 201
Nametil, *Mozambique* 15°44′ S, 39°24′ E 224
Namgia, *India* 31°46′ N, 78°41′ E 188
Namib Desert, *Angola* 15°54′ S, 12°10′ E 220
Namibe, *Angola* 15°14′ S, 12°10′ E 220
Namibe, adm. division, *Angola* 16°24′ S, 11°50′ E 220
Namibia 21°53′ S, 15°16′ E 220
Namib-Naukluft Park, *Namibia* 25°49′ S, 15°21′ E 227
Namies, *S. Af.* 29°17′ S, 19°11′ E 227
Namīn, *Iran* 38°29′ N, 48°30′ E 195
Namiquipa, *Mex.* 29°14′ N, 107°25′ W 92

Namjagbarwa Feng, peak, China 29°37′ N, 94°55′ E 188
Namji, S. Korea 35°23′ N, 128°29′ E 200
Namlea, Indonesia 3°16′ S, 127°1′ E 192
Namling, China 29°42′ N, 89°3′ E 197
Namoi, river, Austral. 30°32′ S, 147°10′ E 231
Nāmolokama Mountain, peak, Hawai'i, U.S. 22°7′ N, 159°33′ W 99
Namoluk Atoll 5°35′ N, 150°28′ E 192
Namonuito Atoll, North Pacific Ocean 8°43′ N, 149°21′ E 192
Nampa, Can. 56°3′ N, 117°9′ W 108
Nampa, Idaho, U.S. 43°32′ N, 116°34′ W 82
Nampala, Mali 15°15′ N, 5°34′ W 222
Namp'o, N. Korea 38°43′ N, 125°25′ E 200
Nampō Shotō, islands, North Pacific Ocean 30°47′ N, 138°20′ E 190
Nampula, Mozambique 15°8′ S, 39°17′ E 224
Nampula, adm. division, Mozambique 15°0′ S, 37°41′ E 224
Namsos, Nor. 64°29′ N, 11°41′ E 160
Namsskogan, Nor. 64°55′ N, 13°12′ E 152
Namtsy, Russ. 62°41′ N, 129°32′ E 160
Namtu, Myanmar 23°1′ N, 97°27′ E 202
Namu, Can. 51°50′ N, 127°49′ W 108
Namuli, peak, Mozambique 15°26′ S, 36°59′ E 224
Namuno, Mozambique 13°31′ S, 38°52′ E 224
Namur, Belg. 50°28′ N, 4°51′ E 167
Namur Lake, Can. 57°18′ N, 113°21′ W 108
Namuruputh, Kenya 4°31′ N, 35°54′ E 224
Namutoni, Namibia 18°51′ S, 16°57′ E 220
Namwala, Zambia 15°46′ S, 26°25′ E 224
Namwon, S. Korea 35°23′ N, 127°23′ E 200
Namyang, N. Korea 40°44′ N, 129°17′ E 200
Nan, Thai. 18°48′ N, 100°45′ E 202
Nan Hulsan Hu, lake, China 36°42′ N, 94°42′ E 188
Nan, river, Thai. 18°37′ N, 100°46′ E 202
Nana, river, Cen. Af. Rep. 5°48′ N, 15°21′ E 218
Nanaimo, Can. 49°9′ N, 123°57′ W 100
Nanakru, Liberia 4°52′ N, 8°45′ W 222
Nanam, Korea 41°41′ N, 129°39′ E 200
Nan'an, China 24°55′ N, 118°22′ E 198
Nanao, Japan 37°2′ N, 136°56′ E 201
Nanbu, China 31°20′ N, 106°0′ E 198
Nanchang, China 28°41′ N, 115°54′ E 198
Nancheng, China 27°33′ N, 116°37′ E 198
Nanchong, China 30°49′ N, 106°2′ E 198
Nanchuan, China 29°11′ N, 107°3′ E 198
Ñancorainza, Bol. 20°41′ S, 63°28′ W 137
Nancy, Fr. 48°41′ N, 6°11′ E 163
Nanda Devi, peak, India 30°22′ N, 79°52′ E 197
Nandan, China 24°57′ N, 107°30′ E 198
Nanded, India 19°11′ N, 77°19′ E 188
Nanfen, China 41°8′ N, 123°48′ E 200
Nanfeng, China 27°13′ N, 116°25′ E 198
Nang, China 29°5′ N, 93°6′ E 188
Nanga Parbat, peak, Pak. 35°13′ N, 74°28′ E 186
Nangade, Mozambique 11°6′ S, 39°43′ E 224
Nangapinoh, Indonesia 0°21′ N, 111°38′ E 192
Nangin, Myanmar 10°32′ N, 98°29′ E 202
Nangis, Fr. 48°33′ N, 3°0′ E 163
Nangnim, N. Korea 40°57′ N, 127°8′ E 200
Nangong, China 37°18′ N, 115°23′ E 198
Nangqên, China 32°15′ N, 96°28′ E 188
Nangtud, Mount, peak, Philippines 11°16′ N, 122°6′ E 203
Nanika Lake, lake, Can. 53°45′ N, 128°5′ W 108
Nanjiang, China 32°24′ N, 106°46′ E 198
Nanjing, China 32°5′ N, 118°48′ E 198
Nanjing, China 24°22′ N, 117°16′ E 198
Nankang, China 25°39′ N, 114°41′ E 198
Nankoku, Japan 33°34′ N, 133°38′ E 201
Nanle, China 36°3′ N, 115°11′ E 198
Nanning, China 22°49′ N, 108°19′ E 198
Nanortalik 60°13′ N, 45°14′ W 106
Nanpara, India 27°50′ N, 81°30′ E 197
Nanping, China 42°18′ N, 129°12′ E 200
Nanping, China 26°37′ N, 118°4′ E 198
Nanri Dao, island, China 24°53′ N, 119°22′ E 198
Nansan Dao, island, China 21°1′ N, 110°37′ E 198
Nansei Shotō (Ryukyu Islands), East China Sea 25°0′ N, 125°56′ E 190
Nansen Basin, Arctic Ocean 85°0′ N, 78°46′ E 255
Nansen Land 82°0′ N, 43°58′ W 246
Nansen Sound 80°31′ N, 104°17′ W 72
Nansio, Tanzania 2°7′ S, 33°4′ E 224
Nantais, Lac, lake, Can. 61°33′ N, 76°5′ W 246
Nantes, Fr. 47°12′ N, 1°36′ W 150
Nanteuil-le-Haudouin, Fr. 49°8′ N, 2°48′ E 163
Nanticoke, Pa., U.S. 41°11′ N, 76°1′ W 110
Nanton, Can. 50°20′ N, 113°47′ W 108
Nantong, China 32°2′ N, 120°54′ E 198
Nantucket, Mass., U.S. 41°16′ N, 70°7′ W 104
Nantucket Inlet 74°39′ S, 66°32′ W 248
Nantucket Island, Mass., U.S. 41°22′ N, 70°2′ W 104
Nantucket Sound 41°26′ N, 70°19′ W 104
Nantulo, Mozambique 12°30′ S, 39°1′ E 224
Nantwich, U.K. 53°3′ N, 2°31′ W 162
Nanuque, Braz. 17°49′ S, 40°21′ W 138
Nanusa, Kepulauan, islands, Philippine Sea 4°57′ N, 126°54′ E 203
Nanxi, China 28°51′ N, 104°56′ E 198
Nanxian, China 29°23′ N, 112°23′ E 198
Nanxiong, China 25°6′ N, 114°15′ E 198
Nanyang, China 33°1′ N, 112°34′ E 198
Nanyuki, Kenya 1°58′ S, 37°4′ E 224
Nanzhang, China 31°47′ N, 111°50′ E 198
Nanzhila, Zambia 16°6′ S, 26°1′ E 224
Nao, Cabo de La, Sp. 38°30′ N, 0°10′ E 214
Naococane, Lac, lake, Can. 52°47′ N, 71°20′ W 111
Naozhou Dao, island, China 20°51′ N, 110°39′ E 198
Napa, Calif., U.S. 38°18′ N, 122°19′ W 100
Napá, Mozambique 13°17′ S, 39°3′ E 224
Napaimiut, Alas., U.S. 61°32′ N, 158°41′ W 98
Napaleofú, Arg. 37°38′ S, 58°46′ W 139
Napalkovo, Russ. 70°3′ N, 73°54′ E 169
Napanee, Can. 44°14′ N, 76°59′ W 82
Napas, Russ. 59°48′ N, 81°57′ E 169
Napasoq 65°4′ N, 52°21′ W 106
Napenay, Arg. 26°44′ S, 60°38′ W 139
Naperville, Ill., U.S. 41°46′ N, 88°9′ W 102
Napier, N.Z. 39°30′ S, 176°54′ E 240
Napier Bay 11°54′ S, 131°12′ E 231
Naples, Fla., U.S. 26°9′ N, 81°48′ W 105
Naples, Me., U.S. 43°57′ N, 70°37′ W 104
Naples, Tex., U.S. 33°11′ N, 94°41′ W 103
Naples see Napoli, It. 40°51′ N, 14°15′ E 156
Napo, China 23°21′ N, 105°50′ E 198
Napo, river, Ecua. 1°14′ S, 77°33′ W 136
Napo, river, Peru 2°38′ S, 74°29′ W 122
Napoleon, N. Dak., U.S. 46°29′ N, 99°47′ W 90
Napoleon, Ohio, U.S. 41°22′ N, 84°8′ W 102
Napoleonville, La., U.S. 29°55′ N, 91°3′ W 103
Napoli (Naples), It. 40°51′ N, 14°15′ E 156
Nappanee, Ind., U.S. 41°26′ N, 86°1′ W 102
Nāpu'ukūlua, peak, Hawai'i, U.S. 19°42′ N, 155°40′ W 99
Naqoura, Leb. 33°7′ N, 35°8′ E 194
Nara, Japan 34°42′ N, 135°50′ E 201
Nara, Mali 15°10′ N, 7°18′ W 222
Nara, adm. division, Japan 34°17′ N, 135°40′ E 201
Nara, river, Pak. 24°46′ N, 69°35′ E 186
Nara Visa, N. Mex., U.S. 35°36′ N, 103°6′ W 92
Narach, Belarus 54°55′ N, 26°41′ E 166
Narach, Vozyera, lake, Belarus 54°52′ N, 26°17′ E 166
Na'rān, Israel 33°2′ N, 35°42′ E 194
Naranbulag, Mongolia 49°14′ N, 113°19′ E 198
Narang, Afghan. 34°44′ N, 70°57′ E 186
Narasannapeta, India 18°24′ N, 84°5′ E 188
Narasapur, India 16°27′ N, 81°40′ E 188
Narathiwat, Thai. 6°26′ N, 101°49′ E 196
Narayanganj, Bangladesh 23°26′ N, 90°40′ E 197
Nærbø, Nor. 58°40′ N, 5°38′ E 152
Narbonne, Fr. 43°10′ N, 2°59′ E 164
Narcondam Island, India 13°28′ N, 94°19′ E 188
Nardīn, Iran 37°0′ N, 55°57′ E 180
Naré, Arg. 30°58′ S, 60°28′ W 139
Nares Land 81°45′ N, 46°0′ W 72
Nares Plain, North Atlantic Ocean 22°43′ N, 63°8′ W 253
Narib, Namibia 24°12′ S, 17°46′ E 227
Naricual, Venez. 10°2′ N, 64°37′ W 116
Narimanabad, Azerb. 38°51′ N, 48°50′ E 195
Narin, river, China 36°20′ N, 92°32′ E 188
Nariño, adm. division, Col. 1°27′ N, 78°30′ W 136
Narlı, Turk. 37°25′ N, 37°8′ E 156
Narmada, river, India 22°56′ N, 78°26′ E 197
Narodnaya, Gora, peak, Russ. 65°6′ N, 59°49′ E 154
Narok, Kenya 1°6′ S, 35°50′ E 224
Narowlya, Belarus 51°44′ N, 29°38′ E 158
Nærøy, Nor. 64°48′ N, 11°16′ E 152
Närpiö see Närpes, Fin. 62°27′ N, 21°18′ E 152
Narragansett Pier, R.I., U.S. 41°25′ N, 71°28′ W 104
Narran Lake, lake, Austral. 30°0′ S, 146°18′ E 230
Narrogin, Austral. 32°56′ S, 117°11′ E 231
Narsaq 60°59′ N, 46°0′ W 246
Narsarsuaq 61°10′ N, 45°21′ W 106
Narsimhapur, India 22°56′ N, 79°12′ E 197
Narsinghgarh, India 23°41′ N, 77°5′ E 197
Narsipatnam, India 17°39′ N, 82°37′ E 188
Nart, Mongolia 49°8′ N, 105°27′ E 198
Narta, Croatia 45°49′ N, 16°47′ E 168
Nartháki, Óros, peak, Gr. 39°12′ N, 22°20′ E 156
Nartkala, Russ. 43°32′ N, 43°53′ E 195
Naruko, Japan 38°45′ N, 140°43′ E 201
Naruto, Japan 34°10′ N, 134°34′ E 201
Narva, Est. 59°21′ N, 28°8′ E 154
Narva Jõesuu, Est. 59°26′ N, 28°1′ E 166
Narvacan, Philippines 17°26′ N, 120°28′ E 203
Narvik, Nor. 68°16′ N, 17°45′ E 160
Narvskoye Vodokhranilishche, lake, Russ. 59°17′ N, 27°33′ E 166
Narwana, India 29°36′ N, 76°8′ E 197
Nar'yan Mar, Russ. 67°43′ N, 53°6′ E 169
Narym, Russ. 58°57′ N, 81°41′ E 169
Naryn, Kyrg. 41°24′ N, 76°2′ E 184
Naryn Khuduk, Russ. 45°26′ N, 46°32′ E 158
Naryn Qum, Kaz. 48°1′ N, 47°52′ E 184
Naryn, river, Kyrg. 41°47′ N, 73°27′ E 197
Narynqol, Kaz. 42°41′ N, 80°11′ E 184
Naryshkino, Russ. 52°55′ N, 35°46′ E 154
Näs, Nor. 62°57′ N, 14°33′ E 152
Nasa, peak, Nor. 66°28′ N, 15°13′ E 152
Nasarawa, Nig. 8°29′ N, 7°41′ E 222
Nasca, Peru 14°53′ S, 74°58′ W 137
Nasca Ridge, South Pacific Ocean 20°50′ S, 79°49′ W 253
Naseby 1645, battle, U.K. 52°23′ N, 0°59′ E 162
Naselle, Wash., U.S. 46°20′ N, 123°49′ W 100
Nash, Tex., U.S. 33°25′ N, 94°9′ W 103
Nashua, Iowa, U.S. 42°56′ N, 92°33′ W 94
Nashua, Mont., U.S. 48°8′ N, 106°24′ W 90
Nashville, Ark., U.S. 33°54′ N, 93°51′ W 96
Nashville, Ga., U.S. 31°11′ N, 83°15′ W 96
Nashville, Ind., U.S. 39°12′ N, 86°15′ W 102
Nashville, Mich., U.S. 42°35′ N, 85°5′ W 102
Nashville, Mo., U.S. 38°20′ N, 89°23′ W 94
Nashville, Tenn., U.S. 36°7′ N, 86°54′ W 96
Nashwaaksis, Can. 45°58′ N, 66°42′ W 94
Našice, Croatia 45°29′ N, 18°5′ E 168
Näsijärvi, lake, Fin. 61°42′ N, 23°24′ E 166
Nasik, India 19°59′ N, 73°46′ E 188
Nasir, Sudan 8°36′ N, 33°4′ E 224
Nasirabad, India 26°16′ N, 74°44′ E 186
Nasiriyah see An Nāşirīyah, Iraq 31°5′ N, 46°11′ E 180
Naskaupi, river, Can. 54°6′ N, 62°58′ W 111
Nasri, spring, Mauritania 19°49′ N, 15°52′ W 222
Nass, river, Can. 56°14′ N, 128°29′ W 108
Nassau, Bahamas 25°4′ N, 77°23′ W 118
Nassau, Ger. 50°19′ N, 7°48′ E 167
Nassau, N.Y., U.S. 42°30′ N, 73°37′ W 104
Nassau, island, American Samoa, U.S. 11°34′ S, 165°33′ W 252
Nassawadox, Va., U.S. 37°28′ N, 75°52′ W 96
Nasser, Lake, Egypt 23°18′ N, 32°21′ E 182
Nassian, Côte d'Ivoire 8°29′ N, 3°29′ W 222
Nässjö, Nor. 57°38′ N, 14°41′ E 152
Nastapoka Islands, islands, Hudson Bay 57°26′ N, 76°40′ W 106
Nastätten, Ger. 50°12′ N, 7°51′ E 167
Næstved, Den. 55°13′ N, 11°45′ E 152
Nasukoin Mountain, peak, Mont., U.S. 48°46′ N, 114°39′ W 90
Nasva, Russ. 56°34′ N, 30°13′ E 166
Näsviken, Nor. 61°43′ N, 16°49′ E 152
Naszály, peak, Hung. 47°50′ N, 19°8′ E 168
Nat, river, Can. 48°49′ N, 82°8′ W 94
Nata, Botswana 20°15′ S, 26°5′ E 227
Natá, Pan. 8°20′ N, 80°31′ W 115
Nata, river, Botswana 19°53′ S, 26°31′ E 224
Natal, Braz. 5°49′ S, 35°12′ W 132
Natal, Braz. 7°0′ S, 60°19′ W 130
Natal, Indonesia 0°36′ N, 99°7′ E 196
Natal'inskiy, Russ. 61°13′ N, 172°5′ E 160
Naţanz, Iran 33°31′ N, 51°55′ E 180
Natara, Russ. 68°19′ N, 124°1′ E 160
Natashquan, Can. 50°11′ N, 61°48′ W 106
Natashquan, Pointe de, Can. 49°58′ N, 61°45′ W 111
Natashquan, river, Can. 52°21′ N, 63°26′ W 111
Natchitoches, La., U.S. 31°45′ N, 93°5′ W 103
Natera, Mex. 22°39′ N, 102°7′ W 114
Natick, Mass., U.S. 42°17′ N, 71°21′ W 104
Natih, oil field, Oman 22°22′ N, 56°41′ E 182
Nation, river, Can. 55°12′ N, 124°23′ W 108
National, Wash., U.S. 46°45′ N, 122°4′ W 100
National Bison Range, site, Mont., U.S. 47°18′ N, 114°20′ W 90
National City, Calif., U.S. 32°40′ N, 117°7′ W 101
National Park, N.Z. 39°13′ S, 175°23′ E 240
Natitiai, Gebel, peak, Egypt 23°2′ N, 34°20′ E 182
Natividade, Braz. 11°41′ S, 47°48′ W 130
Natkyizin, Myanmar 14°55′ N, 97°57′ E 202
Natogami Lake, lake, Can. 50°11′ N, 81°5′ W 94
Natoma, Kans., U.S. 39°11′ N, 99°2′ W 90
Nator, Bangladesh 24°20′ N, 88°54′ E 197
Nattavaara, Nor. 66°44′ N, 20°54′ E 152
Natuna Besar, island, Indonesia 3°37′ N, 108°21′ E 196
Natuna Besar, Kepulauan, islands, Indonesia 4°7′ N, 107°49′ E 196
Natuna Selatan, Kepulauan, islands, South China Sea 2°45′ N, 107°49′ E 196
Naturaliste, Cape, Austral. 33°25′ S, 113°28′ E 230
Naturaliste Plateau, Indian Ocean 34°20′ S, 112°15′ E 254
Naturita, Colo., U.S. 38°12′ N, 108°34′ W 90
Naturno, It. 46°40′ N, 10°59′ E 167
Naubinway, Mich., U.S. 46°5′ N, 85°28′ W 94
Nauchas, Namibia 23°41′ S, 16°20′ E 227
Naufrage, Pointe au, Can. 49°52′ N, 63°31′ W 111
Naugatuck, Conn., U.S. 41°29′ N, 73°4′ W 104
Nauhcampatépetl see Cofre de Perote, peak, Mex. 19°27′ N, 97°13′ W 114
Naujoji Vilnia, Lith. 54°42′ N, 25°24′ E 166
Naulila, Angola 17°12′ S, 14°40′ E 220
Naumburg, Ger. 51°8′ N, 11°48′ E 152
Naumburg, Ger. 51°14′ N, 9°10′ E 167
Naunak, Russ. 58°58′ N, 80°11′ E 169
Naungpale, Myanmar 19°32′ N, 97°6′ E 202
Nā'ūr, Jordan 31°52′ N, 35°49′ E 194
Naurskaya, Russ. 43°33′ N, 45°21′ E 195
Nauru 0°32′ N, 166°55′ E 242
Naushahra, India 33°9′ N, 74°13′ E 186
Naushki, Russ. 50°33′ N, 106°15′ E 190
Naushon Island, Mass., U.S. 41°31′ N, 70°45′ W 104
Nauta, Peru 4°29′ S, 73°37′ W 130
Nautla, Mex. 20°9′ N, 96°47′ W 114
Nautla, river, Mex. 20°7′ N, 97°14′ W 114
Nautsi, Russ. 68°58′ N, 29°0′ E 152
Nauvoo, Mo., U.S. 40°32′ N, 91°23′ W 94
Nava, Mex. 28°24′ N, 100°46′ W 92
Navabelitsa, Belarus 52°22′ N, 31°8′ E 158
Navadwip, India 23°22′ N, 88°18′ E 197
Navahrudak, Belarus 53°36′ N, 25°50′ E 152
Naval, Sp. 42°11′ N, 0°9′ E 164
Naval Submarine Base, Conn., U.S. 41°24′ N, 72°7′ W 104
Navalvillar de Pelea, Sp. 39°5′ N, 5°28′ W 164
Navan (An Uaimh), Ire. 53°38′ N, 6°42′ W 150
Navapolatsk, Belarus 55°30′ N, 28°35′ E 152
Navarin, Mys, Russ. 62°4′ N, 179°6′ E 160
Navarino, Isla, island, Chile 55°25′ S, 67°12′ W 134
Navarra, adm. division, Sp. 42°41′ N, 2°13′ W 164
Navarrenx, Fr. 43°20′ N, 0°47′ E 164
Navarro, Peru 6°20′ S, 75°47′ W 130
Navàs, Sp. 41°54′ N, 1°52′ E 164
Navasota, Tex., U.S. 30°22′ N, 96°5′ W 96
Navassa Island, U.S. 18°25′ N, 75°2′ W 116
Navayel'nya, Belarus 53°29′ N, 25°32′ E 152
Nave, It. 45°35′ N, 10°16′ E 167
Navesti, river, Est. 58°31′ N, 25°1′ E 166
Navia, Arg. 34°46′ S, 66°35′ W 134
Navidad, Chile 34°1′ S, 71°51′ W 134
Navlakhi, India 22°55′ N, 70°31′ E 186
Navlya, Russ. 52°48′ N, 34°32′ E 154
Navoiy, Uzb. 40°6′ N, 65°22′ E 197
Navojoa, Mex. 27°4′ N, 109°27′ W 112
Navrongo, Ghana 10°53′ N, 1°8′ W 222
Navsari, India 20°56′ N, 72°57′ E 186
Nawa, Japan 35°29′ N, 133°30′ E 201
Nawá, Syr. 32°53′ N, 36°3′ E 194
Nawabganj, Bangladesh 24°30′ N, 88°18′ E 197
Nawabganj, India 26°55′ N, 81°14′ E 197
Nawabshah, Pak. 26°15′ N, 68°25′ E 186
Nawada, India 24°51′ N, 85°31′ E 197
Nawah, Afghan. 32°19′ N, 67°52′ E 186
Nawalgarh, India 27°49′ N, 75°16′ E 197
Nawapara, India 20°49′ N, 82°32′ E 188
Naworth Castle, site, U.K. 54°56′ N, 2°48′ W 150
Naxçıvan, Azerb. 39°12′ N, 45°23′ E 195
Naxçıvan, adm. division, Azerb. 39°23′ N, 45°1′ E 195
Naxi, China 28°47′ N, 105°27′ E 198
Náxos, island, Gr. 37°10′ N, 25°35′ E 180
Naxos, ruin(s), It. 37°48′ N, 15°9′ E 156
Nay, Fr. 43°10′ N, 0°16′ E 164
Nāy Band, Iran 32°27′ N, 57°41′ E 186
Nāy Band, Iran 27°22′ N, 52°37′ E 196
Nay, Mui, Vietnam 12°52′ N, 109°29′ E 202
Naya, Col. 3°10′ N, 77°22′ W 136
Nayar, Mex. 22°15′ N, 104°31′ W 114
Nayarit, Mex. 32°20′ N, 115°20′ W 92
Nayarit, adm. division, Mex. 21°46′ N, 105°30′ W 114
Nayba, Russ. 70°43′ N, 130°46′ E 173
Nay Pyi Taw, Myanmar 19°47′ N, 96°8′ E 202
Nazaré, Port. 39°34′ N, 9°5′ W 150
Nazareno, Mex. 25°24′ N, 103°26′ W 114
Nazareth, Ky., U.S. 37°50′ N, 85°29′ W 96
Nazareth see Naẓerat, Israel 32°42′ N, 35°18′ E 194
Nazas, Mex. 25°14′ N, 104°7′ W 114
Nazas, river, Mex. 25°8′ N, 104°32′ W 114
Naze, The, U.K. 51°52′ N, 1°11′ E 162
Naẓerat (Nazareth), Israel 32°42′ N, 35°18′ E 194
Nāzīk, Iran 38°59′ N, 45°0′ E 195
Nazik Gölü, lake, Turk. 38°50′ N, 42°6′ E 195
Nazilli, Turk. 37°55′ N, 28°20′ E 156
Nazımiye, Turk. 39°10′ N, 39°48′ E 195
Nazimovo, Russ. 59°30′ N, 90°52′ E 169
Nazino, Russ. 60°8′ N, 78°55′ E 169
Nazir Hat, Bangladesh 22°35′ N, 91°46′ E 197
Naziya, Russ. 59°49′ N, 31°35′ E 152
Nazko, Can. 52°59′ N, 123°39′ W 108
Nazko, river, Can. 52°54′ N, 123°47′ W 108
Nazrēt, Eth. 8°31′ N, 39°14′ E 224
Nazyvayevsk, Russ. 55°33′ N, 71°24′ E 184
Nchelenge, Zambia 9°21′ S, 28°48′ E 224
Ncheu, Malawi 14°50′ S, 34°40′ E 224
Ncojane, Botswana 23°4′ S, 20°14′ E 227
Ndala, Tanzania 4°45′ S, 33°15′ E 224
N'dalatando, Angola 9°18′ S, 14°54′ E 218
Ndali, Benin 9°50′ N, 2°46′ E 222
Ndande, Senegal 15°17′ N, 16°28′ W 222
Ndélé, Cen. Af. Rep. 8°23′ N, 20°37′ E 218
Ndikiniméki, Cameroon 4°41′ N, 10°49′ E 222
N'Djamena, Chad 12°5′ N, 14°53′ E 218
Ndjolé, Gabon 0°11′ N, 10°41′ E 218
Ndola, Zambia 13°1′ S, 28°39′ E 224
Ndop, Cameroon 5°57′ N, 10°23′ E 222
Ndu, Dem. Rep. of the Congo 4°39′ N, 22°49′ E 218
Ndumbwe, Tanzania 10°15′ S, 39°56′ E 224
Ndumo, S. Af. 26°56′ S, 32°14′ E 227
Nduye, Dem. Rep. of the Congo 1°47′ N, 28°59′ E 224
Né, river, Fr. 45°27′ N, 0°21′ E 150
Neah Bay, Wash., U.S. 48°20′ N, 124°39′ W 100
Neamţ, adm. division, Rom. 47°4′ N, 25°44′ E 156
Near Islands, Bering Sea 53°10′ N, 170°29′ E 160
Nebbou, Burkina Faso 11°19′ N, 1°55′ W 222
Nebdino, Russ. 64°11′ N, 48°4′ E 154
Nebel, Ger. 54°39′ N, 8°22′ E 152
Nebelhorn, peak, Ger. 47°23′ N, 10°15′ E 156
Nebitdag see Balkanabat, Turkm. 39°31′ N, 54°21′ E 180
Neblina, Pico da, peak, Venez. 0°44′ N, 66°8′ W 136
Nebo, La., U.S. 31°34′ N, 92°9′ W 103
Nebo, Mount, peak, Utah, U.S. 39°47′ N, 111°50′ W 90
Nebo, Mount see Nabā, Jabal, peak, Jordan 31°45′ N, 35°43′ E 194
Nebolchi, Russ. 59°6′ N, 33°25′ E 154
Nebraska, adm. division, Nebr., U.S. 41°15′ N, 101°2′ W 90
Nebraska City, Nebr., U.S. 40°40′ N, 95°52′ W 94
Nebrodi, Monti, It. 37°55′ N, 14°11′ E 156
Necedah, Wis., U.S. 44°1′ N, 90°5′ W 102
Neches, Tex., U.S. 31°50′ N, 95°30′ W 103
Neches, river, Tex., U.S. 31°38′ N, 95°16′ W 103
Nechí, Col. 8°4′ N, 74°49′ W 136
Nechi, river, Col. 7°14′ N, 75°17′ W 136
Nechiou, Tun. 34°19′ N, 8°58′ E 156
Nechisar National Park, Eth. 5°50′ N, 37°30′ E 206
Necochea, Arg. 38°33′ S, 58°48′ W 139
Necoclí, Col. 8°27′ N, 76°46′ W 136
Necuto, Angola 4°54′ S, 12°36′ E 218
Nederrijn, river, Neth. 51°55′ N, 5°14′ E 167
Nêdong, China 29°13′ N, 91°44′ E 197
Nedvědice, Czech Rep. 49°26′ N, 16°19′ E 152
Needle Mountain, peak, Wyo., U.S. 44°2′ N, 109°42′ W 90
Needles, Calif., U.S. 34°50′ N, 114°38′ W 101
Needles, The, peak, Calif., U.S. 36°6′ N, 118°32′ W 101
Neenah, Wis., U.S. 44°9′ N, 88°29′ W 102
Neenoshe Reservoir, lake, Colo., U.S. 38°20′ N, 103°2′ W 90
Neepawa, Can. 50°16′ N, 99°29′ W 90
Neermoor, Ger. 53°18′ N, 7°26′ E 163
Neerpelt, Belg. 51°13′ N, 5°25′ E 167
Nefasi, Eritrea 15°15′ N, 39°3′ E 182
Nefedova, Russ. 58°49′ N, 72°38′ E 169
Nefta, Tun. 33°52′ N, 7°53′ E 214
Neftçala, Azerb. 39°23′ N, 49°14′ E 195

Neftegorsk, Russ. 44°19' N, 39°40' E 158
Neftekamsk, Russ. 56°4' N, 54°32' E 154
Neftekumsk, Russ. 44°43' N, 45°5' E 158
Nefteyugansk, Russ. 61°3' N, 72°41' E 169
Nega Nega, Zambia 15°52' S, 28°0' E 220
Negage, Angola 7°47' S, 15°16' E 218
Negaunee, Mich., U.S. 46°30' N, 87°36' W 94
Negev, region, Israel 30°27' N, 34°30' E 194
Negoiul, peak, Rom. 45°34' N, 24°28' E 156
Negola, Angola 14°10' S, 14°28' E 220
Negomano, Mozambique 11°25' S, 38°31' E 224
Negombo, Sri Lanka 7°13' N, 79°53' E 188
Negotin, Serb. 44°13' N, 22°31' E 168
Negotka, Russ. 59°41' N, 80°40' E 169
Negra, Cordillera, Peru 9°45' S, 78°20' W 130
Negra, Laguna, lake, Uru. 34°7' S, 54°12' W 139
Negra, Loma, peak, Sp. 42°3' N, 1°25' W 164
Negra, Punta, Peru 5°56' S, 82°20' W 130
Negra, Serra, Braz. 6°46' S, 47°5' W 130
Negra, Serranía, Bol. 13°39' S, 61°23' W 132
Negreiros, Chile 19°53' S, 69°53' W 137
Negreşti-Oaş, Rom. 47°52' N, 23°25' E 168
Negría, Col. 4°43' N, 76°55' W 136
Negrillos, Bol. 18°50' S, 68°40' W 137
Negrine, Alg. 34°27' N, 7°30' E 214
Negro Mountain, Md., U.S. 39°41' N, 79°27' W 94
Negro, Río, adm. division, Arg. 39°34' S, 64°37' W 139
Negro, river, Arg. 39°44' S, 65°18' W 134
Negro, river, Bol. 14°45' S, 62°49' W 132
Negro, river, Bol. 10°26' S, 65°45' W 137
Negro, river, Braz. 5°22' S, 71°33' W 130
Negro, river, Braz. 0°23' N, 64°46' W 123
Negro, river, Braz. 19°21' S, 57°26' W 132
Negro, river, Guatemala 15°21' N, 91°12' W 115
Negro, river, Parag. 24°5' S, 59°11' W 132
Negro, river, Uru. 32°14' S, 54°53' W 139
Negros, island, Philippines 9°1' N, 121°30' E 192
Negru Vodă, Rom. 43°49' N, 28°12' E 156
Nehalem, Oreg., U.S. 45°42' N, 123°54' W 100
Nehalem, river, Oreg., U.S. 45°45' N, 123°41' W 100
Nehbandān, Iran 31°31' N, 60°4' E 180
Nehe, China 48°30' N, 124°54' E 198
Neheim-HÜsten, Ger. 51°26' N, 7°59' E 167
Nei Mongol, adm. division, China 42°32' N, 114°22' E 198
Neiba, Dom. Rep. 18°27' N, 71°26' W 116
Neihart, Mont., U.S. 46°54' N, 110°45' W 90
Neijiang, China 29°35' N, 105°2' E 198
Neilburg, Can. 52°51' N, 109°37' W 108
Neillsville, Wis., U.S. 44°32' N, 90°35' W 94
Neiqiu, China 37°18' N, 114°31' E 198
Neiva, Col. 2°55' N, 75°17' W 136
Nejanilini Lake, Can. 59°38' N, 98°13' W 108
Nejo, Eth. 9°27' N, 35°28' E 224
Nekalagba, Dem. Rep. of the Congo 2°49' N, 27°57' E 224
Nékaounié, Côte d'Ivoire 5°6' N, 7°27' W 222
Nek'emtē (Lekemt), Eth. 9°2' N, 36°33' E 224
Nekhayevskiy, Russ. 50°23' N, 41°38' E 158
Nekonda, India 17°46' N, 79°47' E 188
Nekoosa, Wis., U.S. 44°18' N, 89°55' W 110
Neksø, Den. 55°3' N, 15°7' E 152
Nelas, Port. 40°31' N, 7°53' W 150
Nelaug, Nor. 58°39' N, 8°38' E 152
Nelidovo, Russ. 56°13' N, 32°55' E 154
Neligh, Nebr., U.S. 42°6' N, 98°2' W 90
Nel'kan, Russ. 57°47' N, 135°57' E 160
Nellimo, Fin. 68°49' N, 28°15' E 152
Nellis Air Force Base, Nev., U.S. 36°13' N, 115°5' W 101
Nellore, India 14°24' N, 79°56' E 188
Nelson, Can. 49°28' N, 117°18' W 90
Nelson, Nebr., U.S. 40°11' N, 98°5' W 90
Nelson, Nev., U.S. 35°42' N, 114°50' W 101
Nelson, Pa., U.S. 41°58' N, 77°14' W 94
Nelson, U.K. 53°50' N, 2°12' W 162
Nelson Forks, Can. 59°30' N, 123°55' W 108
Nelson House, Can. 55°48' N, 98°54' W 108
Nelson Island, Antarctica 62°35' S, 59°3' W 134
Nelson Lagoon, Bristol Bay 55°59' N, 161°14' W 98
Nelson Lake, lake, Wis., U.S. 46°2' N, 91°51' W 94
Nelson Reservoir, lake, Mont., U.S. 48°28' N, 108°15' W 90
Nelson, river, Can. 56°7' N, 95°20' W 106
Nelsons Island, U.K. 5°38' S, 72°12' E 188
Nelsonville, Ohio, U.S. 39°27' N, 82°15' W 102
Nelspruit, S. Af. 25°30' S, 31°0' E 227
Nem, river, Russ. 61°20' N, 55°54' E 154
Néma, Mauritania 16°36' N, 7°13' W 222
Nema, Russ. 57°31' N, 50°35' E 154
Neman, Russ. 55°1' N, 22°1' E 166
Nembe, Nig. 4°33' N, 6°25' E 222
Nemeiben Lake, Can. 55°16' N, 106°14' W 108
Nemenčinė, Lith. 54°51' N, 25°28' E 166
Nementcha, Monts des, Alg. 34°57' N, 5°55' E 214
Nëmerçkë, Mal, Alban. 40°9' N, 19°57' E 156
Nemila, Bosn. and Herzg. 44°18' N, 17°53' E 168
Nemiscau, Can. 51°23' N, 77°0' W 82
Nemor, river, China 48°24' N, 125°22' E 198
Nemours, Fr. 48°15' N, 2°41' E 163
Nemrut Gölü, lake, Turk. 38°36' N, 42°1' E 195
Nemunas, river, Lith. 54°11' N, 24°4' E 166
Nen, river, China 47°45' N, 124°13' E 198
Nene, river, U.K. 52°21' N, 0°36' E 162
Nenets, adm. division, Russ. 66°30' N, 45°3' E 169
Nenjiang, China 49°11' N, 125°14' E 198
Neno, Malawi 15°26' S, 34°38' E 224
Neodesha, Kans., U.S. 37°24' N, 95°41' W 96
Neoga, Ill., U.S. 39°18' N, 88°27' W 102
Neosho, Mo., U.S. 36°51' N, 94°22' W 96
Neosho, river, Kans., U.S. 38°3' N, 95°56' W 80
Ne'ot ha Kikkar, Israel 30°55' N, 35°21' E 194
Nepa, Russ. 59°19' N, 108°22' E 160
Nepal 28°11' N, 83°31' E 188
Nepalganj, Nepal 28°6' N, 81°40' E 197
Nepean, Can. 45°20' N, 75°44' W 94
Nephi, Utah, U.S. 39°42' N, 111°49' W 92
Nephin, peak, Ire. 54°0' N, 9°29' W 150
Nepoko, river, Dem. Rep. of the Congo 2°15' N, 28°25' E 224
Neponset, Ill., U.S. 41°18' N, 89°47' W 102
Neptune, N.J., U.S. 40°12' N, 74°4' W 94
Neptune Islands, islands, Great Australian Bight 35°42' S, 133°49' E 230
Nerău, Rom. 45°58' N, 20°32' E 168
Nerchinsk, Russ. 52°0' N, 116°30' E 190
Nerdva, Russ. 58°44' N, 55°5' E 154
Nerekhta, Russ. 57°25' N, 40°32' E 154
Nereta, Latv. 56°12' N, 25°19' E 166
Neretva, river, Bosn. and Herzg. 43°33' N, 18°5' E 168
Nerezine, Croatia 44°40' N, 14°23' E 156
Neriquinha, Angola 15°54' S, 21°37' E 220
Neris, river, Lith. 55°2' N, 24°18' E 166
Nerja, Sp. 36°44' N, 3°53' W 164
Nérondes, Fr. 46°59' N, 2°48' E 150
Neroy, Russ. 54°31' N, 97°40' E 190
Neroyka, Gora, peak, Russ. 64°35' N, 59°18' E 154
Nerva, Sp. 37°41' N, 6°34' W 164
Neryungri, Russ. 56°43' N, 124°31' E 160
Nes, Neth. 53°26' N, 5°47' E 163
Nes, Nor. 60°33' N, 9°56' E 152
Nes', Russ. 66°37' N, 44°48' E 154
Nesbyen, Nor. 60°33' N, 9°7' E 152
Nesebür (Mesemvria), Bulg. 42°39' N, 27°44' E 156
Neshkan, Russ. 67°0' N, 172°56' W 98
Neshkoro, Wis., U.S. 43°56' N, 89°14' W 102
Neskaupstaður, Ice. 65°7' N, 13°46' W 143
Nesle, Fr. 49°45' N, 2°54' E 163
Nesna, Nor. 66°11' N, 13°0' E 152
Nespelem, Wash., U.S. 48°9' N, 118°59' W 90
Ness City, Kans., U.S. 38°27' N, 99°55' W 90
Nesseby, Nor. 70°9' N, 28°51' E 152
Nesselrode, Mount, peak, Can. 58°57' N, 134°28' W 108
Nestaocano, river, Can. 49°33' N, 73°34' W 94
Nesterov, Russ. 54°38' N, 22°34' E 166
Nestokhoríou, ruin(s), Gr. 41°18' N, 24°6' E 156
Nestor Falls, Can. 49°5' N, 93°55' W 90
Netanya, Israel 32°19' N, 34°51' E 194
Netherlands 52°20' N, 5°27' E 163
Netla, Can. 60°59' N, 123°18' W 108
Nett Lake, Minn., U.S. 48°4' N, 93°30' W 94
Nettancourt, Fr. 48°53' N, 4°55' E 163
Nettetal, Ger. 51°18' N, 6°11' E 167
Nettichi, river, Can. 51°35' N, 81°41' W 110
Nettilling Lake, Can. 67°30' N, 71°20' W 246
Netzahualcóyotl, Mex. 19°21' N, 99°3' W 114
Neu Kaliss, Ger. 53°9' N, 11°19' E 152
Neuchâtel, Switz. 46°59' N, 6°55' E 150
Neuenhaus, Ger. 52°30' N, 6°58' E 163
Neuenkirchen, Ger. 53°14' N, 8°31' E 163
Neuerburg, Ger. 50°0' N, 6°18' E 167
Neufahrn, Ger. 48°44' N, 12°10' E 152
Neufchâteau, Fr. 49°26' N, 4°1' E 163
Neufchâtel, Fr. 49°43' N, 1°26' E 163
Neugablonz, Ger. 47°55' N, 10°38' E 152
Neuhaus, Ger. 50°31' N, 11°8' E 152
Neuhof, Ger. 50°27' N, 9°37' E 167
Neuillé-Pont-Pierre, Fr. 47°32' N, 0°32' E 150
Neuilly-Saint-Front, Fr. 49°9' N, 3°14' E 163
Neu-Isenburg, Ger. 50°2' N, 8°41' E 167
Neukirchen, Ger. 50°52' N, 9°22' E 167
Neumagen-Dhron, Ger. 49°51' N, 6°54' E 167
Neumarkt, Aust. 47°4' N, 14°25' E 156
Neumarkt, Aust. 48°16' N, 13°43' E 152
Neumayer, Germany, station, Antarctica 70°36' S, 8°23' W 248
Neumünster, Ger. 54°4' N, 9°59' E 152
Neun, river, Laos 20°4' N, 103°52' E 202
Neunkirchen, Aust. 47°42' N, 16°4' E 168
Neunkirchen, Ger. 49°19' N, 7°10' E 163
Neuquén, Arg. 38°57' S, 68°6' W 134
Neuquén, adm. division, Arg. 39°6' S, 71°18' W 134
Neureut, Ger. 49°2' N, 8°22' E 163
Neuse River, N.C., U.S. 35°26' N, 78°9' W 80
Neusiedl, Aust. 47°57' N, 16°50' E 168
Neuss, Ger. 51°11' N, 6°42' E 167
Neuvic, Fr. 45°5' N, 0°28' E 150
Neuville, Fr. 45°52' N, 4°51' E 150
Neuville-lès-Dieppe, Fr. 49°55' N, 1°6' E 163
Neuwied, Ger. 50°25' N, 7°27' E 167
Nevada, Iowa, U.S. 41°59' N, 93°27' W 94
Nevada, Mo., U.S. 37°49' N, 94°21' W 96
Nevada, adm. division, Nev., U.S. 39°15' N, 117°48' W 92
Nevada, Sierra, Calif., U.S. 37°27' N, 119°49' W 100
Nevada, Sierra, Sp. 36°53' N, 3°49' W 164
Nevado de Toluca National Park, Mex. 19°1' N, 100°9' W 72
Neve, Serra da, peak, Angola 13°55' S, 13°27' E 220
Nevel', Russ. 56°1' N, 30°0' E 166
Nevel'sk, Russ. 46°42' N, 141°59' E 190
Never, Russ. 53°56' N, 124°27' E 190
Nevers, Fr. 46°59' N, 3°9' E 150
Neves, Braz. 22°49' S, 43°2' W 138
Nevesinje, Bosn. and Herzg. 43°15' N, 18°5' E 168
Nevėžis, river, Lith. 55°26' N, 24°7' E 166
Nevinnomyssk, Russ. 44°39' N, 42°1' E 158
Nevis, Ben, peak, U.K. 56°46' N, 5°7' W 150
Nevis, island, Saint Kitts and Nevis 17°8' N, 62°35' W 118
Nevşehir, Turk. 38°35' N, 34°41' E 156
Nev'yansk, Russ. 57°32' N, 60°13' E 154
New Aiyansh, Can. 55°14' N, 129°4' W 108
New Albany, Ind., U.S. 38°17' N, 85°49' W 94
New Albany, Miss., U.S. 34°28' N, 89°4' W 112
New Amsterdam, Guyana 6°12' N, 57°30' W 130
New Augusta, Miss., U.S. 31°11' N, 89°1' W 103
New Baltimore, Mich., U.S. 42°39' N, 82°44' W 102
New Baltimore, N.Y., U.S. 42°26' N, 73°48' W 104
New Bedford, Mass., U.S. 41°38' N, 70°57' W 104
New Berlin, Wis., U.S. 42°59' N, 88°7' W 102
New Bern, N.C., U.S. 35°6' N, 77°5' W 96
New Boston, N.H., U.S. 42°57' N, 71°42' W 104
New Boston, Ohio, U.S. 38°45' N, 82°54' W 94
New Boston, Tex., U.S. 33°27' N, 94°27' W 103
New Braunfels, Tex., U.S. 29°41' N, 98°7' W 92
New Bremen, Ohio, U.S. 40°25' N, 84°23' W 102
New Britain, Conn., U.S. 41°39' N, 72°47' W 104
New Britain, island, P.N.G. 6°33' S, 151°20' E 192
New Brunswick, N.J., U.S. 40°27' N, 74°29' W 82
New Brunswick, adm. division, Can. 46°41' N, 66°53' W 94
New Buckenham, U.K. 52°28' N, 1°4' E 162
New Buffalo, Mich., U.S. 41°47' N, 86°44' W 102
New Caledonia Basin, South Pacific Ocean 30°55' S, 165°34' E 252
New Caledonia, island, Fr. 21°22' S, 165°30' E 252
New Canaan, Conn., U.S. 41°8' N, 73°30' W 104
New Caney, Tex., U.S. 30°7' N, 95°13' W 103
New Carlisle, Can. 48°0' N, 65°21' W 94
New Castle, Ind., U.S. 39°55' N, 85°22' W 102
New Castle, Pa., U.S. 41°0' N, 80°21' W 94
New City, N.Y., U.S. 41°8' N, 74°0' W 104
New Concord, Ohio, U.S. 39°59' N, 81°44' W 102
New Cuyama, Calif., U.S. 34°56' N, 119°42' W 100
New Delhi, India 28°33' N, 77°3' E 197
New Denver, Can. 49°59' N, 117°23' W 90
New Durham, N.H., U.S. 43°25' N, 71°11' W 104
New England, N. Dak., U.S. 46°32' N, 102°52' W 90
New England Range, Austral. 30°48' S, 150°30' E 230
New England Seamounts, North Atlantic Ocean 38°16' N, 62°9' W 253
New Fairfield, Conn., U.S. 41°26' N, 73°30' W 104
New Forest, region, U.K. 50°47' N, 1°45' W 162
New Forest National Park, U.K. 50°52' N, 1°35' W 162
New Georgia Group, islands, Solomon Sea 8°5' S, 157°19' E 242
New Georgia, island, Solomon Islands 8°20' S, 157°40' E 242
New Georgia Sound (The Slot) 8°11' S, 158°30' E 242
New Glasgow, Can. 45°34' N, 62°40' W 111
New Gloucester, Me., U.S. 43°57' N, 70°17' W 104
New Goshen, Ind., U.S. 39°34' N, 87°28' W 102
New Guinea, island, Indonesia 4°27' S, 131°42' E 192
New Guni, Nig. 9°43' N, 6°56' E 222
New Hamburg, Can. 43°22' N, 80°41' W 102
New Hampshire, adm. division, N.H., U.S. 43°31' N, 71°50' W 104
New Hampton, N.H., U.S. 43°36' N, 71°40' W 104
New Hanover, island, P.N.G. 2°3' S, 149°5' E 192
New Harbor, Me., U.S. 43°52' N, 69°30' W 111
New Hartford, Conn., U.S. 41°52' N, 72°59' W 104
New Haven, Conn., U.S. 41°18' N, 72°56' W 104
New Haven, Ind., U.S. 41°3' N, 85°1' W 102
New Haven, N.Y., U.S. 43°28' N, 76°19' W 94
New Haven, Vt., U.S. 44°7' N, 73°10' W 104
New Hebrides Trench, South Pacific Ocean 23°47' S, 172°15' E 252
New Hebron, Miss., U.S. 31°43' N, 89°59' W 103
New Holstein, Wis., U.S. 43°56' N, 88°6' W 102
New Iberia, La., U.S. 29°58' N, 91°49' W 103
New Ipswich, N.H., U.S. 42°45' N, 71°52' W 104
New Ireland, island, P.N.G. 3°27' S, 149°43' E 192
New Island, New Island 51°50' S, 62°10' W 134
New Jersey, adm. division, N.J., U.S. 41°2' N, 74°51' W 94
New Lebanon, N.Y., U.S. 42°27' N, 73°25' W 104
New Lenox, Ill., U.S. 41°29' N, 87°58' W 102
New Lexington, Ohio, U.S. 39°41' N, 82°12' W 102
New Lisbon, Wis., U.S. 43°51' N, 90°11' W 102
New Liskeard, Can. 47°30' N, 79°41' W 94
New London, Conn., U.S. 41°20' N, 72°7' W 104
New London, N.H., U.S. 43°24' N, 71°59' W 104
New London, Ohio, U.S. 41°4' N, 82°24' W 102
New London, Tex., U.S. 32°14' N, 94°57' W 103
New London, Wis., U.S. 44°23' N, 88°46' W 110
New Madrid, Mo., U.S. 36°35' N, 89°31' W 96
New Market, Ind., U.S. 39°57' N, 86°56' W 102
New Matamoras, Ohio, U.S. 39°31' N, 81°4' W 102
New Meadows, Idaho, U.S. 44°57' N, 116°16' W 90
New Mexico, adm. division, N. Mex., U.S. 34°43' N, 106°25' W 92
New Miami, Ohio, U.S. 39°25' N, 84°32' W 102
New Milford, Conn., U.S. 41°34' N, 73°25' W 104
New Orleans, La., U.S. 29°56' N, 90°5' W 103
New Osnaburgh, Can. 51°12' N, 90°12' W 110
New Paltz, N.Y., U.S. 41°44' N, 74°5' W 104
New Paris, Ohio, U.S. 39°51' N, 84°47' W 102
New Philadelphia, Ohio, U.S. 40°28' N, 81°26' W 102
New Plymouth, Idaho, U.S. 43°57' N, 116°50' W 90
New Plymouth, N.Z. 39°6' S, 174°6' E 240
New Point, Ind., U.S. 39°17' N, 85°20' W 102
New Port Richey, Fla., U.S. 28°15' N, 82°43' W 105
New Prague, Minn., U.S. 44°31' N, 93°36' W 94
New Providence, island, Bahamas 25°1' N, 77°26' W 118
New Radnor, U.K. 52°14' N, 3°9' W 162
New Richmond, Can. 48°10' N, 65°53' W 94
New Richmond, Ohio, U.S. 38°56' N, 84°16' W 102
New Richmond, Wis., U.S. 45°7' N, 92°33' W 94
New, river, Calif., U.S. 33°5' N, 115°43' W 101
New, river, W. Va., U.S. 37°51' N, 81°3' W 94
New Roads, La., U.S. 30°41' N, 91°27' W 103
New Rochelle, N.Y., U.S. 40°55' N, 73°48' W 104
New Rockford, N. Dak., U.S. 47°39' N, 99°10' W 90
New Romney, U.K. 50°59' N, 0°56' E 162
New Salem, Mass., U.S. 42°30' N, 72°20' W 104
New Salem, N. Dak., U.S. 46°49' N, 101°27' W 90
New Schwabenland, region, Antarctica 73°46' S, 13°38' W 248
New Shoreham, R.I., U.S. 41°10' N, 71°34' W 104
New Siberian Islands see Novosi Birskiye Ostrova, Russ. 76°14' N, 142°6' E 160
New Smyrna Beach, Fla., U.S. 29°0' N, 80°56' W 105
New South Wales, adm. division, Austral. 32°28' S, 147°11' E 231
New Summerfield, Tex., U.S. 31°57' N, 95°5' W 103
New Town, N. Dak., U.S. 47°57' N, 102°30' W 90
New Ulm, Minn., U.S. 44°18' N, 94°29' W 90
New Washington, Ind., U.S. 38°33' N, 85°33' W 102
New Waterford, Can. 46°14' N, 60°6' W 111
New Waverly, Tex., U.S. 30°31' N, 95°29' W 103
New Willard, Tex., U.S. 30°46' N, 94°53' W 103
New Windsor, N.Y., U.S. 41°28' N, 74°3' W 104
New York, N.Y., U.S. 40°43' N, 74°1' W 104
New York, adm. division, N.Y., U.S. 42°56' N, 76°33' W 94
New York Mountains, Calif., U.S. 35°22' N, 115°20' W 101
New York Mountains, Calif., U.S. 35°22' N, 115°26' W 80
New Zealand 42°2' S, 173°5' E 240
Newala, Tanzania 10°58' S, 39°16' E 224
Newark, Ark., U.S. 35°41' N, 91°26' W 96
Newark, Ill., U.S. 41°32' N, 88°35' W 102
Newark, N.J., U.S. 40°43' N, 74°12' W 94
Newark, N.Y., U.S. 43°2' N, 77°6' W 94
Newark, Ohio, U.S. 40°3' N, 82°25' W 102
Newark, U.K. 53°4' N, 0°49' E 162
Newaygo, Mich., U.S. 43°24' N, 85°48' W 102
Newbald, U.K. 53°49' N, 0°38' E 162
Newbern, Ala., U.S. 32°35' N, 87°32' W 103
Newbern, Tenn., U.S. 36°6' N, 89°17' W 96
Newberry, Fla., U.S. 29°38' N, 82°37' W 105
Newberry, Mich., U.S. 46°21' N, 85°31' W 94
Newberry Springs, Calif., U.S. 34°49' N, 116°42' W 101
Newbrook, Can. 54°18' N, 112°58' W 108
Newburgh, N.Y., U.S. 41°30' N, 74°2' W 104
Newbury, U.K. 51°23' N, 1°20' W 162
Newbury, Vt., U.S. 44°4' N, 72°4' W 104
Newburyport, Mass., U.S. 42°48' N, 70°53' W 104
Newcastle, Can. 47°0' N, 65°35' W 94
Newcastle, S. Af. 27°46' S, 29°55' E 227
Newcastle, Tex., U.S. 33°10' N, 98°44' W 92
Newcastle, U.K. 54°12' N, 5°55' W 150
Newcastle, U.K. 54°58' N, 1°38' W 150
Newcastle, Wyo., U.S. 43°49' N, 104°12' W 90
Newcastle Bay 10°58' S, 141°25' E 230
Newcastle under Lyme, U.K. 53°0' N, 2°15' W 162
Newcastle Waters, Austral. 17°23' S, 133°23' E 231
Newcomb, N.Y., U.S. 43°57' N, 74°11' W 104
Newcomb, Tenn., U.S. 36°32' N, 84°10' W 96
Newcomerstown, Ohio, U.S. 40°16' N, 81°36' W 102
Newell, Ark., U.S. 33°8' N, 92°45' W 103
Newell, S. Dak., U.S. 44°42' N, 103°25' W 90
Newell, Lake, Can. 50°19' N, 112°29' W 90
Newellton, La., U.S. 32°3' N, 91°16' W 103
Newenham, Cape, Alas., U.S. 58°18' N, 162°19' W 106
Newenham, Cape, Alas., U.S. 58°38' N, 164°32' W 98
Newfields, N.H., U.S. 43°2' N, 70°57' W 104
Newfoundland and Labrador, adm. division, Can. 48°5' N, 58°29' W 111
Newfoundland, Island of, Can. 48°58' N, 53°21' W 106
Newgrange Mound, ruin(s), Ire. 53°40' N, 6°36' W 150
Newhalem, Wash., U.S. 48°40' N, 121°17' W 100
Newhalen, Alas., U.S. 59°39' N, 155°1' W 98
Newhaven, U.K. 50°47' N, 4°238' E 162
Newington, Conn., U.S. 41°41' N, 72°44' W 104
Newkirk, N. Mex., U.S. 35°4' N, 104°16' W 92
Newkirk, Okla., U.S. 36°52' N, 97°3' W 92
Newllano, La., U.S. 31°5' N, 93°17' W 103
Newman, Calif., U.S. 37°18' N, 121°3' W 100
Newman, Ill., U.S. 39°47' N, 88°0' W 102
Newman Island, island, Antarctica 75°13' S, 146°2' W 248
Newman, Mount, peak, Austral. 23°17' S, 119°19' E 230
Newmarket, Can. 44°2' N, 79°28' W 94
Newmarket, N.H., U.S. 43°4' N, 70°57' W 104
Newmarket, U.K. 52°14' N, 0°24' E 162
Newnan, Ga., U.S. 33°22' N, 84°48' W 112
Newport, Ark., U.S. 35°34' N, 91°18' W 82
Newport, Ind., U.S. 39°51' N, 87°25' W 102
Newport, Mich., U.S. 41°59' N, 83°18' W 102
Newport, N.H., U.S. 43°22' N, 72°11' W 104
Newport, Oreg., U.S. 44°38' N, 124°5' W 82
Newport, R.I., U.S. 41°29' N, 71°19' W 104
Newport, Tenn., U.S. 35°57' N, 83°12' W 96
Newport, U.K. 50°41' N, 1°18' W 162
Newport, U.K. 51°35' N, 3°0' W 162
Newport, U.K. 52°45' N, 2°23' W 162
Newport, Vt., U.S. 44°56' N, 72°13' W 82
Newport, Wash., U.S. 48°10' N, 117°4' W 108
Newport Beach, Calif., U.S. 33°38' N, 117°57' W 101
Newport News, Va., U.S. 36°58' N, 76°26' W 94
Newport Pagnell, U.K. 52°4' N, 0°44' E 162
Newry, Me., U.S. 44°29' N, 70°48' W 104
Newry, S.C., U.S. 34°43' N, 82°56' W 96
Newsome, Tex., U.S. 32°57' N, 95°8' W 103
Newtok, Alas., U.S. 60°57' N, 164°37' W 98
Newton, Ill., U.S. 38°58' N, 88°11' W 102
Newton, Iowa, U.S. 41°41' N, 93°3' W 94
Newton, Kans., U.S. 38°2' N, 97°21' W 90
Newton, Mass., U.S. 42°19' N, 71°15' W 104
Newton, Miss., U.S. 32°18' N, 89°9' W 103
Newton, Mo., U.S. 38°58' N, 88°11' W 94
Newton, Tex., U.S. 30°49' N, 93°46' W 103
Newton Falls, Ohio, U.S. 41°10' N, 80°58' W 102

Newtown, Conn., U.S. 41°24′ N, 73°19′ W 104
Newtown, U.K. 52°30′ N, 3°18′ W 162
New-Wes-Valley, Can. 49°9′ N, 53°35′ W 111
Nexpa, river, Mex. 18°7′ N, 102°40′ W 114
Neya, Russ. 58°17′ N, 43°52′ E 154
Neyrīz, Iran 29°12′ N, 54°18′ E 196
Neyshābūr, Iran 36°12′ N, 58°51′ E 180
Neyto, Ozero, lake, Russ. 69°51′ N, 68°36′ E 169
Neyvo Shaytanskiy, Russ. 57°46′ N, 61°14′ E 154
Nez Perce Pass, Mont., U.S. 45°42′ N, 114°31′ W 90
Nezperce, Idaho, U.S. 46°13′ N, 116°14′ W 90
N'Gabé, Congo 3°14′ S, 16°8′ E 218
Ngahere, N.Z. 42°25′ S, 171°27′ E 240
Ngambé, Cameroon 4°15′ N, 10°39′ E 222
Ngamda, China 31°5′ N, 96°37′ E 188
Ngamring, China 29°17′ N, 87°11′ E 197
Ngangla Ringco, lake, China 31°40′ N, 82°35′ E 188
Nganglong Kangri, peak, China 32°50′ N, 80°41′ E 188
Ngangzê Co, lake, China 30°56′ N, 86°20′ E 197
N'Gao, Congo 2°30′ S, 15°45′ E 218
Ngao, Thai. 18°46′ N, 99°57′ E 202
Ngaoundal, Cameroon 6°26′ N, 13°25′ E 218
Ngaoundéré, Cameroon 7°16′ N, 13°34′ E 218
Ngaputaw, Myanmar 16°31′ N, 94°42′ E 188
Ngara, Tanzania 2°31′ S, 30°39′ E 224
Ngaruawahia, N.Z. 37°43′ S, 175°10′ E 240
Ngauruhoe, Mount, peak, N.Z. 39°12′ S, 175°32′ E 240
Ngayu, river, Dem. Rep. of the Congo 1°53′ N, 27°25′ E 224
Ngcheangel, island, Palau 8°4′ N, 134°43′ E 242
Ngeaur see Angaur, island, Palau 7°0′ N, 134°0′ E 242
Ngerengere, Tanzania 6°42′ S, 38°7′ E 224
Ngeruktabel (Urukthapel), island, Palau 7°13′ N, 134°24′ E 242
Nggatokae, island, Solomon Islands 8°45′ S, 158°10′ E 242
Nghia Lo, Vietnam 21°37′ N, 104°28′ E 202
Ngoïla, Cameroon 2°45′ N, 14°0′ E 218
Ngoko, Congo 0°35′ N, 15°21′ E 218
Ngola Shankou, pass, China 35°30′ N, 99°28′ E 188
Ngomba, Tanzania 8°25′ S, 32°54′ E 224
Ngomeni, Ras, Kenya 2°59′ S, 40°14′ E 224
Ngong, Kenya 1°23′ S, 36°40′ E 224
Ngop, Sudan 6°13′ N, 30°10′ E 224
Ngoqumaima, China 32°30′ N, 86°51′ E 188
Ngorno-Karabakh, special sovereignty, Asia 39°59′ N, 46°23′ E 195
Ngorongoro Crater, peak, Tanzania 3°15′ S, 35°31′ E 224
Ngote, Dem. Rep. of the Congo 2°12′ N, 30°48′ E 224
Ngoto, Cen. Af. Rep. 4°4′ N, 17°18′ E 218
Ngouo, Mont, peak, Cen. Af. Rep. 7°55′ N, 24°32′ E 224
Ngouri, Chad 13°39′ N, 15°23′ E 216
Ngourti, Niger 15°19′ N, 13°11′ E 216
Ngoywa, Tanzania 5°55′ S, 32°47′ E 224
Ngozi, Burundi 2°56′ S, 29°47′ E 224
Ngudu, Tanzania 2°56′ S, 33°21′ E 224
Nguigmi, Niger 14°17′ N, 13°6′ E 216
Ngukurr, Austral. 14°44′ S, 134°46′ E 238
Ngulu Atoll, F.S.M. 8°42′ N, 134°55′ E 192
Ngum, river, Laos 18°47′ N, 102°47′ E 202
N'gungo, Angola 11°47′ S, 14°9′ E 220
Nguni, Kenya 0°49′ N, 38°17′ E 224
Nguru, Nig. 12°53′ N, 10°28′ E 222
Ngurumahiga, Tanzania 10°18′ S, 37°57′ E 224
Nha Trang, Vietnam 12°15′ N, 109°10′ E 202
Nhamundá, Braz. 2°13′ S, 56°44′ W 130
Nhamundá, river, Braz. 1°33′ S, 58°0′ W 132
Nhecolândia, Braz. 19°15′ S, 57°1′ W 132
Nho Quan, Vietnam 20°20′ N, 105°45′ E 202
Nhulunbuy, Austral. 12°18′ S, 136°48′ E 238
Nia Nia, Dem. Rep. of the Congo 1°29′ N, 27°40′ E 224
Niabembe, Dem. Rep. of the Congo 2°11′ S, 27°40′ E 224
Niadi, Dem. Rep. of the Congo 4°25′ S, 18°50′ E 218
Niafounké, Mali 15°56′ N, 4°1′ W 222
Niagassola, Guinea 12°20′ N, 9°8′ W 222
Niamey, Niger 13°29′ N, 2°0′ E 222
Niandan Koro, Guinea 11°6′ N, 9°14′ W 222
Niangara, Dem. Rep. of the Congo 3°41′ N, 27°53′ E 224
Niangay, Lac, lake, Mali 15°54′ N, 3°22′ W 222
Niangoloko, Burkina Faso 10°17′ N, 4°56′ W 222
Niantic, Conn., U.S. 41°19′ N, 72°12′ W 104
Niantic, Ill., U.S. 39°50′ N, 89°10′ W 102
Nianzishan, China 47°33′ N, 122°54′ E 198
Niapidou, Côte d'Ivoire 5°18′ N, 6°3′ W 222
Niapu, Dem. Rep. of the Congo 2°24′ N, 26°32′ E 224
Niari, river, Congo 3°33′ S, 12°45′ E 218
Nias, island, Indonesia 0°26′ N, 97°33′ E 196
Niassa, adm. division, Mozambique 12°52′ S, 35°24′ E 224
Niaza, spring, Mauritania 18°13′ N, 11°0′ W 222
Nīca, Latv. 56°21′ N, 21°1′ E 166
Nicaragua 12°38′ N, 85°49′ W 115
Nicaragua, Lago de, Nicar. 11°30′ N, 85°30′ W 116
Nice, Fr. 43°42′ N, 7°15′ E 165
Nichihara, Japan 34°31′ N, 131°51′ E 201
Nichinan, Japan 31°36′ N, 131°21′ E 201
Nicholasville, Ky., U.S. 37°52′ N, 84°34′ W 96
Nicholls' Town, Bahamas 25°7′ N, 78°2′ W 96
Nichollstown and Berry Islands, adm. division, Bahamas 25°47′ N, 78°22′ W 96
Nicholson, Can. 47°58′ N, 83°46′ W 94
Nickel Centre, Can. 46°33′ N, 80°52′ W 94
Nickelsdorf, Aust. 47°56′ N, 17°4′ E 168
Nickerson, Kans., U.S. 38°8′ N, 98°6′ W 90
Nickol Bay 20°40′ S, 115°56′ E 230
Nicobar Islands, Andaman Sea 8°59′ N, 93°39′ E 192
Nicolás Bravo, Mex. 24°21′ N, 104°44′ W 114
Nicolet, Can. 46°13′ N, 72°37′ W 94
Nicopolis, ruin(s), Gr. 38°59′ N, 20°37′ E 156
Nicopolis see Suşehri, Turk. 40°8′ N, 38°5′ E 180
Nicosia see Lefkosia, Cyprus 35°9′ N, 33°18′ E 194
Nicotera, It. 38°34′ N, 15°55′ E 156
Nicoya, C.R. 10°8′ N, 85°26′ W 115
Nicuadala, Mozambique 17°38′ S, 36°48′ E 224
Nida, Russ. 55°19′ N, 21°2′ E 166
Nidda, Ger. 50°24′ N, 9°1′ E 167
Niddatal, Ger. 50°17′ N, 8°48′ E 167
Nidder, river, Ger. 50°22′ N, 9°3′ E 167
Nidže, Maced. 41°1′ N, 21°41′ E 156
Nidzh, Azerb. 40°57′ N, 47°39′ E 195
Niebla, Sp. 37°21′ N, 6°42′ W 164
Niechorze, Pol. 54°5′ N, 15°4′ E 152
Nied, river, Fr. 49°5′ N, 6°20′ E 163
Nieddu, Monte, peak, It. 40°44′ N, 9°30′ E 156
Niederaula, Ger. 50°48′ N, 9°35′ E 167
Niederbronn, Fr. 48°57′ N, 7°38′ E 163
Niedere Tauern, Aust. 47°11′ N, 13°24′ E 156
Niedoradz, Pol. 51°52′ N, 15°40′ E 152
Niéjirane, spring, Mauritania 17°32′ N, 9°51′ W 222
Niem, Cen. Af. Rep. 6°5′ N, 15°15′ E 218
Niemba, Dem. Rep. of the Congo 5°59′ S, 28°24′ E 224
Niéna, Mali 11°26′ N, 6°21′ W 222
Niers, river, Ger. 51°41′ N, 5°58′ E 167
Nierstein, Ger. 49°52′ N, 8°20′ E 167
Nieuw Amsterdam, Suriname 5°50′ N, 55°6′ W 130
Nieuwe Pekela, Neth. 53°4′ N, 6°56′ E 163
Nieuwpoort, Belg. 51°7′ N, 2°44′ E 163
Nieves, Bol. 14°5′ S, 65°54′ W 137
Nieves, Mex. 24°0′ N, 103°2′ W 114
Nif, Indonesia 3°19′ S, 130°34′ E 192
Niğde, Turk. 37°58′ N, 34°42′ E 180
Niger 17°56′ N, 8°41′ E 216
Niger Delta, Nig. 5°29′ N, 6°7′ E 222
Niger, river, Africa 5°54′ N, 6°33′ E 222
Nigeria 9°25′ N, 6°46′ E 218
Nightingale Island see Bach Long Vi, Dao, Vietnam 19°46′ N, 107°30′ E 198
Nihonmatsu, Japan 37°35′ N, 140°26′ E 201
Niigata, Japan 37°55′ N, 139°5′ E 201
Niigata, adm. division, Japan 37°27′ N, 138°42′ E 201
Niihama, Japan 33°56′ N, 133°17′ E 201
Ni'ihau, island, Hawai'i, U.S. 21°36′ N, 160°11′ W 99
Niimi, Japan 35°0′ N, 133°28′ E 201
Niitsu, Japan 37°47′ N, 139°8′ E 201
Nijar, Sp. 36°57′ N, 2°13′ W 164
Nijmegen, Neth. 51°50′ N, 5°51′ E 167
Nikel', Russ. 69°24′ N, 30°10′ E 152
Nikiniki, Indonesia 9°49′ S, 124°28′ E 192
Nikiski, Gulf of Alaska 60°43′ N, 151°18′ W 98
Nikitin Seamount, Indian Ocean 3°48′ S, 82°58′ E 254
Nikki, Benin 9°56′ N, 3°9′ E 222
Nikkō, Japan 36°43′ N, 139°37′ E 201
Nikkō National Park, Japan 37°3′ N, 139°40′ E 201
Nikolai, Alas., U.S. 63°0′ N, 154°11′ W 98
Nikolayevo, Russ. 58°15′ N, 29°28′ E 166
Nikolayevsk, Russ. 50°3′ N, 45°33′ E 158
Nikolayevsk na Amure, Russ. 53°14′ N, 140°36′ E 190
Nikolo Berezovka, Russ. 56°6′ N, 54°18′ E 154
Nikol'sk, Russ. 53°41′ N, 46°7′ E 154
Nikol'sk, Russ. 59°30′ N, 45°32′ E 154
Nikol'skoye, Russ. 52°4′ N, 55°42′ E 154
Nikol'skoye, Russ. 47°43′ N, 46°21′ E 158
Nikol'skoye, Russ. 55°13′ N, 165°54′ E 160
Nikonga, river, Tanzania 4°2′ S, 31°30′ E 224
Nikopol', Ukr. 47°34′ N, 34°24′ E 156
Nikpey, Iran 36°52′ N, 48°12′ E 195
Niksar, Turk. 40°35′ N, 36°57′ E 156
Nīkshahr, Iran 26°13′ N, 60°13′ E 182
Nikšić, Mont. 42°46′ N, 18°56′ E 168
Nikulino, Russ. 60°21′ N, 90°1′ E 169
Niland, Calif., U.S. 33°14′ N, 115°32′ W 101
Nilandu Atoll, Maldives 2°56′ N, 72°16′ E 188
Nilandu, island, Maldives 0°27′ N, 73°24′ E 188
Nile, river, Africa 27°17′ N, 31°18′ E 206
Niles, Mich., U.S. 41°48′ N, 86°15′ W 102
Niles, Ohio, U.S. 41°10′ N, 80°45′ W 94
Nili, Alg. 33°24′ N, 3°2′ E 214
Nilka, China 43°47′ N, 82°38′ E 184
Nilsen, Mount, peak, Antarctica 77°54′ S, 154°11′ W 248
Nilsen Plateau, Antarctica 86°27′ S, 180°0′ E 248
Nilsiä, Fin. 63°10′ N, 28°0′ E 152
Nimach, India 24°27′ N, 74°51′ E 188
Nimba Mountains, Guinea 8°22′ N, 9°5′ W 222
Nimbahera, India 24°38′ N, 74°40′ E 188
Nimberra Well, spring, Austral. 23°6′ S, 123°18′ E 230
Nîmes, Fr. 43°49′ N, 4°22′ E 214
Nimfai, Gr. 39°45′ N, 19°47′ E 156
Nimule, Sudan 3°34′ N, 32°5′ E 224
Nin, Croatia 44°14′ N, 15°9′ E 156
Ninayeri, Nicar. 14°27′ N, 83°18′ W 115
Ninda, Angola 14°54′ S, 21°25′ E 220
Nine Degree Channel 8°40′ N, 71°55′ E 188
Ninemile Peak, Nev., U.S. 39°8′ N, 116°20′ W 90
Ninety East Ridge, Indian Ocean 8°11′ S, 88°50′ E 254
Ninety Mile Beach, N.Z. 35°3′ S, 172°43′ E 240
Nineveh, ruin(s), Iraq 36°21′ N, 42°59′ E 195
Ninfas, Punta, Arg. 43°10′ S, 64°20′ W 134
Ning'an, China 44°20′ N, 129°32′ E 190
Ningbo, China 29°54′ N, 121°29′ E 198
Ningcheng, China 41°34′ N, 119°20′ E 198
Ningde, China 26°40′ N, 119°31′ E 198
Ningdu, China 26°26′ N, 115°55′ E 198
Ningguo, China 30°34′ N, 119°1′ E 198
Ningi, Nig. 11°3′ N, 9°32′ E 222
Ningming, China 22°5′ N, 107°1′ E 198
Ningshan, China 33°20′ N, 108°19′ E 198
Ningwu, China 39°0′ N, 112°13′ E 198
Ningxia, adm. division, China 36°46′ N, 105°17′ E 198
Ningyuan, China 25°36′ N, 111°56′ E 198
Ninh Binh, Vietnam 20°14′ N, 105°56′ E 198
Ninh Hoa, Vietnam 12°30′ N, 109°8′ E 202
Ninigo Group, islands, South Pacific Ocean 0°49′ N, 142°30′ E 192
Ninigo Islands, islands, South Pacific Ocean 1°10′ S, 142°49′ E 192
Ninilchik, Gulf of Alaska 60°3′ N, 151°39′ W 98
Nioaque, Braz. 21°9′ S, 55°50′ W 132
Niobrara, river, Nebr., U.S. 42°37′ N, 102°2′ W 90
Nioka, Dem. Rep. of the Congo 2°8′ N, 30°39′ E 224
Nioki, Dem. Rep. of the Congo 2°44′ S, 17°38′ E 218
Niokolo-Koba National Park, Senegal 13°2′ N, 13°30′ W 222
Niono, Mali 14°16′ N, 6°0′ W 222
Nioro du Sahel, Mali 15°14′ N, 9°38′ W 222
Niort, Fr. 46°19′ N, 0°28′ E 150
Niout, spring, Mauritania 16°3′ N, 6°52′ W 222
Nipa, oil field, Venez. 9°6′ N, 64°8′ W 116
Nipani, India 16°24′ N, 74°23′ E 188
Nipawin, Can. 53°21′ N, 104°1′ W 108
Nipigon, Can. 49°1′ N, 88°16′ W 94
Nipigon Bay 48°50′ N, 89°13′ W 80
Nipigon, Lake, Can. 50°12′ N, 88°35′ W 94
Nipin, river, Can. 55°24′ N, 109°25′ W 108
Nipissing, Lake, Can. 46°12′ N, 80°13′ W 80
Nipomo, Calif., U.S. 35°2′ N, 120°29′ W 100
Nipple, The, peak, Can. 49°56′ N, 121°38′ W 100
Nipton, Calif., U.S. 35°27′ N, 115°17′ W 101
Niquelândia, Braz. 14°33′ S, 48°30′ W 138
Niquero, Cuba 20°2′ N, 77°34′ W 115
Nīr, Iran 38°3′ N, 47°59′ E 195
Nir Yizḥaq, Israel 31°14′ N, 34°21′ E 194
Nir'am, Israel 31°30′ N, 34°34′ E 194
Nirasaki, Japan 35°41′ N, 138°27′ E 201
Ñire Có, Arg. 37°0′ S, 68°28′ W 134
Nirji see Morin Dawa, China 48°27′ N, 124°30′ E 198
Nirmal, India 19°6′ N, 78°20′ E 188
Nirmali, India 26°18′ N, 86°34′ E 197
Niš, Serb. 43°18′ N, 21°54′ E 168
Niṣāb, Saudi Arabia 29°8′ N, 44°44′ E 180
Niṣāb, Yemen 14°31′ N, 46°33′ E 182
Nišava, river, Serb. 43°18′ N, 22°7′ E 168
Nishi Nasuno, Japan 36°52′ N, 139°58′ E 201
Nishikō, Japan 32°36′ N, 130°27′ E 201
Nishinomiya, Japan 34°44′ N, 135°18′ E 201
Nishio, Japan 34°50′ N, 137°4′ E 201
Nishiwaki, Japan 34°58′ N, 134°57′ E 201
Nishtūn, Yemen 15°48′ N, 52°10′ E 182
Niska, Fin. 64°35′ N, 26°33′ E 152
Niskayuna, N.Y., U.S. 42°45′ N, 73°51′ W 104
Nissedal, Nor. 59°9′ N, 8°30′ E 152
Nissi, Est. 59°4′ N, 24°17′ E 166
Nissilä, Fin. 63°56′ N, 26°48′ E 152
Nisswa, Minn., U.S. 46°30′ N, 94°18′ W 90
Niṭā', Saudi Arabia 27°10′ N, 48°23′ E 196
Nītaure, Latv. 57°3′ N, 25°7′ E 166
Nitchequon, Can. 53°12′ N, 70°53′ W 111
Niterói, Braz. 22°56′ S, 43°3′ W 138
Nitmiluk National Park, Austral. 14°16′ S, 132°7′ E 238
Nitra, Slovakia 48°18′ N, 18°6′ E 168
Nitransky, adm. division, Slovakia 48°10′ N, 17°51′ E 152
Nitro, W. Va., U.S. 38°25′ N, 81°51′ W 94
Nitsa, river, Russ. 57°45′ N, 63°3′ E 154
Niue, island, N.Z. 18°58′ S, 169°55′ W 238
Niut, peak, Indonesia 0°59′ N, 109°50′ E 196
Niutou Shan, island, China 28°54′ N, 121°49′ E 198
Niuxintai, China 41°20′ N, 123°55′ E 200
Niva, Fin. 65°9′ N, 28°21′ E 152
Niva, Russ. 61°36′ N, 30°14′ E 166
Nivala, Fin. 63°54′ N, 24°55′ E 152
Nivelles, Belg. 50°35′ N, 4°19′ E 163
Nivernais, region, Fr. 47°30′ N, 3°17′ E 165
Nivshera, Russ. 62°24′ N, 53°1′ E 154
Nixon, Tex., U.S. 29°15′ N, 97°45′ W 92
Nizamabad, India 18°40′ N, 78°5′ E 188
Nizamghat, India 28°14′ N, 95°43′ E 188
Nizao, Dom. Rep. 18°14′ N, 70°13′ W 116
Nizhnekamsk, Russ. 55°33′ N, 51°53′ E 154
Nizhneshadrino, Russ. 59°53′ N, 90°38′ E 169
Nizhneudinsk, Russ. 54°53′ N, 99°14′ E 190
Nizhnevartovsk, Russ. 60°54′ N, 76°35′ E 169
Nizhniy Baskunchak, Russ. 48°11′ N, 46°42′ E 158
Nizhniy Lomov, Russ. 53°30′ N, 43°40′ E 154
Nizhniy Novgorod, Russ. 56°15′ N, 44°0′ E 154
Nizhniy Novgorod, adm. division, Russ. 56°0′ N, 43°9′ E 154
Nizhniy Tagil, Russ. 57°56′ N, 59°59′ E 154
Nizhniy Ufaley, Russ. 55°56′ N, 60°3′ E 154
Nizhniye Nikulyasy, Russ. 60°27′ N, 30°44′ E 152
Nizhniye Sergi, Russ. 56°40′ N, 59°16′ E 154
Nizhnyaya Mgla, Russ. 66°29′ N, 44°27′ E 154
Nizhnyaya Omra, Russ. 62°46′ N, 55°51′ E 154
Nizhnyaya Pesha, Russ. 66°46′ N, 47°38′ E 154
Nizhnyaya Salda, Russ. 58°5′ N, 60°44′ E 154
Nizhnyaya Tunguska, river, Russ. 64°30′ N, 90°34′ E 169
Nizhnyaya Tura, Russ. 58°41′ N, 59°49′ E 154
Nizhnyaya Voch', Russ. 61°12′ N, 54°11′ E 154
Nizhyn, Ukr. 51°2′ N, 31°53′ E 158
Nizi, Dem. Rep. of the Congo 1°44′ N, 30°17′ E 224
Nizip, Turk. 36°58′ N, 37°50′ E 180
Nizke Tatry, Slovakia 48°51′ N, 19°24′ E 152
Nizwá, Oman 22°55′ N, 57°31′ E 182
Nizza Monferrato, It. 44°46′ N, 8°21′ E 167
Nizzana (El'Auja), Israel 30°52′ N, 34°25′ E 194
Njazidja (Grande Comore), island, Comoros 11°46′ S, 43°35′ E 220
Njegoš, peak, Mont. 42°54′ N, 18°43′ E 168
Njegoševo, Serb. 45°45′ N, 19°44′ E 168
Njombe, Tanzania 9°22′ S, 34°45′ E 224
Njombe, river, Tanzania 7°22′ S, 34°8′ E 224
Njunnesvarre, peak, Nor. 68°45′ N, 19°17′ E 152
Njurunda, Nor. 62°14′ N, 17°20′ E 152
Nkambe, Cameroon 6°29′ N, 10°43′ E 222
Nkawkaw, Ghana 6°33′ N, 0°46′ E 222
Nkayi, Zimb. 19°3′ S, 28°55′ E 224
Nkhata Bay, Malawi 11°35′ S, 34°17′ E 224
Nkhotakota, Malawi 12°56′ S, 34°15′ E 224
Nkhunga, Malawi 12°29′ S, 34°3′ E 224
Nkongsamba, Cameroon 4°53′ N, 9°56′ E 222
Nkoul, Cameroon 3°30′ N, 13°33′ E 218
Nkululu, river, Tanzania 6°19′ S, 32°39′ E 224
Nkundi, Tanzania 7°50′ S, 31°25′ E 224
Nkurenkuru, Namibia 17°39′ S, 18°36′ E 220
Nkusi, river, Uganda 1°8′ N, 30°56′ E 224
No, Lake, Sudan 9°22′ N, 30°7′ E 224
Noamundi, India 22°11′ N, 85°31′ E 197
Noarvas, peak, Nor. 68°47′ N, 24°35′ E 152
Noatak, Alas., U.S. 67°29′ N, 163°5′ W 98
Noatak, river, Alas., U.S. 68°4′ N, 159°51′ W 98
Nobeoka, Japan 32°35′ N, 131°39′ E 201
Noble, Ill., U.S. 38°41′ N, 88°14′ W 102
Noble, La., U.S. 31°40′ N, 93°42′ W 103
Noblesville, Ind., U.S. 40°2′ N, 86°0′ W 102
Nobska Point, Mass., U.S. 41°28′ N, 70°40′ W 104
Nocatee, Fla., U.S. 27°10′ N, 81°53′ W 105
Noce, river, It. 46°16′ N, 10°59′ E 167
Noceto, It. 44°48′ N, 10°10′ E 167
Nochistlán, Mex. 21°20′ N, 102°52′ W 114
Nochixtlán, Mex. 17°26′ N, 97°14′ W 114
Nocona, Tex., U.S. 33°46′ N, 97°42′ W 92
Nodales, Bahía de los 48°5′ S, 67°43′ W 134
Nodaway, river, Iowa, U.S. 40°1′ N, 95°9′ W 80
Noel Kempff Mercado National Park, Bol. 14°31′ S, 62°11′ W 132
Noel, Mount, peak, Can. 50°43′ N, 122°56′ W 90
Noelville, Can. 46°7′ N, 80°26′ W 94
Nofre, Peña, peak, Sp. 42°0′ N, 7°26′ W 150
Nogales, Ariz., U.S. 31°21′ N, 110°57′ W 112
Nogales, Mex. 31°17′ N, 110°57′ W 92
Nogara, It. 45°10′ N, 11°3′ E 167
Nōgata, Japan 33°43′ N, 130°42′ E 200
Nogayskaya Step', Russ. 44°29′ N, 46°3′ E 180
Nogayty, Kaz. 45°17′ N, 55°55′ E 158
Nogent-le-Roi, Fr. 48°38′ N, 1°32′ E 163
Nogent-le-Rotrou, Fr. 48°19′ N, 0°49′ E 163
Nogent-sur-Seine, Fr. 48°29′ N, 3°30′ E 163
Noginsk, Russ. 64°25′ N, 91°16′ E 169
Nogliki, Russ. 51°47′ N, 143°4′ E 190
Nógrád, adm. division, Hung. 47°58′ N, 19°1′ E 156
Nohar, India 29°11′ N, 74°47′ E 186
Nohfelden, Ger. 49°34′ N, 7°8′ E 163
Nohona o Hae, peak, Hawai'i, U.S. 19°54′ N, 155°44′ W 99
Noia, Sp. 42°47′ N, 8°55′ W 150
Noir, Isla, island, Chile 54°23′ S, 74°10′ W 134
Noire, Montagne, peak, Fr. 43°25′ N, 2°25′ E 165
Noire, river, Can. 46°46′ N, 77°41′ W 94
Noires, Montagnes, Fr. 48°2′ N, 4°9′ W 150
Nojima Zaki, Japan 34°45′ N, 139°53′ E 201
Nok Kundi, Pak. 28°49′ N, 62°47′ E 182
Nokaneng, Botswana 19°41′ S, 22°11′ E 220
Nokara, Mali 15°10′ N, 2°24′ W 222
Nokia, Fin. 61°28′ N, 23°31′ E 166
Nokola, Russ. 61°10′ N, 38°51′ E 154
Nokomis, Can. 51°30′ N, 105°2′ W 90
Nokomis, Ill., U.S. 39°17′ N, 89°17′ W 102
Nokou, Chad 14°35′ N, 14°45′ E 216
Nola, Cen. Af. Rep. 3°42′ N, 16°5′ E 218
Noli, It. 44°12′ N, 8°25′ E 167
Nolinsk, Russ. 57°33′ N, 49°57′ E 154
Noma Misaki, Japan 31°16′ N, 129°55′ E 201
Nomans Land, island, Mass., U.S. 41°11′ N, 70°52′ W 104
Nomansland Point, Can. 52°1′ N, 81°2′ W 110
Nombre de Dios, Mex. 23°49′ N, 104°14′ W 114
Nombre de Dios, Mex. 28°42′ N, 106°7′ W 92
Nome, Alas., U.S. 64°25′ N, 165°28′ W 98
Nome, Tex., U.S. 30°1′ N, 94°26′ W 103
Nome Lake, Can. 59°38′ N, 131°35′ W 108
Nomgon, Mongolia 42°52′ N, 104°53′ E 198
Nomhon, China 36°22′ N, 96°26′ E 188
Nomhon, river, China 36°31′ N, 96°27′ E 188
Nomo Saki, Japan 32°28′ N, 129°35′ E 201
Nomoneas, island, F.S.M. 7°25′ N, 151°52′ E 242
Nomwin Atoll, F.S.M. 9°13′ N, 150°41′ E 192
Nonancourt, Fr. 48°46′ N, 1°12′ E 163
Nonburg, Russ. 65°33′ N, 50°32′ E 154
Nondalton, Alas., U.S. 59°56′ N, 155°0′ W 98
Nong Khai, Thai. 17°52′ N, 102°44′ E 202
Nong'an, China 44°27′ N, 125°11′ E 198
Nongoma, S. Af. 27°54′ S, 31°37′ E 227
Nongpoh, India 25°51′ N, 91°51′ E 197
Nono, Eth. 8°30′ N, 37°22′ E 224
Nonoava, Mex. 27°28′ N, 106°44′ W 112
Nonsan, S. Korea 36°11′ N, 127°6′ E 200
Nonthaburi, Thai. 13°53′ N, 100°31′ E 202
Noonan, N. Dak., U.S. 48°52′ N, 103°1′ W 108
Noord Beveland, Neth. 51°33′ N, 3°42′ E 163
Noordoewer, Namibia 28°44′ S, 17°37′ E 227
Noormarkku, Fin. 61°35′ N, 21°51′ E 166
Nootka, Can. 49°37′ N, 126°39′ W 90
Nopah Range, Calif., U.S. 36°4′ N, 116°10′ W 101
Nóqui, Angola 5°55′ S, 13°28′ E 218
Nora, Ill., U.S. 42°26′ N, 89°57′ W 102
Nora, Nor. 59°30′ N, 14°59′ E 152
Nora, island, Eritrea 16°4′ N, 39°43′ E 182
Nora, ruin(s), It. 38°59′ N, 8°55′ E 156
Norak, Taj. 38°23′ N, 69°21′ E 197
Norberg, Nor. 60°3′ N, 15°54′ E 152
Norco, La., U.S. 29°59′ N, 90°25′ W 103
Nord 81°43′ N, 17°32′ W 246
Nord Frøya, Nor. 63°45′ N, 8°47′ E 152
Nord, Petit lac du, lake, Can. 50°46′ N, 67°57′ W 111
Nordaustlandet, island, Nor. 80°34′ N, 5°48′ E 160

Norddalsfjord, Nor. 61°39' N, 5°22' E 152
Norddeich, Ger. 53°37' N, 7°10' E 163
Nordegg (Brazeau), Can. 52°28' N, 116°7' W 108
Norden, Ger. 53°36' N, 7°11' E 163
Norderney, Ger. 53°42' N, 7°9' E 163
Nordfold, Nor. 67°45' N, 15°11' E 152
Nordhordland, region, North Sea 60°50' N, 4°39' E 152
Nordhorn, Ger. 52°26' N, 7°3' E 163
Nordkapp (North Cape), Nor. 71°6' N, 25°55' E 152
Nordkinnhalvøya, Nor. 70°45' N, 26°37' E 152
Nord-Kivu, adm. division, Dem. Rep. of the Congo 0°10' N, 28°8' E 224
Nordli, Nor. 64°28' N, 13°36' E 152
Nordmaling, Nor. 63°33' N, 19°30' E 152
Nordøstrundingen 80°22' N, 30°36' W 72
Nordøyan, islands, Norwegian Sea 64°47' N, 9°13' E 152
Nordøyane, islands, Nor. 62°38' N, 4°46' E 152
Nordoyar, islands, Norwegian Sea 62°30' N, 9°12' W 72
Nord-Pas-De-Calais, adm. division, Fr. 50°24' N, 1°57' E 150
Nordreisa, Nor. 69°46' N, 21°2' E 152
Nordvik, Nor. 66°7' N, 12°31' E 152
Nordvik, Russ. 73°59' N, 111°16' E 160
Norfolk, Conn., U.S. 41°59' N, 73°12' W 104
Norfolk, Nebr., U.S. 42°0' N, 97°26' W 90
Norfolk, Va., U.S. 36°51' N, 76°17' W 96
Norfolk Island, Australia 29°0' S, 168°0' E
Norfolk Ridge, South Pacific Ocean 27°44' S, 167°48' E 252
Norfork Lake, Ark., U.S. 36°16' N, 93°15' W 80
Nori, Russ. 66°11' N, 72°31' E 169
Noril'sk, Russ. 69°20' N, 88°8' E 169
Normal, Ill., U.S. 40°30' N, 88°59' W 102
Norman, Okla., U.S. 35°11' N, 97°27' W 92
Norman Wells, Can. 65°18' N, 126°44' W 98
Normanby Island, P.N.G. 9°58' S, 151°19' E 192
Normandin, Can. 48°49' N, 72°31' W 94
Normandy, Tex., U.S. 28°53' N, 100°35' W 96
Normandy, region, Fr. 48°57' N, 0°46' E 163
Normanton, Austral. 17°46' S, 141°10' E 238
Normétal, Can. 49°0' N, 79°23' W 94
Norphlet, Ark., U.S. 33°17' N, 92°40' W 103
Ñorquincó, Arg. 41°50' S, 70°51' W 134
Norra Storfjället, peak, Nor. 65°51' N, 15°10' E 152
Norrby, Nor. 64°25' N, 15°37' E 152
Nørresundby, Den. 57°3' N, 9°55' E 150
Norrfors, Nor. 63°46' N, 18°59' E 152
Norrhult, Nor. 57°7' N, 15°9' E 152
Norris Lake, lake, Tenn., U.S. 36°18' N, 84°3' W 94
Norrköping, Nor. 58°33' N, 16°9' E 152
Norrland, region, Sw. 61°29' N, 17°15' E 166
Norrtälje, Sw. 59°45' N, 18°39' E 166
Norseman, Austral. 32°12' S, 121°47' E 231
Norske Øer, islands, Norske Øer 78°33' N, 16°48' W 246
Norte, adm. division, Braz. 4°51' S, 37°14' W 132
Norte, Cabo, Braz. 1°44' N, 49°56' W 130
Norte, Cayo 18°50' N, 87°32' W 115
Norte de Santander, adm. division, Col. 8°18' N, 73°17' W 136
Norte, Punta, Arg. 36°18' S, 56°43' W 139
Norte, Punta, Arg. 50°51' S, 69°6' W 134
Norte, Serra do, Braz. 10°18' S, 59°11' W 130
Nortelândia, Braz. 14°29' S, 56°48' W 132
Nörten-Hardenberg, Ger. 51°37' N, 9°57' E 167
North Adams, Mass., U.S. 42°41' N, 73°7' W 104
North Albanian Alps, Alban. 42°31' N, 19°47' E 168
North America 25°0' N, 112°0' W 73
North Amherst, Mass., U.S. 42°24' N, 72°32' W 104
North Andaman, island, India 13°28' N, 91°39' E 188
North Andover, Mass., U.S. 42°41' N, 71°9' W 104
North Anson, Me., U.S. 44°51' N, 69°55' W 94
North Atlantic Ocean 20°33' N, 74°33' W 253
North Augusta, S.C., U.S. 33°30' N, 81°59' W 96
North Aulatsivik Island, Can. 59°49' N, 63°58' W 106
North Australian Basin, Indian Ocean 14°56' S, 117°17' E 254
North Baldy, peak, Wash., U.S. 48°31' N, 117°14' W 90
North Baltimore, Ohio, U.S. 41°10' N, 83°40' W 102
North Barrule, peak 54°16' N, 4°29' W 150
North Battleford, Can. 52°47' N, 108°19' W 108
North Bay, Can. 46°18' N, 79°27' W 94
North Belcher Islands, islands, Hudson Bay 56°39' N, 83°25' W 106
North Bend, Can. 49°52' N, 121°27' W 100
North Bend, Wash., U.S. 47°28' N, 121°47' W 100
North Bennington, Vt., U.S. 42°55' N, 73°15' W 104
North Berwick, Me., U.S. 43°18' N, 70°44' W 104
North Bimini, island, Bahamas 25°46' N, 79°29' W 105
North Bonneville, Wash., U.S. 45°38' N, 121°58' W 100
North Boston, N.Y., U.S. 42°40' N, 78°48' W 110
North Bradley, Mich., U.S. 43°41' N, 84°29' W 102
North Branch, Mich., U.S. 43°13' N, 83°9' W 102
North Branch, Minn., U.S. 45°30' N, 92°59' W 94
North Branford, Conn., U.S. 41°19' N, 72°47' W 104
North Bridgton, Me., U.S. 44°6' N, 70°43' W 104
North Caicos, island, North Caicos 22°1' N, 72°1' W 80
North Canton, Ohio, U.S. 40°52' N, 81°24' W 102
North, Cape, Antarctica 70°15' S, 169°9' E 248
North, Cape, Can. 47°2' N, 60°54' W 111
North Cape, Can. 46°59' N, 64°47' W 111
North Cape, N.Z. 34°24' S, 172°51' E 240
North Cape May, N.J., U.S. 38°58' N, 74°58' W 94
North Cape see Horn, Ice. 66°30' N, 26°3' W 246
North Cape see Nordkapp, Nor. 71°10' N, 25°50' E 152
North Carolina, adm. division, N.C., U.S. 35°44' N, 80°14' W 96
North Carver, Mass., U.S. 41°55' N, 70°49' W 104
North Cascades National Park, Wash., U.S. 48°34' N, 121°27' W 100
North Cat Cay, island, Bahamas 25°32' N, 79°16' W 105
North Channel 45°49' N, 83°42' W 80
North Channel 54°35' N, 5°17' W 150
North Clarendon, Vt., U.S. 43°34' N, 72°59' W 104
North College Hill, Ohio, U.S. 39°12' N, 84°34' W 102
North Conway, N.H., U.S. 44°2' N, 71°8' W 104
North Cowichan, Can. 48°51' N, 123°42' W 100
North Creek, N.Y., U.S. 43°41' N, 74°0' W 104
North Dakota, adm. division, N. Dak., U.S. 47°45' N, 101°21' W 90
North Dartmouth, Mass., U.S. 41°37' N, 71°0' W 104
North Downs, region, U.K. 51°8' N, 0°49' E 162
North Eagle Butte, S. Dak., U.S. 44°59' N, 101°15' W 90
North East Land, island, Nor. 79°53' N, 23°37' E 255
North Edgecomb, Me., U.S. 43°59' N, 69°39' W 104
North Edwards, Calif., U.S. 35°2' N, 117°50' W 101
North Egremont, Mass., U.S. 42°11' N, 73°27' W 104
North Fiji Basin, South Pacific Ocean 17°30' S, 173°11' E 252
North Fond du Lac, Wis., U.S. 43°48' N, 88°30' W 102
North Foreland, Drake Passage 61°14' S, 61°24' W 248
North Foreland, U.K. 51°22' N, 1°25' E 163
North Fork, Calif., U.S. 37°13' N, 119°32' W 100
North Fork, river, Kans., U.S. 39°29' N, 100°4' W 90
North Fort Myers, Fla., U.S. 26°40' N, 81°53' W 105
North Fryeburg, Me., U.S. 44°7' N, 70°59' W 104
North Grosvenor Dale, Conn., U.S. 41°58' N, 71°55' W 104
North Hampton, N.H., U.S. 42°58' N, 70°51' W 104
North Hartland, Vt., U.S. 43°35' N, 72°22' W 104
North Haven, N.Y., U.S. 41°1' N, 72°19' W 104
North Head, Can. 53°43' N, 56°24' W 111
North Head, N.Z. 36°36' S, 173°49' E 240
North Hodge, La., U.S. 32°18' N, 92°43' W 96
North Holland, adm. division, Neth. 53°6' N, 4°6' E 150
North Horr, Kenya 3°18' N, 37°4' E 224
North Hudson, N.Y., U.S. 43°57' N, 73°44' W 104
North Industry, Ohio, U.S. 40°44' N, 81°22' W 102
North Island, Austral. 15°27' S, 136°40' E 230
North Jay, Me., U.S. 44°32' N, 70°15' W 104
North Judson, Ind., U.S. 41°12' N, 86°46' W 102
North Kingstown (Wickford), R.I., U.S. 41°34' N, 71°28' W 104
North Knife Lake, Can. 58°2' N, 97°42' W 108
North La Veta Pass, Colo., U.S. 37°36' N, 105°13' W 90
North Land see Severnaya Zemlya, islands, Russ. 80°20' N, 102°0' E 160
North Las Vegas, Nev., U.S. 36°11' N, 115°9' W 101
North Liberty, Ind., U.S. 41°31' N, 86°26' W 102
North Little Rock, Ark., U.S. 34°47' N, 92°16' W 82
North Loup, river, Nebr., U.S. 42°25' N, 101°5' W 80
North Luangwa National Park, Zambia 11°43' S, 32°2' E 224
North Mamm Peak, Colo., U.S. 39°22' N, 107°57' W 90
North Manchester, Ind., U.S. 40°59' N, 85°46' W 102
North Miami, Fla., U.S. 25°54' N, 80°12' W 105
North Montpelier, Vt., U.S. 44°17' N, 72°28' W 104
North Moose Lake, Can. 54°10' N, 100°33' W 108
North Muskegon, Mich., U.S. 43°15' N, 86°17' W 102
North Myrtle Beach, S.C., U.S. 33°48' N, 78°42' W 96
North Naples, Fla., U.S. 26°13' N, 81°48' W 105
North Negril Point, Jam. 18°23' N, 79°33' W 116
North Orange, Mass., U.S. 42°37' N, 72°17' W 104
North Ossetia-Alania, adm. division, Russ. 42°59' N, 43°49' E 159
North Ossetia-Alania see Severnaya Osetiya-Alaniya, adm. division, Russ. 42°59' N, 43°49' E 195
North Oxford, Mass., U.S. 42°9' N, 71°53' W 104
North Pacific Ocean 22°12' N, 118°57' W 252
North Palisade, peak, Calif., U.S. 37°5' N, 118°34' W 101
North Palmetto Point, Bahamas 25°10' N, 76°10' W 96
North Pass, Colo., U.S. 38°11' N, 106°35' W 90
North Peak, Nev., U.S. 40°39' N, 117°13' W 90
North Pine, Can. 56°24' N, 120°48' W 108
North Platte, Nebr., U.S. 41°10' N, 100°44' W 106
North Platte, river, Wyo., U.S. 42°50' N, 105°34' W 106
North Point, Mich., U.S. 44°49' N, 83°16' W 94
North Port, Fla., U.S. 27°4' N, 82°15' W 105
North Powder, Oreg., U.S. 45°1' N, 117°56' W 90
North Pownal, Vt., U.S. 42°47' N, 73°16' W 104
North Rhine-Westphalia, adm. division, Ger. 51°18' N, 6°44' E 167
North River, Can. 59°0' N, 94°54' W 73
North, river, Can. 53°53' N, 58°14' W 111
North, river, Wash., U.S. 46°48' N, 123°42' W 100
North Salem, N.H., U.S. 42°50' N, 71°15' W 104
North Saskatchewan, river, Can. 52°15' N, 116°35' W 108
North Scituate, Mass., U.S. 42°13' N, 70°48' W 104
North Sea 55°38' N, 2°30' E 150
North Sentinel Island, India 11°29' N, 91°2' E 188
North Shapleigh, Me., U.S. 43°36' N, 70°54' W 104
North Shore, Calif., U.S. 33°31' N, 115°56' W 101
North Shoshone Peak, Nev., U.S. 39°8' N, 117°34' W 90
North Slope, Alas., U.S. 69°31' N, 155°32' W 98
North Springfield, Pa., U.S. 41°59' N, 80°27' W 94
North Springfield, Vt., U.S. 43°19' N, 72°32' W 104
North Star, Can. 56°51' N, 117°39' W 108
North Stradbroke Island, Austral. 28°5' S, 150°57' E 230
North Tawton, U.K. 50°48' N, 3°54' W 162
North Thetford, Vt., U.S. 43°50' N, 72°12' W 104
North Truro, Mass., U.S. 42°2' N, 70°6' W 104
North Turner, Me., U.S. 44°20' N, 70°15' W 104
North Vancouver, Can. 49°19' N, 123°3' W 100
North Vassalboro, Me., U.S. 44°29' N, 69°38' W 104
North Vernon, Ind., U.S. 39°0' N, 85°38' W 102
North Wabasca Lake, Can. 56°2' N, 114°57' W 108
North Walpole, N.H., U.S. 43°8' N, 72°27' W 104
North Walsham, U.K. 52°49' N, 1°22' E 163
North Warren, Pa., U.S. 41°52' N, 79°10' W 110
North Waterford, Me., U.S. 44°13' N, 70°46' W 104
North Webster, Ind., U.S. 41°19' N, 85°42' W 102
North Weddell Ridge see America-Antarctic Ridge, South Atlantic Ocean 59°0' S, 16°0' W 255
North West Cape, Austral. 21°48' S, 114°19' E 230
North West Point, Can. 53°25' N, 60°2' W 111
North West River, Can. 53°34' N, 60°8' W 111
North West Rocks, islands, Caribbean Sea 14°31' N, 80°34' W 115
North Wildwood, N.J., U.S. 39°0' N, 74°48' W 94
North Yolla Bolly Mountains, peak, Calif., U.S. 40°11' N, 123°4' W 90
North York Moors, National Park, U.K. 54°20' N, 1°2' W 162
Northallerton, U.K. 54°20' N, 1°27' W 162
Northam, Austral. 31°41' S, 116°41' E 231
Northam, S. Af. 24°58' S, 27°15' E 227
Northampton, Mass., U.S. 42°18' N, 72°38' W 104
Northampton, U.K. 52°14' N, 0°54' E 162
Northampton, Mount, peak, Antarctica 72°37' S, 169°35' E 248
Northbluff Point, Can. 51°27' N, 80°24' W 110
Northeast Cape, Alas., U.S. 63°5' N, 167°44' W 160
Northeast Greenland National Park, Greenland, Den. 77°0' N, 33°0' W 246
Northeast Pacific Basin, North Pacific Ocean 26°5' N, 145°35' W 252
Northeast Point, Bahamas 22°48' N, 74°14' W 80
Northeast Point, Can. 51°54' N, 55°18' W 111
Northeast Point, Jam. 18°12' N, 76°20' W 115
Northeim, Ger. 51°42' N, 9°59' E 167
Northern, adm. division, Sudan 20°14' N, 31°0' E 182
Northern Bahr Al Ghazal, adm. division, Sudan 9°11' N, 26°10' E 224
Northern Cape, adm. division, S. Af. 30°2' S, 19°39' E 227
Northern Cay, island, Belize 17°21' N, 87°29' W 116
Northern Cyprus, special sovereignty, Cyprus 35°16' N, 32°56' E 194
Northern Darfur, adm. division, Sudan 16°39' N, 23°59' E 226
Northern Head, Can. 46°4' N, 59°46' W 111
Northern Ireland, adm. division, U.K. 54°35' N, 7°41' W 150
Northern Mariana Islands, U.S. 20°7' N, 141°10' E 192
Northern Sierra Madre National Park, Philippines 16°48' N, 121°37' E 203
Northern Territory, adm. division, Austral. 19°14' S, 130°35' E 231
Northfield, Minn., U.S. 44°26' N, 93°8' W 94
Northfield, N.H., U.S. 43°25' N, 71°36' W 104
Northfield, Vt., U.S. 44°8' N, 72°40' W 104
Northfield Falls, Vt., U.S. 44°9' N, 72°39' W 104
Northford, Conn., U.S. 41°23' N, 72°48' W 104
Northport, Ala., U.S. 33°13' N, 87°35' W 103
Northport, Nebr., U.S. 41°41' N, 103°6' W 92
Northport, Wash., U.S. 48°53' N, 117°48' W 90
Northridge, Ohio, U.S. 39°59' N, 83°46' W 102
Northumberland, N.H., U.S. 44°33' N, 71°34' W 104
Northumberland Islands, Coral Sea 22°8' S, 150°56' E 230
Northville, N.Y., U.S. 43°13' N, 74°11' W 104
Northway, Alas., U.S. 62°51' N, 141°59' W 98
North-West, adm. division, S. Af. 26°44' S, 24°15' E 227
Northwest Angle, Minn., U.S. 49°4' N, 95°20' W 90
Northwest Atlantic Mid-Ocean Canyon, North Atlantic Ocean 52°31' N, 45°36' W 253
Northwest Miscou Point, Can. 48°11' N, 65°14' W 94
Northwest Pacific Basin, North Pacific Ocean 39°52' N, 157°39' E 252
Northwest Passages 70°33' N, 125°19' W 72
Northwest Territories, adm. division, Can. 60°25' N, 115°14' W 108
Northwestern Hawaiian Islands, North Pacific Ocean 23°42' N, 165°44' W 99
Northwich, U.K. 53°15' N, 2°31' W 162
Northwind Escarpment, Arctic Ocean 75°55' N, 153°20' W 255
Northwind Ridge, Arctic Ocean 76°13' N, 156°12' W 255
Northwood, N.H., U.S. 43°11' N, 71°10' W 104
Northwood, N. Dak., U.S. 47°43' N, 97°35' W 90
Northwood, Ohio, U.S. 41°35' N, 83°27' W 102
Norton, Kans., U.S. 39°49' N, 99°54' W 90
Norton, Va., U.S. 36°55' N, 82°39' W 94
Norton, Zimb. 17°56' S, 30°40' E 224
Norton Bay 64°20' N, 162°6' W 98
Norton Shores, Mich., U.S. 43°9' N, 86°16' W 102
Norton Sound 63°37' N, 165°6' W 98
Norvalspont, S. Af. 30°38' S, 25°24' E 227
Norvegia, Cape, Antarctica 71°16' S, 18°23' W 248
Norwalk, Calif., U.S. 33°55' N, 118°4' W 101
Norwalk, Conn., U.S. 41°7' N, 73°25' W 104
Norwalk, Ohio, U.S. 41°13' N, 82°37' W 102
Norway, Me., U.S. 44°12' N, 70°33' W 104
Norway, Mich., U.S. 45°47' N, 87°55' W 94
Norway 63°25' N, 10°58' E 152
Norway House, Can. 53°56' N, 97°52' W 108
Norwegian Basin, Norwegian Sea 68°5' N, 1°43' E 255
Norwegian Sea 68°1' N, 5°35' E 152
Norwich, Conn., U.S. 41°31' N, 72°5' W 104
Norwich, N.Y., U.S. 42°31' N, 75°33' W 94
Norwich, U.K. 52°37' N, 1°16' E 162
Norwich, Vt., U.S. 43°42' N, 72°19' W 104
Norwood, Colo., U.S. 38°7' N, 108°17' W 90
Norwood, La., U.S. 30°57' N, 91°7' W 103
Norwood, Mass., U.S. 42°11' N, 71°13' W 104
Norwood, Ohio, U.S. 39°9' N, 84°27' W 94
Noshul', Russ. 60°8' N, 49°35' E 154
Nosivka, Ukr. 50°54' N, 31°38' E 158
Nosok, Russ. 70°8' N, 82°12' E 169
Nosovshchina, Russ. 62°57' N, 37°3' E 154
Noşratābād, Iran 29°51' N, 59°56' E 180
Nosy-Varika, Madagascar 20°33' S, 48°31' E 220
Noszlop, Hung. 47°10' N, 17°26' E 168
Not Ozero, lake, Russ. 66°26' N, 30°49' E 152
Notch Peak, Utah, U.S. 39°7' N, 113°29' W 90
Notikewin, Can. 56°58' N, 117°38' W 108
Notikewin, river, Can. 56°55' N, 119°2' W 108
Nótio Egéo, adm. division, Gr. 37°12' N, 25°30' E 156
Nötö, Fin. 59°57' N, 21°45' E 166
Noto, It. 36°53' N, 15°4' E 156
Noto, Japan 37°19' N, 137°8' E 201
Notodden, Nor. 59°33' N, 9°17' E 152
Notre Dame Bay 49°29' N, 55°32' W 111
Notre Dame de Lourdes, Can. 49°31' N, 98°34' W 90
Notre-Dame-du-Nord, Can. 47°36' N, 79°29' W 94
Notsé, Togo 6°57' N, 1°9' E 222
Nottaway, river, Can. 51°13' N, 78°54' W 80
Nottingham, N.H., U.S. 43°6' N, 71°7' W 104
Nottingham, U.K. 52°57' N, 1°9' W 162
Nottingham Island, Can. 63°12' N, 82°17' W 106
Nottuln, Ger. 51°55' N, 7°21' E 167
Nouabalé-Ndoki National Park, Congo 2°10' N, 16°11' E 218
Nouadhibou (Port Étienne), Mauritania 20°56' N, 17°2' W 222
Nouakchott, Mauritania 18°6' N, 16°11' W 222
Nouamrhar, Mauritania 19°22' N, 16°32' W 222
Nouaoudar, Mauritania 16°46' N, 7°18' W 222
Nouart, Fr. 49°26' N, 5°3' E 163
Nouasser, Mor. 33°22' N, 7°39' W 214
Nouméa, New Caledonia, Fr. 22°11' S, 166°42' E 238
Nouna, Burkina Faso 12°43' N, 3°53' W 222
Noupoort, S. Af. 31°10' S, 24°55' E 227
Nourounba, Mali 12°31' N, 9°8' W 222
Nousu, Fin. 67°10' N, 28°36' E 152
Nouzonville, Fr. 49°47' N, 4°44' E 163
Nova América, Braz. 15°3' S, 50°0' W 138
Nova Andradina, Braz. 22°15' S, 53°21' W 138
Nova Esperança, Braz. 23°10' S, 52°17' W 138
Nova Esperança, Braz. 16°34' S, 43°56' W 138
Nova Friburgo, Braz. 22°18' S, 42°31' W 138
Nova Gorica, Slov. 45°57' N, 13°38' E 167
Nova Gradiška, Croatia 45°15' N, 17°22' E 168
Nova Granada, Braz. 20°32' S, 49°21' W 138
Nova Iguaçu, Braz. 22°45' S, 43°28' W 138
Nova Kakhovka, Ukr. 46°45' N, 33°17' E 156
Nova Kapela, Croatia 45°12' N, 17°36' E 168
Nova Kasaba, Bosn. and Herzg. 44°13' N, 19°7' E 168
Nova Lamego, Guinea-Bissau 12°17' N, 14°16' W 222
Nova Lima, Braz. 19°58' S, 43°51' W 138
Nova Mambone, Mozambique 21°1' S, 34°57' E 227
Nova Nabúri, Mozambique 16°50' S, 38°55' E 224
Nova Odesa, Ukr. 47°21' N, 31°45' E 156
Nova Olinda do Norte, Braz. 3°49' S, 59°2' W 130
Nova Prata, Braz. 28°50' S, 51°35' W 139
Nova Roma, Braz. 13°53' S, 46°59' W 138
Nova Scotia, adm. division, Can. 44°50' N, 65°14' W 111
Nova Sofala, Mozambique 20°10' S, 34°43' E 227
Nova Trento, Braz. 27°20' S, 48°56' W 138
Nova Varoš, Serb. 43°27' N, 19°48' E 168
Nova Venécia, Braz. 18°46' S, 40°26' W 138
Nova Viçosa, Braz. 17°54' S, 39°24' W 138
Novafeltria, It. 43°53' N, 12°17' E 167
Novalukoml', Belarus 54°42' N, 29°11' E 166
Novara, It. 45°26' N, 8°36' E 167
Novato, Calif., U.S. 38°7' N, 122°35' W 100
Novaya Lyalya, Russ. 59°1' N, 60°39' E 154
Novaya Shul'ba, Kaz. 50°32' N, 81°19' E 184
Novaya Sibir', Ostrov, island, Russ. 75°1' N, 151°6' E 160
Novaya Vodolaga, Ukr. 49°44' N, 35°53' E 158
Novaya Zemlya, island, Russ. 70°43' N, 57°35' E 169
Nové Zámky, Slovakia 47°59' N, 18°10' E 168
Novelda, Sp. 38°22' N, 0°47' E 164
Novgorod, adm. division, Russ. 58°2' N, 30°16' E 166
Novgorodka, Russ. 57°2' N, 28°33' E 166
Novhorod-Sivers'kyy, Ukr. 51°58' N, 33°18' E 158
Novi Bečej, Serb. 45°35' N, 20°8' E 168
Novi Kneževac, Serb. 46°2' N, 20°6' E 168
Novi Ligure, It. 44°45' N, 8°47' E 167
Novi Pazar, Bulg. 43°20' N, 27°11' E 158
Novi Pazar, Serb. 43°8' N, 20°31' E 168
Novi Sad, Serb. 45°14' N, 19°46' E 168
Novigrad, Croatia 45°20' N, 13°34' E 167
Novikovo, Russ. 58°9' N, 80°35' E 169
Novilara, It. 43°51' N, 12°55' E 167
Noville Peninsula, Antarctica 71°26' S, 95°25' W 248
Novillero, Mex. 22°21' N, 105°40' W 114
Novinka, Russ. 59°10' N, 30°20' E 166
Novo Acordo, Braz. 10°9' S, 47°20' W 130
Novo Aripuanã, Braz. 5°9' S, 60°21' W 130
Novo Cruzeiro, Braz. 17°29' S, 41°53' W 138
Novo Hamburgo, Braz. 29°42' S, 51°7' W 139
Novo Horizonte, Braz. 21°29' S, 49°15' W 138
Novo Izborsk, Russ. 57°47' N, 27°55' E 166
Novo Paraíso, Braz. 1°15' N, 60°18' W 123
Novo, river, Braz. 4°47' S, 53°49' W 130
Novoagansk, Russ. 61°57' N, 76°26' E 169
Novoaleksandrovsk, Russ. 45°31' N, 41°6' E 158
Novoaltaysk, Russ. 53°27' N, 84°6' E 184
Novoanninskiy, Russ. 50°28' N, 42°42' E 158
Novobogatīnskoe, Kaz. 47°21' N, 51°11' E 158
Novocheremshansk, Russ. 54°21' N, 50°5' E 154
Novodvinsk, Russ. 64°25' N, 40°48' E 154
Novohrad-Volyns'kyy, Ukr. 50°34' N, 27°35' E 152
Novoīshīmskīy, Kaz. 53°13' N, 66°48' E 184
Novokhovansk, Russ. 55°55' N, 29°43' E 166
Novokuybyshevsk, Russ. 53°6' N, 50°0' E 154
Novokuznetsk, Russ. 53°48' N, 87°8' E 184
Novolazarevskaya, Russia, station, Antarctica 70°47' S, 11°39' E 248
Novomalykla, Russ. 54°10' N, 49°50' E 154

Novomichurinsk, *Russ.* 53°59′ N, 39°49′ E 154
Novomikhaylovskoye, *Russ.* 44°15′ N, 38°55′ E 156
Novomoskovsk, *Russ.* 54°3′ N, 38°12′ E 154
Novomoskovs'k, *Ukr.* 48°40′ N, 35°18′ E 158
Novonikolayevskiy, *Russ.* 50°56′ N, 42°20′ E 158
Novonikol'skoye, *Russ.* 49°5′ N, 45°4′ E 158
Novonikol'skoye, *Russ.* 59°43′ N, 79°17′ E 169
Novooleksiyivka, *Ukr.* 46°15′ N, 34°37′ E 156
Novoorsk, *Russ.* 51°23′ N, 58°57′ E 158
Novopokrovskaya, *Russ.* 45°58′ N, 40°37′ E 158
Novopskov, *Ukr.* 49°34′ N, 39°9′ E 158
Novorepnoye, *Russ.* 51°3′ N, 48°21′ E 158
Novorossiysk, *Russ.* 44°46′ N, 37°41′ E 156
Novorybnoye, *Russ.* 72°45′ N, 105°56′ E 160
Novorzhev, *Russ.* 57°1′ N, 29°18′ E 166
Novosel'ye, *Russ.* 58°5′ N, 28°52′ E 166
Novosergiyevka, *Russ.* 52°3′ N, 53°36′ E 158
Novoshakhtinsk, *Russ.* 47°43′ N, 39°57′ E 158
Novosi Birskiye Ostrova (New Siberian Islands), *Russ.* 76°14′ N, 142°6′ E 160
Novosibirsk, *Russ.* 55°3′ N, 83°2′ E 184
Novosibirsk, adm. division, *Russ.* 54°25′ N, 77°40′ E 184
Novosil', *Russ.* 52°57′ N, 37°1′ E 154
Novosil'skiy, Cape, *Antarctica* 68°20′ S, 159°52′ E 248
Novosokol'niki, *Russ.* 56°20′ N, 30°13′ E 154
Novotitarovskaya, *Russ.* 45°16′ N, 39°1′ E 156
Novotroitsk, *Russ.* 51°13′ N, 58°16′ E 158
Novoukrayinka, *Ukr.* 48°21′ N, 31°36′ E 156
Novouzensk, *Russ.* 50°29′ N, 48°7′ E 158
Novovyatsk, *Russ.* 58°28′ N, 49°41′ E 154
Novozhilovskaya, *Russ.* 64°49′ N, 51°24′ E 154
Novozybkov, *Russ.* 52°30′ N, 31°58′ E 154
Novska, *Croatia* 45°19′ N, 16°59′ E 168
Novyy Oskol, *Russ.* 50°46′ N, 37°53′ E 158
Novyy Bor, *Russ.* 66°43′ N, 52°16′ E 154
Novyy Buh, *Ukr.* 47°41′ N, 32°25′ E 156
Novyy Buyan, *Russ.* 53°40′ N, 50°5′ E 154
Novyy Port, *Russ.* 67°40′ N, 72°54′ E 169
Novyy Uoyan, *Russ.* 56°5′ N, 111°38′ E 173
Novyy Urengoy, *Russ.* 65°53′ N, 77°10′ E 169
Novyy Vasyugan, *Russ.* 58°34′ N, 76°25′ E 169
Now Zad, *Afghan.* 32°23′ N, 64°30′ E 186
Nowa Sól, *Pol.* 51°47′ N, 15°43′ E 152
Nowata, *Okla., U.S.* 36°41′ N, 95°39′ W 96
Nowbarān, *Iran* 35°12′ N, 49°40′ E 180
Nowgong, *India* 25°4′ N, 79°26′ E 197
Nowra, *Austral.* 34°49′ S, 150°36′ E 231
Nowshera, *Pak.* 33°57′ N, 72°0′ E 186
Nowy Sącz, *Pol.* 49°40′ N, 20°47′ E 160
Noxapater, *Miss., U.S.* 32°58′ N, 89°4′ W 103
Noxon, *Mont., U.S.* 47°57′ N, 115°47′ W 90
Noxubee, river, *Ala., U.S.* 33°11′ N, 88°47′ W 103
Noy, river, *Laos* 17°6′ N, 105°20′ E 202
Noyabr'sk, *Russ.* 63°12′ N, 75°24′ E 169
Noyes, *Minn., U.S.* 48°57′ N, 97°13′ W 94
Noyo, *Calif., U.S.* 39°25′ N, 123°49′ W 90
Noyo, river, *Calif., U.S.* 39°20′ N, 123°46′ W 90
Noyon, *Fr.* 49°34′ N, 3°0′ E 163
Nsanje (Port Herald), *Malawi* 16°56′ S, 35°13′ E 224
Nsawam, *Ghana* 5°50′ N, 0°21′ E 222
Nsélé, *Gabon* 6°357′ N, 10°10′ E 218
Nsoc, *Equatorial Guinea* 1°13′ N, 11°14′ E 218
Nsontin, *Dem. Rep. of the Congo* 3°9′ S, 17°54′ E 218
Nsukka, *Nig.* 6°51′ N, 7°23′ E 222
Nsumbu National Park, *Zambia* 8°52′ S, 30°7′ E 206
Ntakat, spring, *Mauritania* 16°49′ N, 11°45′ W 222
N'Tima, *Congo* 3°47′ S, 12°3′ E 218
Ntui, *Cameroon* 4°25′ N, 11°36′ E 222
Nu (Salween), river, *Asia* 31°21′ N, 93°34′ E 190
Nu'aymah, *Syr.* 32°38′ N, 36°10′ E 194
Nuba Mountains, *Sudan* 10°45′ N, 30°5′ E 224
Nubia, Lake, *Sudan* 21°56′ N, 30°53′ E 182
Nubian Desert, *Sudan* 20°50′ N, 30°59′ E 182
Nucet, *Rom.* 46°30′ N, 22°35′ E 168
Nucla, *Colo., U.S.* 38°16′ N, 108°33′ W 90
Nüden, *Mongolia* 43°58′ N, 110°37′ E 198
Nueces, river, *Tex., U.S.* 28°12′ N, 98°46′ W 92
Nueltin Lake, *Can.* 59°37′ N, 102°11′ W 106
Nueva Esparta, adm. division, *Venez.* 10°57′ N, 64°24′ W 130
Nueva Galia, *Arg.* 35°6′ S, 65°13′ W 134
Nueva Gerona, *Cuba* 21°53′ N, 82°49′ W 116
Nueva, Isla, island, *Chile* 55°13′ S, 66°24′ W 134
Nueva Palmira, *Uru.* 33°54′ S, 58°20′ W 139
Nueva Rosita, *Mex.* 27°55′ N, 101°12′ W 92
Nuevo Berlín, *Uru.* 32°59′ S, 57°59′ W 139
Nuevo Casas Grandes, *Mex.* 30°24′ N, 107°55′ W 92
Nuevo Delicias, *Mex.* 26°16′ N, 102°48′ W 114
Nuevo Ideal, *Mex.* 24°51′ N, 105°4′ W 114
Nuevo Laredo, *Mex.* 27°28′ N, 99°32′ W 96
Nuevo León, *Mex.* 32°25′ N, 115°14′ W 101
Nuevo León, adm. division, *Mex.* 25°9′ N, 100°14′ W 114
Nuevo Morelos, *Mex.* 22°30′ N, 99°13′ W 114
Nuevo Rocafuerte, *Ecua.* 1°0′ N, 75°27′ W 136
Nuevo Rodríguez, *Mex.* 27°8′ N, 100°4′ W 96
Nugaaleed, Dooxo, *Somalia* 8°39′ N, 47°24′ E 216
Nugruș, Gebel, peak, *Egypt* 24°47′ N, 34°29′ E 182
Nuh, Ras, *Pak.* 24°55′ N, 62°25′ E 182
Nuia, *Est.* 58°5′ N, 25°30′ E 166
Nuijamaa, *Fin.* 60°58′ N, 28°34′ E 166
Nuiqsut, *Alas., U.S.* 70°12′ N, 151°2′ W 98
Nuits, *Fr.* 47°43′ N, 4°11′ E 150
Nukhayb, *Iraq* 32°3′ N, 42°15′ E 180
Nukheila (Merga), spring, *Sudan* 19°3′ N, 26°20′ E 226
Nuku'alofa, *Tonga* 21°8′ S, 175°12′ W 241
Nukumanu Atoll, *South Pacific Ocean* 4°52′ S, 159°33′ E 238
Nukus, *Uzb.* 42°26′ N, 59°39′ E 180
Nulato, *Alas., U.S.* 64°36′ N, 158°12′ W 98
Nules, *Sp.* 39°51′ N, 0°10′ E 164
Nullarbor Plain, *Austral.* 30°43′ S, 125°29′ E 230
Numan, *Nig.* 9°29′ N, 12°5′ E 216
Numata, *Japan* 36°38′ N, 139°2′ E 201
Numazu, *Japan* 35°5′ N, 138°53′ E 201
Numedal, region, *Nor.* 60°8′ N, 8°56′ E 152
Numfoor, island, *Indonesia* 1°23′ S, 134°21′ E 192
Nummi, *Fin.* 60°23′ N, 23°52′ E 166
Numto, *Russ.* 63°30′ N, 71°20′ E 169
Nunap Isua (Kap Farvel) 59°20′ N, 43°43′ W 106
Nunavik 71°32′ N, 56°33′ W 106
Nunavut, adm. division, *Can.* 65°9′ N, 74°23′ W 106
Nunchía, *Col.* 5°35′ N, 72°14′ W 136
Nuneaton, *U.K.* 52°31′ N, 1°27′ W 162
Nuñes, island, *Chile* 53°38′ S, 74°58′ W 134
Nungesser Lake, *Can.* 51°31′ N, 94°27′ W 80
Nungnain Sum, *China* 45°42′ N, 119°0′ E 198
Nungo, *Mozambique* 13°23′ S, 37°46′ E 224
Nunim Lake, lake, *Can.* 59°28′ N, 102°54′ W 108
Nunivak Island, *Alas., U.S.* 59°24′ N, 166°59′ W 98
Nunkiní, *Mex.* 20°21′ N, 90°13′ W 112
Nunligran, *Russ.* 64°51′ N, 175°16′ W 98
Nuñoa, *Peru* 14°31′ S, 70°37′ W 137
Nuoro, *It.* 40°19′ N, 9°19′ E 156
Nuqayr, spring, *Saudi Arabia* 27°50′ N, 48°17′ E 196
Nuquí, *Col.* 5°41′ N, 77°16′ W 136
Nura, river, *Kaz.* 50°28′ N, 71°12′ E 184
Nurki, Mys, *Russ.* 56°29′ N, 138°30′ E 160
Nurlat, *Russ.* 54°26′ N, 50°41′ E 154
Nurmes, *Fin.* 63°31′ N, 29°7′ E 152
Nurmo, *Fin.* 62°49′ N, 22°50′ E 154
Nürnberg, *Ger.* 49°26′ N, 11°0′ E 143
Nurobod, *Uzb.* 39°34′ N, 66°17′ E 197
Nurota, *Uzb.* 40°33′ N, 65°41′ E 197
Nurri, Mount, peak, *Austral.* 31°45′ S, 145°48′ E 230
Nushagak Peninsula, *Alas., U.S.* 58°17′ N, 160°46′ W 98
Nushki, *Pak.* 29°31′ N, 66°3′ E 182
Nut Mountain, *Can.* 52°8′ N, 103°23′ W 108
Nuttby Mountain, peak, *Can.* 45°32′ N, 63°18′ W 111
Nu'uanu Pali Overlook, site, *Hawai'i, U.S.* 21°20′ N, 157°50′ W 99
Nuugaatsiaq 71°35′ N, 53°13′ W 106
Nuuk (Godthåb), *Greenland, Den.* 64°14′ N, 51°38′ W 106
Nuupas, *Fin.* 66°0′ N, 26°19′ E 154
Nuussuaq 70°6′ N, 51°42′ W 106
Nuussuaq (Kraulshavn) 74°9′ N, 57°1′ W 106
Nuwara Eliya, *Sri Lanka* 6°56′ N, 80°47′ E 188
Nuwerus, *S. Af.* 31°8′ S, 18°20′ E 227
Nuyno, *Ukr.* 51°31′ N, 24°53′ E 158
Nuyts Archipelago, islands, *Great Australian Bight* 32°45′ S, 130°56′ E 230
Nwayfadh, *Africa* 24°53′ N, 14°50′ W 214
Nxai Pan National Park, *Botswana* 20°3′ S, 24°40′ E 224
Ny Ålesund, *Nor.* 78°50′ N, 12°1′ E 160
Nyaake, *Liberia* 4°50′ N, 7°36′ W 222
Nyac, *Alas., U.S.* 60°53′ N, 160°7′ W 98
Nyagan', *Russ.* 62°19′ N, 65°34′ E 169
Nyahanga, *Tanzania* 2°22′ S, 33°34′ E 224
Nyainqêntanglha Shan, peak, *China* 30°23′ N, 90°32′ E 197
Nyainrong, *China* 32°2′ N, 92°14′ E 188
Nyakabindi, *Tanzania* 2°37′ S, 33°55′ E 224
Nyakanazi, *Tanzania* 3°6′ S, 31°15′ E 224
Nyåker, *Nor.* 63°47′ N, 19°19′ E 152
Nyakrom, *Ghana* 5°37′ N, 0°48′ E 222
Nyaksimvol', *Russ.* 62°29′ N, 60°51′ E 169
Nyala, *Sudan* 12°2′ N, 24°55′ E 224
Nyalam, *China* 28°11′ N, 85°57′ E 197
Nyamandhlovu, *Zimb.* 19°53′ S, 28°16′ E 224
Nyamapanda, *Zimb.* 16°56′ S, 32°48′ E 224
Nyambiti, *Tanzania* 2°49′ S, 33°24′ E 218
Nyamirembe, *Tanzania* 2°33′ S, 31°42′ E 224
Nyamtumbo, *Tanzania* 10°31′ S, 36°6′ E 224
Nyanding, river, *Sudan* 8°8′ N, 32°18′ E 224
Nyandoma, *Russ.* 61°39′ N, 40°10′ E 154
Nyanga, *Zimb.* 18°11′ S, 32°42′ E 224
Nyanga Nature Reserve, *Congo* 3°2′ S, 11°27′ E 206
Nyangwe, *Dem. Rep. of the Congo* 4°12′ S, 26°11′ E 218
Nyanje, *Zambia* 14°24′ S, 31°47′ E 224
Nyanza Lac, *Burundi* 4°20′ S, 29°36′ E 224
Nyarling, river, *Can.* 60°20′ N, 114°23′ W 108
Nyasa, Lake see Malawi, Lake, *Malawi* 34°30′ S, 12°0′ E 21
Nyashabozh, *Russ.* 65°28′ N, 53°52′ E 154
Nyaunglebin, *Myanmar* 17°58′ N, 96°42′ E 202
Nyazepetrovsk, *Russ.* 56°3′ N, 59°39′ E 154
Nyborg, *Den.* 55°17′ N, 10°47′ E 150
Nyborg, *Nor.* 70°10′ N, 28°36′ E 152
Nybro, *Nor.* 56°45′ N, 15°53′ E 152
Nyda, *Russ.* 66°34′ N, 73°2′ E 169
Nye Mountains, *Antarctica* 68°4′ S, 48°39′ E 248
Nyeboe Land 81°28′ N, 53°44′ W 246
Nyeharelaye, *Belarus* 53°33′ N, 27°4′ E 152
Nyékládháza, *Hung.* 47°59′ N, 20°48′ E 168
Nyeri, *Kenya* 0°26′ N, 36°57′ E 224
Nyerol, *Sudan* 8°40′ N, 32°2′ E 224
Nyika National Park, *Malawi* 11°6′ S, 34°9′ E 224
Nyika Plateau, *Malawi* 10°39′ S, 33°28′ E 224
Nyima, *China* 31°55′ N, 87°49′ E 188
Nyimba, *Zambia* 14°35′ S, 30°50′ E 224
Nyingchi, *China* 29°36′ N, 94°24′ E 188
Nyírábrány, *Hung.* 47°33′ N, 22°3′ E 168
Nyírbátor, *Hung.* 47°49′ N, 22°8′ E 168
Nyíregyháza, *Hung.* 47°56′ N, 21°44′ E 168
Nyiri Desert, *Kenya* 2°23′ S, 37°10′ E 224
Nyiru, Mount, peak, *Kenya* 2°16′ N, 36°42′ E 224
Nykarleby (Uusikaarlepyy), *Fin.* 63°31′ N, 22°32′ E 152
Nykøbing, *Den.* 54°46′ N, 11°53′ E 152
Nykøbing, *Den.* 56°47′ N, 8°49′ E 150
Nykøbing, *Den.* 55°55′ N, 11°39′ E 152
Nyköping, *Nor.* 58°44′ N, 16°59′ E 152
Nylstroom see Modimolle, *S. Af.* 24°44′ S, 28°24′ E 227
Nynäshamn, *Sw.* 58°53′ N, 17°53′ E 166
Nyoma Rap, *India* 33°9′ N, 78°39′ E 188
Nyoman, river, *Belarus* 53°52′ N, 25°34′ E 166
Nyon, *Switz.* 46°25′ N, 6°16′ E 167
Nyrob, *Russ.* 60°44′ N, 56°43′ E 154
Nyrud, *Nor.* 69°9′ N, 29°12′ E 152
Nyrza, *Russ.* 63°27′ N, 43°37′ E 154
Nysa, *Pol.* 50°29′ N, 17°20′ E 152
Nyssa, *Oreg., U.S.* 43°52′ N, 117°1′ W 90
Nytva, *Russ.* 57°56′ N, 55°21′ E 154
Nyukhcha, *Russ.* 63°27′ N, 46°28′ E 154
Nyukka, *Russ.* 66°3′ N, 32°41′ E 152
Nyuksenitsa, *Russ.* 60°24′ N, 44°18′ E 154
Nyunzu, *Dem. Rep. of the Congo* 5°58′ S, 27°57′ E 224
Nyurba, *Russ.* 63°22′ N, 118°13′ E 160
Nyuvchim, *Russ.* 61°22′ N, 50°50′ E 154
Nyzhn'ohirs'kyy, *Ukr.* 45°26′ N, 34°41′ E 156
Nzara, *Sudan* 4°41′ N, 28°14′ E 224
Nzega, *Tanzania* 4°14′ S, 33°11′ E 224
Nzérékoré, *Guinea* 7°38′ N, 8°50′ W 222
N'zeto, *Angola* 7°19′ S, 12°52′ E 218
Nzi, river, *Côte d'Ivoire* 6°6′ N, 4°51′ W 222
Nzo, *Guinea* 7°35′ N, 8°20′ W 222
Nzo, river, *Côte d'Ivoire* 6°49′ N, 7°36′ W 222
Nzoro, *Dem. Rep. of the Congo* 3°14′ N, 29°31′ E 224
Nzoro, river, *Dem. Rep. of the Congo* 3°25′ N, 30°25′ E 224
Nzwani (Anjouan), island, *Comoros* 12°36′ S, 44°15′ E 220

O

Oacoma, *S. Dak., U.S.* 43°47′ N, 99°24′ W 90
Oahe Dam, *S. Dak., U.S.* 44°39′ N, 101°32′ W 82
Oahe, Lake, *N. Dak., U.S.* 45°33′ N, 100°54′ W 80
O'ahu, island, *Hawai'i, U.S.* 21°43′ N, 158°0′ W 99
Oak Bluffs, *Mass., U.S.* 41°27′ N, 70°35′ W 104
Oak Creek, *Colo., U.S.* 40°17′ N, 106°57′ W 90
Oak Grove, *La., U.S.* 32°50′ N, 91°23′ W 103
Oak Harbor, *Ohio, U.S.* 41°30′ N, 83°9′ W 102
Oak Harbor, *Wash., U.S.* 48°17′ N, 122°38′ W 100
Oak Hill, *Fla., U.S.* 28°51′ N, 80°52′ W 105
Oak Hill, *W. Va., U.S.* 37°58′ N, 81°9′ W 94
Oak Lake, *Can.* 49°45′ N, 100°39′ W 90
Oak Lawn, *Ill., U.S.* 41°43′ N, 87°45′ W 102
Oak Park, *Ill., U.S.* 41°53′ N, 87°48′ W 102
Oak Ridge, *La., U.S.* 32°36′ N, 91°46′ W 103
Oak Ridge, *Tenn., U.S.* 36°0′ N, 84°15′ W 96
Oak View, *Calif., U.S.* 34°24′ N, 119°19′ W 100
Oakdale, *Calif., U.S.* 37°45′ N, 120°52′ W 100
Oakdale, *La., U.S.* 30°47′ N, 92°40′ W 103
Oakdale, *Mass., U.S.* 42°23′ N, 71°48′ W 104
Oakengates, *U.K.* 52°41′ N, 2°26′ W 162
Oakes, *N. Dak., U.S.* 46°7′ N, 98°6′ W 90
Oakesdale, *Wash., U.S.* 47°7′ N, 117°15′ W 90
Oakham, *U.K.* 52°39′ N, 0°44′ E 162
Oakhurst, *Calif., U.S.* 37°20′ N, 119°40′ W 100
Oakland, *Calif., U.S.* 37°48′ N, 122°16′ W 100
Oakland, *Ill., U.S.* 39°38′ N, 88°2′ W 102
Oakland, *Iowa, U.S.* 41°17′ N, 95°22′ W 90
Oakland, *Me., U.S.* 44°32′ N, 69°44′ W 104
Oakland, *Nebr., U.S.* 41°48′ N, 96°28′ W 90
Oakland, *Oreg., U.S.* 43°24′ N, 123°18′ W 90
Oakland, *Pa., U.S.* 41°56′ N, 75°38′ W 94
Oakland Park, *Fla., U.S.* 26°10′ N, 80°9′ W 105
Oakley, *Calif., U.S.* 37°59′ N, 121°44′ W 100
Oakley, *Kans., U.S.* 39°7′ N, 100°52′ W 90
Oakridge, *Oreg., U.S.* 43°44′ N, 122°28′ W 90
Oaktown, *Ind., U.S.* 38°51′ N, 87°27′ W 102
Oakura, *N.Z.* 39°10′ S, 173°57′ E 240
Oakville, *Conn., U.S.* 41°35′ N, 73°5′ W 104
Oakville, *Wash., U.S.* 46°48′ N, 123°14′ W 100
Oamaru, *N.Z.* 45°6′ S, 170°57′ E 240
Oaro, *N.Z.* 42°33′ S, 173°28′ E 240
Ōasa, *Japan* 34°45′ N, 132°28′ E 201
Oates Coast, *Antarctica* 69°56′ S, 159°4′ E 248
Oatman, *Ariz., U.S.* 35°0′ N, 114°23′ W 101
Oaxaca, *Mex.* 17°2′ N, 96°46′ W 114
Oaxaca, adm. division, *Mex.* 17°32′ N, 97°22′ W 114
Ob', *Russ.* 54°59′ N, 82°50′ E 184
Ob' Bank, *Greenland Sea* 80°34′ N, 10°39′ W 255
Ob', river, *Russ.* 51°41′ N, 83°0′ E 172
Ob' Tablemount, *Indian Ocean* 52°22′ S, 41°12′ E 255
Oba, *Can.* 49°5′ N, 84°6′ W 94
Oba Lake, *Can.* 48°34′ N, 84°44′ W 94
Obabika Lake, lake, *Can.* 47°3′ N, 80°43′ W 94
Obak, spring, *Sudan* 18°10′ N, 34°51′ E 182
Obala, *Cameroon* 4°12′ N, 11°31′ E 222
Obalj, *Bosn. and Herzg.* 43°27′ N, 18°20′ E 168
Obama, *Japan* 32°44′ N, 130°13′ E 201
Obama, *Japan* 35°28′ N, 135°44′ E 201
Obamsca, Lac, lake, *Can.* 50°23′ N, 78°51′ W 110
Obamsca, river, *Can.* 50°51′ N, 78°50′ W 110
Oban, *U.K.* 56°25′ N, 5°28′ W 150
Obanazawa, *Japan* 38°36′ N, 140°25′ E 201
Obando, *Col.* 3°48′ N, 67°51′ W 136
Obed, *Can.* 53°34′ N, 117°14′ W 108
Obed Wild and Scenic River, *Tenn., U.S.* 35°51′ N, 87°55′ W 80
Oberá, *Arg.* 27°29′ S, 55°10′ W 139
Oberdrauburg, *Aust.* 46°45′ N, 12°58′ E 167
Oberhausen, *Ger.* 51°28′ N, 6°51′ E 167
Oberlin, *Kans., U.S.* 39°49′ N, 100°33′ W 90
Oberlin, *La., U.S.* 30°36′ N, 92°47′ W 103
Oberlin, *Ohio, U.S.* 41°16′ N, 82°13′ W 102
Obernai, *Fr.* 48°27′ N, 7°28′ E 163
Obernburg, *Ger.* 49°50′ N, 9°9′ E 167
Oberpullendorf, *Aust.* 47°30′ N, 16°31′ E 168
Obersuhl, *Ger.* 50°57′ N, 10°1′ E 167
Oberursel, *Ger.* 50°12′ N, 8°33′ E 167
Oberwesel, *Ger.* 50°6′ N, 7°42′ E 167
Obi, *Nig.* 8°20′ N, 8°45′ E 222
Obi, island, *Indonesia* 1°21′ S, 127°18′ E 192
Obi, Kepulauan, islands, *Indonesia* 2°17′ S, 126°42′ E 192
Óbidos, *Braz.* 1°53′ S, 55°32′ W 130
Óbidos, *Port.* 39°21′ N, 9°11′ W 150
Obigarm, *Taj.* 38°43′ N, 69°45′ E 197
Obihiro, *Japan* 42°55′ N, 143°9′ E 190
Obili, *Gabon* 0°42′ N, 14°22′ E 218
Obil'noye, *Russ.* 47°29′ N, 44°20′ E 158
Obion, *Tenn., U.S.* 36°15′ N, 89°12′ W 96
Obispo, Punta, *Chile* 26°45′ S, 71°27′ W 132
Obispo Trejo, *Arg.* 30°47′ S, 63°26′ W 139
Obispos, *Venez.* 8°37′ N, 70°8′ W 136
Oblivskaya, *Russ.* 48°31′ N, 42°25′ E 158
Oblong, *Ill., U.S.* 39°0′ N, 87°54′ W 102
Obluch'ye, *Russ.* 49°6′ N, 131°5′ E 190
Obninsk, *Russ.* 55°4′ N, 36°40′ E 154
Obo, *Cen. Af. Rep.* 5°21′ N, 26°30′ E 224
Obo Liang, *China* 38°48′ N, 92°39′ E 188
Obock, *Djibouti* 11°55′ N, 43°20′ E 182
Obokote, *Dem. Rep. of the Congo* 0°52′ N, 26°19′ E 224
Obol', *Belarus* 55°23′ N, 29°22′ E 166
Obonga Lake, *Can.* 49°58′ N, 89°45′ W 94
Obot, *Alban.* 41°59′ N, 19°25′ E 168
Obouya, *Congo* 0°57′ N, 15°43′ E 218
Oboyan', *Russ.* 51°12′ N, 36°21′ E 158
Obozerskiy, *Russ.* 63°27′ N, 40°24′ E 154
Obra, river, *Pol.* 52°31′ N, 15°33′ E 152
Obre Lake, lake, *Can.* 60°19′ N, 103°25′ W 108
Obreja, *Rom.* 45°28′ N, 22°16′ E 168
Obrenovac, *Serb.* 44°38′ N, 20°10′ E 168
Obrian Peak see Trident Peak, *Nev., U.S.* 41°53′ N, 118°30′ W 90
O'Brien, *Can.* 47°40′ N, 80°45′ W 110
Obruk, *Turk.* 38°8′ N, 33°11′ E 156
Observation Peak, *Calif., U.S.* 40°45′ N, 120°16′ W 90
Obskaya Guba 67°26′ N, 71°48′ E 169
Obuasi, *Ghana* 6°15′ N, 1°40′ W 222
Obubra, *Nig.* 6°2′ N, 8°19′ E 222
Ob'yachevo, *Russ.* 60°21′ N, 49°39′ E 154
Obzor, *Bulg.* 42°49′ N, 27°52′ E 158
Oca, Montes de, *Sp.* 42°24′ N, 3°38′ W 164
Ocala, *Fla., U.S.* 29°10′ N, 82°9′ W 105
Ocampo, *Mex.* 22°49′ N, 99°19′ W 114
Ocampo, *Mex.* 21°36′ N, 101°29′ W 114
Ocaña, *Col.* 8°12′ N, 73°20′ W 136
Ocaña, *Sp.* 39°57′ N, 3°30′ W 164
Occidental, Cordillera, *South America* 4°36′ N, 76°51′ W 122
Occidental, Grand Erg, *Alg.* 30°22′ N, 0°26′ E 214
Ocean Cay, island, *Bahamas* 25°25′ N, 79°26′ W 105
Ocean City, *Md., U.S.* 38°20′ N, 75°6′ W 94
Ocean City, *Wash., U.S.* 47°3′ N, 124°10′ W 100
Ocean Falls, *Can.* 52°22′ N, 127°43′ W 108
Ocean Grove, *Mass., U.S.* 41°43′ N, 71°13′ W 104
Ocean Island see Kure Atoll, *Hawai'i, U.S.* 28°6′ N, 179°12′ W 99
Ocean Lake, lake, *Wyo., U.S.* 43°9′ N, 108°57′ W 90
Ocean Park, *Wash., U.S.* 46°28′ N, 124°3′ W 100
Ocean Springs, *Miss., U.S.* 30°24′ N, 88°50′ W 96
Oceano, *Calif., U.S.* 35°6′ N, 120°37′ W 100
Oceanographer Fracture Zone, *North Atlantic Ocean* 34°28′ N, 33°24′ W 253
Oceanside, *Calif., U.S.* 33°11′ N, 117°23′ W 101
Ochakiv, *Ukr.* 46°41′ N, 31°29′ E 156
Och'amch'ire, *Asia* 42°42′ N, 41°31′ E 195
Ocher, *Russ.* 57°52′ N, 54°49′ E 154
Ōchi, *Japan* 35°4′ N, 132°36′ E 201
Ochobo, *Nig.* 7°10′ N, 7°59′ E 222
Ochogavía, *Sp.* 42°55′ N, 1°6′ W 164
Ochopee, *Fla., U.S.* 25°53′ N, 81°18′ W 105
Ochre River, *Can.* 51°4′ N, 99°48′ W 90
Ochtrup, *Ger.* 52°12′ N, 7°12′ E 163
Ocilla, *Ga., U.S.* 31°35′ N, 83°16′ W 96
Ockelbo, *Nor.* 60°53′ N, 16°42′ E 152
Ocmulgee, river, *Ga., U.S.* 32°46′ N, 83°37′ W 80
Ocnele Mari, *Rom.* 45°5′ N, 24°17′ E 156
Ocnița, *Mold.* 48°23′ N, 27°26′ E 156
Ocoee, *Fla., U.S.* 28°34′ N, 81°33′ W 105
Ocoña, *Peru* 16°27′ S, 73°6′ W 137
Ocoña, river, *Peru* 16°2′ S, 73°19′ W 137
Oconee, Lake, *Ga., U.S.* 33°21′ N, 83°39′ W 96
Oconee, river, *Ga., U.S.* 32°41′ N, 83°14′ W 80
Oconomowoc, *Wis., U.S.* 43°6′ N, 88°30′ W 102
Oconto, *Wis., U.S.* 44°54′ N, 87°52′ W 94
Oconto Falls, *Wis., U.S.* 44°52′ N, 88°8′ W 94
Ocoruro, *Peru* 15°4′ S, 71°8′ W 137
Ocós, *Guatemala* 14°32′ N, 92°12′ W 115
Ocotillo, *Calif., U.S.* 32°44′ N, 116°2′ W 101
Ocotillo Wells, *Calif., U.S.* 33°8′ N, 116°9′ W 101
Ocotlán, *Mex.* 20°21′ N, 102°46′ W 114
Ocoyo, *Peru* 14°3′ S, 75°1′ W 137
Ocracoke, *N.C., U.S.* 35°6′ N, 76°0′ W 96
Ocracoke Inlet 34°49′ N, 75°39′ W 80
Ócsa, *Hung.* 47°17′ N, 19°14′ E 168
Octave, river, *Can.* 48°52′ N, 78°35′ W 94
Ocumare del Tuy, *Venez.* 10°5′ N, 66°47′ W 136
Ocuri, *Bol.* 18°55′ S, 65°52′ W 137
Oda, *Eth.* 6°41′ N, 41°10′ E 224
Oda, *Ghana* 5°55′ N, 1°0′ E 222
Ōda, *Japan* 35°11′ N, 132°30′ E 201
Oda, Jebel, peak, *Sudan* 20°17′ N, 36°32′ E 182
Ōdaejin, *N. Korea* 41°21′ N, 129°47′ E 200
Odanovce, *Serb.* 42°32′ N, 21°41′ E 168
Odawara, *Japan* 35°15′ N, 139°9′ E 201
Odda, *Nor.* 60°5′ N, 6°31′ E 152
Oddur see Xuddur, *Somalia* 4°6′ N, 43°55′ E 218

Odebolt, *Iowa, U.S.* 42° 18′ N, 95° 15′ W 90
Odei, river, *Can.* 56° 18′ N, 98° 57′ W 108
Odell, *Ill., U.S.* 41° 0′ N, 88° 31′ W 102
Odell, *Oreg., U.S.* 45° 36′ N, 121° 33′ W 100
Ödemiş, *Turk.* 38° 13′ N, 27° 56′ E 156
Odendaalsrus, *S. Af.* 27° 53′ S, 26° 39′ E 227
Odense, *Den.* 55° 23′ N, 10° 23′ E 150
Odenwald, *Ger.* 49° 45′ N, 8° 35′ E 167
Oder see Odra, river, *Ger.-Pol.* 51° 37′ N, 16° 16′ E 160
Odesa, *Ukr.* 46° 28′ N, 30° 43′ E 156
Odesdino, *Russ.* 63° 28′ N, 54° 25′ E 154
Odessa, *Tex., U.S.* 31° 49′ N, 102° 22′ W 92
Odessa, *Wash., U.S.* 47° 18′ N, 118° 42′ W 90
Odiel, river, *Sp.* 37° 34′ N, 6° 47′ W 164
Odienné, *Côte d'Ivoire* 9° 31′ N, 7° 34′ W 222
Odin, Mount, peak, *Can.* 50° 32′ N, 118° 14′ W 90
Odolanów, *Pol.* 51° 35′ N, 17° 41′ E 152
Odon, *Ind., U.S.* 38° 50′ N, 87° 0′ W 102
O'Donnell, *Tex., U.S.* 32° 57′ N, 101° 49′ W 92
Odra, river, *Ger.-Pol.* 51° 37′ N, 16° 16′ E 160
Odra, river, *Sp.* 42° 29′ N, 4° 3′ W 164
Odžaci, *Serb.* 45° 29′ N, 19° 16′ E 168
Odžak, *Bosn. and Herzg.* 45° 0′ N, 18° 18′ E 168
Odzala, *Congo* 0° 32′ N, 14° 34′ E 218
Odzala National Park, *Congo* 0° 45′ N, 14° 35′ E 206
Odzi, river, *Zimb.* 19° 11′ S, 32° 22′ E 224
Oecusse see Pante Makasar, *Indonesia* 9° 21′ S, 124° 20′ E 192
Oederan, *Ger.* 50° 51′ N, 13° 10′ E 152
Oeiras, *Braz.* 7° 0′ S, 42° 10′ W 132
Oelde, *Ger.* 51° 49′ N, 8° 7′ E 167
Oelrichs, *S. Dak., U.S.* 43° 10′ N, 103° 15′ W 90
Oelwein, *Iowa, U.S.* 42° 40′ N, 91° 55′ W 94
Oeniadae, ruin(s), *Gr.* 38° 23′ N, 21° 5′ E 156
Oenpelli, *Austral.* 12° 22′ S, 133° 6′ E 238
Oerlenbach, *Ger.* 50° 9′ N, 10° 7′ E 167
Oeta, Mount see Oíti, Óros, peak, *Gr.* 38° 47′ N, 22° 10′ E 156
Of, *Turk.* 40° 57′ N, 40° 17′ E 195
O'Fallon, *Ill., U.S.* 38° 34′ N, 89° 55′ W 102
O'Fallon Creek, river, *Mont., U.S.* 46° 49′ N, 105° 31′ W 90
Ofaqim, *Israel* 31° 19′ N, 34° 37′ E 194
Ofen Pass, *Switz.* 46° 38′ N, 10° 17′ E 167
Offa, *Nig.* 8° 12′ N, 4° 43′ E 222
Offenbach, *Ger.* 50° 5′ N, 8° 46′ E 167
Offutt Air Force Base, *Nebr., U.S.* 41° 5′ N, 96° 0′ W 90
Oficina Dominador, *Chile* 24° 23′ S, 69° 34′ W 132
Oficina, oil field, *Venez.* 8° 43′ N, 64° 27′ W 116
Oficina Santa Fe, *Chile* 21° 52′ S, 69° 37′ W 137
Ofin, river, *Ghana* 6° 26′ N, 2° 7′ W 222
Ofu, island, *United States* 14° 11′ S, 169° 38′ W 241
Ogadēn, region, *Eth.* 6° 45′ N, 42° 8′ E 224
Ōgaki, *Japan* 35° 21′ N, 136° 37′ E 201
Ogallala, *Nebr., U.S.* 41° 7′ N, 101° 44′ W 92
Ogasawara Guntō see Bonin Islands, *North Pacific Ocean* 25° 25′ N, 143° 8′ E 238
Ogbomosho, *Nig.* 8° 10′ N, 4° 16′ E 222
Ogden, *Iowa, U.S.* 42° 0′ N, 94° 2′ W 94
Ogden, *Utah, U.S.* 41° 13′ N, 111° 58′ W 90
Ogden, Mount, peak, *Can.* 58° 25′ N, 133° 32′ W 108
Ogema, *Can.* 49° 33′ N, 104° 56′ W 90
Oggiono, *It.* 45° 46′ N, 9° 19′ E 167
Ogi, *Japan* 37° 49′ N, 138° 16′ E 201
Ogilvie Mountains, *Can.* 64° 46′ N, 139° 9′ W 106
Oglanly, *Turkm.* 39° 52′ N, 54° 22′ E 180
Oglat Beraber, spring, *Alg.* 30° 24′ N, 3° 34′ W 214
Oglat d'Admamlalmat, spring, *Mauritania* 23° 25′ N, 11° 48′ W 214
'Oglât ed Daoud, spring, *Mauritania* 23° 31′ N, 6° 57′ W 214
'Oglât el Fersig, spring, *Mauritania* 21° 49′ N, 6° 21′ W 222
'Oglat el Khnâchîch, spring, *Mali* 21° 51′ N, 3° 59′ W 222
Oglats de Mkhaïzira, spring, *Mauritania* 22° 44′ N, 10° 18′ W 214
Oglesby, *Ill., U.S.* 41° 17′ N, 89° 5′ W 102
Oglethorpe, *Ga., U.S.* 32° 17′ N, 84° 4′ W 96
Oglethorpe, Mount, peak, *Ga., U.S.* 34° 28′ N, 84° 24′ W 96
Ogna, *Nor.* 58° 31′ N, 5° 48′ E 150
Ognev Yar, *Russ.* 58° 21′ N, 76° 30′ E 169
Ognon, river, *Fr.* 47° 17′ N, 5° 59′ E 165
Ogoja, *Nig.* 6° 38′ N, 8° 42′ E 222
Ogoki, *Can.* 51° 40′ N, 85° 52′ W 82
Ogoki Reservoir, lake, *Can.* 50° 50′ N, 89° 14′ W 80
Ogoki, river, *Can.* 51° 5′ N, 86° 10′ W 110
Ögöömör, *Mongolia* 46° 47′ N, 107° 50′ E 198
Ogōri, *Japan* 34° 6′ N, 131° 24′ E 200
Ogou, river, *Togo* 8° 48′ N, 1° 25′ E 222
Ogr, *Sudan* 12° 2′ N, 27° 1′ E 218
Ogražden, *Maced.* 41° 25′ N, 22° 52′ E 168
Ogre, *Latv.* 56° 49′ N, 24° 33′ E 166
Ogre, river, *Latv.* 56° 46′ N, 25° 27′ E 166
'Ogueïlet en Nmâdi, spring, *Mauritania* 19° 45′ N, 11° 1′ W 222
Oguma, *Nig.* 7° 51′ N, 7° 2′ E 222
Ogunquit, *Me., U.S.* 43° 14′ N, 70° 37′ W 104
Ogwashi Uku, *Nig.* 6° 17′ N, 6° 28′ E 222
Ohanet, oil field, *Alg.* 28° 46′ N, 8° 49′ E 214
Ohangoron, *Uzb.* 40° 56′ N, 69° 56′ E 197
Ohau, *N.Z.* 40° 41′ S, 175° 15′ E 240
Óhi, Óros, peak, *Gr.* 38° 3′ N, 24° 23′ E 156
Ohio, *Ill., U.S.* 41° 33′ N, 89° 28′ W 102
Ohio, adm. division, *Ohio, U.S.* 40° 15′ N, 83° 3′ W 102
Ohio City, *Ohio, U.S.* 40° 45′ N, 84° 37′ W 102
Ohio Range, *Antarctica* 85° 4′ S, 101° 32′ W 248
Ohio, river, *U.S.* 37° 37′ N, 87° 7′ W 80
Ōi, river, *Japan* 35° 9′ N, 138° 8′ E 201
Oiapoque, *Braz.* 3° 50′ N, 51° 48′ W 130
Oijärvi, *Fin.* 65° 38′ N, 25° 48′ E 152
Oil City, *La., U.S.* 32° 44′ N, 93° 58′ W 103
Oil City, *Pa., U.S.* 41° 24′ N, 79° 43′ W 94
Oil Islands see Chagos Archipelago, *Indian Ocean* 6° 42′ S, 71° 25′ E 188
Oildale, *Calif., U.S.* 35° 25′ N, 119° 2′ W 101
Oilton, *Okla., U.S.* 36° 3′ N, 96° 35′ W 92
Oilton, *Tex., U.S.* 27° 27′ N, 98° 58′ W 92
Oise, river, *Fr.* 49° 51′ N, 3° 39′ E 163
Ōita, *Japan* 33° 13′ N, 131° 37′ E 201
Ōita, adm. division, *Japan* 33° 42′ N, 131° 34′ E 200
Oíti, Óros (Oeta, Mount), peak, *Gr.* 38° 47′ N, 22° 10′ E 156
Oiticica, *South America* 5° 2′ S, 41° 6′ W 132
Oituz, *Rom.* 46° 6′ N, 26° 23′ E 156
Ojai, *Calif., U.S.* 34° 26′ N, 119° 15′ W 101
Öje, *Nor.* 60° 48′ N, 13° 49′ E 152
Ojeda, *Arg.* 35° 18′ S, 63° 59′ W 139
Ojinaga, *Mex.* 29° 33′ N, 104° 27′ W 92
Ojiya, *Japan* 37° 17′ N, 138° 47′ E 201
Ojo Caliente, *Mex.* 22° 33′ N, 102° 16′ W 114
Ojo de Laguna, *Mex.* 29° 26′ N, 106° 25′ W 92
Ojós, *Sp.* 38° 8′ N, 1° 22′ W 164
Ojos del Salado, Cerro, peak, *Chile* 27° 6′ S, 68° 45′ W 132
Ojuelos de Jalisco, *Mex.* 21° 51′ N, 101° 35′ W 114
Oka, river, *Russ.* 55° 43′ N, 42° 12′ E 154
Oka, river, *Russ.* 53° 14′ N, 36° 17′ E 154
Okaba, *Indonesia* 8° 7′ S, 139° 37′ E 192
Okahandja, *Namibia* 21° 59′ S, 16° 53′ E 227
Okahukura, *N.Z.* 38° 49′ S, 175° 14′ E 240
Okak Islands, *Can.* 57° 32′ N, 65° 21′ W 106
Okakarara, *Namibia* 20° 36′ S, 17° 30′ E 227
Okaloacoochee Slough, marsh, *Fla., U.S.* 26° 26′ N, 80° 42′ W 105
Okanagan Lake, *Can.* 49° 50′ N, 120° 51′ W 80
Okanogan, *Wash., U.S.* 48° 21′ N, 119° 37′ W 90
Okanogan Range, *Wash., U.S.* 48° 48′ N, 120° 27′ W 90
Okány, *Hung.* 46° 53′ N, 21° 21′ E 168
Okaputa, *Namibia* 20° 7′ S, 16° 58′ E 227
Okara, *Pak.* 30° 49′ N, 73° 27′ E 186
Okatjoruu, *Namibia* 19° 38′ S, 18° 34′ E 220
Okaukuejo, *Namibia* 19° 9′ S, 15° 57′ E 220
Okavango Delta, *Botswana* 19° 33′ S, 23° 16′ E 224
Ōkawa, *Japan* 33° 12′ N, 130° 22′ E 201
Okawville, *Ill., U.S.* 38° 25′ N, 89° 33′ W 102
Okaya, *Japan* 36° 4′ N, 138° 2′ E 201
Okayama, *Japan* 34° 38′ N, 133° 53′ E 201
Okayama, adm. division, *Japan* 34° 54′ N, 133° 20′ E 201
Okazaki, *Japan* 34° 56′ N, 137° 10′ E 201
Okcheon, *S. Korea* 36° 18′ N, 127° 34′ E 200
Okeechobee, *Fla., U.S.* 27° 15′ N, 80° 50′ W 105
Okeechobee, Lake, *Fla., U.S.* 26° 57′ N, 80° 59′ W 105
Okeene, *Okla., U.S.* 36° 6′ N, 98° 20′ W 92
Okefenokee Swamp, marsh, *Ga., U.S.* 30° 35′ N, 83° 9′ W 80
Okene, *Nig.* 7° 34′ N, 6° 14′ E 222
Okha, *India* 22° 26′ N, 69° 3′ E 186
Okha, *Russ.* 53° 33′ N, 142° 43′ E 160
Okhaldhunga, *Nepal* 27° 20′ N, 86° 30′ E 197
Okhansk, *Russ.* 57° 42′ N, 55° 19′ E 154
Okhotsk, *Russ.* 59° 26′ N, 143° 20′ E 160
Okhotsk, Sea of 57° 51′ N, 141° 45′ E 160
Okhotskiy Perevoz, *Russ.* 61° 52′ N, 135° 38′ E 160
Okhtyrka, *Ukr.* 50° 19′ N, 34° 55′ E 158
Oki Guntō, islands, *Sea of Japan* 35° 59′ N, 133° 6′ E 201
Okiep, *S. Af.* 29° 36′ S, 17° 52′ E 227
Okinawa, island, *Japan* 26° 22′ N, 128° 16′ E 190
Okino Erabu Shima, island, *Japan* 27° 2′ N, 128° 25′ E 190
Okitipupa, *Nig.* 6° 40′ N, 4° 43′ E 222
Okkang, *N. Korea* 40° 18′ N, 124° 46′ E 200
Oklahoma, adm. division, *Okla., U.S.* 35° 37′ N, 98° 23′ W 96
Oklahoma City, *Okla., U.S.* 35° 25′ N, 97° 36′ W 92
Oklawaha, *Fla., U.S.* 29° 2′ N, 81° 56′ W 105
Okletac, *Serb.* 44° 5′ N, 19° 34′ E 168
Okmulgee, *Okla., U.S.* 35° 36′ N, 95° 58′ W 94
Okolona, *Miss., U.S.* 33° 59′ N, 88° 45′ W 96
Okotoks, *Can.* 50° 44′ N, 113° 59′ W 90
Okounfo, *Benin* 8° 20′ N, 2° 37′ E 222
Okoyo, *Congo* 1° 27′ S, 15° 1′ E 218
Okpara, river, *Africa* 7° 44′ N, 2° 37′ E 222
Okp'yŏng, *N. Korea* 39° 16′ N, 127° 20′ E 200
Oksino, *Russ.* 67° 34′ N, 52° 20′ E 169
Oksovskiy, *Russ.* 62° 36′ N, 39° 56′ E 154
Okstindan, peak, *Nor.* 65° 59′ N, 14° 11′ E 152
Oktyabr'sk, *Kaz.* 49° 26′ N, 57° 25′ E 158
Oktyabr'skīy, *Kaz.* 49° 39′ N, 83° 37′ E 184
Oktyabr'skiy, *Russ.* 55° 5′ N, 60° 10′ E 154
Oktyabr'skiy, *Russ.* 47° 55′ N, 43° 34′ E 158
Oktyabr'skiy, *Russ.* 54° 27′ N, 53° 35′ E 154
Oktyabr'skoe, *Kaz.* 52° 8′ N, 65° 40′ E 184
Oktyabr'skoye, *Russ.* 62° 34′ N, 66° 2′ E 160
Oktyabr'skoye, *Russ.* 52° 23′ N, 55° 37′ E 154
Oktyabr'skoye, *Russ.* 52° 21′ N, 55° 32′ E 184
Okučani, *Croatia* 45° 15′ N, 17° 12′ E 168
Ōkuchi, *Japan* 32° 3′ N, 130° 37′ E 201
Okulovka, *Russ.* 58° 24′ N, 33° 19′ E 154
Okunev Nos, *Russ.* 66° 16′ N, 52° 39′ E 154
Okushiri Tō, island, *Japan* 41° 45′ N, 138° 29′ E 190
Okuta, *Nig.* 9° 12′ N, 3° 15′ E 222
Ola, *Ark., U.S.* 35° 1′ N, 93° 14′ W 96
Ola, *Russ.* 59° 37′ N, 151° 11′ E 160
Ólafsvík, *Ice.* 64° 53′ N, 23° 45′ W 246
Olaine, *Latv.* 56° 48′ N, 23° 57′ E 166
Olancha, *Calif., U.S.* 36° 17′ N, 118° 2′ W 101
Olancha Peak, *Calif., U.S.* 36° 15′ N, 118° 10′ W 101
Olanchito, *Hond.* 15° 28′ N, 86° 35′ W 115
Ölands Norra Udde, *Sw.* 57° 23′ N, 16° 58′ E 152
Ölands Södra Udde, *Sw.* 55° 54′ N, 16° 3′ E 152
Olanga, *Russ.* 66° 9′ N, 30° 35′ E 152
Olary, *Austral.* 32° 16′ S, 140° 20′ E 231
Olasan, spring, *Eth.* 5° 17′ N, 45° 4′ E 218
Olascoaga, *Arg.* 35° 15′ S, 60° 39′ W 139
Olathe, *Kans., U.S.* 38° 51′ N, 94° 49′ W 94
Olavarría, *Arg.* 36° 55′ S, 60° 17′ W 139
Oława, *Pol.* 50° 57′ N, 17° 17′ E 152
Olbia, *It.* 40° 55′ N, 9° 28′ E 214
Old Cove Fort, site, *Utah, U.S.* 38° 39′ N, 112° 38′ W 90
Old Crow, *Can.* 67° 32′ N, 139° 56′ W 73
Old Dongola, ruin(s), *Sudan* 18° 12′ N, 30° 42′ E 226
Old Fort, *Can.* 55° 4′ N, 126° 20′ W 108
Old Man of the Mountain, site, *N.H., U.S.* 44° 10′ N, 71° 44′ W 104
Old Mkushi, *Zambia* 14° 22′ S, 29° 20′ E 224
Old Orchard Beach, *Me., U.S.* 43° 30′ N, 70° 24′ W 104
Old Rhodes Key, island, *Fla., U.S.* 25° 22′ N, 80° 14′ W 105
Old Sarum, ruin(s), *U.K.* 51° 5′ N, 1° 50′ W 162
Old Saybrook, *Conn., U.S.* 41° 17′ N, 72° 23′ W 104
Old Slains Castle, site, *U.K.* 57° 20′ N, 2° 1′ W 150
Old Speck Mountain, peak, *Me., U.S.* 44° 33′ N, 71° 0′ W 104
Old Sturbridge, site, *Mass., U.S.* 42° 5′ N, 72° 8′ W 104
Old Sugar Mill, site, *Hawai'i, U.S.* 21° 30′ N, 157° 53′ W 99
Old Town, *Fla., U.S.* 29° 36′ N, 83° 0′ W 105
Old Wives Lake, *Can.* 50° 3′ N, 106° 39′ W 90
Old Woman Mountains, *Calif., U.S.* 34° 26′ N, 115° 25′ W 101
Oldbury, *U.K.* 52° 29′ N, 2° 1′ W 162
Oldeani, *Tanzania* 3° 20′ S, 35° 34′ E 224
Olden, *Nor.* 61° 50′ N, 6° 49′ E 152
Oldenburg, *Ger.* 53° 8′ N, 8° 13′ E 163
Oldenzaal, *Neth.* 52° 18′ N, 6° 55′ E 163
Oldham, *U.K.* 53° 32′ N, 2° 7′ W 162
Olds, *Can.* 51° 49′ N, 114° 6′ W 90
Olduvai Gorge, site, *Tanzania* 2° 57′ S, 35° 14′ E 224
Öldzeyte Suma, *Mongolia* 44° 33′ N, 106° 10′ E 198
Öldziyt, *Mongolia* 44° 39′ N, 109° 3′ E 198
Olean, *N.Y., U.S.* 42° 4′ N, 78° 27′ W 94
Olecko, *Pol.* 54° 1′ N, 22° 31′ E 166
Olekma, river, *Russ.* 59° 23′ N, 120° 19′ E 160
Olekminsk, *Russ.* 60° 23′ N, 120° 16′ E 160
Oleksandriya, *Ukr.* 50° 44′ N, 26° 20′ E 152
Olema, *Russ.* 64° 28′ N, 46° 2′ E 154
Ølen, *Nor.* 59° 35′ N, 5° 47′ E 152
Olenegorsk, *Russ.* 68° 8′ N, 33° 15′ E 152
Olenek, *Russ.* 68° 30′ N, 112° 22′ E 160
Olenek, river, *Russ.* 66° 59′ N, 107° 5′ E 160
Olenekskiy Zaliv 72° 54′ N, 114° 57′ E 160
Olenino, *Russ.* 56° 12′ N, 33° 37′ E 154
Olenitsa, *Russ.* 66° 26′ N, 35° 13′ E 152
Oleniy, Ostrov, island, *Russ.* 72° 2′ N, 72° 25′ E 160
Olesno, *Pol.* 50° 52′ N, 18° 25′ E 152
Olevs'k, *Ukr.* 51° 13′ N, 27° 40′ E 152
Ølfjellet, peak, *Nor.* 66° 46′ N, 15° 4′ E 152
Olga, Lac, lake, *Can.* 49° 45′ N, 77° 35′ W 94
Olga, Mount see Kata Tjuta, peak, *Austral.* 25° 21′ S, 130° 31′ E 230
Olgastretet 78° 6′ N, 20° 12′ E 160
Ölgiy, *Mongolia* 48° 57′ N, 89° 50′ E 184
Ølgod, *Den.* 55° 48′ N, 8° 35′ E 150
Olhava, *Fin.* 65° 28′ N, 25° 22′ E 152
Oli Qoltyq Sory, marsh, *Kaz.* 45° 20′ N, 53° 31′ E 158
Oli, river, *Nig.* 9° 46′ N, 4° 0′ E 222
Oliete, *Sp.* 40° 59′ N, 0° 41′ E 164
Olifants, river, *S. Af.* 24° 36′ S, 30° 29′ E 227
Olifantshoek, *S. Af.* 27° 58′ S, 22° 42′ E 227
Olimarao Atoll 7° 48′ N, 143° 3′ E 192
Ólimbos, *Gr.* 35° 44′ N, 27° 11′ E 156
Ólimbos, Óros (Olympus), peak, *Gr.* 40° 3′ N, 22° 17′ E 156
Olímpia, *Braz.* 20° 43′ S, 48° 55′ W 138
Olinalá, *Mex.* 17° 48′ N, 98° 51′ W 114
Olinda, *Braz.* 8° 0′ S, 34° 55′ W 132
Olinda Entrance 11° 17′ S, 142° 53′ E 192
Olite, *Sp.* 42° 28′ N, 1° 39′ W 164
Oliva, *Arg.* 32° 3′ S, 63° 33′ W 139
Oliva, *Sp.* 38° 55′ N, 0° 8′ E 164
Oliva de la Frontera, *Sp.* 38° 16′ N, 6° 56′ W 150
Oliveira, *Braz.* 20° 40′ S, 44° 51′ W 138
Oliver, *Can.* 49° 10′ N, 119° 34′ W 90
Oliver Lake, lake, *Can.* 56° 50′ N, 103° 50′ W 108
Olivet, *Mich., U.S.* 42° 27′ N, 84° 55′ W 102
Olivia, *Minn., U.S.* 44° 46′ N, 95° 0′ W 90
Ol'khovka, *Russ.* 49° 51′ N, 44° 31′ E 158
Olla, *La., U.S.* 31° 53′ N, 92° 15′ W 103
Ollachea, *Peru* 13° 49′ S, 70° 32′ W 137
Ollagüe (Oyahue), *Chile* 21° 14′ S, 68° 18′ W 137
Ollagüe, Volcan, peak, *Chile* 21° 19′ S, 68° 20′ W 137
Ollanta, *Peru* 9° 45′ S, 74° 2′ W 137
Ollerton, *U.K.* 53° 11′ N, 1° 2′ W 162
Olmaliq, *Uzb.* 40° 50′ N, 69° 35′ E 197
Olnes, *Alas., U.S.* 65° 5′ N, 147° 40′ W 98
Olney, *Ill., U.S.* 38° 42′ N, 88° 1′ W 82
Olney, *Tex., U.S.* 33° 21′ N, 98° 46′ W 92
Olney, *U.K.* 52° 9′ N, 0° 42′ E 162
Oloibiri, oil field, *Nig.* 4° 39′ N, 6° 16′ E 222
Olomouc, *Czech Rep.* 49° 35′ N, 17° 16′ E 152
Olomoucký, adm. division, *Czech Rep.* 49° 35′ N, 17° 16′ E 152
Olonets, *Russ.* 60° 56′ N, 33° 2′ E 154
Olongapo, *Philippines* 14° 50′ N, 120° 17′ E 203
Olonzac, *Fr.* 43° 16′ N, 2° 42′ E 164
Oloron, *Fr.* 43° 12′ N, 0° 36′ E 164
Oloru, *Nig.* 8° 39′ N, 4° 35′ E 222
Olosega, island, *United States* 14° 11′ S, 169° 36′ W 241
Olot, *Sp.* 42° 11′ N, 2° 28′ E 164
Olovo, *Bosn. and Herzg.* 44° 7′ N, 18° 34′ E 168
Olovyannaya, *Russ.* 50° 54′ N, 115° 24′ E 190
Olovyannaya, *Russ.* 66° 13′ N, 178° 56′ W 98
Oloy, river, *Russ.* 66° 12′ N, 160° 20′ E 160
Olpe, *Ger.* 51° 1′ N, 7° 50′ E 167
Olshammar, *Nor.* 58° 45′ N, 14° 45′ E 152
Olsztyn, *Pol.* 53° 46′ N, 20° 28′ E 166
Olt, adm. division, *Rom.* 44° 11′ N, 24° 12′ E 156
Olt, river, *Rom.* 45° 46′ N, 24° 19′ E 156
Olten, *Switz.* 47° 21′ N, 7° 53′ E 156
Olteni, *Rom.* 44° 11′ N, 25° 18′ E 156
Oltenița, *Rom.* 44° 6′ N, 26° 39′ E 156
Olton, *Tex., U.S.* 34° 9′ N, 102° 8′ W 92
Oltu, *Turk.* 40° 34′ N, 41° 57′ E 195
Oltu, river, *Turk.* 40° 43′ N, 41° 41′ E 195
Oluan Pi, *Taiwan, China* 21° 39′ N, 120° 53′ E 198
Olukonda, *Namibia* 18° 6′ S, 16° 4′ E 220
Ólvega, *Sp.* 41° 45′ N, 1° 59′ W 164
Olvera, *Sp.* 36° 55′ N, 5° 17′ W 164
Olympia, *Wash., U.S.* 47° 1′ N, 122° 56′ W 100
Olympia, ruin(s), *Gr.* 37° 38′ N, 21° 32′ E 156
Olympic Mountains, *Wash., U.S.* 47° 16′ N, 123° 50′ W 100
Olympic National Park, *Wash., U.S.* 48° 0′ N, 125° 7′ W 100
Olympos, peak, *Cyprus* 34° 55′ N, 32° 50′ E 194
Olympus, Mount, peak, *Wash., U.S.* 47° 47′ N, 123° 45′ W 100
Olympus, Mount see Ulu Dağ, peak, *Turk.* 40° 4′ N, 29° 7′ E 156
Olympus see Ólimbos, Óros, peak, *Gr.* 40° 3′ N, 22° 17′ E 156
Olynthus, ruin(s), *Gr.* 40° 16′ N, 23° 17′ E 156
Olyutorskiy, Mys, *Russ.* 59° 44′ N, 170° 18′ E 160
Om', river, *Russ.* 55° 17′ N, 77° 33′ E 184
Oma, *China* 32° 26′ N, 83° 17′ E 188
Oma, *Miss., U.S.* 31° 43′ N, 90° 9′ W 103
Oma, river, *Russ.* 66° 23′ N, 46° 47′ E 154
Ōmachi, *Japan* 36° 30′ N, 137° 51′ E 201
Omae Zaki, *Japan* 34° 29′ N, 138° 14′ E 201
Omaha, *Nebr., U.S.* 41° 15′ N, 95° 58′ W 90
Omaha, *Tex., U.S.* 33° 10′ N, 94° 45′ W 103
Omaha Beach, *Fr.* 49° 17′ N, 1° 13′ W 150
Omak, *Wash., U.S.* 48° 24′ N, 119° 33′ W 90
Omakau, *N.Z.* 45° 5′ S, 169° 38′ E 240
Omakere, *N.Z.* 40° 3′ S, 176° 49′ E 240
Oman 21° 52′ N, 57° 32′ E 182
Oman, Gulf of 24° 46′ N, 57° 23′ E 172
Oman, Gulf of 24° 30′ N, 58° 46′ E 254
Omarama, *N.Z.* 44° 31′ S, 169° 58′ E 240
Omaruru, *Namibia* 21° 27′ S, 15° 55′ E 227
Ombabika, *Can.* 50° 14′ N, 87° 54′ W 94
Ombaïa, *Congo* 2° 24′ S, 13° 10′ E 218
Ombombo, spring, *Namibia* 18° 44′ S, 13° 55′ E 220
Ombwe, *Dem. Rep. of the Congo* 4° 23′ S, 25° 32′ E 224
Omchali, Mys, *Turkm.* 40° 54′ N, 53° 5′ E 158
Omdurman, *Sudan* 15° 36′ N, 32° 27′ E 182
Omegna, *It.* 45° 52′ N, 8° 24′ E 167
Omer, *Mich., U.S.* 44° 3′ N, 83° 51′ W 102
Ometepec, *Mex.* 16° 30′ N, 98° 28′ W 73
Ōmihachiman, *Japan* 35° 6′ N, 136° 5′ E 201
Omihi, *N.Z.* 43° 2′ S, 172° 52′ E 240
Omineca, river, *Can.* 55° 54′ N, 126° 9′ W 108
Omiš, *Croatia* 43° 26′ N, 16° 42′ E 168
Ōmiya, *Japan* 35° 54′ N, 139° 38′ E 201
Ommaney, Cape, *Alas., U.S.* 56° 0′ N, 135° 20′ W 108
Ommen, *Neth.* 52° 31′ N, 6° 24′ E 163
Omo National Park, *Eth.* 5° 39′ N, 35° 20′ E 224
Omo, river, *Eth.* 5° 54′ N, 35° 55′ E 224
Omolon, *Russ.* 65° 10′ N, 160° 34′ E 173
Omolon, river, *Russ.* 69° 30′ N, 155° 38′ E 172
Omoloy, river, *Russ.* 69° 50′ N, 132° 42′ E 160
Omont, *Fr.* 49° 35′ N, 4° 42′ E 163
Omro, *Wis., U.S.* 44° 1′ N, 88° 45′ W 102
Omsk, *Russ.* 54° 58′ N, 73° 26′ E 184
Omsk, adm. division, *Russ.* 54° 44′ N, 72° 20′ E 184
Omsukchan, *Russ.* 62° 29′ N, 155° 44′ E 173
Omu Aran, *Nig.* 8° 9′ N, 5° 6′ E 222
Omul, peak, *Rom.* 45° 26′ N, 25° 22′ E 156
Omullyakhskaya Guba 72° 1′ N, 138° 2′ E 160
Ōmura, *Japan* 32° 54′ N, 129° 58′ E 201
Ōmuta, *Japan* 33° 1′ N, 130° 26′ E 201
Omutninsk, *Russ.* 58° 40′ N, 52° 15′ E 154
Oña, *Sp.* 42° 43′ N, 3° 26′ W 164
Onaga, *Kans., U.S.* 39° 28′ N, 96° 10′ W 90
Onakawana, *Can.* 50° 36′ N, 81° 27′ W 110
Onalaska, *Tex., U.S.* 30° 47′ N, 95° 7′ W 103
Onaman Lake, *Can.* 50° 0′ N, 87° 59′ W 110
Onamia, *Minn., U.S.* 46° 3′ N, 93° 41′ W 94
Onaping Lake, *Can.* 46° 56′ N, 82° 3′ W 94
Onarga, *Ill., U.S.* 40° 42′ N, 88° 1′ W 102
Onatchiway, Lac, lake, *Can.* 48° 59′ N, 71° 46′ W 94
Oñati, *Sp.* 43° 1′ N, 2° 24′ W 164
Onavas, *Mex.* 28° 27′ N, 109° 32′ W 92
Onawa, *Iowa, U.S.* 42° 0′ N, 96° 6′ W 90
Oncativo, *Arg.* 31° 55′ S, 63° 41′ W 139
Onda, *Sp.* 39° 58′ N, 0° 17′ E 164
Ondangwa, *Namibia* 17° 56′ S, 15° 59′ E 220
Ondas, river, *Braz.* 12° 42′ S, 46° 4′ W 132
Ondjiva, *Angola* 17° 6′ S, 15° 39′ E 220
Ondo, *Nig.* 7° 7′ N, 4° 49′ E 222
Ondor Sum, *China* 42° 30′ N, 112° 50′ E 198
Öndörhaan, *Mongolia* 47° 22′ N, 110° 40′ E 198
Öndörhushuu, *Mongolia* 47° 59′ N, 113° 55′ E 198
One and Half Degree Channel 0° 58′ N, 72° 7′ E 188
Oneco, *Conn., U.S.* 41° 41′ N, 71° 49′ W 104
Oneco, *Fla., U.S.* 27° 27′ N, 82° 32′ W 105
Onega, *Russ.* 63° 55′ N, 38° 12′ E 154
Oneida, *N.Y., U.S.* 43° 5′ N, 75° 41′ W 94
Oneida, *Tenn., U.S.* 36° 29′ N, 84° 31′ W 96
Oneida Lake, *N.Y., U.S.* 43° 14′ N, 76° 34′ W 80
O'Neill, *Nebr., U.S.* 42° 26′ N, 98° 40′ W 90
Oneonta, *Ala., U.S.* 33° 56′ N, 86° 29′ W 96
Oneonta, *N.Y., U.S.* 42° 27′ N, 75° 5′ W 94
Onezhskaya Guba 64° 4′ N, 36° 13′ E 154

Onezhskoye Ozero, lake, *Russ.* 60°31′ N, 33°29′ E 160
Ongarue, *N.Z.* 38°43′ S, 175°17′ E 240
Ongcheon, *S. Korea* 36°41′ N, 128°42′ E 200
Ongi, *Mongolia* 45°28′ N, 103°56′ E 198
Ongjin, *N. Korea* 37°55′ N, 125°22′ E 200
Ongniud Qi, *China* 42°56′ N, 118°59′ E 198
Ongoka, *Dem. Rep. of the Congo* 1°24′ S, 26°2′ E 224
Ongole, *India* 15°30′ N, 80°4′ E 188
Ongtustik Qazaqstan, adm. division, *Kaz.* 42°4′ N, 67°24′ E 197
Ongwediva, *Namibia* 17°55′ S, 15°54′ E 220
Oni, *Ga.* 42°33′ N, 43°27′ E 195
Onib, *Sudan* 21°26′ N, 35°16′ E 182
Onitsha, *Nig.* 6°15′ N, 6°46′ E 222
Onizuka Center for International Astronomy, site, *Hawai'i, U.S.* 19°43′ N, 155°29′ W 99
Önjüül, *Mongolia* 46°46′ N, 105°32′ E 198
Onley, *Va., U.S.* 37°41′ N, 75°44′ W 94
Onnela, *Fin.* 69°54′ N, 26°59′ E 152
Ōno, *Japan* 35°58′ N, 136°29′ E 201
Onolimbu, *Indonesia* 1°3′ N, 97°51′ E 196
Onomichi, *Japan* 34°25′ N, 133°12′ E 201
Onon, *Mongolia* 49°9′ N, 112°41′ E 198
Onon, *Mongolia* 48°32′ N, 110°30′ E 198
Onon, river, *Asia* 49°19′ N, 112°28′ E 198
Onoto, *Venez.* 9°36′ N, 65°12′ W 136
Onoway, *Can.* 53°42′ N, 114°13′ W 108
Onsen, *Japan* 35°32′ N, 134°29′ E 201
Onslow, *Austral.* 21°39′ S, 115°7′ E 231
Onsŏng, *N. Korea* 42°57′ N, 129°59′ E 200
Onsugok, *S. Korea* 37°37′ N, 126°28′ E 200
Ontario, *Calif., U.S.* 34°3′ N, 117°40′ W 101
Ontario, *Ohio, U.S.* 40°44′ N, 82°38′ W 102
Ontario, *Oreg., U.S.* 43°58′ N, 116°58′ W 82
Ontario, adm. division, *Can.* 51°1′ N, 90°29′ W 106
Ontario, Lake 43°37′ N, 78°57′ W 80
Ontojärvi, lake, *Fin.* 64°19′ N, 26°24′ E 154
Ontong Java Atoll, islands, *South Pacific Ocean* 7°9′ S, 159°58′ E 238
Ontur, *Sp.* 38°36′ N, 1°30′ W 164
Onuškis, *Lith.* 54°27′ N, 24°36′ E 166
Onyx, *Calif., U.S.* 35°41′ N, 118°15′ W 101
Oodaaq Island, 83°32′ N, 30°53′ W 255
Oodnadatta, *Austral.* 27°34′ S, 135°27′ E 231
Oodweyne, *Somalia* 9°22′ N, 45°5′ E 216
Ooldea, *Austral.* 30°28′ S, 131°50′ E 231
Oolitic, *Ind., U.S.* 38°53′ N, 86°33′ W 102
Oona River, *Can.* 53°57′ N, 130°19′ W 108
Ooruk-Tam, *Kyrg.* 41°26′ N, 76°39′ E 184
Oost Vlieland, *Neth.* 53°17′ N, 5°2′ E 163
Oostburg, *Wis., U.S.* 43°37′ N, 87°48′ W 102
Oostende (Ostend), *Belg.* 51°13′ N, 2°55′ E 163
Oosterhout, *Neth.* 51°39′ N, 4°51′ E 167
Ootsa Lake, *Can.* 53°50′ N, 126°3′ W 108
Opachuanau Lake, lake, *Can.* 56°42′ N, 100°14′ W 108
Opal, *Wyo., U.S.* 41°47′ N, 110°19′ W 92
Opala, *Dem. Rep. of the Congo* 0°38′ N, 24°20′ E 224
Opari, *Sudan* 3°55′ N, 32°5′ E 224
Oparino, *Russ.* 59°52′ N, 48°14′ E 154
Opasatica, Lac, lake, *Can.* 48°1′ N, 79°53′ W 110
Opasatika Lake, lake, *Can.* 49°2′ N, 83°40′ W 94
Opasatika, river, *Can.* 49°32′ N, 82°56′ W 94
Opataca, Lac, lake, *Can.* 50°13′ N, 75°49′ W 94
Opataouaga, Lac, lake, *Can.* 50°19′ N, 77°24′ W 94
Opelika, *Ala., U.S.* 32°38′ N, 85°24′ W 96
Opelousas, *La., U.S.* 30°30′ N, 92°6′ W 103
Opheim, *Mont., U.S.* 48°50′ N, 106°25′ W 90
Ophir, peak, *Indonesia* 8°475′ N, 99°55′ E 196
Ophthalmia Range, *Austral.* 23°24′ S, 118°34′ E 230
Opienge, *Dem. Rep. of the Congo* 0°15′ N, 27°21′ E 224
Opinaca, Réservoir, lake, *Can.* 52°3′ N, 77°47′ W 110
Opinaca, river, *Can.* 52°14′ N, 78°18′ W 106
Opladen, *Ger.* 51°4′ N, 7°0′ E 167
Oploca, *Bol.* 21°22′ S, 65°48′ W 137
Opobo, *Nig.* 4°34′ N, 7°32′ E 222
Opochka, *Russ.* 56°41′ N, 28°40′ E 166
Opoczno, *Pol.* 51°23′ N, 20°15′ E 152
Opodepe, *Mex.* 29°55′ N, 110°38′ W 92
Opole, *Pol.* 50°39′ N, 17°57′ E 152
Opolskie, adm. division, *Pol.* 50°39′ N, 17°57′ E 152
Opornyy, *Kaz.* 46°3′ N, 54°37′ E 158
Oporto see Porto, *Port.* 41°8′ N, 8°38′ W 150
Opotiki, *N.Z.* 38°2′ S, 177°19′ E 240
Opp, *Ala., U.S.* 31°16′ N, 86°15′ W 96
Oppenheim, *Ger.* 49°50′ N, 8°21′ E 167
Oppola, *Russ.* 61°34′ N, 30°19′ E 166
Oprişoru, *Rom.* 44°16′ N, 23°6′ E 168
Opsa, *Belarus* 55°32′ N, 26°49′ E 166
Opua, *N.Z.* 35°21′ S, 174°5′ E 240
Opukhliki, *Russ.* 56°5′ N, 30°9′ E 166
Opunake, *N.Z.* 39°28′ S, 173°51′ E 240
Opuwo, *Namibia* 18°6′ S, 13°50′ E 220
Oqtosh, *Uzb.* 39°55′ N, 65°55′ E 197
Or, Les Îles d' see Hyères, Îles d', islands, *Mediterranean Sea* 42°57′ N, 6°33′ E 165
Or, river, *Asia* 49°38′ N, 58°38′ E 158
Ora, oil field, *Lib.* 28°26′ N, 19°15′ E 216
Oradea, *Rom.* 47°3′ N, 21°57′ E 168
Öræfajökull, glacier, *Ice.* 63°52′ N, 15°30′ W 142
Orahovica, *Croatia* 45°32′ N, 17°54′ E 168
Oral, *Kaz.* 51°12′ N, 51°24′ E 158
Oran, *Alg.* 35°39′ N, 0°38′ E 214
Orange, *Fr.* 44°8′ N, 4°47′ E 214
Orange, *Mass., U.S.* 42°35′ N, 72°19′ W 104
Orange, *Tex., U.S.* 30°5′ N, 93°45′ W 103
Orange, *Va., U.S.* 38°14′ N, 78°7′ W 94
Orange, Cabo, *Braz.* 4°26′ N, 51°35′ W 130
Orange City, *Fla., U.S.* 28°57′ N, 81°19′ W 105
Orange City, *Iowa, U.S.* 42°58′ N, 96°5′ W 90
Orange Cove, *Calif., U.S.* 36°37′ N, 119°20′ W 100
Orange Grove, *Tex., U.S.* 27°56′ N, 97°56′ W 96
Orange (Oranje), river, *Africa* 28°40′ S, 18°39′ E 227
Orange, river, *S. Af.* 30°46′ S, 26°51′ E 227
Orange Walk, *Belize* 18°5′ N, 88°35′ W 115
Orangeburg, *S.C., U.S.* 33°29′ N, 80°51′ W 96
Orangeville, *Can.* 43°55′ N, 80°6′ W 94
Orangeville, *Ill., U.S.* 42°27′ N, 89°39′ W 102
Orango, island, *Guinea-Bissau* 11°1′ N, 16°41′ W 222
Oranienburg, *Ger.* 52°45′ N, 13°14′ E 152
Oranje Gebergte, *Suriname* 3°12′ N, 56°2′ W 130
Oranje see Orange, river, *Africa* 28°40′ S, 18°39′ E 227
Oranjemund, *Namibia* 28°31′ S, 16°25′ E 227
Oranjestad, *Aruba, Neth.* 12°34′ N, 70°2′ W 118
Oranzherei, *Russ.* 45°49′ N, 47°35′ E 158
Orapa, *Botswana* 21°16′ S, 25°17′ E 227
Orari, *N.Z.* 44°9′ S, 171°17′ E 240
Oras, *Philippines* 12°10′ N, 125°26′ E 203
Orašac, *Maced.* 42°3′ N, 21°48′ E 168
Orašje, *Bosn. and Herzg.* 45°1′ N, 18°40′ E 168
Oravais (Oravainen), *Fin.* 63°16′ N, 22°21′ E 152
Orawia, *N.Z.* 46°4′ S, 167°46′ E 240
Orba Co, lake, *China* 34°28′ N, 80°29′ E 188
Örbyhus, *Nor.* 60°13′ N, 17°39′ E 152
Orcadas, station, *Antarctica* 60°46′ S, 44°52′ W 134
Orce, *Sp.* 37°42′ N, 2°29′ W 164
Orcera, *Sp.* 38°18′ N, 2°39′ W 164
Orchard City, *Colo., U.S.* 38°50′ N, 107°58′ W 92
Orchards, *Wash., U.S.* 45°39′ N, 122°34′ W 100
Orchies, *Fr.* 50°28′ N, 3°14′ E 163
Orchomenus, ruin(s), *Gr.* 38°29′ N, 22°50′ E 156
Orcières, *Fr.* 44°41′ N, 6°19′ E 167
Orco, river, *It.* 45°23′ N, 7°25′ E 167
Orcutt, *Calif., U.S.* 34°51′ N, 120°28′ W 100
Ord, *Nebr., U.S.* 41°35′ N, 98°57′ W 90
Ord, Mount, peak, *Austral.* 17°22′ S, 125°22′ E 230
Ord Mountains, *Calif., U.S.* 34°40′ N, 116°49′ W 101
Orda, *Russ.* 57°11′ N, 56°56′ E 154
Orderville, *Utah, U.S.* 37°16′ N, 112°38′ W 92
Ordu, *Turk.* 40°58′ N, 37°51′ E 156
Ordubad, *Asia* 38°53′ N, 46°0′ E 195
Orduña, *Sp.* 42°58′ N, 3°2′ W 164
Orduña, peak, *Sp.* 37°19′ N, 3°33′ W 164
Ordway, *Colo., U.S.* 38°13′ N, 103°46′ W 90
Ordzhonikidze, *Kaz.* 52°27′ N, 61°41′ E 184
Ordzhonikidze, *Ukr.* 47°41′ N, 34°5′ E 156
Ore City, *Tex., U.S.* 32°48′ N, 94°44′ W 103
Orea, *Sp.* 40°32′ N, 1°43′ W 164
Oreana, *Ill., U.S.* 39°56′ N, 88°52′ W 102
Orebić, *Croatia* 42°58′ N, 17°9′ E 168
Örebro, *Nor.* 59°16′ N, 15°10′ E 152
Oredezh, *Russ.* 58°49′ N, 30°20′ E 166
Oregon, *Ohio, U.S.* 41°38′ N, 83°29′ W 102
Oregon, *Wis., U.S.* 42°55′ N, 89°23′ W 102
Oregon, adm. division, *Oreg., U.S.* 43°43′ N, 121°32′ W 90
Oregon Caves National Monument, *Oreg., U.S.* 42°5′ N, 123°29′ W 90
Oregon Dunes National Recreation Area, *Oreg., U.S.* 43°59′ N, 129°37′ W 80
Öregrund, *Sw.* 60°18′ N, 18°22′ E 166
Orekhovo-Zuyevo, *Russ.* 55°49′ N, 38°56′ E 154
Orel, *Russ.* 52°55′ N, 36°4′ E 154
Orel, adm. division, *Russ.* 52°59′ N, 35°55′ E 154
Orellana, *Peru* 6°56′ S, 75°14′ W 130
Orellana la Vieja, *Sp.* 39°0′ N, 5°32′ W 164
Orem, *Utah, U.S.* 40°18′ N, 111°41′ W 90
Ören, *Turk.* 37°1′ N, 27°57′ E 156
Orenburg, *Russ.* 51°47′ N, 55°9′ E 154
Orenburg, adm. division, *Russ.* 52°50′ N, 51°59′ E 154
Orense, *Arg.* 38°41′ S, 59°45′ W 139
Örenşehir, *Turk.* 38°59′ N, 36°40′ E 156
Orford, *N.H., U.S.* 43°54′ N, 72°8′ W 104
Orford, *U.K.* 52°5′ N, 1°31′ E 163
Orford Ness, *U.K.* 52°0′ N, 1°35′ E 163
Orfordville, *N.H., U.S.* 43°52′ N, 72°7′ W 104
Orfordville, *Wis., U.S.* 42°38′ N, 89°15′ W 102
Organ Peak, *N. Mex., U.S.* 32°20′ N, 106°43′ W 82
Organ Pipe Cactus National Monument, *Ariz., U.S.* 32°2′ N, 112°37′ W 80
Organt, *Kaz.* 44°7′ N, 66°46′ E 184
Organyà, *Sp.* 42°12′ N, 1°18′ E 164
Órgiva, *Sp.* 36°53′ N, 3°26′ W 164
Orgon, *Fr.* 43°47′ N, 5°1′ E 150
Orgun, *Afghan.* 32°52′ N, 69°11′ E 186
Orhaneli, *Turk.* 39°54′ N, 28°57′ E 156
Orhangazi, *Turk.* 40°29′ N, 29°17′ E 158
Orhei, *Mold.* 47°22′ N, 28°50′ E 156
Orhi, peak, *Fr.* 42°58′ N, 1°3′ W 164
Orhon, adm. division, *Mongolia* 49°2′ N, 104°5′ E 198
Orhon, river, *Mongolia* 48°34′ N, 104°41′ E 190
Orhontuul, *Mongolia* 48°54′ N, 104°57′ E 198
Oria, *Sp.* 37°29′ N, 2°18′ W 164
Orick, *Calif., U.S.* 41°16′ N, 124°5′ W 92
Oricum see Orikon, ruin(s), *Alban.* 40°17′ N, 19°19′ E 156
Orient, *N.Y., U.S.* 41°8′ N, 72°18′ W 104
Orient, *Wash., U.S.* 48°51′ N, 118°14′ W 90
Orient Point, *N.Y., U.S.* 41°9′ N, 72°20′ W 104
Oriental, Cordillera, *Peru* 5°11′ S, 77°46′ W 130
Oriental, Grand Erg, *Alg.* 29°30′ N, 4°11′ E 214
Orientale, adm. division, *Dem. Rep. of the Congo* 2°6′ N, 26°40′ E 218
Oriente, *Arg.* 38°44′ S, 60°37′ W 139
Oriente, *Braz.* 10°1′ S, 64°7′ W 137
Origny-Sainte-Benoite, *Fr.* 49°50′ N, 3°29′ E 163
Orihuela, *Sp.* 38°4′ N, 0°57′ E 164
Orikhiv, *Ukr.* 47°32′ N, 35°47′ E 156
Orikon (Oricum), ruin(s), *Alban.* 40°17′ N, 19°19′ E 156
Orillia, *Can.* 44°36′ N, 79°25′ W 94
Orimattila, *Fin.* 60°47′ N, 25°42′ E 166
Orinoca, *Bol.* 18°59′ S, 67°15′ W 137
Orinoco, river, *Venez.* 3°9′ N, 65°14′ W 130
Orissa, adm. division, *India* 21°55′ N, 84°41′ E 197
Orissaare, *Est.* 58°32′ N, 23°3′ E 166
Oristano, *It.* 39°54′ N, 8°35′ E 214
Orivesi, *Fin.* 61°40′ N, 24°18′ E 166
Oriximiná, *Braz.* 1°44′ S, 55°54′ W 130
Orizaba, *Mex.* 18°50′ N, 97°6′ W 114
Orizaba, Pico de, peak, *Mex.* 18°59′ N, 97°20′ W 114
Orizona, *Braz.* 17°4′ S, 48°19′ W 138
Orjen, peak, *Mont.* 42°33′ N, 18°30′ E 168
Orkney, *S. Af.* 26°59′ S, 26°38′ E 227
Orkney Islands, *U.K.* 59°28′ N, 6°40′ W 142
Orland, *Calif., U.S.* 39°44′ N, 122°13′ W 90
Orland, *Me., U.S.* 44°34′ N, 68°45′ W 94
Orlando, *Fla., U.S.* 28°32′ N, 81°23′ W 105
Orlando, Capo d', *It.* 38°11′ N, 13°59′ E 156
Orléanais, region, *Fr.* 48°23′ N, 1°15′ E 163
Orléans, *Fr.* 47°54′ N, 1°54′ E 163
Orleans, *Ind., U.S.* 38°39′ N, 86°27′ W 102
Orleans, *Mass., U.S.* 41°46′ N, 70°0′ W 104
Orleans, *Nebr., U.S.* 40°6′ N, 99°27′ W 90
Orlik, *Russ.* 52°36′ N, 99°50′ E 190
Orlová, *Czech Rep.* 49°50′ N, 18°25′ E 152
Orlovat, *Serb.* 45°15′ N, 20°33′ E 168
Orlovka, *Russ.* 56°55′ N, 76°24′ E 169
Orlovskiy, *Russ.* 46°49′ N, 41°56′ E 158
Orlu, *Nig.* 5°45′ N, 7°10′ E 222
Ormara, *Pak.* 25°12′ N, 64°35′ E 182
Ormara, Ras, *Pak.* 25°2′ N, 64°39′ E 182
Ormea, *It.* 44°9′ N, 7°54′ E 167
Ormoc, *Philippines* 11°2′ N, 124°36′ E 203
Ormond, *N.Z.* 38°33′ S, 177°55′ E 240
Ormond Beach, *Fla., U.S.* 29°16′ N, 81°4′ W 105
Ormond by the Sea, *Fla., U.S.* 29°19′ N, 81°4′ W 105
Ormož, *Slov.* 46°24′ N, 16°7′ E 168
Ormskirk, *U.K.* 53°34′ N, 2°53′ W 162
Orne, river, *Fr.* 49°7′ N, 5°44′ E 163
Orneta, *Pol.* 54°5′ N, 20°7′ E 166
Ornö, island, *Sw.* 59°0′ N, 18°32′ E 166
Orno Peak, *Colo., U.S.* 40°3′ N, 107°10′ W 90
Örnsköldsvik, *Nor.* 63°16′ N, 18°43′ E 152
Oro Blanco, *Peru* 3°11′ S, 73°14′ W 136
Oro Grande, *Calif., U.S.* 34°36′ N, 117°21′ W 101
Oro Ingenio, *Bol.* 21°16′ S, 66°1′ W 137
Oro, river, *Mex.* 25°55′ N, 105°18′ W 80
Orobie, Alpi, *It.* 46°18′ N, 9°48′ E 167
Orocopia Mountains, *Calif., U.S.* 33°38′ N, 115°55′ W 101
Orocué, *Col.* 4°47′ N, 71°21′ W 136
Orodara, *Burkina Faso* 10°57′ N, 4°56′ W 222
Orofino, *Idaho, U.S.* 46°29′ N, 116°15′ W 90
Orokam, *Nig.* 7°1′ N, 7°33′ E 222
Oromia, region, *Eth.* 5°54′ N, 38°39′ E 224
Oron, *Israel* 30°54′ N, 35°0′ E 194
Oron, *Nig.* 4°49′ N, 8°12′ E 222
Orono, *Me., U.S.* 44°52′ N, 68°41′ W 111
Oronoquekamp, *Guyana* 2°43′ N, 57°32′ W 130
Orontes see 'Āṣī, river, *Syr.* 35°40′ N, 36°21′ E 194
Oropesa del Mar (Orpesa), *Sp.* 40°5′ N, 0°7′ E 164
Oroquieta, *Philippines* 8°31′ N, 123°46′ E 203
Orós, *Braz.* 6°21′ S, 38°53′ W 132
Oros Áskio, peak, *Gr.* 40°23′ N, 21°28′ E 156
Orosháza, *Hung.* 46°33′ N, 20°40′ E 168
Orosi, *Calif., U.S.* 36°33′ N, 119°18′ W 100
Orotukan, *Russ.* 62°13′ N, 151°26′ E 160
Oroville, *Calif., U.S.* 39°30′ N, 121°35′ W 90
Oroyek, *Russ.* 64°52′ N, 153°22′ E 160
Oroz Betelu, *Sp.* 42°54′ N, 1°19′ W 164
Orqohan, *China* 49°29′ N, 121°22′ E 198
Orr, *Minn., U.S.* 48°2′ N, 92°50′ W 94
Orrs Island, *Me., U.S.* 43°45′ N, 69°59′ W 104
Orrville, *Ohio, U.S.* 40°49′ N, 81°45′ W 102
Orsa, *Nor.* 61°6′ N, 14°35′ E 152
Orsha, *Belarus* 54°31′ N, 30°31′ E 154
Orshanka, *Russ.* 56°54′ N, 47°55′ E 154
Orsk, *Russ.* 51°11′ N, 58°36′ E 158
Örskär, island, *Sw.* 60°31′ N, 18°12′ E 166
Orta, *Turk.* 40°37′ N, 33°6′ E 156
Ortaca, *Turk.* 36°50′ N, 28°45′ E 156
Ortegal, Cabo, *Sp.* 43°46′ N, 7°54′ W 150
Orthez, *Fr.* 43°29′ N, 0°46′ E 164
Orting, *Wash., U.S.* 47°4′ N, 122°13′ W 100
Ortisei, *It.* 46°36′ N, 11°39′ E 167
Orţişoara, *Rom.* 45°58′ N, 21°12′ E 168
Ortiz, *Mex.* 28°17′ N, 110°44′ W 92
Ortiz, *Mex.* 28°14′ N, 105°33′ W 92
Ortiz, *Venez.* 9°35′ N, 67°19′ W 136
Ortles, *It.* 46°22′ N, 10°15′ E 167
Orto Surt, *Russ.* 62°34′ N, 125°4′ E 173
Ortón, river, *Bol.* 11°2′ S, 66°58′ W 137
Ortona, *It.* 42°21′ N, 14°23′ E 156
Ortonville, *Mich., U.S.* 42°51′ N, 83°28′ W 102
Ortonville, *Minn., U.S.* 45°17′ N, 96°27′ W 90
Örträsk, *Nor.* 64°8′ N, 18°59′ E 152
Orūmīyeh, *Iran* 37°30′ N, 44°58′ E 143
Orūmīyeh, Daryācheh-ye (Urmia, Lake), *Iran* 38°7′ N, 45°16′ E 195
Orūmīyeh (Urmia), *Iran* 37°37′ N, 45°4′ E 195
Orungo, *Uganda* 2°0′ N, 33°28′ E 224
Oruro, *Bol.* 17°59′ S, 67°8′ W 137
Oruro, adm. division, *Bol.* 18°53′ S, 68°19′ W 137
Orwell, *Ohio, U.S.* 41°31′ N, 80°52′ W 102
Orwell, *Vt., U.S.* 43°48′ N, 73°19′ W 104
Orxon, river, *China* 48°16′ N, 117°47′ E 198
Orynyn, *Ukr.* 48°44′ N, 26°25′ E 152
Orzinuovi, *It.* 45°24′ N, 9°55′ E 167
Os, *Nor.* 60°11′ N, 5°27′ E 152
Osa, *Russ.* 57°15′ N, 55°32′ E 154
Osage, *Iowa, U.S.* 43°15′ N, 92°49′ W 94
Osage, *Wyo., U.S.* 43°57′ N, 104°25′ W 90
Osage City, *Kans., U.S.* 38°36′ N, 95°50′ W 90
Ōsaka, *Japan* 34°42′ N, 135°32′ E 190
Osaka, *Japan* 35°57′ N, 137°17′ E 201
Ōsaka, *Japan* 34°40′ N, 135°30′ E 201
Ōsaka, adm. division, *Japan* 34°20′ N, 135°21′ E 201
Osakarovka, *Kaz.* 50°34′ N, 72°35′ E 184
Osakis, *Minn., U.S.* 45°50′ N, 95°11′ W 90
Osan, *S. Korea* 37°8′ N, 127°4′ E 200
Osawatomie, *Kans., U.S.* 38°28′ N, 94°57′ W 94
Osborn Plateau, *Indian Ocean* 14°42′ S, 86°43′ E 254
Osborne, *Kans., U.S.* 39°25′ N, 98°43′ W 90
Osby, *Nor.* 56°23′ N, 13°57′ E 152
Oscar Ii Coast, *Antarctica* 65°25′ S, 61°36′ W 134
Osceola, *Iowa, U.S.* 41°2′ N, 93°45′ W 94
Osečina, *Serb.* 44°22′ N, 19°35′ E 168
Ösel see Saaremaa, island, *Est.* 58°32′ N, 21°21′ E 166
Osel'ki, *Russ.* 60°14′ N, 30°26′ E 166
Osen, *Nor.* 64°18′ N, 10°31′ E 152
Osgood, *Ind., U.S.* 39°7′ N, 85°17′ W 102
Osgood Mountains, *Nev., U.S.* 41°3′ N, 117°37′ W 90
Osh, *Kyrg.* 40°31′ N, 72°49′ E 197
Oshakati, *Namibia* 17°54′ S, 15°48′ E 220
Oshawa, *Can.* 43°53′ N, 78°50′ W 94
Oshikango, *Namibia* 17°28′ S, 15°52′ E 220
Ōshima, *Japan* 34°44′ N, 139°21′ E 201
Oshkosh, *Nebr., U.S.* 41°24′ N, 102°22′ W 90
Oshkosh, *Wis., U.S.* 44°1′ N, 88°33′ W 102
Oshkur'ya, *Russ.* 66°0′ N, 56°40′ E 154
Oshogbo, *Nig.* 7°50′ N, 4°35′ E 222
Oshta, *Russ.* 60°49′ N, 35°33′ E 154
Oshwe, *Dem. Rep. of the Congo* 3°27′ S, 19°29′ E 218
Osian, *India* 26°41′ N, 72°55′ E 186
Osijek, *Croatia* 45°32′ N, 18°40′ E 168
Osilinka, river, *Can.* 56°4′ N, 125°26′ W 108
Osinovka, *Russ.* 56°33′ N, 102°11′ E 160
Osinovo, *Russ.* 61°18′ N, 89°49′ E 169
Oskaloosa, *Iowa, U.S.* 41°17′ N, 92°38′ W 94
Öskemen (Ust' Kamenogorsk), *Kaz.* 49°59′ N, 82°38′ E 184
Oskoba, *Russ.* 60°20′ N, 100°33′ E 160
Oskol, river, *Russ.* 50°34′ N, 37°37′ E 158
Oslo, *Minn., U.S.* 48°10′ N, 97°8′ W 90
Oslo, *Nor.* 59°53′ N, 10°33′ E 152
Oslob, *Philippines* 9°32′ N, 123°23′ E 203
Osma, *Sp.* 41°34′ N, 3°6′ W 164
Osmancık, *Turk.* 40°58′ N, 34°47′ E 156
Osmaniye, *Turk.* 37°4′ N, 36°13′ E 156
Os'mino, *Russ.* 59°1′ N, 29°7′ E 166
Osmus Saar, island, *Est.* 59°9′ N, 23°14′ E 166
Osnabrück, *Ger.* 52°16′ N, 8°2′ E 163
Osnaburgh House, *Can.* 51°8′ N, 90°17′ W 110
Oso, *Wash., U.S.* 48°16′ N, 121°56′ W 100
Oso, river, *Dem. Rep. of the Congo* 1°0′ N, 27°43′ E 224
Osogovske Planina, *Maced.* 42°2′ N, 22°2′ E 168
Osor, *Croatia* 44°42′ N, 14°23′ E 156
Osório, *Braz.* 29°54′ S, 50°17′ W 134
Osorno, *Chile* 40°34′ S, 73°9′ W 134
Osorno, *Sp.* 42°24′ N, 4°22′ W 150
Osoyoos, *Can.* 49°1′ N, 119°30′ W 108
Ospika, river, *Can.* 57°3′ N, 124°28′ W 108
Osprey, *Fla., U.S.* 27°12′ N, 82°28′ W 105
Oss, *Neth.* 51°45′ N, 5°31′ E 167
Ossa, Mount, peak, *Austral.* 41°53′ S, 145°50′ E 230
Óssa, Óros, peak, *Gr.* 39°47′ N, 22°36′ E 156
Ossabaw Island, *Ga., U.S.* 31°36′ N, 81°3′ W 112
Osse, river, *Nig.* 7°44′ N, 5°58′ E 222
Osselé, *Congo* 1°26′ S, 15°19′ E 218
Osseo, *Wis., U.S.* 44°33′ N, 91°13′ W 94
Ossian, *Ind., U.S.* 40°52′ N, 85°10′ W 102
Ossining, *N.Y., U.S.* 41°9′ N, 73°52′ W 104
Ossipee, *N.H., U.S.* 43°40′ N, 71°8′ W 104
Ossjøen, lake, *Nor.* 61°10′ N, 11°24′ E 152
Ossokmanuan Reservoir, lake, *Can.* 52°59′ N, 66°19′ W 111
Ossora, *Russ.* 59°14′ N, 163°0′ E 160
Ostaboningue, Lac, lake, *Can.* 47°7′ N, 79°36′ W 94
Ostashkov, *Russ.* 57°7′ N, 33°12′ E 154
Östavall, *Nor.* 62°25′ N, 15°29′ E 152
Ostbevern, *Ger.* 52°2′ N, 7°50′ E 167
Ostellato, *It.* 44°44′ N, 11°56′ E 167
Ostend see Oostende, *Belg.* 51°13′ N, 2°55′ E 163
Østerdalen, *Nor.* 61°50′ N, 10°47′ E 152
Östergarnsholme, island, *Sw.* 57°25′ N, 19°1′ E 166
Osterode, *Ger.* 51°44′ N, 10°13′ E 167
Östersund, *Nor.* 63°10′ N, 14°40′ E 152
Osterville, *Mass., U.S.* 41°37′ N, 70°24′ W 104
Östhammar, *Sw.* 60°14′ N, 18°18′ E 166
Ostheim, *Ger.* 50°27′ N, 10°13′ E 167
Ostiglia, *It.* 45°3′ N, 11°8′ E 167
Östra Kvarken 63°31′ N, 20°16′ E 152
Ostrava, *Czech Rep.* 49°49′ N, 18°15′ E 152
Ostro, *Pol.* 53°4′ N, 21°33′ E 152
Ostróda, *Pol.* 53°41′ N, 19°58′ E 152
Ostrov, *Russ.* 57°21′ N, 28°21′ E 166
Ostrov, *Russ.* 58°28′ N, 28°37′ E 166
Ostrov Russkiy, island, *Russ.* 76°38′ N, 89°18′ E 160
Ostrovtsy, *Russ.* 58°23′ N, 27°42′ E 166
Ostrožac, *Bosn. and Herzg.* 43°40′ N, 17°50′ E 168
Ostuni, *It.* 40°43′ N, 17°35′ E 156
O'sullivan Lake, lake, *Can.* 50°22′ N, 87°38′ W 110
Osuna, *Sp.* 37°14′ N, 5°7′ W 164
Osvaldo Cruz, *Braz.* 21°47′ S, 50°52′ W 138
Oswego, *N.Y., U.S.* 43°26′ N, 76°32′ W 110
Oswestry, *U.K.* 52°51′ N, 3°4′ W 162
Osyka, *Miss., U.S.* 31°0′ N, 90°30′ W 103
Ota, *Japan* 35°56′ N, 136°3′ E 201
Ōta, *Japan* 36°16′ N, 139°24′ E 201
Ōta, river, *Japan* 34°29′ N, 132°11′ E 201
Otaci, *Mold.* 48°25′ N, 27°47′ E 152
Ōtake, *Japan* 34°12′ N, 132°13′ E 200
Otaki, *N.Z.* 40°46′ S, 175°8′ E 240
Otanmäki, *Fin.* 64°4′ N, 27°4′ E 152
Otar, *Kaz.* 43°31′ N, 75°12′ E 184

Otare, Cerro, peak, *Col.* 1°43′ N, 72°49′ W 136
Otaru, *Japan* 43°12′ N, 140°49′ E 190
Otatara, *N.Z.* 46°27′ S, 168°18′ E 240
Otautau, *N.Z.* 46°11′ S, 167°58′ E 240
Otava, *Fin.* 61°37′ N, 27°2′ E 166
Otavalo, *Ecua.* 0°11′ N, 78°24′ W 136
Otavi, *Namibia* 19°39′ S, 17°19′ E 220
Otawara, *Japan* 36°49′ N, 140°1′ E 201
Otay, *Calif., U.S.* 32°36′ N, 117°6′ W 101
Otchinjau, *Angola* 16°30′ S, 13°56′ E 220
Otelec, *Rom.* 45°36′ N, 20°50′ E 168
Oţelu Roşu, *Rom.* 45°30′ N, 22°23′ E 168
Otematata, *N.Z.* 44°37′ S, 170°11′ E 240
Otepää, *Est.* 58°2′ N, 26°29′ E 166
Oteros, river, *Mex.* 27°19′ N, 108°36′ W 80
Othello, *Wash., U.S.* 46°48′ N, 119°11′ W 90
Otherside, river, *Can.* 59°5′ N, 107°21′ W 108
Óthris, Óros, *Gr.* 38°57′ N, 22°19′ E 156
Oti, river, *Ghana* 8°32′ N, 8°476′ E 222
Otinapa, *Mex.* 24°0′ N, 105°1′ W 114
Otira, *N.Z.* 42°50′ S, 171°33′ E 240
Otis, *Colo., U.S.* 40°9′ N, 102°58′ W 90
Otis, *Mass., U.S.* 42°11′ N, 73°6′ W 104
Otisco, *Ind., U.S.* 38°32′ N, 85°39′ W 102
Otish, Monts, peak, *Can.* 52°17′ N, 70°36′ W 111
Otjikondo, *Namibia* 19°52′ S, 15°29′ E 220
Otjimbingwe, *Namibia* 22°19′ S, 16°7′ E 227
Otjivero, *Namibia* 22°16′ S, 17°51′ E 227
Otjiwarongo, *Namibia* 20°27′ S, 16°39′ E 227
Otley, *U.K.* 53°54′ N, 1°41′ W 162
Otmök, *Kyrg.* 42°11′ N, 73°16′ E 197
Otog Qi, *China* 39°6′ N, 107°58′ E 198
Otok, *Croatia* 45°8′ N, 18°51′ E 168
Otok, *Croatia* 43°41′ N, 16°43′ E 168
Otoka, *Bosn. and Herzg.* 44°57′ N, 16°8′ E 168
Otorohanga, *N.Z.* 38°11′ S, 175°13′ E 240
Otoskwin, river, *Can.* 51°48′ N, 90°58′ W 80
Otosquen, *Can.* 53°16′ N, 102°1′ W 108
Otradnaya, *Russ.* 44°22′ N, 41°27′ E 158
Otradnoye, *Russ.* 51°59′ N, 156°39′ E 160
Otradnoye, *Russ.* 56°13′ N, 30°3′ E 166
Otradnyy, *Russ.* 53°24′ N, 51°26′ E 154
Otranto, Capo d′, *It.* 40°2′ N, 18°31′ E 156
Otsego, *Mich., U.S.* 42°26′ N, 85°42′ W 102
Ōtsu, *Japan* 35°1′ N, 135°51′ E 201
Otta, *Nig.* 6°44′ N, 3°13′ E 222
Ottawa, *Can.* 45°22′ N, 75°50′ W 94
Ottawa, *Ill., U.S.* 41°20′ N, 88°51′ W 102
Ottawa, *Kans., U.S.* 38°34′ N, 95°17′ W 94
Ottawa, *Mo., U.S.* 41°20′ N, 88°51′ W 110
Ottawa, *Ohio, U.S.* 41°1′ N, 84°3′ W 102
Ottawa Islands, islands, *Can.* 59°8′ N, 83°8′ W 106
Ottenby, *Sw.* 56°14′ N, 16°26′ E 152
Otter Creek, *Fla., U.S.* 29°19′ N, 82°47′ W 105
Otter Head, *Can.* 47°53′ N, 86°14′ W 94
Otter Rapids, *Can.* 50°11′ N, 81°40′ W 94
Otterbein, *Ind., U.S.* 40°29′ N, 87°6′ W 102
Otterndorf, *Ger.* 53°48′ N, 8°54′ E 152
Ottoville, *Ohio, U.S.* 40°55′ N, 84°20′ W 102
Otú, *Col.* 6°55′ N, 74°45′ W 136
Otukpa, *Nig.* 7°4′ N, 7°40′ E 222
Otukpo, *Nig.* 7°12′ N, 8°9′ E 222
Otumpa, *Arg.* 27°20′ S, 62°16′ W 139
Otynya, *Ukr.* 48°43′ N, 24°49′ E 152
Ötztal Alps, *Aust.* 46°46′ N, 10°36′ E 167
Ou Nua, *Laos* 22°16′ N, 101°48′ E 202
Ou, river, *Laos* 21°49′ N, 102°6′ E 202
Ouachita, Lake, *Ark., U.S.* 34°41′ N, 93°59′ W 80
Ouachita Mountains, *Ark., U.S.* 34°26′ N, 95°36′ W 96
Ouachita, river, *La., U.S.* 32°16′ N, 92°10′ W 103
Ouadane, *Mauritania* 20°57′ N, 11°37′ W 222
Ouadda, *Cen. Af. Rep.* 8°4′ N, 22°24′ E 218
Ouagadougou, *Burkina Faso* 12°19′ N, 1°43′ W 222
Ouagama, Lac, lake, *Can.* 50°37′ N, 77°43′ W 110
Ouahigouya, *Burkina Faso* 13°34′ N, 2°26′ W 222
Ouaka, river, *Cen. Af. Rep.* 5°11′ N, 19°49′ E 218
Oualâta, *Mauritania* 17°18′ N, 7°2′ W 222
Oualâta, Dahr, *Mauritania* 17°41′ N, 8°22′ W 222
Oualidia, *Mor.* 32°43′ N, 9°4′ W 214
Ouallam, *Niger* 14°22′ N, 1°59′ E 222
Ouan Taredert, oil field, *Alg.* 27°26′ N, 9°29′ E 214
Oua-n-Ahaggar, Tassili, *Alg.* 21°14′ N, 4°57′ E 222
Ouanda Djallé, *Cen. Af. Rep.* 8°52′ N, 22°48′ E 218
Ouandjia, *Cen. Af. Rep.* 9°17′ N, 22°40′ E 218
Ouando, *Cen. Af. Rep.* 5°58′ N, 25°45′ E 224
Ouango, *Cen. Af. Rep.* 4°20′ N, 22°29′ E 218
Ouaouizarht, *Mor.* 32°12′ N, 6°23′ W 214
Ouarane, *Mauritania* 20°48′ N, 11°23′ W 222
Ouargaye, *Burkina Faso* 11°31′ N, 2°119′ E 222
Ouargla, *Alg.* 31°56′ N, 5°20′ E 214
Ouarkoye, *Burkina Faso* 12°6′ N, 3°41′ W 222
Ouarkziz, Jebel, *Mor.* 28°10′ N, 9°37′ W 214
Ouarra, river, *Cen. Af. Rep.* 5°49′ N, 25°48′ E 224
Ouarsenis, Djebel, peak, *Alg.* 35°52′ N, 1°34′ E 150
Ouas Ouas, spring, *Mali* 16°6′ N, 1°20′ E 222
Ouasiemsca, river, *Can.* 49°43′ N, 73°11′ W 111
Ouassane, spring, *Mauritania* 17°56′ N, 13°13′ W 222
Ouassou, *Guinea* 10°2′ N, 13°45′ W 222
Ouche, river, *Fr.* 47°15′ N, 4°48′ E 165
Ouchennane, spring, *Mali* 17°23′ N, 1°59′ E 222
Ouddorp, *Neth.* 51°48′ N, 3°55′ E 163
Oude Rijn, river, *Neth.* 52°12′ N, 4°26′ E 163
Oudeïka, spring, *Mali* 17°27′ N, 1°42′ W 222
Oudenaarde, *Belg.* 50°50′ N, 3°36′ E 163
Oudeschild, *Neth.* 53°2′ N, 4°50′ E 163
Oudon, *Fr.* 47°21′ N, 1°19′ W 150
Oudtshoorn, *S. Af.* 33°35′ S, 22°11′ E 227
Oued Laou, *Mor.* 35°26′ N, 5°6′ W 150
Oued Lili, *Alg.* 35°30′ N, 1°16′ E 150
Oued Rhiou, *Alg.* 35°57′ N, 0°55′ E 164
Oued Taria, *Alg.* 35°6′ N, 9°535′ E 150
Oued Tlelat, *Alg.* 35°32′ N, 0°28′ E 150
Oueïba, spring, *Chad* 18°24′ N, 23°18′ E 226
Oueïta, spring, *Chad* 17°43′ N, 20°42′ E 216
Ouella, spring, *Niger* 14°39′ N, 3°53′ E 222
Ouellé, *Côte d′Ivoire* 7°14′ N, 4°2′ W 222
Ouémé, river, *Benin* 8°19′ N, 2°11′ E 222
Ouescapis, Lac, lake, *Can.* 50°15′ N, 77°36′ W 94
Ouessa, *Burkina Faso* 11°3′ N, 2°48′ W 222
Ouesso, *Congo* 1°51′ N, 16°2′ E 218
Ouest, Pointe, *Haiti* 18°51′ N, 74°1′ W 116
Ouest, Pointe de l′ (Coupé Cap), *Fr.* 46°48′ N, 57°0′ W 111
Ouffet, *Belg.* 50°26′ N, 5°26′ E 167
Oufrane, *Alg.* 28°31′ N, 0°10′ E 214
Ougarta, *Alg.* 29°40′ N, 2°16′ W 214
Ougrée, *Belg.* 50°35′ N, 5°33′ E 167
Ouidah, *Benin* 6°23′ N, 2°5′ E 222
Oujaf, spring, *Mauritania* 17°50′ N, 7°54′ W 222
Oujda, *Mor.* 34°38′ N, 1°55′ W 214
Oujeft, *Mauritania* 20°2′ N, 13°4′ W 222
Oulad el Abed, *Tun.* 35°59′ N, 10°17′ E 156
Oulad Hammou, *Mor.* 35°7′ N, 6°9′ W 150
Oulad Saïd, *Alg.* 29°27′ N, 0°15′ E 214
Oulainen, *Fin.* 64°15′ N, 24°44′ E 152
Ould Mouloud, spring, *Alg.* 23°46′ N, 0°9′ E 214
Ouled Amar, *Alg.* 35°27′ N, 5°8′ E 150
Ouled Djellal, *Alg.* 34°23′ N, 5°3′ E 214
Oulou, river, *Cen. Af. Rep.* 10°27′ N, 22°30′ E 218
Oulton Broad, *U.K.* 52°27′ N, 1°41′ E 163
Oulton Lake, lake, *Can.* 60°45′ N, 111°53′ W 108
Oulu, *Fin.* 64°59′ N, 25°47′ E 160
Oulu (Uleåborg), *Fin.* 65°0′ N, 25°25′ E 152
Oulx, *It.* 45°1′ N, 6°51′ E 167
Oum Chalouba, *Chad* 15°47′ N, 20°45′ E 216
Oum er Rbia, Oued, river, *Mor.* 32°10′ N, 8°13′ W 142
Oum Hadjer, *Chad* 13°15′ N, 19°40′ E 216
Oum Mesgué, *Mauritania* 16°17′ N, 7°15′ W 222
Oumache, *Alg.* 34°40′ N, 5°42′ E 214
Oumé, *Côte d′Ivoire* 6°17′ N, 5°25′ W 222
Oumm el A′sel, spring, *Mali* 23°32′ N, 4°46′ W 214
Oumm el Khez, spring, *Mauritania* 17°7′ N, 11°3′ W 222
Ounasselkä, *Fin.* 67°32′ N, 24°23′ E 152
Oundle, *U.K.* 52°28′ N, 0°29′ E 162
Ounianga Kébir, *Chad* 19°4′ N, 20°31′ E 216
Ounianga Sérir, spring, *Chad* 18°54′ N, 20°54′ E 216
Ounissouli, spring, *Niger* 17°33′ N, 12°3′ E 222
Ouolodo, *Mali* 13°13′ N, 7°55′ W 222
Ourafane, *Niger* 14°2′ N, 8°8′ E 222
Ouray, *Utah, U.S.* 40°5′ N, 109°41′ W 90
Ouray, Mount, peak, *Colo., U.S.* 38°24′ N, 106°18′ W 90
Ourense, *Sp.* 42°19′ N, 7°53′ W 150
Ouri, *Chad* 21°35′ N, 19°13′ E 216
Ourinhos, *Braz.* 22°58′ S, 49°52′ W 138
Ouro, *Braz.* 8°13′ S, 46°14′ W 130
Ouro Preto, *Braz.* 20°24′ S, 43°31′ W 138
Ouro Prêto, river, *Braz.* 10°44′ S, 64°28′ W 137
Ours, Cap de l′, *Can.* 49°36′ N, 62°30′ W 111
Oursi, *Burkina Faso* 14°40′ N, 4°238′ E 222
Ourthe, river, *Belg.* 50°11′ N, 5°34′ E 167
Ouse, river, *U.K.* 54°4′ N, 1°21′ W 162
Oust, *Fr.* 42°51′ N, 1°12′ E 164
Outardes Quatre, Réservoir, lake, *Can.* 49°34′ N, 70°50′ W 94
Outat Oulad el Hajj, *Mor.* 33°25′ N, 3°44′ W 214
Outeniqua Mountains, *S. Af.* 33°49′ S, 22°28′ E 227
Outer Banks, islands, *North Atlantic Ocean* 35°28′ N, 75°25′ W 96
Outer Santa Barbara Channel 33°9′ N, 118°41′ W 101
Outjo, *Namibia* 20°7′ S, 16°10′ E 227
Outlook, *Can.* 51°29′ N, 107°5′ W 90
Outokumpu, *Fin.* 62°43′ N, 29°0′ E 152
Outram Island, *India* 12°17′ N, 93°14′ E 188
Outtaye, *Mali* 14°28′ N, 8°23′ W 222
Ovacık, *Turk.* 39°21′ N, 39°12′ E 195
Ovada, *It.* 44°38′ N, 8°39′ E 167
Oval Peak, *Wash., U.S.* 48°15′ N, 120°31′ W 90
Ovalle, *Chile* 30°35′ S, 71°14′ W 134
Ovalo, *Tex., U.S.* 32°10′ N, 99°50′ W 92
Ovamboland, region, *Namibia* 19°53′ S, 15°29′ E 227
Ovana, Cerro, peak, *Venez.* 4°37′ N, 67°4′ W 136
Ovar, *Port.* 40°51′ N, 8°40′ W 150
Overath, *Ger.* 50°56′ N, 7°16′ E 167
Øverbygd, *Nor.* 69°0′ N, 19°7′ E 152
Overflowing River, *Can.* 53°6′ N, 101°10′ W 108
Overland Park, *Kans., U.S.* 38°56′ N, 94°41′ W 94
Overland Pass, *Nev., U.S.* 40°1′ N, 115°36′ W 90
Övermark (Ylimarkku), *Fin.* 62°35′ N, 21°25′ E 152
Overpelt, *Belg.* 51°11′ N, 5°24′ E 167
Överstjuktan, lake, *Nor.* 65°39′ N, 15°22′ E 152
Overstrand, *U.K.* 52°54′ N, 1°20′ E 162
Overton, *Nev., U.S.* 36°32′ N, 114°27′ W 101
Overton, *Tex., U.S.* 32°16′ N, 94°59′ W 103
Overton, *U.K.* 52°57′ N, 2°55′ W 162
Överum, *Nor.* 58°0′ N, 16°17′ E 152
Ovett, *Miss., U.S.* 31°27′ N, 89°1′ W 103
Ovid, *Colo., U.S.* 40°57′ N, 102°23′ W 90
Ovid, *Mich., U.S.* 43°0′ N, 84°22′ W 102
Oviedo, *Sp.* 43°21′ N, 5°51′ W 150
Ovišì, *Latv.* 57°29′ N, 21°33′ E 166
Ovoot, *Mongolia* 45°20′ N, 113°38′ E 198
Övör-Ereen, *Mongolia* 49°16′ N, 112°25′ E 198
Ovruch, *Ukr.* 51°19′ N, 28°52′ E 152
Owaka, *N.Z.* 46°28′ S, 169°42′ E 240
Owando, *Congo* 0°33′ N, 15°53′ E 218
Owaneco, *Ill., U.S.* 39°28′ N, 89°12′ W 102
Owase, *Japan* 34°3′ N, 136°12′ E 201
Owbeh, *Afghan.* 34°26′ N, 63°10′ E 186
Owego, *N.Y., U.S.* 42°6′ N, 76°17′ W 94
Owen Falls Dam, *Uganda* 0°5′ N, 33°1′ E 224
Owen Fracture Zone, *Arabian Sea* 11°9′ N, 57°40′ E 254
Owen, Mount, peak, *N.Z.* 41°34′ S, 172°28′ E 240
Owen River, *N.Z.* 41°42′ S, 172°27′ E 240
Owen Sound, *Can.* 44°34′ N, 80°56′ W 94
Owen Stanley Range, *P.N.G.* 8°34′ S, 147°0′ E 192
Owens Peak, *Calif., U.S.* 35°44′ N, 118°2′ W 101
Owensboro, *Ky., U.S.* 37°45′ N, 87°7′ W 96
Owensburg, *Ind., U.S.* 38°55′ N, 86°44′ W 102
Owensville, *Mo., U.S.* 38°20′ N, 91°30′ W 94
Owenton, *Ky., U.S.* 38°31′ N, 84°50′ W 102
Owerri, *Nig.* 5°30′ N, 7°0′ E 222
Owickeno, *Can.* 51°41′ N, 127°16′ W 108
Owl Creek Mountains, *Wyo., U.S.* 43°36′ N, 109°5′ W 90
Owlshead Mountains, *Calif., U.S.* 35°46′ N, 116°46′ W 101
Owo, *Nig.* 6°28′ N, 7°43′ E 222
Owo, *Nig.* 7°15′ N, 5°36′ E 222
Owosso, *Mich., U.S.* 43°0′ N, 84°8′ W 102
Owschlag, *Ger.* 54°24′ N, 9°35′ E 150
Owyhee, *Nev., U.S.* 41°57′ N, 116°6′ W 90
Owyhee Mountains, *Idaho, U.S.* 43°10′ N, 116°45′ W 90
Owyhee, river, *Idaho, U.S.* 42°25′ N, 117°4′ W 106
Ox Mountains, the see Gamph, Slieve, *Ire.* 54°2′ N, 9°28′ W 150
Öxarfjörður 66°6′ N, 20°0′ W 142
Oxbow Dam, *U.S.* 45°1′ N, 116°55′ W 90
Oxford, *Kans., U.S.* 37°15′ N, 97°11′ W 90
Oxford, *Me., U.S.* 44°7′ N, 70°30′ W 104
Oxford, *Mich., U.S.* 42°48′ N, 83°16′ W 102
Oxford, *Miss., U.S.* 34°20′ N, 89°31′ W 96
Oxford, *Nebr., U.S.* 40°14′ N, 99°39′ W 90
Oxford, *N.Z.* 43°19′ S, 172°11′ E 240
Oxford, *Ohio, U.S.* 39°30′ N, 84°45′ W 102
Oxford, *U.K.* 51°44′ N, 1°16′ W 162
Oxford, *Wis., U.S.* 43°46′ N, 89°33′ W 102
Oxford House, *Can.* 54°54′ N, 95°17′ W 108
Oxford Peak, *Idaho, U.S.* 42°17′ N, 112°10′ W 90
Oxnard, *Calif., U.S.* 34°11′ N, 119°12′ W 101
Oxus see Ab-e Vakhan, river, *Afghan.* 37°8′ N, 72°26′ E 186
Oya, *Malaysia* 2°47′ N, 111°52′ E 192
Oyahue see Ollagüe, *Chile* 21°14′ S, 68°18′ W 137
Oyan, *Kaz.* 50°44′ N, 50°23′ E 158
Øye, *Nor.* 62°11′ N, 6°39′ E 152
Oyé Yeska, spring, *Chad* 18°36′ N, 19°31′ E 216
Oyem, *Gabon* 1°35′ N, 11°36′ E 207
Oyen, *Can.* 51°22′ N, 110°29′ W 90
Øygarden Group, islands, *Indian Ocean* 66°53′ S, 57°43′ E 248
Oymyakon, *Russ.* 63°25′ N, 142°41′ E 160
Oyo, *Congo* 1°10′ S, 15°59′ E 218
Oyo, *Nig.* 7°54′ N, 3°57′ E 222
Oyo, *Sudan* 21°56′ N, 36°12′ E 182
Oyonnax, *Fr.* 46°15′ N, 5°38′ E 150
Oyster Bay, *N.Y., U.S.* 40°52′ N, 73°32′ W 104
Oyster River, *Can.* 49°53′ N, 125°8′ W 100
Oysterville, *Wash., U.S.* 46°32′ N, 124°2′ W 100
Oyyl, *Kaz.* 49°4′ N, 54°38′ E 158
Özalp, *Turk.* 38°38′ N, 43°57′ E 195
Ozamis, *Philippines* 8°13′ N, 123°50′ E 203
Ozark, *Ala., U.S.* 31°27′ N, 85°39′ W 96
Ozark, *Ark., U.S.* 35°28′ N, 93°51′ W 96
Ozark, *Mo., U.S.* 37°0′ N, 93°11′ W 96
Ozark National Scenic Riverways, *Mo., U.S.* 37°0′ N, 96°4′ W 80
Ozark Plateau, *Mo., U.S.* 35°31′ N, 93°28′ W 96
Ozen, *Kaz.* 43°27′ N, 53°3′ E 158
Ozernovskiy, *Russ.* 51°32′ N, 156°34′ E 160
Ozernoy, Mys, *Russ.* 57°26′ N, 163°12′ E 160
Ozernyy, *Russ.* 55°30′ N, 32°29′ E 154
Ozernyy, *Russ.* 51°6′ N, 60°57′ E 158
Ozernyy, *Russ.* 66°23′ N, 179°3′ W 98
Ozersk, *Russ.* 54°25′ N, 21°58′ E 166
Ozery, *Russ.* 54°52′ N, 38°30′ E 154
Ozgon, *Kyrg.* 40°45′ N, 73°18′ E 197
Ozhiski Lake, *Can.* 51°57′ N, 89°4′ W 110
Ozhogino, *Russ.* 68°59′ N, 147°39′ E 160
Ozieri, *It.* 40°35′ N, 9°1′ E 156
Ozinki, *Russ.* 51°11′ N, 49°46′ E 158
Ozoli, *Latv.* 57°38′ N, 24°55′ E 166
Ozona, *Tex., U.S.* 30°41′ N, 101°12′ W 92
Ozorków, *Pol.* 51°57′ N, 19°17′ E 152
Ozrinići, *Mont.* 42°44′ N, 19°0′ E 168
Ōzu, *Japan* 33°30′ N, 132°32′ E 201
Ozurget′i, *Ga.* 41°54′ N, 42°0′ E 195

P

Pa Kha, *Vietnam* 22°34′ N, 104°16′ E 202
Pa Mong Dam, *Asia* 18°10′ N, 101°26′ E 202
Pa Sak, river, *Thai.* 15°27′ N, 101°2′ E 202
Paakkola, *Fin.* 66°0′ N, 24°40′ E 152
Paamiut (Frederikshåb) 62°4′ N, 49°33′ W 106
Paarl, *S. Af.* 33°45′ S, 18°55′ E 227
Paavola, *Fin.* 64°35′ N, 25°9′ E 152
Paberžė, *Lith.* 54°56′ N, 25°14′ E 166
Pabo, *Uganda* 2°58′ N, 32°7′ E 224
Pabradė, *Lith.* 54°59′ N, 25°43′ E 166
Pac, *Alban.* 42°17′ N, 20°12′ E 168
Pacaás Novos National Park, *Braz.* 11°14′ S, 63°35′ W 137
Pacaás Novos, river, *Braz.* 11°13′ S, 65°5′ W 137
Pacaás Novos, Serra dos, *Braz.* 10°27′ S, 64°29′ W 130
Pacahuaras, river, *Bol.* 10°25′ S, 66°13′ W 137
Pacajus, *Braz.* 4°14′ S, 38°30′ W 132
Pacanów, *Pol.* 50°24′ N, 21°2′ E 152
Pacaraima, Sierra, *Venez.* 4°3′ N, 63°19′ W 130
Pacasmayo, *Peru* 7°23′ S, 79°35′ W 130
Pacaya, *Peru* 10°9′ S, 74°7′ W 137
Paceco, *It.* 37°58′ N, 12°32′ E 156
Pacheco Pass, *Calif., U.S.* 37°4′ N, 121°14′ W 100
Pachelma, *Russ.* 53°18′ N, 43°20′ E 154
Pachena Point, *Can.* 48°44′ N, 125°5′ W 100
Pachía, *Peru* 17°56′ S, 70°9′ W 137
Pachuca, *Mex.* 20°6′ N, 98°48′ W 114
Pachuta, *Miss., U.S.* 32°1′ N, 88°53′ W 103
Pacific, *Can.* 54°44′ N, 128°20′ W 108
Pacific Beach, *Wash., U.S.* 47°10′ N, 124°11′ W 100
Pacific Crest Trail, *U.S.* 47°55′ N, 121°14′ W 100
Pacific Grove, *Calif., U.S.* 36°36′ N, 121°56′ W 100
Pacific Missile Test Center, *Calif., U.S.* 34°6′ N, 119°10′ W 101
Pacific Ocean 35°4′ N, 122°0′ W 252
Pacific Rim National Park Reserve, *Can.* 48°38′ N, 124°46′ W 100
Pacifica, *Calif., U.S.* 37°37′ N, 122°30′ W 100
Pacific-Antarctic Ridge, *South Pacific Ocean* 63°11′ S, 161°29′ W 255
Pačir, *Serb.* 45°54′ N, 19°26′ E 168
Packwood, *Wash., U.S.* 46°35′ N, 121°41′ W 100
Pacov, *Czech Rep.* 49°27′ N, 14°59′ E 152
Padada, *Philippines* 6°41′ N, 125°21′ E 203
Padang, *Indonesia* 3°2′ N, 105°42′ E 196
Padang, *Indonesia* 0°55′ N, 100°22′ E 196
Padang Endau, *Malaysia* 2°39′ N, 103°38′ E 196
Padang, island, *Indonesia* 0°55′ N, 101°49′ E 196
Padangpanjang, *Indonesia* 0°28′ N, 100°23′ E 196
Padangsidempuan, *Indonesia* 1°23′ N, 99°17′ E 196
Padany, *Russ.* 63°17′ N, 33°24′ E 152
Padas, river, *Malaysia* 4°40′ N, 115°43′ E 203
Padasjoki, *Fin.* 61°20′ N, 25°15′ E 166
Padauiri, river, *Braz.* 0°59′ N, 64°48′ W 130
Padcaya, *Bol.* 21°52′ S, 64°48′ W 137
Paddle Prairie, *Can.* 57°55′ N, 117°27′ W 108
Paden City, *W. Va., U.S.* 39°35′ N, 80°56′ W 102
Paderborn, *Ger.* 51°43′ N, 8°45′ E 167
Padeş, peak, *Rom.* 45°39′ N, 22°18′ E 168
Padilla, *Bol.* 19°17′ S, 64°21′ W 137
Padina, *Serb.* 45°7′ N, 20°44′ E 168
Padirac, site, *Fr.* 44°51′ N, 1°42′ E 165
Padlei, *Can.* 61°56′ N, 96°42′ W 73
Padloping Island, *Can.* 67°11′ N, 62°19′ W 246
Padova (Padua), *It.* 45°24′ N, 11°52′ E 167
Padrauna, *India* 26°52′ N, 83°58′ E 197
Padre Island National Seashore, *Gulf of Mexico* 27°4′ N, 97°18′ W 96
Padrela, Serra da, *Port.* 41°35′ N, 7°53′ W 150
Padsvillye, *Belarus* 55°10′ N, 27°57′ E 166
Padua see Padova, *It.* 45°24′ N, 11°52′ E 167
Paducah, *Ky., U.S.* 37°4′ N, 88°37′ W 96
Paducah, *Tex., U.S.* 34°0′ N, 100°19′ W 92
Padul, *Sp.* 37°1′ N, 3°37′ W 164
Padun, *Russ.* 68°37′ N, 31°48′ E 152
Padwa, *India* 18°23′ N, 82°41′ E 188
Paech′ŏn, *N. Korea* 37°58′ N, 126°18′ E 200
Paektu-san, peak, *N. Korea* 41°58′ N, 128°4′ E 200
Paeroa, *N.Z.* 37°22′ S, 175°40′ E 240
Paesana, *It.* 44°41′ N, 7°16′ E 167
Paestum, ruin(s), *It.* 40°24′ N, 14°54′ E 156
Páez, *Col.* 2°37′ N, 75°59′ W 136
Pafúri, *Mozambique* 22°27′ S, 31°23′ E 227
Paga Conta, *Braz.* 4°58′ S, 54°37′ W 130
Pagadian, *Philippines* 7°52′ N, 123°25′ E 203
Pagan, island, *Pagan* 18°7′ N, 144°58′ E 192
Pagasae, ruin(s), *Gr.* 39°18′ N, 22°49′ E 156
Pagashi, river, *Can.* 51°31′ N, 83°51′ W 110
Pagato, river, *Can.* 56°4′ N, 102°44′ W 108
Page, *N. Dak., U.S.* 47°9′ N, 97°35′ W 90
Pagėgiai, *Lith.* 55°8′ N, 21°54′ E 166
Pager, river, *Uganda* 3°18′ N, 33°13′ E 224
Paghman, *Afghan.* 34°38′ N, 68°57′ E 186
Pagiriai, *Lith.* 55°21′ N, 24°20′ E 166
Pago Pago, *American Samoa, U.S.* 14°14′ S, 170°42′ W 241
Pagoda Peak, *Colo., U.S.* 40°7′ N, 107°26′ W 90
Pagoda Point, *Myanmar* 15°59′ N, 94°14′ E 202
Paguchi Lake, lake, *Can.* 49°31′ N, 92°2′ W 94
Pagwa River, *Can.* 50°1′ N, 85°12′ W 94
Pagwachuan Lake, lake, *Can.* 49°40′ N, 86°46′ W 94
Pah Rah Range, *Nev., U.S.* 39°42′ N, 119°42′ W 90
Pahang, river, *Malaysia* 3°19′ N, 102°37′ E 196
Paharpur, *Pak.* 32°5′ N, 71°1′ E 186
Pahokee, *Fla., U.S.* 26°49′ N, 80°40′ W 105
Pahranagat Range, *Nev., U.S.* 37°6′ N, 115°19′ W 101
Pahranagat Valley, *Nev., U.S.* 37°11′ N, 115°11′ W 101
Pahrock Range, *Nev., U.S.* 38°1′ N, 115°7′ W 90
Pah-rum Peak, *Nev., U.S.* 40°22′ N, 119°40′ W 90
Pahrump, *Nev., U.S.* 36°12′ N, 116°0′ W 101
Pahute Mesa, *Nev., U.S.* 37°12′ N, 116°41′ W 92
Pai, *Thai.* 19°18′ N, 98°23′ E 202
Paiaguás, *Braz.* 18°24′ S, 57°9′ W 132
Paicines, *Calif., U.S.* 36°43′ N, 121°17′ W 100
Paide, *Est.* 58°53′ N, 25°33′ E 166
Paige, *Tex., U.S.* 30°11′ N, 97°7′ W 96
Paihia, *N.Z.* 35°20′ S, 174°4′ E 240
Paiján, *Peru* 7°44′ S, 79°18′ W 130
Päijänne, lake, *Fin.* 61°36′ N, 25°27′ E 166
Pailĭn City, *Cambodia* 12°52′ N, 102°37′ E 202
Paimio, *Fin.* 60°26′ N, 22°41′ E 166
Paimpol, *Fr.* 48°47′ N, 3°4′ W 150
Painan, *Indonesia* 1°19′ S, 100°34′ E 196
Paincourtville, *La., U.S.* 29°58′ N, 91°4′ W 103
Paine, Cerro, peak, *Chile* 51°0′ S, 73°13′ W 134
Painesville, *Ohio, U.S.* 41°42′ N, 81°15′ W 102
Paint Lake, *Can.* 55°23′ N, 98°23′ W 108
Paint Rock, *Tex., U.S.* 31°29′ N, 99°56′ W 92
Painted Desert, *Ariz., U.S.* 36°17′ N, 111°0′ W 92
Painter, Mount, peak, *Austral.* 30°19′ S, 139°7′ E 230
Paintsville, *Ky., U.S.* 37°49′ N, 82°49′ W 94
Paisley, *Oreg., U.S.* 42°41′ N, 120°33′ W 90

Paistunturit, peak, *Fin.* 69°35′ N, 26°13′ E 152
Paita, *Peru* 5°0′ S, 81°9′ W 130
Pajala, *Nor.* 67°12′ N, 23°22′ E 152
Pajares, Puerto de, pass, *Sp.* 43°0′ N, 5°47′ W 150
Pajarito, *N. Mex., U.S.* 34°59′ N, 106°42′ W 92
Pajaro, *Calif., U.S.* 36°52′ N, 121°45′ W 100
Pájaro, *Col.* 11°40′ N, 72°40′ W 136
Pajule, *Uganda* 2°56′ N, 32°54′ E 224
Pajusti, *Est.* 59°15′ N, 26°22′ E 166
Pak Nam Chumphon, *Thai.* 10°22′ N, 99°16′ E 202
Pak Phanang, *Thai.* 8°22′ N, 100°13′ E 202
Pakaraima Mountains, *Guyana* 5°59′ N, 60°35′ W 130
Pakaur, *India* 24°36′ N, 87°50′ E 197
Pakawau, *N.Z.* 40°38′ S, 172°40′ E 240
Pakbèng, *Laos* 19°55′ N, 101°11′ E 202
Pakch'ŏn, *N. Korea* 39°43′ N, 125°36′ E 200
Pakhtusovo, *Russ.* 74°23′ N, 59°40′ E 160
Paki, *Nig.* 11°28′ N, 8°10′ E 222
Pakipaki, *N.Z.* 39°42′ S, 176°46′ E 240
Pakistan 33°52′ N, 73°37′ E 186
Pakleni Otoci, island, *Croatia* 43°10′ N, 15°56′ E 168
Pakokku, *Myanmar* 21°24′ N, 95°5′ E 202
Pakotai, *N.Z.* 35°43′ S, 173°54′ E 240
Pak-Ou, *Laos* 20°5′ N, 102°13′ E 202
Pakowki Lake, *Can.* 49°12′ N, 111°36′ W 90
Pakpattan, *Pak.* 30°22′ N, 73°22′ E 186
Pakrac, *Croatia* 45°26′ N, 17°12′ E 168
Pakruojis, *Lith.* 55°58′ N, 23°51′ E 166
Pakwach, *Uganda* 2°25′ N, 31°28′ E 224
Pakxan, *Laos* 18°23′ N, 103°40′ E 202
Pal Lahara, *India* 21°26′ N, 85°12′ E 188
Pala, *Calif., U.S.* 33°22′ N, 117°6′ W 101
Pala, *Chad* 9°23′ N, 14°55′ E 216
Pala, *Myanmar* 12°51′ N, 98°39′ E 202
Palabek, *Uganda* 3°27′ N, 32°34′ E 224
Palacios, *Tex., U.S.* 28°42′ N, 96°13′ W 96
Palaeopolis, ruin(s), *Gr.* 40°28′ N, 25°24′ E 156
Palafrugell, *Sp.* 41°54′ N, 3°9′ E 164
Palagruža (Pelagosa), island, *Croatia* 42°25′ N, 16°0′ E 168
Palaichori, *Cyprus* 34°55′ N, 33°4′ E 194
Palaiseau, *Fr.* 48°41′ N, 2°14′ E 163
Palamau National Park, *India* 23°45′ N, 84°9′ E 197
Palamós, *Sp.* 41°50′ N, 3°7′ E 164
Palana, *Russ.* 59°7′ N, 160°9′ E 160
Palanan, *Philippines* 17°4′ N, 122°25′ E 203
Palanga, *Lith.* 55°54′ N, 21°4′ E 166
Palani, *India* 10°27′ N, 77°30′ E 188
Palanpur, *India* 24°10′ N, 72°26′ E 186
Palapag, *Philippines* 12°33′ N, 125°7′ E 203
Palapye, *Botswana* 22°30′ S, 27°5′ E 227
Palar, river, *India* 12°46′ N, 79°11′ E 188
Palatia, ruin(s), *Gr.* 35°51′ N, 27°9′ E 156
Palatka, *Fla., U.S.* 29°38′ N, 81°39′ W 105
Palatka, *Russ.* 60°13′ N, 150°51′ E 160
Palau 5°28′ N, 132°55′ E 242
Palau Trench, *North Pacific Ocean* 4°9′ N, 133°9′ E 254
Palauig, *Philippines* 15°26′ N, 119°55′ E 203
Palauk, *Myanmar* 13°16′ N, 98°38′ E 202
Palaw, *Myanmar* 12°58′ N, 98°39′ E 202
Palawan, island, *Philippines* 8°51′ N, 116°11′ E 192
Palawan Trough, *South China Sea* 9°2′ N, 116°31′ E 254
Palazzo San Gervasio, *It.* 40°56′ N, 15°59′ E 156
Palazzolo sull'Oglio, *It.* 45°36′ N, 9°51′ E 167
Paldiski, *Est.* 59°20′ N, 24°2′ E 166
Pale, *Bosn. and Herzg.* 43°49′ N, 18°34′ E 168
Pale, ruin(s), *Gr.* 38°10′ N, 20°18′ E 156
Palel, *India* 24°27′ N, 94°3′ E 188
Paleleh, *Indonesia* 1°2′ N, 121°53′ E 192
Paleliu (Beliliou), island, *Palau* 7°0′ N, 134°15′ E 242
Palembang, *Indonesia* 2°59′ S, 104°39′ E 192
Palen Mountains, *Calif., U.S.* 33°47′ N, 115°10′ W 101
Palencia, *Sp.* 42°0′ N, 4°33′ W 150
Palenque National Park, *Mex.* 17°29′ N, 92°9′ W 115
Palenque, ruin(s), *Mex.* 17°28′ N, 92°8′ W 115
Palermo, *Col.* 0°24′ N, 73°29′ W 136
Palermo, *It.* 38°8′ N, 13°20′ E 156
Palestina, *Chile* 23°52′ S, 69°47′ W 132
Palestina, *Mex.* 29°8′ N, 100°59′ W 92
Palestine, *Ill., U.S.* 39°0′ N, 87°37′ W 102
Palestine, *Tex., U.S.* 31°44′ N, 95°38′ W 103
Paletwa, *Myanmar* 21°19′ N, 92°46′ E 188
Palgrave, Mount, peak, *Austral.* 23°25′ S, 115°46′ E 230
Palgrave Point, *Namibia* 20°47′ S, 12°44′ E 220
Pali, *India* 25°46′ N, 73°21′ E 186
Pali, river, *Sri Lanka* 9°4′ N, 79°55′ E 188
Palian, *Thai.* 7°13′ N, 99°40′ E 196
Palić, *Serb.* 46°5′ N, 19°46′ E 168
Palikir, *F.S.M.* 6°57′ N, 158°10′ E 242
Palimbang, *Philippines* 6°15′ N, 124°12′ E 203
Palinuro, Capo, *It.* 39°56′ N, 14°28′ E 156
Palisade, *Colo., U.S.* 39°7′ N, 108°22′ W 90
Palisade, *Nebr., U.S.* 40°20′ N, 101°7′ W 90
Palisade Glacier, *Calif., U.S.* 37°3′ N, 118°46′ W 101
Palizada, *Mex.* 18°14′ N, 92°8′ W 115
Pälkäne, *Fin.* 61°20′ N, 24°14′ E 166
Palkino, *Russ.* 57°32′ N, 28°0′ E 166
Pallasovka, *Russ.* 50°2′ N, 46°51′ E 158
Pallës, Bishti i, *Alban.* 41°20′ N, 18°42′ E 156
Palling, *Can.* 54°21′ N, 125°55′ W 108
Palliser, Cape, *N.Z.* 41°49′ S, 174°57′ E 240
Palm Bay, *Fla., U.S.* 28°2′ N, 80°37′ W 105
Palm Beach, *Fla., U.S.* 26°42′ N, 80°3′ W 105
Palm Beach Gardens, *Fla., U.S.* 26°50′ N, 80°8′ W 105
Palm Coast, *Fla., U.S.* 29°30′ N, 81°11′ W 105
Palm Harbor, *Fla., U.S.* 28°3′ N, 82°45′ W 105
Palm Islands, *Coral Sea* 18°27′ S, 146°34′ E 230
Palm Point, *Nig.* 4°9′ N, 5°30′ E 222
Palm Springs, *Calif., U.S.* 33°51′ N, 116°33′ W 101
Palm Springs, *Fla., U.S.* 26°38′ N, 80°7′ W 105
Palma, *Mozambique* 10°46′ S, 40°29′ E 224
Palma, *Sp.* 39°40′ N, 2°37′ E 143
Palma de Mallorca, *Sp.* 39°34′ N, 2°39′ E 150
Palma del Río, *Sp.* 37°42′ N, 5°17′ W 164
Palma, river, *Braz.* 12°27′ S, 47°55′ W 130
Palma Sola, *Venez.* 10°33′ N, 68°34′ W 136
Palmaner, *India* 13°12′ N, 78°45′ E 188
Palmanova, *It.* 45°54′ N, 13°18′ E 167
Palmar Sur, *C.R.* 8°57′ N, 83°27′ W 115
Palmares, *Braz.* 10°27′ S, 67°47′ W 137
Palmares, *Braz.* 8°38′ S, 35°34′ W 132
Palmarito, *Venez.* 7°38′ N, 70°9′ W 136
Palmas, *Braz.* 26°28′ S, 52°1′ W 139
Palmas, *Braz.* 10°11′ S, 48°18′ W 130
Palmas, Cape 4°10′ N, 7°35′ W 222
Palmas de Monte Alto, *Braz.* 14°19′ S, 43°7′ W 138
Palmdale, *Calif., U.S.* 34°35′ N, 118°8′ W 101
Palmdale, *Fla., U.S.* 26°56′ N, 81°19′ W 105
Palmeira das Missões, *Braz.* 27°54′ S, 53°18′ W 139
Palmeira dos Índios, *Braz.* 9°25′ S, 36°37′ W 132
Palmeirante, *Braz.* 7°49′ S, 47°55′ W 130
Palmela, *Port.* 38°33′ N, 8°55′ W 150
Palmer, *Alas., U.S.* 61°31′ N, 149°10′ W 98
Palmer, *Mass., U.S.* 42°9′ N, 72°20′ W 104
Palmer Archipelago, islands, *Weddell Sea* 63°51′ S, 63°17′ W 134
Palmer Land, region, *Antarctica* 69°25′ S, 65°11′ W 248
Palmer, river, *Austral.* 16°10′ S, 142°53′ E 230
Palmer, station, *Antarctica* 64°48′ S, 64°0′ W 134
Palmerston, *Can.* 43°49′ N, 80°50′ W 102
Palmerston, *N.Z.* 45°30′ S, 170°43′ E 240
Palmerston North, *N.Z.* 40°23′ S, 175°36′ E 240
Palmertown, *Conn., U.S.* 41°26′ N, 72°8′ W 104
Palmetto, *Fla., U.S.* 27°31′ N, 82°33′ W 105
Palmillas, *Mex.* 23°17′ N, 99°34′ W 114
Palmira, *Col.* 3°29′ N, 76°18′ W 136
Palmira, *Venez.* 8°49′ N, 72°24′ W 136
Palmitas, *Uru.* 33°31′ S, 57°48′ W 139
Palmyra, *Ill., U.S.* 39°25′ N, 90°0′ W 102
Palmyra, *Mo., U.S.* 39°47′ N, 91°33′ W 94
Palmyras Point, *India* 20°32′ N, 87°4′ E 188
Palo Alto, *Calif., U.S.* 37°27′ N, 122°11′ W 100
Palo Duro Canyon, *Tex., U.S.* 34°39′ N, 101°35′ W 92
Palo Negro, *Arg.* 29°39′ S, 62°10′ W 139
Palo Negro, *Col.* 1°29′ N, 72°20′ W 136
Palo Verde, *Calif., U.S.* 33°25′ N, 114°45′ W 101
Paloh, *Indonesia* 1°45′ N, 109°17′ E 196
Paloich, *Sudan* 10°27′ N, 32°32′ E 224
Palojärvi, *Fin.* 63°22′ N, 28°43′ E 152
Palokoski, *Fin.* 66°51′ N, 25°23′ E 152
Palomar Mountain, peak, *Calif., U.S.* 33°21′ N, 116°53′ W 101
Palomas, *Mex.* 31°41′ N, 107°37′ W 92
Palopo, *Indonesia* 3°0′ S, 120°10′ E 192
Palos, Cabo de, *Sp.* 37°38′ N, 0°42′ E 164
Palouse Hills, *Wash., U.S.* 47°11′ N, 117°57′ W 90
Palouse, river, *Wash., U.S.* 46°37′ N, 118°22′ W 90
Palpa, *Peru* 14°35′ S, 75°11′ W 132
Palpa, *Peru* 11°30′ S, 77°7′ W 130
Palpana, Cerro, peak, *Chile* 21°34′ S, 68°37′ W 137
Paltamo, *Fin.* 64°24′ N, 27°45′ E 152
Pältsa, peak, *Nor.* 69°0′ N, 20°2′ E 152
Palu, *Indonesia* 0°54′ N, 119°51′ E 238
Palu, *Turk.* 38°42′ N, 39°56′ E 195
Paluan, *Philippines* 13°27′ N, 120°28′ E 203
Palwal, *India* 28°8′ N, 77°19′ E 197
Pama, *Burkina Faso* 11°14′ N, 0°42′ E 222
Pama, river, *Cen. Af. Rep.* 4°42′ N, 17°8′ E 218
Pamekasan, *Indonesia* 7°13′ S, 113°28′ E 192
Pamiers, *Fr.* 43°6′ N, 1°36′ E 164
Pamir, river, *Taj.* 37°15′ N, 72°46′ E 184
Pamirs, *Taj.* 37°33′ N, 72°10′ E 190
Pamirsky National Park, *Taj.* 39°0′ N, 72°0′ E 197
Pamoni, *Venez.* 2°49′ N, 65°54′ W 136
Pampa, *Tex., U.S.* 35°30′ N, 100°58′ W 92
Pampa de los Guanacos, *Arg.* 26°15′ S, 61°54′ W 139
Pampa del Indio, *Arg.* 26°3′ S, 59°55′ W 139
Pampa del Infierno, *Arg.* 26°30′ S, 61°12′ W 139
Pampa Grande, *Bol.* 18°7′ S, 64°7′ W 137
Pampaļi, *Latv.* 56°32′ N, 22°11′ E 166
Pamparato, *It.* 44°15′ N, 7°55′ E 167
Pampas, *Peru* 12°20′ S, 74°58′ W 137
Pampeiro, *Braz.* 30°31′ S, 55°18′ W 139
Pamplona, *Col.* 7°25′ N, 72°37′ W 136
Pamplona (Iruña), *Sp.* 42°47′ N, 1°40′ W 164
Pamzal, *India* 34°13′ N, 78°47′ E 188
Pan de Azúcar, *Bol.* 21°56′ S, 67°28′ W 137
Pan de Azúcar, *Uru.* 34°48′ S, 55°16′ W 139
Pana, *Ill., U.S.* 39°23′ N, 89°5′ W 102
Pana Tinai, island, *P.N.G.* 11°9′ S, 153°5′ E 230
Panabá, *Mex.* 21°17′ N, 88°17′ W 112
Panaca, *Nev., U.S.* 37°47′ N, 114°24′ W 92
Panacea, *Fla., U.S.* 30°2′ N, 84°23′ W 96
Panadura, *Sri Lanka* 6°41′ N, 79°56′ E 188
Panahaïkó, Óros, peak, *Gr.* 38°10′ N, 21°47′ E 156
Panaji, *India* 15°27′ N, 73°51′ E 188
Panama, *Okla., U.S.* 35°8′ N, 94°41′ W 96
Panama 8°20′ N, 81°0′ W 115
Panama, *Sri Lanka* 6°45′ N, 81°48′ E 188
Panamá, Bahía de 8°46′ N, 80°20′ W 115
Panama Basin, *North Pacific Ocean* 2°47′ N, 83°11′ W 252
Panama City, *Fla., U.S.* 30°9′ N, 85°40′ W 96
Panama City, *Pan.* 8°58′ N, 79°39′ W 115
Panamá, Golfo de 7°45′ N, 80°2′ W 115
Panamá Viejo, ruin(s), *Pan.* 8°59′ N, 79°33′ W 115
Panambi, *Braz.* 28°20′ S, 53°29′ W 139
Panamint Range, *Calif., U.S.* 36°18′ N, 117°20′ W 101
Panamint Springs, *Calif., U.S.* 36°20′ N, 117°29′ W 101
Panamint Valley, *Calif., U.S.* 36°3′ N, 117°25′ W 101
Panay, island, *Philippines* 10°6′ N, 121°16′ E 192
Pancake Range, *Nev., U.S.* 38°34′ N, 116°13′ W 90
Pančevo, *Serb.* 44°52′ N, 20°38′ E 156
Pančićev Vrh, peak, *Kos.* 43°15′ N, 20°47′ E 168
Pancorbo, *Sp.* 42°37′ N, 3°6′ W 164
Pancurbatu, *Indonesia* 3°29′ N, 98°37′ E 196
Panda, *Mozambique* 24°0′ S, 34°42′ E 227
Pandan, *Philippines* 14°3′ N, 124°10′ E 203
Pandan, *Philippines* 11°41′ N, 122°6′ E 203
Pandėlys, *Lith.* 56°0′ N, 25°12′ E 166
Pando, *Uru.* 34°41′ S, 55°57′ W 139
Pando, adm. division, *Bol.* 10°53′ S, 67°31′ W 137
Pandora Entrance 11°42′ S, 143°12′ E 230
Panetolikó, Óros, peak, *Gr.* 38°40′ N, 21°30′ E 156
Panevėžys, *Lith.* 55°42′ N, 24°20′ E 166
Panfilovo, *Russ.* 50°22′ N, 42°50′ E 158
Panga, *Dem. Rep. of the Congo* 1°50′ N, 26°23′ E 224
Pangala, *Congo* 3°20′ S, 14°34′ E 218
Pangani, *Tanzania* 5°23′ S, 38°59′ E 224
Panganiban (Payo), *Philippines* 13°56′ N, 124°17′ E 203
Pangéo, Óros, *Gr.* 40°51′ N, 23°44′ E 156
Panghyŏn, *N. Korea* 39°52′ N, 125°14′ E 200
Pangi, *Dem. Rep. of the Congo* 3°14′ S, 26°39′ E 224
Pangkalanbrandan, *Indonesia* 4°2′ N, 98°18′ E 196
Pangkalanbuun, *Indonesia* 2°44′ S, 111°31′ E 192
Pangkalankotabaru, *Indonesia* 0°7′ N, 100°43′ E 196
Pangkalpinang, *Indonesia* 2°3′ S, 106°2′ E 192
Pangkor, island, *Malaysia* 4°4′ N, 100°3′ E 196
Pangnirtung, *Can.* 66°7′ N, 65°46′ W 106
Panguitch, *Utah, U.S.* 37°48′ N, 112°25′ W 82
Panguma, *Sierra Leone* 8°9′ N, 11°8′ W 222
Panguru, *N.Z.* 35°24′ S, 173°22′ E 240
Pangutaran, *Philippines* 6°20′ N, 120°33′ E 203
Panhandle, *Tex., U.S.* 35°20′ N, 101°23′ W 92
Pania Mutombo, *Dem. Rep. of the Congo* 5°13′ S, 23°52′ E 224
Pānī'au, peak, *Hawai'i, U.S.* 21°55′ N, 160°8′ W 99
Panié, Mount, peak 20°39′ S, 164°24′ E 238
Panipat, *India* 29°23′ N, 77°0′ E 197
Panj, *Taj.* 37°14′ N, 69°6′ E 186
Panj, river, *Asia* 37°40′ N, 71°30′ E 197
Panjab, *Afghan.* 34°23′ N, 67°6′ E 186
Panjakent, *Taj.* 39°28′ N, 67°32′ E 197
Panjang, island, *Indonesia* 2°48′ N, 108°57′ E 196
Panjang, oil field, *Strait of Malacca* 4°10′ N, 98°14′ E 196
Panjgur, *Pak.* 26°55′ N, 64°7′ E 182
Pankakoski, *Fin.* 63°17′ N, 30°8′ E 152
Pankow, *Ger.* 52°35′ N, 13°25′ E 152
Pankshin, *Nig.* 9°18′ N, 9°24′ E 222
Panmunjom, site, *N. Korea* 37°56′ N, 126°34′ E 200
Panna, *India* 24°42′ N, 80°12′ E 197
Pannonhalma, *Hung.* 47°32′ N, 17°48′ E 168
Panny, river, *Can.* 57°17′ N, 114°41′ W 108
Pano Lefkara, *Cyprus* 34°52′ N, 33°18′ E 194
Pano Panagia, *Cyprus* 34°55′ N, 32°37′ E 194
Pano Platres, *Cyprus* 34°52′ N, 32°51′ E 194
Panoche Pass, *Calif., U.S.* 36°37′ N, 121°1′ W 100
Panola, *Ala., U.S.* 32°58′ N, 88°15′ W 103
Panolik, *Russ.* 60°23′ N, 101°25′ E 173
Panorama, *Braz.* 21°19′ S, 51°51′ W 138
Panozero, *Russ.* 64°57′ N, 32°50′ E 152
P'anp'yŏng, *N. Korea* 40°26′ N, 125°50′ E 200
Panshi, *China* 42°55′ N, 126°3′ E 200
Pantanal Matogrossense National Park, *Braz.* 17°45′ S, 58°17′ W 132
Pantar, island, *Indonesia* 8°15′ S, 123°28′ E 192
Pante Makasar (Oecusse), *Indonesia* 9°21′ S, 124°20′ E 192
Pantelleria, island, *It.* 36°47′ N, 10°43′ E 216
Pantepec, *Mex.* 20°35′ N, 97°55′ W 114
Pantoja, *Peru* 0°59′ N, 75°11′ W 136
Pantonlabu, *Indonesia* 5°7′ N, 97°26′ E 196
Pantyy, *Russ.* 62°27′ N, 48°55′ E 154
Pánuco, *Mex.* 22°1′ N, 98°11′ W 114
Pánuco, river, *Mex.* 21°56′ N, 98°25′ W 114
Panyam, *Nig.* 9°23′ N, 9°12′ E 222
Panza Range, La, *Calif., U.S.* 35°22′ N, 120°19′ W 100
Panzhihua, *China* 26°21′ N, 101°45′ E 190
Panzi, *Dem. Rep. of the Congo* 7°17′ S, 18°0′ E 218
Pao, river, *Thai.* 17°1′ N, 103°9′ E 202
Pao, river, *Venez.* 8°23′ N, 64°24′ W 116
Paola, *It.* 39°22′ N, 16°2′ E 156
Paola, *Kans., U.S.* 38°33′ N, 94°52′ W 94
Paoli, *Ind., U.S.* 38°33′ N, 86°28′ W 102
Paonia, *Colo., U.S.* 38°51′ N, 107°35′ W 90
Paoua, *Cen. Af. Rep.* 7°12′ N, 16°25′ E 218
Paoziyan, *China* 41°19′ N, 125°24′ E 200
Pap, *Sudan* 6°6′ N, 31°12′ E 224
Pápa, *Hung.* 47°19′ N, 17°28′ E 168
Pāpā Heiau, site, *Hawai'i, U.S.* 21°9′ N, 156°48′ W 99
Papakura, *N.Z.* 37°4′ S, 174°58′ E 240
Papanoa, *Mex.* 17°16′ N, 101°2′ W 114
Papanoa, Morro de, *Mex.* 17°15′ N, 101°1′ W 114
Papantla, *Mex.* 20°26′ N, 97°19′ W 114
Paparoa, *N.Z.* 36°7′ S, 174°15′ E 240
Papeete, *French Polynesia, Fr.* 17°32′ S, 149°35′ W 241
Papenburg, *Ger.* 53°5′ N, 7°23′ E 163
Paphos, *Cyprus* 34°45′ N, 32°24′ E 194
Papigochic, river, *Mex.* 29°0′ N, 108°1′ W 80
Papíkio, peak, *Gr.* 41°12′ N, 25°13′ E 156
Papilė, *Lith.* 56°9′ N, 22°46′ E 166
Papua, Gulf of 8°59′ S, 144°26′ E 192
Papua New Guinea 6°34′ S, 142°53′ E 192
Papuk, *Croatia* 45°32′ N, 17°20′ E 168
Papun, *Myanmar* 18°4′ N, 97°26′ E 202
Papuri, river, *Braz.* 0°36′ N, 70°11′ W 136
Pará, adm. division, *Braz.* 4°16′ S, 53°14′ W 130
Paracale, *Philippines* 14°16′ N, 122°47′ E 203
Paracari, river, *Braz.* 4°42′ S, 57°55′ W 132
Paracas, Península, *Peru* 13°53′ S, 77°45′ W 130
Paracatu, *Braz.* 17°16′ S, 46°52′ W 138
Paracatu, river, *Braz.* 17°25′ S, 46°35′ W 138
Paracel Islands, islands, *South China Sea* 16°38′ N, 111°40′ E 192
Parachinar, *Pak.* 33°52′ N, 70°8′ E 186
Parachute, *Colo., U.S.* 39°27′ N, 108°4′ W 90
Paraćin, *Serb.* 43°51′ N, 21°24′ E 168
Paracuru, *Braz.* 3°25′ S, 39°7′ W 132
Parád, *Hung.* 47°54′ N, 20°2′ E 168
Parada, Punta, *Peru* 15°37′ S, 75°39′ W 132
Paradas, *Sp.* 37°17′ N, 5°31′ W 150
Paradis, *Can.* 48°14′ N, 76°35′ W 94
Paradise, *Calif., U.S.* 39°45′ N, 121°39′ W 90
Paradise, *Mich., U.S.* 46°37′ N, 85°4′ W 94
Paradise, *Mont., U.S.* 47°22′ N, 114°49′ W 90
Paradise, *Nev., U.S.* 36°5′ N, 115°9′ W 101
Paradise Valley, *Nev., U.S.* 41°29′ N, 117°32′ W 90
Paraf'yanava, *Belarus* 54°52′ N, 27°35′ E 166
Paragon Lake, lake, *Can.* 58°16′ N, 97°49′ W 108
Paragould, *Ark., U.S.* 36°3′ N, 90°29′ W 94
Paraguá, river, *Bol.* 15°1′ S, 61°6′ W 132
Paragua, river, *Venez.* 5°37′ N, 63°43′ W 130
Paraguaçu Paulista, *Braz.* 22°26′ S, 50°39′ W 138
Paraguaçu, river, *Braz.* 13°10′ S, 40°53′ W 138
Paraguai, river, *South America* 20°11′ S, 58°21′ W 132
Paraguaipoa, *Venez.* 11°21′ N, 72°0′ W 136
Paraguaná, Península de, *Venez.* 12°6′ N, 70°25′ W 116
Paraguaná, Península de, *Venez.* 12°3′ N, 70°14′ W 136
Paraguarí, *Parag.* 25°38′ S, 57°9′ W 132
Paraguay 23°21′ S, 59°9′ W 132
Paraíba, adm. division, *Braz.* 7°3′ S, 38°22′ W 132
Parainen see Pargas, *Fin.* 60°17′ N, 22°17′ E 166
Paraíso, *Braz.* 19°3′ S, 53°2′ W 138
Paraíso, *Braz.* 6°41′ S, 59°1′ W 130
Paraíso, *Mex.* 18°24′ N, 93°14′ W 115
Paraíso do Tocantins, *Braz.* 10°15′ S, 48°57′ W 132
Parakhonsk, *Belarus* 52°13′ N, 26°26′ E 152
Parakou, *Benin* 9°19′ N, 2°36′ E 222
Paralimni, *Cyprus* 35°2′ N, 33°58′ E 194
Paramaribo, *Suriname* 5°42′ N, 55°27′ W 130
Paramé, *Fr.* 48°39′ N, 2°0′ W 150
Paramera, Sierra de la, *Sp.* 40°22′ N, 5°33′ W 150
Paramillo National Park, *Col.* 7°21′ N, 76°14′ W 136
Paramirim, *Braz.* 13°27′ S, 42°16′ W 138
Paraná, adm. division, *Braz.* 24°35′ S, 51°41′ W 132
Paraná, *Arg.* 31°46′ S, 60°31′ W 139
Paranã, *Braz.* 12°35′ S, 47°50′ W 130
Paraná, river, *Arg.* 29°37′ S, 58°49′ W 123
Paranaguá, *Braz.* 25°34′ S, 48°33′ W 138
Paranaíba, *Braz.* 19°40′ S, 51°13′ W 138
Paranaíba, river, *Braz.* 19°34′ S, 51°11′ W 138
Paranaiguara, *Braz.* 18°53′ S, 50°33′ W 138
Paranaíta, river, *Braz.* 9°31′ S, 56°55′ W 130
Paranapanema, river, *Braz.* 22°26′ S, 52°17′ W 138
Paranapiacaba, Serra do, *Braz.* 24°13′ S, 49°11′ W 132
Paranavaí, *Braz.* 23°4′ S, 52°37′ W 138
Parang, *Philippines* 5°58′ N, 120°53′ E 203
Parapetí, river, *Bol.* 20°14′ S, 63°34′ W 137
Parás, *Mex.* 26°27′ N, 99°31′ W 114
Parati, *Braz.* 23°13′ S, 44°45′ W 132
Paratinga, *Braz.* 12°43′ S, 43°11′ W 138
Parauapebas, river, *Braz.* 7°0′ S, 50°16′ W 130
Parauaquara, Serra, peak, *Braz.* 1°34′ S, 53°13′ W 130
Paraúna, *Braz.* 17°4′ S, 50°28′ W 138
Parbati, river, *India* 24°46′ N, 77°3′ E 197
Parbhani, *India* 19°15′ N, 76°45′ E 188
Parbig, *Russ.* 57°11′ N, 81°29′ E 169
Parcines, *It.* 46°41′ N, 11°4′ E 167
Parczew, *Pol.* 51°38′ N, 22°53′ E 152
Pardés Hanna-Karkur, *Israel* 32°28′ N, 34°58′ E 194
Pardilla, *Sp.* 41°32′ N, 3°43′ W 164
Pardo, river, *Braz.* 20°59′ S, 53°16′ W 138
Pardo, river, *Braz.* 15°49′ S, 42°6′ W 138
Pardo, river, *Braz.* 21°32′ S, 46°54′ W 138
Pardo, river, *Braz.* 15°29′ S, 45°7′ W 138
Pardubice, *Czech Rep.* 50°1′ N, 15°47′ E 152
Pardubický, adm. division, *Czech Rep.* 49°50′ N, 16°5′ E 152
Pare Mountains, *Tanzania* 3°29′ S, 37°42′ E 224
Parec, Serra dos, *Braz.* 9°47′ S, 64°10′ W 137
Parechcha, *Belarus* 53°51′ N, 24°8′ E 166
Parecis, *Braz.* 13°34′ S, 55°55′ W 123
Parecis, river, *Braz.* 13°39′ S, 57°13′ W 130
Paren', *Russ.* 62°24′ N, 162°51′ E 160
Parent, *Can.* 47°56′ N, 74°38′ W 94
Parent, Lac, lake, *Can.* 48°44′ N, 77°24′ W 94
Parepare, *Indonesia* 4°0′ S, 119°37′ E 192
Pargas (Parainen), *Fin.* 60°17′ N, 22°17′ E 166
Pargny, *Fr.* 48°45′ N, 4°48′ E 163
Parguaza, *Venez.* 6°24′ N, 67°5′ W 136
Paria, *Bol.* 17°52′ S, 67°1′ W 137
Paria, Gulf of 10°13′ N, 62°40′ W 116
Paria, Península de, *Venez.* 10°47′ N, 62°56′ W 116
Pariacaca, Cerro, peak, *Peru* 11°58′ S, 76°5′ W 130
Pariaman, *Indonesia* 0°36′ N, 100°8′ E 196
Paricá, Lago, lake, *Braz.* 1°54′ S, 66°4′ W 136
Paricutín, Volcán, peak, *Mex.* 19°28′ N, 102°21′ W 114
Parida, Isla, island, *Pan.* 7°48′ N, 82°24′ W 115
Parika, *Guyana* 6°47′ N, 58°27′ W 130
Parikkala, *Fin.* 61°31′ N, 29°30′ E 166
Parima, river, *Braz.* 2°30′ N, 63°49′ W 130
Parima, Serra, *Braz.* 3°17′ N, 64°33′ W 130
Parima-Tapirapecó National Park, *Venez.* 1°56′ N, 65°41′ W 136
Pariñas, Punta, *Peru* 4°31′ S, 82°26′ W 130
Parintins, *Braz.* 2°42′ S, 56°48′ W 130
Paris, *Ark., U.S.* 35°16′ N, 93°45′ W 96
Paris, *Fr.* 48°52′ N, 2°17′ E 163
Paris, *Ill., U.S.* 39°36′ N, 87°42′ W 102
Paris, *Ky., U.S.* 38°12′ N, 84°16′ W 94
Paris, *Me., U.S.* 44°16′ N, 70°30′ W 104
Paris, *Mo., U.S.* 39°28′ N, 92°1′ W 94
Paris, *Mo., U.S.* 39°36′ N, 87°42′ W 94

Paris, *Tenn., U.S.* 36° 17′ N, 88° 20′ W 96
Paris, *Tex., U.S.* 33° 38′ N, 95° 32′ W 96
Parismina, *C.R.* 10° 15′ N, 83° 22′ W 115
Parit Buntar, *Malaysia* 5° 6′ N, 100° 29′ E 196
Parita, *Pan.* 8° 0′ N, 80° 32′ W 115
Park Falls, *Wis., U.S.* 45° 55′ N, 90° 28′ W 94
Park Range, *Colo., U.S.* 40° 43′ N, 106° 47′ W 90
Park Rapids, *Minn., U.S.* 46° 54′ N, 95° 5′ W 90
Park River, *N. Dak., U.S.* 48° 21′ N, 97° 47′ W 90
Parkajoki, *Nor.* 67° 42′ N, 23° 24′ E 152
Parkal, *India* 18° 11′ N, 79° 42′ E 188
Parkano, *Fin.* 62° 0′ N, 22° 58′ E 166
Parkdale, *Ark., U.S.* 33° 6′ N, 91° 33′ W 103
Parker, *Ariz., U.S.* 34° 8′ N, 114° 18′ W 101
Parker, *S. Dak., U.S.* 43° 22′ N, 97° 8′ W 90
Parker Dam, *Calif., U.S.* 34° 16′ N, 114° 10′ W 101
Parker Dam, *Calif., U.S.* 34° 19′ N, 114° 16′ W 101
Parkersburg, *W. Va., U.S.* 39° 15′ N, 81° 34′ W 102
Parkhill, *Can.* 43° 9′ N, 81° 41′ W 102
Parkin, *Ark., U.S.* 35° 14′ N, 90° 34′ W 96
Parkland, *Wash., U.S.* 47° 7′ N, 122° 26′ W 100
Parks, *La., U.S.* 30° 11′ N, 91° 51′ W 103
Parks Lake, lake, *Can.* 49° 25′ N, 87° 58′ W 110
Parksley, *Va., U.S.* 37° 46′ N, 75° 40′ W 94
Parkston, *S. Dak., U.S.* 43° 22′ N, 97° 59′ W 90
Parksville, *Can.* 49° 18′ N, 124° 19′ W 100
Parkumäki, *Fin.* 61° 56′ N, 28° 27′ E 166
Parkview Mountain, peak, *Colo., U.S.* 40° 18′ N, 106° 12′ W 90
Parli, *India* 18° 51′ N, 76° 31′ E 188
Parlier, *Calif., U.S.* 36° 36′ N, 119° 33′ W 101
Parma, *Idaho, U.S.* 43° 46′ N, 116° 57′ W 90
Parma, *It.* 44° 47′ N, 10° 20′ E 167
Parma, *Mich., U.S.* 42° 14′ N, 84° 36′ W 102
Parma, *Ohio, U.S.* 41° 23′ N, 81° 42′ W 94
Parma, river, *It.* 44° 25′ N, 10° 3′ E 167
Parnaguá, *Braz.* 10° 16′ S, 44° 36′ W 132
Parnaíba, *Braz.* 2° 58′ S, 41° 45′ W 132
Parnaíba, river, *Braz.* 8° 21′ S, 45° 45′ W 130
Parnamirim, *Braz.* 8° 8′ S, 39° 35′ W 132
Parnarama, *Braz.* 5° 43′ S, 43° 9′ W 132
Parnassós National Park, *Gr.* 38° 29′ N, 22° 26′ E 180
Parnassós, peak, *Gr.* 38° 31′ N, 22° 32′ E 156
Parnassus, *N.Z.* 42° 42′ S, 173° 17′ E 240
Párnitha National Park, *Gr.* 38° 8′ N, 23° 38′ E 156
Párnitha, Óros, peak, *Gr.* 38° 10′ N, 23° 38′ E 156
Párnonas, Óros, *Gr.* 37° 22′ N, 22° 31′ E 156
Pärnu, *Est.* 58° 23′ N, 24° 29′ E 166
Pärnu Jaagupi, *Est.* 58° 36′ N, 24° 27′ E 166
Pärnu Laht 58° 18′ N, 24° 7′ E 166
Pärnu, river, *Est.* 58° 45′ N, 25° 16′ E 166
Paroho, lake, *S. Korea* 38° 8′ N, 127° 41′ E 200
Páros, *Gr.* 37° 4′ N, 25° 9′ E 156
Páros, island, *Gr.* 36° 50′ N, 24° 52′ E 180
Parowan, *Utah, U.S.* 37° 50′ N, 112° 49′ W 92
Parr, Cape 81° 8′ S, 171° 43′ E 248
Parral, *Chile* 36° 7′ S, 71° 52′ W 134
Parras de la Fuente, *Mex.* 25° 25′ N, 102° 12′ W 114
Parris Island, *S.C., U.S.* 32° 5′ N, 80° 27′ W 112
Parrish, *Fla., U.S.* 27° 35′ N, 82° 25′ W 105
Parrs Halt, *Botswana* 23° 22′ S, 27° 16′ E 227
Parry, Cape, *Can.* 69° 59′ N, 124° 19′ W 106
Parry, Cape, *Can.* 70° 11′ N, 126° 24′ W 98
Parry Islands, *Foxe Basin* 74° 19′ N, 107° 51′ W 106
Parry, Kap 76° 58′ N, 75° 51′ W 106
Parry, Kap, *Traill Ø* 72° 1′ N, 21° 53′ W 246
Parry Peninsula, *Can.* 69° 48′ N, 125° 21′ W 98
Parry Sound, *Can.* 45° 20′ N, 80° 2′ W 94
Parshall, *N. Dak., U.S.* 47° 57′ N, 102° 10′ W 90
Parsi, oil field, *Iran* 31° 0′ N, 49° 54′ E 180
Parsnip Peak, *Nev., U.S.* 38° 8′ N, 114° 25′ W 90
Parsnip Peak, *Oreg., U.S.* 42° 50′ N, 117° 11′ W 90
Parsnip, river, *Can.* 54° 34′ N, 122° 18′ W 108
Parsons, *Kans., U.S.* 37° 19′ N, 95° 16′ W 96
Pårtefjället, peak, *Nor.* 67° 9′ N, 17° 29′ E 152
Partridge Bay 53° 8′ N, 56° 28′ W 111
Partridge, river, *Can.* 50° 50′ N, 80° 23′ W 110
Parú, river, *Venez.* 4° 34′ N, 66° 7′ W 136
Parucito, river, *Venez.* 5° 2′ N, 66° 8′ W 136
Paruro, *Peru* 13° 48′ S, 71° 51′ W 137
P'arvani, Tba, lake, *Ga.* 41° 23′ N, 43° 28′ E 195
Parvatipuram, *India* 18° 45′ N, 83° 26′ E 188
Paryang, *China* 30° 11′ N, 83° 20′ E 197
Parychy, *Belarus* 52° 46′ N, 29° 29′ E 152
Parys, *S. Af.* 26° 58′ S, 27° 27′ E 227
Pasadena, *Calif., U.S.* 34° 8′ N, 118° 11′ W 101
Pasadena, *Tex., U.S.* 29° 41′ N, 95° 12′ W 103
Pasado, Cabo, *Ecua.* 0° 22′ N, 81° 24′ W 130
Pasaje, *Ecua.* 3° 28′ S, 79° 49′ W 130
Pasaje (Juramento), river, *Arg.* 28° 44′ S, 62° 58′ W 139
P'asanauri, *Ga.* 42° 19′ N, 44° 37′ E 195
Pascagoula, *Miss., U.S.* 30° 21′ N, 88° 32′ W 103
Paşcani, *Rom.* 47° 14′ N, 26° 42′ E 156
Pasco, *Wash., U.S.* 46° 13′ N, 119° 5′ W 90
Pasco, adm. division, *Peru* 10° 15′ S, 74° 55′ W 137
Pascoag, *R.I., U.S.* 41° 57′ N, 71° 43′ W 104
Pascoal, Monte, peak, *Braz.* 16° 53′ S, 39° 25′ W 138
Pascua, Isla de see Easter Island, *Chile* 27° 0′ S, 109° 0′ W 241
Pasewalk, *Ger.* 53° 30′ N, 13° 59′ E 152
Pasfield Lake, *Can.* 58° 24′ N, 105° 44′ W 108
Pasha, river, *Russ.* 59° 46′ N, 34° 4′ E 154
Pashiya, *Russ.* 58° 26′ N, 58° 22′ E 154
Pashskiy Perevoz, *Russ.* 60° 23′ N, 33° 8′ E 154
Pasinler, *Turk.* 39° 59′ N, 41° 40′ E 195
Pasir Mas, *Malaysia* 6° 3′ N, 102° 7′ E 196
Pasir Puteh, *Malaysia* 5° 50′ N, 102° 23′ E 196
Paskwachi Bay 57° 14′ N, 102° 46′ W 108
Pasley, Cape, *Austral.* 34° 26′ S, 123° 41′ E 231
Pasni, *Pak.* 25° 15′ N, 63° 26′ E 182
Paso de los Libres, *Arg.* 29° 40′ S, 57° 9′ W 139
Paso de los Toros, *Uru.* 32° 46′ S, 56° 31′ W 139
Paso de Ovejas, *Mex.* 19° 16′ N, 96° 26′ W 114
Paso Robles, *Calif., U.S.* 35° 37′ N, 120° 42′ W 100
Pasorapa, *Bol.* 18° 21′ S, 64° 39′ W 137
Pasque Island, *Mass., U.S.* 41° 27′ N, 70° 53′ W 104
Pass Christian, *Miss., U.S.* 30° 18′ N, 89° 15′ W 103
Passadumkeag Mountain, peak, *Me., U.S.* 45° 6′ N, 68° 28′ W 94
Passat Nunatak, peak, *Antarctica* 71° 25′ S, 4° 12′ W 248
Passau, *Ger.* 48° 33′ N, 13° 28′ E 152
Passero, Capo, *It.* 36° 39′ N, 15° 9′ E 216
Passo Fundo, *Braz.* 28° 16′ S, 52° 27′ W 139
Passos, *Braz.* 20° 43′ S, 46° 37′ W 138
Pastavy, *Belarus* 55° 7′ N, 26° 50′ E 166
Pastaza, river, *Ecua.* 2° 3′ S, 76° 53′ W 130
Pastaza, river, *Peru* 4° 29′ S, 76° 33′ W 130
Pasteur, *Arg.* 35° 7′ S, 62° 14′ W 139
Pasto, *Col.* 1° 13′ N, 77° 17′ W 136
Pastora Peak, *Ariz., U.S.* 36° 46′ N, 109° 14′ W 92
Pastos Bons, *Braz.* 6° 38′ S, 44° 5′ W 132
Pastrana, *Sp.* 40° 24′ N, 2° 56′ W 150
Pasvalys, *Lith.* 56° 3′ N, 24° 22′ E 166
Pasvik, *Nor.* 69° 47′ N, 30° 32′ E 152
Pašvitinys, *Lith.* 56° 9′ N, 23° 47′ E 166
Pásztó, *Hung.* 47° 54′ N, 19° 43′ E 168
Pata, *Cen. Af. Rep.* 8° 2′ N, 21° 28′ E 218
Patagonia, *Ariz., U.S.* 31° 31′ N, 110° 45′ W 92
Patamisk, Lac, lake, *Can.* 52° 52′ N, 71° 43′ W 111
Patan, *India* 23° 50′ N, 72° 7′ E 186
Patan, *India* 17° 24′ N, 73° 55′ E 188
Patan, *India* 23° 16′ N, 79° 43′ E 197
Patan see Lalitpur, *Nepal* 27° 36′ N, 85° 22′ E 197
Patani, *Indonesia* 0° 15′ N, 128° 46′ E 192
Patara Shiraki, *Ga.* 41° 17′ N, 46° 20′ E 195
Patchogue, *N.Y., U.S.* 40° 45′ N, 73° 1′ W 104
Pate Island, *Kenya* 2° 16′ S, 41° 4′ E 224
Pategi, *Nig.* 8° 43′ N, 5° 44′ E 222
Pateley Bridge, *U.K.* 54° 5′ N, 1° 45′ W 162
Patensie, *S. Af.* 33° 46′ S, 24° 48′ E 227
Paternion, *Aust.* 46° 43′ N, 13° 40′ E 167
Paterson, *N.J., U.S.* 40° 53′ N, 74° 11′ W 82
Paterson Range, *Austral.* 21° 46′ S, 121° 56′ E 230
Pathankot, *India* 32° 16′ N, 75° 42′ E 186
Pathein, *Myanmar* 16° 44′ N, 94° 45′ E 202
Pathfinder Dam, *Wyo., U.S.* 42° 28′ N, 106° 49′ W 90
Pathum Thani, *Thai.* 14° 1′ N, 100° 31′ E 202
Pati, river, *Braz.* 3° 40′ S, 67° 54′ W 136
Patiala, *India* 30° 19′ N, 76° 22′ E 197
Pativilca, *Peru* 10° 42′ S, 77° 47′ W 130
Pátmos, *Gr.* 37° 18′ N, 26° 33′ E 156
Patna, *India* 25° 33′ N, 85° 5′ E 197
Patnos, *Turk.* 39° 13′ N, 42° 52′ E 195
Pató, *Col.* 7° 27′ N, 74° 55′ W 136
Patoka, *Ill., U.S.* 38° 44′ N, 89° 6′ W 102
Patoka, *Ind., U.S.* 38° 24′ N, 87° 36′ W 94
Patos, *Braz.* 7° 0′ S, 37° 15′ W 132
Patos de Minas, *Braz.* 18° 36′ S, 46° 30′ W 138
Patos, Lagoa dos, lake, *Braz.* 31° 15′ S, 51° 35′ W 139
Patos, Laguna de, lake, *Mex.* 30° 41′ N, 107° 3′ W 92
Patos, Ponta dos, *Braz.* 2° 59′ S, 39° 40′ W 132
Pátra, *Gr.* 38° 12′ N, 21° 47′ E 180
Patrae see Pátra, *Gr.* 38° 14′ N, 21° 43′ E 156
Patricio Lynch, Isla, island, *Chile* 48° 27′ S, 77° 53′ W 134
Patrick Air Force Base, *Fla., U.S.* 28° 14′ N, 80° 39′ W 105
Patrick, Croagh, peak, *Ire.* 53° 44′ N, 9° 46′ W 150
Patrick Point, peak, *Antarctica* 73° 36′ S, 66° 6′ E 248
Patrimonio, *Braz.* 19° 30′ S, 48° 31′ W 138
Patrington, *U.K.* 53° 40′ N, 7° 419′ W 162
Patriot, *Ind., U.S.* 38° 50′ N, 84° 49′ W 102
Patrocínio, *Braz.* 18° 57′ S, 46° 58′ W 138
Pattani, *Thai.* 6° 50′ N, 101° 16′ E 196
Patten, *Me., U.S.* 45° 59′ N, 68° 27′ W 94
Patterson, *Calif., U.S.* 37° 28′ N, 121° 9′ W 100
Patterson Lake, lake, *Can.* 57° 37′ N, 109° 54′ W 108
Patterson, Mount, peak, *Calif., U.S.* 38° 25′ N, 119° 24′ W 90
Patterson Mountain, peak, *Calif., U.S.* 36° 58′ N, 119° 6′ W 101
Patti, *India* 31° 16′ N, 74° 53′ E 186
Pattison, *Miss., U.S.* 31° 53′ N, 90° 53′ W 103
Patton Seamounts, *North Pacific Ocean* 54° 12′ N, 150° 21′ W 252
Pattullo, Mount, peak, *Can.* 56° 13′ N, 129° 48′ W 108
Patu, *Braz.* 6° 8′ S, 37° 38′ W 132
Patuakhali, *Bangladesh* 22° 18′ N, 90° 19′ E 197
Patuanak, *Can.* 55° 55′ N, 107° 44′ W 108
Patuca National Park, *Hond.* 14° 27′ N, 85° 53′ W 115
Patuca, river, *Hond.* 14° 16′ N, 85° 54′ W 115
Pătulele, *Rom.* 44° 20′ N, 22° 47′ E 168
Patutahi, *N.Z.* 38° 38′ S, 177° 52′ E 240
Patuxent River Naval Air Test Center, *Md., U.S.* 38° 16′ N, 76° 29′ W 94
Pátzcuaro, *Mex.* 19° 28′ N, 101° 37′ W 114
Pátzcuaro, Laguna de, lake, *Mex.* 19° 30′ N, 102° 3′ W 114
Pau, *Fr.* 43° 18′ N, 0° 22′ E 164
Pau d'Arco, river, *Braz.* 8° 20′ S, 50° 41′ W 132
Paucarbamba, *Peru* 12° 27′ S, 74° 37′ W 137
Paucartambo, *Peru* 13° 22′ S, 71° 36′ W 137
Pauillac, *Fr.* 45° 12′ N, 0° 46′ E 150
Pauini, *Braz.* 7° 45′ S, 67° 2′ W 130
Pauini, river, *Braz.* 2° 33′ S, 63° 52′ W 130
Pauini, river, *Braz.* 7° 42′ S, 67° 48′ W 130
Pauini, river, *Braz.* 8° 5′ S, 69° 34′ W 130
Paulatuk, *Can.* 69° 26′ N, 124° 6′ W 98
Paulding, *Miss., U.S.* 32° 0′ N, 89° 1′ W 103
Paulding, *Ohio, U.S.* 41° 7′ N, 84° 35′ W 102
Pauléoula, *Côte d'Ivoire* 5° 45′ N, 7° 24′ W 222
Paulilatino, *It.* 40° 5′ N, 8° 47′ E 156
Paulina Peak, *Oreg., U.S.* 43° 40′ N, 121° 21′ W 90
Pauline, Mount, peak, *Can.* 53° 31′ N, 119° 59′ W 108
Paulis see Isiro, *Dem. Rep. of the Congo* 2° 43′ N, 27° 39′ E 224
Paulista, *Braz.* 7° 56′ S, 34° 59′ W 132
Paulistana, *Braz.* 8° 10′ S, 41° 9′ W 132
Paull Lake, lake, *Can.* 56° 8′ N, 105° 11′ W 108
Paullo, *It.* 45° 25′ N, 9° 23′ E 167
Paulo Afonso, *Braz.* 9° 24′ S, 38° 16′ W 132
Pauls Valley, *Okla., U.S.* 34° 43′ N, 97° 13′ W 92
Pauma Valley, *Calif., U.S.* 33° 18′ N, 117° 0′ W 101
Paungde, *Myanmar* 18° 30′ N, 95° 29′ E 202
Pauni, *India* 20° 45′ N, 79° 37′ E 188
Pauri, *India* 30° 9′ N, 78° 48′ E 197
Pausa, *Peru* 15° 19′ S, 73° 22′ W 137
Pauto, river, *Col.* 5° 21′ N, 71° 31′ W 136
Pavão, *Braz.* 17° 25′ S, 41° 5′ W 138
Pavda, *Russ.* 59° 17′ N, 59° 29′ E 154
Pāveh, *Iran* 35° 4′ N, 46° 21′ E 180
Pavia, *It.* 45° 11′ N, 9° 9′ E 167
Pavia, *Port.* 38° 52′ N, 8° 2′ W 150
Pavie, *Fr.* 43° 36′ N, 0° 35′ E 150
Pavillion, *Wyo., U.S.* 43° 14′ N, 108° 42′ W 90
Pavilly, *Fr.* 49° 34′ N, 0° 57′ E 163
Pāvilosta, *Latv.* 56° 53′ N, 21° 11′ E 166
Pavino, *Russ.* 59° 7′ N, 46° 9′ E 154
Pavlica, *Serb.* 43° 20′ N, 20° 39′ E 168
Pavlodar, *Kaz.* 52° 17′ N, 76° 57′ E 184
Pavlodar, adm. division, *Kaz.* 52° 5′ N, 74° 35′ E 184
Pavlof Volcano, peak, *Alas., U.S.* 55° 23′ N, 162° 4′ W 98
Pavlohrad, *Ukr.* 48° 32′ N, 35° 52′ E 158
Pavlovac, *Croatia* 45° 43′ N, 17° 1′ E 168
Pavlovka, *Russ.* 53° 5′ N, 51° 17′ E 154
Pavlovka, *Russ.* 52° 39′ N, 47° 13′ E 158
Pavlovo, *Russ.* 55° 55′ N, 43° 8′ E 154
Pavlovsk, *Russ.* 50° 27′ N, 40° 6′ E 158
Pavlovskaya, *Russ.* 46° 8′ N, 39° 44′ E 158
Pavullo nel Frignano, *It.* 44° 20′ N, 10° 49′ E 167
Pavy, *Russ.* 58° 2′ N, 29° 30′ E 166
Paw Paw, *Mich., U.S.* 42° 13′ N, 85° 53′ W 94
Pawarenga, *N.Z.* 35° 24′ S, 173° 15′ E 240
Pawcatuck, *Conn., U.S.* 41° 22′ N, 71° 51′ W 104
Pawhuska, *Okla., U.S.* 36° 39′ N, 96° 20′ W 92
Pawlet, *Vt., U.S.* 43° 20′ N, 73° 12′ W 104
Pawleys Island, *S.C., U.S.* 33° 25′ N, 79° 8′ W 96
Pawling, *N.Y., U.S.* 41° 33′ N, 73° 37′ W 104
Pawnee, *Okla., U.S.* 36° 18′ N, 96° 48′ W 92
Pawnee Buttes, peak, *Colo., U.S.* 40° 49′ N, 104° 4′ W 90
Pawnee City, *Nebr., U.S.* 40° 5′ N, 96° 10′ W 90
Pawnee Creek, river, *Colo., U.S.* 40° 31′ N, 104° 0′ W 90
Pawonków, *Pol.* 50° 41′ N, 18° 35′ E 152
Pawtucket, *R.I., U.S.* 41° 52′ N, 71° 24′ W 104
Paxí, *Gr.* 39° 11′ N, 20° 10′ E 156
Paxtakor, *Uzb.* 40° 22′ N, 67° 59′ E 197
Paxton, *Ill., U.S.* 40° 27′ N, 88° 6′ W 102
Paxton, *Mass., U.S.* 42° 18′ N, 71° 56′ W 104
Paxton, *Mo., U.S.* 40° 27′ N, 88° 6′ W 94
Paxton, *Nebr., U.S.* 41° 7′ N, 101° 23′ W 90
Payakumbuh, *Indonesia* 0° 13′ N, 100° 37′ E 196
Payar, *Senegal* 14° 24′ N, 14° 32′ W 222
Payas, peak, *Hond.* 15° 43′ N, 85° 0′ W 115
Payer Mountains, *Antarctica* 71° 54′ S, 15° 30′ E 248
Payerne, *Switz.* 46° 49′ N, 6° 57′ E 167
Payette, *Idaho, U.S.* 44° 2′ N, 116° 53′ W 82
Payne, *Ohio, U.S.* 41° 4′ N, 84° 44′ W 102
Payne, Lac, lake, *Can.* 59° 34′ N, 75° 34′ W 106
Payne, Mount, peak, *Peru* 12° 19′ S, 73° 39′ W 137
Paynesville, *Minn., U.S.* 45° 20′ N, 94° 44′ W 90
Payo see Panganiban, *Philippines* 13° 56′ N, 124° 17′ E 203
Pays de La Loire, adm. division, *Fr.* 47° 34′ N, 1° 59′ W 150
Paysandú, *Uru.* 32° 21′ S, 58° 2′ W 139
Payshanba, *Uzb.* 39° 54′ N, 66° 16′ E 197
Payson, *Ariz., U.S.* 34° 13′ N, 111° 19′ W 92
Payson, *Utah, U.S.* 40° 1′ N, 111° 43′ W 90
Paz, *Braz.* 25° 41′ S, 52° 11′ W 138
Paz de Ariporo, *Col.* 5° 50′ N, 71° 51′ W 136
Paz de Río, *Col.* 5° 59′ N, 72° 46′ W 136
Paz, river, *Braz.* 9° 26′ S, 52° 2′ W 130
Pazar, *Turk.* 40° 16′ N, 36° 16′ E 156
Pazar, *Turk.* 41° 10′ N, 40° 52′ E 195
Pazar, *Turk.* 40° 17′ N, 32° 42′ E 156
Pazarcık, *Turk.* 37° 29′ N, 37° 19′ E 156
Pazardzhik, *Bulg.* 42° 12′ N, 24° 19′ E 156
Pazña, *Bol.* 18° 38′ S, 66° 56′ W 137
Pčinja, river, *Maced.* 41° 46′ N, 21° 48′ E 156
Pe, *Myanmar* 13° 27′ N, 98° 30′ E 202
Pe Ell, *Wash., U.S.* 46° 32′ N, 123° 18′ W 100
Peabody, *Kans., U.S.* 38° 9′ N, 97° 7′ W 94
Peabody, *Mass., U.S.* 42° 31′ N, 70° 56′ W 104
Peace Dale, *R.I., U.S.* 41° 27′ N, 71° 31′ W 104
Peace Garden, *N. Dak., U.S.* 48° 58′ N, 100° 9′ W 90
Peace River, *Can.* 56° 14′ N, 117° 15′ W 108
Peace, river, *Can.* 57° 16′ N, 116° 57′ W 108
Peace, river, *Fla., U.S.* 27° 11′ N, 81° 54′ W 105
Peach Springs, *Ariz., U.S.* 35° 31′ N, 113° 25′ W 101
Peaima Falls, *Guyana* 6° 23′ N, 61° 16′ W 130
Peak District National Park, *U.K.* 51° 21′ N, 1° 50′ W 150
Peaked Mountain, *Me., U.S.* 46° 33′ N, 68° 54′ W 94
Peale, Mount, peak, *Utah, U.S.* 38° 25′ N, 109° 18′ W 90
Peard Bay 70° 39′ N, 160° 16′ W 98
Pearisburg, *Va., U.S.* 37° 18′ N, 80° 44′ W 96
Pearl and Hermes Atoll, islands, *North Pacific Ocean* 26° 30′ N, 179° 37′ E 238
Pearl Peak, *Nev., U.S.* 40° 13′ N, 115° 37′ W 90
Pearl River, *La., U.S.* 30° 21′ N, 89° 45′ W 103
Pearl, river, *Miss., U.S.* 30° 46′ N, 89° 41′ W 103
Pearland, *Tex., U.S.* 29° 32′ N, 95° 17′ W 103
Pearsall, *Tex., U.S.* 28° 53′ N, 99° 6′ W 92
Pearse Canal 54° 48′ N, 130° 40′ W 108
Pearson, *Ga., U.S.* 31° 17′ N, 82° 51′ W 96
Pearston, *S. Af.* 32° 36′ S, 25° 8′ E 227
Peary Land 83° 29′ N, 42° 51′ W 72
Pease, river, *Tex., U.S.* 34° 21′ N, 100° 39′ W 80
Peawanuk, *Can.* 55° 3′ N, 85° 34′ W 106
Pebane, *Mozambique* 17° 16′ S, 38° 11′ E 224
Pebas, *Peru* 3° 19′ S, 71° 51′ W 136
Pebble Beach, *Calif., U.S.* 36° 34′ N, 121° 58′ W 100
Pebble Island, *Pebble Island* 51° 9′ S, 60° 3′ W 248
Peć see Peja, *Kosovo* 42° 40′ N, 20° 17′ E 168
Pecan Island, *La., U.S.* 29° 38′ N, 92° 26′ W 103
Peçanha, *Braz.* 18° 34′ S, 42° 35′ W 138
Pécel, *Hung.* 47° 29′ N, 19° 20′ E 168
Pechenga, *Russ.* 69° 32′ N, 31° 11′ E 152
Pechina, *Sp.* 36° 54′ N, 2° 26′ W 164
Pechora, *Russ.* 65° 8′ N, 57° 11′ E 154
Pechora, river, *Russ.* 65° 40′ N, 56° 56′ E 154
Pechorskaya Guba 68° 13′ N, 50° 14′ E 246
Pechorskaya Nizmennost', *Russ.* 64° 53′ N, 51° 55′ E 154
Pechorskoye More 69° 0′ N, 53° 8′ E 246
Pechory, *Russ.* 57° 48′ N, 27° 36′ E 166
Pecica, *Rom.* 46° 10′ N, 21° 4′ E 168
Peciu Nou, *Rom.* 45° 36′ N, 21° 4′ E 168
Peck, Mount, peak, *Can.* 58° 17′ N, 124° 52′ W 108
Pecka, *Serb.* 44° 18′ N, 19° 32′ E 168
Peconic, *N.Y., U.S.* 41° 2′ N, 72° 28′ W 104
Pecora, Capo, *It.* 39° 23′ N, 7° 46′ E 156
Pecos, *N. Mex., U.S.* 35° 34′ N, 105° 41′ W 92
Pecos, *Tex., U.S.* 31° 24′ N, 103° 30′ W 92
Pecos, river, *U.S.* 35° 7′ N, 105° 5′ W 92
Pécs, *Hung.* 46° 4′ N, 18° 13′ E 168
Pécsvárad, *Hung.* 46° 8′ N, 18° 25′ E 168
Peddapalli, *India* 18° 36′ N, 79° 23′ E 188
Pededze, river, *Latv.* 57° 11′ N, 27° 6′ E 166
Pedernales, *Venez.* 9° 54′ N, 62° 16′ W 116
Pedja, river, *Est.* 58° 28′ N, 26° 13′ E 166
Pêdo Pass, *China* 29° 24′ N, 83° 24′ E 197
Pedra Azul, *Braz.* 16° 3′ S, 41° 16′ W 138
Pedra de Amolar, *Braz.* 10° 34′ S, 46° 25′ W 130
Pedras Altas, *Braz.* 31° 44′ S, 53° 32′ W 139
Pedras Negras, *Braz.* 12° 49′ S, 62° 54′ W 130
Pedregal, *Venez.* 11° 2′ N, 70° 8′ W 136
Pedreiras, *Braz.* 4° 34′ S, 44° 41′ W 132
Pedrera, *Sp.* 37° 13′ N, 4° 55′ W 164
Pedriceña, *Mex.* 25° 5′ N, 103° 49′ W 114
Pedro Afonso, *Braz.* 8° 59′ S, 48° 10′ W 130
Pedro Bay, *Alas., U.S.* 59° 47′ N, 154° 7′ W 98
Pedro Cays, islands, *Caribbean Sea* 16° 52′ N, 77° 47′ W 115
Pedro de Valdivia, *Chile* 22° 37′ S, 69° 44′ W 137
Pedro González, Isla, island, *Pan.* 8° 23′ N, 80° 13′ W 115
Pedro Juan Caballero, *Parag.* 22° 36′ S, 55° 46′ W 132
Pedro Luro, *Arg.* 39° 31′ S, 62° 42′ W 139
Pedro Montoya, *Mex.* 21° 38′ N, 99° 49′ W 114
Pedro Muñoz, *Sp.* 39° 23′ N, 2° 57′ W 164
Pedro Osório, *Braz.* 31° 52′ S, 52° 48′ W 139
Pedro R. Fernández, *Arg.* 28° 44′ S, 58° 39′ W 139
Pedroso, Sierra del, *Sp.* 38° 27′ N, 5° 51′ W 164
Pee Dee, river, *S.C., U.S.* 34° 48′ N, 79° 52′ W 80
Peebles, *Ohio, U.S.* 38° 56′ N, 83° 25′ W 102
Peekskill, *N.Y., U.S.* 41° 16′ N, 73° 56′ W 104
Peel, river, *Can.* 65° 54′ N, 137° 18′ W 98
Peene, *U.K.* 51° 7′ N, 1° 14′ E 162
Peeples Valley, *Ariz., U.S.* 34° 15′ N, 112° 44′ W 92
Peerless Lake, *Can.* 56° 41′ N, 115° 8′ W 108
Peetz, *Colo., U.S.* 40° 57′ N, 103° 8′ W 90
Pego, *Sp.* 38° 49′ N, 0° 7′ E 164
Pegtymel', river, *Russ.* 69° 51′ N, 173° 25′ E 160
Pegyshdor, *Russ.* 63° 26′ N, 50° 35′ E 154
Pehčevo, *Maced.* 41° 45′ N, 22° 54′ E 168
Pehuajó, *Arg.* 35° 47′ S, 61° 54′ W 139
Peine, *Ger.* 52° 19′ N, 10° 13′ E 152
Peixe, *Braz.* 12° 5′ S, 48° 35′ W 130
Peixe, river, *Braz.* 27° 25′ S, 51° 52′ W 139
Peixe, river, *Braz.* 14° 42′ S, 50° 46′ W 138
Peja (Peć), *Kosovo* 42° 40′ N, 20° 17′ E 168
Pek, river, *Serb.* 44° 34′ N, 21° 34′ E 168
Pekalongan, *Indonesia* 7° 1′ S, 109° 38′ E 192
Pekan, *Malaysia* 3° 30′ N, 103° 24′ E 196
Pekanbaru, *Indonesia* 0° 32′ N, 101° 27′ E 196
Pekin, *Ill., U.S.* 40° 33′ N, 89° 39′ W 102
Peking see Beijing, *China* 39° 52′ N, 116° 9′ E 198
Pekkala, *Fin.* 66° 21′ N, 26° 52′ E 152
Pelado, peak, *Sp.* 39° 44′ N, 1° 27′ W 150
Pelagie, Isole, islands, *Mediterranean Sea* 35° 6′ N, 12° 12′ E 156
Pelagosa see Palagruža, island, *Croatia* 42° 25′ N, 16° 0′ E 168
Pelahatchie, *Miss., U.S.* 32° 18′ N, 89° 48′ W 103
Pelalawan, *Indonesia* 0° 29′ N, 102° 6′ E 196
Pelat, Mont, peak, *Fr.* 44° 16′ N, 6° 39′ E 165
Peldoaivi, peak, *Fin.* 69° 10′ N, 26° 25′ E 152
Peleaga, peak, *Rom.* 45° 21′ N, 22° 52′ E 168
Pelechuco, *Bol.* 14° 52′ S, 69° 4′ W 137
Peleduy, *Russ.* 59° 45′ N, 112° 45′ E 160
Pelee Island, *Can.* 41° 44′ N, 82° 40′ W 102
Pelée, Montagne, peak, *Martinique* 14° 47′ N, 61° 15′ W 116
Pelendria, *Cyprus* 34° 53′ N, 32° 58′ E 194
Peleng, island, *Indonesia* 2° 0′ S, 122° 52′ E 192
Pelham, *Ga., U.S.* 31° 7′ N, 84° 9′ W 96
Pelham, *Mass., U.S.* 42° 23′ N, 72° 25′ W 104
Pelican, *Alas., U.S.* 57° 58′ N, 136° 14′ W 98
Pelican, *La., U.S.* 31° 52′ N, 93° 36′ W 103
Pelican Lake, lake, *Can.* 52° 24′ N, 100° 48′ W 108
Pelican Mountain, peak, *Can.* 55° 36′ N, 113° 53′ W 108
Pelican Narrows, *Can.* 55° 12′ N, 102° 56′ W 108
Pelican Point, *Namibia* 22° 55′ S, 13° 55′ E 220
Pelican Portage, *Can.* 55° 41′ N, 112° 36′ W 108
Pelican Rapids, *Can.* 52° 43′ N, 100° 44′ W 108
Pelican Rapids, *Minn., U.S.* 46° 32′ N, 96° 5′ W 94
Pelinéo, Óros, peak, *Gr.* 38° 33′ N, 25° 56′ E 156
Pelister National Park, *Maced.* 40° 29′ N, 21° 15′ E 180

Pelister, peak, *Maced.* 40°59′ N, 21°7′ E 156
Pelješac, *Croatia* 42°58′ N, 17°6′ E 168
Pella, *S. Af.* 29°3′ S, 19°9′ E 227
Pellegrini, *Arg.* 36°18′ S, 63°9′ W 139
Pello, *Fin.* 66°47′ N, 24°0′ E 152
Pelly, *Can.* 51°50′ N, 101°56′ W 90
Pelly Crossing, *Can.* 62°53′ N, 136°34′ W 98
Pelly, river, *Can.* 61°45′ N, 131°16′ W 98
Pelokehn, *Liberia* 5°34′ N, 8°8′ W 222
Peloponnesus, *Gr.* 38°2′ N, 21°53′ E 180
Peloponnisos, adm. division, *Gr.* 36°51′ N, 22°29′ E 156
Peloritani, Monti, *It.* 38°0′ N, 14°49′ E 156
Pelotas, *Braz.* 31°44′ S, 52°19′ W 139
Pelotas, river, *Braz.* 27°42′ S, 51°25′ W 139
Pelplin, *Pol.* 53°55′ N, 18°42′ E 166
Pelsart Group, islands, *Indian Ocean* 29°25′ S, 112°14′ E 230
Peltovuoma, *Fin.* 68°22′ N, 24°11′ E 152
Pelusium, ruin(s), *Egypt* 31°0′ N, 32°29′ E 194
Pelvoux, Massif du, *Fr.* 44°50′ N, 6°9′ E 165
Pelyatka, *Russ.* 69°59′ N, 82°13′ E 169
Pelym, *Russ.* 59°40′ N, 63°5′ E 154
Pelym, river, *Russ.* 60°42′ N, 62°22′ E 154
Pemache, river, *Can.* 47°29′ N, 83°50′ W 110
Pemaquid Point, *Me., U.S.* 43°37′ N, 69°34′ W 94
Pematang, *Indonesia* 0°10′ N, 102°6′ E 196
Pematangsiantar, *Indonesia* 3°2′ N, 99°7′ E 196
Pemba, *Mozambique* 13°2′ S, 40°33′ E 224
Pemba, *Zambia* 16°32′ S, 27°20′ E 224
Pemba Island, *Tanzania* 5°7′ S, 39°54′ E 224
Pemberton, *Can.* 50°19′ N, 122°49′ W 100
Pembina, *N. Dak., U.S.* 48°56′ N, 97°17′ W 90
Pembina Hills, *Can.* 49°27′ N, 98°58′ W 90
Pembina, oil field, *Can.* 53°6′ N, 115°14′ W 108
Pembina, river, *North America* 53°4′ N, 116°13′ W 108
Pembroke, *Can.* 45°50′ N, 77°7′ W 110
Pembroke, *Ga., U.S.* 32°8′ N, 81°38′ W 96
Pembroke, *N.H., U.S.* 43°8′ N, 71°28′ W 104
Pembroke, Cape, *East Falkland* 51°49′ S, 57°42′ W 134
Pembrokeshire Coast National Park, *U.K.* 51°50′ N, 5°5′ W 150
Peña Blanca, Cerro, peak, *Pan.* 8°39′ N, 80°40′ W 115
Peña de Francia, Sierra de, *Sp.* 40°32′ N, 6°47′ W 150
Peña Grande, *Sp.* 40°28′ N, 3°45′ W 164
Penã Negra, Paso de, pass, *Chile* 28°14′ S, 69°28′ W 132
Peña, Sierra de, *Sp.* 42°27′ N, 1°0′ E 164
Penalva, *Braz.* 3°18′ S, 45°13′ W 132
Penápolis, *Braz.* 21°24′ S, 50°7′ W 138
Peñarroya, peak, *Sp.* 40°22′ N, 0°43′ E 164
Penarth, *U.K.* 51°26′ N, 3°10′ W 162
Peñas Blancas, *Nicar.* 11°13′ N, 85°36′ W 115
Peñas, Cabo de, *Sp.* 43°39′ N, 6°7′ W 150
Peñas de San Pedro, *Sp.* 38°43′ N, 2°0′ W 150
Pencarreg, *U.K.* 52°4′ N, 4°8′ W 162
Pench National Park, *India* 21°40′ N, 79°30′ E 197
Penck, Cape 66°6′ S, 84°17′ E 248
Pendé, river, *Cen. Af. Rep.* 6°38′ N, 15°51′ E 218
Pendéli, peak, *Gr.* 38°4′ N, 23°48′ E 156
Pendembu, *Sierra Leone* 8°3′ N, 10°42′ W 222
Pender, *Nebr., U.S.* 42°5′ N, 96°43′ W 90
Pender Bay 17°0′ S, 122°19′ E 230
Pendjari National Park, *Benin* 11°17′ N, 1°27′ E 222
Pendleton, *Ind., U.S.* 39°59′ N, 85°44′ W 102
Pendleton, *Oreg., U.S.* 45°38′ N, 118°48′ W 90
Pendleton, Mount, peak, *Can.* 59°12′ N, 129°29′ W 108
Pendroy, *Mont., U.S.* 48°2′ N, 112°19′ W 90
Penebangan, island, *Indonesia* 1°7′ S, 108°41′ E 196
Penedo, *Braz.* 10°15′ S, 36°36′ W 132
Penetanguishene, *Can.* 44°45′ N, 79°56′ W 94
Penge, *Dem. Rep. of the Congo* 5°32′ S, 24°36′ E 224
Penghu (Pescadores), islands, *Taiwan, China* 23°30′ N, 119°30′ E 191
Penglai, *China* 37°47′ N, 120°49′ E 198
Pengshui, *China* 29°18′ N, 108°14′ E 198
Pengxi, *China* 30°45′ N, 105°42′ E 198
Penha do Tapaua, *Braz.* 5°48′ S, 64°29′ W 130
Penhold, *Can.* 52°7′ N, 113°53′ W 90
Peniche, *Port.* 39°20′ N, 9°23′ W 214
Peninga, *Russ.* 63°33′ N, 31°35′ E 152
Península de Paría National Park, *Caribbean Sea* 10°37′ N, 62°36′ W 122
Peñíscola, *Sp.* 40°21′ N, 0°23′ E 164
Penitente, Serra do, *Braz.* 9°3′ S, 46°49′ W 130
Pénjamo, *Mex.* 20°25′ N, 101°44′ W 114
Penmaenmawr, *U.K.* 53°16′ N, 3°55′ W 162
Penmarc'h, Pointe de, *Fr.* 47°29′ N, 4°56′ W 150
Penmon, *U.K.* 53°18′ N, 4°3′ W 162
Penn Yan, *N.Y., U.S.* 42°40′ N, 77°4′ W 94
Penna, Punta della, *It.* 42°11′ N, 14°44′ E 156
Pennabilli, *It.* 43°49′ N, 12°15′ E 167
Pennant Point, *Can.* 44°20′ N, 63°44′ W 111
Pennask Lake, *Can.* 49°56′ N, 120°44′ W 90
Pennask Mountain, peak, *Can.* 49°52′ N, 120°12′ W 90
Pennell Coast, *Antarctica* 70°51′ S, 173°14′ E 248
Pennine Alps, *Switz.* 46°13′ N, 7°29′ E 165
Pennines, The, *U.K.* 54°14′ N, 2°15′ W 162
Pennino, Monte, peak, *It.* 43°5′ N, 12°48′ E 156
Pennsboro, *W. Va., U.S.* 39°16′ N, 80°58′ W 102
Pennsylvania, adm. division, *Pa., U.S.* 41°46′ N, 79°36′ W 94
Pennville, *Ind., U.S.* 40°29′ N, 85°9′ W 102
Penny, *Can.* 53°50′ N, 121°17′ W 108
Penny Point 80°25′ S, 170°23′ E 248
Pennycutaway, river, *Can.* 56°7′ N, 94°14′ W 108
Peno, *Russ.* 56°56′ N, 32°47′ E 154
Penobscot Bay 44°8′ N, 69°6′ W 80
Penong, *Austral.* 31°57′ S, 132°59′ E 231
Penrith, *U.K.* 54°40′ N, 2°46′ W 162
Penryn, *Calif., U.S.* 38°51′ N, 121°11′ W 90
Pensacola, *Fla., U.S.* 30°24′ N, 87°13′ W 96
Pensacola Mountains, *Antarctica* 85°14′ S, 76°52′ W 248
Penticton, *Can.* 49°27′ N, 119°33′ W 106
Pentland Hills, *U.K.* 55°48′ N, 3°57′ W 150
Pentland Skerries, islands, *North Sea* 58°23′ N, 2°50′ W 150
Pentwater, *Mich., U.S.* 43°46′ N, 86°25′ W 102
Penunjok, Tanjong, *Malaysia* 4°1′ N, 103°30′ E 196
Penwell, *Tex., U.S.* 31°43′ N, 102°36′ W 92
Penza, *Russ.* 53°9′ N, 45°3′ E 154
Penza, adm. division, *Russ.* 53°28′ N, 43°26′ E 154
Penzance, *U.K.* 50°7′ N, 5°33′ W 150
Peoples Creek, river, *Mont., U.S.* 48°5′ N, 109°10′ W 108
Peoria, *Ariz., U.S.* 33°34′ N, 112°14′ W 92
Peoria, *Ill., U.S.* 40°40′ N, 89°37′ W 102
Peotillos, *Mex.* 22°28′ N, 100°37′ W 114
Peotone, *Ill., U.S.* 41°19′ N, 87°47′ W 102
Pepe'ekeo, *Hawai'i, U.S.* 19°50′ N, 155°7′ W 99
Pepel, *Sierra Leone* 8°37′ N, 13°4′ W 222
Pephnos, ruin(s), *Gr.* 36°47′ N, 22°13′ E 156
Pequeña, Punta, *Mex.* 26°6′ N, 113°34′ W 112
Pequop Mountains, *Nev., U.S.* 40°40′ N, 114°44′ W 90
Pera, *Cyprus* 35°1′ N, 33°15′ E 194
Perälä, *Fin.* 62°27′ N, 21°36′ E 152
Peralada, *Sp.* 42°18′ N, 3°1′ E 164
Perales de Alfambra, *Sp.* 40°37′ N, 1°0′ E 164
Peramiho, *Tanzania* 10°38′ S, 35°28′ E 224
Peranka, *Fin.* 65°21′ N, 29°1′ E 154
Peräposio, *Fin.* 66°11′ N, 27°52′ E 154
Perast, *Mont.* 42°29′ N, 18°42′ E 168
Perati, ruin(s), *Aegean Sea* 37°54′ N, 23°56′ E 156
Percé, *Can.* 48°30′ N, 64°15′ W 111
Perce Point, *Antarctica* 72°48′ S, 78°20′ W 248
Perch Bay 58°2′ N, 102°23′ W 108
Perche, region, *Fr.* 48°50′ N, 0°46′ E 163
Percy Isles, islands, *Coral Sea* 21°39′ S, 150°29′ E 230
Perdido, *Ala., U.S.* 30°59′ N, 87°37′ W 103
Perdido, Monte, peak, *Sp.* 42°39′ N, 1°59′ W 164
Perdido, river, *U.S.* 30°45′ N, 87°38′ W 103
Perdizes, *Braz.* 19°22′ S, 47°19′ W 138
Perechitsy, *Russ.* 58°48′ N, 30°3′ E 166
Perechyn, *Ukr.* 48°43′ N, 22°26′ E 152
Pereira, *Col.* 4°45′ N, 75°42′ W 136
Pereira Barreto, *Braz.* 20°38′ S, 51°6′ W 138
Perelazovskiy, *Russ.* 49°8′ N, 42°25′ E 158
Perelyub, *Russ.* 51°51′ N, 50°21′ E 158
Peremennyy, Cape, *Antarctica* 65°57′ S, 109°36′ E 248
Peremetnoe, *Kaz.* 51°11′ N, 50°53′ E 158
Pereslavl' Zalesskiy, *Russ.* 56°44′ N, 38°50′ E 154
Perevolotskiy, *Russ.* 51°51′ N, 54°12′ E 158
Pereyaslav-Khmel'nyts'kyy, *Ukr.* 50°3′ N, 31°33′ E 158
Pérez, Isla, island, *Mex.* 22°17′ N, 89°57′ W 116
Perga, ruin(s), *Turk.* 36°59′ N, 30°44′ E 156
Pergamino, *Arg.* 33°57′ S, 60°34′ W 139
Perham, *Minn., U.S.* 46°34′ N, 95°35′ W 90
Perhentian Besar, island, *Malaysia* 5°58′ N, 102°37′ E 196
Perho, *Fin.* 63°13′ N, 24°21′ E 152
Peri Mirim, *Braz.* 2°41′ S, 44°53′ W 132
Periam, *Rom.* 46°2′ N, 20°54′ E 168
Péribonka, Lac, lake, *Can.* 49°55′ N, 71°53′ W 94
Péribonka, river, *Can.* 48°50′ N, 71°20′ W 111
Perico, *Arg.* 24°24′ S, 65°7′ W 134
Peridot, *Ariz., U.S.* 33°19′ N, 110°27′ W 92
Perigoso, Canal 3°177′ S, 50°35′ W 130
Perijá National Park, *Venez.* 9°15′ N, 73°18′ W 136
Perijá, Sierra de, *Venez.* 10°10′ N, 73°20′ W 136
Perim see Barīm, island, *Yemen* 12°36′ N, 42°32′ E 182
Períssa, *Gr.* 36°20′ N, 25°27′ E 156
Perito Moreno, *Arg.* 46°35′ S, 70°55′ W 134
Perito Moreno National Park, *Arg.* 48°0′ S, 72°42′ W 122
Peritoró, *Braz.* 4°17′ S, 44°21′ W 132
Perkins, *Okla., U.S.* 35°57′ N, 97°2′ W 92
Perkinston, *Miss., U.S.* 30°45′ N, 89°7′ W 103
Perkinsville, *Vt., U.S.* 43°22′ N, 72°32′ W 104
Perković, *Croatia* 43°40′ N, 16°5′ E 168
Perky, *Fla., U.S.* 24°38′ N, 81°34′ W 105
Perl, *Ger.* 49°28′ N, 6°23′ E 163
Perla, *Ark., U.S.* 34°20′ N, 92°47′ W 96
Perlas, Laguna de 12°24′ N, 83°56′ W 115
Perlevka, *Russ.* 51°50′ N, 38°47′ E 158
Perm', *Russ.* 57°57′ N, 56°14′ E 154
Perm', adm. division, *Russ.* 58°50′ N, 56°13′ E 154
Permas, *Russ.* 59°19′ N, 45°36′ E 154
Pernaja see Pernå, *Fin.* 60°26′ N, 26°2′ E 166
Pernambuco, adm. division, *Braz.* 8°41′ S, 38°59′ W 132
Pernambuco Plain, *South Atlantic Ocean* 7°10′ S, 25°50′ W 253
Pernik, *Bulg.* 42°36′ N, 23°2′ E 168
Pernik, adm. division, *Bulg.* 42°31′ N, 22°44′ E 168
Perniö, *Fin.* 60°11′ N, 23°6′ E 166
Pernitz, *Aust.* 47°54′ N, 15°57′ E 168
Peron Islands, *Joseph Bonaparte Gulf* 13°19′ S, 128°31′ E 230
Peronit Burnu, *Turk.* 41°23′ N, 41°2′ E 195
Péronne, *Fr.* 49°55′ N, 2°55′ E 163
Peros Banhos, atoll, *Indian Ocean* 5°16′ S, 71°8′ E 188
Perosa Argentina, *It.* 44°57′ N, 7°12′ E 167
Perote, *Mex.* 19°31′ N, 97°16′ W 114
Perouse Strait, La 45°35′ N, 139°41′ E 160
Perow, *Can.* 54°31′ N, 126°27′ W 108
Perpignan, *Fr.* 42°41′ N, 2°53′ E 164
Perrault Falls, *Can.* 50°19′ N, 93°10′ W 90
Perrault Lake, lake, *Can.* 50°14′ N, 93°36′ W 90
Perrine, *Fla., U.S.* 25°36′ N, 80°22′ W 105
Perris, *Calif., U.S.* 33°47′ N, 117°16′ W 101
Perros-Guirec, *Fr.* 48°48′ N, 3°28′ W 150
Perry, *Fla., U.S.* 30°5′ N, 83°34′ W 96
Perry, *Ga., U.S.* 32°27′ N, 83°44′ W 96
Perry, *Iowa, U.S.* 41°49′ N, 94°6′ W 94
Perry, *Mich., U.S.* 42°49′ N, 84°12′ W 102
Perry, *Ohio, U.S.* 41°44′ N, 81°7′ W 102
Perry, *Okla., U.S.* 36°15′ N, 97°17′ W 92
Perry, *Utah, U.S.* 41°27′ N, 112°1′ W 90
Perry Island, *Foxe Basin* 67°49′ N, 102°21′ W 106
Perrysburg, *Ohio, U.S.* 41°32′ N, 83°38′ W 102
Perryton, *Tex., U.S.* 36°22′ N, 100°49′ W 92
Perşembe, *Turk.* 41°4′ N, 37°45′ E 156
Persepolis, ruin(s), *Iran* 30°2′ N, 52°54′ E 196
Pershore, *U.K.* 52°6′ N, 2°5′ W 162
Persian Gulf 26°40′ N, 51°30′ E 196
Pertek, *Turk.* 38°52′ N, 39°19′ E 195
Perth, *Austral.* 31°57′ S, 115°32′ E 231
Perth, *Can.* 44°54′ N, 76°16′ W 94
Perth-Andover, *Can.* 46°43′ N, 67°42′ W 94
Pertominsk, *Russ.* 64°47′ N, 38°20′ E 154
Pertunmaa, *Fin.* 61°30′ N, 26°28′ E 166
Peru, *Ill., U.S.* 41°19′ N, 89°8′ W 102
Peru, *Ind., U.S.* 40°45′ N, 86°4′ W 102
Peru, *Me., U.S.* 44°30′ N, 70°26′ W 104
Peru, *Mo., U.S.* 41°19′ N, 89°8′ W 94
Peru, *Nebr., U.S.* 40°28′ N, 95°44′ W 94
Peru, *N.Y., U.S.* 44°34′ N, 73°34′ W 104
Peru 8°44′ S, 77°9′ W 130
Peru, *Vt., U.S.* 43°14′ N, 72°54′ W 104
Peru Basin, *South Pacific Ocean* 11°59′ S, 88°41′ W 252
Peru-Chile Trench, *South Pacific Ocean* 18°8′ S, 73°12′ W 253
Perugia, *It.* 43°6′ N, 12°23′ E 156
Perugorría, *Arg.* 29°20′ S, 58°34′ W 139
Péruwelz, *Belg.* 50°29′ N, 3°35′ E 163
Pervari, *Turk.* 37°53′ N, 42°32′ E 195
Pervomaevka, *Kaz.* 42°5′ N, 69°52′ E 197
Pervomaysk, *Russ.* 54°49′ N, 43°49′ E 154
Pervomays'k, *Ukr.* 48°4′ N, 30°58′ E 156
Pervomayskīy, *Kaz.* 50°14′ N, 81°58′ E 184
Pervomayskiy, *Russ.* 53°15′ N, 40°14′ E 154
Pervomayskiy, *Russ.* 59°33′ N, 61°23′ E 154
Pervomayskiy, *Russ.* 51°29′ N, 55°4′ E 158
Pervomayskoye, *Russ.* 51°26′ N, 47°40′ E 158
Pervomayskoye, *Russ.* 57°4′ N, 86°21′ E 169
Pervoural'sk, *Russ.* 56°56′ N, 59°57′ E 154
Pervyy Kuril'skiy Proliv 50°43′ N, 153°5′ E 160
Pesaro, *It.* 43°54′ N, 12°55′ E 167
Pescadero, *Calif., U.S.* 37°14′ N, 122°24′ W 100
Pescadores see Penghu, islands, *Taiwan, China* 23°30′ N, 119°30′ E 191
Pescara, *It.* 42°27′ N, 14°13′ E 156
Peschanyy, Mys, *Kaz.* 43°2′ N, 50°52′ E 195
Peschici, *It.* 41°56′ N, 16°1′ E 168
Peschiera, *It.* 45°26′ N, 10°40′ E 167
Pesha, river, *Russ.* 66°28′ N, 48°19′ E 154
Peshawar, *Pak.* 34°0′ N, 71°35′ E 186
Peshawarun, ruin(s), *Afghan.* 31°29′ N, 61°31′ E 186
Peshtigo, *Wis., U.S.* 45°3′ N, 87°47′ W 94
Peski, *Russ.* 51°13′ N, 42°29′ E 158
Peskovka, *Russ.* 59°1′ N, 52°25′ E 154
Pesochnoye, *Russ.* 58°18′ N, 39°7′ E 154
Pesotum, *Ill., U.S.* 39°54′ N, 88°17′ W 102
Pest, adm. division, *Hung.* 47°13′ N, 18°57′ E 156
Peşteana Jiu, *Rom.* 44°50′ N, 23°18′ E 168
Pestovo, *Russ.* 58°37′ N, 35°50′ E 154
Pestravka, *Russ.* 52°24′ N, 49°56′ E 158
Petah Tiqwa, *Israel* 32°5′ N, 34°53′ E 194
Petäjävesi, *Fin.* 62°14′ N, 25°11′ E 154
Petal, *Miss., U.S.* 31°19′ N, 89°14′ W 103
Petalax (Petolahti), *Fin.* 62°49′ N, 21°24′ E 154
Petaluma, *Calif., U.S.* 38°13′ N, 122°39′ W 100
Pétange, *Lux.* 49°32′ N, 5°51′ E 163
Petare, *Venez.* 10°27′ N, 66°48′ W 116
Petatlán, *Mex.* 17°29′ N, 101°16′ W 114
Petatlán, river, *Mex.* 26°14′ N, 107°46′ W 80
Petatlán, river, *Mex.* 17°20′ N, 101°31′ W 112
Petauke, *Zambia* 14°16′ S, 31°16′ E 224
Petén, region, *Guatemala* 16°4′ N, 90°38′ W 115
Petenwell Lake, *Wis., U.S.* 44°6′ N, 90°16′ W 102
Peter I Island, *Antarctica* 68°58′ S, 90°43′ W 248
Peter Lake, *Can.* 57°11′ N, 104°29′ W 108
Peter Pond Lake, *Can.* 55°58′ N, 111°17′ W 106
Peterbell, *Can.* 48°36′ N, 83°22′ W 94
Peterborough, *Austral.* 32°59′ S, 138°49′ E 231
Peterborough, *Can.* 44°18′ N, 78°21′ W 94
Peterborough, *U.K.* 52°34′ N, 0°15′ E 162
Petermann Bjerg, peak 73°3′ N, 29°0′ W 246
Petermann Gletscher, glacier 78°50′ N, 62°8′ W 72
Petersberg, *Ger.* 50°33′ N, 9°42′ E 167
Petersburg, *Alas., U.S.* 56°36′ N, 132°51′ W 106
Petersburg, *Ill., U.S.* 40°0′ N, 89°51′ W 102
Petersburg, *Ind., U.S.* 38°29′ N, 87°16′ W 102
Petersburg, *Mich., U.S.* 41°53′ N, 83°42′ W 102
Petersburg, *Tex., U.S.* 33°51′ N, 101°36′ W 96
Petersburg, *Va., U.S.* 37°11′ N, 77°23′ W 82
Petersburg, *W. Va., U.S.* 38°59′ N, 79°8′ W 94
Petersburg National Battlefield, *Va., U.S.* 37°12′ N, 77°27′ W 96
Petersfield, *U.K.* 51°0′ N, 0°56′ E 162
Petersham, *Mass., U.S.* 42°29′ N, 72°12′ W 104
Petit Port, *Alg.* 36°11′ N, 0°23′ E 164
Petit-Louango Faunal Reserve, *Gabon* 2°20′ S, 9°17′ E 206
Petitot, river, *Can.* 59°49′ N, 123°28′ W 106
Petitot, river, *Can.* 60°4′ N, 122°43′ W 108
Petkula, *Fin.* 67°40′ N, 26°41′ E 152
Petlad, *India* 22°27′ N, 72°49′ E 186
Petlalcingo, *Mex.* 18°4′ N, 97°55′ W 114
Peto, *Mex.* 20°6′ N, 88°57′ W 115
Petolahti see Petalax, *Fin.* 62°49′ N, 21°24′ E 154
Petoskey, *Mich., U.S.* 45°20′ N, 85°0′ W 82
Petra, Ostrova, islands, *Laptev Sea* 75°41′ N, 108°52′ E 160
Petra, ruin(s), *Jordan* 30°17′ N, 35°23′ E 180
Petra Velikogo, Zaliv 42°40′ N, 131°45′ E 200
Petras, Mount, peak, *Antarctica* 75°47′ S, 127°55′ W 248
Petre, Point, *Can.* 43°38′ N, 77°26′ W 94
Petriano, *It.* 43°46′ N, 12°43′ E 167
Petrich, *Bulg.* 41°24′ N, 23°9′ E 180
Petrified Forest National Park, *Ariz., U.S.* 34°44′ N, 109°45′ W 92
Petrinja, *Croatia* 45°26′ N, 16°16′ E 168
Petrodvorets, *Russ.* 59°49′ N, 29°47′ E 166
Petroglyphs, site, *Hawai'i, U.S.* 19°0′ N, 155°50′ W 99
Petrolândia, *Braz.* 9°1′ S, 38°15′ W 132
Petrólea, *Col.* 8°29′ N, 72°40′ W 136
Petrolia, *Calif., U.S.* 40°19′ N, 124°18′ W 90
Petrolia, *Can.* 42°52′ N, 82°10′ W 102
Petrolia, *Tex., U.S.* 33°59′ N, 98°14′ W 92
Petrolina, *Braz.* 9°20′ S, 40°31′ W 132
Petrolina de Goiás, *Braz.* 16°9′ S, 49°21′ W 138
Petropavlovsk, *Kaz.* 54°51′ N, 69°7′ E 184
Petropavlovsk Kamchatskiy, *Russ.* 53°10′ N, 158°42′ E 160
Petroşani, *Rom.* 45°24′ N, 23°22′ E 168
Petrovac, *Mont.* 42°11′ N, 18°57′ E 168
Petrovac, *Serb.* 44°23′ N, 21°25′ E 168
Petrovaradin, *Serb.* 45°14′ N, 19°52′ E 168
Petrovgrad see Zrenjanin, *Serb.* 45°23′ N, 20°22′ E 168
Petrovići, *Mont.* 42°46′ N, 18°29′ E 168
Petrovsk, *Russ.* 52°19′ N, 45°26′ E 158
Petrovsk Zabaykal'skiy, *Russ.* 51°25′ N, 108°56′ E 190
Petrovskoye, *Russ.* 57°0′ N, 39°11′ E 154
Petrozavodsk, *Russ.* 61°45′ N, 34°23′ E 154
Petrun', *Russ.* 66°27′ N, 60°54′ E 169
Petscapiskau Hill, peak, *Can.* 54°23′ N, 64°34′ W 111
Petten, *Neth.* 52°44′ N, 4°39′ E 163
Petukhovo, *Russ.* 55°5′ N, 67°57′ E 184
Peukankuala, *Indonesia* 4°6′ N, 96°12′ E 196
Peumo, *Chile* 34°22′ S, 71°13′ W 134
Peunasoe, island, *Indonesia* 5°31′ N, 94°35′ E 202
Peuplier, Pointe du, *Can.* 51°13′ N, 79°32′ W 110
Peurasuvanto, *Fin.* 67°48′ N, 26°43′ E 152
Peureulak, *Indonesia* 4°50′ N, 97°53′ E 196
Pevek, *Russ.* 69°40′ N, 170°27′ E 160
Pevensey, *U.K.* 50°49′ N, 0°20′ E 162
Pewsum, *Ger.* 53°26′ N, 7°4′ E 163
Peyia, *Cyprus* 34°53′ N, 32°22′ E 194
Peza, river, *Russ.* 65°37′ N, 46°57′ E 154
Pézenas, *Fr.* 43°27′ N, 3°24′ E 164
Pezmog, *Russ.* 61°53′ N, 51°50′ E 154
Pezu, *Pak.* 32°18′ N, 70°47′ E 186
Pfungstadt, *Ger.* 49°48′ N, 8°35′ E 167
Phaestus, ruin(s), *Gr.* 35°1′ N, 24°42′ E 156
Phalasarna, ruin(s), *Gr.* 35°29′ N, 23°29′ E 156
Phalodi, *India* 27°6′ N, 72°21′ E 186
Phalsbourg, *Fr.* 48°45′ N, 7°14′ E 163
Phan, *Thai.* 19°31′ N, 99°43′ E 202
Phan Ly, *Vietnam* 11°13′ N, 108°34′ E 202
Phan Rang, *Vietnam* 11°34′ N, 108°58′ E 202
Phan Thiet, *Vietnam* 10°56′ N, 108°4′ E 202
Phanae, ruin(s), *Gr.* 38°11′ N, 25°49′ E 156
Phangan, Ko, island, *Thai.* 9°49′ N, 99°43′ E 202
Phangnga, *Thai.* 8°30′ N, 98°32′ E 202
Pharus see Hvar, island, *Croatia* 43°3′ N, 16°47′ E 168
Phato, *Thai.* 9°47′ N, 98°49′ E 202
Phatthalung, *Thai.* 7°38′ N, 100°6′ E 196
Phayao, *Thai.* 19°13′ N, 99°55′ E 202
Phelps, *Tex., U.S.* 30°41′ N, 95°26′ W 103
Phelps Lake, lake, *Can.* 59°10′ N, 103°45′ W 108
Pheneus, ruin(s), *Gr.* 37°53′ N, 22°14′ E 156
Phenix City, *Ala., U.S.* 32°27′ N, 85°1′ W 96
Phetchabun, *Thai.* 16°25′ N, 101°8′ E 202
Phetchaburi, *Thai.* 13°7′ N, 99°55′ E 202
Phiafai, *Laos* 14°49′ N, 105°58′ E 202
Phibun Mangsaban, *Thai.* 15°15′ N, 105°14′ E 202
Phichai, *Thai.* 17°18′ N, 100°6′ E 202
Phichit, *Thai.* 16°25′ N, 100°19′ E 202
Philadelphia, *Miss., U.S.* 32°45′ N, 89°7′ W 103
Philadelphia, *Pa., U.S.* 39°57′ N, 75°11′ W 94
Philadelphia see 'Ammān, *Jordan* 31°56′ N, 35°53′ E 194
Philae, ruin(s), *Egypt* 23°56′ N, 32°44′ E 182
Philbin Inlet 74°5′ S, 113°45′ W 248
Philip, *S. Dak., U.S.* 44°2′ N, 101°41′ W 90
Philip Smith Mountains, *Alas., U.S.* 67°56′ N, 149°31′ W 98
Philippeville, *Belg.* 50°11′ N, 4°32′ E 167
Philippi, *W. Va., U.S.* 39°8′ N, 80°3′ W 94
Philippi, ruin(s), *Gr.* 41°0′ N, 24°10′ E 156
Philippine Basin, *Philippine Sea* 14°23′ N, 128°46′ E 254
Philippine Sea 15°8′ N, 123°42′ E 203
Philippine Trench, *Philippine Sea* 11°16′ N, 127°0′ E 254
Philippines 15°0′ N, 121°0′ E 203
Philippolis, *S. Af.* 30°16′ S, 25°16′ E 227
Philippopolis see Plovdiv, *Bulg.* 42°9′ N, 24°45′ E 156
Philippopolis see Shahbā', *Syr.* 32°51′ N, 36°37′ E 194
Philipstown, *S. Af.* 30°25′ S, 24°27′ E 227
Phillip Bay, Port 38°18′ S, 143°6′ E 230
Phillip Island, island, *Austral.* 38°56′ S, 144°23′ E 230
Phillips, *Tex., U.S.* 35°40′ N, 101°22′ W 92
Phillips, *Wis., U.S.* 45°41′ N, 90°24′ W 94
Phillips, Mount, peak, *Austral.* 24°29′ S, 116°18′ E 230
Phillipsburg, *Kans., U.S.* 39°44′ N, 99°20′ W 92
Phillipsburg, *N.J., U.S.* 40°41′ N, 75°12′ W 110
Philmont, *N.Y., U.S.* 42°14′ N, 73°39′ W 104
Philomath, *Oreg., U.S.* 44°31′ N, 123°22′ W 90
Philomena, *Can.* 55°9′ N, 111°40′ W 108
Phitsanulok, *Thai.* 16°52′ N, 100°12′ E 202
Phnom Bokor National Park, *Cambodia* 10°46′ N, 103°34′ E 172
Phnom Penh, *Cambodia* 11°32′ N, 104°45′ E 202
Pho, Laem, *Thai.* 6°54′ N, 101°24′ E 196
Phoenix, *Ariz., U.S.* 33°25′ N, 112°8′ W 92

Phoenix Islands, *South Pacific Ocean* 4°31′ S, 173°41′ W 238
Phon Phisai, *Thai.* 18°3′ N, 103°6′ E 202
Phong Tho, *Vietnam* 22°32′ N, 103°21′ E 202
Phôngsali, *Laos* 21°44′ N, 102°5′ E 202
Phra Thong, Ko, island, *Thai.* 8°47′ N, 97°49′ E 202
Phraaspa, ruin(s), *Iran* 36°44′ N, 47°18′ E 195
Phrae, *Thai.* 18°9′ N, 100°9′ E 202
Phran Kratai, *Thai.* 16°40′ N, 99°37′ E 202
Phrao, *Thai.* 18°7′ N, 100°7′ E 190
Phrao, *Thai.* 19°24′ N, 99°11′ E 202
Phrom Phiram, *Thai.* 17°3′ N, 100°12′ E 202
Phu Cat, *Vietnam* 14°1′ N, 109°4′ E 202
Phu Loc, *Vietnam* 16°17′ N, 107°53′ E 202
Phu Ly, *Vietnam* 20°33′ N, 105°55′ E 198
Phu My, *Vietnam* 14°12′ N, 109°2′ E 202
Phu Quoc, Dao, island, *Vietnam* 9°53′ N, 103°33′ E 202
Phu Rieng, *Vietnam* 11°42′ N, 106°56′ E 202
Phuket, *Thai.* 7°54′ N, 98°23′ E 202
Phuket, Ko, island, *Thai.* 7°38′ N, 97°55′ E 196
Phum Kompadou, *Cambodia* 13°48′ N, 107°25′ E 202
Phuntsholing, *Bhutan* 26°52′ N, 89°20′ E 197
Phuoc Long, *Vietnam* 9°27′ N, 105°25′ E 202
Phuthaditjhada, *S. Af.* 28°33′ S, 28°47′ E 227
Phutthaisong, *Thai.* 15°28′ N, 102°56′ E 202
Phyarpon, *Myanmar* 16°17′ N, 95°39′ E 202
Pi, *Pol.* 53°8′ N, 16°44′ E 152
Piacenza, *It.* 45°2′ N, 9°40′ E 167
Piacouadie, Lac, lake, *Can.* 51°13′ N, 71°36′ W 111
Piadena, *It.* 45°7′ N, 10°21′ E 167
Piana, *Fr.* 42°14′ N, 8°38′ E 156
Pianello Val Tidone, *It.* 44°56′ N, 9°23′ E 167
Pianguan, *China* 39°27′ N, 111°29′ E 198
Pianoro, *It.* 44°22′ N, 11°20′ E 167
Pianosa, *It.* 42°35′ N, 10°5′ E 156
Piapot, *Can.* 49°58′ N, 109°7′ W 90
Piaseczno, *Pol.* 52°4′ N, 21°1′ E 152
Piatã, *Braz.* 13°13′ S, 41°45′ W 138
Piatra, *Rom.* 43°48′ N, 25°10′ E 156
Piatra Neamţ, *Rom.* 46°56′ N, 26°22′ E 156
Piauí, adm. division, *Braz.* 10°24′ S, 45°55′ W 130
Piauí, Serra do, *Braz.* 9°52′ S, 42°4′ W 132
Piaxtla, river, *Mex.* 23°54′ N, 106°6′ W 114
Piazzi, Isla, island, *Chile* 51°36′ S, 73°59′ W 134
Pibor Post, *Sudan* 6°44′ N, 33°6′ E 224
Pic, river, *Can.* 48°51′ N, 86°10′ W 94
Pica, *Chile* 20°31′ S, 69°22′ W 137
Picacho, *Ariz., U.S.* 32°43′ N, 111°28′ W 92
Picacho Pass, *Ariz., U.S.* 32°37′ N, 111°24′ W 92
Picachos, Cerro dos, peak, *Mex.* 29°21′ N, 114°12′ W 92
Picardie, adm. division, *Fr.* 49°35′ N, 1°44′ E 150
Picardy, region, *Fr.* 49°58′ N, 1°57′ E 163
Picassent, *Sp.* 39°20′ N, 0°29′ E 164
Picayune, *Miss., U.S.* 30°31′ N, 89°40′ W 103
Picerno, *It.* 40°39′ N, 15°38′ E 156
Pichanal, *Arg.* 23°17′ S, 64°13′ W 134
Picher, *Okla., U.S.* 36°57′ N, 94°51′ W 96
Pichhor, *India* 25°56′ N, 78°23′ E 197
Pichilemu, *Chile* 34°25′ S, 72°0′ W 134
Pichilingue, *Mex.* 24°17′ N, 110°20′ W 112
Pickens, *Miss., U.S.* 32°53′ N, 89°59′ W 103
Pickerel Lake, *Can.* 48°33′ N, 91°59′ W 110
Pickering, *U.K.* 54°14′ N, 0°47′ E 162
Pickering Nunatak, peak, *Antarctica* 71°27′ S, 70°58′ E 248
Pickle Crow, *Can.* 51°29′ N, 90°4′ W 110
Pickle Lake, *Can.* 51°28′ N, 90°11′ W 110
Pickton, *Tex., U.S.* 33°1′ N, 95°23′ W 103
Pico da Neblina National Park, *Braz.* 0°7′ N, 65°34′ W 136
Pico de Orizaba National Park, *Mex.* 19°0′ N, 97°34′ W 72
Pico de Tancítaro National Park, *Mex.* 19°18′ N, 102°43′ W 72
Pico, island, *Port.* 38°21′ N, 28°24′ W 253
Pico Truncado, *Arg.* 46°45′ S, 67°57′ W 134
Picos, *Braz.* 7°6′ S, 41°26′ W 132
Picton, *Can.* 44°0′ N, 77°9′ W 94
Picton, *N.Z.* 41°19′ S, 174°0′ E 240
Pictou, *Can.* 45°41′ N, 62°43′ W 111
Picture Gorge, site, *Oreg., U.S.* 44°32′ N, 119°43′ W 90
Pictured Rocks, *Mich., U.S.* 46°30′ N, 87°10′ W 80
Pictured Rocks National Lakeshore, *Mich., U.S.* 46°12′ N, 92°34′ W 80
Picuris Peak, *N. Mex., U.S.* 36°13′ N, 105°44′ W 92
Pidurutalagala, peak, *Sri Lanka* 6°58′ N, 80°41′ E 188
Piedecuesta, *Col.* 6°58′ N, 73°4′ W 136
Piedmont, *Mo., U.S.* 37°9′ N, 90°42′ W 96
Piedmont, adm. division, *It.* 44°51′ N, 6°58′ E 165
Piedra, *Calif., U.S.* 36°49′ N, 119°23′ W 100
Piedra del Águila, *Arg.* 40°2′ S, 70°6′ W 134
Piedra Lais, *Venez.* 3°6′ N, 65°56′ W 136
Piedra Parada, ruin(s), *Mex.* 16°48′ N, 93°33′ W 115
Piedra Shotel, *Arg.* 44°23′ S, 70°30′ W 134
Piedra Sola, *Uru.* 32°4′ S, 56°19′ W 139
Piedrabuena, *Sp.* 39°2′ N, 4°11′ W 164
Piedras Blancas, Point, *Calif., U.S.* 35°41′ N, 121°29′ W 100
Piedras Negras, *Mex.* 28°40′ N, 100°31′ W 92
Piedras Negras, ruin(s), *Guatemala* 17°11′ N, 91°23′ W 115
Piedras, Punta, *Arg.* 35°25′ S, 57°9′ W 139
Piedras, river, *Peru* 11°22′ S, 70°42′ W 137
Piedritas, *Arg.* 34°47′ S, 62°58′ W 139
Piedruja, *Latv.* 55°47′ N, 27°26′ E 166
Pieksämäki, *Fin.* 62°16′ N, 27°7′ E 154
Piendamó, *Col.* 2°38′ N, 76°33′ W 136
Pieniężno, *Pol.* 54°13′ N, 20°8′ E 166
Pierce, *Idaho, U.S.* 46°28′ N, 115°47′ W 90
Pierce, *Nebr., U.S.* 42°11′ N, 97°32′ W 90
Piéria, Óros, *Gr.* 40°7′ N, 22°3′ E 156
Pierre, *S. Dak., U.S.* 44°21′ N, 100°26′ W 90
Pierre Lake, lake, *Can.* 49°28′ N, 81°6′ W 94
Pierrefonds, *Fr.* 49°20′ N, 2°58′ E 163
Pierrelatte, *Fr.* 44°22′ N, 4°41′ E 150
Pierson, *Fla., U.S.* 29°14′ N, 81°28′ W 105
Piet Retief, *S. Af.* 27°1′ S, 30°45′ E 227
Pietarsaari see Jakobstad, *Fin.* 63°39′ N, 22°39′ E 152
Pietermaritzburg, *S. Af.* 29°35′ S, 30°21′ E 227
Pietersburg see Polokwane, *S. Af.* 23°54′ S, 29°26′ E 227
Pietro Verri, *Somalia* 3°20′ N, 45°39′ E 218
Pietrosu, peak, *Rom.* 47°5′ N, 25°4′ E 156
Pietrosul, peak, *Rom.* 47°34′ N, 24°32′ E 156
Pieve d'Alpago, *It.* 46°9′ N, 12°20′ E 167
Pieve di Cadore, *It.* 46°25′ N, 12°20′ E 167
Pigailoe (West Fayu Atoll) 8°36′ N, 146°3′ E 192
Pigeon, *Mich., U.S.* 43°49′ N, 83°16′ W 102
Pigeon Cove, *Mass., U.S.* 42°40′ N, 70°38′ W 104
Pigeon Lake, *Can.* 53°2′ N, 114°24′ W 108
Pigeon Point, *Lake Superior* 47°46′ N, 89°36′ W 94
Pigeon, river, *Can.* 52°13′ N, 96°58′ W 108
Piggott, *Ark., U.S.* 36°22′ N, 90°12′ W 96
Pigüé, *Arg.* 37°37′ S, 62°23′ W 139
Pihlava, *Fin.* 61°32′ N, 21°36′ E 166
Pihtipudas, *Fin.* 63°21′ N, 25°32′ E 154
Pihuamo, *Mex.* 19°15′ N, 103°22′ W 114
Pihyŏn, *N. Korea* 40°0′ N, 124°35′ E 200
Piʻilanihale Heiau, site, *Hawaiʻi, U.S.* 20°47′ N, 156°6′ W 99
Pijijiapan, *Mex.* 15°40′ N, 93°15′ W 115
Pikalevo, *Russ.* 59°33′ N, 34°5′ E 154
Pikangikum, *Can.* 51°48′ N, 93°57′ W 82
Pike, river, *Wis., U.S.* 45°31′ N, 88°3′ W 94
Pikelot, island, *F.S.M.* 8°17′ N, 147°41′ E 192
Pikes Peak, *Colo., U.S.* 38°49′ N, 105°7′ W 90
Piketberg, *S. Af.* 32°54′ S, 18°43′ E 227
Piketon, *Ohio, U.S.* 39°3′ N, 83°1′ W 102
Pikeville, *Ky., U.S.* 37°29′ N, 82°32′ W 96
Pikounda, *Congo* 0°30′ N, 16°38′ E 218
Pikwitonei, *Can.* 55°35′ N, 97°12′ W 108
Pila, *Arg.* 36°2′ S, 58°10′ W 139
Pila, peak, *Sp.* 38°15′ N, 1°14′ W 164
Pilani, *India* 28°21′ N, 75°37′ E 197
Pilão Arcado, *Braz.* 9°57′ S, 42°32′ W 132
Pilar, *Arg.* 31°26′ S, 61°16′ W 139
Pilar, *Parag.* 26°51′ S, 58°16′ W 139
Pilar, Cabo, *Chile* 52°46′ S, 76°6′ W 134
Pilatovica, peak, *Europe* 43°7′ N, 20°54′ E 168
Pilaya, river, *Bol.* 21°13′ S, 64°29′ W 137
Pilcaniyeu, *Arg.* 41°9′ S, 70°41′ W 134
Pilcomayo, river, *Bol.* 19°19′ S, 65°2′ W 137
Pil'dozero, *Russ.* 65°40′ N, 33°27′ E 152
Pil'gyn, *Russ.* 69°19′ N, 179°3′ E 98
Pilibhit, *India* 28°37′ N, 79°47′ E 197
Pílio, *Gr.* 38°45′ N, 23°34′ E 156
Pílio, Óros, peak, *Gr.* 39°25′ N, 22°58′ E 156
Pillcopata, *Peru* 13°5′ S, 71°11′ W 137
Pilling, *U.K.* 53°55′ N, 2°55′ W 162
Pilón, river, *Mex.* 25°15′ N, 100°31′ W 114
Pilón-Lajas National Park, *Bol.* 14°51′ S, 66°41′ W 137
Pílos, *Gr.* 36°54′ N, 21°41′ E 156
Pilot Butte, peak, *Oreg., U.S.* 44°3′ N, 121°20′ W 90
Pilot Knob, *Mo., U.S.* 37°37′ N, 90°39′ W 96
Pilot Knob, peak, *Ark., U.S.* 35°33′ N, 93°20′ W 96
Pilot Knob, peak, *Idaho, U.S.* 45°52′ N, 115°47′ W 90
Pilot Mound, *Can.* 49°12′ N, 98°55′ W 108
Pilot Peak, *Nev., U.S.* 38°20′ N, 118°4′ W 90
Pilot Peak, *Nev., U.S.* 41°0′ N, 114°9′ W 90
Pilot Peak, *Wyo., U.S.* 44°57′ N, 109°59′ W 90
Pilot Point, *Alas., U.S.* 57°31′ N, 157°38′ W 98
Pilottown, *La., U.S.* 29°11′ N, 89°15′ W 103
Pilsen see Plzeň, *Czech Rep.* 49°44′ N, 13°23′ E 152
Pil'skaya Guba, *Russ.* 66°47′ N, 34°12′ E 152
Piltene, *Latv.* 57°13′ N, 21°40′ E 166
Pil'tun, Zaliv 52°48′ N, 141°39′ E 160
Pim, river, *Russ.* 62°20′ N, 71°29′ E 169
Pimenta Bueno, *Braz.* 11°41′ S, 61°15′ W 130
Piña, *Pan.* 9°16′ N, 80°2′ W 130
Pinacate, Cerro del, peak, *Mex.* 31°44′ N, 113°35′ W 92
Pinang (Penang), island, *Malaysia* 5°14′ N, 99°44′ E 196
Pinangah, *Malaysia* 5°15′ N, 116°48′ E 203
Pinar del Río, *Cuba* 22°25′ N, 83°43′ W 116
Pinar del Río, adm. division, *Cuba* 22°33′ N, 83°55′ W 116
Pinar del Río, island, *Cuba* 23°1′ N, 83°27′ W 116
Pınarbaşı, *Turk.* 38°42′ N, 36°24′ E 156
Pinardville, *N.H., U.S.* 42°59′ N, 71°31′ W 104
Pinas, *Arg.* 31°9′ S, 65°28′ W 134
Pinatubo, Mount, peak, *Philippines* 15°5′ N, 120°1′ E 238
Pinawa, *Can.* 50°8′ N, 95°52′ W 90
Pincehely, *Hung.* 46°41′ N, 18°25′ E 168
Pincén, *Arg.* 34°51′ S, 63°55′ W 139
Pincher, *Can.* 49°31′ N, 113°57′ W 90
Pincher Creek, *Can.* 49°28′ N, 113°56′ W 90
Pinchi Lake, lake, *Can.* 54°32′ N, 124°49′ W 108
Pinckney, *Mich., U.S.* 42°26′ N, 83°57′ W 102
Pinconning, *Mich., U.S.* 43°50′ N, 83°59′ W 102
Pîncota, *Rom.* 46°20′ N, 21°43′ E 168
Pindamonhangaba, *Braz.* 22°57′ S, 45°27′ W 138
Pinders Point, *Bahamas* 26°27′ N, 78°42′ W 105
Pindi Bhattian, *Pak.* 31°54′ N, 73°14′ E 186
Pindi Gheb, *Pak.* 33°14′ N, 72°17′ E 186
Píndos, peak, *Gr.* 39°18′ N, 21°28′ E 156
Pindus Mountains, *Gr.* 39°54′ N, 20°40′ E 156
Pine Bluff, *Ark., U.S.* 34°12′ N, 92°1′ W 96
Pine Bluffs, *Wyo., U.S.* 41°11′ N, 104°5′ W 90
Pine, Cape, *Can.* 46°38′ N, 54°6′ W 111
Pine City, *Minn., U.S.* 45°47′ N, 93°0′ W 94
Pine Creek, *Austral.* 13°51′ S, 131°51′ E 231
Pine Falls, *Can.* 50°31′ N, 96°17′ W 108
Pine Flat, *Calif., U.S.* 35°52′ N, 118°39′ W 101
Pine Flat Lake, *Calif., U.S.* 36°50′ N, 119°32′ W 101
Pine Forest Range, *Nev., U.S.* 41°41′ N, 119°7′ W 90
Pine Hill, *Ala., U.S.* 31°58′ N, 87°35′ W 103
Pine Hills, *Fla., U.S.* 28°34′ N, 81°28′ W 105
Pine Island, *Fla., U.S.* 26°37′ N, 82°25′ W 105
Pine Island Bay 74°36′ S, 97°34′ W 248
Pine Mountain, *Ky., U.S.* 37°17′ N, 82°36′ W 96
Pine Mountain, peak, *Calif., U.S.* 35°41′ N, 121°9′ W 100
Pine Mountain, peak, *Calif., U.S.* 35°33′ N, 118°49′ W 101
Pine Pass, *Can.* 55°23′ N, 122°41′ W 108
Pine Plains, *N.Y., U.S.* 41°58′ N, 73°40′ W 104
Pine Point, *Can.* 60°46′ N, 114°19′ W 73
Pine Point, *Can.* 60°46′ N, 114°22′ W 108
Pine Point, *Me., U.S.* 43°32′ N, 70°21′ W 104
Pine River, *Can.* 51°46′ N, 100°33′ W 90
Pine River, *Can.* 55°55′ N, 107°28′ W 108
Pine River, *Minn., U.S.* 46°42′ N, 94°25′ W 90
Pine, river, *Can.* 55°52′ N, 121°7′ W 108
Pine, river, *Mich., U.S.* 44°1′ N, 85°39′ W 102
Pine Valley, *Can.* 55°38′ N, 122°10′ W 108
Pinecrest, *Calif., U.S.* 38°11′ N, 120°1′ W 100
Pinedale, *Calif., U.S.* 36°50′ N, 119°48′ W 92
Pinega, *Russ.* 64°43′ N, 43°19′ E 154
Pinega, river, *Russ.* 63°44′ N, 45°11′ E 154
Pinehouse Lake, *Can.* 55°33′ N, 107°14′ W 108
Pinehouse Lake, *Can.* 55°30′ N, 106°37′ W 108
Pinehurst, *Ga., U.S.* 32°11′ N, 83°46′ W 96
Pinehurst, *N.C., U.S.* 35°11′ N, 79°29′ W 96
Pineland, *Tex., U.S.* 31°14′ N, 93°58′ W 103
Pinellas Park, *Fla., U.S.* 27°51′ N, 82°42′ W 105
Pinerolo, *It.* 44°53′ N, 7°20′ E 167
Pinetown, *S. Af.* 29°49′ S, 30°46′ E 227
Pineville, *Ky., U.S.* 36°44′ N, 83°43′ W 96
Pineville, *La., U.S.* 31°18′ N, 92°26′ W 103
Piney, *Fr.* 48°22′ N, 4°19′ E 163
Piney Buttes, *Mont., U.S.* 47°27′ N, 107°14′ W 90
Piney Point, *Fla., U.S.* 29°46′ N, 83°35′ W 105
Piney Woods, *Miss., U.S.* 32°2′ N, 89°59′ W 103
Ping, river, *Thai.* 16°8′ N, 99°46′ E 202
Pingba, *China* 26°26′ N, 106°14′ E 198
Pingchang, *China* 31°35′ N, 107°4′ E 198
Pingdingshan, *China* 33°44′ N, 113°19′ E 198
Pingdu, *China* 36°49′ N, 119°58′ E 198
Pinggang, *China* 42°56′ N, 124°50′ E 200
Pingguo, *China* 23°18′ N, 107°34′ E 198
Pingjiang, *China* 28°45′ N, 113°37′ E 198
Pingle, *China* 24°35′ N, 110°41′ E 198
Pingli, *China* 32°29′ N, 109°24′ E 198
Pingliang, *China* 35°31′ N, 106°39′ E 198
Pinglu, *China* 39°31′ N, 112°17′ E 198
Pinglu, *China* 34°53′ N, 111°12′ E 198
Pingluo, *China* 38°57′ N, 106°33′ E 198
Pingnan, *China* 23°34′ N, 110°23′ E 198
Pingquan, *China* 41°2′ N, 118°39′ E 198
Pingsha, *China* 22°2′ N, 113°12′ E 198
Pingtan, *China* 25°28′ N, 119°51′ E 198
Pingtang, *China* 25°50′ N, 107°17′ E 198
Pingtung, *Taiwan, China* 22°43′ N, 120°31′ E 198
Pingwu, *China* 32°28′ N, 104°34′ E 198
Pingxiang, *China* 27°41′ N, 113°48′ E 198
Pingxiang, *China* 22°5′ N, 106°44′ E 198
Pingyang, *China* 27°37′ N, 120°33′ E 198
Pingyao, *China* 37°15′ N, 112°9′ E 198
Pingyi, *China* 35°28′ N, 117°39′ E 198
Pingyin, *China* 36°18′ N, 116°26′ E 198
Pingyuan, *China* 24°32′ N, 115°52′ E 198
Pinhal, *Braz.* 22°13′ S, 46°47′ W 138
Pinhão, *Braz.* 25°42′ S, 51°38′ W 138
Pinheiro, *Braz.* 2°31′ S, 45°7′ W 132
Pinheiro Machado, *Braz.* 31°37′ S, 53°22′ W 139
Pinhuã, river, *Braz.* 7°4′ S, 66°0′ W 130
Pini, island, *Indonesia* 0°6′ N, 98°51′ E 196
Pink Mountain, *Can.* 57°4′ N, 122°36′ W 108
Pink, river, *Can.* 56°39′ N, 104°24′ W 108
Pinkafeld, *Aust.* 47°21′ N, 16°8′ E 168
Pinlaung, *Myanmar* 20°7′ N, 96°42′ E 202
Pinleibu, *Myanmar* 24°1′ N, 95°22′ E 188
Pinnacles National Monument, *Calif., U.S.* 36°27′ N, 121°20′ W 100
Pino Hachado, Paso de, pass, *Chile* 38°34′ S, 70°54′ W 134
Pinola, *Miss., U.S.* 31°52′ N, 89°58′ W 103
Pinon Hills, *Calif., U.S.* 34°26′ N, 117°39′ W 101
Pinos, *Mex.* 22°17′ N, 101°34′ W 114
Pinos, Mount, peak, *Calif., U.S.* 34°48′ N, 119°11′ W 101
Pinos, Point, *Calif., U.S.* 36°38′ N, 122°3′ W 100
Pinos-Puente, *Sp.* 37°15′ N, 3°46′ W 150
Pinotepa Nacional, *Mex.* 16°20′ N, 98°2′ W 112
Pins, Pointe aux, *Can.* 42°6′ N, 81°50′ W 102
Pinsk, *Belarus* 52°7′ N, 26°6′ E 152
Pinsk Marshes, *Belarus* 52°39′ N, 25°28′ E 142
Pinta, Sierra, *Ariz., U.S.* 32°27′ N, 113°48′ W 101
Pinta, Sierra, *Mex.* 31°26′ N, 115°33′ W 112
Pintados, *Chile* 20°37′ S, 69°38′ W 137
Pintasan, *Malaysia* 5°27′ N, 117°40′ E 203
Pinto, *Arg.* 29°9′ S, 62°40′ W 139
Pinto, *Sp.* 40°14′ N, 3°42′ W 164
Pinto Butte, peak, *Can.* 49°18′ N, 107°30′ W 90
Pinto Mountains, *Calif., U.S.* 34°4′ N, 115°57′ W 101
Pintoyacu, river, *Peru* 2°58′ S, 74°37′ W 136
Pintwater Range, *Nev., U.S.* 36°42′ N, 115°35′ W 101
Pinyon Pines, *Calif., U.S.* 33°35′ N, 116°29′ W 101
Pinyug, *Russ.* 60°15′ N, 47°45′ E 154
Pioche, *Nev., U.S.* 37°55′ N, 114°27′ W 92
Piombino, *It.* 42°56′ N, 10°32′ E 156
Pioneer, *La., U.S.* 32°43′ N, 91°26′ W 103
Pioneer, *Ohio, U.S.* 41°40′ N, 84°33′ W 102
Pioneer Fracture Zone, *North Pacific Ocean* 37°39′ N, 139°49′ W 252
Pioneer Mountains, *Idaho, U.S.* 43°34′ N, 114°3′ W 90
Pioneer Mountains, *Mont., U.S.* 45°30′ N, 113°21′ W 90
Pioneer Point, *Calif., U.S.* 35°47′ N, 117°23′ W 101
Pioneer Tank, spring, *Austral.* 31°47′ S, 123°48′ E 230
Pioner, Ostrov, island, *Russ.* 79°38′ N, 99°4′ E 246
Pionki, *Pol.* 51°29′ N, 21°25′ E 152
Piorini, Lago, lake, *Braz.* 3°38′ S, 63°31′ W 130
Piorini, river, *Braz.* 2°34′ S, 64°7′ W 130
Piotrków Trybunalski, *Pol.* 51°23′ N, 19°41′ E 152
Piove di Sacco, *It.* 45°18′ N, 12°1′ E 167
Pipar, *India* 26°20′ N, 73°33′ E 186
Piparia, *India* 21°55′ N, 77°22′ E 197
Piper City, *Ill., U.S.* 40°45′ N, 88°12′ W 102
Piper, oil field, *North Sea* 58°26′ N, 0°10′ E 150
Pipestone, *Minn., U.S.* 43°58′ N, 96°19′ W 94
Pipestone Lake, lake, *Can.* 48°59′ N, 94°9′ W 90
Pipestone, river, *Can.* 57°57′ N, 106°36′ W 108
Pipinas, *Arg.* 35°32′ S, 57°21′ W 139
Pipmuacan, Réservoir, lake, *Can.* 49°28′ N, 71°47′ W 94
Piqua, *Ohio, U.S.* 40°7′ N, 84°16′ W 102
Piquiá, *Braz.* 1°49′ S, 66°8′ W 136
Piquiri, river, *Braz.* 24°58′ S, 52°42′ W 138
Pira, *Benin* 8°30′ N, 1°44′ E 222
Piracanjuba, *Braz.* 17°21′ S, 49°2′ W 138
Piracicaba, *Braz.* 22°45′ S, 47°38′ W 138
Piracuruca, *Braz.* 3°56′ S, 41°42′ W 132
Piraeus see Pireás, *Gr.* 37°57′ N, 23°38′ E 156
Piraí do Sul, *Braz.* 24°34′ S, 49°57′ W 138
Piraju, *Braz.* 23°15′ S, 49°25′ W 138
Pirajuí, *Braz.* 22°1′ S, 49°28′ W 138
Piran, *Slov.* 45°31′ N, 13°35′ E 167
Pirané, *Arg.* 25°45′ S, 59°6′ W 132
Piranhas, *Braz.* 16°34′ S, 51°49′ W 138
Piranhas, *Braz.* 9°37′ S, 37°45′ W 132
Pirapora, *Braz.* 17°22′ S, 44°55′ W 138
Pirarajá, *Uru.* 33°45′ S, 54°44′ W 139
Piratuba, *Braz.* 27°27′ S, 51°48′ W 139
Piray, river, *Bol.* 16°49′ S, 63°37′ W 137
Pire Goureye, *Senegal* 15°2′ N, 16°34′ W 222
Pireás, *Gr.* 37°57′ N, 23°36′ E 180
Pireás (Piraeus), *Gr.* 37°57′ N, 23°38′ E 156
Pirenópolis, *Braz.* 15°55′ S, 49°0′ W 138
Pires do Rio, *Braz.* 17°20′ S, 48°17′ W 138
Pírgos, *Gr.* 37°38′ N, 21°26′ E 216
Piriá, river, *Braz.* 2°10′ S, 46°28′ W 130
Piriápolis, *Uru.* 34°53′ S, 55°16′ W 139
Pirin, *Bulg.* 41°21′ N, 23°26′ E 156
Pirin National Park, *Bulg.* 41°37′ N, 22°39′ E 180
Piripiri, *Braz.* 4°17′ S, 41°49′ W 132
Piritu, *Venez.* 9°22′ N, 69°15′ W 136
Pirna, *Ger.* 50°58′ N, 13°56′ E 152
Pirojpur, *Bangladesh* 22°35′ N, 89°58′ E 197
Pirot, *Serb.* 43°8′ N, 22°34′ E 168
Pirre, Cerro, peak, *Pan.* 7°47′ N, 77°49′ W 136
Pirsagat, river, *Azerb.* 40°28′ N, 48°40′ E 195
Pirtleville, *Ariz., U.S.* 31°22′ N, 109°34′ W 92
Pirttikylä see Pörtom, *Fin.* 62°41′ N, 21°35′ E 154
Piru, *Calif., U.S.* 34°25′ N, 118°48′ W 101
Piru, *Indonesia* 3°6′ S, 128°7′ E 192
Pisa, *It.* 43°44′ N, 10°24′ E 167
Pisac, *Peru* 13°27′ S, 71°50′ W 137
Pisagua, *Chile* 19°37′ S, 70°14′ W 137
Pisarovina, *Croatia* 45°35′ N, 15°51′ E 168
Pisco, *Peru* 13°45′ S, 76°12′ W 130
Písek, *Czech Rep.* 49°17′ N, 14°8′ E 152
Pisgah Crater, *Calif., U.S.* 34°44′ N, 116°23′ W 101
Pisgah, Mount, peak, *Oreg., U.S.* 44°26′ N, 120°20′ W 90
Pishan (Guma), *China* 37°39′ N, 78°22′ E 184
Pishcha, *Ukr.* 51°35′ N, 23°47′ E 158
Pīshīn, *Iran* 26°4′ N, 61°46′ E 182
Pishin, *Pak.* 30°34′ N, 67°2′ E 186
Pishin Lora, river, *Pak.* 29°14′ N, 65°33′ E 186
Piskom, *Uzb.* 41°53′ N, 70°19′ E 197
Pismo Beach, *Calif., U.S.* 35°9′ N, 120°39′ W 100
Pis'moguba, *Russ.* 64°33′ N, 31°50′ E 152
Pisogne, *It.* 45°48′ N, 10°6′ E 167
Pissouri, *Cyprus* 34°39′ N, 32°42′ E 194
Pisté, *Mex.* 20°42′ N, 88°38′ W 116
Pistoia, *It.* 43°55′ N, 10°55′ E 156
Pisz, *Pol.* 53°37′ N, 21°46′ E 152
Piszczac, *Pol.* 51°58′ N, 23°22′ E 152
Pit, river, *Calif., U.S.* 41°25′ N, 121°5′ W 90
Pita, *Guinea* 11°3′ N, 12°26′ W 222
Pitaga, *Can.* 52°26′ N, 65°48′ W 111
Pitanga, *Braz.* 24°45′ S, 51°47′ W 138
Pitangui, *Braz.* 19°41′ S, 44°54′ W 138
Pitcairn Island, *U.K.* 25°5′ S, 130°6′ W 241
Piteå, *Nor.* 65°19′ N, 21°29′ E 152
Piteşti, *Rom.* 44°52′ N, 24°52′ E 156
Pithiviers, *Fr.* 48°9′ N, 2°15′ E 163
Pithora, *India* 21°15′ N, 82°30′ E 188
Pithoragarh, *India* 29°36′ N, 80°12′ E 197
Pitkin, *La., U.S.* 30°54′ N, 92°57′ W 103
Pitkyaranta, *Russ.* 61°31′ N, 31°33′ E 152
Pitlochrie, *Can.* 55°0′ N, 111°45′ W 108
Pitlyar, *Russ.* 65°50′ N, 66°4′ E 169
Pitman, river, *Can.* 57°53′ N, 128°36′ W 108
Pitomača, *Croatia* 45°57′ N, 17°15′ E 168
Pitre, Isle au, island, *La., U.S.* 30°1′ N, 89°11′ W 103
Pitsligo Castle, site, *U.K.* 57°39′ N, 2°13′ W 150
Pitt Island, *Can.* 53°37′ N, 130°52′ W 98
Pitt Island, island, *Can.* 53°43′ N, 129°56′ W 106
Pitt Lake, *Can.* 49°22′ N, 122°43′ W 100
Pittsboro, *Miss., U.S.* 33°55′ N, 89°20′ W 96
Pittsburg, *Calif., U.S.* 38°1′ N, 121°54′ W 100
Pittsburg, *Kans., U.S.* 37°23′ N, 94°42′ W 96
Pittsburg, *Tex., U.S.* 32°59′ N, 94°59′ W 103
Pittsburgh, *Pa., U.S.* 40°26′ N, 79°59′ W 94
Pittsfield, *Mass., U.S.* 42°26′ N, 73°16′ W 104
Pittsfield, *Mo., U.S.* 39°35′ N, 90°49′ W 94
Pittsfield, *N.H., U.S.* 43°18′ N, 71°20′ W 104
Pittsfield, *Vt., U.S.* 43°46′ N, 72°49′ W 104

Pittsford, *Vt., U.S.* 43°42′ N, 73°2′ W 104
Pittston, *Pa., U.S.* 41°18′ N, 75°48′ W 94
Piua Petrii, *Rom.* 44°41′ N, 27°51′ E 156
Piũí, *Braz.* 20°31′ S, 45°57′ W 138
Piura, *Peru* 5°6′ S, 80°40′ W 130
Piura, adm. division, *Peru* 4°50′ S, 81°6′ W 130
Piute Pass, *Calif., U.S.* 37°14′ N, 118°41′ W 101
Piute Peak, *Calif., U.S.* 35°26′ N, 118°26′ W 101
Piute Valley, *Calif., U.S.* 35°1′ N, 114°54′ W 101
Piva, river, *Mont.* 43°8′ N, 18°52′ E 168
Pivabiska, river, *Can.* 49°53′ N, 83°45′ W 94
Pivdennyy Buh, river, *Ukr.* 48°3′ N, 30°39′ E 158
Pivka, *Slov.* 45°41′ N, 14°11′ E 156
Pivot Mountain, peak, *Can.* 54°0′ N, 133°6′ W 108
Pixariá Óros, peak, *Gr.* 38°42′ N, 23°34′ E 156
Pixian, *China* 34°17′ N, 117°58′ E 198
Pixley, *Calif., U.S.* 35°58′ N, 119°18′ W 100
Pizacoma, *Peru* 16°57′ S, 69°22′ W 137
Pizarra, *Sp.* 36°45′ N, 4°43′ W 164
Pizhma, river, *Russ.* 64°37′ N, 51°1′ E 154
Placentia, *Can.* 47°12′ N, 54°0′ W 111
Placentia Point, *Belize* 16°26′ N, 88°21′ W 115
Placer, *Philippines* 9°40′ N, 125°35′ E 203
Placerville, *Calif., U.S.* 38°44′ N, 120°47′ W 82
Placid, Lake, *Fla., U.S.* 27°14′ N, 81°27′ W 105
Placid Lake, *Mont., U.S.* 47°3′ N, 114°1′ W 90
Placida, *Fla., U.S.* 26°51′ N, 82°17′ W 105
Plácido de Castro, *Braz.* 10°19′ S, 67°11′ W 137
Plačkovica, *Maced.* 41°44′ N, 22°13′ E 168
Plahn, *Liberia* 5°20′ N, 8°51′ W 222
Plain, *Wis., U.S.* 43°16′ N, 90°3′ W 102
Plain, Cape, *South Atlantic Ocean* 34°50′ S, 7°54′ E 253
Plain City, *Ohio, U.S.* 40°5′ N, 83°17′ W 102
Plain Dealing, *La., U.S.* 32°53′ N, 93°42′ W 103
Plainfield, *Conn., U.S.* 41°40′ N, 71°56′ W 104
Plainfield, *Ind., U.S.* 39°41′ N, 86°24′ W 102
Plainfield, *Mass., U.S.* 42°30′ N, 72°56′ W 104
Plainfield, *Vt., U.S.* 44°16′ N, 72°27′ W 104
Plains, *Kans., U.S.* 37°15′ N, 100°36′ W 92
Plains, *Mont., U.S.* 47°26′ N, 114°54′ W 90
Plains, *Pa., U.S.* 41°16′ N, 75°51′ W 110
Plains, *Tex., U.S.* 33°9′ N, 102°50′ W 92
Plainview, *Nebr., U.S.* 42°19′ N, 97°49′ W 90
Plainview, *Tex., U.S.* 34°10′ N, 101°43′ W 92
Plainwell, *Mich., U.S.* 42°26′ N, 85°37′ W 110
Plaistow, *N.H., U.S.* 42°49′ N, 71°6′ W 104
Pláka, *Gr.* 40°0′ N, 25°25′ E 156
Plakoti, Cape 35°32′ N, 34°1′ E 194
Plan, *Sp.* 42°34′ N, 0°20′ E 164
Plana, *Bosn. and Herzg.* 42°57′ N, 18°24′ E 168
Plana Cays (French Cays), islands, *North Atlantic Ocean* 22°41′ N, 73°33′ W 116
Plana o Nueva Tabarca, Isla, island, *Sp.* 38°5′ N, 0°28′ E 164
Planada, *Calif., U.S.* 37°17′ N, 120°20′ W 100
Planeta Rica, *Col.* 8°25′ N, 75°35′ W 116
Planinica, *Serb.* 43°49′ N, 22°7′ E 168
Plano, *Ill., U.S.* 41°39′ N, 88°33′ W 102
Plano, *Tex., U.S.* 33°0′ N, 96°42′ W 96
Plant City, *Fla., U.S.* 28°1′ N, 82°7′ W 105
Plantation, *Fla., U.S.* 26°8′ N, 80°15′ W 105
Plantation Key, island, *Fla., U.S.* 25°16′ N, 80°41′ W 105
Plantsite, *Ariz., U.S.* 33°2′ N, 109°18′ W 92
Plaquemine, *La., U.S.* 30°16′ N, 91°15′ W 103
Plasencia, *Sp.* 40°2′ N, 6°5′ W 150
Plaški, *Croatia* 45°4′ N, 15°20′ E 156
Plassen, *Nor.* 61°8′ N, 12°29′ E 152
Plast, *Russ.* 54°22′ N, 60°43′ E 154
Plaster City, *Calif., U.S.* 32°47′ N, 115°52′ W 101
Plaster Rock, *Can.* 46°54′ N, 67°24′ W 111
Plata, Punta, *Chile* 25°1′ S, 71°10′ W 132
Plata, Río de la, *South America* 35°34′ S, 57°6′ W 139
Plataea 479 B.C., battle, *Gr.* 38°11′ N, 23°9′ E 156
Platanal, *Venez.* 2°22′ N, 64°58′ W 130
Plátano, river, *Hond.* 15°18′ N, 85°2′ W 116
Plateau, *Can.* 48°57′ N, 108°46′ W 90
Plateau Station (closed), site, *Antarctica* 80°37′ S, 36°13′ E 248
Platen, Kapp, *Nor.* 80°28′ N, 23°58′ E 160
Plateros, *Mex.* 23°13′ N, 102°52′ W 114
Plato, *Col.* 9°46′ N, 74°47′ W 136
Platte, *S. Dak., U.S.* 43°21′ N, 98°51′ W 90
Platte, river, *Nebr., U.S.* 40°56′ N, 100°48′ W 80
Platteville, *Wis., U.S.* 42°43′ N, 90°28′ W 94
Plattsburg, *Mo., U.S.* 39°32′ N, 94°27′ W 94
Plattsmouth, *Nebr., U.S.* 40°59′ N, 95°53′ W 94
Plauen, *Ger.* 50°30′ N, 12°8′ E 152
Plav, *Mont.* 42°35′ N, 19°56′ E 168
Plavča Draga, *Croatia* 45°2′ N, 15°23′ E 156
Pļaviņas, *Latv.* 56°36′ N, 25°42′ E 166
Plavnica, *Mont.* 42°17′ N, 19°13′ E 168
Plavsk, *Russ.* 53°40′ N, 37°19′ E 154
Playa Grande, *Mex.* 31°8′ N, 114°56′ W 92
Playa Lauro Villar, *Mex.* 25°52′ N, 97°10′ W 114
Playa los Corchos, *Mex.* 21°41′ N, 105°28′ W 114
Playa Vicente, *Mex.* 17°49′ N, 95°49′ W 114
Playa Vicente, river, *Mex.* 17°50′ N, 95°40′ W 114
Playas, *Ecua.* 2°43′ S, 80°22′ W 130
Playas de Rosarito, *Mex.* 32°20′ N, 117°4′ W 92
Pleasant Grove, *Utah, U.S.* 40°21′ N, 111°43′ W 90
Pleasant Hill, *La., U.S.* 31°47′ N, 93°31′ W 103
Pleasant Point, *N.Z.* 44°17′ S, 171°8′ E 240
Pleasant Valley, *N.Y., U.S.* 41°44′ N, 73°51′ W 104
Pleasanton, *Calif., U.S.* 37°39′ N, 121°52′ W 100
Pleasanton, *Kans., U.S.* 38°10′ N, 94°42′ W 94
Pleasanton, *Tex., U.S.* 28°56′ N, 98°30′ W 96
Pleasantville, *N.J., U.S.* 39°23′ N, 74°33′ W 94
Pleiku, *Vietnam* 14°2′ N, 107°48′ E 192
Pleniţa, *Rom.* 44°12′ N, 23°13′ E 168
Plentywood, *Mont., U.S.* 48°45′ N, 104°34′ W 90
Plentzia, *Sp.* 43°23′ N, 2°58′ W 164
Plesetsk, *Russ.* 62°43′ N, 40°18′ E 154
Plesetsk Cosmodrome, spaceport, *Russ.* 62°17′ N, 39°54′ E 160
Plessisville, *Can.* 46°13′ N, 71°47′ W 94
Pleternica, *Croatia* 45°16′ N, 17°47′ E 168
Plétipi, Lac, lake, *Can.* 51°43′ N, 70°26′ W 111
Plettenberg, *Ger.* 51°13′ N, 7°52′ E 167
Pleuron, ruin(s), *Gr.* 38°23′ N, 21°18′ E 156
Pleven, *Bulg.* 43°25′ N, 24°37′ E 156
Pleven, adm. division, *Bulg.* 43°34′ N, 24°18′ E 156
Plevna, *Mont., U.S.* 46°23′ N, 104°33′ W 90
Plibo, *Liberia* 4°38′ N, 7°42′ W 222
Plješevica, *Croatia* 44°42′ N, 15°49′ E 168
Pljevlja, *Mont.* 43°21′ N, 19°20′ E 168
Ploče, *Croatia* 43°2′ N, 17°26′ E 168
Ploieşti, *Rom.* 44°57′ N, 26°1′ E 156
Plomb du Cantal, peak, *Fr.* 45°3′ N, 2°43′ E 165
Płonsk, *Pol.* 52°32′ N, 19°41′ E 152
Plopiş, Munţii, *Rom.* 47°12′ N, 22°17′ E 168
Plotnikovo, *Russ.* 56°50′ N, 83°15′ E 169
Plougastel, *Fr.* 48°22′ N, 4°22′ W 150
Plovdiv, *Bulg.* 42°5′ N, 24°45′ E 180
Plovdiv, adm. division, *Bulg.* 42°0′ N, 24°30′ E 156
Plovdiv (Philippopolis), *Bulg.* 42°9′ N, 24°45′ E 156
Plugari, *Rom.* 47°28′ N, 27°6′ E 158
Plum, *Pa., U.S.* 40°29′ N, 79°46′ W 94
Plum Island, *Mass., U.S.* 42°44′ N, 70°48′ W 104
Plum Island, *N.Y., U.S.* 41°9′ N, 72°10′ W 104
Plummer, *Idaho, U.S.* 47°18′ N, 116°54′ W 90
Plumtree, *Zimb.* 20°30′ S, 27°47′ E 227
Plungė, *Lith.* 55°55′ N, 21°52′ E 166
Pluscarden Abbey, site, *U.K.* 57°35′ N, 3°33′ W 150
Plyeshchanitsy, *Belarus* 54°26′ N, 27°49′ E 166
Plymouth, *Conn., U.S.* 41°40′ N, 73°3′ W 104
Plymouth, *Ind., U.S.* 41°20′ N, 86°19′ W 102
Plymouth, *Mass., U.S.* 41°57′ N, 70°41′ W 104
Plymouth, *Montserrat* 16°44′ N, 62°14′ W 116
Plymouth, *N.C., U.S.* 35°51′ N, 76°46′ W 96
Plymouth, *Ohio, U.S.* 40°58′ N, 82°40′ W 102
Plymouth, *U.K.* 50°29′ N, 4°11′ W 143
Plymouth, *Wash., U.S.* 45°56′ N, 119°22′ W 90
Plymouth, *Wis., U.S.* 43°44′ N, 88°0′ W 102
Plympton, *Mass., U.S.* 41°57′ N, 70°50′ W 104
Plyussa, *Russ.* 58°25′ N, 29°20′ E 166
Plyussa, river, *Russ.* 58°47′ N, 27°53′ E 154
Plzeň (Pilsen), *Czech Rep.* 49°44′ N, 13°23′ E 152
Plzeňský, adm. division, *Czech Rep.* 49°46′ N, 12°31′ E 152
Pnevo, *Russ.* 58°13′ N, 27°33′ E 166
Pô, *Burkina Faso* 11°9′ N, 1°12′ W 222
Po di Volano, river, *It.* 44°44′ N, 11°57′ E 167
Po, river, *It.* 45°7′ N, 9°19′ E 167
Pobé, *Benin* 7°2′ N, 2°39′ E 222
Pobeda, Gora, peak, *Russ.* 65°15′ N, 145°7′ E 160
Pobedy Peak (Jengish Chokusu, Victory Peak), *China* 42°2′ N, 80°3′ E 184
Pocahontas, *Ark., U.S.* 36°14′ N, 90°59′ W 96
Pocahontas, *Can.* 53°11′ N, 117°56′ W 108
Pocahontas, *Ill., U.S.* 38°48′ N, 89°32′ W 102
Pocahontas, *Iowa, U.S.* 42°43′ N, 94°41′ W 94
Pocasset, *Mass., U.S.* 41°41′ N, 70°37′ W 104
Pocatello, *Idaho, U.S.* 42°53′ N, 112°26′ W 90
Pochala, *Sudan* 7°11′ N, 34°2′ E 224
Pochep, *Russ.* 52°53′ N, 33°25′ E 154
Pochinok, *Russ.* 54°24′ N, 32°30′ E 154
Pochutla, *Mex.* 15°44′ N, 96°28′ W 112
Pocklington, *U.K.* 53°55′ N, 0°48′ E 162
Poções, *Braz.* 14°34′ S, 40°21′ W 138
Pocolo, *Angola* 15°45′ S, 13°41′ E 220
Pocoma, *Peru* 17°29′ S, 71°23′ W 137
Poconé, *Braz.* 16°17′ S, 56°39′ W 132
Pocono Mountains, *Pa., U.S.* 41°21′ N, 75°15′ W 94
Poços de Caldas, *Braz.* 21°47′ S, 46°35′ W 138
Podareš, *Maced.* 41°37′ N, 22°32′ E 168
Podberez′ye, *Russ.* 56°57′ N, 30°40′ E 152
Podborov′ye, *Russ.* 57°52′ N, 28°35′ E 166
Podchinnyy, *Russ.* 50°49′ N, 45°13′ E 158
Poddor′ye, *Russ.* 57°27′ N, 31°6′ E 152
Podgora, *Croatia* 43°14′ N, 17°4′ E 168
Podgorac, *Serb.* 43°56′ N, 21°57′ E 168
Podgorica, *Mont.* 42°25′ N, 19°11′ E 168
Podgornoye, *Russ.* 57°45′ N, 82°46′ E 169
Podhum, *Bosn. and Herzg.* 43°42′ N, 16°58′ E 168
Podil′s′ka Vysochyna, *Ukr.* 48°46′ N, 25°47′ E 152
Podkamennaya Tunguska, river, *Russ.* 61°52′ N, 89°40′ E 160
Podkarpackie, adm. division, *Pol.* 50°9′ N, 21°13′ E 152
Podlaskie, adm. division, *Pol.* 54°9′ N, 22°33′ E 166
Podlesnoye, *Russ.* 51°46′ N, 47°3′ E 158
Podnovlje, *Bosn. and Herzg.* 44°56′ N, 18°5′ E 168
Podocarpus National Park, *Ecua.* 4°22′ S, 79°17′ W 122
Podoleni, *Rom.* 46°47′ N, 26°37′ E 156
Podol′sk, *Russ.* 55°23′ N, 37°31′ E 154
Podor, *Senegal* 16°38′ N, 15°0′ W 222
Podosinovets, *Russ.* 60°17′ N, 47°3′ E 154
Podporozh′ye, *Russ.* 60°52′ N, 34°12′ E 154
Podravska Slatina, *Croatia* 45°41′ N, 17°40′ E 168
Podromanija, *Bosn. and Herzg.* 43°55′ N, 18°45′ E 168
Podsosan′ye (Zvoz), *Russ.* 63°17′ N, 42°2′ E 154
Podtesovo, *Russ.* 58°36′ N, 92°11′ E 169
Podyuga, *Russ.* 61°6′ N, 40°49′ E 154
Pofadder, *S. Af.* 29°8′ S, 19°22′ E 227
Poggio Rusco, *It.* 44°59′ N, 11°6′ E 167
Pogi, *Russ.* 59°31′ N, 30°35′ E 166
Pogny, *Fr.* 48°51′ N, 4°29′ E 163
Pogŏ, *N. Korea* 40°42′ N, 128°54′ E 200
Pogorelets, *Russ.* 65°26′ N, 45°5′ E 154
Pogost, *Belarus* 52°50′ N, 27°40′ E 152
Pogromnoye, *Russ.* 52°35′ N, 52°28′ E 154
P′oha, *N. Korea* 40°58′ N, 129°43′ E 200
Pohang, *S. Korea* 36°2′ N, 129°22′ E 200
Pohja see Pojo, *Fin.* 60°5′ N, 23°31′ E 166
Pohnpei (Ponape), island, *F.S.M.* 6°55′ N, 158°15′ E 242
Pohorje, *Slov.* 46°25′ N, 15°37′ E 168
Poiana Mare, *Rom.* 43°55′ N, 23°4′ E 168
Poiana Ruscă, Munţii, *Rom.* 45°36′ N, 22°18′ E 168
Poie, *Dem. Rep. of the Congo* 2°52′ S, 23°11′ E 218
Poim, *Russ.* 53°0′ N, 43°7′ E 154
Poincaré, Lac, lake, *Can.* 51°43′ N, 58°54′ W 111
Poinsett, Cape, *Antarctica* 65°27′ S, 117°42′ E 248
Point Baker, *Alas., U.S.* 56°19′ N, 133°32′ W 108
Point, China, *Calif., U.S.* 32°44′ N, 118°33′ W 101
Point Coulomb National Park, *Austral.* 17°22′ S, 121°55′ E 238
Point Edward, *Can.* 42°59′ N, 82°24′ W 102
Point Hope, *Alas., U.S.* 68°19′ N, 166°40′ W 98
Point Judith, *R.I., U.S.* 41°21′ N, 71°30′ W 104
Point Lake, *Can.* 64°58′ N, 113°44′ W 106
Point Lay, *Alas., U.S.* 69°46′ N, 163°10′ W 73
Point Pedro, *Sri Lanka* 9°49′ N, 80°14′ E 188
Point Pelee National Park, *Can.* 41°53′ N, 82°56′ W 102
Point Pleasant, *W. Va., U.S.* 38°50′ N, 82°9′ W 102
Point Reyes National Seashore, *Calif., U.S.* 38°16′ N, 127°9′ W 80
Point Roberts, *Can.* 48°58′ N, 123°4′ W 100
Pointe a la Hache, *La., U.S.* 29°34′ N, 89°49′ W 103
Pointe, Lac de la, lake, *Can.* 52°42′ N, 70°54′ W 111
Pointe-à-Gravois, *Haiti* 17°54′ N, 74°4′ W 116
Pointe-à-Pitre, *Grande-Terre* 16°15′ N, 61°31′ W 116
Pointe-au-Pic, *Can.* 47°36′ N, 70°10′ W 94
Pointe-aux-Anglais, *Can.* 49°40′ N, 67°12′ W 111
Pointe-Noire, *Congo* 4°49′ S, 11°50′ E 218
Poipet, *Cambodia* 13°40′ N, 102°37′ E 202
Poissons, *Fr.* 48°24′ N, 5°12′ E 163
Poissy, *Fr.* 48°56′ N, 2°3′ E 163
Poitiers, *Fr.* 46°34′ N, 0°19′ E 150
Poitou, region, *Fr.* 46°19′ N, 1°0′ E 165
Poitou-Charentes, adm. division, *Fr.* 46°13′ N, 0°37′ E 150
Poix, *Fr.* 49°46′ N, 1°58′ E 163
Poix-Terron, *Fr.* 49°38′ N, 4°39′ E 163
Pojo, *Bol.* 17°47′ S, 64°53′ W 137
Pojo (Pohja), *Fin.* 60°5′ N, 23°31′ E 166
Pokcha, *Russ.* 62°56′ N, 56°11′ E 154
Pokeno, *N.Z.* 37°15′ S, 175°3′ E 240
Pokhara, *Nepal* 28°17′ N, 83°58′ E 197
Pokhvistnevo, *Russ.* 53°38′ N, 52°4′ E 154
Pokka, *Fin.* 68°9′ N, 25°47′ E 152
Poko, *Dem. Rep. of the Congo* 3°7′ N, 26°53′ E 224
Pokrashevo, *Belarus* 53°11′ N, 27°33′ E 152
Pokrovsk Ural′skiy, *Russ.* 60°7′ N, 59°48′ E 154
Pokshen′ga, river, *Russ.* 63°31′ N, 43°43′ E 154
Pokupsko, *Croatia* 45°29′ N, 16°0′ E 168
Pola, *Philippines* 13°10′ N, 121°25′ E 203
Pola, *Russ.* 57°54′ N, 31°50′ E 154
Polače, *Croatia* 42°46′ N, 17°22′ E 168
Polān, *Iran* 25°32′ N, 61°11′ E 182
Poland 51°58′ N, 18°31′ E 152
Polar Plateau, *Antarctica* 88°4′ S, 20°29′ W 248
Polatlı, *Turk.* 39°34′ N, 32°9′ E 156
Polatsk, *Belarus* 55°29′ N, 28°47′ E 166
Polch, *Ger.* 50°17′ N, 7°18′ E 163
Polcirkeln, *Nor.* 66°33′ N, 20°58′ E 152
Pol-e Khomri, *Afghan.* 35°56′ N, 68°50′ E 186
Pole Plain, *Arctic Ocean* 83°54′ N, 131°5′ E 255
Polesella, *It.* 44°58′ N, 11°46′ E 167
Polessk, *Russ.* 54°50′ N, 21°2′ E 166
Poletica, Mount, peak, *Alas., U.S.* 59°4′ N, 134°43′ W 98
Polevskoy, *Russ.* 56°26′ N, 60°13′ E 154
Poli, *Cameroon* 8°26′ N, 13°14′ E 218
Poligus, *Russ.* 62°0′ N, 94°40′ E 169
Polikarpovskoye, *Russ.* 70°41′ N, 82°13′ E 169
Polillo Islands, *Philippine Sea* 14°33′ N, 121°54′ E 203
Polis, *Cyprus* 35°2′ N, 32°25′ E 194
Polje, *Bosn. and Herzg.* 44°59′ N, 17°57′ E 168
Polkville, *Miss., U.S.* 32°10′ N, 89°42′ W 103
Pollachi, *India* 10°40′ N, 77°1′ E 188
Pöllau, *Aust.* 47°18′ N, 15°49′ E 168
Pollino, Monte, peak, *It.* 39°53′ N, 16°8′ E 156
Pollock, *La., U.S.* 31°30′ N, 92°26′ W 103
Pollock, *S. Dak., U.S.* 45°52′ N, 100°19′ W 90
Pollok, *Tex., U.S.* 31°26′ N, 94°52′ W 103
Pollos, *Sp.* 41°25′ N, 5°9′ W 150
Polna, *Russ.* 58°27′ N, 28°8′ E 166
Polnovat, *Russ.* 63°47′ N, 66°2′ E 169
Polo, *Ill., U.S.* 41°58′ N, 89°35′ W 102
Polohy, *Ukr.* 47°26′ N, 36°14′ E 156
Polokwane (Pietersburg), *S. Af.* 23°54′ S, 29°26′ E 227
Polom, *Russ.* 59°11′ N, 50°54′ E 154
Polonne, *Ukr.* 50°5′ N, 27°31′ E 152
Polson, *Mont., U.S.* 47°38′ N, 114°12′ W 82
Poltava, *Ukr.* 49°36′ N, 34°29′ E 158
Poltavka, *Russ.* 54°19′ N, 71°47′ E 184
Põltsamaa, *Est.* 58°38′ N, 25°55′ E 166
Polunochnoye, *Russ.* 60°51′ N, 60°26′ E 154
Polur, *India* 12°32′ N, 79°7′ E 188
Poluy, *Russ.* 65°5′ N, 69°7′ E 169
Põlva, *Est.* 58°2′ N, 27°2′ E 166
Polvadera, *N. Mex., U.S.* 34°12′ N, 106°55′ W 92
Polyarnoye, *Russ.* 71°1′ N, 149°0′ E 160
Polyarnyy, *Russ.* 69°11′ N, 33°27′ E 152
Polyarnyy, *Russ.* 69°8′ N, 178°45′ E 98
Polyarnyy Krug, *Russ.* 66°26′ N, 32°51′ E 154
Polyarnyye Zori, *Russ.* 67°19′ N, 32°27′ E 152
Polynesian Cultural Center, site, *Hawai'i, U.S.* 21°37′ N, 157°58′ W 99
Polyrrhenia, ruin(s), *Gr.* 35°25′ N, 23°35′ E 156
Pomabamba, *Peru* 8°52′ S, 77°28′ W 130
Pomarão, *Port.* 37°33′ N, 7°33′ W 150
Pomarkku, *Fin.* 61°40′ N, 22°1′ E 166
Pómaro, *Mex.* 18°17′ N, 103°18′ W 114
Pomáz, *Hung.* 47°38′ N, 19°1′ E 168
Pombal, *Braz.* 6°47′ S, 37°48′ W 132
Pomene, *Mozambique* 22°53′ S, 35°29′ E 220
Pomerania, region, *Pol.* 54°38′ N, 18°22′ E 166
Pomeroy, *Ohio, U.S.* 39°1′ N, 82°2′ W 102
Pomeroy, *Wash., U.S.* 46°28′ N, 117°37′ W 90
Pomichna, *Ukr.* 48°15′ N, 31°31′ E 156
Pomona, *Calif., U.S.* 34°3′ N, 117°46′ W 101
Pomona Park, *Fla., U.S.* 29°29′ N, 81°36′ W 105
Pomorskie, adm. division, *Pol.* 53°54′ N, 18°28′ E 166
Pomos Point, *Cyprus* 35°9′ N, 32°27′ E 194
Pomovaara, peak, *Fin.* 67°54′ N, 26°14′ E 152
Pomozdino, *Russ.* 62°10′ N, 54°10′ E 154
Pompano Beach, *Fla., U.S.* 26°14′ N, 80°9′ W 105
Pompéia, *Braz.* 22°8′ S, 50°12′ W 138
Pompeii, ruin(s), *It.* 40°45′ N, 14°24′ E 156
Pompeiopolis, ruin(s), *Turk.* 36°43′ N, 34°26′ E 156
Pompéu, *Braz.* 19°14′ S, 45°0′ W 138
Pompeys Pillar, *Mont., U.S.* 45°57′ N, 107°56′ W 90
Pompeys Pillar National Monument, *Mont., U.S.* 45°58′ N, 108°2′ W 90
Pomuq, *Uzb.* 39°1′ N, 65°0′ E 197
Ponape see Pohnpei, island, *F.S.M.* 6°55′ N, 158°15′ E 242
Ponca City, *Okla., U.S.* 36°40′ N, 97°7′ W 82
Ponce 18°1′ N, 66°37′ W 116
Ponce de Leon Bay 25°20′ N, 81°22′ W 105
Ponchatoula, *La., U.S.* 30°25′ N, 90°26′ W 103
Poncheville, Lac, lake, *Can.* 50°8′ N, 77°36′ W 94
Poncin, *Fr.* 46°5′ N, 5°24′ E 156
Poncitlán, *Mex.* 20°22′ N, 102°57′ W 114
Pond, *Calif., U.S.* 35°43′ N, 119°21′ W 100
Pond Creek, *Okla., U.S.* 36°39′ N, 97°48′ W 92
Pond Inlet, *Can.* 72°36′ N, 77°53′ W 73
Pondicherry see Puducherry, *India* 11°56′ N, 79°47′ E 188
Ponferrada, *Sp.* 42°33′ N, 6°37′ W 150
Pong, *Thai.* 19°12′ N, 100°15′ E 202
Pongaroa, *N.Z.* 40°34′ S, 176°13′ E 240
Pongo, river, *Sudan* 7°39′ N, 27°11′ E 224
Pon′goma, *Russ.* 65°19′ N, 34°15′ E 152
Ponlei, *Cambodia* 12°26′ N, 104°27′ E 202
Ponoka, *Can.* 52°40′ N, 113°40′ W 108
Ponomarevka, *Russ.* 53°18′ N, 54°10′ E 154
Ponoy, *Russ.* 67°4′ N, 40°59′ E 154
Ponoy, river, *Russ.* 66°59′ N, 38°23′ E 154
Pons, *Fr.* 45°34′ N, 0°33′ E 150
Pont Canavese, *It.* 45°25′ N, 7°36′ E 167
Ponta Delgada, *Port.* 37°40′ N, 25°51′ W 207
Ponta Grossa, *Braz.* 25°6′ S, 50°9′ W 138
Ponta Porã, *Braz.* 22°32′ S, 55°40′ W 132
Pontalina, *Braz.* 17°34′ S, 49°29′ W 138
Pont-à-Mousson, *Fr.* 48°54′ N, 6°2′ E 163
Pontarlier, *Fr.* 46°54′ N, 6°19′ E 156
Pontassieve, *It.* 43°47′ N, 11°25′ E 167
Pontax, river, *Can.* 51°50′ N, 77°1′ W 110
Pontchartrain, Lake, *La., U.S.* 30°10′ N, 90°24′ W 103
Pontchâteau, *Fr.* 47°26′ N, 2°7′ W 150
Ponte Branca, *Braz.* 16°25′ S, 52°42′ W 138
Ponte de Lima, *Port.* 41°45′ N, 8°37′ W 150
Ponte di Legno, *It.* 46°16′ N, 10°29′ E 167
Ponte Firme, *Braz.* 18°4′ S, 46°26′ W 138
Ponte Nova, *Braz.* 20°25′ S, 42°53′ W 138
Ponteareas, *Sp.* 42°9′ N, 8°31′ W 150
Pontedecimo, *It.* 44°30′ N, 8°55′ E 167
Pontedera, *It.* 43°39′ N, 10°36′ E 156
Pontefract, *U.K.* 53°41′ N, 1°18′ W 162
Ponteix, *Can.* 49°43′ N, 107°28′ W 90
Pontevedra, *Sp.* 42°24′ N, 8°39′ W 150
Pontiac, *Ill., U.S.* 40°52′ N, 88°38′ W 102
Pontiac, *Mich., U.S.* 42°37′ N, 83°18′ W 102
Pontiac, *Mo., U.S.* 40°52′ N, 88°38′ W 94
Pontian Kechil, *Malaysia* 1°29′ N, 103°23′ E 196
Pontianak, *Indonesia* 3°178′ S, 109°18′ E 196
Pontoise, *Fr.* 49°3′ N, 2°4′ E 163
Ponton, *Can.* 54°37′ N, 99°11′ W 108
Ponton, river, *Can.* 58°26′ N, 116°3′ W 108
Pontós, *Sp.* 42°10′ N, 2°54′ E 164
Pontrieux, *Fr.* 48°41′ N, 3°10′ W 150
Ponts, *Sp.* 41°54′ N, 1°11′ E 164
Pont-Sainte-Maxence, *Fr.* 49°18′ N, 2°37′ E 163
Pont-sur-Yonne, *Fr.* 48°16′ N, 3°12′ E 163
Pontypool, *U.K.* 51°41′ N, 3°3′ W 162
Ponyri, *Russ.* 52°17′ N, 36°17′ E 158
Ponziane, Isole, islands, *Tyrrhenian Sea* 40°46′ N, 12°1′ E 156
Ponzone, *It.* 44°35′ N, 8°29′ E 167
Poole, *U.K.* 50°43′ N, 1°59′ W 162
Poondinna, Mount, peak, *Austral.* 27°22′ S, 129°46′ E 230
Poopó, *Bol.* 18°23′ S, 66°59′ W 137
Poopó, Lago, lake, *Bol.* 18°59′ S, 67°12′ W 137
Pōōsapea, *Est.* 59°12′ N, 23°29′ E 166
Popa, Isla, island, *Pan.* 8°12′ N, 82°18′ W 115
Popayán, *Col.* 2°23′ N, 76°37′ W 136
Pope, *Latv.* 57°23′ N, 21°50′ E 166
Poperinge, *Belg.* 50°51′ N, 2°43′ E 163
Popham Beach, *Me., U.S.* 43°44′ N, 69°48′ W 104
Popigay, *Russ.* 72°1′ N, 110°58′ E 160
Poplar, *Calif., U.S.* 36°3′ N, 119°10′ W 101
Poplar, *Mont., U.S.* 48°5′ N, 105°11′ W 90
Poplar Bluff, *Mo., U.S.* 36°45′ N, 90°24′ W 96
Poplar Point, *Can.* 52°54′ N, 97°53′ W 108
Poplar, river, *Can.* 61°22′ N, 121°44′ W 108
Poplar, river, *Can.* 52°27′ N, 95°49′ W 108
Poplarville, *Miss., U.S.* 30°50′ N, 89°33′ W 103
Popocatépetl, peak, *Mex.* 19°0′ N, 98°40′ W 114
Popokabaka, *Dem. Rep. of the Congo* 5°41′ S, 16°36′ E 218
Popovača, *Croatia* 45°34′ N, 16°37′ E 168
Poppi, *It.* 43°43′ N, 11°44′ E 167

Poprad, *Slovakia* 49°3′ N, 20°18′ E 152
Pŏptong, *N. Korea* 38°58′ N, 127°4′ E 200
Populonia, *It.* 42°58′ N, 10°30′ E 156
Por Chaman, *Afghan.* 33°10′ N, 63°52′ E 186
Porangahau, *N.Z.* 40°19′ S, 176°38′ E 240
Porangatu, *Braz.* 13°30′ S, 49°12′ W 138
Porazava, *Belarus* 52°56′ N, 24°21′ E 152
Porbandar, *India* 21°39′ N, 69°37′ E 186
Porcher Island, *Can.* 54°1′ N, 130°53′ W 98
Porco, *Bol.* 19°50′ S, 66°1′ W 137
Porcos, river, *Braz.* 13°5′ S, 45°10′ W 138
Porcuna, *Sp.* 37°53′ N, 4°12′ W 164
Porcupine, Cape, *Can.* 53°57′ N, 57°8′ W 111
Porcupine Hill, peak, *Can.* 53°42′ N, 61°5′ W 111
Porcupine Mountains, peak, *Mich., U.S.* 46°43′ N, 89°52′ W 94
Porcupine Plain, *Can.* 52°35′ N, 103°16′ W 108
Porcupine Plain, *North Atlantic Ocean* 47°55′ N, 15°54′ W 253
Porcupine, river, *Can.* 66°51′ N, 144°4′ W 106
Pordenone, *It.* 45°57′ N, 12°39′ E 167
Pordim, *Bulg.* 43°22′ N, 24°50′ E 156
Poreč, *Croatia* 45°13′ N, 13°36′ E 167
Porecatu, *Braz.* 22°47′ S, 51°28′ W 138
Poretskoye, *Russ.* 55°11′ N, 46°19′ E 154
Pórfido, Punta, *Arg.* 41°56′ S, 64°57′ W 134
Porga, *Benin* 11°0′ N, 0°58′ E 222
Porgho, *Mali* 16°34′ N, 6°356′ W 222
Pori (Björneborg), *Fin.* 61°26′ N, 21°44′ E 166
Porirua, *N.Z.* 41°10′ S, 174°51′ E 240
Porjus, *Nor.* 66°56′ N, 19°50′ E 152
Porkhov, *Russ.* 57°44′ N, 29°39′ E 166
Porkkala, *Fin.* 59°58′ N, 24°24′ E 166
Porlock, *U.K.* 51°12′ N, 3°35′ W 162
Porog, *Russ.* 62°1′ N, 56°40′ E 154
Poroma, *Bol.* 18°30′ S, 65°34′ W 137
Poronaysk, *Russ.* 49°15′ N, 143°0′ E 190
Poronin, *Pol.* 49°20′ N, 20°0′ E 152
Poroslyany, *Belarus* 52°39′ N, 24°21′ E 152
Porosozero, *Russ.* 62°43′ N, 32°44′ E 152
Poroszló, *Hung.* 47°38′ N, 20°38′ E 168
Porozhsk, *Russ.* 63°56′ N, 53°41′ E 154
Porpoise Bay 66°28′ S, 128°20′ E 255
Porsangerhalvøya, *Nor.* 70°46′ N, 23°56′ E 152
Porsuk, river, *Turk.* 39°30′ N, 29°57′ E 156
Port Alberni, *Can.* 49°14′ N, 124°48′ W 100
Port Albert, *Can.* 43°52′ N, 81°42′ W 102
Port Alexander, *Alas., U.S.* 56°15′ N, 134°41′ W 108
Port Alfred, *S. Af.* 33°35′ S, 26°52′ E 227
Port Alice, *Can.* 50°22′ N, 127°26′ W 90
Port Allen, *La., U.S.* 30°27′ N, 91°14′ W 103
Port Alsworth, *Alas., U.S.* 60°11′ N, 154°20′ W 98
Port Angeles, *Wash., U.S.* 48°5′ N, 123°26′ W 100
Port Antonio, *Jam.* 18°10′ N, 76°27′ W 115
Port Arthur, *Tex., U.S.* 29°53′ N, 93°56′ W 103
Port Arthur see Lüshun, *China* 38°52′ N, 121°16′ E 198
Port Austin, *Mich., U.S.* 44°2′ N, 83°0′ W 102
Port Barre, *La., U.S.* 30°32′ N, 91°58′ W 103
Port Bay, Port au 48°38′ N, 59°28′ W 111
Port Beaufort, *S. Af.* 34°21′ S, 20°46′ E 227
Port Bell, *Uganda* 0°16′ N, 32°36′ E 224
Port Blair, *India* 11°44′ N, 92°52′ E 188
Port Blanford, *Can.* 48°21′ N, 54°11′ W 111
Port Bolivar, *Tex., U.S.* 29°21′ N, 94°46′ W 103
Port Bouet, *Côte d'Ivoire* 5°16′ N, 3°59′ W 222
Port Bruce, *Can.* 42°38′ N, 81°1′ W 102
Port Burwell, *Can.* 42°38′ N, 80°47′ W 102
Port Burwell, *Can.* 60°19′ N, 64°39′ W 106
Port Canning, *India* 22°18′ N, 88°38′ E 197
Port Carling, *Can.* 45°6′ N, 79°33′ W 94
Port Chalmers, *N.Z.* 45°48′ S, 170°36′ E 240
Port Charlotte, *Fla., U.S.* 26°59′ N, 82°5′ W 105
Port Clements, *Can.* 53°41′ N, 132°11′ W 108
Port Clinton, *Ohio, U.S.* 41°29′ N, 82°57′ W 102
Port Colborne, *Can.* 42°52′ N, 79°15′ W 110
Port Coquitlam, *Can.* 49°15′ N, 122°46′ W 100
Port de Sóller, *Sp.* 39°47′ N, 2°42′ E 164
Port Dickson, *Malaysia* 2°35′ N, 101°48′ E 196
Port Dover, *Can.* 42°46′ N, 80°11′ W 94
Port Eads, *La., U.S.* 29°1′ N, 89°9′ W 103
Port Edward, *Can.* 54°13′ N, 130°16′ W 108
Port Edwards, *Wis., U.S.* 44°20′ N, 89°53′ W 110
Port Elgin, *Can.* 44°25′ N, 81°23′ W 94
Port Elizabeth, *S. Af.* 33°56′ S, 25°34′ E 227
Port Étienne see Nouadhibou, *Mauritania* 20°56′ N, 17°2′ W 222
Port Ewen, *N.Y., U.S.* 41°53′ N, 74°0′ W 104
Port Fitzroy, *N.Z.* 36°11′ S, 175°22′ E 240
Port Gamble, *Wash., U.S.* 47°49′ N, 122°37′ W 100
Port Gibson, *Miss., U.S.* 31°57′ N, 91°0′ W 103
Port Harcourt, *Nig.* 4°46′ N, 7°0′ E 222
Port Hardy, *Can.* 50°43′ N, 127°32′ W 108
Port Hawkesbury, *Can.* 45°36′ N, 61°22′ W 111
Port Henry, *N.Y., U.S.* 44°2′ N, 73°29′ W 104
Port Herald see Nsanje, *Malawi* 16°56′ S, 35°13′ E 224
Port Hope, *Can.* 43°56′ N, 78°19′ W 94
Port Hope, *Mich., U.S.* 43°56′ N, 82°44′ W 102
Port Hueneme, *Calif., U.S.* 34°9′ N, 119°12′ W 101
Port Huron, *Mich., U.S.* 42°57′ N, 82°28′ W 102
Port Isabel, *Tex., U.S.* 26°5′ N, 97°13′ W 114
Port Jefferson, *N.Y., U.S.* 40°56′ N, 73°4′ W 104
Port Jervis, *N.Y., U.S.* 41°22′ N, 74°42′ W 110
Port Joinville, *Fr.* 46°43′ N, 2°22′ W 150
Port Kaituma, *Guyana* 7°47′ N, 59°55′ W 116
Port Katon, *Russ.* 46°51′ N, 38°44′ E 156
Port Kelang, *Malaysia* 2°58′ N, 101°26′ E 196
Port Láirge see Waterford, *Ire.* 52°15′ N, 7°8′ W 150
Port Laoise, *Ire.* 53°2′ N, 7°18′ W 150
Port Lavaca, *Tex., U.S.* 28°35′ N, 96°37′ W 96
Port Lions, *Alas., U.S.* 57°50′ N, 152°56′ W 98
Port Loko, *Sierra Leone* 8°46′ N, 12°47′ W 222
Port Louis, *Mauritius* 20°9′ S, 57°30′ E 22
Port Lyautey see Kenitra, *Mor.* 34°17′ N, 6°37′ W 214
Port Mansfield, *Tex., U.S.* 26°33′ N, 97°26′ W 114
Port Maria, *Jam.* 18°21′ N, 76°54′ W 115
Port McNeill, *Can.* 50°33′ N, 127°6′ W 90
Port McNicoll, *Can.* 44°44′ N, 79°48′ W 94
Port Moody, *Can.* 49°15′ N, 122°51′ W 100
Port Moresby, *P.N.G.* 9°30′ S, 146°47′ E 230
Port Neches, *Tex., U.S.* 29°58′ N, 93°57′ W 103
Port Neville, *Can.* 50°29′ N, 126°2′ W 90
Port Nolloth, *S. Af.* 29°15′ S, 16°52′ E 227
Port O'Connor, *Tex., U.S.* 28°26′ N, 96°26′ W 96
Port Ontario, *N.Y., U.S.* 43°33′ N, 76°12′ W 94
Port Orange, *Fla., U.S.* 29°7′ N, 81°0′ W 105
Port Orchard, *Wash., U.S.* 47°30′ N, 122°39′ W 100
Port Pirie, *Austral.* 33°12′ S, 138°0′ E 231
Port Renfrew, *Can.* 48°32′ N, 124°25′ W 100
Port Royal, *S.C., U.S.* 32°22′ N, 80°42′ W 96
Port Royal National Historic Site, *Can.* 44°42′ N, 65°43′ W 111
Port Said see Bûr Saʻîd, *Egypt* 31°15′ N, 32°18′ E 194
Port Saint Joe, *Fla., U.S.* 29°48′ N, 85°17′ W 96
Port Saint Johns, *S. Af.* 31°39′ S, 29°30′ E 227
Port Saint Lucie, *Fla., U.S.* 27°20′ N, 80°18′ W 105
Port Salerno, *Fla., U.S.* 27°7′ N, 80°13′ W 105
Port Sanilac, *Mich., U.S.* 43°25′ N, 82°34′ W 102
Port Saunders, *Can.* 50°38′ N, 57°18′ W 111
Port Shepstone, *S. Af.* 30°44′ S, 30°25′ E 227
Port Simpson, *Can.* 54°32′ N, 130°25′ W 108
Port Stanley, *Can.* 42°39′ N, 81°14′ W 102
Port Sudan, *Sudan* 19°38′ N, 37°11′ E 182
Port Sulphur, *La., U.S.* 29°28′ N, 89°42′ W 103
Port Talbot, *Can.* 42°38′ N, 81°20′ W 102
Port Talbot, *U.K.* 51°35′ N, 3°46′ W 162
Port Townsend, *Wash., U.S.* 48°6′ N, 122°47′ W 100
Port Vladimir, *Russ.* 69°25′ N, 33°6′ E 152
Port Washington, *N.Y., U.S.* 40°49′ N, 73°42′ W 104
Port Washington, *Wis., U.S.* 43°23′ N, 87°53′ W 102
Port Weld, *Malaysia* 4°50′ N, 100°37′ E 196
Port William, *Alas., U.S.* 58°29′ N, 152°38′ W 98
Portachuelo, *Bol.* 17°23′ S, 63°30′ W 132
Portadown, *U.K.* 54°24′ N, 6°27′ W 150
Portage, *Ind., U.S.* 41°33′ N, 87°11′ W 102
Portage, *Mich., U.S.* 42°11′ N, 85°36′ W 102
Portage, *Wis., U.S.* 43°31′ N, 89°27′ W 102
Portage Creek, *Alas., U.S.* 58°52′ N, 157°44′ W 98
Portage la Prairie, *Can.* 49°58′ N, 98°19′ W 108
Portageville, *Mo., U.S.* 36°25′ N, 89°42′ W 96
Portal, *N. Dak., U.S.* 48°57′ N, 102°35′ W 90
Portalegre, *Port.* 39°17′ N, 7°26′ W 150
Portalegre, adm. division, *Port.* 39°3′ N, 8°10′ W 150
Portales, *N. Mex., U.S.* 34°10′ N, 103°21′ W 92
Port-à-Piment, *Haiti* 18°16′ N, 74°8′ W 115
Port-au-Prince, *Haiti* 18°31′ N, 72°29′ W 116
Port-Bergé see Boriziny, *Madagascar* 15°35′ S, 47°43′ E 220
Portbou, *Sp.* 42°25′ N, 3°9′ E 164
Port-Cartier, *Can.* 50°1′ N, 66°51′ W 111
Port-Cartier, *Can.* 50°2′ N, 66°54′ W 106
Port-Daniel, *Can.* 48°10′ N, 64°59′ W 94
Porteirinha, *Braz.* 15°45′ S, 43°4′ W 138
Portel, *Braz.* 1°59′ S, 50°48′ W 130
Portela, *Braz.* 21°39′ S, 42°0′ W 138
Portendick, *Mauritania* 18°34′ N, 16°7′ W 222
Porter, *Me., U.S.* 43°47′ N, 70°56′ W 104
Porter, *Tex., U.S.* 30°4′ N, 95°14′ W 103
Porter Lake, *Can.* 56°13′ N, 107°56′ W 108
Porter Lake, lake, *Can.* 61°40′ N, 108°34′ W 108
Porterdale, *Ga., U.S.* 33°33′ N, 83°54′ W 96
Porterville, *Calif., U.S.* 36°5′ N, 119°2′ W 101
Porterville, *Miss., U.S.* 32°40′ N, 88°29′ W 103
Porterville, *S. Af.* 33°1′ S, 19°1′ E 227
Portete, Bahía de 12°12′ N, 72°32′ W 136
Port-Gentil, *Gabon* 1°9′ S, 8°53′ E 207
Porthcawl, *U.K.* 51°28′ N, 3°42′ W 162
Port-İliç, *Azerb.* 38°51′ N, 48°47′ E 195
Portimão, *Port.* 37°6′ N, 8°36′ W 214
Portishead, *U.K.* 51°28′ N, 2°46′ W 162
Portland, *Ark., U.S.* 33°13′ N, 91°31′ W 103
Portland, *Conn., U.S.* 41°34′ N, 72°39′ W 104
Portland, *Ind., U.S.* 40°26′ N, 84°58′ W 102
Portland, *Me., U.S.* 43°39′ N, 70°16′ W 104
Portland, *Mich., U.S.* 42°51′ N, 84°55′ W 102
Portland, *N. Dak., U.S.* 47°28′ N, 97°24′ W 90
Portland, *Oreg., U.S.* 45°30′ N, 122°43′ W 90
Portland, *Tenn., U.S.* 36°34′ N, 86°31′ W 96
Portland Inlet 54°43′ N, 131°3′ W 108
Portland Point, *Jam.* 17°35′ N, 77°7′ W 115
Port-la-Nouvelle, *Fr.* 43°0′ N, 3°1′ E 164
Port-Menier, *Can.* 49°48′ N, 64°22′ W 106
Portneuf, Lac, lake, *Can.* 49°9′ N, 70°56′ W 94
Portneuf-sur-Mer, *Can.* 48°36′ N, 69°8′ W 111
Porto, *Braz.* 3°54′ S, 42°44′ W 132
Porto, *Fr.* 42°16′ N, 8°42′ E 156
Porto, *Port.* 41°13′ N, 8°32′ W 150
Porto Acre, *Braz.* 9°37′ S, 67°33′ W 137
Porto, adm. division, *Port.* 41°12′ N, 8°44′ W 150
Porto Alegre, *Braz.* 21°34′ S, 53°33′ W 132
Porto Alegre, *Braz.* 9°0′ S, 67°51′ W 137
Porto Alegre, *Braz.* 4°24′ S, 52°47′ W 130
Porto Alegre, *Braz.* 30°3′ S, 51°10′ W 139
Porto Amboim, *Angola* 10°44′ S, 13°47′ E 220
Porto Artur, *Braz.* 13°5′ S, 55°5′ W 130
Porto de Moz, *Braz.* 1°45′ S, 52°13′ W 130
Porto de Pedras, *Braz.* 9°10′ S, 35°20′ W 132
Porto do Son, *Sp.* 42°42′ N, 9°0′ W 150
Porto dos Gaúchos, *Braz.* 11°30′ S, 57°23′ W 130
Porto Empedocle, *It.* 37°18′ N, 13°31′ E 156
Porto Esperança, *Braz.* 19°37′ S, 57°26′ W 132
Porto Esperidião, *Braz.* 15°50′ S, 58°31′ W 132
Porto Franco, *Braz.* 6°23′ S, 47°24′ W 130
Porto Garibaldi, *It.* 44°40′ N, 12°13′ E 167
Porto Grande, *Braz.* 0°42′ N, 51°25′ W 130
Porto Levante, *It.* 45°3′ N, 12°21′ E 167
Porto Levante, *It.* 38°25′ N, 14°56′ E 156
Porto Lucena, *Braz.* 27°53′ S, 55°1′ W 132
Porto Murtinho, *Braz.* 21°42′ S, 57°54′ W 132
Porto Nacional, *Braz.* 10°43′ S, 48°24′ W 130
Porto (Oporto), *Port.* 41°8′ N, 8°38′ W 150
Porto San Giorgio, *It.* 43°10′ N, 13°47′ E 156
Porto Santana, *Braz.* 1°59′ S, 51°11′ W 130
Porto Santo Stefano, *It.* 42°26′ N, 11°6′ E 156
Porto São José, *Braz.* 22°44′ S, 53°12′ W 138
Porto Tolle, *It.* 44°56′ N, 12°19′ E 167
Porto Velho, *Braz.* 8°43′ S, 63°53′ W 137
Portobelo, *Pan.* 9°33′ N, 79°39′ W 115
Portobelo National Park, *Pan.* 9°33′ N, 79°41′ W 115
Portofino, *It.* 44°18′ N, 9°12′ E 167
Port of Spain, *Trinidad and Tobago* 10°40′ N, 61°32′ W 118
Portogruaro, *It.* 45°45′ N, 12°50′ E 167
Portola, *Calif., U.S.* 39°48′ N, 120°29′ W 90
Pörtom (Pirttikylä), *Fin.* 62°41′ N, 21°35′ E 154
Portomaggiore, *It.* 44°41′ N, 11°47′ E 167
Porto-Novo, *Benin* 6°31′ N, 2°31′ E 222
Portorož, *Slov.* 45°30′ N, 13°37′ E 167
Porto-Vecchio, *Fr.* 41°35′ N, 9°17′ E 156
Portovenere, *It.* 44°3′ N, 9°50′ E 167
Portoviejo, *Ecua.* 1°11′ S, 80°19′ W 130
Port-Sainte-Marie, *Fr.* 44°14′ N, 0°23′ E 150
Portsmouth, *N.H., U.S.* 43°4′ N, 70°46′ W 104
Portsmouth, *N.C., U.S.* 35°4′ N, 76°5′ W 96
Portsmouth, *Ohio, U.S.* 38°44′ N, 82°59′ W 102
Portsmouth, *R.I., U.S.* 41°35′ N, 71°16′ W 104
Portsmouth, *U.K.* 50°47′ N, 1°6′ W 162
Portsmouth, *Va., U.S.* 36°49′ N, 76°19′ W 96
Port-sur-Saône, *Fr.* 47°41′ N, 6°2′ E 156
Portugal 38°56′ N, 8°33′ W 150
Portugués, *Peru* 8°21′ S, 78°5′ W 130
Portuguesa, adm. division, *Venez.* 8°51′ N, 69°58′ W 136
Portuguesa, river, *Venez.* 8°45′ N, 69°2′ W 136
Port-Vendres, *Fr.* 42°30′ N, 3°5′ E 164
Port Vila, *Vanuatu* 17°41′ S, 167°55′ E 243
Porvenir, *Bol.* 11°15′ S, 68°45′ W 137
Porvenir, *Chile* 53°14′ S, 70°21′ W 134
Porvoo (Borgå), *Fin.* 60°23′ N, 25°40′ E 166
Por'ya Guba, *Russ.* 66°45′ N, 33°48′ E 154
Porz, *Ger.* 50°53′ N, 7°3′ E 167
Porzuna, *Sp.* 39°8′ N, 4°9′ W 164
Posadas, *Arg.* 27°25′ S, 55°55′ W 139
Posadas, *Sp.* 37°48′ N, 5°6′ W 164
Posadowsky Bay 66°58′ S, 88°27′ E 248
Poshekhon'ye Volodarsk, *Russ.* 58°29′ N, 39°11′ E 154
Poshkokagan, river, *Can.* 49°19′ N, 89°35′ W 94
Posht-e Bādām, *Iran* 32°57′ N, 55°19′ E 180
Posidium, ruin(s), *Gr.* 35°28′ N, 27°9′ E 156
Posio, *Fin.* 66°5′ N, 28°7′ E 154
Poso, *Indonesia* 1°27′ S, 120°44′ E 192
Poso Creek, river, *Calif., U.S.* 35°37′ N, 119°9′ W 101
Posof, *Turk.* 41°30′ N, 42°42′ E 195
Pospelkova, *Russ.* 59°27′ N, 60°53′ E 154
Posse, *Braz.* 14°8′ S, 46°23′ W 138
Possel, *Cen. Af. Rep.* 5°4′ N, 19°14′ E 218
Possession Island, *Namibia* 27°13′ S, 15°14′ E 227
Possession Islands, *Ross Sea* 71°53′ S, 178°9′ E 248
Post Falls, *Idaho, U.S.* 47°41′ N, 116°56′ W 90
Post Mills, *Vt., U.S.* 43°53′ N, 72°17′ W 104
Posta de San Martín, *Arg.* 33°11′ S, 60°29′ W 139
Poste, Baie du, lake, *Can.* 50°39′ N, 73°51′ W 110
Postmasburg, *S. Af.* 28°23′ S, 23°5′ E 227
Posto Alto Maniçauá, *Braz.* 11°19′ S, 54°44′ W 130
Posto Bobonaza, *Peru* 2°40′ S, 76°36′ W 136
Posto Cunambo, *Peru* 2°9′ S, 76°1′ W 136
Poston, *Ariz., U.S.* 33°58′ N, 114°25′ W 101
Postville, *Iowa, U.S.* 43°4′ N, 91°34′ W 94
Posušje, *Bosn. and Herzg.* 43°27′ N, 17°18′ E 168
Pos'yet, *Russ.* 42°40′ N, 130°49′ E 200
Pot Mountain, peak, *Idaho, U.S.* 46°41′ N, 115°30′ W 90
Potamós, *Gr.* 35°52′ N, 23°16′ E 156
Potapovo, *Russ.* 68°40′ N, 86°26′ E 169
Potchefstroom, *S. Af.* 26°45′ S, 27°1′ E 227
Poté, *Braz.* 17°50′ S, 41°53′ W 138
Poteau, *Okla., U.S.* 35°0′ N, 94°38′ W 96
Poteet, *Tex., U.S.* 29°1′ N, 98°34′ W 96
Potenza, *It.* 40°38′ N, 15°48′ E 156
Potenza Picena, *It.* 43°21′ N, 13°37′ E 156
Potgietersrus see Mokopane, *S. Af.* 24°9′ S, 28°59′ E 227
Poth, *Tex., U.S.* 29°3′ N, 98°5′ W 92
P'ot'i, *Ga.* 42°7′ N, 41°38′ E 195
Potidaea, ruin(s), *Aegean Sea* 40°11′ N, 23°14′ E 156
Potiskum, *Nig.* 11°42′ N, 11°5′ E 222
Potlatch, *Idaho, U.S.* 46°54′ N, 116°56′ W 90
Potlogi, *Rom.* 44°34′ N, 25°35′ E 156
Potoci, *Bosn. and Herzg.* 43°23′ N, 17°53′ E 168
Potomac, *Ill., U.S.* 40°17′ N, 87°48′ W 102
Potosí, *Bol.* 19°37′ S, 65°37′ W 123
Potosí, *Bol.* 19°36′ S, 65°44′ W 137
Potosi, *Mo., U.S.* 37°55′ N, 90°47′ W 94
Potosí, *Nicar.* 12°58′ N, 87°30′ W 115
Potosí, adm. division, *Bol.* 20°39′ S, 67°39′ W 137
Potosi Mountain, peak, *Nev., U.S.* 35°56′ N, 115°32′ W 101
Potosí, river, *Mex.* 24°45′ N, 100°17′ W 114
Potrerillo, Paso de, pass, *Chile* 29°24′ S, 70°0′ W 132
Potrerillos, *Chile* 26°25′ S, 69°30′ W 132
Potsdam, *Ger.* 52°24′ N, 13°3′ E 152
Potsdam, *N.Y., U.S.* 44°40′ N, 75°0′ W 94
Pottendorf, *Aust.* 47°54′ N, 16°22′ E 168
Potter, *Nebr., U.S.* 41°13′ N, 103°20′ W 90
Pottersville, *N.Y., U.S.* 43°43′ N, 73°50′ W 104
Potterville, *Mich., U.S.* 42°36′ N, 84°45′ W 102
Potton, *U.K.* 52°7′ N, 0°13′ E 162
Pouancé, *Fr.* 47°43′ N, 1°11′ W 150
Poughkeepsie, *N.Y., U.S.* 41°41′ N, 73°55′ W 104
Poulan, *Ga., U.S.* 31°30′ N, 83°48′ W 96
Poulsbo, *Wash., U.S.* 47°43′ N, 122°39′ W 100
Poultney, *Vt., U.S.* 43°31′ N, 73°15′ W 104
Poulton le Fylde, *U.K.* 53°50′ N, 3°0′ W 162
Pouma, *Cameroon* 3°55′ N, 10°37′ E 222
Pourri, Mont, peak, *Fr.* 45°31′ N, 6°50′ E 165
Pouso Alegre, *Braz.* 22°13′ S, 45°56′ W 138
Pouss, *Cameroon* 10°50′ N, 15°0′ E 216
Poussu, *Fin.* 65°47′ N, 29°18′ E 152
Poutrincourt, Lac, lake, *Can.* 49°4′ N, 74°48′ W 94
Povenets, *Russ.* 62°51′ N, 34°52′ E 154
Povlen, *Serb.* 44°6′ N, 19°31′ E 168
Povorino, *Russ.* 51°9′ N, 42°12′ E 158
Povors'k, *Ukr.* 51°16′ N, 25°7′ E 152
Povungnituk, Baie de 59°33′ N, 79°35′ W 106
Poway, *Calif., U.S.* 32°57′ N, 117°3′ W 101
Powder River, *Wyo., U.S.* 43°1′ N, 106°59′ W 90
Powder, river, *Mont., U.S.* 44°58′ N, 105°46′ W 90
Powder River Pass, *Wyo., U.S.* 44°7′ N, 107°6′ W 90
Powder, river, *Wyo., U.S.* 45°2′ N, 105°33′ W 80
Powderly, *Ky., U.S.* 37°13′ N, 87°10′ W 96
Powell, *Wyo., U.S.* 44°43′ N, 108°46′ W 90
Powell Butte, *Oreg., U.S.* 44°13′ N, 121°3′ W 90
Powell Lake, *Can.* 50°2′ N, 124°32′ W 100
Powell Peak, *Ariz., U.S.* 34°39′ N, 114°28′ W 92
Powell River, *Can.* 49°52′ N, 124°30′ W 100
Powers Lake, *N. Dak., U.S.* 48°33′ N, 102°39′ W 90
Powerview, *Can.* 50°30′ N, 96°14′ W 90
Powhatan, *La., U.S.* 31°51′ N, 93°13′ W 103
Pownal Center, *Vt., U.S.* 42°47′ N, 73°14′ W 104
Poxoréo, *Braz.* 15°52′ S, 54°24′ W 132
Poygan, Lake, *Wis., U.S.* 44°8′ N, 89°5′ W 102
Poygan, Lake, *Wis., U.S.* 44°4′ N, 89°16′ W 110
Pöytyä, *Fin.* 60°45′ N, 22°37′ E 166
Poza Rica, *Mex.* 20°32′ N, 97°26′ W 114
Pozantı, *Turk.* 37°24′ N, 34°51′ E 156
Požarevac, *Serb.* 44°37′ N, 21°10′ E 168
Pozas de Santa Ana, *Mex.* 22°47′ N, 100°29′ W 114
Požega, *Serb.* 43°9′ N, 20°24′ E 168
Pozheg, *Russ.* 61°58′ N, 54°20′ E 154
Pozhva, *Russ.* 59°6′ N, 56°5′ E 154
Poznań, *Pol.* 52°24′ N, 16°55′ E 152
Pozo Alcón, *Sp.* 37°42′ N, 2°56′ W 164
Pozo Almonte, *Chile* 20°16′ S, 69°50′ W 137
Pozo Borrado, *Arg.* 28°55′ S, 61°43′ W 139
Pozo Colorado, *Parag.* 23°29′ S, 58°52′ W 132
Pozoblanco, *Sp.* 38°22′ N, 4°52′ W 164
Pozohondo, *Sp.* 38°43′ N, 1°55′ W 164
Pozos, *Mex.* 21°12′ N, 100°30′ W 114
Pozzallo, *It.* 36°44′ N, 14°51′ E 156
Pra, river, *Ghana* 5°4′ N, 1°41′ W 222
Prača, *Bosn. and Herzg.* 43°46′ N, 18°45′ E 168
Prachin Buri, *Thai.* 14°2′ N, 101°22′ E 202
Prachuap Khiri Khan, *Thai.* 11°48′ N, 99°46′ E 202
Prádena, *Sp.* 41°7′ N, 3°42′ W 164
Prado, *Braz.* 17°20′ S, 39°15′ W 132
Praesus, ruin(s), *Gr.* 35°5′ N, 25°59′ E 156
Prague see Praha, *Czech Rep.* 50°4′ N, 14°17′ E 152
Praha, adm. division, *Czech Rep.* 50°0′ N, 14°10′ E 152
Praha (Prague), *Czech Rep.* 50°4′ N, 14°17′ E 152
Prahova, adm. division, *Rom.* 45°2′ N, 25°43′ E 156
Prahovo, *Serb.* 44°16′ N, 22°34′ E 168
Prai, *Malaysia* 5°20′ N, 100°25′ E 196
Praia Grande, *Braz.* 29°11′ S, 49°56′ W 138
Prainha, *Braz.* 7°18′ S, 60°32′ W 130
Prainha, *Braz.* 1°48′ S, 53°32′ W 130
Prairie City, *Oreg., U.S.* 44°27′ N, 118°44′ W 90
Prairie du Chien, *Wis., U.S.* 43°1′ N, 91°10′ W 82
Prairie du Sac, *Wis., U.S.* 43°16′ N, 89°43′ W 102
Prairie River, *Can.* 52°51′ N, 102°59′ W 108
Prairieton, *Ind., U.S.* 39°22′ N, 87°28′ W 102
Pran Buri, *Thai.* 12°21′ N, 99°56′ E 202
Prangli, island, *Est.* 59°33′ N, 24°48′ E 166
Pranjani, *Serb.* 44°1′ N, 20°11′ E 168
Prapat, *Indonesia* 2°42′ N, 98°56′ E 196
Prata, *Braz.* 19°19′ S, 48°57′ W 138
Prata, river, *Braz.* 19°0′ S, 49°44′ W 138
Pratas Islands see Dongsha, *Taiwan, China* 20°43′ N, 116°42′ E 199
Prato, *It.* 43°53′ N, 11°4′ E 167
Pratt, *Kans., U.S.* 37°38′ N, 98°46′ W 90
Pratt Guyot, *North Pacific Ocean* 56°10′ N, 142°51′ W 252
Pravdinsk, *Russ.* 54°27′ N, 20°53′ E 166
Prawle Point, *U.K.* 50°2′ N, 3°56′ W 150
Prazaroki, *Belarus* 55°18′ N, 28°13′ E 166
Predazzo, *It.* 46°18′ N, 11°37′ E 167
Predejane, *Serb.* 42°50′ N, 22°9′ E 168
Predigtstuhl, peak, *Ger.* 47°40′ N, 12°48′ E 156
Predlitz, *Aust.* 47°3′ N, 13°55′ E 156
Preeceville, *Can.* 51°57′ N, 102°40′ W 108
Preetz, *Ger.* 54°14′ N, 10°17′ E 152
Pregolya, river, *Russ.* 54°38′ N, 21°24′ E 166
Pregonero, *Venez.* 7°59′ N, 71°46′ W 136
Pregrada, *Croatia* 46°10′ N, 15°45′ E 168
Preila, *Russ.* 55°23′ N, 21°3′ E 166
Preiļi, *Latv.* 56°17′ N, 26°44′ E 166
Prek Kak, *Cambodia* 12°14′ N, 105°30′ E 202
Prešovský, adm. division, *Slovakia* 49°8′ N, 20°7′ E 152
Prelate, *Can.* 50°51′ N, 109°24′ W 90
Preljina, *Serb.* 43°55′ N, 20°25′ E 168
Prelog, *Croatia* 46°20′ N, 16°37′ E 168
Premont, *Tex., U.S.* 27°21′ N, 98°7′ W 92
Prenj, *Bosn. and Herzg.* 43°34′ N, 17°45′ E 168
Prentice, *Wis., U.S.* 45°31′ N, 90°19′ W 94
Prentiss, *Miss., U.S.* 31°35′ N, 89°51′ W 103
Preparis North Channel 14°59′ N, 91°25′ E 188
Preparis South Channel 14°17′ N, 92°20′ E 188

Prepolac, *Serb.* 43° 0′ N, 21° 13′ E 168
Přerov, *Czech Rep.* 49° 27′ N, 17° 26′ E 152
Presa de la Amistad, *Mex.* 29° 23′ N, 101° 7′ W 112
Prescott, *Ariz., U.S.* 34° 32′ N, 112° 30′ W 112
Prescott, *Ark., U.S.* 33° 47′ N, 93° 23′ W 96
Prescott, *Can.* 44° 43′ N, 75° 32′ W 94
Prescott, *Mich., U.S.* 44° 11′ N, 83° 56′ W 102
Prescott, *Wash., U.S.* 46° 17′ N, 118° 19′ W 90
Preseli, Mynydd, peak, *U.K.* 51° 56′ N, 4° 51′ W 150
Preševo, *Serb.* 42° 17′ N, 21° 39′ E 168
Presho, *S. Dak., U.S.* 43° 53′ N, 100° 5′ W 90
Presidante Eduardo Frei, station, *Antarctica* 62° 12′ S, 59° 5′ W 134
Presidencia Roca, *Arg.* 26° 9′ S, 59° 37′ W 139
Presidente de la Plaza, *Arg.* 27° 0′ S, 59° 50′ W 139
Presidente Dutra, *Braz.* 5° 17′ S, 44° 31′ W 132
Presidente Eduardo Frei, Chile, station, *Antarctica* 62° 12′ S, 59° 5′ W 248
Presidente Epitácio, *Braz.* 21° 49′ S, 52° 8′ W 138
Presidente Olegário, *Braz.* 18° 25′ S, 46° 27′ W 138
Presidente Prudente, *Braz.* 22° 9′ S, 51° 25′ W 138
Presidente Roque Sáenz Peña, *Arg.* 26° 47′ S, 60° 27′ W 139
Presidente Venceslau, *Braz.* 21° 52′ S, 51° 53′ W 138
Presidential Range, *N.H., U.S.* 44° 20′ N, 71° 22′ W 104
Presidio, *Tex., U.S.* 29° 32′ N, 104° 22′ W 92
Presidio, river, *Mex.* 23° 50′ N, 105° 56′ W 114
Presidios, *Mex.* 25° 16′ N, 105° 37′ W 114
Presnovka, *Kaz.* 54° 38′ N, 67° 9′ E 184
Prešov, *Slovakia* 48° 59′ N, 21° 14′ E 152
Prešovský, adm. division, *Slovakia* 49° 10′ N, 21° 15′ E 152
Prespa, peak, *Bulg.* 41° 41′ N, 24° 45′ E 156
Presque Isle, *Me., U.S.* 46° 41′ N, 68° 8′ W 106
Presque Isle, *Mich., U.S.* 45° 19′ N, 83° 28′ W 94
Presque Isle, *Pa., U.S.* 42° 9′ N, 80° 19′ W 94
Presqu'île d'Ampasindava, *Madagascar* 13° 32′ S, 46° 47′ E 220
Pressburg see Bratislava, *Slovakia* 48° 7′ N, 16° 57′ E 152
Prestatyn, *U.K.* 53° 20′ N, 3° 24′ W 162
Prestea, *Ghana* 5° 25′ N, 2° 10′ W 222
Presteigne, *U.K.* 52° 15′ N, 3° 0′ W 162
Presto, *Bol.* 18° 55′ S, 64° 58′ W 137
Preston, *Idaho, U.S.* 42° 6′ N, 111° 53′ W 92
Preston, *Minn., U.S.* 43° 40′ N, 92° 6′ W 94
Preston, *Mo., U.S.* 37° 55′ N, 93° 13′ W 96
Preston, *U.K.* 53° 46′ N, 2° 42′ W 162
Preston City, *Conn., U.S.* 41° 31′ N, 71° 59′ W 104
Preston Peak, *Calif., U.S.* 41° 49′ N, 123° 42′ W 90
Prestonsburg, *Ky., U.S.* 37° 40′ N, 82° 46′ W 94
Prêto, river, *Braz.* 16° 38′ S, 46° 44′ W 138
Pretoria (Tshwane), *S. Af.* 25° 48′ S, 28° 3′ E 227
Prey Nop, *Cambodia* 10° 39′ N, 103° 46′ E 202
Prey Veng, *Cambodia* 11° 29′ N, 105° 17′ E 202
Priansus, ruin(s), *Gr.* 34° 58′ N, 25° 10′ E 156
Pribilof Islands, *Anadyrskiy Zaliv* 56° 57′ N, 169° 25′ W 98
Pribinić, *Bosn. and Herzg.* 44° 37′ N, 17° 41′ E 168
Priboj, *Serb.* 42° 37′ N, 22° 0′ E 168
Priboj, *Serb.* 43° 35′ N, 19° 31′ E 168
Price, *Tex., U.S.* 32° 7′ N, 94° 57′ W 103
Price, *Utah, U.S.* 39° 35′ N, 110° 49′ W 90
Price, Cape, *India* 13° 35′ N, 93° 8′ E 188
Prichard, *Ala., U.S.* 30° 43′ N, 88° 5′ W 103
Pridvorje, *Croatia* 42° 32′ N, 18° 20′ E 168
Priego de Córdoba, *Sp.* 37° 26′ N, 4° 12′ W 164
Priekule, *Lith.* 55° 34′ N, 21° 18′ E 166
Prienai, *Lith.* 54° 38′ N, 23° 55′ E 166
Prieska, *S. Af.* 29° 41′ S, 22° 43′ E 227
Priest River, *Idaho, U.S.* 48° 10′ N, 116° 56′ W 90
Priestly Mountain, peak, *Me., U.S.* 46° 31′ N, 69° 30′ W 94
Prieta, Peña, peak, *Sp.* 42° 59′ N, 4° 46′ W 150
Prigorodnyy, *Kaz.* 52° 13′ N, 61° 19′ E 158
Prijedor, *Bosn. and Herzg.* 44° 58′ N, 16° 43′ E 168
Prijepolje, *Serb.* 43° 22′ N, 19° 39′ E 168
Prilep, *Maced.* 41° 19′ N, 21° 35′ E 180
Priluka, *Bosn. and Herzg.* 43° 52′ N, 16° 56′ E 168
Prim, Point, *Can.* 45° 58′ N, 63° 38′ W 111
Primavera, *Braz.* 0° 57′ N, 47° 1′ W 130
Primeira Cruz, *Braz.* 2° 31′ S, 43° 25′ W 132
Primero de la Vega, *Sp.* 36° 41′ N, 4° 29′ W 164
Primolano, *It.* 45° 58′ N, 11° 43′ E 167
Primorsk, *Russ.* 54° 44′ N, 20° 0′ E 166
Primorsk, *Russ.* 60° 22′ N, 28° 36′ E 166
Primorsko Akhtarsk, *Russ.* 46° 5′ N, 38° 10′ E 156
Primošten, *Croatia* 43° 35′ N, 15° 55′ E 168
Primrose Lake, *Can.* 54° 46′ N, 110° 37′ W 108
Prince Albert, *Can.* 53° 10′ N, 105° 46′ W 108
Prince Albert, *S. Af.* 33° 15′ S, 22° 2′ E 227
Prince Albert Mountains, *Antarctica* 75° 43′ S, 179° 49′ E 248
Prince Albert National Park, *Can.* 53° 40′ N, 106° 52′ W 108
Prince Albert Peninsula, *Can.* 72° 24′ N, 124° 18′ W 106
Prince Albert Sound 70° 23′ N, 110° 14′ W 246
Prince Alfred, Cape, *Can.* 74° 7′ N, 132° 53′ W 106
Prince Charles Island, *Can.* 67° 18′ N, 84° 1′ W 106
Prince Charles's Cave, site 57° 26′ N, 6° 16′ W 150
Prince Edward Fracture Zone, *Indian Ocean* 44° 27′ S, 35° 49′ E 254
Prince Edward Island, *Can.* 46° 35′ N, 62° 1′ W 106
Prince Edward Island, adm. division, *Can.* 46° 18′ N, 63° 31′ W 111
Prince Edward Islands, *Indian Ocean* 46° 47′ S, 37° 53′ E 254
Prince George, *Can.* 53° 44′ N, 122° 48′ W 106
Prince Gustaf Adolf Sea 78° 44′ N, 105° 4′ W 246
Prince of Wales Island, *Alas., U.S.* 55° 18′ N, 135° 26′ W 98
Prince of Wales Island, *Austral.* 11° 18′ S, 141° 21′ E 192
Prince of Wales Island, *Can.* 71° 17′ N, 103° 2′ W 106
Prince of Wales Strait 72° 19′ N, 120° 33′ W 72
Prince Patrick Island, *Can.* 75° 38′ N, 126° 11′ W 106
Prince Regent Inlet 72° 52′ N, 90° 5′ W 246
Prince Regent Nature Reserve, *Austral.* 15° 39′ S, 124° 56′ E 238
Prince Rupert, *Can.* 54° 17′ N, 130° 19′ W 108
Prince William Forest Park, *Va., U.S.* 38° 34′ N, 77° 27′ W 94
Prince William Sound 60° 4′ N, 147° 27′ W 98
Princess Anne, *Md., U.S.* 38° 12′ N, 75° 41′ W 94
Princess Astrid Coast, *Antarctica* 71° 37′ S, 4° 26′ E 248
Princess Martha Coast, *Antarctica* 75° 5′ S, 27° 22′ W 248
Princess Ragnhild Coast, *Antarctica* 70° 44′ S, 23° 46′ E 248
Princeton, *Can.* 49° 25′ N, 120° 32′ W 90
Princeton, *Ill., U.S.* 41° 22′ N, 89° 27′ W 102
Princeton, *Mo., U.S.* 40° 23′ N, 93° 35′ W 94
Princeton, *N.J., U.S.* 40° 20′ N, 74° 40′ W 94
Princeton, *Wis., U.S.* 43° 51′ N, 89° 8′ W 102
Princeville, *Ill., U.S.* 40° 55′ N, 89° 45′ W 102
Principe Channel 53° 21′ N, 130° 24′ W 108
Príncipe da Beira, *Braz.* 12° 28′ S, 64° 24′ W 137
Príncipe, island, *Sao Tome and Principe* 1° 21′ N, 6° 33′ E 214
Prineville, *Oreg., U.S.* 44° 17′ N, 120° 50′ W 82
Prins Karls Forland, island, *Nor.* 78° 53′ N, 3° 57′ W 246
Prinzapolka, *Nicar.* 13° 22′ N, 83° 36′ W 115
Prior, Cabo 43° 31′ N, 8° 38′ W 150
Priozersk, *Russ.* 61° 2′ N, 30° 7′ E 166
Priozerskoye, *Russ.* 45° 15′ N, 44° 49′ E 158
Prisaca, *Rom.* 45° 52′ N, 26° 47′ E 158
Prishtina (Priština), *Kos.* 42° 40′ N, 21° 10′ E 168
Prislop, Pasul, pass, *Rom.* 47° 36′ N, 24° 53′ E 152
Priština see Prishtina, *Kos.* 42° 40′ N, 21° 10′ E 168
Pritchett, *Colo., U.S.* 37° 22′ N, 102° 52′ W 92
Pritzwalk, *Ger.* 53° 10′ N, 12° 11′ E 152
Privlaka, *Croatia* 44° 15′ N, 15° 6′ E 156
Privodino, *Russ.* 61° 4′ N, 46° 34′ E 154
Privolzhsk, *Russ.* 57° 21′ N, 41° 17′ E 154
Privolzhskaya Vozvyshennost', *Russ.* 53° 31′ N, 46° 34′ E 154
Privolzhskiy, *Russ.* 51° 19′ N, 46° 6′ E 158
Privolzh'ye, *Russ.* 52° 51′ N, 48° 39′ E 154
Priyutnoye, *Russ.* 46° 3′ N, 43° 20′ E 158
Prizren, *Kos.* 42° 13′ N, 20° 43′ E 168
Prizzi, *It.* 37° 44′ N, 13° 26′ E 156
Prnjavor, *Bosn. and Herzg.* 44° 51′ N, 17° 39′ E 168
Prnjavor, *Serb.* 44° 41′ N, 19° 23′ E 168
Proberta, *Calif., U.S.* 40° 5′ N, 122° 11′ W 90
Probizhna, *Ukr.* 49° 0′ N, 25° 58′ E 152
Probstzella, *Ger.* 50° 32′ N, 11° 24′ E 152
Proctor, *Minn., U.S.* 46° 45′ N, 92° 15′ W 94
Proctor, *Vt., U.S.* 43° 39′ N, 73° 4′ W 104
Proddatur, *India* 14° 44′ N, 78° 35′ E 188
Prodromi, *Cyprus* 35° 1′ N, 32° 23′ E 194
Progreso, *Mex.* 21° 17′ N, 89° 40′ W 116
Progress, Russia, station, *Antarctica* 69° 33′ S, 76° 34′ E 248
Progresso, *Braz.* 9° 47′ S, 71° 44′ W 137
Prokhladnyy, *Russ.* 43° 44′ N, 44° 0′ E 195
Prokhorkino, *Russ.* 59° 30′ N, 79° 28′ E 169
Prokop'yevsk, *Russ.* 53° 53′ N, 86° 49′ E 184
Prokuplje, *Serb.* 43° 14′ N, 21° 35′ E 168
Proletarsk, *Russ.* 46° 41′ N, 41° 35′ E 158
Proletarskiy, *Russ.* 50° 46′ N, 35° 49′ E 158
Prolivy, *Russ.* 67° 6′ N, 32° 14′ E 152
Prolog, *Bosn. and Herzg.* 43° 46′ N, 16° 49′ E 168
Promissão, *Braz.* 18° 18′ S, 55° 40′ W 132
Promyshlennyy, *Kaz.* 51° 7′ N, 71° 35′ E 184
Pronsfeld, *Ger.* 50° 9′ N, 6° 20′ E 167
Prophet River, *Can.* 58° 5′ N, 122° 45′ W 108
Prophet, river, *Can.* 57° 34′ N, 124° 5′ W 108
Prophetstown, *Ill., U.S.* 41° 40′ N, 89° 57′ W 102
Propriá, *Braz.* 10° 16′ S, 36° 52′ W 132
Prorva, *Kaz.* 45° 56′ N, 53° 17′ E 158
Prosek, *Alban.* 41° 44′ N, 19° 56′ E 168
Prosperity, *W. Va., U.S.* 37° 49′ N, 81° 13′ W 94
Prosser, *Wash., U.S.* 46° 10′ N, 119° 47′ W 90
Protection, *Kans., U.S.* 37° 11′ N, 99° 30′ W 92
Protem, *S. Af.* 34° 14′ S, 20° 4′ E 227
Prouts Neck, *Me., U.S.* 43° 31′ N, 70° 20′ W 104
Provencal, *La., U.S.* 31° 38′ N, 93° 13′ W 103
Provence, region, *Fr.* 43° 11′ N, 5° 35′ E 165
Provence-Alpes-Côte D'Azur, adm. division, *Fr.* 43° 54′ N, 4° 52′ E 150
Proves, *It.* 46° 28′ N, 11° 1′ E 167
Providence, *Ky., U.S.* 37° 23′ N, 87° 46′ W 96
Providence, *R.I., U.S.* 41° 49′ N, 71° 27′ W 104
Providence Island, *Seychelles* 9° 32′ S, 51° 7′ E 218
Providence Mountains, *Calif., U.S.* 35° 1′ N, 115° 35′ W 101
Providencia, Isla de, island, *Col.* 13° 4′ N, 82° 8′ W 115
Providência, Serra da, *Braz.* 10° 43′ S, 61° 36′ W 130
Provideniya, *Russ.* 64° 31′ N, 173° 8′ W 98
Provincetown, *Mass., U.S.* 42° 2′ N, 70° 12′ W 104
Provins, *Fr.* 48° 33′ N, 3° 17′ E 163
Provo, *Serb.* 44° 40′ N, 19° 54′ E 168
Provo, *Utah, U.S.* 40° 14′ N, 111° 38′ W 90
Provost, *Can.* 52° 21′ N, 110° 16′ W 108
Prozor, *Bosn. and Herzg.* 43° 47′ N, 17° 36′ E 168
Prudentópolis, *Braz.* 25° 15′ S, 51° 0′ W 138
Prudhoe Bay, *Alas., U.S.* 70° 12′ N, 148° 22′ W 98
Prud'homme, *Can.* 52° 20′ N, 105° 54′ W 108
Prüm, *Ger.* 50° 12′ N, 6° 24′ E 167
Prüm, river, *Ger.* 50° 8′ N, 6° 17′ E 167
Pruna, *Sp.* 36° 58′ N, 5° 14′ W 164
Prundeni, *Rom.* 44° 45′ N, 24° 14′ E 156
Prusac, *Bosn. and Herzg.* 44° 5′ N, 17° 23′ E 168
Prussia, region, *Pol.* 54° 29′ N, 19° 50′ E 166
Pruszcz Gdański, *Pol.* 54° 16′ N, 18° 36′ E 166
Prut, river, *Ukr.* 48° 18′ N, 26° 2′ E 158
Pryazha, *Russ.* 61° 41′ N, 33° 41′ E 154
Prydz Bay 69° 36′ S, 73° 49′ E 248
Pryluky, *Ukr.* 50° 34′ N, 32° 26′ E 158
Prymors'k, *Ukr.* 46° 43′ N, 36° 17′ E 156
Prymors'ke, *Ukr.* 46° 23′ N, 35° 19′ E 156
Pryor, *Okla., U.S.* 36° 17′ N, 95° 19′ W 94
Pryor Mountains, *Mont., U.S.* 45° 17′ N, 108° 32′ W 90
Prypyats', river, *Belarus* 51° 39′ N, 29° 36′ E 158
Przemyśl, *Pol.* 49° 45′ N, 22° 47′ E 152
Przeradz, *Pol.* 53° 46′ N, 16° 33′ E 152
Przerośl, *Pol.* 54° 14′ N, 22° 38′ E 166
Przeworsk, *Pol.* 50° 3′ N, 22° 32′ E 152
Przytu, *Pol.* 53° 22′ N, 22° 17′ E 152
Psará, *Gr.* 38° 32′ N, 25° 33′ E 156
Psiloreítis see Ídi, Óros, peak, *Gr.* 35° 12′ N, 24° 41′ E 156
Pskov, *Russ.* 57° 49′ N, 28° 22′ E 166
Pskov, adm. division, *Russ.* 57° 21′ N, 28° 27′ E 166
Ps'ol, river, *Ukr.* 49° 17′ N, 33° 25′ E 158
Psunj, peak, *Croatia* 45° 22′ N, 17° 17′ E 168
Ptsich, river, *Belarus* 53° 51′ N, 27° 4′ E 152
Ptuj, *Slov.* 46° 25′ N, 15° 52′ E 168
Pua, *Thai.* 19° 14′ N, 100° 53′ E 202
Puán, *Arg.* 37° 35′ S, 62° 47′ W 139
Puarent', Ozero, lake, *Russ.* 68° 44′ N, 33° 7′ E 152
Pubei, *China* 22° 15′ N, 109° 31′ E 198
Puca Barranca, *Peru* 2° 43′ S, 73° 32′ W 136
Puca Urco, *Peru* 2° 22′ S, 71° 54′ W 136
Pucacuro, river, *Peru* 2° 55′ S, 75° 18′ W 136
Pucallpa, *Peru* 8° 25′ S, 74° 36′ W 137
Pucará, *Bol.* 18° 44′ S, 64° 18′ W 137
Pucará, *Peru* 15° 6′ S, 70° 24′ W 137
Pucarani, *Bol.* 16° 24′ S, 68° 30′ W 137
Pucheng, *China* 34° 56′ N, 109° 34′ E 198
Pucheng, *China* 27° 58′ N, 118° 30′ E 198
Puckett, *Miss., U.S.* 32° 3′ N, 89° 46′ W 103
Pudasjärvi, *Fin.* 65° 24′ N, 26° 52′ E 152
Pudem, *Russ.* 58° 18′ N, 52° 15′ E 154
Pudimoe, *S. Af.* 27° 26′ S, 24° 42′ E 227
Pudino, *Russ.* 57° 35′ N, 79° 26′ E 169
Pudozh, *Russ.* 61° 49′ N, 36° 38′ E 154
Pudu, *Indonesia* 0° 25′ N, 102° 16′ E 196
Puducherry, adm. division, *India* 11° 44′ N, 79° 20′ E 188
Puducherry (Pondicherry), *India* 11° 56′ N, 79° 47′ E 188
Pudukkottai, *India* 10° 25′ N, 78° 48′ E 188
Puebla, *Mex.* 18° 59′ N, 98° 16′ W 114
Puebla, adm. division, *Mex.* 18° 51′ N, 98° 31′ W 114
Puebla de Alcocer, *Sp.* 38° 59′ N, 5° 16′ W 150
Puebla de Don Rodrigo, *Sp.* 39° 4′ N, 4° 38′ W 164
Pueblo, *Colo., U.S.* 38° 17′ N, 104° 39′ W 90
Pueblo Bonito, site, *N. Mex., U.S.* 36° 3′ N, 108° 2′ W 92
Pueblo Mountains, *Oreg., U.S.* 42° 14′ N, 118° 57′ W 90
Pueblo Nuevo, *Mex.* 23° 23′ N, 105° 21′ W 114
Pueblo Nuevo, *Peru* 16° 44′ S, 72° 27′ W 137
Pueblo Nuevo, *Venez.* 11° 57′ N, 69° 57′ W 136
Pueblo Nuevo Tiquisate, *Guatemala* 14° 15′ N, 91° 22′ W 115
Puelches, *Arg.* 38° 9′ S, 65° 56′ W 134
Puente de Ixtla, *Mex.* 18° 35′ N, 99° 21′ W 114
Puente la Reina (Gares), *Sp.* 42° 39′ N, 1° 49′ W 164
Puente-Genil, *Sp.* 37° 23′ N, 4° 47′ W 164
Pu'er, *China* 22° 56′ N, 101° 3′ E 202
Puertecitos, *Mex.* 30° 14′ N, 114° 41′ W 92
Puerto Acosta, *Bol.* 15° 34′ S, 69° 15′ W 137
Puerto Aisén, *Chile* 45° 25′ S, 72° 59′ W 123
Puerto Alegre, *Peru* 8° 44′ S, 74° 14′ W 130
Puerto Alfonso, *Col.* 2° 13′ S, 71° 2′ W 136
Puerto América, *Peru* 4° 42′ S, 77° 3′ W 130
Puerto Ángel, *Mex.* 15° 39′ N, 96° 31′ W 112
Puerto Arista, *Mex.* 15° 58′ N, 93° 50′ W 115
Puerto Armuelles, *Pan.* 8° 18′ N, 82° 51′ W 115
Puerto Asís, *Col.* 0° 27′ N, 76° 32′ W 136
Puerto Aurora, *Peru* 2° 12′ S, 74° 18′ W 136
Puerto Ayacucho, *Venez.* 5° 37′ N, 67° 32′ W 136
Puerto Ayora, *Ecua.* 0° 45′ N, 90° 20′ W 130
Puerto Bahía Negra, *Parag.* 20° 12′ S, 58° 14′ W 132
Puerto Baquerizo Moreno, *Ecua.* 0° 57′ N, 89° 27′ W 130
Puerto Barrios, *Guatemala* 15° 42′ N, 88° 36′ W 115
Puerto Belgrano, *Arg.* 38° 53′ S, 62° 6′ W 139
Puerto Bermúdez, *Peru* 10° 19′ S, 74° 54′ W 137
Puerto Berrío, *Col.* 6° 28′ N, 74° 26′ W 136
Puerto Boy, *Col.* 0° 11′ N, 74° 53′ W 136
Puerto Cabello, *Venez.* 10° 27′ N, 68° 1′ W 136
Puerto Cabezas, *Nicar.* 14° 2′ N, 83° 24′ W 115
Puerto Cahuinari, *Col.* 1° 26′ S, 70° 44′ W 136
Puerto Capaz see El Jabha, *Mor.* 35° 12′ N, 4° 40′ W 150
Puerto Carabuco, *Bol.* 15° 44′ S, 69° 5′ W 137
Puerto Carlos, *Col.* 1° 41′ S, 71° 52′ W 136
Puerto Carlos, *Peru* 12° 57′ S, 70° 15′ W 137
Puerto Carranza, *Col.* 2° 38′ S, 70° 11′ W 136
Puerto Carreño, *Col.* 6° 9′ N, 67° 25′ W 136
Puerto Chicama, *Peru* 7° 43′ S, 79° 26′ W 130
Puerto Coig, *Arg.* 50° 54′ S, 69° 13′ W 134
Puerto Colombia, *Col.* 10° 57′ N, 74° 57′ W 136
Puerto Copal, *Peru* 3° 1′ S, 74° 46′ W 136
Puerto Córdoba, *Col.* 1° 20′ S, 69° 53′ W 136
Puerto Cortés, *Hond.* 15° 49′ N, 87° 56′ W 116
Puerto Cumarebo, *Venez.* 11° 27′ N, 69° 22′ W 136
Puerto Curaray, *Peru* 2° 26′ S, 74° 7′ W 136
Puerto de Lomas, *Peru* 15° 34′ S, 74° 50′ W 137
Puerto de Luna, *N. Mex., U.S.* 34° 49′ N, 104° 37′ W 92
Puerto de Nutrias, *Venez.* 8° 5′ N, 69° 20′ W 136
Puerto de Santa Cruz, *Sp.* 39° 18′ N, 5° 51′ W 164
Puerto Deseado, *Arg.* 47° 43′ S, 65° 55′ W 134
Puerto El Triunfo, *El Salv.* 13° 16′ N, 88° 34′ W 115
Puerto Escondido, *Col.* 9° 2′ N, 76° 15′ W 136
Puerto Escondido, *Mex.* 15° 52′ N, 97° 6′ W 112
Puerto Estrella, *Col.* 12° 19′ N, 71° 20′ W 136
Puerto Francisco de Orellana, *Ecua.* 0° 30′ N, 77° 2′ W 136
Puerto Frey, *Bol.* 14° 44′ S, 61° 10′ W 132
Puerto General Ovando, *Bol.* 9° 51′ S, 65° 39′ W 137
Puerto Grether, *Bol.* 17° 14′ S, 64° 23′ W 137
Puerto Heath, *Bol.* 12° 33′ S, 68° 39′ W 137
Puerto Huitoto, *Col.* 0° 16′ N, 74° 3′ W 136
Puerto Inírida, *Col.* 3° 44′ N, 67° 53′ W 136
Puerto Iradier, *Equatorial Guinea* 1° 6′ N, 9° 43′ E 218
Puerto Jiménez, *C.R.* 8° 32′ N, 83° 19′ W 115
Puerto La Concordia, *Col.* 2° 38′ N, 72° 49′ W 136
Puerto La Cruz, *Venez.* 10° 12′ N, 64° 39′ W 130
Puerto La Esperanza, *Parag.* 22° 0′ S, 58° 3′ W 132
Puerto La Paz, *Arg.* 22° 29′ S, 62° 24′ W 132
Puerto La Victoria, *Parag.* 22° 17′ S, 57° 58′ W 132
Puerto Lápice, *Sp.* 39° 19′ N, 3° 29′ W 164
Puerto Leguízamo, *Col.* 0° 11′ N, 74° 47′ W 136
Puerto Leigue, *Bol.* 14° 19′ S, 64° 53′ W 137
Puerto Lempira, *Hond.* 15° 10′ N, 83° 47′ W 115
Puerto Libertad, *Mex.* 29° 55′ N, 112° 41′ W 92
Puerto Limón, *Col.* 1° 0′ N, 76° 32′ W 136
Puerto Limón, *C.R.* 9° 45′ N, 83° 4′ W 123
Puerto Limón, *C.R.* 9° 59′ N, 83° 2′ W 115
Puerto Lobos, *Mex.* 30° 16′ N, 112° 51′ W 92
Puerto Lobos (Arroyo Verde), *Arg.* 42° 2′ S, 65° 5′ W 134
Puerto López, *Col.* 4° 6′ N, 72° 59′ W 136
Puerto López (Tucacas), *Col.* 11° 56′ N, 71° 18′ W 136
Puerto Lumbreras, *Sp.* 37° 33′ N, 1° 50′ W 164
Puerto Macaco, *Col.* 2° 0′ N, 71° 5′ W 136
Puerto Madryn, *Arg.* 42° 53′ S, 64° 59′ W 123
Puerto Maldonado, *Peru* 12° 39′ S, 69° 13′ W 137
Puerto Mamoré, *Bol.* 16° 43′ S, 64° 51′ W 137
Puerto Miraña, *Col.* 1° 21′ S, 70° 20′ W 136
Puerto Mirando, *Venez.* 10° 46′ N, 71° 34′ W 116
Puerto Montt, *Chile* 41° 29′ S, 72° 58′ W 134
Puerto Morazán, *Nicar.* 12° 50′ N, 87° 10′ W 115
Puerto Morelos, *Mex.* 20° 50′ N, 86° 56′ W 116
Puerto Mutis see Bahía Solano, *Col.* 6° 12′ N, 77° 25′ W 136
Puerto Napo, *Ecua.* 1° 7′ S, 77° 52′ W 136
Puerto Naré, *Col.* 6° 9′ N, 74° 37′ W 136
Puerto Natales, *Chile* 51° 39′ S, 72° 29′ W 134
Puerto Nuevo, *Col.* 5° 43′ N, 70° 1′ W 136
Puerto Obaldía, *Col.* 8° 40′ N, 77° 25′ W 115
Puerto Olaya, *Col.* 6° 29′ N, 74° 22′ W 136
Puerto Páez, *Venez.* 6° 14′ N, 67° 23′ W 136
Puerto Pardo, *Peru* 12° 33′ S, 68° 48′ W 137
Puerto Patiño, *Bol.* 16° 36′ S, 65° 50′ W 137
Puerto Peñasco, *Mex.* 31° 18′ N, 113° 33′ W 92
Puerto Pinasco, *Parag.* 22° 36′ S, 57° 52′ W 132
Puerto Piracuacito, *Arg.* 28° 11′ S, 59° 10′ W 139
Puerto Píritu, *Venez.* 10° 3′ N, 65° 3′ W 116
Puerto Pizarro, *Col.* 0° 16′ N, 73° 28′ W 136
Puerto Plata, *Dom. Rep.* 19° 46′ N, 70° 41′ W 116
Puerto Portillo, *Peru* 9° 46′ S, 72° 46′ W 137
Puerto Prado, *Peru* 11° 11′ S, 74° 20′ W 137
Puerto Princesa, *Philippines* 9° 44′ N, 118° 45′ E 203
Puerto Príncipe, *Col.* 0° 27′ N, 75° 9′ W 136
Puerto Real, *Sp.* 36° 31′ N, 6° 12′ W 164
Puerto Rico, *Bol.* 11° 8′ S, 67° 35′ W 137
Puerto Rico, *Col.* 2° 33′ N, 74° 14′ W 136
Puerto Rico, adm. division, *U.S.* 18° 13′ N, 66° 29′ W 118
Puerto Rico Trench, *North Atlantic Ocean* 19° 41′ N, 63° 30′ W 253
Puerto Rondón, *Col.* 6° 19′ N, 71° 7′ W 136
Puerto Salgar, *Col.* 5° 28′ N, 74° 38′ W 136
Puerto Salvatierra, *Peru* 3° 34′ S, 76° 31′ W 136
Puerto San Augustín, *Peru* 2° 45′ S, 71° 25′ W 136
Puerto San Francisquito, *Mex.* 28° 24′ N, 112° 54′ W 92
Puerto San José, *Guatemala* 13° 56′ N, 90° 50′ W 115
Puerto San Julián, *Arg.* 49° 17′ S, 67° 46′ W 134
Puerto Sandino, *Nicar.* 12° 10′ N, 86° 44′ W 115
Puerto Santa Cruz, *Arg.* 50° 0′ S, 68° 33′ W 134
Puerto Saucedo, *Bol.* 14° 1′ S, 62° 50′ W 130
Puerto Siles, *Bol.* 12° 47′ S, 65° 7′ W 137
Puerto Socorro, *Col.* 2° 48′ S, 69° 59′ W 136
Puerto Tejada, *Col.* 3° 14′ N, 76° 25′ W 136
Puerto Tirol, *Arg.* 27° 22′ S, 59° 6′ W 139
Puerto Tres Palmas, *Parag.* 21° 43′ S, 57° 59′ W 132
Puerto Umbría, *Col.* 0° 47′ N, 76° 35′ W 136
Puerto Vallarta, *Mex.* 20° 35′ N, 105° 16′ W 114
Puerto Velarde, *Bol.* 16° 31′ S, 63° 41′ W 137
Puerto Velasco Ibarra, *Ecua.* 1° 22′ S, 90° 33′ W 130
Puerto Villamil, *Ecua.* 0° 55′ N, 90° 57′ W 130
Puerto Villarroel, *Bol.* 16° 54′ S, 64° 49′ W 137
Puerto Villazón, *Bol.* 13° 29′ S, 61° 56′ W 130
Puerto Wilches, *Col.* 7° 20′ N, 73° 52′ W 136
Puertollano, *Sp.* 38° 41′ N, 4° 7′ W 164
Pueşti, *Rom.* 46° 24′ N, 27° 30′ E 156
Puesto Arturo, *Peru* 1° 51′ S, 73° 20′ W 136
Pugachev, *Russ.* 52° 1′ N, 48° 48′ E 158
Pugal, *India* 28° 30′ N, 72° 49′ E 186
Puget Sound 47° 46′ N, 123° 32′ W 80
Puget-Théniers, *Fr.* 43° 57′ N, 6° 52′ E 167
Puglia, adm. division, *It.* 41° 12′ N, 15° 15′ E 156
Pugŏ, *N. Korea* 42° 2′ N, 129° 58′ E 200
Puhja, *Est.* 58° 19′ N, 26° 18′ E 166
Pui, *Rom.* 45° 31′ N, 23° 6′ E 168
Puig Major, peak, *Sp.* 39° 47′ N, 2° 45′ E 164
Puigcerdà, *Fr.* 42° 25′ N, 1° 55′ E 164
Puigmal d'Err, peak, *Sp.* 42° 22′ N, 2° 3′ E 164
Puig-reig, *Sp.* 41° 57′ N, 1° 52′ E 164
Puiseaux, *Fr.* 48° 11′ N, 2° 28′ E 163
Pujehun, *Sierra Leone* 7° 21′ N, 11° 44′ W 222
Pujiang, *China* 29° 30′ N, 119° 55′ E 198
Pujŏn, *N. Korea* 40° 26′ N, 127° 37′ E 200
Pujŏn, river, *N. Korea* 40° 54′ N, 127° 33′ E 200
Puka, *Est.* 58° 3′ N, 26° 13′ E 166
Puka see Pukë, *Alban.* 42° 2′ N, 19° 53′ E 168
Pukaki, Lake, *N.Z.* 44° 7′ S, 169° 48′ E 240
Pukapuka Atoll (Danger Islands), *South Pacific Ocean* 10° 35′ S, 167° 12′ W 238
Pukapuka, island, *Fr.* 14° 46′ S, 138° 53′ W 252
Pukari, *Russ.* 65° 58′ N, 30° 1′ E 152
Pukaskwa National Park, *Can.* 48° 16′ N, 88° 31′ W 94

Pukatawagan, *Can.* 55°45′ N, 101°17′ W 108
Pukchin, *N. Korea* 40°12′ N, 125°44′ E 200
Pukch'ŏng, *N. Korea* 40°14′ N, 128°21′ E 200
Pukë (Puka), *Alban.* 42°2′ N, 19°53′ E 168
Pukeashun Mountain, peak, *Can.* 51°12′ N, 119°19′ W 90
Pukehou, *N.Z.* 39°51′ S, 176°38′ E 240
Pukekohe, *N.Z.* 37°13′ S, 174°53′ E 240
Pukemiro, *N.Z.* 37°38′ S, 175°0′ E 240
Pukovac, *Serb.* 43°10′ N, 21°50′ E 168
Puksa, *Russ.* 62°35′ N, 40°20′ E 154
Puksoozero, *Russ.* 62°36′ N, 40°34′ E 154
Pula, Capo di, *It.* 38°53′ N, 8°59′ E 156
Pulacayo, *Bol.* 20°28′ S, 66°40′ W 137
Pulaj, *Alban.* 41°53′ N, 19°23′ E 168
Pulandian, *China* 39°25′ N, 122°2′ E 198
Pulap Atoll 7°29′ N, 150°1′ E 192
Pular, Cerro, peak, *Chile* 24°12′ S, 68°12′ W 132
Pulaski, *N.Y., U.S.* 43°34′ N, 76°8′ W 94
Pulaski, *Tenn., U.S.* 35°10′ N, 87°1′ W 96
Pulaski, *Va., U.S.* 37°2′ N, 80°47′ W 96
Pulaukijang, *Indonesia* 0°42′ N, 103°11′ E 196
Pulheim, *Ger.* 51°0′ N, 6°47′ E 167
Puli, *Taiwan, China* 23°52′ N, 120°57′ E 198
Pulkkila, *Fin.* 64°16′ N, 25°50′ E 152
Pullen Island, island, *Antarctica* 73°2′ S, 63°3′ W 248
Pullman, *Mich., U.S.* 42°28′ N, 86°5′ W 102
Pullman, *Wash., U.S.* 46°44′ N, 117°10′ W 90
Pullo, *Peru* 15°15′ S, 73°50′ W 137
Pulog, Mount, peak, *Philippines* 16°35′ N, 120°49′ E 203
Pulozero, *Russ.* 68°21′ N, 33°18′ E 152
Pulpí, *Sp.* 37°24′ N, 1°44′ W 164
Púlpito, Punta, *Mex.* 26°33′ N, 111°32′ W 112
Pülümür, *Turk.* 39°29′ N, 39°53′ E 195
Puluwat Atoll 6°50′ N, 149°57′ E 192
Puma Yumco, lake, *China* 28°40′ N, 90°6′ E 197
Pummanki, *Russ.* 69°46′ N, 31°53′ E 152
Pumpsaint, *U.K.* 52°1′ N, 3°56′ W 162
Puna, *Arg.* 27°47′ S, 62°30′ W 139
Puná, Isla, island, *Ecua.* 3°11′ S, 80°46′ W 130
Puna, region, *Hawai'i, U.S.* 19°32′ N, 155°23′ W 99
Punakha, *Bhutan* 27°37′ N, 89°51′ E 197
Punata, *Bol.* 17°35′ S, 65°47′ W 137
Punch, *India* 33°46′ N, 74°6′ E 186
Punchaw, *Can.* 53°27′ N, 123°15′ W 108
Pune, *India* 18°30′ N, 73°53′ E 188
Pungan, *Uzb.* 40°47′ N, 70°55′ E 197
P'ungch'ŏn see Kwail, *N. Korea* 38°25′ N, 125°1′ E 200
Punggi, *S. Korea* 36°51′ N, 128°32′ E 200
Punilla, Cordillera de la, *Chile* 29°37′ S, 71°36′ W 134
Punitaqui, *Chile* 30°50′ S, 71°17′ W 134
Punjab, adm. division, *India* 30°2′ N, 74°58′ E 197
Punjab, adm. division, *Pak.* 30°51′ N, 71°22′ E 186
Punkaharju, *Fin.* 61°47′ N, 29°18′ E 166
Puno, *Peru* 15°53′ S, 70°1′ W 137
Puno, adm. division, *Peru* 15°4′ S, 70°39′ W 137
Punta Abreojos, *Mex.* 26°44′ N, 113°38′ W 112
Punta Alta, *Arg.* 38°49′ S, 62°4′ W 139
Punta Arenas, *Chile* 53°6′ S, 70°56′ W 134
Punta Cardón, *Venez.* 11°38′ N, 70°13′ W 136
Punta de Bombón, *Peru* 17°13′ S, 71°46′ W 137
Punta de Díaz, *Chile* 28°3′ S, 70°38′ W 132
Punta del Este, *Uru.* 34°58′ S, 54°58′ W 139
Punta Gorda, *Fla., U.S.* 26°55′ N, 82°2′ W 105
Punta Gorda, *Nicar.* 11°31′ N, 83°48′ W 115
Punta Gorda, river, *Nicar.* 11°45′ N, 84°16′ W 115
Punta Indio, *Arg.* 35°21′ S, 57°18′ W 139
Punta La Marmora, peak, *It.* 39°58′ N, 9°14′ E 156
Punta Maldonado, *Mex.* 16°19′ N, 98°33′ W 112
Punta Prieta, *Mex.* 28°54′ N, 114°21′ W 92
Punta Skala, *Croatia* 44°11′ N, 15°8′ E 156
Puntarenas, *C.R.* 9°59′ N, 84°50′ W 115
Punto Fijo, *Venez.* 11°41′ N, 70°14′ W 136
Puntzi Lake, lake, *Can.* 52°10′ N, 124°26′ W 108
Punxsutawney, *Pa., U.S.* 40°56′ N, 78°59′ W 94
Puok, *Cambodia* 13°28′ N, 103°46′ E 202
Puokio, *Fin.* 64°44′ N, 27°16′ E 152
Puolanka, *Fin.* 64°50′ N, 27°36′ E 152
Puqi, *China* 29°38′ N, 113°51′ E 198
Puquina, *Peru* 16°40′ S, 71°11′ W 137
Puquio, *Peru* 14°43′ S, 74°9′ W 137
Puračić, *Bosn. and Herzg.* 44°33′ N, 18°28′ E 168
Puranpur, *India* 28°31′ N, 80°7′ E 197
Purari, river, *P.N.G.* 7°1′ S, 144°29′ E 192
Purcell, *Okla., U.S.* 35°0′ N, 97°22′ W 92
Purcell Mountains, *Can.* 48°59′ N, 116°12′ W 108
Purchena, *Sp.* 37°19′ N, 2°22′ W 164
Purdy Islands, *Bismarck Sea* 3°3′ S, 144°14′ E 192
Purépero, *Mex.* 19°53′ N, 102°1′ W 114
Puri, *Angola* 7°43′ S, 15°40′ E 218
Puri, *India* 19°48′ N, 85°49′ E 188
Purificación, *Mex.* 19°42′ N, 104°39′ W 114
Purikari Neem, *Est.* 59°39′ N, 25°21′ E 166
Purmerend, *Neth.* 52°30′ N, 4°56′ E 163
Purnema, *Russ.* 64°24′ N, 37°21′ E 154
Purnia, *India* 25°45′ N, 87°28′ E 197
Purnululu National Park, *Austral.* 17°30′ S, 128°16′ E 238
Pursat, *Cambodia* 12°35′ N, 103°48′ E 202
Puruándiro, *Mex.* 20°4′ N, 101°31′ W 114
Puruê, river, *Braz.* 2°12′ S, 68°30′ W 136
Purukcahu, *Indonesia* 0°34′ N, 114°29′ E 192
Purulia, *India* 23°20′ N, 86°21′ E 197
Purus, river, *Braz.* 9°3′ S, 69°52′ W 132
Purvis, *Miss., U.S.* 31°7′ N, 89°24′ W 103
Puryŏng, *N. Korea* 42°3′ N, 129°41′ E 200
Pusad, *India* 19°53′ N, 77°34′ E 188
Pusan see Busan, *S. Korea* 35°6′ N, 129°3′ E 200
Pushkin, *Russ.* 59°41′ N, 30°21′ E 152
Pushkino, *Russ.* 51°12′ N, 46°55′ E 158
Pushkinskiye Gory, *Russ.* 57°1′ N, 28°53′ E 166
Pusi, *Peru* 15°30′ S, 69°58′ W 137
Püspökladány, *Hung.* 47°18′ N, 21°7′ E 168
Püssi, *Est.* 59°20′ N, 27°2′ E 166
Pusticamica, Lac, lake, *Can.* 49°19′ N, 77°6′ W 110
Pustoshka, *Russ.* 56°19′ N, 29°28′ E 166
Pusztamérges, *Hung.* 46°19′ N, 19°41′ E 168
Puta, *Azerb.* 40°19′ N, 49°38′ E 195
Putahow Lake, lake, *Can.* 59°50′ N, 101°15′ W 108
Putao, *Myanmar* 27°23′ N, 97°19′ E 190
Putari, Lagoa, lake, *Braz.* 13°3′ S, 61°54′ W 130
Putaruru, *N.Z.* 38°3′ S, 175°46′ E 240
Putian, *China* 25°26′ N, 119°3′ E 198
Putilovo, *Russ.* 59°22′ N, 44°35′ E 154
Putina, *Peru* 14°57′ S, 69°54′ W 137
Put-in-Bay, *Ohio, U.S.* 41°39′ N, 82°48′ W 102
Putla, *Mex.* 17°0′ N, 97°56′ W 112
Put'Lenina, *Russ.* 68°28′ N, 107°40′ E 173
Putna, *Rom.* 47°52′ N, 25°37′ E 156
Putnam, *Conn., U.S.* 41°54′ N, 71°55′ W 104
Putnam, *Dem. Rep. of the Congo* 1°25′ N, 28°34′ E 224
Putorana, Plato, *Russ.* 68°46′ N, 91°28′ E 169
Putorino, *N.Z.* 39°8′ S, 177°1′ E 240
Putre, *Chile* 18°14′ S, 69°37′ W 137
Putsonderwater, *S. Af.* 29°12′ S, 21°50′ E 227
Puttalam, *Sri Lanka* 8°2′ N, 79°51′ E 188
Putten, *Neth.* 52°14′ N, 5°36′ E 163
Puttur, *India* 12°44′ N, 75°12′ E 188
Puttur, *India* 13°27′ N, 79°33′ E 188
Putu Range, *Liberia* 5°32′ N, 7°50′ W 222
Putumayo, *Ecua.* 9°535′ N, 75°53′ W 136
Putumayo, adm. division, *Col.* 0°34′ N, 77°9′ W 136
Putumayo, river, *South America* 2°52′ S, 73°10′ W 122
Putussibau, *Indonesia* 0°52′ N, 112°51′ E 192
Pu'u Kūlua, peak, *Hawai'i, U.S.* 19°31′ N, 155°29′ W 99
Pu'u Lehua, peak, *Hawai'i, U.S.* 19°33′ N, 155°51′ W 99
Pu'u Maka'ala, peak, *Hawai'i, U.S.* 19°31′ N, 155°17′ W 99
Pu'u Mākanaka, peak, *Hawai'i, U.S.* 19°50′ N, 155°29′ W 99
Pu'uhonua O Hōnaunau National Historical Park (City of Refuge National Historical Park), *Hawai'i, U.S.* 19°24′ N, 155°57′ W 99
Pu'ukoholā Heiau National Historic Site, *Hawai'i, U.S.* 20°1′ N, 155°52′ W 99
Puulavesi, lake, *Fin.* 61°41′ N, 26°26′ E 166
Puumala, *Fin.* 61°31′ N, 28°9′ E 166
Pu'uomahuka Heiau, site, *Hawai'i, U.S.* 21°38′ N, 158°6′ W 99
Puvirnituq, *Can.* 60°5′ N, 77°15′ W 73
Puxian, *China* 36°24′ N, 111°5′ E 198
Puyallup, *Wash., U.S.* 47°9′ N, 122°18′ W 100
Puyang, *China* 35°41′ N, 114°58′ E 198
Puylaurens, *Fr.* 43°34′ N, 2°0′ E 150
Puyo, *Ecua.* 1°36′ S, 78°4′ W 136
Puyoô-Bellocq-Ramous, *Fr.* 43°32′ N, 0°55′ E 164
Puysegur Point, *N.Z.* 46°21′ S, 166°20′ E 240
Pwani, adm. division, *Tanzania* 7°19′ S, 38°26′ E 224
Pweto, *Zambia* 8°29′ S, 28°52′ E 224
Pwllheli, *U.K.* 52°53′ N, 4°25′ W 150
Pyakupur, river, *Russ.* 63°23′ N, 73°59′ E 169
Pyalitsa, *Russ.* 66°14′ N, 39°28′ E 154
Pyal'ma, *Russ.* 62°24′ N, 35°58′ E 154
P'yana, river, *Russ.* 55°26′ N, 44°27′ E 154
Pyasina, river, *Russ.* 71°11′ N, 90°11′ E 160
Pyasino, Ozero, lake, *Russ.* 69°58′ N, 86°36′ E 169
Pyasinskiy Zaliv 73°39′ N, 78°4′ E 160
Pyatigorsk, *Russ.* 44°4′ N, 43°6′ E 158
Pyatīmarskoe, *Kaz.* 49°31′ N, 50°28′ E 158
P'yatykhatky, *Ukr.* 48°24′ N, 33°40′ E 156
Pyay, *Myanmar* 18°51′ N, 95°14′ E 202
Pydna 168 B.C., battle, *Gr.* 40°22′ N, 22°27′ E 156
Pyeongchang, *S. Korea* 37°21′ N, 128°23′ E 200
Pyeonghae, *S. Korea* 36°43′ N, 129°28′ E 200
Pyeongtaek, *S. Korea* 36°57′ N, 127°7′ E 200
Pyetrikaw, *Belarus* 52°8′ N, 28°34′ E 152
Pyhajärvi, lake, *Fin.* 60°59′ N, 21°55′ E 166
Pyhäjoki, *Fin.* 64°27′ N, 24°13′ E 152
Pyhämaa, *Fin.* 60°56′ N, 21°20′ E 166
Pyhäntä, *Fin.* 64°5′ N, 26°18′ E 152
Pyhäsalmi, *Fin.* 63°40′ N, 25°54′ E 152
Pyhäselkä, *Fin.* 62°24′ N, 29°56′ E 152
Pyhätunturi, peak, *Fin.* 66°59′ N, 26°56′ E 152
Pyhtää (Pyttis), *Fin.* 60°29′ N, 26°33′ E 166
Pyinkayaing, *Myanmar* 15°58′ N, 94°25′ E 202
Pyinmanaa, *Myanmar* 19°46′ N, 96°10′ E 202
Pyin-U-Lwin, *Myanmar* 22°1′ N, 96°27′ E 202
Pylos, ruin(s), *Ionian Sea* 36°56′ N, 21°34′ E 156
P'yŏngyang, *N. Korea* 39°1′ N, 125°45′ E 200
P'yŏngsan, *N. Korea* 38°20′ N, 126°24′ E 200
P'yŏngsan, *N. Korea* 40°36′ N, 127°57′ E 200
P'yŏng-sŏng, *N. Korea* 39°13′ N, 125°52′ E 200
P'yŏngwŏn, *N. Korea* 39°18′ N, 125°37′ E 200
Pyote, *Tex., U.S.* 31°31′ N, 103°8′ W 92
Pyramid Lake, *Nev., U.S.* 39°50′ N, 120°31′ W 80
Pyramid Mountain, peak, *Can.* 58°52′ N, 130°0′ W 108
Pyramid Peak, *Calif., U.S.* 36°22′ N, 116°40′ W 101
Pyrds Bay 68°45′ S, 74°19′ E 255
Pyrenees, *Sp.* 43°7′ N, 1°10′ E 165
Pyrrha, ruin(s), *Gr.* 39°8′ N, 26°12′ E 156
Pyryatyn, *Ukr.* 50°12′ N, 32°30′ E 158
Pyshchug, *Russ.* 58°52′ N, 45°43′ E 154
Pyshma, *Russ.* 56°58′ N, 63°13′ E 154
Pytalovo, *Russ.* 57°3′ N, 27°52′ E 166
Pýthion, *Gr.* 41°22′ N, 26°36′ E 156
Pyttegga, peak, *Nor.* 62°11′ N, 7°34′ E 152
Pyttis see Pyhtää, *Fin.* 60°29′ N, 26°33′ E 166
Pyu, *Myanmar* 18°30′ N, 96°25′ E 202

Q

Qaa, *Leb.* 34°22′ N, 36°29′ E 194
Qaanaaq (Thule) 77°32′ N, 69°13′ W 106
Qabanbay, *Kaz.* 45°49′ N, 80°36′ E 184
Qabb Ilyās, *Leb.* 33°47′ N, 35°49′ E 194
Qades, *Afghan.* 34°48′ N, 63°26′ E 186
Qāḑub, *Yemen* 12°37′ N, 53°50′ E 182
Qā'emshahr, *Iran* 36°30′ N, 52°55′ E 186
Qā'en, *Iran* 33°44′ N, 59°14′ E 180
Qagan Nur, *China* 43°18′ N, 112°57′ E 198
Qagan Nur, lake, *China* 43°18′ N, 114°17′ E 198
Qagcaka, *China* 32°33′ N, 81°52′ E 188
Qahar Youyi Houqi, *China* 41°28′ N, 113°11′ E 198
Qahar Youyi Zhongqi, *China* 41°15′ N, 112°36′ E 198
Qaharir, oil field, *Oman* 17°55′ N, 55°30′ E 182
Qaidam Pendi, *China* 37°41′ N, 91°15′ E 188
Qaidam, river, *China* 36°29′ N, 97°23′ E 188
Qairouan, *Tun.* 35°40′ N, 10°5′ E 156
Qaiyara, oil field, *Iraq* 35°43′ N, 43°6′ E 180
Qal 'at al Ḩasā, ruin(s), *Jordan* 30°49′ N, 35°53′ E 194
Qala 'en Nahl, *Sudan* 13°36′ N, 34°55′ E 182
Qalaa Kebira, *Tun.* 35°53′ N, 10°31′ E 156
Qalansīyah, *Yemen* 12°38′ N, 53°26′ E 182
Qalat, *Afghan.* 32°8′ N, 66°58′ E 186
Qal'at al Azlam, ruin(s), *Saudi Arabia* 27°3′ N, 35°55′ E 180
Qal'at al Maḑīq, *Syr.* 35°25′ N, 36°22′ E 194
Qal'at Bīshah, *Saudi Arabia* 19°59′ N, 42°37′ E 182
Qal'at Şahyūn, ruin(s), *Syr.* 35°34′ N, 36°0′ E 194
Qal'at Şālī', ruin(s), *Syr.* 35°33′ N, 35°59′ E 156
Qal'eh-ye Bar Panj, *Afghan.* 37°32′ N, 71°27′ E 184
Qal'eh-ye Now, *Afghan.* 34°57′ N, 63°11′ E 186
Qal'eh-ye Saber, *Afghan.* 34°3′ N, 69°4′ E 186
Qal'eh-ye Sarkari, *Afghan.* 35°51′ N, 67°16′ E 186
Qalhāt, *Oman* 22°40′ N, 59°20′ E 182
Qallabat, *Sudan* 12°56′ N, 36°6′ E 182
Qalqaman, *Kaz.* 51°57′ N, 76°4′ E 184
Qalqīlyah, *West Bank, Israel* 32°11′ N, 34°58′ E 194
Qaltat Bū as Su'ūd, spring, *Lib.* 27°39′ N, 18°13′ E 216
Qalzhat, *Kaz.* 43°32′ N, 80°35′ E 184
Qamar, Ghubbat al 15°45′ N, 52°17′ E 182
Qamashi, *Uzb.* 38°49′ N, 66°27′ E 197
Qamata, *S. Af.* 32°0′ S, 27°26′ E 227
Qamdo, *China* 31°10′ N, 97°6′ E 188
Qamīnis, *Lib.* 31°39′ N, 20°1′ E 216
Qamystybas, *Kaz.* 46°13′ N, 61°58′ E 184
Qanā, *Saudi Arabia* 27°44′ N, 41°30′ E 180
Qanawāt, *Syr.* 32°45′ N, 36°36′ E 194
Qandala, *Somalia* 11°23′ N, 49°50′ E 216
Qanshenggel, *Kaz.* 44°18′ N, 75°30′ E 184
Qapqal, *China* 43°49′ N, 81°18′ E 184
Qapshaghay, *Kaz.* 43°54′ N, 77°6′ E 184
Qaqortoq (Julianehåb) 60°47′ N, 46°7′ W 106
Qâra, *Egypt* 29°38′ N, 26°32′ E 180
Qarabey, *Kaz.* 48°46′ N, 53°2′ E 158
Qarabulaq, *Kaz.* 44°53′ N, 78°28′ E 184
Qarabulaq, *Kaz.* 42°32′ N, 69°49′ E 197
Qarabutaq, *Kaz.* 49°57′ N, 60°7′ E 158
Qaraghandy, *Kaz.* 49°49′ N, 73°9′ E 184
Qaraghandy, adm. division, *Kaz.* 48°3′ N, 68°19′ E 184
Qaraghayly, *Kaz.* 49°20′ N, 75°43′ E 184
Qārah, *Syr.* 34°9′ N, 36°44′ E 194
Qarah Bagh, *Afghan.* 33°9′ N, 68°10′ E 186
Qaraoba, *Kaz.* 47°0′ N, 56°14′ E 158
Qaraqalpakstan, *Uzb.* 44°49′ N, 56°10′ E 158
Qarasū, *Kaz.* 52°39′ N, 65°30′ E 184
Qaratal, river, *Kaz.* 45°59′ N, 77°1′ E 184
Qarataū, *Kaz.* 43°5′ N, 70°28′ E 184
Qarataū Zhotasy, *Kaz.* 42°32′ N, 70°38′ E 197
Qaratöbe, *Kaz.* 49°43′ N, 53°26′ E 158
Qaratoghay, *Kaz.* 48°24′ N, 84°29′ E 184
Qaraton, *Kaz.* 46°20′ N, 53°35′ E 158
Qaraūt, *Kaz.* 48°56′ N, 79°15′ E 184
Qarazhal, *Kaz.* 48°1′ N, 70°49′ E 184
Qarazhar, *Kaz.* 47°45′ N, 56°8′ E 158
Qardho, *Somalia* 9°30′ N, 49°7′ E 216
Qareh, river, *Iran* 38°31′ N, 47°57′ E 195
Qarghaly, *Kaz.* 50°18′ N, 57°17′ E 158
Qarn Alam, oil field, *Oman* 20°59′ N, 57°3′ E 182
Qarokŭl, lake, *Taj.* 39°5′ N, 73°10′ E 197
Qarqan, river, *China* 38°25′ N, 86°14′ E 188
Qarqan, river, *China* 38°31′ N, 85°47′ E 190
Qarqaraly, *Kaz.* 49°29′ N, 75°23′ E 184
Qarsaqbay, *Kaz.* 47°47′ N, 66°37′ E 184
Qarshi, *Uzb.* 38°51′ N, 65°48′ E 197
Qarṭabā, *Leb.* 34°5′ N, 35°51′ E 194
Qaryah al 'Ulyā, *Saudi Arabia* 27°32′ N, 47°40′ E 196
Qaryat abu Nujaym, *Lib.* 30°34′ N, 15°21′ E 216
Qaryat al Qaddā'iyah, *Lib.* 31°21′ N, 15°13′ E 216
Qaryat az Zuwaytīnah, *Lib.* 30°56′ N, 20°8′ E 216
Qaryat Shumaykh, *Lib.* 31°21′ N, 17°57′ E 216
Qarynzharyq, desert, *Kaz.* 42°45′ N, 53°31′ E 180
Qasigiannguit (Christianshåb) 68°47′ N, 51°7′ W 106
Qāsim, *Syr.* 32°59′ N, 36°3′ E 194
Qaskeleng, *Kaz.* 43°12′ N, 76°39′ E 184
Qaşr al Azraq, ruin(s), *Jordan* 31°51′ N, 36°46′ E 194
Qaşr al Ḩallābāt, ruin(s), *Jordan* 32°3′ N, 36°19′ E 194
Qaşr al Ḩammām, ruin(s), *Jordan* 31°31′ N, 36°8′ E 194
Qaşr al Kharānah, ruin(s), *Jordan* 31°43′ N, 36°26′ E 194
Qaşr al Mushayyish, ruin(s), *Jordan* 30°54′ N, 36°5′ E 194
Qaşr 'Amrah, ruin(s), *Jordan* 31°47′ N, 36°32′ E 194
Qaşr ash Shaqqah, ruin(s), *Lib.* 30°48′ N, 24°52′ E 180
Qaşr at Ţūbah, ruin(s), *Jordan* 31°18′ N, 36°31′ E 194
Qaşr Bū Hādī, ruin(s), *Lib.* 31°3′ N, 16°20′ E 216
Qaşr Burqu', ruin(s), *Jordan* 32°34′ N, 37°48′ E 180
Qaşr Farâfra, *Egypt* 27°2′ N, 27°58′ E 180
Qaşr Ḩamām, *Saudi Arabia* 20°47′ N, 45°51′ E 182
Qaşr Ibrîm, ruin(s), *Egypt* 22°30′ N, 31°51′ E 182
Qaşr-e Qand, *Iran* 26°11′ N, 60°50′ E 182
Qaşr-e Shīrīn, *Iran* 34°31′ N, 45°34′ E 180
Qasserine (Kasserine), *Tun.* 35°9′ N, 8°51′ E 156
Qatar 25°0′ N, 51°0′ E 196
Qattara Depression see Qaţâra, Munkhafad el, *Egypt* 29°32′ N, 26°42′ E 180
Qaţţâra, Munkhafad el (Qattara Depression), *Egypt* 29°32′ N, 26°42′ E 180
Qaţţâra, spring, *Egypt* 30°10′ N, 27°9′ E 180
Qax, *Azerb.* 41°25′ N, 46°55′ E 195
Qaynar, *Kaz.* 49°16′ N, 77°29′ E 184
Qazakh, *Azerb.* 41°5′ N, 45°21′ E 195
Qazaly, *Kaz.* 45°49′ N, 62°7′ E 184
Qazaq Shyghanaghy 42°42′ N, 51°45′ E 158
Qazbegi, *Ga.* 42°38′ N, 44°40′ E 195
Qazimämmäd, *Azerb.* 40°2′ N, 48°54′ E 195
Qazvīn, *Iran* 36°18′ N, 49°59′ E 195
Qazyqurt, *Kaz.* 41°48′ N, 69°27′ E 197
Qeissan, *Sudan* 10°47′ N, 34°48′ E 224
Qelibia, *Tun.* 36°51′ N, 11°5′ E 156
Qemult'a, *Asia* 42°26′ N, 43°47′ E 158
Qena, *Egypt* 26°12′ N, 32°40′ E 180
Qeqertarsuaq (Disko), island, *Den.* 69°31′ N, 62°11′ W 106
Qeqertarsuaq (Godhavn), *Den.* 69°15′ N, 53°30′ W 106
Qeqertarsuatsiaat (Fiskenæsset), *Den.* 63°6′ N, 50°43′ W 106
Qeren Naftali, peak, *Israel* 33°3′ N, 35°30′ E 194
Qerqenah Islands, *Tun.* 35°1′ N, 11°13′ E 214
Qertassi see Qirţâs, ruin(s), *Egypt* 23°39′ N, 32°43′ E 182
Qeshm, *Iran* 26°55′ N, 56°12′ E 196
Qeshm, island, *Iran* 26°36′ N, 56°3′ E 180
Qeys, island, *Iran* 26°22′ N, 53°46′ E 180
Qeysar, *Afghan.* 35°42′ N, 64°14′ E 186
Qezel Owzan, river, *Iran* 37°3′ N, 48°34′ E 195
Qian Gorlos, *China* 45°3′ N, 124°48′ E 198
Qian'an, *China* 44°58′ N, 124°4′ E 198
Qianxi, *China* 27°3′ N, 106°2′ E 198
Qianxian, *China* 34°31′ N, 108°15′ E 198
Qianyang, *China* 34°38′ N, 107°6′ E 198
Qiaowan, *China* 40°35′ N, 96°43′ E 188
Qibā', *Saudi Arabia* 27°22′ N, 44°23′ E 180
Qidaogou, *China* 41°32′ N, 126°21′ E 200
Qidong, *China* 31°48′ N, 121°38′ E 198
Qidong, *China* 26°44′ N, 112°8′ E 198
Qiemo, *China* 38°12′ N, 85°18′ E 190
Qijiang, *China* 28°58′ N, 106°38′ E 198
Qikiqtarjuaq (Broughton Island), *Can.* 67°30′ N, 63°52′ W 73
Qila Ladgasht, *Pak.* 27°49′ N, 63°0′ E 182
Qila Safed, *Pak.* 28°58′ N, 61°35′ E 182
Qilian Shan, *China* 39°14′ N, 96°43′ E 188
Qimen, *China* 29°51′ N, 117°40′ E 198
Qimusseriarsuaq 75°28′ N, 66°10′ W 106
Qin'an, *China* 34°51′ N, 105°40′ E 198
Qing, river, *China* 30°28′ N, 110°40′ E 198
Qing'an, *China* 46°53′ N, 127°30′ E 198
Qingchengzi, *China* 40°43′ N, 123°37′ E 200
Qingdao, *China* 36°5′ N, 120°24′ E 198
Qinggang, *China* 46°40′ N, 126°7′ E 198
Qinghai, adm. division, *China* 35°28′ N, 92°33′ E 188
Qinghai Hu, lake, *China* 36°45′ N, 99°5′ E 190
Qinghe, *China* 42°32′ N, 124°9′ E 200
Qingjian, *China* 37°8′ N, 110°11′ E 198
Qingjiang, *China* 28°1′ N, 115°30′ E 198
Qingshuihe, *China* 33°42′ N, 97°4′ E 188
Qingshuihe, *China* 39°54′ N, 111°40′ E 198
Qingtian, *China* 28°10′ N, 120°17′ E 198
Qingtongxia, *China* 38°4′ N, 106°3′ E 198
Qingxu, *China* 37°36′ N, 112°19′ E 198
Qingyang, *China* 36°2′ N, 107°54′ E 198
Qingyuan, *China* 42°6′ N, 124°52′ E 200
Qingyuan, *China* 23°40′ N, 113°2′ E 198
Qinhuangdao, *China* 39°56′ N, 119°36′ E 198
Qinxian, *China* 36°45′ N, 112°42′ E 198
Qinzhou, *China* 21°56′ N, 108°34′ E 198
Qionghai, *China* 19°14′ N, 110°31′ E 198
Qiqihar, *China* 47°21′ N, 123°59′ E 198
Qira, *China* 37°2′ N, 80°54′ E 184
Qir'awn, Bu'ayrat al, lake, *Leb.* 33°34′ N, 35°35′ E 194
Qirţâs (Qertassi), ruin(s), *Egypt* 23°39′ N, 32°43′ E 182
Qiryat Arba', *West Bank, Israel* 31°32′ N, 35°7′ E 194
Qiryat Ata, *Israel* 32°47′ N, 35°6′ E 194
Qiryat Gat, *Israel* 31°36′ N, 34°46′ E 194
Qiryat Mal'akhi, *Israel* 31°43′ N, 34°43′ E 194
Qiryat Motzkin, *Israel* 32°49′ N, 35°3′ E 194
Qiryat Shemona, *Israel* 33°12′ N, 35°34′ E 194
Qishn, *Yemen* 15°26′ N, 51°39′ E 182
Qitaihe, *China* 45°49′ N, 130°52′ E 238
Qixia, *China* 37°16′ N, 120°47′ E 198
Qīyaly, *Kaz.* 54°11′ N, 69°37′ E 184
Qiyang, *China* 26°38′ N, 111°48′ E 198
Qızılağac Körfäzi 39°6′ N, 48°36′ E 195
Qizilcha, *Uzb.* 40°42′ N, 66°11′ E 197
Qizilqum, *Uzb.* 41°58′ N, 64°9′ E 197
Qiziltepa, *Uzb.* 40°1′ N, 64°50′ E 197
Qobda, *Kaz.* 50°8′ N, 55°37′ E 158
Qoghaly, *Kaz.* 44°25′ N, 78°37′ E 184
Qoghir see K2, peak, *Pak.* 35°51′ N, 76°25′ E 186
Qom (Qum), *Iran* 34°39′ N, 50°50′ E 180
Qom, river, *Iran* 34°17′ N, 50°22′ E 180
Qomolangma see Everest, Mount, peak, *China-Nepal* 28°0′ N, 86°53′ E 197
Qonaqkänd, *Azerb.* 41°3′ N, 48°36′ E 195
Qonggyai, *China* 29°5′ N, 91°37′ E 197
Qongyrat, *Kaz.* 46°59′ N, 74°57′ E 184
Qoornoq 64°33′ N, 51°9′ W 106
Qoow, *Somalia* 11°11′ N, 48°57′ E 216

Qo'qon, *Uzb.* 40°31′ N, 70°55′ E 197
Qorakŭl, *Uzb.* 39°30′ N, 63°51′ E 197
Qorday, *Kaz.* 43°17′ N, 74°54′ E 184
Qorghalzhyn, *Kaz.* 50°36′ N, 69°50′ E 184
Qorovulbozor, *Uzb.* 39°31′ N, 64°51′ E 197
Qorsaq, *Kaz.* 47°0′ N, 53°18′ E 158
Qorveh, *Iran* 35°11′ N, 47°44′ E 180
Qoryaale, *Somalia* 7°28′ N, 49°11′ E 218
Qo'shrabot, *Uzb.* 40°15′ N, 66°39′ E 197
Qosköl, *Kaz.* 49°36′ N, 67°3′ E 184
Qosshaghyl, *Kaz.* 46°54′ N, 53°54′ E 158
Qostanay, *Kaz.* 53°13′ N, 63°35′ E 184
Qostanay, adm. division, *Kaz.* 52°2′ N, 60°25′ E 154
Qotanqaraghay, *Kaz.* 49°10′ N, 85°36′ E 184
Qoton, *Somalia* 9°30′ N, 50°27′ E 216
Qoţūr, *Iran* 38°27′ N, 44°23′ E 195
Qoubaiyat, *Leb.* 34°34′ N, 36°17′ E 194
Qsar Ghilan, *Tun.* 33°3′ N, 9°35′ E 216
Qsour Essaf, *Tun.* 35°26′ N, 10°58′ E 156
Qu' Appelle Valley Dam, *Can.* 50°47′ N, 106°26′ W 90
Quail Mountains, *Calif., U.S.* 35°39′ N, 117°1′ W 101
Quakenbrück, *Ger.* 52°40′ N, 7°58′ E 163
Qualicum Beach, *Can.* 49°20′ N, 124°26′ W 100
Quan Hoa, *Vietnam* 20°25′ N, 105°7′ E 202
Quanah, *Tex., U.S.* 34°16′ N, 99°45′ W 92
Quang Ngai, *Vietnam* 15°7′ N, 108°47′ E 202
Quang Tri, *Vietnam* 16°44′ N, 107°12′ E 202
Quannan, *China* 24°41′ N, 114°28′ E 198
Quantz Lake, *Can.* 51°7′ N, 85°56′ W 110
Quanzhou, *China* 25°59′ N, 111°4′ E 198
Quanzhou, *China* 24°58′ N, 118°36′ E 198
Qu'Appelle, *Can.* 50°32′ N, 103°54′ W 90
Qu'Appelle, river, *Can.* 50°40′ N, 103°48′ W 108
Quaraí, *Braz.* 30°25′ S, 56°24′ W 139
Quaraí, river, *South America* 30°8′ S, 57°11′ W 139
Quaritoufoulout, spring, *Mali* 16°14′ N, 3°17′ E 222
Quartz Hill, *Calif., U.S.* 34°39′ N, 118°14′ W 101
Quartzite Mountain, peak, *Nev., U.S.* 37°29′ N, 116°25′ W 92
Quartzsite, *Ariz., U.S.* 33°39′ N, 114°15′ W 101
Quatsino, *Can.* 50°32′ N, 127°38′ W 90
Quba, *Azerb.* 41°20′ N, 48°32′ E 195
Qūchān, *Iran* 37°4′ N, 58°29′ E 180
Que Son, *Vietnam* 15°40′ N, 108°13′ E 202
Québec, *Can.* 46°47′ N, 71°22′ W 94
Quebec, adm. division, *Can.* 53°50′ N, 76°4′ W 106
Quebracho, *Uru.* 31°57′ S, 57°52′ W 139
Quebracho Coto, *Arg.* 26°20′ S, 64°28′ W 132
Quedal, Cabo, *Chile* 41°11′ S, 75°34′ W 134
Queen Bess, Mount, peak, *Can.* 51°15′ N, 124°39′ W 90
Queen Charlotte Islands see Haida Gwaii, *Can.* 53°6′ N, 132°30′ W 98
Queen Charlotte Sound 51°46′ N, 130°1′ W 108
Queen City, *Tex., U.S.* 33°8′ N, 94°10′ W 103
Queen Elizabeth Islands, *Northwest Passage* 76°21′ N, 116°41′ W 106
Queen Elizabeth National Park, *Uganda* 0°25′ N, 30°10′ E 224
Queen Elizabeth Shelf, *Arctic Ocean* 80°30′ N, 100°0′ W 255
Queen Mary Coast, *Antarctica* 69°42′ S, 97°55′ E 248
Queen Maud Gulf 67°52′ N, 102°7′ W 106
Queen Maud Land, region, *Antarctica* 76°48′ S, 8°55′ E 248
Queen Maud Mountains, *Antarctica* 86°1′ S, 141°33′ W 248
Queen Victoria's Profile, site, *Hawai'i, U.S.* 21°55′ N, 159°27′ W 99
Queens Channel 75°46′ N, 100°43′ W 106
Queens Sound 51°48′ N, 128°37′ W 108
Queensbury, *U.K.* 53°46′ N, 1°52′ W 162
Queensland, adm. division, *Austral.* 23°32′ S, 140°33′ E 231
Queenstown, *Austral.* 42°3′ S, 145°33′ E 231
Queenstown, *N.Z.* 45°1′ S, 168°39′ E 240
Queenstown, *S. Af.* 31°54′ S, 26°45′ E 207
Queenstown, *S. Af.* 31°53′ S, 26°51′ E 227
Queets, *Wash., U.S.* 47°31′ N, 124°20′ W 100
Queets, river, *Wash., U.S.* 47°28′ N, 124°16′ W 100
Queimadas, *Braz.* 11°2′ S, 39°38′ W 132
Quela, *Angola* 9°17′ S, 17°4′ E 218
Quelimane, *Mozambique* 17°55′ S, 36°52′ E 224
Quellón, *Chile* 43°6′ S, 73°39′ W 134
Quelo, *Angola* 6°28′ S, 12°48′ E 218
Quemado, *N. Mex., U.S.* 34°19′ N, 108°29′ W 92
Quemado, *Tex., U.S.* 28°56′ N, 100°37′ W 92
Quemado de Güines, *Cuba* 22°47′ N, 80°15′ W 116
Quembo, river, *Angola* 13°59′ S, 19°30′ E 220
Quemoy see Kinmen, island, *Taiwan, China* 24°23′ N, 118°32′ E 198
Quemú Quemú, *Arg.* 36°4′ S, 63°33′ W 139
Quentin, *Miss., U.S.* 31°29′ N, 90°45′ W 103
Quequén, *Arg.* 38°31′ S, 58°43′ W 139
Quequeña, *Peru* 16°36′ S, 71°26′ W 137
Querco, *Peru* 13°53′ S, 74°52′ W 137
Quercy, *Fr.* 44°40′ N, 1°10′ E 165
Querétaro, *Mex.* 20°34′ N, 100°27′ W 114
Querétaro, adm. division, *Mex.* 20°44′ N, 100°33′ W 114
Quesada, *Sp.* 37°51′ N, 3°5′ W 164
Queshan, *China* 32°46′ N, 114°2′ E 198
Quesnel, *Can.* 52°59′ N, 122°21′ W 106
Quesnel Lake, lake, *Can.* 52°41′ N, 121°20′ W 108
Quetico Lake, lake, *Can.* 48°32′ N, 92°24′ W 94
Quetta, *Pak.* 30°13′ N, 67°5′ E 186
Quetzaltenango, *Guatemala* 14°50′ N, 91°31′ W 115
Queulat National Park, *Chile* 44°30′ S, 72°44′ W 122
Queule, *Chile* 39°18′ S, 73°12′ W 134
Quevedo, *Ecua.* 1°8′ S, 79°37′ W 130
Quevedo, Península de, *Mex.* 23°56′ N, 108°18′ W 112
Quévillon, Lac, lake, *Can.* 49°2′ N, 77°31′ W 94
Quezon, *Philippines* 9°15′ N, 118°2′ E 203
Quezon City, *Philippines* 14°43′ N, 121°1′ E 203
Qufār, *Saudi Arabia* 27°24′ N, 41°40′ E 180
Qufu, *China* 35°34′ N, 116°54′ E 198
Qui Nhon, *Vietnam* 13°47′ N, 109°12′ E 202
Quibala, *Angola* 10°45′ S, 14°58′ E 220
Quibaxe, *Angola* 8°30′ S, 14°36′ E 220
Quibdó, *Col.* 5°40′ N, 76°38′ W 136
Quibell, *Can.* 49°57′ N, 93°26′ W 90
Quiberon, Presqu'île de, *Fr.* 47°32′ N, 3°9′ W 150
Quicabo, *Angola* 8°20′ S, 13°47′ E 220
Quick, *Can.* 54°35′ N, 126°58′ W 108
Quigley, *Can.* 56°5′ N, 110°55′ W 108
Quiĭama National Park, *Angola* 9°57′ S, 13°20′ E 206
Quiindy, *Parag.* 26°0′ S, 57°14′ W 139
Quilá, *Mex.* 24°23′ N, 107°13′ W 112
Quilán, Isla, island, *Chile* 43°34′ S, 74°35′ W 134
Quilcene, *Wash., U.S.* 47°48′ N, 122°53′ W 100
Quilengues, *Angola* 14°6′ S, 14°3′ E 220
Quill Lake, *Can.* 52°4′ N, 104°16′ W 108
Quillabamba, *Peru* 12°50′ S, 72°43′ W 137
Quillacollo, *Bol.* 17°29′ S, 66°13′ W 137
Quillagua, *Chile* 21°40′ S, 69°33′ W 137
Quillaicillo, *Chile* 31°24′ S, 71°37′ W 134
Quillan, *Fr.* 42°52′ N, 2°9′ E 164
Quilpie, *Austral.* 26°37′ S, 144°15′ E 231
Quilpué, *Chile* 33°3′ S, 71°26′ W 134
Quimbele, *Angola* 6°32′ S, 16°10′ E 218
Quime, *Bol.* 17°5′ S, 67°18′ W 137
Quimili, *Arg.* 27°38′ S, 62°25′ W 139
Quimistán, *Hond.* 15°22′ N, 88°22′ W 116
Quinault, *Wash., U.S.* 47°26′ N, 123°51′ W 100
Quinault, river, *Wash., U.S.* 47°22′ N, 124°9′ W 100
Quince Mil, *Peru* 13°15′ S, 70°44′ W 137
Quincy, *Fla., U.S.* 30°34′ N, 84°35′ W 96
Quincy, *Mass., U.S.* 42°14′ N, 71°1′ W 104
Quincy, *Mich., U.S.* 41°56′ N, 84°54′ W 102
Quincy, *Mo., U.S.* 39°55′ N, 91°25′ W 94
Quincy, *Oreg., U.S.* 46°7′ N, 123°10′ W 100
Quines, *Arg.* 32°15′ S, 65°48′ W 134
Quinga, *Mozambique* 15°49′ S, 40°11′ E 224
Quinhagak, *Alas., U.S.* 59°41′ N, 161°45′ W 106
Quinigua, Serranía, peak, *Venez.* 4°19′ N, 65°41′ W 136
Quintana Roo, adm. division, *Mex.* 19°18′ N, 88°58′ W 115
Quintanar de la Orden, *Sp.* 39°35′ N, 3°2′ W 164
Quinter, *Kans., U.S.* 39°3′ N, 100°14′ W 90
Quintette Mountain, peak, *Can.* 54°51′ N, 120°59′ W 108
Quintin, *Fr.* 48°24′ N, 2°55′ W 150
Quinto, *Sp.* 41°24′ N, 0°31′ E 164
Quinzau, *Angola* 6°50′ S, 12°43′ E 218
Quionga, *Mozambique* 10°37′ S, 40°33′ E 224
Quiquibey, river, *Bol.* 14°48′ S, 67°39′ W 137
Quiriguá, ruin(s), *Guatemala* 15°15′ N, 89°10′ W 115
Quirima, *Angola* 10°49′ S, 18°4′ E 220
Quirinópolis, *Braz.* 18°35′ S, 50°32′ W 138
Quirke Lake, *Can.* 46°27′ N, 83°4′ W 94
Quiroga, *Arg.* 35°18′ S, 61°27′ W 139
Quiroga, Punta, *Arg.* 42°23′ S, 66°1′ W 134
Quirusillas, *Bol.* 18°23′ S, 63°57′ W 137
Quisiro, *Venez.* 10°56′ N, 71°18′ W 136
Quissanga, *Mozambique* 12°24′ S, 40°30′ E 224
Quissico, *Mozambique* 24°40′ S, 34°43′ E 227
Quitapa, *Angola* 10°23′ S, 18°11′ E 220
Quitaque, *Tex., U.S.* 34°21′ N, 101°4′ W 92
Quiterajo, *Mozambique* 11°45′ S, 40°27′ E 224
Quitilipi, *Arg.* 26°53′ S, 60°13′ W 139
Quitman, *Ga., U.S.* 30°46′ N, 83°34′ W 96
Quitman, *La., U.S.* 32°20′ N, 92°44′ W 103
Quitman, *Miss., U.S.* 32°2′ N, 88°43′ W 103
Quitman, *Tex., U.S.* 32°47′ N, 95°27′ W 103
Quito, *Ecua.* 0°17′ N, 78°49′ W 130
Quitor, *Chile* 22°50′ S, 68°14′ W 137
Quitovac, *Mex.* 31°30′ N, 112°45′ W 92
Quixadá, *Braz.* 4°56′ S, 39°4′ W 132
Quixaxe, *Mozambique* 15°16′ S, 40°9′ E 224
Qujiang, *China* 24°38′ N, 113°34′ E 198
Qulan (Lŭgovoy), *Kaz.* 42°54′ N, 72°44′ E 184
Qulandy, *Kaz.* 46°6′ N, 59°28′ E 184
Qulbān Layyah, spring, *Iraq* 29°47′ N, 46°1′ E 196
Qullissat, *Den.* 70°3′ N, 53°2′ W 106
Qulsary, *Kaz.* 46°58′ N, 54°1′ E 158
Qum see Qom, *Iran* 34°39′ N, 50°50′ E 180
Qumarlêb, *China* 34°27′ N, 95°24′ E 188
Qumsay, *Kaz.* 49°27′ N, 58°25′ E 158
Qunayyah, *Syr.* 34°30′ N, 37°1′ E 194
Quneitra see Al Qunayţirah, *Syr.* 33°7′ N, 35°49′ E 194
Qŭnghirot, *Uzb.* 43°1′ N, 58°50′ E 180
Qu'nyido, *China* 31°18′ N, 97°58′ E 188
Quogue, *N.Y., U.S.* 40°49′ N, 72°36′ W 104
Quoin Point, *S. Af.* 35°3′ S, 19°34′ E 227
Quorn, *Can.* 49°25′ N, 90°54′ W 94
Qurayyāt, *Oman* 23°16′ N, 58°54′ E 182
Qŭrghonteppa, *Taj.* 37°49′ N, 68°48′ E 197
Quryq, *Kaz.* 43°11′ N, 51°41′ E 158
Qûş, *Egypt* 25°54′ N, 32°44′ E 182
Qusar, *Azerb.* 41°24′ N, 48°27′ E 195
Quşeir, *Egypt* 26°8′ N, 34°13′ E 180
Qusmuryn, *Kaz.* 52°27′ N, 64°37′ E 184
Qusum, *China* 29°5′ N, 92°12′ E 197
Quthing, *Lesotho* 30°25′ S, 27°41′ E 227
Quttinirpaaq National Park, *Can.* 81°58′ N, 73°8′ W 72
Quwo, *China* 35°40′ N, 111°27′ E 198
Quxian, *China* 30°51′ N, 106°52′ E 198
Qüxü, *China* 29°21′ N, 90°39′ E 197
Quy Chau, *Vietnam* 19°32′ N, 105°7′ E 202
Quzhou, *China* 36°49′ N, 114°53′ E 198
Quzhou, *China* 28°56′ N, 118°49′ E 198
Qvareli, *Ga.* 41°57′ N, 45°48′ E 195
Qyyq, *Kaz.* 43°46′ N, 70°57′ E 184
Qyzan, *Kaz.* 44°56′ N, 52°45′ E 158
Qyzylkayyn, *Kaz.* 45°47′ N, 80°14′ E 184
Qyzylorda, *Kaz.* 44°49′ N, 65°34′ E 184
Qyzylorda, adm. division, *Kaz.* 42°40′ N, 66°6′ E 197
Qyzylorda, adm. division, *Kaz.* 44°54′ N, 61°41′ E 184
Qyzylqaq Köli, lake, *Kaz.* 53°27′ N, 73°13′ E 184
Qyzylzhar, *Kaz.* 48°17′ N, 69°38′ E 184

R

Raab, river, *Aust.* 47°2′ N, 15°40′ E 168
Raahe (Brahestad), *Fin.* 64°41′ N, 24°27′ E 152
Raanujärvi, *Fin.* 66°39′ N, 24°41′ E 152
Raate, *Fin.* 64°47′ N, 29°43′ E 152
Rab, *Croatia* 44°46′ N, 14°45′ E 156
Raba, *Indonesia* 8°31′ S, 118°52′ E 192
Rába, river, *Hung.* 47°26′ N, 17°10′ E 168
Rábahidvég, *Hung.* 47°4′ N, 16°45′ E 168
Rabai, *Kenya* 3°54′ S, 39°35′ E 224
Rabak, *Sudan* 13°6′ N, 32°46′ E 182
Rabast, Cap de, *Can.* 49°59′ N, 64°15′ W 111
Rabastens, *Fr.* 43°48′ N, 1°42′ E 150
Rabastens, *Fr.* 43°23′ N, 0°8′ E 164
Rabat, *Mor.* 33°53′ N, 7°7′ W 214
Rabaul, *P.N.G.* 4°15′ S, 152°8′ E 238
Rabbit Ears Pass, *Colo., U.S.* 40°22′ N, 106°38′ W 90
Rabbit Lake, *Can.* 53°8′ N, 107°46′ W 108
Rabbit, river, *Can.* 59°25′ N, 127°17′ W 108
Rabga Pass, *China* 27°51′ N, 87°33′ E 197
Rābigh, *Saudi Arabia* 22°48′ N, 39°0′ E 182
Rabrovo, *Serb.* 44°33′ N, 21°32′ E 168
Rabyānah, spring, *Lib.* 24°16′ N, 21°57′ E 216
Răcăşdia, *Rom.* 44°59′ N, 21°37′ E 168
Racconigi, *It.* 44°45′ N, 7°41′ E 167
Raccoon Point, *La., U.S.* 28°58′ N, 91°7′ W 103
Race, Cape, *Can.* 46°41′ N, 53°15′ W 111
Race Point, *Mass., U.S.* 42°3′ N, 70°21′ W 104
Race Point, *N.Y., U.S.* 41°11′ N, 72°2′ W 104
Race, The 41°11′ N, 72°9′ W 104
Raceland, *La., U.S.* 29°42′ N, 90°37′ W 103
Rach Gia, *Vietnam* 10°1′ N, 105°5′ E 202
Raciąż, *Pol.* 52°46′ N, 20°5′ E 152
Racine, *Wis., U.S.* 42°42′ N, 87°48′ W 102
Racing, river, *Can.* 58°36′ N, 125°4′ W 108
Raco, *Mich., U.S.* 46°22′ N, 84°44′ W 94
Raczki, *Pol.* 53°58′ N, 22°46′ E 166
Radan, *Serb.* 43°1′ N, 21°22′ E 168
Radashkovichy, *Belarus* 54°9′ N, 27°14′ E 166
Rădăuţi, *Rom.* 47°50′ N, 25°55′ E 152
Radcliff, *Ky., U.S.* 37°50′ N, 85°57′ W 96
Radebeul, *Ger.* 51°6′ N, 13°37′ E 152
Radford, *Va., U.S.* 37°6′ N, 80°35′ W 96
Radhanpur, *India* 23°49′ N, 71°38′ E 186
Radio Beacon, site, *Can.* 43°55′ N, 60°7′ W 111
Radishchevo, *Russ.* 52°49′ N, 47°52′ E 154
Radisson, *Can.* 52°28′ N, 107°23′ W 108
Radisson, *Can.* 53°44′ N, 77°40′ W 106
Raditsa Krylovka, *Russ.* 53°17′ N, 34°23′ E 154
Radlinski, Mount, peak, *Antarctica* 82°22′ S, 102°9′ W 248
Radna, *Rom.* 46°6′ N, 21°42′ E 168
Radojevo, *Serb.* 45°44′ N, 20°47′ E 168
Radolfzell, *Ger.* 47°44′ N, 8°57′ E 150
Radom, *Pol.* 51°23′ N, 21°9′ E 152
Radom, *Sudan* 9°49′ N, 24°50′ E 224
Radom National Park, *Sudan* 9°1′ N, 23°41′ E 224
Radomiru, *Rom.* 44°8′ N, 24°10′ E 156
Radomsko, *Pol.* 51°4′ N, 19°27′ E 152
Radomyshl', *Ukr.* 50°29′ N, 29°19′ E 158
Radovići, *Mont.* 42°23′ N, 18°40′ E 168
Radoviš, *Maced.* 41°38′ N, 22°27′ E 168
Radstock, *U.K.* 51°17′ N, 2°27′ W 162
Raduzhnyy, *Russ.* 62°0′ N, 77°39′ E 169
Radviliškis, *Lith.* 55°47′ N, 23°30′ E 166
Radville, *Can.* 49°26′ N, 104°19′ W 90
Raḑwá, Jabal, peak, *Saudi Arabia* 24°32′ N, 38°11′ E 182
Radway, *Can.* 54°3′ N, 112°57′ W 108
Radziwiłłówka, *Pol.* 52°22′ N, 23°1′ E 152
Rae Bareli, *India* 26°13′ N, 81°14′ E 197
Rae Isthmus, *Can.* 66°53′ N, 91°0′ W 106
Rae, Mount, peak, *Can.* 50°36′ N, 115°4′ W 90
Rae, river, *Can.* 68°7′ N, 118°55′ W 98
Rae-Edzo see Behchok, *Can.* 62°42′ N, 116°26′ W 106
Raesfeld, *Ger.* 51°46′ N, 6°51′ E 167
Raetihi, *N.Z.* 39°27′ S, 175°15′ E 240
Rāf, Jabal, peak, *Saudi Arabia* 29°12′ N, 39°47′ E 180
Rafaela, *Arg.* 31°14′ S, 61°27′ W 139
Rafa', *Gaza Strip, Israel* 31°16′ N, 34°15′ E 194
Rafaï, *Cen. Af. Rep.* 4°58′ N, 23°58′ E 224
Rafalivka, *Ukr.* 51°18′ N, 25°55′ E 152
Rafḩā', *Saudi Arabia* 29°41′ N, 43°31′ E 180
Rafsanjān, *Iran* 30°22′ N, 56°5′ E 196
Raft River Mountains, *Utah, U.S.* 41°48′ N, 113°46′ W 90
Rafter, *Can.* 55°38′ N, 101°11′ W 108
Rafz, *Switz.* 47°36′ N, 8°32′ E 150
Raga, *Sudan* 8°25′ N, 25°39′ E 224
Raga, river, *Sudan* 8°11′ N, 25°30′ E 224
Ragachow, *Belarus* 53°5′ N, 30°9′ E 154
Ragag, *Sudan* 10°56′ N, 24°45′ E 224
Ragauka, *Latv.* 56°41′ N, 27°24′ E 166
Ragay Gulf 13°35′ N, 122°30′ E 203
Ragged, Mount, peak, *Austral.* 33°29′ S, 123°13′ E 230
Raglan, *N.Z.* 37°51′ S, 174°54′ E 240
Ragley, *La., U.S.* 30°29′ N, 93°15′ W 103
Raguba, oil field, *Lib.* 29°1′ N, 18°57′ E 216
Ragunda, *Nor.* 63°3′ N, 16°23′ E 154
Ragusa, *It.* 36°54′ N, 14°42′ E 216
Ragusa see Dubrovnik, *Croatia* 42°38′ N, 18°5′ E 156
Rahad el Berdi, *Sudan* 11°16′ N, 23°52′ E 224
Raheita, *Eritrea* 12°43′ N, 43°5′ E 218
Rahib, Jebel, peak, *Sudan* 17°41′ N, 27°5′ E 226
Rahimyar Khan, *Pak.* 28°24′ N, 70°18′ E 186
Rahotu, *N.Z.* 39°20′ S, 173°49′ E 240
Rahuri, *India* 19°25′ N, 74°38′ E 188
Raíces, *Arg.* 31°53′ S, 59°14′ W 139
Raichur, *India* 16°12′ N, 77°20′ E 188
Raiganj, *India* 25°35′ N, 88°6′ E 197
Raigarh, *India* 21°54′ N, 83°22′ E 197
Rakiura National Park, *N.Z.* 47°25′ S, 168°23′ E 240
Railroad Flat, *Calif., U.S.* 38°20′ N, 120°32′ W 100
Railroad Pass, *Nev., U.S.* 39°22′ N, 117°25′ W 90
Rainbach, *Aust.* 48°33′ N, 14°28′ E 156
Rainbow, *Calif., U.S.* 33°24′ N, 117°10′ W 101
Rainbow Falls, site, *Hawai'i, U.S.* 19°42′ N, 155°10′ W 99
Rainbow Lake, *Can.* 58°28′ N, 119°29′ W 108
Rainbow Springs, site, *Fla., U.S.* 29°6′ N, 82°27′ W 105
Rainer, *Minn., U.S.* 48°35′ N, 93°21′ W 94
Rainier, *Oreg., U.S.* 46°4′ N, 122°57′ W 100
Rainier, Mount, peak, *Wash., U.S.* 46°49′ N, 121°49′ W 100
Rainy Lake, *Can.* 48°41′ N, 94°17′ W 80
Rainy River, *Can.* 48°44′ N, 94°34′ W 90
Rainy, river, *Can.* 48°31′ N, 94°41′ W 82
Raippaluoto see Replot, *Fin.* 63°13′ N, 21°24′ E 152
Raipur, *India* 21°15′ N, 81°38′ E 188
Rairakhol, *India* 21°4′ N, 84°20′ E 188
Ra's, *Saudi Arabia* 23°33′ N, 38°37′ E 182
Raisduoddarhalde, peak, *Nor.* 69°19′ N, 21°11′ E 152
Raisin, *Calif., U.S.* 36°36′ N, 119°55′ W 101
Raisinghnagar, *India* 29°31′ N, 73°27′ E 186
Raisio, *Fin.* 60°28′ N, 22°10′ E 166
Raj Samund, *India* 25°1′ N, 73°51′ E 186
Raja, *Est.* 58°46′ N, 26°53′ E 166
Raja, Ujung, *Indonesia* 3°30′ N, 96°14′ E 196
Rajada, *Braz.* 8°46′ S, 40°50′ W 132
Rajahmundry, *India* 17°0′ N, 81°48′ E 190
Rajamäki, *Fin.* 60°30′ N, 24°44′ E 166
Rajampet, *India* 14°11′ N, 79°8′ E 188
Rajanpur, *Pak.* 29°8′ N, 70°21′ E 186
Rajasthan, adm. division, *India* 26°20′ N, 70°59′ E 186
Rajasthan Canal, *India* 28°0′ N, 72°30′ E 186
Rajbari, *Bangladesh* 23°40′ N, 89°36′ E 197
Rajgarh, *India* 28°38′ N, 75°24′ E 197
Rajin (Raseon), *N. Korea* 42°15′ N, 130°19′ E 200
Rajka, *Hung.* 47°59′ N, 17°12′ E 168
Rajkot, *India* 22°17′ N, 70°46′ E 186
Rajshahi, *Bangladesh* 24°21′ N, 88°33′ E 197
Raka, river, *China* 29°23′ N, 85°57′ E 197
Rakai, *Uganda* 0°43′ N, 31°22′ E 224
Rakaia, *N.Z.* 43°46′ S, 172°0′ E 240
Rakamaz, *Hung.* 48°6′ N, 21°27′ E 152
Rakaposhi, peak, *Pak.* 36°7′ N, 74°22′ E 186
Rakaw, *Belarus* 53°58′ N, 27°2′ E 166
Rakhshan, river, *Pak.* 26°58′ N, 63°58′ E 186
Rakhyūt, *Oman* 16°41′ N, 53°18′ E 182
Rakisvaara, peak, *Nor.* 68°13′ N, 20°6′ E 152
Rakke, *Est.* 58°58′ N, 26°13′ E 166
Rakops, *Botswana* 21°3′ S, 24°24′ E 227
Rakovitsa, *Bulg.* 43°46′ N, 22°27′ E 168
Rakovo, *Bulg.* 42°5′ N, 22°43′ E 168
Rakow, *Ger.* 54°2′ N, 13°2′ E 152
Rakula, *Russ.* 63°42′ N, 41°36′ E 154
Rakulka, *Russ.* 61°50′ N, 45°19′ E 154
Rakvere, *Est.* 59°20′ N, 26°19′ E 166
Raleigh, *Miss., U.S.* 32°1′ N, 89°31′ W 103
Raleigh, *N.C., U.S.* 35°45′ N, 78°43′ W 96
Ralik Chain, islands, *North Pacific Ocean* 7°28′ N, 166°35′ E 238
Ralja, *Serb.* 44°33′ N, 20°32′ E 168
Ralls, *Tex., U.S.* 33°39′ N, 101°23′ W 92
Ralston, *Can.* 50°15′ N, 111°12′ W 90
Rām Allāh, *West Bank, Israel* 31°53′ N, 35°11′ E 194
Rama, *Israel* 32°56′ N, 35°22′ E 194
Rama, *Nicar.* 12°10′ N, 84°10′ W 115
Ramādī Barrage, dam, *Iraq* 33°39′ N, 42°10′ E 180
Ramage Point 73°23′ S, 115°8′ W 248
Ramah, *Colo., U.S.* 39°6′ N, 104°11′ W 92
Ramah, *N. Mex., U.S.* 35°7′ N, 108°29′ W 92
Ramales de la Victoria, *Sp.* 43°14′ N, 3°30′ W 164
Ramalho, Serra do, *Braz.* 14°0′ S, 44°39′ W 132
Ramallo, *Arg.* 33°31′ S, 60°1′ W 139
Raman, *Thai.* 6°24′ N, 101°22′ E 196
Raman, oil field, *Turk.* 37°45′ N, 41°29′ E 195
Ramanava, *Belarus* 53°56′ N, 24°37′ E 166
Ramanuj Ganj, *India* 23°46′ N, 83°39′ E 197
Ramat Magshimim, *Israel* 32°51′ N, 35°49′ E 194
Ramatlabama, *Botswana* 25°38′ S, 25°31′ E 227
Rambau, Lac, lake, *Can.* 53°39′ N, 70°45′ W 111
Rambouillet, *Fr.* 48°38′ N, 1°49′ E 163
Rambutyo, island, *P.N.G.* 2°44′ S, 147°51′ E 192
Ramea, *Can.* 47°31′ N, 57°24′ W 111
Ramerupt, *Fr.* 48°30′ N, 4°17′ E 163
Rameshki, *Russ.* 57°18′ N, 36°1′ E 154
Ramgarh, *India* 23°35′ N, 85°32′ E 197
Ramgarh, *India* 27°22′ N, 70°29′ E 186
Ramírez, Isla, island, *Chile* 51°49′ S, 76°41′ W 134
Rāmis, river, *Eth.* 8°27′ N, 41°27′ E 224
Ramla, *Israel* 31°55′ N, 34°52′ E 194
Ramlu, peak, *Eritrea* 13°22′ N, 41°38′ E 182
Ramnagar, *India* 25°14′ N, 83°3′ E 197
Ramnagar, *India* 29°24′ N, 79°6′ E 197
Ramnäs, *Nor.* 59°46′ N, 16°10′ E 152
Râmnicu Vâlcea, *Rom.* 45°7′ N, 24°21′ E 156
Ramon', *Russ.* 51°52′ N, 39°13′ E 158
Ramon, Har, peak, *Israel* 30°29′ N, 34°36′ E 194
Ramón Santamarina, *Arg.* 38°28′ S, 59°21′ W 139
Ramón Trigo, *Uru.* 32°21′ S, 54°39′ W 139
Ramona, *Calif., U.S.* 33°2′ N, 116°53′ W 101

Ramonal, Mex. 18°25′ N, 88°34′ W 115
Ramore, Can. 48°26′ N, 80°20′ W 94
Ramos, Mex. 22°48′ N, 101°56′ W 114
Ramos Arizpe, Mex. 25°32′ N, 100°57′ W 114
Ramos, oil field, Arg. 22°41′ S, 64°15′ W 137
Ramos, river, Mex. 25°13′ N, 105°19′ W 114
Ramotswa, Botswana 24°52′ S, 25°47′ E 227
Rampart, Alas., U.S. 65°19′ N, 150°13′ W 98
Ramparts, river, Can. 66°25′ N, 130°46′ W 98
Rampur, India 28°46′ N, 79°3′ E 197
Rampur Hat, India 24°9′ N, 87°48′ E 197
Ramsay, Mich., U.S. 46°28′ N, 90°1′ W 94
Ramsele, Nor. 63°31′ N, 16°29′ E 152
Ramsey, Ill., U.S. 39°8′ N, 89°6′ W 102
Ramsey, N.J., U.S. 41°3′ N, 74°9′ W 104
Ramsey Lake, Can. 47°9′ N, 82°46′ W 110
Ramsgate, U.K. 51°20′ N, 1°24′ E 163
Ramsjö, Nor. 62°11′ N, 15°38′ E 152
Ramu, Kenya 3°50′ N, 41°13′ E 224
Ramu, river, P.N.G. 5°7′ S, 144°53′ E 192
Ramvik, Nor. 62°48′ N, 17°49′ E 152
Rana, Cerro, peak, Col. 3°34′ N, 68°9′ W 136
Ranaghat, India 23°7′ N, 88°35′ E 197
Ranai, Indonesia 3°59′ N, 108°23′ E 196
Ranau, Malaysia 5°57′ N, 116°41′ E 203
Rancagua, Chile 34°11′ S, 70°50′ W 134
Rance, Belg. 50°7′ N, 4°17′ E 163
Rancharia, Braz. 22°14′ S, 50°56′ W 138
Rancheria, river, Can. 60°0′ N, 130°57′ W 108
Ranchester, Wyo., U.S. 44°54′ N, 107°10′ W 90
Ranchi, India 23°22′ N, 85°19′ E 197
Ranchita, Calif., U.S. 33°13′ N, 116°33′ W 101
Rancho California, Calif., U.S. 33°30′ N, 117°11′ W 101
Rancho Cordova, Calif., U.S. 38°35′ N, 121°19′ W 92
Rancho de Caça dos Tapiúnas, Braz. 10°50′ S, 56°2′ W 130
Rancho Mirage, Calif., U.S. 33°43′ N, 116°26′ W 101
Rancho Santa Fe, Calif., U.S. 33°1′ N, 117°13′ W 101
Ranchos de Taos, N. Mex., U.S. 36°20′ N, 105°37′ W 92
Randa, Nig. 9°7′ N, 8°27′ E 222
Randers, Den. 56°27′ N, 10°0′ E 152
Randers Fjord 56°32′ N, 9°59′ E 152
Randijaur, lake, Nor. 66°41′ N, 18°35′ E 152
Randle, Wash., U.S. 46°31′ N, 121°59′ W 100
Randolph, Me., U.S. 44°14′ N, 69°46′ W 104
Randolph, Nebr., U.S. 42°21′ N, 97°21′ W 90
Randolph, N.H., U.S. 44°22′ N, 71°17′ W 104
Randolph, Utah, U.S. 41°40′ N, 111°11′ W 90
Randolph, Vt., U.S. 43°55′ N, 72°41′ W 104
Randolph, Wis., U.S. 43°32′ N, 89°0′ W 102
Randolph Air Force Base, Tex., U.S. 29°28′ N, 98°21′ W 92
Randolph Center, Vt., U.S. 43°56′ N, 72°37′ W 104
Random Lake, Wis., U.S. 43°32′ N, 87°58′ W 102
Randsburg, Calif., U.S. 35°21′ N, 117°41′ W 101
Råneå, Nor. 65°51′ N, 22°16′ E 152
Ranérou, Senegal 15°19′ N, 14°0′ W 222
Ranfurly, N.Z. 45°8′ S, 170°6′ E 240
Rangae, Thai. 6°19′ N, 101°45′ E 196
Rangamati, Bangladesh 22°37′ N, 92°7′ E 188
Rangeley, Me., U.S. 44°57′ N, 70°40′ W 94
Rangely, Colo., U.S. 40°4′ N, 108°48′ W 90
Ranger, Tex., U.S. 32°27′ N, 98°41′ W 92
Rangiora, N.Z. 43°20′ S, 172°34′ E 240
Rangkŭl, Taj. 38°27′ N, 74°25′ E 184
Rangoon see Yangon, Myanmar 16°45′ N, 96°0′ E 202
Rangpur, Bangladesh 25°41′ N, 89°12′ E 197
Rangsang, island, Indonesia 1°1′ N, 103°5′ E 196
Raniganj, India 23°37′ N, 87°7′ E 197
Ranikhet, India 29°40′ N, 79°25′ E 197
Rāniyah, Iraq 36°15′ N, 44°52′ E 195
Rankin, Tex., U.S. 31°12′ N, 101°57′ W 92
Rankin Inlet, Can. 62°50′ N, 92°9′ W 106
Rankūs, Syr. 33°45′ N, 36°22′ E 194
Rann of Kutch 23°59′ N, 69°56′ E 186
Rano, Nig. 11°32′ N, 8°34′ E 222
Ranohira, Madagascar 22°36′ S, 45°22′ E 220
Ranomafana, Madagascar 24°33′ S, 46°59′ E 220
Ranomafana, Madagascar 21°13′ S, 47°23′ E 220
Ranomena, Madagascar 23°24′ S, 47°16′ E 220
Ranong, Thai. 9°54′ N, 98°38′ E 192
Ranongga (Ganongga), island, Solomon Islands 8°5′ S, 156°30′ E 242
Ranot, Thai. 7°48′ N, 100°20′ E 196
Ransiki, Indonesia 1°27′ S, 134°2′ E 192
Ransom, Ill., U.S. 41°9′ N, 88°39′ W 102
Rantasalmi, Fin. 62°2′ N, 28°15′ E 166
Rantau, oil field, Indonesia 4°23′ N, 98°7′ E 196
Rantauprapat, Indonesia 2°6′ N, 99°50′ E 196
Rantoul, Ill., U.S. 40°18′ N, 88°9′ W 102
Rantsila, Fin. 64°30′ N, 25°37′ E 152
Ranua, Fin. 65°53′ N, 26°30′ E 152
Rao, Senegal 15°56′ N, 16°26′ W 222
Raoui, Erg er, Alg. 30°3′ N, 3°41′ W 214
Rapahoe, N.Z. 42°23′ S, 171°17′ E 240
Raper, Cabo 46°54′ S, 77°3′ W 134
Raper, Cape, Can. 69°39′ N, 67°9′ W 106
Rapid City, Can. 50°9′ N, 100°3′ W 90
Rapid City, S. Dak., U.S. 44°3′ N, 103°15′ W 90
Rapid River, Mich., U.S. 45°55′ N, 86°59′ W 94
Rapid, river, Minn., U.S. 48°16′ N, 95°2′ W 90
Räpina, Est. 58°6′ N, 27°27′ E 166
Rapla, Est. 59°0′ N, 24°47′ E 166
Rappahannock, river, Va., U.S. 38°36′ N, 77°58′ W 80
Rápulo, river, Bol. 14°24′ S, 66°30′ W 137
Raqiq, ruin(s), Israel 31°16′ N, 34°39′ E 194
Rara National Park, Nepal 29°29′ N, 81°58′ E 197
Rarotonga, island, N.Z. 21°14′ S, 159°47′ W 241
Ra's Abū Madd, Saudi Arabia 24°44′ N, 37°10′ E 182
Ra's Abū Qumayyiş, Saudi Arabia 24°33′ N, 51°30′ E 196
Ra's al Arḑ, Kuwait 29°19′ N, 48°8′ E 196
Ra's al 'Ayn, Syr. 36°49′ N, 40°7′ E 195
Ra's al Basīt 35°52′ N, 35°13′ E 156
Ra's al Bayyāḑah, Leb. 33°9′ N, 35°0′ E 194
Ra's al Ḩadd, Oman 22°33′ N, 59°46′ E 182
Ra's al Hilāl, Lib. 33°2′ N, 22°7′ E 216
Ra's al Kalb, Yemen 13°55′ N, 48°41′ E 182
Ra's al Khaymah, U.A.E. 25°45′ N, 55°57′ E 196
Ra's al Madrakah, Oman 18°59′ N, 56°39′ E 182
Ra's al Mil′, Lib. 32°1′ N, 24°56′ E 180
Ra's al Mish'āb, Saudi Arabia 28°9′ N, 48°36′ E 196
Ra's al Qulay'ah, Kuwait 28°53′ N, 48°17′ E 196
Ra's al Unūf, Lib. 30°31′ N, 18°31′ E 216
Ra's 'Āmir, Lib. 33°2′ N, 20°43′ E 216
Ra's an Naqb, Jordan 29°57′ N, 35°32′ E 180
Ra's as Sa'dīyāt, Leb. 33°41′ N, 35°14′ E 194
Ra's ash Shaqq, Leb. 34°19′ N, 35°34′ E 194
Ra's ash Sharbatāt, Oman 17°42′ N, 56°21′ E 182
Ra's aţ Ţarfā, Saudi Arabia 16°55′ N, 41°35′ E 182
Ra's at Tīn, Lib. 32°41′ N, 23°5′ E 180
Ra's az Zawr, Saudi Arabia 27°28′ N, 49°0′ E 196
Ra's Ba'labakk, Leb. 34°15′ N, 36°24′ E 194
Ra's Ḑarbat 'Alī, Oman 16°42′ N, 52°15′ E 182
Râs el 'Ish, Egypt 31°8′ N, 32°17′ E 194
Râs el Ma, Alg. 36°7′ N, 5°31′ E 150
Râs el Ma, Alg. 34°29′ N, 0°48′ E 214
Râs el Mâ, Mali 16°36′ N, 4°38′ W 222
Ra's Fartak, Yemen 15°38′ N, 51°28′ E 182
Râs Ghârib, Egypt 28°21′ N, 33°0′ E 180
Râs Ghârib, oil field, Egypt 27°56′ N, 32°47′ E 143
Ra's Ḩāţibah, Saudi Arabia 21°55′ N, 38°6′ E 182
Ra's Ibn Hāni′, Syr. 35°35′ N, 35°44′ E 194
Ra's Jibsh, Oman 21°28′ N, 58°38′ E 182
Ra's Mirbāţ, Oman 16°48′ N, 54°46′ E 182
Ras Muhammad National Park, Egypt 27°44′ N, 33°47′ E 182
Ra's Musandam, Oman 26°18′ N, 56°29′ E 196
Ra's Shamrah, site, Mediterranean Sea 35°35′ N, 35°41′ E 156
Ra's Shamrah (Ugarit), site, Syr. 35°33′ N, 35°44′ E 194
Ra's Sharwayn, Yemen 15°11′ N, 51°29′ E 182
Ra's Shū'ab, Yemen 12°24′ N, 52°34′ E 182
Ra's Tannūrah, Saudi Arabia 26°39′ N, 50°7′ E 196
Rasa, Punta, Arg. 40°51′ S, 62°17′ W 134
Raseiniai, Lith. 55°22′ N, 23°5′ E 166
Raseon see Rajin , N. Korea 42°15′ N, 130°19′ E 200
Rashaant, Mongolia 45°21′ N, 106°14′ E 198
Rashad, Sudan 11°51′ N, 31°4′ E 216
Rāshayyā, Leb. 33°29′ N, 35°50′ E 194
Rashi, oil field, Iraq 30°9′ N, 47°1′ E 196
Rashîd (Rosetta), Egypt 31°23′ N, 30°21′ E 180
Rasht, Iran 37°15′ N, 49°32′ E 195
Raška, Serb. 43°17′ N, 20°36′ E 168
Raška, river, Serb. 43°7′ N, 20°35′ E 168
Rasony, Belarus 55°52′ N, 28°50′ E 166
Rasovo, Bulg. 43°42′ N, 23°14′ E 168
Răspopeni, Mold. 47°45′ N, 28°37′ E 156
Rasskazovo, Russ. 52°37′ N, 41°49′ E 158
Rastatt, Ger. 48°50′ N, 8°10′ E 150
Rastede, Ger. 53°14′ N, 8°11′ E 163
Rastigaissa, peak, Nor. 69°58′ N, 26°5′ E 152
Rastu, Rom. 43°53′ N, 23°17′ E 168
Rasua Garhi, Nepal 28°18′ N, 85°24′ E 197
Rat, island, Alas., U.S. 51°33′ N, 177°41′ E 160
Rat Islands, Bering Sea 51°41′ N, 174°8′ E 160
Rat Lake, lake, Can. 56°23′ N, 99°38′ W 108
Rat Rapids, Can. 51°10′ N, 90°13′ W 110
Rat, river, Can. 56°8′ N, 99°19′ W 108
Rat, river, Wis., U.S. 45°33′ N, 88°38′ W 94
Rata, N.Z. 40°0′ S, 175°30′ E 240
Rataje, Serb. 43°28′ N, 21°7′ E 168
Ratak Chain, islands, North Pacific Ocean 9°43′ N, 169°11′ E 238
Ratamka, Belarus 53°54′ N, 27°21′ E 166
Ratangarh, India 28°3′ N, 74°38′ E 186
Ratanpur, India 22°18′ N, 82°10′ E 197
Ratcliff, Tex., U.S. 31°22′ N, 95°8′ W 103
Rath, India 25°35′ N, 79°34′ E 197
Rätikon, Switz. 46°55′ N, 9°41′ E 167
Ratina, Serb. 43°42′ N, 20°44′ E 168
Ratlam, India 23°18′ N, 75°1′ E 188
Ratnagiri, India 17°0′ N, 73°19′ E 188
Ratne, Ukr. 51°38′ N, 24°32′ E 152
Raton, N. Mex., U.S. 36°53′ N, 104°27′ W 92
Raton Pass, N. Mex., U.S. 36°58′ N, 104°29′ W 92
Ratta, Russ. 63°34′ N, 83°50′ E 169
Rattlesnake Hills, Wash., U.S. 46°30′ N, 120°25′ W 90
Rattlesnake Hills, Wyo., U.S. 42°50′ N, 107°40′ W 90
Rättvik, Nor. 60°52′ N, 15°6′ E 152
Ratz, Mount, peak, Can. 57°23′ N, 132°27′ W 108
Raub, Malaysia 3°47′ N, 101°50′ E 196
Rauch, Arg. 36°47′ S, 59°8′ W 139
Raudal Yupurari (Devils Cataract), fall(s), Col. 0°58′ N, 71°28′ W 136
Raudhatain, oil field, Kuwait 29°51′ N, 47°39′ E 196
Rauer Islands, Indian Ocean 68°54′ S, 74°26′ E 248
Raufarhöfn, Ice. 66°28′ N, 16°5′ W 143
Raul Soares, Braz. 20°7′ S, 42°29′ W 138
Rauma, Fin. 61°7′ N, 21°29′ E 166
Rauna, Latv. 57°19′ N, 25°37′ E 166
Raupunga, N.Z. 39°3′ S, 177°8′ E 240
Raurkela, India 22°14′ N, 84°57′ E 197
Rautas, Nor. 67°59′ N, 19°53′ E 152
Rautavaara, Fin. 63°28′ N, 28°15′ E 152
Rautio, Fin. 64°4′ N, 24°10′ E 154
Rautjärvi, Fin. 61°16′ N, 29°7′ E 166
Ravānsar, Iran 34°43′ N, 46°41′ E 180
Rāvar, Iran 31°12′ N, 56°55′ E 180
Ravelo, Bol. 18°51′ S, 65°36′ W 137
Ravena, N.Y., U.S. 42°28′ N, 73°50′ W 104
Ravenglass, U.K. 54°21′ N, 3°24′ W 162
Ravenna, It. 44°24′ N, 12°11′ E 167
Ravenna, Ky., U.S. 37°40′ N, 83°57′ W 94
Ravenna, Nebr., U.S. 41°1′ N, 98°55′ W 90
Ravenna, Ohio, U.S. 41°8′ N, 81°14′ W 102
Ravensthorpe, Austral. 33°35′ S, 120°1′ E 231
Ravenswood, W. Va., U.S. 38°56′ N, 81°46′ W 94
Ravi, river, Pak. 30°34′ N, 71°52′ E 186
Ravn, Kap 68°9′ N, 28°16′ W 246
Ravna Banja, Serb. 42°45′ N, 21°40′ E 168
Ravne, Slov. 46°31′ N, 14°57′ E 156
Ravno, Bosn. and Herzg. 43°50′ N, 17°22′ E 168
Rawa Aopa Watumohai National Park, Indonesia 4°22′ S, 121°38′ E 238
Rāwah, Iraq 34°30′ N, 41°55′ E 180
Rawalpindi, Pak. 33°31′ N, 73°4′ E 186
Rawandoz, Iraq 36°39′ N, 44°31′ E 195
Rawene, N.Z. 35°26′ S, 173°30′ E 240
Raw'ah, Saudi Arabia 19°28′ N, 41°44′ E 182
Rawhide Lake, Can. 46°36′ N, 83°11′ W 94
Rawi, Ko, island, Thai. 6°36′ N, 98°58′ E 196
Rawicz, Pol. 51°36′ N, 16°52′ E 152
Rawley Point, Wis., U.S. 44°7′ N, 87°30′ W 102
Rawlinna, Austral. 31°0′ S, 125°19′ E 231
Rawlins, Wyo., U.S. 41°48′ N, 107°14′ W 90
Rawlinson Range, Austral. 25°29′ S, 127°57′ E 230
Rawson, Arg. 43°16′ S, 65°7′ W 134
Rawtenstall, U.K. 53°42′ N, 2°17′ W 162
Raxaul, India 26°58′ N, 84°48′ E 197
Ray, N. Dak., U.S. 48°19′ N, 103°11′ W 90
Ray, Cape, Can. 47°39′ N, 59°56′ W 111
Raya, peak, Indonesia 0°40′ N, 112°25′ E 192
Rayachoti, India 14°2′ N, 78°46′ E 188
Rayagada, India 19°10′ N, 83°24′ E 188
Rayakoski, Russ. 68°56′ N, 28°44′ E 152
Raychikhinsk, Russ. 49°52′ N, 129°24′ E 190
Rayevskiy, Russ. 54°4′ N, 54°54′ E 154
Raymond, Calif., U.S. 37°13′ N, 119°56′ W 100
Raymond, Can. 49°27′ N, 112°40′ W 90
Raymond, N.H., U.S. 43°2′ N, 71°12′ W 104
Raymond, Wash., U.S. 46°41′ N, 123°44′ W 100
Raymondville, Tex., U.S. 26°28′ N, 97°47′ W 114
Raymore, Can. 51°24′ N, 104°31′ W 90
Rayna, India 23°2′ N, 87°52′ E 197
Rayne, La., U.S. 30°13′ N, 92°17′ W 103
Rayner Peak, Antarctica 67°30′ S, 55°30′ E 248
Raynham Center, Mass., U.S. 41°55′ N, 71°4′ W 104
Rayón, Mex. 29°42′ N, 110°34′ W 92
Rayón, Mex. 21°49′ N, 99°39′ W 114
Rayón National Park, Mex. 19°58′ N, 100°9′ W 112
Rayong, Thai. 12°41′ N, 101°18′ E 202
Rayside-Balfour, Can. 46°35′ N, 81°11′ W 94
Rayville, La., U.S. 32°27′ N, 91°46′ W 103
Raz, Pointe du, Fr. 47°46′ N, 4°59′ W 150
Razan, Iran 35°24′ N, 49°2′ E 180
Ražana, Serb. 44°5′ N, 19°54′ E 168
Ražanj, Serb. 43°40′ N, 21°32′ E 168
Razbojna, Serb. 43°19′ N, 21°10′ E 168
Razgrad, Bulg. 43°33′ N, 26°31′ E 156
Razgrad, adm. division, Bulg. 43°33′ N, 26°7′ E 156
Razhanka, Belarus 53°31′ N, 24°46′ E 158
Razzaza Lake, Iraq 32°54′ N, 42°53′ E 180
Re, Cu Lao, island, Vietnam 15°15′ N, 109°10′ E 202
Readfield, Me., U.S. 44°23′ N, 69°59′ W 104
Reading, Mich., U.S. 41°49′ N, 84°46′ W 102
Reading, Ohio, U.S. 39°13′ N, 84°27′ W 102
Reading, U.K. 51°27′ N, 0°57′ E 162
Readsboro, Vt., U.S. 42°46′ N, 72°58′ W 104
Real, Cordillera, Bol. 17°2′ S, 67°51′ W 132
Real del Castillo, Mex. 31°55′ N, 116°20′ W 92
Realicó, Arg. 35°2′ S, 64°14′ W 134
Ream, Cambodia 10°30′ N, 103°39′ E 202
Rębków, Pol. 51°52′ N, 21°33′ E 152
Rebojo, Cachoeira do, fall(s), Braz. 9°44′ S, 59°8′ W 130
Reboly, Russ. 63°49′ N, 30°47′ E 152
Rebouças, Braz. 25°37′ S, 50°42′ W 138
Rebun Tō, island, Japan 45°31′ N, 139°42′ E 190
Recalada, Isla, island, Chile 53°26′ S, 76°1′ W 134
Recalde, Arg. 36°41′ S, 61°9′ W 139
Recaş, Rom. 45°48′ N, 21°30′ E 168
Recherche, Archipelago of the, islands, Great Australian Bight 34°52′ S, 120°32′ E 230
Rechytsa, Belarus 52°19′ N, 30°26′ E 154
Recife, Braz. 8°4′ S, 34°57′ W 132
Recife, Cape, S. Af. 34°19′ S, 25°42′ E 227
Recklinghausen, Ger. 51°36′ N, 7°12′ E 167
Recoaro Terme, It. 45°43′ N, 11°13′ E 167
Reconquista, Arg. 29°10′ S, 59°39′ W 139
Recreo, Arg. 29°17′ S, 65°6′ W 134
Recsk, Hung. 47°55′ N, 20°7′ E 168
Red Bay, Ala., U.S. 34°26′ N, 88°8′ W 96
Red Bay, Can. 51°44′ N, 56°26′ W 111
Red Bluff, Calif., U.S. 40°11′ N, 122°16′ W 106
Red Cedar Lake, lake, Can. 46°38′ N, 80°30′ W 94
Red Cinder, peak, Calif., U.S. 40°29′ N, 121°20′ W 90
Red Cliff, Wis., U.S. 46°51′ N, 90°49′ W 94
Red Cloud, Nebr., U.S. 40°4′ N, 98°33′ W 90
Red Deer, Can. 52°13′ N, 113°48′ W 108
Red Deer Lake, lake, Can. 52°56′ N, 101°58′ W 108
Red Deer Point, Can. 52°4′ N, 99°51′ W 108
Red Deer, river, Can. 51°41′ N, 115°26′ W 108
Red Devil, Alas., U.S. 61°48′ N, 157°13′ W 73
Red Hill see Pu'u 'Ula'ula, peak, Hawai'i, U.S. 20°42′ N, 156°18′ W 99
Red Hill, site, Va., U.S. 37°0′ N, 78°58′ W 96
Red Hills, Kans., U.S. 37°28′ N, 99°23′ W 90
Red Hook, N.Y., U.S. 41°59′ N, 73°53′ W 104
Red Indian Lake, Can. 48°41′ N, 57°34′ W 111
Red Lake, Can. 51°0′ N, 93°50′ W 90
Red Lake, Can. 50°55′ N, 95°1′ W 80
Red Lake, Minn., U.S. 47°50′ N, 95°1′ W 90
Red Lake Falls, Minn., U.S. 47°50′ N, 96°18′ W 90
Red Lake Road, Can. 49°57′ N, 93°23′ W 90
Red Lick, Miss., U.S. 31°46′ N, 90°58′ W 103
Red Mountain, Calif., U.S. 35°21′ N, 117°38′ W 101
Red Mountain, peak, Calif., U.S. 41°30′ N, 124°0′ W 90
Red Mountain, peak, Mont., U.S. 47°4′ N, 112°49′ W 90
Red Oak, Iowa, U.S. 40°59′ N, 95°12′ W 94
Red Pass, Can. 52°57′ N, 119°3′ W 108
Red, river, Can. 59°17′ N, 128°11′ W 108
Red, river, Can. 49°16′ N, 97°12′ W 90
Red, river, La., U.S. 31°11′ N, 92°26′ W 103
Red, river, Okla., U.S. 33°56′ N, 97°49′ W 80
Red, river, Tenn., U.S. 36°26′ N, 87°15′ W 96
Red Rock, Can. 48°56′ N, 88°16′ W 94
Red Sea 18°15′ N, 39°26′ E 182
Red Sea, adm. division, Sudan 19°37′ N, 35°5′ E 182
Red Sucker Lake, Can. 54°8′ N, 93°38′ W 108
Red Wing, Minn., U.S. 44°32′ N, 92°32′ W 94
Redang, island, Malaysia 5°44′ N, 103°4′ E 196
Redcar, U.K. 54°36′ N, 1°5′ W 162
Redcliff, Can. 50°4′ N, 110°46′ W 90
Redcliff, Zimb. 19°3′ S, 29°47′ E 224
Redcliffe, Mount, peak, Austral. 28°27′ S, 121°20′ E 230
Reddell, La., U.S. 30°39′ N, 92°26′ W 103
Reddick, Fla., U.S. 29°22′ N, 82°12′ W 105
Redding, Calif., U.S. 40°35′ N, 122°24′ W 90
Redding, Conn., U.S. 41°18′ N, 73°23′ W 104
Redditch, U.K. 52°18′ N, 1°57′ W 162
Redeyef, Tun. 34°21′ N, 8°7′ E 214
Redfield, S. Dak., U.S. 44°51′ N, 98°33′ W 90
Redgranite, Wis., U.S. 44°1′ N, 89°6′ W 102
Rédics, Hung. 46°36′ N, 16°29′ E 168
Redig, S. Dak., U.S. 45°15′ N, 103°33′ W 90
Redkey, Ind., U.S. 40°20′ N, 85°9′ W 102
Redknife, river, Can. 60°49′ N, 119°41′ W 108
Redlands, Calif., U.S. 34°3′ N, 117°13′ W 101
Redmon, Ill., U.S. 39°38′ N, 87°52′ W 102
Redmond, Oreg., U.S. 44°16′ N, 121°9′ W 238
Redmond, Wash., U.S. 47°39′ N, 122°7′ W 100
Redon, Fr. 47°39′ N, 2°7′ W 150
Redonda Islands, Strait of Georgia 50°12′ N, 124°55′ W 100
Redonda, Punta, Arg. 41°8′ S, 62°40′ W 134
Redondeados, Mex. 25°51′ N, 106°48′ W 114
Redondo, Port. 38°38′ N, 7°34′ W 150
Redondo Beach, Calif., U.S. 33°50′ N, 118°24′ W 101
Redondo, Pico, peak, Braz. 2°29′ N, 63°33′ W 130
Redoubt Volcano, peak, Alas., U.S. 60°28′ N, 152°55′ W 98
Redvers, Can. 49°34′ N, 101°43′ W 90
Redwater, Can. 53°57′ N, 113°7′ W 108
Redwater, Tex., U.S. 33°21′ N, 94°16′ W 103
Redwood, Miss., U.S. 32°29′ N, 90°48′ W 103
Redwood City, Calif., U.S. 37°29′ N, 122°15′ W 100
Redwood Empire, region, Calif., U.S. 39°43′ N, 123°40′ W 92
Redwood National Park, Calif., U.S. 41°20′ N, 126°3′ W 92
Reed City, Mich., U.S. 43°52′ N, 85°31′ W 102
Reeder, N. Dak., U.S. 46°6′ N, 102°57′ W 90
Reedley, Calif., U.S. 36°35′ N, 119°28′ W 100
Reedsburg, Wis., U.S. 43°32′ N, 90°1′ W 102
Reedsport, Oreg., U.S. 43°41′ N, 124°6′ W 90
Reedsville, Wis., U.S. 44°9′ N, 87°58′ W 102
Reefton, N.Z. 42°7′ S, 171°52′ E 240
Rees, Ger. 51°45′ N, 6°24′ E 167
Reese, Mich., U.S. 43°26′ N, 83°42′ W 102
Reeth, U.K. 54°23′ N, 1°57′ W 162
Reeves, La., U.S. 30°30′ N, 93°4′ W 103
Refahiye, Turk. 39°53′ N, 38°47′ E 180
Reform, Ala., U.S. 33°21′ N, 88°1′ W 103
Refuge Cove, Can. 50°7′ N, 124°50′ W 100
Refugio, Tex., U.S. 28°18′ N, 97°17′ W 96
Regbat, region, Alg. 26°23′ N, 6°14′ W 214
Regência, Braz. 19°40′ S, 39°54′ W 138
Regência, Pontal de, Braz. 20°0′ S, 39°48′ W 138
Regeneração, Braz. 6°16′ S, 42°43′ W 132
Regensburg, Ger. 49°0′ N, 12°6′ E 152
Reggane, Alg. 26°42′ N, 0°8′ E 214
Reggio di Calabria, It. 38°13′ N, 15°40′ E 143
Regina, Can. 50°26′ N, 104°46′ W 90
Régina, South America 4°21′ N, 52°11′ W 130
Registro, Braz. 24°30′ S, 47°48′ W 138
Registro do Araguaia, Braz. 15°45′ S, 51°47′ W 138
Regocijo, Mex. 23°39′ N, 105°9′ W 114
Regozero, Russ. 65°30′ N, 31°17′ E 152
Rehoboth, Namibia 23°18′ S, 17°3′ E 227
Reḥovot, Israel 31°53′ N, 34°48′ E 194
Reïbell see Ksar Chellala, Alg. 35°12′ N, 2°19′ E 150
Reidsville, Ga., U.S. 32°4′ N, 82°7′ W 96
Reidsville, N.C., U.S. 36°21′ N, 79°41′ W 94
Reigate, U.K. 51°14′ N, 0°13′ E 162
Reims, Fr. 49°15′ N, 4°2′ E 163
Reina Adelaida, Archipiélago, islands, Chile 52°7′ S, 78°46′ W 134
Reina, Jardines de la, islands, Caribbean Sea 20°13′ N, 79°3′ W 115
Reinbolt Hills, Antarctica 71°11′ S, 72°8′ E 248
Reindeer Lake, Can. 57°3′ N, 111°32′ W 72
Reine, Nor. 67°55′ N, 13°4′ E 152
Reinga, Cape, N.Z. 34°27′ S, 172°19′ E 240
Reinhardswald, Ger. 51°28′ N, 9°23′ E 167
Reinosa, Sp. 43°0′ N, 4°9′ W 150
Reira, spring, Sudan 15°19′ N, 34°38′ E 182
Reisjärvi, Fin. 63°36′ N, 24°52′ E 154
Reitz, S. Af. 27°50′ S, 28°24′ E 227
Rejaf, Sudan 4°43′ N, 31°33′ E 224
Rekavice, Bosn. and Herzg. 44°40′ N, 17°7′ E 168
Reken, Ger. 51°50′ N, 7°3′ E 167
Rekinniki, Russ. 60°45′ N, 163°30′ E 160
Rekovac, Serb. 43°51′ N, 21°6′ E 168
Rėkyva, lake, Lith. 55°51′ N, 23°5′ E 166

Reliance, *Can.* 62°44′ N, 109°4′ W 106
Reliance, *Wyo., U.S.* 41°40′ N, 109°11′ W 90
Relizane, *Alg.* 35°44′ N, 0°33′ E 150
Remada, *Tun.* 32°21′ N, 10°24′ E 216
Remagen, *Ger.* 50°34′ N, 7°13′ E 167
Remansão, *Braz.* 4°28′ S, 49°35′ W 130
Remanso, *Braz.* 9°34′ S, 42°8′ W 132
Remarkables, The, peak, *N.Z.* 45°6′ S, 168°45′ E 240
Remate de Males, *Braz.* 4°25′ S, 70°13′ W 130
Remecó, *Arg.* 37°39′ S, 63°37′ W 139
Remer, *Minn., U.S.* 47°2′ N, 93°56′ W 90
Remeshk, *Iran* 26°48′ N, 58°51′ E 196
Remich, *Lux.* 49°33′ N, 6°21′ E 163
Remington, *Ind., U.S.* 40°45′ N, 87°10′ W 102
Rémire, *South America* 4°54′ N, 52°17′ W 130
Remmel Mountain, peak, *Wash., U.S.* 48°54′ N, 120°17′ W 90
Remontnoye, *Russ.* 46°30′ N, 43°34′ E 158
Remscheid, *Ger.* 51°10′ N, 7°11′ E 167
Remus, *Mich., U.S.* 43°36′ N, 85°9′ W 102
Rena, *Nor.* 61°8′ N, 11°19′ E 152
Renascença, *Braz.* 3°51′ S, 66°30′ W 130
Renaud Island, *Antarctica* 65°34′ S, 68°9′ W 134
Renca, *Arg.* 32°47′ S, 65°19′ W 134
Rencēni, *Latv.* 57°43′ N, 25°23′ E 166
Renda, *Latv.* 57°3′ N, 22°15′ E 166
Rendakoma, *Eth.* 14°25′ N, 40°2′ E 182
Rendova, island, *Solomon Islands* 8°35′ S, 157°15′ E 242
Renfrew, *Can.* 45°28′ N, 76°43′ W 94
Rengat, *Indonesia* 0°23′ N, 102°30′ E 196
Renholmen, *Nor.* 65°0′ N, 21°20′ E 152
Renhuai, *China* 27°46′ N, 106°24′ E 198
Reni, *India* 28°40′ N, 75°4′ E 186
Renison, *Can.* 50°58′ N, 81°9′ W 110
Renk, *Sudan* 11°44′ N, 32°48′ E 182
Renko, *Fin.* 60°53′ N, 24°16′ E 166
Rennell, island, *Solomon Islands* 11°41′ S, 160°19′ E 242
Rennell Sound 53°18′ N, 132°59′ W 108
Rennerod, *Ger.* 50°36′ N, 8°3′ E 167
Rennes, *Fr.* 48°6′ N, 1°42′ W 150
Reno, *Nev., U.S.* 39°32′ N, 119°50′ W 90
Reno, river, *It.* 44°34′ N, 11°58′ E 167
Rensselaer, *Ind., U.S.* 40°56′ N, 87°10′ W 102
Rensselaer, *N.Y., U.S.* 42°37′ N, 73°45′ W 104
Rentería, *Sp.* 43°17′ N, 1°54′ W 164
Renton, *Wash., U.S.* 47°28′ N, 122°14′ W 100
Renville, *Minn., U.S.* 44°46′ N, 95°13′ W 90
Reo, *Indonesia* 8°26′ S, 120°26′ E 192
Répcelak, *Hung.* 47°25′ N, 17°1′ E 168
Repino, *Russ.* 60°10′ N, 29°52′ E 166
Replot (Raippaluoto), *Fin.* 63°13′ N, 21°24′ E 152
Reposaari, *Fin.* 61°36′ N, 21°25′ E 166
Repparfjord, *Nor.* 70°26′ N, 24°19′ E 152
Republic, *Mich., U.S.* 46°24′ N, 87°58′ W 94
Republic, *Ohio, U.S.* 41°6′ N, 83°1′ W 102
Republican, river, *Nebr., U.S.* 40°17′ N, 100°48′ W 80
Repulse Bay, *Can.* 66°39′ N, 86°29′ W 73
Requa, *Calif., U.S.* 41°32′ N, 124°4′ W 90
Requena, *Peru* 5°5′ S, 73°50′ W 130
Requena, *Sp.* 39°30′ N, 1°7′ W 164
Requeña, *Venez.* 7°58′ N, 65°33′ W 136
Reşadiye, *Turk.* 40°23′ N, 37°19′ E 156
Resavica, *Serb.* 44°1′ N, 21°34′ E 168
Rescue, Punta, *Chile* 46°16′ S, 76°41′ W 134
Resende, *Braz.* 22°29′ S, 44°22′ W 138
Reserva, *Braz.* 24°41′ S, 50°55′ W 138
Reserve, *N. Mex., U.S.* 33°41′ N, 108°46′ W 92
Reshadat, oil field, *Persian Gulf* 25°57′ N, 52°43′ E 196
Reshety, *Russ.* 57°8′ N, 28°27′ E 166
Resia, *It.* 46°49′ N, 10°32′ E 167
Resistencia, *Arg.* 27°27′ S, 59°2′ W 139
Reşiţa, *Rom.* 45°18′ N, 21°53′ E 168
Resolute, *Can.* 74°39′ N, 94°58′ W 73
Resolution Island, *Can.* 61°20′ N, 64°59′ W 106
Restigouche, *Can.* 48°1′ N, 66°43′ W 94
Reston, *Can.* 49°32′ N, 101°7′ W 90
Restrepo, *Col.* 4°14′ N, 73°34′ W 136
Reszel, *Pol.* 54°2′ N, 21°8′ E 166
Retalhuleu, *Guatemala* 14°32′ N, 91°40′ W 115
Retezat, Munţii, *Rom.* 45°19′ N, 22°47′ E 168
Rethel, *Fr.* 49°30′ N, 4°21′ E 163
Rethondes, *Fr.* 49°24′ N, 2°56′ E 163
Reti, *Pak.* 28°4′ N, 69°49′ E 186
Retno, *Russ.* 57°59′ N, 30°12′ E 166
Rétság, *Hung.* 47°54′ N, 19°9′ E 168
Return Point, *Antarctica* 60°50′ S, 47°56′ W 134
Réunion, island, *Fr.* 21°9′ S, 55°35′ E 254
Reus, *Sp.* 41°8′ N, 1°6′ E 164
Reva, *S. Dak., U.S.* 45°32′ N, 103°6′ W 90
Reval see Tallinn, *Est.* 59°23′ N, 24°37′ E 166
Revda, *Russ.* 67°58′ N, 34°30′ E 152
Revda, *Russ.* 56°47′ N, 59°56′ E 154
Reveille Peak, *Nev., U.S.* 37°50′ N, 116°13′ W 90
Revelle Inlet 68°43′ S, 66°23′ W 248
Revelstoke, *Can.* 51°0′ N, 118°12′ W 90
Révfülöp, *Hung.* 46°50′ N, 17°38′ E 168
Revigny, *Fr.* 48°50′ N, 4°59′ E 163
Revillagigedo, Islas, islands, *North Pacific Ocean* 18°28′ N, 113°41′ W 112
Revin, *Fr.* 49°55′ N, 4°38′ E 163
Revivim, *Israel* 31°1′ N, 34°43′ E 194
Rewa, *India* 24°31′ N, 81°19′ E 197
Rex, Mount, peak, *Antarctica* 74°52′ S, 76°39′ W 248
Rexburg, *Idaho, U.S.* 43°49′ N, 111°48′ W 90
Rexford, *Mont., U.S.* 48°52′ N, 115°10′ W 90
Rexton, *Mich., U.S.* 46°9′ N, 85°15′ W 110
Rey, *Iran* 35°34′ N, 51°30′ E 180
Rey Bouba, *Cameroon* 8°38′ N, 14°12′ E 218
Rey, Isla del, island, *Pan.* 8°7′ N, 79°3′ W 115
Rey, river, *Cameroon* 8°10′ N, 14°26′ E 218
Reyes, *Bol.* 14°22′ S, 67°25′ W 137
Reyes, Point 38°2′ N, 123°22′ W 90
Reyes, Punta, *Col.* 2°40′ N, 78°24′ W 136
Reykjanes Ridge, *North Atlantic Ocean* 59°58′ N, 29°41′ W 253
Reykjavík, *Ice.* 64°4′ N, 22°23′ W 143
Reynoldsburg, *Ohio, U.S.* 39°56′ N, 82°49′ W 102
Rēzekne, *Latv.* 56°29′ N, 27°19′ E 166
Rezh, *Russ.* 57°23′ N, 61°22′ E 154
Rezh, river, *Russ.* 57°26′ N, 60°57′ E 154
Rezovo, *Bulg.* 41°59′ N, 28°1′ E 156
Rgotina, *Serb.* 44°0′ N, 22°16′ E 168
Rhaetian Alps, *Switz.* 46°22′ N, 9°21′ E 167
Rhafsaï, *Mor.* 34°39′ N, 4°55′ W 214
Rhame, *N. Dak., U.S.* 46°13′ N, 103°40′ W 90
Rhamnus, ruin(s), *Gr.* 38°12′ N, 23°56′ E 156
Rhayader, *U.K.* 52°17′ N, 3°31′ W 162
Rheda-Wiedenbrück, *Ger.* 51°51′ N, 8°17′ E 167
Rhede, *Ger.* 51°50′ N, 6°42′ E 167
Rheden, *Neth.* 52°0′ N, 6°3′ E 167
Rhein, river, *Ger.* 51°47′ N, 6°15′ E 167
Rheinbach, *Ger.* 50°37′ N, 6°57′ E 167
Rheinbrohl, *Ger.* 50°29′ N, 7°21′ E 167
Rheine, *Ger.* 52°16′ N, 7°26′ E 163
Rheinland-Palatinate, adm. division, *Ger.* 49°50′ N, 6°34′ E 150
Rhemilès, spring, *Alg.* 28°28′ N, 4°22′ W 214
Rhens, *Ger.* 50°16′ N, 7°37′ E 167
Rheydt, *Ger.* 51°9′ N, 6°26′ E 167
Rhinebeck, *N.Y., U.S.* 41°55′ N, 73°55′ W 104
Rhinelander, *Wis., U.S.* 45°38′ N, 89°23′ W 94
Rhineland-Palatinate, adm. division, *Ger.* 50°15′ N, 6°36′ E 167
Rhino Camp, *Uganda* 2°58′ N, 31°23′ E 224
Rhinocolura see El 'Arîsh, *Egypt* 31°6′ N, 33°46′ E 194
Rhiou, river, *Alg.* 35°59′ N, 0°58′ E 150
Rhir, Cap, *Mor.* 30°41′ N, 10°44′ W 214
Rho, *It.* 45°32′ N, 9°1′ E 167
Rhode Island, adm. division, *R.I., U.S.* 41°45′ N, 71°46′ W 104
Rhode Island Sound 41°14′ N, 71°13′ W 104
Rhodes Peak, *Idaho, U.S.* 46°38′ N, 114°53′ W 90
Rhodes see Ródos, *Gr.* 36°25′ N, 28°13′ E 156
Rhodes see Ródos, adm. division, *Gr.* 35°58′ N, 27°21′ E 156
Rhodes see Ródos, island, *Gr.* 35°44′ N, 27°53′ E 156
Rhodope Mountains, *Bulg.* 41°50′ N, 23°44′ E 156
Rhön, *Ger.* 50°36′ N, 9°54′ E 167
Rhône, river, *Europe* 46°10′ N, 7°16′ E 165
Rhône-Alpes, adm. division, *Fr.* 45°24′ N, 5°32′ E 156
Rhône-Alpes, adm. division, *Fr.* 45°41′ N, 4°23′ E 150
Rhourd el Baguel, oil field, *Alg.* 31°25′ N, 6°40′ E 214
Rhyl, *U.K.* 53°18′ N, 3°29′ W 162
Riachão, *Braz.* 7°22′ S, 46°41′ W 130
Riacho de Santana, *Braz.* 13°37′ S, 42°59′ W 138
Riachos, Isla de los, island, *Arg.* 40°12′ S, 62°5′ W 134
Rialma, *Braz.* 15°21′ S, 49°34′ W 138
Rialto, *Calif., U.S.* 34°6′ N, 117°23′ W 101
Rianápolis, *Braz.* 15°31′ S, 49°28′ W 138
Riangnom, *Sudan* 9°53′ N, 30°1′ E 224
Riaño, *Sp.* 42°57′ N, 5°2′ W 150
Riasi, *India* 33°4′ N, 74°51′ E 186
Riau, Kepulauan, islands, *South China Sea* 0°25′ N, 103°59′ E 196
Riaza, *Sp.* 41°16′ N, 3°29′ W 164
Rib Lake, *Wis., U.S.* 45°19′ N, 90°13′ W 94
Rib Mountain, peak, *Wis., U.S.* 44°54′ N, 89°47′ W 94
Riba de Saelices, *Sp.* 40°54′ N, 2°18′ W 164
Ribadavia, *Sp.* 42°16′ N, 8°11′ W 150
Ribadeo, *Sp.* 43°31′ N, 7°4′ W 150
Riba-roja d'Ebre, *Sp.* 41°13′ N, 0°28′ E 164
Ribarska Banja, *Serb.* 43°25′ N, 21°32′ E 168
Ribas do Rio Pardo, *Braz.* 20°27′ S, 53°49′ W 132
Ribáuè, *Mozambique* 14°57′ S, 38°21′ E 220
Ribe, *Den.* 55°19′ N, 8°45′ E 150
Ribécourt-Dreslincourt, *Fr.* 49°30′ N, 2°55′ E 163
Ribeira, *Braz.* 24°41′ S, 49°0′ W 138
Ribeira do Pombal, *Braz.* 10°49′ S, 38°34′ W 132
Ribeira, river, *Braz.* 24°43′ S, 48°18′ W 138
Ribeirão, *Braz.* 8°30′ S, 35°20′ W 132
Ribeirão do Salto, *Braz.* 15°48′ S, 40°17′ W 138
Ribeirão Preto, *Braz.* 21°11′ S, 47°50′ W 138
Ribemont, *Fr.* 49°47′ N, 3°27′ E 163
Riberalta, *Bol.* 11°2′ S, 66°7′ W 137
Ribes de Freser, *Sp.* 42°18′ N, 2°9′ E 164
Riblah, *Syr.* 34°27′ N, 36°33′ E 194
Rîbniţa, *Mold.* 47°44′ N, 29°0′ E 156
Ricardo Flores Magón, *Mex.* 29°56′ N, 106°58′ W 92
Ricaurte, *Col.* 1°10′ S, 70°14′ W 136
Riccione, *It.* 43°58′ N, 12°38′ E 167
Rice Lake, *Wis., U.S.* 45°30′ N, 91°45′ W 94
Rice Mountain, peak, *N.H., U.S.* 44°50′ N, 71°20′ W 94
Rice Valley, *Calif., U.S.* 34°1′ N, 114°52′ W 101
Rich, *Mor.* 32°20′ N, 4°31′ W 214
Rich Creek, *Va., U.S.* 37°22′ N, 80°50′ W 96
Rich Hill, *Mo., U.S.* 38°4′ N, 94°22′ W 94
Richan, *Can.* 49°59′ N, 92°49′ W 94
Richard Collinson Inlet 72°42′ N, 114°48′ W 106
Richard Toll, *Senegal* 16°28′ N, 15°44′ W 222
Richards Bay, *S. Af.* 28°48′ S, 32°6′ E 227
Richards Island, *Can.* 69°12′ N, 136°58′ W 98
Richardson Lake, *Can.* 58°18′ N, 111°58′ W 108
Richardson Mountains, *Can.* 68°35′ N, 136°39′ W 98
Richardson, river, *Can.* 58°6′ N, 111°0′ W 108
Richardton, *N. Dak., U.S.* 46°52′ N, 102°20′ W 90
Riche, Pointe, *Can.* 50°43′ N, 58°9′ W 111
Richey, *Mont., U.S.* 47°37′ N, 105°6′ W 90
Richfield, *Utah, U.S.* 38°46′ N, 112°5′ W 92
Richford, *Vt., U.S.* 44°59′ N, 72°41′ W 94
Richgrove, *Calif., U.S.* 35°48′ N, 119°7′ W 101
Richibucto, *Can.* 46°40′ N, 64°53′ W 111
Richland, *Wash., U.S.* 46°21′ N, 119°20′ W 246
Richland Center, *Wis., U.S.* 43°19′ N, 90°23′ W 94
Richland Springs, *Tex., U.S.* 31°15′ N, 98°57′ W 92
Richlands, *Va., U.S.* 37°5′ N, 81°49′ W 94
Richmond, *Austral.* 33°37′ S, 150°48′ E 231
Richmond, *Calif., U.S.* 37°56′ N, 122°21′ W 100
Richmond, *Can.* 45°39′ N, 72°8′ W 111
Richmond, *Can.* 49°9′ N, 123°10′ W 100
Richmond, *Ill., U.S.* 42°28′ N, 88°18′ W 102
Richmond, *Ind., U.S.* 39°48′ N, 84°52′ W 102
Richmond, *Ky., U.S.* 37°43′ N, 84°18′ W 96
Richmond, *Me., U.S.* 44°5′ N, 69°49′ W 104
Richmond, *Mass., U.S.* 42°21′ N, 73°23′ W 104
Richmond, *Mo., U.S.* 39°16′ N, 93°58′ W 94
Richmond, *Mo., U.S.* 42°28′ N, 88°18′ W 94
Richmond, *N.H., U.S.* 42°44′ N, 72°17′ W 104
Richmond, *S. Af.* 29°54′ S, 30°15′ E 227
Richmond, *S. Af.* 31°26′ S, 23°56′ E 227
Richmond, *U.K.* 54°24′ N, 1°45′ W 162
Richmond, *Vt., U.S.* 44°24′ N, 73°0′ W 104
Richmond, *Va., U.S.* 37°30′ N, 77°33′ W 94
Richmond Dale, *Ohio, U.S.* 39°12′ N, 82°49′ W 102
Richmond Hill, *Can.* 43°53′ N, 79°26′ W 94
Richtersveld National Park, *S. Af.* 28°14′ S, 16°16′ E 227
Richton, *Miss., U.S.* 31°20′ N, 88°56′ W 103
Richwood, *Ohio, U.S.* 40°25′ N, 83°17′ W 102
Ricla, *Sp.* 41°30′ N, 1°25′ W 164
Rico, *Colo., U.S.* 37°41′ N, 108°2′ W 92
Ridā', *Yemen* 14°26′ N, 44°49′ E 182
Ridanna, *It.* 46°54′ N, 11°17′ E 167
Riddell Nunataks, *Antarctica* 70°25′ S, 56°25′ E 248
Ridder, *Kaz.* 50°16′ N, 83°30′ E 190
Ridder (Leninogorsk), *Kaz.* 50°21′ N, 83°32′ E 184
Riddle, *Idaho, U.S.* 42°12′ N, 116°7′ W 90
Riderwood, *Ala., U.S.* 32°8′ N, 88°20′ W 103
Ridge Farm, *Ill., U.S.* 39°53′ N, 87°39′ W 102
Ridge, river, *Can.* 50°24′ N, 83°51′ W 110
Ridgecrest, *Calif., U.S.* 35°37′ N, 117°41′ W 101
Ridgefield, *Conn., U.S.* 41°17′ N, 73°30′ W 104
Ridgefield, *Wash., U.S.* 45°48′ N, 122°44′ W 100
Ridgeland, *Miss., U.S.* 32°24′ N, 90°9′ W 103
Ridgetown, *Can.* 42°25′ N, 81°53′ W 102
Ridgeville, *Ind., U.S.* 40°16′ N, 85°2′ W 102
Ridgewood, *N.J., U.S.* 40°58′ N, 74°8′ W 104
Riding Mountain National Park, *Can.* 50°49′ N, 101°3′ W 108
Riding Rocks, islands, *North Atlantic Ocean* 24°56′ N, 79°6′ W 116
Riedlingen, *Ger.* 48°9′ N, 9°29′ E 156
Rieneck, *Ger.* 50°5′ N, 9°39′ E 167
Ries, region, *Ger.* 48°44′ N, 10°30′ E 152
Riesco, Isla, island, *Chile* 52°41′ S, 71°24′ W 134
Rietavas, *Lith.* 55°44′ N, 21°56′ E 166
Rietberg, *Ger.* 51°47′ N, 8°25′ E 167
Rietfontein, *Namibia* 26°46′ S, 19°59′ E 227
Rievaulx, *U.K.* 54°15′ N, 1°7′ W 162
Riffe Lake, *Wash., U.S.* 46°28′ N, 122°21′ W 100
Rifle, *Colo., U.S.* 39°31′ N, 107°47′ W 90
Rig Rig, *Chad* 14°16′ N, 14°21′ E 216
Rīga, *Latv.* 56°55′ N, 24°1′ E 166
Riga, Gulf of 57°41′ N, 23°20′ E 166
Rīgān, *Iran* 28°38′ N, 59°3′ E 196
Riggins, *Idaho, U.S.* 45°24′ N, 116°19′ W 90
Rigolet, *Can.* 54°11′ N, 58°24′ W 111
Riguldi, *Est.* 59°6′ N, 23°31′ E 166
Rihand Dam, *India* 23°55′ N, 82°11′ E 197
Riihimäki, *Fin.* 60°44′ N, 24°44′ E 166
Riipi, *Fin.* 67°19′ N, 26°3′ E 152
Riiser-Larsen, Mount, peak, *Antarctica* 66°44′ S, 50°12′ E 248
Riisipere, *Est.* 59°6′ N, 24°17′ E 166
Riistavesi, *Fin.* 62°53′ N, 28°6′ E 154
Rifto, *Mex.* 32°5′ N, 114°55′ W 92
Rijau, *Nig.* 11°4′ N, 5°14′ E 222
Rijeća, *Bosn. and Herzg.* 44°1′ N, 18°40′ E 168
Rijeka (Fiume), *Croatia* 45°20′ N, 14°26′ E 156
Rijssen, *Neth.* 52°18′ N, 6°30′ E 163
Rila, *Bulg.* 41°59′ N, 23°11′ E 168
Rila, *Bulg.* 42°7′ N, 23°8′ E 168
Rila National Park, *Bulg.* 41°47′ N, 22°39′ E 180
Riley, *Kans., U.S.* 39°16′ N, 96°50′ W 90
Rilly, *Fr.* 49°9′ N, 4°2′ E 163
Rimā', Jabal ar, peak, *Jordan* 32°18′ N, 36°51′ E 194
Rimbey, *Can.* 52°37′ N, 114°14′ W 108
Rimbo, *Sw.* 59°44′ N, 18°21′ E 166
Rimini, *It.* 44°2′ N, 12°33′ E 167
Rîmnicu Sărat, *Rom.* 45°23′ N, 27°3′ E 156
Rimouski, *Can.* 48°26′ N, 68°31′ W 94
Rimpar, *Ger.* 49°51′ N, 9°57′ E 167
Rimrock, *Wash., U.S.* 46°39′ N, 121°8′ W 100
Rinbung, *China* 29°15′ N, 89°57′ E 197
Rinca, island, *Indonesia* 9°14′ S, 119°36′ E 192
Rincão, *Braz.* 21°33′ S, 48°5′ W 138
Rînceni, *Rom.* 46°23′ N, 28°7′ E 158
Rincon, *Ga., U.S.* 32°17′ N, 81°14′ W 96
Rincon, *N. Mex., U.S.* 32°40′ N, 107°5′ W 92
Rincón, Cerro, peak, *Arg.* 24°6′ S, 67°30′ W 132
Rincon de Guayabitos, *Mex.* 21°0′ N, 105°20′ W 114
Rincón de Romos, *Mex.* 22°13′ N, 102°19′ W 114
Rincón de Soto, *Sp.* 42°13′ N, 1°51′ W 164
Rincón del Atuel, *Arg.* 34°44′ S, 68°23′ W 134
Rincón del Bonete, *Uru.* 32°54′ S, 56°26′ W 139
Rincón del Bonete, Lago, lake, *Uru.* 32°30′ S, 56°26′ W 139
Rincón Hondo, *Venez.* 7°24′ N, 69°6′ W 136
Rincona, *Sp.* 37°11′ N, 4°28′ W 164
Rinconada, *Arg.* 22°27′ S, 66°13′ W 137
Rindge, *N.H., U.S.* 42°44′ N, 72°1′ W 104
Ringgold, *La., U.S.* 32°18′ N, 93°17′ W 103
Ringim, *Nig.* 12°9′ N, 9°9′ E 222
Ringkøbing, *Den.* 56°5′ N, 8°13′ E 150
Ringwood, *U.K.* 50°51′ N, 1°47′ W 162
Rini, spring, *Mauritania* 16°57′ N, 6°58′ W 222
Rinns Point 55°29′ N, 6°45′ W 150
Rio, *Fla., U.S.* 27°13′ N, 80°15′ W 105
Rio Abiseo National Park, *Peru* 8°0′ S, 77°34′ W 122
Rio Azul, *Braz.* 25°45′ S, 50°48′ W 138
Rio Branco, *Braz.* 9°58′ S, 67°49′ W 137
Río Branco, *Uru.* 32°34′ S, 53°23′ W 139
Rio Branco do Sul, *Braz.* 25°10′ S, 49°21′ W 138
Río Bravo, *Mex.* 26°0′ N, 98°8′ W 114
Rio Bravo del Norte see Rio Grande, river, *North America* 28°13′ N, 99°43′ W 80
Rio Brilhante, *Braz.* 21°50′ S, 54°32′ W 132
Río Bueno, *Chile* 40°20′ S, 72°59′ W 134
Río Caribe, *Venez.* 10°40′ N, 63°7′ W 116
Río Chico, *Venez.* 10°21′ N, 65°59′ W 136
Rio Claro, *Braz.* 22°26′ S, 47°35′ W 138
Río Colorado, *Arg.* 39°1′ S, 64°5′ W 139
Río Corrientes, *Ecua.* 2°22′ S, 76°23′ W 136
Río Cuarto, *Arg.* 33°10′ S, 64°21′ W 134
Rio das Mortes see Manso, river, *Braz.* 15°20′ S, 53°1′ W 138
Rio de Contas, *Braz.* 13°34′ S, 41°51′ W 138
Rio de Janeiro, *Braz.* 22°53′ S, 43°15′ W 138
Rio de Janeiro, adm. division, *Braz.* 22°4′ S, 42°44′ W 138
Río de Jesús, *Pan.* 7°59′ N, 81°10′ W 115
Rio do Prado, *Braz.* 16°37′ S, 40°34′ W 138
Rio do Sul, *Braz.* 27°17′ S, 49°39′ W 138
Río Gallegos, *Arg.* 51°37′ S, 69°17′ W 134
Río Grande, *Arg.* 53°50′ S, 67°48′ W 123
Río Grande, *Bol.* 20°52′ S, 67°16′ W 137
Rio Grande, *Braz.* 32°1′ S, 52°11′ W 139
Río Grande, *Mex.* 23°47′ N, 103°2′ W 114
Rio Grande City, *Tex., U.S.* 26°24′ N, 98°49′ W 114
Río Grande de Matagalpa, river, *Nicar.* 13°21′ N, 84°20′ W 115
Rio Grande do Norte, adm. division, *Braz.* 5°27′ S, 37°44′ W 132
Rio Grande do Sul, adm. division, *Braz.* 28°37′ S, 53°52′ W 138
Rio Grande (Río Bravo del Norte), river, *North America* 28°13′ N, 99°43′ W 80
Rio Grande Rise, *South Atlantic Ocean* 31°19′ S, 35°27′ W 253
Rio Grande Wild and Scenic River, *Tex., U.S.* 29°51′ N, 102°10′ W 96
Río Muerto, *Arg.* 26°19′ S, 61°40′ W 139
Río Mulatos, *Bol.* 19°42′ S, 66°48′ W 137
Río Muni, region, *Equatorial Guinea* 1°40′ N, 9°49′ E 218
Rio Negro, *Braz.* 26°4′ S, 49°45′ W 138
Rio Pardo, *Braz.* 29°59′ S, 52°25′ W 139
Rio Pardo de Minas, *Braz.* 15°39′ S, 42°35′ W 138
Río Pico, *Arg.* 44°12′ S, 71°24′ W 134
Río Pilcomayo National Park, *Arg.* 25°17′ S, 58°18′ W 122
Rio Pomba, *Braz.* 21°17′ S, 43°11′ W 138
Río Sucio, *Col.* 5°25′ N, 75°42′ W 136
Río Tercero, *Arg.* 32°13′ S, 64°8′ W 134
Río Tigre, *Ecua.* 2°7′ S, 76°4′ W 136
Rio Tinto, *Braz.* 6°48′ S, 35°5′ W 132
Rio Tuba, *Philippines* 8°33′ N, 117°26′ E 203
Rio Verde, *Braz.* 17°50′ S, 50°57′ W 138
Río Verde, *Chile* 52°34′ S, 71°28′ W 134
Río Verde, *Mex.* 21°53′ N, 100°0′ W 114
Rio Verde de Mato Grosso, *Braz.* 18°57′ S, 54°53′ W 132
Rio Vista, *Calif., U.S.* 38°9′ N, 121°43′ W 100
Riobamba, *Ecua.* 1°47′ S, 78°47′ W 130
Riogordo, *Sp.* 36°54′ N, 4°18′ W 164
Ríohacha, *Col.* 11°29′ N, 72°55′ W 136
Riom, *Fr.* 45°54′ N, 3°6′ E 150
Riomaggiore, *It.* 44°5′ N, 9°45′ E 167
Rion-des-Landes, *Fr.* 43°56′ N, 0°57′ E 150
Rionegro, *Col.* 6°10′ N, 75°21′ W 136
Rioni, river, *Ga.* 42°29′ N, 43°10′ E 195
Ríosucio, *Col.* 7°29′ N, 77°9′ W 136
Riou Lake, lake, *Can.* 59°2′ N, 106°56′ W 108
Riozinho, *Braz.* 9°32′ S, 66°51′ W 137
Riozinho, river, *Braz.* 3°7′ S, 67°7′ W 136
Riozinho, river, *Braz.* 8°22′ S, 52°3′ W 130
Ripanj, *Serb.* 44°38′ N, 20°30′ E 168
Riparius, *N.Y., U.S.* 43°39′ N, 73°55′ W 104
Ripley, *Calif., U.S.* 33°31′ N, 114°40′ W 101
Ripley, *Can.* 44°3′ N, 81°34′ W 102
Ripley, *Miss., U.S.* 34°42′ N, 88°58′ W 96
Ripley, *Ohio, U.S.* 38°43′ N, 83°49′ W 102
Ripley, *U.K.* 53°3′ N, 1°25′ W 162
Ripoll, *Sp.* 42°12′ N, 2°11′ E 164
Ripon, *Calif., U.S.* 37°44′ N, 121°8′ W 100
Ripon, *U.K.* 54°8′ N, 1°32′ W 162
Ripon, *Wis., U.S.* 43°50′ N, 88°50′ W 102
Ripple Mountain, peak, *Can.* 49°0′ N, 117°10′ W 90
Risaralda, adm. division, *South America* 5°9′ N, 76°8′ W 136
Risbäck, *Nor.* 64°41′ N, 15°31′ E 154
Rīshahr, *Iran* 28°50′ N, 50°55′ E 196
Rishikesh, *India* 30°8′ N, 78°18′ E 197
Rishiri Tō, island, *Japan* 44°52′ N, 140°18′ E 190
Rishon Leẕiyyon, *Israel* 31°57′ N, 34°47′ E 194
Rising Star, *Tex., U.S.* 32°5′ N, 98°59′ W 92
Rising Sun, *Ind., U.S.* 38°56′ N, 84°52′ W 102
Rissani, *Mor.* 31°18′ N, 4°15′ W 214
Risti, *Est.* 58°59′ N, 24°3′ E 166
Ristiina, *Fin.* 61°29′ N, 27°14′ E 166
Ristna, *Est.* 58°53′ N, 21°42′ E 166
Risum-Lindholm, *Ger.* 54°46′ N, 8°52′ E 150
Ritscher Upland, *Antarctica* 74°5′ S, 11°15′ W 248
Ritter, Mount, peak, *Calif., U.S.* 37°41′ N, 119°15′ W 100
Rittman, *Ohio, U.S.* 40°57′ N, 81°47′ W 102
Ritva, *Fin.* 65°29′ N, 26°32′ E 152
Ritzville, *Wash., U.S.* 47°6′ N, 118°24′ W 90
Riva del Garda, *It.* 45°53′ N, 10°50′ E 167
Rivadavia, *Arg.* 35°28′ S, 62°58′ W 139

Rivadavia, Arg. 33°12' S, 68°29' W 134
Rivarolo Canavese, It. 45°19' N, 7°43' E 167
Rivas, Nicar. 11°26' N, 85°51' W 115
River Cess, Liberia 5°26' N, 9°35' W 222
River Jordan, Can. 48°25' N, 124°2' W 100
River Nile, adm. division, Sudan 18°30' N, 32°31' E 182
Rivera, Arg. 37°12' S, 63°13' W 139
Rivera, Uru. 30°53' S, 55°35' W 139
Riverbank, Calif., U.S. 37°43' N, 120°58' W 100
Riverdale, Calif., U.S. 36°25' N, 119°53' W 100
Riverdale, N. Dak., U.S. 47°28' N, 101°23' W 90
Riverhead, N.Y., U.S. 40°55' N, 72°39' W 104
Riverhurst, Can. 50°54' N, 106°53' W 90
Riverina, region, Austral. 33°35' S, 146°11' E 230
Rivero, Isla, island, Chile 45°34' S, 75°39' W 134
Rivers, Can. 50°2' N, 100°15' W 90
Riversdale, N.Z. 45°56' S, 168°45' E 240
Riversdale, S. Af. 34°5' S, 21°14' E 220
Riverside, Calif., U.S. 33°59' N, 117°24' W 101
Riverside, Tex., U.S. 30°50' N, 95°24' W 103
Riverside, Wash., U.S. 48°29' N, 119°32' W 90
Riverton, Can. 50°58' N, 97°1' W 90
Riverton, Conn., U.S. 41°57' N, 73°1' W 104
Riverton, Ill., U.S. 39°50' N, 89°32' W 102
Riverton, Wyo., U.S. 43°1' N, 108°23' W 90
Riverview, Can. 46°2' N, 64°49' W 111
Rivesaltes, Fr. 42°45' N, 2°51' E 164
Riviera, Ariz., U.S. 35°5' N, 114°37' W 101
Riviera Beach, Fla., U.S. 26°46' N, 80°5' W 105
Riviera, region, Mediterranean Sea 43°21' N, 6°39' E 165
Rivière au Serpent, river, Can. 50°29' N, 71°42' W 110
Rivière aux Rats, river, Can. 49°9' N, 72°14' W 94
Rivière-de-la-Chaloupe, site, Gulf of St. Lawrence 49°8' N, 62°35' W 111
Rivière-du-Loup, Can. 47°48' N, 69°34' W 94
Rivne, Ukr. 50°37' N, 26°13' E 152
Rivoli, It. 45°3' N, 7°30' E 167
Riwaka, N.Z. 41°6' S, 172°59' E 240
Riwoqê, China 31°8' N, 96°33' E 188
Riyadh see Ar Riyāḑ, Saudi Arabia 24°35' N, 46°35' E 186
Rīyāq, Leb. 33°51' N, 36°0' E 194
Rize, Turk. 41°2' N, 40°29' E 195
Rizhao, China 35°26' N, 119°27' E 198
Rizokarpaso (Dipkarpaz), Cyprus 35°36' N, 34°22' E 194
Rizzuto, Capo, It. 38°48' N, 17°8' E 156
Rkiz, Lac, lake, Mauritania 16°55' N, 15°26' W 222
Roa, Sp. 41°41' N, 3°57' W 164
Roachdale, Ind., U.S. 39°50' N, 86°48' W 102
Road Town, Tortola 18°27' N, 64°38' W 116
Roan, Nor. 64°10' N, 10°14' E 152
Roan Cliffs, Colo., U.S. 39°38' N, 108°13' W 90
Roan Cliffs, Utah, U.S. 39°29' N, 110°17' W 90
Roan Plateau, Colo., U.S. 39°44' N, 108°50' W 90
Roann, Ind., U.S. 40°54' N, 85°54' W 102
Roanne, Fr. 46°1' N, 4°3' E 150
Roanoke, Ind., U.S. 40°57' N, 85°23' W 102
Roanoke, La., U.S. 30°13' N, 92°46' W 103
Roanoke Island, N.C., U.S. 35°46' N, 75°34' W 80
Roatán, Isla de, island, Hond. 16°13' N, 86°24' W 115
Robaa Ouled Yahia, Tun. 36°5' N, 9°34' E 156
Robāṭ-e Khān, Iran 33°21' N, 56°4' E 180
Robāţ-e Tork, Iran 33°45' N, 50°51' E 180
Robbins Island, Austral. 41°2' S, 142°8' E 230
Robe, Mount, peak, Austral. 31°41' S, 141°7' E 230
Robeline, La., U.S. 31°40' N, 93°19' W 103
Robert, Cap, Can. 49°29' N, 62°18' W 111
Robert, Cape, Antarctica 66°26' S, 137°47' E 248
Robert Lee, Tex., U.S. 31°53' N, 100°28' W 92
Roberts, Arg. 35°8' S, 61°59' W 139
Roberts, Idaho, U.S. 43°43' N, 112°7' W 90
Roberts, Ill., U.S. 40°37' N, 88°11' W 102
Roberts Butte, peak, Antarctica 72°35' S, 160°47' E 248
Roberts Creek Mountain, peak, Nev., U.S. 39°51' N, 116°23' W 90
Roberts Knoll, peak, Antarctica 71°27' S, 3°40' W 248
Roberts Mountain, peak, Wyo., U.S. 42°54' N, 109°22' W 90
Roberts, Point, Wash., U.S. 48°53' N, 122°45' W 80
Robertsdale, Ala., U.S. 30°32' N, 87°42' W 103
Robertsganj, India 24°40' N, 83°2' E 197
Robertson, S. Af. 33°48' S, 19°53' E 227
Robertson Island, Antarctica 65°11' S, 59°19' W 134
Robertsport, Liberia 6°40' N, 11°22' W 222
Roberval, Can. 48°28' N, 72°15' W 82
Robin Hood's Bay, U.K. 54°26' N, 0°33' E 162
Robinson, Ill., U.S. 39°0' N, 87°44' W 102
Robinson Range, Austral. 26°23' S, 118°37' E 230
Robinsons, Me., U.S. 46°28' N, 67°50' W 111
Roblin, Can. 51°14' N, 101°22' W 90
Roboré, Bol. 18°25' S, 59°43' W 132
Robsart, Can. 49°23' N, 109°17' W 90
Robson, Can. 49°20' N, 117°41' W 90
Robson, Mount, peak, Can. 53°5' N, 119°16' W 108
Roby, Tex., U.S. 32°44' N, 100°23' W 92
Roca Partida, Isla, island, Isla Roca Partida 19°1' N, 112°48' W 112
Roca Partida, Punta, Mex. 18°43' N, 95°14' W 114
Rocamadour, Fr. 44°46' N, 1°38' E 214
Rocas, Atol das, island, Atol das Rocas 4°5' S, 33°47' W 132
Rocchetta Ligure, It. 44°42' N, 9°3' E 167
Rocha, Uru. 34°30' S, 54°20' W 139
Rochdale, Mass., U.S. 42°11' N, 71°55' W 104
Rochdale, U.K. 53°37' N, 2°9' W 162
Rochefort, Belg. 50°9' N, 5°13' E 167
Rochegda, Russ. 62°42' N, 43°27' E 154
Rochelle, Ga., U.S. 31°56' N, 83°28' W 96
Rochelle, Ill., U.S. 41°55' N, 89°5' W 102
Rocher, Lac, lake, Can. 50°28' N, 77°0' W 110
Roches, Lac des, lake, Can. 51°30' N, 120°54' W 90
Rochester, Can. 54°22' N, 113°26' W 108
Rochester, Ill., U.S. 39°44' N, 89°32' W 102
Rochester, Ind., U.S. 41°3' N, 86°13' W 102
Rochester, Minn., U.S. 44°1' N, 92°30' W 94
Rochester, N.H., U.S. 43°18' N, 70°59' W 104
Rochester, N.Y., U.S. 43°9' N, 77°37' W 110
Rochester, Pa., U.S. 40°41' N, 80°17' W 94
Rochester, U.K. 51°22' N, 0°28' E 162
Rochester, Vt., U.S. 43°52' N, 72°49' W 104
Rochester, Wash., U.S. 46°48' N, 123°5' W 100
Rock Falls, Ill., U.S. 41°45' N, 89°42' W 102
Rock Hill, S.C., U.S. 34°55' N, 81°2' W 96
Rock Island, Mo., U.S. 41°29' N, 90°34' W 110
Rock Lake, N. Dak., U.S. 48°45' N, 99°15' W 90
Rock Rapids, Iowa, U.S. 43°24' N, 96°11' W 90
Rock River, Wyo., U.S. 41°44' N, 105°58' W 90
Rock, river, Can. 60°24' N, 127°14' W 108
Rock, river, Wis., U.S. 42°48' N, 89°12' W 102
Rock Sound, Bahamas 24°55' N, 76°10' W 96
Rock Springs, Mont., U.S. 46°47' N, 106°16' W 90
Rock Springs, Wyo., U.S. 41°38' N, 109°14' W 106
Rockall, island, U.K. 57°36' N, 13°41' W 253
Rockdale, Ill., U.S. 41°29' N, 88°7' W 102
Rockefeller Plateau, Antarctica 79°52' S, 104°57' W 248
Rockenhausen, Ger. 49°37' N, 7°48' E 163
Rockford, Ill., U.S. 42°16' N, 89°4' W 102
Rockford, Mich., U.S. 43°7' N, 85°33' W 102
Rockford, Ohio, U.S. 40°40' N, 84°39' W 102
Rockglen, Can. 49°10' N, 105°58' W 90
Rockingham, Austral. 32°19' S, 115°45' E 231
Rockingham, N.C., U.S. 34°55' N, 79°48' W 96
Rockingham, Vt., U.S. 43°11' N, 72°30' W 104
Rockland, Can. 45°32' N, 75°18' W 94
Rockland, Idaho, U.S. 42°35' N, 112°52' W 90
Rockland, Mass., U.S. 42°7' N, 70°55' W 104
Rockledge, Fla., U.S. 28°19' N, 80°44' W 105
Rockport, Calif., U.S. 39°44' N, 123°50' W 90
Rockport, Ind., U.S. 37°52' N, 87°4' W 94
Rockport, Me., U.S. 44°11' N, 69°5' W 94
Rockport, Tex., U.S. 28°0' N, 97°4' W 96
Rockport, Wash., U.S. 48°29' N, 121°36' W 100
Rocksprings, Tex., U.S. 30°0' N, 100°13' W 92
Rockton, Ill., U.S. 42°27' N, 89°5' W 102
Rockville, Ind., U.S. 39°45' N, 87°14' W 102
Rockville, N.Z. 40°46' S, 172°39' E 240
Rockwell City, Iowa, U.S. 42°23' N, 94°38' W 94
Rockwood, Tenn., U.S. 35°52' N, 84°41' W 96
Rocky Ford, Colo., U.S. 38°3' N, 103°44' W 90
Rocky Hill, Conn., U.S. 41°39' N, 72°39' W 104
Rocky Lane, Can. 58°29' N, 116°23' W 108
Rocky Mount, N.C., U.S. 35°55' N, 77°48' W 96
Rocky Mountain House, Can. 52°21' N, 114°53' W 108
Rocky Mountain National Park, Colo., U.S. 40°33' N, 105°37' W 80
Rocky Mountain, peak, Mont., U.S. 47°46' N, 112°52' W 90
Rocky Mountains, Mont., U.S. 45°5' N, 114°26' W 72
Rocky Point, Calif., U.S. 41°9' N, 124°26' W 90
Rocky Point, Namibia 19°6' S, 12°1' E 220
Rocky Point, N.Y., U.S. 40°56' N, 72°56' W 104
Roda de Isabena, Sp. 42°16' N, 0°31' E 164
Rødby, Den. 54°42' N, 11°23' E 152
Roddickton, Can. 50°51' N, 56°7' W 111
Rodel 57°44' N, 6°58' W 150
Rodeo, Arg. 30°13' S, 69°7' W 134
Rodeo, Mex. 25°8' N, 104°35' W 114
Rodeo, N. Mex., U.S. 31°50' N, 109°1' W 92
Rodessa, La., U.S. 32°57' N, 94°1' W 103
Rodez, Fr. 44°21' N, 2°35' E 150
Rodi Garganico, It. 41°55' N, 15°54' E 156
Rodino, Russ. 52°28' N, 80°18' E 184
Rodnei, Munţii, Rom. 47°28' N, 24°19' E 156
Rodney, Can. 42°33' N, 81°41' W 102
Rodniki, Kaz. 49°9' N, 58°22' E 158
Rodniki, Russ. 57°5' N, 41°39' E 154
Rodnīkovka, Kaz. 50°39' N, 57°8' E 158
Rodonit, Kepi i, Alban. 41°27' N, 19°15' E 168
Ródos, Gr. 36°20' N, 28°10' E 180
Ródos (Rhodes), Gr. 36°25' N, 28°13' E 156
Ródos (Rhodes), adm. division, Gr. 35°58' N, 27°21' E 156
Ródos (Rhodes), island, Gr. 35°44' N, 27°53' E 156
Rødøy, Nor. 66°39' N, 13°3' E 152
Rodrigues, Braz. 6°34' S, 73°12' W 130
Rodrigues, island, Mauritius 19°45' S, 63°25' E 254
Rodrigues Ridge, Indian Ocean 19°45' S, 62°11' E 254
Roebourne, Austral. 20°46' S, 117°6' E 231
Roebuck Bay 18°13' S, 120°59' E 230
Roes Welcome Sound 64°30' N, 89°28' W 106
Roeselare, Belg. 50°56' N, 3°7' E 163
Roetgen, Ger. 50°38' N, 6°11' E 167
Rogagua, Lago, lake, Bol. 13°40' S, 67°19' W 137
Rogaguado, Bol. 13°46' S, 64°44' W 137
Rogaguado, Laguna, lake, Bol. 12°56' S, 65°54' W 137
Rogaguado, Laguna, lake, Bol. 12°56' S, 66°43' W 130
Roganville, Tex., U.S. 30°47' N, 93°55' W 103
Rogatica, Bosn. and Herzg. 43°48' N, 19°0' E 168
Rogers, Ark., U.S. 36°18' N, 94°7' W 96
Rogers, Conn., U.S. 41°50' N, 71°55' W 104
Rogers, Tex., U.S. 30°54' N, 97°13' W 96
Rogers City, Mich., U.S. 45°25' N, 83°50' W 94
Rogers, Mount, peak, Va., U.S. 36°38' N, 81°38' W 96
Rogerson, Idaho, U.S. 42°13' N, 114°36' W 90
Rogersville, Tenn., U.S. 36°23' N, 83°1' W 94
Rognan, Nor. 67°5' N, 15°19' E 152
Rogun, Taj. 38°46' N, 69°51' E 197
Roha, India 18°25' N, 73°8' E 188
Rohault, Lac, lake, Can. 49°22' N, 74°51' W 94
Rohia, Tun. 35°39' N, 9°3' E 156
Röhlingen, Ger. 48°56' N, 10°11' E 152
Rohnerville, Calif., U.S. 40°34' N, 124°9' W 92
Rohri, Pak. 27°38' N, 68°59' E 186
Rohtak, India 28°54' N, 76°34' E 188
Rohtasgarh, India 24°36' N, 83°56' E 197
Roi Et, Thai. 16°3' N, 103°41' E 202
Roja, Latv. 57°30' N, 22°46' E 166
Roja, Punta, Sp. 38°26' N, 1°36' E 150
Rojas, Arg. 34°14' S, 60°41' W 139
Rojo, Cabo 17°49' N, 67°45' W 116
Rojo, Cabo, Mex. 21°36' N, 97°23' W 114
Rokan, river, Indonesia 0°57' N, 100°36' E 196
Rokeby National Park, Austral. 14°1' S, 142°34' E 238
Rokel, river, Sierra Leone 8°54' N, 11°46' W 222
Rokhmoyva, Gora, peak, Russ. 66°51' N, 29°2' E 152
Rokiškis, Lith. 55°57' N, 25°34' E 166
Rokytne, Ukr. 51°16' N, 27°11' E 152
Rola Co, lake, China 35°17' N, 87°51' E 188
Rolde, Neth. 52°59' N, 6°37' E 163
Rolette, N. Dak., U.S. 48°38' N, 99°52' W 90
Roll, Ariz., U.S. 32°44' N, 113°59' W 101
Rolla, Can. 55°53' N, 120°10' W 108
Rolla, Mo., U.S. 37°56' N, 91°46' W 96
Rolla, N. Dak., U.S. 48°50' N, 99°38' W 90
Rolle, Switz. 46°29' N, 6°21' E 167
Rolleston, N.Z. 43°35' S, 172°21' E 240
Rolling Fork, Miss., U.S. 32°53' N, 90°53' W 103
Rollins, Mont., U.S. 47°53' N, 114°12' W 90
Rom, Sudan 10°46' N, 32°30' E 182
Roma, Austral. 26°34' S, 148°47' E 231
Roma (Rome), It. 41°52' N, 12°21' E 156
Romain, Cape, S.C., U.S. 32°54' N, 79°32' W 96
Romakloster, Sw. 57°28' N, 18°28' E 166
Roma-Los Saenz, Tex., U.S. 26°26' N, 98°59' W 96
Roman, Rom. 46°56' N, 26°56' E 156
Romanche Fracture Zone, North Atlantic Ocean 0°8' N, 16°37' W 253
Romang, Arg. 29°29' S, 59°50' W 139
Românî, Egypt 31°0' N, 32°38' E 194
Romania 45°51' N, 24°6' E 156
Romanija, peak, Bosn. and Herzg. 43°51' N, 18°37' E 168
Roman-Kosh, peak, Ukr. 44°37' N, 34°8' E 156
Romano, Cape, Fla., U.S. 25°54' N, 82°1' W 105
Romano, Cayo, island, Cuba 22°0' N, 77°36' W 116
Romanovce, Maced. 42°4' N, 21°40' E 168
Romanovka, Russ. 53°14' N, 112°47' E 238
Romanovka, Russ. 51°43' N, 42°44' E 158
Romans, Fr. 45°3' N, 5°3' E 150
Romanzof, Cape, Alas., U.S. 61°29' N, 168°48' W 98
Romblon, Philippines 12°35' N, 122°17' E 203
Rome, Ga., U.S. 34°15' N, 85°10' W 96
Rome, N.Y., U.S. 43°13' N, 75°28' W 94
Rome City, Ind., U.S. 41°29' N, 85°23' W 102
Rome see Roma, It. 41°52' N, 12°21' E 156
Romeo, Mich., U.S. 42°47' N, 83°1' W 102
Romford, U.K. 51°34' N, 0°10' E 162
Romilly, Fr. 48°31' N, 3°44' E 163
Romiton, Uzb. 39°56' N, 64°22' E 197
Rommani, Mor. 33°33' N, 6°42' W 143
Romnaes, Mount, peak, Antarctica 71°30' S, 23°33' E 248
Romney Marsh, U.K. 50°59' N, 0°45' E 162
Romny, Ukr. 50°45' N, 33°28' E 158
Romodanovo, Russ. 54°25' N, 45°22' E 154
Romont, Switz. 46°42' N, 6°54' E 167
Romsdal, Nor. 62°26' N, 7°43' E 152
Romsey, U.K. 50°59' N, 1°30' W 162
Røn, Nor. 61°3' N, 9°3' E 152
Ron, Mui, Vietnam 17°57' N, 106°33' E 198
Ronald, Wash., U.S. 47°13' N, 121°2' W 100
Ronan, Mont., U.S. 47°30' N, 114°7' W 90
Roncade, It. 45°37' N, 12°21' E 167
Roncador, Serra do, Braz. 11°42' S, 52°48' W 130
Ronceverte, W. Va., U.S. 37°45' N, 80°28' W 94
Ronchamp, Fr. 47°42' N, 6°37' E 150
Ronda, Sp. 36°44' N, 5°9' W 150
Rondane, peak, Nor. 61°54' N, 9°43' E 152
Rønde, Den. 56°18' N, 10°28' E 150
Rondón, Col. 6°15' N, 71°7' W 136
Rondônia, adm. division, Braz. 10°29' S, 65°14' W 137
Rondonópolis, Braz. 16°29' S, 54°37' W 132
Rong, Koh, island, Cambodia 10°41' N, 102°33' E 202
Rong Kwang, Thai. 18°22' N, 100°19' E 202
Rong'an, China 25°16' N, 109°18' E 198
Rongcheng (Yatou), China 37°10' N, 122°26' E 198
Rongjiang, China 25°56' N, 108°27' E 198
Rongshui, China 25°4' N, 109°12' E 198
Rõngu, Est. 58°7' N, 26°13' E 166
Rongxian, China 22°50' N, 110°33' E 198
Ronkonkoma, N.Y., U.S. 40°49' N, 73°9' W 104
Ronne Ice Shelf, Antarctica 77°54' S, 68°27' W 248
Rönnskär, Nor. 64°39' N, 21°15' E 152
Ronse, Belg. 50°44' N, 3°35' E 163
Ronuro, river, Braz. 13°7' S, 54°31' W 130
Roodhouse, Mo., U.S. 39°28' N, 90°22' W 94
Roof Butte, peak, Ariz., U.S. 36°26' N, 109°9' W 92
Roosendaal, Neth. 51°32' N, 4°28' E 167
Roosevelt, Utah, U.S. 40°17' N, 110°0' W 92
Roosevelt Island, Antarctica 78°13' S, 162°49' W 248
Roosevelt, Mount, peak, Can. 58°24' N, 125°29' W 108
Rooslepa, Est. 59°11' N, 23°29' E 166
Root, river, Can. 62°50' N, 124°50' W 98
Root, river, Minn., U.S. 43°32' N, 92°10' W 80
Ropaži, Latv. 56°56' N, 24°40' E 166
Ropcha, Russ. 63°2' N, 52°29' E 154
Roper, river, Austral. 15°13' S, 134°30' E 230
Ropi, Fin. 68°36' N, 21°46' E 152
Ropotovo, Maced. 41°28' N, 21°22' E 168
Roquefort, Fr. 44°1' N, 0°19' E 150
Roquetes, Sp. 40°49' N, 0°29' E 164
Roraima, adm. division, Braz. 2°16' N, 63°20' W 130
Roraima, Mount, peak, Venez. 5°12' N, 60°51' W 130
Rorketon, Can. 51°23' N, 99°35' W 90
Rørstad, Nor. 67°34' N, 15°13' E 152
Rosa, Zambia 9°40' S, 31°21' E 224
Rosa, Monte, peak, Switz. 45°56' N, 7°49' E 165
Rosa, Punta, Mex. 26°31' N, 110°22' W 112
Rosales, Arg. 34°10' S, 63°10' W 139
Rosales, Mex. 28°9' N, 105°33' W 92
Rosalia, Wash., U.S. 47°13' N, 117°22' W 90
Rosamond, Calif., U.S. 34°51' N, 118°11' W 101
Rosamorada, Mex. 22°7' N, 105°12' W 114
Rosario, Arg. 32°56' S, 60°41' W 139
Rosário, Braz. 2°57' S, 44°16' W 132
Rosario, Mex. 23°0' N, 105°54' W 114
Rosario, Parag. 24°26' S, 57°7' W 132
Rosario, Uru. 34°19' S, 57°19' W 139
Rosario, Venez. 10°18' N, 72°24' W 136
Rosario, Bahía del 29°53' N, 116°22' W 92
Rosario, Cayo del, island, Cuba 21°10' N, 82°0' W 116
Rosario de Lerma, Arg. 24°58' S, 65°36' W 134
Rosario del Tala, Arg. 32°18' S, 59°6' W 139
Rosário do Sul, Braz. 30°16' S, 54°58' W 139
Rosário d'Oeste, Braz. 14°51' S, 56°26' W 132
Rosarito, Mex. 26°29' N, 111°40' W 112
Rosas, Col. 2°13' N, 76°45' W 136
Roscoe, Tex., U.S. 32°26' N, 100°34' W 92
Roscoff, Fr. 48°43' N, 4°0' W 150
Roscommon, Ire. 53°38' N, 8°12' W 150
Roscommon, Mich., U.S. 44°29' N, 84°36' W 94
Rose Blanche, Can. 47°36' N, 58°41' W 111
Rose Harbour, Can. 52°6' N, 131°5' W 108
Rose Lake, Can. 54°24' N, 126°4' W 108
Rose Point, Can. 54°8' N, 131°39' W 108
Rose Prairie, Can. 56°29' N, 120°50' W 108
Rose Valley, Can. 52°16' N, 103°48' W 108
Roseau, Dominica 15°16' N, 61°31' W 116
Roseau, Minn., U.S. 48°49' N, 95°49' W 90
Roseau, river, North America 48°57' N, 96°21' W 94
Rosebud, Mont., U.S. 46°15' N, 106°27' W 90
Rosebud Mountains, Mont., U.S. 45°21' N, 107°15' W 90
Rosebud Peak, Nev., U.S. 40°48' N, 118°45' W 90
Roseburg, Oreg., U.S. 43°12' N, 123°20' W 82
Rosebush, Mich., U.S. 43°42' N, 84°46' W 102
Rosedale, Ind., U.S. 39°37' N, 87°17' W 102
Rosée, Belg. 50°13' N, 4°40' E 167
Roseires Dam, Sudan 11°39' N, 34°2' E 182
Roseland, La., U.S. 30°45' N, 90°31' W 103
Roselawn, Ind., U.S. 41°8' N, 87°19' W 102
Roselend, Lac de, lake, Fr. 45°40' N, 6°28' E 165
Rosenberg, Tex., U.S. 29°32' N, 95°49' W 96
Rosendal, Nor. 59°59' N, 5°59' E 152
Rosendale, N.Y., U.S. 41°50' N, 74°7' W 104
Rosepine, La., U.S. 30°54' N, 93°18' W 103
Roseto degli Abruzzi, It. 42°39' N, 14°0' E 156
Rosetown, Can. 51°33' N, 108°0' W 90
Rosetta see Rashîd, Egypt 31°23' N, 30°21' E 180
Roseville, Calif., U.S. 38°44' N, 121°19' W 90
Roseville, Mich., U.S. 42°29' N, 82°57' W 94
Roseville, Ohio, U.S. 39°48' N, 82°5' W 102
Rosharon, Tex., U.S. 29°20' N, 95°27' W 103
Roshchino, Russ. 60°14' N, 29°36' E 166
Rosholt, S. Dak., U.S. 45°51' N, 96°45' W 90
Roshtkala, Taj. 37°13' N, 71°48' E 186
Rosignol, Guyana 6°9' N, 57°35' W 130
Roşiori de Vede, Rom. 44°6' N, 24°56' E 143
Roskilde, Den. 55°37' N, 12°4' E 152
Roslavl', Russ. 53°54' N, 32°55' E 154
Roslyn, Wash., U.S. 47°12' N, 121°0' W 90
Rösrath, Ger. 50°53' N, 7°10' E 163
Ross, N.Z. 42°55' S, 170°49' E 240
Ross Bethio, Senegal 16°17' N, 16°11' W 214
Ross Dam, Wash., U.S. 48°50' N, 121°5' W 82
Ross Ice Shelf, Antarctica 81°35' S, 166°21' W 248
Ross Island, island, Antarctica 77°2' S, 171°48' E 248
Ross Lake National Recreation Area, Wash., U.S. 48°43' N, 121°28' W 100
Ross, Mount, peak, N.Z. 41°29' S, 175°17' E 240
Ross on Wye, U.K. 51°55' N, 2°35' W 162
Ross River, Can. 61°56' N, 132°32' W 98
Ross, river, Can. 62°6' N, 131°21' W 98
Ross Sea 74°54' S, 179°17' E 248
Rossburn, Can. 50°40' N, 100°49' W 90
Rosscarbery, Ire. 51°35' N, 9°2' W 150
Rossel Island, island, P.N.G. 11°15' S, 154°4' E 192
Rosses, The, Ire. 54°46' N, 8°16' W 150
Rossignol, Lac, lake, Can. 52°41' N, 74°1' W 111
Rossini Point 73°0' S, 74°12' W 248
Rossland, Can. 49°3' N, 117°50' W 82
Rosso, Mauritania 16°34' N, 15°52' W 222
Rosso, Capo, Fr. 42°9' N, 7°58' E 156
Rossosh', Russ. 50°13' N, 39°32' E 158
Rossville, Ill., U.S. 40°22' N, 87°39' W 102
Rossville, Ind., U.S. 40°24' N, 86°36' W 102
Røst Bank, Norwegian Sea 67°47' N, 12°7' E 255
Rosthern, Can. 52°39' N, 106°20' W 108
Rostock, Ger. 54°5' N, 12°7' E 152
Rostov, Russ. 57°12' N, 39°19' E 154
Rostov, adm. division, Russ. 47°19' N, 38°14' E 156
Rostov na Donu, Russ. 47°13' N, 39°42' E 156
Rostuša, Maced. 41°36' N, 20°35' E 168
Røsvassbukt, Nor. 65°52' N, 14°4' E 152
Roswell, N. Mex., U.S. 33°23' N, 104°32' W 92
Rota, Sp. 36°37' N, 6°22' W 164
Rotan, Tex., U.S. 32°50' N, 100°29' W 92
Rotenburg, Ger. 51°0' N, 9°43' E 167
Rothaargebirge, Ger. 51°4' N, 8°8' E 167
Rothera, U.K., station, Antarctica 67°32' S, 68°18' W 248
Rotherham, N.Z. 42°44' S, 172°56' E 240
Rotherham, U.K. 53°26' N, 1°22' W 162
Rothschild Island, Antarctica 69°22' S, 77°37' W 248

Roti, island, *Indonesia* 11°14′ S, 122°38′ E 192
Rotondo, Monte, peak, *Fr.* 42°12′ N, 8°59′ E 156
Rotorua, *N.Z.* 38°9′ S, 176°13′ E 240
Rotterdam, *Neth.* 51°54′ N, 4°29′ E 167
Rotterdam, *N.Y., U.S.* 42°48′ N, 74°0′ W 104
Rottneros, *Nor.* 59°49′ N, 13°5′ E 152
Rottnest Island, *Austral.* 32°39′ S, 114°32′ E 230
Rottumeroog, island, *Neth.* 53°29′ N, 6°32′ E 163
Rottumerplaat, island, *Neth.* 53°31′ N, 5°57′ E 163
Roubaix, *Fr.* 50°41′ N, 3°10′ E 163
Rouen, *Fr.* 49°26′ N, 1°6′ E 163
Rõuge, *Est.* 57°44′ N, 26°53′ E 166
Rouge, Pointe 49°20′ N, 68°5′ W 94
Rouina, *Alg.* 36°14′ N, 1°48′ E 150
Roumila, *Alg.* 37°2′ N, 6°20′ E 150
Round Mount, peak, *Austral.* 30°22′ S, 152°2′ E 230
Round Pond, *Me., U.S.* 43°57′ N, 69°28′ W 94
Round Rock, *Tex., U.S.* 30°29′ N, 97°41′ W 92
Roundstone, *Ire.* 53°23′ N, 9°57′ W 150
Roundup, *Mont., U.S.* 46°25′ N, 108°33′ W 90
Roura, *South America* 4°46′ N, 52°20′ W 130
Rous, Península, *Chile* 55°23′ S, 71°22′ W 134
Rouses Point, *N.Y., U.S.* 44°58′ N, 73°24′ W 94
Rouseville, *Pa., U.S.* 41°27′ N, 79°42′ W 110
Roussillon, region, *Fr.* 42°51′ N, 2°39′ E 165
Rouxville, *S. Af.* 30°25′ S, 26°50′ E 227
Rouyn-Noranda, *Can.* 48°14′ N, 79°2′ W 110
Rovaniemi, *Fin.* 66°26′ N, 25°38′ E 160
Rovde, *Nor.* 62°9′ N, 5°44′ E 152
Rovdino, *Russ.* 61°41′ N, 42°35′ E 154
Roven'ki, *Russ.* 49°58′ N, 38°54′ E 158
Rover, Mount, peak, *Can.* 66°38′ N, 141°0′ W 98
Rovereto, *It.* 45°53′ N, 11°3′ E 167
Roversi, *Arg.* 27°35′ S, 61°58′ W 139
Rovieng, *Cambodia* 13°21′ N, 105°5′ E 202
Rovigo, *It.* 45°4′ N, 11°47′ E 167
Rovinj, *Croatia* 45°5′ N, 13°38′ E 167
Rovišće, *Croatia* 45°56′ N, 16°43′ E 168
Rovkuly, *Russ.* 64°2′ N, 30°47′ E 152
Rovnoye, *Russ.* 50°43′ N, 46°5′ E 158
Rovuma, river, *Africa* 11°46′ S, 37°36′ E 224
Rowan Lake, *Can.* 49°15′ N, 94°4′ W 94
Rowd-e Lurah, river, *Afghan.* 31°31′ N, 66°49′ E 186
Rowletts, *Ky., U.S.* 37°13′ N, 85°54′ W 96
Rowley, *Mass., U.S.* 42°42′ N, 70°53′ W 104
Rowley Island, *Can.* 68°35′ N, 80°9′ W 106
Roxa, island, *Guinea-Bissau* 11°9′ N, 15°37′ W 222
Roxas, *Philippines* 10°18′ N, 119°16′ E 203
Roxas, *Philippines* 17°5′ N, 121°36′ E 203
Roxas, *Philippines* 11°33′ N, 122°43′ E 203
Roxas, *Philippines* 12°36′ N, 121°30′ E 203
Roxburgh, *N.Z.* 45°33′ S, 169°17′ E 240
Roxbury, *Vt., U.S.* 44°5′ N, 72°44′ W 104
Roxen, lake, *Nor.* 58°26′ N, 15°14′ E 152
Roxo, Cap, *Senegal* 12°26′ N, 17°12′ W 222
Roy, *Mont., U.S.* 47°18′ N, 108°58′ W 90
Roy, *N. Mex., U.S.* 35°56′ N, 104°13′ W 92
Roy, *Utah, U.S.* 41°9′ N, 112°1′ W 92
Royal Center, *Ind., U.S.* 40°51′ N, 86°30′ W 102
Royal Chitwan National Park, *Nepal* 27°14′ N, 83°51′ E 197
Royal Gorge, site, *Colo., U.S.* 38°27′ N, 105°26′ W 90
Royal Manas National Park, *Bhutan* 26°37′ N, 91°8′ E 197
Royal Natal National Park, *S. Af.* 28°52′ S, 28°0′ E 227
Royale, Isle, island, *Mich., U.S.* 47°37′ N, 89°34′ W 80
Royalton, *Vt., U.S.* 43°49′ N, 72°34′ W 104
Royalty, *Tex., U.S.* 31°21′ N, 102°52′ W 92
Royan, *Fr.* 45°39′ N, 1°3′ W 150
Roye, *Fr.* 49°41′ N, 2°48′ E 163
Røyrvik, *Nor.* 64°53′ N, 13°31′ E 152
Royston, *Can.* 49°38′ N, 124°57′ W 100
Royston, *U.K.* 52°2′ N, 1°59′ W 162
Rožaje, *Mont.* 42°50′ N, 20°9′ E 168
Rožanj, peak, *Serb.* 44°17′ N, 19°24′ E 168
Rožanstvo, *Serb.* 43°43′ N, 19°50′ E 168
Rozdil'na, *Ukr.* 46°53′ N, 30°3′ E 156
Rozewie, Przylądek, *Pol.* 54°51′ N, 17°52′ E 152
Rozhdestvenskoye, *Russ.* 58°7′ N, 45°38′ E 154
Rozhyshche, *Ukr.* 50°54′ N, 25°15′ E 152
Rozívka, *Ukr.* 47°21′ N, 37°3′ E 156
Rožňava, *Slovakia* 48°39′ N, 20°32′ E 152
Roznov, *Rom.* 46°51′ N, 26°29′ E 158
Rozoy, *Fr.* 49°42′ N, 4°7′ E 163
Roztocze, *Pol.* 50°37′ N, 22°29′ E 152
Rrëshen, *Alban.* 41°47′ N, 19°54′ E 168
Rtanj, mountains, *Serb.* 43°50′ N, 21°42′ E 168
Rtishchevo, *Russ.* 52°15′ N, 43°48′ E 158
Ruabon, *U.K.* 52°59′ N, 3°2′ W 162
Ruacaná Falls, *Angola* 17°54′ S, 12°59′ E 220
Ruaha, *Tanzania* 7°23′ S, 36°34′ E 224
Ruaha National Park, *Tanzania* 7°47′ S, 34°17′ E 224
Ruakituri, *N.Z.* 38°45′ S, 177°24′ E 240
Ruapehu, Mount, peak, *N.Z.* 39°20′ S, 175°28′ E 240
Ruatahuna, *N.Z.* 38°38′ S, 176°58′ E 240
Ruatoria, *N.Z.* 37°55′ S, 178°19′ E 240
Ruawai, *N.Z.* 36°9′ S, 174°2′ E 240
Rubafu, *Tanzania* 1°5′ S, 31°51′ E 224
Rubel', *Belarus* 51°57′ N, 27°5′ E 152
Rubene, *Latv.* 57°27′ N, 25°13′ E 166
Rubeži, *Mont.* 42°46′ N, 19°1′ E 168
Rubi, river, *Dem. Rep. of the Congo* 2°33′ N, 25°16′ E 224
Rubiataba, *Braz.* 15°11′ S, 49°51′ W 138
Rubielos de Mora, *Sp.* 40°10′ N, 0°40′ E 164
Rubim, *Braz.* 16°23′ S, 40°33′ W 138
Rubin, Mount, peak, *Antarctica* 73°31′ S, 64°58′ E 248
Rubio, *Venez.* 7°41′ N, 72°23′ W 136
Rubio, peak, *Sp.* 41°25′ N, 3°51′ W 164
Rubondo Island National Park, *Tanzania* 2°31′ S, 32°6′ E 224
Rubtsovsk, *Russ.* 51°31′ N, 81°11′ E 184
Ruby, *Alas., U.S.* 64°33′ N, 155°34′ W 98
Ruby Beach, site, *Wash., U.S.* 47°42′ N, 124°27′ W 100
Ruby Dome, peak, *Nev., U.S.* 40°36′ N, 115°33′ W 90
Ruby Mountains, *Nev., U.S.* 40°30′ N, 115°37′ W 90
Ruby Range, *Mont., U.S.* 44°58′ N, 112°50′ W 90
Rucava, *Latv.* 56°9′ N, 21°8′ E 166
Ruch'i, *Russ.* 66°2′ N, 41°6′ E 154
Ruch'i Karel'skiye, *Russ.* 66°59′ N, 32°10′ E 152
Ruda, *Pol.* 53°35′ N, 22°30′ E 152
Rudall River National Park, *Austral.* 22°34′ S, 122°13′ E 238
Rudan, *Iran* 27°26′ N, 57°18′ E 196
Rudauli, *India* 26°44′ N, 81°45′ E 188
Rudawka, *Pol.* 53°51′ N, 23°29′ E 166
Rudbar, *Afghan.* 30°6′ N, 62°37′ E 186
Rūdbār, *Iran* 36°50′ N, 49°21′ E 195
Rudinice, *Mont.* 43°4′ N, 18°50′ E 168
Rūdiškės, *Lith.* 54°30′ N, 24°48′ E 166
Rudky, *Ukr.* 49°38′ N, 23°28′ E 152
Rudne, *Ukr.* 49°50′ N, 23°51′ E 152
Rudnica, *Serb.* 43°13′ N, 20°43′ E 168
Rūdnīchnyy, *Kaz.* 44°39′ N, 78°55′ E 184
Rudnichnyy, *Russ.* 59°39′ N, 52°32′ E 154
Rudnichnyy, *Russ.* 59°40′ N, 60°17′ E 154
Rudnik, *Serb.* 44°3′ N, 20°26′ E 168
Rudnik, peak, *Serb.* 44°8′ N, 20°28′ E 168
Rudno, *Russ.* 58°57′ N, 28°15′ E 166
Rudnya, *Russ.* 54°57′ N, 31°11′ E 154
Rūdnyy, *Kaz.* 52°58′ N, 63°5′ E 184
Rudo, *Bosn. and Herzg.* 43°37′ N, 19°22′ E 168
Rudolf, Lake see Turkana, Lake, *Kenya* 2°32′ N, 34°10′ E 206
Rudolph, Ostrov, island, *Russ.* 81°54′ N, 59°19′ E 160
Rudong, *China* 32°18′ N, 121°11′ E 198
Rudyard, *Mich., U.S.* 46°13′ N, 84°36′ W 94
Rudzyensk, *Belarus* 53°35′ N, 27°53′ E 152
Rue, *Fr.* 50°15′ N, 1°39′ E 163
Rufa'a, *Sudan* 14°44′ N, 33°23′ E 182
Rufiji, river, *Tanzania* 8°14′ S, 37°49′ E 224
Rufino, *Arg.* 34°16′ S, 62°41′ W 139
Rufisque, *Senegal* 14°45′ N, 16°56′ W 214
Rufunsa, *Zambia* 15°4′ S, 29°36′ E 224
Rugāji, *Latv.* 57°0′ N, 27°4′ E 166
Rugby, *N. Dak., U.S.* 48°20′ N, 100°0′ W 90
Rugby, *U.K.* 52°22′ N, 1°16′ W 162
Rugei, oil field, *Kuwait* 29°10′ N, 46°47′ E 196
Rugeley, *U.K.* 52°45′ N, 1°57′ W 162
Rugozero, *Russ.* 64°5′ N, 32°42′ E 152
Ruhengeri, *Rwanda* 1°32′ S, 29°36′ E 224
Ruhla, *Ger.* 50°53′ N, 10°21′ E 167
Ruhnu Saar, island, *Est.* 57°41′ N, 23°5′ E 166
Ruhr, region, *Ger.* 51°38′ N, 7°7′ E 167
Ruhr, river, *Ger.* 51°21′ N, 8°10′ E 167
Ruhuhu, river, *Tanzania* 10°16′ S, 34°54′ E 224
Ruhuna National Park, *Sri Lanka* 6°21′ N, 81°4′ E 172
Rui Barbosa, *Braz.* 12°18′ S, 40°27′ W 132
Rui'an, *China* 27°45′ N, 120°39′ E 198
Ruidosa, *Tex., U.S.* 29°58′ N, 104°41′ W 92
Ruidoso, *N. Mex., U.S.* 33°19′ N, 105°41′ W 92
Ruidoso Downs, *N. Mex., U.S.* 33°19′ N, 105°35′ W 92
Ruijin, *China* 25°50′ N, 116°0′ E 198
Ruinas de Numancia, ruin(s), *Sp.* 41°48′ N, 2°30′ W 164
Ruinen, *Neth.* 52°45′ N, 6°21′ E 163
Ruiru, *Kenya* 1°9′ S, 36°56′ E 224
Ruivo, Pico, peak, *Port.* 32°38′ N, 17°4′ W 214
Ruíz, *Mex.* 21°57′ N, 105°8′ W 114
Ruj, peak, *Bulg.* 42°50′ N, 22°32′ E 168
Rujen, peak, *Maced.* 42°8′ N, 22°28′ E 168
Rūjiena, *Latv.* 57°54′ N, 25°18′ E 166
Ruker, Mount, peak, *Antarctica* 73°47′ S, 63°43′ E 248
Ruki, river, *Dem. Rep. of the Congo* 2°0′ N, 18°32′ E 218
Rukungiri, *Uganda* 0°51′ N, 29°55′ E 224
Rukwa, adm. division, *Tanzania* 6°54′ S, 30°38′ E 224
Rukwa, Lake, *Tanzania* 8°0′ S, 32°25′ E 224
Rule, *Tex., U.S.* 33°10′ N, 99°54′ W 92
Rum Cay, island, *Bahamas* 23°32′ N, 74°47′ W 116
Rum, river, *Minn., U.S.* 45°43′ N, 93°41′ W 94
Ruma, *Serb.* 45°0′ N, 19°49′ E 168
Rumā', *Saudi Arabia* 25°34′ N, 47°11′ E 196
Rumaila, oil field, *Iraq* 30°15′ N, 47°23′ E 196
Rumaylah, 'Urūqar, *Saudi Arabia* 23°47′ N, 47°58′ E 196
Rumaysh, *Leb.* 33°4′ N, 35°21′ E 194
Rumbek, *Sudan* 6°47′ N, 29°38′ E 224
Rumford, *Me., U.S.* 44°32′ N, 70°33′ W 104
Rumia, *Pol.* 54°34′ N, 18°24′ E 152
Rumija, peak, *Mont.* 42°5′ N, 19°9′ E 168
Rumilly, *Fr.* 45°51′ N, 5°56′ E 150
Rumney, *N.H., U.S.* 43°48′ N, 71°50′ W 104
Rumo, *Fin.* 63°49′ N, 28°31′ E 152
Rumonge, *Burundi* 3°59′ S, 29°24′ E 218
Rumphi, *Malawi* 11°1′ S, 33°49′ E 224
Rumput, peak, *Indonesia* 1°44′ N, 109°35′ E 196
Rumuruti, *Kenya* 0°15′ N, 36°32′ E 224
Runan, *China* 33°0′ N, 114°19′ E 198
Runaway, Cape, *N.Z.* 37°32′ S, 177°29′ E 240
Runcorn, *U.K.* 53°19′ N, 2°44′ W 162
Runde, river, *Zimb.* 21°15′ S, 31°22′ E 227
Rundeng, *Indonesia* 2°41′ N, 97°48′ E 196
Rundēni, *Latv.* 56°15′ N, 27°50′ E 166
Rundu, *Namibia* 17°54′ S, 19°44′ E 220
Rundvik, *Nor.* 63°30′ N, 19°24′ E 152
Runere, *Tanzania* 3°7′ S, 33°15′ E 224
Runge, *Tex., U.S.* 28°52′ N, 97°43′ W 92
Rungu, *Dem. Rep. of the Congo* 3°12′ N, 27°54′ E 224
Rungwa, *Tanzania* 6°58′ S, 33°32′ E 224
Rungwa Game Reserve, *Tanzania* 7°5′ S, 33°52′ E 206
Rungwa, river, *Tanzania* 7°24′ S, 32°3′ E 224
Rungwe Mountain, peak, *Tanzania* 9°5′ S, 33°58′ E 224
Runib, oil field, *Oman* 18°45′ N, 56°6′ E 182
Ruokolahti, *Fin.* 61°17′ N, 28°49′ E 166
Ruoqiang, *China* 39°6′ N, 88°12′ E 188
Ruovesi, *Fin.* 61°57′ N, 24°0′ E 166
Rupanco, Lago, lake, *Chile* 40°49′ S, 73°42′ W 134
Rupara, *Namibia* 17°52′ S, 19°7′ E 220
Rupat, island, *Indonesia* 1°59′ N, 101°48′ E 196
Rupert, *Idaho, U.S.* 42°38′ N, 113°40′ W 90
Rupert, *Vt., U.S.* 43°15′ N, 73°14′ W 104
Rupert, Baie de 51°24′ N, 80°18′ W 80
Rupert Creek, river, *Can.* 57°18′ N, 93°20′ W 108
Ruponda, *Tanzania* 10°17′ S, 38°41′ E 224
Ruppert Coast, *Antarctica* 75°24′ S, 126°21′ W 248
Rur, river, *Ger.* 50°36′ N, 6°29′ E 167
Rurrenabaque, *Bol.* 14°30′ S, 67°34′ W 137
Rusambo, *Zimb.* 16°36′ S, 32°12′ E 224
Rušani, *Croatia* 45°53′ N, 17°32′ E 168
Rusanova, *Russ.* 69°32′ N, 63°38′ E 169
Rusanova, Zaliv 74°43′ N, 55°55′ E 160
Rusanovo, *Russ.* 70°35′ N, 56°13′ E 169
Rusape, *Zimb.* 18°34′ S, 32°8′ E 224
Ruse, *Bulg.* 43°50′ N, 25°57′ E 156
Ruse, adm. division, *Bulg.* 43°32′ N, 25°31′ E 156
Rushan, *Taj.* 37°57′ N, 71°37′ E 197
Rushden, *U.K.* 52°17′ N, 0°36′ E 162
Rushford, *Minn., U.S.* 43°48′ N, 91°45′ W 110
Rushville, *Ind., U.S.* 39°36′ N, 85°28′ W 102
Rushville, *Mo., U.S.* 40°6′ N, 90°33′ W 94
Rushville, *Nebr., U.S.* 42°42′ N, 102°29′ W 90
Rusizi, river, *Africa* 2°44′ S, 29°0′ E 224
Rusk, *Tex., U.S.* 31°46′ N, 95°9′ W 103
Ruskie Piaski, *Pol.* 50°48′ N, 23°6′ E 152
Rusksträsk, *Nor.* 64°49′ N, 18°44′ E 152
Rusnė, *Lith.* 55°18′ N, 21°19′ E 166
Rusoma, *Russ.* 64°45′ N, 45°53′ E 154
Rušonu Ezers, lake, *Latv.* 56°12′ N, 26°49′ E 166
Russas, *Braz.* 4°58′ S, 37°59′ W 132
Russell, *Can.* 50°47′ N, 101°17′ W 90
Russell, *Kans., U.S.* 38°52′ N, 98°52′ W 90
Russell, *Ky., U.S.* 38°31′ N, 82°43′ W 94
Russell, Cape, *Antarctica* 74°37′ S, 169°23′ E 248
Russell Cave National Monument, *Ala., U.S.* 34°57′ N, 85°52′ W 96
Russell Fiord 59°52′ N, 140°33′ W 98
Russell Island, island, *Can.* 73°57′ N, 103°15′ W 106
Russell Islands, *Solomon Sea* 9°5′ S, 159°10′ E 242
Russell Lake, *Can.* 57°22′ N, 105°59′ W 108
Russell Lake, lake, *Can.* 56°9′ N, 102°6′ W 108
Russell, Mount, peak, *Austral.* 23°17′ S, 130°14′ E 230
Russells Point, *Ohio, U.S.* 40°27′ N, 83°54′ W 102
Russellville, *Ala., U.S.* 34°30′ N, 87°43′ W 96
Russellville, *Ark., U.S.* 35°15′ N, 93°8′ W 96
Russellville, *Ky., U.S.* 36°50′ N, 86°54′ W 96
Rüsselsheim, *Ger.* 49°59′ N, 8°24′ E 167
Russi, *It.* 44°22′ N, 12°2′ E 167
Russia 65°0′ N, 97°26′ E 160
Russian Fort Elizabeth State Historical Park, *Hawai'i, U.S.* 21°56′ N, 159°42′ W 99
Russian Mission, *Alas., U.S.* 61°46′ N, 161°26′ W 98
Russian Peak, *Calif., U.S.* 41°16′ N, 123°3′ W 90
Russiaville, *Ind., U.S.* 40°25′ N, 86°16′ W 102
Russkaya Gavan', *Russ.* 76°5′ N, 62°55′ E 160
Russkaya Polyana, *Russ.* 53°47′ N, 73°50′ E 184
Russkiy, Ostrov, island, *Russ.* 77°12′ N, 88°39′ E 160
Russum, *Miss., U.S.* 31°52′ N, 91°1′ W 103
Rust'avi, *Ga.* 41°32′ N, 45°0′ E 195
Rustenburg, *S. Af.* 25°41′ S, 27°13′ E 227
Ruston, *La., U.S.* 32°30′ N, 92°39′ W 103
Rutana, *Burundi* 3°57′ S, 29°59′ E 224
Rütenbrock, *Ger.* 52°50′ N, 7°6′ E 163
Ruteng, *Indonesia* 8°32′ S, 120°28′ E 238
Ruth, *Miss., U.S.* 31°22′ N, 90°20′ W 103
Ruth, *Nev., U.S.* 39°17′ N, 115°0′ W 90
Rüthen, *Ger.* 51°27′ N, 8°25′ E 167
Rutheron, *N. Mex., U.S.* 36°43′ N, 106°36′ W 92
Ruthin, *U.K.* 53°6′ N, 3°17′ W 162
Rutland, *Ohio, U.S.* 39°2′ N, 82°8′ W 102
Rutland, *Vt., U.S.* 43°36′ N, 72°59′ W 104
Rutland Island, *India* 11°11′ N, 91°46′ E 188
Rutledge Lake, lake, *Can.* 61°32′ N, 111°30′ W 108
Rutledge, river, *Can.* 61°13′ N, 112°19′ W 108
Rutshuru, *Dem. Rep. of the Congo* 1°13′ S, 29°26′ E 224
Ruurlo, *Neth.* 52°5′ N, 6°27′ E 163
Ruvozero, *Russ.* 66°27′ N, 30°44′ E 152
Ruvu, *Tanzania* 6°46′ S, 38°43′ E 224
Ruvu, river, *Tanzania* 7°24′ S, 38°14′ E 218
Ruvuma, adm. division, *Tanzania* 11°2′ S, 35°25′ E 224
Ruvuma, river, *Africa* 11°25′ S, 38°25′ E 224
Ruwe, *Dem. Rep. of the Congo* 10°39′ S, 25°29′ E 224
Ruwenzori, *Uganda* 0°12′ N, 29°58′ E 224
Ruwenzori Mountain National Park, *Dem. Rep. of the Congo* 0°20′ N, 29°40′ E 206
Ruwer, *Ger.* 49°46′ N, 6°43′ E 167
Ruzayevka, *Russ.* 54°2′ N, 44°52′ E 154
Ruzhany, *Belarus* 52°52′ N, 24°53′ E 152
Rwanda 2°4′ S, 29°53′ E 224
Rwindi, *Dem. Rep. of the Congo* 0°47′ N, 29°16′ E 224
Ryabovo, *Russ.* 61°33′ N, 47°54′ E 154
Ryan, *Okla., U.S.* 34°0′ N, 97°57′ W 92
Ryasna, *Belarus* 54°38′ N, 29°53′ E 166
Ryazan', *Russ.* 54°36′ N, 39°43′ E 154
Ryazan', adm. division, *Russ.* 54°26′ N, 39°28′ E 154
Ryazhsk, *Russ.* 53°40′ N, 40°4′ E 154
Rybach'e, *Kaz.* 46°29′ N, 81°34′ E 184
Rybachiy, *Russ.* 55°9′ N, 20°49′ E 166
Rybachiy, Poluostrov, *Russ.* 69°50′ N, 28°33′ E 152
Rybinsk, *Russ.* 58°1′ N, 38°49′ E 154
Rybinskoye Vodokhranilishche, lake, *Russ.* 58°29′ N, 37°45′ E 154
Rybnaya Sloboda, *Russ.* 55°28′ N, 50°2′ E 154
Rybnik, *Pol.* 50°4′ N, 18°33′ E 152
Rycroft, *Can.* 55°44′ N, 118°43′ W 108
Ryderwood, *Wash., U.S.* 46°21′ N, 123°3′ W 100
Rye, *Colo., U.S.* 37°55′ N, 104°57′ W 90
Rye, *N.H., U.S.* 43°0′ N, 70°47′ W 104
Rye, *N.Y., U.S.* 40°58′ N, 73°42′ W 104
Rye, *U.K.* 50°57′ N, 0°44′ E 162
Rye, river, *U.K.* 54°11′ N, 0°58′ E 162
Ryegate, *Mont., U.S.* 46°17′ N, 109°17′ W 90
Ryfylke, region, *Nor.* 59°16′ N, 5°53′ E 152
Rykovo, *Russ.* 56°9′ N, 28°51′ E 166
Ryley, *Can.* 53°16′ N, 112°27′ W 108
Ryl'sk, *Russ.* 51°32′ N, 34°38′ E 158
Rymättylä, *Fin.* 60°21′ N, 21°55′ E 166
Ryn, *Pol.* 53°55′ N, 21°32′ E 166
Rynda, *Russ.* 68°51′ N, 36°49′ E 152
Ryōtsu, *Japan* 38°6′ N, 138°26′ E 201
Rypin, *Pol.* 53°4′ N, 19°25′ E 152
Rysy, peak, *Slovakia* 49°10′ N, 19°58′ E 152
Rytel, *Pol.* 53°45′ N, 17°48′ E 152
Ryūjin, *Japan* 33°57′ N, 135°33′ E 201
Ryukyu Trench, *Philippine Sea* 25°33′ N, 129°7′ E 254
Rzeszów, *Pol.* 50°1′ N, 22°0′ E 152
Rzhev, *Russ.* 56°14′ N, 34°24′ E 154

S

's Hertogenbosch, *Neth.* 51°41′ N, 5°18′ E 167
Sa, *Thai.* 18°39′ N, 100°42′ E 202
Sa Dec, *Vietnam* 10°16′ N, 105°45′ E 202
Sa Pobla, *Sp.* 39°45′ N, 3°1′ E 164
Sa Vileta, *Sp.* 39°35′ N, 2°37′ E 150
Saa, *Cameroon* 4°20′ N, 11°26′ E 222
Saacow, *Somalia* 1°39′ N, 42°28′ E 224
Sa'ādatābād, *Iran* 27°58′ N, 55°55′ E 196
Saales, *Fr.* 48°20′ N, 7°6′ E 163
Saanen, *Switz.* 46°29′ N, 7°16′ E 167
Saanich, *Can.* 48°26′ N, 123°22′ W 100
Saarbrücken, *Ger.* 49°14′ N, 6°58′ E 163
Saarburg, *Ger.* 49°36′ N, 6°33′ E 163
Sääre, *Est.* 57°55′ N, 22°2′ E 166
Saaremaa (Ösel), island, *Est.* 58°32′ N, 21°21′ E 166
Saarenkylä, *Fin.* 63°16′ N, 25°2′ E 152
Saari, *Fin.* 61°38′ N, 29°45′ E 166
Saarijärvi, *Fin.* 62°42′ N, 25°12′ E 152
Saariselkä, *Fin.* 68°5′ N, 27°26′ E 152
Saarland, adm. division, *Ger.* 49°21′ N, 6°36′ E 163
Saarlouis, *Ger.* 49°18′ N, 6°45′ E 163
Sa'ata, *Sudan* 12°41′ N, 29°33′ E 216
Saatta, *Eritrea* 16°28′ N, 37°22′ E 182
Saavedra, *Arg.* 37°46′ S, 62°21′ W 139
Sab' Ābār, *Syr.* 33°43′ N, 37°40′ E 180
Saba, island, *Neth.* 17°39′ N, 63°12′ W 116
Šabac, *Serb.* 44°44′ N, 19°41′ E 168
Sabadell, *Sp.* 41°33′ N, 2°5′ E 164
Sabae, *Japan* 35°56′ N, 136°11′ E 201
Sabah, region, *Malaysia* 4°57′ N, 115°59′ E 203
Sabán, oil field, *Venez.* 9°7′ N, 65°53′ W 136
Sabana, *Col.* 3°48′ N, 70°58′ W 136
Sabana, Archipiélago de, *North Atlantic Ocean* 23°19′ N, 80°40′ W 116
Sabana de La Mar, *Dom. Rep.* 19°2′ N, 69°24′ W 116
Sabanalarga, *Col.* 10°36′ N, 74°56′ W 115
Sabancuy, *Mex.* 18°57′ N, 91°12′ W 115
Sabang, *Indonesia* 0°9′ N, 119°53′ E 192
Sabang, *Indonesia* 5°54′ N, 95°19′ E 196
Şabanözü, *Turk.* 40°29′ N, 33°16′ E 156
Sabará, *Braz.* 19°52′ S, 43°47′ W 138
Sabarei, *Kenya* 4°17′ N, 36°56′ E 224
Sabasţīyah, *West Bank, Israel* 32°16′ N, 35°11′ E 194
Sabattus, *Me., U.S.* 44°7′ N, 70°7′ W 104
Sabattus Pond, lake, *Me., U.S.* 44°9′ N, 70°16′ W 104
Sabaudia, *It.* 41°18′ N, 13°2′ E 156
Sabaya, *Bol.* 19°3′ S, 68°24′ W 137
Sabbathday Lake, *Me., U.S.* 43°59′ N, 70°23′ W 104
Sabderat, *Eritrea* 15°23′ N, 36°38′ E 182
Sabetha, *Kans., U.S.* 39°53′ N, 95°48′ W 90
Şab'ā, *Jordan* 32°19′ N, 36°30′ E 194
Sabhā, *Lib.* 27°5′ N, 14°26′ E 216
Şab'ah, *Saudi Arabia* 23°13′ N, 44°40′ E 182
Sabidana, Jebel, peak, *Sudan* 18°3′ N, 36°41′ E 182
Sabie, *S. Af.* 25°6′ S, 30°49′ E 227
Sabile, *Latv.* 57°3′ N, 22°33′ E 166
Sabina, *Ohio, U.S.* 39°29′ N, 83°37′ W 102
Sabinal, *Mex.* 30°55′ N, 107°35′ W 92
Sabinal, *Tex., U.S.* 29°18′ N, 99°28′ W 92
Sabinal, Cayo, island, *Cuba* 21°41′ N, 77°10′ W 116
Sabinal, Punta del, *Sp.* 36°31′ N, 2°42′ W 164
Sabiñánigo, *Sp.* 42°30′ N, 0°23′ E 164
Sabinas Hidalgo, *Mex.* 26°30′ N, 100°11′ W 114
Sabine, *Tex., U.S.* 29°41′ N, 93°53′ W 103
Sabine Pass, *Tex., U.S.* 29°43′ N, 93°54′ W 103
Sabine, river, *U.S.* 30°33′ N, 93°40′ W 103
Sabiote, *Sp.* 38°4′ N, 3°18′ W 164
Sabitsy, *Russ.* 58°49′ N, 29°17′ E 166
Sablayan, *Philippines* 12°50′ N, 120°48′ E 203
Sable, Cape, *Can.* 43°19′ N, 65°36′ W 111
Sable, Cape, *Fla., U.S.* 25°12′ N, 81°24′ W 105
Sable Island, *Can.* 43°40′ N, 61°10′ W 106
Sable, Lac du, lake, *Can.* 54°20′ N, 68°9′ W 111
Sables, Lac des, lake, *Can.* 48°14′ N, 70°17′ W 111
Sabonkafi, *Niger* 14°37′ N, 8°42′ E 222
Sabrina Coast, *Antarctica* 68°56′ S, 121°18′ E 248
Sabriyah, oil field, *Kuwait* 29°50′ N, 47°49′ E 196
Sabtang, island, *Philippines* 20°13′ N, 121°21′ E 198
Sabun, river, *Russ.* 62°8′ N, 81°15′ E 169
Sabunçu, *Azerb.* 40°28′ N, 50°0′ E 180
Şabyā, *Saudi Arabia* 17°7′ N, 42°36′ E 182
Sabzawar see Shindand, *Afghan.* 33°17′ N, 62°11′ E 186

Sabzevār, Iran 36°16′ N, 57°40′ E 180
Sac City, Iowa, U.S. 42°24′ N, 95°1′ W 90
Sacaca, Bol. 18°7′ S, 66°24′ W 137
Sacajawea Peak, Oreg., U.S. 45°13′ N, 117°23′ W 90
Sacanta, Arg. 31°42′ S, 63°4′ W 139
Săcăşeni, Rom. 47°27′ N, 22°40′ E 168
Sachene, Col. 1°52′ N, 74°2′ W 136
Sacheon, S. Korea 34°56′ N, 128°6′ E 200
Sachigo, river, Can. 54°51′ N, 90°58′ W 106
Sachs Harbour, Can. 71°56′ N, 124°42′ W 106
Sacile, It. 45°57′ N, 12°30′ E 167
Sackets Harbor, N.Y., U.S. 43°56′ N, 76°8′ W 94
Sackville, Can. 45°52′ N, 64°23′ W 111
Saco, Me., U.S. 43°30′ N, 70°27′ W 104
Saco, Mont., U.S. 48°26′ N, 107°17′ W 90
Sacramento, Braz. 19°53′ S, 47°30′ W 138
Sacramento, Calif., U.S. 38°31′ N, 121°35′ W 90
Sacramento, Mex. 26°59′ N, 101°44′ W 82
Sacramento Mountains, N. Mex., U.S. 32°32′ N, 105°43′ W 92
Sacramento Pass, Nev., U.S. 39°8′ N, 114°21′ W 90
Sacramento Valley, Calif., U.S. 38°16′ N, 121°56′ W 100
Sacratif, Cabo, Sp. 36°34′ N, 3°28′ W 164
Sacromonte National Park, Mex. 19°16′ N, 98°58′ W 72
Săcueni, Rom. 47°20′ N, 22°6′ E 168
Sacul, Tex., U.S. 31°49′ N, 94°55′ W 103
Sacuriuiná, river, Braz. 14°4′ S, 57°45′ W 130
Şadad, Syr. 34°18′ N, 36°55′ E 194
Şa'dah, Yemen 16°57′ N, 43°45′ E 182
Saddat ash Shuqqah, Yemen 18°36′ N, 50°29′ E 182
Saddle Mountain, peak, Idaho, U.S. 43°54′ N, 113°2′ W 90
Saddle Mountains, Wash., U.S. 46°44′ N, 119°47′ W 90
Saddle Peak, India 13°9′ N, 92°56′ E 188
Saddle Peak, Mont., U.S. 45°46′ N, 111°3′ W 90
Saddleback Mountain, peak, Me., U.S. 46°24′ N, 68°9′ W 94
Şad', Oman 17°4′ N, 55°4′ E 182
Sadiola, Mali 13°55′ N, 11°43′ W 222
Sadiqabad, Pak. 28°14′ N, 70°3′ E 186
Sado, island, Japan 38°11′ N, 137°23′ E 190
Sadovoye, Russ. 47°45′ N, 44°27′ E 158
Sadská, Czech Rep. 50°8′ N, 14°58′ E 152
Sa'dun, Sudan 11°18′ N, 25°11′ E 224
Sädvaluspen, Nor. 66°26′ N, 16°43′ E 152
Sae Islands, South Pacific Ocean 0°42′ N, 144°26′ E 192
Saebyŏl, N. Korea 42°49′ N, 130°11′ E 200
Saelices, Sp. 39°54′ N, 2°49′ W 164
Şafājah, Saudi Arabia 26°17′ N, 38°44′ E 180
Safaniya, oil field, Persian Gulf 28°2′ N, 48°44′ E 196
Şafarābād, Iran 39°2′ N, 47°27′ E 195
Säffle, Nor. 59°7′ N, 12°52′ E 152
Safford, Ala., U.S. 32°16′ N, 87°22′ W 103
Safford, Ariz., U.S. 32°48′ N, 109°42′ W 112
Saffron Walden, U.K. 52°1′ N, 0°14′ E 162
Safi, Mor. 32°17′ N, 9°13′ W 214
Safia, Hamada, Mali 23°5′ N, 5°11′ W 214
Şāfītā, Syr. 34°49′ N, 36°7′ E 194
Safonovo, Russ. 55°4′ N, 33°16′ E 154
Safonovo, Russ. 65°42′ N, 47°34′ E 154
Safranbolu, Turk. 41°14′ N, 32°41′ E 156
Şafwān, Iraq 30°6′ N, 47°43′ E 196
Sag Harbor, N.Y., U.S. 40°59′ N, 72°18′ W 104
Saga, China 29°23′ N, 85°25′ E 197
Saga, Japan 33°4′ N, 133°4′ E 201
Saga, Japan 33°15′ N, 130°18′ E 201
Saga, adm. division, Japan 33°17′ N, 129°52′ E 201
Sagae, Japan 38°23′ N, 140°16′ E 201
Sagaing, Myanmar 21°56′ N, 95°56′ E 202
Sagamore, Mass., U.S. 41°45′ N, 70°33′ W 104
Sagamore Beach, Mass., U.S. 41°47′ N, 70°32′ W 104
Saganaga Lake, Can. 48°12′ N, 91°24′ W 94
Sagar, India 14°9′ N, 75°3′ E 188
Sagar (Saugor), India 23°50′ N, 78°45′ E 188
Sagara, Japan 34°41′ N, 138°11′ E 201
Sagard, Ger. 54°32′ N, 13°33′ E 152
Sagarejo, Ga. 41°44′ N, 45°17′ E 195
Sagarmāthā see Everest, Mount, peak, China-Nepal 28°0′ N, 86°53′ E 197
Sagastyr, Russ. 73°18′ N, 126°45′ E 160
Saghyz, Kaz. 48°16′ N, 54°55′ E 158
Saginaw, Mich., U.S. 43°24′ N, 83°56′ W 102
Saginaw Bay 43°28′ N, 84°8′ W 80
Saginaw Point, Mich., U.S. 47°50′ N, 88°41′ W 94
Sagleipie, Liberia 6°52′ N, 8°50′ W 222
Saglek Bay 58°17′ N, 63°17′ W 106
Sagra, peak, Sp. 37°56′ N, 2°36′ W 164
Sagres, Ponta de, Port. 36°40′ N, 8°56′ W 150
Sagu, Myanmar 20°19′ N, 94°41′ E 202
Şagu, Rom. 46°4′ N, 21°17′ E 168
Saguache, Colo., U.S. 38°5′ N, 106°8′ W 90
Saguaro National Park, Ariz., U.S. 32°16′ N, 113°14′ W 80
Saguenay, Can. 48°23′ N, 71°14′ W 94
Saguenay, river, Can. 48°5′ N, 71°39′ W 80
Sagunto-Sagunt, Sp. 39°40′ N, 0°17′ E 150
Sagwon, Alas., U.S. 69°23′ N, 148°42′ W 98
Sa'gya, China 28°53′ N, 88°4′ E 197
Sagyndyk, Mys, Kaz. 43°50′ N, 50°14′ E 158
Sahagún, Col. 8°58′ N, 75°27′ W 136
Sahagún, Sp. 42°22′ N, 5°3′ W 150
Şa'am, Oman 24°8′ N, 56°52′ E 196
Sahara, Africa 33°57′ N, 8°18′ E 214
Saharanpur, India 29°56′ N, 77°34′ E 197
Saharsa, India 25°51′ N, 86°34′ E 197
Sahasinaka, Madagascar 21°49′ S, 47°49′ E 220
Sahaswan, India 28°3′ N, 78°46′ E 197
Sahel, region, Africa 15°2′ N, 3°51′ W 206
Sahiwal, Pak. 31°58′ N, 72°22′ E 186
Sahiwal, Pak. 30°39′ N, 73°7′ E 186
Şa'rā' Awbārī, Lib. 28°22′ N, 10°13′ E 142
Şa'rā' Marzūq, Lib. 24°58′ N, 12°3′ E 216
Sahtaneh, river, Can. 59°1′ N, 122°22′ W 108
Sahuaripa, Mex. 29°2′ N, 109°14′ W 92
Sahuayo, Mex. 20°3′ N, 102°44′ W 114
Sai Buri, Thai. 6°42′ N, 101°38′ E 196
Saibi, Indonesia 1°20′ S, 98°50′ E 196
Sa'id Bundas, Sudan 8°28′ N, 24°39′ E 224
Saïda, Alg. 34°48′ N, 0°9′ E 214
Saida (Sidon), Leb. 33°33′ N, 35°22′ E 194
Saidpur, Bangladesh 25°47′ N, 88°52′ E 197
Saidpur, India 25°32′ N, 83°14′ E 197
Saidu, Pak. 34°44′ N, 72°26′ E 186
Saigon see Ho Chi Minh City, Vietnam 10°48′ N, 106°40′ E 202
Saih Nihayda, oil field, Oman 21°18′ N, 57°5′ E 182
Saija, Fin. 67°5′ N, 28°49′ E 152
Saijō, Japan 33°53′ N, 133°10′ E 201
Saijō, Japan 34°56′ N, 133°7′ E 201
Saikai National Park, Japan 33°23′ N, 129°42′ E 201
Saiki, Japan 32°57′ N, 131°53′ E 201
Saillagouse-Llo, Fr. 42°27′ N, 2°1′ E 164
Sailolof, Indonesia 1°7′ S, 130°44′ E 192
Sailu, India 19°25′ N, 76°28′ E 188
Saima, China 40°58′ N, 124°15′ E 200
Saimbeyli, Turk. 37°58′ N, 36°5′ E 156
Saín Alto, Mex. 23°32′ N, 103°14′ W 114
Saint Agnes Head, U.K. 50°20′ N, 5°33′ W 150
Saint Alban's, Can. 47°51′ N, 55°52′ W 111
Saint Albans, U.K. 51°44′ N, 0°21′ E 162
Saint Albans, Vt., U.S. 44°48′ N, 73°6′ W 94
Saint Albans Bay, Vt., U.S. 44°48′ N, 73°9′ W 110
Saint Alban's Head, English Channel 50°16′ N, 2°21′ W 150
Saint Albert, Can. 53°37′ N, 113°39′ W 108
Saint André, Cap, Madagascar 16°13′ S, 43°55′ E 220
Saint Andrew Bay 30°2′ N, 86°50′ W 80
Saint Andrews, Can. 45°4′ N, 67°4′ W 94
Saint Andrews, N.Z. 44°32′ S, 171°10′ E 240
Saint Anne, Ill., U.S. 41°1′ N, 87°43′ W 102
Saint Ann's Bay, Jam. 18°25′ N, 77°14′ W 116
Saint Ann's Head, U.K. 51°23′ N, 5°31′ W 150
Saint Anthony, Can. 51°20′ N, 55°38′ W 106
Saint Anthony, Idaho, U.S. 43°57′ N, 111°41′ W 90
Saint Augustine, Fla., U.S. 29°52′ N, 81°20′ W 105
Saint Augustine, Fla., U.S. 29°52′ N, 81°20′ W 73
Saint Bees Head, U.K. 54°30′ N, 3°46′ W 162
Saint Bernard, Philippines 10°17′ N, 125°10′ E 203
Saint Blaize, Cape, S. Af. 34°33′ S, 22°12′ E 227
Saint Boniface, Can. 49°52′ N, 97°3′ W 90
Saint Bride, Mount, peak, Can. 51°30′ N, 116°3′ W 90
Saint Catharines, Can. 43°8′ N, 79°14′ W 94
Saint Catherines Island, Ga., U.S. 31°25′ N, 81°7′ W 112
Saint Catherine's Point 50°16′ N, 1°17′ W 150
Saint Charles, Idaho, U.S. 42°8′ N, 111°24′ W 90
Saint Charles, Mich., U.S. 43°16′ N, 84°8′ W 102
Saint Charles, Minn., U.S. 43°57′ N, 92°4′ W 94
Saint Charles, Mo., U.S. 38°46′ N, 90°31′ W 94
Saint Christopher see Saint Kitts, island, Saint Kitts and Nevis 17°21′ N, 62°47′ W 118
Saint Clair, Mich., U.S. 42°48′ N, 82°30′ W 94
Saint Clair, Mo., U.S. 38°20′ N, 91°0′ W 94
Saint Clair, Pa., U.S. 40°42′ N, 76°12′ W 94
Saint Clair Shores, Mich., U.S. 42°28′ N, 82°53′ W 102
Saint Cloud, Fla., U.S. 28°15′ N, 81°18′ W 105
Saint Cloud, Minn., U.S. 45°32′ N, 94°21′ W 106
Saint Croix, Can. 45°33′ N, 67°24′ W 94
Saint Croix Falls, Wis., U.S. 45°23′ N, 92°38′ W 94
Saint Croix Island International Historic Site, Me., U.S. 45°6′ N, 67°14′ W 111
Saint Croix, island, U.S. 17°43′ N, 64°47′ W 118
Saint Croix National Scenic Riverway, Wis., U.S. 45°54′ N, 92°44′ W 110
Saint David, Ill., U.S. 40°28′ N, 90°4′ W 102
Saint David Island, U.K. 32°30′ N, 64°41′ W 118
Saint David's, U.K. 51°52′ N, 5°16′ W 150
Saint Edward, Nebr., U.S. 41°33′ N, 97°52′ W 90
Saint Elias, Mount, peak, Alas., U.S. 60°11′ N, 141°6′ W 98
Saint Elias Mountains, Can. 59°29′ N, 138°43′ W 98
Saint Elmo, Ala., U.S. 30°28′ N, 88°16′ W 103
Saint Elmo, Ill., U.S. 39°1′ N, 88°51′ W 102
Saint Eustatius, island, Neth. 17°24′ N, 63°48′ W 116
Saint Francis, Ark., U.S. 36°26′ N, 90°9′ W 96
Saint Francis, S. Dak., U.S. 43°8′ N, 100°55′ W 90
Saint Francis, Wis., U.S. 42°58′ N, 87°53′ W 102
Saint Francis Bay 34°9′ S, 24°27′ E 227
Saint Francis, Cape, Can. 47°49′ N, 53°40′ W 111
Saint Francis, Cape, S. Af. 34°36′ S, 24°27′ E 227
Saint Francis, river, Ark., U.S. 34°57′ N, 90°30′ W 80
Saint Francisville, Ill., U.S. 38°35′ N, 87°39′ W 102
Saint Francisville, La., U.S. 30°45′ N, 91°23′ W 103
Saint François Mountains, Mo., U.S. 37°20′ N, 90°59′ W 96
Saint George, Anadyrskiy Zaliv 56°35′ N, 169°34′ W 98
Saint George, Can. 45°7′ N, 66°50′ W 94
Saint George, S.C., U.S. 33°10′ N, 80°34′ W 96
Saint George, Utah, U.S. 37°6′ N, 113°33′ W 101
Saint George, Cape, Can. 48°23′ N, 60°23′ W 111
Saint George, Cape, Fla., U.S. 29°29′ N, 85°1′ W 96
Saint George, Cape, P.N.G. 5°1′ S, 152°57′ E 192
Saint George's, Can. 48°24′ N, 58°28′ W 111
Saint George's, Grenada 12°1′ N, 61°50′ W 116
Saint Georges Bay 45°38′ N, 61°49′ W 111
Saint George's Channel 52°2′ N, 6°25′ W 150
Saint Gregory, Cape, Can. 49°26′ N, 59°21′ W 111
Saint Gregory, Mount, peak, Can. 49°18′ N, 58°17′ W 111
Saint Helen, Lake, Mich., U.S. 44°19′ N, 84°57′ W 94
Saint Helena, island, U.K. 15°59′ S, 5°45′ W 253
Saint Helena, Mount, peak, Calif., U.S. 38°39′ N, 122°43′ W 90
Saint Helena Sound 32°21′ N, 81°48′ W 80
Saint Helens, Oreg., U.S. 45°50′ N, 122°49′ W 100
Saint Helens, U.K. 53°27′ N, 2°45′ W 162
Saint Helens, Mount, peak, Wash., U.S. 46°11′ N, 122°14′ W 100
Saint Helier, U.K. 49°11′ N, 2°6′ W 150
Saint Ignace, Mich., U.S. 45°51′ N, 84°44′ W 94
Saint Ives, U.K. 52°19′ N, 0°3′ E 162
Saint James, Mo., U.S. 37°59′ N, 91°37′ W 94
Saint James, Cape, Can. 51°40′ N, 131°26′ W 108
Saint James City, Fla., U.S. 26°29′ N, 82°5′ W 105
Saint John, Can. 45°16′ N, 66°5′ W 94
Saint John, Kans., U.S. 38°0′ N, 98°46′ W 90
Saint John, N. Dak., U.S. 48°55′ N, 99°44′ W 108
Saint John Bay 50°50′ N, 57°41′ W 111
Saint John, Cape, Can. 50°0′ N, 55°30′ W 111
Saint John, island, Virgin Is., U.S. 18°21′ N, 64°44′ W 118
Saint John's, Antigua and Barbuda 17°6′ N, 61°59′ W 116
Saint Johns, Ariz., U.S. 34°29′ N, 109°22′ W 92
Saint John's, Can. 47°22′ N, 53°3′ W 107
Saint Johns, Mich., U.S. 43°0′ N, 84°34′ W 102
Saint Joseph, La., U.S. 31°54′ N, 91°15′ W 103
Saint Joseph, Mich., U.S. 42°5′ N, 86°29′ W 102
Saint Joseph, Mo., U.S. 39°45′ N, 94°54′ W 82
Saint Joseph, Lake, Can. 50°49′ N, 92°26′ W 110
Saint Joseph Point, Fla., U.S. 29°46′ N, 86°14′ W 96
Saint Kitts and Nevis, islands, Caribbean Sea 17°16′ N, 62°41′ W 118
Saint Kitts (Saint Christopher), island, Saint Kitts and Nevis 17°21′ N, 62°47′ W 118
Saint Landrey, La., U.S. 30°50′ N, 92°16′ W 103
Saint Laurent, Can. 50°24′ N, 97°56′ W 90
Saint Lawrence, Can. 46°54′ N, 55°24′ W 111
Saint Lawrence, S. Dak., U.S. 44°30′ N, 98°57′ W 90
Saint Lawrence, Gulf of 46°56′ N, 63°44′ W 111
Saint Lawrence Island, Alas., U.S. 62°43′ N, 171°35′ W 98
Saint Lawrence Islands National Park, Can. 44°20′ N, 76°10′ W 110
Saint Lawrence River, river, Can. 49°0′ N, 69°0′ W 111
Saint Lawrence Seaway, Lake Ontario 44°20′ N, 75°7′ W 80
Saint Leo, Fla., U.S. 28°20′ N, 82°15′ W 105
Saint Lewis, river, Can. 52°7′ N, 57°9′ W 111
Saint Louis, Mich., U.S. 43°22′ N, 84°37′ W 102
Saint Louis, Mo., U.S. 38°38′ N, 90°28′ W 73
Saint Lucia, Cape, S. Af. 28°31′ S, 31°58′ E 227
Saint Lucia 13°53′ N, 60°68′ W 116
Saint Lucia Channel 14°11′ N, 61°40′ W 116
Saint Lucie, Fla., U.S. 27°29′ N, 80°21′ W 105
Saint Lucie Canal, Fla., U.S. 26°59′ N, 80°23′ W 105
Saint Marks, Fla., U.S. 30°8′ N, 84°13′ W 96
Saint Martin, island, Fr. 18°3′ N, 63°4′ W 116
Saint Martin, Lake, Can. 51°40′ N, 98°53′ W 108
Saint Martinville, La., U.S. 30°6′ N, 91°51′ W 103
Saint Mary, Cape, Can. 44°5′ N, 66°35′ W 94
Saint Mary Peak, Austral. 31°33′ S, 138°20′ E 230
Saint Marys, Can. 43°15′ N, 81°8′ W 102
Saint Marys, Ga., U.S. 30°43′ N, 81°34′ W 96
Saint Marys, Kans., U.S. 39°10′ N, 96°5′ W 92
Saint Marys, Ohio, U.S. 40°31′ N, 84°24′ W 102
Saint Marys Bay 44°20′ N, 66°15′ W 111
Saint Mary's, Cape, Can. 46°43′ N, 55°22′ W 111
Saint Marys City, Md., U.S. 38°10′ N, 76°26′ W 94
Saint Matthew Island, Alas., U.S. 60°27′ N, 172°55′ W 98
Saint Matthews, S.C., U.S. 33°39′ N, 80°47′ W 96
Saint Michael, Alas., U.S. 63°24′ N, 162°1′ W 106
Saint Michael's Mount, site, English Channel 50°6′ N, 5°35′ W 150
Saint Nazianz, Wis., U.S. 44°0′ N, 87°56′ W 102
Saint Neots, U.K. 52°13′ N, 0°15′ E 162
Saint Ninian's Cave, site, U.K. 54°41′ N, 4°31′ W 150
Saint Norbert, Can. 49°48′ N, 97°10′ W 90
Saint Ouen 49°13′ N, 2°14′ W 150
Saint Paris, Ohio, U.S. 40°6′ N, 83°58′ W 102
Saint Paul, Anadyrskiy Zaliv 57°8′ N, 170°16′ W 98
Saint Paul, Can. 53°58′ N, 111°19′ W 108
Saint Paul, Minn., U.S. 44°58′ N, 93°28′ W 106
Saint Paul, Nebr., U.S. 41°12′ N, 98°28′ W 90
Saint Paul, Cape, Ghana 5°42′ N, 0°57′ E 222
Saint Paul Island, Can. 47°15′ N, 61°15′ W 80
Saint Pauls, N.C., U.S. 34°48′ N, 79°0′ W 96
Saint Peter, Minn., U.S. 44°18′ N, 93°59′ W 94
Saint Peter and Saint Paul Rocks, islands, North Atlantic Ocean 0°54′ N, 29°27′ W 253
Saint Peter Port, U.K. 49°27′ N, 2°32′ W 150
Saint Peters, Can. 45°39′ N, 60°53′ W 111
Saint Petersburg, Fla., U.S. 27°47′ N, 82°39′ W 105
Saint Petersburg see Sankt-Peterburg, Russ. 59°55′ N, 30°17′ E 166
Saint Pierre and Miquelon, Fr. 47°5′ N, 56°49′ W 111
Saint Pierre Island, Seychelles 9°16′ S, 50°11′ E 218
Saint Pierre-Jolys, Can. 49°25′ N, 97°1′ W 90
Saint Sébastien, Cap, Madagascar 12°29′ S, 47°49′ E 220
Saint Simons Island, Ga., U.S. 31°8′ N, 81°24′ W 96
Saint Stephen, Can. 45°11′ N, 67°15′ W 82
Saint Stephen, S.C., U.S. 33°23′ N, 79°56′ W 96
Saint Terese, Alas., U.S. 58°28′ N, 134°46′ W 108
Saint Thomas, Can. 42°47′ N, 81°11′ W 102
Saint Thomas, N. Dak., U.S. 48°35′ N, 97°27′ W 90
Saint Thomas, island, U.S. 18°21′ N, 64°56′ W 118
Saint Vincent, Minn., U.S. 48°55′ N, 97°13′ W 90
Saint Vincent and the Grenadines 13°15′ N, 61°12′ W 116
Saint Vincent, Cap, Madagascar 21°58′ S, 42°31′ E 220
Saint Vincent Island, Fla., U.S. 29°8′ N, 85°32′ W 112
Saint Vith, Belg. 50°16′ N, 6°7′ E 167
Saint Walburg, Can. 53°38′ N, 109°12′ W 108
Saint-Agapit, Can. 46°33′ N, 71°26′ W 94
Saint-Amand, Fr. 50°26′ N, 3°24′ E 163
Saint-Amand-Montrond, Fr. 46°43′ N, 2°29′ E 150
Saint-Augustin, Can. 51°14′ N, 58°42′ W 106
Saint-Avold, Fr. 49°6′ N, 6°42′ E 163
Saint-Barthélemy, island, Fr. 17°55′ N, 62°55′ W 117
Saint-Brice, Fr. 45°52′ N, 0°57′ E 150
Saint-Brieuc, Fr. 48°30′ N, 2°50′ W 143
Saint-Denis, Can. 47°28′ N, 69°56′ W 94
Saint-Denis, Fr. 46°2′ N, 1°25′ W 150
Saint-Denis, Indian Ocean 20°54′ S, 55°25′ E 207
Saint-Denis, Réunion 20°55′ S, 55°25′ E 220
Saint-Dié, Fr. 48°17′ N, 6°57′ E 163
Saint-Dizier, Fr. 48°39′ N, 4°56′ E 163
Saint-Dizier, Fr. 48°39′ N, 4°57′ E 143
Sainte Agathe, Can. 49°33′ N, 97°13′ W 90
Sainte Anne, Can. 49°38′ N, 96°40′ W 90
Sainte Marie, Gabon 3°50′ S, 11°2′ E 218
Sainte Marie, Ill., U.S. 38°55′ N, 88°2′ W 102
Sainte Marie, Cap, Madagascar 26°14′ S, 44°46′ E 220
Sainte Marie, Nosy, island, Madagascar 16°50′ S, 50°3′ E 220
Sainte Rose du Lac, Can. 51°3′ N, 99°31′ W 90
Sainte-Agathe-des-Monts, Can. 46°2′ N, 74°18′ W 110
Sainte-Anne, Lac, lake, Can. 50°12′ N, 68°19′ W 111
Sainte-Anne-de-Beaupré, Can. 47°0′ N, 70°59′ W 94
Sainte-Anne-de-Madawaska, Can. 47°15′ N, 68°3′ W 111
Sainte-Anne-des-Monts, Can. 49°6′ N, 66°30′ W 111
Sainte-Anne-du-Lac, Can. 46°51′ N, 75°22′ W 94
Sainte-Marie, Can. 46°26′ N, 71°1′ W 94
Sainte-Marie, Martinique 14°45′ N, 61°1′ W 116
Sainte-Maxime, Fr. 43°18′ N, 6°37′ E 150
Sainte-Menehould, Fr. 49°5′ N, 4°54′ E 163
Saintes, Les, islands, Caribbean Sea 15°44′ N, 62°30′ W 116
Saint-Étienne, Fr. 45°26′ N, 4°23′ E 150
Saint-Étienne-du-Rouvray, Fr. 49°21′ N, 1°5′ E 163
Saint-Félicien, Can. 48°38′ N, 72°27′ W 94
Saint-Gaudens National Historic Site, N.H., U.S. 43°29′ N, 72°24′ W 104
Saint-Georges, Can. 46°37′ N, 72°40′ W 111
Saint-Georges, Can. 46°6′ N, 70°40′ W 94
Saint-Georges, South America 3°54′ N, 51°51′ W 130
Saint-Germain, Fr. 48°53′ N, 2°5′ E 163
Saint-Hilaire-de-Riez, Fr. 46°43′ N, 1°58′ W 150
Saint-Hyacinthe, Can. 45°36′ N, 72°59′ W 110
Saint-Jacques, Can. 45°56′ N, 73°35′ W 94
Saint-Jean, South America 5°23′ N, 54°6′ W 130
Saint-Jean, Lac, lake, Can. 48°35′ N, 72°56′ W 80
Saint-Jean, Lac, lake, Can. 48°33′ N, 73°30′ W 106
Saint-Jean-de-Luz, Fr. 43°22′ N, 1°40′ W 164
Saint-Jean-de-Maurienne, Fr. 45°16′ N, 6°19′ E 167
Saint-Jean-Pied-de-Port, Fr. 43°9′ N, 1°16′ W 164
Saint-Jean-sur-Richelieu, Can. 45°17′ N, 73°17′ W 94
Saint-Joseph-de-Beauce, Can. 46°18′ N, 70°53′ W 111
Saint-Jovite, Can. 46°7′ N, 74°36′ W 94
Saint-Julien, Fr. 46°8′ N, 6°4′ E 167
Saint-Just-en-Chausée, Fr. 49°30′ N, 2°26′ E 163
Saint-Laurent du Maroni, South America 5°23′ N, 53°57′ W 123
Saint-Laurent du Maroni, South America 5°30′ N, 54°1′ W 130
Saint-Léonard, Can. 47°9′ N, 67°55′ W 94
Saint-Louis, Senegal 15°54′ N, 16°22′ W 207
Saint-Lys, Fr. 43°30′ N, 1°10′ E 164
Saint-Malo, Fr. 48°39′ N, 2°1′ W 150
Saint-Marc, Haiti 19°8′ N, 72°43′ W 116
Saint-Marcel, Mont, peak, South America 2°21′ N, 53°7′ W 130
Saint-Martory, Fr. 43°8′ N, 0°55′ E 164
Saint-Mathieu, Pointe de, Fr. 47°32′ N, 10°13′ W 143
Saint-Michel, Fr. 49°54′ N, 4°8′ E 163
Saint-Mihiel, Fr. 48°53′ N, 5°32′ E 163
Saint-Nazaire, Fr. 47°16′ N, 2°13′ W 150
Saint-Nicolas-de-Port, Fr. 48°37′ N, 6°18′ E 163
Saint-Octave-de-Metis, Can. 48°35′ N, 68°6′ W 111
Saint-Omer, Fr. 50°45′ N, 2°15′ E 163
Saint-Pacôme, Can. 47°23′ N, 69°57′ W 94
Saint-Pascal, Can. 47°30′ N, 69°49′ W 111
Saint-Paul, Fr. 44°31′ N, 6°44′ E 167
Saint-Paul, island, Fr. 38°36′ S, 77°34′ E 254
Saint-Paul-de-Fenouillet, Fr. 42°48′ N, 2°28′ E 164
Saint-Pierre 46°46′ N, 56°11′ W 111
Saint-Pierre, Fr. 45°57′ N, 1°20′ W 150
Saint-Pierre, Pointe, Can. 48°32′ N, 64°10′ W 111
Saint-Pol, Fr. 50°21′ N, 2°22′ E 163
Saint-Pol-de-Léon, Fr. 48°41′ N, 4°0′ W 150
Saint-Pons, Fr. 43°28′ N, 2°45′ E 164
Saint-Quentin, Fr. 49°51′ N, 3°16′ E 163
Saint-Quentin, Pointe de, Fr. 50°16′ N, 1°11′ E 163
Saint-Romain, Can. 45°46′ N, 71°7′ W 94
Saint-Servan, Fr. 48°37′ N, 2°1′ W 150
Saint-Siméon, Can. 47°49′ N, 69°54′ W 94
Saint-Tite, Can. 46°43′ N, 72°34′ W 94
Saint-Valéry-sur-Somme, Fr. 50°10′ N, 1°37′ E 163
Saint-Vallier, Fr. 43°41′ N, 6°50′ E 167
Saint-Vincent, It. 45°45′ N, 7°39′ E 167
Saint-Vincent-de-Tyrosse, Fr. 43°39′ N, 1°20′ W 150
Saint-Vivien, Fr. 45°25′ N, 1°3′ W 150
Saipan, island, U.S. 15°11′ N, 145°45′ E 242
Saissac, Fr. 43°21′ N, 2°9′ E 164
Saitama, adm. division, Japan 35°53′ N, 138°44′ E 201
Saito, Japan 32°5′ N, 131°23′ E 201
Sajama, Bol. 18°8′ S, 69°0′ W 137
Sajama, Nevado, peak, Bol. 18°9′ S, 68°58′ W 137
Saka, Kenya 0°10′ N, 39°23′ E 224
Sakai, Japan 34°35′ N, 135°28′ E 201
Sakaide, Japan 34°18′ N, 133°51′ E 201
Sakaiminato, Japan 35°30′ N, 133°13′ E 201
Sakākah, Saudi Arabia 29°55′ N, 40°15′ E 180
Sakakawea, Lake, N. Dak., U.S. 48°18′ N, 102°54′ W 90
Sakal, Senegal 15°52′ N, 16°15′ W 222
Sakalilo, Tanzania 8°8′ S, 31°59′ E 224
Sakami, Can. 53°36′ N, 76°8′ W 106
Sakami, Lac, lake, Can. 53°9′ N, 78°17′ W 106

Sakami, river, *Can.* 53°6′ N, 73°14′ W 111
Sakania, *Dem. Rep. of the Congo* 12°48′ S, 28°31′ E 224
Säkar, *Turkm.* 38°55′ N, 63°41′ E 197
Sakarya, river, *Turk.* 40°3′ N, 30°33′ E 156
Sakata, *Japan* 38°50′ N, 139°53′ E 190
Sakçagöze, *Turk.* 37°10′ N, 36°52′ E 156
Sakchu, *N. Korea* 40°22′ N, 125°2′ E 200
Sakha, adm. division, *Russ.* 65°15′ N, 125°44′ E 160
Sakhalin, adm. division, *Russ.* 44°21′ N, 147°1′ E 160
Sakhalin, Ostrov, island, *Russ.* 50°36′ N, 143°44′ E 190
Sakhalinskiy Zaliv 53°48′ N, 139°32′ E 160
Sakhar, *Afghan.* 32°54′ N, 65°32′ E 186
Şäki, *Azerb.* 41°12′ N, 47°9′ E 195
Šakiai, *Lith.* 54°57′ N, 23°1′ E 166
Sakinohama, *Japan* 33°24′ N, 134°11′ E 201
Sakishima Shotō, islands, *East China Sea* 22°44′ N, 124°24′ E 238
Sakmara, *Russ.* 52°1′ N, 55°21′ E 158
Sa-koi, *Myanmar* 19°54′ N, 97°1′ E 202
Sakon Nakhon, *Thai.* 17°13′ N, 103°59′ E 202
Sakora, *Mali* 14°10′ N, 9°21′ W 222
Sakrand, *Pak.* 26°10′ N, 68°16′ E 186
Sakrivier, *S. Af.* 30°53′ S, 20°25′ E 227
Saku, *Japan* 36°13′ N, 138°25′ E 201
Saky, *Ukr.* 45°8′ N, 33°35′ E 156
Säkylä, *Fin.* 61°2′ N, 22°19′ E 166
Sal Mountains, La, *Utah, U.S.* 38°24′ N, 109°18′ W 90
Sal, Punta, *Hond.* 15°53′ N, 87°37′ W 115
Sal, river, *Russ.* 47°22′ N, 43°19′ E 184
Sal, river, *Russ.* 47°12′ N, 41°50′ E 158
Sala, *Eritrea* 16°56′ N, 37°25′ E 182
Sala, *Nor.* 59°54′ N, 16°34′ E 152
Šal'a, *Slovakia* 48°9′ N, 17°52′ E 152
Salaberry-de-Valleyfield, *Can.* 45°16′ N, 74°9′ W 110
Sălacea, *Rom.* 47°26′ N, 22°18′ E 168
Salacgrīva, *Latv.* 57°44′ N, 24°20′ E 166
Saladas, *Arg.* 28°16′ S, 58°37′ W 139
Saladillo, *Arg.* 35°39′ S, 59°47′ W 139
Saladillo, river, *Arg.* 28°47′ S, 64°10′ W 134
Salado, river, *Arg.* 29°28′ S, 62°14′ W 139
Salado, river, *Arg.* 35°50′ S, 57°49′ W 139
Salado, river, *Arg.* 36°1′ S, 66°45′ W 134
Salado, river, *Mex.* 26°57′ N, 99°51′ W 96
Salaga, *Ghana* 8°33′ N, 0°32′ E 222
Salagle, *Somalia* 1°48′ N, 42°17′ E 224
Şala' ad Dīn, *Iraq* 36°23′ N, 44°8′ E 195
Salahīyah, *Syr.* 35°0′ N, 37°3′ E 194
Salahmi, *Fin.* 63°47′ N, 26°53′ E 152
Salair, *Russ.* 54°11′ N, 85°49′ E 184
Sălaj, adm. division, *Rom.* 47°1′ N, 22°45′ E 156
Salal, *Chad* 14°49′ N, 17°14′ E 216
Salala, *Sudan* 21°15′ N, 36°16′ E 182
Salālah, *Oman* 17°2′ N, 54°6′ E 182
Salamanca, *Chile* 31°46′ S, 71°1′ W 134
Salamanca, *Mex.* 20°34′ N, 101°12′ W 114
Salamanca, *Sp.* 40°58′ N, 5°38′ W 214
Salamis 480 B.C., battle, *Aegean Sea* 37°56′ N, 23°25′ E 156
Salamis, ruin(s) 35°10′ N, 33°51′ E 194
Salang, Kowtal-e, pass, *Afghan.* 35°21′ N, 69°5′ E 186
Salangen, *Nor.* 68°51′ N, 17°51′ E 152
Salantai, *Lith.* 56°2′ N, 21°34′ E 166
Sălard, *Rom.* 47°13′ N, 22°1′ E 168
Salardú, *Sp.* 42°42′ N, 0°55′ E 164
Salaš, *Serb.* 44°6′ N, 22°19′ E 168
Salas de Bureba, *Sp.* 42°41′ N, 3°29′ W 164
Salas de los Infantes, *Sp.* 42°0′ N, 3°17′ W 164
Salaspils, *Latv.* 56°52′ N, 24°18′ E 166
Salavat, *Russ.* 53°22′ N, 55°51′ E 154
Salaverry, *Peru* 8°13′ S, 78°57′ W 123
Salavina, *Arg.* 28°48′ S, 63°26′ W 139
Salawati, island, *Indonesia* 1°28′ S, 129°43′ E 192
Salay, *Philippines* 8°53′ N, 124°50′ E 203
Salay Gómez Ridge, *South Pacific Ocean* 26°4′ S, 95°15′ W 252
Sala-y-Gómez, Isla, island, *Chile* 26°25′ S, 105°19′ W 252
Salbris, *Fr.* 47°25′ N, 2°2′ E 150
Šalčininkai, *Lith.* 54°19′ N, 25°22′ E 166
Sălciua de Jos, *Rom.* 46°24′ N, 23°27′ E 168
Saldanha, *S. Af.* 32°59′ S, 17°55′ E 220
Saldé, *Senegal* 16°9′ N, 13°59′ W 222
Saldungaray, *Arg.* 38°13′ S, 61°48′ W 139
Saldus, *Latv.* 56°38′ N, 22°28′ E 166
Sale, *Austral.* 38°6′ S, 147°3′ E 231
Sale, *U.K.* 53°25′ N, 2°20′ W 162
Salekhard, *Russ.* 66°29′ N, 66°46′ E 169
Salem, *Ark., U.S.* 36°21′ N, 91°49′ W 96
Salem, *Conn., U.S.* 41°29′ N, 72°17′ W 104
Salem, *Fla., U.S.* 29°52′ N, 83°26′ W 105
Salem, *India* 11°37′ N, 78°10′ E 188
Salem, *Ind., U.S.* 38°36′ N, 86°6′ W 102
Salem, *Mo., U.S.* 37°37′ N, 91°32′ W 96
Salem, *N.H., U.S.* 42°47′ N, 71°13′ W 104
Salem, *N.Y., U.S.* 43°10′ N, 73°21′ W 104
Salem, *Ohio, U.S.* 40°53′ N, 80°51′ W 102
Salem, *Oreg., U.S.* 44°55′ N, 123°8′ W 90
Salem, *S. Dak., U.S.* 43°42′ N, 97°24′ W 90
Salem, *Sw.* 59°14′ N, 17°47′ E 166
Salem, *Va., U.S.* 37°17′ N, 80°4′ W 96
Salem, *W. Va., U.S.* 39°16′ N, 80°34′ W 94
Sälen, *Nor.* 61°10′ N, 13°13′ E 152
Salford, *U.K.* 53°28′ N, 2°19′ W 162
Salgótarján, *Hung.* 48°5′ N, 19°49′ E 168
Salgueiro, *Braz.* 8°8′ S, 39°7′ W 132
Salhus, *Nor.* 60°30′ N, 5°16′ E 152
Sali, *Alg.* 26°58′ N, 2°118′ W 214
Salida, *Calif., U.S.* 37°42′ N, 121°6′ W 100
Salida, *Colo., U.S.* 38°32′ N, 106°2′ W 82
Salies-du-Salat, *Fr.* 43°6′ N, 0°56′ E 164
Şalīf, *Yemen* 15°18′ N, 42°41′ E 182
Salihorsk, *Belarus* 52°47′ N, 27°29′ E 158
Salima, *Malawi* 13°46′ S, 34°24′ E 224
Salin, *Myanmar* 20°35′ N, 94°39′ E 202
Salina, *Kans., U.S.* 38°49′ N, 97°38′ W 94
Salina, *Utah, U.S.* 38°57′ N, 111°52′ W 90
Salinas, *Braz.* 16°11′ S, 42°22′ W 138
Salinas, *Calif., U.S.* 36°40′ N, 121°40′ W 100
Salinas, *Ecua.* 2°17′ S, 80°56′ W 130
Salinas, *Mex.* 22°36′ N, 101°43′ W 114
Salinas de Añana, *Sp.* 42°48′ N, 2°59′ W 164
Salinas de G. Mendoza, *Bol.* 19°39′ S, 67°43′ W 137
Salinas, Ponta das, *Angola* 12°55′ S, 12°20′ E 220
Salinas Pueblo Missions National Monument, *N. Mex., U.S.* 34°31′ N, 106°43′ W 92
Salinas, Sierra de, *Calif., U.S.* 36°20′ N, 121°30′ W 100
Salinas Victoria, *Mex.* 25°57′ N, 100°18′ W 114
Saline, *La., U.S.* 32°9′ N, 92°59′ W 103
Saline, *Mich., U.S.* 42°9′ N, 83°48′ W 102
Saline, river, *Ark., U.S.* 33°9′ N, 92°6′ W 103
Saline, river, *Kans., U.S.* 39°0′ N, 99°22′ W 90
Saline, river, *La., U.S.* 32°20′ N, 93°2′ W 103
Saline Valley, *Calif., U.S.* 36°47′ N, 117°55′ W 101
Salines, Point, *Grenada* 11°53′ N, 62°36′ W 116
Salinópolis, *Braz.* 0°38′ N, 47°19′ W 130
Salisbury, *Conn., U.S.* 41°59′ N, 73°26′ W 104
Salisbury, *N.H., U.S.* 43°22′ N, 71°44′ W 104
Salisbury, *U.K.* 51°4′ N, 1°47′ W 162
Salisbury, *Vt., U.S.* 43°53′ N, 73°7′ W 104
Salisbury Island, *Can.* 63°31′ N, 76°33′ W 106
Salisbury, Mount, peak, *Alas., U.S.* 69°7′ N, 146°30′ W 98
Salisbury Plain, *U.K.* 51°18′ N, 2°5′ W 162
Salisbury Sound 57°16′ N, 136°9′ W 108
Salish Mountains, *Mont., U.S.* 48°30′ N, 115°8′ W 90
Salish Sea, 48°56′ N, 123°3′ W 100
Săliște, *Rom.* 45°48′ N, 23°54′ E 156
Şalkhad, *Syr.* 32°29′ N, 36°43′ E 194
Salkum, *Wash., U.S.* 46°30′ N, 122°39′ W 100
Salla, *Fin.* 66°49′ N, 28°39′ E 152
Sallanches, *Fr.* 45°56′ N, 6°37′ E 167
Sallent, *Sp.* 41°50′ N, 1°54′ E 164
Sallent de Gállego, *Sp.* 42°46′ N, 0°20′ E 164
Salliqueló, *Arg.* 36°45′ S, 62°57′ W 139
Sallis, *Miss., U.S.* 33°0′ N, 89°47′ W 103
Sallisaw, *Okla., U.S.* 35°26′ N, 94°47′ W 96
Sallom, *Sudan* 19°23′ N, 37°3′ E 182
Salluit, *Can.* 62°11′ N, 75°42′ W 106
Salmās, *Iran* 38°17′ N, 44°44′ E 195
Salme, *Est.* 58°9′ N, 22°14′ E 166
Salmerón, *Sp.* 40°33′ N, 2°30′ W 164
Salmi, *Russ.* 61°21′ N, 31°56′ E 152
Salmo, *Can.* 49°11′ N, 117°17′ W 90
Salmon, *Idaho, U.S.* 45°9′ N, 113°54′ W 90
Salmon Arm, *Can.* 50°41′ N, 119°17′ W 90
Salmon Falls Creek Reservoir, lake, *Idaho, U.S.* 42°19′ N, 118°19′ W 80
Salmon Mountain, peak, *Idaho, U.S.* 45°34′ N, 114°56′ W 90
Salmon Mountains, *Calif., U.S.* 41°7′ N, 123°27′ W 90
Salmon, river, *Idaho, U.S.* 45°31′ N, 116°2′ W 106
Salmon River Mountains, *Idaho, U.S.* 45°9′ N, 116°18′ W 90
Salo, *Cen. Af. Rep.* 3°23′ N, 16°8′ E 218
Salo, *Fin.* 60°23′ N, 23°5′ E 166
Salò, *It.* 45°37′ N, 10°31′ E 167
Salobelyak, *Russ.* 57°8′ N, 48°5′ E 154
Salole, *Eth.* 4°27′ N, 39°33′ E 224
Salome, *Ariz., U.S.* 33°46′ N, 113°36′ W 101
Salomon Islands, *Indian Ocean* 5°16′ S, 72°22′ E 188
Salon, *Fr.* 43°38′ N, 5°5′ E 150
Salonae see Solin, *Croatia* 43°32′ N, 16°28′ E 168
Salonga National Park, *Dem. Rep. of the Congo* 3°0′ S, 20°3′ E 218
Salonga, river, *Dem. Rep. of the Congo* 1°6′ S, 20°36′ E 218
Salonica see Thessaloníki, *Gr.* 40°38′ N, 22°57′ E 156
Salonta, *Rom.* 46°48′ N, 21°42′ E 168
Salor, river, *Sp.* 39°19′ N, 6°20′ W 164
Salou, Cap de, *Sp.* 40°53′ N, 1°8′ E 164
Salpausselkä, *Fin.* 61°19′ N, 28°51′ E 166
Salsberry Pass, *Calif., U.S.* 35°55′ N, 116°26′ W 101
Salses, *Fr.* 42°49′ N, 2°53′ E 164
Sălsig, *Rom.* 47°30′ N, 23°19′ E 168
Sal'sk, *Russ.* 46°27′ N, 41°26′ E 158
Salsomaggiore Terme, *It.* 44°48′ N, 9°58′ E 167
Salt, *Sp.* 41°57′ N, 2°47′ E 164
Salt Fork Brazos, river, *Tex., U.S.* 33°9′ N, 101°34′ W 80
Salt Fork Red, river, *Tex., U.S.* 35°5′ N, 100°57′ W 112
Salt Lake, *Calif., U.S.* 36°41′ N, 117°58′ W 101
Salt Lake City, *Utah, U.S.* 40°43′ N, 111°59′ W 90
Salt River, *Can.* 60°6′ N, 112°22′ W 108
Salt, river, *Can.* 59°36′ N, 112°15′ W 108
Salt, river, *Mo., U.S.* 39°29′ N, 91°35′ W 94
Salt River Range, *Wyo., U.S.* 42°53′ N, 111°5′ W 90
Salta, *Arg.* 24°47′ S, 65°25′ W 132
Saltburn by the Sea, *U.K.* 54°35′ N, 0°59′ E 162
Saltcoats, *Can.* 51°2′ N, 102°11′ W 90
Saltdal, *Nor.* 67°4′ N, 15°24′ E 152
Saltee Islands, *Ire.* 51°49′ N, 6°37′ W 150
Saltfleetby Saint Peter, *U.K.* 53°23′ N, 0°10′ E 162
Saltillo, *Mex.* 25°23′ N, 101°5′ W 114
Salto, *Arg.* 34°18′ S, 60°16′ W 139
Salto, *Uru.* 31°22′ S, 57°55′ W 139
Salto Angostura I, fall(s), *Col.* 1°59′ N, 73°53′ W 136
Salto Angostura Ii, fall(s), *Col.* 2°11′ N, 73°35′ W 136
Salto Angostura Iii, fall(s), *Col.* 2°54′ N, 72°16′ W 136
Salto del Guairá, *Parag.* 24°3′ S, 54°19′ W 132
Salto Grande, *Braz.* 22°54′ S, 50°0′ W 138
Salto, river, *Mex.* 22°12′ N, 99°19′ W 114
Saltoluokta, *Nor.* 67°23′ N, 18°31′ E 152
Salton City, *Calif., U.S.* 33°16′ N, 115°58′ W 101
Salton Sea Beach, *Calif., U.S.* 33°20′ N, 116°0′ W 101
Salton Sea, lake, *Calif., U.S.* 33°19′ N, 115°53′ W 101
Saltoro Kangri, peak, *Pak.* 35°22′ N, 76°45′ E 188
Saltpond, *Ghana* 5°14′ N, 1°5′ W 222
Saltsjöbaden, *Sw.* 59°15′ N, 18°15′ E 166
Saltspring Island, *Can.* 48°48′ N, 123°16′ W 100
Saltvik, *Fin.* 60°15′ N, 20°3′ E 166
Saluda, *S.C., U.S.* 34°0′ N, 81°47′ W 96
Saluggia, *It.* 45°13′ N, 8°0′ E 167
Salûm, *Egypt* 31°33′ N, 25°11′ E 180
Salur, *India* 18°31′ N, 83°12′ E 188
Saluzzo, *It.* 44°38′ N, 7°30′ E 167
Salvacañete, *Sp.* 40°5′ N, 1°31′ W 164
Salvador (Bahia), *Braz.* 12°59′ S, 38°28′ W 132
Salvador Mazza, *Arg.* 22°5′ S, 63°48′ W 137
Salvage Islands see Selvagens, Ilhas, *North Atlantic Ocean* 30°18′ N, 16°15′ W 214
Salvaterra, *Braz.* 0°46′ N, 48°33′ W 130
Salvatierra, *Mex.* 20°11′ N, 100°54′ W 114
Salvatierra, *Sp.* 42°50′ N, 2°23′ W 150
Salwá, Daw'at 24°39′ N, 49°59′ E 196
Salween see Nu, river, *Asia* 31°21′ N, 93°34′ E 190
Salween see Thanlwin, river, *Asia* 21°45′ N, 98°44′ E 202
Salyan, *Azerb.* 39°36′ N, 48°58′ E 195
Salyan, *Azerb.* 41°3′ N, 49°6′ E 180
Salyersville, *Ky., U.S.* 37°44′ N, 83°4′ W 96
Salym, *Russ.* 60°6′ N, 71°26′ E 169
Salzbrunn, *Namibia* 24°24′ S, 17°57′ E 227
Salzburg, *Aust.* 47°49′ N, 13°3′ E 156
Salzgitter, *Ger.* 52°2′ N, 10°22′ E 152
Salzkammergut, region, *Aust.* 47°39′ N, 12°48′ E 156
Salzkotten, *Ger.* 51°40′ N, 8°36′ E 167
Sam, *India* 26°47′ N, 70°34′ E 186
Sam Rayburn Reservoir, lake, *Tex., U.S.* 31°3′ N, 95°0′ W 103
Sam Son, *Vietnam* 19°45′ N, 105°52′ E 198
Sama, river, *Peru* 18°1′ S, 70°36′ W 137
Samah, oil field, *Lib.* 28°7′ N, 19°0′ E 216
Samā', spring, *Saudi Arabia* 29°2′ N, 45°26′ E 196
Samaipata, *Bol.* 18°13′ S, 63°52′ W 137
Samâlût, *Egypt* 28°16′ N, 30°39′ E 180
Samaná, *Dom. Rep.* 19°12′ N, 69°20′ W 116
Samaná, Cabo, *Dom. Rep.* 19°12′ N, 69°7′ W 116
Samana Cay, island, *Bahamas* 23°10′ N, 74°2′ W 116
Samandağı (Seleucia), *Turk.* 36°4′ N, 35°57′ E 156
Samanga, *Tanzania* 8°20′ S, 39°13′ E 224
Samaqua, river, *Can.* 49°53′ N, 72°31′ W 94
Samar, *Jordan* 32°39′ N, 35°48′ E 194
Samar, island, *Philippines* 12°14′ N, 125°25′ E 192
Samara, *Russ.* 53°14′ N, 50°14′ E 154
Samara, adm. division, *Russ.* 53°31′ N, 49°15′ E 154
Samara, river, *Russ.* 52°22′ N, 53°17′ E 184
Samarai, *P.N.G.* 10°38′ S, 150°40′ E 231
Samaria Mountain, peak, *Idaho, U.S.* 42°4′ N, 112°26′ W 90
Samariapo, *Venez.* 5°10′ N, 67°44′ W 136
Samarinda, *Indonesia* 0°30′ N, 117°7′ E 192
Samarqand, *Uzb.* 39°39′ N, 67°0′ E 197
Sāmarrā', *Iraq* 34°17′ N, 43°52′ E 180
Samarskoe, *Kaz.* 49°1′ N, 83°23′ E 184
Samarskoye, *Russ.* 46°57′ N, 39°38′ E 156
Samastipur, *India* 25°50′ N, 85°47′ E 197
Samatiguila, *Côte d'Ivoire* 9°49′ N, 7°35′ W 222
Samaúma, *Braz.* 0°8′ N, 69°16′ W 136
Samaúma, *Braz.* 8°43′ S, 67°22′ W 130
Samawah see As Samāwah, *Iraq* 31°15′ N, 45°15′ E 180
Samba, *Burkina Faso* 12°40′ N, 2°26′ W 222
Samba, *Gabon* 1°4′ S, 10°41′ E 218
Samba, *India* 32°33′ N, 75°9′ E 188
Sambalpur, *India* 21°29′ N, 83°59′ E 188
Sambalpur, *India* 20°18′ N, 81°2′ E 188
Sambas, *Indonesia* 1°22′ N, 109°17′ E 196
Sambava, *Madagascar* 14°19′ S, 50°8′ E 220
Sambhal, *India* 28°32′ N, 78°34′ E 197
Sambhar, *India* 26°54′ N, 75°13′ E 197
Sambiase, *It.* 38°58′ N, 16°15′ E 156
Sambir, *Ukr.* 49°30′ N, 23°11′ E 152
Sambolabbo, *Cameroon* 7°3′ N, 11°57′ E 218
Samborombón, Bahía 34°27′ S, 58°24′ W 134
Samburg, *Russ.* 66°52′ N, 78°20′ E 169
Samburu Reserve, *Kenya* 0°37′ N, 37°34′ E 224
Samcheok, *S. Korea* 37°27′ N, 129°9′ E 200
Samdari, *India* 25°49′ N, 72°34′ E 186
Samdŭng, *N. Korea* 38°59′ N, 126°12′ E 200
Same, *Tanzania* 4°5′ S, 37°44′ E 224
Samedan, *Switz.* 46°33′ N, 9°52′ E 167
Samer, *Fr.* 50°38′ N, 1°45′ E 163
Samfya, *Zambia* 11°21′ S, 29°30′ E 224
Samgi, *N. Korea* 40°27′ N, 128°20′ E 200
Samho, *N. Korea* 39°55′ N, 127°51′ E 200
Şāmiţah, *Saudi Arabia* 16°35′ N, 42°55′ E 182
Sammatti, *Fin.* 60°18′ N, 23°48′ E 166
Samnangjin, *S. Korea* 35°24′ N, 128°51′ E 200
Samnū, *Lib.* 27°17′ N, 14°52′ E 216
Samnye, *S. Korea* 35°54′ N, 127°5′ E 200
Samoa, *Calif., U.S.* 40°48′ N, 124°11′ W 90
Samoa 13°50′ S, 172°8′ W 241
Samoa, islands, *South Pacific Ocean* 13°58′ S, 175°18′ W 238
Samoded, *Russ.* 63°37′ N, 40°30′ E 154
Samoëns, *Fr.* 46°5′ N, 6°43′ E 167
Samokov, *Maced.* 41°40′ N, 21°8′ E 168
Samolva, *Russ.* 58°15′ N, 27°37′ E 166
Samorogouan, *Burkina Faso* 11°24′ N, 4°58′ W 222
Samoš, *Serb.* 45°12′ N, 20°47′ E 168
Sámos, island, *Gr.* 37°50′ N, 26°34′ E 180
Samos, ruin(s), *Gr.* 37°40′ N, 26°51′ E 156
Samothráki, island, *Gr.* 40°31′ N, 25°17′ E 180
Samoylovka, *Russ.* 51°8′ N, 43°44′ E 158
Sampa, *Ghana* 7°58′ N, 2°43′ W 222
Sampacho, *Arg.* 33°24′ S, 64°43′ W 134
Samparha Koura, *Mali* 14°38′ N, 8°5′ W 222
Samper de Calanda, *Sp.* 41°10′ N, 0°23′ E 164
Sampit, *Indonesia* 2°32′ S, 112°46′ E 192
Samp'o, *N. Korea* 41°1′ N, 127°9′ E 200
Sam'po, *N. Korea* 41°13′ N, 129°42′ E 200
Sampwe, *Dem. Rep. of the Congo* 9°20′ S, 27°23′ E 224
Samrē, *Eth.* 13°10′ N, 39°12′ E 182
Samro, Ozero, lake, *Russ.* 58°58′ N, 28°36′ E 166
Samrong, *Cambodia* 14°12′ N, 103°34′ E 202
Samsŏ, *N. Korea* 41°17′ N, 127°39′ E 200
Samsu, *N. Korea* 41°18′ N, 128°2′ E 200
Samsun, *Turk.* 41°13′ N, 36°13′ E 143
Samsun (Amisus), *Turk.* 41°17′ N, 36°20′ E 158
Samthar, *India* 25°51′ N, 78°55′ E 197
Samtredia, *Ga.* 42°9′ N, 42°22′ E 195
Samuel, Mount, peak, *Austral.* 19°42′ S, 133°57′ E 230
Samuhú, *Arg.* 27°30′ S, 60°30′ W 139
Samui, Ko, island, *Thai.* 9°15′ N, 99°59′ E 202
Samur, river, *Europe* 41°22′ N, 47°38′ E 195
Samus', *Russ.* 56°46′ N, 84°47′ E 169
Samut Prakan, *Thai.* 13°36′ N, 100°36′ E 202
Samut Songkhram, *Thai.* 13°26′ N, 100°2′ E 202
San, *Mali* 13°17′ N, 4°56′ W 222
San Adrián, Cabo, *Sp.* 43°1′ N, 8°54′ W 150
San Agustín, *Col.* 1°53′ N, 76°18′ W 136
San Agustin, Cape, *Philippines* 6°17′ N, 126°14′ E 203
San Agustín de Valle Fértil, *Arg.* 30°39′ S, 67°35′ W 134
San Ambrosio Island, *Chile* 26°14′ S, 79°39′ W 253
San Andreas, *Calif., U.S.* 38°11′ N, 120°42′ W 100
San Andrés, *Bol.* 15°2′ S, 64°28′ W 137
San Andrés, Isla de, island, *Col.* 12°23′ N, 82°18′ W 115
San Andrés, Laguna de 22°40′ N, 98°25′ W 114
San Andrés Tuxtla, *Mex.* 18°25′ N, 95°12′ W 114
San Angelo, *Tex., U.S.* 31°27′ N, 100°26′ W 92
San Anselmo, *Calif., U.S.* 37°58′ N, 122°35′ W 100
San Antero, *Col.* 9°21′ N, 75°46′ W 136
San Antonio, *Bol.* 14°56′ S, 64°32′ W 137
San Antonio, *Col.* 1°48′ N, 78°19′ W 136
San Antonio, *Peru* 3°45′ S, 74°25′ W 136
San Antonio, *Tex., U.S.* 29°25′ N, 98°30′ W 92
San Antonio, *Venez.* 3°29′ N, 66°46′ W 136
San Antonio Bay 28°9′ N, 96°58′ W 112
San Antonio, Cabo, *Arg.* 36°48′ S, 57°6′ W 139
San Antonio da Cachoeira, *Braz.* 0°39′ N, 52°31′ W 130
San Antonio de Areco, *Arg.* 34°15′ S, 59°27′ W 139
San Antonio de Bravo, *Tex., U.S.* 30°11′ N, 104°42′ W 92
San Antonio de Caparo, *Venez.* 7°32′ N, 71°31′ W 136
San Antonio de las Alazanas, *Mex.* 25°15′ N, 100°35′ W 114
San Antonio de los Cobres, *Arg.* 24°11′ S, 66°23′ W 132
San Antonio, Lake, *Calif., U.S.* 35°49′ N, 121°4′ W 100
San Antonio, Mount, peak, *Calif., U.S.* 34°17′ N, 117°42′ W 101
San Antonio Mountain, peak, *Tex., U.S.* 31°56′ N, 105°38′ W 92
San Antonio Mountains, *Nev., U.S.* 38°9′ N, 117°34′ W 90
San Antonio, Punta, *Mex.* 29°28′ N, 116°4′ W 92
San Antonio, river, *Tex., U.S.* 29°18′ N, 99°13′ W 80
San Antonio, Sierra de, *Mex.* 30°9′ N, 110°53′ W 112
San Ardo, *Calif., U.S.* 36°1′ N, 120°55′ W 100
San Asensio, *Sp.* 42°29′ N, 2°45′ W 164
San Augustine, *Tex., U.S.* 31°30′ N, 94°7′ W 103
San Bartolo, *Peru* 12°28′ S, 76°48′ W 130
San Benedetto Po, *It.* 45°2′ N, 10°55′ E 167
San Benedicto, Isla, island, *Isla San Benedicto* 19°4′ N, 110°53′ W 112
San Benito, *Tex., U.S.* 26°6′ N, 97°37′ W 114
San Benito, Islas, islands, *North Pacific Ocean* 28°23′ N, 116°19′ W 112
San Benito Mountain, peak, *Calif., U.S.* 36°21′ N, 120°42′ W 100
San Bernardino, *Calif., U.S.* 34°6′ N, 117°18′ W 101
San Bernardino Mountains, *Calif., U.S.* 34°12′ N, 117°25′ W 101
San Bernardino Strait 12°35′ N, 123°0′ E 192
San Bernardo, *Chile* 33°36′ S, 70°45′ W 134
San Bernardo, *Mex.* 25°59′ N, 105°28′ W 114
San Blas, *Mex.* 21°33′ N, 105°17′ W 114
San Blas, *Mex.* 27°26′ N, 101°45′ W 96
San Blas, Archipiélago de, *North America* 9°22′ N, 78°6′ W 115
San Blas, Cape, *Fla., U.S.* 29°33′ N, 85°57′ W 96
San Bonifacio, *It.* 45°23′ N, 11°17′ E 167
San Borja, *Bol.* 14°51′ S, 66°52′ W 137
San Borja, Sierra de, *Mex.* 29°34′ N, 115°3′ W 112
San Buenaventura, *Bol.* 14°33′ S, 67°38′ W 137
San Candido, *It.* 46°43′ N, 12°17′ E 167
San Carlos, *Arg.* 27°45′ S, 55°58′ W 139
San Carlos, *Arg.* 25°57′ S, 65°57′ W 134
San Carlos, *Chile* 36°24′ S, 71°59′ W 134
San Carlos, *Mex.* 29°0′ N, 100°54′ W 92
San Carlos, *Mex.* 24°33′ N, 98°56′ W 114
San Carlos, *Mex.* 27°59′ N, 111°4′ W 112
San Carlos, *Mex.* 24°46′ N, 112°6′ W 112
San Carlos, *Nicar.* 11°8′ N, 84°46′ W 115
San Carlos, *Philippines* 15°55′ N, 120°19′ E 203
San Carlos, *Philippines* 10°27′ N, 123°22′ E 203
San Carlos, *Uru.* 34°48′ S, 54°56′ W 139
San Carlos, *Venez.* 9°39′ N, 68°36′ W 136
San Carlos, *Venez.* 1°56′ N, 66°59′ W 123
San Carlos Centro, *Arg.* 31°44′ S, 61°4′ W 139
San Carlos de Bolívar, *Arg.* 36°13′ S, 61°6′ W 139
San Carlos de Río Negro, *Venez.* 1°52′ N, 67°2′ W 136
San Carlos, Mesa de, peak, *Mex.* 29°37′ N, 115°25′ W 92
San Carlos, Punta, *Mex.* 29°17′ N, 115°44′ W 92
San Cayetano, *Arg.* 38°21′ S, 59°37′ W 139
San Clemente, *Calif., U.S.* 33°25′ N, 117°38′ W 101

San Clemente, island, *Calif., U.S.* 32°46′ N, 118°22′ W 101
San Cosme, *Arg.* 27°22′ S, 58°33′ W 139
San Cosme y Damián, *Parag.* 27°18′ S, 56°20′ W 139
San Cristóbal, *Arg.* 30°17′ S, 61°14′ W 139
San Cristóbal, *Bol.* 21°6′ S, 67°10′ W 137
San Cristóbal, *Col.* 2°18′ S, 73°2′ W 136
San Cristóbal, *Venez.* 7°44′ N, 72°14′ W 136
San Cristóbal, Isla, island, *Ecua.* 0°45′ N, 89°16′ W 130
San Cristobal, island, *Solomon Islands* 10°35′ S, 161°45′ E 242
San Cristóbal Verapaz, *Guatemala* 15°23′ N, 90°26′ W 115
San Custodio, *Venez.* 1°35′ N, 66°13′ W 136
San Diego, *Calif., U.S.* 32°43′ N, 117°11′ W 101
San Diego, *Tex., U.S.* 27°45′ N, 98°14′ W 92
San Diego, Cabo, *Arg.* 54°30′ S, 65°11′ W 134
San Donà di Piave, *It.* 45°38′ N, 12°33′ E 167
San Estanislao, *Parag.* 24°39′ S, 56°29′ W 132
San Esteban, *Hond.* 15°17′ N, 85°52′ W 115
San Esteban de Gormaz, *Sp.* 41°34′ N, 3°13′ W 164
San Esteban de Litera, *Sp.* 41°54′ N, 0°19′ E 164
San Esteban, island, *Mex.* 28°29′ N, 112°33′ W 112
San Felice sul Panaro, *It.* 44°50′ N, 11°8′ E 167
San Felipe, *Col.* 1°51′ N, 67°5′ W 136
San Felipe, *Mex.* 21°27′ N, 101°14′ W 114
San Felipe, *Tex., U.S.* 29°47′ N, 96°6′ W 96
San Felipe, *Venez.* 10°18′ N, 68°46′ W 136
San Felipe, Cayos de, *Caribbean Sea* 21°35′ N, 84°7′ W 116
San Felipe, peak, *Mex.* 17°8′ N, 96°43′ W 114
San Félix, *Venez.* 8°5′ N, 72°15′ W 136
San Félix Island, *Chile* 26°7′ S, 80°18′ W 253
San Fermín, Punta, *Mex.* 30°19′ N, 114°38′ W 92
San Fernando, *Calif., U.S.* 34°17′ N, 118°27′ W 101
San Fernando, *Mex.* 24°50′ N, 98°9′ W 114
San Fernando, *Philippines* 15°1′ N, 120°40′ E 203
San Fernando, *Philippines* 16°38′ N, 120°20′ E 203
San Fernando, *Sp.* 36°27′ N, 6°12′ W 164
San Fernando, *Trinidad and Tobago* 10°16′ N, 61°26′ W 116
San Fernando de Apure, *Venez.* 7°51′ N, 67°30′ W 136
San Fernando de Atabapo, *Venez.* 3°59′ N, 67°42′ W 136
San Fernando, river, *Mex.* 25°12′ N, 98°37′ W 114
San Francisco, *Arg.* 31°27′ S, 62°6′ W 139
San Francisco, *Bol.* 15°18′ S, 65°35′ W 137
San Francisco, *Calif., U.S.* 37°46′ N, 122°26′ W 100
San Francisco, *Col.* 1°10′ N, 76°58′ W 136
San Francisco, *Mex.* 30°49′ N, 112°37′ W 92
San Francisco Bay 37°36′ N, 122°19′ W 100
San Francisco, Cabo de, *Ecua.* 0°33′ N, 81°47′ W 130
San Francisco de Bellocq, *Arg.* 38°42′ S, 60°2′ W 139
San Francisco de Conchos, *Mex.* 27°35′ N, 105°18′ W 112
San Francisco de la Paz, *Hond.* 14°55′ N, 86°4′ W 115
San Francisco de Macorís, *Dom. Rep.* 19°16′ N, 70°15′ W 116
San Francisco de Paula, Cabo, *Arg.* 49°56′ S, 67°41′ W 134
San Francisco del Monte de Oro, *Arg.* 32°36′ S, 66°7′ W 134
San Francisco del Oro, *Mex.* 26°51′ N, 105°51′ W 112
San Francisco del Rincón, *Mex.* 21°0′ N, 101°52′ W 114
San Francisco Mountain, *Ariz., U.S.* 35°17′ N, 111°58′ W 92
San Francisco Mountain, peak, *Ariz., U.S.* 35°19′ N, 111°47′ W 112
San Francisco, Paso de, pass, *Chile* 26°53′ S, 68°22′ W 132
San Gabriel, *Ecua.* 0°34′ N, 78°0′ W 136
San Gabriel Mountains, *Calif., U.S.* 34°24′ N, 118°19′ W 101
San Germán 18°4′ N, 67°4′ W 116
San Gervàs, peak, *Sp.* 42°17′ N, 0°47′ E 164
San Gregorio, *Arg.* 34°21′ S, 62°2′ W 139
San Gregorio, *Uru.* 32°36′ S, 55°50′ W 139
San Guillermo, *Arg.* 30°22′ S, 61°55′ W 139
San Hipólito, Punta, *Mex.* 26°55′ N, 115°40′ W 112
San Ignacio, *Arg.* 27°15′ S, 55°33′ W 132
San Ignacio, *Belize* 17°9′ N, 89°7′ W 115
San Ignacio, *Bol.* 16°29′ S, 61°0′ W 132
San Ignacio, *Bol.* 14°58′ S, 65°38′ W 137
San Ignacio, *Mex.* 23°56′ N, 106°26′ W 114
San Ignacio, *Mex.* 27°18′ N, 112°55′ W 112
San Ignacio, *Parag.* 26°51′ S, 56°58′ W 139
San Ignacio, *Peru* 14°5′ S, 68°58′ W 137
San Ignacio, *Peru* 5°2′ S, 79°0′ W 130
San Ildefonso, Cape, *Philippines* 15°40′ N, 122°1′ E 203
San In Kaigan National Park, *Japan* 35°30′ N, 134°30′ E 201
San Isidro, *Peru* 4°55′ S, 76°17′ W 130
San Jacinto, *Calif., U.S.* 33°47′ N, 116°59′ W 101
San Jacinto Mountains, *Calif., U.S.* 33°47′ N, 116°41′ W 101
San Jaime, *Arg.* 30°17′ S, 58°21′ W 139
San Javier, *Arg.* 30°33′ S, 59°58′ W 139
San Javier, *Arg.* 27°52′ S, 55°9′ W 139
San Javier, *Bol.* 14°38′ S, 64°42′ W 137
San Javier, *Bol.* 16°28′ S, 62°37′ W 132
San Javier, *Mex.* 28°36′ N, 109°45′ W 92
San Javier, *Sp.* 37°48′ N, 0°51′ E 164
San Javier, *Uru.* 32°40′ S, 58°5′ W 139
San Jerónimo, *Mex.* 17°7′ N, 100°28′ W 114
San Jerónimo, *Peru* 7°52′ S, 74°53′ W 130
San Joaquín, *Bol.* 13°8′ S, 64°51′ W 137
San Joaquin, *Calif., U.S.* 36°36′ N, 120°12′ W 100
San Joaquin Valley, *Calif., U.S.* 35°29′ N, 119°46′ W 100
San Jon, *N. Mex., U.S.* 35°6′ N, 103°20′ W 92
San Jorge, *Arg.* 31°54′ S, 61°49′ W 139
San Jorge, *Nicar.* 11°26′ N, 85°48′ W 115
San Jorge, Bahía 31°0′ N, 113°17′ W 92
San Jorge, Golfo 46°26′ S, 68°15′ W 134
San Jorge, Golfo 46°19′ S, 69°42′ W 122
San Jorge, Golfo 45°51′ S, 70°25′ W 123
San Jorge, Gulf of 46°6′ S, 66°41′ W 253
San Jorge, river, *Col.* 7°40′ N, 75°55′ W 115
San José, *Arg.* 27°45′ S, 55°46′ W 139
San Jose, *Calif., U.S.* 37°19′ N, 121°54′ W 100
San José, *Col.* 2°37′ S, 68°3′ W 136
San José, *C.R.* 9°54′ N, 84°11′ W 115
San Jose, *Ill., U.S.* 40°18′ N, 89°37′ W 102
San José, *Peru* 14°44′ S, 70°10′ W 137
San José, *Peru* 3°29′ S, 76°33′ W 136
San Jose, *Philippines* 12°22′ N, 121°4′ E 203
San Jose, *Philippines* 15°48′ N, 120°57′ E 203
San Jose, *Philippines* 10°45′ N, 121°57′ E 203
San José, *Venez.* 4°36′ N, 67°49′ W 136
San José de Amacuro, *Venez.* 8°28′ N, 60°29′ W 116
San José de Chiquitos, *Bol.* 17°50′ S, 60°44′ W 132
San José de Feliciano, *Arg.* 30°20′ S, 58°44′ W 139
San José de Jáchal, *Arg.* 30°15′ S, 68°46′ W 134
San José de Mayo, *Uru.* 34°21′ S, 56°42′ W 139
San José de Ocuné, *Col.* 4°15′ N, 70°22′ W 136
San José de Raíces, *Mex.* 24°33′ N, 100°14′ W 114
San José del Guaviare, *Col.* 2°32′ N, 72°39′ W 136
San José, Isla, island, *Mex.* 24°52′ N, 110°30′ W 112
San José, Isla, island, *Pan.* 7°54′ N, 79°26′ W 115
San José, Punta, *Mex.* 31°9′ N, 116°39′ W 92
San José, Serranía de, *Bol.* 18°20′ S, 61°26′ W 132
San Juan, *Arg.* 31°33′ S, 68°34′ W 134
San Juan, *Col.* 8°45′ N, 76°32′ W 136
San Juan, *Dom. Rep.* 18°48′ N, 71°13′ W 116
San Juan, *Tex., U.S.* 26°13′ N, 98°9′ W 114
San Juan, *Trinidad and Tobago* 10°39′ N, 61°28′ W 118
San Juan, *P.R., U.S.* 18°28′ N, 66°6′ W 118
San Juan, adm. division, *Arg.* 31°19′ S, 70°15′ W 134
San Juan Bautista, *Calif., U.S.* 36°50′ N, 121°33′ W 100
San Juan Bautista, *Parag.* 26°40′ S, 57°10′ W 139
San Juan, Cabo, *Arg.* 54°47′ S, 63°46′ W 134
San Juan, Cabo, *Equatorial Guinea* 1°10′ N, 9°1′ E 218
San Juan Capistrano, *Calif., U.S.* 33°30′ N, 117°41′ W 101
San Juan de Guadalupe, *Mex.* 24°35′ N, 102°46′ W 114
San Juan de Lima, Punta, *Mex.* 18°26′ N, 105°17′ W 112
San Juan de los Cayos, *Venez.* 11°9′ N, 68°28′ W 136
San Juan de los Lagos, *Mex.* 21°14′ N, 102°19′ W 114
San Juan de los Morros, *Venez.* 9°51′ N, 67°23′ W 136
San Juan de Sabinas, *Mex.* 27°50′ N, 101°7′ W 92
San Juan del Cesar, *Col.* 10°46′ N, 72°59′ W 136
San Juan del Norte, *Nicar.* 10°53′ N, 83°42′ W 115
San Juan del Río, *Mex.* 24°45′ N, 104°27′ W 114
San Juan del Río, *Mex.* 20°22′ N, 100°1′ W 114
San Juan del Sur, *Nicar.* 11°14′ N, 85°51′ W 115
San Juan Island National Historical Park, *Wash., U.S.* 48°35′ N, 123°10′ W 100
San Juan Islands, *Hecate Strait* 48°16′ N, 122°29′ W 80
San Juan Mountains, *Colo., U.S.* 38°0′ N, 107°58′ W 90
San Juan Neembucú, *Parag.* 26°41′ S, 57°59′ W 139
San Juan Nepomuceno, *Col.* 9°55′ N, 75°6′ W 136
San Juan Nepomuceno, *Parag.* 26°8′ S, 55°53′ W 139
San Juan, Punta, *El Salv.* 12°58′ N, 89°31′ W 130
San Juan, Punta, *El Salv.* 13°1′ N, 88°32′ W 116
San Juan, Punta, *Mex.* 18°20′ N, 94°54′ W 112
San Juan, river, *Can.* 48°36′ N, 124°5′ W 100
San Juan, river, *Col.* 4°14′ N, 77°13′ W 136
San Juan, river, *Mex.* 25°32′ N, 99°22′ W 114
San Juan, river, *Nicar.* 10°51′ N, 84°27′ W 115
San Juanico, Punta, *Mex.* 25°54′ N, 113°36′ W 112
San Juanito, *Mex.* 27°58′ N, 107°36′ W 112
San Just, Sierra de, *Sp.* 40°44′ N, 1°2′ W 164
San Justo, *Arg.* 34°42′ S, 58°33′ W 139
San Justo, *Arg.* 30°46′ S, 60°34′ W 139
San Lázaro, Cabo, *Mex.* 24°50′ N, 113°42′ W 112
San Leandro, *Calif., U.S.* 37°42′ N, 122°9′ W 100
San Leo, *It.* 43°53′ N, 12°21′ E 167
San Leonardo de Yagüe, *Sp.* 41°49′ N, 3°5′ W 164
San Lorenzo, *Arg.* 28°7′ S, 58°46′ W 139
San Lorenzo, *Arg.* 32°44′ S, 60°44′ W 139
San Lorenzo, *Bol.* 11°53′ S, 66°52′ W 137
San Lorenzo, *Bol.* 21°29′ S, 64°47′ W 137
San Lorenzo, *Bol.* 15°25′ S, 65°52′ W 137
San Lorenzo, *Col.* 6°59′ N, 71°31′ W 136
San Lorenzo, *Ecua.* 1°14′ N, 78°58′ W 130
San Lorenzo, *Hond.* 13°24′ N, 87°27′ W 115
San Lorenzo, *Mex.* 29°47′ N, 107°7′ W 92
San Lorenzo, *Mex.* 25°31′ N, 102°11′ W 114
San Lorenzo, *Parag.* 25°22′ S, 57°30′ W 134
San Lorenzo, *Peru* 11°28′ S, 69°20′ W 137
San Lorenzo al Mare, *It.* 43°51′ N, 7°57′ E 167
San Lorenzo, Isla, island, *Peru* 12°9′ S, 78°36′ W 130
San Lorenzo, island, *Mex.* 28°34′ N, 113°59′ W 112
San Lorenzo, river, *Mex.* 25°34′ N, 99°6′ W 114
San Lorenzo, river, *Mex.* 24°21′ N, 106°55′ W 114
San Lorenzo, ruin(s), *Mex.* 17°42′ N, 94°52′ W 114
San Lucas, *Bol.* 20°5′ S, 65°9′ W 137
San Lucas, *Calif., U.S.* 36°8′ N, 121°2′ W 100
San Lucas, *Mex.* 22°32′ N, 104°27′ W 114
San Lucas, Cabo, *Mex.* 22°40′ N, 109°52′ W 112
San Luis, *Arg.* 33°20′ S, 66°20′ W 134
San Luis, *Colo., U.S.* 37°11′ N, 105°26′ W 92
San Luis, *Guatemala* 16°12′ N, 89°28′ W 116
San Luis, *Mex.* 32°29′ N, 114°47′ W 101
San Luis, adm. division, *Arg.* 33°41′ S, 66°59′ W 134
San Luis de la Paz, *Mex.* 21°18′ N, 100°30′ W 114
San Luis de Palenque, *Col.* 5°23′ N, 71°39′ W 136
San Luis del Cordero, *Mex.* 25°23′ N, 104°18′ W 114
San Luis del Palmar, *Arg.* 27°32′ S, 58°32′ W 139
San Luis, Isla, island, *Mex.* 29°50′ N, 114°25′ W 112
San Luis, Lago de, lake, *Bol.* 13°53′ S, 64°33′ W 137
San Luis Obispo, *Calif., U.S.* 35°17′ N, 120°41′ W 100
San Luis Peak, *Colo., U.S.* 37°58′ N, 107°1′ W 90
San Luis Potosí, *Mex.* 22°6′ N, 101°3′ W 114
San Luis Potosí, adm. division, *Mex.* 22°40′ N, 101°25′ W 114
San Luis Río Colorado, *Mex.* 32°27′ N, 114°48′ W 101
San Luis Valley, *Colo., U.S.* 38°1′ N, 106°15′ W 90
San Marcial, Punta, *Mex.* 25°20′ N, 111°2′ W 112
San Marco, Capo, *It.* 37°24′ N, 12°27′ E 156
San Marcos, *Arg.* 32°37′ S, 62°29′ W 139
San Marcos, *Calif., U.S.* 33°8′ N, 117°11′ W 101
San Marcos, *Col.* 8°39′ N, 75°8′ W 136
San Marcos, *Tex., U.S.* 29°51′ N, 97°56′ W 96
San Marcos, Isla, island, *Mex.* 27°12′ N, 112°2′ W 112
San Marino 43°54′ N, 12°11′ E 156
San Marino, *San Marino* 43°55′ N, 12°24′ E 167
San Martín, *Arg.* 33°6′ S, 68°29′ W 134
San Martin, *Calif., U.S.* 37°4′ N, 121°38′ W 100
San Martín, *Col.* 3°41′ N, 73°43′ W 136
San Martín, *Mex.* 21°20′ N, 98°39′ W 114
San Martín, adm. division, *Peru* 6°45′ S, 77°36′ W 130
San Martín, Argentina, station, *Antarctica* 68°16′ S, 67°5′ W 248
San Martin, Cape, *Calif., U.S.* 35°47′ N, 121°39′ W 100
San Martín, Isla, island, *Mex.* 30°27′ N, 117°21′ W 112
San Martín, river, *Bol.* 15°1′ S, 62°19′ W 132
San Mateo, *Calif., U.S.* 37°33′ N, 122°20′ W 100
San Mateo, *Peru* 3°53′ S, 71°37′ W 130
San Mateo, *Venez.* 9°45′ N, 64°35′ W 116
San Mateo del Mar, *Mex.* 16°13′ N, 94°59′ W 112
San Mateo Peak, *N. Mex., U.S.* 33°36′ N, 107°30′ W 92
San Matías, *Bol.* 16°25′ S, 58°23′ W 132
San Matías, Golfo 41°24′ S, 64°56′ W 134
San Miguel, *Arg.* 28°0′ S, 57°35′ W 139
San Miguel, *Bol.* 13°59′ S, 65°25′ W 137
San Miguel, *Calif., U.S.* 35°45′ N, 120°43′ W 100
San Miguel, *Col.* 0°16′ N, 76°32′ W 136
San Miguel, *El Salv.* 13°27′ N, 88°13′ W 115
San Miguel, *N. Mex., U.S.* 32°9′ N, 106°44′ W 92
San Miguel, *Peru* 13°2′ S, 74°1′ W 137
San Miguel, *Venez.* 2°39′ N, 67°28′ W 136
San Miguel Bay 13°48′ N, 122°39′ E 203
San Miguel de Allende, *Mex.* 20°53′ N, 100°45′ W 114
San Miguel de Horcasitas, *Mex.* 29°28′ N, 110°44′ W 92
San Miguel de Huachi, *Bol.* 15°43′ S, 67°15′ W 137
San Miguel de Salinas, *Sp.* 37°58′ N, 0°48′ E 164
San Miguel de Tucumán, *Arg.* 26°51′ S, 65°14′ W 132
San Miguel del Monte, *Arg.* 35°25′ S, 58°48′ W 139
San Miguel, island, *Calif., U.S.* 34°3′ N, 120°43′ W 100
San Miguel, river, *Mex.* 29°30′ N, 110°29′ W 92
San Miguel (San Pablo), river, *Bol.* 14°3′ S, 64°2′ W 137
San Miguel Zapotitlán, *Mex.* 25°55′ N, 109°4′ W 112
San Miguelito, *Bol.* 11°40′ S, 68°28′ W 137
San Narciso, *Philippines* 15°3′ N, 120°5′ E 203
San Nicolás, *Arg.* 33°23′ S, 60°13′ W 139
San Nicolás, *Mex.* 24°54′ N, 105°27′ W 114
San Nicolás, *Mex.* 24°40′ N, 98°48′ W 114
San Nicolas, *Philippines* 18°11′ N, 120°34′ E 203
San Nicolas, island, *Calif., U.S.* 33°16′ N, 119°46′ W 101
San Pablo, *Arg.* 54°14′ S, 66°47′ W 134
San Pablo, *Bol.* 21°43′ S, 66°37′ W 137
San Pablo, *Bol.* 15°44′ S, 63°15′ W 137
San Pablo, *Philippines* 14°3′ N, 121°18′ E 203
San Pablo Bay 38°3′ N, 122°32′ W 100
San Pablo, Punta, *Mex.* 27°16′ N, 115°54′ W 112
San Pablo see San Miguel, river, *Bol.* 14°3′ S, 64°2′ W 137
San Patricio, *N. Mex., U.S.* 33°24′ N, 105°20′ W 92
San Pedro, *Arg.* 24°22′ S, 64°58′ W 132
San Pedro, *Arg.* 26°38′ S, 54°11′ W 139
San Pedro, *Arg.* 33°42′ S, 59°41′ W 139
San Pedro, *Belize* 17°56′ N, 87°59′ W 116
San Pedro, *Bol.* 14°23′ S, 64°50′ W 137
San Pedro, *Bol.* 16°49′ S, 62°32′ W 132
San Pedro, *Bol.* 16°17′ S, 68°53′ W 137
San Pedro, *Mex.* 27°0′ N, 109°38′ W 112
San Pedro, *Mex.* 22°12′ N, 100°48′ W 114
San Pedro, *Mex.* 29°20′ N, 104°54′ W 92
San Pedro Carchá, *Guatemala* 15°28′ N, 90°16′ W 115
San Pedro Channel 33°34′ N, 118°43′ W 101
San Pedro Corralitos, *Mex.* 30°43′ N, 107°41′ W 92
San Pedro de Arimena, *Col.* 4°35′ N, 71°37′ W 136
San Pedro de Atacama, *Chile* 22°55′ S, 68°15′ W 137
San Pedro de Curahuara, *Bol.* 17°41′ S, 68°3′ W 137
San Pedro de las Colonias, *Mex.* 25°44′ N, 102°59′ W 114
San Pedro de Lloc, *Peru* 7°25′ S, 79°28′ W 130
San Pedro de Macorís, *Dom. Rep.* 18°28′ N, 69°17′ W 116
San Pedro del Gallo, *Mex.* 25°32′ N, 104°18′ W 114
San Pedro del Norte, *Nicar.* 13°4′ N, 84°44′ W 115
San Pedro del Paraná, *Parag.* 26°46′ S, 56°13′ W 139
San Pedro del Pinatar, *Sp.* 37°49′ N, 0°48′ E 164
San Pedro Lagunillas, *Mex.* 21°13′ N, 104°45′ W 114
San Pedro Mártir, Sierra, *Mex.* 31°12′ N, 115°38′ W 112
San Pedro, Punta, *Chile* 25°36′ S, 71°15′ W 132
San Pedro, Sierra de, *Sp.* 39°20′ N, 6°54′ W 164
San Pedro Sula, *Hond.* 15°29′ N, 88°1′ W 115
San Quintín, Cabo, *Mex.* 30°5′ N, 116°22′ W 92
San Rafael, *Arg.* 34°33′ S, 68°12′ W 123
San Rafael, *Bol.* 16°48′ S, 60°36′ W 132
San Rafael, *Calif., U.S.* 37°57′ N, 122°33′ W 100
San Rafael, *Col.* 6°1′ N, 69°47′ W 136
San Rafael, *Venez.* 10°57′ N, 71°47′ W 136
San Rafael, Bahía 28°25′ N, 113°20′ W 92
San Rafael, Cabo, *Dom. Rep.* 19°2′ N, 68°53′ W 116
San Rafael de Atamaica, *Venez.* 7°31′ N, 67°24′ W 136
San Rafael Knob, peak, *Utah, U.S.* 38°48′ N, 110°56′ W 90
San Rafael Mountains, *Calif., U.S.* 34°47′ N, 120°9′ W 100
San Rafael National Park, *Parag.* 26°23′ S, 55°42′ W 139
San Ramón, *Bol.* 13°23′ S, 64°43′ W 137
San Ramón, *Uru.* 34°18′ S, 55°56′ W 139
San Ramón de la Nueva Orán, *Arg.* 23°7′ S, 64°22′ W 132
San Remo, *It.* 43°49′ N, 7°46′ E 150
San, river, *Cambodia* 13°36′ N, 106°36′ E 202
San Roque, *Arg.* 28°34′ S, 58°42′ W 139
San Roque, *Sp.* 36°12′ N, 5°26′ W 164
San Saba, *Tex., U.S.* 31°10′ N, 98°43′ W 92
San Saba, river, *Tex., U.S.* 30°35′ N, 100°42′ W 112
San Salvador, *Arg.* 31°37′ S, 58°31′ W 139
San Salvador, *El Salv.* 13°40′ N, 89°21′ W 115
San Salvador, *Peru* 2°26′ S, 71°20′ W 136
San Salvador and Rum Cay, adm. division, *Bahamas* 24°35′ N, 76°23′ W 96
San Salvador de Jujuy, *Arg.* 24°13′ S, 65°21′ W 132
San Salvador (Watling), island, *Bahamas* 23°41′ N, 74°29′ W 116
San Sebastián, *Arg.* 53°15′ S, 68°30′ W 134
San Sebastián, Cabo, *Arg.* 53°32′ S, 68°2′ W 134
San Severo, *It.* 41°41′ N, 15°23′ E 156
San Silvestre, oil field, *Venez.* 8°21′ N, 70°10′ W 136
San Simeon, *Calif., U.S.* 35°39′ N, 121°13′ W 100
San Simon, *Ariz., U.S.* 32°15′ N, 109°13′ W 92
San Sosti, *It.* 39°39′ N, 16°1′ E 156
San Telmo, *Mex.* 30°56′ N, 116°6′ W 92
San Tiburcio, *Mex.* 24°9′ N, 101°28′ W 114
San Vicente, *Mex.* 31°17′ N, 116°14′ W 92
San Vicente, *Mex.* 24°8′ N, 100°55′ W 114
San Vicente, *Venez.* 4°56′ N, 67°45′ W 130
San Vicente de Cañete (Cañete), *Peru* 13°5′ S, 76°23′ W 130
San Vicente del Caguán, *Col.* 2°7′ N, 74°48′ W 136
San Vincenzo, *It.* 38°48′ N, 15°12′ E 156
San Vito al Tagliamento, *It.* 45°54′ N, 12°51′ E 167
San Ygnacio, *Tex., U.S.* 27°4′ N, 99°24′ W 96
Şan'ā' (Sanaa), *Yemen* 15°22′ N, 44°3′ E 182
Sanaa see Şan'ā', *Yemen* 15°22′ N, 44°3′ E 182
Sanad, *Serb.* 45°59′ N, 20°7′ E 168
SANAE IV, South Africa, station, *Antarctica* 71°40′ S, 2°49′ W 247
Şanāfīr, island, *Egypt* 27°50′ N, 34°43′ E 180
Sanam, *Niger* 14°54′ N, 4°20′ E 222
Sanana, island, *Indonesia* 2°39′ S, 126°5′ E 192
Sanandaj, *Iran* 35°20′ N, 46°59′ E 180
Sanandita, *Bol.* 21°40′ S, 63°38′ W 137
Sananduva, *Braz.* 27°59′ S, 51°49′ W 139
Sanāw, *Yemen* 17°50′ N, 51°4′ E 182
Sanawad, *India* 22°10′ N, 76°4′ E 197
Şanawbar, *Syr.* 35°28′ N, 35°53′ E 194
Sanbornville, *N.H., U.S.* 43°33′ N, 71°3′ W 104
Sanchahe, *China* 44°58′ N, 126°1′ E 198
Sanchakou, *China* 39°55′ N, 78°27′ E 184
Sanchor, *India* 24°48′ N, 71°46′ E 186
Sanchursk, *Russ.* 56°54′ N, 47°18′ E 154
Sancti Spíritus, *Cuba* 21°55′ N, 79°28′ W 116
Sancti Spíritus, adm. division, *Cuba* 21°50′ N, 79°47′ W 116
Sancti Spíritus, island, *Cuba* 21°32′ N, 80°49′ W 116
Sancy, Puy de, peak, *Fr.* 45°31′ N, 2°46′ E 165
Sand Hill, river, *Minn., U.S.* 47°26′ N, 97°3′ W 94
Sand Hills, *Calif., U.S.* 32°58′ N, 115°9′ W 101
Sand Hills, *Nebr., U.S.* 42°16′ N, 101°38′ W 90
Sand Lake, *Can.* 49°2′ N, 95°16′ W 94
Sand Lake, *Mich., U.S.* 43°17′ N, 85°31′ W 102
Sand Lake, *Minn., U.S.* 47°34′ N, 94°27′ W 90
Sand Point, *Lake Huron* 43°50′ N, 83°40′ W 102
Sand, river, *Can.* 54°44′ N, 111°6′ W 108
Sand Sea of Calanscio see Kalanshiyū ar Ramlī al Kabīr, Sarīr, *Lib.* 28°52′ N, 23°25′ E 180
Sand Springs, *Mont., U.S.* 47°4′ N, 107°29′ W 90
Sand Springs, *Okla., U.S.* 36°7′ N, 96°6′ W 96
Sandakan, *Malaysia* 5°53′ N, 118°6′ E 203
Sandalo, Capo, *It.* 39°3′ N, 7°38′ E 156
Sandaré, *Mali* 14°41′ N, 10°19′ W 222
Sandbach, *U.K.* 53°8′ N, 2°22′ W 162
Sandborn, *Ind., U.S.* 38°53′ N, 87°12′ W 102
Sande, *Nor.* 62°14′ N, 5°27′ E 152
Sandeid, *Nor.* 59°33′ N, 5°50′ E 152
Sandercock Nunataks, *Antarctica* 69°7′ S, 42°3′ E 248
Sanderk, *Iran* 26°52′ N, 57°30′ E 196
Sanders, *Ariz., U.S.* 35°12′ N, 109°20′ W 92
Sanders, *Ky., U.S.* 38°39′ N, 84°57′ W 102
Sanderson, *Tex., U.S.* 30°8′ N, 102°23′ W 92
Sandersville, *Ga., U.S.* 32°58′ N, 82°49′ W 96
Sandersville, *Miss., U.S.* 31°46′ N, 89°3′ W 103
Sandford Lake, lake, *Can.* 49°5′ N, 92°11′ W 110
Sandgate, *U.K.* 51°4′ N, 1°8′ E 162
Sandhammaren, *Nor.* 55°23′ N, 14°12′ E 152
Sandhamn, *Sw.* 59°16′ N, 18°53′ E 166
Sandia, *Peru* 14°18′ S, 69°29′ W 137
Sandia Crest, peak, *N. Mex., U.S.* 35°12′ N, 106°31′ W 92
Sandıklı, *Turk.* 38°27′ N, 30°15′ E 156
Sandila, *India* 27°3′ N, 80°30′ E 197
Sandknölen, peak, *Nor.* 64°6′ N, 14°16′ E 152
Sandnes, *Nor.* 58°50′ N, 5°45′ E 152
Sandnessjøen, *Nor.* 66°0′ N, 12°37′ E 152
Sandoa, *Dem. Rep. of the Congo* 9°42′ S, 22°54′ E 218
Sandoval, *Ill., U.S.* 38°36′ N, 89°7′ W 102
Sandoval, Boca de 25°0′ N, 97°58′ W 114
Sandovo, *Russ.* 58°25′ N, 36°30′ E 154
Sandow, Mount, peak, *Antarctica* 67°28′ S, 100°53′ E 248
Sandoway, *Myanmar* 18°37′ N, 94°12′ E 173
Sandpoint, *Idaho, U.S.* 48°15′ N, 116°34′ W 108
Sandringham, *U.K.* 52°49′ N, 0°31′ E 162
Sands Key, island, *Fla., U.S.* 25°29′ N, 80°11′ W 105
Sandspit, *Can.* 53°14′ N, 131°52′ W 108
Sandstad, *Nor.* 63°30′ N, 9°3′ E 152
Sandstone, *Minn., U.S.* 46°7′ N, 92°54′ W 94
Sandtop, Cap, *Can.* 49°13′ N, 61°43′ W 111
Sandu, *China* 26°0′ N, 107°51′ E 198
Sandusky, *Mich., U.S.* 43°24′ N, 82°49′ W 102

Sandusky, *Ohio, U.S.* 41°26′ N, 82°41′ W 94
Sandusky, river, *Ohio, U.S.* 41°4′ N, 83°8′ W 102
Sandvika, *Nor.* 59°53′ N, 10°29′ E 152
Sandviken, *Nor.* 60°37′ N, 16°49′ E 152
Sandwich, *Mass., U.S.* 41°45′ N, 70°30′ W 104
Sandwich, *Mo., U.S.* 41°38′ N, 88°37′ W 94
Sandwich Bay 23°21′ S, 13°35′ E 220
Sandwich Mountain, peak, *N.H., U.S.* 43°53′ N, 71°32′ W 104
Sandwip, *Bangladesh* 22°30′ N, 91°28′ E 197
Sandy, *Nev., U.S.* 35°47′ N, 115°37′ W 101
Sandy, *U.K.* 52°8′ N, 0°18′ E 162
Sandy, *Utah, U.S.* 40°34′ N, 111°52′ W 90
Sandy Bar, *Can.* 52°25′ N, 97°23′ W 108
Sandy Bay, *Can.* 55°31′ N, 102°21′ W 108
Sandy Hook, *N.J., U.S.* 40°2′ N, 73°56′ W 80
Sandy Lake, *Can.* 56°58′ N, 107°17′ W 108
Sandy Lake, *Can.* 53°6′ N, 93°25′ W 82
Sandy Narrows, *Can.* 55°2′ N, 103°4′ W 108
Sandy Point 41°13′ N, 71°29′ W 104
Sandy Point, *Bahamas* 26°0′ N, 77°24′ W 96
Sånfjället, peak, *Nor.* 62°15′ N, 13°23′ E 152
Sanford, *Fla., U.S.* 28°47′ N, 81°17′ W 105
Sanford, *Me., U.S.* 43°26′ N, 70°47′ W 104
Sanford, *Mich., U.S.* 43°39′ N, 84°22′ W 102
Sanford, *Miss., U.S.* 31°28′ N, 89°26′ W 103
Sanford, *N.C., U.S.* 35°28′ N, 79°12′ W 96
Sanford, Mount, peak, *Alas., U.S.* 62°11′ N, 144°19′ W 98
Sang Bast, *Iran* 35°58′ N, 59°46′ E 180
Sanga, *Angola* 11°8′ S, 15°25′ E 220
Sanga, *Burkina Faso* 11°11′ N, 0°8′ E 222
Sanga, *Mali* 14°26′ N, 3°19′ W 222
Sangar, *Russ.* 64°2′ N, 127°21′ E 160
Sangardo, *Guinea* 9°23′ N, 10°14′ W 222
Sangaréd, *Guinea* 11°3′ N, 13°46′ W 222
Sangay National Park, *Ecua.* 1°58′ S, 78°42′ W 122
Sangay, peak, *Ecua.* 2°5′ S, 78°29′ W 136
Sangayan, Isla de, island, *Peru* 14°5′ S, 77°5′ W 130
Sangbé, *Cameroon* 6°1′ N, 12°28′ E 218
Sangbu, *S. Korea* 35°33′ N, 128°17′ E 200
Sang-e Masheh, *Afghan.* 33°16′ N, 67°7′ E 186
Sanger, *Calif., U.S.* 36°42′ N, 119°34′ W 100
Sanger, *Tex., U.S.* 33°21′ N, 97°9′ W 92
Sanggan, river, *China* 39°44′ N, 113°30′ E 198
Sanggou Wan 37°0′ N, 122°2′ E 198
Sanghar, *Pak.* 26°3′ N, 68°58′ E 186
Sangihe, Kepulauan, islands, *Molucca Sea* 2°38′ N, 125°59′ E 192
Sangiyn Dalay, *Mongolia* 46°0′ N, 104°58′ E 198
Sangju, *S. Korea* 36°23′ N, 128°11′ E 200
Sangkhla, *Thai.* 15°7′ N, 98°32′ E 202
Sangkulirang, *Indonesia* 0°56′ N, 117°52′ E 192
Sangla, *Pak.* 31°45′ N, 73°21′ E 186
Sangni, *N. Korea* 40°58′ N, 128°7′ E 200
Sangre de Cristo Mountains, *N. Mex., U.S.* 35°28′ N, 105°41′ W 112
Sangri, *China* 29°20′ N, 92°10′ E 197
Sangt'ong, *N. Korea* 40°5′ N, 127°20′ E 200
Sangue, river, *Braz.* 11°2′ S, 58°36′ W 130
Sanguinaires, Îles, islands, *Mediterranean Sea* 41°50′ N, 7°26′ E 156
Sangvor, *Taj.* 38°41′ N, 71°21′ E 197
Sangwŏn, *N. Korea* 38°50′ N, 126°6′ E 200
Sangzhi, *China* 29°24′ N, 110°10′ E 198
Sanhecun, *China* 42°30′ N, 129°42′ E 200
Sanibel Island, *Fla., U.S.* 26°20′ N, 82°10′ W 105
Sanikiluaq, *Can.* 56°20′ N, 79°9′ W 73
Saniquellie, *Liberia* 7°16′ N, 8°41′ W 222
Sanislău, *Rom.* 47°39′ N, 22°21′ E 168
Sāniyat ad Daffah, spring, *Lib.* 30°5′ N, 24°13′ E 180
Sanje, *Uganda* 0°50′ N, 31°29′ E 224
Sanjeong, *S. Korea* 34°21′ N, 126°33′ E 200
Sanjiang, *China* 25°52′ N, 109°39′ E 198
Sanjō, *Japan* 37°38′ N, 138°58′ E 201
Sankaty Head, *Mass., U.S.* 41°16′ N, 69°58′ W 104
Sankeyushu, *China* 41°44′ N, 125°21′ E 200
Sankt Augustin, *Ger.* 50°45′ N, 7°10′ E 167
Sankt Goar, *Ger.* 50°8′ N, 7°41′ E 167
Sankt Ingbert, *Ger.* 49°16′ N, 7°6′ E 163
Sankt Michael, *Aust.* 47°7′ N, 16°15′ E 168
Sankt Moritz, *Switz.* 46°30′ N, 9°49′ E 167
Sankt Pölten, *Aust.* 48°11′ N, 15°38′ E 143
Sankt Pölten, *Aust.* 48°12′ N, 15°37′ E 152
Sankt Ruprecht, *Aust.* 47°10′ N, 15°40′ E 168
Sankt Wendel, *Ger.* 49°27′ N, 7°10′ E 163
Sankt-Maurice, *Switz.* 46°13′ N, 7°1′ E 167
Sankt-Peterburg, adm. division, *Russ.* 59°55′ N, 30°15′ E 166
Sankt-Peterburg (Saint Petersburg, Leningrad), *Russ.* 59°55′ N, 30°17′ E 166
Sankuru, river, *Dem. Rep. of the Congo* 4°3′ S, 21°26′ E 218
Sankuru, river, *Dem. Rep. of the Congo* 5°56′ S, 23°37′ E 224
Şanlıurfa (Edessa), *Turk.* 37°6′ N, 38°45′ E 180
Sanlúcar de Barrameda, *Sp.* 36°46′ N, 6°22′ W 164
Sanmenxia, *China* 34°45′ N, 111°12′ E 198
Sanming, *China* 26°9′ N, 117°34′ E 198
Sannazzaro, *It.* 45°6′ N, 8°54′ E 167
Sannikova, Proliv 74°30′ N, 145°34′ E 246
Sano, *Japan* 36°18′ N, 139°36′ E 201
Sanquianga National Park, *Col.* 2°25′ N, 78°40′ W 122
Sans Sault Rapids, fall(s), *Can.* 65°13′ N, 128°46′ W 98
Sansanding, *Mali* 13°45′ N, 6°1′ W 222
Sansane, *Niger* 13°50′ N, 1°37′ E 222
Sansha, *China* 26°58′ N, 120°12′ E 198
Sanshui, *China* 23°10′ N, 112°55′ E 198
Sansui, *China* 27°1′ N, 108°40′ E 198
Sant' Antioco, island, *It.* 38°27′ N, 7°30′ E 214
Sant Antoni de Portmany, *Sp.* 38°58′ N, 1°17′ E 150
Sant Celoni, *Sp.* 41°41′ N, 2°29′ E 164
Sant Feliu de Guíxols, *Sp.* 41°46′ N, 3°1′ E 164
Sant Francesc de Formentera, *Sp.* 38°41′ N, 1°25′ E 150
Sant Jaume d'Enveja, *Sp.* 40°41′ N, 0°43′ E 164
Sant Joan d'Alacant, *Sp.* 38°23′ N, 0°26′ E 164
Sant Josep, *Sp.* 38°55′ N, 1°17′ E 150
Sant Llorenç de Morunys, *Sp.* 42°8′ N, 1°34′ E 164
Sant Quirze de Besora, *Sp.* 42°6′ N, 2°13′ E 164
Santa, *Peru* 9°2′ S, 78°38′ W 130
Santa Amelia, *Guatemala* 16°14′ N, 90°3′ W 115
Santa Ana, *Bol.* 15°32′ S, 67°30′ W 137
Santa Ana, *Calif., U.S.* 33°45′ N, 117°53′ W 101
Santa Ana, *El Salv.* 13°59′ N, 89°33′ W 115
Santa Ana, *Mex.* 30°32′ N, 111°6′ W 92
Santa Ana, *Philippines* 18°29′ N, 122°9′ E 203
Santa Ana, island, *Solomon Islands* 10°50′ S, 162°30′ E 242
Santa Ana Mountains, *Calif., U.S.* 33°40′ N, 117°36′ W 101
Santa Ana, river, *Venez.* 9°32′ N, 72°47′ W 116
Santa Barbara, *Calif., U.S.* 34°25′ N, 119°44′ W 100
Santa Bárbara, *Mex.* 26°47′ N, 105°50′ W 112
Santa Bárbara, *Peru* 12°53′ S, 75°2′ W 130
Santa Bàrbara, *Sp.* 40°42′ N, 0°30′ E 164
Santa Bárbara, *Venez.* 3°54′ N, 67°5′ W 136
Santa Bárbara, *Venez.* 7°47′ N, 71°12′ W 136
Santa Barbara Channel 34°13′ N, 120°27′ W 100
Santa Barbara, island, *Calif., U.S.* 33°29′ N, 119°23′ W 101
Santa Bárbara, peak, *Sp.* 37°22′ N, 2°53′ W 164
Santa Catalina, *Arg.* 21°57′ S, 66°4′ W 137
Santa Catalina, *Pan.* 8°46′ N, 81°19′ W 115
Santa Catalina, Isla, island, *Mex.* 25°30′ N, 110°46′ W 112
Santa Catalina, island, *Calif., U.S.* 33°25′ N, 118°23′ W 101
Santa Catalina, island, *Solomon Islands* 10°53′ S, 162°30′ E 242
Santa Catarina, *Mex.* 25°39′ N, 100°29′ W 114
Santa Catarina, adm. division, *Braz.* 26°54′ S, 53°39′ W 139
Santa Catarina, Ilha de, island, *Braz.* 27°57′ S, 48°22′ W 132
Santa Clara, *Calif., U.S.* 37°21′ N, 121°57′ W 100
Santa Clara, *Col.* 2°45′ S, 69°43′ W 136
Santa Clara, *Cuba* 22°26′ N, 79°57′ W 116
Santa Clara, *Mex.* 24°27′ N, 103°22′ W 114
Santa Clara, *Mex.* 29°16′ N, 107°2′ W 92
Santa Clara, *Uru.* 32°55′ S, 54°58′ W 139
Santa Clara, *Utah, U.S.* 37°8′ N, 113°39′ W 101
Santa Clarita, *Calif., U.S.* 34°25′ N, 118°34′ W 101
Santa Claus Mountain, peak, *Can.* 54°11′ N, 61°31′ W 111
Santa Clotilde, *Peru* 2°32′ S, 73°41′ W 136
Santa Cruz, *Angola* 6°59′ S, 16°17′ E 218
Santa Cruz, *Bol.* 17°48′ S, 63°13′ W 137
Santa Cruz, *Braz.* 6°1′ S, 72°25′ W 130
Santa Cruz, *Calif., U.S.* 36°58′ N, 122°3′ W 100
Santa Cruz, *Mex.* 31°12′ N, 110°38′ W 92
Santa Cruz, *Philippines* 17°5′ N, 120°27′ E 203
Santa Cruz, *Philippines* 13°6′ N, 120°45′ E 203
Santa Cruz, *Philippines* 14°16′ N, 121°24′ E 203
Santa Cruz, *Philippines* 15°47′ N, 119°55′ E 203
Santa Cruz, *Venez.* 8°2′ N, 64°26′ W 130
Santa Cruz, adm. division, *Arg.* 48°26′ S, 71°7′ W 134
Santa Cruz, adm. division, *Bol.* 17°36′ S, 64°15′ W 137
Santa Cruz Cabrália, *Braz.* 16°18′ S, 39°3′ W 132
Santa Cruz Channel 33°57′ N, 120°5′ W 101
Santa Cruz de la Zarza, *Sp.* 39°59′ N, 3°13′ W 164
Santa Cruz de Moya, *Sp.* 39°57′ N, 1°17′ W 164
Santa Cruz de Mudela, *Sp.* 38°39′ N, 3°28′ W 164
Santa Cruz del Norte, *Cuba* 23°8′ N, 81°55′ W 112
Santa Cruz del Sur, *Cuba* 20°43′ N, 77°59′ W 116
Santa Cruz do Arai, *Braz.* 0°36′ N, 49°12′ W 130
Santa Cruz do Rio Pardo, *Braz.* 22°53′ S, 49°39′ W 138
Santa Cruz do Sul, *Braz.* 29°42′ S, 52°23′ W 139
Santa Cruz, Isla, island, *Ecua.* 0°40′ N, 90°9′ W 130
Santa Cruz, island, *Calif., U.S.* 34°4′ N, 119°42′ W 100
Santa Cruz Islands, *Coral Sea* 11°42′ S, 166°19′ E 238
Santa Cruz Mountains, *Calif., U.S.* 37°16′ N, 122°4′ W 100
Santa Elena, *Arg.* 30°56′ S, 59°46′ W 139
Santa Elena, *Ecua.* 2°18′ S, 80°48′ W 130
Santa Elena, *Mex.* 27°57′ N, 104°0′ W 92
Santa Elena, *Venez.* 4°36′ N, 61°7′ W 130
Santa Elena, Cabo, *C.R.* 10°50′ N, 87°0′ W 115
Santa Eulalia, *Sp.* 40°33′ N, 1°19′ W 164
Santa Eulalia del Río, *Sp.* 38°58′ N, 1°32′ E 150
Santa Fe, *Arg.* 31°37′ S, 60°42′ W 139
Santa Fe, *N. Mex., U.S.* 35°40′ N, 106°2′ W 92
Santa Fe, *Philippines* 12°10′ N, 121°59′ E 203
Santa Fé, *Sp.* 37°11′ N, 3°43′ W 164
Santa Fe, adm. division, *Arg.* 30°54′ S, 61°46′ W 139
Santa Filomena, *Braz.* 9°7′ S, 45°54′ W 130
Santa Helena, *Braz.* 24°56′ S, 54°26′ W 132
Santa Helena, *Braz.* 5°13′ S, 56°20′ W 130
Santa Helena de Goiás, *Braz.* 17°49′ S, 50°33′ W 138
Santa Inês, *Braz.* 3°43′ S, 45°26′ W 130
Santa Inês, *Braz.* 13°22′ S, 39°49′ W 138
Santa Inés, Isla, island, *Chile* 53°50′ S, 75°22′ W 134
Santa Inés, peak, *Sp.* 38°31′ N, 5°40′ W 164
Santa Isabel, *Arg.* 36°15′ S, 66°54′ W 134
Santa Isabel, *Arg.* 33°55′ S, 61°40′ W 139
Santa Isabel, *Venez.* 1°20′ N, 65°49′ W 136
Santa Isabel do Morro, *Braz.* 11°32′ S, 50°43′ W 130
Santa Isabel, Ilha Grande de, island, *Braz.* 3°25′ S, 42°32′ W 132
Santa Isabel, island, *Solomon Islands* 8°5′ S, 159°10′ E 242
Santa Juana, *Venez.* 7°0′ N, 67°33′ W 136
Santa Júlia, *Braz.* 7°48′ S, 58°14′ W 130
Santa Julia, *Col.* 1°34′ S, 72°18′ W 136
Santa Juliana, *Braz.* 19°19′ S, 47°32′ W 138
Santa Kurutze Kanpezu, *Sp.* 42°39′ N, 2°21′ W 164
Santa Lucía, *Arg.* 28°59′ S, 59°8′ W 139
Santa Lucía, *Nicar.* 12°30′ N, 85°41′ W 115
Santa Lucía, *Uru.* 34°28′ S, 56°22′ W 139
Santa Lucia Range, *Calif., U.S.* 35°58′ N, 121°22′ W 100
Santa Magdalena, *Arg.* 34°32′ S, 63°54′ W 139
Santa Margarita, *Calif., U.S.* 35°23′ N, 120°38′ W 100
Santa Margarita, Isla, island, *Mex.* 24°9′ N, 112°57′ W 112
Santa María, *Arg.* 26°43′ S, 66°2′ W 132
Santa Maria, *Braz.* 1°45′ S, 58°36′ W 130
Santa Maria, *Braz.* 2°57′ S, 60°25′ W 130
Santa Maria, *Braz.* 29°44′ S, 53°48′ W 139
Santa Maria, *Calif., U.S.* 34°57′ N, 120°27′ W 100
Santa María, *Peru* 1°25′ S, 74°38′ W 136
Santa Maria, *Switz.* 46°35′ N, 10°24′ E 167
Santa Maria, *Zambia* 11°9′ S, 29°58′ E 224
Santa María, Bahía 24°57′ N, 109°16′ W 80
Santa María, Cabo, *Uru.* 34°59′ S, 54°11′ W 139
Santa Maria, Cape, *Bahamas* 23°44′ N, 75°18′ W 80
Santa María, Cayo, island, *Cuba* 22°42′ N, 78°57′ W 116
Santa Maria da Vitória, *Braz.* 13°23′ S, 44°14′ W 138
Santa María de Huerta, *Sp.* 41°15′ N, 2°11′ W 164
Santa María de Ipire, *Venez.* 8°48′ N, 65°20′ W 136
Santa María de los Ángeles, *Mex.* 22°10′ N, 103°12′ W 114
Santa María de Nanay, *Peru* 3°54′ S, 73°45′ W 130
Santa María de Otáez, *Mex.* 24°40′ N, 106°0′ W 114
Santa María del Oro, *Mex.* 25°55′ N, 105°19′ W 114
Santa María del Oro, *Mex.* 21°20′ N, 104°36′ W 114
Santa María del Río, *Mex.* 21°47′ N, 100°44′ W 114
Santa Maria do Suaçuí, *Braz.* 18°12′ S, 42°26′ W 138
Santa María, Isla, island, *Chile* 37°8′ S, 75°29′ W 134
Santa María, Isla, island, *Ecua.* 1°54′ S, 90°21′ W 130
Santa María, river, *Mex.* 21°47′ N, 100°34′ W 114
Santa Marta, *Col.* 11°11′ N, 74°14′ W 136
Santa Marta, *Sp.* 38°36′ N, 6°38′ W 164
Santa Marta Grande, Cabo de, *Braz.* 28°34′ S, 48°43′ W 134
Santa Monica Mountains, *Calif., U.S.* 34°8′ N, 118°55′ W 101
Santa Olalla del Cala, *Sp.* 37°54′ N, 6°15′ W 164
Santa Pola, *Sp.* 38°11′ N, 0°34′ E 164
Santa Rita, *Col.* 4°54′ N, 68°22′ W 136
Santa Rita, *Venez.* 8°6′ N, 66°17′ W 136
Santa Rita, *Venez.* 10°33′ N, 71°32′ W 116
Santa Rita do Araguaia, *Braz.* 17°22′ S, 53°14′ W 138
Santa Rita do Weil, *Braz.* 3°31′ S, 69°20′ W 136
Santa Rita Park, *Calif., U.S.* 37°2′ N, 120°36′ W 100
Santa, river, *Peru* 8°55′ S, 78°46′ W 130
Santa Rosa, *Arg.* 28°3′ S, 67°37′ W 132
Santa Rosa, *Arg.* 36°37′ S, 64°18′ W 139
Santa Rosa, *Arg.* 40°0′ S, 66°33′ W 134
Santa Rosa, *Arg.* 32°21′ S, 65°9′ W 134
Santa Rosa, *Ariz., U.S.* 32°19′ N, 112°2′ W 92
Santa Rosa, *Bol.* 14°13′ S, 66°54′ W 137
Santa Rosa, *Bol.* 11°41′ S, 65°14′ W 137
Santa Rosa, *Bol.* 10°38′ S, 67°24′ W 137
Santa Rosa, *Braz.* 15°6′ S, 47°15′ W 138
Santa Rosa, *Braz.* 27°53′ S, 54°31′ W 139
Santa Rosa, *Calif., U.S.* 38°26′ N, 122°42′ W 90
Santa Rosa, *N. Mex., U.S.* 34°55′ N, 104°41′ W 92
Santa Rosa, *Peru* 14°39′ S, 70°46′ W 137
Santa Rosa, *Peru* 3°48′ S, 76°26′ W 136
Santa Rosa, *Peru* 3°1′ S, 73°13′ W 136
Santa Rosa, *Venez.* 8°30′ N, 69°43′ W 136
Santa Rosa de Amanadona, *Venez.* 1°25′ N, 66°53′ W 136
Santa Rosa de Cop'an, *Hond.* 14°46′ N, 88°46′ W 115
Santa Rosa de Río Primero, *Arg.* 31°9′ S, 63°22′ W 139
Santa Rosa do Purus, *Peru* 9°28′ S, 70°33′ W 137
Santa Rosa, island, *Calif., U.S.* 34°3′ N, 120°7′ W 100
Santa Rosa Mountains, *Calif., U.S.* 33°29′ N, 116°25′ W 101
Santa Rosa National Park, *North Pacific Ocean* 10°46′ N, 85°46′ W 115
Santa Rosa Peak, *Nev., U.S.* 41°33′ N, 117°46′ W 90
Santa Rosa Range, *Nev., U.S.* 41°50′ N, 117°39′ W 90
Santa Rosalía, *Mex.* 27°20′ N, 112°17′ W 82
Santa Rosalía, *Venez.* 7°25′ N, 65°42′ W 136
Santa Rosalíita, *Mex.* 28°40′ N, 114°19′ W 92
Santa Sylvina, *Arg.* 27°47′ S, 61°8′ W 139
Santa Teresa, *Arg.* 33°27′ S, 60°46′ W 139
Santa Teresa, *Braz.* 13°42′ S, 49°3′ W 138
Santa Teresa, *Mex.* 25°18′ N, 97°52′ W 114
Santa Teresa, river, *Braz.* 13°39′ S, 49°1′ W 138
Santa Terezinha, *Braz.* 10°28′ S, 50°35′ W 130
Santa Victoria, *Arg.* 22°16′ S, 62°45′ W 132
Santa Victoria, *Arg.* 22°16′ S, 64°59′ W 137
Santa Vitória do Palmar, *Braz.* 33°31′ S, 53°20′ W 139
Santa Ynez, *Calif., U.S.* 34°37′ N, 120°6′ W 100
Santa Ynez Mountains, *Calif., U.S.* 34°32′ N, 120°28′ W 100
Santai, *China* 31°2′ N, 105°0′ E 198
Santalpur, *India* 23°47′ N, 71°12′ E 186
Santana, *Braz.* 12°59′ S, 44°5′ W 138
Santana do Araguaia, *Braz.* 8°52′ S, 49°45′ W 130
Santana do Livramento, *Braz.* 30°53′ S, 55°29′ W 139
Santana, river, *Braz.* 10°0′ S, 51°14′ W 130
Santander, *Col.* 2°58′ N, 76°30′ W 136
Santander, *Sp.* 43°23′ N, 3°59′ W 214
Santander, *Sp.* 43°27′ N, 3°49′ W 164
Santander, adm. division, *Col.* 6°30′ N, 74°20′ W 136
Santander Jiménez, *Mex.* 24°11′ N, 98°30′ W 114
Sant'Angelo Lodigiano, *It.* 45°13′ N, 9°24′ E 167
Santanilla, Islas, islands, *Caribbean Sea* 17°40′ N, 84°22′ W 115
Santanyí, *Sp.* 39°20′ N, 3°7′ E 150
Santarcangelo di Romagna, *It.* 44°3′ N, 12°26′ E 167
Santarém, *Braz.* 2°29′ S, 54°48′ W 130
Santarém, *Port.* 39°13′ N, 8°42′ W 150
Santarém, adm. division, *Port.* 39°17′ N, 8°59′ W 150
Santaren Channel 23°42′ N, 79°35′ W 96
Santee, *Calif., U.S.* 32°50′ N, 116°59′ W 101
Santee Point 33°1′ N, 79°15′ W 96
Santee, river, *S.C., U.S.* 33°36′ N, 80°10′ W 80
Santena, *It.* 44°57′ N, 7°46′ E 167
Santhià, *It.* 45°22′ N, 8°10′ E 167
Santiago, *Bol.* 18°26′ S, 59°34′ W 132
Santiago, *Braz.* 29°12′ S, 54°50′ W 139
Santiago, *Chile* 33°30′ S, 70°56′ W 134
Santiago, *Mex.* 25°24′ N, 100°7′ W 114
Santiago, Cerro, peak, *Pan.* 8°32′ N, 81°48′ W 115
Santiago de Compostela, *Sp.* 42°51′ N, 8°34′ W 150
Santiago de Cuba, *Cuba* 20°1′ N, 75°50′ W 115
Santiago de Cuba, adm. division, *Cuba* 20°11′ N, 76°25′ W 115
Santiago de la Peña, *Mex.* 20°53′ N, 97°24′ W 114
Santiago del Estero, *Arg.* 27°48′ S, 64°19′ W 132
Santiago del Estero, adm. division, *Arg.* 28°2′ S, 63°30′ W 139
Santiago, Isla, island, *Ecua.* 0°21′ N, 90°34′ W 130
Santiago Mountains, *Tex., U.S.* 29°59′ N, 103°28′ W 92
Santiago Papasquiaro, *Mex.* 25°1′ N, 105°28′ W 114
Santiago, Region Metropolitana de, adm. division, *Chile* 33°45′ S, 72°16′ W 134
Santiago, Serranía de, *Bol.* 17°57′ S, 60°30′ W 132
Santiago Tuxtla, *Mex.* 18°27′ N, 95°19′ W 114
Santiaguillo, Laguna de, lake, *Mex.* 24°56′ N, 105°40′ W 81
Santiam Pass, *Oreg., U.S.* 44°24′ N, 121°52′ W 90
Santillana, *Sp.* 43°23′ N, 4°6′ W 164
Santo Amaro, *Braz.* 12°31′ S, 38°44′ W 132
Santo Anastácio, *Braz.* 21°58′ S, 51°42′ W 138
Santo André, *Braz.* 23°39′ S, 46°32′ W 138
Santo Ângelo, *Braz.* 28°22′ S, 54°18′ W 139
Santo Antônio, *Braz.* 2°0′ N, 68°29′ W 136
Santo Antônio do Içá, *Braz.* 3°5′ S, 67°58′ W 136
Santo Corazón, *Bol.* 18°0′ S, 58°49′ W 132
Santo Domingo, *Dom. Rep.* 18°26′ N, 70°3′ W 116
Santo Domingo, *Mex.* 23°18′ N, 101°44′ W 114
Santo Domingo de Acobamba, *Peru* 11°49′ S, 74°45′ W 137
Santo Domingo de los Colorados, *Ecua.* 0°16′ N, 79°13′ W 130
Santo Domingo Pueblo, *N. Mex., U.S.* 35°30′ N, 106°22′ W 92
Santo Hipólito, *Braz.* 18°17′ S, 44°16′ W 138
Santo Stefano, *It.* 44°32′ N, 9°26′ E 167
Santo Tomás, *Mex.* 31°32′ N, 116°25′ W 92
Santo Tomás, *Peru* 14°30′ S, 72°5′ W 137
Santo Tomás, Punta, *Mex.* 31°16′ N, 117°0′ W 92
Santo Tomé, *Arg.* 31°41′ S, 60°46′ W 139
Santo Tomé, *Arg.* 28°33′ S, 56°4′ W 139
Santok, *Pol.* 52°45′ N, 15°25′ E 152
Santong, river, *China* 42°4′ N, 125°59′ E 200
Santopitar, peak, *Sp.* 36°47′ N, 4°20′ W 164
Santos, *Braz.* 23°56′ S, 46°21′ W 138
Santos Dumont, *Braz.* 21°28′ S, 43°32′ W 138
Santos Dumont, *Braz.* 6°28′ S, 68°16′ W 130
Santos Plateau, *South Atlantic Ocean* 26°36′ S, 43°17′ W 253
Santos, Sierra de los, *Sp.* 37°57′ N, 5°14′ W 164
Santovenia de Pisuerga, *Sp.* 41°40′ N, 4°42′ W 150
Santuario del Moncayo, peak, *Sp.* 41°46′ N, 1°54′ W 164
Santurtzi, *Sp.* 43°18′ N, 3°2′ W 164
Sanya, *China* 18°13′ N, 109°30′ E 198
Sanyō-Onoda, *Japan* 33°58′ N, 131°11′ E 200
Sanyuan, *China* 34°38′ N, 108°56′ E 198
Sanza Pombo, *Angola* 7°21′ S, 15°59′ E 218
São Benedito, river, *Braz.* 9°16′ S, 57°29′ W 132
São Bento, *Braz.* 2°43′ S, 44°47′ W 132
São Borja, *Braz.* 28°41′ S, 56°3′ W 139
São Carlos, *Braz.* 22°2′ S, 47°55′ W 138
São Cristóvão, *Braz.* 11°2′ S, 37°11′ W 132
São Domingos, *Braz.* 19°14′ S, 40°38′ W 138
São Domingos, *Braz.* 13°24′ S, 46°23′ W 138
São Domingos, *Guinea-Bissau* 12°23′ N, 16°9′ W 222
São Fé de Minas, *Braz.* 16°42′ S, 45°25′ W 138
São Félix do Xingu, *Braz.* 6°39′ S, 52°0′ W 130
São Fidélis, *Braz.* 21°41′ S, 41°47′ W 138
São Francisco, *Braz.* 15°58′ S, 44°54′ W 138
São Francisco de Sales, *Braz.* 19°53′ S, 49°47′ W 138
São Francisco do Sul, *Braz.* 26°16′ S, 48°34′ W 138
São Francisco, Ilha de, island, *Braz.* 26°22′ S, 48°27′ W 132
São Francisco, river, *Braz.* 14°13′ S, 43°40′ W 138
São Gabriel, *Braz.* 30°22′ S, 54°20′ W 139
São Gabriel da Cachoeira, *Braz.* 0°8′ N, 67°5′ W 136
São Gabriel de Goiás, *Braz.* 15°13′ S, 47°34′ W 138
São Geraldo do Araguaia, *Braz.* 6°21′ S, 48°35′ W 130
São Gonçalo do Abaete, *Braz.* 18°21′ S, 45°52′ W 138
Sao Hill, *Tanzania* 8°23′ S, 35°13′ E 224
São João, *Guinea-Bissau* 11°36′ N, 15°26′ W 222
São João da Aliança, *Braz.* 14°44′ S, 47°31′ W 138
São João da Barra, *Braz.* 21°41′ S, 41°3′ W 138
São João da Boa Vista, *Braz.* 21°58′ S, 46°48′ W 138
São João da Ponte, *Braz.* 15°58′ S, 44°0′ W 138
São João de Cortes, *Braz.* 2°11′ S, 44°30′ W 132
São João del Rei, *Braz.* 21°9′ S, 44°16′ W 138
São João do Araguaia, *Braz.* 5°26′ S, 48°46′ W 130
São João do Paraíso, *Braz.* 15°21′ S, 42°6′ W 138
São João do Piauí, *Braz.* 8°22′ S, 42°14′ W 132
São João, Serra de, *Braz.* 8°22′ S, 62°44′ W 130
São Joaquim, *Braz.* 28°20′ S, 49°57′ W 138
São Joaquim, *Braz.* 2°119′ S, 67°19′ W 136
São Joaquim da Barra, *Braz.* 20°37′ S, 47°53′ W 138
São Joaquim National Park, *Braz.* 28°18′ S, 49°50′ W 138
São José, *Braz.* 9°40′ S, 67°10′ W 137
São José, *Braz.* 27°37′ S, 48°38′ W 138
São José de Anauá, *Braz.* 1°2′ N, 61°27′ W 130
São José do Norte, *Braz.* 32°2′ S, 52°3′ W 139

São José do Rio Pardo, *Braz.* 21°37′ S, 46°56′ W 138
São José do Rio Preto, *Braz.* 20°49′ S, 49°22′ W 138
São José dos Campos, *Braz.* 23°12′ S, 45°51′ W 138
São José dos Pinhais, *Braz.* 25°32′ S, 49°11′ W 138
São Leopoldo, *Braz.* 29°45′ S, 51°12′ W 139
São Lourenço, *Braz.* 22°8′ S, 45°4′ W 138
São Lourenço do Sul, *Braz.* 31°20′ S, 51°58′ W 139
São Luís, *Braz.* 2°33′ S, 44°15′ W 132
São Luís de Montes Belos, *Braz.* 16°33′ S, 50°21′ W 138
São Luís do Tocantins, *Braz.* 14°19′ S, 48°0′ W 138
São Luís Gonzaga, *Braz.* 28°27′ S, 54°59′ W 139
São Luís, Ilha de, island, *Braz.* 2°45′ S, 44°0′ W 132
São Manuel see Teles Pires, river, *Braz.* 9°30′ S, 55°14′ W 122
São Marcelino, *Braz.* 0°53′ N, 67°15′ W 136
São Marcos, river, *Braz.* 18°1′ S, 47°33′ W 138
São Mateus, *Braz.* 18°45′ S, 39°53′ W 138
São Mateus do Sul, *Braz.* 25°52′ S, 50°25′ W 138
São Miguel do Araguaia, *Braz.* 13°22′ S, 50°16′ W 138
São Miguel, river, *Braz.* 12°27′ S, 63°14′ W 132
São Paulo, *Braz.* 23°33′ S, 46°36′ W 138
São Paulo, adm. division, *Braz.* 21°42′ S, 49°43′ W 138
São Paulo de Olivença, *Braz.* 3°31′ S, 68°49′ W 136
São Pedro, *Braz.* 0°19′ N, 66°50′ W 136
São Pedro, *Braz.* 22°34′ S, 47°56′ W 138
São Pedro, *Braz.* 3°6′ S, 68°54′ W 136
São Raimundo do Araguaia, *Braz.* 5°40′ S, 48°14′ W 130
São Raimundo Nonato, *Braz.* 9°2′ S, 42°43′ W 132
São Romão, *Braz.* 5°51′ S, 67°48′ W 130
São Romão, *Braz.* 16°22′ S, 45°8′ W 138
São Roque do Paraguaçu, *Braz.* 12°54′ S, 38°54′ W 132
São Salvador, *Braz.* 7°28′ S, 73°13′ W 130
São Sebastião, *Braz.* 23°48′ S, 45°27′ W 138
São Sebastião do Paraíso, *Braz.* 20°55′ S, 46°59′ W 138
São Sebastião dos Poções, *Braz.* 14°34′ S, 44°24′ W 138
São Sebastião, Ilha de, island, *Braz.* 24°18′ S, 45°10′ W 132
São Sebastião, Ponta, *Mozambique* 22°35′ S, 35°29′ E 220
Sao Tome and Principe 1°0′ N, 7°0′ E 214
São Tomé, island, *Sao Tome and Principe* 0°12′ N, 6°39′ E 214
São Tomé, river, *Braz.* 8°29′ S, 57°57′ W 130
São Tomé & Principe 0°10′ N, 6°32′ E 218
São Vicente, *Braz.* 10°38′ S, 69°28′ W 137
São Vicente, *Braz.* 24°0′ S, 46°24′ W 138
São Vicente, Cabo de, *Port.* 36°57′ N, 11°3′ W 214
São Vicente do Sul, *Braz.* 29°42′ S, 54°43′ W 139
Saona, Isla, island, *Dom. Rep.* 17°48′ N, 68°52′ W 116
Saône, river, *Fr.* 45°58′ N, 4°39′ E 165
Saône, river, *Fr.* 47°32′ N, 5°41′ E 165
Saonek, *Indonesia* 0°23′ N, 130°43′ E 192
Saoner, *India* 21°22′ N, 78°54′ E 188
Saous, spring, *Mali* 17°45′ N, 5°296′ W 222
Sap, Tonle, lake, *Cambodia* 13°6′ N, 103°45′ E 202
Sapahaqui, *Bol.* 17°0′ S, 67°55′ W 137
Sapanca, *Turk.* 40°41′ N, 30°16′ E 156
Sapateiro, Lago, lake, *Braz.* 2°18′ S, 67°8′ W 136
Sapele, *Nig.* 5°59′ N, 5°41′ E 222
Şaphane Dağı, peak, *Turk.* 39°2′ N, 29°13′ E 156
Sapo, Serranía del, *Pan.* 7°38′ N, 78°2′ W 136
Sappada, *It.* 46°34′ N, 12°41′ E 167
Sapphire Mountains, *Mont., U.S.* 46°4′ N, 113°55′ W 90
Sappho, *Wash., U.S.* 48°3′ N, 124°18′ W 100
Sapporo, *Japan* 43°14′ N, 141°18′ E 190
Sapri, *It.* 40°5′ N, 15°37′ E 156
Sapt Kosi, river, *India* 26°10′ N, 86°44′ E 197
Sapulpa, *Okla., U.S.* 35°58′ N, 96°6′ W 96
Saqqez, *Iran* 36°17′ N, 46°14′ E 195
Šar Planina, *Maced.* 41°54′ N, 20°43′ E 168
Sara, *Burkina Faso* 11°44′ N, 3°50′ W 222
Sarāb, *Iran* 37°58′ N, 47°32′ E 195
Saraburi, *Thai.* 14°33′ N, 100°57′ E 202
Saraféré, *Mali* 15°48′ N, 3°42′ W 222
Sarahs, *Turkm.* 36°31′ N, 61°13′ E 180
Sarai, *Russ.* 53°41′ N, 40°58′ E 154
Sarajevo, *Bosn. and Herzg.* 43°51′ N, 18°22′ E 168
Sarakhs, *Iran* 36°33′ N, 61°4′ E 180
Saraktash, *Russ.* 51°46′ N, 56°16′ E 158
Sarala, *Côte d'Ivoire* 8°34′ N, 4°40′ W 222
Saraland, *Ala., U.S.* 30°48′ N, 88°4′ W 103
Saralzhyn, *Kaz.* 49°11′ N, 48°54′ E 158
Sarana, *Russ.* 56°29′ N, 57°46′ E 154
Saranac, *Mich., U.S.* 42°54′ N, 85°13′ W 102
Saranac Lake, *N.Y., U.S.* 44°19′ N, 74°9′ W 104
Saranda, *Tanzania* 5°41′ S, 34°56′ E 224
Sarandi, *Braz.* 27°58′ S, 52°56′ W 139
Sarandí del Yi, *Uru.* 33°19′ S, 55°39′ W 139
Sarandí Grande, *Uru.* 33°45′ S, 56°21′ W 139
Sarangani Bay 5°52′ N, 125°4′ E 203
Sarangani Islands, islands, *Philippine Sea* 4°20′ N, 123°17′ E 192
Saranpaul′, *Russ.* 64°15′ N, 60°53′ E 169
Saransk, *Russ.* 54°9′ N, 45°7′ E 154
Sarapul, *Russ.* 56°28′ N, 53°47′ E 154
Sarasota, *Fla., U.S.* 27°21′ N, 82°31′ W 105
Saratoga, *Tex., U.S.* 30°17′ N, 94°32′ W 103
Saratoga, *Wyo., U.S.* 41°27′ N, 106°48′ W 90
Saratoga National Historical Park, *N.Y., U.S.* 42°58′ N, 73°42′ W 104
Saratoga Springs, *N.Y., U.S.* 43°4′ N, 73°48′ W 104
Saratoga Table, *Antarctica* 84°9′ S, 45°38′ W 248
Saratok, *Malaysia* 1°45′ N, 111°21′ E 192
Saratov, *Russ.* 51°29′ N, 45°56′ E 158
Saratov, adm. division, *Russ.* 52°44′ N, 47°53′ E 154
Saravan, *Laos* 15°43′ N, 106°22′ E 202
Sarawak, region, *Malaysia* 4°47′ N, 114°58′ E 203
Saray, *Turk.* 41°25′ N, 27°54′ E 156
Saray, *Turk.* 38°39′ N, 44°9′ E 195
Saraya, *Senegal* 12°51′ N, 11°47′ W 222
Sarayacu, *Ecua.* 1°48′ S, 77°31′ W 136
Sarayköy, *Turk.* 37°55′ N, 28°54′ E 156
Sarbāz, *Iran* 26°34′ N, 61°15′ E 182
Sarbīsheh, *Iran* 32°32′ N, 59°48′ E 180
Sárbogárd, *Hung.* 46°52′ N, 18°37′ E 168
Sarca, river, *It.* 46°4′ N, 10°49′ E 167
Sarco, *Chile* 28°49′ S, 71°26′ W 134
Sardão, Cabo, *Port.* 37°26′ N, 9°10′ W 150
Sardarshahr, *India* 28°26′ N, 74°29′ E 186
Sardegna (Sardinia), adm. division, *It.* 39°58′ N, 8°28′ E 156
Sardinal, *C.R.* 10°30′ N, 85°40′ W 115
Sardinia, island, *It.* 40°44′ N, 5°41′ E 143
Sardinia see Sardegna, adm. division, *It.* 39°58′ N, 8°28′ E 156
Sardis, *Miss., U.S.* 34°26′ N, 89°55′ W 96
Sardis Lake, lake, *Okla., U.S.* 34°39′ N, 95°42′ W 96
Sardis, ruin(s), *Turk.* 38°27′ N, 27°55′ E 156
Sar-e Pol, *Afghan.* 36°12′ N, 65°55′ E 186
Sarepta, *La., U.S.* 32°52′ N, 93°27′ W 103
Sargent, *Nebr., U.S.* 41°38′ N, 99°23′ W 90
Sargento Lores, *Peru* 3°48′ S, 74°33′ W 136
Sargo Plateau, *Arctic Ocean* 78°14′ N, 175°5′ W 255
Sargodha, *Pak.* 32°5′ N, 72°45′ E 186
Sarh, *Chad* 9°0′ N, 18°12′ E 207
Sar'add, *Afghan.* 36°57′ N, 73°29′ E 186
Sarhro, Jebel, *Mor.* 30°53′ N, 6°8′ W 214
Sārī, *Iran* 36°34′ N, 53°3′ E 180
Sariá, island, *Gr.* 35°52′ N, 26°48′ E 180
Sariã, river, *Braz.* 6°57′ S, 66°15′ W 130
Sáric, *Mex.* 31°7′ N, 111°25′ W 92
Sarigan, island, *Sarigan* 16°46′ N, 144°50′ E 192
Sarıgöl, *Turk.* 38°14′ N, 28°40′ E 156
Sarıkamış, *Turk.* 40°20′ N, 42°35′ E 195
Sarikei, *Malaysia* 2°3′ N, 111°33′ E 192
Sarimoy, *Uzb.* 41°4′ N, 62°0′ E 180
Sariñena, *Sp.* 41°47′ N, 0°10′ E 164
Sarinleey, *Somalia* 2°24′ N, 42°16′ E 224
Sarīr, oil field, *Lib.* 27°36′ N, 22°18′ E 216
Sariwŏn, *N. Korea* 38°29′ N, 125°45′ E 200
Sarıyer, *Turk.* 41°10′ N, 29°1′ E 156
Sarız, *Turk.* 38°28′ N, 36°29′ E 156
Sarjektjåkko, peak, *Nor.* 67°26′ N, 17°33′ E 152
Särkelä, *Fin.* 65°39′ N, 27°42′ E 152
Sarkhan, oil field, *Iran* 33°19′ N, 47°42′ E 180
Şarkîkaraağaç, *Turk.* 38°4′ N, 31°22′ E 156
Särkisalo, *Fin.* 62°47′ N, 26°6′ E 154
Şarkışla, *Turk.* 39°20′ N, 36°24′ E 156
Şarköy, *Turk.* 40°36′ N, 27°4′ E 156
Sarles, *N. Dak., U.S.* 48°55′ N, 99°2′ W 90
Sarman Didinte, *Eth.* 10°32′ N, 42°28′ E 224
Sărmăşag, *Rom.* 47°20′ N, 22°51′ E 168
Sarmi, *Indonesia* 1°50′ S, 138°40′ E 192
Sarmiento, *Arg.* 45°35′ S, 69°9′ W 134
Särna, *Nor.* 61°41′ N, 13°5′ E 152
Sarnen, *Switz.* 46°54′ N, 8°14′ E 167
Sarnia, *Can.* 42°57′ N, 82°23′ W 102
Sarny, *Ukr.* 51°19′ N, 26°36′ E 152
Särö, *Nor.* 57°31′ N, 11°57′ E 152
Saronno, *It.* 45°37′ N, 9°1′ E 167
Sárospatak, *Hung.* 48°20′ N, 21°33′ E 152
Sarowbi, *Afghan.* 34°35′ N, 69°48′ E 186
Sarpa, *Russ.* 47°2′ N, 45°27′ E 158
Sarpa, Ozero, lake, *Russ.* 47°12′ N, 45°10′ E 158
Sarqan, *Kaz.* 45°25′ N, 79°54′ E 184
Sarracín, *Sp.* 42°14′ N, 3°42′ W 164
Sarralbe, *Fr.* 49°0′ N, 7°3′ E 163
Sarrebourg, *Fr.* 48°44′ N, 7°3′ E 163
Sarreguemines, *Fr.* 49°7′ N, 7°4′ E 163
Sarre-Union, *Fr.* 48°56′ N, 7°5′ E 163
Sarria, *Sp.* 42°47′ N, 7°26′ W 214
Sarrión, *Sp.* 40°7′ N, 0°49′ E 164
Sars, *Russ.* 56°33′ N, 57°17′ E 154
Sarsang, *Iraq* 37°5′ N, 43°13′ E 195
Sarsina, *It.* 43°56′ N, 12°8′ E 167
Sarstoon, river, *North America* 15°56′ N, 89°29′ W 115
Sartène, *Fr.* 41°37′ N, 8°59′ E 156
Sarto, *Col.* 4°54′ N, 70°10′ W 136
Särur, *Asia* 39°33′ N, 44°57′ E 195
Sárvár, *Hung.* 47°15′ N, 16°55′ E 168
Sárvíz, river, *Hung.* 46°33′ N, 18°35′ E 168
Saryaghash, *Kaz.* 41°23′ N, 69°2′ E 197
Sary-Bee, *Kyrg.* 40°36′ N, 73°54′ E 197
Sarych, Mys, *Ukr.* 44°18′ N, 32°56′ E 156
Saryg Sep, *Russ.* 51°32′ N, 95°43′ E 190
Sarykemer, *Kaz.* 42°55′ N, 71°25′ E 184
Sarykenggir, river, *Kaz.* 49°16′ N, 67°24′ E 184
Saryköl, *Kaz.* 53°19′ N, 65°32′ E 184
Sary-Mogol, *Kyrg.* 39°40′ N, 72°57′ E 197
Saryözek, *Kaz.* 44°21′ N, 77°56′ E 184
Saryqamys, *Kaz.* 45°57′ N, 53°31′ E 158
Saryqopa Köli, lake, *Kaz.* 50°17′ N, 63°20′ E 184
Sarysay, *Kaz.* 48°24′ N, 60°32′ E 184
Saryshaghan, *Kaz.* 46°3′ N, 73°33′ E 184
Sarysu, river, *Kaz.* 46°47′ N, 67°16′ E 184
Sary-Tash, *Kyrg.* 39°42′ N, 73°15′ E 197
Saryzhal, *Kaz.* 49°36′ N, 78°45′ E 184
Saryzhaz, *Kaz.* 42°54′ N, 79°39′ E 184
Sarzana, *It.* 44°6′ N, 9°58′ E 167
Sas de Còrdoba, *Arg.* 31°38′ S, 63°50′ W 139
Sas van Gent, *Neth.* 51°13′ N, 3°48′ E 163
Sa'sa', *Syr.* 33°18′ N, 36°1′ E 194
Sasaginnigak Lake, lake, *Can.* 51°29′ N, 96°23′ W 108
Sasak, *Indonesia* 4°238′ N, 99°41′ E 196
Sasaram, *India* 24°56′ N, 84°0′ E 197
Sasca Montană, *Rom.* 44°52′ N, 21°44′ E 168
Sásd, *Hung.* 46°15′ N, 18°6′ E 168
Sasebo, *Japan* 33°10′ N, 129°43′ E 201
Saser Kangri, peak, *India* 34°49′ N, 77°37′ E 188
Saskatchewan, adm. division, *Can.* 53°56′ N, 110°0′ W 106
Saskatoon, *Can.* 52°8′ N, 106°40′ W 108
Sason, *Turk.* 38°19′ N, 41°26′ E 195
Sasovo, *Russ.* 54°18′ N, 41°53′ E 154
Sass, river, *Can.* 60°13′ N, 113°18′ W 108
Sassafras Mountain, peak, *N.C., U.S.* 35°2′ N, 82°52′ W 96
Sassan, oil field, *Iraq* 36°24′ N, 42°15′ E 195
Sassandra, *Côte d'Ivoire* 4°58′ N, 6°6′ W 222
Sassari, *It.* 40°43′ N, 8°34′ E 156
Sassello, *It.* 44°29′ N, 8°29′ E 167
Sassnitz, *Ger.* 54°31′ N, 13°39′ E 160
Sasstown, *Liberia* 4°46′ N, 8°26′ W 222
Sassulko, Goz, *Cen. Af. Rep.* 10°59′ N, 23°22′ E 224
Sassuolo, *It.* 44°33′ N, 10°47′ E 167
Sástago, *Sp.* 41°18′ N, 0°22′ E 164
Sastre, *Arg.* 31°46′ S, 61°49′ W 139
Sasyk-Kel, *Taj.* 37°39′ N, 73°10′ E 197
Sasykoli, *Russ.* 47°27′ N, 47°2′ E 158
Sata Misaki, *Japan* 30°28′ N, 129°42′ E 190
Satadougou Tintiba, *Mali* 12°39′ N, 11°25′ W 222
Satala, ruin(s), *Turk.* 40°1′ N, 39°31′ E 195
Satama Sakoura, *Côte d'Ivoire* 7°53′ N, 4°19′ W 222
Sataniv, *Ukr.* 49°15′ N, 26°14′ E 152
Satanta, *Kans., U.S.* 37°25′ N, 101°0′ W 92
Satara, *India* 17°41′ N, 73°58′ E 188
Satartia, *Miss., U.S.* 32°39′ N, 90°32′ W 103
Satawan Atoll 5°14′ N, 150°47′ E 192
Sätbaev, *Kaz.* 47°54′ N, 67°30′ E 184
Satellite Beach, *Fla., U.S.* 28°9′ N, 80°37′ W 105
Säter, *Nor.* 60°20′ N, 15°42′ E 152
Satevó, *Mex.* 27°56′ N, 106°6′ W 92
Saticoy, *Calif., U.S.* 34°17′ N, 119°10′ W 101
Satilla, river, *Ga., U.S.* 31°32′ N, 83°4′ W 80
Satipo, *Peru* 11°15′ S, 74°42′ W 137
Satka, *Russ.* 55°5′ N, 59°6′ E 154
Satna, *India* 24°34′ N, 80°49′ E 197
Sato, *Japan* 37°25′ N, 137°2′ E 201
Sato, *Japan* 31°50′ N, 129°54′ E 201
Šator, peak, *Bosn. and Herzg.* 44°9′ N, 16°35′ E 168
Satpura National Park, *India* 22°30′ N, 78°12′ E 197
Sattahip, *Thai.* 12°41′ N, 100°53′ E 202
Satu Mare, *Rom.* 47°47′ N, 22°54′ E 168
Satu Mare, adm. division, *Rom.* 48°5′ N, 22°59′ E 152
Satun, *Thai.* 6°35′ N, 100°3′ E 196
Sauce, *Arg.* 30°4′ S, 58°45′ W 139
Saucier, *Miss., U.S.* 30°37′ N, 89°7′ W 103
Saūdakent, *Kaz.* 43°42′ N, 69°55′ E 184
Sauđárkrókur, *Ice.* 65°43′ N, 19°41′ W 246
Saudi Arabia 23°44′ N, 43°56′ E 182
Sauêruiná, river, *Braz.* 11°36′ S, 58°51′ W 132
Saugatuck, *Mich., U.S.* 42°39′ N, 86°11′ W 102
Saugor see Sagar, *India* 23°50′ N, 78°45′ E 188
Sauk Centre, *Minn., U.S.* 45°46′ N, 94°57′ W 82
Sauk City, *Wis., U.S.* 43°15′ N, 89°44′ W 102
Sauk Rapids, *Minn., U.S.* 45°35′ N, 94°11′ W 90
Sauk, river, *Wash., U.S.* 48°16′ N, 121°41′ W 100
Saukville, *Wis., U.S.* 43°22′ N, 87°58′ W 102
Saulkrasti, *Latv.* 57°16′ N, 24°25′ E 166
Sault Sainte Marie, *Can.* 46°35′ N, 84°18′ W 106
Sault Sainte Marie, *Mich., U.S.* 46°29′ N, 84°22′ W 94
Saūmalköl, *Kaz.* 53°18′ N, 68°8′ E 184
Saumlaki, *Indonesia* 7°58′ S, 131°10′ E 192
Saundatti, *India* 15°46′ N, 75°6′ E 188
Saunders Coast, *South Pacific Ocean* 76°48′ S, 132°37′ W 248
Saunders Mount, peak, *Antarctica* 76°46′ S, 144°52′ W 248
Saunders, Mount, peak, *Antarctica* 85°40′ S, 163°7′ E 248
Saurimo, *Angola* 9°38′ S, 20°25′ E 218
Sauris, *It.* 46°27′ N, 12°42′ E 167
Sautar, *Angola* 11°6′ S, 18°27′ E 220
Sauterelles, Lac aux, lake, *Can.* 51°58′ N, 65°8′ W 111
Sava, river, *Croatia* 45°46′ N, 15°48′ E 168
Savage, *Mont., U.S.* 47°25′ N, 104°22′ W 90
Savai'i, island, *Samoa* 13°38′ S, 172°38′ W 241
Savalou, *Benin* 7°57′ N, 1°57′ E 222
Savanna, *Ill., U.S.* 42°5′ N, 90°9′ W 102
Savannah, *Ga., U.S.* 32°3′ N, 81°6′ W 96
Savannah, *Mo., U.S.* 39°55′ N, 94°50′ W 94
Savannah, river, *U.S.* 33°27′ N, 82°1′ W 80
Savannakhét, *Laos* 16°32′ N, 104°46′ E 202
Savanna-la-Mar, *Jam.* 18°14′ N, 78°8′ W 115
Savant Lake, *Can.* 50°14′ N, 90°42′ W 110
Savant Lake, *Can.* 50°14′ N, 90°42′ W 94
Savanur, *India* 14°58′ N, 75°20′ E 188
Savar Kundla, *India* 21°21′ N, 71°17′ E 186
Savaştepe, *Turk.* 39°22′ N, 27°38′ E 156
Savé, *Benin* 8°4′ N, 2°27′ E 222
Save, river, *Africa* 21°16′ S, 32°29′ E 207
Save, river, *Fr.* 43°40′ N, 1°10′ E 165
Sāveh, *Iran* 35°3′ N, 50°19′ E 180
Savelugu, *Ghana* 9°37′ N, 0°51′ E 222
Saverdun, *Fr.* 43°13′ N, 1°33′ E 164
Saverne, *Fr.* 48°44′ N, 7°21′ E 163
Savigliano, *It.* 44°37′ N, 7°39′ E 167
Savignano sul Rubicone, *It.* 44°6′ N, 12°24′ E 156
Savignone, *It.* 44°33′ N, 8°59′ E 167
Savinobor, *Russ.* 63°35′ N, 56°27′ E 154
Savio, river, *It.* 44°8′ N, 12°11′ E 167
Săvîrşin, *Rom.* 46°1′ N, 22°14′ E 168
Savissivik 75°59′ N, 64°51′ W 246
Savitaipale, *Fin.* 61°11′ N, 27°40′ E 166
Šavnik, *Mont.* 42°56′ N, 19°5′ E 168
Savona, *It.* 44°18′ N, 8°28′ E 167
Savonlinna, *Fin.* 61°51′ N, 28°51′ E 166
Savonranta, *Fin.* 62°9′ N, 29°11′ E 152
Savoy, *Ill., U.S.* 40°3′ N, 88°15′ W 102
Savoy, *Mass., U.S.* 42°33′ N, 73°2′ W 104
Savoy, region, *Fr.* 45°19′ N, 6°12′ E 165
Şavşat, *Turk.* 41°15′ N, 42°20′ E 195
Savu Sea 9°59′ S, 121°35′ E 192
Savudrija, *Croatia* 45°29′ N, 13°30′ E 167
Savukoski, *Fin.* 67°18′ N, 28°6′ E 152
Savur, *Turk.* 37°32′ N, 40°56′ E 195
Saw, *Myanmar* 21°12′ N, 94°5′ E 202
Sawada, *Japan* 38°0′ N, 138°20′ E 201
Sawahlunto, *Indonesia* 0°40′ N, 100°47′ E 196
Sawai Madhopur, *India* 26°0′ N, 76°25′ E 197
Sawankhalok, *Thai.* 17°19′ N, 99°51′ E 202
Sawara, *Japan* 35°52′ N, 140°31′ E 201
Sawārah Tūkā, *Iraq* 37°0′ N, 43°6′ E 195
Sawatch Range, *Colo., U.S.* 39°21′ N, 106°52′ W 90
Sawdā', Jabal as, *Lib.* 29°0′ N, 14°26′ E 216
Sawdā', Qurnat as, peak, *Leb.* 34°18′ N, 36°5′ E 194
Sawe, *Indian Ocean* 1°31′ N, 97°23′ E 196
Sawi, *Thai.* 10°13′ N, 99°6′ E 202
Sāwinnū, ruin(s), *Lib.* 30°59′ N, 20°45′ E 216
Sawkanah, *Lib.* 29°6′ N, 15°45′ E 216
Sawla, *Ghana* 9°16′ N, 2°26′ W 222
Sawn Lake, *Can.* 56°57′ N, 116°29′ W 108
Şawqirah, *Oman* 18°5′ N, 56°29′ E 182
Şawqirah, Ghubbat 18°31′ N, 56°2′ E 182
Sawtooth Mountains, *Minn., U.S.* 47°35′ N, 91°23′ W 94
Sawtooth National Recreation Area, *Idaho, U.S.* 43°42′ N, 121°19′ W 80
Sawtooth Range, *Idaho, U.S.* 44°7′ N, 115°16′ W 90
Sawu, island, *Indonesia* 10°33′ S, 122°2′ E 192
Sawyer, *Mich., U.S.* 41°52′ N, 86°35′ W 102
Sawyer Bay 41°3′ S, 145°0′ E 230
Sax, *Sp.* 38°31′ N, 0°51′ E 164
Saxmundham, *U.K.* 52°12′ N, 1°28′ E 163
Saxnäs, *Nor.* 64°56′ N, 15°17′ E 152
Saxony, adm. division, *Ger.* 51°7′ N, 12°33′ E 152
Saxony-Anhalt, adm. division, *Ger.* 52°38′ N, 10°57′ E 152
Saxtons River, *Vt., U.S.* 43°8′ N, 72°31′ W 104
Say, *Niger* 13°5′ N, 2°18′ E 222
Sayak, *Kaz.* 47°0′ N, 77°24′ E 184
Sayanogorsk, *Russ.* 52°48′ N, 91°19′ E 190
Sayat, *Turkm.* 38°47′ N, 63°53′ E 197
Saybrook, *Ill., U.S.* 40°25′ N, 88°32′ W 102
Şaydnāyā, *Syr.* 33°41′ N, 36°22′ E 194
Say'ūt, *Yemen* 15°15′ N, 51°15′ E 182
Saylac, *Somalia* 11°16′ N, 43°27′ E 216
Säyneinen, *Fin.* 63°10′ N, 28°24′ E 152
Saynshand (Buyant-Uhaa), *Mongolia* 44°51′ N, 110°9′ E 190
Sayötesh, *Kaz.* 44°18′ N, 53°33′ E 158
Sayqyn, *Kaz.* 48°48′ N, 46°47′ E 158
Sayram Hu, lake, *China* 44°27′ N, 80°40′ E 184
Sayre, *Okla., U.S.* 35°16′ N, 99°39′ W 92
Sayre, *Pa., U.S.* 41°58′ N, 76°32′ W 94
Sayrob, *Uzb.* 38°2′ N, 67°0′ E 197
Sayula, *Mex.* 19°52′ N, 103°37′ W 114
Sayula, *Mex.* 17°51′ N, 94°58′ W 114
Sayulita, *Mex.* 20°51′ N, 105°28′ W 114
Sayville, *N.Y., U.S.* 40°44′ N, 73°5′ W 104
Sbaa, *Alg.* 28°14′ N, 0°11′ E 214
Sbikha, *Tun.* 35°56′ N, 10°1′ E 156
Scafell Pike, peak, *U.K.* 54°26′ N, 3°15′ W 162
Scalea, *It.* 39°49′ N, 15°47′ E 156
Scammon Bay, *Alas., U.S.* 61°50′ N, 165°35′ W 98
Scandia, *Kans., U.S.* 39°46′ N, 97°47′ W 90
Scandiano, *It.* 44°36′ N, 10°41′ E 167
Scanzano Ionico, *It.* 40°15′ N, 16°42′ E 156
Scapegoat Mountain, peak, *Mont., U.S.* 47°16′ N, 112°55′ W 90
Scappoose, *Oreg., U.S.* 45°44′ N, 122°52′ W 100
Scaraben, peak, *U.K.* 58°12′ N, 3°43′ W 150
Scarborough, *Me., U.S.* 43°34′ N, 70°19′ W 104
Scarborough, *U.K.* 54°16′ N, 0°26′ E 162
Scardona see Skradin, *Croatia* 43°49′ N, 15°54′ E 168
Scargill, *N.Z.* 42°58′ S, 172°57′ E 240
Scauri, *It.* 36°45′ N, 11°59′ E 156
Sceale Bay 33°7′ S, 132°54′ E 230
Sceaux, *Fr.* 48°46′ N, 2°18′ E 163
Šćedro, island, *Croatia* 43°2′ N, 16°29′ E 168
Schagen, *Neth.* 52°47′ N, 4°46′ E 163
Schaghticoke, *N.Y., U.S.* 42°54′ N, 73°36′ W 104
Schefferville, *Can.* 54°51′ N, 67°3′ W 106
Schela, *Rom.* 45°9′ N, 23°18′ E 168
Schell Creek Range, *Nev., U.S.* 39°34′ N, 114°51′ W 90
Schenectady, *N.Y., U.S.* 42°48′ N, 73°57′ W 104
Scherfede, *Ger.* 51°31′ N, 9°2′ E 167
Scherhorn, peak, *Switz.* 46°47′ N, 8°47′ E 167
Schertz, *Tex., U.S.* 29°31′ N, 98°16′ W 92
Schiermonnikoog, island, *Neth.* 53°25′ N, 6°1′ E 163
Schillighörn 53°39′ N, 7°51′ E 163
Schilpario, *It.* 46°1′ N, 10°9′ E 167
Schio, *It.* 45°43′ N, 11°21′ E 167
Schirmeck, *Fr.* 48°28′ N, 7°12′ E 163
Schleiden, *Ger.* 50°31′ N, 6°28′ E 167
Schleswig-Holstein, adm. division, *Ger.* 54°2′ N, 9°4′ E 150
Schlitz, *Ger.* 50°40′ N, 9°33′ E 167
Schlossbach, Cape, *Antarctica* 75°51′ S, 61°41′ W 248
Schlüchtern, *Ger.* 50°20′ N, 9°31′ E 167
Schmallenberg, *Ger.* 51°9′ N, 8°16′ E 167
Schmelz, *Ger.* 49°26′ N, 6°51′ E 163
Schmücke, peak, *Ger.* 51°13′ N, 11°12′ E 152
Schofield, *Wis., U.S.* 44°54′ N, 89°36′ W 110
Schofield Barracks, *Hawai'i, U.S.* 21°29′ N, 158°7′ W 99
Schönecken, *Ger.* 50°9′ N, 6°28′ E 167
Schonungen, *Ger.* 50°3′ N, 10°17′ E 167
Schoolcraft, *Mich., U.S.* 42°6′ N, 85°38′ W 102
Schortens, *Ger.* 53°31′ N, 7°57′ E 163
Schotten, *Ger.* 50°30′ N, 9°7′ E 167
Schouten Islands, islands, *Bismarck Sea* 3°8′ S, 142°32′ E 192
Schreiber, *Can.* 48°48′ N, 87°15′ W 110
Schreiner Peak, *Oreg., U.S.* 44°52′ N, 122°8′ W 90

Schroeder, *Minn., U.S.* 47°32′ N, 90°56′ W 110
Schroon Lake, *N.Y., U.S.* 43°50′ N, 73°47′ W 104
Schubert Inlet 71°7′ S, 72°22′ W 248
Schuler, *Can.* 50°20′ N, 110°5′ W 90
Schull, *Ire.* 51°31′ N, 9°33′ W 150
Schumacher, *Can.* 48°29′ N, 81°17′ W 94
Schüttorf, *Ger.* 52°19′ N, 7°14′ E 163
Schuyler, *Nebr., U.S.* 41°26′ N, 97°4′ W 92
Schuylerville, *N.Y., U.S.* 43°5′ N, 73°36′ W 104
Schwaben, region, *Ger.* 48°8′ N, 7°50′ E 163
Schwäbische Alb, *Ger.* 48°9′ N, 8°23′ E 150
Schwalmstadt, *Ger.* 50°55′ N, 9°12′ E 167
Schwarzwald, region, *Ger.* 48°6′ N, 7°38′ E 163
Schweich, *Ger.* 49°49′ N, 6°45′ E 167
Schweinfurt, *Ger.* 50°2′ N, 10°13′ E 167
Schweizer Reneke, *S. Af.* 27°11′ S, 25°18′ E 227
Schwerin, *Ger.* 53°38′ N, 11°25′ E 152
Schwerte, *Ger.* 51°26′ N, 7°33′ E 167
Schwob Peak, *Antarctica* 75°50′ S, 127°59′ W 248
Scicli, *It.* 36°47′ N, 14°42′ E 156
Scilly, Isles of, islands, *Celtic Sea* 49°48′ N, 6°58′ W 150
Scînteia, *Rom.* 46°55′ N, 27°34′ E 156
Scione, ruin(s), *Gr.* 39°56′ N, 23°26′ E 156
Scioto, river, *Ohio, U.S.* 40°26′ N, 83°16′ W 102
Scipio, *Utah, U.S.* 39°14′ N, 112°6′ W 90
Scituate, *Mass., U.S.* 42°11′ N, 70°44′ W 104
Scobey, *Mont., U.S.* 48°46′ N, 105°26′ W 90
Scooba, *Miss., U.S.* 32°47′ N, 88°30′ W 103
Scoresby Land 71°45′ N, 24°3′ W 246
Scoresby Sund 70°5′ N, 31°35′ W 72
Scoresbysund see Ittoqqortoormiit 70°26′ N, 21°53′ W 246
Scorpion Bight 32°38′ S, 126°15′ E 230
Scorton, *U.K.* 54°24′ N, 1°37′ W 162
Scotch Corner, *U.K.* 54°26′ N, 1°41′ W 162
Scotia, *Calif., U.S.* 40°28′ N, 124°6′ W 92
Scotia, *N.Y., U.S.* 42°49′ N, 73°59′ W 104
Scotia Sea 56°22′ S, 49°38′ W 134
Scotland, *S. Dak., U.S.* 43°6′ N, 97°43′ W 90
Scotland, adm. division, *U.K.* 56°50′ N, 5°37′ W 150
Scotland Neck, *N.C., U.S.* 36°7′ N, 77°26′ W 96
Scotlandville, *La., U.S.* 30°30′ N, 91°12′ W 103
Scotstown, *Can.* 45°31′ N, 71°17′ W 111
Scott, *Can.* 52°21′ N, 108°51′ W 108
Scott, *La., U.S.* 30°13′ N, 92°6′ W 96
Scott Air Force Base, *Ill., U.S.* 38°31′ N, 89°54′ W 102
Scott Bar Mountains, *Calif., U.S.* 41°51′ N, 123°0′ W 90
Scott Base, New Zealand, station, *Antarctica* 77°52′ S, 166°44′ E 248
Scott, Cape, *Can.* 50°35′ N, 128°45′ W 90
Scott City, *Kans., U.S.* 38°29′ N, 100°55′ W 90
Scott Coast, *Antarctica* 76°20′ S, 169°0′ E 248
Scott Island, *South Pacific Ocean* 67°24′ S, 179°50′ E 255
Scott Islands, *North Pacific Ocean* 50°18′ N, 130°51′ W 106
Scott, Mount, peak, *Oreg., U.S.* 42°54′ N, 122°7′ W 90
Scott Mountains, *Antarctica* 67°31′ S, 49°49′ E 248
Scott Mountains, *Calif., U.S.* 41°14′ N, 122°55′ W 90
Scott Nunataks, *Antarctica* 77°13′ S, 156°24′ W 248
Scott Point, *Mich., U.S.* 45°47′ N, 86°0′ W 94
Scottburgh, *S. Af.* 30°17′ S, 30°41′ E 227
Scotts Valley, *Calif., U.S.* 37°3′ N, 122°2′ W 100
Scottsbluff, *Nebr., U.S.* 41°51′ N, 103°39′ W 82
Scottsboro, *Ala., U.S.* 34°39′ N, 86°1′ W 96
Scottsburg, *Ind., U.S.* 38°41′ N, 85°46′ W 102
Scottsville, *Ky., U.S.* 36°44′ N, 86°12′ W 96
Scottville, *Mich., U.S.* 43°57′ N, 86°17′ W 102
Scourie, *U.K.* 58°21′ N, 5°9′ W 150
Scout Mountain, peak, *Idaho, U.S.* 42°40′ N, 112°24′ W 90
Scranton, *Pa., U.S.* 41°24′ N, 75°40′ W 94
Scranton, *S.C., U.S.* 33°54′ N, 79°46′ W 96
Scribner, *Nebr., U.S.* 41°38′ N, 96°41′ W 90
Scudder, *Can.* 41°48′ N, 82°38′ W 102
Scugog, Lake, *Can.* 44°7′ N, 79°16′ W 110
Scullin Monolith, peak, *Antarctica* 67°52′ S, 66°27′ E 248
Scunthorpe, *U.K.* 53°34′ N, 0°40′ E 162
Scuol, *Switz.* 46°48′ N, 10°17′ E 167
Scutari see Shkodër, *Alban.* 42°4′ N, 19°30′ E 168
Sea Gull Lake, lake, *Minn., U.S.* 48°5′ N, 91°4′ W 110
Sea Island, *Ga., U.S.* 31°10′ N, 81°22′ W 96
Sea Lion Islands, *Scotia Sea* 52°42′ S, 58°40′ W 134
Seabrook, *N.H., U.S.* 42°53′ N, 70°53′ W 104
Seabrook, *Tex., U.S.* 29°34′ N, 95°1′ W 103
Seacliff, *N.Z.* 45°41′ S, 170°37′ E 240
Seadrift, *Tex., U.S.* 28°24′ N, 96°43′ W 96
Seaford, *Del., U.S.* 38°38′ N, 75°37′ W 94
Seaford, *U.K.* 50°46′ N, 9°535′ E 162
Seaforth, *Can.* 43°33′ N, 81°24′ W 102
Seagraves, *Tex., U.S.* 32°55′ N, 102°34′ W 92
Seaham, *U.K.* 54°50′ N, 1°21′ W 162
Seal Bay 71°46′ S, 14°44′ W 248
Seal, Cape, *S. Af.* 34°21′ S, 23°27′ E 227
Seal Islands, *Scotia Sea* 60°59′ S, 56°17′ W 134
Seal Nunataks 64°59′ S, 60°8′ W 248
Seal, river, *Can.* 58°50′ N, 96°21′ W 108
Sealy, *Tex., U.S.* 29°45′ N, 96°9′ W 96
Seaman, *Ohio, U.S.* 38°55′ N, 83°34′ W 102
Seaman Range, *Nev., U.S.* 37°57′ N, 115°22′ W 90
Searchlight, *Nev., U.S.* 35°27′ N, 114°56′ W 101
Searcy, *Ark., U.S.* 35°14′ N, 91°47′ W 112
Seascale, *U.K.* 54°24′ N, 3°29′ W 162
Seaside, *Calif., U.S.* 36°36′ N, 121°52′ W 100
Seaside, *Oreg., U.S.* 45°59′ N, 123°54′ W 100
Seaside Park, *N.J., U.S.* 39°54′ N, 74°6′ W 94
Seattle, *Wash., U.S.* 47°35′ N, 122°19′ W 100
Seaview, *Wash., U.S.* 46°18′ N, 124°3′ W 100
Sebago Lake, *Me., U.S.* 43°50′ N, 70°38′ W 104
Sebago Lake, *Me., U.S.* 43°45′ N, 70°32′ W 104
Sebanga, oil field, *Indonesia* 1°16′ N, 101°10′ E 196
Sebastian, *Fla., U.S.* 27°48′ N, 80°29′ W 105
Sebastian, Cape, *Oreg., U.S.* 42°18′ N, 124°56′ W 90
Sebastián Elcano, *Arg.* 30°10′ S, 63°38′ W 139
Sebastián Vizcaíno, Bahía 28°3′ N, 115°1′ W 92
Sebastopol, *Calif., U.S.* 38°24′ N, 122°50′ W 100
Sebastopol, *Miss., U.S.* 32°33′ N, 89°21′ W 103
Sebba, *Burkina Faso* 13°26′ N, 0°30′ E 222
Sébé, river, *Gabon* 0°56′ N, 13°15′ E 218
Seben, *Turk.* 40°24′ N, 31°33′ E 156
Seberi, *Braz.* 27°43′ S, 53°19′ W 139
Seberi, Cerro, peak, *Mex.* 27°46′ N, 110°21′ W 112
Sebeşului, Munţii, *Rom.* 45°34′ N, 23°9′ E 168
Sebeta, Rabt, *Africa* 23°59′ N, 14°47′ W 214
Sebewaing, *Mich., U.S.* 43°43′ N, 83°26′ W 102
Sebezh, *Russ.* 56°17′ N, 28°29′ E 166
Sebina, *Botswana* 20°53′ S, 27°13′ E 227
Sebiş, *Rom.* 46°23′ N, 22°10′ E 168
Sebring, *Fla., U.S.* 27°30′ N, 81°26′ W 105
Sečanj, *Serb.* 45°22′ N, 20°47′ E 168
Sechelt, *Can.* 49°28′ N, 123°46′ W 100
Sechura, *Peru* 5°30′ S, 80°51′ W 130
Sechura, Desierto de, *Peru* 6°10′ S, 82°8′ W 130
Seclin, *Fr.* 50°32′ N, 3°1′ E 163
Second Mesa, *Ariz., U.S.* 35°46′ N, 110°30′ W 92
Secret Pass, *Nev., U.S.* 40°50′ N, 115°12′ W 90
Secunderabad, *India* 17°28′ N, 78°28′ E 188
Securé, river, *Bol.* 15°44′ S, 65°44′ W 137
Seda, *Latv.* 57°39′ N, 25°44′ E 166
Seda, *Lith.* 56°9′ N, 22°4′ E 166
Sedalia, *Mo., U.S.* 38°41′ N, 93°14′ W 94
Sedan, *Fr.* 49°42′ N, 4°56′ E 163
Sedano, *Sp.* 42°42′ N, 3°44′ W 164
Sedbergh, *U.K.* 54°19′ N, 2°32′ W 162
Seddon, *N.Z.* 41°43′ S, 174°3′ E 240
Seddon, Kap 75°11′ N, 58°11′ W 106
Seddonville, *N.Z.* 41°35′ S, 171°58′ E 240
Sedé Boqér, *Israel* 30°51′ N, 34°47′ E 194
Sedeh, *Iran* 33°20′ N, 59°16′ E 180
Sederot, *Israel* 31°31′ N, 34°36′ E 194
Sedgemoor 1685, battle, *U.K.* 51°8′ N, 2°56′ W 162
Sédhiou, *Senegal* 12°43′ N, 15°33′ W 222
Sedlare, *Serb.* 44°12′ N, 21°16′ E 168
Sedley, *Can.* 50°9′ N, 104°2′ W 90
Sedom, *Israel* 31°4′ N, 35°23′ E 194
Sedro Woolley, *Wash., U.S.* 48°30′ N, 122°15′ W 100
Šeduva, *Lith.* 55°44′ N, 23°44′ E 166
Seeheim, *Namibia* 26°50′ S, 17°46′ E 227
Seeis, *Namibia* 22°28′ S, 17°34′ E 227
Seekonk, *Mass., U.S.* 41°48′ N, 71°21′ W 104
Seeley, *Calif., U.S.* 32°47′ N, 115°42′ W 101
Seelig, Mount, peak, *Antarctica* 82°14′ S, 102°46′ W 248
Seelow, *Ger.* 52°32′ N, 14°22′ E 152
Seelyville, *Ind., U.S.* 39°29′ N, 87°16′ W 102
Seemade, *Somalia* 7°9′ N, 48°31′ E 218
Sefare, *Botswana* 23°0′ S, 27°27′ E 227
Sefophe, *Botswana* 22°16′ S, 27°59′ E 227
Sefrou, *Mor.* 33°51′ N, 4°53′ W 214
Seg Ozero, lake, *Russ.* 63°15′ N, 33°33′ E 154
Segag, *Eth.* 7°32′ N, 42°55′ E 218
Ségala, *Mali* 14°35′ N, 10°58′ W 222
Segamat, *Malaysia* 2°33′ N, 102°49′ E 196
Segbana, *Benin* 10°57′ N, 3°38′ E 222
Segesta, ruin(s), *It.* 37°54′ N, 12°43′ E 156
Segezha, *Russ.* 63°45′ N, 34°16′ E 154
Segorbe, *Sp.* 39°50′ N, 0°30′ E 164
Ségou, *Mali* 13°25′ N, 6°16′ W 222
Segovia, *Sp.* 40°55′ N, 4°8′ W 150
Séguédine, *Niger* 20°17′ N, 12°55′ E 216
Séguéla, *Côte d'Ivoire* 7°53′ N, 6°40′ W 222
Séguéla, *Mali* 14°6′ N, 6°44′ W 222
Seguin, *Tex., U.S.* 29°33′ N, 97°58′ W 92
Segura, Sierra de, *Sp.* 37°58′ N, 2°57′ W 164
Sehithwa, *Botswana* 20°26′ S, 22°39′ E 227
Sehnkwehn, *Liberia* 5°13′ N, 9°32′ W 222
Sehore, *India* 23°11′ N, 77°5′ E 197
Seibal, ruin(s), *Guatemala* 16°28′ N, 90°13′ W 115
Seida, *Nor.* 70°12′ N, 28°6′ E 152
Seiling, *Okla., U.S.* 36°8′ N, 98°56′ W 92
Seine, river, *Fr.* 48°9′ N, 4°21′ E 165
Seine, river, *Fr.* 49°4′ N, 1°35′ E 163
Seini, *Rom.* 47°44′ N, 23°16′ E 168
Seira, *Sp.* 42°28′ N, 0°26′ E 164
Sejenane, *Tun.* 37°4′ N, 9°15′ E 156
Sejny, *Pol.* 54°5′ N, 23°20′ E 166
Seke, *Tanzania* 3°19′ S, 33°30′ E 224
Seke Banza, *Dem. Rep. of the Congo* 5°20′ S, 13°15′ E 218
Seken Seyfüllīn, *Kaz.* 48°50′ N, 72°48′ E 184
Sekenke, *Tanzania* 4°17′ S, 34°9′ E 224
Sekhira, *Tun.* 34°21′ N, 10°4′ E 156
Sekikawa, *Japan* 38°5′ N, 139°33′ E 201
Sekiu, *Wash., U.S.* 48°14′ N, 124°20′ W 100
Sekondi-Takoradi, *Ghana* 4°58′ N, 1°45′ W 222
Sekseūil, *Kaz.* 47°4′ N, 61°9′ E 184
Sekulići, *Mont.* 42°33′ N, 19°9′ E 168
Sela Dingay, *Eth.* 9°55′ N, 39°37′ E 224
Selama, *Malaysia* 5°12′ N, 100°43′ E 196
Selaru, island, *Indonesia* 8°39′ S, 130°27′ E 192
Selatpampang, *Indonesia* 0°13′ N, 109°8′ E 196
Selawik, *Alas., U.S.* 66°28′ N, 160°0′ W 98
Selayar, island, *Indonesia* 6°45′ S, 119°37′ E 192
Selby, *S. Dak., U.S.* 45°30′ N, 100°3′ W 90
Selby, *U.K.* 53°47′ N, 1°4′ W 162
Selce, *Maced.* 42°3′ N, 20°55′ E 168
Selden, *Kans., U.S.* 39°32′ N, 100°34′ W 90
Selden, *N.Y., U.S.* 40°52′ N, 73°3′ W 104
Seldovia, *Alas., U.S.* 59°19′ N, 151°43′ W 98
Selebi Phikwe, *Botswana* 21°59′ S, 27°52′ E 227
Selečka Planina, *Maced.* 41°14′ N, 21°7′ E 156
Selendi, *Turk.* 38°46′ N, 28°51′ E 156
Selenge, adm. division, *Mongolia* 49°12′ N, 105°4′ E 198
Selenge, river, *Mongolia* 48°15′ N, 99°37′ E 172
Selenge, river, *Mongolia* 49°25′ N, 103°10′ E 190
Sélestat, *Fr.* 48°16′ N, 7°27′ E 163
Seleucia see Samandağı, *Turk.* 36°4′ N, 35°57′ E 156
Selevac, *Serb.* 44°29′ N, 20°52′ E 168
Seleznevo, *Russ.* 60°45′ N, 28°37′ E 166
Selfridge, *N. Dak., U.S.* 46°2′ N, 100°57′ W 90
Selib, *Russ.* 63°47′ N, 48°28′ E 154
Sélibaby, *Mauritania* 15°9′ N, 12°13′ W 222
Seliger, Ozero, lake, *Russ.* 57°16′ N, 32°32′ E 154
Seligman, *Ariz., U.S.* 35°19′ N, 112°52′ W 92
Selima Oasis, *Sudan* 21°22′ N, 29°21′ E 226
Selinde, *Russ.* 57°16′ N, 132°39′ E 173
Selinus, ruin(s), *It.* 37°34′ N, 12°43′ E 156
Selitrennoye, *Russ.* 47°9′ N, 47°23′ E 158
Seliyarovo, *Russ.* 61°17′ N, 70°16′ E 169
Selizharovo, *Russ.* 56°50′ N, 33°38′ E 154
Selje, *Nor.* 62°3′ N, 5°22′ E 152
Selkirk, *Can.* 50°8′ N, 96°54′ W 90
Selkirk Mountains, *Can.* 51°22′ N, 117°56′ W 108
Selles, *Fr.* 47°16′ N, 1°33′ E 150
Sells, *Ariz., U.S.* 31°54′ N, 111°52′ W 92
Sellye, *Hung.* 45°51′ N, 17°51′ E 168
Selma, *Ala., U.S.* 32°24′ N, 87°1′ W 96
Selma, *Calif., U.S.* 36°34′ N, 119°37′ W 100
Selma, *N.C., U.S.* 35°32′ N, 78°18′ W 96
Selmer, *Tenn., U.S.* 35°9′ N, 88°35′ W 96
Selous Game Reserve, *Tanzania* 9°29′ S, 36°6′ E 224
Selous, Mount, peak, *Can.* 62°56′ N, 132°38′ W 98
Sel'tso, *Russ.* 63°19′ N, 41°23′ E 154
Selty, *Russ.* 57°19′ N, 52°8′ E 169
Seluan, island, *Indonesia* 4°1′ N, 107°25′ E 196
Selva, *Arg.* 29°45′ S, 62°3′ W 139
Selvagens, Ilhas (Salvage Islands), *North Atlantic Ocean* 30°18′ N, 16°15′ W 214
Selwyn Mountains, *Can.* 62°26′ N, 129°39′ W 98
Selwyn Range, *Austral.* 21°1′ S, 139°47′ E 230
Selyatyn, *Ukr.* 47°51′ N, 25°11′ E 156
Semarang, *Indonesia* 7°5′ S, 110°15′ E 192
Sembé, *Congo* 1°38′ N, 14°37′ E 218
Sembo, *Eth.* 7°32′ N, 36°37′ E 224
Şemdinli, *Turk.* 37°18′ N, 44°31′ E 195
Semenov, *Russ.* 56°45′ N, 44°35′ E 154
Semepalatinsk see Semey, *Kaz.* 50°23′ N, 80°14′ E 184
Semeru, peak, *Indonesia* 8°5′ S, 112°44′ E 192
Semey (Semepalatinsk), *Kaz.* 50°23′ N, 80°14′ E 184
Semichi Islands, islands, *Alas., U.S.* 52°28′ N, 175°7′ E 160
Sémien, *Côte d'Ivoire* 7°33′ N, 7°9′ W 222
Semiluki, *Russ.* 51°40′ N, 38°58′ E 158
Seminary, *Miss., U.S.* 31°33′ N, 89°29′ W 103
Seminole, *Okla., U.S.* 35°13′ N, 96°41′ W 96
Seminole, *Tex., U.S.* 32°43′ N, 102°38′ W 92
Sémit, spring, *Mali* 16°43′ N, 0°41′ E 222
Semizovac, *Bosn. and Herzg.* 43°55′ N, 18°17′ E 168
Semmé, *Senegal* 15°11′ N, 13°0′ W 222
Semmens Lake, lake, *Can.* 54°57′ N, 94°50′ W 108
Semmering, pass, *Aust.* 47°37′ N, 15°47′ E 168
Semmes, *Ala., U.S.* 30°46′ N, 88°15′ W 103
Semna West, ruin(s), *Sudan* 21°30′ N, 30°49′ E 182
Semnān, *Iran* 35°36′ N, 53°26′ E 180
Semzha, *Russ.* 66°9′ N, 44°11′ E 154
Sen, river, *Cambodia* 13°50′ N, 104°36′ E 202
Sena, *Bol.* 11°31′ S, 67°11′ W 137
Sena, *Mozambique* 17°27′ S, 34°59′ E 224
Sena, *Sp.* 41°42′ N, 3°177′ W 164
Sena Madureira, *Braz.* 9°8′ S, 68°41′ W 137
Senador José Porfírio, *Braz.* 2°39′ S, 51°56′ W 130
Senaja, *Malaysia* 6°50′ N, 117°3′ E 203
Senanga, *Zambia* 16°8′ S, 23°16′ E 220
Senatobia, *Miss., U.S.* 34°37′ N, 89°58′ W 96
Sendai, *Japan* 38°16′ N, 140°53′ E 201
Senden, *Ger.* 51°51′ N, 7°29′ E 167
Sendenhorst, *Ger.* 51°50′ N, 7°49′ E 167
Senec, *Slovakia* 48°13′ N, 17°24′ E 152
Seneca, *Ill., U.S.* 41°19′ N, 88°38′ W 102
Seneca, *Kans., U.S.* 39°48′ N, 96°4′ W 90
Seneca, *Oreg., U.S.* 44°8′ N, 118°58′ W 90
Seneca, *Pa., U.S.* 41°23′ N, 79°42′ W 110
Seneca, *S.C., U.S.* 34°40′ N, 82°58′ W 96
Seneca Rocks, site, *W. Va., U.S.* 38°48′ N, 79°31′ W 82
Senecaville Lake, *Ohio, U.S.* 39°52′ N, 81°41′ W 102
Senegal 15°10′ N, 15°27′ W 214
Sénégal, river, *Africa* 16°36′ N, 15°57′ W 206
Seneki, *Ga.* 42°16′ N, 42°4′ E 195
Senetosa, Punta di, *Fr.* 41°29′ N, 7°54′ E 156
Senftenberg, *Ger.* 51°31′ N, 13°59′ E 152
Sengés, *Braz.* 24°7′ S, 49°29′ W 138
Sengiley, *Russ.* 53°54′ N, 48°47′ E 154
Senguerr, river, *Arg.* 45°3′ S, 71°6′ W 134
Sengwa, river, *Zimb.* 18°24′ S, 28°11′ E 224
Senhor do Bonfim, *Braz.* 10°27′ S, 40°11′ W 132
Senigallia, *It.* 43°42′ N, 13°12′ E 167
Senkobo, *Zambia* 17°38′ S, 25°54′ E 224
Senlin Shan, peak, *China* 43°10′ N, 130°35′ E 200
Senlis, *Fr.* 49°12′ N, 2°35′ E 163
Senmonorom, *Cambodia* 12°37′ N, 107°14′ E 202
Sennar, *Sudan* 13°31′ N, 33°34′ E 182
Senneterre, *Can.* 48°24′ N, 77°16′ W 94
Sénoudébou, *Senegal* 14°21′ N, 12°18′ W 222
Senozero, *Russ.* 66°9′ N, 31°44′ E 154
Sens, *Fr.* 48°11′ N, 3°17′ E 163
Sensuntepeque, *El Salv.* 13°52′ N, 88°38′ W 116
Senta, *Serb.* 45°55′ N, 20°4′ E 168
Sentein, *Fr.* 42°52′ N, 0°55′ E 164
Sentinel, *Okla., U.S.* 35°7′ N, 99°10′ W 96
Sentinel Peak, *Can.* 54°53′ N, 122°4′ W 108
Senyavin Islands, *North Pacific Ocean* 7°29′ N, 156°35′ E 238
Seocheon, *S. Korea* 36°4′ N, 126°43′ E 200
Seogwipo, *S. Korea* 33°18′ N, 126°35′ E 198
Seokjeong, *S. Korea* 34°53′ N, 127°0′ E 200
Seomjin, river, *S. Korea* 35°11′ N, 127°28′ E 200
Seonbong, *N. Korea* 42°20′ N, 130°25′ E 200
Seongnae, *S. Korea* 36°30′ N, 129°26′ E 200
Seoni, *India* 22°5′ N, 79°33′ E 197
Seoni Malwa, *India* 22°27′ N, 77°28′ E 197
Seonsan, *S. Korea* 36°13′ N, 128°19′ E 200
Seosan, *S. Korea* 36°45′ N, 126°26′ E 200
Seoul, *S. Korea* 37°33′ N, 126°54′ E 200
Sepahua, *Peru* 11°7′ S, 73°4′ W 137
Separation Point, *Can.* 53°36′ N, 57°26′ W 111
Sepatini, river, *Braz.* 8°4′ S, 66°6′ W 132
Sept Îles, Les, islands, *English Channel* 48°57′ N, 3°38′ W 150
Sept-Îles, *Can.* 50°11′ N, 66°22′ W 111
Sepupa, *Botswana* 18°48′ S, 22°10′ E 220
Sequim, *Wash., U.S.* 48°3′ N, 123°6′ W 100
Serafimovich, *Russ.* 49°32′ N, 42°41′ E 158
Seraing, *Belg.* 50°35′ N, 5°30′ E 167
Seram, *India* 17°11′ N, 77°18′ E 188
Serang, *Indonesia* 6°13′ S, 106°7′ E 192
Serasan, island, *Indonesia* 2°24′ N, 108°36′ E 196
Seraya, island, *Indonesia* 2°33′ N, 108°11′ E 196
Sërba, *Eth.* 13°12′ N, 40°32′ E 182
Serbia 43°45′ N, 20°29′ E 168
Sercaia, *Rom.* 45°50′ N, 25°9′ E 158
Serdeles see Al 'Uwaynāt, *Lib.* 25°47′ N, 10°33′ E 216
Serdo, *Eth.* 11°54′ N, 41°19′ E 182
Serdobol see Sortavala, *Russ.* 61°42′ N, 30°39′ E 166
Serdobsk, *Russ.* 52°28′ N, 44°13′ E 158
Serebryanka, *Russ.* 57°6′ N, 70°43′ E 169
Serebryansk, *Kaz.* 49°42′ N, 83°21′ E 184
Seredka, *Russ.* 58°8′ N, 28°10′ E 166
Şereflikoçhisar, *Turk.* 38°54′ N, 33°32′ E 156
Seregno, *It.* 45°38′ N, 9°12′ E 167
Seremban, *Malaysia* 2°45′ N, 101°55′ E 196
Serena, *Ill., U.S.* 41°28′ N, 88°44′ W 102
Serengeti National Park, *Tanzania* 2°26′ S, 34°26′ E 224
Serengeti Plain, *Tanzania* 1°51′ S, 35°12′ E 224
Serenje, *Zambia* 13°16′ S, 30°14′ E 224
Serere, *Uganda* 1°29′ N, 33°25′ E 224
Séres, *Gr.* 41°5′ N, 23°31′ E 180
Serg Ozero, lake, *Russ.* 66°45′ N, 36°13′ E 154
Ser'ga, *Russ.* 57°47′ N, 57°1′ E 154
Sergach, *Russ.* 55°31′ N, 45°33′ E 154
Sergeant Robinson, Mount, peak, *Alas., U.S.* 61°33′ N, 148°2′ W 98
Sergeevka, *Kaz.* 53°53′ N, 67°23′ E 184
Sergeyevo, *Russ.* 57°17′ N, 86°6′ E 169
Sergino, *Russ.* 62°37′ N, 65°34′ E 169
Sergipe, adm. division, *Braz.* 9°54′ S, 37°48′ W 132
Sergiyev Posad, *Russ.* 56°19′ N, 38°7′ E 154
Seria, *Brunei* 4°35′ N, 114°25′ E 192
Serian, *Malaysia* 1°3′ N, 110°33′ E 192
Seribudolok, *Indonesia* 2°56′ N, 98°36′ E 196
Sérifontaine, *Fr.* 49°21′ N, 1°46′ E 163
Sérignan, *Fr.* 43°16′ N, 3°15′ E 164
Serik, *Turk.* 36°54′ N, 31°5′ E 156
Seringa, Serra da, *Braz.* 7°31′ S, 51°0′ W 130
Seripe, *Ghana* 8°55′ N, 2°24′ W 222
Serkovo, *Russ.* 66°35′ N, 88°25′ E 169
Sermata, island, *Indonesia* 8°38′ S, 128°59′ E 192
Sermyle, ruin(s), *Gr.* 40°13′ N, 23°27′ E 156
Sernur, *Russ.* 56°57′ N, 49°12′ E 154
Séro, *Mali* 14°49′ N, 11°4′ W 222
Seroglazovka, *Russ.* 46°56′ N, 47°27′ E 158
Serón, *Sp.* 37°19′ N, 2°31′ W 164
Seronera, *Tanzania* 2°28′ S, 34°50′ E 224
Serov, *Russ.* 59°38′ N, 60°37′ E 154
Serowe, *Botswana* 22°23′ S, 26°42′ E 227
Serpent's Mouth 9°50′ N, 62°13′ W 116
Serpukhov, *Russ.* 54°54′ N, 37°22′ E 154
Serra Bonita, *Braz.* 15°16′ S, 46°50′ W 138
Serra da Bocaina National Park, *Braz.* 23°22′ S, 44°57′ W 122
Serra da Canastra National Park, *Braz.* 20°24′ S, 46°53′ W 138
Serra da Capivara National Park, *Braz.* 8°44′ S, 42°32′ W 122
Serra das Araras, *Braz.* 15°34′ S, 45°24′ W 138
Serra do Divisor National Park, *Braz.* 9°11′ S, 73°16′ W 137
Serra do Espinhaço, *Braz.* 17°53′ S, 43°58′ W 138
Serra do Navio, *Braz.* 0°57′ N, 52°5′ W 130
Serra Dourada, *Braz.* 12°45′ S, 43°59′ W 138
Serrado Roncador, *Braz.* 14°7′ S, 53°7′ W 138
Serranía de la Macarena National Park, *Col.* 2°33′ N, 73°56′ W 136
Serranía de La Neblina National Park, *Venez.* 1°4′ N, 66°23′ W 136
Serrano, *Arg.* 34°29′ S, 63°33′ W 139
Serre, river, *Fr.* 49°41′ N, 3°44′ E 163
Serrezuela, *Arg.* 30°39′ S, 65°23′ W 134
Serrinha, *Braz.* 11°40′ S, 39°3′ W 132
Serro, *Braz.* 18°38′ S, 43°25′ W 138
Sertã, *Port.* 39°47′ N, 8°7′ W 150
Sertânia, *Braz.* 8°5′ S, 37°16′ W 132
Sertanópolis, *Braz.* 23°5′ S, 51°6′ W 138
Serti, *Nig.* 7°30′ N, 11°20′ E 222
Serui, *Indonesia* 1°48′ S, 136°11′ E 192
Serule, *Botswana* 21°58′ S, 27°13′ E 227
Sêrxü, *China* 33°0′ N, 98°5′ E 188
Seryesik-Atyraū Qumy, *Kaz.* 46°3′ N, 75°39′ E 184
Sesa, *Dem. Rep. of the Congo* 7°2′ S, 26°7′ E 224
Sese Islands, *Uganda* 0°34′ N, 32°5′ E 224
Seseganaga Lake, *Can.* 49°54′ N, 91°13′ W 94
Sesfontein, *Namibia* 19°10′ S, 13°36′ E 220
Sesheke, *Zambia* 17°28′ S, 24°17′ E 224
Seskar, Ostrov, island, *Russ.* 60°0′ N, 28°26′ E 166

Seskarö, *Sw.* 65°43' N, 23°43' E 152
Sessa, *Angola* 13°57' S, 20°37' E 220
Séssao, spring, *Mali* 16°59' N, 4°5' E 222
Sestino, *It.* 43°43' N, 12°16' E 167
Sesto Calende, *It.* 45°44' N, 8°37' E 167
Sesto Fiorentino, *It.* 43°50' N, 11°12' E 167
Sesto San Giovanni, *It.* 45°32' N, 9°14' E 167
Šeštokai, *Lith.* 54°21' N, 23°26' E 166
Sestola, *It.* 44°13' N, 10°45' E 167
Sestri Ponente, *It.* 44°25' N, 8°52' E 167
Sestroretsk, *Russ.* 60°4' N, 29°55' E 166
Šeta, *Lith.* 55°16' N, 24°13' E 166
Sete, *Angola* 14°56' S, 21°44' E 220
Sète, *Fr.* 43°24' N, 3°40' E 164
Sete Lagoas, *Braz.* 19°27' S, 44°16' W 138
Sete Quedas, Cachoeira das, fall(s), *Braz.* 9°42' S, 56°32' W 130
Setenil, *Sp.* 36°51' N, 5°11' W 164
Setesdal, region, *Nor.* 58°58' N, 7°4' E 152
Sétif, *Alg.* 36°13' N, 5°25' E 150
Setit, river, *Africa* 14°20' N, 37°5' E 182
Seto, *Japan* 35°10' N, 137°6' E 201
Setonaikai National Park, *Japan* 34°16' N, 134°16' E 201
Settat, *Mor.* 33°2' N, 7°38' W 214
Setté Cama, *Gabon* 2°32' S, 9°46' E 218
Settle, *U.K.* 54°4' N, 2°16' W 162
Setúbal, *Port.* 38°31' N, 8°54' W 150
Setúbal, adm. division, *Port.* 38°28' N, 8°42' W 150
Seul Choix Point, *Mich., U.S.* 45°39' N, 86°8' W 110
Seul, Lac, lake, *Can.* 50°33' N, 93°10' W 80
Seulimeum, *Indonesia* 5°21' N, 95°33' E 202
Seumanyam, *Indonesia* 3°47' N, 96°37' E 196
Sevan, *Arm.* 40°33' N, 44°56' E 195
Sevan National Park, *Arm.* 40°21' N, 45°12' E 195
Sevana Lich, lake, *Arm.* 40°14' N, 45°15' E 195
Sevar, *Bulg.* 43°50' N, 26°36' E 156
Sevaruyo, *Bol.* 19°26' S, 66°53' W 137
Sevastopol', *Ukr.* 44°34' N, 33°28' E 156
Seven Heads, *Ire.* 51°22' N, 8°41' W 150
Seven Sisters Peaks, *Can.* 54°56' N, 128°18' W 108
Seven Stones, islands, *Celtic Sea* 50°5' N, 7°11' W 150
Seven Troughs Range, *Nev., U.S.* 40°36' N, 118°57' W 90
Sevenoaks, *U.K.* 51°16' N, 0°11' E 162
Severn y ye Uvaly, *Russ.* 59°38' N, 46°36' E 169
Severnaya Dvina, river, *Russ.* 64°32' N, 43°16' E 154
Severnaya Osetiya-Alaniya (North Ossetia), adm. division, *Russ.* 42°59' N, 43°49' E 195
Severnaya, river, *Russ.* 63°21' N, 41°46' E 154
Severnaya, river, *Russ.* 63°21' N, 40°44' E 246
Severnaya Zemlya (North Land), islands, *Russ.* 80°22' N, 102°0' E 160
Severnoye, *Russ.* 56°21' N, 78°15' E 169
Severnoye Ust'ye, *Russ.* 57°34' N, 30°16' E 166
Severnyy, *Russ.* 67°39' N, 64°18' E 169
Severnyy Kommunar, *Russ.* 58°21' N, 54°4' E 154
Severnyy Mayak, *Russ.* 65°19' N, 43°39' E 154
Severnyye Uvaly, *Russ.* 60°56' N, 51°45' E 154
Severo Kuril'sk, *Russ.* 50°35' N, 155°59' E 160
Severo Yeniseyskiy, *Russ.* 60°23' N, 93°13' E 169
Severobaykal'sk, *Russ.* 55°49' N, 109°7' E 190
Severodvinsk, *Russ.* 64°34' N, 39°52' E 154
Severomuysk, *Russ.* 56°20' N, 113°25' E 190
Severoural'sk, *Russ.* 60°10' N, 59°55' E 154
Seversk, *Russ.* 56°39' N, 84°51' E 169
Sevettijärvi, *Fin.* 69°32' N, 28°35' E 152
Sevier Desert, *Utah, U.S.* 39°38' N, 113°0' W 90
Sevier, river, *Utah, U.S.* 38°27' N, 112°24' W 80
Sevilla, *Col.* 4°14' N, 75°57' W 136
Sevilla, *Sp.* 37°22' N, 5°58' W 214
Sevilla (Seville), *Sp.* 37°23' N, 6°0' W 164
Seville, *Fla., U.S.* 29°18' N, 81°29' W 105
Seville see Sevilla, *Sp.* 37°23' N, 6°0' W 164
Sevnica, *Slov.* 46°0' N, 15°18' E 156
Sevsk, *Russ.* 52°7' N, 34°30' E 158
Seward, *Alas., U.S.* 60°2' N, 149°33' W 98
Seward, *Nebr., U.S.* 40°53' N, 97°6' W 90
Seward Peninsula, *Alas., U.S.* 67°2' N, 167°43' W 160
Seward Peninsula, *Alas., U.S.* 65°17' N, 165°10' W 98
Sexsmith, *Can.* 55°20' N, 118°47' W 108
Sexton Mountain Pass, *Oreg., U.S.* 42°34' N, 123°25' W 90
Seyakha, *Russ.* 70°8' N, 72°28' E 169
Seychelles 8°7' S, 51°26' E 173
Seydi, *Turkm.* 39°25' N, 62°55' E 184
Seydişehir, *Turk.* 37°24' N, 31°51' E 156
Seyitgazi, *Turk.* 39°27' N, 30°41' E 156
Seym, river, *Russ.* 51°24' N, 36°36' E 158
Seym, river, *Ukr.* 51°19' N, 33°0' E 158
Seymchan, *Russ.* 62°55' N, 152°12' E 160
Seymour, *Conn., U.S.* 41°23' N, 73°5' W 104
Seymour, *Ind., U.S.* 38°57' N, 85°54' W 102
Seymour, *Tex., U.S.* 33°34' N, 99°16' W 92
Seymour, *Wis., U.S.* 44°30' N, 88°20' W 94
Seymour Island, *Antarctica* 64°25' S, 56°33' W 134
Seyne, *Fr.* 44°21' N, 6°19' E 167
Sézanne, *Fr.* 48°43' N, 3°44' E 163
Sfax, *Tun.* 34°48' N, 10°46' E 156
Sferracavallo, Capo, *It.* 39°44' N, 9°42' E 156
Sfîntu Gheorghe, *Rom.* 45°52' N, 25°47' E 156
Sfizef, *Alg.* 35°13' N, 0°15' E 150
Sha, river, *China* 26°5' N, 117°4' E 198
Shaanxi, adm. division, *China* 37°13' N, 107°48' E 198
Shabasha, *Sudan* 14°7' N, 32°11' E 226
Shabla, *Bulg.* 43°33' N, 28°32' E 156
Shabla, Nos, *Bulg.* 43°34' N, 28°38' E 156
Shabogamo Lake, *Can.* 53°13' N, 67°3' W 111
Shabunda, *Dem. Rep. of the Congo* 2°41' S, 27°19' E 224
Shaburovo, *Russ.* 59°40' N, 62°8' E 154
Shabwah, *Yemen* 15°21' N, 47°5' E 182
Shache (Yarkant), *China* 38°27' N, 77°17' E 184
Shackleton Base (historic), site, *Weddell Sea* 78°21' S, 37°47' W 248
Shackleton Coast, *Antarctica* 82°30' S, 179°30' E 248
Shadehill Reservoir, lake, *S. Dak., U.S.* 45°46' N, 102°37' W 90
Shadrinsk, *Russ.* 56°5' N, 63°40' E 184
Shaduzup, *Myanmar* 25°56' N, 96°40' E 188
Shadyside, *Ohio, U.S.* 39°57' N, 80°46' W 94
Sha'f, *Syr.* 32°36' N, 36°50' E 194
Shafer Peak, *Antarctica* 73°56' S, 163°9' E 248
Shafter, *Calif., U.S.* 35°30' N, 119°18' W 100
Shaftesbury, *U.K.* 51°0' N, 2°12' W 162
Shaftsbury, *Vt., U.S.* 43°0' N, 73°12' W 104
Shag Rocks, islands, *Scotia Sea* 54°7' S, 42°46' W 134
Shagamu, *Nig.* 7°0' N, 3°37' E 222
Shaghan, *Kaz.* 50°34' N, 79°13' E 184
Shah Bandar, *Pak.* 24°10' N, 67°58' E 186
Shah Juy, *Afghan.* 32°31' N, 67°28' E 186
Shah Malan, *Afghan.* 31°11' N, 64°5' E 186
Shahabad, *India* 27°38' N, 79°54' E 197
Shahabad, *India* 25°16' N, 77°10' E 197
Shahbā' (Philippopolis), *Syr.* 32°51' N, 36°37' E 194
Shahdadkot, *Pak.* 27°51' N, 67°55' E 186
Shahdol, *India* 23°18' N, 81°22' E 197
Shahgarh, *India* 27°6' N, 69°58' E 186
Sha''āt (Cyrene), *Lib.* 32°50' N, 21°50' E 216
Shahimardan, *Uzb.* 39°56' N, 71°45' E 197
Shāhīn Dezh, *Iran* 36°46' N, 46°35' E 195
Shahjahanpur, *India* 27°51' N, 79°54' E 197
Shahpur, *Pak.* 28°42' N, 68°22' E 186
Shahpura, *India* 23°11' N, 80°43' E 197
Shahrak, *Afghan.* 34°11' N, 64°24' E 186
Shahr-e Bābak, *Iran* 30°7' N, 55°9' E 196
Shahr-e Kord, *Iran* 32°19' N, 50°51' E 180
Shahr-e Monjan, *Afghan.* 36°2' N, 70°58' E 186
Shahrezā, *Iran* 32°1' N, 51°51' E 180
Shahrisabz, *Uzb.* 39°5' N, 66°51' E 197
Shahriston, *Taj.* 39°46' N, 68°52' E 197
Shahrtuz, *Taj.* 37°14' N, 68°9' E 186
Shāhrūd, *Iran* 36°27' N, 54°59' E 180
Shaim, *Russ.* 60°15' N, 64°16' E 169
Shajapur, *India* 23°24' N, 76°16' E 197
Shakawe, *Botswana* 18°25' S, 21°48' E 220
Shaker Heights, *Ohio, U.S.* 41°26' N, 81°34' W 102
Shakespeare Cliff, *U.K.* 51°6' N, 1°21' E 163
Shakhbuz, *Asia* 39°24' N, 45°34' E 195
Shakhtakhty, *Asia* 39°19' N, 45°7' E 195
Shakhtīnsk, *Kaz.* 49°44' N, 72°37' E 184
Shakhty, *Russ.* 47°40' N, 40°9' E 156
Shakhun'ya, *Russ.* 57°39' N, 46°41' E 154
Shaki, *Nig.* 8°40' N, 3°23' E 222
Shâkir, Gezîrat, island, *Egypt* 27°25' N, 32°57' E 180
Shalaamboot, *Somalia* 1°38' N, 44°41' E 218
Shalakusha, *Russ.* 62°11' N, 40°18' E 154
Shalë, *Alban.* 42°18' N, 19°48' E 168
Shali, *Russ.* 43°6' N, 45°52' E 195
Shaling, *China* 41°19' N, 123°5' E 200
Shalkar Yega Kara, Ozero, lake, *Russ.* 50°39' N, 59°7' E 158
Shallowater, *Tex., U.S.* 33°41' N, 101°59' W 92
Shalqar, *Kaz.* 50°29' N, 51°49' E 158
Shalqar, *Kaz.* 47°50' N, 59°39' E 158
Shalqar Köli, lake, *Kaz.* 50°35' N, 51°20' E 158
Shalqīya, *Kaz.* 47°15' N, 70°38' E 184
Shal'skiy, *Russ.* 61°48' N, 36°4' E 154
Shām, Jabal ash, peak, *Oman* 23°10' N, 57°11' E 182
Shamattawa, *Can.* 55°59' N, 91°53' W 106
Shambe, *Sudan* 7°5' N, 30°43' E 224
Shamīl, *Iran* 27°28' N, 56°53' E 196
Shamkhor, *Azerb.* 40°49' N, 46°0' E 195
Shammar, Jabal, *Saudi Arabia* 27°8' N, 40°8' E 180
Shamokin, *Pa., U.S.* 40°47' N, 76°34' W 94
Shamrock, *Fla., U.S.* 29°38' N, 83°11' W 105
Shamrock, *Tex., U.S.* 35°12' N, 100°15' W 92
Shamva, *Zimb.* 17°21' S, 31°34' E 224
Shanchengzhen, *China* 42°22' N, 125°27' E 200
Shandon, *Calif., U.S.* 35°39' N, 120°24' W 100
Shandong, adm. division, *China* 36°25' N, 116°37' E 198
Shandur Pass, *Pak.* 36°3' N, 72°31' E 186
Shangalowe, *Dem. Rep. of the Congo* 10°50' S, 26°30' E 224
Shangaly, *Russ.* 61°8' N, 43°18' E 154
Shangani, *Zimb.* 19°48' S, 29°21' E 224
Shangcai, *China* 33°17' N, 114°17' E 198
Shangcheng, *China* 31°48' N, 115°23' E 198
Shangchuan Dao, island, *China* 21°31' N, 112°51' E 198
Shangdu, *China* 41°35' N, 113°33' E 198
Shanghai, *China* 31°15' N, 121°27' E 198
Shanghang, *China* 24°58' N, 116°21' E 198
Shanghekou, *China* 40°25' N, 124°49' E 200
Shanglin, *China* 23°29' N, 108°35' E 198
Shangnan, *China* 33°32' N, 110°55' E 198
Shangombo, *Zambia* 16°20' S, 22°7' E 220
Shangqiu, *China* 34°27' N, 115°34' E 198
Shangrao, *China* 28°27' N, 117°56' E 198
Shangri-La, *China* 27°52' N, 99°40' E 190
Shangsi, *China* 22°12' N, 107°57' E 198
Shangxian, *China* 33°55' N, 109°56' E 198
Shangyi, *China* 41°5' N, 113°58' E 198
Shangyou, *China* 25°50' N, 114°30' E 198
Shangyou Shuiku, lake, *China* 40°24' N, 79°49' E 184
Shangzhi, *China* 45°12' N, 127°53' E 198
Shani, *Nig.* 10°12' N, 12°5' E 218
Shanidar Cave, ruin(s), *Iraq* 36°48' N, 44°8' E 195
Shaniko, *Oreg., U.S.* 44°59' N, 120°46' W 90
Shannock, *R.I., U.S.* 41°26' N, 71°39' W 104
Shannon, *Ill., U.S.* 42°8' N, 89°44' W 102
Shannon, *Ire.* 52°52' N, 8°49' W 143
Shannon, *Miss., U.S.* 34°6' N, 88°43' W 96
Shannon, *N.Z.* 40°35' S, 175°25' E 240
Shannon Airport, *Ire.* 52°40' N, 9°8' W 150
Shannon, island, *Shannon* 75°18' N, 17°23' W 246
Shannon, Lake, *Wash., U.S.* 48°35' N, 121°58' W 100
Shantarskiye Ostrova, islands, *Russ.* 54°31' N, 138°48' E 160
Shantou (Swatow), *China* 23°23' N, 116°40' E 198
Shanwa, *Tanzania* 3°8' S, 33°45' E 224
Shanxi, adm. division, *China* 38°43' N, 111°16' E 198
Shanxian, *China* 34°49' N, 116°5' E 198
Shanyang, *China* 33°33' N, 109°54' E 198
Shanyin, *China* 39°29' N, 112°51' E 198
Shanyincheng, *China* 39°24' N, 112°56' E 198
Shaoguan, *China* 24°52' N, 113°32' E 198
Shaowu, *China* 27°14' N, 117°27' E 198
Shaoxing, *China* 29°59' N, 120°34' E 198
Shaoyang, *China* 27°15' N, 111°29' E 198
Shap, *U.K.* 54°32' N, 2°41' W 162
Shapa, *China* 21°32' N, 111°28' E 198
Shapleigh, *Me., U.S.* 43°33' N, 70°52' W 104
Shaqlāwah, *Iraq* 36°24' N, 44°16' E 195
Shaqqā, *Syr.* 32°53' N, 36°41' E 194
Shaqrā', *Saudi Arabia* 25°12' N, 45°18' E 182
Shaqrā', *Yemen* 13°24' N, 45°41' E 182
Shar, *Kaz.* 49°37' N, 81°1' E 184
Shār, Jabal, peak, *Saudi Arabia* 27°36' N, 35°40' E 180
Shar Space Launch Center, spaceport, *India* 13°36' N, 80°5' E 188
Sharafkhāneh, *Iran* 38°17' N, 45°26' E 195
Sharbaqty, *Kaz.* 52°30' N, 78°11' E 184
Sharbatāt, *Oman* 17°53' N, 56°18' E 182
Shardara, *Kaz.* 41°16' N, 67°54' E 197
Sharg'un, *Uzb.* 38°21' N, 68°0' E 197
Sharhulsan, *Mongolia* 44°37' N, 104°1' E 198
Sharjah, *U.A.E.* 25°21' N, 55°24' E 196
Shark Bay 25°46' S, 113°18' E 230
Sharkan, *Russ.* 57°15' N, 53°54' E 154
Sharkowshchyna, *Belarus* 55°22' N, 27°24' E 166
Sharlawuk, *Turkm.* 38°14' N, 55°42' E 180
Sharlyk, *Russ.* 52°55' N, 54°46' E 154
Sharon, *Conn., U.S.* 41°52' N, 73°29' W 104
Sharon, *Mass., U.S.* 42°7' N, 71°11' W 104
Sharon, *Pa., U.S.* 41°13' N, 80°31' W 94
Sharon, *Vt., U.S.* 43°47' N, 72°28' W 104
Sharon, *Wis., U.S.* 42°30' N, 88°44' W 102
Sharon Springs, *Kans., U.S.* 38°53' N, 101°46' W 90
Sharp Top, peak, *Oreg., U.S.* 42°50' N, 120°34' W 90
Sharpe, Lake, *S. Dak., U.S.* 43°9' N, 99°14' W 80
Sharr Mountains National Park, *Kosovo* 42°7' N, 20°50' E 168
Sharuhen, ruin(s), *Israel* 31°15' N, 34°26' E 194
Shar'ya, *Russ.* 58°20' N, 45°34' E 154
Sharypovo, *Russ.* 55°34' N, 89°15' E 169
Shasha, *Eth.* 6°28' N, 35°55' E 224
Shashe, river, *Africa* 21°47' S, 28°27' E 227
Shashemenē, *Eth.* 7°12' N, 38°32' E 224
Shashi, *China* 30°22' N, 112°18' E 198
Shass Mountain, peak, *Can.* 54°25' N, 124°58' W 108
Shasta, Mount, peak, *Calif., U.S.* 41°24' N, 122°18' W 90
Shatsk, *Belarus* 53°25' N, 27°42' E 152
Shatsk, *Russ.* 54°0' N, 41°39' E 154
Shats'k, *Ukr.* 51°27' N, 23°54' E 152
Shatskiy Rise, *North Pacific Ocean* 34°16' N, 160°36' E 252
Shattuck, *Okla., U.S.* 36°15' N, 99°53' W 92
Shatura, *Russ.* 55°33' N, 39°31' E 154
Shaumyani, *Ga.* 41°20' N, 44°44' E 195
Shaunavon, *Can.* 49°37' N, 108°26' W 90
Shaver Lake, *Calif., U.S.* 37°6' N, 119°20' W 100
Shaverki, *Russ.* 63°14' N, 31°27' E 154
Shaviklde, peak, *Ga.* 42°14' N, 45°35' E 195
Shaw, *Miss., U.S.* 33°35' N, 90°47' W 96
Shaw Air Force Base, *S.C., U.S.* 33°57' N, 80°33' W 96
Shaw Island, *Austral.* 20°22' S, 149°7' E 230
Shawan, *China* 44°20' N, 85°39' E 184
Shawano, *Wis., U.S.* 44°46' N, 88°37' W 94
Shawinigan, *Can.* 46°33' N, 72°46' W 94
Shawnee, *Ohio, U.S.* 39°35' N, 82°13' W 102
Shawnee, *Wyo., U.S.* 42°44' N, 105°1' W 90
Shawnigan Lake, *Can.* 48°38' N, 123°37' W 100
Shaxian, *China* 26°24' N, 117°44' E 198
Shaxrixon, *Uzb.* 40°41' N, 72°4' E 197
Shaybah, oil field, *Saudi Arabia* 22°23' N, 53°55' E 182
Shaybārā, island, *Saudi Arabia* 25°25' N, 36°3' E 182
Shâyib el Banât, Gebel, peak, *Egypt* 26°58' N, 33°22' E 180
Shaykh, Jabal ash (Hermon, Mount), peak, *Leb.* 33°24' N, 35°49' E 194
Shaykh Miskīn, *Syr.* 32°50' N, 36°10' E 194
Shaykh 'Uthmān, *Yemen* 12°52' N, 44°59' E 182
Shaymak, *Taj.* 37°29' N, 74°51' E 184
Shayrāt, *Syr.* 34°29' N, 36°57' E 194
Shaytanovka, *Russ.* 62°2' N, 58°6' E 154
Shchekino, *Russ.* 53°59' N, 37°33' E 154
Shchel'yabozh, *Russ.* 66°17' N, 56°23' E 154
Shchel'yayur, *Russ.* 65°18' N, 53°26' E 154
Shchigry, *Russ.* 51°49' N, 36°57' E 158
Shchuch'ye, *Russ.* 67°6' N, 68°36' E 169
Shchūchīnsk, *Kaz.* 52°52' N, 70°14' E 184
Shchurovo, *Russ.* 55°1' N, 38°49' E 154
Shchurovychi, *Ukr.* 50°16' N, 25°0' E 152
Shchyrets', *Ukr.* 49°38' N, 23°50' E 152
Shchytkavichy, *Belarus* 53°13' N, 27°58' E 154
Shebar, Kowtal-e, pass, *Afghan.* 34°57' N, 68°9' E 186
Shebekino, *Russ.* 50°24' N, 36°56' E 158
Shebele, river, *Eth.* 5°47' N, 42°0' E 207
Sheberghan, *Afghan.* 36°40' N, 65°46' E 186
Sheboya, *Peru* 9°59' S, 74°8' W 137
Sheboygan, *Wis., U.S.* 43°45' N, 87°44' W 102
Shediac, *Can.* 46°12' N, 64°32' W 111
Shedin Peak, *Can.* 55°56' N, 127°36' W 108
Shedok, *Russ.* 44°12' N, 40°44' E 158
Sheenjek, river, *Alas., U.S.* 66°50' N, 144°27' W 98
Sheep Hole Mountains, *Calif., U.S.* 34°21' N, 115°45' W 101
Sheep Mountain, peak, *Colo., U.S.* 39°54' N, 107°13' W 90
Sheep Mountain, peak, *Mont., U.S.* 45°4' N, 110°46' W 90
Sheep Peak, *Nev., U.S.* 36°34' N, 115°18' W 101
Sheep Range, *Nev., U.S.* 36°44' N, 115°13' W 101
Sheepeater Mountain, peak, *Idaho, U.S.* 45°22' N, 115°25' W 90
Sheep's Head, *Ire.* 51°22' N, 10°11' W 150
Sheerness, *U.K.* 51°25' N, 0°45' E 162
Sheet Harbour, *Can.* 44°56' N, 62°32' W 111
Sheffield, *Ala., U.S.* 34°45' N, 87°41' W 96
Sheffield, *Ill., U.S.* 41°21' N, 89°44' W 102
Sheffield, *Mass., U.S.* 42°6' N, 73°22' W 104
Sheffield, *Tex., U.S.* 30°40' N, 101°49' W 92
Sheffield, *U.K.* 53°22' N, 1°28' W 162
Sheguiandah, *Can.* 45°54' N, 81°55' W 94
Sheikh Idris, *Sudan* 11°45' N, 33°28' E 182
Sheksna, *Russ.* 59°11' N, 38°29' E 154
Shelagskiy, Mys, *Russ.* 69°48' N, 174°42' E 160
Shelburn, *Ind., U.S.* 39°10' N, 87°24' W 102
Shelburne, *Can.* 43°44' N, 65°20' W 111
Shelburne, *Vt., U.S.* 44°22' N, 73°15' W 104
Shelburne Falls, *Vt., U.S.* 44°21' N, 73°13' W 104
Shelby, *Ind., U.S.* 41°11' N, 87°21' W 102
Shelby, *Mich., U.S.* 43°36' N, 86°21' W 102
Shelby, *Mont., U.S.* 48°28' N, 111°51' W 90
Shelby, *Ohio, U.S.* 40°51' N, 82°39' W 102
Shelbyville, *Ill., U.S.* 39°23' N, 88°48' W 102
Shelbyville, *Ind., U.S.* 39°30' N, 85°46' W 102
Shelbyville, *Tex., U.S.* 31°44' N, 94°5' W 103
Sheldon, *Ill., U.S.* 40°45' N, 87°34' W 102
Sheldon, *Iowa, U.S.* 43°10' N, 95°51' W 94
Sheldrake, *Can.* 50°16' N, 64°54' W 111
Shelikhova, Zaliv 61°11' N, 158°34' E 160
Shelikof Strait 58°3' N, 154°5' W 98
Shell Beach, *Guyana* 8°8' N, 59°42' W 116
Shell Lake, *Can.* 53°17' N, 107°1' W 108
Shell Lake, *Wis., U.S.* 45°44' N, 91°57' W 94
Shell Mountain, peak, *Calif., U.S.* 40°5' N, 123°10' W 90
Shellbrook, *Can.* 53°13' N, 106°24' W 108
Shellem, *Nig.* 9°57' N, 12°2' E 218
Shellman, *Ga., U.S.* 31°45' N, 84°37' W 96
Shellrock Peak, *Idaho, U.S.* 44°56' N, 115°1' W 90
Shelokhovskaya, *Russ.* 61°54' N, 39°3' E 154
Shelter Island, *N.Y., U.S.* 41°3' N, 72°21' W 104
Shelton, *Conn., U.S.* 41°18' N, 73°6' W 104
Shelton, *Wash., U.S.* 47°11' N, 123°7' W 100
Sheltozero, *Russ.* 61°20' N, 35°25' E 154
Shemakha, *Azerb.* 40°37' N, 48°37' E 195
Shemonaīkha, *Kaz.* 50°38' N, 81°55' E 184
Shëmri, *Alban.* 42°6' N, 20°13' E 168
Shenandoah, *Pa., U.S.* 40°49' N, 76°13' W 94
Shenandoah Mountain, *Va., U.S.* 38°29' N, 79°32' W 94
Shenandoah National Park, *Va., U.S.* 37°29' N, 79°36' W 80
Shenchi, *China* 39°4' N, 112°10' E 198
Shendam, *Nig.* 8°53' N, 9°29' E 222
Shendi, *Sudan* 16°39' N, 33°24' E 182
Shenge, *Sierra Leone* 7°54' N, 12°57' W 222
Shëngjin, *Alban.* 41°49' N, 19°34' E 168
Shengli Daban, pass, *China* 43°6' N, 86°48' E 184
Shengxian, *China* 29°39' N, 120°44' E 198
Shenkursk, *Russ.* 62°4' N, 42°58' E 154
Shenmu, *China* 38°51' N, 110°31' E 198
Shennongjia, *China* 31°44' N, 110°45' E 198
Shenqiu, *China* 33°27' N, 115°6' E 198
Shenton, Mount, peak, *Austral.* 28°1' S, 123°11' E 230
Shenyang, *China* 41°49' N, 123°28' E 200
Shenzhen, *China* 22°34' N, 114°7' E 198
Sheopur, *India* 25°41' N, 76°43' E 197
Shepard Island, *Antarctica* 73°49' S, 134°36' W 248
Shepetivka, *Ukr.* 50°10' N, 27°4' E 152
Shepherd, *Mich., U.S.* 43°30' N, 84°42' W 102
Shepherd, *Tex., U.S.* 30°29' N, 94°59' W 103
Shepparton, *Austral.* 36°23' S, 145°27' E 231
Sherada, *Eth.* 7°17' N, 36°29' E 224
Sherborne, *U.K.* 50°56' N, 2°31' W 162
Sherbro Island, *Sierra Leone* 7°8' N, 12°52' W 222
Sherbrooke, *Can.* 45°24' N, 71°56' W 94
Sherburn, *Minn., U.S.* 43°38' N, 94°44' W 90
Sherda, spring, *Chad* 20°10' N, 16°43' E 216
Shereiq, *Sudan* 18°44' N, 33°36' E 182
Sherghati, *India* 24°33' N, 84°49' E 197
Shergui Island, *Tun.* 34°39' N, 11°21' E 216
Sheridan, *Ill., U.S.* 41°31' N, 88°41' W 102
Sheridan, *Ind., U.S.* 40°7' N, 86°13' W 102
Sheridan, *Mich., U.S.* 43°12' N, 85°5' W 102
Sheridan, *Wyo., U.S.* 44°47' N, 106°56' W 90
Sheridan, Cape, *Can.* 81°51' N, 73°43' W 246
Sheringham, *U.K.* 52°56' N, 1°12' E 162
Sherkaly, *Russ.* 62°48' N, 65°41' E 169
Sherman, *Me., U.S.* 45°51' N, 68°25' W 94
Sherman, *Tex., U.S.* 33°37' N, 96°36' W 96
Sherman Island, island, *Antarctica* 72°20' S, 100°58' W 248
Sherman Mountain, peak, *Nev., U.S.* 40°6' N, 115°40' W 90
Sherman Peak, *Calif., U.S.* 36°0' N, 118°26' W 101
Sherman Peak, *Idaho, U.S.* 42°28' N, 111°38' W 90
Sherman Peak, *Idaho, U.S.* 44°31' N, 114°44' W 90
Sherobod, *Uzb.* 37°39' N, 67°1' E 197
Sherridon, *Can.* 55°6' N, 101°6' W 108
Sherwood, *N. Dak., U.S.* 48°57' N, 101°40' W 108
Sherwood Forest, *U.K.* 53°14' N, 1°13' W 162
Sherwood Lake, *Can.* 60°48' N, 104°14' W 108
Sherwood Peak, *Calif., U.S.* 39°30' N, 123°36' W 90
Sheshea, river, *Peru* 9°26' S, 73°51' W 137
Sheslay, river, *Can.* 58°27' N, 132°15' W 108

Shestakovo, *Russ.* 58°55′ N, 50°9′ E 154
Shethanei Lake, *Can.* 58°47′ N, 98°24′ W 108
Shetland Islands, *North Atlantic Ocean* 61°2′ N, 3°52′ W 72
Shetlands Islands, *U.K.* 60°53′ N, 3°18′ W 142
Shetpe, *Kaz.* 44°9′ N, 52°6′ E 158
Shetrunja, peak, *India* 21°26′ N, 71°41′ E 186
Shewa Gīmīra, *Eth.* 6°59′ N, 35°49′ E 224
Shexian, *China* 29°52′ N, 118°26′ E 198
Sheyang, *China* 33°45′ N, 120°15′ E 198
Sheyenne, *N. Dak., U.S.* 47°48′ N, 99°8′ W 90
Sheyenne, river, *N. Dak., U.S.* 47°40′ N, 98°56′ W 90
Sheyenne, river, *N. Dak., U.S.* 46°26′ N, 97°38′ W 90
Sheykhabad, *Afghan.* 34°6′ N, 68°45′ E 186
Sh'īm, *Leb.* 33°38′ N, 35°29′ E 194
Shibām, *Yemen* 15°54′ N, 48°36′ E 182
Shibata, *Japan* 37°57′ N, 139°20′ E 201
Shibîn el Kôm, *Egypt* 30°34′ N, 30°57′ E 180
Shibing, *China* 27°0′ N, 108°4′ E 198
Shibukawa, *Japan* 36°29′ N, 138°59′ E 201
Shibushi, *Japan* 31°27′ N, 131°5′ E 201
Shicheng, *China* 26°21′ N, 116°16′ E 198
Shidao, *China* 36°55′ N, 122°25′ E 198
Shiderti, *Kaz.* 51°40′ N, 74°27′ E 184
Shidler, *Okla., U.S.* 36°45′ N, 96°40′ W 92
Shiega, *Ghana* 10°42′ N, 0°44′ E 222
Shīeli, *Kaz.* 44°9′ N, 66°44′ E 184
Shi'erdaogou, *China* 41°30′ N, 127°35′ E 200
Shifnal, *U.K.* 52°39′ N, 2°22′ W 162
Shiga, *Japan* 37°1′ N, 136°46′ E 201
Shiga, adm. division, *Japan* 35°12′ N, 135°52′ E 201
Shiguai, *China* 40°42′ N, 110°17′ E 198
Shi'an, *Yemen* 17°41′ N, 52°27′ E 182
Shihezi, *China* 44°17′ N, 86°1′ E 184
Shiikh, *Somalia* 9°55′ N, 45°12′ E 216
Shijiazhuang, *China* 38°5′ N, 114°30′ E 198
Shikag Lake, lake, *Can.* 49°41′ N, 91°15′ W 94
Shikarpur, *Pak.* 27°53′ N, 68°42′ E 186
Shikoku, island, *Japan* 32°22′ N, 133°0′ E 190
Shilabo, *Eth.* 6°5′ N, 44°45′ E 218
Shildon, *U.K.* 54°38′ N, 1°40′ W 162
Shīli, *Kaz.* 50°34′ N, 62°34′ E 184
Shiliguri, *India* 26°43′ N, 88°28′ E 190
Shilik, *Kaz.* 43°34′ N, 78°12′ E 184
Shiliu see Changjiang, *China* 19°13′ N, 109°2′ E 198
Shiliyn Bogd Uul, peak, *Mongolia* 45°26′ N, 114°24′ E 198
Shilka, *Russ.* 51°54′ N, 116°0′ E 238
Shilka, river, *Russ.* 52°45′ N, 119°25′ E 190
Shilla, peak, *Nepal* 32°22′ N, 78°4′ E 188
Shillong, *India* 25°32′ N, 91°52′ E 197
Shiloh, ruin(s), *West Bank, Israel* 32°2′ N, 35°15′ E 194
Shilou, *China* 37°2′ N, 110°47′ E 198
Shilovo, *Russ.* 54°17′ N, 40°50′ E 154
Shimabara, *Japan* 32°46′ N, 130°20′ E 201
Shimada, *Japan* 34°50′ N, 138°11′ E 201
Shimane, adm. division, *Japan* 34°32′ N, 131°43′ E 200
Shimanovsk, *Russ.* 52°4′ N, 127°46′ E 190
Shimen, *China* 29°36′ N, 111°24′ E 198
Shimizu, *Japan* 35°0′ N, 138°28′ E 201
Shimminato, *Japan* 36°46′ N, 137°5′ E 201
Shimoda, *Japan* 32°57′ N, 132°58′ E 201
Shimoda, *Japan* 34°41′ N, 138°58′ E 201
Shimoga, *India* 13°55′ N, 75°33′ E 188
Shimokoshiki, *Japan* 31°38′ N, 129°43′ E 201
Shimoni, *Kenya* 4°35′ S, 39°22′ E 224
Shimonoseki, *Japan* 33°58′ N, 130°56′ E 200
Shimotsu, *Japan* 34°7′ N, 135°8′ E 201
Shimozero, *Russ.* 60°29′ N, 35°37′ E 154
Shimsk, *Russ.* 58°13′ N, 30°44′ E 152
Shīn, *Syr.* 34°46′ N, 36°26′ E 194
Shināș, *Oman* 24°45′ N, 56°25′ E 196
Shindand (Sabzawar), *Afghan.* 33°17′ N, 62°11′ E 186
Shiner, *Tex., U.S.* 29°25′ N, 97°11′ W 96
Shingū, *Japan* 33°41′ N, 135°58′ E 201
Shinjō, *Japan* 38°46′ N, 140°18′ E 201
Shinkafi, *Nig.* 13°3′ N, 6°30′ E 222
Shinkay, *Afghan.* 31°54′ N, 67°27′ E 186
Shinkolobwe, *Dem. Rep. of the Congo* 11°3′ S, 26°36′ E 224
Shinnston, *W. Va., U.S.* 39°23′ N, 80°18′ W 94
Shinonoi, *Japan* 36°35′ N, 138°9′ E 201
Shinshār, *Syr.* 34°36′ N, 36°43′ E 194
Shinyanga, *Tanzania* 3°42′ S, 33°26′ E 224
Shinyanga, adm. division, *Tanzania* 3°36′ S, 31°46′ E 224
Shiogama, *Japan* 38°19′ N, 141°0′ E 201
Shiono Misaki, *Japan* 33°17′ N, 135°45′ E 201
Shionomachi, *Japan* 38°19′ N, 139°33′ E 201
Ship Island, *Miss., U.S.* 30°9′ N, 88°55′ W 103
Shiping, *China* 23°41′ N, 102°26′ E 202
Shipitsino, *Russ.* 61°17′ N, 46°32′ E 154
Shipki La, pass, *China* 31°51′ N, 78°43′ E 188
Shipley, *U.K.* 53°49′ N, 1°47′ W 162
Shippagan, *Can.* 47°44′ N, 64°44′ W 94
Shiprock, *N. Mex., U.S.* 36°46′ N, 108°42′ W 82
Shipu, *China* 29°12′ N, 121°52′ E 198
Shipunovo, *Russ.* 52°15′ N, 82°24′ E 184
Shiqian, *China* 27°30′ N, 108°14′ E 198
Shiqiao, *China* 31°21′ N, 107°4′ E 198
Shiqijie, *China* 42°56′ N, 128°29′ E 200
Shiquan, *China* 33°4′ N, 108°15′ E 198
Shiquanhe, *China* 32°29′ N, 79°48′ E 188
Shir Khan, *Afghan.* 37°9′ N, 68°40′ E 186
Shīr Kūh, peak, *Iran* 31°35′ N, 54°0′ E 180
Shirakawa, *Japan* 37°6′ N, 140°12′ E 201
Shirase Coast, *Antarctica* 79°5′ S, 139°50′ W 248
Shirati, *Tanzania* 1°11′ S, 34°0′ E 224
Shīrāz, *Iran* 29°40′ N, 52°29′ E 196
Shirbîn, *Egypt* 31°12′ N, 31°30′ E 180
Shire, river, *Malawi* 16°0′ S, 34°49′ E 224
Shireet, *Mongolia* 45°42′ N, 112°21′ E 198
Shiren, *China* 41°57′ N, 126°38′ E 200
Shiringushi, *Russ.* 53°47′ N, 42°44′ E 154
Shirkent National Park, *Taj.* 38°46′ N, 68°25′ E 197
Shirley, *Ind., U.S.* 39°52′ N, 85°34′ W 102
Shirley, *N.Y., U.S.* 40°48′ N, 72°53′ W 104
Shirley, Mount, peak, *Antarctica* 75°30′ S, 141°18′ W 248
Shirley Mountains, *Wyo., U.S.* 42°8′ N, 106°39′ W 90
Shiroishi, *Japan* 38°0′ N, 140°37′ E 201
Shirone, *Japan* 37°45′ N, 139°0′ E 201
Shirotori, *Japan* 35°52′ N, 136°53′ E 201
Shīrvān, *Iran* 37°27′ N, 57°56′ E 180
Shiryayevo, *Russ.* 59°58′ N, 46°17′ E 154
Shishaldin Volcano, peak, *Alas., U.S.* 54°39′ N, 164°14′ W 98
Shishmaref, *Alas., U.S.* 66°12′ N, 166°3′ W 98
Shishou, *China* 29°39′ N, 112°24′ E 198
Shitai, *China* 30°12′ N, 117°26′ E 198
Shiv, *India* 26°11′ N, 71°17′ E 186
Shivpuri, *India* 25°26′ N, 77°39′ E 197
Shiwa Ngandu, *Zambia* 11°10′ S, 31°44′ E 224
Shixian, *China* 43°5′ N, 129°47′ E 200
Shiyan, *China* 32°39′ N, 110°48′ E 198
Shizhu, *China* 29°59′ N, 108°9′ E 198
Shizui, *China* 43°3′ N, 126°9′ E 200
Shizuishan, *China* 39°19′ N, 106°44′ E 198
Shizuishan (Dawukou), *China* 39°4′ N, 106°25′ E 198
Shizuoka, *Japan* 34°57′ N, 138°23′ E 201
Shizuoka, adm. division, *Japan* 35°4′ N, 137°51′ E 201
Shklow, *Belarus* 54°14′ N, 30°19′ E 154
Shkodër (Scutari), *Alban.* 42°4′ N, 19°30′ E 168
Shkunovka, *Russ.* 50°45′ N, 55°23′ E 158
Shmoylovo, *Russ.* 57°35′ N, 28°52′ E 166
Shoal Lake, *Can.* 50°27′ N, 100°36′ W 90
Shoals, *Ind., U.S.* 38°39′ N, 86°47′ W 102
Shoals, Isles of, islands, *Gulf of Maine* 42°56′ N, 70°34′ W 104
Shoalwater, Cape, *Wash., U.S.* 46°38′ N, 124°24′ W 100
Shōbara, *Japan* 34°50′ N, 133°2′ E 201
Shocha, *Russ.* 63°9′ N, 46°50′ E 154
Shoe Cove Point, *Can.* 48°56′ N, 53°37′ W 111
Shoeburyness, *U.K.* 51°31′ N, 0°47′ E 162
Shokal'skogo, Proliv 78°34′ N, 90°29′ E 160
Sholapur, *India* 17°40′ N, 75°52′ E 188
Shollar, *Azerb.* 41°37′ N, 48°39′ E 195
Shombozero, *Russ.* 65°18′ N, 32°18′ E 152
Shomvukva, *Russ.* 63°41′ N, 51°50′ E 154
Shonga, *Nig.* 9°5′ N, 5°7′ E 222
Shonzhy, *Kaz.* 43°31′ N, 79°28′ E 184
Shoqpar, *Kaz.* 43°49′ N, 74°21′ E 184
Sho'rchi, *Uzb.* 37°42′ N, 67°31′ E 197
Shoreham, *Vt., U.S.* 43°53′ N, 73°19′ W 104
Shoreham by Sea, *U.K.* 50°50′ N, 0°17′ E 162
Shorewood, *Wis., U.S.* 43°4′ N, 87°53′ W 102
Shorobe, *Botswana* 19°46′ S, 23°42′ E 224
Shortland, island, *Solomon Islands* 7°5′ S, 155°40′ E 242
Shortland Islands, *Solomon Sea* 7°0′ S, 155°49′ E 242
Shoshone, *Calif., U.S.* 35°58′ N, 116°17′ W 101
Shoshone Mountains, *Nev., U.S.* 38°54′ N, 117°37′ W 90
Shoshone Range, *Nev., U.S.* 40°34′ N, 116°58′ W 90
Shoshong, *Botswana* 23°1′ S, 26°27′ E 227
Shoshoni, *Wyo., U.S.* 43°14′ N, 108°7′ W 90
Shostka, *Ukr.* 51°49′ N, 33°33′ E 158
Shotor Khun Kowtal, pass, *Afghan.* 34°25′ N, 64°54′ E 186
Shoval, *Israel* 31°24′ N, 34°43′ E 194
Showak, *Sudan* 14°22′ N, 35°46′ E 182
Shoyna, *Russ.* 67°47′ N, 44°12′ E 169
Shpola, *Ukr.* 49°1′ N, 31°32′ E 158
Shreve, *Ohio, U.S.* 40°40′ N, 82°2′ W 102
Shreveport, *La., U.S.* 32°29′ N, 93°46′ W 103
Shrewsbury, *U.K.* 52°42′ N, 2°45′ W 162
Shri Mohangarh, *India* 27°15′ N, 71°14′ E 186
Shrub Oak, *N.Y., U.S.* 41°18′ N, 73°51′ W 104
Shtërpca (Štrpce), *Kosovo* 42°15′ N, 21°2′ E 168
Shtime, *Kosovo* 42°27′ N, 21°3′ E 168
Shū, *Kaz.* 43°35′ N, 73°45′ E 190
Shū, river, *Kaz.* 44°51′ N, 70°15′ E 190
Shuangcheng, *China* 45°22′ N, 126°19′ E 198
Shuangchengzi, *China* 40°18′ N, 99°45′ E 190
Shuangjiang, *China* 23°29′ N, 99°48′ E 202
Shuangliao, *China* 43°31′ N, 123°27′ E 198
Shuangyang, *China* 43°32′ N, 125°42′ E 198
Shuangyashan, *China* 46°41′ N, 131°11′ E 238
Shubarakköl, *Kaz.* 49°7′ N, 68°46′ E 184
Shubarquduyq, *Kaz.* 49°8′ N, 56°26′ E 158
Shubarshī, *Kaz.* 48°35′ N, 57°17′ E 158
Shubuta, *Miss., U.S.* 31°51′ N, 88°42′ W 103
Shucheng, *China* 31°26′ N, 116°56′ E 198
Shudino, *Russ.* 61°41′ N, 48°9′ E 154
Shufu, *China* 39°22′ N, 75°44′ E 184
Shugozero, *Russ.* 59°55′ N, 34°16′ E 154
Shukpa Kunzang, *India* 34°22′ N, 78°21′ E 188
Shuksan, Mount, peak, *Wash., U.S.* 48°48′ N, 121°38′ W 100
Shulan, *China* 44°25′ N, 126°58′ E 198
Shulaps Peak, *Can.* 50°57′ N, 122°37′ W 90
Shule, *China* 39°23′ N, 76°3′ E 184
Shullsburg, *Wis., U.S.* 42°34′ N, 90°14′ W 102
Shumagin Islands, *Gulf of Alaska* 54°23′ N, 161°29′ W 98
Shumanay, *Uzb.* 42°35′ N, 58°59′ E 180
Shumen (Kolarovgrad), *Bulg.* 43°16′ N, 26°55′ E 156
Shumerlya, *Russ.* 55°29′ N, 46°29′ E 154
Shumikha, *Russ.* 55°13′ N, 63°16′ E 184
Shumilina, *Belarus* 55°21′ N, 29°41′ E 166
Shunchang, *China* 26°50′ N, 117°47′ E 198
Shun'ga, *Russ.* 62°34′ N, 34°59′ E 154
Shungnak, *Alas., U.S.* 66°47′ N, 157°12′ W 98
Shungopavi, *Ariz., U.S.* 35°48′ N, 110°31′ W 92
Shuozhou, *China* 39°18′ N, 112°26′ E 198
Shupenzë, *Alban.* 41°31′ N, 20°25′ E 168
Shuqualak, *Miss., U.S.* 32°57′ N, 88°34′ W 103
Shūr Gaz, *Iran* 29°9′ N, 59°21′ E 180
Shuraabad, *Azerb.* 40°49′ N, 49°27′ E 195
Shūrāb, *Iran* 33°42′ N, 56°32′ E 180
Shurma, *Russ.* 56°56′ N, 50°24′ E 154
Shurob, *Taj.* 40°4′ N, 70°32′ E 197
Shurugwi, *Zimb.* 19°40′ S, 29°58′ E 224
Shuryshkary, *Russ.* 65°56′ N, 65°25′ E 169
Shūsf, *Iran* 31°47′ N, 60°5′ E 180
Shushan, *N.Y., U.S.* 43°5′ N, 73°21′ W 104
Shushenskoye, *Russ.* 53°19′ N, 92°2′ E 184
Shūshtar, *Iran* 32°1′ N, 48°55′ E 180
Shuya, *Russ.* 56°50′ N, 41°21′ E 154
Shuya, *Russ.* 61°58′ N, 34°19′ E 154
Shuyak Island, *Alas., U.S.* 58°22′ N, 152°19′ W 98
Shuyang, *China* 34°8′ N, 118°50′ E 198
Shuyskoye, *Russ.* 59°21′ N, 40°58′ E 154
Shwebo, *Myanmar* 22°33′ N, 95°44′ E 202
Shwegu, *Myanmar* 24°10′ N, 96°45′ E 188
Shwegyin, *Myanmar* 17°56′ N, 96°52′ E 202
Shweli, river, *Asia* 23°29′ N, 97°5′ E 202
Shyghys Qazaqstan, adm. division, *Kaz.* 48°56′ N, 80°14′ E 184
Shymkent, *Kaz.* 42°17′ N, 69°34′ E 197
Shyngghyriau, *Kaz.* 51°5′ N, 54°3′ E 158
Shyok, river, *India* 35°1′ N, 76°45′ E 188
Siabu, *Indonesia* 1°1′ N, 99°29′ E 196
Sīah Chashmeh, *Iran* 39°4′ N, 44°26′ E 195
Sialkot, *Pak.* 32°27′ N, 74°33′ E 186
Sianów, *Pol.* 54°13′ N, 16°18′ E 152
Siantan, island, *Indonesia* 3°6′ N, 106°18′ E 196
Siapa, river, *Venez.* 1°57′ N, 66°5′ W 136
Siargao, island, *Philippines* 9°56′ N, 126°9′ E 192
Siasconset, *Mass., U.S.* 41°15′ N, 69°59′ W 104
Siasi, *Philippines* 5°35′ N, 120°49′ E 203
Siaton, *Philippines* 9°4′ N, 123°2′ E 203
Šiaulėnai, *Lith.* 55°40′ N, 23°24′ E 166
Šiauliai, *Lith.* 55°55′ N, 23°17′ E 166
Sibâ'i, Gebel el, peak, *Egypt* 25°42′ N, 34°3′ E 182
Sibari, *It.* 39°45′ N, 16°27′ E 156
Sibay, *Russ.* 52°44′ N, 58°37′ E 154
Sibaya, Lake, *S. Af.* 27°27′ S, 32°5′ E 227
Sibbald, Cape, *Antarctica* 73°46′ S, 172°14′ E 248
Sibbo (Sippo), *Fin.* 60°22′ N, 25°13′ E 166
Šibenik, *Croatia* 43°44′ N, 15°53′ E 168
Siberia, region, *Russ.* 68°9′ N, 99°54′ E 172
Siberut, island, *Indonesia* 1°23′ S, 99°7′ E 196
Siberut National Park, *Indonesia* 1°17′ S, 98°20′ E 172
Siberut, Selat 0°52′ N, 98°4′ E 196
Sibi, *Pak.* 29°37′ N, 67°53′ E 186
Sibigo, *Indonesia* 2°49′ N, 95°53′ E 196
Sibiloi National Park, *Kenya* 3°55′ N, 36°36′ E 224
Sibirskiy, *Russ.* 60°36′ N, 69°51′ E 169
Sibiryakova, Ostrov, island, *Russ.* 72°47′ N, 79°54′ E 160
Sibiti, *Congo* 3°42′ S, 13°18′ E 218
Sibiu, *Rom.* 45°49′ N, 24°8′ E 156
Sibiu, adm. division, *Rom.* 45°38′ N, 23°39′ E 156
Sibley, *La., U.S.* 32°31′ N, 93°18′ W 103
Sibolga, *Indonesia* 1°46′ N, 98°48′ E 196
Siborongborong, *Indonesia* 2°14′ N, 98°59′ E 196
Șibot, *Rom.* 45°56′ N, 23°20′ E 168
Sibsagar, *India* 27°0′ N, 94°38′ E 188
Sibsey, *U.K.* 53°2′ N, 2°119′ E 162
Sibu, *Malaysia* 2°18′ N, 111°51′ E 192
Sibu, island, *Malaysia* 2°9′ N, 104°6′ E 196
Sibuco, *Philippines* 7°20′ N, 122°4′ E 203
Sibut, *Cen. Af. Rep.* 5°42′ N, 19°5′ E 218
Sibuyan Sea 12°34′ N, 122°29′ E 203
Siby, *Mali* 12°23′ N, 8°20′ W 222
Sicapoo, Mount, peak, *Philippines* 18°1′ N, 120°51′ E 203
Sicasica, *Bol.* 17°24′ S, 67°48′ W 137
Sichuan, adm. division, *China* 31°1′ N, 105°8′ E 198
Sicié, Cap, *Fr.* 42°57′ N, 5°44′ E 165
Sicilia (Sicily), adm. division, *It.* 37°28′ N, 13°21′ E 156
Sicily Island, *La., U.S.* 31°49′ N, 91°41′ W 103
Sicily, island, *It.* 36°26′ N, 14°37′ E 156
Sicilia see Sicily, adm. division, *Sicily* 38°18′ N, 12°49′ E 156
Sico, river, *Hond.* 15°38′ N, 85°43′ W 115
Sicuani, *Peru* 14°19′ S, 71°12′ W 137
Sicyon, ruin(s), *Gr.* 37°58′ N, 22°38′ E 156
Šid, *Serb.* 45°7′ N, 19°13′ E 168
Sidaogou, *China* 41°44′ N, 127°5′ E 200
Sidaouet, *Niger* 18°32′ N, 8°4′ E 222
Sidas, *Indonesia* 0°23′ N, 109°42′ E 196
Siddhapur, *India* 23°56′ N, 72°22′ E 186
Side, ruin(s), *Mediterranean Sea* 36°43′ N, 31°17′ E 156
Sideby (Siipyy), *Fin.* 62°1′ N, 21°19′ E 166
Sideia, island, *P.N.G.* 10°56′ S, 150°17′ E 192
Sidéradougou, *Burkina Faso* 10°39′ N, 4°16′ W 222
Sidi Aïch, *Alg.* 36°36′ N, 4°42′ E 150
Sidi Aïssa, *Alg.* 35°52′ N, 3°46′ E 150
Sidi Akacha, *Alg.* 36°27′ N, 1°18′ E 150
Sidi Ali, *Alg.* 36°5′ N, 0°25′ E 150
Sidi Amar, *Alg.* 36°32′ N, 2°18′ E 150
Sîdi Barrâni, *Egypt* 31°39′ N, 25°57′ E 180
Sidi Bel Abbès, *Alg.* 35°10′ N, 0°38′ E 150
Sidi Bel Atar, *Alg.* 36°1′ N, 0°16′ E 164
Sidi Bernous, Djebel, peak, *Alg.* 36°20′ N, 1°31′ E 150
Sidi bou Haous, *Alg.* 32°4′ N, 2°3′ E 214
Sidi Bouzid, *Tun.* 35°2′ N, 9°29′ E 156
Sidi Daoud, *Alg.* 36°50′ N, 3°51′ E 150
Sidi el Hadj bou Haous, *Alg.* 31°38′ N, 2°0′ E 214
Sidi el Hadj Zaoui, *Alg.* 28°17′ N, 4°36′ E 214
Sidi Hosni, *Alg.* 35°28′ N, 1°35′ E 150
Sidi Ifni, *Mor.* 29°21′ N, 10°10′ W 214
Sidi Kada, *Alg.* 35°19′ N, 0°19′ E 150
Sidi Lakhdar, *Alg.* 36°9′ N, 0°26′ E 164
Sîdi 'Omar, *Egypt* 31°24′ N, 24°55′ E 180
Siding Spring Observatory, *Austral.* 31°21′ S, 148°51′ E 230
Sidlaw Hills, *U.K.* 56°22′ N, 3°17′ W 150
Sidley, Mount, peak, *Antarctica* 76°57′ S, 125°31′ W 248
Sidney, *Can.* 48°38′ N, 123°24′ W 100
Sidney, *Iowa, U.S.* 40°44′ N, 95°39′ W 90
Sidney, *Mont., U.S.* 47°40′ N, 104°11′ W 90
Sidney, *Nebr., U.S.* 41°8′ N, 103°0′ W 90
Sidney, *N.Y., U.S.* 42°18′ N, 75°24′ W 94
Sidney, *Ohio, U.S.* 40°17′ N, 84°9′ W 102
Sido, *Mali* 11°41′ N, 7°36′ W 222
Sidoktaya, *Myanmar* 20°27′ N, 94°13′ E 202
Sidon, *Miss., U.S.* 33°23′ N, 90°13′ W 103
Sidon see Saida, *Leb.* 33°33′ N, 35°22′ E 194
Sidorovsk, *Russ.* 66°34′ N, 82°24′ E 169
Sidra, Gulf of 31°40′ N, 16°22′ E 142
Sidra see Surt, *Lib.* 31°12′ N, 16°32′ E 216
Siedlce, *Pol.* 52°10′ N, 22°16′ E 152
Siegal, Mount, peak, *Nev., U.S.* 38°53′ N, 119°36′ W 90
Siegburg, *Ger.* 50°48′ N, 7°11′ E 167
Siegen, *Ger.* 50°53′ N, 8°1′ E 167
Siem Pang, *Cambodia* 14°9′ N, 106°19′ E 202
Siem Reap, *Cambodia* 13°24′ N, 103°51′ E 202
Siempurgo, *Côte d'Ivoire* 9°31′ N, 6°13′ W 222
Siena, *It.* 43°20′ N, 11°19′ E 214
Sieppijärvi, *Fin.* 67°8′ N, 23°56′ E 152
Sieradz, *Pol.* 51°35′ N, 18°43′ E 152
Sierck, *Fr.* 49°25′ N, 6°21′ E 163
Sierra Blanca, *Tex., U.S.* 31°9′ N, 105°22′ W 92
Sierra Colorada, *Arg.* 40°35′ S, 67°46′ W 134
Sierra de San Pedro Mártir National Park, *Mex.* 30°58′ N, 115°45′ W 238
Sierra Gorda, *Chile* 22°54′ S, 69°22′ W 137
Sierra Grande, *Arg.* 41°35′ S, 65°22′ W 134
Sierra Leone 8°30′ N, 12°17′ W 214
Sierra Leone Rise, *North Atlantic Ocean* 5°17′ N, 20°42′ W 253
Sierra Madre Mountains, *Calif., U.S.* 34°57′ N, 120°5′ W 100
Sierra Madre Occidental, *Mex.* 25°42′ N, 106°57′ W 114
Sierra Madre Oriental, *Mex.* 23°10′ N, 100°33′ W 114
Sierra Mojada, *Mex.* 27°18′ N, 103°42′ W 112
Sierra Nevada de Santa Marta National Park, *Col.* 11°19′ N, 74°8′ W 130
Sierra Nevada National Park, *Venez.* 8°41′ N, 71°26′ W 136
Sierra Vista, *Ariz., U.S.* 31°33′ N, 110°18′ W 92
Sierre, *Switz.* 46°18′ N, 7°31′ E 167
Sieruela, *Sp.* 38°58′ N, 5°3′ W 164
Siesta Key, island, *Fla., U.S.* 27°10′ N, 82°37′ W 105
Siete Aguas, *Sp.* 39°28′ N, 0°56′ E 164
Șieu, *Rom.* 47°0′ N, 24°36′ E 156
Sif Fatima, spring, *Alg.* 31°6′ N, 8°40′ E 214
Sifié, *Côte d'Ivoire* 7°54′ N, 6°56′ W 222
Sífnos, island, *Gr.* 36°51′ N, 24°9′ E 180
Sifton, *Can.* 51°22′ N, 100°8′ W 90
Sifton Pass, *Can.* 57°53′ N, 126°10′ W 108
Sig, *Russ.* 65°34′ N, 34°9′ E 152
Sigdal, *Nor.* 60°3′ N, 9°37′ E 152
Sigean, *Fr.* 43°1′ N, 2°56′ E 164
Sigep, *Indonesia* 0°59′ N, 98°49′ E 196
Sighnaghi, *Ga.* 41°37′ N, 45°55′ E 195
Siglan, *Russ.* 59°17′ N, 152°31′ E 173
Sigli, *Indonesia* 5°23′ N, 95°55′ E 196
Siglufjörður, *Ice.* 66°10′ N, 19°5′ W 143
Sigmaringen, *Ger.* 48°4′ N, 9°12′ E 152
Signai, site, *Can.* 48°18′ N, 76°55′ W 94
Signal Hill, peak, *Austral.* 21°59′ S, 139°52′ E 230
Signal Peak, *Ariz., U.S.* 33°21′ N, 114°8′ W 101
Signy Island, *Antarctica* 61°0′ S, 46°55′ W 134
Signy-le-Petit, *Fr.* 49°53′ N, 4°17′ E 163
Sigourney, *Iowa, U.S.* 41°20′ N, 92°12′ W 94
Sigovo, *Russ.* 62°39′ N, 87°2′ E 169
Sigre, river, *Hond.* 15°21′ N, 84°51′ W 115
Sigüenza, *Sp.* 41°3′ N, 2°40′ W 164
Siguiri, *Guinea* 11°27′ N, 9°11′ W 222
Sigulda, *Latv.* 57°8′ N, 24°51′ E 166
Sihanoukville, *Cambodia* 10°38′ N, 103°32′ E 202
Sihor, *India* 21°42′ N, 71°56′ E 186
Sihora, *India* 23°29′ N, 80°7′ E 197
Siikainen, *Fin.* 61°51′ N, 21°47′ E 166
Siilinjärvi, *Fin.* 63°3′ N, 27°38′ E 152
Siipyy see Sideby, *Fin.* 62°1′ N, 21°19′ E 166
Siirt, *Turk.* 37°54′ N, 41°57′ E 195
Sikanni Chief, *Can.* 57°15′ N, 122°44′ W 108
Sikanni Chief, river, *Can.* 57°26′ N, 122°27′ W 108
Sikar, *India* 27°36′ N, 75°10′ E 197
Sikasso, *Mali* 11°19′ N, 5°41′ W 222
Sikeå, *Nor.* 64°9′ N, 20°55′ E 152
Sikes, *La., U.S.* 32°3′ N, 92°31′ W 103
Sikeston, *Mo., U.S.* 36°51′ N, 89°35′ W 96
Sikhote Alin', Khrebet 43°1′ N, 132°36′ E 200
Síkinos, island, *Gr.* 36°44′ N, 24°37′ E 180
Sikkim, adm. division, *India* 27°29′ N, 88°6′ E 197
Siklós, *Hung.* 45°50′ N, 18°17′ E 168
Siknäs, *Nor.* 65°50′ N, 22°40′ E 152
Sikonda, *Hung.* 46°9′ N, 18°14′ E 168
Sikonge, *Tanzania* 5°36′ S, 32°47′ E 224
Siksjö, *Nor.* 64°21′ N, 17°47′ E 152
Siktyakh, *Russ.* 69°51′ N, 124°43′ E 160
Sikuati, *Malaysia* 6°54′ N, 116°40′ E 203
Sila, La, *It.* 39°31′ N, 16°21′ E 156
Silacayoapan, *Mex.* 17°29′ N, 98°9′ W 114
Šilalė, *Lith.* 55°29′ N, 22°10′ E 166
Silandro, *It.* 46°37′ N, 10°47′ E 167
Silao, *Mex.* 20°54′ N, 101°26′ W 114
Silas, *Ala., U.S.* 31°46′ N, 88°20′ W 103
Šilderi, *Latv.* 56°51′ N, 22°10′ E 166
Șile, *Turk.* 41°10′ N, 29°36′ E 156
Silesia, region, *Pol.* 49°36′ N, 17°59′ E 152
Silet, *Alg.* 22°39′ N, 4°34′ E 214

Siletitengi Köli, lake, *Kaz.* 53°9′ N, 72°22′ E 184
Siliana, *Alg.* 36°32′ N, 6°17′ E 150
Silifke, *Turk.* 36°20′ N, 33°55′ E 156
Silil, spring, *Somalia* 10°52′ N, 43°18′ E 182
Siling Co, lake, *China* 31°37′ N, 88°26′ E 188
Silistra, *Bulg.* 44°5′ N, 27°15′ E 156
Silistra, adm. division, *Bulg.* 43°56′ N, 26°22′ E 156
Silivri, *Turk.* 41°5′ N, 28°14′ E 156
Silkeborg, *Den.* 56°8′ N, 9°31′ E 150
Silla, *Sp.* 39°21′ N, 0°24′ E 164
Sillamäe, *Est.* 59°22′ N, 27°43′ E 166
Silli, *Burkina Faso* 11°35′ N, 2°30′ W 222
Silliman, Mount, peak, *Calif., U.S.* 36°37′ N, 118°44′ W 101
Silloth, *U.K.* 54°52′ N, 3°23′ W 162
Sílo, peak, *Gr.* 41°9′ N, 25°51′ E 156
Silogui, *Indonesia* 1°12′ S, 98°58′ E 196
Silopi, *Turk.* 37°14′ N, 42°17′ E 195
Silsbee, *Tex., U.S.* 30°19′ N, 94°11′ W 103
Silt Lake, *Can.* 60°2′ N, 119°18′ W 108
Siltou, spring, *Chad* 16°51′ N, 15°42′ E 216
Siluas, *Indonesia* 1°17′ N, 109°49′ E 196
Šilutė, *Lith.* 55°22′ N, 21°28′ E 166
Silvan, *Turk.* 38°8′ N, 41°3′ E 195
Silvânia, *Braz.* 16°42′ S, 48°37′ W 138
Silvassa, *India* 20°16′ N, 73°3′ E 186
Silver Bay, *Minn., U.S.* 47°17′ N, 91°17′ W 110
Silver City, *Idaho, U.S.* 43°1′ N, 116°46′ W 90
Silver City, *Miss., U.S.* 33°4′ N, 90°31′ W 103
Silver City, *Nev., U.S.* 39°15′ N, 119°39′ W 90
Silver City, *N. Mex., U.S.* 32°45′ N, 108°18′ W 112
Silver Cliff, *Colo., U.S.* 38°8′ N, 105°26′ W 90
Silver Creek, *Miss., U.S.* 31°34′ N, 89°59′ W 103
Silver Lake, *Ind., U.S.* 41°3′ N, 85°53′ W 102
Silver Lake, *N.H., U.S.* 43°53′ N, 71°11′ W 104
Silver Peak, *Nev., U.S.* 37°45′ N, 117°39′ W 92
Silver Run Peak, *Mont., U.S.* 45°5′ N, 109°37′ W 90
Silver Springs, *Fla., U.S.* 29°12′ N, 82°4′ W 105
Silver Star Mountain, peak, *Can.* 50°21′ N, 119°9′ W 90
Silver Zone Pass, *Nev., U.S.* 40°56′ N, 114°21′ W 90
Silverthrone, Mount, peak, *Alas., U.S.* 63°6′ N, 150°53′ W 98
Silverthrone Mountain, peak, *Can.* 51°29′ N, 126°10′ W 108
Silverton, *Colo., U.S.* 37°48′ N, 107°40′ W 82
Silverton, *Tex., U.S.* 34°27′ N, 101°19′ W 92
Silves, *Braz.* 2°52′ S, 58°14′ W 130
Silvretta, *Aust.* 46°49′ N, 9°58′ E 167
Silwa Baḥari, *Egypt* 24°42′ N, 32°55′ E 182
Sim, *Russ.* 54°59′ N, 57°39′ E 154
Sim, Cap, *Mor.* 31°25′ N, 10°40′ W 214
Simaleke-hilir, *Indonesia* 1°10′ S, 98°37′ E 196
Sim'ān, Jabal, *Syr.* 36°31′ N, 36°38′ E 156
Simao, *China* 22°37′ N, 101°12′ E 202
Şīmareh, river, *Iran* 33°25′ N, 46°51′ E 180
Simav, *Turk.* 39°4′ N, 28°58′ E 156
Simav, river, *Turk.* 39°17′ N, 28°15′ E 156
Simba, *Dem. Rep. of the Congo* 0°36′ N, 22°56′ E 218
Simbo, island, *Solomon Islands* 8°17′ S, 156°30′ E 242
Simcoe, *Can.* 42°49′ N, 80°18′ W 94
Simcoe, Lake, *Can.* 44°27′ N, 79°55′ W 80
Simcoe Mountains, peak, *Wash., U.S.* 45°57′ N, 120°55′ W 90
Simdega, *India* 22°35′ N, 84°30′ E 197
Simeria, *Rom.* 45°50′ N, 23°1′ E 168
Simeulue, island, *Indonesia* 2°43′ N, 95°5′ E 196
Simferopol', *Ukr.* 44°57′ N, 34°1′ E 156
Simhana, *China* 39°40′ N, 73°57′ E 197
Sími, *Gr.* 36°36′ N, 27°49′ E 156
Simi Valley, *Calif., U.S.* 34°16′ N, 118°46′ W 101
Simikot, *Nepal* 29°59′ N, 81°51′ E 197
Simin Han, *Bosn. and Herzg.* 44°32′ N, 18°44′ E 168
Simití, *Col.* 7°57′ N, 73°59′ W 136
Simla, *Colo., U.S.* 39°8′ N, 104°6′ W 92
Simla, *Nepal* 31°8′ N, 77°9′ E 197
Şimleu Silvaniei, *Rom.* 47°14′ N, 22°50′ E 168
Simme, river, *Switz.* 46°34′ N, 7°25′ E 165
Simmern, *Ger.* 49°58′ N, 7°30′ E 167
Simmesport, *La., U.S.* 30°57′ N, 91°50′ W 103
Simojärvi, *Fin.* 65°55′ N, 27°7′ E 152
Simojovel, *Mex.* 17°9′ N, 92°44′ W 115
Simola, *Fin.* 60°54′ N, 28°7′ E 166
Simón Bolívar, *Mex.* 24°39′ N, 103°15′ W 114
Simonette, river, *Can.* 54°1′ N, 118°37′ W 108
Simonhouse, *Can.* 54°26′ N, 101°24′ W 108
Simon's Town, *S. Af.* 34°12′ S, 18°25′ E 227
Simontornya, *Hung.* 46°45′ N, 18°32′ E 168
Simpang, *Indonesia* 0°9′ N, 103°16′ E 196
Simpang, *Indonesia* 1°15′ S, 104°5′ E 196
Simpele, *Fin.* 61°25′ N, 29°20′ E 166
Simplício Mendes, *Braz.* 7°51′ S, 41°55′ W 132
Simplon Pass, *Switz.* 46°15′ N, 8°1′ E 167
Simpson, *La., U.S.* 31°14′ N, 93°1′ W 103
Simpson, *Pa., U.S.* 41°34′ N, 75°29′ W 94
Simpson Desert, *Austral.* 25°28′ S, 135°47′ E 230
Simpson Hill, peak, *Austral.* 26°34′ S, 126°21′ E 230
Simpson Lake, *Can.* 60°47′ N, 129°44′ W 108
Simpson Park Mountains, *Nev., U.S.* 39°45′ N, 116°58′ W 90
Simpson Peninsula, *Can.* 68°27′ N, 91°51′ W 106
Simrishamn, *Nor.* 55°32′ N, 14°20′ E 152
Sims Lake, *Can.* 53°59′ N, 66°28′ W 111
Simsboro, *La., U.S.* 32°31′ N, 92°49′ W 103
Simushir, island, *Russ.* 46°43′ N, 152°15′ E 190
Sina, *Peru* 14°34′ S, 69°16′ W 137
Sinabang, *Indonesia* 2°29′ N, 96°20′ E 196
Sinabung, peak, *Indonesia* 3°11′ N, 98°17′ E 196
Sinai, *Egypt* 30°23′ N, 33°2′ E 194
Sinai, Mount see Mûsa, Gebel, peak, *Egypt* 28°30′ N, 33°54′ E 226
Sinal, Morro do, *Braz.* 10°41′ S, 55°37′ W 130
Sinaloa, adm. division, *Mex.* 23°42′ N, 106°50′ W 114
Sinaloa, river, *Mex.* 25°46′ N, 108°25′ W 80
Sinamaica, *Venez.* 11°6′ N, 71°53′ W 136
Sinan, *China* 27°56′ N, 108°13′ E 198
Sînandrei, *Rom.* 45°52′ N, 21°10′ E 168
Sinanju, *N. Korea* 39°35′ N, 125°36′ E 200
Sinäwin, *Lib.* 31°4′ N, 10°37′ E 216
Sinbang-ni, *N. Korea* 41°5′ N, 127°28′ E 200
Sincelejo, *Col.* 9°16′ N, 75°26′ W 136
Sincennes, Lac, lake, *Can.* 47°27′ N, 74°27′ W 94
Sinch'ang, *N. Korea* 40°7′ N, 128°28′ E 200
Sinch'ang, *N. Korea* 39°23′ N, 126°7′ E 200
Sinchiyacu, *Peru* 3°11′ S, 76°44′ W 136
Sinch'ŏn, *N. Korea* 38°21′ N, 125°29′ E 200
Sinclair, *Wyo., U.S.* 41°46′ N, 107°6′ W 90
Sinclair, Lake, *Ga., U.S.* 33°12′ N, 83°57′ W 112
Sindangan, *Philippines* 8°16′ N, 123°0′ E 203
Sindara, *Gabon* 1°4′ S, 10°37′ E 218
Sindeni, *Tanzania* 5°18′ S, 38°15′ E 224
Sindèr, *Niger* 14°14′ N, 1°14′ E 222
Sindeya, *Russ.* 60°5′ N, 61°29′ E 154
Sindh, adm. division, *Pak.* 25°54′ N, 68°3′ E 186
Sindi, *Est.* 58°22′ N, 24°39′ E 166
Sindi, *Sudan* 14°22′ N, 25°48′ E 226
Sindri, *India* 23°40′ N, 86°30′ E 197
Sinegorskiy, *Russ.* 47°56′ N, 40°49′ E 158
Sines, *Port.* 37°57′ N, 8°52′ W 150
Sines, Cabo de, *Port.* 37°42′ N, 9°11′ W 150
Sinfra, *Côte d'Ivoire* 6°31′ N, 5°55′ W 222
Sing Buri, *Thai.* 14°53′ N, 100°23′ E 202
Singa, *Sudan* 13°8′ N, 33°56′ E 182
Singapore, *Singapore* 1°16′ N, 103°43′ E 196
Singer, *La., U.S.* 30°38′ N, 93°25′ W 103
Sîngerei, *Mold.* 47°38′ N, 28°8′ E 158
Singida, *Tanzania* 4°49′ S, 34°43′ E 224
Singida, adm. division, *Tanzania* 6°0′ S, 34°4′ E 224
Singing Tower, site, *Fla., U.S.* 27°55′ N, 81°36′ W 105
Singkawang, *Indonesia* 0°55′ N, 108°58′ E 196
Singkep, island, *Indonesia* 0°38′ N, 104°36′ E 196
Singkil, *Indonesia* 2°19′ N, 97°46′ E 196
Singkuang, *Indonesia* 1°6′ N, 98°57′ E 196
Singleton, Mount, peak, *Austral.* 22°5′ S, 130°37′ E 230
Singö, island, *Sw.* 60°10′ N, 18°46′ E 166
Singoli, *India* 24°58′ N, 75°18′ E 188
Singtam, *India* 27°17′ N, 88°29′ E 197
Singu, *Myanmar* 22°34′ N, 96°0′ E 202
Singus, ruin(s), *Gr.* 40°9′ N, 23°41′ E 156
Sin'gye, *N. Korea* 38°30′ N, 126°32′ E 200
Singye Dzong, *Bhutan* 28°0′ N, 91°18′ E 197
Sinhŭng, *N. Korea* 40°11′ N, 127°36′ E 200
Sini Vrŭkh, peak, *Bulg.* 41°49′ N, 24°56′ E 156
Sinianka-Minia Game Reserve, *Chad* 10°5′ N, 17°4′ E 218
Şinīf'ah, *Jordan* 30°50′ N, 35°33′ E 194
Sinj, *Croatia* 43°42′ N, 16°37′ E 168
Sinjajevina, mountains, *Mont.* 43°0′ N, 19°6′ E 168
Sinjār, *Iraq* 36°20′ N, 41°53′ E 195
Sinkat, *Sudan* 18°51′ N, 36°48′ E 182
Sinkiang, region 38°43′ N, 73°57′ E 197
Sinkiang, region, *China* 46°12′ N, 83°11′ E 184
Sinking Spring, *Ohio, U.S.* 39°3′ N, 83°24′ W 102
Sin-le-Noble, *Fr.* 50°20′ N, 3°7′ E 163
Sinnamary, *South America* 5°23′ N, 52°57′ W 130
Sinnar, adm. division, *Sudan* 12°44′ N, 33°18′ E 182
Sinntal, *Ger.* 50°18′ N, 9°38′ E 167
Sinnûris, *Egypt* 29°25′ N, 30°50′ E 180
Sinop, *Braz.* 11°55′ S, 55°35′ W 130
Sinop, *Turk.* 41°53′ N, 34°57′ E 143
Sinop Burnu, *Turk.* 42°1′ N, 35°14′ E 156
Sinop (Sinope), *Turk.* 42°1′ N, 35°8′ E 156
Sinope see Sinop, *Turk.* 42°1′ N, 35°8′ E 156
Sinp'a see Kimjŏngsuk, *N. Korea* 41°24′ N, 127°48′ E 200
Sinp'o, *N. Korea* 40°1′ N, 128°13′ E 200
Sinsang, *N. Korea* 39°39′ N, 127°25′ E 200
Sinsk, *Russ.* 61°9′ N, 126°40′ E 160
Sint Andries, *Belg.* 51°11′ N, 3°11′ E 163
Sint Georgen, *Ger.* 48°7′ N, 8°19′ E 152
Sint Mang, *Ger.* 47°43′ N, 10°20′ E 152
Sint Maarten, island, *Neth.* 18°2′ N, 63°4′ W 116
Sint Truiden, *Belg.* 50°48′ N, 5°11′ E 167
Sîntana, *Rom.* 46°20′ N, 21°31′ E 168
Sintang, *Indonesia* 4°238′ N, 111°27′ E 192
Sinton, *Tex., U.S.* 28°1′ N, 97°30′ W 96
Sintuya, *Peru* 12°44′ S, 71°17′ W 137
Sinú, river, *Col.* 7°52′ N, 76°16′ W 136
Sinŭiju, *N. Korea* 40°3′ N, 124°23′ E 200
Sinujiif, *Somalia* 8°32′ N, 48°59′ E 216
Sinwŏn, *N. Korea* 38°12′ N, 125°43′ E 200
Sinyaya, river, *Latv.* 56°26′ N, 28°2′ E 166
Sinzig, *Ger.* 50°32′ N, 7°15′ E 163
Sió, river, *Hung.* 46°48′ N, 18°13′ E 168
Sióagárd, *Hung.* 46°23′ N, 18°39′ E 168
Siocon, *Philippines* 7°45′ N, 122°8′ E 203
Siófok, *Hung.* 46°54′ N, 18°5′ E 168
Sioma, *Zambia* 16°41′ S, 23°30′ E 224
Sioma Ngwezi National Park, *Zambia* 17°7′ S, 23°42′ E 224
Sion, *Switz.* 46°14′ N, 7°20′ E 167
Siorapaluk 77°50′ N, 70°37′ W 246
Sioux City, *Iowa, U.S.* 42°29′ N, 96°26′ W 82
Sioux Falls, *S. Dak., U.S.* 43°31′ N, 96°44′ W 90
Sioux Lookout, *Can.* 50°5′ N, 91°51′ W 82
Sioux Narrows, *Can.* 49°25′ N, 94°7′ W 90
Sioux Rapids, *Iowa, U.S.* 42°52′ N, 95°10′ W 90
Sipalay, *Philippines* 9°45′ N, 122°24′ E 203
Šipan, island, *Croatia* 42°44′ N, 17°54′ E 168
Sipapo, Cerro, peak, *Venez.* 4°51′ N, 67°15′ W 136
Sipapo, river, *Venez.* 4°35′ N, 67°40′ W 136
Siphanqeni, *S. Af.* 31°5′ S, 29°29′ E 227
Siping, *China* 43°8′ N, 124°22′ E 200
Sipirok, *Indonesia* 1°37′ N, 99°17′ E 196
Sipiwesk, *Can.* 55°28′ N, 97°25′ W 108
Siple Coast, *Antarctica* 83°0′ S, 148°28′ W 248
Siple Island, *Antarctica* 72°30′ S, 127°21′ W 248
Siple, Mount, peak, *Antarctica* 73°20′ S, 126°3′ W 248
Šipovo, *Bosn. and Herzg.* 44°17′ N, 17°4′ E 168
Sippo see Sibbo, *Fin.* 60°22′ N, 25°13′ E 166
Šiprage, *Bosn. and Herzg.* 44°27′ N, 17°33′ E 168
Sipsey, river, *Ala., U.S.* 33°25′ N, 87°46′ W 103
Sipura, island, *Indonesia* 2°5′ S, 99°22′ E 192
Siqueros, *Mex.* 23°18′ N, 106°15′ W 114
Siquia, river, *Nicar.* 12°31′ N, 84°32′ W 115
Siquijor, *Philippines* 9°13′ N, 123°29′ E 203
Siquisique, *Venez.* 10°31′ N, 69°46′ W 136
Sir Alexander, Mount, peak, *Can.* 53°55′ N, 120°29′ W 108
Şīr Banī Yās, island, *U.A.E.* 24°23′ N, 52°28′ E 182
Sir Douglas, Mount, peak, *Can.* 50°43′ N, 115°25′ W 90
Sir Edward Pellew Group, islands, *Austral.* 15°27′ S, 136°56′ E 230
Sir Francis Drake, Mount, peak, *Can.* 50°48′ N, 124°54′ W 90
Sir Graham Moore Islands, *Austral.* 13°44′ S, 124°3′ E 230
Sir James Macbrien, Mount, peak, *Can.* 61°57′ N, 129°1′ W 72
Sir Sandford, Mount, peak, *Can.* 51°40′ N, 117°58′ W 90
Sir Thomas, Mount, peak, *Austral.* 27°13′ S, 129°31′ E 230
Sira, *India* 13°44′ N, 76°56′ E 188
Siracusa, *It.* 37°3′ N, 15°14′ E 216
Siracusa (Syracuse), *It.* 37°3′ N, 15°17′ E 156
Sirajganj, *Bangladesh* 24°22′ N, 89°39′ E 197
Şiran, *Turk.* 40°12′ N, 39°8′ E 195
Sirba, river, *Burkina Faso* 12°25′ N, 0°32′ E 222
Sirdaryo, *Uzb.* 40°50′ N, 68°39′ E 197
Sīrē, *Eth.* 8°14′ N, 39°27′ E 224
Sīrē, *Eth.* 9°1′ N, 36°53′ E 224
Sireniki, *Russ.* 64°30′ N, 173°50′ W 98
Sirghāyā, *Syr.* 33°48′ N, 36°9′ E 194
Siri, Cape, *P.N.G.* 11°54′ S, 153°3′ E 192
Siri, Gebel, peak, *Egypt* 22°6′ N, 31°3′ E 182
Sīrīk, *Iran* 26°32′ N, 57°9′ E 196
Sirino, Monte, peak, *It.* 40°7′ N, 15°44′ E 156
Sīrjan, *Iran* 29°29′ N, 55°40′ E 196
Sirkka, *Fin.* 67°48′ N, 24°47′ E 152
Sirma, *Nor.* 70°1′ N, 27°21′ E 152
Sirmilik National Park, *Can.* 73°2′ N, 83°20′ W 72
Şırnak, *Turk.* 37°30′ N, 42°23′ E 195
Siro, Jebel, peak, *Sudan* 14°22′ N, 24°16′ E 226
Sirohi, *India* 24°52′ N, 72°52′ E 186
Široki Brijeg, *Bosn. and Herzg.* 43°22′ N, 17°35′ E 168
Sirombu, *Indonesia* 1°0′ N, 97°23′ E 196
Sīrrī, island, *Iran* 25°47′ N, 54°21′ E 180
Sirsa, *India* 29°32′ N, 75°4′ E 186
Sirur, *India* 18°49′ N, 74°23′ E 188
Şirvan, *Turk.* 38°1′ N, 42°0′ E 195
Širvintos, *Lith.* 55°1′ N, 24°56′ E 166
Sisak, *Croatia* 45°27′ N, 16°22′ E 168
Sisal, *Mex.* 21°9′ N, 90°6′ W 116
Sishen, *S. Af.* 27°47′ S, 23°3′ E 227
Sisian, *Arm.* 39°32′ N, 46°2′ E 195
Sisib Lake, lake, *Can.* 52°34′ N, 99°41′ W 108
Sisimiut (Holsteinsborg) 66°56′ N, 53°43′ W 106
Siskiyou Mountains, *Calif., U.S.* 41°51′ N, 123°44′ W 90
Sisophon, *Cambodia* 13°37′ N, 102°58′ E 202
Sisquoc, *Calif., U.S.* 34°52′ N, 120°19′ W 100
Sisseton, *S. Dak., U.S.* 45°38′ N, 97°5′ W 90
Sissonne, *Fr.* 49°34′ N, 3°53′ E 163
Sīstān, Daryācheh-ye, lake, *Iran* 30°44′ N, 60°36′ E 186
Sīstān, region, *Iran* 32°6′ N, 59°49′ E 180
Sister Bay, *Wis., U.S.* 45°11′ N, 87°7′ W 110
Sistersville, *W. Va., U.S.* 39°32′ N, 81°0′ W 102
Sitampiky, *Madagascar* 16°41′ S, 46°8′ E 220
Sitapur, *India* 27°33′ N, 80°42′ E 197
Siteki, *Swaziland* 26°23′ S, 31°56′ E 227
Sitges, *Sp.* 41°14′ N, 1°48′ E 164
Sithonía, *Gr.* 40°12′ N, 23°39′ E 156
Sitía, *Gr.* 35°9′ N, 26°6′ E 180
Sitidgi Lake, *Can.* 68°28′ N, 134°8′ W 98
Sítio da Abadia, *Braz.* 14°51′ S, 46°15′ W 138
Sítio do Mato, *Braz.* 13°5′ S, 43°30′ W 138
Sitka, *Alas., U.S.* 57°6′ N, 135°14′ W 73
Sitka National Historical Park, *Alas., U.S.* 57°2′ N, 135°18′ W 108
Sitkalidak Island, *Alas., U.S.* 56°43′ N, 153°12′ W 106
Sitkovo, *Russ.* 69°7′ N, 86°19′ E 169
Sitra, spring, *Egypt* 28°43′ N, 26°53′ E 180
Sittard, *Neth.* 51°0′ N, 5°50′ E 167
Sittingbourne, *U.K.* 51°19′ N, 0°43′ E 162
Sittong, river, *Myanmar* 19°24′ N, 96°14′ E 202
Sittwe, *Myanmar* 20°12′ N, 92°52′ E 188
Siuna, *Nicar.* 13°44′ N, 84°46′ W 115
Siuri, *India* 23°51′ N, 87°31′ E 197
Siv. Donets, river, *Ukr.* 49°25′ N, 36°31′ E 158
Sivac, *Serb.* 45°41′ N, 19°23′ E 168
Sivas, *Turk.* 39°45′ N, 37°0′ E 156
Siverek, *Turk.* 37°43′ N, 39°19′ E 195
Siverić, *Croatia* 43°52′ N, 16°11′ E 168
Siverskiy, *Russ.* 59°20′ N, 30°5′ E 166
Sivil, peak, *Sp.* 42°12′ N, 6°36′ W 164
Sivrihisar, *Turk.* 39°27′ N, 31°31′ E 156
Sivuchiy, Mys, *Russ.* 56°56′ N, 162°44′ E 160
Sivulya, Hora, peak, *Ukr.* 48°31′ N, 24°2′ E 152
Sîwa, *Egypt* 29°13′ N, 25°33′ E 180
Siwan, *India* 26°11′ N, 84°21′ E 197
Sixaola, *Pan.* 9°30′ N, 82°37′ W 115
Sixian, *China* 33°30′ N, 117°53′ E 198
Siyal Islands, *Red Sea* 22°17′ N, 35°39′ E 182
Siyäzän, *Azerb.* 41°4′ N, 49°5′ E 195
Siziwang Qi, *China* 41°33′ N, 111°46′ E 198
Sjenica, *Serb.* 43°15′ N, 19°59′ E 168
Sjoa, *Nor.* 61°41′ N, 9°34′ E 152
Sjoutnäs, *Nor.* 64°35′ N, 14°54′ E 152
Sjøvegan, *Nor.* 68°53′ N, 17°50′ E 152
Skadovs'k, *Ukr.* 46°8′ N, 32°54′ E 156
Skaftung, *Fin.* 62°6′ N, 21°18′ E 152
Skagen, *Den.* 57°42′ N, 10°33′ E 150
Skagens Odde, *Den.* 57°30′ N, 10°37′ E 150
Skagerrak, strait 57°52′ N, 7°50′ E 152
Skaget, peak, *Nor.* 61°16′ N, 9°3′ E 152
Skagit, river, *Wash., U.S.* 48°31′ N, 122°3′ W 100
Skagway, *Alas., U.S.* 59°26′ N, 135°19′ W 108
Skaistkalne, *Latv.* 56°23′ N, 24°38′ E 166
Skala-Podil's'ka, *Ukr.* 48°50′ N, 26°11′ E 156
Skamokawa, *Wash., U.S.* 46°15′ N, 123°27′ W 100
Skånevik, *Nor.* 59°43′ N, 5°54′ E 152
Skänninge, *Nor.* 58°22′ N, 15°3′ E 152
Skærbæk, *Den.* 55°9′ N, 8°44′ E 150
Skardu, *Pak.* 35°17′ N, 75°39′ E 186
Skærfjorden 77°13′ N, 24°16′ W 246
Skärhamn, *Sw.* 57°59′ N, 11°33′ E 150
Skarnes, *Nor.* 60°14′ N, 11°41′ E 152
Skarvdalsegga, peak, *Nor.* 62°4′ N, 7°55′ E 152
Skattkärr, *Nor.* 59°24′ N, 13°38′ E 152
Skaudvilė, *Lith.* 55°24′ N, 22°34′ E 166
Skaymat, *Africa* 24°29′ N, 15°7′ W 214
Skebo, *Sw.* 59°57′ N, 18°33′ E 166
Skeena Crossing, *Can.* 55°4′ N, 127°48′ W 108
Skeena Mountains, *Can.* 56°49′ N, 129°31′ W 98
Skeena, river, *Can.* 55°21′ N, 127°45′ W 108
Skegness, *U.K.* 53°8′ N, 0°20′ E 162
Skeldon, *Guyana* 5°46′ N, 57°12′ W 130
Skeleton Coast Park, *Namibia* 17°59′ S, 10°48′ E 220
Skeleton Coast, region, *Namibia* 17°31′ S, 11°47′ E 220
Skellefteå, *Nor.* 64°45′ N, 20°53′ E 152
Skelleftehamn, *Nor.* 64°40′ N, 21°14′ E 152
Skender Vakuf, *Bosn. and Herzg.* 44°29′ N, 17°22′ E 168
Skënderaj (Srbica), *Kosovo* 42°44′ N, 20°46′ E 168
Skępe, *Pol.* 52°51′ N, 19°21′ E 152
Skerries, *Ire.* 53°33′ N, 6°8′ W 150
Ski, *Nor.* 59°43′ N, 10°51′ E 152
Skiatook, *Okla., U.S.* 36°21′ N, 96°0′ W 96
Skibo Castle, site, *U.K.* 57°51′ N, 4°16′ W 150
Skibotn, *Nor.* 69°23′ N, 20°21′ E 152
Skidal', *Belarus* 53°35′ N, 24°14′ E 152
Skiddaw, peak, *U.K.* 54°38′ N, 3°11′ W 162
Skidmore, *Tex., U.S.* 28°14′ N, 97°41′ W 92
Skidmore, Mount, peak, *Antarctica* 80°29′ S, 29°26′ W 248
Skien, *Nor.* 59°13′ N, 9°32′ E 160
Skihist Mountain, peak, *Can.* 50°10′ N, 121°59′ W 108
Skillingaryd, *Nor.* 57°25′ N, 14°4′ E 152
Skipskjolen, peak, *Nor.* 70°20′ N, 29°32′ E 152
Skipton, *U.K.* 53°57′ N, 2°1′ W 162
Skíros, island, *Gr.* 38°57′ N, 24°31′ E 180
Skive, *Den.* 56°33′ N, 9°0′ E 150
Skjåk, *Nor.* 61°52′ N, 8°21′ E 152
Skjern, *Den.* 55°56′ N, 8°27′ E 150
Skjern Å, river, *Den.* 55°50′ N, 8°41′ E 152
Skjervøy, *Nor.* 70°1′ N, 20°59′ E 152
Sklad, *Russ.* 71°53′ N, 123°21′ E 160
Sklinna, islands, *Norwegian Sea* 65°8′ N, 9°53′ E 152
Skodje, *Nor.* 62°29′ N, 6°42′ E 152
Skokie, *Ill., U.S.* 42°1′ N, 87°44′ W 102
Skokowa, *Pol.* 51°23′ N, 16°52′ E 152
Skole, *Ukr.* 49°2′ N, 23°31′ E 152
Skönvik, *Nor.* 62°26′ N, 17°17′ E 152
Skopin, *Russ.* 53°50′ N, 39°30′ E 154
Skopje, *Maced.* 41°58′ N, 21°21′ E 168
Skotoúsa, *Gr.* 41°7′ N, 23°23′ E 156
Skövde, *Nor.* 58°22′ N, 13°48′ E 152
Skovorodino, *Russ.* 53°52′ N, 123°53′ E 190
Skowhegan, *Me., U.S.* 44°43′ N, 69°44′ W 82
Skrad, *Croatia* 45°25′ N, 14°53′ E 156
Skradin (Scardona), *Croatia* 43°49′ N, 15°54′ E 168
Skrīveri, *Latv.* 56°37′ N, 25°7′ E 166
Skrunda, *Latv.* 56°39′ N, 21°58′ E 166
Skudeneshavn, *Nor.* 59°9′ N, 5°15′ E 152
Skulerud, *Nor.* 59°40′ N, 11°32′ E 152
Skull Mountain, peak, *Nev., U.S.* 36°46′ N, 116°13′ W 101
Skultuna, *Nor.* 59°42′ N, 16°25′ E 152
Skuodas, *Lith.* 56°15′ N, 21°32′ E 166
Skutskär, *Sw.* 60°38′ N, 17°23′ E 166
Skvyra, *Ukr.* 49°44′ N, 29°47′ E 158
Skwentna, *Alas., U.S.* 61°48′ N, 151°17′ W 98
Skykomish, *Wash., U.S.* 47°41′ N, 121°22′ W 100
Skykomish, river, *Wash., U.S.* 47°48′ N, 121°58′ W 100
Slagelse, *Den.* 55°23′ N, 11°22′ E 152
Slagle, *La., U.S.* 31°11′ N, 93°9′ W 103
Slains Castle, site, *U.K.* 57°24′ N, 1°57′ W 150
Slakovci, *Croatia* 45°13′ N, 18°55′ E 168
Slano, *Croatia* 42°46′ N, 17°52′ E 168
Slantsy, *Russ.* 59°5′ N, 28°0′ E 166
Slaný, *Czech Rep.* 50°13′ N, 14°4′ E 152
Śląskie, adm. division, *Pol.* 50°19′ N, 18°25′ E 152
Slate Islands, *Can.* 48°29′ N, 87°23′ W 94
Slate Mountain, peak, *Calif., U.S.* 40°48′ N, 120°57′ W 90
Slate Range, *Calif., U.S.* 35°49′ N, 117°22′ W 101
Slater, *Mo., U.S.* 39°12′ N, 93°4′ W 94
Slatersville, *R.I., U.S.* 41°59′ N, 71°35′ W 104
Slatina, *Bosn. and Herzg.* 44°49′ N, 17°16′ E 168
Slatina, *Bosn. and Herzg.* 44°57′ N, 18°26′ E 168
Slatina, *Rom.* 44°27′ N, 24°21′ E 156
Slatina Timiş, *Rom.* 45°15′ N, 22°16′ E 168
Slatinski Drenovac, *Croatia* 45°32′ N, 17°42′ E 168
Slaton, *Tex., U.S.* 33°25′ N, 101°39′ W 92
Slave Coast, region, *Nig.* 5°48′ N, 5°8′ E 222
Slave Lake, *Can.* 55°17′ N, 114°47′ W 108
Slave Point, *Can.* 61°1′ N, 115°56′ W 108
Slave, river, *Can.* 59°1′ N, 111°30′ W 106

Slavgorod, Belarus 53°23' N, 31°1' E 154
Slavgorod, Russ. 52°59' N, 78°47' E 184
Slavinja, Serb. 43°8' N, 22°52' E 168
Slavkovichi, Russ. 57°37' N, 29°4' E 166
Slavonia, region, Croatia 45°20' N, 16°50' E 168
Slavonice, Czech Rep. 48°59' N, 15°21' E 152
Slavonski Kobaš, Croatia 45°6' N, 17°44' E 168
Slavuta, Ukr. 50°18' N, 26°53' E 152
Slavyanka, Russ. 42°51' N, 131°22' E 200
Slavyansk na Kubani, Russ. 45°17' N, 38°3' E 156
Slayton, Minn., U.S. 43°57' N, 95°45' W 94
Sleaford, U.K. 52°59' N, 0°25' E 162
Sleat, Point of 56°43' N, 6°3' W 150
Sled Lake, lake, Can. 54°22' N, 107°42' W 108
Sleeper Islands, islands, Can. 57°9' N, 82°37' W 106
Sleepy Eye, Minn., U.S. 44°16' N, 94°44' W 94
Ślesin, Pol. 53°10' N, 17°42' E 152
Slide Mountain, peak, N.Y., U.S. 41°58' N, 74°29' W 94
Slidell, La., U.S. 30°14' N, 89°47' W 103
Sliedrecht, Neth. 51°49' N, 4°45' E 167
Slievemore, peak, Ire. 53°59' N, 10°10' W 150
Slievenamon, peak, Ire. 52°24' N, 7°40' W 150
Sligo, Ire. 54°15' N, 8°29' W 150
Slim Buttes, peak, S. Dak., U.S. 45°21' N, 103°16' W 90
Slinger, Wis., U.S. 43°19' N, 88°17' W 102
Slingerlands, N.Y., U.S. 42°37' N, 73°53' W 104
Slite, Sw. 57°42' N, 18°47' E 166
Sliven, Bulg. 42°40' N, 26°18' E 156
Sliven, adm. division, Bulg. 42°40' N, 25°52' E 156
Slivnica, Serb. 42°58' N, 22°45' E 168
Slivnitsa, Bulg. 42°51' N, 23°2' E 168
Sljeme, peak, Croatia 45°54' N, 15°55' E 168
Sloan, Nev., U.S. 35°56' N, 115°14' W 101
Slobodchikovo, Russ. 61°45' N, 48°16' E 154
Slobodskoy, Russ. 58°46' N, 50°10' E 169
Slobozia, Rom. 44°34' N, 27°21' E 156
Slocan, Can. 49°45' N, 117°28' W 90
Sloka, Latv. 56°57' N, 23°37' E 166
Słomniki, Pol. 50°14' N, 20°6' E 152
Slonim, Belarus 53°4' N, 25°18' E 152
Slotten, Nor. 70°44' N, 24°33' E 152
Slottsbron, Nor. 59°18' N, 13°3' E 152
Slough, U.K. 51°31' N, 0°37' E 162
Slovakia 48°50' N, 18°49' E 152
Sloveni, Belarus 54°20' N, 29°35' E 166
Slovenia 46°4' N, 14°46' E 156
Slov"yans'k, Ukr. 48°51' N, 37°37' E 158
Sludka, Russ. 61°56' N, 50°12' E 154
Sludka, Russ. 59°22' N, 49°43' E 154
Sluis, Neth. 51°18' N, 3°23' E 163
Slumbering Hills, Nev., U.S. 41°16' N, 118°18' W 90
Slŭnchev Bryag, Bulg. 42°41' N, 27°42' E 156
Słupca, Pol. 52°17' N, 17°52' E 152
Słupsk, Pol. 54°21' N, 16°40' E 152
Slussfors, Nor. 65°26' N, 16°14' E 152
Slutsk, Belarus 53°0' N, 27°33' E 152
Slyudyanka, Russ. 51°32' N, 103°50' E 190
Smackover, Ark., U.S. 33°20' N, 92°44' W 103
Smalininkai, Lith. 55°4' N, 22°35' E 166
Small Lake, lake, Can. 57°40' N, 97°46' W 108
Small Point, Me., U.S. 43°38' N, 69°52' W 104
Smalltree Lake, lake, Can. 61°0' N, 105°43' W 108
Smallwood Reservoir, lake, Can. 53°25' N, 70°28' W 106
Smalyavichy, Belarus 54°1' N, 28°5' E 166
Smara, Africa 26°45' N, 11°43' W 214
Smarhon', Belarus 54°29' N, 26°22' E 166
Smederevo, Serb. 44°39' N, 20°55' E 168
Smedjebacken, Nor. 60°6' N, 15°23' E 152
Smeïda see Taoudenni, Mali 22°41' N, 3°59' W 214
Śmigiel, Pol. 52°0' N, 16°31' E 152
Smila, Ukr. 49°15' N, 31°48' E 160
Smilavichy, Belarus 53°46' N, 28°2' E 152
Smilde, Neth. 52°56' N, 6°28' E 163
Smiltene, Latv. 57°25' N, 25°52' E 166
Smirnovo, Kaz. 54°30' N, 69°26' E 184
Smith, Can. 55°8' N, 114°3' W 108
Smith Arm 66°9' N, 124°31' W 98
Smith Bay 70°41' N, 155°33' W 98
Smith Bay 76°54' N, 81°57' W 106
Smith Canyon, Colo., U.S. 37°23' N, 103°35' W 92
Smith Center, Kans., U.S. 39°46' N, 98°47' W 90
Smith Island, Antarctica 62°54' S, 63°41' W 134
Smith Island, Can. 60°21' N, 80°16' W 106
Smith, Mount, peak, Eth. 6°15' N, 36°15' E 224
Smith River, Can. 59°52' N, 126°26' W 108
Smith Sound 51°10' N, 128°2' W 108
Smith Sound 78°12' N, 79°48' W 246
Smithboro, Ill., U.S. 38°53' N, 89°21' W 102
Smithdale, Miss., U.S. 31°19' N, 90°41' W 103
Smithers, Can. 54°44' N, 127°15' W 106
Smithers, W. Va., U.S. 38°10' N, 81°19' W 94
Smithfield, N.C., U.S. 35°30' N, 78°21' W 96
Smithfield, S. Af. 30°12' S, 26°32' E 227
Smiths Falls, Can. 44°54' N, 75°58' W 82
Smithtown, N.Y., U.S. 40°51' N, 73°12' W 104
Smithville, W. Va., U.S. 39°4' N, 81°6' W 102
Smoke Creek Desert, Nev., U.S. 40°32' N, 120°5' W 90
Smokey, Cape, Can. 46°30' N, 60°22' W 111
Smokvica, Croatia 42°54' N, 16°52' E 168
Smoky Falls, Can. 50°3' N, 82°11' W 94
Smoky Hill, river, Kans., U.S. 38°41' N, 99°5' W 90
Smoky Hills, Kans., U.S. 39°16' N, 99°19' W 90
Smoky Lake, Can. 54°6' N, 112°28' W 108
Smoky Mountains, Idaho, U.S. 43°40' N, 114°50' W 90
Smoky, river, Can. 53°52' N, 119°16' W 108
Smoky, river, Can. 55°21' N, 118°10' W 108
Smolensk, Russ. 54°48' N, 32°7' E 154
Smolensk, adm. division, Russ. 54°59' N, 31°37' E 154
Smolijana, Bosn. and Herzg. 44°37' N, 16°25' E 168
Smólikas, peak, Gr. 40°4' N, 20°51' E 156
Smolyan, Bulg. 41°35' N, 24°40' E 156
Smolyan, adm. division, Bulg. 41°37' N, 24°7' E 156
Smolyanovtsi, Bulg. 43°31' N, 22°59' E 168
Smooth Rock Falls, Can. 49°17' N, 81°38' W 94
Smyley Island, Antarctica 72°41' S, 82°11' W 248
Smyrna see İzmir, Turk. 38°24' N, 27°8' E 156
Snaefell, peak 54°14' N, 4°33' W 150
Snaght, Slieve, peak, Ire. 55°10' N, 7°27' W 150
Snake Falls, Can. 50°50' N, 93°26' W 90
Snake Range, Nev., U.S. 39°18' N, 114°25' W 90
Snake River, Can. 59°5' N, 122°26' W 108
Snake, river, Can. 65°50' N, 133°4' W 98
Snake River Plain, Idaho, U.S. 43°24' N, 116°24' W 90
Snake, river, U.S. 43°5' N, 116°27' W 90
Snappertuna, Fin. 59°59' N, 23°39' E 166
Snare Lake, Can. 58°25' N, 108°18' W 108
Snare, river, Can. 58°23' N, 107°39' W 108
Snåsa, Nor. 64°13' N, 12°20' E 152
Sneek, Neth. 53°1' N, 5°40' E 163
Snelland, U.K. 53°18' N, 0°24' E 162
Snelling, Calif., U.S. 37°31' N, 120°28' W 100
Snettisham, U.K. 52°52' N, 0°30' E 162
Snezhnogorsk, Russ. 68°6' N, 87°36' E 169
Snezhnoye, Russ. 65°27' N, 173°3' E 160
Sněžka, peak, Czech Rep. 50°43' N, 15°37' E 152
Snihurivka, Ukr. 47°5' N, 32°48' E 156
Snilfjord, Nor. 63°23' N, 9°30' E 152
Snipe Keys, islands, Gulf of Mexico 24°43' N, 81°46' W 105
Snøhetta, peak, Nor. 62°18' N, 9°9' E 152
Snohomish, Wash., U.S. 47°54' N, 122°6' W 100
Snonuten, peak, Nor. 59°29' N, 6°45' E 152
Snoqualmie, Wash., U.S. 47°30' N, 121°50' W 100
Snoqualmie Pass, Wash., U.S. 47°24' N, 121°25' W 100
Snov, river, Ukr. 51°34' N, 31°44' E 158
Snover, Mich., U.S. 43°27' N, 82°58' W 102
Snow Hill Island, Antarctica 64°55' S, 56°59' W 134
Snow Island, Antarctica 62°42' S, 61°37' W 134
Snow Lake, Can. 54°52' N, 100°3' W 108
Snow, Mount, peak, Vt., U.S. 42°57' N, 72°57' W 104
Snow Mountain, peak, Calif., U.S. 39°22' N, 122°51' W 90
Snow Mountain, peak, Me., U.S. 45°16' N, 70°48' W 94
Snow Peak, Wash., U.S. 48°33' N, 118°33' W 90
Snowbird Lake, Can. 60°37' N, 103°28' W 108
Snowden, Can. 53°29' N, 104°40' W 108
Snowdon, peak, U.K. 53°4' N, 4°6' W 162
Snowflake, Ariz., U.S. 34°30' N, 110°5' W 92
Snowmass Mountain, peak, Colo., U.S. 39°7' N, 107°10' W 90
Snowshoe Peak, Mont., U.S. 48°11' N, 115°46' W 90
Snowy Mountains, Austral. 36°23' S, 147°16' E 230
Snuol, Cambodia 12°6' N, 106°24' E 202
Snyder, Colo., U.S. 40°19' N, 103°37' W 90
Snyder, Okla., U.S. 34°38' N, 98°58' W 92
Snyder, Tex., U.S. 32°41' N, 100°54' W 92
Soala see Sokolo, Mali 14°45' N, 6°7' W 222
Soanierana-Ivongo, Madagascar 16°54' S, 49°33' E 220
Soatá, Col. 6°19' N, 72°42' W 136
Soavinandriana, Madagascar 19°11' S, 46°44' E 220
Soba, Nig. 10°57' N, 8°5' E 222
Sobat, river, Sudan 8°53' N, 32°30' E 224
Soberania National Park, Pan. 9°9' N, 79°51' W 115
Sobernheim, Ger. 49°46' N, 7°39' E 167
Sobinka, Russ. 55°58' N, 40°1' E 154
Sobolev, Russ. 51°54' N, 51°41' E 158
Sobozo, spring, Niger 21°10' N, 14°47' E 222
Sobral, Braz. 3°41' S, 40°23' W 132
Sobti, spring, Mali 22°45' N, 1°46' W 214
Soc Trang, Vietnam 9°36' N, 105°57' E 202
Socha, Col. 5°59' N, 72°41' W 136
Sochaczew, Pol. 52°13' N, 20°14' E 152
Sochi, Russ. 43°36' N, 39°46' E 195
Society Islands, South Pacific Ocean 17°21' S, 152°59' W 238
Socompa, Chile 24°25' S, 68°21' W 132
Socorro, N. Mex., U.S. 34°2' N, 106°53' W 82
Socorro, Isla, island, Isla Socorro 18°28' N, 111°0' W 112
Socotra (Suquṭrá), island, Yemen 12°19' N, 54°12' E 182
Socovos, Sp. 38°20' N, 1°59' W 164
Socuéllamos, Sp. 39°17' N, 2°48' W 164
Soda Creek, Can. 52°20' N, 122°16' W 108
Soda Lake, Calif., U.S. 35°12' N, 120°2' W 100
Soda Mountains, Calif., U.S. 35°16' N, 116°20' W 101
Soda Peak, Wash., U.S. 45°51' N, 122°6' W 100
Sodankylä, Fin. 67°25' N, 26°33' E 152
Söderhamn, Nor. 61°18' N, 17°0' E 152
Södertälje, Nor. 59°10' N, 17°34' E 152
Sodiri, Sudan 14°23' N, 29°8' E 226
Sodo, Eth. 6°49' N, 37°46' E 224
Södra Kvarken 60°17' N, 18°40' E 166
Södra Storfjället, peak, Nor. 65°36' N, 14°36' E 152
Södra Sunderbyn, Nor. 65°39' N, 21°56' E 152
Södra Vi, Nor. 57°44' N, 15°46' E 152
Sodus, Mich., U.S. 42°1' N, 86°22' W 102
Soekmekaar see Morebeng, S. Af. 23°30' S, 29°56' E 227
Soela Väin 58°37' N, 22°8' E 166
Soest, Ger. 51°34' N, 8°6' E 167
Sofala, adm. division, Mozambique 18°26' S, 34°1' E 224
Sofara, Mali 14°1' N, 4°15' W 222
Sofi, Sudan 14°8' N, 35°51' E 226
Sofi, Tanzania 8°47' S, 36°9' E 224
Sofia see Sofiya, Bulg. 42°41' N, 23°12' E 156
Sofiya, adm. division, Bulg. 42°51' N, 22°47' E 168
Sofiya (Sofia), Bulg. 42°41' N, 23°12' E 156
Sofiya-Grad, adm. division, Bulg. 42°35' N, 23°7' E 156
Sofporog, Russ. 65°48' N, 31°28' E 152
Sof'yanga, Russ. 65°52' N, 31°17' E 152
Sog, China 31°51' N, 93°40' E 188
Soga, Tanzania 6°47' S, 38°55' E 224
Sogamoso, Col. 5°41' N, 72°56' W 136
Sogata, Eth. 5°41' N, 35°8' E 224
Sögel, Ger. 52°50' N, 7°32' E 163
Sogod, Philippines 10°24' N, 125°0' E 203
Sogolle, spring, Chad 15°20' N, 15°20' E 216
Sogra, Russ. 62°49' N, 47°28' E 169
Sogra, Russ. 62°39' N, 46°16' E 154
Söğüt, Turk. 40°0' N, 30°10' E 180
Söğüt Gölü, lake, Turk. 37°4' N, 29°39' E 156
Sohâg, Egypt 26°33' N, 31°35' E 180
Soham, U.K. 52°19' N, 0°20' E 162
Soheuksando, island, S. Korea 34°7' N, 124°32' E 198
Sohm Plain, North Atlantic Ocean 37°43' N, 53°36' W 253
Sŏhŭng, N. Korea 38°28' N, 126°10' E 200
Soignies, Belg. 50°35' N, 4°4' E 163
Şoimuş, Rom. 45°55' N, 22°55' E 168
Soissons, Fr. 49°22' N, 3°18' E 163
Sōja, Japan 34°40' N, 133°45' E 201
Sojat, India 25°54' N, 73°42' E 186
Sok, river, Russ. 53°53' N, 51°16' E 154
Sokcho, S. Korea 38°13' N, 128°34' E 200
Söke, Turk. 37°44' N, 27°22' E 156
Sokhumi (Sukhum), Rep. of Georgia 43°0' N, 41°55' E 195
Soko Banja, Serb. 43°38' N, 21°51' E 168
Sokodé, Togo 8°57' N, 1°8' E 214
Sokol, Russ. 59°28' N, 40°12' E 154
Sokolac, Bosn. and Herzg. 43°56' N, 18°49' E 168
Sokolarci, Maced. 41°54' N, 22°17' E 168
Sokółka, Pol. 53°24' N, 23°29' E 152
Sokolo (Soala), Mali 14°45' N, 6°7' W 222
Sokolovka, Kaz. 55°9' N, 69°11' E 184
Sokolovo, Russ. 65°21' N, 57°1' E 154
Sokol'skoye, Russ. 57°8' N, 43°13' E 154
Sokoto, Nig. 13°1' N, 5°13' E 222
Soksa, N. Korea 40°38' N, 127°17' E 200
Sokuluk, Kyrg. 42°51' N, 74°23' E 184
Sol, Costa del, Sp. 36°34' N, 4°40' W 164
Sol de Julio, Arg. 29°33' S, 63°27' W 139
Sol, river, Braz. 6°42' S, 67°47' W 130
Solana Beach, Calif., U.S. 32°59' N, 117°17' W 101
Solano, Venez. 1°56' N, 66°56' W 136
Solano, Punta, Col. 6°16' N, 77°53' W 136
Solberg, Nor. 63°47' N, 17°38' E 152
Solberget, peak, Nor. 63°47' N, 17°27' E 152
Solec, Pol. 51°8' N, 21°45' E 152
Soledad, Arg. 30°38' S, 60°55' W 139
Soledad, Calif., U.S. 36°25' N, 121°20' W 100
Soledad, Col. 10°52' N, 74°48' W 136
Soledad, Peru 3°32' S, 77°49' W 136
Soledad, Venez. 8°11' N, 63°33' W 116
Soledad de Doblado, Mex. 19°3' N, 96°25' W 114
Soledad Pass, Calif., U.S. 34°30' N, 118°9' W 101
Soledade, Braz. 28°50' S, 52°32' W 139
Soledade, Braz. 6°38' S, 69°9' W 130
Solhan, Turk. 38°57' N, 41°3' E 195
Soliera, It. 44°44' N, 10°55' E 167
Soligalich, Russ. 59°5' N, 42°16' E 154
Solignano, It. 44°38' N, 9°58' E 156
Solikamsk, Russ. 59°38' N, 56°45' E 154
Solimões (Amazonas), river, Braz. 2°50' S, 66°35' W 122
Solin (Salonae), Croatia 43°32' N, 16°28' E 168
Solingen, Ger. 51°9' N, 7°5' E 167
Sollefteå, Nor. 63°9' N, 17°15' E 152
Solling, Ger. 51°43' N, 9°23' E 167
Sol'lletsk, Russ. 51°9' N, 55°2' E 158
Solms, Ger. 50°31' N, 8°24' E 167
Solna, Sw. 59°22' N, 17°58' E 166
Solnechnogorsk, Russ. 56°9' N, 37°0' E 154
Solobkivtsi, Ukr. 49°3' N, 26°54' E 152
Solodcha, Russ. 49°37' N, 44°18' E 158
Solok, Indonesia 0°47' N, 100°39' E 196
Sololo, Kenya 3°27' N, 38°34' E 224
Solomennoye, Russ. 61°50' N, 34°19' E 154
Solomon, Can. 53°21' N, 117°56' W 108
Solomon, Kans., U.S. 38°53' N, 97°22' W 90
Solomon Islands 10°21' S, 162°22' E 242
Solomon Islands, South Pacific Ocean 10°55' S, 162°35' E 238
Solomon, river, Kans., U.S. 39°41' N, 99°17' W 90
Solomon Sea 6°43' S, 150°46' E 238
Solon Springs, Wis., U.S. 46°21' N, 91°50' W 94
Solotcha, Russ. 54°47' N, 39°49' E 154
Solothurn, Switz. 47°12' N, 7°31' E 150
Solovetskiye Ostrova, islands, Beloye More 64°40' N, 35°18' E 154
Solsona, Sp. 41°59' N, 1°31' E 164
Solstad, Nor. 65°10' N, 12°8' E 152
Solt, Hung. 46°47' N, 19°1' E 168
Šolta, island, Croatia 43°18' N, 16°9' E 168
Soltan Bagh, Afghan. 33°19' N, 68°39' E 186
Solṭānābād, Iran 36°24' N, 57°56' E 180
Solṭānābād, Iran 31°2' N, 49°44' E 186
Soltan-e Bakva, Afghan. 32°18' N, 62°58' E 186
Soltüstik Qazaqstan, adm. division, Kaz. 53°58' N, 67°52' E 184
Soltvadkert, Hung. 46°34' N, 19°25' E 168
Solund, Nor. 61°4' N, 4°50' E 152
Solunska Glava, peak, Maced. 41°41' N, 21°21' E 168
Soluntum, ruin(s), It. 38°5' N, 13°25' E 156
Sol'vychegodsk, Russ. 61°21' N, 46°59' E 154
Solwezi, Zambia 12°13' S, 26°24' E 224
Solyanka, Russ. 51°28' N, 50°7' E 158
Soma, Turk. 39°10' N, 27°35' E 156
Somabhula, Zimb. 19°43' S, 29°40' E 224
Somali Basin, Indian Ocean 0°21' N, 51°48' E 254
Somali, region, Eth. 4°34' N, 42°4' E 224
Somalia 4°7' N, 45°14' E 218
Somaliland, special sovereignty, Somalia 10°26' N, 42°54' E 216
Sombor, Serb. 45°45' N, 19°7' E 168
Sombrerete, Mex. 23°36' N, 103°39' W 112
Sombrero, island, Sombrero 18°38' N, 63°21' W 116
Somero, Fin. 60°35' N, 23°29' E 166
Somers, Mont., U.S. 48°3' N, 114°15' W 108
Somers Point, N.J., U.S. 39°19' N, 74°36' W 94
Somerset, Can. 49°23' N, 98°40' W 94
Somerset, Colo., U.S. 38°56' N, 107°28' W 90
Somerset, Ky., U.S. 37°4' N, 84°36' W 96
Somerset, Mass., U.S. 41°46' N, 71°8' W 104
Somerset, Ohio, U.S. 39°48' N, 82°19' W 102
Somerset, Pa., U.S. 40°0' N, 79°5' W 94
Somerset Center, Mich., U.S. 42°2' N, 84°26' W 102
Somerset East, S. Af. 32°45' S, 25°33' E 227
Somerset Island, Can. 71°22' N, 92°26' W 106
Somerton, Ariz., U.S. 32°35' N, 114°43' W 101
Somerville, Mass., U.S. 42°23' N, 71°6' W 104
Somerville, Tenn., U.S. 35°14' N, 89°21' W 96
Somerville, Tex., U.S. 30°19' N, 96°32' W 96
Sommepy-Tahure, Fr. 49°15' N, 4°32' E 163
Sommesous, Fr. 48°44' N, 4°12' E 163
Somogy, adm. division, Hung. 46°31' N, 17°13' E 156
Somonauk, Ill., U.S. 41°37' N, 88°42' W 102
Somotillo, Nicar. 13°1' N, 86°53' W 115
Sompa, Est. 59°20' N, 27°20' E 166
Somuncurá, Meseta de, Arg. 41°27' S, 69°4' W 134
Son, Con, islands, South China Sea 8°29' N, 106°16' E 202
Son Ha, Vietnam 15°3' N, 108°33' E 202
Son Hoa, Vietnam 13°4' N, 108°58' E 202
Son Islands, Con, South China Sea 6°2' N, 107°2' E 238
Son, river, India 24°23' N, 82°1' E 197
Son, river, India 25°22' N, 84°42' E 197
Son, river, India 23°50' N, 81°25' E 190
Son Tay, Vietnam 21°7' N, 105°29' E 202
Sŏnch'ŏn, N. Korea 39°47' N, 124°53' E 200
Soncillo, Sp. 42°57' N, 3°48' W 164
Soncino, It. 45°24' N, 9°51' E 167
Sondalo, It. 46°19' N, 10°17' E 167
Sondheimer, La., U.S. 32°32' N, 91°10' W 103
Sondrio, It. 46°10' N, 9°51' E 167
Song, Nig. 9°49' N, 12°36' E 216
Song Cau, Vietnam 13°28' N, 109°11' E 202
Song Ma, Vietnam 21°4' N, 103°42' E 202
Songea, Tanzania 10°42' S, 35°39' E 224
Songeons, Fr. 49°32' N, 1°51' E 163
Songhua Hu, lake, China 43°3' N, 126°28' E 200
Songhua, river, China 46°3' N, 129°18' E 190
Songjiang, China 30°59' N, 121°13' E 198
Songjianghe, China 42°8' N, 127°30' E 200
Sŏngjin see Kimch'aek, N. Korea 40°38' N, 129°11' E 200
Songkhla, Thai. 7°10' N, 100°35' E 196
Songkhram, river, Thai. 18°7' N, 103°29' E 202
Song-Köl, lake, Kyrg. 41°49' N, 74°39' E 184
Songnim, N. Korea 38°44' N, 125°39' E 200
Songo, Angola 7°23' S, 14°51' E 218
Songo Songo Island, Tanzania 8°29' S, 39°25' E 224
Songshuzhen, China 42°2' N, 127°6' E 200
Songxi, China 27°35' N, 118°47' E 198
Songxian, China 34°10' N, 112°4' E 198
Songzi, China 30°10' N, 111°45' E 198
Sonhat, India 23°29' N, 82°32' E 197
Sonid Youqi, China 42°51' N, 112°35' E 198
Sonid Zuoqi, China 43°49' N, 113°43' E 198
Sonipat, India 28°57' N, 77°1' E 188
Sonkovo, Russ. 57°45' N, 37°9' E 154
Sonmiani, Pak. 25°25' N, 66°32' E 186
Sonmiani Bay 25°14' N, 65°37' E 186
Sonoyta, Mex. 31°52' N, 112°51' W 92
Sonoita, river, Mex. 31°15' N, 113°23' W 92
Sonoma, Calif., U.S. 38°17' N, 122°28' W 100
Sonoma Peak, Nev., U.S. 40°50' N, 117°42' W 90
Sonoma Range, Nev., U.S. 40°45' N, 117°50' W 90
Sonora, Calif., U.S. 37°58' N, 120°23' W 100
Sonora, Tex., U.S. 30°32' N, 100°38' W 92
Sonora, adm. division, Mex. 30°11' N, 111°25' W 92
Sonora Pass, Calif., U.S. 38°19' N, 119°39' W 100
Sonora Peak, Calif., U.S. 38°21' N, 119°41' W 100
Sonoran Desert, Ariz., U.S. 33°27' N, 115°27' W 101
Sonqor, Iran 34°45' N, 47°35' E 180
Sonsón, Col. 5°40' N, 75°16' W 136
Sonsonate, El Salv. 13°44' N, 89°44' W 115
Sonsoro, Benin 11°7' N, 2°46' E 222
Sonsorol Islands, Philippine Sea 5°19' N, 129°32' E 192
Sonta, Serb. 45°35' N, 19°6' E 168
Sontra, Ger. 51°4' N, 9°56' E 167
Sooke, Can. 48°21' N, 123°43' W 100
Soomaa National Park, Est. 58°23' N, 24°42' E 166
Sopachuy, Bol. 19°30' S, 64°36' W 137
Soperton, Ga., U.S. 32°22' N, 82°36' W 96
Sopo, river, Sudan 7°50' N, 25°52' E 224
Sopochnoye, Russ. 56°1' N, 156°4' E 160
Sopot, Pol. 54°25' N, 18°33' E 166
Sopron, Hung. 47°40' N, 16°36' E 168
Šopsko Rudare, Maced. 42°4' N, 22°0' E 168
Sopur, India 34°18' N, 74°30' E 186
Soquel, Calif., U.S. 37°0' N, 121°57' W 100
Sør Flatanger, Nor. 64°26' N, 10°46' E 152
Sør Varanger, region, Nor. 69°54' N, 29°6' E 152
Sorata, Bol. 15°46' S, 68°43' W 137
Soratte, Monte, peak, It. 42°13' N, 12°25' E 156
Sorbas, Sp. 37°5' N, 2°8' W 164
Sore, Fr. 44°19' N, 0°35' E 150
Sorel, Can. 46°1' N, 73°6' W 110
Soresina, It. 45°17' N, 9°50' E 167
Sørfjord, Nor. 66°29' N, 13°17' E 152
Sorgun, Turk. 39°49' N, 35°10' E 156
Soria, Sp. 41°45' N, 2°30' W 164
Soriano, Uru. 33°25' S, 58°16' W 139
Sorkwity, Pol. 53°49' N, 21°10' E 166

Sorø, *Den.* 55°26′ N, 11°34′ E 152
Sorocaba, *Braz.* 23°30′ S, 47°30′ W 138
Sorochinsk, *Russ.* 52°25′ N, 53°9′ E 154
Sorol Atoll 8°24′ N, 141°13′ E 192
Sorong, *Indonesia* 0°52′ N, 131°12′ E 192
Soroti, *Uganda* 1°41′ N, 33°35′ E 224
Soroti Station, *Uganda* 1°45′ N, 33°37′ E 224
Sorotona, *Côte d'Ivoire* 7°59′ N, 7°9′ W 222
Sørøyane, islands, *Nor.* 62°10′ N, 4°15′ E 152
Sorqudyq, *Kaz.* 46°30′ N, 59°4′ E 158
Sørreisa, *Nor.* 69°10′ N, 18°5′ E 152
Sorrento, *La., U.S.* 30°9′ N, 90°52′ W 103
Sorsatunturi, peak, *Fin.* 67°23′ N, 29°27′ E 152
Sorsele, *Nor.* 65°31′ N, 17°32′ E 152
Sorsk, *Russ.* 54°2′ N, 90°14′ E 184
Sorsogon, *Philippines* 13°0′ N, 124°0′ E 203
Sort, *Sp.* 42°24′ N, 1°6′ E 164
Sortavala, *Russ.* 61°38′ N, 30°35′ E 160
Sortavala (Serdobol), *Russ.* 61°42′ N, 30°39′ E 166
Sortland, *Nor.* 68°41′ N, 15°24′ E 152
Sørumsand, *Nor.* 59°58′ N, 11°14′ E 152
Sørvær, *Nor.* 70°37′ N, 22°0′ E 152
Sõrve Poolsaar, *Est.* 58°4′ N, 21°39′ E 166
Sõrve Säär, *Est.* 57°47′ N, 21°52′ E 166
Sørvika, *Nor.* 62°25′ N, 11°51′ E 152
Sos del Rey Católico, *Sp.* 42°29′ N, 1°13′ W 164
Sosaq, *Kaz.* 44°9′ N, 68°28′ E 184
Soscumica, Lac, lake, *Can.* 50°15′ N, 78°17′ W 110
Sosna, river, *Russ.* 52°20′ N, 38°2′ E 158
Sosnogorsk, *Russ.* 63°35′ N, 54°0′ E 154
Sosnovets, *Russ.* 64°26′ N, 34°20′ E 152
Sosnovka, *Russ.* 66°30′ N, 40°25′ E 154
Sosnovka, *Russ.* 56°15′ N, 51°21′ E 154
Sosnovka, *Russ.* 53°12′ N, 41°18′ E 154
Sosnovka, *Russ.* 56°11′ N, 47°11′ E 154
Sosnovo, *Russ.* 60°33′ N, 30°15′ E 166
Sosnovyy Bor, *Russ.* 59°54′ N, 29°7′ E 166
Sosnowica, *Pol.* 51°30′ N, 23°4′ E 152
Soso, *Miss., U.S.* 31°45′ N, 89°16′ W 103
Sospel, *Fr.* 43°52′ N, 7°26′ E 150
Sospirolo, *It.* 46°7′ N, 12°3′ E 167
Sosso, *Cen. Af. Rep.* 3°58′ N, 15°32′ E 218
Sos'va, *Russ.* 59°12′ N, 61°45′ E 154
Sos'va, *Russ.* 63°42′ N, 61°56′ E 169
Sotataival, *Fin.* 67°44′ N, 28°52′ E 152
Soteir, spring, *Sudan* 17°3′ N, 30°27′ E 182
Sotério, river, *Braz.* 11°36′ S, 64°36′ W 137
Sotik, *Kenya* 0°41′ N, 35°4′ E 224
Sotkamo, *Fin.* 64°7′ N, 28°22′ E 152
Soto la Marina, *Mex.* 23°44′ N, 98°12′ W 114
Sotsgorodok, *Russ.* 50°8′ N, 38°4′ E 158
Sottunga 60°6′ N, 20°40′ E 166
Sotuélamos, *Sp.* 39°2′ N, 2°35′ W 164
Sotuf, Adrar, *Africa* 21°9′ N, 15°55′ W 222
Souanké, *Congo* 2°2′ N, 14°2′ E 218
Soubré, *Côte d'Ivoire* 5°46′ N, 6°37′ W 222
Soudan, *Minn., U.S.* 47°48′ N, 92°14′ W 94
Souffay, *Congo* 2°4′ N, 14°54′ E 218
Souilly, *Fr.* 49°1′ N, 5°17′ E 163
Souk Ahras, *Alg.* 36°17′ N, 7°58′ E 156
Souk el Arba du Rharb, *Mor.* 34°42′ N, 6°2′ W 214
Soulac-sur-Mer, *Fr.* 45°30′ N, 1°9′ W 150
Soultz-sous-Forêts, *Fr.* 48°56′ N, 7°52′ E 163
Soumoulou, *Fr.* 43°15′ N, 0°11′ E 164
Sounding Lake, *Can.* 52°10′ N, 110°55′ W 108
Soúnion, ruin(s), *Gr.* 37°38′ N, 23°55′ E 156
Sountel, spring, *Niger* 16°50′ N, 11°37′ E 222
Souppes, *Fr.* 48°10′ N, 2°43′ E 163
Sour, *Alg.* 35°59′ N, 0°19′ E 164
Sour Lake, *Tex., U.S.* 30°7′ N, 94°25′ W 103
Soûr (Tyre), *Leb.* 33°16′ N, 35°12′ E 194
Soure, *Braz.* 0°42′ N, 48°31′ W 130
Soure, *Port.* 40°3′ N, 8°38′ W 150
Souris, *Can.* 46°21′ N, 62°15′ W 111
Souris, *Can.* 49°38′ N, 100°15′ W 90
Souris, river, *Can.-U.S.* 49°11′ N, 101°9′ W 80
Sous, Oued, river, *Mor.* 30°2′ N, 9°37′ W 142
Sousa, *Braz.* 6°48′ S, 38°9′ W 132
Sousse, *Tun.* 35°49′ N, 10°35′ E 156
South Africa 29°13′ S, 23°21′ E 227
South America 37°0′ S, 58°0′ W 123
South Andaman, island, *India* 12°10′ N, 91°34′ E 188
South Atlantic Ocean 66°37′ S, 30°53′ W 253
South Aulatsivik Island, *Can.* 56°52′ N, 64°48′ W 106
South Australia, adm. division, *Austral.* 29°25′ S, 133°4′ E 231
South Australian Basin, *Great Australian Bight* 37°26′ S, 128°11′ E 254
South Baldy, peak, *N. Mex., U.S.* 33°58′ N, 107°16′ W 92
South Baldy, peak, *Wash., U.S.* 48°24′ N, 117°13′ W 90
South Barre, *Mass., U.S.* 42°22′ N, 72°6′ W 104
South Barre, *Vt., U.S.* 44°10′ N, 72°31′ W 104
South Barrule, peak 54°8′ N, 4°47′ W 150
South Bay, *Fla., U.S.* 26°39′ N, 80°43′ W 105
South Baymouth, *Can.* 45°34′ N, 82°0′ W 94
South Beloit, *Ill., U.S.* 42°28′ N, 89°3′ W 102
South Bend, *Ind., U.S.* 41°39′ N, 86°15′ W 102
South Bend, *Wash., U.S.* 46°38′ N, 123°47′ W 100
South Bentinck Arm 52°4′ N, 127°5′ W 108
South Berwick, *Me., U.S.* 43°13′ N, 70°49′ W 104
South Bimini, island, *Bahamas* 25°39′ N, 79°34′ W 105
South Bruny Island, island, *Austral.* 43°8′ S, 145°12′ E 230
South Burlington, *Vt., U.S.* 44°27′ N, 73°10′ W 104
South Carolina, adm. division, *S.C., U.S.* 34°13′ N, 81°30′ W 96
South Cat Cay, island, *Bahamas* 25°30′ N, 79°34′ W 105
South Chatham, *N.H., U.S.* 44°6′ N, 71°1′ W 104
South China Sea 9°35′ N, 110°49′ E 192
South Cle Elum, *Wash., U.S.* 47°9′ N, 120°58′ W 100
South Dakota, adm. division, *S. Dak., U.S.* 44°43′ N, 101°5′ W 90
South Daytona, *Fla., U.S.* 29°10′ N, 81°1′ W 105
South Deerfield, *Mass., U.S.* 42°28′ N, 72°37′ W 104
South Dorset, *Vt., U.S.* 43°13′ N, 73°5′ W 104
South Dos Palos, *Calif., U.S.* 36°57′ N, 120°40′ W 101
South Downs, region, *U.K.* 50°55′ N, 1°10′ W 162
South Downs National Park, *U.K.* 50°55′ N, 0°30′ W 162
South Egremont, *Mass., U.S.* 42°9′ N, 73°25′ W 104
South Elgin, *Ill., U.S.* 41°59′ N, 88°19′ W 102
South Fiji Basin, *South Pacific Ocean* 27°11′ S, 176°32′ E 252
South Fork Kern, river, *Calif., U.S.* 36°17′ N, 118°16′ W 101
South Fork Moreau, river, *S. Dak., U.S.* 45°6′ N, 104°14′ W 90
South Fork Mountain, *Calif., U.S.* 40°32′ N, 123°50′ W 90
South Fulton, *Tenn., U.S.* 36°28′ N, 88°52′ W 96
South Georgia, island, *U.K.* 54°19′ S, 39°36′ W 134
South Govç, adm. division, *Mongolia* 43°16′ N, 104°29′ E 198
South Hadley, *Mass., U.S.* 42°15′ N, 72°35′ W 104
South Hamilton, *Mass., U.S.* 42°36′ N, 70°53′ W 104
South Hangay, adm. division, *Mongolia* 45°20′ N, 102°36′ E 198
South Haven, *Mich., U.S.* 42°23′ N, 86°16′ W 102
South Head, *Can.* 49°4′ N, 59°4′ W 111
South Henik Lake, lake, *Can.* 61°26′ N, 99°59′ W 106
South Horr, *Kenya* 2°12′ N, 36°53′ E 224
South Indian Lake, *Can.* 56°46′ N, 98°54′ W 108
South Island National Park, *Kenya* 2°31′ N, 36°32′ E 224
South Jacksonville, *Mo., U.S.* 39°41′ N, 90°15′ W 94
South Knife Lake, lake, *Can.* 58°11′ N, 97°8′ W 108
South Korea 35°16′ N, 126°48′ E 238
South Lee, *Mass., U.S.* 42°16′ N, 73°18′ W 104
South Loup, river, *Nebr., U.S.* 41°19′ N, 100°42′ W 80
South Luangwa National Park, *Zambia* 13°7′ S, 31°5′ E 224
South Male Atoll, *Maldives* 3°43′ N, 72°38′ E 188
South Mansfield, *La., U.S.* 31°59′ N, 93°44′ W 103
South Milwaukee, *Wis., U.S.* 42°54′ N, 87°53′ W 102
South Molton, *U.K.* 51°1′ N, 3°50′ W 162
South Mountain, peak, *Idaho, U.S.* 42°44′ N, 117°0′ W 90
South Nahanni, river, *Can.* 61°12′ N, 124°28′ W 246
South Negril Point, *Jam.* 18°15′ N, 79°22′ W 115
South Orkney Islands, *Scotia Sea* 60°22′ S, 46°55′ W 134
South Orleans, *Mass., U.S.* 41°44′ N, 70°0′ W 104
South Ossetia, special sovereignty, *Ga.* 42°13′ N, 43°45′ E 195
South Pacific Ocean 31°20′ S, 86°12′ W 252
South Paris, *Me., U.S.* 44°13′ N, 70°32′ W 104
South Pass, *Wyo., U.S.* 42°21′ N, 108°55′ W 90
South Point, *Can.* 46°43′ N, 60°17′ W 111
South Point, *Mich., U.S.* 44°42′ N, 83°39′ W 94
South Point see Kalae, *Hawai'i, U.S.* 18°40′ N, 155°43′ W 99
South Porcupine, *Can.* 48°27′ N, 81°10′ W 106
South Portland, *Me., U.S.* 43°38′ N, 70°15′ W 104
South River, *Can.* 45°50′ N, 79°22′ W 82
South Royalton, *Vt., U.S.* 43°48′ N, 72°32′ W 104
South Ryegate, *Vt., U.S.* 44°11′ N, 72°9′ W 104
South Saskatchewan, river, *Can.* 50°21′ N, 110°52′ W 106
South Seal, river, *Can.* 57°49′ N, 99°40′ W 108
South Shaftsbury, *Vt., U.S.* 42°56′ N, 73°14′ W 104
South Shetland Islands, *Drake Passage* 62°7′ S, 56°55′ W 134
South Shore, *Ky., U.S.* 38°42′ N, 82°58′ W 102
South Shoshone Peak, *Nev., U.S.* 39°3′ N, 117°39′ W 90
South Sioux City, *Nebr., U.S.* 42°26′ N, 96°25′ W 90
South Sudan, region, *Sudan* 7°6′ N, 30°40′ E 224
South Superior, *Wyo., U.S.* 41°44′ N, 108°57′ W 92
South Tamworth, *N.H., U.S.* 43°49′ N, 71°18′ W 104
South Tasman Rise, *South Pacific Ocean* 47°59′ S, 148°46′ E 252
South Wabasca Lake, *Can.* 55°53′ N, 114°29′ W 108
South Weare, *N.H., U.S.* 43°3′ N, 71°43′ W 104
South Wellesley Islands, *Austral.* 17°51′ S, 139°47′ E 230
South Wellfleet, *Mass., U.S.* 41°55′ N, 70°0′ W 104
South Wellington, *Can.* 49°5′ N, 123°53′ W 100
South West Island, *Austral.* 16°26′ S, 135°45′ E 230
South Weymouth Naval Air Station, *Mass., U.S.* 42°8′ N, 70°58′ W 104
South Whitley, *Ind., U.S.* 41°4′ N, 85°38′ W 102
South Windham, *Conn., U.S.* 41°40′ N, 72°11′ W 104
South Windsor, *Conn., U.S.* 41°48′ N, 72°38′ W 104
South Woodbury, *Vt., U.S.* 44°24′ N, 72°26′ W 104
South Woodstock, *Conn., U.S.* 41°55′ N, 71°58′ W 104
South Woodstock, *Vt., U.S.* 43°33′ N, 72°33′ W 104
South Yarmouth, *Mass., U.S.* 41°39′ N, 70°12′ W 104
South Yolla Bolly Mountains, peak, *Calif., U.S.* 40°1′ N, 122°57′ W 90
South Zanesville, *Ohio, U.S.* 39°53′ N, 82°1′ W 102
Southampton, *N.Y., U.S.* 40°53′ N, 72°24′ W 104
Southampton, *U.K.* 50°54′ N, 1°25′ W 162
Southampton, Cape, *Can.* 61°57′ N, 87°52′ W 106
Southampton Island, *Can.* 65°3′ N, 90°41′ W 106
Southaven, *Miss., U.S.* 34°57′ N, 90°1′ W 96
Southbank, *Can.* 53°59′ N, 125°47′ W 108
Southbridge, *Mass., U.S.* 42°4′ N, 72°3′ W 104
Southbury, *Conn., U.S.* 41°28′ N, 73°13′ W 104
Southeast Indian Ridge, *Indian Ocean* 47°18′ S, 98°12′ E 254
Southeast Pacific Basin, *South Pacific Ocean* 47°50′ S, 90°49′ W 252
Southeast Point 41°5′ N, 71°26′ W 104
Southend, *Can.* 56°20′ N, 103°17′ W 108
Southend-on-Sea, *U.K.* 51°32′ N, 0°42′ E 162
Southern Alps, *N.Z.* 44°16′ S, 168°12′ E 240
Southern Darfur, adm. division, *Sudan* 10°34′ N, 23°30′ E 224
Southern Indian Lake, *Can.* 57°40′ N, 100°23′ W 108
Southern Indian Lake, lake, *Can.* 56°10′ N, 100°54′ W 106
Southern Kordofan, adm. division, *Sudan* 11°5′ N, 29°45′ E 224
Southern National Park, *Sudan* 6°25′ N, 27°55′ E 224
Southern Ocean 248
Southern Uplands, *U.K.* 55°19′ N, 4°36′ W 150
Southey, *Can.* 50°56′ N, 104°31′ W 90
Southfield, *Mass., U.S.* 42°5′ N, 73°15′ W 104
Southington, *Conn., U.S.* 41°35′ N, 72°53′ W 104
Southminster, *U.K.* 51°40′ N, 0°49′ E 162
Southold, *N.Y., U.S.* 41°4′ N, 72°26′ W 104
Southport, *Fla., U.S.* 30°17′ N, 85°38′ W 96
Southport, *N.Y., U.S.* 42°3′ N, 76°50′ W 94
Southport, *N.C., U.S.* 33°55′ N, 78°2′ W 96
Southport, *U.K.* 53°38′ N, 3°1′ W 162
Southwell, *U.K.* 53°4′ N, 0°58′ E 162
Southwest Indian Ridge, *Indian Ocean* 39°49′ S, 48°6′ E 254
Southwest Pacific Basin, *South Pacific Ocean* 40°58′ S, 149°1′ W 252
Southwest Point, *Bahamas* 25°45′ N, 77°12′ W 96
Southwold, *U.K.* 52°19′ N, 1°40′ E 163
Soutpansberg, peak, *S. Af.* 23°2′ S, 29°20′ E 227
Souvannakhili, *Laos* 15°25′ N, 105°48′ E 202
Soveja, *Rom.* 45°59′ N, 26°39′ E 158
Sovetsk, *Russ.* 55°4′ N, 21°52′ E 166
Sovetsk, *Russ.* 57°35′ N, 49°3′ E 154
Sovetskaya Gavan', *Russ.* 48°54′ N, 140°9′ E 238
Sovetskaya Rechka, *Russ.* 66°41′ N, 83°37′ E 169
Sovetskiy, *Russ.* 60°30′ N, 28°41′ E 166
Sovetskiy, *Russ.* 61°26′ N, 63°15′ E 169
Sovetskoye, *Russ.* 47°16′ N, 44°28′ E 158
So'x, *Uzb.* 40°0′ N, 71°7′ E 197
Soy, *Belg.* 50°16′ N, 5°30′ E 167
Soyala, *Russ.* 64°28′ N, 43°21′ E 154
Soyana, river, *Russ.* 65°35′ N, 42°11′ E 154
Soymigora, *Russ.* 63°9′ N, 51°50′ E 154
Soyo, *Angola* 6°12′ S, 12°20′ E 218
Soyopa, *Mex.* 28°45′ N, 109°40′ W 92
Sozh, river, *Belarus* 52°13′ N, 30°59′ E 158
Sozimskiy, *Russ.* 59°44′ N, 52°17′ E 154
Sozopol (Apollonia), *Bulg.* 42°25′ N, 27°42′ E 156
Spa, *Belg.* 50°30′ N, 5°52′ E 167
Spa, *Pol.* 51°32′ N, 20°8′ E 152
Spaatz Island, *Antarctica* 74°21′ S, 75°18′ W 248
Spackenkill, *N.Y., U.S.* 41°38′ N, 73°56′ W 104
Spain 40°34′ N, 3°17′ W 150
Spalatum see Split, *Croatia* 43°30′ N, 16°26′ E 168
Spalding, *Nebr., U.S.* 41°40′ N, 98°22′ W 90
Spalding, *U.K.* 52°47′ N, 0°9′ E 162
Spanish Fork, *Utah, U.S.* 40°5′ N, 111°37′ W 90
Spanish Head 53°51′ N, 5°7′ W 150
Spanish Peak, *Oreg., U.S.* 44°22′ N, 119°51′ W 90
Spanish Peaks, *Colo., U.S.* 37°9′ N, 104°56′ W 92
Spanish Town, *Jam.* 17°59′ N, 76°59′ W 115
Spann, Mount, peak, *Antarctica* 82°4′ S, 42°47′ W 248
Sparkman, *Ark., U.S.* 33°54′ N, 92°51′ W 96
Sparks, *Ga., U.S.* 31°9′ N, 83°26′ W 96
Sparks Lake, lake, *Can.* 61°11′ N, 110°10′ W 108
Sparland, *Ill., U.S.* 41°0′ N, 89°28′ W 102
Sparta, *Can.* 42°41′ N, 81°5′ W 102
Sparta, *Ga., U.S.* 33°16′ N, 82°58′ W 96
Sparta, *Mo., U.S.* 38°6′ N, 89°42′ W 94
Sparta, *Tenn., U.S.* 35°55′ N, 85°28′ W 96
Sparta, *Wis., U.S.* 43°57′ N, 90°49′ W 94
Spartanburg, *S.C., U.S.* 34°57′ N, 81°56′ W 96
Spartel, Cap, *Mor.* 35°50′ N, 7°13′ W 214
Spartivento, Capo, *It.* 37°51′ N, 16°6′ E 156
Spartivento, Capo, *It.* 38°47′ N, 8°52′ E 156
Sparwood, *Can.* 49°44′ N, 114°53′ W 90
Spas Demensk, *Russ.* 54°28′ N, 34°3′ E 154
Spas Klepiki, *Russ.* 55°9′ N, 40°11′ E 154
Spasporub, *Russ.* 60°39′ N, 48°57′ E 154
Spassk, *Russ.* 52°47′ N, 87°48′ E 184
Spassk Dal'niy, *Russ.* 44°38′ N, 132°48′ E 160
Spatsizi, river, *Can.* 57°14′ N, 128°35′ W 108
Spearfish, *S. Dak., U.S.* 44°28′ N, 103°53′ W 82
Spearman, *Tex., U.S.* 36°10′ N, 101°12′ W 92
Spearsville, *La., U.S.* 32°54′ N, 92°36′ W 103
Specter Range, *Nev., U.S.* 36°41′ N, 116°17′ W 101
Speedway, *Ind., U.S.* 39°47′ N, 86°14′ W 102
Speedwell Island, *Speedwell Island* 52°55′ S, 59°49′ W 248
Speicher, *Ger.* 49°56′ N, 6°39′ E 167
Speightstown, *Barbados* 13°12′ N, 59°37′ W 116
Spencer, *Idaho, U.S.* 44°20′ N, 112°10′ W 90
Spencer, *Ind., U.S.* 39°17′ N, 86°47′ W 102
Spencer, *Iowa, U.S.* 43°8′ N, 95°9′ W 90
Spencer, *Nebr., U.S.* 42°51′ N, 98°43′ W 90
Spencer, *W. Va., U.S.* 38°48′ N, 81°23′ W 94
Spencer, Cape, *Austral.* 35°9′ S, 136°35′ E 231
Spencer Gulf 34°27′ S, 135°22′ E 230
Spencerville, *Ohio, U.S.* 40°41′ N, 84°21′ W 102
Spences Bridge, *Can.* 50°24′ N, 121°21′ W 108
Spennymoor, *U.K.* 54°42′ N, 1°37′ W 162
Sperlonga, *It.* 41°16′ N, 13°26′ E 156
Sperone, Capo, *It.* 38°54′ N, 7°43′ E 156
Sperrin Mountains, *U.K.* 54°46′ N, 7°48′ W 150
Spessart, *Ger.* 50°7′ N, 9°7′ E 167
Spezand, *Pak.* 29°58′ N, 66°59′ E 186
Spicer Islands, islands, *Can.* 67°44′ N, 80°35′ W 106
Spickard, Mount, peak, *Wash., U.S.* 48°57′ N, 121°17′ W 100
Spieden, Cape 66°10′ S, 129°48′ E 248
Spiess Seamount, *South Atlantic Ocean* 55°29′ S, 1°19′ W 255
Spiez, *Switz.* 46°41′ N, 7°40′ E 167
Spike Mountain, peak, *Alas., U.S.* 67°26′ N, 142°2′ W 98
Spilsby, *U.K.* 53°10′ N, 9°535′ E 162
Spin Buldak, *Afghan.* 31°1′ N, 66°27′ E 186
Spincourt, *Fr.* 49°19′ N, 5°39′ E 163
Spind, *Nor.* 58°5′ N, 6°54′ E 150
Špionica, *Bosn. and Herzg.* 44°45′ N, 18°31′ E 168
Spirit Lake, *Iowa, U.S.* 43°24′ N, 95°7′ W 90
Spirit Lake, *Wash., U.S.* 46°15′ N, 122°19′ W 100
Spirit River, *Can.* 55°46′ N, 118°50′ W 108
Spiritwood, *Can.* 53°21′ N, 107°28′ W 108
Spiro, *Okla., U.S.* 35°12′ N, 94°38′ W 96
Spirovo, *Russ.* 57°24′ N, 35°0′ E 154
Spišská Nová Ves, *Slovakia* 48°56′ N, 20°33′ E 152
Spitsbergen Fracture Zone, *Greenland Sea* 81°13′ N, 3°8′ W 255
Spitsbergen, island, *Nor.* 77°10′ N, 3°50′ E 160
Spittal, *Aust.* 46°48′ N, 13°29′ E 167
Splendora, *Tex., U.S.* 30°12′ N, 95°10′ W 103
Split, Cape, *Can.* 45°20′ N, 64°27′ W 111
Split Lake, *Can.* 56°14′ N, 96°11′ W 108
Split Peak, *Nev., U.S.* 41°48′ N, 118°31′ W 90
Split (Spalatum), *Croatia* 43°30′ N, 16°26′ E 168
Splügen, *Switz.* 46°33′ N, 9°17′ E 167
Splügen Pass, *Switz.* 46°31′ N, 9°19′ E 167
Spogi, *Latv.* 56°3′ N, 26°43′ E 166
Spokane, *Wash., U.S.* 47°40′ N, 117°27′ W 90
Spokane, Mount, peak, *Wash., U.S.* 47°53′ N, 117°12′ W 90
Spokane, river, *Wash., U.S.* 47°57′ N, 118°41′ W 80
Spooner, *Wis., U.S.* 45°49′ N, 91°54′ W 94
Sporyy Navolok, Mys, *Russ.* 75°20′ N, 44°26′ E 172
Spotted Range, *Nev., U.S.* 36°45′ N, 115°53′ W 101
Sprague, *Can.* 49°1′ N, 95°36′ W 90
Sprague, *Wash., U.S.* 47°16′ N, 117°59′ W 90
Spranger, Mount, peak, *Can.* 52°53′ N, 120°50′ W 108
Spratly Islands, *South China Sea* 11°51′ N, 112°52′ E 238
Spray, *Oreg., U.S.* 44°49′ N, 119°48′ W 90
Spremberg, *Ger.* 51°34′ N, 14°21′ E 152
Spring, *Tex., U.S.* 30°3′ N, 95°25′ W 103
Spring Butte, peak, *Oreg., U.S.* 43°30′ N, 121°26′ W 90
Spring Glen, *Utah, U.S.* 39°39′ N, 110°51′ W 92
Spring Green, *Wis., U.S.* 43°10′ N, 90°4′ W 102
Spring Grove, *Minn., U.S.* 43°33′ N, 91°39′ W 94
Spring Hill, *Fla., U.S.* 28°26′ N, 82°36′ W 105
Spring Lake, *Mich., U.S.* 43°3′ N, 86°10′ W 94
Spring Mountains, *Nev., U.S.* 36°22′ N, 115°51′ W 101
Spring Point, *Can.* 59°24′ N, 109°46′ W 108
Spring Valley, *N.Y., U.S.* 41°6′ N, 74°3′ W 104
Springbok, *S. Af.* 29°41′ S, 17°52′ E 227
Springdale, *Ark., U.S.* 36°10′ N, 94°9′ W 96
Springdale, *Can.* 49°30′ N, 56°6′ W 111
Springdale, *Ohio, U.S.* 39°16′ N, 84°29′ W 102
Springer, *N. Mex., U.S.* 36°21′ N, 104°36′ W 92
Springer Mountain, peak, *Ga., U.S.* 34°37′ N, 84°17′ W 96
Springfield, *Colo., U.S.* 37°23′ N, 102°37′ W 92
Springfield, *Fla., U.S.* 30°8′ N, 85°36′ W 96
Springfield, *Idaho, U.S.* 43°5′ N, 112°41′ W 90
Springfield, *Ill., U.S.* 39°47′ N, 89°41′ W 102
Springfield, *La., U.S.* 30°24′ N, 90°33′ W 103
Springfield, *Mass., U.S.* 42°6′ N, 72°36′ W 104
Springfield, *Minn., U.S.* 44°13′ N, 95°0′ W 90
Springfield, *Mo., U.S.* 37°12′ N, 93°18′ W 96
Springfield, *N.Z.* 43°21′ S, 171°55′ E 240
Springfield, *Ohio, U.S.* 39°54′ N, 83°48′ W 102
Springfield, *Oreg., U.S.* 44°2′ N, 123°1′ W 90
Springfield, *S. Dak., U.S.* 42°50′ N, 97°55′ W 90
Springfield, *Tenn., U.S.* 36°30′ N, 86°52′ W 94
Springfield, *Vt., U.S.* 43°17′ N, 72°29′ W 104
Springfontein, *S. Af.* 30°16′ S, 25°42′ E 227
Springhill, *Can.* 45°38′ N, 64°5′ W 111
Springhill, *La., U.S.* 32°59′ N, 93°28′ W 103
Springport, *Mich., U.S.* 42°22′ N, 84°42′ W 102
Springvale, *Me., U.S.* 43°27′ N, 70°49′ W 104
Springview, *Nebr., U.S.* 42°48′ N, 99°46′ W 90
Springville, *Calif., U.S.* 36°8′ N, 118°50′ W 101
Spruce Home, *Can.* 53°23′ N, 105°46′ W 108
Spruce Knob, peak, *W. Va., U.S.* 38°41′ N, 79°37′ W 94
Spruce Knob-Seneca Rocks National Recreation Area, *W. Va., U.S.* 38°49′ N, 87°57′ W 80
Spruce Mountain, peak, *Nev., U.S.* 40°32′ N, 114°54′ W 90
Spruce Pine, *N.C., U.S.* 35°55′ N, 82°5′ W 96
Spry, *Pa., U.S.* 39°54′ N, 76°41′ W 94
Spulico, Capo, *It.* 39°57′ N, 16°40′ E 156
Spur, *Tex., U.S.* 33°27′ N, 100°51′ W 92
Spurger, *Tex., U.S.* 30°40′ N, 94°11′ W 103
Spurn Head, *U.K.* 53°30′ N, 0°7′ E 162
Spuž, *Mont.* 42°31′ N, 19°13′ E 168
Spuzzum, *Can.* 49°41′ N, 121°26′ W 100
Squamish, *Can.* 49°42′ N, 123°8′ W 100
Squamish, river, *Can.* 50°7′ N, 123°20′ W 100
Square Islands, *Can.* 52°43′ N, 55°51′ W 111
Squires, Mount, peak, *Austral.* 26°15′ S, 127°12′ E 230
Squirrel, river, *Can.* 50°25′ N, 84°20′ W 110
Srbac, *Bosn. and Herzg.* 45°5′ N, 17°31′ E 168
Srbica see Skënderaj, *Kosovo* 42°44′ N, 20°46′ E 168
Srbobran, *Serb.* 45°33′ N, 19°47′ E 168
Sre Umbell, *Cambodia* 11°6′ N, 103°45′ E 202
Srebrenica, *Bosn. and Herzg.* 44°6′ N, 19°19′ E 168
Sredinnyy Khrebet, *Russ.* 57°35′ N, 160°3′ E 160
Srednekolymsk, *Russ.* 67°27′ N, 153°21′ E 160
Sredneye Bugayevo, *Russ.* 66°0′ N, 52°28′ E 154
Srednyaya Olekma, *Russ.* 55°20′ N, 120°33′ E 190
Sremska Mitrovica, *Serb.* 44°58′ N, 19°37′ E 168
Sremska Rača, *Serb.* 44°54′ N, 19°19′ E 168
Sremski Karlovci, *Serb.* 45°11′ N, 19°55′ E 168
Sretensk, *Russ.* 52°17′ N, 117°45′ E 190

Sri Jayewardenepura Kotte, *Sri Lanka* 6°54′ N, 79°57′ E 188
Sri Kalahasti, *India* 13°46′ N, 79°40′ E 188
Sri Lanka 7°26′ N, 80°15′ E 188
Sri Madhopur, *India* 27°28′ N, 75°37′ E 197
Srikakulam, *India* 18°17′ N, 83°55′ E 188
Srinagar, *India* 34°7′ N, 74°48′ E 186
Srivardhan, *India* 18°5′ N, 73°0′ E 188
Srnetica, *Bosn. and Herzg.* 44°26′ N, 16°35′ E 168
Srokowo, *Pol.* 54°11′ N, 21°31′ E 166
Srpska Crnja, *Serb.* 45°43′ N, 20°42′ E 168
Srpski Itebej, *Serb.* 45°34′ N, 20°43′ E 168
Ssanggyo, *N. Korea* 37°46′ N, 125°26′ E 200
Staaten River National Park, *Austral.* 16°39′ S, 142°26′ E 238
Staberhuk, *Kattegat* 54°18′ N, 10°48′ E 152
Stack, Ben, peak, *U.K.* 58°19′ N, 5°5′ W 150
Stade, *Ger.* 53°36′ N, 9°28′ E 150
Städjan, peak, *Nor.* 61°54′ N, 12°44′ E 152
Stadskanaal, *Neth.* 52°59′ N, 6°57′ E 163
Stadtallendorf, *Ger.* 50°49′ N, 9°0′ E 167
Stadtkyll, *Ger.* 50°20′ N, 6°32′ E 167
Stadtlohn, *Ger.* 51°59′ N, 6°54′ E 167
Stafford, *Kans., U.S.* 37°56′ N, 98°36′ W 90
Stafford, *U.K.* 52°47′ N, 2°7′ W 162
Stafford Springs, *Conn., U.S.* 41°57′ N, 72°19′ W 104
Staffordsville, *Ky., U.S.* 37°49′ N, 82°51′ W 94
Stage Road Pass, *Oreg., U.S.* 42°43′ N, 123°22′ W 90
Stagira, ruin(s), *Gr.* 40°31′ N, 23°38′ E 156
Stagnone, Isole dello, islands, *Mediterranean Sea* 37°35′ N, 11°52′ E 156
Staicele, *Latv.* 57°51′ N, 24°44′ E 166
Staigue Fort, site, *Ire.* 51°47′ N, 10°7′ W 150
Staines, *U.K.* 51°26′ N, 0°31′ E 162
Staithes, *U.K.* 54°33′ N, 0°48′ E 162
Stalać, *Serb.* 43°41′ N, 21°25′ E 168
Staldzene, *Latv.* 57°25′ N, 21°35′ E 166
Stalham, *U.K.* 52°46′ N, 1°31′ E 163
Stalingrad see Volgograd, *Russ.* 48°46′ N, 44°28′ E 158
Stallo, *Miss., U.S.* 32°53′ N, 89°6′ W 103
Stallworthy, Cape, *Can.* 81°41′ N, 95°15′ W 246
Stalowa Wola, *Pol.* 50°33′ N, 22°2′ E 152
Stamford, *Conn., U.S.* 41°2′ N, 73°33′ W 104
Stamford, *N.Y., U.S.* 42°24′ N, 74°39′ W 110
Stamford, *Tex., U.S.* 32°55′ N, 99°49′ W 92
Stamford, *U.K.* 52°39′ N, 0°29′ E 162
Stamford Bridge, *U.K.* 53°59′ N, 0°55′ E 162
Stamovo, *Bulg.* 42°26′ N, 25°50′ E 156
Stampriet, *Namibia* 24°18′ S, 18°23′ E 227
Stamps, *Ark., U.S.* 33°21′ N, 93°31′ W 103
Stanberry, *Mo., U.S.* 40°12′ N, 94°32′ W 94
Standerton, *S. Af.* 26°57′ S, 29°13′ E 227
Standish, *Me., U.S.* 43°43′ N, 70°33′ W 104
Standish, *Mich., U.S.* 43°58′ N, 83°58′ W 102
Standish Ranges, *Austral.* 21°44′ S, 138°59′ E 230
Stanfield, *Oreg., U.S.* 45°46′ N, 119°14′ W 90
Stanford, *Ky., U.S.* 37°31′ N, 84°40′ W 94
Stanford, *Mont., U.S.* 47°7′ N, 110°14′ W 90
Stånga, *Sw.* 57°16′ N, 18°27′ E 166
Stanger, *S. Af.* 29°21′ S, 31°15′ E 227
Staniard Creek, *Bahamas* 24°50′ N, 77°55′ W 96
Stanišić, *Serb.* 45°55′ N, 19°9′ E 168
Staňkov, *Czech Rep.* 49°33′ N, 13°4′ E 152
Stanley, *Can.* 46°16′ N, 66°45′ W 111
Stanley, *Falk. Is., U.K.* 51°42′ S, 57°52′ W 134
Stanley, *Idaho, U.S.* 44°12′ N, 114°56′ W 90
Stanley, *N. Dak., U.S.* 48°17′ N, 102°24′ W 90
Stanley, *Wis., U.S.* 44°57′ N, 90°56′ W 94
Stanley Falls see Boyoma Falls, *Dem. Rep. of the Congo* 0°14′ N, 25°9′ E 224
Stanley Mission, *Can.* 55°25′ N, 104°30′ W 108
Stanley, Mount, peak, *Austral.* 22°50′ S, 130°28′ E 230
Stanley, Mount, peak, *Austral.* 40°6′ S, 143°46′ E 230
Stanley Peak, *Can.* 51°11′ N, 116°6′ W 90
Stanleyville see Kisangani, *Dem. Rep. of the Congo* 0°33′ N, 25°16′ E 224
Stanovoy Khrebet, *Russ.* 54°46′ N, 122°14′ E 190
Stanton, *Mich., U.S.* 43°17′ N, 85°5′ W 102
Stanton, *Tex., U.S.* 32°7′ N, 101°47′ W 92
Stanwick, *U.K.* 52°20′ N, 0°33′ E 162
Stanwood, *Wash., U.S.* 48°13′ N, 122°23′ W 100
Staphorst, *Neth.* 52°39′ N, 6°12′ E 163
Staples, *Minn., U.S.* 46°20′ N, 94°48′ W 90
Stapleton, *Nebr., U.S.* 41°28′ N, 100°31′ W 90
Star, *Miss., U.S.* 32°5′ N, 90°2′ W 103
Star City, *Ark., U.S.* 33°56′ N, 91°51′ W 96
Star City, *Ind., U.S.* 40°58′ N, 86°34′ W 102
Star Peak, *Nev., U.S.* 40°31′ N, 118°16′ W 90
Star Valley, *Wyo., U.S.* 42°38′ N, 111°3′ W 90
Stara Moravica, *Serb.* 45°52′ N, 19°28′ E 168
Stara Pazova, *Serb.* 44°58′ N, 20°9′ E 168
Stara Ushytsya, *Ukr.* 48°34′ N, 27°5′ E 152
Stara Vyzhivka, *Ukr.* 51°25′ N, 24°25′ E 152
Stara Zagora, *Bulg.* 42°25′ N, 25°36′ E 156
Stara Zagora, adm. division, *Bulg.* 42°39′ N, 25°6′ E 156
Staraya, *Russ.* 70°56′ N, 112°20′ E 173
Staraya Poltavka, *Russ.* 50°28′ N, 46°26′ E 158
Staraya Russa, *Russ.* 57°56′ N, 31°23′ E 152
Starbuck, *Wash., U.S.* 46°30′ N, 118°8′ W 90
Stare Pole, *Pol.* 54°3′ N, 19°11′ E 166
Stargard Szczeciński, *Pol.* 53°19′ N, 15°1′ E 152
Stari Bar, *Mont.* 42°6′ N, 19°8′ E 168
Stari Mikanovci, *Croatia* 45°15′ N, 18°33′ E 168
Starigrad, *Croatia* 43°10′ N, 16°35′ E 168
Staritsa, *Belarus* 53°14′ N, 27°15′ E 154
Staritsa, *Russ.* 56°28′ N, 34°56′ E 154
Starke, *Fla., U.S.* 29°56′ N, 82°8′ W 96
Starks, *La., U.S.* 30°17′ N, 93°40′ W 103
Starksboro, *Vt., U.S.* 44°13′ N, 73°4′ W 104
Starkville, *Colo., U.S.* 37°7′ N, 104°33′ W 92
Starkville, *Miss., U.S.* 33°26′ N, 88°48′ W 103
Starobaltachevo, *Russ.* 56°1′ N, 55°56′ E 154
Starobil's'k, *Ukr.* 49°18′ N, 38°53′ E 158
Starobin, *Belarus* 52°42′ N, 27°27′ E 152
Starodub, *Russ.* 52°31′ N, 32°51′ E 154
Starokostyantyniv, *Ukr.* 49°44′ N, 27°12′ E 152
Starominskaya, *Russ.* 46°32′ N, 39°1′ E 156
Staropol'ye, *Russ.* 59°1′ N, 28°34′ E 166
Starorybnoye, *Russ.* 72°48′ N, 104°49′ E 173
Staroshcherbinovskaya, *Russ.* 46°37′ N, 38°38′ E 156
Staroye Syalo, *Belarus* 55°17′ N, 29°58′ E 166
Start Point, *English Channel* 50°2′ N, 3°37′ W 150
Starvyy Karabutak, *Kaz.* 49°49′ N, 59°54′ E 158
Staryy Biryuzyak, *Russ.* 44°45′ N, 46°47′ E 158
Staryy Krym, *Ukr.* 45°1′ N, 35°0′ E 156
Staryy Kryvyn, *Ukr.* 50°21′ N, 26°42′ E 152
Staryy Nadym, *Russ.* 65°36′ N, 72°50′ E 169
Staryy Oskol, *Russ.* 51°17′ N, 37°45′ E 158
Staryy Sambir, *Ukr.* 49°23′ N, 22°55′ E 152
Staszów, *Pol.* 50°33′ N, 21°10′ E 152
State Line, *Miss., U.S.* 31°24′ N, 88°28′ W 103
Staten Island, *N.Y., U.S.* 40°27′ N, 74°6′ W 104
Staten Island see de los Estados, Isla, *Arg.* 55°28′ S, 64°48′ W 134
Statesboro, *Ga., U.S.* 32°25′ N, 81°47′ W 112
Station 10, *Sudan* 19°41′ N, 33°8′ E 182
Station 5, *Sudan* 21°2′ N, 32°19′ E 182
Station 6, *Sudan* 20°44′ N, 32°30′ E 182
Staunton, *Ill., U.S.* 39°0′ N, 89°47′ W 102
Staunton, *Va., U.S.* 38°8′ N, 79°5′ W 94
Stavanger, *Nor.* 58°56′ N, 5°43′ E 152
Stave Lake, *Can.* 49°18′ N, 122°30′ W 100
Stavelot, *Belg.* 50°23′ N, 5°56′ E 167
Stavely, *Can.* 50°10′ N, 113°39′ W 90
Staveren, *Neth.* 52°53′ N, 5°22′ E 163
Stavnoye, *Ukr.* 48°56′ N, 22°42′ E 156
Stavropol', *Russ.* 45°3′ N, 41°58′ E 158
Stavropol', adm. division, *Russ.* 45°26′ N, 41°12′ E 160
Stawiski, *Pol.* 53°22′ N, 22°8′ E 154
Stayner, *Can.* 44°24′ N, 80°6′ W 110
Steamboat, *Can.* 58°40′ N, 123°45′ W 108
Steamboat Mountain, peak, *Wyo., U.S.* 41°57′ N, 109°2′ W 90
Stederdorf, *Ger.* 52°21′ N, 10°13′ E 150
Steele, *N. Dak., U.S.* 46°50′ N, 99°56′ W 108
Steele Island, island, *Antarctica* 71°8′ S, 60°19′ W 248
Steelpoort, *S. Af.* 24°46′ S, 30°11′ E 227
Steelton, *Pa., U.S.* 40°13′ N, 76°51′ W 94
Steelville, *Mo., U.S.* 37°57′ N, 91°21′ W 96
Steen River, *Can.* 59°39′ N, 117°11′ W 108
Steen, river, *Can.* 59°17′ N, 118°21′ W 108
Steens Mountain, *Oreg., U.S.* 43°21′ N, 118°14′ W 90
Steensby Inlet 69°57′ N, 81°26′ W 106
Steenstrup Gletscher, glacier 74°42′ N, 64°7′ W 106
Steenwijk, *Neth.* 52°46′ N, 6°6′ E 163
Steep Rock, *Can.* 51°26′ N, 98°48′ W 90
Steep Rock Lake, *Can.* 48°49′ N, 91°38′ W 94
Steers Head 81°45′ S, 164°32′ W 248
Stefansson Island, island, *Can.* 73°43′ N, 112°11′ W 106
Stege, *Den.* 54°59′ N, 12°17′ E 152
Steger, *Ill., U.S.* 41°27′ N, 87°38′ W 102
Steigen, *Nor.* 67°55′ N, 14°58′ E 152
Steigerwald, *Ger.* 49°45′ N, 10°17′ E 167
Stein Pass, *Ger.* 47°39′ N, 12°45′ E 152
Stein, river, *Can.* 50°10′ N, 122°21′ W 90
Steinau, *Ger.* 50°18′ N, 9°27′ E 167
Steinbach, *Can.* 49°31′ N, 96°42′ W 90
Steinfeld, *Ger.* 52°36′ N, 8°13′ E 163
Steinfort, *Lux.* 49°39′ N, 5°55′ E 163
Steinfurt, *Ger.* 52°8′ N, 7°19′ E 163
Steinhatchee, *Fla., U.S.* 29°40′ N, 83°24′ W 105
Steinhausen, *Namibia* 21°49′ S, 18°15′ E 227
Steinkjer, *Nor.* 63°57′ N, 11°44′ E 160
Steinkopf, *S. Af.* 29°15′ S, 17°42′ E 227
Stellaland, region, *S. Af.* 27°19′ S, 24°2′ E 227
Stelle, *Ger.* 53°22′ N, 10°6′ E 152
Stellenbosch, *S. Af.* 33°55′ S, 18°48′ E 227
Stelvio, Passo dello, *It.* 46°31′ N, 10°26′ E 167
Stenay, *Fr.* 49°29′ N, 5°11′ E 163
Stende, *Latv.* 57°8′ N, 22°32′ E 166
Stenstorp, *Nor.* 58°15′ N, 13°41′ E 152
Stenträsk, *Nor.* 66°19′ N, 19°50′ E 152
Stepanakert (Xankändi), *Asia* 39°48′ N, 46°43′ E 195
Step'anavan, *Arm.* 41°0′ N, 44°21′ E 195
Stepanci, *Maced.* 41°29′ N, 21°38′ E 168
Stephen, *Minn., U.S.* 48°26′ N, 96°53′ W 94
Stephens, *Ark., U.S.* 33°23′ N, 93°5′ W 103
Stephens Lake, lake, *Can.* 56°42′ N, 94°17′ W 108
Stephens Passage 57°46′ N, 134°48′ W 108
Stephens, Port 32°50′ S, 150°48′ E 230
Stephenson, *Mich., U.S.* 45°24′ N, 87°36′ W 94
Stephenson, Mount, peak, *Antarctica* 69°49′ S, 70°21′ W 248
Stephenville, *Can.* 48°31′ N, 58°39′ W 106
Stephenville, *Tex., U.S.* 32°13′ N, 98°13′ W 92
Stepnogorsk, *Kaz.* 52°23′ N, 71°54′ E 184
Stepnoye, *Russ.* 44°15′ N, 44°32′ E 158
Stepnyak, *Kaz.* 52°49′ N, 70°47′ E 184
Stepojevac, *Serb.* 44°30′ N, 20°18′ E 168
Steptoe Butte, peak, *Wash., U.S.* 46°59′ N, 117°24′ W 900
Stereá Eláda, adm. division, *Gr.* 38°54′ N, 22°26′ E 156
Sterling, *Colo., U.S.* 40°37′ N, 103°14′ W 90
Sterling, *Ill., U.S.* 41°47′ N, 89°42′ W 102
Sterling, *Kans., U.S.* 38°12′ N, 98°13′ W 90
Sterling, *Mich., U.S.* 44°1′ N, 84°2′ W 102
Sterling, *Mo., U.S.* 41°47′ N, 89°42′ W 94
Sterling, *N. Dak., U.S.* 46°48′ N, 100°18′ W 90
Sterling City, *Tex., U.S.* 31°49′ N, 101°0′ W 92
Sterlington, *La., U.S.* 32°40′ N, 92°5′ W 103
Sterlitamak, *Russ.* 53°39′ N, 55°53′ E 154
Stettler, *Can.* 52°19′ N, 112°42′ W 108
Stevenage, *U.K.* 51°54′ N, 0°13′ E 162
Stevens Point, *Wis., U.S.* 44°31′ N, 89°35′ W 94
Stevenson, *Wash., U.S.* 45°41′ N, 121°54′ W 100
Stevenson Lake, lake, *Can.* 53°54′ N, 96°43′ W 108
Stevenson Mountain, peak, *Oreg., U.S.* 44°33′ N, 120°32′ W 90
Stevensville, *Mich., U.S.* 42°0′ N, 86°30′ W 102
Stewardson, *Ill., U.S.* 39°15′ N, 88°39′ W 102
Stewart, *Can.* 55°56′ N, 130°1′ W 108
Stewart, *Miss., U.S.* 33°25′ N, 89°26′ W 103
Stewart, *Ohio, U.S.* 39°18′ N, 81°54′ W 102
Stewart Crossing, *Can.* 63°27′ N, 136°41′ W 98
Stewart, Isla, island, *Chile* 54°51′ S, 72°56′ W 134
Stewart Islands, *South Pacific Ocean* 8°0′ S, 163°3′ E 238
Stewart River, *Can.* 63°21′ N, 139°26′ W 98
Steynsburg, *S. Af.* 31°18′ S, 25°47′ E 227
Steyr, *Aust.* 48°2′ N, 14°24′ E 152
Steytlerville, *S. Af.* 33°20′ S, 24°18′ E 227
Stia, *It.* 43°48′ N, 11°41′ E 167
Stickney, *S. Dak., U.S.* 43°34′ N, 98°26′ W 90
Stiene, *Latv.* 57°23′ N, 24°33′ E 166
Stiens, *Neth.* 53°15′ N, 5°44′ E 163
Stigler, *Okla., U.S.* 35°13′ N, 95°9′ W 96
Stih, Hora, peak, *Ukr.* 48°35′ N, 23°12′ E 152
Stikine, river, *Can.* 57°15′ N, 131°59′ W 108
Stikine, river, *Can.* 58°11′ N, 130°31′ W 98
Stikine, river, *Can.* 58°0′ N, 129°22′ W 108
Stillman Valley, *Ill., U.S.* 42°6′ N, 89°11′ W 102
Stillwater, *Can.* 49°46′ N, 124°17′ W 100
Stillwater, *Minn., U.S.* 45°2′ N, 92°50′ W 94
Stillwater, *N.Y., U.S.* 42°56′ N, 73°40′ W 104
Stillwater, *Okla., U.S.* 36°5′ N, 97°2′ W 92
Stillwater Range, *Nev., U.S.* 39°59′ N, 118°14′ W 90
Stilo, Punta, *It.* 38°27′ N, 16°35′ E 156
Stilton, *U.K.* 52°29′ N, 0°17′ E 162
Stilwell, *Okla., U.S.* 35°46′ N, 94°38′ W 96
Stine Mountain, peak, *Mont., U.S.* 45°41′ N, 113°11′ W 90
Stinear, Mount, peak, *Antarctica* 73°18′ S, 66°2′ E 248
Stinkingwater Pass, *Oreg., U.S.* 43°42′ N, 118°32′ W 90
Stinnett, *Tex., U.S.* 35°47′ N, 101°27′ W 92
Stinson Lake, *N.H., U.S.* 43°51′ N, 71°50′ W 104
Štip, *Maced.* 41°44′ N, 22°11′ E 168
Stiring-Wendel, *Fr.* 49°12′ N, 6°55′ E 163
Stirling Island, *Solomon Islands* 7°20′ S, 155°30′ E 242
Stirling, Mount, peak, *Nev., U.S.* 36°26′ N, 116°1′ W 101
Stobi, ruin(s), *Maced.* 41°31′ N, 21°54′ E 168
Stock Route, *Austral.* 19°46′ S, 126°40′ E 231
Stockbridge, *Mass., U.S.* 42°16′ N, 73°20′ W 104
Stockbridge, *Mich., U.S.* 42°25′ N, 84°11′ W 102
Stockbridge, *U.K.* 51°6′ N, 1°29′ W 162
Stockbridge, *Vt., U.S.* 43°47′ N, 72°46′ W 104
Stockdale, *Tex., U.S.* 29°13′ N, 97°57′ W 96
Stockholm, *Sw.* 59°19′ N, 17°55′ E 166
Stockport, *U.K.* 53°23′ N, 2°10′ W 162
Stockton, *Ala., U.S.* 30°58′ N, 87°51′ W 103
Stockton, *Calif., U.S.* 37°57′ N, 121°17′ W 100
Stockton, *Ill., U.S.* 42°20′ N, 90°1′ W 102
Stockton, *Kans., U.S.* 39°26′ N, 99°17′ W 90
Stockton, *Mo., U.S.* 37°40′ N, 93°48′ W 94
Stockton on Tees, *U.K.* 54°34′ N, 1°20′ W 162
Stockwell, *Ind., U.S.* 40°16′ N, 86°46′ W 102
Stoddard, *N.H., U.S.* 43°4′ N, 72°8′ W 104
Støde, *Nor.* 62°24′ N, 16°33′ E 152
Stogovo, *Maced.* 41°28′ N, 20°32′ E 168
Stoke, *N.Z.* 41°21′ S, 173°14′ E 240
Stoke Ferry, *U.K.* 52°34′ N, 0°31′ E 162
Stoke on Trent, *U.K.* 53°0′ N, 2°11′ W 162
Stokes, Bahía 54°9′ S, 73°50′ W 134
Stokes, Mount, peak, *N.Z.* 41°8′ S, 174°2′ E 240
Stokesay, *U.K.* 52°25′ N, 2°50′ W 162
Stoksund, *Nor.* 64°2′ N, 10°4′ E 152
Stolac, *Bosn. and Herzg.* 43°3′ N, 17°57′ E 168
Stolberg, *Ger.* 50°46′ N, 6°12′ E 167
Stolbovo, *Russ.* 55°59′ N, 30°1′ E 166
Stolbovoy, Ostrov, island, *Russ.* 73°52′ N, 128°4′ E 160
Stolin, *Belarus* 51°53′ N, 26°49′ E 152
Stöllet, *Nor.* 60°23′ N, 13°16′ E 152
Stolnici, *Rom.* 44°35′ N, 24°47′ E 156
Stone, *U.K.* 52°54′ N, 2°8′ W 162
Stone Lake, lake, *Can.* 50°34′ N, 87°51′ W 110
Stonehenge, site, *U.K.* 51°9′ N, 1°51′ W 162
Stoner, *Can.* 53°38′ N, 122°40′ W 108
Stonewall, *Can.* 50°7′ N, 97°19′ W 108
Stonewall, *La., U.S.* 32°16′ N, 93°50′ W 103
Stonewall, *Miss., U.S.* 32°7′ N, 88°46′ W 103
Stonglandet, *Nor.* 69°5′ N, 17°12′ E 152
Stonington, *Ill., U.S.* 39°37′ N, 89°12′ W 102
Stony Brook, *N.Y., U.S.* 40°55′ N, 73°9′ W 104
Stony Creek, *N.Y., U.S.* 43°25′ N, 73°57′ W 104
Stony Lake, *Can.* 58°53′ N, 99°17′ W 108
Stony Plain, *Can.* 53°31′ N, 114°3′ W 108
Stony Point, *N.Y., U.S.* 43°39′ N, 76°34′ W 94
Stony Point, *N.Y., U.S.* 41°13′ N, 74°0′ W 104
Stony Rapids, *Can.* 59°10′ N, 106°0′ W 106
Stony River, *Alas., U.S.* 61°48′ N, 156°33′ W 98
Stooping, river, *Can.* 51°19′ N, 82°32′ W 110
Støren, *Nor.* 63°0′ N, 10°18′ E 152
Storfjord, *Nor.* 69°16′ N, 19°59′ E 152
Storfjorden 77°20′ N, 7°31′ E 172
Storkerson Bay 72°55′ N, 128°56′ W 106
Storlien, *Nor.* 63°18′ N, 12°7′ E 152
Storm Berg, peak, *S. Af.* 31°22′ S, 26°27′ E 227
Storm King Mountain, peak, *Colo., U.S.* 37°55′ N, 106°29′ W 90
Storm Lake, *Iowa, U.S.* 42°38′ N, 95°13′ W 90
Storozhevsk, *Russ.* 61°56′ N, 52°20′ E 154
Storr, The, peak 57°29′ N, 6°18′ W 150
Storriten, peak, *Nor.* 68°6′ N, 17°7′ E 152
Storrs, *Conn., U.S.* 41°48′ N, 72°16′ W 104
Storsjö, *Nor.* 62°47′ N, 13°2′ E 152
Storskavlen, peak, *Nor.* 60°44′ N, 7°10′ E 152
Storuman, *Nor.* 65°5′ N, 17°6′ E 152
Storvätteshågna, peak, *Nor.* 62°7′ N, 12°21′ E 152
Storvik, *Nor.* 60°34′ N, 16°28′ E 152
Story, *Wyo., U.S.* 44°34′ N, 106°53′ W 90
Story City, *Iowa, U.S.* 42°11′ N, 93°36′ W 94
Stoughton, *Can.* 49°40′ N, 103°4′ W 90
Stoughton, *Wis., U.S.* 42°54′ N, 89°12′ W 102
Stour, river, *U.K.* 51°58′ N, 0°47′ E 162
Stourbridge, *U.K.* 52°27′ N, 2°9′ W 162
Stourport on Severn, *U.K.* 52°20′ N, 2°16′ W 162
Stovepipe Wells, *Calif., U.S.* 36°36′ N, 117°10′ W 101
Stow, *Ohio, U.S.* 41°8′ N, 81°26′ W 94
Stow on the Wold, *U.K.* 51°55′ N, 1°44′ W 162
Stowbtsy, *Belarus* 53°29′ N, 26°45′ E 154
Stowe, *Vt., U.S.* 44°27′ N, 72°42′ W 104
Stowell, *Tex., U.S.* 29°46′ N, 94°24′ W 103
Stowmarket, *U.K.* 52°11′ N, 0°59′ E 162
Stoyaniv, *Ukr.* 50°22′ N, 24°39′ E 158
Stradella, *It.* 45°4′ N, 9°17′ E 167
Straldzha, *Bulg.* 42°36′ N, 26°41′ E 158
Stralsund, *Ger.* 54°16′ N, 13°4′ E 160
Strand, *S. Af.* 34°6′ S, 18°51′ E 227
Strandebarm, *Nor.* 60°16′ N, 5°59′ E 152
Strasbourg, *Can.* 51°3′ N, 104°57′ W 90
Strasbourg, *Fr.* 48°34′ N, 7°44′ E 163
Strasburg, *N. Dak., U.S.* 46°7′ N, 100°11′ W 90
Strasburg, *Ohio, U.S.* 40°35′ N, 81°32′ W 102
Strasburg, *Va., U.S.* 38°59′ N, 78°22′ W 94
Strășeni, *Mold.* 47°7′ N, 28°38′ E 156
Strata Florida, *U.K.* 52°16′ N, 3°50′ W 162
Stratford, *Calif., U.S.* 36°11′ N, 119°50′ W 100
Stratford, *Can.* 43°21′ N, 80°58′ W 102
Stratford, *Conn., U.S.* 41°11′ N, 73°9′ W 104
Stratford, *Tex., U.S.* 36°19′ N, 102°5′ W 92
Stratford upon Avon, *U.K.* 52°11′ N, 1°44′ W 162
Strathcona, Mount, peak, *Antarctica* 67°24′ S, 99°40′ E 248
Strathmore, *Calif., U.S.* 36°9′ N, 119°5′ W 101
Strathmore, *Can.* 51°2′ N, 113°25′ W 90
Strathmore, *U.K.* 56°24′ N, 3°37′ W 150
Strathnaver, *Can.* 53°20′ N, 122°33′ W 108
Strathroy, *Can.* 42°56′ N, 81°36′ W 102
Stratobowl, *S. Dak., U.S.* 43°58′ N, 103°25′ W 90
Stratonicea, ruin(s), *Gr.* 40°30′ N, 23°42′ E 156
Stratton, *Colo., U.S.* 39°17′ N, 102°36′ W 90
Stratton, *Me., U.S.* 45°8′ N, 70°27′ W 111
Stratton, *Nebr., U.S.* 40°8′ N, 101°14′ W 90
Stratus, ruin(s), *Gr.* 38°40′ N, 21°12′ E 156
Straubing, *Ger.* 48°52′ N, 12°34′ E 152
Straw Peak, *Calif., U.S.* 35°37′ N, 117°14′ W 101
Strawberry, *Calif., U.S.* 38°12′ N, 120°2′ W 100
Strawberry Mountain, peak, *Oreg., U.S.* 44°18′ N, 118°48′ W 90
Strawn, *Ill., U.S.* 40°38′ N, 88°24′ W 102
Strawn, *Tex., U.S.* 32°32′ N, 98°31′ W 92
Strážske, *Slovakia* 48°51′ N, 21°50′ E 156
Streaky Bay, *Austral.* 32°51′ S, 134°11′ E 231
Streatfield Lake, lake, *Can.* 52°7′ N, 86°30′ W 110
Streator, *Ill., U.S.* 41°7′ N, 88°50′ W 102
Středočeský, adm. division, *Czech Rep.* 49°52′ N, 13°50′ E 152
Streeter, *N. Dak., U.S.* 46°38′ N, 99°23′ W 90
Strehaia, *Rom.* 44°37′ N, 23°12′ E 168
Strekov, *Slovakia* 47°53′ N, 18°26′ E 168
Strel'na, *Russ.* 66°5′ N, 38°28′ E 154
Strel'skaya, *Russ.* 59°28′ N, 47°40′ E 154
Strenči, *Latv.* 57°37′ N, 25°40′ E 166
Stresa, *It.* 45°53′ N, 8°32′ E 167
Strezhevoy, *Russ.* 60°41′ N, 77°21′ E 169
Strickland, river, *P.N.G.* 7°53′ S, 141°4′ E 192
Strilki, *Ukr.* 49°18′ N, 22°53′ E 152
Strimasund, *Nor.* 66°3′ N, 14°54′ E 152
Strizhi, *Russ.* 58°23′ N, 49°2′ E 154
Strizivojna, *Croatia* 45°13′ N, 18°24′ E 168
Strmica, *Croatia* 44°8′ N, 16°14′ E 168
Stroeder, *Arg.* 40°12′ S, 62°36′ W 134
Strofádes, Nísoi, islands, *Ionian Sea* 37°9′ N, 20°20′ E 156
Ströhen, *Ger.* 52°32′ N, 8°41′ E 163
Stromberg, *Ger.* 49°57′ N, 7°46′ E 167
Stromsburg, *Nebr., U.S.* 41°6′ N, 97°37′ W 90
Strömsnäsbruk, *Nor.* 56°32′ N, 13°43′ E 152
Strömstad, *Nor.* 58°56′ N, 11°12′ E 152
Strömsund, *Nor.* 63°51′ N, 15°33′ E 152
Strong, *Ark., U.S.* 33°5′ N, 92°22′ W 103
Stroud, *Okla., U.S.* 35°42′ N, 96°40′ W 92
Stroud, *U.K.* 51°44′ N, 2°13′ W 162
Stroudsburg, *Pa., U.S.* 40°59′ N, 75°13′ W 94
Štrpce see Shtërpca, *Kosovo* 42°15′ N, 21°2′ E 168
Struer, *Den.* 56°28′ N, 8°34′ E 150
Strugi-Krasnyye, *Russ.* 58°16′ N, 29°6′ E 166
Strumica, *Maced.* 41°26′ N, 22°37′ E 168
Struthers, *Ohio, U.S.* 41°2′ N, 80°36′ W 94
Stružec, *Croatia* 45°30′ N, 16°32′ E 168
Strydenburg, *S. Af.* 29°58′ S, 23°40′ E 227
Stryker, *Ohio, U.S.* 41°29′ N, 84°25′ W 102
Stryy, *Ukr.* 49°14′ N, 23°50′ E 152
Strzelce Opolskie, *Pol.* 50°31′ N, 18°19′ E 152
Stuart, *Fla., U.S.* 27°11′ N, 80°14′ W 105
Stuart, *Iowa, U.S.* 41°30′ N, 94°20′ W 94
Stuart, *Nebr., U.S.* 42°34′ N, 99°9′ W 90
Stuart, *Va., U.S.* 36°38′ N, 80°17′ W 94
Stuart Bluff Range, *Austral.* 22°37′ S, 131°45′ E 231
Stuart Island, *Alas., U.S.* 63°34′ N, 163°8′ W 98
Stuart Lake, lake, *Can.* 54°8′ N, 124°56′ W 106
Stuart Range, *Austral.* 28°48′ S, 134°5′ E 230
Stuart, river, *Can.* 54°16′ N, 124°4′ W 108
Stubbenkammer 54°29′ N, 13°54′ E 152

Stubica, *Serb.* 43°56′ N, 21°29′ E 168
Štubik, *Serb.* 44°16′ N, 22°21′ E 168
Studholme Junction, *N.Z.* 44°45′ S, 171°7′ E 240
Stugun, *Nor.* 63°10′ N, 15°39′ E 154
Stumpy Point, *N.C., U.S.* 35°43′ N, 75°46′ W 96
Stupart, river, *Can.* 55°25′ N, 94°34′ W 108
Stupino, *Russ.* 54°53′ N, 38°2′ E 154
Sturbridge, *Mass., U.S.* 42°6′ N, 72°5′ W 104
Sturgeon Bay 51°59′ N, 98°31′ W 108
Sturgeon Falls, *Can.* 46°22′ N, 79°53′ W 94
Sturgeon Lake, *Can.* 50°1′ N, 91°23′ W 110
Sturgeon Landing, *Can.* 54°17′ N, 101°52′ W 108
Sturgeon Point, *Mich., U.S.* 44°32′ N, 83°15′ W 110
Sturgeon, river, *Can.* 50°14′ N, 94°26′ W 90
Sturgis, *Can.* 51°55′ N, 102°33′ W 90
Sturgis, *Ky., U.S.* 37°32′ N, 87°59′ W 96
Sturgis, *Mich., U.S.* 41°47′ N, 85°25′ W 102
Sturgis, *Miss., U.S.* 33°19′ N, 89°3′ W 103
Sturgis, *S. Dak., U.S.* 44°23′ N, 103°31′ W 90
Štúrovo, *Slovakia* 47°48′ N, 18°42′ E 168
Sturt Stony Desert, *Austral.* 26°37′ S, 139°38′ E 230
Sturtevant, *Wis., U.S.* 42°41′ N, 87°54′ W 102
Stuttgart, *Ark., U.S.* 34°30′ N, 91°36′ W 82
Stuttgart, *Ger.* 48°47′ N, 9°11′ E 150
Styx, river, *Ala., U.S.* 30°49′ N, 87°44′ W 103
Suakin, *Sudan* 19°5′ N, 37°16′ E 182
Suakin Archipelago, islands, *Red Sea* 18°49′ N, 37°56′ E 182
Suao, *Taiwan, China* 24°27′ N, 121°45′ E 198
Suaqui Grande, *Mex.* 28°24′ N, 109°54′ W 92
Suardi, *Arg.* 30°29′ S, 61°56′ W 139
Subačius, *Lith.* 55°45′ N, 24°46′ E 166
Subaşı Dağı, peak, *Turk.* 38°22′ N, 41°30′ E 195
Subata, *Latv.* 56°0′ N, 25°54′ E 166
Subcetate, *Rom.* 45°36′ N, 23°0′ E 168
Subei, *China* 39°30′ N, 94°57′ E 188
Subeita, ruin(s), *Israel* 30°53′ N, 34°35′ E 194
Subi, island, *Indonesia* 3°3′ N, 108°52′ E 196
Sublette, *Ill., U.S.* 41°38′ N, 89°14′ W 102
Sublette, *Kans., U.S.* 37°28′ N, 100°51′ W 92
Sublime, Point, peak, *Ariz., U.S.* 36°10′ N, 112°18′ W 92
Subotica, *Serb.* 46°5′ N, 19°40′ E 168
Subugo, peak, *Kenya* 1°40′ S, 35°44′ E 224
Suceava, *Rom.* 47°38′ N, 26°15′ E 152
Suceava, adm. division, *Rom.* 47°27′ N, 25°9′ E 156
Sučevići, *Croatia* 44°16′ N, 16°4′ E 168
Suchdol, *Czech Rep.* 48°53′ N, 14°52′ E 152
Suchixtepec, *Mex.* 16°4′ N, 96°28′ W 112
Suchowola, *Pol.* 51°42′ N, 22°43′ E 152
Sucio, river, *Col.* 7°26′ N, 77°3′ W 136
Sucre, *Bol.* 19°3′ S, 65°22′ W 137
Sucre, *Col.* 8°52′ N, 74°44′ W 136
Sucre, *Col.* 1°48′ N, 75°40′ W 136
Sucre, adm. division, *Col.* 8°42′ N, 75°15′ W 136
Sucre, adm. division, *Venez.* 10°19′ N, 63°47′ W 116
Sucuaro, *Col.* 4°32′ N, 68°50′ W 136
Sucunduri, river, *Braz.* 5°30′ S, 59°32′ W 130
Sucunduri, river, *Braz.* 9°5′ S, 58°59′ W 132
Sućuraj, *Croatia* 43°6′ N, 17°9′ E 168
Sucuriú, river, *Braz.* 18°42′ S, 52°0′ W 138
Sud Kivu, adm. division, *Dem. Rep. of the Congo* 3°59′ S, 28°18′ E 218
Sud, Pointe du, *Can.* 48°58′ N, 62°57′ W 111
Suda, *Russ.* 59°7′ N, 37°29′ E 154
Suda, river, *Russ.* 59°33′ N, 36°18′ E 154
Sudak, *Ukr.* 44°51′ N, 34°54′ E 156
Sudan 13°26′ N, 24°57′ E 207
Sudan, *Tex., U.S.* 34°3′ N, 102°32′ W 92
Suday, *Russ.* 58°59′ N, 43°9′ E 154
Sudbury see Greater Sudbury, *Can.* 46°29′ N, 81°0′ W 95
Sudbury, *Mass., U.S.* 42°22′ N, 71°26′ W 104
Sudbury, *U.K.* 52°2′ N, 0°43′ E 162
Suddie, *Guyana* 7°3′ N, 58°33′ W 130
Sudeten, *Pol.* 50°58′ N, 14°40′ E 152
Sud-Kivu, adm. division, *Dem. Rep. of the Congo* 3°17′ N, 27°56′ E 218
Sud-Ouest, Pointe du, *Can.* 49°20′ N, 64°50′ W 111
Sudr, *Egypt* 29°38′ N, 32°42′ E 180
Suđuroy, island, *Suđuroy* 61°26′ N, 10°6′ W 142
Sudzha, *Russ.* 51°10′ N, 35°18′ E 158
Sue, Mys, *Kaz.* 41°34′ N, 52°11′ E 158
Sue, river, *Sudan* 7°1′ N, 28°7′ E 224
Sueca, *Sp.* 39°11′ N, 0°19′ E 150
Suehn, *Liberia* 6°31′ N, 10°43′ W 222
Sueyoshi, *Japan* 31°39′ N, 131°1′ E 201
Suez Canal, *Egypt* 30°19′ N, 32°20′ E 206
Suez see El Suweis, *Egypt* 30°1′ N, 32°26′ E 180
Sūf, *Jordan* 32°18′ N, 35°50′ E 194
Şufaynah, *Saudi Arabia* 23°5′ N, 40°36′ E 182
Suffield, *Can.* 50°12′ N, 111°10′ W 90
Suffield, *Conn., U.S.* 41°58′ N, 72°39′ W 104
Suffolk, *Va., U.S.* 36°43′ N, 76°35′ W 96
Şūfīān, *Iran* 38°18′ N, 46°0′ E 195
Sugar City, *Colo., U.S.* 38°14′ N, 103°40′ W 90
Sugar City, *Idaho, U.S.* 43°52′ N, 111°45′ W 90
Sugar Hill, *N.H., U.S.* 44°12′ N, 71°48′ W 104
Sugarbush Hill, peak, *Wis., U.S.* 45°31′ N, 88°55′ W 94
Sugarcreek, *Ohio, U.S.* 40°29′ N, 81°37′ W 102
Sugarloaf Key, island, *Fla., U.S.* 24°44′ N, 81°39′ W 105
Sugarloaf Mountain, peak, *Me., U.S.* 45°0′ N, 70°23′ W 94
Sugarloaf Mountain, peak, *N.H., U.S.* 44°43′ N, 71°33′ W 94
Suggi Lake, lake, *Can.* 54°20′ N, 103°12′ W 108
Suğla Gölü, lake, *Turk.* 37°18′ N, 31°44′ E 180
Sugut, river, *Malaysia* 6°0′ N, 117°8′ E 203
Sugut, Tanjong, *Malaysia* 6°25′ N, 117°46′ E 203
Suhai Hu, lake, *China* 38°49′ N, 93°36′ E 188
Şu'ār, *Oman* 24°19′ N, 56°44′ E 196
Sühbaatar, *Mongolia* 50°14′ N, 106°13′ E 198
Sühbaatar, adm. division, *Mongolia* 46°0′ N, 111°56′ E 198
Suheli Par 10°5′ N, 71°16′ E 188
Suhopolje, *Croatia* 45°46′ N, 17°29′ E 168
Şuhut, *Turk.* 38°31′ N, 30°32′ E 156
Sui, *Pak.* 28°38′ N, 69°18′ E 186
Šuica, *Bosn. and Herzg.* 43°49′ N, 17°10′ E 168
Suichang, *China* 28°36′ N, 119°15′ E 198
Suichuan, *China* 26°20′ N, 114°33′ E 198
Suide, *China* 37°28′ N, 110°14′ E 198
Suihua, *China* 46°38′ N, 127°2′ E 198
Suileng, *China* 47°14′ N, 127°11′ E 198
Suining, *China* 33°53′ N, 117°58′ E 198
Suining, *China* 26°38′ N, 110°11′ E 198
Suippes, *Fr.* 49°8′ N, 4°32′ E 163
Suisun City, *Calif., U.S.* 38°13′ N, 122°3′ W 100
Suixi, *China* 33°51′ N, 116°48′ E 198
Suixi, *China* 21°23′ N, 110°14′ E 202
Suiyang, *China* 27°57′ N, 107°10′ E 198
Suizhong, *China* 40°19′ N, 120°19′ E 198
Suizhou, *China* 31°45′ N, 113°20′ E 198
Sujangarh, *India* 27°42′ N, 74°29′ E 186
Sukabumi, *Indonesia* 6°59′ S, 106°51′ E 192
Sukagawa, *Japan* 37°17′ N, 140°21′ E 201
Sukau, *Malaysia* 5°33′ N, 118°16′ E 203
Sukch'ŏn, *N. Korea* 39°24′ N, 125°38′ E 200
Sukeva, *Fin.* 63°49′ N, 27°21′ E 152
Sukhaya Tunguska, *Russ.* 65°3′ N, 88°4′ E 169
Sukhinichi, *Russ.* 54°3′ N, 35°24′ E 154
Sukhona, river, *Russ.* 60°0′ N, 42°51′ E 160
Sukhona, river, *Russ.* 60°19′ N, 44°4′ E 154
Sukhothai, *Thai.* 17°4′ N, 99°49′ E 202
Sukhoy Nos, Mys, *Russ.* 73°37′ N, 46°36′ E 160
Sukhum see Sokhumi, *Rep. of Georgia* 43°0′ N, 41°55′ E 195
Sukkertoppen see Maniitsoq 65°26′ N, 53°0′ W 106
Sukkur, *Pak.* 27°45′ N, 68°55′ E 186
Sukon, Ko, island, *Thai.* 7°0′ N, 98°57′ E 196
Suksun, *Russ.* 57°9′ N, 57°26′ E 154
Sukumo, *Japan* 32°56′ N, 132°41′ E 201
Sukunka, river, *Can.* 55°9′ N, 121°33′ W 108
Šula, *Mont.* 43°23′ N, 19°4′ E 168
Sula, Kepulauan, islands, *Banda Sea* 1°49′ S, 124°12′ E 192
Sula, river, *Russ.* 66°58′ N, 50°14′ E 169
Sula, river, *Ukr.* 50°48′ N, 33°36′ E 158
Sulaco, river, *Hond.* 15°4′ N, 87°41′ W 115
Sulak, *Russ.* 43°18′ N, 47°35′ E 195
Sulak, *Russ.* 51°50′ N, 48°23′ E 184
Sulanheer, *Mongolia* 42°42′ N, 109°24′ E 198
Sulat, *Philippines* 11°48′ N, 125°26′ E 203
Sulawesi (Celebes), island, *Indonesia* 2°0′ S, 121°0′ E 192
Sulb, ruin(s), *Sudan* 20°23′ N, 30°12′ E 226
Sulechów, *Pol.* 52°5′ N, 15°38′ E 152
Suleya, *Russ.* 55°14′ N, 58°46′ E 154
Süleymanlı, *Turk.* 37°52′ N, 36°49′ E 156
Sulgrave, *U.K.* 52°5′ N, 1°13′ W 162
Sulima, *Sierra Leone* 6°57′ N, 11°32′ W 222
Sulina, *Rom.* 45°9′ N, 29°38′ E 156
Sulitjelma, peak, *Nor.* 67°7′ N, 16°13′ E 152
Sulkava, *Fin.* 61°46′ N, 28°21′ E 166
Sull Basin, *Sulu Sea* 8°31′ N, 120°28′ E 254
Sullivan, *Ill., U.S.* 39°35′ N, 88°37′ W 102
Sullivan, *Ind., U.S.* 39°5′ N, 87°25′ W 102
Sullivan, *Mo., U.S.* 38°12′ N, 91°10′ W 94
Sullivan Bay, *Can.* 50°51′ N, 126°47′ W 90
Sullivan Lake, *Can.* 52°1′ N, 112°19′ W 90
Sulphur, *La., U.S.* 30°12′ N, 93°23′ W 103
Sulphur, *Okla., U.S.* 34°29′ N, 96°58′ W 92
Sulphur Point, *Can.* 60°56′ N, 114°51′ W 108
Sulphur, river, *Tex., U.S.* 33°23′ N, 95°13′ W 103
Sulphur Springs, *Tex., U.S.* 33°7′ N, 95°36′ W 103
Sultan Kheyl, *Afghan.* 33°50′ N, 68°42′ E 186
Sultanhanı, *Turk.* 38°14′ N, 33°33′ E 156
Sultanpur, *India* 26°14′ N, 82°3′ E 197
Sul'tsa, *Russ.* 63°28′ N, 46°0′ E 154
Sulu Archipelago, islands, *Sulu Sea* 5°31′ N, 121°16′ E 203
Sulu Sea 7°57′ N, 119°4′ E 192
Sülüklü, *Turk.* 38°52′ N, 32°22′ E 156
Suluova, *Turk.* 40°48′ N, 35°41′ E 156
Sulūq, *Lib.* 31°39′ N, 20°15′ E 216
Sulütöbe, *Kaz.* 44°39′ N, 66°1′ E 184
Sulz, *Ger.* 48°21′ N, 8°36′ E 150
Sumaco Napo Galeras National Park, *Ecua.* 0°49′ N, 78°13′ W 136
Sumampa, *Arg.* 29°22′ S, 63°30′ W 139
Sumapaz National Park, *Col.* 3°40′ N, 74°55′ W 136
Sumarokovo, *Russ.* 61°36′ N, 89°38′ E 169
Sumas, *Wash., U.S.* 48°59′ N, 122°17′ W 100
Sumatra, island, *Indonesia* 4°43′ S, 105°52′ E 192
Šumava, *Czech Rep.* 49°13′ N, 13°12′ E 152
Sumba, island, *Indonesia* 10°3′ S, 117°57′ E 192
Sumbar, river, *Turkm.* 38°12′ N, 55°30′ E 180
Sumbawa, island, *Indonesia* 8°13′ S, 117°31′ E 192
Sumbawanga, *Tanzania* 7°56′ S, 31°37′ E 224
Sumbay, *Peru* 16°0′ S, 71°22′ W 137
Sumbe, *Angola* 11°15′ S, 13°53′ E 220
Sumbuya, *Sierra Leone* 7°39′ N, 11°58′ W 222
Sumé, *Braz.* 7°39′ S, 36°53′ W 132
Sümeg, *Hung.* 46°57′ N, 17°17′ E 168
Sumeih, *Sudan* 9°47′ N, 27°34′ E 224
Sumiton, *Ala., U.S.* 33°44′ N, 87°3′ W 96
Sümiyn Bulag, *Mongolia* 49°38′ N, 114°59′ E 198
Sumkino, *Russ.* 58°3′ N, 68°14′ E 169
Summer Lake, *Oreg., U.S.* 42°45′ N, 121°49′ W 80
Summerfield, *La., U.S.* 32°53′ N, 92°50′ W 103
Summerfield, *Ohio, U.S.* 39°47′ N, 81°20′ W 102
Summerland, *Calif., U.S.* 34°25′ N, 119°37′ W 101
Summerland, *Can.* 49°36′ N, 119°40′ W 108
Summerland Key, *Fla., U.S.* 24°39′ N, 81°27′ W 105
Summerside, *Can.* 46°23′ N, 63°47′ W 111
Summersville, *W. Va., U.S.* 38°16′ N, 80°52′ W 94
Summerville, *S.C., U.S.* 33°0′ N, 80°11′ W 96
Summit, *Miss., U.S.* 31°16′ N, 90°28′ W 103
Summit, *Sudan* 18°47′ N, 36°48′ E 182
Summit Lake, *Can.* 58°39′ N, 124°39′ W 108
Summit Lake, *Can.* 54°16′ N, 122°37′ W 108
Summit Mountain, peak, *Nev., U.S.* 39°21′ N, 116°33′ W 90
Summitville, *Ind., U.S.* 40°20′ N, 85°39′ W 102
Sumner, Lake, *N. Mex., U.S.* 34°36′ N, 105°23′ W 80
Sumner Strait 56°10′ N, 134°28′ W 108
Sumprabum, *Myanmar* 26°35′ N, 97°32′ E 188
Sumqayıt, *Azerb.* 40°36′ N, 49°36′ E 195
Sumrall, *Miss., U.S.* 31°24′ N, 89°33′ W 103
Sumsa, *Fin.* 64°14′ N, 29°50′ E 152
Sumskiy Posad, *Russ.* 64°14′ N, 35°22′ E 154
Sumter, *S.C., U.S.* 33°54′ N, 80°23′ W 82
Sumy, *Ukr.* 50°55′ N, 34°46′ E 158
Sun, *La., U.S.* 30°38′ N, 89°54′ W 103
Sun City, *Calif., U.S.* 33°43′ N, 117°13′ W 101
Sun City, *S. Af.* 25°20′ S, 27°0′ E 227
Sun Kosi, river, *Nepal* 27°20′ N, 85°44′ E 197
Sun Prairie, *Wis., U.S.* 43°11′ N, 89°14′ W 102
Sun, river, *Mont., U.S.* 47°24′ N, 112°20′ W 90
Sun, river, *Mont., U.S.* 47°55′ N, 113°15′ W 80
Suna, *Russ.* 57°50′ N, 50°10′ E 154
Suna, river, *Russ.* 62°38′ N, 32°38′ E 152
Sunan, *N. Korea* 39°11′ N, 125°42′ E 200
Sunapee, *N.H., U.S.* 43°23′ N, 72°5′ W 104
Sunburst, *Mont., U.S.* 48°52′ N, 111°57′ W 90
Sunbury, *Ohio, U.S.* 40°14′ N, 82°52′ W 102
Sunbury, *Pa., U.S.* 40°51′ N, 76°48′ W 94
Sunchales, *Arg.* 30°58′ S, 61°34′ W 139
Suncho Corral, *Arg.* 27°57′ S, 63°27′ W 139
Sunch'ŏn, *N. Korea* 39°21′ N, 126°1′ E 200
Sund, *Fin.* 60°14′ N, 20°5′ E 166
Sunda Shelf, *South China Sea* 5°0′ N, 107°0′ E 254
Sunda Trench see Java Trench, *Indian Ocean* 10°30′ S, 110°0′ E 254
Sundance, *Wyo., U.S.* 44°22′ N, 104°23′ W 90
Sundargarh, *India* 22°6′ N, 84°4′ E 197
Sunderland, *U.K.* 54°54′ N, 1°24′ W 162
Sunderland, *Vt., U.S.* 43°6′ N, 73°6′ W 104
Sundern, *Ger.* 51°19′ N, 8°0′ E 167
Sündiken Dăg, peak, *Turk.* 39°57′ N, 31°2′ E 156
Sundown, *Tex., U.S.* 33°26′ N, 102°30′ W 92
Sundridge, *Can.* 45°45′ N, 79°25′ W 94
Sundsvall, *Nor.* 62°22′ N, 17°15′ E 152
Sunflower, Mount, peak, *Kans., U.S.* 41°55′ N, 101°28′ W 90
Sungai Petani, *Malaysia* 5°37′ N, 100°29′ E 196
Sungaidareh, *Indonesia* 0°57′ N, 101°31′ E 196
Sungaiguntung, *Indonesia* 0°19′ N, 103°37′ E 196
Sŭngam, *N. Korea* 41°39′ N, 129°40′ E 200
Sungikai, *Sudan* 12°19′ N, 29°47′ E 218
Sungurlu, *Turk.* 40°9′ N, 34°23′ E 156
Suni, *Sudan* 13°3′ N, 24°27′ E 226
Sunja, *Croatia* 45°21′ N, 16°33′ E 168
Sunjiapuzi, *China* 42°0′ N, 126°38′ E 200
Sunman, *Ind., U.S.* 39°13′ N, 85°6′ W 102
Sunne, *Nor.* 59°51′ N, 13°6′ E 152
Sunnhordland, region, *North Sea* 59°51′ N, 5°0′ E 152
Sunniland, *Fla., U.S.* 26°15′ N, 81°21′ W 105
Sunnmøre, region, *Nor.* 62°8′ N, 5°42′ E 152
Sunnyvale, *Calif., U.S.* 37°22′ N, 122°2′ W 100
Sunray, *Tex., U.S.* 36°0′ N, 101°50′ W 92
Sunrise, *Wyo., U.S.* 42°19′ N, 104°42′ W 90
Sunrise Peak, *Wash., U.S.* 46°18′ N, 121°48′ W 100
Sunsas, Serranía de, *Bol.* 18°7′ S, 59°38′ W 132
Sunset, *La., U.S.* 30°23′ N, 92°5′ W 103
Sunset Peak, *Mont., U.S.* 44°50′ N, 112°13′ W 90
Sunset Prairie, *Can.* 55°49′ N, 120°48′ W 108
Suntar, *Russ.* 62°9′ N, 117°28′ E 160
Suntaži, *Latv.* 56°52′ N, 24°55′ E 166
Suntsar, *Pak.* 25°26′ N, 62°2′ E 182
Sunwu, *China* 49°24′ N, 127°21′ E 198
Sunyani, *Ghana* 7°21′ N, 2°22′ W 222
Suō Nada 33°46′ N, 131°13′ E 200
Suolahti, *Fin.* 62°33′ N, 25°49′ E 152
Suomenniemi, *Fin.* 61°19′ N, 27°26′ E 166
Suomenselkä, *Fin.* 61°47′ N, 23°16′ E 166
Suomussalmi, *Fin.* 64°53′ N, 29°3′ E 152
Suonenjoki, *Fin.* 62°36′ N, 27°4′ E 152
Suorsa Pää, peak, *Fin.* 68°32′ N, 28°16′ E 152
Suorva, *Nor.* 67°32′ N, 18°15′ E 152
Suoyarvi, *Russ.* 62°6′ N, 32°22′ E 152
Superior, *Ariz., U.S.* 33°17′ N, 111°6′ W 92
Superior, *Nebr., U.S.* 40°0′ N, 98°5′ W 90
Superior, *Wis., U.S.* 46°42′ N, 92°5′ W 94
Superior, *Wyo., U.S.* 41°46′ N, 108°58′ W 90
Superior, Lake 47°32′ N, 89°30′ W 110
Superstition Mountains, *Ariz., U.S.* 33°22′ N, 111°40′ W 92
Supetar, *Croatia* 43°22′ N, 16°32′ E 168
Süphan Dağı, peak, *Turk.* 38°54′ N, 42°45′ E 195
Supiori, island, *Indonesia* 0°31′ N, 135°18′ E 192
Sūq Suwayq, *Saudi Arabia* 24°21′ N, 38°27′ E 182
Suqa el Gamal, *Sudan* 12°48′ N, 27°39′ E 216
Suquṭrá see Socotra, island, *Yemen* 12°19′ N, 54°12′ E 182
Şūr, *Oman* 22°31′ N, 59°32′ E 182
Sur, Point, *Calif., U.S.* 36°13′ N, 121°58′ W 100
Sur, Punta, *Arg.* 37°5′ S, 56°40′ W 134
Sura, river, *Russ.* 53°23′ N, 45°15′ E 154
Sura, river, *Russ.* 53°16′ N, 46°16′ E 154
Surab, *Pak.* 28°29′ N, 66°19′ E 186
Surabaya, *Indonesia* 7°19′ S, 112°37′ E 192
Surahammar, *Nor.* 59°42′ N, 16°11′ E 152
Sūrak, *Iran* 25°41′ N, 58°49′ E 196
Surakarta, *Indonesia* 7°30′ S, 110°35′ E 192
Surama, *Venez.* 6°57′ N, 63°19′ W 130
Şūrān, *Syr.* 35°17′ N, 36°44′ E 194
Surar, *Eth.* 7°30′ N, 40°53′ E 224
Surat, *India* 21°11′ N, 72°51′ E 186
Surat Thani (Ban Don), *Thai.* 9°7′ N, 99°20′ E 202
Suraxanı, *Azerb.* 40°26′ N, 50°1′ E 195
Surazh, *Russ.* 52°59′ N, 32°25′ E 154
Surduc, *Rom.* 47°15′ N, 23°22′ E 168
Surdulica, *Serb.* 42°41′ N, 22°10′ E 168
Surendranagar, *India* 22°39′ N, 71°39′ E 186
Surfside, *Mass., U.S.* 41°14′ N, 70°6′ W 104
Surgidero de Batabanó, *Cuba* 22°42′ N, 82°16′ W 112
Surgut, *Russ.* 61°15′ N, 73°19′ E 169
Surgut, *Russ.* 53°55′ N, 51°6′ E 154
Surgutikha, *Russ.* 63°49′ N, 87°18′ E 169
Surianu, peak, *Rom.* 45°34′ N, 23°25′ E 156
Surigao, *Philippines* 9°47′ N, 125°30′ E 203
Surimena, *Col.* 3°51′ N, 73°16′ W 136
Surin, *Thai.* 14°53′ N, 103°28′ E 202
Surin Nua, Ko, island, *Thai.* 9°22′ N, 96°58′ E 202
Suriname 4°0′ N, 55°51′ W 122
Sürmene, *Turk.* 40°55′ N, 40°5′ E 195
Surovikino, *Russ.* 48°37′ N, 42°45′ E 158
Surovni, *Belarus* 55°31′ N, 29°38′ E 166
Surprise Lake, lake, *Can.* 59°37′ N, 134°3′ W 108
Surrey, *Can.* 49°11′ N, 122°54′ W 100
Sursee, *Switz.* 47°10′ N, 8°7′ E 156
Sursk, *Russ.* 53°2′ N, 45°45′ E 154
Surskoye, *Russ.* 54°29′ N, 46°44′ E 154
Surt (Sidra), *Lib.* 31°12′ N, 16°32′ E 216
Surtanahu, *Pak.* 26°22′ N, 70°3′ E 186
Surte, *Nor.* 57°50′ N, 12°1′ E 152
Surtsey, island, *Iceland* 63°16′ N, 20°29′ W 253
Surud Cad, Buuraha, peak, *Somalia* 10°38′ N, 47°9′ E 218
Surumu, river, *Braz.* 4°11′ N, 61°30′ W 130
Susa, *It.* 45°7′ N, 7°2′ E 167
Susa, *Japan* 34°36′ N, 131°36′ E 200
Sušac, island, *Croatia* 42°46′ N, 16°25′ E 168
Sūsah (Apollonia), *Lib.* 32°52′ N, 21°59′ E 143
Susaki, *Japan* 33°23′ N, 133°16′ E 201
Sūsangerd, *Iran* 31°29′ N, 48°15′ E 216
Susanino, *Russ.* 58°8′ N, 41°38′ E 154
Suşehri (Nicopolis), *Turk.* 40°8′ N, 38°5′ E 180
Susitna, *Alas., U.S.* 61°31′ N, 150°30′ W 98
Susitna, river, *Alas., U.S.* 62°30′ N, 147°57′ W 98
Suslonger, *Russ.* 56°18′ N, 48°14′ E 154
Susoh, *Indonesia* 3°44′ N, 96°48′ E 196
Suspiro, *Braz.* 30°39′ S, 54°23′ W 139
Susques, *Arg.* 23°25′ S, 66°32′ W 132
Sussex, *Can.* 45°42′ N, 65°31′ W 94
Sustut Peak, *Can.* 56°33′ N, 126°42′ W 108
Sustut, river, *Can.* 56°15′ N, 127°9′ W 108
Susuman, *Russ.* 62°56′ N, 147°27′ E 160
Susurluk, *Turk.* 39°54′ N, 28°8′ E 156
Susz, *Pol.* 53°43′ N, 19°20′ E 152
Sutak, *India* 33°7′ N, 77°34′ E 188
Sutatenza, *Col.* 5°2′ N, 73°24′ W 136
Sütçüler, *Turk.* 37°29′ N, 30°58′ E 156
Sutherland, *Nebr., U.S.* 41°9′ N, 101°9′ W 90
Sutherland, *S. Af.* 32°23′ S, 20°38′ E 227
Sutherlin, *Oreg., U.S.* 43°22′ N, 123°20′ W 90
Sutjesca National Park, *Bosn. and Herzg.* 43°16′ N, 18°28′ E 168
Sutlej, river, *Pak.* 29°35′ N, 72°12′ E 186
Sutorman, *Mont.* 42°10′ N, 19°7′ E 168
Sutter Buttes, peak, *Calif., U.S.* 39°11′ N, 121°55′ W 90
Sutter Creek, *Calif., U.S.* 38°22′ N, 120°49′ W 100
Sutton, *Nebr., U.S.* 40°35′ N, 97°51′ W 90
Sutton Coldfield, *U.K.* 52°33′ N, 1°50′ W 162
Sutton on Sea, *U.K.* 53°18′ N, 0°16′ E 162
Sutton, river, *Can.* 54°19′ N, 84°35′ W 106
Sutwik Island, *Alas., U.S.* 56°8′ N, 157°43′ W 98
Suure-Jaani, *Est.* 58°31′ N, 25°27′ E 166
Suva, *Fiji* 18°12′ S, 178°26′ E 242
Suva Gora, *Maced.* 41°54′ N, 21°2′ E 168
Suva Planina, *Serb.* 43°14′ N, 21°58′ E 168
Suvadiva Atoll (Huvadu), *Maldives* 0°39′ N, 72°35′ E 188
Suvainiškis, *Lith.* 56°9′ N, 25°15′ E 166
Suvorov, *Russ.* 54°8′ N, 36°29′ E 154
Suwa, *Eritrea* 14°12′ N, 41°8′ E 182
Suwa, *Japan* 36°3′ N, 138°8′ E 201
Suwałki, *Pol.* 54°6′ N, 22°57′ E 166
Suwannaphum, *Thai.* 15°35′ N, 103°47′ E 202
Suwannee, *Fla., U.S.* 29°19′ N, 83°9′ W 105
Suwannee, river, *Fla., U.S.* 29°20′ N, 83°1′ W 105
Suwannee Sound 29°11′ N, 83°18′ W 105
Şuwaylī', *Jordan* 32°1′ N, 35°50′ E 194
Suwon, *S. Korea* 37°16′ N, 127°1′ E 200
Suydam, Mount, peak, *Antarctica* 84°32′ S, 67°31′ W 248
Suyevat, *Russ.* 61°36′ N, 60°30′ E 154
Süyqbulaq, *Kaz.* 49°50′ N, 80°48′ E 184
Suyutkino, *Russ.* 44°10′ N, 47°12′ E 158
Suzaka, *Japan* 36°39′ N, 138°18′ E 201
Suzhou, *China* 31°22′ N, 120°38′ E 198
Suzhou, *China* 39°31′ N, 98°39′ E 173
Suzhou, *China* 33°38′ N, 116°56′ E 198
Suzu (Iida), *Japan* 37°26′ N, 137°15′ E 201
Suzu Misaki, *Japan* 37°32′ N, 137°21′ E 201
Suzuka, *Japan* 34°52′ N, 136°36′ E 201
Suzun, *Russ.* 53°47′ N, 82°27′ E 184
Suzzara, *It.* 44°59′ N, 10°45′ E 167
Svalbard, islands, *Barents Sea* 76°55′ N, 20°18′ E 246
Svalbard, islands, *Barents Sea* 78°21′ N, 22°28′ E 255
Svaneke, *Den.* 55°7′ N, 15°7′ E 152
Svanstein, *Nor.* 66°39′ N, 23°49′ E 152
Svarta (Mustio), *Fin.* 60°8′ N, 23°51′ E 166
Svatove, *Ukr.* 49°25′ N, 38°12′ E 158
Svatsum, *Nor.* 61°18′ N, 9°50′ E 152
Svay Chek, *Cambodia* 13°53′ N, 103°1′ E 202

Svay Rieng, *Cambodia* 11°5' N, 105°46' E 202
Svealand, region, *Sw.* 60°4' N, 17°28' E 166
Svecha, *Russ.* 58°16' N, 47°30' E 154
Svėdasai, *Lith.* 55°40' N, 25°21' E 166
Švėkšna, *Lith.* 55°31' N, 21°36' E 166
Švenčionėliai, *Lith.* 55°10' N, 26°0' E 166
Švenčionys, *Lith.* 55°9' N, 26°11' E 166
Svendborg, *Den.* 55°3' N, 10°36' E 152
Šventoji, *Lith.* 56°1' N, 21°6' E 166
Sverdlovs'k, *Ukr.* 48°6' N, 39°41' E 158
Sverdlovsk, adm. division, *Russ.* 58°42' N, 60°3' E 154
Sverdrup Islands, *Foxe Basin* 77°45' N, 99°50' W 106
Sverdrup Mountains, *Antarctica* 72°33' S, 3°0' W 248
Svēte, river, *Latv.* 56°22' N, 23°26' E 166
Sveti Đorđe, *Mont.* 41°57' N, 19°20' E 168
Sveti Nikola, *Mont.* 41°53' N, 19°21' E 168
Sveti Nikola, Prokhod, pass, *Bulg.* 43°27' N, 22°34' E 168
Sveti Nikole, *Maced.* 41°51' N, 21°57' E 168
Sveti Stefan, *Mont.* 42°14' N, 18°53' E 168
Světlá, *Czech Rep.* 49°40' N, 15°24' E 152
Svetlaya, *Russ.* 46°36' N, 138°10' E 190
Svetlogorsk, *Russ.* 54°55' N, 20°9' E 166
Svetlogorsk, *Russ.* 66°47' N, 88°30' E 169
Svetlograd, *Russ.* 45°18' N, 42°42' E 158
Svetlyy, *Russ.* 54°40' N, 20°6' E 166
Svetogorsk, *Russ.* 61°6' N, 28°51' E 166
Svetozar Miletić, *Serb.* 45°50' N, 19°12' E 168
Svilaja, *Croatia* 43°48' N, 16°18' E 168
Svilajnac, *Serb.* 44°14' N, 21°11' E 168
Svilengrad, *Bulg.* 41°46' N, 26°11' E 158
Svir, *Belarus* 54°50' N, 26°22' E 166
Svir', river, *Russ.* 60°32' N, 33°2' E 154
Sviritsa, *Russ.* 60°28' N, 32°51' E 154
Svir'stroy, *Russ.* 60°47' N, 33°48' E 154
Svislach, *Belarus* 53°2' N, 24°5' E 152
Svitavy, *Czech Rep.* 49°45' N, 16°29' E 152
Svobodny Cosmodrome, spaceport, *Russ.* 51°43' N, 128°9' E 190
Svobodnyy, *Russ.* 51°27' N, 128°5' E 238
Svodna, *Bosn. and Herzg.* 45°3' N, 16°31' E 168
Svolvær, *Nor.* 68°16' N, 14°14' E 160
Svrljig, *Serb.* 43°24' N, 22°7' E 168
Svrljiške Planina, *Serb.* 43°16' N, 22°16' E 168
Svyataya Anna Fan, *Arctic Ocean* 84°7' N, 59°47' E 255
Svyataya Anna Trough, *Kara Sea* 80°7' N, 71°25' E 255
Svyatitsa, *Belarus* 52°44' N, 26°1' E 154
Svyatoy Nos, Mys, *Russ.* 72°24' N, 133°19' E 160
Svyetlahorsk, *Belarus* 52°34' N, 29°48' E 154
Swa Tenda, *Dem. Rep. of the Congo* 7°12' S, 17°5' E 218
Swadlincote, *U.K.* 52°45' N, 1°34' W 162
Swaffham, *U.K.* 52°38' N, 0°41' E 162
Swain Post, *Can.* 51°17' N, 92°40' W 110
Swains Island, *U.S.* 11°4' S, 171°10' W 252
Swainsboro, *Ga., U.S.* 32°35' N, 82°21' W 96
Swakopmund, *Namibia* 22°31' S, 14°28' E 207
Swale, river, *U.K.* 54°23' N, 1°51' W 162
Swampscott, *Mass., U.S.* 42°28' N, 70°56' W 104
Swan Hills, *Can.* 54°43' N, 115°35' W 108
Swan Lake, *S. Dak., U.S.* 45°14' N, 100°18' W 90
Swan Lake, lake, *Can.* 55°45' N, 129°7' W 108
Swan Range, *Mont., U.S.* 47°43' N, 113°44' W 90
Swan River, *Can.* 52°4' N, 101°15' W 108
Swan, river, *Can.* 52°16' N, 102°16' W 108
Swanquarter, *N.C., U.S.* 35°24' N, 76°21' W 96
Swansea (Abertawe), *U.K.* 51°37' N, 3°57' W 162
Swanton, *Ohio, U.S.* 41°35' N, 83°53' W 102
Swanzey, *N.H., U.S.* 42°51' N, 72°18' W 104
Swartmodder, *S. Af.* 28°5' S, 20°34' E 227
Swartruggens, *S. Af.* 25°41' S, 26°41' E 227
Swartz, *La., U.S.* 32°33' N, 91°59' W 103
Swarzędz, *Pol.* 52°24' N, 17°4' E 152
Swasey Peak, *Utah, U.S.* 39°22' N, 113°23' W 90
Swat, river, *Pak.* 34°46' N, 72°24' E 186
Swatow see Shantou, *China* 23°23' N, 116°40' E 198
Swaziland 26°31' S, 31°28' E 227
Sweden 63°13' N, 16°14' E 152
Swedru, *Ghana* 5°32' N, 0°44' E 222
Sweeney Mountains, *Antarctica* 74°37' S, 74°59' W 248
Sweet Home, *Oreg., U.S.* 44°22' N, 122°44' W 90
Sweetgrass, *Mont., U.S.* 48°58' N, 111°59' W 90
Sweetwater, *Tenn., U.S.* 35°35' N, 84°28' W 96
Sweetwater, *Tex., U.S.* 32°27' N, 100°24' W 96
Sweetwater Summit, pass, *Nev., U.S.* 38°30' N, 119°14' W 100
Świdwin, *Pol.* 53°45' N, 15°47' E 152
Świebodzin, *Pol.* 52°15' N, 15°31' E 152
Świętokrzyskie, *Pol.* 51°5' N, 19°47' E 152
Świętokrzyskie, adm. division, *Pol.* 50°51' N, 19°47' E 152
Swift Current, *Can.* 50°17' N, 107°49' W 90
Swift River, *Can.* 60°2' N, 131°13' W 108
Swift, river, *Can.* 59°57' N, 131°54' W 108
Swindon, *U.K.* 51°33' N, 1°47' W 162
Świnoujście, *Pol.* 53°54' N, 14°14' E 152
Switz City, *Ind., U.S.* 39°1' N, 87°3' W 102
Switzerland 46°48' N, 7°57' E 156
Syamzha, *Russ.* 60°3' N, 41°9' E 154
Syanno, *Belarus* 54°48' N, 29°46' E 166
Syas', river, *Russ.* 59°47' N, 32°43' E 154
Syas'stroy, *Russ.* 60°7' N, 32°41' E 154
Syava, *Russ.* 58°0' N, 46°21' E 154
Sycamore, *Ga., U.S.* 31°39' N, 83°38' W 96
Sycamore, *Ill., U.S.* 41°59' N, 88°41' W 102
Sycamore, *Ohio, U.S.* 40°56' N, 83°10' W 102
Sycewice, *Pol.* 54°25' N, 16°51' E 152
Sychevka, *Russ.* 55°49' N, 34°21' E 154
Sydney, *Austral.* 33°56' S, 150°50' E 230
Sydney, *Can.* 46°8' N, 60°11' W 111
Sydney Lake, *Can.* 50°40' N, 94°47' W 90
Syelishcha, *Belarus* 53°0' N, 27°23' E 154
Syghyndy, *Kaz.* 43°45' N, 51°4' E 195
Syktyvkar, *Russ.* 61°44' N, 50°56' E 154
Sylacauga, *Ala., U.S.* 33°9' N, 86°20' W 112
Sylarna, peak, *Nor.* 62°59' N, 12°5' E 152
Sylhet, *Bangladesh* 24°53' N, 91°53' E 197
Sylte, *Nor.* 62°50' N, 7°15' E 152
Sylva, *Russ.* 58°1' N, 56°46' E 154
Sylvan Lake, *Can.* 52°18' N, 114°7' W 108
Sylvan Pass, *Wyo., U.S.* 44°27' N, 110°8' W 90
Sylvania, *Ga., U.S.* 32°43' N, 81°39' W 96
Sylvania, *Ohio, U.S.* 41°42' N, 83°42' W 102
Sylvester, *Tex., U.S.* 32°43' N, 100°17' W 92
Sylvester, Mount, peak, *Can.* 48°9' N, 55°11' W 111
Sylvia, Mount, peak, *Can.* 58°5' N, 124°32' W 108
Sym, *Russ.* 60°19' N, 88°25' E 169
Sym, river, *Russ.* 60°42' N, 87°3' E 169
Synel'nykove, *Ukr.* 48°18' N, 35°32' E 158
Syngyrli, Mys, *Kaz.* 41°54' N, 51°54' E 158
Synnfjell, peak, *Nor.* 61°3' N, 9°40' E 152
Synnot, Mount, peak, *Austral.* 16°43' S, 125°3' E 230
Synya, *Russ.* 65°23' N, 58°1' E 154
Syowa, Japan, station, *Antarctica* 69°0' S, 39°36' E 248
Syr Darya, river, *Kaz.* 44°30' N, 65°40' E 184
Syracuse, *Ind., U.S.* 41°25' N, 85°45' W 102
Syracuse, *Kans., U.S.* 37°59' N, 101°45' W 90
Syracuse, *Nebr., U.S.* 40°38' N, 96°11' W 90
Syracuse, *N.Y., U.S.* 43°3' N, 76°10' W 94
Syracuse see Siracusa, *It.* 37°3' N, 15°17' E 156
Syria 34°59' N, 38°11' E 180
Syrian Desert, *Iraq* 32°22' N, 37°50' E 180
Syrian Gates, pass, *Turk.* 36°28' N, 36°12' E 156
Sýrna, island, *Gr.* 36°13' N, 26°43' E 180
Sysert', *Russ.* 56°30' N, 60°50' E 154
Sysmä, *Fin.* 61°29' N, 25°38' E 166
Sysola, river, *Russ.* 61°2' N, 50°31' E 154
Systyg Khem, *Russ.* 52°52' N, 95°43' E 190
Sytomino, *Russ.* 61°18' N, 71°21' E 169
Syumsi, *Russ.* 57°5' N, 51°42' E 154
Syuneysale, *Russ.* 66°54' N, 71°23' E 169
Syutkya, peak, *Bulg.* 41°52' N, 23°56' E 156
Syzran', *Russ.* 53°11' N, 48°33' E 154
Szabadszállás, *Hung.* 46°51' N, 19°13' E 168
Szabolcs-Szatmár-Bereg, adm. division, *Hung.* 48°6' N, 21°43' E 156
Szamotuły, *Pol.* 52°36' N, 16°34' E 152
Szarvas, *Hung.* 46°52' N, 20°33' E 168
Szczebra, *Pol.* 53°55' N, 22°57' E 166
Szczecin, *Pol.* 53°25' N, 14°33' E 152
Szczecinek, *Pol.* 53°42' N, 16°42' E 152
Szczuczyn, *Pol.* 53°33' N, 22°14' E 152
Szeged, *Hung.* 46°15' N, 20°8' E 168
Szeghalom, *Hung.* 47°1' N, 21°9' E 168
Szegvár, *Hung.* 46°35' N, 20°14' E 168
Székesfehérvár, *Hung.* 47°11' N, 18°25' E 168
Szekszárd, *Hung.* 46°20' N, 18°42' E 168
Szentendre, *Hung.* 47°39' N, 19°6' E 168
Szentes, *Hung.* 46°39' N, 20°16' E 168
Szentgotthárd, *Hung.* 46°56' N, 16°16' E 168
Szentl orinc, *Hung.* 46°2' N, 17°59' E 168
Szepietowo, *Pol.* 52°51' N, 22°31' E 152
Szigetvár, *Hung.* 46°2' N, 17°48' E 168
Szikszó, *Hung.* 48°12' N, 20°56' E 152
Szob, *Hung.* 47°48' N, 18°54' E 168
Szolnok, *Hung.* 47°11' N, 20°11' E 168
Szombathely, *Hung.* 47°14' N, 16°39' E 168
Szőny, *Hung.* 47°44' N, 18°10' E 168
Szőreg, *Hung.* 46°12' N, 20°12' E 168
Sztum, *Pol.* 53°54' N, 19°0' E 166
Sztutowo, *Pol.* 54°19' N, 19°9' E 166
Szulok, *Hung.* 46°3' N, 17°32' E 168
Szypliszki, *Pol.* 54°14' N, 23°5' E 166

T

Ta La, *Vietnam* 11°26' N, 107°26' E 202
Taalintehdas see Dalsbruk, *Fin.* 60°1' N, 22°31' E 166
Taavetti, *Fin.* 60°54' N, 27°31' E 166
Tab, *Hung.* 46°43' N, 18°1' E 168
Tabacal, *Arg.* 23°14' S, 64°16' W 132
Ţābah, *Saudi Arabia* 27°3' N, 42°11' E 180
Tabalak, *Niger* 15°3' N, 6°0' E 222
Tabane Lake, lake, *Can.* 60°33' N, 102°21' W 108
Tabankort, spring, *Mali* 17°49' N, 0°15' E 222
Tabanovce, *Maced.* 42°11' N, 21°42' E 168
Ţabaqat Fa'l, *Jordan* 32°26' N, 35°36' E 194
Tabar Islands, islands, *P.N.G.* 2°35' S, 152°4' E 192
Ţabas, *Iran* 33°35' N, 56°54' E 180
Ţabas, *Iran* 32°49' N, 60°13' E 180
Tabasará, Serranía de, *Pan.* 8°29' N, 81°39' W 115
Tabasco, *Mex.* 21°51' N, 102°55' W 114
Tabasco, adm. division, *Mex.* 18°12' N, 93°42' W 115
Tabatinga, Serra da, *Braz.* 10°53' S, 45°27' W 130
Tabelbala, *Alg.* 29°25' N, 3°15' W 143
Tabelkoza, *Alg.* 29°46' N, 0°44' E 214
Tabelot, *Niger* 17°34' N, 8°55' E 222
Taber, *Can.* 49°46' N, 112°8' W 90
Tabernas, *Sp.* 37°2' N, 2°24' W 164
Tabili, *Dem. Rep. of the Congo* 0°6' N, 27°59' E 224
Tablas Strait 12°28' N, 121°16' E 203
Tablat, *Alg.* 36°24' N, 3°19' E 150
Table, Cap de la, *Can.* 49°21' N, 61°51' W 111
Table Head, *Can.* 51°59' N, 55°45' W 111
Table Hill, peak, *Austral.* 14°33' S, 129°35' E 230
Table Mountain, peak, *Alas., U.S.* 68°12' N, 144°2' W 98
Table Mountain, peak, *S. Dak., U.S.* 45°51' N, 103°46' W 90
Table Point, *Can.* 50°23' N, 58°21' W 111
Table Rock, *Nebr., U.S.* 40°9' N, 96°5' W 94
Taboose Pass, *Calif., U.S.* 36°59' N, 118°26' W 101
Tábor, *Czech Rep.* 49°25' N, 14°38' E 152
Tabor, *Russ.* 71°9' N, 150°45' E 160
Tabor City, *N.C., U.S.* 34°8' N, 78°54' W 96
Tabora, *Tanzania* 5°2' S, 32°49' E 224
Tabora, adm. division, *Tanzania* 5°32' S, 31°41' E 224
Tabory, *Russ.* 58°31' N, 64°28' E 154
Taboshar, *Taj.* 40°35' N, 69°37' E 197
Tabou, *Côte d'Ivoire* 4°33' N, 7°22' W 222
Tabrīz, *Iran* 38°4' N, 46°16' E 195
Tabūk, *Saudi Arabia* 28°23' N, 36°34' E 180
Tabuleiro, *Braz.* 5°7' S, 58°28' W 130
Tabusintac Bay 47°18' N, 65°36' W 111
Tabusintac, river, *Can.* 47°11' N, 65°51' W 94
Tabuyung, *Indonesia* 0°51' N, 98°59' E 196
Täby, *Sw.* 59°29' N, 18°2' E 166
Tacalé, *Braz.* 1°37' N, 54°46' W 130
Tacámbaro, *Mex.* 19°13' N, 101°28' W 114
Tacaná, Volcán, peak, *Mex.* 15°8' N, 92°14' W 115
Tacheng, *China* 46°41' N, 83°5' E 184
Tachichilte, Isla de, island, *Mex.* 24°40' N, 109°13' W 112
Tachikawa, *Japan* 35°41' N, 139°25' E 201
Táchira, adm. division, *Venez.* 7°32' N, 72°29' W 136
Tacloban, *Philippines* 11°13' N, 125°0' E 203
Tacna, *Ariz., U.S.* 32°41' N, 113°58' W 101
Tacna, *Col.* 2°25' S, 70°38' W 136
Tacna, *Peru* 18°2' S, 70°14' W 137
Tacna, adm. division, *Peru* 17°46' S, 70°53' W 137
Taco Pozo, *Arg.* 25°38' S, 63°16' W 132
Tacoma, *Wash., U.S.* 47°13' N, 122°26' W 100
Tacuarembó, *Uru.* 31°45' S, 55°59' W 139
Tacubaya, *Mex.* 25°38' N, 103°2' W 114
Tacupeto, *Mex.* 28°47' N, 109°9' W 92
Tadami, *Japan* 37°21' N, 139°18' E 201
Tadcaster, *U.K.* 53°53' N, 1°15' W 162
Tadebyayakha, *Russ.* 70°26' N, 74°21' E 169
Tadélaka, spring, *Niger* 15°29' N, 7°57' E 222
Tademaït, Plateau du, *Alg.* 28°24' N, 1°10' E 214
Tadjakant, *Mauritania* 18°36' N, 14°34' W 222
Tadjetaret, spring, *Alg.* 22°39' N, 7°52' E 214
Tadjmout, *Alg.* 25°32' N, 3°42' E 214
Tadjoura, *Djibouti* 11°43' N, 42°54' E 216
Tadmor, *N.Z.* 41°28' S, 172°46' E 240
Tadmur, *Syr.* 34°32' N, 38°19' E 180
Tadoba National Park, *India* 20°18' N, 79°12' E 188
Tadoule Lake, *Can.* 58°32' N, 99°4' W 108
Tadoussac, *Can.* 48°8' N, 69°43' W 94
Taean, *S. Korea* 36°44' N, 126°18' E 200
T'aech'ŏn, *N. Korea* 39°55' N, 125°29' E 200
Taedong, *N. Korea* 40°37' N, 125°27' E 200
Taedong, river, *N. Korea* 39°51' N, 126°37' E 200
Taegu see Daegu, *S. Korea* 35°51' N, 128°37' E 200
Taegwan, *N. Korea* 40°11' N, 125°10' E 200
Taehŭng, *N. Korea* 40°5' N, 126°56' E 200
Taejŏn see Daejeon, *S. Korea* 36°18' N, 127°27' E 200
Taenarum see Akrotírio Ténaro, *Gr.* 36°13' N, 21°38' E 156
Ta'erqi, *China* 48°1' N, 121°5' E 198
T'aet'an, *N. Korea* 38°2' N, 125°18' E 200
Tafalla, *Sp.* 42°31' N, 1°41' W 164
Tafara, *Mali* 15°38' N, 11°22' W 222
Tafarit, Cap, *Mauritania* 20°0' N, 16°12' W 222
Ţafas, *Syr.* 32°43' N, 36°3' E 194
Tafí Viejo, *Arg.* 26°46' S, 65°16' W 134
Tafiré, *Côte d'Ivoire* 9°4' N, 5°10' W 222
Tafraout, *Mor.* 29°43' N, 8°59' W 214
Taft, *Calif., U.S.* 35°8' N, 119°29' W 100
Taft, *Tex., U.S.* 27°57' N, 97°23' W 96
Taftān, Kūh-e, peak, *Iran* 28°37' N, 61°7' E 182
Tagama, region, *Niger* 15°46' N, 7°16' E 222
Taganrog, *Russ.* 47°14' N, 38°51' E 156
Taganrogskiy Zaliv 47°0' N, 38°41' E 158
Tagant, region, *Mauritania* 17°21' N, 12°13' W 222
Tagarma, *China* 38°1' N, 75°5' E 184
Tagawa, *Japan* 33°37' N, 130°49' E 201
Tagbilaran, *Philippines* 9°40' N, 123°52' E 203
Taggafadi, *Niger* 18°31' N, 9°14' E 222
Taggia, *It.* 43°51' N, 7°50' E 167
Taghit, *Alg.* 30°58' N, 2 0' W 214
Tagil, river, *Russ.* 58°14' N, 61°20' E 154
Tagish, *Can.* 60°20' N, 134°22' W 108
Taglio di Po, *It.* 45°0' N, 12°10' E 167
Tagnout Chaggueret, spring, *Mali* 21°15' N, 0°48' E 222
Tagounit, *Mor.* 29°57' N, 5°39' W 214
Tagtabazar, *Turkm.* 35°55' N, 62°56' E 186
Tagua, *Bol.* 19°54' S, 67°44' W 137
Taguedoufat, spring, *Niger* 16°8' N, 8°24' E 222
Tagula, island, *P.N.G.* 11°20' S, 153°16' E 192
Tagum, *Philippines* 7°30' N, 125°47' E 203
Tagus see Tajo, river, *Sp.* 39°56' N, 6°57' W 214
Tahaetkun Mountain, peak, *Can.* 50°15' N, 119°49' W 90
Tahakopa, *N.Z.* 46°31' S, 169°22' E 240
Tahala, *Mor.* 34°6' N, 4°25' W 214
Tahan, peak, *Malaysia* 4°37' N, 102°8' E 196
Tahat, Mount, peak, *Alg.* 23°15' N, 5°23' E 214
Ţāherī, *Iran* 27°43' N, 52°22' E 196
Tahiti, island, *French Polynesia, Fr.* 17°38' S, 149°25' W 241
Tahkoluoto, *Fin.* 61°37' N, 21°25' E 166
Tahkuna Nina, *Est.* 59°5' N, 22°35' E 166
Tahlequah, *Okla., U.S.* 35°53' N, 94°59' W 96
Tahltan, *Can.* 58°1' N, 131°1' W 108
Tahltan Lake, *Can.* 57°56' N, 132°22' W 108
Tahoe City, *Calif., U.S.* 39°10' N, 120°10' W 90
Tahoka, *Tex., U.S.* 33°8' N, 101°49' W 92
Taholah, *Wash., U.S.* 47°18' N, 124°17' W 100
Tahoua, *Niger* 14°54' N, 5°17' E 222
Tahquamenon, river, *Mich., U.S.* 46°27' N, 86°7' W 94
Tahsis, *Can.* 49°55' N, 126°40' W 90
Tahtalı Dağ, peak, *Turk.* 38°45' N, 36°42' E 156
Tahtalıdağı, peak, *Turk.* 36°30' N, 30°22' E 156
Tahuamanu, river, *Bol.* 11°13' S, 68°47' W 137
Tahuamanu, river, *Peru* 11°7' S, 70°52' W 137
Tahuna, *Indonesia* 3°41' N, 125°26' E 192
Taï, *Côte d'Ivoire* 5°49' N, 7°28' W 222
Tai Hu, lake, *China* 31°13' N, 120°0' E 198
Taï National Park, *Côte d'Ivoire* 5°49' N, 7°11' W 222
Tai'an, *China* 36°12' N, 117°8' E 198
Taibai, *China* 34°0' N, 107°19' E 198
Taibei see Taipei, *Taiwan, China* 24°58' N, 121°21' E 198
Taibilla, Sierra de, *Sp.* 37°57' N, 2°28' W 164
Taibus Qi, *China* 41°52' N, 115°15' E 198
T'aichung, *Taiwan, China* 24°7' N, 120°41' E 198
Taigbe, *Sierra Leone* 7°25' N, 12°23' W 222
Taígetos, Óros, *Gr.* 37°10' N, 22°10' E 156
Taigu, *China* 37°26' N, 112°30' E 198
Taihape, *N.Z.* 39°42' S, 175°46' E 240
Taihe, *China* 26°47' N, 114°50' E 198
Taihe, *China* 33°12' N, 115°36' E 198
Taihu, *China* 30°26' N, 116°15' E 198
Taikkyee, *Myanmar* 17°20' N, 95°56' E 202
Tailai, *China* 46°18' N, 123°27' E 198
Taim, *Braz.* 32°30' S, 52°38' W 139
Taïmana, *Mali* 13°55' N, 6°45' W 222
Tain, *Fr.* 45°4' N, 4°50' E 150
Tainan, *Taiwan, China* 22°59' N, 120°12' E 198
Taining, *China* 26°56' N, 117°7' E 198
Taiobeiras, *Braz.* 15°49' S, 42°15' W 138
Taipale, *Fin.* 62°38' N, 29°9' E 152
Taipei, *Taiwan, China* 24°58' N, 121°21' E 199
Taiping, *Malaysia* 4°51' N, 100°44' E 196
Taiping Ling, peak, *China* 47°35' N, 120°26' E 198
Taipingshao, *China* 40°53' N, 125°12' E 200
Taipudia, *India* 27°49' N, 94°35' E 188
Taira, *Japan* 37°2' N, 140°52' E 201
Tairua, *N.Z.* 37°0' S, 175°50' E 240
Taisha, *Japan* 35°22' N, 132°41' E 201
Taishan, *China* 22°16' N, 112°43' E 198
Taitao, Cabo, *Chile* 46°0' S, 76°26' W 134
Taitao, Peninsula de, *South America* 46°27' S, 75°28' W 134
Taitung, *Taiwan, China* 22°44' N, 121°6' E 198
Taivalkoski, *Fin.* 65°34' N, 28°13' E 152
Taivassalo, *Fin.* 60°33' N, 21°36' E 166
Taiwan, special sovereignty, *China* 23°41' N, 120°53' E 198
Taiwan, island, *Taiwan, China* 24°25' N, 121°54' E 198
Taiwan Strait 23°49' N, 118°3' E 198
Taiyara, *Sudan* 13°8' N, 30°45' E 226
Taiyuan, *China* 37°52' N, 112°35' E 198
Taiyuan Space Launch Center, spaceport, *China* 37°33' N, 112°32' E 198
Taizhou, *China* 32°30' N, 119°55' E 198
Ta'izz, *Yemen* 13°35' N, 44°1' E 182
Tajar'ī, *Lib.* 24°21' N, 14°12' E 216
Tajerouine, *Tun.* 35°53' N, 8°33' E 156
Tajikistan 38°32' N, 69°13' E 184
Tajima, *Japan* 37°11' N, 139°46' E 201
Tajimi, *Japan* 35°18' N, 137°10' E 201
Tajo, river, *Sp.* 40°5' N, 3°6' W 164
Tajo (Tagus), river, *Sp.* 39°56' N, 6°57' W 214
Tajrīsh, *Iran* 35°52' N, 51°35' E 180
Tajumulco, Volcán, peak, *Guatemala* 15°0' N, 92°0' W 115
Tak, *Thai.* 16°52' N, 99°7' E 202
Takāb, *Iran* 36°27' N, 47°5' E 195
Takaba, *Kenya* 3°20' N, 40°10' E 224
Takahashi, *Japan* 34°48' N, 133°37' E 201
Takahe, Mount, peak, *Antarctica* 76°12' S, 111°45' W 248
Takajō, *Japan* 31°47' N, 131°7' E 201
Takaka, *N.Z.* 40°54' S, 172°50' E 240
Takamatsu, *Japan* 34°20' N, 134°2' E 201
Takamori, *Japan* 32°48' N, 131°7' E 201
Takanabe, *Japan* 32°7' N, 131°29' E 201
Takaoka, *Japan* 36°44' N, 137°1' E 201
Takapau, *N.Z.* 40°4' S, 176°22' E 240
Takasaki, *Japan* 36°18' N, 139°0' E 201
Takatsu, *Japan* 34°40' N, 131°48' E 200
Takaungu, *Kenya* 3°43' S, 39°51' E 224
Tā-kaw, *Myanmar* 21°15' N, 98°39' E 202
Takayama, *Japan* 36°8' N, 137°16' E 201
Takefu, *Japan* 35°53' N, 136°10' E 201
Takengon, *Indonesia* 4°38' N, 96°49' E 196
Takeo, *Cambodia* 10°58' N, 104°47' E 202
Takeo, *Japan* 33°11' N, 130°1' E 201
Tākestān, *Iran* 36°6' N, 49°39' E 180
Taketa, *Japan* 32°57' N, 131°24' E 201
Takhiatosh, *Uzb.* 42°20' N, 59°36' E 180
Takhini, *Can.* 60°51' N, 135°25' W 108
Takhta, *Russ.* 45°51' N, 41°58' E 158
Takiéta, *Niger* 13°41' N, 8°31' E 222
Takijuq Lake, *Can.* 66°22' N, 115°33' W 106
Takipy, *Can.* 55°24' N, 100°58' W 108
Takla Lake, *Can.* 55°9' N, 126°12' W 108
Takla Landing, *Can.* 55°28' N, 125°59' W 108
Taklimakan Shamo, *China* 39°27' N, 77°39' E 184
Takotna, *Alas., U.S.* 62°59' N, 156°4' W 98
Taksa Bor, *Russ.* 67°4' N, 34°40' E 152
Taku, river, *Can.* 58°39' N, 133°35' W 108
Takua Pa, *Thai.* 8°53' N, 98°20' E 202
Takum, *India* 27°48' N, 93°37' E 188
Takum, *Nig.* 7°13' N, 9°57' E 222
Takwa, river, *Can.* 51°32' N, 72°10' W 110
Tal, *Pak.* 35°28' N, 72°14' E 186
Tala, *Mex.* 20°38' N, 103°40' W 114
Tala, *Tun.* 35°32' N, 8°38' E 156
Talachyn, *Belarus* 54°24' N, 29°42' E 166
Talaimannar, *Sri Lanka* 9°6' N, 79°42' E 188
Talak, region, *Niger* 18°15' N, 4°51' E 222
Talara, *Peru* 4°37' S, 81°13' W 123
Talas, *Kyrg.* 42°27' N, 72°33' E 197

Talas, river, *Kyrg.* 42°37′ N, 71°44′ E 197
Talâta, *Egypt* 30°35′ N, 32°20′ E 194
Talata Mafara, *Nig.* 12°33′ N, 6°2′ E 222
Talaud, Kepulauan, islands, *Philippine Sea* 4°1′ N, 127°6′ E 192
Talavera de la Reina, *Sp.* 39°57′ N, 4°51′ W 150
Talavera la Real, *Sp.* 38°52′ N, 6°48′ W 164
Talayón, peak, *Sp.* 37°32′ N, 1°34′ W 164
Talayuelas, *Sp.* 39°51′ N, 1°17′ W 164
Talbahat, *India* 25°2′ N, 78°27′ E 197
Talbert, Sillon de, *English Channel* 48°54′ N, 3°10′ W 150
Talbot, Cape, *Austral.* 13°51′ S, 123°45′ E 172
Talbot, Mount, peak, *Austral.* 26°10′ S, 126°25′ E 230
Talca, *Chile* 35°25′ S, 71°41′ W 134
Talcahuano, *Chile* 36°45′ S, 73°7′ W 134
Talco, *Tex., U.S.* 33°20′ N, 95°6′ W 103
Taldyq, *Kaz.* 49°18′ N, 59°52′ E 158
Taldyqorghan, *Kaz.* 44°59′ N, 78°22′ E 184
Taleex, *Somalia* 9°10′ N, 48°25′ E 216
Talgarth, *U.K.* 51°59′ N, 3°13′ W 162
Talguharai, *Sudan* 18°14′ N, 35°52′ E 182
Tali Post, *Sudan* 5°54′ N, 30°48′ E 224
Taliabu, island, *Indonesia* 2°2′ S, 124°26′ E 192
Talibong, Ko, island, *Thai.* 7°10′ N, 98°36′ E 196
Talitsa, *Russ.* 61°8′ N, 60°28′ E 154
Talitsa, *Russ.* 58°2′ N, 51°32′ E 154
Talitsa, *Russ.* 56°59′ N, 63°44′ E 154
Talkot, *Nepal* 29°33′ N, 81°18′ E 197
Tall Abū Ẓahir, *Iraq* 36°50′ N, 42°23′ E 195
Tall 'Afar, *Iraq* 36°22′ N, 42°19′ E 195
Tall as Sulṭān, ruin(s), *West Bank, Israel* 31°52′ N, 35°24′ E 194
Tall Birāk, *Syr.* 36°39′ N, 41°6′ E 195
Tall Bīsah, *Syr.* 34°50′ N, 36°43′ E 194
Tall Ḥalaf, ruin(s), *Syr.* 36°46′ N, 40°1′ E 195
Tall Kalakh, *Syr.* 34°40′ N, 36°16′ E 194
Tall Kayf, *Iraq* 36°30′ N, 43°1′ E 195
Tall Kūjik, *Syr.* 36°48′ N, 42°1′ E 195
Tall Tamir, *Syr.* 36°38′ N, 40°25′ E 195
Tall Trees Grove, site, *Calif., U.S.* 41°12′ N, 124°4′ W 90
Tallahassee, *Fla., U.S.* 30°24′ N, 84°23′ W 96
Tallaringa Well, spring, *Austral.* 29°0′ S, 133°24′ E 230
Tallassee, *Ala., U.S.* 32°31′ N, 85°54′ W 96
Tällberg, *Nor.* 60°48′ N, 14°59′ E 152
Talley, *U.K.* 51°58′ N, 3°59′ W 162
Tallinn (Reval), *Est.* 59°23′ N, 24°37′ E 166
Tallmadge, *Ohio, U.S.* 41°5′ N, 81°26′ W 102
Tallulah, *La., U.S.* 32°23′ N, 91°12′ W 103
Talmage, *Calif., U.S.* 39°8′ N, 123°10′ W 90
Talmine, *Alg.* 29°21′ N, 0°29′ E 214
Talnakh, *Russ.* 69°28′ N, 88°34′ E 169
Tal'ne, *Ukr.* 48°51′ N, 30°49′ E 158
Talo, peak, *Eth.* 10°38′ N, 37°55′ E 224
Talodi, *Sudan* 10°35′ N, 30°24′ E 224
Taloga, *Okla., U.S.* 36°1′ N, 98°58′ W 92
Talon, *Russ.* 59°47′ N, 148°39′ E 173
Taloqan, *Afghan.* 36°45′ N, 69°31′ E 186
Talorha, *Mauritania* 18°52′ N, 12°23′ W 222
Talos Dome, *Antarctica* 73°6′ S, 161°47′ E 248
Taloyoak, *Can.* 69°25′ N, 93°20′ W 106
Talpa de Allende, *Mex.* 20°26′ N, 104°50′ W 114
Talshand, *Mongolia* 45°20′ N, 97°55′ E 190
Talsi, *Latv.* 57°14′ N, 22°34′ E 166
Talsint, *Mor.* 32°34′ N, 3°27′ W 214
Taltal, *Chile* 25°25′ S, 70°30′ W 132
Taltson, river, *Can.* 60°34′ N, 111°59′ W 108
Talu, *Indonesia* 0°14′ N, 100°0′ E 196
Taluk, *Indonesia* 0°30′ N, 101°33′ E 196
Talvik, *Nor.* 70°2′ N, 22°54′ E 152
Talybont, *U.K.* 52°28′ N, 3°59′ W 162
Talyllyn, *U.K.* 52°38′ N, 3°53′ W 162
Tam Ky, *Vietnam* 15°34′ N, 108°29′ E 202
Tam Quan, *Vietnam* 14°34′ N, 109°1′ E 202
Tamada, spring, *Alg.* 21°37′ N, 3°10′ E 222
Tamala, *Russ.* 52°32′ N, 43°14′ E 158
Tamalameque, *Col.* 8°51′ N, 73°48′ W 136
Tamale, *Ghana* 9°24′ N, 0°52′ E 222
Tamale Port see Yapei, *Ghana* 9°10′ N, 1°11′ W 222
Taman', *Russ.* 45°13′ N, 36°40′ E 156
Taman Negara National Park, *Malaysia* 4°30′ N, 102°51′ E 196
Tamana, *Japan* 32°55′ N, 130°33′ E 201
Tamanar, *Mor.* 30°59′ N, 9°41′ W 214
Tamánco, *Peru* 5°48′ S, 74°18′ W 130
Tamano, *Japan* 34°29′ N, 133°55′ E 201
Tamanrasset, *Alg.* 22°48′ N, 5°18′ E 207
Támara, *Col.* 5°47′ N, 72°10′ W 136
Tamarugal, Pampa del, *Chile* 20°34′ S, 69°24′ W 132
Tamashima, *Japan* 34°32′ N, 133°39′ E 201
Tamási, *Hung.* 46°38′ N, 18°16′ E 168
Tamaulipas, adm. division, *Mex.* 24°20′ N, 99°35′ W 114
Tamaulipas, Sierra de, *Mex.* 23°9′ N, 98°45′ W 112
Tamaya, river, *Peru* 8°59′ S, 74°11′ W 137
Tamayya, *Africa* 23°56′ N, 15°42′ W 214
Tamazula, *Mex.* 19°39′ N, 103°15′ W 114
Tamazula, *Mex.* 24°55′ N, 106°57′ W 114
Tamazulapan, *Mex.* 17°38′ N, 97°34′ W 114
Tamazunchale, *Mex.* 21°12′ N, 98°48′ W 114
Tambach, *Kenya* 0°35′ N, 35°33′ E 224
Tambacounda, *Senegal* 13°46′ N, 13°43′ W 222
Tambaga, *Mali* 13°0′ N, 9°53′ W 222
Tambaqui, *Braz.* 5°15′ S, 62°50′ W 130
Tambelan Besar, island, *Indonesia* 0°49′ N, 106°57′ E 196
Tambey, *Russ.* 71°30′ N, 71°56′ E 173
Tambo de Mora, *Peru* 13°32′ S, 76°12′ W 130
Tambo, river, *Peru* 10°48′ S, 73°53′ W 137
Tambo, river, *Peru* 17°4′ S, 71°21′ W 137
Tamboril, *Braz.* 4°50′ S, 40°22′ W 132
Tambov, *Russ.* 52°41′ N, 41°19′ E 154
Tambov, adm. division, *Russ.* 53°5′ N, 40°14′ E 154
Tambunan, *Malaysia* 5°41′ N, 116°20′ E 203
Tambura, *Sudan* 5°34′ N, 27°29′ E 218
Tamchaket, *Mauritania* 17°16′ N, 10°44′ W 222
Tamel Aike, *Arg.* 48°18′ S, 70°57′ W 134
Tamesí, river, *Mex.* 22°26′ N, 98°27′ W 114
Tamesna, region, *Niger* 18°45′ N, 4°10′ E 222
Tamgak, Adrar, peak, *Niger* 19°11′ N, 8°37′ E 222
Tamgrout, *Mor.* 30°19′ N, 5°45′ W 214
Tamgué, *Guinea* 12°18′ N, 12°21′ W 222
Tamiahua, *Mex.* 21°14′ N, 97°27′ W 114
Tamiahua, Laguna de 21°29′ N, 98°2′ W 114
Tamil Nadu, adm. division, *India* 9°23′ N, 77°23′ E 188
Tamīnah, *Lib.* 32°16′ N, 15°3′ E 216
Tamins, *Switz.* 46°50′ N, 9°23′ E 167
Tamitatoala (Batovi), river, *Braz.* 14°11′ S, 53°58′ W 132
Tamitsa, *Russ.* 64°10′ N, 38°5′ E 154
Tammerfors see Tampere, *Fin.* 61°29′ N, 23°43′ E 166
Tammisaari see Ekenäs, *Fin.* 59°58′ N, 23°26′ E 166
Tampa, *Fla., U.S.* 27°58′ N, 82°26′ W 105
Tampa Bay 27°37′ N, 83°17′ W 80
Tampere, *Fin.* 61°23′ N, 23°51′ E 160
Tampere (Tammerfors), *Fin.* 61°29′ N, 23°43′ E 166
Tampico, *Ill., U.S.* 41°37′ N, 89°48′ W 102
Tampico, *Mex.* 22°11′ N, 97°51′ W 112
Tampin, *Malaysia* 2°29′ N, 102°12′ E 196
Tamrida see Hadīboh, *Yemen* 12°37′ N, 53°49′ E 173
Tamsagbulag, *Mongolia* 47°13′ N, 117°15′ E 198
Tamsalu, *Est.* 59°7′ N, 26°5′ E 166
Tamshiyacu, *Peru* 4°1′ S, 73°6′ W 130
Tamu, *Myanmar* 24°10′ N, 94°19′ E 188
Tamuín, *Mex.* 21°59′ N, 98°46′ W 114
Tamuning, *U.S.* 13°28′ N, 144°46′ E 242
Tamur, river, *Nepal* 26°56′ N, 87°39′ E 197
Tamworth, *N.H., U.S.* 43°51′ N, 71°17′ W 104
Tamworth, *U.K.* 52°39′ N, 1°42′ W 162
Tan An, *Vietnam* 10°32′ N, 106°25′ E 202
Tan Quang, *Vietnam* 22°30′ N, 104°51′ E 202
Tana, *Nor.* 70°27′ N, 28°15′ E 152
Tana, Lake, *Eth.* 11°57′ N, 35°26′ E 206
Tana, river, *Europe* 68°26′ N, 25°33′ E 160
Tana, river, *Kenya* 1°37′ S, 40°7′ E 224
Tanabe, *Japan* 33°43′ N, 135°23′ E 201
Tanacross, *Alas., U.S.* 63°14′ N, 143°23′ W 98
Tanafjorden 70°37′ N, 25°20′ E 160
Tanaga, island, *Alas., U.S.* 51°25′ N, 178°58′ W 160
Tanagra, ruin(s), *Gr.* 38°19′ N, 23°26′ E 156
Tanagura, *Japan* 37°1′ N, 140°23′ E 201
Tanah Merah, *Malaysia* 5°48′ N, 102°7′ E 196
Tanahbala, island, *Indonesia* 0°38′ N, 97°40′ E 196
Tanahgrogot, *Indonesia* 1°56′ S, 116°11′ E 192
Tanahmasa, island, *Indonesia* 0°18′ N, 98°33′ E 196
Tanahmerah, *Indonesia* 3°44′ N, 117°33′ E 192
Tanahmerah, *Indonesia* 6°14′ S, 140°17′ E 192
Tanakpur, *India* 29°4′ N, 80°3′ E 197
Tanalyk, river, *Russ.* 52°38′ N, 58°2′ E 154
Tanama, river, *Russ.* 69°45′ N, 78°33′ E 169
Tanami Desert, *Austral.* 19°13′ S, 130°40′ E 230
Tanami, Mount, peak, *Austral.* 19°59′ S, 129°25′ E 230
Tanana, *Alas., U.S.* 65°3′ N, 152°16′ W 98
Tanana, river, *Alas., U.S.* 63°31′ N, 144°53′ W 98
Tancheng, *China* 34°36′ N, 118°23′ E 198
Tanch'ŏn, *N. Korea* 40°26′ N, 128°56′ E 200
Tanda, *India* 26°31′ N, 82°38′ E 197
Ţăndărei, *Rom.* 44°38′ N, 27°39′ E 156
Tandaué, river, *Angola* 15°55′ S, 16°59′ E 220
Tandik, *Malaysia* 6°37′ N, 116°52′ E 203
Tandil, *Arg.* 37°20′ S, 59°11′ W 139
Tandil, Sierra del, *Arg.* 37°52′ S, 59°49′ W 134
Tando Allahyar, *Pak.* 25°29′ N, 68°45′ E 186
Tando Muhammad Khan, *Pak.* 25°10′ N, 68°34′ E 186
Tandur, *India* 19°9′ N, 79°28′ E 188
Tandur, *India* 17°16′ N, 77°34′ E 188
Tanega Shima, island, *Japan* 30°14′ N, 131°3′ E 190
Tanegashima Space Center, spaceport, *Japan* 30°37′ N, 130°50′ E 190
Tanezrouft, region, *Alg.* 21°41′ N, 2°31′ W 222
Tang Paloch, *Cambodia* 12°3′ N, 104°21′ E 202
Tanga, *Tanzania* 5°6′ S, 39°4′ E 224
Tanga, adm. division, *Tanzania* 5°32′ S, 37°29′ E 224
Tangail, *Bangladesh* 24°13′ N, 89°54′ E 197
Tangaza, *Nig.* 13°21′ N, 4°55′ E 222
Tange Promontory, *Antarctica* 67°10′ S, 40°56′ E 248
Tanger (Tangier), *Mor.* 35°47′ N, 5°46′ W 150
Tanggu, *China* 39°4′ N, 117°40′ E 198
Tanggula Shan, *China* 32°34′ N, 90°26′ E 188
Tanggula Shankou, pass, *China* 32°52′ N, 91°57′ E 188
Tanggulashan (Tuotuoheyan), *China* 34°10′ N, 92°24′ E 188
Tanghe, *China* 32°38′ N, 112°53′ E 198
Tangi, *India* 19°53′ N, 85°23′ E 188
Tangier see Tanger, *Mor.* 35°47′ N, 5°46′ W 150
Tangipahoa, *La., U.S.* 30°52′ N, 90°31′ W 103
Tanglewood, site, *Mass., U.S.* 42°20′ N, 73°21′ W 104
Tangmai, *China* 30°6′ N, 95°7′ E 188
Tango, *Japan* 35°42′ N, 135°6′ E 201
Tangra Yumco, lake, *China* 30°46′ N, 85°46′ E 197
Tangse, *Indonesia* 5°3′ N, 95°55′ E 196
Tangshan, *China* 39°34′ N, 118°10′ E 198
Tanguiéta, *Benin* 10°38′ N, 1°16′ E 222
Tanguro, river, *Braz.* 12°42′ S, 52°30′ W 138
Tanh Linh, *Vietnam* 11°6′ N, 107°41′ E 202
Tanimbar, Kepulauan, islands, *Banda Sea* 10°2′ S, 131°4′ E 238
Tanimbar, Kepulauan, islands, *Indonesia* 7°56′ S, 132°5′ E 192
Taninges, *Fr.* 46°6′ N, 6°35′ E 167
Tanintharyi, *Myanmar* 12°3′ N, 98°59′ E 202
Taniyama, *Japan* 31°29′ N, 130°30′ E 201
Tanjay, *Philippines* 9°31′ N, 123°7′ E 203
Tanjung Puting National Park, *Indonesia* 3°4′ S, 111°39′ E 238
Tanjungbalai, *Indonesia* 2°59′ N, 99°48′ E 196
Tanjungkarang-Telubketung, *Indonesia* 5°28′ S, 105°7′ E 192
Tanjungpandan, *Indonesia* 2°45′ S, 107°40′ E 192
Tanjungpinang, *Indonesia* 0°54′ N, 104°29′ E 196
Tanjungpura, *Indonesia* 3°56′ N, 98°24′ E 196
Tanjungredep, *Indonesia* 2°10′ N, 117°18′ E 192
Tanjungselor, *Indonesia* 2°53′ N, 117°16′ E 192
Tank, *Pak.* 32°10′ N, 70°25′ E 186
Tankapirtti, *Fin.* 68°15′ N, 27°15′ E 152
Ta-n-Kena, *Alg.* 26°33′ N, 9°36′ E 214
Tankovo, *Russ.* 60°38′ N, 89°47′ E 169
Tann, *Ger.* 50°38′ N, 10°1′ E 167
Tännäs, *Nor.* 62°26′ N, 12°39′ E 152
Tannersville, *N.Y., U.S.* 42°11′ N, 74°9′ W 104
Tannila, *Fin.* 65°27′ N, 26°0′ E 152
Tannin, *Can.* 49°39′ N, 91°1′ W 94
Tannur, ruin(s), *Jordan* 30°57′ N, 35°40′ E 194
Tano, river, *Ghana* 6°13′ N, 2°45′ W 222
Tanobato, *Indonesia* 0°46′ N, 99°32′ E 196
Tanot, *India* 27°47′ N, 70°19′ E 186
Tanoûchert, spring, *Mauritania* 20°46′ N, 11°51′ W 222
Tanoudert, *Mauritania* 20°10′ N, 16°10′ W 222
Tânout, *Niger* 14°57′ N, 8°50′ E 222
Tanquián, *Mex.* 21°35′ N, 98°40′ W 114
Ṭanṭa, *Egypt* 30°46′ N, 30°58′ E 180
Tantabin, *Myanmar* 18°50′ N, 96°26′ E 202
Tantallon Castle, site, *U.K.* 56°2′ N, 2°45′ W 150
Tan-Tan, *Mor.* 28°25′ N, 11°9′ W 214
Tantonville, *Fr.* 48°27′ N, 6°8′ E 163
Tantoyuca, *Mex.* 21°19′ N, 98°14′ W 114
Tanus, *Fr.* 44°6′ N, 2°18′ E 150
Tanyang, *S. Korea* 36°55′ N, 128°20′ E 200
Tanzania 6°44′ S, 33°1′ E 224
Tao, Ko, island, *Thai.* 10°6′ N, 99°39′ E 202
Tao'er, river, *China* 45°25′ N, 123°5′ E 198
Taojiang, *China* 28°31′ N, 112°5′ E 198
Taokest, peak, *Mauritania* 18°6′ N, 9°32′ W 222
Taole, *China* 38°47′ N, 106°44′ E 198
Taonan, *China* 45°19′ N, 122°47′ E 198
Taos, *N. Mex., U.S.* 36°24′ N, 105°34′ W 92
Taoudenni (Smeïda), *Mali* 22°41′ N, 3°59′ W 214
Taoujafet, spring, *Mauritania* 18°53′ N, 11°50′ W 222
Taourirt, *Alg.* 26°43′ N, 0°13′ E 214
Taourirt, *Mor.* 34°27′ N, 2°51′ W 214
Taoussa, *Mali* 16°56′ N, 0°33′ E 222
Taouz, *Mor.* 30°57′ N, 3°58′ W 214
Taoyuan, *China* 28°54′ N, 111°28′ E 198
Taoyüan, *Taiwan, China* 24°58′ N, 121°14′ E 198
Tapa, *Est.* 59°14′ N, 25°56′ E 166
Tapachula, *Mex.* 14°54′ N, 92°16′ W 115
Tapah, *Malaysia* 4°11′ N, 101°16′ E 196
Tapajós, river, *Braz.* 4°53′ S, 55°51′ W 123
Tapaktuan, *Indonesia* 3°17′ N, 97°11′ E 196
Tapalquén, *Arg.* 36°22′ S, 60°5′ W 139
Tapanui, *N.Z.* 45°57′ S, 169°17′ E 240
Tapauá, river, *Braz.* 6°23′ S, 65°55′ W 130
Tapawera, *N.Z.* 41°23′ S, 172°50′ E 240
Tapera, *Braz.* 28°37′ S, 52°55′ W 139
Tapera, river, *Braz.* 0°22′ N, 61°45′ W 130
Tapes, *Braz.* 30°40′ S, 51°27′ W 139
Tapeta, *Liberia* 6°20′ N, 8°54′ W 222
Taphan Hin, *Thai.* 16°19′ N, 100°27′ E 202
Tapi, river, *India* 21°17′ N, 73°33′ E 186
Tapiola, *Fin.* 60°9′ N, 24°48′ E 166
Tápiószele, *Hung.* 47°20′ N, 19°53′ E 168
Tapira, *Braz.* 1°20′ N, 68°3′ W 136
Tapirapecó, Sierra, *Venez.* 1°27′ N, 65°2′ W 130
Tapley Mountains, *Antarctica* 84°46′ S, 134°49′ W 248
Tapol, *Chad* 8°31′ N, 15°34′ E 218
Tapolca, *Hung.* 46°52′ N, 17°27′ E 168
Tappahannock, *Va., U.S.* 37°55′ N, 76°53′ W 94
Tapuaenuku, peak, *N.Z.* 42°2′ S, 173°35′ E 240
Tapul, *Philippines* 5°45′ N, 120°53′ E 203
Tapurucuará, *Braz.* 0°27′ N, 65°6′ W 130
Ţaqah, *Oman* 17°3′ N, 54°22′ E 182
Taquara, *Braz.* 29°39′ S, 50°48′ W 139
Taquari, river, *Braz.* 18°45′ S, 57°2′ W 132
Tar, *Croatia* 45°18′ N, 13°37′ E 167
Tar, river, *N.C., U.S.* 36°12′ N, 78°32′ W 80
Tara, *Russ.* 56°50′ N, 74°26′ E 169
Tara, *Zambia* 16°57′ S, 26°45′ E 224
Tara, Hill of, peak, *Ire.* 53°33′ N, 6°44′ W 150
Tara National Park, *Serb.* 43°49′ N, 19°20′ E 168
Tara, river, *Russ.* 56°17′ N, 76°25′ E 169
Taraba, river, *Nig.* 7°55′ N, 10°57′ E 222
Tarabuco, *Bol.* 19°8′ S, 64°58′ W 137
Ţarābulus (Tripoli), *Leb.* 34°22′ N, 35°53′ E 216
Ţarābulus (Tripoli), *Lib.* 32°37′ N, 12°35′ E 216
Taraclia, *Mold.* 46°33′ N, 29°7′ E 156
Taraco, *Peru* 15°21′ S, 69°58′ W 137
Taradale, *N.Z.* 39°32′ S, 176°50′ E 240
Taragi, *Japan* 32°15′ N, 130°56′ E 201
Taragma, *Sudan* 16°42′ N, 33°36′ E 182
Tarairí, *Bol.* 21°9′ S, 63°31′ W 137
Tarakan, *Indonesia* 3°22′ N, 117°29′ E 192
Taran, Mys, *Russ.* 54°56′ N, 19°42′ E 166
Taranaki, Mount (Egmont, Mount), peak, *N.Z.* 39°20′ S, 173°58′ E 240
Tarancón, *Sp.* 40°0′ N, 3°1′ W 164
Tarangire National Park, *Tanzania* 4°20′ S, 35°41′ E 224
Taranto, *It.* 40°27′ N, 17°13′ E 156
Tarapacá, *Chile* 19°56′ S, 69°35′ W 137
Tarapacá, *Col.* 2°56′ S, 69°44′ W 136
Tarapacá, adm. division, *Chile* 19°30′ S, 70°16′ W 137
Tarapoto, *Peru* 6°31′ S, 76°21′ W 123
Taraquá, *Braz.* 7°416′ N, 68°25′ W 136
Tarare, *Fr.* 45°53′ N, 4°25′ E 150
Tarasa Dwip, island, *India* 8°24′ N, 91°59′ E 188
Tarascon, *Fr.* 42°50′ N, 1°35′ E 150
Tarasovo, *Russ.* 66°16′ N, 46°43′ E 154
Tarasp, *Switz.* 46°45′ N, 10°13′ E 167
Tarat, *Alg.* 26°7′ N, 9°22′ E 214
Tarata, *Bol.* 17°39′ S, 65°53′ W 137
Tarata, *Peru* 17°33′ S, 70°3′ W 137
Taratakbuluh, *Indonesia* 0°25′ N, 101°26′ E 196
Tarauacá, *Braz.* 8°12′ S, 70°48′ W 130
Tarauacá, river, *Braz.* 7°43′ S, 70°59′ W 130
Tarawa (Bairiki), *Kiribati* 1°15′ N, 169°58′ E 242
Tarawa, island, *Kiribati* 1°30′ N, 173°0′ E 242
Tarawera, *N.Z.* 39°3′ S, 176°34′ E 240
Tarawera, Mount, peak, *N.Z.* 38°15′ S, 176°27′ E 240
Taraz, *Kaz.* 42°52′ N, 71°23′ E 197
Tarazit, Massif de, *Niger* 19°41′ N, 7°25′ E 222
Tarazit, spring, *Niger* 20°3′ N, 8°18′ E 222
Tarazona, *Sp.* 41°53′ N, 1°45′ W 164
Tarazona de la Mancha, *Sp.* 39°15′ N, 1°56′ W 164
Tarbagatay Zhotasy, *Kaz.* 47°15′ N, 81°21′ E 184
Tarbaj, *Kenya* 2°8′ N, 40°5′ E 224
Tarbes, *Fr.* 43°13′ N, 0°4′ E 164
Tarboro, *N.C., U.S.* 35°54′ N, 77°34′ W 96
Tarcău, Munţii, *Rom.* 46°42′ N, 25°42′ E 156
Tarcento, *It.* 46°12′ N, 13°14′ E 167
Tarčin, *Bosn. and Herzg.* 43°48′ N, 18°6′ E 168
Tarcoola, *Austral.* 30°44′ S, 134°34′ E 231
Tardajos, *Sp.* 42°20′ N, 3°50′ W 164
Tardienta, *Sp.* 41°58′ N, 0°32′ E 164
Tärendö, *Nor.* 67°9′ N, 22°35′ E 152
Tareraimbu, Cachoeira do, fall(s), *Braz.* 7°51′ S, 53°36′ W 130
Tarfaya (Villa Bens), *Mor.* 27°55′ N, 12°54′ W 214
Targane, spring, *Niger* 16°32′ N, 5°43′ E 222
Targhee Pass, *Mont., U.S.* 44°39′ N, 111°17′ W 90
Târgu Mureş, *Rom.* 46°33′ N, 24°33′ E 156
Tarhaouhaout (Fort Motylinski), *Alg.* 22°38′ N, 5°55′ E 214
Tarhmert, *Niger* 18°45′ N, 8°51′ E 222
Tarhūnī, Jabal at, peak, *Lib.* 22°9′ N, 22°14′ E 216
Tariana, *Braz.* 0°24′ N, 68°46′ W 136
Târié, spring, *Mauritania* 20°8′ N, 11°37′ W 222
Ţarīf, *U.A.E.* 24°1′ N, 53°44′ E 196
Tarifa, *Sp.* 36°0′ N, 5°37′ W 164
Tarifa, Punta de, *Sp.* 35°51′ N, 5°36′ W 164
Tariffville, *Conn., U.S.* 41°53′ N, 72°47′ W 104
Tarija, *Bol.* 21°34′ S, 64°44′ W 137
Tarija, adm. division, *Bol.* 21°51′ S, 64°52′ W 137
Tarik Ibn Ziad, *Alg.* 35°59′ N, 2°9′ E 150
Tarīm, *Yemen* 16°5′ N, 49°1′ E 182
Tarim, river, *China* 40°9′ N, 80°48′ E 190
Tarime, *Tanzania* 1°20′ S, 34°26′ E 224
Taringamotu, *N.Z.* 38°51′ S, 175°16′ E 240
Taritatu, river, *Indonesia* 2°42′ S, 138°14′ E 192
Tarka, *Niger* 14°36′ N, 7°54′ E 222
Tarkastad, *S. Af.* 32°2′ S, 26°14′ E 227
Tarkhankut, Mys, *Ukr.* 45°24′ N, 31°29′ E 156
Tarkhoj, *Afghan.* 35°22′ N, 66°36′ E 186
Tarkio, *Mo., U.S.* 40°25′ N, 95°23′ W 90
Tarko Sale, *Russ.* 64°52′ N, 77°50′ E 169
Tarkwa, *Ghana* 5°19′ N, 1°56′ W 222
Tarlac, *Philippines* 15°30′ N, 120°35′ E 203
Tarm, *Den.* 55°53′ N, 8°29′ E 150
Tarma, *Peru* 3°23′ S, 71°45′ W 136
Tarn, Bahía 47°57′ S, 75°13′ W 134
Tarn, river, *Fr.* 43°47′ N, 1°35′ E 165
Tarnak, river, *Afghan.* 31°51′ N, 66°45′ E 186
Tarnogskiy Gorodok, *Russ.* 60°27′ N, 43°38′ E 154
Tarnów, *Pol.* 50°0′ N, 20°59′ E 152
Tarnya, *Russ.* 62°5′ N, 42°24′ E 154
Ţārom, *Iran* 28°8′ N, 55°43′ E 196
Tarou, spring, *Chad* 20°41′ N, 19°14′ E 216
Tarpon Springs, *Fla., U.S.* 28°8′ N, 82°44′ W 105
Tarporley, *U.K.* 53°9′ N, 2°38′ W 162
Tarragona, *Sp.* 41°7′ N, 1°15′ E 164
Tarras, *N.Z.* 44°50′ S, 169°25′ E 240
Tàrrega, *Sp.* 41°38′ N, 1°8′ E 164
Tarrekaise, peak, *Nor.* 67°1′ N, 17°14′ E 152
Tarrytown, *N.Y., U.S.* 41°3′ N, 73°52′ W 104
Tarsus, *Turk.* 36°53′ N, 34°53′ E 156
Tart, *China* 37°4′ N, 92°51′ E 188
Tartagal, *Arg.* 28°37′ S, 59°53′ W 139
Tartagal, *Arg.* 22°29′ S, 63°53′ W 137
Tartar Strait 47°18′ N, 139°16′ E 238
Tartas, river, *Russ.* 56°24′ N, 78°32′ E 169
Tartu, *Est.* 58°21′ N, 26°40′ E 166
Ţarţūs (Tortosa), *Syr.* 34°53′ N, 35°53′ E 194
Tarumizu, *Japan* 31°28′ N, 130°43′ E 201
Tarusa, *Russ.* 54°42′ N, 37°10′ E 154
Tarutao, Ko, island, *Thai.* 6°38′ N, 99°41′ E 196
Tarutung, *Indonesia* 2°0′ N, 98°56′ E 196
Tarvisio, *It.* 46°30′ N, 13°34′ E 156
Tasa, *N. Korea* 39°49′ N, 124°23′ E 200
Tasajera, Sierra de la, *Mex.* 29°34′ N, 105°52′ W 112
Tasāwah, *Lib.* 26°2′ N, 13°31′ E 216
Taschereau, *Can.* 48°40′ N, 78°43′ W 110
Tascosa, *Tex., U.S.* 35°28′ N, 102°14′ W 92
Taseko Mountain, peak, *Can.* 51°13′ N, 123°36′ W 90
Taseko, river, *Can.* 51°45′ N, 123°40′ W 108
Tashanta, *Russ.* 49°41′ N, 89°10′ E 184
Tashk, Daryācheh-ye, lake, *Iran* 29°46′ N, 53°13′ E 196
Tashkent see Toshkent, *Uzb.* 41°18′ N, 69°10′ E 197
Tash-Kömür, *Kyrg.* 41°23′ N, 72°15′ E 197
Tashla, *Russ.* 51°46′ N, 52°44′ E 158
Tashota, *Can.* 50°14′ N, 87°40′ W 94
Tashtagol, *Russ.* 52°48′ N, 88°0′ E 184
Tashtyp, *Russ.* 52°49′ N, 89°56′ E 184
Tasiilaq 65°39′ N, 37°48′ W 106
Tasikmalaya, *Indonesia* 7°21′ S, 108°12′ E 238
Tasiusaq 73°22′ N, 56°3′ W 106
Tåsjö, *Nor.* 64°12′ N, 15°56′ E 152
Tåsjön, lake, *Nor.* 64°20′ N, 15°12′ E 152

Task, *Niger* 14°54' N, 10°43' E 222
Taskan, *Russ.* 63°14' N, 150°29' E 160
Tasker, *Niger* 15°12' N, 10°46' E 222
Taskesken, *Kaz.* 47°14' N, 80°45' E 184
Taskinigup Falls, *Can.* 55°24' N, 99°0' W 108
Taşköprü, *Turk.* 41°30' N, 34°12' E 156
Tasman, *N.Z.* 41°14' S, 173°2' E 240
Tasman Fracture Zone, *South Pacific Ocean* 52°43' S, 147°43' E 255
Tasman Peninsula, *Austral.* 42°49' S, 147°14' E 230
Tasman Plain, *Tasman Sea* 35°46' S, 153°34' E 252
Tasman Sea 37°36' S, 153°44' E 231
Tasmania, adm. division, *Austral.* 42°4' S, 145°43' E 231
Tăşnad, *Rom.* 47°27' N, 22°36' E 168
Taşova, *Turk.* 40°47' N, 36°19' E 156
Tass, *Hung.* 47°1' N, 19°2' E 168
Tassara, *Niger* 16°49' N, 5°29' E 222
Tassialouc, Lac, lake, *Can.* 58°58' N, 76°3' W 106
Tassili-n-Ajjer National Park, *Alg.* 25°43' N, 7°49' E 214
Tassili-n-Ajjer, region, *Alg.* 25°32' N, 7°10' E 214
Tasso Fragoso, *Braz.* 8°30' S, 45°46' W 130
Tast, Lac du, lake, *Can.* 50°58' N, 77°53' W 110
Tasty-Taldy, *Kaz.* 50°43' N, 66°37' E 184
Tata, *Mor.* 29°45' N, 7°59' W 214
Tatabánya, *Hung.* 47°32' N, 18°26' E 168
Tatalin, river, *China* 37°33' N, 96°17' E 188
Tatar Strait 48°40' N, 136°53' E 172
Tatarbunary, *Ukr.* 45°49' N, 29°35' E 156
Tatarsk, *Russ.* 55°10' N, 75°59' E 184
Tatarskiy Proliv 50°55' N, 141°25' E 190
Tatarstan, adm. division, *Russ.* 55°18' N, 48°59' E 154
Tatau, island, *P.N.G.* 2°42' S, 151°9' E 192
Tate, *Ga., U.S.* 34°24' N, 84°24' W 96
Tatebayashi, *Japan* 36°14' N, 139°32' E 201
Tateyama, *Japan* 34°58' N, 139°52' E 201
Tathlina Lake, *Can.* 60°31' N, 118°6' W 108
Tathlīth, *Saudi Arabia* 19°30' N, 43°30' E 182
Tatishchevo, *Russ.* 51°39' N, 45°35' E 158
Tatkon, *Myanmar* 20°8' N, 96°14' E 202
Tatlatui Lake, lake, *Can.* 56°53' N, 127°53' W 108
Tatlayoko Lake, *Can.* 51°34' N, 125°6' W 108
Tatman Mountain, peak, *Wyo., U.S.* 44°16' N, 108°33' W 90
Tatnam, Cape, *Can.* 57°19' N, 90°49' W 106
Tatoosh Island, *Wash., U.S.* 48°17' N, 124°55' W 100
Tatrang, *China* 38°35' N, 85°50' E 184
Tatrart, spring, *Mauritania* 17°32' N, 10°21' W 222
Tatry, *Pol.* 49°7' N, 19°22' E 152
Tatsamenie Lake, *Can.* 58°19' N, 133°15' W 108
Tattershall, *U.K.* 53°4' N, 0°12' E 162
Tätti, *Kaz.* 43°12' N, 73°20' E 184
Tatuí, *Braz.* 23°22' S, 47°50' W 138
Tatuke, *Liberia* 5°9' N, 8°17' W 222
Tatum, *N. Mex., U.S.* 33°14' N, 103°19' W 92
Tatum, *Tex., U.S.* 32°18' N, 94°32' W 103
Tatvan, *Turk.* 38°30' N, 42°14' E 195
Tau, island, *U.S.* 14°14' S, 169°29' W 241
Tauá, *Braz.* 6°2' S, 40°24' W 132
Tauapeçaçu, *Braz.* 2°41' S, 60°57' W 130
Taubaté, *Braz.* 23°3' S, 45°34' W 138
Tauern, Hohe, *Aust.* 46°51' N, 12°14' E 167
Taulabé National Monument, *Hond.* 14°42' N, 88°3' W 115
Taum Sauk Mountain, peak, *Mo., U.S.* 37°32' N, 90°48' W 96
Taumarunui, *N.Z.* 38°54' S, 175°17' E 240
Taumatawhakatangihangakoauauotamateapokaiwhenuakitanatahu, peak, *N.Z.* 40°21' S, 176°29' E 240
Taung, *S. Af.* 27°33' S, 24°47' E 227
Taunggok, *Myanmar* 18°51' N, 94°15' E 202
Taungoo, *Myanmar* 18°58' N, 96°23' E 202
Taungup Pass, *Myanmar* 18°40' N, 94°45' E 202
Taunsa, *Pak.* 30°42' N, 70°40' E 186
Taunsa Barrage, dam, *Pak.* 30°13' N, 70°38' E 186
Taunton, *Mass., U.S.* 41°54' N, 71°6' W 104
Taunton, *U.K.* 51°0' N, 3°7' W 162
Taunus, *Ger.* 50°18' N, 7°54' E 167
Taunusstein, *Ger.* 50°8' N, 8°11' E 167
Taupo, *N.Z.* 38°43' S, 176°7' E 240
Tauragė, *Lith.* 55°15' N, 22°17' E 166
Tauramena, *Col.* 5°1' N, 72°45' W 136
Taureau, Réservoir, lake, *Can.* 46°45' N, 74°23' W 94
Taurus see Toros Dağlar, *Turk.* 36°29' N, 32°7' E 156
Taūshyq, *Kaz.* 44°17' N, 51°18' E 158
Tauste, *Sp.* 41°55' N, 1°16' W 164
Tauyskaya Guba 59°1' N, 147°41' E 160
Tavankut, *Serb.* 46°2' N, 19°29' E 168
Tavares, *Braz.* 31°13' S, 51°0' W 139
Tavares, *Fla., U.S.* 28°48' N, 81°45' W 105
Tavas, *Turk.* 37°34' N, 29°3' E 156
Tavda, *Russ.* 57°58' N, 65°19' E 160
Tavda, river, *Russ.* 59°37' N, 62°54' E 154
Tavernes de la Valldigna, *Sp.* 39°4' N, 0°16' E 164
Tavernier, *Fla., U.S.* 25°1' N, 80°32' W 105
Taveta, *Kenya* 3°25' S, 37°40' E 218
Taveta, *Tanzania* 9°2' S, 35°32' E 224
Taviche, *Mex.* 16°43' N, 96°35' W 112
Tavistock, *Can.* 43°19' N, 80°49' W 102
Tavoy Point, *Myanmar* 13°31' N, 97°43' E 202
Tavricheskoye, *Russ.* 54°32' N, 73°36' E 184
Tavşanlı, *Turk.* 39°33' N, 29°30' E 156
Tawai, *India* 27°46' N, 96°46' E 188
Tawake, *Liberia* 5°10' N, 7°38' W 222
Tawang, *India* 27°36' N, 91°51' E 197
Tawau, *Malaysia* 4°19' N, 117°53' E 192
Taweisha, *Sudan* 12°14' N, 26°39' E 216
Tawi Tawi, island, *Philippines* 5°14' N, 119°31' E 192
Tawu, *Taiwan, China* 22°22' N, 120°52' E 198
Ţāwūq, *Iraq* 35°9' N, 44°26' E 180
Tāwurghā', *Lib.* 32°5' N, 15°8' E 216
Taxco, *Mex.* 18°32' N, 99°37' W 114
Taxila, ruin(s), *Pak.* 33°43' N, 72°38' E 186
Taxkorgan, *China* 37°48' N, 75°9' E 184
Tay Ninh, *Vietnam* 11°18' N, 106°4' E 202
Tay, river, *Can.* 62°38' N, 133°39' W 98
Tayabas Bay 13°36' N, 121°40' E 203
Tayarte, spring, *Alg.* 23°6' N, 0°20' E 214
Tayeeglow, *Somalia* 4°1' N, 44°31' E 218
Tayga, *Russ.* 56°3' N, 85°46' E 169
Taygonos, Poluostrov, *Russ.* 62°44' N, 159°36' E 160
Tayildara, *Taj.* 38°40' N, 70°31' E 197
Taylakova, *Russ.* 59°11' N, 74°0' E 169
Taylor, *Ariz., U.S.* 34°28' N, 110°5' W 92
Taylor, *Ark., U.S.* 33°6' N, 93°28' W 103
Taylor, *Tex., U.S.* 30°33' N, 97°24' W 96
Taylor, Mount, peak, *N. Mex., U.S.* 35°14' N, 107°42' W 92
Taylor Mountain, peak, *Idaho, U.S.* 44°52' N, 114°17' W 90
Taylor Mountains, peak, *Alas., U.S.* 60°47' N, 157°45' W 98
Taylors Head, *Can.* 44°41' N, 62°34' W 111
Taylorsville, *Ind., U.S.* 39°17' N, 85°57' W 102
Taylorsville, *Miss., U.S.* 31°50' N, 89°26' W 103
Taylorville, *Ill., U.S.* 39°32' N, 89°18' W 102
Taymā', *Saudi Arabia* 27°36' N, 38°28' E 180
Taymura, river, *Russ.* 63°11' N, 99°3' E 160
Taymylyr, *Russ.* 72°29' N, 122°5' E 160
Taymyr, adm. division, *Russ.* 68°43' N, 85°44' E 169
Taymyr, Ozero, lake, *Russ.* 74°33' N, 99°13' E 160
Taymyr, Poluostrov, *Russ.* 75°28' N, 84°4' E 160
Taypaq, *Kaz.* 48°57' N, 51°47' E 158
Tayshet, *Russ.* 55°57' N, 98°2' E 160
Taytay, *Philippines* 10°47' N, 119°31' E 203
Ţayyebāt, *Iran* 34°50' N, 60°47' E 180
Tayynsha, *Kaz.* 53°49' N, 69°25' E 160
Taz, river, *Russ.* 64°55' N, 81°39' E 169
Taz, river, *Russ.* 63°43' N, 84°32' E 169
Taza, *Mor.* 34°15' N, 4°4' W 214
Tazadite, spring, *Mali* 24°32' N, 4°56' W 214
Taze, *Myanmar* 22°57' N, 95°25' E 202
Tazin Lake, *Can.* 59°50' N, 110°4' W 108
Tazin, river, *Can.* 59°41' N, 108°48' W 108
Tazin, river, *Can.* 60°21' N, 110°59' W 108
Tāzirbū, *Lib.* 25°47' N, 21°2' E 216
Tazolé, *Niger* 17°12' N, 9°10' E 222
Tazouikert, spring, *Mali* 21°32' N, 1°19' W 222
Tazovskaya Guba 68°46' N, 74°22' E 169
Tazovskiy, *Russ.* 67°21' N, 78°43' E 169
Tazzaït, spring, *Alg.* 26°57' N, 5°55' E 214
Tazzarine, *Mor.* 30°46' N, 5°34' W 214
Tbilisi, *Ga.* 41°42' N, 44°42' E 195
Tbilisskaya, *Russ.* 45°22' N, 40°7' E 158
Tchamba, *Togo* 8°56' N, 1°22' E 222
Tchaourou, *Benin* 8°54' N, 2°35' E 222
Tchentlo Lake, *Can.* 55°11' N, 125°26' W 108
Tchibanga, *Gabon* 2°58' S, 10°56' E 207
Tchié, spring, *Chad* 17°6' N, 18°53' E 216
Tchin-Tabaradène, *Niger* 15°45' N, 5°38' E 222
Tchula, *Miss., U.S.* 33°9' N, 90°14' W 103
Te Anau, *N.Z.* 45°26' S, 167°44' E 240
Te Anau, Lake, *N.Z.* 45°12' S, 167°25' E 240
Te Araroa, *N.Z.* 37°40' S, 178°20' E 240
Te Aroha, *N.Z.* 37°33' S, 175°43' E 240
Te Hapua, *N.Z.* 34°32' S, 172°54' E 240
Te Kaha, *N.Z.* 37°46' S, 177°41' E 240
Te Kao, *N.Z.* 34°40' S, 172°57' E 240
Te Karaka, *N.Z.* 38°29' S, 177°51' E 240
Te Kauwhata, *N.Z.* 37°25' S, 175°9' E 240
Te Kopuru, *N.Z.* 36°3' S, 173°55' E 240
Te Kuiti, *N.Z.* 38°23' S, 175°8' E 240
Te Pohue, *N.Z.* 39°16' S, 176°42' E 240
Te Puia Springs, *N.Z.* 38°3' S, 178°18' E 240
Te Puke, *N.Z.* 37°48' S, 176°19' E 240
Te Teko, *N.Z.* 38°3' S, 176°47' E 240
Tea, river, *Braz.* 0°37' N, 65°37' W 136
Teacapan, *Mex.* 22°33' N, 105°44' W 114
Teague, *Tex., U.S.* 31°36' N, 96°17' W 96
Teapa, *Mex.* 17°32' N, 92°57' W 115
Teapot Dome, peak, *Wyo., U.S.* 43°13' N, 106°16' W 90
Tearce, *Maced.* 42°4' N, 21°3' E 168
Teba, *Sp.* 36°59' N, 4°56' W 164
Ţebea, *Rom.* 46°10' N, 22°45' E 168
Teberda, *Russ.* 43°27' N, 41°42' E 195
Tébessa, *Alg.* 35°23' N, 8°8' E 156
Tebicuary, river, *Parag.* 26°29' S, 58°1' W 139
Tebingtinggi, *Indonesia* 3°19' N, 99°8' E 196
Tebingtinggi, island, *Indonesia* 0°36' N, 102°10' E 196
Teboursouq, *Tun.* 36°26' N, 9°14' E 216
Tebra, river, *Latv.* 56°53' N, 21°20' E 152
Tebulosmta, peak, *Russ.* 42°34' N, 45°21' E 195
Tecalitlán, *Mex.* 19°27' N, 103°18' W 114
Tecate, *Mex.* 32°34' N, 116°39' W 101
Techa, river, *Russ.* 55°37' N, 61°59' E 154
Tecolotlán, *Mex.* 20°12' N, 104°3' W 114
Tecomán, *Mex.* 18°54' N, 103°53' W 112
Tecopa, *Calif., U.S.* 35°50' N, 116°14' W 101
Tecopa Hot Springs, *Calif., U.S.* 35°52' N, 116°14' W 101
Tecoripa, *Mex.* 28°36' N, 109°56' W 92
Tecozautla, *Mex.* 20°31' N, 99°38' W 114
Tecpan, *Mex.* 17°11' N, 100°38' W 114
Tecuala, *Mex.* 22°23' N, 105°29' W 114
Tecumseh, *Can.* 42°17' N, 82°53' W 102
Tecumseh, *Mich., U.S.* 42°0' N, 83°57' W 102
Ted Ceidaar Dabole, *Somalia* 4°21' N, 43°56' E 218
Teerijärvi see Terjärv, *Fin.* 63°32' N, 23°29' E 154
Tefé, *Braz.* 3°29' S, 64°46' W 123
Tefé, river, *Braz.* 3°50' S, 65°20' W 130
Tefenni, *Turk.* 37°17' N, 29°46' E 156
Tegalhusi, *Sudan* 15°29' N, 36°14' E 182
Tegea, ruin(s), *Gr.* 37°27' N, 22°19' E 156
Tegelen, *Neth.* 51°20' N, 6°8' E 167
Tegina, *Nig.* 10°3' N, 6°11' E 222
Tégouma, spring, *Niger* 15°42' N, 9°15' E 222
Tegucigalpa, *Hond.* 14°3' N, 87°21' W 115
Teguidda-n-Tessoumt, *Niger* 17°26' N, 6°38' E 222
Tegul'det, *Russ.* 57°18' N, 88°16' E 169
Tehachapi, *Calif., U.S.* 35°8' N, 118°28' W 101
Tehachapi Mountains, *Calif., U.S.* 34°56' N, 118°40' W 101
Tehachapi Pass, *Calif., U.S.* 35°6' N, 118°18' W 101
Tehama, *Calif., U.S.* 40°1' N, 122°8' W 92
Tehamiyam, *Sudan* 18°19' N, 36°28' E 182
Tehek Lake, *Can.* 65°13' N, 97°17' W 106
Téhini, *Côte d'Ivoire* 9°36' N, 3°41' W 222
Tehrān, *Iran* 35°41' N, 51°20' E 180
Tehuacán, *Mex.* 18°25' N, 97°25' W 114
Tehuantepec, Istmo de, *Mex.* 17°38' N, 95°8' W 114
Tehuantepec, Golfo de 15°10' N, 96°44' W 73
Teide, Pico de, peak, *Sp.* 28°12' N, 16°47' W 214
Teifi, river, *U.K.* 52°6' N, 4°40' W 150
Teisko, *Fin.* 61°40' N, 23°47' E 166
Teixeiro, *Sp.* 43°5' N, 8°4' W 150
Tejen, *Turkm.* 37°23' N, 60°30' E 180
Tejo, river, *Braz.* 9°12' S, 72°23' W 137
Tejo, river, *Port.* 39°28' N, 8°16' W 150
Tejon Pass, *Calif., U.S.* 34°47' N, 118°53' W 101
Teju, *India* 27°54' N, 96°11' E 188
Tejupan, Punta, *Mex.* 18°21' N, 103°32' W 114
Tejupilco, *Mex.* 18°52' N, 100°9' W 114
Tekamah, *Nebr., U.S.* 41°45' N, 96°13' W 90
Tekax, *Mex.* 20°11' N, 89°18' W 112
Tekes, *China* 43°11' N, 81°50' E 184
Tekes, river, *Asia* 42°55' N, 80°31' E 184
Tekezē, river, *Eth.* 13°44' N, 38°33' E 182
Tekiliktag, peak, *China* 36°31' N, 80°15' E 184
Tekirdağ, *Turk.* 40°58' N, 27°30' E 156
Tekirova, *Turk.* 36°29' N, 30°29' E 156
Tekkali, *India* 18°37' N, 84°13' E 188
Tekman, *Turk.* 39°37' N, 41°30' E 195
Teknaf, *Bangladesh* 20°52' N, 92°16' E 188
Tekoa, *Wash., U.S.* 47°13' N, 117°6' W 90
Tekro, spring, *Chad* 19°29' N, 20°56' E 216
Tel Aviv-Yafo, *Israel* 32°2' N, 34°45' E 194
Tel Jemmeh, ruin(s), *Israel* 31°22' N, 34°24' E 194
Tela, *Hond.* 15°45' N, 87°26' W 115
Télabit, *Mali* 19°4' N, 0°56' E 222
Telaga, island, *Indonesia* 3°10' N, 105°42' E 196
Telataipale, *Fin.* 61°37' N, 28°36' E 166
T'elavi, *Ga.* 41°55' N, 45°28' E 195
Tele, river, *Dem. Rep. of the Congo* 2°29' N, 24°31' E 224
Telegraph Creek, *Can.* 57°55' N, 131°12' W 108
Telêmaco Borba, *Braz.* 24°25' S, 50°38' W 138
Telemark, region, *Nor.* 59°13' N, 7°55' E 152
Teleneşti, *Mold.* 47°29' N, 28°21' E 156
Teleorman, adm. division, *Rom.* 43°47' N, 24°43' E 156
Telerhteba, Djebel, peak, *Alg.* 24°11' N, 6°46' E 214
Teles Pires (São Manuel), river, *Braz.* 9°30' S, 55°14' W 122
Telescope Peak, *Calif., U.S.* 36°9' N, 117°8' W 101
Teletskoye Ozero, lake, *Russ.* 51°38' N, 86°38' E 184
Telfel, spring, *Mali* 19°49' N, 3°39' W 222
Telford, *U.K.* 52°40' N, 2°29' W 162
Telgte, *Ger.* 51°58' N, 7°46' E 167
Télimélé, *Guinea* 10°54' N, 13°5' W 222
Telixtlahuaca, *Mex.* 17°15' N, 96°51' W 114
Teljo, Jebel, peak, *Sudan* 14°40' N, 25°52' E 226
Telkwa, *Can.* 54°40' N, 127°7' W 108
Tell City, *Ind., U.S.* 37°56' N, 86°45' W 96
Tell el 'Amârna, ruin(s), *Egypt* 27°39' N, 30°48' E 180
Tell Tayinat, ruin(s), *Turk.* 36°14' N, 36°16' E 156
Tellicherry see Thalassery, *India* 11°45' N, 75°29' E 188
Tellier, *Arg.* 47°37' S, 66°4' W 134
Telluride, *Colo., U.S.* 37°56' N, 107°50' W 92
Telo, *Indonesia* 2°118' S, 98°15' E 196
Teloloapan, *Mex.* 18°20' N, 99°53' W 114
Telsen, *Arg.* 42°28' S, 66°51' W 134
Telšiai, *Lith.* 55°59' N, 22°14' E 166
Teluk Intan, *Malaysia* 4°1' N, 101°1' E 196
Telukbutun, *Indonesia* 4°14' N, 108°13' E 196
Telukdalem, *Indonesia* 0°37' N, 97°48' E 196
Tema, *Ghana* 5°41' N, 2°0' E 222
Temagami, Lake, *Can.* 46°59' N, 80°43' W 110
Tembenchi, *Russ.* 64°56' N, 99°16' E 246
Tembenchi, river, *Russ.* 66°3' N, 94°53' E 169
Témbi, *Gr.* 39°46' N, 22°18' E 156
Tembilahan, *Indonesia* 0°19' N, 103°8' E 196
Temblor Range, *Calif., U.S.* 35°28' N, 120°5' W 100
Teme, river, *U.K.* 52°17' N, 2°29' W 162
Temecula, *Calif., U.S.* 33°29' N, 117°10' W 101
Temerin, *Serb.* 45°23' N, 19°53' E 168
Temerloh, *Malaysia* 3°28' N, 102°23' E 196
Temiang, island, *Indonesia* 2°57' N, 106°9' E 196
Temir, *Kaz.* 49°8' N, 57°7' E 158
Temir, *Kaz.* 42°48' N, 68°26' E 197
Temirgoyevskaya, *Russ.* 45°6' N, 40°15' E 158
Temirtaū, *Kaz.* 50°5' N, 72°53' E 185
Temirtau, *Russ.* 53°9' N, 87°35' E 184
Témiscamie, Lac, lake, *Can.* 51°6' N, 72°55' W 110
Témiscaming, *Can.* 46°44' N, 79°6' W 94
Temnikov, *Russ.* 54°38' N, 43°16' E 154
Temósachic, *Mex.* 28°57' N, 107°50' W 92
Tempe, *Ariz., U.S.* 33°24' N, 111°58' W 112
Tempestad, *Peru* 1°20' S, 74°56' W 136
Temple, *N.H., U.S.* 42°48' N, 71°51' W 104
Temple, *Okla., U.S.* 34°14' N, 98°14' W 92
Temple, *Tex., U.S.* 31°5' N, 97°20' W 96
Temple Bar, *Ariz., U.S.* 36°0' N, 114°20' W 101
Temple, Mount, peak, *Can.* 51°20' N, 116°17' W 90
Templeman, Mount, peak, *Can.* 50°40' N, 117°19' W 90
Templeton, *Calif., U.S.* 35°33' N, 120°44' W 100
Templeton, *Mass., U.S.* 42°33' N, 72°5' W 104
Tempoal, *Mex.* 21°31' N, 98°26' W 114
Tempué, *Angola* 13°30' S, 18°50' E 220
Temryuk, *Russ.* 45°18' N, 37°24' E 156
Temryukskiy Zaliv 45°23' N, 37°2' E 158
Temse, *Belg.* 51°7' N, 4°12' E 163
Temuco, *Chile* 38°43' S, 72°39' W 134
Temuka, *N.Z.* 44°15' S, 171°18' E 240
Ten Degree Channel 9°44' N, 91°13' E 188
Ten Sleep, *Wyo., U.S.* 44°1' N, 107°26' W 90
Ten Thousand Islands, *Gulf of Mexico* 25°48' N, 81°41' W 105
Tena, *Ecua.* 1°4' S, 77°55' W 136
Tenabo, Mount, peak, *Nev., U.S.* 40°9' N, 116°42' W 90
Tenaha, *Tex., U.S.* 31°55' N, 94°15' W 103
Tenakee Springs, *Alas., U.S.* 57°48' N, 135°11' W 108
Tenala, *Fin.* 60°2' N, 23°17' E 166
Tenamaxtlán, *Mex.* 20°11' N, 104°10' W 114
Tenancingo, *Mex.* 18°56' N, 99°38' W 114
Tenay, *Fr.* 45°55' N, 5°30' E 156
Tenbury, *U.K.* 52°17' N, 2°36' W 162
Tendaho, *Eth.* 11°39' N, 40°56' E 182
Tende, *Fr.* 44°5' N, 7°34' E 167
Tendelti, *Sudan* 13°0' N, 31°52' E 182
Tendō, *Japan* 38°22' N, 140°22' E 201
Tendoy Mountains, *Mont., U.S.* 44°49' N, 113°6' W 90
Tendrara, *Mor.* 33°5' N, 2°0' W 214
Tendürek Dağı, peak, *Turk.* 39°20' N, 43°50' E 195
Tenekert, spring, *Mali* 17°48' N, 3°9' E 222
Ténenkou, *Mali* 14°28' N, 4°57' W 222
Ténéré, *Niger* 19°23' N, 9°29' E 222
Ténéré du Tafassâsset, region, *Niger* 20°49' N, 9°47' E 222
Ténéré, ḥErg du, *Niger* 17°10' N, 9°47' E 222
Tenerife, island, *Sp.* 28°32' N, 16°3' W 214
Ténès, *Alg.* 36°30' N, 1°18' E 150
Tenexpa, *Mex.* 17°10' N, 100°43' W 114
Teng'aopu, *China* 41°5' N, 122°48' E 200
Tengchong, *China* 25°3' N, 98°26' E 190
Tengge, *Kaz.* 43°16' N, 52°46' E 158
Tengiz, oil field, *Kaz.* 46°7' N, 53°23' E 158
Tengizy Köli, lake, *Kaz.* 50°11' N, 68°11' E 184
Tengxian, *China* 23°16' N, 110°51' E 198
Tengzhou, *China* 35°5' N, 117°9' E 198
Teniente Origone, *Arg.* 39°6' S, 62°35' W 139
Tenino, *Wash., U.S.* 46°50' N, 122°52' W 100
Tenke, *Dem. Rep. of the Congo* 10°36' S, 26°10' E 224
Tenkeli, *Russ.* 70°10' N, 140°46' E 160
Tenkergynpil'gyn, Laguna 68°29' N, 178°36' E 98
Ten'ki, *Russ.* 55°24' N, 48°54' E 154
Tenkodogo, *Burkina Faso* 11°46' N, 0°22' E 222
Tenlaa, *India* 7°1' N, 93°58' E 188
Tennant Creek, *Austral.* 19°38' S, 134°13' E 231
Tennessee, adm. division, *Tenn., U.S.* 35°41' N, 87°31' W 96
Tennessee Pass, *Colo., U.S.* 39°20' N, 106°19' W 90
Tenojoki, river, *Europe* 68°54' N, 25°39' E 160
Tenosique, *Mex.* 17°28' N, 91°26' W 116
Tenryū, river, *Japan* 35°7' N, 137°41' E 201
Tensas, river, *La., U.S.* 32°8' N, 91°21' W 103
Tensaw, *Ala., U.S.* 31°8' N, 87°48' W 103
Tentane, *Mauritania* 19°55' N, 13°3' W 222
Teocaltiche, *Mex.* 21°25' N, 102°34' W 114
Teodelina, *Arg.* 34°12' S, 61°34' W 139
Teófilo Otoni, *Braz.* 17°49' S, 41°32' W 138
Teofipol', *Ukr.* 49°49' N, 26°24' E 152
Teolo, *It.* 45°20' N, 11°40' E 167
Teora, *It.* 40°52' N, 15°16' E 156
Teotepec, Cerro, peak, *Mex.* 17°26' N, 100°13' W 114
Teotihuacan, ruin(s), *Mex.* 19°40' N, 98°57' W 114
Tepache, *Mex.* 29°31' N, 109°31' W 92
Tepalcatepec, *Mex.* 19°10' N, 102°52' W 114
Tepalcatepec, river, *Mex.* 19°0' N, 102°44' W 114
Tepatitlán, *Mex.* 20°48' N, 102°47' W 114
Tepe Gawra, ruin(s), *Iraq* 36°32' N, 43°7' E 195
Tepe Musyan, ruin(s), *Iran* 32°34' N, 47°9' E 180
Tepe, mountain, *Serb.* 42°43' N, 21°31' E 168
Tepechitlán, *Mex.* 21°38' N, 103°19' W 114
Tepecoacuilco, *Mex.* 18°16' N, 99°29' W 114
Tepehuanes, *Mex.* 25°21' N, 105°42' W 114
Tepeji de Ocampo, *Mex.* 19°52' N, 99°20' W 114
Tepetongo, *Mex.* 22°27' N, 103°8' W 114
Tepic, *Mex.* 21°29' N, 104°57' W 114
Tepich, *Mex.* 20°17' N, 88°14' W 115
Tepoca, Cabo, *Mex.* 30°4' N, 113°13' W 92
Teposcolula, *Mex.* 17°29' N, 97°31' W 114
Tequila, *Mex.* 20°53' N, 103°49' W 114
Tequisquiapan, *Mex.* 20°30' N, 99°54' W 114
Ter Apel, *Neth.* 52°52' N, 7°4' E 163
T'er, river, *Eth.* 7°14' N, 41°49' E 224
Têra, *Niger* 13°59' N, 0°46' E 222
Teradomari, *Japan* 37°37' N, 138°47' E 201
Terakeka, *Sudan* 5°25' N, 31°43' E 224
Teramo, *It.* 42°39' N, 13°42' E 156
Tercan, *Turk.* 39°47' N, 40°22' E 195
Teregova, *Rom.* 45°7' N, 22°18' E 168
Terek, river, *Russ.* 43°24' N, 46°17' E 195
Terekhovka, *Belarus* 52°10' N, 31°30' E 158
Terekli Mekteb, *Russ.* 44°9' N, 45°53' E 158
Terekty, *Kaz.* 48°22' N, 85°39' E 184
Terempa, *Indonesia* 3°14' N, 106°12' E 196
Terengözek, *Kaz.* 45°2' N, 64°59' E 184
Terenos, *Braz.* 20°24' S, 54°51' W 132
Tereressene, spring, *Mali* 16°55' N, 2°39' E 222
Teresa Cristina, *Braz.* 24°52' S, 51°6' W 138
Teresina, *Braz.* 5°3' S, 42°48' W 132
Teresinha, *Braz.* 0°57' N, 52°1' W 130
Teresita, *Peru* 12°35' S, 73°47' W 137
Terezino Polje, *Croatia* 45°56' N, 17°27' E 168
Tergnier, *Fr.* 49°39' N, 3°17' E 163
Terhazza, ruin(s), *Mali* 23°34' N, 5°9' W 214
Teriberka, *Russ.* 69°10' N, 35°9' E 152

Teriberskiy, Mys, *Russ.* 69° 1' N, 35° 15' E 152
Terisaqqan, river, *Kaz.* 51° 22' N, 67° 25' E 184
Terjärv (Teerijärvi), *Fin.* 63° 32' N, 23° 29' E 154
Terkezi, spring, *Chad* 18° 24' N, 21° 28' E 216
Termas de Río Hondo, *Arg.* 27° 29' S, 64° 52' W 134
Terme, *Turk.* 41° 12' N, 36° 57' E 156
Termini Imerese, *It.* 37° 58' N, 13° 41' E 156
Terminus Mountain, peak, *Can.* 58° 46' N, 127° 12' W 108
Termit, *Niger* 16° 5' N, 11° 11' E 222
Termit, Massif de, *Niger* 16° 8' N, 10° 42' E 222
Termit, spring, *Niger* 15° 58' N, 11° 15' E 206
Termita, *Russ.* 45° 5' N, 45° 14' E 158
Termit-Kaoboul, *Niger* 15° 37' N, 11° 26' E 222
Termiz, *Uzb.* 37° 14' N, 67° 16' E 186
Termoli, *It.* 41° 59' N, 14° 59' E 156
Termópilas, *Peru* 10° 41' S, 73° 53' W 137
Ternate, *Indonesia* 0° 41' N, 127° 25' E 192
Terneuzen, *Neth.* 51° 19' N, 3° 50' E 163
Terney, *Russ.* 45° 6' N, 136° 31' E 190
Terni, *It.* 42° 34' N, 12° 39' E 156
Ternitz, *Aust.* 47° 43' N, 16° 0' E 168
Ternopil', *Ukr.* 49° 31' N, 25° 35' E 152
Terpeniya, Mys, *Russ.* 48° 8' N, 144° 42' E 190
Terpeniya, Zaliv 47° 55' N, 142° 48' E 190
Terra Bella, *Calif., U.S.* 35° 58' N, 119° 3' W 101
Terra Nova Bay, Italy, station, *Antarctica* 74° 45' S, 163° 39' E 248
Terra Nova National Park, *Can.* 48° 30' N, 54° 55' W 111
Terrace, *Can.* 54° 31' N, 128° 36' W 108
Terrace Bay, *Can.* 48° 47' N, 87° 6' W 94
Terracina, *It.* 41° 18' N, 13° 14' E 156
Terralba, *It.* 39° 42' N, 8° 37' E 214
Terrassa, *Sp.* 41° 33' N, 2° 1' E 164
Terre Haute, *Ind., U.S.* 39° 27' N, 87° 25' W 102
Terrebonne Bay 29° 1' N, 90° 39' W 96
Terrecht, region, *Mali* 20° 26' N, 0° 35' E 222
Terrell, *Tex., U.S.* 32° 45' N, 96° 18' W 112
Terry, *Miss., U.S.* 32° 4' N, 90° 18' W 103
Terry, *Mont., U.S.* 46° 46' N, 105° 20' W 90
Terry Peak, *S. Dak., U.S.* 44° 18' N, 103° 55' W 90
Terschelling, island, *Neth.* 53° 27' N, 5° 7' E 163
Tertenia, *It.* 39° 40' N, 9° 33' E 156
Teru, *Pak.* 36° 8' N, 72° 48' E 186
Teruel, *Sp.* 40° 19' N, 1° 9' W 214
Tervo, *Fin.* 62° 55' N, 26° 41' E 152
Tešanj, *Bosn. and Herzg.* 44° 36' N, 17° 59' E 168
Teshi, *Ghana* 5° 37' N, 7° 415' W 222
Teshi, river, *Nig.* 9° 17' N, 4° 3' E 222
Tešica, *Serb.* 43° 25' N, 21° 45' E 168
Teslić, *Bosn. and Herzg.* 44° 36' N, 17° 50' E 168
Teslin, *Can.* 60° 13' N, 132° 47' W 108
Teslin Lake, *Can.* 59° 45' N, 132° 58' W 108
Teslin, river, *Can.* 59° 16' N, 132° 5' W 108
Tesouro, *Braz.* 16° 7' S, 53° 33' W 132
Tesovo Netyl'skiy, *Russ.* 58° 56' N, 31° 8' E 152
Tessalit, *Mali* 20° 12' N, 0° 58' E 222
Tessaoua, *Niger* 13° 47' N, 7° 57' E 222
Tessenberg, *Aust.* 46° 45' N, 12° 28' E 167
Tessenei, *Eritrea* 15° 6' N, 36° 39' E 182
Tessier, Lac, lake, *Can.* 48° 10' N, 75° 44' W 94
Tessounfat, spring, *Mali* 20° 51' N, 0° 37' E 222
Tét, *Hung.* 47° 30' N, 17° 31' E 168
Tetas, Punta, *Chile* 23° 28' S, 71° 8' W 132
Tétat ed Douaïr, *Alg.* 35° 59' N, 2° 53' E 150
Tete, *Mozambique* 16° 13' S, 33° 34' E 224
Tete, adm. division, *Mozambique* 15° 27' S, 31° 58' E 224
Tête Jaune Cache, *Can.* 52° 57' N, 119° 26' W 108
Tetepare, island, *Solomon Islands* 8° 45' S, 157° 30' E 242
Tetford, *U.K.* 53° 15' N, 2° 119' E 162
Tethul, river, *Can.* 60° 30' N, 112° 25' W 108
Tetlin, *Alas., U.S.* 63° 9' N, 142° 29' W 98
Tetney, *U.K.* 53° 29' N, 0° 1' E 162
Teton Pass, *Wyo., U.S.* 43° 30' N, 110° 58' W 90
Teton Range, *Wyo., U.S.* 43° 29' N, 110° 59' W 90
Teton, river, *Mont., U.S.* 47° 56' N, 111° 43' W 90
Tétouan (Tetuán), *Mor.* 35° 35' N, 5° 23' W 150
Tetovo, *Maced.* 42° 1' N, 20° 58' E 168
Tetrino, *Russ.* 66° 5' N, 38° 6' E 154
Tetuán see Tétouan, *Mor.* 35° 35' N, 5° 23' W 150
Tetyushi, *Russ.* 54° 56' N, 48° 44' E 154
Teuco, river, *Arg.* 24° 41' S, 61° 45' W 132
Teul, *Mex.* 21° 27' N, 103° 29' W 114
Teulada, Capo, *It.* 38° 48' N, 7° 59' E 156
Teulon, *Can.* 50° 23' N, 97° 18' W 90
Teutopolis, *Ill., U.S.* 39° 7' N, 88° 29' W 102
Teutschenthal, *Ger.* 51° 27' N, 11° 48' E 152
Teuva, *Fin.* 62° 28' N, 21° 41' E 152
Teverya (Tiberias), *Israel* 32° 47' N, 35° 31' E 194
Tewantin, *Austral.* 26° 26' S, 153° 2' E 231
Tewkesbury, *U.K.* 51° 59' N, 2° 9' W 162
Texada Island, *Can.* 49° 38' N, 124° 16' W 100
Texarkana, *Ark., U.S.* 33° 24' N, 94° 3' W 103
Texas, adm. division, *Tex., U.S.* 31° 8' N, 101° 3' W 82
Texas City, *Tex., U.S.* 29° 21' N, 94° 54' W 103
Texas Point, *Tex., U.S.* 29° 34' N, 93° 54' W 103
Texcoco, *Mex.* 19° 27' N, 99° 15' W 112
Texel, island, *Neth.* 53° 5' N, 4° 33' E 163
Texhoma, *Okla., U.S.* 36° 30' N, 101° 47' W 92
Texico, *Tex., U.S.* 34° 23' N, 103° 4' W 92
Texline, *Tex., U.S.* 36° 22' N, 103° 2' W 92
Texon, *Tex., U.S.* 31° 11' N, 101° 41' W 92
Teya, *Russ.* 60° 20' N, 92° 46' E 169
Teykovo, *Russ.* 56° 52' N, 40° 27' E 154
Teylan, *Afghan.* 35° 34' N, 64° 49' E 186
Teziutlán, *Mex.* 19° 48' N, 97° 23' W 114
Tezontepec, *Mex.* 19° 50' N, 98° 48' W 114
Tezpur, *India* 26° 43' N, 92° 45' E 188
Tezzeron Lake, *Can.* 54° 38' N, 125° 6' W 108
Tfaritiy, *Africa* 26° 11' N, 10° 34' W 214
Tha Li, *Thai.* 17° 39' N, 101° 23' E 202
Tha, river, *Laos* 21° 6' N, 101° 15' E 202
Tha Sala, *Thai.* 8° 40' N, 99° 56' E 202
Thaba Nchu, *S. Af.* 29° 14' S, 26° 48' E 227
Thabaung, *Myanmar* 17° 4' N, 94° 46' E 202
Thabazimbi, *S. Af.* 24° 38' S, 27° 23' E 227
Thādiq, *Saudi Arabia* 25° 16' N, 45° 53' E 182
Thaga Pass, *India* 31° 26' N, 79° 8' E 188
Thagyettaw, *Myanmar* 13° 46' N, 98° 8' E 202
Thai Binh, *Vietnam* 20° 27' N, 106° 20' E 198
Thai Hoa, *Vietnam* 19° 20' N, 105° 26' E 202
Thai Nguyen, *Vietnam* 21° 35' N, 105° 50' E 198
Thailand 15° 33' N, 101° 6' E 202
Thailand, Gulf of 9° 44' N, 101° 14' E 202
Thal, *Pak.* 33° 22' N, 70° 38' E 186
Thalabarivat, *Cambodia* 13° 35' N, 105° 56' E 202
Thalassery (Tellicherry), *India* 11° 45' N, 75° 29' E 188
Thamad Bū Ḩashīshah, spring, *Lib.* 26° 23' N, 18° 44' E 216
Thamarīt, *Oman* 17° 38' N, 54° 1' E 182
Thames, *N.Z.* 37° 10' S, 175° 34' E 240
Thames, river, *Can.* 42° 16' N, 82° 26' W 102
Thamesville, *Can.* 42° 32' N, 81° 57' W 102
Thamūd, *Yemen* 17° 18' N, 49° 55' E 182
Thane, *India* 19° 12' N, 72° 56' E 188
Thanggu, *India* 27° 53' N, 88° 36' E 197
Thanh Hoa, *Vietnam* 19° 48' N, 105° 44' E 202
Thanh Tri, *Vietnam* 9° 26' N, 105° 43' E 202
Thanlwin (Salween), river, *Asia* 21° 45' N, 98° 44' E 202
Thann, *Fr.* 47° 48' N, 7° 5' E 150
Thaon-les-Vosges, *Fr.* 48° 14' N, 6° 25' E 163
Thap Lan National Park, *Thai.* 14° 1' N, 102° 29' E 202
Thar Desert (Great Indian Desert), *India-Pak.* 27° 30' N, 69° 30' E 187
Tharabwin, *Myanmar* 12° 19' N, 99° 3' E 202
Tharad, *India* 24° 24' N, 71° 41' E 186
Tharrawaddy, *Myanmar* 17° 40' N, 95° 47' E 202
Tharros, ruin(s), *It.* 39° 52' N, 8° 21' E 156
Tharthār Lake, *Iraq* 33° 57' N, 42° 50' E 180
Thássos, island, *Gr.* 40° 26' N, 24° 36' E 180
That Khe, *Vietnam* 22° 18' N, 106° 30' E 198
That Phanom, *Thai.* 16° 58' N, 104° 42' E 202
Thatcher, *Ariz., U.S.* 32° 50' N, 109° 45' W 92
Thaton, *Myanmar* 16° 56' N, 97° 21' E 202
Thatta, *Pak.* 24° 45' N, 67° 55' E 186
Thaungdut, *Myanmar* 24° 25' N, 94° 37' E 188
Thawatti, *Myanmar* 19° 31' N, 96° 12' E 202
Thaxted, *U.K.* 51° 56' N, 0° 21' E 162
Thayawthadangyi Kyun, island, *Myanmar* 12° 20' N, 96° 28' E 202
Thayer, *Ill., U.S.* 39° 32' N, 89° 45' W 102
Thayer, *Mo., U.S.* 36° 31' N, 91° 33' W 96
Thayetchaung, *Myanmar* 13° 52' N, 98° 16' E 202
The Alley, *Jam.* 17° 47' N, 77° 16' W 115
The Brothers see Al Ikhwān, islands, *Yemen* 11° 24' N, 52° 52' E 182
The Caterthuns, ruin(s), *U.K.* 56° 46' N, 2° 53' W 150
The Curragh, site, *Ire.* 53° 8' N, 6° 56' W 150
The Dalles, *Oreg., U.S.* 45° 34' N, 121° 11' W 90
The English Company's Islands, *Arafura Sea* 11° 39' S, 136° 42' E 230
The Four Archers, site, *Austral.* 15° 30' S, 135° 13' E 230
The Hague see Den Haag, *Neth.* 52° 5' N, 4° 18' E 167
The Mumbles, *U.K.* 51° 34' N, 4° 0' W 162
The Ovens, site, *Can.* 44° 18' N, 64° 23' W 111
The Pas, *Can.* 53° 47' N, 101° 17' W 108
The Plains, *Ohio, U.S.* 39° 21' N, 82° 8' W 102
The Rivals see Yr Eifl, peak, *U.K.* 52° 57' N, 4° 32' W 150
The Slot see New Georgia Sound 8° 11' S, 158° 30' E 242
The Two Rivers, *Can.* 55° 45' N, 103° 15' W 108
The Valley, *Anguilla* 18° 13' N, 63° 4' W 116
The Woodlands, *Tex., U.S.* 30° 10' N, 95° 28' W 103
Theano Point, *Can.* 47° 10' N, 84° 40' W 110
Thebes, ruin(s), *Egypt* 25° 40' N, 32° 2' E 206
Thedford, *Can.* 43° 9' N, 81° 51' W 102
Thedford, *Nebr., U.S.* 41° 58' N, 100° 35' W 90
Thekulthili Lake, *Can.* 61° 2' N, 110° 46' W 108
Thelon, river, *Can.* 63° 20' N, 104° 51' W 106
Thenon, *Fr.* 45° 8' N, 1° 4' E 150
Theo, Mount, peak, *Austral.* 21° 23' S, 131° 9' E 230
Théodat, Lac, lake, *Can.* 50° 53' N, 76° 41' W 110
Theodore Roosevelt National Park, Elkhorn Ranch Site, *N. Dak., U.S.* 47° 12' N, 103° 45' W 90
Theodore Roosevelt National Park, North Unit, *N. Dak., U.S.* 47° 17' N, 105° 57' W 80
Theodore Roosevelt, river, *Braz.* 11° 28' S, 60° 30' W 130
Thepha, *Thai.* 6° 51' N, 100° 56' E 196
Thera, ruin(s), *Gr.* 36° 20' N, 25° 23' E 156
Therien, *Can.* 54° 13' N, 111° 17' W 108
Thermal, *Calif., U.S.* 33° 38' N, 116° 9' W 101
Thermiá, ruin(s), *Gr.* 41° 27' N, 24° 20' E 156
Thermopolis, *Wyo., U.S.* 43° 38' N, 108° 13' W 90
Thermopylae 480 B.C., battle, *Gr.* 38° 47' N, 22° 27' E 156
Thermum, ruin(s), *Gr.* 38° 33' N, 21° 36' E 156
Thessalía, adm. division, *Gr.* 39° 19' N, 21° 28' E 156
Thessalon, *Can.* 46° 16' N, 83° 34' W 94
Thessaloníki (Salonica), *Gr.* 40° 38' N, 22° 57' E 156
Thetford, *U.K.* 52° 25' N, 0° 45' E 162
Thetford Mines, *Can.* 46° 4' N, 71° 18' W 111
Theux, *Belg.* 50° 31' N, 5° 48' E 167
Thiaucourt, *Fr.* 48° 57' N, 5° 50' E 163
Thibodaux, *La., U.S.* 29° 46' N, 90° 50' W 103
Thicket Portage, *Can.* 55° 18' N, 97° 42' W 108
Thief River Falls, *Minn., U.S.* 48° 6' N, 96° 13' W 90
Thielsen, Mount, peak, *Oreg., U.S.* 43° 8' N, 122° 9' W 90
Thiene, *It.* 45° 42' N, 11° 28' E 167
Thiès, *Senegal* 14° 48' N, 16° 41' W 222
Thignica, ruin(s), *Tun.* 36° 31' N, 9° 15' E 156
Thika, *Kenya* 1° 3' S, 37° 4' E 224
Thilogne, *Senegal* 15° 57' N, 13° 40' W 222
Thimphu, *Bhutan* 27° 32' N, 89° 31' E 197
Thinahtea Lake, *Can.* 59° 40' N, 121° 4' W 108
Thio, *Eritrea* 14° 36' N, 40° 54' E 182
Thionville, *Fr.* 49° 22' N, 6° 9' E 163
Thiou, *Burkina Faso* 13° 47' N, 2° 42' W 222
Thíra, island, *Gr.* 36° 11' N, 25° 9' E 180
Thirsk, *U.K.* 54° 14' N, 1° 21' W 162
Thiruvananthapuram see Trivandrum, *India* 8° 28' N, 76° 56' E 188
Thisted, *Den.* 56° 57' N, 8° 40' E 150
Thistle Island, island, *Austral.* 35° 8' S, 134° 33' E 230
Thíva, *Gr.* 38° 20' N, 23° 20' E 180
Thiviers, *Fr.* 45° 24' N, 0° 55' E 150
Thlewiaza, river, *Can.* 60° 54' N, 99° 1' W 108
Tho Chu, Dao, island, *Vietnam* 9° 2' N, 103° 21' E 202
Thoa, river, *Can.* 60° 39' N, 108° 55' W 108
Thoen, *Thai.* 17° 37' N, 99° 10' E 202
Thohoyandou, *S. Af.* 22° 58' S, 30° 25' E 227
Tholey, *Ger.* 49° 29' N, 7° 5' E 163
Thomas, *Okla., U.S.* 35° 43' N, 98° 44' W 92
Thomas Mountains, *Antarctica* 76° 11' S, 75° 43' W 248
Thomaston, *Ala., U.S.* 32° 15' N, 87° 37' W 103
Thomaston, *Ga., U.S.* 32° 53' N, 84° 19' W 96
Thomaston, *Me., U.S.* 44° 4' N, 69° 12' W 94
Thomasville, *Ala., U.S.* 31° 55' N, 87° 44' W 103
Thomasville, *Ga., U.S.* 30° 49' N, 83° 59' W 96
Thomasville, *N.C., U.S.* 35° 52' N, 80° 6' W 96
Thompson, *Can.* 55° 44' N, 97° 51' W 108
Thompson, *Utah, U.S.* 38° 58' N, 109° 43' W 90
Thompson Lake, *Me., U.S.* 44° 1' N, 70° 41' W 104
Thompson Peak, *Calif., U.S.* 40° 59' N, 123° 9' W 90
Thompson Peak, *Mont., U.S.* 47° 43' N, 114° 56' W 90
Thompson Point, *Can.* 58° 14' N, 93° 0' W 108
Thompson, river, *Can.* 49° 56' N, 121° 12' W 80
Thomson, *Ill., U.S.* 41° 57' N, 90° 6' W 102
Thomson, Mount, peak, *Austral.* 24° 1' S, 115° 37' E 230
Thon Buri, *Thai.* 13° 39' N, 100° 25' E 202
Thongwa, *Myanmar* 16° 46' N, 96° 35' E 202
Thonotosassa, *Fla., U.S.* 28° 4' N, 82° 18' W 105
Thorenc, *Fr.* 43° 47' N, 6° 49' E 167
Thorhild, *Can.* 54° 9' N, 113° 8' W 108
Thornaby on Tees, *U.K.* 54° 33' N, 1° 19' W 162
Thornapple, river, *Mich., U.S.* 42° 40' N, 85° 22' W 102
Thornbury, *Can.* 44° 33' N, 80° 27' W 94
Thornbury, *N.Z.* 46° 18' S, 168° 6' E 240
Thornbury, *U.K.* 51° 37' N, 2° 31' W 162
Thorndale, *Tex., U.S.* 30° 35' N, 97° 12' W 96
Thorne, *U.K.* 53° 36' N, 0° 59' E 162
Thorne Bay, *Alas., U.S.* 55° 42' N, 132° 35' W 98
Thornton, *Calif., U.S.* 38° 13' N, 121° 26' W 100
Thornton, *W. Va., U.S.* 39° 20' N, 79° 57' W 94
Thorp, *Wash., U.S.* 47° 2' N, 120° 42' W 90
Thorp, *Wis., U.S.* 44° 57' N, 90° 49' W 94
Thouars, *Fr.* 46° 59' N, 0° 14' E 150
Thousand Oaks, *Calif., U.S.* 34° 11' N, 118° 53' W 101
Thrapston, *U.K.* 52° 23' N, 0° 31' E 162
Three Brothers, islands, *Indian Ocean* 5° 55' S, 69° 39' E 188
Three Brothers Mountain, peak, *Can.* 49° 8' N, 120° 51' W 90
Three Cocks, *U.K.* 52° 1' N, 3° 12' W 162
Three Fingered Jack, peak, *Oreg., U.S.* 44° 27' N, 121° 56' W 90
Three Forks, *Mont., U.S.* 45° 52' N, 111° 34' W 90
Three Hills, *Can.* 51° 43' N, 113° 17' W 90
Three Lakes, *Wis., U.S.* 45° 48' N, 89° 10' W 94
Three Oaks, *Mich., U.S.* 41° 47' N, 86° 36' W 102
Three Pagodas Pass, *Thai.* 15° 19' N, 98° 24' E 202
Three Points, *Calif., U.S.* 34° 44' N, 118° 37' W 101
Three Points, Cape 4° 29' N, 3° 5' W 222
Three Rivers, *Calif., U.S.* 36° 26' N, 118° 55' W 101
Three Rivers, *Mass., U.S.* 42° 10' N, 72° 23' W 104
Three Rivers, *Mich., U.S.* 41° 56' N, 85° 38' W 102
Three Rivers, *Tex., U.S.* 28° 27' N, 98° 11' W 92
Three Sisters, *S. Af.* 31° 53' S, 23° 5' E 227
Three Sisters Islands, *Solomon Sea* 10° 11' S, 161° 55' E 242
Three Sisters, peak, *Oreg., U.S.* 44° 4' N, 121° 51' W 90
Thrissur see Trichur, *India* 10° 31' N, 76° 11' E 188
Throckmorton, *Tex., U.S.* 33° 10' N, 99° 11' W 92
Throssell Range, *Austral.* 21° 43' S, 120° 55' E 230
Thu, Cu Lao, island, *Vietnam* 10° 16' N, 108° 52' E 202
Thugga, ruin(s), *Tun.* 36° 24' N, 9° 7' E 156
Thuin, *Belg.* 50° 20' N, 4° 17' E 163
Thulaythiwāt, Tilāl ath, peak, *Jordan* 30° 58' N, 36° 38' E 194
Thule Air Base 76° 28' N, 69° 3' W 106
Thule see Qaanaaq 77° 32' N, 69° 13' W 106
Thuli, river, *Zimb.* 21° 21' S, 28° 59' E 227
Thun, *Switz.* 46° 44' N, 7° 36' E 167
Thunder Bay, *Can.* 48° 24' N, 89° 14' W 94
Thunder Hills, *Can.* 54° 19' N, 106° 33' W 108
Thuner See, lake, *Switz.* 46° 42' N, 7° 28' E 165
Thung Song, *Thai.* 8° 10' N, 99° 41' E 202
Thüringer Wald, *Ger.* 50° 54' N, 10° 1' E 167
Thuringia, adm. division, *Ger.* 50° 46' N, 9° 58' E 167
Thurston Island, *Antarctica* 72° 13' S, 98° 45' W 255
Thusis, *Switz.* 46° 42' N, 9° 25' E 167
Thutade Lake, *Can.* 56° 46' N, 127° 52' W 108
Thyborøn, *Den.* 56° 41' N, 8° 10' E 150
Thynne, Mount, peak, *Can.* 49° 41' N, 120° 57' W 100
Thyou, *Burkina Faso* 11° 55' N, 2° 14' W 222
Tiago, *Braz.* 0° 59' N, 57° 1' W 130
Tian Head, *Can.* 53° 38' N, 133° 34' W 108
Tian Shan 40° 8' N, 71° 21' E 197
Tianbaoshan, *China* 42° 57' N, 128° 56' E 200
Tiandeng, *China* 23° 3' N, 107° 6' E 198
Tiandong, *China* 23° 33' N, 107° 6' E 198
Tian'e, *China* 25° 0' N, 107° 9' E 198
Tianguá, *Braz.* 3° 43' S, 41° 0' W 132
Tianjin, *China* 38° 52' N, 117° 15' E 190
Tianjin, adm. division, *China* 39° 47' N, 117° 15' E 190
Tianjin (Tientsin), *China* 39° 3' N, 117° 9' E 198
Tianjun, *China* 37° 18' N, 99° 0' E 188
Tianlin, *China* 24° 16' N, 106° 14' E 198
Tianmen, *China* 30° 40' N, 113° 10' E 198
Tianshan see Ar Horqin Qi, *China* 43° 55' N, 120° 7' E 198
Tianshifu, *China* 41° 14' N, 124° 19' E 200
Tianshui, *China* 34° 36' N, 105° 42' E 198
Tianyang, *China* 23° 45' N, 106° 51' E 198
Tianzhu, *China* 26° 56' N, 109° 11' E 198
Tiaret, *Alg.* 35° 21' N, 1° 19' E 150
Tiaret, spring, *Tun.* 30° 56' N, 10° 6' E 214
Tiaski, *Senegal* 15° 40' N, 14° 18' W 222
Tiassalé, *Côte d'Ivoire* 5° 49' N, 4° 53' W 222
Tib, Ras el, *Tun.* 36° 57' N, 10° 31' E 156
Tibagi, *Braz.* 24° 31' S, 50° 27' W 138
Tibagi, river, *Braz.* 23° 51' S, 50° 44' W 138
Tibasti, Sarīr, *Lib.* 22° 48' N, 15° 52' E 216
Tibati, *Cameroon* 6° 23' N, 12° 36' E 218
Tibbie, *Ala., U.S.* 31° 21' N, 88° 15' W 103
Tibé, Pic de, peak, *Guinea* 8° 49' N, 8° 58' W 222
Tiber Dam, *Mont., U.S.* 48° 8' N, 111° 8' W 90
Tiberias see Teverya, *Israel* 32° 47' N, 35° 31' E 194
Tibesti, *Chad* 19° 48' N, 17° 13' E 216
Tibet see Xizang, adm. division, *China* 29° 28' N, 87° 1' E 197
Tibet, Plateau of, *China* 33° 55' N, 81° 5' E 172
Tibeysale, *Russ.* 67° 3' N, 79° 31' E 169
Tibidabo, peak, *Sp.* 41° 24' N, 2° 6' E 164
Tibiri, *Niger* 13° 5' N, 3° 55' E 222
Tibiri, *Niger* 13° 34' N, 7° 3' E 222
Ţibleş, Munţii, *Rom.* 47° 31' N, 23° 48' E 156
Ţibleş, peak, *Rom.* 47° 30' N, 24° 11' E 156
Tibnine, *Leb.* 33° 11' N, 35° 24' E 194
Tibrikot, *Nepal* 29° 0' N, 82° 50' E 197
Tibú, *Col.* 8° 37' N, 72° 42' W 136
Tiburon, *Calif., U.S.* 37° 52' N, 122° 29' W 100
Tiburón, Cabo, *Col.* 8° 41' N, 77° 31' W 136
Tiburón, Isla, island, *Mex.* 28° 30' N, 112° 28' W 80
Tichégami, river, *Can.* 51° 50' N, 73° 58' W 110
Tîchît, *Mauritania* 18° 28' N, 9° 30' W 222
Tîchît, Dahr, *Mauritania* 18° 36' N, 10° 27' W 214
Ticonderoga, *N.Y., U.S.* 43° 50' N, 73° 26' W 104
Ticouapé, *Can.* 48° 42' N, 72° 30' W 94
Ticul, *Mex.* 20° 23' N, 89° 33' W 115
Tide Lake, *Can.* 50° 33' N, 111° 32' W 108
Tidikelt, region, *Alg.* 26° 28' N, 1° 9' E 214
Tidjidit, Erg, *Alg.* 23° 32' N, 0° 8' E 214
Tidjikdja, *Mauritania* 18° 30' N, 11° 27' W 207
Tidra, Île, island, *Mauritania* 19° 47' N, 16° 46' W 222
Tiébissou, *Côte d'Ivoire* 7° 5' N, 5° 14' W 222
Tiechang, *China* 41° 40' N, 126° 13' E 200
Tiehnpo, *Liberia* 5° 13' N, 8° 6' W 222
Tiel, *Neth.* 51° 53' N, 5° 25' E 167
Tiel, *Senegal* 14° 55' N, 15° 2' W 222
Tieli, *China* 47° 3' N, 128° 3' E 198
Tieling, *China* 42° 17' N, 123° 51' E 200
Tielt, *Belg.* 51° 0' N, 3° 19' E 163
Tien Yen, *Vietnam* 21° 20' N, 107° 21' E 198
Tienen, *Belg.* 50° 48' N, 4° 55' E 167
Tiensuu, *Fin.* 65° 35' N, 25° 59' E 152
Tientsin see Tianjin, *China* 39° 3' N, 117° 9' E 198
Tiéré, *Mali* 11° 54' N, 5° 26' W 222
Tiermas, *Sp.* 42° 37' N, 1° 7' W 164
Tieroko, peak, *Chad* 20° 46' N, 17° 43' E 216
Tierp, *Sw.* 60° 20' N, 17° 29' E 166
Tierra Blanca, *Mex.* 18° 26' N, 96° 20' W 114
Tierra Colorada, *Mex.* 17° 9' N, 99° 32' W 114
Tierra del Fuego, Isla Grande de, island, *Arg.-Chile* 53° 3' S, 68° 33' W 248
Tierra del Fuego-Antártida e Islas Atlántico Sur, adm. division, *Arg.* 53° 44' S, 70° 49' W 134
Tietê, river, *Braz.* 23° 28' S, 46° 16' W 138
Tiffany Mountain, peak, *Wash., U.S.* 48° 38' N, 120° 1' W 90
Tiffin, *Ohio, U.S.* 41° 6' N, 83° 11' W 102
Tífristós, peak, *Gr.* 38° 56' N, 21° 44' E 156
Tifton, *Ga., U.S.* 31° 27' N, 83° 31' W 96
Tigharry 57° 37' N, 7° 29' W 150
Tighennif, *Alg.* 35° 24' N, 0° 20' E 150
Tigil', *Russ.* 57° 51' N, 158° 45' E 160
Tignère, *Cameroon* 7° 20' N, 12° 39' E 218
Tigray, region, *Eth.* 13° 57' N, 36° 41' E 182
Tigre, river, *Peru* 3° 28' S, 74° 47' W 136
Tigre, river, *Venez.* 8° 56' N, 63° 10' W 116
Tigris (Dicle, Dijlah), river, *Iraq* 32° 8' N, 46° 36' E 180
Tiguent, *Mauritania* 17° 17' N, 16° 7' W 222
Tiguentourine, oil field, *Alg.* 27° 44' N, 9° 4' E 214
Tiguidit, Falaise de, region, *Niger* 16° 40' N, 6° 58' E 222
Tigyaing, *Myanmar* 23° 45' N, 96° 3' E 202
Tīh, Gebel el, *Egypt* 29° 35' N, 33° 0' E 180
Tihany, *Hung.* 46° 54' N, 17° 53' E 168
Tihosuco, *Mex.* 20° 12' N, 88° 26' W 115
Tihuatlán, *Mex.* 20° 41' N, 97° 33' W 114
Tijamré, spring, *Mauritania* 20° 18' N, 11° 16' W 222
Tijesno, *Croatia* 43° 47' N, 15° 38' E 156
Tijola, *Sp.* 37° 19' N, 2° 26' W 164
Tijti, spring, *Mauritania* 17° 52' N, 7° 15' W 222
Tijuana, *Mex.* 32° 31' N, 117° 4' W 101
Tijucas, *Braz.* 27° 16' S, 48° 39' W 138
Tijucas do Sul, *Braz.* 25° 57' S, 49° 12' W 138
Tikal National Park, *Guatemala* 17° 13' N, 90° 10' W 115
Tikamgarh, *India* 24° 44' N, 78° 50' E 197
Tikanlik, *China* 40° 40' N, 87° 40' E 188
Tikaré, *Burkina Faso* 13° 16' N, 1° 44' W 222
Tikattane, *Mauritania* 19° 2' N, 16° 15' W 222
Tikhmanga, *Russ.* 61° 14' N, 38° 31' E 154
Tikhoretsk, *Russ.* 45° 52' N, 40° 5' E 158
Tikhtozero, *Russ.* 65° 33' N, 30° 31' E 154

Tikhvin, *Russ.* 59°38′ N, 33°32′ E 154
Tikitiki, *N.Z.* 37°48′ S, 178°23′ E 240
Tikkurila, *Fin.* 60°16′ N, 24°58′ E 166
Tiko, *Cameroon* 4°5′ N, 9°21′ E 222
Tikshozero, *Russ.* 64°6′ N, 31°47′ E 152
Tikshozero, *Russ.* 66°0′ N, 32°23′ E 152
Tiksi, *Russ.* 71°22′ N, 128°46′ E 160
Tilaiya Dam, *India* 24°20′ N, 85°35′ E 197
Tilamuta, *Indonesia* 0°34′ N, 122°17′ E 192
Tilatou, *Alg.* 35°19′ N, 5°47′ E 150
Tilburg, *Neth.* 51°33′ N, 5°4′ E 163
Tilbury, *Can.* 42°15′ N, 82°27′ W 102
Tilbury, *U.K.* 51°27′ N, 0°21′ E 162
Til-Châtel, *Fr.* 47°30′ N, 5°9′ E 150
Tilden, *Nebr., U.S.* 42°1′ N, 97°50′ W 90
Tileagd, *Rom.* 47°3′ N, 22°14′ E 168
Tilemsoun, *Mor.* 28°13′ N, 10°57′ W 214
Tilichiki, *Russ.* 60°28′ N, 165°53′ E 160
Tillabéri, *Niger* 14°12′ N, 1°26′ E 222
Tillamook, *Oreg., U.S.* 45°27′ N, 123°51′ W 90
Tillamook Head, *Oreg., U.S.* 45°56′ N, 124°9′ W 100
Tillanchang Dwip, island, *India* 8°34′ N, 93°43′ E 188
Tillia, *Niger* 15°53′ N, 4°35′ E 222
Tilloo Cay, island, *Bahamas* 26°33′ N, 76°56′ W 116
Tillson, *N.Y., U.S.* 41°49′ N, 74°5′ W 104
Tillsonburg, *Can.* 42°51′ N, 80°43′ W 102
Tilos, island, *Gr.* 36°24′ N, 27°25′ E 180
Tilpa, *Austral.* 30°56′ S, 144°26′ E 231
Tilrhemt, *Alg.* 33°11′ N, 3°21′ E 214
Tiltagals, *Latv.* 56°33′ N, 26°39′ E 166
Tilton, *Ill., U.S.* 40°5′ N, 87°40′ W 102
Tilton, *N.H., U.S.* 43°26′ N, 71°36′ W 104
Tilža, *Latv.* 56°53′ N, 27°21′ E 166
Tim, *Russ.* 51°34′ N, 37°9′ E 158
Ţima, *Egypt* 26°55′ N, 31°21′ E 180
Timanskiy Kryazh, *Russ.* 65°21′ N, 50°38′ E 154
Timaru, *N.Z.* 44°24′ S, 171°13′ E 240
Timashevo, *Russ.* 53°22′ N, 51°5′ E 154
Timashevsk, *Russ.* 45°40′ N, 38°58′ E 156
Timbáki, *Gr.* 35°2′ N, 24°44′ E 180
Timbalier Bay 29°8′ N, 90°33′ W 103
Timbalier Island, *La., U.S.* 28°57′ N, 90°34′ W 103
Timbedgha, *Mauritania* 16°16′ N, 8°12′ W 222
Timber, *Oreg., U.S.* 45°42′ N, 123°19′ W 100
Timber Bay, *Can.* 54°9′ N, 105°40′ W 108
Timber Lake, *S. Dak., U.S.* 45°25′ N, 101°6′ W 90
Timber Mountain, peak, *Calif., U.S.* 41°37′ N, 121°23′ W 90
Timber Mountain, peak, *Nev., U.S.* 37°2′ N, 116°30′ W 101
Timbío, *Col.* 2°17′ N, 76°43′ W 136
Timbiquí, *Col.* 2°41′ N, 77°45′ W 136
Timbo, *Guinea* 10°37′ N, 11°52′ W 222
Timbo, *Liberia* 5°31′ N, 9°42′ W 222
Timbuktu see Tombouctou, *Mali* 16°44′ N, 3°2′ W 222
Timeïaouine, spring, *Alg.* 20°28′ N, 1°48′ E 222
Timellouline, spring, *Alg.* 29°15′ N, 8°55′ E 214
Timerein, *Sudan* 16°58′ N, 36°29′ E 182
Timétrine, region, *Mali* 19°15′ N, 1°20′ W 222
Tímfi, Óros, peak, *Gr.* 39°58′ N, 20°43′ E 156
Timgad, ruin(s), *Alg.* 35°25′ N, 6°21′ E 150
Timia, *Niger* 18°3′ N, 8°39′ E 222
Timiş, adm. division, *Rom.* 45°49′ N, 20°44′ E 156
Timimoun, *Alg.* 29°6′ N, 0°13′ E 207
Timiris, Cap (Mirik), *Mauritania* 19°28′ N, 16°53′ W 222
Timiryazevskiy, *Russ.* 56°28′ N, 84°44′ E 169
Timiskaming, Lake, *Can.* 47°15′ N, 80°13′ W 94
Timişoara, *Rom.* 45°46′ N, 21°14′ E 168
Timkapaul′, *Russ.* 61°29′ N, 62°16′ E 169
Timmiarmiut 62°33′ N, 42°19′ W 106
Timmins, *Can.* 48°29′ N, 81°16′ W 82
Timms Hill, peak, *Wis., U.S.* 45°25′ N, 90°16′ W 94
Timon, *Braz.* 5°6′ S, 42°53′ W 132
Timor, island, *Indonesia* 9°36′ S, 122°49′ E 192
Timor Sea 11°14′ S, 126°40′ E 192
Timor-Leste (East Timor) 9°0′ S, 125°0′ E 192
Timote, *Arg.* 35°20′ S, 62°15′ W 139
Timpanogos Cave National Monument, *Utah, U.S.* 40°25′ N, 111°46′ W 90
Timpson, *Tex., U.S.* 31°53′ N, 94°23′ W 103
Timrå, *Nor.* 62°28′ N, 17°17′ E 152
Tin Féraré, spring, *Mali* 15°6′ N, 0°53′ E 222
Tin Fouye, oil field, *Alg.* 28°31′ N, 7°20′ E 214
Tin Mountain, peak, *Calif., U.S.* 36°52′ N, 117°33′ W 92
Tîna, Khalîg el 31°3′ N, 32°35′ E 194
Tina, Mont, peak, *Dem. Rep. of the Congo* 2°56′ N, 28°32′ E 224
Tinaca Point, *Philippines* 5°25′ N, 125°1′ E 203
Tinaco, *Venez.* 9°41′ N, 68°28′ W 136
Ti-n-Assamert, spring, *Mali* 16°12′ N, 0°30′ E 222
Ti-n-Brahim, spring, *Mauritania* 19°31′ N, 15°58′ W 222
Tinca, *Rom.* 46°46′ N, 21°58′ E 168
Tinde see Jomu, *Tanzania* 3°53′ S, 33°11′ E 224
Ti-n-Deïla, spring, *Mauritania* 17°59′ N, 15°32′ W 222
Tindel, spring, *Mauritania* 17°0′ N, 12°57′ W 222
Tindouf, *Alg.* 27°43′ N, 8°9′ W 143
Tiné, *Chad* 14°59′ N, 22°47′ E 216
Ti-n-Essako, spring, *Mali* 18°25′ N, 2°29′ E 222
Ti-n-Ethisane, spring, *Mali* 19°2′ N, 0°50′ E 222
Tinfouchy, spring, *Alg.* 28°53′ N, 5°49′ W 214
Tinfunque National Park, *Parag.* 24°3′ S, 60°28′ W 122
Tinggi, island, *Malaysia* 2°21′ N, 103°58′ E 196
Tingo María National Park, *Peru* 9°13′ S, 76°11′ W 130
Tingréla, *Côte d'Ivoire* 10°30′ N, 6°25′ W 222
Tingri (Xêgar), *China* 28°40′ N, 87°3′ E 197
Tingsryd, *Nor.* 56°31′ N, 14°59′ E 152
Tingstäde, *Sw.* 57°44′ N, 18°36′ E 166
Tinkisso, river, *Guinea* 11°27′ N, 10°6′ W 222
Tinn, *Nor.* 59°58′ N, 8°44′ E 152
Tinniswood, Mount, peak, *Can.* 50°18′ N, 123°52′ W 100
Tinogasta, *Arg.* 28°5′ S, 67°34′ W 132
Tinombo, *Indonesia* 0°24′ N, 120°13′ E 192
Ti-n-Orfane, *Mali* 16°30′ N, 2°15′ W 222
Tiñoso, Cabo, *Sp.* 37°25′ N, 1°15′ W 164
Ti-n-Rerhoh, spring, *Alg.* 20°45′ N, 4°1′ E 222
Tinrhert, Hamada de, *Lib.* 28°3′ N, 6°55′ E 206
Tinsley, *Miss., U.S.* 32°42′ N, 90°28′ W 103
Tinsukia, *India* 27°29′ N, 95°22′ E 188
Tintagel (King Arthur's Castle), site, *U.K.* 50°39′ N, 4°49′ W 150
Tintane, spring, *Mauritania* 20°51′ N, 16°32′ W 222
Ti-n-Taourdi, spring, *Alg.* 22°46′ N, 8°0′ E 214
Tintina, *Arg.* 27°1′ S, 62°43′ W 139
Tinto Hills, peak, *U.K.* 55°34′ N, 3°47′ W 150
Ti-n-Toumma, region, *Niger* 16°27′ N, 12°0′ E 222
Tinui, *N.Z.* 40°54′ S, 176°5′ E 240
Ti-n-Zaouâtene (Fort Pierre Bordes), *Alg.* 19°58′ N, 2°57′ E 222
Tioga, *La., U.S.* 31°22′ N, 92°26′ W 103
Tioga, *N. Dak., U.S.* 48°23′ N, 102°57′ W 90
Tioga Pass, *Calif., U.S.* 37°54′ N, 119°16′ W 100
Tioman, peak, *Malaysia* 2°47′ N, 104°4′ E 196
Tionaga, *Can.* 48°5′ N, 82°6′ W 94
Tip Top Mountain, peak, *Can.* 48°16′ N, 86°4′ W 94
Tipitapa, *Nicar.* 12°9′ N, 86°4′ W 115
Tipp City, *Ohio, U.S.* 39°57′ N, 84°10′ W 102
Tippecanoe, *Ind., U.S.* 41°11′ N, 86°7′ W 102
Tipton, *Calif., U.S.* 36°3′ N, 119°20′ W 100
Tipton, *Ind., U.S.* 40°17′ N, 86°2′ W 102
Tipton, *Iowa, U.S.* 41°45′ N, 91°8′ W 110
Tipton, *Mich., U.S.* 42°0′ N, 84°4′ W 102
Tipton, *Okla., U.S.* 34°28′ N, 99°9′ W 92
Tipton, Mount, peak, *Ariz., U.S.* 35°31′ N, 114°13′ W 101
Tipuani, *Bol.* 15°35′ S, 68°0′ W 137
Tiputini, river, *Ecua.* 1°6′ S, 77°6′ W 136
Tiquicheo, *Mex.* 18°52′ N, 100°45′ W 114
Tiquié, river, *Braz.* 0°7′ N, 69°41′ W 136
Tir Pol, *Afghan.* 34°38′ N, 61°20′ E 180
Tiracambu, Serra do, *Braz.* 3°36′ S, 46°54′ W 130
Tīrān, island, *Egypt* 27°57′ N, 34°5′ E 180
Tirana see Tiranë, *Alban.* 41°19′ N, 19°41′ E 156
Tiranë (Tirana), *Alban.* 41°19′ N, 19°41′ E 156
Tirano, *It.* 46°12′ N, 10°9′ E 167
Tiraspol, *Mold.* 46°49′ N, 29°37′ E 156
Tirat Karmel, *Israel* 32°45′ N, 34°58′ E 194
Tire, *Turk.* 38°3′ N, 27°42′ E 156
Tiream, *Rom.* 47°37′ N, 22°29′ E 168
Tirebolu, *Turk.* 41°0′ N, 38°46′ E 195
Tirest, spring, *Mali* 20°21′ N, 1°6′ E 222
Tîrgovişte, *Rom.* 44°57′ N, 25°26′ E 156
Tîrgu Jiu, *Rom.* 45°1′ N, 23°18′ E 168
Tîrguşor, *Rom.* 44°28′ N, 28°24′ E 158
Tirich Mir, peak, *Pak.* 36°16′ N, 71°46′ E 186
Tiririne, spring, *Alg.* 23°34′ N, 8°31′ E 214
Tirlyanskiy, *Russ.* 54°14′ N, 58°28′ E 154
Tîrnova, *Mold.* 48°9′ N, 27°39′ E 152
Tîrnova, *Rom.* 45°19′ N, 21°59′ E 168
Tiroungoulou, *Cen. Af. Rep.* 9°34′ N, 22°8′ E 216
Tirthahalli, *India* 13°42′ N, 75°14′ E 188
Tiruchchirappalli, *India* 10°48′ N, 78°41′ E 188
Tirunelveli, *India* 8°44′ N, 77°40′ E 188
Tiruntán, *Peru* 7°56′ S, 74°56′ W 130
Tiryns, ruin(s), *Gr.* 37°35′ N, 22°42′ E 156
Tisaiyanvilai, *India* 8°20′ N, 77°49′ E 188
Tisdale, *Can.* 52°50′ N, 104°4′ W 108
Tishomingo, *Okla., U.S.* 34°13′ N, 96°40′ W 92
Tiskilwa, *Ill., U.S.* 41°17′ N, 89°31′ W 102
Tissamaharama, *Sri Lanka* 6°17′ N, 81°18′ E 188
Tissemsilt, *Alg.* 35°36′ N, 1°49′ E 150
Tissint, *Mor.* 29°53′ N, 7°20′ W 214
Tista, river, *India* 25°59′ N, 89°9′ E 197
Tisul′, *Russ.* 55°43′ N, 88°25′ E 169
Tisza, river, *Hung.* 46°31′ N, 20°4′ E 156
Tiszacsege, *Hung.* 47°40′ N, 20°58′ E 168
Tiszaföldvár, *Hung.* 46°59′ N, 20°15′ E 168
Tiszafüred, *Hung.* 47°37′ N, 20°45′ E 168
Tiszakürt, *Hung.* 46°53′ N, 20°8′ E 168
Tiszanána, *Hung.* 47°32′ N, 20°32′ E 168
Tiszaug, *Hung.* 46°50′ N, 20°2′ E 168
Tiszaújváros, *Hung.* 47°53′ N, 21°2′ E 168
Tit, *Alg.* 26°56′ N, 1°30′ E 214
Titaf, *Alg.* 27°27′ N, 0°12′ E 214
Titan Dome, *Antarctica* 88°11′ S, 165°43′ W 248
Titel, *Serb.* 45°12′ N, 20°17′ E 168
Titicaca, Lago, lake, *Peru* 15°34′ S, 70°43′ W 122
Titu, *Rom.* 44°40′ N, 25°31′ E 158
Titule, *Dem. Rep. of the Congo* 3°12′ N, 25°32′ E 224
Titusville, *Fla., U.S.* 28°36′ N, 80°50′ W 105
Titusville, *Pa., U.S.* 41°37′ N, 79°41′ W 94
Tivaouane, *Senegal* 14°57′ N, 16°38′ W 222
Tivat, *Mont.* 42°26′ N, 18°41′ E 168
Tiverton, *U.K.* 50°54′ N, 3°28′ W 162
Tivissa, *Sp.* 41°2′ N, 0°44′ E 164
Tivoli, *N.Y., U.S.* 42°3′ N, 73°55′ W 104
Tiwai Point, *N.Z.* 46°35′ S, 168°23′ E 240
Tiwanacu, *Bol.* 16°38′ S, 68°43′ W 137
Tixtla, *Mex.* 17°32′ N, 99°23′ W 114
Tizayuca, *Mex.* 19°49′ N, 98°57′ W 114
Tizi Ouzou, *Alg.* 36°42′ N, 4°3′ E 150
Tizimín, *Mex.* 21°7′ N, 88°11′ W 116
Tiznit, *Mor.* 29°42′ N, 9°45′ W 214
Tjåmotis, *Nor.* 66°54′ N, 18°39′ E 152
Tlacotalpan, *Mex.* 18°37′ N, 95°40′ W 114
Tlahualilo de Zaragoza, *Mex.* 26°6′ N, 103°27′ W 114
Tlajomulco, *Mex.* 20°27′ N, 103°28′ W 114
Tlalnepantla, *Mex.* 19°31′ N, 99°11′ W 114
Tlapa, *Mex.* 17°31′ N, 98°34′ W 114
Tlapacoyan, *Mex.* 19°57′ N, 97°13′ W 114
Tlaquepaque, *Mex.* 20°37′ N, 103°19′ W 112
Tlaxcala, *Mex.* 19°15′ N, 98°19′ W 114
Tlaxcala, adm. division, *Mex.* 19°30′ N, 98°38′ W 114
Tlaxiaco, *Mex.* 17°15′ N, 97°42′ W 114
Tlell, *Can.* 53°36′ N, 131°59′ W 108
Tlemcen, *Alg.* 34°51′ N, 1°18′ W 214
Tleta, *Alg.* 36°47′ N, 5°52′ E 150
Tlīsan, spring, *Lib.* 28°27′ N, 17°28′ E 216
Tlyarata, *Russ.* 42°3′ N, 46°22′ E 195
Tmassah, *Lib.* 26°22′ N, 15°46′ E 216
Tni Haïa, spring, *Alg.* 24°20′ N, 2°45′ W 214
Toad River, *Can.* 58°50′ N, 125°15′ W 108
Toadlena, *N. Mex., U.S.* 36°13′ N, 108°53′ W 92
Toahayana, *Mex.* 26°8′ N, 107°42′ W 112
Toamasina, *Madagascar* 18°8′ S, 49°22′ E 220
Toana Range, *Nev., U.S.* 40°45′ N, 114°29′ W 90
Toano, *It.* 44°22′ N, 10°33′ E 167
Toast, *N.C., U.S.* 36°28′ N, 80°39′ W 96
Toay, *Arg.* 36°41′ S, 64°23′ W 134
Toba, *Japan* 34°27′ N, 136°51′ E 201
Toba, Danau, lake, *Indonesia* 2°47′ N, 98°39′ E 196
Toba Inlet 50°19′ N, 124°52′ W 90
Toba, river, *Can.* 50°35′ N, 124°16′ W 108
Tobacco Root Mountains, *Mont., U.S.* 45°25′ N, 112°19′ W 90
Tobago, island, *Trinidad and Tobago* 11°13′ N, 60°39′ W 118
Tobarra, *Sp.* 38°35′ N, 1°42′ W 164
Tobelo, *Indonesia* 1°41′ N, 127°54′ E 192
Tobermory 56°37′ N, 6°5′ W 150
Tobermory, *Can.* 45°13′ N, 81°40′ W 94
Tobin, Mount, peak, *Nev., U.S.* 40°22′ N, 117°37′ W 90
Tobli, *Liberia* 6°16′ N, 8°33′ W 222
Toboali, *Indonesia* 3°3′ S, 106°26′ E 192
Tobol, river, *Russ.* 56°41′ N, 66°37′ E 169
Tobol′sk, *Russ.* 58°14′ N, 68°22′ E 169
Tobruk see Ţubruq, *Lib.* 32°3′ N, 23°57′ E 216
Tobseda, *Russ.* 68°31′ N, 52°47′ E 160
Toby, Mount, peak, *Mass., U.S.* 42°28′ N, 72°34′ W 104
Tobyl, *Kaz.* 52°41′ N, 62°39′ E 184
Tobyl, river, *Kaz.* 53°48′ N, 63°50′ E 184
Tobysh, river, *Russ.* 66°21′ N, 50°21′ E 154
Tocantínia, *Braz.* 9°36′ S, 48°23′ W 130
Tocantinópolis, *Braz.* 6°19′ S, 47°28′ W 130
Tocantins, adm. division, *Braz.* 12°57′ S, 48°39′ W 138
Tocantins, river, *Braz.* 5°23′ S, 56°13′ W 132
Tocantins, river, *Braz.* 11°43′ S, 48°39′ W 130
Toccoa, *Ga., U.S.* 34°33′ N, 83°20′ W 96
Tochigi, adm. division, *Japan* 36°37′ N, 139°24′ E 201
Tochio, *Japan* 37°28′ N, 138°59′ E 201
Toco, *Chile* 22°5′ S, 69°41′ W 137
Toconao, *Chile* 23°12′ S, 68°2′ W 132
Tocopilla, *Chile* 22°8′ S, 70°13′ W 137
Tocuyo de la Costa, *Venez.* 11°1′ N, 68°25′ W 136
Tocuyo, river, *Venez.* 10°43′ N, 69°31′ W 136
Todal, *Nor.* 62°48′ N, 8°44′ E 152
Todd, *Alas., U.S.* 57°29′ N, 135°5′ W 108
Todenyang, *Kenya* 4°27′ N, 35°53′ E 224
Todireni, *Rom.* 47°36′ N, 27°5′ E 156
Todmorden, *U.K.* 53°43′ N, 2°6′ W 162
Todo Santos, *Peru* 1°16′ S, 73°47′ W 136
Todorovo, *Bulg.* 43°43′ N, 26°55′ E 156
Todos Santos, *Bol.* 16°49′ S, 65°10′ W 137
Todos Santos, *Mex.* 23°26′ N, 110°13′ W 112
Toe Head 57°49′ N, 7°32′ W 150
Tofield, *Can.* 53°21′ N, 112°40′ W 108
Tofino, *Can.* 49°6′ N, 125°52′ W 82
Töfsingdalens National Park, *Nor.* 62°11′ N, 12°23′ E 152
Tōgane, *Japan* 35°30′ N, 140°19′ E 201
Togi, *Japan* 37°7′ N, 136°44′ E 201
Togiak, *Alas., U.S.* 59°3′ N, 160°25′ W 106
Togian, Kepulauan, islands, *Indonesia* 0°10′ N, 122°30′ E 192
Togliatti see Tol′yatti, *Russ.* 53°30′ N, 49°34′ E 154
Togni, *Sudan* 18°2′ N, 35°9′ E 182
Tognuf, *Eritrea* 16°8′ N, 37°23′ E 182
Togo, *Can.* 51°24′ N, 101°37′ W 90
Togo 8°41′ N, 1°2′ E 214
Togobala, *Guinea* 9°16′ N, 7°57′ W 222
Togtoh, *China* 40°17′ N, 111°8′ E 198
Togur, *Russ.* 58°21′ N, 82°43′ E 169
Togüsken, *Kaz.* 43°34′ N, 67°24′ E 184
Togwotee Pass, *Wyo., U.S.* 43°44′ N, 110°3′ W 90
Togyz, *Kaz.* 47°36′ N, 60°30′ E 184
Tohatchi, *N. Mex., U.S.* 35°51′ N, 108°46′ W 92
Tohma, river, *Turk.* 38°58′ N, 37°29′ E 156
Tohogne, *Belg.* 50°22′ N, 5°29′ E 167
Toholampi, *Fin.* 63°45′ N, 24°11′ E 152
Töhöm, *Mongolia* 44°26′ N, 108°17′ E 198
Toibalawe, *India* 10°35′ N, 92°39′ E 188
Toijala, *Fin.* 61°9′ N, 23°52′ E 166
Toinya, *Sudan* 6°16′ N, 29°42′ E 224
Toiyabe Range, *Nev., U.S.* 39°23′ N, 117°19′ W 90
Tok, river, *Russ.* 52°40′ N, 52°27′ E 154
Tōkamachi, *Japan* 37°6′ N, 138°45′ E 201
Tokar, *Sudan* 18°26′ N, 37°41′ E 182
Tokara Rettō, islands, *East China Sea* 29°46′ N, 128°15′ E 190
Tokat, *Turk.* 40°18′ N, 36°34′ E 156
Tŏkch'ŏn, *N. Korea* 39°44′ N, 126°18′ E 200
Tokeland, *Wash., U.S.* 46°41′ N, 123°59′ W 100
Tokelau, islands, *N.Z.* 8°1′ S, 173°11′ W 238
Tokewanna Peak, *Utah, U.S.* 40°47′ N, 110°42′ W 90
Tokhtamysh, *Taj.* 37°49′ N, 74°40′ E 184
Toki, *Japan* 35°21′ N, 137°13′ E 201
Tokmak, *Ukr.* 47°12′ N, 35°45′ E 156
Tokmok, *Kyrg.* 42°48′ N, 75°17′ E 184
Toko, *N.Z.* 39°21′ S, 174°22′ E 240
Tokomaru Bay, *N.Z.* 38°8′ S, 178°17′ E 240
Tokoroa, *N.Z.* 38°15′ S, 175°52′ E 240
Toksova, *Russ.* 60°9′ N, 30°31′ E 166
Toksu see Xinhe, *China* 41°35′ N, 82°38′ E 184
Toktogul Reservoir, lake, *Kyrg.* 41°50′ N, 72°37′ E 197
Tokuno Shima, island, *Japan* 27°22′ N, 129°2′ E 190
Tokushima, *Japan* 34°4′ N, 134°32′ E 201
Tokushima, adm. division, *Japan* 33°53′ N, 133°42′ E 201
Tokuyama, *Japan* 34°4′ N, 131°50′ E 200
Tōkyō, *Japan* 35°39′ N, 139°40′ E 201
Tōkyō, adm. division, *Japan* 35°38′ N, 139°16′ E 201
Tolaga Bay, *N.Z.* 38°21′ S, 178°17′ E 240
Tôlañaro, *Madagascar* 24°56′ S, 46°58′ E 207
Tolbo, *Mongolia* 48°22′ N, 90°16′ E 184
Tolchin, Mount, peak, *Antarctica* 85°6′ S, 67°14′ W 248
Töle Bī, *Kaz.* 43°36′ N, 73°47′ E 184
Toledo, *Braz.* 24°41′ S, 53°46′ W 132
Toledo, *Braz.* 5°56′ S, 73°6′ W 130
Toledo, *Ill., U.S.* 39°16′ N, 88°15′ W 102
Toledo, *Iowa, U.S.* 41°59′ N, 92°35′ W 94
Toledo, *Ohio, U.S.* 41°38′ N, 83°32′ W 102
Toledo, *Sp.* 39°52′ N, 4°2′ W 164
Toledo, *Wash., U.S.* 46°25′ N, 122°52′ W 100
Toledo Bend Reservoir, lake, *La., U.S.* 31°49′ N, 93°56′ W 103
Toledo, Montes de, *Sp.* 39°29′ N, 4°52′ W 164
Tolentino, *It.* 43°12′ N, 13°16′ E 156
Tolentino, *Mex.* 22°14′ N, 100°34′ W 114
Tolhuaca National Park, *Chile* 38°8′ S, 71°55′ W 134
Tol′yatti (Togliatti), *Russia* 53°30′ N, 49°34′ E 154
Toli, *China* 45°47′ N, 83°40′ E 184
Toliara, *Madagascar* 23°18′ S, 43°50′ E 207
Tolima, adm. division, *Col.* 4°1′ N, 75°40′ W 136
Tolitoli, *Indonesia* 1°5′ N, 120°45′ E 192
Tol′ka, *Russ.* 63°57′ N, 82°2′ E 169
Tolkaboua, *Burkina Faso* 10°11′ N, 2°59′ W 222
Tolkmicko, *Pol.* 54°18′ N, 19°32′ E 166
Tollhouse, *Calif., U.S.* 37°1′ N, 119°25′ W 100
Tollimarjon, *Uzb.* 38°17′ N, 65°33′ E 197
Tollya, Zaliv 76°15′ N, 98°2′ E 160
Tolmachevo, *Russ.* 58°51′ N, 29°52′ E 166
Tolmin, *Slov.* 46°11′ N, 13°44′ E 167
Tolna, *Hung.* 46°25′ N, 18°46′ E 168
Tolna, adm. division, *Hung.* 46°26′ N, 18°4′ E 156
Tolo, Teluk 2°28′ S, 121°52′ E 192
Tolono, *Ill., U.S.* 39°58′ N, 88°16′ W 102
Tolosa, *Sp.* 43°8′ N, 2°3′ W 164
Tolstoi, *Can.* 49°5′ N, 96°49′ W 90
Toltén, *Chile* 39°12′ S, 73°13′ W 134
Tolti, *Pak.* 35°0′ N, 76°6′ E 186
Tolú, *Col.* 9°31′ N, 75°34′ W 136
Toluca, *Ill., U.S.* 41°0′ N, 89°8′ W 102
Toluca, *Mex.* 19°14′ N, 99°43′ W 114
Toluca, *Mo., U.S.* 41°0′ N, 89°8′ W 94
Tom Burke, *S. Af.* 23°5′ S, 27°59′ E 227
Tom, Mount, peak, *Mass., U.S.* 42°14′ N, 72°41′ W 104
Tom Price, *Austral.* 22°41′ S, 117°49′ E 238
Tom′, river, *Russ.* 55°15′ N, 85°0′ E 160
Tom White, Mount, peak, *Alas., U.S.* 60°38′ N, 143°50′ W 98
Tomah, *Wis., U.S.* 43°58′ N, 90°30′ W 94
Tomahawk, *Wis., U.S.* 45°27′ N, 89°43′ W 94
Tomales Point, *Calif., U.S.* 38°13′ N, 122°57′ W 90
Tomar, *Braz.* 0°25′ N, 63°54′ W 130
Tómaros, peak, *Gr.* 39°28′ N, 20°43′ E 156
Tomás Barrón, *Bol.* 17°41′ S, 67°29′ W 137
Tomás Gomensoro, *Uru.* 30°24′ S, 57°27′ W 139
Tomaševo, *Mont.* 43°4′ N, 19°39′ E 168
Tomashevka, *Belarus* 51°32′ N, 23°35′ E 152
Tomatin, *U.K.* 57°20′ N, 4°0′ W 150
Tomatlán, *Mex.* 19°56′ N, 105°17′ W 114
Tomatlán, river, *Mex.* 19°46′ N, 105°21′ W 114
Tombador, Serra do, *Braz.* 10°46′ S, 58°16′ W 130
Tombe, *Sudan* 5°47′ N, 31°39′ E 224
Tombigbee, river, *Ala., U.S.* 31°46′ N, 88°8′ W 103
Tomboco, *Angola* 6°51′ S, 13°17′ E 218
Tombos, *Braz.* 20°54′ S, 42°3′ W 138
Tombouctou (Timbuktu), *Mali* 16°44′ N, 3°2′ W 222
Tombstone, *Ariz., U.S.* 31°41′ N, 110°4′ W 112
Tombstone Mountain, peak, *Can.* 64°19′ N, 138°47′ W 98
Tombua, *Angola* 15°52′ S, 11°50′ E 220
Tomdibuloq, *Uzb.* 41°45′ N, 64°39′ E 197
Tomé, *Chile* 36°35′ S, 72°57′ W 134
Tomelloso, *Sp.* 39°9′ N, 3°2′ W 164
Tomini, Teluk 0°22′ N, 120°27′ E 192
Tomislavgrad, *Bosn. and Herzg.* 43°40′ N, 17°12′ E 168
Tommot, *Russ.* 58°59′ N, 126°27′ E 160
Tomo, river, *Col.* 5°29′ N, 68°18′ W 136
Tomorit, Maja e, peak, *Alban.* 40°41′ N, 20°4′ E 156
Tompa, *Hung.* 46°11′ N, 19°32′ E 168
Tompkinsville, *Ky., U.S.* 36°41′ N, 85°42′ W 96
Tomsino, *Russ.* 56°26′ N, 28°32′ E 166
Tomsk, *Russ.* 56°30′ N, 85°3′ E 169
Tomsk, adm. division, *Russ.* 58°34′ N, 80°3′ E 169
Tonalá, *Mex.* 16°4′ N, 93°46′ W 115
Tonale, Passo del, *It.* 46°16′ N, 10°34′ E 167
Tonami, *Japan* 36°37′ N, 136°56′ E 201
Tonantins, *Braz.* 2°45′ S, 67°46′ W 136
Tonantins, river, *Braz.* 2°26′ S, 68°35′ W 136
Tonasket, *Wash., U.S.* 48°41′ N, 119°27′ W 90
Tonbridge, *U.K.* 51°11′ N, 0°16′ E 162
Tondi Kiwindi, *Niger* 14°40′ N, 1°51′ E 222
Tondou, Massif du, *Cen. Af. Rep.* 7°50′ N, 23°43′ E 224
Tonekābon, *Iran* 36°47′ N, 50°54′ E 180
Toney Mount, peak, *Antarctica* 75°44′ S, 115°16′ W 248
Tonga 22°46′ S, 174°39′ W 238
Tonga, *Sudan* 9°30′ N, 31°3′ E 224
Tonga, islands, *South Pacific Ocean* 20°25′ S, 173°49′ W 238
Tonga Trench, *South Pacific Ocean* 21°53′ S, 172°51′ W 252
Tong'an, *China* 24°43′ N, 118°9′ E 198
Tongatapu Group, islands, *Tonga* 22°46′ S, 174°39′ W 238
Tongatapu, island, *Tonga* 21°11′ S, 175°11′ W 241

Tongcheng, *China* 31°3′ N, 116°56′ E 198
Tongchuan, *China* 35°7′ N, 109°9′ E 198
Tongdao, *China* 26°9′ N, 109°45′ E 198
Tongeren, *Belg.* 50°46′ N, 5°27′ E 167
Tonghe, *China* 46°0′ N, 128°45′ E 198
Tonghua, *China* 41°42′ N, 125°54′ E 200
Tonghua (Kuaidamao), *China* 41°41′ N, 125°45′ E 200
Tongjiang, *China* 31°59′ N, 107°14′ E 198
Tongjosŏn-man 39°23′ N, 128°10′ E 200
Tongliang, *China* 29°50′ N, 106°4′ E 198
Tongliao, *China* 43°35′ N, 122°17′ E 198
Tongling, *China* 30°53′ N, 117°48′ E 198
Tonglu, *China* 29°47′ N, 119°37′ E 198
Tongnae, *S. Korea* 35°11′ N, 129°6′ E 200
Tongobory, *Madagascar* 23°28′ S, 44°18′ E 220
Tongren, *China* 27°45′ N, 109°13′ E 198
Tongshi, *China* 18°43′ N, 109°29′ E 198
Tongtian, river, *China* 33°51′ N, 93°30′ E 190
Tongue of the Ocean 23°55′ N, 77°32′ W 96
Tongue, river, *Mont., U.S.* 45°47′ N, 106°6′ W 90
Tongwei, *China* 35°14′ N, 105°12′ E 198
Tongxian, *China* 39°52′ N, 116°38′ E 198
Tongxin, *China* 37°1′ N, 105°53′ E 198
Tongyeong, *S. Korea* 34°50′ N, 128°26′ E 200
Tongyu, *China* 44°47′ N, 123°4′ E 198
Tongyuanpu, *China* 40°47′ N, 123°57′ E 200
Tongzi, *China* 28°8′ N, 106°48′ E 198
Tonica, *Ill., U.S.* 41°12′ N, 89°4′ W 102
Tonichí, *Mex.* 28°35′ N, 109°33′ W 92
Tönisvorst, *Ger.* 51°18′ N, 6°30′ E 167
Tonj, *Sudan* 7°16′ N, 28°45′ E 224
Tonj see Ibba, river, *Sudan* 6°16′ N, 28°21′ E 224
Tonk, *India* 26°9′ N, 75°48′ E 197
Tonkawa, *Okla., U.S.* 36°39′ N, 97°18′ W 92
Tonkin, Gulf of 19°38′ N, 107°25′ E 190
Tonneins, *Fr.* 44°23′ N, 0°17′ E 150
Tonopah, *Nev., U.S.* 38°4′ N, 117°15′ W 92
Tonota, *Botswana* 21°30′ S, 27°26′ E 227
Tønsberg, *Nor.* 59°16′ N, 10°26′ E 152
Tonsina, *Alas., U.S.* 61°38′ N, 145°11′ W 98
Tonto National Monument, *Ariz., U.S.* 33°37′ N, 111°10′ W 92
Tonya, *Turk.* 40°52′ N, 39°15′ E 195
Tooele, *Utah, U.S.* 40°32′ N, 112°14′ W 106
Toora Khem, *Russ.* 52°29′ N, 96°34′ E 190
Toore, *Somalia* 1°21′ N, 44°22′ E 218
Tootsi, *Est.* 58°34′ N, 24°47′ E 166
Topaz Mountain, peak, *Utah, U.S.* 39°41′ N, 113°11′ W 90
Topeka, *Kans., U.S.* 38°59′ N, 95°48′ W 90
Topia, *Mex.* 25°9′ N, 106°33′ W 114
Topki, *Russ.* 55°15′ N, 85°43′ E 169
Topley, *Can.* 54°31′ N, 126°20′ W 108
Topley Landing, *Can.* 54°47′ N, 126°11′ W 108
Topli Do, *Serb.* 43°20′ N, 22°40′ E 168
Topocalma, Punta, *Chile* 34°15′ S, 73°58′ W 134
Topock, *Ariz., U.S.* 34°42′ N, 114°28′ W 101
Topolobampo, Bahía de 25°32′ N, 110°21′ W 80
Topolovăţu Mare, *Rom.* 45°47′ N, 21°38′ E 168
Toppenish, *Wash., U.S.* 46°21′ N, 120°20′ W 90
Topsfield, *Mass., U.S.* 42°38′ N, 70°58′ W 104
Topsham, *Me., U.S.* 43°55′ N, 69°58′ W 104
Toquepala, *Peru* 17°18′ S, 70°35′ W 137
Toquima Range, *Nev., U.S.* 39°28′ N, 116°59′ W 90
Tor, *Eth.* 7°48′ N, 33°32′ E 224
Tor Bay 45°10′ N, 61°39′ W 111
Torà, *Sp.* 41°48′ N, 1°23′ E 164
Toragay, oil field, *Azerb.* 40°9′ N, 49°21′ E 195
Toranou, *Côte d'Ivoire* 8°48′ N, 7°47′ W 222
Torata, *Peru* 17°7′ S, 70°51′ W 137
Torbalı, *Turk.* 38°10′ N, 27°20′ E 156
Torbat-e Ḩeydarīyeh, *Iran* 35°17′ N, 59°13′ E 180
Torbat-e Jām, *Iran* 35°16′ N, 60°34′ E 180
Torbay, *U.K.* 50°27′ N, 3°34′ W 150
Torbert, Mount, peak, *Antarctica* 83°32′ S, 55°58′ W 248
Torch, river, *Can.* 53°33′ N, 104°9′ W 108
Torchiara, *It.* 40°19′ N, 15°2′ E 156
Torda, *Serb.* 45°35′ N, 20°26′ E 168
Tordesilos, *Sp.* 40°39′ N, 1°35′ W 164
Töre, *Nor.* 65°54′ N, 22°39′ E 152
Töreboda, *Nor.* 58°41′ N, 14°7′ E 152
Torelló, *Sp.* 42°2′ N, 2°15′ E 164
Torere, *N.Z.* 37°59′ S, 177°30′ E 240
Torez, *Ukr.* 47°59′ N, 38°37′ E 158
Torgau, *Ger.* 51°34′ N, 12°59′ E 152
Torghay, *Kaz.* 49°46′ N, 63°35′ E 184
Torghay, river, *Kaz.* 48°34′ N, 62°27′ E 184
Torhout, *Belg.* 51°3′ N, 3°6′ E 163
Torija, *Sp.* 40°44′ N, 3°2′ W 164
Torino (Turin), *It.* 45°4′ N, 7°40′ E 167
Torit, *Sudan* 4°24′ N, 32°33′ E 224
Torixoréu, *Braz.* 16°13′ S, 52°31′ W 138
Torkovichi, *Russ.* 58°53′ N, 30°26′ E 166
Torma, *Est.* 58°47′ N, 26°43′ E 166
Tormac, *Rom.* 45°31′ N, 21°30′ E 168
Tornado Mountain, peak, *Can.* 49°56′ N, 114°45′ W 90
Torneå see Tornio, *Fin.* 65°51′ N, 24°7′ E 154
Torneträsk, lake, *Nor.* 67°53′ N, 19°22′ E 152
Torngat Mountains, *Can.* 59°30′ N, 64°3′ W 106
Tornillo, *Tex., U.S.* 31°26′ N, 106°5′ W 92
Tornio (Torneå), *Fin.* 65°51′ N, 24°7′ E 154
Tornquist, *Arg.* 38°6′ S, 62°15′ W 139
Toro, *Nig.* 10°2′ N, 9°3′ E 222
Toro, *Sp.* 41°31′ N, 5°25′ W 150
Toro Doum, spring, *Chad* 16°31′ N, 16°37′ E 216
Toro Peak, *Calif., U.S.* 33°31′ N, 116°28′ W 101
Torodi, *Niger* 13°18′ N, 1°42′ E 222
Torodo, *Mali* 14°33′ N, 8°52′ W 222
Törökszentmiklos, *Hung.* 47°10′ N, 20°26′ E 168
Torom, *Russ.* 54°20′ N, 135°47′ E 190
Torone, ruin(s), *Gr.* 40°0′ N, 23°43′ E 156
Toronto, *Can.* 43°39′ N, 79°29′ W 94
Toronto, *Kans., U.S.* 37°46′ N, 95°57′ W 94
Toropalca, *Bol.* 20°25′ S, 65°49′ W 137
Toropets, *Russ.* 56°29′ N, 31°39′ E 154
Tororo, *Uganda* 0°39′ N, 34°12′ E 224
Toros Dağlar (Taurus), *Turk.* 36°29′ N, 32°7′ E 156
Toros Dağları, *Turk.* 36°26′ N, 32°15′ E 180
Torotoro, *Bol.* 18°7′ S, 65°50′ W 137
Torquato Severo, *Braz.* 31°4′ S, 54°14′ W 139
Torra Bay, *Namibia* 20°17′ S, 13°15′ E 220
Torrance, *Calif., U.S.* 33°50′ N, 118°21′ W 101
Torre Astura, *It.* 41°25′ N, 12°44′ E 156
Torre de Moncorvo, *Port.* 41°9′ N, 7°4′ W 150
Torre Pacheco, *Sp.* 37°43′ N, 0°58′ E 164
Torreblanca, *Sp.* 40°12′ N, 0°10′ E 164
Torre-Cardela, *Sp.* 37°31′ N, 3°21′ W 164
Torrecilla en Cameros, *Sp.* 42°15′ N, 2°38′ W 164
Torredelcampo, *Sp.* 37°46′ N, 3°54′ W 164
Torredonjimeno, *Sp.* 37°46′ N, 3°58′ W 164
Torrelaguna, *Sp.* 40°49′ N, 3°32′ W 164
Torremolinos, *Sp.* 36°37′ N, 4°31′ W 164
Torrent, *Arg.* 28°49′ S, 56°28′ W 139
Torrent, *Sp.* 39°26′ N, 0°28′ E 164
Torrenueva, *Sp.* 38°39′ N, 3°22′ W 164
Torreón, *Mex.* 25°31′ N, 103°26′ W 114
Torreón de Cañas, *Mex.* 26°22′ N, 105°16′ W 114
Torres, *Mex.* 28°45′ N, 110°46′ W 92
Torres del Paine National Park, *Chile* 51°6′ S, 73°25′ W 122
Torres Islands, *South Pacific Ocean* 14°42′ S, 164°17′ E 238
Torres Strait 9°40′ S, 141°19′ E 231
Torrevieja, *Sp.* 37°58′ N, 0°41′ E 164
Torrijo, *Sp.* 41°29′ N, 1°53′ W 164
Torrijos, *Sp.* 39°59′ N, 4°17′ W 150
Torrington, *Conn., U.S.* 41°47′ N, 73°8′ W 104
Torrington, *Wyo., U.S.* 42°4′ N, 104°11′ W 90
Torroella de Montgrí, *Sp.* 42°2′ N, 3°7′ E 164
Torrox, *Sp.* 36°45′ N, 3°58′ W 164
Torsås, *Nor.* 56°25′ N, 15°58′ E 152
Tórshavn 62°10′ N, 6°53′ W 143
Torsken, *Nor.* 69°21′ N, 17°8′ E 152
Tortola, island, *British Virgin Is., U.K.* 18°26′ N, 64°38′ W 118
Tortolì, *It.* 39°55′ N, 9°36′ E 214
Tortona, *It.* 44°53′ N, 8°52′ E 167
Tortosa, *Sp.* 40°50′ N, 0°34′ E 214
Tortosa, Cap de, *Sp.* 40°29′ N, 0°59′ E 143
Tortosa see Ţarţūs, *Syr.* 34°53′ N, 35°53′ E 194
Tortue, Île de la, island, *Haiti* 20°9′ N, 73°9′ W 116
Tortuguero, *C.R.* 10°33′ N, 83°32′ W 115
Tortum, *Turk.* 40°19′ N, 41°34′ E 195
Ţorūd, *Iran* 35°26′ N, 55°6′ E 180
Torul, *Turk.* 40°35′ N, 39°18′ E 195
Tõrva, *Est.* 57°59′ N, 25°54′ E 166
Torzhok, *Russ.* 57°0′ N, 34°57′ E 154
Tosa, *Japan* 33°30′ N, 133°25′ E 201
Tosa Wan 33°16′ N, 133°37′ E 201
Tosamaganga, *Tanzania* 7°50′ S, 35°35′ E 224
T'osan, *N. Korea* 38°17′ N, 126°43′ E 200
Tosanachi, *Mex.* 28°32′ N, 108°3′ W 92
Tosashimizu, *Japan* 32°46′ N, 132°55′ E 201
Tosayamada, *Japan* 33°37′ N, 133°40′ E 201
Tosca, *S. Af.* 26°9′ S, 23°51′ E 227
Tosca, Punta, *Mex.* 24°19′ N, 112°36′ W 112
Toshkent (Tashkent), *Uzb.* 41°18′ N, 69°10′ E 197
Toson Hu, lake, *China* 37°3′ N, 96°15′ E 188
Tossa de Mar, *Sp.* 41°43′ N, 2°55′ E 164
Tostado, *Arg.* 29°13′ S, 61°48′ W 139
Tõstamaa, *Est.* 58°19′ N, 23°56′ E 166
Tostuya, *Russ.* 73°10′ N, 113°42′ E 173
Tosu, *Japan* 33°22′ N, 130°31′ E 201
Tosya, *Turk.* 41°1′ N, 34°1′ E 156
Toszek, *Pol.* 50°26′ N, 18°31′ E 152
Totana, *Sp.* 37°46′ N, 1°31′ W 164
Totara, *N.Z.* 45°9′ S, 170°52′ E 240
Totatiche, *Mex.* 21°55′ N, 103°27′ W 114
Toten, region, *Nor.* 60°41′ N, 10°37′ E 152
Toteng, *Botswana* 20°23′ S, 22°57′ E 227
Tôtes, *Fr.* 49°40′ N, 1°2′ E 163
Tótkomlós, *Hung.* 46°24′ N, 20°45′ E 168
Tot'ma, *Russ.* 59°58′ N, 42°48′ E 154
Totness (Coronie), *Suriname* 5°49′ N, 56°18′ W 130
Tôto, *Angola* 7°11′ S, 14°18′ E 218
Totogan Lake, lake, *Can.* 52°3′ N, 89°35′ W 110
Totokro, *Côte d'Ivoire* 7°10′ N, 5°8′ W 222
Totolapan, *Mex.* 18°7′ N, 100°23′ W 114
Totora, *Bol.* 17°47′ S, 65°9′ W 137
Totoras, *Arg.* 32°37′ S, 61°9′ W 139
Totskoye, *Russ.* 52°31′ N, 52°43′ E 154
Tottori, *Japan* 35°27′ N, 134°14′ E 201
Tottori, adm. division, *Japan* 35°19′ N, 133°25′ E 201
Touba, *Côte d'Ivoire* 8°12′ N, 7°41′ W 222
Touba, *Senegal* 14°52′ N, 15°49′ W 222
Toubakouta, *Senegal* 13°48′ N, 16°22′ W 222
Toubkal, Jebel, peak, *Mor.* 31°3′ N, 8°6′ W 214
Toueïla, spring, *Mauritania* 18°24′ N, 15°46′ W 222
Toueyyirât, spring, *Mali* 17°57′ N, 3°16′ W 222
Toufourine, spring, *Mali* 24°38′ N, 4°43′ W 214
Tougan, *Burkina Faso* 13°4′ N, 3°6′ W 222
Touggourt, *Alg.* 32°58′ N, 5°58′ E 207
Tougouri, *Burkina Faso* 13°18′ N, 0°34′ E 222
Tougouya, *Burkina Faso* 13°27′ N, 2°5′ W 222
Tougué, *Guinea* 11°26′ N, 11°42′ W 222
Touila, spring, *Mauritania* 25°56′ N, 6°22′ W 214
Toukoto, *Mali* 13°29′ N, 9°52′ W 222
Toul, *Fr.* 48°39′ N, 5°52′ E 163
Toulépleu, *Côte d'Ivoire* 6°27′ N, 8°24′ W 222
Touliu, *Taiwan, China* 23°40′ N, 120°31′ E 198
Toulon, *Fr.* 43°7′ N, 5°55′ E 150
Toulon, *Ill., U.S.* 41°5′ N, 89°52′ W 102
Toulouse, *Fr.* 43°35′ N, 1°27′ E 164
Toumania, *Guinea* 10°24′ N, 10°50′ W 222
Toumbélaga, spring, *Niger* 15°52′ N, 7°48′ E 222
Toummo, *Lib.* 22°39′ N, 14°11′ E 216
Toumodi, *Côte d'Ivoire* 6°28′ N, 5°2′ W 222
Toungad, *Mauritania* 20°4′ N, 13°9′ W 222
Toungo, *Nig.* 8°3′ N, 12°2′ E 218
Touraine, region, *Fr.* 47°35′ N, 0°56′ E 165
Tourassine, ruin(s), *Mauritania* 24°40′ N, 11°36′ W 214
Tourba, *Chad* 12°53′ N, 15°17′ E 216
Tourbe, Pointe de la, *Can.* 49°14′ N, 64°15′ W 111
Tourcoing, *Fr.* 50°43′ N, 3°9′ E 163
Tourine, spring, *Mauritania* 22°31′ N, 11°53′ W 214
Tournai, *Belg.* 50°35′ N, 3°23′ E 163
Tournan, *Fr.* 48°44′ N, 2°46′ E 163
Tournus, *Fr.* 46°34′ N, 4°53′ E 150
Touros, *Braz.* 5°14′ S, 35°29′ W 132
Touroua, *Cameroon* 9°0′ N, 12°58′ E 216
Tours, *Fr.* 47°23′ N, 0°41′ E 150
Toury, *Fr.* 48°11′ N, 1°55′ E 163
Touside, Pic, peak, *Chad* 21°1′ N, 16°19′ E 216
Tovar, *Venez.* 8°20′ N, 71°48′ W 136
Tovarkovskiy, *Russ.* 53°39′ N, 38°13′ E 154
Tovik, *Nor.* 68°40′ N, 16°54′ E 152
Tovste, *Ukr.* 48°50′ N, 25°43′ E 156
Tovuz, *Azerb.* 40°58′ N, 45°35′ E 195
Towanda, *Pa., U.S.* 41°45′ N, 76°28′ W 94
Towcester, *U.K.* 52°7′ N, 1°0′ E 162
Tower, *Minn., U.S.* 47°47′ N, 92°17′ W 110
Tower Hill, *Ill., U.S.* 39°22′ N, 88°58′ W 102
Tower Island, *Antarctica* 63°32′ S, 61°29′ W 134
Tower Mountain, peak, *Oreg., U.S.* 45°2′ N, 118°40′ W 90
Towne Pass, *Calif., U.S.* 36°23′ N, 117°18′ W 101
Towner, *N. Dak., U.S.* 48°19′ N, 100°25′ W 90
Townsend, *Mass., U.S.* 42°39′ N, 71°43′ W 104
Townsend, *Mont., U.S.* 46°17′ N, 111°30′ W 90
Townsend, *Va., U.S.* 37°10′ N, 75°58′ W 96
Townshend, *Vt., U.S.* 43°2′ N, 72°41′ W 104
Townshend Island, island, *Austral.* 22°30′ S, 150°37′ E 230
Towot, *Sudan* 6°12′ N, 34°22′ E 224
Towraghondi, *Afghan.* 35°13′ N, 62°15′ E 186
Towrzi, *Afghan.* 30°10′ N, 66°2′ E 186
Towuti, Danau, lake, *Indonesia* 2°51′ S, 120°29′ E 192
Toxkan, river, *China* 40°55′ N, 76°50′ E 184
Toyah, *Tex., U.S.* 31°17′ N, 103°48′ W 92
Toyahvale, *Tex., U.S.* 30°55′ N, 103°47′ W 92
Toyama, *Japan* 36°41′ N, 137°14′ E 201
Toyama, adm. division, *Japan* 36°32′ N, 136°50′ E 201
Toyama Wan 36°50′ N, 137°8′ E 201
Toyohashi, *Japan* 34°44′ N, 137°23′ E 201
Toyooka, *Japan* 35°31′ N, 134°47′ E 201
Toyoura, *Japan* 34°9′ N, 130°56′ E 200
To'ytepa, *Uzb.* 41°2′ N, 69°21′ E 197
Tozeur, *Tun.* 33°54′ N, 8°1′ E 143
Tozeur, spring, *Chad* 18°9′ N, 18°22′ E 216
Tpig, *Russ.* 41°45′ N, 47°36′ E 195
Tqvarch'eli, *Asia* 42°49′ N, 41°41′ E 195
Traben-Trarbach, *Ger.* 49°57′ N, 7°7′ E 167
Trablous (Tripoli), *Leb.* 34°26′ N, 35°50′ E 194
Trabzon, *Turk.* 40°58′ N, 39°41′ E 195
Trachonas 35°12′ N, 33°20′ E 194
Tracy, *Calif., U.S.* 37°44′ N, 121°27′ W 100
Tracy, *Can.* 46°0′ N, 73°10′ W 111
Tracy, *Minn., U.S.* 44°12′ N, 95°38′ W 90
Tracy Arm 57°52′ N, 134°8′ W 108
Tradate, *It.* 45°43′ N, 8°54′ E 167
Trade Lake, lake, *Can.* 55°19′ N, 104°14′ W 108
Trade Town, *Liberia* 5°41′ N, 9°51′ W 222
Trädet, *Nor.* 57°58′ N, 13°32′ E 152
Trading, river, *Can.* 51°33′ N, 89°29′ W 110
Traeger Hills, peak, *Austral.* 23°53′ S, 124°26′ E 230
Traer, *Iowa, U.S.* 42°10′ N, 92°28′ W 94
Trafalgar, *Ind., U.S.* 39°24′ N, 86°9′ W 102
Trafalgar, Cabo, *Sp.* 36°5′ N, 6°14′ W 164
Trafford, Lake, *Fla., U.S.* 26°25′ N, 81°37′ W 105
Tragacete, *Sp.* 40°19′ N, 1°52′ W 164
Traian, *Rom.* 45°10′ N, 27°44′ E 156
Tráighlí see Tralee, *Ire.* 52°16′ N, 9°42′ W 150
Trail, *Can.* 49°6′ N, 117°44′ W 90
Traill Ø, island, *Traill Ø* 72°17′ N, 28°9′ W 246
Trainor Lake, *Can.* 60°26′ N, 120°43′ W 108
Traíra Taraira, river, *South America* 5°296′ S, 69°56′ W 136
Trakai National Park, *Lith.* 54°37′ N, 24°35′ E 166
Tralake, *Miss., U.S.* 33°14′ N, 90°48′ W 103
Tralee (Tráighlí), *Ire.* 52°16′ N, 9°42′ W 150
Tramonti di Sopra, *It.* 46°18′ N, 12°47′ E 167
Træna, islands, *Norwegian Sea* 66°33′ N, 11°1′ E 152
Tranås, *Nor.* 58°2′ N, 14°58′ E 152
Tranebjerg, *Den.* 55°49′ N, 10°34′ E 150
Trang, *Thai.* 7°35′ N, 99°38′ E 196
Trangan, island, *Indonesia* 7°9′ S, 133°3′ E 192
Tranqueras, *Uru.* 31°13′ S, 55°43′ W 139
Tranquillity, *Calif., U.S.* 36°38′ N, 120°16′ W 100
Tranquitas, oil field, *Arg.* 22°41′ S, 64°0′ W 137
Trans-Baikal, adm. division, *Russ.* 52°8′ N, 113°31′ E 161
Transantarctic Mountains, *Antarctica* 81°39′ S, 40°42′ W 248
Transcona, *Can.* 49°52′ N, 96°58′ W 90
Transdniestria, special sovereignty, *Mold.* 48°6′ N, 27°46′ E 152
Transit Hill, peak, *Austral.* 15°21′ S, 129°21′ E 230
Transylvania, region, *Rom.* 46°2′ N, 22°9′ E 168
Transylvanian Alps, *Rom.* 44°55′ N, 22°35′ E 168
Trapper Peak, *Mont., U.S.* 45°51′ N, 114°26′ W 80
Trarza, region, *Mauritania* 17°53′ N, 15°24′ W 222
Trascău, Munţii, *Rom.* 46°14′ N, 23°13′ E 168
Trashigang, *Bhutan* 27°16′ N, 91°33′ E 188
Trasury Islands, *Solomon Sea* 7°20′ S, 155°30′ E 242
Trat, *Thai.* 12°15′ N, 102°31′ E 202
Trauira, Ilha da, island, *Braz.* 1°34′ S, 46°34′ W 130
Travemünde, *Ger.* 53°58′ N, 10°52′ E 150
Traver, *Calif., U.S.* 36°27′ N, 119°30′ W 100
Travers Reservoir, lake, *Can.* 50°9′ N, 113°19′ W 90
Travis Air Force Base, *Calif., U.S.* 38°14′ N, 121°59′ W 100
Travnik, *Bosn. and Herzg.* 44°14′ N, 17°41′ E 168
Trawsfynydd, *U.K.* 52°54′ N, 3°54′ W 162
Trbunje, *Serb.* 43°15′ N, 21°16′ E 168
Trebinje, *Bosn. and Herzg.* 42°43′ N, 18°19′ E 168
Trebujena, *Sp.* 36°51′ N, 6°11′ W 164
Trecate, *It.* 45°25′ N, 8°43′ E 167
Trecenta, *It.* 45°1′ N, 11°28′ E 167
Treetops, site, *Kenya* 0°24′ N, 36°41′ E 224
Treffurt, *Ger.* 51°8′ N, 10°14′ E 167
Tregaron, *U.K.* 52°12′ N, 3°55′ W 162
Tregrosse Islets, islands, *Coral Sea* 18°3′ S, 149°35′ E 230
Treinta y Tres, *Uru.* 33°13′ S, 54°22′ W 139
Treis-Karden, *Ger.* 50°10′ N, 7°18′ E 167
Treklyano, *Bulg.* 42°32′ N, 22°36′ E 168
Trelawney, *Zimb.* 17°31′ S, 30°28′ E 224
Trelleborg, *Nor.* 55°22′ N, 13°8′ E 152
Tremblant, Mount, peak, *Can.* 46°13′ N, 74°40′ W 94
Tremiti, Isole, islands, *Adriatic Sea* 42°11′ N, 15°36′ E 156
Tremont, *Ill., U.S.* 40°30′ N, 89°30′ W 102
Tremp, *Sp.* 42°9′ N, 0°52′ E 164
Trenary, *Mich., U.S.* 46°11′ N, 86°58′ W 94
Trenche, river, *Can.* 48°43′ N, 73°43′ W 94
Trenčianský, adm. division, *Slovakia* 48°52′ N, 18°3′ E 156
Trenčín, *Slovakia* 48°52′ N, 18°3′ E 152
Trenque Lauquen, *Arg.* 35°57′ S, 62°42′ W 139
Trent, river, *U.K.* 53°33′ N, 0°46′ E 162
Trent, river, *U.K.* 53°1′ N, 2°10′ W 162
Trentino-Alto Adige, adm. division, *It.* 46°32′ N, 10°41′ E 167
Trento, *It.* 46°4′ N, 11°8′ E 167
Trenton, *Can.* 44°6′ N, 77°35′ W 110
Trenton, *Fla., U.S.* 29°36′ N, 82°50′ W 105
Trenton, *Mich., U.S.* 42°8′ N, 83°12′ W 102
Trenton, *Nebr., U.S.* 40°10′ N, 101°1′ W 90
Trenton, *N.J., U.S.* 40°11′ N, 74°53′ W 94
Trepassey, *Can.* 46°43′ N, 53°22′ W 111
Tres Arboles, *Uru.* 32°26′ S, 56°43′ W 139
Tres Arroyos, *Arg.* 38°23′ S, 60°14′ W 139
Três Corações, *Braz.* 21°42′ S, 45°14′ W 138
Tres Cruces, Cerro, peak, *Mex.* 15°26′ N, 92°32′ W 115
Tres Esquinas, *Col.* 0°43′ N, 75°14′ W 136
Tres Isletas, *Arg.* 26°20′ S, 60°25′ W 139
Três Lagoas, *Braz.* 20°47′ S, 51°44′ W 138
Tres Lagos, *Arg.* 49°36′ S, 71°30′ W 134
Tres Lomas, *Arg.* 36°28′ S, 62°51′ W 139
Três Marias Dam, *Braz.* 18°6′ S, 45°17′ W 138
Tres Montes, Península, *Chile* 47°7′ S, 77°36′ W 134
Três Passos, *Braz.* 27°28′ S, 53°58′ W 139
Tres Picos, *Arg.* 38°18′ S, 62°14′ W 139
Tres Pinos, *Calif., U.S.* 36°47′ N, 121°20′ W 100
Três Pontas, *Braz.* 21°24′ S, 45°29′ W 138
Tres Pozos, *Arg.* 28°23′ S, 62°15′ W 139
Tres Puntas, Cabo, *Arg.* 47°1′ S, 65°54′ W 134
Tres Puntas, Cabo de, *Guatemala* 15°59′ N, 88°44′ W 115
Três Rios, *Braz.* 22°5′ S, 43°14′ W 138
Tres Valles, *Mex.* 18°14′ N, 96°8′ W 114
Tres Zapotes, ruin(s), *Mex.* 18°26′ N, 95°32′ W 114
Treskavica, *Bosn. and Herzg.* 43°39′ N, 18°12′ E 168
Trespaderne, *Sp.* 42°47′ N, 3°25′ W 164
Tretower, *U.K.* 51°52′ N, 3°11′ W 162
Treungen, *Nor.* 58°59′ N, 8°29′ E 152
Trêve, Lac la, lake, *Can.* 49°55′ N, 76°5′ W 94
Treviglio, *It.* 45°30′ N, 9°35′ E 167
Treviño, *Sp.* 42°43′ N, 2°45′ W 164
Treviso, *It.* 45°39′ N, 12°13′ E 167
Trgovište, *Serb.* 42°22′ N, 22°6′ E 168
Tria, islands, *Aegean Sea* 36°9′ N, 26°46′ E 156
Triánda (Ialysus), *Gr.* 36°24′ N, 28°10′ E 156
Triangle, *Zimb.* 21°3′ S, 31°33′ E 227
Triángulo Oeste, islands, *Gulf of Mexico* 21°5′ N, 93°24′ W 112
Triángulo Sur, islands, *Gulf of Mexico* 20°49′ N, 92°7′ W 112
Triberg, *Ger.* 48°7′ N, 8°14′ E 152
Tribune, *Kans., U.S.* 38°28′ N, 101°46′ W 90
Tricase, *It.* 39°55′ N, 18°21′ E 156
Trichur (Thrissur), *India* 10°31′ N, 76°11′ E 188
Trident Peak (Obrian Peak), *Nev., U.S.* 41°53′ N, 118°30′ W 90
Trie, *Fr.* 43°19′ N, 0°21′ E 164
Trier, *Ger.* 49°45′ N, 6°39′ E 163
Trieste, *It.* 45°38′ N, 13°45′ E 167
Trigal, *Bol.* 18°18′ S, 64°14′ W 137
Triglav, peak, *Slov.* 46°22′ N, 13°46′ E 156
Trigo Mountains, *Ariz., U.S.* 33°7′ N, 114°37′ W 101
Trijebovo, *Bosn. and Herzg.* 44°30′ N, 17°4′ E 168
Tríkala, *Gr.* 39°32′ N, 21°46′ E 180
Trikomo (Iskele), *N. Cyprus, Cyprus.* 35°17′ N, 33°53′ E 194
Trikora, Puncak, peak, *Indonesia* 4°10′ S, 138°25′ E 192
Trilby, *Fla., U.S.* 28°26′ N, 82°14′ W 105
Trilj, *Croatia* 43°37′ N, 16°42′ E 168
Trillo, *Sp.* 40°42′ N, 2°36′ W 164
Trilsbeck Lake, lake, *Can.* 50°46′ N, 84°38′ W 110
Trincomalee, *Sri Lanka* 8°34′ N, 81°14′ E 188
Trindade, *Braz.* 16°41′ S, 49°30′ W 138
Trindade, island, *Braz.* 20°45′ S, 30°23′ W 132
Trinidad, *Bol.* 14°49′ S, 64°48′ W 137
Trinidad, *Colo., U.S.* 37°10′ N, 104°29′ W 92
Trinidad, *Uru.* 33°32′ S, 56°54′ W 139
Trinidad and Tobago 10°41′ N, 61°3′ W 118

Trinidad Head, *Calif., U.S.* 40°52′ N, 124°27′ W 90
Trinidad, Isla, island, *Arg.* 39°21′ S, 61°52′ W 134
Trinidad, island, *Trinidad and Tobago* 10°8′ N, 60°56′ W 116
Trinidad, island, *Trinidad and Tobago* 10°25′ N, 61°14′ W 118
Trinity, *Tex., U.S.* 30°55′ N, 95°23′ W 103
Trinity Bay 47°57′ N, 54°30′ W 106
Trinity Island, island, *Antarctica* 64°12′ S, 61°28′ W 248
Trinity Islands, *Alas., U.S.* 55°55′ N, 155°52′ W 98
Trinity Mountains, *Calif., U.S.* 40°56′ N, 122°47′ W 90
Trinity Range, *Nev., U.S.* 40°23′ N, 118°49′ W 90
Trinity, river, *Calif., U.S.* 40°38′ N, 123°37′ W 80
Trinity, river, *Tex., U.S.* 30°26′ N, 94°56′ W 103
Trinkitat, *Sudan* 18°37′ N, 37°41′ E 182
Trino, *It.* 45°12′ N, 8°17′ E 167
Trinway, *Ohio, U.S.* 40°8′ N, 82°1′ W 102
Trion, *Ga., U.S.* 34°31′ N, 85°19′ W 96
Triora, *It.* 43°59′ N, 7°46′ E 167
Trípoli, *Gr.* 37°31′ N, 22°22′ E 156
Tripoli see Ţarābulus, *Lib.* 32°37′ N, 12°35′ E 216
Tripoli see Trablous, *Leb.* 34°26′ N, 35°50′ E 194
Tripolitania, region, *Lib.* 30°23′ N, 11°4′ E 214
Tripp, *S. Dak., U.S.* 43°11′ N, 97°58′ W 90
Tripura, adm. division, *India* 23°47′ N, 91°18′ E 197
Tristan da Cunha Group, islands, *South Atlantic Ocean* 36°47′ S, 14°34′ W 206
Tristao, Îles, islands, *North Atlantic Ocean* 10°23′ N, 15°45′ W 222
Triunfo, river, *Braz.* 6°38′ S, 53°18′ W 130
Trivandrum (Thiruvananthapuram), *India* 8°28′ N, 76°56′ E 188
Trivento, *It.* 41°46′ N, 14°32′ E 156
Trn, *Bosn. and Herzg.* 44°50′ N, 17°13′ E 168
Trnava, *Slovakia* 48°22′ N, 17°35′ E 152
Trnavský, adm. division, *Slovakia* 48°34′ N, 16°56′ E 152
Trnovo, *Bosn. and Herzg.* 43°39′ N, 18°27′ E 168
Trobriand Islands, *P.N.G.* 8°14′ S, 150°59′ E 238
Trobriand Islands, *Solomon Sea* 7°51′ S, 149°6′ E 192
Trochu, *Can.* 51°51′ N, 113°14′ W 90
Troebratskīy, *Kaz.* 54°19′ N, 66°7′ E 184
Troezen, ruin(s), *Gr.* 37°29′ N, 23°16′ E 156
Trofīmovka, *Kaz.* 53°27′ N, 76°59′ E 184
Trofors, *Nor.* 65°32′ N, 13°19′ E 152
Troilus, Lac, lake, *Can.* 50°53′ N, 75°5′ W 110
Troisdorf, *Ger.* 50°49′ N, 7°8′ E 167
Trois-Pistoles, *Can.* 48°6′ N, 69°9′ W 94
Trois-Ponts, *Belg.* 50°24′ N, 4°42′ E 167
Trois-Rivières, *Can.* 46°20′ N, 72°34′ W 94
Troisvierges, *Lux.* 50°7′ N, 6°0′ E 167
Troitsk, *Russ.* 54°9′ N, 61°32′ E 154
Troitskiy, *Russ.* 57°5′ N, 63°42′ E 154
Troitsko Pechorsk, *Russ.* 62°42′ N, 56°7′ E 154
Troitskoye, *Russ.* 46°22′ N, 44°11′ E 158
Troitskoye, *Russ.* 52°19′ N, 56°16′ E 154
Troitskoye, *Russ.* 53°1′ N, 84°43′ E 184
Troll, Norway, station, *Antarctica* 71°50′ S, 2°56′ E 248
Trolla, spring, *Chad* 15°26′ N, 14°48′ E 216
Troll-heimen, *Nor.* 62°57′ N, 8°39′ E 152
Trombas, *Braz.* 13°29′ S, 48°47′ W 138
Tromelin Island, *Fr.* 15°58′ S, 54°27′ E 254
Tromsø, *Nor.* 69°38′ N, 18°53′ E 152
Tron, peak, *Nor.* 62°9′ N, 10°34′ E 152
Trona, *Calif., U.S.* 35°45′ N, 117°24′ W 101
Troncon, *Mex.* 23°29′ N, 104°20′ W 114
Trondheim, *Nor.* 63°23′ N, 10°27′ E 152
Trondheimsfjorden 63°25′ N, 5°22′ E 142
Trones, *Nor.* 64°45′ N, 12°50′ E 152
Trönninge, *Nor.* 56°38′ N, 12°57′ E 152
Troodos Mountains, *Cyprus* 34°58′ N, 32°24′ E 194
Tropea, *It.* 38°41′ N, 15°53′ E 156
Tropic, *Utah, U.S.* 37°37′ N, 112°4′ W 92
Tropojë, *Alban.* 42°24′ N, 20°9′ E 168
Trosa, *Nor.* 58°54′ N, 17°29′ E 152
Trosh, *Russ.* 66°22′ N, 55°59′ E 154
Troškūnai, *Lith.* 55°35′ N, 24°52′ E 166
Trostan, peak, *U.K.* 55°1′ N, 6°16′ W 150
Trostyanets′, *Ukr.* 50°28′ N, 34°57′ E 158
Trotternish, region 57°35′ N, 6°46′ W 150
Trotwood, *Ohio, U.S.* 39°47′ N, 84°19′ W 102
Troup, *Tex., U.S.* 32°8′ N, 95°8′ W 103
Troup Head 57°42′ N, 2°42′ W 150
Trout, *La., U.S.* 31°41′ N, 92°12′ W 103
Trout Creek, *Can.* 45°59′ N, 79°21′ W 94
Trout Lake, *Can.* 50°39′ N, 117°33′ W 90
Trout Lake, *Can.* 51°10′ N, 93°47′ W 110
Trout Lake, *Can.* 60°25′ N, 121°11′ W 108
Trout Lake, *Minn., U.S.* 47°55′ N, 92°47′ W 94
Trout Lake, *Wash., U.S.* 45°58′ N, 121°32′ W 100
Trout Lake, lake, *Can.* 51°6′ N, 94°18′ W 106
Trout Peak, *Wyo., U.S.* 44°34′ N, 109°37′ W 90
Trout, river, *Can.* 60°58′ N, 120°45′ W 108
Trout, river, *Can.* 56°18′ N, 114°30′ W 108
Troutdale, *Oreg., U.S.* 45°32′ N, 122°25′ W 90
Trouville, *Fr.* 49°21′ N, 8°475′ E 150
Trowbridge, *U.K.* 51°18′ N, 2°12′ W 162
Troy, *Ala., U.S.* 31°48′ N, 85°59′ W 96
Troy, *Mich., U.S.* 42°34′ N, 83°9′ W 102
Troy, *Mo., U.S.* 38°58′ N, 90°59′ W 94
Troy, *Mont., U.S.* 48°26′ N, 115°54′ W 90
Troy, *N.H., U.S.* 42°49′ N, 72°12′ W 104
Troy, *N.Y., U.S.* 42°43′ N, 73°42′ W 104
Troy, *N.C., U.S.* 35°21′ N, 79°55′ W 96
Troy, *Ohio, U.S.* 40°1′ N, 84°13′ W 102
Troy Peak, *Nev., U.S.* 38°18′ N, 115°35′ W 90
Troy, ruin(s), *Turk.* 39°56′ N, 26°7′ E 156
Troyes, *Fr.* 48°17′ N, 4°4′ E 163
Trozadero, *Peru* 3°0′ S, 76°47′ W 136
Trpezi, *Mont.* 42°53′ N, 20°0′ E 168
Trubar, *Bosn. and Herzg.* 44°21′ N, 16°13′ E 168
Trubchevsk, *Russ.* 52°33′ N, 33°49′ E 158
Truckee, *Calif., U.S.* 39°19′ N, 120°12′ W 90
Trudfront, *Russ.* 45°53′ N, 47°40′ E 158
Trufant, *Mich., U.S.* 43°17′ N, 85°21′ W 102
Trujillo, *Hond.* 15°54′ N, 85°59′ W 115
Trujillo, *Peru* 8°8′ S, 79°2′ W 130
Trujillo, *Sp.* 39°27′ N, 5°53′ W 164
Trujillo, *Venez.* 9°20′ N, 70°27′ W 136
Trujillo, adm. division, *Venez.* 9°26′ N, 71°6′ W 136
Trujillo Alto, *U.S.* 18°21′ N, 66°0′ W 118
Truk Islands see Chuuk, islands, *F.S.M.* 7°44′ N, 152°5′ E 242
Trumbull, *Conn., U.S.* 41°14′ N, 73°12′ W 104
Trumbull, Mount, peak, *Ariz., U.S.* 36°23′ N, 113°12′ W 92
Trumon, *Indonesia* 2°51′ N, 97°36′ E 196
Trŭn, *Bulg.* 42°49′ N, 22°37′ E 168
Truro, *Can.* 45°21′ N, 63°17′ W 111
Truro, *Mass., U.S.* 41°59′ N, 70°4′ W 104
Truşeşti, *Rom.* 47°45′ N, 27°1′ E 152
Trutch, *Can.* 57°44′ N, 122°57′ W 108
Truth or Consequences, *N. Mex., U.S.* 33°8′ N, 107°15′ W 92
Trutnov, *Czech Rep.* 50°33′ N, 15°54′ E 152
Truxton, *Ariz., U.S.* 35°29′ N, 113°33′ W 101
Trwyn Cilan, *U.K.* 52°36′ N, 4°52′ W 150
Tryphena, *N.Z.* 36°19′ S, 175°27′ E 240
Trysil, *Nor.* 61°19′ N, 12°15′ E 152
Trzcianka, *Pol.* 53°1′ N, 16°27′ E 152
Trzebież, *Pol.* 53°39′ N, 14°31′ E 152
Trzemeszno, *Pol.* 52°33′ N, 17°49′ E 152
Tsacha Lake, *Can.* 52°59′ N, 125°26′ W 108
Tsada, *Cyprus* 34°50′ N, 32°28′ E 194
Tsagaanders, *Mongolia* 48°5′ N, 114°21′ E 198
Tsagaangol, *Mongolia* 49°1′ N, 89°3′ E 184
Tsagaannuur, *Mongolia* 49°28′ N, 89°39′ E 184
Tsagan Aman, *Russ.* 47°30′ N, 46°37′ E 158
Ts′ageri, *Ga.* 42°36′ N, 42°42′ E 195
Tsagveri, *Ga.* 41°48′ N, 43°27′ E 195
Tsaka La, pass, *India* 33°20′ N, 78°50′ E 188
Tsalka, *Ga.* 41°34′ N, 44°3′ E 195
Tsao see Tsau, *Botswana* 20°13′ S, 22°23′ E 227
Tsapel′ka, *Russ.* 58°2′ N, 28°57′ E 166
Tsaratanana, Massif du, *Madagascar* 14°17′ S, 48°37′ E 220
Tsarevo, *Bulg.* 42°10′ N, 27°51′ E 158
Tsau (Tsao), *Botswana* 20°13′ S, 22°23′ E 227
Tsavo, *Kenya* 3°3′ S, 38°29′ E 224
Tsavo National Park, *Kenya* 2°59′ S, 39°7′ E 218
Tsavo, river, *Kenya* 3°15′ S, 37°42′ E 224
Tsawisis, *Namibia* 26°16′ S, 18°8′ E 227
Tsayta Lake, lake, *Can.* 55°23′ N, 125°57′ W 108
Tschaukaib, *Namibia* 26°37′ S, 15°36′ E 227
Tschida, Lake, *N. Dak., U.S.* 46°33′ N, 102°24′ W 90
Tselina, *Russ.* 46°33′ N, 40°59′ E 158
Tsenogora, *Russ.* 64°55′ N, 46°34′ E 154
Tserovo, *Bulg.* 42°21′ N, 24°3′ E 156
Tses, *Namibia* 25°53′ S, 18°3′ E 227
Tsetsegnuur, *Mongolia* 46°32′ N, 93°6′ E 190
Tsetseng, *Botswana* 23°32′ S, 23°6′ E 227
Tsetserleg, *Mongolia* 47°28′ N, 101°24′ E 198
Tsévié, *Togo* 6°28′ N, 1°12′ E 222
Tshabong, *Botswana* 26°4′ S, 22°27′ E 227
Tshane, *Botswana* 24°3′ S, 21°53′ E 227
Tshela, *Dem. Rep. of the Congo* 5°1′ S, 12°52′ E 218
Tshibamba, *Dem. Rep. of the Congo* 9°7′ S, 22°31′ E 218
Tshikapa, *Dem. Rep. of the Congo* 6°25′ S, 20°50′ E 218
Tshilenge, *Dem. Rep. of the Congo* 6°17′ S, 23°45′ E 224
Tshilongo, *Dem. Rep. of the Congo* 10°31′ S, 26°0′ E 224
Tshinota, *Dem. Rep. of the Congo* 7°2′ S, 20°55′ E 218
Tshinsenda, *Dem. Rep. of the Congo* 12°18′ S, 27°56′ E 224
Tshisenga, *Dem. Rep. of the Congo* 7°17′ S, 22°0′ E 218
Tsholotsho, *Zimb.* 19°47′ S, 27°45′ E 224
Tshootsha, *Botswana* 22°5′ S, 20°54′ E 227
Tshopo, river, *Dem. Rep. of the Congo* 0°26′ N, 26°42′ E 224
Tshuapa, river, *Dem. Rep. of the Congo* 2°15′ S, 24°11′ E 224
Tshumbe, *Dem. Rep. of the Congo* 4°10′ S, 24°21′ E 218
Tshwane see Pretoria, *S. Af.* 25°48′ S, 28°3′ E 227
Tsiigehtchic, *Can.* 67°25′ N, 133°35′ W 98
Tsil′ma, river, *Russ.* 65°29′ N, 51°1′ E 154
Tsimanampetsotsa, Lac, lake, *Madagascar* 24°15′ S, 42°16′ E 220
Tsimkavichy, *Belarus* 53°4′ N, 27°0′ E 152
Tsimlyansk, *Russ.* 47°37′ N, 41°58′ E 158
Tsinjomitondraka, *Madagascar* 15°40′ S, 47°9′ E 220
Tsintsabis, *Namibia* 18°43′ S, 17°58′ E 220
Tsiombe, *Madagascar* 25°17′ S, 45°32′ E 220
Tsipikan, *Russ.* 54°57′ N, 113°20′ E 190
Tsiteli Tskaro, *Ga.* 41°24′ N, 46°8′ E 180
Tsitondroina, *Madagascar* 21°16′ S, 46°0′ E 220
Tsitsikamma Forest and Coastal National Park, *Indian Ocean* 34°5′ S, 23°29′ E 206
Tsivory, *Madagascar* 24°3′ S, 46°6′ E 220
Tsna, river, *Russ.* 53°52′ N, 41°47′ E 154
Tsnori, *Ga.* 41°36′ N, 45°57′ E 195
Tsomog, *Mongolia* 45°53′ N, 109°8′ E 198
Tsoohor, *Mongolia* 43°16′ N, 104°5′ E 198
Tsu, *Japan* 34°42′ N, 136°31′ E 201
Tsu Lake, lake, *Can.* 60°38′ N, 112°18′ W 108
Tsubame, *Japan* 37°39′ N, 138°56′ E 201
Tsubata, *Japan* 36°40′ N, 136°43′ E 201
Tsuchiura, *Japan* 36°5′ N, 140°12′ E 201
Tsugaru Kaikyō 41°4′ N, 138°25′ E 190
Tsukumi, *Japan* 33°3′ N, 131°51′ E 201
Tsuma, *Japan* 36°12′ N, 133°14′ E 201
Tsumeb, *Namibia* 19°16′ S, 17°41′ E 220
Tsumis Park, *Namibia* 23°42′ S, 17°25′ E 227
Tsumkwe, *Namibia* 19°38′ S, 20°35′ E 220
Tsunō, *Japan* 32°14′ N, 131°33′ E 201
Tsuru, *Japan* 35°32′ N, 138°54′ E 201
Tsuruga, *Japan* 35°37′ N, 136°4′ E 201
Tsurugi, *Japan* 36°27′ N, 136°37′ E 201
Tsuruoka, *Japan* 38°43′ N, 139°50′ E 201
Tsurusaki, *Japan* 33°14′ N, 131°41′ E 201
Tsushima, *Japan* 35°9′ N, 136°44′ E 201
Tsushima, *Japan* 33°6′ N, 132°31′ E 201
Tsushima Strait 33°56′ N, 125°37′ E 198
Tsutsu, *Japan* 34°7′ N, 129°11′ E 200
Tsuyama, *Japan* 35°4′ N, 134°0′ E 201
Tsyp Navolok, *Russ.* 69°42′ N, 33°5′ E 152
Tsyurupyns′k, *Ukr.* 46°37′ N, 32°43′ E 156
Tua, *Dem. Rep. of the Congo* 3°42′ S, 16°36′ E 218
Tuai, *N.Z.* 38°51′ S, 177°9′ E 240
Tuakau, *N.Z.* 37°17′ S, 174°58′ E 240
Tual, *Indonesia* 5°46′ S, 132°37′ E 192
Tuan Giao, *Vietnam* 21°45′ N, 103°19′ E 202
Tuangku, island, *Indonesia* 2°9′ N, 97°18′ E 196
Tuapí, *Nicar.* 14°8′ N, 83°19′ W 115
Tuapse, *Russ.* 44°6′ N, 39°4′ E 156
Tuaran, *Malaysia* 6°12′ N, 116°14′ E 203
Tuba City, *Ariz., U.S.* 36°8′ N, 111°15′ W 92
Tuban, *Indonesia* 7°3′ S, 111°53′ E 192
Tubarão, *Braz.* 28°32′ S, 49°0′ W 138
Ţūbās, *West Bank, Israel* 32°19′ N, 35°21′ E 194
Tubinskiy, *Russ.* 52°54′ N, 58°10′ E 154
Tubmanburg, *Liberia* 6°47′ N, 10°53′ W 222
Tubod, *Philippines* 8°3′ N, 123°48′ E 203
Ţubruq (Tobruk), *Lib.* 32°3′ N, 23°57′ E 216
Tubuai Islands see Austral Islands, *South Pacific Ocean* 21°30′ S, 152°33′ W 238
Tubutama, *Mex.* 30°53′ N, 111°29′ W 92
Tucacas, *Venez.* 10°47′ N, 68°21′ W 136
Tucacas see Puerto López, *Col.* 11°56′ N, 71°18′ W 136
Tucano, *Braz.* 10°58′ S, 38°49′ W 132
Tucavaca, *Bol.* 18°39′ S, 58°58′ W 132
Tuchomie, *Pol.* 54°7′ N, 17°21′ E 152
Tuckerman, *Ark., U.S.* 35°43′ N, 91°13′ W 96
Tuckernuck Island, *Mass., U.S.* 41°16′ N, 70°36′ W 104
Tuckerton, *N.J., U.S.* 39°35′ N, 74°21′ W 94
Tucki Mountain, peak, *Calif., U.S.* 36°29′ N, 117°13′ W 92
Tucson, *Ariz., U.S.* 32°14′ N, 110°58′ W 92
Tucumán, adm. division, *Arg.* 26°30′ S, 66°11′ W 132
Tucumcari, *N. Mex., U.S.* 35°10′ N, 103°44′ W 92
Tucupita, *Venez.* 9°5′ N, 62°5′ W 116
Tucuruí, *Braz.* 3°44′ S, 49°46′ W 130
Tuczno, *Pol.* 53°11′ N, 16°9′ E 152
Tudela, *Sp.* 42°3′ N, 1°37′ W 164
Tudulinna, *Est.* 59°1′ N, 27°1′ E 166
Ţufay′, *Saudi Arabia* 26°49′ N, 49°39′ E 196
Tuffé, *Fr.* 48°6′ N, 0°30′ E 150
Tufts Plain, *North Pacific Ocean* 44°55′ N, 143°12′ W 252
Tughyl, *Kaz.* 47°42′ N, 84°11′ E 184
Tuguegarao, *Philippines* 17°38′ N, 121°42′ E 203
Tugur, *Russ.* 53°46′ N, 136°38′ E 190
Tui, *Sp.* 42°2′ N, 8°41′ W 214
Tuichi, river, *Bol.* 14°14′ S, 68°23′ W 137
Tuitán, *Mex.* 23°59′ N, 104°15′ W 114
Tukan, *Russ.* 53°52′ N, 57°26′ E 154
Tukayyid, spring, *Iraq* 29°45′ N, 45°38′ E 196
Tukchi, *Russ.* 57°28′ N, 139°21′ E 173
Tukhkala, *Russ.* 65°41′ N, 30°41′ E 152
Tukhlya, *Ukr.* 48°52′ N, 23°30′ E 152
Tukita, *Can.* 64°53′ N, 125°16′ W 106
Tūkrah, *Lib.* 32°32′ N, 20°34′ E 216
Tuktoyaktuk, *Can.* 69°24′ N, 133°11′ W 73
Tuktut Nogait National Park, *Can.* 68°46′ N, 123°49′ W 98
Tukums, *Latv.* 56°58′ N, 23°7′ E 166
Tukuyu, *Tanzania* 9°17′ S, 33°39′ E 224
Tula, *Mex.* 22°58′ N, 99°43′ W 114
Tula, *Mex.* 20°1′ N, 99°27′ W 112
Tula, *Russ.* 54°10′ N, 37°36′ E 154
Tula, adm. division, *Russ.* 53°58′ N, 36°48′ E 154
Tula de Allende, *Mex.* 20°0′ N, 99°21′ W 114
Tulak, *Afghan.* 33°56′ N, 63°38′ E 186
Tulameen, *Can.* 49°32′ N, 120°47′ W 90
Tulancingo, *Mex.* 20°2′ N, 98°22′ W 114
Tulare, *Calif., U.S.* 36°13′ N, 119°21′ W 100
Tulare, *Serb.* 42°48′ N, 21°27′ E 168
Tularosa Valley, *N. Mex., U.S.* 33°7′ N, 106°27′ W 92
Tulcán, *Ecua.* 0°44′ N, 77°57′ W 136
Tulcea, *Rom.* 45°10′ N, 28°47′ E 156
Tulcea, adm. division, *Rom.* 44°58′ N, 28°9′ E 156
Tul′chyn, *Ukr.* 48°40′ N, 28°57′ E 156
Tülen Araldary, islands, *Caspian Sea* 44°43′ N, 49°2′ E 180
Tuli, *Zimb.* 21°55′ S, 29°14′ E 227
Tulia, *Tex., U.S.* 34°30′ N, 101°47′ W 92
Tulita, *Can.* 64°56′ N, 125°23′ W 98
Tulivaara, *Russ.* 63°37′ N, 30°26′ E 154
Ţūlkarm, *West Bank, Israel* 32°18′ N, 35°1′ E 194
Tülkibas, *Kaz.* 42°28′ N, 70°19′ E 197
Tullahoma, *Tenn., U.S.* 35°21′ N, 86°13′ W 96
Tullamore, *Ire.* 53°15′ N, 7°30′ W 150
Tulloch Reservoir, lake, *Calif., U.S.* 37°52′ N, 120°46′ W 100
Tullos, *La., U.S.* 31°48′ N, 92°20′ W 103
Tully Lake, *Mass., U.S.* 42°38′ N, 72°21′ W 104
Tulpan, *Russ.* 61°23′ N, 57°22′ E 154
Tulsa, *Okla., U.S.* 36°8′ N, 95°59′ W 96
Tulsequah, *Can.* 58°36′ N, 133°36′ W 108
Tuluá, *Col.* 4°4′ N, 76°13′ W 136
Tuluksak, *Alas., U.S.* 61°4′ N, 160°59′ W 98
Tulum National Park, *Mex.* 20°8′ N, 87°35′ W 115
Tulum, ruin(s), *Mex.* 20°11′ N, 87°36′ W 115
Tulun, *Russ.* 54°40′ N, 100°27′ E 160
Tuma, *Russ.* 55°8′ N, 40°34′ E 154
Tuma, river, *Nicar.* 13°20′ N, 85°36′ W 115
Tumacácori National Historical Park, *Ariz., U.S.* 31°34′ N, 111°2′ W 92
Tumaco, *Col.* 1°39′ N, 78°37′ W 123
Tumanskaya, *Russ.* 64°3′ N, 178°9′ E 73
Tumany, *Russ.* 60°57′ N, 155°46′ E 160
Tumba, *Dem. Rep. of the Congo* 3°10′ S, 23°35′ E 224
Tumbes, *Peru* 3°39′ S, 80°25′ W 130
Tumble Mountain, peak, *Mont., U.S.* 45°17′ N, 110°6′ W 90
Tumbledown Mountain, peak, *Me., U.S.* 45°26′ N, 70°33′ W 94
Tumbler Ridge, *Can.* 55°3′ N, 121°0′ W 108
Tumcha, *Russ.* 66°34′ N, 30°46′ E 152
Tumd Youqi, *China* 40°31′ N, 110°31′ E 198
Tumd Zuoqi, *China* 40°44′ N, 111°8′ E 198
Tumeka Lake, *Can.* 57°11′ N, 130°21′ W 108
Tumen, *China* 42°57′ N, 129°49′ E 200
Tumen, river, *Asia* 42°2′ N, 128°35′ E 200
Tumeremo, *Venez.* 7°18′ N, 61°30′ W 130
Tumiã, river, *Braz.* 8°15′ S, 66°37′ W 132
Tumiritinga, *Braz.* 19°0′ S, 41°39′ W 138
Tumpat, *Malaysia* 6°11′ N, 102°8′ E 196
Tumu, *Ghana* 10°51′ N, 2°0′ W 222
Tumucumaque National Park, *Braz.* 1°51′ N, 56°1′ W 130
Tumucumaque, Serra de, *Braz.* 0°45′ N, 55°55′ W 130
Tumupasa, *Bol.* 14°11′ S, 67°55′ W 137
Tumusla, *Bol.* 20°32′ S, 65°41′ W 137
Tumwater, *Wash., U.S.* 46°59′ N, 122°55′ W 100
Tuna, *Ghana* 9°29′ N, 2°27′ W 222
Tunapuna, *Trinidad and Tobago* 10°37′ N, 61°24′ W 118
Tunas, *Braz.* 25°1′ S, 49°6′ W 138
Tunas, Sierra de las, *Mex.* 30°5′ N, 107°50′ W 112
Tunbridge, *Vt., U.S.* 43°53′ N, 72°30′ W 104
Tunbridge Wells, *U.K.* 51°7′ N, 0°15′ E 162
Tunceli, *Turk.* 39°5′ N, 39°31′ E 195
Tunchang, *China* 19°21′ N, 110°4′ E 202
Tünchel, *Mongolia* 48°50′ N, 106°42′ E 198
Tundubai, *Sudan* 14°47′ N, 22°42′ E 216
Tundubai, spring, *Sudan* 18°25′ N, 28°30′ E 226
Tunduma, *Tanzania* 9°19′ S, 32°46′ E 224
Tunduru, *Tanzania* 11°7′ S, 37°22′ E 224
Tunel, *Pol.* 50°25′ N, 19°58′ E 152
Tunga, *Nig.* 8°2′ N, 9°21′ E 222
Tŭngam, *N. Korea* 37°44′ N, 125°26′ E 200
Tungaru, *Sudan* 10°12′ N, 30°45′ E 224
Tungelsta, *Sw.* 59°6′ N, 18°2′ E 166
Tungkang, *Taiwan, China* 22°29′ N, 120°30′ E 198
Tungsten, *Can.* 62°1′ N, 128°21′ W 98
Tunguska Podkamennaya, *Russ.* 61°35′ N, 90°11′ E 169
Tuni, *India* 17°21′ N, 82°32′ E 188
Tunica, *Miss., U.S.* 34°39′ N, 90°24′ W 96
Tunis, *Tun.* 36°46′ N, 10°3′ E 156
Tunisia 34°0′ N, 9°0′ E 214
Tunja, *Col.* 5°32′ N, 73°23′ W 136
Tunkinsky National Park, *Russ.* 51°26′ N, 101°42′ E 172
Tŭnkovo, *Bulg.* 41°42′ N, 25°45′ E 156
Tuntutuliak, *Alas., U.S.* 60°20′ N, 162°38′ W 98
Tununak, *Alas., U.S.* 60°29′ N, 165°20′ W 98
Tunuyán, *Arg.* 33°35′ S, 69°3′ W 134
Tuolumne, *Calif., U.S.* 37°57′ N, 120°15′ W 100
Tuong Duong, *Vietnam* 19°15′ N, 104°23′ E 202
Tuotuo, river, *China* 34°3′ N, 91°7′ E 188
Tuotuoheyan see Tanggulashan, *China* 34°10′ N, 92°24′ E 188
Tup, *Kyrg.* 42°43′ N, 78°21′ E 184
Tupã, *Braz.* 21°56′ S, 50°29′ W 138
Tupaciguara, *Braz.* 18°36′ S, 48°45′ W 138
Tupanciretã, *Braz.* 29°6′ S, 53°50′ W 139
Tuparro, river, *Col.* 4°42′ N, 69°28′ W 136
Tupelo, *Miss., U.S.* 34°15′ N, 88°44′ W 112
Tupi, *Philippines* 6°13′ N, 125°1′ E 203
Tupinambarama, Ilha, *Braz.* 3°24′ S, 58°32′ W 130
Tupiraçaba, *Braz.* 14°34′ S, 48°36′ W 138
Tupitsyno, *Russ.* 58°34′ N, 28°21′ E 166
Tupiza, *Bol.* 21°29′ S, 65°46′ W 137
Tupper, *Can.* 55°31′ N, 120°4′ W 108
Tupper Lake, *N.Y., U.S.* 44°13′ N, 74°29′ W 94
Tüpqaraghan Tübegi, *Kaz.* 44°24′ N, 50°30′ E 180
Tuquan, *China* 45°23′ N, 121°32′ E 198
Túquerres, *Col.* 1°6′ N, 77°39′ W 136
Túr, river, *Hung.* 48°0′ N, 22°23′ E 168
Tura, *Hung.* 47°35′ N, 19°36′ E 168
Tura, *India* 25°26′ N, 90°11′ E 188
Tura, *Russ.* 64°22′ N, 100°29′ E 160
Tura, *Tanzania* 5°28′ S, 33°50′ E 224
Tura, river, *Russ.* 58°20′ N, 62°52′ E 154
Turabah, *Saudi Arabia* 21°12′ N, 41°40′ E 182
Turabah, spring, *Saudi Arabia* 28°12′ N, 42°53′ E 180
Turan Lowland, *Uzb.* 40°50′ N, 57°48′ E 180
Turangi, *N.Z.* 39°1′ S, 175°47′ E 240
Turar Ryskulov, *Kaz.* 42°30′ N, 70°20′ E 197
Turaw, *Belarus* 52°4′ N, 27°44′ E 152
Ţurayf, *Saudi Arabia* 31°39′ N, 38°38′ E 180
Turba, *Est.* 59°3′ N, 24°11′ E 166
Turbaco, *Col.* 10°19′ N, 75°25′ W 136
Turbacz, peak, *Pol.* 49°31′ N, 20°1′ E 152
Turbat, *Pak.* 25°56′ N, 63°6′ E 182
Turbe, *Bosn. and Herzg.* 44°15′ N, 17°35′ E 168
Turbo, *Col.* 8°7′ N, 76°43′ W 136
Turco, *Bol.* 18°14′ S, 68°13′ W 137
Turda, spring, *Sudan* 10°22′ N, 28°33′ E 224
Turégano, *Sp.* 41°9′ N, 4°1′ W 164
Turenki, *Fin.* 60°54′ N, 24°38′ E 166
Tureta, *Nig.* 12°35′ N, 5°35′ E 222
Turgeon, river, *Can.* 49°32′ N, 79°47′ W 94
Tŭrgovishte, *Bulg.* 43°14′ N, 26°34′ E 156
Tŭrgovishte, adm. division, *Bulg.* 43°1′ N, 25°52′ E 156
Turgut, *Turk.* 38°37′ N, 31°47′ E 156
Turhal, *Turk.* 40°23′ N, 36°6′ E 156
Türi, *Est.* 58°47′ N, 25°25′ E 166
Turiaçu, *Braz.* 1°40′ S, 45°25′ W 130

Turin, *Can.* 49°57′ N, 112°33′ W 90
Turin see Torino, *It.* 45°4′ N, 7°40′ E 167
Turinsk, *Russ.* 58°2′ N, 63°35′ E 154
Turinskaya Sloboda, *Russ.* 57°36′ N, 64°21′ E 154
Turjak, *Bosn. and Herzg.* 45°0′ N, 17°10′ E 168
Turkana, Lake (Rudolph, Lake), *Kenya* 2°32′ N, 34°10′ E 206
Turkestan Range, *Uzb.* 39°30′ N, 68°9′ E 184
Túrkeve, *Hung.* 47°6′ N, 20°45′ E 168
Turkey, *Tex., U.S.* 34°22′ N, 100°55′ W 96
Turkey 38°54′ N, 33°55′ E 180
Turki, *Russ.* 51°57′ N, 43°17′ E 158
Türkistan, *Kaz.* 43°17′ N, 68°13′ E 184
Türkmenabat (Chärjew), *Turkm.* 39°4′ N, 63°35′ E 184
Türkmenbaşy, *Turkm.* 40°0′ N, 52°58′ E 180
Turkmenistan 39°37′ N, 57°48′ E 184
Turks and Caicos Islands, *U.K.* 21°58′ N, 72°29′ W 116
Turks Islands, *North Atlantic Ocean* 21°27′ N, 70°58′ W 116
Turku, *Fin.* 60°27′ N, 22°0′ E 160
Turku (Åbo), *Fin.* 60°27′ N, 22°15′ E 166
Turmalina, *Braz.* 17°16′ S, 42°46′ W 138
Turnagain, Cape, *N.Z.* 40°43′ S, 176°35′ E 240
Turnberry, *Can.* 53°26′ N, 101°42′ W 108
Turneffe Islands, *Caribbean Sea* 17°35′ N, 87°42′ W 115
Turner, *Me., U.S.* 44°15′ N, 70°16′ W 104
Turner, *Mont., U.S.* 48°49′ N, 108°25′ W 90
Turner Mountain, peak, *Calif., U.S.* 40°17′ N, 121°43′ W 90
Turners Falls, *Mass., U.S.* 42°35′ N, 72°34′ W 104
Turnertown, *Tex., U.S.* 32°11′ N, 94°58′ W 103
Turnhout, *Belg.* 51°19′ N, 4°56′ E 167
Turnu, *Rom.* 46°16′ N, 21°6′ E 168
Turnu Roşu, Pasul, pass, *Rom.* 45°34′ N, 24°14′ E 156
Turobin, *Pol.* 50°48′ N, 22°44′ E 152
Turpan, *China* 43°3′ N, 89°14′ E 190
Turpan Depression, *China* 42°8′ N, 91°23′ E 190
Turquino, Pico, peak, *Cuba* 19°58′ N, 76°56′ W 115
Turre, *Sp.* 37°8′ N, 1°54′ W 164
Tursunzoda, *Taj.* 38°31′ N, 68°19′ E 197
Turt, *Mongolia* 51°22′ N, 100°56′ E 190
Turţ, *Rom.* 47°59′ N, 23°13′ E 168
Turtas, river, *Russ.* 58°37′ N, 69°48′ E 169
Tŭrtkŭl, *Uzb.* 41°32′ N, 61°0′ E 180
Turtle Creek Point, *Fla., U.S.* 29°2′ N, 83°11′ W 105
Turtle Islands, *North Atlantic Ocean* 7°30′ N, 13°42′ W 222
Turtle Mountain, peak, *N. Dak., U.S.* 48°59′ N, 100°31′ W 90
Turtle Mountains, *Calif., U.S.* 34°14′ N, 114°53′ W 101
Turtle, river, *Can.* 49°6′ N, 92°32′ W 110
Turtleford, *Can.* 53°23′ N, 108°58′ W 108
Turugart Pass, *Kyrg.* 40°33′ N, 75°23′ E 184
Turugart, pass, *China* 40°31′ N, 75°21′ E 184
Turukhansk, *Russ.* 65°45′ N, 88°6′ E 169
Turukta, *Russ.* 60°39′ N, 116°3′ E 160
Turvo, *Braz.* 28°59′ S, 49°43′ W 138
Turvo, river, *Braz.* 16°24′ S, 50°11′ W 138
Tur'ya, *Russ.* 62°50′ N, 50°41′ E 154
Turysh, *Kaz.* 45°27′ N, 56°5′ E 158
Turza Wielka, *Pol.* 53°18′ N, 20°4′ E 152
Tuscaloosa, *Ala., U.S.* 33°11′ N, 87°34′ W 103
Tuscany, adm. division, *It.* 44°2′ N, 10°22′ E 167
Tuscarora, *Nev., U.S.* 41°19′ N, 116°14′ W 90
Tuscarora Mountains, *Nev., U.S.* 40°44′ N, 116°22′ W 90
Tuscola, *Ill., U.S.* 39°48′ N, 88°17′ W 102
Tuscola, *Tex., U.S.* 32°12′ N, 99°48′ W 92
Tuscumbia, *Ala., U.S.* 34°43′ N, 87°42′ W 96
Tuskegee, *Ala., U.S.* 32°24′ N, 85°41′ W 96
Tustin, *Mich., U.S.* 44°6′ N, 85°28′ W 102
Tustna, *Nor.* 63°12′ N, 8°7′ E 152
Tutak, *Turk.* 39°30′ N, 42°41′ E 195
Tutayev, *Russ.* 57°52′ N, 39°30′ E 154
Tuticorin, *India* 8°47′ N, 78°6′ E 188
Tutin, *Serb.* 42°59′ N, 20°20′ E 168
Tutira, *N.Z.* 39°13′ S, 176°53′ E 240
Tutoko, Mount, peak, *N.Z.* 44°38′ S, 167°56′ E 240
Tutonchany, *Russ.* 64°14′ N, 93°42′ E 169
Tutshi Lake, lake, *Can.* 59°53′ N, 135°14′ W 108
Tutuaca, river, *Mex.* 29°32′ N, 108°48′ W 80
Tutuala, *Timor-Leste* 8°31′ S, 127°6′ E 192
Tutubu, *Tanzania* 5°29′ S, 32°41′ E 218
Tutuila, *American Samoa, U.S.* 14°20′ S, 170°45′ W 241
Tututepec, *Mex.* 16°6′ N, 97°37′ W 112
Tuul, river, *Mongolia* 47°17′ N, 105°0′ E 198
Tuupovaara, *Fin.* 62°28′ N, 30°37′ E 152
Tuusniemi, *Fin.* 62°48′ N, 28°26′ E 152
Tuvalu 9°0′ S, 179°0′ E 241
Tuve, Mount, peak, *Antarctica* 73°50′ S, 80°43′ W 248
Ţuwayq, Jabal, *Saudi Arabia* 24°12′ N, 46°21′ E 196
Tuxford, *U.K.* 53°13′ N, 0°54′ E 162
Tuxpan, *Mex.* 20°56′ N, 97°24′ W 114
Tuxpan, *Mex.* 19°32′ N, 103°23′ W 114
Tuxpan, *Mex.* 21°55′ N, 105°19′ W 114
Tuxtepec, *Mex.* 18°5′ N, 96°7′ W 114
Tuxtla Gutiérrez, *Mex.* 16°42′ N, 93°14′ W 115
Tuy An, *Vietnam* 13°17′ N, 109°12′ E 202
Tuy Hoa, *Vietnam* 13°4′ N, 109°18′ E 202
Tuya Lake, *Can.* 59°3′ N, 131°11′ W 108
Tuya, river, *Can.* 58°24′ N, 130°35′ W 108
Tuyen Hoa, *Vietnam* 17°51′ N, 106°12′ E 198
Tuyen Quang, *Vietnam* 21°49′ N, 105°11′ E 202
Tuymazy, *Russ.* 54°34′ N, 53°45′ E 154
Tūyserkān, *Iran* 34°30′ N, 48°23′ E 180
Tuz Gölü, lake, *Turk.* 38°40′ N, 33°18′ E 156
Tuzantla, *Mex.* 19°2′ N, 100°23′ W 114
Tuzi, *Mont.* 42°21′ N, 19°19′ E 168
Tuzigoot National Monument, *Ariz., U.S.* 34°46′ N, 112°5′ W 92
Tuzla, *Bosn. and Herzg.* 44°32′ N, 18°39′ E 168
Tuzla Gölü, lake, *Turk.* 38°59′ N, 35°27′ E 156
Tuzluca, *Turk.* 40°3′ N, 43°39′ E 195
Tvedestrand, *Nor.* 58°37′ N, 8°53′ E 152
Tver', *Russ.* 56°50′ N, 35°54′ E 154
Tver', adm. division, *Russ.* 56°49′ N, 33°43′ E 154
Tverrvik, *Nor.* 67°2′ N, 14°31′ E 152
Twain Harte, *Calif., U.S.* 38°1′ N, 120°15′ W 100
Twee Rivieren, *S. Af.* 26°28′ S, 20°31′ E 227
Tweedy Mountain, peak, *Mont., U.S.* 45°27′ N, 113°2′ W 90
Twelve Bens, The, peak, *Ire.* 53°30′ N, 9°56′ W 150
Twentynine Palms, *Calif., U.S.* 34°8′ N, 116°3′ W 101
Twifu Praso, *Ghana* 5°37′ N, 1°32′ W 222
Twillingate, *Can.* 49°38′ N, 54°46′ W 111
Twin Falls, *Idaho, U.S.* 42°34′ N, 114°28′ W 90
Twin Lakes, *Can.* 57°25′ N, 117°31′ W 108
Twin Lakes, *Nebr., U.S.* 42°17′ N, 102°55′ W 90
Twin Lakes Mountain, peak, *Oreg., U.S.* 43°12′ N, 122°42′ W 90
Twin Mountain, *N.H., U.S.* 44°16′ N, 71°33′ W 104
Twin Mountain, peak, *Oreg., U.S.* 44°54′ N, 118°15′ W 90
Twin Peaks, *Idaho, U.S.* 44°35′ N, 114°33′ W 90
Twin Valley, *Minn., U.S.* 47°14′ N, 96°17′ W 90
Twining, *Mich., U.S.* 44°6′ N, 83°49′ W 102
Twisp, *Wash., U.S.* 48°20′ N, 120°9′ W 90
Twitya, river, *Can.* 63°42′ N, 129°33′ W 98
Twizel, *N.Z.* 44°16′ S, 170°6′ E 240
Two Buttes, *Colo., U.S.* 37°33′ N, 102°24′ W 92
Two Buttes, peak, *Colo., U.S.* 37°38′ N, 102°38′ W 90
Two Creeks, *Can.* 54°17′ N, 116°21′ W 108
Two Harbors, *Minn., U.S.* 47°1′ N, 91°41′ W 94
Two Hills, *Can.* 53°42′ N, 111°45′ W 108
Two Ocean Pass, *Wyo., U.S.* 44°1′ N, 110°10′ W 90
Two Rivers, *Wis., U.S.* 44°9′ N, 87°35′ W 102
Two Top Peak, *S. Dak., U.S.* 44°57′ N, 103°41′ W 90
Twofold Bay 37°24′ S, 149°35′ E 230
Tyab, *Iran* 26°58′ N, 57°1′ E 196
Tyanya, *Russ.* 59°0′ N, 119°43′ E 160
Tydal, *Nor.* 63°3′ N, 11°34′ E 152
Tyee, *Queen Charlotte Sound* 57°2′ N, 134°32′ W 108
Tygda, *Russ.* 53°9′ N, 126°19′ E 190
Tyin, *Nor.* 61°13′ N, 8°12′ E 152
Tyler, *Minn., U.S.* 44°15′ N, 96°10′ W 90
Tyler, *Tex., U.S.* 32°20′ N, 95°18′ W 103
Tylertown, *Miss., U.S.* 31°6′ N, 90°9′ W 103
Tym, river, *Russ.* 60°2′ N, 83°35′ E 169
Tymsk, *Russ.* 59°19′ N, 80°23′ E 169
Tynda, *Russ.* 55°10′ N, 124°44′ E 190
Tyndall, *S. Dak., U.S.* 42°58′ N, 97°53′ W 90
Tyndaris, ruin(s), *It.* 38°7′ N, 14°55′ E 156
Tynset, *Nor.* 62°17′ N, 10°45′ E 152
Tyre see Soûr, *Leb.* 33°16′ N, 35°12′ E 194
Tyree, Mount, peak, *Antarctica* 78°25′ S, 87°7′ W 248
Tyrnyauz, *Russ.* 43°24′ N, 42°56′ E 195
Tyrol, region, *It.* 46°1′ N, 10°30′ E 167
Tyrone, *N. Mex., U.S.* 32°43′ N, 108°17′ W 92
Tyrone, *Okla., U.S.* 36°56′ N, 101°6′ W 92
Tyrrhenian Sea 40°7′ N, 11°28′ E 156
Tyrvää, *Fin.* 61°21′ N, 22°51′ E 166
Tysvær, *Nor.* 59°18′ N, 5°28′ E 152
Tytuvėnai, *Lith.* 55°36′ N, 23°9′ E 166
Tyubelyakh, *Russ.* 65°18′ N, 142°53′ E 160
Tyugyuren, *Russ.* 67°12′ N, 142°36′ E 173
Tyukalinsk, *Russ.* 55°52′ N, 72°13′ E 184
Tyukyun, river, *Russ.* 65°42′ N, 118°13′ E 160
Tyulenovo, *Bulg.* 43°31′ N, 28°35′ E 156
Tyul'gan, *Russ.* 52°22′ N, 56°2′ E 154
Tyul'kino, *Russ.* 59°47′ N, 56°30′ E 154
Tyumen', *Russ.* 57°7′ N, 65°32′ E 184
Tyumen', adm. division, *Russ.* 55°59′ N, 66°44′ E 184
Tyung, river, *Russ.* 66°37′ N, 116°51′ E 160
Tyungur, *Russ.* 50°12′ N, 86°38′ E 184
Tyva, adm. division, *Russ.* 50°56′ N, 89°32′ E 184
Tyvoll, *Nor.* 62°43′ N, 11°21′ E 152
Tywyn, *U.K.* 52°34′ N, 4°5′ W 162
Tzintzuntzan, ruin(s), *Mex.* 19°34′ N, 101°37′ W 114

U

U. P. Mammoth Kill Site, *Wyo., U.S.* 41°30′ N, 107°43′ W 90
Uacari, *Braz.* 1°12′ N, 69°26′ W 136
Üälīkhanov, *Kaz.* 52°47′ N, 71°52′ E 184
Uamba, *Angola* 7°21′ S, 16°9′ E 218
Uarandab, *Eth.* 7°8′ N, 44°6′ E 218
Uarirambá, *Braz.* 1°40′ N, 69°26′ W 136
Uatumã, river, *Braz.* 0°2′ N, 59°58′ W 130
Uauá, *Braz.* 9°50′ S, 39°32′ W 132
Uaupés, river, *Braz.* 0°7′ N, 67°56′ W 136
Uaxactún, ruin(s), *Guatemala* 17°20′ N, 89°46′ W 115
Ub, *Serb.* 44°26′ N, 20°4′ E 168
Ubá, *Braz.* 21°7′ S, 42°55′ W 138
Uba, *Nig.* 10°29′ N, 13°12′ E 216
Übach-Palenberg, *Ger.* 50°55′ N, 6°7′ E 167
Ubaitaba, *Braz.* 14°20′ S, 39°18′ W 132
Ubangi, river, *Africa* 4°24′ N, 19°9′ E 206
Ubari see Awbārī, *Lib.* 26°37′ N, 12°45′ E 216
Ubatã, *Braz.* 14°15′ S, 39°28′ W 138
Úbeda, *Sp.* 38°0′ N, 3°22′ W 164
Ubehebe Crater, *Calif., U.S.* 37°1′ N, 117°27′ W 101
Uberaba, *Braz.* 19°44′ S, 47°56′ W 138
Uberlândia, *Braz.* 18°55′ S, 48°20′ W 138
Ubiaja, *Nig.* 6°41′ N, 6°22′ E 222
Ubiatã, *Braz.* 24°33′ S, 53°1′ W 138
Ubierna, *Sp.* 42°28′ N, 3°43′ W 164
Ubinas, *Peru* 16°25′ S, 70°52′ W 137
Ubly, *Mich., U.S.* 43°42′ N, 82°55′ W 102
Ubombo, *S. Af.* 27°32′ S, 32°9′ E 227
Ubon Ratchathani, *Thai.* 15°14′ N, 104°53′ E 202
Ubrique, *Sp.* 36°40′ N, 5°27′ W 164
Ubundu, *Dem. Rep. of the Congo* 0°24′ N, 25°30′ E 224
Ucacha, *Arg.* 33°3′ S, 63°30′ W 139
Üçajy, *Turkm.* 38°4′ N, 62°45′ E 184
Ucar, *Azerb.* 40°31′ N, 47°38′ E 195
Ucayali, adm. division, *Peru* 10°3′ S, 73°40′ W 137
Ucayali, river, *Peru* 6°29′ S, 75°37′ W 122
Uchab, *Namibia* 19°44′ S, 17°47′ E 220
Uchaly, *Russ.* 54°22′ N, 59°24′ E 154
Uchami, *Russ.* 63°49′ N, 96°31′ E 169
Uchami, river, *Russ.* 62°30′ N, 94°55′ E 160
Uchami, river, *Russ.* 62°38′ N, 93°54′ E 169
Uchi Lake, *Can.* 51°4′ N, 92°34′ W 110
Uchiko, *Japan* 33°33′ N, 132°38′ E 201
Uchiza, *Peru* 8°26′ S, 76°24′ W 130
Uchqo'rg'on, *Uzb.* 41°12′ N, 71°59′ E 197
Uchquduq, *Uzb.* 42°6′ N, 63°37′ E 197
Uchsay, *Uzb.* 43°48′ N, 58°56′ E 180
Uchur, river, *Russ.* 56°55′ N, 130°38′ E 160
Ucluelet, *Can.* 48°56′ N, 125°34′ W 90
Ucuriş, *Rom.* 46°37′ N, 21°57′ E 168
Uda, river, *Russ.* 53°59′ N, 133°25′ E 190
Udachnoye, *Russ.* 47°45′ N, 46°51′ E 184
Udachnyy, *Russ.* 66°22′ N, 112°38′ E 173
Udainagar, *India* 22°31′ N, 76°13′ E 197
Udaipur, *India* 24°33′ N, 73°41′ E 186
Udala, *India* 21°35′ N, 86°33′ E 188
Uddevalla, *Nor.* 58°20′ N, 11°56′ E 152
Uder, *Ger.* 51°21′ N, 10°3′ E 167
Udhampur, *India* 32°54′ N, 75°10′ E 186
Udi, *Nig.* 6°19′ N, 7°23′ E 222
Udine, *It.* 46°4′ N, 13°15′ E 167
Udintsev Fracture Zone, *South Pacific Ocean* 52°14′ S, 155°38′ W 252
Udmurtiya, adm. division, *Russ.* 57°3′ N, 51°20′ E 154
Udobnaya, *Russ.* 44°11′ N, 41°30′ E 158
Udomlya, *Russ.* 57°51′ N, 35°5′ E 154
Udorn see Udon Thani, *Thai.* 17°26′ N, 102°46′ E 202
Udovo, *Maced.* 41°21′ N, 22°26′ E 156
Udzungwa Mountain National Park, *Tanzania* 7°50′ S, 36°22′ E 206
Uebonti, *Indonesia* 0°59′ N, 121°35′ E 192
Ueda, *Japan* 36°24′ N, 138°17′ E 201
Uele, river, *Dem. Rep. of the Congo* 3°32′ N, 28°10′ E 224
Uelen, *Russ.* 66°7′ N, 169°51′ W 98
Uel'kal', *Russ.* 65°34′ N, 179°24′ W 98
Uelsen, *Ger.* 52°29′ N, 6°53′ E 163
Ueno, *Japan* 34°44′ N, 136°7′ E 201
Uere, river, *Dem. Rep. of the Congo* 3°44′ N, 25°23′ E 224
Ufa, *Russ.* 54°45′ N, 56°0′ E 154
Ufa, river, *Russ.* 56°29′ N, 58°7′ E 154
Uftyuga, river, *Russ.* 61°36′ N, 46°15′ E 154
Ugāle, *Latv.* 57°15′ N, 22°1′ E 166
Ugalla Game Reserve, *Tanzania* 6°5′ S, 31°39′ E 224
Ugalla, river, *Tanzania* 5°55′ S, 31°20′ E 224
Ugam-Chatkal National Park, *Uzb.* 41°38′ N, 70°0′ E 197
Uganda 1°13′ N, 32°13′ E 224
Uganik, *Gulf of Alaska* 57°45′ N, 153°38′ W 98
Ugarit see Ra's Shamrah, site, *Syr.* 35°33′ N, 35°44′ E 194
Ugleural'skiy, *Russ.* 58°57′ N, 57°36′ E 154
Uglich, *Russ.* 57°27′ N, 38°20′ E 154
Ugljane, *Croatia* 43°33′ N, 16°44′ E 168
Uglovka, *Russ.* 58°15′ N, 33°34′ E 154
Ugol'nyye Kopi, *Russ.* 64°47′ N, 177°47′ E 73
Ugoma, *Dem. Rep. of the Congo* 4°28′ S, 28°25′ E 224
Ugra, river, *Russ.* 54°44′ N, 35°45′ E 154
Ugut, *Russ.* 60°27′ N, 74°6′ E 169
Uhlenhorst, *Namibia* 23°42′ S, 17°53′ E 227
Uhrichsville, *Ohio, U.S.* 40°23′ N, 81°22′ W 102
Uig 58°11′ N, 7°1′ W 150
Uíge, *Angola* 7°37′ S, 15°4′ E 218
Uíge, adm. division, *Angola* 7°15′ S, 14°43′ E 218
Uijeongbu, *S. Korea* 37°43′ N, 127°2′ E 200
Uilpata, peak, *Russ.* 42°42′ N, 43°48′ E 195
Uimaharju, *Fin.* 62°53′ N, 30°13′ E 152
Uinta Mountains, *Utah, U.S.* 40°23′ N, 110°42′ W 90
Uiseong, *S. Korea* 36°19′ N, 128°42′ E 200
Uitenhage, *S. Af.* 33°46′ S, 25°25′ E 220
Uithuizen, *Neth.* 53°24′ N, 6°40′ E 163
Újfehértó, *Hung.* 47°47′ N, 21°41′ E 168
Uji, *Japan* 34°51′ N, 135°51′ E 201
Ujiie, *Japan* 36°40′ N, 139°58′ E 201
Ujiji, *Tanzania* 4°57′ S, 29°40′ E 224
Ujjain, *India* 23°10′ N, 75°47′ E 197
Újszász, *Hung.* 47°17′ N, 20°5′ E 168
Ujung Kulon National Park, *Indian Ocean* 7°5′ S, 104°54′ E 172
Ujung Pandang see Makassar, *Indonesia* 5°11′ S, 119°25′ E 192
Uka, *Russ.* 57°50′ N, 161°48′ E 160
Ukhiya, *Bangladesh* 21°16′ N, 92°7′ E 188
Ukhrul, *India* 25°9′ N, 94°22′ E 188
Ukhta, *Russ.* 63°31′ N, 53°44′ E 169
Ukhvala, *Belarus* 54°5′ N, 29°16′ E 166
Ukia, *Tanzania* 7°43′ S, 31°46′ E 224
Ukiah, *Calif., U.S.* 39°8′ N, 123°14′ W 90
Ukkusiksalik National Park, *Can.* 65°25′ N, 90°48′ W 107
Ukmergė, *Lith.* 55°15′ N, 24°43′ E 166
Ukraine 49°12′ N, 31°23′ E 158
Uktym, *Russ.* 62°38′ N, 49°0′ E 154
Uku, *Angola* 11°27′ S, 14°19′ E 220
Ukulahu, island, *Maldives* 4°11′ N, 71°57′ E 188
Ukuma, *Angola* 12°53′ S, 15°2′ E 220
Ukwaa, *Sudan* 6°41′ N, 34°37′ E 224
Ula, *Turk.* 37°5′ N, 28°24′ E 156
Ulaanbaatar (Ulan Bator), *Mongolia* 47°56′ N, 106°41′ E 198
Ulaangom, *Mongolia* 49°57′ N, 92°3′ E 184
Ulaanjirem, *Mongolia* 45°5′ N, 105°45′ E 190
Ulaan-Uul, *Mongolia* 44°8′ N, 111°15′ E 198
Ulaga, *Russ.* 66°15′ N, 131°36′ E 160
Ulan, *China* 36°55′ N, 98°27′ E 188
Ulan Bator see Ulaanbaatar, *Mongolia* 47°56′ N, 106°41′ E 198
Ulan Erge, *Russ.* 46°15′ N, 44°51′ E 158
Ulan Khol, *Russ.* 45°25′ N, 46°48′ E 158
Ulan Ude, *Russ.* 51°54′ N, 107°30′ E 190
Ulan Ul Hu, lake, *China* 34°51′ N, 89°56′ E 188
Ulanbol, *Kaz.* 44°45′ N, 71°9′ E 184
Ulang, river, *Nicar.* 14°37′ N, 83°51′ W 115
Ulanhot, *China* 46°5′ N, 122°5′ E 198
Ulaş, *Turk.* 39°25′ N, 37°2′ E 156
Ulaya, *Tanzania* 7°3′ S, 36°55′ E 224
Ülbi, *Kaz.* 50°16′ N, 83°23′ E 184
Ulbio, *Braz.* 10°20′ S, 70°24′ W 137
Ulcinj, *Mont.* 41°55′ N, 19°12′ E 168
Uldz, *Mongolia* 48°38′ N, 112°2′ E 198
Uldz, river, *Mongolia* 49°24′ N, 113°23′ E 198
Uleåborg see Oulu, *Fin.* 65°0′ N, 25°25′ E 152
Ulen, *Minn., U.S.* 47°3′ N, 96°17′ W 90
Ulfborg, *Den.* 56°16′ N, 8°17′ E 150
Uliastay, *Mongolia* 47°48′ N, 96°47′ E 190
Ulindi, river, *Dem. Rep. of the Congo* 1°43′ S, 26°5′ E 224
Ulithi Atoll, *F.S.M.* 9°6′ N, 138°40′ E 192
Uljin, *S. Korea* 36°59′ N, 129°24′ E 200
Uljma, *Serb.* 45°2′ N, 21°10′ E 168
Ülken, *Kaz.* 45°12′ N, 73°57′ E 184
Ülken Borsyq Qumy, *Kaz.* 46°18′ N, 58°51′ E 184
Ülkennaryn, *Kaz.* 49°13′ N, 84°31′ E 184
Ulla, *Belarus* 55°12′ N, 29°15′ E 166
Ullared, *Nor.* 57°9′ N, 12°42′ E 152
Ulldecona, *Sp.* 40°35′ N, 0°26′ E 164
Ulleung, *S. Korea* 37°31′ N, 130°55′ E 200
Ulloma, *Bol.* 17°37′ S, 68°29′ W 137
Ullswater, lake, *U.K.* 54°34′ N, 2°59′ W 162
Ulm, *Ger.* 48°24′ N, 9°59′ E 152
Ulmen, *Ger.* 50°12′ N, 6°59′ E 163
Ulmeni, *Rom.* 47°27′ N, 23°19′ E 168
Ulmer, Mount, peak, *Antarctica* 77°32′ S, 87°5′ W 248
Ulog, *Bosn. and Herzg.* 43°24′ N, 18°17′ E 168
Ulrichstein, *Ger.* 50°34′ N, 9°12′ E 167
Ulsan, *S. Korea* 35°33′ N, 129°21′ E 200
Ulsteinvik, *Nor.* 62°20′ N, 5°52′ E 152
Ulu Dağ (Olympus, Mount), peak, *Turk.* 40°4′ N, 29°7′ E 156
Ulubat Gölü, lake, *Turk.* 40°4′ N, 28°7′ E 156
Uluborlu, *Turk.* 38°5′ N, 30°28′ E 156
Ulugan Bay 10°1′ N, 118°25′ E 203
Ulugqat, *China* 39°49′ N, 74°21′ E 197
Uluguru Mountains, *Tanzania* 7°28′ S, 37°2′ E 224
Ulukışla, *Turk.* 37°32′ N, 34°28′ E 156
Ulul, island, *F.S.M.* 8°19′ N, 149°8′ E 192
Ulundi, *S. Af.* 28°17′ S, 31°33′ E 227
Ulungur Hu, lake, *China* 47°14′ N, 86°46′ E 184
Ulungur, river, *China* 46°35′ N, 87°38′ E 184
Ulupō Heiau, site, *Hawai'i, U.S.* 21°22′ N, 157°47′ W 99
Uluru (Ayers Rock), peak, *Austral.* 25°23′ S, 130°52′ E 230
Ulus, *Turk.* 41°36′ N, 32°38′ E 158
Uluyul, river, *Russ.* 57°34′ N, 85°49′ E 169
Ulverston, *U.K.* 54°12′ N, 3°6′ W 162
Ulvöhamn, *Sw.* 63°0′ N, 18°38′ E 152
Ulvvik, *Nor.* 62°40′ N, 17°50′ E 152
Uly Balkan Gershi, *Turkm.* 39°30′ N, 54°0′ E 180
Ul'ya, *Russ.* 58°57′ N, 141°46′ E 160
Ul'yanovka, *Russ.* 59°38′ N, 30°46′ E 166
Ul'yanovsk, *Russ.* 54°19′ N, 48°24′ E 154
Ul'Yanovsk, adm. division, *Russ.* 53°58′ N, 46°12′ E 154
Ül'yanovskīy, *Kaz.* 50°4′ N, 73°47′ E 184
Ulysses, *Kans., U.S.* 37°34′ N, 101°22′ W 90
Ülytaū, *Kaz.* 48°25′ N, 66°48′ E 184
Ulyzhylanshyq, river, *Kaz.* 49°32′ N, 64°32′ E 184
Umag, *Croatia* 45°25′ N, 13°32′ E 167
Umala, *Bol.* 17°22′ S, 67°59′ W 137
Umán, *Mex.* 20°51′ N, 89°46′ W 116
Uman', *Ukr.* 48°44′ N, 30°23′ E 158
Umaria, *India* 23°30′ N, 80°50′ E 197
Umarkot, *Pak.* 25°22′ N, 69°44′ E 186
Umasi La, pass, *India* 33°26′ N, 76°36′ E 186
Umatilla, *Oreg., U.S.* 45°53′ N, 119°22′ W 90
Umb Ozero, lake, *Russ.* 67°35′ N, 34°0′ E 152
Umba, *Russ.* 66°40′ N, 34°16′ E 152
Umbelasha, river, *Sudan* 9°29′ N, 24°3′ E 224
Umberto Primo, *Arg.* 30°54′ S, 61°21′ W 139
Umboi, island, *P.N.G.* 5°59′ S, 147°5′ E 192
Umbria, adm. division, *It.* 42°41′ N, 11°58′ E 156
Umbukta, *Nor.* 66°9′ N, 14°35′ E 152
Umčari, *Serb.* 44°34′ N, 20°44′ E 168
Umeå, *Nor.* 63°49′ N, 20°15′ E 152
Umfors, *Nor.* 65°57′ N, 15°2′ E 152
Umm al 'Abīd, *Lib.* 27°30′ N, 15°1′ E 216
Umm al Arānib, *Lib.* 26°9′ N, 14°45′ E 216
Umm al Qaywayn, *U.A.E.* 25°33′ N, 55°33′ E 196
Umm az Zumūl, spring, *Saudi Arabia* 22°36′ N, 55°20′ E 182
Umm Badr, spring, *Sudan* 14°10′ N, 27°56′ E 226
Umm Bel, *Sudan* 13°31′ N, 28°3′ E 226
Umm Buru, spring, *Sudan* 15°1′ N, 23°45′ E 226
Umm Busha, *Sudan* 13°25′ N, 30°35′ E 226
Umm Dam, *Sudan* 13°46′ N, 30°58′ E 226
Umm Gudair, oil field, *Kuwait* 28°49′ N, 47°39′ E 196
Umm Hagar, *Eritrea* 14°16′ N, 36°37′ E 182
Umm Haraz, *Sudan* 11°57′ N, 23°10′ E 216
Umm Keddada, *Sudan* 13°35′ N, 26°39′ E 226

Umm Lahai, spring, *Sudan* 15°38' N, 25°50' E 226
Umm Lajj, *Saudi Arabia* 25°4' N, 37°15' E 182
Umm Qaşr, *Iraq* 30°2' N, 47°55' E 196
Umm Qays, *Jordan* 32°39' N, 35°40' E 194
Umm Qozein, spring, *Sudan* 14°15' N, 27°16' E 226
Umm Rahau, *Sudan* 18°53' N, 32°0' E 182
Umm Ruwaba, *Sudan* 12°52' N, 31°11' E 216
Umm Sa'īd, *Qatar* 24°58' N, 51°33' E 196
Umm Saiyala, *Sudan* 14°24' N, 31°9' E 226
Umm Shalil, *Sudan* 10°50' N, 23°41' E 224
Umm Shanqa, *Sudan* 13°12' N, 27°11' E 226
Umm Urūmah, island, *Saudi Arabia* 25°48' N, 35°31' E 182
Umniati, *Zimb.* 18°41' S, 29°46' E 224
Umpulo, *Angola* 12°43' S, 17°39' E 220
Umreth, *India* 22°38' N, 73°5' E 186
Umtanum Ridge, *Wash., U.S.* 46°50' N, 120°53' W 90
Umtata, *S. Af.* 31°35' S, 28°41' E 227
Umuahia, *Nig.* 5°33' N, 7°30' E 222
Umuarama, *Braz.* 23°47' S, 53°27' W 138
Umzimkulu, *S. Af.* 30°16' S, 29°58' E 227
Umzimvubu, *S. Af.* 31°31' S, 29°24' E 207
Umzinto, *S. Af.* 30°19' S, 30°36' E 227
Una, *Russ.* 64°36' N, 38°5' E 154
Una, river, *Bosn. and Herzg.* 44°39' N, 16°0' E 168
Unac, river, *Bosn. and Herzg.* 44°22' N, 16°24' E 168
Unadilla, *Ga., U.S.* 32°15' N, 83°45' W 96
Unaí, *Braz.* 16°24' S, 46°54' W 138
Unalakleet, *Alas., U.S.* 63°50' N, 160°39' W 106
Unalaska, *Alas., U.S.* 53°51' N, 166°33' W 238
Unalaska Island, *Alas., U.S.* 53°58' N, 168°29' W 98
Unango, *Mozambique* 12°52' S, 35°25' E 224
Unari, *Fin.* 67°8' N, 25°42' E 152
'Unayzah, *Jordan* 30°28' N, 35°47' E 194
'Unayzah, *Saudi Arabia* 26°5' N, 43°59' E 182
'Unayzah, Jabal, peak, *Iraq* 32°9' N, 39°13' E 180
Uncastillo, *Sp.* 42°21' N, 1°8' W 164
Uncasville, *Conn., U.S.* 41°25' N, 72°7' W 104
Uncía, *Bol.* 18°29' S, 66°39' W 137
Uncompahgre Peak, *Colo., U.S.* 38°3' N, 107°32' W 90
Underberg, *S. Af.* 29°49' S, 29°30' E 227
Underhill, *Vt., U.S.* 44°31' N, 72°57' W 104
Underwood, *N. Dak., U.S.* 47°26' N, 101°9' W 90
Ŭndŏk, *N. Korea* 42°32' N, 130°19' E 200
Unduksa, *Russ.* 65°39' N, 34°4' E 152
Unecha, *Russ.* 52°49' N, 32°44' E 154
Uneiuxi, river, *Braz.* 1°8' S, 66°18' W 136
Ungava Bay 59°10' N, 68°2' W 106
Unggi, *N. Korea* 42°29' N, 130°25' E 190
Unggok, *S. Korea* 34°36' N, 126°2' E 200
Unhŭng, *N. Korea* 41°17' N, 128°31' E 200
União, *Braz.* 4°36' S, 42°52' W 132
União, *Braz.* 9°18' S, 70°58' W 137
União da Vitória, *Braz.* 26°15' S, 51°8' W 139
Unicoi, *Tenn., U.S.* 36°11' N, 82°21' W 96
Unimak Island, *Alas., U.S.* 55°1' N, 164°53' W 98
Union, *La., U.S.* 30°4' N, 90°54' W 103
Union, *Miss., U.S.* 32°34' N, 89°7' W 103
Union, *N.H., U.S.* 43°29' N, 71°3' W 104
Union, *Oreg., U.S.* 45°12' N, 117°52' W 90
Union, *S.C., U.S.* 34°42' N, 81°38' W 96
Union, *Wash., U.S.* 47°19' N, 123°6' W 100
Union Bay, *Can.* 49°34' N, 124°54' W 100
Union City, *Ind., U.S.* 40°11' N, 84°49' W 102
Union City, *Mich., U.S.* 42°4' N, 85°8' W 102
Union City, *Tenn., U.S.* 36°24' N, 89°3' W 96
Unión de Tula, *Mex.* 19°56' N, 104°17' W 114
Union Grove, *Wis., U.S.* 42°41' N, 88°4' W 102
Union, islands, *Caribbean Sea* 12°47' N, 61°42' W 116
Union Pass, *Wyo., U.S.* 43°28' N, 109°51' W 90
Union Springs, *Ala., U.S.* 32°8' N, 85°43' W 96
Uniondale, *S. Af.* 33°40' S, 23°6' E 227
Uniontown, *Ala., U.S.* 32°27' N, 87°32' W 103
Uniontown, *Pa., U.S.* 39°54' N, 79°45' W 94
Unionville, *Mich., U.S.* 43°38' N, 83°28' W 102
United Arab Emirates 24°7' N, 54°35' E 196
United Kingdom 51°54' N, 2°36' W 150
United States 39°40' N, 101°22' W 82
United States Naval Base Guantánamo Bay, *Cuba* 19°53' N, 75°14' W 115
Unity, *Can.* 52°26' N, 109°10' W 108
Unity, adm. division, *Sudan* 8°46' N, 29°13' E 224
Universales, Montes, *Sp.* 40°18' N, 1°37' W 164
University Park, *Iowa, U.S.* 41°16' N, 92°36' W 94
Unknown Lake, *Can.* 58°19' N, 105°10' W 108
Unna, *Ger.* 51°32' N, 7°41' E 167
Unnao, *India* 26°32' N, 80°29' E 197
Ŭnnyul, *N. Korea* 38°29' N, 125°12' E 200
Unsan, *N. Korea* 40°5' N, 125°52' E 200
Unuk, river, *Can.* 56°12' N, 131°1' W 108
Ünye, *Turk.* 41°7' N, 37°16' E 156
Unzen-Amakusa National Park, *Japan* 32°27' N, 130°11' E 201
Unzha, *Russ.* 58°0' N, 44°2' E 154
Uozu, *Japan* 36°49' N, 137°24' E 201
Upemba National Park, *Dem. Rep. of the Congo* 9°6' S, 25°37' E 224
Upernavik 72°49' N, 56°14' W 106
Upernavik Kujalleq 72°9' N, 55°36' W 106
Upham, *N. Dak., U.S.* 48°34' N, 100°45' W 90
Upía, river, *Col.* 4°38' N, 73°10' W 136
Upington, *S. Af.* 28°25' S, 21°13' E 227
Upland, *Calif., U.S.* 34°5' N, 117°40' W 101
Upoloksha, *Russ.* 67°32' N, 31°56' E 152
Upolu, island, *Samoa* 13°56' S, 171°50' W 241
Upper Arlington, *Ohio, U.S.* 40°0' N, 83°3' W 102
Upper Delaware Scenic and Recreational River, *N.Y., U.S.* 41°45' N, 82°49' W 80
Upper Foster Lake, lake, *Can.* 56°48' N, 105°45' W 108
Upper Goose Lake, lake, *Can.* 51°42' N, 93°24' W 110
Upper Laberge, *Can.* 60°57' N, 135°7' W 98
Upper Lake, *Calif., U.S.* 41°45' N, 120°35' W 90
Upper Liard, *Can.* 60°3' N, 128°59' W 108
Upper Missouri River Breaks National Monument, *Mont., U.S.* 47°43' N, 110°27' W 90
Upper Nile, adm. division, *Sudan* 11°36' N, 32°24' E 182
Upper Roslyn Lake, lake, *Can.* 49°14' N, 88°9' W 94
Upper Sandusky, *Ohio, U.S.* 40°48' N, 83°18' W 102
Uppingham, *U.K.* 52°35' N, 0°44' E 162
Upplands Väsby, *Sw.* 59°31' N, 17°52' E 166
Uppsala, *Sw.* 59°51' N, 17°38' E 166
Uprang, *China* 36°36' N, 75°56' E 186
Upstart Bay 19°49' S, 146°34' E 230
Upton, *Wyo., U.S.* 44°5' N, 104°37' W 90
Uqturpan see Wushi, *China* 41°9' N, 79°17' E 184
Urabá, Golfo de 8°18' N, 77°25' W 136
Urad Houqi, *China* 41°30' N, 107°3' E 198
Urad Qianqi, *China* 40°41' N, 108°38' E 198
Urad Zhongqi, *China* 41°33' N, 108°33' E 198
Ural Mountains, *Russ.* 63°37' N, 58°26' E 154
Ural, river, *Kaz.-Russ.* 52°59' N, 58°53' E 154
Urambo, *Tanzania* 5°3' S, 32°4' E 224
Urandi, *Braz.* 14°48' S, 42°40' W 138
Urania, *La., U.S.* 31°51' N, 92°18' W 103
Uranium City, *Can.* 59°33' N, 108°42' W 106
Uraricoera, *Braz.* 3°27' N, 61°1' W 130
Uravan, *Colo., U.S.* 38°23' N, 108°44' W 90
Urawa, *Japan* 35°51' N, 139°39' E 201
Uray, *Russ.* 60°6' N, 65°2' E 169
'Uray'irah, *Saudi Arabia* 25°56' N, 48°53' E 182
Urbana, *Ark., U.S.* 33°8' N, 92°27' W 103
Urbana, *Ill., U.S.* 40°5' N, 88°13' W 102
Urbana, *Ohio, U.S.* 40°6' N, 83°45' W 102
Urbandale, *Iowa, U.S.* 41°37' N, 93°43' W 94
Urbania, *It.* 43°40' N, 12°32' E 156
Urbano Santos, *Braz.* 3°13' S, 43°25' W 132
Urbel, river, *Sp.* 42°40' N, 3°57' W 164
Urbino, *It.* 43°43' N, 12°38' E 167
Urbión, Picos de, *Sp.* 42°5' N, 2°58' W 164
Urcos, *Peru* 13°45' S, 71°40' W 137
Urda, *Sp.* 39°24' N, 3°43' W 164
Urdos, *Fr.* 42°52' N, 0°33' E 164
Ure, river, *U.K.* 54°16' N, 1°49' W 162
Urechcha, *Belarus* 52°56' N, 27°51' E 152
Ureliki, *Russ.* 64°24' N, 173°17' W 98
Uren', *Russ.* 57°27' N, 45°51' E 154
Urengoy, *Russ.* 65°54' N, 78°30' E 169
Urenui, *N.Z.* 39°1' S, 174°26' E 240
Ures, *Mex.* 29°25' N, 110°24' W 92
Urgut, *Uzb.* 39°22' N, 67°18' E 197
Uri, *India* 34°3' N, 74°4' E 188
Uriah, *Ala., U.S.* 31°17' N, 87°30' W 103
Uriah, Mount, peak, *N.Z.* 42°3' S, 171°33' E 240
Uribe, *Col.* 3°13' N, 74°25' W 136
Uribia, *Col.* 11°41' N, 72°17' W 136
Urimán, *Venez.* 5°23' N, 62°43' W 130
Uriondo, *Bol.* 21°42' S, 64°46' W 137
Urique, river, *Mex.* 27°18' N, 107°56' W 80
Uritsk, *Russ.* 59°49' N, 30°8' E 166
Urjala, *Fin.* 61°4' N, 23°31' E 166
Urk, *Neth.* 52°40' N, 5°35' E 163
Úrkút, *Hung.* 47°4' N, 17°38' E 168
Urkut, *Somalia* 3°29' N, 42°44' E 218
Urla, *Turk.* 38°18' N, 26°44' E 156
Urman, *Russ.* 54°53' N, 56°56' E 154
Urmia, Lake see Orūmīyeh, Daryācheh-ye, *Iran* 38°7' N, 45°16' E 195
Urmia see Orūmīyeh, *Iran* 37°37' N, 45°4' E 195
Uroševac see Ferizaj, *Kosovo* 42°22' N, 21°9' E 168
Ŭroteppa see Istaravshan, *Taj.* 39°53' N, 69°0' E 197
Urroz, *Sp.* 42°46' N, 1°29' W 164
Ursus, *Pol.* 52°11' N, 20°50' E 152
Urszulin, *Pol.* 51°23' N, 23°11' E 152
Urt Moron, river, *China* 37°3' N, 93°7' E 188
Uruaçu, *Braz.* 14°33' S, 49°12' W 138
Uruana, *Braz.* 15°33' S, 49°41' W 138
Uruapan, *Mex.* 19°24' N, 102°4' W 114
Urubamba, *Peru* 13°19' S, 72°8' W 130
Urubamba, river, *Peru* 10°42' S, 73°24' W 137
Urubaxi, river, *Braz.* 1°30' S, 64°53' W 130
Urubuquara, Serra, peak, *Braz.* 3°34' S, 52°27' W 130
Uruçanga, *Braz.* 28°32' S, 49°19' W 138
Urucará, *Braz.* 2°31' S, 57°46' W 130
Urucu, river, *Braz.* 4°18' S, 64°15' W 130
Uruçuí, *Braz.* 7°17' S, 44°34' W 132
Uruçuí, Serra do, *Braz.* 9°25' S, 45°41' W 130
Urucuia, *Braz.* 16°8' S, 45°45' W 138
Urucuia, river, *Braz.* 15°33' S, 46°47' W 138
Urucurituba, *Braz.* 2°40' S, 57°39' W 130
Urugi, *Japan* 35°17' N, 137°44' E 201
Uruguai, river, *Braz.* 27°14' S, 54°6' W 139
Uruguaiana, *Braz.* 29°48' S, 57°5' W 139
Uruguay 32°54' S, 55°57' W 139
Uruguay, river, *South America* 27°36' S, 55°4' W 134
Urukthapel see Ngeruktabel, island, *Palau* 7°13' N, 134°24' E 242
Ürümqi, *China* 43°46' N, 87°37' E 184
Urung, *Indonesia* 2°39' N, 96°4' E 196
Urup, island, *Russ.* 45°21' N, 148°49' E 190
Urupá, river, *Braz.* 11°13' S, 62°43' W 130
Urussu, *Russ.* 54°37' N, 53°25' E 154
Urutaí, *Braz.* 17°29' S, 48°11' W 138
Uruti, *N.Z.* 38°59' S, 174°32' E 240
Uruwira, *Tanzania* 6°24' S, 31°22' E 224
Urville, Tanjung d', *Indonesia* 1°31' S, 137°53' E 192
Uryupinsk, *Russ.* 50°47' N, 41°57' E 158
Ürzhar, *Kaz.* 47°4' N, 81°35' E 184
Urzhum, *Russ.* 57°8' N, 50°1' E 154
Us Nuur, Har, lake, *Mongolia* 48°7' N, 91°1' E 190
Usa, *Japan* 33°28' N, 133°26' E 201
Usa, river, *Russ.* 66°8' N, 58°13' E 160
Uşak, *Turk.* 38°40' N, 29°24' E 156
Usakos, *Namibia* 22°2' S, 15°36' E 227
Usambara Mountains, peak, *Tanzania* 4°33' S, 38°15' E 224
Usarp Mountains, *Antarctica* 71°32' S, 161°30' E 248
Ušće, *Serb.* 43°27' N, 20°37' E 168
Used, *Sp.* 41°3' N, 1°33' W 164
Useko, *Tanzania* 5°6' S, 32°33' E 224
Ushachy, *Belarus* 55°10' N, 28°33' E 166
Ushakova, Ostrov, island, *Russ.* 80°20' N, 74°7' E 160
Üsharal, *Kaz.* 46°11' N, 80°54' E 184
'Ushayrah, *Saudi Arabia* 21°43' N, 40°39' E 182
Ushetu, *Tanzania* 4°10' S, 32°16' E 224
Ushibuka, *Japan* 32°12' N, 130°1' E 201
Üshtöbe, *Kaz.* 45°14' N, 77°58' E 184
Ushuaia, *Arg.* 54°43' S, 68°18' W 134
Ushumun, *Russ.* 52°45' N, 126°37' E 190
Usinge, *Tanzania* 5°6' S, 31°16' E 224
Usingen, *Ger.* 50°19' N, 8°32' E 167
Usinsk, *Russ.* 65°58' N, 57°27' E 154
Usk, *Can.* 54°38' N, 128°27' W 108
Usk, river, *U.K.* 51°54' N, 3°17' W 162
Uska, *India* 27°11' N, 83°5' E 197
Uskoplje see Gornji Vakuf, *Bosn. and Herzg.* 43°55' N, 17°33' E 168
Üsküdar, *Turk.* 41°1' N, 29°1' E 156
Uslar, *Ger.* 51°39' N, 9°38' E 167
Usman', *Russ.* 52°0' N, 39°36' E 158
Usmas Ezers, lake, *Latv.* 57°10' N, 21°57' E 166
Usogorsk, *Russ.* 63°25' N, 48°43' E 154
Usol'ye, *Russ.* 59°25' N, 56°35' E 154
Usol'ye Sibirskoye, *Russ.* 52°47' N, 103°33' E 173
Usove, *Ukr.* 51°20' N, 28°5' E 152
Üspenka, *Kaz.* 52°54' N, 77°22' E 184
Uspenovka, *Kaz.* 43°12' N, 74°29' E 184
U.S.S. Arizona Memorial, *Pacific Ocean* 21°21' N, 158°0' W 99
Usson, *Fr.* 42°44' N, 2°5' E 164
Ussuriysk, *Russ.* 43°53' N, 132°4' E 190
Ust' Alekseyevo, *Russ.* 60°28' N, 46°31' E 154
Ust' Baikha, *Russ.* 65°48' N, 86°14' E 169
Ust' Barguzin, *Russ.* 53°29' N, 109°8' E 190
Ust' Bol'sheretsk, *Russ.* 52°58' N, 156°14' E 160
Ust' Buzulukskaya, *Russ.* 50°7' N, 42°5' E 158
Ust' Chaun, *Russ.* 68°42' N, 170°21' E 160
Ust' Chernaya, *Russ.* 60°27' N, 52°41' E 154
Ust' Ilimsk, *Russ.* 57°46' N, 102°17' E 160
Ust' Ilych, *Russ.* 62°31' N, 56°48' E 154
Ust' Ishim, *Russ.* 57°35' N, 71°1' E 160
Ust' Izes, *Russ.* 55°57' N, 76°55' E 184
Ust' Izhma, *Russ.* 65°17' N, 52°58' E 154
Ust' Kalmanka, *Russ.* 52°7' N, 83°28' E 184
Ust' Kamchatsk, *Russ.* 56°18' N, 162°17' E 160
Ust' Kamenogorsk see Öskemen, *Kaz.* 49°59' N, 82°38' E 184
Ust' Kan, *Russ.* 51°2' N, 84°50' E 184
Ust' Kara, *Russ.* 69°11' N, 65°7' E 169
Ust' Katav, *Russ.* 54°56' N, 58°14' E 154
Ust' Khayryuzovo, *Russ.* 57°10' N, 156°50' E 160
Ust' Kosa, *Russ.* 60°12' N, 55°15' E 154
Ust' Kozha, *Russ.* 63°37' N, 38°43' E 154
Ust' Kulom, *Russ.* 61°41' N, 53°46' E 154
Ust' Kurenga, *Russ.* 57°26' N, 75°32' E 169
Ust' Kureyka, *Russ.* 66°25' N, 87°23' E 169
Ust' Kut, *Russ.* 56°55' N, 105°58' E 160
Ust' Kuyga, *Russ.* 70°5' N, 135°32' E 160
Ust' Labinsk, *Russ.* 45°15' N, 39°39' E 158
Ust' Luga, *Russ.* 59°38' N, 28°14' E 166
Ust' Lyzha, *Russ.* 65°42' N, 56°38' E 154
Ust' Maya, *Russ.* 60°29' N, 134°29' E 160
Ust' Mil', *Russ.* 59°45' N, 132°55' E 160
Ust' Nem, *Russ.* 61°38' N, 54°48' E 154
Ust' Nera, *Russ.* 64°31' N, 143°13' E 160
Ust' Nyukzha, *Russ.* 56°25' N, 121°35' E 160
Ust' Olenek, *Russ.* 72°53' N, 119°39' E 160
Ust' Ordynskiy, *Russ.* 52°51' N, 104°47' E 190
Ust' Ordynskiy Buryat, adm. division, *Russ.* 53°23' N, 102°46' E 160
Ust' Ozernoye, *Russ.* 58°53' N, 87°48' E 169
Ust' Paden'ga, *Russ.* 61°51' N, 42°37' E 154
Ust' Pinega, *Russ.* 64°10' N, 42°2' E 154
Ust' Pit, *Russ.* 58°59' N, 91°53' E 169
Ust' Port, *Russ.* 69°44' N, 84°25' E 169
Ust' Shchugor, *Russ.* 64°18' N, 57°30' E 154
Ust' Shonosha, *Russ.* 61°11' N, 41°16' E 154
Ust' Tara, *Russ.* 56°40' N, 74°46' E 169
Ust' Tareya, *Russ.* 73°22' N, 90°50' E 160
Ust' Tigil', *Russ.* 57°56' N, 158°12' E 173
Ust' Tsil'ma, *Russ.* 65°26' N, 52°11' E 154
Ust' Ulagan, *Russ.* 50°41' N, 87°57' E 184
Ust' Uls, *Russ.* 60°35' N, 58°28' E 154
Ust' Un'ya, *Russ.* 61°49' N, 57°51' E 154
Ust' Ura, *Russ.* 63°7' N, 44°48' E 154
Ust' Usa, *Russ.* 65°59' N, 56°59' E 154
Ust' Vayen'ga, *Russ.* 63°0' N, 42°44' E 154
Ust' Voya, *Russ.* 64°28' N, 57°37' E 154
Ust' Voyampolka, *Russ.* 58°30' N, 159°20' E 160
Ust' Vym', *Russ.* 62°15' N, 50°25' E 154
Ust' Yegralyaga, *Russ.* 62°27' N, 59°4' E 154
Ust' Yudoma, *Russ.* 59°14' N, 135°9' E 160
Ustaoset, *Nor.* 60°30' N, 8°0' E 152
Ust'-Dolyssy, *Russ.* 56°9' N, 29°42' E 166
Ústecký, adm. division, *Czech Rep.* 50°30' N, 13°50' E 152
Ústí nad Labem, *Czech Rep.* 50°39' N, 14°2' E 152
Ustica, *It.* 38°42' N, 13°11' E 156
Ustiprača, *Bosn. and Herzg.* 43°42' N, 19°6' E 168
Ustrem, *Russ.* 64°18' N, 65°28' E 169
Ust'ye, *Russ.* 59°38' N, 39°40' E 154
Ustyluh, *Ukr.* 50°51' N, 24°9' E 158
Ustyurt Plateau, *Uzb.* 42°38' N, 55°45' E 158
Ustyuzhna, *Russ.* 58°49' N, 36°29' E 154
Usu, *China* 44°27' N, 84°41' E 184
Usuki, *Japan* 33°7' N, 131°47' E 201
Usure, *Tanzania* 4°39' S, 34°19' E 224
Us'va, *Russ.* 58°41' N, 57°39' E 154
Usvyaty, *Russ.* 55°44' N, 30°49' E 154
Utah, adm. division, *Utah, U.S.* 39°29' N, 112°5' W 92
Utah Beach, *Fr.* 49°24' N, 1°36' W 150
Utajärvi, *Fin.* 64°44' N, 26°23' E 152
'Utaybah, *Syr.* 33°29' N, 36°36' E 194
Utegi, *Tanzania* 1°23' S, 34°13' E 224
Utembo, river, *Angola* 16°30' S, 21°27' E 220
Utena, *Lith.* 55°29' N, 25°35' E 166
Utete, *Tanzania* 8°0' S, 38°46' E 224
Uthai Thani, *Thai.* 15°21' N, 100°2' E 202
Uthal, *Pak.* 25°45' N, 66°38' E 186
Uthina, ruin(s), *Tun.* 36°36' N, 10°5' E 156
Utiariti, *Braz.* 13°3' S, 58°21' W 130
Utica, *Ill., U.S.* 41°20' N, 89°1' W 102
Utica, *Miss., U.S.* 32°6' N, 90°38' W 103
Utica, *Mo., U.S.* 41°20' N, 89°1' W 110
Utica, *N.Y., U.S.* 43°6' N, 75°14' W 94
Utica, *Ohio, U.S.* 40°13' N, 82°26' W 102
Utica, ruin(s), *Tun.* 37°3' N, 9°57' E 156
Utiel, *Sp.* 39°34' N, 1°13' W 164
Utiku, *N.Z.* 39°47' S, 175°50' E 240
Utikuma, river, *Can.* 56°5' N, 115°18' W 108
Utila, Isla de, island, *Hond.* 16°8' N, 87°17' W 115
Utkholok, *Russ.* 57°35' N, 157°8' E 173
Uto, *Japan* 32°41' N, 130°41' E 201
Utö, island, *Sw.* 58°54' N, 18°19' E 166
Utonkon, *Nig.* 6°55' N, 8°3' E 222
Utraula, *India* 27°17' N, 82°23' E 197
Utrecht, *Neth.* 52°4' N, 5°6' E 167
Utrecht, *S. Af.* 27°40' S, 30°18' E 227
Utrera, *Sp.* 37°11' N, 5°48' W 164
Utroya, river, *Russ.* 57°8' N, 28°15' E 166
Utsunomiya, *Japan* 36°33' N, 139°52' E 201
Utta, *Russ.* 46°20' N, 45°55' E 158
Uttar Pradesh, adm. division, *India* 27°12' N, 79°59' E 197
Uttaradit, *Thai.* 17°39' N, 100°5' E 202
Uttarakhand, adm. division, *India* 29°54' N, 78°19' E 197
Uttoxeter, *U.K.* 52°53' N, 1°53' W 162
Utuado 18°15' N, 66°44' W 116
Utubulak, *China* 46°51' N, 86°26' E 184
Utukok, river, *Alas., U.S.* 69°53' N, 161°22' W 98
Uubulan, *Mongolia* 48°36' N, 101°54' E 198
Uummannaq 70°36' N, 52°9' W 106
Uummannaq, island, *Uummannaq* 62°51' N, 41°19' W 106
Uummannaq Kangerlua 70°45' N, 56°41' W 106
Uurainen, *Fin.* 62°29' N, 25°25' E 152
Uusikaarlepyy see Nykarleby, *Fin.* 63°31' N, 22°32' E 152
Uusikaupunki, *Fin.* 60°47' N, 21°24' E 166
Uva, *Russ.* 56°57' N, 52°15' E 154
Uvá, river, *Col.* 3°38' N, 70°3' W 136
Uvac, river, *Serb.* 43°33' N, 19°38' E 168
Uvalde, *Tex., U.S.* 29°11' N, 99°47' W 92
Uvarovo, *Russ.* 51°57' N, 42°9' E 158
Uvat, *Russ.* 59°4' N, 68°52' E 169
Uvel'skiy, *Russ.* 54°29' N, 61°19' E 154
Uvinza, *Tanzania* 5°4' S, 30°20' E 224
Uvira, *Dem. Rep. of the Congo* 3°27' S, 29°4' E 224
Uvs, adm. division, *Mongolia* 49°54' N, 90°12' E 184
Uvs Nuur, lake, *Mongolia* 50°29' N, 90°48' E 172
Uwajima, *Japan* 33°12' N, 132°33' E 201
'Uweinat, Jebel (Al 'Uwaynāt), peak, *Sudan* 21°51' N, 24°58' E 226
Uwi, island, *Indonesia* 1°5' N, 107°5' E 196
Uxbridge, *Mass., U.S.* 42°4' N, 71°39' W 104
Uxin Qi (Dabqig), *China* 38°24' N, 108°59' E 198
Uxmal, ruin(s), *Mex.* 20°17' N, 89°54' W 115
Uy, river, *Russ.* 54°11' N, 60°11' E 154
Uyar, *Russ.* 55°40' N, 94°17' E 160
Üydzin, *Mongolia* 44°7' N, 107°1' E 198
Uyo, *Nig.* 5°3' N, 7°56' E 222
Uyowa, *Tanzania* 4°33' S, 32°1' E 224
Uyuni, *Bol.* 20°33' S, 66°55' W 137
Uza, river, *Russ.* 52°48' N, 45°39' E 158
Užava, *Latv.* 57°14' N, 21°27' E 166
Užava, river, *Latv.* 57°8' N, 21°24' E 166
Uzbekistan 41°0' N, 63°0' E 184
Uzbel Shankou, pass, *China* 38°39' N, 73°48' E 197
Uzcudún, *Arg.* 44°13' S, 66°7' W 134
Uzdin, *Serb.* 45°12' N, 20°37' E 168
Uzhur, *Russ.* 55°21' N, 89°52' E 169
Užice, *Serb.* 43°51' N, 19°50' E 168
Uzlovaya, *Russ.* 53°57' N, 38°8' E 154
Üzümlü, *Turk.* 36°44' N, 29°13' E 156
Uzunköprü, *Turk.* 41°14' N, 26°39' E 156
Užventis, *Lith.* 55°46' N, 22°39' E 166
Uzynaghash, *Kaz.* 43°14' N, 76°16' E 184
Uzynköl, *Kaz.* 53°57' N, 64°52' E 184

V

Vääksy, *Fin.* 61°9' N, 25°32' E 166
Vaal, river, *S. Af.* 26°51' S, 29°39' E 227
Vaala, *Fin.* 64°33' N, 26°48' E 152
Vaals, *Neth.* 50°46' N, 6°0' E 167
Vääna, *Est.* 59°22' N, 24°23' E 166
Vaasa, *Fin.* 63°4' N, 21°42' E 160
Vaasa (Vasa), *Fin.* 63°5' N, 21°37' E 152
Vabalninkas, *Lith.* 55°58' N, 24°43' E 166
Vác, *Hung.* 47°45' N, 19°10' E 168
Vacaria, *Braz.* 28°28' S, 50°55' W 139
Vacaville, *Calif., U.S.* 38°21' N, 122°0' W 100

Vacha, *Ger.* 50°49′ N, 10°1′ E 167
Väddö, *Sw.* 60°0′ N, 18°49′ E 166
Vader, *Wash., U.S.* 46°23′ N, 122°58′ W 100
Vadheim, *Nor.* 61°12′ N, 5°49′ E 152
Vadodara, *India* 22°17′ N, 73°13′ E 186
Vadsø, *Nor.* 70°10′ N, 29°50′ E 160
Vaduz, *Liech.* 47°6′ N, 9°22′ E 156
Vaga, river, *Russ.* 61°42′ N, 42°48′ E 154
Vagan, *Bosn. and Herzg.* 44°10′ N, 17°9′ E 168
Vagay, river, *Russ.* 56°29′ N, 68°53′ E 169
Vågen, *Nor.* 64°39′ N, 13°43′ E 152
Vahdat (Kofarnihon), *Taj.* 38°32′ N, 69°1′ E 197
Vaiaku, *Tuvalu* 80°31′ S, 179°11′ E 241
Vaiden, *Miss., U.S.* 33°17′ N, 89°45′ W 103
Väike Maarja, *Est.* 59°5′ N, 26°15′ E 166
Vailly, *Fr.* 49°24′ N, 3°30′ E 163
Vainikkala, *Fin.* 60°51′ N, 28°18′ E 166
Vaiņode, *Latv.* 56°25′ N, 21°50′ E 166
Vakh, river, *Russ.* 60°45′ N, 79°42′ E 160
Vakh, river, *Russ.* 61°22′ N, 83°43′ E 169
Vakhsh, river, *Taj.* 37°50′ N, 68°58′ E 197
Vakhtan, *Russ.* 57°56′ N, 46°45′ E 154
Vál, *Hung.* 47°20′ N, 18°39′ E 168
Val Grande National Park, *It.* 45°57′ N, 8°7′ E 167
Val Marie, *Can.* 49°13′ N, 107°45′ W 90
Val Verde Park, *Calif., U.S.* 34°27′ N, 118°41′ W 101
Vala, river, *Russ.* 56°41′ N, 52°16′ E 154
Valaam, *Russ.* 61°21′ N, 30°58′ E 166
Valaichchenai, *Sri Lanka* 7°54′ N, 81°34′ E 188
Valaku, *Tuvalu* 8°31′ S, 179°11′ E 241
Valamaz, *Russ.* 57°32′ N, 52°8′ E 154
Valatie, *N.Y., U.S.* 42°24′ N, 73°41′ W 104
Valberg, *Nor.* 68°11′ N, 13°56′ E 152
Vâlcani, *Rom.* 46°0′ N, 20°23′ E 168
Valcarlos see Luzaide, *Fr.* 43°5′ N, 1°19′ W 164
Vâlcea, adm. division, *Rom.* 44°57′ N, 23°47′ E 156
Valcheta, *Arg.* 40°39′ S, 66°11′ W 134
Valday, *Russ.* 57°57′ N, 33°15′ E 154
Valdayskaya Vozvyshennost′, *Russ.* 56°12′ N, 30°12′ E 152
Valdemārpils, *Latv.* 57°21′ N, 22°34′ E 166
Valdepeñas, *Sp.* 38°45′ N, 3°23′ W 164
Valderrobres, *Sp.* 40°51′ N, 0°8′ E 164
Valders, *Wis., U.S.* 44°3′ N, 87°53′ W 102
Valdés, Península, *Arg.* 42°42′ S, 64°40′ W 134
Valdez, *Ecua.* 1°10′ N, 79°11′ W 130
Valdivia, *Chile* 39°47′ S, 73°17′ W 134
Valdivia, *Col.* 7°4′ N, 75°28′ W 136
Valdivia, *Sp.* 39°1′ N, 5°42′ W 164
Val-d'Or, *Can.* 48°7′ N, 77°48′ W 94
Valdosta, *Ga., U.S.* 30°49′ N, 83°17′ W 96
Valdres, region, *Nor.* 60°44′ N, 8°54′ E 152
Vale, *Oreg., U.S.* 43°59′ N, 117°16′ W 90
Valea lui Mihai, *Rom.* 47°31′ N, 22°8′ E 168
Valea Vişeului, *Rom.* 47°54′ N, 24°10′ E 156
Valemount, *Can.* 52°49′ N, 119°16′ W 108
Valença, *Braz.* 13°23′ S, 39°9′ W 132
Valença, *Port.* 41°56′ N, 8°40′ W 214
Valence, *Fr.* 44°56′ N, 4°55′ E 143
Valencia, *Calif., U.S.* 34°23′ N, 118°34′ W 101
Valencia, *Sp.* 39°28′ N, 0°23′ E 164
Valencia, *Venez.* 10°9′ N, 67°59′ W 136
Valencia, adm. division, *Sp.* 40°10′ N, 0°26′ E 164
Valencia, Golfo de 39°40′ N, 0°51′ E 150
Valenciennes, *Fr.* 50°20′ N, 3°32′ E 163
Valentine, *Ariz., U.S.* 35°24′ N, 113°40′ W 101
Valentine, *Nebr., U.S.* 42°50′ N, 100°34′ W 90
Valentine, *Tex., U.S.* 30°33′ N, 104°29′ W 92
Valentine, Cape, *Antarctica* 61°6′ S, 55°0′ W 134
Valenza, *It.* 45°0′ N, 8°38′ E 167
Våler, *Nor.* 60°40′ N, 11°49′ E 152
Valera, *Venez.* 9°17′ N, 70°39′ W 136
Valestrand, *Nor.* 59°40′ N, 5°26′ E 152
Valets, Lac, lake, *Can.* 48°30′ N, 76°55′ W 94
Valga, *Est.* 57°45′ N, 26°3′ E 166
Valier, *Mo., U.S.* 38°0′ N, 89°3′ W 94
Valier, *Mont., U.S.* 48°17′ N, 112°16′ W 90
Valjala, *Est.* 58°24′ N, 22°46′ E 166
Valjok, *Nor.* 69°41′ N, 25°54′ E 152
Valka, *Latv.* 57°45′ N, 25°59′ E 166
Valkeakoski, *Fin.* 61°16′ N, 23°59′ E 166
Valkenswaard, *Neth.* 51°20′ N, 5°26′ E 167
Valkyrie Dome, *Antarctica* 76°20′ S, 28°43′ E 248
Valla, *Nor.* 59°1′ N, 16°20′ E 152
Valladares, *Mex.* 26°54′ N, 100°39′ W 96
Valladolid, *Mex.* 20°41′ N, 88°13′ W 116
Valladolid, *Sp.* 41°38′ N, 4°44′ W 150
Valladolid de los Bimviles, *Equatorial Guinea* 1°50′ N, 10°42′ E 218
Vallard, Lac, lake, *Can.* 52°49′ N, 69°26′ W 111
Valle, *Nor.* 59°11′ N, 7°32′ E 152
Valle Crucis Abbey, site, *U.K.* 52°59′ N, 3°13′ W 162
Valle d'Aosta, adm. division, *It.* 45°49′ N, 7°2′ E 165
Valle de Banderas, *Mex.* 20°47′ N, 105°17′ W 114
Valle de Bravo, *Mex.* 19°9′ N, 100°8′ W 114
Valle de la Pascua, *Venez.* 9°12′ N, 66°2′ W 136
Valle de Santiago, *Mex.* 20°22′ N, 101°11′ W 114
Valle de Zaragoza, *Mex.* 27°26′ N, 105°49′ W 112
Valle del Cauca, adm. division, *Col.* 3°59′ N, 78°23′ W 130
Valle del Cauca, adm. division, *Col.* 3°38′ N, 76°58′ W 136
Valle Fértil, Sierra del, *Arg.* 30°20′ S, 68°17′ W 134
Valle Hermoso, *Mex.* 25°40′ N, 97°48′ W 114
Vallecillo, *Mex.* 26°39′ N, 99°58′ W 114
Vallecito Mountains, *Calif., U.S.* 33°5′ N, 116°22′ W 101
Valledupar, *Col.* 10°26′ N, 73°15′ W 136
Vallegrande, *Bol.* 18°32′ S, 64°12′ W 137
Vallejo, *Calif., U.S.* 38°5′ N, 122°15′ W 100
Vallendar, *Ger.* 50°24′ N, 7°37′ E 167
Valletta, *Malta* 35°52′ N, 14°23′ E 156
Valley, *Miss., U.S.* 32°45′ N, 90°30′ W 103
Valley City, *N. Dak., U.S.* 46°54′ N, 98°2′ W 90
Valley Falls, *R.I., U.S.* 41°54′ N, 71°24′ W 104
Valley Head, *Philippines* 17°53′ N, 122°13′ E 203
Valley Mills, *Tex., U.S.* 31°38′ N, 97°28′ W 92
Valley Park, *Miss., U.S.* 32°38′ N, 90°53′ W 103
Valley Pass, *Nev., U.S.* 41°8′ N, 114°26′ W 90
Valley Springs, *Calif., U.S.* 38°11′ N, 120°51′ W 100
Valleyview, *Can.* 55°3′ N, 117°19′ W 108
Vallibona, *Sp.* 40°35′ N, 6°357′ E 164
Vallo della Lucania, *It.* 40°14′ N, 15°16′ E 156
Vallorbe, *Switz.* 46°42′ N, 6°23′ E 167
Valls, *Sp.* 41°17′ N, 1°15′ E 164
Valmeyer, *Mo., U.S.* 38°16′ N, 90°19′ W 94
Valmiera, *Latv.* 57°31′ N, 25°23′ E 166
Valmy, *Fr.* 49°5′ N, 4°48′ E 163
Valozhyn, *Belarus* 54°4′ N, 26°31′ E 166
Valparaíso, *Braz.* 21°16′ S, 50°55′ W 138
Valparaíso, *Chile* 33°5′ S, 71°40′ W 134
Valparaíso, *Col.* 1°10′ N, 75°44′ W 136
Valparaiso, *Ind., U.S.* 41°27′ N, 87°3′ W 102
Valparaíso, *Mex.* 22°46′ N, 103°35′ W 114
Valparaíso, adm. division, *Chile* 33°23′ S, 71°33′ W 134
Valpovo, *Croatia* 45°38′ N, 18°24′ E 168
Vals, *Fr.* 44°40′ N, 4°21′ E 150
Vals, Tanjung, *Indonesia* 8°24′ S, 136°6′ E 192
Valsad, *India* 20°35′ N, 72°56′ E 188
Valsjöbyn, *Nor.* 64°4′ N, 14°5′ E 152
Valstagna, *It.* 45°52′ N, 11°41′ E 167
Valtimo, *Fin.* 63°39′ N, 28°48′ E 152
Valuyevka, *Russ.* 46°39′ N, 43°40′ E 158
Valuyki, *Russ.* 50°13′ N, 38°4′ E 158
Valvær, islands, *Norwegian Sea* 66°51′ N, 11°54′ E 152
Valverde del Camino, *Sp.* 37°34′ N, 6°46′ W 164
Valyntsy, *Belarus* 55°42′ N, 28°10′ E 166
Vammala, *Fin.* 61°19′ N, 22°53′ E 166
Vámospércs, *Hung.* 47°31′ N, 21°54′ E 168
Vampula, *Fin.* 60°59′ N, 22°41′ E 166
Van, *Tex., U.S.* 32°30′ N, 95°37′ W 103
Van, *Turk.* 38°27′ N, 43°18′ E 195
Van Alstyne, *Tex., U.S.* 33°25′ N, 96°35′ W 96
Van Blommestein Meer, lake, *Suriname* 4°38′ N, 56°23′ W 130
Van Buren, *Ark., U.S.* 35°24′ N, 94°21′ W 96
Van Buren, *Ind., U.S.* 40°36′ N, 85°30′ W 102
Van Buren, *Me., U.S.* 47°8′ N, 67°57′ W 94
Van Gölü, lake, *Turk.* 38°34′ N, 42°36′ E 195
Van Hoa, *Vietnam* 21°11′ N, 107°33′ E 198
Van Horn, *Tex., U.S.* 31°1′ N, 104°51′ W 82
Van, Lake, *Turk.* 38°10′ N, 41°15′ E 206
Van Ninh, *Vietnam* 12°42′ N, 109°12′ E 202
Van Tassell, *Wyo., U.S.* 42°40′ N, 104°5′ W 90
Van Wert, *Ohio, U.S.* 40°51′ N, 84°36′ W 102
Van Yen, *Vietnam* 21°6′ N, 104°41′ E 202
Vanadzor, *Arm.* 40°47′ N, 44°28′ E 195
Vanaja, *Fin.* 60°58′ N, 24°29′ E 166
Vananda, *Can.* 49°44′ N, 124°32′ W 100
Vanavara, *Russ.* 60°22′ N, 102°12′ E 160
Vanceboro, *Me., U.S.* 45°33′ N, 67°28′ W 94
Vanceburg, *Ky., U.S.* 38°34′ N, 83°19′ W 102
Vancorum, *Colo., U.S.* 38°14′ N, 108°37′ W 90
Vancouver, *Can.* 49°16′ N, 123°7′ W 100
Vancouver, *Wash., U.S.* 45°37′ N, 122°41′ W 100
Vancouver Island, *Can.* 49°11′ N, 123°48′ W 100
Vandalia, *Ill., U.S.* 38°57′ N, 89°6′ W 102
Vandalia, *Ohio, U.S.* 39°52′ N, 84°12′ W 102
Vandenberg Air Force Base, *Calif., U.S.* 34°43′ N, 120°38′ W 100
Vandenberg Village, *Calif., U.S.* 34°42′ N, 120°29′ W 100
Vanderlin Island, *Austral.* 15°49′ S, 137°10′ E 230
Vändra, *Est.* 58°38′ N, 25°1′ E 166
Vandúzi, *Mozambique* 19°0′ S, 33°17′ E 224
Vandysh, *Russ.* 61°20′ N, 40°12′ E 154
Vanegas, *Mex.* 23°49′ N, 100°53′ W 114
Vänern, lake, *Sw.* 58°24′ N, 11°45′ E 160
Vang, Mount, peak, *Antarctica* 73°58′ S, 69°22′ W 248
Vanga, *Kenya* 4°38′ S, 39°12′ E 224
Vangaindrano, *Madagascar* 23°22′ S, 47°35′ E 220
Vangozero, *Russ.* 65°34′ N, 33°18′ E 152
Vanguard, *Can.* 49°54′ N, 107°18′ W 90
Vangunu, island, *Solomon Islands* 8°41′ S, 158°0′ E 242
Vangviang, *Laos* 18°56′ N, 102°27′ E 202
Vanikolo Islands, *Solomon Islands* 12°49′ S, 164°8′ E 238
Vanino, *Russ.* 49°4′ N, 140°3′ E 190
Vaniyambadi, *India* 12°40′ N, 78°37′ E 188
Vanj, *Taj.* 38°21′ N, 71°23′ E 197
Vankarem, *Russ.* 67°44′ N, 175°59′ W 98
Vännäs, *Nor.* 63°54′ N, 19°44′ E 152
Vannes, *Fr.* 47°40′ N, 2°51′ W 143
Vanoise, Massif de la, *Fr.* 45°18′ N, 6°25′ E 165
Vanrhynsdorp, *S. Af.* 31°37′ S, 18°41′ E 227
Vansbro, *Nor.* 60°29′ N, 14°9′ E 152
Vanscoy, *Can.* 52°0′ N, 106°59′ W 90
Vansittart Bay 14°4′ S, 125°1′ E 230
Vansittart Island, island, *Can.* 66°8′ N, 84°9′ W 106
Vanua Levu, island, *Fiji* 16°41′ S, 179°10′ E 242
Vanuatu 17°41′ S, 167°55′ E 243
Vanwyksvlei, *S. Af.* 30°22′ S, 21°48′ E 227
Vanzetur, *Russ.* 63°31′ N, 64°52′ E 169
Vanzevat, *Russ.* 64°15′ N, 65°15′ E 169
Vanzhil' Kynak, *Russ.* 60°23′ N, 84°17′ E 169
Vanzylsrus, *S. Af.* 26°52′ S, 22°3′ E 227
Var, river, *Fr.* 43°54′ N, 7°7′ E 165
Vara, *Nor.* 58°14′ N, 12°55′ E 152
Varades, *Fr.* 47°23′ N, 1°2′ W 150
Varakļāni, *Latv.* 56°36′ N, 26°45′ E 166
Varalé, *Côte d'Ivoire* 9°39′ N, 3°18′ W 222
Varāmīn, *Iran* 35°21′ N, 51°40′ E 180
Varanasi (Banaras), *India* 25°18′ N, 82°57′ E 197
Varangerfjorden 69°48′ N, 26°7′ E 142
Varangerhalvøya, *Nor.* 70°11′ N, 28°10′ E 152
Varapayeva, *Belarus* 55°8′ N, 27°10′ E 166
Varaždin, *Croatia* 46°19′ N, 16°20′ E 168
Varazze, *It.* 44°21′ N, 8°34′ E 167
Vardar, river, *Maced.* 41°21′ N, 22°7′ E 180
Varde, *Den.* 55°37′ N, 8°27′ E 150
Vårdö, *Fin.* 60°14′ N, 20°21′ E 166
Vardø, *Nor.* 70°20′ N, 31°16′ E 160
Varel, *Ger.* 53°23′ N, 8°9′ E 163
Varėna, *Lith.* 54°13′ N, 24°34′ E 166
Varengeville, *Fr.* 49°54′ N, 0°58′ E 163
Varennes, *Fr.* 49°13′ N, 5°0′ E 163
Vareš, *Bosn. and Herzg.* 44°10′ N, 18°18′ E 168
Varese, *It.* 45°49′ N, 8°50′ E 167
Varese, *It.* 44°22′ N, 9°37′ E 167
Vårgårda, *Nor.* 58°1′ N, 12°46′ E 152
Varginha, *Braz.* 21°35′ S, 45°27′ W 138
Varilhes, *Fr.* 43°2′ N, 1°37′ E 164
Varitino, *Russ.* 57°10′ N, 29°33′ E 166
Varkaus, *Fin.* 62°18′ N, 27°48′ E 152
Värmlandsnäs, *Nor.* 58°49′ N, 12°24′ E 152
Varna, *Bulg.* 43°12′ N, 27°55′ E 156
Varna, *Russ.* 53°26′ N, 60°48′ E 154
Varna, adm. division, *Bulg.* 42°56′ N, 27°20′ E 156
Varnado, *La., U.S.* 30°52′ N, 89°50′ W 103
Värnamo, *Nor.* 57°11′ N, 14°0′ E 152
Varnavino, *Russ.* 57°24′ N, 45°3′ E 154
Varnek, *Russ.* 69°47′ N, 60°9′ E 169
Varniai, *Lith.* 55°45′ N, 22°22′ E 166
Varonichy, *Belarus* 54°59′ N, 28°36′ E 166
Varosha 35°6′ N, 33°56′ E 194
Városl od, *Hung.* 47°8′ N, 17°39′ E 168
Várpalota, *Hung.* 47°11′ N, 18°9′ E 168
Värska, *Est.* 57°56′ N, 27°37′ E 166
Varstu, *Est.* 57°37′ N, 26°38′ E 166
Vårtejeni, *Mold.* 47°59′ N, 28°33′ E 152
Vartius, *Fin.* 64°29′ N, 29°57′ E 152
Varto, *Turk.* 39°10′ N, 41°27′ E 195
Varvarin, *Serb.* 43°43′ N, 21°21′ E 168
Várzea da Palma, *Braz.* 17°34′ S, 44°43′ W 138
Várzea Grande, *Braz.* 15°38′ S, 56°13′ W 132
Várzea, river, *Braz.* 27°27′ S, 53°7′ W 139
Varzelândia, *Braz.* 15°44′ S, 44°4′ W 138
Varzi, *It.* 44°49′ N, 9°12′ E 167
Varzino, *Russ.* 68°19′ N, 38°20′ E 169
Varzo, *It.* 46°13′ N, 8°16′ E 167
Varzob, *Taj.* 38°43′ N, 68°49′ E 197
Varzuga, *Russ.* 66°22′ N, 36°28′ E 154
Vas, adm. division, *Hung.* 47°0′ N, 16°31′ E 156
Vasa see Vaasa, *Fin.* 63°5′ N, 21°37′ E 152
Vasalemma, *Est.* 59°13′ N, 24°15′ E 166
Vaşcău, *Rom.* 46°28′ N, 22°31′ E 168
Vashka, river, *Russ.* 64°11′ N, 46°16′ E 154
Vasilevo, *Maced.* 41°29′ N, 22°37′ E 168
Vasiliko, *Cyprus* 34°43′ N, 33°17′ E 194
Vasilishki, *Belarus* 53°46′ N, 24°50′ E 152
Vasil'ki, *Russ.* 56°27′ N, 29°28′ E 166
Vasil'yevo, *Russ.* 55°49′ N, 48°45′ E 154
Vasis, *Russ.* 57°23′ N, 74°47′ E 169
Vaskelovo, *Russ.* 60°22′ N, 30°25′ E 166
Vasknarva, *Est.* 58°59′ N, 27°42′ E 166
Vaskút, *Hung.* 46°6′ N, 18°59′ E 168
Vaslui, *Rom.* 46°38′ N, 27°44′ E 156
Vaslui, adm. division, *Rom.* 46°32′ N, 27°23′ E 156
Vassar, *Mich., U.S.* 43°21′ N, 83°35′ W 102
Vassilítsa, Óros, peak, *Gr.* 40°1′ N, 21°0′ E 156
Västerås, *Nor.* 59°36′ N, 16°32′ E 152
Västervik, *Nor.* 57°44′ N, 16°36′ E 152
Vasto, *It.* 42°6′ N, 14°42′ E 156
Vasvár, *Hung.* 47°2′ N, 16°49′ E 168
Vasyl'kiv, *Ukr.* 50°12′ N, 30°27′ E 158
Vasyl'kivka, *Ukr.* 48°14′ N, 36°6′ E 158
Vasyugan, river, *Russ.* 59°10′ N, 77°11′ E 169
Vata, *Rom.* 46°11′ N, 22°37′ E 168
Vathí, *Gr.* 37°44′ N, 26°59′ E 156
Váthia, *Gr.* 36°28′ N, 22°27′ E 156
Vatican City 41°54′ N, 12°26′ E 156
Vatili 35°7′ N, 33°38′ E 194
Vatin, *Serb.* 45°13′ N, 21°17′ E 168
Vatnajökull, glacier, *Ice.* 64°28′ N, 25°0′ W 142
Vatneyri, *Ice.* 65°37′ N, 23°57′ W 143
Vatomandry, *Madagascar* 19°20′ S, 48°57′ E 220
Vatry, *Fr.* 48°48′ N, 4°14′ E 163
Vatutin, *Ukr.* 49°2′ N, 31°10′ E 158
Vaucouleurs, *Fr.* 48°36′ N, 5°39′ E 163
Vaughn, *Mont., U.S.* 47°32′ N, 111°34′ W 90
Vaupés, adm. division, *Col.* 0°39′ N, 71°23′ W 136
Vauxhall, *Can.* 50°3′ N, 112°7′ W 90
Vavincourt, *Fr.* 48°49′ N, 5°12′ E 163
Vavla, *Cyprus* 34°50′ N, 33°16′ E 194
Vavoua, *Côte d'Ivoire* 7°19′ N, 6°29′ W 222
Vavozh, *Russ.* 56°46′ N, 51°55′ E 154
Vawkavysk, *Belarus* 53°9′ N, 24°29′ E 154
Vaxholm, *Sw.* 59°23′ N, 18°18′ E 166
Växjö, *Sw.* 56°51′ N, 14°50′ E 160
Vaygach, Ostrov, island, *Russ.* 70°25′ N, 59°19′ E 169
Vazante, *Braz.* 18°2′ S, 46°56′ W 138
Vazhgort, *Russ.* 64°5′ N, 46°54′ E 154
Veazie, *Me., U.S.* 44°50′ N, 68°43′ W 94
Veblen, *S. Dak., U.S.* 45°50′ N, 97°19′ W 90
Vecāki, *Latv.* 57°4′ N, 24°6′ E 166
Vecchiano, *It.* 43°47′ N, 10°23′ E 167
Vecsés, *Hung.* 47°23′ N, 19°18′ E 168
Vedeno, *Russ.* 42°54′ N, 46°5′ E 195
Vedia, *Arg.* 34°29′ S, 61°34′ W 139
Veedersburg, *Ind., U.S.* 40°6′ N, 87°17′ W 102
Vega, *Nor.* 65°39′ N, 11°56′ E 152
Vega, *Tex., U.S.* 35°13′ N, 102°25′ W 92
Vega de Alatorre, *Mex.* 19°59′ N, 96°38′ W 114
Vega Island, *Antarctica* 63°58′ S, 57°4′ W 134
Vegesack, *Ger.* 53°10′ N, 8°38′ E 163
Veghel, *Neth.* 51°36′ N, 5°32′ E 167
Vegreville, *Can.* 53°29′ N, 112°6′ W 108
Vehmaa, *Fin.* 60°40′ N, 21°38′ E 166
Vehmasjärvi, *Fin.* 63°35′ N, 27°53′ E 152
Veines, *Nor.* 70°37′ N, 26°34′ E 152
Veio, ruin(s), *It.* 42°0′ N, 12°16′ E 156
Vejen, *Den.* 55°28′ N, 9°8′ E 152
Vejer de la Frontera, *Sp.* 36°14′ N, 5°58′ W 164
Vejle, *Den.* 55°42′ N, 9°31′ E 150
Vel', river, *Russ.* 63°42′ N, 55°26′ E 154
Vela, Cabo de la, *Col.* 12°6′ N, 72°55′ W 116
Vela Luka, *Croatia* 42°56′ N, 16°42′ E 168
Velarde, *N. Mex., U.S.* 36°9′ N, 105°58′ W 92
Velardeña, *Mex.* 25°2′ N, 103°43′ W 114
Velas, Cabo, *C.R.* 10°24′ N, 86°30′ W 115
Velasco, Sierra de, *Arg.* 28°27′ S, 67°31′ W 132
Velay, Monts du, *Fr.* 45°4′ N, 3°39′ E 165
Velázquez, *Uru.* 34°3′ S, 54°18′ W 139
Velbert, *Ger.* 51°20′ N, 7°2′ E 167
Velebit, *Croatia* 44°16′ N, 15°50′ E 168
Veles, *Maced.* 41°43′ N, 21°47′ E 168
Vélez, *Col.* 6°0′ N, 73°42′ W 136
Vélez Blanco, *Sp.* 37°41′ N, 2°5′ W 164
Velež, peak, *Bosn. and Herzg.* 43°19′ N, 17°58′ E 168
Vélez Rubio, *Sp.* 37°38′ N, 2°4′ W 164
Velhas, river, *Braz.* 18°49′ S, 44°7′ W 138
Velia, ruin(s), *It.* 40°9′ N, 15°5′ E 156
Velika, *Croatia* 45°27′ N, 17°39′ E 168
Velika Drenova, *Serb.* 43°37′ N, 21°8′ E 168
Velika Gorica, *Croatia* 45°43′ N, 16°4′ E 168
Velika Kladuša, *Bosn. and Herzg.* 45°10′ N, 15°48′ E 168
Velika Ljubuša, peak, *Bosn. and Herzg.* 43°44′ N, 17°21′ E 168
Velika Plana, *Serb.* 44°19′ N, 21°2′ E 168
Velikaya, river, *Russ.* 64°12′ N, 176°12′ E 160
Velikaya, river, *Russ.* 57°32′ N, 28°7′ E 166
Veliki Drvenik, island, *Croatia* 43°27′ N, 15°54′ E 168
Veliki Popović, *Serb.* 44°6′ N, 21°20′ E 168
Veliki Snežnik, peak, *Slov.* 45°35′ N, 14°20′ E 156
Veliki Troglav, peak, *Bosn. and Herzg.* 43°56′ N, 16°33′ E 168
Veliki Zdenci, *Croatia* 45°39′ N, 17°5′ E 168
Velikiy Novgorod, *Russ.* 58°30′ N, 31°21′ E 152
Velikiy Ustyug, *Russ.* 60°47′ N, 46°24′ E 154
Velikiye Luki, *Russ.* 56°20′ N, 30°38′ E 152
Veliko Gradište, *Serb.* 44°45′ N, 21°30′ E 168
Veliko Tŭrnovo, *Bulg.* 43°4′ N, 25°38′ E 156
Veliko Tŭrnovo, adm. division, *Bulg.* 43°17′ N, 25°17′ E 156
Velikoye Ozero, *Russ.* 62°32′ N, 37°44′ E 154
Vélingara, *Senegal* 13°9′ N, 14°9′ W 222
Vélingara, *Senegal* 15°0′ N, 14°43′ W 222
Velino, Monte, peak, *It.* 42°8′ N, 13°19′ E 156
Velizh, *Russ.* 55°35′ N, 31°13′ E 154
Velizhany, *Russ.* 57°32′ N, 65°49′ E 169
Vel'ká Ida, *Slovakia* 48°35′ N, 21°9′ E 156
Vella Lavella, island, *Solomon Islands* 7°45′ S, 156°34′ E 242
Vellberg, *Ger.* 49°5′ N, 9°52′ E 152
Vellore, *India* 12°54′ N, 79°8′ E 188
Vel'mo, river, *Russ.* 60°32′ N, 93°42′ E 169
Velp, *Neth.* 51°59′ N, 5°57′ E 167
Vels, *Russ.* 60°44′ N, 58°50′ E 154
Vel'sk, *Russ.* 61°2′ N, 42°2′ E 154
Velva, *N. Dak., U.S.* 48°1′ N, 100°58′ W 90
Vema Fracture Zone, *North Atlantic Ocean* 12°13′ N, 44°53′ W 253
Vemdalen, *Nor.* 62°26′ N, 13°49′ E 152
Venable Ice Shelf, *Antarctica* 73°35′ S, 92°3′ W 248
Venado, *Mex.* 22°54′ N, 101°6′ W 114
Venado, Isla del, island, *Nicar.* 11°52′ N, 83°41′ W 115
Venado Tuerto, *Arg.* 33°45′ S, 61°57′ W 139
Venamo, Cerro, peak, *Venez.* 5°54′ N, 61°32′ W 130
Venango, *Nebr., U.S.* 40°45′ N, 102°3′ W 90
Venaria, *It.* 45°7′ N, 7°37′ E 167
Venceslau Braz, *Braz.* 23°51′ S, 49°49′ W 138
Vendenga, *Russ.* 63°33′ N, 47°50′ E 154
Vendeuvre, *Fr.* 48°13′ N, 4°27′ E 163
Venecia, *Col.* 5°58′ N, 75°44′ W 136
Venejärvi, *Fin.* 67°15′ N, 24°13′ E 152
Veneto, adm. division, *It.* 45°41′ N, 11°27′ E 167
Venev, *Russ.* 54°21′ N, 38°18′ E 154
Venezia (Venice), *It.* 45°25′ N, 12°19′ E 167
Venezuela 7°0′ N, 66°0′ W 130
Venezuela, Golfo de 11°18′ N, 71°31′ W 136
Vengerovo, *Russ.* 55°38′ N, 76°52′ E 184
Veniaminof, Mount, peak, *Alas., U.S.* 56°11′ N, 159°26′ W 98
Venice, *Fla., U.S.* 27°6′ N, 82°25′ W 105
Venice, *La., U.S.* 29°16′ N, 89°22′ W 103
Venice, Gulf of 44°47′ N, 12°35′ E 167
Venice see Venezia, *It.* 45°25′ N, 12°19′ E 167
Venlo, *Neth.* 51°22′ N, 6°10′ E 167
Vennesund, *Nor.* 65°13′ N, 12°4′ E 152
Venray, *Neth.* 51°31′ N, 5°57′ E 167
Venta del Olivo, *Sp.* 38°19′ N, 1°29′ W 164
Venta, river, *Lith.* 55°46′ N, 22°51′ E 166
Ventana, Sierra de la, *Arg.* 38°15′ S, 62°54′ W 134
Ventavon, *Fr.* 44°22′ N, 5°54′ E 156
Ventersdorp, *S. Af.* 26°21′ S, 26°47′ E 227
Ventotene, *It.* 40°48′ N, 13°25′ E 156
Ventoux, Mont, peak, *Fr.* 44°9′ N, 5°15′ E 165
Vents, Lac des, lake, *Can.* 49°28′ N, 75°25′ W 94
Ventspils, *Latv.* 57°21′ N, 21°31′ E 166
Ventuari, river, *Venez.* 5°7′ N, 65°59′ W 136
Ventuari, river, *Venez.* 4°1′ N, 66°50′ W 136
Ventura, *Calif., U.S.* 34°17′ N, 119°19′ W 100
Venus, *Fla., U.S.* 27°4′ N, 81°22′ W 105
Venustiano Carranza, *Mex.* 16°19′ N, 92°35′ W 115
Venustiano Carranza, *Mex.* 19°45′ N, 103°46′ W 114

Venustiano Carranza, Presa, lake, Mex. 27°32' N, 101°46' W 80
Vepriai, Lith. 55°9' N, 24°32' E 166
Vera, Arg. 29°26' S, 60°12' W 139
Vera, Okla., U.S. 36°26' N, 95°53' W 96
Vera, Sp. 37°14' N, 1°52' W 164
Vera y Pintado, Arg. 30°7' S, 60°21' W 139
Veracruz, Mex. 19°9' N, 96°9' W 114
Veracruz, adm. division, Mex. 19°32' N, 97°21' W 114
Verba, Ukr. 50°15' N, 25°35' E 152
Verbania, It. 45°56' N, 8°33' E 167
Vercelli, It. 45°19' N, 8°24' E 167
Verçinin Tepesi, peak, Turk. 40°42' N, 40°51' E 195
Verdalsøra, Nor. 63°47' N, 11°29' E 152
Verde, Laguna, lake, Arg. 42°38' S, 69°8' W 134
Verde, Península, Arg. 39°35' S, 62°4' W 139
Verde, river, Braz. 19°2' S, 53°33' W 132
Verde, river, Mex. 26°39' N, 107°18' W 80
Verde, river, Parag. 23°0' S, 59°40' W 132
Verdi Inlet 71°43' S, 77°30' W 248
Verdigre, Nebr., U.S. 42°35' N, 98°4' W 90
Verdon, river, Fr. 43°54' N, 6°34' E 165
Verdun, Fr. 49°10' N, 5°23' E 163
Vereeniging, S. Af. 26°42' S, 27°54' E 227
Vereshchagino, Russ. 64°9' N, 87°41' E 169
Vereshchagino, Russ. 58°6' N, 54°43' E 154
Verga, Cap, Guinea 10°10' N, 15°6' W 222
Vergara, Chile 22°28' S, 69°39' W 137
Vergara, Uru. 32°57' S, 53°58' W 139
Vergato, It. 44°16' N, 11°4' E 167
Vergel Ondara, Sp. 38°48' N, 1°59' E 164
Vergennes, Vt., U.S. 44°9' N, 73°16' W 104
Véria, Gr. 40°31' N, 22°12' E 180
Verín, Sp. 41°55' N, 7°28' W 150
Veríssimo, Braz. 19°42' S, 48°20' W 138
Verkhneimbatsk, Russ. 63°8' N, 88°0' E 169
Verkhnetulomskiy, Russ. 68°39' N, 31°38' E 152
Verkhneural'sk, Russ. 53°55' N, 59°12' E 154
Verkhnevilyuysk, Russ. 63°26' N, 120°13' E 173
Verkhniy Baskunchak, Russ. 48°13' N, 46°37' E 158
Verkhniy Mamon, Russ. 50°12' N, 40°19' E 158
Verkhniy Tagil, Russ. 57°25' N, 59°55' E 154
Verkhniy Ufaley, Russ. 56°3' N, 60°16' E 154
Verkhnyaya Inta, Russ. 66°0' N, 60°16' E 154
Verkhnyaya Pesha, Russ. 66°34' N, 47°51' E 154
Verkhnyaya Pyshma, Russ. 56°58' N, 60°36' E 154
Verkhnyaya Salda, Russ. 58°4' N, 60°34' E 154
Verkhnyaya Sinyachikha, Russ. 57°59' N, 61°36' E 154
Verkhnyaya Taymyra, river, Russ. 72°53' N, 91°25' E 160
Verkhnyaya Tura, Russ. 58°23' N, 59°52' E 154
Verkhnyaya Zolotitsa, Russ. 65°41' N, 40°3' E 154
Verkholuz'ye, Russ. 59°55' N, 48°36' E 154
Verkhoshizhem'ye, Russ. 58°0' N, 49°6' E 154
Verkhotur'ye, Russ. 58°53' N, 60°50' E 154
Verkhovazh'ye, Russ. 60°45' N, 42°0' E 154
Verkhov'ye, Russ. 52°47' N, 37°15' E 158
Verkhoyansk, Russ. 67°27' N, 133°35' E 160
Verkhoyanskiy Khrebet, Russ. 64°49' N, 117°28' E 160
Verkhozim, Russ. 52°54' N, 46°26' E 154
Vermelho, river, Braz. 15°20' S, 51°16' W 138
Vermeş, Rom. 45°32' N, 21°40' E 168
Vermilion, Can. 53°19' N, 110°49' W 108
Vermilion, Ohio, U.S. 41°24' N, 82°22' W 102
Vermilion Bay 29°42' N, 92°3' W 103
Vermilion Bay, Can. 49°51' N, 93°24' W 82
Vermilion Range, Minn., U.S. 48°0' N, 91°38' W 94
Vermillion, S. Dak., U.S. 42°45' N, 96°57' W 90
Vermillion, river, Can. 47°18' N, 73°23' W 94
Vérmio, Óros, Gr. 40°47' N, 21°55' E 156
Vermont, adm. division, Vt., U.S. 43°48' N, 73°7' W 104
Vermontville, N.Y., U.S. 44°26' N, 74°5' W 104
Vermosh, Alban. 42°35' N, 19°42' E 168
Vernadsky, station, Antarctica 65°23' S, 64°14' W 134
Verneuil, Fr. 48°44' N, 0°54' E 163
Vérno, Óros, peak, Gr. 40°38' N, 21°18' E 156
Vernon, Ala., U.S. 33°44' N, 88°6' W 96
Vernon, Can. 50°15' N, 119°15' W 90
Vernon, Fr. 49°5' N, 1°27' E 163
Vernon, Ill., U.S. 38°48' N, 89°5' W 102
Vernon, Ind., U.S. 38°59' N, 85°36' W 102
Vernon, Tex., U.S. 34°8' N, 99°18' W 92
Vernon, Vt., U.S. 42°46' N, 72°32' W 104
Vernonia, Oreg., U.S. 45°51' N, 123°13' W 100
Vero Beach, Fla., U.S. 27°38' N, 80°24' W 105
Verona, Ill., U.S. 41°12' N, 88°30' W 102
Verona, It. 45°25' N, 11°0' E 167
Verona, Ky., U.S. 38°48' N, 84°40' W 102
Verona, Mich., U.S. 43°47' N, 82°53' W 102
Verona, Wis., U.S. 42°58' N, 89°32' W 102
Verónica, Arg. 35°24' S, 57°21' W 139
Verrabotn, Nor. 63°47' N, 10°32' E 152
Verrès, It. 45°40' N, 7°42' E 167
Verret, Lake, La., U.S. 29°50' N, 91°21' W 103
Versailles, Fr. 48°48' N, 2°8' E 163
Versailles, Ky., U.S. 38°2' N, 84°44' W 94
Versailles, Ohio, U.S. 40°12' N, 84°29' W 102
Vershina, Russ. 60°57' N, 62°5' E 154
Vershino Darasunskiy, Russ. 52°23' N, 115°29' E 190
Vershire, Vt., U.S. 43°58' N, 72°20' W 104
Versmold, Ger. 52°2' N, 8°10' E 167
Vert, Cap, Senegal 14°45' N, 17°37' W 222
Verte, river, Can. 47°48' N, 68°34' W 94
Vértes, Hung. 47°23' N, 18°11' E 168
Verviers, Belg. 50°35' N, 5°51' E 167
Vervins, Fr. 49°50' N, 3°54' E 163
Verwood, U.K. 50°52' N, 1°53' W 162
Verzy, Fr. 49°9' N, 4°9' E 163
Vesanto, Fin. 62°55' N, 26°22' E 152
Veselí nad Moravou, Czech Rep. 48°57' N, 17°23' E 152
Veselovskoye, Russ. 53°57' N, 78°43' E 184
Veselyy, Russ. 47°2' N, 40°42' E 158
Veshenskaya, Russ. 49°37' N, 41°36' E 158
Veslyana, Russ. 63°1' N, 51°0' E 154
Veslyana, river, Russ. 60°28' N, 52°52' E 154
Vesnitsk, Belarus 55°4' N, 28°19' E 166
Vesoul, Fr. 47°37' N, 6°8' E 150
Vesterålen, islands, Norwegian Sea 68°51' N, 14°50' E 152
Vesterø Havn, Den. 57°16' N, 10°55' E 152
Vestfjorden 67°53' N, 11°40' E 142
Vestfold Hills, Antarctica 68°26' S, 79°17' E 248
Vestmannaeyjar, islands, Ice. 62°44' N, 27°0' W 142
Vestnes, Nor. 62°36' N, 7°4' E 152
Vestone, It. 45°43' N, 10°23' E 167
Vesuvio, peak, It. 40°44' N, 14°15' E 143
Ves'yegonsk, Russ. 58°37' N, 37°17' E 154
Veszprém, Hung. 47°5' N, 17°55' E 168
Veszprém, adm. division, Hung. 47°8' N, 17°13' E 156
Veszprémvarsány, Hung. 47°25' N, 17°51' E 168
Vetluga, Russ. 57°51' N, 45°49' E 154
Vetluga, river, Russ. 57°33' N, 45°22' E 154
Vetluzhskiy, Russ. 57°8' N, 45°10' E 154
Vetly, Ukr. 51°52' N, 25°6' E 152
Vetto, It. 44°28' N, 10°19' E 167
Vettore, Monte, peak, It. 42°49' N, 13°10' E 156
Veules-les-Roses, Fr. 49°51' N, 0°46' E 163
Veum, Nor. 59°17' N, 8°5' E 152
Veurne (Furnes), Belg. 51°4' N, 2°40' E 150
Vevay, Ind., U.S. 38°44' N, 85°4' W 102
Vevelstad, Nor. 65°41' N, 12°27' E 152
Veveno, river, Sudan 6°5' N, 32°27' E 224
Vevey, Switz. 46°28' N, 6°50' E 167
Vévi, Gr. 40°46' N, 21°36' E 156
Veynes, Fr. 44°32' N, 5°48' E 150
Vézelise, Fr. 48°29' N, 6°4' E 163
Vezhen, peak, Bulg. 42°44' N, 24°20' E 156
Vezirköprü, Turk. 41°8' N, 35°27' E 156
Viacha, Bol. 16°42' S, 68°21' W 137
Viadana, It. 44°55' N, 10°32' E 167
Viale, Arg. 31°52' S, 60°2' W 139
Viamonte, Arg. 33°46' S, 63°4' W 139
Viana, Braz. 3°14' S, 45°4' W 132
Viana do Castelo, Port. 41°41' N, 8°50' W 150
Viana Do Castelo, adm. division, Port. 41°59' N, 8°49' W 150
Vianden, Lux. 49°55' N, 6°11' E 167
Viangchan (Vientiane), Laos 17°56' N, 102°32' E 202
Viareggio, It. 43°52' N, 10°15' E 167
Viaur, river, Fr. 44°5' N, 2°10' E 165
Vibank, Can. 50°19' N, 103°57' W 108
Viborg, Den. 56°26' N, 9°23' E 150
Vic, Sp. 41°55' N, 2°14' E 164
Vicálvaro, Sp. 40°23' N, 3°35' W 164
Vicdessos, Fr. 42°46' N, 1°28' E 164
Vicente Guerrero, Mex. 30°45' N, 115°59' W 112
Vicente Guerrero, Mex. 23°44' N, 103°59' W 114
Vicente Guerrero, Presa, lake, Mex. 23°56' N, 99°20' W 114
Vicente Pérez Rosales National Park, Chile 41°13' S, 72°34' W 122
Vicenza, It. 45°33' N, 11°33' E 167
Vic-Fézensac, Fr. 43°45' N, 0°17' E 150
Vichada, adm. division, Col. 4°52' N, 70°21' W 136
Vichada, river, Col. 4°55' N, 68°23' W 136
Vichadero, Uru. 31°48' S, 54°42' W 139
Vichuga, Russ. 57°11' N, 41°56' E 154
Vichy, Fr. 46°5' N, 3°7' E 143
Vici, Okla., U.S. 36°8' N, 99°18' W 96
Vick, La., U.S. 31°13' N, 92°6' W 103
Vicksburg, Mich., U.S. 42°7' N, 85°32' W 102
Vicksburg, Miss., U.S. 32°18' N, 90°53' W 103
Vicksburg National Military Park, La., U.S. 32°20' N, 90°56' W 103
Viçosa, Braz. 20°45' S, 42°53' W 138
Vicovu de Sus, Rom. 47°55' N, 25°40' E 158
Victor, Idaho, U.S. 43°35' N, 111°6' W 90
Victor Harbor, Austral. 35°33' S, 138°36' E 231
Victor, Mount, peak, Antarctica 72°39' S, 30°58' E 248
Víctor Rosales, Mex. 22°57' N, 102°42' W 114
Victoria, Arg. 32°36' S, 60°10' W 139
Victoria, Can. 48°24' N, 123°23' W 100
Victoria, Chile 38°14' S, 72°20' W 134
Victoria, Ill., U.S. 41°1' N, 90°7' W 102
Victoria, Philippines 15°34' N, 120°40' E 203
Victoria, Seychelles 4°53' S, 54°51' E 172
Victoria, Tex., U.S. 28°47' N, 97°0' W 96
Victoria, Va., U.S. 36°59' N, 78°14' W 96
Victoria, adm. division, Austral. 36°44' S, 141°23' E 231
Victoria Beach, Can. 50°40' N, 96°33' W 90
Victoria Falls, Zimb. 17°21' S, 20°52' E 207
Victoria Falls National Park, Zimb. 17°55' S, 25°40' E 225
Victoria, Grand lac, lake, Can. 47°33' N, 78°19' W 94
Victoria, Isla, island, Chile 45°18' S, 73°44' W 134
Victoria Island, Can. 70°18' N, 121°1' W 106
Victoria, Lake, Africa 1°23' S, 30°40' E 218
Victoria Land, region, Antarctica 74°59' S, 162°2' E 248
Victoria, Mount, peak, Myanmar 21°27' N, 93°33' E 190
Victoria, Mount, peak, P.N.G. 8°54' S, 147°21' E 192
Victoria Strait 68°57' N, 101°27' W 106
Victoria West, S. Af. 31°24' S, 23°5' E 227
Victoriaville, Can. 46°3' N, 71°59' W 94
Victorica, Arg. 36°14' S, 65°25' W 134
Victorino, Venez. 2°49' N, 67°49' W 136
Victorio Peak, Tex., U.S. 31°17' N, 104°57' W 92
Victorville, Calif., U.S. 34°32' N, 117°19' W 101
Victory Peak see Pobedy Peak, China 42°2' N, 80°3' E 184
Vidal, Calif., U.S. 34°7' N, 114°31' W 101
Vidal, Peru 2°38' S, 73°29' W 136
Vidal Gormaz, Isla, island, Chile 52°17' S, 76°29' W 134
Vidalia, Ga., U.S. 32°12' N, 82°25' W 96
Videira, Braz. 27°1' S, 51°9' W 139
Videla, Arg. 30°57' S, 60°41' W 139
Videle, Rom. 44°17' N, 25°32' E 158
Vidin, Bulg. 43°59' N, 22°51' E 168
Vidin, adm. division, Bulg. 43°42' N, 22°24' E 168
Vidisha (Bhilsa), India 23°32' N, 77°51' E 197
Vidlitsa, Russ. 61°10' N, 32°28' E 152
Vidor, Tex., U.S. 30°6' N, 94°1' W 103
Vidriži, Latv. 57°19' N, 24°36' E 166
Vidsel, Nor. 65°50' N, 20°28' E 152
Vidzibor, Belarus 51°58' N, 26°47' E 152
Vidzy, Belarus 55°24' N, 26°37' E 166
Vidz'yuyar, Russ. 60°52' N, 51°19' E 154
Vie, river, Fr. 46°36' N, 1°55' W 150
Viedma, Arg. 40°51' S, 63°1' W 134
Viedma, Lago, lake, Arg. 49°34' S, 73°52' W 134
Vieja, Sierra, Tex., U.S. 30°42' N, 105°1' W 92
Viejo, Cerro, peak, Mex. 30°16' N, 112°23' W 92
Viekšniai, Lith. 56°15' N, 22°31' E 166
Vielha, Sp. 42°41' N, 0°47' E 164
Vielsalm, Belg. 50°16' N, 5°55' E 167
Vienna, Ga., U.S. 32°5' N, 83°48' W 96
Vienna, Mo., U.S. 37°25' N, 88°53' W 96
Vienna, W. Va., U.S. 39°19' N, 81°33' W 102
Vienna see Wien, Aust. 48°10' N, 16°14' E 152
Vienne, Fr. 45°31' N, 4°52' E 150
Vientiane, Laos 17°53' N, 101°53' E 172
Vientiane see Viangchan, Laos 17°56' N, 102°32' E 202
Vieques, island, U.S. 18°8' N, 65°26' W 118
Viersen, Ger. 51°15' N, 6°23' E 167
Viesca, Mex. 25°21' N, 102°48' W 114
Vieste, It. 41°52' N, 16°10' E 156
Vieste, Latv. 56°20' N, 25°34' E 166
Vietnam 21°0' N, 105°0' E 202
Vieux-Fort, Can. 51°25' N, 57°49' W 111
Vievis, Lith. 54°45' N, 24°48' E 166
Vif, Fr. 45°2' N, 5°39' E 150
Vigan, Philippines 17°33' N, 120°24' E 203
Vigeois, Fr. 45°22' N, 1°30' E 150
Vigevano, It. 45°18' N, 8°50' E 167
Vigía, Cabo, Arg. 48°46' S, 66°49' W 134
Vigía Chico, Mex. 19°46' N, 87°38' W 116
Vignacourt, Fr. 50°0' N, 2°11' E 163
Vignal, Lac, lake, Can. 53°15' N, 68°51' W 111
Vignale, It. 45°0' N, 8°24' E 167
Vignemale, Pic de, peak, Fr. 42°46' N, 0°11' E 164
Vignola, It. 44°29' N, 11°0' E 167
Vigo, Sp. 42°13' N, 8°45' W 150
Vigone, It. 44°50' N, 7°29' E 167
Vihanti, Fin. 64°29' N, 24°58' E 152
Vihorlat, peak, Slovakia 48°53' N, 22°0' E 152
Viiala, Fin. 61°12' N, 23°43' E 166
Viiksimo, Fin. 64°13' N, 30°26' E 154
Viipuri see Vyborg, Russ. 60°41' N, 28°45' E 166
Viiri, Fin. 66°23' N, 26°38' E 152
Vijayadurg, India 16°31' N, 73°19' E 188
Vijayanagar, ruin(s), India 15°16' N, 76°17' E 188
Vijayawada, India 16°34' N, 80°33' E 190
Vík, Ice. 63°28' N, 18°59' W 143
Vika, Fin. 66°35' N, 26°23' E 152
Vikhren, peak, Bulg. 41°45' N, 23°19' E 156
Viking, Can. 53°5' N, 111°48' W 108
Vikna, islands, Norwegian Sea 64°56' N, 9°48' E 152
Vikulovo, Russ. 56°47' N, 70°37' E 169
Vila Bela da Santíssima Trindade, Braz. 15°1' S, 59°57' W 132
Vila Bittencourt, Braz. 1°21' S, 69°23' W 136
Vila Conceição, Braz. 0°8' N, 63°55' W 130
Vila Coutinho, Mozambique 14°34' S, 34°18' E 224
Vila da Maganja, Mozambique 17°19' S, 37°31' E 224
Vila de Moura, Port. 38°7' N, 7°29' W 214
Vila de Sagres, Port. 37°0' N, 8°57' W 150
Vila do Conde, Port. 41°20' N, 8°45' W 150
Vila Gamito, Mozambique 14°11' S, 33°0' E 224
Vila Gomes da Costa, Mozambique 24°19' S, 33°39' E 227
Vila Junqueiro, Mozambique 15°29' S, 36°58' E 224
Vila Luísa, Mozambique 25°42' S, 32°40' E 227
Vila Machado, Mozambique 19°20' S, 34°13' E 224
Vila Murtinho, Braz. 10°23' S, 65°17' W 137
Vila Nova de Foz Côa, Port. 41°4' N, 7°10' W 150
Vila Nova de Gaia, Port. 41°6' N, 8°39' W 150
Vila Paiva de Andrada, Mozambique 18°40' S, 34°4' E 224
Vila Real, Port. 41°17' N, 7°46' W 150
Vila Real, adm. division, Port. 41°23' N, 7°55' W 150
Vila Real de Santo António, Port. 37°12' N, 7°36' W 214
Vila Vasco da Gama, Mozambique 14°54' S, 32°15' E 224
Vila Velha, Braz. 3°15' N, 51°15' W 130
Vila Velha (Espírito Santo), Braz. 20°25' S, 40°21' W 138
Vilafranca del Penedès, Sp. 41°20' N, 1°41' E 164
Viļaka, Latv. 57°10' N, 27°37' E 166
Vilaller, Sp. 42°26' N, 0°42' E 164
Vilán, Cabo, Sp. 43°10' N, 9°27' W 150
Viļāni, Latv. 56°32' N, 26°56' E 166
Vilanova i la Geltrú, Sp. 41°12' N, 1°43' E 164
Vilar Formoso, Port. 40°36' N, 6°52' W 150
Vilcabamba, Cordillera, Peru 13°0' S, 73°16' W 130
Vilcabamba, ruin(s), Peru 13°7' S, 73°25' W 137
Vileyka, Belarus 54°30' N, 26°54' E 166
Vil'gort, Russ. 60°35' N, 56°25' E 154
Vil'gort, Russ. 61°37' N, 50°49' E 154
Vilhelmina, Nor. 64°37' N, 16°38' E 152
Vilhena, Braz. 12°42' S, 60°9' W 130
Viliya, Ukr. 50°11' N, 26°17' E 152
Viliya, river, Belarus 54°49' N, 25°58' E 166
Viljandi, Est. 58°20' N, 25°33' E 166
Vilkaviškis, Lith. 54°40' N, 23°1' E 166
Vil'kitskogo, Proliv 76°58' N, 84°44' E 172
Villa Abecia, Bol. 21°0' S, 65°24' W 137
Villa Ahumada, Mex. 30°36' N, 106°32' W 92
Villa Alberdi, Arg. 27°35' S, 65°37' W 134
Villa Ana, Arg. 28°28' S, 59°37' W 139
Villa Ángela, Arg. 27°34' S, 60°43' W 139
Villa Bella, Bol. 10°29' S, 65°24' W 137
Villa Bens see Tarfaya, Mor. 27°55' N, 12°54' W 214
Villa Berthet, Arg. 27°16' S, 60°25' W 139
Villa Cañás, Arg. 34°1' S, 61°37' W 139
Villa Clara, adm. division, Cuba 22°39' N, 80°15' W 116
Villa Clara, island, Cuba 23°7' N, 80°39' W 116
Villa Constitución, Arg. 33°16' S, 60°19' W 139
Villa Cuauhtémoc, Mex. 22°9' N, 97°49' W 114
Villa de Cos, Mex. 23°17' N, 102°21' W 114
Villa de Guadalupe, Mex. 23°20' N, 100°46' W 114
Villa de Hidalgo, Mex. 22°24' N, 100°41' W 114
Villa de María, Arg. 29°54' S, 63°42' W 139
Villa de San Antonio, Hond. 14°20' N, 87°36' W 115
Villa del Río, Sp. 37°59' N, 4°19' W 164
Villa del Rosario, Arg. 31°37' S, 63°32' W 139
Villa Dolores, Arg. 31°56' S, 65°9' W 134
Villa Elisa, Arg. 32°9' S, 58°23' W 139
Villa Escobedo, Mex. 27°1' N, 105°47' W 112
Villa Florida, Parag. 26°26' S, 57°6' W 139
Villa Grove, Ill., U.S. 39°52' N, 88°11' W 102
Villa Guerrero, Mex. 21°57' N, 103°35' W 114
Villa Guillermina, Arg. 28°13' S, 59°29' W 139
Villa Hayes, Parag. 25°5' S, 57°33' W 132
Villa Hernandarias, Arg. 31°15' S, 59°58' W 139
Villa Hidalgo, Mex. 26°14' N, 104°54' W 114
Villa Ingavi (Caiza), Bol. 21°47' S, 63°33' W 137
Villa Iris, Arg. 38°12' S, 63°13' W 139
Villa Jesús María, Mex. 28°11' N, 114°3' W 92
Villa Juan José Pérez, Bol. 15°16' S, 69°4' W 137
Villa Juárez, Mex. 22°18' N, 100°16' W 114
Villa Mainero, Mex. 24°33' N, 99°38' W 114
Villa María, Arg. 32°25' S, 63°14' W 139
Villa Martín, Bol. 20°47' S, 67°41' W 137
Villa Minetti, Arg. 28°37' S, 61°39' W 139
Villa Nueva, Arg. 32°29' S, 63°15' W 139
Villa Ocampo, Arg. 28°28' S, 59°22' W 139
Villa Ocampo, Mex. 26°26' N, 105°30' W 114
Villa O'Higgins, Chile 48°28' S, 72°38' W 134
Villa Ojo de Agua, Arg. 29°27' S, 63°45' W 139
Villa Oliva, Parag. 26°0' S, 57°50' W 139
Villa Opicina, It. 45°41' N, 13°46' E 156
Villa Orestes Pereyra, Mex. 26°28' N, 105°40' W 114
Villa Pesqueira, Mex. 29°6' N, 109°57' W 92
Villa Ramírez, Arg. 32°10' S, 60°12' W 139
Villa Regina, Arg. 39°7' S, 67°7' W 134
Villa San José, Arg. 32°12' S, 58°12' W 139
Villa Serrano, Bol. 19°5' S, 64°25' W 137
Villa Talavera, Bol. 19°48' S, 65°23' W 137
Villa Tunari, Bol. 17°0' S, 65°28' W 137
Villa Unión, Arg. 29°25' S, 62°47' W 139
Villa Unión, Arg. 29°18' S, 68°12' W 134
Villa Unión, Mex. 23°10' N, 106°14' W 114
Villa Unión, Mex. 23°58' N, 104°3' W 114
Villa Unión, Mex. 28°12' N, 100°45' W 92
Villa Vaca Guzmán, Bol. 19°57' S, 63°48' W 137
Villacañas, Sp. 39°37' N, 3°20' W 164
Villacarrillo, Sp. 38°6' N, 3°5' W 164
Villach, Aust. 46°36' N, 13°50' E 156
Villada, Sp. 42°14' N, 4°58' W 150
Villadossola, It. 46°3' N, 8°14' E 167
Villafeliche, Sp. 41°12' N, 1°30' W 164
Villafranca, Sp. 42°16' N, 1°45' W 164
Villafranca de los Barros, Sp. 38°34' N, 6°20' W 164
Villafranca del Cid, Sp. 40°25' N, 0°17' E 164
Villafranca di Verona, It. 45°21' N, 10°51' E 167
Villagrán, Mex. 24°28' N, 99°30' W 114
Villaguay, Arg. 31°51' S, 59°1' W 139
Villaharta, Sp. 38°7' N, 4°55' W 164
Villahermosa, Mex. 17°56' N, 93°2' W 115
Villahermosa, Sp. 38°45' N, 2°52' W 164
Villajoyosa (La Vila Joiosa), Sp. 38°29' N, 0°14' E 164
Villaldama, Mex. 26°29' N, 100°27' W 114
Villalonga, Arg. 39°54' S, 62°36' W 139
Villamartín, Sp. 36°52' N, 5°39' W 164
Villamontes, Bol. 21°15' S, 63°33' W 137
Villanueva, Mex. 22°21' N, 102°54' W 114
Villanueva, N. Mex., U.S. 35°16' N, 105°22' W 92
Villanueva de Castellón, Sp. 39°4' N, 0°31' E 164
Villanueva de la Concepción, Sp. 36°55' N, 4°33' W 164
Villanueva de la Jara, Sp. 39°26' N, 1°58' W 164
Villanueva de la Serena, Sp. 38°58' N, 5°48' W 164
Villanueva de los Infantes, Sp. 38°44' N, 3°2' W 164
Villanueva del Arzobispo, Sp. 38°10' N, 3°0' W 164
Villanueva del Duque, Sp. 38°23' N, 5°1' W 164
Villanueva del Río y Minas, Sp. 37°39' N, 5°43' W 164
Villány, Hung. 45°52' N, 18°27' E 168
Villapalacios, Sp. 38°34' N, 2°38' W 164
Villaputzu, It. 39°27' N, 9°35' E 156
Villaquejida, Sp. 42°8' N, 5°36' W 150
Villar del Rey, Sp. 39°8' N, 6°51' W 164
Villarcayo, Sp. 42°55' N, 3°34' W 164
Villarino, Punta, Arg. 41°0' S, 64°58' W 134
Villarrica, Parag. 25°45' S, 56°27' W 132
Villarrica National Park, Chile 39°24' S, 72°10' W 134
Villarrobledo, Sp. 39°15' N, 2°37' W 164
Villarroya de la Sierra, Sp. 41°28' N, 1°48' W 164
Villasayas, Sp. 41°20' N, 2°37' W 164
Villavicencio, Col. 4°8' N, 73°40' W 136
Villaviciosa de Córdoba, Sp. 38°4' N, 5°1' W 164
Villavieja, Col. 3°13' N, 75°13' W 136
Villazón, Bol. 22°7' S, 65°39' W 137
Villé, Fr. 48°19' N, 7°17' E 163
Ville Platte, La., U.S. 30°40' N, 92°17' W 103
Villebon, Lac, lake, Can. 47°54' N, 77°50' W 94
Villefranche, Fr. 45°59' N, 4°43' E 150
Villefranche, Fr. 47°17' N, 1°46' E 150
Villefranche-de-Lauragais, Fr. 43°23' N, 1°43' E 164

Villel, *Sp.* 40°13′ N, 1°13′ W 164
Villemaur, *Fr.* 48°15′ N, 3°45′ E 163
Villena, *Sp.* 38°37′ N, 0°53′ E 164
Villenauxe, *Fr.* 48°35′ N, 3°32′ E 163
Villeneuve-Saint-Georges, *Fr.* 48°43′ N, 2°26′ E 163
Villers-Bretonneux, *Fr.* 49°52′ N, 2°30′ E 163
Villerupt, *Fr.* 49°27′ N, 5°55′ E 163
Villiers, *S. Af.* 27°7′ S, 28°36′ E 227
Villisca, *Iowa, U.S.* 40°56′ N, 94°59′ W 94
Villupuram, *India* 11°56′ N, 79°30′ E 188
Vilna, *Can.* 54°6′ N, 111°56′ W 108
Vilnius, *Lith.* 54°38′ N, 25°12′ E 166
Vilppula, *Fin.* 62°1′ N, 24°25′ E 166
Vilsandi National Park, *Est.* 58°21′ N, 21°36′ E 166
Vilsandi Saar, island, *Est.* 58°23′ N, 21°35′ E 166
Vilshofen, *Ger.* 48°37′ N, 13°11′ E 152
Vilusi, *Mont.* 42°42′ N, 18°35′ E 168
Vilvoorde, *Belg.* 50°55′ N, 4°26′ E 167
Vilyuy, river, *Russ.* 62°48′ N, 120°41′ E 172
Vilyuy, river, *Russ.* 64°45′ N, 108°36′ E 160
Vilyuy, river, *Russ.* 63°0′ N, 115°4′ E 160
Vilyuysk, *Russ.* 63°38′ N, 121°30′ E 160
Vilyuyskoye Plato, *Russ.* 66°22′ N, 99°40′ E 172
Vilyuyskoye Vodokhranilishche, lake, *Russ.* 63°5′ N, 101°50′ E 172
Vimioso, *Port.* 41°34′ N, 6°32′ W 150
Vimpeli, *Fin.* 63°9′ N, 23°46′ E 152
Vina, *Calif., U.S.* 39°56′ N, 122°4′ W 90
Vina, *Serb.* 43°37′ N, 22°8′ E 168
Vinalhaven, *Me., U.S.* 44°2′ N, 68°50′ W 94
Vinaròs, *Sp.* 40°27′ N, 0°27′ E 150
Vinça, *Fr.* 42°39′ N, 2°29′ E 164
Vincennes, *Ind., U.S.* 38°40′ N, 87°31′ W 102
Vincent Lake, lake, *Can.* 50°34′ N, 91°27′ W 110
Vinchina, *Arg.* 28°46′ S, 68°14′ W 134
Vindeln, *Nor.* 64°11′ N, 19°43′ E 152
Vindrey, *Russ.* 54°15′ N, 43°0′ E 154
Vinegar Hill, peak, *Oreg., U.S.* 44°41′ N, 118°39′ W 90
Vineta, *Namibia* 22°34′ S, 14°30′ E 220
Vineyard Sound 41°24′ N, 70°48′ W 104
Vinga, *Rom.* 46°1′ N, 21°12′ E 168
Vinh, *Vietnam* 18°42′ N, 105°38′ E 202
Vinh Chau, *Vietnam* 9°21′ N, 105°59′ E 202
Vinh Long, *Vietnam* 10°13′ N, 105°57′ E 202
Vinica, *Maced.* 41°53′ N, 22°30′ E 168
Vinita, *Okla., U.S.* 36°37′ N, 95°10′ W 96
Vinje, *Nor.* 59°38′ N, 7°51′ E 152
Vinjeøra, *Nor.* 63°12′ N, 8°58′ E 152
Vînju Mare, *Rom.* 44°25′ N, 22°53′ E 168
Vinkovci, *Croatia* 45°16′ N, 18°46′ E 168
Vinnytsya, *Ukr.* 49°12′ N, 28°37′ E 152
Vinson Massif, peak, *Antarctica* 78°33′ S, 86°54′ W 248
Vinton, *Iowa, U.S.* 42°9′ N, 92°2′ W 110
Vinton, *La., U.S.* 30°11′ N, 93°36′ W 103
Violet Grove, *Can.* 53°8′ N, 115°4′ W 108
Vipiteno, *It.* 46°54′ N, 11°25′ E 167
Vir, *Taj.* 37°42′ N, 72°11′ E 197
Virac, *Philippines* 13°33′ N, 124°13′ E 203
Virachei, *Cambodia* 14°0′ N, 106°46′ E 202
Virachey National Park, *Cambodia* 14°12′ N, 106°23′ E 202
Viramgam, *India* 23°5′ N, 72°3′ E 186
Virandozero, *Russ.* 64°1′ N, 36°7′ E 154
Viranşehir, *Turk.* 37°12′ N, 39°46′ E 195
Virbalis, *Lith.* 54°38′ N, 22°48′ E 166
Virden, *Can.* 49°51′ N, 100°57′ W 90
Virden, *Ill., U.S.* 39°29′ N, 89°46′ W 102
Virden, *Mo., U.S.* 39°29′ N, 89°46′ W 94
Vire, *Fr.* 48°50′ N, 0°54′ E 150
Vireši, *Latv.* 57°27′ N, 26°21′ E 166
Vîrfurile, *Rom.* 46°18′ N, 22°33′ E 168
Virgem da Lapa, *Braz.* 16°48′ S, 42°23′ W 138
Virgin Gorda, island, *U.K.* 18°28′ N, 64°26′ W 118
Virgin Islands, *Caribbean Sea* 18°4′ N, 64°50′ W 118
Virgin Islands, adm. division, *U.S.* 18°20′ N, 64°50′ W 118
Virgin Mountains, *Nev., U.S.* 36°39′ N, 114°12′ W 101
Virgin, river, *Can.* 57°0′ N, 108°9′ W 108
Virgin, river, *Nev., U.S.* 36°39′ N, 114°20′ W 101
Virginia, *Minn., U.S.* 47°31′ N, 92°35′ W 82
Virginia, *S. Af.* 28°11′ S, 26°51′ E 227
Virginia, adm. division, *Va., U.S.* 37°56′ N, 79°15′ W 94
Virginia Beach, *Va., U.S.* 36°50′ N, 76°0′ W 94
Virginia Falls, *Can.* 61°52′ N, 128°14′ W 98
Virgolândia, *Braz.* 18°29′ S, 42°18′ W 138
Virje, *Croatia* 46°3′ N, 16°58′ E 168
Virmutjoki, *Fin.* 61°20′ N, 28°44′ E 166
Virojoki, *Fin.* 60°34′ N, 27°40′ E 166
Virolahti, *Fin.* 60°30′ N, 27°40′ E 166
Virovitica, *Croatia* 45°49′ N, 17°24′ E 168
Virpazar, *Mont.* 42°15′ N, 19°5′ E 168
Virrat, *Fin.* 62°12′ N, 23°43′ E 154
Vîrşolţ, *Rom.* 47°12′ N, 22°55′ E 168
Virtaniemi, *Russ.* 68°53′ N, 28°27′ E 152
Virton, *Belg.* 49°34′ N, 5°32′ E 163
Virtsu, *Est.* 58°33′ N, 23°30′ E 166
Virú, *Peru* 8°28′ S, 78°46′ W 130
Viru Roela, *Est.* 59°9′ N, 26°35′ E 166
Viru-Jaagupi, *Est.* 59°14′ N, 26°27′ E 166
Virunga, *Dem. Rep. of the Congo* 1°1′ S, 29°0′ E 224
Virunga National Park, *Dem. Rep. of the Congo* 0°40′ N, 29°47′ E 224
Vis, *Croatia* 43°2′ N, 16°10′ E 168
Vis (Lissa), island, *Croatia* 42°57′ N, 16°5′ E 168
Visaginas, *Lith.* 55°34′ N, 26°23′ E 166
Visalia, *Calif., U.S.* 36°20′ N, 119°18′ W 100
Visayan Sea 11°27′ N, 123°36′ E 203
Visbek, *Ger.* 52°50′ N, 8°19′ E 163
Visby, *Sw.* 57°37′ N, 18°17′ E 166
Visconde do Rio Branco, *Braz.* 2°54′ S, 69°39′ W 136
Viscount Melville Sound 74°17′ N, 105°54′ W 255
Visé, *Belg.* 50°44′ N, 5°42′ E 167
Višegrad, *Bosn. and Herzg.* 43°47′ N, 19°18′ E 168
Visegrád, *Hung.* 47°46′ N, 18°59′ E 168
Viseu, *Braz.* 1°13′ S, 46°10′ W 130
Viseu, *Port.* 40°39′ N, 7°56′ W 150
Viseu, adm. division, *Port.* 40°41′ N, 8°16′ W 150
Vishakhapatnam, *India* 17°44′ N, 83°18′ E 188
Vishera, river, *Russ.* 61°4′ N, 58°44′ E 154
Višķi, *Latv.* 56°1′ N, 26°46′ E 166
Vislanda, *Nor.* 56°46′ N, 14°25′ E 152
Viso del Marqués, *Sp.* 38°30′ N, 3°34′ W 164
Viso, Monte, peak, *It.* 44°39′ N, 7°4′ E 165
Visoko, *Bosn. and Herzg.* 43°58′ N, 18°9′ E 168
Visp, *Switz.* 46°17′ N, 7°53′ E 167
Vista, *Calif., U.S.* 33°12′ N, 117°16′ W 101
Vista Alegre, *Braz.* 4°21′ S, 56°17′ W 130
Vista Alegre, *Braz.* 6°18′ S, 68°10′ W 130
Vista Alegre, *Braz.* 1°27′ N, 68°14′ W 136
Vista, Cerro, peak, *N. Mex., U.S.* 36°13′ N, 105°29′ W 92
Vistula Lagoon, *Pol.-Russ.* 54°20′ N, 19°32′ E 166
Vital Lake, lake, *Can.* 61°31′ N, 108°33′ W 108
Vitån, river, *Nor.* 66°17′ N, 21°49′ E 152
Viterbo, *It.* 42°25′ N, 12°5′ E 214
Viti Levu, island, *Fiji* 17°50′ S, 178°0′ E 242
Vitichi, *Bol.* 20°16′ S, 65°29′ W 137
Vitim, *Russ.* 59°27′ N, 112°22′ E 160
Vitim, river, *Russ.* 53°53′ N, 114°38′ E 190
Vitina, *Bosn. and Herzg.* 43°13′ N, 17°29′ E 168
Vitor, *Chile* 18°48′ S, 70°22′ W 137
Vítor, *Peru* 16°29′ S, 71°48′ W 137
Vitória, *Braz.* 20°17′ S, 40°18′ W 138
Vitória, *Braz.* 2°56′ S, 52°3′ W 130
Vitória da Conquista, *Braz.* 14°52′ S, 40°52′ W 138
Vitória Seamount, *South Atlantic Ocean* 20°20′ S, 37°0′ W 253
Vitoria-Gasteiz, *Sp.* 42°50′ N, 2°41′ W 164
Vitorog, peak, *Bosn. and Herzg.* 44°6′ N, 17°2′ E 168
Vitry-le-François, *Fr.* 48°43′ N, 4°35′ E 163
Vitsyebsk, *Belarus* 55°12′ N, 30°20′ E 152
Vittangi, *Nor.* 67°40′ N, 21°37′ E 152
Vittel, *Fr.* 48°12′ N, 5°58′ E 163
Vittoria, *It.* 36°57′ N, 14°31′ E 156
Vittorio Veneto, *It.* 45°58′ N, 12°16′ E 167
Vitvattnet, *Nor.* 66°3′ N, 23°9′ E 152
Vityaz Trench, *South Pacific Ocean* 11°20′ S, 174°17′ E 252
Viveiro, *Sp.* 43°36′ N, 7°38′ W 214
Viver, *Sp.* 39°55′ N, 0°36′ E 164
Vivi, Ozero, lake, *Russ.* 66°19′ N, 92°55′ E 169
Vivi, river, *Russ.* 65°5′ N, 96°4′ E 169
Vivian, *La., U.S.* 32°51′ N, 93°59′ W 103
Vivoratá, *Arg.* 37°41′ S, 57°42′ W 139
Vizcachas, Meseta de las, *Arg.* 50°35′ S, 73°58′ W 134
Vizcaíno, Cape, *Calif., U.S.* 39°45′ N, 124°16′ W 90
Vizcaíno, Desierto de, *Mex.* 27°41′ N, 113°54′ W 112
Vizcaíno, Sierra, *Mex.* 27°31′ N, 114°24′ W 112
Vize, *Turk.* 41°34′ N, 27°45′ E 156
Vizhas, *Russ.* 66°38′ N, 45°50′ E 154
Vizhay, *Russ.* 61°14′ N, 60°13′ E 154
Vizhevo, *Russ.* 64°41′ N, 43°55′ E 154
Vizianagaram, *India* 18°5′ N, 83°24′ E 188
Vizinga, *Russ.* 61°6′ N, 50°6′ E 154
Vlădeasa, peak, *Rom.* 46°44′ N, 22°46′ E 168
Vladičin Han, *Serb.* 42°42′ N, 22°3′ E 168
Vladikavkaz, *Russ.* 43°0′ N, 44°44′ E 195
Vladimir, *Russ.* 56°9′ N, 40°19′ E 154
Vladimir, adm. division, *Russ.* 56°2′ N, 39°15′ E 154
Vladimirci, *Serb.* 44°35′ N, 19°46′ E 168
Vladimirovac, *Serb.* 45°1′ N, 20°52′ E 168
Vladimirovka, *Russ.* 60°48′ N, 30°28′ E 166
Vladimirskiy Tupik, *Russ.* 55°40′ N, 33°25′ E 154
Vladivostok, *Russ.* 43°8′ N, 131°54′ E 200
Vlasenica, *Bosn. and Herzg.* 44°11′ N, 18°55′ E 168
Vlašić, *Bosn. and Herzg.* 44°18′ N, 17°21′ E 168
Vlasinje, *Bosn. and Herzg.* 44°26′ N, 17°12′ E 168
Vlasotince, *Serb.* 42°57′ N, 22°7′ E 168
Vlčany, *Slovakia* 48°0′ N, 17°57′ E 168
Vlieland, island, *Neth.* 53°18′ N, 4°49′ E 163
Vlissingen (Flushing), *Neth.* 51°27′ N, 3°34′ E 163
Vltava, river, *Czech Rep.* 49°29′ N, 14°4′ E 152
Vobkent, *Uzb.* 40°1′ N, 64°33′ E 197
Voćin, *Croatia* 45°37′ N, 17°31′ E 168
Voden, *Bulg.* 42°4′ N, 26°54′ E 156
Vodil, *Uzb.* 40°9′ N, 71°44′ E 197
Vodl Ozero, lake, *Russ.* 62°16′ N, 36°18′ E 154
Vodnyy, *Russ.* 63°31′ N, 53°28′ E 154
Voerde, *Ger.* 51°36′ N, 6°40′ E 167
Vogan, *Togo* 6°21′ N, 1°30′ E 222
Vogelsberg, *Ger.* 50°40′ N, 8°44′ E 167
Voghera, *It.* 44°58′ N, 9°0′ E 167
Võhandu, river, *Est.* 57°46′ N, 27°7′ E 166
Vohipeno, *Madagascar* 22°21′ S, 47°53′ E 220
Võhma, *Est.* 58°36′ N, 25°32′ E 166
Võhma, *Est.* 58°31′ N, 22°20′ E 166
Vöhringen, *Ger.* 48°16′ N, 10°4′ E 152
Voi, *Kenya* 3°23′ S, 38°35′ E 224
Void-Vacon, *Fr.* 48°41′ N, 5°36′ E 163
Voikoski, *Fin.* 61°14′ N, 26°47′ E 166
Vóïo, Óros, peak, *Gr.* 40°16′ N, 20°59′ E 156
Voislova, *Rom.* 45°31′ N, 22°27′ E 168
Voiteg, *Rom.* 45°28′ N, 21°14′ E 156
Vojmån, *Nor.* 64°47′ N, 16°48′ E 152
Vojmsjön, lake, *Nor.* 64°51′ N, 16°2′ E 152
Vojvodina, region, *Serb.* 45°21′ N, 19°4′ E 168
Voknavolok, *Russ.* 64°56′ N, 30°33′ E 152
Voláda, *Gr.* 35°32′ N, 27°11′ E 156
Volán Domuyo, peak, *Arg.* 36°44′ S, 70°47′ W 122
Volborg, *Mont., U.S.* 45°49′ N, 105°40′ W 90
Volcán, *Arg.* 23°54′ S, 65°29′ W 132
Volcán Isluga National Park, *Chile* 19°20′ S, 69°19′ W 122
Volcán Masaya National Park, *Nicar.* 11°56′ N, 86°13′ W 115
Volcán Nevado de Colima National Park, *Mex.* 19°27′ N, 103°57′ W 72
Volcán Poás National Park, *C.R.* 10°11′ N, 84°19′ W 115
Volcano Islands (Kazan Rettō), islands, *Philippine Sea* 23°11′ N, 139°38′ E 190
Volcano Peak, *Calif., U.S.* 35°57′ N, 117°53′ W 101
Volchansk, *Russ.* 59°57′ N, 60°3′ E 154
Voldi, *Est.* 58°32′ N, 26°35′ E 166
Vol'dino, *Russ.* 62°15′ N, 54°8′ E 154
Volga, *Russ.* 57°57′ N, 38°22′ E 154
Volga, *S. Dak., U.S.* 44°17′ N, 96°57′ W 90
Volga, river, *Russ.* 55°48′ N, 44°12′ E 160
Volga-Don Canal, *Russ.* 48°33′ N, 43°47′ E 158
Volgodonsk, *Russ.* 47°30′ N, 42°2′ E 158
Volgograd, adm. division, *Russ.* 49°28′ N, 42°54′ E 158
Volgograd (Stalingrad), *Russ.* 48°46′ N, 44°28′ E 158
Volgogradskoye Vodokhranilishche, lake, *Russ.* 50°16′ N, 45°9′ E 158
Volgorechensk, *Russ.* 57°27′ N, 41°16′ E 154
Volímes, *Gr.* 37°52′ N, 20°39′ E 156
Volintiri, *Mold.* 46°26′ N, 29°35′ E 156
Volkach, *Ger.* 49°51′ N, 10°13′ E 167
Volkhov, *Russ.* 59°55′ N, 32°25′ E 154
Volkhov, river, *Russ.* 58°34′ N, 31°39′ E 154
Volksrust, *S. Af.* 27°22′ S, 29°50′ E 227
Vollenhove, *Neth.* 52°40′ N, 5°58′ E 163
Volma, *Belarus* 53°52′ N, 26°57′ E 166
Volnovakha, *Ukr.* 47°36′ N, 37°29′ E 156
Volochanka, *Russ.* 71°2′ N, 94°36′ E 160
Volochys'k, *Ukr.* 49°30′ N, 26°11′ E 152
Volodarsk, *Russ.* 56°13′ N, 43°11′ E 154
Volodskaya, *Russ.* 62°22′ N, 41°56′ E 154
Vologda, *Russ.* 59°10′ N, 39°48′ E 154
Vologda, adm. division, *Russ.* 59°52′ N, 39°27′ E 154
Voloki, *Belarus* 54°35′ N, 28°11′ E 166
Volokonovka, *Russ.* 50°29′ N, 37°51′ E 158
Volonga, *Russ.* 67°3′ N, 47°52′ E 169
Vólos, *Gr.* 39°24′ N, 22°55′ E 180
Voloshka, *Russ.* 61°19′ N, 40°2′ E 154
Voloshovo, *Russ.* 58°42′ N, 29°17′ E 166
Volosovo, *Russ.* 59°26′ N, 29°28′ E 166
Volovo, *Russ.* 53°32′ N, 38°0′ E 154
Voloyarvi, *Russ.* 60°17′ N, 30°46′ E 166
Vol'sk, *Russ.* 52°5′ N, 47°22′ E 158
Volta, *Calif., U.S.* 37°5′ N, 120°56′ W 100
Volta, Lake, *Ghana* 8°15′ N, 1°21′ W 214
Volta Redonda, *Braz.* 22°27′ S, 44°6′ W 138
Volterra, *It.* 43°24′ N, 10°50′ E 156
Volubilis, ruin(s), *Mor.* 34°6′ N, 5°46′ W 214
Voluntown, *Conn., U.S.* 41°34′ N, 71°52′ W 104
Volzhsk, *Russ.* 55°52′ N, 48°25′ E 154
Volzhskiy, *Russ.* 48°49′ N, 44°50′ E 184
Vonavona, island, *Solomon Islands* 8°17′ S, 157°0′ E 242
Vonda, *Can.* 52°19′ N, 106°5′ W 108
Vondrozo, *Madagascar* 22°49′ S, 47°19′ E 220
Võnnu, *Est.* 58°16′ N, 27°3′ E 166
Voo, *Kenya* 1°41′ S, 38°20′ E 224
Voranava, *Belarus* 54°8′ N, 25°18′ E 166
Vorder-rhein, river, *Switz.* 46°40′ N, 8°52′ E 167
Vordingborg, *Den.* 55°0′ N, 11°55′ E 152
Vóreio Egéo, adm. division, *Gr.* 38°45′ N, 26°0′ E 156
Vorga, *Russ.* 53°42′ N, 32°45′ E 154
Vóries Sporádes, islands, *Aegean Sea* 39°8′ N, 23°37′ E 180
Voring Plateau, *Norwegian Sea* 67°13′ N, 4°23′ E 255
Vorkuta, *Russ.* 67°25′ N, 64°4′ E 169
Vorlich, Ben, peak, *U.K.* 56°20′ N, 4°20′ W 150
Vormsi, island, *Est.* 59°3′ N, 23°1′ E 166
Vorogovo, *Russ.* 60°57′ N, 89°25′ E 169
Vorona, river, *Russ.* 52°8′ N, 42°26′ E 158
Voronech', *Belarus* 55°18′ N, 28°35′ E 166
Voronezh, *Russ.* 51°38′ N, 39°11′ E 158
Voronezh, adm. division, *Russ.* 50°50′ N, 38°58′ E 158
Voronezh, river, *Russ.* 52°21′ N, 39°31′ E 158
Vorontsovka, *Russ.* 59°37′ N, 60°12′ E 154
Vorontsovo, *Russ.* 57°18′ N, 28°42′ E 166
Vorontsovo, *Russ.* 71°40′ N, 83°35′ E 160
Voron'ye, *Russ.* 68°28′ N, 35°22′ E 152
Vorposten Peak, *Antarctica* 71°31′ S, 14°56′ E 248
Vorskla, river, *Ukr.* 49°36′ N, 34°40′ E 158
Vørterkaka Nunatak, peak, *Antarctica* 72°42′ S, 27°23′ E 248
Võrts Järv, lake, *Est.* 58°19′ N, 25°43′ E 166
Võru, *Est.* 57°49′ N, 27°0′ E 166
Vorukh, *Taj.* 39°50′ N, 70°34′ E 197
Vosburg, *S. Af.* 30°35′ S, 22°49′ E 227
Vose, *Taj.* 37°46′ N, 69°41′ E 197
Vosges, *Fr.* 48°57′ N, 6°56′ E 163
Voskresensk, *Russ.* 55°19′ N, 38°43′ E 154
Voskresenskoye, *Russ.* 56°48′ N, 45°28′ E 154
Voskresenskoye, *Russ.* 59°25′ N, 37°56′ E 154
Voskresenskoye, *Russ.* 53°8′ N, 56°4′ E 154
Voss, *Nor.* 60°37′ N, 6°22′ E 152
Vostochnaya Guba, *Russ.* 67°24′ N, 32°38′ E 152
Vostok, Russia, station, *Antarctica* 78°31′ S, 107°1′ E 248
Võsu, *Est.* 59°33′ N, 25°56′ E 166
Votaw, *Tex., U.S.* 30°24′ N, 94°41′ W 103
Votice, *Czech Rep.* 49°38′ N, 14°37′ E 152
Votkinsk, *Russ.* 57°0′ N, 53°55′ E 154
Votuporanga, *Braz.* 20°25′ S, 49°59′ W 138
Voulgára, peak, *Gr.* 39°5′ N, 21°50′ E 156
Voulx, *Fr.* 48°14′ N, 2°59′ E 163
Vounása, peak, *Gr.* 39°56′ N, 21°41′ E 156
Voúrnios, Óros, *Gr.* 40°3′ N, 21°16′ E 156
Vouziers, *Fr.* 49°23′ N, 4°43′ E 163
Vovchans'k, *Ukr.* 50°16′ N, 36°57′ E 158
Voves, *Fr.* 48°15′ N, 1°38′ E 163
Vovodo, river, *Cen. Af. Rep.* 5°59′ N, 24°33′ E 218
Vowchyn, *Belarus* 52°17′ N, 23°17′ E 152
Voyageurs National Park, *Minn., U.S.* 48°14′ N, 94°58′ W 94
Voynitsa, *Russ.* 65°9′ N, 30°18′ E 152
Voyvozh, *Russ.* 62°54′ N, 55°5′ E 154
Vozhayel', *Russ.* 62°50′ N, 51°22′ E 154
Vozhe, Ozero, lake, *Russ.* 60°35′ N, 38°36′ E 154
Vozhega, *Russ.* 60°27′ N, 40°10′ E 154
Vozhgora, *Russ.* 64°34′ N, 48°21′ E 154
Vozhma, *Russ.* 58°55′ N, 46°47′ E 154
Vozh'yel', *Russ.* 63°14′ N, 49°37′ E 154
Voznesens'k, *Ukr.* 47°36′ N, 31°21′ E 156
Voznesen'ye, *Russ.* 61°1′ N, 35°30′ E 154
Vozvyahenka, *Kaz.* 54°28′ N, 70°52′ E 184
Vrachíonas, peak, *Gr.* 37°49′ N, 20°39′ E 156
Vrancea, adm. division, *Rom.* 45°41′ N, 26°29′ E 156
Vrancei, Munţii, *Rom.* 45°49′ N, 25°55′ E 156
Vrang, *Taj.* 37°1′ N, 72°22′ E 186
Vrangelya, Ostrov (Wrangel Island), island, *Russ.* 71°29′ N, 175°23′ E 160
Vranica, peak, *Bosn. and Herzg.* 43°56′ N, 17°40′ E 168
Vranje, *Serb.* 42°33′ N, 21°54′ E 168
Vranjska Banja, *Serb.* 42°32′ N, 22°1′ E 168
Vratsa, *Bulg.* 43°12′ N, 23°33′ E 156
Vratsa, adm. division, *Bulg.* 43°18′ N, 23°27′ E 156
Vrbanja, *Croatia* 44°58′ N, 18°55′ E 168
Vrbas, *Serb.* 45°33′ N, 19°38′ E 168
Vrbnik, *Croatia* 44°0′ N, 16°9′ E 168
Vrbnik, *Croatia* 45°4′ N, 14°39′ E 156
Vrboska, *Croatia* 43°9′ N, 16°40′ E 156
Vrbovec, *Croatia* 45°53′ N, 16°25′ E 168
Vrčin, *Serb.* 44°40′ N, 20°33′ E 168
Vrdnik, *Serb.* 45°7′ N, 19°47′ E 168
Vrede, *S. Af.* 27°27′ S, 29°8′ E 227
Vreden, *Ger.* 52°2′ N, 6°49′ E 167
Vredenburg, *S. Af.* 32°55′ S, 17°58′ E 227
Vrginmost, *Croatia* 45°20′ N, 15°52′ E 168
Vrgorac, *Croatia* 43°11′ N, 17°22′ E 168
Vrlika, *Croatia* 43°55′ N, 16°24′ E 168
Vrnograč, *Bosn. and Herzg.* 45°9′ N, 15°57′ E 168
Vršac, *Serb.* 45°7′ N, 21°18′ E 168
Vrtoče, *Bosn. and Herzg.* 44°38′ N, 16°10′ E 168
Vryburg, *S. Af.* 26°59′ S, 24°42′ E 227
Vryheid, *S. Af.* 27°48′ S, 30°45′ E 227
Vsevolodo Blagodatskiy, *Russ.* 60°28′ N, 59°59′ E 154
Vsheli, *Russ.* 58°10′ N, 29°50′ E 166
Vu Liet, *Vietnam* 18°42′ N, 105°22′ E 202
Vučitrn see Vushtrria, *Kos.* 42°49′ N, 20°58′ E 168
Vučja Luka, *Bosn. and Herzg.* 43°55′ N, 18°31′ E 168
Vučje, *Serb.* 42°51′ N, 21°54′ E 168
Vught, *Neth.* 51°38′ N, 5°17′ E 167
Vuka, river, *Croatia* 45°27′ N, 18°32′ E 168
Vuktyl, *Russ.* 63°54′ N, 57°28′ E 154
Vulcan, *Can.* 50°24′ N, 113°16′ W 90
Vulcan, *Rom.* 45°22′ N, 23°18′ E 168
Vulci, ruin(s), *It.* 42°23′ N, 11°31′ E 156
Vung Tau, *Vietnam* 10°21′ N, 107°4′ E 202
Vuntut National Park, *Can.* 68°11′ N, 139°49′ W 98
Vuoggatjålme, *Nor.* 66°33′ N, 16°21′ E 152
Vuohijärvi, *Fin.* 61°4′ N, 26°47′ E 166
Vuohijärvi, lake, *Fin.* 61°7′ N, 26°20′ E 166
Vuokatti, *Fin.* 64°7′ N, 28°13′ E 152
Vuollerim, *Nor.* 66°25′ N, 20°36′ E 152
Vuonislahti, *Fin.* 63°8′ N, 29°59′ E 152
Vuotso, *Fin.* 68°5′ N, 27°6′ E 152
Vurnary, *Russ.* 55°28′ N, 47°1′ E 154
Vushtrria (Vučitrn), *Kos.* 42°49′ N, 20°58′ E 168
Vwawa, *Tanzania* 9°6′ S, 32°55′ E 224
Vyartsilya, *Russ.* 62°10′ N, 30°41′ E 152
Vyatka, river, *Russ.* 59°20′ N, 52°0′ E 154
Vyatskiye Polyany, *Russ.* 56°11′ N, 51°11′ E 154
Vyazemskiy, *Russ.* 47°31′ N, 134°46′ E 190
Vyaz'ma, *Russ.* 55°13′ N, 34°21′ E 154
Vyazniki, *Russ.* 56°14′ N, 42°9′ E 154
Vybor, *Russ.* 57°13′ N, 29°7′ E 166
Vyborg (Viipuri), *Russ.* 60°41′ N, 28°45′ E 166
Vyborovo, *Russ.* 58°19′ N, 29°0′ E 166
Vychegda, river, *Russ.* 61°31′ N, 48°11′ E 154
Vyderta, *Ukr.* 51°43′ N, 25°1′ E 152
Vyerkhnyadzvinsk, *Belarus* 55°46′ N, 27°56′ E 166
Vyetryna, *Belarus* 55°24′ N, 28°26′ E 166
Vyg Ozero, lake, *Russ.* 63°48′ N, 33°40′ E 152
Vyksa, *Russ.* 55°18′ N, 42°12′ E 154
Vylkove, *Ukr.* 45°26′ N, 29°35′ E 156
Vylok, *Ukr.* 48°6′ N, 22°50′ E 156
Vym', river, *Russ.* 62°41′ N, 50°53′ E 154
Vym', river, *Russ.* 63°22′ N, 51°36′ E 154
Vymsk, *Russ.* 60°24′ N, 48°19′ E 154
Vyritsa, *Russ.* 59°24′ N, 30°17′ E 166
Vyshhorod, *Ukr.* 50°32′ N, 30°35′ E 158
Vyshniy Volochek, *Russ.* 57°34′ N, 34°38′ E 154
Vysočina, adm. division, *Czech Rep.* 49°10′ N, 15°21′ E 152
Vysokaye, *Belarus* 52°21′ N, 23°20′ E 152
Vysokovsk, *Russ.* 56°17′ N, 36°31′ E 154
Vysotsk, *Russ.* 60°36′ N, 28°34′ E 166
Vysotskoye, *Russ.* 56°49′ N, 29°1′ E 166
Vytegra, *Russ.* 61°1′ N, 36°30′ E 154

W

"W" National Park, *Benin* 11°49′ N, 2°27′ E 222
Wa, *Ghana* 10°2′ N, 2°30′ W 222
Wa, *Pol.* 50°45′ N, 16°16′ E 152
Waajid, *Somalia* 3°47′ N, 43°16′ E 218
Waal, river, *Neth.* 51°54′ N, 5°35′ E 167
Waalwijk, *Neth.* 51°41′ N, 5°5′ E 167

Waas, Mount, peak, *Utah, U.S.* 38°31′ N, 109°19′ W 90
Waʻat, *Sudan* 8°8′ N, 32°7′ E 224
Wababimiga Lake, *Can.* 50°18′ N, 87°9′ W 94
Wabakimi Lake, *Can.* 50°34′ N, 90°20′ W 110
Wabana, *Can.* 47°38′ N, 52°56′ W 111
Wabasca, river, *Can.* 56°15′ N, 113°42′ W 108
Wabasca-Desmarais, *Can.* 55°59′ N, 113°52′ W 108
Wabash, *Ind., U.S.* 40°48′ N, 85°50′ W 102
Wabash, river, *Ind., U.S.* 40°48′ N, 85°14′ W 102
Wabasha, *Minn., U.S.* 44°21′ N, 92°3′ W 110
Wabassi, river, *Can.* 51°46′ N, 87°39′ W 110
Wabasso, *Fla., U.S.* 27°44′ N, 80°27′ W 105
Wabē Gestro, river, *Eth.* 5°53′ N, 41°38′ E 224
Wabē Shebelē, river, *Eth.* 7°25′ N, 39°36′ E 224
Wabern, *Ger.* 51°6′ N, 9°21′ E 167
Wabimeig Lake, *Can.* 51°26′ N, 86°15′ W 110
Waboose Dam, *Can.* 50°51′ N, 88°0′ W 110
Wabowden, *Can.* 54°54′ N, 98°38′ W 108
Wabuk Point, *Can.* 55°18′ N, 87°23′ W 106
W.A.C. Bennett Dam, *Can.* 55°51′ N, 123°2′ W 108
Waccasassa Bay 29°6′ N, 82°54′ W 105
Wächtersbach, *Ger.* 50°15′ N, 9°17′ E 167
Waco, *Can.* 51°26′ N, 65°36′ W 111
Waco, *Tex., U.S.* 31°31′ N, 97°8′ W 96
Waconichi, Lac, lake, *Can.* 50°5′ N, 74°39′ W 94
Wad Abu Nahl, *Sudan* 13°6′ N, 34°53′ E 182
Wad Banda, *Sudan* 13°4′ N, 27°56′ E 216
Wad el Haddad, *Sudan* 13°48′ N, 33°30′ E 182
Wad Hamid, *Sudan* 16°27′ N, 32°45′ E 182
Wad Medani, *Sudan* 14°23′ N, 33°29′ E 182
Wadamago, *Somalia* 8°52′ N, 46°15′ E 216
Wadayama, *Japan* 35°19′ N, 134°48′ E 201
Waddān, *Lib.* 29°10′ N, 16°6′ E 216
Waddenzee 53°5′ N, 4°54′ E 163
Waddington, *N.Y., U.S.* 44°51′ N, 75°13′ W 94
Waddington, Mount, peak, *Can.* 51°22′ N, 125°21′ W 90
Wadena, *Can.* 51°56′ N, 103°48′ W 90
Wadena, *Minn., U.S.* 46°25′ N, 95°9′ W 94
Wadersloh, *Ger.* 51°44′ N, 8°14′ E 167
Wādī al Masīlah, river, *Yemen* 16°12′ N, 49°33′ E 182
Wādī as Sīr, *Jordan* 31°56′ N, 35°48′ E 194
Wâdi Gimâl, Gezîrat, island, *Egypt* 24°30′ N, 33°51′ E 182
Wadi Halfa, *Sudan* 21°46′ N, 31°20′ E 182
Wādīas Sir ḩān, *Saudi Arabia* 31°38′ N, 37°3′ E 194
Wadsworth, *Nev., U.S.* 39°38′ N, 119°19′ W 90
Wadsworth, *Ohio, U.S.* 41°0′ N, 81°44′ W 102
Wadu, island, *Maldives* 5°44′ N, 72°17′ E 188
Waelder, *Tex., U.S.* 29°40′ N, 97°18′ W 96
Waesche, Mount, peak, *Antarctica* 77°3′ S, 126°15′ W 248
Wafangdian, *China* 39°39′ N, 121°59′ E 198
Wafania, *Dem. Rep. of the Congo* 1°23′ S, 20°19′ E 218
Wafra, oil field, *Kuwait* 28°34′ N, 47°52′ E 196
Wagenia Fisheries, site, *Dem. Rep. of the Congo* 0°25′ N, 25°17′ E 224
Wageningen, *Neth.* 51°58′ N, 5°39′ E 167
Wager Bay 65°25′ N, 90°48′ W 106
Wager, Isla, island, *Chile* 47°34′ S, 75°43′ W 134
Waglisla, *Can.* 52°10′ N, 128°10′ W 108
Wagner, *S. Dak., U.S.* 43°3′ N, 98°19′ W 90
Wagner Nunatak, peak, *Antarctica* 83°59′ S, 68°23′ W 248
Wagon Mound, *N. Mex., U.S.* 36°0′ N, 104°43′ W 92
Wagontire Mountain, peak, *Oreg., U.S.* 43°20′ N, 119°58′ W 90
Wah Wah Range, *Utah, U.S.* 38°29′ N, 113°52′ W 90
Waha, oil field, *Lib.* 28°2′ N, 19°46′ E 216
Wahaʻula Heiau, site, *Hawaiʻi, U.S.* 19°19′ N, 155°5′ W 99
Wahoo, *Nebr., U.S.* 41°12′ N, 96°38′ W 90
Wahpeton, *N. Dak., U.S.* 46°15′ N, 96°38′ W 90
Wai, *India* 17°58′ N, 73°55′ E 188
Waiʻaleʻale, peak, *Hawaiʻi, U.S.* 22°4′ N, 159°33′ W 99
Wāīas Sir'ān, *Jordan* 31°26′ N, 36°56′ E 194
Waiau, *N.Z.* 42°40′ S, 173°3′ E 240
Waiau, river, *N.Z.* 45°42′ S, 167°34′ E 240
Waigeo, island, *Indonesia* 7°416′ N, 130°3′ E 192
Waihi, *N.Z.* 37°23′ S, 175°50′ E 240
Waihola, *N.Z.* 46°3′ S, 170°7′ E 240
Waikabubak, *Indonesia* 9°39′ S, 119°20′ E 192
Waikanae, *N.Z.* 40°54′ S, 175°6′ E 240
Waikawa, *N.Z.* 46°38′ S, 169°6′ E 240
Waikiwi, *N.Z.* 46°24′ S, 168°20′ E 240
Waikouaiti, *N.Z.* 45°35′ S, 170°40′ E 240
Waimamaku, *N.Z.* 35°34′ S, 173°28′ E 240
Waimangaroa, *N.Z.* 41°45′ S, 171°45′ E 240
Waimarama, *N.Z.* 39°49′ S, 176°58′ E 240
Waimate, *N.Z.* 44°45′ S, 171°2′ E 240
Wainfleet All Saints, *U.K.* 53°7′ N, 0°14′ E 162
Waingapu, *Indonesia* 9°41′ S, 120°4′ E 192
Waini Point, *Guyana* 8°25′ N, 59°51′ W 116
Wainwright, *Alas., U.S.* 70°37′ N, 160°3′ W 246
Wainwright, *Can.* 52°50′ N, 110°51′ W 108
Waiohonu Petroglyphs, site, *Hawaiʻi, U.S.* 20°42′ N, 156°3′ W 99
Waiʻoli Mission, site, *Hawaiʻi, U.S.* 22°11′ N, 159°33′ W 99
Waiotira, *N.Z.* 35°57′ S, 174°12′ E 240
Waiouru, *N.Z.* 39°30′ S, 175°40′ E 240
Waipahi, *N.Z.* 46°9′ S, 169°14′ E 240
Waipara, *N.Z.* 43°4′ S, 172°45′ E 240
Waipawa, *N.Z.* 39°58′ S, 176°35′ E 240
Waipu, *N.Z.* 36°0′ S, 174°26′ E 240
Waipukurau, *N.Z.* 40°1′ S, 176°35′ E 240
Wairau Valley, *N.Z.* 41°36′ S, 173°31′ E 240
Wairoa, *N.Z.* 39°4′ S, 177°23′ E 240
Waitahanui, *N.Z.* 38°48′ S, 176°5′ E 240
Waitakaruru, *N.Z.* 37°16′ S, 175°24′ E 240
Waitakere, *N.Z.* 36°52′ S, 174°37′ E 240
Waitara, *N.Z.* 39°2′ S, 174°13′ E 240
Waitati, *N.Z.* 45°46′ S, 170°34′ E 240
Waite, Cape, *Antarctica* 72°42′ S, 103°44′ W 248
Waitoa, *N.Z.* 37°36′ S, 175°39′ E 240
Waitomo Caves, site, *N.Z.* 38°18′ S, 175°2′ E 240
Waitotara, *N.Z.* 39°49′ S, 174°43′ E 240
Wajima, *Japan* 37°23′ N, 136°53′ E 201
Wajir, *Kenya* 1°42′ N, 40°2′ E 224
Waka, *Dem. Rep. of the Congo* 0°50′ N, 20°3′ E 218
Waka, *Dem. Rep. of the Congo* 0°58′ N, 20°13′ E 218
Waka, *Eth.* 7°5′ N, 37°18′ E 224
Wakami Lake, *Can.* 47°27′ N, 83°25′ W 94
Wakasa, *Japan* 35°18′ N, 134°22′ E 201
Wakasa Wan 35°32′ N, 135°31′ E 201
Wakaw, *Can.* 52°39′ N, 105°45′ W 108
Wakayama, *Japan* 34°12′ N, 135°10′ E 201
Wakayama, adm. division, *Japan* 34°13′ N, 135°16′ E 201
Wake Forest, *N.C., U.S.* 35°58′ N, 78°31′ W 96
Wake Island, *U.S.* 19°19′ N, 166°31′ E 252
Wakeeney, *Kans., U.S.* 39°0′ N, 99°54′ W 90
Wakefield, *Bhutan, U.S.* 39°11′ N, 97°2′ W 90
Wakefield, *Mich., U.S.* 46°28′ N, 89°57′ W 94
Wakefield, *Nebr., U.S.* 42°15′ N, 96°52′ W 94
Wakefield, *R.I., U.S.* 41°26′ N, 71°30′ W 104
Wakefield, *U.K.* 53°41′ N, 1°30′ W 162
Wakema, *Myanmar* 16°36′ N, 95°9′ E 202
Wakenaam Island, *Guyana* 6°59′ N, 58°35′ W 130
Wakkanai, *Japan* 45°18′ N, 141°48′ E 190
Wakkerstroom, *S. Af.* 27°20′ S, 30°7′ E 227
Wakuach, Lac, lake, *Can.* 55°34′ N, 69°29′ W 106
Wakulla Springs, site, *Fla., U.S.* 30°12′ N, 84°23′ W 96
Walachia, region, *Rom.* 44°28′ N, 22°46′ E 168
Walberswick, *U.K.* 52°18′ N, 1°39′ E 163
Walcott, *Can.* 54°30′ N, 126°54′ W 108
Walcott Inlet 16°45′ S, 123°56′ E 230
Waldbröl, *Ger.* 50°52′ N, 7°36′ E 167
Waldeck, *Ger.* 51°12′ N, 9°4′ E 167
Walden, *Vt., U.S.* 44°26′ N, 72°14′ W 104
Waldfischbach-Burgalben, *Ger.* 49°16′ N, 7°38′ E 163
Waldheim, *Can.* 52°37′ N, 106°39′ W 108
Waldo, *Ark., U.S.* 33°20′ N, 93°18′ W 103
Waldo, *Fla., U.S.* 29°47′ N, 82°11′ W 105
Waldport, *Oreg., U.S.* 44°23′ N, 124°3′ W 90
Waldron, *Ark., U.S.* 34°52′ N, 94°6′ W 96
Waldron, *Ind., U.S.* 39°27′ N, 85°40′ W 102
Waldron, Cape, *Antarctica* 66°15′ S, 119°43′ E 248
Wales, *Alas., U.S.* 65°31′ N, 168°7′ W 98
Wales, *Mass., U.S.* 42°3′ N, 72°11′ W 104
Wales, adm. division, *U.K.* 52°21′ N, 3°52′ W 162
Wales Island, island, *Can.* 67°38′ N, 89°20′ W 106
Walewale, *Ghana* 10°21′ N, 0°49′ E 222
Walgreen Coast, *Antarctica* 75°29′ S, 102°49′ W 248
Walhalla, *Mich., U.S.* 43°56′ N, 86°7′ W 102
Walhalla, *N. Dak., U.S.* 48°54′ N, 97°56′ W 90
Walhalla, *S.C., U.S.* 34°45′ N, 83°5′ W 96
Walikale, *Dem. Rep. of the Congo* 1°30′ S, 28°5′ E 224
Walker, *La., U.S.* 30°29′ N, 90°52′ W 103
Walker, *Mich., U.S.* 42°59′ N, 85°43′ W 102
Walker, *Minn., U.S.* 47°4′ N, 94°37′ W 90
Walker, Lac, lake, *Can.* 50°24′ N, 67°30′ W 111
Walker Lake, *Nev., U.S.* 38°38′ N, 119°38′ W 80
Walker Lake, lake, *Can.* 54°36′ N, 97°31′ W 108
Walker Pass, *Calif., U.S.* 35°39′ N, 118°3′ W 101
Walkerton, *Can.* 44°7′ N, 81°9′ W 102
Walkerton, *Ind., U.S.* 41°28′ N, 86°29′ W 102
Walkerville, *Mich., U.S.* 43°42′ N, 86°7′ W 102
Wall, *S. Dak., U.S.* 43°59′ N, 102°16′ W 90
Wall, Mount, peak, *Austral.* 22°50′ S, 116°37′ E 230
Walla Walla, *Wash., U.S.* 46°4′ N, 118°22′ W 106
Wallabi Group, islands, *Indian Ocean* 28°15′ S, 113°42′ E 230
Wallace, *Idaho, U.S.* 47°26′ N, 115°54′ W 82
Wallace, *Nebr., U.S.* 40°50′ N, 101°11′ W 90
Wallace, *N.C., U.S.* 34°44′ N, 78°0′ W 96
Wallace Mountain, peak, *Can.* 54°55′ N, 115°56′ W 108
Wallaceburg, *Can.* 42°34′ N, 82°22′ W 102
Wallaroo, *Austral.* 33°55′ S, 137°39′ E 231
Wallasey, *U.K.* 53°25′ N, 3°2′ W 162
Walldorf, *Ger.* 50°36′ N, 10°23′ E 167
Wallenhorst, *Ger.* 52°20′ N, 7°59′ E 163
Wallingford, *Conn., U.S.* 41°27′ N, 72°50′ W 104
Wallingford, *Vt., U.S.* 43°28′ N, 72°59′ W 104
Wallis, Îles, islands, *South Pacific Ocean* 14°55′ S, 177°49′ W 238
Wallops Island, *Va., U.S.* 37°25′ N, 75°20′ W 80
Wallowa Mountains, *Oreg., U.S.* 45°28′ N, 117°49′ W 90
Walmer, *U.K.* 51°12′ N, 1°23′ E 163
Walnum, Mount, peak, *Antarctica* 72°8′ S, 23°50′ E 248
Walnut, *Ill., U.S.* 41°33′ N, 89°36′ W 102
Walnut Cove, *N.C., U.S.* 36°18′ N, 80°10′ W 94
Walnut Grove, *Calif., U.S.* 38°13′ N, 121°32′ W 100
Walnut Grove, *Miss., U.S.* 32°34′ N, 89°28′ W 103
Walnut Ridge, *Ark., U.S.* 36°3′ N, 90°58′ W 96
Walong, *India* 28°10′ N, 97°0′ E 188
Walpi, *Ariz., U.S.* 35°49′ N, 110°24′ W 92
Walpole, *Mass., U.S.* 42°5′ N, 71°16′ W 104
Walpole, *N.H., U.S.* 43°4′ N, 72°26′ W 104
Walsall, *U.K.* 52°35′ N, 2°0′ W 162
Walsenburg, *Colo., U.S.* 37°37′ N, 104°48′ W 92
Walsh, *Colo., U.S.* 37°22′ N, 102°17′ W 92
Walsingham, *U.K.* 52°53′ N, 0°52′ E 163
Walt Disney World, *Fla., U.S.* 28°23′ N, 81°34′ W 105
Walterboro, *S.C., U.S.* 32°54′ N, 80°41′ W 96
Walters Shoal, *Indian Ocean* 33°25′ S, 43°32′ E 254
Waltham, *Mass., U.S.* 42°22′ N, 71°15′ W 104
Walton, *Ind., U.S.* 40°39′ N, 86°14′ W 102
Walton, *Ky., U.S.* 38°51′ N, 84°36′ W 102
Walton, *N.Y., U.S.* 42°10′ N, 75°9′ W 94
Walton on the Naze, *U.K.* 51°50′ N, 1°15′ E 163
Walvis Bay, *Namibia* 23°0′ S, 14°33′ E 207
Walvis Ridge, *South Atlantic Ocean* 26°7′ S, 5°31′ E 253
Walyahmoning Rock, peak, *Austral.* 30°41′ S, 118°32′ E 230
Wamac, *Ill., U.S.* 38°29′ N, 89°8′ W 102
Wamba, *Dem. Rep. of the Congo* 1°37′ S, 22°28′ E 218
Wamba, *Dem. Rep. of the Congo* 2°9′ N, 27°57′ E 218
Wamba, *Nig.* 8°55′ N, 8°35′ E 222
Wampú, river, *Hond.* 15°0′ N, 85°36′ W 115
Wampusirpi, *Hond.* 15°11′ N, 84°38′ W 115
Wamsutter, *Wyo., U.S.* 41°40′ N, 107°58′ W 90
Wana, *Pak.* 32°19′ N, 69°40′ E 188
Wan'an, *China* 26°28′ N, 114°46′ E 198
Wandel Sea 82°11′ N, 24°59′ W 246
Wandering River, *Can.* 55°9′ N, 112°27′ W 108
Wando, *S. Korea* 34°17′ N, 126°47′ E 200
Wanfried, *Ger.* 51°11′ N, 10°10′ E 167
Wang Kai, *Sudan* 9°3′ N, 29°29′ E 224
Wang, river, *Thai.* 17°37′ N, 99°18′ E 202
Wanganui, *N.Z.* 39°57′ S, 175°2′ E 240
Wangcang, *China* 32°17′ N, 106°21′ E 198
Wangda see Zogang, *China* 29°42′ N, 97°53′ E 188
Wangdiphodrang, *Bhutan* 27°30′ N, 89°54′ E 197
Wangdu, *China* 38°40′ N, 115°6′ E 198
Wangkui, *China* 46°50′ N, 126°30′ E 198
Wangmo, *China* 25°10′ N, 106°6′ E 198
Wangou, *China* 42°4′ N, 126°56′ E 200
Wangpan Yang 30°22′ N, 120°37′ E 198
Wanham, *Can.* 55°43′ N, 118°22′ W 108
Wani, *India* 20°2′ N, 78°57′ E 188
Wanie Rukula, *Dem. Rep. of the Congo* 0°12′ N, 25°35′ E 224
Wankaner, *India* 22°35′ N, 70°56′ E 186
Wanning, *China* 18°48′ N, 110°19′ E 198
Wanow, *Afghan.* 32°37′ N, 65°55′ E 186
Wantage, *U.K.* 51°35′ N, 1°26′ W 162
Wantagh, *N.Y., U.S.* 40°40′ N, 73°30′ W 104
Wanxian, *China* 30°47′ N, 108°17′ E 198
Wanyuan, *China* 32°5′ N, 108°7′ E 198
Wanzai, *China* 28°5′ N, 114°27′ E 198
Wapakoneta, *Ohio, U.S.* 40°33′ N, 84°11′ W 102
Wapata Lake, lake, *Can.* 58°46′ N, 106°16′ W 108
Wapawekka Lake, lake, *Can.* 54°49′ N, 105°23′ W 108
Wapella, *Can.* 50°17′ N, 102°0′ W 90
Wapello, *Iowa, U.S.* 41°10′ N, 91°12′ W 110
Wapesi, river, *Can.* 50°25′ N, 92°17′ W 110
Wapiti, river, *Can.* 54°43′ N, 119°50′ W 108
Wapou, *Côte d'Ivoire* 4°38′ N, 7°12′ W 222
Wappingers Falls, *N.Y., U.S.* 41°35′ N, 73°56′ W 104
Wapta Icefield, glacier, *Can.* 51°44′ N, 117°0′ W 108
Wapusk National Park, *Can.* 57°35′ N, 93°37′ W 108
War, *W. Va., U.S.* 37°18′ N, 81°42′ W 96
War Galoh, *Somalia* 6°15′ N, 47°36′ E 218
Warab, *Sudan* 8°2′ N, 28°35′ E 224
Warab, adm. division, *Sudan* 7°50′ N, 28°24′ E 224
Warangal, *India* 17°59′ N, 79°33′ E 188
Warburg, *Ger.* 51°29′ N, 9°8′ E 167
Ward, *N.Z.* 41°51′ S, 174°7′ E 240
Ward Cove, *Alas., U.S.* 55°26′ N, 131°46′ W 108
Ward Hill, peak 58°52′ N, 3°28′ W 150
Ward, Mount, peak, *Antarctica* 71°45′ S, 66°36′ W 248
Ward Mountain, peak, *Nev., U.S.* 39°5′ N, 115°0′ W 90
Warden, *S. Af.* 27°53′ S, 28°55′ E 227
Warden, *Wash., U.S.* 46°56′ N, 119°3′ W 90
Wardenburg, *Ger.* 53°4′ N, 8°12′ E 163
Wardha, *India* 20°43′ N, 78°36′ E 188
Ward's Stone, peak, *U.K.* 54°1′ N, 2°40′ W 162
Wardsboro, *Vt., U.S.* 43°2′ N, 72°48′ W 104
Ware, *Can.* 57°26′ N, 125°37′ W 108
Ware, *Mass., U.S.* 42°15′ N, 72°15′ W 104
Ware Shoals, *S.C., U.S.* 34°23′ N, 82°16′ W 96
Waregem, *Belg.* 50°53′ N, 3°26′ E 163
Wareham, *Mass., U.S.* 41°45′ N, 70°45′ W 104
Warehouse Point, *Conn., U.S.* 41°55′ N, 72°37′ W 104
Waremme, *Belg.* 50°41′ N, 5°14′ E 167
Waren, *Indonesia* 2°27′ S, 136°18′ E 192
Warendorf, *Ger.* 51°57′ N, 7°59′ E 167
Warffum, *Neth.* 53°23′ N, 6°34′ E 163
Warka, *Pol.* 51°47′ N, 21°11′ E 152
Warkworth, *U.K.* 55°20′ N, 1°37′ W 150
Warlubie, *Pol.* 53°35′ N, 18°37′ E 152
Warm Springs, *Ga., U.S.* 32°53′ N, 84°41′ W 96
Warman, *Can.* 52°17′ N, 106°34′ W 108
Warmbad, *Namibia* 28°28′ S, 18°45′ E 227
Warmbaths see Bela-Bela, *S. Af.* 24°55′ S, 28°16′ E 227
Warmeriville, *Fr.* 49°21′ N, 4°13′ E 163
Warmińsko-Mazurskie, adm. division, *Pol.* 53°57′ N, 19°25′ E 152
Warminster, *U.K.* 51°12′ N, 2°12′ W 162
Warner, *Can.* 49°16′ N, 112°12′ W 90
Warner, *N.H., U.S.* 43°16′ N, 71°49′ W 104
Warner, Mount, peak, *Can.* 51°4′ N, 123°17′ W 90
Warner Mountains, *Calif., U.S.* 41°1′ N, 120°16′ W 90
Warner Robins, *Ga., U.S.* 32°32′ N, 83°36′ W 112
Warner Valley, *Oreg., U.S.* 42°48′ N, 119°59′ W 90
Warnes, *Arg.* 34°54′ S, 60°30′ W 139
Warora, *India* 20°13′ N, 79°0′ E 188
Warralu, *Sudan* 8°10′ N, 27°17′ E 224
Warrego Range, *Austral.* 25°4′ S, 145°24′ E 230
Warren, *Ark., U.S.* 33°35′ N, 92°5′ W 96
Warren, *Ill., U.S.* 42°29′ N, 89°59′ W 102
Warren, *Ind., U.S.* 40°40′ N, 85°25′ W 102
Warren, *Mich., U.S.* 42°30′ N, 83°3′ W 102
Warren, *Minn., U.S.* 48°9′ N, 96°47′ W 90
Warren, *Ohio, U.S.* 41°13′ N, 80°48′ W 102
Warren, *Oreg., U.S.* 45°48′ N, 122°52′ W 100
Warren, *Pa., U.S.* 41°51′ N, 79°10′ W 94
Warren, *R.I., U.S.* 41°43′ N, 71°17′ W 104
Warren, *Tex., U.S.* 30°36′ N, 94°24′ W 103
Warren, *Vt., U.S.* 44°6′ N, 72°52′ W 104
Warren Landing, *Can.* 53°41′ N, 97°56′ W 108
Warren Peak, *Calif., U.S.* 41°21′ N, 120°19′ W 90
Warren Point, *Can.* 69°43′ N, 134°16′ W 98
Warrender, Cape, *Can.* 74°24′ N, 80°17′ W 106
Warrensburg, *N.Y., U.S.* 43°29′ N, 73°47′ W 104
Warrenton, *Ga., U.S.* 33°23′ N, 82°40′ W 96
Warrenton, *Oreg., U.S.* 46°9′ N, 123°55′ W 100
Warrenton, *S. Af.* 28°11′ S, 24°50′ E 227
Warri, *Nig.* 5°32′ N, 5°42′ E 222
Warrington, *U.K.* 53°23′ N, 2°36′ W 162
Warrnambool, *Austral.* 38°21′ S, 142°29′ E 231
Warroad, *Minn., U.S.* 48°53′ N, 95°22′ W 90
Warsaw, *Ind., U.S.* 41°13′ N, 85°51′ W 102
Warsaw, *Ky., U.S.* 38°45′ N, 84°54′ W 102
Warsaw, *N.C., U.S.* 34°59′ N, 78°6′ W 96
Warsaw, *Ohio, U.S.* 40°20′ N, 82°1′ W 102
Warsaw see Warszawa, *Pol.* 52°12′ N, 20°50′ E 152
Warshiikh, *Somalia* 2°15′ N, 45°53′ E 218
Warsop, *U.K.* 53°12′ N, 1°9′ W 162
Warstein, *Ger.* 51°26′ N, 8°20′ E 167
Warszawa (Warsaw), *Pol.* 52°12′ N, 20°50′ E 152
Warton, *U.K.* 53°44′ N, 2°54′ W 162
Warwick, *Austral.* 28°12′ S, 152°3′ E 231
Warwick, *R.I., U.S.* 41°41′ N, 71°23′ W 104
Warwick, *U.K.* 52°16′ N, 1°36′ W 162
Wasagu, *Nig.* 11°20′ N, 5°51′ E 222
Wasam, *Pak.* 36°32′ N, 72°53′ E 186
Wasatch Range, *Utah, U.S.* 39°56′ N, 111°51′ W 90
Wasco, *Calif., U.S.* 35°36′ N, 119°21′ W 100
Wasco, *Oreg., U.S.* 45°34′ N, 120°43′ W 90
Wase, *Nig.* 9°5′ N, 9°58′ E 222
Wase, river, *Nig.* 9°8′ N, 9°47′ E 222
Waseca, *Minn., U.S.* 44°3′ N, 93°33′ W 82
Wash, The 52°55′ N, 0°9′ E 162
Washakie Needles, peak, *Wyo., U.S.* 43°44′ N, 109°17′ W 90
Washburn, *Ill., U.S.* 40°54′ N, 89°18′ W 102
Washburn, *N. Dak., U.S.* 47°17′ N, 101°4′ W 108
Washburn, Mount, peak, *Wyo., U.S.* 44°46′ N, 110°31′ W 90
Washington, *D.C., U.S.* 38°52′ N, 77°9′ W 94
Washington, *Ga., U.S.* 33°43′ N, 82°45′ W 96
Washington, *Ill., U.S.* 40°41′ N, 89°25′ W 102
Washington, *Ind., U.S.* 38°39′ N, 87°10′ W 102
Washington, *Kans., U.S.* 39°48′ N, 97°3′ W 90
Washington, *Ky., U.S.* 38°36′ N, 83°49′ W 102
Washington, *Md., U.S.* 38°38′ N, 77°41′ W 72
Washington, *Miss., U.S.* 31°34′ N, 91°18′ W 96
Washington, *Mo., U.S.* 38°32′ N, 91°0′ W 94
Washington, *N.H., U.S.* 43°10′ N, 72°7′ W 104
Washington, *N.C., U.S.* 35°33′ N, 77°4′ W 96
Washington, *Pa., U.S.* 40°8′ N, 80°15′ W 82
Washington, *R.I., U.S.* 41°40′ N, 71°35′ W 104
Washington, *Utah, U.S.* 37°7′ N, 113°31′ W 101
Washington, *Wis., U.S.* 45°23′ N, 86°55′ W 94
Washington, adm. division, *Wash., U.S.* 47°10′ N, 122°22′ W 90
Washington, Cape, *Antarctica* 74°14′ S, 172°22′ E 248
Washington Court House, *Ohio, U.S.* 39°32′ N, 83°26′ W 102
Washington Depot, *Conn., U.S.* 41°38′ N, 73°20′ W 104
Washington Land 80°27′ N, 66°2′ W 246
Washington, Mount, peak, *N.H., U.S.* 44°15′ N, 71°20′ W 104
Washington, Mount, peak, *Oreg., U.S.* 44°18′ N, 121°56′ W 90
Washita, river, *Okla., U.S.* 35°38′ N, 99°16′ W 80
Washita, river, *Tex., U.S.* 35°36′ N, 100°25′ W 96
Washtucna, *Wash., U.S.* 46°44′ N, 118°20′ W 90
Wasior, *Indonesia* 2°39′ S, 134°28′ E 192
Wasipe, *Ghana* 8°33′ N, 2°14′ W 222
Waskaganish, *Can.* 51°27′ N, 78°42′ W 82
Waskaiowaka Lake, *Can.* 56°28′ N, 97°29′ W 108
Waskesiu Lake, *Can.* 53°55′ N, 106°2′ W 108
Waskom, *Tex., U.S.* 32°29′ N, 94°5′ W 103
Wasselonne, *Fr.* 48°37′ N, 7°26′ E 163
Wasserkuppe, peak, *Ger.* 50°29′ N, 9°54′ E 167
Wassuk Range, *Nev., U.S.* 38°57′ N, 118°59′ W 90
Wassy, *Fr.* 48°30′ N, 4°56′ E 163
Waswanipi, Lac, lake, *Can.* 49°22′ N, 77°51′ W 80
Waţá al Khān, *Syr.* 35°40′ N, 36°3′ E 194
Watamu Marine National Park, *Kenya* 3°20′ S, 39°58′ E 224
Watapi Lake, lake, *Can.* 55°18′ N, 110°3′ W 108
Watari, *Japan* 38°2′ N, 140°51′ E 201
Watch Hill, *R.I., U.S.* 41°18′ N, 71°52′ W 104
Watchet, *U.K.* 51°10′ N, 3°19′ W 162
Water Cays, islands, *North Atlantic Ocean* 23°36′ N, 79°7′ W 80
Waterboro, *Me., U.S.* 43°32′ N, 70°43′ W 104
Waterbury, *Conn., U.S.* 41°33′ N, 73°3′ W 104
Waterbury, *Vt., U.S.* 44°19′ N, 72°46′ W 104
Waterbury Center, *Vt., U.S.* 44°22′ N, 72°44′ W 104
Waterbury Lake, lake, *Can.* 58°2′ N, 105°7′ W 108
Wateree Lake, *S.C., U.S.* 34°20′ N, 81°49′ W 80
Waterford, *Calif., U.S.* 37°38′ N, 120°47′ W 100
Waterford, *Conn., U.S.* 41°20′ N, 72°9′ W 104
Waterford, *Wis., U.S.* 42°46′ N, 88°14′ W 102
Waterford (Port Láirge), *Ire.* 52°15′ N, 7°8′ W 150
Waterfound, river, *Can.* 58°27′ N, 104°45′ W 108
Waterloo, *Can.* 45°20′ N, 72°33′ W 94
Waterloo, *Can.* 43°27′ N, 80°32′ W 94
Waterloo, *Ind., U.S.* 41°25′ N, 85°2′ W 102
Waterloo, *Iowa, U.S.* 42°28′ N, 92°22′ W 94
Waterloo, *Mo., U.S.* 38°19′ N, 90°9′ W 94
Waterloo, *Sierra Leone* 8°20′ N, 13°4′ W 222
Waterloo, *Wis., U.S.* 43°10′ N, 89°0′ W 102
Waterman, *Ill., U.S.* 41°45′ N, 88°48′ W 102
Waterman, Isla, island, *Chile* 55°22′ S, 71°46′ W 134
Waterproof, *La., U.S.* 31°47′ N, 91°24′ W 103
Watersmeet, *Mich., U.S.* 46°16′ N, 89°11′ W 94
Waterton Lakes National Park, *Can.* 49°4′ N, 113°35′ W 80
Watertown, *Conn., U.S.* 41°36′ N, 73°7′ W 104
Watertown, *N.Y., U.S.* 43°58′ N, 75°55′ W 94
Watertown, *S. Dak., U.S.* 44°52′ N, 97°7′ W 90

Watertown, *Wis., U.S.* 43°10' N, 88°43' W 102
Waterval Boven, *S. Af.* 25°40' S, 30°17' E 227
Waterville, *Kans., U.S.* 39°40' N, 96°45' W 90
Waterville, *Me., U.S.* 44°32' N, 69°39' W 104
Waterville, *Minn., U.S.* 44°11' N, 93°35' W 94
Waterville, *Ohio, U.S.* 41°29' N, 83°44' W 102
Waterville, *Wash., U.S.* 47°38' N, 120°5' W 90
Waterville Valley, *N.H., U.S.* 43°57' N, 71°31' W 104
Watervliet, *Mich., U.S.* 42°10' N, 86°15' W 102
Watervliet, *N.Y., U.S.* 42°43' N, 73°44' W 104
Watford, *Can.* 42°56' N, 81°52' W 102
Watford, *U.K.* 51°39' N, 0°25' E 162
Watford City, *N. Dak., U.S.* 47°47' N, 103°18' W 90
Wathaman Lake, lake, *Can.* 56°56' N, 104°28' W 108
Wathena, *Kans., U.S.* 39°44' N, 94°57' W 94
Watino, *Can.* 55°41' N, 117°41' W 108
Watling see San Salvador, island, *Bahamas* 23°41' N, 74°29' W 116
Watonga, *Okla., U.S.* 35°49' N, 98°24' W 92
Watrous, *Can.* 51°41' N, 105°29' W 90
Watrous, *N. Mex., U.S.* 35°46' N, 104°59' W 92
Watsa, *Dem. Rep. of the Congo* 2°59' N, 29°31' E 224
Watseka, *Ill., U.S.* 40°45' N, 87°44' W 102
Watsi Kengo, *Dem. Rep. of the Congo* 0°47' N, 20°31' E 218
Watson, *Can.* 52°7' N, 104°32' W 108
Watson Lake, *Can.* 60°6' N, 128°46' W 98
Watsonville, *Calif., U.S.* 36°54' N, 121°46' W 100
Watton, *U.K.* 52°33' N, 0°51' E 162
Wattwil, *Switz.* 47°19' N, 9°5' E 156
Wau, *P.N.G.* 7°22' S, 146°41' E 192
Wau, *Sudan* 7°39' N, 27°58' E 224
Wau, river, *Sudan* 6°8' N, 27°1' E 224
Waubay, *S. Dak., U.S.* 45°18' N, 97°19' W 90
Wauchula, *Fla., U.S.* 27°33' N, 81°49' W 105
Waucoba Mountain, peak, *Calif., U.S.* 37°1' N, 118°3' W 101
Waugh, *Can.* 49°37' N, 95°13' W 90
Waukena, *Calif., U.S.* 36°8' N, 119°31' W 100
Waukesha, *Wis., U.S.* 43°1' N, 88°14' W 102
Waupaca, *Wis., U.S.* 44°20' N, 89°6' W 94
Waupun, *Wis., U.S.* 43°37' N, 88°44' W 102
Wauregan, *Conn., U.S.* 41°44' N, 71°55' W 104
Waurika, *Okla., U.S.* 34°8' N, 97°59' W 96
Wausa, *Nebr., U.S.* 42°29' N, 97°33' W 90
Wausau, *Wis., U.S.* 44°56' N, 89°37' W 94
Wauseon, *Ohio, U.S.* 41°32' N, 84°9' W 102
Wautoma, *Wis., U.S.* 44°4' N, 89°18' W 102
Wauwinet, *Mass., U.S.* 41°19' N, 70°0' W 104
Waveland, *Miss., U.S.* 30°16' N, 89°23' W 103
Waverley, *N.Z.* 39°47' S, 174°37' E 240
Waverly, *Ill., U.S.* 39°34' N, 89°58' W 102
Waverly, *Iowa, U.S.* 42°42' N, 92°29' W 94
Waverly, *Nebr., U.S.* 40°54' N, 96°33' W 90
Waverly, *N.Y., U.S.* 42°0' N, 76°33' W 110
Waverly, *Ohio, U.S.* 39°6' N, 83°0' W 102
Waverly, *Va., U.S.* 37°2' N, 77°6' W 96
Wavre, *Belg.* 50°42' N, 4°36' E 167
Wāw al Kabīr, *Lib.* 25°20' N, 16°43' E 216
Wāw an Nāmūs, spring, *Lib.* 24°58' N, 17°46' E 216
Wawa, *Can.* 47°59' N, 84°47' W 94
Wawa, *Nig.* 9°54' N, 4°24' E 222
Wawa, river, *Nicar.* 14°1' N, 84°24' W 115
Wawagosic, river, *Can.* 50°6' N, 79°5' W 94
Wawona, *Calif., U.S.* 37°32' N, 119°40' W 100
Waxahachie, *Tex., U.S.* 32°23' N, 96°51' W 96
Waxweiler, *Ger.* 50°5' N, 6°22' E 167
Waxxari, *China* 38°46' N, 87°29' E 188
Way Archipelago, islands, *Antarctica* 66°37' S, 147°19' E 248
Way Kambas National Park, *Indonesia* 5°4' S, 105°20' E 172
Wayagamac, Lac, lake, *Can.* 47°20' N, 73°14' W 94
Waycross, *Ga., U.S.* 31°11' N, 82°23' W 112
Wayland, *Mich., U.S.* 42°39' N, 85°39' W 102
Wayne, *Can.* 51°24' N, 112°42' W 90
Wayne, *Me., U.S.* 44°20' N, 70°4' W 104
Wayne, *Nebr., U.S.* 42°12' N, 97°1' W 90
Wayne, *Ohio, U.S.* 41°17' N, 83°29' W 102
Waynesboro, *Ga., U.S.* 33°4' N, 82°2' W 96
Waynesboro, *Miss., U.S.* 31°40' N, 88°38' W 103
Waynesboro, *Tenn., U.S.* 35°19' N, 87°45' W 96
Waynesboro, *Va., U.S.* 38°4' N, 78°54' W 94
Waynoka, *Okla., U.S.* 36°34' N, 98°54' W 92
Wayside, *Miss., U.S.* 33°14' N, 91°2' W 103
Waza, *Cameroon* 11°24' N, 14°35' E 216
Waza National Park, *Cameroon* 11°12' N, 14°21' E 206
Wazay, *Afghan.* 33°18' N, 69°27' E 186
Wāzin, *Lib.* 31°57' N, 10°42' E 214
Wazirabad, *Pak.* 32°24' N, 74°8' E 186
We, island, *Indonesia* 5°52' N, 95°22' E 196
Weagamow Lake, *Can.* 52°59' N, 91°20' W 82
Weald, The, region, *U.K.* 51°0' N, 0°17' E 162
Weare, *N.H., U.S.* 43°5' N, 71°45' W 104
Wearhead, *U.K.* 54°45' N, 2°14' W 162
Weatherford, *Okla., U.S.* 35°30' N, 98°43' W 92
Weatherford, *Tex., U.S.* 32°46' N, 97°48' W 112
Weaver Lake, lake, *Can.* 52°42' N, 97°13' W 108
Webb, *Can.* 50°10' N, 108°13' W 90
Webb City, *Okla., U.S.* 36°47' N, 96°42' W 92
Webbwood, *Can.* 46°16' N, 81°53' W 94
Weber Inlet 72°27' S, 74°30' W 248
Weber Ridge, peak, *Antarctica* 84°21' S, 65°15' W 248
Webster, *Fla., U.S.* 28°36' N, 82°4' W 105
Webster, *Mass., U.S.* 42°2' N, 71°53' W 104
Webster, *N.H., U.S.* 43°19' N, 71°44' W 104
Webster, *S. Dak., U.S.* 45°18' N, 97°32' W 90
Webster City, *Iowa, U.S.* 42°26' N, 93°50' W 94
Weda, *Indonesia* 0°22' N, 127°46' E 192
Weddell Island, *Falk. Is., U.K.* 51°50' S, 64°6' W 134
Weddell Plain, *South Atlantic Ocean* 62°46' S, 4°49' W 255
Weddell Sea 65°39' S, 58°34' W 134
Wedge Mountain, peak, *Can.* 50°7' N, 122°53' W 108
Weed, *Calif., U.S.* 41°25' N, 122°24' W 92
Weed Patch, *Calif., U.S.* 35°13' N, 118°56' W 101
Weed Patch Hill, peak, *Ind., U.S.* 39°8' N, 86°16' W 102
Weekapaug, *R.I., U.S.* 41°19' N, 71°46' W 104
Weekes, *Can.* 52°33' N, 102°54' W 108
Weeki Wachee, *Fla., U.S.* 28°31' N, 82°34' W 105
Weeki Wachee Springs, site, *Fla., U.S.* 28°29' N, 82°37' W 105
Weems, Mount, peak, *Antarctica* 77°25' S, 87°1' W 248
Weende, *Ger.* 51°33' N, 9°56' E 167
Weener, *Ger.* 53°10' N, 7°21' E 163
Weert, *Neth.* 51°14' N, 5°41' E 167
Weeze, *Ger.* 51°37' N, 6°12' E 167
Wegīdī, *Eth.* 9°25' N, 38°23' E 224
Wei, river, *China* 34°27' N, 109°55' E 198
Weichang, *China* 41°54' N, 117°43' E 198
Weiden, *Ger.* 49°40' N, 12°9' E 152
Weidman, *Mich., U.S.* 43°40' N, 84°58' W 102
Weifang, *China* 36°42' N, 119°5' E 198
Weihai, *China* 37°29' N, 122°8' E 198
Weilburg, *Ger.* 50°29' N, 8°15' E 167
Weilmünster, *Ger.* 50°27' N, 8°22' E 167
Weimar, *Tex., U.S.* 29°41' N, 96°47' W 96
Weinan, *China* 34°30' N, 109°28' E 198
Weipa, *Austral.* 12°41' S, 142°4' E 238
Weir, *Miss., U.S.* 33°14' N, 89°17' W 103
Weir, river, *Can.* 56°58' N, 93°45' W 108
Weirsdale, *Fla., U.S.* 28°58' N, 81°55' W 105
Weirton, *W. Va., U.S.* 40°23' N, 80°37' W 94
Weiser, *Idaho, U.S.* 44°15' N, 116°59' W 90
Weishan, *China* 34°47' N, 117°11' E 198
Weisshorn, peak, *Switz.* 46°6' N, 7°39' E 165
Weissmies, peak, *Switz.* 46°7' N, 8°0' E 167
Weitra, *Aust.* 48°42' N, 14°54' E 156
Weitzel Lake, lake, *Can.* 57°39' N, 107°11' W 108
Weixin, *China* 27°49' N, 105°3' E 198
Weiya, *China* 42°7' N, 94°41' E 190
Weizhou Dao, island, *China* 20°44' N, 108°55' E 198
Wekusko, *Can.* 54°30' N, 99°46' W 108
Wekusko Lake, lake, *Can.* 54°39' N, 100°27' W 108
Wel Jara, spring, *Kenya* 0°28' N, 40°53' E 224
Welaka, *Fla., U.S.* 29°28' N, 81°40' W 105
Welbeck Abbey, site, *U.K.* 53°16' N, 1°10' W 162
Welch, *W. Va., U.S.* 37°26' N, 81°36' W 96
Welcome Mount, peak, *Antarctica* 72°13' S, 160°40' E 248
Weldiya, *Eth.* 11°48' N, 39°33' E 182
Weldon, *Calif., U.S.* 35°39' N, 118°18' W 101
Weldon, *Ill., U.S.* 40°6' N, 88°45' W 102
Weldon, *N.C., U.S.* 36°24' N, 77°36' W 96
Weldon, *Tex., U.S.* 31°0' N, 95°34' W 103
Welel, Tulu, peak, *Eth.* 8°51' N, 34°44' E 224
Welk'īt'ē, *Eth.* 8°15' N, 37°48' E 224
Welkom, *S. Af.* 28°1' S, 26°41' E 227
Welland, *Can.* 42°52' N, 79°22' W 82
Wellesley, *Mass., U.S.* 42°17' N, 71°18' W 104
Wellesley Islands, *Gulf of Carpentaria* 16°33' S, 137°4' E 230
Wellfleet, *Mass., U.S.* 41°56' N, 70°3' W 104
Wellingborough, *U.K.* 52°18' N, 0°42' E 162
Wellington, *Colo., U.S.* 40°42' N, 105°1' W 90
Wellington, *Ill., U.S.* 40°31' N, 87°41' W 102
Wellington, *N.Z.* 41°18' S, 174°39' E 240
Wellington, *Ohio, U.S.* 41°9' N, 82°13' W 102
Wellington, *S. Af.* 33°38' S, 18°59' E 227
Wellington, *Tex., U.S.* 34°50' N, 100°14' W 96
Wellington, *U.K.* 50°58' N, 3°13' W 162
Wellington Channel 74°55' N, 95°14' W 106
Wellington, Isla, island, *Chile* 49°48' S, 74°23' W 134
Wells, *Can.* 53°5' N, 121°36' W 108
Wells, *Me., U.S.* 43°19' N, 70°35' W 104
Wells, *Mich., U.S.* 45°46' N, 87°5' W 94
Wells, *Nev., U.S.* 41°6' N, 114°58' W 90
Wells, *Tex., U.S.* 31°28' N, 94°57' W 103
Wells, *Vt., U.S.* 43°24' N, 73°13' W 104
Wells next the Sea, *U.K.* 52°56' N, 0°51' E 162
Wells River, *Vt., U.S.* 44°8' N, 72°4' W 104
Wellsboro, *Pa., U.S.* 41°44' N, 77°19' W 82
Wellsford, *N.Z.* 36°18' S, 174°31' E 240
Wellston, *Mich., U.S.* 44°12' N, 85°57' W 102
Wellston, *Ohio, U.S.* 39°6' N, 82°32' W 102
Wellsville, *N.Y., U.S.* 42°7' N, 77°58' W 94
Wellsville, *Ohio, U.S.* 40°35' N, 80°39' W 94
Wellton, *Ariz., U.S.* 32°39' N, 114°10' W 101
Welmel, river, *Eth.* 6°7' N, 40°6' E 224
Wels, *Aust.* 48°9' N, 14°1' E 152
Welsh, *La., U.S.* 30°13' N, 92°50' W 96
Welshpool, *U.K.* 52°39' N, 3°9' W 162
Welwel, *Eth.* 7°6' N, 45°23' E 218
Welwyn Garden City, *U.K.* 51°49' N, 0°14' E 162
Wem, *U.K.* 52°51' N, 2°43' W 162
Wembley, *Can.* 55°10' N, 119°9' W 108
Wenatchee, *Wash., U.S.* 47°24' N, 120°19' W 90
Wenatchee Mountains, *Wash., U.S.* 47°34' N, 121°49' W 100
Wenchang, *China* 19°36' N, 110°43' E 198
Wencheng, *China* 27°45' N, 120°3' E 198
Wenchi, *Ghana* 7°45' N, 2°8' W 222
Wendelstein, peak, *Ger.* 47°40' N, 11°55' E 156
Wenden, *Ariz., U.S.* 33°48' N, 113°33' W 101
Wendeng, *China* 37°11' N, 122°6' E 198
Wendo, *Eth.* 6°38' N, 38°21' E 224
Wendover, *Utah, U.S.* 40°43' N, 114°1' W 90
Wenduine, *Belg.* 51°16' N, 3°4' E 163
Wenebegon Lake, *Can.* 47°21' N, 83°46' W 94
Wengyuan, *China* 24°14' N, 114°6' E 198
Wenling, *China* 28°19' N, 121°24' E 198
Wenona, *Ill., U.S.* 41°3' N, 89°4' W 102
Wenquan, *China* 33°4' N, 91°54' E 188
Wenquan, *China* 44°50' N, 80°57' E 184
Wenshan, *China* 23°25' N, 104°18' E 202
Wensu, *China* 41°16' N, 80°15' E 184
Wentworth, *N.H., U.S.* 43°51' N, 71°55' W 104
Wentzel Lake, lake, *Can.* 59°0' N, 115°2' W 108
Wentzel, river, *Can.* 58°53' N, 114°49' W 108
Wenxian, *China* 32°56' N, 104°40' E 198
Wenzhou, *China* 27°57' N, 120°44' E 198
Weobley, *U.K.* 52°9' N, 2°54' W 162
Wepener, *S. Af.* 29°45' S, 27°0' E 227
Wepusko Bay 56°59' N, 102°57' W 108
Werbkowice, *Pol.* 50°44' N, 23°46' E 152
Werda, *Botswana* 25°17' S, 23°14' E 227
Werdau, *Ger.* 50°44' N, 12°23' E 152
Werdēr, *Eth.* 7°0' N, 45°17' E 218
Werder, *Ger.* 52°22' N, 12°56' E 152
Werdohl, *Ger.* 51°15' N, 7°45' E 167
Were Īlu, *Eth.* 10°35' N, 39°31' E 224
Werl, *Ger.* 51°33' N, 7°54' E 167
Wermelskirchen, *Ger.* 51°8' N, 7°13' E 167
Werne, *Ger.* 51°39' N, 7°37' E 167
Werneck, *Ger.* 49°59' N, 10°5' E 167
Werota, *Eth.* 11°45' N, 37°31' E 182
Wertheim, *Ger.* 49°44' N, 9°30' E 167
Wervik, *Belg.* 50°47' N, 3°1' E 163
Wesel, *Ger.* 51°39' N, 6°36' E 167
Wesergebirge, *Ger.* 52°6' N, 8°54' E 150
Weskan, *Kans., U.S.* 38°51' N, 101°58' W 90
Weslaco, *Tex., U.S.* 26°9' N, 98°1' W 96
Wesleyville, *Pa., U.S.* 42°7' N, 80°2' W 110
Wessel Islands, *Arafura Sea* 10°56' S, 135°48' E 192
Wesseling, *Ger.* 50°48' N, 6°58' E 167
Wessex, region, *U.K.* 51°28' N, 2°20' W 162
Wessington, *S. Dak., U.S.* 44°26' N, 98°43' W 90
Wessington Springs, *S. Dak., U.S.* 44°3' N, 98°34' W 90
Wesson, *Ark., U.S.* 33°5' N, 92°47' W 103
Wesson, *Miss., U.S.* 31°41' N, 90°25' W 103
West, *Miss., U.S.* 33°10' N, 89°48' W 103
West, *Tex., U.S.* 31°46' N, 97°5' W 92
West Acton, *Mass., U.S.* 42°28' N, 71°29' W 104
West Allis, *Wis., U.S.* 43°0' N, 88°2' W 102
West Baldwin, *Me., U.S.* 43°49' N, 70°47' W 104
West Bank, special sovereignty, *Israel* 31°22' N, 35°0' E 194
West Bay 29°12' N, 95°8' W 103
West Bay 28°59' N, 89°38' W 103
West Bay, *Fla., U.S.* 30°17' N, 85°52' W 96
West Bend, *Wis., U.S.* 43°24' N, 88°13' W 102
West Bengal, adm. division, *India* 24°8' N, 87°45' E 197
West Berlin, *Vt., U.S.* 44°11' N, 72°38' W 104
West Beskids, *Pol.* 49°32' N, 18°33' E 152
West Bethel, *Me., U.S.* 44°23' N, 70°52' W 104
West Boylston, *Mass., U.S.* 42°21' N, 71°48' W 104
West Braintree, *Vt., U.S.* 43°58' N, 72°46' W 104
West Branch, *Iowa, U.S.* 41°40' N, 91°21' W 110
West Branch, *Mich., U.S.* 44°17' N, 84°14' W 94
West Bridgford, *U.K.* 52°55' N, 1°7' W 162
West Bromwich, *U.K.* 52°30' N, 2°0' W 162
West Burlington, *Iowa, U.S.* 40°49' N, 91°10' W 110
West Butte, peak, *Mont., U.S.* 48°54' N, 111°38' W 90
West Buxton, *Me., U.S.* 43°39' N, 70°36' W 104
West Caicos, island, *West Caicos* 21°35' N, 72°57' W 116
West Camp, *N.Y., U.S.* 42°6' N, 73°57' W 104
West Campton, *N.H., U.S.* 43°50' N, 71°41' W 104
West Caroline Basin, *North Pacific Ocean* 3°16' N, 136°56' E 254
West Carrollton City, *Ohio, U.S.* 39°39' N, 84°15' W 102
West Castleton, *Vt., U.S.* 43°39' N, 73°15' W 104
West Chicago, *Ill., U.S.* 41°52' N, 88°12' W 102
West Coal, river, *Can.* 61°12' N, 128°15' W 108
West Cornwall, *Conn., U.S.* 41°52' N, 73°22' W 104
West Danville, *Vt., U.S.* 44°24' N, 72°12' W 104
West Des Moines, *Iowa, U.S.* 41°33' N, 93°44' W 94
West Dummerston, *Vt., U.S.* 42°55' N, 72°38' W 104
West Elk Peak, *Colo., U.S.* 38°42' N, 107°17' W 90
West End, *Bahamas* 26°40' N, 78°57' W 105
West End Point, *Bahamas* 26°41' N, 78°58' W 105
West End Point, *Little Cayman* 19°40' N, 81°6' W 115
West Falkland, island, *Falk. Is., U.K.* 51°34' S, 62°18' W 134
West Fayu Atoll see Pigailoe 8°36' N, 146°3' E 192
West Frankfort, *Mo., U.S.* 37°53' N, 88°55' W 96
West Glacier, *Mont., U.S.* 48°27' N, 113°59' W 108
West Gouldsboro, *Me., U.S.* 44°27' N, 68°6' W 111
West Granville, *Mass., U.S.* 42°4' N, 72°57' W 104
West Group, islands, *Great Australian Bight* 33°43' S, 120°1' E 230
West Ham, *U.K.* 51°30' N, 1°59' E 162
West Hartford, *Conn., U.S.* 41°45' N, 72°45' W 104
West Haven, *Conn., U.S.* 41°16' N, 72°57' W 104
West Hazleton, *Pa., U.S.* 40°57' N, 76°1' W 94
West Helena, *Ark., U.S.* 34°32' N, 90°40' W 96
West Hurley, *N.Y., U.S.* 41°59' N, 74°7' W 104
West Ice Shelf, *Antarctica* 66°37' S, 86°47' E 248
West Island, *Austral.* 15°45' S, 135°31' E 231
West Jefferson, *Ohio, U.S.* 39°55' N, 83°16' W 102
West Keal, *U.K.* 53°8' N, 0°2' E 162
West Lafayette, *Ohio, U.S.* 40°16' N, 81°45' W 102
West Liberty, *Ky., U.S.* 37°55' N, 83°16' W 94
West Liberty, *Ohio, U.S.* 40°15' N, 83°46' W 102
West Lorne, *Can.* 42°35' N, 81°36' W 102
West Lunga National Park, *Zambia* 12°45' S, 24°52' E 224
West Lunga National Park, *Zambia* 13°10' S, 24°22' E 206
West Lunga, river, *Zambia* 12°14' S, 24°21' E 220
West Mariana Basin, *Philippine Sea* 17°0' N, 138°57' E 254
West Milton, *Ohio, U.S.* 39°56' N, 84°20' W 102
West Monroe, *La., U.S.* 32°29' N, 92°9' W 103
West Newfield, *Me., U.S.* 43°38' N, 70°56' W 104
West Nicholson, *Zimb.* 21°2' S, 29°18' E 227
West Ossipee, *N.H., U.S.* 43°49' N, 71°13' W 104
West Palm Beach, *Fla., U.S.* 26°43' N, 80°5' W 105
West Paris, *Me., U.S.* 44°19' N, 70°35' W 104
West Park, *N.Y., U.S.* 41°47' N, 73°59' W 104
West Pawlet, *Vt., U.S.* 43°21' N, 73°16' W 104
West Peru, *Me., U.S.* 44°30' N, 70°29' W 104
West Pittston, *Pa., U.S.* 41°19' N, 75°49' W 94
West Plains, *Mo., U.S.* 36°43' N, 91°52' W 96
West Point 43°55' N, 60°58' W 111
West Point, *Calif., U.S.* 38°23' N, 120°33' W 100
West Point, *Can.* 46°37' N, 64°23' W 111
West Point, *Ky., U.S.* 37°59' N, 85°58' W 94
West Point, *Me., U.S.* 43°45' N, 69°52' W 104
West Point, *Miss., U.S.* 33°35' N, 88°39' W 96
West Point, *N.Y., U.S.* 41°23' N, 73°59' W 104
West Point, *Va., U.S.* 37°32' N, 76°48' W 94
West Portsmouth, *Ohio, U.S.* 38°45' N, 83°2' W 102
West Quoddy Head, *Me., U.S.* 44°49' N, 66°55' W 111
West Rumney, *N.H., U.S.* 43°48' N, 71°53' W 104
West Salem, *Ill., U.S.* 38°31' N, 88°1' W 102
West Southport, *Me., U.S.* 43°49' N, 69°41' W 104
West Spanish Peak, *Colo., U.S.* 37°19' N, 105°4' W 80
West Tanfield, *U.K.* 54°12' N, 1°35' W 162
West Tavaputs Plateau, *Utah, U.S.* 39°48' N, 110°44' W 90
West Terre Haute, *Ind., U.S.* 39°27' N, 87°27' W 102
West Terschelling, *Neth.* 53°21' N, 5°12' E 163
West Thornton, *N.H., U.S.* 43°56' N, 71°42' W 104
West Topsham, *Vt., U.S.* 44°6' N, 72°19' W 104
West Townsend, *Mass., U.S.* 42°40' N, 71°45' W 104
West Union, *Ill., U.S.* 39°12' N, 87°40' W 102
West Union, *Iowa, U.S.* 42°57' N, 91°47' W 110
West Virginia, adm. division, *W. Va., U.S.* 38°34' N, 81°18' W 94
West Wareham, *Mass., U.S.* 41°47' N, 70°46' W 104
West Webster, *N.Y., U.S.* 43°12' N, 77°30' W 94
West Wendover, *Nev., U.S.* 40°43' N, 114°4' W 90
West Woodstock, *Vt., U.S.* 43°36' N, 72°34' W 104
West Yarmouth, *Mass., U.S.* 41°38' N, 70°15' W 104
Westbrook, *Conn., U.S.* 41°16' N, 72°27' W 104
Westbrook, *Me., U.S.* 43°40' N, 70°22' W 104
Westbrook, *Tex., U.S.* 32°21' N, 101°1' W 92
Westbury, *U.K.* 51°15' N, 2°11' W 162
Westend, *Calif., U.S.* 35°41' N, 117°24' W 101
Westerburg, *Ger.* 50°33' N, 7°58' E 167
Westerlo, *N.Y., U.S.* 42°30' N, 74°4' W 104
Westerly, *R.I., U.S.* 41°22' N, 71°50' W 104
Western Australia, adm. division, *Austral.* 25°2' S, 118°22' E 231
Western Bahr Al Ghazal, adm. division, *Sudan* 7°22' N, 25°15' E 224
Western Cape, adm. division, *S. Af.* 33°0' S, 19°18' E 227
Western Darfur, adm. division, *Sudan* 14°27' N, 23°55' E 226
Western Desert, *Egypt* 29°2' N, 24°32' E 142
Western Equatoria, adm. division, *Sudan* 5°29' N, 27°18' E 224
Western Ghats, *India* 21°0' N, 73°17' E 186
Western Head, *Can.* 49°34' N, 58°48' W 111
Western Kordofan, adm. division, *Sudan* 10°39' N, 27°40' E 224
Western Port, *Austral.* 38°38' S, 143°33' E 230
Western Sahara, special sovereignty, *Mor.* 21°39' N, 13°57' W 222
Western Thebes, ruin(s), *Egypt* 25°43' N, 32°25' E 182
Westerschelde 51°21' N, 3°54' E 163
Westerville, *Ohio, U.S.* 40°7' N, 82°55' W 102
Westerwald, *Ger.* 50°33' N, 7°25' E 167
Westfield, *N.Y., U.S.* 42°19' N, 79°35' W 110
Westfield, *Tex., U.S.* 30°0' N, 95°25' W 103
Westfield, *Wis., U.S.* 43°53' N, 89°30' W 102
Westhampton Beach, *N.Y., U.S.* 40°48' N, 72°39' W 104
Westhope, *N. Dak., U.S.* 48°53' N, 101°3' W 90
Westlake, *La., U.S.* 30°13' N, 93°16' W 103
Westland (Tai Poutini) National Park, *N.Z.* 43°26' S, 168°39' E 240
Westley, *Calif., U.S.* 37°32' N, 121°13' W 100
Westlock, *Can.* 54°9' N, 113°52' W 108
Westminster, *Colo., U.S.* 39°50' N, 105°3' W 90
Westminster, *Vt., U.S.* 43°3' N, 72°28' W 104
Westmorland, *Calif., U.S.* 33°2' N, 115°38' W 101
Weston, *Malaysia* 5°14' N, 115°36' E 203
Weston, *Mo., U.S.* 39°24' N, 94°55' W 94
Weston, *Oreg., U.S.* 45°47' N, 118°26' W 90
Weston, *Vt., U.S.* 43°17' N, 72°48' W 104
Weston, *W. Va., U.S.* 39°2' N, 80°28' W 94
Weston-super-Mare, *U.K.* 51°19' N, 2°58' W 162
Westonzoyland, *U.K.* 51°6' N, 2°56' W 162
Westover, *W. Va., U.S.* 39°37' N, 79°59' W 94
Westoverledingen, *Ger.* 53°9' N, 7°27' E 163
Westpoint, *Ind., U.S.* 40°20' N, 87°3' W 102
Westport, *Calif., U.S.* 39°38' N, 123°47' W 90
Westport, *Conn., U.S.* 41°8' N, 73°22' W 104
Westport, *Ind., U.S.* 39°10' N, 85°34' W 102
Westport, *N.Y., U.S.* 44°10' N, 73°28' W 104
Westport, *N.Z.* 41°47' S, 171°38' E 240
Westport, *Wash., U.S.* 46°52' N, 124°7' W 100
Westport Point, *Mass., U.S.* 41°31' N, 71°6' W 104
Westray, *Can.* 53°35' N, 101°23' W 108
Westree, *Can.* 47°25' N, 81°33' W 94
Westville, *Ill., U.S.* 40°2' N, 87°38' W 102
Westward Ho!, *U.K.* 51°2' N, 4°13' W 150
Westwego, *La., U.S.* 29°54' N, 90°9' W 103
Westwood, *Calif., U.S.* 40°18' N, 121°0' W 92

Wesuwe, *Ger.* 52°45′ N, 7°12′ E 163
Wetar, island, *Indonesia* 7°40′ S, 126°18′ E 192
Wetaskiwin, *Can.* 52°57′ N, 113°23′ W 108
Wete, *Tanzania* 5°1′ S, 39°45′ E 224
Wetetnagami, Lac, lake, *Can.* 48°53′ N, 76°59′ W 94
Wetherby, *U.K.* 53°56′ N, 1°23′ W 162
Wethersfield, *Conn., U.S.* 41°42′ N, 72°41′ W 104
Wetter, *Ger.* 50°53′ N, 8°42′ E 167
Wetteren, *Belg.* 50°59′ N, 3°53′ E 163
Wettringen, *Ger.* 52°12′ N, 7°19′ E 163
Wetumka, *Okla., U.S.* 35°13′ N, 96°14′ W 96
Wetzlar, *Ger.* 50°33′ N, 8°29′ E 167
Wevertown, *N.Y., U.S.* 43°37′ N, 73°58′ W 104
Wewak, *P.N.G.* 3°36′ S, 143°37′ E 238
Wewoka, *Okla., U.S.* 35°7′ N, 96°29′ W 92
Wexford, *Ire.* 52°20′ N, 6°29′ W 150
Weybourne, *U.K.* 52°56′ N, 1°8′ E 162
Weybridge, *Vt., U.S.* 44°3′ N, 73°13′ W 104
Weyburn, *Can.* 49°39′ N, 103°52′ W 90
Weymouth, *Mass., U.S.* 42°13′ N, 70°57′ W 104
Weymouth Bay 12°36′ S, 142°4′ E 230
Whakapara, *N.Z.* 35°33′ S, 174°16′ E 240
Whakapunake, peak, *N.Z.* 38°50′ S, 177°31′ E 240
Whakatane, *N.Z.* 37°59′ S, 177°0′ E 240
Whale Bay 56°34′ N, 135°35′ W 108
Whale Cay, island, *Bahamas* 25°27′ N, 78°38′ W 80
Whale Cove, *Can.* 62°28′ N, 92°59′ W 73
Whangara, *N.Z.* 38°33′ S, 178°12′ E 240
Whangarei, *N.Z.* 35°46′ S, 174°18′ E 240
Wharfe, river, *U.K.* 53°55′ N, 1°21′ W 162
Wharton, *Tex., U.S.* 29°18′ N, 96°6′ W 96
Wharton Basin, *Indian Ocean* 20°5′ S, 100°10′ E 254
Wharton, Mount, peak, *Antarctica* 81°1′ S, 158°48′ E 248
Wharton, Peninsula, *Chile* 49°34′ S, 76°33′ W 134
Whataroa, *N.Z.* 43°17′ S, 170°21′ E 240
Whatcom, Lake, *Wash., U.S.* 48°41′ N, 122°34′ W 100
Whatley, *Ala., U.S.* 31°38′ N, 87°42′ W 103
Whatshan Lake, lake, *Can.* 50°0′ N, 118°40′ W 90
Wheatland, *Ind., U.S.* 38°39′ N, 87°19′ W 102
Wheatland, *Wyo., U.S.* 42°3′ N, 104°58′ W 90
Wheatley, *Can.* 42°6′ N, 82°28′ W 102
Wheaton, *Ill., U.S.* 41°51′ N, 88°6′ W 102
Wheaton, *Minn., U.S.* 45°47′ N, 96°30′ W 90
Wheeler, *Kans., U.S.* 39°45′ N, 101°43′ W 90
Wheeler, *Oreg., U.S.* 45°40′ N, 123°53′ W 100
Wheeler, *Tex., U.S.* 35°26′ N, 100°17′ W 92
Wheeler Mountain, peak, *Nev., U.S.* 41°16′ N, 116°7′ W 90
Wheeler Peak, *Nev., U.S.* 38°58′ N, 114°23′ W 90
Wheeler Peak, *N. Mex., U.S.* 36°32′ N, 105°29′ W 92
Wheeling, *W. Va., U.S.* 40°3′ N, 80°43′ W 94
Wheelwright, *Arg.* 33°49′ S, 61°12′ W 139
Whinham, Mount, peak, *Austral.* 26°5′ S, 129°59′ E 230
Whipple, Mount, peak, *Can.* 56°36′ N, 131°44′ W 108
Whipple Observatory, site, *Ariz., U.S.* 31°41′ N, 110°57′ W 92
Whirlwind Lake, *Can.* 60°15′ N, 109°15′ W 108
Whiskey Jack Lake, *Can.* 58°24′ N, 102°28′ W 108
Whistler, *Can.* 50°7′ N, 122°59′ W 100
Whitby, *U.K.* 54°29′ N, 0°38′ E 162
Whitchurch, *U.K.* 52°58′ N, 2°41′ W 162
Whitchurch, *U.K.* 51°13′ N, 1°21′ W 162
White Bay 49°57′ N, 56°42′ W 111
White Butte, peak, *N. Dak., U.S.* 46°22′ N, 103°23′ W 90
White Cap Mountain, peak, *Me., U.S.* 45°32′ N, 69°20′ W 94
White Castle, *La., U.S.* 30°9′ N, 91°9′ W 103
White City, *Fla., U.S.* 27°23′ N, 80°20′ W 105
White Cloud, *Mich., U.S.* 43°33′ N, 85°47′ W 102
White Deer, *Tex., U.S.* 35°24′ N, 101°11′ W 92
White Hall, *Ark., U.S.* 34°16′ N, 92°5′ W 96
White Heath, *Ill., U.S.* 40°4′ N, 88°30′ W 102
White Hills, *Ariz., U.S.* 35°47′ N, 114°27′ W 101
White Horse Beach, *Mass., U.S.* 41°55′ N, 70°35′ W 104
White Horse Pass, *Nev., U.S.* 40°20′ N, 114°15′ W 90
White Island, *Antarctica* 78°9′ S, 175°55′ E 248
White Island, *Antarctica* 66°45′ S, 45°32′ E 248
White Island, island, *Can.* 66°2′ N, 88°7′ W 246
White Lake, *La., U.S.* 29°41′ N, 92°41′ W 103
White Mount Peak, *Calif., U.S.* 37°37′ N, 118°21′ W 92
White Mountain, *Alas., U.S.* 64°40′ N, 163°26′ W 98
White Mountains, *Calif., U.S.* 37°10′ N, 118°10′ W 80
White Mountains, *Calif., U.S.* 37°46′ N, 118°28′ W 90
White Mountains, *N.H., U.S.* 44°2′ N, 72°0′ W 104
White Mountains National Park, *Austral.* 20°38′ S, 144°43′ E 238
White Nile, adm. division, *Sudan* 13°33′ N, 31°53′ E 182
White Nile Dam, *Sudan* 14°56′ N, 31°53′ E 226
White Oak, *Tex., U.S.* 32°32′ N, 94°52′ W 103
White Otter Lake, lake, *Can.* 49°3′ N, 92°29′ W 94
White Pigeon, *Mich., U.S.* 41°47′ N, 85°38′ W 102
White Pine Peak, *Utah, U.S.* 38°50′ N, 112°18′ W 90
White Pine Range, *Nev., U.S.* 39°4′ N, 115°37′ W 90
White Plains, *N.Y., U.S.* 41°1′ N, 73°47′ W 104
White River, *Can.* 48°35′ N, 85°16′ W 94
White River, *S. Dak., U.S.* 43°34′ N, 100°45′ W 90
White, river, *Ark., U.S.* 36°2′ N, 92°6′ W 80
White, river, *Ark., U.S.* 34°42′ N, 91°43′ W 80
White, river, *Can.* 48°30′ N, 86°2′ W 94
White, river, *Can.* 63°13′ N, 140°3′ W 98
White, river, *Colo., U.S.* 40°8′ N, 108°49′ W 90
White, river, *Colo., U.S.* 39°50′ N, 108°56′ W 80
White River Junction, *Vt., U.S.* 43°38′ N, 72°20′ W 104
White, river, *Nebr., U.S.* 42°55′ N, 103°10′ W 90
White River Plateau, *Colo., U.S.* 39°50′ N, 107°54′ W 90
White, river, *S. Dak., U.S.* 43°41′ N, 102°24′ W 82
White, river, *S. Dak., U.S.* 43°34′ N, 99°56′ W 90
White, river, *Tex., U.S.* 34°5′ N, 101°57′ W 112
White, river, *Utah, U.S.* 39°50′ N, 109°27′ W 90
White Rock, *Can.* 49°2′ N, 122°48′ W 100
White Rock Peak, *Nev., U.S.* 38°14′ N, 114°11′ W 90
White Rock, peak, *Oreg., U.S.* 43°6′ N, 123°7′ W 90
White Salmon, *Wash., U.S.* 45°43′ N, 121°30′ W 100
White Sands National Monument, *N. Mex., U.S.* 32°54′ N, 106°5′ W 80
White Sea see Beloye More 63°17′ N, 35°24′ E 160
White Volta, river, *Ghana* 9°39′ N, 0°54′ E 222
Whitecap Mountain, peak, *Can.* 50°42′ N, 122°36′ W 90
Whiteclay Lake, lake, *Can.* 50°49′ N, 89°14′ W 110
Whitecourt, *Can.* 54°7′ N, 115°42′ W 108
Whiteface Mountain, peak, *N.Y., U.S.* 44°21′ N, 73°56′ W 104
Whiteface, river, *Minn., U.S.* 47°4′ N, 92°51′ W 94
Whitefield, *Me., U.S.* 44°9′ N, 69°39′ W 104
Whitefield, *N.H., U.S.* 44°22′ N, 71°37′ W 104
Whitefish, *Mont., U.S.* 48°23′ N, 114°21′ W 90
Whitefish Bay, *Wis., U.S.* 43°6′ N, 87°55′ W 102
Whitefish Lake, lake, *Can.* 48°12′ N, 90°30′ W 110
Whitefish Point, *Mich., U.S.* 46°35′ N, 84°56′ W 94
Whitefish Range, *Mont., U.S.* 48°59′ N, 114°56′ W 90
Whitefish, river, *Can.* 60°42′ N, 125°12′ W 108
Whitehall, *Mich., U.S.* 43°22′ N, 86°21′ W 102
Whitehall, *Mont., U.S.* 45°51′ N, 112°6′ W 90
Whitehall, *N.Y., U.S.* 43°32′ N, 73°26′ W 104
Whitehall, *Ohio, U.S.* 39°57′ N, 82°53′ W 102
Whitehall, *Wis., U.S.* 44°21′ N, 91°20′ W 94
Whitehaven, *U.K.* 54°33′ N, 3°35′ W 162
Whitehorse, *Can.* 60°43′ N, 135°20′ W 98
Whitehouse, *Tex., U.S.* 32°12′ N, 95°14′ W 103
Whitemouth, *Can.* 49°55′ N, 95°59′ W 90
Whitemud, river, *Can.* 56°32′ N, 118°28′ W 108
Whiten Head, *U.K.* 58°36′ N, 4°54′ W 150
Whiteriver, *Ariz., U.S.* 33°50′ N, 109°58′ W 92
Whitesand, river, *Can.* 59°50′ N, 115°54′ W 108
Whitesboro, *Tex., U.S.* 33°38′ N, 96°55′ W 92
Whitesburg, *Ky., U.S.* 37°7′ N, 82°49′ W 94
Whitetail, *Mont., U.S.* 48°52′ N, 105°12′ W 90
Whiteville, *N.C., U.S.* 34°19′ N, 78°43′ W 96
Whiteville, *Tenn., U.S.* 35°18′ N, 89°9′ W 96
Whitewater, *Mont., U.S.* 48°44′ N, 107°37′ W 90
Whitewater, *Wis., U.S.* 42°50′ N, 88°45′ W 102
Whitewater Bay 25°16′ N, 81°13′ W 105
Whitewater Lake, *Can.* 50°42′ N, 89°52′ W 110
Whitewood, *Can.* 50°19′ N, 102°17′ W 90
Whitianga, *N.Z.* 36°50′ S, 175°40′ E 240
Whiting, *Vt., U.S.* 43°51′ N, 73°13′ W 104
Whiting, river, *Can.* 58°2′ N, 133°46′ W 108
Whitingham, *Vt., U.S.* 42°47′ N, 72°54′ W 104
Whitley Gardens, *Calif., U.S.* 35°39′ N, 120°32′ W 101
Whitman, *Nebr., U.S.* 42°1′ N, 101°32′ W 90
Whitmire, *S.C., U.S.* 34°29′ N, 81°37′ W 96
Whitney, Lake, *Tex., U.S.* 31°56′ N, 98°22′ W 80
Whitney, Mount, peak, *Calif., U.S.* 36°34′ N, 118°20′ W 101
Whitstable, *U.K.* 51°21′ N, 1°2′ E 162
Whitsunday Island National Park, *Austral.* 20°21′ S, 148°39′ E 238
Whittemore, *Mich., U.S.* 44°13′ N, 83°48′ W 102
Whittier, *Alas., U.S.* 60°40′ N, 148°51′ W 98
Whittier, *Calif., U.S.* 33°58′ N, 118°3′ W 101
Whittle, Cap, *Can.* 50°6′ N, 60°13′ W 111
Whittlesey, *U.K.* 52°32′ N, 0°8′ E 162
Wholdaia Lake, *Can.* 60°42′ N, 105°15′ W 108
Whyalla, *Austral.* 33°0′ S, 137°33′ E 231
Wiarton, *Can.* 44°43′ N, 81°9′ W 94
Wibaux, *Mont., U.S.* 46°57′ N, 104°13′ W 90
Wichita, *Kans., U.S.* 37°39′ N, 97°20′ W 90
Wichita Falls, *Tex., U.S.* 33°52′ N, 98°30′ W 92
Wichita, river, *Tex., U.S.* 33°47′ N, 99°19′ W 80
Wick, *U.K.* 58°27′ N, 3°9′ W 143
Wickede, *Ger.* 51°30′ N, 7°52′ E 167
Wickenburg, *Ariz., U.S.* 33°58′ N, 112°47′ W 112
Wickford see North Kingstown, *R.I., U.S.* 41°34′ N, 71°28′ W 104
Wickliffe, *Ky., U.S.* 36°58′ N, 89°4′ W 96
Wickliffe, *Ohio, U.S.* 41°35′ N, 81°28′ W 102
Wicklow, *Ire.* 52°58′ N, 6°4′ W 150
Wicklow Mountains, *Ire.* 53°1′ N, 6°59′ W 150
Wickrath, *Ger.* 51°7′ N, 6°24′ E 167
Widerøe, Mount, peak, *Antarctica* 72°7′ S, 22°53′ E 248
Widnes, *U.K.* 53°21′ N, 2°44′ W 162
Wiehl, *Ger.* 50°56′ N, 7°32′ E 167
Wielbark, *Pol.* 53°23′ N, 20°55′ E 152
Wielkopolskie, adm. division, *Pol.* 52°11′ N, 15°54′ E 152
Wien (Vienna), *Aust.* 48°10′ N, 16°14′ E 152
Wiener Neustadt, *Aust.* 47°48′ N, 16°14′ E 168
Wierden, *Neth.* 52°21′ N, 6°35′ E 163
Wiergate, *Tex., U.S.* 30°59′ N, 93°43′ W 103
Wiesbaden, *Ger.* 50°4′ N, 8°13′ E 167
Wiesmoor, *Ger.* 53°24′ N, 7°44′ E 163
Wieżyca, peak, *Pol.* 54°13′ N, 18°2′ E 152
Wigan, *U.K.* 53°32′ N, 2°38′ W 162
Wiggins, *Miss., U.S.* 30°50′ N, 89°6′ W 103
Wignes Lake, *Can.* 60°11′ N, 106°37′ W 108
Wigton, *U.K.* 54°49′ N, 3°10′ W 162
Wikieup, *Ariz., U.S.* 34°43′ N, 113°37′ W 101
Wil, *Switz.* 47°27′ N, 9°2′ E 156
Wilberforce, Cape, *Austral.* 11°50′ S, 136°37′ E 192
Wilbur, *Wash., U.S.* 47°44′ N, 118°42′ W 90
Wilcox, *Can.* 50°5′ N, 104°45′ W 90
Wilczek, Zemlya, islands, *Russ.* 79°47′ N, 64°40′ E 160
Wild, Cape, *Antarctica* 67°58′ S, 152°38′ E 248
Wild Rice, river, *Minn., U.S.* 46°57′ N, 96°45′ W 94
Wild Rose, *Wis., U.S.* 44°10′ N, 89°16′ W 102
Wildcat Peak, *Nev., U.S.* 39°0′ N, 116°55′ W 90
Wilder, *Vt., U.S.* 43°40′ N, 72°19′ W 104
Wildflicken, *Ger.* 50°23′ N, 9°55′ E 167
Wildomar, *Calif., U.S.* 33°36′ N, 117°17′ W 101
Wildon, *Aust.* 46°52′ N, 15°28′ E 156
Wildrose, *N. Dak., U.S.* 48°37′ N, 103°12′ W 90
Wildspitze, peak, *Aust.* 46°53′ N, 10°48′ E 167
Wildwood, *Can.* 53°35′ N, 115°16′ W 108
Wildwood, *Fla., U.S.* 28°51′ N, 82°3′ W 105
Wildwood, *N.J., U.S.* 38°59′ N, 74°50′ W 94
Wiley, *Colo., U.S.* 38°9′ N, 102°43′ W 90
Wilhelm, Mount, peak, *P.N.G.* 5°48′ S, 144°54′ E 192
Wilhelmina Gebergte, *Suriname* 3°44′ N, 56°34′ W 130
Wilhelmshaven, *Ger.* 53°31′ N, 8°8′ E 163
Wilhelmstal, *Namibia* 21°53′ S, 16°31′ E 227
Wilkes, U.S., station, *Antarctica* 66°5′ S, 110°43′ E 248
Wilkesboro, *N.C., U.S.* 36°8′ N, 81°10′ W 96
Wilkesland, region, *Antarctica* 69°56′ S, 132°51′ E 248
Wilkie, *Can.* 52°25′ N, 108°43′ W 108
Wilkinson, *Miss., U.S.* 31°13′ N, 91°14′ W 103
Will, Mount, peak, *Can.* 57°31′ N, 128°55′ W 108
Willacoochee, *Ga., U.S.* 31°20′ N, 83°3′ W 96
Willapa, *Wash., U.S.* 46°40′ N, 123°40′ W 100
Willapa Bay 46°32′ N, 125°1′ W 80
Willapa Bay, *Wash., U.S.* 46°40′ N, 124°4′ W 100
Willapa Hills, *Wash., U.S.* 46°20′ N, 123°12′ W 100
Willard, *N. Mex., U.S.* 34°35′ N, 106°2′ W 92
Willard, *Ohio, U.S.* 41°2′ N, 82°44′ W 102
Willaumez Peninsula, *P.N.G.* 5°15′ S, 149°24′ E 192
Willcox, *Ariz., U.S.* 32°14′ N, 109°51′ W 112
Willebroek, *Belg.* 51°2′ N, 4°21′ E 163
Willemstad, *Neth. Antilles, Neth.* 51°41′ N, 4°25′ E 167
William Lake, lake, *Can.* 53°49′ N, 99°46′ W 108
William Point, *Can.* 58°55′ N, 109°47′ W 108
William, river, *Can.* 58°9′ N, 109°0′ W 108
Williams, *Ariz., U.S.* 35°13′ N, 112°11′ W 82
Williams, *Calif., U.S.* 39°9′ N, 122°10′ W 90
Williams, *Ind., U.S.* 38°48′ N, 86°39′ W 102
Williams, *Minn., U.S.* 48°44′ N, 94°58′ W 90
Williams Bay, *Wis., U.S.* 42°34′ N, 88°33′ W 102
Williams Island, *Bahamas* 24°33′ N, 78°35′ W 105
Williams Lake, *Can.* 51°46′ N, 91°23′ W 110
Williams Lake, *Can.* 52°6′ N, 122°5′ W 106
Williams, Point, *Antarctica* 67°54′ S, 68°26′ E 248
Williamsburg, *Ky., U.S.* 36°44′ N, 84°10′ W 96
Williamsburg, *Mass., U.S.* 42°23′ N, 72°43′ W 104
Williamsburg, *Ohio, U.S.* 39°3′ N, 84°4′ W 102
Williamsburg, *Va., U.S.* 37°16′ N, 76°43′ W 94
Williamsfield, *Ill., U.S.* 40°54′ N, 90°2′ W 102
Williamson, *W. Va., U.S.* 37°40′ N, 82°17′ W 96
Williamson, Mount, peak, *Calif., U.S.* 36°39′ N, 118°21′ W 101
Williamsport, *Ind., U.S.* 40°16′ N, 87°18′ W 102
Williamsport, *Ohio, U.S.* 39°34′ N, 83°7′ W 102
Williamsport, *Pa., U.S.* 41°14′ N, 77°1′ W 94
Williamstown, *Ky., U.S.* 38°37′ N, 84°34′ W 102
Williamstown, *Vt., U.S.* 44°7′ N, 72°33′ W 104
Williamstown, *W. Va., U.S.* 39°23′ N, 81°28′ W 102
Williamsville, *Ill., U.S.* 39°56′ N, 89°33′ W 102
Willich, *Ger.* 51°15′ N, 6°33′ E 167
Willimantic, *Conn., U.S.* 41°42′ N, 72°13′ W 104
Willingdon, Mount, peak, *Can.* 51°46′ N, 116°20′ W 90
Willis, *Tex., U.S.* 30°24′ N, 95°28′ W 103
Willis Islands, *Scotia Sea* 53°50′ S, 39°43′ W 134
Willis Islets, islands, *Coral Sea* 15°9′ S, 149°13′ E 230
Williston, *Fla., U.S.* 29°22′ N, 82°28′ W 105
Williston, *N. Dak., U.S.* 48°7′ N, 103°39′ W 90
Williston, *S. Af.* 31°19′ S, 20°53′ E 227
Williston Lake, *Can.* 55°59′ N, 124°26′ W 108
Willits, *Calif., U.S.* 39°24′ N, 123°22′ W 90
Willmar, *Minn., U.S.* 45°6′ N, 95°3′ W 90
Willoughby, *U.K.* 53°13′ N, 0°12′ E 162
Willow, *Alas., U.S.* 61°44′ N, 150°4′ W 98
Willow Bunch, *Can.* 49°22′ N, 105°38′ W 90
Willow City, *N. Dak., U.S.* 48°34′ N, 100°19′ W 94
Willow Hill, *Ill., U.S.* 38°58′ N, 88°1′ W 102
Willow Island, *Nebr., U.S.* 40°53′ N, 100°5′ W 90
Willow Reservoir, lake, *Wis., U.S.* 45°42′ N, 90°22′ W 94
Willow River, *Can.* 54°2′ N, 122°31′ W 108
Willow Springs, *Mo., U.S.* 36°58′ N, 91°59′ W 96
Willowick, *Ohio, U.S.* 41°37′ N, 81°28′ W 102
Willowmore, *S. Af.* 33°17′ S, 23°29′ E 227
Willows, *Calif., U.S.* 39°31′ N, 122°13′ W 92
Wills Point, *Tex., U.S.* 32°41′ N, 96°1′ W 96
Willsboro, *N.Y., U.S.* 44°21′ N, 73°25′ W 104
Wilmer, *Ala., U.S.* 30°49′ N, 88°21′ W 103
Wilmer, *Can.* 50°32′ N, 116°4′ W 108
Wilmette, *Ill., U.S.* 42°4′ N, 87°42′ W 102
Wilmington, *Del., U.S.* 39°45′ N, 75°33′ W 94
Wilmington, *Ill., U.S.* 41°18′ N, 88°8′ W 102
Wilmington, *N.Y., U.S.* 44°23′ N, 73°50′ W 104
Wilmington, *N.C., U.S.* 34°14′ N, 77°55′ W 73
Wilmington, *Ohio, U.S.* 39°26′ N, 83°49′ W 102
Wilmington, *Vt., U.S.* 42°51′ N, 72°52′ W 104
Wilmot, *Ark., U.S.* 33°2′ N, 91°35′ W 103
Wilmot, *S. Dak., U.S.* 45°23′ N, 96°53′ W 90
Wilmot Flat, *N.H., U.S.* 43°25′ N, 71°54′ W 104
Wilmslow, *U.K.* 53°19′ N, 2°14′ W 162
Wilpattu National Park, *Sri Lanka* 8°19′ N, 79°37′ E 172
Wilsall, *Mont., U.S.* 45°58′ N, 110°40′ W 90
Wilseyville, *Calif., U.S.* 38°22′ N, 120°32′ W 100
Wilson, *Ark., U.S.* 35°33′ N, 90°3′ W 96
Wilson, *Kans., U.S.* 38°48′ N, 98°29′ W 92
Wilson, *La., U.S.* 30°54′ N, 91°7′ W 103
Wilson, *N.C., U.S.* 35°42′ N, 77°56′ W 96
Wilson, *Okla., U.S.* 34°8′ N, 97°25′ W 92
Wilson, *Tex., U.S.* 33°18′ N, 101°44′ W 92
Wilson Creek, *Wash., U.S.* 47°25′ N, 119°8′ W 90
Wilson Creek Range, *Nev., U.S.* 38°23′ N, 114°38′ W 90
Wilson Inlet 35°22′ S, 116°46′ E 230
Wilson, Mount, peak, *Colo., U.S.* 37°49′ N, 108°4′ W 92
Wilson, Mount, peak, *Nev., U.S.* 38°13′ N, 114°28′ W 90
Wilson, Mount, peak, *Oreg., U.S.* 45°2′ N, 121°45′ W 90
Wilsonville, *Ill., U.S.* 39°3′ N, 89°51′ W 102
Wilton, *Conn., U.S.* 41°11′ N, 73°27′ W 104
Wilton, *N.H., U.S.* 42°50′ N, 71°45′ W 104
Wilton, *N. Dak., U.S.* 47°8′ N, 100°49′ W 90
Wilton, *U.K.* 51°5′ N, 1°53′ W 162
Wilton, river, *Austral.* 13°31′ S, 133°56′ E 231
Wiluna, *Austral.* 26°36′ S, 120°13′ E 231
Wimauma, *Fla., U.S.* 27°43′ N, 82°17′ W 105
Wimbledon, *U.K.* 51°25′ N, 0°13′ E 162
Wimereux, *Fr.* 50°46′ N, 1°37′ E 163
Winam 0°21′ N, 34°13′ E 224
Winamac, *Ind., U.S.* 41°2′ N, 86°37′ W 102
Winburg, *S. Af.* 28°33′ S, 26°58′ E 227
Wincanton, *U.K.* 51°3′ N, 2°25′ W 162
Winchelsea, *U.K.* 50°55′ N, 0°43′ E 162
Winchelsea Island, *Austral.* 13°36′ S, 136°22′ E 230
Winchendon, *Mass., U.S.* 42°40′ N, 72°4′ W 104
Winchester, *Calif., U.S.* 33°42′ N, 117°6′ W 101
Winchester, *Ind., U.S.* 40°10′ N, 84°59′ W 102
Winchester, *N.H., U.S.* 42°45′ N, 72°23′ W 104
Winchester, *Ohio, U.S.* 38°55′ N, 83°38′ W 102
Winchester, *U.K.* 51°3′ N, 1°19′ W 162
Winchester, *Va., U.S.* 39°10′ N, 78°10′ W 94
Winchester Bay 43°35′ N, 125°25′ W 80
Wind Cave National Park, *S. Dak., U.S.* 43°29′ N, 103°16′ W 80
Wind Point, *Wis., U.S.* 42°46′ N, 87°46′ W 102
Wind, river, *Can.* 65°23′ N, 135°18′ W 98
Wind River Peak, *Wyo., U.S.* 42°42′ N, 109°13′ W 90
Wind River Range, *Wyo., U.S.* 42°39′ N, 109°21′ W 90
Wind, river, *Wyo., U.S.* 43°22′ N, 109°9′ W 80
Windeck, *Ger.* 50°48′ N, 7°36′ E 167
Winder, *Ga., U.S.* 33°58′ N, 83°44′ W 96
Windermere, *U.K.* 54°22′ N, 2°54′ W 162
Windfall, *Can.* 54°9′ N, 116°18′ W 108
Windfall, *Ind., U.S.* 40°21′ N, 85°58′ W 102
Windham, *Conn., U.S.* 41°41′ N, 72°10′ W 104
Windhoek, *Namibia* 22°34′ S, 16°56′ E 227
Windigo, river, *Can.* 48°22′ N, 73°33′ W 94
Windmill Islands, *Indian Ocean* 66°40′ S, 114°44′ E 248
Windom, *Minn., U.S.* 43°51′ N, 95°7′ W 90
Windom Peak, *Colo., U.S.* 37°36′ N, 107°41′ W 92
Window Rock, *Ariz., U.S.* 35°41′ N, 109°3′ W 92
Winds, Bay of 66°11′ S, 99°28′ E 248
Windsor, *Can.* 45°34′ N, 72°1′ W 94
Windsor, *Can.* 42°18′ N, 83°1′ W 102
Windsor, *Can.* 44°59′ N, 64°8′ W 111
Windsor, *Colo., U.S.* 40°28′ N, 104°55′ W 90
Windsor, *Conn., U.S.* 41°50′ N, 72°39′ W 104
Windsor, *Ill., U.S.* 39°25′ N, 88°36′ W 102
Windsor, *Mo., U.S.* 38°31′ N, 93°31′ W 94
Windsor, *N.C., U.S.* 35°59′ N, 77°0′ W 96
Windsor, *U.K.* 51°28′ N, 0°37′ E 162
Windsor, *Vt., U.S.* 43°28′ N, 72°24′ W 104
Windsorton, *S. Af.* 28°21′ S, 24°39′ E 227
Windward Islands, *Caribbean Sea* 13°41′ N, 61°20′ W 116
Windy Lake, *Can.* 60°18′ N, 100°44′ W 108
Windy Peak, *Wash., U.S.* 48°54′ N, 120°3′ W 90
Windy Point, *Can.* 50°56′ N, 55°48′ W 111
Winefred Lake, *Can.* 55°25′ N, 111°16′ W 108
Winfall, *N.C., U.S.* 36°13′ N, 76°29′ W 96
Winfield, *Can.* 52°56′ N, 114°27′ W 108
Winfield, *Tex., U.S.* 33°9′ N, 95°7′ W 103
Wingham, *Can.* 43°53′ N, 81°19′ W 102
Winifred, *Mont., U.S.* 47°31′ N, 109°23′ W 90
Winifreda, *Arg.* 36°15′ S, 64°15′ W 139
Winisk Lake, *Can.* 52°49′ N, 88°29′ W 80
Winisk, river, *Can.* 54°27′ N, 86°26′ W 106
Wink, *Tex., U.S.* 31°43′ N, 103°9′ W 92
Winkleigh, *U.K.* 50°51′ N, 3°57′ W 162
Winkler, *Can.* 49°10′ N, 97°56′ W 94
Winlock, *Wash., U.S.* 46°28′ N, 122°56′ W 100
Winn, *Me., U.S.* 45°28′ N, 68°23′ W 94
Winneba, *Ghana* 5°22′ N, 0°40′ E 222
Winnebago, *Ill., U.S.* 42°15′ N, 89°15′ W 102
Winnebago, *Minn., U.S.* 43°45′ N, 94°10′ W 94
Winnebago, Lake, *Wis., U.S.* 43°50′ N, 88°27′ W 102
Winneconne, *Wis., U.S.* 44°6′ N, 88°45′ W 102
Winner, *S. Dak., U.S.* 43°21′ N, 99°52′ W 90
Winnetka, *Ill., U.S.* 42°6′ N, 87°44′ W 102
Winnfield, *La., U.S.* 31°54′ N, 92°39′ W 103
Winnibigoshish, Lake, *Minn., U.S.* 47°21′ N, 96°1′ W 80
Winnie, *Tex., U.S.* 29°48′ N, 94°23′ W 103
Winnipeg, *Can.* 49°53′ N, 97°19′ W 90
Winnipeg Beach, *Can.* 50°29′ N, 97°2′ W 90
Winnipeg, Lake, *Can.* 53°1′ N, 98°32′ W 80
Winnipegosis, *Can.* 51°39′ N, 99°57′ W 90
Winnipegosis, Lake, *Can.* 52°3′ N, 99°36′ W 80
Winnisquam, *N.H., U.S.* 43°30′ N, 71°32′ W 104
Winnsboro, *La., U.S.* 32°9′ N, 91°44′ W 103
Winnsboro, *S.C., U.S.* 34°21′ N, 81°5′ W 96
Winnsboro, *Tex., U.S.* 32°57′ N, 95°17′ W 103
Winokapau Lake, *Can.* 53°13′ N, 63°41′ W 111
Winona, *Kans., U.S.* 39°3′ N, 101°15′ W 90
Winona, *Minn., U.S.* 44°2′ N, 91°38′ W 94
Winona, *Miss., U.S.* 33°27′ N, 89°44′ W 103
Winona, *Tex., U.S.* 32°29′ N, 95°10′ W 103
Winona Lake, *Ind., U.S.* 41°12′ N, 85°49′ W 94
Winschoten, *Neth.* 53°8′ N, 7°1′ E 163
Winsen, *Ger.* 53°22′ N, 10°12′ E 150
Winsford, *U.K.* 53°11′ N, 2°32′ W 162
Winslow, *Ariz., U.S.* 35°1′ N, 110°41′ W 92
Winslow, *Me., U.S.* 44°32′ N, 69°38′ W 94
Winstead, *S. Af.* 28°51′ S, 22°8′ E 227
Winsted, *Conn., U.S.* 41°55′ N, 73°4′ W 104
Winter Harbour, *Can.* 50°30′ N, 128°4′ W 90
Winter Haven, *Fla., U.S.* 28°1′ N, 81°44′ W 105
Winter Park, *Fla., U.S.* 28°35′ N, 81°22′ W 105
Winterberg, *Ger.* 51°11′ N, 8°32′ E 167
Winterhaven, *Calif., U.S.* 32°44′ N, 114°40′ W 101
Wintering Lake, lake, *Can.* 49°23′ N, 87°51′ W 94
Winters, *Tex., U.S.* 31°56′ N, 99°58′ W 96

Winterswijk, *Neth.* 51°58' N, 6°43' E 167
Winterton on Sea, *U.K.* 52°43' N, 1°41' E 163
Winterville, *Miss., U.S.* 33°29' N, 91°3' W 103
Winthrop, *Mass., U.S.* 42°22' N, 71°0' W 104
Winthrop, *Minn., U.S.* 44°32' N, 94°23' W 90
Winthrop, *Wash., U.S.* 48°27' N, 120°10' W 108
Winthrop Harbor, *Ill., U.S.* 42°28' N, 87°50' W 102
Winton, *Austral.* 22°25' S, 143°2' E 238
Winton, *Calif., U.S.* 37°23' N, 120°38' W 100
Winton, *Minn., U.S.* 47°54' N, 91°49' W 94
Winton, *N.Z.* 46°9' S, 168°18' E 240
Wipperfürth, *Ger.* 51°7' N, 7°23' E 163
Wis, river, *Pol.* 53°7' N, 18°11' E 142
Wis, river, *Pol.* 50°1' N, 20°37' E 152
Wisbech, *U.K.* 52°39' N, 0°9' E 162
Wiscasset, *Me., U.S.* 44°0' N, 69°41' W 94
Wisconsin, adm. division, *Wis., U.S.* 44°20' N, 91°11' W 94
Wisconsin Dells, *Wis., U.S.* 43°37' N, 89°46' W 102
Wisconsin, Lake, *Wis., U.S.* 43°21' N, 89°53' W 102
Wisconsin Range, *Antarctica* 84°42' S, 105°9' W 248
Wisconsin Rapids, *Wis., U.S.* 44°23' N, 89°50' W 110
Wisconsin, river, *Wis., U.S.* 42°45' N, 91°14' W 80
Wise Bay 82°34' S, 170°4' E 248
Wiseman, *Alas., U.S.* 67°18' N, 150°16' W 98
Wishek, *N. Dak., U.S.* 46°14' N, 99°35' W 90
Wishram, *Wash., U.S.* 45°39' N, 120°58' W 100
Wisner, *La., U.S.* 31°58' N, 91°39' W 103
Wissen, *Ger.* 50°46' N, 7°43' E 167
Wistaria, *Can.* 53°51' N, 126°18' W 108
Witbank, *S. Af.* 25°53' S, 29°11' E 227
Witdraai, *S. Af.* 27°1' S, 20°41' E 227
Witham, *U.K.* 51°48' N, 0°38' E 162
Witherbee, *N.Y., U.S.* 44°5' N, 73°33' W 104
Withernsea, *U.K.* 53°43' N, 3°179' E 162
Witney, *U.K.* 51°47' N, 1°29' W 162
Witry-lès-Reims, *Fr.* 49°17' N, 4°7' E 163
Witt, *Ill., U.S.* 39°14' N, 89°21' W 102
Wittdün, *Ger.* 54°37' N, 8°23' E 150
Witten, *Ger.* 51°25' N, 7°19' E 167
Witten, *S. Dak., U.S.* 43°25' N, 100°6' W 90
Wittenberge, *Ger.* 53°3' N, 11°43' E 160
Wittlich, *Ger.* 49°59' N, 6°54' E 167
Wittmund, *Ger.* 53°34' N, 7°47' E 163
Wittow, *Ger.* 54°38' N, 13°6' E 152
Witu, *Kenya* 2°23' S, 40°26' E 224
Witu Islands, islands, *Bismarck Sea* 4°24' S, 148°22' E 192
Witvlei, *Namibia* 22°24' S, 18°32' E 227
Witzenhausen, *Ger.* 51°20' N, 9°51' E 167
Wivenhoe, *Can.* 56°11' N, 95°11' W 108
Wiwŏn, *N. Korea* 40°53' N, 126°2' E 200
Wiżajny, *Pol.* 54°21' N, 22°52' E 166
Włocławek, *Pol.* 52°38' N, 19°4' E 152
Włodawa, *Pol.* 51°32' N, 23°31' E 152
Woburn, *Mass., U.S.* 42°28' N, 71°10' W 104
Woc, *Pol.* 54°16' N, 18°45' E 166
Wofford Heights, *Calif., U.S.* 35°43' N, 118°28' W 101
Wokam, island, *Indonesia* 5°44' S, 134°34' E 192
Woking, *Can.* 55°34' N, 118°47' W 108
Woking, *U.K.* 51°18' N, 0°35' E 162
Wokingham, *U.K.* 51°22' N, 0°52' E 162
Wolcott, *Ind., U.S.* 40°45' N, 87°3' W 102
Wolds, The, *U.K.* 53°56' N, 0°40' E 162
Woleai Atoll, *F.M.S.* 7°26' N, 141°37' E 192
Wolf Creek, *Mont., U.S.* 46°58' N, 112°3' W 90
Wolf Creek Pass, *Colo., U.S.* 37°29' N, 106°49' W 90
Wolf Lake, *Can.* 60°38' N, 132°17' W 108
Wolf Lake, *Mich., U.S.* 43°14' N, 86°7' W 102
Wolf Mountains, *Mont., U.S.* 45°9' N, 107°18' W 90
Wolf, river, *Miss., U.S.* 30°33' N, 89°23' W 103
Wolf, river, *Wis., U.S.* 45°17' N, 89°0' W 94
Wolfau, *Aust.* 47°15' N, 16°5' E 168
Wolfeboro, *N.H., U.S.* 43°34' N, 71°13' W 104
Wolfeboro Falls, *N.H., U.S.* 43°35' N, 71°13' W 104
Wolfen, *Ger.* 51°40' N, 12°16' E 152
Wolfforth, *Tex., U.S.* 33°29' N, 102°1' W 92
Wolfhagen, *Ger.* 51°19' N, 9°10' E 167
Wolfsburg, *Ger.* 52°25' N, 10°47' E 152
Wolfstein, *Ger.* 49°34' N, 7°36' E 163
Wolin, *Pol.* 53°51' N, 14°36' E 152
Wollaston Forland 74°31' N, 18°52' W 246
Wollaston, Islas, islands, *Chile* 56°6' S, 67°3' W 134
Wollaston Lake, *Can.* 57°56' N, 103°5' W 73
Wollaston Peninsula, *Can.* 69°41' N, 121°29' W 106
Wollongong, *Austral.* 34°24' S, 150°50' E 231
Wöllstein, *Ger.* 49°48' N, 7°57' E 167
Wolmaransstad, *S. Af.* 27°13' S, 25°58' E 227
Wolseley, *Can.* 50°25' N, 103°17' W 90
Wolsingham, *U.K.* 54°44' N, 1°54' W 162
Wolsztyn, *Pol.* 52°7' N, 16°7' E 152
Wolvega, *Neth.* 52°52' N, 6°0' E 163
Wolverhampton, *U.K.* 52°35' N, 2°9' W 162
Wolverine, river, *Can.* 57°46' N, 116°59' W 108
Wolverton, *U.K.* 52°3' N, 0°49' E 162
Wondong, *S. Korea* 34°21' N, 126°42' E 200
Wonewoc, *Wis., U.S.* 43°38' N, 90°12' W 102
Wonga Wongué National Park, *Gabon* 0°29' N, 9°13' E 206
Wonju, *S. Korea* 37°19' N, 127°57' E 200
Wonotobo Vallen, fall(s), *Suriname* 4°22' N, 58°6' W 130
Wonowon, *Can.* 56°43' N, 121°48' W 108
Wŏnsan, *N. Korea* 39°8' N, 127°24' E 200
Wonyulgunna Hill, peak, *Austral.* 24°53' S, 119°34' E 230
Wood Buffalo National Park, *Can.* 59°16' N, 114°1' W 72
Wood Lake, *Nebr., U.S.* 42°37' N, 100°15' W 90
Wood Lake, lake, *Can.* 55°13' N, 103°45' W 108
Wood, Mount, peak, *Mont., U.S.* 45°14' N, 109°53' W 90
Wood River, *Nebr., U.S.* 40°48' N, 98°37' W 90
Wood, river, *Can.* 49°22' N, 107°21' W 80
Woodah, Isle, island, *Austral.* 13°20' S, 134°37' E 230
Woodall Mountain, peak, *Miss., U.S.* 34°43' N, 88°18' W 96
Woodbine, *Ky., U.S.* 36°53' N, 84°6' W 96
Woodbridge, *Calif., U.S.* 38°8' N, 121°19' W 100
Woodbridge, *U.K.* 52°5' N, 1°17' E 162
Woodburn, *Ind., U.S.* 41°6' N, 84°51' W 102
Woodburn, *Oreg., U.S.* 45°7' N, 122°51' W 90
Woodbury, *Conn., U.S.* 41°32' N, 73°13' W 104
Woodbury, *N.J., U.S.* 39°50' N, 75°11' W 94
Woodcock, Mount, peak, *Austral.* 19°17' S, 133°51' E 230
Woodhall Spa, *U.K.* 53°9' N, 0°13' E 162
Woodlake, *Calif., U.S.* 36°25' N, 119°7' W 101
Woodland, *Calif., U.S.* 38°40' N, 121°47' W 90
Woodland, *Wash., U.S.* 45°53' N, 122°46' W 100
Woodlark, island, *P.N.G.* 9°5' S, 153°2' E 192
Woodmont, *Conn., U.S.* 41°13' N, 73°0' W 104
Woodpecker, *Can.* 53°30' N, 122°39' W 108
Woodridge, *Can.* 49°15' N, 96°9' W 90
Woodroffe, Mount, peak, *Austral.* 26°23' S, 131°32' E 230
Woodruff, *Utah, U.S.* 41°31' N, 111°10' W 90
Woods, Lake of the, *Can.* 49°4' N, 96°1' W 106
Woodsboro, *Tex., U.S.* 28°13' N, 97°19' W 96
Woodsfield, *Ohio, U.S.* 39°44' N, 81°7' W 102
Woodstock, *Can.* 43°7' N, 80°44' W 102
Woodstock, *Can.* 46°9' N, 67°36' W 94
Woodstock, *Ill., U.S.* 42°18' N, 88°26' W 102
Woodstock, *N.Y., U.S.* 42°2' N, 74°8' W 104
Woodstock, *U.K.* 51°50' N, 1°22' W 162
Woodstock, *Vt., U.S.* 43°37' N, 72°31' W 104
Woodsville, *N.H., U.S.* 44°8' N, 72°3' W 104
Woodville, *Calif., U.S.* 36°5' N, 119°13' W 101
Woodville, *Ga., U.S.* 33°39' N, 83°7' W 96
Woodville, *Miss., U.S.* 31°4' N, 91°18' W 103
Woodville, *Tex., U.S.* 30°45' N, 94°26' W 103
Woodward, *Okla., U.S.* 36°24' N, 99°23' W 96
Woodworth, *La., U.S.* 31°8' N, 92°31' W 103
Woody, *Calif., U.S.* 35°42' N, 118°51' W 101
Woody Point, *Can.* 49°30' N, 57°56' W 111
Woollard, Mount, peak, *Antarctica* 80°27' S, 95°39' W 248
Woollett, Lac, lake, *Can.* 51°22' N, 74°22' W 110
Woolpit, *U.K.* 52°13' N, 0°53' E 162
Woolwich, *Me., U.S.* 43°55' N, 69°49' W 104
Woolwich, *U.K.* 51°29' N, 6°357' E 162
Woomera, *Austral.* 31°13' S, 136°55' E 231
Woonsocket, *S. Dak., U.S.* 44°2' N, 98°18' W 90
Wooster, *Ohio, U.S.* 40°47' N, 81°56' W 102
Woosung, *Ill., U.S.* 41°53' N, 89°33' W 102
Worbis, *Ger.* 51°25' N, 10°21' E 167
Worcester, *Mass., U.S.* 42°16' N, 71°48' W 104
Worcester, *S. Af.* 33°38' S, 19°23' E 227
Worcester, *U.K.* 52°11' N, 2°12' W 162
Worden, *Mont., U.S.* 45°57' N, 108°10' W 90
Wordie Nunatak, peak, *Antarctica* 66°19' S, 51°16' E 248
Workington, *U.K.* 54°38' N, 3°33' W 162
Worksop, *U.K.* 53°17' N, 1°8' W 162
Worland, *Wyo., U.S.* 44°0' N, 107°56' W 90
World's View Hill, site, *Zimb.* 20°31' S, 28°29' E 227
World War II Valor in the Pacific National Monument, *Calif., U.S.* 41°53' N, 121°22' W 90
World War II Valor in the Pacific National Monument, *Hawai'i, U.S.* 21°21' N, 157°57' W 99
Wormeldange, *Lux.* 49°37' N, 6°24' E 163
Woronoco, *Mass., U.S.* 42°9' N, 72°51' W 104
Wörrstadt, *Ger.* 49°49' N, 8°6' E 167
Worsley, *Can.* 56°33' N, 119°8' W 108
Wörth, *Ger.* 49°47' N, 9°10' E 167
Wortham, *Tex., U.S.* 31°45' N, 96°28' W 96
Worthing, *U.K.* 50°49' N, 0°23' E 162
Worthington, *Ind., U.S.* 39°6' N, 86°59' W 102
Worthington, *Minn., U.S.* 43°35' N, 95°37' W 90
Worthington, *Ohio, U.S.* 40°5' N, 83°0' W 102
Worthington Peak, *Nev., U.S.* 37°54' N, 115°42' W 90
Worthville, *Ky., U.S.* 38°36' N, 85°4' W 102
Wosi, *Indonesia* 0°10' N, 127°46' E 192
Woumbou, *Cameroon* 5°15' N, 14°14' E 218
Wounta, Laguna de, lake, *Nicar.* 13°34' N, 84°18' W 115
Wour, *Chad* 21°21' N, 15°57' E 216
Wowoni, island, *Indonesia* 4°20' S, 123°14' E 192
Woyla, river, *Indonesia* 4°21' N, 96°4' E 196
Wragby, *U.K.* 53°16' N, 0°19' E 162
Wrangel Island see Vrangelya, Ostrov, island, *Russ.* 71°29' N, 175°23' E 160
Wrangel Plain, *Arctic Ocean* 81°41' N, 157°4' E 255
Wrangell, *Alas., U.S.* 56°28' N, 132°25' W 108
Wrangell Mountains, *Alas., U.S.* 61°51' N, 144°32' W 98
Wrangell-Saint Elias National Park and Preserve, *Alas., U.S.* 62°15' N, 143°49' W 98
Wray, *Colo., U.S.* 40°3' N, 102°14' W 90
Wreck Point, *S. Af.* 29°7' S, 16°12' E 227
Wrekin, The, peak, *U.K.* 52°39' N, 2°36' W 162
Wren, *Ala., U.S.* 34°25' N, 87°17' W 96
Wrens, *Ga., U.S.* 33°11' N, 82°24' W 96
Wrexham, *U.K.* 53°2' N, 2°59' W 162
Wright, *Philippines* 11°47' N, 125°1' E 203
Wright, *Wyo., U.S.* 43°42' N, 105°32' W 90
Wright Hill, peak, *Antarctica* 79°36' S, 159°27' E 248
Wright, Mont, peak, *Can.* 52°43' N, 67°27' W 111
Wright Patman Lake, *Ark., U.S.* 33°1' N, 94°59' W 80
Wright-Patterson Air Force Base, *Ohio, U.S.* 39°48' N, 84°6' W 102
Wrightsville Beach, *N.C., U.S.* 34°12' N, 77°49' W 96
Wrightwood, *Calif., U.S.* 34°21' N, 117°39' W 101
Wrigley, *Can.* 63°19' N, 123°21' W 98
Wrigley Gulf 73°35' S, 126°58' W 248
Wrington, *U.K.* 51°21' N, 2°46' W 162
Wroc, *Pol.* 51°6' N, 17°0' E 152
Wrong Lake, lake, *Can.* 52°34' N, 96°38' W 108
Wronki, *Pol.* 52°42' N, 16°23' E 152
Wroxeter, *Can.* 43°51' N, 81°11' W 102
Wroxham, *U.K.* 52°43' N, 1°24' E 163
Wroxton, *Can.* 51°12' N, 101°54' W 90
Wroxton, *U.K.* 52°4' N, 1°25' W 162
Wu, river, *China* 28°38' N, 108°25' E 198
Wu, river, *China* 27°14' N, 108°4' E 190
Wu'an, *China* 36°42' N, 114°13' E 198
Wubu, *China* 37°27' N, 110°40' E 198
Wuchang, *China* 44°55' N, 127°8' E 198
Wuchuan, *China* 41°7' N, 111°33' E 198
Wuchuan, *China* 28°26' N, 108°1' E 198
Wuchuan, *China* 21°24' N, 110°47' E 198
Wuda, *China* 39°33' N, 106°44' E 198
Wudalianchi, *China* 48°38' N, 126°10' E 198
Wudaogou, *China* 42°5' N, 125°51' E 200
Wudaoliang, *China* 35°13' N, 93°2' E 188
Wudi, *China* 37°45' N, 117°35' E 198
Wudu, *China* 33°25' N, 104°54' E 198
Wufeng, *China* 30°14' N, 110°40' E 198
Wugang, *China* 26°44' N, 110°34' E 198
Wugong, *China* 34°17' N, 108°11' E 198
Wuhai, *China* 39°39' N, 106°50' E 198
Wuhan, *China* 30°30' N, 114°21' E 198
Wuhe, *China* 33°9' N, 117°55' E 198
Wuhu, *China* 31°23' N, 118°26' E 198
Wūjang, *China* 33°36' N, 79°54' E 188
Wukari, *Nig.* 7°49' N, 9°48' E 222
Wulff Land 81°57' N, 58°19' W 246
Wuli, *China* 34°22' N, 92°45' E 188
Wulian, *China* 35°44' N, 119°13' E 198
Wulongbei, *China* 40°15' N, 124°15' E 200
Wum, *Cameroon* 6°19' N, 10°3' E 222
Wuming, *China* 23°8' N, 108°18' E 198
Wun Shwai, *Sudan* 8°1' N, 29°24' E 224
Wuning, *China* 29°18' N, 115°1' E 198
Wünnenberg, *Ger.* 51°30' N, 8°43' E 167
Wunstorf, *Ger.* 52°25' N, 9°26' E 152
Wuping, *China* 25°4' N, 116°4' E 198
Wuppertal, *Ger.* 51°16' N, 7°10' E 167
Wuqi, *China* 36°57' N, 108°14' E 198
Wuqia, *China* 39°45' N, 75°6' E 184
Wuqing, *China* 39°25' N, 117°0' E 198
Wurno, *Nig.* 13°14' N, 5°27' E 222
Würselen, *Ger.* 50°49' N, 6°7' E 163
Würzburg, *Ger.* 49°47' N, 9°56' E 167
Wusa'a, *Sudan* 13°0' N, 32°31' E 182
Wushan, *China* 31°6' N, 109°51' E 198
Wushi (Uqturpan), *China* 41°9' N, 79°17' E 184
Wutai, *China* 38°41' N, 113°11' E 198
Wuvulu Island, *P.N.G.* 2°23' S, 142°45' E 192
Wuwei, *China* 38°0' N, 102°55' E 190
Wuwei, *China* 31°17' N, 117°47' E 198
Wuxi, *China* 31°23' N, 109°36' E 198
Wuxi, *China* 31°37' N, 120°18' E 198
Wuxue, *China* 29°54' N, 115°33' E 198
Wuyi Shan, *China* 26°4' N, 116°25' E 198
Wuyiling, *China* 48°37' N, 129°21' E 198
Wuyuan, *China* 41°4' N, 108°19' E 198
Wuzhai, *China* 38°54' N, 111°49' E 198
Wuzhong, *China* 38°1' N, 106°12' E 198
Wuzhou, *China* 23°34' N, 111°21' E 198
Wyandotte, *Mich., U.S.* 42°11' N, 83°11' W 102
Wyanet, *Ill., U.S.* 41°22' N, 89°34' W 102
Wye, river, *U.K.* 52°15' N, 3°30' W 162
Wyemandoo, peak, *Austral.* 28°36' S, 118°19' E 230
Wylatowo, *Pol.* 52°36' N, 17°55' E 152
Wymondham, *U.K.* 52°34' N, 1°6' E 163
Wymore, *Nebr., U.S.* 40°5' N, 96°40' W 90
Wyndham, *Austral.* 15°29' S, 128°14' E 238
Wyndmere, *N. Dak., U.S.* 46°15' N, 97°10' W 90
Wynne, *Ark., U.S.* 35°12' N, 90°49' W 96
Wynnewood, *Okla., U.S.* 34°37' N, 97°9' W 96
Wynyard, *Can.* 51°45' N, 104°11' W 90
Wyoming, *Can.* 42°56' N, 82°7' W 102
Wyoming, *Ill., U.S.* 41°3' N, 89°47' W 102
Wyoming, adm. division, *Wyo., U.S.* 42°49' N, 108°38' W 90
Wyoming Peak, *Wyo., U.S.* 42°36' N, 110°43' W 90
Wyoming Range, *Wyo., U.S.* 42°46' N, 110°47' W 90
Wysox, *Pa., U.S.* 41°46' N, 76°25' W 110
Wytheville, *Va., U.S.* 36°56' N, 81°6' W 96
Wyville Thomson Ridge, *North Atlantic Ocean* 59°30' N, 10°10' W 253
Wyvis, Ben, peak, *U.K.* 57°39' N, 4°41' W 150

X

X, Rock, *Antarctica* 66°2' S, 138°54' E 248
Xá Muteba, *Angola* 9°33' S, 17°49' E 218
Xaafuun, *Somalia* 10°21' N, 51°18' E 216
Xaafuun, Raas, *Somalia* 10°26' N, 51°28' E 216
Xàbia see Jávea, *Sp.* 38°47' N, 0°9' E 164
Xaçmaz, *Azerb.* 41°27' N, 48°49' E 195
Xaignabouri, *Laos* 19°16' N, 101°43' E 202
Xainza, *China* 30°57' N, 88°37' E 197
Xaitongmoin, *China* 29°27' N, 88°9' E 188
Xai-Xai, *Mozambique* 25°3' S, 33°39' E 227
Xalapa, *Mex.* 19°28' N, 96°59' W 114
Xalin, *Somalia* 9°5' N, 48°37' E 216
Xam Nua, *Laos* 20°27' N, 104°0' E 202
Xamure, *Somalia* 7°11' N, 48°56' E 218
Xamure, spring, *Somalia* 7°12' N, 48°55' E 216
Xangongo, *Angola* 16°45' S, 15°0' E 220
Xankändi see Stepanakert, *Asia* 39°48' N, 46°43' E 195
Xanten, *Ger.* 51°39' N, 6°27' E 167
Xánthi, *Gr.* 41°8' N, 24°54' E 180
Xanthus, ruin(s), *Turk.* 36°19' N, 29°12' E 156
Xanxerê, *Braz.* 26°52' S, 52°25' W 138
Xapecó, river, *Braz.* 26°39' S, 52°30' W 139
Xapuri, *Braz.* 10°42' S, 68°32' W 137
Xapuri, river, *Braz.* 10°43' S, 69°13' W 137
Xar Moron, river, *China* 43°17' N, 119°27' E 198
Xarardheere, *Somalia* 4°38' N, 47°53' E 218
Xassengue, *Angola* 10°26' S, 18°33' E 220
Xàtiva, *Sp.* 38°58' N, 0°31' E 164
Xavantina, *Braz.* 21°15' S, 52°50' W 138
Xayar, *China* 41°14' N, 82°51' E 184
Xcalak National Park, *Mex.* 18°20' N, 88°6' W 72
Xêgar see Tingri, *China* 28°40' N, 87°3' E 197
Xèng, river, *Laos* 20°10' N, 102°44' E 202
Xenia, *Ill., U.S.* 38°37' N, 88°38' W 102
Xenia, *Ohio, U.S.* 39°41' N, 83°56' W 102
Xépôn, *Laos* 16°41' N, 106°15' E 202
Xeriuini, river, *Braz.* 0°50' N, 62°15' W 130
Xhora, *S. Af.* 31°59' S, 28°39' E 227
Xi Ujimqin Qi, *China* 44°36' N, 117°36' E 198
Xiachuan Dao, island, *China* 21°17' N, 112°22' E 198
Xiajiang, *China* 27°35' N, 115°3' E 198
Xiamen (Amoy), *China* 24°25' N, 118°6' E 198
Xi'an, *China* 34°17' N, 108°57' E 198
Xianfeng, *China* 29°41' N, 109°8' E 198
Xiang, river, *China* 26°33' N, 112°13' E 198
Xiangfan, *China* 32°6' N, 112°2' E 198
Xianggang see Hong Kong, island, *China* 21°55' N, 114°15' E 198
Xianghuang Qi (Hobot Xar), *China* 42°11' N, 113°53' E 198
Xiangkhoang, *Laos* 19°20' N, 103°23' E 202
Xiangning, *China* 35°57' N, 110°48' E 198
Xiangshan, *China* 29°26' N, 121°52' E 198
Xiangtan, *China* 27°54' N, 112°51' E 198
Xiangyin, *China* 28°42' N, 112°50' E 198
Xianju, *China* 28°53' N, 120°43' E 198
Xiantao, *China* 30°19' N, 113°26' E 198
Xianyou, *China* 25°22' N, 118°42' E 198
Xiaogan, *China* 30°55' N, 113°55' E 198
Xiaojiang, *China* 27°33' N, 120°28' E 198
Xiaoshan, *China* 30°8' N, 120°18' E 198
Xiaoyi, *China* 37°7' N, 111°46' E 198
Xiapu, *China* 26°53' N, 119°59' E 198
Xichang, *China* 27°53' N, 102°16' E 190
Xichang Space Launch Center, spaceport, *China* 28°13' N, 101°49' E 190
Xichú, *Mex.* 21°23' N, 100°5' W 114
Xichuan, *China* 33°10' N, 111°31' E 198
Xicoténcatl, *Mex.* 22°58' N, 98°56' W 114
Xicotepec de Juárez, *Mex.* 20°16' N, 97°57' W 114
Xié, river, *Braz.* 1°12' N, 67°15' W 136
Xiejia, *China* 42°23' N, 125°43' E 200
Xifeng, *China* 42°45' N, 124°39' E 200
Xifeng, *China* 35°47' N, 107°39' E 198
Xigazê, *China* 29°13' N, 88°53' E 190
Xihe, *China* 33°59' N, 105°16' E 198
Xihu, *China* 40°33' N, 95°1' E 188
Xiis, *Somalia* 10°47' N, 46°52' E 216
Xiji, *China* 36°0' N, 105°43' E 198
Xijir Ulan Hu, lake, *China* 35°9' N, 89°12' E 188
Xiliao, river, *China* 43°45' N, 122°32' E 198
Xilinhot, *China* 43°56' N, 116°8' E 198
Xilitla, *Mex.* 21°23' N, 98°58' W 114
Ximeng, *China* 22°43' N, 99°25' E 202
Xin Barag Youqi, *China* 48°39' N, 116°47' E 198
Xin Barag Zuoqi, *China* 48°10' N, 118°13' E 198
Xin Hot see Abag Qi, *China* 44°1' N, 114°56' E 198
Xinavane, *Mozambique* 25°2' S, 32°47' E 227
Xinbin, *China* 41°43' N, 125°4' E 200
Xincai, *China* 32°46' N, 114°53' E 198
Xincheng, *China* 38°32' N, 106°11' E 198
Xinchengzi, *China* 42°4' N, 123°33' E 200
Xinfeng, *China* 25°24' N, 114°54' E 198
Xinfeng, *China* 24°1' N, 114°10' E 198
Xing'an, *China* 25°33' N, 110°37' E 198
Xingcheng, *China* 40°39' N, 120°46' E 198
Xingdi, *China* 41°17' N, 87°58' E 188
Xinge, *Angola* 9°47' S, 19°11' E 220
Xinghe, *China* 40°51' N, 113°54' E 198
Xinghua, *China* 32°56' N, 119°53' E 198
Xingning, *China* 24°6' N, 115°43' E 198
Xingshan, *China* 31°22' N, 110°44' E 198
Xingtai, *China* 37°1' N, 114°31' E 198
Xingu, river, *Braz.* 5°8' S, 54°18' W 122
Xingxian, *China* 38°28' N, 111°3' E 198
Xingyi, *China* 25°1' N, 105°8' E 190
Xingzi, *China* 29°27' N, 115°59' E 198
Xinhe, *China* 37°31' N, 115°13' E 198
Xinhe (Toksu), *China* 41°35' N, 82°38' E 184
Xinhuang, *China* 27°20' N, 109°17' E 198
Xinhui, *China* 22°26' N, 113°1' E 198
Xining, *China* 36°30' N, 101°51' E 190
Xinji, *China* 37°56' N, 115°15' E 198
Xinjiang, *China* 35°38' N, 111°12' E 198
Xinjiang, adm. division, *China* 41°27' N, 81°29' E 184
Xinmin, *China* 41°59' N, 122°49' E 200
Xinning, *China* 26°28' N, 110°48' E 198
Xinpu see Lianyungang, *China* 34°38' N, 119°14' E 198
Xinshao, *China* 27°21' N, 111°28' E 198
Xinwen, *China* 35°53' N, 117°43' E 198
Xinxiang, *China* 35°12' N, 113°48' E 198
Xinxing, *China* 22°43' N, 112°9' E 198
Xinyang, *China* 32°9' N, 114°6' E 198
Xinye, *China* 32°31' N, 112°26' E 198
Xinyi, *China* 34°19' N, 118°20' E 198
Xinyu, *China* 27°46' N, 114°52' E 198
Xinyuan, *China* 43°25' N, 83°25' E 184
Xinzhou, *China* 38°24' N, 112°45' E 198
Xique Xique, *Braz.* 10°51' S, 42°43' W 132
Xiruá, river, *Braz.* 7°19' S, 68°34' W 130

Xishui, *China* 30°27′ N, 115°13′ E 198
Xishui, *China* 28°20′ N, 106°11′ E 198
Xiushan, *China* 28°25′ N, 108°59′ E 198
Xiushui, *China* 29°4′ N, 114°30′ E 198
Xiuyan, *China* 40°16′ N, 123°15′ E 200
Xiuying, *China* 19°59′ N, 110°12′ E 198
Xixia, *China* 33°21′ N, 111°30′ E 198
Xixian, *China* 32°22′ N, 114°41′ E 198
Xixiang, *China* 33°4′ N, 107°44′ E 198
Xizang (Tibet), adm. division, *China* 29°28′ N, 87°1′ E 197
Xizhong Dao, island, *China* 39°8′ N, 121°11′ E 198
Xocavand see Martuni, *Azerb.* 39°48′ N, 47°5′ E 195
Xochihuehuetlán, *Mex.* 17°54′ N, 98°28′ W 114
Xorkol, *China* 38°52′ N, 91°10′ E 188
Xpuhil, ruin(s), *Mex.* 18°31′ N, 89°33′ W 115
Xu, river, *China* 28°10′ N, 116°2′ E 198
Xuan Loc, *Vietnam* 10°56′ N, 107°14′ E 202
Xuan'en, *China* 30°1′ N, 109°28′ E 198
Xuanhan, *China* 31°21′ N, 107°36′ E 198
Xuanhua, *China* 40°38′ N, 115°5′ E 198
Xuanzhou, *China* 30°54′ N, 118°46′ E 198
Xuchang, *China* 34°3′ N, 113°49′ E 198
Xudat, *Azerb.* 41°37′ N, 48°41′ E 195
Xuddur (Oddur), *Somalia* 4°6′ N, 43°55′ E 218
Xudun, *Somalia* 9°3′ N, 47°29′ E 216
Xugou, *China* 34°41′ N, 119°23′ E 198
Xulun Hoh see Zhenglan Qi, *China* 42°13′ N, 116°2′ E 198
Xümatang, *China* 33°52′ N, 97°21′ E 188
Xunwu, *China* 24°52′ N, 115°37′ E 198
Xunyang, *China* 32°53′ N, 109°22′ E 198
Xunyi, *China* 35°10′ N, 108°18′ E 198
Xupu, *China* 27°56′ N, 110°35′ E 198
Xuwen, *China* 20°18′ N, 110°9′ E 198
Xuyong, *China* 28°9′ N, 105°28′ E 198
Xuzhou, *China* 34°16′ N, 117°7′ E 198
Xylofagou, *Cyprus* 34°58′ N, 33°50′ E 194

Y

Yaak, *Mont., U.S.* 48°49′ N, 115°43′ W 90
Yaak, river, *Can.* 48°43′ N, 116°2′ W 90
Ya'an, *China* 30°2′ N, 103°1′ E 190
Yabassi, *Cameroon* 4°25′ N, 9°58′ E 222
Yabēlo, *Eth.* 4°51′ N, 38°8′ E 224
Yablunyts'kyy, Pereval, pass, *Ukr.* 48°17′ N, 24°27′ E 152
Yabrīn, spring, *Saudi Arabia* 23°11′ N, 48°57′ E 182
Yabrūd, *Syr.* 33°58′ N, 36°38′ E 194
Yachi, river, *China* 26°59′ N, 106°14′ E 198
Yacimiento Río Turbio, *Arg.* 51°35′ S, 72°21′ W 134
Yaco, *Bol.* 17°13′ S, 67°34′ W 137
Yaco, river, *Peru* 10°47′ S, 70°49′ W 137
Yacolt, *Wash., U.S.* 45°51′ N, 122°25′ W 100
Yacuma, river, *Bol.* 14°6′ S, 66°36′ W 137
Yadgir, *India* 16°46′ N, 77°8′ E 188
Yaenengu, *Dem. Rep. of the Congo* 2°27′ N, 23°11′ E 218
Yag, river, *China* 34°0′ N, 93°55′ E 188
Yağca, *Turk.* 37°1′ N, 30°32′ E 156
Yagodnoye, *Russ.* 62°34′ N, 149°33′ E 160
Yagoua, *Cameroon* 10°22′ N, 15°14′ E 216
Yagradagzê Shan, peak, *China* 35°8′ N, 95°34′ E 188
Yaguarón, river, *South America* 32°0′ S, 54°1′ W 139
Yaguas, river, *Peru* 3°11′ S, 71°2′ W 136
Yahia Lehouas, *Alg.* 35°36′ N, 4°55′ E 150
Yahk, *Can.* 49°5′ N, 116°7′ W 90
Yahualica, *Mex.* 21°9′ N, 102°54′ W 114
Yahuma, *Dem. Rep. of the Congo* 1°5′ N, 23°5′ E 218
Yahyalı, *Turk.* 38°5′ N, 35°21′ E 156
Yainax Butte, peak, *Oreg., U.S.* 42°19′ N, 121°20′ W 90
Yaita, *Japan* 36°47′ N, 139°56′ E 201
Yaizu, *Japan* 34°51′ N, 138°18′ E 201
Yakeshi, *China* 49°15′ N, 120°43′ E 198
Yakima, *Wash., U.S.* 46°35′ N, 120°30′ W 90
Yakkabog', *Uzb.* 39°1′ N, 66°41′ E 197
Yakmach, *Pak.* 28°43′ N, 63°48′ E 182
Yakoma, *Dem. Rep. of the Congo* 4°2′ N, 22°21′ E 218
Yakossi, *Cen. Af. Rep.* 5°37′ N, 23°22′ E 218
Yakotoko, *Cen. Af. Rep.* 5°20′ N, 25°16′ E 224
Yaksha, *Russ.* 61°49′ N, 56°50′ E 154
Yaku Shima, island, *Japan* 29°39′ N, 130°35′ E 190
Yakusu, *Dem. Rep. of the Congo* 0°35′ N, 25°1′ E 224
Yakutsk, *Russ.* 62°2′ N, 129°36′ E 160
Yala, *Ghana* 10°7′ N, 1°52′ W 222
Yala, *Sri Lanka* 6°22′ N, 81°31′ E 188
Yala, *Thai.* 6°30′ N, 101°16′ E 196
Yalagüina, *Nicar.* 13°28′ N, 86°28′ W 115
Yale, *Can.* 49°34′ N, 121°26′ W 100
Yale, *Mich., U.S.* 43°8′ N, 82°47′ W 102
Yale, *Okla., U.S.* 36°5′ N, 96°41′ W 92
Yale Dam, *Wash., U.S.* 45°59′ N, 122°25′ W 100
Yali, *Dem. Rep. of the Congo* 1°59′ N, 21°5′ E 218
Yaligimba, *Dem. Rep. of the Congo* 2°11′ N, 22°54′ E 218
Yalinga, *Cen. Af. Rep.* 6°30′ N, 23°19′ E 218
Yalkubul, Punta, *Mex.* 21°34′ N, 89°27′ W 116
Yalova, *Turk.* 40°38′ N, 29°15′ E 156
Yalta, *Ukr.* 44°30′ N, 34°5′ E 156
Yalu, river, *Asia* 41°46′ N, 128°2′ E 200
Yalutorovsk, *Russ.* 56°40′ N, 66°11′ E 169
Yalvaç, *Turk.* 38°17′ N, 31°9′ E 156
Yamada, *Japan* 33°33′ N, 130°45′ E 201
Yamaga, *Japan* 33°0′ N, 130°41′ E 201
Yamagata, *Japan* 38°15′ N, 140°20′ E 201
Yamagata, adm. division, *Japan* 38°22′ N, 139°45′ E 201
Yamaguchi, *Japan* 34°11′ N, 131°29′ E 200
Yamaguchi, adm. division, *Japan* 34°6′ N, 131°0′ E 200
Yamal, Poluostrov, *Russ.* 70°23′ N, 70°9′ E 169
Yamal-Nenets, adm. division, *Russ.* 66°22′ N, 74°2′ E 160
Yamanaka, *Japan* 36°14′ N, 136°22′ E 201
Yamanashi, adm. division, *Japan* 35°30′ N, 138°17′ E 201
Yamato Mountains, *Antarctica* 71°23′ S, 36°56′ E 248
Yambio, *Sudan* 4°32′ N, 28°24′ E 224
Yambol, *Bulg.* 42°29′ N, 26°30′ E 156
Yambol, adm. division, *Bulg.* 42°12′ N, 26°17′ E 156
Yamburg, *Russ.* 68°18′ N, 77°12′ E 169
Yamdena, island, *Indonesia* 7°13′ S, 131°2′ E 192
Yamethinn, *Myanmar* 20°26′ N, 96°7′ E 202
Yamkino, *Russ.* 57°53′ N, 29°17′ E 166
Yamm, *Russ.* 58°24′ N, 28°4′ E 166
Yammaw, *Myanmar* 26°15′ N, 97°42′ E 188
Yamoussoukro, *Côte d'Ivoire* 6°44′ N, 5°24′ W 222
Yampa, river, *Colo., U.S.* 40°33′ N, 108°7′ W 92
Yampil', *Ukr.* 48°14′ N, 28°20′ E 156
Yampol', *Ukr.* 49°57′ N, 26°16′ E 152
Yamsay Mountain, peak, *Oreg., U.S.* 42°55′ N, 121°27′ W 90
Yamsk, *Russ.* 59°35′ N, 153°56′ E 160
Yamuna, river, *India* 29°23′ N, 77°4′ E 190
Yamzho Yumco, lake, *China* 28°59′ N, 90°26′ E 197
Yana, *Sierra Leone* 9°43′ N, 12°22′ W 222
Yana, river, *Russ.* 69°54′ N, 135°39′ E 160
Yanachaga Chemillén National Park, *Peru* 10°31′ S, 75°37′ W 122
Yanagawa, *Japan* 33°9′ N, 130°24′ E 201
Yanai, *Japan* 33°58′ N, 132°7′ E 201
Yanam, *India* 16°45′ N, 82°5′ E 190
Yan'an, *China* 36°33′ N, 109°28′ E 198
Yanaoca, *Peru* 14°15′ S, 71°25′ W 137
Yanaul, *Russ.* 56°16′ N, 55°4′ E 154
Yanbu'al Ba'r, *Saudi Arabia* 24°5′ N, 38°4′ E 182
Yanchang, *China* 36°36′ N, 110°3′ E 198
Yancheng, *China* 33°21′ N, 120°6′ E 198
Yanchi, *China* 37°46′ N, 107°20′ E 198
Yanchuan, *China* 36°50′ N, 110°10′ E 198
Yandoon, *Myanmar* 17°3′ N, 95°37′ E 202
Yanfolila, *Mali* 11°11′ N, 8°10′ W 222
Yangambi, *Dem. Rep. of the Congo* 0°47′ N, 24°25′ E 224
Yangarey, *Russ.* 68°43′ N, 61°29′ E 169
Yangasso, *Mali* 13°4′ N, 5°20′ W 222
Yangbajain, *China* 30°11′ N, 90°29′ E 197
Yangchun, *China* 22°8′ N, 111°47′ E 198
Yanggu, *S. Korea* 38°7′ N, 127°59′ E 200
Yanghe, *China* 40°4′ N, 123°25′ E 200
Yangi-Nishon, *Uzb.* 38°37′ N, 65°40′ E 197
Yangiqishloq, *Uzb.* 40°25′ N, 67°13′ E 197
Yangiyer, *Uzb.* 40°12′ N, 68°51′ E 197
Yangiyŭl, *Uzb.* 41°9′ N, 69°4′ E 197
Yangjiang, *China* 21°50′ N, 111°59′ E 198
Yangon (Rangoon), *Myanmar* 16°45′ N, 96°0′ E 202
Yangory, *Russ.* 62°46′ N, 37°48′ E 154
Yangou Gala, *Cen. Af. Rep.* 7°21′ N, 20°11′ E 218
Yangquan, *China* 37°52′ N, 113°36′ E 198
Yangsan, *S. Korea* 35°20′ N, 129°3′ E 200
Yangshan, *China* 24°29′ N, 112°39′ E 198
Yangshuo, *China* 24°45′ N, 110°26′ E 198
Yangtze, lake, *China* 30°23′ N, 106°28′ E 172
Yangtze, river, *China* 27°59′ N, 104°57′ E 172
Yangtze see Jinsha, river, *China* 25°47′ N, 103°15′ E 190
Yangtze, Source of the, *China* 33°16′ N, 90°53′ E 188
Yangudi Rassa National Park, *Eth.* 10°46′ N, 41°7′ E 224
Yangxian, *China* 33°13′ N, 107°31′ E 198
Yangxin, *China* 29°51′ N, 115°6′ E 198
Yangyang, *S. Korea* 38°5′ N, 128°37′ E 200
Yangyuan, *China* 40°7′ N, 114°8′ E 198
Yangzhou, *China* 32°25′ N, 119°27′ E 198
Yangzishao, *China* 42°25′ N, 126°7′ E 200
Yanhe, *China* 28°32′ N, 108°25′ E 198
Yanis'yarvi, Ozero, lake, *Russ.* 61°52′ N, 29°54′ E 152
Yanji, *China* 42°55′ N, 129°27′ E 200
Yanji (Longjing), *China* 42°46′ N, 129°24′ E 200
Yankari National Park, *Nig.* 9°47′ N, 9°50′ E 222
Yankeetown, *Fla., U.S.* 29°2′ N, 82°44′ W 105
Yankovichi, *Belarus* 55°47′ N, 28°48′ E 166
Yankton, *S. Dak., U.S.* 42°51′ N, 97°24′ W 90
Yanonge, *Dem. Rep. of the Congo* 0°33′ N, 24°39′ E 224
Yanqi, *China* 42°8′ N, 86°39′ E 184
Yanrakynnot, *Russ.* 64°59′ N, 172°39′ W 98
Yanshan, *China* 38°4′ N, 117°13′ E 198
Yanshan, *China* 23°32′ N, 104°20′ E 202
Yanshan, *China* 28°16′ N, 117°38′ E 198
Yanshou, *China* 45°30′ N, 128°21′ E 198
Yanskiy, *Russ.* 68°22′ N, 135°8′ E 160
Yantai, *China* 37°32′ N, 121°21′ E 198
Yantarnyy, *Russ.* 54°51′ N, 19°56′ E 166
Yao, *Japan* 34°38′ N, 135°35′ E 201
Yaoundé, *Cameroon* 3°55′ N, 11°24′ E 222
Yaoxian, *China* 34°59′ N, 109°0′ E 198
Yap Islands, *Philippine Sea* 9°43′ N, 136°10′ E 192
Yap Trench, *North Pacific Ocean* 7°20′ N, 137°57′ E 254
Yapacana National Park, *Venez.* 3°44′ N, 66°47′ W 136
Yapacani, river, *Bol.* 15°52′ S, 64°33′ W 137
Yapei (Tamale Port), *Ghana* 9°10′ N, 1°11′ W 222
Yapele, *Dem. Rep. of the Congo* 0°12′ N, 24°25′ E 224
Yapen, island, *Indonesia* 1°32′ S, 135°43′ E 192
Yapeyú, *Arg.* 29°26′ S, 56°53′ W 139
Yaptiksale, *Russ.* 69°20′ N, 72°36′ E 169
Yaqui, river, *Mex.* 28°10′ N, 110°3′ W 112
Yaquina Head, *Oreg., U.S.* 44°29′ N, 124°22′ W 90
Yar, *Russ.* 58°13′ N, 52°9′ E 154
Yar Sale, *Russ.* 66°49′ N, 70°48′ E 169
Yaracuy, adm. division, *Venez.* 10°25′ N, 69°4′ W 136
Yaraka, *Austral.* 24°54′ S, 144°4′ E 231
Yaralıgöz, peak, *Turk.* 41°45′ N, 34°1′ E 156
Yaransk, *Russ.* 57°18′ N, 47°57′ E 154
Yarda, spring, *Chad* 18°31′ N, 18°58′ E 216
Yardımcı Burnu, *Turk.* 36°6′ N, 30°26′ E 156
Yardymly, *Azerb.* 38°54′ N, 48°14′ E 195
Yarega, *Russ.* 63°26′ N, 53°35′ E 154
Yaren, *Nauru* 0°33′ N, 166°55′ E 242
Yarenga, *Russ.* 62°43′ N, 49°33′ E 154
Yarensk, *Russ.* 62°10′ N, 49°11′ E 154
Yarí, river, *Col.* 0°20′ N, 72°50′ W 136
Yarīm, *Yemen* 14°17′ N, 44°24′ E 182
Yarkant, river, *China* 37°58′ N, 76°14′ E 184
Yarkant see Shache, *China* 38°27′ N, 77°17′ E 184
Yarkul', *Russ.* 54°36′ N, 77°17′ E 184
Yarma, *Turk.* 37°49′ N, 32°53′ E 156
Yarmouth, *Can.* 43°48′ N, 66°8′ W 94
Yarmouth, *Me., U.S.* 43°47′ N, 70°12′ W 104
Yarnema, *Russ.* 62°59′ N, 39°23′ E 154
Yaroslavl', *Russ.* 57°34′ N, 39°48′ E 154
Yaroslavl', adm. division, *Russ.* 57°40′ N, 37°38′ E 154
Yaroto, Ozera, lake, *Russ.* 67°59′ N, 70°25′ E 169
Yarozero, *Russ.* 60°27′ N, 38°35′ E 154
Yartsevo, *Russ.* 60°9′ N, 90°14′ E 169
Yarumal, *Col.* 6°58′ N, 75°26′ W 136
Yary, *Russ.* 68°50′ N, 66°41′ E 169
Yashalta, *Russ.* 46°18′ N, 42°6′ E 158
Yashchera, *Russ.* 59°8′ N, 29°54′ E 166
Yashi, *Nig.* 12°21′ N, 7°55′ E 222
Yashichu, *China* 37°25′ N, 75°22′ E 184
Yashikera, *Nig.* 9°44′ N, 3°29′ E 222
Yashkino, *Russ.* 52°41′ N, 53°30′ E 154
Yashkul', *Russ.* 46°8′ N, 45°18′ E 158
Yasnoye, *Russ.* 55°11′ N, 21°31′ E 166
Yasnyy, *Russ.* 51°5′ N, 59°53′ E 158
Yasothon, *Thai.* 15°48′ N, 104°9′ E 202
Yasugi, *Japan* 35°24′ N, 133°15′ E 201
Yāsūj, *Iran* 30°39′ N, 51°35′ E 180
Yasun Burnu, *Turk.* 41°10′ N, 37°6′ E 156
Yasuní National Park, *Ecua.* 0°57′ N, 76°27′ W 136
Yata, *Bol.* 13°20′ S, 66°48′ W 137
Yata, *Braz.* 10°40′ S, 65°21′ W 137
Yata, river, *Bol.* 11°14′ S, 65°43′ W 137
Yata, river, *Cen. Af. Rep.* 10°13′ N, 23°2′ E 218
Yatakala, *Niger* 14°47′ N, 0°22′ E 222
Yates Center, *Kans., U.S.* 37°51′ N, 95°44′ W 96
Yates City, *Ill., U.S.* 40°45′ N, 90°1′ W 102
Yates, river, *Can.* 59°31′ N, 116°31′ W 108
Yatina, *Bol.* 20°46′ S, 64°45′ W 137
Yatou see Rongcheng, *China* 37°10′ N, 122°26′ E 198
Yatsushiro, *Japan* 32°30′ N, 130°36′ E 201
Yatta Plateau, *Kenya* 1°52′ S, 37°52′ E 224
Yauca, *Peru* 15°42′ S, 74°31′ W 137
Yauca, river, *Peru* 15°13′ S, 74°7′ W 137
Yauna Moloca, *Col.* 0°55′ N, 70°9′ W 136
Yaupi, *Ecua.* 2°55′ S, 77°53′ W 136
Yauri (Espinar), *Peru* 14°51′ S, 71°24′ W 137
Yautepec, *Mex.* 18°51′ N, 99°2′ W 114
Yavarate, *Col.* 0°38′ N, 69°13′ W 136
Yavarí Mirim, river, *Peru* 5°10′ S, 73°8′ W 130
Yavaros, *Mex.* 26°42′ N, 109°33′ W 112
Yavatmal, *India* 20°23′ N, 78°7′ E 188
Yavero, river, *Peru* 12°25′ S, 72°51′ W 137
Yavi, *Arg.* 22°10′ S, 65°30′ W 137
Yavita, *Venez.* 2°53′ N, 67°28′ W 136
Yavlenka, *Kaz.* 54°17′ N, 68°22′ E 184
Yavne, *Israel* 31°51′ N, 34°44′ E 194
Yavoriv, *Ukr.* 49°56′ N, 23°22′ E 152
Yavr, river, *Russ.* 68°14′ N, 29°36′ E 152
Yawatahama, *Japan* 33°26′ N, 132°25′ E 201
Yawnghwe, *Myanmar* 20°40′ N, 96°57′ E 202
Yawri Bay 8°3′ N, 13°19′ W 222
Yaxchilán, ruin(s), *Mex.* 16°50′ N, 91°7′ W 115
Yaya, *Russ.* 56°11′ N, 86°22′ E 169
Yaynangyoung, *Myanmar* 20°28′ N, 94°54′ E 202
Yayuan, *China* 41°42′ N, 126°9′ E 200
Yayva, *Russ.* 59°19′ N, 57°21′ E 154
Yazd, *Iran* 31°53′ N, 54°26′ E 180
Yazdān, *Iran* 33°34′ N, 60°53′ E 180
Yazevets, *Russ.* 65°44′ N, 46°27′ E 154
Yazhma, *Russ.* 66°57′ N, 44°43′ E 154
Yazılıkaya, *Turk.* 39°11′ N, 30°42′ E 156
Yazlıca Dağı, peak, *Turk.* 37°45′ N, 42°27′ E 195
Yazno, *Russ.* 56°2′ N, 29°18′ E 166
Yazoo City, *Miss., U.S.* 32°50′ N, 90°26′ W 103
Yazoo, river, *Miss., U.S.* 32°33′ N, 90°50′ W 103
Yazykovo, *Russ.* 54°16′ N, 47°27′ E 154
Ybakoura, spring, *Chad* 22°6′ N, 15°44′ E 216
Ye, *Myanmar* 15°15′ N, 97°50′ E 202
Yebbi Bou, *Chad* 21°0′ N, 18°8′ E 216
Yebyu, *Myanmar* 14°16′ N, 98°8′ E 202
Yecheng (Kargilik), *China* 37°52′ N, 77°31′ E 184
Yecheon, *S. Korea* 36°38′ N, 128°26′ E 200
Yecla, *Sp.* 38°36′ N, 1°7′ W 164
Yécora, *Mex.* 28°22′ N, 108°58′ W 92
Yédri, spring, *Chad* 22°11′ N, 17°25′ E 216
Yeed, *Somalia* 4°28′ N, 43°5′ E 218
Yefremov, *Russ.* 53°8′ N, 38°4′ E 154
Yeggueba, spring, *Niger* 19°52′ N, 12°53′ E 222
Yegorovskaya, *Russ.* 65°43′ N, 52°3′ E 154
Yegor'yevsk, *Russ.* 55°22′ N, 39°1′ E 154
Yegozero, *Russ.* 62°44′ N, 36°38′ E 154
Yegros, *Parag.* 26°23′ S, 56°24′ W 139
Yeguas, Sierra de, *Sp.* 37°8′ N, 4°58′ W 164
Yei, *Sudan* 4°3′ N, 30°40′ E 224
Yei, river, *Sudan* 5°11′ N, 30°17′ E 224
Yeji, *Ghana* 8°11′ N, 0°43′ E 222
Yekaterinburg, *Russ.* 56°49′ N, 60°35′ E 154
Yekaterinovka, *Russ.* 52°1′ N, 44°23′ E 158
Yekepa, *Liberia* 7°26′ N, 8°34′ W 222
Yekhrimyanvara, *Russ.* 64°32′ N, 30°9′ E 152
Yekī, *Eth.* 7°10′ N, 35°17′ E 224
Yekia Nerba, spring, *Chad* 16°14′ N, 17°38′ E 216
Yelabuga, *Russ.* 55°46′ N, 52°6′ E 154
Yelan', *Russ.* 50°56′ N, 43°46′ E 158
Yelan Kolenovskiy, *Russ.* 51°8′ N, 41°14′ E 158
Yelapa, *Mex.* 20°28′ N, 105°29′ W 114
Yelat'ma, *Russ.* 54°56′ N, 41°44′ E 154
Yelets, *Russ.* 52°37′ N, 38°27′ E 158
Yeletskiy, *Russ.* 67°3′ N, 64°0′ E 169
Yelizarovo, *Russ.* 61°22′ N, 68°18′ E 169
Yelizavety, Mys, *Russ.* 54°19′ N, 142°29′ E 160
Yelkhovka, *Russ.* 53°50′ N, 50°16′ E 154
Yellandu, *India* 17°34′ N, 80°18′ E 188
Yellow Butte, peak, *Oreg., U.S.* 43°31′ N, 123°29′ W 90
Yellow Grass, *Can.* 49°47′ N, 104°10′ W 90
Yellow Sea 36°17′ N, 121°47′ E 190
Yellow see Huang, river, *China* 37°14′ N, 104°6′ E 198
Yellowknife, *Can.* 62°27′ N, 114°50′ W 106
Yellowstone, river, *Mont., U.S.* 47°11′ N, 104°31′ W 90
Yelm, *Wash., U.S.* 46°55′ N, 122°37′ W 90
Yel'nya, *Russ.* 54°36′ N, 33°14′ E 154
Yeloguy, river, *Russ.* 61°32′ N, 85°41′ E 169
Yel'sk, *Belarus* 51°47′ N, 29°14′ E 152
Yelva, river, *Russ.* 63°26′ N, 50°49′ E 154
Yelverton Bay 81°31′ N, 98°43′ W 72
Yelwa, *Nig.* 10°52′ N, 4°45′ E 222
Yemanzhelinsk, *Russ.* 54°45′ N, 61°21′ E 154
Yemaotai, *China* 42°20′ N, 122°54′ E 200
Yemassee, *S.C., U.S.* 32°41′ N, 80°51′ W 96
Yembo, *Eth.* 8°17′ N, 35°56′ E 224
Yemel'yanovka, *Russ.* 63°54′ N, 30°56′ E 152
Yemen 15°57′ N, 48°3′ E 182
Yemetsk, *Russ.* 63°29′ N, 41°48′ E 154
Yemtsa, *Russ.* 63°4′ N, 40°22′ E 154
Yen, *Cameroon* 2°28′ N, 12°42′ E 218
Yen Bai, *Vietnam* 21°44′ N, 104°52′ E 202
Yena, *Russ.* 67°36′ N, 31°9′ E 152
Yenakiyeve, *Ukr.* 48°12′ N, 38°12′ E 158
Yenanma, *Myanmar* 19°46′ N, 94°49′ E 202
Yendéré, *Burkina Faso* 10°12′ N, 4°59′ W 222
Yendi, *Ghana* 9°24′ N, 4°237′ W 222
Yenge, river, *Dem. Rep. of the Congo* 1°46′ S, 21°21′ E 218
Yengisar, *China* 38°55′ N, 76°9′ E 184
Yéni, *Niger* 13°27′ N, 3°0′ E 222
Yeniçağa, *Turk.* 40°47′ N, 32°0′ E 156
Yenice, *Turk.* 39°18′ N, 32°41′ E 156
Yeniceoba, *Turk.* 38°51′ N, 32°46′ E 156
Yenisey, river, *Russ.* 51°38′ N, 92°28′ E 190
Yeniseysk, *Russ.* 58°21′ N, 92°10′ E 160
Yeniseyskiy Zaliv 72°20′ N, 75°5′ E 160
Yenyuka, *Russ.* 57°53′ N, 121°44′ E 160
Yeo, river, *U.K.* 51°0′ N, 2°45′ W 162
Yeoju, *S. Korea* 37°17′ N, 127°38′ E 200
Yeola, *India* 20°1′ N, 74°29′ E 188
Yeoncheon, *S. Korea* 38°5′ N, 127°5′ E 200
Yeongam, *S. Korea* 34°46′ N, 126°41′ E 200
Yeongdeok, *S. Korea* 36°24′ N, 129°25′ E 200
Yeongdong, *S. Korea* 36°9′ N, 127°47′ E 200
Yeonggwang, *S. Korea* 35°14′ N, 126°30′ E 200
Yeongju, *S. Korea* 36°48′ N, 128°38′ E 200
Yeongwol, *S. Korea* 37°11′ N, 128°28′ E 200
Yeosu, *S. Korea* 34°45′ N, 127°45′ E 200
Yeovil, *U.K.* 50°56′ N, 2°38′ W 162
Yepes, *Sp.* 39°54′ N, 3°38′ W 164
Yepómera, *Mex.* 29°2′ N, 107°51′ W 92
Yerakhtur, *Russ.* 54°40′ N, 41°5′ E 154
Yerbent, *Turkm.* 39°16′ N, 58°35′ E 180
Yerbogachen, *Russ.* 61°19′ N, 108°10′ E 160
Yerema, *Russ.* 60°24′ N, 107°56′ E 173
Yerevan, *Arm.* 40°8′ N, 44°24′ E 195
Yerington, *Nev., U.S.* 38°59′ N, 119°11′ W 90
Yerköy, *Turk.* 39°37′ N, 34°28′ E 156
Yermak Plateau, *Greenland Sea* 80°41′ N, 6°9′ E 255
Yermak Point, *Antarctica* 70°15′ S, 160°38′ E 248
Yermakovo, *Russ.* 66°31′ N, 86°5′ E 169
Yermilovka, *Russ.* 57°39′ N, 72°59′ E 169
Yermitsa, *Russ.* 66°56′ N, 52°14′ E 169
Yermo, *Calif., U.S.* 34°54′ N, 116°50′ W 101
Yermo, *Mex.* 26°23′ N, 104°3′ W 114
Yeroḥam, *Israel* 30°58′ N, 34°54′ E 194
Yeropol, *Russ.* 65°21′ N, 168°41′ E 160
Yershov, *Russ.* 51°19′ N, 48°18′ E 158
Yershovo, *Russ.* 57°57′ N, 28°11′ E 166
Yerushalayim see Jerusalem, *Israel* 31°46′ N, 35°9′ E 194
Yesan, *S. Korea* 36°40′ N, 126°51′ E 200
Yeşilırmak, river, *Turk.* 41°22′ N, 36°28′ E 156
Yeşilova, *Turk.* 37°29′ N, 29°45′ E 156
Yeşilyazı, *Turk.* 39°19′ N, 39°4′ E 195
Yessey, *Russ.* 68°28′ N, 102°1′ E 160
Yeste, *Sp.* 38°21′ N, 2°19′ W 164
Yetti, region, *Mauritania* 26°6′ N, 8°10′ W 214
Ye-u, *Myanmar* 22°46′ N, 95°24′ E 202
Yevgashchino, *Russ.* 56°24′ N, 74°39′ E 169
Yevlax, *Azerb.* 40°36′ N, 47°8′ E 195
Yevpatoriya, *Ukr.* 45°12′ N, 33°19′ E 156
Yevstratovskiy, *Russ.* 50°9′ N, 39°49′ E 158
Yexian, *China* 37°11′ N, 119°57′ E 198
Yeysk, *Russ.* 46°41′ N, 38°11′ E 156
Yezerishche, *Belarus* 55°49′ N, 30°3′ E 166
Ygatimí, *Parag.* 24°7′ S, 55°39′ W 132
Yi, river, *China* 35°6′ N, 118°35′ E 198
Yí, river, *Uru.* 33°33′ S, 56°20′ W 139
Yi'an, *China* 47°57′ N, 125°20′ E 198
Yibin, *China* 28°39′ N, 104°21′ E 190
Yibug Caka, lake, *China* 32°51′ N, 85°54′ E 188
Yichang, *China* 30°42′ N, 111°22′ E 198
Yicheng, *China* 31°41′ N, 112°12′ E 198
Yichuan, *China* 36°3′ N, 110°9′ E 198
Yichun, *China* 27°45′ N, 114°23′ E 198
Yichun, *China* 47°43′ N, 128°58′ E 198
Yifag, *Eth.* 12°2′ N, 37°44′ E 182
Yigo, *U.S.* 13°31′ N, 144°52′ E 242
Yijun, *China* 35°24′ N, 109°3′ E 198
Yila, *Liberia* 6°46′ N, 9°13′ W 222
Yilan, *China* 46°16′ N, 129°44′ E 190
Yıldız Dağları, peak, *Turk.* 41°46′ N, 27°31′ E 156
Yıldızeli, *Turk.* 39°51′ N, 36°35′ E 156

Yilehuli Shan, *China* 51°24′ N, 118°51′ E 190
Yiliang, *China* 24°50′ N, 102°55′ E 190
Yinan, *China* 35°32′ N, 118°29′ E 198
Yinchuan, *China* 38°29′ N, 106°21′ E 198
Yingcheng, *China* 30°56′ N, 113°31′ E 198
Yingcheng, *China* 44°7′ N, 125°56′ E 198
Yingchengzi, *China* 43°11′ N, 125°29′ E 200
Yingde, *China* 24°4′ N, 113°20′ E 198
Yingkou, *China* 40°39′ N, 122°12′ E 198
Yingshan, *China* 31°34′ N, 113°49′ E 198
Yingshang, *China* 32°36′ N, 116°14′ E 198
Yingxian, *China* 39°32′ N, 113°13′ E 198
Yining, *China* 43°51′ N, 81°28′ E 184
Yinmabin, *Myanmar* 22°8′ N, 94°52′ E 202
Yi'ong, river, *China* 30°27′ N, 93°53′ E 188
Yirga 'Alem, *Eth.* 6°45′ N, 38°20′ E 224
Yirol, *Sudan* 6°34′ N, 30°30′ E 224
Yirshi, *China* 47°16′ N, 119°48′ E 198
Yishan, *China* 24°26′ N, 108°40′ E 198
Yishui, *China* 35°45′ N, 118°40′ E 198
Yitong, *China* 43°19′ N, 125°14′ E 198
Yitulihe, *China* 50°41′ N, 121°36′ E 238
Yiwu, *China* 29°18′ N, 120°3′ E 198
Yixian, *China* 41°31′ N, 121°17′ E 198
Yixing, *China* 31°21′ N, 119°48′ E 198
Yiyang, *China* 28°41′ N, 112°22′ E 198
Yiyuan, *China* 36°11′ N, 118°8′ E 198
Ylämaa, *Fin.* 60°47′ N, 27°58′ E 166
Yläne, *Fin.* 60°52′ N, 22°24′ E 166
Yli Ii, *Fin.* 65°22′ N, 25°47′ E 152
Ylihärmä, *Fin.* 63°7′ N, 22°45′ E 152
Ylikiiminki, *Fin.* 65°1′ N, 26°6′ E 152
Ylimarkku see Övermark, *Fin.* 62°35′ N, 21°25′ E 152
Ylitornio, *Fin.* 66°19′ N, 23°41′ E 152
Ylivieska, *Fin.* 64°3′ N, 24°28′ E 152
Ylivuokki, *Fin.* 64°38′ N, 29°42′ E 154
Yllästunturi, peak, *Fin.* 67°33′ N, 24°4′ E 152
Ÿnderbor, *Kaz.* 48°23′ N, 51°31′ E 158
Yndin, *Russ.* 61°22′ N, 55°11′ E 154
Yoakum, *Tex., U.S.* 29°17′ N, 97°9′ W 96
Yobuko, *Japan* 33°31′ N, 129°54′ E 201
Yog Point, *Philippines* 14°6′ N, 124°13′ E 203
Yogyakarta, *Indonesia* 7°49′ S, 110°19′ E 238
Yoho National Park, *Can.* 51°20′ N, 116°51′ W 238
Yojoa, Lago de, lake, *Hond.* 14°50′ N, 88°31′ W 116
Yok Don National Park, *Vietnam* 12°50′ N, 107°15′ E 238
Yoka, *Japan* 35°23′ N, 134°44′ E 201
Yokadouma, *Cameroon* 3°40′ N, 15°5′ E 218
Yokkaichi, *Japan* 34°57′ N, 136°38′ E 201
Yoko, *Cameroon* 5°30′ N, 12°20′ E 218
Yokohama, *Japan* 35°26′ N, 139°37′ E 201
Yokosuka, *Japan* 35°15′ N, 139°39′ E 201
Yola, *Nig.* 9°12′ N, 12°30′ E 216
Yolombo, *Dem. Rep. of the Congo* 1°37′ S, 23°11′ E 218
Yolöten, *Turkm.* 37°16′ N, 62°20′ E 186
Yom, river, *Thai.* 18°0′ N, 99°38′ E 202
Yombiro, *Guinea* 9°3′ N, 10°20′ W 222
Yomra, *Turk.* 40°57′ N, 39°50′ E 195
Yon, river, *Fr.* 46°36′ N, 1°35′ W 150
Yonago, *Japan* 35°24′ N, 133°21′ E 201
Yonaguni Jima, island, *Japan* 24°16′ N, 122°27′ E 198
Yŏnan, *N. Korea* 37°54′ N, 126°9′ E 200
Yonezawa, *Japan* 37°54′ N, 140°5′ E 201
Yongama, *Dem. Rep. of the Congo* 2°19′ S, 24°34′ E 224
Yongamp'o, *N. Korea* 39°55′ N, 124°19′ E 200
Yong'an, *China* 25°57′ N, 117°25′ E 198
Yŏngbyŏn, *N. Korea* 39°49′ N, 125°48′ E 200
Yongch'ŏn, *N. Korea* 39°58′ N, 124°24′ E 200
Yongchuan, *China* 29°19′ N, 105°55′ E 198
Yongchun, *China* 25°19′ N, 118°17′ E 198
Yongfu, *China* 25°0′ N, 110°3′ E 198
Yŏngjŏ, *N. Korea* 41°23′ N, 127°4′ E 200
Yongkang, *China* 28°55′ N, 120°3′ E 198
Yongning, *China* 22°41′ N, 108°30′ E 198
Yongning, *China* 38°18′ N, 106°15′ E 198
Yongo, *Dem. Rep. of the Congo* 1°37′ S, 21°50′ E 218
Yongshun, *China* 29°1′ N, 109°51′ E 198
Yongtai, *China* 25°52′ N, 118°57′ E 198
Yongxin, *China* 27°0′ N, 114°16′ E 198
Yongxing, *China* 26°7′ N, 112°55′ E 198
Yongxiu, *China* 29°4′ N, 115°46′ E 198
Yongzhou, *China* 26°15′ N, 111°36′ E 198
Yonkers, *N.Y., U.S.* 40°56′ N, 73°54′ W 104
Yonne, river, *Fr.* 48°22′ N, 3°1′ E 163
Yŏnp'o, *N. Korea* 39°47′ N, 127°30′ E 200
Yŏnsa, *N. Korea* 41°52′ N, 129°0′ E 200
Yŏnsan, *N. Korea* 38°51′ N, 126°14′ E 200
Yonza, *Bol.* 20°39′ S, 68°3′ W 137
Yopal, *Col.* 5°16′ N, 72°19′ W 136
Yopurga, *China* 39°16′ N, 76°40′ E 184
Yoqne'am, *Israel* 32°39′ N, 35°5′ E 194
York, *Ala., U.S.* 32°28′ N, 88°19′ W 103
York, *Nebr., U.S.* 40°51′ N, 97°36′ W 90
York, *Pa., U.S.* 39°57′ N, 76°43′ W 94
York, *U.K.* 53°58′ N, 1°5′ W 162
York, Cape, *Austral.* 10°37′ S, 142°35′ E 192
York Factory National Historic Site, *Can.* 57°1′ N, 92°24′ W 108
York Harbor, *Me., U.S.* 43°8′ N, 70°39′ W 104
York, Kap 75°35′ N, 70°18′ W 106
York Peninsula, Cape, *Austral.* 11°46′ S, 141°22′ E 192
York, river, *Va., U.S.* 37°40′ N, 77°21′ W 80
York Village, *Me., U.S.* 43°8′ N, 70°40′ W 104
Yorkton, *Can.* 51°12′ N, 102°29′ W 90
Yorktown, *Ark., U.S.* 34°0′ N, 91°50′ W 96
Yorktown, *Tex., U.S.* 28°58′ N, 97°30′ W 92
Yorktown, *Va., U.S.* 37°13′ N, 76°32′ W 94
Yoro, *Hond.* 15°8′ N, 87°7′ W 115
Yoro, *Mali* 14°17′ N, 2°11′ W 222
Yorosso, *Mali* 12°23′ N, 4°48′ W 222
Yortan Tepe, ruin(s), *Turk.* 38°58′ N, 27°20′ E 156
Yosemite National Park, *Calif., U.S.* 37°52′ N, 119°49′ W 100
Yosemite Valley, *Calif., U.S.* 37°41′ N, 119°34′ W 100
Yosemite Village, *Calif., U.S.* 37°45′ N, 119°36′ W 100
Yoshida, *Japan* 34°39′ N, 132°42′ E 201
Yoshii, river, *Japan* 35°4′ N, 133°55′ E 201
Yoshino-Kumano National Park, *Japan* 33°57′ N, 135°45′ E 201
Yoshiwara, *Japan* 35°9′ N, 138°42′ E 201
Yoshkar Ola, *Russ.* 56°38′ N, 47°52′ E 154
Yost, *Utah, U.S.* 41°57′ N, 113°32′ W 90
Yotala, *Bol.* 19°11′ S, 65°18′ W 137
You, river, *China* 23°34′ N, 107°15′ E 198
Youbou, *Can.* 48°53′ N, 124°14′ W 100
Youhao, *China* 47°54′ N, 128°48′ E 198
Youkou, *Côte d'Ivoire* 5°14′ N, 7°18′ W 222
Youkounkoun, *Guinea* 12°32′ N, 13°9′ W 214
Young, *Uru.* 32°43′ S, 57°39′ W 139
Young, Mount, peak, *Austral.* 15°14′ S, 135°37′ E 230
Youngstown, *Can.* 51°32′ N, 111°12′ W 90
Youngstown, *Ohio, U.S.* 41°5′ N, 80°38′ W 110
Younts Peak, *Wyo., U.S.* 43°57′ N, 109°57′ W 90
Yountville, *Calif., U.S.* 38°24′ N, 122°22′ W 100
Youshashan, *China* 38°11′ N, 90°59′ E 188
Youssoufia, *Mor.* 32°16′ N, 8°33′ W 214
Youxian, *China* 27°3′ N, 113°18′ E 198
Youyang, *China* 28°50′ N, 108°45′ E 198
Yovan, *Taj.* 38°21′ N, 69°7′ E 197
Yovkovo, *Bulg.* 43°47′ N, 28°6′ E 158
Yoxford, *U.K.* 52°15′ N, 1°30′ E 163
Yozgat, *Turk.* 39°48′ N, 34°48′ E 156
Ypé Jhú, *Parag.* 23°57′ S, 55°28′ W 132
Ypres see Ieper, *Belg.* 50°50′ N, 2°53′ E 163
Ypsilanti, *Mich., U.S.* 42°13′ N, 83°38′ W 102
Yr Eifl (The Rivals), peak, *U.K.* 52°57′ N, 4°32′ W 150
Yreka, *Calif., U.S.* 41°42′ N, 122°39′ W 106
Yrghyz, *Kaz.* 48°37′ N, 61°15′ E 184
Yrghyz, river, *Kaz.* 48°49′ N, 60°3′ E 158
Ysabel Channel 2°11′ S, 148°53′ E 192
Ystad, *Nor.* 55°25′ N, 13°48′ E 152
Ystrad Mynach, *U.K.* 51°38′ N, 3°14′ W 162
Ysyk-Köl, lake, *Kyrg.* 42°29′ N, 77°1′ E 184
Yu, river, *China* 22°32′ N, 109°18′ E 198
Yü Shan, peak, *Taiwan, China* 23°31′ N, 120°56′ E 198
Yuan, river, *China* 28°32′ N, 110°33′ E 198
Yuanbaoshan, *China* 42°13′ N, 119°15′ E 198
Yuanjiang, *China* 23°33′ N, 101°53′ E 202
Yüanli, *Taiwan, China* 24°26′ N, 120°41′ E 198
Yüanlin, *Taiwan, China* 23°52′ N, 120°35′ E 198
Yuanqu, *China* 35°21′ N, 111°40′ E 198
Yuba Pass, *Calif., U.S.* 39°37′ N, 120°29′ W 90
Yūbari, *Japan* 43°5′ N, 142°3′ E 190
Yubdo, *Eth.* 8°57′ N, 35°26′ E 224
Yubineto, river, *Peru* 0°38′ N, 74°56′ W 136
Yucaipa, *Calif., U.S.* 34°2′ N, 117°3′ W 101
Yucatán, adm. division, *Mex.* 19°0′ N, 90°49′ W 112
Yucca, *Ariz., U.S.* 34°52′ N, 114°10′ W 101
Yucca Flat, *Nev., U.S.* 37°9′ N, 116°8′ W 101
Yucca House National Monument, *Colo., U.S.* 37°14′ N, 108°46′ W 92
Yucca Mountain, peak, *Nev., U.S.* 36°56′ N, 116°32′ W 101
Yucca Valley, *Calif., U.S.* 34°7′ N, 116°28′ W 101
Yucheng, *China* 36°57′ N, 116°42′ E 198
Yuci, *China* 37°41′ N, 112°42′ E 198
Yucuyácua, Cerro, peak, *Mex.* 17°7′ N, 97°43′ W 114
Yudino, *Russ.* 55°48′ N, 48°53′ E 154
Yueyang, *China* 29°22′ N, 113°6′ E 198
Yug, *Russ.* 57°43′ N, 56°8′ E 154
Yug, river, *Russ.* 60°31′ N, 46°57′ E 154
Yugan, *China* 28°41′ N, 116°38′ E 198
Yugorenok, *Russ.* 59°54′ N, 137°38′ E 160
Yugyd Va National Park, *Russ.* 65°15′ N, 59°11′ E 169
Yuhuan Dao, island, *China* 28°16′ N, 120°24′ E 198
Yukhnov, *Russ.* 54°43′ N, 35°16′ E 154
Yukon, river, *Can.-U.S.* 64°54′ N, 154°10′ W 98
Yukon, adm. division, *Can.* 63°10′ N, 137°18′ W 98
Yukon-Charley Rivers National Preserve, *Alas., U.S.* 65°8′ N, 143°40′ W 98
Yüksekova, *Turk.* 37°34′ N, 44°12′ E 195
Yukspor, Gora, peak, *Russ.* 68°9′ N, 32°14′ E 152
Yukuhashi, *Japan* 33°42′ N, 130°59′ E 200
Yula, river, *Russ.* 63°38′ N, 44°14′ E 154
Yuldybayevo, *Russ.* 52°20′ N, 57°47′ E 154
Yuli, *China* 41°24′ N, 86°16′ E 184
Yuli, *Nig.* 9°43′ N, 10°17′ E 222
Yüli, *Taiwan, China* 23°20′ N, 121°15′ E 198
Yulin, *China* 22°38′ N, 110°6′ E 198
Yulin, *China* 38°22′ N, 109°48′ E 198
Yuma, *Ariz., U.S.* 32°42′ N, 114°37′ W 101
Yuma, *Colo., U.S.* 40°7′ N, 102°44′ W 90
Yuma, *Russ.* 65°6′ N, 33°15′ E 152
Yuma Desert, *Ariz., U.S.* 32°17′ N, 114°46′ W 92
Yumaguzino, *Russ.* 52°55′ N, 56°16′ E 154
Yumari, Cerro, peak, *Venez.* 4°20′ N, 66°52′ W 136
Yumbe, *Uganda* 3°27′ N, 31°16′ E 224
Yumbi, *Dem. Rep. of the Congo* 1°16′ S, 26°17′ E 224
Yumen, *China* 39°54′ N, 97°41′ E 190
Yumin, *China* 45°59′ N, 82°57′ E 184
Yumurtalık, *Turk.* 36°46′ N, 35°45′ E 156
Yunan, *China* 23°12′ N, 111°27′ E 198
Yuncheng, *China* 35°2′ N, 110°57′ E 198
Yunguyo, *Peru* 16°20′ S, 69°6′ W 137
Yūnīn, *Leb.* 34°4′ N, 36°17′ E 194
Yunnan, adm. division, *China* 23°6′ N, 100°55′ E 202
Yunotsu, *Japan* 35°5′ N, 132°22′ E 201
Yunquera de Henares, *Sp.* 40°44′ N, 3°11′ W 164
Yunxi, *China* 32°59′ N, 110°26′ E 198
Yunxian, *China* 32°54′ N, 110°49′ E 198
Yunyang, *China* 31°1′ N, 108°37′ E 198
Yup'yŏng, *N. Korea* 41°47′ N, 128°51′ E 200
Yuquan, *China* 45°23′ N, 127°7′ E 198
Yura, river, *Bol.* 19°58′ S, 66°13′ W 137
Yurécuaro, *Mex.* 20°19′ N, 102°17′ W 114
Yurga, *Russ.* 55°42′ N, 84°54′ E 169
Yuribey, *Russ.* 71°3′ N, 77°2′ E 169
Yurimaguas, *Peru* 5°55′ S, 76°9′ W 130
Yurkino, *Russ.* 68°46′ N, 32°20′ E 152
Yurla, *Russ.* 59°19′ N, 54°21′ E 154
Yuroma, *Russ.* 65°11′ N, 45°34′ E 154
Yurovsk, *Russ.* 59°25′ N, 69°8′ E 169
Yur'ya, *Russ.* 59°3′ N, 49°19′ E 154
Yur'yev Pol'skiy, *Russ.* 56°30′ N, 39°39′ E 154
Yur'yevets, *Russ.* 57°17′ N, 43°3′ E 154
Yuryuzan', *Russ.* 54°51′ N, 58°30′ E 154
Yuscarán, *Hond.* 13°54′ N, 86°49′ W 115
Yushan, *China* 28°45′ N, 118°14′ E 198
Yushkozero, *Russ.* 64°44′ N, 32°3′ E 152
Yushu, *China* 33°1′ N, 96°54′ E 188
Yushu, *China* 44°48′ N, 126°31′ E 198
Yusta, *Russ.* 47°5′ N, 46°17′ E 158
Yusufeli, *Turk.* 40°55′ N, 41°37′ E 195
Yus'va, *Russ.* 58°57′ N, 55°1′ E 154
Yutian, *China* 36°54′ N, 81°34′ E 190
Yutian, *China* 39°53′ N, 117°47′ E 198
Yutian (Keriya), *China* 36°55′ N, 81°36′ E 184
Yuty, *Parag.* 26°31′ S, 56°10′ W 139
Yuxi, *China* 24°21′ N, 102°36′ E 190
Yuxian, *China* 38°6′ N, 113°25′ E 198
Yuzawa, *Japan* 36°56′ N, 138°48′ E 201
Yuzha, *Russ.* 56°34′ N, 41°59′ E 154
Yuzhno Sakhalinsk, *Russ.* 46°59′ N, 142°35′ E 190
Yuzhnoural'sk, *Russ.* 54°27′ N, 61°12′ E 154
Yuzhnyy, *Kaz.* 49°17′ N, 72°58′ E 184
Yuzhnyy, *Russ.* 45°46′ N, 45°36′ E 158
Yuzhnyy, Mys, *Russ.* 57°36′ N, 153°7′ E 160
Yuzhong, *China* 35°54′ N, 104°8′ E 198
Yverdon-les-Bains, *Switz.* 46°46′ N, 6°38′ E 167
Yvetot, *Fr.* 49°36′ N, 0°45′ E 163

Z

Za, river, *China* 33°3′ N, 95°13′ E 188
Zaamin National Park, *Uzb.* 39°33′ N, 68°6′ E 197
Zaanstad, *Neth.* 52°26′ N, 4°49′ E 163
Zab, *Pol.* 53°0′ N, 23°19′ E 154
Zāb al Kabīr (Great Zab), river, *Iraq* 36°32′ N, 43°40′ E 195
Zabalats', *Belarus* 53°56′ N, 24°47′ E 166
Žabalj, *Serb.* 45°22′ N, 20°3′ E 168
Žabari, *Serb.* 44°21′ N, 21°12′ E 168
Zabaykal'sk, *Russ.* 49°41′ N, 117°22′ E 198
Zaberezh', *Belarus* 53°56′ N, 26°13′ E 166
Zabīd, *Yemen* 14°10′ N, 43°17′ E 182
Zablaće, *Serb.* 43°50′ N, 20°26′ E 168
Žabljak, *Mont.* 43°9′ N, 19°7′ E 168
Zabok, *Croatia* 46°2′ N, 15°53′ E 168
Zābol, *Iran* 31°1′ N, 61°34′ E 186
Zābolī, *Iran* 27°6′ N, 61°43′ E 182
Zabolottsi, *Ukr.* 50°0′ N, 24°58′ E 152
Zabolottya, *Ukr.* 51°36′ N, 24°14′ E 152
Zabré, *Burkina Faso* 11°10′ N, 0°41′ E 222
Zabrežje, *Serb.* 44°40′ N, 20°12′ E 168
Zabu, *Egypt* 28°22′ N, 28°55′ E 180
Zabūrūn'e, *Kaz.* 46°45′ N, 50°9′ E 158
Zacapa, *Guatemala* 14°58′ N, 89°34′ W 115
Zacapu, *Mex.* 19°47′ N, 101°48′ W 114
Zacatecas, *Mex.* 22°45′ N, 102°40′ W 114
Zacatecas, adm. division, *Mex.* 23°33′ N, 103°44′ W 114
Zacatepec, *Mex.* 17°10′ N, 95°51′ W 114
Zaccar Rherbi, Djebel, peak, *Alg.* 36°19′ N, 2°8′ E 150
Zachary, *La., U.S.* 30°38′ N, 91°11′ W 103
Zachodnio-Pomorskie, adm. division, *Pol.* 53°37′ N, 14°39′ E 152
Zacoalco, *Mex.* 20°14′ N, 103°34′ W 114
Zacualtipán, *Mex.* 20°38′ N, 98°39′ W 114
Zadar, *Croatia* 44°8′ N, 15°16′ E 143
Zadar (Zara), *Croatia* 44°6′ N, 15°14′ E 156
Zadawa, *Nig.* 11°28′ N, 10°18′ E 222
Zadetkale Kyun, island, *Myanmar* 10°1′ N, 97°11′ E 202
Zadetkyi Kyun, island, *Myanmar* 9°32′ N, 98°6′ E 202
Zadoi, *China* 33°4′ N, 95°4′ E 188
Zadonsk, *Russ.* 52°19′ N, 38°51′ E 158
Za'farâna, *Egypt* 29°6′ N, 32°36′ E 180
Zafarobod, *Uzb.* 40°32′ N, 65°0′ E 197
Zafirovo, *Bulg.* 43°59′ N, 26°48′ E 158
Zafóra, islands, *Aegean Sea* 36°4′ N, 25°55′ E 156
Zafra, *Sp.* 38°25′ N, 6°27′ W 164
Zafrilla, *Sp.* 40°11′ N, 1°37′ W 164
Żagań, *Pol.* 51°36′ N, 15°18′ E 152
Žagarė, *Lith.* 56°21′ N, 23°15′ E 166
Zagazig, *Egypt* 30°36′ N, 31°29′ E 180
Zaghouan, *Tun.* 36°23′ N, 10°9′ E 156
Zagnanado, *Benin* 7°15′ N, 2°20′ E 222
Zagne, *Côte d'Ivoire* 6°8′ N, 7°29′ W 222
Zagor, *Bosn. and Herzg.* 43°40′ N, 18°34′ E 168
Zagora, *Mor.* 30°19′ N, 5°54′ W 214
Zagreb, *Croatia* 45°47′ N, 15°55′ E 168
Zagros Mountains see Zāgros, Kūhhā-ye, *Iran* 36°37′ N, 45°23′ E 195
Žagubica, *Serb.* 44°12′ N, 21°47′ E 168
Zagvozd, *Croatia* 43°22′ N, 17°2′ E 168
Za'gya, river, *China* 32°20′ N, 89°27′ E 188
Zahana, *Alg.* 35°30′ N, 0°25′ E 150
Zaháro, *Gr.* 37°29′ N, 21°38′ E 156
Zāhedān, *Iran* 29°29′ N, 60°53′ E 182
Za'lah, *Leb.* 33°50′ N, 35°54′ E 194
Ẓahrān, *Saudi Arabia* 17°41′ N, 43°24′ E 182
Zahrisht, *Alban.* 42°12′ N, 20°20′ E 168
Zaidín, *Sp.* 41°35′ N, 0°16′ E 164
Zainsk, *Russ.* 55°18′ N, 52°7′ E 184
Zaire, adm. division, *Angola* 7°36′ S, 13°1′ E 218
Zaječar, *Serb.* 43°53′ N, 22°17′ E 168
Zajta, *Hung.* 47°53′ N, 22°48′ E 168
Zaka, *Zimb.* 20°20′ S, 31°29′ E 227
Zakamensk, *Russ.* 50°22′ N, 103°22′ E 190
Zákány, *Hung.* 46°16′ N, 16°57′ E 168
Zakataly, *Azerb.* 41°38′ N, 46°37′ E 195
Zakho, *Iraq* 37°8′ N, 42°34′ E 195
Zakhodnyaya Dzvina, river, *Belarus* 54°48′ N, 30°6′ E 154
Zakhrebetnoye, *Russ.* 68°57′ N, 36°27′ E 152
Zákinthos, *Gr.* 37°45′ N, 20°51′ E 216
Zákinthos, island, *Gr.* 37°48′ N, 19°27′ E 216
Zakīyah, *Syr.* 33°19′ N, 36°8′ E 194
Zakouma National Park, *Chad* 10°24′ N, 19°17′ E 218
Zakum, oil field, *Persian Gulf* 24°46′ N, 53°41′ E 196
Zakwaski Mountain, peak, *Can.* 50°8′ N, 121°24′ W 108
Zala, *Angola* 7°52′ S, 14°2′ E 218
Zala, adm. division, *Hung.* 46°34′ N, 16°29′ E 156
Zalaegerszeg, *Hung.* 46°49′ N, 16°51′ E 168
Zalalöv o, *Hung.* 46°50′ N, 16°36′ E 168
Zalamea la Real, *Sp.* 37°40′ N, 6°40′ W 164
Zalanga, *Nig.* 10°36′ N, 10°10′ E 222
Zalangoye, *Congo* 1°22′ N, 14°48′ E 218
Zalantun, *China* 48°2′ N, 122°47′ E 198
Zalau, *Nig.* 10°22′ N, 8°59′ E 222
Zalău, *Rom.* 47°10′ N, 23°4′ E 168
Žalec, *Slov.* 46°15′ N, 15°8′ E 156
Ẓalim, *Saudi Arabia* 22°41′ N, 42°11′ E 182
Zalingei, *Sudan* 12°52′ N, 23°29′ E 216
Zalishchyky, *Ukr.* 48°38′ N, 25°44′ E 152
Zalṭan, oil field, *Lib.* 28°47′ N, 19°44′ E 216
Zalve, *Latv.* 56°19′ N, 25°14′ E 166
Zama, *Miss., U.S.* 32°56′ N, 89°22′ W 103
Zama Lake, *Can.* 58°46′ N, 119°27′ W 108
Zamarte, *Pol.* 53°35′ N, 17°29′ E 152
Žamberk, *Czech Rep.* 50°4′ N, 16°27′ E 152
Zambezi, *Zambia* 13°33′ S, 23°9′ E 220
Zambezi National Park, *Zimb.* 18°30′ S, 25°12′ E 224
Zambezi, river, *Zambia* 16°33′ S, 23°28′ E 220
Zambézia, adm. division, *Mozambique* 16°33′ S, 35°52′ E 224
Zambia 15°2′ S, 26°18′ E 220
Zamboanga, *Philippines* 6°58′ N, 122°3′ E 203
Zamboanguita, *Philippines* 9°9′ N, 123°11′ E 203
Zâmbuè, *Mozambique* 15°9′ S, 30°47′ E 224
Zamezhnaya, *Russ.* 65°0′ N, 51°50′ E 154
Zamoge, *Eth.* 12°56′ N, 37°19′ E 182
Zamora, *Ecua.* 4°2′ S, 79°0′ W 130
Zamora, *Mex.* 19°59′ N, 102°17′ W 114
Zamora, *Sp.* 41°30′ N, 5°46′ W 150
Zamość, *Pol.* 50°42′ N, 23°14′ E 152
Zamošša, *Belarus* 55°30′ N, 27°3′ E 166
Zamostoch'ye, *Belarus* 53°51′ N, 28°26′ E 166
Zamsheva, *Russ.* 59°4′ N, 89°14′ E 169
Zamuro, Sierra del, *Venez.* 4°48′ N, 63°53′ W 130
Zam'yany, *Russ.* 46°46′ N, 47°35′ E 158
Zanda, *China* 31°29′ N, 79°47′ E 188
Zandvoort, *Neth.* 52°22′ N, 4°31′ E 163
Zanesville, *Ohio, U.S.* 39°56′ N, 82°1′ W 102
Zangeza Bay 57°56′ N, 102°46′ W 108
Zanjān, *Iran* 36°42′ N, 48°29′ E 195
Zanjón, river, *Mex.* 29°24′ N, 110°58′ W 80
Zantiguila, *Mali* 11°37′ N, 5°21′ W 222
Zanzibar, *Tanzania* 6°7′ S, 39°16′ E 224
Zanzibar Island, *Tanzania* 6°36′ S, 39°36′ E 224
Zaouatallaz, *Alg.* 24°53′ N, 8°24′ E 214
Zaouiet Azmour, *Tun.* 36°55′ N, 11°0′ E 156
Zaoyang, *China* 32°6′ N, 112°43′ E 198
Zaozhuang, *China* 34°54′ N, 117°33′ E 198
Zapadnaya Dvina, *Russ.* 56°15′ N, 32°4′ E 154
Zapadno Sibirskaya Ravnina 61°31′ N, 62°50′ E 154
Zapala, *Arg.* 38°54′ S, 70°2′ W 123
Zapata, *Tex., U.S.* 26°53′ N, 99°16′ W 96
Zapata, Península de, *Cuba* 22°23′ N, 82°2′ W 116
Zapatoca, *Col.* 6°47′ N, 73°16′ W 136
Zapiga, *Chile* 19°38′ S, 70°4′ W 137
Zapiola Ridge, *South Atlantic Ocean* 45°8′ S, 42°14′ W 253
Zapolyarnyy, *Russ.* 69°25′ N, 30°49′ E 152
Zapol'ye, *Russ.* 58°38′ N, 29°11′ E 166
Zaporizhzhya, *Ukr.* 47°48′ N, 35°11′ E 158
Zaporozhskoye, *Russ.* 60°33′ N, 30°32′ E 166
Zapotiltic, *Mex.* 19°36′ N, 103°26′ W 114
Zapug, *China* 33°16′ N, 80°51′ E 188
Zar, spring, *Mauritania* 18°0′ N, 14°39′ W 222
Zara, *Turk.* 39°54′ N, 37°44′ E 156
Zara see Zadar, *Croatia* 44°6′ N, 15°14′ E 156
Zarafshon, *Taj.* 39°8′ N, 68°39′ E 197
Zarafshon, *Uzb.* 41°31′ N, 64°14′ E 197
Zarafshon Range, *Taj.* 39°13′ N, 66°58′ E 184
Zarafshon, river, *Taj.* 39°20′ N, 69°7′ E 197
Zaragoza, *Col.* 7°28′ N, 74°49′ W 136
Zaragoza, *Mex.* 31°36′ N, 106°23′ W 112
Zaragoza, *Mex.* 28°28′ N, 100°56′ W 92
Zaragoza, *Mex.* 23°57′ N, 99°46′ W 114
Zaragoza, *Mex.* 22°0′ N, 100°45′ W 114
Zaragoza, *Sp.* 41°34′ N, 1°0′ E 214
Zarand, *Iran* 30°46′ N, 56°38′ E 180
Zarand, Munţii, *Rom.* 46°8′ N, 22°4′ E 168
Zaranou, *Côte d'Ivoire* 6°23′ N, 3°23′ W 222
Zarasai, *Lith.* 55°44′ N, 26°16′ E 166
Zárate, *Arg.* 34°6′ S, 59°1′ W 139
Zarautz, *Sp.* 43°15′ N, 2°12′ W 164
Zaraysk, *Russ.* 54°45′ N, 38°52′ E 154
Zaraza, *Venez.* 9°20′ N, 65°21′ W 136
Zarcilla de Ramos, *Sp.* 37°50′ N, 1°53′ W 164
Zard Kūh, peak, *Iran* 32°21′ N, 49°58′ E 180
Zarech'ye, *Belarus* 54°8′ N, 29°49′ E 166

Zarghun Shahr, *Afghan.* 32°49′ N, 68°26′ E 186
Zaria, *Nig.* 11°2′ N, 7°43′ E 222
Zarichne, *Ukr.* 51°48′ N, 26°7′ E 152
Zaris Berge, *Namibia* 24°22′ S, 16°10′ E 227
Zarit, spring, *Mali* 16°4′ N, 3°50′ E 222
Żarnów, *Pol.* 51°14′ N, 20°11′ E 152
Zarqan, *Iran* 29°46′ N, 52°47′ E 196
Zarrarah, oil field, *U.A.E.* 22°42′ N, 54°2′ E 182
Zarubikha, *Russ.* 69°18′ N, 34°14′ E 152
Zarubino, *Russ.* 42°38′ N, 131°4′ E 200
Zaruma, *Ecua.* 3°49′ S, 79°37′ W 130
Żary, *Pol.* 51°37′ N, 15°8′ E 152
Zarya, Poluostrov, *Russ.* 75°5′ N, 70°47′ E 172
Zarzaïtine, oil field, *Alg.* 28°5′ N, 9°40′ E 214
Zarzal, *Col.* 4°21′ N, 76°6′ W 136
Zarzis, *Tun.* 33°31′ N, 11°5′ E 214
Zashaghan, *Kaz.* 51°9′ N, 51°20′ E 158
Zasheyek, *Russ.* 66°15′ N, 31°4′ E 152
Zaskevichi, *Belarus* 54°23′ N, 26°35′ E 166
Zaslawye, *Belarus* 54°0′ N, 27°14′ E 166
Zaslonava, *Belarus* 54°51′ N, 28°59′ E 166
Zastron, *S. Af.* 30°18′ S, 27°4′ E 227
Zatish'ye, *Russ.* 66°10′ N, 158°50′ E 160
Zatobyl, *Kaz.* 53°11′ N, 63°42′ E 184
Zatoka, *Ukr.* 46°4′ N, 30°28′ E 156
Zaturtsi, *Ukr.* 50°45′ N, 24°50′ E 152
Zavala, *Bosn. and Herzg.* 42°49′ N, 17°58′ E 168
Zavalla, *Tex., U.S.* 31°9′ N, 94°26′ W 103
Zavetnoye, *Russ.* 47°3′ N, 43°49′ E 158
Zavidovići, *Bosn. and Herzg.* 44°27′ N, 18°7′ E 168
Zavlaka, *Serb.* 44°27′ N, 19°29′ E 168
Zavolzhsk, *Russ.* 57°32′ N, 42°9′ E 154
Zav'yalovo, *Russ.* 56°47′ N, 53°24′ E 154
Zāwiyat al Mukhaylá, *Lib.* 32°11′ N, 22°17′ E 216
Zāwiyat Masūs, *Lib.* 31°33′ N, 21°0′ E 216
Zāwyet Shammâs, *Egypt* 31°28′ N, 26°27′ E 180
Zayāki Jangal, *Pak.* 27°52′ N, 65°49′ E 182
Zaymah, *Saudi Arabia* 21°36′ N, 40°8′ E 182
Zaysan, *Kaz.* 47°27′ N, 84°52′ E 184
Zaysan Köli, lake, *Kaz.* 47°57′ N, 83°47′ E 184
Zayü, *China* 28°37′ N, 97°30′ E 188
Zboriv, *Ukr.* 49°40′ N, 25°7′ E 152
Ždala, *Croatia* 46°9′ N, 17°7′ E 168
Zdolbuniv, *Ukr.* 50°31′ N, 26°14′ E 152
Zdziechowice, *Pol.* 50°47′ N, 22°7′ E 152
Zéalé, *Côte d'Ivoire* 6°51′ N, 8°9′ W 222
Zebla, Jebel, peak, *Tun.* 36°48′ N, 9°11′ E 156
Zednes, peak, *Mauritania* 23°44′ N, 10°46′ W 214
Zeeland, *Mich., U.S.* 42°48′ N, 86°1′ W 102
Ze'elim, *Israel* 31°12′ N, 34°31′ E 194
Zeerust, *S. Af.* 25°34′ S, 26°3′ E 227
Zefat, *Israel* 32°58′ N, 35°29′ E 194
Zeidab, *Sudan* 17°25′ N, 33°54′ E 182
Zeil, Mount, peak, *Austral.* 23°27′ S, 132°11′ E 230
Zeist, *Neth.* 52°5′ N, 5°14′ E 163
Zeitûn, *Egypt* 29°9′ N, 25°47′ E 180
Zejmen, *Alban.* 41°42′ N, 19°41′ E 168
Zela see Zile, *Turk.* 40°19′ N, 35°53′ E 156
Zelenchukskaya, *Russ.* 43°51′ N, 41°27′ E 195
Zelenikovo, *Maced.* 41°53′ N, 21°34′ E 168
Zelenoborskiy, *Russ.* 66°48′ N, 32°19′ E 152
Zelenoe, *Kaz.* 48°2′ N, 51°34′ E 158
Zelenogorsk, *Russ.* 60°11′ N, 29°42′ E 166
Zelenogradsk, *Russ.* 54°56′ N, 20°27′ E 166
Zelenokumsk, *Russ.* 44°22′ N, 43°55′ E 158
Zelfana, *Alg.* 32°27′ N, 4°5′ E 214
Zelina, *Croatia* 45°58′ N, 16°15′ E 168
Željin, *Serb.* 43°29′ N, 20°39′ E 168
Zell, *Ger.* 49°48′ N, 9°51′ E 167
Zell, *Ger.* 50°1′ N, 7°10′ E 167
Zellingen, *Ger.* 49°53′ N, 9°49′ E 167
Zellwood, *Fla., U.S.* 28°43′ N, 81°37′ W 105
Zeltiņi, *Latv.* 57°20′ N, 26°45′ E 166
Zel'va, *Belarus* 53°8′ N, 24°48′ E 152
Želva, *Lith.* 55°13′ N, 25°5′ E 166
Zemaitija National Park, *Lith.* 55°58′ N, 21°54′ E 166
Zemē, *Eth.* 9°53′ N, 37°45′ E 224
Zemen, *Bulg.* 42°29′ N, 22°45′ E 168
Zemetchino, *Russ.* 53°27′ N, 42°34′ E 154
Zemio, *Cen. Af. Rep.* 5°4′ N, 25°6′ E 224
Zemlya Frantsa Iosifa, islands, *Barents Sea* 82°32′ N, 4°43′ E 173
Zemlya Frantsa Iosifa see Franz Josef Land, islands, *Barents Sea* 82°32′ N, 4°43′ E 172
Zemongo, *Cen. Af. Rep.* 7°4′ N, 24°54′ E 224
Zempoala (Cempoala), ruin(s), *Mex.* 19°23′ N, 96°28′ W 114
Zempoaltepec, Cerro, peak, *Mex.* 17°8′ N, 96°2′ W 114
Zemun, *Serb.* 44°49′ N, 20°25′ E 168
Zencirli, site, *Turk.* 37°6′ N, 36°36′ E 156
Zengfeng Shan, peak, *China* 42°22′ N, 128°42′ E 200
Zenica, *Bosn. and Herzg.* 44°12′ N, 17°52′ E 168
Zenith Plateau, *Indian Ocean* 22°32′ S, 104°34′ E 254
Zenobia Peak, *Colo., U.S.* 40°35′ N, 108°57′ W 90
Zenobia, ruin(s), *Syr.* 35°39′ N, 39°45′ E 180
Zentsūji, *Japan* 34°14′ N, 133°47′ E 201
Zenza do Itombe, *Angola* 9°17′ S, 14°14′ E 218
Zenzontepec, *Mex.* 16°32′ N, 97°31′ W 112
Zepa, *Bosn. and Herzg.* 43°56′ N, 19°8′ E 168
Žepče, *Bosn. and Herzg.* 44°26′ N, 18°2′ E 168
Zephyrhills, *Fla., U.S.* 28°13′ N, 82°11′ W 105
Zepu, *China* 38°12′ N, 77°18′ E 184
Żerczyce, *Pol.* 52°28′ N, 23°3′ E 152
Zerendi, *Kaz.* 52°53′ N, 69°9′ E 184
Zerf, *Ger.* 49°35′ N, 6°41′ E 163
Zerhamra, *Alg.* 29°57′ N, 2°29′ W 214
Zerind, *Rom.* 46°38′ N, 21°32′ E 168
Zermatt, *Switz.* 46°1′ N, 7°44′ E 167
Zernez, *Switz.* 46°42′ N, 10°5′ E 167
Zernograd, *Russ.* 46°50′ N, 40°18′ E 158
Zerqan, *Alban.* 41°30′ N, 20°21′ E 168
Zestap'oni, *Ga.* 42°3′ N, 43°2′ E 195
Zetel, *Ger.* 53°25′ N, 7°59′ E 163
Zevio, *It.* 45°21′ N, 11°7′ E 167
Zeya, *Russ.* 53°51′ N, 127°9′ E 190
Zeysk, *Russ.* 54°51′ N, 129°16′ E 173
Zgharta, *Leb.* 34°23′ N, 35°54′ E 156
Zgierz, *Pol.* 51°50′ N, 19°25′ E 152
Zhabinka, *Belarus* 52°12′ N, 24°0′ E 152
Zhabye, *Ukr.* 48°9′ N, 24°48′ E 152
Zhag'yab, *China* 30°37′ N, 97°35′ E 188
Zhalangash, *Kaz.* 43°2′ N, 78°38′ E 184
Zhalauly, *Kaz.* 48°1′ N, 61°12′ E 184
Zhaldama, *Kaz.* 50°26′ N, 65°39′ E 184
Zhalpaqtal, *Kaz.* 49°40′ N, 49°28′ E 158
Zhaltyr, *Kaz.* 51°38′ N, 69°51′ E 184
Zhambyl, *Kaz.* 47°9′ N, 71°8′ E 184
Zhambyl, adm. division, *Kaz.* 42°45′ N, 70°19′ E 197
Zhanadarīya, *Kaz.* 44°43′ N, 64°45′ E 184
Zhanang, *China* 29°16′ N, 91°18′ E 197
Zhanaqala, *Kaz.* 44°46′ N, 63°11′ E 184
Zhanbīke, *Kaz.* 47°2′ N, 55°7′ E 158
Zhanga Qazan, *Kaz.* 48°57′ N, 49°35′ E 158
Zhangaly, *Kaz.* 47°2′ N, 50°46′ E 158
Zhangaözen, *Kaz.* 43°20′ N, 52°46′ E 158
Zhangaqala, *Kaz.* 49°13′ N, 50°19′ E 158
Zhangaqīma, *Kaz.* 51°36′ N, 67°35′ E 184
Zhangbei, *China* 41°11′ N, 114°40′ E 198
Zhangjiakou, *China* 40°48′ N, 114°51′ E 198
Zhangping, *China* 25°18′ N, 117°24′ E 198
Zhangpu, *China* 24°4′ N, 117°36′ E 198
Zhangwu, *China* 42°24′ N, 122°34′ E 200
Zhangye, *China* 38°51′ N, 100°33′ E 190
Zhangzhou, *China* 24°29′ N, 117°36′ E 198
Zhangzi, *China* 36°6′ N, 112°51′ E 198
Zhanhua, *China* 37°44′ N, 118°10′ E 198
Zhänibek, *Kaz.* 49°24′ N, 46°50′ E 158
Zhanjiang, *China* 21°10′ N, 110°20′ E 198
Zhansügirov, *Kaz.* 45°21′ N, 79°28′ E 184
Zhāntöbe, *Kaz.* 44°43′ N, 68°50′ E 184
Zhanyi, *China* 25°41′ N, 103°44′ E 190
Zhao'an, *China* 23°42′ N, 117°9′ E 198
Zhaodong, *China* 46°3′ N, 125°57′ E 198
Zhaosu, *China* 43°7′ N, 81°1′ E 184
Zhaotong, *China* 27°19′ N, 103°38′ E 190
Zhaoyuan, *China* 45°29′ N, 125°6′ E 198
Zhaozhou, *China* 45°41′ N, 125°17′ E 198
Zhapo, *China* 21°35′ N, 111°52′ E 198
Zhaqsy, *Kaz.* 51°55′ N, 67°20′ E 184
Zharbulaq, *Kaz.* 46°4′ N, 82°4′ E 184
Zharkamys, *Kaz.* 47°56′ N, 56°21′ E 158
Zharkent, *Kaz.* 44°8′ N, 79°58′ E 184
Zharkovskiy, *Russ.* 55°52′ N, 32°20′ E 154
Zharma, *Kaz.* 48°47′ N, 80°51′ E 184
Zharman Köli, lake, *Kaz.* 51°32′ N, 63°36′ E 184
Zharmysh, *Kaz.* 44°8′ N, 52°24′ E 158
Zhashui, *China* 33°42′ N, 109°7′ E 198
Zhaslyk, *Uzb.* 43°53′ N, 57°41′ E 158
Zhaxi Co, lake, *China* 32°5′ N, 84°27′ E 188
Zhayylma, *Kaz.* 51°33′ N, 61°39′ E 184
Zhayyq, river, *Kaz.* 50°40′ N, 51°12′ E 158
Zhdanov, *Azerb.* 39°47′ N, 47°36′ E 195
Zhecheng, *China* 34°3′ N, 115°16′ E 198
Zhejiang, adm. division, *China* 28°7′ N, 120°50′ E 198
Zhelezīnka, *Kaz.* 53°38′ N, 75°13′ E 184
Zheleznodorozhnyy, *Russ.* 54°20′ N, 21°16′ E 166
Zheleznodorozhnyy, *Russ.* 62°33′ N, 50°59′ E 154
Zheleznogorsk, *Russ.* 52°17′ N, 35°20′ E 158
Zheleznovodsk, *Russ.* 44°10′ N, 43°3′ E 158
Zhem, river, *Kaz.* 47°13′ N, 55°32′ E 160
Zhemgang, *Bhutan* 27°7′ N, 90°45′ E 197
Zhen'an, *China* 33°25′ N, 109°7′ E 198
Zhenba, *China* 32°32′ N, 107°53′ E 198
Zhenfeng, *China* 25°21′ N, 105°42′ E 198
Zheng'an, *China* 28°35′ N, 107°22′ E 198
Zhenghe, *China* 27°23′ N, 118°51′ E 198
Zhenglan Qi (Xulun Hoh), *China* 42°13′ N, 116°2′ E 198
Zhengxiangbai Qi, *China* 42°15′ N, 115°3′ E 198
Zhengzhou (Chengchow), *China* 34°46′ N, 113°36′ E 198
Zhenjiang, *China* 32°10′ N, 119°25′ E 198
Zhenlai, *China* 45°48′ N, 123°11′ E 198
Zhenning, *China* 26°5′ N, 105°44′ E 198
Zhenping, *China* 31°58′ N, 109°30′ E 198
Zhenping, *China* 33°4′ N, 112°16′ E 198
Zhenyuan, *China* 23°50′ N, 100°50′ E 202
Zhenyuan, *China* 27°3′ N, 108°26′ E 198
Zhenyuan, *China* 35°43′ N, 107°13′ E 198
Zherdevka, *Russ.* 51°52′ N, 41°21′ E 158
Zherino, *Belarus* 54°50′ N, 29°24′ E 166
Zheshart, *Russ.* 62°4′ N, 49°36′ E 154
Zhetibay, *Kaz.* 43°33′ N, 52°4′ E 158
Zhetiger, *Kaz.* 43°40′ N, 77°6′ E 184
Zhetiqara, *Kaz.* 52°11′ N, 61°13′ E 158
Zhezdi, *Kaz.* 48°2′ N, 67°1′ E 184
Zhezkent, *Kaz.* 50°54′ N, 81°24′ E 184
Zhezqazghan, *Kaz.* 47°46′ N, 67°31′ E 190
Zhicheng, *China* 30°18′ N, 111°28′ E 198
Zhidan, *China* 36°49′ N, 108°45′ E 198
Zhidoi, *China* 33°54′ N, 95°38′ E 188
Zhigalovo, *Russ.* 54°44′ N, 104°58′ E 160
Zhigansk, *Russ.* 66°44′ N, 123°6′ E 160
Zhigulevsk, *Russ.* 53°26′ N, 49°37′ E 158
Zhijiang, *China* 27°28′ N, 109°42′ E 198
Zhilichi, *Belarus* 53°28′ N, 24°8′ E 152
Zhilikhovo, *Belarus* 52°55′ N, 27°3′ E 152
Zhilinda, *Russ.* 70°9′ N, 113°46′ E 160
Zhirnovsk, *Russ.* 50°58′ N, 44°47′ E 158
Zhitkovo, *Russ.* 60°41′ N, 29°19′ E 166
Zhizdra, *Russ.* 53°41′ N, 34°49′ E 154
Zhlobin, *Belarus* 52°52′ N, 30°6′ E 154
Zhmerynka, *Ukr.* 49°3′ N, 28°19′ E 152
Zhob, *Pak.* 31°20′ N, 69°30′ E 186
Zhob, river, *Pak.* 30°50′ N, 68°17′ E 186
Zhodzina, *Belarus* 54°7′ N, 28°20′ E 166
Zhokhova, island, *Russ.* 76°1′ N, 152°19′ E 255
Zholymbet, *Kaz.* 51°45′ N, 71°44′ E 184
Zhongba, *China* 29°41′ N, 84°13′ E 197
Zhongning, *China* 37°30′ N, 105°38′ E 198
Zhongshan, *China* 24°28′ N, 111°17′ E 198
Zhongshan, China, station, *Antarctica* 69°24′ S, 76°11′ E 248
Zhongwei, *China* 37°32′ N, 105°9′ E 198
Zhongxian, *China* 30°21′ N, 107°57′ E 198
Zhongxiang, *China* 31°8′ N, 112°34′ E 198
Zhosaly, *Kaz.* 45°29′ N, 64°5′ E 184
Zhoukou, *China* 33°34′ N, 114°43′ E 198
Zhoushan Dao, island, *China* 30°5′ N, 122°19′ E 198
Zhovten', *Ukr.* 49°1′ N, 24°46′ E 152
Zhovti Vody, *Ukr.* 48°23′ N, 33°29′ E 156
Zhovtneve, *Ukr.* 46°53′ N, 32°1′ E 156
Zhuanghe, *China* 39°42′ N, 122°57′ E 200
Zhuanglang, *China* 35°11′ N, 106°2′ E 198
Zhucheng, *China* 36°3′ N, 119°26′ E 198
Zhugqu, *China* 33°40′ N, 104°15′ E 198
Zhuji, *China* 29°44′ N, 120°10′ E 198
Zhukovka, *Russ.* 53°29′ N, 33°49′ E 154
Zhumysker, *Kaz.* 47°5′ N, 51°48′ E 158
Zhuolu, *China* 40°23′ N, 115°10′ E 198
Zhuozhou, *China* 39°29′ N, 115°57′ E 198
Zhuozi, *China* 40°55′ N, 112°36′ E 198
Zhuozi Shan, peak, *China* 39°39′ N, 106°54′ E 198
Zhur (Žur), *Kosovo* 42°10′ N, 20°36′ E 168
Zhuryn, *Kaz.* 49°18′ N, 57°33′ E 158
Zhushan, *China* 32°16′ N, 110°14′ E 198
Zhuxi, *China* 32°20′ N, 109°42′ E 198
Zhuzhou, *China* 27°50′ N, 113°12′ E 198
Zhympity, *Kaz.* 50°15′ N, 52°37′ E 158
Zhytomyr, *Ukr.* 50°15′ N, 28°40′ E 152
Zi, river, *China* 32°39′ N, 96°11′ E 188
Zi, river, *China* 28°25′ N, 111°8′ E 198
Zibak, *Afghan.* 36°32′ N, 71°25′ E 186
Zibo, *China* 36°49′ N, 118°6′ E 198
Zichang, *China* 37°7′ N, 109°39′ E 198
Zierikzee, *Neth.* 51°39′ N, 3°55′ E 163
Žiežmariai, *Lith.* 54°49′ N, 24°25′ E 166
Zigana Geçidi, pass, *Turk.* 40°37′ N, 39°21′ E 195
Zigey, *Chad* 14°43′ N, 15°46′ E 216
Zigong, *China* 29°25′ N, 104°50′ E 198
Zigui, *China* 31°2′ N, 110°40′ E 198
Ziguinchor, *Senegal* 12°31′ N, 16°13′ W 222
Zihuatanejo, *Mex.* 17°36′ N, 101°33′ W 114
Zikhron Ya'aqov, *Israel* 32°33′ N, 34°57′ E 194
Zilair, *Russ.* 52°12′ N, 57°21′ E 154
Zile (Zela), *Turk.* 40°19′ N, 35°53′ E 156
Žilina, *Slovakia* 49°13′ N, 18°45′ E 152
Žilinský, adm. division, *Slovakia* 49°13′ N, 18°45′ E 152
Zillah, *Lib.* 28°32′ N, 17°33′ E 216
Zillah, *Wash., U.S.* 46°23′ N, 120°17′ W 90
Zilupe, *Latv.* 56°22′ N, 28°6′ E 166
Zima, *Russ.* 53°59′ N, 101°50′ E 190
Zimapán, *Mex.* 20°42′ N, 99°23′ W 114
Zimatlán, *Mex.* 16°51′ N, 96°45′ W 112
Zimba, *Zambia* 17°19′ S, 26°9′ E 224
Zimbabwe 19°5′ S, 29°8′ E 220
Zimmi, *Sierra Leone* 7°16′ N, 11°18′ W 222
Zimnicea, *Rom.* 43°41′ N, 25°20′ E 180
Zimovniki, *Russ.* 47°5′ N, 42°21′ E 158
Zina, *Cameroon* 11°16′ N, 14°56′ E 216
Zinapécuaro, *Mex.* 19°51′ N, 100°49′ W 114
Zinave National Park, *Mozambique* 21°47′ S, 33°31′ E 227
Zinder, *Niger* 13°46′ N, 8°59′ E 222
Zinguinasso, *Côte d'Ivoire* 10°3′ N, 6°22′ W 222
Zinjibār, *Yemen* 13°7′ N, 45°19′ E 182
Zion, *Ill., U.S.* 42°27′ N, 87°49′ W 102
Zion National Park, *Utah, U.S.* 37°15′ N, 114°31′ W 80
Zionsville, *Ind., U.S.* 39°57′ N, 86°17′ W 102
Zipaquirá, *Col.* 5°2′ N, 74°0′ W 136
Zirc, *Hung.* 47°15′ N, 17°53′ E 168
Žirče, *Serb.* 43°1′ N, 20°22′ E 168
Zirkel, Mount, peak, *Colo., U.S.* 40°49′ N, 106°44′ W 90
Zirkūh, island, *U.A.E.* 24°45′ N, 52°44′ E 182
Zitácuaro, *Mex.* 19°24′ N, 100°23′ W 114
Zitlala, *Mex.* 17°40′ N, 99°11′ W 114
Zitong, *China* 31°41′ N, 105°8′ E 198
Zitundo, *Mozambique* 26°37′ S, 32°53′ E 227
Živinice, *Bosn. and Herzg.* 44°28′ N, 18°38′ E 168
Zixi, *China* 27°39′ N, 117°2′ E 198
Zixing, *China* 26°0′ N, 113°21′ E 198
Ziya, river, *China* 38°30′ N, 116°41′ E 198
Ziyang, *China* 30°8′ N, 104°35′ E 198
Ziyang, *China* 32°34′ N, 108°33′ E 198
Ziyuan, *China* 26°2′ N, 110°41′ E 198
Ziyun, *China* 25°43′ N, 106°6′ E 198
Zizhou, *China* 37°37′ N, 110°5′ E 198
Zlatar, *Croatia* 46°6′ N, 16°4′ E 168
Zlatna, *Rom.* 46°7′ N, 23°15′ E 168
Zlatoust, *Russ.* 55°12′ N, 59°40′ E 154
Zlín, *Czech Rep.* 49°12′ N, 17°41′ E 152
Zlínský, adm. division, *Czech Rep.* 49°19′ N, 17°33′ E 152
Zlot, *Serb.* 44°1′ N, 21°59′ E 168
Zmeinogorsk, *Russ.* 51°10′ N, 82°17′ E 184
Żmigród, *Pol.* 51°28′ N, 16°55′ E 152
Zmiyev, *Ukr.* 49°40′ N, 36°18′ E 158
Znamenka, *Kaz.* 50°2′ N, 79°31′ E 184
Znamensk, *Russ.* 54°35′ N, 21°12′ E 166
Znam'yanka, *Ukr.* 48°43′ N, 32°39′ E 158
Zobia, *Dem. Rep. of the Congo* 3°0′ N, 25°58′ E 224
Zóbuè, *Mozambique* 15°35′ S, 34°24′ E 224
Zocca, *It.* 44°21′ N, 10°59′ E 167
Zodoke, *Liberia* 4°44′ N, 8°8′ W 214
Zoetermeer, *Neth.* 52°4′ N, 4°30′ E 163
Zofar, *Israel* 30°28′ N, 35°9′ E 194
Zogang (Wangda), *China* 29°42′ N, 97°53′ E 188
Zohor, *Slovakia* 48°18′ N, 16°59′ E 152
Zolfo Springs, *Fla., U.S.* 27°30′ N, 81°47′ W 105
Zolochiv, *Ukr.* 50°19′ N, 35°58′ E 158
Zolochiv, *Ukr.* 49°48′ N, 24°54′ E 152
Zolotarevka, *Russ.* 53°3′ N, 45°19′ E 154
Zolotonosha, *Ukr.* 49°38′ N, 32°3′ E 158
Zomba, *Malawi* 15°22′ S, 35°20′ E 224
Zongga see Gyirong, *China* 28°59′ N, 85°16′ E 197
Zongo, *Dem. Rep. of the Congo* 4°16′ N, 18°36′ E 218
Zonguldak, *Turk.* 41°27′ N, 31°48′ E 156
Zonhoven, *Belg.* 50°59′ N, 5°22′ E 167
Zoo Baba, spring, *Niger* 18°12′ N, 13°3′ E 222
Zoquiapan y Anexas National Park, *Mex.* 19°14′ N, 99°2′ W 72
Zor Dağ, peak, *Turk.* 39°43′ N, 43°53′ E 195
Zorita, *Sp.* 39°17′ N, 5°42′ W 164
Zorritos, *Peru* 3°45′ S, 80°40′ W 130
Żory, *Pol.* 50°3′ N, 18°41′ E 152
Zorzor, *Liberia* 7°41′ N, 9°28′ W 222
Zouar, *Chad* 20°28′ N, 16°31′ E 216
Zoucheng, *China* 35°24′ N, 117°0′ E 198
Zoug, *Africa* 21°37′ N, 14°9′ W 222
Zouîrat, *Mauritania* 22°46′ N, 12°27′ W 214
Zoushi, *China* 29°4′ N, 111°35′ E 198
Zoutkamp, *Neth.* 53°20′ N, 6°18′ E 163
Zrenjanin (Petrovgrad), *Serb.* 45°23′ N, 20°22′ E 168
Zrin, *Croatia* 45°11′ N, 16°24′ E 168
Zsira, *Hung.* 47°27′ N, 16°41′ E 168
Zubia, *Sp.* 37°7′ N, 3°35′ W 164
Zubovo, *Russ.* 60°16′ N, 37°0′ E 154
Zubtsov, *Russ.* 56°11′ N, 34°39′ E 154
Zudañez, *Bol.* 19°2′ S, 64°48′ W 137
Zuénoula, *Côte d'Ivoire* 7°21′ N, 6°3′ W 222
Zuera, *Sp.* 41°52′ N, 0°48′ E 164
Zufre, *Sp.* 37°49′ N, 6°21′ W 164
Zugdidi, *Ga.* 42°30′ N, 41°52′ E 195
Zugspitze, peak, *Aust.* 47°23′ N, 10°54′ E 156
Zuidhorn, *Neth.* 53°14′ N, 6°24′ E 163
Zújar, *Sp.* 37°32′ N, 2°51′ W 164
Zula, *Eritrea* 15°12′ N, 39°39′ E 182
Zulia, adm. division, *Venez.* 9°34′ N, 73°2′ W 136
Zülpich, *Ger.* 50°41′ N, 6°38′ E 167
Zululand, region, *S. Af.* 27°12′ S, 31°44′ E 227
Zumaia, *Sp.* 43°17′ N, 2°15′ W 150
Žumberačka Gora, *Slov.* 45°39′ N, 14°43′ E 156
Zumbo, *Mozambique* 15°37′ S, 30°28′ E 224
Zumpango, *Mex.* 19°45′ N, 99°3′ W 114
Zunape, *Col.* 4°12′ N, 70°28′ W 136
Zungeru, *Nig.* 9°47′ N, 6°9′ E 222
Zunhua, *China* 40°14′ N, 117°56′ E 198
Zuni, *N. Mex., U.S.* 35°4′ N, 108°51′ W 92
Zunyi, *China* 27°40′ N, 106°53′ E 198
Zuo, river, *China* 22°21′ N, 107°31′ E 198
Zuoz, *Switz.* 46°36′ N, 9°56′ E 167
Županja, *Croatia* 45°4′ N, 18°41′ E 168
Zūq Mīkhā'īl, *Leb.* 33°58′ N, 35°36′ E 194
Žur see Zhur, *Kosovo* 42°10′ N, 20°36′ E 168
Zūrābād, *Iran* 38°47′ N, 44°32′ E 195
Żurawica, *Pol.* 49°48′ N, 22°47′ E 152
Zureiqa, *Sudan* 13°32′ N, 32°1′ E 226
Zurich, *Can.* 43°25′ N, 81°37′ W 102
Zürich, *Switz.* 47°22′ N, 8°31′ E 150
Zuru, *Nig.* 11°24′ N, 5°12′ E 222
Zutiua, river, *Braz.* 5°8′ S, 46°19′ W 130
Zuwārah, *Lib.* 32°57′ N, 12°2′ E 216
Zuyevka, *Russ.* 58°24′ N, 51°15′ E 154
Zvenyhorodka, *Ukr.* 49°5′ N, 31°6′ E 158
Zvishavane, *Zimb.* 20°20′ S, 30°2′ E 227
Zvolen, *Slovakia* 48°34′ N, 19°7′ E 156
Zvonce, *Serb.* 42°55′ N, 22°34′ E 168
Zvornik, *Bosn. and Herzg.* 44°24′ N, 19°5′ E 168
Zvoz see Podsosan'ye, *Russ.* 63°17′ N, 42°2′ E 154
Zwedru, *Liberia* 5°57′ N, 8°9′ W 222
Zweibrücken, *Ger.* 49°14′ N, 7°21′ E 163
Zwickau, *Ger.* 50°43′ N, 12°29′ E 152
Zwijndrecht, *Neth.* 51°48′ N, 4°39′ E 167
Zwinge, *Ger.* 51°32′ N, 10°22′ E 167
Zwoleń, *Pol.* 51°21′ N, 21°34′ E 152
Zwolle, *La., U.S.* 31°36′ N, 93°39′ W 103
Zwolle, *Neth.* 52°31′ N, 6°5′ E 163
Zyembin, *Belarus* 54°21′ N, 28°11′ E 166
Zygi, *Cyprus* 34°43′ N, 33°19′ E 194
Żyrardów, *Pol.* 52°2′ N, 20°24′ E 152
Zyrya, *Azerb.* 40°22′ N, 50°16′ E 195
Zyryanka, *Russ.* 65°51′ N, 150°31′ E 160
Zyryanovo, *Russ.* 63°39′ N, 87°27′ E 169
Zyryanovsk, *Kaz.* 49°45′ N, 84°18′ E 184

Appendix

NATIONAL GEOGRAPHIC SOCIETY'S PLACE-NAMES POLICY

In keeping with the National Geographic Society's 123-year chartered purpose as a not-for-profit scientific and educational organization, the Society's cartographic policy is one of portraying de facto situations; that is, to portray to the best of our judgment a current reality. National Geographic strives to be apolitical, to consult multiple authoritative sources, and to make independent decisions based on extensive research. When there are conflicting or variant names, National Geographic does not purport to be the arbiter or determiner of a single name, but simply tries to provide the reader of the map sufficient information in which the reality of conflicting naming claims can be presented. International boundaries and disputed territories, where scale permits, reflect de facto status at the time of publication of our maps and atlases.

The Society's policy for naming geographic features is governed by a representative council of Society cartographers. This council meets frequently to assess available information about naming issues and, based on the best information and research available, seeks to make an independent judgment about future changes or clarifications on its maps, as well as to correct any errors. It is the policy of the Society to correct any errors as quickly as possible on the next published version of a particular map or atlas.

Depending on the type of map (whether physical or political), the Society uses either conventional (English) or local-language spellings, or, where space permits, a combination of both. For example, when a commonly recognized form of a well-known place-name, such as Bombay, differs from the official national form — Mumbai—the conventional form is listed in parenthesis: Mumbai (Bombay). The Society does not follow any single source in making its naming determinations. Decisions regarding the naming assigned to geographic places, locations, bodies of water, and the like are checked against a number of external entities, including: the U.S. Board on Geographic Names; recognized reference books such as encyclopedias, dictionaries, geographical dictionaries, other atlases, independent academic texts and other similar sources; international bodies such as the United Nations, the European Union, and the like; as well as the policies of individual governmental entities. Names commonly recognized as alternatives or variants by such sources are often used on our maps. In such instances, the primary name is determined by using the form recognized by the de facto controlling country of the area, or by using the generally held conventional form of the name. On occasion, where warranted and where space permits, explanatory notes stating the basis or context of a recognized variant naming are provided. Current examples of the application of this variant naming policy are: Falkland Islands (Islas Malvinas); Sea of Japan (East Sea).

National Geographic Maps frequently applies a secondary place-name in parenthesis ( ) after a recognized primary form of a place-name. This treatment is used even when the primary name is more widely recognized, provided that the variant name is used widely enough that National Geographic considers the inclusion of both to have real reference and educational value for the users of its products. Some instances of this use and examples are listed below.

CONVENTIONAL NAMES:

Used when the commonly recognized English-language form (conventional) of a well-known place-name differs from the official national form. The conventional form is listed in parenthesis. Conventional names are recognized as an official variant form for a place-name by multiple reference sources. On physical maps only the conventional form is generally used.

Roma (Rome)
Mumbai (Bombay)
Ghazzah (Gaza City)
El Qâhira (Cairo)
Wien (Vienna)

If a feature crosses over multiple countries (usually a river), the official national form is labeled within that specific country, with the conventional in parentheses. As the feature moves into another country, then that country's official form is used as the primary name.

Donau (Danube)
Duna (Danube)
Dunaj (Danube)
Dunărea (Danube)
Dunav (Danube)
Dunay (Danube)

HISTORIC NAMES:

Given same treatment as conventional names.

Istanbul (Constantinople)
Guangzhou (Canton)
Volgograd (Stalingrad)

VARIANT NAMES:

Similar to conventional names, but are not necessarily officially recognized as an official variant. Often used by the media.

Al Fallūjah (Fallujah)
Gebel Mûsa (Mount Sinai)

NAMES WITH SHARED POSSESSION:

When a name (usually a border mountain) is jointly controlled by more then one country and has multiple official names, the general rule is to list the conventional name first and then list the official names together in parentheses. Order of the secondary names can vary. The country that is the main subject of the map would be first. If both countries are the subject of the map, the names are listed in order of the country.

Mount Everest (Sagarmāthā, Qomolangma):
for a map of South Asia when Nepal is the map subject.
Mount Everest (Qomolangma, Sagarmāthā):
for a map of China or when both countries are the map subject.

DISPUTED NAMES:

When a name has differing forms recognized by different countries. The primary name is determined by using the form recognized by the de facto controlling country of the area, or using the generally held conventional form of the name.

CYPRUS:

Nicosia (Lefkosia, Lefkoşa)
Famagusta (Ammochostos, Gazimagusa)

DOKDO:

Dokdo (Takeshima, Liancourt Rocks)

SOUTHERN KURIL ISLANDS:

Iturup (Etorofu)
Kunashir (Kunashiri)

OTHER FEATURES:

English Channel (La Manche)
Falkland Islands (Islas Malvinas)
Sea of Japan (East Sea)

POSSESSION LABELS:

National Geographic Maps applies possession labels in red type to non-contiguous territorial areas (generally islands), identifying the country that has political control of it. Where an area is controlled by one country but is also claimed by another, a red note explains the dispute

Falkland Islands (Islas Malvinas) United Kingdom
Administered by United Kingdom (claimed by Argentina)

Senkaku Shotō (Diaoyu Islands) Japan
Administered by Japan (claimed by China and Taiwan)

MAP NOTES:

Where scale permits, explanatory notes, as those listed below, are added to our maps to explain the current political situation of disputed possessions or territories.

ABKHAZIA
Separatists defeated Georgian troops to gain control of this region in 1993—negotiations continue on resolving the conflict.

ABU MUSA
Island is claimed by Iran and U.A.E. and jointly administered by them.

DIVIDED CYPRUS
Cyprus was partitioned in 1974 following a coup backed by Greece and an invasion by Turkey. The island is composed of a Greek Cypriot south with an internationally recognized government and a Turkish Cypriot north (gray) with a government recognized only by Turkey. The UN patrols the dividing line and works toward reunification of the island.

KASHMIR
India and Pakistan both claim Kashmir—a disputed region of some 10 million people. India administers only the area south of the line of control; Pakistan controls northwestern Kashmir. China took eastern Kashmir from India in a 1962 war.

KOSOVO
On February 17, 2008, Kosovo declared its independence. Serbia still claims it as a province.

KURIL ISLANDS
The southern Kuril Islands of Iturup (Etorofu), Kunashir (Kunashiri), Shikotan, and the Habomai group were lost by Japan to the Soviet Union in 1945. Japan continues to claim these Russian-administered islands.

NAGORNO-KARABAKH
Since a 1994 cease-fire between Azerbaijani and Armenian forces, ethnic Armenians have controlled Nagorno-Karabakh and surrounding areas (gray). Azerbaijan continues to claim this disputed region.

PALESTINE
The bounds of the historical region of Palestine have varied through time, but it is generally agreed that the land between the Mediterranean Sea and the Jordan River constitutes its core.

PARACEL ISLANDS
Occupied by China in 1974, which calls them Xisha Qundao; claimed by Vietnam, which calls them Hoàng Sa.

SOMALILAND
In 1991 the Somali National Movement declared Somaliland an independent republic (in gray) with Hargeysa as the capital. It is not internationally recognized.

SOUTH OSSETIA
Georgia lost control of South Ossetia in 1992. Georgia tried to retake South Ossetia in 2008 but was defeated by Russian forces.

SOUTHERN SUDAN
In January 2011, the people of Southern Sudan voted to form a new independent country to be named South Sudan. It is scheduled to become the newest nation on July 9, 2011.

TAIWAN
The People's Republic of China claims Taiwan as its 23rd province. Taiwan's government (Republic of China) maintains that there are two political entities. The islands of Dongsha, Kinmen, Matsu, and Penghu are administered by Taiwan.

TRANSDNIESTRIA
Since the break-up of the Soviet Union, Ukrainian and Russian minorities have been struggling for independence from Moldova.

WEST BANK & GAZA STRIP
Captured by Israel in the 1967 Six Day War, a 1993 peace agreement gives areas of the West Bank and Gaza limited Palestinian autonomy. The future for these autonomous areas and 3 million Palestinians is subject to Israeli-Palestinian negotiations.

WESTERN SAHARA
Western Sahara, formerly Spanish Sahara, was divided by Morocco and Mauritania in 1976. Morocco has administered the territory since Mauritania's withdrawal in August 1979. The United Nations does not recognize this annexation, and Western Sahara remains in dispute.

ABBREVIATIONS

A. — Arroio, Arroyo
A.C.T. — Australian Capital Territory
A.F.B. — Air Force Base
A.F.S. — Air Force Station
A.R.B. — Air Reserve Base
Adm. — Administrative
Af. — Africa
Afghan. — Afghanistan
Ala. — Alabama
Alas. — Alaska
Alban. — Albania
Alg. — Algeria
Alta. — Alberta
Amer. — America-n
Amzns. — Amazonas
Anch. — Anchorage
And. & Nic. — Andaman and Nicobar Islands
And. Prad. — Andhra Pradesh
Antil. — Antilles
Arch. — Archipelago, Archipiélago
Arg. — Argentina
Ariz. — Arizona
Ark. — Arkansas
Arkh. — Arkhangel'sk
Arm. — Armenia
Arun. Prad. — Arunachal Pradesh
Astrak. — Astrakhan'
Atl. Oc. — Atlantic Ocean
Aust. — Austria
Austral. — Australia
Auton. — Autonomous
Azerb. — Azerbaijan
B. — Baai, Baía, Baie, Bahía, Bay, Bugt-en, Buḩayrat
B. Aires — Buenos Aires
B.C. — British Columbia
B. Qazaq. — Batys Qazaqstan
Bashk. — Bashkortostan
Belg. — Belgium
Bol. — Bolivia
Bol. — Bol'sh-oy, -aya, -oye
Bosn. & Herzg. — Bosnia and Herzegovina
Br. — Branch
Braz. — Brazil
Bulg. — Bulgaria
Burya. — Buryatiya
C. — Cabo, Cap, Cape, Capo
C.H. — Court House
C.P. — Conservation Park
C.R. — Costa Rica
C.S.I. Terr. — Coral Sea Islands Territory
Cach. — Cachoeira
Calif. — California
Can. — Canada
Cap. — Capitán
Catam. — Catamarca
Cd. — Ciudad
Cen. Af. Rep. — Central African Republic
Cga. — Ciénaga
Chan. — Channel
Chand. — Chandigarh
Chap. — Chapada
Chech. — Chechnya
Chely. — Chelyabinsk
Chhat. — Chhattīsgarh
Chongq. — Chongqing Shi
Chuk. — Chukotskiy
Chuv. — Chuvashiya
Chyrv. — Chyrvony, -aya, -aye
Cmte. — Comandante
Cnel. — Coronel
Co.-s. — Cerro-s
Col. — Colombia
Colo. — Colorado
Conn. — Connecticut
Cord. — Cordillera
Corr. — Corrientes
Cr. — Creek, Crique
D. — Danau
D. & Diu — Daman and Diu
D. & Nagar — Dadra and Nagar Haveli
D.C. — District of Columbia
D.F. — Distrito Federal
Del. — Delaware
Dem. — Democratic
Den. — Denmark
Dist. — District, Distrito
Dom. Rep. — Dominican Republic
Dr. — Doctor
Dz. — Dzong
E. — East-ern
E. Ríos — Entre Ríos
E. Santo — Espírito Santo
Ea. — Estancia
Ecua. — Ecuador
El Salv. — El Salvador
Emb. — Embalse
Eng. — England
Ens. — Ensenada
Entr. — Entrance
Eq. — Equatorial
Esc. — Escarpment
Est. — Estación
Est. — Estonia
Ét. — Étang
Eth. — Ethiopia
Eur. — Europe
Ez. — Ezers
F. — Fiume
F.S.M. — Federated States of Micronesia
Falk. Is. — Falkland Islands
Fd. — Fiord, Fiordo, Fjord
Fed. — Federal, Federation
Fin. — Finland
Fk. — Fork
Fla. — Florida
Fn. — Fortín
Fr. — France, French
Ft. — Fort
Fy. — Ferry
F.Z. — Fracture zone
G. — Golfe, Golfo, Gulf
G. Altay — Gorno-Altay
G.R. — Game Reserve
Ga. — Georgia
Geb. — Gebergte, Gebirge
Gen. — General
Ger. — Germany
Gez. — Gezîra-t, Gezîret
Gezr. — Gezâir
Gl. — Glacier, Gletscher
Gob. — Gobernador
Gr. — Greece,
Gr. — Gross-er
Gral. — General
Gt. — Great-er
Guang. — Guangdong
H.K. — Hong Kong
Hbr. — Harbor, Harbour
Hdqrs. — Headquarters
Heilong. — Heilongjiang
Hi. Prad. — Himachal Pradesh
Hist. — Historic, -al
Hond. — Honduras
Hts. — Heights
Hung. — Hungary
Hwy. — Highway
I.H.S. — International Historic Site
I.-s. — Île-s, Ilha-s, Isla-s, Island-s, Isle, Isol-a, -e
Ice. — Iceland
Ig. — Igarapé
Igr. — Ingeniero
Ill. — Illinois
Ind. — Indiana
Ind. Oc. — Indian Ocean
Ingush. — Ingushetiya
Intl. — International
Ire. — Ireland
It. — Italy
J. — Järvi, Joki
J. & Kash. — Jammu and Kashmir
J.A.R. — Jewish Autonomous Region
Jab., Jeb. — Jabal, Jebel
Jam. — Jamaica
Jct. — Jonction, Junction
Jez. — Jezero, Jezioro
Jhark. — Jharkhand
K. — Kanal
K. Balka. — Kabardino-Balkariya
K. Cherk. — Karachayevo-Cherkesiya
K. Mansi — Khanty-Mansi
Kalin. — Kaliningrad
Kalmy. — Kalmykiya
Kamchat. — Kamchatka
Kans. — Kansas
Karna. — Karnataka
Kaz. — Kazakhstan
Kemer. — Kemerovo
Kep. — Kepulauan
Kh. — Khor
Khabar. — Khabarovsk
Khak. — Khakasiya
Khr. — Khrebet
Km. — Kilómetro
Kól. — Kólpos
Kör. — Körfez,-i
Kos. — Kosovo
Kr. — Krasn-yy, -aya, -oye
Krasnod. — Krasnodar
Krasnoy. — Krasnoyarsk
Ky. — Kentucky
Kyrg. — Kyrgyzstan
L. — Lac, Lago, Lake, Límni, Loch, Lough
La. — Louisiana
Lag. — Laguna
Lakshad. — Lakshadweep
Latv. — Latvia
Ldg. — Landing
Leb. — Lebanon
Lib. — Libya
Liech. — Liechtenstein
Lith. — Lithuania
Lux. — Luxembourg
Mal. — Mal-y-y, -aya, -aye
M.C.A.S. — Marine Corps Air Station
M. Gerais — Minas Gerais
M. Grosso — Mato Grosso
M. Grosso S. — Mato Grosso do Sul
M. Prad. — Madhya Pradesh
Maced. — Macedonia
Mahar. — Maharashtra
Man. — Manitoba
Mangg. — Mangghystaū
Maran. — Maranhão
Mass. — Massachusetts
Md. — Maryland
Me. — Maine
Medit. Sea — Mediterranean Sea
Meghal. — Meghalaya
Mex. — Mexico
Mgne. — Montagne
Mich. — Michigan
Minn. — Minnesota
Miss. — Mississippi
Mo. — Missouri
Mold. — Moldova
Mon. — Monument
Mont. — Montana
Mor. — Morocco
Mord. — Mordoviya
Mt.-s. — Mont-s, Mount-ain-s
Mte.-s. — Monte-s
Mti., Mtii. — Munţi-i
Mun. — Municipal
Murm. — Murmansk
N. — North-ern
N.A.S. — Naval Air Station
N.B. — National Battlefield
N.B. — New Brunswick
N.B.P. — National Battlefield Park
N.B.S. — National Battlefield Site
N.C. — National Cemetery
N.C. — North Carolina
N.C.A. — National Conservation Area
N. Dak. — North Dakota
N.E. — North East
N.H. — New Hampshire
N.H.P. — National Historic, -al Park
N.H.S. — National Historic Site
N. Ire. — Northern Ireland
N.J. — New Jersey
N.L. — National Lakeshore
N.M. — National Monument
N.M.P. — National Military Park
N. Mem. — National Memorial
N. Mem. P. — National Memorial Park
N. Mex. — New Mexico
N. Mongol — Nei Mongol
N.P. — National Park
N.R. — Nature Reserve
N.R.A. — National Recreation Area
N.S. — Nova Scotia
N.S.R. — National Scenic Riverway
N.S.R.A. — National Seashore Recreational Area
N.S.T. — National Scenic Trail
N.S.W. — New South Wales
N.T. — Northern Territory
N.T.C. — Naval Training Center
N.T.S. — Naval Training Station
N.V.M. — National Volcanic Monument
N.W.T. — Northwest Territories
N.Y. — New York
N.Z. — New Zealand
Nat. Mem. — National Memorial
Nat. Mon. — National Monument
Nat. Park — National Park
Nebr. — Nebraska
Neth. — Netherlands
Nev. — Nevada, Nevado
Nfld. & Lab. — Newfoundland and Labrador
Nicar. — Nicaragua
Niz. Nov. — Nizhniy Novogorod
Nizh. — Nizhn-iy, -yaya, -eye
Nor. — Norway
Nov. — Nov-yy, -aya, -aye, -oye
Novg. — Novgorod
Novo. — Novosibirsk
Nr. — Nørre
O. — Ostrov, Oued
Oc. — Ocean
Of. — Oficina
Okla. — Oklahoma
Ong. Qazaq. — Ongtüstik Qazaqstan
Ont. — Ontario
Ør. — Øster
Oreg. — Oregon
Orenb. — Orenburg
Oz. — Ozero
P. — Paso, Pass, Passo
P.E.I. — Prince Edward Island
P.N.G. — Papua New Guinea
P.R. — Puerto Rico
Pa. — Pennsylvania
Pac. Oc. — Pacific Ocean
Pak. — Pakistan
Pan. — Panama
Pant. — Pantano
Parag. — Paraguay
Parq. Nac. — Parque Nacional
Pass. — Passage
Peg. — Pegunungan
Pen. — Peninsula, Péninsule
Per. — Pereval
Pern. — Pernambuco
Pivd. — Pivdennyy
Pk. — Peak
Pl. — Planina
Plat. — Plateau
Pol. — Poland
Pol. — Poluostrov
Por. — Porog
Port. — Portugal
Pres. — Presidente
Prov. — Province, Provincial
Pt.-e. — Point-e
Pta. — Ponta, Punta
Pto. — Puerto
Q. — Quebrada
Qarag. — Qaraghandy
Qnsld. — Queensland
Que. — Quebec
Qyzyl. — Qyzylorda
R. — Río, River, Rivière
R.R. — Railroad
R. Gr. Norte — Rio Grande do Norte
R. Gr. Sul — Rio Grande do Sul
R.I. — Rhode Island
R. Jan. — Rio de Janeiro
R. Negro — Río Negro
Ra.-s. — Range-s
Raja. — Rajasthan
Reg. — Region
Rep. — Republic
Res. — Reservoir, Reserve, Reservatório
Rk. — Rock
Rom. — Romania
Russ. — Russia
S. — South-ern
S.A.R. — Special Administrative Region
S. Aust. — South Australia
S.C. — South Carolina
S. Dak. — South Dakota
S. Estero — Santiago del Estero
S. Ossetia — South Ossetia
S. Paulo — São Paulo
S.W. — Southwest
Sa.-s. — Serra, Sierra-s
Sal. — Salar, Salina
Sask. — Saskatchewan
Scot. — Scotland
Sd. — Sound, Sund
Sel. — Selat
Ser. — Serranía
Serb. — Serbia
Sev. — Severn-yy, -aya, -oye
Sev. Oset. — Severnaya Osetiya-Alaniya
Sgt. — Sargento
Shand. — Shandong
Shy. Qazaq. — Shyghys Qazaqstan
Sk. — Shankou
Slov. — Slovenia
Smt.-s — Seamount-s
Solt. Qazaq. — Soltüstik Qazaqstan
Sp. — Spain, Spanish
Spr.-s. — Spring-s
Sq. — Square
Sr. — Sønder
St.-e. — Saint-e, Sankt, Sint
St. Peter. — Saint Petersburg
Sta., Sto. — Santa, Station, Santo
Sta. Cata. — Santa Catarina
Sta. Cruz. — Santa Cruz
Stavr. — Stavropol'
Str.-s. — Straat, Strait-s
Sv. — Svyat-oy, -aya, -oye
Sverd. — Sverdlovsk
Sw. — Sweden
Switz. — Switzerland
Syr. — Syria
T. Fuego — Tierra del Fuego
T. Nadu — Tamil Nadu
Taj. — Tajikistan
Tartar. — Tartarstan
Tas. — Tasmania
Tel. — Teluk
Tenn. — Tennessee
Terr. — Territory
Tex. — Texas
Tg. — Tanjung
Thai. — Thailand
Tmt.-s — Tablemount-s
Tocant. — Tocantins
Trin. — Trinidad
Tun. — Tunisia
Turk. — Turkey
Turkm. — Turkmenistan
U.A.E. — United Arab Emirates
U.K. — United Kingdom
U. Prad. — Uttar Pradesh
U.S. — United States
Udmur. — Udmurtiya
Uj. — Ujung
Ukr. — Ukraine
Ulyan. — Ul'yanovsk
Uru. — Uruguay
Uttar. — Uttarakhand
Uzb. — Uzbekistan
Va. — Virginia
Val. — Valle
Vdkhr. — Vodokhranil-ishche
Vdskh. — Vodoskhovy-shche
Venez. — Venezuela
Verkh. — Verkhn-iy, -yaya, -eye
Vic. — Victoria
Vol. — Volcán, Volcano
Volg. — Volgograd
Voz. — Vozyera, -yero, -yera
Vozv. — Vozvyshennost'
Vr. — Vester
Vt. — Vermont
Vyal. — Vyaliki, -ikaya,-ikaye
W. — Wadi, Wâdi, Wādī, Webi
W. — West-ern
W. Aust. — Western Australia
W. Bengal — West Bengal
W.H. — Water Hole
W. Va. — West Virginia
Wash. — Washington
Wis. — Wisconsin
Wyo. — Wyoming
Yar. — Yarymadasy
Yaro. — Yaroslavl'
Yu. — Yuzhn-yy, -aya, -oye
Zakh. — Zakhod-ni, -nyaya, -nye
Zal. — Zaliv
Zap. — Zapadn-yy, -aya, -oye
Zimb. — Zimbabwe

Geographic Comparisons

The Earth

MASS:	5,973,600,000,000,000,000,000 metric tons
TOTAL AREA:	510,066,000 sq km
LAND AREA:	148,647,000 sq km (29.1%)
WATER AREA:	361,419,000 sq km (70.9%)
POPULATION 2010:	6,908,688,000

The Continents

	Area (sq km)	Percent of Land
Asia	44,570,000	30.0
Africa	30,065,000	20.2
North America	24,474,000	16.5
South America	17,819,000	12.0
Antarctica	13,209,000	8.9
Europe	9,947,000	6.7
Australia	7,692,000	5.2

Highest Point on Each Continent

	Meters
Mount Everest, Asia	8,850
Cerro Aconcagua, South America	6,959
Mount McKinley (Denali), North America	6,194
Kilimanjaro, Africa	5,895
El'brus, Europe	5,642
Vinson Massif, Antarctica	4,897
Mount Kosciuszko, Australia	2,228

Lowest Surface Point on Each Continent

	Meters
Dead Sea, Asia	-422
Lake Assal, Africa	-156
Laguna del Carbón, South America	-105
Death Valley, North America	-86
Caspian Sea, Europe	-28
Lake Eyre, Australia	-16
Bentley Subglacial Trench, Antarctica	-2,555

Population of Each Continent, 2010

	Population	Percent of World Total
Asia	4,167,000,000	60.3
Africa	1,033,000,000	15.0
Europe	733,000,000	10.6
North America	547,000,000	7.9
South America	393,000,000	5.7
Australia	22,000,000	0.3
Islands of the Pacific	14,000,000	0.2

The Oceans

	Area (sq km)	Percent of Earth's Water Area
Pacific	169,479,000	46.8
Atlantic	91,526,400	25.3
Indian	74,694,800	20.6
Arctic	13,960,100	3.9

Deepest Point in Each Ocean

	Meters
Challenger Deep, Pacific Ocean	-10,971
Puerto Rico Trench, Atlantic Ocean	-8,605
Java Trench, Indian Ocean	-7,125
Molloy Deep, Arctic Ocean	-5,669

Major Seas

	Area (sq km)	Average Depth (meters)
Coral Sea	4,184,000	2,471
South China Sea	3,596,000	1,180
Caribbean Sea	2,834,000	2,596
Bering Sea	2,520,000	1,832
Mediterranean Sea	2,469,000	1,572
Sea of Okhotsk	1,625,000	814
Gulf of Mexico	1,532,000	1,544
Norwegian Sea	1,425,000	1,768
Greenland Sea	1,158,000	1,443
Sea of Japan (East Sea)	1,008,000	1,647

Longest Rivers

	Length (km)
Nile, Africa	7,081
Amazon, South America	6,679
Chang Jiang (Yangtze), Asia	6,244
Mississippi-Missouri, North America	6,083
Yenisey-Angara, Asia	5,810
Huang (Yellow), Asia	5,778
Ob-Irtysh, Asia	5,520
Amur, Asia	5,504
Lena, Asia	5,150
Congo, Africa	5,118

Metric Conversion Tables

SYMBOL	WHEN YOU KNOW	MULTIPLY BY	TO FIND	SYMBOL
		LENGTH		
cm	centimeters	0.393701	inches	in
m	meters	3.280840	feet	ft
m	meters	1.093613	yards	yd
km	kilometers	0.621371	miles	mi
		AREA		
cm²	square centimeters	0.155000	square inches	in²
m²	square meters	10.76391	square feet	ft²
m²	square meters	1.195990	square yards	yd²
km²	square kilometers	0.386102	square miles	mi²
ha	hectares	2.471054	acres	--
		MASS		
g	grams	0.035274	ounces	oz
kg	kilograms	2.204623	pounds	lb
t	metric tons	1.102311	short tons	--
		VOLUME		
mL	milliliters	0.061024	cubic inches	in³
mL	milliliters	0.033814	liquid ounces	liq oz
L	liters	2.113376	pints	pt
L	liters	1.056688	quarts	qt
L	liters	0.264172	gallons	gal
m³	cubic meters	35.31467	cubic feet	ft³
m³	cubic meters	1.307951	cubic yards	yd³
		TEMPERATURE		
°C	degrees Celsius (centigrade)	9/5 (1.8) then add 32	degrees Fahrenheit	°F

SYMBOL	WHEN YOU KNOW	MULTIPLY BY	TO FIND	SYMBOL
		LENGTH		
in	inches	2.54	centimeters	cm
ft	feet	0.3048	meters	m
yd	yards	0.9144	meters	m
mi	miles	1.609344	kilometers	km
		AREA		
in²	square inches	6.4516	square centimeters	cm²
ft²	square feet	0.092903	square meters	m²
yd²	square yards	0.836127	square meters	m²
mi²	square miles	2.589988	square kilometers	km²
--	acres	0.404686	hectares	ha
		MASS		
oz	ounces	28.349523	grams	g
lb	pounds	0.453592	kilograms	kg
--	short tons	0.907185	metric tons	t
		VOLUME		
in³	cubic inches	16.387064	milliliters	mL
liq oz	liquid ounces	29.57353	milliliters	mL
pt	pints	0.473176	liters	L
qt	quarts	0.946353	liters	L
gal	gallons	3.785412	liters	L
ft³	cubic feet	0.028317	cubic meters	m³
yd³	cubic yards	0.764555	cubic meters	m³
		TEMPERATURE		
°F	degrees Fahrenheit	5/9 (.555) after subtracting 32	degrees Celsius (centigrade)	°C

Aaglet — well
Aain — spring
Aauinat — spring
Āb — river, water
Ache — stream
Açude — reservoir
Ada,-sı — island
Adrar — mountain-s, plateau
Aguada — dry lake bed
Aguelt — water hole, well
'Ain, Aïn — spring, well
Aïoun-et — spring-s, well
Aivi — mountain
Akra, Akrotírio — cape, promontory
Alb — mountain, ridge
Alföld — plain
Alin' — mountain range
Alpe-n, -s — mountain-s
Altiplanicie — high plain, plateau
Alto — hill-s, mountain-s, ridge
Älv-en — river
Āmba — hill, mountain
Anou — well
Anse — bay, inlet
Ao — bay, cove, estuary
Ap — cape, point
Archipel, Archipiélago — archipelago
Arcipelago, Arkhipelag — archipelago
Arquipélago — archipelago
Arrecife-s — reef-s
Arroio, Arroyo — brook, gully, rivulet, stream
Ås — ridge
Ava — channel
Aylagy — gulf
'Ayn — spring, well
Ba — intermittent stream, river
Baai — bay, cove, lagoon
Bāb — gate, strait
Badia — bay
Bælt — strait
Bagh — bay
Bahar — drainage basin
Bahía — bay
Bahr, Baḩr — bay, lake, river, sea, wadi
Baía, Baie — bay
Bajo-s — shoal-s
Ban — village
Bañado-s — flooded area, wamp-s
Banc, Banco-s — bank-s, sandbank-s, shoal-s
Band — lake
Bandao — peninsula
Baño-s — hot spring-s, spa
Baraj-ı — dam, reservoir
Barra — bar, sandbank
Barrage, Barragem — dam, lake, reservoir
Barranca — gorge, ravine
Bazar — marketplace
Belentligi — plateau
Ben, Beinn — mountain
Belt — strait
Bereg — bank, coast, shore
Berg,-e — mountain-s
Bil — lake
Biq'at — plain, valley
Bir, Bîr, Bi'r — spring, well
Birket — lake, pool, swamp
Bjerg-e — mountain-s, range
Boca, Bocca — channel, river, mouth
Bocht — bay
Bodden — bay
Boğaz, -ı — strait
Bögeni — reservoir
Boka — gulf, mouth
Bol'sh-oy, -aya, -oye — big
Bolsón — inland basin
Boubairet — lagoon, lake
Bras — arm, branch of a stream
Braţ, -ul — arm, branch of a stream
Bræ-er — glacier
Bre, -en — glacier, ice cap
Bredning — bay, broad water
Bruch — marsh
Bucht — bay
Bugt-en — bay
Buḩayrat, Buheirat — lagoon, lake, marsh
Bukhta, Bukta, Bukt-en — bay
Bulak, Bulaq — spring
Bum — hill, mountain
Burnu, Burun — cape, point
Busen — gulf
Buuraha — hill-s, mountain-s
Büyük — big, large
Cabeza-s — head-s, summit-s
Cabo — cape
Cachoeira — rapids, waterfall
Cal — hill, peak
Caleta — cove, inlet
Campo-s — field-s, flat country
Canal — canal, channel, strait
Caño — channel, stream
Cao Nguyen — mountain, plateau
Cap, Capo — cape
Capitán — captain
Càrn — mountain
Castillo — castle, fort
Catarata-s — cataract-s, waterfall-s
Causse — upland
Çay — brook, stream
Cay-s, Cayo-s — island-s, key-s, shoal-s
Cerro-s — hill-s, peak-s
Chaîne, Chaînons — mountain chain, range
Chapada-s — plateau, upland-s
Chedo — archipelago
Chenal — river channel
Chersónisos — peninsula
Chhung — bay
Chi — lake
Chiang — bay
Chiao — cape, point, rock
Ch'ih — lake
Chink — escarpment
Chott — intermittent salt lake, salt marsh
Chou — island
Ch'ü — canal
Ch'üntao — archipelago, islands
Chute-s — cataract-s, waterfall-s
Chyrvony, -aya, -aye — red
Ciénaga — marsh
Cima — mountain, peak, summit
Ciudad — city
Co — lake
Col — pass
Collina, Colline — hill, mountains
Con — island
Cordillera — mountain chain
Corno — mountain, peak
Coronel — colonel
Corredeira — cascade, rapids
Costa — coast
Côte — coast, slope
Coxilha, Cuchilla — range of low hills
Crique — creek, stream
Csatorna — canal, channel
Cul de Sac — bay, inlet
Da — great, greater
Daban — pass
Dağ, -ı, Dagh — mountain
Dağlar, -ı — mountains
Dahr — cliff, mesa
Dake — mountain, peak
Dal-en — valley
Dala — steppe
Dan — cape, point
Danau — lake
Dao — island
Dar'ya — lake, river
Daryācheh — lake, marshy lake
Dasht — desert, plain
Dawan — pass
Dawḩat — bay, cove, inlet
Deniz, -i — sea
Dent-s — peak-s
Deo — pass
Desēt — hummock, island, land-tied island
Desierto — desert
Détroit — channel, strait
Dhar — hills, ridge, tableland
Ding — mountain
Distrito — district
Djebel — mountain, range
Do — island-s, rock-s
Doi — hill, mountain
Dome — ice dome
Dong — village
Dooxo — floodplain
Dzong — castle, fortress
Eiland-en — island-s
Eilean — island
Ejland — island-s
Elv — river
Embalse — lake, reservoir
Emi — mountain, rock
Enseada, Ensenada — bay, cove
Ér — rivulet, stream
Erg — sand dune region
Est — east
Estación — railroad station
Estany — lagoon, lake
Estero — estuary, inlet, lagoon, marsh
Estrecho — strait
Étang — lake, pond
Eylandt — island
Ežeras — lake
Ezers — lake
Falaise — cliff, escarpment
Farvand-et — channel, sound
Fell — mountain
Feng — mount, peak
Fiord-o — inlet, sound
Firn — snowfield
Fiume — river
Fjäll-et — mountain
Fjällen — mountains
Fjärd-en — fjord
Fjarđar, Fjörđur — fjord
Fjeld-e — mountain-s, nunatak-s
Fjell-ene — mountain-s
Fjöll — mountain-s
Fjord-en — inlet, fjord
Fleuve — river
Fljót — large river
Flói — bay, marshland
Foci — river mouths
Főcsatorna — principal canal
Foko — point
Förde — fjord, gulf, inlet
Forsen — rapids, waterfall
Fortaleza — fort, fortress
Fortín — fortified post
Foss-en — waterfall
Foum — pass, passage
Foz — mouth of a river
Fuerte — fort, fortress
Fwafwate — waterfalls
Gacan-ka — hill, peak
Gal — pond, spring, water hole, well
Gang — harbor
Gangri — peak, range
Gaoyuan — plateau
Garaet, Gara'et — lake, lake bed, salt lake
Gardaneh — pass
Garet — hill, mountain
Gat — channel
Gata — bay, inlet, lake
Gattet — channel, strait
Gaud — depression, saline tract
Gave — mountain stream
Gebel — mountain-s, range
Gebergte — mountain range
Gebirge — mountains, range
Geçidi — mountain pass, passage
Geçit — mountain pass, passage
Gezâir — islands
Gezîra-t, Gezîret — island, peninsula
Ghats — mountain range
Ghubb-at, -et — bay, gulf
Giri — mountain
Gjiri — bay
Gletscher — glacier
Gobernador — governor
Gobi — desert
Gol — river, stream
Göl, -ü — lake
Golets — mountain, peak
Golf, -e, -o — gulf
Gor-a, -y, Gór-a, -y — mountain,-s
Got — point
Gowd — depression
Goz — sand ridge
Gran, -de — great, large
Gryada — mountains, ridge
Guan — pass
Guba — bay, gulf
Guelta — well
Guntō — archipelago
Gunung — mountain
Gura — mouth, passage
Guyot — table mount
Ḩadabat — plateau
Haehyŏp — strait
Haff — lagoon
Hai — lake, sea
Haihsia — strait
Haixia — channel, strait
Hakau — reef, rock
Hakuchi — anchorage
Halvø, Halvøy-a — peninsula
Hama — beach
Hamada, Ḩammādah — rocky desert
Hamn — harbor, port
Hāmūn, Hamun — depression, lake
Hana — cape, point
Hantō — peninsula
Har — hill, mound, mountain
Ḩarrat — lava field
Hasi, Hassi — spring, well
Hauteur — elevation, height
Hav-et — sea
Havn, Havre — harbor, port
Hawr — lake, marsh
Hāyk' — lake, reservoir
He — canal, lake, river
Hegy, -ség — mountain, -s, range
Heiau — temple
Hoek — hook, point
Hög-en — high, hill
Höhe, -n — height, high
Høj — height, hill
Holm, -e, Holmene — island-s, islet -s
Ḩolot — dunes
Hon — island-s
Hor-a, -y — mountain, -s
Horn — horn, peak
Houma — point
Hoved — headland, peninsula, point
Hraun — lava field
Hsü — island
Hu — lake, reservoir
Huk — cape, point
Hüyük — hill, mound
Idehan — sand dunes
Igarapé — creek, stream
Île-s, Ilha-s, Illa-s, Îlot-s — island-s, islet-s
Îlet, Ilhéu-s — islet, -s
Irhil — mountain-s
'Irq — sand dune-s
Isblink — glacier, ice field
Is-en — glacier
Isebræ — glacier
Isfjord — ice fjord
Iskappe — ice cap
Isla-s, Islote — island-s, islet
Isol-a, -e — island, -s
Isstrøm — glacier, ice field
Istmo — isthmus
Iwa — island, islet, rock
Jabal, Jebel — mountain-s, range
Järv, -i, Jaure, Javrre — lake
Jazā'ir, Jazīrat, Jazīreh — island-s
Jehīl — lake
Jezero, Jezioro — lake
Jiang — river, stream
Jiao — cape
Jibāl — hill, mountain, ridge
Jima — island-s, rock-s
Jøkel, Jökull — glacier, ice cap
Joki, Jokka — river
Jökulsá — river from a glacier
Jūn — bay
Kaap — cape
Kap, Kapp — cape
Kafr — village
Kaikyō — channel, strait
Kaise — mountain
Kaiwan — bay, gulf, sea
Kanal — canal, channel
Kangerlua — fjord
Kangri — mountain, peak
Kavīr — salt desert
Kefar — village
Kënet' — lagoon, lake
Kep — cape, point
Kepulauan — archipelago, islands
Khalīg, Khalīj — bay, gulf
Khirb-at, -et — ancient site, ruins
Khrebet — mountain range
Kinh — canal
Klint — bluff, cliff
Kō — bay, cove, harbor
Ko — island, lake
Koh — island, mountain, range
Köl-i — lake
Kólpos — gulf
Kong — king, mountain
Körfez, -i — bay, gulf
Kosa — spit of land
Kou — estuary, river mouth
Kowtal-e — pass
Kronprince — crown prince
Krasn-yy, -aya, -oye — red
Kryazh — mountain range, ridge
Kuala — estuary, river mouth
Kuan — mountain pass
Kūh, Kūhhā — mountain-s, range
Kul', Kuli — lake
Kum — sandy desert
Kundo — archipelago
Kuppe — hill-s, mountain-s
Kust — coast, shore
Kyst — coast
Kyun — island
La — pass
Lac, Lac-ul, -us — lake
Lae — cape, point
Lago, -a — lagoon, lake
Lagoen, Lagune — lagoon
Laguna-s — lagoon-s, lake-s
Laht — bay, gulf, harbor
Laje — reef, rock ledge
Laut — sea
Lednik — glacier
Leida — channel
Lhari — mountain
Li — village
Liedao — archipelago, islands
Liehtao — archipelago, islands
Lille — little, small
Liman-ı — bay, estuary
Límni — lake
Ling — mountain-s, range
Linn — pool, waterfall
Lintasan — passage
Liqen — lake
Llano-s — plain-s

Loch, Lough — lake, arm of the sea
Loma-s — hill-s, knoll-s

Mal — mountain, range
Mal-yy, -aya, -oye — little, small
Mamarr — pass, path
Man — bay
Mar, Mare — large lake, sea
Marsa, Marsá — bay, inlet
Masabb — mouth of river
Massif — mountain-s
Mauna — mountain
Mēda — plain
Meer — lake, sea
Melkosopochnik — undulating plain
Mesa, Meseta — plateau, tableland
Mierzeja — sandspit
Minami — south
Mios — island
Misaki — cape, peninsula, point
Mochun — passage
Molsron — harbor
Mong — town, village
Mont-e, -i, -ii, -s — mount, -ain, -s
Montagne, -s — mount, -ain, -s
Montaña, -s — mountain, -s
More — sea
Morne — hill, peak
Morro — bluff, headland, hill
Motu, -s — islands
Mouïet — well
Mouillage — anchorage
Muang — town, village
Mui — cape, point
Mull — headland, promontory
Munkhafad — depression
Munte — mountain
Munţi-i — mountains
Muong — town, village
Mynydd — mountain
Mys — cape

Nacional — national
Nada — gulf, sea
Næs, Näs — cape, point
Nafūd — area of dunes, desert
Nagor'ye — mountain range, plateau
Nahar, Nahr — river, stream
Nakhon — town
Namakzār — salt waste
Ne — island, reef, rock-s
Neem — cape, point, promontory
Nes, Ness — peninsula, point
Nevado-s — snow-capped mountain-s
Nez — cape, promontory
Ni — village
Nísi, Nísia, Nisís, Nísoi — island-s, islet-s
Nisídhes — islets
Nizhn-iy, -yaya, -eye — lower
Nizmennost' — low country
Noord — north
Nord-re — north-ern
Nørre — north-ern
Nos — cape, nose, point
Nosy — island, reef, rock
Nov-yy, -aya, -aye, -oye — new
Nudo — mountain
Numa — lake
Nunaa — area, region
Nunaat — area, island
Nunatak, -s, -ker — peak-s surrounded by ice cap
Nur — lake, salt lake
Nuruu — mountain range, ridge
Nut-en — peak
Nuur — lake

O-n, Ø-er — island-s
Oblast' — administrative division
Oblast' — province, region
Oceanus — ocean
Odde-n — cape, point
Øer-ne — islands
Oglat — group of wells
Oguilet — well
Ór-os, -i — mountain, -s
Órmos — bay, port
Ort — place, point
Øst-er — east
Ostrov, -a, Ostrv-o, -a — island, -s
Otoci, Otok — islands, island
Ouadi, Oued — river, watercourse
Øy-a — island
Øyane — islands
Ozer-o, -a — lake, -s

Pää — mountain, point
Palus — marsh
Pampa-s — grassy plain-s
Pantà — lake, reservoir
Pantanal — marsh, swamp
Pao, P'ao — lake
Parbat — mountain
Parque — park
Pas, -ul — pass
Paso, Passo — pass
Passe — channel, pass
Pasul — pass
Pedra — rock
Pegunungan — mountain range
Pellg — bay, bight
Peña — cliff, rock
Pendi — basin
Penedo-s — rock-s
Péninsule — peninsula
Peñón — point, rock
Pereval — mountain pass
Pertuis — strait
Peski — sands, sandy region
Phnom — hill, mountain, range
Phou — mountain range
Phu — mountain
Piana-o — plain
Pic, Pik, Piz — peak
Picacho — mountain, peak
Pico-s — peak-s
Pistyll — waterfall
Piton-s — peak-s
Pivdennyy — southern
Plaja, Playa — beach, inlet, shore
Planalto, Plato — plateau
Planina — mountain, plateau
Plassen — lake
Ploskogor'ye — plateau, upland
Pointe — point
Polder — reclaimed land
Poluostrov — peninsula
Pongo — water gap
Ponta, -l — cape, point
Ponte — bridge
Poolsaar — peninsula
Portezuelo — pass
Porto — port
Poulo — island
Praia — beach, seashore
Presa — reservoir
Presidente — president
Presqu'île — peninsula
Prins — prince
Prinsesse — princess
Prokhod — pass
Proliv — strait
Promontorio — promontory
Průsmyk — mountain pass
Przylądek — cape
Puerto — bay, pass, port
Pulao — island-s
Pulau, Pulo — island
Puncak — peak, summit, top
Punt, Punta, -n — point, -s
Pun — peak
Pu'u — hill, mountain
Puy — peak

Qā' — depression, marsh, mud flat
Qal'at — fort
Qal'eh — castle, fort
Qanâ — canal
Qārat — hill-s, mountain-s
Qaşr — castle, fort, hill
Qila — fort
Qiryat — settlement, suburb
Qolleh — peak
Qooriga — anchorage, bay
Qoz — dunes, sand ridge
Qu — canal
Quebrada — ravine, stream
Qullai — peak, summit
Qum — desert, sand
Qundao — archipelago, islands
Qurayyāt — hills

Raas — cape, point
Rabt — hill
Rada — roadstead
Rade — anchorage, roadstead
Rags — point
Ramat — hill, mountain
Rand — ridge of hills
Rann — swamp
Raqaba — wadi, watercourse
Ras, Râs, Ra's — cape
Ravnina — plain
Récif-s — reef-s
Regreg — marsh
Represa — reservoir
Reservatório — reservoir
Restinga — barrier, sand area
Rettō — chain of islands
Ri — mountain range, village
Ría — estuary
Ribeirão — stream
Río, Rio — river
Roca-s — cliff, rock-s
Roche-r, -s — rock-s
Rosh — mountain, point
Rt — cape, point
Rubha — headland
Rupes — scarp

Saar — island
Saari, Sari — island
Sabkha-t, Sabkhet — lagoon, marsh, salt lake
Sagar — lake, sea
Sahara, Şaḩrā' — desert
Sahl — plain
Saki — cape, point
Salar — salt flat
Salina — salt pan
Salin-as, -es — salt flat-s, salt marsh-es
Salto — waterfall
Sammyaku — mountain range
San — hill, mountain
San, -ta, -to — saint
Sandur — sandy area
Sankt — saint
Sanmaek — mountain range
São — saint
Sarīr — gravel desert
Sasso — mountain, stone
Savane — savanna
Scoglio — reef, rock
Se — reef, rock-s, shoal-s
Sebjet — salt lake, salt marsh
Sebkha — salt lake, salt marsh
Sebkhet — lagoon, salt lake
See — lake, sea
Selat — strait
Selkä — lake, ridge
Semenanjung — peninsula
Sen — mountain
Seno — bay, gulf
Sermeq — glacier
Sermia — glacier
Serra, Serranía — range of hills or mountains
Severn-yy, -aya, -oye — northern
Sgùrr — peak
Sha — island, shoal
Sha'īb — ravine, watercourse
Shamo — desert
Shan — island-s, mountain-s, range
Shankou — mountain pass
Shanmo — mountain range
Sharm — cove, creek, harbor
Shatt, Shaţţ — large river
Shi — administrative division
Shi — municipality
Shima — island-s, rock-s
Shō — island, reef, rock
Shotō — archipelago
Shott — intermittent salt lake
Shuiku — reservoir
Shuitao — channel
Shyghanaghy — bay, gulf
Sierra — mountain range
Silsilesi — mountain chain, ridge
Sint — saint
Sinus — bay, sea
Sjö-n — lake
Skarv-et — barren mountain
Skerry — rock
Slieve — mountain
Sø-er — lake-s
Sønder, Søndre — south-ern
Sopka — conical mountain, volcano
Sor — lake, salt lake
Sør, Sör — south-ern
Sory — salt lake, salt marsh
Spitz-e — peak, point, top
Sredn-iy, -yaya, -eye — central, middle
Stagno — lake, pond
Stantsiya — station
Stausee — reservoir
Stenón — channel, strait
Step'-i — steppe-s
Štít — summit, top
Stor-e — big, great
Straat — strait
Straum-en — current-s
Strelka — spit of land
Stretet, Stretto — strait
Su — reef, river, rock, stream
Sud — south
Sudo — channel, strait
Suidō — channel, strait
Şummān — rocky desert
Sund — sound, strait
Sunden — channel, inlet, sound
Svyat-oy, -aya, -oye — holy, saint
Sziget — island

Tagh — mountain-s
Tall — hill, mound
T'an — lake
Tanezrouft — desert
Tang — plain, steppe
Tangi — peninsula, point
Tanjong, Tanjung — cape, point
Tao — island-s
Tarso — hill-s, mountain-s
Tassili — plateau, upland
Tau — mountain-s, range
Taūy — hills, mountains
Tchabal — mountain-s
Te Ava — tidal flat
Tel-l — hill, mound
Telok, Teluk — bay
Tepe, -si — hill, peak
Tepuí — mesa, mountain
Terara — hill, mountain, peak
Testa — bluff, head
Thale — lake
Thang — plain, steppe
Tien — lake
Tierra — land, region
Ting — hill, mountain
Tir'at — canal
Tó — lake, pool
To, Tō — island-s, rock-s
Tonle — lake
Tope — hill, mountain, peak
Top-pen — peak-s
Träsk — bog, lake
Tso — lake
Tsui — cape, point
Tübegi — peninsula
Tulu — hill, mountain
Tunturi-t — hill-s, mountain-s

Uad — wadi, watercourse
Udde-m — point
Ujong, Ujung — cape, point
Umi — bay, lagoon, lake
Ura — bay, inlet, lake
'Urūq — dune area
Uul, Uula — mountain, range
'Uyûn — springs

Vaara — mountain
Vaart — canal
Vær — fishing station
Vaïn — channel, strait
Valle, Vallée — valley, wadi
Vallen — waterfall
Valli — lagoon, lake
Vallis — valley
Vanua — land
Varre — mountain
Vatn, Vatten, Vatnet — lake, water
Veld — grassland, plain
Verkhn-iy, -yaya, -eye — higher, upper
Vesi — lake, water
Vest-er — west
Via — road
Vidda — plateau
Vig, Vík, Vik, -en — bay, cove
Vinh — bay, gulf
Vodokhranilishche — reservoir
Vodoskhovyshche — reservoir
Volcan, Volcán — volcano
Vostochn-yy, -aya, -oye — eastern
Vötn — stream
Vozvyshennost' — plateau, upland
Vozyera, -yero, -yera — lake-s
Vrchovina — mountains
Vrch-y — mountain-s
Vrh — hill, mountain
Vrŭkh — mountain
Vyaliki, -ikaya, -ikaye — big, large
Vysočina — highland

Wabē — stream
Wadi, Wâdi, Wādī — valley, watercourse
Wâhât, Wāḩat — oasis
Wald — forest, wood
Wan — bay, gulf
Water — harbor
Webi — stream
Wiek — cove, inlet

Xia — gorge, strait
Xiao — lesser, little

Yanchi — salt lake
Yang — ocean
Yarymadasy — peninsula
Yazovir — reservoir
Yŏlto — island group
Yoma — mountain range
Yü — island
Yumco — lake
Yunhe — canal
Yuzhn-yy, -aya, -oye — southern

Zaki — cape, point
Zaliv — bay, gulf
Zan — mountain, ridge
Zangbo — river, stream
Zapadn-yy, -aya, -oye — western
Zatoka — bay, gulf
Zee — bay, sea
Zemlya — land
Zhotasy — mountains

POPULATION OF URBAN AGGLOMERATIONS WITH 750,000 INHABITANTS OR MORE

URBAN AGGLOMERATION	COUNTRY	POPULATION
Tokyo	Japan	36,669,000
Delhi	India	22,157,000
São Paulo	Brazil	20,262,000
Mumbai (Bombay)	India	20,041,000
Mexico City	Mexico	19,460,000
New York-Newark	U.S.	19,425,000
Shanghai	China	16,575,000
Kolkata (Calcutta)	India	15,552,000
Dhaka	Bangladesh	14,648,000
Karachi	Pakistan	13,125,000
Buenos Aires	Argentina	13,074,000
Los Angeles-Long Beach-Santa Ana	U.S.	12,762,000
Beijing	China	12,385,000
Rio de Janeiro	Brazil	11,950,000
Manila	Philippines	11,628,000
Osaka-Kobe	Japan	11,337,000
Cairo	Egypt	11,001,000
Lagos	Nigeria	10,578,000
Moscow	Russia	10,550,000
Istanbul	Turkey	10,525,000
Paris	France	10,485,000
Seoul	South Korea	9,773,000
Chongqing	China	9,401,000
Jakarta	Indonesia	9,210,000
Chicago	U.S.	9,204,000
Shenzhen	China	9,005,000
Lima	Peru	8,941,000
Guangzhou, Guangdong	China	8,884,000
Kinshasa	Dem. Rep. of the Congo	8,754,000
London	U.K.	8,631,000
Bogotá	Colombia	8,500,000
Tianjin	China	7,884,000
Wuhan	China	7,681,000
Chennai (Madras)	India	7,547,000
Tehran	Iran	7,241,000
Bangalore	India	7,218,000
Lahore	Pakistan	7,132,000
Hong Kong, Hong Kong S.A.R.	China	7,069,000
Bangkok	Thailand	6,976,000
Hyderabad	India	6,751,000
Ho Chi Minh City	Vietnam	6,167,000
Santiago	Chile	5,952,000
Baghdad	Iraq	5,891,000
Belo Horizonte	Brazil	5,852,000
Madrid	Spain	5,851,000
Miami	U.S.	5,750,000
Ahmadabad	India	5,717,000
Philadelphia	U.S.	5,626,000
Toronto	Canada	5,449,000
Dongguan, Guangdong	China	5,347,000
Khartoum	Sudan	5,172,000
Shenyang	China	5,166,000
Barcelona	Spain	5,083,000
Pune (Poona)	India	5,002,000
Foshan	China	4,969,000
Chittagong	Bangladesh	4,962,000
Chengdu	China	4,961,000
Dallas-Fort Worth	U.S.	4,951,000
Riyadh	Saudi Arabia	4,848,000
Singapore	Singapore	4,837,000
Luanda	Angola	4,772,000
Xi'an, Shaanxi	China	4,747,000
Atlanta	U.S.	4,691,000
Houston	U.S.	4,605,000
Boston	U.S.	4,593,000
St. Petersburg	Russia	4,575,000
Nanjing, Jiangsu	China	4,519,000
Washington, D.C.	U.S.	4,460,000
Sydney	Australia	4,429,000
Guadalajara	Mexico	4,402,000
Alexandria	Egypt	4,387,000
Yangon	Myanmar	4,350,000
Haerbin	China	4,251,000
Detroit	U.S.	4,200,000
Surat	India	4,168,000
Abidjan	Côte d'Ivoire	4,125,000
Pôrto Alegre	Brazil	4,092,000
Salvador	Brazil	3,918,000
Ankara	Turkey	3,906,000
Brasília	Brazil	3,905,000
Monterrey	Mexico	3,896,000
Recife	Brazil	3,871,000
Hangzhou	China	3,860,000
Melbourne	Australia	3,853,000
Montréal	Canada	3,783,000
Kabul	Afghanistan	3,731,000
Fortaleza	Brazil	3,719,000
Phoenix-Mesa	U.S.	3,684,000
Johannesburg	South Africa	3,670,000
Changchun	China	3,597,000
Medellín	Colombia	3,594,000
San Francisco-Oakland	U.S.	3,541,000
Nairobi	Kenya	3,523,000
Shantou	China	3,502,000
Curitiba	Brazil	3,462,000
Berlin	Germany	3,450,000
Busan	South Korea	3,425,000
Cape Town	South Africa	3,405,000
Kano	Nigeria	3,395,000
Kanpur	India	3,364,000
Rome	Italy	3,362,000
Dar es Salaam	Tanzania	3,349,000
Qingdao	China	3,323,000
Dalian	China	3,306,000
Casablanca	Morocco	3,284,000
Tel Aviv-Jaffa	Israel	3,272,000
Nagoya	Japan	3,267,000
Athens	Greece	3,257,000
Jinan, Shandong	China	3,237,000
Jiddah	Saudi Arabia	3,234,000
Ekurhuleni (East Rand)	S. Africa	3,202,000
Seattle	U.S.	3,171,000
Taiyuan, Shanxi	China	3,154,000
Jaipur	India	3,131,000
Kunming	China	3,116,000
Caracas	Venezuela	3,090,000
Aleppo	Syria	3,087,000
San Diego	U.S.	2,999,000
Milan	Italy	2,967,000
Zhengzhou	China	2,966,000
Addis Ababa	Ethiopia	2,930,000
Durban	South Africa	2,879,000
Lucknow	India	2,873,000
Dakar	Senegal	2,863,000
Faisalabad	Pakistan	2,849,000
Ibadan	Nigeria	2,837,000
P'yongyang	North Korea	2,833,000
Lisbon	Portugal	2,824,000
Campinas	Brazil	2,818,000
Fukuoka-Kitakyushu	Japan	2,816,000
Hanoi	Vietnam	2,814,000
Kiev	Ukraine	2,805,000
Algiers	Algeria	2,800,000
Fuzhou, Fujian	China	2,787,000
San Juan	Puerto Rico	2,743,000
Izmir	Turkey	2,723,000
Nanchang	China	2,701,000
Minneapolis-St. Paul	U.S.	2,693,000
Guayaquil	Ecuador	2,690,000
Sapporo	Japan	2,687,000
Wuxi, Jiangsu	China	2,682,000
Wenzhou	China	2,659,000
Mashhad	Iran	2,652,000
Taipei	China	2,633,000
Nagpur	India	2,607,000
Damascus	Syria	2,597,000
Incheon	South Korea	2,583,000
Surabaya	Indonesia	2,509,000
Shijiazhuang	China	2,487,000
Daegu	South Korea	2,458,000
Zibo	China	2,456,000
Changsha, Hunan	China	2,415,000
Bandung	Indonesia	2,412,000
Hefei	China	2,404,000
Cali	Colombia	2,401,000
Ürümqi	China	2,398,000
Suzhou, Jiangsu	China	2,398,000
Denver-Aurora	U.S.	2,394,000
Tampa-St. Petersburg	U.S.	2,387,000
Sendai	Japan	2,376,000
Sana'a'	Yemen	2,342,000
Accra	Ghana	2,342,000
Patna	India	2,321,000
Baltimore	U.S.	2,320,000
Puebla	Mexico	2,315,000
Kuwait City	Kuwait	2,305,000
Birmingham	U.K.	2,302,000
Lanzhou	China	2,285,000
Naples	Italy	2,276,000
St. Louis	U.S.	2,259,000
Manchester	U.K.	2,253,000
Vancouver	Canada	2,220,000
Ningbo	China	2,217,000
Zhongshan	China	2,211,000
Tashkent	Uzbekistan	2,210,000
Xiamen	China	2,207,000
Maracaibo	Venezuela	2,192,000
Belém	Brazil	2,191,000
Santo Domingo	Dom. Rep.	2,180,000
Indore	India	2,173,000
Guiyang	China	2,154,000
Goiânia	Brazil	2,146,000
Port-au-Prince	Haiti	2,143,000
Xuzhou	China	2,142,000
Medan	Indonesia	2,131,000
Havana	Cuba	2,130,000
Douala	Cameroon	2,125,000
Nanning	China	2,096,000
Hiroshima	Japan	2,081,000
Changzhou, Jiangsu	China	2,062,000
Asunción	Paraguay	2,030,000
Rawalpindi	Pakistan	2,026,000
Abuja	Nigeria	1,995,000
Baku	Azerbaijan	1,972,000
Brisbane	Australia	1,970,000
Hai Phòng	Vietnam	1,970,000
Portland	U.S.	1,944,000
Cleveland	U.S.	1,942,000
Beirut	Lebanon	1,937,000
Bucharest	Romania	1,934,000
Baotou	China	1,932,000
Las Vegas	U.S.	1,916,000
Ouagadougou	Burkina Faso	1,908,000
Bruxelles-Brussel	Belgium	1,904,000
Jilin	China	1,888,000
Pittsburgh	U.S.	1,887,000
Antananarivo	Madagascar	1,879,000
Vadodara	India	1,872,000
Tangshan, Hebei	China	1,870,000
Barranquilla	Colombia	1,867,000
Minsk	Belarus	1,852,000
Grande Vitória	Brazil	1,848,000
Quito	Ecuador	1,846,000
Bhopal	India	1,843,000
Kumasi	Ghana	1,834,000
Baixada Santista	Brazil	1,819,000
Riverside-San Bernardino	U.S.	1,807,000
Coimbatore	India	1,807,000
Kyoto	Japan	1,804,000
Rabat	Morocco	1,802,000
Yaoundé	Cameroon	1,801,000
Hamburg	Germany	1,786,000
Manaus	Brazil	1,775,000
Valencia	Venezuela	1,770,000
Ludhiana	India	1,760,000
Esfahan	Iran	1,742,000
San Jose	U.S.	1,718,000
Warsaw	Poland	1,712,000
Budapest	Hungary	1,706,000
Vienna	Austria	1,706,000
Agra	India	1,703,000
Bamako	Mali	1,699,000
Weifang	China	1,698,000
Cincinnati	U.S.	1,686,000
Khulna	Bangladesh	1,682,000
La Paz	Bolivia	1,673,000
Lomé	Togo	1,667,000
Turin	Italy	1,665,000
Tijuana	Mexico	1,664,000
Anshan, Liaoning	China	1,663,000
Sacramento	U.S.	1,660,000
Multan	Pakistan	1,659,000
Maputo	Mozambique	1,655,000
Conakry	Guinea	1,653,000
Gujranwala	Pakistan	1,652,000
Santa Cruz	Bolivia	1,649,000
Montevideo	Uruguay	1,635,000
Harare	Zimbabwe	1,632,000
Visakhapatnam	India	1,625,000
Kaohsiung	China	1,611,000
Kochi (Cochin)	India	1,610,000
Perth	Australia	1,599,000
Kampala	Uganda	1,598,000
Hyderabad	Pakistan	1,590,000
Hohhot	China	1,589,000
Nashik	India	1,588,000
Bursa	Turkey	1,588,000
Qiqihaer	China	1,588,000
Haikou	China	1,586,000
Karaj	Iran	1,584,000
Toluca de Lerdo	Mexico	1,582,000
León de los Aldamas	Mexico	1,571,000
Dubai	U.A.E.	1,567,000
San Salvador	El Salvador	1,565,000
Phnom Penh	Cambodia	1,562,000
Kaduna	Nigeria	1,561,000
West Yorkshire	U.K.	1,547,000
Daqing	China	1,546,000
Lubumbashi	Dem. Rep. of the Congo	1,543,000
Luoyang	China	1,539,000
Virginia Beach	U.S.	1,534,000
Yantai	China	1,526,000
San Antonio	U.S.	1,521,000
Kuala Lumpur	Malaysia	1,519,000
Davao	Philippines	1,519,000
Kansas City	U.S.	1,513,000
Daejon	South Korea	1,509,000
Mogadishu	Somalia	1,500,000
Meerut	India	1,494,000
Córdoba	Argentina	1,493,000
Indianapolis	U.S.	1,490,000
Mbuji-Mayi	Dem. Rep. of the Congo	1,488,000
Mecca	Saudi Arabia	1,484,000
Tabriz	Iran	1,483,000
Gwangju	South Korea	1,476,000
Marseille-Aix-en-Provence	France	1,469,000
Lyon	France	1,468,000
San José	Costa Rica	1,461,000
Kharkiv	Ukraine	1,453,000
Lusaka	Zambia	1,451,000
Mosul	Iraq	1,447,000
Varanasi (Benares)	India	1,432,000
Pretoria	South Africa	1,429,000
Milwaukee	U.S.	1,428,000
Linyi, Shandong	China	1,427,000
Nantong	China	1,423,000
Asansol	India	1,423,000
Peshawar	Pakistan	1,422,000

Urban Agglomeration	Country	Population
Auckland	New Zealand	1,404,000
Orlando	U.S.	1,400,000
Xiangfan, Hubei	China	1,399,000
Novosibirsk	Russia	1,397,000
Huainan	China	1,396,000
Ciudad Juárez	Mexico	1,394,000
Jamshedpur	India	1,387,000
Huizhou	China	1,384,000
Almaty	Kazakhstan	1,383,000
Panama City	Panama	1,378,000
Fushun, Liaoning	China	1,378,000
Jabalpur	India	1,367,000
Madurai	India	1,365,000
Adana	Turkey	1,361,000
Rajkot	India	1,357,000
Porto	Portugal	1,355,000
Liuzhou	China	1,352,000
Munich	Germany	1,349,000
Yekaterinburg	Russia	1,344,000
Taizhou, Zhejiang	China	1,338,000
Dhanbad	India	1,328,000
Homs	Syria	1,328,000
Brazzaville	Congo	1,323,000
Providence	U.S.	1,317,000
Natal	Brazil	1,316,000
Columbus, Ohio	U.S.	1,313,000
Benin City	Nigeria	1,302,000
Shiraz	Iran	1,299,000
Amritsar	India	1,297,000
Semarang	Indonesia	1,296,000
Ujung Pandang	Indonesia	1,294,000
Yancheng, Jiangsu	China	1,289,000
Stockholm	Sweden	1,285,000
Grande São Luís	Brazil	1,283,000
Allahabad	India	1,277,000
Nizhniy Novgorod	Russia	1,267,000
Xining	China	1,261,000
Zhuhai	China	1,252,000
Taichung	China	1,251,000
Datong, Shanxi	China	1,251,000
Handan	China	1,249,000
Palembang	Indonesia	1,244,000
Taian, Shandong	China	1,239,000
Rosario	Argentina	1,231,000
Srinagar	India	1,216,000
Austin	U.S.	1,215,000
Baoding	China	1,213,000
Vijayawada	India	1,207,000
Torreón	Mexico	1,199,000
Aurangabad	India	1,198,000
Sofia	Bulgaria	1,196,000
Maceió	Brazil	1,192,000
Copenhagen	Denmark	1,186,000
Calgary	Canada	1,182,000
Ottawa-Gatineau	Canada	1,182,000
Barquisimeto	Venezuela	1,180,000
Zaozhuang	China	1,175,000
Durg-Bhilainagar	India	1,172,000
Glasgow	U.K.	1,170,000
Adelaide	Australia	1,168,000
Prague	Czech Republic	1,162,000
Zurich	Switzerland	1,150,000
Vereeniging	South Africa	1,143,000
Kazan	Russia	1,140,000
Solapur	India	1,133,000
Suweon	South Korea	1,132,000
Samara	Russia	1,131,000
Anyang	China	1,130,000
Klang	Malaysia	1,128,000
Omsk	Russia	1,124,000
Tbilisi	Georgia	1,120,000
Ranchi	India	1,119,000
Memphis	U.S.	1,117,000
Belgrade	Serbia	1,117,000
Helsinki	Finland	1,117,000
Edmonton	Canada	1,113,000
Yerevan	Armenia	1,112,000
Gaziantep	Turkey	1,109,000
Tripoli	Libya	1,108,000
Amman	Jordan	1,105,000
Port Harcourt	Nigeria	1,104,000
Guatemala City	Guatemala	1,104,000
Medina	Saudi Arabia	1,104,000
Jiangmen	China	1,103,000
Hengyang	China	1,099,000
Dublin	Ireland	1,099,000
Yueyang	China	1,096,000
Chelyabinsk	Russia	1,094,000
Bucaramanga	Colombia	1,092,000
Putian	China	1,085,000
Ulsan	South Korea	1,081,000
Yangzhou	China	1,080,000
Jining, Shandong	China	1,077,000
Norte/Nordeste Catarinense	Brazil	1,069,000
Quanzhou	China	1,068,000
Port Elizabeth	South Africa	1,068,000
Fès	Morocco	1,065,000
Jodhpur	India	1,061,000
Ahvaz	Iran	1,060,000
Maracay	Venezuela	1,057,000
Bridgeport-Stamford	U.S.	1,055,000
Guwahati (Gauhati)	India	1,053,000
Florianópolis	Brazil	1,049,000
Chandigarh	India	1,049,000
Amsterdam	Netherlands	1,049,000
San Luis Potosí	Mexico	1,049,000
Niamey	Niger	1,048,000
Rostov-on-Don	Russia	1,046,000
Buffalo	U.S.	1,045,000
Bogor	Indonesia	1,044,000
Zhangjiakou	China	1,043,000
Charlotte	U.S.	1,043,000
Jixi, Heilongjiang	China	1,042,000
Qom	Iran	1,042,000
Jingzhou	China	1,039,000
Gwalior	India	1,039,000
Kathmandu	Nepal	1,037,000
Haifa	Israel	1,036,000
Huambo	Angola	1,034,000
Mandalay	Myanmar	1,034,000
Lille	France	1,033,000
Ogbomosho	Nigeria	1,032,000
Querétaro	Mexico	1,031,000
Tegucigalpa	Honduras	1,028,000
Zhuzhou	China	1,025,000
Pingdingshan, Henan	China	1,024,000
Nay Pyi Taw	Myanmar	1,024,000
Ufa	Russia	1,023,000
Jacksonville, Florida	U.S.	1,022,000
Xianyang, Shaanxi	China	1,019,000
Xinxiang	China	1,016,000
João Pessoa	Brazil	1,015,000
Mérida	Mexico	1,015,000
Rotterdam	Netherlands	1,010,000
Tiruchirappalli	India	1,010,000
Erbil	Iraq	1,009,000
Odesa	Ukraine	1,009,000
Zhenjiang, Jiangsu	China	1,007,000
Kozhikode (Calicut)	India	1,007,000
Thiruvananthapuram	India	1,006,000
Mianyang, Sichuan	China	1,006,000
Dnipropetrovsk	Ukraine	1,004,000
Mombasa	Kenya	1,003,000
Cologne	Germany	1,001,000
Johore Bharu	Malaysia	999,000
Huai'an	China	998,000
Salt Lake City	U.S.	997,000
Zhanjiang	China	996,000
Guilin	China	991,000
Perm	Russia	982,000
Louisville	U.S.	979,000
Konya	Turkey	978,000
Volgograd	Russia	977,000
Nice-Cannes	France	977,000
Maiduguri	Nigeria	970,000
Benxi	China	969,000
Ulaanbaatar	Mongolia	966,000
Donetsk	Ukraine	966,000
Antwerpen	Belgium	965,000
Zaria	Nigeria	963,000
Cartagena	Colombia	962,000
Huaibei	China	962,000
Krasnoyarsk	Russia	961,000
Goyang	South Korea	961,000
Yichang	China	959,000
Seongnam	South Korea	955,000
Dongying	China	949,000
Hubli-Dharwad	India	946,000
Managua	Nicaragua	944,000
Richmond	U.S.	944,000
Raipur	India	943,000
Mysore	India	942,000
Hartford	U.S.	942,000
Kigali	Rwanda	939,000
Mexicali	Mexico	934,000
Salem	India	932,000
Marrakech	Morocco	928,000
Aguascalientes	Mexico	926,000
Xiangtan, Hunan	China	926,000
Basra	Iraq	923,000
Zigong	China	918,000
Mendoza	Argentina	917,000
Jalandhar	India	917,000
Bengbu	China	914,000
Toulouse	France	912,000
Bhubaneswar	India	912,000
Puning	China	911,000
Nashville-Davidson	U.S.	911,000
Yinchuan	China	911,000
Bucheon	South Korea	909,000
Wuhu, Anhui	China	908,000
Ad-Dammam	Saudi Arabia	902,000
Freetown	Sierra Leone	901,000
Jiaozuo	China	900,000
Teresina	Brazil	900,000
Hamah	Syria	897,000
Qinhuangdao	China	893,000
Newcastle upon Tyne	U.K.	891,000
Lufeng	China	889,000
Oslo	Norway	888,000
Yamoussoukro	Côte d'Ivoire	885,000
Kota	India	884,000
Neijiang	China	883,000
Kananga	Dem. Rep. of the Congo	878,000
Rajshahi	Bangladesh	878,000
Lianyungang	China	878,000
Palermo	Italy	875,000
Fuyang	China	874,000
Valparaíso	Chile	873,000
Bareilly	India	868,000
Nanyang, Henan	China	867,000
Lilongwe	Malawi	865,000
Bishkek	Kyrgyzstan	864,000
Aligarh	India	863,000
Cebu	Philippines	860,000
Bhiwandi	India	859,000
Jinjiang	China	858,000
New Orleans	U.S.	858,000
Jammu	India	857,000
Jinzhou	China	857,000
Blantyre-Limbe	Malawi	856,000
Islamabad	Pakistan	856,000
Jieyang	China	855,000
Zamboanga	Philippines	854,000
Tucson	U.S.	853,000
Shaoxing	China	853,000
Luzhou	China	850,000
Changde	China	849,000
Yingkou	China	848,000
Moradabad	India	845,000
Shaoguan	China	845,000
Cotonou	Benin	844,000
Zunyi	China	843,000
Voronezh	Russia	842,000
Chifeng	China	842,000
Quetta	Pakistan	841,000
Chihuahua	Mexico	840,000
Antalya	Turkey	838,000
Da Nang - CP	Vietnam	838,000
Bordeaux	France	838,000
Thessaloniki	Greece	837,000
Kermanshah	Iran	837,000
Culiacán	Mexico	836,000
Sulaimaniya	Iraq	836,000
Ilorin	Nigeria	835,000
Vientiane	Laos	831,000
San Miguel de Tucumán	Argentina	831,000
N'Djaména	Chad	829,000
Monrovia	Liberia	827,000
Saratov	Russia	822,000
Fuxin	China	821,000
Yiyang, Hunan	China	820,000
Liverpool	U.K.	819,000
Jiamusi	China	817,000
Rizhao	China	816,000
Valencia	Spain	814,000
Londrina	Brazil	814,000
Panjin	China	813,000
Kisangani	Dem. Rep. of the Congo	812,000
Oklahoma City	U.S.	812,000
Honolulu	U.S.	812,000
Sharjah	U.A.E.	809,000
Nanchong	China	808,000
Maoming	China	803,000
Jos	Nigeria	802,000
Saltillo	Mexico	801,000
Dayton	U.S.	800,000
Bandar Lampung	Indonesia	799,000
Dandong	China	795,000
Tiruppur	India	795,000
Taizhou, Jiangsu	China	795,000
Huludao	China	795,000
Matola	Mozambique	793,000
Arequipa	Peru	789,000
McAllen	U.S.	789,000
Tanger	Morocco	788,000
Malang	Indonesia	786,000
Aba	Nigeria	785,000
Agadir	Morocco	783,000
Mudanjiang	China	783,000
Aracaju	Brazil	782,000
Jerusalem	Israel	782,000
Cixi	China	781,000
Hermosillo	Mexico	781,000
Rochester	U.S.	780,000
El Paso	U.S.	779,000
Yichun, Heilongjiang	China	779,000
Tainan	China	777,000
Zaporizhzhya	Ukraine	775,000
Cúcuta	Colombia	774,000
Cuiabá	Brazil	772,000
Oran	Algeria	770,000
Raleigh	U.S.	769,000
Pekan Baru	Indonesia	769,000
Tunis	Tunisia	767,000
Tampico	Mexico	761,000
Krakow	Poland	756,000

Credits and Sources

COVER

GLOBES (left to right, back cover to front): **Topography and Bathymetry:** Land relief from SRTM30 DEMs with Natural Earth vegetation drape; Ocean relief from ETOPO2 data, rendered by Tibor G. Tóth/Tóth Graphix. **True-Color Land Surface:** NASA, Blue Marble: Next Generation, Terra, Earth Observatory System (EOS). **Terrestrial Ecoregions:** WWF. **Lights at Night:** NASA/NGDC; DMSP; Tibor G. Tóth/Tóth Graphix. **Average Sea Surface Temperature:** MODIS data, NASA/GSFC. **True-Color Land and Bathymetry:** Land data from NASA's Blue Marble imagery; Ocean bathymetry data from NGDC's ETOPO2. **Human Footprint:** Human Footprint Project, WCS and the Center for International Earth Science Information Network (CIESIN). **Biosphere:** Gene Carl Feldman, SeaWIFs, NASA/GSFC; ORBIMAGE. **Land Cover:** AVHRR data from University of Maryland's Global Land Cover Facility. **Land Cover and Bathymetry:** AVHRR and ETOPO2 data processed by Robert Stacey, WorldSat International Inc. **Population Density:** CIESIN's Gridded Population of the World (GPWv3); Centro Internacional de Agricultura Tropical (CIAT). **Political Boundaries:** © National Geographic Society.

FULL-TITLE SPREAD, PAGES 2–3

Same as cover, see above.

PREFACE, PAGE 4

World map: Lights at Night, 2009 NOAA/NGDC; DMSP.

WORLD FROM ABOVE, PAGES 14–15

CONSULTANT: Robert Stacey,
WorldSat International Inc.

Aerial Photographs: Washington, D.C.: National Capital Planning Commission and District of Columbia, processed by Photo Science, Gaithersburg, Maryland. **Rio de Janeiro radar imagery:** Data by Canadian Space Agency, processed by Radarsat International. **Other Rio de Janeiro imagery:** Landsat/Thermal, Near Infrared, Visible data from Brazilian Ministry of Science and Technology's National Institute for Space Research, processed by Stephen W. Stetson, Systems for World Surveillance. **Globes:** Nimbus satellite data processed by Laboratory for Oceans and Ice, NASA/GSFC; **North America map:** Landsat, AVHRR, and Lights at Night data rendered by Robert Stacey, WorldSat International Inc.; NOAA/NGDC; DMSP. **Beaufort Sea imagery:** Landsat, SPOT, and RADARSAT data processed by Canada Centre for Remote Sensing. **North Carolina Flooding imagery:** RADARSAT ScanSAR data processed by Canada Centre for Remote Sensing. **Southern California Wildfire imagery:** Landsat-5 data courtesy of USGS. **Ancient Footpaths, Arenal, Costa Rica imagery:** NASA/MSFC.

GEOSPATIAL CONCEPTS, PAGES 16–17

CONSULTANT: Steven Steinberg,
Humboldt State University

California map series: © National Geographic Society. **Urban Planning image:** Community Cartography. **Transportation Planning image:** Caliper Corporation. **Emergency Management image:** CalMAST and the San Bernadino County Sheriff used ESRI's ArcGIS technology to visualize a 3-D flyover of the Old and Grand Prix Fire perimeters (data provided courtesy of CalMAST and USGS). **Demographic/Census image:** Courtesy of CBS News and ESRI. **Health image:** Copyright © 2001–2005 ESRI. All rights reserved. Used by permission. **Conservation image:** National Zoological Park, Smithsonian Institution.

Physical and Political Maps and Editorial Content

UNITED STATES GOVERNMENT

Central Intelligence Agency
Departments of economic development in each state
Library of Congress, Geography and Map Division
National Aeronautics and Space Administration (NASA)
- Earth Observatory System (EOS)
- Goddard Space Flight Center (GSFC)
- Marshall Space Flight Center (MSFC)

National Geospatial-Intelligence Agency (NGA)
- Hydrographic and Topographic Center

Naval Research Laboratory
U.S. Board on Geographic Names (BGN)
U.S. Department of Agriculture (USDA)
U.S. Department of Commerce
Bureau of Census
Bureau of Economic Affairs
National Oceanic and Atmospheric Administration (NOAA)
- National Marine Fisheries Service (NMFS)
- National Environmental Satellite, Data, and Information Service (NESDIS)
- National Climatic Data Center (NCDC)
- National Geophysical Data Center (NGDC)
- National Ocean Service (NOS)

U.S. Department of Defense
- Air Force Space & Missile Systems Center (SMC)
- Defense Meteorological Satellite Program (DMSP)

U.S. Department of Interior
- Bureau of Land Management (BLM)
- Geological Survey (USGS)
- National Biological Survey
- EROS Data Center
- National Park Service
- National Wetlands Research Center
- Office of Territories

U.S. Department of State
U.S. Naval Oceanographic Office
U.S. Navy/NOAA Joint Ice Center

GOVERNMENT OF CANADA

Department of Energy, Mines and Resource
Canadian Permanent Committee on Geographic Names
Government du Québec
- Commission de Toponymie

Offices of provincial premiers and of commissioners of the territories
Statistics Canada

OTHER

Embassies and statistical agencies of foreign nations
International Astronomical Union Working Group for Planetary System Nomenclature
International Telecommunication Union (ITU)
Norwegian Polar Institute
Population Reference Bureau (PRB)
Scripps Institution of Oceanography
Sea Around Us project
State Economic Agencies
United Nations (UN)
- Cartography Unit, Map Library, Department of Technical Cooperation, Documentation, Reference and Terminology Section
- Department of Economic and Social Affairs, Statistics Division
- Environmental Program (UNEP), World Conservation Monitoring Centre (WCMC), Protected Areas Program
- Food and Agriculture Organization (FAO)
- Global Resources Information Database (GRID)
- United Nations High Commission on Refugees (UNHCR)

University of Cambridge, Scott Polar Research Institute
Wildlife Conservation Society (WCS)
- Human Footprint Project

Wisconsin Demographic Services Center
World Bank
- Map Library, Statistical Office
- World Development Indicators

World Health Organization (WHO)
World Resources Institute (WRI), Global Forest Watch
World Wildlife Fund (WWF)

World Thematic Maps and Editorial Content

OVERALL CONSULTANT

Roger M. Downs,
Pennsylvania State University

WORLD OPENER, PAGES 18–19

LAYERS (top to bottom): **Land Cover:** Boston University Department of Geography and Environment Global Land Cover Project. Source data provided by NASA's Moderate Resolution Imaging Spectraradiometer. Available online at http://modis.gsfc.nasa.gov. **Population Density and Global Shipping Routes:** Population data from LandScan 2008™, Oak Ridge National Laboratory (ORNL) / UT-Battelle, LLC. Shipping routes from Halpern et al, "A Global Map of Human Impact on Marine Ecosystems," *Science* (15 Feb. 2008): Vol. 319, no. 5865, pp. 948–952. **Ocean Chlorophyll:** NASA Earth Observatory. **Agriculture Mosaic, Global Fisheries:** Land data from Ramankutty, N., A.T. Evan, C. Monfreda and J.A. Foley. "Farming the planet. Part 1: The Geographic Distribution of Global Agriculture Lands in the Year 2000." Global Biochemical Cycles (2007), Vol. 22, GB1022, doi:10.1029/2007GB002947. Ocean data from The Sea Around Us Project/Pauly, D.: *The Sea Around Us Project*: Documenting and Communicating Global Fisheries Impacts on Marine Ecosystems," Ambio 36 (2007): 290–295. Available online at www.seaaroundus.org. **Sea Surface Temperature (SST):** NASA/MODIS. **ETOPO1:** Amante, C. and B. W. Eakins, ETOPO1 1 Arc-Minute Global Relief Model: Procedures, Data Sources and Analysis. NOAA Technical Memorandum NESDIS NGDC-24, 19 pp, March 2009.

PLATE TECTONICS, PAGES 24–25

CONSULTANT: Seth Stein,
Northwestern University

Paleogeography images: Ron Blakey, Northern Arizona University. **Earth Tectonics map:** Seth Stein, Northwestern University; USGS Earthquake Hazard Program; Smithsonian Institution's Global Volcanism Program; NOAA/National Geophysical Data Center's Significant Earthquake Database. **Tectonic block diagrams:** Susan Sanford.

GEOMORPHOLOGY, PAGES 26–27

CONSULTANT: Stephen Cunha,
Humboldt State University

Eolian Landforms diagrams: Chris Orr. **World Landforms map:** © National Geographic Society. PHOTOS: **Crater Lake, Oregon:** James Balog. **Misti Volcano, Peru:** Stefano Scata, Getty Images. **Mount Fuji, Japan:** George Mobley. **Isle of Skye, Scotland:** Wilfried Krecicwost, Getty Images. **Southern China:** James Blair. **Namibia:** Natphotos/Getty Images. **Blyde River Canyon, South Africa:** Natphotos/Getty Images. **Victoria, Australia:** Rob Brander. **Kejimkujik Lake, Nova Scotia:** Douglas Grant, Parks Canada. **Mississippi River Delta, Louisiana:** SPOT Image/Photo Researchers; (CNES). **Meteor Crater, Arizona:** Adriel Heisey. **Fluvial Landforms and Glacial Landforms diagrams:** Steven Fick. **Eolian Landforms, Watersheds, and Ice Age maps:** © National Geographic Society.

EARTH'S SURFACE, PAGES 28–29

CONSULTANTS: Peter Sloss, NOAA;
Jonathan T. Overpeck and Jeremy L. Weiss, Department of Geosciences, The University of Arizona

Maps and cross-section diagram: data from Tom Patterson's CleanTOPO2 (edited SRTM30 Plus), © National Geographic Society.

CLIMATE, PAGES 30–31

CONSULTANT: John Oliver,
Indiana State University

Hadley Cells artwork: Don Foley, NASA. **Seasons diagram:** Shusei Nagaoka. **Modified Köppen classification map:** © H. J. de Blij, P. O. Muller, and John Wiley & Sons, Inc. **Seasonal Temperature maps:** Barbara Summey, NASA/GSFC Visualization Analysis Laboratory. **Mean Annual Precipitation map:** Data from NOAA/NESDIS/NCDC/Satellite Data Services Division (SDSD), compiled by UNEP-GRID.

WEATHER, PAGES 32–33

CONSULTANT: John Oliver,
Indiana State University

Pressure and Predominant Winds maps: NOAA/Cooperative Institute for Research in Environmental Sciences (CIRES) Climate Diagnostic Center; National Centers for Environmental Prediction (NCEP)/National Center for Atmospheric Research (NCAR) Reanalysis Project Data. **Oceans and Cyclones map:** NASA; NOAA. **El Niño/La Niña globes:** TOPEX/Poseidon satellite data from NASA, Jet Propulsion Laboratory (JPL), California Institute of Technology. **Cyclonic Activity diagrams:** Don Foley. **How Weather Happens artwork:** Robert Hynes.

BIOSPHERE, PAGES 34–35

CONSULTANT: Gene Carl Feldman,
SeaWIFs, NASA/Goddard Space Flight Center

Biosphere map: Gene Carl Feldman, SeaWIFs, NASA/Goddard Space Flight Center. **Ocean Circulation map:** Don Foley. **Our Layered Ocean artwork:** Don Foley. **Water and Carbon Cycle artwork:** Edward S. Gazsi.

WATER, PAGES 36–37

CONSULTANT: Aaron Wolf,
Oregon State University

Water Availability map: Dobson, et al. LandScan 2000; Vörösmarty, et al., River Discharge Database, Version 1.1 (RivDIS v1.0 supplement); Gleick, Peter: Water Conflict Chronology, http://www.worldwater.org/conflict/index.html. **Access to Fresh Water map:** World Health Organization World Health Statistics, 2010. **Water Withdrawal graphs:** AQUASTAT-FAO, http://www.fao.org/nr/aquastat. **Water by Volume graphs:** Peter Gleick, Pacific Institute.

LAND COVER, PAGES 38–39

CONSULTANTS: Mark Friedl,
Global Land Cover Project, Boston University
and Paul Davis, University of Maryland
Global Land Cover Facility

Global Land Cover imagery: Boston University Department of Geography and Environment Global Land Cover Project. Source data provided by NASA's Moderate Resolution Imaging Spectraradiometer. PHOTOS: **Evergreen Needleleaf Forest:** Tom and Pat Leeson, Photo Researchers. **Evergreen Broadleaf Forest:** Michael Nichols, National Geographic Society Image Collection. **Deciduous Needleleaf Forest:** Stephen Krasemann, PhotoResearchers. **Deciduous Broadleaf Forest:** Rod Planck, Photo Researchers. **Mixed Forest:** Jim Steinberg, Photo Researchers. **Woody Savanna:** Matthew Hansen. **Savanna:** Gregory Dimijian, Photo Researchers. **Closed Shrubland:** Sharon G. Johnson. **Open Shrubland:** Georg Gerster, Photo Researchers. **Grassland:** Rod Planck, Photo Researchers. **Cropland:** Jim Richardson. **Barren/Sparsely Vegetated:** George Steinmetz. **Urban and Built-up:** Steve McCurry. **Cropland/Natural Vegetation Mosaic:** Robert Estall/CORBIS. **Wetland:** James Randklev/Getty Images. **Snow and Ice:** B.&C. Alexander, Photo Researchers.

BIODIVERSITY, PAGES 40–41

CONSULTANT: John Kupter,
University of South Carolina

Terrestrial and Aquatic Ecoregions maps: Conservation Science Program, World Wildlife Fund—U.S. **Threatened Mammals and Birds graph:** IUCN Red List. **Biodiversity Hotspots and Status of Biodiversity map:** Conservation International. PHOTOS: **The Bering Sea:** Stephen Krasemann, Getty Images. **Southeastern United States Rivers and Streams:** Kevin Schafer Photography. **The Amazon River and Flooded Forests:** Flip Nicklin, Minden Pictures. **Rift Valley Lakes:** John Ginstina, Getty Images. **Eastern Himalayan Broadleaf and Conifer Forests:** ZSSD, Minden Pictures. **Sulu-Sulawesi Seas:** Fred Bavendam, Minden Pictures.

LAND USE, PAGES 42–43

CONSULTANT: Navin Ramankutty,
McGill University.

Land Use map: Jonathan Foley, Navin Ramankutty, Billie Leff, Center for Sustainability and the Global Environment, University of Wisconsin—Madison. **Bolivia Deforestation; Black Hills Fire Damage; Saudi Arabia Agricultural Development images:** Landsat-5 satellite data courtesy of USGS. **Aral Sea Shoreline images:** NASA's Earth Observatory.

HUMAN POPULATION, PAGES 44–45

CONSULTANT: Carl Haub,
Population Reference Bureau.

Population Density map: Source: Landscan 2009™ Population Dataset created by UT-Battelle, LLC, the management and operating contractor of the Oak Ridge National Laboratory acting on behalf of the U.S. Department of Energy under Contract No. DE-AC05-00OR22725. **Cartogram:** World Population Prospects, 2008 Revision; CIA World Factbook. **Population Pyramids:** International Data Base (IDB), U.S. Census Bureau. **Regional Population Growth graph:** © National Geographic Society.

POPULATION TRENDS, PAGES 46–47

CONSULTANT: Carl Haub,
Population Reference Bureau

Fertility, Infant Mortality, and Life Expectancy maps: PRB. **Urban Population and Urban Growth:** UN Department of Economic and Social Affairs, Population Division, World Urbanization Prospects, 2009 Revision.

CULTURE, PAGES 48–49

CONSULTANT: Bernard Comrie,
Max Planck Institute for Revolutionary
Anthropology and Dennis Cosgrove,
University of California, Los Angeles

Major Religions and World Languages maps and graphs: © National Geographic Society; **Religious Adherence graphs:** World Christian Database, Center for the Study of Global Christianity, Gordon-Conwell Theological Seminary and CIA World Factbook. **Imagery, Jerusalem, Mecca, Allahabad:** IKONOS satellite data, courtesy of Space Imaging. **Struggling Cultures map:** Moseley, Christopher (ed.). 2010. Atlas of the World's Languages in Danger, 3rd ed. Paris, UNESCO Publishing. Online version: http://www.unesco.org/culture/en/endangeredlanguages/atlas.

HEALTH AND LITERACY, PAGES 50–51

CONSULTANT: Michael Reich,
Harvard University

Causes of Death, Cardiovascular Deaths, Physicians maps: WHO (World Health Organization). **HIV/AIDS map:** Population Reference Bureau's World Population Data Sheet and CIA World Factbook. **Malaria map:** Malaria Atlas Project; http://www.map.ox.ac.uk. **Calorie supply per capita map:** World Resources Institute (Earthtrends). **Percentage of Population Undernourished map:** The State of Food Insecurity in the World, 2009 (FAO). **Literacy Rate map:** PRB. **Male and Female Literacy Rates graph:** CIA World Factbook.

FOOD, PAGES 52–53

CONSULTANT: Gil Latz,
Portland State University

Cereals, Roots and Tubers, Sugar-bearing Crops, Pulses, Oil-bearing Crops: Harvested Area and Yields of 175 Crops (M3-Crops Data) from www.geog.mcgill.ca/~nramankutty/Datasets/Datasets.html. **Livestock map:** Global Livestock Production Health Atlas (GLiPHA), FAO. **World Diet graphs:** FAOSTAT Food Balance Sheets. **Fisheries and Aquaculture map:** The Sea Around Us project, Fisheries Centre, University of British Columbia; FAO. **Genetically Modified Agriculture map:** International Service for the Acquisition of Agri-Biotech Applications, isaaa.org. ISAAA Brief 42-2010: Executive Summary. Global Status of Commercialized Biotech/GM Crops: 2010.

ECONOMY, PAGES 54–55

CONSULTANT: Amy Glasmeier,
Pennsylvania State University.

Cartogram: CIA World Factbook; World Bank. **GDP per Capita graph:** CIA World Factbook. **Real GDP Growth graph:** CIA World Factbook. GNI per capita map: World Bank. **Labor Migration and GDP PPP per Capita map:** CIA World Factbook; Institute for the Study of International Migration, Georgetown University. **World Employment map:** CIA World Factbook.

TRADE AND GLOBALIZATION, PAGES 56–57

CONSULTANT: Amy Glasmeier,
Pennsylvania State University

Trade Flow map: World Bank's World Development Indicators; World Federation of Exchanges; World Trade Organization's International Trade Statistics; International Trade Centre's Trade by Commodity Statistics 2001–2010. **Trade Blocs map:** World Trade Organization's Regional Trade Agreements Information System (RTA-IS). **World Debt map:** World Bank's WDI database. **Growth of Trade map:** World Trade Organzation's International Trade Statistics 2010. **Merchandise imports/exports graphs:** CIA World Factbook.

TRANSPORTATION, PAGES 58–59

CONSULTANT: Jean-Paul Rodrigue,
Hofstra University

Airline Passenger Volume map: OAG Aviation Solutions/National Geographic Maps. **World's Busiest Airports list:** Airports Council International, airports.org. Passenger Traffic 2009 Final. **World's Largest Ports list:** American Association of Port Authorities, aapa-ports.org. World Port Rankings (2009). **Road and Rail Network Density maps:** World Bank, worldbank.org. World Development Indicators Online (WDI). **Shipping Map:** American Association of Port Authorities, aapa-ports.org. World Port Rankings (2009).

COMMUNICATION, PAGES 60–61

CONSULTANT: Greg Downey,
University of Wisconsin—Madison

Communications Satellites graphic: Union of Concerned Scientists, ucsusa.org. UCS Satellite Database. **Mapping the Internet:** Hal Burch and Bill Cheswick, Lumeta Corporation Patent(s) Pending & Copyright © Lumeta Corporation 2006. All Rights Reserved. **Internet Explosion map:** CIA World Factbook; ITU (International Telecommunication Union) World Telecommunication/ICT Indicators Database. **Rise of the Mobile Phone graph:** ITU World Telecommunication/ICT Indicators Database. **Connecting the Planet map:** International Cable Protection Committee Cable Database and ITU World Telecommunication/ICT Indicators Database.

ENERGY, PAGES 62–63

CONSULTANT: Barry D. Solomon,
Michigan Technological University

Annual Energy and Major Energy Deposits map: Energy Information Administration, U.S. Department of Energy: www.eia.doe.gov; International Petroleum Encyclopedia. **Renewable Energy and World Oil Supply graphs:** Energy Information Administration, U.S. Department of Energy. **Flow of Oil Worldwide:** BP Statistical Review of World Energy, June 2010. PHOTOS:
Continued on next page

Hydropower: Jim Richardson. **Nuclear:** Mark Burnett, Photo Researchers. **Solar:** Courtesy National Renewable Energy Lab. **Wind:** John Mead, Science Photo Library/Photo Researchers. **Geothermal:** Science Photo Library/Photo Researchers.

DEFENSE AND CONFLICT, PAGES 64–65

CONSULTANT: Monty G. Marshall, Center for Systemic Peace and Center for Global Policy, George Mason University

Regime Type and Active Military map: Monty Marshall, Center for Systemic Peace (www.systemicpeace.org); International Institute for Strategic Studies; *The Military Balance 2010*. **Uprooted People graph:** United Nations High Commission on Refugees (www.unhcr.org). **Defense Spending map:** CIA World Factbook; International Institute of Strategic Studies. **Biological and Chemical Weapons maps:** Center for Nonproliferation Studies, Monterey Institute of International Studies; Organisation for the Prohibition of Chemical Weapons. **Nuclear Weapons map:** Carnegie Endowment for International Peace; Henry Stimson Center.

ENVIRONMENT, PAGES 66–67

CONSULTANT: Tania del Mar López Marrero, Pennsylvania State University

Habitat Loss map: Lara Hansen, Adam Markham, WWF. **Deforestation map:** Global Forest Watch, World Resources Institute. **Threatened Oceans map:** NOAA/NMFS; UNEP-WCMC. **Risk of Desertification map:** USDA Global Desertification Vulnerability Map. **Ozone Depletion maps:** NASA. **Atmospheric Carbon Dioxide graph:** Dr. Pieter Tans, NOAA/ESRL (www.esrl.noaa.gov/gmd/ccgg/trends/) and Dr. Ralph Keeling, Scripps Institution of Oceanography (scrippsco2.ucsd.edu/). **Polar Ice Cap map:** National Snow and Ice Data Center. **Pollution map:** © National Geographic Society. Shipping routes from Halpern et al.; see citation for pp. 18–19.

PROTECTED AREAS, PAGES 68–69

CONSULTANTS: Philip Dearden, University of Victoria and Eric Sanderson, Wildlife Conservation Society

Protected Areas Worldwide graph: © National Geographic Society; UNEP-WCMC. **Wildest Biomes map:** © Wildlife Conservation Society (WCS) and Center for International Earth Science Information Network (CIESIN). PHOTOS: **Hawai'i Volcanoes N.P., U.S.:** Bryan Lowry, Seapics.com. **Galápagos, N.P., Ecuador:** Cristina G. Mittermeier. **Arches N.P., Western U.S.:** Art Wolfe. **Madidi N.P., Bolivia:** Joel Sartore. **Amazon Basin, Brazil:** Michael Nichols. **Arctic Regions:** Flip Nicklin. **Sareks N.P., Sweden:** Jan-Peter Lahall. **African Reserves:** Beverly Joubert, National Geographic Television and Film. **Wolong Nature Reserve, China:** Daniel J. Cox, Natural Exposures. **Kamchatka Peninsula, Russia:** Sarah Leen. **Gunung Palung N.P., Indonesia:** Tim Laman. **Australia and New Zealand:** Art Wolfe. **Protected Areas Worldwide map:** WDPA Consortium, World Database on Protected Areas. Copyright © World Conservation Union (IUCN); UNEP-WCMC.

Continental Thematic Section

CHAPTER OPENERS

Continental images (pp. 70–71, 120–121, 140–141, 170–171, 204–205; 228–229, 244–245): Landsat, AVHRR, Lights at Night data rendered by Robert Stacey, WorldSat International Inc.; NOAA/NGDC; DMSP.
To "paint" the images of continents, polar regions, and oceans which open the chapters, data from multiple passes of numerous satellites, Space Shuttle, and sonar soundings—recorded at varying scales and levels of resolution—were combined digitally to form mosaics. This level of detail, rendered cloud free, captured nighttime lights of populated areas, flares from natural gas burning above oil wells, and lights from fishing fleets. The images were further enhanced and blended to approximate true color. Shaded relief, as if the sun were shining from the northwest, was added for realism, and elevation was exaggerated twenty times to make variations in elevation easily visible. The images were then reproduced as if viewed from space.

NATURAL WORLD

North America, pages 74–75; United States, pages 84–85; South America, pages 124–125; Europe, pages 144–145; Asia, pages 174–175; Africa, pages 208–209; Australia and Oceania, pages 232–233: **Global Land Cover imagery:** Boston University Department of Geography and Environment Global Land Cover Project. Source data provided by NASA's Moderate Resolution Imaging Spectraradiometer. **Modified Köppen Climate maps:** © H. J. de Blij, P. O. Muller, and John Wiley & Sons, Inc. **Natural Hazards maps:** USGS Earthquake Hazard Program; Smithsonian Institution's Global Volcanism Program; National Geophysical Data Center/World Data Center (NGDC/WDC) Historical Tsunami Database; Lights at Night data, DMSP. **Water Availability maps:** Aaron Wolf, Oregon State University. **Climagraphs:** National Climatic Data Center, NOAA. **U.S. Federal Lands map:** National Park Service, Bureau of Land Management; USDA Forest Service; U.S. Fish and Wildlife Service; Bureau of Indian Affairs; Department of Defense; Department of Energy; NOAA; Natural Earth Vector dataset.

HUMAN WORLD

North America, pages 76–77; South America, pages 126–127; Europe, pages 146–147; Asia, pages 176–177; Africa, pages 210–211; Australia & Oceania, pages 234–235: **Population Density maps:** Source: Landscan 2009™ Population Dataset created by UT-Battelle, LLC, the management and operating contractor of the Oak Ridge National Laboratory acting on behalf of the U.S. Department of Energy under Contract No. DE-AC05-00OR22725. **Percent Population Change 2000–2050 maps:** PRB 2010 World Population Data Sheet. **Urbanization maps:** UN Department of Economic and Social Affairs, Population Division, World Urbanization Prospects, 2009 Revision. **Languages maps:** © National Geographic Society. **Population Pyramids:** International Data Base (IDB), U.S. Census Bureau.

United States, pages 86–87: **Most Prevalent Religious Group, by County map:** Data for Major Religious Families by Counties of the United States, 2000 from "Religious Congregations and Membership in the United States 2000," Dale E. Jones, et. al. Nashville, TN: Glenmary Research Center. © 2002 Association of Statisticians of American Religious Bodies. All rights reserved. **Percentage Foreign Born; Percent Change in U.S. Population 2000–2010;** and **U.S. Population Density by County maps:** U.S. Census Bureau.

ECONOMIC WORLD

North America, pages 78–79; South America, pages 128–129; Europe, pages 148–149; Asia, pages 178–179; Africa, pages 212–213; Australia & Oceania, pages 236–237: **Land Use maps:** Jonathan Foley, Navin Ramankutty, Billie Leff, Center for Sustainability and the Global Environment, University of Wisconsin—Madison. **Per Capita Energy Consumption maps:** EIA (U.S. Energy Information Administration). **GDP by Sector maps:** CIA World Factbook. **People Living on Less than $2 per Day maps:** PRB 2010 World Population Data Sheet. **Imports/Exports graphs:** International Trade Centre, Trade Map (www.trademap.org).

U.S., pages 88–89: **Manufacturing Employment, Service Employment, Farm Area, and Median Income by County maps:** U.S. Census Bureau/American Community Survey, with assistance from Phil Wells, Wisconsin Demographic Services Center.

Other

GEOGRAPHIC INFORMATION

DAVID DIVINS, NOAA/NGDC
ROBERT FISHER, Scripps Institute of Oceanography
CARL HAUB, Population Reference Bureau
MARTIN JAKOBSSON, University of New Hampshire
CHARLES O'REILLY, Canadian Hydrographic Service
RON SALVASON, Canadian Hydrographic Service
HANS WERNER SCHENKE, Alfred Wegener Institute for Polar and Marine Research

OCEANS, PAGES 250–251

All globes: Gregory W. Shirah, NASA/GSFC Scientific Visualization Studio; David W. Pierce, Scripps Institution of Oceanography. *The speed and direction of ocean currents can be computed from small variations in the height of the sea surface just as the speed and direction of the wind is computed from surface air pressure differences. Satellite-derived images depict a ten-year average of the hills and valleys, or shape, of the changing ocean surface. These undulations range over a few meters in height, and flow occurs along the color contours. The vectors (white arrows) show ocean velocity caused exclusively by the effect of wind on the top layer of the ocean (called the Ekman Drift). Estimates of the Ekman Drift are used by ocean researchers to determine the shape of the sea surface and as a component of the overall surface current (which also includes thermal, saline, tidal, and wave-driven components).*

COMPARISONS & CONVERSIONS, PAGE 391

Statistical Information: The Columbia Gazetteer of the World; Encyclopedia Britannica; The World Almanac and Book of Facts; United Nations Department of Economic & Social Affairs: Population Division.

Additional Source Information

Blakey, Ron. *Global Paleogeography*. Available online at http://www2.nau.edu/rcb7/globaltext2.html.

Boston University Department of Geography and Environment Global Land Cover Project. Source data from NASA/MODIS. Available online at www-modis.bu.edu/landcover/index.html.

BP Statistical Review of World Energy. Available online at www.bp.com.

Busby, Rebecca L., ed. *International Petroleum Encyclopedia*. Tulsa, Oklahoma: Penwell Corporation.

Central Intelligence Agency. *The World Factbook*. Washington, D.C. Available online at https://www.cia.gov.

Cohen, Saul. *The Columbia Gazetteer of the World*. New York: Columbia University Press.

de Blij, H. J. and Peter O. Muller. *Geography: Realms, Regions, and Concepts, 12th ed.* New York: John Wiley & Sons, Inc., 2006.

de Blij, H. J., Peter O. Muller, and Richard S. Williams, Jr. Physical Geography: *The Global Environment. 3rd ref. ed.* New York: Oxford University Press, 2004.

Encyclopedia Britannica. Chicago, Illinois: Available online at www.britannica.com.

Energy Information Administration. *International Energy Annual (IEA)*. Washington, D.C.: Department of Energy. Available online at www.eia.doe.gov/iea.

FAO (Food and Agriculture Organization of the United Nations):

Review of Water Resources by Country. Available online at www.fao.org/ag/agl/aglw/aquastat/water_res.

FAO Statistical Yearbook
Available online at www.fao.org/WAICENT/FAOINFO/ECONOMIC/ESS/yearbook.
Data from FAOSTAT: www.faostat.fao.org.

The State of Food Insecurity in the World (SOFI): Eradicating World Hunger-Key to achieving the Millennium Development Goals. Rome: FAO, Available online at www.fao.org/SOF/sofi/en.

The State of World Fisheries and Aquaculture (SOFIA). Available online at www.fao.org/sof/sofia/index_en.htm.

The State of the World's Forests. Available online at www.fao.org/forestry/en/

Foley, J. A., R. DeFries, G. P. Asner, C. Barford, G. Bonan, S. R. Carpenter, F. S. Chapin, M. T. Coe, G. C. Daily, H. K. Gibbs, J. H. Helkowski, T. Holloway, E. A. Howard, C. J. Kucharik, C. Monfreda, J. A. Patz, I. C. Prentice, N. Ramankutty, and P. K. Snyder. "Global Consequences of Land Use." *Science* (22 July 2005), 570–574.

Gleick, Peter. *The World's Water: The Biennial Report on Freshwater Resources.*
Available online at www.worldwater.org.

Goddard, Ives, Vol. ed. *Handbook of North American Indians.* Vol. 17, Languages. Washington, D.C.: Smithsonian Institution, 1996.

Jones, Dale E., Sherri Doty, Clifford Grammich, James E. Horsch, Richard Houseal, Mac Lynn, John P. Marcum, Kenneth M. Sanchagrin, and Richard H. Taylor. *Religious Congregations and Membership in the United States 2000: An Enumeration by Region, State and County Based on Data Reported by 149 Religious Bodies.* Nashville, TN: Glenmary Research Center, 2002.

Hackett, James, ed., International Institute for Strategic Studies. *The Military Balance 2010*. London: Routledge.

ISAAA (International Service for the Acquisition of Agri-Biotech Applications). "ISAAA Brief 42-2010: Executive Summary. Global Status of Commercialized Biotech/GM Crops: 2010." Available online at www.isaaa.org.

Mackay, J, and G. Mensah, eds. *Atlas of Heart Disease and Stroke*. Geneva, Switzerland: World Health Organization. Available online at www.who.int/cardiovascular_diseases/resources/atlas/en.

Monfreda et al. (2008), "Farming the planet: 2. Geographic distribution of crop areas, yields, physiological types, and net primary production in the year 2000." *Global Biogeochemical Cycles*, Vol.22, GB1022, doi:10.1029/2007GB002947.

Morrell, Virginia. "California's Wild Crusade." *National Geographic* (February 2006), 2–35.

National Geographic Maps:

"Danger Zones: Earthquake Risk-A Global View." Supplement map, April 2006.

"Humans and Habitats: Cultural Extinctions Loom." EarthPulse feature, September 2001.

"Millennium in Maps: Biodiversity." Supplement map, February 1999.

"Millennium in Maps: Cultures." Supplement map, June 1999.

"State of the Planet: A World Transformed." Supplement map, September 2002.

Oliver, John E. and John Hidore. *Climatology: An Atmospheric Science.* N.Y.: Prentice Hall, 2001.

Olson, D. M. and E. Dinerstein. 1998. "The Global 200: A representation approach to conserving the earth's most biologically valuable ecoregions." *Conservation Biology* (1998), 502–515.

Olson, D. M., E. Dinerstein, E. D. Wikramanayake, N. D. Burgess, G. V. N. Powell, E. C. Underwood, J. A. D'Amico, I. Itoua, H. E. Strand, J. C. Morrison, C. J. Loucks, T. F. Allnutt, T. H. Ricketts, Y. Kura, J. F. Lamoreux, W. W. Wettengel, P. Hedao, and K. R. Kassem. "Terrestrial Ecoregions of the World: A New Map of Life on Earth." *BioScience* (2001), 933–938.

Overpeck J. T., B. L. Otto-Bliesner, G. H. Miller, D. R. Muhs, R. B. Alley, and J. T. Kiehl. "Paleoclimatic evidence for future ice-sheet instability and rapid sea-level rise." *Science* (24 March 2006), 1747–50.

Natural Earth Vector map data, available online at www.naturalearthdata.com.

Patterson, Tom. CleanTOPO2. Available online at www.shadedrelief.com/cleantopo2/

Population Reference Bureau. *2010 World Population Data Sheet*. Washington, D.C. Available online at www.prb.org.

Sarmiento, Jorge L. and Nicolas Gruber. "Sinks for Anthropogenic Carbon." *Physics Today* (August 2002), 30–36.

Simons, Lewis M. "Weapons of Mass Destruction." *National Geographic* (February 2006), 2–35.

UNEP One Planet Many People: *Atlas of Our Changing Environment.* UNEP/DEWAL/GRID. Available online at: http://na.unep.net/atlas/

UNESCO *Atlas of the World's Languages in Danger, 3rd ed.* Paris, UNESCO Publishing. Available online at www.unesco.org/culture/en/endangeredlanguages/atlas.

United Nations, Department of Economic and Social Affairs, Population Division. *International Migration, 2002*. New York, NY: October 2002. Available online at www.un.org/esa/population/publications.

United Nations. *World Population Prospects: The 2008 Revision*. New York, NY: United Nations, 2009. Available online at http://esa.un.org/unpp/

United Nations. *World Urbanization Prospects: The 2009 Revision*. New York, NY: United Nations, 2010. Available online at http://esa.un.org/unpd/wup/index.htm.

WDPA Consortium. World Database on Protected Areas. Cambridge, U.K.: World Conservation Union (IUCN) and UNEP-World Conservation Monitoring Centre (UNEP-WCMC). Available online at www.wdpa.org/

Wilford, John Noble. "Revolutions in Mapping." *National Geographic* (February 1998), 6–39.

The World Almanac and Book of Facts. New York: World Almanac Education Group.

World Bank. *World Development Indicators*. Washington, D.C.: The World Bank Group. Available online at www.data.worldbank.org.

World Health Organization (WHO), UNICEF, and Roll Back Malaria (RBM). *World Malaria Report.* WHO: Geneva, Switzerland. Available online at www.rbm.who.int/wmr2005.

World Trade Organization. *International Trade Statistics*. Geneva, Switzerland: World Trade Organization. Available online at www.wto.org.

Online Sources

Central Intelligence Agency
www.cia.gov

Conservation International
www.conservation.org

El Niño/La Niña (TOPEX/Poseidon and Jason-1 data)
sealevel.jpl.nasa.gov

Energy Information Agency
www.eia.doe.gov

Food and Agriculture Organization of the UN (FAO)
www.fao.org

International Telecommunication Union (ITU)
www.itu.int

National Aeronautics and Space Administration
www.nasa.gov

National Atmospheric and Oceanic Administration
www.noaa.gov

National Climatic Data Center
www.ncdc.noaa.gov

National Geophysical Data Center
www.ngdc.noaa.gov/

National Park Service
www.nps.gov

Ozone hole
www.gsfc.nasa.gov

Pacific Institute-The World's Water
www.worldwater.org

Population Reference Bureau
www.prb.org

The Smithsonian Global Volcanism Program
www.volcano.si.edu

United Nations
www.un.org

UNEP Global Resources Information Database (GRID)
www.grid.unep.ch/data/index

UNEP-World Conservation Monitoring Centre
www.unep-wcmc.org

UNESCO
www.unesco.org

U.S. Geological Survey
www.usgs.gov

World Bank
www.worldbank.org

World Conservation Union
www.iucn.org

World Health Organization
www.who.int

World Resources Institute
www.wri.org

World Wildlife Fund
www.worldwildlife.org

NATIONAL GEOGRAPHIC

Collegiate Atlas of the World

SECOND EDITION

Published by the National Geographic Society
John M. Fahey, Jr., *Chairman of the Board and Chief Executive Officer*
Timothy T. Kelly, *President*
Declan Moore, *Executive Vice President; President, Publishing*
Melina Gerosa Bellows, *Executive Vice President, Chief Creative Officer, Books, Kids, and Family*

Prepared by the Book Division
Barbara Brownell Grogan, *Vice President and Editor in Chief*
Jonathan Halling, *Design Director, Books and Children's Publishing*
Marianne R. Koszorus, *Director of Design*
R. Gary Colbert, *Production Director*
Jennifer A. Thornton, *Managing Editor*
Meredith C. Wilcox, *Administrative Director, Illustrations*

Staff for This Second Edition Atlas
Carl Mehler, *Project Editor and Director of Maps*
Matthew W. Chwastyk, *Designer and Map Production Manager*
Laura McCormick, David B. Miller, Scott A. Zillmer *Map Editors*
Michael McNey, Gregory Ugiansky, and XNR Productions, *Map Research and Production*
Melissa Farris, Greg Ugiansky, *Cover Design*

Manufacturing and Quality Management
Christopher A. Liedel, *Chief Financial Officer*
Phillip L. Schlosser, *Senior Vice President*
Chris Brown, *Technical Director*
Nicole Elliott, *Manager*
Rachel Faulise, *Manager*
Robert L. Barr, *Manager*

Atlas printed and bound by Courier Kendallville, Inc.
Case cover and dust jacket printed by Moore Langen

National Geographic Maps
Charles D. Regan, Jr., *Vice President, General Manager, NG Maps*
Kevin P. Allen, *Vice President, Mapping Services*

National Geographic Maps Staff
Juan José Valdés, *Project Manager, Director of Editorial and Research*
Richard W. Bullington, *Director of GIS*
Debbie J. Gibbons, *Director of Production*
James E. McClelland, Jr., *Senior Production Cartographer*
Stephen P. Wells, *Map Production*
Maureen J. Flynn, Julie A. Ibinson, *Map Editors*
Evan Feeney, Alissa M. Ferry, Ewa K. Wieslaw, *Interns*

Additional Staff
Glenn C. Caillouet, *Map Production*
Nicholas P. Rosenbach, *Map Editor*
Mapping Specialists Limited, *Production*

The National Geographic Society is one of the world's largest nonprofit scientific and educational organizations. Founded in 1888 to "increase and diffuse geographic knowledge," the Society works to inspire people to care about the planet. National Geographic reflects the world through its magazines, television programs, films, music and radio, books, DVDs, maps, exhibitions, live events, school publishing programs, interactive media and merchandise. *National Geographic* magazine, the Society's official journal, published in English and 33 local-language editions, is read by more than 40 million people each month. The National Geographic Channel reaches 370 million households in 34 languages in 168 countries. National Geographic Digital Media receives more than 15 million visitors a month. National Geographic has funded more than 9,600 scientific research, conservation and exploration projects and supports an education program promoting geography literacy. For more information, visit www.nationalgeographic.com.

For more information, please call 1-800-NGS LINE (647-5463) or write to the following address:

National Geographic Society
1145 17th Street N.W.
Washington, D.C. 20036-4688 U.S.A.

For information about special discounts for bulk purchases, please contact National Geographic Books Special Sales: ngspecsales@ngs.org

For rights or permissions inquiries, please contact National Geographic Books Subsidiary Rights: ngbookrights@ngs.org

ISBN: 978-1-4262-0839-3

Printed in the U.S.A.
11/CK-CML/1

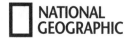

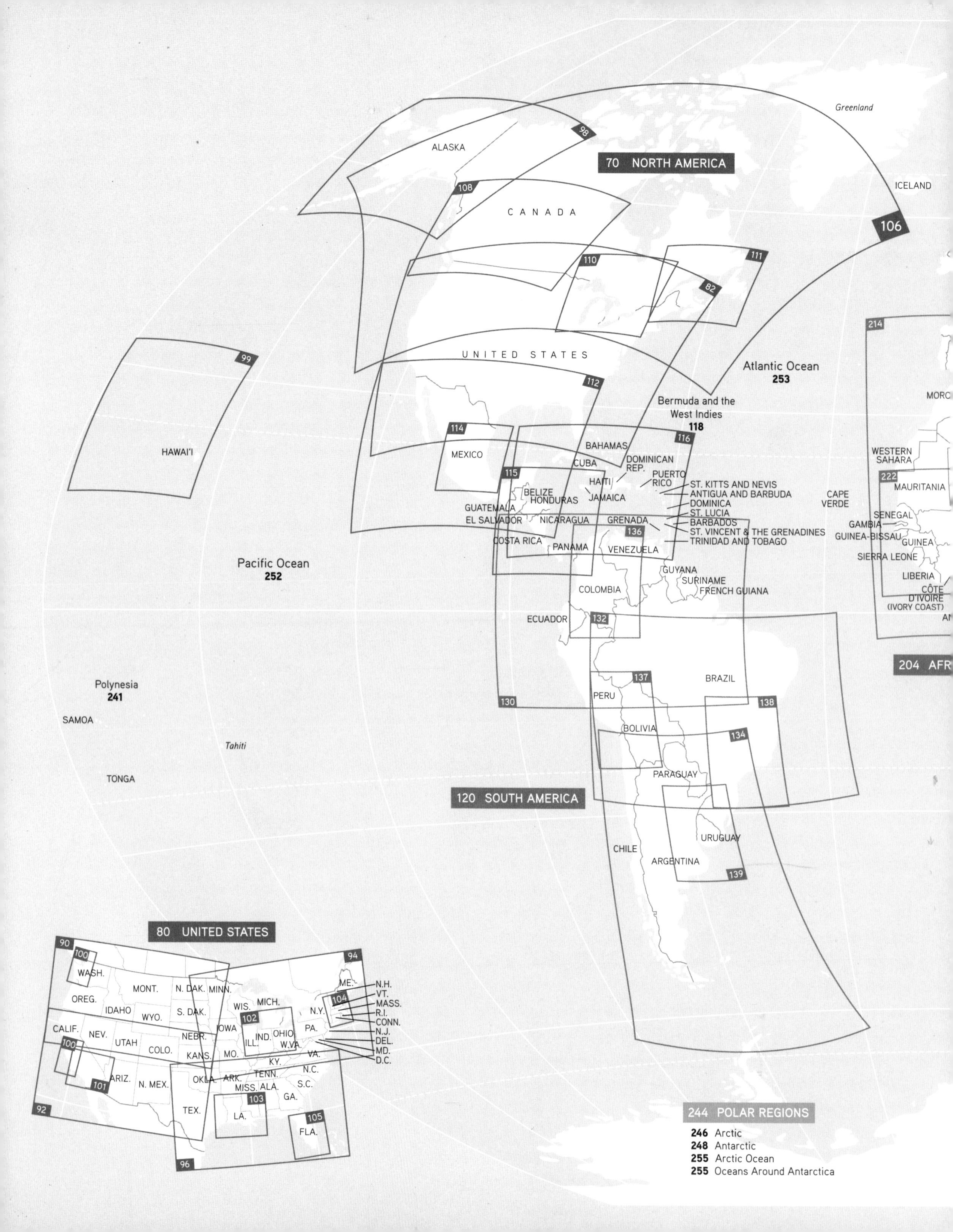
70 NORTH AMERICA
ALASKA
98
108
CANADA
Greenland
ICELAND
106
110
111
82
UNITED STATES
Atlantic Ocean
253
99
HAWAI'I
112
Bermuda and the West Indies
118
114
116
MEXICO
BAHAMAS
DOMINICAN REP.
CUBA
PUERTO RICO
115
HAITI
JAMAICA
BELIZE
HONDURAS
ST. KITTS AND NEVIS
ANTIGUA AND BARBUDA
DOMINICA
ST. LUCIA
BARBADOS
ST. VINCENT & THE GRENADINES
TRINIDAD AND TOBAGO
GUATEMALA
EL SALVADOR
NICARAGUA
GRENADA
136
COSTA RICA
PANAMA
VENEZUELA
Pacific Ocean
252
GUYANA
SURINAME
FRENCH GUIANA
COLOMBIA
ECUADOR
132
BRAZIL
137
PERU
130
138
BOLIVIA
134
PARAGUAY
120 SOUTH AMERICA
URUGUAY
CHILE
ARGENTINA
139
Polynesia
241
SAMOA
Tahiti
TONGA
214
MORC
WESTERN SAHARA
222
MAURITANIA
CAPE VERDE
SENEGAL
GAMBIA
GUINEA-BISSAU
GUINEA
SIERRA LEONE
LIBERIA
CÔTE D'IVOIRE (IVORY COAST)
204 AFR
80 UNITED STATES
90
100
94
WASH.
MONT.
N. DAK.
MINN.
ME.
OREG.
IDAHO
WYO.
S. DAK.
WIS.
MICH.
N.Y.
104
N.H.
VT.
MASS.
R.I.
CONN.
N.J.
DEL.
MD.
D.C.
102
CALIF.
NEV.
UTAH
COLO.
NEBR.
IOWA
ILL.
IND.
OHIO
PA.
W.VA.
VA.
100
KANS.
MO.
KY.
N.C.
101
ARIZ.
N. MEX.
OKLA.
ARK.
TENN.
S.C.
MISS.
ALA.
GA.
103
TEX.
LA.
105
FLA.
92
96
244 POLAR REGIONS
246 Arctic
248 Antarctic
255 Arctic Ocean
255 Oceans Around Antarctica